NOVELISTS

AND PROSE WRITERS

Great Writers of the English Language

Poets

Novelists and Prose Writers

Dramatists

GREAT WRITERS OF THE ENGLISH LANGUAGE

NOVELISTS

AND PROSE WRITERS

EDITOR
JAMES VINSON

ASSOCIATE EDITOR
D. L. KIRKPATRICK

ST. MARTIN'S PRESS
NEW YORK

All rights reserved. For information write:
ST. MARTIN'S PRESS
175 Fifth Avenue
New York, New York 10010

ISBN 0–312–34624–7
Library of Congress Catalog Card Number 78–78302

Typeset by Computacomp (UK) Ltd.,
Fort William, Scotland

CONTENTS

EDITOR'S NOTE

The selection of writers included in this book is based on the recommendations of the advisers listed on page ix.

The entry for each writer consists of a biography, a complete list of his published books, a selected list of published bibliographies and critical studies on the writer, and a signed critical essay on his work.

In the biographies, details of education, military service, and marriage(s) are generally given before the usual chronological summary of the life of the writer; awards and honours are given last.

The Publications section is meant to include all book publications, though as a rule broadsheets, single sermons and lectures, minor pamphlets, exhibition catalogues, etc. are omitted. Under the heading Collections, we have listed the most recent collections of the complete works and those of individual genres (verse, plays, novels, stories, and letters); only those collections which have some editorial authority and were issued after the writer's death are listed; on-going editions are indicated by a dash after the date of publication; often a general selection from the writer's works or a selection from the works in the individual genres listed above is included.

Titles are given in modern spelling, though the essayists were allowed to use original spelling for titles and quotations; often the titles are "short." The date given is that of the first book publication, which often followed the first periodical or anthology publication by some time; we have listed the actual year of publication, often different from that given on the title-page. No attempt has been made to indicate which works were published anonymously or pseudonymously, or which works of fiction were published in more than one volume. We have listed plays which were produced but not published, but only since 1700; librettos and musical plays are listed along with the other plays; no attempt has been made to list lost or unverified plays. Reprints of books (including facsimile editions) and revivals of plays are not listed unless a revision or change of title is involved. The most recent edited version of individual works is included if it supersedes the collected edition cited.

In the essays, short references to critical remarks refer to items cited in the Publications section or in the Reading List. Introductions, memoirs, editorial matter, etc. in works cited in the Publications section are not repeated in the Reading List.

We would like to thank the advisers and contributors for their patience and help.

ADVISERS

Walter Allen
F. W. Bateson
Bernard Bergonzi
Earle Birney
Ruby Cohn
Allen Curnow
Warren French
John C. Gerber
Roma Gill
Daniel Hoffman
C. Hugh Holman
Louis James
A. Norman Jeffares
Lewis Leary
David Lodge

W. H. New
Roy Harvey Pearce
George Perkins
John M. Reilly
H. Winston Rhodes
Pat Rogers
Gāmini Salgādo
C. K. Stead
James Sutherland
Derek A. Traversi
Gerald Weales
Margaret Willy
James Woodress
Judith Wright

CONTRIBUTORS

Peter Alcock
Walter Allen
David D. Anderson
W. E. K. Anderson
James Angle
Leonard R. N. Ashley
James C. Austin
Gillian Avery
John Barnes
Martin C. Battestin
Miriam J. Benkovitz
George N. Bennett
Gabriel Bergonzi
Dominic J. Bisignano
Jean Frantz Blackall
Edward A. Bloom
Lynn Z. Bloom
Joseph Blotner
Walter Bode
Vernon Bogdanor
Theophilus E. M. Boll
Margaret Bottrall
Ronald Bottrall
J. S. Bratton
Neville Braybrooke
Alan Brissenden
Lawrence R. Broer
Ashley Brown
Lloyd W. Brown
Mary Brown

Martin Bucco
R. A. Burchell
Ian Campbell
Geoffrey Carnall
Frederic I. Carpenter
Janice M. Cauwels
John R. Clark
A. O. J. Cockshut
Hennig Cohen
Morton N. Cohen
Ruby Cohn
John Colmer
R. A. Copland
Neil Corcoran
Martha Heasley Cox
Patricia Craddock
Patricia Craig
Curtis Dahl
Walter R. Davis
Michael DePorte
Elizabeth Story Donno
Dennis G. Donovan
J. A. Downie
Charles Doyle
R. P. Draper
Geoffrey Dutton
Louise Duus
Peter Easingwood
Anne Henry Ehrenpreis
Clayton L. Eichelberger

Chester E. Eisinger
Brian Elliott
Patrick Evans
Charles Fanning
Philip José Farmer
Peter Faulkner
Ian Fletcher
Joseph M. Flora
Herbert Foltinek
Edward Halsey Foster
G. S. Fraser
R. B. D. French
Warren French
John C. Gerber
Winifred Gérin
Roma Gill
Barbara Gitenstein
Clarence A. Glasrud
Ian A. Gordon
Lois Gordon
Dorothy Green
Roger Lancelyn Green
Ian Greenlees
Ernest Griffin
Andrew Gurr
William F. Halloran
Clive Hart
Gwynneth Hatton
William J. Heim
Jack Hicks
William Higgins
J. C. Hilson
Bert Hitchcock
Jacqueline Hoefer
Daniel Hoffman
Jan Hokenson
C. Hugh Holman
Derek Hudson
William J. Hyde
M. Thomas Inge
Randolph Ivy
A. Norman Jeffares
Estelle C. Jelinek
Jay Jernigan
Lawrence Jones
M. K. Joseph
Nancy C. Joyner
Martin Kallich
Bruce Kellner
Gary Kelly
Malcolm Kelsall
Peter Kemp
Burton Kendle
I. T. Ker

Brian Kiernan
Kimball King
Keneth Kinnamon
Chirantan Kulshrestha
Lewis Leary
Margaret B. Lewis
Maurice Lindsay
Bruce A. Lohof
George C. Longest
John Lucas
Townsend Ludington
Douglas S. Mack
Brent MacLaine
Norman Macleod
Frank MacShane
David Madden
Hena Maes-Jelinek
Derek Mahon
Suzanne Marrs
W. J. McCormack
David McCracken
Paul D. McGlynn
Howard McNaughton
Stephen Medcalf
Christian H. Moe
Jack B. Moore
Rayburn S. Moore
Margery Morgan
J. E. Morpurgo
Katharine M. Morsberger
Robert E. Morsberger
John Muirhead
John M. Munro
I. B. Nadel
Bruce Nesbitt
Francis M. Nevins, Jr.
Alastair Niven
Brady Nordland
Robert Nye
George O'Brien
Thomas F. O'Donnell
B. C. Oliver-Morden
Malcolm Page
C. A. Patrides
William Peden
Barbara M. Perkins
George Perkins
Kirsten Holst Petersen
F. B. Pinion
Arthur Pollard
Edward Martin Potoker
Peter Quartermain
Eric Quayle
Gloria Rawlinson

C. J. Rawson
John Q. Reed
Ian Reid
John M. Reilly
Sylvia Lyons Render
William D. Reynolds
Robert F. Richards
John Richetti
Donald A. Ringe
Pat Rogers
Earl Rovit
James E. Ruoff
Anna Rutherford
A. J. Sambrook
Stewart F. Sanderson
George Brandon Saul
Arnold T. Schwab
Daniel R. Schwarz
Brian W. M. Scobie
Brocard Sewell
Per Seyersted
J. N. Sharma
Joanne Shattock
Alan R. Shucard
David J. Smith
Elton E. Smith
Esther Marian Greenwell Smith
Rowland Smith
Stan Smith
Martin Stannard
Madeleine B. Stern
Edward Stokes
David Stouck

W. J. Stuckey
John Sutherland
Wesley D. Sweetser
G. T. Tanselle
Ned Thomas
Peter Thomson
Ann Thwaite
E. W. F. Tomlin
Clarence Tracy
James Trainer
Simon Trussler
William M. Tydeman
Stephen Wall
Mark I. Wallach
Richard Walser
George Walsh
Marcus Walsh
William Walsh
Alan Warner
Val Warner
Harold H. Watts
Gerald Weales
Sybil B. Weir
P. D. Westbrook
John Stuart Williams
Margaret Willy
T. J. Winnifrith
Maurice Wohlgelernter
Peter Wolfe
George Woodcock
James Woodress
George J. Worth
Kenneth Young

NOVELISTS

AND PROSE WRITERS

Peter Abrahams
Chinua Achebe
Henry Adams
Joseph Addison
George Ade
James Agee
Conrad Aiken
William Harrison Ainsworth
Louisa May Alcott
Richard Aldington
Horatio Alger
Nelson Algren
James Lane Allen
Kingsley Amis
Mulk Raj Anand
Sherwood Anderson
Michael Arlen
Timothy Shay Arthur
Gertrude Atherton
Louis Auchincloss
Jane Austen

Francis Bacon
Robert Bage
James Baldwin
Joseph G. Baldwin
R. M. Ballantyne
John Banim
Maurice Baring
Sabine Baring-Gould
Djuna Barnes
John Barth
Donald Barthelme
H. E. Bates
L. Frank Baum
Samuel Beckett
William Beckford
Max Beerbohm
Edward Bellamy
Saul Bellow
Ludwig Bemelmans
Robert Benchley
Arnold Bennett
E. F. Benson
Stella Benson
Walter Besant
Ambrose Bierce
R. D. Blackmore
Maxwell Bodenheim
Rolf Boldrewood
George Borrow
James Boswell
Elizabeth Bowen
Paul Bowles

James Boyd
Martin Boyd
H. H. Boyesen
Kay Boyle
Roger Boyle
Hugh Henry Brackenridge
Mary Elizabeth Braddon
Roark Bradford
John Braine
Louis Bromfield
Anne Brontë
Charlotte Brontë
Emily Brontë
Charles Brockden Brown
Tom Brown
William Wells Brown
Sir Thomas Browne
John Buchan
Pearl S. Buck
Edward Bulwer-Lytton
John Bunyan
Edmund Burke
Frances Hodgson Burnett
Fanny Burney
Edgar Rice Burroughs
William S. Burroughs
Robert Burton
Samuel Butler

James Branch Cabell
George Washington Cable
Abraham Cahan
James M. Cain
Erskine Caldwell
Hortense Calisher
Morley Callaghan
Truman Capote
William Carleton
Thomas Carlyle
Lewis Carroll
Joyce Cary
Willa Cather
Raymond Chandler
John Cheever
Charles Waddell Chesnutt
G. K. Chesterton
Kate Chopin
Agatha Christie
Winston Churchill
Walter Van Tilburg Clark
Marcus Clarke
John Cleland
William Cobbett
Wilkie Collins

Ivy Compton-Burnett
Joseph Conrad
John Esten Cooke
James Fenimore Cooper
A. E. Coppard
Marie Corelli
James Courage
James Gould Cozzens
Stephen Crane
F. Marion Crawford

Edward Dahlberg
Richard Henry Dana, Jr.
Robertson Davies
Dan Davin
Rebecca Harding Davis
Richard Harding Davis
Daniel Defoe
John William De Forest
Margaret Deland
Mazo de la Roche
Floyd Dell
Thomas Deloney
William De Morgan
Thomas De Quincey
Charles Dickens
Benjamin Disraeli
Ignatius Donnelly
John Dos Passos
Norman Douglas
Arthur Conan Doyle
Theodore Dreiser
W. E. B. Du Bois
Maurice Duggan
Daphne du Maurier
George du Maurier
Finley Peter Dunne
Lawrence Durrell

Maria Edgeworth
Pierce Egan
Edward Eggleston
Cyprian Ekwensi
George Eliot
Ralph Ellison
Ralph Waldo Emerson

James T. Farrell
William Faulkner
Edna Ferber
Susan Ferrier
Henry Fielding
Sarah Fielding
Roderick Finlayson

Ronald Firbank
Vardis Fisher
F. Scott Fitzgerald
Ian Fleming
Ford Madox Ford
C. S. Forester
E. M. Forster
Hannah Foster
Janet Frame
Waldo Frank
Harold Frederic
Mary E. Wilkins Freeman
Henry Blake Fuller
Joseph Furphy

William Gaddis
Zona Gale
John Galsworthy
John Galt
Erle Stanley Gardner
Hamlin Garland
David Garnett
Elizabeth Gaskell
William Gerhardie
Edward Gibbon
Lewis Grassic Gibbon
George Gissing
Ellen Glasgow
William Godwin
Michael Gold
William Golding
Oliver Goldsmith
Paul Goodman
Nadine Gordimer
Caroline Gordon
Catherine Gore
R. B. Cunninghame Graham
Kenneth Grahame
Richard Graves
Robert Graves
Henry Green
Graham Greene
Robert Greene
Zane Grey
Gerald Griffin
Edith Searle Grossman
George Grossmith
Frederick Philip Grove
Neil M. Gunn

H. Rider Haggard
Thomas Chandler Haliburton
Dashiell Hammett
James Hanley

Thomas Hardy
George Washington Harris
Joel Chandler Harris
Wilson Harris
Bret Harte
L. P. Hartley
John Hawkes
Nathaniel Hawthorne
Eliza Haywood
William Hazlitt
Lafcadio Hearn
Joseph Heller
Ernest Hemingway
O. Henry
G. A. Henty
Xavier Herbert
Joseph Hergesheimer
Robert Herrick
DuBose Heyward
Thomas Hobbes
James Hogg
Thomas Holcroft
Oliver Wendell Holmes
Theodore Hook
Johnson Jones Hooper
Anthony Hope
E. W. Howe
William Dean Howells
W. H. Hudson
Richard Hughes
Thomas Hughes
James Huneker
Leigh Hunt
Zora Neale Hurston
Aldous Huxley
Robin Hyde

Elizabeth Inchbald
Joseph Holt Ingraham
Washington Irving
Christopher Isherwood

Helen Hunt Jackson
Shirley Jackson
W. W. Jacobs
Henry James
M. R. James
Richard Jefferies
Jerome K. Jerome
Sarah Orne Jewett
Ruth Prawer Jhabvala
Pamela Hansford Johnson
Samuel Johnson
James Jones

James Joyce

Anna Kavan
Thomas Keneally
John Pendleton Kennedy
Jack Kerouac
Charles Kingsley
Henry Kingsley
Rudyard Kipling
Joseph Kirkland
Arthur Koestler
Jerzy Kosinski

Oliver La Farge
Charles Lamb
George Lamming
Walter Savage Landor
Ring Lardner
Margaret Laurence
Mary Lavin
D. H. Lawrence
Henry Lawson
Stephen Leacock
John Lee
Sheridan Le Fanu
Rosamond Lehmann
Charlotte Lennox
Doris Lessing
Charles Lever
Ada Leverson
C. S. Lewis
Matthew Gregory Lewis
Sinclair Lewis
Wyndham Lewis
Jack Lindsay
Eric Linklater
Ross Lockridge
Thomas Lodge
Jack London
Augustus Baldwin Longstreet
H. P. Lovecraft
Samuel Lover
Malcolm Lowry
John Lyly
Andrew Lytle

Rose Macaulay
Thomas Babington Macaulay
George MacDonald
Arthur Machen
Colin MacInnes
Compton Mackenzie
Henry Mackenzie
Hugh MacLennan

5

Norman Mailer
Roger Mais
Bernard Malamud
William Hurrell Mallock
Thomas Malory
Jane Mander
Delariviere Manley
Olivia Manning
Katherine Mansfield
John P. Marquand
Don Marquis
Frederick Marryat
Ngaio Marsh
Harriet Martineau
A. E. W. Mason
Charles Robert Maturin
W. Somerset Maugham
Mary McCarthy
Carson McCullers
Herman Melville
H. L. Mencken
George Meredith
Henry Miller
A. A. Milne
Donald Grant Mitchell
Margaret Mitchell
S. Weir Mitchell
Nancy Mitford
Edgar Mittelholzer
Brian Moore
George Moore
John Moore
Hannah More
Charles Morgan
Sydney Owenson, Lady Morgan
Christopher Morley
Wright Morris
Arthur Morrison
Willard Motley
John Mulgan
Dinah Maria Mulock
Iris Murdoch
Mary Noailles Murfree
L. H. Myers

Vladimir Nabokov
V. S. Naipaul
R. K. Narayan
Petroleum V. Nasby
Thomas Nashe
John Neal
P. H. Newby
John Henry Newman
Anaïs Nin

Frank Norris

Fitz-James O'Brien
Flann O'Brien
Flannery O'Connor
Frank O'Connor
Seán O'Faoláin
Liam O'Flaherty
John O'Hara
Margaret Oliphant
Amelia Opie
George Orwell
Ouida

Thomas Nelson Page
Vance Palmer
Robert Paltock
Dorothy Parker
Walter Pater
Alan Paton
James Kirke Paulding
Thomas Love Peacock
Mervyn Peake
Walker Percy
S. J. Perelman
David Graham Phillips
William Plomer
Edgar Allan Poe
Hal Porter
Katherine Anne Porter
Anthony Powell
J. F. Powers
John Cowper Powys
T. F. Powys
J. B. Priestley
V. S. Pritchett
James Purdy
Thomas Pynchon

Ellery Queen
Arthur Quiller-Couch

Ann Radcliffe
Raja Rao
Marjorie Kinnan Rawlings
Charles Reade
Clara Reeve
Vic Reid
Mary Renault
Jean Rhys
Barnaby Rich
Dorothy Richardson
Henry Handel Richardson
Samuel Richardson

Mordecai Richler
Conrad Richter
Mary Roberts Rinehart
Elizabeth Madox Roberts
Kenneth Roberts
Frederick Rolfe
O. E. Rølvaag
Martin Ross
Sinclair Ross
Henry Roth
Philip Roth
Susanna Rowson
Steele Rudd
Damon Runyon
John Ruskin
Mark Rutherford

Saki
J. D. Salinger
Edgar Saltus
William Sansom
George Santayana
Frank Sargeson
William Saroyan
Henry Savary
Dorothy L. Sayers
Olive Schreiner
Sir Walter Scott
Catharine Maria Sedgwick
Samuel Selvon
Maurice Shadbolt
William Sharp
Henry Wheeler Shaw
Mary Shelley
Joseph Henry Shorthouse
Sir Philip Sidney
Alan Sillitoe
William Gilmore Simms
May Sinclair
Upton Sinclair
Isaac Bashevis Singer
Charlotte Smith
Seba Smith
Tobias Smollett
C. P. Snow
Edith Somerville
Muriel Spark
Jean Stafford
Christina Stead
Richard Steele
Wilbur Daniel Steele
Gertrude Stein
John Steinbeck
Laurence Sterne

Robert Louis Stevenson
Bram Stoker
David Storey
Rex Stout
Randolph Stow
Harriet Beecher Stowe
T. S. Stribling
L. A. G. Strong
William Styron
Ruth Suckow
R. S. Surtees
Jonathan Swift

Booth Tarkington
Elizabeth Taylor
Kylie Tennant
William Makepeace Thackeray
Henry David Thoreau
Thomas Bangs Thorpe

James Thurber
J. R. R. Tolkien
Jean Toomer
Albion W. Tourgée
B. Traven
Robert Tressell
Lionel Trilling
Anthony Trollope
Amos Tutuola
Mark Twain

John Updike
Edward Upward

Laurens van der Post
Carl Van Vechten
Gore Vidal
Kurt Vonnegut, Jr.

Edgar Wallace
Lew Wallace
Edward Lewis Wallant
Horace Walpole
Hugh Walpole
Izaak Walton
Artemus Ward
Mrs. Humphry Ward
Charles Dudley Warner
Rex Warner
Sylvia Townsend Warner
Robert Penn Warren
Price Warung
Evelyn Waugh
Denton Welch

H. G. Wells
Eudora Welty
Glenway Wescott
Nathanael West
Rebecca West
Edith Wharton
E. B. White
Patrick White
T. H. White
Thornton Wilder
Charles Williams
Henry Williamson
Nathaniel Parker Willis
Angus Wilson

Edmund Wilson
Ethel Wilson
Owen Wister
P. G. Wodehouse
Thomas Wolfe
Virginia Woolf
Constance Fenimore Woolson
Richard Wright

Frank Yerby
Charlotte Yonge

Israel Zangwill

ABRAHAMS, Peter (Henry).   South African.   Born in Vrededorp, near Johannesburg, 19 March 1919. Educated at Church of England mission schools in South Africa. Married 1) Dorothy Pennington in 1942 (divorced, 1948); 2) Daphne Elizabeth Miller in 1948, one son and two daughters. Worked in South Africa as a kitchen helper, porter and clerk, also as an editor in Durban; seaman, 1939–41; settled in England, 1941–56, and lived in France, 1948–50; regular contributor to *The Observer*, London, and the *Herald Tribune*, New York and Paris, 1952–64; emigrated to Jamaica, 1956: Editor, *West Indian Economist*, and Controller, "West Indian News" program, Jamaica, 1958–62. Lives in St. Andrews, Jamaica.

PUBLICATIONS

Fiction

> *Dark Testament* (stories).   1942.
> *Song of the City*.   1945.
> *Mine Boy*.   1946.
> *The Path of Thunder*.   1948.
> *Wild Conquest*.   1950.
> *A Wreath for Udomo*.   1956.
> *A Night of Their Own*.   1965.
> *This Island Now*.   1966.

Verse

> *A Blackman Speaks of Freedom! Poems*.   1938(?).
> *Here, Friend*.   N.d.

Other

> *Return to Goli* (reportage).   1953.
> *Tell Freedom: Memories of Africa*.   1954.
> *Jamaica: An Island Mosaic*.   1957.
> *The World of Mankind*, with others.   1962.

Reading List: *Abrahams* by Michael Wade, 1972.

*   *   *

Peter Abrahams has spent more of his life outside South Africa than in it (he left there in 1939 when he was twenty years of age) but the impact of the South African system on him in his formative years has been such that with one exception all his work has been set in Africa and deals with racial conflict, oppression, economic injustice, and social and political deprivation. The one exception is *This Island Now*, which is set in Jamaica. It is easy to see why Peter Abrahams chose Jamaica, for, given the conditions which exist there, he is able to explore the same themes which concern him and show them at work in a slightly different setting.

His most successful writing is to be found in his non-fiction, particularly in his autobiography, *Tell Freedom*. Here he describes his early life in South Africa, the frustrations

9

and humiliations he suffered, and the growing disillusionment until he reached the decision that he must leave. What adds an extra dimension to this work is "the portrait of the artist as a young man" flavour which it possesses. The incompatability of art and apartheid was a major factor in his choice of exile.

His fiction deals with familiar South African themes: the boy who leaves the village for the town (*Mine Boy*), the dilemma of the coloured (*The Path of Thunder*). He moves away from the expected in *Wild Conquest*, which deals with the Great Trek and the clash between the Boers and the Matabele, and in *A Wreath for Udomo*, which is set in a fictitious African state in 1956 (Ghana comes most readily to mind).

Abrahams never makes facile judgements, the truth is rarely simple. For example, Boer and Matabele alike are criticized in *Wild Conquest*, and in *A Wreath for Udomo* there are no easy solutions to the dilemmas facing the leader of a newly independent African state. Abrahams's greatest weakness lies in his depiction of character. They lack psychological depth and tend to become romanticized mouth-pieces for Abrahams's ideas. It is almost certain that his reputation as an artist is likely to decrease and his main interest will be as a phenomenon of literary history.

—Anna Rutherford

ACHEBE, Chinua. Nigerian. Born Albert Chinualumogu in Ogidi, East Central State, 16 November 1930. Educated at the Government College, Umuahia, 1944–47; University College, Ibadan, 1948–53, B.A. (London) 1953. Married Christie Okoli in 1961; two sons and two daughters. Talks Producer, Lagos, 1954–57, Controller, Enugu, 1958–61, and Director, Lagos, 1961–66, Nigerian Broadcasting Corporation; Co-Founder, with Christopher Okigbo, and Chairman, Citadel Books Ltd., Enugu, 1967. Since 1967, Senior Research Fellow, University of Nigeria, Nsukka. Visiting Professor, University of Massachusetts, Amherst, 1972–73, University of Connecticut, Storrs, 1975. Founding Editor, Heinemann African Writers series, 1962–72, and since 1970 Director, Heinemann Educational Books (Nigeria) Ltd., and Nwankwo-Ifejika Ltd., publishers, Enugu. Since 1971, Editor, *Okike*, a Nigerian journal of new writing. Travelled to the United States, with Gabriel Okara and Cyprian Ekwensi, to seek help for Biafra, 1969. Member, University of Lagos Council, 1966; Chairman, Society of Nigerian Authors, 1966. Since 1971, Member of the East Central State Library Board. Recipient: Margaret Wrong Memorial Prize, 1959; Nigerian National Trophy, 1960; Rockefeller Fellowship, 1960; UNESCO Fellowship, 1963; Commonwealth Poetry Prize, 1973; Neil Gunn International Fellowship, 1974. D.Litt.: University of Stirling, Scotland, 1974; University of Southampton, Hampshire, 1974. Honorary Fellow, Modern Language Association of America, 1974; Fellow, Ghana Association of Writers, 1975. Lives in Nigeria.

PUBLICATIONS

Fiction

Things Fall Apart. 1958.
No Longer at Ease. 1960.
The Sacrificial Egg and Other Stories. 1962.
Arrow of God. 1964.

A Man of the People.   1966.
Girls at War (stories).   1972.

Verse

Beware Soul-Brother and Other Poems.   1971; revised edition, 1972.
Christmas in Biafra and Other Poems.   1973.

Other

Chike and the River (juvenile).   1966.
How the Leopard Got His Claws (juvenile).   1972.
Morning Yet on Creation Day.   1975.
In Person: Achebe, Awooner, and Soyinka at the University of Washington.   1975.

Editor, *The Insider: Stories of War and Peace from Nigeria.*   1971.

Bibliography: in *Africana Library Journal,* Spring 1970.

Reading List: *The Novels of Achebe* by G. D. Killam, 1969; *Achebe* by Arthur Ravenscroft, 1969; *Achebe* by David Carroll, 1970; *Achebe* edited by Bernth Lindfors and C. L. Innes, 1978.

*   *   *

Chinua Achebe published four novels between 1958 and 1966, but since that time has turned to short stories and poetry. The turbulent history of Nigeria in the last ten years may explain this shift, especially as Achebe is an Ibo and thus sadly involved in the Biafran war. Some of Achebe's novels, while they are obviously relevant to the confused situation in Nigeria today, are also impressive records of Nigeria's past.

In *Things Fall Apart,* perhaps his most impressive work, Achebe describes the fall of Okonkwo, a tribal chieftain unable to accommodate himself to the new values brought in by English missionaries. While Achebe is careful not to take sides in the conflict between African and European values, the tragedy of Okonkwo is such that we are sympathetic to his side, especially as the African code of behaviour is shown to be more fluid than that of the missionaries. It is Okonkwo's failure to recognize this fluidity which causes his downfall. In *No Longer at Ease,* we see Okonkwo's grandson Obi, living in the 1950's, in a similar dilemma as he tries to reconcile the claims of his African tribe and the lessons he has learnt in Europe. *No Longer at Ease,* a slight work, shows Obi's decline into corruption, a decline never satisfactorily explained. In *Arrow of God,* Achebe returns to the past, this time to the 1920's when Nigerian tribal life has to accommodate itself to the colonial administration. Both Ezeulu, the tribal priest, and Winterbottom, the Colonial administrator, fail because they try to impose their own rigid deterministic philosophy on an intransigent world. In *A Man of the People,* we have the familiar conflict between the virtuous but priggish narrator Odih and the corrupt but charming politician Nanga as they struggle for power in a newly independent state. Corruption wins, and the conclusion of the novel is a pessimistic one. Achebe is a little uncertain in his use of the first person narrative in the last novel, but all his novels are stylistically effective, especially in the use of dialogue, where the subtle variation of stately African phrases, their slightly absurd literal translations, pidgin English, and the formal English of administrators and missionaries serve to point the conflicts he is describing.

—T. J. Winnifrith

ADAMS, Henry (Brooks). American. Born in Boston, Massachusetts, 16 February 1838; great grandson of John Adams, grandson of John Quincy Adams, and son of the writer Charles Francis Adams. Educated at Harvard University, Cambridge, Massachusetts, 1854–58, A.B. 1858; studied law at the University of Berlin, 1858–59. Married Marian Hooper in 1872 (died, 1885). Lived in Dresden, 1859–60; travelled in Italy, writing for the *Boston Courier*, 1860; Private Secretary to his father, when Congressman from Massachusetts, in Washington, D.C., 1860–61, and when Minister to the Court of St. James, London, 1861–68; lived in Washington, D.C., and again in London, contributing to various American periodicals, 1869; Editor, *North American Review*, Boston, and Assistant Professor of History, Harvard University, 1870–76; settled in Washington, D.C.; in later life spent six months in each year in France. LL.D.: Western Reserve University, Cleveland, 1892. Member, American Academy of Arts and Letters. *Died 26 March 1918.*

PUBLICATIONS

Collections

 Letters, edited by Worthington Chauncey Ford. 2 vols., 1930–38.
 A Henry Adams Reader, edited by Elizabeth Stevenson. 1958.
 The Education of Henry Adams and Other Selected Writings, edited by Edward N.
  Saveth. 1965.

Fiction

 Democracy: An American Novel. 1880.
 Esther. 1884.

Other

 Chapters of Erie and Other Essays, with Charles Francis Adams, Jr. 1871.
 Essays in Anglo-Saxon Law. 1876.
 The Life of Albert Gallatin. 1879.
 John Randolph. 1882; revised edition, 1883.
 History of the United States of America During the Administration of Jefferson and
  Madison. 9 vols., 1889–91; abridged version edited by Herbert Agar, as *The
  Formative Years*, 2 vols., 1947.
 Historical Essays. 1891.
 Memoirs of Marau, Last Queen of Tahiti. 1893; as *Memoirs of Arii*, 1901; edited by
  Robert E. Spiller, as *Tahiti: Memoirs of Arii Taimai*, 1947.
 Recognition of Cuban Independence. 1896.
 Mont-Saint-Michel and Chartres. 1904; revised edition, 1912.
 The Education of Henry Adams: An Autobiography. 1907; edited by Ernest Samuels,
  1974.
 A Letter to American Teachers of History. 1910.
 The Life of George Cabot Lodge. 1911.
 The Degradation of the Democratic Dogma. 1919.
 Letters to a Neice and Prayer to the Virgin of Chartres, edited by Worthington Chauncey
  Ford. 1920.
 Henry Adams and His Friends: A Collection of His Unpublished Letters, edited by Harold
  Dean Cater. 1947.

Selected Letters, edited by Newton Arvin. 1951.
The Great Secession Winter of 1860–61 and Other Essays, edited by George Hochfield. 1958.

Editor, *Documents Relating to New England Federalism 1800–1815.* 1877.
Editor, *The Writings of Albert Gallatin.* 3 vols., 1879.
Editor, with Clara Louise Hay, *Letters of John Hay and Extracts from Diary.* 3 vols., 1908.

Reading List: *The Young Henry Adams, Adams: The Middle Years,* and *Adams: The Major Phase* by Ernest Samuels, 1948–64; *The Mind and Art of Adams* by J. C. Levenson, 1957; *Adams* by George Hochfield, 1962; *The Suspension of Adams: A Study of Manner and Matter* by Vern Wager, 1969; *A Formula of His Own: Adams's Literary Experiment* by John Conder, 1970; *Symbol and Idea in Adams* by Melvin E. Lyon, 1970; *Adams* by Louis Auchincloss, 1971; *Adams* by James G. Murray, 1974; *The Force So Much Closer Home: Adams and the Adams Family* by Earl N. Harbert, 1977.

* * *

Standing in much the same relation to American culture in the latter half of the 19th century that Emerson did to the earlier period, Adams might be said to have made a distinguished and melancholy career out of being the right sensibility for the wrong time and place. Dedicated to public service but shunted to the sidelines, genuinely committed to the orderly development of democratic processes but disillusioned by the post-Civil War expansionism that has been called "The Big Barbecue," Adams gradually contracted the sphere of his idealism, his sociality, and the generosity of his responses to a diminished center of bleak pessimism. Even so, this proved to be a sufficient base on which was built a noteworthy career as teacher (Harvard University), editor (*North American Review*), novelist (*Democracy* and *Esther*), and historian. The two novels deal with pressing issues of the period, the growth of business in government and the strength of science in terms of religious dogma. It is, however, in his twin meditations, *Mont-Saint-Michel and Chartres* and *The Education of Henry Adams,* that his erudition and mastery of the ironic mode fuse with a sombre lyricism to produce a pair of eccentric masterpieces that combine autobiography, philosophy of history, and saturnine prophecy.

Respectively subtitled "A Study of Thirteenth-Century Unity" and "A Study of Twentieth-Century Multiplicity," the books establish the figures of the virgin and the dynamo as the historically dominant symbols of forces that shape the values, the social organization, and the concepts of personality in both time-periods. The replacement of the former by the latter, in Adams's view, exemplifies what he believed to be the scientific principle of the acceleration of history. In these terms he attempts to understand and explain the loss of stable certitudes, the increased fragmentation of social groups, and the new burden of impotence and isolation on the individual psyche. Adams doubtless believed that his own shattered private life was an accurate reflection of this larger social and metaphysical explosion, and this personal despair lends a tone of mordant authority to his prose which almost precisely counters the accents of Emerson's optimism. Brilliant, acerbic, and unsparing in its effort to conduct a grim cultural biopsy, Adams's work consummately articulates the outrage of the Genteel Tradition and stands as a major formulation of the ideology that would later be expressed by such alienated writers as Eliot and Pound.

—Earl Rovit

ADDISON, Joseph. English. Born in Milston, Wiltshire, 1 May 1672. Educated at schools in Amesbury, Salisbury, and Lichfield; Charterhouse, London, where he met Richard Steele; Queen's College, Oxford, 1687–89, and Magdalen College, Oxford, 1689–93, M.A. 1693. Married Charlotte, Dowager Countess of Warwick, 1716. Fellow of Magdalen College, 1698–1711; received government pension, 1699, and travelled in France, Italy, Germany, and Holland, 1699–1704: served under Prince Eugene in Italy as a "Secretary from the King," 1702; settled in London; member of the Kit-Cat Club, and embarked on a political career in the service of the Whigs: Commissioner of Appeal in Excise, 1704–08; Under-Secretary of State, 1705; Secretary to Lord Halifax on his mission to Hanover, 1707; Member of Parliament for Lostwithiel, 1708–10, and for Malmesbury, 1710 until the end of his life; Secretary to Lord Wharton, Lord Lieutenant of Ireland, 1708–10; Editor, *Whig Examiner*, 1710; contributor to Steele's *Tatler*, 1709–11, and Co-Editor, with Steele, and major contributor to *Spectator*, 1711–12, then sole Editor of the revived *Spectator*, 1714; contributor to Steele's *Guardian*, 1713; purchased the estate of Bilton, near Rugby, 1713; after accession of George I, Secretary to Earl of Sunderland, as Lord Lieutenant of Ireland, 1714–15; appointed a commissioner for trade and the colonies, 1715; Editor, *The Freeholder*, London, 1715–16; Secretary of State in the Sunderland cabinet, 1717–18. *Died 17 June 1719.*

PUBLICATIONS

Collections

   Miscellaneous Works, edited by Adolph C. Guthkelch.   2 vols., 1914.
   Letters, edited by Walter Graham.   1941.

Essays and Prose Works

   Remarks on Several Parts of Italy.   1705; revised edition, 1718.
   The Present State of the War and the Necessity of an Augmentation Considered.   1708.
   The Tatler, with Steele.   4 vols., 1710–11; edited by G. A. Aitken, 4 vols., 1898–99;
      selections edited by L. Gibbs, 1953.
   The Spectator, with Steele.   8 vols., 1712–15; edited by D. F. Bond, 5 vols., 1965;
      selections edited by R. J. Allen, 1957.
   The Late Trial and Conviction of Count Tariff.   1713.
   The Guardian, with others.   2 vols., 1714; edited by Alexander Chalmers, 1802.
   The Free-Holder; or, Political Essays.   1716.
   A Dissertation upon the Most Celebrated Roman Poets.   1718.
   The Old Whig.   1720.
   Miscellanies in Verse and Prose.   1725.
   A Discourse on Ancient and Modern Learning.   1734.
   Critical Essays from The Spectator, edited by D. F. Bond.   1970.

Plays

   Rosamond, music by Thomas Clayton (produced 1707).   1707.
   Cato (produced 1713).   1713.
   The Drummer; or, The Haunted House (produced 1716).   1716.

Verse

   A Poem to His Majesty.   1695.

The Campaign. 1705.
Poems on Several Occasions. 1719.
The Christian Poet: A Miscellany of Divine Poems. 1728.

Other Works

Works, edited by Thomas Tickell. 4 vols., 1721.

Editor, *Musarum Anglicanarum*, vol. 2. 1699.

Reading List: *The Life of Addison* by Peter Smithers, 1954, revised edition, 1968; *Steele, Addison, and Their Periodical Essays* by Arthur R. Humphreys, 1959; *The Cultural Milieu of Addison's Literary Criticism* by Lee A. Elioscff, 1963; *Natur und Landschaft bei Addison* by Hans J. Possin, 1965; *Addison's Sociable Animal* by Edward A. and Lillian D. Bloom, 1971.

*   *   *

Joseph Addison's high reputation in the eighteenth and nineteenth centuries was based upon his essays for *The Spectator* (1711–12), a daily periodical edited in conjunction with Richard Steele, but to which Addison was the major contributor. It was revived in 1714 entirely under Addison's control (nos. 556–635). *The Spectator* derived from Steele's *The Tatler* (1709–11), for which Addison wrote, and led on to *The Guardian* (1713). It is an invidious task to distinguish between the two writers, especially in their application of wit to the reform of manners, and in the sharp particularity with which they describe the contemporary scene.

Addison, however, was the more philosophical moralist. The lay sermons which distinguish the Saturday papers in *The Spectator* were his. So too were the major series of critical essays. The character of Sir Roger de Coverley, although invented by Steele, was especially developed by Addison (nos. 106–31), and the limpid elegance of Addison's studied but easy style has generally been preferred to Steele's more careless manner.

Their relationship began at Charterhouse School, and continued at Oxford and in the Kit-Cat Club where many of the leading wits and Whigs gathered under the auspices of Jacob Tonson the publisher. Addison's pretentions to a serious career, however, were weightier than Steele's. He spent twelve years at Oxford where he had achieved considerable distinction, becoming a fellow of Magdalen. Thereafter his political career in the service of the Whig party led him to high office as Secretary of State (and to his marriage with the Dowager Countess of Warwick). Thus many of his works, for instance, "The Dialogues upon Ancient Medals" and *Remarks on Italy*, have a strong scholarly bias, and the most famous of his plays, the tragedy *Cato*, combines classical learning with a strong political bias, for the celebration of the Roman Republic was taken by his friends as an indictment of the tyrannical pretentions of the Tory Jacobites and praise of the Whig hero, the Duke of Marlborough (also the subject of Addison's best known poem *The Campaign*). At the end of his life it was politics which led to his estrangement from Steele (see *The Old Whig*) and may even have prompted Pope's long-delayed satiric portrait of Addison as Atticus in *An Epistle to Dr. Arbuthnot* (1735), although the original cause of that quarrel probably derived from Pope's belief that Addison was sponsoring a rival translation of Homer. Addison's last major venture into periodical journalism, *The Freeholder* (1715–16) is Party propaganda, and even in *The Spectator*, where the editors deliberately avoided political controversy, the de Coverley papers contain a political barb fleshed with humour. Although the rustic squire is almost always amiable and charms the reader, the sentimental comedy only partially conceals the fact that Sir Roger is of the wrong political persuasion, and is a man to whom no one would entrust public affairs, or private business.

The main stream of Addison's career, therefore, was not literary, and his major creative work as an essayist may be viewed as merely the cultural embellishment of a man of affairs. *The Spectator* essays especially were written in the enforced idleness subsequent on the Whigs' fall from power in 1710. Whereas in the eighteenth and nineteenth centuries Addison was frequently invoked as a model of style, and his advice as a moralist was consciously pursued, more recently his easy-going lightness of touch has encouraged the view that his is merely the dilettante manner of the school of *belles lettres*.

Addison's declared aim, however, was to digest substantial learning into simple form, to clarify complex arguments, and, while sustaining that firm moral tone which earned him the sobriquet of "the parson in a tie-wig," to relate moral concerns to the everyday business of society with good humour and wit. He saw himself in the tradition of Horatian satire – a humanistic tradition in which the man of affairs and the man of letters were familiar companions, and in which even the most important philosophical matters were handled without pedantry: "I have brought Philosophy out of Closets and Libraries, Schools and Colleges, to dwell in Clubs and Assemblies, at Tea-Tables, and in Coffee-Houses" (*Spectator* 10). His papers on "The Pleasures of the Imagination" provide the clearest and most pregnant account available of a major aesthetic and psychological concern of the time, and the elaborated criticism of *Paradise Lost* is not only one of the most important early assessments of Milton's poem, but shows also Addison's deep concern with the relation between ethical and literary matters. Such serious preoccupations are matched with a lively and detailed presentation of the everyday scene in his social and satiric essays which challenge comparison with any of the novelists of the time.

Bacon, Montaigne, and Temple are among Addison's models, and periodicals like the *Mercure Galant* in France and Motteux's *Gentleman's Journal* in England suggest earlier analogies to *The Spectator*, but it was Addison especially who established the periodical essay as one of the major artistic genres of the century. Among numerous imitations were Johnson's *The Idler* and *The Rambler*, Hawkesworth's *The Adventurer*, and Dodsley's and Moore's *The World*.

—Malcolm Kelsall

ADE, George.   American.   Born in Kentland, Indiana, 9 February 1866. Educated at local schools, and Purdue University, Lafayette, Indiana, 1883–87 (Editor, *Purdue*), B.S. 1887. Reporter, Lafayette *Morning News*, 1888, and Lafayette *Call*, 1888–90; worked for the Chicago *Morning News*, later *News-Record*, then the *Record*, 1890–1900: from 1893 collaborated with cartoonist John T. McCutcheon on a daily illustrated column about Chicago life; settled on a farm near Brook, Indiana, 1904. Delegate, Republican National Convention, 1908; Trustee, Purdue University, 1908–15, and promoted the Ross-Ade Stadium at Purdue, 1923–24; Grand Consul, Sigma Chi fraternity, 1909; Director of Publicity, Indiana State Council of Defense, 1917–18; Member, Indiana Commission for the Chicago World's Fair, 1933. L.H.D.: Purdue University, 1926; LL.D.: Indiana University, Bloomington, 1927. Member, National Institute of Arts and Letters, 1908. *Died 16 May 1944.*

PUBLICATIONS

Collections

The *America of Ade: Fables, Short Stories, Essays*, edited by Jean Shepherd.   1960.
Letters, edited by Terence Tobin.   1973.

Fiction

Artie. 1896.
Pink Marsh. 1897.
Doc' Horne. 1899.
Fables in Slang. 1900.
More Fables. 1900.
Forty Modern Fables. 1901.
The Girl Proposition. 1902.
People You Know. 1903.
Circus Day. 1903.
Handsome Cyril. 1903.
Clarence Allen. 1903.
In Babel. 1903.
Rollo Johnson. 1904.
Breaking into Society. 1904.
True Bills. 1904.
In Pastures New. 1906.
The Slim Princess. 1907.
I Knew Him When— . 1910.
Hoosier Hand Book. 1911.
Knocking the Neighbors. 1912.
Ade's Fables. 1914.
Hand-Made Fables. 1920.
Single Blessedness and Other Observations. 1922.
Stay with Me Flagons. 1922.
Bang! Bang! 1928.

Plays

The Back-Stair Investigation (produced 1897).
The Night of the Fourth (produced 1901).
The Sultan of Sulu, music by Alfred G. Wathall (produced 1902). 1903.
The County Chairman (produced 1903). 1924.
Peggy from Paris, music by William Loraine (produced 1903).
Bird Center: Cap Fry's Birthday Party (produced 1904).
The Sho-Gun, music by Gustav Luders (produced 1904).
The College Widow (produced 1904). 1924.
Just Out of College (produced 1905). 1924.
The Bad Samaritan (produced 1905).
Marse Covington (produced 1906). 1918.
Artie (produced 1907).
Father and the Boys (produced 1908). 1924.
Mrs. Peckham's Carouse (produced 1908).
The Fair Co-ed, music by Gustav Luders (produced 1909).
The City Chap (produced 1910).
U.S. Minister Bedloe (produced 1910).
The Old Town (produced 1910).
The Mayor and the Manicure (produced 1912). 1923.
Nettie (produced 1914). 1923.
Speaking to Father. 1923.
The Persecuted Wife, in *Liberty,* 4 July 1925.
The Willing Performer, in *The Country Gentleman,* February 1928.

Aunt Fanny from Chautaugua.   1949.

Screenplays: many short films, and the following: *Our Leading Citizen,* with Waldemar Young, 1922; *Back Home and Broke,* with J. Clarkson Miller, 1922; *Woman-Proof,* with Tom Geraghty, 1923; *The Confidence Man,* with others, 1924.

Verse

Verses and Jingles.   1911.

Other

The Old-Time Saloon (essays).   1931.
Revived Remarks on Mark Twain, edited by George Hiram Brownell.   1936.
One Afternoon with Mark Twain.   1939.

Editor, *An Invitation to You and Your Folks, from Jim and Some More of the Home Folks.*   1916.

Bibliography: *A Bibliography of Ade* by Dorothy R. Russo, 1947.

Reading List: *Ade, Warmhearted Satirist* by Fred C. Kelly, 1947; *Ade* by Lee Coyle, 1964; "Ade: The City Uncle" by Edmund Wilson, in *The Bit Between My Teeth,* 1965.

*   *   *

Born in a small Indiana town in 1866, George Ade grew up fascinated with the talk around main-street shops and country stores. While attending Purdue College (later University) he became an avid theater-goer, rarely missing a minstrel show or musical comedy at the Lafayette Opera House. Not surprisingly, transcribing speech and writing plays became his lucrative livelihood. Following a stint as a hometown newspaper man, Ade went up to Chicago in 1890 to join his friend, the cartoonist John T. McCutcheon, on the *Chicago Morning News.*
    In 1893 these two collaborated on a daily illustrated column, "All Roads Lead to the World's Fair," a potpourri of interviews and observations centered on the Columbian Exposition. After the Fair closed, their column continued as "Stories of the Streets and of the Town." Taking all Chicago as their province, Ade and McCutcheon described urban life and common speech in hundreds of vivid sketches. Stylistically, Ade experimented in the "Stories" with straight narrative, light verse, dramatic dialogue, and various ethnic dialects. The pieces were popular enough to be saved and sold in eight paperback collections between 1894 and 1900. Ade also extracted three recurring characters, stitched their scattered appearances into sustained narratives, and published the results as *Artie, Pink Marsh,* and *Doc' Horne.* The title characters were, respectively, a brash street-wise office worker, a black shoeshine boy in a basement barbershop, and a genial yarn-spinner living at the Alfalfa European Hotel. Not coherent enough to be considered novels, these books remain important as pioneering realistic transcriptions of urban vernacular voices – particularly Artie's colorful slang and Pink's northern Negro dialect.
    Ade's best work is in his "Fables in Slang," the first of which appeared in the "Streets and Towns" column in 1897 after Ade had asked himself, "why not retain the archaic form and the stilted manner of composition [of the fable] and, for purposes of novelty, permit the language to be 'fly,' modern, undignified, quite up to the moment?" (Fred C. Kelly, *George*

Ade, p. 136). The fables became a regular Saturday feature, and were soon syndicated and collected into book form. Nine additional collections followed, the last in 1920. Most of Ade's fables were gently satiric exempla of pretension and folly, set in Mid-Western small towns or in Chicago, and capped by incongruous, undercutting moral tag lines. They follow his earlier work in reproducing familiar character types and common street talk. His master stroke was the use of capital letters for comic and ironic emphasis of the tendency of such talk toward platitudes and slang. (For example: "One morning a Modern Solomon, who had been chosen to preside as Judge in a divorce Mill, climbed to his Perch and unbuttoned his Vest for the Wearisome Grind.") The fables brought to literary visibility a host of ordinary people: the bombastic preacher and the travelling salesman, college students, bohemian writers and fast-talking vaudevillians, and numbers of country folk lost in the city. They are valuable as a microcosm of Mid-Western, middle-class life at the turn of the century. More important, Ade's use of the vernacular instead of genteel-academic English provided a shot of vitality to the language, and helped make it more flexible for the next generation of American writers.

During his most productive decade, 1900–10, Ade also wrote over a dozen plays. Three were very successful on Broadway: *The Sultan of Sulu*, a musical-comedy satire on American assumption of the "white man's burden" in the South Pacific; *The County Chairman*, a comedy-drama about politics in the rural Mid-West; and his best play, *The College Widow*, which introduced college life and football to the American stage.

—Charles Fanning

AGEE, James. American. Born in Knoxville, Tennessee, 27 November 1909. Educated at Phillips Exeter Acadmy, New Hampshire; Harvard University, Canfbridge, Massachusetts, 1928–32, B.A. 1932. Settled in New York City, 1932; staff writer for the Luce publications *Fortune* and *Time*, 1932–48; Film Reviewer for *Time*, 1941–48; Film Critic, *The Nation*, 1943–48. Recipient: National Institute of Arts and Letters award, 1949; Pulitzer Prize, 1958. *Died 16 May 1955.*

PUBLICATIONS

Collections

  Collected Poems, edited by Robert Fitzgerald.   1968.
  Collected Short Prose, edited by Robert Fitzgerald.   1968.

Fiction

  The Morning Watch.   1951.
  A Death in the Family.   1957.
  Four Early Stories, edited by Elena Harap.   1964.

Plays

  Agee on Film: Five Film Scripts (includes *The Blue Hotel, The African Queen, The Bride Comes to Yellow Sky, The Night of the Hunter, Noa Noa*).   1960.

Screenplays: *The Quiet One* (documentary), 1949; *The African Queen*, with John Huston, 1951; *The Bride Comes to Yellow Sky* (in *Face to Face*), 1953; *White Man* (documentary), 1953; *The Night of the Hunter*, 1955.

Verse

Permit Me Voyage.   1934.

Other

Let Us Now Praise Famous Men: Three Tenant Families, photographs by Walker Evans. 1941.
Agee on Film: Reviews and Comments.   1958.
Letters to Father Flye.   1962; revised edition, 1971.
A Way of Seeing: Photographs of New York, photographs by Helen Levitt.   1965.

Reading List: *Agee* by Peter H. Ohlin, 1966; *Remembering Agee* edited by David Madden, 1974; *The Restless Journey of Agee* by Genevieve Moreau, 1977.

*   *   *

In 1941 James Agee and the photographer Walker Evans published *Let Us Now Praise Famous Men*. A long, journalistic piece that would become the central fixture of Agee's critical fame, the book was the result of eight months that he and Evans had spent in Alabama sympathetically chronicling in prose and photographs the daily lives of sharecropper families in the deep South.

Prior to the appearance of *Let Us Now Praise Famous Men*, Agee had published a book of poetry, *Permit Me Voyage*, as well as many magazine articles – most of them anonymously – as a member of the staff of *Fortune*. He had also begun writing film criticism for *Time*, an activity which he continued for *The Nation* and which signaled the beginnings of a deep involvement with cinema, not only as an out-spoken critic of the medium but also as a writer of highly detailed screenplays.

Let Us Now Praise Famous Men and his film work aside, Agee is best remembered for his novels, *The Morning Watch* and *A Death in the Family*, which was published two years after his death and for which he was posthumously awarded the Pulitzer Prize. Largely autobiographical, both novels reveal the influence in Agee's life and work of two elemental facts of his childhood: the death of his father when Agee was six years old, and the religious piety of his mother, a piety with which he would constantly struggle. *The Morning Watch*, for instance, is the story of a young student at a religious school who grows away from orthodoxy toward self-awareness and, eventually, alienation. And in *A Death in the Family* the young protagonist's father has been killed in an automobile accident – as Agee's own father had been killed – leaving the boy and his family to cope with his absence, even as had the Agee family.

Many critics have felt that Agee failed to reach the artistic achievement that was his birthright. Never one to settle on a particular genre, they point out, he chose instead to do all: poetry, journalism, fiction, criticism, screenplays. And never one to care for his own health, he lived, as film director John Huston wrote, as though "body destruction was implicit in his make-up." Still, James Agee achieved much in his forty-five years, and his premature death meant, finally, that his greatest fame would have to come posthumously.

—Bruce A. Lohof

AIKEN, Conrad (Potter). American. Born in Savannah, Georgia, 5 August 1889. Educated at Middlesex School, Concord, Massachusetts; Harvard University, Cambridge, Massachusetts (President, *Harvard Advodate*), 1907–12. A.B. 1912. Married 1) Jessie McDonald in 1912 (divorced, 1929), one son, two daughters; 2) Clarice Lorenz, 1930 (divorced, 1937); 3) Mary Hoover, 1937. Contributing Editor, *The Dial*, New York, 1916–19; American Correspondent, *Athenaeum*, London, 1919–25, and *London Mercury*, 1921–22; London Correspondent, *The New Yorker*, 1933–36. Instructor, Harvard University, 1927–28. Fellow, 1948, and Consultant in Poetry, 1950–52, Library of Congress, Washington, D.C. Recipient: Pulitzer Prize, 1930; Shelley Memorial Prize, 1930; Guggenheim Fellowship, 1934; Bryher Award, 1952; National Book Award, 1954; Bollingen Prize, 1956; Academy of American Poets Fellowship, 1957; National Institute of Arts and Letters Gold Medal, 1958; Huntington Hartford Foundation Award, 1961; Brandeis University Creative Arts Award, 1966; National Medal for Literature, 1969. Member, American Academy of Arts and Letters, 1957. *Died 17 August 1973.*

PUBLICATIONS

Collections

   Selected Letters, edited by Joseph Killorin.   1978.

Fiction

   Bring! Bring! and Other Stories.   1925.
   Blue Voyage.   1927.
   Costumes by Eros.   1928.
   Gehenna.   1930.
   Great Circle.   1933.
   Among the Lost People (stories).   1934.
   King Coffin.   1935.
   A Heart for the Gods of Mexico.   1939.
   Conversation; or, Pilgrims' Progress.   1940; as *The Conversation*, 1948.
   The Short Stories.   1950.
   The Collected Short Stories.   1960.
   The Collected Novels.   1964.

Verse

   Earth Triumphant and Other Tales in Verse.   1914.
   The Jig of Forslin: A Symphony.   1916.
   Turns and Movies and Other Tales in Verse.   1916.
   Nocturne of Remembered Spring and Other Poems.   1917.
   The Charnal Rose, Senlin: A Biography, and Other Poems.   1918.
   The House of Dust: A Symphony.   1920.
   Punch: The Immortal Liar.   1921.
   The Pilgrimage of Festus.   1923.
   Priapus and the Pool and Other Poems.   1925.
   (Poems), edited by Louis Untermeyer.   1927.
   Prelude.   1929.

Selected Poems. 1929.
John Deth, A Metaphysical Legend, and Other Poems. 1930.
Preludes for Memnon. 1931.
The Coming Forth by Day of Osiris Jones. 1931.
Landscape West of Eden. 1934.
Time in the Rock: Preludes to Definition. 1936.
And in the Human Heart. 1940.
Brownstone Eclogues and Other Poems. 1942.
The Soldier. 1944.
The Kid. 1947.
The Divine Pilgrim. 1949.
Skylight One: Fifteen Poems. 1949.
Collected Poems. 1953.
A Letter from Li Po and Other Poems. 1955.
The Flute Player. 1956.
Sheepfold Hill: 15 Poems. 1958.
Selected Poems. 1961.
The Morning Song of Lord Zero: Poems Old and New. 1963.
A Seizure of Limericks. 1964.
Thee. 1967.
The Clerk's Journal: An Undergraduate Poem, Together with a Brief Memoir of Dean LeBaron Russell Briggs, T. S. Eliot, and Harvard, in 1911. 1971.
Collected Poems 1916–1970. 1971.

Play

Mr. Arcularis (produced 1949). 1957.

Other

Scepticisms: Notes on Contemporary Poetry. 1919.
Ushant: An Essay (autobiography). 1952.
A Reviewer's ABC: Collected Criticism from 1916 to the Present, edited by Rufus A. Blanshard. 1958; as *Collected Criticism,* 1968.
Cats and Bats and Things with Wings (juvenile). 1965.
Tom, Sue, and the Clock (juvenile). 1966.

Editor, *Modern American Poets.* 1922; as *Twentieth Century American Poetry,* 1944; revised edition, 1963.
Editor, *Selected Poems of Emily Dickinson.* 1924.
Editor, *American Poetry, 1671–1928: A Comprehensive Anthology.* 1929; as *A Comprehensive Anthology of American Poetry, 1944.*
Editor, with William Rose Benét. *An Anthology of Famous English and American Poetry.* 1945.

Reading List: *Aiken: A Life of His Art* by Jay Martin, 1962; *Aiken* by Frederick J. Hoffman, 1962; *Aiken* by Reuel Denney, 1964.

*   *   *

Characteristically, Conrad Aiken himself raises the essential critical problem in a note he wrote in 1917: "It is difficult to place Conrad Aiken in the poetic firmament, so difficult that one sometimes wonders whether he deserves a place there at all" (*Collected Criticism*). The problem is further complicated by the fact that Aiken was not only a poet, but also a respected novelist and critic. The list of his admirers is persuasive: R. P. Blackmur, Allen Tate, Malcolm Lowry all find in him one of the central voices of his age. Yet to the contemporary reader such claims are likely to seem excessive.

About the scope of his ambition there can be no doubt. Five long, complicated novels; many lengthy poetic sequences, or "symphonies," dealing with themes as varied, and as large, as the history of America (*The Kid*), the importance of his Puritan heritage ("Mayflower"), the problems of the self encountering the realities of love and death (*Preludes for Memnon* and *The Coming Forth by Day of Osiris Jones*): all testify to the courageous attempt to convey a rich, complex life in a wide-ranging, always technically experimental art.

The centre of this art lies in the difficultly maintained balance between aesthetic purity and formal perfection on the one hand, and the menacing chaos of terrifying experience on the other. It is tempting to relate this to Aiken's very early experience as a child when he discovered the bodies of his parents after a mutual suicide pact: this moment is placed at the centre of his long autobiographical essay *Ushant*. This deeply buried memory may also have encouraged Aiken's passionate interest in Freud. The five novels show this interest everywhere: the hero of *Blue Voyage*, Demarest, is on a voyage of self-discovery through journey, quest, and dream. This novel, like *Great Circle* – which Freud himself admired – is an elaborate metaphor for the author's psychic search, the exploration of his own consciousness. At their best, the novels find a language for disturbing, hidden states of the psyche: the combination of thriller form and psychoanalytic imagery in *King Coffin* is uniquely memorable. But too often the novels slip into vagueness and imprecision. As Frederick J. Hoffman has observed, their separate parts fail *quite* to cohere. The lack of adequate characterisation, and the over-literariness of the enterprise, are at odds with our valid expectations of prose fiction. It is significant then that Aiken's "autobiography," *Ushant*, should seem to so many of his critics his finest achievement in prose. Here, Aiken as writer, and his literary friends, including Eliot and Pound, are at the centre of a "fictionalised" account of the author's life. Apart from its other intrinsic interests, this quite extraordinary, unclassifiable work is justified, almost alone, by the majestic sweep and lyrical seductiveness of Aiken's rhetoric.

It is this majestic rhetoric that one also recognises in the poetry: Malcolm Lowry referred to Aiken as "the truest and most direct descendant of our own great Elizabethans" (*Wake 11*, 1952). This quality is immediately apparent in *Preludes for Memnon*:

> What dignity can death bestow on us,
> Who kiss beneath a street lamp, or hold hands
> Half hidden in a taxi, or replete
> With coffee, figs and Barsac make our way
> To a dark bedroom in a wormworn house?

The combination here of the common and quotidian – street lamp, taxi, coffee – with noble, "Elizabethan" cadences, is the characteristic Aiken manner. It is a manner that frequently skirts parody and pastiche, but equally often rises to a rich, solemn verbal music. In poem after poem in his enormous output, Aiken sustains a long, flowing musical line, celebrating, as in "Landscape West of Eden," the capacity of language to order the chaos of the unaccomodated self. What one misses, however, in too much of this poetry, and what contributes to a certain lack of *energy* in the verse, is any intense verbal particularity, or, often, the sense of real feeling significantly expressed. In *Time in the Rock*, one of his most ambitious pieces, there is little sense of any real pressure or urgency behind the words; they have a tendency, as it were, to slip off the edge of the page as we read: nothing seems to make it all *cohere*.

His more objective, "dramatic" poems, like *The Kid* and "Mayflower," with their incorporation of historical and legendary material and their evocations of New England landscape and geography, are perhaps more valuable, in the end, than his lyrical self-communings. The contemporary reader is also likely to be more drawn to the lighter side of Aiken: in a poem like "Blues for Ruby Matrix" the rhetoric remains, but allied now to a delightful sexiness and tenderness.

Whatever the mode, however, there is always in Aiken, even if only residually, that sense of horror, of terror, and of death – "The sombre note that gives the chord its power," as he puts it in "Palimpsest" – that gives the best poetry its capacity to hurt and wound us. When, in *Preludes for Memnon*, he defines the role of the poet, Aiken finds a definition that takes full note of this fundamental ground-bass of his own work; the poet is one who

> by imagination [apes]
> God, the supreme poet of despair ...
> Knowing the rank intolerable taste of death,
> And walking dead on the still living earth.

—Neil Corcoran

AINSWORTH, William Harrison. English. Born in Manchester, 4 February 1805. Educated at Manchester Grammar School; articled to a Manchester solicitor, 1821–24; subsequently studied law in London, 1824–26. Married Anne Frances Ebers in 1826; three daughters. Publisher, in London, 1826–28; visited Switzerland and Italy, 1830; successful as a novelist from 1834; also, Editor, *Bentley's Miscellany*, London, 1839–41; Editor and Publisher, *Ainsworth's Magazine*, London, 1842–54, *The New Monthly Magazine*, London, 1845–70, and *Bentley's Miscellany*, 1854–68. *Died 3 January 1882.*

PUBLICATIONS

Fiction

December Tales, with others.   1823.
The Boetian.   1824.
Sir John Chiverton, with J. P. Aston.   1826.
Rookwood.   1834.
Crichton.   1837; revised edition, 1849; as *The Admirable Crichton*, 1927.
Jack Sheppard.   1839.
The Tower of London.   1840.
Guy Fawkes; or, The Gunpowder Treason.   1841.
Old Saint Paul's : A Tale of the Plague and the Fire.   1841.
The Miser's Daughter.   1842.
Windsor Castle.   1843.
Saint James's; or, The Court of Queen Anne.   1844.
James the Second; or, The Revolution of 1688.   1848.
The Lancashire Witches.   1849.

The Star-Chamber.   1854.
The Flitch of Bacon; or, The Custom of Dunmow.   1854.
The Spendthrift.   1857.
Mervyn Clitheroe.   1858.
Ovingdean Grange.   1860.
The Constable of the Tower.   1861.
The Lord Mayor of London; or, City Life in the Last Century.   1862.
Cardinal Pole; or, The Days of Philip and Mary.   1863.
John Law the Projector.   1864.
The Spanish Match; or, Charles Stuart at Madrid.   1865.
Auriol; or, The Elixir of Life.   1865.
The Constable de Bourbon.   1866.
Old Court.   1867.
Myddleton Pomfret.   1868.
Hilary St. Ives.   1870.
The South-Sea Bubble.   1871.
Talbot Harland.   1871.
Tower Hill.   1871.
Boscobel; or, The Royal Oak.   1872.
The Good Old Times: The Story of the Manchester Rebels of '45.   1873; as *The Manchester Rebels of the Fatal '45*, 1874.
Merry England; or, Nobles and Serfs.   1874.
The Goldsmith's Wife.   1875.
Preston Fight; or, The Insurrection of 1715.   1875.
Chetwynd Calverley.   1876.
The Leaguer of Lathom.   1876.
The Fall of Somerset.   1877.
Beatrice Tyldesley.   1878.
Beau Nash; or, Bath in the Eighteenth Century.   1879.
Stanley Brereton.   1881.

Verse

Poems by Cheviot Tichburn.   1822; as *The Maid's Revenge, and A Summer Evening's Tale, with Other Poems;* 1823; as *Works of Cheviot Tichburn,* 1825.
Monody on the Death of John Philip Kemble.   1823.
A Summer Evening Tale.   1825.
Letters from Cockney Lands.   1826.
May Fair.   1827.
Ballads, Romantic, Fantastical, and Humorous.   1855; revised edition, 1872.
The Combat of the Thirty, from a Breton Lay of the Fourteenth Century.   1859.

Other

Consideration on the Best Means of Affording Immediate Relief to the Operative Classes in the Manufacturing Districts.   1826.

Editor, *Modern Chivalry; or, A New Orlando Furioso,* by Catherine Gore.   1843.

Bibliography: *A Bibliographical Catalogue of the Published Novels and Ballads of Ainsworth* by Harold Locke, 1925.

Reading List: *Ainsworth and His Friends* by S. M. Ellis, 2 vols., 1911; *The Newgate Novel* by K. Hollingsworth, 1963; *Ainsworth* by George J. Worth, 1972.

*   *   *

Early in a long career, William Harrison Ainsworth established himself as one of the most popular Victorian novelists, responding to and helping to shape the nineteenth-century taste for historical, Gothic, and rogue fiction. His best work is to be found in such books as *Rookwood, Jack Sheppard, The Tower of London, Old Saint Paul's,* and *Windsor Castle,* but he went on wiriting, to diminishing acclaim, for nearly four more decades, finally producing forty-one novels.

Ainsworth often wrote in haste, and he lacked some of the chief artistic endowments of his major contemporaries. But the best of his novels still make rewarding reading. Each confronts the reader with a crowded, contentious, self-contained fictional world of great vitality, in the process teaching us much about the historical period it treats, and also about our own age – and ourselves. He was especially skillful at depicting man's perpetual craving for power. How power is won and, once won, how it is exercised were subjects to which he returned time and again. But Ainsworth also showed how loss of power, over oneself or others, can bring one to ruin: a very painful sort of ruin, generally, because he was under no illusion about the charity and mercy that man extends to his fellows.

Especially in his historical novels, Ainsworth demonstrates a remarkable fascination with the pomp and pageantry of court and castle. But it is clear that these are merely the outward ornaments of a world that is cruel and violent at the core, a harsh fact that seems to make it all the more urgent to retain what we can of convention and ceremonial and what little there may be of human compassion. More than the general run of nineteenth-century novelists, Ainsworth recognized the pervasiveness of the irrational side of human nature and the insistent drives to which it gives rise. Along with his ability to tell a gripping story and bring the past to vivid life, this surprisingly modern awareness gives Ainsworth a strong claim on our attention.

—George J. Worth

ALCOTT, Louisa May.   American.   Born in Germantown, Philadelphia, Pennsylvania, 29 November 1832; daughter of the philosopher Amos Bronson Alcott; grew up in Boston, and later in Concord, Massachusetts. Educated at home by her father, with instruction from Thoreau, Emerson, and Theodore Parker. Began to write for publication, 1848; also worked as a teacher, seamstress, and domestic servant to support her family; army nurse at the Union Hospital, Georgetown, Washington, D.C. during the Civil War, 1861–63; visited Europe, 1865; Editor of the children's magazine *Merry's Museum,* 1867; visited Europe, 1870, then settled in Boston. *Died 6 March 1888.*

PUBLICATIONS

Collections

   Glimpses of Louisa: A Centennial Sampling of the Best Short Stories. edited by Cornelia
      Meigs.   1968.

Fiction

> *Flower Fables.* 1855.
> *The Rose Family: A Fairy Tale.* 1864.
> *On Picket Duty and Other Tales.* 1864.
> *Moods.* 1865; revised edition, 1882.
> *Morning-Glories and Other Stories.* 1867.
> *The Mysterious Key and What It Opened.* 1867.
> *Three Proverb Stories.* 1868.
> *Kitty's Class Day.* 1868.
> *Aunt Kipp.* 1868.
> *Psyche's Art.* 1868.
> *Little Women; or, Meg, Jo, Beth, and Amy.* 2 vols., 1868–69; as *Little Women and Good Wives*, 1871.
> *An Old-Fashioned Girl.* 1870.
> *Will's Wonder Book.* 1870.
> *Little Men: Life at Plumfield with Jo's Boys.* 1871.
> *V.V.; or, Plots and Counterplots.* 1871.
> *Aunt Jo's Scrap-Bag: My Boys, Shawl-Straps, Cupid and Chow-Chow, My Girls, Jimmy's Cruise in the Pinafore, An Old-Fashioned Thanksgiving.* 6 vols., 1872–82.
> *Work: A Story of Experience.* 1873.
> *Beginning Again, Being a Continuation of "Work."* 1875.
> *Eight Cousins; or, The Aunt-Hill.* 1875.
> *Silver Pitchers, and Independence: A Centennial Love Story.* 1876; as *Silver Pitchers and Other Stories*, 1876.
> *Rose in Bloom: A Sequel to "Eight Cousins."* 1876.
> *A Modern Mephistopheles.* 1877.
> *Under the Lilacs.* 1877.
> *Meadow Blossoms.* 1879.
> *Water Cresses.* 1879.
> *Jack and Jill: A Village Story.* 1880.
> *Proverb Stories.* 1882.
> *Spinning-Wheel Stories.* 1884.
> *Jo's Boys and How They Turned Out.* 1886.
> *Lulu's Library: A Christmas Dream, The Frost King, Recollections.* 3 vols., 1886–89.
> *A Garland for Girls.* 1888.
> *A Modern Mephistopheles, and A Whisper in the Dark.* 1889.
> *Louisa's Wonder Book: An Unknown Alcott Juvenile*, edited by Madeleine B. Stern. 1975.
> *Behind a Mask: The Unknown Thrillers*, edited by Madeleine B. Stern. 1975.
> *Plots and Counterplots: More Unknown Thrillers*, edited by Madeleine B. Stern. 1976.

Plays

> *Comic Tragedies Written by "Jo" and "Meg" and Acted by the "Little Women,"* edited by A. B. Pratt. 1893.

Other

> *Hospital Sketches.* 1863; revised edition, as *Hospital Sketches and Camp and Fireside Stories*, 1869.
> *Nelly's Hospital.* 1868.

Something to Do. 1873.
A Glorious Fourth. 1887.
What It Cost. 1887.
Jimmy's Lecture. 1887.
Alcott: Her Life, Letters, and Journals, edited by Ednah D. Cheney. 1889.
Recollections of My Childhood's Days. 1890.
A Sprig of Andromeda: A Letter on the Death of Henry David Thoreau, edited by John L.
Cooley. 1962.

Bibliography: in *Bibliography of American Literature* by Jacob Blanck, 1955; in *Louisa's Wonder Book* edited by Madeleine B. Stern, 1975.

Reading List: *Alcott* by Madeleine B. Stern, 1950; *Alcott* by Cathering O. Peare, 1950; *Miss Alcott of Concord* by Marjorie Worthington, 1958; *Alcott and the American Family Story* by Cornelia Meigs, 1970; *Louisa May: A Modern Biography of Alcott* by Martha Saxton, 1977.

*   *   *

Louisa May Alcott's reputation as one of America's best-loved writers is based upon *Little Women*, a domestic novel for girls which is also appealing to adults. *Little Women* reflects the Alcott family background of high-minded idealism while it glosses over the Alcott family problems. Its characters, the four March girls, were drawn from those of the author and her sisters, its scenes from the New England where she had grown up, and many of its episodes from those she and her family had experienced, although the literary influence of Bunyan, Dickens, Carlyle, Hawthorne, Emerson, Theodore Parker, and Thoreau may be traced.

In the creation of *Little Women*, Alcott was something of a pioneer, using her own life as the basis of a juvenile novel, and achieving a realistic but wholesome picture of family life with which readers could readily identify. The Alcott poverty was sentimentalized, the eccentric Alcott father was an adumbrated shadow; yet the core of the domestic drama was apparent. Reported simply and directly in a style that applied her injunction, "Never use a long word, when a short one will do as well," the narrative embodied the simple facts and persons of a family, and so filled a gap in the literature of adolescence and domesticity.

There is no doubt that *Little Women* was the author's masterpiece. It had been preceded by a succession of literary efforts and experiments that gave Alcott a wide range of professional experience before she undertook her domestic novel. Her first published book, *Flower Fables*, consisted of "legends of faery land" and was dedicated to Emerson's daughter Ellen, for whom the tales were originally created. Her first novel, *Moods*, was a narrative of stormy violence, death, and intellectual love in which she attempted to apply Emerson's remark "Life is a train of moods like a string of beads." On and off she worked on an autobiographical, feminist novel, *Success*, subsequently renamed *Work: A Story of Experience.*

The Alcott bibliography encompasses nearly three hundred books, articles, novels, short stories, and poems, many of which appeared in the periodicals of the day. They were written in a variety of literary genres: stories of sweetness and light; dramatic narratives of strong-minded women; realistic episodes of Civil War life based upon her experience as a nurse; pseudonymous blood-and-thunder thrillers of revenge and passion whose leading character was usually a manipulating and vindictive woman. From the exigencies of serialization she developed the skills of cliff-hanger and page-turner. By 1868, when she began *Little Women*, she had produced a broad spectrum of stories from tales of virtue rewarded to tales of vice unpunished.

Little Women was followed by a succession of wholesome domestic narratives, the so-called *Little Women Series*, in which the author continued to supply a persistent demand. More or less autobiographical in origin, perceptive in their characterizations of adolescents, all are in a sense sequels of *Little Women* though none quite rises to its level. *An Old-*

Fashioned Girl is a domestic drama in reverse, exposing the fashionable absurdities of one home in contrast with the wholesome domesticity of another. *Eight Cousins* exalts the family hearth again, and *Jack and Jill* enlarges upon the theme of domesticity, describing the home life of a New England village rather than of a single family.

An exception to this preoccupation with domestic life was *A Modern Mephistopheles*. Here Alcott exploited a theme of Goethe in a novel that reverted to the sensationalism of her earlier thrillers. "Enjoyed doing it," she wrote in her journal, "being tired of providing moral pap for the young."

Alcott was a far more complex writer than has been recognized. Drawn to a variety of literary themes and techniques, she eschewed most of them in favor of the domestic novel she had perfected. Motivated by the "inspiration of necessity," she became a victim of her own success. She has inevitably achieved fame as the "Children's Friend" and the author of a single masterpiece. Thanks to its psychological perceptions, its realistic characterizations, and its honest domesticity, *Little Women* has become an embodiment of the American home at its best. As the *Boston Herald* commented after her death: "When the family history, out of which this remarkable authorship grew, shall be told to the public, it will be apparent that few New England homes have ever had closer converse with the great things of human destiny than that of the Alcotts." Imbedded in the domestic novel *Little Women* are "the great things of human destiny," for there the particular has been transmuted into the universal.

—Madeleine B. Stern

ALDINGTON, Richard.   English.   Born in Hampshire, 8 July 1892. Educated at Dover College; University College, University of London. Served in the Army, in France, 1916–18. Married 1) the poet Hilda Doolittle ("H.D.") in 1913 (divorced, 1937), one step-daughter; 2) Netta McCulloch Patmore in 1938, one daughter. Editor, *The Egoist*, London, 1914–17; assisted Ford Madox Ford with the *English Review*, and T. S. Eliot with *The Criterion*; critic of French literature for the *Times Literary Supplement*. Lived in France, 1928–36, in the United States, 1939–46, and again in France, 1946–62. Recipient: Black Memorial Prize, for biography, 1947. *Died 27 July 1962.*

PUBLICATIONS

Fiction

    Death of a Hero.   1929; revised edition, 1930.
    Roads to Glory (stories).   1930.
    Two Stories.   1930.
    At All Costs (stories).   1930.
    Last Straws (stories).   1930.
    The Colonel's Daughter.   1931.
    Stepping Heavenward: A Record.   1931.
    Soft Answers (stories).   1932.
    All Men Are Enemies: A Romance.   1933.
    Women Must Work.   1934.

Very Heaven.   1937.
Seven Against Reeves: A Comedy-Farce.   1938.
Rejected Guest.   1939.
The Romance of Casanova.   1946.

Play

Life of a Lady, with Derek Patmore.   1936.

Verse

Images (1910 1915).   1915; as, *Images Old and New*,1916.
Reverie: A Little Book of Poems for H.D.   1917.
The Love of Myrrhine and Konallis, and Other Prose Poems.   1917.
Images of War.   1919; revised edition, 1919.
Images of Desire.   1919.
Images.   1919.
War and Love (1915 1918).   1919.
Collected Poems 1915 1923.   1923; revised edition, 1928.
Exile and Other Poems.   1923.
A Fool i' the Forest: A Phantasmagoria.   1924.
Love and the Luxembourg.   1930; as *A Dream in the Luxembourg*,1930.
Movietones, Invented and Set Down 1928 1929.   1932.
The Eaten Heart.   1933.
The Poems.   1934.
Life Quest.   1935.
The Crystal World.   1937.
Complete Poems.   1948.

Other

Literary Studies and Reviews.   1924.
Voltaire.   1925.
French Studies and Reviews.   1926.
D. H. Lawrence: An Indiscretion.   1927.
Rémy de Gourmont: A Modern Man of Letters.   1928.
Balls and Another Book for Suppression.   1930.
The Squire.   1934.
Artifex: Sketches and Ideas.   1935.
Life for Life's Sake: A Book of Reminiscences.   1941.
The Duke, Being an Account of the Life and Achievements of the 1st Duke of Wellington.   1943; as *Wellington*, 1946.
Jane Austen.   1948.
Four English Portraits 1801 1851.   1948.
The Strange Life of Charles Waterton 1782 1865.   1949.
D. H. Lawrence: An Appreciation.   1950.
D. H. Lawrence: Portrait of a Genius But....   1950.
Pinorman: Recollections of Norman Douglas, Pino Orioli, and Charles Prentice.   1954.
A. E. Housman and W. B. Yeats: Two Lectures.   1955.
Lawrence l'Imposteur: T. E. Lawrence, The Legend and the Man.   1954; as *Lawrence of Arabia: A Biographical Inquiry*, 1955.

Introduction to Mistral. 1956.
Frauds. 1957.
A Tourist's Rome. 1957.
Portrait of a Rebel: The Life and Works of Robert Louis Stevenson. 1957.
D. H. Lawrence in Selbstzeugnissen und Bilddokumenten. 1961.
Selected Critical Writings 1928 60, edited by Alister Kershaw. 1970.
A Passionate Prodigality: Letters to Alan Bird, edited by Miriam J. Benkovitz. 1976.

Editor and Translator, *A Book of "Characters" from Theophrastus and Other Authors.* 1924.
Editor and Translator, *Letters of Madame de Sevigné.* 1927.
Editor and Translator, *Letters of Voltaire and Frederick the Great.* 1927.
Editor, *The Private Life of the Marshall Duke of Richelieu.* 1927.
Editor, *Memoirs of the Duc de Lausun.* 1928.
Editor and Translator, *Fifty Romance Lyric Poems.* 1928.
Editor, with Guiseppe Orioli, *Last Poems,* by D. H. Lawrence. 1932.
Editor, *Selected Poems,* by D. H. Lawrence. 1934.
Editor, *The Spirit of Place: An Anthology Compiled from the Prose of D. H. Lawrence.* 1935.
Editor, *The Viking Book of Poetry of the English-Speaking World.* 1941.
Editor, *The Portable Oscar Wilde.* 1946; as *Selected Writings,* 1946.
Editor and Translator, *Great French Romances.* 1946.
Editor, *Selected Works,* by Walter Pater. 1948.
Editor, *The Religion of Beauty: Selections from the Aesthetes.* 1950.
Editor, *Selected Letters of D. H. Lawrence.* 1950.
Editor, *Selected Essays,* by D. H. Lawrence. 1950

Translator, *The Poems of Anyte of Tegea.* 1915.
Translator, *Latin Poems of the Renaissance.* 1915.
Translator, *The Little Demon,* by Feodor Sogolub. 1916.
Translator, *The Garland of Months,* by Folgore Da San Gemignano. 1917.
Translator, *Greek Songs in the Manner of Anacreon.* 1919.
Translator, *The Poems of Meleager of Gadara.* 1920.
Translator, *Medallions in Clay.* 1921.
Translator, *The Good-Humoured Ladies,* by Goldoni. 1922.
Translator, *French Comedies of the XVIIIth Century.* 1923.
Translator, *Voyages to the Moon and the Sun,* by Cyrano de Bergerac. 1923.
Translator, *Dangerous Acquaintances,* by Choderlos de Laclos. 1924.
Translator, *Sturley,* by Pierre Custot. 1924.
Translator, *The Mystery of the Nativity.* 1924.
Translator, *The Fifteen Joys of Marriage, Ascribed to Antoine De La Sale.* 1926.
Translator, *Candide and Other Romances,* by Voltaire. 1927.
Translator, *Letters of Voltaire and Madame du Deffland.* 1927.
Translator, *The Great Betrayal,* by Julien Benda. 1928.
Translator, *Rémy de Gourmont: Selections from All His Works.* 1929.
Translator, *Alcestis,* by Euripides. 1930.
Translator, *The Decameron of Giovanni Boccaccio.* 1930.
Translator, *Letters to the Amazon,* by Rémy de Gourmont. 1931.
Translator, *Aurelia,* by Gérard de Nerval. 1932.
Translator, *A Wreath for San Gemignano.* 1945.
Translator, with Delano Ames, *Larousse Encyclopedia of Mythology.* 1959.

Bibliography: *A Bibliography of the Works of Aldington 1915 1948* by Alister Kershaw, 1950; *A Checklist of the Letters of Aldington* by Norman T. Gates, 1977.

31

Reading List: *Aldington, An Englishman* by Thomas MacGreevy, 1931; *Aldington: An Intimate Portrait* edited by Alister Kershaw and Frederic-Jacques Temple, 1965; *Aldington* by M. V. Urnov, 1968; *The Poetry of Aldington: A Critique, Evaluation, and Anthology of Uncollected Poems* by Norman T. Gates, 1974.

*   *   *

For a writer who distinguished himself in so many different ways, Richard Aldington is surprisingly under-rated today. When still very young, he began to make his name as the leading English Imagist poet. Within a short time he had also begun to produce first-rate translations of the Greek and Latin poets, Voltaire, Cyrano de Bergerac, Marivaux, Laclos, Gérard de Nerval, Goldoni, and, especially, Rémy de Gourmont. A gifted editor, Aldington worked on several important periodicals in the 1910's and 1920's, but his exceptional talents perhaps are best displayed in the variety of books he edited. *The Viking Book of Poetry of the English-Speaking World* may be singled out for its being especially influential. His introduction to *The Portable Oscar Wilde* is one his finest sustained pieces of criticism. The range and depth of his critical writings are further displayed in *Selected Critical Writings 1928 60* and the uncollected contributions to the *Times Literary Supplement* and elsewhere.

Long before he became widely known as an anthologist and critic, however, Aldington had made an international reputation as a novelist. During his period as a front-line soldier in the First World War, he was gassed and apparently suffered some form of shell-shock. His fictional response to the war, *Death of a Hero*, was a best-seller, widely regarded as the most brilliant novel in English to derive from the horrors of life on the front. For two decades Aldington sustained a substantial reputation as a novelist; his other most successful novel is probably *All Men Are Enemies*.

In the last two decades of his life, Aldington made yet another reputation, as a biographer. His work on the Duke of Wellington was awarded the Black Memorial Prize, and his works on D. H. Lawrence are still read. Two other biographical works, however, *Pinorman* and *Lawrence of Arabia*, excited enough animosity to damage Aldington's reputation. In Britain, especially, reaction to these books may have been partly responsible for the poverty and loneliness of the last few years of his life. The controversy over Lawrence of Arabia is still alive today.

Whatever his current reputation in the English-speaking world, there can be no doubt that, in a widely varied career, Aldington made remarkable achievements in at least four literary genres. Even in a climate of opinion highly unfavourable to Aldington, one obituarist was able to write of him as "an English literary all-rounder of formidable genius, one of the truly independent, creative minds of the age."

—Charles Doyle

ALGER, Horatio (Jr.) American. Born in Revere, Massachusetts, 13 January 1834. Educated at Gates Academy; Harvard University, Cambridge, Massachusetts, graduated 1854; Harvard Divinity School, graduated 1860. Teacher and journalist, 1854–57; lived in Paris, 1860–61; private tutor in Cambridge, Massachusetts, 1861–64; ordained minister, Unitarian church in Brewster, Massachusetts, 1864, but resigned in 1866 and moved to New York City to devote himself to literature; lived in New York, 1866–96: Chaplain, Newsboy's Lodging House, from 1866; lived in Natick, Massachusetts, 1896 until his death. *Died 18 July 1899.*

PUBLICATIONS

Collections

   Alger Street: The Poetry, edited by Gilbert K. Westgard, II.   1964.

Fiction

   Bertha's Christmas Vision: An Autumn Sheaf (stories and verse).   1856.
   Frank's Campaign; or, What Boys Can Do on the Farm for the Camp.   1864.
   Paul Prescott's Charge.   1865.
   Helen Ford.   1866.
   Timothy Crump's Ward; or, The New Year's Loan, and What Came of It.   1866;
      revised edition, as *Jack's Ward; or, The Boy Guardian,* 1875.
   Charlie Codman's Cruise.   1867; as *Bill Sturdy; or, The Cruise of Shipwrecked Charlie,*
      1903(?).
   Fame and Fortune; or, The Progress of Richard Hunter.   1868.
   Ragged Dick; or, Street Life in New York with the Boot-Blacks.   1868.
   Luck and Pluck; or, John Oakley's Inheritance.   1869.
   Mark, The Match Boy; or, Richard Hunter's Ward.   1869.
   Rough and Ready; or, Life among the New York Newsboys.   1869.
   Ben, The Luggage Boy; or, Among the Wharves.   1870.
   Rufus and Rose; or, The Fortunes of Rough and Ready.   1870.
   Sink or Swim; or, Harry Raymond's Resolve.   1870; as *Paddle Your Own Canoe,*
      1903(?).
   Paul the Peddler; or, The Adventures of a Young Street Merchant.   1871.
   Strong and Steady; or, Paddle Your Own Canoe.   1871.
   Tattered Tom; or, The Story of a Street Arab.   1871.
   Phil, The Fiddler; or, The Story of a Young Street Musician.   1872.
   Slow and Sure; or, From the Street to the Shop.   1872.
   Strive and Succeed; or, The Progress of Walter Conrad.   1872.
   Bound to Rise; or, Harry Walton's Motto.   1873.
   Try and Trust; or, The Story of a Bound Boy.   1873; as *Trials and Adventures of
      Herbert Mason,* 1903(?).
   Brave and Bold; or, The Adventures of a Factory Boy.   1874.
   Julius; or, The Street Boy Out West.   1874.
   Risen from the Ranks; or, Harry Walton's Success.   1874.
   Herbert Carter's Legacy; or, The Inventor's Son.   1875; as *George Carter's Legacy,*
      1903(?).
   The Young Outlaw; or, Adrift in the Streets.   1875.
   Sam's Chance, and How He Improved It.   1876.
   Shifting for Himself; or, Gilbert Greyson's Fortunes.   1876.
   Wait and Hope; or, Ben Bradford's Motto.   1877.
   The Western Boy; or, The Road to Success.   1878; as *Tom, The Bootblack,* 1880.
   The Young Adventurer; or, Tom's Trip Across the Plains.   1878.
   The Telegraph Boy.   1879; as *The District Telegraph Boy,* N.d.
   The Young Explorer; or, Among the Sierras.   1880.
   Tony, The Hero.   1880; as *Tony, The Tramp,* 1910(?).
   The Train Boy.   1882; revised edition, 1883.
   Ben's Nugget; or, A Boy's Search for Fortune: A Story of the Pacific Coast.   1882.
   Dan, The Detective.   1883; as *Dan the Newsboy,* 1893; as *Dutiful Dan, The Brave Boy
      Detective,* 1903(?).
   The Young Circus Rider; or, The Mystery of Robert Rudd.   1883.

Do and Dare; or, A Brave Boy's Fight for Fortune. 1884.
Hector's Inheritance; or, The Boys of Smith Institute. 1885.
Helping Himself; or, Grant Thornton's Ambition. 1886.
Joe's Luck; or, A Boy's Adventure in California. 1887.
Frank Fowler, The Cash Boy. 1887.
Number 91; or, The Adventures of a New York Telegraph Boy. 1887.
The Story Boy; or, The Fortunes of Ben Barclay. 1887; as *Ben Barclay's Courage,*
    1904.
Bob Burton; or, The Young Ranchman of the Missouri. 1888.
The Errand Boy. 1888.
The Merchant's Crime. 1888; as *Ralph Raymond's Heir,* 1892.
Tom Temple's Career. 1888.
Tom Thatcher's Fortune. 1888.
Tom Tracy. 1888.
The Young Acrobat of the Great North American Circus. 1888.
Luke Walton; or, The Chicago Newsboy. 1889.
Mark Stanton; or, Both Sides of the Continent. 1890.
Ned Newton; or, The Fortunes of a New York Bootblack. 1890.
A New York Boy. 1890.
The Odds Against Him; or, Carl Crawford's Experience. 1890; as *Driven from Home,*
    n.d.
Struggling Upward; or, Luke Larkin's Luck. 1890.
Dean Dunham. 1890.
The Erie Train Boy. 1890.
$500; or, Jacob Marlowe's Secret. 1890; as *The Five Hundred Dollar Check,* 1891.
Digging for Gold: A Story of California. 1892.
The Young Boatman of Pine Point. 1892.
Facing the World; or, The Haps and Mishaps of Harry Vane. 1893.
In a New World; or, Among the Gold-Fields of Australia. 1893; as *The Nugget Finders,*
    1894; as *Val Vane's Victory; or, Well Won,* 1903(?).
Only an Irish Boy; or, Andy Burke's Fortunes and Misfortunes. 1894.
Victor Vane, The Young Secretary. 1894.
Adrift in the City; or, Oliver Conrad's Plucky Fight. 1895.
The Disagreeable Woman: A Social Mystery. 1895.
Frank Hunter's Peril. 1896.
The Young Salesman. 1896.
Walter Sherwood's Probation. 1897.
Frank and Fearless; or, The Fortunes of Jasper Kent. 1897.
The Young Bank Messenger. 1898.
A Boy's Fortune; or, The Strange Adventures of Ben Baker. 1898.
Rupert's Ambition. 1899.
Jed, The Poorhouse Boy. 1899.
Mark Mason's Victory; or, The Trails and Triumphs of a Telegraph Boy. 1899.
A Debt of Honor: The Story of Gerald Lane's Success in the Far West. 1900.
Falling in with Fortune; or, The Experiences of a Young Secretary, completed by
    Edward Stratemeyer. 1900.
Out for Business; or, Robert Frost's Strange Career, completed by Edward
    Stratemeyer. 1900.
Ben Bruce: Scenes in the Life of a Bowery Newsboy. 1901.
Lester's Luck. 1901.
Making His Mark. 1901.
Nelson the Newsboy; or, Afloat in New York, completed by Edward Stratemeyer. 1901.
Striving for Fortune; or, Walter Griffith's Trials and Successes. 1901; as *Walter
    Griffith,* 1901.

Tom Brace: Who He Was and How He Fared. 1901.
Young Captain Jack; or, The Son of a Soldier, completed by Edward
    Stratemeyer. 1901.
Andy Grant's Pluck. 1902.
A Rolling Stone; or, The Adventures of a Wanderer. 1902; as *Wren Winter's Triumph,*
    1902.
Tom Turner's Legacy: The Story of How He Secured It. 1902.
The World Before Him. 1902.
Bernard Brooks' Adventures: The Story of a Brave Boy's Trials. 1903.
Chester Rand; or, A New Path to Fortune. 1903.
Forging Ahead. 1903; as *Andy Gordon,* 1905.
Adrift in New York. 1904.
Finding a Fortune. 1904; as *The Tin Box,* 1905(?).
Jerry, The Backwoods Boy; or, The Parkhurst Treasure, completed by Edward
    Stratemeyer. 1904.
Lost at Sea; or, Robert Roscoe's Strange Cruise, completed by Edward
    Stratemeyer. 1904.
From Farm to Fortune; or, Nat Nason's Strange Experience, completed by Edward
    Stratemeyer. 1905.
Mark Manning's Mission; or, The Story of a Shoe Factory Boy. 1905.
The Young Book Agent; or, Frank Hardy's Road to Success, completed by Edward
    Stratemeyer. 1905.
Joe the Hotel Boy; or, Winning Out by Pluck, completed by Edward Stratemeyer. 1906.
Randy of the River; or, The Adventures of a Young Deckhand, completed by Edward
    Stratemeyer. 1906.
The Young Musician. 1906.
In Search of Treasure: The Story of Guy's Eventful Voyage. 1907.
Wait and Win: The Story of Jack Drummond's Pluck. 1908.
Robert Coverdale's Struggle; or, On the Wave of Success. 1910.

Verse

Grand'ther Baldwin's Thanksgiving with Other Ballads and Poems. 1875.

Other

Nothing to Do: A Tilt at Our Best Society. 1857.
*From Canal Boy to President; or, The Boyhood and Manhood of James A.
    Garfield.* 1881.
*From Farm Boy to Senator, Being the History of the Boyhood and Manhood of Daniel
    Webster.* 1882.
Abraham Lincoln, The Backwoods Boy. 1883.

Bibliography: *Road to Success: The Bibliography of the Works of Alger* by Ralph D. Gardner,
1971.

Reading List: *From Rags to Riches: Alger and the American Dream* by John W. Tebbel,
1963.

*   *   *

In 1867 Horatio Alger, failed preacher and school master, entered upon a literary career which eventually produced more than a hundred so-called boy's novels, thereby becoming one of the most successful writers in history. Indeed, so successful was he that his name has entered the language to signify the rags-to-riches American hero who, though born in dire straits, follows a virtuous and diligent life to a position of wealth and influence.

So prodigious an output necessarily dictated that Alger's characters were little more than caricatures, heroes with faces that "indicated a frank, sincere nature" (as in *The World Before Him*), and villains "with shifty black eyes and thin lips, shaded by a dark moustache" (*Adrift in New York*). His plots also inevitably located an impoverished but ingenuous lad, often an orphan, in a hostile environment, usually the city. There, possessed of those virtues which have become synonymous with the Alger myth – optimism, ambition, thrift, and self-reliance – the lad matured toward an adulthood of power, affluence, and respectability.

This conventional reading of the Alger stories and the myth to which they gave birth is, however, somewhat misleading. For to the more careful reader Alger's novels carry a more ambiguous message. First, it is not simply individual virtue but virtue in the face of good fortune that brings success to Alger's boys. Thus, as the typical story unfolds, the hero chances to save the millionaire's grandson from drowning or to find and return the lost bag of bank notes. In a sense, then, the cultivation of virtue is really a ritual of purification which prepares Alger's hero for the providential moment when he will be tried and found not wanting. Luck, no less than pluck – not to mention virtue – figures deeply in the success of the Alger hero. Second, the Alger hero's virtues are often compromised by their countervailing vices. Thrift, for instance, routinely gives way to a profligate visit to the theater or a spendthrift ride on a ferry boat, and self-reliance is often submerged in the desire for security and dependence.

Alger's heroes, in short, are not of the unalloyed virtue that the myth would have one believe. And virtue itself, compromised as it is, is routinely abetted by dumb luck. Still, Alger's name lives in the language as a synonym for virtue rewarded. And Alger himself, a novelist of admittedly modest abilities, has been eclipsed by his own name in the minds of the millions who have never read his work.

—Bruce A. Lohof

ALGREN, Nelson. American. Born in Detroit, Michigan, 28 March 1909. Educated at the University of Illinois, Urbana, 1928–31, B.S. in journalism 1931. Served in the United States Army Medical Corps, 1942–45. Married in 1936 (divorced, 1940); married Betty Ann Jones in 1965 (divorced, 1967). Worked as a salesman, migratory worker, carnival shill, and part-owner of a gas station, 1931–35; for the Works Progress Administration (WPA), 1936–40; for the Venereal Disease Program of the Chicago Board of Health, 1941–42. Editor, with Jack Conroy, *The New Anvil*, Chicago, 1939–41. Teacher of creative writing, University of Iowa, Iowa City, 1967, and University of Florida, Gainesville, 1974. Recipient: National Institute of Arts and Letters grant, 1947; Newberry Library Fellowship, 1947; National Book Award, 1950; American Academy of Arts and Letters Award of Merit, 1974. Lives in Chicago.

PUBLICATIONS

Fiction

Somebody in Boots. 1935; as *The Jungle*, n.d.

Never Come Morning. 1942.
The Neon Wilderness (stories). 1946.
The Man with the Golden Arm. 1949.
A Walk on the Wild Side. 1956.
The Last Carousel (stories). 1973.

Other

Chicago: City on the Make. 1951.
*Who Lost an American? Being a Guide to the Seamier Sides of New York City, Inner
London, Paris, Dublin, Barcelona, Seville, Almeria, Istanbul, Crete and Chicago,
Illinois.* 1963.
Conversations with Algren, with H. E. F. Donohue. 1964.
Notes from a Sea-Diary: Hemingway All the Way. 1965.

Editor, *Algren's Own Book of Lonesome Monsters.* 1962.

Bibliography: *Algren: A Checklist* by Kenneth G. McCollum, 1973.

Reading List: *Algren* by Martha Heasley Cox and R. W. Chatterton, 1975.

*   *   *

Four novels, some fifty short stories, numerous sketches, essays, poems, travel books, book
reviews and other literary criticism produced over a period of more than forty years assure
Nelson Algren a place in American literature. Chicago, where Algren lived for much of his
life, is the setting for most of his work. Characters, themes, symbols, and imagery, as well as
the Chicago settings, recur throughout his canon as he becomes the spokesman for the
derelicts, professional tramps, prostitutes, addicts, convicts, prize-fighters, and baseball
players who inhabit his city jungle, "The Neon Wilderness," as he titled one of his collection
of short stories. While most of Algren's characters speak the dialogue of the gutter, his style
varies from staccato reporting to the richly poetic passages that have gained him the title "the
poet of the Chicago slums." His books contain much offbeat information revealed with satire,
irony, humor, and farce.

His first novel, *Somebody in Boots*, is a "Depression novel," a chronicle of poverty and
failure dedicated to "those innumerable thousands: the homeless boys of America." His
second, *Never Come Morning*, is a story of rape and murder with a doomed Chicago Polish
boxer as its hero. His best known work, however, is his third novel *The Man with the Golden
Arm*, which won him the first National Book Award. In this book, written two decades
before drug addiction became a national dilemma, Algren fictionalized the world of the drug
addict with as yet unsurpassed authority and impact.

His last novel, *A Walk on the Wild Side*, the result of an attempt to rework *Somebody in
Boots*, is Algren's favorite work as well as that of most of his later critics. Though Algren
once maintained that no one has understood *A Walk on the Wild Side* – a book, he says, of a
kind never before written, "an American fantasy – a poem written to an American beat as
truly as *Huckleberry Finn*" – the novel is now acclaimed for its prophetic qualities and for its
influence on later novels and films, particularly the novel and film *Midnight Cowboy* and the
film *Easy Rider*.

—Martha Heasley Cox

ALLEN, James Lane. American. Born near Lexington, Kentucky, 21 December 1849. Educated at Transylvania Academy, Lexington, 1866–68; Kentucky University, now Transylvania University, Lexington, 1868–72, 1875–77, B.A. (honors) 1872, M.A. 1887. Taught at a district school in Fort Springs, Kentucky, 1872–73, and at a high school in Richmond, Missouri, 1873–74; teacher at his own school in Lexington, Missouri, 1875; Principal, Transylvania Academy, 1878–80; Professor of Latin, Bethany College, West Virginia, 1880–83; opened and taught at a private school in Lexington, Kentucky, 1883–85; thereafter a full-time writer; settled in New York City, 1893; lived in Europe, 1894, 1900, 1909. M.A.: Bethany College, 1880; LL.D.: Kentucky University, 1898. *Died 18 February 1925.*

PUBLICATIONS

Collections

    A Kentucky Cardinal, Aftermath, and Other Selected Works, edited by William K. Bottorff. 1967.

Fiction

    Flute and Violin and Other Kentucky Tales and Romances. 1891.
    John Gray: A Kentucky Tale of the Olden Time. 1893.
    A Kentucky Cardinal. 1895.
    Aftermath. 1896.
    Summer in Arcady: A Tale of Nature. 1896.
    The Choir Invisible. 1897; revised edition, 1898.
    The Reign of Law: A Tale of the Kentucky Hemp Fields. 1900; as *The Increasing Purpose,* 1900.
    The Mettle of the Pasture. 1903.
    The Bride of the Mistletoe. 1909.
    The Doctor's Christmas Eve. 1910.
    The Heroine in Bronze; or, A Portrait of a Girl: A Pastoral of the City. 1912.
    The Last Christmas Tree: An Idyll of Immortality. 1914.
    The Sword of Youth. 1915.
    A Cathedral Singer. 1916.
    The Kentucky Warbler. 1918.
    The Emblems of Fidelity: A Comedy in Letters. 1919.
    The Alabaster Box (stories). 1923.
    The Landmark (stories). 1925.

Other

    The Blue-Grass Region of Kentucky and Other Kentucky Articles. 1892.
    Chimney Corner Graduates. 1900.

Bibliography: in *Bibliography of American Literature* by Jacob Blanck, 1955.

Reading List: *Allen* by John Wilson Townsend, 1927; *Allen and the Genteel Tradition* by Grant C. Knight, 1935; *Allen* by William K. Bottorff, 1964.

James Lane Allen was ideally suited to purveying the kind of story and novel demanded by the popular reading audience of the 1890's. Because of his evangelical religious orthodoxy, his innate Southern chivalry, and his readings in Hawthorne, Eliot, Thackeray, and Dickens, he demonstrated the rigorous moral control so often admired by conservative readers of the *fin de siècle*.

Although Allen wrote during an era of fiction that is generally regarded as realistic, he himself is remembered as a Romantic local colorist under the influence of Wordsworth, Thoreau, and Audubon, who tended to idealize Nature by pointing out the "spiritual sustenance" nature offers (William K. Bottorff). Allen's settings were often in the central Kentucky landscape he knew so well.

There are essentially four groups of works in the Allen canon (see H. A. Toulmin, Jr., *Social Historians*). The first group sprang naturally from the disposition of a local colorist: a distinctive, sympathetic treatment of Kentucky life as in *Flute and Violin and Other Kentucky Tales* and *The Blue-Grass Region of Kentucky*. The second group constitutes a limited philosophical growth in its treatment of nature as in *A Kentucky Cardinal* and *Aftermath*. The third group champions the doctrines of evolution and the consequences of circumstance as in *Summer in Arcady*, *The Reign of Law*, and *The Mettle of the Pasture*. The fourth vein of Allen's writings is the historical problem novel as in *The Choir Invisible*.

It is to *Flute and Violin and Other Kentucky Tales* that the avid Allen reader returns. Three distinct weaknesses, however, become apparent in this early Allen collection – sentimentality, an excessively adorned style, and a Puritanic point of view that weaves, as Grant C. Knight says, "allegories and symbols into the pattern of the narratives." The title story has enjoyed considerable popularity owing to its sentimental portrayal of the Reverend James Moore who communes on his flute with the fatherless waif David, who plays the violin. The Dickensian character complements are marked.

A Kentucky Cardinal is a love story set against the beauties of the rural Kentucky landscape just outside Lexington. The hero, Adam Moss, may well be Allen's finest and most Thoreau-like character. *The Choir Invisible*, a poorly unified work, sought to create a gentleman "in buckskins." The novel, set in Kentucky in 1795, is comparable to Eliot and Thackeray in its morality, humor, and pathos.

Allen's work began a marked decline early in the twentieth century, *The Mettle of the Pasture* had a mixed critical reception. *The Bride of the Mistletoe* and *The Doctor's Christmas Eve* met with indifference and disapproval, and his later works are all but forgotten.

Today's readers and critics will find it difficult to agree with Edmund Gosse's 1888 letter to Joseph B. Gilder that Allen's was "A pen possessed of every accomplishment." The contemporary literary historian will agree, however, that Allen's writings constitute some of the best moments of American local color. Allen may be regarded as the supreme Southern Victorian in his medievalism, in his moral and didactic inclination, in his desire to experiment, and in his eclecticism. As Bottorff notes, from Hawthorne Allen drew his psychology, morality, and complexity, from Thoreau he learned his transcendentalism, and from James the complexity of his psychological probings.

—George C. Longest

AMIS, Kingsley (William). English. Born in London, 16 April 1922. Educated at the City of London School; St John's College, Oxford, M.A. Served as an Officer in the Royal Corps of Signals, 1942–45. Married 1) Hilary Ann Bardwell in 1948 (divorced, 1965), two sons, including the writer Martin Amis, and one daughter; 2) the novelist Elizabeth Jane

Howard in 1965. Lecturer in English, University College, Swansea, 1949–61; Fellow in English, Peterhouse, Cambridge, 1961–63. Visiting Fellow in Creative Writing, Princeton University, New Jersey, 1958–59; Visiting Professor, Vanderbilt University, Nashville, Tennessee, 1967–68. Recipient: Maugham Award, 1955.

PUBLICATIONS

Fiction

> *Lucky Jim.* 1954.
> *That Uncertain Feeling.* 1955.
> *I Like It Here.* 1958.
> *Take a Girl Like You.* 1960.
> *My Enemy's Enemy* (stories). 1962.
> *One Fat Englishman.* 1963.
> *The Egyptologists,* with Robert Conquest. 1965.
> *The Anti-Death League.* 1966.
> *I Want It Now.* 1968.
> *Colonel Sun: A James Bond Adventure.* 1968.
> *The Green Man.* 1969.
> *Girl, 20.* 1971.
> *Dear Illusion.* 1972.
> *The Riverside Villas Murder.* 1973.
> *Ending Up.* 1974.
> *The Alteration.* 1976.
> *Jake's Thing.* 1978.

Plays

Radio Play: *Something Strange,* 1962.

Television Plays: *A Question about Hell,* 1964; *The Importance of Being Harry,* 1971; *Dr. Watson and the Darkwater Hall Mystery,* 1974; *See What You've Done* (*Softly, Softly* series), 1974; *We Are All Guilty* (*Against the Crowd* series), 1975.

Verse

> *Bright November.* 1947.
> *A Frame of Mind.* 1953.
> *A Case of Samples: Poems 1946 1956.* 1956.
> *The Evans Country.* 1962.
> *A Look round the Estate: Poems 1957 1967.* 1967.

Other

> *Socialism and the Intellectuals.* 1957.
> *New Maps of Hell: A Survey of Science Fiction.* 1960.

The James Bond Dossier. 1965.
Lucky Jim's Politics. 1968.
What Became of Jane Austen? and Other Essays. 1970.
On Drink. 1973.
Kipling and His World. 1975.

Editor, with James Michie, *Oxford Poetry 1949.* 1949.
Editor, with Robert Conquest, *Spectrum: A Science Fiction Anthology.* 1961 (and later volumes).
Editor, *Selected Short Stories of Chesterton.* 1972.
Editor, *Tennyson.* 1973.
Editor, *Harold's Years: The Harold Wilson Era.* 1977.
Editor, *The New Oxford Book of Light Verse.* 1978.
Editor, *The Faber Popular Reciter* (verse anthology). 1978.

Bibliography: *Amis: A Checklist* by Jack Benoit Gohn, 1976.

Reading List: *Language of Fiction* by David Lodge, 1966; *The Reaction Against Experiment: A Study of the English Novel 1950 1960* by Rubin Rabinovitz, 1967.

*   *   *

Kingsley Amis's high reputation rests on his craftsmanship, on a linguistic resourcefulness that does without modernist experiment, and on a traditional concern for being readable. However innovative it might be – and Amis's new departures constantly extend his range – a new Amis novel guarantees a story about recognizable characters and events, involving clearly defined themes, and punctiliously written. Besides that, with perhaps a couple of exceptions (*The Anti-Death League* and *The Alteration* – and even these not completely so), Amis's novels are inventive comedies, ironic or satiric, reflecting everyday experience. Writing that is entertaining and that generally keeps faith with the reading public has ensured a popular standing that is more stable than any journalistic success, such as the "Angry Young Men" label of the 1950's.

Amis's work is not easily pigeon-holed. A useful rule-of-thumb (suggested by Amis himself) is to note that, from their order of publication, his even-numbered novels are more serious and considered than the odd-numbered ones. *That Uncertain Feeling* (number 2) is about marital fidelity; *Take a Girl Like You* (4), in rich detail, explores the changing social mores of the late 1950's; *The Anti-Death League* (6), most serious of all, looks at the nihilistic consequences of the fact of death. In contrast, *I Like It Here* (3) is generally (perhaps mistakenly) regarded as slight; *One Fat Englishman* (5) and *I Want It Now* (7) seem merely to take old themes into newer, exotic settings. But more and more, and indeed from the very beginning, seriousness and comedy intermingle brilliantly. *Lucky Jim*, for all its fondly-remembered farce, had things to say about integrity, and Amis's ninth novel, *Girl, 20*, while indulging in swipes at environmental tattiness, trendiness, and the bogus in general, also deals with the need for responsibility.

More and more, Amis's novels have been recognized examples of fictional sub-genres – though always of course with an individual treatment. He has attempted the contemporary spy thriller (*Colonel Sun* – a James Bond story); a ghost story (*The Green Man*) with elements that recall both Henry James (linguistic ambiguity) and M. R. James (antiquarian texts and evil spirits); a classic 1930's crime mystery with a highly individual detective, and wonderfully evocative of both genre and period (*The Riverside Villas Murder*); and, most recently, a thoughtful science-fiction exercise, set in an alternative world which depends on the Reformation never having occurred (*The Alteration*). Even *Ending Up* looks like a very special attempt at the type of geriatric novel familiar from the work of Elizabeth Taylor and William Trevor.

Another feature of Amis's recent work is a growing sophistication in developing individual narrative stances, particularly with first-person narratives. Yandell, the "no nonsense" narrator of *Girl, 20*, seems always to get things exactly wrong. Maurice Allington's narrative of *The Green Man* seems so cunningly contrived as to turn questions about an ambiguous content into ones about form. But even an early work like *That Uncertain Feeling* used a detached first-person narrator who spoke of himself in third-person terms. Indeed, it could be a mistake not to credit Amis with a possibly long-standing devotion to narrative versatility, even narrative audacity.

The concerns and themes of Amis's fiction can sometimes be seen to link closely with his poems, though poetry is now a minor activity. His verse is of a piece with his fiction – as might be expected with influences from Graves and Empson – with irony, satiric intentions, and a habit of nonplussing the reader.

—Norman Macleod

ANAND, Mulk Raj. Indian. Born in Peshawar, 12 December 1905. Educated at Khalsa College, Amritsar; Punjab University, 1921–24, B.A. (honours) 1924; University College, University of London, 1926–29; Cambridge University, 1929–30; League of Nations School of Intellectual Cooperation, Geneva, 1930–32. Married 1) the actress Kathleen Van Gelder in 1939 (divorced, 1948); 2) the dancer Shirin Vajifdar in 1950, one daughter. Lecturer, School of Intellectual Cooperation, Summer 1930, and Workers Educational Association, London, intermittently 1932–45; has also taught at the universities of Punjab, of Banares, Varanasai, and of Rajasthan, Jaipur, 1948–66: Tagore Professor of Literature and Fine Art, University of Punjab, 1963–66; Visiting Professor, Institute of Advanced Studies, Simla, 1967–68. Fine Art Chairman, Lalit Kala Akademi (National Academy of Art), New Delhi, 1965–70. Since 1946, Editor of *Marg* magazine, Bombay. Since 1970, President of the Lokayata Trust, for creating a community and cultural centre in Hauz Khas village, New Delhi. Recipient: Leverhulme Fellowship, 1940–42; World Peace Council prize, 1952; Padma Bhushan, India, 1968. Member, Indian Academy of Letters. Lives in Bombay.

PUBLICATIONS

Fiction

The Lost Child and Other Stories.   1934.
Untouchable.   1935.
Coolie.   1936; revised edition, 1972.
Two Leaves and a Bud.   1937.
The Village.   1939.
Lament on the Death of a Master of Arts.   1939.
Across the Black Waters.   1940.
The Sword and the Sickle.   1942.
The Barber's Trade Union and Other Stories.   1944.
The Big Heart.   1945.
The Tractor and the Corn Goddess and Other Stories.   1947.
Seven Summers: The Story of an Indian Childhood.   1951.
The Private Life of an Indian Prince.   1953; revised edition, 1970.
Reflections on the Golden Bed (stories).   1954.

The Road.   1962.
The Old Woman and the Cow.   1963.
Death of a Hero.   1964.
The Power of Darkness.   1966.
Morning Face.   1968.

Play

India Speaks (produced 1943).

Other

Persian Painting.   1930.
Curries and Other Indian Dishes.   1932.
The Golden Breath: Studies in Five Poets of the New India.   1933.
The Hindu View of Art.   1933; revised edition, 1957.
Apology for Heroism: An Essay in Search of a Faith.   1934.
Letters on India.   1942.
Indian Fairy Tales: Retold (juvenile).   1946.
On Education.   1947.
The Bride's Book of Beauty, with K. N. Hutheesing.   1947.
The Story of India (juvenile).   1948.
The King Emperor's English; or, The Role of the English Language in the Free India.   1948.
Lines Written to an Indian Air: Essays.   1949.
Indian Theatre.   1950.
The Story of Man (juvenile).   1954.
More Indian Fairy Tales (juvenile).   1956.
Kama Kala: Some Notes on the Philososphical Basis of Hindu Erotic Sculpture.   1958.
India in Colour.   1959.
Homage to Khajuraho, with Stella Kramrisch.   1960.
Is There a Contemporary Indian Civilization?   1963.
The Volcano: Lectures on the Painting of Rabindranath Tagore.   1968.
Annals of Childhood.   1968.
Ajunta, photographs by R. R. Bhurdwaj.   1971.
Seven Summers.   1972.

Editor, *Marx and Engels on India.*   1933.
Editor, with Iqbal Singh, *Indian Short Stories.*   1947.
Editor, *Introduction to Indian Art,* by A. K. Coomaraswamy.   1956.
Editor, *Experiments: Contemporary Indian Short Stories.*   1968.

Reading List: *Anand: A Critical Essay,* 1948, and *The Lotus and the Elephant,* 1954, both by Jack Lindsay; *An Ideal of Man in Anand's Novels* by D. Riemenschneider, 1969; *Anand: The Man and the Novelist* by Margaret Berry, 1970; *Anand: A Study of His Fiction in Humanist Perspective* by G. S. Gupta, 1975; *So Many Freedoms: A Study of the Major Fiction of Anand* by Saros Cowasgee, 1978.

*   *   *

Mulk Raj Anand is the most controversial of the Indian writers writing in English, and, along with R. K. Narayan, the best known.

He is a socially committed writer, and, though he denies the influence of Marx on his writing (he calls himself a rational humanist), there can be little doubt that his writing is to a certain extent influenced by Marxist theories. An advocate of equality and universal brotherhood, he believes in man's latent goodness which will triumph over evil given the right conditions. And it is socialism alone which can provide the right conditions for man's total development.

Anand's characters invariably fall into three classes: the victims, who are usually the protagonists; the oppressors, those who oppose change and progress; and the good men. Under the last category fall the social workers, the labour leaders, all those who believe in progress and can see how modern science can improve the lot of the sufferers and help bring about the equality of all men. One feels in all his work his deep compassion for others and his understanding of, to quote his own words, "the dignity of weakness of others."

Anand is a prolific writer; apart from some twenty works of fiction he has written an almost equal number of works of non-fiction on subjects which range from Persian painting to Indian food. He has also begun a seven-volume autobiography. His best work is the fiction produced in the 1930's and 1940's, *Untouchable, Coolie*, the trilogy *The Village, Across the Black Waters*, and *The Sword and the Sickle*, and *The Private Life of an Indian Prince* (written in 1948 though not published until 1953).

Most socially committed novelists have a tendency towards didacticism; the artist becomes the propagandist, style is sacrificed for the message. Anand does not escape these failings; Bonamy Dobrée once criticized him for substituting "emotions for criticism," but in the above mentioned works he avoids most of the pitfalls. They are his most successful attempts at combining the role of artist and social critic.

—Anna Rutherford

ANDERSON, Sherwood (Berton). American. Born in Camden, Ohio, 13 September 1876. Educated at a high school in Clyde, Ohio; Wittenberg Academy, Springfield, Ohio, 1899–1900. Served in the United States Army in Cuba during the Spanish-American War, 1898–99. Married 1) Cornelia Pratt Lane in 1904 (divorced, 1916), two sons and one daughter; 2) Tennessee Claflin Mitchell in 1916 (divorced, 1924); 3) Elizabeth Prall in 1924 (divorced, 1932); 4) Eleanor Copenhaver in 1933. Worked in a produce warehouse in Chicago, 1896–97; Advertising Copywriter, Long-Critchfield Company, Chicago, 1900–05; President, United Factories Company, Cleveland, 1906, and Anderson Manufacturing Company, paint manufacturers, Elyria, Ohio, 1907–12; free-lance copywriter, then full-time writer, Chicago, 1913–23; visited France and England, 1921; lived in New Orleans, 1923–24; settled on a farm near Marion, Virginia, 1925: Publisher of the *Smyth County News* and *Marion Democrat* from 1927; travelled extensively in the United States in the mid 1930's reporting on depression life. Member, National Institute of Arts and Letters, 1937. *Died 8 March 1941.*

PUBLICATIONS

Collections

Anderson Reader, edited by Paul Rosenfeld. 1947.

Letters, edited by Howard Mumford Jones and Walter B. Rideout.   1953.
Short Stories, edited by Maxwell Geismar.   1962.

Fiction

Windy McPherson's Son.   1916.
Marching Men.   1917; edited by Ray Lewis White, 1972.
Winesburg, Ohio: A Group of Tales of Ohio Small Town Life.   1919.
Poor White.   1920.
The Triumph of the Egg and Other Stories.   1921.
Many Marriages.   1923.
Horses and Men (stories).   1923.
Dark Laughter.   1925.
Alice, and The Lost Novel (stories).   1929.
Beyond Desire.   1932.
Death in the Woods and Other Stories.   1933.
Kit Brandon: A Portrait.   1936.

Plays

Winesburg (produced 1934).   In *Winesburg and Others,* 1937.
Mother (produced ?).   In *Winesburg and Others,* 1937.
Winesburg and Others (includes *The Triumph of the Egg,* dramatized by Raymond
    O'Neil; *Mother, They Married Later*).   1937.
Textiles, in *Contemporary One-Act Plays,* edited by William Kozlenko.   1938.
Above Suspicion (broadcast 1941).   In *The Free Company Presents,* edited by James
    Boyd, 1941.

Radio Play: *Above Suspicion,* 1941.

Other

Mid-American Chants.   1918.
A Story Teller's Story.   1924; edited by Ray Lewis White, 1968.
The Modern Writer.   1925.
Notebook.   1926.
Tar: A Midwest Childhood.   1926; edited by Ray Lewis White, 1969.
A New Testament.   1927.
Hello Towns!   1929.
Nearer the Grass Roots.   1929.
The American County Fair.   1930.
Perhaps Women.   1931.
No Swank.   1934.
Puzzled America.   1935.
A Writer's Conception of Realism.   1939.
Home Town.   1940.
Memoirs.   1942; edited by Ray Lewis White, 1969.
Return to Winesburg (essays), edited by Ray Lewis White.   1967.
The Buck Fever Papers, edited by Welford Dunaway Taylor.   1971.
France and Anderson: Paris Notebook 1921, edited by Michael Fanning.   1976.

Bibliography: *Anderson: A Bibliography* by Eugene P. Sheehy and Kenneth A. Lohf, 1960; *Merrill Checklist of Anderson* by Ray Lewis White, 1969.

Reading List: *Anderson: His Life and Work* by James E. Schevill, 1951; *Anderson* by Irving Howe, 1951; *Anderson* by Brom Weber, 1964; *Anderson* by Rex Burbank, 1964; *The Achievement of Anderson: Essays in Criticism* edited by Ray Lewis White, 1966; *Anderson: An Introduction and Interpretation* by David D. Anderson, 1967; *The Road to Winesburg: A Mosaic of the Imaginative Life of Anderson* by William A. Sutton, 1972; *Anderson: A Collection of Critical Essays* edited by Walter B. Rideout, 1974; *Anderson* by Welford Dunaway Taylor, 1977.

*   *   *

In an interview for the *Paris Review* (Spring 1956), William Faulkner stated that Sherwood Anderson was "the father of my generation of American writers and the tradition of American writing which our successors will carry on." Anderson's importance in literary history is accurately summed up in Faulkner's statement, for Anderson is a seminal figure whose prose style has had a significant impact on the direction of American literature in the twentieth century. As a boy from a small town in Ohio Anderson fell under the spell of Twain's *Huckleberry Finn* with its innocent narrator and non-literary, vernacular style. Later, as an aspiring writer in Chicago and New York, he became fascinated with Gertrude Stein's attempt to use language as a plastic medium, the way an artist uses paints. These influences on Anderson resulted in the development of a simple, concrete style close to the rhythms of American speech, a style which left an indelible imprint on the prose of Hemingway and his followers.

Anderson also developed a number of characteristically American themes in his fiction. The celebration of youth and innocence is one of those distinguishing features of American writing, and Anderson, raised in the middle west before the turn of the century, celebrates small-town life in the days of the horse and buggy. A boy's wonder and innocent joy in rural life, his love of horses and the open countryside, his admiration for the craftsmen of the village are all part of a nostalgic vein running through Anderson's writing. But Anderson, raised in poverty, was intimate with another side of American life, one which he eventually termed "grotesque." As a young man he observed the people of his town caught in a struggle for material wealth and cowed by a repressive Puritan ethic and consequently wrote with great feeling about people like his parents whose lives were made wretched by their society's values. Anderson is very sensitive in his fiction to movement, to the restlessness of the individual and to the movements of peoples within the ever-changing fabric of society. He documents America's transition from a rural to an industrial society, and in several books he represents Americans, working in factories, as trapped in a form of living death. He saw the great masses of working Americans as alienated from creative work, and he pondered the artist's role in reawakening his countrymen to more meaningful forms of life.

Anderson's influence and reputation, however, outweigh his actual achievement as a writer. He published seven novels, but critics are not agreed that any one of the novels is wholly successful. The first, *Windy McPherson's Son*, which at the outset effectively recreates something of Anderson's own youth, particularly his relation to his father, becomes a rambling, incoherent narrative about a man's quest for a family and meaningful work. *Marching Men* is an ideological novel with a cranky and finally incoherent vision of men marching for the betterment of humankind. *Poor White*, which dramatizes the industrialization of America, is usually considered the best of the novels, but the charges of diffuseness and unnecessary repetition are not without some justification. Critics generally feel Anderson's worst novel is *Many Marriages*, the story of a man on the point of giving up his business and family in order to escape what has become for him a living death. Anderson himself walked out on his family and a successful career in order to become a writer, which explains perhaps his own fondness for *Many Marriages*. The other novels, *Dark Laughter*,

Beyond Desire, and *Kit Brandon* all contain interesting variations on the theme of the individual's quest for a more vital existence, but none of these books succeeds completely in terms of characterization and especially plot. More valuable and interesting are Anderson's autobiographical writings, *A Story Teller's Story*, *Tar: A Midwest Childhood*, and the posthumous *Memoirs*, all of which fictionalize to a degree the actual events of Anderson's life and reveal the contrary and powerful impulses of the writer's imagination.

Anderson's success as a fiction writer, however, is undisputed in the short story form, and all the collections he published contain at least one or two first rate pieces. Stories such as "I Want to Know Why," "I'm a Fool," and "The Man Who Became a Woman" in which Anderson employs an innocent narrator and a simple, direct style have a unified purpose and effect that is lacking in all the longer fictions. These are initiation stories wherein a youth, usually an innocent boy from the country who loves horses, is awakened to fear, sexual guilt, and a knowledge of his own limitations. "Death in the Woods" is another short masterpiece; it describes a peasant woman's work-burdened existence with a simplicity and sureness of craft that have made critics compare it with the best of Turgenev's stories.

But the book for which Anderson will always be best known is *Winesburg, Ohio*, a cycle of stories about lonely people in a small midwestern town. Anderson originally titled it "The Book of the Grotesque" and in these stories he portrays with both compassion and clinical accuracy the secret lives of people who have been irreparably thwarted and frustrated in different ways. The narrator explains by means of a dream vision that the characters have become grotesque because they have chosen to believe in a single truth. Whether they believe in love, virginity, or godliness, the truth becomes a lie because such a narrow view distorts reality and tragically cuts people off from each other. The grotesques, caught up in their obsessive beliefs, are unable to communicate their ideas and feelings to each other. For example, a farmer consumed with the idea of being a Biblical patriarch so confuses and terrifies his only grandson in a ritual of sacrifice that the boy runs away forever. A young man, obsessed with the idea that he is "queer," hopelessly different from other people, breaks into a frantic dance and physically strikes out at his one sympathetic listener. A shy woman, who has waited many years for the return of her lover, one night in desperation runs naked across her front lawn in the rain. Appearing in several stories is the young newspaper reporter, George Willard, to whom some of the grotesques tell their story. George's mother, one of the aliens of the town, finds an ultimate release from her frustration and loneliness through death, but before she dies she prays that some day her son will "express something" for them both, that he will redeem their lives through art. The mother gives the book a tragic cast, for her prayer cannot be answered. The artists in *Winesburg, Ohio* are ineffectual figures, often persons the least capable of expressing themselves. George Willard at the end of the book leaves Winesburg and we can assume he has written the stories we have read, but he has not been able to "save" his people because the underlying insight in his book is that each man lives by a truth and no one can fully understand or express that truth for someone else.

Anderson once assessed himself as "the minor author of a minor masterpiece," and one recognizes here an author's startlingly accurate self-assessment. But what the author's statement does not comprehend is the powerful influence Anderson had on other writers like Hemingway and Faulkner and on the course of American literature as a whole.

—David Stouck

ARLEN, Michael. British. Born Dikran Kouyoumdjian in Rustchuk, Bulgaria, 16 November 1895; emigrated to England; naturalized as Michael Arlen, 1922. Educated at Malvern College, Worcestershire; briefly studied medicine at the University of Edinburgh. Served as Civil Defense Public Relations Officer in the West Midlands, 1940–41. Married Atalanta, daughter of Count Mercati, in 1928; one son and one daughter. Full-time writer from 1920; settled in Cannes, 1928–39; writer in Hollywood, 1942–44; thereafter settled in New York City. *Died 23 June 1956.*

PUBLICATIONS

Fiction

The London Venture. 1920.
The Romantic Lady and Other Stories. 1921.
Piracy: A Romantic Chronicle of These Days. 1922.
These Charming People (stories). 1923; selection as *The Man with the Broken Nose and Other Stories,* 1927.
The Green Hat: A Romance for a Few People. 1924.
May Fair, In Which Are Told the Last Adventures of These Charming People (stories). 1925; selection as *The Ace of Cads and Other Stories,* 1925.
Ghost Stories. 1927.
Young Men in Love. 1927.
Lily Christine. 1928.
Babes in the Wood (stories). 1929.
The Ancient Sin and Other Stories. 1930.
Men Dislike Women. 1931.
A Young Man Comes to London. 1932.
The Short Stories. 1933.
Man's Mortality. 1933.
Hell! Said the Duchess: A Bed-Time Story. 1934.
The Crooked Coronet and Other Misrepresentations of the Real Facts of Life. 1937.
Flying Dutchman. 1939.

Plays

Dear Father: A Comedy about Nothing (produced 1924).
The Green Hat, from his own novel (produced 1925). 1925.
The Zoo, with Winchell Smith (produced 1927). 1927.
Good Loser, with Walter Hackett (produced 1931). 1933.

Reading List: *Arlen: Kritiker der Englischen Gesellschaft* by H. C. Guggenbühl, 1937.

*   *   *

When Michael Arlen began writing in the early 1920's he soon became a literary phenomenon. "No-one," says Collins's advertisement for *The Green Hat,* "has gained a greater or swifter reputation since the war" – and it was true. The contemporary literary scene, governed by the old guard (Bennett, Galsworthy, Shaw, and Wells) and the *avant-garde* (Proust, Joyce, Lawrence, and Woolf), allowed little room for intelligent "light reading." It was this gap that Arlen filled and the refreshing influence of his work was reflected in the reviews: "Pure coquetry, of course, but what perfect technique"; "For sheer wit and cynicism Mr. Arlen stands alone"; "Mr. Arlen has a fatally intimate knowledge of the wily ways of women"; "A delightful atmosphere of irresponsibility and freedom"; "Mr. Arlen has invented a new kind of literary cocktail."

The critics who disliked Firbank's foppishness, who now thought Wilde and George Moore passé, and who found Norman Douglas "dangerous," could revel in Arlen because he was "vivid, amusing, intensely modern, and intensely clever." In fact, he was distinctly less ingenious than Wilde and did nothing to develop Firbank's experiments in fictional technique, so important to the novelist who was to eclipse Arlen as a popular humourist in the 1930's, Evelyn Waugh. The key to his astounding popularity is his "modernity" – he talked freely, if in veiled terms, of sex, cocktail parties, and the young, rich, irresponsible, speed-crazed generation with the urbanity of a literary man of the world. He was the chronicler of new Mayfair.

The style is often verbose, as complex as Thackeray or Dickens, yet it cleverly eschews serious intent. Always there is the implicit awareness of the silliness of writing books. He does not, except in *The Green Hat* and the short stories (and then rather gratuitously), deal in complex plots. Neither does he project the doom-laden images of the *avant-garde*. His attitude in the 1920's was that of a precocious after-dinner speaker whose primary objective was to entertain, and he did this by indulging his audience's thirst for luxury and excitement in confections of mock-serious language. It is not surprising that, to the calloused post-war generation, he became a temporary darling.

But for all his "modernity," many of his characters seem almost to belong to Thackeray's world of bucks and rogues, English roses and *femmes fatales*. Arlen wrote "romances" for an educated and optimistic middle-class public who could accept the rather snobbish escapism in terms of a parody of Victorian values. Iris Storm, a partial portrait of Nancy Cunard, became an archetype for many other fictional heroines of the period – Hemingway's Brett Ashley and Waugh's stream of intelligent, sexually-liberated, careless female protagonists: Margot Beste-Chetwynde, Nina Blount, Brenda Last, Virginia Troy. Of the novels, only *The Green Hat* still merits serious consideration, but, even so, its plot is disastrously melodramatic and coy when compared with the abrasive revolutionary tactics of Lawrence or Joyce.

In the more serious *Men Dislike Women*, he revealed himself as a shallow thinker and, for all his irony and bravado, little removed from either the traditional lady romantic novelist or the snappy detective story writer. When the flamboyant, linguistic tricks were dropped altogether in *Man's Mortality*, an "Utopian" vision in which the future world is governed by "International Aircraft and Airways," the plot struggles awkwardly to a naive moral conclusion and the characterisation rises little above that of a boy's adventure story. Even the idea was unoriginal (compare Kipling's "As Easy as A.B.C.").

Unlike Waugh, when he abandoned his whimsical precocity in response to the dour 1930's, he failed to provide incisive social commentary. It is the combination of enthusiasm and worldliness which creates the distinctive atmosphere of his early works, but when the naivety and flippancy of the Mayfair voice began to pale before the various threats of the Depression, Communism, and Fascism, his work shrank in importance and has never returned to favour.

—Martim Stannard

ARTHUR, Timothy Shay. American. Born in Newburgh, New York, 6 June 1809; moved with his family to Baltimore, 1817. Briefly attended Baltimore public schools; largely self-educated. Married Ellen Alden in 1836; five sons and two daughters. Watchmaker's apprentice, then worked as a clerk in a Baltimore counting room; Western Agent for a Baltimore bank, 1833; member of the editorial staff of various Baltimore journals, including the *Athenaeum* and *Saturday Visitor*, 1834–38; Co-Editor, *Baltimore Literary Magazine*,

1838–40; Editor, *Baltimore Merchant*, 1840; moved to Philadelphia, 1841, and became a writer for *Saturday Courier*, *Graham's Magazine*, and *Godey's Lady's Book*; established *Arthur's Ladies' Magazine*, 1845; Founder and Publisher, *Arthur's Home Gazette* (*Arthur's Home Magazine* from 1853), 1852 until his death; published the juvenile periodical *Children's Hour*, from 1867, and *Once a Month*, 1869–70. Member, Executive Committee, Centennial Exhibition, 1876. *Died 6 March 1885.*

PUBLICATIONS

Fiction

Insubordination: An American Story of Real Life. 1841.
Tired of Housekeeping. 1842.
Six Nights with the Washingtonians (stories). 1842; as *The Tavern-Keeper's Victims*, 1860.
Bell Martin; or, The Heiress. 1843.
Fanny Dale; or, The First Year after Marriage. 1843.
The Tailor's Apprentice: A Story of Cruelty and Oppression. 1843.
The Little Pilgrims: A Sequel to The Tailor's Apprentice. 1843.
Madeline; or, A Daughter's Love, and Other Tales. 1843.
Making a Sensation and Other Tales. 1843.
The Ruined Family and Other Tales. 1843.
Swearing Off and Other Tales. 1843.
The Seamstress. 1843.
The Stolen Wife. 1843.
Sweethearts and Wives; or, Before and after Marriage. 1843.
The Two Merchants. 1843.
The Village Doctors and Other Tales. 1843.
Cecilia Howard; or, The Young Lady Who Had Finished Her Education. 1844.
Pride or Principle   Which Makes the Lady? 1844.
Family Pride; or, The Palace and the Poor House. 1844.
Hints and Helps for the Home Circle; or, The Mother's Friend. 1844.
Hiram Elwood, The Banker; or, Like Father Like Son. 1844.
The Martyr Wife. 1844.
Prose Fictions Written for the Illustration of True Principles. 1844.
The Ruined Gamester; or, Two Eras in My Life. 1844.
The Two Sisters; or, Life's Changes. 1844.
The Maiden. 1845.
The Wife. 1845.
Anna Milnor, The Young Lady Who Was Not Punctual, and Other Tales. 1845.
The Heiress. 1845.
The Club Room and Other Temperance Tales. 1845.
Married and Single; or, Marriage and Celibacy Contrasted. 1845.
Lovers and Husbands. 1845.
Tales from Real Life. 1845.
The Two Husbands and Other Tales. 1845.
The Mother. 1846.
Random Recollections of an Old Doctor. 1846.
The Beautiful Widow. 1847.
Improving Stories for the Young. 1847.
Keeping Up Appearances. 1847.

Riches Have Wings. 1847.

The Young Lady at Home. 1847.

The Young Music Teacher and Other Tales. 1847.

Agnes; or The Possessed: A Revelation of Mesmerism. 1848.

Debtor and Creditor. 1848.

The Lost Children. 1848.

Retiring from Business; or, The Rich Man's Error. 1848.

Love in a Cottage. 1848.

Rising in the World. 1848.

Lucy Sanford: A Story of the Heart. 1848.

Making Haste to Be Rich. 1848.

The Three Eras of a Woman's Life (includes *The Maiden, The Wife, The Mother*). 1848.

Love in High Life. 1849.

Mary Moreton; or, The Broken Promise. 1849.

Sketches of Life and Character. 1849.

Alice Mellville; or, The Indiscretion; Mary Ellis; or, The Runaway Match. 1850.

All for the Best; or, The Old Peppermint Man. 1850.

The Debtor's Daughter. 1850.

The Divorced Wife. 1850.

Golden Grains from Life's Harvest Field. 1850.

Illustrated Temperance Tales. 1850.

The Lights and Shadows of Real Life. 1850.

The Orphan Children. 1850.

Pride and Prudence; or, The Married Sisters. 1850.

Tales of Domestic Life. 1850.

True Riches and Other Tales. 1850.

The Two Brides. 1850.

The Young Artist; or, The Dream of Italy. 1850.

The Two Wives. 1851.

The Banker's Wife. 1851.

Lessons in Life for All Who Will Read Them. 1851.

Off-Hand Sketches. 1851.

Seed-Time and Harvest (stories). 1851.

Stories for My Young Friends, Parents, Young Housekeepers. 3 vols., 1851.

The Way to Prosper; or, In Union There Is Strength and Other Tales. 1851.

Woman's Trials (stories). 1851.

Words for the Wise (stories). 1851.

Confessions of a House-Keeper. 1852.

Home Scenes and Home Influences. 1852.

The Tried and the Tempted. 1852.

Cedardale. 1852.

Pierre the Organ-Boy and Other Stories. 1852.

The Poor Wood-Cutter and Other Stories. 1852.

Jessie Hampton. 1852.

Uncle Ben's New Year's Gift. 1852.

The Ways of Providence (stories). 1852.

Confessions of a Housekeeper. 1852; revised edition, as *Trials and Confessions of an American Housekeeper*, 1854; as *Ups and Downs*, 1857.

Who Are Happiest? and Other Stories. 1852.

Who Is Greatest? and Other Stories. 1852.

Before and After the Election; or, The Political Experiences of Mr. Patrick Murphy. 1853.

Finger Posts on the Way of Life. 1853.

The Fireside Angel. 1853.
Haven't-Time and Don't-Be-in-a-Hurry and Other Stories. 1853.
Heart-Histories and Life-Pictures. 1853.
Home Lights and Shadows. 1853.
The Home Mission. 1853.
The Iron Rule; or, Tyranny in the Household. 1853.
The Lady at Home. 1853.
The Last Penny and Other Stories. 1853.
Leaves from the Book of Human Life. 1853.
Maggy's Baby and Other Stories. 1853.
Married Life: Its Shadows and Sunshine (stories). 1852.
The Old Man's Bride. 1853.
Sparing to Spend; or, The Loftons and Pinkertons. 1853.
The Wounded Boy and Other Stories. 1853.
Ten Nights in a Bar-Room and What I Saw There. 1854; edited by H. Hugh Holman,
    with *In His Steps* by Charles M. Sheldon, 1966.
The Angel of the Household. 1954.
Shadows and Sunbeams. 1854.
Leaves from the Book of Human Life. 1855.
The Good Time Coming. 1855.
The Hand But Not the Heart. 1855.
What Can Woman Do? 1855.
The Withered Heart. 1857.
The Hand But Not the Heart; or, The Life-Trials of Jessie Loring. 1858.
The Angel and the Demon: A Tale of Modern Spiritualism. 1858.
The Little Bound-Boy. 1858.
Lizzy Glenn; or, The Trials of a Seamstress. 1859.
The Allen House; or, Twenty Years Ago and Now. 1860.
Aunt Mary's Preserving Kettle. 1863.
Nancy Wimble. 1863.
Hidden Wings and Other Stories. 1864.
Light on Shadowed Paths. 1864.
Out in the World. 1864.
Sunshine at Home and Other Stories. 1864.
Sowing the Wind and Other Stories. 1865.
Home-Heroes, Saints, and Martyrs. 1865.
Nothing But Money. 1865.
What Came Afterwards. 1865.
Life's Crosses and How to Meet Them. 1865.
Our Neighbors in the Corner House. 1866.
The Lost Bride; or, The Astrologer's Prophecy Fulfilled. 1866.
Blind Nelly's Boy and Other Stories. 1867.
After the Storm. 1868.
The Peacemaker and Other Stories. 1869.
After a Shadow and Other Stories. 1869.
Not Anything for Peace and Other Stories. 1869.
Heroes of the Household. 1869.
Rainy Day at Home. 1869.
The Seen and the Unseen. 1869.
Anna Lee. 1869.
Beacon Lights. 1869.
Tom Blinn's Temperance Society and Other Tales. 1870.
Idle Hands and Other Stories. 1871.
Orange Blossoms, Fresh and Faded (stories). 1871.

The Wonderful Story of Gentle Hand and Other Stories. 1871.
Grace Myers' Sewing Machine and Other Tales. 1872.
Cast Adrift. 1872.
Three Years in a Man-Trap. 1872.
Comforted. 1873.
Woman to the Rescue: A Story of the New Crusade. 1874.
The Power of Kindness and Other Stories. 1875.
Danger; or, Wounded in the House of a Friend. 1875.
The Latimer Family. 1877.
The Wife's Engagement Ring. 1877.
The Bar-Rooms at Brantley. 1877.
The Mill and the Tavern. 1878.
The Strike at Jivoli Mills and What Came of It. 1879.
Saved as by Fire. 1881.
Death-Dealing Gold. 1890.
The Little Savoyard and Other Stories. 1891.
Two Little Girls and What They Did. 1899.
Won by Waiting. N.d.

Other

A Christmas Box for the Sons and Daughters of Temperance. 1847.
Advice to Young Men on Their Duties and Conduct in Life. 1847; *Advice to Young Ladies,* 1848.
The Young Wife: A Manual of Moral, Religious, and Domestic Duties. 1847.
Wreaths of Friendship: A Gift for the Young, with Francis Channing Woodworth. 1849.
A Wheat Sheaf, Gathered from Our Own Field, with Francis Channing Woodworth. 1851.
Our Little Harry and Other Poems and Stories. 1852.
The History of Georgia, Illinois, Kentucky, New Jersey, New York, Ohio, Pennsylvania, Vermont, Virginia, with W. H. Carpenter. 10 vols., 1852–54.
The String of Pearls for Boys and Girls, with Francis Channing Woodworth. 1853.
Steps Towards Heaven (sermons). 1858.
Growler's Income Tax. 1864.
Talks with a Philosopher on the Ways of God and Man. 1871.
Strong Drink: The Curse and the Cure. 1877.
Feet and Wings; or, Among the Beasts and Birds. 1880.
Adventures by Sea and Land. 1890.
Sow Well and Reap Well: A Book for the Young. N.d.
Story Sermons. N.d.
Talks with a Child on the Beatitudes. N.d.

Editor, with W. H. Carpenter, *The Baltimore Book.* 1838.
Editor, *The Sons of Temperance Offering.* 2 vols., 1849–50.
Editor, *The Brilliant: A Gift-Book.* 1850.
Editor, *The Crystal Fount for All Seasons.* 1850.
Editor, *The Temperance Gift.* 1854.
Editor, *The Temperance Offering.* 1854.
Editor, *Friends and Neighbors; or, Two Ways of Living in the World.* 1856.
Editor, *The Mother's Rule.* 1856.
Editor, *Our Homes.* 1856.
Editor, *The True Path and How to Walk Therein.* 1856.

Editor, *The Wedding Guest.* 1856.
Editor, *Words of Cheer for the Tempted, The Toiling, and the Sorrowing.* 1856.
Editor, *Orange Blossoms.* 1857.
Editor, *The Boys' and Girls' Treasury.* 1859.
Editor, *Little Gems from the Children's Hour.* 1875.
Editor, *The Prattler.* 1876.
Editor, *The My Books.* 1877.
Editor, *The Budget: A Book for Boys and Girls.* 1877.
Editor, *The Playmate.* 1878.
Editor, *Lucy Grey and Other Stories.* 1880.
Editor, *Sophy and Prince.* 1881.
Editor, *Friendship's Token.* N.d.

*   *   *

Timothy Shay Arthur is likely to be recalled today as the author of *Ten Nights in a Bar-Room*, the popular melodrama about a small-town miller turned saloon-keeper who brings misfortune upon his family and community, until the killing of his daughter by drunken brawlers saves him and the town for temperance (which to Arthur meant total prohibition). Actually he did not write the play, which was one of the most often performed on the American stage during the late nineteenth century and which still survives, though now it is usually burlesqued; the dramatization was prepared by William W. Pratt from Arthur's novel. Nor did Arthur devote himself before the Civil War exclusively to the temperance cause, although he enjoyed his first success with *Six Nights with the Washingtonians*, tales about the work of this noble band that sought to redeem drunkards through "moral suasion." After gaining experience as a contributor to literary magazines and then as co-editor of several short-lived publications in Baltimore from 1834 to 1840, he moved to Philadelphia, where, after several earlier experiments in finding the profitable format for a journal devoted to "the good, the true, and the beautiful," he founded in 1852 *Arthur's Home Magazine*, which he edited until his death.

During these years he wrote about a hundred novels and uncounted short stories, most of which appeared first either in his magazines or the many gift-books that he edited. Before the Civil War, the majority of these tales were thinly fictionalized guides to young people getting married and setting up a home and business. *The Three Eras of a Woman's Life* was only the most ambitious of about two dozen that advised maiden, wife and mother on the woman's proper "sphere" and duties. *Debtor and Creditor* was one of many that warned against unsound business practices; but Arthur was also one of the first American novelists, even before the age of the Robber Barons, to condemn unscrupulous business practices growing out of a greed for gain in an unexpectedly bleak and cynical novel like *Nothing But Money*. Arthur was also a member of the Church of the New Jerusalem, as the followers of Emmanuel Swedenborg called themselves; and he expounded the doctrines of the church in novels like *The Good Time Coming*, an attempt to dissuade egotistical people from reckless courses. He also, surprisingly, pioneered in fiction dealing with divorce – then a scandalous subject. *The Hand But Not the Heart*, *After the Storm*, and *Out in the World* castigate hasty marriage and easy divorce, but grant that legal separation may be necessitated by a spouse's philandering or intemperance.

After the Civil War left him disheartened about his fellow Americans, he devoted his fiction largely to the temperance crusade, growing through *Three Years in a Man-Trap*, *Woman to the Rescue*, and *The Bar-Rooms at Brantley* constantly more hysterical in his denunciation of the evils of drink and shriller in his demands for legal prohibition rather than a reliance upon self-reform. These works in print or on the stage, however, failed to enjoy the success of his earlier writings.

—Warren French

ATHERTON, Gertrude (Franklin, née Horn). American. Born in San Francisco, California, 30 October 1857. Educated in private schools in California and Kentucky. Married George H. Bowen Atherton in 1876 (died, 1887). After her husband's death travelled extensively and lived in Europe; in later life returned to San Francisco. Trustee, San Francisco Public Library; Member, San Francisco Art Commission. President, American National Academy of Literature, 1934; Chairman of Letters, League of American Pen Women, 1939; President, Northern California Section of P.E.N. Recipient: International Academy of Letters and Sciences of Italy Gold Medal. D.Litt.: Mills College, Oakland, California, 1935; LL.D.: University of California, Berkeley, 1937. Chevalier, Legion of Honor, 1925; Honorary Member, Institut Littéraire et Artistique de France. *Died 14 June 1948.*

PUBLICATIONS

Fiction

What Dreams May Come. 1888.
Hermia Suydam. 1889; as *Hermia, An American Woman,* 1889.
Los Cerritos: A Romance of the Modern Time. 1890.
A Question of Time. 1891.
The Doomswoman. 1893.
Before the Gringo Came. 1894; revised edition, as *The Splendid Idle Forties: Stories of Old California,* 1902.
A Whirl Asunder. 1895.
His Fortunate Grace. 1897.
Patience Sparhawk and Her Times. 1897.
American Wives and English Husbands. 1898; revised edition, as *Transplanted,* 1919.
The Californians. 1898; revised edition, 1935.
The Valiant Runaways. 1898.
A Daughter of the Vine. 1899.
Senator North. 1900.
The Aristocrats, Being the Impressions of the Lady Helen Pole During Her Sojourn in the Great North Woods. 1901.
The Conqueror, Being the True and Romantic Story of Alexander Hamilton. 1902.
Heart of Hyacinth. 1903.
Mrs. Pendleton's Four-in-Hand. 1903.
Rulers of Kings. 1904.
The Bell in the Fog and Other Stories. 1905.
The Travelling Thirds. 1905.
Rezánov. 1906.
Ancestors. 1907.
The Gorgeous Isle: A Romance: Scene, Nevis, B.W.I., 1842. 1908.
Tower of Ivory. 1910.
Julia France and Her Times. 1912.
Perch of the Devil. 1914.
Mrs. Balfame. 1916.
The White Morning: A Novel of the Power of the German Women in Wartime. 1918.
The Avalanche: A Mystery Story. 1919.
The Sisters-in-Law: A Novel of Our Time. 1921.
Sleeping Fires. 1922; as *Dormant Fires,* 1922.
Black Oxen. 1923.

The Crystal Cup. 1925.
The Immortal Marriage. 1927.
The Jealous Gods: A Processional Novel of the Fifth Century B.C. (Concerning One Alcibiades). 1928; as *Vengeful Gods*, 1928.
Dido, Queen of Hearts. 1929.
The Sophisticates. 1931.
The Foghorn: Stories. 1934.
Golden Peacock. 1936.
Rezánov and Doña Concha. 1937.
The House of Lee. 1940.
The Horn of Life. 1942.

Play

Screenplay: *Don't Neglect Your Wife,* with Louis Sherwin, 1921.

Other

California: An Intimate History. 1914.
Life in the War Zone. 1916.
The Living Present (essays). 1917.
Adventures of a Novelist (autobiography). 1932.
Can Women Be Gentlemen? (essays). 1938.
Golden Gate Country. 1945.
My San Francisco: A Wayward Biography. 1946.

Editor, *A Few of Hamilton's Letters, Including His Description of the Great West Indian Hurricane of 1772.* 1903.

Bibliography: "A Checklist of the Writings of and about Atherton" by Charlotte S. McClure, in *American Literary Realism 1870 1910,* Spring 1976.

Reading List: *Atherton* by Joseph H. Jackson, 1940.

*   *   *

Gertrude Atherton was a popular and prolific writer, publishing nearly forty novels, several volumes of short stories, three collections of essays, a history of California, two books about San Francisco, a selection of Alexander Hamilton's letters, and numerous uncollected articles. Although her novels lack great artistic merit, they are significant for the literary historian because they helped to free American literature from the shackles of Victorian prudery. From the beginning of her career, Atherton rejected the Victorian myths about woman's moral superiority and sexual imbecility. Her heroines are sensual, egotistical, and intellectually ambitious. They seek an identity based on their own needs and talents rather than on the attributes society ascribed to women. Her treatment of female sexuality in particular gained her considerable critical attention both in America and in England; liberal critics singled her out for her "fearless treatment of the problems of sex," while conservatives screamed that she exalted "the morals of the barn-yard into a social ideal" and accelerated "the corruption of private life and the destruction of the family relation."

Atherton's California fiction is of particular interest to the cultural historian, focussing, as it does, on the effects of the "gringo" coming to power at the expense of the Mexican aristocracy. Her best novel, *The Californians*, effectively analyzes the conflict between the heritages of Hispanic indolence and pride and Yankee shrewdness and pragmatism. In this novel, Atherton's conception of her heroine is firmly rooted in her knowledge of the patriarchal, restrictive Spanish tradition as well as the shallow ambiance of San Francisco society. However, in many of her other California novels, Atherton romanticizes her subject matter. As Kevin Starr points out in *Americans and the California Dream*, Atherton speaks for the California elite which, on the one hand, mourned the loss of the Arcadian existence of the Hispanic settlers, but, on the other hand, repudiated that existence as inimical to the progress of the state.

In most of her fiction, Atherton sensationalized and romanticized her subject matter. Thus, the heroine of *Patience Sparhawk and Her Times* is wrongly convicted of her husband's murder, the heroine of *Black Oxen* is a rejuvenated fifty-eight year old woman who falls in love with a man in his thirties, and the heroine of *The Immortal Marriage* is Aspasia, whom Atherton presents not as a prostitute, but as Pericles' beloved wife, supremely beautiful and intelligent enough to provoke admiration from men such as Sophocles and Socrates. Despite Atherton's artistic shortcomings, her lifelong concern with the contribution of women to civilization as well as her fictional observation of fifty years of America's social history suggests that her work deserves further examination by literary and cultural historians.

—Sybil B. Weir

AUCHINCLOSS, Louis (Stanton). American. Born in Lawrence, New York, 27 September 1917. Educated at Groton School, Connecticut, graduated 1935; Yale University, New Haven, Connecticut, 1935–38; University of Virginia Law School, Charlottesville, LL.B. 1941; admitted to the New York Bar, 1941. Served in the United States Naval Reserve, 1941–45: Lieutenant. Married Adele Lawrence in 1957; three sons. Associate Lawyer, Sullivan and Cromwell, New York, 1941–51. Associate, 1954–58, and since 1958 Partner, Hawkins, Delafield and Wood, New York. Since 1966, President of the Museum of the City of New York. Trustee, Josiah Macy Jr. Foundation, New York; Member of the Executive Committee, Association of the Bar of New York City; Member of the Administrative Committee, Dumbarton Oaks Research Library and Collection, Washington, D.C. Litt.D.: New York University, 1974. Member, National Institute of Arts and Letters. Lives in New York City.

PUBLICATIONS

Fiction

The Indifferent Children. 1947.
The Injustice Collectors (stories). 1950.
Sybil. 1952.
A Law for the Lion. 1953.
The Romantic Egoists: A Reflection in Eight Minutes. 1954.
The Great World and Timothy Colt. 1956.

Venus in Sparta. 1958.
Pursuit of the Prodigal. 1959.
The House of Five Talents. 1960.
Portrait in Brownstone. 1962.
Powers of Attorney (stories). 1963.
The Rector of Justin. 1964.
The Embezzler. 1966.
Tales of Manhattan. 1967.
A World of Profit. 1968.
Second Chance (stories). 1970.
I Come as a Thief. 1972.
The Partners. 1974.
The Winthrop Covenant. 1976.
The Dark Lady. 1977.
The Country Cousin. 1978.

Play

The Club Bedroom (produced 1967).

Other

Edith Wharton. 1961.
Reflections of a Jacobite. 1961.
Ellen Glasgow. 1964.
Pioneers and Caretakers: A Study of 9 American Women Novelists. 1965.
Motiveless Malignity (on Shakespeare). 1969.
Henry Adams. 1971.
Edith Wharton: A Woman in Her Time. 1971.
Richelieu. 1972.
A Writer's Capital (autobiography). 1974.
Reading Henry James. 1975.

Editor, *An Edith Wharton Reader.* 1965.
Editor, *Fables of Wit and Elegance.* 1972.

Bibliography: *Auchincloss and His Critics: A Bibliographical Record* by Jackson R. Bryer, 1977.

*   *   *

Louis Auchincloss is a successor to Edith Wharton as a chronicler of the New York aristocracy. In this role he necessarily imbues his novels with an elegiac tone as he observes the passing beauties of the city and the fading power of the white Anglo-Saxon Protestants of old family and old money who can no longer sustain their position of dominance. His principal subject is thus the manners and morals, the money and marriages, the families and houses, the schools and games, the language and arts of the New York aristocracy as he traces its rise, observes its present crisis, and meditates its possible fall and disappearance. The point of vantage from which he often observes the aristocracy is that of the lawyer who serves and frequently belongs to this class.
The idea of good family stands in an uneasy relation to money in Auchincloss's fiction.

Auchincloss dramatizes the dilemma of the American aristocracy by showing that it is necessary to possess money to belong to this class but fatal to one's standing within the class to pursue money. People who have connections with those who are still in trade cannot themselves fully qualify as gentlemen, as the opportunistic Mr. Dale in *The Great World and Timothy Colt* shows. On the other hand, Auchincloss is clearly critical of those aristocrats like Bertie Millinder or Percy Prime who do nothing constructive and are engaged simply in the spending of money. Auchincloss recognizes that the family is the most important of aristocratic institutions and that its place in its class is guaranteed by the conservation of its resources. This task of preserving the family wealth falls to the lawyers, and his fiction is rich in the complexities, both moral and financial, of fiduciary responsibility; *Venus in Sparta* is a novel in point.

Auchincloss fully exploits the conflict between the marriage arranged for the good of the family, often by strong women, and romantic or sexual impulses that are destructive of purely social goals, as *Portrait in Brownstone* illustrates. Sex and love are enemies to the organicism of conservative societies, in which the will of the individual is vested in the whole. Auchincloss observes the workings of this organic notion in the structure of family and marriage as well as in institutions like the school and the club. Such institutions preserve a way of life and protect those who live by it from those on the outside who do not.

Auchincloss's fiction does more than present us with a mere record of the institutions that support the American aristocracy. The dramatic interest in his novels and whatever larger importance may be accorded them lies in his recognition that the entire class is in jeopardy and that individual aristocrats are often failures. Sometimes Auchincloss sees problems arising within the context of aristocracy itself, as when individual will or desire comes in conflict with the organicism; perhaps Reese Parmalee, in *Pursuit of the Prodigal*, makes the most significant rebellion of all Auchincloss's characters, but he is rejecting a decadent aristocracy and not aristocracy itself. But the real failures are those aristocrats who suffer, as so many of Auchincloss's male characters do, from a sense of inadequacy and insecurity that leads them to self-destructiveness. They are not strong and tough-fibred, as so many of the women are; they seem too fastidious and over-civilized, and they are failing the idea of society and their class. *A World of Profit* is the most explicit recognition of this failure.

Auchincloss has made his record of the New York aristocracy in a style which is clear and simple, occasionally elegant and brilliant, and sometimes self-consciously allusive. He has a gift for comedy of manners, which he has not sufficiently cultivated, and a fine model in Oscar Wilde. Yet among his faults as a novelist, especially evident because of the particular genre he has chosen, is a failure to give the reader a richness of detail. Furthermore, he sometimes loses control of his novels and permits action to overwhelm theme. The most serious criticism to be made of his work is that while he does indeed pose moral dilemmas for his characters, he too easily resolves their problems for them. He has given us, on balance, a full enough record of upper class life in New York, but he has fallen short of the most penetrating and meaningful kinds of social insight that the best of the novelists of manners offer.

—Chester E. Eisinger

AUSTEN, Jane. English. Born in Steventon, near Basingstoke, Hampshire, 16 December 1775. Educated at a school in Reading, and privately. Lived a retired life with her family in Steventon, 1775–1800, Bath, 1801–06, Southampton, 1806–09, and Chawton, Hampshire, 1809–17. *Died 18 July 1817.*

PUBLICATIONS

Collections

Works, edited by R. W. Chapman.   6 vols., 1923–54.
Letters, edited by R. W. Chapman.   2 vols., 1932; revised edition, 1952; selection, 1955.
Shorter Works (selections), edited by Richard Church.   1963.

Fiction

Sense and Sensibility.   1811; edited by Claire Lamont, 1970.
Pride and Prejudice.   1813; edited by F. W. Bradbrook, 1975.
Mansfield Park.   1814; edited by John Lucas, 1970.
Emma.   1816; edited by David Lodge, 1971.
Northanger Abbey, and Persuasion.   1818; edited by John Davie, 1971.
Love and Freindship (sic), edited by G. K. Chesterton.   1922.
The Watsons, edited by A. B. Walkley.   1923; edited by Q. D. Leavis, with *Sense and Sensibility,* 1958.
Lady Susan, edited by R. W. Chapman.   1925; edited by Q. D. Leavis, with *Sense and Sensibility,* 1958.
Sanditon: Fragment of a Novel, edited by R. W. Chapman.   1925.
Volume the First, edited by R. W. Chapman.   1933.
Volume the Third, edited by R. W. Chapman.   1951.
Volume the Second, edited by B. C. Southam.   1963.

Other

Three Evening Prayers, edited by W. M. Roth.   1940.

Bibliography: *Austen: A Critical Bibliography* by R. W. Chapman, 1953.

Reading List: *Austen: Facts and Problems* by R. W. Chapman, 1948; *Austen: Irony as Defense and Discovery* by Marvin Mudrick, 1952; *Austen's Novels: A Study in Structure* by Andrew H. Wright, 1953, revised edition, 1964; *Austen's Novels: The Fabric of Dialogue* by H. S. Babb, 1962; *The Novels of Austen* by Robert Liddell, 1963; *Austen: A Collection of Critical Essays* edited by Ian Watt, 1963; *Austen: A Study of Her Artistic Development* by A. Walton Litz, 1965; *Austen: The Six Novels* by W. A. Craik, 1965; *Austen and Her Predecessors* by F. W. Bradbrook, 1966; *Austen: Critical Essays* edited by B. C. Southam, 1968; *Austen* by Douglas Bush, 1975; *Austen, Woman and Writer* by Joan Rees, 1976.

*   *   *

Jane Austen raises in a peculiarly difficult form the question "What do we mean by originality?" How is it that we can say with equal truth that she is one of the most traditional and one of the most original of all our great writers? Indeed, she is traditional in several different senses. First, she has the general assumption that the wisdom of our ancestors is justified in the experience of each generation, and (if he has the wit to see it) of each person. She would have thought any kind of innovation in religion or morality merely foolish. How could anything that was fundamentally true once ever cease to be fundamentally true? She would have thought it quite as absurd to suggest that one day apples would fall off the trees upwards as that truth, honesty, kindness, moderation, or humility could ever be outmoded. Then she was traditional too in the narrower context of English literary culture. She was steeped from early years in the writings of the Augustan classics. She accepted both their appeal to authority and tradition and their appeal to experience. She rejoiced especially in the wise synthesis of tradition and experience achieved by Johnson in his essays. She accepted without questioning the way of life of the very last generation of country squires who were truly local in their interests and concerns, and truly feudal in their social assumptions. Thirty years after her death it is a very different squirearchy that meets us in the pages of the early Victorians. Factories, railways, and Reform had brought irrevocable changes.

She was less completely traditional in her attitude to her predecessors in the art of the novel. She read them eagerly but with discrimination, sometimes with amused contempt, which can be seen not only in *Northanger Abbey* but even more in her earliest adolescent scribblings. But from Richardson, the greatest of her predecessors in fiction, she learnt how minute and subtle were the psychological possibilities open to the novelist, and from her best feminine predecessors that there was no need for the restricted social world of women to be an obstacle to the production of major art.

English literature, even in its Augustan phase, is not characteristically a product of the classical spirit, by which I mean the determination to see life steadily and whole, to understand the causes and consequences of things, and to allow personal tastes and preferences as little influence as possible. The writings of Dryden, Swift, and Johnson are steeped in personal enthusiasms and antipathies. Perhaps we should have to go back as far as Ben Jonson to find a great English writer as detached as Austen from the material of her art. Inevitably, this affected the use she made of her reading of earlier novelists. She delighted in Richardson's psychological minuteness and subtlety, and entirely shared his conviction that the domestic and feminine affords opportunities for art as rich and varied as any offered by the world of public affairs and adventures. But she rejected or did not require the exciting melodrama of his plots, and always maintained a much wider emotional distance from her heroines than he had done from Pamela and Clarissa. She had no need of any artificial excitement. She would have rejected as merely stupid Hardy's idea that unless a novelist has an unusual and exciting tale to tell (like the Ancient Mariner) he had better be silent. It is one of her most basic assumptions that ordinary humdrum daily life contains all the profundities of life, its agonizing dilemmas, its joys and disappointments, its moral dangers, and its spiritual opportunities. Nothing is dull for those who understand; even dulness and stupidity are fascinating to those gifted with the spirit of comedy.

The society of which she writes is well-meaning on the whole, decorous, and corrupt. Its decorousness may tend to mask its corruption. But the corruption is there. In *Mansfield Park*, Sir Thomas Bertram, a dignified and conscientious squire, sees no incongruity at all in selling the family living to pay his son's gambling debts; and when his second son is ordained, there is a general flurry of surprise and self-congratulation on all sides when it is decided that he should actually reside in his parish. No doubt considerations like this led Cardinal Newman, in one of the very few adverse criticisms of Jane Austen that do not merely reveal the limitations of the critic, to complain that she "has not a dream of the high Catholic ethos." Indeed, her moral standards are puzzling, both to those who base their attitudes upon the Sermon on the Mount and to those who are influenced by romantic individualism and hatred of respectable conventions. Her standards are at once moderate and exacting. She has no idea of sanctity or of any extraordinary flights of virtue. But she is ruthless in condemning those who fail to be honest, truthful, responsible, and kind. It never occurs to her that Mr. Knightley need have any higher aspirations than to be a good squire, a generous neighbour, and, in due course, a faithful husband. But nor does it ever occur to her to excuse Emma for being rude to Miss Bates, because she was hot and out of temper, because she did not really understand how much pain she was causing, or for any of the dozen reasons with which most people would try to reduce such an offence to the dimensions of a peccadillo if they had themselves been guilty of it. Jane Austen is at once easygoing and inexorable. And it is noticeable that, comparatively easy of attainment as they may seem to be, her standards do find almost every character wanting. Mr. Knightley is no exception. His normally sound moral judgment is deflected by the jealousy he feels when he imagines that Emma is in love with Frank Churchill. In an amusing and very typical aside we are told that his view of Frank's character changed completely in the half hour during which he discovered that it was he himself that Emma really loved. Similarly, the best and most appealing of all Jane Austen's heroines, Anne Elliot, is caught out when her own obsession with Captain Wentworth leads her to suppose that Lady Russell is watching him too, when in fact she has her eye fixed on an attractive shop window.

Both these failings in characters generally admirable reflect Jane Austen's intense concern with objective truth, which includes both exact self-knowledge and realism about the character and conduct of others. Knightley fails, momentarily, in both, Anne in the second only. Many more examples could be given of this ruthless pursuit of truth and uncompromising criticism of all those, however admirable otherwise, who relax even for a moment their desire to avoid self-deception. This fierce love of truth, this determination to follow it even when it is unpalatable or threatening, is one reason why Jane Austen is a challenging and disturbing writer. Other reasons are her acute sense of comedy which often makes the perceptive reader blush for himself, and her pervasive sense of the limits of human foresight. Many of her characters are clever, but almost all are either self-deceived, or much mistaken in their assessment of events, or both. A careful reading of Jane Austen should be a humbling as well as an exhilarating experience.

The exhilaration will come from the deadly accuracy of her humour and the beautiful exactness of her plots. Every character in the books is an independent being; we never feel, as we often do in the novels even of her greatest Victorian successors, that the character has for the moment become a ventriloquist's dummy. Yet the histories of all these independent beings converge into one grand, simple effect. In her less great books, *Northanger Abbey*, *Pride and Prejudice*, and *Sense and Sensibility*, there are few loose ends; in her greatest, *Emma*, *Mansfield Park*, and *Persuasion*, almost none at all. She is ruthlessly classical on a large scale as on a small. Her sentences do not waste a word and her books do not waste a scene or a character. Her career was short; no more than six years separate her first book from her death at the age of forty-one. But in that time she established beyond question her claim to be one of the two or three greatest English novelists.

—A. O. J. Cockshut

BACON, Francis; Baron Verulam; Viscount St. Albans. English. Born in London, 22 January 1561; elder brother of the diplomatist Anthony Bacon. Educated at Trinity College, Cambridge, 1573–76; Gray's Inn, London, 1576, 1579–82; called to the Bar, 1582. Married Alice Barnham in 1606. Accompanied Sir Amyas Paulet, as Ambassador to France, 1576–79; Member of Parliament for Melcombe Regis, Dorset, 1584, Taunton, 1586, Liverpool, 1589, Middlesex, 1593, Southampton, 1597, Ipswich, 1604, and Cambridge University, 1614; enjoyed the patronage of the Earl of Essex from 1591, and advised him to undertake suppression of Tyrone's rebellion in Ireland, 1598, but later took part in the trial for treason against him, 1601; one of the Queen's learned Counsel, 1595–1603, and King's Counsel from 1604; commissioner for the union of Scotland and England, 1603; Solicitor-General, 1607–13; Attorney-General, 1613–17; Privy Councillor, 1616; Lord Keeper, 1617–18, and Lord Chancellor, 1618; accused of bribery, confessed to general guilt, and stripped of offices, 1621; later pardoned by the king. Knighted, 1603; created Baron Verulam, 1618, and Viscount St. Albans, 1621. *Died 9 April 1626.*

PUBLICATIONS

Collections

> *Works* (including life and letters), edited by James Spedding, R. L. Ellis, and D. D. Heath. 14 vols., 1857–74.
> *Essays, Advancement of Learning, New Atlantis, and Other Pieces,* edited by R. F. Jones. 1937.
> *The New Organon and Related Writings,* edited by F. H. Anderson. 1960.

Prose

> *Essays.* 1597; revised edition, 1612, 1625.
> *A Declaration of the Treasons Committed by Essex.* 1601.
> *A Brief Discourse Touching the Happy Union of the Kingdoms of England and Scotland.* 1603.
> *His Apology in Certain Imputations Concerning Essex.* 1604.
> *Certain Considerations Touching the Church of England.* 1604.
> *Of the Proficience and Advancement of Learning, Divine and Humane.* 1605; translated into Latin as *De Augmentis Scientiarum,* 1623; as *The Advancement of Learning,* 1640.
> *De Sapientia Veterum.* 1609.
> *The Charge Touching Duels.* 1614.
> *Novum Organum: Summi Angliae Cancellarii Instauratio Magna.* 1620.
> *The History of the Reign of Henry VII.* 1622.
> *Historia Naturalis et Experimentalis: [Historia Ventorum].* 1622.
> *Historia Vitae et Mortis.* 1623.
> *Sylva Sylvarum; or, A Natural History in Ten Centuries* (includes *The New Atlantis: A Work Unfinished*). 1626.
> *Considerations Touching a War with Spain.* 1629.
> *Certain Miscellany Works.* 1629.
> *The Lawyer's Light; or, A Due Direction for the Study of the Law.* 1629.
> *The Elements of the Common Laws of England.* 1630.
> *Cases of Treason.* 1641.
> *The Confession of Faith.* 1641.

Three Speeches. 1641.
The Learned Reading upon the Statute of Uses. 1642.
Remains. 1648; as *The Mirror of State and Eloquence,* 1656.
Scripta in Naturali et Universali Philosophia. 1653.
Resuscitatio; or, Bringing into Public Light Several Pieces of the Works Hitherto Sleeping, edited by William Rawley. 2 vols., 1657–70.
Opuscula Varia Posthuma, edited by William Rawley. 1658.
Baconiana; or, Certain Genuine Remains. 1679.

Editor, *Apothegms New and Old.* 1625.

Translator, *Certain Psalms* (verse). 1625.

Bibliography: *Bacon: A Bibliography of His Works and of Baconiana to the Year 1750* by R. W. Gibson, 1950.

Reading List: *Bacon on Communication and Rhetoric,* 1943, and *Bacon on the Nature of Man,* 1967, both by Karl R. Wallace; *Bacon: His Life and Thought* by F. H. Anderson, 1962; *Bacon and Renaissance Prose* by B. Vickers, 1968; *Peace among the Willows: The Political Philosophy of Bacon* by H. B. White, 1968; *Bacon: Discovery and the Art of Discourse* by Lisa Jardine, 1975; *Bacon and the Style of Science* by James Stephens, 1975; *Bacon: A Political Biography* by Joel J. Epstein, 1977.

*   *   *

Francis Bacon's main interest lay in matters of interpretation, interpretation of nature in his scientific works, of human constructs in his work on myth and history, of human experience in his essays. *The Advancement of Learning* was devoted to an inventory of human learning in order to discover the deficiencies in history (a result of the faculty of memory), poetry (imagination), and philosophy (reason), and the main hindrances to its advancement, chief among which were the tendencies of his time to create circular fictions (by means of final causation, analogy, the syllogism, and systems) which reduced a mysterious nature to the ordered forms of the mind itself. And so, later in *The New Organon,* when he had narrowed his scope to natural philosophy Bacon had come to realize that the hindrances to the interpretation of nature lay in the human mind itself, which tends to impose order on phenomena (Idols of the Tribe) and does so by its selection of operations and interests (Cave), its use of words (Marketplace), and its construction of philosophical systems (Theater); this tendency he intended to counteract by the inductive method, in which human reason was restrained by strict method, the chief element of which was the use of negative instances which deliberately frustrated the mind's rage for order, in the service of accurate interpretation. What Bacon was after in *The Great Instauration* (of which *The New Organon* formed the second of its six parts, a greatly expanded version of the *Advancement* the first) was the invention of "new models to understand new things," or the discovery of "a new myth for thought," which must now be seen as the reproduction of nature in the human mind instead of the mind proliferating itself outward (Elizabeth Sewell, *The Orphic Voice*). Such a "new model" was created by translating the "common logic" of words into a new logic of things, so that invention or finding arguments became finding experiments (Part 3), judgment or constructing arguments and refuting sophisms became the operating of scientific method and restricting the human mind (*New Organon,* Part 2), memory became the setting out of discoveries in tables (Part 4), and so on.

The *Instauration* was never pushed to completion, but scattered images throughout suggest that it was informed by the grand vision of repairing the Fall, which had caused a divorce between the human mind and nature and had caused the mind to turn in on itself; Bacon's method would rectify the senses by experiment, would "re-marry" the purged senses to the mind, rectify the mind by the inductive method, then "re-marry" the mind to nature and hence lead man to the Adamic state in which his investigations would be like playing with the God of created nature. *The New Atlantis* is Bacon's visionary myth of the completion of the *Instauration*; in it, the pious and charitable actions of Bensalem proceed from a model of the mind (Salomon's House) rectified by the inductive method so as to become an accurate mirror of God's Creation. For Bacon, myth and image prescinded the logic of words in a way different from the inductive method but complementary to it; hence in his book of myth interpretation, *The Wisdom of the Ancients*, he presented pagan myth as the pathway to things, closer to experience and the true interpretation of political, moral, and natural matters than philosophy, both in its focus and in its imitative method (see Sewell). Of considerable importance to the understanding of Bacon's science of interpretation is *The History of the Reign of King Henry VII*, long admired for its vigorous prose style and its relentless drive to discover the true causes of human events.

Bacon's *Essays* exhibit an informal operation of the inductive method as applied to the interpretation of human experience. They exist in three versions. The slim volume of 1597 contains ten essays in the aphoristic form recommended by the *Advancement* whereby, in order to lead readers to discover things for themselves, only direct observations are admitted and such things as illustrations, examples, and transitions are excluded. Their style is curt or Senecan (in reaction to the Ciceronian periodic style which Bacon considered one of the diseases of learning), sparing of modifiers and connectives, pulling concepts into juxtaposition by parallelism and antithesis. In their insistence on the empirical basis of experience, they teach the usefulness and limits of interpretation, and their aphoristic manner mirrors their matter. The edition of 1612 was much expanded: it contained revisions of the original essays and twenty-eight new ones, and expanded the scope of subjects treated beyond mere civil issues to morality and the life of man in general (love, death, fortune); the style is now less curt, more antithetical, imagistic, and suggestive; and the essays are more fully formed, either by symmetry (the revised "Of Studies") or by contrast, as when two parts revolve around a large contrast in subject or point of view ("Of Nobility"). The final edition of 1625 contains fifty-eight essays; its range of subjects is expanded still more to include manners as well as civil and moral matters; its style is more relaxed, full of images, illustrations, examples, even personal reminiscences; and the essays show a greater fulness and coherence of structure, often made explicit by formal subdivisions ("Of Friendship"). This is a fully unified volume, containing cross-references and paired essays ("Of Building" and "Of Gardens," "Of Beauty" and "Of Deformity," "Of Envy" and "Of Love").

Bacon's *Essays* are designed to make the reader examine rather than accept ideas, and most precepts therein are therefore provisional and occasionally disturbing. Their keynote is tonal complexity – the usefulness of a practice as well as its corruptions ("Of Usury"), moral judgment offered then blocked ("Of Negotiating"), contempt for a habit changing to precepts for using it ("Of Cunning"), full entrance into an amoral point of view ending with sudden moral judgment ("Of Simulation"). As an essay proceeds it tends to offer constant re-evaluation of its subject, whether it be in the form of a series of associative links, as in "Of Delays," or a two-part structure balancing excessive and moderate views of a subject in the high and middle styles respectively ("Of Adversity"). "Of Truth" is one of the finest examples of such subtle re-evaluation; it starts with a consideration of the difficulty of seeking truth but then shifts to the divine imperative to follow truth no matter what the consequences; the shift is accomplished imagistically by moving from man-made half-lights to the full light of Creation, syntactically from a loose style to a series of tight tripartite sentences, and allusively from our life as it now seems to us (after Pilate's denial) to our life as God sees it from Creation to Fall to the Second Coming evoked by its last sentence.

—Walter R. Davis

BAGE, Robert. English. Born in Darley, Derbyshire, 29 February 1728. Educated at a common school in Darley; subsequently trained in his father's paper-making business; in later life studied with a private tutor in Birmingham. Married in 1751; three sons. Established a paper mill at Elford, near Tamworth, soon after his marriage, and continued to manage the business until his death; also a partner in an iron manufactory, 1765–79; began writing in 1781. *Died 1 September 1801.*

PUBLICATIONS

Fiction

Mount Henneth. 1782.
Barham Downs. 1784.
The Fair Syrian. 1787.
James Wallace. 1788.
Man As He Is. 1792.
Hermsprong; or, Man As He Is Not. 1796; edited by Vaughan Wilkins, 1951.

*   *   *

If Robert Bage is an underrated novelist it is perhaps his own fault. He pretended that he only turned to novel-writing in middle age in order to satisfy his daughters' demands for new gowns, and then he persisted in turning out at regular intervals novels that were so entertaining that he was bound to be considered merely a talented amateur, working successfully in the vein of Fielding and Smollett. In fact, Bage continued rather than repeated the work of his predecessors in the comic novel tradition, and succeeded in adapting that tradition to the tastes, ideas, issues, and attitudes of the Age of Sensibility and the decades of the French and American Revolutions. Yet Bage was always, though in the best sense, provincial. Far removed from the life of literary London, he had to give his own intellectual and comic vitality to fictional techniques and forms perfected by others, and put them to serving his own interests, ideas, and vision of man and society. For his novels are crammed with references to new developments in science and technology (Bage was a paper manufacturer and member of the Derby Philosophical Society), to English, Irish, American, and French politics, to the philosophical, aesthetic, and religious issues of the day, to the condition of women, and to the standard subjects of social satire – luxury, fashion, "improvement," social climbing, and snobbery. All this Bage cast in the comic novel conventions of his day, coloured with his own tolerant and benevolent outlook on human folly. The seriousness of his work, then, is revealed in its overall unity, just as each of his novels has a unity of tone and theme rather than of plot and construction. And his seriousness is also demonstrated by his continual development and mastery of his chosen repertoire of conventions and techniques, and by his continual adaptation of that repertoire to ever new issues and ideas.

There is a continuous development in skill and scope from *Mount Henneth* to *Man As He Is*, and it is really only *Hermsprong; or, Man As He Is Not*, written after the French Revolution had caused a conservative reaction in England, that Bage's satire acquired a sharper bite, and a more radical view of social relations. For this reason, it is this last novel which has most to offer now, although its predecessor, *Man As He Is*, is a more copious comic fiction. Sceptical and tolerant, benevolent and satiric, comic and humane, Bage's novels manage to reconcile qualities and conventions usually at odds in the fiction of that time, and it is this unity which is perhaps his best claim to originality and to our continued interest.

—Gary Kelly

BALDWIN, James (Arthur). American. Born in New York City, 2 August 1924. Educated at Public School 139, Harlem, New York, and DeWitt Clinton High School, Bronx, New York. Lived in Europe, mainly in Paris, 1948–56. Member, Actors Studio, New York; National Advisory Board of CORE (Congress on Racial Equality); and National Committee for a Sane Nuclear Policy. Recipient: Saxton Fellowship, 1945; Rosenwald Fellowship, 1948; Guggenheim Fellowship, 1954; National Institute of Arts and Letters grant, 1956; Ford Fellowship, 1958; National Conference of Christians and Jews Brotherhood Award, 1962; George Polk Award, 1963; Foreign Drama Critics Award, 1964. D.Litt.: University of British Columbia, Vancouver, 1964. Member, National Institute of Arts and Letters, 1964. Lives in New York City.

PUBLICATIONS

Fiction

    Go Tell It on the Mountain. 1953.
    Giovanni's Room. 1956.
    Another Country. 1962.
    Going to Meet the Man (stories). 1965.
    Tell Me How Long the Train's Been Gone. 1968.
    If Beale Street Could Talk. 1974.

Plays

    The Amen Corner (produced 1955). 1965.
    Blues for Mr. Charlie (produced 1964). 1964
    One Day, When I Was Lost: A Scenario Based on "The Autobiography of Malcolm X." 1972.
    A Deed from the King of Spain (produced 1974).

    Screenplay: *The Inheritance,* 1973.

Other

    Notes of a Native Son. 1955.
    Nobody Knows My Name: More Notes of a Native Son. 1961.
    The Fire Next Time. 1963.
    Nothing Personal, with Richard Avedon. 1964.
    A Rap on Race, with Margaret Mead. 1971.
    No Name in the Street. 1971.
    A Dialogue: James Baldwin and Nikki Giovanni. 1973.
    Little Man, Little Man (juvenile). 1976.
    The Devil Finds Work: An Essay. 1976.

Bibliography: "James Baldwin: A Checklist, 1947–1962" by Kathleen A. Kindt, and "James Baldwin: A Bibliography, 1947–1962" by Russell G. Fischer, both in *Bulletin of Bibliography,* January–April 1965; "James Baldwin: A Checklist, 1963–67" by Fred L. Standley, in *Bulletin of Bibliography,* May–August 1968.

Reading List: *The Furious Passage of Baldwin* by Ferm M. Eckman, 1966; *Baldwin: A Critical Study* by Stanley Macebuh, 1973; *Baldwin: A Collection of Critical Essays* edited by Keneth Kinnamon, 1974; *Baldwin: A Critical Evaluation* edited by Therman B. O'Daniel, 1977.

*   *   *

James Baldwin's major theme has always been identity or its denial. He develops the complex personal and social dimensions of this theme in four main subjects: church, self, city, and race. The result is a substantial body of writing in fiction, drama, and the personal essay characterized by intense feeling, stylistic eloquence, and social urgency.

As Baldwin was making his first adolescent efforts to write, he was simultaneously preaching in store-front churches in Harlem. Of brief duration, his religious vocation both satisfied his need to prove his worth to his father and complicated his intellectual development. Seeming to simplify personal problems, his religious commitment actually generated tensions that were to make Baldwin an eloquent critic of Christianity, especially its pernicious social effects, as well as a witness of its emotional power and richness. The enduring fictional achievement of Baldwin's involvement with the church is his brilliant first novel, *Go Tell It on the Mountain*. By means of a carefully crafted tripartite structure, rich characterizations, and a distinctive stylistic voice, Baldwin tells the story not only of John Grimes, a Harlem youth undergoing a personal and religious crisis, but also of his stepfather, Gabriel; his stepfather's sister, Florence; and his mother, Elizabeth. With historical scope as well as personal immediacy, the author shows how sex, race, and religion affect the lives of these worshippers in The Temple of the Fire Baptized. Religious experience is conveyed to the reader with overwhelming emotional power, but he is also forced to recognize how it erodes social reality or even, in the case of Gabriel, becomes a means of oppression. The critique of the church is carried further in the play *The Amen Corner*, in which a fanatical woman preacher substitutes her small church for the love of her husband. Narrowly fulfilling, but in the final analysis life-denying, religion must be abandoned, Baldwin implies, if the self is to be realized.

Many of Baldwin's best early essays and stories – "Autobiographical Notes," "Notes of a Native Son," "Stranger in the Village," "The Discovery of What It Means to Be an American," "Previous Condition," "The Rockpile," "The Outing" – concern his search for self. His second novel, *Giovanni's Room*, explores the theme mainly as it relates to love and sexuality. David, an American expatriate in France, must choose between his mistress Hella and his lover Giovanni. By rejecting Giovanni, David denies his true homosexual self and his deepest feeling for another person in favor of socially sanctioned heterosexuality. As Baldwin develops it, the choice is also between America and Europe, conformity and freedom, safety and the risks necessary to realize love. In search of psychological security, David instead precipitates chaos and tragedy for himself, Hella, and Giovanni.

Both *Go Tell It on the Mountain* and *Giovanni's Room* express social concerns, but their emphasis is on psychological conflict. In his third novel, *Another Country*, Baldwin gives greater attention to the city itself as both the arena and the cause of personal problems. The New York setting of this novel, seething with hatred, corruption, and moral disarray, dooms the characters who inhabit its inhuman confines. The most obvious victim is Rufus Scott, a disconsolate black jazz musician who commits suicide at the end of the long first chapter, but the other seven major characters also suffer as they struggle to assuage their guilt and satisfy their craving for love in the unloving urban environment. Some of these concerns appear in the splendid earlier story, "Sonny's Blues" (1957), where, however, racial suffering in the northern city is controlled, expressed, and thus to some degree transcended through music. In his recent novel *If Beale Street Could Talk*, Baldwin again tries to transcend the hostility of urban life, this time through a story of young love, but his effort is vitiated by sentimentality and problems of fictional technique.

With few exceptions, most of Baldwin's books have dealt in one way or another with race and racism. From youthful disengagement he has moved through commitment to interracial efforts to achieve civil rights to black nationalism to bitter prophecies of racial vengeance on the white West. *The Fire Next Time* is an eloquent statement of militant intergrationism, but the play *Blues for Mister Charlie* expresses a deeper racial outrage and a diminished but not entirely abandoned hope for improvement. The social pathology revealed in this drama of race relations in the South derives from psychosexual origins much more than from political or economic causes. The shift from the nonviolent mode of resistance to racism to the advocacy of violence as the appropriate means of black self-defense begins in the play, and receives a stronger endorsement in the idealized portrait of Christopher, a fierce young black nationalist, in the novel *Tell Me How Long the Train's Been Gone*. The protagonist of this novel, a middle-aged actor named Leo Proudhammer, is an autobiographical character whose experience Baldwin sentimentalizes tiresomely, but in the autobiographical material of the tough-minded *No Name in the Street* the author avoids self-pity. Shifting back and forth between private experience and the public history of the violence-wracked sixties, Baldwin offers in this work a sad and embittered testimony on race and racism. Quite different in its restrained tone and deliberately flat rhetoric from the hortatory *The Fire Next Time*, it is equally impressive.

By comparison Baldwin's recent books – a film scenario, film criticism, transcripts of conversations, a children's book – are minor efforts. He may yet produce the genuinely major novel for which stylistic resources, his capacity for feeling, and his thematic breadth equip him. In any event, as a master of the personal essay, as racial commentator, and as a gifted if uneven novelist and short story writer, James Baldwin has been one of the indispensable writers of the third quarter of the twentieth century.

—Keneth Kinnamon

BALDWIN, Joseph G(lover). American. Born in Winchester, Virginia, in January 1815. Received no formal education; self-taught in law. Married Sidney White in 1839; six children. Began practice of law in DeKalb, Mississippi, 1836; moved to Gainesville, Alabama, 1839; Whig Member of the Alabama Legislature, 1844–49; lived in Livingston, Alabama, 1850–53; law partner of Philip Phillips in Mobile, Alabama, 1853–54; moved to San Francisco, 1854, and practised law there; served as Associate Justice, California Supreme Court, 1858–62, then returned to private practice. *Died 30 September 1864*.

PUBLICATIONS

Fiction

  The Flush Times of Alabama and Mississippi: A Series of Sketches.   1853; edited by William A. Owens, 1957.

Other

  Party Leaders: Sketches of Jefferson, Hamilton, Jackson, Clay, Randolph of Roanoke. 1855.

Bibliography: in *Bibliography of American Literature* by Jacob Blanck, 1955.

Reading List: "Baldwin: Humorist or Moralist?" by Eugene Current-Garcia, in *Frontier Humorists: Critical Essays* edited by M. Thomas Inge, 1975.

* * *

Although well known to American literary scholars for *The Flush Times of Alabama and Mississippi*, Joseph G. Baldwin has been little studied. As the title itself suggests, *Flush Times* constitutes an attempt to re-create in the *native* American tradition of the Old Southwest humorists a day and age with which Baldwin was well acquainted: an "age of litigation in a lawless country," as Eugene Current-Garcia says. A closer examination both of the author's life and the text of his work, however, suggests that Baldwin, in addition to being frontier humorist, is a serious "moralist" who employs traditional conventions such as satire and irony in his exposure of the vices and weaknesses of mankind, thus bridging the gap between native Southwest humor and the older literary conventions of European art.

While Baldwin's purpose was doubtlessly moral, his generic forte was essays and sketches rather than short stories. His literary models were, in all probability, Lamb and Dickens. His best character types remain self-important Virginians, inexperienced lawyers, and garrulous narrators. Two characters in particular are notable, Ovid Bolus, Esq., a truly artful liar, and Colonel Simon Suggs, Jr., to Current-Garcia the "symbol of his time, the epitome of a lawless, acquisitive society which had raised fraud and corruption to the level of 'super-Spartan roguery.' "

Nineteenth-century sensibilities extended, by contemporary standards, odd shadows. As a practicing attorney, Baldwin no doubt felt some sense of embarrassment over his authorship of *Flush Times*, a work which many American Victorians would have considered inconsequential. In order to demonstrate his talents for more "serious" writing, Baldwin published in 1855 *Party Leaders*, which is rarely read today. Containing sketches of political leaders like Jefferson, Hamilton, Jackson, Clay, and Randolph, the book is motivated by the author's biographical and historical impulse and emphasizes moral instruction at the expense of humor.

Had Baldwin not died as suddenly as he did, he might well have become, as his wife believed, the Thucydides of the Civil War. In any event, his accomplishments as frontier humorist, as moralist, and as essayist continue to be admired by readers.

—George C. Longest

BALLANTYNE, R(obert) M(ichael). Scottish. Born in Edinburgh, 24 April 1825. Educated at Edinburgh Academy, 1835–37, and privately. Ensign, 1858, and Captain, 1860, in the Edinburgh Volunteers. Married Jane Dickson Grant in 1866; four sons and two daughters. Apprentice Clerk, Hudson's Bay Company, Canada, 1841–47; Clerk, North British Railway Company, Edinburgh, 1847–49; member of staff, Alexander Cowan and Company, paper makers, Edinburgh, 1849; Junior Partner, Thomas Constable and Company, printers, Edinburgh, 1849–55; lecturer and free-lance writer from 1855; lived in Harrow after 1883. *Died 8 February 1894.*

Fiction

Snowflakes and Sunbeams; or, The Young Fur Trader: A Tale of the Far North. 1856.
Three Little Kittens. 1856.
Ungava: A Tale of Esquimeaux-Land. 1857.
The Coral Island: A Tale of the Pacific Ocean. 1857.
Mister Fox. 1857.
My Mother. 1857; as *Chit-Chat by a Penitent Cat,* 1874.
The Butterfly's Ball and the Grasshopper's Feast. 1857.
The Life of a Ship from the Launch to the Wreck. 1857.
The Robber Kitten. 1858.
Martin Rattler; or, A Boy's Adventures in the Forests of Brazil. 1858.
The World of Ice; or, Adventures in the Polar Regions. 1859.
Mee-a-ow! or, Good Advice to Cats and Kittens. 1859.
The Dog Crusoe: A Tale of the Western Prairies. 1861; as *The Dog Crusoe and His Master,* 1869.
The Gorilla Hunters: A Tale of the Wilds of Africa. 1861.
The Golden Dream; or, Adventures in the Far West. 1861.
The Red Eric; or, The Whaler's Last Cruise: A Tale. 1861.
The Wild Man of the West: A Tale of the Rocky Mountains. 1862.
Gascoyne, The Sandal-Wood Trader: A Tale of the Pacific. 1863.
Fighting the Whales; or, Doings and Dangers on a Fishing Cruise. 1863.
Away in the Wilderness; or, Life among the Red Indians and the Fur-Traders. 1863.
Fast in the Ice; or, Adventures in the Polar Region. 1863.
The Lifeboat: A Tale of Our Coast Heroes. 1864.
Chasing the Sun; or, Rambles in Norway. 1864.
Freaks on the Fells; or, Three Months' Rustication, and Why I Did Not Become a Sailor. 1864.
The Lighthouse, Being the Story of a Great Fight Between Man and the Sea. 1865.
Shifting Winds: A Tough Yarn. 1866.
Fighting the Flames: A Tale of the London Fire Brigade. 1867.
Silver Lake; or, Lost in the Snow. 1867.
Deep Down: A Tale of the Cornish Mines. 1868.
Erling the Bold: A Tale of the Norse Sea-Kings. 1869.
Sunk at Sea; or, The Adventures of Wandering Will in the Pacific. 1869.
Lost in the Forest; or, Wandering Will's Adventures in South America. 1869.
Over the Rocky Mountains; or, Wandering Will in the Land of the Red Skin. 1869.
Saved by the Lifeboat: A Tale of Wreck and Rescue on the Coast. 1869,
The Cannibal Islands; or, Captain Cook's Adventures in the South Seas. 1869.
Hunting the Lions; or, The Land of the Negro. 1869.
Digging for Gold; or, Adventures in California. 1869.
Up in the Clouds; or, Balloon Voyages. 1869.
The Battle and the Breeze; or, The Fights and Fancies of a British Tar. 1869.
The Floating Light of the Goodwin Sands: A Tale. 1870.
The Iron Horse; or, Life on the Line: A Tale of the Grand National Trunk Railway. 1871.
The Pioneers: A Tale of the Western Wilderness, Illustrative of the Adventures and Discoveries of Sir Alexander Mackenzie. 1872.
The Norsemen in the West; or, America Before Columbus: A Tale. 1872.
Life in the Red Brigade. 1873.
Black Ivory: A Tale of Adventure among the Slavers of East Africa. 1873.

The Pirate City: An Algerine Tale. 1874.
Rivers of Ice: A Tale Illustrative of Alpine Adventure and Glacier Action. 1875.
The Story of the Rock; or, Building on the Eddystone. 1875.
Under the Waves; or, Diving in Deep Waters: A Tale. 1876.
The Settler and the Savage: A Tale of Peace and War in South Africa. 1876.
In the Track of the Troops: A Tale of Modern War. 1878.
Jarwin and Cuffy: A Tale. 1878.
Philosopher Jack: A Tale of the Southern Seas. 1879.
The Lonely Island; or, The Refuge of the Mutineers. 1880.
Post Haste: A Tale of Her Majesty's Mails. 1880.
The Red Man's Revenge: A Tale of the Red River Flood. 1880.
My Doggie and I. 1881.
The Giant of the North; or, Poking Around the Pole. 1881.
The Battery and the Boiler; or, Adventures in the Laying of Submarine Electric Cables. 1882.
The Kitten Pilgrims; or, Great Battles and Grand Victories. 1882.
Dusty Diamonds Cut and Polished: A Tale of City-Arab Life and Adventure. 1883.
Battles with the Sea; or, Heroes of the Lifeboat and Rocket. 1883.
The Thorogood Family. 1883.
The Madman and the Pirate. 1883.
The Young Trawler: A Story of Life and Death and Rescue on the North Sea. 1884.
Twice Bought: A Tale of the Oregon Gold Fields. 1884.
The Rover of the Andes: A Tale of Adventure in South America. 1885.
The Island Queen; or, Dethroned by Fire and Water: A Tale of the Southern Hemisphere. 1885.
Red Rooney; or, The Last of the Crew. 1886.
The Prairie Chief: A Tale. 1886.
The Lively Poll: A Tale of the North Sea. 1886.
The Big Otter: A Tale of the Great Nor'west. 1887.
The Fugitives; or, The Tyrant Queen of Madagascar. 1887.
Blue Lights; or, Hot Work in the Soudan: A Tale of Soldier Life in Several of Its Phases. 1888.
The Middy and the Moors: An Algerine Story. 1888; as *Slave of the Moors*, 1950.
The Crew of the Water Wagtail: A Story of Newfoundland. 1889.
The Eagle Cliff: A Tale of the Western Isles. 1889.
Blown to Bits; or, The Lonely Man of Rakata: A Tale of the Malay Peninsula. 1889.
The Garret and the Garden; or, Low Life High Up, and Jeff Benson; or, The Young Coastguardsman. 1890.
Charlie to the Rescue: A Tale of the Sea and the Rockies. 1890.
The Buffalo Runners: A Tale of the Red River Plain. 1891.
The Coxwain's Bride; or, The Rising Tide: A Tale of the Sea, and Other Tales. 1891.
The Hot Swamp: A Romance of Old Albion. 1892.
Hunted and Harried: A Tale of the Scottish Covenanters. 1892.
The Walrus Hunters: A Romance of the Realms of Ice. 1893.
Reuben's Luck: A Tale of the Wild North. 1896.

Other

Hudson's Bay; or, Every-Day Life in the Wilds of North America. 1848.
The Northern Coasts of America, and the Hudson's Bay Territories: A Narrative of Discovery and Adventure, by Patrick Fraser Tytler, with continuation by Ballantyne. 1853.
Handbook to the New Gold Fields: A Full Account of the Richness and Extent of the Fraser and Thompson River Gold Mines. 1858.

Environs and Vicinity of Edinburgh. 1859.
Ships: The Great Eastern and Lesser Crafts. 1859.
The Lakes of Killarney. 1859.
How Not to Do It: A Manual for the Awkward Squad; or, A Handbook of Directions Written for the Instruction of Raw Recruits in Our Rifle Volunteer Regiments. 1859.
Discovery and Adventure in the Polar Seas and Regions, by Sir John Leslie and Hugh Murray, with continuation by Ballantyne. 1860.
The Volunteer Levee; or, The Remarkable Experiences of Ensign Sopht. 1860.
Ensign Sopht's Volunteer Almanack for 1861. 1861.
Man on the Ocean. 1862; revised edition, 1874.
Photographs of Edinburgh, with Archibald Burns. 1868.
Our Seamen: An Appeal. 1873.
The Ocean and Its Wonders. 1874.
Six Months at the Cape; or, Letters to Periwinkle from South Africa. 1878.
The Collected Works of Ensign Sopht, Late of the Volunteers. 1881.
Personal Reminiscences in Book-Making. 1893.

Editor, *Naughty Boys; or, The Sufferings of Mr. Delteil,* by Champfleury, translated by Jane Ballantyne. 1855.

Bibliography: *Ballantyne: A Bibliography of First Editions* by Eric Quayle, 1968.

Reading List: *Ballantyne the Brave: A Victorian Writer and His Family* by Eric Quayle, 1967.

*   *   *

R. M. Ballantyne was one of the first writers of fictional adventure tales to study original material on whatever geographical location his stories used. G. A. Henty, another adventure writer of the same period, used historical backgrounds in the manner of Sir Walter Scott; Ballantyne lived in whatever environment his plot was to deal with. Thus for *The Lifeboat,* he lived at Deal with a lifeboat crew; for *The Lighthouse,* he spent several uncomfortable weeks in the Bell Rock Lighthouse; for *Fighting the Flames,* he stayed with the London Fire Brigade, waiting for the bells to signal a fire; for *Deep Down,* he lived with the tin-miners of St. Just, Cornwall, for over three months. He endured weeks of sea-sickness on the Gull Lightship for *The Floating Light of the Goodwin Sands,* and he acted as fireman on board the tender of the London-Edinburgh express for *The Iron Horse.* The result of these and similar expeditions was a series of well over a hundred juvenile novels with a realism never before seen in works for teenage boys.

His first novel was *Snowflakes and Sunbeams* in 1856; a year later, with *The Coral Island,* he made his name as the foremost writer of adventure stories. *Coral Island* was the book R. L. Stevenson acknowledged as the formative influence on his own love of the South Seas which eventually led to his writing *Treasure Island,* with its dedicatory reference to "Ballantyne the Brave."

Ballantyne's weakness as a writer lay in his being strait-jacketed by his puritanism. Unlike Stevenson, he was unable to give his readers a romantic and exciting story that was not laced through with moralising. Too often the action in his tales slowed to a halt while his young hero fell on his knees for a stint of evangelistic soliloquizing. Nevertheless, for the children of middle- and working-class families Ballantyne opened up an exciting vista of a world spiced with romance and danger waiting to be explored. Boys in the late Victorian age learned more geography from reading his books than from their teachers, just as they learned much of their history from Henty.

Ballantyne used a well-tried formula – giving full rein to youthful emotions within the strict bounds of what then passed for Christian morality. He wrote for the age in which he lived, portraying a world in which the good were terribly good and terribly British, and the bad were terribly bad and spoke with foreign accents. To have suggested otherwise was quite unthinkable.

—Eric Quayle

BANIM, John. Irish. Born in Kilkenny, 3 April 1798; brother of the writer Michael Banim. Educated locally; subsequently studied art at the drawing academy of the Royal Dublin Society. Married in 1821; one daughter. Drawing teacher in Kilkenny; settled in Dublin, 1820, and thereafter devoted himself to literature; moved to London, 1822, and contributed to various periodicals, most notably the *Literary Register*; lived abroad for his health, 1829–35; returned to Kilkenny, 1835. Granted Civil List pension, 1836. *Died 13 August 1842.*

PUBLICATIONS

Fiction (with Michael Banim)

Tales of the O'Hara Family (*Crohoore of the Billhook, The Fetches, John Doe*).   1825; second series (*The Nowlans, Peter of the Castle*). 1826.
The Boyne Water.   1826.
The Anglo-Irish of the Nineteenth Century.   1828; as *Lord Clangore*, 1865.
The Croppy.   1828.
The Denounced; or, The Last Baron of Crana.   1830.
The Smuggler.   1831.
The Ghost-Hunter and His Family.   1833; as *Joe Wilson's Ghost*, 1913.
The Mayor of Wind-Gap, with *Canvassing* by Miss Martin of Ballynahinch.   1835.
The Bit o' Writin' and Other Tales.   1838.
Father Connell.   1842.

Plays

Damon and Pythias, revised by R. L. Sheil (produced 1821).   1821.
Sylla, from a play by V. J. E. de Jouy (produced 1826).
The Sergeant's Wife, music by John Godd (produced 1827).   1855(?).
The Ghost Hunter, from his own story (produced 1833).
The Duchess of Ormond (produced 1836).

Verse

The Celt's Paradise, in Four Duans.   1821.
Chaunt of the Cholera: Songs for Ireland, with Michael Banim.   1831.

Other

Revelations of the Dead Alive (essays).   1824; as *London and Its Eccentricities in the Year 2023,* 1845.

Bibliography: in *XIX Century Fiction: A Bibliographical Record* by Michael Sadleir, 2 vols., 1951.

Reading List: *The Life of Banim* by P. J. Murray, 1857; *John and Michael Banim: A Study in the Development of the Anglo-Irish Novel* by Mark D. Hawthorne, 1975.

*   *   *

In his day, John Banim had his poetry praised by Sir Walter Scott, a tragedy produced successfully at Covent Garden, and was a prolific member, until his health gave way, of that hard-living and overworked band of Irish journalists (prominent among them were William Maginn and Gerald Griffin) involved in the burgeoning London literary periodical trade. He is best remembered now for *Tales of the O'Hara Family,* written in collaboration with his brother Michael, a rather less talented writer who did not pursue a professional literary career.

The tales were intended to do for Ireland what Scott's fiction had done for his native land. From a documentary point of view they achieved some success. Lower levels of contemporary Irish life – peasants, bailiffs, and priests – were portrayed more intimately than ever before. But here any similarity with Scott's work ends. The tales contain the substance of history, but nothing like an adequate fictional rendering of an historical sense. For the most part the subject matter is portrayed in either sombre, or lurid, shades. Violence, often presented with maximum gothic effect, is endemic. The style is frequently strident and overheated. While such effects depict a certain truth about the psychological atmosphere of the life found in a realm of contemporary Ireland – interlaced as they are with the lore and superstitions of the people – the picture lacks the sense Scott's work offers of a whole view judiciously reached. Once Banim's work moves beyond its chosen realm, to depict life in a higher class, for example, it quickly becomes vapid and stilted. Because it achieves some degree of psychological differentiation, and a sense of depth and completeness of view, *The Nowlans* is probably the most successful of the tales. The nearest John Banim comes to emulating Scott is in his novel of the Jacobite war, *The Boyne Water,* which provides an understanding of that conflict's issues but in its prolixity makes the narrative disproportioned and unresolved. There is throughout Banim's work a distinct sense of the impossible situation as an archetype of experience, a reading of contemporary history possibly reinforced by the author's own physical and emotional suffering.

Michael Banim's contribution to the tales is not negligible, both in his provision of local colour for his London-based brother and in his actual artistic contribution. As to the extent of the latter there is a certain amount of scholarly conjecture. It is likely that John took final editorial responsibility, however, a view substantiated by the poor quality of the work Michael produced after his brother's death, the best-known piece being *The Town of the Cascades* (1864).

—George O'Brien

BARING, Maurice. English. Born in London, 27 April 1874; fourth son of the first Lord Revelstoke. Educated at Eton College; Trinity College, Cambridge. Served in the Royal Flying Corps in World War I: Major, 1917; O.B.E. (Officer, Order of the British Empire), 1918. Entered the diplomatic service in 1898, and served in Paris, Copenhagen, and Rome, and at the Foreign Office, London, 1903 until he left the service in 1904; Correspondent for the *Morning Post* in Manchuria, 1904–05, Russia, 1905–08, and Constantinople, 1909; Editor, with Hilaire Belloc, *North Street Gazette*, 1910; Correspondent for *The Times* in the Balkans, 1912. Honorary Wing Commander, Royal Air Force, 1925; Fellow, and Member of the Academic Committee, Royal Society of Literature; Chevalier, Legion of Honor. *Died 14 December 1945.*

PUBLICATIONS

Collections

>*Baring Restored: Selections from His Work*, edited by Paul Horgan. 1970.

Fiction

>*Orpheus in Mayfair and Other Stories and Sketches.* 1909.
>*Dead Letters.* 1910.
>*The Glass Mender and Other Stories.* 1910; as *The Blue Rose Fairy Book*, 1911.
>*Lost Diaries.* 1913.
>*Passing By.* 1921.
>*Overlooked.* 1922.
>*A Triangle: Passages from Three Notebooks.* 1923.
>*C.* 1924.
>*Half a Minute's Silence and Other Stories.* 1925.
>*Cat's Cradle.* 1925.
>*Daphne Adeane.* 1926.
>*Tinker's Leave.* 1927.
>*Comfortless Memory.* 1928.
>*When They Love.* 1928.
>*The Coat Without Seam.* 1929.
>*Robert Peckham.* 1930.
>*Friday's Business.* 1932.
>*The Lonely Lady of Dulwich.* 1934.
>*Darby and Joan.* 1935.

Plays

>*Gaston de Foix and Other Plays* (includes *Dusk, Tristram and Iseult*). 1903; revised version of *Gaston de Foix*, 1913.
>*Mahasena.* 1905.
>*Desiderio.* 1906.
>*Proserpine: A Masque.* 1908.
>*The Grey Stocking* (produced 1908). In *The Grey Stocking ...*, 1911.
>*The Green Elephant* (produced 1911). In *The Grey Stocking ...*, 1911.
>*The Grey Stocking and Other Plays.* 1911.
>*The Double Game* (produced 1912). In *The Grey Stocking ...*, 1911.

Diminutive Dramas (22 plays). 1911.
Catherine Carr (produced 1912). In *Diminutive Dramas*, 1911.
The Blue Harlequin (produced 1924). In *Diminutive Dramas*, 1911.
Lucullus's Dinner Party (produced 1924). In *Diminutive Dramas*, 1911.
Calpurnia's Dinner Party (produced 1924). In *Diminutive Dramas*, 1911.
The Aulis Difficulty (produced 1928). In *Diminutive Dramas*, 1911.
Palamon and Arcite: A Play for Puppets. 1913.
Manfroy. 1920.
His Majesty's Embassy and Other Plays (includes *Manfroy, June and After*). 1923.
Fantasio, from a play by Alfred de Musset. 1927.

Verse

Pastels and Other Rhymes. 1891.
Poems. 1897.
Hildesheim: Quatre Pastiches. 1899.
The Black Prince and Other Poems. 1902.
Poems. 2 vols. with same title, 1905.
Sonnets and Short Poems. 1906.
Collected Poems. 1911; revised edition, 1925.
Sonnets. 1914.
Fifty Sonnets. 1915.
In Memoriam Auberon Herbert. 1917.
Poems 1914–17. 1918; as *Poems 1914–19*, 1920.
Poems 1892–1929. 1929; as *Selected Poems*, 1930.

Other

Damozel Blanche and Other Faery Tales. 1891.
The Story of Forget-Me-Not and Lily of the Valley (juvenile). 1905.
With the Russians in Manchuria. 1905.
A Year in Russia. 1907; revised edition, 1917.
Russian Essays and Stories. 1908.
Landmarks in Russian Literature. 1910.
The Russian People. 1911.
Letters from the Near East 1909 and 1912. 1913.
What I Saw in Russia. 1913; revised edition, 1927.
Round the World in Any Number of Days. 1914.
The Mainsprings of Russia. 1914.
The R.F.C. Alphabet. 1915.
An Outline of Russian Literature. 1915.
Translations Found in a Commonplace Book. 1916; as *Translations Ancient and Modern*, 1918.
R.F.C.H.Q. 1914–18. 1920.
The Puppet Show of Memory (autobiography). 1922.
Punch and Judy and Other Essays. 1924.
French Literature. 1927.
Per Ardua 1914–1918. 1928.
In My End Is My Beginning (on Mary Queen of Scots). 1931.
Lost Lectures; or, The Fruits of Experience. 1932.
Sarah Bernhardt. 1933.
Unreliable History (includes *Diminutive Dramas, Dead Letters, Lost Diaries*). 1934.

Have You Anything to Declare? A Notebook with Commentaries. 1936.
Baring: A Postscript, edited by Laura Lovat. 1947.

Editor, *English Landscape: An Anthology.* 1916.
Editor, *The Oxford Book of Russian Verse.* 1924.
Editor, *Algae: An Anthology of Phrases.* 1928.

Translator, *Thoughts on Art and Life,* by Leonardo da Vinci. 1906.
Translator, *Last Days at Tsarskoe Selo, Being the Personal Notes and Memoirs of Count Paul Benckendoff.* 1927.
Translator, *Poems from Pushkin.* 1931.
Translator, *Russian Lyrics.* 1943.

Bibliography: *A Bibliography of the First Editions of the Works of Baring* by Leslie Chaundy, 1925.

Reading List: *Baring* by L. Chaigne, 1935; *Baring* by Ethel Smyth, 1938; "Baring, Novelist: A Reappraisal" by David Lodge, in *Dublin Review,* 1960.

*   *   *

Maurice Baring was a novelist and short-story writer, an essayist and journalist, a poet and playwright, a diplomat and war correspondent. He wrote with ease and showed his breeding. His sense of finish can be glimpsed in Paul Horgan's *Baring Restored,* but for the full flavor one must go to his best poetry and to such works as *A Triangle, Cat's Cradle, Daphne Adeane, Robert Peckham,* and *The Lonely Lady of Dulwich.* His genuine talent is seen best in works of limited scope, where his finesse and subtle charm can compensate for lack of structure and substance. He is at home with small things, seen in such poems as the fine World War I elegy "In Memoriam: A. H.," "Julian Grenfell," and "Elegy on the Death of Juliet's Cat." Like Max Beerbohm, he is often saved from preciosity by a sense of humor which evokes a sophisticated smile (*The Puppet Show of Memory*), though he can also raise a guffaw (in *Dead Letters* and *Lost Diaries*).

Unlike most other essayists and novelists of his period, he was a man of action: he reported both the Russo-Japanese War and the First Balkan War from the front, and served in the Royal Flying Corps in World War I. His reporting was notable for its fine sense of historical background. This perhaps helps give a nice sense of period to such novels as *Passing By* and *Friday's Business.*

Baring, however, is more notable for his style. George Sampson (in *The Concise Cambridge History of English Literature,* 1948) calls *Have You Anything to Declare* "an odd combination of commonplace-book and confession, presenting with sincere and unaffected comment the passages from great literature that have travelled with him as 'spiritual luggage' through the journey of life. The choice and the criticism are both exquisite...." Writers such as Baring are, unfortunately but firmly, quite out of fashion. Spiritual Luggage is definitely Not Wanted on the Voyage.

—Leonard R. N. Ashley

BARING-GOULD, Sabine.   English.   Born at Dix's Fields, Exeter, Devon, 28 January 1834. Educated privately, mainly abroad, and at Clare College, Cambridge, 1853–56, B.A. 1856. Married Grace Taylor in 1868 (died, 1916); five sons and nine daughters. Assistant Master at the choir school of St. Barnabas's Church, Pimlico, London, 1857, and at Hurstpierpoint College, Sussex, 1857–64; ordained deacon, 1864, and priest, 1865; Curate of Horbury, Yorkshire, 1864–66; Vicar, Dalton, Yorkshire, 1866–71; Editor, *The Sacristy* magazine, 1871–73; Rector of East Mersea, Essex, 1871–81, and Lew-Trenchard, Devon, 1881 until his death. President, Devonshire Association, 1896. Honorary Fellow, Clare College, 1918. Wrote numerous hymns, including "Onward Christian Soldiers." *Died 2 January 1924.*

PUBLICATIONS

Fiction

The Path of the Just: Tales of Holy Men and Children.   1857.
Through Flood and Flame.   1868.
In Exitu Israel.   1870.
Mehalah: A Story of the Salt Marshes.   1880; edited by C. A. McIntyre, 1950.
John Herring.   1883.
Court Royal.   1886.
Little Tu'penny.   1887.
Jack Frost's Little Prisoners.   1887.
Red Spider.   1887.
The Gaverocks.   1887.
Richard Cable, The Lightshipman.   1888.
Eve.   1888.
The Pennycomequicks.   1889.
Arminell.   1890.
Jacquetta and Other Stories.   1890.
Urith.   1891.
Margery of Quether and Other Stories.   1891.
In the Roar of the Sea.   1892.
Through All the Changing Scenes of Life.   1892.
Mrs. Curgenven of Curgenven.   1893.
Cheap Jack Zita.   1893.
The Icelander's Sword; or, The Story of Oraefadal.   1894.
Kitty Alone.   1894.
The Queen of Love.   1894.
Noémi.   1895.
Dartmoor Idylls.   1896.
The Broom-Squire.   1896.
Perpetua.   1897.
Guavas the Tinner.   1897.
Bladys of the Stewponey.   1897.
Domitia.   1898.
Pabo the Priest.   1899.
Furze Bloom: Tales of the Western Moors.   1899.
Winefred.   1900.
In a Quiet Village (stories).   1900.
The Forbishers.   1901.

Royal Georgie. 1901.
Nebo the Nailer. 1902.
Miss Quillet. 1902.
Chris of All-Sorts. 1903.
Siegfried. 1904.
In Dewisland. 1904.
Monsieur Pichelmère and Other Stories. 1905.

Play

The Red Spider, music by Learmont Drysdale, from the novel by Baring-Gould (produced 1898).

Verse

The Silver Store, Collected from Medieval, Christian, and Jewish Mines. 1868; revised edition, 1887, 1898.

Other

Iceland: Its Scenes and Sagas. 1863.
The Book of Were Wolves. 1865.
Post-Medieval Preachers. 1865.
Curious Myths of the Middle Ages. 2 vols., 1866–68.
Curiosities of the Olden Times. 1869; revised edition, 1896.
The Golden Gate: A Manual. 3 vols., 1869–70.
The Origin and Development of Religious Belief. 2 vols., 1869–70.
Legends of Old Testament Characters. 2 vols., 1871.
One Hundred Sermon Sketches for Extempore Preachers. 1871.
The Lives of the Saints. 17 vols., 1872–89; revised edition, 16 vols., 1897–98.
Village Conferences on the Creed. 1873.
How to Save Fuel. 1874.
Yorkshire Oddities, Incidents, and Strange Events. 2 vols., 1874.
The Lost and Hostile Gospels: An Essay on the Toledoth Jeschu and the Petrine and Pauline Gospels. 1874.
Some Modern Difficulties: Nine Lectures. 1875.
The Vicar of Morwenstow: Life of R. S. Hawker. 1876; revised edition, 1876, 1899.
The Mystery of Suffering: Six Lectures. 1877.
Germany Past and Present. 2 vols., 1879.
Sermons to Children. 2 vols., 1879–1907.
The Preacher's Pocket: A Packet of Sermons. 1880.
The Village Pulpit: Sermon Outlines. 2 vols., 1881.
The Seven Last Words: A Course of Sermons. 1884.
Our Parish Church: Twenty Addresses to Children. 1885.
The Passion of Jesus. 1885.
The Birth of Jesus: Eight Discourses. 1885.
Nazareth to Capernum: Ten Lectures. 1886.
Germany. 1886; revised edition, 1905.
The Trials of Jesus: Seven Discourses for Lent. 1886.
The Way of Sorrows. 1887.
Our Inheritance: An Account of the Eucharistic Service in the First Three Centuries. 1888.

The Death and Resurrection of Jesus: Ten Lectures. 1888.
Grettir the Outlaw (juvenile). 1889.
Historic Oddities and Strange Events. 2 vols., 1889–91.
Old County Life. 1890.
Conscience and Sin: Daily Meditations for Lent. 1890.
My Prague Pig and Other Stories for Children. 1890.
The Church in Germany, edited by P. H. Ditchfield. 1891.
In Troubadour Land: Provence and Languedoc. 1891.
Wagner's Parsifal at Baireuth. 1892.
The Tragedy of the Caesars. 2 vols., 1892.
Strange Survivals: Some Chapters in the History of Man. 1892.
A Book of Fairy Tales Retold. 1894.
The Deserts of Southern France. 2 vols., 1894.
The Life of Napoleon Bonaparte. 1897.
A Study of St. Paul. 1897.
The Sunday Round: Plain Village Sermons. 4 vols.,1898–99.
An Armory of the Western Counties, from Unpublished Manuscripts of the 16th Century,
    with R. W. Twigge. 1898.
An Old English Home and its Dependencies. 1898.
A Book of the West: Introduction to Devon and Cornwall. 2 vols., 1899.
The Crock of Gold (juvenile). 1899.
Virgin Saints and Martyrs. 1900.
A Book of Dartmoor, Brittany, North Wales, South Wales, the Riviera, the Rhine, the
    Cevennes, the Pyrenees. 8 vols., 1900–07.
Brittany. 1902.
A Coronation Souvenir. 1902.
Amazing Adventures. 1903.
A Book of Ghosts. 1904.
A Memorial of Lord Nelson. 1905.
Lives of the British Saints, with J. Fisher. 1907.
The Restitution of All Things; or, The Hope That Is Before Us. 1907.
Devon. 1907.
Devonshire Characters and Strange Events. 1908.
A Baring-Gould Continuous Reader, edited by G. H. Rose. 1908.
Cornish Characters and Strange Events. 1909.
A History of Sarawak under Its Two White Rajahs 1839–1908, with C. A.
    Bampfylde. 1909.
Cornwall. 1910.
Family Names and Their Story. 1910.
The Land of Teck and Its Neighbourhood. 1911.
Cliff Castles and Cave Dwellings of Europe. 1911.
Sheepstor. 1912.
A Book of Folk-Lore. 1913.
The Church Revival. 1914.
Thoughts of Baring-Gould, edited by H. B. Elliott. 1917.
The Evangelical Revival. 1920.
Early Reminiscences 1834–64. 1923.
My Last Few Words (sermons). 1924.
Further Reminiscences 1864–94. 1925.

Editor, *Songs and Ballads of the West.* 4 vols., 1889–91.
Editor, with H. Fleetwood Sheppard, *A Garland of Country Song: English Folk*
    Song. 1895.
Editor, *English Minstrelsie.* 8 vols., 1895–99.

Editor, *Old English Fairy Tales*. 1895.
Editor, *A Book of Nursery Songs and Rhymes*. 1895.
Editor, *Selected Works*, by St. Francis de Sales. 1907.

Translator, *Ernestine*, by Wilhelmine von Hillern. 1879.

Reading List: *Onward Christian Soldier: A Life of Baring-Gould* by William Purcell, 1957; "The Stature of Baring-Gould as a Novelist" by William J. Hyde in *Nineteenth Century Fiction 15*, 1961; *Baring-Gould, Writer and Folklorist* by B. H. C. Dickinson, 1970.

                    *   *   *

   When Sabine Baring-Gould's *Mehalah* appeared in 1880, it drew praise from critics as a novel of promise and power. Swinburne found it the only work which might "challenge the comparison" with *Wuthering Heights*. The high promise remained unfulfilled, but in output – novels of country life, hymns, saints' lives, folklore, folk songs, travel books, reminiscences – Baring-Gould's career would dwarf that of most major novelists.
   The chief virtue of Baring-Gould's novels is, in his own critical terms, their "colour." First there is color of setting, the tangible atmosphere of regions like the Essex salt marshes or the Devonshire moors, and the occupations of the land from which the character of the people derives. Then there is color of character, by which he meant visibly striking figures grouped harmoniously in their environment. Many of his characters, especially women in the title roles and hero-villains such as Elijah Rebow, Farmer Drownlands, and "Captain Cruel" Coppinger, have enormous vitality. Young women were Baring-Gould's specialty. His preference for a heroine was usually a lower-class girl, orphaned or burdened with a helpless parent. Set amidst the grasping rivalries and passions of a male world, she displays uninhibited and thoroughly unconventional self-reliance.
   "The character of the scenery and the character of the people determine the character of the tale." Plot was subordinate in Baring-Gould's critical intentions, yet as his output grew, he was accused of employing melodramatic formulas and self-plagiarism of characters, probably to satisfy expectations of typical novel readers "whose whole aim is distraction." Swinburne and, later, Barrie questioned unnecessary violence in his plots, but Baring-Gould was convinced of "an innate cruelty in human nature which neither Christianity, nor education, nor teetotalism will eradicate." The resultant starkness often does seem right, though interrupted sometimes by inharmonious comedy. Some virtue derives even from his faults, for Baring-Gould scarcely ever grows dull.
   "There is no veneer in my work," the narrator of "Margery of Quether" asserts. Unvarnished realism is preferred, especially in the short stories, where anecdotes are not shaped by an artist so much as transcribed from the author's observations. A troubled sleeper at the Warren Inn is fascinated by moonlight illuminating an old oak chest in his room, until he looks inside the chest and discovers a corpse. Morning brings a simple explanation from his hostess: "it's only old vayther. The frost be that hard, the snow that deep, us can't carr'n yet awhile to Lydford churchyard to bury'n so us has salted'n in" (*Dartmoor Idylls*).
   "If only Mr. Baring-Gould wrote less, what fine work might he not turn out!" (*Athenaeum*, 9 December 1893). The preacher, however, preferred serving God to carefully cultivating his art. With a profusion of novels he could reach the widest possible readership, "to please, perhaps to instruct." Baring-Gould is much more than a third-rate novelist – one with many first-rate talents which he persisted in exploiting in his own way.

                                                              —William J. Hyde

BARNES, Djuna (Chappell). American. Born in Cornwall-on-Hudson, New York, 12 June 1892. Privately educated; studied art at the Pratt Institute, Brooklyn, New York, and the Art Students' League, New York. Journalist and illustrator, 1913–31; full-time writer since 1931; also an artist: exhibited at Art of This Century Gallery, New York, 1946. Has lived in Paris and London. Trustee, New York Committee, Dag Hammarskjöld Foundation. Member, National Institute of Arts and Letters. Lives in New York City.

PUBLICATIONS

Fiction

The Book of Repulsive Women (stories). 1915.
A Book (stories, verse, and plays). 1923; augmented edition, as *A Night among the Horses*, 1929; shortened version, stories only, as *Spillway*, 1962.
Ryder. 1928.
Nightwood. 1936.
Vagaries Malicieux: Two Stories. 1974.

Plays

Three from the Earth (produced 1919). In *A Book*, 1923.
Kurzy of the Sea (produced 1919).
An Irish Triangle (produced 1919). In *Playboy*, 1921.
To the Dogs, in *A Book*. 1923.
The Dove (produced 1926). In *A Book*, 1923.
She Tells Her Daughter, in *Smart Set*, 1923.
The Antiphon (produced 1961). 1958.

Other

Ladies Almanack: Showing Their Signs and Their Tides; Their Moon and Their Changes; The Seasons as It Is with Them; Their Eclipses and Equinoxes; As Well as a Full Record of Diurnal and Nocturnal Distempers Written and Illustrated by a Lady of Fashion. 1928.
Selected Works. 1962.

Bibliography: *Barnes: A Bibliography* by Douglas Messerli, 1976.

Reading List: *The Art of Barnes: Duality and Damnation* by Louis F. Kannenstine, 1977.

* * *

Djuna Barnes, a woman of striking beauty, was one of the original members of the Theater Guild and acted in New York in plays by Tolstoi and Paul Claudel in the early 1920's. By the late 1930's the publication of her novel *Nightwood*, with an enthusiastic introduction by T. S. Eliot, had led to her being considered the most important woman novelist living in Paris. In the fiction of Anaïs Nin she appears frequently as "Djuna," and David Gascoyne's poem "Noctambules" carries the dedication "Hommage à Djuna Barnes." When her play *The*

Antiphon was published, Edwin Muir declared that it was "one of the greatest things written in our times." Yet, despite such high praise, her books have become collectors' items rather than popular successes.

Nightwood is about the obsession of two American women for each other in the 1920's. Their Paris is not the Paris of Scott Fitzgerald, but that of Romaine Brooks, Natalie Clifford Barney, and the circle of "Amazonians" which surrounded them. Norah Flood, one of the protagonists of the novel, arranges publicity from time to time for Denckman Circus, and she also runs a *salon*. Some thirty years before, Dr. Matthew O'Connor assisted at her birth; now living in Paris, he has given way to his homosexual-transvestite urges. He is called one night from a cafe to a nearby hotel to attend Robin Vote, a boyish young woman who has had a collapse. The doctor takes along with him his drinking companion, Baron Felix Volkbein, who falls in love with Robin and subsequently marries her. In due course Robin bears him a son, but she cannot stand the course of marriage and starts an affair with Norah. A passionate and tempestuous sequence of events follows and Robin's promiscuity nearly unhinges Norah's mind. Her old friend the doctor sits with her through the night boozing and pouring forth great streams of disconnected thoughts of life, literature, and the vagaries of the human condition. Had the novel been adapted for radio, the role of the doctor was one that Dylan Thomas aspired to play.

The Antiphon, written in blank verse, recalls a Jacobean closet drama:

> You have such sons
> Would mate the pennies on a dead man's eyes
> To breed the sexton's fee.

But the setting is modern and takes place in England during the second World War. Augusta Burley betrays her aristocratic lineage by marrying a coarse, uncultivated Mormon from Salem, by whom she has three sons and a daughter. Now a widow, she arranges a reunion at Burley Hall for the whole family. Yet nothing is what it seems. For as two of the brothers and their sister await their third brother, he enjoys himself at their expense disguised as "a coachman." Recriminations and suppressed violence cause the two identified sons to plan a matricide, while their sister acts as inquisitor to her mother for marrying her father. Finally incensed by the desertion of her two sons, the mother turns on her daughter to kill her and brings about her own death at the same time. The original production of this powerful play – by the Royal Dramatic Theatre of Stockholm in 1961 – was in a translation by Dag Hammarskjöld.

Djuna Barnes has also illustrated books and written poems, short stories, and other plays. *Ladies Almanack*, which she brought out anonymously in Paris, created a minor *succès de scandale* in the 1920's. A number of lesbians are gently mocked – among them Radclyffe Hall (Lady Buck-and-Balk), Natalie Clifford Barney (Evangeline Musset), and Lady Una Troubridge (Tilly-Tweed-in-Blood).

—Neville Braybrooke

BARTH, John (Simmons). American. Born in Cambridge, Maryland, 27 May 1930. Educated at the Juilliard School of Music, New York; Johns Hopkins University, Baltimore, A.B. 1951, M.A. 1952. Married 1) Anne Strickland in 1951, one daughter and two sons; 2) Shelley Rosenberg in 1970. Junior Instructor in English, Johns Hopkins University, 1951–53; Instructor to Associate Professor of English, Pennsylvania State University.

University Park, 1953–65; Professor of English, State University of New York at Buffalo, 1965–73. Since 1973, Professor of English and Creative Writing, Johns Hopkins University. Recipient: Brandeis University Creative Arts Award, 1965; Rockefeller grant, 1965; National Institute of Arts and Letters grant, 1966; National Book Award, 1973. Litt.D.: University of Maryland, College Park, 1969. Lives in Baltimore.

PUBLICATIONS

Fiction

The Floating Opera. 1956; revised edition, 1967.
The End of the Road. 1958; revised edition, 1967.
The Sot-Weed Factor. 1960; revised edition, 1967.
Giles Goat-Boy; or, The Revised New Syllabus. 1966.
Lost in the Funhouse: Fiction for Print, Tape, Live Voice (stories). 1968.
Chimera (stories). 1972.

Bibliography: *Barth: A Descriptive Primary and Annotated Secondary Bibliography* by Joseph Weixlmann, 1975.

Reading List: *Barth* by Gerhard Joseph, 1969; *Barth: The Comic Sublimity of Paradox* by Jac Tharpe, 1974; *Barth: An Introduction* by David Morrell, 1977

*   *   *

Highly susceptible to the sport of metaphysical games and passionately attracted to the conundrums of self-consciousness, John Barth has moved steadily away from the objective and realistic toward myth and unashamed fable. His first two novels, *The Floating Opera* and *The End of the Road* — novels which he has claimed to be twin explorations of the comic and tragic aspects of philosophical nihilism — fall well within the conventions of realism. But his next novel, *The Sot-Weed Factor*, takes an entirely different direction. It is framed on a gigantic scale of multiple plots, disguises, coincidences, intrigues, and deceptions, and it is written in an exuberant and constantly inventive pastiche of 17th-century prose style. Mingling history, legend, fiction, and outrageous lie in a bawdy, funny, and learned parody of the initiation-and-quest novel, *The Sot-Weed Factor* purports to chronicle the life and career of Ebenezer Cooke, Poet-Laureate of Maryland. Partly a reinterpretation of the primal fall from innocence, and partly a re-examination of the rich ambiguities in the archetypal American experience, it is both a dazzling *tour de force* and a major contribution to the novel of fabulation.

Barth is even more ambitious in scope and substance in *Giles Goat-Boy*. In this gargantuan spoof, he attempts to fuse myth, allegory, satire, parody, and the conventions of science-fiction to produce a comically revised New Testament which will expose the fictive sources of all myths while leaving a new one in their place. Although the novel inevitably falls short of its excessive aims, its relative failure — it goes on too long and its plot becomes mechanical — is still a significant and startling achievement. In *Lost in the Fun House* and *Chimera*, he has withdrawn into an increasingly abstract and cerebral style, deliberately focusing on the naked process of story-telling itself as a subject — if not a substitute — for telling stories. The results are curiously mixed: over-clever, strained, whimsical, desperate, terrifying, boring, and funny. Whether these works represent a temporary exhaustion of Barth's imaginative energies or are, instead, a necessary and courageous phase in his development as a major writer, there is little doubt that his literary intelligence and mastery of language place him in the forefront of his generation of writers.

—Earl Rovit

BARTHELME, Donald. American. Born in Philadelphia, Pennsylvania, 7 April 1931. Served in the United States Army. Married to Birgit Barthelme; one daughter. Museum Director, Houston, in the mid-1950's. Visiting Professor, Boston University, 1973, and City College of New York, 1974–75. Formerly, Managing Editor, *Location* magazine, New York. Recipient: Guggenheim Fellowship, 1966; National Book Award, 1972; National Institute of Arts and Letters Morton Dauwen Zabel Award, 1972. Lives in New York City.

PUBLICATIONS

Fiction

Come Back, Dr. Caligari (stories). 1964.
Snow White. 1967.
Unspeakable Practices, Unnatural Acts (stories). 1968.
City Life (stories). 1971.
Sadness (stories). 1972.
Guilty Pleasures (stories). 1974.
The Dead Father. 1975.
Amateurs (stories). 1976.

Other

The Slightly Irregular Fire Engine; or, The Hithering Dithering Djinn (juvenile). 1972.

*   *   *

Since the American publication of two volumes of fictions by Argentinian Jorge Luis Borges in 1962, an interest in short, highly self-conscious, directly philosophical fiction has become apparent in the United States. Donald Barthelme is perhaps the best exemplar of this strain of fiction. His best work to date has been in the short story (for lack of a more expansive term), particularly in the sub-strain "metafiction," a term coined by William Gass. Like Borges, the Americans John Barth, Gass, and Robert Coover, and the Italian Italo Calvino, Barthelme has little interest in mimetic fiction which works from the bedrock of the "real" world. Instead of protracted social or psychological studies, he busies himself with very short, often truncated and discontinuous, literary pieces that depend on other literary works, philosophy, film, pop culture, and high art for their fictional matrices. There is throughout his work a suspicion of received morality or attitude, indeed of any unself-conscious and sustained human construct – including fiction. Thus his works are brief, constantly shifting in tone and style, reliant as much on the juxtaposition and reverberation of image and language in modern poetry and on the open randomness and "objectness" of the collage and much modern art as on traditional fictional technique.

Barthelme's first work, *Come Back, Dr. Caligari*, was very well-reviewed, but one notes the bewilderment of critics who searched for "meaning" in his work. His best works have been collections of short fiction; of these, *City Life* and *Sadness* are most sustained in imagination and execution.

While Barthelme has little interest in miming reality, he does have a recurrent interest in modern consciousness, particularly as manifested in urban Americans. He issues elegant fictional reports on the state of consciousness in "The City," and, indeed, the daily sorrowful, maddening minutiae of city life – tattered marriages, the loss of innocence, the failure of love, the absurd hope of social or political "progress," the torrent of stimulation by the media – comprise the stuff of his reports. "The City" is dangerous and confusing, and is finally a configuration of human consciousness: "It heaves and palpitates. It is multi-dimensional and has a mayor. To describe it takes many hundreds of thousands of words. Our muck is only a part of a much greater muck – the nation state – which is itself the creation of that muck of mucks, human consciousness" ("City Life").

Indeed, the human urban condition is Barthelme's major subject, and like his city, his vision can certainly appear bleak and pessimistic. Endlessly self-conscious (his narrators offer clues as to the significance of their tales), satiric and parodic (Barthelme's liberated *Snow White* is hilarious), a mournful connoisseur of the many flavors of metaphysical *malaise* and *angst* of our time (a character "pickets" the human condition in an early story: "THE HUMAN CONDITION: WHY DOES IT HAVE TO BE THAT WAY?"), he can often seem depressing and negative. Yet his wit and humor are a delight, and his stylistic command is among the most deft of writers in English in our time.

Barthelme demands a creative reader, and he offers his own best apologia in writing on the work of Samuel Beckett: "His pessimism is the premise necessary to a marvelous pedantic high-wire performance, the wire itself supporting a comic turn of endless virtuosity. No one who writes as well as Beckett can be said to be doing anything but celebrating life."

—Jack Hicks

BATES, H(erbert) E(rnest). English. Born in Rushden, Northamptonshire, 16 May 1905. Educated at the Grammar School, Kettering, until 1921. Served in the Royal Air Force, 1941–45: Squadron Leader. Married Marjorie Helen Cox in 1931; two sons and two daughters. Prior to 1926 worked as a provincial journalist and warehouse clerk. Fellow, Royal Society of Literature, 1950; resigned, 1963. C.B.E (Commander, Order of the British Empire), 1973. *Died 29 January 1974.*

PUBLICATIONS

Fiction

The Two Sisters. 1926.
The Seekers (stories). 1926.

The Spring Song, and In View of the Fact That …: Two Stories.   1927.
Day's End and Other Stories.   1928.
Seven Tales and Alexander.   1929.
Catherine Foster.   1929.
The Tree (story).   1930.
The Hessian Prisoner (story).   1930.
Mrs. Esmond's Life (story).   1930.
A Threshing Day (stories).   1931.
Charlotte's Row.   1931.
The Fallow Land.   1932.
The Story Without an End, and The Country Doctor.   1932.
A German Idyll (story).   1932.
The Black Boxer: Tales.   1932.
Sally Go round the Moon (story).   1932.
The House with the Apricot and Two Other Tales.   1933.
The Woman Who Had Imagination and Other Stories.   1934.
Thirty Tales.   1934.
The Duet (story).   1935.
The Poacher.   1935.
Cut and Come Again: Fourteen Stories.   1935.
A House of Women.   1936.
Something Short and Sweet: Stories.   1937.
"Spella Ho."   1938.
I Am Not Myself (story).   1939.
The Flying Goat: Stories.   1939.
My Uncle Silas: Stories.   1939.
Country Tales: Collected Short Stories.   1940.
The Beauty of the Dead and Other Stories.   1940.
The Bride Comes to Evensford (story).   1943.
Fair Stood the Wind for France.   1944.
The Cruise of "The Breadwinner."   1946.
The Purple Plain.   1947.
Thirty-One Selected Tales.   1947.
The Bride Comes to Evensford and Other Tales.   1949.
The Jacaranda Tree.   1949.
Dear Life.   1949.
The Scarlet Sword.   1950.
Selected Short Stories.   1951.
Twenty Tales.   1951.
Colonel Julian and Other Stories.   1951.
Love for Lydia.   1952.
The Nature of Love: Three Short Novels.   1953.
The Feast of July.   1954.
The Daffodil Sky (stories).   1955.
The Sleepless Moon.   1956.
Death of a Huntsman: Four Short Novels.   1957; as *Summer in Salandar*, 1957.
Selected Stories.   1957.
Sugar for the Horse (stories).   1957.
The Darling Buds of May.   1958.
A Breath of French Air.   1959.
The Watercress Girl and Other Stories.   1959.
When the Green Woods Laugh.   1960; as *Hark, Hark, the Lark!*, 1961.
An Aspidistra in Babylon: Four Novellas.   1960; as *The Grapes of Paradise: Four Short
     Novels*, 1960.

Now Sleeps the Crimson Petal and Other Stories. 1961; as *The Enchantress and Other Stories,* 1961.
The Day of the Tortoise. 1961.
The Golden Oriole: Five Novellas. 1962.
A Crown of Wild Myrtle. 1962.
Oh! To Be in England. 1963.
Seven by Five: Stories 1926–1961. 1963; as *The Best of Bates,* 1963.
A Moment in Time. 1964.
The Fabulous Mrs. V. (stories). 1964.
The Wedding Party (stories). 1965.
The Distant Horns of Summer. 1967.
The Wild Cherry Tree (stories). 1968.
The Four Beauties (stories). 1968.
A Little of What You Fancy. 1970.
The Triple Echo. 1970.
The Song of the Wren (stories). 1972.
The Good Corn and Other Stories, edited by Geoffrey Halson. 1974.
H. E. Bates (selected stories), edited by Alan Cattell. 1975.
The Poison Ladies and Other Stories, edited by Mike Poulton. 1976.
The Yellow Meads of Asphodel (stories). 1976.

Plays

The Last Bread. 1926.
The Day of Glory (produced 1946). 1945.

Screenplay: *The Loves of Joanna Godden,* with Angus Macphail, 1947.

Other

Flowers and Faces. 1935.
Through the Woods: The English Woodland – April to April. 1936.
Down the River (essays). 1937.
The Seasons and the Gardener: A Book for Children. 1940.
The Modern Short Story: A Critical Survey. 1941.
In the Heart of the Country. 1942.
The Greatest People in the World and Other Stories. 1942; as *There's Something in the Air,* 1943.
How Sleep the Brave and other Stories. 1943.
O! More Than Happy Countryman. 1943; revised edition, as *The Country Heart* (includes *In the Heart of the Country*), 1949.
Something in the Air: Stories by Flying Officer X. 1944.
There's Freedom in the Air: The Official Story of the Allied Air Forces from the Occupied Countries. 1944.
The Tinkers of Elstow. 1946(?).
Edward Garnett (biography). 1950.
Flower Gardening: A Reader's Guide. 1950.
The Country of White Clover (essays). 1952.
The Face of England. 1952.
Pastoral on Paper. 1956.
Achilles the Donkey (juvenile). 1962.
Achilles and Diana (juvenile). 1963.

Achilles and the Twins (juvenile).   1964.
The White Admiral (juvenile).   1968.
The Vanished World (autobiography).   1969.
The Blossoming World (autobiography).   1971.
A Love of Flowers (autobiography).   1971.
The World in Ripeness (autobiography).   1972.
A Fountain of Flowers (on gardening).   1974.

*   *   *

Accomplished and prolific in various literary forms, H. E. Bates was above all an acknowledged master of the short story. His long and distinguished career extended over five decades, ending only with his posthumous *The Yellow Meads of Asphodel*. His exquisitely wrought early mood-pieces and prose-poems, showing little concern with plot or complexities of characterization, seemed to be chiefly in the Chekhovian tradition. Bates himself, however, claimed Maupassant as the initial influence. The development of his interest in the intricacies of human nature, and in the techniques of narrative, can be seen in its maturity in such a volume as *The Daffodil Sky*, giving substance to the lyricism which remained a constant element in his work, and demonstrating an equal debt to the disciplines of both his masters.

The war brought a whole dimension of fresh experience for fictional exploration. Hitherto in his short stories, and novels like *The Fallow Land* and *The Poacher*, Bates had written almost exclusively about rural life, portraying it with the fidelity of the countryman's intimate, unsentimental knowledge of its characters, customs, and changing conditions. Now his creative range was immeasurably broadened beyond his native scene. His experiences as a squadron-leader in the R.A.F. are reflected in the tales of service life published under the pseudonym of "Flying Officer X", and the best-selling novels *Fair Stood the Wind for France* and *The Cruise of "The Breadwinner*." Later, Burma and India provided material for the exotic landscapes and dramatic events of *The Purple Plain, The Jacaranda Tree*, and *The Scarlet Sword*. This enlargement of background was matched by a corresponding growth in psychological penetration and a richer variety of character and predicament. Bates's human interest embraces spiritually displaced persons like Colonel Julian and the Captain in "The Flag," the tough Irish nurse in Burma of "Time Expired," the crippled Indian girl of "A Place in the Heart," the pretensions of middle-class English country society, the disenchantments of middle age. To all he brings a gift of compassionate involvement and sense of the underlying sadness of existence. That his tone is not invariably sombre may be seen from the comedy of the Uncle Silas stories and the zestful adventures of the happy-go-lucky Larkin family in *The Darling Buds of May* and its successors.

It is Bates's pictures of country life which remain most memorably in the minds of his admirers. His landscapes glow with the warmth and clarity – the figures in them are delineated with something of the elemental and timeless simplicity – of a canvas by Millet. The slow cycle of the seasons in fields, lanes, woods, and villages in which his humble folk – cottagers, farm labourers, small shopkeepers, vagrants – enact their poignant, often inarticulate joys and troubles, disappointments and hopes, is evoked with a quivering, sensuous actuality, economy of style, and precision of atmospheric detail unsurpassed by any modern painter of the English countryside.

—Margaret Willy

BAUM, L(yman) Frank. American. Born in Chittenango, New York, 15 May 1856. Educated at schools in Syracuse, New York, and Peekskill Military Academy, New York. Married Maud Gage in 1882; four sons. Reporter, New York *World*, 1873–75; Founding Editor, *New Era*, Bradford, Pennsylvania, 1876; actor (as Louis F. Baum and George Brooks), theatre manager, and producer, New York and on tour; poultry farmer in the 1880's; salesman, Baum's Castorine axle grease, 1886–88; Owner, Baum's Bazaar general store, Aberdeen, Dakota Territory, 1888–90; Editor, *Saturday Pioneer*, Aberdeen, 1890–91; Reporter, Chicago *Post*, and Buyer, Siegel Cooper and Company, Chicago, and Salesman, Pitkin and Brooks, Chicago, 1891–97; Founder, National Association of Window Trimmers, 1897, and Founding Editor and Publisher, *The Show Window* magazine, Chicago, 1897–1902; Founding Director, Oz Film Manufacturing Company, Los Angeles, 1914. *Died 6 May 1919.*

PUBLICATIONS

Fiction

A New Wonderland. 1900: as *The Surprising Adventures of the Magical Monarch of Mo,* 1903.
The Wonderful Wizard of Oz. 1900; as *The New Wizard of Oz,* 1903.
Dot and Tot of Merryland. 1901.
The Master Key: An Electrical Fairy Tale. 1901.
The Life and Adventures of Santa Claus. 1902.
The Enchanted Island of Yew. 1903.
The Marvelous Land of Oz. 1904.
Queen Zixi of Ix. 1905.
The Woggle-Bug Book. 1905.
The Fate of a Crown. 1905.
Daughters of Destiny. 1906.
John Dough and the Cherub. 1906.
Annabel. 1906.
Sam Steele's Adventures on Land and Sea. 1906; as *The Boy Fortune Hunters in Alaska,* 1908.
Aunt Jane's Nieces. 1906.
Aunt Jane's Nieces Abroad. 1906.
Twinkle Tales. 6 vols., 1906; as *Twinkle and Chubbins,* 1911.
Tamawaca Folks. 1907.
Ozma of Oz. 1907; as *Princess Ozma of Oz,* 1942.
Sam Steele's Adventures in Panama. 1907; as *The Boy Fortune Hunters in Panama,* 1908.
Policeman Bluejay. 1907; as *Babes in Birdland,* 1911.
The Last Egyptian. 1908.
Dorothy and the Wizard in Oz. 1908.
The Boy Fortune Hunters in Egypt. 1908.
Aunt Jane's Nieces at Millville. 1908.
The Road to Oz. 1909.
The Boy Fortune Hunters in China. 1909.
Aunt Jane's Nieces at Work. 1909.
The Emerald City of Oz. 1910.
The Boy Fortune Hunters in Yucatan. 1910.
Aunt Jane's Nieces in Society. 1910.

The Sea Fairies. 1911.
The Daring Twins. 1911.
The Boy Fortune Hunters in the South Seas. 1911.
Aunt Jane's Nieces and Uncle John. 1911.
The Flying Girl. 1911.
Sky Island. 1912.
Phoebe Daring. 1912.
Aunt Jane's Nieces on Vacation. 1912.
The Flying Girl and Her Chum. 1912.
The Patchwork Girl of Oz. 1913.
Aunt Jane's Nieces on the Ranch. 1913.
The Little Wizard Series. 6 vols., 1913; as *Little Wizard Stories of Oz*, 1914.
Tik-Tok of Oz. 1914.
Aunt Jane's Nieces Out West. 1914.
The Scarecrow of Oz. 1915.
Aunt Jane's Nieces in the Red Cross. 1915.
Rinkitink in Oz. 1916.
The Snuggle Tales. 6 vols., 1916–17; as *Oz-Man Tales*, 6 vols,. 1920.
Mary Louise. 1916.
Mary Louise in the Country. 1916.
The Lost Princess of Oz. 1917.
Mary Louise Solves a Mystery. 1917.
The Tin Woodman of Oz. 1918.
Mary Louise and the Liberty Girls. 1918.
Mary Louise Adopts a Soldier. 1919.
The Magic of Oz. 1919.
Glinda of Oz. 1920.
Jaglon and the Tiger Fairies. 1953.
A Kidnapped Santa Claus. 1961.

Plays

The Maid of Arran, music and lyrics by Baum, from the novel *A Princess of Thule* by
    William Black (produced 1882).
Matches (produced 1882).
Kilmourne; or, O'Connor's Dream (produced 1883).
The Wizard of Oz, music by Paul Tietjens, lyrics by Baum, from the story by Baum
    (produced 1902); revised version, as *There Is Something New under the Sun*
    (produced 1903).
The Woggle-Bug, music by Frederic Chapin, from the story *The Marvelous Land of Oz*
    by Baum (produced 1905).
The Tik-Tok Man of Oz, music by Louis F. Gottschalk, from the story by Baum
    (produced 1913).
Stagecraft: The Adventures of a Strictly Moral Man, music by Louis F. Gottschalk
    (produced 1914).
The Uplift of Lucifer; or, Raising Hell, music by Louis F. Gottschalk (produced
    1915). Edited by Manuel Weltman, 1963.
The Uplifters' Minstrels, music by Byron Gay (produced 1916).
The Orpheus Road Company, music by Louis F. Gottschalk (produced 1917).

Screenplays: *The Fairylogue and Radio-Plays*, 1908–09; *The Patchwork Girl of Oz*,
1914, *The Babes in the Wood*, 1914; *The Last Egyptian*, 1914; *The New Wizard of Oz*,
1915.

Verse

> *By the Candelabra's Glare.* 1898.
> *Father Goose, His Book.* 1899.
> *The Army Alphabet.* 1900.
> *The Navy Alphabet.* 1900.
> *The Songs of Father Goose,* music by Alberta N. Hall. 1900.
> *Father Goose's Year Book: Quaint Quacks and Feathery Shafts for Mature Children.* 1907.

Other

> *The Book of the Hamburgs: A Brief Treatise upon the Mating, Rearing, and Management of the Different Varieties of Hamburgs.* 1886.
> *Mother Goose in Prose.* 1897.
> *The Art of Decorating Dry Goods Windows and Interiors.* 1900.
> *American Fairy Tales.* 1901; augmented edition, 1908.
> *Baum's Juvenile Speaker* (miscellany). 1910; as *Baum's Own Book for Children,* 1912.
> *Our Landlandy* (newspaper columns). 1941.

Bibliography: *Bibliographia Oziana* by Peter E. Hanff and Douglas G. Greene, 1976.

Reading List: *The Wizard of Oz and Who He Was* edited by Russel Nye and Martin Gardner, 1957; *To Please a Child: A Biography of Baum* by Frank Joslyn Baum and Russell P. MacFall, 1961; *The Annotated Wizard of Oz* edited by Michael Patrick Hearn, 1973 (includes bibliography); *Wonderful Wizard Marvelous Land* by Raylyn Moore, 1974.

*   *   *

L. Frank Baum's *The Wonderful Wizard of Oz,* illustrated by W. W. Denslow, is his masterpiece. It made him famous and, with its 13 sequels, has established him as a classic writer of children's stories.

The Wonderful Wizard of Oz was a novelty in children's books at the time it was published, lacking the didactic, moralizing, and stilted tone so common. Its characters spoke the American vernacular; its plot was simple but intriguing and well-structured. Moreover, Baum created five characters worthy to stand with Lewis Carroll's. Dorothy and the Wizard, and the three non-human characters (the Tin Woodman, the Scarecrow, and the Cowardly Lion), are all archetypes yet sharply distinguished individuals. The quest of the Scarecrow for brains, the Woodman for a heart, and the Lion for courage, qualities they already possessed but did not know how to use, is the stuff of which classics are made. All have become literary figures as instantly recognizable as Alice and Peter Pan.

The Wizard was also Baum's most successful, though not his best, example of what he called the American or modernized fairy tale. Responding to ideas expressed by Hamlin Garland and others, he intended to write fantasies which would be distinct from the European and New England tradition. They would recognize the existence and importance of the industry, technology, and social concepts of the dawning 20th century. He did incorporate mechanical gadgets (particularly electricity, which fascinated him) into his works – *The Master Key: An Electrical Fairy Tale* is the best example – and dealt with such modern concepts as Populism. But in general his ambition to create a new genre was only partly successful. Though the visitors to Oz were American, the country itself was as foreign as James Branch Cabell's Poictesme or Swift's Lilliput. Furthermore, he often used such traditional fairy tale paraphernalia as witches, gnomes, talking animals, and wishing caps.

What many consider his best book, *Queen Zixi of Ix*, is entirely derived from European children's literature, though it contains many imaginative novelties.

Baum tired of his Oz series. But just as public demand kept Doyle writing his Sherlock Holmes stories when he would have preferred to concentrate on his more "serious" works, so it kept Baum at his Oz tales, though he did write many other children's books, few of them fantasies. Though written "to please a child" (Baum's phrase), the Oz books have also been popular with adults, who recognize subtleties which escaped them as children. *The Wonderful Wizard of Oz* is still popular, and now seems to have passed the judgment of time.

—Philip José Farmer

BECKETT, Samuel (Barclay). Irish. Born in Foxrock, County Dublin, 13 April 1906. Educated at Portora Royal School, Enniskillen, County Fermanagh; Trinity College, Dublin, B.A. in French and Italian 1927, M.A. 1931. Worked at the Irish Red Cross Hospital, St. Lô, France, 1945. Married Suzanne Dechevaux-Dumesnil in 1948. Lecturer in English, Ecole Normale Supérieure, Paris, 1928–30; Lecturer in French, Trinity College, Dublin, 1930–32. Closely associated with James Joyce in Paris in the late 1920's and 1930's. Settled in Paris in 1937, and has written chiefly in French since 1945; translates his own work into English. Recipient: *Evening Standard* award, 1955; Obie Award, 1958, 1960, 1962, 1964; Italia Prize. 1959; Prix Formentor, 1959; International Publishers Prize, 1961; Prix Filmcritice, 1965; Tours Film Prize, 1966; Nobel Prize for Literature, 1969. D.Litt.: University of Dublin, 1959. Member, American Academy of Arts and Letters, 1968. Lives in Paris.

PUBLICATIONS

Fiction and Texts

> *More Pricks Than Kicks* (stories).   1934.
> *Murphy*.   1938.
> *Molloy* (in French).   1951; translated by the author and Patrick Bowles, 1955.
> *Malone Meurt*.   1951; as *Malone Dies, 1956*.
> *L'Innommable*.   1953; as *The Unnamable, 1958*.
> *Watt* (in English).   1953.
> *Nouvelles et Textes pour Rien*.   1955; as *Stories and Texts for Nothing*,   1967.
> *From an Abandoned Work*.   1958.
> *Comment C'Est*.   1961; as *How It Is, 1961*.
> *Imagination Morte Imaginez*.   1965; as *Imagination Dead Imagine, 1965*.
> *Assez*.   1966; as *Enough*, in *No's Knife, 1967*.
> *Bing*.   1966; as *Ping*, in *No's Knife, 1967*.
> *No's Knife: Selected Shorter Prose 1945–1966*.   1967.
> *L'Issue*.   1968.
> *Sans*.   1969; as *Lessness, 1971*.
> *Mercier et Camier*.   1970; as *Mercier and Camier*,   1974.
> *Sejour*.   1970.
> *Premier Amour*.   1970; as *First Love, 1973*.

Le Depeupleur. 1971; as *The Lost Ones,* 1972.
The North. 1973.
First Love and Other Shorts. 1974.
Fizzles. 1976.
For to End Yet Again and Other Fizzles. 1977.
Four Novellas. 1977.
Six Residua. 1978.

Plays

Le Kid, with Georges Pelorson (produced 1931).
En Attendant Godot (produced 1953). 1952; as *Waiting for Godot: Tragicomedy* (produced 1955), 1954.
Fin de Partie, Suivi de Acte sans Paroles (produced 1957). 1957; as *Endgame, Followed by Act Without Words* (*Endgame* produced 1958, *Act Without Words* produced 1960), 1958.
All That Fall (broadcast 1957). 1957.
Krapp's Last Tape (produced 1958). With *Embers,* 1959.
Embers (broadcast 1959). With *Krapp's Last Tape,* 1959.
Act Without Words II (produced 1959). In *Krapp's Last Tape and Other Dramatic Pieces,* 1960.
Happy Days (produced 1961). 1961; bilingual edition edited by James Knowlson, 1978.
Words and Music (broadcast 1962). In *Play,* 1964.
Cascando (in French, broadcast 1963). 1963; in English (broadcast 1964; produced on stage 1970), in *Play,* 1964.
Play (produced 1963). 1964.
Eh Joe (televised 1966). In *Eh Joe and Other Writings,* 1967.
Come and Go: Dramaticule (produced 1966). 1967.
Film. 1969.
Breath (produced 1970). In *Breath and Other Shorts,* 1971.
Not I (produced 1972). 1973.
That Time (produced 1976). 1976.
Footfalls (produced 1976). 1976.
Tryst (televised 1976). In *Ends and Odd,* 1976.
Ends and Odd: Dramatic Pieces. 1976.

Screenplay: *Film,* 1965.

Radio Plays: *All That Fall,* 1957; *Embers,* 1959; *The Old Tune,* 1960; *Words and Music,* 1962; *Cascando,* 1963.

Television Plays: *Eh Joe,* 1966; *Tryst,* 1976; *Shades* (*Ghost Trio, Not I, ... But the Clouds ...*), 1977.

Verse

Whoroscope. 1930.
Echo's Bones and Other Precipitates. 1935.
Gedichte (collected poems in English and French, with German translations) 1959.
Poems in English. 1961.
Collected Poems in English and French. 1977.

Other

Proust. 1931; with *Three Dialogues with Georges Duthuit,* 1965.
Bram van Welde, with Georges Duthuit and J. Putman.   1958.
A Beckett Reader. 1967.
I Can't Go On: A Selection from the Work of Beckett, edited by Richard W.
   Seaver.   1976.

Translator, *Anthology of Mexican Poetry,* edited by Octavio Paz.   1958.
Translator, *La Manivelle/The Old Tune,* by Robert Pinget.   1960.
Translator, *Zone,* by Guillaume Apollinaire.   1960.
Translator, *Drunken Boat,* by Arthur Rimbaud, edited by James Knowlson and Felix
   Leakey.   1977.

Bibliography: *Beckett: His Work and His Critics: An Essay in Bibliography* by Raymond
Felderman and John Fletcher, 1970.

Reading List: "Beckett Issue" of *Perspective 11,* 1959, and of *Modern Drama 9,* 1966 both
edited by Ruby Cohn, and *Beckett: The Comic Gamut,* 1962, and *Back to Beckett,* 1973, both
by Cohn; *Beckett: A Critical Study* by Hugh Kenner, 1961, revised edition, 1968; *Beckett* by
William York Tindall, 1964; *The Novels of Beckett* by John Fletcher, 1964; *Beckett: A
Collection of Critical Essays* edited by Martin Esslin, 1965; *Beckett at Sixty: A Festschrift*
edited by John Calder, 1967; *Beckett* by Ronald Hayman, 1968; *Beckett / Beckett* by Vivian
Mercier, 1978; *Beckett: A Biography* by Deirdre Bair, 1978; *Beckett: The Critical Heritage*
edited by Lawrence Graver and Raymond Felderman, 1978.

                              *   *   *

    No living author in English or French has molded words so skillfully in fiction and drama,
while paradoxically protesting his own failure. Better appreciated as a playwright, Beckett
himself has taken deepest pains with his fiction – most of it originally written in French but
self-translated into his native English. Most of his drama, in contrast, was translated into
French from English. "English is a good theatre language," he has said, "because of its
concreteness, its close relationship between thing and vocable." Two languages and two
genres have been indelibly marked by Beckett's vision – a reaching toward human essence or
elemental being.
    Beckett broke into print in 1929 with a piece on *Finnegans Wake,* written at Joyce's
request, with a pastiche dialogue on contraception in Ireland, with a cryptic short story
"Assumption." Supercilious mannerism mars the three pieces, and yet they predict Beckett's
generic variety. From 1929 to 1977 no year has passed without his contribution to some
literary or theatre genre: nearly half a century of creative activity, however his characters
may yearn for indolence.
    In the early 1930's, in English, Beckett wavered between obscure verse and satiric short
fiction, publishing a volume of each. At about the time he settled in Paris, he published his
first English novel, *Murphy* – traditional in its coherence and comic omniscience. It was
perceptively reviewed by Dylan Thomas: "[*Murphy*] is serious because it is, mainly, the study
of a complex and oddly tragic character who cannot reconcile the unreality of the seen world
with the reality of the unseen, and who, through scorn and neglect of 'normal' society, drifts
into the society of the certified abnormal in his search for 'a little world.' " The sentence also
describes Beckett's next very untraditional novel, *Watt,* and it is relevant too to Beckett's
French fiction, where "the seen world" recedes toward a vanishing point.
    Watt is a less finished but more important novel than *Murphy* because it predicts the
anarchic immediacy of most of the French fiction. Watt carries the Beckettian burden of

solitude, attracted and rejected as he is by the inscrutable Mr. Knott. A would-be Cartesian, Watt thinks in order to try to be, but his French successors, adopting the language of Descartes, will try *not* to think in order to be. Beckett revised *Watt* several times during a four-year period in which he fled from his Paris home to a Free French farm. Back in Paris, forty years old when World War II ended, Beckett wrote with prolific zest, producing four long stories, four novels, and two plays. He has never again attained such fluidity.

The French fiction, considered by many to be his most important work, is a shifting soulscape painted by a narrating "I." But "I"'s identity changes in the stories, in the novels, and in the works that grow out of them — *Texts for Nothing* and *How It Is.* The story narrators are nameless social outcasts, old and ill, inventing their ways of survival. Conflict and climax do not structure these alogical cumulations of passionate language. But common to all of them is the overriding sense that they are stories.

The reach toward formal fiction is inherited by the novel heroes Molloy, Moran, Malone, and the Unnamable — four narrators of three books that Beckett himself calls a trilogy. Molloy seeks his mother, and Moran seeks Molloy; both write an account of a fruitless search. Malone writes so as to fill the time of his dying. The Unnamable disowns the written for the spoken discourse, whosoever the voice that speaks it. Even more aural is *How It Is*, whose narrator/narrated tries to order chaos through a few images, many numbers, and skeletal story remnants rising from ubiquitous mud. Probably the most difficult sustained work in the Beckett canon, *How It Is* invents a language rhythmically if not lexically, a language that conveys the body's movements through its mud and the mind's movements through its mud. After *How It Is* Beckett discarded first-person fiction and assumed resolute objectivity for the short rending fictions of the late 1960's.

It is a critical convenience to discuss Beckett's fiction and drama as though each had an independent development, but this is inaccurate. Not only did Beckett zigzag from drama to fiction and back (from 1948 to 1971, at any rate), but he frequently translated in the one genre while producing original work in the other. He himself has stated that drama is a relaxation for him: "You have a definite space and people in this space. That's relaxing." In relaxation he has created a spate of works in dramatic form; the list of those published and/or produced includes fourteen plays for the stage, six for radio, three for television, two mime plays, and one film script.

The stage images are at once visually arresting and metaphysically meaningful: two frayed comedians by a tree, a throned and shabby ruler with two ashbins, a prattling blonde buried in the ground, an unkempt old man bent over a tape recorder, three grey faces atop three grey urns, three stately faceless women, a mouth adrift in the dark, a whitehaired head turned up to the light, "a faint tangle of pale grey tatters." The radio plays introduce a rare verbal music to the medium. The television plays are at once paintings through the camera eye and soul searches beyond the camera's power.

Though Beckett does not speak of a stage trilogy, one might so view his three full-evening plays, *Waiting for Godot, Endgame, Happy Days.* All three are plays in which the main action is waiting; all three are plays in which the stage day is ending without quite coming to an end. A Beckett baptism, however, might well begin with simpler pieces. In *Breath* a faint cry signals an increase of light and breath to a maximum in about ten seconds, holds for five seconds, and fades to the cry "*as before.*" Vagitus and death-rattle are barely distinguishable in the black depths of eternity. This Beckett obsession is dramatized far more memorably in the plays of the 1970's. *Not I* embraces an asyntactical incantation of a life from premature birth to compulsive speech at age seventy, that biblical terminus. *That Time* looks back on three ages of man, finally giving to dust the pronouncement of human brevity. *Footfalls* paces through human pain, unable to escape it even beyond the grave, but always and forever revolving it all in the mind.

Brief as human life may be, Beckett theatricalizes it. The mime plays do this in almost allegorical fashion, the first teaching its arotagonist what Beckett in *Proust* calls the "oblation of desire," and the second demonstrating the repetitive futility of contrasting life-processes. *Come and Go*, less absolute than *Breath*, links childhood and age in a beautifully regular pattern; it is the first of several Beckett stage plays to dramatize the mystery at the heart of being. With the exception of *Not I*, Beckett's stage plays end in a stasis that confirms mystery.

Though Beckett's recent plays hover at death's threshold, he is more widely known for the theater trilogy that is absorbed in life. *Happy Days* implies courage even as Winnie sinks ever deeper into that old extinguisher, the earth. *Endgame*'s four characters reflect on each expiring moment. Liveliest of all Beckett's plays, and living on many stages in many languages is that contemporary classic, *Waiting for Godot*.

The impact of *Godot* is immediate; the impact of *Godot* is inexhaustible. Vaudeville turns are threaded on philosophic nihilism and a classico-Christian tradition. The seed of *Godot* is Luke's account of the crucifixion, as summarized by St. Augustine: "Do not despair: one of the thieves was saved. Do not presume: one of the thieves was damned." The two thieves are Vladimir and Estragon; the two thieves are Pozzo and Lucky; the two thieves are Godot's boy and his brother. On the stage, characters divide into two inseparable couples; action divides into two repetitive acts. The two friends are conscientious about trying to live through each disappointing evening, for Godot may always come tomorrow. In the meantime they volley routines with Wimbledon finesse. In their dogged invention lies the delight of *Godot*. Each act ends: "Well shall we go?" "Yes, let's go," but the friends "*do not move*." They do not move, but they have moved audiences and readers the world over.

—Ruby Cohn

BECKFORD, William. English. Born in Fonthill, Wiltshire, 29 September 1759. Educated privately; studied music with Mozart; studied in Geneva, 1777–78. Married Lady Margaret Gordon in 1783 (died, 1786); two daughters. Inherited vast family fortune, 1770; visited the Low Countries and Italy, 1780, 1782; lived in Switzerland, 1783–86; Member of Parliament for Wells, 1784–90, and Hindon, 1790–94; settled near Cintra, Portugal, 1794–96; built Fonthill Abbey, 1796, and lived there until 1822, amassing a collection of books, art objects, and curios; again served as Member of Parliament for Hindon, 1806–20; moved to Bath, 1822; built Lansdowne Tower, Bath. *Died 2 May 1844.*

PUBLICATIONS

Fiction

An Arabian Tale, translated by Samuel Henley.   1786; as *Vathek* (in French), 1787; revised edition, 1816; edited by R. H. Lonsdale, 1970.
Modern Novel Writing; or, The Elegant Enthusiast.   1796.
Azemia: A Descriptive and Sentimental Novel.   1797.
The Episodes of Vathek, edited by Frank T. Marzials.   1912.

Other

Biographical Memoirs of Extraordinary Painters.   1780.
Dreams, Waking Thoughts, and Incidents in a Series of Letters from Various Parts of Europe.   1783; edited by Guy Chapman, as *The Travel Diaries 1*, 1928.

Epitaphs. 1825.

Italy, with Sketches of Spain and Portugal. 2 vols., 1834; revised edition, 1834; edited by Guy Chapman, as *The Travel Diaries 2,* 1928.

Recollections of an Excursion to the Monasteries of Alcobaca and Batalha. 1835; revised edition, 1840; edited by A. Parreaux, 1956.

The Vision; Liber Veritatis, edited by Guy Chapman. 1930

Journal in Portugal and Spain 1787 88, edited by Boyd Alexander. 1954.

Life at Fonthill 1807 22, from the Correspondence, translated and edited by Boyd Alexander. 1957.

Translator, *The Story of Al Raoui: A Tale from the Arabic.* 1799; revised edition 1799.

Bibliography: *A Bibliography of Beckford* by Guy Chapman, 1930.

Reading List: *Beckford* by Guy Chapman, 1937; *Beckford, A. de Vathek* by A. Parreaux, 1960; *England's Wealthiest Son: A Study of Beckford* by Boyd Alexander, 1962; *Beckford* by Robert J. Gemmett, 1977.

*   *   *

William Beckford's fame rests on the bizarre, pseudo-Oriental tale *Vathek* – some would say, on the last ten to twelve pages of the book, when the caliph Vathek and the beautiful Nouronihar descend into the subterranean caverns of Istakar to meet the Prince of Darkness, Eblis, and their doom of hatred and unrelenting fire in their hearts. Yet even without *Vathek* Beckford would have a minor place in English literary history, if not for his clever mixture of art criticism and parody (in *Biographical Memoirs*) or his later satires on gothic and sentimental novels (in *Modern Novel Writing* and *Azemia*), then certainly for his romantic travel books about Italy and Portugal. *Dreams, Waking Thoughts, and Incidents,* suppressed at his mother's request and later republished in abridged form as *Italy,* best displays what Beckford called "my visionary way of gazing." It is not so much a description of place as an artful record of impressions and sensations, in response to people, places, and especially landscapes, which had a powerful effect on Beckford's imagination.

The genius of this eccentric collector and dilettante – "England's wealthiest son," in Byron's phrase – is clearly strongest, however, in *Vathek* and in the three *Episodes* intended to accompany the tale but not published until 1912. The English prose is not, in fact, Beckford's: he wrote the tale in French, sent it to his friend, Rev. Samuel Henley, who translated it and, against Beckford's strict orders, published it himself in 1786 as a translation of an anonymous Arabic tale. Although Vathek, with Faustian curiosity, seeks knowledge and experience at any expense, Beckford is not interested in his moral choices but in the spectacle of Vathek's pursuit of gratification. The eternal childishness and innocence of the boy Gulchenrouz has its appeal in Beckford's world, but the passionate life of Vathek leads him (and the reader) into another world of repulsive cripples and beautiful women, of black magic and ardent love, of sadism and voluptuous sweetness, and finally into a Hell of exhaustion and torment which Borges aptly called "the first truly atrocious Hell in literature."

—David McCracken

BEERBOHM, Sir (Henry) Max(imilian). English. Born in Kensington, London, 24 August 1872; half-brother of the actor-manager Sir Herbert Beerbohm Tree. Educated at Charterhouse, London; Merton College, Oxford, left without taking a degree. Married 1) Florence Kahn in 1910 (died, 1951); 2) Elisabeth Jungmann in 1956. Contributed to *The Spirit Lamp*, Oxford, 1893, and to various periodicals, including *The Yellow Book*, London, 1894; travelled in the United States, 1895; Drama Critic, *The Saturday Review* London, 1898–1910; lived in Rapallo, Italy, except for the world wars, from 1911. Also an artist: exhibited caricatures at the Carfax Gallery, 1910. LL.D.: University of Edinburgh, 1930. Honorary Fellow, Merton College, 1945. Knighted, 1939. *Died 20 May 1956.*

PUBLICATIONS

Collections

> *The Incomparable Max: A Selection*, edited by S. C. Roberts.   1962.
> *The Bodley Head Beerbohm*, edited by David Cecil.   1970.

Fiction

> *The Happy Hypocrite: A Fairy Tale for Tired Men.*   1897.
> *Zuleika Dobson; or, An Oxford Love Story.*   1911.
> *A Christmas Garland.*   1912; revised edition, 1950.
> *Seven Men.*   1919; as *Seven Men and Two Others*, 1950.
> *The Dreadful Dragon of Hay Hill.*   1928.

Plays

> *The Happy Hypocrite*, from his own story (produced 1900).
> *The Fly on the Wheel*, with S. Murray Carson (produced 1902).
> *A Social Success* (produced 1913).

Verse

> *Max in Verse: Rhymes and Parodies*, edited by J. G. Riewald.   1963.

Other

> *Works* (essays).   1896.
> *More.*   1899.
> *Yet Again.*   1909.
> *And Even Now.*   1920.
> *Works.*   10 vols., 1922–28.
> *A Peep into the Past.*   1923.
> *Around Theatres.*   2 vols., 1924.
> *The Guerdon.*   1925.
> *A Variety of Things.*   1928.
> *Mainly on the Air.*   1946; revised edition, 1957.

Selected Essays, edited by N. L. Clay. 1958.
Letters to Reggie Turner, edited by Rupert Hart-Davis. 1969.
More Theatres 1898–1903, edited by Rupert Hart-Davis. 1969.
Last Theatres 1904–1910, edited by Rupert Hart-Davis. 1970.
A Peep into the Past and Other Prose Pieces, edited by Rupert Hart-Davis. 1972.
Max and Will: Letters of Beerbohm and William Rothenstein, edited by Mary Lago and Karl Beckson. 1975.
Literary Caricatures from Homer to Huxley, edited by J. G. Riewald. 1977.

Editor, *Herbert Beerbohm Tree: Some Memories of Him and His Art.* 1920.

Drawings: *Caricatures of Twenty-Five Gentlemen,* 1896; *The Poets' Corner,* 1904, revised edition, 1943; *A Book of Caricatures,* 1907; *Cartoons: The Second Childhood of John Bull,* 1911; *Fifty Caricatures,* 1913; *A Survey,* 1921; *Rossetti and His Circle,* 1922; *Things Old and New,* 1923; *Observations,* 1925; *Max's Nineties: Drawings 1892–99,* 1958; *Caricatures from the Collection of the Ashmolean Museum,* 1958.

Bibliography: *A Bibliography of the Works of Beerbohm* by A. E. Gallatin and L. M. Oliver, 1952.

Reading List: *Beerbohm, Man and Writer: A Critical Analysis with a Brief Life and a Bibliography* by J. G. Riewald, 1953; *Conversations with Max* by S. N. Behrman, 1960, as *Portrait of Max,* 1960; *Max: A Biography* by David Cecil, 1964; *The Surprise of Excellence: Modern Essays on Beerbohm* edited by J. G. Riewald, 1974.

*   *   *

Max Beerbohm was properly definitive about himself: "My gifts are small. I've used them very well and discreetly, never straining them and the result is that I've made a charming little reputation." But they are gifts, if of narrow scope, and diffused through fiction, essay, verse, drama and caricature. Far from being oppressed by a multiplicity of talents, Max deployed them with the same skill and tact that he displayed in the conduct of his life.

Although it has become the mode to praise the later Beerbohm, his best work is essentially of the dandiacal *fin de siècle,* both in theme and tone. In every medium he was essentially a parodist, a brilliant parasite, paying the homage of languor to vitality. The early essays, best read in their periodical rather then their volume form, fall readily into the pedantries, colloquialism, insolent paradoxes, French tags (not always correctly set as Whistler pointed out – indeed *suspecte* to employ one of Max's favoured epithets) of the period. The title *Works* with the joke of *apparatus criticus* and the declaration that at twenty- two he was out-moded – that he belonged to the Beardsley period – both have as much defence as defiance about them, while the second is almost true. *Zuleika Dobson,* his one attempt at sustained prose, includes broad satire on "New" women as fatal Women, the Wildean "decadence," Pre-Raphaelitism, but Max always burns what he adores. Though the novel has brilliant passages, its texture is hardly as rich as Firbank's or as absorbing as early Waugh's.

His theatrical criticism, founded not on formal theory but on the thin elegance of his taste, subtly reflects the boredom Max felt in its production. It acutely exposes the limitations of his sensibility: he fell for the earlier Stephen Phillips, exalted Peter Pan, could find little positive in Duse, and remained uneasy about Ibsen and indeed all realist drama. About Shakespeare, he is absurd without being funny: the master was far too raw, though *The Tempest* was approved as the masterpiece of a Jacobean Barrie. Max did, however, admire Gordon Craig, and his enthusiasm for Aristophanes is tonic, though the problem of translation seems not to have disturbed him (he might have managed all but the lyrical altitudes rather decently himself). His own verse is highly competent and like his better prose satire survives the ephemerality of its victims.

His enthusiasms predictably were for the notable stylisers of life: Meredith, Pater, Wilde, James; but his own essays in this direction tended to bloodless fantasy: *The Dreadful Dragon of Hay Hill* and *The Happy Hypocrite* have distinctly flaked. *Seven Men* is perennially engaging, particularly "Savonarola Brown," a parody of Victorian neo-Shakesperian drama and that definitive portrait of the nineties *poète maudit*, Enoch Soames, with the stock properties of Inverness cape, absinthe, catholic diabolism, and morbidity. Max's reminiscences of the period are always shrewd and entertaining, particularly the knowing "Peep into the Past" which reflects his continued fascination with Wilde. It remains regrettable that he wrote no formally informal account of the period in which he matured and to which he so firmly belongs.

The humour and wit of the prose are most masterfully vented in the caricatures where the captions are even more pungent than the exaggerated features and gestures in which he so lightly imprisons his distinguished or faded victims. The phrase he applied to Whistler's malicious prose settles felicitously upon himself: "You may shed a tear over the flies, if you will, I am content to laud the amber." Wilde declared that the Gods had bestowed upon Max the gift of perpetual old age; but in the drawings it is rather the child's ruthless perception of incongruity that is immediately striking.

Like all true decadents, Max was obsessed by the aesthetics of failure, and this probably accounts for his literary creativity dying early; the later essays are often amusing; the broadcasts are all conversational elegance; but in a more dangerous world Max occasionally touched on real issues and became palely fantastic, sentimental, banal, reactionary. After 1910 he had little to say and said it, though *Seven Men* and the acute parodies of *A Christmas Garland* must obviously be excepted.

It is pleasantly ironic that having published his *Works* in his twenty-fourth year to ridicule the pomps of scholarship, Max himself should have become the target of relentless annotation. He appears as minuscular Goethe in the hushed pages of S. N. Behrman, while his slenderest hack work and most casual letters have been published and lingeringly footnoted. The fugitive parodies of his earlier career, however, do deserve scholarly attention. Max has been over-rated but should survive his adulators as at least a minimal classic.

—Ian Fletcher

BELLAMY, Edward. American. Born in Chicopee Falls, Massachusetts, 26 March 1850, and lived there for most of his life. Educated at local schools; Union College, Schenectady, New York, 1867–68; travelled and studied in Germany, 1868–69; studied law: admitted to the Massachusetts Bar, 1871, but never practised. Married Emma Sanderson in 1882. Associate Editor, *Union*, Springfield, Massachusetts; Editorial Writer, *Evening Post*, New York, 1878; Founder, with his brother, Springfield *Daily News*, 1880; after 1885 devoted himself to writing and propagation of Socialist ideas: lectured throughout the United States; founded *New Nation*, Boston, 1891. *Died 22 May 1898.*

PUBLICATIONS

Fiction

Six to One: A Nantucket Idyl. 1878.
Dr. Heidenhoff's Process. 1880.
Miss Ludington's Sister: A Romance of Immortality. 1884.
Looking Backward 2000–1887. 1888; edited by John L. Thomas, 1967.
Equality. 1897.
The Blindman's World and Other Stories. 1898.
The Duke of Stockbridge: A Romance of Shays' Rebellion, edited by Francis Bellamy. 1900; edited by Joseph Schiffman, 1962.

Other

Bellamy Speaks Again! Articles, Public Addresses, Letters. 1937.
Talks on Nationalism. 1938.
The Religion of Solidarity, edited by Arthur E. Morgan. 1940.
Selected Writings on Religion and Society, edited by Joseph Schiffman. 1955.

Bibliography: in *Bibliography of American Literature* by Jacob Blanck, 1955.

Reading List: *Bellamy,* 1944, and *The Philosophy of Bellamy,* 1945, both by Arthur E. Morgan; *The Year 2000* by Sylvia E. Bowman, 1958; *Bellamy, Novelist and Reformer* by Daniel Aaron and Harry Levin, 1968.

*   *   *

Edward Bellamy is known chiefly for his Utopian romance *Looking Backward: 2000–1887,* which within a short time after its publication sold over one million copies. The purpose of the book was to offer a blueprint of what Bellamy considered to be an ideal society. To make his presentation more palatable to the general reader, he encased it in a romantic plot: A young Bostonian after a hypnotic sleep of 113 years awakens in the year 2000 to discover a totally transformed social and economic order. Falling in love with a girl descended from his fiancée of 1887, he learns from her father, a physician, the details of the state socialism that has replaced the laissez-faire capitalism that obtained before his long sleep. Under the new order all commerce, industry and other economic and professional activities have been nationalized into one vast, interlocking enterprise. All men and women between the ages of twenty-one and forty-five are required to engage in work suitable to their abilities and, when possible, to their tastes; and all, no matter what occupation they may be in, receive the same wages. Superior ability and productivity are rewarded by social recognition and by assignment to positions of leadership. After the age of forty-five all are retired and are free to do what they wish.

Looking Backward is one of a number of books expressing the dissatisfaction of many Americans with the conditions of labor, the rise of monopolies, and the political corruption that characterized the second half of the nineteenth century. But Bellamy's book enjoyed a greater popularity and exerted a stronger influence than any other, with the possible exception of Henry George's *Progress and Poverty* (1879). Bellamy called his program Nationalism, and in the 1890's many Nationalist Clubs were formed and began to wield a political influence, most notably on the newly formed and temporarily quite powerful Populist Party. As a sequel to *Looking Backward,* Bellamy wrote *Equality,* which he finished shortly before his death. But by this time the Nationalist movement was losing its momentum, though Bellamy's ideas continued to be an influence on later reform efforts. Bellamy's most lasting contribution, as one critic has put it, was in fostering "an attitude toward social change." For example, many of the innovations of the New Deal had been suggested and made familiar to the public by Bellamy's book.

Bellamy's literary career was not confined solely to reformist writing. He was an able newspaper and magazine editor and the author of unpolitical fiction. Several of his novels, among them *Dr. Heidenhoff's Process* and *Miss Ludington's Sister* received favorable notice in their day; and his *The Duke of Stockbridge* (serialized 1879) has been called, perhaps extravagantly, "one of the greatest historical novels." Dealing with the revolt in 1786 and 1787 of Massachusetts farmers who were overburdened with debt and taxes and ruthlessly exploited by lawyers, merchants, and bankers, this book provides early evidence of Bellamy's concern with social and economic injustice – a concern that doubtless had its origin in his early awareness of the exploitation of workers in the Massachusetts mill town in which he grew up.

—P. D. Westbrook

BELLOW, Saul. American. Born in Lachine, Quebec, Canada, 10 June 1915; grew up in Montreal; moved with his family to Chicago, 1924. Educated at the University of Chicago, 1933–35; Northwestern University, Evanston, Illinois, 1935–37, B.S. (honors) in sociology and anthropology 1937; did graduate work in anthropology at the University of Wisconsin, Madison, 1937. Served in the United States Merchant Marine, 1944–45. Married 1) Anita Goshkin in 1937 (divorced), one son; 2) Alexandra Tschacbasov in 1956 (divorced), one son; 3) Susan Glassman in 1961, one son. Teacher, Pestalozzi-Froebel Teachers College, Chicago, 1938–42; Member of the Editorial Department, "Great Books" Project, *Encyclopaedia Britannica*, Chicago, 1943–46; Instructor, 1946, and Assistant Professor English, 1948–49, University of Minnesota, Minneapolis; Visiting Lecturer, New York University, 1950–52; Creative Writing Fellow, Princeton University, New Jersey, 1952–53; Member of the English faculty, Bard College, Annandale-on-Hudson, New York, 1953–54; Associate Professor of English, University of Minnesota, 1954–59; Visiting Professor of English, University of Puerto Rico, Rio Piedras, 1961. Since 1962, Professor, Committee on Social Thought, University of Chicago. Co-Founding Editor, *The Noble Savage*, Cleveland, 1960–62. Fellow, Academy for Policy Study, 1966; Fellow, Branford College, Yale University, New Haven, Connecticut. Recipient: Guggenheim Fellowship, 1948, 1955; National Institute of Arts and Letters grant, 1952; National Book Award, 1954, 1965, 1971; Ford Foundation grant, 1959, 1960; Friends of Literature award, 1960; James L. Dow Award, 1964; Prix International de Littérature, France, 1965; Jewish Heritage Award, 1968; Nobel Prize for Literature, 1976; Pulitzer Prize, 1976; American Academy of Arts and Letters Gold Medal, 1977. D. Litt.: Northwestern University, 1962; Bard College, 1963. Member, National Institute of Arts and Letters. Lives in Chicago.

PUBLICATIONS

Fiction

Dangling Man. 1944.
The Victim. 1947.
The Adventures of Augie March. 1953.

Seize the Day, with Three Short Stories and a One-Act Play. 1956.
Henderson the Rain King. 1959.
Herzog. 1964.
Mosby's Memoirs and Other Stories. 1968.
Mr. Sammler's Planet. 1970.
Humboldt's Gift. 1975.

Plays

The Wrecker (televised, 1964). In *Seize the Day* ..., 1956.
The Last Analysis (produced 1964). 1965.
Under the Weather (includes *Out from Under, A Wen, Orange Soufflé*) (produced 1966;
    as *The Bellow Plays*, produced 1966). *A Wen* and *Orange Soufflé* in *Traverse Plays*,
    1967.

Other

Dessins, by Jess Reichek; text by Bellow and C. Zervos. 1960.
*Like You're Nobody: The Letters of Louis Gallo to Bellow, 1961–62, Plus Oedipus-
    Schmoedipus, The Story That Started It All.* 1966.
The Future of the Moon. 1970.
The Portable Bellow, edited by Gabriel Josipovici. 1974.
To Jerusalem and Back: A Personal Account. 1976.

Editor, *Great Jewish Short Stories.* 1963.

Translator, with others, *Gimpel the Fool and Other Stories*, by Isaac Bashevis
    Singer. 1957.

Bibliography: *Bellow: A Comprehensive Bibliography* by B. A. Sokoloff and Mark E. Posner,
1973; *Bellow, His Works and His Critics: An Annotated International Bibliography* by
Marianne Nault, 1977.

Reading List: *Bellow* by Tony Tanner, 1965; *Bellow* by Earl Rovit, 1967, and *Bellow: A
Collection of Critical Essays* edited by Rovit, 1974; *Bellow: A Critical Essay* by Robert
Detweiler, 1967; *The Novels of Bellow: An Introduction* by Keith Michael Opdahl, 1967;
Bellow and the Critics edited by Irving Malin, 1967, and *Bellow's Fiction* by Malin, 1969;
Bellow: In Defense of Man by John Jacob Clayton, 1968; *Bellow* by Robert R. Dutton, 1971;
Bellow's Enigmatic Laughter by Sarah Blacher Cohen, 1974; *Whence the Power? The Artistry
and Humanity of Bellow* by M. Gilbert Porter, 1974.

*   *   *

Since 1976, when he received the Nobel Prize for Literature, Saul Bellow has been assured
an important position in American literature. This position was not new for the Chicago
writer. For the past twenty years, at least since the publication of his popular *Adventures of
Augie March*, Bellow has been heralded as the major spokesman of realism in America, as the
most articulate voice for humanism in America, as the most sophisticated comedian of the
modern predicament, and even as the one on whose shoulders has fallen the mantle of genius
previously worn by William Faulkner. No matter how exaggerated these evaluations might
seem, Bellow is surely one of the major American novelists of the past twenty years.

It is as a novelist that he assumes his important position. However, Bellow also writes essays, short stories, and plays. Most of his non-fiction is a clarification of his view of the duties of novelist and human being. For Bellow fiction should be basically realistic; it should not obscure the human condition, but should delve deeply into the psychological idiosyncrasies that explain an individual act. *To Jerusalem and Back* relates a visit to Israel less for the purpose of providing an answer to the Middle East question than for the fascinating personalized portraits of individuals. It is not sociology, but psychology.

Most of the short pieces that appear in journals are sections of novels in progress, but some of these short pieces have remained as short stories, the best of which have been collected in *Mosby's Memoirs and Other Stories*. Perhaps the best of these tales in relation to his major work is "The Old System," a short story that approaches one of Bellow's significant themes: the conflict between modern Jewish man and his ageless ties to a Jewish past. The plays of Saul Bellow, especially the one-act sketches, barely hint at the power of his novels. *The Last Analysis*, a full-length work, is his best attempt in this genre. The fragmentation, confusion, and discomfort of modern life color the play as much as they do the novels.

Bellow's first novel, *Dangling Man*, is a diary of a young man awaiting induction into the army during World War II. Joseph quits his job, planning to relax and read before being subjected to the rigors of army life. Instead, the period becomes one of inaction and meaninglessness. Joseph begins to question the value of his friendships, the meaning of his family, and finally even the goodness of life. After months of stultification, existence seems absurd; relief comes in the promise of the regimentation of military life. Joseph no longer awaits induction; he enlists.

The Victim is similar to the previous novel in atmosphere and tone, but dissimilar in form. Asa Leventhal is plagued by family responsibilities, human responsibilities, and anti-Semitism. He is the victim. But in his treatment, or rather his acceptance, of his major tormentor, Kirby Allbee, Asa victimizes his tormentor and himself. The bleak picture of human irrationality, death, and sorrow is broken only by the end of an unbearably hot summer, the return of Asa's wife, and the philosophy of humanism that is spoken by the Yiddishist Schlossberg. These reprieves assure Asa's escape.

The Adventures of Augie March was the novel that thrust Bellow before the American public as a major writer. An exuberant picaresque tale of a Chicago boy, born to a retarded mother, *Augie March* bespeaks an American innocence and joy in existence that Bellow seemed shy of in his first novels. This joyousness is not, however, unadulterated. Augie is a Jewish bastard who must learn to fend for himself in the confused and constantly changing world that was America in the 1940's: he encounters abortion, political manipulation, the black-market, and sexual perversion. In the face of all of this, Augie can still laugh.

Seize the Day, a novella, tells of a middle-aged Wilky Adler forced to recognize the aimlessness of his life. Always a failure in his father's eyes, Wilky tries to establish an independent identity by attaining what his father most admires – wealth. Wilky is, of course, an abysmal failure, though he learns the valuelessness of money. His epiphany is of his shared humanity with all man. The beauty of humanity is not revealed in the predatory stalking for materialistic gain, but rather in the prayer over the corpse of a stranger.

Henderson the Rain King is a fantasy of a trip to an Africa of the spirit. Here in the continent that saw the first man evolve, Eugene Henderson tries to return to essentials. Henderson leaves America as a man who feels his soul gnawed at by a demanding voice crying "I want! I want!" By the time he returns from Africa, after encountering the primitive power that is in a lion and in an African tribal king, he assumes the status of human being, with all its grace and goodness. His desires to do good for others, his love for his family and wife, are directed now so that he can accept the joy of existence. Suffering is no longer his only means of definition.

In *Herzog*, Bellow created a character that caught the consciousness of the American intellectual of the 1960's. Moses Elkanah Herzog, on the brink of divorce (for the second time) and professional suicide, begins to develop his naturally reflective nature to the point of insanity. He writes letters, letters to his friends, to his family, to famous people both dead and alive, even notes to himself. These attempts to come to terms with his changing self-image center especially on his feeling for his Jewish past. During his adult life, Moses has been a Jew totally assimilated into the Christian intellectual world; he has learned the history of the Christian West; he has accepted the precepts of the Christian philosophers and theologians; and he has taken a Christian wife. Suddenly, this life begins to disintegrate. Before Herzog can attain any equanimity he must learn how to balance his present individuality with his past tradition.

In *Mr. Sammler's Planet*, the conflict between past and present is again a concern of the novelist, but with many added ambiguities. Arthur Sammler, representative of the Old World, survivor of the Holocaust, is divorced from his Jewish past. He is one who admires and studies the Christian ideals of the West. In America, his benefactor and nephew, Elya Bruner, a gynecologist who got rich by doing illegal abortions for the Mafia, is the representative of the Old World patterns. He is the one who, despite his flaws, follows the ideals of humanism that was the backbone of the East European *shtetl*. Only at the end of the novel can Sammler articulate the beauty that he sees in his nephew. In most of the novel, Sammler is suffering life in New York, dodging nymphomaniacs, pickpockets, exhibitionists, violent madmen, and schizophrenics. In the face of such disruption of morals, his own delicacy is not the answer; Elya's goodness is the only philosophy that provides order.

Humboldt's Gift relates the growth of a dilettante writer, Charlie Citrine, who must learn the true value of his mad mentor, Von Humboldt Fleischer (a personalized portrait of the poet Delmore Schwartz). As a young man, Charlie worships the charismatic Humboldt. Moving East to follow his god, Charlie becomes a friend and colleague of the poet. Only after Charlie's success on Broadway do the two writers part – Humboldt accusing Charlie of stealing his personality for the hero of his play. This big, funny, and poignant novel centers on the young man's reflections on Humboldt and on his true value as an artist and mentor. Through flashbacks Citrine reveals the despair and paranoia that destroy his idol. The persistence of Humboldt's spiritual presence in Charlie's later life, long after the poet's death, bespeaks the importance of Humboldt to Charlie.

The gift that the mentor leaves is really twofold. The most obvious gift is the absurd play that will probably become a great success as a film. But more importantly, Humboldt serves as an exemplum for Charlie's own life. The reflection of later years gradually reveals that Humboldt is indeed mad; he was a genius who was driven insane and finally killed by his own unwritten poems. He was one who misused his talents. After this realization, Charlie is able to accept the memory of Humboldt. The reburial of the poet's body is a significant rite of passage for Charlie. No longer is he possessed by his mentor's personality.

The variety and power of Bellow's novels assure him a place in American literature. When Bellow resists the term "Jewish writer," it is because his art is not a chauvinistic and narrow one. But as readers we must not be misled by his resistance to this term: he is most assuredly a writer whose style, characters, form, and humor derive in large part from his Jewish past.

—Barbara Gitenstein

BEMELMANS, Ludwig. American. Born in Meran, Austria, now Merano, Italy, 27 April 1898; emigrated to the United States in 1914; naturalized, 1918. Educated at schools in Regensburg and Rothenburg, Bavaria. Served in the United States Army during World War I. Married Madeline Freund in 1935; one daughter. Worked as a hotel clerk and restaurant proprietor in New York City; writer for *The New Yorker*; also an artist: works exhibited in principal galleries in the United States and abroad. Recipient: American Library Association Caldecott Medal, 1954. *Died 1 October 1962.*

PUBLICATIONS

Fiction

> *I Love You, I Love You, I Love You* (stories).   1942.
> *Now I Lay Me Down to Sleep.*   1943.
> *The Blue Danube.*   1945.
> *Dirty Eddie.*   1947.
> *The Eye of God.*   1947; as *The Snow Mountain,* 1950.
> *The Woman of My Life.*   1957.
> *Are You Hungry, Are You Cold.*   1960.
> *The Street Where the Heart Lies.*   1963.

Other

> *Hansi* (juvenile).   1934
> *The Golden Basket* (juvenile).   1936.
> *The Castle Number Nine* (juvenile).   1937.
> *My War with the United States.*   1937.
> *Life Class.*   1938.
> *Quito Express* (juvenile).   1938.
> *Madeline* (juvenile).   1938.
> *Small Beer.*   1939.
> *Fifi* (juvenile).   1940.
> *At Your Service: The Way of Life in a Hotel.*   1941.
> *The Donkey Inside.*   1941.
> *Hotel Splendide.*   1941.
> *Rosebud* (juvenile).   1942.
> *Hotel Bemelmans.*   1946.
> *A Tale of Two Glimps* (juvenile).   1947.
> *The Best of Times: An Account of Europe Revisited.*   1948.
> *Sunshine* (juvenile).   1950.
> *How to Travel Incognito.*   1952.
> *The Happy Place* (juvenile).   1952.
> *Madeline's Rescue* (juvenile).   1953.
> *Father, Dear Father* (autobiography).   1953.
> *The High World* (juvenile).   1954.
> *Parsley* (juvenile).   1955.
> *To the One I Love the Best.*   1955.
> *The World of Bemelmans.*   1955.
> *Madeline and the Bad Hat* (juvenile).   1956.
> *My Life in Art.*   1958.
> *Madeline and the Gypsies* (juvenile).   1959.
> *Welcome Home!* (juvenile).   1960.
> *How to Have Europe All to Yourself.*   1960.
> *Italian Holiday.*   1961.
> *Madeline in London* (juvenile).   1961.
> *Marina* (juvenile).   1962.
> *On Board Noah's Ark.*   1962.
> *La Bonne Table* (writings and drawings), edited by Donald and Eleanor Friede. 1964.

> Editor, *Holiday in France.*   1957.

*   *   *

William McFee once wrote of Ludwig Bemelmans, the writer, stage designer, illustrator and painter, that he was "one of those fortunate writers who have all the reviewers ranged on one side, rooting for him." I must at the outset confess myself one of that number. Whether chronicling the adventures of Madeline, the irrepressible little French *gamine*, or reporting his own adventures as "El Señor Bnelemaas" in Ecuador (*The Donkey Inside*) or as a waiter (in *Hotel Splendide*), he is delightful. He always wanted to be a painter (despite his family's belief that all artists are "hunger candidates") and only wrote because he had insomnia, but in his acerb and risible little essays, even more than in his drawings, every line is precisely *right*.

To him happen all the most fabulous things. He meets "Mr. Sigsag" of the Hotel Splendide and a host of other charming eccentrics. Just for him a war breaks out (*My War with the United States*) to galvanize a gallery of characters into action. He encounters a little girl who contrives to make her schoolmates livid with jealousy by having an appendix operation. For him tables and chairs have something droll about them. For him people do the most ludicrous things. The world ("I regard it as a curiousity") is funny and he has only to report it (*I Love You, I Love You, I Love You*). He claimed he had no imagination.

Bemelmans is always satirical, but at his best when his unquenchable good humor is given free play, as in the novel *Now I Lay Me Down to Sleep* or the collection of *New Yorker* essays *Small Beer*. It is hard not to gush when mentioning his works. But his delightful humor disarms criticism.

—Leonard R. N. Ashley

BENCHLEY, Robert (Charles). American. Born in Worcester, Massachusetts, 15 September 1889. Educated at Worcester High School, 1904–07; Phillips Exeter Academy, New Hampshire, 1907–08; Harvard University, Cambridge, Massachusetts (member of the Board of Editors of *Lampoon*), 1908–12, B.A. 1913. Married Gertrude Darling in 1914; two sons, including the writer Nathaniel Benchley. Worked for the Boston Museum of Fine Art, 1912, and for Curtis Publishing Company, 1912–14 (Editor of the house journal *Obiter Dicta*); did welfare work in Boston and New York, 1914; worked in advertising, then as a reporter for the New York *Tribune* and *Tribune* magazine, 1916–17; Drama Critic, *Vanity Fair*, New York, 1917; journalist and office worker in Washington, D.C., 1918; Managing Editor of *Vanity Fair*, 1919–20; Columnist, New York *World*, 1920–21; Drama Critic, 1920–24, and Editor, 1924–29, *Life* magazine, New York; Columnist, 1925–40, and Drama Critic, 1929–40, *The New Yorker*; Columnist for King Features Syndicate, 1933–36. Also an actor: stage debut, 1923; also wrote and starred in 48 motion pictures, 1928–45; radio broadcaster from 1938. Recipient: Academy Award, for short film, 1935. *Died 21 November 1945.*

PUBLICATIONS

Essays and Sketches

Of All Things! 1921.
Love Conquers All. 1922.
Pluck and Luck. 1925.

The Early Worm. 1927.
The Bridges of Binding. 1928.
20,000 Leagues under the Sea; or, David Copperfield. 1928.
The Treasurer's Report and Other Aspects of Community Singing. 1930.
No Poems; or, Around the World Backwards and Sideways. 1932.
From Bed to Worse; or, Comforting Thoughts about the Bison. 1934.
Why Does Nobody Collect Me? 1935.
My Ten Years in a Quandary and How They Grew. 1936.
After 1903 — What? 1938.
Inside Benchley (selection). 1942.
Benchley Beside Himself. 1943.
One Minute Please. 1945.
Benchley   or Else! 1947.
Chips off the Old Benchley. 1949.
The "Reel" Benchley, edited by George Hornby. 1950.
The Bedside Manner; or, No More Nightmares. 1952.
The Benchley Roundup, edited by Nathaniel Benchley. 1954.
Benchley Lost and Found: 39 Fugitive Pieces. 1970.

Reading List: *Benchley: A Biography* by Nathaniel Benchley, 1955; *Benchley* by Norris W. Yates, 1968.

*   *   *

After the customary false starts, forays into advertising and personnel work, Robert Benchley, like most of the American humorists of his generation, found his way to journalism. He began as a reporter for the New York *Tribune* in 1916, and within a few years became editor, columnist, or occasional contributor to *Collier's, Vanity Fair,* the New York *World, Life, The Bookman,* and *The New Yorker.* Aside from his comic writing, his most sustained work in the magazines was as a drama reviewer, primarily for *Life* and *The New Yorker,* and as a press critic, in which capacity he used a pseudonym, Guy Fawkes, and initiated "The Wayward Press" department in *The New Yorker.* His first book, *Of All Things!,* was published in 1921 and between that time and his death in 1945, some dozen more volumes appeared, all of them collections of pieces written for magazines or newspapers. Some of the later ones, like *Benchley Beside Himself,* cannibalize earlier collections.

In a letter to his mother written in 1922, E. B. White called *Of All Things!* "about as funny as anything there is on the market today," and, in a letter to Walter Blair in 1964, he admitted that he imitated Benchley in his early work. That writers like White and James Thurber, who so early found their own authentic voices, were influenced by Benchley is evidence not simply of the pervasiveness of his subject matter — the little indignities of daily life which have always beset humorists — but of the quality of his prose. Benchley could, like Frank Sullivan, rise to complete nonsense, but most of the time he wrote simple, deceptively rational sentences in which a judicious choice of adjective or a demanding parenthesis could turn the sentence, the whole piece, a conventional way of thinking inside out.

Benchley early developed a firm comic personality, created a character who sometimes appears in the pieces, is more often the voice that creates them. His persona became a Benchley after-image, through the Gluyas Williams illustrations for his books and the bumbling character he played in movie shorts and in feature films. As he emerges in Benchley's writing, the character is more than the conventional little man so loved by humorists, cartoonists, and politicians. He is both vain and ponderous, using his own self-esteem as the banana peel on which to slip; he is easily embarrassed, but he will snarl — a bit tentatively — if he is cornered by too preposterous an assault from social usage. His ordinary antagonists are things like pigeons, roadmaps, ocean liners, Christmas, but there are hints of darker enemies, as in "My Trouble" in which he asks, "Do all boys of 46 stop breathing when they go to bed?" This disquieting undertone emerges infrequently in Benchley's work; for the most part, his confused and confusing other self is satisfied to worry a pomposity or a platitude to death and in the process leave the reader laughing.

—Gerald Weales

BENNETT, (Enoch) Arnold. English. Born in Hanley, Staffordshire, 27 May 1867. Educated at Burslem Endowed School, and Middle School, Newcastle under Lyme; studied law and worked as a clerk in his father's law firm, 1885–88; articled to the firm of Le Brasseur and Oakley, solicitors, London, 1888–93. Married Marguerite Soulie in 1907 (separated, 1921); associated with the actress Dorothy Cheston by whom he had a daughter. Worked, while in his father's law firm, as a free-lance journalist for *The Staffordshire Sentinel*; Assistant Editor, 1893–96, and Editor, 1896–1900, of the weekly journal *Woman*, London; full-time writer from 1900; lived in Paris and Fontainebleau, France, 1902–12; contributed to the *New Age*, London, 1908–11; settled in Thorpe-le-Soken, Essex, 1912; during First World War engaged in propaganda journalism and served on various public committees; in charge of British propaganda in France, and subsequently served as head of the British propaganda organization, 1918; lived in London, 1919 until his death; Partner, with Sir Nigel Playfair and Alistair Tayler, in the management of the Lyric Theatre, London; contributed a weekly column to the *Evening Standard*, London. Recipient: Black Memorial Prize, 1924. *Died 27 March 1931.*

PUBLICATIONS

Collections

  Letters, edited by James G. Hepburn.   3 vols., 1966–70.

Fiction

  A Man from the North.   1898.
  The Grand Babylon Hotel: A Fantasia on Modern Themes.   1902; as *T. Racksole & Daughter*, 1902.
  Anna of the Five Towns.   1902.
  The Gates of Wrath: A Melodrama.   1903.
  Leonora.   1903.
  A Great Man: A Frolic.   1904.
  Teresa of Watling Street: A Fantasia on Modern Themes.   1904.
  Tales of the Five Towns.   1905.
  The Boot of Cities, Being the Adventures of a Millionaire in Search of Joy: A Fantasia (stories).   1905; revised edition, 1917.
  Sacred and Profane Love.   1905; revised edition, as *The Book of Carlotta*, 1911.
  Hugo: A Fantasia on Modern Themes.   1906.

Whom God Hath Joined. 1906.

The Sinews of War: A Romance of London and the Sea, with Eden Phillpotts. 1906; as *Doubloons,* 1906.

The Ghost: A Fantasia on Modern Themes. 1907.

The Grim Smile of the Five Towns (stories). 1907.

The City of Pleasure: A Fantasia on Modern Themes. 1907.

The Statue, with Eden Phillpotts. 1908.

Buried Alive: A Tale of These Days. 1908.

The Old Wives' Tale. 1908.

The Glimpse: An Adventure of the Soul. 1909.

Helen with the High Hand: An Idyllic Diversion. 1910.

Clayhanger. 1910; *Hilda Lessways,* 1911; *These Twain,* 1915; complete edition, as *The Clayhanger Family,* 1925.

The Card: A Story of Adventure in the Five Towns. 1911; as *Dendry the Audacious,* 1911.

The Matador of the Five Towns and Other Stories. 1912.

The Regent: A Five Towns Story of Adventure in London. 1913; as *The Old Adam,* 1913.

The Price of Love. 1914.

The Lion's Share. 1916.

The Pretty Lady. 1918.

The Roll-Call. 1918.

Mr. Prohack. 1922.

Lilian. 1922.

Riceyman Steps. 1923.

Elsie and the Child: A Tale of Riceyman Steps, and Other Stories. 1924.

Lord Raingo. 1926.

The Vanguard: A Fantasia. 1927; as *The Strange Vanguard,* 1928.

The Woman Who Stole Everything and Other Stories. 1927.

Accident. 1929.

Piccadilly: Story of the Film. 1929.

Imperial Palace. 1930.

The Night Visitor and Other Stories. 1931.

Dream of Destiny: An Unfinished Novel, and Venus Rising From the Sea. 1932; as *Stroke of Luck, and Dream of Destiny,* 1932.

Plays

Rosalys: A Music Play for Girls, music by J. Brown (produced 1898). In *La Jeunesse de Bennett* by M. Locherbie-Goff, 1939.

Polite Farces for the Drawing-Room (includes *The Stepmother, A Good Woman, A Question of Sex*). 1899.

A Good Woman (as *Rivals for Rosamund,* produced 1914). In *Polite Farces,* 1899.

Cupid and Commonsense, from his own novel *Anna of the Five Towns* (produced 1908). 1909.

What the Public Wants (produced 1909). 1909.

The Honeymoon (produced 1911). 1911.

Milestones, with Edward Knoblock (produced 1912). 1912.

The Great Adventure, from his own novel *Buried Alive* (produced 1912). 1913.

The Title (produced 1918). 1918.

Judith (produced 1919). 1919; revised version, music by Eugene Goossens (produced 1929), 1929.

Sacred and Profane Love, from his own novel (produced 1919). 1919.

The Love Match (produced 1922). 1922.

Body and Soul (produced 1922). 1922.

Don Juan de Marana. 1923; revised version, music by Eugene Goossens (produced 1937), 1935.

London Life, with Edward Knoblock (produced 1924). 1924.

The Bright Island (produced 1925), 1924.

Flora (produced 1927). In *Five Three-Act Plays,* 1933.

Mr. Prohack, with Edward Knoblock, from the novel by Bennett (produced 1927). 1927.

The Return Journey (produced 1928). 1928.

The Snake-Charmer, in *Eight One-Act Plays.* 1933.

The Ides of March, with F. Adcock, in *One-Act Plays for Stage and Study 8.* 1934.

Screenplay: *Piccadilly,* 1929.

Other

Journalism for Women: A Practical Guide. 1898.

Fame and Fiction: An Inquiry into Certain Popularities. 1901.

How to Become an Author: A Practical Guide. 1903.

The Truth about an Author. 1903.

Things That Have Interested Me, Being Leaves from a Journal. 3 vols., 1906–09; new series, 3 vols., 1921–26.

The Reasonable Life, Being Hints for Men and Women. 1907; revised edition, as *Mental Efficiency,* 1911.

How to Live on 24 Hours a Day. 1908.

The Human Machine. 1908.

Literary Taste: How to Form It. 1909; edited by Frank Swinnerton, 1937.

The Present Crisis: Plain Words to Plain Men. 1910.

The Feast of St. Friend. 1911; as *Friendship and Happiness,* 1914.

Those United States. 1912; as *Your United States,* 1912.

Paris Nights and Other Impressions of Places and People. 1913.

The Plain Man and His Wife. 1913; as *Married Life,* 1913; as *Marriage,* 1916.

From the Log of the Velsa. 1914.

Liberty! A Statement of the British Case. 1914.

The Author's Craft. 1914.

Over There: War Scenes on the Western Front. 1915.

Books and Persons, Being Comments on a Past Epoch 1908 11. 1917.

Self and Self-Management: Essays about Existing. 1918.

Our Women: Chapters on the Sex-Discord. 1920.

How to Make the Best of Life. 1923.

Works (Minerva Edition). 7 vols., 1926.

The Savour of Life: Essays in Gusto. 1928.

Mediterranean Scenes: Rome, Greece, Constaninople. 1928.

The Religious Interregnum. 1929.

Journal 1929. 1930; as *Journal of Things New and Old,* 1930.

Journals 1896 1928, edited by Newman Flower. 3 vols., 1932–33; edited by Frank Swinnerton, 1954.

Bennett and H. G. Wells: A Record of Personal and Literary Friendship, edited by Harris Wilson. 1960.

Florentine Journal 1st April 25th May 1910. 1967.

The Author's Craft and Other Critical Writings, edited by Samuel Hynes. 1968.

Evening Standard Years: Books and Persons 1926 1931, edited by Andrew Mylett. 1974.

Bibliography: *Bennett: A Bibliography* by Norman Emery, 1967.

Reading List: *Bennett* by Walter Allen, 1948; *Bennett*, 1950, revised edition, 1961, and *Bennett: A Last Word*, 1978, both by Frank Swinnerton; *Bennett: Primitivism and Taste* by James Hall, 1959; *The Art of Bennett* by James G. Hepburn, 1963; *Writer by Trade: A View of Bennett* by Dudley Barker, 1966; *The Master: A Study of Bennett* by Oswald H. Davis, 1966; *Bennett* by John Wain, 1967; *Bennett* (biography) by Margaret Drabble, 1974; *Bennett: A Study of His Fiction* by John Lucas, 1975.

*   *   *

Arnold Bennett is by far the best of those British novelists who grew up during the latter half of the nineteenth century, and fell under the spell of the French naturalists. Bennett was an avowed admirer of Zola and Maupassant, and his first published piece of fiction, "A Letter Home," which was published in the *Yellow Book*, is positively modish in its arid, pessimistic manner. It is a manner which no doubt owes something to George Moore and Gissing, as well as to their French models, and the same is true of Bennett's first novel, *A Man from the North*. Published in 1898, *A Man from the North* is a fastidiously written account of a would-be literary man who encounters the fringe of London literary life, but whose attempts to break into the real world of writing founder and die. He ends by making a loveless marriage and retreating into penny-pinching suburban life.

A Man from the North was followed by *Anna of the Five Towns*, a novel which differs from its predecessor not simply in the fact that Bennett is more at home writing about the Potteries where he was born and brought up, but because the novel is less in the grip of literary theory, and consequently has more real life to it. As I have pointed out in my *Arnold Bennett: A Study of His Fiction*, by this time Bennett had discovered Chekhov; the discovery was of colossal importance to him, for it encouraged him to explore the ways individuals struggled against the iron grip of circumstance, and without ever condescending to them, or studying them with pretended scientific objectivity (features integral to naturalism). Thus *Anna* is a most moving study of a girl who lives for others, who is scarcely ever able to consult her own wishes or loves, and who allows herself to be married off to Henry Mynors, a handsome and upright noncomformist lay preacher and business man whom she does not love. Bennett is extraordinarily successful in communicating the emotional pallor of Anna's life, and equally successful in providing the context in which she moves, and by which she is largely conditioned. Indeed, it seems proper to note here that Bennett is one of the great provincial novelists.

After the critical success of *Anna of the Five Towns*, Bennett settled for writing a series of novels about the Potteries, culminating in the *Clayhanger* trilogy. Yet during this same period, between 1900 and 1914, he was also scribbling away at a succession of potboilers in expectation of making piles of money from them. Accordingly, they are written with both eyes firmly fixed on the market: sensation novels, cheap rogue-thrillers that imitate the world of Raffles, detective novels, novels of international intrigue, and so on. Perhaps the best known of these, though not the best, is *The Grand Babylon Hotel*. None of them made Bennett a great deal of money. Indeed, by a pleasing irony his substantial fortune – and he did strike it rich – came from his serious fiction. (The plays he wrote had a fair measure of success, but none was a box-office smash.)

Not all Bennett's serious fiction is successful. And it is sometimes difficult to know when he is being "serious." For example, *Sacred and Profane Love*, about a "passionate woman," Carlotta, and her love affairs, must be the worst novel ever written by a major novelist. (Not even Elinor Glyn wrote a dafter fiction.) Yet *Leonora* is a moving study of a failed marriage, and *Whom God Hath Joined*, another study of a failed marriage, has as good scenes between its men and women as any that Edwardian fiction can show.

But of course the great triumph of this period of Bennett's writing is *The Old Wives' Tale*. It is hardly too much to say that by any standards this is a great novel. Its loving, attentive study of the Baines sisters, stay-at-home Constance, fly-away Sophia, is flawlessly handled, as is the way Bennett writes of the people who surround them: Constance's husband, Samuel Povey, and her selfish, modestly talented son, Cyril; Sophia's ne'er-do-well husband, Gerald; and other, minor characters of the five towns. It is a novel in which Bennett never puts a foot wrong, and in which the writing reaches a level which he was never again to achieve.

Yet having said this, one must hasten to add that the first of the *Clayhanger* trilogy is very nearly as good. Indeed, in some ways it is more challenging. This is because Bennett writes in such detail about work, public houses, meeting-halls: writes, that is, about a man's world, as he had written about a woman's in *The Old Wives' Tale*. The relationship between Edwin Clayhanger and his tyrannical father, Darius, is managed with a rare tact and sympathy, so that one never loses sympathy with Darius, for all his brow-beating overbearing ways (Anna's father is, by comparison, a monster of unthinking selfishness). Darius's slow decline into imbecility and his undignified death are made intensely moving, just because Bennett has succeeded in persuading us of the old man's reality, his physical and psychological aches, feelings, joys. And Bennett is also wonderfully good on Edwin's growing love for the young, spiky Hilda Lessways and his cooling affection for Janet Orgreave, and on the way in which the Orgreave family represent an oasis of culture for a soul-starved provincial boy. Unfortunately, the two subsequent novels are not so good. *Hilda Lessways*, is, indeed, a poor piece of work, and, although Bennett recovers his stride in *These Twain*, he doesn't get back to the level of *Clayhanger* itself.

The best of the remaining novels about the five towns is not *The Card*, which, popular though it is, I find to be a cheap, cynically comic performance, but *The Price of Love*, a tenderly affectionate novel about a young girl's readiness to make a marriage work with an utterly undeserving, vain, selfish, shallow husband.

Bennett wrote about the war in *The Roll-Call* and, much more impressively, *The Pretty Lady*. There followed some more potboilers, including the insufferable *Mr. Prohack*. But then Bennett once more succeeded with *Riceyman Steps*, a finely judged account of the progress and death of a miser's marriage, in which he managed the considerable feat of making the miser, Mr. Earlforward, credible and sympathetic. *Lord Raingo* followed, a perversely impressive study of an empty, conventional public man and his slow death, then the partly good, partly appallingly bad *Accident*. *Imperial Palace* has been neglected unjustly, since it contains one of Bennett's best studies of a woman, Gracie Savott, a flapper, but one with unsuspected depths, a kind he had been trying to capture in his fiction right through the 1920's.

Bennett's career was a long and distinguished one. Although his greatest work undoubtedly comes before the first war it is unfair, as many critics have done, to write off his later fiction. It may not be the equal of *Old Wives' Tale*, but it is impressive in its own right. Certainly, there is not much in the 1920's that can equal it.

—John Lucas

BENSON, E(dward) F(rederic). English. Born at Wellington College, Shropshire, 24 July 1867; son of E. W. Benson, afterwards Archbishop of Canterbury; brother of the writer A. C. Benson. Educated at Marlborough College (Editor of the *Marlburian*); King's College, Cambridge (exhibitioner, 1888; scholar, 1890; Wortz Student; Prendergast and Craven Student), first-class honours degree, 1891. Member of the staff of the British School of Archaeology, Athens, 1892–95, and the Society for the Promotion of Hellenic Studies, in Egypt, 1895; full-time writer from 1895; settled in Rye, Sussex: Mayor of Rye, 1934–37. Honorary Fellow, Magdalene College, Cambridge, 1938. *Died 29 February 1940.*

Fiction

Dodo. 1893.
A Double Overture (stories). 1894.
The Rubicon. 1894.
The Judgment Books. 1895.
Limitations. 1896.
The Babe, B.A. 1896.
The Vintage. 1898.
The Money Market. 1898.
The Capsina. 1899.
Mammon and Co. 1899.
The Princess Sophia. 1900.
The Luck of the Vails. 1901.
Scarlet and Hyssop. 1902.
The Book of Months. 1903.
The Valkyries. 1903.
The Relentless City. 1903.
An Act in a Backwater. 1903.
The Challoners. 1904.
The Angel of Pain. 1905.
The Image in the Sand. 1905
Paul. 1906.
The House of Defence. 1906.
Sheaves. 1907.
The Blotting Book. 1908.
The Climber. 1908.
A Reaping. 1909.
Daisy's Aunt. 1910; as *The Fascinating Mrs. Halton,* 1910.
Margery. 1910.
The Osbornes. 1910.
Juggernaut. 1911.
Account Rendered. 1911.
Mrs. Ames. 1912.
The Room in the Tower and Other Stories. 1912.
The Weaker Vessel. 1913.
Dodo's Daughter. 1913.
Thorley Weir. 1913.
Dodo the Second. 1914.
Arundel. 1914.
The Oakleyites. 1915.
David Blaize. 1916.
Mike. 1916; as *Michael,* 1916.
The Freaks of Mayfair. 1916.
Robin Linnet. 1916.
An Autumn Sowing. 1916.
Mr. Teddy. 1917; as *The Tortoise,* 1917.
Up and Down. 1918.
David Blaize and the Blue Door. 1918.
Across the Stream. 1919.
The Countess of Lowndes Square and Other Stories. 1920.

Queen Lucia. 1920.
Lovers and Friends. 1921.
Dodo Wonders. 1921.
Miss Mapp. 1922.
Peter. 1922.
Colin. 1923.
Visible and Invisible (stories). 1923.
David of King's. 1924.
Alan. 1924.
Rex. 1925.
Colin II. 1925.
Mezzanine. 1926.
Pharisees and Publicans. 1926.
Lucia in London. 1927.
Spook Stories. 1928.
Paying Guests. 1929.
The Step. 1930.
The Inheritor. 1930.
Mapp and Lucia. 1931.
Secret Lives. 1932.
As We Are: A Modern Revue. 1932.
Travail of Gold. 1933.
More Spook Stories. 1934.
Ravens' Brood. 1934.
Lucia's Progress. 1935; as The Worshipful Lucia, 1935.
Old London. 1937.
Trouble for Lucia. 1939.

Plays

Aunt Jeannie. 1902.
Dodo: A Detail of Yesterday, from his own novel (produced 1905).
The Friend in the Garden (produced 1906).
Westward Ho!, music by Philip Napier Miles, from the novel by Charles Kingsley
   (produced 1913).
Dinner for Eight (produced 1915). 1915.
The Luck of the Vails, from his own novel (produced 1928).

Other

Six Common Things. 1893.
Daily Training, with E. H. Miles. 1902.
The Mad Annual, edited by E. H. Miles. 1903.
Two Generations. 1904.
Diversions Day by Day, with E. H. Miles. 1905.
English Figure Skating. 1908.
Bensoniana. 1912.
Winter Sports in Switzerland. 1913.
Deutschland über Allah. 1917.
Poland and Mittel-Europa. 1918.
The White Eagle of Poland. 1918.
Crescent and Iron Cross. 1918.

Our Family Affairs 1867–1896.   1920.
Mother.   1925.
Sir Francis Drake.   1927.
The Life of Alcibiades.   1928.
Ferdinand Magellan.   1929.
The Male Impersonator.   1929.
As We Were: A Victorian Peep-Show (autobiography).   1930.
Charlotte Brontë.   1932.
King Edward VII.   1933.
The Outbreak of War 1914.   1933.
Queen Victoria.   1935.
The Kaiser and English Relations.   1936.
Queen Victoria's Daughters.   1938.
Final Edition: Informal Autobiography.   1940.

Editor, with E. H. Miles, *A Book of Golf.*   1903.
Editor, with E. H. Miles, *The Cricket of Abel, Hirst and Shrewsbury.*   1903.
Editor, *Henry James: Letters to A. C. Benson and Auguste Monod.*   1930.

*   *   *

E. F. Benson was one of three sons of a somewhat unpopular Archbishop of Canterbury, all of whom wrote with excessive copiousness. Alone of the three, E. F. Benson had a certain destructively observant wit, and his Lucia novels, which have lately been reprinted, may be considered a small masterpiece of light comedy set in a leisurely world of elegant small-town rivalries. That world has vanished but it remains permanently alive in Benson's pages as a study of the importance of pettiness. Lucia herself, with her scraps of Italian, her carefully rehearsed piano duets, her patient and long suffering husband George, the ambition which is crowned by the Mayorship of a small town, her mixture of practical shrewdness and self-important silliness, is an unforgettable comic character. The rest of Benson's work is slight and flimsy though always written with buoyancy. *As We Were* is a superficial but interesting and often malicious book of reminiscences.

—G. S. Fraser

BENSON, Stella. English. Born in Much Wenlock, Shropshire, 6 January 1892. Educated privately. Married John O'Gorman Anderson in 1921. Involved in the woman's suffrage campaign c. 1914; during World War I did social work in Hoxton, East London; went to America for her health, 1918; went to China with her husband, 1921, and lived there, apart from visits to England, for the remainder of her life. Recipient: Royal Society of Literature Benson Medal, 1932; Femina Vie Heureuse Prize, 1932. *Died 6 December 1933.*

PUBLICATIONS

Fiction

I Pose.   1915.
This Is the End.   1917.

Living Alone. 1919.
The Poor Man. 1922.
Pipers and a Dancer. 1924.
The Awakening: A Fantasy (story). 1925.
Goodbye, Stranger. 1926.
The Man Who Missed the 'bus (story). 1928.
The Far-Away Bride. 1930; as *Tobit Transplanted,* 1931.
Hope Against Hope and Other Stories. 1931.
Christmas Formula and Other Stories. 1932.
Mundos: An Unfinished Novel. 1935.
Collected Short Stories. 1936.

Play

Kwan-Yin. 1922.

Verse

Twenty. 1918.
Poems. 1935.

Other

The Little World (travel). 1925.
Worlds Within World (travel). 1928.

Editor, *Come to Eleuthera; or, New Lands for Old.* 1929(?).
Editor, *Pull Devil Pull Baker,* by Nicolas de Toulouse Lautrec de Savine. 1933.

Bibliography: in *Ten Contemporaries* by John Gawsworth, 1933.

Reading List: *Benson* by Phyllis Bottome, 1934; *Portrait of Benson* by R. E. Roberts, 1939.

*   *   *

Stella Benson, in the eyes of one critic, is a "highly original novelist whose tragic view of life is artfully disposed behind a facade of remarkable comic wit." Her novels focus on the anguish resulting from a failure of communication, or, as one of her characters says, "Everyone ... here translates instead of understanding what I say...."

Benson was concerned with "the point of view of people as people." She explored this idea in her first novel, *I Pose*, where the two themes that occupied her writing are enunciated: the failure of communication between two people, resulting in alienation and tragedy, and the theme of the expatriate or colonialist. Her second novel, *This Is the End*, deals with personal tragedy in the wake of World War I. When Benson wrote of her experiences in America in *The Poor Man*, she had to defend herself against a storm of protest: "The American culture *that reaches us in Europe and Asia* consists of short cuts to bad art – of which the movie, the gramophone, the radio, the lusciously illustrated Home Magazine are superficial manifestations." The narrow provincialism and the intellectually stagnant life of the colonialist form the content of her next two novels: *Pipers and a Dancer* and *Goodbye, Stranger.* The last named is probably the most brilliantly developed of all her novels; it combines her fine sense of tragedy with her biting, comic wit.

The novel that brought her fame and wider recognition was *Tobit Transplanted* for which she won the Femina Vie Heureuse Prize. Although the book is a retelling of the biblical story of Tobias, Benson successfully transfers the scene to Manchuria and Korea among the White Russians who settled in that area.

At her death, she left an unfinished novel *Mundos*; in it, she returned to the themes of alienation and colonialism. The civil servants of the island of Mundos do not understand the people they govern any more than they understand themselves. The violent story swells beneath a facade of tea parties and seemingly innocent encounters. The novel's architectonic design can be compared with Joseph Conrad's best work.

—Dominic J. Bisignano

BESANT, Sir Walter. English. Born in Portsmouth, Hampshire, 14 August 1836. Educated at King's College, University of London; Christ's College, Cambridge (scholar and Prizeman exhibitioner), BA. 1859. Married Mary Foster-Barham in 1895. Senior Professor, Royal College of Mauritius, 1861–67; Secretary, 1868–85, and Honorary Secretary, 1885–1901, Palestine Exploration Fund. Advocate of social reform in the East End of London: helped found the People's Palace at Mile End. A Founder, 1884, and first Chairman, 1884–85, and, again, 1887–92, Society of Authors. Fellow, Society of Antiquaries, 1894. Knighted, 1895. *Died 9 June 1901.*

PUBLICATIONS

Fiction

> *Ready-Money Mortiboy*, with James Rice.   1872.
> *My Little Girl*, with James Rice.   1873.
> *With Harp and Crown*, with James Rice.   1875.
> *The Golden Butterfly*, with James Rice.   1876.
> *The Case of Mr. Lucraft and Other Tales*, with James Rice.   1876.
> *This Son of Vulcan*, with James Rice.   1876.
> *Such a Good Man!*, with James Rice.   1877.
> *The Monks of Thelema*, with James Rice.   1878.
> *By Celia's Arbour*, with James Rice.   1878.
> *'Twas in Trafalgar's Bay and Other Stories*, with James Rice.   1879.
> *The Seamy Side*, with James Rice.   1880.
> *The Chaplain of the Fleet*, with James Rice.   1881.
> *Sir Richard Whittington*, with James Rice.   1881.
> *The Ten Years' Tenant and Other Stories*, with James Rice.   1881.
> *The Revolt of Man*.   1882.
> *All Sorts and Conditions of Men*.   1882.
> *All in a Garden Fair*.   1883.
> *The Captain's Room*.   1883.
> *Dorothy Foster*.   1884.
> *Uncle Jack* (stories).   1885.

Children of Gibeon. 1886.
Katherine Regina. 1887.
The World Went Very Well Then. 1887.
Herr Paulus. 1888.
The Inner House. 1888.
The Bell of St. Paul's. 1889.
For Faith and Freedom. 1889.
The Doubts of Dives. 1889.
To Call Her Mine. 1889.
Armorel of Lyonesse. 1890.
The Demoniac. 1890.
The Holy Rose. 1890.
Blind Love, by Wilkie Collins, completed by Besant. 1890.
St. Katherine's by the Tower. 1891.
Verbena Camellia Stephanotis (stories and essays). 1892.
The Ivory Gate. 1892.
Beyond the Dreams of Avarice. 1895.
In Deacon's Orders (stories). 1895.
The City of Refuge. 1896.
The Master Craftsman. 1896.
A Fountain Sealed. 1897.
The Changeling. 1898.
The Orange-Girl. 1899.
The Alabaster Box. 1900.
The Fourth Gentleman. 1900.
The Lady of Lynn. 1901.
A Five Years' Tryst and Other Stories. 1902.
No Other Way. 1902.

Plays

Ready-Money, with James Rice, from their own novel. 1875.
Such a Good Man, with James Rice, from their own novel (produced 1879).
The Charm, with W. H. Pollock (produced 1884).   In *The Charm* ..., 1896.
The Ballad Monger, with W. H. Pollock (produced 1887).
The Charm and Other Drawing Room Plays, with W. H. Pollock. 1896.

Other

Studies in Early French Poetry. 1868.
Jerusalem: The City of Herod and Saladin, with E. H. Palmer. 1871.
When George III Was King. 1872.
The French Humorists. 1873.
Constantinople, with W. J. Brodribb. 1879.
Gaspard de Coligny. 1879.
Rabelais. 1879.
The Life and Achievements of E. H. Palmer. 1883.
Life in an Hospital: An East End Chapter. 1883.
Twenty-One Years' Work 1865–86. 1886; revised edition, 1895.
The Eulogy of Richard Jefferies. 1888.
Fifty Years Ago. 1888.
Captain Cook. 1890.

121

London. 1892.
The History of London. 1893.
The Society of Authors. 1893.
Westminster. 1895.
The Rise of the Empire. 1897.
The Pen and the Book. 1899.
South London. 1899.
East London. 1901.
The Story of King Alfred. 1901.
The Strand District, with Geraldine Mitton. 1902.
Autobiography. 1902.
London in the Eighteenth Century. 1902.
London in the Time of the Stuarts. 1903.
As We Are and As We May Be. 1903.
Essays and Historiettes. 1903.
The Thames. 1903.
London in the Time of the Tudors. 1904.
Medieval London. 2 vols., 1906.
Early London: Prehistoric, Roman, Saxon, and Norman. 1908.
London in the Nineteenth Century. 1909.
London South of the Thames. 1912.
Bourbon Journal, August 1863. 1933.

Editor, with R. J. Griffiths, *Stewart's Local Examination Series.* 17 vols., 1877–82.
Editor, *The Literary Remains of C. F. T. Drake.* 1877.
Editor, with E. H. Palmer, *The Survey of Western Palestine,* by C. R. Conder. 1881.
Editor, *Readings in Rabelais.* 1883.
Editor, *The Fascination of London Series,* with Geraldine Mitton. 12 vols., 1902–08.
Editor, *The Survey of London.* 10 vols., 1901–12.

Reading List: "Besant, Novelist" by F. W. Boege, in *English Fiction in Transition 2,* 1959; "Besant on the Art of the Novel" by E. Boll, in *English Fiction in Transition 2,* 1959

*   *   *

Although Sir Walter Besant is probably the best remembered as the author of an essay on the art of fiction which brought Henry James to reply in one of the greatest essays ever written on the subject, Besant was, in his own day, a highly popular author who had his say on many issues of importance, and who was first president of the Society of Authors. An admirer of Zola, and something of a socialist, Besant wrote two widely acclaimed novels about working-class London, *All Sorts and Conditions of Men* and *Children of Gibeon.* These two works of the 1880's had a colossal influence on contemporaries, so much so indeed that Besant's recommendation for a people's palace of pleasures became a reality when in 1887 Sir Edmund Currie, taking *All Sorts and Conditions of Men* as his textbook, began a subscription which resulted in a "palace" of sorts being built.

During the same decade Besant was at work in other areas. *The Revolt of Man* is a satire on feminism, and as such it anticipates his hostile reaction to Ibsen's *The Doll's House.* In his article "The Doll's House – and After" (*English Illustrated Magazine,* January 1890), Besant conjured up a picture of the effects on Nora's family of her desertion. Her husband has degenerated into a drunkard, her son turns to a life of crime, and her daughter ends in suicide. For a man with socialist sympathies, Besant was stridently conventional about the role of women in public and private life. This is evident in another of his popular successes, *Dorothy Foster,* an historical novel which is really no more than "costume" history, and which treats the fortunes of its heroine in a sugary, romantic-sentimental manner. (It is no accident that Besant should have been an enthusiastic admirer of Anthony Hope's *The Prisoner of Zenda*.)

More substantial, perhaps, is *All in a Garden Fair*, a novel about the literary life, which Gissing admired and which may have had some influence over Gissing's novel on the subject, *New Grub Street*. *New Grub Street* is a much better novel than *All in a Garden Fair*, perhaps because Gissing was a more serious and dedicated admirer of Zola than Besant was, and his naturalism seems more authentic.

Besant, indeed, never seems to be wholly serious in his avowals of support for either naturalism or socialism. I do not find it surprising that he should have written the mawkish little tale *The Ivory Gate*, which shows a lawyer who in his business hours is very lawyer-like – tough, legalistic, dry – but who in his hours of relaxation becomes the very model of benevolence, overflowing with the milk of human kindness, and ready to put his money where his mouth is. *The Ivory Gate* owes something to *A Christmas Carol*, and perhaps to the Cheerybles of *Nicholas Nickleby*.

Besant also had a highly successful literary partnership with James Rice. In 1872 he and Rice published *Ready-Money Mortiboy*, the popularity of which resulted in a series of twelve novels. On the whole, Besant's gifts were too readily deployed in tailoring books to meet audience demand. Yet *All Sorts and Conditions of Men* retains its interest, and *Children of Gibeon* is a decent if comparatively undistinguished contribution to fiction about working-class London and the possibilities of social revolution, matters which so engaged people's attention during the 1880's.

—John Lucas

BIERCE, Ambrose (Gwinnet).   American.   Born in Meigs County, Ohio, 24 June 1842. Educated at high school in Warsaw, Indiana; Kentucky Military Institute, 1859–60. Served in the Ninth Indiana Infantry Regiment of the Union Army during the Civil War, 1861–65: Major. Married Mollie Day in 1871 (divorced, 1905); two sons and one daughter. Printer's Devil, *Northern Indianan* (anti-slavery paper), 1857–59; United States Treasury aide, Alabama, 1865; served on a military expedition, Omaha to San Francisco, 1866–67; worked for the Sub-Treasury, San Francisco, 1867–68; Editor, *News Letter*, San Francisco, 1868–72; in London, 1872–76: member of the staff of *Fun*, 1872–75, and Editor of *The Lantern*, 1875; returned to San Francisco: worked for the United States Mint, from 1875, Columnist for *The Sunday Examiner*, 1876–97; Associate Editor of *The Argonaut*, 1877–79; Agent, Black Hills Placer Mining Company, Rockerville, Dakota Territory, 1880; Editor of *The Wasp*, San Francisco, 1881–86; lived in Washington, D.C., 1900–13: Washington Correspondent for the New York *American* until 1906; member of staff of *The Cosmopolitan*, Washington, 1905–09; travelled in Mexico, 1913–14: served in Villa's forces and was killed in action at the Battle of Ojinaga. *Died (probably 11 January) in 1914*.

PUBLICATIONS

Collections

> *Collected Works*, edited by Walter Neale.   12 vols., 1909–12.
> *The Letters*, edited by Bertha Clark Pope.   1921.

Complete Short Stories, edited by Ernest Jerome Hopkins. 1970.
Stories and Fables, edited by Edward Wagenknecht. 1977.

Fiction

The Fiend's Delight. 1873.
Nuggets and Dust Panned Out in California. 1873.
Cobwebs from an Empty Skull. 1873.
The Dance of Death, with Thomas A. Harcourt. 1877; revised edition, 1877.
Tales of Soldiers and Civilians. 1891; as In the Midst of Life, 1892; revised edition, 1898.
The Monk and the Hangman's Daughter, from a translation by Gustav Adolph Danziger of a story by Richard Voss. 1892.
Can Such Things Be? 1893.
Fantastic Fables. 1899.
Battleships and Ghosts. 1931.

Verse

Black Beetles in Amber. 1892.
Shapes of Clay. 1903.

Other

The Cynic's Word Book. 1906; as The Devil's Dictionary, 1911; revised edition by Ernest Jerome Hopkins, as The Enlarged Devil's Dictionary, 1967.
Write It Right: A Little Black-List of Literary Faults. 1909.
Twenty-One Letters, edited by Samual Loveman. 1922.
Selections from Prattle, edited by Carroll D. Hall. 1936.

Bibliography: Bierce: A Bibliography by Vincent Starrett, 1929; in Bibliography of American Literature by Jacob Blanck, 1955.

Reading List: Bierce: A Biography by Carey McWilliams, 1929; Bierce, The Devil's Lexicographer, 1951, and Bierce and the Black Hills, 1956, both by Paul Fatout; Bierce by Robert A. Wiggins, 1964; The Short Stories of Bierce: A Study in Polarity by Stuart C. Woodruff, 1965; Bierce: A Biography by Richard O'Connor, 1967; Bierce by Mary E. Grenander, 1971.

*   *   *

Though not widely read today, Ambrose Bierce is a familiar name in American letters. After several years of distinguished soldiering in the Civil War, the almost completely self-taught Bierce turned to journalism and ended up being one of the most colourful figures in late 19th- and early 20th-century journalism in America. In San Francisco, where he spent most of his life, he was a newspaper editor and columnist, and delighted in exposing hypocrisy and stupidity in private and public life. Besides his witty and pungent journalistic writing, Bierce produced a sizeable body of short stories and essays, and also some verse, chiefly occasional and satiric. His literary reputation, however, must depend upon the stories collected in Tales of Soldiers and Civilians, such as "The Occurrence at Owl Creek Bridge," in which Bierce skilfully uses suspense not as a mere melodramatic devise but logically and calculatingly to wind up the bizarre incidents concerning a young man about to be executed. In other stories, like "One of the Missing," there is perhaps a heavier use of coincidence than most readers would accept unprotestingly.

If young Bierce dealt in the tall-tale and broad Western humour, the older Bierce was a master of sardonic humour and mordant but often sparkling wit. Perhaps the best specimen of these qualities as well as of his life-long cynicism is to be found, outside his journalism, in *The Devil's Dictionary*, a book quoted universally even though many that quote from it may not be aware of the author's identity. As a serious literary writer Bierce belongs to – and has helped perpetuate (in however small a measure) – the tradition of the absurd and grotesque in American writing. There is in him a marked interest in abnormal or intensified psychological states and a persistent hostility to the realistic mode. One will look in vain for a range of emotional experience in his writing and consequently for the depth of serious feeling usually associated with great literature. But for his picturesque personality and his contribution as a committed and hard-hitting journalist, and as a writer of some excellent stories, Bierce is an enduring figure in the history of American literature.

—J. N. Sharma

BILLINGS, Josh.   See SHAW, Henry Wheeler.

BLACKMORE, R(ichard) D(oddridge).   English.   Born in Longworth, Berkshire, 7 June 1825. Educated at Blundell's School, Tiverton; Exeter College, Oxford, matriculated 1843, B.A. 1847, M.A. 1852; worked as a tutor in the family of Sir Samuel Scott of Sundridge Park, Kent, then entered the Middle Temple, London: called to the Bar, 1852. Married Lucy Pinto Leite in 1852 (died). Settled in London; practised as a conveyancer, but gave up the law because of ill-health; Classical Master, Wellesley House School, Twickenham Common, Middlesex, 1853; built Gomer House on extensive grounds at Teddington, Middlesex, 1858, settled there, and supported himself as a market gardener. *Died 20 January 1900.*

PUBLICATIONS

Fiction

   Clara Vaughan.   1864; revised edition, 1872.
   Cradock Nowell.   1866; revised edition, 1873.
   Lorna Doone: A Romance of Exmoor.   1869; edited by R. O. Morris, 1920.
   The Maid of Sker.   1872.
   Alice Lorraine.   1875; revised edition, 1876.

Cripps the Carrier. 1876.
Erema; or, My Father's Sin. 1877.
Mary Anerley. 1880.
Christowell. 1882.
The Remarkable History of Sir Thomas Upmore Bart, M.P. 1884.
Springhaven. 1887.
Kit and Kitty. 1890.
Perlycross. 1894.
Tales from the Telling-House. 1896.
Dariel. 1897.

Verse

Poems. 1854.
Epullia. 1854.
The Bugle of the Black Sea; or, The British in the East. 1855.
The Fate of Franklin. 1860.
Fringilla: Some Tales in Verse. 1895.

Other

Figaro at Hastings, St. Leonards. 1877.
Humour, Wit, and Satire. 1885.
Fotheringay and Mary Queen of Scots. 1886.
Betrothal Ring of Mary Queen of Scots 1565: A Description of the Darnley Ring. 1887.
Argyll's Highlands; or, MacCailein Mor and the Lords of Lorne, with Traditional Tales, edited by J. Mackay. 1902.

Translator, *The Farm and Fruit of Old: The First and Second Georgics of Virgil.* 1862.
Translator, *The Georgics of Virgil.* 1871; edited by R. S. Conway, 1932.

Reading List: *Blackmore: His Life and Novels* by Q. C. Burris, 1930; *Blackmore, The Author of Lorna Doone* by W. H. Dunn, 1956 (includes bibliography; supplement by J. A. Carter in *Notes and Queries*, August 1962); *The Last Victorian: Blackmore and His Novels* by Kenneth Budd, 1960.

*   *   *

Lorna Doone is the only novel by which R. D. Blackmore is now remembered, although he wrote fourteen others, beginning with *Clara Vaughan* in 1864, while living a quiet life in the house he built himself in Teddington. The appeal of *Lorna Doone* lies in its combination of an exciting story, a good deal of historical colour from the time of Monmouth's rising, and a genuine feeling for the landscape of Exmoor. It may be related to other "regional" novels like those of Scott and Hardy, but it has a robust and passionate, if at times melodramatic, atmosphere of its own.

Blackmore had some difficulty in getting *Lorna Doone* published, and at first it did not sell well, but the publication of a cheaper one-volume edition changed the situation. He himself thought that the novel owed some of its success to the fact that its appearance coincided with Queen Victoria's giving permission to her daughter Princess Louise to marry the Marquis of Lorne. It came to be believed that the novel concerned Lord Lorne's ancestors, and this encouraged many to read it out of curiosity. However this may be, the romantic story of the high-born Lorna and her lowly but ardent lover, John Ridd, embodies an archetypal romantic situation which may have had particular appeal in the changing society of the nineteenth century. Blackmore based his novel on memories of stories told by his grandfather, who used to ride across Exmoor to preach on alternate Sundays while rector of Oare, and on published accounts of the Doone family, in whose historical reality he firmly believed. The landscape descriptions present the moor as a place of mystery, and visitors attracted to the area apparently complained – according to Waldo Dunn's biography – that the moor was less dramatic and awe-inspiring than the novel had led them to believe. Blackmore's reasonable explanation, in a letter to the editor of Baedeker's *Handbook of Great Britain* in 1887, was that he "romanced" simply "for the uses of my story." And he did so to excellent effect.

Some of his later novels, like *The Maid of Sker* (Blackmore's own favourite) and *Springhaven*, also combine landscape and passion in ways that make their neglect surprising. How much the success of *Lorna Doone* owed to the Victorian tendency – which it encouraged – to equate the West Country with a particular quality of Englishness is hard to calculate, but its continuing appeal suggests the strength of the central romantic story. It is a classic of middlebrow literature, and representative of a significant tradition romanticising specific parts of the English countryside.

—Peter Faulkner

BLAIR, Eric Arthur. See **ORWELL, George.**

BODENHEIM, Maxwell. American. Born in Hermanville, Mississippi, 26 May 1892. Self-educated; studied law and art in Chicago. Joined the Army, 1909; jailed for desertion and discharged, 1911. Married 1) Minna Schein in 1918 (divorced, 1938), one son; 2) Grace Finan in 1939 (died, 1950); 3) Ruth Fagan in 1951. Travelled in the Southwest, 1911–12; lived in Chicago, 1914; settled in New York City, 1915; writer for the *Literary Times*, Chicago, 1923–24; worked for the Federal Writers Project, 1939–40 (fired for being a communist). *Died 7 February 1954.*

PUBLICATIONS

Fiction

Blackguard. 1923.
Crazy Man. 1924.
Cutie, A Warm Mamma, with Ben Hecht. 1924.
Replenishing Jessica. 1925.

127

Ninth Avenue. 1926.
Georgie May. 1928.
Sixty Seconds. 1929.
A Virtuous Girl. 1930.
Naked on Roller Skates 1930.
Duke Herring. 1931.
6 A.M. 1932.
Run, Sheep, Run. 1932.
New York Madness. 1933.
Slow Vision. 1934.

Plays

Knot Holes (produced 1917).
The Gentle Furniture Shop (produced 1917).   In *Drama 10,* 1920

Verse

Minna and Myself. 1918.
Advice. 1920.
Introducing Irony: A Book of Poetic Short Stories and Poems. 1922.
Against This Age. 1923.
The Sardonic Arm. 1923.
Returning to Emotion. 1927.
The King of Spain. 1928.
Bringing Jazz! 1930.
Lights in the Valley. 1942.
Selected Poems 1914–44. 1946.

Other

My Life and Loves in Greenwich Village. 1954.

Reading List: *Bodenheim* by Jack B. Moore, 1970.

*   *   *

Maxwell Bodenheim's slow but steady and determined pursuit of self-destruction, and the frequently giddy capers he cut while parading (at first) and then lurching around New York's literary scene, have almost completely obscured his solid if inconsistent achievements as a writer. Easily forgotten, because buried under an avalanche of anecdotes, novels, and plays by other writers about his escapades during the Jazz Age and Great Depression years, is the undoubted evidence that he was sometimes a very powerful, often an innovative, and nearly always a fascinating poet-novelist of the world that ultimately passed him by.

Bodenheim's social and literary criticism is perhaps the least well known aspect of his literary career. Ezra Pound wanted to have published Bodenheim's "whole blooming book" on aesthetics although (or perhaps because) Pound claimed only he and a few other writers would understand it. In fact only a few chapters of the book were ever printed, and these were published separately as essays. As a reviewer for many of the leading journals of the 1920's, he championed the work of such contemporaries as Conrad Aiken, Wallace Stevens, and William Carlos Williams; lambasted what he considered the sham pastoralism in modern fiction where "young men lie upon their backs in cornfields and feel oppressed by their bodies"; and tilted with the very popular and he felt often fake Freudianism of his times for trumpeting that "sex underlies all human motives and is the basis of all creations." He also sought out new writers. When he was one of the editors of the avant-garde little magazine *Others* he went out of his way to praise and secure publication for the very young Hart Crane.

From 1923 to 1934 he published some dozen novels, which, together with the poetry he wrote around the same period, refute the idea that he crippled himself as a writer simply through dissipating his resources in sordid adventures. He was by no means a major novelist, for his works lack artistic control. Too often he used the form as a way to settle personal scores, or, worse, did not attend strictly enough to technical details of his craft. He sometimes seemed more intent upon setting down striking phrases than in constructing a coherent and compelling story. But most of the novels display solid and significant attainments: the touching comic (and autobiographic) portrait of the young artist in *Blackguard*; the sad, sordid decline of the prostitute Georgie May; the urban nightmare of *Ninth Avenue*; the parade of numbed derelicts that sleepwalk through *Slow Vision*, his Depression novel.

Bodenheim's artistic reputation rests most solidly upon his poetry, and his ultimate failure to become a first-rate poet is probably the saddest element of his professional career. Bodenheim was early considered one of the most promising writers taking part in the American literary renaissance of the 1910's: Harriet Monroe and Margaret Anderson, editors of the two most influential literary magazines of the day, both strove to be the first to announce the arrival of his genius. Conrad Aiken and William Carlos Williams were only two of the many writers who, though sometimes appalled by his antics, highly praised his poetry. Among his chief virtues as a poet were his ability to compose beautiful and exotic images and to weave them harmoniously into the texture of a unified poem, such as "Death." He could also write harshly and effectively about the ugliness of modern city life, as in "Summer Evening: New York Subway Station." His jazz poems, such as those in *Bringing Jazz!*, were interesting experiments in a form one critic said had been successfully employed only by one other poet – T. S. Eliot.

Bodenheim's artistic death, which long preceded his physical death, was lamentable, for he never came close to attaining the greatness his early promise and ability seemed to predict. Yet he accomplished far more than his relatively obscure reputation today would suggest.

—Jack B. Moore

BOLDREWOOD, Rolf. Pseudonym for Thomas Alexander Browne. Australian. Born in London, England, 6 August 1826; emigrated to Australia 1831. Educated at O'Connell Street Dame School, Sydney; W. T. Cape's private academy, Sydney; Sydney College, 1835–41; tutored by Rev. David Boyd, Melbourne. Married Margaret Maria Riley in 1861; five daughters and four sons. Pioneer squatter (i.e., grazier), 1844–63 in the western district of Victoria; sheepfarmer and Justice of Peace in Narrandera, New South Wales, 1864–69; gave up farming 1869; Police Magistrate, Gulgong, New South Wales, 1871; Goldfield's Commissioner, 1872, and later District Coroner, Gulgong, until 1881; Police Magistrate, Dubbo, New South Wales, 1881–84, and Armidale, New South Wales, 1884; Chairman, Land Licensing Board, Albury, New South Wales, 1885–87, and Police Magistrate and Mining Warden, Albury, 1887–95; settled in Melbourne, 1895. *Died 11 March 1915.*

PUBLICATIONS

Collections

The Portable Boldrewood, edited by Alan Brissenden.   1978.

Fiction

Ups and Downs: A Story of Australian Life.   1878; as *The Squatter's Dream,* 1890.
*Robbery under Arms: A Story of Life and Adventure in the Bush and in the Goldfields of
    Australia.*   1888; revised edition, 1889.
The Miner's Right: A Tale of the Australian Goldfields.   1890.
A Colonial Reformer.   1890.
A Sydney-Side Saxon.   1891.
Nevermore.   1892.
A Modern Buccaneer.   1894.
The Sphinx of Eaglehawk: A Tale of Old Bendigo.   1895.
The Crooked Stick; or, Pollie's Probation.   1895.
The Sealskin Cloak.   1896.
My Run Home.   1897.
Plain Living: A Bush Idyll.   1898.
A Romance of Canvas Town and Other Stories.   1898.
"War to the Knife"; or, Tangata Maori.   1899.
Babes in the Bush.   1899.
In Bad Company and Other Stories.   1901.
The Ghost Camp; or, The Avengers.   1902.
The Last Chance: A Tale of the Golden West.   1905.

Other

S. W. Silver's Australian Grazier's Guide.   2 vols., 1879–81.
Old Melbourne Memories.   1884; revised edition, 1886; edited by C. E. Sayers, 1969.

Bibliography: *Boldrewood: An Annotated Bibliography, Checklist, and Chronology* by Keast
Burke, 1956.

Reading List: *Boldrewood* by T. Inglis Moore, 1968; *Boldrewood* by Alan Brissenden, 1972.

*   *   *

T. A. Browne began writing (as Rolf Boldrewood) in middle life to supplement a depleted
income and repay debts to relatives, drawing on his experience as a squatter and his
unbounded admiration for the novels of Scott. Most of his work was first printed in weekly
periodicals (12 of his 16 novels originally appeared as serials). His good-natured attitude to
life was expressed in six pastoral romances and ten adventure stories; material for several of
these – the best are *The Miner's Right* and *Nevermore* – derived from his life on the goldfields.
    Browne often fictionalized historical events with success, especially in *Robbery under
Arms*, an exciting tale of bushrangers which has remained popular. Its hero, Captain
Starlight, and the Marstons – old Ben, an ex-convict, and his sons Dick and Jim – steal cattle,
rob a bank, raid homesteads, and hold up a rich gold escort. Though generally successful, the

outlaws plan to escape to America. On their way to take ship from Queensland, they are betrayed. Starlight and Jim are shot dead, and Dick, the teller of the tale, is condemned to hang. Dick's sentence is commuted, and, on his release, he marries the faithful Grace Storefield and they take up a new life on a cattle station.

The novel succeeds where others by Browne fail because its structure is tight but varied and the action is depicted vividly. Most of all, through choosing an ill-educated colonial as his narrator, Browne was able to restrain his usually weak, florid style. He was the first to use the Australian vernacular in this way for a novel, and the first to present Australian-born colonials as main characters. The Marstons are a foil for the noble Englishman Starlight, a dashing Byronic figure who is a master of manners, wit, and disguise. Important historically, the novel is also good reading. Others, e.g., *A Colonial Reformer, A Sydney-Side Saxon*, and a volume of reminiscences, *Old Melbourne Memories*, have value more as sources of social history than as lively writing.

Politically conservative, Browne disagreed with the nationalistic mood of Australia in the 1890's and refused to write for its chief voice, the *Bulletin*. He was patriotic, but ambiguously so, lauding the colonial life with its opportunities for wealth and its physical excellence, while firmly believing a noble lineage and an ancestral home to be ultimately desirable. His most vigorous characters are the native-born men and women of *Robbery under Arms*; his most vivid writing is in the descriptions, seen through Dick Marston's eyes, of the Australian bush and the gang's exploits. While the novel lacks the depth of vision of Marcus Clarke's *For the Term of His Natural Life* and the consistency of Henry Kingsley's *Geoffry Hamlyn*, it is more distinctively Australian than either in its depiction of the relationship between the young colonials and the immigrant landowners, in the swinging gusto of its narration, and particularly in its language.

—Alan Brissenden

BORROW, George (Henry). English. Born in East Dereham, Norfolk, 5 July 1803. Educated at Norwich Grammar School, 1816–18; articled to a firm of Norwich solicitors, 1818–23. Married Mary Clarke in 1840. Worked as a hack writer to the publisher Sir Richard Phillips, London, 1824; travelled throughout England, often with groups of gypsies, 1825–32; Agent of the Bible Society: travelled to St. Petersburg, 1833–35, and in Spain, Portugal, and Morocco, 1835–39; also, Foreign Correspondent of the *Morning Herald*, 1837–39; lived at Oulton Broad, Norfolk, from 1840. *Died 26 July 1881.*

PUBLICATIONS

Collections

Works, edited by Clement K. Shorter. 16 vols., 1923–24.

Fiction

Tales of the Wild and Wonderful. 1825.
Lavengro: The Scholar, The Gypsy, The Priest. 1851; edited by Walter Starkie, 1961.
The Romany Rye: A Sequel to Lavengro. 1857; edited by Walter Starkie, 1949.

Other

The Zincali; or, An Account of the Gypsies of Spain, with an Original Collection of Their Songs and Poetry and a Copious Dictionary of Their Language. 2 vols., 1841; edited by Walter Starkie, 1961.

The Bible in Spain; or, The Journeys, Adventures, and Imprisonments of an Englishman in an Attempt to Circulate the Scriptures in the Peninsula. 3 vols., 1843; supplementary chapter, 1913; edited by Peter Quennell, 1959.

Wild Wales: Its People, Language, and Scenery. 3 vols., 1862.

Romano Lavo-Lil: Word-Book of the Romany; or, English Gypsy Language. 1874.

Letters to the British and Foreign Bible Society, edited by T. H. Darlow. 1911.

Letters to His Wife, Mary Borrow. 1913.

Letters to His Mother, Ann Borrow, and Other Correspondents. 1913.

Celtic Bards, Chiefs, and Kings, edited by H. G. Wright. 1928.

Editor, *Celebrated Trials and Remarkable Cases of Criminal Jurisprudence from the Earliest Records to 1825.* 6 vols., 1825.

Editor, *Evangelioa San Lucasen Guissan,* by Oteiza. 1838.

Translator, *Faustus,* by F. M. von Klinger. 1825.

Translator, *Romantic Ballads.* 1826.

Translator, *Targum; or, Metrical Translations from Thirty Languages and Dialects.* 1835.

Translator, *The Talisman,* by Pushkin. 1835.

Translator, *Embéo e Majaró Lucas.* 1837.

Translator, *The Sleeping Bard; or, Visions of the World, Death, and Hell,* by Elis Wynne. 1860.

Translator, *The Turkish Jester; or, The Pleasantries of Cogia Nasr Eddin Effendi.* 1844.

Translator, *The Death of Balder,* by Johannes Ewald. 1889.

Translator, *Russian Popular Tales.* 1904.

Translator, *The Gold Horns,* by A. G. Ohlenschläger. 1913.

Translator, *Welsh Poems and Ballads,* edited by Ernest Rhys. 1915.

Translator, *Ballads of All Nations: A Selection,* edited by R. Brinsley Johnson. 1927.

Bibliography: *A Bibliography of the Writings in Prose and Verse of Borrow* by T. J. Wise, 1914.

Reading List: *Life, Writings, and Correspondence of Borrow* by W. I. Knapp, 2 vols., 1899; *Borrow* by M. D. Armstrong, 1950; *Gypsy Borrow* by B. Vesey-Fitzgerald, 1953; *Borrow, Vagabond, Polyglotte, Agent Biblique, Ecrivain* by R. Fréchet, 1956 (includes bibliography); *Borrow* by Robert Meyers, 1966.

*   *   *

Though he laid claims to be considered as a novelist, George Borrow was essentially a writer of what was later to be known as travel literature. Some of his work openly purports to be of this kind; but even *Lavengro* and *The Romany Rye,* though usually described as picaresque novels, are really romanticised excursions in autobiography thinly disguised in the trappings of first-person singular narrative fiction. His literary work is to an unusual extent a direct projection of his own personality, a re-creation of his particular quiddity.

His father's itinerant life as a recruiting officer may have encouraged footloose propensities in the son, and certainly meant that his early schooling was erratic. Though he became a considerable philologist, familiar with over thirty languages and dialects and a pioneer in the study of Gypsy languages and customs, he also developed, like many self-taught scholars, a strong didactic strain which perpetually informs his writing. Fortunately he gained his education as much in the streets and market-places, in stable-yards, boxing-rings, and Gypsy camps, as in the school-room, library, or solicitor's office in which he served a brief apprenticeship; but though this give him rich, unusual, and fascinating material to write about, his readers must be prepared to accept a recurrent note of assertive punditry in Borrow's work.

Only Borrow specialists are likely to turn to his earlier publications, translations of *Faustus* and Danish ballads, the volume *Targum* which contains metrical translations from thirty languages, and the six volumes of *Celebrated Trials*, which can be dismissed as hack work. Equally, his translation of St. Luke's Gospel into Caló (the dialect of Spanish Gypsies) and his important *Romano Lavo-Lil*, or Romany word-book, are of interest mainly to philologists and folklorists. But *The Zincali*, with its vivid description of Spanish Gypsy life and customs, and *The Bible in Spain*, one of the most evocative of all descriptions of that country and its manners, are still among the best reading for the traveller in Spain. Borrow's attempts to portray the life of English Gypsies and travelling folk in *Lavengro* and *The Romany Rye* are less successful. Because he was unable to distance himself sufficiently from his material as a novelist, his characters fail to achieve independent reality within a fictional world: the narrative and the dialogue tend to reflect in monochrome Borrow's own colloquial if lively style and tone of voice. His was an egocentric and wayward talent, achieving its best expression in his travel books, including *Wild Wales*, an affectionate description of a walking holiday which is fit to stand beside *The Bible in Spain*.

—Stewart F. Sanderson

BOSWELL, James. Scottish. Born in Edinburgh, 29 October 1740. Educated at Edinburgh High School, and the University of Edinburgh; studied law at the University of Glasgow, and at the University of Utrecht, 1764; admitted an advocate, 1765; admitted to the Scottish Bar, 1766. Married Margaret Montgomerie in 1769 (died, 1789); seven children. Met Samuel Johnson in London, 1763; made a tour of the Continent, and visited Voltaire and Rousseau, 1764–66; practised law in Edinburgh from 1769; frequent visitor to London: a member of Dr. Johnson's Literary Club, 1773; escorted Johnson on a tour of the Highlands and Hebrides, 1773; Contributor (as "The Hypochondriack") to *London Magazine*, 1777–83; abandoned his Scottish practice, moved his family to London, entered the Middle Temple, and was admitted to the English Bar, 1788, but never practised: thereafter worked on his biography of Johnson. *Died 19 May 1795.*

PUBLICATIONS

Collections

Letters, edited by C. B. Tinker.   2 vols., 1924.
Private Papers from Malahide Castle, edited by Geoffrey Scott and Frederick A. Pottle.   18 vols., 1928–34.
Yale Edition of the Private Papers, edited by F. W. Hilles and others.   1951–; research edition, 1966–.

Fiction and Prose

A View of the Edinburgh Theatre During the Summer Season 1759. 1760.
Observations on Foote's The Minor. 1760.
Critical Strictures on Elvira by David Malloch, with Andrew Erskine and George
   Dempster. 1763; edited by Frederick A. Pottle, 1952.
The Essence of the Douglas Cause. 1767.
Dorando: A Spanish Tale. 1767.
*An Account of Corsica: The Journal of a Tour to That Island, and Memoirs of Pascal
   Paoli.* 1768; in Yale Edition, 1955.
Reflections on the Late Alarming Bankruptcies in Scotland. 1772.
A Letter to the People of Scotland on the Present State of the Nation. 1784.
*A Letter to the People of Scotland on the Attempt to Infringe the Articles of the
   Union.* 1785.
The Journal of a Tour to the Hebrides with Samuel Johnson. 1785; in Yale Edition,
   1961.
The Life of Samuel Johnson. 2 vols., 1791; revised edition, 1793, 1799; edited by R.
   W. Chapman, 1953.
Letters to W. J. Temple, edited by Philip Francis. 1857; edited by T. Seccombe, 1908.
Boswelliana: The Commonplace Book, edited by C. Rogers. 1874.
Boswell's Consultation Book. 1922.
Notebook 1776–77, edited by R. W. Chapman. 1923.

Editor, *British Essays in Favour of the Brave Corsicans.* 1768.

Verse

*An Elegy on the Death of an Amiable Young Lady, with an Epistle from Menalcus to
   Lycidas.* 1761.
An Ode to Tragedy. 1761.
The Cub at Newmarket: A Tale. 1762.
*Ode by Dr. Samuel Johnson to Mrs. Thrale upon Their Supposed Approaching
   Nuptials.* 1784.
No Abolition of Slavery; or, The Universal Empire of Love. 1791.
Boswell's Book of Bad Verse (A Verse Self-Portrait); or, Love Poems and Other Verses,
   edited by Jack Werner. 1974.

Bibliography: *The Literary Career of Boswell* by Frederick A. Pottle, 1929; *The Private
Papers of Boswell from Malahide Castle: A Catalogue* by Frederick A. and M. S. Pottle, 1931.

Reading List: *The Highland Jaunt,* 1954, and *Corsica Boswell,* 1966, both by Moray
McLaren; *Boswell* by P. A. W. Collins, 1956; *Boswell's Political Career* by Frank Brady,
1965; *Boswell* by Alfred R. Brooks, 1972; *Boswell and His World* by David Daiches, 1975.

*   *   *

The appreciation of James Boswell as a figure of independent literary status has been
considerably advanced in this century by the publication of a remarkable collection of his
personal papers, following the discovery of them at Malahide Castle near Dublin and at
Fettercairn House in Kincardineshire. We now know that Boswell kept, from 1758, and
elaborately from 1762, a journal of his personal life, recording his experiences in London in
1762–63, his studies in Holland in 1763–64, his travels in Germany, Switzerland, Italy, and
France in 1764–66, and his later life in Scotland. It was Boswell's usual practice to make brief

daily memoranda of events and reflections; these were the raw materials out of which he would make, some few days later, his journals. As a consequence the journals are not merely accidental aggregations of material, but the products of a conscious process of composition. They were generally written with an audience of some kind in mind. The particularly lively London journal was written for Boswell's friend John Johnston and sent to him in weekly parcels. The journals of Boswell's continental travels show at many points Boswell's intention to make out of them a travel-book, and indeed he published, in 1768, his *Account of Corsica*, which both describes his experiences on the island and is a work of propaganda in the cause of Pasquale de Paoli's independent Corsica.

The journals are a colourful and intimate first-hand account of England, Scotland, and continental Europe in the late eighteenth century, covering a remarkable spectrum of life, from the courts of European rulers (Boswell earned the personal friendship of the Margrave of Baden-Durlach, for example) to encounters with street girls. They are also a spiritual autobiography of one of the period's most remarkable personalities, showing Boswell searching for religious truth, attempting with the most partial success to lead a moral life, fighting his melancholia, and finding in his meetings, and friendships, with such great men of his time as Johnson, Voltaire, and Rousseau models of thought and action. If the journals resemble the mid-eighteenth century novel in their explorations of individual experience (Boswell is of kin perhaps to Sterne's half-fictional Yorick), they resemble fiction too in their shaping and heightening of experience. Boswell's accounts of his interviews with Rousseau in Môtiers, and of his affair with "Louisa" in London, for example, are fully-realised actions. The recriminatory scene of parting with Louisa is a marvellous moment of comic drama, presented in animated and polished dialogue. There is in Boswell a pervading sense of the identity of life and literature: "I should live no more than I can record."

The most important experience in Boswell's life was his friendship with Samuel Johnson, and from that friendship his most important literary work arose. Boswell was only twenty-two when he first met Johnson in London in May 1763, and he lived in Johnson's company only intermittently in the twenty-one years before Johnson's death in 1784, but in the *Journal of a Tour to the Hebrides*, published as an account of the journey he had persuaded Johnson to take with him in 1773, and in the monumental *Life* of Johnson itself, he produced a biographical record which is not only scholarly and complete, but also a considerable imaginative achievement. Boswell's writings on Johnson put into practice his belief, shared with Johnson himself, that biography must include all available details: "Every thing relative to so great a man is worth observing." The *Life* and Hebridean *Journal* are together a storehouse of the opinions of Johnson on all subjects, and a portrait of the man down to the fit of his clothes and his method of eating fish. The portrait is drawn both from a variety of documentary materials, and from an ordered shaping and selection of memoranda taken at the time of the events they describe, a method essentially the same as that of the journals, though the *Life* and Hebridean narrative, as published works, are at a further stage of refinement. The Johnson here presented, though a true image of the intellect and personality of the real man, is, like the Boswell of the journals, to some extent a created persona. Shorthand notes of Johnson's conversations are reconstructed, in Boswell's version of a consistent Johnsonian style. Episodes are made dramatic, notably the meeting of Johnson with the politician John Wilkes on the 15th of May 1776, an occasion of which Boswell was himself in real life the playwright. Boswell found in Johnson a subject as interesting as himself, and, as in the journals, turned personality into art.

—Marcus Walsh

BOWEN, Elizabeth (Dorothea Cole). Irish. Born in Dublin, 7 June 1899. Educated at day school in Folkestone, and at Downe House School, Kent. Worked in a shell-shock hospital in Dublin in the last year of World War I; worked for the Ministry of Information, London, during World War II. Married Alan Charles Cameron in 1923 (died, 1952). Reviewer, *The Tatler*, 1941; Member of the Editorial Board, *London Magazine*, 1954–61. Recipient: Black Memorial Prize, 1970. D.Litt.: Trinity College, Dublin, 1948; Oxford University, 1956. Member, Irish Academy of Letters; Companion of Literature, Royal Society of Literature, 1965; Honorary Member, American Academy of Arts and Letters. C.B.E. (Commander, Order of the British Empire), 1948. *Died 22 February 1973.*

PUBLICATIONS

Fiction

Encounters: Stories. 1923.
Ann Lee's and Other Stories. 1926.
The Hotel. 1927.
Joining Charles and Other Stories. 1929.
The Last September. 1929.
Friends and Relations. 1931.
To the North. 1932.
The Cat Jumps and Other Stories. 1934.
The House in Paris. 1935.
The Death of the Heart. 1938.
Look at All Those Roses: Short Stories. 1941.
The Demon Lover and Other Stories. 1945; as *Ivy Gripped the Steps and Other Stories,* 1946.
Selected Stories, edited by R. Moore. 1946.
The Heat of the Day. 1949.
A World of Love. 1955.
Stories. 1959.
The Little Girls. 1964.
A Day in the Dark and Other Stories. 1965.
Eva Trout; or, Changing Scenes. 1969.

Plays

Anthony Trollope: A New Judgement (broadcast, 1945). 1946.
Castle Anna, with John Perry (produced 1948).

Other

Bowen's Court (family history). 1942.
English Novelists. 1942.
Seven Winters. 1942; as *Seven Winters: Memories of a Dublin Childhood,* 1943.
Why Do I Write? An Exchange of Views Between Bowen, Graham Greene, and V. S Pritchett. 1948.
Collected Impressions. 1950.
The Shelbourne: A Centre in Dublin Life for More Than a Century. 1951; as *The Shelbourne Hotel,* 1951.

A Time in Rome.   1960.
After-Thought: Pieces about Writing.   1962.
The Good Tiger (juvenile).   1965.
Pictures and Conversations.   1975.

Editor, *The Faber Book of Modern Stories.*   1937.
Editor, *Stories,* by Katherine Mansfield.   1956; as *34 Short Stories,* 1957.

Reading List: *Bowen* by Jocelyn Brooke, 1952; *Bowen: An Introduction to Her Novels* by William Heath, 1961; *Bowen* by Allan E. Austin, 1971; *Bowen* by Edwin T. Kinney, 1974; *Bowen: Portrait of a Writer* by Victoria Glendinning, 1977.

*   *   *

Elizabeth Bowen's special distinction is that, in an age of experiment and uncertainty in the technique of fiction, she continued the tradition of the nineteenth-century novel. To continue the tradition of a past age always involves the danger of forgoing originality, and writing a mere pastiche of past models. There are many eminently forgettable novels that are only Dickens-and-water. Elizabeth Bowen avoided this for several reasons. The first is her Anglo-Irish background. She wrote more about England than about Ireland; but, in her English just as much as in her Irish scenes, one is aware that the English class system, the English language, and traditional English assumptions all look a little different from the Irish shore. In particular, that special loneliness of the privileged English landowners, fond, perhaps, of the Irish people, but never fully understanding them, is a poignant presence in several of her books. It is especially strong in books, like *The Heat of the Day,* which mix English and Irish scenes. The English patriot, shut away in Ireland and hampered by Irish neutrality in the war against Hitler, is one of her most touching and original portraits.

She also balanced her traditional technique with a lively interest in the contemporary. *The Death of the Heart,* perhaps her best-remembered book, takes its point from a particular phase in the varying history of the upbringing of the adolescent girl. A Victorian girl, or one of the 1970's, could not have just the experience that Portia has. Elizabeth Bowen's work, taken as a whole, is an excellent illustration of the fact that social comedy needs to be done again in every generation, because the substance with which it deals has changed.

Finally, if her methods are partly borrowed, her characters are very much her own. Where her predecessors, even the greatest, had often used caricature in their comic and satirical scenes, she prefers understatement. Thus the magnificent managing, leisured woman in *To the North,* Lady Waters, who was "quick to detect situations that did not exist," remains always within the bounds of the credible, with many easy opportunities for obvious comedy eschewed. She is basically the same kind of woman as Dickens's Mrs. Jellyby, but she does not really much remind us of her; she is too completely credible and too firmly anchored in the inter-war years.

One of the most admirable things about Elizabeth Bowen is the way she avoided the traditional dilemma of the woman novelist – either to risk narrowness of effect by restricting herself to "feminine" and domestic subjects, or to risk unreality and overemphasis by writing about the man's world. Almost as much as Jane Austen, she avoided describing men alone together. The vast majority of her chapters are written from some feminine point of view, in that the reader is sharing the consciousness of one of the female characters. But she did not restrict herself to the domestic. Violence in Ireland, spying and treachery in wartime England, are convincingly shown, and none the less vividly because she shows a woman's view of them or their effect on a woman's life. On the whole her male characters are as well drawn as her female. This is notable, because there are some very distinguished women novelists (Mrs. Gaskell, for instance) about whom one would hesitate to say that.

In her early books, such as *The Hotel* and *Friends and Relations,* she was learning her trade. In a few detailed comic scenes they show the grasp of her more mature books, but they fail to make a convincing total impression. Her middle period, including *To the North* (her most poignant book), *The Death of the Heart*, and *The Heat of the Day* (her best-sustained and most exciting plot), is certainly her best. Her later books are not without merit, and she retains the power to make us laugh. But *A World of Love* and *The Little Girls* suffer from an over-elaborate prose style, and a tendency to linger longer on a single episode than the wisdom and interest of the comments made on it justify. The sharp impressions conveyed in earlier books are now a little blurred.

Finally, it should be noted that her short stories are an integral part of her work, and not, as in so many novelists, a kind of relaxation. In these her methods are not much different; she avoids the common technique of concentrating the whole effect in a single startling episode. The longer stories often read almost like short novels or parts of novels.

—A. O. J. Cockshut

BOWLES, Paul (Frederick). American. Born in New York City, 30 December 1910. Educated at the University of Virginia, Charlottesville, 1928–29; studied music with Aaron Copland in New York and Berlin, 1930–32, and with Virgil Thomson in Paris, 1933–34. Married the writer Jane Sydney Auer (i.e., Jane Bowles) in 1938 (died, 1973). Music Critic, *New York Herald Tribune*, 1942–46; also composer. Recipient: Guggenheim Fellowship, 1941; National Institute of Arts and Letters grant, 1950; Rockefeller grant, 1959; Translation Center grant, 1975. Since 1952 has lived in Tangier.

PUBLICATIONS

Fiction

The Sheltering Sky. 1949.
The Delicate Prey and Other Stories. 1950.
A Little Stone: Stories. 1950.
Let It Come Down. 1952.
The Spider's House. 1955.
The Hours after Noon. 1959.
A Hundred Camels in the Courtyard (stories). 1962.
Up above the World. 1966.
The Time of Friendship (stories). 1967.
Pages from Cold Point and Other Stories. 1968.
Three Tales. 1975.

Play

Senso, with Tennessee Williams, in *Two Screenplays*, by Luigi Visconti. 1970.

Screenplay: *Senso* (*The Wanton Countess*, English dialogue), with Tennessee Williams, 1949.

Verse

Scenes. 1968.
The Thicket of Spring: Poems 1926–1969. 1972.

Other

Yallah (travel). 1956.
Their Heads Are Green (travel). 1963; as *Their Heads Are Green and Their Hands Are Blue,* 1963.
Without Stopping: An Autobiography. 1972.

Editor, with Mohammed Mrabet, and Translator, *The Boy Who Set the Fire and Other Stories.* 1973.

Translator, *No Exit,* by Jean-Paul Sartre. 1946.
Translator, *The Lost Trail of the Sahara,* by Roger Frison-Roche. 1962.
Translator, *A Life Full of Holes,* by Driss ben Hamed Charhadi. 1964.
Translator, *Love with a Few Hairs,* by Mohammed Mrabet. 1967.
Translator, *The Lemon,* by Mohammed Mrabet. 1969.
Translator, *Mhashish,* by Mohammed Mrabet. 1969.
Translator, *For Bread Alone,* by Mohamed Choukri. 1974.
Translator, *Jean Genet in Tangier,* by Mohamed Choukri. 1974.
Translator, *Look and Move On,* by Mohammed Mrabet. 1975.
Translator, *Harmless Poisons, Blameless Sins,* by Mohammed Mrabet. 1976.

Reading List: "Bowles and the Natural Man" by Oliver Evans, in *Recent American Fiction,* 1963; *Bowles: The Illumination of North Africa* by Lawrence D. Stewart, 1974.

*   *   *

A prolific writer of music, Paul Bowles did not commit himself seriously to writing fiction until after the Second World War, when he was in his mid-thirties and living in New York after many years spent in North Africa. He has described the period as "the Atomic Age" (*The Sheltering Sky*), and his characters are appropriate to a period of fear and desolation – most are empty, deracinated, and hopeless, the hollow men of T. S. Eliot, as Chester Eisinger has described them (*Fiction of the Forties,* 1965).

His first novel, *The Sheltering Sky,* may be taken as typical of most of his fiction. In it, three young Americans, a married couple and a male friend, have left fashionable New York for adventure in North Africa. There, they move steadily into the Sahara, leaving their morality, sense of purpose, and identities further behind them as they move from town to town. They become separated: Porter Moresby dies of typhoid after a horrifying vision of blood and excrement; his wife, Kit, a neurotic socialite, eventually loses her sanity after living with Arabs. Only their companion, Tunner, survives, left with the task of escorting the remnant of the woman he loves back to civilization. Some critics would agree with the reaction of Doubleday, the publishers who commissioned but then rejected the novel on the grounds that it lacked coherence and purpose. It is a charge that could be brought against several of his stories, which seem full of gratuitous violence and emptiness, as well as his second novel, *Let It Come Down,* which follows the steady degeneration of a single American, Dyar, in North Africa – he too moves steadily away from civilization and morality and toward murder and violence, ending with nothing but confirmation of his basic nature.

But what such a critical response ignores is the virility and vigour of the native life that is

139

so central to Bowles's writing, which needs his apathetic Europeans and Americans to make a contrast with his vision of authenticity. Every native in his fiction is as much an individual as each European and American is not. His third novel, *The Spider's House*, is probably more successful than the first two because it gives considerable weight to such a native – Amar, the Moroccan youth who shares the story with a couple of Americans. Details and rituals of native life come into the foreground and the novel is given a liveliness and colour that is rather lacking in the others. His fourth novel, *Up above the World*, although set in Central America, is another disintegration into violence and death, and there is probably more satisfaction to be gained from Bowles's recent translations of stories told by pre-literate Moroccan story-tellers, in which the patterns of native life are once more dominant.

—Patrick Evans

———————

BOYD, James.   American.   Born in Harrisburg, Pennsylvania, 2 July 1888. Educated at Hill School, Pottstown, Pennsylvania, 1901–06; Princeton University, New Jersey 1906–10, B.A. 1910; Trinity College, Cambridge, 1910–12. Served in the New York Infantry, 1916, as a Red Cross volunteer, 1917, and in the United States Army Ambulance Service, in Italy and France, 1917–19: Lieutenant. Married Katharine Lamont in 1917; two sons and one daughter. Staff writer and cartoonist, Harrisburg *Patriot*, 1910; teacher of English and French at the Harrisburg Academy, 1912–14; Member of the editorial staff of *Country Life in America*, 1916; settled on a family farm in Southern Pines, North Carolina, 1919: Owner and Editor, *Southern Pines Pilot*, 1941–44. Founder and first National Chairman, Free Company of Players, 1941. Member, National Institute of Arts and Letters, 1937; Society of American Historians, 1939. *Died 25 February 1944.*

PUBLICATIONS

Fiction

Drums.   1925.
Marching On.   1927.
Long Hunt.   1930.
Roll River.   1933.
Bitter Creek.   1939.
Old Pines and Other Stories.   1952.

Play

One More Free Man (broadcast 1941).   In *The Free Company Presents*, 1941.

Verse

Eighteen Poems.   1944.

Other

Mr. Hugh David MacWhirr Looks after His $1.00 Investment in the Pilot Newspaper (sketches). 1943.

Editor, The Free Company Presents: A Collection of Plays about the Meaning of America. 1941.

Reading List: Boyd by David E. Whisnant, 1972.

*   *   *

In the 1920's James Boyd was in the forefront of those who set about revitalizing and reconditioning the American historical novel, which had lapsed into romantic clichés and suspect authenticity. His deliberate apprenticeship in professional writing consisted of a series of experimental short stories testing his ability to master such techniques as dialogue, mood, and setting. Though his research for sketching in the Revolutionary milieu of Drums was facilitated by the availability of archival depositories then being developed and enlarged, he went a step further by uncovering period documents on his own and by visiting the scenes about which he would write. His authoritative historicity was never questioned. But Boyd's principal contribution to the historical novel was an emphasis on a "psychological realism" overlying the romantic conventions and accuracy of detail. For example, in Drums, Boyd's most highly acclaimed work, the ambivalent loyalties of the backwoodsman Johnny Fraser during the dislocations of the American Revolution, and his slow development from an acceptance of British rule in the Colonies to his realization that change is inevitable, are never subsidiary to events, which instead are used to support the demands of characterization and motivation. From the hinterlands of North Carolina to the famed battle between the Serapis and John Paul Jones's Bonhomme Richard, the incidents of history are mere background to the novelist's multi-dimensional portrait of his hero.

In Marching On, it is from the point of view of the Confederate infantryman James Fraser, descendant of Johnny Fraser, that the Civil War is seen as "a rich man's war but a poor man's fight." In addition to such climactic chapters as that narrating James's participation in the Battle of Antietam, the novel provides social commentary in depicting and contrasting the lower segments of Southern life, Fraser's middle class, and the landed aristocrats. Often criticized is Boyd's yielding to romantic practice in allowing his hero at war's end to marry the planter's daughter. Long Hunt, though it required as much research in gathering historical minutiae as did Boyd's first two books, is more properly defined as a frontier novel of the 1790's when settlers moved from North Carolina across the mountains into Indian territory and on to the Mississippi River. Roll River was a change in pace. In it Boyd wrote from personal observation of the shifting values among four generations of a proud, wealthy family in the city of Midian (the author's native Harrisburg, Pennsylvania). Bitter Creek is a cowboy "western" to which Boyd, as in the other books, applied his gift for psychological analysis.

His biographer wrote that Boyd saw man as "first of all a creature of history whose problems had to be understood in historical depth." His books, especially the two war novels which profited from his battlefield experience in World War I, were so highly regarded as exemplary of the "new" American historical novels that their other virtues have been for the most part overlooked by readers and critics alike.

—Richard Walser

BOYD, Martin (à Beckett). Australian. Born in Lucerne, Switzerland, of Australian parents, 10 June 1893; grew up in Melbourne. Educated at Trinity Grammar School, Kew, Victoria; St. John's Theological College, Melbourne; trained as an architect, but never practised. Served as a Lieutenant in The Buffs Regiment, 1916; Observer, Royal Flying Corps, 1917; Pilot, Royal Air Force, 1918. Settled in London, 1919; member of a religious community for a time; thereafter a full-time writer; reviewer for the *Times Literary Supplement*, London, 1931–40; returned to Australia briefly, 1948, came back to England, then settled in Rome. Also a painter: one-man shows, Cambridge, 1964, Melbourne, 1967. Recipient: Australian Literary Society Gold Medal, 1928, 1956. *Died 3 June 1972.*

PUBLICATIONS

Fiction

> *Love Gods.* 1925.
> *Brangane: A Memoir.* 1926; as *The Aristocrat: A Memoir,* 1927.
> *The Montforts.* 1928; as *Madeleine Heritage,* 1928; revised edition, 1963.
> *Scandal of Spring.* 1934.
> *The Lemon Farm.* 1935.
> *The Picnic.* 1937.
> *Night of the Party.* 1938.
> *Nuns in Jeopardy.* 1940.
> *Lucinda Brayford.* 1946.
> *Such Pleasure.* 1949; as *Bridget Malwyn,* 1949.
> *The Cardboard Crown.* 1952.
> *A Difficult Young Man.* 1955.
> *Outbreak of Love.* 1957.
> *When Blackbirds Sing.* 1962.
> *The Teatime of Love: The Clarification of Miss Stilby.* 1969.

Verse

> *Retrospect.* 1920.

Other

> *The Painted Princess: A Fairy Story* (juvenile). 1936.
> *A Single Flame* (autobiography). 1939.
> *Much Else in Italy: A Subjective Travel Book.* 1958.
> *Day of My Delight* (autobiography). 1965.
> *Why They Walk Out: An Essay in Seven Parts.* 1970.

Bibliography: *Boyd* by Brenda Niall, 1978.

Reading List: *Boyd* by Kathleen Fitzpatrick, 1963; *Boyd* by Brenda Niall, 1974.

*   *   *

In Martin Boyd many literary impulses meet, but the last impression is old-fashioned. There is a *pot-pourri* fragrance in his writing, but it is a fragrance of spice, not of sentiment. His professed concern was for what he called artistic truth; but it is doubtful if he could have conceived of that without a humanizing abundance of romantic humour. Humour is with him crossed with both sympathy and criticism: he is in effect an ironist.

In him many loyalties conflict; but if there were no contradictions there would be less life and vigour in the irony. His first family inheritance was the old, basic colonial conflict: were the Australians Englishmen in exile, a stockbroker-professional-Government House aristocracy, or were they mental republicans articulating the new world? Boyd himself was capable of varying moods, as an Australian Englishman, as aesthete and sceptic, snob and anti-snob, fantasist and realist. As an artist he trusts more than most to spontaneity and intuition, believing that the imagination when truly excited cannot go seriously wrong. On the whole his style justified that trust, though his books have a certain amiable sprawl – especially the collective Langton chronicle, which, being discursively conceived, is perhaps a little too leisurely. His shorter novels are well-made; the more ambitious tend to be overburdened with material (*The Montforts, Lucinda Brayford*) or to be architecturally shaky, however full of attractive nooks and crannies. In the case of the Langton series, it is the family material itself that holds the work in proportion.

Apart from structural considerations Boyd's style is highly personal. A man of strong and at times obstinate opinions, not incapable of bias and prejudice if touched on a sensitive spot (he would hear no good, for instance, of Winston Churchill), he nevertheless possessed a humour which invariably distinguished his best writing. Perhaps, like Joseph Furphy (with whom he had little else in common), he could be called a humourist in the tradition of Sterne, Steele, or Goldsmith – or his own à Beckett great-uncle who edited *Punch*. He approves the eighteenth-century virtues, detests the eighteenth-century sins (hypocrisy, false dealing, rapacity), as well as colonial philistinism or any form of artistic insincerity. To read him as he intends, one must be able to distinguish between iniquities and peccadilloes. Austin's scandalous life with Hetty, for example, monstrous as Aunt Mildred thinks it, is not condemned because it is passionate and human; but Mildred's ("Aunt Mildew's") mean opinion is, because it is arid and insensitive. Dominic's riding his horse into the house is merely a brave and bold defiance of cold, dead convention; but Dominic's allowing the horse to die of neglect is a black mark against him. And Wolfie is condemned not for the adultery involved in sleeping with the floozy who is the "subject" of his beautiful musical tone-poems, but for being coarse enough to leave his socks on in bed.

These values may seem odd in a Melbourne context, but their conservatism is attractive and enlivening. It is one of the ways in which Boyd contrives to convey in his novels a pervading sense of continuity, something piquant in the survival of the half-forgotten past into the not-yet-too-clearly-defined present. So in effect it happens that time is always a cogent factor in Martin Boyd's imaginative world: time, that is, as a present experience, never merely as mere historical order or sequence. The essence of Boyd is imagination, sympathy, and humanity. The books have certain wandering weaknesses, but they never lack life. The truth that he sought – artistic truth – is the major cause of their never-failing warmth.

—Brian Elliott

BOYESEN, H(jalmar) H(jorth). American. Born in Frederiksvarn, Norway, 23 September 1848; emigrated to the United States, 1869. Educated at the Latin School, Dramen; Christiania Gymnasium; University of Leipzig; University of Christiania, Ph.D. 1868. Married Elizabeth Keen in 1874. Editor, Norwegian weekly *Fremad* (Forward), Chicago, 1869; Tutor in Greek and Latin, Urbana University, Ohio, 1870–73; Professor of

German, Cornell University, Ithaca, New York, 1874–80; Member of the German faculty, 1880–82, Gebhard Professor of German, 1882–90, and Professor of Germanic Languages and Literatures, 1890–95, Columbia University, New York. *Died 4 October 1895.*

PUBLICATIONS

Fiction

Gunnar: A Tale of Norse Life. 1874.
A Norseman's Pilgrimage. 1875.
Tales from Two Hemispheres. 1876.
Falconberg. 1879.
Ilka on the Hill-Top and Other Stories. 1881.
Queen Titania (stories). 1881.
A Daughter of the Philistines. 1883.
The Light of Her Countenance. 1889.
Vagabond Tales. 1889.
The Mammon of Unrighteousness. 1891.
The Golden Calf. 1892.
Social Strugglers. 1893.

Play

Alpine Roses, from his own story *Ilka on the Hill-Top* (produced 1884). 1884.

Verse

Idyls of Norway and Other Poems. 1882.

Other

Goethe and Schiller: Their Lives and Works. 1879.
The Story of Norway. 1886.
The Modern Vikings: Stories of Life and Sport in the Norseland (juvenile). 1887.
Against Heavy Odds: A Tale of Norse Heroism (juvenile). 1890.
Essays on German Literature. 1892.
Boyhood in Norway: Stories of Boy-Life in the Land of the Midnight Sun (juvenile). 1892; as *The Battle of the Rafts and Other Stories,* 1893.
Norseland Tales (juvenile). 1894.
A Commentary on the Works of Henrik Ibsen. 1894.
Literary and Social Silhouettes. 1894.
Essays on Scandinavian Literature. 1894.

Reading List: *Boyesen* by Clarence A. Glasrud, 1963; "Boyseen: Outer Success, Inner Failure" by Per Seyersted, in *Americana Norvegica 1* edited by Sigmund Skard and Henry H. Wasser, 1966.

*   *   *

H. H. Boyesen published his first novel, *Gunnar*, in 1874, five years after he came to the United States and mastered English. This romantic Norwegian idyl was influenced by Bjørnstierne Bjørnson's early fiction; Boyesen's success with this first effort was due in large part to his friendship with William Dean Howells, who helped polish the manuscript and serialized the story in the *Atlantic Monthly*. But though he was unquestionably a romantic by nature and early influence, Boyesen became a realist by conviction; with Howells he read and admired Turgenev and Tolstoy. Boyesen met Turgenev in Paris in 1873, with an introduction from a German critic; and Boyesen's second novel, *A Norseman's Pilgrimage*, was dedicated to Turgenev. Howells declined this romantically autobiographical story, warning the author that he was too hungry for publication; ten years elapsed before Turgenev approved one of the realistic stories Boyesen sent him ("A Dangerous Virtue").

Boyesen became one of America's best known teachers and lecturers. His *Goethe and Schiller*, essentially an English re-working of German scholarship and criticism, went into ten editions. His three collections of essays on German and Scandinavian literature published in the 1890's are magazine pieces, usually reprinted without revision. Boyesen was a literary journalist and popularizer, not a scholar and critic. But he was an important European-American liaison man who argued persuasively that Americans were so subservient to British literature that they ignored Goethe and Ibsen.

Boyesen's hundreds of articles, essays, and short stories show that he became "a magazinist" who depended on the income from such writing, but they also reflect his changing experience and convictions. His articles and stories on Norwegian-Americans, including the novel *Falconberg*, are not convincing because he had little contact with his fellow immigrants. But Boyesen lived in New York for fifteen years, on Fifth Avenue and at Southampton; and he was both fascinated and repelled by the social world of the newly rich.

He became sharply critical of American political and financial corruption, arguing that the American novelist was duty-bound to document and criticize American problems; and he tried to do this in such novels as *The Golden Calf* and *Social Strugglers*. For such efforts he was berated as an ungrateful foreigner and blamed for abandoning the idyllic vein of *Gunnar*. But Boyesen was consistent in his views, whether they were expressed in novels, essays, or speeches: when he died suddenly and unexpectedly in 1895, he was arguing vehemently for more realistic and responsible American fiction, citing the "high water mark" of realism established by the new Scandinavian writers.

In his long battle with the "purveyors of romance," Boyesen identified the American girl as the enemy of serious writing. She was "the Iron Madonna" who strangled the American novelist in her fond embrace, because magazine editors and book publishers knew she was the reader and arbiter they must satisfy. The beautiful, vivacious, and independent girls Boyesen found in America had fascinated him from his first arrival. He married one of them, and his subsequent efforts to augment a professor's salary by ceaseless writing and lecturing dissipated his talents and shortened his life. It seems significant that such girls frustrate their Norwegian-born admirers in his earliest fiction, dominate their parents in later stories (*A Daughter of the Philistines*), and victimize their husbands, notably in his most ambitious *Mammon of Unrighteousness*.

—Clarence A. Glasrud

BOYLE, Kay. American. Born in St. Paul, Minnesota, 19 February 1903. Studied violin at the Cincinnati Conservatory of Music, and agriculture at the Ohio Mechanics Institute, 1917–19. Married 1) Richard Brault in 1923 (divorced), one daughter; 2) Laurence Vail in 1931 (divorced, 1943), three daughters; 3) Baron Joseph von Franckenstein (died, 1963), one daughter and one son. Lived in Europe for 30 years before and after the Second World War.

Foreign Correspondent, *The New Yorker*, 1946–54. Lecturer, New School for Social Research, New York, 1962; Fellow, Wesleyan University, Middletown, Connecticut, 1963; Professor of English, San Francisco State College, 1963–72; Director, New York Writers Conference, Wagner College, New York, 1964; Fellow, Radcliffe Institute for Independent Study, Cambridge, Massachusetts, 1965; Writer-in-Residence, Hollins College, Virginia, 1970–71. Recipient: Guggenheim Fellowship, 1934, 1961; O. Henry Award, 1935, 1941; California Literary Medal Award, 1971. D. Litt.: Columbia College, Chicago, 1971. Member, National Institute of Arts and Letters, 1958. Lives in New York City.

PUBLICATIONS

Fiction

> *Short Stories.* 1929.
> *Wedding Day and Other Stories.* 1930.
> *Plagued by the Nightingale.* 1931.
> *Year Before Last.* 1932.
> *The First Lover and Other Stories.* 1933.
> *Gentlemen, I Address You Privately.* 1933.
> *My Next Bride.* 1934.
> *The White Horses of Vienna and Other Stories.* 1936.
> *Death of a Man.* 1936.
> *Monday Night.* 1938.
> *The Crazy Hunter: Three Short Novels.* 1940; as *The Crazy Hunter and Other Stories*, 1940.
> *Primer for Combat.* 1942.
> *Avalanche.* 1944.
> *Thirty Stories.* 1946.
> *A Frenchman Must Die.* 1946.
> *1939.* 1948.
> *His Human Majesty.* 1949.
> *The Smoking Mountain: Stories of Post-War Germany.* 1951.
> *The Seagull on the Step.* 1955.
> *Three Short Novels.* 1958.
> *Generation Without Farewell.* 1960.
> *Nothing Ever Breaks Except the Heart.* 1966.
> *The Underground Woman.* 1975.

Verse

> *A Statement.* 1932.
> *A Glad Day.* 1938.
> *American Citizen: Naturalized in Leadville, Colorado.* 1944.
> *Collected Poems.* 1962.
> *Testament for My Students.* 1970.

Other

> *The Youngest Camel* (juvenile). 1939; revised edition, 1959.

Breaking the Silence: Why a Mother Tells Her Son about the Nazi Era.   1962.
Pinky: The Cat Who Liked to Sleep (juvenile).   1966.
Pinky in Persia (juvenile).   1968.
Being Geniuses Together, with Robert McAlmon.   1968.
The Long Walk at San Francisco State and Other Essays.   1970.
Four Visions of America, with others.   1977.

Editor, with Laurence Vail and Nina Conarain, *365 Days.*   1936.
Editor, *The Autobiography of Emanuel Carnevali.*   1967.
Editor, *Enough of Dying! An Anthology of Peace Writings.*   1972.

Translator, *Don Juan,* by Joseph Delteil.   1931.
Translator, *Mr. Knife, Miss Fork,* by René Crevel.   1931.
Translator, *The Devil in the Flesh,* by Raymond Radiguet.   1932.

Acted as ghost-writer for the books *Relations and Complications, Being the Recollections of H. H. the Dayang Muda of Sarawak,* by Gladys Palmer Brooke, 1929, and *Yellow Dusk,* by Bettina Bedwell, 1937.

Reading List: "Boyle" by Richard C. Carpenter, in *College English 15,* November 1953; "Boyle's Fiction" by Harry T. Moore, in *Kenyon Review,* Spring 1960.

*   *   *

What is most memorable in Kay Boyle's fiction are specific scenes – the sight of the sea tide building and crashing through the mouth of a river; a young man, sick with tuberculosis, leaning over a basin to vomit blood; a bus-driver arguing recklessly with his passengers while the bus careens along a cliff road; a run-over dog pulling itself forward, as its spilled-out entrails drag and turn white in the dust; Americans and Germans waiting over real fox holes in a German forest, ready to club the young foxes as they come out, and underground, moving through the tunnels, now near, now distant, the sound of the yelping pack and pursuing dog.

Miss Boyle's concern here is to heighten our responses to these events. She asks us not only to respond to the vivid and extreme sensations which they present, but to see them in sharp moral and aesthetic terms, as beautiful or dangerous or agonizingly brutal.

It is this intense kind of involvement that Miss Boyle asks from us generally. She offers very little neutral ground on which we may look at these scenes on our own. The youthful idealists, who play a major role in her novels, will give us, I think, the right emotional cues for appreciating her work. Inexperienced in the ways of the world, their feelings are open and unmitigated; they do not quite believe in evil and yet they are deeply troubled by pain and injustice. Bridget, Victoria John, Mary Farrant, Milly Roberts – young Americans whose destinies are connected with Europe – are such figures. If the fictional situation would seem to echo James, there are major differences in its development, for Kay Boyle's morality is active rather than introspective.

Indeed, whether her heroes be young Americans in Europe or former German soldiers, they express themselves in concrete acts. What her heroes have in common is the courage to act – it is the only thing people ever remember, one character says. But action is, of course, no guarantee of success. Involved in every human venture, it would seem, are elements that bring about its destruction. Those elements may be physical in nature – not malevolent but merely indifferent – stupid accident, or man's incapacity to make a social world that is supportive and helpful.

Thus, in *Plagued by the Nightingale,* the closely-bound world of a French family becomes so destructive that three daughters and a son wait desperately for an escape. Only Charlotte, the fourth daughter, loves her richly domestic life and her place within the family; and only Charlotte is deprived of it by death. In *Year Before Last*, Martin, a young poet, dying of tuberculosis, and Eve, his aunt, are bound together by their dedication to art. Yet the emotion that shapes their lives is Eve's cruel jealousy of Hanah, whom Martin loves and who would shield him from the agonies of poverty and illness. In *My Next Bride*, the artist, Sorrel, uses the common funds of the art colony to buy a magnificent and expensive automobile. In this shallow attempt to escape poverty and ugliness, he betrays the destitute craftsmen who work for him, as well as the artistic creed he has professed to live by.

Miss Boyle's novels have, I think, a potentially tragic feeling. The qualities she projects in her strongest characters – courage to act as a counter to failure, energy rather than hopeless despair – offer this possibility. Very often, it seems wasted, for although Miss Boyle insists upon courageous action, the possible choices she sees in such action are limited. Also, perhaps equally harmful, these choices do not necessarily grow out of the fictional situation; they seem fixed from the beginning. It is for this reason, perhaps, that her characters sometimes take unreal positions – in *Avalanche*, the mountain men are total in their dedication to a good cause, the German agent, total in his dedication to a bad one; in *The Seagull on the Step*, the doctor commits melodramatic villanies, the teacher-reformer, heroic deeds; in *Generation Without Farewell*, the American colonel is brutal and gross, his wife and daughter are gentle and sensitive. Such extreme divisions in realistic novels are unconvincing.

What gives her work strength is but her understanding that our human connections lie finally in our limitations, most of all in our common mortality. From the beginning, she has had this kind of knowledge.

At moments we see it expressed with startling clarity. In her first novel, Charlotte's family is hastily called to her bedside. Those who have waited through the day – Charlotte's young children, her sisters – make their way through the dark, wet fall night, to Charlotte's house, up the great stairs and to her room. There, they wait in silence until the door is opened, and the children walk "calmly into the roar of Charlotte's death." In her most recent novel of post-war Germany, a power shovel in downtown Frankfurt accidentally unearths an underground air raid shelter and releases a single survivor, entombed there since the war. As the mad, tattered figure runs wildly across the upturned ground, bewildered by his resurrection, any ideals we may hold about nationality, military success, moral justification, diminish into nothingness. Only a sense of our common inhumanity persists.

—Jacqueline Hoefer

BOYLE, Roger; Baron Broghill; 1st Earl of Orrery.   Irish.   Born in Lismore, 25 April 1621. Educated at Trinity College, Dublin; may have studied at Oxford University. Married Lady Margaret Howard in 1641; two sons and five daughters. Travelled in France and Italy for several years after leaving university, then went to England, and commanded the Earl of Northumberland's troops in the Scottish expedition; returned home to Ireland at the time of the rebellion, 1641: under the Earl of Cork took part in the defence of Lismore, and held a command at the battle of Liscarrol, 1642; served under the parliamentarians, 1647–48, but continued to support the Royalist, and later the Restoration, cause, until offered a general's command by Cromwell in the war against the Irish, 1650; after the defeat of the Irish appointed Governor of Munster, and given control of various estates in Ireland, including Blarney Castle; served the Commonwealth government as Member of Parliament for Cork, 1654, and for Edinburgh, 1656, as Lord President of the Council, 1656, as a Member of the House of Lords, 1657, and as one of Cromwell's special council; after death of Cromwell concluded that Richard Cromwell's attempts to consolidate the government were hopeless: obtained command of Munster, and with Sir Charles Coote, secured Ireland for Charles II; served as Lord President of Munster until 1668; appointed a Lord Justice of Ireland, 1660; Member of Parliament for Arundel, 1661; impeached by the House of Commons for taxing without the king's authority, 1668, which proceedings were stopped by the King's proroguing Parliament. Created Baron Broghill, 1627; Earl of Orrery, 1660. *Died 16 October 1679.*

PUBLICATIONS

Collections

   Dramatic Works, edited by William S. Clark, II.   2 vols., 1937.

Fiction

   Parthenissa.   6 vols., 1654–69.
   English Adventures.   1676.
   The Martyrdom of Theodora and Didymus.   1687.

Plays

   The General (as *Altamire,* produced 1663; as *The General,* produced 1664).   Edited by
      J. O. Halliwell, 1853.
   Henry the Fifth (produced 1664).   With *Mustapha,* 1668.
   Mustapha, Son of Solyman the Magnificent (produced 1665).   With *Henry the Fifth,*
      1668; edited by Bonamy Dobrée, in *Five Heroic Plays,* 1960.
   The Black Prince (produced 1667).   In *Two New Tragedies,* 1669.
   Tryphon (produced 1668).   In *Two New Tragedies,* 1669.
   Guzman (produced 1669).   1693.
   Mr. Anthony (produced 1669).   1690.
   Herod the Great, in *Six Plays.*   1694.
   King Saul.   1703.
   Zoroastres, in *Dramatic Works.*   1937.

Verse

   Poems on Most of the Festivals of the Church.   1681.

Other

   A Treatise of the Art of War.   1677.
   A Collection of the State Letters.   1742.

Reading List: "An Unheroic Dramatist" by Graham Greene, in *The Lost Childhood and Other Essays,* 1951; *Boyle* by Kathleen M. Lynch, 1965.

*   *   *

Despite the opinion of Graham Greene – "Roger Boyle ... is one of the great bores of literature" – the First Earl of Orrery remains a fascinating representative of Cavalier culture. Nobleman, statesman, servant of the Stuart kings and of Cromwell, he also found time to pursue a career as a man of letters. His plays, which include the first important attempts to introduce rhymed heroic tragedy on the English stage, were admired by Dryden and Davenant, and retained some popularity after the Restoration.

His contemporaries also knew him as the author of a work which has proved less accessible to posterity – *Parthenissa,* one of the earliest and best English experiments with long heroic romance in the manner of such French salon-writers as La Calprenède and the de Scudérys. Orrery points out in his Preface that the book is a deliberate amalgam of history and fiction, real and imaginary people, because "Historyes are for the most Part but mixt Romances, and yet the Pure Romance Part, may be as Instructive as, if not more than, the Historicall." Like its French models, *Parthenissa* interlaces pseudo-philosophical dialogues on Platonic love and honour with descriptions of action – the pageantry of tournaments, and battles on land and sea. It is structured around the intersecting stories of four pairs of high-born lovers, of whom Parthenissa and Artabanes are the most important. The couples assemble at the Temple of Hierophanus in Syria to consult the oracle, and there exchange tales of trials in love and friendship, and hazards in war, in a prose which, though sometimes florid, often has a pleasing dignity and serenity. Orrery's aim was to bring all of his lovers to felicity, but the romance remained unfinished, and only one of the stories is resolved.

—J. C. Hilson

BRACKENRIDGE, Hugh Henry. American. Born in Kintyre, near Campbeltown, Argyll, Scotland, in 1748; emigrated with his family to a farm in York County, Pennsylvania, 1753. Educated at the College of New Jersey, now Princeton University, 1768–71, B.A. 1771, M.A. 1774; studied law under Samuel Chase in Annapolis, Maryland, 1780. Chaplain in Washington's army during the Revolutionary War, 1776–78. Married 1) Miss Montgomery in 1785, one son; 2) Sabina Wolfe in 1790, two sons and one daughter. Teacher in the public school in Gunpowder Falls, Maryland, 1763–67, and at Somerset Academy, Back Creek, Maryland, 1772; Founding Editor, *United States Magazine,* Philadelphia, 1779; moved to Pittsburgh, and practised law there, 1781–99: Founder, *Pittsburgh Gazette,* 1786; Pennsylvania State Assemblyman, 1786–88; established Pittsburgh Academy, 1787, and the first bookshop in Pittsburgh, 1789; Justice of the Pennsylvania Supreme Court, 1799–1816. *Died 25 June 1816.*

PUBLICATIONS

Collections

A Brackenridge Reader, edited by Daniel Marder.   1970.

Fiction

> *Modern Chivalry.*   6 vols., 1792–1805; revised edition, 1815, 1819; edited by Claude
> Milton Newlin, 1937.

Plays

> *The Battle of Bunkers Hill.*   1776.
> *The Death of General Montgomery at the Siege of Quebec.*   1777.

Verse

> *A Poem on the Rising Glory of America,* with Philip Freneau.   1772.
> *A Poem on Divine Revelation.*   1774.
> *An Epistle to Walter Scott.*   1811(?).

Other

> *Six Political Discourses Founded on the Scriptures.*   1778.
> *An Eulogium of the Brave Men Who Have Fallen in the Contest with Great
> Britain.*   1779.
> *Incidents of the Insurrection in the Western Parts of Pennsylvania in 1794.*   1795; edited
> by Daniel Marder, 1972.
> *The Standard of Liberty.*   1802.
> *Gazette Publications* (miscellany).   1806.
> *Law Miscellanies.*   1814.

> Editor, *Narratives of a Late Expedition Against the Indians.*   1783.

Bibliography: in *Bibliography of American Literature* by Jacob Blanck, 1955.

Reading List: *The Life and Writings of Brackenridge* by Claude Milton Newlin, 1932;
Brackenridge by Daniel Marder, 1967.

*   *   *

Although Hugh Henry Brackenridge wrote in a number of different genres – poetry,
drama, and non-fictional prose – his one real claim to our attention today is for the first part
of *Modern Chivalry,* an extended piece of satiric fiction published in four volumes between
1792 and 1797. It can hardly be called a novel. The narrative line is thin, merely holding
together a series of episodes involving a modern American Quixote, Captain John Farrago,
and his Irish servant, Teague O'Regan, as they travel together on the western frontier and
later visit the city of Philadelphia. It moves toward no climax in either plot or meaning, but
merely illustrates through their adventures various failings of American democracy.

But if *Modern Chivalry* is weak in both narrative and thematic development, it is strong in
its realistic pictures of frontier life and manners – exaggerated though they may be for satiric
purposes – and in the simple, straightforward style through which both the incidents and the
authorial discussions of them are presented. Various kinds of dialect – Irish, Scotch, and
Negro – are well reproduced in its pages, and, though the characters may not be fully
developed, they are sharply and skillfully sketched through their language and actions. Thus,
the book has often been justly praised as an early piece of American realism.

It is also important for what it has to say about the theory and practice of American democracy. Most of the satire is directed against the Teague O'Regans, ignorant and ambitious men who are eager to accept honors and positions for which they are not qualified, and against an electorate that will put such men in office. But the book is not anti-democratic. It attacks as well those men of wealth or inherited position who are no more suited to rule, and members of organizations who admit unqualified persons to their ranks. What the book affirms is the basic principle of democracy: that positions of leadership should be given only to men of ability and integrity, qualities that may appear at any level of society, but which must be developed through education.

Only this first part is wholly successful. Brackenridge published the second in 1804–05 and extended the work yet again in the edition of 1815. His satiric touch was gone, however, and with it much of the charm of the book. The second part even lacks the narrative line of the first and becomes, in effect, an endlessly redundant lecture. It more than doubles the size of *Modern Chivalry*, but it does not add appreciably to what Brackenridge had accomplished in the 1790's.

—Donald A. Ringe

BRADDON, Mary Elizabeth. English. Born in London, 4 October 1835. Educated privately. Lived with the publisher John Maxwell in the 1860's, married him in 1874 (died); two daughters and three sons, including the novelists W. B Maxwell and Gerald Maxwell. Appeared on the stage during the 1850's as Mary Seaton; full-time writer from 1860; became wealthy as a result of the success of *Lady Audley's Secret*, 1862; contributed to various London magazines, and edited *Belgravia* from 1866, the *Belgravia Annual* from 1867, and the *Mistletoe Bough*, 1878–92. *Died 4 February 1915.*

PUBLICATIONS

Fiction

Three Times Dead; or, The Secret of the Heath. 1854; as *The Trail of the Serpent*, 1861.
The Lady Lisle. 1861.
The Captain of the Vulture. 1862.
Lady Audley's Secret. 1862.
Ralph the Bailiff and Other Tales. 1862; augmented edition, 1866(?).
Eleanor's Victory. 1863.
Aurora Floyd. 1863.
John Marchmont's Legacy. 1863.
The Doctor's Wife. 1864.
Henry Dunbar: The Story of an Outcast. 1864.
Only a Clod. 1865.
Sir Jasper's Tenant. 1865.
The Lady's Mile. 1866.
Birds of Prey. 1867.

Rupert Godwin. 1867.
Dead-Sea Fruit. 1868.
Charlotte's Inheritance. 1868.
Run to Earth. 1868.
Fenton's Quest. 1871.
The Lovels of Arden. 1871.
Robert Ainsleigh. 1872.
To the Bitter End. 1872.
Lucius Davoren; or, Publicans and Sinners. 1873.
Milly Darrell and Other Tales. 1873.
Strangers and Pilgrims. 1873.
Taken at the Flood. 1874.
Lost for Love. 1874.
Hostages to Fortune. 1875.
A Strange World. 1875.
Dead Men's Shoes. 1876.
Joshua Haggard's Daughter. 1876.
The Black Band; or, Mysteries of Midnight. 1877.
Weavers and Weft and Other Tales. 1877.
An Open Verdict. 1878.
The Cloven Foot. 1879.
Vixen. 1879.
Just As I Am. 1880.
The Story of Barbara. 1880.
Asphodel. 1881.
Mount Royal. 1882.
Flower and Weed. 1882.
Phantom Fortune. 1883.
Married in Haste. 1883.
The Golden Calf. 1883.
Under the Red Flag. 1883.
Flower and Weed and Other Tales. 1884.
Ishmael. 1884; as *An Ishmaelite*, 1884.
Wyllard's Weird. 1885.
One Thing Needful, and Cut by the County. 1886.
Mohawks. 1886.
Like and Unlike. 1887.
The Fatal Three. 1888.
The Day Will Come. 1889.
One Life, One Love. 1890.
Gerard; or, The World, The Flesh, and the Devil. 1891.
The Venetians. 1892.
All along the River (stories). 1893.
Thou Art the Man. 1894.
The Christmas Hirelings. 1894.
Sons of the Fire. 1895.
London Pride; or, When the World Was Younger. 1896.
Under Love's Rule. 1897.
Rough Justice. 1898.
In High Places. 1898.
His Darling Sin. 1899.
The Infidel: A Story of the Great Revival. 1900.
The Conflict. 1903.
A Lost Eden. 1904.

    The Rose of Life. 1905.
    The White House. 1906.
    Her Convict. 1907.
    Dead Love Has Chains. 1907.
    During Her Majesty's Pleasure. 1908.
    Our Adversary. 1909.
    Beyond These Voices. 1910.
    The Green Curtain. 1911.
    Miranda. 1913.
    Mary. 1916.

Plays

    The Loves of Arcadia (produced 1860).
    The Model Husband (produced 1868).
    Griselda; or, The Patient Wife (produced 1873).
    Genevieve (produced 1874).
    The Missing Witness. 1880.
    Dross; or, The Root of Evil. 1882.
    Married Beneath Him. 1882.
    Marjorie Daw. 1882.
    For Better, For Worse (produced 1890).

Verse

    Garibaldi and Other Poems. 1861.

Other

    Boscastle, Cornwall: An English Engadine. 1881.

    Editor, *The Summer Tourist: A Book for Long and Short Journeys.* 1871.
    Editor, *Aladdin; or, The Wonderful Lamp.* 1880.

Reading List: *Things Past* by Michael Sadleir, 1944; *The Novels of Braddon* by B. M. Nyberg (unpublished dissertation, University of Colorado), 1965; *A Literature of Their Own* by Elaine Showalter, 1977; *Sensational Victorian: The Life and Fiction of Braddon* by Robert Lee Wolff, 1978 (includes bibliography).

*   *   *

    Mary Elizabeth Braddon's literary career spanned nearly sixty years and included the publication of more than seventy novels under her own name, a large quantity of anonymous and pseudonymous work, and the editorship of several periodicals, most notably *Belgravia*; but it was as the author of a single immensely popular novel, *Lady Audley's Secret*, that she was primarily famous among her contemporaries and is remembered today.
    Along with Wilkie Collins's *The Woman in White* and Mrs. Henry Wood's *East Lynne*, *Lady Audley's Secret* inaugurated the vogue of the Sensation Novel, a controversial sub-genre that dominated the popular fiction of the 1860's. Initially, some reviewers applauded the exciting, well-made plots characteristic of the form, but as the decade progressed they

became increasingly critical of the Sensation Novel's plot-dominance, its emphasis on crime and encouragement of sympathy for morally ambiguous characters, and its lack of realism despite its contemporary settings. Miss Braddon was especially criticized for the lurid melodrama of her work and her relatively frank depiction of passionate and criminal women; and, indeed, of all the Sensation Novelists she gave hostile reviewers the most opportunities, publishing seventeen novels, almost all of them sensational, in eight years. This extraordinary productivity stemmed in part from an abundant creative energy which characterized Miss Braddon's entire career, but it was also due at least in part to the sensational quality of her private life. Her relationship with John Maxwell, an enterprising publisher with five children and a wife in an asylum, involved her in his financial difficulties throughout the mid-1860's.

After 1870, Miss Braddon's domestic life (she and Maxwell were able to marry in 1874) and her novels assumed a calmer character. The humor, sharp social observation, and interest in character, only intermittent in her early work, became the leading characteristics of the later. Observing this, Michael Sadleir has argued that Miss Braddon was more than a "mere sensationalist," and that her reputation was distorted by her youthful success. In his excellent dissertation, the most extended discussion of Miss Braddon's work, B. M. Nyberg contends that her Sensation Novels are neither her best nor, considering her career as a whole, her most characteristic work; he points to *The Infidel* among her historical novels, *Strangers and Pilgrims* among her novels of manners, and *The Rose of Life* among her character novels as a more suitable basis for her literary reputation. Sadleir and Nyberg are surely right that Miss Braddon's early fame obscured her later achievement; but it is also true that her early novels attracted attention and praise from readers as diverse as Thackeray, Rossetti, Robert Louis Stevenson, and the middle-class patrons of Mudie's, and that *Lady Audley's Secret*, which helped to establish an important sub-genre and a new feminine type, perhaps understandably secured her place in literary history.

—Randolph Ivy

BRADFORD, Roark. American. Born in Lauderdale County, Tennessee, 21 August 1896. Educated in local schools. Served in the Artillery Reserve of the United States Army, 1917–20: Lieutenant; United States Navy Reserve, assigned to the Bureau of Aeronautics Training Literature Division, Navy Department, Washington, D.C., 1942–45. Married Mary Rose Himler; one son. Reporter, Atlanta *Georgian*, 1920–22, *Telegraph*, Macon, Georgia, 1923, and the *Daily Advertiser*, Lafayette, Louisiana, 1923; Night City Editor, later Sunday Editor, *Times Picayune*, New Orleans, 1924–26; full-time writer from 1929. Recipient: O. Henry Award, 1927. Member, National Institute of Arts and Letters. *Died 13 November 1948*.

PUBLICATIONS

Fiction

Ol' Man Adam an' His Chillun. 1928.
This Side of Jordan. 1929.

155

Ol' King David and the Philistine Boys.   1930.
John Henry.   1931.
Kingdom Coming.   1933.
Let the Band Play Dixie and Other Stories.   1934.
The Three-Headed Angel.   1937.

Plays

How Come Christmas: A Modern Morality.   1930.
John Henry, music by Jacques Wolfe, from the story by Bradford.   1939.

Other

The Green Roller (miscellany).   1949.

*   *   *

To read the stories and novels of Roark Bradford is to enter into a world separated from us by time, space, and especially by temperament. In his depiction of the life on southern plantations, the white man's world fades into the background, becoming no more nor less important than the plowing of fields or the picking of cotton. Bradford wrote of the southern black out of a deep respect and love, which, coupled with his uncanny gift for imitating dialectical speech, makes his writing altogether unique in a white man.

Bradford turned to writing full-time in 1927, concerning himself not with philosophical or moral evalutions of the Negro's life, but rather with the reality of his situation, and the problems of coping with it. His prose, like his characters, is simple and direct, even childlike, but never sentimental. Death can come quickly and unromantically to them, and when it does, they face it with the deep faith that was a part of the author himself, up until his death in 1948.

Above all, "Brad" was a storyteller. His work vibrates with the strong, simple rhythms of speech, whether in his realistic novels or in his modern myths like *John Henry*: "The night John Henry was born the moon was copper-colored and the sky was black.... Forked lightning cleaved the air and the earth trembled like a leaf. The panthers squalled in the brake like a baby and the Mississippi ran upstream a thousand miles."

Bradford won the O. Henry prize in 1927 with his second published short story, "Child of God." His retelling of Biblical stories, *Ol' Man Adam and His Chillun*, was adapted for the stage by Marc Connelly, and became the highly successful play *The Green Pastures*.

—Walter Bode

BRAINE, John (Gerard).   English.   Born in Bradford, Yorkshire, 13 April 1922. Educated at St. Bede's Grammar School, Bradford; Leeds School of Librarianship, A.L.A. 1949. Served as a telegraphist in the Royal Navy, 1942–43. Married Helen Patricia Wood in 1955; one son and three daughters. Assistant Librarian, Bingley, Yorkshire Public Library, 1940–51; freelance writer in London and Yorkshire, 1951–54; Branch Librarian, Northumberland County Library, 1954–56, and West Riding County Library at Darton, 1956–57. Full-time writer since 1957. Toured the United States, 1959, 1964. Member, BBC North Regional Advisory Council, 1960–64. Lives in Woking, Surrey.

PUBLICATIONS

Fiction

> *Room at the Top.* 1957.
> *The Vodi* 1959; as *From the Hand of the Hunter*, 1960.
> *Life at the Top.* 1962.
> *The Jealous God.* 1964.
> *The Crying Game.* 1968.
> *Stay with Me till Morning.* 1970; as *The View from Tower Hill*, 1971.
> *The Queen of a Distant Country.* 1972.
> *The Pious Agent.* 1975.
> *Waiting for Sheila.* 1976.
> *The Only Game in Town.* 1976.
> *Finger of Fire.* 1977.

Plays

> *The Desert in the Mirror* (produced 1951).

> Television Plays: *Man at the Top* series, 1970, 1972; *Waiting for Sheila*, 1977; *Queen of a Distant Country*, 1978.

Other

> *Writing a Novel.* 1974.
> *J. B. Priestley.* 1978.

Reading List: *Braine* by James W. Lee, 1968.

*   *   *

John Braine's powerful first novel, *Room at the Top*, made its young author relatively rich and famous. The internationally successful motion picture it became put him at the very top and, in a sense, he has been trying to hold on to his place there ever since.

Room at the Top probed and evaluated a problem still persisting in Britain: the class struggle. Braine's working-class hero, Joe Lampton, is the creation of the post-World War II British welfare state. He reaches for his piece of the pie and gets it, but his triumph turns sour as he becomes aware that he has achieved success at the expense of his self-respect. A sad rather than "angry" young man, Lampton metamorphoses, somewhat like John Braine, into a conservative, tradition-respecting person. Notable in *Room at the Top* is Braine's careful picture of Great Britain in the late 1940's and early 1950's. His sense of locale, revealed in the details of West Riding, its industry and millionaires, its speech and values, is superb. His style here, as in some of his early writing, seems pointedly American in its emphasis on taut dialogue and on the Americanized culture of post-war Britain (Cadillacs and Coca-Colas). His involvement with the tangible – everything with a hard, clear edge – shows.

While Braine's first novel was preoccupied with success, his second (and favorite), *The Vodi*, is a study in failure. Neither widely acclaimed nor read, it has, indeed, more weaknesses than strengths. Its *leitmotiv* – that man must accept responsibility if he is to reap reward – is banal; its flashbacks are clumsy; its pace is interrupted by too many shifts in focus.

Life at the Top continues the story of Joe Lampton. After its publication, many readers and critics felt that Braine's career had begun to show a disconcerting resemblance to that of John O'Hara who, in his preoccupation with wealth, sex, class, and a boozy kind of religiosity, tended to keep rewriting his first book. But Braine's reputation was partly salvaged with *The Jealous God*. Himself "a cradle Catholic," Braine wrote a novel excellent in its exposition of Irish-Catholic life in Protestant Yorkshire. In *The Crying Game* Braine further exhibits stress in developing new material. Significantly influenced by Graham Greene, it concerns both the honestly and dishonestly corrupt. In the end, honesty and sentimentality about middle-class, provincial, Catholic virtues prevail.

The distance, philosophically, socially, and stylistically, from *Room at the Top* to *The Crying Game* is not very great. Two later novels, *Stay with Me till Morning* and *The Queen of a Distant Country*, have not added to or detracted from Braine's reputation as a writer. They have signaled, however, a definite shift to the right: a sharper contempt for progressives and an ongoing enthusiasm for materialism. If Braine has not fulfilled his early promise, he has continued vital, strong as a stylist, and expert in relating his characters to their settings.

—Edward Martin Potoker

BROMFIELD, Louis. American. Born in Mansfield, Ohio, 27 December 1896. Educated at Cornell University Agricultural College, Ithaca, New York, 1914–15; School of Journalism, Columbia University, New York, 1916, honorary war degree 1920. Served in the American Ambulance Corps, with the 34th and 168th divisions of the French Army, 1917–19: Croix de Guerre. Married Mary Appleton Wood in 1921 (died, 1952); three daughters. Reporter, City News Service and Associated Press, New York, 1920–22; Editor and/or Critic for *Musical America*, *The Bookman*, and *Time*, also worked as an assistant to a theatrical producer and as Advertising Manager of Putnam's, publishers, all New York, 1922–25; lived in Senlis, France, 1925–38; settled on a farm in Richland County, Ohio, 1939, and lived there until his death. President, Emergency Committee for the American Wounded in Spain,1938. Director, United States Chamber of Commerce. Recipient: Pulitzer Prize, 1927. LL.D: Marshall College, Huntington, West Virginia; Parsons College, Fairfield, Iowa; Litt.D.: Ohio Northern University, Ada. Chevalier, Legion of Honor, 1939. Member, National Institute of Arts and Letters. *Died 18 March 1956.*

PUBLICATIONS

Fiction

The Green Bay Tree. 1924.
Possession. 1925; as *Lilli Barr*, 1926.
Early Autumn. 1926.
A Good Woman. 1927.
The Strange Case of Miss Annie Spragg. 1928.
Awake and Rehearse (stories). 1929.
Tabloid News (stories). 1930.
Twenty-Four Hours. 1930.

A Modern Hero. 1932.
The Farm. 1933.
Here Today and Gone Tomorrow: Four Short Novels. 1934.
The Man Who Had Everything. 1935.
It Had to Happen. 1936.
The Rains Came: A Novel of Modern India. 1937.
It Takes All Kinds (omnibus). 1939.
Night in Bombay. 1940.
Wild Is the River. 1941.
Until the Day Break. 1942.
Mrs. Parkington. 1943.
Bitter Lotus. 1944.
What Became of Anna Bolton. 1944.
The World We Live In: Stories. 1944.
Colorado. 1947.
Kenny. 1947.
McLeod's Folly. 1948.
The Wild Country. 1948.
Mr. Smith. 1951.

Plays

The House of Women, from his novel The Green Bay Tree (produced 1927).
DeLuxe, with John Gearnon (produced 1934).
Times Have Changed (produced 1935).

Screenplay: Brigham Young – Frontiersman, with Lamar Trotti, 1940.

Other

The Work of Robert Nathan. 1927.
England, A Dying Oligarchy. 1939.
Pleasant Valley. 1945.
A Few Brass Tacks. 1946.
Malabar Farm. 1948.
Out of the Earth. 1950.
The Wealth of the Soil. 1952.
A New Pattern for a Tired World. 1954.
From My Experience: The Pleasures and Miseries of Life on a Farm. 1955.
Animals and Other People. 1955.
Walt Disney's Vanishing Prairie. 1956(?).

Reading List: Bromfield and His Books by Morrison Brown, 1956; Bromfield by David D. Anderson, 1964.

*   *   *

One of the most promising young American novelists of the 1920's, Louis Bromfield fell into critical disfavor in the early 1930's, a condition that prevailed until his death in 1956, in spite of a continued prodigious production of novels and short stories and a remarkable popular success. To assess his contributions to American literature is not difficult; the many literary shortcomings that prevented the fulfillment of his early literary promise are sufficient to keep him out of the first rank of American novelists. But at the same time he deserves a better literary fate than he has received: his effective style, his character portrayal, and his narrative technique are consistently strong, and his interpretations of American life are effective and intelligent.

The themes with which he dealt are significant: the decline of American individualism and agrarian democracy and the growth of industrialism; the unique role of the strong woman in American life; the egalitarian philosophy that permits a young person to rise above his origins. In his use of them in his work he came close to the essence of American life as thoughtful Americans know it. That he did not go on to chronicle the rise of an industrial democracy, as the Marxist critics of the 1930's demanded, but attempted instead to return to the past, contributed to the demise of his reputation, but it resulted in some of his best works, those in which he develops his major themes effectively as he reiterates the values upon which the country was built and emphasizes the need to return to those values in an increasingly materialistic age.

Among his substantial literary contributions must be included his four panel novels, *The Green Bay Tree*, *Possession*, *Early Autumn*, and *A Good Woman*, which document in human terms the impact of sweeping social changes and perverted values in the early years of this century. These novels also illustrate his literary talents: a forthright, literate style; character portrayal that is human and intense; and a strong narrative technique. To these novels must be added *The Farm*, his best single work, *Twenty-Four Hours*, a remarkably controlled work in spite of its lapses, and *The Rains Came*, the most dramatic and philosophically unified of his work. Of his later work, *Mrs. Parkington* is an intensely human portrait of a magnificent American woman, and *The Wild Country* comes close to a definitive expression of the American Midwestern experience in transition from frontier to civilization.

One must recognize, too, his contributions to the literature of nature, folklore, and agriculture. Most of the best of his folklore and nature writing is included in *Animals and Other People*, while *Pleasant Valley* and *Malabar Farm* indicate what technical writing may achieve when it is lively, imaginative, and literate.

Unfortunately, Bromfield still suffers from the fact that he has received little objective criticism. The unfair criticisms of the early 1930's have discouraged later critics from looking at his work clearly and coherently. He wrote too well too easily, and his early critical and commercial successes proved ultimately to be adverse. But in almost all of his work he wrote well and he constructed human, memorable characters and situations. These are not common abilities in any age.

—David D. Anderson

BRONTË, Anne. English. Born in Thornton, Yorkshire, 17 March 1820; sister of Charlotte Brontë, *q.v.*, and Emily Brontë, *q.v.*; moved with her family to Haworth, Yorkshire, 1820, and lived there for the rest of her life. Educated at home, and at Miss Wooler's School, Roehead, later at Dewsbury Moor, Yorkshire, 1835–37. Governess to the Ingham family at Blake Hall, 1839, and to the Robinson family at Thorpe Green, 1841–45. *Died 28 May 1849.*

PUBLICATIONS

Collections

> *Complete Poems*, edited by C. K. Shorter.   1923.
> *The Shakespeare Head Brontë*, edited by T. J. Wise and J. A. Symington.   19 vols.,
>   1932–38.

Fiction

> *Agnes Grey*, with *Wuthering Heights*, by Emily Brontë.   1847; edited by Herbert Van
>   Thal, 1966.
> *The Tenant of Wildfell Hall.*   1848.

Verse

> *Poems*, with Charlotte and Emily Brontë.   1846.
> *Self-Communion*, edited by T. J. Wise.   1900.
> *Dreams and Other Poems.*   1917.

Bibliography: *A Bibliography of the Writings in Prose and Verse of the Brontë Family* by T. J. Wise, 1917.

Reading List: *Brontë* by Winifred Gérin, 1959; *Brontë* by Ada Harrison and Derek Stanford, 1959. For other works, see the entry for Charlotte Brontë.

*   *   *

But for the impetus given her by her sisters' example, Anne Brontë might never have sought self-expression in writing fiction. As a child, led on by the enthusiasm of her favourite sister, Emily, she joined in writing some of the "Gondal" saga scripts; but her true talent lay in poetry, for which she had a life-long love. Mostly written in the prosody of hymns, and influenced by the thought and style of Cowper and Wordsworth, her favourite poets, she made no claim to originality. Writing poetry was for her the most natural outlet for the two strongest emotions of her life: religion and her love of Nature. She found consolation for the trials and sorrows of her life in the one; and her keenest joy in the other. The lines "Written on a Windy Day" are not only typical of her simple, unforced style, but evidence of her close observation of Nature's moods:

> My soul is awakened, my spirit is soaring
> And carried aloft on the wings of the breeze;
> For above and around me the wild wind is roaring,
> Arousing to rapture the earth and the seas.
>
> The long withered grass in the sunshine is glancing,
> The bare trees are tossing their branches on high;
> The dead leaves, beneath them, are merrily dancing,
> The white clouds are scudding across the blue sky.

161

> I wish I could see how the ocean is lashing
> The foam of its billows to whirlwinds of spray;
> I wish I could see how its proud waves are dashing
> And hear the roar of their thunder to-day!

Life dealt hardly with her: William Weightman, the man she could have loved and married, died young of cholera, and she mourned his loss in some memorably haunting lines that have found their place in the anthologies. Hers was a naturally elegiac talent.

Her first novel, *Agnes Grey*, was the relation of her experiences in her two posts as governess. It was highly rated by George Moore, who said of it (*Conversations in Ebury Street*, 1930) that it was "the most perfect prose narrative in English literature.... As simple and as beautiful as a muslin dress ... the one story in which style, characters and subject are in perfect keeping ...," a judgement not shared by the generality of critics and readers despite the artless charm of the writing and the imprint of truth in the incidents.

Branwell Brontë, the highly gifted brother of the Brontës, died of a mixture of drink and drugs at thirty-one after untold mental and physical suffering. Anne Brontë felt it her duty to describe unflinchingly, in *The Tenant of Wildfell Hall*, the degradation and horror of such a ruin and its effects on the family of the victim. In her novel she traces the slow degrees of Arthur Huntingdon's destruction, and the courage of his wife, Helen, in leaving him so as to rescue their son from his influence. This made scandalous reading at the time, with its strong plea for the rights of married women to protection from such husbands, and to financial independence; but its very boldness ensured the book's success. It was, with *Jane Eyre*, in the best-seller class in the Circulating Libraries. At the same time, the author's love and pity and her deep faith speak eloquently on behalf of the sinner whose death she records as the inevitable "Wages of Sin." Huntingdon's wife, who returns to nurse him through the final stages of his decay, sitting by him through his last moments, proclaims the faith the author herself strongly held – not generally accepted at the time in evangelical circles – of ultimate salvation, even for such as he: "none can imagine the miseries, bodily and mental, of that death-bed! How could I endure to think that that poor trembling soul was hurried away to everlasting torment? It would drive me mad! But, thank God, I have hope ... that through whatever purging fires the erring spirit may have to pass, whatever fate awaits it, still, it is not lost, and God, who hateth nothing that He hath made, will bless it in the end."

—Winifred Gérin

BRONTË, Charlotte. English. Born in Thornton, Yorkshire, 21 April 1816; sister of Anne Brontë, *q.v.*, and Emily Brontë, *q.v.*; moved with her family to Haworth, Yorkshire, 1820, and lived there for the rest of her life. Educated at home, at a school for clergymen's daughters, Cowan Bridge, Yorkshire, 1824–25, Miss Wooler's School, Roehead, Yorkshire, 1831–32, and at the Pensionnat Heger, Brussels, 1842. Married Arthur Bell Nicholls in 1854. Teacher at Miss Wooler's School, Roehead, later at Dewsbury Moor, Yorkshire, 1835–37, 1838; Governess to the Sidgwick family of Stonegappe, Yorkshire, 1839, and the White family of Rawdon, Yorkshire, 1841; Teacher at the Pensionnat Heger, 1843; successful as a novelist from 1847. *Died 31 March 1855.*

Publications

Collections

> *The Complete Poems*, edited by C. K. Shorter. 1923.
> *The Shakespeare Head Brontë*, edited by T. J. Wise and J. A. Symington. 19 vols., 1932–38.

Fiction

> *Jane Eyre: An Autobiography.* 1847; edited by Margaret Smith, 1973.
> *Shirley.* 1849; edited by Andrew and Judith Hook, 1974.
> *Villette.* 1853; edited by Margaret Lane, 1957.
> *The Professor.* 1857.
> *The Adventures of Ernest Alembert: A Fairy tale*, edited by T. J. Wise. 1896.
> *The Moores*, edited by W. R. Nicoll, with *Jane Eyre.* 1902.
> *The Four Wishes: A Fairy Tale*, edited by C. K. Shorter. 1918.
> *Napoleon and the Spectre: A Ghost Story.* 1919.
> *The Twelve Adventurers and Other Stories*, edited by C. W. Hatfield. 1925.
> *The Spell: An Extravaganza*, edited by G. E. MacLean. 1931.
> *Legends of Angria*, edited by Fannie E. Ratchford and W. C. De Vane. 1933.
> *The Search after Hapiness: A Tale*, edited by T. A. J. Burnett. 1969.
> *Five Novelettes*, edited by Winifred Gérin. 1971.
> *Two Tales: The Secret and Lily Hart*, edited by William Holtz. 1978.

Verse

> *Poems*, with Anne and Emily Brontë. 1846.
> *Richard Coeur de Lion and Blondel*, edited by C. K. Shorter. 1912.
> *Saul and Other Poems.* 1913.
> *The Violet*, edited by C. K. Shorter. 1916.
> *The Red Cross Knight and Other Poems.* 1917.
> *The Swiss Emigrant's Return and Other Poems.* 1917.
> *Latest Gleanings*, edited by C. K. Shorter. 1918.
> *Darius Codomannus.* 1920.

Bibliography: *A Bibliography of the Writings in Prose and Verse of the Brontë Family* by T. J. Wise, 1917.

Reading List: *The Brontës' Web of Childhood* by Fannie E. Ratchford, 1941; *The Accents of Persuasion: Brontë's Novels* by R. B. Martin, 1966; *Their Proper Sphere: A Study of the Brontë Sisters as Early Victorian Female Novelists* by I. S. Ewbank, 1966; *Brontë: The Evolution of Genius* by Winifred Gérin, 1967; *The Brontës: A Collection of Critical Essays* edited by Ian Gregor, 1970; *The Brontës and Their Background: Romance and Reality* by Tom Winnifrith, 1973; *Brontë: A Psychosexual Study of Her Novels* by Charles Burkhart, 1973; *The Brontës: The Critical Heritage* edited by Miriam Allott, 1974; *Charlotte: The Foreign Vision of Brontë* by Enid L. Duthie, 1975; *Brontë: The Self Conceived* by Helene Moglen, 1976.

*   *   *

Limited in her formative years to the region and residents of her father's Yorkshire moorland parish, Charlotte Brontë was essentially influenced by her reading in the periodical literature of the day – *Blackwood's Magazine*, in particular – and the leading poets of the Romantic Revival – Byron, Scott, Southey, Campbell. Her strong imagination was stimulated far in advance of her experience of life, and resulted in a precocious talent for writing. From the age of twelve she was continuously writing stories, dramas, verses, and critiques, the apprenticeship for her adult writings. Consequently, her work forms one continuous whole, the major works on which her fame rests to-day – *Jane Eyre, Shirley, Villette, The Professor* – being as securely rooted in the juvenilia as in the subsequent experiences of her life.

Her writing is marked throughout by intensity, intensity of vision in the descriptive passages, intensity of feeling in the emotional scenes. The passionate involvement of the individual in every situation endows her work, like that of her sister Emily, with the quality of poetry, even in the medium of prose. Her childish writings already show the two distinct characteristics of her work as a whole: the closely observed, scrupulously factual relation of domestic detail and the extravagant adventures of the spirit in which she ranged as in a fantasy world, whose scenario and setting were supplied by any book she happened to be reading at the time, *The Travels of Mungo Park*, say or *The Arabian Nights*. Two constant themes overlapped from the juvenilia into the adult writings: the theme of the Rival Brothers, and the theme of the Orphan Girl. The first of these originated with the Wellesley brothers, Wellington's sons, who were the protagonists of the young Brontës' earliest tales, their substitute identities. The brothers' inveterate enmity formed the main-spring of Charlotte's Angrian cycle of tales for ten years and more. Under modified identities they appear in *The Professor* as the Crimsworth brothers, and in *Shirley* as Robert and Louis Moore. Stranger still, they appear again in one of Charlotte's last sketches, "Willie Ellin," as though the potentiality of the subject still remained un-resolved. The conception of a fragile, friendless, often orphaned, girl, whose struggles in a hostile society could reflect Charlotte's own painful experiences as governess, became central to the development of her plot-patterns in the adolescent novelettes; Mina Laury, Caroline Vernon, and Elizabeth Hastings are the recognisable prototypes of their illustrious successors Jane Eyre, Lucy Snowe, and Frances Henri, the first governess-heroines in Victorian literature.

Jane Eyre became a best-seller overnight. It tells the story of an orphan girl, educated in a charitable Institution, Lowood, and engaged as governess at Thornfield Hall. There she is exposed to some heart-searching experiences in her relations with her employer, Mr. Rochester, who is, unknown to her, a married man with a mad wife. The depth of her involvement and the honesty of her mind made this love-story startling in its day, and still profoundly true in human terms to-day.

The theme of unrequited love, so central to the plots of the adolescent juvenilia, is again present in *Shirley*. What weakens the interest is the duplication of the situation: there are two pairs of lovers, Caroline Helstone and Robert Moore, Shirley Keeldar and Louis Moore. The second pair of lovers would be redundant were it not for the character of Shirley, who was reputed to be an attempt to portray Emily Brontë after her death, an act of piety that was doomed to failure. The real subject of the book is Caroline's unhappy love, which is explored with exemplary delicacy and reticence.

Of all Charlotte Brontë's novels, *Villette* is the most ambitious in scale, the richest in character, the most mature in experience. It is set in a Brussels boarding-school, closely resembling the Pensionnat Heger where the author spent two years; the heroine, Lucy Snowe, is an orphan, without relatives or friends other than a godmother, Mrs. Bretton, and her son, Dr. John Graham Bretton. Her isolation is essential to the subject of the book. It makes Lucy exceptionally vulnerable to suffering or to kindness of any sort; she responds, both to Dr. Bretton's and Professor Emanuel's kindness, with all the intensity of a lonely heart. It is again the theme of unrequited love, such as the author herself suffered for her Belgian master, the married M. Heger. In the novel there is no legal barrier to Lucy's happiness, only the jealousy of the school's Directrice, the superbly realised Mme. Beck. The emotional climate of the book is tempestuous throughout, progressing from stormy scene to stormy scene with a climax of electrical excitement that called on all the author's reserves of consummate story-telling. *Villette* is not only Charlotte Brontë's masterpiece, but one of the great Victorian novels. Here, once again, use is made throughout of natural forces at work, to heighten the sense of fate directing human destinies.

Written before all the rest of the Brontë novels, and rejected by successive publishers throughout the author's life, *The Professor* was posthumously published. In its use of a male first-person narrator, and in the revival of the Enemy-Brothers theme, the book harks back to the juvenilia. It is saved, however, by the charm of the heroine, Frances Henri, who, in Mrs. Gaskell's opinion, was "the most charming woman she ever drew," and by some humorously observed Brussels characters and scenes that foreshadow the triumph of *Villette*.

The novels are not only autobiographical in setting, but in the character and situation of the protagonists. Her heroines are marked by a code of honour and a personal fastidiousness of taste characteristic of the author herself; this, while exposing them to great mental suffering, also allows them no facile road to fulfilment and happiness. Jane Eyre, Lucy Snowe, and Shirley Keeldar are endowed with a quality of mind, a strength of will, a capacity for love that differentiates them fundamentally from the general productions of contemporary lady-novelists; they are portrayed with total honesty and courage. Charlotte Brontë and her sister Anne were among the first women novelists to claim equality between women and men in the right to declare their love. It is Jane Eyre who declares her love to Rochester before he makes his sentiments plain to her, and, by doing so, greatly shocked the first readers of the book. "Do you think, because I am poor, obscure, plain, and little, I am soulless and heartless?" she cries, believing Rochester about to marry another woman and to dismiss her; "You think wrong! – I have as much soul as you, – and full as much heart! And if God had gifted me with some beauty, and much wealth, I should have made it as hard for you to leave me, as it is now for me to leave you. I am not talking to you now through the medium of custom, conventionalities, nor even of mortal flesh: – it is my spirit that addresses your spirit; just as if both had passed through the grave, and we stood at God's feet, – equal, – as we are!"

A further distinctive element in the novels is the role given to nature in affecting the affairs of man. Writing in a wild and beautiful region in closest contact with the changing elements at all seasons of the year, Charlotte Brontë, not surprisingly, shows the influence of natural phenomena on the human situation, and uses it as a device in the plot. Witness the Aurora Borealis in *Villette* that influences Lucy Snowe to go to London, the storm that forces her to seek shelter in Ste. Gudule to make her Confession, and the storm in *Jane Eyre* that rends the old chestnut tree in presage of her broken marriage. In such passages as these, and in countless others, the poetic character of the inspiration is plainly seen, enriching the total vision of the novels with a spiritual quality that is as integral a part of their content as the narrative impetus of their plots.

—Winifred Gérin

BRONTË, Emily (Jane).   English.   Born in Thornton, Yorkshire, 30 July 1818; sister of Anne Brontë, *q.v.*, and Charlotte Brontë, *q.v.*; moved with her family to Haworth, Yorkshire, 1820, and lived there for the rest of her life. Educated at home, at a school for clergymen's daughters, Cowan Bridge, Yorkshire, 1824–25, Miss Wooler's School, Roehead, Yorkshire, 1835; Pensionnat Heger, Brussels, 1842. Taught in a school at Law Hill, Halifax, 1837–38. *Died 19 December 1848.*

PUBLICATIONS

Collections

Complete Works, edited by C. K. Shorter and W. R. Nicoll.   2 vols., 1910–11.
The Shakespeare Head Brontë, edited by T. J. Wise and J. A. Symington.   19 vols., 1932–38.
Complete Poems, edited by C. W. Hatfield.   1941.
Poems, edited by Rosemary Hartill.   1973.

Fiction

Wuthering Heights, with *Agnes Grey*, by Anne Brontë.   1847.

Verse

Poems, with Anne and Charlotte Brontë.   1846.
Two Poems, edited by Fannie E. Ratchford.   1934.
Gondal Poems, edited by Helen Brown and Joan Mott.   1938.
Gondal's Queen: A Novel in Verse, edited by Fannie E. Ratchford.   1955.

Other

Five Essays Written in French, translated by Lorine White Nagel, edited by Fannie E. Ratchford.   1948.

Bibliography: *A Bibliography of the Writings in Prose and Verse of the Brontë Family* by T. J. Wise, 1917.

Reading List: *Bronte: Her Life and Work* by Muriel Spark and Derek Stanford, 1953; *Bronte* by Winifred Gérin, 1971; *Brontë: A Critical Anthology* edited by Jean-Pierre Petit, 1973; *The Mind of Brontë* by Herbert Dingle, 1974. For other works, see the entry for Charlotte Brontë.

*   *   *

Emily Brontë's reputation might appear at first sight disproportionate to her meagre output: one novel and 193 poems. Their quality, however, is unique, so visionary and powerful as to rank her indisputedly among the writers of genius.

Few influences on her writing can be traced. She was a very private person, rejecting such contacts with the world as were offered her through her sister Charlotte and her London publishers. Though her work has many affinities with the English Metaphysical poets, Traherne and Vaughan in particular, there is no evidence that she ever read them. Her reading was, on her own showing, very limited, very desultory, and without method. She reproached herself repeatedly in her diary papers for the want of "regularity" in her studies. She knew the romantic poets, Wordsworth especially, and Shakespeare, whom she often quotes. She had little schooling, falling ill whenever sent from home. All the source of her health and happiness, and the inspiration of her writing, were the moors that stretch twenty miles round about her home, Haworth, where she spent her whole life. Her intimate knowledge of the moors at all seasons of the year, and of the wild-life inhabiting them, gave her all the stimulus she needed to enrich her imagination and inspire her writing.

The nature of her poetry and of her one novel — *Wuthering Heights* — is profoundly metaphysical, nourished by the visions that she undoubtedly experienced and was able to describe with all the clarity of facts perceived. The following lines are drawn from a poem about a young captive who awaits her liberator. As with much of her poetic imagery, the awaited visitant is not a corporeal but a spiritual presence.

> He comes with western winds, with evening's wandering airs,
> With that clear dusk of heaven that brings the thickest stars;
> Winds take a pensive tone, and stars a tender fire,
> And visions rise and change which kill me with desire....
>
> But first a hush of peace, a soundless calm descends;
> The struggle of distress and fierce impatience ends;
> Mute music soothes my breast — unuttered harmony
> That I could never dream till earth was lost to me.
>
> Then dawns the Invisible, the Unseen itself reveals;
> My outward sense is gone, my inward essence feels —
> Its wings are almost free, its home, its harbour found;
> Measuring the gulf it stoops and dares the final bound!
>
> Oh, dreadful is the check — intense the agony
> When the ear begins to hear and the eye begins to see;
> When the pulse begins to throb, the brain to think again,
> The soul to feel the flesh and the flesh to feel the chain!

The religious terminology of much of Emily Brontë's poetry does not obscure the fact that hers was no conventional religion (despite her father's calling). So far as her intensely personal beliefs can be defined, she was a Pantheist, seeing all life as One — the Visible and the Invisible, the human, the elemental, the animal and vegetable all imbued with the same spiritual forces.

She made a marked distinction between her personal and her Gondal poetry by transcribing them in two separate and clearly marked notebooks. Through the Gondal poems runs a dramatic Saga relating to the royal houses of Angora and Almedore, who contended for the thrones of the island kingdoms of Gondal and Gaaldine, the location of the drama; the principal theme is the love-hate relationship binding the Queen of Angora, Augusta Geraldine Almeda, to her various lovers, primarily Julius Brenzaida. Under cover of this scenario, begun in childhood, Emily Brontë found the substitute identities and the adventurous actions lacking in her life, the freedom that her spirit craved. Freedom was, for her, a pre-condition of life. As she wrote in one of her personal poems:

> And if I pray, the only prayer
> That moves my lips for me
> Is — "Leave me the heart that now I bear
> And give me liberty.
>
> Yes, as my swift days near their goal
> 'Tis all that I implore —
> Through life and death, a chainless soul
> With courage to endure."

The situations of which she wrote in the Gondal poems, often describing passionate love relations, led her early readers to suppose them autobiographical, revealing a real-life love affair. Their true context in the Gondal Saga, however, has dispelled this notion for good (the known circumstances of her life leave no room for such a relationship), though the "love-poems," like the famous lament "Cold in the earth," when placed in their right context, are seen to resemble the subject of *Wuthering Heights* so closely as to show the overall unity of her creative work.

For years before the writing of *Wuthering Heights*, the Gondal poems dealt with an orphan boy, "black of mien, savage in disposition," passionately involved with a fair girl, his superior in social standing, the very situation of Heathcliff and Catherine Earnshaw in the novel. Emily Brontë's belief in the indissoluble nature of earthly love, first treated in the poems, found its complete expression in the novel, where even the separation of death is shown as powerless to sever a spiritual connection. Catherine Earnshaw gives utterance to this Credo early in the novel when Heathcliff runs away and she is urged to forget him and make a suitable marriage with Edgar Linton: "... my great thought in living is [Heathcliff]. If all else perished, and *he* remained, I should still continue to be; and if all else remained, and he were annihilated, the universe would turn to a mighty stranger; I should not seem a part of it.... My love for Heathcliff resembles the eternal rocks beneath.... Nelly, I *am* Heathcliff!" Catherine's faith is shown as justified in the novel's end where Heathcliff even desecrates her grave so as to be buried with her; and their ghosts are ultimately seen, wandering freely together upon the hillside. The death of Heathcliff, self-induced by his longing for Catherine, is one of the most powerful and daring climaxes in English fiction.

The boldness of the conception that man is the master of his own fate is matched by her last poem, "No coward soul is mine." Addressed to the "God within my breast," she makes her declaration of faith in the universal nature of the soul inhabiting each individual:

> Though Earth and moon were gone
> And suns and universes ceased to be
> And thou wert left alone
> Every Existence would exist in thee
>
> There is not room for Death
> Nor atom that his might could render void
> Since thou art Being and Breath
> And what thou art may never be destroyed.

That is the metaphysical message of *Wuthering Heights*: the indestructibility of the spirit. Such a subject was so far removed from the general run of Victorian fiction – it belonged, if anywhere, to the Gothic tradition, still being followed by Mary Shelley with her *Valperga* (1823) in Emily Brontë's childhood – that it explains the novel's failure when first published. Only two critics, Sydney Dobell and Swinburne, praised it (in 1850 and 1883 respectively), too late to bring recognition to the author in her lifetime.

The book's curious and lasting appeal rests upon a number of qualities: the unflagging excitement of the plot; the wild moorland setting and the splendour of the descriptions; the originality of the characters; the unearthly, not to say ghostly atmosphere created by the interplay of the elements in the affairs of men; the homely background of the old house, The Heights, in which the decaying fortunes of the Earnshaw family are – literally – played out, gambled away, by the last of the line. The author's close familiarity with the local rustic types, the fiercely independent hill-farmers living about the moors, enabled her to create the old curmudgeon Joseph, the general factotum to the family, with both humour and fidelity: his permanent ill-humour and girding condemnation of his associates as all destined for Hell fire, faithfully portrays the primitive attitudes left in the wake of the Methodist Revival in Yorkshire; and acts as a counter-balance to the gothic atmosphere of much of the plot and the high Romanticism of the larger-than-life hero and heroine, Heathcliff and Catherine. In creating such a character as Joseph, Emily Brontë showed that, undoubted visionary as she was, she also had her feet firmly planted on earth.

—Winifred Gérin

BROWN, Charles Brockden. American. Born in Philadelphia, Pennsylvania, 17 January 1771. Educated at the Friends' Latin School, Philadelphia, 1781–86; studied law in the office of Alexander Wilcocks, Philadelphia, 1787–92, but never practised. Married Elizabeth Linn in 1804; three sons and one daughter. Lived in New York, associated with the Friendly Society there, 1798–1801: edited the society's *Monthly Magazine and American Review*, 1799–1800; returned to Philadelphia, and worked in his brother's importing business, 1800–06, and as an independent trader, 1807–10; also Editor of the *Literary Magazine*, 1803–07, and the *American Register*, 1807–10. *Died 22 February 1810.*

PUBLICATIONS

Collections

Novels. 7 vols., 1827.

Fiction

Wieland; or, The Transformation: An American Tale. 1798; edited by Fred Lewis Pattee, with *Memoirs of Carwin*, 1926.
Ormond; or, The Secret Witness. 1799; edited by Ernest Marchand, 1937.
Arthur Mervyn; or, Memoirs of the Year 1793. 2 vols., 1799–1800; edited by Warner Berthoff, 1962.
Edgar Huntly; or, Memoirs of a Sleep-Walker. 1799; edited by David Lee Clark, 1928.
Clara Howard. 1801; as *Philip Stanley; or, The Enthusiasm of Love*, 1807.
Jane Talbot. 1801.
Carwin the Biloquist and Other American Tales and Pieces. 1822.

Other

Alcuin: A Dialogue. 1798; edited by Lee R. Edwards, 1971.
An Address to the Government on the Cession of Louisiana to the French. 1803; revised edition, 1803.
Monroe's Embassy. 1803.
An Address on the Utility and Justice of Restrictions upon Foreign Commerce. 1809.
The Rhapsodist and Other Uncollected Writings, edited by Harry R. Warfel. 1943.

Translator, *A View of the Soil and Climate of the United States of America*, by C. F. Volney. 1804.

Bibliography: in *Bibliography of American Literature* by Jacob Blanck, 1955; "A Census of the Works of Brown" by Sydney J. Krause and Jane Nieset, in *Serif 3*, 1966.

Reading List: *The Life of Brown* by William Dunlap, 2 vols., 1815; *Brown, American Gothic Novelist* by Harry R. Warfel, 1949; *Brown, Pioneer Voice of America* by David Lee Clark, 1952; *Brown* by Donald A. Ringe, 1966.

                                   *   *   *

When Charles Brockden Brown began to write fiction in the latter half of the 1790's, he turned for his models to the popular novels of his time: the Gothic romances of England and Germany, the sentimental tale of seduction, and the novel of purpose. All of these types of fiction had a strong influence on the young American, and each of his six novels can be classified under one or more of these headings. But however much he may have learned from his wide reading, Brown was no mere imitator. He shaped his models to his own artistic ends and turned even such unpromising forms as the Gothic and sentimental romance into vehicles for the development of important themes. He left his indelible mark on everything he wrote.

A major characteristic of Brown's fiction is its intense intellectuality. Though *Wieland* and *Ormond* may both be viewed as tales of seduction, and *Wieland* and *Edgar Huntly* as tales of terror, all three carry a weight of thematic meaning not commonly found in the sentimental or Gothic romance. Sensationalist psychology, theories of education, and the sources of mania are major concerns in *Wieland*; utopian theories, the proper training for women, and the place of religion in education in *Ormond*; and benevolist principles in *Edgar Huntly*. Other of Brown's books are equally intellectual. Benevolist theory also appears in *Arthur Mervyn*, a book modeled on William Godwin's *Caleb Williams*, and Godwinian rationalism clashes with religion in *Jane Talbot*, a sentimental romance.

This is not to say that Brown in a propagandist. He used his fiction, as one critic has observed, not for the exposition, but for the discovery of ideas, which he puts to the test through the actions of his characters. The mistakes that the mad Theodore Wieland, the distraught Clara Wieland, and the rationalistic Henry Pleyel make in attempting to act on the basis of misinterpreted sensations, and the disaster that Edgar Huntly causes by acting on benevolist principles well illustrate Brown's technique. He forces the reader to examine the ideas in the context of the action, but he draws no conclusion himself. Indeed, since all of his books are first-person narrations, told through the voices of one or more characters or through a series of letters, the reader must often penetrate the psychology of the narrator before he can discover the thematic meaning embodied in the action.

In *Ormond*, the point of view causes relatively little trouble, for the story is told in a straightforward manner by a rational character who, throughout most of the book, plays no major role in the action. In other novels, however, where the protagonists tell their own stories, the problem can be difficult. Blessed with an innocent face and a glib tongue, Arthur Mervyn always presents himself in a favorable light, but he exists in a world where appearances are often deceiving, and his actions seem to belie the purity of motive that he consistently attributes to himself. He is, therefore, extremely difficult to penetrate, and critics are divided over the meaning of his experience. The protagonists in *Wieland* and *Edgar Huntly* present a different problem, for both are mentally disturbed. Clara Wieland lapses into madness in the course of her narrative, and Edgar Huntly is driven by strange compulsions from the very first pages of the book. Both narrators are, presumably, brought back to sanity by the close of their stories, but neither is easy for the reader to plumb.

In both of these Gothic tales, however, Brown found effective means for revealing the mental state of his disturbed narrators. Through the use of enclosures in *Wieland* – the temple, the summerhouse, and Clara's room and closet – he suggests the isolation and introspection of all the Wielands, including Clara; through the labyrinthine paths and deep cave in *Edgar Huntly*, he projects his protagonist's mental journey and withdrawal into himself. Other devices, too – Clara's dream, Edgar Huntly's somnambulism, and the appearance of his double, Clithero Edny – help the reader to understand their psychology. All of these were excellent inventions that function well in their respective books. Through them, Brown helped to establish the kind of psychological Gothic that became so popular throughout the nineteenth century in the works of Poe, Hawthorne, and even James.

Brown's position at the head of that tradition accounts for part of the interest he generates among readers today, but his historical importance is not his only claim to attention. Though he never wrote a wholly satisfactory novel – even his best books are marred by structural flaws and a defective style – he achieved so great an intellectual and imaginative intensity in such works as *Wieland, Edgar Huntly*, and *Arthur Mervyn* that one can forgive the weaknesses for the strengths. All are told by protagonists whose psychological state fascinates, and the tales they recount appeal to both the intellect and the emotions of the reader. The ideas Brown explores are always interesting, and the means he found to reveal the psychology of the narrators and to advance the action are absorbing. Though a hasty and careless writer – he hurried all six of his novels through the press in about three years – Brown instilled in the best of his books a vitality yet apparent almost two centuries after they were written.

—Donald A. Ringe

BROWN, Tom (Thomas Brown). English. Born in Shifnal, Shropshire, in 1663. Educated at Newport School, Shropshire; Christ Church, Oxford, 1678–85, left without taking a degree. Usher in a school in Kingston-upon-Thames, and subsequently Headmaster of Kingston Grammar School, for three years; settled in London, and supported himself as a hack writer and translator; started the *Lacedaemonian Mercury* c. 1691; notorious for his licentious life and for the animosity of his feuds with, among others, Sir Richard Blackmore and John Dryden. *Died 16 June 1704.*

PUBLICATIONS

Fiction, Sketches, and Dialogues

The Reason of Mr. Bays Changing his Religion, Considered in a Dialogue Between Crites, Eugenius, and Mr. Bays. 1688; part 2, 1690; part 3, 1690.
The Reasons of the New Convert's Taking the Oaths to the Present Government. 1691.
Wit for Money; or, Poet Stutter. 1691.
Novus Reformator Vapulans; or, The Welsh Levite Tossed in a Blanket. 1691.
Physic Lies a Bleeding; or, The Apothecary Turned Doctor. 1697.
Amusements Serious and Comical, Calculated for the Meridian of London. 1700; edited by A. L. Hayward, 1927.
Laconics; or, New Maxims of State and Conversation, with others. 1701.
Advice to the Kentish Long-Tails, by the Wise Men of Gotham. 1701.
Letters from the Dead to the Living, with others. 3 vols., 1702–03.
The Dying Thoughts and Last Reflections, in a Letter to a Friend. 1704.
A Collection of All the Dialogues. 1704.

A Legacy for the Ladies; or, Characters of the Women of the Age, with *A Comical View of London and Westminster,* by Ned Ward.   1705.
Azarias: A Sermon Held Forth in a Quakers Meeting.   1710.
Twenty-Two Select Colloquies by Erasmus, to Which Are Added Seven More Dialogues.   1711.

Play

The Stage-Beaux Tossed in a Blanket; or, Hypocrisy Alamode, Exposed in a True Picture of Jerry.   1704.

Verse

The Weasels: A Satrical Fable.   1691.
The Moralist; or, A Satire upon the Sects.   1691.
Commendatory Verses on the Author of The Two Arthurs, and The Satire Against Wit, with others.   1700; revised edition, 1702.
A Description of Mr. D[ryden]n's Funeral.   1700.
The Mourning Poet.   1703.

Other

A Collection of Miscellany Poems, Letters, etc.   1699; revised edition, 1700.
Works.   2 vols., 1707; revised edition, 3 vols., 1708; 4 vols., 1711–12; 5 vols., 1719–20.

Editor, *The Lives of All the Princes of Orange,* by L. Aubery du Maurier.   1693.
Editor, with Charles Gildon, *Familiar Letters,* by Rochester, Otway, and Katherine Philips.   2 vols., 1697.
Editor, *Miscellanea Aulica; or, A Collection of State Treatises.*   1702.
Editor, *The Adventures of Lindamira.*   1702; as *The Lover's Secretary,* 1713.
Editor, *The Miscellaneous Works of the Duke of Buckingham.*   2 vols., 1704.

Translator, *Memoirs of the Court of Spain,* by Marie d'Aulnoy.   1692.
Translator, *The Life of Cardinal Richelieu,* by A. J. Du Plessis.   1695.
Translator, *A New and Easy Method to Understand the Roman History,* by Abbé de Fourcroy.   1695.
Translator, *Twelve Dissertations Out of Jean Le Clerc's Genesis.*   1696.
Translator, *Seven New Colloquies,* by Erasmus.   1699.
Translator, *Select Epistles Out of Cicero.*   1702.
Translator, *The Circe,* by G. B. Gelli.   1702.
Translator, *Justin's History of the World, Being an Abridgement of Trogus Pompeius' Phillipic History.*   1702.
Translator, *France and Spain Naturally Enemies,* by Carlos García.   1704.
Translator, *A Looking-Glass for Married People,* by L. de Gaya.   1704.

Reading List: *Brown of Facetious Memory* by Benjamin Boyce, 1939; *Brown e le Origini del Saggio di Costume* by Edrige Schulte, 1969.

*   *   *

While living, Tom Brown was considered a *"Pestilence* of Wit"; once dead, his was a "facetious Memory." One detractor, in the *Discommendatory Verses* (1700), went so far as to insist. "But this I dare affirm, without a Lie,/His *Epigrams* are only *born* to *die*." Curiously enough, this anonymous slanderer was dead wrong, for Brown is best remembered for his supposedly spontaneous epigram (see Martial, I, 32) against Dr. John Fell, Dean of Christ Church while Brown was at Oxford:

> I do not love thee, Dr. Fell,
> The reason why I cannot tell;
> But this I know, and know full well,
> I do not love thee, Dr. Fell.

To be sure, Brown was a prolific, scurrilous, witty and brash minor writer, but he was nonetheless a writer of considerable significance.

In an era witnessing the decline of the nobility's patronage, and the corresponding rise of a middle-class reading audience, Tom Brown is a pure specimen of the hackney writer, an educated multifarious scribbler, offering himself and almost any subject to virtually every bidder – for hire. The genteel and the squeamish might label such efforts "prostitution," but they will have, somewhat uncomfortably, to admit Dryden, Defoe, Addison, Swift, Fielding, and Johnson among that company.

If most often unsteady and impecunious throughout his London-based life, Brown was nevertheless imaginative, diligent, and workmanlike. His voluminous productions include Tory and Anglican pamphlets, catches and lampoons, pieces for the magazines (*The Gentleman's Journal* and *The London Mercury*), translations (of Lucian, Lucretius, Cicero, Cervantes, Gelli, Scarron, Le Clerc, Mme. d'Aulnoy, Fontenelle, and Saint-Evremond), historical and biographical works (on Richelieu, on Roman history, on the ancient Druids), a satire upon Louis XIV, and contributions to the highly popular poetical miscellanies of his day (including the *Poems on Affairs of State*). Almost single-handedly, he roused the wits to war against that duncical physician and epical poet, Sir Richard Blackmore, producing the caustic *Commendatory Verses on the Author of the Two Arthurs*.

Most importantly, Tom Brown should be remembered for his share (Part III) of the *Laconics; or, New Maxims of State and Conversation*, where his terse reflections on the nature of politics and life are insightful and occasionally profound; for his hand in the epistolary novel (long before Richardson), *The Adventures of Lindamira*; for his *Letters from the Dead to the Living* – in the tradition of Lucian, Rabelais, Quevedo, Erasmus, Fontenelle (see Frederick Keener, *English Dialogues of the Dead*, 1973). Above all stands his *Amusements Serious and Comical*, presenting in pert and gusty documentary prose a tour with an hypothetical Indian of the sights and lurid alleyways of old London. Utilizing the traditions of satire, the polemic, the epistle, the "Character," and the jest-book, Brown forges a rough and ready journalism that was destined to help play a role in shaping subsequent prose and the English novel as well. For the rest, he views the world, *cum grano salis*, as being no better than it should be (*Letters from the Dead*):

> We have nothing new here, because we are under the sun. Wise men keep company with one another; fools write and fools read; the booksellers have the advantage ...; some pragmatical fellows set up for politicians; others think they have merit because they have money. Cheats prosper, drunkenness is a little rebuked in the pulpit ...; people marry that don't love one the other, and your old mistress Melisinda goes to church constantly, prays devoutly, sings psalms gravely, hears sermons attentively, receives the sacrament monthly, lies with her footman nightly, and rails against lewdness and hypocrisy from morning till night.

—John R. Clark

BROWN, William Wells. American. Born in Lexington, Kentucky, c. 1816; son of a slave owner, George Higgins, and one of his slaves. Married a free Black woman in 1834; two daughters. Taken to St. Louis as a boy and hired out on a steamboat; subsequently employed in the printshop of the editor of the *St. Louis Times*, then again hired out on a steamboat; escaped from slavery to Ohio and assumed the name of a man who befriended him, 1834; worked as a steward on steamboats on Lake Erie; occasional lecturer for anti-slavery societies in New York and Massachusetts, 1843–49, and associated with various other reform movements in the United States: represented the American Peace Society at the Peace Congress in Paris, 1849; travelled in Europe, 1849–54, and studied medicine abroad. *Died 6 November 1884.*

PUBLICATIONS

Fiction

Clotel; or, The President's Daughter: A Narrative of Slave Life in the United States. 1853; another version published as *Clotelle: A Tale of the Southern States,* 1864; edited by W. Edward Farrison, with *Narrative of Brown,* 1969.

Plays

Experience; or, How to Give a Northern Man a Backbone. 1856.
The Escape; or, A Leap for Freedom. 1858.

Other

Narrative of William Wells Brown, A Fugitive Slave. 1847; revised edition, 1848, 1849; edited by W. Edward Farrison, with *Clotel,* 1969.
Three Years in Europe; or, Places I Have Seen and People I Have Met. 1852; revised edition, as *The American Fugitive in Europe,* 1855.
The Black Man: His Antecedents, His Genius, and His Achievements. 1863; revised edition, 1863.
The Negro in the American Rebellion: His Heroism and His Fidelity. 1867.
The Rising Son: or, The Antecedents and Advancement of the Colored Race. 1874.
My Southern Home; or, The South and Its People. 1880(?).

Editor, *The Anti-Slavery Harp: A Collection of Songs for Anti-Slavery Meetings.* 1848.

Reading List: *Brown, Author and Reformer* by W. Edward Farrison, 1969 (includes bibiliography).

*   *   *

Born a slave in Kentucky, William Wells Brown was schooled by the "peculiar institution" for life-long work as a reformer. Within two years of his own escape from bondage in 1834, he was conducting others to freedom on the underground railroad, and by the 1850's he was among the most famous abolitionists in Europe as well as America.

Crusaders then as now employed every medium available to their talents to advance their cause. In this company, Brown was remarkable, for besides oration and documentary reports he also produced a novel, a European travel book, plays, several historical studies, and reflective memoirs. The novel, *Clotel*, the travel book, *Three Years in Europe*, and the five-act drama, *The Escape*, are first examples of their type written by a black American. Together with the range of his other writings they assure Brown a place in American literary history.

Brown's narrative of his life in slavery was a best-seller. His novel found a broad audience by virtue of its appearance in several versions, and his histories and recollections went through multiple editions. Their contemporary appeal seems to have been due largely to their reaffirmation of standard arguments in their use of familiar literary conventions.

Yet it is precisely the evident redundancy in his work that accounts for Brown's present significance. In his autobiography, Brown's first published book, he describes his master as stealing him as soon as he was born. His mother, he explains, bore seven children by seven different men, including a white relative of the master, who fathered William. Each infant was claimed by the master as his property without regard to lineage or paternal affection. William and his mother tried to escape slavery but were caught, and his mother sold into the Deep South "to die on a ... plantation!" Later, when he made his way alone to freedom in Ohio, he joined the name his mother had given him with that of Wells Brown, his first white friend and surrogate father. These autobiographical facts reveal the terms in which Brown saw destiny. Thus, his fiction centers upon mulatto characters whose very existence images violation and relates incidents where neither blood, race, nor intimacy prevent subjugation. Carried into non-fiction, where he argued the case for equality on the basis of achievement and service, Brown adapts his motifs into a plea for reconciliation within the human family.

It is repeated examination of fate in an America where essential humanity is divided by brutal practive that gives Brown continued importance. For this first black man of letters established in literature the prevalent Afro-American concern with identity.

—John M. Reilly

BROWNE, Charles Farrar. See **WARD, Artemus.**

BROWNE, Sir Thomas. English. Born in London, 19 October 1605. Educated at Winchester College, 1616–23; Broadgates Hall, now Pembroke College, Oxford, matriculated 1623, B.A. 1626, M.A. 1629; studied medicine at the University of Leyden, M.D. 1633; granted Oxford M.D. 1637. Married Dorothy Mileham in 1641; twelve children. Practised medicine in Norwich, 1637 until the end of his life. Knighted, 1671. *Died 19 October 1682.*

PUBLICATIONS

Collections

Works, edited by Geoffrey Keynes. 6 vols., 1928–31; revised edition, 4 vols., 1964.
The Major Works, edited by C. A. Patrides. 1977.

Prose

Religio Medici.   1642; revised edition, 1643.
*Pseudodoxia Epidemica; or, Enquiries into Very Many Received Tenets and Commonly
    Presumed Truths.*   1646; revised edition, 1650, 1658, 1669, 1669, 1672.
*Hydriotaphia, Urn-Burial; or, A Discourse of the Sepulchral Urns Lately Found in
    Norfolk, Together with The Garden of Cyrus; or, The Quincuncial Lozenge, or Network
    Plantations of the Ancients, Artificially, Naturally, Mystically Considered.*   1658.
Certain Miscellany Tracts, edited by Archbishop Tenison.   1683.
Posthumous Works.   1712.
Christian Morals, edited by John Jeffery.   1716.
Notes and Letters on the Natural History of Norfolk, edited by Thomas
    Southwell.   1902.

Bibliography: *A Bibliography of Browne* by Geoffrey Keynes, 1924; revised edition, 1968.

Reading List: *Science and Imagination in Browne* by Egon S. Merton, 1949; *Browne: A
Doctor's Life of Science and Faith* by J. S. Finch, 1950; *Browne: A Biographical and Critical
Study* by Frank L. Huntley, 1962; *Browne: A Man of Achievement in Literature* by Joan
Bennett, 1962; *Studies in Browne* by Robert Ralston Cawley and Gen Yost, 1965; *The
Strategy of Truth: A Study of Browne* by Leonard Nathanson, 1967.

                                *   *   *

The narrator in Sir Thomas Browne's *Religio Medici* describes his life as "a miracle of
thirty yeares, which to relate, were not a History, but a peece of Poetry, and would sound to
common eares like a fable." But Browne's own life was certainly not a poem, much less a
miracle. The fable must instead be sought in the works of his fertile imagination.

Browne's style depends on the generalisation he ventures in *Religio Medici* ("The Religion
of a Physician") that man is "naturally inclined unto Rhythme." Such rhythm implied for
Browne the existence of an ultimate order which, emanating from the One, is diversified into
the Many – witness in the first instance the diverse yet harmonious aspects of the created
universe, and in the second the variable yet unified tonal range of the given work of art. In
this respect Browne's characteristic "doublets" – his sequentially arranged synonymous
words or parallel phrases – may not be considered in isolation since they form part of his
intention to create effects which, cumulatively, assert the all-pervasive presence of order. The
basic principle he articulated in the penultimate paragraph of *The Garden of Cyrus* applies as
much to style as to the theme delineated: "All things began in order, so shall they end, and so
shall they begin again; according to the ordainer of order and mysticall Mathematicks of the
City of Heaven." For Browne no less than for many of his contemporaries such as Herbert,
language is sacramental in that its several units inclusive of words are sufficiently emblematic
or allusive to intimate the divine through the profane. The attitude is characteristic not of
Christians generally but of Christian Platonists in particular.

Browne wore his Platonism with casual abandon, it is true. But as *Religio Medici* confirms
explicitly enough, Platonism had in any case been adapted in the symbolic form it had
assumed ever since the advent of the legendary Hermes Trismegistus, the supposed Egyptian
author of widely venerated works believed to have predated Plato although actually written
in the second century A.D. The fundamental Hermetic concept of "hieroglyphics" led
Browne to accept, in *Religio Medici,* that "this visible world is but a picture of the invisible,"
itself but a different way of affirming the presence of a transcendent principle as stated in
Christian Morals: "The Hand of Providence writes often by Abbreviatures, Hieroglyphicks
or short Characters." Confirmation of this principle in *Religio Medici* is ample, and may most
evidently be discerned in the assertion of the vertical order inherent in the Scale of Nature and

the horizontal order of history that extends from the creation through the Last Judgement.

Pseudodoxia Epidemica ("Vulgar Errors") demonstrates through its several amendments Browne's unfailing commitment to the latest developments in various disciplines. The method is vital; the constant appeal to the triad of experience, reason, and authority, proclaims that Browne had, like Bacon, intended to suggest the best possible ways to journey through the labyrinthine routes that lead to truth. Even while annihilating "vulgar errors," however, he was responding to them through the rhythms of his prose. His major scientific treatise is, all too obviously, articulated in aesthetic terms.

The connexion between the jointly published *Hydriotaphia* and *The Garden of Cyrus* has been described as "nexus through contrast": the two works are related in that "the obsession of death in one, is balanced by the celebration of life in the other," even as "accident is opposed to design, body to soul, time to space, ignorance to knowledge, substance to form, darkness to light, mutability to immutabilty" (see Huntley, *Browne*). *Hydriotaphia* poses the problem of the incomprehensible physical evil of death, to resolve it at last through the haunting rhythms of its final paragraphs where death is subsumed within the larger vision of immortality. *The Garden of Cyrus* extends the awareness of the other work, save that here the tonal range tends constantly toward a joyous whimsey. The underlying purpose remains serious in the extreme, however. It coincides with Browne's sustained concern to establish "how nature Geometrizeth, and observeth order in all things." His ultimate aspiration was clearly the attainment of harmony: the rhythm within the universe as within art.

—C. A. Patrides

BROWNE, Thomas Alexander.   See BOLDREWOOD, Rolf.

BUCHAN, John; 1st Baron Tweedsmuir of Elsfield.   Scottish.   Born in Broughton Green, Peebles-shire, 26 August 1875. Educated at the University of Glasgow; Brasenose College, Oxford (scholar, 1895; Stanhope Prize, 1897; Newdigate Prize, 1898; President of the Union, 1899), B.A. (honours) 1899; called to the Bar, Middle Temple, London, 1901. Served on the Headquarters Staff of the British Army in France, as temporary Lieutenant Colonel, 1916–17; Director of Information under the Prime Minister, 1917–18. Married Susan Charlotte Grosvenor in 1907; three sons and one daughter. Private Secretary to the High Commissioner for South Africa, Lord Milner, 1901–03; Director of Nelson, publishers, London, from 1903; Conservative Member of Parliament for the Scottish Universities, 1927–35; Lord High Commissioner to the Church of Scotland, 1933, 1934; Governor-General of Canada, 1935–40; Privy Councillor, 1937. Curator, Oxford University Chest, 1924–30; President, Scottish History Society, 1929–33; Bencher of the Middle Temple, 1935; Chancellor of the University of Edinburgh, 1937–40; Justice of the Peace, Peebles-shire and Oxfordshire. Recipient: Black Memorial Prize, 1929. D.C.L.: Oxford University; LL.D.: University of Glasgow; University of St. Andrews; University of Edinburgh; McGill University, Montreal; University of Toronto; University of Manitoba, Winnipeg; Harvard

University, Cambridge, Massachusetts; Yale University, New Haven, Connecticut; D.Litt.: Columbia University, New York; University of British Columbia, Vancouver; McMaster University, Hamilton, Ontario. Honorary Fellow, Brasenose College, Oxford. Companion of Honour, 1932; created Baron Tweedsmuir, 1935; G.C.M.G. (Knight Grand Cross, Order of St. Michael and St. George), 1935; G.C.V.O. (Knight Grand Cross, Royal Victorian Order), 1939. *Died 11 February 1940.*

PUBLICATIONS

Fiction

Sir Quixote of the Moors. 1895.
John Burnet of Barns. 1898.
Grey Weather: Moorland Tales of My Own People. 1899.
A Lost Lady of Old Years. 1899.
The Half-Hearted. 1900.
The Watcher by the Threshold and Other Tales. 1902; augmented edition, 1918.
Prester John. 1910; as *The Great Diamond Pipe*, 1910.
The Moon Endureth: Tales and Fancies. 1912.
The Thirty-Nine Steps. 1915.
Salute to Adventurers. 1915.
Ordeal by Marriage: An Eclogue. 1915.
The Power-House. 1916.
Greenmantle. 1916.
Mr. Standfast. 1918.
The Path of the King. 1921.
Huntingtower. 1922.
Midwinter: Certain Travellers in Old England. 1923.
The Three Hostages. 1924.
John Macnab. 1925.
The Dancing Floor. 1926.
Witch Wood. 1927.
The Runagates Club. 1928.
The Courts of the Morning. 1929.
Castle Gay. 1930.
The Blanket of the Dark. 1931.
The Gap in the Curtain. 1932.
The Magic Walking-Stick. 1932.
A Prince of the Captivity. 1933.
The Free Fishers. 1934.
The House of the Four Winds. 1935.
The Island of Sheep. 1936; as *The Man from the Norlands*, 1936.
Sick Heart River. 1941; as *Mountain Meadow*, 1941.
The Long Traverse. 1941; as *Lake of Gold*, 1941.

Play

Screenplay: *The Battles of Coronel and Falkland Islands*, with Harry Engholm and Merritt Crawford, 1927.

Verse

> *The Pilgrim Fathers.* 1898.
> *Poems, Scots and English.* 1917; revised edition, 1936.

Other

> *Scholar Gipsies.* 1896.
> *Sir Walter Raleigh.* 1897.
> *Brasenose College.* 1898.
> *The African Colony: Studies in the Reconstruction.* 1903.
> *The Law Relating to the Taxation of Foreign Income.* 1905.
> *Some Eighteenth Century Byways and Other Essays.* 1908.
> *A Lodge in the Wilderness.* 1906.
> *Sir Walter Raleigh* (juvenile). 1911.
> *The Marquis of Montrose.* 1913.
> *Andrew Jameson, Lord Ardwall.* 1913.
> *Britain's War by Land.* 1915.
> *Nelson's History of the War.* 24 vols., 1915–19; as *A History of the Great War,* 4 vols., 1921–22.
> *The Achievement of France.* 1915.
> *The British Front in the West.* 1916.
> *These for Remembrance.* 1919.
> *The Island of Sheep,* with Susan Buchan. 1919.
> *The Battle-Honours of Scotland 1914–18.* 1919.
> *The History of the South African Forces in France.* 1920.
> *Francis and Riversdale Grenfell: A Memoir.* 1920.
> *A Book of Escapes and Hurried Journeys.* 1922.
> *The Last Secrets: The Final Mysteries of Exploration.* 1923.
> *Days to Remember: The British Empire in the Great War,* with Henry Newbolt. 1923.
> *Lord Minto: A Memoir.* 1924.
> *The History of the Royal Scots Fusiliers 1678–1918.* 1925.
> *The Man and the Book: Sir Walter Scott.* 1925.
> *Homilies and Recreations.* 1926.
> *The Fifteenth – Scottish – Division 1914–1919,* with John Stewart. 1926.
> *Montrose.* 1928.
> *The Kirk in Scotland 1560–1929.* 1930.
> *The Novel and the Fairy Tale.* 1931.
> *Sir Walter Scott.* 1932.
> *Julius Caesar.* 1932.
> *The Massacre of Glencoe.* 1933.
> *Gordon at Khartoum.* 1934.
> *Oliver Cromwell.* 1934.
> *Men and Deeds.* 1935.
> *The King's Grace 1910–35* (on George V). 1935.
> *Augustus.* 1937.
> *Presbyterianism Yesterday, Today, and Tomorrow.* 1938.
> *Memory Hold-the-Door.* 1940; as *Pilgrim's Way: An Essay in Recollection,* 1940.
> *Comments and Characters,* edited by W. Forbes Gray. 1940.
> *Canadian Occasions* (lectures). 1940.

> Editor, *Essays and Apothegms,* by Francis Bacon. 1894.
> Editor, *Musa Piscatrix.* 1896.

Editor, *The Long Road to Victory*. 1920.
Editor, *Great Hours in Sport*. 1921.
Editor, *Miscellanies*, by Archibald Primrose, Earl of Rosebery. 1921.
Editor, *A History of English Literature*. 1923.
Editor, *The Nations of Today: A New History of the World*. 12 vols., 1923–24.
Editor, *The Northern Muse: An Anthology of Scots Vernacular Poetry*. 1924.
Editor, *Modern Short Stories*. 1926.

Bibliography: *Buchan: A Bibliography* by Archibald Hanna, 1953; by J. R. Cox, in *English Literature in Transition*, 1966, 1967.

Reading List: *Buchan, by His Wife and Friends*, 1947; *Buchan, Writer* by A. C. Turner, 1949; *Clubland Heroes* by Richard Usborne, 1952, revised edition, 1974; *Buchan: A Biography* by Janet Adam Smith, 1965; *The Interpreter's House: A Critical Assessment of the Works of Buchan* by David Daniell, 1975.

*   *   *

John Buchan's reputation, like that of Scott's, has suffered from his novels' appeal to youth. Regarding him as a novelist of adventure, and remembering him later for swashbuckling travel yarns and vivid (and undeniably excellent) description of scenery, whether the Scottish beach of Birkcaple in *Prester John*, the Middle East of *Greenmantle*, or the Canada of *Sick Heart River*, the ordinary reader gives him too little credit for his remarkable width of achievement as poet and anthologist, critic, journalist, and reviewer – all this, along with a prodigious output of fiction, crammed into the intervals of leisure in a professional life which would have absorbed the energies of two others.

Buchan was a traveller. He fought his way to the top of his profession in law, he reached the highest levels of government and diplomatic service, and he moved freely in a world which was threatened by depression and war. He certainly did provide entertainment and, where it was wanted, escapism, his plots frequently based on accurate personal observation of the Scottish borders, Oxfordshire, South Africa, North America. His reading was as extensive as his travels, and results in intelligent writing about tribal loyalties in *Prester John*, brilliant investigation of the psychology of the belief in witchcraft which can take over a whole community – in *Witch Wood* – as thoroughly as can a political dream, like the Jacobite loyalties inspiring *Midwinter*. This last is a little-read but very professional historical novel a long way after *Redgauntlet*, trying to revive the historical experience of being involved *in* a Jacobite rebellion in the making, rather than looking back on it with cool historical judgement.

It is not easy to point to the "best" in such a writer, though clearly he was still breaking new ground, and writing disturbing and very adult novels, towards his death. Perhaps the most challenging of his books in this respect is the very late *Sick Heart River*, only thinly disguised autobiography in places, the story of a dying civil servant and public figure who goes to find his own Heart of Darkness in the wilds of Canada. He finds not Conradian horror, but a kind of peace: not new life, but a calmer approach to death, an approach devoted to helping an Indian tribe shake off the infections of a spreading European civilisation, and find again the will to live a distinctive life instead of accepting extinction. It still has the power to disturb, not only our own views of colonisation and the settlement of Canada, but our view of Buchan as an upper-class establishment figure who made writing a profitable sideline. The variety and the extent of his work demand a fuller and more informed assessment, a process now clearly under way.

—Ian Campbell

BUCK, Pearl S(ydenstricker). American. Born in Hillsboro, West Virginia, 26 June 1892; daughter of Presbyterian missionaries in China. Educated at boarding school in Shanghai, China, 1907–09; Randolph-Macon Women's College, Lynchburg, Virginia, B.A. 1914 (Phi Beta Kappa); Cornell University, Ithaca, New York, M.A. 1926. Married 1) the missionary John Lossing Buck in 1917 (divorced, 1935), one daughter; 2) the publisher Richard J. Walsh in 1935 (died, 1960); eight adopted children. Taught psychology at Randolph-Macon Women's College, 1914; taught English at the University of Nanking, 1921–31, Southeastern University, Nanking, 1925–27, and Chung Yang University, Nanking, 1928–31; returned to the United States, 1935; Co-Editor, *Asia* magazine, New York, 1941–46; Founder and Director, East and West Association, 1941–51; Founder, Welcome House, an adoption agency, 1949, and the Pearl S. Buck Foundation, 1964; Member of the Board of Directors, Weather Engineering Corporation of America, Manchester, New Hampshire, 1966. Recipient: Pulitzer Prize, 1932; Howells Medal, 1935; Nobel Prize for Literature, 1938; National Conference of Christians and Jews Brotherhood Award, 1955; President's Commission on Employment of the Physically Handicapped Citation, 1958; Women's National Book Association Skinner Award, 1960; ELA Award in Literature, 1969. M.A.: Yale University, New Haven, Connecticut, 1933; D.Litt.: University of West Virginia, Morgantown, 1940; St. Lawrence University, Canton, New York, 1942; Delaware Valley College, Doylestown, Pennsylvania, 1965; LL.D.: Howard University, Washington, D.C., 1942; Muhlenberg College, Allentown, Pennsylvania, 1966; L.H.D.: Lincoln University, Pennsylvania, 1953; Woman's Medical College of Philadelphia, 1954; University of Pittsburgh, 1960; Bethany College, West Virginia, 1963; Hahnemann Medical College, Philadelphia, 1966; Rutgers University, New Brunswick, New Jersey, 1969; D.Mus.: Combs College of Music, Philadelphia, 1962; D.H.: West Virginia State College, Institute, 1963. Member, American Academy of Arts and Letters. *Died 6 March 1973.*

Publications

Fiction

East Wind: West Wind. 1930.
The Good Earth. 1931.
Sons. 1932.
The First Wife and Other Stories. 1933.
The Mother. 1934.
A House Divided. 1935.
This Proud Heart. 1938.
The Patriot. 1939.
Other Gods: An American Legend. 1940.
Today and Forever: Stories of China. 1941.
China Sky. 1942.
Dragon Seed. 1942.
The Promise. 1943.
China Flight. 1945.
The Townsman. 1945.
Portrait of a-Marriage. 1945.
Pavilion of Women. 1946.
The Angry Wife. 1947.
Far and Near: Stories of Japan, China, and America. 1948.
Peony. 1948; as *The Bondmaid,* 1949.
Kinfolk. 1949.

The Long Love. 1949.
God's Men. 1950.
The Hidden Flower. 1952.
Satan Never Sleeps. 1952.
Bright Procession. 1952.
Come, My Beloved. 1953.
Voices in the House. 1953.
Imperial Women. 1954.
Letter from Peking. 1957.
Command the Morning. 1959.
Fourteen Stories. 1961; as *With a Delicate Air and Other Stories,* 1962.
Hearts Come Home and Other Stories. 1962.
The Living Reed. 1963.
Stories of China. 1964.
Death in the Castle. 1965.
The Time Is Noon. 1967.
The New Year. 1968.
The Good Deed and Other Stories of Asia, Past and Present. 1969.
The Three Daughters of Madame Liang. 1969.
Mandala. 1970.
The Goddess Abides. 1972.
All under Heaven. 1973.
The Rainbow. 1974.
Book of Christmas (stories). 1974.
East and West (stories). 1975.
Secrets of the Heart. 1976.
The Lovers and Other Stories. 1977.

Plays

Flight into China (produced 1939).
Sun Yat Sen: A Play, Preceded by a Lecture by Dr. Hu-Shih. 1944(?).
China to America (radio play), in *Free World Theatre,* edited by Arch Oboler and
    Stephen Longstreet. 1944.
Will This Earth Hold? (radio play), in *Radio Drama in Action,* edited by Erik
    Barnouw. 1945.
The First Wife (produced 1945).
A Desert Incident (produced 1959).
Christine, with Charles K. Peck, Jr., music by Sammy Fain, from the book *My Indian
    Family* by Hilda Wernher (produced 1960).
The Guide, from the novel by R. K. Narayan (produced 1965).

Screenplays: *The Big Wave,* 1962, and *The Guide,* 1965, both with Ted Danielewski.

Verse

Words of Love. 1974.

Other

The Young Revolutionist (juvenile). 1932.

Is There a Case for Foreign Missions? 1932.
East and West and the Novel: Sources of the Early Chinese Novel. 1932.
The Exile (biography). 1936.
Fighting Angel: Portrait of a Soul (biography). 1936.
Stories for Little Children. 1940.
When Fun Begins (juvenile). 1941
Of Men and Women. 1941.
American Unity and Asia. 1942; as *Asia and Democracy*, 1943.
The Chinese Children Next Door (juvenile). 1942.
The Water Buffalo Children (juvenile). 1943.
What America Means to Me. 1943.
The Dragon Fish (juvenile). 1944.
Talk about Russia, with Masha Scott. 1945.
Tell the People: Talks with James Yen about the Mass Education Movement. 1945.
Yu Lan: Flying Boy of China (juvenile). 1945.
How It Happens: Talk about the German People, 1914–1933, with Erna von Pustau. 1947.
The Big Wave (juvenile). 1947.
American Argument, with Eslanda Goode Robeson. 1949.
One Bright Day (juvenile). 1950; as *One Bright Day and Other Stories for Children*, 1952.
The Child Who Never Grew. 1950.
The Man Who Changed China: The Story of Sun Yat Sen (juvenile). 1953.
My Several Worlds (autobiography). 1954.
The Beech Tree (juvenile). 1954.
Johnny Jack and His Beginnings (juvenile). 1954.
Christmas Miniature (juvenile). 1957; as *The Christmas Mouse*, 1958.
Friend to Friend, with Carlos P. Romulo. 1958.
The Delights of Learning. 1960.
The Christmas Ghost (juvenile). 1960.
A Bridge for Passing (autobiography). 1962.
The Joy of Children. 1964.
Welcome Child (juvenile). 1964.
The Gifts They Bring: Our Debts to the Mentally Retarded, with Gweneth T. Zarfoss. 1965.
Children for Adoption. 1965.
The Big Fight (juvenile). 1965.
The People of Japan. 1966.
For Spacious Skies: Journey in Dialogue, with Theodore F. Harris. 1966.
The Little Fox in the Middle (juvenile). 1966.
My Mother's House, with others. 1966.
To My Daughters, With Love. 1967.
Matthew, Mark, Luke, and John (juvenile). 1967.
The People of China. 1968.
The Kennedy Women: A Personal Appraisal. 1970.
China as I See It, edited by Theodore F. Harris. 1970.
The Story Bible. 1971.
The Chinese Storyteller (juvenile). 1971.
China Past and Present. 1972.
A Community Success Story: The Founding of the Pearl Buck Center. 1972.
Oriental Cookbook. 1972.
A Gift for the Children (juvenile). 1973.
Mrs. Sterling's Problem (juvenile). 1973.

Editor, *China in Black and White: An Album of Woodcuts by Contemporary Chinese Artists.* 1945.
Editor, *Fairy Tales of the Orient.* 1965.

Translator, *All Men Are Brothers,* by Shui Hu Chan. 2 vols., 1933.

Reading List: *Buck* by Paul A. Doyle, 1965; *Buck: A Biography* by Theodore F. Harris, 2 vols., 1969–71.

*   *   *

The amount and variety of Pearl S. Buck's writing and the strong correlation between her writing and her life make critical analysis complex. She admired the work of such naturalists as Zola and Dreiser and often emphasized the power of nature and culture, but she was never sordid nor pessimistic, and her realistic details of places, events, and people are organized around such romantic tenets as individuality, the nobility of common people, the corrupting influence of wealth and cities, and the universal interest in "love." Her years in China, her missionary connections, her exposure to many marital situations, and her humanitarian projects furnished both the material and the themes of her stories. And while her masterpiece, *The Good Earth,* and the biographies of her parents, *The Exile* and *Fighting Angel,* are almost universally rated as classics, much of the rest of her work is of uneven artistic merit.

The Good Earth achieves a perfect blending of appropriate diction, informative detail, epic structure, and universal themes. Such semi-biblical lines as "I am with child," and such "Chinese" lines as "There is this woman of mine," are held together with such thematic lines as: "He had no articulate thought of anything; there was only this perfect sympathy of movement, of turning this earth of theirs over and over to the sun, this earth which formed their home and fed their bodies and made their gods." Occasionally there are poetic lines as delicate as a Chinese painting: "A small soft wind blew gently from the east, a wind mild and murmurous and full of rain." While she used a similar style in her other Chinese books, she both modernized and Americanized the language when appropriate.

The Good Earth is the "epic" of a "rags-to-riches" farmer-hero of Old China, practicing his native customs but experiencing the universal drama of birth and death, prosperity and famine, work and sex, tradition and change. The plot is structured by Wang's relationship to three wives – and to his land. The "good" wives sympathize with his love of the land; the "bad" wife hates the land. Like nearly all of Miss Buck's male characters, Wang is inept in human relations, controlled by forces he never understands, yet capable of resisting social pressure and remaining loyal to personal qualities of honesty and kindness. In contrast, nearly all of her female characters are wiser, or craftier, than the men they are destined to serve – an "autobiographical" point of view especially apparent in *This Proud Heart, Pavilion of Women, Peony,* and *Letter from Peking.*

Throughout her writing she portrays religion, slavery, economic tyranny, war, and government as capable of being manipulated by individuals. And although she occasionally generalizes about settings or classes, her character development is consistent, the variety of her "solutions" credible. Certainly her informative handling of cultural conflicts has served her overriding purposes, freedom and reconciliation.

—Esther Marian Greenwell Smith

BULWER-LYTTON, Edward (George Earle); 1st Baron Lytton of Knebworth. English. Born in London, 25 May 1803. Educated at Dr. Ruddock's School in Fulham, London; Dr. Hooker's School at Rottingdean, Sussex; with a Mr. Wallington, Ealing, London, 1818–20; Trinity College, Cambridge (pensioner), 1822, and Trinity Hall, Cambridge (fellow-commoner; Chancellor's Medal for verse, 1825), 1822–25, B.A. 1826, M.A. 1835. Married Rosina Doyle Wheeler in 1827 (separated, 1836); one daughter and one son. Visited Paris, 1825, and thereafter divided his time between London and Paris; settled at Woodcot House, near Pangbourne, Berkshire, 1827, and supported himself by writing for various magazines, including *Quarterly Review, Keepsakes,* and *Books of Beauty*; settled in London, 1829; Editor, *New Monthly Magazine,* London, 1831–33; Liberal Member of Parliament for St. Ives, Cornwall, 1831, and for Lincoln, 1832–41: active supporter of stronger copyright laws and of the removal of taxes on literature; published, with others, *The Monthly Chronicle,* London, 1841; succeeded to the family estate at Knebworth, 1843; travelled abroad, 1849; Conservative Member of Parliament for Hertfordshire, 1852 until his elevation to the peerage, 1866: Secretary for the Colonies, 1858–59. Lord Rector of the University of Glasgow, 1856, 1858. LL.D.: Cambridge University, 1864. Created Baron Lytton, 1866. *Died 18 January 1873.*

PUBLICATIONS

Fiction

Falkland. 1827; edited by Herbert Van Thal, 1967.
Pelham. 1828; revised edition, 1839; edited by Jerome J. McGann, 1972.
The Disowned. 1828.
Devereux. 1829.
Paul Clifford. 1830.
Eugene Aram. 1832.
Asmodeus at Large. 1833.
Godolphin. 1833.
The Last Days of Pompeii. 1834; revised edition, 1835; edited by Edgar Johnson, 1956.
The Pilgrims of the Rhine. 1834.
Rienzi, The Last of the Roman Tribunes. 1835.
Ernest Maltravers. 1837.
Leila; or, The Siege of Granada. 1837.
Alice; or, The Mysteries. 1838.
Calderon, The Courtier. 1838.
Night and Morning. 1841.
Zanoni. 1842.
The Last of the Barons. 1843; edited by F. C. Romilly, 1913.
Lucretia; or, The Children of Night. 1846.
Harold, The Last of the Saxon Kings. 1848; edited by G. L. Gomme, 1906.
The Caxtons: A Family Picture. 1849.
My Novel; or, Varieties in English Life. 1852.
The Haunted and the Haunters. 1857.
What Will He Do with It? 1859.
A Strange Story. 1862; revised edition, 1863.
The Coming Race. 1871.
Kenelm Chillingly: His Adventures and Opinions. 1873.
The Parisians. 1873.
Pausanias the Spartan, edited by Bulwer-Lytton's son. 1876.

Plays

The Duchess de la Vallière (produced 1837).   1836.
The Lady of Lyons; or, Love and Pride (produced 1838).   1838.
Richelieu; or, The Conspiracy (produced 1839).   1839.
The Sea-Captain; or, The Birth-Right (produced 1839).   1839.
Money (produced 1840).   1840.
Not So Bad as We Seem; or, Many Sides to a Character (produced 1851).   1851.
The Rightful Heir (produced 1868).   1868.
Walpole; or, Every Man Has His Price.   1869.
The House of Darnley Court, revised by Charles F. Coghlan (produced 1877).
Junius Brutus; or, The Household Gods (produced 1885).

Verse

Ismael: An Oriental Tale.   1820.
Delmour; or, A Tale of a Sylphid and Other Poems.   1823.
Sculpture.   1825.
Weeds and Wild Flowers.   1826.
O'Neill; or, The Rebel.   1827.
The Siamese Twins: A Satirical Tale.   1831.
Eva, The Ill-Omened Marriage, and Other Poems.   1842.
Poems, edited by C. D. Macleod.   1845.
The New Timon.   1846.
King Arthur: An Epic Poem.   3 vols., 1848–49; revised edition, 1870.
Poetical Works.   1859; revised edition, 1865, 1873.
St. Stephen's.   1860.
The Boatman.   1864.
Lost Tales of Miletus.   1866.

Other

England and the English.   2 vols., 1833; edited by Standish Meachum, 1970.
A Letter to a Late Cabinet Minster on the Present Crisis.   1834.
The Student: A Series of Papers.   2 vols., 1835.
Athens: Its Rise and Fall.   2 vols., 1837.
Critical and Miscellaneous Works.   2 vols., 1841.
Confessions of a Water-Patient.   1846.
A Word to the Public.   1847.
Letters to John Bull Esquire.   1851.
Poetical and Dramatic Works.   5 vols., 1852–54.
Caxtonia: A Series of Essays on Life, Literature, and Manners.   2 vols., 1863.
Miscellaneous Prose Works.   3 vols., 1868.
Speeches.   2 vols., 1874.
Works.   37 vols., 1873–77.
Quarterly Essays.   1875.
Letters to His Wife, edited by Louisa Devey.   1884.
Pamphlets and Sketches.   1887.
Letters to Macready.   1911.
Bulwer and Macready: A Chronicle of the Early Victorian Theatre, edited by Charles H.
   Shattuck.   1958.

Editor, *Literary Remains of William Hazlitt.* 2 vols., 1836.

Translator, *The Poems and Ballads of Schiller.* 2 vols., 1844.
Translator, *The Odes and Epodes of Horace.* 1869.

Bibliography: *XIX Century Fiction* by Michael Sadleir, 2 vols., 1951.

Reading List: *Life, Letters, and Literary Remains,* edited by Earl of Lytton, 2 vols., 1883; *The Life of Lytton,* 2 vols., 1913, and *Bulwer-Lytton,* 1948, both by V. A. G. R. B. Lytton; *Bulwer-Lytton's Novels and Isis Unveiled* by S. B. Liljegren, 1957; *The Newgate Novel 1830–1847* by Keith Hollingsworth, 1963; "Bulwer-Lytton" by Curtis Dahl, in *Victorian Fiction* edited by Lionel Stevenson, 1964; *Bulwer-Lytton: The Fiction of New Regions* by Allen Conrad Christensen, 1977.

*   *   *

"The padded man – that wears the stays – / Who killed the girls and thrilled the boys / With dandy pathos when you wrote" – so in his biting satiric poem "The New Timon and the Poets" Tennyson characterized Edward Bulwer-Lytton, and the description had enough truth in it to cut. Both as a person and as a writer Bulwer was often stiff, affected, prolix, melodramatic, sentimental. But, as in more generous moods Tennyson and almost all his contemporaries would have admitted, this harsh judgment was far too severe and ignored the central role that Bulwer played in earlier Victorian literature. Indeed, no Victorian novelist had a more creatively stimulating influence on his fellow writers than Bulwer-Lytton. None opened so many new paths in fiction for them to follow. His *Pelham* set the character for the "silver-fork" novel of high life and offered the ideal target for Carlyle's *Sartor Resartus*; *Paul Clifford*, *Eugene Aram*, and *Lucretia* effectively established the "Newgate novel" of crime and criminals; *The Last Days of Pompeii* popularized the archaeological novel; *Rienzi*, *Harold*, and *The Last of the Barons* brought careful historical research and contemporary political reference into the English historical novel; *The Caxtons* and *What Will He Do with It?* encouraged the trend toward domestic realism; *Zanoni* and *A Strange Story* made important the novel of the occult; *The Coming Race* is central in the tradition of the utopian science-fiction novel. Dickens, Thackeray, George Eliot, Collins, and others owe him a tremendous debt.

But Bulwer-Lytton's merits are not historical only. He won a huge popularity with a wide reading public from the parlors of England to the backwoods of America. He wrote effective satires, such as *The New Timon*, and graceful essays. He was influential as a critic and as editor of *The New Monthly Magazine*. His *England and the English* was one of the most acute critiques of English culture and society. He had a moderate success as a politician and as a political pamphleteer. Though his epic and lyric poetry, his translations, and his historical writings are rightly forgotten, his plays *The Lady of Lyons* and *Richelieu*, written for the great actor-manager Macready, held the boards into the twentieth century, and still have vitality. Moreover, after a period of denigration, his fiction is gaining more and more critical respect. For behind the too frequently obfuscating diction, wordiness, and generality of his style, there are keen philosophical, political, and moral thought and a sound though currently unfashionable concept of literary art. He has much to say to the reader who will fight through his verbiage, and a number of his novels are still readable today as fascinating and exciting fiction. Though his once brilliant general fame has waned, the "padded man," whose own wife once vengefully accused him of trying to get rid of her by shutting her up in a madhouse but who held the respect and friendship of most of the English literary world of his time, still rightly deserves his just share of praise.

—Curtis Dahl

BUNYAN, John. English. Born in Elstow, Bedfordshire, baptized 30 November 1628. Educated in the village school in Elstow and, possibly, at Bedford Grammar School. Served in the Parliamentary Army, 1644–46. Married 1) c. 1648 (his wife died, 1656), two sons and two daughters; 2) Elizabeth Bunyan in 1659, one son and one daughter. Practised the family trade of tinker, in Elstow and the surrounding area, from 1646; joined a nonconformist church in Bedford, 1653; moved to Bedford, 1655, and began preaching, 1656; ordained, 1657, and quickly became famous as a travelling preacher; indicted for preaching at Eaton Socon, 1658; imprisoned in Bedford Gaol for preaching without a license, 1660–66, 1666–72; licensed to preach, 1672; pastor of the nonconformist congregation in Bedford, 1678 until his death; also preached throughout Bedfordshire and beyond; Chaplain to the Lord Mayor of London, 1688. *Died 31 August 1688.*

PUBLICATIONS

Collections

Complete Works, edited by George Offor.   3 vols., 1860–62.
Miscellaneous Works, edited by Roger Sharrock.   2 vols. (of 13), 1976–78.

Fiction

The Pilgrim's Progress from This World to That Which Is to Come.   1678; revised
    edition, 1679; part 2, 1684; edited by Roger Sharrock, with *Grace Abounding,* 1966.
The Life and Death of Mr. Badman.   1680; edited by G. B. Harrison, 1928.
The Holy War Made by Shaddai upon Diabolus.   1682; edited by Thomas Patrick
    Murphy, 1975.
The Heavenly Footman.   1698; edited by Henri A. Talon, in *God's Knotty Log,* 1961.

Verse

Profitable Meditations Fitted to Man's Different Condition.   1661(?).
A Discourse of the Building of the House of God.   1688.

Other

Some Gospel Truths Opened According to the Scriptures.   1656.
A Vindication of Some Gospel Truths Opened.   1657.
A Few Sighs from Hell; or, The Groans of a Damned Soul.   1658.
The Doctrine of the Law and Grace Unfolded.   1659; edited by Richard L. Greaves, in
    Miscellaneous Works 2, 1976.
I Will Pray with the Spirit and I Will Pray with the Understanding Also.   1663; edited by
    Richard L. Greaves, in *Miscellaneous Works 2,* 1976.
Christian Behaviour; or, The Fruits of True Christianity.   1663.
A Map Showing the Order and Causes of Salvation and Damnation.   1664(?).
One Thing Is Needful; or, Serious Meditations upon the Four Last Things.   1665(?).
The Holy City; or, The New Jerusalem.   1665.
The Resurrection of the Dead.   1665(?).
Grace Abounding to the Chief of Sinners; or, A Brief and Faithful Relation of the Mercy of

God to His Poor Servant John Bunyan. 1666; revised edition, 1772(?); edited by Roger Sharrock, with *Pilgrim's Progress,* 1966.
A Confession of My Faith and a Reason for My Practice. 1672.
A Defence of the Doctrine of Justification by Faith in Jesus Christ. 1672.
Differences in Judgment about Water Baptism. 1673.
The Barren Fig Tree; or, The Doom and Downfall of the Fruitless Professor. 1673.
Reprobation Asserted; or, The Doctrine of Eternal Election and Reprobation Promiscuously Handled. 1674(?).
Light for Them That Sit in Darkness. 1675.
Instruction for the Ignorant. 1675.
The Strait Gate; or, Great Difficulty in Going to Heaven. 1676.
Come and Welcome, to Jesus Christ. 1678.
A Treatise of the Fear of God. 1679.
The Greatness of the Soul and Unspeakableness of the Loss Thereof. 1683.
A Case of Conscience Resolved. 1683.
A Holy Life, The Beauty of Christianity. 1684.
Seasonable Counsel; or, Advice to Sufferers. 1684.
A Discourse upon the Pharisee and the Publican. 1685.
Questions about the Nature and Perpetuity of the Seventh-Day Sabbath. 1685.
A Book for Boys and Girls; or, Country Rhymes for Children. 1686; as *Divine Emblems,* 1724; edited by E. S. Buchanan, 1928.
Good News for the Vilest of Men (includes verse). 1688; as *The Jerusalem Sinner Saved,* 1697.
The Advocateship of Jesus Christ Clearly Explained and Largely Improved. 1688; as *The Work of Jesus Christ as an Advocate,* 1688.
The Water of Life. 1688.
Solomon's Temple Spiritualized; or, Gospel Light Fetched Out of the Temple at Jerusalem. 1688.
The Acceptable Sacrifice. 1689.
Works, edited by Ebenezer Chandler and John Wilson. 1692.
A Relation of the Imprisonment of Bunyan. 1765.

Bibliography: *A Bibliography of the Works of Bunyan* by F. M. Harrison, 1932.

Reading List: *Bunyan: His Life, Times, and Work* by John Brown, 1885, revised by F. M. Harrison, 1928; *Bunyan: A Study in Personality* by F. M. Harrison, 1928; *Bunyan, Mechanick, Preacher* by William York Tindall, 1934; *Bunyan: L'Homme et l'Oeuvre* by Henri A. Talon, 1948; *Bunyan* by Roger Sharrock, 1954; *Bunyan: A Study in Narrative Technique* by Charles Baird, 1977.

*   *   *

It was once widely believed that John Bunyan was an ignorant rustic whose crude allegories and meditations were inspired by evangelical tracts, the Authorized Version, and the Holy Spirit. This misconception may have resulted in part from the calculated pose of Bunyan himself, who, like Robert Burns, was inclined to dramatize himself as the egalitarian spokesman of the common man. In reality, in spite of his humble origins, lack of formal education, and unexalted occupations of tinker, soldier, and "mechanic" Baptist preacher, Bunyan was an accomplished student of medieval pulpit literature, patristic writings, emblem books, Spenser's *Faerie Queene,* Milton's poetry, and the whole range of Reformation theological works by Luther, Zwingli, Calvin, and many others. Whether by self-training or instinct, moreover, he was an astute logician and masterful prose stylist, as is evidenced by his first two polemical tracts, *Some Gospel Truths Opened* and *A Vindication of Some Gospel*

Truths Opened, both composed in refutation of Bunyan's Quaker neighbors in Bedford. Both tracts set forth the Reformation tenets he was to flesh out in allegory and characterizations in his later writings for ordinary readers – the priesthood of all believers, the autonomy of Scripture, predestination, total depravity, and salvation by faith alone. These were commonplace Protestant doctrines, hardly original with Bunyan, who was not an innovative theologian or even a very original religious thinker, but they were simple ideas he was able to render in powerfully affective narratives, and in a time when such ideas, fired in the crucible of widespread religious persecutions, struck Bunyan's readers with great emotional force. Essentially a preacher, he knew how to reach out from his pulpit and touch the nerves and hearts of a vast congregation of simple, uneducated listeners.

His disarming directness and candor are apparent in his extraordinary and immensely popular autobiography *Grace Abounding to the Chief of Sinners* written during the twelve years he spent in prison for unlicensed preaching. Like St. Augustine's *Confessions*, it charts the progress of the author through despair and alienation to joyous reconciliation, and its one abiding message is deceptively simple: "Take hope, my readers, because I, chief among sinners, have experienced God's light." In the first part he describes his arduous, faltering trek to conversion; in the second his equally agonizing decision to enter the ministry. The first part is populated by characters as vivid and lively as any in Fielding or Dickens – his uncomprehending, tawdry parents; village toughs and roisterers; rough companions among Cromwell's pikemen; and his saintly wife, who read to him from soul-awakening evangelical tracts like *The Plain Man's Pathway to Happiness*. Compelling for its graphic literary qualities, *Grace Abounding*, is equally fascinating as a study in the psychopathology of guilt. Behind the visible characters and events looms the vacillating spirit, lurching from despair to ecstasy, from sinful bondage to the sudden release of vindication, from feelings of depravity to glowing transcendence. After an inspiring Sunday sermon, Bunyan joys in the conviction that he is surely among the Elect; at the next moment the sight of a pretty ankle or the tantalizing scent from a tavern door sends his spirit plummeting to Satan's carnal regions. Can he truly be predestined for Election if his weak flesh responds so easily to worldly temptations? Frail men long for a sign to end their doubts, but Scripture tells them there will be no sign, only the agony of pursuit that tests a wavering faith. Thus *Grace Abounding* is a poignant account of all the cruel afflictions of the Puritan experience.

Bunyan's next classic, *The Pilgrim's Progress*, is in the same direct, unpretentious style, but employs allegorical characterizations and narrative. If Spenser had fashioned his *Faerie Queene* for the edification of Queen Elizabeth's courtly gentlemen, Bunyan composed his *Pilgrim's Progress* for the spiritual inspiration of God's humblest Christians, and the amazing popularity of the work attests to Bunyan's keen awareness of the emotional needs of his readers. Not content with Milton's "fit audience, though few," Bunyan strives to reach the masses with a plain allegory devoid of theological complexities. His myth, based on the age-old device of the journey, describes his hero Christian's struggle to achieve salvation (the Celestial City) amid a world filled with such easily recognized threats to the soul as Vanity Fair and Giant Despair. Obviously Bunyan had read Book I of the *Faerie Queene* and stripped Spenser's allegory of its courtly equipage and philosophical complexities. The plain truth plainly told is Bunyan's guiding principle, embellished artistically by his sure sense of drama and talent for concrete, evocative description. *Pilgrim's Progress* is replete with what in modern parlance is called subliminal communication; through massing of associative images, Bunyan, to an extent even greater than that of Spenser, can make his readers *feel* the ugliness of vice and the beauties of virtue. Bunyan's deceptively simple style, consisting of a sonorous, rhythmic syntax clothed in images from folklore and the Bible, endured with the masses until the decline of religious sentiment in the twentieth century, when his *Pilgrim's Progress* was forgotten by the masses and first appreciated by the literati.

In his *Life and Death of Mr. Badman* Bunyan combines medieval exemplum, allegory, and dialogue, the last much favored for theological disputation. The work was intended as a companion-piece to *Pilgrim's Progress*. Whereas the story of Christian and his wife is a success tale depicting the various stages on the ascent to salvation, the narrative of Mr.

Badman shows all the sordid steps in the descent to damnation. Bunyan's preface "To the Courteous Reader" makes clear that his story is intended to illustrate the awesome universality of human depravity, the terrifying finality of original sin. The dialogue that follows is between Mr. Wiseman, who relates Mr. Badman's sinful life, and Mr. Attentive, who provides questions enabling Wiseman to expand into details and interpretations at various points of the narrative. *The Life and Death of Mr. Badman* is patently less effective as literature than *Pilgrim's Progress* because, first, the dialogue form in the service of narration appears forced and artificial, always lapsing into sermonizing; and second, the fact that Mr. Badman is totally depraved from birth, totally beyond any possibility of redemption, gives the story a static, repetitious effect. Mr. Badman has none of Faustus's capacity for virtue; indeed, Bunyan's obligation to prove the ineluctible power of original sin prevents him from portraying a flexible, multi-dimensional anti-hero responding to experience. Hence Mr. Badman is not shaped by experience but doomed by hereditary curse; his actions are narrowly restricted to a somewhat tedious repetition of the Seven Deadly Sins. It would appear that in this work, at least, Bunyan's role as Baptist preacher wholly committed to expounding the doctrine of original sin prevented him from exercising his natural genius as a writer.

Bunyan's voluminous works include not only autobiography and allegorical fiction but children's verse, sermons, meditations, and theological tracts. A self-educated evangelist with an astonishing range of interests, he saw his religious faith as applicable to every human activity, and his one abiding goal as a writer was to communicate his clear vision of God.

—James E. Ruoff

BURKE, Edmund. Irish. Born in Dublin, 12 January 1729. Educated at Abraham Shackleton's school in Ballitore, County Kildare, 1741–43; Trinity College, Dublin, 1744–48, B.A. 1748; entered the Middle Temple, London, 1750; left the law for literary work, 1755. Married Jane Nugent in 1756; two sons. Settled in London: Editor, *Annual Register*, 1759–66, and contributor to it until 1788; Private Secretary to William Gerard Hamilton, 1759–64: accompanied him to Ireland, 1763–64, and received a pension on Hamilton's retirement, 1764; Whig Member of Parliament for Wendover, 1765–74, Bristol, 1774–80, and for Malton, Yorkshire, 1781–94: Private Secretary to the Marquis of Rockingham, 1765; attacked administrations of Chatham and Grafton, especially their handling of the American question, 1767; vigorously opposed policies of the Tory government, 1769; succeeded in convincing Parliament to publicize its proceedings, 1771; attacked the North ministry's handling of affairs, 1774–75, and strongly advocated peace with the American colonies, 1775–76; advocated economic reform in the public services and limitations on the slave trade, 1780; by his attacks on the conduct of the American war, forced North to resign, 1781–82; in new Whig government served as Paymaster-General of the Forces, under Rockingham, 1782, and Portland, 1783, but was never given a Cabinet post; advocated self-government for Ireland, 1782; drafted the government's East India bill, 1783; involved in the impeachment of Warren Hastings of the East India Company, 1786–95; passed over by Fox ministry in forming a new Cabinet, but supported Fox in upholding the right of the Prince of Wales to regency, 1788; supported Wilberforce in advocating abolition of the slave trade, 1788–89; spoke against French democracy, 1790; quarrelled with Fox and the Whigs, 1791, and advised support for Pitt and the Tories, 1792; retired from Parliament, 1794. Lord Rector, University of Glasgow, 1784, 1785; encouraged foundation of Maynooth College, 1795; established school for sons of French refugees at Penn, Buckinghamshire, 1796. LL.D.: Dublin University, 1891. Granted government pension, 1794. *Died 9 July 1797.*

PUBLICATIONS

Collections

Works, edited by French Laurence and Walker King.   8 vols., 1792–1827.
Select Works, edited by E. J. Payne.   3 vols., 1874–78.
Correspondence, edited by T. W. Copeland.   10 vols., 1958–77.
Selected Writings and Speeches, edited by P. J. Stanlis.   1963.

Prose

A Vindication of Natural Society in a Letter.   1756.
An Account of the European Settlements in America, by William Burke, revised by Edmund Burke.   2 vols., 1757.
A Philosophical Enquiry into the Origin of Our Ideas of the Sublime and Beautiful.   1757.
An Essay Towards an Abridgement of the English History.   1757.
A Short Account of a Late Short Administration.   1766.
Observations on a Late State of the Nation.   1769.
Thoughts on the Cause of the Present Discontents.   1770.
Reflections on the Revolution in France.   1790; edited by Conor Cruise O'Brien, 1969.
Two Letters on the French Revolution.   1791.
An Appeal from the New to the Old Whigs.   1791.
Report from the Committee of the House of Commons on the Trial of Warren Hastings.   1794.
Thoughts on the Prospect of a Regicide Peace.   1796.
Three Memorials on French Affairs Written 1791, 1792, and 1793.   1797.
Thoughts and Details on Scarcity.   1800.
The Catholic Claims.   1807.
Speeches in the House of Commons and in Westminster Hall.   4 vols., 1816.
Epistolary Correspondence of Burke and French Laurence.   1827.
Letters, Speeches, and Tracts on Irish Affairs, edited by Matthew Arnold.   1881.
Burke's Politics: Selected Writings and Speeches on Reform, Revolution, and War, edited by R. J. S. Hoffman and P. Levack.   1949.
A Note-Book, edited by W. V. F. Somerset.   1957.
The Philosophy of Burke: A Selection, edited by Louis I. Bredvold and R. G. Ross.   1960.

Editor, *The Annual Register.*   8 vols., 1759–66.
Editor, *J. P. Brissot to His Constituents*, translated by William Burke.   1794.

Bibliography: *A Bibliography of Burke 1748–1968* by P. J. Stanlis, 1972.

Reading List: *Burke and His Literary Friends* by Donald C. Bryant, 1939; *Burke* by Harold Laski, 1947; *Our Eminent Friend Burke: Six Essays* by T. W. Copeland, 1949; *The Moral Basis of Burke's Political Thought* by Charles Parkin, 1956; *Burke* by T. E. Utley, 1957; *Burke and the Natural Law* by P. J. Stanlis, 1958; *Burke: The Practical Imagination* by G. W. Chapman, 1967; *Burke* edited by Isaac Kramnick, 1974; *The Rage of Burke: Portrait of an Ambivalent Conservative* by Isaac Kramnick, 1977.

*   *   *

Edmund Burke's achievement in literature and thought may be considered under three rubrics: criticism, politics, and rhetorical style. His *Philosophical Enquiry into the Origin of Our Ideas of the Sublime and Beautiful*, an apparently anomalous work in the canon of one so deeply committed to Parliamentary affairs, is the product of his early intellectual endeavours before he sought to make his political fortune. Burke never again wrote so substantially about critical problems, although he did continue to show a lively interest in literature, as demonstrated, for example, by his reviews in the *Annual Register*, his connections with Samuel Johnson and other members of the Literary Club, and his patronage of George Crabbe.

In the *Enquiry*, Burke distinguishes between the two esthetic states, the sublime and the beautiful, on the basis of their psychological origins, particularly in sensation. Burke grounds the sublime upon the complex feeling of "delight," which, unlike ordinary or simple pleasure, results from the removal of pain or danger; and, unlike pleasure, is characterized by feelings of awe, surprise, and a tranquillity tinged with a sense of horror. Whatever excites a kind of "delightful horror," those ideas of pain and danger which permit, as it were, an esthetic distance, not the actual circumstances themselves, is an "efficient" cause of the sublime. Ideas, then, that generate the sublime effect are all terrifying, for terror is its ruling principle: vacuity, obscurity, darkness, solitude, silence, infinity, vastness, difficulty, negligent ruggedness, magnificence, massive solidity, and power.

For his theory of the beautiful, Burke grounds this esthetic state upon the pleasure of love, some quality in beautiful objects, he believes, causing love. The specific qualities of beauty, relative to those of sublimity, are smallness, smoothness, gradual variation, delicacy, and clear bright colors. Burke denies, however, that proportion, perfection, and fitness are ingredients of the beautiful. In the history of criticism, Burke's theory of the beautiful is less significant than that of the sublime – and much less original.

Burke's originality in this treatise consists in his elaborating a distinction between sublimity and beauty, a contrast that was significant to the development of the complex of ideas and qualities constituting Romanticism. But his esthetics, like affective and romantic theory, raises more questions than it settles, for it does not explore meaningfully normative problems of value.

In political thought and practice, Burke is significant for two great contributions to our time – for establishing the concept, structure, and function of modern political parties and, in this connection, developing the possibility of a continuing loyal Opposition; and for systematically illuminating the principles of modern conservatism. The first, the idea of open parties as legitimate vehicles of constitutional government, is proposed in *Thoughts on the Cause of the Present Discontents*. Here Burke argues for the need of a political party to counteract the King's influence in Parliament, as he raises serious objections to attempts to fortify and extend the royal prerogative, theorizes over a court cabal or secret "double cabinet," and criticizes the "King's friends" who constituted it. From 1770 to 1782, through the period of the American troubles, Burke was the party whip of the Rockingham Whigs in the House of Commons, and kept its members from abandoning their role as Opposition to the King.

Burke's conservative social and political philosphy remained the same from his first work, *A Vindication of Natural Society*, to his last group of publications on French affairs, including the celebrated *Reflections on the Revolution in France* and the essay in which he summarizes and defends his career in politics, *A Letter to a Noble Lord*. In the *Vindication*, Burke ironically demonstrates the absurdity of Bolingbroke's principles of natural religion by showing that if they were applied to civilized government as they had been to religion they would justify the destruction of civilized society and a return to "natural society" with as much validity as they had justified the adoption of natural religion.

Burke detested the deists for the unrelenting rigor in which they pursued nature as an ideal norm of value without considering the practical effect upon the structure of society. Believing that it is equally natural for man to live in accordance with tradition and law, to form social groups and develop a civilized and hierarchal order, Burke attacked those abstract perfectionists who wished to reform society by returning romantically to what he thought was an unreal state of nature. On the contrary, he asserted in his polemical *Appeal from the New to the Old Whigs,* "Art is man's nature." Therefore he passionately attacked not only deists and rationalists in his *Reflections* and his other writings on French Revolutionary ideals, but all levellers who wished to destroy long-established traditions and institutions made venerable by continued use in the course of time, while they asserted their hopes for equality and natural rights. Moreover, Burke was consistently sceptical of metaphysical reason when it pretended to be exact and conclusive in social affairs. He preferred to abide by the norms of prudence and moderation, guided by natural law, established precedents and patterns of behavior. Even in his great speeches on American Taxation (1774) and Conciliation with the Colonies (1775), Burke took a stand against the Parliamentary majority on prudential grounds.

As he responded to the controversial issues and events at the end of the eighteenth century, Burke hammered out a philosophy of political conservatism, the basic principles being the doctrine of aristocratic trusteeship – that is, civil authority must be restricted to men "of permanent property"; the sacredness of prescriptive rights – the hereditary principle of succession is necessary for social stability and order, and tradition and precedent are more significant than innovation; the utility of an established church – an alliance of civil government and the church is necessary for maintaining social order; and the positive value of a hereditary monarchy – monarchy protects liberty from the tyranny of the majority or democracy. With some modification, these principles have proved to be adaptable to nineteenth- and twentieth-century conservatism, thereby demonstrating their durability.

Finally, Burke is notable for the Baroque pomp and splendor of his oratory. In Parliamentary affairs, Burke was an experienced and skilful speaker who, if not always persuasive, was always fascinating for the sublimity of his discourse. Impassioned, rich in imagery and literary allusion, learned, and thoughtful, many of his speeches have become oratorical classics, those on America and on India and the impeachment of Warren Hastings being particularly outstanding. Similarly, the style of his written essays meant for the eye rather than the ear, like the *Reflections,* is characterized by a splendid manly vigor, a rhetorical audacity appropriate to the challenges presented by his compelling argument.

—Martin Kallich

BURNETT, Frances (Eliza) Hodgson.   American.   Born in Cheetham Hill, Manchester, England, 24 November 1849; emigrated with her parents to Knoxville, Tennessee, 1865; naturalized, 1905. Educated in schools in Manchester. Married 1) Dr. Swan Moses Burnett in 1873 (divorced, 1898), two sons; 2) Stephen Townesend in 1900 (separated, 1901; died, 1914). Full-time writer from 1866; lived in Europe, 1875–77; settled in Washington, D.C., 1877; lived in England, 1898–1901, then settled near Plandome Park on Long Island. *Died 29 October 1924.*

PUBLICATIONS

Fiction

Surly Tim and Other Stories. 1877.
Theo: A Love Story. 1877.
Pretty Polly Pemberton: A Love Story. 1877.
That Lass o' Lowries. 1877.
Dolly: A Love Story. 1877; as *Vagabondia*, 1883.
Kathleen: A Love Story. 1878.
Miss Crespigny: A Love Story. 1878.
Earlier Stories. 1878; second series, 1878.
A Quiet Life, and The Tide on the Moaning Bar. 1878.
Our Neighbour Opposite. 1878.
Jarl's Daughter and Other Stories. 1879.
Natalie and Other Stories. 1879.
Haworth's. 1879.
Louisiana. 1880.
A Fair Barbarian. 1881.
Through One Administration. 1883.
Little Lord Fauntleroy. 1886.
A Woman's Will; or, Miss Defarge. 1887.
Sara Crewe; or, What Happened at Miss Minchin's. 1887.
Editha's Burglar. 1888.
The Fortunes of Philippa Fairfax. 1888.
The Pretty Sister of José. 1889.
Little Saint Elizabeth and Other Stories. 1890.
Children I Have Known. 1892; as *Giovanni and the Other: Children Who Have Made Stories*, 1894.
The Captain's Youngest and Other Stories. 1894; as *Piccino and Other Child Stories*, 1894.
Two Little Pilgrims' Progress: A Story of the City Beautiful. 1895.
A Lady of Quality. 1896.
His Grace of Osmonde. 1897.
In Connection with the De Willoughby Claim. 1899.
The Making of a Marchioness. 1901; revised edition, 1901.
The Methods of Lady Walderhurst. 1901.
In the Closed Room. 1904.
A Little Princess, Being the Whole Story of Sara Crewe Now Told for the First Time. 1905.
Racketty Packetty House. 1905.
The Dawn of a Tomorrow. 1906.
The Troubles of Queen Silver-Bell. 1906.
The Cozy Lion, as Told by Queen Crosspatch. 1907.
The Spring Cleaning, as Told by Queen Crosspatch. 1908.
The Shuttle. 1908.
The Good Wolf. 1908.
Barty Crusoe and His Man Saturday. 1909.
The Land of the Blue Flower. 1909.
The Secret Garden. 1911.
My Robin. 1912.
T. Tembarom. 1913.
The Lost Prince. 1915.

The Way to the House of Santa Claus: A Christmas Story. 1916.
Little Hunchback Zia. 1916.
The White People. 1917.
The Head of the House of Coombe. 1922.
Robin. 1922.

Plays

That Lass o' Lowries, with Julian Magnus, from the novel by Burnett (produced 1878).
Esmeralda, with William Gillette (produced 1881; as *Young Folks' Ways,* produced
    1883). 1882.
The Real Little Lord Fauntleroy, from her own novel (produced 1888).
Phyllis, from her own novel *The Fortunes of Philippa Fairfax* (produced 1889).
Editha's Burglar, with Stephen Townesend, from the novel by Burnett (produced 1890;
    as *Nixie,* produced 1890).
The Showman's Daughter, with Stephen Townesend (produced 1891).
The First Gentleman of Europe, with Constance Fletcher (produced 1897).
A Lady of Quality, with Stephen Townesend, from the novel by Burnett (produced
    1897).
A Little Princess, from her own novel *Sara Crewe* (as *A Little Unfairy Princess,* produced
    1902; as *A Little Princess,* produced 1903).   In *Treasury of Plays for Children,* edited
    by Montrose J. Moses, 1921.
The Pretty Sister of José, from her own novel (produced 1903).
That Man and I, from her own novel *In Connection with the De Willoughby Claim*
    (produced 1903).
The Dawn of a Tomorrow, from her own novel (produced 1909).
Racketty Packetty House, from her own novel (produced 1912).

Other

The Drury Lane Boys' Club. 1892.
The One I Knew Best of All: A Memory of the Mind of a Child (autobiography). 1893.
In the Garden. 1925.

Reading List: *Mrs. Ewing, Mrs. Molesworth, and Mrs. Burnett* by Marghanita Laski, 1950;
Waiting for the Party: The Life of Burnett by Ann Thwaite, 1974.

*   *   *

When Frances Hodgson Burnett died in 1924, *The Times'* obituary writer praised her work
in helping to bring about the 1911 Copyright Act but decided that it was almost solely by her
"idyll of child life" *Little Lord Fauntleroy* that Mrs. Burnett would be remembered. *Times*
readers rushed to deny that her claims to permanence were so limited. Some of her adult
novels were mentioned and, of course, *The Secret Garden.* In fact, since her death, her three
major children's books, *Fauntleroy, A Little Princess,* and *The Secret Garden,* have never
been out of print. *Fauntleroy* made an immediate impact on its first publication. Along with
King Solomon's Mines and *War and Peace* it was one of the best-selling novels of 1886 in
America, read by old and young alike. The descriptions of the "handsome, blooming, curly-
headed little fellow" may be nauseating to today's taste but it remains an excellent story.
    Its wild success changed Mrs. Burnett's career. Up till this time, she had been gradually
establishing herself as a serious and important novelist. In 1877 her American publisher,

Scribner, wrote to her English publisher, Warne, "She is considered by good judges as the 'Coming Woman' in literature." The *Boston Transcript* wrote of her first full-length novel, *That Lass o' Lowries*: "We know of no more powerful work from a woman's hand in the English language, not even excepting the best of George Eliot." Both this novel and *Haworth's* were set in industrial Lancashire with a liberal use of the dialect which had fascinated her even as a young child in Manchester.

Through One Administration, her last adult novel before *Fauntleroy*, is a considerable achievement, proving that Mrs. Burnett was indeed much more than the romantic middle-brow novelist her later books suggest. It was not the love between Bertha Amory and Tredennis that interested her; it was the lack of love between Bertha and Richard Amory. And the novel's picture of Washington lobbying, of machinations and intrigues, is vivid and convincing. It was at this time (in an article in the July 1883 issue of *The Century*) that Mrs. Burnett was named as one of the five writers in America "who hold the front rank today in general estimation." Then came *Fauntleroy*, a great deal of money and a pattern of writing which had to keep pace with her new way of life – large houses, numerous crossings of the Atlantic, and a constant demand for her talents.

The most interesting of her later adult books are *A Woman's Will*, her autobiography, *The One I Knew the Best of All*, *The Shuttle*, and *The Making of a Marchioness*, In Marghanita Laski's words, the last is a "fairy story diluted with unromantic realism," and it is that realistic treatment of its period which gives it its special appeal today.

Much of the appeal of her children's story *A Little Princess* is its period charm. But its incredible coincidences do not conceal Mrs. Burnett's understanding of children. Sara is real in an unreal story. *The Secret Garden* has real children in a real story. Two unhappy children are convincingly transformed, not by outside intervention but by their own determination. It is a book which made no great impact on publication, but it has steadily established itself as one of the few real classics of children's literature.

—Ann Thwaite

BURNEY, Fanny (Frances Burney). English. Born in King's Lynn, Norfolk, 13 June 1752; moved with her family to London, 1760. Married the French officer Alexandre d'Arblay in 1793 (died, 1818); one son and one daughter. From 1778 member of the London literary circle of Mrs. Thrale: a friend of Johnson, Burke, Sheridan, and Garrick; Second Keeper of the Robes to Queen Charlotte, 1786 until she retired with a pension, 1791; lived in France, 1802–12, 1814–15; thereafter lived in retirement in London. *Died 6 January 1840.*

PUBLICATIONS

Collections

Journals and Letters, edited by Joyce Hemlow and others.   1972—

Fiction

Evelina; or, The History of a Young Lady's Entrance into the World.   1778; edited by Edward A. Bloom, 1968.

197

Cecilia; or, Memoirs of an Heiress.   1782; edited by R. B. Johnson, 1893.
Camilla; or, A Picture of Youth.   1796; revised edition, 1802; edited by Edward A. and
   Lillian D. Bloom, 1972.
The Wanderer; or, Female Difficulties.   1814.

Play

Edwy and Elgiva (produced 1795).   Edited by Miriam J. Benkovitz, 1957.

Other

Brief Reflections Relative to the Emigrant French Clergy.   1793.
Memoirs of Dr. Burney.   3 vols., 1832.
Diary and Letters 1778–1840, edited by Charlotte Frances Barrett.   7 vols., 1842–46;
   edited by Austin Dobson, 6 vols., 1904–05; selections edited by John Wain, 1960.
The Early Diary 1768–78, edited by Annie Raine Ellis.   2 vols., 1889; revised
   edition, 1907.

Reading List: *Poets and Story-Tellers* by David Cecil, 1949; *The History of Fanny Burney* by
Joyce Hemlow, 1958; *Burney, Novelist: A Study in Technique* by Eugene White, 1960;
Burney by Michael E. Adelstein, 1968.

*   *   *

A novel, as conceived by Fanny Burney, "is, or it ought to be a picture of supposed, but
natural and probable human existence. It holds, therefore, in its hands our best affections; it
exercises our imaginations; it points out the path of honour; and gives to juvenile credulity
knowledge of the world, without ruin, or repentance; and the lessons of experience, without
its tears." This, essentially, was the critical creed to which she adhered with the tenacity of
absolute conviction. The limitations are self-evident, but within them – even granting often
flawed textures of character and incident – she wrought stories that have delighted readers for
two hundred years since publication of *Evelina.* Fiction was Fanny Burney's private world of
imagination transposed into a filtered reality, peculiar to her ethos, which she equated with
moral truthfulness. It was a truthfulness sometimes too high-flown for pragmatic tastes.
Nevertheless it was compounded of respect for traditional Christian values and a sense that
these values must be confirmed by individual experience, growth, and self-identity. Each of
her young heroines – Evelina, Cecilia, Camilla, Juliet – is subjected to the rites of social
initiation as the requisite for private discovery. Simultaneously each heroine emerges from
the seclusion of self, stirring in sympathetic readers the pangs and joys of maturing.
Avowedly didactic, thus, Fanny Burney was in palpable control of the feeling heart.
    Although she never quite shook off the bias inculcated in proper young females that novels
were morally suspect, she was unable to resist either the compulsion of her own creative
spirit or the lure of literary fame and fortune. At least in her first two novels – *Evelina* and
Cecilia – she wrote with a passionate intensity that conveys the sense of necessity indigenous
in all good if not necessarily great art. And she wrote about human fallibility and nobility,
about poignant and comic experience, in such a way as to encase her truths in the agreeably
disguised symbols of highly entertaining narration. There is an organic impulse in the earlier
novels – a union of wisdom and invention – that has insured Fanny Burney's permanent
niche in literary history. By common consent she is an important transitional novelist,
carrying on the traditions of Richardson, Fielding, and Smollett while creating a modest
tradition of her own, and then passing that on to Jane Austen.

The architectonics of fiction never engaged her as much as its potential for edification. Certainly she was no bold innovator in structure. Having employed, and quite successfully, the epistolary format of *Evelina*, she was content thereafter to write in the more conventional episodic manner of the omniscient author. The capacious, sometimes melodramatic, structures of *Cecilia*, *Camilla*, and *The Wanderer* were better suited to authorial exhortation than were the subjective letters (even when penned by a persona like the Reverend Mr. Villars). That tendency toward didactic statement, increasingly apparent after *Evelina*, was in part deference to public taste. But it was also symptomatic of the author's view of her own craft. Periodically, however, she flashes forth in scenes whose comic dialogue remind us that Fanny Burney was dramatically talented. In at least two of her plays (unfortunately never produced) she reveals the kind of comic spirit which brightens some of the somber restraint of *Cecilia* and *The Wanderer*. Balancing that disposition toward the hortatory, therefore, is an attractive strain of wit and satire. Comic mischance, social stumbling, any manners indeed which reveal the vulgar posturings of such commoners as the Branghtons, Mrs. Mittin and Mr. Dubster, sailors and shopkeepers, are the entertaining if implicitly cruel resources of a snobbish author.

Fops and well-born cads are also targets in these novels. And they, like the vulgarians, are important to the diversity which constitutes Fanny Burney's often complex plots and informs an almost central theme: youthful innocence, often orphaned, must come to virtuous maturity despite the temptations and bad examples which confront it constantly. The heroine is especially vulnerable when, like Cecilia or Juliet, she is stranded in an alien society without financial means of her own. A Burney heroine, however, is endowed with innate goodness which causes her not only to withstand ultimate temptation but to learn from it. Some, like Evelina and Camilla, err frequently and are humiliated. But through error they gradually discover the prudence that comes with maturity, and they are assisted by the benevolent concern of guardian figures and their future husbands.

The rewards for prudent conduct may stretch belief, but they are the essence of much that we hold dear in the fairy-tale ethic. In Fanny Burney's ideal world, an excellent marriage, freedom from financial care, and the lasting love of parent or guardian become the zenith of social well-being. The rascals retreat in confusion, but they have served their purpose, giving "to juvenile credulity knowledge of the world, without ruin, or repentance; and the lessons of experience, without its tears."

—Edward A. Bloom

BURROUGHS, Edgar Rice. American. Born in Chicago, Illinois, 1 September 1875. Educated at the Harvard School, Chicago, 1888–91; Phillips Academy, Andover, Massachusetts, 1891–92; Michigan Military Academy, Orchard Lake, 1892–95. Served in the United States 7th Cavalry, 1896–97; Illinois Reserve Militia, 1918–19. Married 1) Emma Centennia Hulbert in 1900 (divorced, 1934), two sons and one daughter; 2) Florence Dearholt in 1935 (divorced, 1942). Instructor and Assistant Commandant, Michigan Military Academy, 1895–96; owner of a stationery store, Pocatello, Idaho, 1898; worked in his father's American Battery Company, Chicago, 1899–1903; joined his brother's Sweetser-Burroughs Mining Company, Idaho, 1903–04; railroad policeman, Oregon Short Line Railroad Company, Salt Lake City, 1904; Manager of the Stenographic Department, Sears, Roebuck and Company, Chicago, 1906–08; Partner, Burroughs and Dentzer, advertising contractors, Chicago, 1908–09; Office Manager, Physicians Co-Operative Association, Chicago, 1909; Partner, Stace-Burroughs Company, salesmanship firm, Chicago, 1909;

worked for Champlain Yardley Company, stationers, Chicago, 1910–11; Manager, System Service Bureau, Chicago, 1912–13; free-lance writer after 1913: formed Edgar Rice Burroughs Inc., publishers, 1913; Burroughs-Tarzan Enterprises, 1934–39, and Burroughs-Tarzan Pictures, 1934–37; lived in California after 1919; Mayor of Malibu Beach, 1933; also United Press Correspondent in the Pacific during World War II, and Columnist ("Laugh It Off"), *Honolulu Advertiser*, 1941–42, 1945. *Died 19 March 1950.*

PUBLICATIONS

Fiction

Tarzan of the Apes. 1914.
The Return of Tarzan. 1915.
The Beasts of Tarzan. 1916.
The Son of Tarzan. 1917.
A Princess of Mars. 1917.
Tarzan and the Jewels of Opar. 1918.
The Gods of Mars. 1918.
Jungle Tales of Tarzan. 1919.
The Warlord of Mars. 1919.
Tarzan the Untamed (stories). 1920.
Thuvia, Maid of Mars. 1920.
Tarzan the Terrible. 1921.
The Mucker (stories). 1921; as *The Mucker* and *The Man Without a Soul* 2 vols., 1922.
The Chessmen of Mars. 1922.
At the Earth's Core. 1922.
Tarzan and the Golden Lion. 1923.
The Girl from Hollywood. 1923.
Pellucidar. 1923.
Tarzan and the Ant Men. 1924.
The Land That Time Forgot (stories). 1924.
The Bandit of Hell's Bend. 1925.
The Eternal Lover (stories). 1925; as *The Eternal Savage.* 1963.
The Cave Girl (stories). 1925.
The Mad King (stories). 1926.
The Moon Maid (stories). 1926; as *The Moon Men,* 1962.
The Tarzan Twins (juvenile). 1927.
The Outlaw of Torn. 1927.
The War Chief. 1927.
Tarzan, Lord of the Jungle. 1928.
The Master Mind of Mars. 1928.
Tarzan and the Lost Empire. 1929.
The Monster Men. 1929.
Tarzan at the Earth's Core. 1930.
Tanar of Pellucidar. 1930.
Tarzan the Invincible. 1931.
A Fighting Man of Mars. 1931.
Tarzan Triumphant. 1932.
Jungle Girl. 1932; as *The Land of Hidden Men,* 1963.
Tarzan and the City of Gold. 1933.
Apache Devil. 1933.

Tarzan and the Lion-Man. 1934.
Pirates of Venus. 1934.
Tarzan and the Leopard Man. 1935.
Lost on Venus. 1935.
Tarzan and the Tarzan Twins with Jad-Bal-Ja, The Golden Lion (juvenile). 1936.
Tarzan's Quest. 1936.
Swords of Mars. 1936.
The Oakdale Affair; The Rider. 1937.
Back to the Stone Age. 1937.
Tarzan and the Forbidden City. 1938.
The Lad and the Lion. 1938.
Tarzan the Magnificent (stories). 1939.
Carson of Venus. 1939.
The Deputy Sheriff of Comanche County. 1940.
Synthetic Men of Mars. 1940.
Land of Terror. 1944.
Escape on Venus (stories). 1946.
Tarzan and the Foreign Legion. 1947.
Llana of Gathol (stories). 1948.
Beyond Thirty (story). 1955.
The Man-Eater (story). 1955.
The Lost Continent (stories). 1963.
Savage Pellucidar (stories). 1963.
Escape on Venus (stories). 1964.
Tales of Three Planets. 1964.
John Carter of Mars (stories). 1964.
Beyond the Farthest Star. 1964.
Tarzan and the Castaways (stories). 1964.
Tarzan and the Madman. 1964.
The Girl from Farris's. 1965.
The Efficiency Expert. 1966.
I Am a Barbarian. 1967.
Pirate Blood. 1970.

Other

Official Guide of the Tarzan Clans of America. 1939.

Reading List: *Explorers of the Infinite* by Sam Moskowitz, 1963; *Burroughs, Master of Adventure* by Richard A. Lupoff, 1965; *Burroughs, The Man Who Created Tarzan* by Irwin Porges, 1975 (includes bibliography).

*   *   *

When almost 36 years old, with a wife and three children, disappointed in his military and various business careers, Edgar Rice Burroughs decided to try fiction-writing. His first sale, later printed in hardcovers as *A Princess of Mars*, was serialized in *All-Story Magazine* in 1912. The first of a series still immensely popular, the novel illustrates most of the strengths and weaknesses of his works. Fast-paced, colorful, and often strikingly imaginative, it stimulates the sense of wonder, especially of children and juveniles. The one-dimensional characters are either evil or good, and the use of coincidence is abused. Though his "Barsoomian" cultures are vividly presented, they are not developed in depth. The historical novel that he next wrote, *The Outlaw of Torn*, and his "realistic" stories, notably those of crime and corruption in Chicago and Hollywood, illustrate his failure to be convincing at anything other than fantasy. Tales set on Mars, in darkest Africa, or in earth's centre, worlds which neither he nor his readers knew much about, were never-never lands that he could deal with.

Burroughs is best known as the creator of Tarzan, son of an English nobleman, Lord Greystoke, raised from the age of one in the African jungle by language-using great apes. Critics have maintained that Burroughs wrote *Tarzan of the Apes* to demonstrate his belief in the superiority of heredity over environment, and especially of the superior heredity of the British nobility. In one sense they are correct. Tarzan's human genes gave him an intelligence superior to the apes'; they gave him an innate curiosity and drive which would have taken him out of any ghetto or other underprivileged community he had been born into. But in the final analysis it was the environment which molded Tarzan's character. Raised as a feral child, he is a classic example of the outsider, one who has an objective view of human society because he has not imbibed its irrationalities along with his mother's milk. Through Tarzan's eyes, Burroughs satirizes Homo sapiens, as he did through some of his other heroes, notably Carson Napier of the "Venus" series.

However, Burroughs's ape-man is more than a Voltairean observer or noble savage. Though he regards pre-literates as superior in their way of life to civilized peoples, he is never quite human. He is, when in the jungle, free of the mundane, drab, wearing, and often tragic restrictions of tribal or civilized life. It is his being a law unto himself and his extreme closeness to nature which have been part of his appeal. But Burroughs, though unconsciously, also gave him most of the attributes of the pre-literate and classical hero of fairy tale, legend, and mythology, including the Trickster. He is the last of the Golden Age heroes, a literary character who reflects the archetypal images and feelings of the unconscious mind noted by Carl Jung and Joseph Campbell.

Like Arthur Conan Doyle, Burroughs had the gift of writing adventure stories with an indefinable quality that made them endure while thousands of similar novels dropped into oblivion. Like Doyle he created a classical fictional character of whom he wearied. The later Tarzan novels, in fact all of his works written in the latter part of his career, show a flagging invention, repetitiveness of plot and incident, excess of coincidences and improbabilities, and failure to develop fully promising themes.

He never thought of himself as anything but a commercial writer of romances. His works betray the biases, conservatisms, and timidities of his social class and times, and his style is old-fashioned. With the exception of Tarzan and a few others, his characters are cardboard. His genius was in the creation of the archetypal feral Tarzan and the writing of many pseudo-scientific romances which have enthralled generations of young readers, many of whom have remained loyal to him through their middle age.

—Philip José Farmer

BURROUGHS, William S(eward).   American.   Born in St. Louis, Missouri, 5 February 1914. Educated at Los Alamos Ranch School, New Mexico; Harvard University, Cambridge, Massachusetts, A.B. in anthropology 1936; studied medicine at the University of Vienna, and at Mexico City College, 1948–50. Served in the United States Army, 1942. Married Jean Vollmer in 1945 (died); one son. Has worked as a journalist, private detective, and bartender; now a full-time writer. Heroin addict, 1944–57. Recipient: National Institute of Arts and Letters award, 1975. Lived for many years in Tangier; now lives in New York City.

Publications

Fiction

Junkie: Confessions of an Unredeemed Drug Addict, with *Narcotic Agent*, by Maurice
    Helbront. 1953.
The Naked Lunch. 1959; as *Naked Lunch*, 1962.
The Soft Machine. 1961.
The Ticket That Exploded. 1962; revised edition, 1963.
Dead Fingers Talk. 1963.
Nova Express. 1964.
Speed. 1970.
The Wild Boys: A Book of the Dead. 1971.
Port of Saints. 1973.
Exterminator! 1974.
Short Novels. 1978.
Ah Pook Is Here and Other Texts. 1978.

Plays

The Last Words of Dutch Schultz: A Fiction in the Form of a Film Script. 1970.

Screenplay: *Towers Open Fire*, 1963.

Verse

Minutes to Go: Poems, with others. 1968.

Other

The Exterminator, with Brion Gysin. 1960.
The Yage Letters, with Allen Ginsberg. 1963.
Roosevelt after Inauguration. 1964.
Valentine's Day Reading. 1965.
Time. 1965.
Health Bulletin: APO–33. 1965.
*APO–33 Bulletin: A Metabolic Regulator: A Report on the Synthesis of the Amorphine
    Formula*, edited by Mary Beach and Claude Pelieu. 1966.
So Who Owns Death TV?, with Claude Pelieu and Carl Weissner. 1967.
The Dead Star. 1969.
Ali's Smile. 1969.
Fernseh-Tuberkulose, with Claude Pelieu and Carl Weissner. 1969.
Entretiens avec Burroughs, by Daniel Odier. 1969; translated as *The Job: Interviews
    with Burroughs*, 1970; revised edition, 1974.
The Third Mind. 1970.
The Braille Film: With a Counterscript by Burroughs, by Carl Weissner. 1970.
Electronic Revolution 1970–71. 1971.
Brion Gysin Let the Mice In, with Brion Gysin and Ian Somerville, edited by
    Somerville. 1973.
The Electronic Generation. 1973.

White Subway, edited by James Pennington.   1974.
Smack: Two Tape Transcripts, with Eric Mottram.   1975.
Sidetripping, with Charles Gatewood.   1975.
The Book of Breeething.   1976.
Lasers.   1976.
The Third Mind, with Brion Gysin.   1978.

Bibliography: *A Descriptive Catalogue of the Burroughs Archives*, edited by Miles Associates, 1973; *Burroughs: An Annotated Bibliography of His Works and Criticism* by Michael B. Goodman, 1975.

Reading List: *Burroughs: The Algebra of Need* by Eric Mottram, 1971.

*   *   *

There are two fields of experience central to the life and work of William Burroughs. They mark points at which criticism of his work must begin, and around which controversy has swirled. Scion of the Burroughs Machine family, he has travelled for most of his adult life (only recently settling in New York), during which he became addicted to heroin in 1944, remaining so across three continents and fourteen years. His addiction and cure (the last and presumably final in 1957) have provided the controlling metaphor for an *oeuvre* of cosmic dimensions.

The second area of concern is, like Burroughs's opiate addiction, an extended series of drug experiences. In 1953, he journeyed to the Peruvian Amazon expressly for the purpose of taking *yage*, a mescaline-like natural hallucinogen used sacramentally by the Indians of the region. These and subsequent psychedelic experiences provided not only primary materials for *Naked Lunch*, *The Soft Machine* and *The Ticket That Exploded*, but served to expand and intensify his vision beyond the relative solipsism of "junk."

For Burroughs's most fervent admirers he has become a cult figure: an international underworld traveller, a gifted teacher, a universal personage reborn, at least partially, from innumerable deaths, returned to speak and write of his experiences. For this group, his life is an example and his writing is a report, a formal statement of an entire life-style. He is a beatific figure, the madman-saint, like de Sade, Artaud, Céline and his contemporary Genet. His life is a message, as Alan Ansen writes unabashedly: "In the case of Burroughs, the writing is only a by-product, however brilliant, of a force. What I am writing is not only a paean to a writer; it is also a variant of hagiography." His detractors are equally enthusiastic: George Garrett speaks for John Wain, George Steiner, Anaïs Nin, and others when he complains: "Do we have to become connoisseurs of vomit? Is the world doing so badly a job at tearing itself apart that it needs the aid of gifted writers to finish it off?"

The indelible image of the heroin addict is presented in Burroughs's first work, *Junkie* – the addict slumped nodding in his chair or out on the street, waiting, making his ruins public. The rhetoric of this small book has the economy and force of needle and spoon, and its initial sociological value is as reportage, in the lucid pictures of the addict world. But more, in the linking of the heroin addict with the metaphysical condition of the "enslaved" condition of modern man, it establishes the single radical image from which Burroughs's "new mythology for the space age" develops.

The Naked Lunch is Burroughs's most famous work. Admitted for publication to the United States after several famous obscenity trials, "composed" with aid from his friends Allen Ginsberg and Jack Kerouac, the novel is a series of fantastic episodes arranged in collage form, the whole being held together by a mantic and comic narrative voice that turns matters inevitably to the theme of human control. *Naked Lunch* becomes increasingly disjointed and surrealistic in technique, and it displays the misogynist/homosexual concerns and the satiric comic vision that have become his signatures.

Subsequent longer works, especially *The Soft Machine* and *The Ticket That Exploded*, have ranged from anthropological pre-history to the uncertain future of dystopian science fiction, but share a predilection for radical linquistic and textual experiment: the "cut-up," the "fold in," and similar dislocations. As revealed in *The Job: Interviews with William Burroughs* (Daniel Odier), Burroughs's recent interests have been less in fiction than in the possibilities for human growth – evidenced especially in his fascination with out-of-body experience and psychobiology. His most recent fiction, *Exterminator!* and *The Wild Boys*, is more accessible than much of his previous work, but no less unsettling. John Tytell, for one, suggests that *The Wild Boys* is Burroughs's best work since *The Naked Lunch*.

The piercing of flesh by the needle, the body by the phallus, the rending of language and – finally – the physical cosmos itself, these are transformations. William Burroughs's endless, cranky linguistic experiments – with cut-ups, fold-ins, the shattering of images, sentences and words, with nightclub routines and carnival "drums" and surreal war and sex fantasies – flawed and confusing as they can be, I see as an attempt to use The Word itself to negate its own power, to lay bare the multiple prisons of corporeal existence, the passage of time, the deceits of language, the illusions of individual consciousness, the endless charades of mass social and political existence.

—Jack Hicks

BURTON, Robert.   English.   Born in Lindley, Leicestershire, 8 February 1577. Educated at Sutton Coldfield School, Warwickshire; Nuneaton Grammar School, Warwickshire; Brasenose College, Oxford, 1593–99; elected student of Christ Church, Oxford, 1599, and took the degree of B.D. 1614. Presented to the Christ Church living of St. Thomas, Oxford, 1616, also served as Rector of Seagrave, Leicestershire, 1630–40. *Died 25 January 1640.*

PUBLICATIONS

Prose

The Anatomy of Melancholy, What It Is.   1621; revised edition, 1624, 1628, 1632, 1638, 1651(?); edited by Holbrook Jackson, 1932.

Play

Philosophaster (produced 1618).   In *Philosophaster, Poemata,* 1862; translated by Paul Jordan-Smith, 1931.

Other

Philosophaster, Poemata, edited by W. E. Buckley.   1862.
Philosophaster, with an English Translation, and Minor Writings in Prose and Verse, edited by Paul Jordan-Smith.   1931.

Reading List: *Bibliographia Burtoniana: A Study of Burton's Anatomy of Melancholy* by Paul Jordan-Smith, 1931 (includes bibliography); *Burton's Knowledge of English Poetry* by H. J. Gottlieb, 1937; *The Anatomy of Burton's England* by W. R. Mueller, 1952; *Sanity in Bedlam: A Study of Burton's Anatomy of Melancholy* by Lawrence Babb, 1959; *Burton et l'Anatomie de la Melancholie* by J. R. Simon, 1964.

*   *   *

In 1621 Robert Burton published *The Anatomy of Melancholy*, in a thick quarto format. With a brief, uncluttered preface and a short postscript it is a rather unpretentious volume, not at all reminiscent of the carefully outlined, elaborately prefaced book with which we usually associate Burton. Ostensibly a medical treatise which purported to examine fully the causes, symptoms, and cures of the dreaded disease − melancholy − his work was an immediate success and according to legend its publisher Henry Cripps "got an estate by it." A minister by profession, a physician by inclination, and thought by many to be a prose stylist by accident, Burton revised and expanded the *Anatomy* five times. From the first through the sixth editions the *Anatomy* grew from approximately 300,000 to 480,000 words. Although he deleted some words and phrases, and revised some sentences, the most important change is the additions, especially those made between the first and second editions. It is clear that in the process of expanding, Burton very early lost interest in the purely medical aspects of his subject and became increasingly fascinated with the ramifications of melancholy, especially as applied to love and religion. In addition, the short postscript of the first edition is incorporated into a greatly expanded preface, entitled "Democritus Junior to the Reader," in which Burton reveals the purpose of his volume, together with the development of a major persona of the book. The use of Democritus is a key to understanding the tone and meaning of the *Anatomy*. To Burton's seventeenth-century audience Democritus was known as the "laughing philosopher," a satiric, witty observer of the foibles of human nature. But Burton is not consistent in his use of the persona. Frequently, he simply drops the mask and speaks straightforwardly and autobiographically. Occasionally, his persona in no way resembles Democritus.

On first reading the *Anatomy*, one has the impression that Burton has read everything that he could get his hands on and then commented on it in his volume. The margins fairly bristle with references to authorities, and his offhand, casual remarks about his own prose style suggest the idea that he gave little serious thought to the organization and method of the *Anatomy*. Consequently, until the twentieth century Burton was thought to have written a brilliant compendium of digressions, a hodge-podge of interesting but unrelated comments, ranging from the creation of a utopia to a detailed listing of the miseries of scholars, from a delightful discussion of the pleasures of travel and sightseeing − "A Digression of Air" − to a sermon on the most serious form of seventeenth-century melancholy − religious despair. A rich mine of anecdotes and strange tales, the *Anatomy* was deservedly popular during the seventeenth, eighteenth, and nineteenth centuries, exerting an important influence on such diverse authors as John Ford, Swift, Johnson, Sterne, Lamb, Keats, Thackeray, and Melville. Although an important source for numerous writers he was not taken seriously as a thinker or prose stylist. Considered an interesting eccentric, he was best characterized in Lamb's words as the "fantasticke, old great man."

In our century, criticism has focused on the artistry and unity of the *Anatomy*. Critics have discovered that Burton (despite his open disclaimers) was a much more careful prose stylist than once was thought to be the case. They have seen that, like any artist, Burton subtly varies his style to suit his purposes. There is a clearly defined "medical style" which contrasts markedly with the exuberant rhetoric of "Love Melancholy," and the eloquent pulpit strains of "Religious Melancholy."

Scholars have rightly noted that what may appear at first glance haphazard and ill-organized possesses a unity which binds the work together. They have observed (according to their inclinations) Burton's clear indebtedness to several satirical traditions, all of which suggest a unity of tone which was earlier overlooked. But the most fruitful approach to studying the unity of the *Anatomy* has been the belated recognition that Renaissance concepts of aesthetic unity allow for a much greater diversity of parts than do modern concepts of unity; in short, the Renaissance concept of unity is encyclopedic rather than "organic."

At the moment, there is much critical interest in Burton. His considerable position as a prose stylist is secure; his reputation as a thinker is growing. The Anglican minister and amateur physician remains an important seventeenth-century literary figure.

—Dennis G. Donovan

BUTLER, Samuel. English. Born at Langar Rectory, near Bingham, Nottinghamshire, 4 December 1835. Educated at Shrewsbury School, Shropshire, 1848–54; St. John's College, Cambridge, 1854–58, B.A. (honours) 1858; abandoned intention of taking holy orders; studied painting at Heatherley's School, London, 1865. Sheep farmer in the Rangitata district of New Zealand, 1859–64; returned to England, and settled in London, 1864; exhibited paintings at the Royal Academy, London, 1868–76; studied and composed music, including the cantata *Narcissus*, 1888, and the oratorio *Ulysses*, 1904. *Died 18 June 1902.*

PUBLICATIONS

Collections

   Works, edited by H. F. Jones and A. T. Bartholomew. 20 vols., 1923–26.
   The Essential Butler, edited by G. D. H. Cole. 1950.

Fiction

   Erewhon; or, Over the Range. 1872; revised edition, 1872, 1901; edited by Peter Mudford, 1970.
   Erewhon Revisited Twenty Years Later. 1901.
   The Way of All Flesh, edited by R. A. Streatfeild. 1903; edited by James Cochrane, 1966.

Verse

   Seven Sonnets and a Psalm of Montreal, edited by R. A. Streatfeild. 1904.

Other

   A First Year in Canterbury Settlement. 1863; revised edition, edited by R. A. Streatfeild, 1917; edited by A. C. Brassington and P. B. Maling, 1964.
   The Evidence for the Resurrection of Jesus Christ As Given by the Four Evangelists. 1865.

The Fair Haven: A Work in Defence of the Miraculous Element in Our Lord's Ministry upon Earth.   1873; edited by G. Bullett, 1938.
Life and Habit: An Essay after a Completer View of Evolution.   1877.
Evolution Old and New.   1879.
Unconscious Memory.   1880.
Alps and Sanctuaries of Piedmont and the Canton Ticino.   1881.
Selections from Previous Works.   1884.
Holbein's Dance.   1886.
Luck or Cunning as the Main Means of Organic Modifications?   1886.
Ex Voto: An Account of the Sacro Monte or New Jerusalem at Varallo-Sesia.   1888; revised edition, 1889.
On the Trapanese Origin of the Odyssey.   1893.
The Life and Letters of Dr. Samuel Butler.   2 vols., 1896.
The Authoress of the Odyssey.   1897.
Shakespeare's Sonnets Reconsidered, and in Part Rearranged.   1899.
Essays on Life, Art, and Science, edited by R. A. Streatfeild.   1904.
Note-Books: Selections, edited by H. F. Jones.   1912; *Butleriana,* edited by A. T. Bartholomew, 1932; *Further Extracts,* edited by A. T. Bartholomew, 1934; *Selections,* edited by Geoffrey Keynes and Brian Hill, 1951.
God the Known and God the Unknown, edited by R. A. Streatfeild.   1909.
The Humour of Homer and Other Essays, edited by R. A. Streatfeild.   1913.
Letters Between Butler and Miss E. M. A. Savage, edited by Geoffrey Keynes and Brian Hill.   1935.
Correspondence of Butler and His Sister May, edited by Daniel F. Howard.   1962.
The Family Letters 1841–1886, edited by Arnold Silver.   1962.

Translator, *The Iliad and Odyssey of Homer.*   2 vols., 1898–1900; edited by L. R. Loomis, 2 vols., 1942–44.
Translator, *Hesiod's Works and Days.*   1924.

Bibliography: *The Career of Butler: A Bibliography* by S. B. Harkness, 1955.

Reading List: *Butler: A Memoir* by H. F. Jones, 1919; *The Triple Thinkers* by Edmund Wilson, 1938; *Butler and the Way of All Flesh* by G. D. H. Cole, 1947; *Butler* by P. N. Furbank, 1948; *Darwin and Butler: Two Versions of Evolution* by Basil Willey, 1960; *Butler* by Lee E. Holt, 1964.

*   *   *

Samuel Butler was one of the most independent minds of the later nineteenth century: his interest in social ideas links him with such Victorian sages as Carlyle, Ruskin, and Arnold, but his preference for irony and paradox brings him close to Bernard Shaw and Oscar Wilde. The fact that he is so hard to classify would undoubtedly have pleased him, but it may account for the varied and fluctuating assessments of his importance.

Erewhon is his most stimulating book. A story in the tradition of *Gulliver's Travels,* it uses its conventional Evangelical protagonist Higgs and his adventures to raise many significant lines of thought – a possible analogy between crime and disease, the inauthenticity of much contemporary religious observance, the abstractness of upper-class Classical education, the dangers of mechanisation, the extravagances of moral dogma, and, above all, the hold of conventions on the mind. And Butler does all this in a highly entertaining way. He clearly saw himself as a free-thinker, and his mission as to challenge, by argument and irony, the conventional wisdom of his day. Above all, his insight into the extent to which human beliefs are the products of social environment is impressive, especially at a time when thinkers were apt to believe in absolutes. He writes of an Erewhonian judge: "He could not emanicpate himself from, nay, it did not even occur to him to feel, the bondage of the ideas in which he had been born and bred." Butler's distinction was his awareness of the awaiting bondage.

In some cases Butler's determination not to be dragooned into orthodoxy led him to extravagances of his own. Many would feel that this is true of his protracted campaign against Darwin's idea of evolution. In a series of books including *Life and Habit*, *Unconscious Memory*, and *Luck or Cunning*, Butler argued that the evolutionary process was directed by some kind of life-force. He thus introduced a new and complicating note into the controversy between Science and Religion. Sometimes his love of heterodoxy led him to attack accepted assumptions irresponsibly, but there was usually enough behind his arguments to make attention to them an enlivening experience. In *The Authoress of the Odyssey* he argued from internal evidence that the poet must have been a woman, and in *Shakespeare's Sonnets* that they were addressed to a plebeian lover.

His *Note-Books* perhaps best reveal the wide range of his interests, but his best-known book is *The Way of All Flesh* which, published posthumously in 1903, dealt a massive blow to the Victorian family ideal. In it Butler mixes autobiography with experiences of his own ideas, thoroughly debunking the attitudes represented by the father, Theobald Pontifex. The book had a liberating effect on many young writers of the time, and its attitude to Victorianism underlies the criticisms of the 1920's. The early scenes have great vividness, but there are elements of complacency in the later part which mark Butler's limitations. He lived very much to himself and this comes out in the somewhat inhuman ideal which is propounded at the end. The comment made on Ernest Pontifex shows, however, a just awareness on Butler's part of how he was regarded: "With the general public he is not a favourite. He is admitted to have talent, but it is considered generally to be of a queer, unpractical kind, and no matter how serious he is, he is always accused of being in jest." Butler's jests often retain for the modern reader an interest which can no longer be accorded to the conventional wisdom of the age which he strove to educate by his paradoxes.

—Peter Faulkner

CABELL, James Branch. American. Born in Richmond, Virginia, 14 April 1879. Educated at the College of William and Mary, Williamsburg, Virginia, A.B. 1898. Married 1) Priscilla Bradley Shepherd in 1939 (died, 1949), one son; 2) Margaret Waller Freeman in 1950. Instructor in Greek and French at the College of William and Mary while an undergraduate, 1896–97; worked in the pressroom of the Richmond, Virginia *Times*, 1898; member of staff of the New York *Herald*, 1899–1901, and the Richmond *News*, 1901; engaged in genealogical research in America and Europe, 1901–11; coal miner in West Virginia, 1911–13; Genealogist for the Virginia Society of Colonial Wars, 1916–28, and the Virginia Sons of the American Revolution, 1917–24; Editor, Virginia War History Commission, 1919–26; silent editor, *The Reviewer*, Richmond, 1921; one of the editors of *The American Spectator*, 1932–35. President, Virginia Writers Association, 1918–21. Member, National Institute of Arts and Letters. *Died 5 May 1958.*

PUBLICATIONS

Collections

The Letters, edited by Edward Wagenknecht. 1975.

Fiction

The Eagle's Shadow. 1904; revised edition, 1923.
The Line of Love (stories). 1905; revised edition, 1921.
Gallantry (stories). 1907; revised edition, 1922.
Chivalry (stories). 1909.
The Cords of Vanity. 1909; revised edition, 1920.
The Soul of Melicent. 1913; revised edition, as *Domnei*, 1920.
The Rivet in Grandfather's Neck. 1915.
The Certain Hour (stories). 1916.
The Cream of the Jest. 1917; revised edition, 1923.
Beyond Life. 1919.
Jurgen. 1919.
Figures of Earth. 1921.
The High Place. 1923.
The Silver Stallion. 1926.
The Music from Behind the Moon (stories). 1926.
Something about Eve. 1927.
The Works (revised editions). 18 vols., 1927–30.
The White Robe (stories). 1928.
The Way of Ecben. 1929.
Smirt: An Urbane Nightmare. 1934.
Smith: A Sylvan Interlude. 1935.
Smire: An Acceptance in the Third Person. 1937.
The King Was in His Counting House. 1938.
Hamlet Had an Uncle. 1940.
The First Gentleman of America. 1942.
There Were Two Pirates. 1946.
The Witch-Woman (includes *The Music from Behind the Moon, The Way of Ecben, The White Robe*). 1948.
The Devil's Own Dear Son. 1949.

Play

> *The Jewel Merchants.*   1921.

Verse

> *From the Hidden Way.*   1916; revised edition, 1924.
> *Ballades from the Hidden Way.*   1928.
> *Sonnets from Antan.*   1929.

Other

> *Branchiana* (genealogy).   1907.
> *Branch of Abingdon.*   1911.
> *The Majors and Their Marriages.*   1915.
> *The Judging of Jurgen.*   1920.
> *Jurgen and the Censor.*   1920.
> *Taboo: A Legend Retold from the Dirghic of Saevius Nicanor.*   1921.
> *Joseph Hergesheimer.*   1921.
> *The Lineage of Lichfield: An Essay in Eugenics.*   1922.
> *Straws and Prayer-Books.*   1924.
> *Some of Us: An Essay in Epitaphs.*   1930.
> *Townsend of Lichfield.*   1930.
> *Between Dawn and Sunrise: Selections,* edited by John Macy.   1930.
> *These Restless Heads: A Trilogy of Romantics.*   1932.
> *Special Delivery: A Packet of Replies.*   1933.
> *Ladies and Gentlemen: A Parcel of Reconsiderations.*   1934.
> *Preface to the Past.*   1936.
> *The Nightmare Has Triplets: An Author's Note on Smire.*   1937.
> *On Ellen Glasgow.*   1938.
> *The St. John: A Parade of Diversities.*   1943.
> *Let Me Lie.*   1947.
> *Quiet, Please.*   1952.
> *As I Remember It: Some Epilogues in Recollection.*   1955.
> *Between Friends: Letters of Cabell and Others,* edited by Padraic Colum and Margaret
>   Freeman Cabell.   1962.

Bibliography: *Cabell: A Complete Bibliography* by James N. Hall, 1974.

Reading List: *No Place on Earth: Ellen Glasgow, Cabell, and Richmond-in-Virginia* by Louis D. Rubin, Jr., 1959; *Cabell* by Joe Lee Davis, 1962; *Jesting Moses: A Study in Cabellian Comedy* by Arvin R. Wells, 1962; *Cabell: The Dream and the Reality* by Desmond Tarrant, 1967; *Cabell: Three Essays* by Carl Van Doren, H. L. Mencken, and Hugh Walpole, 1967.

*   *   *

Reckoned in the top echelon of American writers throughout the 1920's, James Branch Cabell has never regained the prestige he then knew. But even during the decade of his greatest fame, Cabell was outside the mainstream. While his contemporaries found increasing fascination with life in their period and used the standard of critical realism to treat the immediate, Cabell's preference was for romance and myth. He defined his preference brilliantly in *Beyond Life* and reiterated it in essays and romances throughout his long career. He avowed "the auctorial virtues of distinction and clarity, of beauty and symmetry, of tenderness and truth and urbanity."

Cabell's tastes, like his ancestry, were aristocratic and mannered. The elegant prose style he perfected was appropriate to his Virginia roots and his subject matter. It is ironic that so cultivated a writer with a specialized appeal became so popular. One important reason was that Cabell was almost the only sign of hope H. L. Mencken could find that the culture of the post-Civil War South was not to be damned totally, and Mencken made very loud noises about Cabell's work. More important was Cabell's novel *Jurgen*, the tale of a medieval pawnbroker in Cabell's mythical kingdom of Poictesme. Jurgen was ever willing to do the gentlemanly thing, and word got around that Cabell's book was lascivious. It was suppressed in 1920, but Cabell's cause rallied the foes of censorship, ensuring booming sales. The novel, which certainly has its Rabelaisian touches, was exonerated in 1922.

Jurgen is a part of Cabell's most ambitious and most important work, the eighteen-volume "Biography of the Life of Manuel." Dom Manuel is the founder of Poictesme, and his followers and offspring (legitimate and otherwise) inherit his legend and face the same tensions between the dream (the dynamic illusion) and the frustrating reality of everyday life. The most brilliant of the Romances besides *Jurgen* are *Figures of Earth, The Silver Stallion, The High Place*, and *Something about Eve*. Cabell revised his earlier Romances of Virginia as later volumes of the Biography because they, too, were illustrative of the attitudes of Chivalry, Gallantry, and Poetry treated in the more famous books. Virginia and Poictesme have much in common.

After the completion of the Biography, Cabell published for a time under the name Branch Cabell, to symbolize the completion of his grand design and perhaps in recognition of the end of the era of his greatest fame. During the years of the Great Depression and World War II, Cabell tenaciously followed his own ideals and eschewed the contemporary. A trilogy of high satire (*Smirt, Smith, Smire*) treated the dream life of the writer, mirroring the dream experience more fully than anything Cabell had written previously. Another trilogy dealt with murder, conquest, and intrigue in Hamlet's Denmark, the family circle of Cosimo dei Medici, and the Virginia of Nemattanon, an Indian Prince during the time of the Spanish conquests. A final trilogy explored Florida's legendary past.

Cabell then focused attention on his own life with several volumes of reminiscences and assessments of his career and those of many of his contemporaries. He viewed his progress with humor and detachment. His professed goal was to write beautifully of beautiful happenings. Although he can certainly sting his readers with a sense of reality, it seems clear that writing gave him great joy. He wrote mainly for himself, he tells us, but he did so with such humor and insight that he insures himself a loyal group of enthusiasts.

—Joseph M. Flora

CABLE, George Washington. American. Born in New Orleans, Louisiana, 12 October 1844. Educated in the New Orleans public schools until 1859; largely self-taught. Served in the 4th Mississippi Cavalry during the Civil War, 1863–65. Married 1) Louise Stewart Bartlett in 1869 (died, 1904), six daughters and one son; 2) Eva C. Stevenson in 1906 (died, 1923); 3) Hanna Cowing in 1923. Worked as a state surveyor in Louisiana, 1865–66; incapacitated by malaria, 1866–68; Reporter and Columnist ("Drop Shot") for the New Orleans *Picayune*, 1869; Accountant and Correspondence Clerk for A. C. Black and Company, cotton factors, New Orleans, 1869–79; full-time writer from 1879; settled in

Northampton, Massachusetts, 1885; thereafter made yearly tours of the United States, reading his own works; organized the Home-Culture Club in Northampton, 1886, renamed the Northampton People's Institute, 1909; published the journals *The Letter*, 1892–96, and *The Symposium*, 1896. A.M: Yale University, New Haven, Connecticut, 1883; D.Litt.: Washington and Lee University, Lexington, Virginia, 1882; Yale University, 1901; Bowdoin College, Brunswick, Maine, 1904. Member, American Academy of Arts and Letters. *Died 31 January 1925.*

PUBLICATIONS

Collections

   Creoles and Cajuns: Stories of Old Louisiana, edited by Arlin Turner.   1959.

Fiction

   Old Creole Days (stories).   1879.
   The Grandissimes: A Story of Creole Life.   1880.
   Madame Delphine.   1881.
   Dr. Sevier.   1884.
   Madame Delphine, Carancro, Grande Pointe.   1887.
   Bonaventure: A Prose Pastoral of Acadian Louisiana.   1888.
   Strange True Stories of Louisiana.   1889.
   John March, Southerner.   1894.
   Strong Hearts.   1899.
   The Cavalier.   1901.
   Père Raphaël.   1901.
   Bylow Hill.   1902.
   Kincaid's Battery.   1908.
   "Posson Jone' " and Père Raphaël.   1909.
   Gideon's Band: A Tale of the Mississippi.   1914.
   The Amateur Garden.   1914.
   The Flower of the Chapdelaines.   1918.
   Lovers of Louisiana (Today).   1918.

Other

   The Creoles of Louisiana.   1884.
   The Silent South.   1885.
   The Negro Question.   1890.
   A Busy Man's Bible.   1891.
   A Memory of Roswell Smith.   1892.
   A Southerner Looks at Negro Discrimination: Selected Writings, edited by Isabel Cable
      Manes.   1946.
   Twins of Genius: Letters of Mark Twain, Cable, and Others, edited by Guy A.
      Cardwell.   1953.
   The Negro Question: A Selection of Writings on Civil Rights in the South, edited by Arlin
      Turner.   1958.
   Mark Twain and Cable: The Record of a Literary Friendship, edited by Arlin
      Turner.   1960.

Bibliography: in *Bibliography of American Literature* by Jacob Blanck, 1957.

Reading List: *Cable: His Life and Letters* by Lucy Leffingwell Cable Bikle, 1928; *Cable: A Study of His Early Life and Work* by Kjell Ekström, 1950; *Cable: A Biography* by Arlin Turner, 1956; *Cable: The Northampton Years*, 1959, and *Cable*, 1962, both by Philip Butcher; *Cable: The Life and Times of a Southern Heretic* by Louis D. Rubin, Jr., 1969.

*   *   *

George Washington Cable was one of the first progressive writers of the "New South." His father's German background and his mother's New England protestantism contributed to his own sense of isolation in a community whose leaders were primarily French and Catholic. Cable's position as an outsider may have stimulated his interest in sociological problems and made him more sensitive to the needs of minorities, especially Southern blacks. His father's untimely death and the Civil War prevented him from completing his formal education, but he was always an avid reader and enjoyed writing. In his late twenties he took a part-time job on the *New Orleans Picayune*, where his "Drop Shot" column, though occasionally controversial, was well received. At this time Cable began writing a series of short stories, and was discovered by Scribner's Edward King, who was touring Louisiana in search of materials for his "Great South" series. Although Scribner's rejected "Bibi," Cable's story of a tormented slave-prince, on the grounds of its unpleasant subject matter, they published his character sketch of an old Creole, " 'Sieur George," in 1873. Richard Watson Gilder, editor of *Scribner's Monthly* and the *Century*, considered Cable one of his leading local colorists, who would contribute to Gilder's plan for reconciling the North and South through literature. H. H. Boyesen also took an interest in Cable's writing and initiated a correspondence helpful to the latter's career.

In 1879 Cable's *Old Creole Days*, a collection of short stories, was published, and the first installments of *The Grandissimes*, which incorporated the "Bibi" materials, appeared in *Scribner's Monthly*. In 1880 *The Grandissimes* was published in book form, as was *Madame Delphine*, a novella. These two books represent Cable's highest achievement, anticipating the complex drama of Faulkner's works. Each deals with racial injustice, the continuing problems caused by exploitation of the black community, and the Creoles' resistance to social change. He described the lush, exotic world of the deep South unknown to most Americans. Topics considered off limits to the genteel authors of the Tidewater region or the wholesome humorists of the Piedmont are insightfully probed: miscegenation, the cruelties of the *Code Noire*, and the arrogance and indolence of the aristocracy.

By 1882 Cable began a full-time career as a writer, completing *Dr. Sevier*, a serious novel dealing with prison reform, which was followed by a *Century Magazine* exposé, "The Convict Lease System in the Southern States," and a history, *The Creoles of Louisiana*. These three works, openly polemical, offended Gilder and caused tremendous resentment throughout the South. A reading tour with Mark Twain brought Cable some additional income and popularity, but his increasingly fervent publications on the Negro's dilemma, especially "A Freedman's Case in Equity" and *The Silent South*, made him notorious in New Orleans, and he eventually settled in Northampton, Massachusetts.

There Cable organized the Home-Culture clubs, racially integrated reading groups designed to raise the educational level of average citizens. The success of the movement was due in part to the national atmosphere of self-improvement and upward mobility in the last quarter of the nineteenth century.

When Cable was fifty he published *John March, Southerner*, an ambiguous portrait of a Southern aristocrat during the reconstruction era. As in his earlier fiction he examined outmoded conceptions of chivalry and honor, racial injustice, and anachronistic social and political attitudes. This was his last attempt at social satire. He continued to be an outspoken essayist, but his fiction became unashamedly romantic. The public taste of the period and his editors reinforced his tendency toward sentimentalism. *The Cavalier* was Cable's greatest popular success. He even overcame his Calvinistic distrust of the stage and authorized a dramatic version of the novel, starring Julia Marlowe. Energetic until the end, he wrote three novels in his seventies and shaped an optimistic vision of technological progress in the New South and the eventual integration of the races.

Perhaps because he remained too dependent on the family magazine audience and the taste of his editors, Cable did not live up to his early potential as a major Southern writer. Nevertheless, in his best fiction he transcended the limitations of the local color genre and revealed a daring and prophetic intelligence.

—Kimball King

CAHAN, Abraham. American. Born in Vilna, Russia, 7 July 1860; emigrated to the United States, 1882, later naturalized. Educated at the Teachers' Institute, Vilna; later attended a law school in New York. Married Anna Braunstein in 1887. Settled in New York; staff member, *Commercial Advertiser*, New York, 1897–1901; Editor of the Yiddish newspaper *Forverts* (*Jewish Daily Forward*) for more than 40 years. *Died 31 August 1951.*

PUBLICATIONS

Fiction

Yekl: A Tale of the New York Ghetto. 1896.
The Imported Bridegroom and Other Stories of the New York Ghetto. 1898.
The White Terror and the Red: A Novel of Revolutionary Russia. 1905.
The Rise of David Levinsky. 1917.

Other

Historye fun die Fereinigte Staaten (in Yiddish). 2 vols., 1910–12.
Bleter fun Mayn Lebn (in Yiddish). 5 vols., 1926–31; as *The Education of Cahan*, 2 vols., 1969.

Editor, *Hear the Other Side: A Symposium of Democratic Socialist Opinion.* 1934.

Bibliography: *Cahan: Bibliography* by Ephim H. Jeshurin, 1941.

Reading List: *From the Ghetto: The Fiction of Cahan* by Jules Chametzky, 1977.

* * *

Abraham Cahan is perhaps more notable for his leadership in the Yiddish-speaking community of the Lower East Side than he is for any of his English prose. For more than forty years, he was the editor of the popular Yiddish newspaper *Forverts*. As such he guided the immigrant Jewish populace in their Americanization. His editorials, his Yiddish fiction, and his work as a union organizer – all bespoke his socialist, didactic prejudices.

It was not until 1895 that he published his first short story in English. However, at least as early as the 1880's he was contributing non-fiction prose to the *New York World* and the *New*

York Sun and Press. In these pieces Cahan introduced the East Side ghetto to non-Jewish America. In the career of Cahan, however, these articles are not as important as the writing he did in the offices of the *Commercial Advertiser* (1897–1901). The relationship between Cahan and his colleagues on the English newspaper was mutually beneficial: Hutchins Hapgood and Lincoln Steffens learned of the intellectual turmoil and excitement of the Lower East Side; Cahan learned more sophisticated techniques of journalism.

Before his tenure on the *Commercial Advertiser*, Cahan had published only two short stories and a novella in English. These three pieces are local-color treatments of immigrant life. Cahan adds a strong moralizing temperament, the socialist criticism of the dehumanization of capitalism.

Cahan never turned from this socialist didacticism. But his later fiction more successfully subsumes this purpose under an aesthetic control. He also became more interested in presenting the dilemma of his old world immigrants in modern America. Their struggles result from the conflict between the teachings and expectations of the past and the realities and threats of the present. In short story form, Cahan's most successful treatment of this conflict is "The Imported Bridegroom," a tale of the repercussions of the modern world vision on Jews in different stages of alienation from their Jewish past.

It is, however, the novel *The Rise of David Levinsky* that assures Cahan a significance in American literature. Past ideals and present desires plague the rise of this Silas Lapham. The title clearly alludes to the famous novel of William Dean Howells, Cahan's favorite American writer and one of his staunchest supporters and mentors in the American literary establishment. The story of David is different from that of Silas: unlike the Protestant version of the rags to riches hero, Cahan's hero never effects a moral rise, never learns to balance his present reality with his past expectations.

Cahan's novel is one of the most powerful about immigrant life in America and one of the most telling portraits of the joylessness of the moneyed life without spiritual fulfilment. After this great success, Cahan seemed to have finished his discourse with English-speaking America. The rest of his career was centered on the *Forverts* and his autobiography in Yiddish.

—Barbara Gitenstein

CAIN, James M(allahan). American. Born in Annapolis, Maryland, 1 July 1892. Educated at Washington College, Chestertown, Maryland, A.B. 1910, A.M. 1917. Served as a private in the 79th Division of the American Expeditionary Forces, 1918–19; Editor of the *Lorraine Cross*, the official newspaper of the 79th Division, 1919. Married 1) Mary Rebekah Clough in 1920 (divorced); 2) Elina Sjosted Tyszecka in 1927 (divorced); 3) Aileen Pringle in 1944 (divorced); 4) Florence Macbeth Whitwell in 1947 (died). Staff Member, *Baltimore American*, 1917–18; Reporter, *Baltimore Sun*, 1919–23; Professor of Journalism, St. John's College, Annapolis, Maryland, 1923–24; Editorial Writer, *New York World*, 1924–31; full-time writer from 1931; screenwriter, in Hollywood, 1932–48. Recipient: Mystery Writers of America Grand Master Award, 1969. *Died 27 October 1977.*

PUBLICATIONS

Fiction

The Postman Always Rings Twice. 1934.
Serenade. 1937.

Mildred Pierce. 1941.
Love's Lovely Counterfeit. 1942.
Three of a Kind: Career in C Major, The Embezzler, Double Indemnity. 1943.
Past All Dishonor. 1946.
The Butterfly. 1947.
The Sinful Woman. 1947.
The Moth. 1948.
Jealous Woman. 1950.
The Root of His Evil. 1951.
Galatea. 1953.
Mignon. 1962.
The Magician's Wife. 1965.
Rainbow's End. 1975.
The Institute. 1976.

Plays

Hero; Hemp; Red, White, and Blue; Trial by Jury; Theological Interlude; Citizenship; Will of the People (short plays), in *American Mercury* 6 to *29*, 1926–29.
The Postman Always Rings Twice, from his own novel (produced 1936).
Algiers (screenplay), with John Howard Lawson, in *Foremost Films of 1938,* edited by Frank Vreeland. 1939.

Screenplays: *Algiers,* with John Howard Lawson, 1938; *Stand Up and Fight,* with others, 1939; *When Tomorrow Comes,* with Dwight Taylor, 1939; *Gypsy Wildcat,* with others, 1944; *Everybody Does It,* with Nunnally Johnson, 1949.

Other

Our Government. 1930.

Editor, *For Men Only: A Collection of Short Stories.* 1944.

Reading List: "Man under Sentence of Death: The Novels of Cain" by Joyce Carol Oates, in *Tough Guy Writers of the Thirties* edited by David Madden, 1967; *Cain* by David Madden 1970.

*   *   *

James M. Cain is the twenty-minute egg of the hard-boiled school. The tough-guy novel made a lasting impact on "serious" American and European fiction; for instance, Albert Camus admitted that *The Postman Always Rings Twice* was a model for *The Stranger.*

Cain has said that he has always had only one story to tell: a love story. "I write of the wish that comes true, for some reason a terrifying concept ... I think my stories have some quality of the opening of a forbidden box." The act of forcing the wish to come true isolates Cain's obsessed lovers from society and places them on what he calls a "love-rack."

If Cain's "heels and harpies" are to consummate and prolong their sexual passion, they must commit a crime. Frank Chambers and Cora in *The Postman* must murder Cora's husband; in *Serenade,* Juana must slaughter Winston Hawes, a homosexual symphony conductor, to ensure the sexual salvation of her lover, Howard Sharp, an opera singer; sex and money are the motives in Walter's and Phyllis's murder of her husband in *Double*

Indemnity; in *The Butterfly*, when his apparently incestuous lust for his daughter Kady is threatened, Jess Tyler, a West Virginia farmer, shoots Moke Blue.

In his novels dealing with criminal love, even in his romances *Career in C Major* and *Galatea* and his historical novels *Past All Dishonor* and *Mignon*, Cain effectively dramatizes profound insights into the American character and scene and into the way American dreams degenerate into nightmares. In his novels of character, *Mildred Pierce* and *The Moth*, set in the depression years, his scrutiny is most direct. Physically and often intellectually aggressive, Cain's audacious American male is an inside-dopester equipped with great know-how in many areas (even food, music, and the art of biography); but self-dramatizing inclinations, a suppressed sentimentality, and a misconceived American romanticism and optimism often defeat him. The female is realistic, ruthless, materialistic, and sensitive to minor social taboos even while violating major laws. A deadly pair, they are more often destroyed by their own sexual and materialistic overreaching than by the police. In their total commitment to each other, severing all ties to other people, Cain's lovers experience a blazing, self-consuming flash of self-deceptive purity and hideous innocence.

Without style and technique, Cain's rich and fascinating subject matter, energized by imagination and controlled by formula, would lack sustaining power. A few characters and a simple plot with a first-person narrator – that is the magic combination of a Cain "natural," producing a style like the "metal of an automatic," a pace like "a motorcycle," and a sense of immediacy that hypnotizes the reader. The first person narration enables Cain to use basic technical devices with special skill and appropriateness. His distinctive dialog is especially powerful when it is all of a piece with the cold objectivity and immediacy of the arrogant, commanding first-person voice. Cain, whose conscious intention is to "cast a spell on the beholder," has stated that he developed "the habit of needling a story at the least hint of a breakdown," striving for a "rising coefficient of intensity."

Cain would never use the term "existential," but as a consequence of his primary intention to tell a story superbly well, he has created an objective, disinterested, often pessimistic view of life that is simultaneously terrifying and starkly beautiful.

—David Madden

CALDWELL, Erskine (Preston).   American.   Born in Moreland, Georgia, 17 December 1903. Educated at Erskine College, Due West, South Carolina, 1920–21; University of Virginia, Charlottesville, 1922, 1925–26; University of Pennsylvania, Philadelphia, 1924. Married 1) Helen Lannigan in 1925 (divorced), two sons and one daughter; 2) the photographer Margaret Bourke-White in 1939 (divorced, 1942); 3) June Johnson in 1942, one son; 4) Virginia Moffett in 1957. Reporter, *Atlanta Journal*, Georgia, 1925; screenwriter in Hollywood, 1930–34, 1942–43; Foreign Correspondent in Mexico, Spain, Czechoslovakia, Russia, and China, 1938–41; Editor, American Folkways series, 1941–55. Member, National Institute of Arts and Letters. Lives in Dunedin, Florida.

PUBLICATIONS

Fiction

The Bastard.   1930.
Poor Fool.   1930.

American Earth (stories).   1931; as *A Swell-Looking Girl*, 1959.
Mama's Little Girl (story).   1932.
Tobacco Road.   1932.
Message for Genevieve (story).   1933.
God's Little Acre.   1933.
We Are the Living: Brief Stories.   1933.
Journeyman.   1935; revised edition, 1938.
Kneel to the Rising Sun and Other Stories.   1935.
The Sacrilege of Alan Kent (story).   1936.
Southways: Stories.   1938.
Trouble in July.   1940.
Jackpot: The Short Stories.   1940.
All Night Long: A Novel of Guerrilla Warfare in Russia.   1942.
Georgia Boy (stories).   1943.
Stories by Caldwell: 24 Representative Stories, edited by Henry Seidel Canby.   1944.
Tragic Ground.   1944.
A House in the Uplands.   1946.
The Caldwell Caravan: Novels and Stories.   1946.
The Sure Hand of God.   1947.
This Very Earth.   1948.
Place Called Estherville.   1949.
Episode in Palmetto.   1950.
A Lamp for Nightfall.   1952.
The Courting of Susie Brown.   1952.
The Complete Stories.   1953.
Love and Money.   1954.
Gretta.   1955.
Gulf Coast Stories.   1956.
Certain Women (stories).   1957.
Claudelle Inglish.   1958.
When You Think of Me (stories).   1959.
Men and Women: 22 Stories.   1961.
Jenny by Nature.   1961.
Close to Home.   1962.
The Last Night of Summer.   1963.
Miss Mama Aimee.   1967.
Summertime Island.   1968.
The Weather Shelter.   1969.
The Earnshaw Neighborhood.   1971.
Annette.   1973.

Plays

Screenplays: *A Nation Dances*, 1943; *Volcano*, 1953.

Other

Tenant Farmer.   1935.
Some American People.   1935.
You Have Seen Their Faces, with Margaret Bourke-White.   1937.
North of the Danube, with Margaret Bourke-White.   1939.
Say! Is This the U.S.A.?, with Margaret Bourke-White.   1941.

All-Out on the Road to Smolensk. 1942; as *Moscow under Fire; A Wartime Diary, 1941,* 1942.
Russia at War, with Margaret Bourke-White. 1942.
The Humorous Side of Caldwell, edited by Robert Cantwell. 1951.
Call It Experience: The Years of Learning How to Write. 1951.
Molly Cottontail (juvenile). 1958.
Around about America. 1964.
In Search of Bisco. 1965.
The Deer at Our House (juvenile). 1966.
In the Shadow of the Steeple. 1967.
Deep South: Memory and Observation (includes *In the Shadow of the Steeple*). 1968.
Writing in America. 1968.
Afternoons in Mid-America. 1976.

Reading List: *The Southern Poor-White from Lubberland to Tobacco Road* by Shields McIlwaine, 1939; *Caldwell* by James Korges, 1969.

*   *   *

The degenerate side of life that Erskine Caldwell exploited so successfully in 1932 in *Tobacco Road* extends back some two hundred years in Southern life, suggesting some kinship between his work and that of the frontier humorists. A hallmark of Caldwell's exploitation of Southern folk and folkways is his use of what Shields McIlwaine calls "idiotic gravity," emanating from characters who are in dead earnest in their sometimes misguided, if not perverted, commitment.

Caldwell's humorous approach to the seaminess and poverty of Southern life, whether in *Tobacco Road, God's Little Acre,* or *Georgia Boy,* accounts for his avoidance of the melodramatic and banal. As Robert Cantwell has suggested (*Georgia Review,* 1957), Caldwell's comic treatment of materials makes the poverty of his characters "unforgettable."

In terms of literary tradition, it is Caldwell's Chaucerian treatment of sex that places his novels in the mainstream of the *fabliau,* McIlwaine noting that the author's poor whites like Ty Ty Walden (*God's Little Acre*) and Jeeter Lester (*Tobacco Road*) enjoy the "game of sex without self consciousness." Cantwell, moreover, points out that Caldwell's sexual scenes normally have witnesses — visitors, Negroes peering over fences, etc. — thus suggesting an initiation process. Caldwell's frank treatment of sex marks in the 1930's a major shift in popular literature. After the success of *Tobacco Road* — especially in resisting suppression — similar works by later writers became a staple of commercial fiction. But, with the exception of *Trouble in July* (1940), few of Caldwell's own novels after *God's Little Acre* add to his stature as a creative artist.

In an equally important sense the Caldwell canon owes much to the tradition of naturalism in American writing. Thus Caldwell's characters — oppressed by barren land, mill life, heredity, or other circumstances beyond their control — fail to perceive any solution in flight. The author, moreover, creates with some consistency character after character who is a victim of his heredity and/or environment. Jeeter Lester (*Tobacco Road*), for example, is but the inevitable outcome of one hundred years of family degeneration and disintegration, whereas Ty Ty Walden's degeneracy (*God's Little Acre*) is owed to a "perverted idealism" (McIlwaine).

Current criticism of Caldwell's work, however, places it in the American Gothic vein. The author's use of deformed and sometimes mentally deficient and perverted characters defines his purpose. In *Tobacco Road* one is confronted by a grandmother consumed by pellagra, in *God's Little Acre* by Pluto's obesity, and in *Tragic Ground* by Bubber's permanent grin. Whereas eighteenth and nineteenth-century Gothicists exploited setting and the supernatural as vehicles, both Caldwell and Faulkner turned Southern sociology and misshapen

220

personalities into effective Gothic pronouncements concerning the quality of modern life.

The Complete Stories reveals the author's true métier: Southern settings, disenfranchised Blacks and poor whites, a depression background. "Candy-Man Beechum," his most frequently anthologized story, presents the artist at his best: passionate in his commitment to social values, primitive in his rhythmic articulation, and genuine in the sense of uncontrolled fate that he evokes.

—George C. Longest

CALISHER, Hortense. American. Born in New York City, 20 December 1911. Educated at Barnard College, New York, A.B. 1932. Married Curtis Harnack in 1959; two children by a previous marriage. Adjunct Professor of English, Barnard College, 1956–57; Visiting Professor, University of Iowa, Iowa City, 1957, 1959–60, Stanford University, California, 1958, Sarah Lawrence College, Bronxville, New York, 1962, and Brandeis University, Waltham, Massachusetts, 1963–64; Adjunct Professor of English, Columbia University, New York, 1968–70; Clark Lecturer, Scripps College, Claremont, California, 1969; Visiting Professor, State University of New York at Buffalo, 1971–72, and Bennington College, Vermont, 1977–78. Recipient: Guggenheim Fellowship, 1952, 1955; Department of State American Specialists grant, 1958; National Institute of Arts and Letters grant, 1967; National Endowment for the Arts Award, 1967. Member, National Institute of Arts and Letters, 1977.

PUBLICATIONS

Fiction

In the Absence of Angels: Stories. 1952.
False Entry. 1962.
Tale for the Mirror: A Novella and Other Stories. 1963.
Textures of Life. 1963.
Extreme Magic: A Novella and Other Stories. 1964.
Journal from Ellipsia. 1965.
The Railway Police, and The Last Trolley Ride (two novellas). 1966.
The New Yorkers. 1969.
Queenie. 1971.
Standard Dreaming. 1972.
Eagle Eye. 1973.
The Collected Stories. 1975.
On Keeping Women. 1977.

Other

Herself (memoir). 1972.

*　　*　　*

Hortense Calisher may be too demanding to find a wide audience, despite her remarkable perceptions and formidable talent. She marks an elliptical narrative with subtle, verbal humor and penetrating examinations of the heart. The patient reader is always richly rewarded.

Her shorter fiction is probably more successful than her full-length novels. The mandarin precision in the telling is better sustained in "an apocalypse, served in a very small cup," in Calisher's own definition of a story. Her range is astonishing: as serious as children confronting death by way of professional mourners; as levitous as a dinner party at which the women suddenly decide to remove their blouses. In *Extreme Magic* two people suffering from the intensity of emotional scars find solace in each other's pain and memory, singled out for the implication in the title of this novella. In another, *The Railway Police* – which is, perhaps, Calisher's most powerful work – a woman abandons the artificial identity represented by her collection of elaborate wigs in order to face the world with a bald skull.

Textures of Life, an early novel, represents Calisher at her most accessible: a conventional, even romantic plot salvaged from the ordinary by a vast intelligence and compassion. *False Entry* and *The New Yorkers*, loosely connected novels of rich complexity in both plot and narrative, contain brilliant set pieces – the Ku Klux Klan section in the former, the childhood story of a Hungarian immigrant in the latter – but are probably too prolix for most readers. *Journal from Ellipsia*, which "only the uninitiate still call science fiction," has an interplanetary Gulliver as heroine and sometime narrator. *Queenie*, a verbal *tour de force*, is Calisher's sexual fable in answer to Portnoy, by way of Colette and a 1970's bawdy of immaculate taste.

Calisher's autobiography, *Herself*, discloses less about Calisher than about her view of art, including, in "Pushing Around the Pantheon," an entertaining and enlightening discussion of sexuality in literature in relation to the masculine and feminine roles tradition has imposed on writers. "The magic is in her writing," Marya Mannes has written, "the marvel is in her range."

—Bruce Kellner

CALLAGHAN, Morley (Edward).   Canadian.   Born in Toronto, Ontario, 22 September 1903. Educated at St. Michael's College, University of Toronto, B.A. 1925; Osgoode Hall Law School, Toronto, LL.B. 1928; admitted to the Ontario Bar, 1928. Worked with the Royal Canadian Navy on assignment for the National Film Board during World War II; travelled across Canada as Chairman of the radio forum "Of Things to Come," 1944. Married Lorette Florence Dee in 1929; two sons. Worked on the Toronto *Star* while a student; full-time writer since 1928; lived in Paris, 1928–29. Recipient: Governor-General's Award, 1952; Lorne Pierce Medal, 1960; Canada Council Medal, 1966; Molson Prize, 1969; Royal Bank of Canada Award, 1970. LL.D.: University of Western Ontario, London, 1965. Lives in Toronto.

PUBLICATIONS

Fiction

> *Strange Fugitive.*   1928.
> *A Native Argosy.*   1929.
> *It's Never Over.*   1930.

A Broken Journey. 1932.
Such Is My Beloved. 1934.
They Shall Inherit the Earth. 1935.
Now That April's Here and Other Stories. 1936.
More Joy in Heaven. 1937.
The Varsity Story. 1948.
The Loved and the Lost. 1951.
Stories. 2 vols., 1959–67.
The Many Colored Coat. 1960.
A Passion in Rome. 1961.
An Autumn Penitent. 1973.
A Fine and Private Place. 1975.
Close to the Sun Again. 1977.

Plays

Turn Again Home (produced 1940; as *Going Home,* produced 1950).
To Tell the Truth (produced 1949).

Other

No Man's Meat. 1931.
Luke Baldwin's Vow (juvenile). 1948.
That Summer in Paris: Memories of Tangled Friendships with Hemingway, Fitzgerald,
     and Some Others. 1963.
Winter. 1974.

Reading List: *Callaghan* by Victor Hoar, 1969; *The Style of Innocence: A Study of Hemingway and Callaghan* by Fraser Sutherland, 1972.

*   *   *

Morley Callaghan's achievement has moved in a majestically cyclic manner, from an early period of gauche apprentice work to a time when he found his true talent in the superb short stories and tense moralistic novellas that led Edmund Wilson to liken him, perhaps over-generously, to Chekhov and Turgenev. This was during the 1930's. From the 1950's through the early 1970's, Callaghan strove to turn himself from a writer of sparse *récits* into a novelist in the full-figured nineteenth-century manner, and failed. Finally, in 1977, at the age of 74 with a novella entitled *Close to the Sun Again,* he returned to the manner of those sparse fictions he wrote forty years ago, and the result was success and renewal.

Callaghan has written very little that is not fiction. During the years when he found it hard to earn a living by fiction, he appeared on quiz shows and did other radio work in preference to becoming involved in journalism and teaching, as most other Canadian writers did in his time. But he did write two plays, which had short runs but were never published, and among his best books is the fragment of autobiography, *That Summer in Paris,* which appeared during one of his fallow periods, and which told of the period in the late 1920's when he spent eight months in the French capital, associating with Hemingway, whom he had known when they both worked for the Toronto *Star,* Joyce, and Fitzgerald.

That Summer in Paris is not only an evocative memoir, written with a laconic vividness characteristic of Callaghan at his best. It is also interesting as the only book setting out his aim of writing a direct and non-metaphorical prose that will show things as they are and put no literary screen between the reader and the characters. It was a theory similar to Orwell's idea of "prose like a window pane," but, like most such dogmas, it was carried out only imperfectly in practice, for even the sparsest of Callaghan's novels tends to be dominated by a symbolic structure in which the towers of the Catholic church, which plays so potent a role in his imagination, are notably present at crucial times.

Though it provided unhappy glimpses of his literary heroes, the period described in *That Summer in Paris* was a crucial one in Callaghan's development, which is perhaps why he remembered it so vividly. He had already published a novel, *Strange Fugitive*, about a weak man's involvement through vanity in a gangland where he is destroyed, and had written *It's Never Over* about the effects on a man's family and friends of his execution for murder. These novels, and also *A Broken Journey* were gauche, tentative, and implausible, and it seemed as though Callaghan — whose bittersweet ironical tales had appeared in *Native Argosy* — was essentially a short story writer.

Then, in the mid-1930's, he turned to a quite different kind of novel. He was certainly affected by the tragic circumstances of the depression, but the books he produced were moral parables rather than political tracts, and gained great strength from the fact that Callaghan evidently knew what he wanted to attain and was in full command of the means he needed. In the three novels of this time — *Such Is My Beloved* (about a priest who helps prostitutes), *They Shall Inherit the Earth* (about a son who lets his father be ruined because of a false suspicion of murder) and *More Joy in Heaven* (about a reformed criminal destroyed by former associations) — the characters move, through the curious limbo of suspended existence that the depression created for so many people, towards their almost classic fates. The biblical titles are only half ironical; though Callaghan rejected conventional morality in action, he did not reject Christian charity as such, and indeed suggested that it might in the end be superior to the revolutionary doctrines some of his characters project. In each of the novels there is a leading character who acts with personal integrity and is destroyed by the conventional morality of society and its institutions.

In his trio of post-World War II books — *The Loved and the Lost, The Many Colored Coat,* and *A Passion in Rome* — he attempted a lusher, decorated style, and adopted the more complex form of the classic realist novel. But he used the equipment of a writer of short stories and novellas, with a consequent corruption of style, an offending of credibility. Both *The Loved and the Lost* and *A Passion in Rome* fail in the unity of conception and force of moral passion that distinguished such books as *They Shall Inherit the Earth. The Many Colored Coat* comes nearer the 1930's novels, at least in spirit, but it is too long and over-written for its simple theme. In 1975 Callaghan reached the end of this long phase in his career by producing an almost autobiographical novel, *A Fine and Public Place*, about an unjustly neglected novelist; it is really a kind of *apologia pro vita sua*, and a somewhat embarrassing one in its lack of emotional control.

In 1977 Callaghan finally broke away from his attempt to become a realist novelist, and, in a splendid novella, *Close to the Sun Again*, worked out in concise form and vibrant prose a tale of amnesia and recollection at the point of death. A powerful tycoon is the central figure, and the main theme is the idea that the will to power only develops among men when their natural impulses are suppressed and their personal defeats come to dominate them. Touch a powerful man and you find an emotional cripple. It is a remarkable book for a man in his seventies to have written, and a fine instance of the resilience of the creative urge.

—George Woodcock

CAPOTE, Truman. American. Born in New Orleans, Louisiana, 30 September 1924. Educated at Trinity School and St. John's Academy, New York; Greenwich High School, Connecticut. Worked in the Art Department, also wrote for "Talk of the Town," *The New Yorker* magazine; now a full-time writer. Recipient: O. Henry Award, 1946, 1948, 1951; National Institute of Arts and Letters grant, 1959; Edgar Allan Poe Award, 1966; Emmy Award, for television adaptation, 1967. Member, National Institute of Arts and Letters. Lives in New York City.

PUBLICATIONS

Fiction

Other Voices, Other Rooms. 1948.
A Tree of Night and Other Stories. 1949.
The Grass Harp. 1951.
Breakfast at Tiffany's: A Short Novel and 3 Stories. 1958.
A Christmas Memory. 1966.

Plays

The Grass Harp (produced 1952). 1952.
House of Flowers, music by Harold Arlen (produced 1954). 1968.
The Thanksgiving Visitor. 1968.
Trilogy: An Experiment in Multimedia, with Eleanor Perry. 1969.

Screenplays: *Beat the Devil*, with John Huston 1953; *Indiscretion of an American Wife*, with others, 1954; *The Innocents*, with William Archibald and John Mortimer, 1961; *Trilogy*, with Eleanor Perry, 1969.

Other

Local Color. 1950.
The Muses Are Heard: An Account. 1956.
Observations, with Richard Avedon. 1959.
Selected Writings, edited by Mark Schorer. 1963.
In Cold Blood: A True Account of a Multiple Murder and Its Consequences. 1966.
The Dogs Bark: Public People and Private Places. 1973.
Then It All Came Down: Criminal Justice Today Discussed by Police, Criminals, and Correction Officers, with Comments by Capote. 1976.

Reading List: *The Worlds of Capote* by William L. Nance, 1970.

*   *   *

Few contemporary writers project a public image as compelling or as enduring as that of Truman Capote. John W. Aldridge in *After the Lost Generation*, for example, compared the popular image of Capote to that of Hemingway and Byron, noting that the author's publishers exploited him in order to reinforce the reader's "impression of fragile aestheticism" evident in his works. Certainly Capote's personal idiosyncrasies and the superficial effects of the style and atmosphere of his work have done much to enhance his popular following.

Although the art of Truman Capote speaks directly to his own day and age, the best of it is rooted in nineteenth-century American literary traditions reflected in Hawthorne and James. Like Hawthorne, for example, his work focuses upon the dichotomy of good and evil, light and dark. Capote's craft, moreover, is that of the romance as defined by James. Dream symbolism adds to the gothic impact of the author's resonance.

Recent critics have tended to divide Capote's works into two fictional modes, the nocturnal and the daylight, or the dark and the light. The light Capote fiction tends to take place in a public world (*The Grass Harp*) and reveals an often aggressive social order. The daylight fiction, moreover, is keynoted by a realistic, colloquial, often funny, first-person narrative (*Breakfast at Tiffany's*). The nocturnal, by contrast, is manifest in the dreamlike, detached, inverted, third-person narrative focusing on an inner complex world, often approaching the surreal as in *Other Voices, Other Rooms*.

Because of the romance tradition implicit in his work, Capote's characters are rooted in gothic narcissism. As an instance of that narcissism, a major Capote theme is the discovery of one's *real* identity. In the author's use of the supernatural, a character often confronts his alter ego, as in *Other Voices, Other Rooms*. The tree house in *The Grass Harp* becomes a place for wish fulfilment, a refuge for fighting off the hypocrisy of the social order. Even Holly Golightly's rebellion in *Breakfast at Tiffany's* suggests a degree of self-love. The more recent *In Cold Blood* emphasizes the nocturnal motif, the use of the modern Gothic, and the skillful manipulation of narcissus. This last book, an experiment with what has been called the non-fiction novel, is an excellent example of Capote's skillful penetration of the nightmarish enigma of evil, suggesting again his kinship to Hawthorne, Melville, and James.

—George C. Longest

CARLETON, William. Irish. Born in Prillisk, Clogher, County Tyrone, 4 March 1794. Educated at various district schools, and at a classical school in Donagh, County Monaghan, 1814–16. Married; two sons. Settled in Dublin: worked as a taxidermist and as a tutor; contributed to the *Christian Examiner* and the *Dublin University Magazine*; full-time writer from 1830. Granted government pension, 1848. *Died 30 January 1869.*

PUBLICATIONS

Fiction

Father Butler; The Lough Dearg Pilgrim; Being Sketches of Irish Manners. 1829.
Traits and Stories of the Irish Peasantry. 1830; second series, 1833; as *Irish Life and Character*, 1860; edited by F. A. Niccolls, 1911.
Tales of Ireland. 1834.
Fardorougha the Miser; or, The Convicts of Lisnamona. 1839.
The Fawn of Spring-Vale, The Clarionet, and Other Tales. 1841; as *Jane Sinclair*, 1843; as *The Clarionet, The Dead Boxer, and Barney Branagan*, 1850.
Parry Sastha; or, The History of Paddy Go-Easy and His Wife Nancy. 1845.

Rody the Rover; or, The Ribbonman.   1845.
The Battle of the Factions and Other Tales of Ireland.   1845.
Tales and Sketches Illustrating the Character of the Irish Peasantry.   1845; as *Irish Life and Character,* 1855.
Valentine M'Clutchey, The Irish Agent; or, The Chronicles of the Castle Cumber Property.   1845.
Art Maguire; or, The Broken Pledge.   1845.
The Black Prophet: A Tale of Irish Famine.   1847.
The Emigrants of Ahadarra: A Tale of Irish Life.   1848.
The Tithe Proctor, Being a Tale of the Tithe Rebellion in Ireland.   1849.
The Irishman at Home: Characteristic Sketches of the Irish Peasantry.   1849.
Red Hall; or, The Baronet's Daughter.   1852; as *The Black Baronet,* 1858.
The Squanders of Castle Squander.   1852.
Willy Reilly and His Dear Coleen Bawn.   1855.
Alley Sheridan and Other Stories.   1858.
The Evil Eye; or, The Black Spectre.   1860.
Redmond Count O'Hanlon, The Irish Rapparee: An Historical Tale.   1862.
The Silver Acre and Other Tales.   1862.
The Double Prophecy; or, Trials of the Heart.   1862.
The Poor Scholar, Frank Martin and the Fairies, The Country Dancing Master, and Other Irish Tales.   1869.
The Fair of Emyvale, and The Master and the Scholar.   1870.
The Red-Haired Man's Wife.   1889.

Other

The Life of Carleton, Being His Autobiography and Letters, continued by D. J. O'Donoghue.   2 vols., 1896.

Reading List: *Poor Scholar: A Study of the Works and Days of Carleton* by Benedict Kiely, 1947.

*   *   *

Patrick Kavanagh, who claimed in a BBC talk that William Carleton was one of the two great native writers of Ireland (the other being James Joyce) also remarked in his preface to Carleton's *Autobiography* (1968) that "he wrote two books and a great deal of melodramatic trash." The two books he refers to are the *Autobiography* itself and *Traits and Stories of the Irish Peasantry.*

The *Autobiography,* which Carleton left unfinished, was first published in 1896 long after his death. It tells the story, in vigorous and straightforward prose, of his early life and wanderings as a hedge-scholar. *Traits and Stories* contains a large collection of stories and descriptive sketches of Irish peasant life in the days before the great famine. They tell of courting, weddings, faction fights, and pilgrimages. Carleton reproduces, in amusing and racy dialogue, the speech of the people, with tags of Irish interspersed, and he attempts by his spelling to suggest the Irish brogue. Some of the stories, such as "The Poor Scholar," are dark and sombre, but the most characteristic are humorous. A priest describing a roasting goose in "Denis O'Shaughnessy Going to Maynooth" remarks: "it was such a goose as a priest's corpse might get up on its elbow to look at, and exclaim 'Avourneen machree, it's a thousand pities that I'm not living to have a cut at you!' "

There is much excellent and amusing writing in *Traits and Stories,* and the whole collection is a valuable source-book of social history, but Carleton was an uneven and an uneducated writer. He is often ponderous, melodramatic, or crudely moralizing. These faults are even more glaring in his novels. He wrote a great many, of which the best known are *Fardorougha the Miser*, *Valentine M'Clutchey*, *The Irish Agent*, *The Black Prophet: A Tale of Irish Famine*, and *The Tithe Proctor*. Melodramatic they certainly are, but it is unfair to dismiss them as trash. There are passages of sombre power that reveal the harsh lives of the Irish peasants with truth and passion.

—Alan Warner

CARLYLE, Thomas. Scottish. Born in Ecclefechan, Dumfriesshire, 4 December 1795. Educated at Ecclefechan School; Annan Academy, 1805–09; University of Edinburgh, 1809–13, B.A. 1813; studied for the ministry of the Church of Scotland, 1813–18; also studied Scottish law, 1819. Married Jane Baillie Welsh in 1826 (died, 1866). Mathematics teacher at Annan Academy, 1814–16, and Kirkcaldy Grammar School, 1816–18; settled in Edinburgh, 1818–22: worked as a private teacher, and wrote for the *Edinburgh Encyclopaedia*; tutor to Charles Buller, 1822–23; full-time writer from 1824; lived at Hoddam Hill, 1825, and again in Edinburgh, 1826–27; contributed to the *Edinburgh Review*, 1827; lived at Craigenputtock, 1828–34; settled in Cheyne Walk, Chelsea, London, 1834, and lived there for the rest of his life; gave a course of public lectures, 1837–40. Lord Rector, University of Edinburgh, 1866. Recipient: Prussian Order of Merit, 1874. Declined a baronetcy from Disraeli. *Died 5 February 1881.*

PUBLICATIONS

Collections

> *Works*, edited by H. D. Traill.   30 vols., 1896–99.
> *Selected Works*, edited by Julian Symons.   1955.

Fiction

> *Sartor Resartus: The Life and Opinions of Herr Teufelsdröckh.*   1836; edited by C. F. Harrold, 1937.
> *Wotton Reinfred: A Romance*, in *Last Words*.   1892.

Other

> *The Life of Schiller.*   1825.
> *The French Revolution.*   3 vols., 1837; edited by C. F. Harrold, 1937.
> *Critical and Miscellaneous Essays.*   4 vols., 1838.
> *Chartism.*   1840.
> *On Heroes, Hero-Worship, and the Heroic in History: Six Lectures.*   1841; edited by H. M. Buller, 2 vols., 1926.
> *Past and Present.*   1843; edited by Richard D. Altick, 1965.

Letters and Speeches of Cromwell, with Elucidations.   2 vols., 1845; revised edition, 3 vols., 1846; edited by W. A. Shaw, 1907.

Latter-Day Pamphlets (The Present Time, Model Prisons, Downing Street, The New Downing Street, Stump-Orator, Parliaments, Hudson's Statue, Jesuitism).   8 vols., 1850.

The Life of John Sterling.   1851; edited by William Hale White, 1907.

Passages Selected from the Writings, edited by T. Ballantyne.   1855.

Collected Works.   16 vols., 1857–58.

The History of Friedrich II of Prussia, Called Frederick the Great.   6 vols., 1858–65; abridged edition by A. M. D. Hughes, 1916.

The Early Kings of Norway, An Essay on the Portraits of John Knox.   1875.

Characteristics.   1877.

The Carlyle Anthology, edited by Edward Barrett.   1876.

Reminiscences, edited by J. A. Froude.   2 vols., 1881.

Letters to Mrs. Basil Montagu and B. W. Procter, edited by Anne Benson Procter.   1881.

Reminiscences of My Irish Journey in 1849.   1882.

Last Words on Trades-Unions, Promoterism, and the Signs of the Times, edited by John Carlyle Aitken.   1882.

The Correspondence of Carlyle and Emerson, edited by Charles Eliot Norton.   1883; revised edition, 1886; edited by J. Slater, 1964.

Early Letters 1814–36, edited by Charles Eliot Norton.   4 vols. 1886–88.

Correspondence Between Goethe and Carlyle, edited by Charles Eliot Norton.   1887; edited by G. Hecht, 1913.

Lectures on the History of Literature 1838, edited by J. R. Greene.   1892.

Last Words: Wotton Reinfred: A Romance, Excursion (Futile Enough) to Paris, Letters.   1892.

Rescued Essays, edited by Percy Newberry.   1892.

Historical Sketches of Notable Persons and Events in the Reigns of James I and Charles I, edited by Alexander Carlyle.   1898.

Two Note Books from 23 March 1822 to 16 May 1832, edited by Charles Eliot Norton.   1898.

Letters to His Youngest Sister, edited by C. T. Copeland.   1899.

Collectanea 1821–55, edited by Samuel Arthur Jones.   1903.

New Letters, edited by Alexander Carlyle.   2 vols., 1904.

Unpublished Letters, edited by F. Harrison.   1907.

Love Letters of Carlyle and Jane Welsh, edited by Alexander Carlyle.   2 vols., 1909.

Letters to William Allingham.   1911.

Letters to John Stuart Mill, John Sterling, and Robert Browning, edited by Alexander Carlyle.   1923.

Journey to Germany, Autumn 1858, edited by R. A. E. Brooks.   1940.

Letters to William Graham, edited by John Graham, Jr.   1950.

Unfinished History of German Literature, edited by Hill Shine.   1951.

Letters to His Wife, edited by Trudy Bliss.   1953.

Letters to His Brother Alexander, with Related Family Letters, edited by Edwin W. Marrs, Jr.   1968.

Collected Letters of Thomas and Jane Carlyle, edited by Charles Richard Sanders and Kenneth F. Fielding.   7 vols., 1970–77.

Translator, *Elements of Geometry and Trigonometry,* by A. M. Legendre.   1824.

Translator, *Wilhelm Meister's Apprenticeship,* by Goethe.   3 vols., 1824; revised edition, with *Wilhelm Meister's Travels,* 1839; edited by N. H. Dole, 1901.

Translator, *German Romance: Specimens of Its Chief Authors with Biographical and Critical Notices.*   4 vols., 1827.

Bibliography: *A Bibliography of Carlyle's Writings with Ana* by I. W. Dyer, 1928.

Reading List: *Carlyle* by J. A. Froude, 4 vols., 1882–84; *Life of Carlyle* by D. A. Wilson, 6 vols., 1923–34; *Carlyle: The Life and Ideas of a Prophet* by Julian Symons, 1952; *Carlyle* by David Gascoyne, 1952; *Victorian Sage* by John Holloway, 1953; *The Boundaries of Fiction: Carlyle, Macaulay, Newman* by George L. Levine, 1968; *Carlyle* by Ian Campbell, 1974; *The Seventh Hero: Carlyle and the Theory of Radical Activism* by Philip Rosenberg, 1974.

*   *   *

Thomas Carlyle's was a long and influential career; his important and seminal essays, particularly "Signs of the Times" (1829), and "Characteristics" (1831), earned him a small but influential body of admirers, including Mill and Emerson, and with the publication of *Sartor Resartus* and *The French Revolution*, and the delivery of some notable lectures (particularly *Heroes and Hero-Worship*), his fame spread throughout the English-speaking nineteenth-century world. Even earlier he had had modest but important success as a translator of German literature and populariser of German thought; from the influence of Goethe, whom he much admired, and from salvaged parts of the childhood Christianity with which his pious parents had surrounded him, a creed which he never left behind despite abandoning their wish that he enter the Church, he synthesised a "message" for his times which gave him something of the status of hero and prophet.

The Carlylean message was strongly outlined and uncomplicated. It stressed the importance of work, of obedience to elected rulers and leaders of society (who would, in a God-controlled world, turn out to be worthy of such obedience in the long run), the importance of submission and of order. Carlyle was haunted by the spectre of societal collapse, convinced that the French Revolution and its consequent barbarities could happen again in a Victorian Britain which seemed to be changing daily in appearance, social patterns, interpersonal obligations, personal and public expressions of faith. Against this change, swift and too close for rational assessment, he put a strong, simple structure of moral injunction, and justified it by copious historical example.

Carlyle the historian looked to the past with scrupulous professional care (though many of his interpretations are now discredited), but he also saw there a commentary on the present, and a guide to the future. In *Past and Present* he drew a pointed parallel between a monastic order and a disordered contemporary industrial Britain. In *Chartism* he elaborated on the surrender on the part of the rulers and rich, the surrender of their obligations to rule, to run the country, to create wealth and work. Instead he lambasts them as he does throughout his work, for idleness, pseudo-scientific "laissez faire" economics, the treatment of people as cyphers to be bought and sold as units of labour in the hated "cash nexus." These are the weaknesses which loosen the structure of society, these and false philanthropy, misplaced liberalism, deliberate refusal to see the lessons of history – or to see in history the lessons Carlyle saw.

His blazing style, its compounds being Biblical English, Shakespeare, multiplex allusions from an international acquaintance with literature, German syntax in imitation, and a huge vocabulary part Scots, part English, part coined, did much to popularise his views. His range of tone was amazing: he could sustain immense historical narrative (in *Frederick* or *Cromwell*), social invective ("Shooting Niagara," "The Nigger Question," *Latter-Day Pamphlets*), moving biographical tribute (*Reminiscences, John Sterling*). Along with his wife, Jane, who throughout was an indispensable companion and inspiration, he was a correspondent of rare gifts; their surviving letters will fill over 30 volumes of the ongoing scholarly edition in progress from Duke and Edinburgh universities.

Jane's death in 1866 halted Carlyle's production of public writing almost totally, and his declining years were spent as a sage, a rallying-point for many readers of all ages who saw in him a man who had fought out a viable philosophical and ethical position from the collapse of earlier belief, and chronicled it memorably in *Sartor Resartus*. They saw hope in his example, and they found his strong message a simple one to embrace. Others, particularly the liberals, moved further and further from him as his views hardened, particularly his distaste for what he saw as a premature and hasty emancipation of West Indian slaves, before the economy could take the consequent violent readjustment. Carlyle's view was that priority lay with the maintenance of order and production, not with the rights of the individual. It was an unpopular view.

In private, he wrote on after Jane's death, brilliant letters, and the *Reminiscences*, exercising his astonishing photographic memory in reliving happier early years. These remain, with *The French Revolution*, the most engaging introduction to his work, which is copious, uneven, and shamefully unavailable in any complete critical edition. Recent criticism has achieved a more steady and unbiassed estimate of him, after accusations of marital trouble, proto-fascism, insincerity, and the like, inevitable after the death of a legend like The Sage of Chelsea. He takes his place as a precursor of many of the most important themes in the works of Dickens, Mrs. Gaskell, George Eliot, John Forster, a host of Victorian eminent writers; the Carlyles had an enormous circle of acquaintance in literary Scotland and England. His influential years were spent in Chelsea, his arrival (1834) predating almost all the well-known Victorian works, his death (1881) making him one of the last of the great. He was central, indispensable; critical reassessment and wider acquaintance with his work will help the necessary objective evaluation which he now needs most of all.

—Ian Campbell

CARROLL, Lewis. Pseudonym for Charles Lutwidge Dodgson. English. Born in Daresbury, Cheshire, 27 January 1832. Educated at a school in Richmond, Surrey, 1844–46; Rugby School, 1846–49; Christ Church, Oxford (Boultor Scholar, 1851), B.A. (first-class honours) in mathematics 1854, M.A. 1857; ordained, 1861. Fellow of Christ Church from 1855: Master of the House and Sub-Librarian, 1855; Bostock Scholar, 1855; Lecturer in Mathematics, 1856–81; Curator of the Common Room, 1882–92. *Died 14 January 1898.*

PUBLICATIONS

Collections

The Collected Verse, edited by J. F. McDermott.   1929.
The Complete Works.   1939.
The Works, edited by Roger Lancelyn Green.   1965.
*Alice in Wonderland: Authoritative Texts of Alice's Adventures in Wonderland, Through
    the Looking-Glass, The Hunting of the Snark*, edited by Donald J. Gray.   1971.
The Poems, edited by Myra Cohn Livingston.   1973.
The Letters, edited by Morton N. Cohen.   2 vols., 1978.

Fiction

Alice's Adventures in Wonderland.   1865; revised edition, 1886, 1897; edited by Roger
    Lancelyn Green, 1965.

Through the Looking-Glass, and What Alice Found There.   1871; revised edition, 1897.
Alice's Adventures Underground.   1886; edited by Martin Gardner, 1965.
The Nursery Alice.   1889; edited by Martin Gardner, 1966.

Verse

Phantasmagoria and Other Poems.   1869.
The Hunting of the Snark: An Agony in Eight Fits.   1876; edited by Martin Gardner, 1962.
Rhyme? and Reason?   1883.
Sylvie and Bruno.   1889.
Sylvie and Bruno Concluded.   1893.
Three Sunsets and Other Poems.   1898.
For the Train: Five Poems and a Tale, edited by Hugh J. Schonfield.   1932.

Other

The Fifth Book of Euclid Treated Algebraically.   1858; revised edition, 1868.
A Syllabus of Plane Algebraical Geometry, part 1.   1860.
Notes on the First Two Books of Euclid.   1860.
Notes on the First Part of Algebra.   1861.
The Formulae of Plane Trigonometry.   1861.
An Index to "In Memoriam."   1862.
The Enunciations of the Propositions and Corollaries with Questions in Euclid, Books 1 and 2.   1863; revised edition, 1873.
A Guide to the Mathematical Student, part 1.   1864.
Notes by an Oxford Chiel (The Dynamics of a Particle, with an Excursus on the New Method of Evaluation as Applied to Pi; Facts, Figures, and Fancies Relating to the Elections to the Hebdomadal Council; The New Belfrey of Christ Church, Oxford; The Vision of the Three T's: A Threnody; The Blank Cheque: A Fable).   5 vols., 1865–74.
An Elementary Treatise on Determinants.   1867.
Algebraic Formulae for Responsions.   1868.
Algebraic Formulae and Rules.   1870.
Enunciations, Euclid, 1–4.   1873.
Preliminary Algebra, and Euclid, Book 5.   1874.
Suggestions as to the Best Methods of Taking Votes.   1874.
Some Popular Fallacies about Vivisection.   1875.
Doublets: A Word Puzzle.   1879.
Euclid and His Modern Rivals.   1879; revised edition, 1885.
Lawn Tennis Tournaments: The True Method of Assigning Prizes.   1883.
Twelve Months in a Curatorship, by One Who Has Tried.   1884; revised edition, 1884.
The Principles of Parliamentary Representation.   1884.
A Tangled Tale: A Series of Mathematical Questions.   1885.
Three Years in a Curatorship.   1886.
The Game of Logic.   1886.
Curiosa Mathematica.   2 vols., 1888–93.
Symbolic Logic, part 1.   1896.
The Carroll Picture Book: A Selection from the Unpublished Writings and Drawings, edited by Stuart Dodgson Collingwood.   1899; as *Diversions and Digressions,* 1961.
Feeding the Mind.   1907.
Some Rare Carrolliana.   1924.
Six Letters, edited by W. Partington.   1924.

Novelty and Romancement. 1925.
Tour in 1867. 1928; as *The Russian Journal,* edited by J. F. McDermott, in *The Russian Journal and Other Selections,* 1935.
Two Letters to Marion. 1932.
The Rectory Umbrella, and Misch-Masch, edited by F. Milner. 1932.
Logical Nonsense, edited by Philip C. Blackburn and Lionel White. 1934.
The Russian Journal and Other Selections, edited by J. F. McDermott. 1935.
How the Boots Got Left Behind. 1943.
The Diaries, edited by Roger Lancelyn Green. 2 vols., 1954.
Carroll Observed: A Collection of Unpublished Photographs, Drawings, Poetry, and New Essays, edited by Edward Guiliano. 1976.
Symbolic Logic, parts 1–2, edited by W. W. Bartley, III. 1977.

Editor, *Euclid, Books 1–2.* 1875; revised edition, 1882.
Editor, *The Rectory Magazine.* 1976.

Bibliography: *A Handbook of the Literature of Dodgson* by S. H. Williams and F. Madan, 1931, additions by Madan, 1935.

Reading List: *Life of Carroll* by Langford Reed, 1932; *Carroll* by Derek Hudson, 1954, revised edition, 1975; *Carroll,* 1960, and *The Carroll Handbook,* 1962, both by Roger Lancelyn Green; *The Annotated Alice* edited by Martin Gardner, 1960; *Language and Carroll* by Robert D. Sutherland, 1970; *Play, Games, and Sport: The Literary Voice of Carroll* by Kathleen Blake, 1974; *Carroll and His World* by John Pudney, 1976; *Carroll: Fragments of a Looking-Glass* by Jean Gattégno, 1976.

*   *   *

If one takes the Christian names of Charles Lutwidge Dodgson and reverses them, then translates them into and out of Latin, the result is, or may be, Lewis Carroll. Some such process of transformation by logical steps takes place too between the mathematical treatises which were written in the real name, and the fantasy of Lewis Carroll. The transformation of orthodox mathematics into wonderland is a passage through the looking glass, where all is still logically related, but seen in reverse. The link is clear in the satires, published in Dodgson's name, on the University of Oxford and its works, under such titles as *New Method of Evaluation of Pi,* and the Carroll books which sought to make mathematics and logic accessible to children, whether in the form of puzzles and games, like *A Tangled Tale* and *The Game of Logic,* or directly, in *Symbolic Logic.*

No external evidence is needed, in fact, to reveal that the Alice books and Carroll's poems in *Phantasmagoria* and *The Hunting of the Snark* are the work of a mathematical logician. Given the premises which they adopt, everything about them conforms strictly to logic: I cannot have more tea if I have had none already, and Alice's answer to the Mad Hatter is not pert but pertinent. In *The Hunting of the Snark,* in particular, the nonsense is so compellingly clear and apparently full of meaning that much scholarly effort (sanctioned, one must suppose, by Carroll's frank admission that he did not know what it meant himself) has been expended on inventing meanings for it to be full of. The verses have the internal consistency – of verse. By a stunningly simple manoeuvre Carroll has taken some of the outer structures of poetry – a particular stanza form, a chorus, some incremental repetition, alliterative naming – and stood them up like a stiff suit of clothes full only of their own shape. The process is related to parody, but the result is paradoxically a comic effect which seems, because it is so abstractly conceived, to belong to some realm of pure freedom and delight. Strictly verbal consistency frees the invention from all more solid and earthbound constraints.

In the Alice books too the appearance of a divine freedom, complete originality and imaginative free play is achieved by the transformation of the known and familiar world of the child, including her books and lessons and good manners and pets, by a species of literary parody, combined with logical games. The people and creatures Alice meets are often recognisably based on the acquaintances of Alice Liddell, to whom the stories were told; but every Victorian child had access to the sources of many other parts of the books. The rhymes are parodies of familiar nursery poems by Dr. Watts and others, or, even more effectively, of adult songs and poems whose incomprehensible original words would have floated over the heads of children in Victorian drawing rooms, and were now delightfully set down for them, making sense at last. The persons encountered, who demand of Alice everchanging, mysterious forms of politeness, reflect the complex adult social world, with its formal phrases and apparently meaningless rules especially designed to plague the young. Carroll's logical extensions of the formulae of social behaviour are very like the kinds of unsuccessful attempt to understand literally what is going on that all children apply to the world around them, especially if it is governed by very formal conventions.

There are a certain clarity and hardness in Alice's logical world which appeal to the modern reader, as reflecting our notion of the innocence of the child – she is direct, positive, innocent of degrading emotional display, self-dramatisation, deceit, and role-playing which burgeon all around her; she is constantly attempting to make rational sense of the messy world of other people's emotions. Carroll too set much store by childish innocence: indeed, out of his responsiveness to the uncomplicated, prepubescent affection of his child friends, which he preferred to the taxing world of adult emotions, has sprung the modern view of him as latent paedophile, a kind of response which could be felt to justify his suspicion of the murky adult imagination. When, however, he made conscious statements of his notion of child innocence, it became narrowly Victorian and very like the central premise of his friend and fellow-fantasist George MacDonald. His outrage at child actors saying "Damme" in a production of *H.M.S. Pinafore* now seems merely a curious instance of double thinking in a man who loved theatre and took his little friends to see all kinds of shows involving the exploitation of wretched theatrical children for the sake of whimsy; but the angel-children in the Sylvie and Bruno books, and particularly Bruno's seraphic baby-talk, are very difficult for the modern reader to accept. These late books, despite some good fantasy figures and some of the best of Carroll's verse, are often made tedious by moralising as well as by the sentimentality of Bruno and his talk. It is perhaps not so strange that the success of *Alice* should have made Carroll too conscious of his responsibilities as a writer for children; and it was then inevitable that he should have reverted to the moulds of moral fiction from which *Alice* had been so excitingly altered.

—J. S. Bratton

CARY, (Arthur) Joyce (Lunel). English. Born in Londonderry, Northern Ireland, 7 December 1888. Educated at Hurstleigh School, Tunbridge Wells, Kent; Clifton College, Bristol; Edinburgh Art School; Trinity College, Oxford. Served in the British Red Cross with the Montenegrin Battalion in the Balkan War, 1912–13, and with the Nigerian Regiment in the Cameroons Campaign, 1915–16. Married Gertrude Ogilvie in 1916 (died, 1949); four sons. Joined the Nigerian Political Service, 1913: Magistrate and Executive Officer, 1913–20; settled in Oxford, 1920. Clark Lecturer, Cambridge University, 1956. Recipient: Black Memorial Prize, 1942. LL.D.: University of Edinburgh, 1953. *Died 29 March 1957.*

PUBLICATIONS

Fiction

Aissa Saved. 1932.
An American Visitor. 1933.
The African Witch. 1936.
Castle Corner. 1938.
Mister Johnson. 1939.
Charley Is My Darling. 1940.
A House of Children. 1941.
Herself Surprised. 1941; *To Be a Pilgrim,* 1942; *The Horse's Mouth,* 1944 (augmented edition, edited by Andrew Wright, 1957); complete version, as *First Trilogy,* 1958.
The Moonlight. 1946.
A Fearful Joy. 1949.
Prisoner of Grace. 1952.
Except the Lord. 1953.
Not Honour More. 1955.
The Old Strife at Plant's (unpublished chapter from *The Horse's Mouth*). 1956.
The Captive and the Free, edited by W. Davin. 1959.
Spring Song and Other Stories. 1960.
Cock Jarvis, edited by Alan Bishop. 1974.

Plays

Screenplays: *Men of Two Worlds,* 1946; *Secret People,* with others, 1952.

Verse

Verse. 1908.
Marching Soldier. 1945.
The Drunken Sailor: A Ballad-Epic. 1947.

Other

Power in Men. 1939.
The Case for African Freedom. 1941; revised edition, 1944.
Process of Real Freedom. 1943.
Britain and West Africa. 1946; revised edition, 1947.
Art and Reality: Ways of the Creative Process. 1958.
Memoir of the Bobotes. 1960.
The Case for African Freedom and Other Writings on Africa, edited by C. Fyfe. 1962.
Selected Essays, edited by Alan Bishop. 1976.

Bibliography: "Cary: A Checklist of Criticism" by P. J. Reed, in *Bulletin of Bibliography 25,* 1968; "Cary's Published Writings" by B. Fisher, in *Bodleian Record 8,* 1970.

Reading List: *Cary* by Walter Allen, 1953, revised edition, 1963; *Cary: A Preface to His Novels* by Andrew Wright, 1958; *The Indeterminate World: A Study of the Novels of Cary* by Robert Bloom, 1962; *Cary's Africa* by M. M. Mahood, 1964; *Cary* by William Van

O'Connor, 1966; *Cary: A Biography* by Malcolm Foster, 1968; *Cary: The Developing Style* by Jack Wolkenfeld, 1968; *Cary* by R. W. Noble, 1973; *Cary and the Novel of Africa* by Michael Echeruo, 1973.

*   *   *

Joyce Cary's African novels, *Aissa Saved, An American Visitor, The African Witch,* and *Mister Johnson,* deal with issues of religion and freedom and are acted out against a turbulent background. Aissa alternates between Christianity and her local religion; the American visitor Marie Hasluck has a romantic, indeed naive, belief in man's goodness; she is naturally opposed to the traditional values of the District Officer, Bewsher. She is, however, a thin figure, representative of an idea — anarchic rebellion against law in the name of Freedom — rather than a fully realised character, such as Elizabeth Aladai, the witch who exerts power through her personality and her rhetoric. *Mister Johnson,* ultimately a tragic comedy, is the best of the African novels, where the difference of values between the administrator, Rudbeck, and his exuberant, devoted servant, Mr. Johnson, has a tragic outcome, Mr. Johnson bound remorselessly to the circle of fortune's wheel. The style here is simple, less urgent than in the earlier novels, but much more effective. These novels are not designed to exhibit Africa, to examine colonialism; it is true that they have an exhilaration, a violence, a touch of the fabulous, but Cary's concern is with some of the fundamentals of human behaviour. He sets these novels in the Africa he saw in his particular idiosyncratic way because he was there, because he saw there at first-hand the tensions between tribal and western society, and because his interpretation of Africa permitted him a dramatic setting and themes for his examination of human beings in universal situations.

Charley Is My Darling is the story of a Cockney evacuee in the West country, an investigation of the delinquency involved in growing up. *Castle Corner,* an overcrowded, somewhat fragmented book, shows an Anglo-Irish family buffeted by history. *A House of Children,* a superb evocation of Cary's own childhood holidays in Donegal, explores the sense of timelessness given by ample space and displays a sensitive, convincing understanding of children, all communicated in a luminous, limpid prose.

Herself Surprised, To Be a Pilgrim, and *The Horse's Mouth* are inter-related; they show the two opposing masculine types of creator and preserver, and the Blakean woman, sexual temptress, instinctively maternal, destructively domestic, typified in Sara Monday. Gulley Jimson, the romantic artist in *The Horse's Mouth,* is creative man with all his concentrated drive and romantic damn-the-consequences attitudes. His antithesis is Thomas Wilsher, who represents traditional, conserving man; he dominates *To Be a Pilgrim* as Sara had *Herself Surprised,* and finally he realises change must come.

The Moonlight is a chronicle of two generations of women and their conflicting attitudes to life, clashing in the inevitable alienation of morals, religion, social attitudes. Despite its speed of narration and lack of realism, *A Fearful Joy* is more successful; it centres upon Tabitha Basket, and Dick Bonser, the attractive rogue who animates her.

The political trilogy consisting of *Prisoner of Grace, Except the Lord,* and *Not Honour More* shows the differing claims upon Nina — Cary's best woman character — of Chester Nimmo and James Latter. In the first novel Nina defends Nimmo's career; he is the adjuster, the compromiser, the political animal. In the second Nimmo, now a peer, but nonetheless an old defeated politician, tells of his early life, his conviction that the present world has lost by abandoning its religious principles. Latter is a soldier, fanatical, simple and ultimately dangerously stupid; he is a fighting animal who finally murders Nina. Nimmo remains a character who represents Cary's questions about life: can a creative, free individual survive in a changing world? Is Nimmo's manipulative managerial relativity, his flexibility, to be condoned?

Cary had his own personal answer. Originally trained as an artist, he became an administrator in Nigeria, and then, as his vast manuscripts indicate, a tireless craftsman. He edited, rejected, rewrote. And he himself believed in morality, in fixed personal values as opposed to political fluidity, in affection and ambition as opposed to anxiety and arrogance, in the freedom to choose. In his novels, his short fiction, his poems and essays, he celebrated these beliefs.

—A. Norman Jeffares

CATHER, Willa (Sibert). American. Born in Back Creek Valley, near Winchester, Virginia, 7 December 1873; moved with her family to a farm near Red Cloud, Nebraska, 1883. Educated at Red Cloud High School, graduated 1890; preparatory school in Lincoln, Nebraska, 1891; University of Nebraska, Lincoln, 1891–95, B.A. 1895. Member of the editorial staff, *Home Monthly*, Pittsburgh, 1896; Telegraph Editor and Drama Critic, *Pittsburgh Leader*, 1897–1901; Latin and English Teacher, Central High School, Pittsburgh, 1901–03; English Teacher, Allegheny High School, Pittsburgh, 1903–06; Editor, *McClure's Magazine*, New York, 1906–12; full-time writer from 1912. Recipient: Pulitzer Prize, 1923; Howells Medal, 1930; Prix Femina Américaine, 1933; National Institute of Arts and Letters Gold Medal, 1944. Litt.D.: University of Nebraska, 1917; University of Michigan, Ann Arbor, 1922; Columbia University, New York, 1928; Yale University, New Haven, Connecticut, 1929; Princeton University, New Jersey, 1931; D.L.: Creighton University, Omaha, Nebraska, 1928; University of California, Berkeley, 1931. Member, American Academy of Arts and Letters. *Died 24 April 1947.*

PUBLICATIONS

Fiction

The Troll Garden (stories). 1905.
Alexander's Bridge. 1912.
O Pioneers! 1913.
The Song of the Lark. 1915.
My Antonia. 1918.
Youth and the Bright Medusa. 1920.
One of Ours. 1922.
A Lost Lady. 1923.
The Professor's House. 1925.
My Mortal Enemy. 1926.
Death Comes for the Archbishop. 1927.
Shadows on the Rock. 1931.
The Fear That Walks by Noonday (stories). 1931.
Obscure Destinies (stories). 1932.
Lucy Gayheart. 1935.
Novels and Stories. 13 vols., 1937–41.
Sapphira and the Slave Girl. 1940.
The Old Beauty and Others. 1948.

Early Stories, edited by Mildred R. Bennett.   1957.
Collected Short Fiction 1892–1912, edited by Virginia Faulkner.   1965.
Uncle Valentine and Other Stories: Uncollected Fiction 1915–29, edited by Bernice Slote.   1973.

Verse

April Twilights.   1903.
April Twilights and Other Poems.   1923; revised edition, 1933; edited by Bernice Slote, 1962.

Other

My Autobiography, by S. S. McClure.   1914 (ghost-written by Cather).
Not Under Forty.   1936.
On Writing: Critical Studies on Writing as an Art.   1949.
Writings from Cather's Campus Years, edited by James R. Shively.   1950.
Cather in Europe: Her Own Story of the First Journey, edited by George N. Kates.   1956.
The Kingdom of Art: Cather's First Principles and Critical Principles 1893–1896, edited by Bernice Slote.   1966.
The World and the Parish: Cather's Articles and Reviews 1893–1902, edited by William M. Curtin.   2 vols., 1970.

Editor, *The Life of Mary Baker G. Eddy, and the History of Christian Science*, by Georgine Milmine.   1909.
Editor, *The Best Stories of Sarah Orne Jewett.*   2 vols., 1925.

Bibliography: *Cather: A Checklist of Her Published Writing* by JoAnna Lothrop, 1975.

Reading List: *Cather: A Critical Introduction* by David Daiches, 1951; *Cather: A Critical Biography* by E. K. Brown, completed by Leon Edel, 1953; *The World of Cather* by Mildred R. Bennett, 1961; *Cather* by Dorothy Van Ghent, 1964; *Cather and Her Critics* edited by James Schroeter, 1967; *Cather: Her Life and Art* by James Woodress, 1970; *Cather: A Pictorial Memoir* by Bernice Slote, 1973; *Cather's Imagination* by David Stouck, 1975; *Cather* by Philip L. Gerber, 1975.

*   *   *

Willa Cather, who now can be ranked as one of the most important American woman writers of the first half of this century, is best known for her novels and stories depicting the early years of Nebraska. Her range is considerably broader, however, and also includes notable work laid in the American Southwest, Quebec, and Virginia. Her reputation is based on an extraordinary ability to capture the sense of place and a meticulous craftsmanship that combines a very clear prose style with effective use of myth and symbol. In an age when authors were increasingly able to exploit their literary talents in the market-place Cather displayed an awesome dedication to her art. She wrote slowly and carefully, consistently refused to allow her works to be anthologized, dramatized, or sold in paperback editions, and when she died she had produced twelve novels and at least 55 stories of consistently high quality.
  Cather served a long literary apprenticeship before she was able to cut loose from

journalism and devote her time exclusively to writing. Her ideas and values, however, were formed early, as the recently published volumes of her early newspaper writings show. During her early years of journalism and teaching she wrote mostly short fiction, producing 45 stories before 1912, when she resigned from her editorship of *McClure's Magazine*. These stories, which show a slowly maturing talent, explore themes and subjects that she later employed in her novels. Her first book, however, was *April Twilights*, a volume of verse published while she was teaching high school in Pittsburgh. Her first fiction was a collection of stories, *The Troll Garden*. These stories deal in various ways with the artist and society and show a strong Jamesian influence. They also make use of western material, particularly "A Sculptor's Funeral" and "A Wagner Matinee," but the tone of these last is more akin to the revolt-from-the-village strain in early 20th-century American literature than Cather's later work celebrating the land in novels like *O Pioneers!* and *My Ántonia*.

In 1911 Cather took a leave from *McClure's* and wrote "The Bohemian Girl," a long story that uses for the first time in a nostalgic and affirmative manner the memories of her early years on a Nebraska farm and in the prairie village of Red Cloud. She blends a realistic use of detail with a romantic sensibility in a very successful story that encouraged her to plunge into full-length novels of the same genre. Even before writing "The Bohemian Girl," however, she had published her first novel, *Alexander's Bridge*, but, despite the fact that it is a well-written work of considerable interest, she later deprecated the book and regarded it as a false start. The novel is very Jamesian, takes place in Boston and London, and concerns a bridge-builder whose bridge, like his character, contains a fatal flaw. The story ends with the collapse of the bridge and the death of the protagonist.

O Pioneers!, *The Song of the Lark*, *My Ántonia*, *One of Ours*, and *A Lost Lady* are laid entirely or in part in Nebraska, and form the basis for Cather's identification with that part of the United States. It is important to note that she began using this material nearly two decades after she had left Nebraska to live in the East. By then the youthful experience was ripe and ready for artistic employment. In a 1925 introduction to the stories of Sarah Orne Jewett, who had been her friend and a literary influence, she quoted from a letter from Jewett: "The thing that teases the mind over and over for years, and at last gets itself put down rightly on paper – whether little or great, it belongs to literature." This was a literary principle in which Cather thoroughly believed, and it places Cather closer to Wordsworth with his view of poetry as "emotion recollected in tranquility" than it does to the realists or naturalists of the late 19th and early 20th centuries like Howells, Garland, or Dreiser, who "worked up" their materials.

O Pioneers! is the story of Alexandra Bergson, a Swedish immigrant who tames the wild land in the pioneer days of Nebraska. Alexandra's life is a success story told with a loving affirmation of the beauty of the land and the value of the pioneer struggle. The novel is not all light, however, as two of Alexandra's brothers turn out to be mean-spirited materialists and her beloved younger brother dies at the hand of a Czech farmer whose wife he has fallen in love with. *The Song of the Lark* combines Cather's memories of her young life in Red Cloud with her great interest in music and in particular the Wagnerian soprano Olive Fremstad, who had grown up in an immigrant family in Minnesota. Thus the youth of the singer is Cather's own youth and the career of the artist is a fictionalized biography of Olive Fremstad. *My Ántonia*, regarded by many readers as Cather's best novel, creates a memorable character in a Bohemian immigrant heroine who had her prototype in a childhood friend. This story is told retrospectively by a male narrator whose experience growing up on a farm and in the town of Black Hawk (Red Cloud) parallels Cather's own life. Again the same sense of place is evoked memorably, and the land and its pioneer settlers are presented with a haunting nostalgia. The book is episodic in character, which is typical of Cather, and contains stories within stories. The novel is carefully constructed, however, and given an organic form that suits the material.

One of Ours is less successful, though the early parts of the novel laid in Nebraska create a vivid picture of life on a Nebraska farm and in a college town like Lincoln where Cather attended the university. The story was suggested by the life of her cousin who was killed in

France during the First World War. Ironically, this novel won a Pulitzer Prize and brought Cather handsome royalties for the first time. She returned to an all-Nebraska setting in *A Lost Lady*, and again evoked childhood memories in the creation of Captain and Mrs. Forrester, the chief characters. The setting is again a fictionalized Red Cloud, and the story of the lost lady, who is a sort of Nebraskan Emma Bovary, is told from the perspective of a boy growing up in the small town. This novel demonstrates the literary technique that Cather explains in her essay "The Novel Démeublé." It is a work of about 50,000 words in which all the excess detail is stripped away. "The higher processes of art are all processes of simplification," she wrote. She also was fond of quoting Dumas *père*, who once had said that to make a drama all "a man needed [was] one passion, and four walls."

The Professor's House is a different sort of novel from the Nebraska stories. It's the tale of a middle-aged professor of history who loses the will to live and barely escapes death. Although he had won an important literary prize and apparently had everything to live for, he is profoundly depressed by the materialism of his family and his culture. There is a good deal of autobiography in this novel, for Cather, too, felt that for her "the world broke in two in 1922 or thereabouts." There is a long tale inserted in the middle of this novel, "Tom Outland's Story," that evokes the ancient civilization of the Mesa Verde Indians in sharp contrast to the 1920's and also reflects Cather's growing interest in the Southwest.

Her most significant use of the Southwest came two years later in *Death Comes for the Archbishop*, the novel that she thought her best. It creates in episodic form the life of Jean Latour, the first bishop of New Mexico. She long had been fascinated by the story of the Catholic church in the Southwest, and had begun visiting the area as early as 1912. When she ran across a letter collection that gave her a clear account of the real Bishop Lamy's career in New Mexico in the 19th century, she found her story and produced a distinguished historical novel. Much of the detail is fiction and it is romanticized, but the material does not do violence to history or to the historical characters it recreates. The work represents Cather at the peak of her creative powers.

Two more historical novels followed, *Shadows on the Rock* and *Sapphira and the Slave Girl*, and Cather after 1927 seemed to take refuge in writing about the past. *Shadows* is a story of Quebec at the end of the 17th century, a novel that is dramatically thin but pictorially rich. *Sapphira*, the only novel Cather ever wrote about her native Virginia, takes place in the Shenandoah Valley before the Civil War and deals with an incident of family history, her grandmother's successful efforts to help a slave escape to Canada.

—James Woodress

CHANDLER, Raymond (Thornton). American. Born in Chicago, Illinois, 23 July 1888; moved to England with his mother: naturalized British subject, 1907; again became an American citizen, 1956. Educated in a local school in Upper Norwood, London; Dulwich College, London, 1900–05; studied in France and Germany, 1905–07. Served in the Canadian Army, 1917–18, and in the Royal Air Force, 1918–19. Married Pearl Cecily Hurlburt in 1924 (died, 1954). Worked in the supply and accounting departments of the Admiralty, London, 1907; Reporter for the *Daily Express*, London, and the *Western Gazette*, Bristol, 1908–12; returned to the United States, 1912; worked in St. Louis, then on a ranch and in a sporting goods firm in California; accountant and bookkeeper at the Los Angeles Creamery, 1912–17; worked in a bank in San Francisco, 1919; worked for the *Daily Express*, Los Angeles, 1919; Bookkeeper, then Auditor, Dabney Oil Syndicate, Los Angeles, 1922–32; full-time writer from 1933. President, Mystery Writers of America, 1959. Recipient: Edgar Allan Poe Award, 1946, 1955. *Died 26 March 1959.*

PUBLICATIONS

Fiction

> *The Big Sleep.* 1939.
> *Farewell, My Lovely.* 1940.
> *The High Window.* 1942.
> *The Lady in the Lake.* 1943.
> *Five Murderers* (stories). 1944.
> *Five Sinister Characters* (stories). 1945.
> *Finger Man and Other Stories.* 1946.
> *The Little Sister.* 1949.
> *The Simple Art of Murder* (stories). 1950.
> *The Long Goodbye.* 1953.
> *Playback.* 1958.
> *Killer in the Rain* (stories). 1964.

Plays

> *Double Indemnity*, with Billy Wilder, in *Best Film Plays 1945*, edited by John Gassner
> and Dudley Nichols. 1946.
> *The Blue Dahlia* (screenplay). 1976.

> Screenplays: *And Now Tomorrow*, with Frank Partos, 1944; *Double Indemnity*, with
> Billy Wilder, 1944; *The Unseen*, with Hagar Wilde and Ken Englund, 1945; *The Blue
> Dahlia*, 1946; *Strangers on a Train*, with Czenzi Ormonde and Whitfield Cook, 1951.

Other

> *Chandler Speaking*, edited by Dorothy Gardiner and Kathrine Sorley Walker. 1962.
> *Chandler Before Marlowe: Chandler's Early Prose and Poetry 1908–1912*, edited by
> Matthew J. Bruccoli. 1973.
> *The Notebooks of Chandler, and English Summer: A Gothic Romance*, edited by Frank
> MacShane. 1976.

Bibliography: *Chandler · A Checklist* by Matthew J. Bruccoli, 1968.

Reading List: *Down These Mean Streets a Man Must Go* by Philip Durham, 1963; *Chandler
on Screen* by Stephen Pendo, 1976; *The Life of Chandler* by Frank MacShane, 1976.

*   *   *

Raymond Chandler first attempted a literary career in London in his early twenties, when
he unsuccessfully tried to establish himself as a poet and critic. Twenty years later, after
losing his important job with an oil company because of his drinking, he tried again, writing
stories for pulp magazines, notably *Black Mask*. This time he was immediately successful,
and, along with Dashiell Hammett, became the principal champion of the "hard-boiled"
school of detective fiction.

Chandler was scornful of the English school of detective fiction which, as he said in a
famous remark, was an "affair of the upper classes, the week-end house party and the vicar's

rose garden." He believed that crime fiction should deal with real criminals and should employ the language actually used by murderers and policemen. Chandler used what he called the "objective method" which assures authenticity. At the same time, his work has a strong emotional center that is capable of illuminating "an utterly unexpected range of sensitivity."

In 1939, he published *The Big Sleep*, his first novel. In quick succession he published *Farewell, My Lovely*, *The High Window*, and *The Lady in the Lake*, reworking material from his earlier stories. Chandler's novels are narrated by the central character, Philip Marlowe, an idealistic and romantic detective who is also tough and cynical. The books are dramatic and funny: Chandler's prose is formal but his vocabulary is full of the slang of his characters. The prose is a mirror of the political and financial corruption that lies under the bland surface of California life. Chandler was the first to give Los Angeles a literary identity.

During the 1940's and early 1950's, Chandler wrote movie scripts in Hollywood, notably *Double Indemnity* (with Billy Wilder), *The Blue Dahlia*, and *Strangers on a Train*. Chandler disliked Hollywood, but earned enough money to retire with his wife, Cissy, to La Jolla, where he returned to fiction, writing *The Little Sister* and his most ambitious novel, *The Long Goodbye*. This book is a conscious effort to stretch the conventions of the detective novel so as to convert it into a general work of fiction. It brings crime fiction to the highest level it has attained in modern times. Chandler also wrote an essay, "The Simple Art of Murder," which places his work in the context of other crime novelists. It attempts to justify his blend of idealism and realism and may be considered his literary testament. He also wrote incisively about Hollywood.

Following the death of his wife, Chandler spent much time in England, where he became a celebrity, acknowledged as a master of contemporary fiction. Nevertheless, he was lonely and withdrawn, and succeeded in writing only one further novel, *Playback*. Since his death his stature has continued to grow, and he is now generally considered to be among the most important American novelists of his time.

—Frank MacShane

CHEEVER, John.   American.   Born in Quincy, Massachusetts, 27 May 1912. Educated at the Thayer Academy. Served in the United States Army in World War II. Married Mary M. Winternitz in 1941; one daughter and two sons. Taught at Barnard College, New York, 1956–57; Visiting Professor of Creative Writing, Boston University, 1974–75. Recipient: Guggenheim Fellowship, 1951; Benjamin Franklin Award, 1955; O. Henry Award, 1956, 1964; National Institute of Arts and Letters grant, 1956; National Book Award, 1958; Howells Medal, 1965. Member, National Institute of Arts and Letters. Lives in Ossining, New York.

PUBLICATIONS

Fiction

The Way Some People Live: A Book of Stories.   1943.
The Enormous Radio and Other Stories.   1953.
The Wapshot Chronicle.   1957.
The Housebreaker of Shady Hill and Other Stories.   1958.

Some People, Places, and Things That Will Not Appear in My Next Novel. 1961.
The Brigadier and the Golf Widow (stories). 1964.
The Wapshot Scandal. 1964.
Bullet Park. 1969.
The World of Apples (stories). 1973.
Falconer. 1977.
The Stories. 1978.

Reading List: *Cheever* by Samuel Coale, 1977.

*   *   *

John Cheever has made his mark as a chronicler of a modern American sensibility that is well-educated, disoriented, and generally bitter toward the situations, sexual and cultural, in which it finds itself. That sensibility is usually represented as able to look back on an earlier generation in which moral codes were fixed and confident; that fixity and confidence almost constitute a romantic backdrop against which the frustrations of current life play out their inconclusive courses. These courses are often presented in short stories which combine the irony of sheer event with Cheever's own comments on what is happening – happening to persons who endure the events rather than understand them. For example, one story, "The Swimmer" (in *The Brigadier and the Golf Widow*), illustrates the texture and scope of many a Cheever tale. A man decides, for reasons that he does not clearly understand, to reach his home by swimming through all the private pools that extend toward his own home and pool. In the course of his feat, no more sensible than climbing the Himalayas, the swimmer has contact, ironic for Cheever and his readers, with several aspects of the swimmer's society. And at the end, the swimmer arrives at his own pool, only to find his own house empty; there is no explanation of this shocking conclusion. The man's dismay is but an intensification of the pressures that set him on his way.

Novels allow Cheever to explore at greater length destinies no more controlled and intelligible than the afternoon efforts of the swimmer. Two closely related novels, *The Wapshot Chronicle* and *The Wapshot Scandal*, represent the decline of a "good family" in a small New England community; the modest certainties of an older generation ravel out in the adventures of two sons as they wander from job to job and from one sexual relation to another. Stories loosely connected with the fates of the two young men ornament the novels and illustrate the impact of conspicuous wealth, American go-getting, scientific research, and the soft life that lies in wait for most Cheever characters. *Bullet Park* presents these themes with more rigor as they apply to two men, Hammer and Nailles. In Nailles appears a man who is fairly content with the disintegrating Zion where he finds himself. In Hammer, Cheever offers a man whose wealth and success create in him only a nameless bitterness. It is a bitterness that leads Hammer to an envy of the complacent Nailles, whose unconsidered contentment he tries to destroy; Hammer attempts to crucify Nailles' son.

Is this the end of the road? *Falconer* seems to say "Not necessarily." Farragut, the hero of this novel, has one of the bitterest experiences that Cheever has contrived. The man is a drug addict who has been sent to prison for the murder of his brother. In a highly unified narrative, Farragut experiences the heartless pressures of the prison system, goes through the routine inhumanity, homosexuality, and sheer boredom of prison life – and has enough energy left to contrive his escape into a world whose qualities are not necessarily superior to the concentrated hell of the prison. Farragut's will to persist, to continue in a life made up of the absurdities that society and fate and Cheever contrive, sums up the counsel that Cheever offers. It is a counsel offered with a skill that is ingenious and deft; it is a counsel immersed in an auctorial consciousness that is condescending rather than sympathetic.

—Harold H. Watts

CHESNUTT, Charles Waddell. American. Born in Cleveland, Ohio, 20 June 1858; moved with his family to North Carolina, 1865. Educated privately, and in local schools; largely self-taught. Married Susan U. Perry in 1878; four children. Taught in the North Carolina public schools, 1874–81; Principal, State Normal School, Fayetteville, North Carolina, 1881–83; newspaper reporter in New York, 1884; returned to Cleveland, 1885, and thereafter worked as a court stenographer for the rest of his life; admitted to the Ohio Bar, 1887. Recipient: Spingarn Medal, 1928. *Died 15 November 1932.*

PUBLICATIONS

Collections

The Short Fiction, edited by Sylvia Lyons Render. 1974.

Fiction

The Conjure Woman (stories). 1899.
The Wife of His Youth and Other Stories of the Color Line. 1899.
The House Behind the Cedars. 1900.
The Marrow of Tradition. 1901.
The Colonel's Dream. 1905.

Other

Frederick Douglass. 1899.

Bibliography: "Secondary Studies on the Fiction of Chesnutt" by Joan Cunningham, and "The Works of Chesnutt: A Checklist" by William L. Andrews, both in *Bulletin of Bibliography,* January 1976.

Reading List: *Chesnutt, Pioneer of the Color Line* by Helen M. Chesnutt, 1952; *Chesnutt, America's First Great Black Novelist* by J. Noel Heermance, 1974; *I Choose Black: The Crusade of Chesnutt* by Frances Richardson Keller, 1978.

*   *   *

Charles Waddell Chesnutt, a "voluntary Negro," reflects in his writings major inter- and intraracial tensions of the nineteenth-century United States. Beginning and ending his life in Cleveland, Ohio, and from age seven to twenty-five living in North Carolina, he found the major motivations and materials of his works in his own life and that of contemporaries or immediate forebears on both sides of the Mason-Dixon line. Chesnutt's preoccupations with the problems of powerless blacks and poor whites is doubtless a reflection not only of the trauma which marked his own poverty-stricken youth but also of the resultant resolve to improve the quality of life for all those denied access to the fullness of American life because of color and/or class.

Chesnutt's fiction ranges in form from simple tale to highly plotted novel, in mood from comic to tragic. The subject matter reflects the major contemporary concerns of Afro-Americans. However, the general reading public, primarily white, rejected Chesnutt's increasingly explicit advocacy of equal rights for blacks and other under-privileged citizens.

Consequently, after *The Colonel's Dream* in 1905, Chesnutt terminated his writing career.

By that time, however, Chesnutt had won a permanent place in American literary history, especially for his short fiction. His unqualified rating as a conscious, accomplished author by critics such as William Dean Howells and George Washington Cable was unprecedented for an Afro-American prose writer. His works, usually presented from a black perspective, are historically and sociologically accurate as well as aesthetically satisfying and ethically admirable. Chesnutt is recognized as "the first real Negro novelist," "the pioneer of the color line," and the first American writer not only to use the folk tale for social protest but also to extensively characterize Afro-Americans.

Subsequently Chesnutt used his increasing influence otherwise to improve the status of his fellow blacks. In recognition of his achievements, the National Association for the Advancement of Colored People awarded him its annual Spingarn Medal in 1928. Upon Chesnutt's death in 1932, a friend recapitulated accurately: "His great contribution in letters is a monument to our race and ... to our national life."

—Sylvia Lyons Render

CHESTERTON, G(ilbert) K(eith). English. Born in London, 28 May 1874. Educated at Colet Court School, London; St. Paul's School, London (Editor, *The Debater*, 1891–93), 1887–92; Slade School of Art, London, 1893–96. Worked for the London publishers Redway, 1896, and T. Fisher Unwin, 1896–1902; weekly contributor to the *Daily News*, London, 1901–13, and the *Illustrated London News*, 1905–36; Co-Editor, *Eye Witness*, London, 1911–12, and Editor, *New Witness*, 1912–23; regular contributor to the *Daily Herald*, London, 1913–14; leader of the Distributist movement after the war, and subsequently President of the Distributist League; convert to Roman Catholicism, 1922; Editor, with H. Jackson and R. B. Johnson, Readers' Classics series, 1922; Editor, *G. K.'s Weekly*, 1925–36; Lecturer, Notre Dame University, Indiana, 1930; radio broadcaster in the 1930's. Also an illustrator: illustrated some of his own works and books by Hilaire Belloc and E. C. Bentley. Honorary degrees: Edinburgh, Dublin, and Notre Dame universities. Fellow, Royal Society of Literature. Knight Commander with Star, Order of St. Gregory the Great, 1934. *Died 14 June 1936.*

PUBLICATIONS

Collections

Selected Stories, edited by Kingsley Amis.   1972.
Greybeards at Play and Other Comic Verse, edited by John Sullivan.   1974.
Plays, edited by D. J. Conlon.   1976.

Fiction

The Tremendous Adventures of Major Brown.   1903.
The Napoleon of Notting Hill.   1904.
The Club of Queer Trades.   1905.
The Man Who Was Thursday: A Nightmare.   1908.
The Ball and the Cross.   1909.
The Innocence of Father Brown.   1911.
Manalive.   1912.
The Flying Inn.   1914.

The Wisdom of Father Brown. 1914.
The Man Who Knew Too Much and Other Stories. 1922.
Tales of the Long Bow. 1925.
The Incredulity of Father Brown. 1926.
The Return of Don Quixote. 1927.
The Secret of Father Brown. 1927.
The Sword of Wood. 1928.
The Poet and the Lunatics: Episodes in the Life of Gabriel Gale. 1929.
Four Faultless Felons. 1930.
The Scandal of Father Brown. 1935.
The Paradoxes of Mr. Pond. 1936.

Plays

Magic: A Fantastic Comedy (produced 1913). 1913.
The Judgment of Dr. Johnson (produced 1932). 1927.
The Surprise (produced 1953). 1952.

Verse

Greybeards at Play: Literature and Art for Old Gentlemen: Rhymes and Sketches. 1900.
The Wild Knight and Other Poems. 1900; revised edition, 1914.
The Ballad of the White Horse. 1911.
Poems. 1915.
Wine, Water, and Song. 1915.
Old King Cole. 1920.
The Ballad of St. Barbara and Other Verses. 1922.
The Queen of Seven Swords. 1926.
Collected Poems. 1927; revised edition, 1933.

Other

The Defendant. 1901.
Twelve Types. 1902; as *Varied Types*, 1903.
Robert Browning. 1903.
G. F. Watts. 1904.
Heretics. 1905.
All Things Considered. 1908.
Orthodoxy. 1909.
George Bernard Shaw. 1909.
Tremendous Trifles. 1909.
What's Wrong with the World? 1910.
Alarms and Discussions. 1910.
William Blake. 1910.
The Ultimate Lie. 1910.
Appreciations and Criticisms of the Works of Dickens. 1911.
A Defence of Nonsense and Other Essays. 1911.
The Future of Religion. 1911.
A Miscellany of Men. 1912.
The Victorian Age in Literature. 1913.
The Barbarism of Berlin. 1914; revised edition, as *The Appetite of Tyranny*, 1915.
London. 1914.

Prussian Versus Belgian Culture. 1914.
The So-Called Belgian Bargain. 1915.
The Crimes of England. 1915.
Temperance and the Great Alliance. 1916.
A Shilling for My Thoughts, edited by E. V. Lucas. 1916.
Lord Kitchener. 1917.
A Short History of England. 1917.
Utopia of Usurers and Other Essays. 1917.
How to Help Annexation. 1918.
Irish Impressions. 1919.
The Superstition of Divorce. 1920.
The Uses of Diversity. 1920.
The New Jerusalem. 1920.
Eugenics and Other Evils. 1922.
What I Saw in America. 1922.
Fancies Versus Fads. 1923.
St. Francis of Assisi. 1923.
The End of the Roman Road: A Pageant of Wayfarers. 1924.
The Superstitions of the Sceptic. 1925.
The Everlasting Man. 1925.
William Cobbett. 1925.
The Outline of Sanity. 1926.
The Catholic Church and Conversion. 1926.
(Selected Works). 9 vols., 1926.
A Gleaming Cohort (miscellany), edited by E. V. Lucas. 1926.
Social Reform Versus Birth Control. 1927.
Robert Louis Stevenson. 1927.
Generally Speaking. 1928.
Do We Agree? A Debate, with George Bernard Shaw. 1928.
G. K. C. as M. C. (introductions), edited by J. P. de Fonseka. 1929.
The Thing. 1929.
The Resurrection of Rome. 1930.
Come to Think of It. 1930.
At the Sign of the World's End. 1930.
Is There a Return to Religion? with E. Haldeman Julius. 1931.
All Is Grist. 1931.
Chaucer. 1932.
Sidelights on New London and Newer York and Other Essays. 1932.
Christendom in Dublin. 1932.
All I Survey. 1933.
St. Thomas Aquinas. 1933.
Avowals and Denials. 1934.
The Well and the Shallows. 1935.
Stories, Essays, and Poems. 1935.
As I Was Saying. 1936.
Autobiography. 1936.
The Legend of the Sword. 1936.
The Man Who Was Chesterton, edited by R. T. Bond. 1937.
The Coloured Lands (miscellany). 1938.
The End of the Armistice, edited by Dorothy Collins. 1949.
The Common Man. 1950.
A Handful of Authors: Essays on Books and Writers, edited by Dorothy Collins. 1953.
The Glass Walking-Stick and Other Essays from the Illustrated London News 1905–36, edited by Dorothy Collins. 1955.

Lunacy and Letters (essays from the *Daily News*, 1901–11), edited by Dorothy
   Collins.   1958.
The Man Who Was Orthodox: A Selection from the Uncollected Writings, edited by A. L.
   Maycock.   1963.
The Spice of Life and Other Essays, edited by Dorothy Collins.   1964.
Chesterton: A Selection from His Non-Fictional Prose, edited by W. H. Auden.   1970.
Chesterton on Shakespeare, edited by Dorothy Collins.   1971.

Editor, *Thackeray* (selections).   1909.
Editor, with Alice Meynell, *Samuel Johnson* (selections).   1911.
Editor, *Essays by Divers Hands*.   1926.
Editor, *G. K.'s* (miscellany from   *G. K.'s Weekly*).   1934.

Bibliography: *Chesterton: A Bibliography* by John Sullivan, 1958, supplement, 1968.

Reading List: *Chesterton*, 1943, and *Return to Chesterton*, 1952, both by Maisie Ward;
Paradox in Chesterton by Hugh Kenner, 1947; *Chesterton*, 1950, and *The Mind of Chesterton*,
1970, both by Christopher Hollis; *Chesterton: Man and Mask* by Garry Wills, 1961;
Chesterton: A Biography by Dudley Barker, 1973; *Chesterton* by Laurence J. Clipper, 1974;
The Novels of Chesterton: A Study in Art and Propaganda by Ian Boyd, 1975; *Chesterton,
Radical Populist* by Margaret Canovan, 1977.

*   *   *

There is magic in Chesterton's social, literary, and theological criticism. He had just the
taste for paradox, just the love of argument, just the touch of robust humor, just the right
mixture of the hilarious and the hortatory that makes for popular leading articles. Now he
looks rather old-fashioned, a belle-lettrist. His social criticism, in works like *Heretics* and
What's Wrong with the World, though lucid, is dated. His poetry fares better, whether
partisan or rhetorical. There may be a few who recall the thrill the noise "Lepanto" made in
the head of a small boy; and "The Donkey" is justly famous. Much of his controversial
writing is still interesting, even if his views on free love and free trade, good catholics and bad
Jews, and other touchy subjects are irritating to a modern reader. Like H. L. Mencken, he can
still interest us in old forgotten battles.
   As long as one is not allergic to a mixture of ideology and fiction, of propaganda and art, he
can enjoy Chesterton's fiction, the best of which is *The Man Who Was Thursday*. One ought
to begin by reading the Father Brown stories, perhaps starting with "The Man in the
Passage." It is in the stories that one sees the best of that Chestertonian paradox about which
Hugh Kenner wrote an entire book. If one thinks detective fiction needs an excuse, one can
read the "Defence of Detective Sories" in *The Defendant*. Father Brown, a little round priest
with a little round hat, is a great creation, with a subtle spiritual intuition as near at hand as
his umbrella. He is the supreme creation of the multi-faceted Chesterton. Indeed, I am
intolerant of other views – but then, as Chesterton said, "tolerance is the virtue of the man
without conviction."

—Leonard R. N. Ashley

CHOPIN, Kate (O'Flaherty).   American.   Born in St. Louis, Missouri, 8 February 1851.
Educated at the Sacred Heart Convent, St. Louis, graduated 1868. Married Oscar Chopin in
1870 (died, 1882); five sons and one daughter. Lived in New Orleans, 1870–80, then on her
husband's plantation in Cloutierville, Louisiana, 1880–82; returned to St. Louis after her
husband's death; began writing in 1888. *Died 22 August 1904.*

PUBLICATIONS

Collections

Complete Works, edited by Per Seyersted. 1969.
The Awakening and Other Stories, edited by Lewis Leary. 1970.

Fiction

At Fault. 1890.
Bayou Folk (stories). 1894.
A Night in Acadie. 1897.
The Awakening. 1899.

Bibliography: in *Bibliography of American Literature* by Jacob Blanck, 1957; *Edith Wharton and Chopin: A Reference Guide* by Marlene Spring, 1976.

Reading List: *Chopin and Her Creole Stories* by Daniel S. Rankin, 1932; *The American 1890's: Life and Times of a Lost Generation* by Larzer Ziff, 1966; *Chopin: A Critical Biography* by Per Seyersted, 1969.

*   *   *

In 1894, when Kate Chopin published *Bayou Folk*, a collection of Louisiana stories, she was greeted as an outstanding local color writer. In 1899, when she brought out *The Awakening*, a novel which in certain respects is an American *Madame Bovary*, she so shocked the public that some libraries banned the book. As a result, her creative spirit was stifled, and, when she died in 1904, she was forgotten. But in 1969, when *The Complete Works of Kate Chopin* appeared, the time was ripe for a reassessment and revival of this writer. Today she is recognized both as a literary artist of the American realist movement and as a particularly significant commentator on the female experience.

Chopin grew up in the French atmosphere of her mother's family in St. Louis, and she married a Creole, and lived in New Orleans and on a Louisiana plantation for 13 years. Her *oeuvre* consists of two novels and about 100 stories. Nearly all she wrote is set in Louisiana, and she makes the atmosphere of this picturesque state creep into our senses, with the enchanting physical setting and the charming peculiarities of the Creoles, Cajuns, and blacks of the region.

But she used local color discreetly, and it was never an end in itself to her; rather, her interest was general human nature. As a child she had been taught to face life without fear and embarrassment and to observe people without judging them. She did not believe in idealism, and she disliked moral reformers. In her first novel, *At Fault*, she lets a woman (who has forced a man to remarry his divorced drunkard wife in order to redeem her) come to the conclusion that no one has the right to submit others to the "exacting and ignorant rule of ... moral conventionalities."

From an early age she was an avid reader, with a particular interest in books dealing with women's position. She was especially influenced by Maupassant, probably because she felt he spoke secretly to her with his frank treatments of the hidden life of women. This fitted in with her own ambition, which was to portray especially the lives of women, as truthfully and openly as America would permit. Her first extant story deals with a "feminine" or traditional heroine who submissively leaves it to the man to decide her fate, and the second with an "emancipated" woman who insists on deciding herself about her own life. Most of her later heroines are variations on these two types. She often wrote about them in pairs, thus keeping up a kind of balanced dialogue between traditional and emancipationist women.

As Chopin gained in self-confidence, she became more daring in her descriptions of unconventional women. When she had just been nationally praised for *Bayou Folk* she wrote

"The Story of an Hour," a tale about a woman who, when told that her husband has suddenly died, whispers "free, free, free!" A few weeks later the author in a sense answered this extreme example of the self-assertive woman with an entry in her diary, where she wrote that could she get her husband back, she would have been willing to give up "the past ten years of my growth – my real growth."

Chopin's ultimate examples of the feminine and the emancipated woman are found in *The Awakening*. Adèle Ratignolle strikingly illustrates the patriarchal ideal of the self-forgetting woman. A Creole and a Catholic, she is likened to a "Faultless Madonna" and described as a "mother-woman," that is, one of those who live for and through their family and who consider it "a holy privilege to efface themselves as individuals." She is a perfect foil for Edna Pontellier, an American married to a New Orleans Creole and the mother of two, who says: "I would give up the unessential; I would ... give my life for my children; but I wouldn't give myself." What she means by this becomes clear as she gradually awakens to a self-assertion both in the physical and spiritual field. Like Emma Bovary, she becomes estranged from her husband, neglects her children, has lovers, and finally takes her life. But while Emma acts out roles inherited from romantic literature and gains little self-knowledge, Edna outgrows her romantic notions and learns "to look with her own eyes [and] to apprehend the deeper undercurrents of life."

She realizes that the physical side of love can live apart from the spiritual one, and that sex is a basic force which – in the guise of romantic emotions – drives us blindly on toward procreation. She understands that, for her, a return to the submission and self-delusion of the past is impossible. She refuses to let the children "drag her into the soul's slavery for the rest of her days," but she finally accepts a responsibility not to give them a bad name and takes her life. While defeated by her environment, she is also victorious: finally understanding her own nature and her situation as a woman, she exerts her inner freedom by assuming sole responsibility for her life.

The critics had to concede that, artistically, *The Awakening* is a small masterpiece. But just as with Dreiser's *Sister Carrie* a year later, they could not accept an author who in no way condemns such a heroine. Larzer Ziff has said of Chopin's silence after this setback that it was "a loss to American letters of the order of the untimely deaths of Crane and Norris." Today *The Awakening* is available in some eight editions, and with this novel and her best stories Kate Chopin seems assured a permanent place in American literature.

—Per Seyersted

CHRISTIE, Dame Agatha (Mary Clarissa, née Miller). English. Born in Torquay, Devon, 15 September 1890. Educated privately at home; studied singing and piano in Paris. Married 1) Colonel Archibald Christie in 1914 (divorced, 1928), one daughter; 2) the archaeologist Max Mallowan in 1930. Served as a Voluntary Aid Detachment nurse in a Red Cross Hospital in Torquay during World War I, and worked in the dispensary of University College Hospital, London, during World War II; also assisted her husband on excavations in Iraq and Syria and on the Assyrian cities. Recipient: Mystery Writers of America Grand Master Award, 1954; New York Drama Critics Circle Award, 1955. D.Litt.: University of Exeter, 1961. Fellow, Royal Society of Literature, 1950. C.B.E. (Commander, Order of the British Empire), 1956; D.B.E. (Dame Commander, Order of the British Empire), 1971. *Died 12 January 1976.*

PUBLICATIONS

Fiction

The Mysterious Affair at Styles: A Detective Story. 1920.
The Secret Adversary. 1922.
The Murder on the Links. 1923.
Poirot Investigates (stories). 1924.
The Man in the Brown Suit. 1924.
The Secret of Chimneys. 1925.
The Murder of Roger Ackroyd. 1926.
The Big Four. 1927.
The Mystery of the Blue Train. 1928.
The Seven Dials Mystery. 1929.
Partners in Crime (stories). 1929.
The Underdog, with *Blackman's Wood,* by E. Phillips Oppenheim. 1929; as *Two
    Thrillers,* 1936.
The Mysterious Mr. Quin (story). 1930; as *The Passing of Mr. Quin,* n.d.
The Murder at the Vicarage. 1930.
Giants' Bread. 1930.
The Sittaford Mystery. 1931; as *The Murder at Hazelmoor,* 1931.
Peril at End House. 1932.
The Thirteen Problems (stories). 1932; as *The Tuesday Club Murders,* 1933; as *Miss
    Marple and the Thirteen Problems,* 1953.
The Hound of Death and Other Stories. 1933.
Lord Edgware Dies. 1933; as *Thirteen at Dinner,* 1933.
Parker Pyne Investigates (stories). 1934; as *Mr. Parker Pyne, Detective,* 1934.
The Listerdale Mystery and Other Stories. 1934.
Why Didn't They Ask Evans? 1934; as *The Boomerang Clue,* 1935.
Murder on the Orient Express. 1934; as *Murder on the Calais Coach,* 1934.
Murder in Three Acts. 1934; as *Three Act Tragedy,* 1935.
Unfinished Portrait. 1934.
Death in the Clouds. 1935; as *Death in the Air,* 1935.
The A.B.C. Murders: A New Poirot Mystery. 1936.
Cards on the Table. 1936.
Murder in Mesopotamia. 1936.
Death on the Nile. 1937.
Dumb Witness. 1937; as *Poirot Loses a Client,* 1937; as *Murder at Littlegreen House,*
    n.d.; as *Mystery at Littlegreen House* n.d.
Murder in the Mews and Other Stories. 1937; as *Dead Man's Mirror and Other Stories,*
    1937.
Appointment with Death: A Poirot Mystery. 1938.
Hercule Poirot's Christmas. 1938; as *Murder for Christmas,* 1939; as *A Holiday for
    Murder,* 1947.
The Regatta Mystery and Other Stories. 1939; as *Poirot and the Regatta Mystery,* 1943.
Murder Is Easy. 1939; as *Easy to Kill,* 1939.
Ten Little Niggers. 1939; as *And Then There Were None,* 1940; as *Ten Little Indians,*
    n.d.; as *The Nursery Rhyme Murders,* n.d.
One, Two, Buckle My Shoe. 1940; as *The Patriotic Murders,* 1941.
Sad Cypress. 1941.
Evil under the Sun. 1941.
N or M? The New Mystery. 1941.
The Body in the Library. 1942.

The Moving Finger.   1942.
Five Little Pigs.   1942; as *Murder in Retrospect,* 1942.
Death Comes as the End.   1942.
Towards Zero.   1944; as *Come and Be Hanged,* n.d.
Absent in the Spring.   1944.
Sparkling Cyanide.   1945; as *Remembered Death,* 1945.
The Hollow: A Hercule Poirot Mystery.   1946.
The Labours of Hercules: Short Stories.   1947; as *Labors of Hercules: New Adventures in Crime by Hercule Poirot,* 1947.
The Witness for the Prosecution and Other Stories.   1948.
Taken at the Flood.   1948; as *There Is a Tide ...,* 1948.
The Rose and the Yew Tree.   1948.
Crooked House.   1949.
The Mousetrap and Other Stories.   1949; as *Three Blind Mice and Other Stories,* 1950.
A Murder Is Announced.   1950.
The Under Dog and Other Stories.   1951.
They Came to Baghdad.   1951.
Blood Will Tell.   1951; as *Mrs. McGinty's Dead,* 1952.
They Do It with Mirrors.   1952; as *Murder with Mirrors,* 1952.
A Daughter's a Daughter.   1952.
After the Funeral.   1953; as *Funerals Are Fatal,* 1953; as *Murder at the Gallop,* 1963.
A Pocket Full of Rye.   1953.
Destination Unknown.   1954; as *So Many Steps to Death,* 1955.
Hickory, Dickory, Dock.   1955; as *Hickory, Dickory, Death,* 1955.
Dead Man's Folly.   1956.
The Burden.   1956.
4:50 from Paddington.   1957; as *What Mrs. McGillicuddy Saw!,* 1957; as *Murder She Said,* 1961.
Ordeal by Innocence.   1958.
Cat among the Pigeons.   1959.
The Adventures of the Christmas Pudding, and Selection of Entrées (stories).   1960.
Double Sin and Other Stories.   1961.
13 for Luck: A Selection of Mystery for Young Readers.   1961.
The Pale Horse.   1961.
The Mirror Crack'd from Side to Side.   1962; as *The Mirror Crack'd,* 1963.
The Clocks.   1963.
A Caribbean Mystery.   1964.
Star over Bethlehem and Other Stories.   1965.
Surprize! Surprize! A Collection of Mystery Stories with Unexpected Endings.   1965.
13 Clues for Miss Marple: A Collection of Mystery Stories.   1965.
At Bertram's Hotel.   1965.
Third Girl.   1966.
Endless Night.   1967.
By the Pricking of My Thumbs.   1968.
Hallowe'en Party.   1969.
Passenger to Frankfurt.   1970.
Nemesis.   1971.
The Golden Ball and Other Stories.   1971.
Elephants Can Remember.   1972.
Postern of Fate.   1973.
Hercule Poirot's Early Cases.   1974.
Curtain: Hercule Poirot's Last Case.   1975.
Sleeping Murder.   1976.

Plays

Black Coffee (produced 1930).   1934.
Ten Little Niggers, from her own novel (produced 1943).   1944; as Ten Little Indians (produced 1944), 1946.
Appointment with Death, from her own novel (produced 1945).   1945.
Murder on the Nile, from her own novel (as Hidden Horizon, produced 1945; as Murder on the Nile, produced 1946).   1948.
The Hollow, from her own novel (produced 1951).   1952.
The Mousetrap, from her story "Three Blind Mice" (broadcast 1952; revised version, produced 1952).   1956.
Witness for the Prosecution, from her own story (produced 1953).   1954.
Spider's Web (produced 1954).   1957.
Towards Zero, with Gerald Verner, from her own novel (produced 1956).   1957.
Verdict (produced 1958).   1958.
The Unexpected Guest (produced 1958).   1958.
Go Back for Murder, from her novel Five Little Pigs (produced 1960).   1960.
Rule of Three: Afternoon at the Seaside, The Patient, The Rats (produced 1962).   1963.
Fiddlers Three (produced 1971).
Akhnaton.   1973.
The Mousetrap and Other Plays.   1978.

Radio Plays: Behind the Screen (serial), with others, 1930; Scoop (serial), with others, 1931; The Mousetrap, 1952; Personal Call, 1960.

Verse

The Road of Dreams.   1925.
Poems.   1973.

Other

Come Tell Me How You Live (travel).   1946.
An Autobiography.   1977.

Reading List: Christie: Mistress of Mystery by G. C. Ramsey, 1967 (includes bibliography); Christie: First Lady of Crime edited by H. R. F. Keating, 1977; The Mystery of Christie by Gwen Robyns, 1978.

*   *   *

Agatha Christie is almost without rival as a writer of detective stories. Her phenomenal output of over seventy novels, a large collection of short stories, and several successful plays (including The Mousetrap, which has run without interruption in London since 1952) should be sufficient to ensure her a mention in any encyclopaedia of literature. As a novelist, however, Agatha Christie has far less claim to fame. Unlike her contemporary, Simenon, Christie seems to have little interest in the world in which she lived. All her novels have a curiously period air, and some early works, such as The Seven Dials Mystery, with its bright young things, beautiful Balkan spies, and sinister anarchists, are almost embarrassing to read. Even the later novels, in their dated village setting, are hardly a reflection of post-war Britain, though there are occasional disquieting hints that the old order is changing. Her two main detectives, the Belgian Hercule Poirot and Miss Marple, are almost entirely featureless, apart from a few irritating personal eccentricities, and Christie does not seem interested in character development, the other people in her novels, guilty and innocent alike, being stereotypes, dancing like puppets in the hands of both detective writer and detective alike. Setting the intellectual puzzle of guessing who the murderer is through a skilful but never unfair use of false clues is obviously more interesting to Miss Christie than investigating the moral issue of what makes people take to crime or even whether murder is in some senses justifiable. The later question is at any rate raised in the famous early novel *Murder on the Orient Express* and the unjustly neglected *Curtain*, but is hardly considered in *The Murder of Roger Ackroyd* and *Ten Little Niggers*, brilliant though these works are as detective stories.

—T. J. Winnifrith

CHURCHILL, Winston. American. Born in St. Louis, Missouri, 10 November 1871. Educated at Smith Academy, St. Louis, 1879–88; United States Naval Academy, Annapolis, Maryland, 1890–94; naval cadet on the cruiser *San Francisco*, New York Navy Yard, 1894. Married Mabel Harlakenden Hall in 1895 (died, 1945); one daughter and two sons. Editor, *Army and Navy Journal*, New York, 1894; Managing Editor, *Cosmopolitan* magazine, New York, 1895; full-time writer from 1895; served as Republican Member of the New Hampshire Legislature for Cornish, 1903–05, and as Delegate for New Hampshire, Republican National Convention, Chicago, 1904; Progressive Party Candidate for the New Hampshire governorship, 1912; toured European battle fronts, and wrote for *Scribner's* magazine, New York, 1917–18. President, Authors League of America, 1913. *Died 12 March 1947.*

PUBLICATIONS

Fiction

The Celebrity: An Episode. 1898.
Richard Carvel. 1899.
The Crisis. 1901.
Mr. Keegan's Elopement (stories). 1903.
The Crossing. 1904.
Coniston. 1906.
Mr. Crewe's Career. 1908.
A Modern Chronicle. 1910.
The Inside of the Cup. 1913.
A Far Country. 1915.
The Dwelling-Place of Light. 1917.
The Faith of Frances Craniford (story). 1917.

Plays

The Title-Mart (produced 1905). 1905.
Dr. Jonathan. 1919.

Other

> *A Traveller in War-Time, with an Essay on the American Contribution and the Democratic Idea.* 1918.
> *The Green Bay Tree.* 1920.
> *The Uncharted Way: The Psychology of the Gospel Doctrine.* 1940.

Reading List: *The Romantic Compromise in the Novels of Churchill* by Charles C. Walcutt, 1951; *Churchill* by Warren I. Titus, 1963.

*   *   *

Winston Churchill was a gifted storyteller who became very popular with well-researched but episodic romances concerning the American Revolution in *Richard Carvel*, the Civil War in *The Crisis*, and the settlement of Tennessee and Kentucky in *The Crossing*. Drawing upon his personal experience as a legislator and candidate for gubernatorial nomination in New Hampshire, Churchill then became a more serious social critic in *Coniston*, a novel about political bossism. The boss, Jethro Bass (based on a real political figure, Ruel Durkee), is a complex mixture of good and evil who in part manipulates the system, and is in part a product of it. He is probably Churchill's best developed and most human character. *Mr. Crewe's Career* does not so much concern the bumbling political efforts of the amateur politician Humphrey Crewe (said by Churchill to be a self-satire) as it concerns the corrupting influence of the railroad and other industries on the state legislature and the courts. Churchill mars these two novels by resolving the conflicts with a marriage between a daughter and a son of the opposing major figures. Although this device was supposed to show how the dynamism of industry could be combined with the idealism of politics, it actually leaves the essential differences of the two views unsettled, and reflects Churchill's mild "Progressive" approach in these novels (he was a friend and admirer of Roosevelt's).

Churchill first evidenced in his fiction a concern for religion in *The Inside of the Cup*, a novel which concerns a clergyman of an unspecified persuasion (Churchill was an active Episcopal layman) who comes to see the necessity for preaching a social gospel rather than a purely "spiritual" one. Although he meets resistance from a slum-landlord in his congregation, the minister makes many converts to his position and remains in the good graces of his church. The novel is therefore less hard-hitting than, say, Sheldon's *In His Steps*. *A Far Country* deals even more forcefully with the conflict Churchill saw between Christianity and capitalism and with society's ill-treatment of unwed mothers. Churchill lent his pen to the propaganda effort during the First World War, but immediately afterward returned in *Dr. Jonathan* to call for more social justice and a more equitable distribution of wealth.

Churchill's popularity had been declining gradually since he forsook the historical romance, but in 1920 he found himself almost without an audience. He then devoted twenty years to research in psychology and theology before publishing a non-fiction reinterpretation of the world and of the Bible, *The Uncharted Way*. Churchill did not think his analysis of history as the conflict between the "moral" self and the "technical" self, the generous and selfish side of each man, would be immediately understood, but looked to future generations for vindication.

—William Higgins

CLARK, Walter Van Tilburg. American. Born in East Orland, Maine, 3 August 1909. Educated at the University of Nevada, Reno, B.A. 1931, M.A. 1932; University of Vermont, Burlington, M.A. 1934. Married Barbara Frances Morse in 1933 (died), one son and one daughter. Taught in high schools in Cazenovia and Rye, New York, 1936–45; Associate Professor of English, University of Montana, Missoula, 1953–56; Professor of English and Creative Writing, San Francisco State College, 1956–62; Fellow in Fiction, Center for Advanced Studies, Wesleyan University, Middletown, Connecticut, 1960–61; Writer-in-Residence, University of Nevada, 1962–71. Recipient: O. Henry Award, 1945. D.Litt.: Colgate University, Hamilton, New York, 1958; University of Nevada, 1969. *Died 11 November 1971.*

PUBLICATIONS

Fiction

> *The Ox-Bow Incident.* 1940.
> *The City of Trembling Leaves.* 1945; as *Tim Hazard,* 1951.
> *The Track of the Cat.* 1949.
> *The Watchful Gods and Other Stories.* 1950.

Verse

> *Christmas Comes to Hjalsen, Reno.* 1930.
> *Ten Women in Gale's House and Shorter Poems.* 1932.

Other

> Editor, *The Journals of Alfred Doten, 1849–1903.* 3 vols. 1974.

Bibliography: "Clark: A Bibliography" by Richard Etulain, in *South Dakota Review,* Autumn 1965.

Reading List: *Clark* by Max Westbrook, 1969; *Clark* by Lawrence L. Lee, 1973.

*   *   *

The place of Walter Van Tilburg Clark in literary history rests on two of his three novels, *The Ox-Bow Incident* and *The Track of the Cat.* If that perch is narrow, it is also firm, not merely because both were made into memorable motion pictures, but, more importantly, because both are sensitive psychological studies of great impact.

Taken as a parable of fascism at the time of its writing, *The Ox-Bow Incident,* set in the American West, is a powerful examination of leadership and mob violence. Against a dry-tinder backdrop of lassitude reminiscent of the setting of Faulkner's "dry September," the men of Bridger's Wells need only an act of violence and the imposition of a strong will to be ignited into a flaming mob. The point is that violence triumphs by default; that a single-minded person can take charge and use the vast energy latent in boredom and resentment for evil as long as no one will take steps sufficient to stop him.

Four years after his jejune second novel, *The City of Trembling Leaves,* Clark published his second successful novel, *The Track of the Cat*. Much more self-consciously artistic than *The Ox-Bow Incident*, the novel uses as its focus a mountain lion that becomes, literally and symbolically, the *bête noire* of the men who are tracking it. In the death of the two men, there is penetrating insight into human character: one, the overbearing realist, cannot cope with the mythic dimensions of the cat and falls from a cliff in fear of it; the other, the arch romantic, forgets the cat's deadly reality and is struck down.

Clark's problem as a novelist resides in his inability to proportion characters appropriately to plot. He invests no one in *The Track of the Cat*, for example, with stature commensurate with the great task of hunting the real and mythic beast. His characters are sometimes sententious. But in his two fine western novels, he largely overcomes the problem by sheer narrative force and by showing his audience some revealing habits of the human animal.

—Alan R. Shucard

CLARKE, Marcus (Andrew Hislop). English. Born in Kensington, London, 24 April 1846. Educated at Cholmeley Grammar School, Highgate, London, 1858–62. Married Marion Dunn in 1869; six children. Emigrated to Australia, 1863: worked in a Melbourne bank, 1863–65; lived at an agricultural station on the Wimmera River, to learn farming, 1865–67; abandoned intention to become a farmer, and went to Melbourne: contributor to *The Age*, and Columnist ("Peripatetic Philosopher"), *Australasian*, 1867–70; Owner and Editor, *Colonial Monthly*, 1868–69; Editor, *Australian Journal*, 1870; Secretary to the Trustees, 1870, Sub-Librarian, 1873, and Assistant Librarian, 1876–81, Melbourne Public Library; Columnist ("Atticus"), *Leader*, from 1877; declared insolvent in 1874 and 1881. A Founder, The Yorick Club, 1868. *Died 2 August 1881.*

PUBLICATIONS

Collections

A Clarke Reader, edited by Bill Wannan.   1963.
(*Selections*), edited by Michael Wilding.   1976.

Fiction

Long Odds.   1869; as *Heavy Odds*, 1896.
Holiday Peak and Other Tales.   1873.
His Natural Life.   1874; as *For the Term of His Natural Life*, 1885; edited by Stephen Murray-Smith, 1970.
'Twixt Shadow and Shine: An Australian Story of Christmas.   1875.
Four Stories High.   1877.
The Man with the Oblong Box.   1878.
The Mystery of Major Molineaux, and Human Repetends.   1881.
The Conscientious Stranger: A Bullocktown Idyll.   1881.
Sensational Tales.   1886.

Chidiock Tichbourne; or, The Catholic Conspiracy. 1893.
Australian Tales. 1896.

Plays

Goody Two Shoes and Little Boy Blue. 1870.
Twinkle, Twinkle, Little Star; or, Harlequin Jack Frost, Little Tom Tucker, and the Old Woman That Lived in a Shoe. 1873.
Reverses. 1876.
Alfred the Great, with H. Keiley. 1876.
The Happy Land, from the play *The Wicked World* by W. S. Gilbert (produced 1880).

Other pantomimes, with R. P. Whitworth.

Other

The Peripatetic Philosopher. 1869.
Old Tales of a Young Country. 1871.
The Future Australian Race. 1877.
Civilization Without Delusion. 1880.
What Is Religion? A Controversy. 1895.
Stories of Australia in the Early Days. 1897.
Colonial City: High and Low Life: Selected Journalism. edited by L. T. Hergenhan. 1972.

Editor, *History of the Continent of Australia and the Island of Tasmania (1787–1870).* 1877.
Editor, *We 5: A Book for the Season.* 1879.
Editor, *Poems*, by Adam Lindsay Gordon. 1887.

Reading List: *Clarke* by Brian Elliott, 1858; *Clarke* by Michael Wilding, 1978.

*   *   *

As Brian Elliott says, "Marcus Clarke was the most facile, most gifted, most charming writer in Australia in his day and generation." In his journalism, he captured the spirit of the times with vividness and immediacy. With laconic ambivalence and wit, he simultaneously deprecated and exalted many elements of the Australian character, such as contempt for culture and authority. In the process he lowered his own standards of taste at the same time as he raised the standards of Australian journalism. Much of his work from the *Argus* and other papers remains uncollected.

Clarke, like Dickens, first published his tales and novels in the papers to which he contributed and which he sometimes edited. His *Old Tales of a Young Country*, mainly published in the *Australasian* at earlier dates, are admittedly compilations from pamphlets, books, and government records, but he has endowed them with such literary quality and creative insight that they have become the focal source for most of the highlights of colonial Australian history: the landing of the First Fleet in Sydney Cove, the destiny of the swell-mob pickpocket George Barrington, William Huckley's survival among the aborigines for thirty-two years, Captain Bligh and the Rum Rebellion, Michael Howe's activities as a bush-ranger, Jorgenson's checkered career from King of Iceland to prisoner in Van Diemen's Land, the make-up of early newspapers, the life of the settlers, the closing of Macquarie Harbour as a penal settlement, mutinies, shipwrecks, land speculation, and much more.

Clarke's novel *Long Odds*, first printed in the *Colonial Monthly*, is a fast-paced melodrama, not entirely unmotivated, involving a young Australian in London; but it is for *His Natural Life*, rewritten and drastically abridged from the *Australian Journal* version and reprinted dozens of times under the title of *For the Term of His Natural Life*, that he is chiefly remembered. A psychological romance with elements of the macabre – cannibalism and torture – the work emphasizes the brutal effect of the convict system upon the human spirit. Its virtue, despite the exaggerations of unnatural punishments, is Clarke's fidelity to the theme of the progressive degeneration of an innocent human being subjected to barbaric cruelty, which gradually destroys all glimmerings of hope, turns his mind into a hard shell of sullen obduracy, goads him into perverse rebellion, and, finally, drives him to the brink of insanity. The work is more of a requiem than a classic, the last word which can be said about an unjust system which had been buried years before and which Clarke himself (in "Port Arthur Visited, 1870") admitted had "only the smell of it left." Still Clarke's concern was not with the already obsolete system of transportation of felons, but, on a humanistic level, like Hugo and Dostoevsky, with the forces of good and evil embroiling his central characters in a "tempest of the soul."

Clarke also wrote for the Australian theatre – largely pantomimes, translations, and adaptations – to supplement his income; but these works are negligible. As Brian Elliott concludes, "It is as a colonial journalist and the writer of one book that Marcus Clarke has a claim to the remembered."

—Wesley D. Sweetser

CLELAND, John. English. Born in England; baptized in Kingston-upon-Thames, Surrey, 24 September 1710. Educated at Westminster School, London, 1721–23. Worked for the East India Company, in Bombay, 1728–40: foot soldier in the East India Company's Militia, 1728; attorney in the Bombay Mayor's Court, 1730; Writer in the Civil Service, 1731; Factor, 1734; in charge of the Mahim Customhouse, 1737; Secretary for Portuguese Affairs, 1737; Junior Merchant, 1737; Secretary of the Council, 1738–40; retired from the company and returned to London, 1741; imprisoned for debt, in Fleet Prison, 1748–49; freelance writer from 1749; regular contributor to the *Monthly Review*, 1749–51, and to the *Public Advertiser*, 1765–87; political writer for Lord Bute's ministry in the early 1760's. *Died 23 January 1789.*

PUBLICATIONS

Fiction

Memoirs of a Woman of Pleasure.   2 vols., 1748–49; revised edition, as *Memoirs of Fanny Hill,* 1750; edited by Peter Quennell, 1963.
Memoirs of a Coxcomb; or, The History of Sir William Delamere.   1751.
The Surprises of Love, Exemplified in the Romance of a Day, and Other Stories.   1764; revised edition, 1765.
The Woman of Honour.   1768.

Plays

Titus Vespasian, from a play by Metastasio.   1754.
The Ladies' Subscription.   1755.
Tombo-Chiqui; or, The American Savage, from a play by L. F. Delisle de la
   Drévetière.   1758.

Other

Institutes of Health.   1761.
The Way to Things by Words and to Words by Things.   1766.
Specimen of an Etymological Vocabulary.   1768; *Additional Articles*, 1769.

Reading List: "*Fanny Hill* and Materialism" by Leo Braudy, in *Eighteenth-Century Studies 4*,
1970; " 'The Most Interesting Moving Picture': *Fanny Hill* and Comedy" by Malcolm
Bradbury, in *Possibilities*, 1973; *Cleland: Images of a Life* by William H. Epstein, 1974.

*   *   *

In the British Library catalogue, John Cleland's name carries that most damning of literary
labels, "Miscellaneous Writer"; and his reputation would probably have remained interred in
the common grave of Grub-street were it not for the notoriety achieved, in its own time and
ours, by his first novel, *Memoirs of a Woman of Pleasure* – better known as *Fanny Hill*.
Cleland's later career reads remarkably like a scenario for the archetypal hack: he tried his
hand at drama, and had one play (*Titus Vespasian*) rejected by Garrick; attempted to repeat
his success in fiction, but managed only a thin follow-up to *Fanny Hill* (*Memoirs of a
Coxcomb*), a standard exercise in epistolary fiction (*The Woman of Honour*), and short
sentimental tales (*The Surprises of Love*); and eventually subsided into literary and political
journalism. Nothing else that he wrote repeated the extraordinary *éclat* of *Fanny Hill*.
   The case of *Fanny Hill* is one in which the literary historian owes a debt to the pornophile.
After the novel's initial prosecution for obscenity in 1749, it went underground, retaining
popularity chiefly among connoisseurs of erotica, and finally re-emerged in the wake of the
liberalisation of book-censorship laws in the 1960's. Its open publication in 1963 stimulated
reassessment by scholars and critics, and led to a more accurate placing of *Fanny Hill* in the
contexts of mid-eighteenth-century fiction and thought rather than in the pornographic
tradition: for example, Leo Braudy demonstrated that the novel may be seen as an
embodiment of philosophical materialism, and Malcolm Bradbury that it is "about aesthetics
as well as about sex."
   Fanny Hill is certainly a novel of considerable comic dexterity and linguistic dash. It
consists of the heroine's retrospective account, in two long letters to a friend, of her career as
a "woman of pleasure." She belongs in that fictional enclave of embattled young provincial
girls isolated in a bewildering, predatory society: she is (self-consciously) part of the
sisterhood that includes Defoe's Moll Flanders, Hogarth's Moll Hackabout, and Richardson's
Pamela and Clarissa – and there are thematic and verbal echoes of these throughout her
narrative. On her arrival in London from Liverpool, she is snapped up by a bawd as a novice
prostitute, but before her confirmation in the profession she falls in love with the handsome
Charles, and runs off with him. However, Charles is forced by his father to leave England,
and Fanny then becomes a high-class whore, and the latter half of the novel is largely an
account of her sexual experiences in this role. Finally, she is reunited with the returned
Charles in marriage. The novel therefore comprises two interlocking structures: the carnal-
picaresque, in which Fanny witnesses and/or participates in, a series of polymorphous sexual
episodes – with the picara's customary delight in her profession; and the sentimental-

romantic, in which Fanny's first love is also her last. The relationship between Fanny and Charles is complete because it unites love *and* lust: as Fanny says, Charles makes her "happy ... by the heart, happy by the senses." This romantic perfection is comically underlined when Fanny flouts the eighteenth-century fictional convention whereby narrator and reader discreetly halt at the boudoir door on the wedding-night: Fanny insists on displaying the *full* joys of the marriage-bed.

—J. C. Hilson

CLEMENS, Samuel Langhorne. See **TWAIN, Mark**.

COBBETT, William. English. Born in Farnham, Surrey, 9 March 1763. Largely self-taught. Worked as a solicitor's clerk in London, 1783, then joined the 54th Foot, and served at Chatham, Kent, 1784, then as a corporal and sergeant-major in Nova Scotia and New Brunswick, 1784–91. Married Ann Reid in 1792; seven children. Teacher in Philadelphia, 1792–96; bookseller and publisher on the loyalist side, Philadelphia, 1796–1800; began the monthly *The Censor*, 1796, and its successor, the daily newspaper *Porcupine's Gazette*, 1797–99; prosecuted for libel, moved to New York, started a new magazine, *The Rush-Light*, then abandoned the project and returned to England, 1800; Editor, *The Porcupine*, London, 1801–02; proprietor of a bookshop in Pall Mall, 1801–03; Founder/Editor, *Cobbett's Weekly Political Register*, 1802 until his death; farmer in Botley, Hampshire, 1804–17; imprisoned for his criticism of the flogging of militiamen, 1810–12; fled to the United States to avoid arrest: farmed on Long Island, 1817–19; returned to England, 1820; published *Corbett's Evening Post*, 1820; established a seed farm at Kensington, 1821; stood as candidate for Parliament for Coventry, 1821, and Preston, 1826; tried for sedition, 1831; Member of Parliament for Oldham, 1832–34. *Died 18 June 1835.*

PUBLICATIONS

Collections

 The Opinions of Cobbett, edited by G. D. H. and Margaret Cole. 1944.
 Letters, edited by Gerald Duff. 1974.

Prose (selection)

 Le Tuteur Anglais; ou, Grammaire Regulière de la Langue Anglaise. 1795.
 The Works of Peter Porcupine. 1795.
 The Life and Adventures of Peter Porcupine. 1796; as *The Life of Cobbett*, 1809.
 The Life of Thomas Paine. 1796.

Porcupine's Works (reprints pamphlets and periodical writings). 2 vols., 1797; revised edition, 12 vols., 1801.

A Collection of the Facts and Observations Relative to the Peace with Bonaparte. 1801.

Cobbett's Political Register (periodical with varying title). 89 vols., 1802–35.

The Political Proteus: A View of the Public Character and Conduct of R. B. Sheridan. 1804.

Letters on the Late War Between the United States and Great Britain. 1815.

The Pride of Britannia Humbled. 1815.

Paper Against Gold and Glory Against Prosperity; or, An Account of the Rise, Progress, Extent, and Present State of the Funds and of the Paper-Money of Great Britain. 2 vols., 1815; revised edition, 1821.

A Year's Residence in the United States of America. 3 vols., 1818–19.

A Grammar of the English Language. 1818; revised edition, 1823.

A Letter from the Queen to the King. 1820.

The American Gardener. 1821.

Sermons. 1822.

Cottage Economy. 1822.

Collective Commentaries. 1822.

A French Grammar. 1824.

A History of the Protestant "Reformation" in England and Ireland. 2 vols., 1826–27.

Poor Man's Friend. 5 vols., 1826–27.

The Woodlands. 1828.

The English Gardener. 1828.

A Treatise on Cobbett's Corn. 1828; revised edition, 1831.

The Emigrant's Guide. 1829.

On the Present Prospects of Merchants, Traders, and Farmers, and on the State of the Country in General (lectures). 1829.

Three Lectures on the State of the Country. 1830.

Good Friday; or, The Murder of Jesus Christ by the Jews. 1830.

Rural Rides. 1830; *Tour in Scotland*, 1832; edited by G. D. H. and Margaret Cole, 3 vols., 1930.

Advice to Young Men and (Incidentally) to Young Women in the Middle and Higher Ranks of Life. 1830.

Eleven Lectures on the French and Belgian Revolutions, and English Boroughmongering. 1830.

History of the Regency and Reign of King George the Fourth. 2 vols., 1834.

Two-Penny Trash; or, Politics for the Poor. 2 vols., 1831–32.

A Spelling Book. 1831.

Manchester Lectures in Support of His Fourteen Reform Propositions. 1832.

A Geographical Dictionary of England and Wales. 1832.

The Speeches of Cobbett, M.P. for Oldham. 2 vols., 1833.

A New French and English Dictionary. 2 vols., 1833.

Three Lectures on the Political State of Ireland. 1834.

Legacy to Labourers. 1835.

Legacy to Parsons. 1835.

Selections from Cobbett's Political Works, edited by John Morgan and James Paul Cobbett. 6 vols., 1835–37.

Legacy to Peel. 1836.

Legacy to Lords, edited by William Cobbett, Jr. 1863.

Thomas Paine: A Sketch of His Life and Character, in *The Life of Thomas Paine* by Moncure Daniel Conway. 1892.

A History of the Last Hundred Days of Freedom, edited by J. L. Hammond. 1921.

Life and Adventures of Peter Porcupine with Other Records of His Early Career in England and America, edited by G. D. H. Cole. 1927.

The Progress of a Plough-Boy to a Seat in Parliament, edited by William Reitzel. 1933.
Letters to Edward Thornton 1797 to 1800, edited by G. D. H. Cole. 1937.

Plays

Big O. and Sir Glory; or, Leisure to Laugh. 1825.
Mexico; or, The Patriot Bondholders, in *Political Register*, 1830.
Surplus Population and Poor-Law Bill. 1835(?).

Verse

French Arrogance; or, The Cat Let Out of the Bag. 1798.

Other Works

Editor, *An Answer to Paine's Rights of Man*, by Henry Mackenzie. 1796.
Editor, *The History of Jacobinism*, by William Playfair. 1796.
Editor, *A View of the Causes and Consequences of the Present War with France*, by Thomas Erskine. 1797.
Editor, *Observations on the Dispute Between the United States and France*, by Robert Goodloe Harper and others. 1798.
Editor, *A Treatise on the Culture and Management of Fruit Trees*, by William Forsyth. 1802.
Editor, *Spirit of the Public Journals for the Year 1804.* 1805.
Editor, with John Wright and Thomas Bayley Howell, *Complete Collection of State Trials.* 33 vols., 1809–26 (Cobbett was co-editor until 1812 only).
Editor, *An Essay on Sheep*, by R. R. Livingston. 1811.
Editor, *The Horse-Hoeing Husbandry*, by Jethro Tull. 1822.
Editor, *The Curse of Paper-Money and Banking; or, A Short History of Banking in the United States*, by William M. Gouge. 1833.
Editor, *Life of Andrew Jackson*, by John Henry Eaton. 1834.

Translator, *Impeachment of Mr. Lafayette.* 1793.
Translator, *A Compendium of the Law of Nations*, by G. F. Von Martens. 1795.
Translator, *A Topographical and Political Description of the Spanish Port of Saint Domingo*, by M. L. E. Moreau de Saint-Mery. 1796.
Translator, *The Empire of Germany*, by Jean Gabriel Peltier. 1803.
Translator, *Elements of the Roman History* (bilingual edition), by J. H. Sievrac. 1828.
Translator, *An Abridged History of the Emperors* (bilingual edition), by J. H. Sievrac. 1829.

Bibliography: *Cobbett: A Bibliographical Account of His Life and Times* by M. L. Pearl, 1953.

Reading List: *Life and Letters of Cobbett* by Lewis Melville, 2 vols., 1913; *The Life of Cobbett* by G. D. H. Cole, 1924, revised edition, 1947; *Cobbett* by W. Baring Pemberton, 1949; *Cobbett* by A. J. Sambrook, 1973; *Cobbett: An Introduction to His Life and Writings* by Simon Booth, 1975.

*   *   *

William Cobbett found his vocation as a political commentator in America in the 1790's when he patriotically opposed Democratic attempts to ally the United States with France in her war against England. In addition to his newspaper *Porcupine's Gazette* he wrote some forty pamphlets, collected later into twelve fat volumes of *Porcupine's Works*; but the most enduring work of those years is *The Life and Adventures of Peter Porcupine*, where Cobbett blends his sense of the unique value of his own life into an attractive, idealized vision of Old England, and, like his Romantic contemporaries in that age of autobiographies, discovers that his own life has a representative significance.

Back in England, Cobbett gradually moved into opposition to the Government, joined the Radicals, and pressed for Parliamentary reform. In this cause he wrote scores of pamphlets, many of which were first published serially in the *Political Register*, the newspaper which he conducted practically single-handed and with a few interruptions (for prison and exile) from 1802 to his death in 1835. He wrote books on many other subjects from grammar to agriculture, all with a marked political bias; his *History of the Protestant "Reformation"* was one of the most widely influential of all the nineteenth-century works which idealized the Middle Ages; but his best writing is to be found in the largely autobiographical *Rural Rides* and *Advice to Young Men*. Cobbett has a political purpose in comparing the condition of England in the 1820's with his idealized view of the 1770's, but his writing about his own childhood conveys an urgent sense of personal wholeness within a landscape of memory. The power, vigour, and beauty of Cobbett's best work, like Wordsworth's, arise from recollected emotion.

—A. J. Sambrook

COLLINS, (William) Wilkie. English. Born in London, 8 January 1824; son of the portrait painter William Collins. Educated at Maida Hill Academy, London; lived with his parents in Italy, 1836–39; articled to the London firm of Antrobus and Company, tea merchants, 1841–46; entered Lincoln's Inn, London, 1846: called to the Bar, 1849. Associated with Caroline Graver, 1859–89; and with Martha Rudd, 1868–89, two daughters and one son. Writer from 1848; also a painter: exhibited at the Royal Academy, 1849; met Charles Dickens, 1851, and contributed to, and assisted Dickens in the editing of, *Household Words*, and its successor *All the Year Round*, 1856–61; toured the United States, giving readings of his works, 1873–74. *Died 23 September 1889.*

PUBLICATIONS

Collections

Tales of Terror and the Supernatural, edited by Herbert van Thal.   1972.

Fiction

Antonia; or, The Fall of Rome.   1850.
Mr. Wray's Cash-Box; or, The Mask and the Mystery.   1851.
Basil: A Story of Modern Life.   1852; revised edition, 1862.
Hide and Seek.   1854; revised edition, 1861.
After Dark.   1856.
The Dead Secret.   1857.

The Queen of Hearts. 1859.
The Woman in White. 1860; edited by Harvey Peter Sucksmith, 1975.
No Name. 1862; edited by Herbert Van Thal, 1967.
Armadale. 1866.
The Moonstone: A Romance. 1868; edited by J. I. M. Stewart, 1966.
Man and Wife. 1870.
Poor Miss Finch. 1872.
The New Magdalen. 1873.
Miss or Mrs.? and Other Stories in Outline. 1873.
The Frozen Deep and Other Stories: Readings and Writings in America. 1874.
The Law and the Lady. 1875.
The Two Destinies. 1876.
A Shocking Story. 1878.
The Haunted Hotel (with *My Lady's Money).* 1878.
A Rogue's Life, From His Birth to His Marriage. 1879.
The Fallen Leaves. 1879.
Jezebel's Daughter. 1880.
The Black Robe. 1881.
Heart and Science. 1883.
I Say No. 1884.
The Evil Genius. 1886.
The Guilty River. 1886.
Little Novels. 1887.
The Legacy of Cain. 1888.
Blind Love, completed by Walter Besant. 1890.
The Lazy Tour of Two Idle Apprentices, No Thoroughfare, The Perils of Certain English Prisoners, with Dickens. 1890.

Plays

A Court Duel (produced 1850).
The Lighthouse, from his own story "Gabriel's Marriage" (produced 1855).
The Frozen Deep (produced 1857). 1866.
The Red Vial (produced 1858).
No Name, with W. B. Bernard, from the novel by Collins (produced 1871). 1863; revised edition, 1870.
Armadale, from his own novel. 1866.
No Thoroughfare, with Dickens, from their own story (produced 1867). 1867; revised version, 1867.
Black and White, with Charles Fechter (produced 1869). 1869.
The Woman in White, from his own novel (produced 1870). 1871.
Man and Wife, from his own novel (produced 1873). 1870.
The New Magdalen (produced 1873). 1873.
Miss Gwilt (produced 1875). 1875.
The Moonstone, from his own novel (produced 1877). 1877.
Rank and Riches (produced 1883).
The Evil Genius (produced 1885).

Other

Memoirs of the Life of William Collins, R.A., with Selections from His Journals and Correspondence. 2 vols., 1848.

Rambles Beyond Railways; or, Notes in Cornwell Taken A-Foot. 1851.
My Miscellanies. 2 vols., 1863.
Considerations on the Copyright Question Addressed to an American Friend. 1880.

Bibliography: *Collins and Reade* by M. L. Parrish, 1940; *Collins and Reade: A Bibliography of Critical Notices and Studies* by F. Cordasco and K. Scott, 1949; "A Collins Check-List" by R. V. Andrew, in *English Studies in Africa 3,* 1960.

Reading List: *Collins: A Biography* by Kenneth Robinson, 1951; *Collins* by Robert Ashley, 1952; *The Life of Collins* by Nuel P. Davis, 1956; *Collins* by William H. Marshall, 1970; *Collins: The Critical Heritage* edited by Norman Page, 1974.

*   *   *

Though one of the most popular novelists in England and America between 1860 and 1889, Wilkie Collins is remembered today primarily for his novels of the 1860's, principally *The Woman in White* and *The Moonstone.* After *Antonia,* his only historical novel, Collins's early work reflects certain lifelong characteristics – an interest in mystery and crime; a talent for foreboding atmosphere, effective description of scene, and intricate plots; and a belief in the romance and drama of real life – characteristics which, along with his bonhomie, made possible a close personal and literary relationship with Dickens. Collins served as assistant editor of Dickens's periodicals from 1856–1861, contributing numerous essays and collaborating with Dickens on several Christmas numbers.

However, despite his ten-year apprenticeship and close association with Dickens, the mature achievement of *The Woman in White* is remarkable. The story itself is a collection of manuscript narratives by individual characters, no one of whom holds all the keys to the complex mystery plot. This device enables Collins legitimately to withhold crucial information and thus heighten suspense while at the same time developing the character of each narrator. Particularly memorable are the villainous Count Fosco and the courageous Marian Halcombe, whose dramatic conflict so gripped the reading public that the publication of each new installment became a social event. Contemporary critics recognized *The Woman in White* as an excellent example (indeed, perhaps initiator) of an emerging and controversial sub-genre, the Sensation Novel, whose merits were debated throughout the decade. With few exceptions, the critics deplored the form's subordination of character to plot, its emphasis on crime and encouragement of sympathy for morally ambiguous characters, its combination of realism and romance, and its melodramatic style; but their strictures did not keep readers of all classes from making the Sensation Novel the dominant sub-genre of the 1860's, with Wilkie Collins its acknowledged master. Collins's next novels, *No Name* and *Armadale,* augment their sensational qualities by employing female Fosco-figures and reveal the centrality of identity mysteries in Collins's work of this period. The loss and recovery of social identity, a theme Collins explored throughout his career, constitutes the formulaic core of his (and others') Sensation Novels and is clearly related to mid-Victorian insecurities. In the characters of Ezra Jennings and Franklin Blake, Collins continues this theme in *The Moonstone,* whose superb plot led T. S. Eliot to call it "the first and greatest of English detective novels."

The marked decline in the quality of Collins's novels after *The Moonstone* is attributed by modern critics to his deteriorating health and subsequent dependence on laudanum, and to the increasing thesis-domination of his work. Among his later novels, *Man and Wife* attacks Scotch marriage laws and athleticism; *The New Magdalen* and *The Fallen Leaves,* society's treatment of reformed prostitutes. Weak though these novels are, they are the natural outgrowth of Collins's earlier thematic concerns, as he now shows society itself, rather than aggressive individualists, to be the principal cause of identity loss. In this development Collins follows the lead of Dickens, but without his range of vision and talent. Still, Collins produced two very fine novels and several others of note, and gave shape to a sub-genre that reflected major preoccupations of mid-Victorian culture. For this, and for his close connection with the many greater and lesser literary lights of his day, he deserves to be remembered.

—Randolph Ivy

COMPTON-BURNETT, Dame Ivy.   English.   Born in Pinner, Middlesex, 5 June 1884. Educated privately, and at Royal Holloway College, University of London, B.A. in classics. Writer from 1911. Recipient: Black Memorial Prize, 1956. D.Litt.: University of Leeds. Companion of Literature, Royal Society of Literature, 1968. C.B.E. (Commander, Order of the British Empire), 1951; D.B.E. (Dame Commander, Order of the British Empire), 1967. *Died 27 August 1969.*

Fiction

Dolores.   1911.
Pastors and Masters: A Study.   1925.
Brothers and Sisters.   1929.
Men and Wives.   1931.
More Women Than Men.   1933.
A House and Its Head.   1935.
Daughters and Sons.   1937.
A Family and a Fortune.   1939.
Parents and Children.   1941.
Elders and Betters.   1944.
Manservant and Maidservant.   1947; as *Bullivant and the Lambs,* 1948.
Two Worlds and Their Ways.   1949.
Darkness and Day.   1951.
The Present and the Past.   1953.
Mother and Son.   1955.
A Father and His Fate.   1957.
A Heritage and Its History.   1959.
The Mighty and Their Fall   1961.
A God and His Gifts.   1963.
The Last and the First.   1971.

Reading List: *Compton-Burnett* by Pamela Hansford Johnson, 1951; *The Novels of Compton-Burnett* by Robert Liddell, 1955; *Compton-Burnett* by Frank Baldanza, 1964; *Compton-Burnett* by Charles Burkhart, 1965; *The Art of Compton-Burnett: A Collection of Critical Essays* edited by Charles Burkhart, 1972; *Ivy and Stevie* (Stevie Smith) by Kay Dick, 1973; *A Compton-Burnett Compendium* by Violet Powell, 1973; *The Life of Compton-Burnett* by Elizabeth Sprigge, 1973; *Ivy When Young: The Early Life of Compton-Burnett* by Hilary Spurling, 1974.

*   *   *

Among the distinguishing features of Ivy Compton-Burnett's novels (apart from the early *Dolores*) are their location in time and place and the handling of character and plot. All are set in late Victorian or Edwardian England; almost all take place in a large country-house, typically inhabited by two or three generations of the minor squirearchy, financially not prospering, whose family relationships are exposed to the shock-waves set up by sudden deaths, remarriages, and births and the subsequent redistribution of income and power. Twice (*More Women Than Men, Two Worlds and Their Ways*) a school setting is used, with a similar structure of dependent human relationships.

Her character-presentation has affinities with drama: the action moves in scenes, almost exclusively dialogue. Description is minimal, usually sufficient to create a memorable visual impression but no more. The self and relationship to others are revealed in public talk at family gatherings, not in private communings. Family meals provide numerous occasions for exposure of tensions and resentments and the dark deeds issuing therefrom. Among the many fraught breakfasts is one where matricide is confessed (*Men and Wives*) and another where mortal illness strikes (*A House and Its Head*). Death itself occurs at dinner (*Daughters and Sons*) and in *Parents and Children* the family gather in the library on the return-as-from-death of the father to hear of attempted bigamy, betrayal of trust, deep deception, and a retaliatory revelation of illegitimacy following adultery. Such events inevitably provoke a rich flow of talk as people adjust to the new situation. This talk is highly-stylised. Typically it is a focused, intensely relevant response to a previous speaker, often brief and witty to the point of epigram.

The deployment of pattern and rhythm in dialogue of this kind echoes the stichomythia of Greek tragedy, and there are other such echoes. There is a choric commentary throughout in the form of guests, servants, and children, and the working out of the plots depends on "discoveries" (adultery and infanticide in *A House and Its Head*, mistaken incest and illegitimate births in *Darkness and Day*, potential incest in *A Heritage and Its History*) and on "reversals" (the heir, fathering a child on his uncle's second wife, disinherits himself in *A House and Its Head* and *A Heritage and Its History*; a lost inheritance leads to a quickly broken engagement in *Daughters and Sons*). The matter of the plots is akin to that of Greek tragedy: family crimes of adultery, murder, suicide, and incest. These formal features, together with the author's straining of plot-events to the edge of credibility and her taste for giving characters literary names (Donne, Edgeworth, Chaucer, Bunyan, Smollett, etc.), draw attention to themselves as artifice and the novels as artefacts. This frees the reader from expecting a rendering of the texture of everyday life, encouraging a spirit of critical detachment. Thus the reader can fully savour the author's concentrated wit and attend to the novel's moral life, which is concerned with man's nature and the social and moral codes by which he attempts to define himself.

Focusing on the family, Compton-Burnett sets up conflicts between the social expectations attached to a role and the self-interested individual who fills it. The multiple nature of the role itself encourages exploitation (e.g., Parent as biological and/or legal fact, and parent as implying provision and protection and sanctioning authority and discipline), and the author introduces outside forces (e.g., death and inheritance, birth and disinheritance) which cause the meaning and stability of the role to be questioned. Further than this, the author displays the overall conflict between what is "natural" and what social and moral codes demand. At surface level, social order prevails; domestic and public rituals are performed by family, servants and neighbours. But what is "natural" frequently erupts, disturbing – though only temporarily – the social order. It is "natural" to seek and enjoy power, to protect oneself, to fulfil sexual appetites; and, given the opportunity, her people act "naturally." There is tragic potentiality when characters are driven by their natures to steal, burn a will, pretend suicide, commit adultery, fratricide, or matricide, and the author acknowledges this, showing understanding of, and even compassion for, the most neurotically-driven characters. But essentially she expresses the comic in showing characters who believe they are only conforming to the demands of their roles in society when they are plainly pleasing themselves.

The gross acts of deception receive public exposure when, in the English country-house murder tradition, the villain is unmasked. The habitual daily acts receive habitual daily commentary from choric and semi-choric commentators: guests, the very young who ask innocent questions, and the older children who, aware of their vulnerability to their elders' selfishness, are shrewd and interested observers. Attention is concentrated on language and the manipulative function of words and phrases like "duty," "living for others," and "my true self." The scrutiny of clichés reveals the imposition of untruths on others ("Better later than never," "She wants nothing but what is good for me," and "Kind hearts are more than coronets"). And since psychological and physical killers shelter behind kinship, words denoting family-relationships are examined exhaustively.

Compton-Burnett shows us a world where conventional social order and public acceptance of Christian morals contain, though not always successfully, seething passions which compel people to deeds violating all the Commandments. Unlike, say, Jane Austen, she does not share with the reader a civilized and humane set of values against which individual conduct is measured. Rather than offer judgement, Compton-Burnett says that this is how it is: people and societies are like that.

Though she sets these novels largely in the 1880's, commenting through them on general human nature, she does show influences of the decades in which she was writing. The role of economic forces in power-structures is apparent in the emphasis placed on money, and there is a specific reference to Engels on the family (*Daughters and Sons*); the conflicts and dilemmas of women and of unmasculine men are dissected with insight; and the inescapable life-long pressure of the family on the psychology of the individual is displayed, often in full-blown neuroses.

These are intelligent novels, patterned and condensed, packed with penetrating observation and unsentimental insight, demanding close attention but yielding to the attentive reader much laughter and much cause for reflection on his laughter.

—Mary Brown

CONRAD, Joseph. British. Born Teodor Josef Konrad Nalecz Korzeniowski in Berdiczew, Podolia, Ukrainian Province of Poland, 6 December 1857; brought up in Cracow; naturalized British subject, 1884. Educated at Cracow, 1868–73. Married Jessie George in 1896; two sons. Merchant seaman from 1874: sailed on a number of French merchant ships to the West Indies until 1876; qualified as an able seaman in England, 1878, and thereafter sailed on British ships in the Orient trade; appointed a master in the British Merchant Marine, 1886, and received first command, 1888; First Mate on the *Torrens*, 1892–93; began writing in 1889: gave up the sea, and retired to England in 1894; settled in Ashford, Kent, 1896. *Died 3 August 1924.*

PUBLICATIONS

Collections

Works (revised by Conrad).   22 vols., 1920–25.
The Portable Conrad, edited by Morton Dauwen Zabel.   1947.

Fiction

Almayer's Folly: A Story of an Eastern River.   1895.
An Outcast of the Islands.   1896.
The Nigger of the "Narcissus": A Tale of the Sea.   1897; as *The Children of the Sea,*
    1897; edited by M. Sutton, 1968.
Tales of Unrest.   1898.
Lord Jim.   1900; edited by T. C. Moser, 1958.
The Inheritors: An Extravagant Story, with Ford Madox Ford.   1901.
Youth: A Narrative, with Two Other Stories.   1902; edited by Morton Dauwen Zabel,
    1959; *Heart of Darkness* edited by Robert Kimbrough, 1972.
Typhoon.   1902.
Typhoon and Other Stories.   1903.
Romance, with Ford Madox Ford.   1903.
Nostromo: A Tale of the Seaboard.   1904.
The Secret Agent: A Simple Tale.   1907.
A Set of Six (stories).   1908.
Under Western Eyes.   1911.
'Twixt Land and Sea: Tales.   1912; *The Secret Sharer* edited by Robert Kimbrough,
    1963.
Chance.   1913.
Victory: An Island Tale.   1915.
Within the Tide: Tales.   1915.
The Shadow-Line: A Confession.   1917.
The Arrow of Gold: A Story Between Two Notes.   1919.
The Tale.   1919.
Prince Roman.   1920.
The Warrior's Soul.   1920.
The Rescue: A Romance of the Shallows.   1920.
The Black Mate: A Story.   1922.
The Rover.   1923.
The Nature of a Crime, with Ford Madox Ford.   1924.
Suspense: A Napoleonic Novel.   1925.
Tales of Hearsay.   1925.
The Sisters (unfinished).   1928.
Complete Short Stories.   1933.

Plays

One Day More, from his own story "Tomorrow" (produced 1905; revised version,
    produced 1918).   1917.
The Secret Agent, from his own novel (produced 1922).   1921.
Laughing Anne, from his own story "Because of the Dollars," with *One Day
    More.*   1923.

Other

The Mirror of the Sea: Memories and Impressions.   1906.
A Personal Record.   1912; as *Some Reminiscences,* 1912.
Notes on Life and Letters.   1921.
Notes on My Books.   1921; as *Prefaces to His Works,* edited by Edward Garnett, 1937.
Last Essays, edited by Richard Curle.   1926.

Letters to His Wife. 1927.

Letters 1895–1924, edited by Edward Garnett. 1928.

Conrad to a Friend: 150 Selected Letters to Richard Curle, edited by Curle.   1928.

Lettres Françaises, edited by Gerard Jean-Aubry.   1930.

Letters to Marguerite Poradowska 1890–1920, edited by John A. Gee and Paul A. Sturm.   1940; edited by R. Rapin (in French), 1966.

Letters to William Blackwood and David S. Meldrum, edited by William Blackburn.   1958.

Conrad's Polish Background: Letters to and from Polish Friends, edited by Zdzislaw Najder.   1964.

Conrad and Warrington Dawson: The Record of a Friendship, edited by D. B. J. Randall.   1968.

Letters to R. B. Cunninghame Graham, edited by C. T. Watts.   1969.

Congo Diary and Other Uncollected Pieces, edited by Zdzislaw Najder.   1977.

Translator, *The Book of Job: A Satirical Comedy,* by Bruno Winawer.   1931.

Bibliography: *A Bibliography of Conrad* by T. G. Ehrsam, 1969.

Reading List: *Conrad: Life and Letters,* 2 vols., 1927, and *The Sea-Dreamer: A Definitive Biography of Conrad,* 1957, both by Gerard Jean-Aubry; *Conrad's Measure of Man* by Paul L. Wiley, 1955; *Conrad the Novelist* by Albert Guerard, 1958; *The Thunder and the Sunshine: A Biography,* 1958, and *The Sea Years of Conrad,* 1965, both by Jerry Allen; *A Reader's Guide to Conrad* by Frederick R. Karl, 1960; *Conrad, Giant in Exile,* 1961, and *The Two Lives of Conrad,* 1965, both by Leo Gurko; *Conrad's Eastern World,* 1966, and *Conrad's Western World,* 1971, both by Norman Sherry; *Conrad: The Critical Heritage* edited by Norman Sherry, 1973; *Conrad: The Modern Imagination* by C. B. Cox, 1974; *Language and Being: Conrad and the Literature of Personality* by Peter J. Glassman, 1976; *Conrad: The Major Phase* by J. Berthoud, 1978.

*   *   *

Only Lawrence and Joyce rank with Joseph Conrad among English and Irish novelists since Hardy. Born in Poland, Conrad was shaped by his memories of political upheaval and the particular struggles of his father who, as an active Polish nationalist under Russian domination, was exiled to Russia where Conrad's mother died. His views of politics and of history were shaped by his despair and indignation at the continuous suppression of Polish freedom. Equally important in shaping his values was his career as an officer in the British Merchant Marine. He admired the solidarity of the crew, the clearly defined responsibilities and discipline of ship life, the hierarchy of command, and the heroic encounters of man with the elements. After he became a novelist, he longed for those values whenever he felt the burdens and complexities of life on land.

It was only in his late thirties that Conrad seriously began his writing career, and, remarkably, he chose English rather than Polish or even French, in which he was fluent. His first two novels, *Almayer's Folly* and *An Outcast of the Islands,* draw upon his merchant marine experience in the Far East. These novels call into question the superiority of white man's civilization to that of the natives. From the outset Conrad wrote about characters who had "soft spots," and "hidden plague spots," by which he meant psychological and moral weaknesses that intrude upon their capacity to act in a morally responsible manner.

Gradually, as he became convinced that objective values were impossible and as he himself was racked by anxiety and self-doubt, he turned to dramatizing a first-person narrator in the process of coming to terms with complex experience. *The Nigger of the "Narcissus"* represents a crucial turning point. He discovered that the tale of a voyage gave him a structure that enabled him to overcome the writing block that haunted him, and that the dramatized first-person voice (which in *The Nigger of the "Narcissus"* alternates with an omniscient voice) enabled him to express his thoughts and values more effectively. *The Nigger of the "Narcissus"* dramatizes a reductive distinction within Conrad's psyche between the evil land, where he was terribly frustrated as he commenced his new career, and his beloved sea, where he felt he had been fairly tested in the comprehensible shipboard life.

Conrad frequently focuses upon the teller rather than the tale. He dramatizes how the consciousness of the speaker is fundamentally changed by his own experience or that of the people he meets. In a method reminiscent of dramatic monologues, the speaker's moral and psychic identity is revealed by the telling. This is the crucial technique in the early Marlow tales, "Youth," "Heart of Darkness," and *Lord Jim*, where the focus is upon Marlow's growth and development. Marlow embodies Conrad's own anxieties and doubts at a time in his life when he felt isolated and doubted his ability to create. Marlow is thus a surrogate for Conrad as well as a dramatic character. For Conrad, as for Hardy, the cosmos is a remorseless process that was indifferent to man's aspirations and needs; Conrad takes particular issue with those, including the Fabians, who believed that man could upwardly evolve toward perfection of the species. As Marlow puts it in "Heart of Darkness," "we live, as we dream – alone." In such a world, objective values are impossible, and each man must discover his own working arrangement. As he wrote in a famous letter, "No man's light is good to any of his fellows.... That's my view of life, – a view that rejects all formulas, dogmas and principles of other people's making. These are only a web of illusions.... Another man's truth is only a dismal lie to me" (G. Jean-Aubry, *Joseph Conrad: Life and Letters*, 1927). In "Heart of Darkness" Marlow encounters Kurtz who has abandoned civilization and begun to participate in nameless atrocities as part of his ivory trade. Marlow's recounting what he learned about himself is as much the focus as Kurtz's astounding conversion from idealism to barbarism in the Congo. Like Kurtz, he has gone to the Congo armed with imperialism's illusions. But gradually Marlow discovers, like Kurtz before him, that the pieties of civilization – the work ethic, imperialism as the emissary of moral enlightenment, the black as the White Man's Burden – are shams; in the Congo, European man is as primitive and savage as the natives, if not more so. When Marlow tells the story, he desperately wants to believe in Kurtz's moral transformation. For that reason he interprets Kurtz's ambiguous "The horror! The horror!" as a renunciation of his past, even though Kurtz might be referring to his capture or the disappointment of his grotesque plans.

After the Marlow tales, Conrad wrote three remarkable political novels – *Nostromo, The Secret Agent*, and *Under Western Eyes*. These novels are almost prophetic in their analysis of twentieth-century political forces, including imperialism, anarchism, and Russian propensity for fanatical political behavior. Paradoxically, they reflect Conrad's disillusionment with politics and his commitment to traditional Western humanism; they show the folly of committing one's self to political ideals at the expense of private relationships. Conrad was sceptical of political theory, and believed that political movements were led by people less motivated by ideals than by unacknowledged psychological needs. In *Nostromo*, Gould's material and political success in a South American country comes at the expense of a potentially vital relationship with his wife. Nostromo, a man of heroic potential, follows the example of the materialists for whom he works and allows greed to corrupt him and to preempt the possibility of his having a private life. Political values often disguise private passions, as in the case of Decoud's commitment to revolution. In *The Secret Agent*, Verloc's personal motives are subsumed by political commitment until life in London is reduced to a bizarre game in which the police and government authorities become complicit with revolutionaries and reactionaries who wish to destroy democratic society, while they ignore poverty and social injustice. Conrad stresses the interrelationship between public amorality and the atrophy of feelings and passion. The omniscient narrator, a satirist who exposes the folly of a world where life is reduced to a Darwinian struggle for survival, stands for positive values of morality, sanity, and compassion. In *Under Western Eyes*, the savagery and irrationality of Russian life are filtered through the mind of a drab, but responsible, kindly, and helpful English language teacher. Gradually, as Russian fanaticism is exposed, the teacher's qualities of balance, moderation, and sensitivity become more attractive. The narrator is an alternative to the Russians like Haldin and Razumov, who idealize their motives and exaggerate their emotions. Russia, which Conrad always resented as a threat to his native Poland's independence, emerges as primitive, violent, and indifferent to private life.

More than his predecessors among British novelists, Conrad stresses that man's conduct was often less the result of conscious decisions than of dimly understood fears, obsessions, and fixations. Thus, in *Lord Jim*, Jim jumps from the *Patna* to save himself, although his entire adult life had been directed towards remaining on ship and behaving heroically. Like Dostoevsky, Conrad was interested in those darker, chaotic impulses that exist beneath the surface of the idealized self which man presents to the world and, often, to himself. Jim reveals his hidden self when he irrationally responds to the outlaw Gentleman Brown's insidious comparisons between themselves and thus jeopardizes the lives of his Patusan friends. As in the case of Gentleman Brown and Kurtz, Conrad often creates a character whose history and situation parallel the protagonist's, but who has a fundamentally different moral character. Perhaps the best example of this is in "The Secret Sharer" where the captain's repressed libidinous self is embodied in the passionate character of Leggatt. While the self-conscious young captain, who has just been assigned his first command, is unable to make any decisions or give an order, Leggatt, as first mate on a ship, has actually killed a crew member in a moment of crisis. Before the captain can assume leadership, he must assimilate some of Leggatt's instinct and passion, but not his atavistic social sense.

The later novels often explore various forms of heterosexual love. *Chance*, the last novel to use Marlow as the narrator, dramatizes how Captain Anthony and Flora are imprisoned by social conventions, and shows how civilization restrains emotional development and contributes to sexual repression. *Victory* shows the folly of a philosophy that does not acknowledge man's urge for personal relationships and human passions. These novels often eschew realism and exploit the allegorical possibilities of romance plots. Conrad's last completed novel, *The Rover*, is a dramatization of his desire for a heroic death as well as his paean to life and love. Of the novels after 1912, perhaps only *The Shadow-Line* approaches his major work. It reaffirms that only by rediscovering traditional values of courage, duty, and responsibility can man succeed in controlling himself within an amoral and often hostile cosmos.

—Daniel R. Schwarz

COOKE, John Esten. American. Born in Winchester, Virginia, 3 November 1830. Educated in schools in Richmond, Virginia; studied law with his father; admitted to the Virginia Bar, 1851. Served as a Captain in the Confederate Army during the Civil War, 1861–65. Married Mary Frances Page in 1867 (died, 1878); three children. Practised law in Richmond, 1851; full-time writer from 1852; moved to an estate near Winchester, 1868, and thereafter devoted himself to both writing and farming. *Died 27 September 1886.*

PUBLICATIONS

Fiction

Leather Stocking and Silk; or, Hunter John Myers and His Times: A Story of the Valley of Virginia. 1854; as *Leather and Silk*, 1892.

The Virginia Comedians; or, Old Days in the Old Dominion.   1854; as *Beatrice Hallam* and *Captain Ralph*, 2 vols., 1892.

Ellie; or, The Human Comedy.   1855.

The Last of the Foresters; or, Humors on the Border: A Story of the Old Virginia Frontier.   1856.

Henry St. John, Gentleman, of "Flower of Hundreds" in the County of Prince George, Virginia: A Tale of 1774–'75.   1859: as *Bonnybel Vane*, 1883; as *Miss Bonnybel*, 1892.

Surry of Eagle's-Nest; or, The Memoirs of a Staff Officer Serving in Virginia.   1866.

Fairfax; or, The Master of Greenway Court: A Chronicle of the Valley of the Shenandoah.   1868; as *Lord Fairfax*, 1888.

Mohun; or, The Last Days of Lee and His Paladins: Final Memories of a Staff Officer Serving in Virginia.   1869.

Hilt to Hilt; or, Days and Nights on the Banks of the Shenandoah in the Autumn of 1864.   1869.

The Heir of Gaymount.   1870.

Hammer and Rapier.   1870.

Out of the Foam.   1871; as *Westbrooke Hall*, 1891.

Doctor Vandyke.   1872.

Her Majesty the Queen.   1873.

Pretty Mrs. Gaston and Other Stories.   1874.

Justin Harley: A Romance of Old Virginia.   1875.

Canolles: The Fortunes of a Partisan of '81.   1877.

Professor Pressensee, Materialist and Inventor.   1878.

Stories of the Old Dominion from the Settlement to the End of the Revolution.   1879.

Mr. Grantley's Idea.   1879.

The Virginia Bohemians.   1880.

Fanchette, by One of Her Admirers.   1883.

My Lady Pokahontas: A True Relation of Virginia.   1885.

The Maurice Mystery.   1885; as *Col. Ross of Piedmont*, 1893.

Other

The Youth of Jefferson; or, A Chronicle of College Scrapes at Williamsburg, in Virginia, A.D. 1764.   1854.

The Life of Stonewall Jackson.   1863; revised edition, as *Stonewall Jackson: A Military Biography*, 1866.

Wearing of the Gray, Being Personal Portraits, Scenes, and Adventures of the War.   1867; edited by Philip Van Doren Stern, 1960.

A Life of Gen. Robert E. Lee.   1871.

Virginia: A History of the People.   1883.

Poe as a Literary Critic, edited by N. Bryllion Fagin.   1946.

Stonewall Jackson and the Old Stonewall Brigade, edited by Richard Barksdale Harwell.   1954.

Outlines from the Outpost, edited by Richard Barksdale Harwell.   1961.

Bibliography: *A Bibliography of the Separate Writings of Cooke* by Oscar Wegelin, 1925; in *Bibliography of American Literature* by Jacob Blanck, 1957.

Reading List: *Cooke, Virginian* by John O. Beaty, 1932.

*   *   *

Although John Esten Cooke, the younger brother of Philip Pendleton Cooke (1816–1850) and cousin of John Pendleton Kennedy (1795–1870), was best known in his own time and afterwards as a writer of long fiction, he was also something of a poet, one of whose fugitive pieces – "The Band in the Pines" – is still occasionally anthologized; a biographer, whose lives of Lee and Stonewall Jackson are worthy of attention but more as accounts of battles than as biography; and a historian, whose *Virginia*, though hardly scholarly according to modern standards, is a pleasant narrative of the early days of the Commonwealth.

Along with stories, sketches, essays, verse, and other contributions to periodicals, Cooke produced at least five novels before the Civil War, four of which are actually historical romances – *Leather Stocking and Silk, The Virginia Comedians, Henry St. John, Gentleman,* and *Fairfax* (serialized in 1859). The second of these is, according to the author, "intended to be a picture of our curiously graded Virginia society just before the Revolution" and included portraits of Patrick Henry and Lewis Hallam's actors in the Williamsburg area. It remains his best work of historical fiction, despite the fact that many of his numerous books on the war are based on his own first-hand experience.

Surry of Eagle's-Nest, the most notable of the war novels and his most popular long fiction, and its sequel, *Mohun,* cover many of the great battles of Lee's army, military actions in which Cooke participated from the first engagement at Bull Run to Appomattox, and priceless material for a novelist. Cooke found it difficult, nevertheless, to fuse fact and fiction in these novels and to refrain, any more than had his predecessors Scott, Cooper, Irving, and Simms, from introducing extraneous materials into his structure, in these particular instances Gothic characters, melodrama, and sub-plots in works that are essentially historical or even realistic. But when, for example, the narrative focuses on Surry and military adventure, it moves swiftly and with eyewitness authority. Though much of Cooke's long fiction now seems romantic and dated, his style remains charming and graceful, his appreciation of the past manifests itself in the ante-bellum work, and his military experience lends authenticity to the best of the Civil War romances.

—Rayburn S. Moore

COOPER, James Fenimore. American. Born in Burlington, New Jersey, 15 September 1789; moved with his family to Cooperstown, New York, 1790. Educated in the village school at Cooperstown; in the household of the rector of St. Peter's, Albany, New York, 1800–02; Yale University, New Haven, Connecticut, 1803–05: dismissed for misconduct; thereafter prepared for a naval career: served on the *Stirling,* 1806–07; commissioned midshipman in the United States Navy, 1808; served on the *Vesuvius,* 1808; for a brief time in command on Lake Champlain, also served on the *Wasp* in the Atlantic, 1809; resigned commission, 1811. Married Susan Augusta DeLancey in 1811; five daughters and two sons. Country gentleman: lived in Mamaroneck, New York, 1811–14, Cooperstown, 1814–17, and Scarsdale, New York, 1817–22; began to write in 1820; lived in New York, 1822–26, and France, 1826–33: United States Consul at Lyons, 1826–29; returned to New York, 1833, and lived in Cooperstown, 1834 until his death. M.A.: Columbia University, New York, 1824. *Died 14 September 1851.*

Collections

Works.   33 vols., 1895–1900.
Representative Selections, edited by Robert E. Spiller.   1936.
Letters and Journals, edited by James Franklin Beard.   6 vols., 1960–68.

Fiction

Precaution.   1820.
The Spy: A Tale of the Neutral Ground.   1821; edited by Tremaine McDowell, 1931.
The Pioneers; or, The Sources of the Susquehanna: A Descriptive Tale.   1823.
Tales for Fifteen; or, Imagination and Heart.   1823.
The Pilot: A Tale of the Sea.   1823.
Lionel Lincoln; or, The Leaguer of Boston.   1825.
The Last of the Mohicans: A Narrative of 1757.   1826; edited by William Charvat, 1958.
The Prairie: A Tale.   1827.
The Red Rover: A Tale.   1827; edited by Warren S. Walker, 1963.
The Borderers: A Tale.   1829; as *The Wept of Wish Ton-Tish,* 1829; as *The Heathcotes,* 1854.
The Water Witch; or, The Skimmer of the Seas: A Tale.   1830.
The Bravo: A Venetian Story.   1831.
The Heidenmauer; or, The Benedictines.   1832.
The Headsman; or, The Abbaye des Vignersons: A Tale.   1833.
The Monikins: A Tale.   1835.
Homeward Bound; or, The Chase: A Tale of the Sea.   1838.
Home as Found.   1838; as *Eve Effingham; or, Home,* 1838.
The Pathfinder; or, The Inland Sea.   1840.
Mercedes of Castile; or, The Voyage to Cathay.   1840.
The Deerslayer; or, The First War-Path: A Tale.   1841; edited by Gregory Paine, 1927.
The Two Admirals: A Tale of the Sea.   1842.
The Jack O'Lantern (Le Feu-Follet); or, The Privateer.   1842; as *The Wing-and-Wing; or, Le Feu-Follet,* 1842.
Le Mouchoir: An Autobiographical Romance.   1843; as *The French Governess; or, The Embroidered Handkerchief,* 1843; edited by George F. Horner and Raymond Adams, as *Autobiography of a Pocket Handkerchief,* 1949.
Wyandotté; or, The Hutted Knoll.   1843.
Afloat and Ashore; or, The Adventures of Miles Wallingford.   1844.
Lucy Harding: A Second Series of Afloat and Ashore.   1844; as *Afloat and Ashore,* vols. 3–4, 1844.
Satanstoe; or, The Family of Littlepage: A Tale of the Colony.   1845; as *Satanstoe; or, The Littlepage Manuscripts,* 1845; edited by Robert E. Spiller and Joseph D. Coppock, 1937.
The Chainbearer; or, The Littlepage Manuscripts.   1845.
Ravensnest; or, The Redskins.   1846; as *The Redskins; or, Indian and Injin, Being the Conclusion of the Littlepage Manuscripts,* 1846.
Mark's Reef; or, The Crater: A Tale of the Pacific.   1847; as *The Crater; or, Vulcan's Peak,* 1847; edited by Thomas Philbrick, 1962.
Captain Spike; or, The Islets of the Gulf.   1848; as *Jack Tier; or, The Florida Reef,* 1848.

The Bee-Hunter; or, The Oak Openings. 1848; as *The Oak Openings*, 1848.
The Sea Lions; or, The Lost Sealers. 1849; edited by Warren S. Walker, 1965.
The Ways of the Hour: A Tale. 1850.
The Lake Gun, edited by Robert E. Spiller. 1932.

Other

Notions of the Americans, Picked Up by a Travelling Bachelor. 2 vols., 1828; as *America and the Americans,* 1836.
Letter to Gen. Lafayette. 1831.
A Letter to His Countrymen. 1834.
Sketches of Switzerland. 2 vols., 1836; as *Excursions in Switzerland,* 1836.
A Residence in France with a Second Visit to Switzerland. 2 vols., 1836; as *Sketches of Switzerland, Part Second,* 1836.
Recollections of Europe. 2 vols., 1837; as *Gleanings in Europe,* 1837.
England, with Sketches of Society in the Metropolis. 2 vols., 1837; as *Gleanings in Europe: England,* 1837.
Excursions in Italy. 2 vols., 1838; as *Gleanings in Europe: Italy,* 1838.
The American Democrat. 1838; edited by George Dekker and Larry Johnston, 1969.
The Chronicles of Cooperstown. 1838.
The History of the Navy of the United States of America. 2 vols., 1839.
The Battle of Lake Erie. 1843.
Ned Myers; or, A Life Before the Mast. 1843.
Lives of Distinguished American Naval Officers. 2 vols., 1846.
The Works, revised by the author. 12 vols., 1849–51.
New York, edited by Dixon Ryan Fox. 1930.
Early Critical Essays 1820–1822, edited by James Franklin Beard. 1955.

Editor, *Elinor Wyllys,* by Susan A. Fenimore Cooper. 1845.

Bibliography: *A Descriptive Bibliography of the Writings of Cooper* by Robert E. Spiller and Philip C. Blackburn, 1934; in *Bibliography of American Literature* by Jacob Blanck, 1957.

Reading List: *Cooper, Critic of His Times,* 1931, and *Cooper,* 1965, both by Robert E. Spiller; *Cooper* by James Grossman, 1949; *Cooper* by Donald A. Ringe, 1962; *Cooper: An Introduction and Interpretation* by Warren S. Walker, 1962; *Cooper, The Novelist* by George Dekker, 1967, as *Cooper, The American Scott,* 1967; *Cooper: The Critical Heritage* edited by George Dekker and J. P. McWilliams, 1973; *A World by Itself: The Pastoral Moment in Cooper's Fiction* by H. Daniel Peck, 1977; *Cooper: A Study of His Life and Imagination* by Stephen Railton, 1978.

*   *   *

James Fenimore Cooper will always be remembered first for his Leatherstocking tales: *The Pioneers, The Last of the Mohicans, The Prairie, The Pathfinder,* and *The Deerslayer.* These five books recount the experiences of an American frontiersman, variously named Deerslayer, Hawkeye, Pathfinder, Leatherstocking, and the trapper, between the early 1740's, when British America was a line of settlements along the Atlantic coast, and 1805–06, when the Lewis and Clark expedition crossed the continent. Though the books were not written in the order of the events they portray, they form, nonetheless, a kind of American epic, concerned not only with the opening of the West, but also with the costs involved in the process: the cutting of the forests, the killing of the game, and the displacement of the Indian. Leatherstocking, a man of the woods, wants to preserve the natural environment and use it only as needed, but by acting as hunter and scout, he opens the wilderness to the very settlers whose wasteful ways he abhors.

Cooper details both the social and moral consequences of the process, and though he laments the fate of the Indian and warns his countrymen against the destruction of their resources, he does not place his values in Leatherstocking alone. He consistently affirms, rather, the Christian civilization that must supplant the wilderness. The problem America faces, these books seem to say, is to insure that the new society will be a just and democratic one, ruled by the most talented and virtuous men who will not needlessly destroy the bounties of nature. To develop the social aspects of his theme, Cooper includes a wide range of characters, both white and Indian, who illustrate the various attitudes that men have toward God, nature, and society, and he uses his physical setting – both dense woods and desolate prairie – to reveal the moral state of his characters and their relation to a transcendent system of value revealed in the landscape – one that Leatherstocking always recognizes, but which too many of his fellow countrymen fail to perceive.

Cooper uses the physical setting to define the social and moral problems in many of his books. The neutral ground in *The Spy*, where contending irregulars fight during the American Revolution, typifies well a moral world where motives and identities are masked and loyalties are uncertain. The isolated frontier settlements in *The Wept of Wish Ton-Tish* and *Wyandotté* clearly represent the islands of peace and order that the colonists try to establish in a moral chaos. Even the sea in the maritime novels functions in a similar fashion. In the two series of *Afloat and Ashore*, it serves a dual purpose as a testing ground for men. Here the right to rule, by virtue of character, training, and knowledge, may be established in the handling of a ship, but here too the weakness of even the most capable men before the power of God may be starkly revealed. Indeed, in *The Crater*, Cooper uses both the sea and the isolated settlement, some islands in the Pacific, to establish the relation between the moral basis of a society and its ability to survive.

Much of Cooper's success as an artist derives from his ability to project his meaning through setting, whether it be a frontier fort in America, a ship at sea, or a part of the European scene: the city of Venice in *The Bravo*, an isolated valley in Germany in *The Heidenmauer*, or the breathtaking landscape of Switzerland in *The Headsman*. That meaning, moreover, is always both moral and social. At times, of course, one or the other aspect may dominate, and, especially in the social criticism, the moral basis may be muted or unexpressed, but it is never completely absent. His attacks on both aristocracy in his three European novels and on the excesses of American democracy in the books that followed derive from his consistent belief that the evils of society are caused by the fallen nature of men, who must humble themselves before God and act, not from economic, but from moral motives if society is ever to escape the wrongs and injustices that have plagued it in the past.

Cooper detested aristocracy wherever he found it and wrote the European novels not merely to attack it in the abstract, but also to make clear the evils of such societies wherever they might appear. Though Cooper was thinking of contemporary England and of the France of Louis Philippe when he wrote these books, he also wished to warn his countrymen that a similar oligarchy, based on commerce, could develop in the United States and subvert its political principles. When he viewed American democracy, on the other hand, he saw a quite different problem. Though the leveling democrat is impelled by an economic motive no less strong than that of the aristocrat, he wishes to remove all distinctions among men and rule, not through a governing class, but through the manipulation of the electoral process. In place of the aristocrat, there appears the demagogue.

Cooper never found a completely suitable means for presenting his criticism of American democracy, and most of his novels attacking the failings of contemporary America do not succeed as fiction. Yet all of them are interesting. In *The Monikins*, he satirized English, American, and French society through a race of monkeys who live in Antarctica, and in *Homeward Bound* and *Home as Found*, he attempted to depict a cross section of American life through the experience of the Effingham family, descendants of the founder of Templeton in *The Pioneers*, who are returning home after a sojourn in Europe. The device gave him the opportunity to attack the leveling democrats and the social climbers, the Anglophiles and the super-patriots of America, while affirming through the Effinghams what true Americans should be. His major characters are rather wooden, however, and though each book has its interest – the adventure parts of the former are very well done – both are rather weak novels.

Cooper did better in some of his later works: the Littlepage series and his final book, *The Ways of the Hour*. Critics have sometimes set the Littlepage series against the Leatherstocking tales to illustrate a bifurcation in Cooper's fiction, but the two series actually complement each other. The Leatherstocking tales, after all, have much to say about American society, and the first two Littlepage books, *Satanstoe* and *The Chainbearer*, contain major frontier episodes. They portray the rise of the Littlepage family during the eighteenth century and their successful struggle to maintain their possessions against both French and Indian invaders and New England squatters. The third book, *The Redskins*, shows them defending their property against insurgent radical democrats in contemporary New York, but the book is too polemical to work as fiction. *The Ways of the Hour*, focused upon a jury trial for murder, is a far more effective treatment of the failings of American democracy.

Not all of Cooper's novels fit into the two main categories for which he is best known: frontier romance and social criticism. A third major type is one he created, the tale of the sea. Cooper's maritime novels cover a wide range, from delightful romantic fictions, like *The Red Rover* and *The Water Witch*, to serious explorations of moral problems, like *The Two Admirals* and *The Wing-and-Wing*. They include the patriotic *The Pilot*, the grim *Jack Tier*, in which all value seems to have been lost, and the deeply religious *The Sea Lions*, which, like *The Oak Openings*, a late tale of the wilderness, makes a strong affirmation of Christian faith. These tales of the sea may appear diverse in theme and tone, but, seen in the broad pattern of Cooper's thirty-year career as a novelist, their relation to his other work is clear. His successful sailors are men who, like Leatherstocking, submit to the God they perceive in the natural setting. Those who fail to do so cause the many evils and injustices that, Cooper believed, always result when men act from selfish motives in this fallen world.

Cooper also wrote a significant amount of good non-fiction. *Notions of the Americans* and *The American Democrat* are sound statements of American beliefs and principles; his five travel volumes (1836–38) not only describe his sojourn abroad, but also make sharp observations on European society; and *The History of the Navy of the United States of America* and *Lives of Distinguished American Naval Officers* are sound historical works. Though Cooper's claim to our attention must always rest on his fiction, these miscellaneous works made a real contribution to nineteenth-century American thought and are still of interest to serious readers today.

—Donald A. Ringe

COPPARD, A(lfred) E(dgar). English. Born in Folkestone, Kent, 4 January 1878; moved with his family to Brighton, 1883. Educated at Lewes Road Boarding School, Brighton, 1883–87; apprenticed to a tailor in Whitechapel, London, 1887–90. Married 1) Lily Annie Richardson in 1905 (died); 2) Winifred May de Kok, one son and one daughter. Had worked as a paraffin vendor's assistant, auctioneer, cheesemonger, soap-agent, and carrier, in Brighton by the time he was twenty; thereafter worked for several years in the offices of an engineering firm; moved to Oxford, 1907: Confidential Clerk, Eagle Ironworks, 1907 until he left the firm for a full-time career as a writer, 1919. *Died 13 January 1957.*

PUBLICATIONS

Collections

Selected Stories. 1972.

Fiction (stories)

Adam and Eve and Pinch Me: Tales. 1921.
Clorinda Walks in Heaven: Tales. 1922.
The Black Dog and Other Stories. 1923.
Fishmonger's Fiddle: Tales. 1925.
The Field of Mustard: Tales. 1926.
Silver Circus: Tales. 1928.
Count Stefan. 1928.
The Gollan. 1929.
The Hundredth Story. 1930.
Pink Furniture: A Tale for Lovely Children with Noble Natures. 1930.
Nixey's Harlequin: Tales. 1931.
Crotty Shinkwin, The Beauty Spot. 1932.
Cheefoo. 1932.
Dunky Fitlow: Tales. 1933.
Ring the Bells of Heaven. 1933.
Emergency Exit. 1934.
Polly Oliver: Tales. 1935.
The Ninepenny Flute: Twenty-One Tales. 1937.
Tapster's Tapestry. 1938.
You Never Know, Do You? and Other Tales. 1939.
Ugly Anna and Other Tales. 1944.
Selected Tales. 1946.
Fearful Pleasures. 1946.
Dark-Eyed Lady: Fourteen Tales. 1947.
Collected Tales. 1948.
Lucy in Her Pink Jacket. 1954.

Verse

Hips and Haws. 1922.
Pelagea and Other Poems. 1926.
Yokohama Garland and Other Poems. 1926.
Collected Poems. 1928.
Easter Day. 1931.
Cherry Ripe. 1935.

Other

Rummy, The Noble Game, with Robert Gibbings. 1932.
It's Me, O Lord! (autobiography). 1957.

Editor, *Songs from Robert Burns.* 1925.

Bibliography: *The Writings of Coppard* by Jacob Schwartz, 1931.

Reading List: *Coppard: His Life and His Poetry* by George Brandon Saul, 1932; *Remarks on the Style of Coppard* by A. Jehin, 1944; *The Lonely Voice: A Study of the Short Story* by Frank O'Connor, 1963.

*   *   *

A. E. Coppard, whom his peer (if not superior) Frank O'Connor regarded as the leading short story writer of their day, is significant as both lyric poet and teller of tales. (His critical bits are unimpressive, as are his book for children, *Pink Furniture*, and his autobiography, *It's Me, O Lord!*) The relatively few lyrics, many in free verse, stirred on publication much division of opinion; the prose tales, rich in lyrical quality, as not only Ford Madox Ford recognized, drew more general approbation. Both categories – which helped make luminous the initial years of the Golden Cockerel Press – have much in common, in concept, metaphor, philosophy, and a fondness for the odd, obsolete, or invented word. But the verse, rich in imagistic qualities stressing the pictorial and descriptive, is especially delightful in evocation of the Elizabethan and Caroline traditions; and it always honors Coppard's belief that poetry should be "instant and simple and clear."

The tales (Coppard's preferred label, since he felt that the only proper approach to the short story was "by way of the folk tale," his model), of which *The Black Dog* and *The Field of Mustard* are in every way clearly superlative as entities, are inevitably as uneven in quality as is apt to be the case with even a dedicated author striving to live by his writing alone. And from *Nixey's Harlequin* on, a certain falling-off in quality seems perceptible, with evidence of what the London *Times Literary Supplement*, reviewing *Ninepenny Flute*, justly called a growing "impulse toward caricature," not to mention an occasional yielding to the purely trivial in subject matter. But there is usually exciting variety, as emphasized by the fairly representative assortment of *Collected Tales*, a mistitled book assembling only thirty-eight pieces.

Coppard's tales, despite tiresomely repeated concerns (as with the *idea* of time) and mannerisms (such as inversions), have at best memorable statement in a rich, nourishing prose pungent with the flavor of the English countryside, especially Berkshire. Their author is always best when preoccupied with what is suggested by George Meredith's phrase "tragic life"; even his humor is often made poignant by strands of tragedy. Bitterly opposed to war and the mistreatment of animals, always concerned with the intimate simplicities of life, humanely tender in brooding over the human scene, especially when children are moving across it, Coppard has moments of ineffectiveness mainly when he essays the metaphysical or (generally) the supernatural, or when he engages in philosophizing which unfortunately tends toward cynical rumination only. But in the main, he proves himself one of the few members of his tribe in the twentieth century to demonstrate anew that the mere unaffected telling of a tale may be a thing of wizard joy to hold "children from play and old men from the chimney corner."

—George Brandon Saul

CORELLI, Marie. Pseudonym for Mary Mackay. English. Born in Bayswater, London, 1 May 1855. Educated privately; studied music, and made debut as a pianist, London, 1884. Writer from 1885; settled in Stratford upon Avon, 1901. *Died 21 April 1924.*

Fiction

A Romance of Two Worlds. 1886.
Vendetta; or, The Story of One Forgotten.   1886.
Thelma. 1887.
Ardath. 1889.
My Wonderful Wife: A Study in Smoke. 1889.
Wormwood. 1890.
The Hired Baby and Other Stories and Social Sketches. 1891.
The Soul of Lilith. 1892.
Barabbas: A Dream of the World's Tragedy.   1893.
The Sorrows of Satan; or, The Strange Adventures of One Geoffrey Tempest,
    Millionaire. 1895.
Cameos: Short Stories. 1896.
The Murder of Delicia. 1896; as Delicia, 1917.
The Mighty Atom. 1896.
Ziska. 1897.
Jane. 1897.
Boy. 1900.
The Master-Christian. 1900.
Temporal Power. 1902.
God's Good Man. 1904.
The Strange Visitation of Josiah McNason.   1904.
The Treasure of Heaven. 1906.
Holy Orders. 1908.
The Devil's Motor. 1910.
The Life Everlasting. 1911.
Innocent: Her Fancy and His Fact. 1914.
Eyes of the Sea. 1917.
The Young Diana. 1918.
My Little Bit. 1919.
The Love of Long Ago and Other Stories. 1920.
The Secret Power. 1921.
Love − and the Philosopher. 1923.

Verse

Poems, edited by Bertha Vyver. 1925.

Other

The Silver Domino; or, Side-Whispers, Social and Literary. 1892.
Patriotism or Self-Advertisement? A Social Note on the War. 1900.
The Greatest Queen in the World: A Tribute to the Majesty of England
    1837−1900. 1900.
A Christmas Greeting of Various Thoughts, Verses, and Fancies. 1901.
The Passing of the Great Queen. 1901.
The Plain Truth of the Stratford-upon-Avon Controversy. 1903.
Free Opinions Freely Expressed on Certain Phases of Modern Social Life and
    Conduct. 1905.

Woman or Suffragette? A Question of National Choice. 1907.
Open Confession to a Man from a Woman. 1924.

Editor, with Percy S. Brentnall and Bertha Vyver, *Stratford upon Avon Guide Book.* 1931.

Reading List: *Corelli: The Life and Death of a Best-Seller* by George Bullock, 1940; *Corelli: The Woman and the Legend* by Eileen Bigland, 1953; *Corelli: The Story of a Friendship* by W. S. Scott, 1955; *Now Barabbas Was a Rotter* (biography) by Brian Masters, 1977.

*   *   *

"Why *can't* I be a Marie Corelli!" Those words were uttered by Anne Sedgwick, a late-nineteenth century novelist of some talent and little popularity. She was contrasting her poor fortunes with those of the most famous best-seller of her day, beside whose achievement even those of Ouida and Elinor Glyn pale into insignificance. Even in 1909, by which time her popularity had begun to fade, her publishers rapidly sold 130,000 copies of her new book, and offered her an advance of £9,500 for the next.

How did she do it? It is not easy to answer that question. Perhaps the nearest we can come to it is by noting the fact that her stories all have an element of sensationalism in them, plus a dose of vague, mystical, other-or-ideal worldly religion; and that this was almost bound to go down well in an age which had not lost its religious impulse, even though the discoveries and arguments of Darwin and his followers had denied that impulse orthodox expression. Queen Victoria herself praised the *Sorrows of Satan*, and Amy Cruse, in *After the Victorians*, points out how often it was used as a text by fashionable preachers of the day. A Father Ignatius praised the novel to a packed congregation at the Portman Rooms, Baker Street, and wrote to Marie Corelli, calling her "a prophet of good things to come in this filthy and materialistic generation." She had thrillingly portrayed, he told her, "the utter misery of being without Christ in life and death, the daring blasphemies of popular poets and other writers, and the consequences in the lives of their readers."

Her choice of living place − Stratford upon Avon − is significant. For it appears that she really did think of herself as a writer in the class of Shakespeare, one whose house would become a literary shrine every bit as much frequented as his. Why should she not choose to live where he had lived? The vanity is touching rather than contemptible. For there was absolutely nothing fraudulent or hypocritical about Marie Corelli. From first to last she believed in her genius, believed, too, in the "reality" of the misty mysticism which blows through the pages of her books. And why should she not, when the entire nation, it seemed, agreed with her valuation of herself? True, there were dissident voices. Critics tended to be unkind. Indeed, after the cruel critical reception given to *Barabbas*, in 1893, Marie Corelli refused to allow any of her books to be sent out for review.

But anyway, criticism did not matter. Suppose a hostile reviewer were to point out the similarity between her *Soul of Lilith* and Rider Haggard's *She*, what then? The hard fact remained that *The Soul of Lilith* sold "by the ton." And suppose that same hostile reviewer were to point out that the end of her greatest best-seller, *The Mighty Atom*, bore a striking resemblance to the ending of *Jude the Obscure*? Marie Corelli could always retort that for many people her novel amounted to a new gospel, and that she had given the little Devon town of Clovelly guide-book fame, "as the scene of Miss Corelli's great novel."

Of course, she isn't a great novelist, she isn't even a good one. But her books are of interest because they clearly reflect opinions, wishes, likes and dislikes that were widely current during the last years of the nineteenth century and the early years of the twentieth. If you want to know what the man on the Clapham omnibus thought of life during those years, Marie Corelli's books will help to tell you.

—John Lucas

CORVO, Baron.   See **ROLFE, Frederick**.

COURAGE, James (Francis).   New Zealander.   Born in Amberley, Canterbury, New Zealand, 9 February 1903. Educated at Christ's College, Christchurch; St. John's College, Oxford. Lived in England 1923 until his death. *Died 5 October 1963.*

PUBLICATIONS

Fiction

> *One House.*   1933.
> *The Fifth Child.*   1948.
> *Desire Without Content.*   1950.
> *Fires in the Distance.*   1952.
> *The Young Have Secrets.*   1954.
> *The Call Home.*   1956.
> *A Way of Love.*   1959.
> *A Visit to Penmorten.*   1961.
> *Such Separate Creatures: Stories,* edited by Charles Brasch.   1973.

Play

> *Private History* (produced 1938).

*   *   *

Although James Courage had aspired to a literary vocation from the time he was an undergraduate at Oxford, his work seldom reached the public (and made no great impression when it did) until he was in his forties. It was with the publication of his second novel, *The Fifth Child*, that he found his most fertile setting – the Canterbury farmland of New Zealand where he had grown up. An unusually large autobiographical element was to be present in all that he subsequently wrote.

The distinguishing mark of the five New Zealand novels is the exploration of disharmonies between an imported set of English middle-class refinements and a colonial bluffness and practicality. Such a conflict is characteristic of a much earlier phase of New Zealand's social history, and it is to be remembered that Courage lived in England from 1923 until his death. Though his novels were appearing well after such poets as A. R. D. Fairburn, Allen Curnow, Charles Brasch and Denis Glover, and such novelists as Robin Hyde, John Mulgan, John Lee, Frank Sargeson, and Dan Davin, had founded a distinctly New Zealand literature, Courage appears unwilling or unable to contribute to this development. By the time his own work began, the New Zealand society he remembers had passed away and the fictional models he works from had been locally supplanted. But the conflict he examines, though it is historically outdated, retains some symbolic force in the study of marital and family strife; for the English gentility is embodied in an unhappy wife, and the colonial crudeness in her husband. A son, often named Walter in the novels and stories, is vulnerably placed between these parents, and the loving allegiance to the mother is matched by a crippling hostility towards the father. A refuge from parental discord is found in the placid wisdom of a grandmother whose acceptance of her new country is graceful and complete.

The Fifth Child, Desire Without Content, and *Fires in the Distance* are all studies in family strife and sexual perplexity for which, as in *The Call Home*, there may be a happy resolution that tends towards the romantic and wishful. Courage is always professionally competent, having learned much from his reading of Forster and Lawrence, particularly in emulating, sometimes a little ineptly, their symbolic use of scene or object.

The Young Have Secrets is usually regarded as Courage's most successful novel. The centre of experience is placed in a ten-year-old boy who, as a boarder in Christchurch, is a puzzled trespasser in adult lives, particularly in their love intrigues. There is a well-drawn range of characters, some of them comic, and a striking representation of place and period (1914) is achieved.

The last two novels have English settings. *A Way of Love* is an ironic, honest and compassionate study of homosexual society; and *A Visit to Penmorten* traces, rather superficially, the recovery of its hero from an Oedipal trauma.

Thirty-two of Courage's short stories survive, and the fifteen of them that have been collected provide a compendious representation of his work in both its New Zealand and its English settings.

—R. A. Copland

COZZENS, James Gould. American. Born in Chicago, Illinois, 19 August 1903. Educated at the Kent School, Connecticut, graduated 1922; Harvard University, Cambridge, Massachusetts, 1922–24. Served in the United States Army Air Force, 1942–45: Major. Married Bernice Beaumgarten in 1927. Schoolteacher, Santa Clara, Cuba, 1925; lived in Europe, 1926–27; Associate Editor, *Fortune* magazine, New York, 1938. Recipient: O. Henry Award, 1936; Pulitzer Prize, 1949; Howells Medal, 1960. Litt.D.: Harvard University, 1952. Member, National Institute of Arts and Letters. *Died 9 August 1978.*

PUBLICATIONS

Fiction

Confusion. 1924.
Michael Scarlett: A History. 1925.
Cock Pit. 1928.
The Son of Perdition. 1929.
S.S. San Pedro: A Tale of the Sea. 1931.
The Last Adam. 1933; as *A Cure of Flesh.* 1933.
Castaway. 1934.
Men and Brethren. 1936.
Ask Me Tomorrow; or, The Pleasant Comedy of Young Fortunatus. 1940.
The Just and the Unjust. 1942.

Guard of Honor.   1948.
By Love Possessed.   1957.
Children and Others (stories).   1964.
Morning Noon and Night.   1968.
A Flower in Her Hair (stories).   1975.

Other

A Rope for Dr. Webster (essay).   1976.

Bibliography: *Cozzens: An Annotated Checklist* by Pierre Michel, 1972; *Cozzens: A Checklist* by James Meriwether, 1973.

Reading List: *Cozzens* by Granville Hicks, 1958; *The Novels of Cozzens* by Frederick Bracher, 1959; *Cozzens: Novelist of Intellect* by Harry John Mooney, Jr., 1963; *Cozzens* by D. E. S. Maxwell, 1964; *Cozzens* by Pierre Michel, 1974.

*   *   *

James Gould Cozzens is a writer whose work offers, with a quiet persistence, an account of American life that is not really duplicated elsewhere. After tentative starts in novels which were modish at the times of their appearance, Cozzens found a stride that carried him off in a more personal direction. The early novel *Confusion* played off the refinement of Europe against the crudity of America, as many novelists of the time were doing. The somewhat later novel, *The Last Adam*, stridently celebrated the lusty and primitive energy of the hero as if he were cousin to the gamekeeper in *Lady Chatterley's Lover.*

But these novels — and *The Last Adam* is excellent in its own right — were apprentice exercises: a cutting-away of underbrush that kept Cozzens from reaching his own territory. This territory is kept strictly to in novels like *The Just and the Unjust* and *By Love Possessed.* It is only apparently departed from in *Men and Brethren*, Cozzens's "clerical" novel with a big-city setting, and *Guard of Honor*, a "war" novel with an army base for its background. Cozzens's domination of his territory has not been difficult; few other American writers have wanted to enter it. Of those who seem to, it is Louis Auchincloss who comes closest to Cozzens; both Auchincloss and Cozzens depict the lives of a privileged minority. But Auchincloss's characters are both more wealthy and more powerful than Cozzens's, "big city" and mobile. In contrast, Cozzens's "right people" are provincial and fixed in their habitations and their careers.

The typical Cozzens heroes, most fully displayed in *The Just and the Unjust* and *By Love Possessed* but represented elsewhere, are the latest members of families that have enjoyed privilege, education, and position for several generations in American towns of medium size. The heroes are at the center of the web of custom and law which continues to hold together the communities they serve, often as lawyers and always as thoughtful and responsible citizens. Both men have fathers who speak of the order they supported in *their* days; the fathers encourage their sons to continue the quiet battle of preserving a way of life that is already old, shadowed by elms and dominated by court-house domes and the law-courts beneath those domes. It is a way of life best enjoyed by people of substance and privilege — a way both misunderstood and resented by those who are "outside the law": Poles, Irish Catholics, and blacks. For these persons, whose drunkenness and violence often take them into the lawyers's offices, the lawyers (and Cozzens the novelist) offer sympathy and comprehension but hardly acceptance; the clients' disorder is part of a more general confusion which is always threatening not just the privileged but the entire community.

This confusion — as most of Cozzens's narratives suggest — can be held back by law and custom; it will not cease. So, in face of the disorder in "alien" behavior and the outbreaks of lust and malice in their own beings, the Cozzens heroes fight and learn while they fight. Their battles are related by Cozzens in such a way that all events, all human deliberations, are bathed in a rationality that is calm and unmilitant; absent from the novels is the self-righteousness of many a novelist whose orientation is liberal. Cozzens has faith in what he says, but the faith is not excessive. Absent also are the transcendental hopes of novelists who have heard a gospel. Cozzens and his heroes are committed to a kind of dubiety, a dubiety both provincial and shrewd. It is a world in which expectations of happiness are both clear and quite modest.

Cozzens's analysis of human motive is sharp. Cozzens and his most perceptive characters – he is not easily to be separated from them – are armed with generations of common sense and desultory talk rather than with the Freudian or Jungian strategies that are useful to many of Cozzens's contemporaries. Cozzens is – differences being allowed for – the Anthony Trollope of the recent American day, judging the life he knows with sharp intelligence rather than dismissing it with contempt or violence.

—Harold H. Watts

CRADDOCK, Charles Egbert. See MURFREE, Mary Noailles.

CRAIK, Mrs. See MULOCK, Dinah Maria.

CRANE, Stephen. American. Born in Newark, New Jersey, 1 November 1871. Educated at schools in Port Jervis, New York, 1878–83, and Asbury Park, New Jersey, 1883–84; Pennington Seminary, 1885–87; Hudson River Institute, and Claverack College, New York, 1888–90; Lafayette College, Easton, Pennsylvania, 1890; Syracuse University, New York, 1891. Lived with Cora Taylor from 1897. Began writing in 1891; settled in New York and worked as a journalist: wrote sketches of New York life for the New York *Press*, 1894; travelled in the American West and Mexico, writing for the Bacheller and Johnson Syndicate, 1895; sent by Bacheller to report on the insurrection in Cuba, 1896; shipwrecked on the voyage, 1897; went to Greece to report the Greco-Turkish War for the New York *Journal*, 1897; settled in England, 1897; reported the Spanish-American War in Cuba for the New York *World*, later for the New York *Journal*, 1898. Tubercular: *Died 5 June 1900.*

Collections

Letters, edited by R. W. Stallman and Lillian Gilkes.   1960.
Works, edited by Fredson Bowers.   10 vols., 1969–75.

Fiction

Maggie, A Girl of the Streets (A Story of New York).   1893.
The Red Badge of Courage: An Episode of the American Civil War.   1895.
George's Mother.   1896.
The Little Regiment and Other Episodes of the American Civil War.   1896.
The Third Violet.   1897.
The Open Boat and Other Tales of Adventure.   1898.
Active Service.   1899.
The Monster and Other Stories.   1899.
Whilomville Stories.   1900.
Wounds in the Rain: War Stories.   1900.
Last Words.   1902.
The O'Ruddy: A Romance, with Robert Barr.   1903.
Sullivan County Sketches, edited by Melvin Schoberlin.   1949; revised edition by R. W. Stallman, as *Sullivan County Tales and Sketches*, 1968.

Play

The Blood of the Martyr.   1940.

Verse

The Black Riders and Other Lines.   1895.
A Souvenir and a Medley: Seven Poems and a Sketch.   1896.
War Is Kind.   1899.

Other

Great Battles of the War.   1901.
Et Cetera: A Collector's Scrap-Book.   1924.
A Battle in Greece.   1936.
Uncollected Writings, edited by Olov W. Fryckstedt.   1963.
The War Despatches, edited by R. W. Stallman and E. R. Hagemann.   1964.
The New York City Sketches and Related Pieces, edited by R. W. Stallman and E. R. Hagemann.   1966.
Notebook, edited by Donald J. and Ellen B. Greiner.   1969.
Crane in the West and Mexico, edited by Joseph Katz.   1970.

Bibliography: *Crane: A Critical Bibliography* by R. W. Stallman, 1972.

Reading List: *Crane* by John Berryman, 1950; *The Poetry of Crane* by Daniel Hoffman, 1957; *Crane* by Edwin H. Cady, 1962; *Crane in England*, 1964, and *Crane, From Parody to Realism*, 1966, both by Eric Solomon; *Crane: A Biography* by R. W. Stallman, 1968; *A Reading of Crane* by Marston LaFrance, 1971; *Crane's Artistry* by Frank Bergon, 1975.

*   *   *

Stephen Crane was a descendant of Methodist ministers and of Revolutionary soldiers. One ancestor was a founder of the city of Newark, New Jersey; a grandfather was a bishop and founder of Syracuse University. His father was a parson, his mother a journalist for religious newspapers. This ancestry of military and civic virtue and literate religious vocation influenced Stephen's responses to experience.

Crane's life was brief; he was dead of tuberculosis before his thirtieth birthday. His career as an author lasted only from 1892 to 1900. Yet he wrote the first naturalistic novel of city life in the United States (*Maggie, A Girl of the Streets*); the greatest novel of the American Civil War, perhaps the best fictional study in English of fear (*The Red Badge of Courage*); and poems which in their avoidance of debilitated Victorian verse conventions seem heralds of the modernist movement (*The Black Riders, War Is Kind*). He wrote incomparable short stories — of shipwreck and survival ("The Open Boat"), of violence in the American West ("The Bride Comes to Yellow Sky," "The Blue Hotel"); a volume of unsentimental local-color stories of a village childhood (*Whilomville Stories*); and a novella ("The Monster") comparable to Ibsen's *An Enemy of the People* in its treatment of alienation and the callousness of society. In addition to these works he was a prolific journalist whose sketches — of war in the Caribbean and the Balkans, of the underside of New York City life, of travels in the American West and Mexico — are stylistically distinguished and raise journalistic occasions to an imaginative intensity close to that in his fiction. Crane was the doomed boy wonder of American literature.

As varied as his subjects were his fictional modes. Critics still debate whether Crane was an impressionist, a realist, a naturalist. With little formal education — he dropped out of college after two semesters, during which he played on the baseball team, smoked cigarettes, and wrote the draft of *Maggie* — he was a natural writer who absorbed from the literature around him the then dominant methods of writing and transformed these with imaginative energy into the instrument of his own purposes. At the time he wrote *Maggie*, his only literary acquaintance was with the Midwestern realist Hamlin Garland. On its appearance William Dean Howells recognized and encouraged the genius of this youth whose work differed so greatly from his own. *The Red Badge* made Crane famous overnight; he was sent by a newspaper syndicate as a correspondent to the Cuban insurrection and the Spanish-American War; later, he covered the war between Greece and Turkey. He went, he said, to test his knowledge in *The Red Badge*. This novel about a conflict that had ended seven years before Crane's birth had been grounded on his experience on the football field, where "the opposing team is the enemy tribe." After seeing war up close, "*The Red Badge*," Crane concluded, "is all right." In fact there were other models beside football: Crane had read Zola's *The Downfall* (*La Débacle*) and Tolstoi's *Sevastopol*; he had studied the reminiscences and memoirs in *The Century Magazine* series "Battles and Leaders of the Civil War"; and he had absorbed and internalized the creed of aesthetic realism held by the war correspondent in Kipling's *The Light That Failed*.

These influences were welded together by a sensibility that found in war the externalization of its obsessive psychological conflicts. There is war everywhere in Crane's work. *Maggie* shows family life in perpetual conflict, the social environment as hostile there as Nature is to the men adrift in "The Open Boat." In "The Blue Hotel," the immigrant Swede, stranded by a blizzard, brings to a frontier outpost the mental image of the violence he expects to find in the West. Crane encapsulated the theme in a brief poem:

289

A man feared that he might find an assassin;
Another that he might find a victim.
One was more wise than the other.

One of his ironic war tales is titled "The Mystery of Heroism." Crane was prepossessed by that mystery; he called *The Red Badge of Courage* "a study of fear." His life was such a study, and a conquest of its subject.

He brought to all of his writings a style at once metaphoric, animistic, striated with color, dense with implication. "An artist," he once wrote, "is nothing but a powerful memory that can move itself at will through certain experiences sideways and every artist must be in some things powerless as a dead snake," thus granting his vocation at once freedom from and subjection to necessity. His influence on later American writers is considerable. His theme of grace under pressure in a masculine world of conflict provided Hemingway with a model, while Crane's metaphoric, ironic style anticipates Flannery O'Connor.

As a poet Crane's work was too fragmentary and his career too brief to affect the glib versifiers of the American 1890's, but after 1912, when the Imagist Movement had begun and the conventions Crane avoided were being defied by the new modernists, he was revived and remembered as a forerunner. His theme is the alienation of man in an uncaring universe. He rebels against the pieties of conventional Christianity, overthrows the rule of its vengeful God, proposes a kinder deity. Certain of his poems, such as "War Is Kind" and "A Man Adrift on a Slim Spar," crystallize the themes of his fiction. This one typifies his parabolic brevity:

A man said to the universe:
"Sir, I exist!"
"However," replied the universe,
"The fact has not created in me
A sense of obligation."

Crane's personal life in the decade of his authorship was as vivid as any of his fictions. As a reporter he frequented the Bowery in New York City, seeking subjects for his sketches. He befriended a woman whom he saw being entrapped by police on a charge of soliciting; after testifying in her defense he was run out of town by the police department. On his way to Cuba to sail aboard the gun-running tug whose shipwreck led him to write "The Open Boat," he met in Jacksonville, Florida, the undivorced wife of a son of the British Governor General of India. Cora Jackson was then the madame of a pleasure parlor. She and Crane lived together as man and wife until his death. Cora went with Stephen to the Balkans as the first woman war correspondent. While in England, as tenants of Morton Frewen's manor house, Brede Place, in Surrey, they entertained Henry James, Joseph Conrad, H. G. Wells, and other notable writers. The preacher's son Stephen Crane lived in notoriety and scandal. He and Cora were spendthrift, always in need of money. His last two years, while sick and dying, were spent desperately in hack work.

Crane remains the most interesting American writer of the nineties. His work is of lasting value; what is local and dated in it (his struggle against the dour God of his fire-eating, Evangelistic background) is subsumed in what anticipates the spiritual negation of the war-torn twentieth century: his sense of the world as a juggernaut of impersonal force against which the precious values of the individual life must be precariously maintained by heroic struggle.

—Daniel Hoffman

CRAWFORD, F(rancis) Marion. American. Born in Bagni di Lucca, Tuscany, Italy, 2 August 1854; son of the sculptor Thomas Crawford. Educated at St. Paul's School, Concord, New Hampshire, 1866–69; Trinity College, Cambridge, 1873; Technische Hochschule, Karlsruhe, Germany, 1874; University of Heidelberg, 1876; Harvard University, Cambridge, Massachusetts, 1881. Married Elizabeth Berdan in 1884; two sons and two daughters. Editor, *Indian Herald*, Allahabad, India, 1879–80; convert to the Roman Catholic Church, 1880; full-time writer from 1882; settled in Sorrento, Italy, 1885, and lived there for the rest of his life. *Died 9 April 1909.*

PUBLICATIONS

Collections

    Novels. 30 vols., 1919.

Fiction

    Mr. Isaacs: A Tale of Modern India. 1882.
    Doctor Claudius: A True Story. 1883.
    To Leeward. 1883.
    A Roman Singer. 1884.
    An American Politician. 1884.
    Zoroaster. 1885.
    A Tale of a Lonely Parish. 1886.
    Saracinesca. 1887.
    Marzio's Crucifix. 1887.
    Paul Patoff. 1887.
    With the Immortals. 1888.
    Greifenstein. 1889.
    Sant' Ilario. 1889.
    A Cigarette-Maker's Romance. 1890.
    Khaled: A Tale of Arabia. 1891.
    The Witch of Prague. 1891.
    The Three Fates. 1892.
    Don Orsino. 1892.
    The Children of the King: A Tale of Southern Italy. 1893.
    Pietro Ghisleri. 1893.
    Marion Darche: A Story Without Comment. 1893.
    Katharine Lauderdale. 1894.
    The Upper Berth (stories). 1894.
    Love in Idleness: A Bar Harbour Tale. 1894.
    Casa Braccio. 1895.
    The Ralstons. 1895.
    Taquisara. 1896.
    Adam Johnstone's Son. 1896.
    A Rose of Yesterday. 1897.
    Corleone: A Tale of Sicily. 1897.
    Via Crucis: A Romance of the Second Crusade. 1899.
    In the Palace of the King: A Love Story of Old Madrid. 1900.
    Marietta, A Maid of Venice. 1901.

291

Cecilia: A Story of Modern Rome. 1902.
Man Overboard! 1903.
The Heart of Rome: A Tale of the "Lost Water." 1903.
Whosoever Shall Offend. 1904.
Soprano: A Portrait. 1905; as *Fair Margaret*, 1905.
A Lady of Rome. 1906.
Arethusa. 1907.
The Little City of Hope: A Christmas Story. 1907.
The Primadonna: A Sequel to Soprano. 1908.
Stradella: An Old Italian Love Tale. 1908.
The Diva's Ruby: A Sequel to Soprano and Primadonna. 1908.
The White Sister. 1909.
The Undesirable Governess. 1910.
Uncanny Tales. 1911; as *Wandering Ghosts*, 1911.

Plays

Doctor Claudius, with Harry St. Maur, from the novel by Crawford (produced 1897).
Francesca Da Rimini (produced 1901). 1902.
The Ideal Wife, from a work by M. Prage (produced 1912).
The White Sister, with Walter Hackett, from the novel by Crawford. 1937.

Other

Our Silver. 1881.
The Novel: What It Is. 1893.
Constaninople. 1895.
Bar Harbor. 1896.
Ave, Roma Immortalis: Studies from the Chronicles of Rome. 2 vols., 1898; revised edition, 1902.
The Rulers of the South, Sicily, Calabria, Malta. 2 vols., 1900; as *Southern Italy and Sicily and the Rulers of the South*, 1905.
Salve Venetia: Gleanings from Venetian History. 2 vols., 1905; as *Venice, The Place and the People*, 1909.

Translator, *The Unknown Life of Christ*, by Nicolai Notovich. 1894.

Reading List: *My Cousin Crawford* by Maud Howe Elliott, 1934; *Crawford* by John Pilkington, Jr., 1964; *The American 1890's: Life and Times of a Lost Generation* by Larzer Ziff, 1966.

*   *   *

F. Marion Crawford was America's most successful novelist at the end of the nineteenth century. He sometimes published three novels a year, simultaneously in New York and London, and Macmillan paid him $10,000 in advance for each of them in the 1890's. All of his 42 novels are marred by haste and a kind of contempt for the esthetics of fiction. In *The Novel: What It Is* Crawford argued that the novel is "an intellectual artistic luxury" that had one essential ingredient, "a story or romance," and one purpose – to entertain. Crawford knew both exotic and lowly places in many lands. He could tell a story easily and naturally, and his fast-moving romances are not impeded by subtleties or significance. He held to traditional values and opposed social, political, and economic change; he upheld the genteel, moral, and ideal in literature and the chivalric code of honor of Christian gentlemen.

The glamor of "the magnificent Marion Crawford," the "Prince of Sorrento," was a factor in his success. He was born in Rome, son of a New England heiress (the sister of Julia Ward Howe) and the Irish-American expatriate sculptor Thomas Crawford, whose circle Hawthorne pictured in *The Marble Faun* (1860). His mother gave her son an international education, designed for an aristocratic genius: private tutors in Rome, St. Paul's School in New Hampshire (which he hated), and additional schooling in England and Germany in preparation for brief periods at Cambridge and Heidelberg. He considered himself both a Roman and an American. He was a linguistic genius and reputedly knew 16 languages. His wide travels gave him a "special and accurate knowledge that created a perfect illusion" (Van Wyck Brooks) of such places as Constantinople (where he was married), St. Petersburg, Munich (where he wrote *A Cigarette-Maker's Romance* and *The Witch of Prague* in 1890), of Iceland and India – as well as Paris, London, and Rome. To a wide audience, many of them attaining great wealth and seeking easy sophistication, Crawford seemed the most cosmopolitan of writers: in a letter to Howells Henry James petulantly called Crawford "a six-penny humbug" – and begged Howells not to betray his jealous outburst!

His first novel *Mr. Isaacs* is the fictional portrait of an enormously wealthy and powerful Persian diamond merchant Crawford had met two years before when he edited a newspaper in Allahabad. With this novel, which anticipated Kipling in its vivid pictures of Indian life, Crawford made himself world famous; Gladstone called it a "literary marvel." Within the same year Crawford published a second semi-biographical novel, *Doctor Claudius*: a Swedish-born Heidelberg Ph.D. inherits an American fortune and marries a Russian countess after saving her inheritance. *A Roman Singer* is based on Crawford's own attempts to become an opera singer. His weakest efforts are the American novels: *An American Politician, Katharine Lauderdale*, and *The Ralstons*. His best are *Saracinesca* and its three sequels, which deal with the Roman social world of his childhood; the others are *Sant' Ilario, Don Orsino*, and *Corleone*. Literary historians exempt these novels from their general condemnation of nineteenth-century melodramatic costume romances and note some other Crawford successes: the English countryside in *A Tale of a Lonely Parish* and the evocation of Phillip II of Spain in *In the Palace of the King*.

—Clarence A. Glasrud

DAHLBERG, Edward. American. Born in Boston, Massachusetts, 22 July 1900; grew up in Kansas City and Cleveland. Educated at the University of California, Berkeley, 1922–23; Columbia University, New York, 1923–25, B.S. in philosophy 1925. Served in World War I. Married 1) Winifred Donlea in 1942; 2) Julia Lawlor in 1967; two children. Writer from 1926; lived in London and Paris, 1926–28; taught at Boston University, 1947; Lecturer in the School of General Education, New York University, 1961–62; Cockefair Professor, 1964–65, and Professor of Language and Literature, 1966, University of Missouri at Kansas City; taught at Columbia University, 1968. Recipient: Longview Foundation Award, 1961; National Institute of Arts and Letters award, 1961; Rockefeller grant, 1965; Ariadne Foundation award, 1970; Cultural Council Foundation award, 1971. Member, National Institute of Arts and Letters, 1968. *Died 27 February 1977.*

PUBLICATIONS

Fiction

>   *Bottom Dogs.*   1929.
>   *From Flushing to Calvary.*   1932.
>   *Kentucky Blue Grass Henry Smith* (story).   1932.
>   *Those Who Perish.*   1934.
>   *Because I Was Flesh.*   1964.
>   *The Olive of Minerva; or, The Comedy of a Cuckold.*   1976.
>   *Bottom Dogs, From Flushing to Calvary, Those Who Perish, and Other Unpublished and Uncollected Works.*   1976.

Verse

>   *Cipango's Hinder Door.*   1965.

Other

>   *Do These Bones Live.*   1941; revised edition, as *Can These Bones Live,* 1960.
>   *Sing, O Barren.*   1947.
>   *The Flea of Sodom.*   1950.
>   *The Sorrows of Priapus.*   1957.
>   *Truth Is More Sacred: A Critical Exchange on Modern Literature,* with Herbert Read.   1961.
>   *Alms for Oblivion: Essays.*   1964.
>   *Reasons of the Heart: Maxims.*   1965.
>   *The Dahlberg Reader.*   1967.
>   *Epitaphs of Our Times: The Letters of Dahlberg.*   1967.
>   *The Leafless American.*   1967.
>   *The Carnal Myth: A Search into Classical Sensuality.*   1968.
>   *The Confessions of Dahlberg.*   1971.
>   *The Gold of Ophir: Travels, Myths and Legends in the New World.*   1972.

Bibliography: *A Bibliography of Dahlberg* by Harold Billings, 1971.

Reading List: *Dahlberg: American Ishmael of Letters* edited by Harold Billings, 1968; *Dahlberg: A Tribute* edited by Jonathan Williams, 1970; *Dahlberg* by Fred Moramarco, 1972.

*   *   *

Edward Dahlberg was the illegitimate son of a lady barber whose hardships and endurance were to be a central subject in his work.

His first book, *Bottom Dogs*, was published with a preface by D. H. Lawrence. Based on his own experience of poverty, it shows the influence of his left-wing political leanings. His next two novels, *From Flushing to Calvary* and *Those Who Perish*, were reportorial pieces of social realism, the first affected by the hardships of the depression, the second by anti-Nazi sentiments, the result of a trip to Germany. For a while, Dahlberg was associated with the Communist Party, but he abandoned politics for aesthetic reasons. He then entered a long period of silence broken only by occasional works of literary criticism such as *Do These Bones Live* and *Sing, O Barren* that examine the heritage of Poe, Thoreau, Melville and other writers, as well as the sexlessness of American literature. Dahlberg's years of study and rumination bore fruit in *Because I Was Flesh*, an autobiography in fictional form. The book is a rewriting of *Bottom Dogs*, but the events and characters are related to literary and mythical antecedents. The prose is aphoristic and affected by classical and Biblical overtones. *Because I Was Flesh* is Dahlberg's most universal book and is already considered a masterpiece of contemporary prose.

In 1965 Dahlberg returned to America after living abroad for many years, mainly in Spain and Ireland. In the last decade of his life, Dahlberg made up for his long silence by publishing on average of a book a year – poems, a collection of aphorisms, essays, fiction, a selection of letters and a literary autobiography entitled *The Confessions of Edward Dahlberg*. Writing in a style reminiscent of Sir Thomas Browne, Dahlberg was a literary Jeremiah, attacking materialism and lamenting the loneliness of human existence. He was also a steadfast foe of modernism, opposed to the work of Faulkner, Hemingway, Pound, Eliot, and Joyce. He felt kinship with Anderson, Dreiser, and William Carlos Williams.

Dahlberg's writing is extremely individualistic, purposefully unfashionable. He thought our age desiccated; he wanted flesh and blood in life as well as literature. He influenced many of his contemporaries but remained an isolated nay-sayer.

—Frank MacShane

————————

DANA, Richard Henry, Jr. American. Born in Cambridge, Massachusetts, 1 August 1815; son of the writer Richard Henry Dana, Sr. Educated at Harvard University, Cambridge, Massachusetts, 1832–34; worked as a sailor on the brig *Pilgrim*, and on the *Alert*, 1834–36; returned to Harvard, 1836–37, graduated 1837; attended Harvard Law School, 1837–40, and taught elocution at Harvard, 1839–40; admitted to the Massachusetts bar, 1840. Married Sarah Watson in 1841; six children. Practised law, specializing in maritime cases, Boston, 1840–78; a Founder, Free Soil Party, 1848; member of the convention for the revision of the Constitution of Massachusetts, 1853; visited England, 1856; United States District Attorney for Massachusetts, 1861–66; visited England again, 1866; Lecturer, Harvard Law School, 1866–68; Member, Massachusetts House of Representatives, and Counsel for the United States in the proceedings against Jefferson Davis, 1867–68; candidate for United States Congress, 1868; appointed minister to England by President Grant, 1876 (appointment not confirmed by the Senate); Senior Counsel for the United States before the Fisheries Commission at Halifax, 1877; lived in Europe, studying and writing on international law, 1878 until his death. Overseer, Harvard University, 1865–77. LL.D.: Harvard University, 1866. *Died 6 January 1882.*

PUBLICATIONS

Prose

> *Two Years Before the Mast: A Personal Narrative of Life at Sea.*   1840; revised edition, 1869; edited by John Haskell Kemble, 1964.
> *The Seaman's Friend.*   1841; as *The Seaman's Manual,* 1841.
> *To Cuba and Back: A Vacation Voyage.*   1859; edited by C. Harvey Gardiner, 1966.
> *Speeches in Stirring Times, and Letters to a Son,* edited by Richard Henry Dana, 3rd.   1910.
> *An Autobiographical Sketch (1815–1842),* edited by Robert F. Metzdorf.   1953.
> *The Journal,* edited by Robert F. Lucis.   1968.

> Editor, *Lectures on Art, and Poems,* by Washington Allston.   2 vols., 1850.
> Editor, *Elements of International Law,* 8th edition, by Henry Wheaton.   1866.

Bibliography: in *Bibliography of American Literature* by Jacob Blanck, 1957.

Reading List: *Dana* by Samuel Shapiro, 1961; *Dana* by Robert L. Gale, 1969.

*   *   *

Richard Henry Dana, Jr., was the author of the best known of three outstanding 19th-century travel books dealing with what were then largely unexplored sections of the American continent. *Two Years Before the Mast* has won a reputation as an adventure story for boys, while the other books, Francis Parkman's *The Oregon Trail* and Lewis Hector Garrard's *Wah-to-yah and the Taos Trail,* survive principally because of their historical, as well as literary, value. Dana would surely have preferred a similar fate for his book; its popularity among boys was a reputation he neither sought nor welcomed.

The popularity of Dana's book among boys is itself curious, for its often complex, if precise, prose might make it seem less desirable than, in particular, *Wah-to-yah,* characterized as it is by a rather colloquial and flowing style. Undoubtedly the major reason for the popularity of Dana's book is its extensive series of high adventures, vividly and objectively described. Parkman and Garrard lived with Indians – but Dana did that and much more. His realistic narrative deals effectively with a wide range of adventures that include not only life on shipboard but also life in what is today the American southwest, then a seemingly exotic region known to most Americans only through rumor. *Two Years Before the Mast* still makes the author's adventures seem exciting and unique, long after the type of customs and way of life he experienced have vanished.

Dana, after the publication of his book, became a lawyer and was never able to duplicate the success of *Two Years Before the Mast.* He published a travel book based on a trip to Canada, and he was the author of a popular handbook for sailors, *The Seaman's Friend,* but neither book has literary interest for readers today.

—Edward Halsey Foster

DAVIES, Robertson. Canadian. Born in Thamesville, Ontario, 28 August 1913. Educated at Upper Canada College, Toronto; Queen's University, Kingston, Ontario; Balliol College, Oxford, 1936–38, B.Litt. 1938. Married Brenda Mathews in 1940; three children. Teacher and actor, Old Vic Theatre School and Repertory Company, London, 1938–40; Literary Editor, *Saturday Night*, Toronto, 1940–42; Editor and Publisher, *Examiner*, Peterborough, Ontario, 1942–63. Since 1960, Professor of English, and since 1962, Master of Massey College, University of Toronto. Formerly, Governor, Stratford Shakespeare Festival, Ontario; Member, Board of Trustees, National Arts Centre. Recipient: Dominion Drama Festival Louis Jouvet Prize, for directing, 1949; Leacock Medal, 1955; Lorne Pierce Medal, 1961; Governor-General's Award, 1973. LL.D.: University of Alberta, Edmonton, 1957; Queen's University, 1962; University of Manitoba, Winnipeg, 1972; D.Litt.: McMaster University, Hamilton, Ontario, 1959; University of Windsor, Ontario, 1971; York University, Toronto, 1973; Memorial University of Newfoundland, St. John's, 1974; University of Western Ontario, London, 1974; McGill University, Montreal, 1974; Trent University, Peterborough, Ontario, 1974; D.C.L.: Bishop's University, Lennoxville, Quebec, 1967; D.C.V.: University of Calgary, Alberta, 1975. Fellow, Royal Society of Canada, 1967. C.C. (Companion, Order of Canada), 1972. Lives in Toronto.

PUBLICATIONS

Fiction

 Tempest-Tost. 1951.
 Leaven of Malice. 1954.
 A Mixture of Frailties. 1958.
 Fifth Business. 1970.
 The Manticore. 1972.
 World of Wonders. 1975.

Plays

 Overlaid (produced 1947). In *Eros at Breakfast and Other Plays,* 1949.
 Voice of the People (produced 1948). In *Eros at Breakfast and Other Plays,* 1949.
 At the Gates of the Righteous (produced 1948). In *Eros at Breakfast and Other Plays,* 1949.
 Hope Deferred (produced 1948). In *Eros at Breakfast and Other Plays,* 1949.
 Fortune My Foe (televised; produced 1948). 1949.
 Eros at Breakfast (produced 1948). In *Eros at Breakfast and Other Plays,* 1949.
 Eros at Breakfast and Other Plays. 1949.
 At My Heart's Core (produced 1950). 1950.
 King Phoenix (produced 1950). In *Hunting Stuart and Other Plays,* 1972.
 A Masque of Aesop (produced 1952). 1952.
 A Jig for the Gypsy (broadcast; produced 1954). 1954.
 Hunting Stuart (produced 1955). In *Hunting Stuart and Other Plays,* 1972.
 Love and Libel; or, The Ogre of the Provincial World, from his novel *Leaven of Malice* (produced 1960).
 A Masque of Mr. Punch (produced 1962). 1963.
 Hunting Stuart and Other Plays (includes *King Phoenix* and *General Confession*). 1972.
 Question Time (produced 1975). 1975.

Radio Plays: *A Jig for the Gypsy*, and others.

Television Plays: *Fortune My Foe, Brothers in the Black Art*, and others.

Other

> *Shakespeare's Boy Actors.*   1939.
> *Shakespeare for Young Players: A Junior Course.*   1942.
> *The Diary of Samuel Marchbanks* (essays).   1947.
> *The Table Talk of Samuel Marchbanks* (essays).   1949.
> *Renown at Stratford: A Record of the Shakespeare Festival in Canada, 1953,* with
>   Tyrone Guthrie and Grant MacDonald.   1953.
> *Twice Have the Trumpets Sounded: A Record of the Stratford Shakespearean Festival in
>   Canada, 1954,* with Tyrone Guthrie.   1954.
> *Thrice the Brinded Cat Hath Mew'd: A Record of the Stratford Shakespearean Festival in
>   Canada, 1955,* with Tyrone Guthrie.   1955.
> *A Voice from the Attic.*   1960.
> *The Personal Art: Reading to Good Purpose.*   1961.
> *Samuel Marchbanks' Almanack.*   1967.
> *Stephen Leacock: Feast of Stephen.*   1970.
> *The Revels History of Drama in English,* vol. 7, with others.   1975.
> *One Half of Davies: Provocative Pronouncements on a Wide Range of Topics.*   1978.

*   *   *

Critics have attempted to read into Robertson Davies's writings a high-flying ambition to construct a parable of the conflict with "the hideous and pervasive forces of materialism." Writing of his own work Davies used Jung's phrase "the Search for the Self" to describe the theme which is central to his novels and to most of his plays. Such pomposities, whether they are expressed by others or by himself, serve only to undervalue Davies by endowing him with the very pretentiousness which from the beginning of his literary career he has set out to destroy. Davies is, in truth, a comic author of considerable skill, conservative in his literary manner but determined to use the sharp edge of satire to reform or to destroy the provincialism which is the prime goal of Canadian society.

His fiction is a small part of his work. He is a sound scholar, a wise critic, a prolific playwright and an elegant essayist, but in these forms only the satirical newspaper columns written in the late 1940's (and collected as *The Diary of Samuel Marchbanks* and *The Table Talk of Samuel Marchbanks*) promised from Davies something more than might come from any other cosmopolitan academic.

Marchbanks, unhesitatingly Canadian and yet unashamedly a twentieth-century successor to Samuel Johnson, applied his caustic fury to the pettiness of life in Canada. For the Salterton trilogy which followed Davies forsook the tradition of Johnson and took over the mantle of Anthony Trollope. Davies's Barchester is Kingston, Ontario, thinly disguised as Salterton. *Tempest-Tost*, the first in the series, is an uproarious travesty of Shakespeare's play. The subsequent novels, *Leaven of Malice* and *A Mixture of Frailties*, are in purpose more solemn and in achievement less satirically brisk, but Davies does not lose his skill in devising romance so that it will serve his purpose as a commentator on Canadian culture.

His second triology also has its origins in small-town Ontario. But Davies's ambitions have become extravagant, and their fulfilment only just short of complete. A snowball thrown by Percy Boyd Staunton at his friend Dunstan Ramsay hits instead the Baptist minister's pregnant wife and so her child, Magnus Eisengrim, is born eighty days too soon: from that simple beginning develops three novels of rare power. *The Fifth Business* belongs primarily to Ramsay, rational and determined, *The Manticore* to Staunton, the man of instinct, and

World of Wonders to the magician Eisengrim. But the distinctive emphasis in each book is little more than a device, a platform from which Davies can range the world of reality, the world of ideas and the other-world of illusion. The theatre, Canada, Passchendaele, circus-life, Switzerland, love, Jungian psychology, London, teaching, myth, the international film industry: there is no logical progression for the catalogue of Davies's concerns in a triology which is at times elegant, often comic and always admirably bold.

—J. E. Morpurgo

DAVIN, Dan(iel Marcus). New Zealander. Born in Invercargill, New Zealand, 1 September 1913. Educated at Marist Brothers School, Invercargill; Sacred Heart College, Auckland; Otago University, Dunedin, M.A. 1936; Balliol College, Oxford (Rhodes Scholar), 1936–39, B.A. 1939, M.A. 1945. Served in the Royal Warwickshire Regiment, 1939–40, and in the New Zealand Division, 1940–45: Major; mentioned in despatches; M.B.E. (Member, Order of the British Empire), 1945. Married Winifred Gonley in 1939; three daughters. Junior Assistant Secretary, 1946–48, and Assistant Secretary, 1948–69, Clarendon Press, Oxford. Since 1970, Deputy Secretary to the Delegates, and since 1974, Director of the Academic Division, Oxford University Press. Fellow of Balliol College, 1965. Fellow of the Royal Society of Arts. Lives in Oxford.

PUBLICATIONS

Fiction

> *Cliffs of Fall.* 1945.
> *The Gorse Blooms Pale* (stories). 1947.
> *For the Rest of Our Lives.* 1947.
> *Roads from Home.* 1949.
> *The Sullen Bell.* 1956.
> *No Remittance.* 1959.
> *Not Here, Not Now.* 1970.
> *Brides of Price.* 1972.
> *Breathing Spaces* (stories). 1975.

Other

> *An Introduction to English Literature,* with John Mulgan. 1947.
> *Crete.* 1953.
> *Writing in New Zealand: The New Zealand Novel,* with W. K. Davin. 1956.
> *Katherine Mansfield in Her Letters.* 1959.
> *Closing Times* (memoirs). 1975.
>
> Editor, *New Zealand Short Stories.* 1953.
> Editor, *Selected Stories,* by Katherine Mansfield. 1953.
> Editor, *English Short Stories of Today: Second Series.* 1958.

Reading List: "Davin: Novelist of Exile" by James Bertram, in *Meanjin 32*, June 1973; "Davin's *Roads from Home*" by H. Winston Rhodes, in *Critical Essays on the New Zealand Novel* edited by Cherry Hankin, 1976; Introduction by Lawrence Jones to *Roads from Home*, 1976.

*   *   *

When he published three novels and a volume of short stories in the first four years following World War II, Dan Davin established himself as the leading New Zealand novelist of his generation. Since then, his devotion to a difficult profession and his continued expatriation have kept him from consolidating that position (he has noted that "the expatriate writer lives on a diminishing capital of deeply felt knowledge"). However, with his gifts as provincial historian, sceptical philosopher, and psychological moralist, he has made a significant contribution to New Zealand fiction.

As a provincial historian with a critical but loving eye, he has captured the Irish Catholic enclave within the Southland community in the 1920's and 1930's, seen against a sharply realised physical background of Invercargill and the surrounding countryside. The Connolly family, of many of the stories in *The Gorse Blooms Pale* and *Breathing Spaces*, and the Hogan family, of *Roads from Home*, most fully exemplify this provincial sub-culture. Richard Kane, in *No Remittance*, provides an outside perspective on it, for he, a charming English scoundrel, marries into it, and the body of the novel is made up of his retrospective account of his struggles with it and absorption into it over a period of fifty years.

In his other novels, Davin shows his Southland characters taking various "roads from home." The shortest road is that to Dunedin and the University of Otago, where the heroes of *Cliffs of Fall* and *Not Here, Not Now* receive their intellectual and sexual initiations and do battle with puritanism in its Scottish Presbyterian rather than its Irish Catholic form. A longer road takes the characters of some of the short stories and of *For the Rest of Our Lives* to the Mediterranean theatre of World War II, where they become part of a special and temporary community of men, the New Zealand Division, whose structure and mores Davin observes as closely as he had those of Irish Southland. For those who survive that journey, the road goes on to England. *The Sullen Bell* pictures expatriate New Zealanders in London trying to start life anew after the intensity and the losses of the war. *Brides of Price* looks at Oxford from the standpoint of a New Zealander long established there, and then brings the hero on a return visit to New Zealand (as do several stories in *Breathing Spaces*).

If the provincial historian in Davin has defined a social environment, the philosopher has defined a larger metaphysical environment. A sceptical, naturalistic philosophy underlies the books and becomes explicit in the meditations of the characters and the author, a vision of man in an indifferent natural universe from which he is estranged by his consciousness but to which he is subject. Man's plight is evident in the sexual impulse which shows us that "we are still creatures of the force that dragged us from the protoplasm to humanity," in the inevitable erosion of all joy and accomplishment by time, and in "the inescapable and unacceptable fact of death."

Davin has said that "for the novelist the web should be important only because it is indispensable to the struggle of the spider and the fly," and in his fiction both the metaphysical and the social webs are there to form the environment against which his characters define themselves. The psychological moralist in Davin focuses on the attempts of those characters to come to terms with nature, society, and a self "that could not exist without other selves" but "could never quite extend to them the priority and autonomy which it instinctively claimed for itself." The stories about childhood and adolescence in Invercargill show the young protagonists awakening to the nature and complexity of self and world. The Southland and Dunedin novels show their young men struggling against the "subtle web of obligation" woven by family and others who would limit their full development of themselves. In *Cliffs of Fall*, Mark Burke, melodramatically Dostoevskian, destroys himself when he attempts to assert his superiority to nature and community by killing his pregnant girl. In *Roads from Home*, John and Ned Hogan are caught in dilemmas in which they painfully realize that their needs inevitably conflict with the needs of others. In *Not Here, Not Now*, Martin Cody tries to reconcile love and ambition, having to face the costs to family, fiancée, and self of his determined drive for a Rhodes Scholarship and the opportunity to develop his talents.

The other novels explore more mature characters' attempts to accomodate themselves to a complex and imperfect world. Such an accomodation requires that one be sceptical and without illusions, but not cynical or despairing. In *For the Rest of Our Lives*, Tony Brandon is destroyed, but Frank Fahey and To O'Dwyer achieve at least an armed truce with existence. In *The Sullen Bell*, Hugh Egan moves beyond despair to a positive acceptance, while Adam Mahon in *Brides of Price*, who has come to believe in nothing "except how complex everything was," arrives at an unexpectedly satisfactory accommodation.

Davin's problem as novelist has been how to bring the social historian, the philosopher, and the psychological moralist together in a structure that is both inclusive and coherent. He has succeeded fully only within the more limited scope of such stories as "Saturday Night" and "The Quiet One." All of the novels are flawed, for in *Cliffs of Fall*, *Roads from Home*, and *The Sullen Bell* melodramatic plotting brings unity at the expense of complexity (the too-neat plotting of *Brides of Price* is carried out more playfully), while *For the Rest of Our Lives*, *No Remittance*, and *Not Here, Not Now* achieve a chronicle-like inclusiveness at the expense of formal coherence. However, in all of the novels there are individual scenes and entire sequences in which Davin brings his gifts together, setting fully developed characters within a convincing social environment, the whole given depth and universality by the philosophic meditations.

—Lawrence Jones

DAVIS, Arthur Hoey.   See **RUDD, Steele.**

DAVIS, Rebecca (Blaine) Harding.   American.   Born in Washington, Pennsylvania, 24 June 1831; moved with her family to Alabama, then to Wheeling, West Virginia. Largely self-educated. Married L. Clarke Davis in 1863 (died, 1904); two sons, including Richard Harding Davis, *q.v.*, and one daughter. Professional writer from 1861; lived in Philadelphia, 1863 until her death; member of the editorial staff of the *New York Tribune* from 1869. *Died 29 September 1910.*

PUBLICATIONS

Fiction

Margret Howth: A Story of Today.   1862.
Dallas Galbraith.   1868.

Waiting for the Verdict. 1868.
Kitty's Choice (stories). 1874(?).
John Andross. 1874.
A Law unto Herself. 1878.
Natasqua. 1886.
Kent Hampden (juvenile). 1892.
Silhouettes of American Life. 1892.
Dr. Warrick's Daughters. 1896.
Frances Waldeaux. 1897.

Other

Pro Aris et Focis: A Plea for Our Altars and Hearths. 1870.
Bits of Gossip. 1904.

Reading List: *The Richard Harding Davis Years: A Biography of a Mother and Son* by Gerald Langford, 1961.

*   *   *

When Rebecca Harding Davis died in 1910, she was remembered in the New York *Times* obituary primarily as the mother of Richard Harding Davis, secondarily as a novelist who had, in 1861, written a story about the "grinding life of the working people" that was so stern in its realism that "many thought the author must be a man." Seventy years after her death, aside from an occasional mention of that story, "Life in the Iron Mills," in literary histories, her work is almost entirely unknown, although in recent years feminist critics such as Tillie Olson have sought to reclaim her from obscurity. Mrs. Davis was not a prolific writer – some dozen works, novels, short stories, and improving essays during a writing career of 40 years – and not a particularly good one. Her plots are slipshod, her prose awkward. Her chief gift lies in the creation of character. But having acknowledged her limitations, a critic must recognize her achievement. She lived for her first thirty-two years the proper life of a middle-class spinster in the frontier industrial town of Wheeling, West Virginia, out of touch with literary circles, restricted in her social contacts. Yet she wrought out of this limited life a coherent theory of literary realism that preceded by a quarter of a century the admonition of William Dean Howells that fiction ought to be true to the life of actual men and women.

In her first, and most important, novel, *Margret Howth: A Story of Today*, she attacks her readers' preference for "idylls delicately tinted." She wants them instead to "dig into this commonplace, this vulgar American life and see what is in it." She finds "a new and awful significance" in the grim underlife of the industrial city where workers live thwarted lives amidst the "white leprosy of poverty." Her heroine, Margret, has been deserted by her fiancé and has gone to work as a bookkeeper in a woolen mill to support her ill and aging parents. The novel is a romance, and ultimately her fiancé is restored to his senses and her arms, but in the course of the narrative, as in "Life in the Iron Mills," Mrs. Davis provides a fully realized image of the oppressive noise, stench, and grime of industrial work. In addition, she creates in Margret a new kind of heroine – plain, blunt, occasionally pettish about the sacrifices she is required to make. Margret is the first of a series of Davis heroines who are, as one is described in a later novel, "built for use and not for show."

Mrs. Davis always wrote about contemporary issues – the Civil War, the problem of the free black, and, in *John Andross* (probably her strongest work), political corruption. Contemporary critics were not kind to her. They found her subjects disagreeable, her prose mawkish, her attitude overly didactic. But one critic, writing in *The Nation* in 1878, acknowledged that despite these flaws she contrived in her "grim and powerful etchings" to evoke the American atmosphere, "its vague excitement, its strife of effort, its varying possibilities." That is an apter summary of her contribution to American letters than the *Times* obituary.

—Louise Duus

DAVIS, Richard Harding. American. Born in Philadelphia, Pennsylvania, 18 April 1864; son of Rebecca Harding Davis, *q.v.* Educated at the Episcopal Academy, Swarthmore, Pennsylvania; Ulrich's Preparatory School, Bethlehem, Pennsylvania; Lehigh University, Bethlehem; Johns Hopkins University, Baltimore. Married 1) Cecil Clark in 1899 (divorced, 1910); 2) Elizabeth G. McEvoy in 1912, one daughter. Journalist from 1886: Reporter, *Philadelphia Record*, 1886, Philadelphia *Press*, 1887–88, and the *New York Sun*, 1889–90; Managing Editor, *Harper's Weekly*, New York, 1890; Correspondent for various newspapers and journals, including *Harper's Monthly*, *New York Sun*, and *Collier's Weekly*, from 1890: covered the Queen's Jubilee in London, Spanish War in Cuba, the Greco-Turkish War, Spanish-American War, Boer War, and the First World War: most widely known reporter of his generation. Fellow of the Royal Geographical Society (U.K.). *Died 11 April 1916.*

PUBLICATIONS

Collections

> *From "Gallegher" to "The Deserter": The Best Stories*, edited by Roger Burlinghame. 1927.

Fiction

> *Gallegher and Other Stories.* 1891.
> *Stories for Boys.* 1891.
> *Van Bibber and Others* (stories). 1892.
> *The Exiles and Other Stories.* 1896.
> *Cinderella and Other Stories.* 1896.
> *Soldiers of Fortune.* 1897.
> *The King's Jackal.* 1898.
> *The Lion and the Unicorn.* 1899.
> *In the Fog.* 1901.
> *Ranson's Folly.* 1902.
> *Captain Macklin, His Memoirs.* 1902.
> *Real Soldiers of Fortune.* 1906.
> *The Scarlet Car.* 1907.
> *Vera the Medium.* 1908.
> *The White Mice.* 1909.
> *Once upon a Time.* 1910.

The Man Who Could Not Lose (stories).   1911.
The Red Cross Girl (stories).   1913.
The Lost Road (stories).   1913.
The Boy Scout (stories).   1914.
Somewhere in France (stories).   1915.
Novels and Stories.   12 vols., 1916.

Plays

The Princess Aline.   1895.
The Dictator (produced 1905).   In *Farces,* 1906.
Miss Civilization, from a story by James Harvey Smith.   1905.
Farces: The Dictator, The Galloper, Miss Civilization.   1906.
A Yankee Tourist, music by Alfred G. Robyn, lyrics by Wallace Irwin (produced ?).
   Music published 1907.
The Consul.   1911.
Blackmail (produced 1912).
Who's Who.   1913.
Peace Manoeuvres.   1914.
The Zone Police.   1914.

Other

The Adventures of My Freshman.   1884.
The West from a Car-Window.   1892.
The Rulers of the Mediterranean.   1894.
Our English Cousins.   1894.
About Paris.   1895.
Three Gringos in Venezuela and Central America.   1896.
Dr. Jameson's Raiders vs. the Johannesburg Reformers.   1897.
Cuba in War Time.   1897.
A Year from a Reporter's Note-Book.   1898.
The Cuban and Puerto Rican Campaigns.   1898.
With Both Armies in South Africa.   1900.
The Congo and Coasts of Africa.   1907.
Notes of a War Correspondent.   1910.
With the Allies.   1914.
The New Sing Sing.   1915.
With the French in France and Salonika.   1916.
Adventures and Letters, edited by Charles Belmont Davis.   1917.

Bibliography: in *Bibliography of American Literature* by Jacob Blanck, 1957.

Reading List: *Davis: His Day* by Fairfax D. Downey, 1933; *The Davis Years: A Biography of a Mother and Son* by Gerald Langford, 1961.

*   *   *

Although the close connection between journalistic and fictional writing in the late 19th century in America has never been adequately analyzed, critics have often claimed that Richard Harding Davis failed as a writer of fiction because he excelled as a journalist. Such a judgment may be less than accurate, for Davis incorporated in his fiction the best qualities of his journalism – his quick recognition of the picturesque, his unerring selection of interest-arousing features, his keen eye for external detail, his easy phrasing of remarkably lively impressionistic passages, his youthful appreciation of adventure and movement. These qualities explain his immense contemporary popularity.

But beneath the pace and vivid detail and youthful verve of Davis's fiction, a certain emptiness bothered the serious critics. Journalistic superficiality and haste were blamed. "Smart and shallow," Ludwig Lewisohn briefly intoned in *Expression in America* (1932); and others had said much the same thing. Davis wrote too much too rapidly. He never probed beneath the surfaces. Although clever, he was unconvincing; although satisfying, never profound. At his best he exhibited impressive dramatic power, but too often the drama drifted into theatricality. His stories always charmed, but they were rarely memorable. Those who waited for Davis's exceptional promise to be fulfilled, waited in vain. "Like many handsome and idolized American college men," wrote Francis Hackett in the *New Republic* (2 March 1918), Davis "never quite graduated." Although his fiction excited, it did not confront or deal meaningfully with those issues of humanity that contribute timelessness to a literary work.

Despite the reluctant acknowledgment of serious literary critics, however, and despite their occasional condescending tributes to Davis as the best of the journalistic novelists, his work was not without value in his own time, nor is it in ours. He was the very symbol of achievement for the mass of Americans at the turn of the century, and so serves as an index to a cultural state. Not only was he the visible embodiment of the exuberant life style of the Strenuous Age, but he was also a vocal exponent of ideals that for many readers pointed direction in their dreams. Further, in both his journalistic and his fictional work, he, perhaps better than any other writer, preserved "for all ages," as Thomas Beer noted in *Liberty* (October 1924), "the adventurous, expansionist spirit of the decades that ushered in the twentieth century, the world war, and our own times."

—Clayton L. Eichelberger

DEFOE, Daniel.   English.   Born in London c. 1660. Educated at Charles Morton's Academy, London. Married Mary Tuffley; seven children. Worked as a hosiery maker, and commission merchant: bankrupt, 1692; associated with a tile works in Tilbury, which failed, 1703; Accountant to the Commissioners of the Glass Duty, 1695–99; pilloried, gaoled, and fined for *The Shortest Way with Dissenters*, 1703–04; political writer and confidential agent for Robert Harley, later Earl of Oxford, 1704–11; Editor of *The Review of the Affairs of France, and of All Europe*, 1704–13; carried out various government commissions and wrote pro-government pamphlets in the 1710's; contributed to various periodicals, and edited *The Manufacturer*, 1720, and *The Director*, 1720–21. *Died 26 April 1731.*

PUBLICATIONS

Collections

  Novels, edited by Sir Walter Scott.   12 vols., 1810.
  Novels and Miscellaneous Works.   20 vols., 1840–41.
  Romances and Narratives, edited by G. A. Aitken.   16 vols., 1895.
  Works, edited by G. H. Maynadier.   16 vols., 1903–04.
  Novels and Selected Writings.   14 vols., 1927–28.

Letters, edited by George Harris Healey.   1955.
Selected Poetry and Prose, edited by M. Schugrue.   1968.
Selected Writings, edited by James T. Boulton.   1975.

Fiction

The Consolidator; or, Memoirs of Sundry Transactions from the World in the Moon.   1705; selections, as *A Journey to the World in the Moon*, 1705, *A Letter from the Man in the Moon*, 1705, and *A Second and More Strange Voyage to the World in the Moon*, 1705.

The Memoirs of Mair, Alexander Ramkins, A Highland Officer.   1718; edited by James T. Boulton, 1970.

The Life and Strange Surprising Adventures of Robinson Crusoe, of York, Mariner.   1719; *Further Adventures*, 1719; part 1 edited by J. Donald Crowley, 1972; edited by Michael Shinagel, 1975.

The King of Pirates, Being an Account of the Famous Enterprises of Captain Avery.   1719.

Memoirs of a Cavalier; or, A Military Journal of the Wars in Germany, and the Wars in England, 1632 to 1648.   1720; edited by James T. Boulton, 1972.

The Life, Adventures, and Piracies of the Famous Captain Singleton.   1720; edited by Shiv Kumar, 1969.

Serious Reflections During the Life and Surprising Adventures of Robinson Crusoe, with His Vision of the Angelic World.   1720.

The History of the Life and Adventures of Mr. Duncan Campbell.   1720; as *The Supernatural Philosopher*, by William Bond, 1728 (perhaps by Bond).

The Fortunes and Misfortunes of the Famous Moll Flanders.   1722; revised edition, 1722, 1723; as *Fortune's Fickle Distribution*, 1730; as *The History of Laetitia Atkins*, 1776; edited by George A. Starr, 1972.

The History and Remarkable Life of the Truly Honourable Col. Jacque, Commonly Called Col. Jack.   1722; edited by Samuel Monk, 1965.

A Journal of the Plague Year, 1665.   1722; as *The History of the Great Plague in London*, 1754; edited by Louis A. Landa, 1969.

The Fortunate Mistress; or, A History of the Life and Vast Variety of Fortunes of Mademoiselle de Beleau, The Lady Roxana, in the Time of King Charles II.   1724; edited by Jane Jack, 1964.

A Narrative of All the Robberies, Escapes, etc. of John Sheppard.   1724; edited by H. Bleackley, in *Jack Sheppard*, 1933.

The History of the Remarkable Life of John Sheppard.   1724; edited by H. Bleackley, in *Jack Sheppard*, 1933.

A New Voyage round the World, by a Course Never Sailed Before.   1724.

The Life of Jonathan Wild, from His Birth to His Death.   1725.

The True and Genuine Account of the Life and Actions of the Late Jonathan Wild.   1725; edited by W. Follett, with *Jonathan Wild* by Henry Fielding, 1926.

The Four Years Voyages of Capt. George Roberts.   1726.

The Memoirs of an English Officer Who Served in the Dutch War in 1672 to the Peace of Utrecht in 1713, by Captain George Carleton.   1728; as *A True and Genuine History of the Last Two Wars*, 1740; as *The Memoirs of Cap. George Carleton*, 1743.

Verse

A New Discovery of an Old Intrigue: A Satire Leveled at Treachery and Ambition.   1691; edited by M. E. Campbell, 1938.

The Character of the Late Dr. Samuel Annesley, by Way of Elegy. 1697.
The Pacificator. 1700.
The True-Born Englishman: A Satire. 1701; revised edition, 1701, 1716.
Reformation of Manners: A Satire. 1702.
The Spanish Descent. 1702.
More Reformation: A Satire upon Himself. 1703.
A Hymn to the Pillory. 1703.
A Hymn to the Funeral Sermon. 1703.
*An Elegy on the Author of The True-Born Englishman, with an Essay on the Late
    Storm.* 1704; as *The Live Man's Elegy,* 1704.
A Hymn to Victory. 1704.
The Double Welcome: A Poem to the Duke of Marlbro. 1705.
The Diet of Poland: A Satire. 1705.
A Hymn to Peace. 1706.
Jure Divino: A Satire. 1706.
Hymn for the Thanksgiving. 1706.
The Vision. 1706.
Caledonia: A Poem in Honour of Scotland and the Scots Nation. 1706.
A Hymn to the Mob. 1715.

Other (a selection)

*The Englishman's Choice and True Interest in a Vigorous Prosecution of the War Against
    France.* 1694.
An Essay upon Projects. 1697; as *Essays upon Several Projects,* 1702.
An Enquiry into the Occasional Conformity of Dissenters. 1698.
*An Argument Showing That a Standing Army Is Not Inconsistent with a Free
    Government.* 1698.
*The Poor Man's Plea for a Reformation of Manners and Suppressing Immorality in the
    Nation.* 1698.
The Two Great Questions Considered. 1700.
The Six Distinguishing Characters of a Parliament-Man. 1701.
The Succession to the Crown of England Considered. 1701.
*Good Advice to the Ladies, Shewing That as the World Goes, and Is Likely to Go, The Best
    Way Is for Them to Keep Unmarried.* 1702; as *A Timely Caution,* 1728.
An Enquiry into Occasional Conformity. 1702.
*The Shortest Way with the Dissenters; or, Proposals for the Establishment of the
    Church.* 1702.
King William's Affection to the Church of England Examined. 1703.
The Shortest Way to Peace and Union. 1703.
A Collection of the Writings. 1703.
A True Collection of the Writings. 1703; revised edition, 1705; vol. 2, 1705.
More Short Ways with the Dissenters. 1704.
*The Storm; or, A Collection of the Most Remarkable Casualties and Disasters Which
    Happened in the Late Dreadful Tempest.* 1704.
Giving Alms No Charity, and Employing the Poor a Grievance to the Nation. 1704.
*The Parallel; or, Persecution of Protestants the Shortest Way to Prevent the Growth of
    Popery in Ireland.* 1705(?).
An Essay at Removing National Prejudices Against a Union with Scotland. 6 vols.,
    1706–07.
A True Relation of the Apparition of One Mrs. Veal. 1706.
The History of the Union of Great Britain. 1709.
*A Collection of the Several Addresses Concerning the Conception and Birth of the
    Pretended Prince of Wales.* 1710.

An Essay upon Public Credit. 1710.

An Essay upon Loans. 1710.

The Secret History of the October Club. 1711; part 2, 1711.

An Essay upon the Trade to Africa. 1711.

An Essay on the South Sea Trade. 1712.

A Defence of the Allies and the Late Ministry; or, Remarks upon the Tories' New Idol. 1712.

Hannibal at the Gates; or, The Progress of Jacobitism, with the Present Danger of the Pretender. 1712; revised edition, 1714.

Memoirs of Count Tariff. 1713.

An Essay on the Treaty of Commerce with France. 1713.

A Brief Account of the Present State of the African Trade. 1713.

Reasons Against the Succession of the House of Hanover. 1713.

And What If the Pretender Should Come? 1713.

An Answer to A Question That No Body Thinks of, viz, But What If the Queen Should Die? 1713.

A Letter to the Dissenters. 1713.

Memoirs of John Duke of Melfort, Being an Account of the Secret Intrigues of the Chevalier de S. George. 1714.

The Secret History of the White Staff. 1714; part 2, 1714; part 3, 1715.

A Secret History of One Year. 1714.

An Appeal to Honour and Justice, Being a True Account of His Conduct in Public Affairs (autobiography). 1715.

The Family Instructor. 2 vols., 1715–18.

The History of the Wars of His Present Majesty Charles XII, King of Sweden. 1715; revised edition, 1720.

Memoirs of the Church of Scotland. 1717.

The Conduct of Robert Walpole from the Beginning of the Reign of Queen Anne. 1717.

A Short View of the Conduct of the King of Sweden. 1717.

Memoirs of the Life and Eminent Conduct of Daniel Williams, D.D. 1718.

A History of the Last Session of the Present Parliament, with a Correct List of Both Houses. 1718.

The History of the Reign of King George. 1718.

The Anatomy of Exchange Alley; or, A System of Stock-Jobbing. 1719.

An Historical Account of the Voyages and Adventures of Sir Walter Raleigh. 1720.

Religious Courtship, Being Historical Discourses on the Necessity of Marrying Religious Husbands and Wives Only. 1722.

Due Preparations for the Plague as Well for Soul as Body. 1722.

An Impartial History of the Life and Actions of Peter Alexowitz, Czar of Muscovy. 1722.

A General History of the Robberies and Murders of the Most Notorious Pirates, by Captain Charles Johnson. 1724; part 2, as *The History of the Pirates*, 1728; edited by Manuel Schonhorn, 1972.

A Tour Thro' the Whole Island of Great Britain. 3 vols., 1724–26; edited by Pat Rogers, 1971.

An Account of the Conduct and Proceedings of the Late John Gow, Alias Smith, Captain of the Late Pirates. 1725; edited by J. R. Russell, 1890.

The Complete English Tradesman, in Familiar Letters. 2 vols., 1725–27.

A Brief Historical Account of the Lives of the Six Notorious Street-Robbers Executed at Kingston. 1726.

An Essay upon Literature; or, An Enquiry into the Antiquity and Original of Letters Proving that the Two Tables Written by the Finger of God in Mount Sinai Was the First Writing in the World. 1726.

The Political History of the Devil. 1726.

Unparalleled Cruelty; or, The Trial of Captain Jeane of Bristol Who Was Convicted for

the Murder of His Cabin-Boy. 1726.
Mere Nature Delineated; or, A Body Without a Soul, Being Observations upon a Young Forester from Germany. 1726.
Some Considerations upon Street-Walkers. 1726.
A System of Magic; or, A History of the Black Art. 1726.
Conjugal Lewdness; or, Matrimonial Whoredom. 1727; as *A Treatise Concerning the Use and Abuse of the Marriage Bed,* 1727; edited by Maximillian E. Novak, 1967.
An Essay on the History and Reality of Apparitions. 1727; as *The Secrets of the Invisible World Disclosed; or, An Universal History of Apparitions,* 1728.
Augusta Triumphans; or, The Way to Make London the Most Flourishing City in the Universe. 1728; revised edition, as *The Generous Projector; or, A Friendly Proposal to Prevent Murder and Other Enormous Abuses,* 1731.
A Plan of the English Commerce, Being a Complete Prospect of the Trade of This Nation as Well the Home Trade as the Foreign. 1728; revised edition, 1730.
Atlas Maritimus and Commercialis; or, A General View of the World So Far as It Relates to Trade and Navigation. 1728.
Madagascar; or, Robert Drury's Journal During Fifteen Years Captivity on That Island, revised and partly written by Defoe. 1729.
The Complete English Gentleman, edited by K. D. Bülbring. 1890.
Of Royall Education: A Fragmentary Treatise, edited by K. D. Bülbring. 1895.
A Review of the Affairs of France, and of All Europe (other minor name changes are used; Defoe's journal covers 1704–13), edited by A. W. Secord. 22 vols., 1938; *Index* by W. L. Payne, 1948.
The Meditations (1681), edited by George Harris Healey. 1946.
The Best of Defoe's Review, edited by W. L. Payne. 1951.
The Versatile Defoe (uncollected non-fiction works), edited by Laura Curtis. 1978.

Editor, *A Collection of Miscellany Letters, Selected Out of Mist's Weekly Journal.* 4 vols., 1722.

Bibliography: *A Checklist of the Writings of Defoe* by J. R. Moore, 1960, revised edition, 1961; *New Cambridge Bibliography of English Literature 2,* 1971; "An Annotated Bibliography of Works about Defoe 1719–1974" by W. L. Payne, 3 parts, in *Bulletin of Bibliography,* 1975.

Reading List: *The Early Masters of English Fiction* by Alan D. McKillop, 1956; *Economics and the Fiction of Defoe,* 1962, and *Defoe and the Nature of Man,* 1963, both by Maximillian E. Novak; *The Rise of the Novel* by Ian Watt, 1963; *Defoe and Spiritual Autobiography,* 1965, and *Defoe and Casuistry,* 1971, both by George A. Starr; *The Reluctant Pilgrim* by J. Paul Hunter, 1966; *Defoe and Middle-Class Gentility* by Michael Shinagel, 1968; *Defoe: A Critical Study* by James Sutherland, 1971; "The Displaced Self in the Novels of Defoe" by Homer O. Brown, in *Journal of English Literary History 38,* 1971; *Defoe: The Critical Heritage* edited by Pat Rogers, 1972; *Defoe and the Novel* by Everett Zimmerman, 1975; *Defoe's Narrative: Situations and Structures* by John J. Richetti, 1975; *Defoe: A Collection of Critical Essays* edited by Max Byrd, 1976.

*   *   *

It is understandable that students of Daniel Defoe should draw attention to the scope and variety of his work – more than 550 separate publications, if we include pamphlets, broadsides, and occasional pieces. His journalism by itself would fill several fat volumes, with the *Review* (1704–13) extending to well over a thousand issues, all from his own hand. He was among the best informed political and economic pamphleteers of his time, and from the time of *The Shortest Way with the Dissenters* (1702) his productions in this area consistently attracted intense national comment and vociferous opposition. His early vein as a satiric poet worked itself out by about 1710, but not before works such as *The True-Born Englishman* and *Jure Divino* had provoked an immense controversy. From the beginning Defoe had the gift of exciting attention. His ghost story *The Apparition of Mrs. Veal* foreshadowed later writings on parapsychology, a century or more prior to the real currency of this genre. His collection of disaster tales, *The Storm*, brings a new actuality and reportorial skill to the conventional mode of "Providence displayed." And, at the very start of his writing career, *An Essay upon Projects* already indicates the breadth of his humanitarian concerns, along with a forceful manner of presentation sharply distinguished from the run of contemporary schemes and proposals.

But equally it is not surprising that the general reading public should have settled on his later work, the novels in particular, as a centre of interest. Something really did change in 1719 when Defoe, rising sixty, produced the first part of *Robinson Crusoe*. Up till then he had been an author of high talent, all too explicably a man famous in his own day who gave little sign of transcending the forms and subject-matter familiar to the contemporary audience. *Robinson Crusoe* is his most deeply original book, though paradoxically it is one with all kinds of roots in earlier modes of literary expression. After its appearance Defoe showed himself regularly a writer of genius. He brought a new purpose and authority to standard forms such as travel books, lives of pirates and criminals, conduct-manuals, sociological tracts, and economic surveys. To this period belongs what may well have been his favourite undertaking, the life of Sir Walter Raleigh (1720). Some of his most characteristic works appeared in a cluster around the middle of the decade. There is the boldly dramatic *General History of the Pyrates*, written under the pseudonym of Captain Charles Johnson, which did more than any other single work to create the image of piracy handed down over many generations. There is the *Tour thro' the Whole Island of Great Britain*, which turns the dull, sub-artistic genre of the guide-book into a wonderfully evocative portrait of the nation. There is still no survey of Britain which conveys so powerfully the sense of a people living and working, of a landscape and a social environment, of a way of life frozen for ever by exact observation and shrewd insight. And there is *The Complete English Tradesman*, a strange, anxious, urgent book: a vocational manual which celebrates the grandeurs of a business community but at the same time explores the miseries of its condition. It is as though an existentialist had rewritten Samuel Smiles. Other works of sharp interest include *A General History of Discoveries and Improvements* and *The Political History of the Devil*. Many people have deplored the fact that Pope saw fit to give Defoe a niche in *The Dunciad* (1728), since we know the poet retained a fair amount of admiration for his victim. Viewing the matter differently, we might instead regret the lost opportunity to instal Defoe as King of the Dunces; he was certainly the individual writer who had brought Grub Street themes and idiom into high literature.

So it is with his masterpiece, indeed. *Robinson Crusoe* can be analysed down to component parts which look like the ingredients for minor art. It draws on many traditions: the narratives of voyages and discoveries which were then so popular, the spiritual guides and manuals of right living, the biographies of puritan converts, the tales of providential escape from natural hazards. Crusoe may be plausibly interpreted as a social misfit, unwisely rebelling against the safe "middle station" to which he was born. He can equally be seen as a lone colonist, improving his state by well-planned industry and prudent measures of self-help. He has been viewed as the embodiment of capitalism, as a figure symbolising the isolation of puritan spirituality, as the precursor of nineteenth-century imperialism, as a type of the prodigal son, and much else. Not all these conflicting interpretations can be wholly correct, since they involve different readings of crucial episodes, such as the "original sin" of running away to sea, or the conversion of Friday. But the book is rich enough to contain a number of overlapping meanings, and it would be rash to discount many of the religious, economic, social, or philosophic ideas which have been discovered. The important thing in the last resort, however, is the extraordinary fictional chemistry which makes a stable compound of so many disparate elements. The heart of the book is to be found in Crusoe's sojourn on the island, particularly his early years of solitude and self-communion. Neither the framing parts of this story, nor the globe-trotting sequel of Crusoe's *Farther Adventures* attains the same power and vibrancy of expression.

If Crusoe is a naturally gregarious man, cast by fate into prolonged isolation, then the heroine of *Moll Flanders* might be described as a natural loner who is destined to float about on the tides of an alien society. Moll wants nothing more than to achieve gentility, or at the very least respectability: but first her sexual misadventures and then her criminal escapades serve to drag her into a marginal condition. The force of the novel derives from this collision in her being; her urge to conformity is cut across by the need to survive in desperate or unconventional ways. She was easily assimilated into the chapbook versions of this story, since her life-history has the diagrammatic clarity favoured in such moralistic narratives. But there is a mysterious dimension to her character, a depth of personality in the acting Moll which the reporting Moll does not seem fully to apprehend. It is this which has made the novel something of a cult in the twentieth century: significantly it was the generation of Joyce and Virginia Woolf which first seized on this added strain of psychological drama.

These two works are Defoe's most famous novels, and deservedly so. His other fiction contains much of interest, but none of the other books quite coheres as do *Crusoe* and *Moll*. For example, *Roxana* mixes several moments of intense nervous energy with some half-hearted melodrama: Defoe does not seem to have been altogether sure how much sympathy (if any) he could afford to invest in the heroine. Again, *Colonel Jack* shows signs of muddled purposes, with excellent evocation of varied social locales (notably a London childhood) and less assurance in depicting inner thoughts and feelings. Defoe was perhaps more at home with the vigorous action which informs the plot of *Captain Singleton*, *Memoirs of a Cavalier*, and *A New Voyage round the World*, the last certainly marking an improvement on the second part of *Crusoe*. There is plenty of external drama, for that matter, in *A Journal of the Plague Year*, but the interest is less narrowly concentrated on such things. Defoe manages to recreate the flurried excitement of a city under siege, and sticks particularly close to the real-life data of the Great Plague. But he deepens the treatment by presenting events through the eyes of a single observer, the saddler H. F., who is involved in the struggle for survival but sufficiently detached to afford a degree of critical detachment. The *Journal* is the most technically adroit among Defoe's works of fiction, with the possible exception of the first part of *Robinson Crusoe*. It avoids the strange *rubato* effects in narrative tempo which impair the structure of other books, and it preserves a more unified angle of vision than, say, *Colonel Jack*.

If we accept that Defoe lives on by virtue of his novels, despite the high merits of the rest of his oeuvre, then it is still difficult to locate with absolute precision the sources of his enduring power. It is not enough to define his themes – for, while the struggle to survive in a hostile environment is a rich vein of interest, such topics are hardly unique to Defoe. And his capacity to dramatise the essential *privacy* of experience, even where an individual like the saddler is caught up in public events, seems to emanate less from a sharply personal vision than from an eclectic blend of the theologies and moralities available to him. He wrote often about ordinary people *in extremis*, but at the level of basic impulse he seems to share the urge of Crusoe and Moll to return to normality at the earliest opportunity. His novels, then, present an unrivalled picture of men and women who reach fulfilment and identity under the severest pressure; but they also dramatise the yearning for a quiet life, even at the cost of losing that fulfilment.

—Pat Rogers

311

DE FOREST, John William. American. Born in Humphreysville, now Seymour, Connecticut, 31 March 1826. Educated in local schools. Married Harriet Silliman Shepard in 1856 (died, 1878); one son. Lived in Syria, 1847–50, then in Florence and Paris; writer from 1856; active soldier during the American Civil War: recruited and became Captain of Company I, 12th Connecticut Volunteers; served as Inspector-General, 1st Division, XIX Corps of the United States Army; commissioned Major, United States Volunteers, 1865; also write descriptions of battle scenes for *Harper's Monthly* during the war; Commanding Captain, Veterans Reserve Corps of Company I, 14th Regiment, after the war; Commander of a district of the Freedmen's Bureau in Greenville, South Carolina, 1866 until mustered out of service, 1868; settled in New Haven, Connecticut, 1869, and thereafter devoted himself to writing; invalid, in hospital, from 1903. A.M.: Amherst College, Massachusetts, 1859. *Died 17 July 1906.*

PUBLICATIONS

Fiction

Seacliff; or, The Mystery of the Westervelts. 1859.
Miss Ravenal's Conversion from Secession to Loyalty. 1867.
Overland. 1871.
Kate Beaumont. 1872.
The Wetherel Affair. 1873.
Honest John Vane. 1875.
Playing the Mischief. 1875.
Justine's Lovers. 1878.
Irene the Missionary. 1879.
The Bloody Chasm. 1881; as *The Oddest of Courtships,* 1882.
A Lover's Revolt. 1898.
Witching Times, edited by Alfred Appel, Jr. 1967.

Verse

The Downing Legends: Stories in Rhyme. 1901.
Poem: Medley and Palestina. 1902.

Other

History of the Indians of Connecticut from the Earliest Known Period to 1850. 1851.
Oriental Acquaintance; or, Letters from Syria. 1856.
European Acquaintance. 1858.
The De Forests of Avesnes (and of New Netherland): A Huguenot Thread in American Colonial History. 1900.
"The First Time under Fire" of the 12th Regiment, Connecticut Volunteers. 1907.
A Volunteer's Adventures: A Union Captain's Record of the Civil War, edited by James H. Croushore. 1946.
A Union Officer in the Reconstruction, edited by James H. Croushore and David Morris Potter. 1948.

Bibliography: "De Forest" by James F. Light, in *American Literary Realism 4*, 1968.

Reading List: *Patriotic Gore* by Edmund Wilson, 1962; *De Forest* by James F. Light, 1965.

*   *   *

John William De Forest was in his own day a prolific but little-read author. Despite the praise of William Dean Howells, nineteenth-century readers, with their love for melodrama and romance, could not accept De Forest's realism. Yet unquestionably De Forest deserves the credit as an innovator that literary critics such as Edmund Wilson and Van Wyck Brooks have accorded him. Three of his novels, *Miss Ravenel's Conversion from Secession to Loyalty*, *Kate Beaumont*, and *Playing the Mischief*, are particularly fine examples of realistic fiction.

In his first published work, *History of the Indians of Connecticut from the Earliest Known Period to 1850*, he demonstrated the objectivity and the penchant for debunking romantic myths which characterize his fictional style. By the time the Civil War began he had written two novels. *Witching Times* is set during the hysteria of the Salem witch trials. *Seacliff*, a country-house novel with a mystery theme, presents Mrs. Westervelt, the first of his wealthy, bored, neurotic middle-aged women. The story is told from a limited first-person point of view, a technique later perfected by Henry James. De Forest also published two travel books, *Oriental Acquaintance* and *European Acquaintance*, during this pre-war period.

The author and his family left Charleston, South Carolina just before Fort Sumter was fired on. In 1862 De Forest, a successful author and a family man of 36, became captain of a company of Connecticut volunteers. This Civil War service became the raw material for a series of magazine articles collected and published posthumously under the title *A Volunteer's Adventures*, and for his most famous novel, *Miss Ravenel's Conversion*. His post-war stint in the Freedmen's Bureau gave him local settings for *Kate Beaumont* and *The Bloody Chasm* and the materials for essays in *A Union Officer in the Reconstruction*.

De Forest's descriptions of war are unemotional, graphic and vivid. Perhaps his maturity at the time he had his wartime experience accounts in part for his dispassionate style, but the same objectivity and ironic detachment characterize all his best fiction. Though the fever pitch of the early war years had been lessened by the tragedy of Bull Run, the war was for most Northern readers still the great crusade; the notion that promotions were ruled by political patronage or that generals caused needless deaths through incompetence were unwelcome dashes of cold water. Descriptions of grim field hospitals with amputated limbs and coagulating blood under the operating table or the dead blackening and bloating in the hot Louisiana sun were too strong for the mass audience.

Howells blamed De Forest's lack of success on the female reader. Certainly it is true that De Forest does not romanticize many female figures in his work. Mrs. La Rue of *Miss Ravenel's Conversion* and Mrs. Chester of *Kate Beaumont* are fading flirts still trying to attract young men. Though Mrs. Chester ultimately goes mad, Mrs. La Rue succeeds in captivating Miss Ravenel's first husband and, after his death, finding another influential lover who helps her to recoup her fortunes lost in the war. Josie Murray of *Playing the Mischief* and Olympia Smiles Vane of *Honest John Vane* manipulate men for material gain with complete success; there may be storm clouds in their futures, but they are secure as the novels end. Even the chaste ingenues like Lily Ravenel and Clara Van Dieman of *Overland* respond passionately to the sexual aspects of the men they marry. The Howells theory has, no doubt, an element of truth in it, but other factors enter in as well.

De Forest suffered as Melville, Hawthorne and others did from the unfavorable condition of the American publishing situation. With no international copyright protection from European rivals and the high volume of sales needed to turn a profit, one after another of De Forest's publishers went bankrupt. De Forest approached his work with the detachment of a scientist; even when exposing the scandal and malfeasance of the war and the Grant era, his tone is clinical and detached. His post-war work eschews sermonizing and he either lets the scene speak for itself or comments with ironic indirection. This lack of passion and subtlety of point of view may have been too demanding for his readers. Moreover, the author's cynicism may have disturbed some readers. There are no gods in his pantheon. Democracy is failing in his Washington novels; the Women's Suffrage movement produces humor but no greatness; romantic love is a delusion better buried, as in *A Lover's Revolt*, in more compelling public issues.

Although occasionally he could not resist the lure of popular taste — *Overland* and *The Bloody Chasm* have highly contrived melodramatic plots — at his best he carefully deflates romantic situations. Josie Murray entraps two Congressional lovers, but the man she really admires escapes one romantic embrace after another, coolly appraising the dangers of committment to an enticing but amoral woman. Nelly Armitage, Kate Beaumont's sister, lured by passion into marriage with a handsome drunkard, is praised for her fortitude in staying with him. She replies, "It is mere hardened callousness and want of feeling. I ceased some time ago to be a woman. I am a species of brute." Captain Colburne, the hero of *Miss Ravenel's Conversion*, is bored during the bombardment of Port Hudson and finds his freed servant is no saintly Uncle Tom, but a pilferer who must be constantly watched. His last novel, *A Lover's Revolt*, demonstrates the conflict between the romantic plot elements he knew the mass audience wanted and the realistic passages he wrote so successfully. The book contains the required love story, but the author's prime concern is the military situation in Boston of 1775–76; the love triangle is mechanically and scantily disposed of.

De Forest wrote many fine stories and novels in the years immediately following the war, and he explored new ground with almost every sally, but his books did not sell. He hoped to leave a standard edition of his work as a "little monument," but no publisher would agree to the venture. Finally this accomplished writer gave up in discouragement; he wrote little during the last two decades of his life.

—Barbara M. Perkins

DELAND, Margaret(ta Wade, née Campbell). American. Born near Allegheny, Pennsylvania, 23 February 1857; orphaned: raised by her aunt and uncle in Manchester, Pennsylvania. Educated in local schools, and at Pelham Priory, New Rochelle, New York, 1873–75; studied art and design at Cooper Union, New York City, 1875–76. Married Lorin F. Deland in 1880 (died, 1917). Assistant Instructor of Drawing and Design, Normal College of the City of New York, later Hunter College, 1876–80; settled in Boston, 1880; with her husband created a hostel, in their home, for unmarried mothers, 1880–84; full-time writer from 1886. Honorary degrees: Rutgers University, New Brunswick, New Jersey, 1917; Tufts College, Medford, Massachusetts, 1920; Bates College, Lewiston, Maine, 1920; Bowdoin College, Brunswick, Maine, 1931. Member, National Institute of Arts and Letters, 1926. *Died 13 January 1945.*

PUBLICATIONS

Fiction

John Ward, Preacher. 1888.
A Summer Day. 1889.

Sidney. 1890.
The Story of a Child. 1892.
Mr. Tommy Dove and Other Stories. 1893.
Philip and His Wife. 1894.
The Wisdom of Fools. 1897.
Old Chester Tales. 1898.
Good for the Soul. 1899.
Dr. Lavendar's People. 1903.
The Awakening of Helena Richie. 1906.
An Encore. 1907.
R. J.'s Mother and Some Other People. 1908.
The Way to Peace. 1910.
The Iron Woman. 1911.
The Voice. 1912.
Partners. 1913.
The Hands of Esau. 1914.
Around Old Chester. 1915.
The Rising Tide. 1916.
The Promises of Alice. 1919.
An Old Chester Secret. 1920.
The Vehement Flame. 1922.
New Friends in Old Chester. 1924.
The Kays. 1926.
Captain Archer's Daughter. 1932.
Old Chester Days. 1937.

Play

Screenplay: *Smouldering Fires,* with others, 1925.

Verse

The Old Garden and Other Verses. 1886.

Other

Florida Days. 1889.
The Common Way. 1904.
Small Things. 1919.
If This Be I, As I Suppose It Be (autobiography). 1935.
Golden Yesterdays (autobiography). 1941.

*   *   *

In 1888 Margaret Deland, who had previously written only one book of poetry, *The Old Garden and Other Verses*, published a novel, *John Ward, Preacher*. A complex, thesis-ridden saga of Puritan zealotry gone rigid and perverse, the book became an infamous best-seller and made its author a celebrity. John Ward, an unreconstructed Calvinist, is married to an Episcopalian woman who, as Percy H. Boynton has written (in *America in Contemporary Fiction*) "is so devoted to her husband that she can ignore his bigotry if only he will permit her to. He believes, however, that the salvation of her soul is more imperative than the survival of his home, sends her away, breaks down under the strain, and dies."

In the years that followed the publication of *John Ward*, Deland moved from the infamous and realistic to the conventional and placid. Her Old Chester pieces – many of which were collected in *Old Chester Tales* and *Dr. Lavendar's People* – for which she is best remembered, told of life in the turn-of-the-century village. Old Chester, a fictionalized Manchester, the small Pennsylvania town in which Deland had spent a part of her childhood, was not drawn with the cynicism of Lewis's Gopher Prairie or the grotesquery of Anderson's Winesburg or even with the zeal of Deland's own *John Ward*. Hers, rather, was an image of small-town Americana both peaceful and homiletic.

Reminiscences of her earlier realism were signaled now and again in Old Chester, however. In *The Awakening of Helena Richie*, for instance, the protagonist comes to the village to escape the drunkenness of her husband and her own adulterous past, only to be revealed by Dr. Lavendar and subsequently shown the path of penitence. And in a sequel, *The Iron Woman*, the awakened Helena leads the next generation away from the realistically portrayed pitfalls of adultery and divorce.

Born before the Civil War, Margaret Deland was a sometimes outspoken defender of marriage, family, and community. But by the time of her death in 1945 one could scarcely imagine that so benign a spokesman had ever been thought provocative. Indeed, the very virtues which she had stood for seemed to be in disarray.

—Bruce A. Lohof

---

de la RAMÉE, Marie Louise.   See **OUIDA.**

---

de la ROCHE, Mazo (Louise).   Canadian.   Born in Newmarket, Ontario, 15 January 1879. Educated at schools in Galt, Ontario, and Toronto; Parkdale Collegiate Institute, Toronto; University of Toronto. Had two adopted daughters. Full-time writer from childhood; lived in Windsor, England, 1929–39; thereafter lived in Toronto. Recipient: Lorne Pierce Medal, 1938; University of Alberta University National Award Medal, 1951. Litt.D.: University of Toronto, 1954. *Died 12 July 1961.*

PUBLICATIONS

Fiction

> *Explorers of the Dawn* (stories).   1922.
> *Possession.*   1923.
> *Delight.*   1926.
> *Jalna.*   1927.

Whiteoaks of Jalna. 1929; as *Whiteoaks,* 1929.
Finch's Fortune. 1931.
Lark Ascending. 1932.
The Thunder of New Wings. 1932.
The Master of Jalna. 1933.
Beside a Norman Tower. 1934.
Young Renny (Jalna – 1906). 1935.
Whiteoak Harvest. 1936.
Growth of a Man. 1938.
The Sacred Bullock and Other Stories of Animals. 1939.
Whiteoak Heritage. 1940.
Wakefield's Course. 1941.
The Two Saplings. 1942.
The Building of Jalna. 1944.
Return to Jalna. 1946.
Mary Wakefield. 1949.
Renny's Daughter. 1951.
A Boy in the House and Other Stories. 1952.
The Whiteoak Brothers: Jalna – 1923. 1953.
Variable Winds at Jalna. 1954.
Centenary at Jalna. 1958.
Morning at Jalna. 1960.

Plays

Low Life (produced 1925). 1925.
Come True (produced 1927).
The Return of the Emigrant (produced 1928). 1929.
Whiteoaks, from her own novel (produced 1936). 1936.
The Mistress of Jalna (produced 1951).

Other

Portrait of a Dog. 1930.
The Very House. 1937.
Quebec, Historic Seaport. 1944.
The Song of Lambert (juvenile). 1955.
Ringing the Changes: An Autobiography. 1957.
Bill and Coo (juvenile). 1958.

Reading List: *de la Roche* by Ronald Hambleton, 1966; *de la Roche* by George Hendrick, 1970.

*   *   *

Mazo de la Roche became a best selling novelist at the age of 48, when her *Jalna* won the first *Atlantic Monthly*-Little Brown prize of $10,000 in 1927. Supported by a wide-ranging American advertising campaign, the novel sold 100,000 copies in three months. To satisfy the demands of a public that expanded to her native Canada and Europe, Miss de la Roche eventually wrote 15 sequels, the last appearing a few months before her death in 1961. By that time, her publishers estimated that nearly nine million hard-cover copies of the *Jalna* novels had been sold.

Miss de la Roche had been a professional writer for twenty-five years when *Jalna* was published, her first story appearing in *Munsey's Magazine* in 1902. A collection of short stories and two novels had been published, but her literary earnings were meager before *Jalna*; and though nineteen non-Jalna books were eventually printed they owe nearly all their success to her Jalna reputation. Many are accounts of children and animals, fiction and non-fiction; this work is neither negligible nor very distinguished.

The Jalna novels are more remarkable for their popular appeal than for their literary merit. *Jalna* and its first two sequels were respectfully received, however. American reviewers in such magazines as the *Nation* and the *Bookman* were impressed by the lively characters and lovely scenery of Southern Ontario. As the sequels multiplied, the Whiteoaks of Jalna were compared to Galsworthy's Forsytes – but it became clear that there was no social significance in Miss de la Roche's fiction. The real ingredients were Dickensian characters, somewhat larger than life-size, sensuous details more romantic than real, and erotic behavior that readers accepted as evidence of virility and strong passions. Her Whiteoak family were English colonial landed gentry, and there was a snob appeal in this escape fiction. Six of the novels examined the family history before the original *Jalna*, which took place in the 1920's. This allowed the author to bring back the lustiest Whiteoak, Adeline, who had dominated *Jalna* in her hundredth year and had died playing backgammon in *Whiteoaks of Jalna*. The family squabbled over her money in *Finch's Fortune*. Thereafter Mazo de la Roche's readers lived with her in a Whiteoak world that preserved in fantasy English colonial life and traditions – at Jalna.

Ringing the Changes: An Autobiography is disappointing in its account of the novelist's creative life and inaccurate in its factual information. The two books on Mazo de la Roche published in the decade following her death agree that she had moved her actual birth date forward six years. More significant are the affirmations of her strong emotional attachment to her cousin and life-long companion, Caroline Clement, and to her father, William Roche. But the chief interest in *Ringing the Changes* is the author's account of "the Play," sometimes called "the Game" – the dream world Mazo de la Roche invented as a child and shared with Caroline Clement. Although "the Play" has been compared to the Angria and Gondal fantasies of the Brontë sisters, even by Miss de la Roche, the characters and episodes of "the Play" were preserved only in the memories of the two girls. *Explorers of the Dawn* was a "marketing" of material from "the Play," according to Ronald Hambleton. To George Hendrick its chief significance is that it "supplied her with overwrought fictional material and kept her an emotional adolescent all her life."

—Clarence A. Glasrud

DELL, Floyd. American. Born in Barry, Illinois, 28 June 1887. Educated in schools in Barry and Quincy, Illinois, and Davenport High School, Iowa. Served in the United States Army, 1918. Married 1) Margery Curry in 1909 (separated, 1913); 2) Berta-Maria Gage in 1919, two sons. Reporter, Davenport *Times*, 1905; Editor, *Tri-City Workers' Magazine*, Davenport, 1906; Reporter, Davenport *Democrat*, 1906, and Chicago *Evening Post*, 1909, and Assistant Editor, 1909–10, Associate Editor, 1910–11, and Editor, 1911–13, of the *Evening Post*'s *Friday Literary Review*; settled in New York, 1913: Associate Editor, *The Masses*, 1914–17, and on editorial board of its successor, *The Liberator*, 1918–21; tried for sedition for his pacifist writings, 1917; full-time writer from 1921; Editor for the WPA (Works Progress Administration), Washington, D.C., 1935–47. *Died 23 July 1969.*

PUBLICATIONS

Fiction

    Moon-Calf. 1920.
    The Briary-Bush. 1921.
    Janet March. 1923; revised edition, 1927.
    This Mad Ideal. 1925.
    Runaway. 1925.
    Love in Greenwich Village (stories and poems). 1926.
    An Old Man's Folly. 1926.
    An Unmarried Father. 1927; as *Little Accident,* 1930.
    Souvenir. 1929.
    Love Without Money. 1931.
    Diana Stair. 1932.
    The Golden Spike. 1934.

Plays

    Human Nature (as *A Five Minute Problem Play,* produced 1913). In *King Arthur's Socks* ..., 1922.
    The Chaste Adventures of Joseph (produced 1914). In *King Arthur's Socks* ..., 1922.
    Ibsen Revisited (produced 1914). In *King Arthur's Socks* ..., 1922.
    Enigma (produced 1915). In *King Arthur's Socks* ..., 1922.
    Legend (as *My Lady's Mirror,* produced 1915). In *King Arthur's Socks* ..., 1922.
    The Rim of the World (produced 1915). In *King Arthur's Socks* ..., 1922.
    King Arthur's Socks (produced 1916). In *King Arthur's Socks* ..., 1922.
    The Angel Intrudes (produced 1917). 1918.
    A Long Time Ago (produced 1917). In *King Arthur's Socks* ..., 1922.
    Sweet-and-Twenty (produced 1918). 1921.
    Poor Harold! (produced 1920). In *King Arthur's Socks* ..., 1922.
    King Arthur's Socks and Other Village Plays. 1922.
    A Little Accident, with Thomas Mitchell, from the novel *An Unmarried Father* by Dell (produced 1928).
    Cloudy with Showers, with Thomas Mitchell (produced 1931).

Other

    Women as World Builders: Studies in Modern Feminism. 1913.
    Were You Ever a Child? 1919.
    Looking at Life. 1924.
    Intellectual Vagabondage: An Apology for the Intelligentsia. 1926.
    The Outline of Marriage. 1926.
    Upton Sinclair: A Study in Social Protest. 1927.
    Love in the Machine Age: A Psychological Study of the Transition from Patriarchal Society. 1930.
    Homecoming: An Autobiography. 1933.
    Children and the Machine Age. 1934.

Editor, *Poems,* by Wilfrid Scawen Blunt. 1923.
Editor, *Poems of Robert Herrick.* 1924.

Editor, *Poems and Prose of William Blake.* 1925.
Editor, with Paul Jordan-Smith, *The Anatomy of Melancholy,* by Robert Burton. 1927.
Editor, *Daughter of the Revolution and Other Stories,* by John Reed. 1927.

Reading List: *Dell* by John D. Hart, 1971.

*   *   *

In a writing career running from 1908 to 1935, Floyd Dell published over twenty books and roughly one thousand periodical pieces. They, like his life, fall into several distinct periods and reflect his connection with many of the important literary movements and intellectual concerns in the United States during the first quarter of the century.

In his Chicago period (1908–13), his output consisted chiefly of book reviews and essays for the *Friday Literary Review* of the *Chicago Evening Post,* which during his editorship found itself at the heart of what has come to be known as the "Chicago renaissance." His brisk and often highly personal discussions for the *Review* championed the "new" literature, introduced the work of many continental novelists, and surveyed current books on socialism and sex; one of his series of articles, "Modern Women," taking up the views of ten feminists, became his first book, *Women as World Builders.*

His Greenwich Village years (1913–20, chronicled nostalgically in prose sketches, short stories, and poetry in *Love in Greenwich Village*) coincided with a period of intense creative and intellectual activity there, and he became one of the leading figures both through his participation in the little theatre movement – several of his short plays gently satirizing the intellectual concerns of the Villagers were collected as *King Arthur's Socks and Other Village Plays* – and his writings as an editor of the socialistic journals *The Masses* and its successor, *The Liberator.* The books that resulted from this writing reflect the dualism both of Dell and of these magazines, which were concerned with art as well as politics and were often as conservative in the former as they were radical in the latter. *Looking at Life* draws together forty short pieces, largely unconnected with socialism; they display an acute intelligence playing lightly and entertainingly, but seldom profoundly, over a wide range of subjects. *Were You Ever a Child?,* based on a series in *The Liberator,* is a plea for educational reform, popularizing the ideas of John Dewey and other educational theorists and presenting them with humor and playfulness (and often in dialogue form). *Intellectual Vagabondage,* based on another series written for *The Liberator* (but after Dell left the Village), is the most important of the three, and is Dell's most ambitious effort at interpreting literature from a social and economic standpoint; with characteristic lightness of touch he traces the historical role of the intelligentsia and then, more significantly, sets forth the "spiritual autobiography" of his own generation, depicting, among other things, the idealistic revolt of youth against the restraints of a commercial world.

This perennial theme of Dell's runs through the novels that he produced during what may be regarded as his third period, the years when he lived at Croton-on-the-Hudson, New York (1920–35). His first – and most famous and best – novel, *Moon-Calf,* draws heavily on his own pre-Chicago years and describes with great sensitivity the intellectual development of a young dreamer and poet; with it he made the analysis of moon-calves, and their adjustment to reality, his own special province. In ten succeeding novels he continued to explore the predicaments of youthful idealists, who in the end find happiness by accepting conventions; like his other writings, these novels are facile and exhibit a keen sense of irony and humour, but they do not fulfill the promise suggested by *Moon-Calf.* The interest in psychological and social problems manifested in the novels reaches its climax in Dell's substantial study of adolescent adjustment, *Love in the Machine Age,* a well-written exposition of the thesis that the neuroses of the modern world are the result of outmoded but still operative patriarchal conventions.

For psychological insight, however, readers are likely to prefer his autobiography,

Homecoming, especially the first half dealing with the years covered fictionally in *Moon-Calf*. As the title implies, the movement of the book and of his life is toward the stability finally found in marriage and a home; but he never lost the ability to write perceptively of youthful rebellion, and the book contains some of his best work. The dust jacket calls it "not Floyd Dell's autobiography but your own," a remark that points to Dell's importance as a representative figure. He will be best remembered as an intelligent and articulate commentator on the characteristic concerns of a sizable segment of his literary generation.

—G. T. Tanselle

DELONEY, Thomas.   English.   Born c. 1543. Very little is known about his life: worked as a silk-weaver, possibly in Norwich; member of the London Clothiers Guild; popular balladeer, especially after the death of William Elderton, c. 1585. *Died c. 1600*

PUBLICATIONS

Collections

Works, edited by F. O. Mann.   1912.
Novels, edited by Merritt E. Lawlis.   1961.

Fiction

The Gentle Craft: A Discourse Showing What Famous Men Have Been Shoemakers in
    Time Past.   1598(?); part 1, 1627; complete version, 1635(?).
Thomas of Reading; or, The Six Worthy Yeomen of the West.   1612 (12th edition).
The Pleasant History of John Winchcomb, Called Jack of Newbery.   1619 (8th edition).

Verse

Three Old Ballads, edited by J. O. Halliwell.   1860.

Other

Editor, Strange Histories of Kings, Princes, Dukes, etc.   1600; revised edition, 1612,
    1631; as The Royal Garland of Love and Delight, 1674.
Editor, The Garland of Good Will.   1628; edited by J. H. Dixon, 1851.

Translator, A Declaration Made by the Archbishop of Cologne upon the Deed of His
    Marriage.   1583.
Translator, The Mirror of Mirth and Pleasant Conceits, by J. B. Des Periers, edited by
    James Woodrow Hassell.   1959.

Reading List: *An Inquiry into Aspects of the Language of Deloney* by T. Dahl, 1951; *Two Elizabethan Writers of Fiction: Thomas Nashe and Deloney* by R. G. Howarth, 1956; *Apology for the Middle Class: The Dramatic Novels of Deloney* by Merritt E. Lawlis, 1960; *Historischer Roman und Realismus: Das Erzählwerk Deloneys* by K. M. Paetzold, 1972.

*   *   *

Though he was England's most popular balladeer in the 1590's, Thomas Deloney's major accomplishment was to articulate in his fiction the dignity and power of hard work, a power reinforced by the blessings of a Protestant Providence. The disappearance or doubtful attribution of many of his ballads makes an assessment of his work in this genre difficult. Ironically, the tradition that Deloney provoked the authorities with a ballad on the scarcity of grain that depicted the Queen in a dialogue of a "very fond and indecent sort" is more interesting than any of his extant ballads, whether versified episodes from Holinshed (*Strange Histories*), or lurid journalistic treatments of contemporary scandals ("The Lamentation of Mr. Pages Wife – of Plimouth, who, being forc'd to wed him, consented to his Murder, for the love of G. Strangwidge; for which they suffered at Barnstable in Devonshire.") Deloney does little to raise the Elizabethan ballad to the level of its medieval ancestor, but his characteristic voice sounds occasionally, as in "A pleasant Dialogue betweene plaine *Truth* and blind *Ignorance*," when a Catholic Ignorance defends his faith in the rustic dialect Deloney was to use brilliantly in his fiction: "Ich care not for this Bible Booke,/tis too big to be true./Our blessed Ladies Psalter,/zhall for my mony go."

Whatever their provenance in the oral tradition that fed these ballads, in Renaissance jest-books, and in his observation of Elizabethan manners, Deloney's four prose narratives published during his last four years constitute his distinctive contribution to English literature and foreshadow the work of later novelists like Defoe. Deloney's embryonic novels, all celebrating the rise to success and the ethics of both individual clothiers and shoemakers and of the crafts collectively, were very popular in his day and were frequently reprinted in the 17th and 18th centuries as the English middle class increased in numbers and influence. Significantly, Deloney addressed *Jack of Newbery* and *The Gentle Craft* to the clothiers and "cordwayners" who are the heroes of these books, rather than to the aristocratic patrons who subsidized and presumably inspired many Renaissance works. He embodies his core myth in the career of Jack, a dedicated weaver who indulges in decorous amusement only on Sundays, and who learns never to carry more than 12 pence to lend to improvident fellow workers. Jack becomes head of the business by marrying his boss's widow, who appreciates his youthful comeliness less than his hard work and leadership potentiality; he creates a world of happy singing workers, and he arms soldiers to defeat cowardly Scottish invaders (foreigners are invariably unattractive in Deloney's xenophobic world). Crowning these achievements, Jack skillfully defends his class against the wily Cardinal Wolsey in a dispute over unfair trade restrictions. He ultimately patronizes many aristocrats and dresses his own retainers in livery, but refuses a title, preferring to "rest in my russet coat, a poore clothier to my dying day." Deloney is ambivalent about aristocrats: they are necessary symbols of traditional order, but their unearned privilege makes more attractive the cheerful and persistent labors of rising workers.

The Gentle Craft (2 parts) teaches that princes have worked proudly at shoemaking since ancient times, a tradition justifying the adjective "gentle," and explaining the comforting adage that "a shoemaker's son is said to be a prince born." The strongest exemplar of the financial and civic success that rewards honest industry is Simon Eyre (part 1), a Dick Whittington variant who rises from country apprentice to Lord Mayor of London. Eyre's pride in his ascent generates an elevated concept of responsibility toward workers, fellow entrepreneurs, and the economic health of the nation.

Thomas of Reading, which traces the careers of several clothiers in the time of Henry I, shows that half the populace worked happily and profitably at the weaving trade: "there were few or no beggars at all; poor people, whom God lightly blesseth with most children, did by means of this occupation, so order them, that by the time that they were come to six or seven years of age, they were able to get their own bread." Though intemperate living sometimes threatens Deloney's businessmen, they profit from their mistakes and from Thomas's gifts sufficiently to return to lucrative operations. Deloney creates no dishonest businessmen, at least not English businessmen; success transforms capitalists into philanthropists: they bequeath money to establish schools, support monasteries, and help young couples begin middle-class existence.

What insures Deloney's effectiveness is not this naively inspirational material, but a lively style that embodies economic growth and social decency in terms familiar to his audience. His homely euphuism domesticates exotic material: "Nay, quoth another, I'll lay my life that as the salamander cannot live without the fire, so Jack cannot live without the smell of his dame's smock"; yet his serious use of Lyly in romantic episodes predictably fails. Strengthening his colloquial tone is the anecdote invented to explain the genesis of familiar figures of speech, such as "St. Hugh's bones" for shoemaker's tools. And he has a talent for dialect, rustic and foreign, often involving malapropisms and often indecent. This humor condescendingly mocks those whose birth bars them from the English middle class. These elements and the illusion of ordinary life ("then shalt thou scoure thy pitchy fingers in a bason of hot water, with an ordinary washing Ball ...") support Deloney's translation of romance and mythic motifs to the ethical and aesthetic equivalents that suit the taste of his audience. Instead of winning princesses and kingdoms in heroic contests against princely rivals, Deloney's heroes aspire prosaically to the hands of mature widows, less for their beauty than for the businesses they control. Romantic love governs only foreigners, fools, and effete aristocrats (when Deloney does attempt a straightforward love theme, it reads like a poor imitation of an episode from a Greene romance). In *The Gentle Craft*, part 2, an apprentice wins his wealthy mistress by performing a variety of dirty kitchen tasks, a domestic version of Hercules' cleaning the Augean stables. Jack of Newbery's rivals vie with gifts of food in a ritual suggesting a childlike belief in the efficacy of material goods to establish the status of the giver and the extent of his devotion. One rival is understandably upset when the widow rejects him: "I never spent a pig and a goose to so bad a purpose before." But the suitors politely refuse the widow's offer to return their gifts: "although we have lost our labors, we have not lost our manners," a response affirming that fusion of public and private decency that characterizes Deloney.

The episodic nature of Deloney's works argues his inability to control plots, perhaps an inheritance from the jest-book tradition, but his good-humored, pragmatic tone unifies otherwise disparate anecdotes. Without Nashe's brilliant style that obviates any criticism of structure, or Greene's anguished personae whose authenticity makes plotting irrelevant, Deloney nevertheless creates a comforting world with a cohesive mood and system of values. Yet, though his fiction has considerable charm and wit, this world is so domestic and practical that the hierarchy of these values occasionally raises inadvertent questions. After an innkeeper and his wife murder Thomas of Reading in a gory episode that foreshadows Macbeth's murder of Duncan, and after Deloney's Providence administers the grimly appropriate punishment, he causes incipient laughter by implying that financial insolvency may be more serious a sin than homicide: "And yet notwithstanding all the money which they had gotten thereby, they prospered not, but at their deaths were found in debt."

—Burton Kendle

DE MORGAN, William (Fend). English. Born in London, 16 November 1839; son of the mathematician Augustus De Morgan. Educated at University College, London; studied art at the Royal Academy School, London, 1859. Married the painter Evelyn Pickering in 1888. Worked in stained glass from 1864; turned his attention to ceramics in 1870, and established a kiln in Cheyne Row, Chelsea, London, 1871; also associated with William Morris in his Fine Art Workmen firm; retired as a potter, 1905; began writing, 1906. *Died 15 January 1917.*

PUBLICATIONS

Fiction

Joseph Vance. 1906.
Alice-for-Short. 1907.
Somehow Good. 1908.
It Never Can Happen Again. 1909.
An Affair of Dishonour. 1910.
A Likely Story. 1911.
When Ghost Meets Ghost. 1914.
The Old Madhouse, completed by Evelyn De Morgan. 1919.
Old Man's Youth, completed by Evelyn De Morgan. 1921.

Other

Report on the Feasibility of a Manufacture of Glazed Pottery in Egypt. 1894.

Reading List: *De Morgan and His Wife* by A. M. W. Stirling, 1922; "The Novels of De Morgan" by Orlo Williams, in *Some Great English Novels*, 1926; *De Morgan* by William Gaunt and M. D. E. Clayton-Stamm, 1971.

*   *   *

A great, original potter, William De Morgan turned novelist only in his sixties, when his factory had gone into liquidation and his artistic career was finished. It is ironic that his writing, taken up as a diversion, should have brought him the popular and financial success which eluded him as an artist.

The mid-Victorian setting of his novels, with their large canvas and humorous portrayal of lower-class London life, has earned him the epithet "Dickensian." By his own admission "Dickens was the master at whose feet" he sat. But the likeness is superficial. Son of a brilliant, unorthodox father and a highly talented mother, and part of an affectionate family, De Morgan did not, as a child, experience the adversity which shaped Dickens's imagination. He was permitted, although not encouraged, to follow his artistic bent when a young man, was happily married to the Pre-Raphaelite painter Evelyn Pickering, and moved in a stimulating circle, numbering among his closest friends William Morris and the Burne-Joneses. He was a man of great personal charm, high-spirited, with a whimsical sense of humour, who relished oddity whether of language, character, or situation and was ready with quip and pun. He possessed a high degree of scientific and inventive ability and an original, independent mind, and, although detesting pretence in life as in art, he was tolerant of his fellow men.

He writes with humour and affection of the London he knew fifty years earlier and brings to vivid life those grimy tenements, alleys, and squares such as Alice-for-short's basement and Sapps Court; against this background move artisans, labourers, women, and children whose racy idiom and Cockney humour and resourcefulness demonstrate De Morgan's creative vitality and irrepressible sense of comedy. Christopher Vance is his masterpiece but perhaps the Wardle household in *When Ghost Meets Ghost* best illustrates his range and, in particular, his sensitive understanding of the very young and the very old. His middle-class families also ring true, especially his heroines: cheerful, affectionate girls with considerable moral strength. Several of these characters can be identified: the memorable Dr. Thorpe was drawn from his father, and in Charles Heath he ridicules himself when a raw artist. Outside these areas he appears ill at ease, and his excursions into the upper social ranks are disastrous.

De Morgan wrote with apparent disregard of advances in contemporary fiction and in many ways belongs to an earlier generation. His novels are long, digressive, and ill-planned; his plots, often hinging on some mystery of identification, are over-elaborate and frequently implausible; his narrative is rarely dramatic (the thrilling capture of Thornton Daverill in *When Ghost Meets Ghost* is a notable exception). The novels' chief originality lies in the tone of mellow reminiscence, and in the presence throughout of their highly individual author who, in a train of asides, speculations, opinions, memories, and reflections, establishes a bond of affection between himself and his reader.

—Gwynneth Hatton

DE QUINCEY, Thomas. English. Born in Manchester, 15 August 1785. Educated at Bath Grammar School, 1796–99; a private school in Winkfield, Wiltshire, 1799–1800; Manchester Grammar School, 1801–02; Worcester College, Oxford, 1803–08, left without taking a degree; entered Middle Temple, London, 1812. Married Margaret Simpson in 1817 (died, 1837), five sons and three daughters. Opium user from 1804; settled in Grasmere, 1809: associated with the Lake Poets, Wordsworth, Coleridge, and Southey; Editor, *Westmorland Gazette*, 1818–19; contributed to the *London Magazine*, 1821–25, and the *Saturday Post* and *Evening Post*, Edinburgh, 1827–28; moved to Edinburgh, 1828: wrote for *Blackwood's Magazine*, 1826–49, and *Tait's Magazine*, 1832–51. *Died 8 December 1859.*

PUBLICATIONS

Collections

Collected Writings, edited by David Masson.   14 vols., 1889–90.

Prose Writings

Confessions of an English Opium Eater.   1822; revised edition, 1865; edited by Alethea Hayter, 1971.
Walladmor: A Novel Freely Translated from the English of Scott and Now Freely Translated into English, by G. W. H. Haering.   2 vols., 1825 (a German forgery).
Klosterheim; or, The Masque.   1832; edited by Dr. Shelton-Mackenzie, 1855.
The Logic of Political Economy.   1844.
Writings, edited by J. T. Fields.   24 vols., 1851–59.
Selections Grave and Gay, revised and arranged by De Quincey.   14 vols., 1853–60.
China.   1857.
Shakespeare: A Biography.   1864.
The Wider Hope: Essays on Future Punishment.   1890.
Uncollected Writings, edited by James Hogg.   2 vols., 1890.
Posthumous Works, edited by A. H. Japp.   2 vols., 1891–93.
De Quincey Memorials, Being Letters and Other Records Here First Published, edited by A. H. Japp.   2 vols., 1891.

A Diary 1803, edited by H. A. Eaton.   1927.
De Quincey at Work, Seen in 130 Letters, edited by W. H. Bonner.   1936.
Dr. Johnson and Lord Chesterfield.   1945.
Recollections of the Lake Poets, edited by Edward Sackville-West.   1948; edited by J. E.
    Jordan, as *Reminiscences of the English Lake Poets*, 1961; edited by David Wright, as
    Recollections of the Lakes and the Lake Poets, 1970.
De Quincey to Wordsworth: A Biography of a Relationship, edited by J. E.
    Jordan.   1962.
*New Essays: His Contributions to the Edinburgh Saturday Post and the Edinburgh
    Evening Post 1827–1828*, edited by Stuart M. Tave.   1966.
De Quincey as Critic, edited by J. E. Jordan.   1973.

Bibliography: *De Quincey: A Bibliography* by J. A. Green, 1908.

Reading List: *A Flame in Sunlight: The Life and Work of De Quincey* by Edward Sackville-West, 1936, edited by J. E. Jordan, 1974; *De Quincey, Literary Critic* by J. E. Jordan, 1952; *De Quincey* by Hugh S. Davies, 1964; *De Quincey: La Vie − L'Homme − L'Oeuvre* by Françoise Moreux, 1964 (includes bibliography); *The Mine and the Mint: Sources for the Writings of De Quincey* by Albert Goldman, 1965; *De Quincey* by Judson S. Lyon, 1969.

*   *   *

Thomas De Quincey shares with Lamb and Hazlitt the distinction of having elevated journalism to a kind of literature. Much of what he wrote was for *Blackwood's*, *Tait's Magazine*, and the *London Magazine*. It could be argued that his style possessed neither the charming oddity, deliberately fostered, of the one, nor the sheer energy of the other. But he shares with both a sharp eye for physical detail and a curiosity about the mainsprings of human conduct.

He worked in the belief that the calling of literature is a noble one, claiming indeed, in his essay on Oliver Goldsmith, that it is not only a fine art, but the highest and most powerful of all the arts. He differentiated between what he called "the literature of *knowledge* and the literature of *power*," the function of the first being to teach and the second to move. The first, however valuable, must inevitably in time be superceded. The second remains "triumphant for ever as long as the language exists in which it speaks." His contrasting examples are a cookery book, giving "something new ... in every paragraph," and *Paradise Lost*, providing "the exercise and expansion to your own latent capacity of sympathy with the infinite."

One of the causes of De Quincey's originality is his interest in his own psychology and its relation to dreams, an interest heightened by his bouts of addiction to opium. By modern Freudian standards, his inquiries into "states of mind and levels of consciousness" may seem elementary, but, allied to his honesty of literary purpose, they give remarkable vividness to *Confessions of an English Opium Eater*, which has remained his most widely read masterpiece, "Autobiography" (1834-53), and "Suspira de Profundis" (1845).

His interest in German metaphysics, resulting in his determination to introduce Kant to English readers, no doubt stimulated a certain transcendental vagueness to which he was prone, and which reflects itself in moments of inflated pretention in an otherwise highly polished style.

His ironic humour is well reflected in "Murder Considered as One of the Fine Arts" (1827). Out of what would seem as transient a subject as "The English Mail Coach" he builds, quite unforgettably, what he describes as one of his "dream fugues," based on a near-miss between the coach and a gig with a girl in it, a glimpse of whom provides the fugue with its counter-subject. Many of his essays reveal his ability to create imaginative reconstructions of incidents in history. The best known, "Joan of Arc," culminates in a passage which illustrates De Quincey's "flying contrapuntal style":

Bishop of Beauvais! thy victim died in fire upon a scaffold – thou upon a down bed. But, for the departing minutes of life, both are oftentimes alike. At the farewell crisis, when the gates of death are opening, and flesh is resting from its struggles, oftentimes the tortured and the torturer have the same truce from carnal torment; both sink together into sleep; together both sometimes kindle into dreams. When the mortal mists were gathering fast upon you two, bishop and shepherd girl – when the pavilions of life were closing up their shadowy curtains about you – let us try, through the gigantic glooms to decipher the flying features of your separate visions.

Not the least valuable of his writings is his *Reminiscences of the English Lake Poets* in which Coleridge (with whom he shared his German metaphysical interests), Southey, and Wordsworth and his sister Dorothy are vividly, and frankly, portrayed. A certain dislike of Wordsworth, which grew up through a coolness between them, comes out in the description of the poet skating "like a cow dancing the cotillion," or impatiently tearing open the pages of a new book with a buttery knife while at table.

The weaknesses of De Quincey's writing are his habit of digression – drawn, perhaps, from his early admiration for the work of Jean-Paul Richter – an over-fondness for exclamatory gesture, and the occasional breaking-off of a subject as if "the printer's devil were waiting at the door" (*A Flame in Sunlight* by Edward Sackville-West, 1936).

Nevertheless, for the 20th-century reader De Quincey is an essayist whose opening sentence is frequently as compelling as presumably it must also have seemed a century and a half ago. His preoccupations, too, remain singularly modern. Through the unlikely medium of journalism, he certainly realised his desire to contribute significantly to England's share of "the literature of *power*."

—Maurice Lindsay

DICKENS, Charles (John Huffam). English. Born in Landport, Portsea, Hampshire, 7 February 1812; moved with his family to London, 1814, Chatham, Kent, 1816, and again to London, 1821. Worked in the office of a blacking factory, Hungerford Market, London, while his family was in debtor's prison; subsequently attended Wellington House Academy, Hampstead, London, 1824–27, and Mr. Dawson's school in Brunswick Square, London, 1827; largely self-educated. Married Catherine Hogarth in 1836 (separated, 1858); seven sons and three daughters. Clerk in a London law office, 1827–28; taught himself shorthand and worked as a shorthand-reporter in the Doctors Commons, 1828–30, and in Parliament for the *True Son*, 1830–32, the *Mirror of Parliament*, 1832–34, and the *Morning Chronicle*, 1835; began contributing articles to the *Monthly Magazine*, 1833, as "Boz," 1834, and to the *Evening Chronicle*, 1835–36; full-time writer from 1836; visited America, 1842; lived in Italy, 1844–45; edited the *Daily News*, London, 1846; lived in Switzerland and Paris, 1846; manager of an amateur theatrical company touring English provincial cities, 1847; Founder-Editor, *Household Words*, London, 1849–59, and its successor, *All the Year Round*, from 1859; toured Britain, reading his works, 1858–59, 1861–63, 1866–67, and 1868–70; toured America, 1867–68. *Died 9 June 1870.*

Collections

Letters, edited by Georgina Hogarth and Mamie Dickens.   3 vols., 1880–82; revised
   edition, edited by Madeleine House and Graham Storey, 1965–
Nonesuch Dickens, edited by Arthur Waugh and others.   23 vols., 1937–38.

Fiction

Sketches by Boz Illustrative of Every-Day Life and Every-Day People.   1836; *New
   Series,* 1836.
The Posthumous Papers of the Pickwick Club.   1837.
Oliver Twist; or, The Parish Boy's Progress.   1838; edited by Kathleen Tillotson,
   1966.
Nicholas Nickleby.   1839; edited by Michael Slater, 1978.
Master Humphrey's Clock: The Old Curiosity Shop, Barnaby Rudge.   3 vols., 1840–41;
   Barnaby Rudge edited by Gordon W. Spence, 1973.
A Christmas Carol, Being a Ghost Story of Christmas.   1843.
Martin Chuzzlewit.   1844.
The Chimes.   1844.
The Cricket on the Hearth: A Fairy Tale of Home.   1845.
The Battle of Life: A Love Story.   1846.
The Haunted Man and the Ghost's Bargain: A Fancy for Christmas Time.   1848.
*Dealings with the Firm of Dombey and Son, Wholesale, Retail, and for
   Exportation.*   1848; edited by Alan Horsman, 1974.
David Copperfield.   1850.
Bleak House.   1853; edited by George Ford and Sylvère Monod, 1977.
Hard Times, for These Times.   1854; edited by George Ford and Sylvère Monod, 1972.
Little Dorrit.   1857; edited by John Holloway, 1967.
A Tale of Two Cities.   1859; edited by Barbara Osbourn, 1957.
Great Expectations.   1861; edited by Louise Stevens, 1966.
Our Mutual Friend.   1865; edited by Stephen Gill, 1971.
The Mystery of Edwin Drood.   1870; edited by Arthur J. Cox, 1974.
Christmas Stories from Household Words and All the Year Round, in *Works* (Charles
   Dickens Edition).   1874.
*The Lazy Tour of Two Idle Apprentices, No Thoroughfare, The Perils of Certain English
   Prisoners,* with Wilkie Collins.   1890.
The Christmas Books, edited by Michael Slater.   1971.

Plays

O'Thello (produced 1833).   In *Nonesuch Dickens,* 1937–38.
The Village Coquettes, music by John Hullah (produced 1836).   1836.
The Strange Gentleman (produced 1836).   1837.
Is She His Wife? or, Something Singular (produced 1837).   1837.
Mr. Nightingale's Diary, with Mark Lemon (produced 1851).   1851.
No Thoroughfare, with Wilkie Collins, from their own story (produced 1867).   1867;
   revised version, 1867.
The Lamplighter.   1879.

Other

American Notes for General Circulation.   2 vols., 1842; edited by John S. Whitely and
 Arnold Goldman, 1972.
Pictures from Italy.   1846.
Works.   17 vols., 1847–67.
A Child's History of England.   3 vols., 1852–54.
The Uncommercial Traveller.   1861.
Speeches Literary and Social, edited by R. H. Shepherd.   1870; revised edition, as The
 Speeches 1841–70, 1884.
Speeches, Letters, and Sayings.   1870.
The Mudfog Papers.   1880.
Plays and Poems, edited by R. H. Shepherd.   2 vols., 1885.
To Be Read at Dusk and Other Stories, Sketches, and Essays, edited by F. G.
 Kitton.   1898.
Miscellaneous Papers, edited by B. W. Matz.   2 vols., 1908.
Speeches, edited by K. J. Fielding.   1960.
Uncollected Writings from Household Words, 1850–1859, edited by Harry
 Stone.   1969.
Household Words: A Weekly Journal 1850–1859, edited by Anne Lohrli.   1974.
The Public Readings, edited by Philip Collins.   1975.

Editor, The Pic Nic Papers.   3 vols., 1841.

Bibliography: The First Editions of the Writings of Dickens by John C. Eckel, 1913, revised
edition, 1932; A Bibliography of the Periodical Works of Dickens by Thomas Hatton and
Arthur H. Cleaver, 1933; A Bibliography of Dickensian Criticism 1836–1975 by R. C.
Churchill, 1976.

Reading List: The Life of Dickens by John Forster, 3 vols., 1872–74, edited by A. J. Hoppé, 2
vols., 1966; The Dickens World by Humphrey House, 1941; Dickens: His Triumph and
Tragedy by Edgar Johnson, 2 vols., 1952, revised edition, 1978; Dickens at Work by
Kathleen Tillotson and John Butt, 1957; Dickens: The World of His Novels by J. Hillis Miller,
1958; The Imagination of Dickens by A. O. J. Cockshut, 1961; The Flint and the Flame: The
Artistry of Dickens by Earle R. Davis, 1963; The Dickens Theatre: A Reassessment of the
Novels by Robert Garis, 1965; Dickens the Novelist by Sylvère Monod, 1968; Dickens the
Novelist by F. R. and Q. D. Leavis, 1970; Dickens: The Critical Heritage edited by Philip
Collins, 1971; A Reader's Guide to Dickens by Philip Hobsbaum, 1973; The Violent Effigy by
John Carey, 1973.

* * *

  The greatness of Charles Dickens is of a peculiar kind, one that should give pause to
highbrows. He was, at the same time, the great popular entertainer and the great artist,
unrivalled in greatness in the rich tradition of the English novel except by Jane Austen.
Moreover, his greatness and his popular appeal are inseparable. We hear a lot – and truly
enough in certain cases – about unappreciated genius. In the generation after Dickens's death,
genius starving in a garret became something of a cliché. The obverse, the successful public
man, read and enjoyed by everybody, but not for many years perceived to be a wonderful
classic genius, was somewhat overlooked. Matthew Arnold enjoyed Dickens like everybody
else, but he could not recognize him as one of the great classics of the age, because he
subconsciously expected that the great classics would be poets. Lord Acton, one of the most
learned men of the age and one of the most omnivorous readers, lamented his own infirmity
in that he returned so much more often to Dickens than to George Eliot. He would have been

surprised, perhaps astonished, that the judgment of posterity would be that Dickens was even greater than George Eliot.

I said that the genius of Dickens and his status as popular entertainer were inseparable. The reasons for this lie deep in the man's nature. He was a born orator and actor. His lifelong enthusiasm for amateur dramatics, and the maniacal intensity with which he read aloud his own works – the excitement of the process may well have contributed to his death at the early age of 58 – were both significant. Like chess-players writers may be divided into those who "play the board" (try to make the best move objectively) and those who "play the man" (try to make the move most effective against a given opponent). Dickens was emphatically of the latter kind. He was never a pure artist. Like a great political orator, he drew strength from his audience; he delighted to please them, he accepted the validity of their judgment. It would never have occurred to him to complain that they were mistaken if some aspect of his art was unappreciated. They were the proper arbiters of his destiny whom he delighted to honour and obey.

In this he was not sycophantic or mercenary. He reverenced them partly because he was so like them. Some great writers are natural solitaries, others are learned and obscure; but Dickens was in many respects the ordinary English man of the middle-class transformed by a unique unrepeatable genius. In his own person he fulfilled and exemplified many dominant myths of the mid-nineteenth century. He was a self-made man, like the heroes of the immensely popular and influential Samuel Smiles. Without proper education, without a loving and secure home, he had made himself a household name by the time he was in his early twenties. In an age more notable perhaps than any other for deep feeling (some might say sentimentality) about childhood, he had been a rejected child, forced to find his own lodgings and earn his own living by the time he was ten years old.

Then, he was typical of his great middle-class public in being a practical man of the world, not particularly bookish, with a double share of the extraordinary exuberant energy and humour of that expansive age. Like his public, he was a bit of a philistine; his views on art were much nearer to those of the crowds who thronged the Royal Academy and admired the accuracy of Frith's *Derby Day* than they were to those of John Ruskin.

Like his public, too, he was interested in reform. Like them he was very certain that reform should work in the direction of reducing aristocratic privilege; like them he was much more dubious about extending middle-class privileges to those lower down. Like them he was very keen on a strong police force and the prevention of crime, and like them he took an unholy delight in the breathless drama of a murder story. He was an unthinking, self-righteous protestant like many of them, and just as intensely insular and as ignorant as they were of the wider European tradition. Sometimes, as in the character of Podsnap in *Our Mutual Friend*, he tried to make fun of some of these English limitations, and at times the satirical humour was excellent. But he shared many of the same characteristics.

Self-knowledge was the least of his attainments. He was sincerely convinced that the breakdown of his marriage was entirely the fault of his unoffending wife, and that he could have lived happily with almost anybody else. But no one else is likely to believe this. Like other popular writers he was deeply melodramatic. But, unlike some, there was nothing cynical or calculating in his melodramatic appeal. He never wrote down to his adoring public. In expressing their aspirations, fears, and prejudices he was simply expressing himself.

Dickens was a man of obsessions, which can be traced all through his work. He was haunted by the idea of the lonely child, because he had been one. He was haunted by the idea of the prison, because his father had been in the debtors' prison. He was deeply obsessed by the thought of violence. These themes and a few others recur constantly; but it would be a complete mistake to suppose that this makes his work repetitive. His development, and like all great artists he developed continually to the end, consists partly in the perpetual deepening and enrichment of these themes. The prison of *Pickwick Papers* is the same debtors' prison as the one in *Little Dorrit* (and the same in which his own father was confined) but as literary experiences the two could hardly be more different, and the later one is immensely the more brilliant and profound. Occasionally, two of his obsessions meet in the same passage, such as the burning of the prison by the mob in *Barnaby Rudge* (prison and violence) or the exclusion of Dorritt at night from her only home, the Marshalsea prison (prison and lonely child). Such passages often have a particularly intense power or pathos.

Balancing this constant recurrence of the same facts and ideas we have his extraordinary inventiveness, variety, and mastery of significant detail. His world is fuller and richer than other novelists' worlds. He squanders enough characters on one novel to last any other novelist for five; and then has just as many swarming into his mind for the next. His hypnotic imagination finds poetry, humour, significance in the most ordinary things. London, that terrifying, amorphous, unadministered, physically filthy Victorian London, which struck intelligent foreign visitors as almost a hell on earth, was his natural home as man and artist. He drew strength and inspiration from his long, solitary walks (often at night) through the dingiest and strangest areas. His pathos, his wild, extravagant humour, his zeal for reform, his serious indignation were all rooted in this vision of the largest and strangest city the world had ever seen, and the one with the most bizarre contrasts.

There is no space here to chart his development in detail. In general one may say that in his early works, up to about 1845, his exuberance, whether comic or melodramatic, predominates. Plots are wildly improbable; coincidences abound; deeds often lack their natural outcome. At times we seem to be almost in the world of "the omnipotence of thought," a kind of fairy-tale, not about princesses, but about orphans and chimney-sweeps and strolling players. *Dombey and Son* (1848) is a landmark of change. The old features are still present in some degree, but so are those that become more and more dominant in his later work, psychological insight, serious thought about society, and above all a sense of the consequences of things and of the complexity of moral choices. In *Nicholas Nickleby*, an early work, two philanthropical brothers diffuse joy and peace all round them by giving away their money. In *Our Mutual Friend*, his last completed novel, Boffin, a kindly man anxious to do good with his large fortune, finds himself thwarted and deceived, and unable to produce beneficial effects. The later books are in places just as funny as the earlier. But the humour is more satirical, even savage. The soaring, high-spirited nonsense of *Pickwick* is gone.

Finally, I would stress the inexhaustible variety of Dickens. In him alone among later English writers, we can, without absurdity, find a likeness to the fecundity of Shakespeare.

— A. O. J. Cockshut

DISRAELI, Benjamin; 1st Earl of Beaconsfield. English. Born in London, 21 December 1804; son of the writer Isaac D'Israeli. Educated at a private school in Walthamstow, London; articled to Swain and Stevenson, solicitors, London, 1821; entered Lincoln's Inn, London, 1824; removed his name, 1831. Married Mrs. Wyndham Lewis in 1839 (died, 1872). Began writing in 1826; toured Spain, Italy, and the Near East, 1828–31; returned to London, and devoted himself to writing, 1831–37; contested the Parliamentary seats of High Wycombe, 1821, 1834, and Taunton, 1835; Conservative Member of Parliament for Maidstone, Kent, 1837–41, Shrewsbury, 1841–47, and Buckinghamshire, 1847 until his elevation to the House of Lords, 1876: Leader of the Young England Party of Conservatives, 1842; Chancellor of the Exchequer in Lord Derby's first government, 1852; Chancellor of the Exchequer and Leader of the House of Commons in Derby's second government, 1858–59; Chancellor of the Exchequer in Derby's third government, 1866–68: introduced and carried Reform Bill, 1867; became Prime Minister on Derby's retirement, 1868; opposed Gladstone's Irish and foreign policies, 1868–73; again Prime Minister, 1874–80: made

Britain half-owner of the Suez Canal, 1875; persuaded Queen Victoria to accept title of Empress of India, 1876, and became a close friend of the Queen; attempted to check Russian influence in Eastern Europe, 1877–78; represented England at the Congress of Berlin, 1878. Created Earl of Beaconsfield, 1876; Knight of the Garter, 1878. *Died 19 April 1881.*

PUBLICATIONS

Collections

   Works, edited by Edmund Gosse.   20 vols., 1904–05.

Fiction

   Rumpel Stiltskin: A Dramatic Spectacle, with W. G. Meredith.   1823; edited by Michael Sadleir, 1952.
   Vivian Grey.   5 vols., 1826–27.
   The Voyage of Captain Popanilla.   1828.
   The Young Duke.   1831.
   Contarini Fleming: A Psychological Autobiography.   1832; as *The Young Venetian,* 1834.
   The Wondrous Tales of Alroy and the Rise of Iskander.   1832; edited by W. S. Northcote, 1906.
   Henrietta Temple.   1837; edited by W. S. Northcote, 1906.
   Venetia; or, The Poet's Daughter.   1837.
   Coningsby; or, The New Generation.   1844.
   Sybil; or, The Two Nations.   1845; edited by Victor Cohen, 1934.
   Tancred; or, The New Crusade.   1847.
   Ixion in Heaven, The Infernal Marriage, Popanilla, Count Alarcos.   1853; edited by W. S. Northcote, 1906.
   Lothair.   1870; edited by Vernon Bogdanor, 1975.
   Novels and Tales.   10 vols., 1870–71.
   Endymion.   1880.
   Tales and Sketches, edited by J. L. Robertson.   1891.

Play

   The Tragedy of Count Alarcos (produced 1868).   1839.

Verse

   The Revolutionary Epick.   1834; revised edition, 1864.
   The Modern Aesop, edited by Michael Sadleir.   1928.

Other

   An Inquiry into the Plans, Progress, and Policy of the American Mining Companies.   1825.

Lawyers and Legislators; or, Notes on the American Mining Companies. 1825.
The Present Stage of Mexico. 1825.
Key to Vivian Grey. 1827.
England and France; or, A Cure for the Ministerial Gallomania. 1832.
What Is He? 1833; revised edition, 1833.
The Crisis Examined. 1834.
Vindication of the English Constitution. 1835.
The Letters of Runnymede, The Spirit of Whiggism. 1836; edited by Francis Bickley, 1923.
Lord George Bentinck: A Political Biography. 1852; revised edition, 1872.
Mr. Disraeli to Colonel Rathbone. 1858.
Church and Queen: Five Speeches 1860–64. 1865.
Speeches on Parliamentary Reform 1848–66, edited by Montagu Corry. 1867.
Speeches on the Conservative Policy of the Last Thirty Years, edited by J. F. Bulley. 1870.
Selected Speeches, edited by T. E. Kebble. 2 vols., 1882.
Home Letters 1830–31, edited by Ralph Disraeli. 1885.
Correspondence with His Sister, edited by Ralph Disraeli. 1886; edited by Augustine Birrell, 1928.
Whigs and Whiggism: Political Writing, edited by William Hutcheon. 1913.
Letters to Lady Bradford and Lady Chesterfield, edited by the Marquis of Zetland. 2 vols., 1929.
The Radical Tory: Disraeli's Political Development Illustrated from His Original Writings and Speeches, edited by H. W. J. Edwards. 1937.
Letters to Frances Anne, Marchioness of Londonderry 1837–61, edited by the Marchioness of Londonderry. 1938.
Tory Democrat: Two Famous Disraeli Speeches, edited by Edward Boyle. 1950.
Notes for an Autobiography, edited by Helen M. Swartz and Marvin Swartz. 1975.

Editor, *The Works of Isaac D'Israeli.* 1858.

Bibliography: *XIX Century Fiction* by Michael Sadleir, 1951; *Disraeli's Novels Reviewed 1826–1968* edited by R. W. Stewart, 1975.

Reading List: *Hours in a Library 2* by Leslie Stephen, 1876; *The Political Novel* by M. E. Speare, 1924; *Disraeli* by Cecil Roth, 1952; *The Victorian Sage* by John Holloway, 1953; *Disraeli* by Paul Bloomfield, 1962; *Disraeli* by Robert Blake, 1966; *Disraeli* by Richard W. Davis, 1976; *Disraeli and His World* by Christopher Hibbert, 1978.

*   *   *

The novels of Benjamin Disraeli are probably little read today, and it is unlikely that anyone who is not interested in politics will turn to them for pleasure. For Disraeli is a prime example of the political novelist. It is not just that he writes, as Trollope does, about political themes, but that his best novels – *Coningsby* and *Endymion* – are political allegories. They express the political ideas through which he hoped to "educate" and transform the Conservative Party of his day; and, through the Conservative Party, England also.

Disraeli's first novel, *Aylmer Papillion,* was published when he was only 19 in 1824; unfortunately only two chapters of it remain. His early novels were written primarily in order to raise the money to satisfy his creditors; and Part 1 of *Vivian Grey,* "as hot and hurried a sketch as ever yet was penned," appeared in 1826 when Disraeli was 21. It proved to be a *succès de scandale* on account of the appearance in it of many characters from contemporary social life whom the reader could amuse himself by identifying. The novel itself however, was a cynical pot-boiler, modelled on the "silver-fork" novel of the day, in the production of which Disraeli's friend Bulwer-Lytton was such a master. *Vivian Grey*'s central theme is the development and political education of a youth who possesses neither political ideals nor moral principles; his only concern is with worldly success — "Why then, the world's mine oyster," claims the epigraph of the book, "which I with sword will open." It was natural for Vivian to be identified with Disraeli himself.

Each of Disraeli's novels seems to display the same basic pattern as *Vivian Grey*, in that its theme is the development of a young man to maturity. Indeed, eight of the novels bear the name of the youth as their title. But what is striking about the novels of Disraeli's maturity — the trilogy *Coningsby*, *Sybil*, and *Tancred*; *Lothair*; and *Endymion* — is the way in which the heroes *differ* from Vivian Grey in seeking something more than worldly success.

As Kathleen Tillotson has noticed (*Novels of the Eighteen-Forties*, 1954), Disraeli's mature heroes "all *think* perhaps ineffectually, ignorantly, fitfully, but in their puzzled or impulsive way they do think, and about their social rights and responsibilities." Coningsby, Charles Egremont in *Sybil*, Tancred, Lothair, and Endymion are concerned at the degradation of the aristocratic ideal typified by the selfishness of great landed magnates such as Coningsby's grandfather Lord Monmouth or Lord Marney in *Sybil*. This degradation has ruined the Conservative Party, once a party of principle, social reform, and devotion to the interests of the people, so that it has become a party of concessionaires and place-seekers whose only *raison d'être* is the spoils of office. As he says in the General Preface to the novels, "no party was national; one was exclusive and odious, and the other liberal and cosmopolitan."

Disraeli's heroes, therefore, seek a social ideal through which they might organise their lives. This ideal is to be found through "the use of ancient forms and the restoration of the past." "That's the true spring of wisdom," Coningsby is told, "meditate over the past." Disraeli sought a re-invigoration of the feudal principle of social responsibility, since in a healthy society, in the relationship between employer and employed, "there must exist other ties than the payment and acceptance of wages." Disraeli's obsession with great houses and aristocratic munificence reflects his view of society. The great houses have a continuous and vital relationship to the past, rooted in the land. They serve a function not only for the family living in them, but also for the hierarchical and intergrated community of which they are the apex. For the ownership of a great house is, ideally, associated with precisely the virtues of generosity and social concern which are needed to regenerate England.

What Disraeli's novels offer then is a clearly thought-out and consistent philosophy of conservatism. His heroes come to understand the nature of conservatism by confronting the different philosophies which seek to explain men's duties, and the mature novels end with the hero at last equipped to face his responsibilities. Coningsby enters Parliament, Egremont in *Sybil* is confident that the seemingly impassable gulf between the two nations — the rich and the poor — can be bridged; Tancred understands that a political renewal cannot occur without a religious revival; and Lothair can assume the duties of a great landowner.

Where the novels end with the marriage of the hero, the symbolic nature of the union is made clear. Coningsby, in marrying Edith Millbank, the daughter of an industrialist, appreciates that the regeneration of the aristocracy depends upon its coming to terms with the rising force of industry; Egremont, by marrying Sybil, acts in accordance with his belief that aristocratic leadership can secure class harmony; and Lothair, in allying himself to Lady Corisande who represents the practical spirit of traditional wisdom, frees himself from the ideological fanaticisms of the Roman Catholic Church and modern nationalism.

Disraeli thus represents a genuine and vital link in the history of English conservative thought — a link between Burke and Coleridge and T. S. Eliot. His view of life was greatly influenced by Burke and Carlyle in that he believed human existence to have an impalpability that is not to be grasped in any set of abstract formulae or rules for living, such as the Utilitarians, for example, attempted to provide. "Utilitarians in politics," Disraeli argued in his early "Mutilated Diary," "are like Unitarians in religion. Both omit Imagination in their systems and Imagination governs mankind." And in *Lothair* Disraeli tells us that the philosophers "accounted for everything, except the only point on which man requires revelation." It is this insistence that life is not to be understood in terms of any dogmatic philosophy that gives Disraeli's novels their characteristic air of exuberance and optimism.

Disraeli was uninterested in the traditional furniture of the English novel. His concern with the development of character was perfunctory and his plots were melodramatic and preposterous. Yet he had a profound insight into political ideas, and succeeded in grafting a novel of political ideas on to the "silver-fork novel." This makes him *sui generis* among novelists writing in the English language.

—Vernon Bogdanor

DODGSON, Charles Lutwidge.   See CARROLL, Lewis.

DONNELLY, Ignatius.   American.   Born in Philadelphia, Pennsylvania, 3 November 1831. Educated at Central High School, Philadelphia, graduated 1849; read law in the office of Benjamin Harris Brewster, Philadelphia: admitted to the Pennsylvania bar, 1852. Married 1) Katharine McCaffrey in 1855 (died, 1894); 2) Marian Hanson in 1898. Moved to Minnesota, 1856: Lieutenant Governor of Minnesota, 1859–63; Republican Member for Minnesota, United States Congress, Washington, D.C., 1863–69; thereafter a liberal Republican, then a Populist: President, National Anti-Monopoly Convention, 1872, and Editor of the *Anti-Monopolist* newspaper, 1874–79; Member of the Minnesota State Senate, 1874–78; Greenback-Democrat candidate for Congress, 1878; thereafter a full-time writer; ran again for Congress, 1884; served as Farmers Alliance Member of the Minnesota State Legislature, 1887, and as President of the State Farmers Alliance of Minnesota; in later years edited *The Representative*, Minneapolis, and again served in the Minnesota Legislature; nominee of the People's Party for Vice-President of the United States, 1898. *Died 1 January 1901.*

PUBLICATIONS

Fiction

   Caesar's Column: A Story of the Twentieth Century.   1890; edited by Walter B. Rideout, 1960.
   Doctor Huguet.   1891.
   The Golden Bottle; or, The Story of Ephraim Benezet of Kansas.   1892.

Verse

   The Mourner's Vision.   1850.

Other

Nininger City. 1856.
The Sonnets of Shakespeare: An Essay. 1859.
Atlantis: The Antediluvian World. 1882; edited by Egerton Sykes, 1949.
Ragnarok: The Age of Fire and Gravel. 1883.
The Great Cryptogram: Francis Bacon's Cipher in the So-Called Shakespeare
     Plays. 1888.
In Memoriam Mrs. Katharine Donnelly. 1895.
The American People's Money. 1895; revised edition, as The Bryan Campaign for the
     American People's Money, 1896.
The Cipher in the Plays and on the Tombstone. 1899.

Bibliography: in Bibliography of American Literature by Jacob Blanck, 1957.

Reading List: North Star Sage: The Story of Donnelly by Oscar M. Sullivan, 1953; Donnelly
by Martin Ridge, 1962.

                            *   *   *

Ignatius Donnelly's works are imaginative, eccentric, and occasionally startling in their
perceptions. Atlantis: The Antediluvian World is an attempt to demonstrate and expand upon
Plato's myth of a great civilization that once supposedly existed near the mouth of the
Mediterranean long before any similarly high culture, an island society suddenly destroyed
by the gods because of its decadence. In his stupifyingly data-crammed book, Donnelly
argued not only that Atlantis actually existed, but that it was "the region where man first rose
from a state of barbarism to civilization." Furthermore, Atlantis was the source of most of the
world's gods, legends, inventions, languages, architectural styles, plants, and animals.
   The book was extremely popular, running through over twenty editions, and it inspired
countless imitators and followers to publish their corroborative findings. Since, as Martin
Gardner says in Fads and Fallacies, there is "not a shred of reliable evidence, geological or
archeological, to support" the myth, this popularity seems a testament to Donnelly's ability
to immerse his readers in an impressively assembled mass of highly interesting but nearly
totally misleading information. Donnelly's argument is dense and the farrago of seemingly
expert testimony he scraped together from a wide variety of library nooks and crannies is
mountainous: his own literary style is far from ornate, however, and though assertive seems
simply the straight-from-the-shoulder truth of a no-nonsense scholar. The work is fun to
read, filled with arcane stories and ingenious, wild yoking of disparate cultural phenomena.
He advances all his evidence quite seriously, including parallel lists showing the similarities
between the Sioux and Danish languages, and hilarious drawings of skulls from Central
America and Egypt artificially deformed in the same fashion. In Ragnarok: The Age of Fire
and Gravel he theorized that long ago the Earth passed through the tail of a giant comet,
producing world-wide catastrophe, "rearings, howlings, ... hissings," and great heat. When
the fires from this heat subsided, an Age of Darkness began, followed by the Ice Age. In The
Great Cryptogram he produced a thousand pages of cipher analyses and lists of parallel
quotations to prove that Francis Bacon wrote Shakespeare's plays. One critic used Donnelly's
de-coding formula to demonstrate that a passage from Hamlet really read "Dou-nill-he, the
author, politician, and mountebanke, will work out the secret of this play. The sage is a
daysie."
   But it would be a distinct mistake to dismiss Donnelly as a crank. He is frequently
fascinating and his forays into scientific theory or literary criticism display impressive if ill-
digested and misguided learning, and sensitivity to literary values. Furthermore, in his fiction
he seriously addressed serious social problems such as the political weakness of the poor (The

Golden Bottle) and racial intolerance (*Doctor Huguet*). *Caesar's Column* is a minor anti-utopian classic predicting class warfare between the economic oppressors and oppressed, forces equally matched in their brutality. Marred only by two silly love stories, the novel accurately depicts many technological horrors of the future – such as air raids – and, more importantly, discusses specific social reforms such as an eight-hour work day and socialized medicine. The book's central image is a grotesque symbol of modern civilization: Caesar's column is a gigantic pillar of dead bodies killed in the slaughter of war.

—Jack B. Moore

DOS PASSOS, John (Roderigo).   American.   Born in Chicago, Illinois, 14 January 1896. Educated at Choate School, Wallingford, Connecticut, 1907–11; Harvard University, Cambridge, Massachusetts (Editor, *Harvard Monthly*), 1912–16, B.A. (cum laude) 1916; studied in Castille, 1916–17. Served with the Norton-Harjes Ambulance Unit in France, 1917, and on Red Cross Ambulance duty in Italy, 1918; served in the United States Medical Corps, 1918–19. Married 1) Katharine F. Smith in 1929 (died, 1947); 2) Elizabeth Hamlin Holdridge in 1950, one daughter. Writer from 1918; lived in Spain and Portugal, 1919; travelled in the Near East with the Near East Relief Organization, 1921; settled in New York, 1922; travelled in Spain, 1923; Co-Founder, *New Masses*, New York, 1926, and contributor until the early 1930's; Founder, New Playwrights Theatre, New York, 1927–28; visited the U.S.S.R., 1928; moved to Provincetown, Massachusetts, 1930; Contributor to *Common Sense*, 1932; screenwriter, in Hollywood, 1934; War Correspondent in the Pacific, and at Nuremburg, 1945, and in South America, 1948, for *Life* magazine, New York. Treasurer, National Committee for the Defense of Political Prisoners, 1931; Chairman, National Committee to Aid Striking Miners, 1931; Treasurer, Campaign for Political Refugees, 1940. Artist: one-man show of sketches, New York, 1937. Recipient: Guggenheim Fellowship, 1939, 1940, 1942; National Institute of Arts and Letters Gold Medal Award, 1957. Member, American Academy of Arts and Letters. *Died 28 September 1970.*

PUBLICATIONS

Fiction

> *One Man's Initiation – 1917.*   1919; as *First Encounter*, 1945.
> *Three Soldiers.*   1921.
> *Streets of Night.*   1923.
> *Manhattan Transfer.*   1925.
> *The 42nd Parallel.*   1930; *1919*, 1932; *The Big Money*, 1936; complete version, as *U.S.A.*, 1938.
> *Adventures of a Young Man.*   1939; *Number One*, 1943; *The Grand Design*, 1949; complete version, as *District of Columbia*, 1952.
> *Most Likely to Succeed.*   1954.
> *The Great Days.*   1958.
> *Mid-Century: A Contemporary Chronicle.*   1961.
> *Century's End.*   1975.

337

Plays

The Garbage Man: A Parade with Shouting (as *The Moon Is a Gong*, produced 1925; as
    The Garbage Man, produced 1926). 1926.
Airways, Inc. (produced 1927). 1928.
Fortune Heights (produced 1933). In *Three Plays*, 1934.
USA: A Dramatic Revue, with Paul Shyre. 1963.

Verse

A Pushcart at the Curb. 1922.

Other

Rosinante to the Road Again. 1922.
Orient Express. 1927.
Facing the Chair: The Story of the Americanization of Two Foreignborn Workmen (on
    Sacco and Vanzetti). 1927.
In All Countries. 1934.
The Villages Are the Heart of Spain. 1937.
Journeys Between Wars. 1938.
The Ground We Stand On: Some Examples from the History of a Political Creed. 1941.
State of the Nation. 1944.
Tour of Duty. 1946.
The Prospect Before Us. 1950.
Life's Picture History of World War II. 1950.
Chosen Country. 1951.
The Head and Heart of Thomas Jefferson. 1954.
The Theme Is Freedom. 1956.
The Men Who Made the Nation. 1957.
Prospects of a Golden Age. 1959.
Mr. Wilson's War. 1962.
Brazil on the Move. 1963.
Thomas Jefferson: The Making of a President (juvenile). 1964.
Occasions and Protests: Essays 1936–1964. 1964.
The Shackles of Power 1801–1826: Three Jeffersonian Decades. 1966.
The Best Times: An Informal Memoir. 1966.
The Portugal Story: Three Decades of Exploration and Discovery. 1969.
Easter Island: Island of Enigmas. 1971.
The Fourteenth Chronicle: Letters and Diaries, edited by Townsend Ludington. 1973.

Editor, *The Living Thoughts of Tom Paine.* 1940.

Translator, *Metropolis*, by Manuel Maples Arce. 1929.
Translator, *Panama*, by Blaise Cendrars. 1931.

Reading List: *Dos Passos* by John H. Wrenn, 1961; *Dos Passos* by Robert Gorham Davis,
1962; *The Fiction of Dos Passos* by John D. Brantley, 1968; *Dos Passos: A Collection of
Critical Essays* edited by Andrew Hook, 1974; *Dos Passos* by George J. Becker, 1974; *Dos
Passos and the Fiction of Despair* by Iain Colley, 1978.

*   *   *

John Dos Passos was involved in many of the episodes that have played an important part in twentieth-century literary history; not surprisingly, these had an important effect on his writing. After a lonely childhood living in Europe and then being a bookish student among advocates of the strenuous life at the Choate School in Wallingford, Connecticut, he went through Harvard University with a number of the writers who became part of the artistic renaissance that started during the period just before World War I. T. S. Eliot was still at Harvard while he was there; E. E. Cummings, Robert Hillyer, and Stewart Mitchell were among his close friends. He drove an ambulance during World War I, then roamed the Continent afterward and passed frequently through the Paris expatriate scene, though he was never truly a part of it. He was a friend of writers like Scott Fitzgerald, Upton Sinclair, Van Wyck Brooks, and a close friend of Archibald MacLeish, Edmund Wilson, and – for a while – Ernest Hemingway, among others. He became deeply involved in political radicalism during the 1920's but was never the activist that his writings made him seem; he interviewed and wrote about the Italian anarchists Sacco and Vanzetti, who had been found guilty of murder on dubious evidence; he worked as a director of a left-wing, experimental drama group, the New Playwrights, in the late 1920's; he traveled to Russia in 1928; he visited the Harlan County, Kentucky, coal mines with Theodore Dreiser in 1931; he experienced the "big money" briefly as a screen writer in Hollywood in 1934; and he went to Spain many times, returning in 1937 with Hemingway to report on the Civil War. During World War II he wrote about the domestic scene, visited the Pacific, and reported on Europe and the war-crimes trials in Germany after the war. In the 1940's and subsequently he took an interest in capitalism – this time viewing it favorably – in Jeffersonian liberalism, and in the development of Latin America.

Although his reputation is not what it was in 1938 when Jean-Paul Sartre declared, "I regard Dos Passos as the greatest writer of our time," his works of fiction, which he came to call chronicles, and his non-fiction continue to be read widely. He is one of the two or three most important political novelists the United States has produced, and certain of his books – in particular *Three Soldiers*, *Manhattan Transfer*, and the three volumes of *U.S.A.* – are landmarks in the nation's literary history. *Three Soldiers* was the first of the significant novels to come from a United States writer's experiences during World War I. *Manhattan Transfer* represents Dos Passos's innovative application to literature of the artistic theories and techniques which emerged during the decades before and after the turn of the century, when a veritable revolution in the arts occurred in Europe and then in the United States. This chronicle of the city incorporates impressionism, expressionism, montage, simultaneity, reportage, and other techniques of "the new" in the arts and is important also for its themes of alienation and loss, as well as for its satiric treatment of the urban scene.

The three volumes of *U.S.A.* are Dos Passos's attempt to employ his techniques of art to chronicle United States civilization from 1900 to the beginning of the Great Depression in 1929. While he was writing *U.S.A.* from 1927 to 1936, he was far to the left politically, although he began turning toward the center by 1934. The trilogy, a panorama of the nation's life from his political perspective, is deeply satiric about business and the materialistic society it had created. The period he was chronicling, he wrote the critic Malcolm Cowley, was a time when the country moved from "competitive" to "monopoly" capitalism.

From being a political leftist, Dos Passos moved toward the right after believing himself personally betrayed by the Communists, a feeling culminating with the execution – he claimed at the hands of the Communists – of his close friend José Robles in Spain in 1937. Betrayal by the Communists became the fate of the hero in his next novel, the distinctly anti-left *Adventures of a Young Man*. Dos Passos's own adventure with the left was over by then; his subsequent chronicles, which dealt with the years until his death, were increasingly strident satires, most of them about the modern liberalism and government bureaucracy that he saw to be the heritage of Franklin Roosevelt's New Deal Administration. A single exception is *Chosen Country* where, through the adventures of an autobiographical hero, Jay Pignatelli, Dos Passos told of his gradual allegiance to the United States and his romance with his first wife, Katharine Smith.

But Dos Passos was not only a novelist. He wrote numerous books of reportage describing his world travels and analyzing the life and politics of his own and other nations. After 1937, he began also to write histories, repeatedly considering the origins of the United States in books such as *The Ground We Stand On, Men Who Made the Nation, Prospects of a Golden Age,* and *Shackles of Power: Three Jeffersonian Decades.* He became fascinated by Thomas Jefferson, who was, in fact, a sort of hero for him; he wrote a biography – *The Head and Heart of Thomas Jefferson* – as well as several other studies of the man and his era. In addition to all these works he wrote a volume of poetry, several plays, and many articles about politics, drama, and art, among other subjects.

In the early 1950's he sympathized with Senator Joseph McCarthy's efforts to ferret Communists out of the government, but did not support McCarthy's methods. In 1964 he applauded Senator Barry Goldwater for the Presidency; yet Dos Passos's conservatism was never the simplistic matter his critics took it to be. Committed to a right-wing support of the United States by 1958, nevertheless he could write to the historian Arthur Schlesinger, Jr.: "It seems to me that there is a myth of the war [World War II] and our position vis-à-vis the rest of the world which has been swallowing us up in an alarming way. Actually, we are disliked and feared by the rest of the world just as Napoleon, and England and Germany have been. At the same time, we have worked up a self-justificatory fantasy about the nobility of our actions and aims." Always critical rather than doctrinaire, Dos Passos wanted to remain independent, something of the anarchist, in his works supporting individual freedoms against bureaucracies and monoliths wherever he saw them while portraying the swirl of life in his chosen country. Granting Dos Passos his political perspectives, the reader can get from his works a remarkably broad chronicle of the twentieth-century United States.

—Townsend Ludington

DOUGLAS, Norman. English. Born George Norman Douglass in Falkenhorst, Thuringen, Austria, 8 December 1868. Educated at Yarlet Hall, Staffordshire, 1878; privately at Mowseley, Warwickshire, 1879–81; Uppingham School, Rutland, 1881–83; Karlsruhe Gymnasium, Germany, 1883–89; Scoones School, London, 1889–93. Married Elizabeth Louisa Fitzgibbon in 1898 (divorced, 1903); two sons. Member of the British Foreign Service, 1893–98: Third Secretary in St. Petersburg, 1894–96; lived in Capri, 1898–1910, and in England, 1910–16: Assistant Editor, *English Review,* London, 1912–16; thereafter lived on the Continent, except for the war years, in Florence, 1922–37, the south of France, 1937–40, Lisbon, 1940–41, and Capri, 1946 until his death. *Died 7 February 1952.*

PUBLICATIONS

Collections

A Selection, edited by D. M. Low.   1955.

Fiction

Unprofessional Tales, with Elsa Douglas.   1901.
South Wind.   1917; revised edition, 1946.

They Went.   1920.
In the Beginning.   1927.
The Angel of Manfredonia.   1929.

Plays

South Wind, with I. C. Tippett, from the novel by Douglas (produced 1923).

Other

Contribution to an Avifauna of Baden.   1894.
Report on the Pumice Stone Industry of the Lipari Islands.   1895.
On the Darwinian Hypothesis of Sexual Selection.   1895.
Materials for a Description of Capri.   10 vols., 1904–15; as *Capri,* 1930.
Siren Land.   1911; revised edition, 1923.
Fountains in the Sand: Rambles among the Oases of Tunisia.   1912; revised edition, 1944.
Old Calabria.   1915.
London Street Games.   1916; revised edition, 1931.
Alone (travel in Italy).   1921.
Together.   1923.
D. H. Lawrence and Maurice Magnus: A Plea for Better Manners.   1924.
Experiments.   1925.
Birds and Beasts of the Greek Anthology.   1927; revised edition, 1928.
How about Europe? Some Footnotes on East and West.   1929; as *Goodbye to Western Culture,* 1930.
One Day.   1929.
Three of Them.   1930.
Paneros: Some Words on Aphrodisiacs and the Like.   1930.
Summer Islands: Ischia and Ponza.   1931.
Looking Back: An Autobiographical Excursion.   2 vols., 1933.
An Almanac.   1941.
Late Harvest (autobiography).   1946; revised edition, 1947.
Footnote on Capri, photographs by Islay Lyons.   1952.

Editor, *Some Limericks.*   1928.
Editor, with Pino Orioli, *Venus in the Kitchen; or, Love's Cookery Book.*   1952

Translator, *The Beaver in Norway,* by A. J. Olsen.   1894.

Bibliography: *A Bibliography of Douglas* by Cecil Woolf, 1954.

Reading List: *Douglas: A Pictorial Record* by Constantine FitzGibbon, 1953; *Douglas: A Critical Study,* 1956, and *Douglas,* 1965, both by R. D. Lindeman; *Douglas* by Ian Greenlees, 1957; *Douglas* by Lewis Leary, 1968; *Douglas: A Biography* by Mark Holloway, 1976.

*   *   *

Norman Douglas's most successful book was his novel *South Wind,* a novel of conversation. The setting is Nepenthe, based on Capri though, as he put it, "the Capri as it always should have been and as it never, alas, yet was or will be." It is written a little in the manner of the novels of Thomas Love Peacock. Some reviewers criticised it because there was no plot. But Douglas replied to this, in *Alone*, when he asserted that "it would be nearer the truth to say that it is nothing but plot. How? You must unconventionalize him and instil into his mind the seeds of doubt and revolt. You must shatter his old notions of what is right ... make the soil receptive to new ideas."

The novel could well be described as a study of the impact made by Italy on an Englishman. Italy certainly has a leavening, softening, and civilizing influence on the northerner. The arteries of the Bishop, Mr. Heard, which have hardened over the years, begin to soften, his conventional point of view becomes less formal, his mind less closed, mainly from his conversations with the hedonist Keith, based on Douglas himself. Slowly but relentlessly Keith converts the Bishop to his views, and Mr. Heard finally begins to notice an unwonted sparkle in the air, something cleansing and clarifying, signifying a new perspective. The novel ends on this note, demonstrating the influence of environment – and such a hedonist as Keith – on an ordinary, conventional human being.

Keith's recipe for happiness is to find everything useful and nothing indispensable, everything wonderful and nothing miraculous, and at the same time to reverence the body and avoid first causes like the plague. But the gaiety and sparkle of the novel are based on other characters, too: Miss Wilberforce (note the irony in the choice of the name), the incurable but happily drunken spinster; Denis, the eternal adolescent, groping his way towards a knowledge of himself; Mr. Parker, the slightly shady, coarse-grained secretary of the local club; Signor Malipizzo, the opportunist, free-thinking judge; and the Russian characters.

Douglas was at his happiest and most delightful in his travel books, especially *Old Calabria* and *Siren Land*. *Old Calabria*, like some of his works on Capri, is erudite and informative. But in all his travel books he was able to expound his philosophy of life, express the many facets of his glittering personality, and indulge in his quest for knowledge. He was further able to record his impressions of the landscape and people he encountered in the course of his travels, along with shrewd digressions on such topics as food and leisure. But, as in *South Wind*, the same dominant personality pervades the books, and his message to today's world is perhaps even more relevant than it was thirty or forty years ago. Just as Douglas was a sun worshipper, so the lesson he has to teach us is radiant with the sunlit atmosphere of the pagan south, and is impregnated with the robust sanity of his outlook.

—Ian Greenlees

DOYLE, Sir Arthur Conan.   Scottish.   Born in Edinburgh, 22 May 1859. Educated at the Hodder School, Lancashire, 1868–70, Stonyhurst College, Lancashire, 1870–75, and the Jesuit School, Feldkirch, Austria, 1875–76; studied medicine at the University of Edinburgh, 1876–81, M.B. 1881, M.D. 1885. Served as Senior Physician to a field hospital in South Africa during the Boer War, 1899–1902; knighted, 1902. Married 1) Louise Hawkins in 1885 (died, 1906), one daughter and one son; 2) Jean Leckie in 1907, two sons and one daughter. Practised medicine in Southsea, 1882–90; full-time writer from 1891; stood for Parliament as Unionist candidate for Central Edinburgh, 1900, and tariff reform candidate for the Hawick Burghs, 1906. LL.D.: University of Edinburgh, 1905. Knight of Grace of the Order of St. John of Jerusalem. *Died 7 July 1930.*

Collections

Great Stories, edited by John Dickson Carr.   1959.

Fiction

A Study in Scarlet.   1888.
The Mystery of Cloomber.   1889.
Micah Clarke.   1889.
Mysteries and Adventures.   1889; as The Gully of Bluemansdyke and Other Stories,
   1893.
The Sign of Four.   1890.
The Captain of the Polestar and Other Tales.   1890.
The Firm of Girdlestone.   1890.
The White Company.   1891; edited by C. Kingsley Williams, 1934.
The Doings of Raffles Haw.   1892.
The Great Shadow.   1892; edited by Guy N. Pocock, 1940.
Beyond the City.   1892.
The Adventures of Sherlock Holmes (stories).   1892.
The Refugees.   1893.
The Memoirs of Sherlock Holmes (stories).   1893.
Round the Red Lamp, Being Facts and Fancies of Medical Life.   1894.
The Parasite.   1894.
The Stark Munro Letters.   1895.
The Exploits of Brigadier Gerard.   1896.
Rodney Stone.   1896; edited by C. Kingsley Williams, 1936.
Uncle Bernac: A Memory of the Empire.   1897.
The Tragedy of the Korosko.   1898.
A Duet, with an Occasional Chorus.   1899.
The Green Flag and Other Stories of War and Sport.   1900.
The Hound of the Baskervilles.   1902.
The Adventures of Gerard.   1903.
The Return of Sherlock Holmes (stories).   1905.
Sir Nigel.   1906.
Round the Fire Stories.   1908.
The Last Galley: Impressions and Tales.   1911.
The Case of Oscar Slater.   1912.
The Lost World.   1912.
The Poison Belt.   1913.
The Valley of Fear.   1915.
His Last Bow: Some Reminiscences of Sherlock Holmes.   1917.
Danger! and Other Stories.   1918.
The Land of Mist.   1926.
The Case-Book of Sherlock Holmes (stories).   1927.
The Maracot Deep and Other Stories.   1929.
Historical Romances.   2 vols., 1931–32.
Strange Studies from Life, edited by Peter Ruber.   1963.
The Annotated Sherlock Holmes, edited by W. S. Baring-Gould.   1968.

Plays

Jane Annie; or, The Good Conduct Prize, with J. M. Barrie, music by Ernest Ford
(produced 1893).   1893.
Foreign Policy (produced 1893).
Waterloo (as *A Story of Waterloo,* produced 1894).   1919(?).
Halves (produced 1899).
Sherlock Holmes, with William Gillette, from works by Doyle (produced 1899).   1922.
A Duet.   1903.
Brigadier Gerard, from his own story (produced 1906).
The Fires of Fate: A Modern Morality (produced 1909).
The House of Temperley (produced 1909).
A Pot of Caviare (produced 1910).   1912.
The Speckled Band (produced 1910).   1912.
The Crown Diamond (produced 1921).

Verse

Songs of Action.   1898.
Songs of the Road.   1911.
The Guards Came Through and Other Poems.   1919.
Collected Poems.   1922.

Other

The Great Boer War.   1900.
The War in South Africa: Its Cause and Conduct.   1902.
Works.   12 vols., 1903.
Through the Magic Door.   1907.
The Crime of the Congo.   1909.
The German War: Sidelights and Reflections.   1914.
To Arms!   1914.
The British Campaign in France and Flanders.   6 vols., 1916–19.
A Visit to Three Fronts, June 1916.   1917.
The New Revelation; or, What Is Spiritualism?   1918.
The Vital Message.   1919.
The Wanderings of a Spiritualist.   1921.
The Case for Spirit Photography, with others.   1922.
The Coming of the Fairies.   1922.
Three of Them.   1923.
Our American Adventure.   1923.
Memories and Adventures.   1924.
Our Second American Adventure.   1924.
The History of Spiritualism.   2 vols., 1926.
Pheneas Speaks: Direct Spirit Communications.   1927.
Our African Winter.   1929.
The Roman Catholic Church.   1929.
The Edge of the Unknown.   1930.

Editor, *The Spiritualist's Reader.*   1924.

Bibliography: *A Bibliographical Catalogue of the Writings of Doyle* by Harold Locke, 1928.

Reading List: *Doyle: His Life and Art* by Hesketh Pearson, 1943, revised edition, 1977; *The Life of Doyle* by John Dickson Carr, 1949; *A Sherlock Holmes Commentary* by D. Martin Dakin, 1972; *The World of Sherlock Holmes* by Michael Harrison, 1973; *The Encyclopedia Sherlockiana* by Jack W. Tracy, 1977.

*   *   *

There are a few characters of fiction who step out of their books and become known almost universally. The literary eminence, or otherwise, of their creators seems to bear no relation to their fame; they range from Scrooge and Peter Pan to the Scarlet Pimpernel and Tarzan of the Apes, and probably the best known of them all is Sherlock Holmes who has been described as "the most famous man who never lived."

Even without Holmes, Sir Arthur Conan Doyle would still hold a reasonably high place in the literature of adventure stories and historical romance — perhaps between Rider Haggard and John Buchan. He himself wished to be remembered by his historical romances, notably *The White Company* and *Sir Nigel*, though these are ponderous compared to his two volumes of Napoleonic short stories, *The Exploits of Brigadier Gerard* and *The Adventures of Gerard*. In Gerard he created a really memorable and living character, a vain French brigadier, as brave as he boasts himself to be, though with an amusing touch of stupidity, who narrates his own exciting adventures in a delightfully flamboyant manner. Gerard is memorable in a way that Sir Nigel Loring and his White Company are not, in spite of Doyle's splendid narrative gift. Doyle's narrative, in fact, makes almost all his fiction eminently readable, and the sheer impetus of breathless adventure in the first half of *The Refugees* rivals Stanley Weyman's best. Besides the Gerard stories Doyle also produced an excellent volume of miscellaneous historical tales, *The Last Galley*, later issued with one additional story as *Tales of Long Ago*, which he considered the best of his unaffiliated short stories. He was certainly a master of the short story of plot rather than character, but, apart from the Holmes and Gerard collections, he was probably at his best with "Tales of Terror and Mystery" and of "Twilight and the Unseen," issued at first in various collections.

In 1912, trying to escape from Sherlock Holmes, Doyle strove to create another memorable character as different from him as possible, and wrote *The Lost World*, the first adventure of the redoubtable Professor Challenger (apparently suggested by Rider Haggard's Professor Higgs in *Queen Sheba's Ring*, 1909), just far enough from caricature to carry conviction. The story is of an expedition to a plateau in South America isolated from the rest of the world, where prehistoric animals and savages in a very early state of development still survive. It is told in a series of reports by the journalist member of the party — an excellent method of creating continual suspense — and remains one of the most popular of Doyle's books, lending itself particularly well to cinematic treatment.

Doyle used Challenger and his companions again in *The Poison Belt* in which they manage to survive an apparent blotting out of all life on Earth, though (as in his earlier story of a modern alchemist, *The Doings of Raffles Haw*) he is unable to exploit his idea to the full as perhaps the early H. G. Wells could have done. The same is true of his dabblings with the supernatural even in as exciting a story as *The Mystery of Cloomber*. By the time he came to introduce his Challenger group to Spiritualism in *The Land of Mist*, he was himself an ardent Spiritualist and produced a mere tract in the form of a novel.

But of course Doyle really lives as an important author by his long and short stories of Mr. Sherlock Holmes, the first private consulting detective, who made his rooms at 221B Baker Street, London so famous that large numbers of letters addressed to a fictitious character at a fictitious address still turn up.

Doyle did not invent the detective story or the detective. There were detectives in the novels of Dickens and Wilkie Collins, and a first "blueprint" for Holmes had admittedly appeared under the name of Dupin in several short stories by Edgar Allan Poe; moreover, M.

Lecoq, an energetic French professional, had been created by Emile Gaboriau – apparently based on the actual detective Vidocq whose *Memoires* had been published in 1828. While these may have suggested conscious or subconscious ideas for the creation of Holmes the only intentional and admitted borrowing was from one of Doyle's professors at Edinburgh University, Dr. Joseph Bell, who was accustomed to detect not only ailments but also profession, antecedents, and other personal information about his patients without them speaking a single word.

The first appearance of Sherlock Holmes, *A Study in Scarlet*, created little stir among critics or readers; the second of the longer adventures, *The Sign of Four*, had more popular success, because Doyle's name had become known through the publication of his first historical romance, *Micah Clarke*, the previous year. But it was not until the *Adventures* began appearing month by month in *The Strand Magazine* in 1891 that Sherlock Holmes took the public by storm. One innovation was that each of the monthly issues included a complete story with the same chief characters instead of a single full-length story cut into monthly parts to which readers of the magazine had become accustomed; but this does not belittle Doyle's achievement in creating the first short detective story with the eccentric detective whose interest for the reader is focused on his mind rather than his soul, and who is accompanied by a companion who is a little more dull-witted than the reader is assumed to be. Doyle, the professional doctor with the scientific and analytic mind, trained to observe and report, but unable to create any but a static and undeveloping character found his perfect *métier* in Holmes and Watson. He also captured the setting and atmosphere of the period and background in a way that created some unexplained spell. This has produced the unique activities of Sherlock Holmes Societies all over the world and a library of Sherlock Holmes literature treating the four long and fifty-six short stories about him as true accounts of a real man's adventures: a kind of playtime research particularly attractive to the academic mind.

Probably most critics agree that *The Hound of the Baskervilles* is Doyle's masterpiece. Many of the short stories, including "The Speckled Band" and "Silver Blaze," are in the same class. Although Doyle describes Holmes as "the most perfect reasoning and observing machine that the world has seen," he was able to create externally a character and a period setting as unique and recognisable as the more deeply drawn characters of the great novelists.

—Roger Lancelyn Green

DREISER, Theodore (Herman Albert). American. Born in Terre Haute, Indiana, 27 August 1871; lived with his family in various Indiana towns; settled in Warsaw, Indiana, 1884. Educated in public schools in Warsaw, Terre Haute, Sullivan, and Evansville, Indiana; Indiana University, Bloomington, 1889–90. Married 1) Sara Osborne White in 1898 (separated, 1909; died, 1942); 2) Helen Patges Richardson in 1944. Worked in a restaurant, and for a hardware company, in Chicago, 1887–89; real estate clerk and collection agent, Chicago, 1890–92; Reporter for the Chicago *Globe*, 1892; Dramatic Editor, St. Louis *Globe-Democrat*, 1892–93; settled in New York, 1895: Editor, *Ev'ry Month*, 1895–96, *Smith's Magazine*, 1905–06, and *Broadway Magazine*, 1906–07; Editor-in-Chief, Butterick Publications, New York, and Editor of Butterick's *Delineator*, 1907–10; Editor, *Bohemian* magazine, 1909–10; full-time writer from 1911; lived in Hollywood, 1919–23; Co-Editor, *American Spectator* magazine, 1932–34; applied for membership in the Communist Party, 1945. Chairman, National Committee for the Defense of Political Prisoners, 1931. Recipient: American Academy of Arts and Letters Award of Merit, 1944. *Died 28 December 1945.*

PUBLICATIONS

Collections

    Letters: A Selection, edited by Robert H. Elias.   3 vols., 1959.
    A Dreiser Reader, edited by James T. Farrell.   1962.
    Selected Poems, edited by Robert P. Saalback.   1969.

Fiction

    Sister Carrie.   1900; edited by Donald Pizer, 1970.
    Jennie Gerhardt.   1911.
    The Financier.   1912.
    The Titan.   1914.
    The "Genius."   1915.
    Free and Other Stories.   1918.
    Twelve Men.   1919.
    An American Tragedy.   1925.
    Chains: Lesser Novels and Stories.   1927.
    A Gallery of Women.   1929.
    Fine Furniture (stories).   1930.
    The Bulwark. 1946.
    The Stoic.   1947.

Plays

    Laughing Gas (produced 1916).   In *Plays,* 1916.
    Plays of the Natural and the Supernatural (includes *The Girl in the Coffin, The Blue Sphere, Laughing Gas, In the Dark, The Spring Recital, The Light in the Window, The Old Ragpicker).*   1916; augmented edition (includes *Phantasmagoria* and *The Count of Progress),* 1926; (includes *The Dream),* 1927; as *Plays, Natural and Supernatural* (includes *The Anaesthetic Revelation),* 1930.
    The Girl in the Coffin (produced 1917).   In *Plays,* 1916.
    The Old Ragpicker (produced 1918).   In *Plays,* 1916.
    The Hand of the Potter (produced 1921).   1919.

Verse

    Moods, Cadenced and Declaimed.   1926; revised edition, 1928; as *Moods Philosophic and Emotional, Cadenced and Declaimed,* 1935.
    The Aspirant.   1929.
    Epitaph.   1930.

Other

    A Traveler at Forty.   1913.
    A Hoosier Holiday.   1916.
    Life, Art, and America.   1917.
    Hey Rub-a-Dub-Dub: A Book of the Mystery and Wonder and Terror of Life.   1920.

A Book about Myself. 1922; as *Newspaper Days,* 1931; *Dawn: A History of Myself,*
    1931; complete version, as *Autobiography,* 2 vols., 1965.
The Color of a Great City (on New York City). 1923.
Dreiser Looks at Russia. 1928; shortened version, as *Dreiser's Russia,* 1928.
My City. 1929.
The Carnegie Works at Pittsburgh. 1929.
Tragic America. 1931.
Tom Mooney. 1933.
America Is Worth Saving. 1941.
Letters to Louise, edited by Louise Campbell. 1959.
Notes on Life, edited by Marguerite Tjader and John J. McAleer. 1974.
A Selection of Uncollected Prose, edited by Donald Pizer. 1977.

Editor, *The Living Thoughts of Thoreau.* 1939.

Bibliography: *Dreiser: A Primary and Secondary Bibliography* by Donald Pizer, 1975.

Reading List: *Dreiser, Apostle of Nature* by Robert H. Elias, 1949, revised edition, 1970; *Dreiser* by Philip L. Gerber, 1964; *Dreiser* by W. A. Swanberg, 1965; *Two Dreisers* by Ellen Moers, 1969; *Dreiser: A Collection of Critical Essays* edited by John Lydenberg, 1971; *Dreiser* by Richard D. Lehan, 1971; *Dreiser* by James Lundquist, 1974; *The Novels of Dreiser: A Critical Study* by Donald Pizer, 1976.

*   *   *

The first major writer to emerge from America's "melting pot" population (his father was a German-Catholic weaver), Theodore Dreiser almost single-handedly created and made respectable a socially oriented fiction that surprisingly complements the romance tradition of Hawthorne and Melville, while expanding the narrowly focused realism of Howells and James. His achievement is vast, paradoxical, and, considering the conditions of his birth and the poverty of his youth, highly unlikely. Personally ungainly, erratically educated, and possessing an unusually shoddy conception of aesthetics, he succeeds through a combination of passionate integrity and a brutal determination to exhaust his material completely. For the first time in American fiction he introduced on an epic scale a literary effort in which the social environment was given a detailed attention equal to, if not greater than, that which was focused on the individual protagonist. His heroes are neither orphans set adrift in a bewildering chaotic world, nor are they archetypal symbols occupying spaces in a moral or allegorical diagram. Instead they are begotten out of concrete family relationships within particular socio-economic situations. And although Dreiser's characters are never the mere pawns of their social and biological circumstances, still they can only be understood in terms of those circumstances. Sex and money have ever been the twin thematic strands out of which novels are built, but Dreiser is the first American novelist to scrutinize these concerns with a consistently unashamed and unaverted gaze. His reluctance to apply moralistic judgments and the spacious compassion with which he views the behavior of his characters infuse his fiction with a vitality and a sense of wonder that transcend by far the mechanical operations of the naturalistic formulas that are sometimes invoked to explain – or explain away – his work.

Partly influenced by Herbert Spencer's interpretation of evolution and excited by the honesty he found in the novels of Balzac, Tolstoy, Zola, and Hardy, Dreiser is, of course, far less intellectual than his intellectual influences. Nearer to the bone he drew upon the chequered adventures of his own large family and his personal experiences as an ill-favored ambitious young man struggling to make good in the big blustering city. With the successes and failures of his brothers and sisters in mind, he had no need of philosophical theory to perceive the sharp disparity between the sanctimonious cant of the pulpit and the popular press and the actual practices of life in the booming economy of the last years of the 19th century. And, perhaps most important, his capacity to project himself autobiographically into such different personalities as Carrie Meeber, Hurstwood, Drouet, Jennie Gerhardt, Frank Cowperwood, and Clyde Griffiths makes his novels both impersonal and personal – wide-scale renderings of American life as viewed from a detached brooding perspective and intimately felt transcriptions of the loneliness, frustration, and burning desire to succeed that torment the sensibilities of the American temperament.

His first novel, *Sister Carrie*, already shows Dreiser in full possession of his powers. The pilgrimage of the eighteen year-old country girl to Chicago and then later to stardom on the New York stage follows the hackneyed scenario of the sentimental fiction (the Horatio Alger-Cinderella fairy tale) that Dreiser knew well as an editor for Butterick publications. But Dreiser does more than simply refuse to disapprove of his amoral heroine; he transforms these stock melodramatic materials into a dispassionate dissection of the factors that conjoin for success and failure in a society where "making" and "being" good are sometimes in radical disalignment. Carrie's rise, Drouet's complacent survival, and Hurstwood's fall are complementary elements in the turbulence of a collective life-force surging and ebbing in accord with its own laws of movement. Man may attempt to resist or try to ride along with the current, but, in terms of his most profoundly cherished ideals, he is alien to the purposes of life and doomed to recurrent and ultimate dissatisfaction.

Sister Carrie introduces the themes that were to preoccupy Dreiser throughout his career and also displays his novelistic techniques in full maturity. Although he has been frequently condemned by critics as a wretched stylist, it might be more accurate to suggest that he simply had no personal style at all. Instead, he absorbed the highly detailed, prolix, occasionally ornate but usually lucid magazine-style of the Mauve Decade and employed it as an impersonal instrument in the fashioning of his fiction. In Dreiser's case, his personal style may be more fruitfully sought in his characteristic use of structure. He built his novels in large narrative blocks, each of them composed of simple sequences of action; these he relates unhurriedly, setting minutely observed detail upon detail like a workman laying bricks. These narrative sequences succeed one another in ponderous waves of relentless motion, suggesting a sense of the irrevocable passage of time, a cumulative weight of authenticity, and a rhythm of inevitability. With the writing of *Sister Carrie*, Dreiser's development as a novelist was complete. In his subsequent novels he might intensify, broaden, or polish aspects of his ideas and craftsmanship, but his work would remain within the same methodology and frame of bemused compassion that constitute his signature in *Sister Carrie*.

After *Jennie Gerhardt* – a curiously neglected novel that turns *Sister Carrie* inside-out, as it were, and presents in its title character the nearest approach to a saint that Dreiser ever made – he produced his study of an American "robber baron" in *The Financier* and *The Titan*. Modeling his protagonist, Frank Cowperwood, on the millionaire Charles T. Yerkes, Dreiser's intention is to show the obverse side of the Darwinian coin – the ruthless Superman, cooly aware of the amoral rules of the game, who stakes his formidable energies in a singleminded drive for power. Utterly persuasive in its grasp of the political and financial minutiae of stock transfers and bond issues, Dreiser's treatment of Cowperwood's career is easily the authoritative – if caricatured – portrait of the American businessman, relentless in his pursuit of wealth and power, but destined to the same frustration as the weak and victimized whom he manipulates.

The last of Dreiser's major novels and perhaps his single most impressive work is *An American Tragedy*. Here Dreiser is at the very peak of his ability, identifying closely with his protagonist, Clyde Griffiths, even as he broods with Olympian resignation over the wretched banality of Clyde's life. Dreiser reveals that life with magisterial authority, piece by painstaking piece, from Clyde's beginnings as a small embarrassed boy walking the city streets with his missionary parents to his final state execution for murder. More like a massive monument that turns in slow-motion before the reader than a literary portrait, *An American Tragedy* patiently and inexorably amasses evidence to show how a weak malleable personality can be so thoroughly molded by his circumstances and by the shallow values of his culture as to become virtually negligible as a generative force in himself. By the end of the novel, the reader so fully understands the elements that have created Clyde that the character himself almost recedes into the landscape of the novel as merely one more passive factor. And although – or because – every relevant fact in his life has been clearly illumined, the reader can no more determine to what extent Clyde is a murderer and to what extent a victim than can Clyde himself.

Dreiser not only wrote long novels, but he was prolific in many genres. Of the poetry, short stories, plays, and non-fiction as well as other novels in his bibliography, we might cite as of special interest *A Book About Myself* and *Dawn*, two volumes of memoirs, *Hey, Rub-A-Dub-Dub!*, a characteristic volume of essays, and *The "Genius"*, his least successful but most nakedly autobiographical novel. Dreiser's stature in American letters is huge, stubborn, and undeniable. As the 19-century Russian novelists are supposed to have climbed out from under Gogol's overcoat, so one might suggest that Dreiser must bear a similar paternal responsibility for the fiction of the 1920's (Anderson, Faulkner, Fitzgerald, Hemingway, Lewis, Wolfe), the 1930's (Farrell, Steinbeck, Wright), and even the 1940's (Bellow, Mailer). There is a sense in which his achievement may seem crude, I suppose, but it required something stronger than gentility to clear a continent in which his successors could pursue their visions of truth unimpeded by the barriers of hypocrisy, reticence, and prudential caution. The momentum of history was in this direction, of course, but yet some of the richness and power of the modern American novel is due to Dreiser's sweeping redefinition of the novelist's task.

—Earl Rovit

DU BOIS, W(illiam) E(dward) B(urghardt).   Ghanaian.   Born in Great Barrington, Massachusetts, 23 February 1868; emigrated to Ghana, 1961; naturalized, 1963. Educated in Great Barrington public schools; Fisk University, Nashville (Editor, *Fisk Herald*), A.B. 1888; Harvard University, Cambridge Massachusetts, A.B. 1890, A.M. 1891, Ph.D. 1895. Married 1) Nina Gomer in 1896 (died, 1950), one son and one daughter; 2) Shirley Graham in 1951. Professor of Greek and Latin, Wilberforce University, Ohio, 1894–96; Assistant Instructor of Sociology, University of Pennsylvania, Philadelphia, 1896–97; Professor of Economics and History, Atlanta University, 1897–1910; Editor, *The Moon Illustrated Weekly*, Memphis, 1906, and *The Horizon*, Washington, D.C., 1907–10; a Founder of the National Association for the Advancement of Colored People, 1910, and Director of Publicity and Research for the NAACP and Editor of the NAACP's magazine *Crisis*, New York, 1910–34; Editor, with A. G. Dill, *The Brownies' Book*, 1920–22; Columnist ("A Forum of Fact and Opinion"), *Pittsburgh Courier*, 1936–38, and ("As the Crow Flies"), *Amsterdam News*, 1939–44; Editor, *Phylon*, Atlanta, 1940–44; Director of the Department of Special Research, NAACP, New York, 1944–48; Columnist ("The Winds of Time"), *Chicago Defender*, 1945–48, and *People's Voice*, 1947–48. Founder, Pan-African Congress, 1900, and the Niagara Movement, 1904; Vice-Chairman, Council on African Affairs, 1949–54. Recipient: Spingarn Medal, 1920; International Peace Prize, 1952. Knight Commander, Liberian Order of African Redemption. Fellow, American Association for the Advancement of Science; Member, National Institute of Arts and Letters. *Died 27 August 1963.*

PUBLICATIONS

Collections

The Seventh Son: The Thoughts and Writings of Du Bois, edited by Julius Lester.   2 vols., 1971.
Correspondence, edited by Herbert Aptheker.   3 vols., 1973–78.

Fiction

The Quest of the Silver Fleece.   1911.
Dark Princess: A Romance.   1928.
The Black Flame: The Ordeal of Mansart.   1957; *Mansart Builds a School*, 1959; *Worlds of Color*, 1961.

Play

The Star of Ethiopia (pageant, produced ?).   1913.

Verse

Selected Poems.   1965.

Other

Suppression of African Slave-Trade to the United States of America 1638–1870.   1896.
The Philadelphia Negro: A Social Study, with *A Report on Domestic Service* by Isabel Eaton.   1899.
Possibilities of the Negro: The Advance Guard of Race.   1903.
Souls of Black Folk: Essays and Sketches.   1903; revised edition, 1953.
Of the Wings of Atlanta.   1904.
The Black Vote of Philadelphia.   1905.
The Negro South and North.   1905.
The Negro in the South, with Booker T. Washington.   1907.
John Brown (biography).   1909.
The Social Evolution of the Black South.   1911.
Disfranchisement.   1912.
The Negro.   1915.
Darkwater: Voices from Within the Veil.   1920.
The Gift of Black Folk: Negroes in the Making of America.   1924.
Africa: Its Geography, People, and Products.   1930.
Africa: Its Place in Modern History.   1930.
Black Reconstruction in America: An Essay.   1935.
A Pageant in Seven Decades 1868–1938.   1938.
Black Folk Then and Now: An Essay in the History and Sociology of the Negro Race.   1939.
The Revelation of Saint Orgne, The Damned.   1939.
Dusk of Dawn: An Essay Toward an Autobiography of a Race Concept.   1940.
Encyclopedia of the Negro: Preparatory Volume.   1945; revised edition, 1946.
Color and Democracy: Colonies and Peace.   1945.
An Appeal to the World.   1947.

The World and Africa. 1947; revised edition, 1965.
In Battle for Peace: The Story of My 83rd Birthday. 1952.
The Story of Benjamin Franklin. 1956.
Africa in Battle Against Colonialism, Racialism, Imperialism. 1960.
An ABC of Color. 1963.
Autobiography. 1968.
The Black North in 1901: A Social Study. 1969.
Du Bois Speaks: Speeches and Addresses 1890–1963, edited by Philip Foner. 2 vols., 1970.
The Emerging Thought of Du Bois (*Crisis* articles), edited by Henry Lee Moon. 1972.
The Education of Black People: Ten Critiques 1906–1960, edited by Herbert Aptheker. 1973.
Book Reviews. 1977.
Du Bois on Sociology and the Black Community, edited by Dan S. Green and Edwin D. Driver. 1978.

Editor, *Atlanta University Publications* (pamphlets published in 1898–1913). 2 vols., 1968–69.

Bibliography: *Annotated Bibliography of the Published Writings of Du Bois* by Herbert Aptheker, 1973.

Reading List: *Du Bois: A Profile* edited by Rayford W. Logan, 1971; *The Art and Imagination of Du Bois* by Arnold Rampersand, 1976.

*   *   *

At the age of 35, in 1903, W. E. B. Du Bois took intellectual leadership of those within the Afro-American world who preferred liberal idealism to compensatory realism. Du Bois was prepared for his role by rigorous training in the traditional liberal arts as well as the newer empirical social sciences. But it was confidence and the moral absolute of truth and a poetic imagination that were to prove the sources of his effectiveness.

Souls of Black Folk, the book in which Du Bois publicly announced his differences with Booker T. Washington, is constructed from first-hand observation, historical research, and reasoned analysis. Its power, however, derives from the images of divided consciousness (souls), a culturally united black nation (folk), and the veil behind which black remained nearly invisible. In a time when Jim Crow shaped perception as much as policy, Du Bois's metaphors represented intellectual liberation, giving blacks a profoundly dignified way of conceiving their own lives and history. The cultural nationalism of *Souls of Black Folk* had been implicit in the earlier study *The Philadelphia Negro,* where Du Bois documented class structure and shared institutions. It reappeared as motivation for the Utopian vision of agricultural cooperatives in *Quest of the Silver Fleece* and the romantic narrative of world-wide organization for colored people in *The Dark Princess.*

Du Bois's well-known commitment to the idea of leadership by a talented tenth has its counterpart in the learned rhetoric of his essays and the grandiose design of his novels. It is no wonder that writing as a critic in *Crisis* he was unsympathetic to the experimentation and modern realism of the younger generation in the Negro Renaissance. Still, he made his own characteristic contribution to the "new Negro." His book *The Negro,* anticipating anti-colonial conferences organized after the First World War, corrected popular impressions that American blacks were without roots by celebrating the African past. Then *Black Reconstruction,* written out of Du Bois's new enthusiasm for Marxism in the 1930's, recovered the significance of black people in the history of the South. Despite limitations of style, these historical re-evaluations initiated a scholarly revisionism comparable to the re-direction of thought in the book *Souls of Black Folk.*

Nearing the end of his life, Du Bois published his most comprehensive treatment of America, *The Black Flame*, a trilogy binding into one narrative an historical account of the years corresponding roughly to his own life and a fictional account of Manuel Mansart. That the plots are meant to inter-relate goes without saying. More to the point is the observation that Du Bois's career, capped by the trilogy, was his most important dialectical demonstration. Seeking to write as truthfully as possible, he became not only a scribe of history but its maker.

—John M. Reilly

DUGGAN, Maurice (Noel). New Zealander. Born in Auckland, 25 November 1922. Educated at the University of Auckland. Married Barbara Platts in 1945; one child. Worked in advertising from 1961; with J. English Wright (Advertising) Ltd., Auckland, 1965 until his death. Recipient: Hubert Church Memorial Award, 1957; Esther Glen Award, 1959; Katherine Mansfield Award, 1959; Robert Burns Fellowship, Otago University, 1960; New Zealand Literary Fund Scholarship, 1966; Freda Buckland Award, 1970. *Died in January 1975.*

PUBLICATIONS

Fiction (stories)

Immanuel's Land. 1956.
New Authors: Short Story 1, with others. 1961.
Summer in the Gravel Pit. 1965.
O'Leary's Orchard and Other Stories. 1970.

Other

Falter Tom and the Water Boy (juvenile). 1957.
The Fabulous McFanes and Other Children's Stories. 1974.

*   *   *

Of his own work, Maurice Duggan modestly wrote, "The output has been small, and I must take what confidence I can from what seem to me small successful things." However, those "small successful things" include some of the finest short stories and novellas ever written in New Zealand, and show the kind of development associated with a major writer.

That development was partially stylistic, a move towards complexity. Such early stories as "A Small Story" (1951) are exercises in controlled simplicity, written, as Duggan said, on the assumption that "If it was to be strong, it had to be simple." In the later novellas and long stories the style becomes more allusive, figurative, dense, as it attempts to evoke the consciousness of complex central characters, for each of whom there is an appropriate idiom – the sad imagist poetry of "Blues for Miss Laverty" (1960), the Beckett-like ravings of Riley in "Riley's Handbook" (1961), the self-conscious raciness of Buster O'Leary in "Along Rideout Road That Summer" (1963), the wry wit of "O'Leary's Orchard" (1967), the elliptical mode of "An Appetite for Flowers" (1967).

The developing style was at the service of a developing moral vision, an imaginative vision that takes us "through the looking-glass, through the superficial fascinations of the mirror-image, past the deceitful gaze to the concentration of the puzzle" so that "the map of the way of our going and of our being may begin to be exposed," in the words of the writer Ben McGoldrick in "The Magsman Miscellany" (published in *Islands*, Winter 1975). That vision focuses on the attempts of the self to find an accommodation with an absurd world in which human relations are both the only possible source of value and the most frequent cause of pain. The early stories present primarily the experience of children and adolescents in a puzzling world of unhappy homes (in the stories of the Lenihan family) and unjust adult authority (in the stories dealing with a Catholic boarding school). The later stories concentrate on adults – the disastrous Lenihan marriage (in "The Deposition" and "The Departure"), the lonely spinster denied any significant human contact ("Blues for Miss Laverty"), the rootless male cutting himself off from life in the fear of commitment ("The Wits of Willie Graves"). All these characters show the difficulty of knowing, without illusions, not only the external world but also the self, for the psyche is "simply the expressive instrument of one's secret desires, wishes made in darkness below the level of consciousness, a repository of half-thoughts and unconscious gestures." If Tryphena Price (in "For the Love of Rupert") and Buster O'Leary show the danger of acting on illusions, the older O'Leary (in "O'Leary's Orchard") and Hilda Preeble (in "An Appetite for Flowers") show the difficulty and pain of moving beyond them without constructing a defence of cynicism. In Duggan's world, life is always painful, not least for those who see most.

—Lawrence Jones

---

du MAURIER, Dame Daphne. English. Born in London, 13 May 1907; daughter of the actor/manager Sir Gerald du Maurier; grand-daughter of George du Maurier, *q.v.* Educated privately and in Paris. Married Lieutenant-General Sir Frederick Browning in 1932 (died, 1965); two daughters and one son. Writer from 1928. Recipient: Mystery Writers of America Grand Master Award, 1978. Fellow, Royal Society of Literature, 1952. D.B.E. (Dame Commander, Order of the British Empire), 1969. Lives in Cornwall.

PUBLICATIONS

Fiction

The Loving Spirit. 1931.
I'll Never Be Young Again. 1932.
The Progress of Julius. 1933.
Jamaica Inn. 1936.
Rebecca. 1938.
Happy Christmas (story). 1940.
Come Wind, Come Weather (stories). 1940.
Frenchman's Creek. 1941.
Hungry Hill. 1943.
Nothing Hurts for Long, and Escorts (stories). 1943.
Consider the Lilies (story). 1943.
Spring Picture (story). 1944.

Leading Lady (story). 1945.
London and Paris (stories). 1945.
The King's General. 1946.
The Parasites. 1949.
My Cousin Rachel. 1951.
The Apple Tree: A Short Novel and Some Stories. 1952; as *Kiss Me Again, Stranger: A Collection of Eight Stories, Long and Short,* 1953.
Mary Anne. 1954.
Early Stories. 1954.
The Scapegoat. 1957.
The Breaking Point: Eight Stories. 1959; as *The Blue Lenses,* 1970.
The Treasury of du Maurier Stories. 1960.
Castle Dor, by Arthur Quiller-Couch, completed by du Maurier. 1962.
The Glass-Blowers. 1963.
The Flight of the Falcon. 1965.
The House on the Strand. 1969.
Not after Midnight (stories). 1971.
Rule Britannia. 1972.
Echoes from the Macabre: Selected Stories. 1976.

Plays

Rebecca, from her own novel (produced 1940). 1940.
The Years Between (produced 1944). 1945.
September Tide (produced 1948). 1949.

Screenplay: *Hungry Hill,* with Terence Young and Francis Crowdry, 1947.

Television Play: *The Breakthrough,* 1976.

Other

Gerald: A Portrait (on Gerald du Maurier). 1934.
The du Mauriers. 1937.
The Infernal World of Branwell Brontë. 1960.
Vanishing Cornwall. 1967.
Golden Lads: Sir Francis Bacon, Anthony Bacon, and Their Friends. 1975.
The Winding Stair: Francis Bacon, His Rise and Fall. 1976.
Growing Pains: The Shaping of a Writer. 1977; as *Myself When Young,* 1977.

Editor, *The Young George du Maurier: A Selection of His Letters 1860–1867.* 1951.
Editor, *Best Stories,* by Phyllis Bottome. 1963.

*   *   *

The novels of Daphne du Maurier span almost half a century, and unlike many of her popular contemporaries she has never become a period piece. Her most famous work, *Rebecca,* with its romantic setting, brooding hero, innocent heroine, frightening housekeeper, and the even more sinister figure of Rebecca herself, does creak a little today, even if one accepts the Gothic conventions which the book follows. Some other novels could be accused of following the same pattern as *Rebecca* – the same interest in romantic settings and Byronic heroes without any corresponding exploitation of human motivation or ordinary life. On the other hand novels with a historical setting such as *Jamaica Inn* and *The King's General*, although still set in "romantic" Cornwall, are more accurate as charts of human behaviour as well as being historically sound.

Miss du Maurier's study of Branwell Brontë is a tribute to her scholarly interest in the past and a careful study of romantic degeneracy; the book is also a reminder that the Brontë sisters were one source of her inspiration as a writer of fiction. Her father, a celebrated actor manager, about whom she wrote lovingly, may explain the theatrical quality of some of her novels, which have been adapted to make exciting films. Some of her later novels, such as *Rule Britannia*, which envisages Britain threatened by an American invasion, and *The Flight of the Falcon*, in which an Italian university tries to re-enact the horrifying splendour of Renaissance Italy, may seem to indicate a further flight from reality, although the latter novel has some splendid insights into the tensions behind academic life, and the former is a useful guide to the gap between generations. It would be a mistake to dismiss Miss du Maurier as a writer of escapist novelettes, even though many readers admire her because she does enable them to forget the tedium of their lives.

—T. J. Winnifrith

---

du MAURIER, George (Louis Palmella Busson). English. Born in Paris, 6 March 1834. Educated at the Pension Froussard, Paris, 1847–51; studied chemistry at University College, London 1851–54, then worked as an analytical chemist, in his own laboratory, London, 1854–56; returned to Paris, and studied art with Gleyre, 1856–57, and under De Keyser and Van Lerius at the Antwerp Academy, 1857–60. Married Emma Wightwick in 1863; two sons and three daughters. Settled in London, 1860, and thereafter worked as an illustrator: contributed to *Once a Week* and *Punch* from 1860, and became a member of the *Punch* table, 1864; illustrated stories for *Cornhill Magazine*, 1863–83; lived in Hampstead, London, 1870 until his death; also a writer from 1891. *Died 6 October 1896.*

PUBLICATIONS

Collections

The Young du Maurier: A Selection of His Letters 1860–1867, edited by Daphne du Maurier. 1951.

Fiction

Peter Ibbetson. 1892.
Trilby. 1894.
The Martian. 1897.

Verse

A Legend of Camelot. 1898.

Other

   Drawings: *English Society at Home,* 1880; *Society Pictures,* 2 vols., 1891; *English Society,* 1897; *Social Pictorial Satire,* 1898.

Reading List: *The du Mauriers* by Daphne du Maurier, 1937; *du Maurier: His Life and Work* by D. P. Whitely, 1948; "du Maurier and the Romantic Novel" by Lionel Stevenson, in *Essays by Divers Hands 30,* 1960; *du Maurier* by Leonée Ormond, 1969.

*   *   *

   George du Maurier in character and achievement can be considered as in some ways resembling a later and minor Thackeray. He knew Paris and the bohemian artistic world of Paris even better than Thackeray did, and his excellent *Punch* cartoons, which beautifully catch the social affectations of the late Victorian period, show that he was a more successful graphic artist than Thackeray if a much less important writer. Yet Thackeray's hasty sketches have sometimes a life and naturalness that du Maurier's delicate penmanship lacks. Similarly, though du Maurier recalls Thackeray in pathos verging dangerously on sentimentality, and in reminiscent humour, he has a kind of staginess (as in the melodramatic character of Svengali in *Trilby*) not found in Thackeray. *Trilby,* his second novel, turned into a successful melodrama with Beerbohm Tree in 1895, was his most famous book. His first, *Peter Ibbetson,* based on dreams, is more personal and original, as is the unfinished story of school memories, *The Martian.* Not a great writer or artist, du Maurier nevertheless catches very skilfully the daydreams of his time.

—G. S. Fraser

<hr>

DUNNE, Finley Peter. American. Born in Chicago, Illinois, 10 July 1867. Educated in Chicago public schools. Married Margaret Abbott in 1902; three sons and one daughter. Journalist from 1885, working for various Chicago newspapers; City Editor, *Chicago Times,* 1891–92; member of the editorial staff of the *Chicago Evening Post* and *Times Herald,* 1892–97; Editor, *Chicago Journal,* 1897–1900; moved to New York, 1900: wrote for *Collier's* and briefly edited the *New York Morning Telegraph*; Editor, with Ida Tarbell and Lincoln Steffens, *The American Magazine,* 1906; edited *Collier's Weekly,* 1918–19. Member, National Institute of Arts and Letters. *Died 24 April 1936.*

PUBLICATIONS

Collections

   Mr. Dooley and the Chicago Irish, edited by Charles Fanning.   1976.
   Mr. Dooley's Chicago, edited by Barbara C. Schaaf.   1977.

Prose

Mr. Dooley in Peace and in War. 1898.
Mr. Dooley in the Hearts of His Countrymen. 1899.
What Dooley Says. 1899.
Mr. Dooley's Philosophy. 1900.
Mr. Dooley's Opinions. 1901.
Observations by Mr. Dooley. 1902.
Dissertations by Mr. Dooley. 1906.
Mr. Dooley Says. 1910.
New Dooley Book. 1911.
Mr. Dooley on Making a Will and Other Necessary Evils. 1919.
Mr. Dooley Remembers: The Informal Memoirs of Dunne, edited by Philip Dunne. 1963.

Reading List: *Mr. Dooley's America: The Life of Dunne* by Elmer Ellis, 1941; *Dunne and Mr. Dooley: The Chicago Years* by Charles Fanning, 1978.

*   *   *

Finley Peter Dunne is best known for having created Mr. Martin Dooley, an aging Irish saloonkeeper from Chicago, who began appearing in a weekly column in the *Chicago Evening Post* in October 1893. Dunne's own parents had been Irish immigrants to Chicago, and he began his journalistic career there in 1884 at age seventeen. After working on six different newspapers, he settled as precocious editorial chairman at the *Post* in 1892. The last in a series of dialect experiments for his creator, Mr. Dooley succeeded Colonel Malachi McNeery, a downtown Chicago barkeep modeled on a friend of Dunne's, who had become a popular *Post* feature during the World's Fair of 1893. Unlike McNeery, Mr. Dooley was placed on Chicago's South Side, in the Irish working-class neighborhood of Bridgeport. Between 1893 and 1898, 215 Dooley pieces appeared in the *Post*. Taken together, they form a coherent body of work, in which a vivid, detailed world comes into existence — that of Bridgeport, a self-contained immigrant culture, with its own customs and ceremonies and a social structure rooted in family, geography, and occupation. Included are memories of Ireland and emigration, descriptions of the daily round of Bridgeport life, and inside narratives of rough-and-tumble politics in a city ward. In addition, other pieces contain wholly serious treatments of suffering and starvation among the poor, the divisive scramble for middle-class respectability, and conflict between immigrant parents and their American children. In these Bridgeport pieces, Dunne contributed to the development of literary realism in America. In depicting this immigrant community and its working-class inhabitants through the medium of Irish vernacular dialect, he gave Chicagoans a weekly example of the realist's faith in the potentiality for serious fiction of common speech and everyday life.

Dunne's career took a sharp turn in 1898, when Mr. Dooley's satirical coverage of the Spanish-American War brought him to the attention of readers outside Chicago. Beginning with his scoop of "Cousin George" Dewey's victory at Manila, Mr. Dooley's reports of military and political bungling during the "splendid little war" were widely reprinted, and national syndication soon followed. By the time Dunne moved to New York in 1900, Mr. Dooley was the most popular figure in American journalism. From this point until World War I, Dunne's gadfly mind ranged over the spectrum of newsworthy events and characters, both national and international: from Teddy Roosevelt's health fads to Andrew Carnegie's passion for libraries; from the invariable silliness of politics to society doings at Newport; from the Boer and Boxer Rebellions to the Negro, Indian, and immigration "problems." Mr. Dooley's perspective was consistently skeptical and critical. The salutary effect of most pieces was the exposure of affectation and hypocrisy through undercutting humor and common sense. The most frequently quoted Dooleyisms indicate this thrust: Teddy Roosevelt's egocentric account of the Rough Riders is retitled, "Alone in Cubia"; Henry Cabot Lodge's imperialist rationale becomes "Take up th' white man's burden an' hand it to th' coons"; a fanatic is defined as "a man that does what he thinks th' Lord wud do if He knew th' facts iv th' case." Although he joined Ida Tarbell and Lincoln Steffens in taking over *The American Magazine* in 1906, Dunne was not himself a progressive reformer. He viewed the world as irrevocably fallen and unimproveable, and many Dooley pieces reflect their author's tendency toward cynicism, pessimism, and fatalism. More pronounced in the early Chicago work than in the lighter national commentary, Dunne's darker side may be explained by his Irish background and his journalist's education into the realities of nineteenth-century urban life.

Mr. Dooley was the first Irish voice in American literature to transcend the confines of "stage Irish" ethnic humor. Dunne's accomplishment divides (at 1898) into two parts: the Chicago pieces, which contain pioneering realistic sketches of an urban immigrant community, and the pieces written for a national audience, which contain some of the best social and political satire ever penned in America.

—Charles Fanning

DURRELL, Lawrence (George). English. Born in Julundur, India, 27 February 1912. Educated at the College of St. Joseph, Darjeeling, India; St. Edmund's School, Canterbury, Kent. Married 1) Nancy Myers in 1935 (divorced, 1947); 2) Eve Cohen in 1947 (divorced); 3) Claude Durrell in 1961 (died, 1967); 4) Ghislaine de Boysson in 1973; two children. Had many varied jobs in early life, including jazz pianist (Blue Peter nightclub, London), automobile racer, and real estate agent; lived in Corfu, 1934–40; Editor, with Henry Miller and Alfred Perlès, *The Booster*, later *Delta*, Paris, 1937–39; taught at the British Institute, Kalamata, Greece, 1940; Foreign Press Service Officer, British Information Office, Cairo, 1941–44, and Press Attaché, British Information Office, Alexandria, 1944–45; also, Columnist for the *Egyptian Gazette*, Cairo, 1941, and Editor, with Robin Fedden and Bernard Spencer, *Personal Landscape*, Cairo, 1942–45; Director of Public Relations for the Dodecanese Islands, Greece, 1946–47; Director of the British Council Institute, Cordoba, Argentina, 1947–48; Press Attaché, British Legation, Belgrade, 1949–52; Special Correspondent in Cyprus for *The Economist*, London, 1953–55; Editor, *Cyprus Review*, Nicosia, 1954–55; Director of Public Relations for the British Government in Cyprus, 1954–56; settled in France, 1957. Recipient: Duff Cooper Memorial Prize, 1957; Prix du Meilleur Livre Etranger, 1959; Black Memorial Prize, 1975. Fellow, Royal Society of Literature, 1954.

PUBLICATIONS

Fiction

Pied Piper of Lovers. 1935.
Panic Spring. 1937.
The Black Book: An Agon. 1938.
Cefalù. 1947; as *The Dark Labyrinth*, 1958.
White Eagles over Serbia. 1957.

Justine, 1957; *Balthazar*, 1958; *Mountolive*, 1958; *Clea*, 1960; complete version, as *The Alexandria Quartet*, 1962.
Esprit de Corps: Sketches from Diplomatic Life.   1957.
Stiff Upper Lip: Life among the Diplomats (stories).   1958.
Sauve Qui Peut (stories).   1966.
Tunc.   1968; *Nunquam*, 1970; complete version, as *The Revolt of Aphrodite*, 1974.
The Best of Antrobus (stories).   1974.
Monsieur; or, The Prince of Darkness.   1975.
Livia; or, Buried Alive.   1978.

Plays

Sappho: A Play in Verse (produced 1959).   1950.
Acte (produced 1961).   1965.
An Irish Faustus: A Morality in Nine Scenes (produced 1966).   1963.

Television Script: *The Lonely Roads*, 1971.

Verse

Quaint Fragment: Poems Written Between the Ages of Sixteen and Nineteen.   1931.
Ten Poems.   1932.
Bromo Bombastes: A Fragment from a Laconic Drama by Gaffer Peaslake.   1933.
Transition.   1934.
Proems: An Anthology of Poems, with others.   1938.
A Private Country.   1943.
Cities, Plains and People.   1946.
Zero, and Asylum in the Snow: Two Excursions into Reality.   1946.
On Seeming to Presume.   1948.
A Landmark Gone.   1949.
Deus Loci.   1950.
Private Drafts.   1955.
The Tree of Idleness and Other Poems.   1955.
Selected Poems.   1956.
Collected Poems.   1960; revised edition, 1968.
Poetry.   1962.
Beccafico Le Becfigue (English, with French translation by F.-J. Temple).   1963.
La Descente du Styx (English, with French translation by F.-J. Temple).   1964.
Selected Poems 1935–63.   1964.
The Ikons and Other Poems.   1966.
The Red Limbo Lingo: A Poetry Notebook for 1968–70.   1971.
On the Suchness of the Old Boy.   1972.
Vega and Other Poems.   1973.
Plant-Magic Man.   1973.
Lifelines.   1974.
Selected Poems, edited by Alan Ross.   1977.

Other

Prospero's Cell: A Guide to the Landscape and Manners of the Island of Corcyra.   1945.
Key to Modern Poetry.   1952; as *A Key to Modern British Poetry*, 1952.

Reflections on a Marine Venus: A Companion to the Landscape of Rhodes. 1953.
Bitter Lemons (on Cyprus). 1957.
Art and Outrage: A Correspondence about Henry Miller Between Alfred Perlès and Durrell, with an Intermission by Henry Miller. 1959.
Durrell and Henry Miller: A Private Correspondence, edited by George Wickes. 1963.
Spirit of Place: Letters and Essays on Travel, edited by Alan G. Thomas. 1969.
Le Grand Suppositoire (a taped biographical interview with Marc Alyn). 1972; as *The Big Supposer,* 1973.
The Happy Rock (on Henry Miller). 1973.
Blue Thirst. 1975.
Sicilian Carousel. 1977.
The Greek Islands. 1978.

Editor, with others, *Personal Landscape: An Anthology of Exile.* 1945.
Editor, *A Henry Miller Reader.* 1959; as *The Best of Henry Miller,* 1960.
Editor, *New Poems, 1963: A P.E.N. Anthology of Contemporary Poetry.* 1963.
Editor, *Lear's Corfu: An Anthology Drawn from the Painter's Letters.* 1965.
Editor, *Wordsworth.* 1973.

Translator, *Six Poems from the Greek of Sekilanos and Seferis.* 1946.
Translator, with Bernard Spencer and Nanos Valaortis, *The King of Asine and Other Poems,* by George Seferis. 1948.
Translator, *The Curious History of Pope Joan,* by Emmanuel Royidis. 1954; revised edition, as *Pope Joan: A Personal Biography,* 1960.

Reading List: *The World of Durrell* edited by Harry T. Moore, 1962; *Durrell* by John Unterecker, 1964; *Durrell* by J. A. Weigel, 1966; *Durrell: A Critical Study* by G. S. Fraser, 1968 (includes bibliography by Alan G. Thomas); *Durrell and the Alexandria Quartet* by Alan Warren Friedman, 1970.

*   *   *

Lawrence Durrell has probably one of the most disputed reputations among contemporary English writers. His poems, which combine a natural sense of word melody with a vivid recreation of the Eastern Mediterranean scene (Greece, Alexandria, the Greek islands), in which he has spent much of his life, are always enjoyable and have been always praised, though few critics have claimed for Durrell the status of a major poet. His travel books, *Prospero's Cell* (about Corfu before the Second World War), *Reflections on a Marine Venus* (about Rhodes after the war), and *Bitter Lemons* (about Cyprus during the troubles) have also won universal approval.

It was the last of these three, in fact, that turned Durrell, in his early forties, from a writer appreciated by a few addicts to a very popular one. *Justine,* published in the same year and rapidly followed by *Balthazar, Mountolive,* and *Clea,* soon to be bound, with some revisions, in one volume as *The Alexandria Quartet,* made him rich as well as famous. (Durrell's early largely autobiographical novel, *The Black Book,* written early in his twenties and published clandestinely in Paris, has a richness and fierceness that might have brought him fame much earlier.) The complex stylish volumes of *The Alexandria Quartet* might be said to have siphoned off one part of Durrell's powers. His other fiction contemporary with it – the high-grade hack work of the Buchanesque thriller *White Eagles over Serbia* and the facetious sketches of embassy life of *Esprit de Corps* and *Stiff Upper Lip* – disappointed his admirers. Durrell's next really ambitious efforts, *Tunc* and its sequel *Nunquam,* seemed, even to many who wanted to admire them, to lack surface plausibility and genuine coherence of theme, and to be not only unevenly written (this is true of *The Alexandria Quartet*) but slackly and tiredly written. There was a great improvement, both in style and in depth of character, in the next serious novel. *Monsieur*, the first of a series.

Nobody would deny Durrell's power at his best, especially in the presentation of the great set scenes of *The Alexandria Quartet*, and in his grotesque humour. What still puzzles readers is whether the implied claim to an arcane "cabalistic" wisdom is justified in the writing, or is in the nature of what Durrell, in his old-fashioned slang of the 1920's, would call a "spoof."

—G. S. Fraser

EDGEWORTH, Maria. Irish/English. Born in Black Bourton, Oxfordshire, 1 January 1767; daughter of the educationist Richard Lovell Edgeworth. Educated in Mrs. Lattaffiere's school in Derby, 1775–80, and at Mrs. Davis's school in London, 1780–82. Lived with her family in Edgeworthtown, Ireland, from 1783, and assisted her father, and later her brother, in running the family estates; collaborated with her father on educational works, 1798–1802; visited France, 1802–03, London, 1803, 1819, and France and Switzerland, 1820–21; thereafter devoted herself to the estate; frequently visited London and made occasional tours of the British Isles. *Died 22 May 1849.*

PUBLICATIONS

Collections

Tales and Novels. 18 vols., 1857.
Selections, edited by G. Griffin. 1918.

Fiction

The Parent's Assistant; or, Stories for Children. 1796; revised edition, 1800.
Castle Rackrent: An Hibernian Tale. 1800; edited by George Watson, 1964.
Early Lessons, with Richard Lovell Edgeworth. 10 vols., 1800–02; edited by L. Valentine, 1875.
Moral Tales for Young People. 1801.
Belinda. 1801; revised edition, 1810; edited by A. T. Ritchie, 1896.
The Mental Thermometer. 1801.
Popular Tales. 1804.
The Modern Griselda. 1805.
Adelaide; or, The Chateau de St. Pierre. 1806.
Leonora. 1806.
Tales of Fashionable Life. 6 vols., 1809–12.
Patronage. 1814; revised edition, in *Tales and Miscellaneous Pieces,* 1825.
Continuation of Early Lessons. 1814.
Harrington, and Ormond. 1817; edited by A. H. Johnson, 1900.
Rosamond: A Sequel to Early Lessons. 1821.
Frank: A Sequel to Early Lessons. 1822.
Harry and Lucy Concluded, Being the Last Part of Early Lessons. 1825.
Tales and Miscellaneous Pieces. 14 vols., 1825.
Helen. 1834; edited by A. T. Ritchie, 1896.

Plays

Love and Law (produced 1810). In *Comic Dramas,* 1817.
Comic Dramas (includes *The Rose, Thistle, and Shamrock; The Two Guardians; Love and Law*). 1817.
Little Plays for Children: The Grinding Organ, Dumb Andy, The Dame School Holiday. 1827.

Other

>Letters for Literary Ladies, to Which Is Added an Essay on the Noble Science of Self-Justification. 1795.
>Practical Education, with Richard Lovell Edgeworth. 1798; as Essays on Practical Education, 1811.
>Essay on Irish Bulls, with Richard Lovell Edgeworth. 1802.
>Essays on Professional Education, with Richard Lovell Edgeworth. 1809.
>Readings on Poetry, with Richard Lovell Edgeworth. 1816.
>Memoirs of Richard Lovell Edgeworth, completed by Maria Edgeworth. 1820.
>Chosen Letters, edited by F. V. Barry. 1931.
>Tour in Connemara and the Martins of Ballinahinch, edited by H. E. Butler. 1950.
>Letters of Edgeworth and Anna Barbauld, edited by Walter Sidney Scott. 1953.
>Letters from England 1813–1844, edited by Christina Colvin. 1971.
>The Education of the Heart: The Correspondence of Rachel Mordecai Lazarus and Edgeworth, edited by Edgar E. MacDonald. 1977.

Bibliography: *Edgeworth: A Bibliographical Tribute* by B. C. Salde, 1937.

Reading List: *Life and Letters of Edgeworth* by A. J. C. Hare, 2 vols., 1894; *Edgeworth* by P. H. Newby, 1950; *The Great Maria: A Portrait* by Elisabeth I. Jones, 1959; *Edgeworth the Novelist* by James Newcomer, 1967; *Edgeworth and the Public Scene: Intellect, Fine Feeling, and Landlordism in the Age of Reform* by Michael C. Hurst, 1969; *Edgeworth's Art of Prose Fiction* by Oleta Harden, 1971; *Edgeworth: A Literary Biography* by Marilyn S. Butler, 1972.

*   *   *

Maria Edgeworth acquired, and to some extent retains, three reputations. With her father, she contributed to the growing literature of education at the end of the eighteenth century, and wrote moral tales designed for young audiences; she was also a significant figure among those minor female novelists who surrounded Jane Austen's ascendant star; finally, she defined and virtually launched the school of Irish fiction which in turn influenced Walter Scott and established (with other Scottish novelists) the regional novel as a serious art-form.

The educational writings are now remembered at a purely academic level, though her training as the author of neat moral allegories should be considered in assessing her work as a whole. The titles of the *Tales of Fashionable Life* reveal her concentration on a singular moral problem or a single character in a specific and limited moral context – "Ennui," "Madame de Fleury," "The Dun." While she can occasionally effect a satirical charge at society with which Jane Austen might agree in principle, the two novelists differ in their methods. Maria Edgeworth retained not only the moral didacticism of the eighteenth century; she was indebted for many of her literary models to authors of the mid-century.

To call her a novelist is, to some extent, to take liberties with the term. Her best fiction was written in the shorter forms. Of the four full-length novels which are not Irish and regional, two – *Belinda* and *Patronage* – had to be extensively and uneasily revised for later editions, while a third, *Helen*, all but marks the end of her writing career. *Patronage* has, to be sure, a broad and impressive social base, and Marilyn Butler has suggested a comparison with *Mansfield Park* which by no means disgraces Maria Edgeworth. But as a contributor to English fiction, she remains firmly in the lower half of the second rank; her work is too calculated in both manner and effect, too mechanical in its methods and objectives, to sustain any profound critical analysis.

It is, of course, as an Irish regional writer that she survives in print. *Castle Rackrent* chronicles the decline of an Irish gentry family through four generations, their misfortune being related by the family retainer, Thady Quirk. Thady's muted dialect speech provides an admirable vehicle for irony, as when he declares of his beloved master's funeral "happy the man who could get but a sight of the hearse." It is significant that the tale was written originally for the amusement of her family, a circumstance which in part explains its diminished didacticism. "Ennui" is a slight affair, and should be read as a trial run for "The Absentee," usually but unfairly relegated to second place by the fame of *Castle Rackrent*. "The Absentee" advances an evident message to its readers, but didacticism is enveloped and transformed by the complex allegorical forms in which Irish history and folklore are interwoven into a "tale of fashionable life." It was "The Absentee" which sent Scott back to the incomplete manuscript of *Waverley* and so assisted at the birth of the historical novel proper. *Ormond*, as if to return the compliment, owes much to Scott; indeed its debt to literature is curiously bound up with its characterisation: the hero's moral development is charted through his reading of *Tom Jones* and *Sir Charles Grandison* – a further indication of Maria Edgeworth's eighteenth-century loyalties.

The Irish work is united and given coherence by its constant attention to the meaning of the past as a constituent of the present; even "Ennui" and "The Absentee," which deal ostensibly with contemporary society, are properly read as historical fiction. The scale of her material as an Irish novelist – the smallness and intimacy of Irish society, together with her inherited experience of political upheavals – suited Maria Edgeworth's abilities and talents. In the Irish fiction, moral worth is seen as directly related to social function, whereas the English novels tend towards abstract moral points.

Despite a reputation as an "ascendancy" novelist, Maria Edgeworth actually occupied a central position in the social system; she belonged to the middle gentry, and shared their insecurity, their Janus-like perspective. This creative ambiguity, unavailable to her as a commentator on English habits, is present in all her Irish work, and no more so than in Thady Quirk's eloquent and damning eulogies. Like Walter Scott her conservatism was a sympathetic one; in her best work, "The Absentee" and *Castle Rackrent*, she looked to history for meaning rather than consolation.

—W. J. McCormack

EGAN, Pierce. English. Born in London in 1772. Married in 1812; one son, the writer Pierce Egan the Younger. Known as a "reporter of sporting events" for various London newspapers by 1812; reporter for the journal printed by E. Young, 1812–23; full-time writer from 1823; Editor, *Pierce Egan's Life in London and Sporting Guide*, weekly newspaper, 1824–27, and *Pierce Egan's Weekly Courier*, 1829. Died 3 August 1849.

PUBLICATIONS

Fiction

Life in London; or, The Day and Night Scenes of Jerry Hawthorn, Esq., and Corinthian
   Tom. 1821.
The Life of an Actor. 1825.
Finish to the Adventures of Tom, Jerry, and Logic in Their Pursuits Through Life In and
   Out of London. 1828; edited by J. C. Hotten, 1871.
The Pilgrims of the Thames in Search of the National! 1838.

Plays

> Tom and Jerry, from his own novel Life in London (produced 1821).
> Life in Dublin (produced 1839).

Verse

> The Show Folks.   1831.
> Matthews's Comic Annual; or, The Snuff-Box and the Leetel Bird.   1831.
> Epsom Races.   1835.

Other

> The Mistress of Royalty; or, The Loves of Florizel and Perdita.   1814.
> Boxiana; or, Sketches of Ancient and Modern Pugilism, vols. 1–3.   1818–21; New Series,
>   2 vols., 1828–29.
> Walks Through Bath.   1819.
> The Key to a Picture of the Fancy.   1819.
> Sporting Anecdotes, Original and Select.   1820.
> The Life and Extraordinary Adventures of S. D. Hayward.   1822.
> The Fancy Togs' Man Versus Young Sadboy, The Milling Quaker.   1823.
> Account of the Trial of J. Thurtell and J. Hunt.   1824.
> Recollections of John Thurtell.   1824.
> Account of the Trial of Mr. Fauntleroy for Forgery.   1824.
> Account of the Trial of Bishop, Williams, and May for Murder.   N.d.
> Anecdotes of the Turf, The Chase, The Ring, and the Stage.   1827.
> Book of Sports and Mirror of Life.   1832.

Reading List: Bucks and Bruisers: Egan and Regency England by J. C. Reid, 1971.

*   *   *

Pierce Egan made his name in 1812 as the author of a history of boxing, issued in monthly parts. Boxiana eventually ran to five volumes, the last published in 1829, and is a high point in sporting journalism. The later volumes record in rapid colloquial prose the fashionable heyday of boxing from the championship victory of "Gentleman" John Jackson in 1795 until his retirement as a coach of the nobility in 1824. Egan knew shorthand, and could revive a fight round-by-round; but Boxiana is socially as well as sportingly alert.

The same is true of Egan's work on his other main interests – crime, city life, and the theatre. He published celebrated accounts of the trials of Hayward, Thurtell and Hunt, and Fauntleroy, and made use of a casual acquaintanceship in adding Recollections of John Thurtell to the less personal courtroom observations. Though clearly fascinated by low-life and high crime, Egan took a moral line against the growing cult of rogue literature. He contributed to it nonetheless. As a practising journalist, he was occupationally committed to doing so. Criminals and criminality are a part of Life in London, which is neither quite a novel nor quite anything else. Ned Ward's London Spy (1698–99) is the model for this hugely successful foray into the high and low life of the city during the Regency. Egan's eye is not on narrative but on the locations, and on the episodes that ensue when Corinthian Tom, together with his friend Bob Logic, undertakes to introduce his Somerset cousin Jerry Hawthorn to London. There is some care in the juxtaposing of contrasting scenes, but the book owed its popularity to its graphic accuracy, to its carefully observed racy slang, and to Egan's appetite for the diversity of city life. A sequel, *Finish to Life in London*, sees the cautionary deaths of Bob and Tom, and Jerry's married retirement to Somerset. *Life in London* fathered a vast, sub-literary family, none of which brought any profit to Egan. His own dramatic version was less effective than William Moncrieff's *Tom and Jerry*, whose sensational run began in November 1821 at the Adelphi, and spread all over the provinces. The "Tom and Jerry" formula had a lasting appeal, independent not only of Egan's text but also of its superb illustration by Robert and George Cruikshank. Egan's last novel, *The Pilgrims of the Thames*, is a variation on it. Its new fastidiousness signals the transition from Regency to Victorian England. *The Life of an Actor*, an old-fashioned picaresque novel, is notable for Theodore Lane's hand-coloured illustrations and for the detailed information it gives about the provincial theatre. This is the world of Vincent Crummles, and the claim that, here and elsewhere, Egan influenced Dickens is plausible. Without Tom and Jerry, Boz might have sketched differently; and Dickens certainly looked to Egan as an expert on thieves' cant.

—Peter Thomson

EGGLESTON, Edward. American. Born in Vevay, Indiana, 10 December 1837. Educated in various Indiana country schools, and at the Amelia Academy, Virginia, 1854–55. Married 1) Lizzie Snider in 1858 (died, 1890), two daughters and one son; 2) Frances E. Goode in 1891. Teacher, Madison, Indiana, 1855; entered the Methodist ministry, 1857: circuit rider in Southeast Indiana, 1856–57; preacher in Minnesota, in Traverse and St. Peter, 1857–58, St. Paul, 1858–60, Stillwater, 1860–61, St. Paul, 1862–63, and Winona, 1864–66; Associate Editor, *The Little Corporal* magazine, and Columnist for the *Evening Journal*, Chicago, 1866–67; Editor, *National Sunday School Teacher*, Chicago, 1867–69; Western (i.e., Chicago) Correspondent, 1867–69, Literary Editor, 1870, and Superintending Editor, 1871, *The Independent*, New York; Editor, *Hearth and Home*, New York, 1871–72; left the Methodist ministry, 1874; Founder and Pastor of the non-sectarian Church of the Christian Endeavor, Brooklyn, New York, 1874 until he retired to devote himself to historical writing, 1879. Co-Founder, Authors' Club, 1882; President, American Historical Association, 1900. D.D.: University of Indiana, Bloomington, 1870; D.H.L.: Allegheny College, Meadville, Pennsylvania, 1893. *Died 2 September 1902.*

PUBLICATIONS

Fiction

Mr. Blake's Walking-Stick: A Christmas Story for Boys and Girls. 1870.
Book of Queer Stories, and Stories Told on a Cellar Door. 1871.
The Hoosier School-Master. 1871; revised edition, 1892.
The End of the World: A Love Story. 1872.
The Mystery of Metropolisville. 1873.
The Circuit Rider: A Tale of the Heroic Age. 1874.
The Schoolmaster's Stories for Boys and Girls. 1874.
Roxy. 1878.
The Hoosier School-Boy. 1882.

Queer Stories for Boys and Girls. 1884.
The Graysons: A Story of Illinois. 1888.
The Faith Doctor: A Story of New York. 1891.
Duffels (collected stories). 1893.

Other

Sunday School Conventions and Institutes. 1867; revised edition, 1870.
The Manual: A Practical Guide to the Sunday-School Work. 1869.
Improved Sunday School Record. 1869.
Tracts for Sunday School Teachers. 1872(?).
Tecumseh and the Shawnee Prophet, with Lillie Eggleston Seelye. 1878.
Pocahontas, with Lillie Eggleston Seelye. 1879; as *The Indian Princess,* 1881.
Brant and Red Jacket, with Lillie Eggleston Seelye. 1879; as *The Rival Warriors, Chiefs of the Five Nations,* 1881.
Montezuma and the Conquest of Mexico, with Lillie Eggleston Seelye. 1880; as *The Mexican Prince,* 1881.
A History of the United States and Its People, for the Use of Schools. 1888.
A First Book in American History. 1889.
Stories of Great Americans for Little Americans: Second Reader Grade.
Stories of American Life and Adventures: Third Reader Grade. 1895.
The Beginners of a Nation. 1896.
The Transit of Civilization from England to America in the Seventeenth Century. 1901.
The New Century History of the United States, edited by G. C. Eggleston. 1904.

Editor, *Christ in Literature.* 1875.
Editor, *Christ in Art.* 1875.
Editor, with Elizabeth Eggleston Seelye, *The Story of Columbus,* 1892.
Editor, with Elizabeth Eggleston Seelye, *The Story of Washington.* 1893.

Bibliography: in *Bibliography of American Literature* by Jacob Blanck, 1959; "Eggleston" by William Peirce Randel, in *American Literary Realism 1,* 1967.

Reading List: *Eggleston, Author of "The Hoosier School-Master,"* 1946, and *Eggleston,* 1963, both by William Peirce Randel.

*   *   *

In 1871 Edward Eggleston, a former Methodist clergyman from Indiana who had become a successful editor of popular magazines for children and adults, published *The Hoosier School-Master,* thereby launching the first of two literary careers for which he is justly famous. In the adventures of a fictional frontier Indiana school-teacher, Eggleston the novelist created a pioneering piece of western dialect fiction, and also contributed seminally to the growth of mid-western realism, a genre which would subsequently be developed by Hamlin Garland.

Written initially for serialization in Eggleston's magazine *Hearth and Home,* with the early installments in print well before the later portions were in outline, *The Hoosier School-Master* has rightly been criticized for its many structural flaws. But Eggleston soon followed with a series of finer though curiously less famous novels in the same realistic vein: *The End of the World,* based upon the Millerite delusion of the 1840's; *The Mystery of Metropolisville,* a poorly constructed but equally realistic saga of boom and bust on the midwestern frontier; *The Circuit Rider,* a novel of remembrance, as the erstwhile preacher Eggleston wrote in its dedication, for his "Comrades of Other Years ... with whom I had the honor to be associate in a frontier ministry"; and *Roxy*, the story of a small-town Ohio girl, thought by some to be Eggleston's best fictional work. Throughout his novels Eggleston sought to portray the commonplace in nineteenth-century American life. As he stated in *The Mystery of Metropolisville*, a novel "needs to be true to human nature in its permanent and essential qualities, and it should truthfully represent ... some form of society."

Given the realistic character of his fiction, it was a short step for Eggleston to his next and final career, that of historian. In 1888 he published his *History of the United States and Its People*. And in 1896 appeared *The Beginners of a Nation*, the first of a projected multi-volume "History of Life in the United States." True to his proclivities as a realist, Eggleston had planned, as he said in 1880, for his history to be "a history of ... the life of the people, the sources of their ideas and habits, the course of their development from beginnings." And had he been able to complete his series he surely would have joined Moses Coit Tyler and John Bach McMaster as one of the great founders of American social history. Unfortunately he came to history too late in life and with too expansive a plan. After publishing the second volume in the series, *The Transit of Civilization*, he died in 1902.

Thus, in history as in literature, Edward Eggleston remains an important but decidedly minor figure.

—Bruce A. Lohof

EKWENSI, Cyprian. Nigerian. Born in Minna, Northern Nigeria, 26 September 1921. Educated at Government College, Ibadan; Achimota College, Ghana; School of Forestry, Ibadan; Higher College, Yaba; Chelsea School of Pharmacy, University of London. Married to Eunice Anyiwo; five children. Lecturer in Biology, Chemistry and English, Igbodi College, Lagos, 1947–49; Lecturer in Pharmacognosy and Pharmaceutics, School of Pharmacy, Lagos, 1949–56; Pharmacist, Nigerian Medical Service, 1956; Head of Features, Nigerian Broadcasting Corporation, 1957–61; Director of Information, Federal Ministry of Information, Lagos, 1961–66. Since 1966, Director of Information Services in Enugu. Travelled to the United States, with Chinua Achebe and Gabriel Okara, to seek help for Biafra, 1969. Chairman, East Central State Library Board, Enugu, 1971; Member, Nigerian Arts Council. Recipient: Dag Hammarskjöld International Award, 1968. Lives in Enugu.

PUBLICATIONS

Fiction

People of the City. 1954.
Jagua Nana. 1961.
Burning Grass: A Story of the Fulani of Northern Nigeria. 1962.
Beautiful Feathers. 1963.
The Rainmaker and Other Stories. 1965.
Lokotown and Other Stories. 1966.
Iska. 1966.
Restless City, and Christmas Gold. 1975.
Survive the Peace. 1976.

Other (juvenile)

When Love Whispers. 1947.
Ikolo the Wrestler and Other Ibo Tales. 1947.
The Leopard's Claw. 1950.
The Drummer Boy. 1960.
The Passport of Mallam Ilia. 1960.
Yaba Roundabout Murder. 1962.
An African Night's Entertainment: A Tale of Vengeance. 1962.
The Great Elephant-Bird. 1965.
Trouble in Form Six. 1966.
The Boa Suitor. 1966.
Juju Rock. 1966.
Coal Camp Boy. 1973.
Samankwe in the Strange Forest. 1973.
The Rainbow-Tinted Scarf and Other Stories. 1975.
Samankwe and the Highway Robbers. 1975.

Reading List: *Ekwensi* by Ernest Emenyonu, 1974.

*   *   *

Cyprian Ekwensi is a prolific writer who covers many genres, novels, short stories, folklore collections, children's stories, and newspaper articles. He is a very popular novelist who writes for the masses.

His literary career started in 1947 when he published the novella *When Love Whispers.* It formed part of the Onitsha Market Literature which flourished after the second World War. Written for and by the newly literate urban masses this literature concerned itself with the problems of adapting to a westernized way of life in the melting-pots of the fast-expanding towns in southern Nigeria. Subjects like romantic love, the generation gap, how to get on in life, and how to avoid the pitfalls of drink and prostitutes were prevalent in this popular literature.

Ekwensi is rooted in this culture, and, although he has written about the life of Fulani cattle-raisers in the North, he is mainly thought of as a writer of city life. His major novels, *People of the City, Jagua Nana,* and *Beautiful Feathers,* are all concerned with the problems of surviving in a big city. Ekwensi has an ambiguous attitude to his subject. On the one hand he is a moralist trying to warn people of the dangers of the city – the bars with their prostitutes, the corrupt politicians and businessmen, the con-men and thieves, the deceitful friends. Ekwensi's city is a jungle in which everybody is on his own, fighting everybody else for survival. On the other hand, Ekwensi is obviously fascinated by the city, particularly its more seedy aspects. This is most obvious in *Jagua Nana.* The main character, Jagua Nana, is a magnificent but ageing prostitute who can still trap men in her favourite haunt, the nightclub "Tropicana"; however, she prefers a young school teacher, Freddy, whom she supports only to be replaced by a younger and more respectable woman.

The books are flawed by contradictions, inconsistencies, improbabilities, heavy sentimentalizing, shallow characterization, and a cliché-ridden English which places Ekwensi squarely among the writers of popular literature, but his historical importance is considerable.

—Kirsten Holst Petersen

ELIOT, George. Pseudonym for Mary Ann or Marian Evans. English. Born at Chilvers Coton, near Nuneaton, Warwickshire, 22 November 1819. Privately educated. Lived with George Henry Lewes, 1854 until he died, 1878; married J. W. Cross in 1880. Took charge of family household after the death of her mother, 1836; moved with her father to Coventry, 1841–49; lived in Geneva, 1849–50; settled in London, 1850, and began to write for the *Westminster Review*: Assistant Editor, 1851–54; lived in Germany, 1854, then returned to England; subsequently settled in Cheyne Walk, Chelsea, London. *Died 22 December 1880.*

PUBLICATIONS

Collections

Works. 21 vols., 1895.
Letters, edited by Gordon Haight. 9 vols., 1954–78.

Fiction

Scenes of Clerical Life (stories). 1858; edited by David Lodge, 1973.
Adam Bede. 1859; edited by John Paterson, 1968.
The Mill on the Floss. 1860; edited by Gordon Haight, 1961.
Silas Marner, The Weaver of Raveloe. 1861; edited by Q. D. Leavis, 1967.
Romola. 1863.
Felix Holt, The Radical. 1866; edited by Peter Coveney, 1972.
Middlemarch: A Study of Provincial Life. 1872; edited by Bert G. Hornback, 1977.
Daniel Deronda. 1876; edited by Barbara Hardy, 1967.

Verse

The Spanish Gypsy. 1868.
How Lisa Loved the King. 1869.
The Legend of Jubal and Other Poems. 1874.
Complete Poems. 1889.

Other

Works. 24 vols., 1878–85.
Impressions of Theophrastus Such. 1879.
Essays and Leaves from a Note-Book, edited by C. L. Lewes. 1884.
Early Essays. 1919.
Essays, edited by T. Pinney. 1963.

Translator, with Mrs. Charles Hennell, *The Life of Jesus Critically Examined*, by D. F. Strauss. 3 vols., 1846; edited by Peter C. Hodgson, 1973.
Translator, *The Essence of Christianity*, by Ludwig Feuerbach. 1854.

Bibliography: *Eliot: A Reference Guide* by Constance M. Fulmer, 1977.

Reading List: *Eliot's Life as Related in Her Letters and Journals* by J. W. Cross, 3 vols., 1885; *Eliot: Her Mind and Art* by Joan Bennett, 1948; *Eliot* by Robert Speaight, 1954; *The Novels of Eliot* by Barbara Hardy, 1959; *The Art of Eliot* by W. J. Harvey, 1961; *Eliot* by Walter Allen, 1964; *A Century of Eliot Criticism* edited by Gordon Haight, 1965; *Eliot: A Biography* by Gordon Haight, 1968; *Critical Essays on Eliot* edited by Barbara Hardy, 1970; *Eliot: The Critical Heritage* edited by D. R. Carroll, 1971; *Eliot: The Emergent Self* by Ruby Redinger, 1975; *Eliot: Her Beliefs and Her Art* by Neil Roberts, 1975; *The Novels of Eliot* by Robert Liddell, 1977.

*   *   *

To many of her admirers during her lifetime, George Eliot, though ranked as a novelist below Dickens and Thackeray, seemed more than a "mere" novelist. She was a maker of the moral law as no novelist had been before her, and despite the unconventional circumstances of her life her position when she died could be paralleled only by Wordsworth's a generation or so earlier. In the decades that followed everything changed. She fell with the great Victorians, and so far as there was interest in her it was largely as a figure in the history of woman's emancipation. Today, all is different again. She still has to yield to Dickens's superior genius but in critical estimation she leads all other Victorian novelists and is seen as the one nineteenth-century English novelist who can be mentioned in the same breath as Tolstoy. In England she is probably over-rated.

She came to the writing of fiction steeped in the advanced thought of Victorian England. She had translated Strauss's *Life of Jesus* and experienced in herself the full force of doubt about religion and the truth of Christianity. She was torn between the old, which she loved, and the new, which won her intellectual assent. She was, indeed, that familiar figure in English life, the radical Tory. Born into the Established Church, she had become a Calvinist Methodist as a girl, and, when intellectual honesty compelled a reluctant agnosticism upon her, it was an agnosticism that laid as remorseless a stress on morals and right behaviour as had the dissent of her youth.

Her beliefs chimed with what seemed to be evidence of the science of the day, of Darwinism as then interpreted. This gave her novels great authority at the time, though later it was to appear dated. It was too mechanistic a view of life to allow her to write tragedy, but by placing the responsibility for a man's life firmly on the moral choices of the individual she changed the nature of the English novel. Character became plot. D. H. Lawrence saw her as the first modern novelist, saying in an early letter that she was the first to start "putting all the action inside."

Her first work of fiction, *Scenes of Clerical Life*, which is made up of three long-short stories, need not detain us. What is good in them George Eliot was to do much better. *Adam Bede*, which appeared a year later, is quite another matter. A key to it is an authorial intrusion in which George Eliot comments on what in fact is one of the qualities of her own art:

> It is for this rare, precious quality of truthfulness that I delight in many Dutch paintings, which lofty-minded people despise. I find a source of delicious sympathy in these faithful pictures of a monotonous homely existence, which has been the fate of so many more among my fellow mortals than a life of pomp or of absolute indigence, of tragic suffering or of world-stirring action.

Here she is stressing the pastoral ambience of the novel, which encloses the moral action; the scenes in Mrs. Poyser's farmhouse, for instance, the harvest supper, and what has been called "the massively slow movement" of the novel in which the rhythms of life and the seasons are beautifully caught. But another key to the novel is contained in the Rev. Mr. Irwine's words: "Consequences are unpitying. Our deeds carry their terrible consequences ... consequences that are hardly ever confined to ourselves." These words define the inner action of the novel:

the fall of Hetty Sorrel, her seduction by Arthur Donnithorne, the effect of this on Adam Bede and his marriage to Dinah Morris.

But the touching, idyllic love-affair of Hetty and Arthur Donnithorne is undercut for us now by the hostile attitude of the author towards sex and sensuality. Nor, though the novel is a wonderful study of the impact of Methodism on English life, can George Eliot be said quite to succeed with Adam Bede and Dinah. The good are notoriously less easy to make convincing or attractive in fiction than the less good.

George Eliot's fiction falls naturally into two parts. *Scenes of Clerical Life, Adam Bede, The Mill on the Floss* and *Silas Marner* were all published between 1858 and 1861. *Romola* (1863) begins her second and more ambitious period, which takes in *Felix Holt, The Radical, Middlemarch*, and *Daniel Deronda*. The speed with which she wrote her first novels shows how near the surface of her mind was the vein of imagination she tapped. To write *The Mill on the Floss* she had only to remember her own childhood, for, though the background and setting have been very much altered, the novel is essentially autobiographical. As a detailed rendering of the growth of a girl to young womanhood, a girl of intellectual distinction and generously ardent feelings, Maggie Tulliver is unsurpassed. Equally brilliant in a different mode is the representation of the Tulliver family and of the Dodsons. They comprise a materialistic world given over entirely to the sense of property, self-regard and pride in family, made palatable to us only by the humour and shrewdness of George Eliot's observation.

Describing the inception of *Silas Marner*, George Eliot noted its Wordsworthian quality. Though she wrote two volumes of verse, it was only in the prose of *Silas Marner* that she achieved poetry. It is indeed of a Wordsworthian order, this story which shows "in a strong light the remedial influences of pure, natural human relations." Only in her own time could she have succeeded in telling the story of Marner without lapsing into sentimentality, and no one could have done so after her. A poor dissenting weaver is betrayed by his friend, accused of theft, loses his future wife, goes into exile in a remote country district, becomes a miser, is robbed of his gold, and in the end brought back into human fellowship by the discovery and adoption of a golden-haired baby girl. It is a small miracle, this novel of redemption; and in the wonderful conversations at the Rainbow Inn it contains George Eliot's finest delineations of rustic characters and her finest humorous writing.

In the fiction of her second period George Eliot wrote only one novel, *Middlemarch*, that can be called a success. *Romola* was an attempt at a historical novel, a recreation of Florence at the end of the fifteenth century and of the career and martyrdom of Savonarola. Enormous pains went to its making. It is crammed with solid and scholarly information and almost totally lacking in life. In writing *Romola* George Eliot had cut herself off from the source of her inspiration, which was the contemplation of the changing scene of the English Midland countryside in her time. She returned to it in *Felix Holt, The Radical*. It contains fine things but is dominated by a plot that is particularly cumbersome, almost impossible to synopsise and turning on points of law relating to inheritance which have baffled most readers. But Harold Transome is a notably impressive character creation, belonging to the company of George Eliot's formidable masculine figures, Lydgate and Grandcourt.

George Eliot's greatest novel is *Middlemarch*, a beautiful composition organised round four major plots, the story of Dorothea Brooke, the story of Lydgate's marriage, the history of Mary Garth, and the fall of the banker Bulstrode, all of them related to one another without strain. Together, they make a network that takes in the whole life and movement of opinion and events in a provincial city and its surrounding country in the years immediately before the first Reform Act of 1832. Two of the characters, Dorothea and Lydgate, are among the finest in fiction, and Dorothea in particular is a great conception. She is, as it were, a heightened Maggie Tulliver, with all Maggie's notability of aspiration but with the advantages of social position, wealth, and independence. The conception of Lydgate falls not far short; and around them are gathered as large and diverse a gallery of characters as exists in any English novel.

The failure of George Eliot's last novel, *Daniel Deronda*, is self-evident. It falls into two parts, that action centred on the imaginatively conceived character of Gwendolen and that centred on Deronda, this latter being propaganda for the establishment of a Zionist state. All the same, the novel is regarded now much more highly than it was because of the brilliance of Gwendolen Harleth as a character-creation. She is utterly different from George Eliot's other great heroines, cold, arrogant, self-willed where they are idealist, warm, and self-sacrificing. And Grandcourt, her nemesis, is no less magisterially drawn. It is plain now that George Eliot died before she had realised the full potentialities of her genius.

One aspect of her genius is shown in the influence she had on later novelists. Hardy and Lawrence are scarcely conceivable without her; a considerable part of Henry James developed out of her; and it has been surmised that *The Mill on the Floss* was in Proust's mind when he was planning *A la recherche du temps perdu*; and her continuing influence and example may be seen in the fiction of such novelists as Angus Wilson and Doris Lessing.

—Walter Allen

ELLISON, Ralph (Waldo). American. Born in Oklahoma City, Oklahoma, 1 March 1914. Educated at a high school in Oklahoma City, and at Tuskegee Institute, Alabama, 1933–36. Served in the United States Merchant Marine, 1943–45. Married Fanny McConnell in 1946. Writer from 1936; Lecturer, Salzburg Seminar in American Studies, 1954; Instructor of Russian and American Literature, Bard College, Annandale-on-Hudson, New York, 1958–61; Alexander White Visiting Professor, University of Chicago, 1961; Visiting Professor of Writing, Rutgers University, New Brunswick, New Jersey, 1962–64; Whittall Lecturer, Library of Congress, Washington, D.C., 1964; Ewing Lecturer, University of California at Los Angeles, 1964; Visiting Fellow in American Studies, Yale University, New Haven, Connecticut, 1966. Since 1970, Albert Schweitzer Professor in the Humanities, New York University. Chairman, Literary Grants Committee, National Institute of Arts and Letters, 1964–67; Member, National Council on the Arts, 1965–67; Member, Carnegie Commission on Educational Television, 1966–67; Member of the Editorial Board, *American Scholar*, Washington, D.C., 1966–69; Honorary Consultant in American Letters, Library of Congress, Washington, D.C., 1966–72. Trustee, John F. Kennedy Center of the Performing Arts, Washington, D.C., New School for Social Research, New York, Bennington College, Vermont, Educational Broadcasting Corporation, and the Colonial Williamsburg Foundation. Recipient: Rosenwald Fellowship, 1945; National Book Award, 1953; National Newspaper Publishers Association Russwarm Award, 1953; National Academy of Arts and Letters Prix de Rome, 1955, 1956; United States Medal of Freedom, 1969. Ph.D. in Humane Letters: Tuskegee Institute, 1963; Litt.D.: Rutgers University, 1966; University of Michigan, Ann Arbor, 1967; Williams College, Williamstown, Massachusetts, 1970; Long Island University, New York, 1971; College of William and Mary, Williamsburg, Virginia, 1972; Wake Forest College, Winston-Salem, North Carolina, 1974; Harvard University, Cambridge, Massachusetts, 1974; L.H.D.: Grinnell College, Iowa, 1967; Adelphi University, Garden City, New York, 1971; University of Maryland, College Park, 1974. Chevalier de l'Ordre des Arts et Lettres, France, 1970. Member, American Academy of Arts and Letters, 1975. Lives in New York City.

Fiction

Invisible Man.   1952.

Other

Shadow and Act (essays).   1964.

Bibliography: "A Bibliography of Ellison's Published Writings" by Bernard Benoit and Michel Fabre, in *Studies in Black Literature 2*, 1971; *The Blinking Eye: Ellison and His American, French, German, and Italian Critics* by Jacqueline Covo, 1974.

Reading List: *Five Black Writers* edited by Donald B. Gibson, 1970; "Ellison Issue" of *C.L.A. Journal 13*, 1970; *Twentieth-Century Interpretations of "Invisible Man"* edited by John M. Reilly, 1970; *The Merrill Studies in "Invisible Man"* edited by Ronald Gottesman, 1971; *Ellison: A Collection of Critical Essays* edited by John Hersey, 1973.

*   *   *

A bookish as well as a musical child, Ralph Ellison began to read some of the classics of modern literature, including *The Waste Land*, while a student at Tuskegee. His literary education was accelerated after he met Richard Wright in 1937. In addition to providing an example of commitment to social and racial justice, Wright helped to persuade Ellison to direct his creative energies to writing, encouraging him to turn to "those works in which writing was discussed as a craft ... to Henry James' prefaces, to Conrad, to Joseph Warren Beach and to the letters of Dostoievsky" (*Shadow and Act*). Despite some later disavowals, Ellison was deeply influenced by Wright's own fiction as well as by his literary tutelage. Such early short stories as "Slick Gonna Learn" and "Mister Toussan'," for example, reveal how carefully Ellison had read Wright's *Uncle Tom's Children*.

When one looks at *Invisible Man*, however, one sees that Ellison's creative consciousness encompasses a vast range of the world's literature. Such modern giants as Eliot, Joyce, Malraux, Hemingway, Pound, Stein, and Faulkner are clearly part of his literary inheritance, but so are the writers of the Harlem Renaissance; the Continental (especially Dostoevsky), British, and American (especially Melville and Twain) masters of nineteenth-century fiction; and his namesake Emerson and other Transcendentalists. Some critics have argued for *The Odyssey* or *The Aeneid* as major influences on Ellison's novel. However allusive, Ellison is also profoundly original, putting his sophisticated technique and literary education to the service of his vision of the racial and human condition in America.

Invisible Man concerns the quest of an unnamed young black man for personal identity and racial community as he travels from South to North, from innocence to experience, from self-deception to knowledge, from a spurious visibility to an existential invisibility. These journeys take place in the immediate context of the late depression, but, as they unfold, their implications extend backward in time to the Reconstruction, slavery, and the founding of the Republic, and outward from the protagonist's self to the social situation of black America and to the very nature of the democratic experiment.

Framed by a prologue and an epilogue set in an underground chamber to which the protagonist has retreated from the chaos of life above ground, the narrative proper begins in the Deep South with his initiation rite into the social order of white supremacy as he graduates from high school and prepares to matriculate at a black college closely resembling

Tuskegee Institute, where he hopes to learn to become a black leader. There the idyllic setting and his personal ambition are disrupted by his naivety, by a northern white capitalist's ambiguous "philanthropy," and by the ruthless self-aggrandizement of Dr. Bledsoe, the black president of the institution. Expelled from college and from the South, the protagonist travels to New York to seek employment in a white-collar position. Unsuccessful in that effort, he undergoes a still more disastrous experience as an industrial worker in the Liberty Paint plant. After these repeated failures in his personal pursuit of success, the protagonist becomes involved with the Brotherhood, a radical political organization paralleling the Communist Party. Here, he hopes, he can achieve self-realization while contributing to social amelioration. But political radicalism fails him – and his race – just as completely as southern segregation and northern employment, and for similar reasons of personal and racial exploitation. When his very physical existence is threatened in a Harlem race riot, he goes underground for sanctuary and reassessment. Ending in the epilogue where it began in the prologue, the narrative completes its circular ("boomerang") structure. Whatever one thinks of the rather forced optimism concerning a possible resurrection and return to the world above ground, the success of which may be viewed as problematical given his repeated rebuffs, the protagonist has at last and at least achieved for himself and for the reader the kind of self-actualization that knowledge of self and society can bring. To that extent he is no longer an invisible man.

Ellison's other published book, *Shadow and Act*, is a prose miscellany deriving some unity from its tripartite arrangement: "The Seer and the Seen" – topics in literature (especially his own career) and folklore; "Sound and the Mainstream" – topics in music, especially the blues and jazz; and "The Shadow and the Act" – black American social and cultural conditions in the context of national patterns. This organization emphasizes the lifelong interests of the author: books, music, and race.

Ellison's long second novel on religion and politics, published excerpts from which indicate high quality, has been in progress for more than two decades. It is clear that Ellison's reputation as a novelist will rest not on an ample *oeuvre* but on the brilliance, verbal dexterity, and mythic and social dimensions of one or two books.

—Keneth Kinnamon

EMERSON, Ralph Waldo. American. Born in Boston, Massachusetts, 25 May 1803. Educated at Harvard University, Cambridge, Massachusetts, graduated 1821; studied for the ministry. Married 1) Ellen Louisa Tucker in 1829 (died, 1831); 2) Lydia Jackson in 1835, one son. Worked for a time as a schoolmaster; Pastor, Old Second Church of Boston (Unitarian), 1829 until he retired from the ministry, 1832; visited Europe, 1832–33; moved to Concord, Massachusetts, 1834: one of the leaders of the Transcendental Club, and contributor to the club's periodical *The Dial*, from 1840; lectured in England, 1847–48. LL.D.: Harvard University, 1866. *Died 27 April 1882.*

PUBLICATIONS

Collections

    Complete Works. 12 vols., 1883–93; edited by Edward Waldo Emerson, 12 vols., 1903–04.

Letters, edited by Ralph L. Rusk.   6 vols., 1939.
The Portable Emerson, edited by Mark Van Doren.   1946.
Collected Works, edited by Alfred R. Ferguson.   1971–

Verse

Poems.   1847.
Selected Poems.   1876.

Other

Nature.   1836; edited by Kenneth W. Cameron, 1940.
Essays.   1841; revised edition, as *Essays: First Series,* 1847; *Second Series,* 1844; revised edition, 1850.
The Young American.   1844.
Nature: An Essay, and Lectures of the Times.   1844.
Orations, Lectures, and Addresses.   1844.
Nature: Addresses and Lectures.   1849.
Representative Men: Seven Lectures.   1850.
English Traits.   1856; edited by Howard Mumford Jones, 1966.
The Conduct of Life.   1860.
Complete Works.   2 vols., 1866.
May-Day and Other Pieces.   1867.
Prose Works.   3 vols., 1868–78(?).
Society and Solitude.   1870.
Letters and Social Aims.   1876.
The Preacher.   1880.
The Correspondence of Carlyle and Emerson 1834–1872, edited by Charles Eliot Norton.   2 vols., 1883; supplement, 1886; edited by Joseph Slater, 1964.
The Senses and the Soul, and Moral Sentiment in Religion: Two Essays.   1884.
Two Unpublished Essays: The Character of Socrates, The Present State of Ethical Philosophy.   1896.
Journals 1820–76, edited by Edward Waldo Emerson and Waldo Emerson Forbes.   10 vols., 1909–14.
Uncollected Writings, edited by Charles C. Bigelow.   1912.
Uncollected Lectures, edited by Clarence Gohdea.   1932.
Young Emerson Speaks: Unpublished Discourses on Many Subjects, edited by Arthur Cushman McGiffert, Jr.   1938.
The Early Lectures, edited by Stephen E. Whicher, Robert E. Spiller, and Wallace. E. Williams.   3 vols., 1959–72.
The Journals and Miscellaneous Notebooks, edited by William H. Gilman.   14 vols. (of 16), 1960–78.

Editor, *Essays and Poems,* by Jones Very.   1839.
Editor, with James Freeman Clarke and W. H. Channing, *Memoirs of Margaret Fuller Ossoli.*   2 vols., 1852.
Editor, *Excursions,* by Henry David Thoreau.   1863.
Editor, *Letters to Various Persons,* by Henry David Thoreau.   1865.
Editor, *Parnassus* (verse anthology).   1875.

Translator, *Vita Nuova,* by Dante, edited by J. Chesley Mathews.   1960.

Bibliography: *A Bibliography of Emerson* by George Willis Cooke, 1908; in *Bibliography of American Literature* by Jacob Blanck, 1959.

Reading List: *The Life of Emerson* by Ralph L. Rusk, 1949; *Spires of Form: A Study of Emerson's Aesthetic Theory* by Vivian C. Hopkins, 1951; *Emerson's Angle of Vision: Man and Nature in American Experience* by Sherman Paul, 1952; *Emerson Handbook* by Frederic I. Carpenter, 1953; *Freedom and Fate: An Inner Life of Emerson* by Stephen E. Whicher, 1953; *Emerson: A Collection of Critical Essays,* edited by Milton R. Konvitz and Stephen E. Whicher, 1962; *Emerson: A Portrait* edited by Carl Bode, 1968; *The Recognition of Emerson: Selected Criticism since 1837* edited by Milton R. Konvitz, 1972; *Emerson: Portrait of a Balanced Soul* by Edward Wagenknecht, 1973; *Emerson as Poet* by Hyatt H. Waggoner, 1974; *Emerson: Prophecy, Metamorphosis, and Influence* edited by David Levin, 1975; *The Slender Human Word: Emerson's Artistry in Prose* by William J. Scheick, 1978.

*   *   *

Ralph Waldo Emerson was the most distinguished of the New England Transcendentalists and one of the most brilliant American poets and thinkers of the nineteenth century. Although Transcendentalism as a mode of Romantic thought has been largely discredited by modern scientific theory, Emerson's essays and poems remain remarkably provocative – and much more tough-minded than they have frequently been given credit for being.

Emerson was not a highly systematic philosopher. His thought was an amalgam from a wide variety of sources: (1) New England religious thought and related English writings of the seventeenth and eighteenth centuries; (2) Scottish realism, which he absorbed principally while at Harvard college; (3) French and English skepticism, the lasting effects of which should not be underestimated; (4) Neo-Platonism, the dominant element in his thought, especially as it was interpreted by the English Romantic poets and the German and French Idealists; (5) Oriental mystical writings, even though he never accepted their fatalism or their concept of transmigration; (6) Yankee pragmatism, which was latent in almost all of his work and which muted his Romantic Idealism, especially in his essays on political and economic affairs. In Coleridge's explanation of Platonic dualism Emerson found the ordering principle for these disparate strands of thought. The discovery of Coleridge's distinction between the Reason and the Understanding brought such a surge of confidence in him that it is hardly an exaggeration to say that it transformed Emerson's life. Certainly it transformed his thinking.

Within one great Unity, he came to believe, there are two levels of reality, the supernatural and the natural. The supernatural is essence, spirit, or Oversoul as Emerson most frequently called it. It is an impersonal force that is eternal, moral, harmonious, and beneficent in tendency. The individual soul is a part of the Oversoul, and man has access to it through his intuition (which like Coleridge Emerson called the Reason, thereby confusing his readers then and now). One of the tendencies of the Oversoul is to express itself in form, hence the world of nature as an emanation of the world of spirit. The individual has access to this secondary level of reality through the senses and the understanding (the rational faculty). To explain the relation between the spiritual and physical levels of being Emerson used such oppositions as One and Many, cause and effect, unity and diversity, object and symbol, reality and appearance, truths and hypothesis, being and becoming. Since laws of correspondence relate the two levels of being, the study of physical laws can generate intuitions of spiritual truths. What especially delighted Emerson about this dualism was that it allowed him to entertain both faith and doubt: to accept the promptings of the intuition without question and yet to view the hypotheses of the understanding as only tentative and hence constantly open to question.

In his earlier essays, Emerson particularly stressed the unlimited potential of the individual. The most notable of these, *Nature* (1836), argues that, although nature serves as commodity, beauty, language, and discipline, its most important function is to excite the intuition so that the individual through a mystical experience becomes aware of the power of the Oversoul residing within him. "Nature always speaks of Spirit. It suggests the absolute." "The American Scholar" (1837) warns that books and scholarship can divert one from seeking the spiritual power within, and the "Divinity School Address" (1838) suggests that historical Christianity can do the same. "Self Reliance" (1844), in metaphor after metaphor, challenges the reader to seek the truths of the Reason: "Trust thyself; every heart vibrates to that iron string." In many respects "Self Reliance" is the capstone of American Romanticism. Later essays are more guarded in announcing the individual's limitless potential. In "Experience" (1844), for example, he admits that such this-world elements as health, temperament, and illusion can prevent one from exploiting all of the vast possibilities asserted in *Nature*. The enormous confidence of his earlier essays dwindles to "Patience and Patience, we shall win at last."

On subjects of public interest, Emerson's philosophical liberalism had to contend with his pragmatism. At most he was a cautious liberal. The Democrats, he thought, had the better causes, the Whigs the better men. Following Adam Smith, he believed that "affairs themselves show the best way they should be handled." So he was for *laissez-faire* and free trade, though he was more of an agrarian than Smith. Of the followers of Smith he rejected the utilitarians and the pessimists, and approved of only the optimists, particularly such members of the American school as Daniel Raymond, A. H. Everett, and Henry C. Carey. Emerson had nothing against wealth *per se*, but was against rule by the wealthy because the wealthy were too likely to be nothing more than materialists, persons without intuitive insight. Rule by an upper class, however, was agreeable to him so long as the upper class consisted of persons who are wise, temperate, and cultivated, persons who have the insight and courage necessary to protect the poor and weak against the predatory. Clearly his thinking did not drift far in the direction of Marxism. Nor was he willing to admit that the socialistic experiments of Owen and Fourier, though he admired their objectives, had the magic key to Utopia. Even the Transcendental experiments at Fruitlands and Brook Farm he believed impractical. Bereft of their romance, he said, they were projects that well might make their participants less intuitive and self-reliant rather than more so. Of the other major reforms of his day, Emerson lectured only in favor of child labor legislation, a public land policy, and the abolition of slavery. The passage of the Fugitive Slave Bill in 1850 made him as angry as he probably ever became on a public issue. More practical than most abolitionists, however, he argued that slavery was basically an economic matter, and that if the Northern church people really wanted to emancipate the slaves they should sell their church silver, buy up the slaves, and themselves set them free. He saw the Civil War not only as necessary for liberating the slave but "a hope for the liberation of American culture."

Emerson's aesthetic theory, to the extent that he had one, is a direct outgrowth of his Idealistic philosophy. As he conceived of it, the great work of art is not an imitation of nature but a symbolization of Truth realized intuitively. It is the result of resigning oneself to the "divine *aura* which breathes through forms." In his most quoted statement on the subject he put it this way: "It is not metres, but a metre-making argument that makes a poem – a thought so passionate and alive that like the spirit of a plant or animal it has an architecture of its own, and adorns nature with a new thing." Thus the poet (or any great artist) must first of all be the Seer, intuitively experiencing the absolutes of the Oversoul, and secondly the Sayer, communicating those absolutes so compellingly that readers are stimulated to have intuitions of their own. Emerson was realistic enough to realize that such a process is not easy. Intuitions fade quickly. And words, being but symbols of symbols, are inadequate even at best to convey them. The most that a writer can do is to suggest his intuitions by a series of half-truths. The greatest writing, therefore, must be provocative, not descriptive or explanatory. Such a conviction lies behind Emerson's epigrammatic prose style and the liberties he takes with poetic conventions.

There is a good reason for considering Emerson as primarily a poet even though one must go to his journals and essays to realize the fullness of his thought. His concentration on the concrete image, the simplicity of his symbols and words, and his willingness within limits to let form follow function were practices that profoundly influenced such widely divergent followers as Whitman and Dickinson and through them much of modern poetry. Many of Emerson's best-known poems, such as "Concord Hymn" and "The Snow Storm," celebrate local events. But his more notable ones give expression to elements of his philosophy. Through the voice of the cosmic force, "Brahma" suggests the enclosure of all diversity in the one great Unity; so does "Each and All" in which the beauty and meaning of "each" is seen to be dependent upon its context, or the "all." "The Problem" contrasts the unlimited freedom of the poet's imagination with the stultifying routine of the "cowed churchman." Perhaps Emerson's most poignant poem is "Threnody," written in two periods after the death of his young son Waldo. The first part, composed immediately after Waldo's death, describes the poet's disillusionment with nature, indeed with the cosmic scheme, which he had spent so many years celebrating. The second part, written several years later, asserts his resurgent confidence. Nathaniel Hawthorne probably spoke for some modern readers when he said that he "admired Emerson as a poet of deep beauty and austere tenderness, but sought nothing from him as a philosopher." Yet his philosophy cannot be dismissed so summarily. It resulted in a freedom of spirit, a respect for the individual human being, a sense of awe and wonder before the inexplicable that many modern readers still find stirring and reassuring.

—John C. Gerber

FARRELL, James T(homas). American. Born in Chicago, Illinois, 27 February 1904. Educated at DePaul University, Chicago, 1924–25; University of Chicago, 1926–29; New York University, 1941. Married 1) Dorothy Butler in 1931 (divorced); 2) Hortense Alden (divorced, 1955), one son; 3) remarried Dorothy Butler in 1955 (separated, 1958). Writer from 1930; Adjunct Professor, St. Peter's College, Jersey City, New Jersey, 1964–65; Writer-in-Residence, Richmond College, Virginia, 1969–70, and Glassboro State College, New Jersey, 1973. Served as Chairman, National Board, Workers Defense League. Recipient: Guggenheim Fellowship, 1936; Messing Award, 1973. D.Litt.: Miami University, Oxford, Ohio, 1968; Columbia College, Chicago, 1974. Member, National Institute of Arts and Letters. Lives in New York City.

PUBLICATIONS

Fiction

Young Lonigan: A Boyhood in Chicago Streets. 1932; *The Young Manhood of Studs Lonigan,* 1934; *Judgment Day,* 1935; complete version, as *Studs Lonigan,* 1935.
Gas-House McGinty. 1933.
Calico Shoes and Other Stories. 1934; as *Seventeen and Other Stories,* 1959.
Guillotine Party and Other Stories. 1935.
Danny O'Neill pentalogy: *A World I Never Made.* 1936; *No Star Is Lost,* 1938; *Father and Son,* 1940 (as *A Father and His Son,* 1943); *My Days of Anger,* 1943; *The Face of Time,* 1953.
Can All This Grandeur Perish? and Other Stories. 1937.
The Short Stories. 1937; as *Fellow Countrymen: Collected Stories,* 1937.
Tommy Gallagher's Crusade. 1939.
Ellen Rogers. 1941.
$1000 a Week and Other Stories. 1942.
Fifteen Selected Stories. 1943.
To Whom It May Concern and Other Stories. 1944.
When Boyhood Dreams Come True. 1946.
More Fellow Countrymen. 1946.
Bernard Carr trilogy: *Bernard Clare.* 1946 (as *Bernard Clayre,* 1948; as *Bernard Carr,* 1952); *The Road Between,* 1949; *Yet Other Waters,* 1952.
The Life Adventurous and Other Stories. 1947.
A Misunderstanding (story). 1949.
An American Dream Girl (stories). 1950.
This Man and This Woman. 1951.
French Girls Are Vicious and Other Stories. 1955.
An Omnibus of Short Stories. 1956.
A Dangerous Woman and Other Stories. 1957.
Saturday Night and Other Stories. 1958.
The Girls at the Sphinx (stories). 1959.
Looking 'em Over (stories). 1960.
Side Street and Other Stories. 1961.
Boarding House Blues. 1961.
Sound of a City. 1962
A Universe of Time:
  The Silence of History. 1963.
  What Time Collects. 1964.
  When Time Was Born. 1966.

  Lonely for the Future. 1966.
  A Brand New Life. 1968.
  Judith. 1969.
  Invisible Swords. 1971.
  Judith and Other Stories. 1973.
  The Dunne Family. 1976.
  The Death of Nora Ryan. 1978.
  Olive and Mary Anne (stories). 1978.
New Year's Eve/1929. 1967.
Childhood Is Not Forever and Other Stories. 1969.

Verse

  The Collected Poems. 1965.

Other

  A Note on Literary Criticism. 1936.
  The League of Frightened Philistines and Other Papers. 1945.
  The Fate of Writing in America. 1946.
  Literature and Morality. 1947.
  The Name Is Fogarty: Private Papers on Public Matters. 1950.
  Reflections at Fifty and Other Essays. 1954.
  *My Baseball Diary: A Famed Author Recalls the Wonderful World of Baseball, Yesterday
   and Today.* 1957.
  It Has Come to Pass (on Israel). 1958.
  Dialogue with John Dewey, with others. 1959.
  Selected Essays, edited by Luna Wolf. 1964.

  Editor, *Prejudices: A Selection,* by H. L. Mencken. 1958.
  Editor, *A Dreiser Reader.* 1962.

Bibliography: *A Bibliography of Farrell's Writings 1921–1957* by Edgar M. Branch, 1959,
supplements in *American Book Collector 11,* 1961, and *17,* 1967.

Reading List: *Farrell* by Edgar M. Branch, 1971.

      *   *   *

  The son and grandson of Irish Catholic working-class laborers, James T. Farrell was raised in a South-Side Chicago neighborhood that became the source for much of his remarkable body of work, which constitutes the greatest sustained production in twentieth-century America of uncompromisingly realistic fiction. Filling, to date, some fifty volumes, this corpus includes four large fictional cycles, three of which are further connected as progressive explorations of their main characters' varying responses to an urban ethnic environment similar to Farrell's. Published between 1932 and 1953, these three related groups are the Studs Lonigan trilogy, the O'Neill-O'Flaherty pentalogy, and the Bernard Carr trilogy.
  Begun with Farrell's first novel, *Young Lonigan,* the first group traces the downward drift to death at twenty-nine of its weak-willed, misguided protagonist. A normally inquisitive boy, Studs shows signs of intelligence, even imagination, in early scenes. And yet he assumes the facile and corrupting "tough guy" values of the Chicago street-corner society to which he

is drawn after graduation from eighth grade. As a partial explanation of the boy's failure of judgment, the trilogy chronicles the breakdown in the twentieth-century city of the previously directing institutions of family, school, and church, and Studs's origin in a well-fixed, middle-class family makes the indictment of urban "spiritual poverty" (Farrell's phrase) all the more severe. The result is a powerful narrative, terrifying in its seemingly inexorable progress to *Judgment Day*, an American tragedy in the Dreiserian mold.

In the O'Neill-O'Flaherty novels, Farrell uses his own family history much more directly. The main figure is Danny O'Neill, a slightly younger contemporary of Studs Lonigan who takes an opposite road – out of Chicago and toward understanding and control of his own life. More intelligent than Studs, Danny is driven by a persistent dream of accomplishment that crystallizes into the desire to be a writer. On the other hand, he also sometimes slips into aimless idling and drinking, and his economic and family situations are potentially dangerous to his normal development. The O'Neills are so poor that some of the children, including Danny, have had to be raised by his mother's parents, the O'Flahertys. This arrangement alienates Danny but provides the pentalogy with a large number of major characters, including his grandfather, Tom O'Flaherty, an aging immigrant teamster, fully evoked in *The Face of Time*, and his grandmother, an archetypal Irish-American matriarch, strong-willed and fiercely maternal, who dominates the early novels of the series. Danny's father, Jim O'Neill, works his way from teamster to shipping clerk, only to be dealt a cruel, decisive blow by a series of paralyzing strokes. His hysterical, hyper-religious wife, Lizz, is no help to him, and in *Father and Son* Jim faces inutility, boredom, and approaching death – but with lonely courage and dignity that make him one of the most memorable characters in Farrell's fiction. Painful attempts at closeness between "father and son," Danny's high school graduation, and Jim's death bring the novel to its climax. In *My Days of Anger*, Danny begins to find his way, through attendance at the University of Chicago, great gulps of reading, and a final decision in 1927 to leave Chicago for New York and a writing career.

Instead of the tight, fatalistic narrative drive of the Lonigan trilogy, the five O'Neill-O'Flaherty novels are diffused and episodic; and in this looser structure is embodied a broader, more open and optimistic, but still unsentimentalized view of urban society. Moreover, in his complex creation of the interrelated lives of the O'Neills and O'Flahertys, Farrell has provided the most thoroughly realized second-generation-immigrant community in American literature.

The Bernard Carr trilogy, published between 1946 and 1952, continues the action of the O'Neill novels in dealing with the young manhood of a working-class Chicago Irishman with literary ambitions who has fled to New York in search of experience and perspective. His ambition is akin to that of Joyce's Stephen Dedalus, with whom Farrell's O'Neill/Carr figure has much in common. In these novels of education, Bernard Carr learns to reject the Catholic Church, his own naive appropriation of Nietzsche, and the Communist Party, all of which he comes to find as threatening to his artistic integrity. His emergence as a successful writer rounds out the Lonigan-O'Neill-Carr connected cycles. The Carr trilogy lacks the rootedness in place and community of the previous Chicago-based novels, but it compensates by providing a vivid rendering of the lives of New York left-wing intellectuals in the 1930's, with particular attention given to their passionate engagement with the question of the relationship between the artist and society.

In addition to his large cycles and a few isolated novels, Farrell has published about two hundred and fifty short stories and novelettes, in which his presentation of twentieth-century life has become even more inclusive. Many stories concern the protagonists of his novels (there are fifty about Danny O'Neill alone); others place new characters in familiar Chicago or New York settings, and still others are set in Europe, especially Paris. True to Farrell's realistic aesthetic, the stories are strong on character revelation and spurn machinations of plot.

Farrell's critical writings also fill several volumes, from *A Note on Literary Criticism* to *Selected Essays*; these contain useful explanations of the relationship between his life and his work, appreciations of writers who have been important to him, including Dreiser, Joyce, and Sherwood Anderson, and declarations of his position as a realist who writes "as part of an attempt to explore the nature of experience."

In 1963 Farrell published *The Silence of History*, his sixteenth novel, and the first of *A Universe of Time*, his fourth and continuing fictional cycle, which, in his heroic projection, will run to thirty volumes. Integrated by the central recurrent character of Eddie Ryan, another Chicago writer, born, like his creator, in 1904, the *Universe* cycle embodies a reassessment of Farrell's life-long concern with the experience of the artist in the modern world, as well as a continuation of the "lifework" that he has defined, in an introduction to the new cycle's sixth unit, *Judith*, as "a panoramic story of our days and years, a story which would continue through as many books as I would be able to write."

Farrell is first and foremost an American realist: fiercely and scrupulously honest, immune to sentimentality, and, in the earlier novels especially, pioneering in his commitment to giving serious literary consideration to the common life in an urban-immigrant-ethnic community. In his later fiction he has gone beyond Chicago and the Irish to explore more widely his most important themes, the possibilities in modern life for self-knowledge, growth, and creativity. His great strengths as a novelist have always been the development of convincing characters, the firm placement of these characters in a detailed, realistic urban setting, and the ability to conceive and carry through monumental fictional cycles. In this vein, Farrell's fullest and most compassionate creation remains Chicago's Irish Catholic South-Side, which emerges in his fiction as a realized world, as whole and coherent as Faulkner's Mississippi.

—Charles Fanning

FAULKNER, William. American. Born William Cuthbert Falkner in New Albany, Mississippi, 25 September 1897; moved with his family to Oxford, Mississippi, 1902. Educated at local schools in Oxford, and at the University of Mississippi, 1919–20. Served in the Royal Canadian Air Force, 1918. Married Estelle Oldham Franklin in 1929; one daughter. Worked in the University Post Office, Oxford, 1921–24; lived in New Orleans briefly, and wrote for the New Orleans *Times-Picayune*, then lived in Paris, and travelled in Italy, Switzerland, and England, 1925; returned to Oxford, 1926: thereafter a full-time writer; screenwriter for Metro-Goldwyn-Mayer, 1932–33, 20th Century Fox, 1935–37, and Warner Brothers, 1942–45; Writer-in-Residence, University of Virginia, Charlottesville, 1957, and part of each year thereafter until his death. Recipient: O. Henry Award, 1939, 1949; Nobel Prize for Literature, 1950; Howells Medal, 1950; National Book Award, 1951, 1955; Pulitzer Prize, 1955, 1963; American Academy of Arts and Letters Gold Medal, 1962. Member, National Institute of Arts and Letters, 1939. *Died 6 July 1962*.

PUBLICATIONS

Collections

The Portable Faulkner, edited by Malcolm Cowley. 1946.
The Faulkner Reader, edited by Saxe Commins. 1954.
Selected Letters, edited by Joseph Blotner. 1977.

Fiction

Soldiers' Pay. 1926.
Mosquitoes. 1927.
Sartoris. 1929; early version, as *Flags in the Dust,* 1973.
The Sound and the Fury. 1929.
As I Lay Dying. 1930.
Sanctuary. 1931.
These Thirteen: Stories. 1931.
Idyll in the Desert. 1931.
Light in August. 1932.
Miss Zilphia Gant. 1932.
Doctor Martino and Other Stories. 1934.
Pylon. 1935.
Absalom, Absalom! 1936.
The Unvanquished. 1938.
The Wild Palms (includes *Old Man*). 1939.
The Hamlet. 1940; excerpt, as *The Long Hot Summer,* 1958.
Go Down, Moses and Other Stories. 1942.
Intruder in the Dust. 1948.
Knight's Gambit (stories). 1949.
Collected Stories. 1950.
Notes on a Horsethief. 1951.
Requiem for a Nun. 1951.
Mirrors of Chartres Street. 1953.
A Fable. 1954.
Big Woods (stories). 1955.
Jealousy and Episode: Two Stories. 1955.
The Town. 1957.
The Mansion. 1959.
The Reivers: A Reminiscence. 1962.
Selected Short Stories. 1962.

Plays

The Big Sleep (screenplay), with Leigh Brackett and Jules Furthman, in *Film Scripts One,* edited by George P. Garrett, O. B. Harrison, Jr., and Jane Gelfmann. 1971.

Screenplays: *Today We Live,* 1933; *The Road to Glory,* with Joel Sayre, 1936; *Slave Ship,* with others, 1937; *Air Force* (uncredited), with Dudley Nichols, 1943; *To Have and Have Not,* with Jules Furthman, 1945; *The Big Sleep,* with Jules Furthman and Leigh Brackett, 1946; *Land of the Pharaohs,* with Harry Kurnitz and Harold Jack Bloom, 1955.

Verse

The Marble Faun. 1924.
This Earth. 1932.
A Green Bough. 1933.

Other

Salmagundi. 1932.
New Orleans Sketches, edited by Ichiro Nishizaki. 1955; revised edition, edited by
Carvel Collins, 1958.
Faulkner's County. 1955.
On Truth and Freedom: Remarks Made During His Manila Visit. 1955(?).
Faulkner at Nagano, edited by Robert A. Jelliffe. 1956.
Faulkner in the University: Class Conferences at the University of Virginia 1957–58,
edited by Frederick L. Gwynn and Joseph Blotner. 1959.
Early Prose and Poetry, edited by Carvel Collins. 1962.
University Pieces, edited by Carvel Collins. 1962.
Faulkner at West Point, edited by Joseph L. Fant. 1964.
The Faulkner-Cowley File: Letters and Memories 1944–1962, edited by Malcolm
Cowley. 1966.
Essays, Speeches, and Public Letters, edited by James B. Meriwether. 1966.
Lion in the Garden: Interviews 1926–1962, edited by James B. Meriwether and Michael
Millgate. 1968.

Bibliography: Faulkner: A Check List, 1957, and The Literary Career of Faulkner, 1961,
both by James B. Meriwether; "Criticism of Faulkner: A Selected Checklist" by Maurice
Beebe, in Modern Fiction Studies 13, 1967; Faulkner, Man Working 1919–1962 by Linton R.
Massey, 1968.

Reading List: Faulkner: A Critical Study by Irving Howe, 1952; The Tangled Fire of
Faulkner by William Van O'Connor, 1954; Faulkner: The Yoknapatawpha Country, 1963,
and Toward Yoknapatawpha and Beyond, 1978, both by Cleanth Brooks; The Novels of
Faulkner by Olga W. Vickery, 1959, revised edition, 1964; Faulkner's People (handbook) by
Robert W. Kirk and Marvin Klotz, 1963; Faulkner: A Collection of Critical Essays edited by
Robert Penn Warren, 1966; The Achievement of Faulkner by Michael Millgate, 1966;
Faulkner's Narrative by Joseph W. Reed, Jr., 1973; Faulkner: A Biography by Joseph
Blotner, 2 vols., 1974; Faulkner: The Critical Heritage edited by John Bassett, 1975; A
Glossary of Faulkner's South by Calvin S. Brown, 1976.

*   *   *

William Faulkner often said that he regarded poetry as the most difficult genre and himself
as a "failed poet." Although he wrote prose quite early, he devoted most of his energy as a
beginning writer to verse, imitating Housman and Swinburne, translating French Symbolist
poets, and coming under the spell of Pound and Eliot. The Marble Faun, however, was a
cycle of pastoral poems, and one of the keys to both the complexity and power of his mature
prose is the carryover of poetic techniques and pastoral imagery into his realistic fiction. In
his Waste Land novel, Soldiers' Pay, he struck the contemporary note of postwar
disillusionment, but in his third, Sartoris, he set his scene in Mississippi and began to mine
the resources of his native region. Conventional in technique, this novel drew upon his own
family, especially Colonel William C. Falkner, in the creation of Colonel John Sartoris and
his troubled descendants. Placed in opposition to them were the Snopeses, a family of landless
whites who had proliferated near Faulkner's fictional town of Jefferson. In their craft,
rapacity, and savagery, they represented the negative aspects of the rise of the new man in the
New South but also perennial facets of human nature castigated by literature's classic
moralists and satirists.
By the time Faulkner began his next novel he had not only read Joyce and imitated Eliot,
he had also composed highly experimental drama and prose tales. All of this exploration and

maturation, together with frustration he felt at repeated rejections of the manuscript of *Sartoris*, combined to produce in his new work a novel of extraordinary power and poetic sensibility. In *The Sound and the Fury* he told the story of the tragic Compson family from four different points of view, employing complex patterns of image and symbol and exploiting the stream of consciousness technique quite as much as Joyce had done. This novel, showing him suddenly at the height of his powers, would later be studied and explicated almost as much as Joyce's *Ulysses*.

In his next two works he employed the Chickasaw name he had chosen for his apocryphal county: Yoknapatawpha. One of these, *Sanctuary*, seemed *grand guignol* to some readers, updated Greek tragedy to others. Its violence and atrocities in a gangland setting, combined with ribald humor and poetic sensibility, constituted a virtuoso performance which gained Faulkner the mass attention which had eluded him. But books such as *As I Lay Dying* repelled many readers, not only because their poor Southern whites seemed strange and often violent, but also because of the technical complexity with which Faulkner presented them, employing fifty-nine separate interior monologues to tell the story of the Bundrens and their disaster-plagued journey undertaken to bury their mother in her family plot.

In novels such as *Light in August* Faulkner continued his exploration of the range of human possibility, not only "the human heart in conflict with itself," but also man in conflict with society, as in the case of Joe Christmas, who does not know whether he is white or black and cannot come to terms with life in either of these worlds. Here Faulkner continued his probing into the psychologies of his characters, their lives deeply determined by their past. Increasingly he employed flashbacks, shifts in chronology, and poetic renderings of perception combined with vivid factual narration and scrupulous use of dialects both black and white.

Now clearly a master of prose fiction, Faulkner published his second and last book of verse, *A Green Bough*, comprising poems written over a decade or more. Embodying several different styles, they showed his versatility but justified his earlier judgment that he was primarily a fiction writer and not a poet. One critic, however, would aptly call him an epic poet in prose.

When *Absalom, Absalom!* appeared (the novel which would challenge *The Sound and the Fury* for pre-eminence), it revealed not only the further exploration of Yoknapatawpha County and its people but also Faulkner's use of the mystery story genre in his attempts to understand history. In part a narrative of the Civil War, it went beyond the regional and the particular to constants in human experience. Like *The Sound and the Fury*, it left some questions unanswered in a kind of aesthetic expression of a principle of indeterminacy in human life and the capacity of literature to represent that life. Continuing his work in shorter fiction, Faulkner depicted his county in the days before the white man came in a sequence of Indian stories which showed his imaginative grasp of another people's culture. Other short stories were later reworked, deepened, and augmented to form novels: *The Unvanquished*, a further tale of the Sartoris family and the South; *The Hamlet*, an account of country people and particularly the Snopeses, whose rise would be further chronicled in *The Town* and *The Mansion*; and *Go Down, Moses*, a narrative of the relations between black and white in Yoknapatawpha County.

A striking quality in his fiction was the interrelationships from book to book, as though the whole panorama of his creation was there in his mind at once, with people, places, and events to be summoned up at will, at times even seeming to obsess him, demanding his creative efforts whether he willed it or not. Nearly twenty years after *Sanctuary* he brought back the ill-starred Temple Drake in a work which explored her partial atonement and that of her husband for their sins in *Sanctuary*. Begun as a play, *Requiem for a Nun* refused to coalesce for Faulkner, and so he turned to narrative prose, introducing each act with a long prologue which set this new drama of passion and murder against the history of Yoknapatawpha County, beginning in the dawn of time and coming up to the present.

Faulkner did not, however, limit himself to settings in Yoknapatawpha, as *A Fable*, set in France during the Great War, testified. More than ten years in the writing, this book was the only one, Faulkner would say, that he had ever written from an idea: what would happen if Christ were to return, giving man his last chance not only for salvation but for survival? His retelling of the story of Christ's Passion and Death during the false armistice on the Western Front was in its way his most explicit statement of his own humanistic faith, using conventional Christian lore as a metaphor. The novel was an ambitious if not wholly successful attempt at a kind of summary statement.

But it was in the Yoknapatawpha novels that his genius found its fullest expression. *The Town* and *The Mansion* completed his chronicle of the rise of the Snopeses and the decline of the Sartoris class, reflecting social changes in the South over the better part of a century yet at the same time remaining faithful to such patterns in other times and other societies. Though these novels had in them something of the same quality of family chronicle as had the earlier *Sartoris*, he continued his technical experimentation, passing the narration from one major character to another and intervening in an omniscient narrative voice when his strategy demanded it. In this latter part of his career, a volume of detective stories and a volume of hunting stories testified to his continuing vigor and versatility. One book, *Intruder in the Dust*, had begun as a detective story, turned into a novel, and evolved as well into a study of racial prejudice and conflict in the South and the process by which a young white boy came to see the humanity of the innocent Negro whom he helped to save from lynching. Faulkner's last book, a kind of valedictory, was a retrospective and often mellow novel, a story of a boy's initiation which was amusing and touching by turns. *The Reivers* showed him once more as master of this domain he had created and exploited as no one had done since Balzac.

Thus it is that he can be called the greatest of modern American novelists. To his strongest admirers he is the greatest of American novelists, a claim that rests upon his prodigious creativity and productivity, his extraordinary mastery of literary techniques, and a breadth of characterization and insight into the human condition which made Yoknapatawpha County a paradigm for the larger world beyond its forests and rivers.

—Joseph Blotner

FERBER, Edna. American. Born in Kalamazoo, Michigan, 15 August 1887. Educated at Ryan High School, Appleton, Wisconsin. Reporter for the Appleton *Daily Crescent* and, subsequently, for the *Milwaukee Journal* and *Chicago Tribune*, 1904–10; full-time writer from 1910; settled in New York; served as a War Correspondent for the United States Army Air Force during World War II. Recipient: Pulitzer Prize, 1924. Litt.D.: Columbia University, New York; Adelphi College, Garden City, New York. Member, National Institute of Arts and Letters. *Died 16 April 1968.*

PUBLICATIONS

Fiction

Dawn O'Hara, The Girl Who Laughed. 1911.
Buttered Side Down (stories). 1912.
Roast Beef, Medium: The Business Adventures of Emma McChesney and Her Son, Jock. 1914.

Personality Plus: Some Experiences of Emma McChesney and Her Son, Jock. 1914.
Emma McChesney & Co. 1915.
Fanny Herself. 1917.
Cheerful, By Request (stories). 1918.
Half Portions (stories). 1920.
The Girls. 1921.
Gigolo (stories). 1922; as *Among Those Present,* 1923.
So Big. 1924.
Show Boat. 1926.
Mother Knows Best. 1927.
Cimarron. 1930; revised edition, 1942.
American Beauty. 1931.
They Brought Their Women (stories). 1933.
Come and Get It. 1935.
Nobody's in Town. 1938.
No Room at the Inn (stories). 1941.
Saratoga Trunk. 1941.
Great Son. 1945.
One Basket: 31 Stories. 1947.
Giant. 1952.
Ice Palace. 1958.

Plays

Our Mrs. McChesney, with George V. Hobart (produced 1905).
$1200 a Year, with Newman Levy. 1920.
Minick, with George S. Kaufman, from the story "Old Man Minick" by Ferber (produced 1924). 1925.
The Eldest: A Drama of American Life. 1925.
The Royal Family, with George S. Kaufman (produced 1927). 1928; as *Theatre Royal* (produced 1935), 1936.
Dinner at Eight with George S. Kaufman (produced 1932). 1932.
Stage Door, with George S. Kaufman (produced 1936). 1936.
The Land Is Bright, with George S. Kaufman (produced 1941). 1946.
Bravo!, with George S. Kaufman (produced 1948). 1949.

Screenplay: *A Gay Old Dog,* 1919.

Other

A Peculiar Treasure (autobiography). 1939.
A Kind of Magic (autobiography). 1963.

Reading List: *Ferber: A Biography* by Julie Goldsmith Gilbert, 1978.

*   *   *

Although many of Edna Ferber's novels were very big best sellers, she acquired among some critics the reputation of being more than an entertainer. Grant Overton, for instance, called her a social critic. It is primarily as a social historian, however, that she made her critical reputation. William Allen White said of her books that there is "no better picture of

America in the first three decades of this century." And it is this aspect of her work – appearing to tell the unvarnished truth about American life – that has most appealed to her serious readers.

Whatever the final judgment about Edna Ferber's work, there is no doubt that her finger was always on the pulse of what many American readers felt or wanted to feel about American life. She had the journalist's gift of "working up" her subject with a minimum of research and often no first-hand experience, though doubtless her earliest books about shrewd, hard-driving working girls came out of her own early career. Books like *Dawn O'Hara*, *Roast Beef, Medium*, and *Emma McChesney & Co.* helped establish her reputation as a writer who knew the facts about American life. She won the Pulitzer Prize in 1924 for *So Big*, a novel dealing with farm life, a subject, she confessed, about which she knew nothing first-hand. Later books were written after quick trips to the locale to get the feel of the territory and gather a few facts.

Cimarron purported to deal with the opening of the Oklahoma Territory and the discovery of oil, *Saratoga Trunk* with the career of a 19th century self-made millionaire (whose exciting life story newspaper reporters refused to believe). *Giant* dealt with the fabulous excesses of the Texas new-rich. But all of these books (regarded by many reviewers as telling the "truth" about American life) and Edna Ferber's two dozen or so other books are all movie-like romances about the lure of money and big-time success, presented with a clever blend of voyeuristic fascination and a satirical undercutting which permits the reader to luxuriate in the fantasy but at the same time feel superior to it.

In addition to romances about working girls, farmers, Oklahoma roustabouts, Indians, and self-made millionaires, Edna Ferber also published several collections of short stories, two autobiographical volumes, and several plays (most written in collaboration with George S. Kaufman). A number of her novels have also been turned into successful stage musicals and motion pictures, *Show Boat* and *Saratoga Trunk* being perhaps the best known. Edna Ferber's popularity and the critical attention she has received suggest that when the definitive study of popular taste in America is written her novels, plays, and short stories will have to be reckoned with.

—W. J. Stuckey

FERRIER, Susan (Edmonstone). Scottish. Born in Edinburgh, 7 September 1782. Educated privately. Writer from 1810; a friend of Sir Walter Scott, whom she visited in 1811, 1829, and 1831; blind in later life. *Died 5 November 1854.*

PUBLICATIONS

Collections

Works, edited by Lady M. Sackville. 4 vols., 1928.

Fiction

Marriage. 1818; revised edition, 1856; edited by Herbert Foltinek, 1971.
The Inheritance. 1824; revised edition, 1857.
Destiny; or, The Chief's Daughter. 1831; revised edition, 1841.

Reading List: *Memoir and Correspondence of Ferrier* by John Ferrier, edited by J. A. Doyle, 1898; *Ferrier of Edinburgh: A Biography* by Aline Grant, 1957; *Ferrier and John Galt* by William M. Parker, 1965.

*   *   *

At first sight, Susan Ferrier's achievement strikes us as a kind of riddle. How could a spinster who spent such an uneventful life produce novels of manners that betray considerable experience combined with a manifest insight into human affairs? True enough, her great contemporary Jane Austen also drew on a limited knowledge of the world, but she, after all, had her share of the egocentricity of the true artist, who absorbs whatever passes his way. Susan Ferrier thought but modestly of her own work, and yet there is something very professional about it, as if she had always correctly assessed her abilities. The secret may lie in her evident good sense, which we are tempted to trace to her background.

A native of Edinburgh, she had inherited something of that city's intellectual alertness and pragmatic way of reasoning. Such a mind will energetically respond to every facet of its environment. At her time Edinburgh social life still had a closeness and coherence that our age discovers only in novels, offering infinite material for the critical faculties. Further impressions were obtained from visits to aristocratic homes, and from her reading. Too clear-headed to turn into a bluestocking, she nevertheless possessed a remarkable knowledge of English and French literature. Her idiosyncratic figures, even when drawn from observation, continue the English tradition of character drawing; the French essayists, on the other hand, taught her to comprehend life in terms of moral and social patterns. This attitude must have suited her well. There is something very natural and obvious about her didacticism. A novel, in her opinion, had to include a sound moral to be worth the telling, but the lesson nowhere becomes a pretext for the tale.

Her common-sense outlook on life made her suspicious of flights of fancy, and she is never at ease when occasionally borrowing a motif from the romance tradition. Conversely, her observant mind and keen sense of humour will inevitably derive an effect from the most commonplace situation. The finest passages in her writings concern everyday events which may not even have an immediate bearing on the progress of the action. This will sometimes move haltingly, for she had little understanding of plotting, but her scenes from high and ordinary life have never failed to amuse. In her time she was commonly assigned to the "Scotch" novelists, although she can usually hold her own even outside her native sphere. What remains most striking about her work is, however, not so much its regional or descriptive character as a tangible element of plain, down-to-earth sense. In a small way she certainly helped to affirm the empirical, realistic quality that has characterized the English novel throughout the ages.

—Herbert Foltinek

FIELDING, Henry. English. Born in Sharpham Park, Glastonbury, Somerset, 22 April 1707; brother of Sarah Fielding, *q.v.* Educated at Eton College; studied letters at the University of Leyden, 1728–29; entered the Middle Temple, London, 1737; called to the Bar, 1740. Married 1) Charlotte Cradock in 1734 (died, 1744); 2) Mary Daniel in 1747. Settled in London, 1727; successful playwright, in London, 1728–37: Author/Manager, Little Theatre, Haymarket, 1737 (theatre closed as a result of Licensing Act); Editor, with James Ralph, *The Champion*, 1739–41; lawyer and novelist from 1740, also writer/editor for *The True Patriot*, 1745–46, *The Jacobite's Journal*, 1747–48, and the *Covent Garden Journal*, 1752; Principal Justice of the Peace for Middlesex and Westminster, 1748; Chairman, Westminster Quarter Sessions, 1749–53. *Died 8 October 1754.*

Collections

Complete Works, edited by W. E. Henley.   16 vols., 1903.
Works (Wesleyan Edition), edited by Martin C. Battestin and others.   1967–

Fiction

An Apology for the Life of Mrs. Shamela Andrews.   1741; edited by A. R. Humphreys,
   with *Joseph Andrews,* 1973.
*The History of the Adventures of Joseph Andrews and of His Friend Mr. Abraham
   Adams.*   1742; revised edition, 1742; edited by Martin C. Battestin, in *Works,* 1967.
The Life of Mr. Jonathan Wild the Great, in *Miscellanies.*   1743; edited by A. R.
   Humphreys and D. Brooks, 1973.
A Journey from This World to the Next, in *Miscellanies.*   1743; edited by Claude J.
   Rawson, 1973.
The History of Tom Jones, A Foundling.   1749; revised edition, 1749, 1750; edited by
   Fredson Bowers and Martin C. Battestin, in *Works,* 2 vols., 1975.
Amelia.   1752; revised edition, in *Works,* 1762; edited by A. R. Humphreys, 1962.

Plays

Love in Several Masques (produced 1728).   1728.
The Temple Beau (produced 1730).   1730.
The Author's Farce, and The Pleasures of the Town (produced 1730).   1730; revised
   version (produced 1734), 1750; 1730 version edited by Charles B. Woods, 1966.
Tom Thumb (produced 1730).   1730; revised version, as *The Tragedy of Tragedies; or,
   The Life and Death of Tom Thumb the Great* (produced 1731), 1731; edited by LeRoy
   J. Morrissey, 1970.
Rape upon Rape; or, The Justice Caught in His Own Trap (produced 1730).   1730;
   revised version, as *The Coffee-House Politician* (produced 1730), 1730.
The Letter-Writers; or, A New Way to Keep a Wife at Home (produced 1731).   1731.
The Welsh Opera; or, The Grey Mare the Better Horse (produced 1731).   1731; as *The
   Genuine Grub Street Opera,* 1731; edited by E. V. Roberts, 1968.
The Lottery (produced 1732).   1732.
The Modern Husband (produced 1732).   1732.
The Covent Garden Tragedy (produced 1732).   1732.
The Old Debauchees (produced 1732).   1732; as *The Debauchees; or, The Jesuit
   Caught,* 1745.
The Mock Doctor; or, The Dumb Lady Cured, from a play by Molière (produced
   1732).   1732; edited by J. Hampden, 1931.
The Miser, from a play by Molière (produced 1733).   1733.
Deborah; or, A Wife for You All (produced 1733).
The Intriguing Chambermaid, from a play by J. F. Regnard (produced 1734).   1734.
Don Quixote in England (produced 1734).   1734.
An Old Man Taught Wisdom; or, The Virgin Unmasked (produced 1735).   1735.
The Universal Gallant; or, The Different Husbands (produced 1735).   1735.
*Pasquin: A Dramatic Satire on the Times, Being the Rehearsal of Two Plays, Viz a
   Comedy Called The Election and a Tragedy Called The Life and Death of Common
   Sense* (produced 1736).   1736; edited by O. M. Brack, Jr., and others, 1973.

Tumble-Down Dick; or, Phaeton in the Suds (produced 1736). 1736.
Eurydice (produced 1737). In *Miscellanies*, 1743.
The Historical Register for the Year 1736 (produced 1737). With *Eurydice Hissed*,
   1737; revised version, 1737; edited by William W. Appleton, 1967.
Eurydice Hissed; or, A Word to the Wise (produced 1737). With *The Historical
   Register*, 1737; revised version 1737; edited by William W. Appleton, 1967.
Plautus, The God of Riches, with W. Young, from a play by Aristophanes. 1742.
Miss Lucy in Town: A Sequel to The Virgin Unmasqued, music by Thomas Arne
   (produced 1742). 1742.
The Wedding Day (produced 1743). In *Miscellanies*, 1743.
Dramatic Works. 2 vols., 1745.
The Fathers; or, The Good-Natured Man (produced 1778). 1778.

Verse

The Masquerade. 1728; edited by C. E. Jones, in *The Female Husband and Other
   Writings*, 1960.
The Vernon-iad. 1741.
Of True Greatness: An Epistle to George Dodington, Esq. 1741.

Other

The Champion; or, The British Mercury. 2 vols., 1741; excerpt edited by S. J. Sackett,
   as *The Voyages of Mr. Job Vinegar*, 1958.
The Opposition: A Vision. 1742.
A Full Vindication of the Duchess Dowager of Marlborough. 1742.
Some Papers Proper to Be Read Before the Royal Society. 1743.
Miscellanies. 3 vols., 1743; vol. 1 edited by Henry Knight Miller, in *Works*, 1972.
An Attempt Toward a Natural History of the Hanover Rat. 1744.
The Charge to the Jury. 1745.
The History of the Present Rebellion in Scotland. 1745; edited by I. K. Fletcher, 1934.
*A Serious Address to the People of Great Britain, in Which the Certain Consequences of
   the Present Rebellion Are Fully Demonstrated*. 1745.
A Dialogue Between the Devil, The Pope, and the Pretender. 1745.
*The Female Husband; or, The Surprising History of Mrs. Mary, Alias Mr. George
   Hamilton, Taken from Her Own Mouth since Her Confinement*. 1746; edited by C. E.
   Jones, in *The Female Husband and Other Writings*, 1960.
*A Dialogue Between a Gentleman of London, Agent for Two Court Candidates, and an
   Honest Alderman of the Country Party*. 1747.
Ovid's Art of Love, Adapted to the Present Times. 1747; as *The Lover's Assistant*, 1759.
*A Proper Answer to a Late Scurrilous Libel, Entitled An Apology for the Conduct of a Late
   Celebrated Second-Rate Minister*. 1747.
A Charge Delivered to the Grand Jury. 1749.
*A True State of the Case of Bosavern Penlez, Who Suffered on Account of the Late Riot in
   the Strand*. 1749.
An Enquiry into the Causes of the Late Increase of Robbers. 1751.
A Plan of the Universal Register Office, with John Fielding. 1752.
*Examples of the Interposition of Providence in the Detection and Punishment of
   Murder*. 1752.
A Proposal for Making an Effectual Provision for the Poor. 1753.
A Clear State of the Case of Elizabeth Canning. 1753.

The Journal of a Voyage to Lisbon.   1755; edited by A. R. Humphreys and D. Brooks, 1973.
The Covent Garden Journal, edited by G. E. Jensen.   1915.
The True Patriot, and The History of Our Own Times, edited by M. A. Locke.   1964.
Criticism, edited by Ioan Williams.   1970.
The Jacobite's Journal, edited by W. B. Coley, in *Works.*   1974.

Translator, *The Military History of Charles XII, King of Sweden,* by M. Gustavus Alderfeld.   3 vols., 1840.

Bibliography: by Martin C. Battestin, in *The English Novel* edited by A. E. Dyson, 1973.

Reading List: *The History of Fielding* by Wilbur L. Cross, 3 vols., 1918; *Fielding the Novelist: A Study in Historical Criticism* by Frederic T. Blanchard, 1926; *Fielding: His Life, Works, and Times* by F. Homes Dudden, 2 vols., 1952; *Fielding* by John Butt, 1954, revised edition, 1959; *The Moral Basis of Fielding's Art* by Martin C. Battestin, 1959; *Essays on Fielding's "Miscellanies"* by Henry Knight Miller, 1961; *Fielding's Social Pamphlets* by Marvin R. Zinker, Jr., 1966; *Fielding and the Language of Irony* by Glenn W. Hatfield, 1968; *Fielding and the Nature of the Novel* by Robert Alter, 1969; *Fielding and the Augustan Ideal under Stress* by Claude J. Rawson, 1972; *Fielding: A Critical Anthology* edited by Claude J. Rawson, 1973; *Fielding's "Tom Jones": The Novelist as Moral Philosopher* by Bernard Harrison, 1975; *Occasional Form: Fielding and the Chains of Circumstance* by J. Paul Hunter, 1975.

*   *   *

Though Henry Fielding is remembered chiefly as a novelist – as, indeed, along with Defoe and Richardson, one of the founders of the modern novel and as the author of one of the dozen or so greatest novels in English, *Tom Jones* – he began his literary career as a poet and a dramatist. A young man of twenty, without much money but with strong family connections to the Whig establishment, he came to London from the West Country in 1727 determined to make his mark as a wit and to solicit the patronage of the Court at a time when, because of the uncertain political climate following the death of George I, a talented writer might expect that his services would be appreciated by the prime minister, Sir Robert Walpole. Contrary to the usual view of Fielding as a staunch and unswerving opponent of Walpole and the Court, his earliest poems and plays reveal that when he was not actively seeking the king's and Walpole's favors he prudently adopted a neutral attitude in politics: to judge from the title of his first published work, *The Coronation: A Poem, and An Ode on the Birthday* (issued in November 1727 but now lost), he began, even in a Cibberian vein, by openly declaring his loyalty to George II; and besides several other poems soliciting Walpole's patronage in 1729–31, he dedicated to the prime minister his most ambitious, if unsuccessful, comedy, *The Modern Husband.* Indeed, as B. L. Goldgar persuasively argues in *Walpole and the Wits* (1976), of the fifteen comedies and farces which Fielding produced between 1728 – when his first play, *Love in Several Masques,* was acted at Drury Lane – and 1734 all but one were calculated shrewdly to amuse the widest possible audience without offending the Court; only in *The Welsh Opera* (1731) – a transparent political allegory satirizing not only Walpole and the leader of the Opposition, but the royal family itself – did he abandon this cautious policy, the result being, predictably, that the play was first withdrawn for revision and then suppressed.

These were the years in which Fielding established himself as London's most popular living playwright. With the exception of *The Modern Husband,* which treats rather too earnestly the disturbing theme of adultery and marital prostitution in high life, his more conventional comedies are entertaining and skillful, but by inviting comparison with the greater works of Congreve and Molière they have suffered the condescension of historians of the drama. No other critic, certainly, has endorsed Shaw's declaration that Fielding was "the greatest practising dramatist, with the single exception of Shakespeare, produced by England between the Middle Ages and the nineteenth century...." Where Fielding did shine was in the lesser modes of farce, burlesque, and satire – in *The Tragedy of Tragedies*, for example, an hilarious travesty of heroic drama, or in *The Author's Farce*, a delightful adaption of the "rehearsal play" concluding with a satiric "puppet show" performed by live actors, a work which in fact anticipates the expressionism of modern experimental drama.

Despite his reputation as the theatrical gadfly of the Court, it was only in the final three years (1734–37) of his dramatic career that Fielding moved, rather hesitantly, into the camp of the Opposition. Though he dedicated *Don Quixote in England* to Chesterfield, who had recently joined their ranks, the political satire in this play – as indeed even in *Pasquin*, which is usually said to be vehemently anti-ministerial – is in fact directed at the venality and incompetence of both parties. Only with *The Historical Register* and its after-piece *Eurydice Hiss'd* did he at last drop the mask of impartiality and, by ridiculing Walpole all too effectively, help to precipitate the Theatrical Licensing Act of 1737, which terminated his career as a playwright.

Forced by an Act of Parliament to abandon the stage, Fielding began preparing for the bar and, to supplement the meager income he would earn as a barrister, enlisted as a hackney author in the Opposition's campaign against Walpole. In this latter capacity, during his editorship of *The Champion* (1739–41), he almost certainly drafted his first work of fiction, *The Life of Jonathan Wild the Great*, a mock biography of an infamous real-life criminal whom he ironically praises for the very qualities of unscrupulous self-aggrandisement by which the prime minister himself had achieved "greatness." This work, however, which Walpole appears to have paid Fielding to suppress, was withheld from publication until 1743, a year after the Great Man's fall from power, when it was issued as part of the *Miscellanies*; by this time Fielding presumably had revised the novel substantially, generalizing the political satire and perhaps expanding the narrative to accommodate the more positive, contrasting element of Wild's relationship with the good-natured Heartfrees. Also included in the *Miscellanies* was *A Journey from This World to the Next*, a satirical fiction done in brisk imitation of Lucian.

It was not politics, however, but a quite remarkable literary event that provoked Fielding into finding his true voice as a novelist. Amused and not a little exasperated by the extraordinary success of Richardson's *Pamela* (1740), Fielding responded first by parodying the novel, hilariously, in *Shamela* (1741) and then by offering in *Joseph Andrews* (1742) his own alternative conception of the art of fiction. Though Fielding's improbably virtuous hero is meant to continue the ridicule of Richardson's indomitable virgin, *Joseph Andrews* is much more than merely another travesty of *Pamela*. Modelled in some respects on Cervantes' masterpiece, it yet enacts Fielding's own original theory of the "comic epic-poem in prose," whose subject is "the true ridiculous" in human nature, exposed in all its variety as Joseph and the amiable quixote Parson Abraham Adams journey homeward through the heart of England. In contrast to the brooding, claustrophobic world evoked in the letters of Richardson's beleaguered maidens, Fielding's is cheerful and expansive, presided over by a genial, omniscient narrator who seems a proper surrogate of that beneficent Providence celebrated by Pope in *An Essay on Man* (1733–34).

In *Joseph Andrews* Fielding founded, as he put it, a "new province of writing." *Tom Jones*, his masterpiece, fulfilled the promise of that ambitious, splendid beginning. Generations of readers have delighted in the comic adventures and nearly disastrous indiscretions of the lusty foundling boy who grows to maturity, discovers the identity of his parents, and marries the beautiful girl he has always loved – a story simple enough in outline, but crowded with entertaining characters, enlivened by the wit and humanity of the narrator, and complicated by the intricacies of an ingenious plot which Coleridge called one of the most perfect in all literature. Like most great books, moreover, *Tom Jones* offers us more than superficial pleasures: it is the realization of its author's profoundest philosophy of life, an artfully constructed model of a world abundant, orderly, and ultimately benign, as the Christian humanist tradition conceived it to be. Thus Fielding declares his subject to be "human nature" and his book to be nothing less than "a great creation of our own." His foundling hero stands for all of us: like the protagonists of romance, he is a kind of wayfaring Everyman who, having been expelled from "Paradise Hall," must through hard experience gain that knowledge of himself which will enable him to be united with the girl, Sophia, whose name signifies Wisdom. *Tom Jones* is, as few books have managed to be, the consummate expression of a particular form and conception of literary art.

With the publication of *Tom Jones* Fielding's life and work entered a new phase. As a reward for his services as publicist for the Pelham administration, he was appointed to the magistracy, an office which he exercised with an energy and diligence that shortened his life. His new role as a public figure, working actively to preserve the peace and to improve the wretched condition of the poor, affected his art in interesting, but most critics would say regrettable, ways. *Amelia*, his last novel, is a very different book from *Tom Jones*: Fielding's tone has become darker, more monitory, in keeping with his subject – no longer the follies of men, but their errors and cupidities and the doubtful efficacy of those institutions, the law and the church, meant to preserve the social order; his narrator less frequently appears upon the stage, and his voice, wavering between anger and a maudlin sentimentality, no longer inspires confidence. Though his ostensible focus is the domestic tribulations of the feckless Captain Booth and his long-suffering wife, Fielding's true intentions are all too patently didactic: scene after scene is calculated to expose the imperfections of the penal laws, the destructiveness of infidelity, the injustices of the patronage system, and the immoralities of an effete and pleasure-loving society. To be sure, *Amelia* is less fun to read than any of Fielding's other novels, but in the starkness and candor of its social commentary it is compelling none the less. It is in fact the first true novel of social protest and reform in England, sounding themes that would not be resumed until the next century.

—Martin C. Battestin

FIELDING, Sarah.   English.   Born in East Stour, Dorset, 8 November 1710; sister of Henry Fielding, *q.v.* Very little is known about her life: educated privately; writer from c. 1740; in later life lived in Ryde, then in Bath. *Died 9 April 1768.*

PUBLICATIONS

Fiction

    The Adventures of David Simple.   5 vols., 1744–53; edited by Malcolm Kelsall, 1969.
    The Governess; or, The Little Female Academy, Being the History of Mrs. Teachum and Her Nine Girls.   1749; edited by Jill E. Grey, 1968.
    The Cry: A New Dramatic Fable, with Jane Collier.   1754.
    The Lives of Cleopatra and Octavia.   1757; edited by R. B. Johnson, 1928.
    The History of the Countess of Dellwyn.   1759.
    The History of Ophelia.   1760.

Other

Translator, *Xenophon's Memoirs of Socrates with the Defence of Socrates.* 1762.

*   *   *

Sarah Fielding was the third sister of Henry Fielding the novelist. Her best known prose fiction is *The Adventures of David Simple*, which obtained the status of a minor classic in the eighteenth century. The second edition of this "Moral Romance," as she called the tale, was extensively revised by her brother. Samuel Richardson's praise of her, in a letter to Sarah, 7 December 1756, is well known: "What a knowledge of the human heart! Well might a critical judge of writing say, as he did to me, that your late brother's knowledge of it was not (fine writer as he was) comparable to yours. His was but as the knowledge of the outside of a clockwork machine, while your's was that of all the finer springs and movements of the inside." The "critical judge" was Samuel Johnson, and an alternative version of the comparison is given in Boswell's *Life of Johnson* where it is applied to Henry Fielding and Richardson.

David Simple is an attempt to blend the variety of incident and wide diversity of character which distinguish her brother's novels with a sententious and sentimental essayist's manner close to that of Steele's *The Tatler*, which she greatly admired. David Simple, disenchanted by the hypocrisy, vanity, and duplicity of the world, sets himself in "his travels through the cities of London and Westminster" to find a true friend, and finds that friendship in marriage to Camilla. True simplicity is shown in the life without affectation, moderate in its desires, and possessed of the few and uncomplicated truths which are the foundation of eighteenth-century practical piety. In a bitterly ironical and tense sequel, however, entitled *Volume the Last*, David is also shown as a simpleton in his naive hopes for happiness and the tale ends with poverty and death.

In addition to producing other novels, Sarah Fielding also wrote a highly successful collection of moral fairy tales for children, *The Governess*, which is an important work in the history of education. She was well versed in classical literature also, and something of a bluestocking. She was a correspondent of Richardson, met figures such as Joseph Warton and Edward Young, and came under the patronage of Henry Fielding's friend, Ralph Allen of Prior Park.

—Malcolm Kelsall

FINLAYSON, Roderick (David). New Zealander. Born in Auckland, 26 April 1904. Educated at the Ponsonby School; Seddon Memorial Technical College, 1918–21; School of Architecture, University of Auckland, 1922–24. Married Ruth Evelyn Taylor in 1936; three daughters and three sons. Architectural draftsman, 1922–28; printing-room assistant, Auckland City Council, 1958–66. Recipient: New Zealand Centennial Prize, 1940. Lives in Manurewa, New Zealand.

PUBLICATIONS

Fiction

Brown Man's Burden (stories).   1938.
Sweet Beulah Land (stories).   1942.
Tidal Creek.   1948.
The Schooner Came to Atia.   1953.
Brown Man's Burden and Later Stories, edited by Bill Pearson.   1973.
Other Lovers (novellas).   1976.

Other

Our Life in This Land (essay).   1940.
The Coming of the Maori.   1955.
The Coming of the Pakeha.   1956.
The Golden Years.   1956.
The Return of the Fugitives.   1957.
Changes in the Pakeha.   1958.
The Maoris of New Zealand, with Joan Smith.   1959.
The New Harvest.   1960.
The Springing Fern (juvenile).   1965.
D'Arcy Cresswell: His Life and Works.   1972.

Reading List: "The Maori and Literature 1938–1965," in *Essays in New Zealand Literature* edited by Wystan Curnow, 1973, and "Attitudes to the Maori in Some Pakeha Fiction," both by Bill Pearson, in *Fretful Sleepers and Other Essays*, 1974; "Narrative Stance in the Early Short Stories of Finlayson" by John Muirhead, in *World Literature Written in English 14*, April 1975.

*   *   *

Roderick Finlayson is a writer with a social thesis that is articulated not only in his fiction, but also in polemical essays – notably *Our Life in This Land*. For the terms of the thesis Finlayson was indebted to the New Zealand poet and sometime visionary D'Arcy Cresswell, whose prose works are a rejection of the scientific spirit of modern society. Finlayson's advocacy of Cresswell's doctrine is apparent in his 1972 study *D'Arcy Cresswell*. But Finlayson drew primarily from his own experience of New Zealand life, particularly during the galvanic years of the depression.

The depression expelled him from the urban white middle class and prompted his reappraisal of its values. Searching for the cause of social collapse, Finlayson eventually "identified the villain as our ruthlessly technological and acquisitive society. Others called it capitalism." He found an alternative creed among the rural Maoris and European subsistence farmers to whom he then turned. He called it the "poetic ideal": "a life dependent on the forces and powers of Nature." When based on a harmonious relationship with the earth, work could be creative, no longer an unwilling enslavement to machines; men would be freed from economic competition, and a sense of community could flourish. Yet already Finlayson recognised the collapse of this ideal with the insinuation of the profit motive into the countryside.

Finlayson's first short stories, published in *Brown Man's Burden* and *Sweet Beulah Land*, observe the decline of the Maori ideal. His was a new insight into Maori experience, eschewing previous literary stereotypes of noble primitive or comically stupid rascal. As Finlayson acknowledges, "no one had touched the life of men and women of flesh and blood in the confusing period between two worlds" – that of the ancient tribal ways, now dying, and that of a painful coercion by the dominant European ethos. The stories explore the tragic and comic ironies of this situation. Such themes are illustrative of Finlayson's social thesis, but he was able to avoid the admonitory tone that marks his essays. Finlayson had a natural affinity with the Maoris, and it enabled him to record their experience as they felt it. This was achieved technically by a narrative style modelled on the Sicilian stories of Giovanni Verga. The author creates a narrative voice that shares the simple dialect of his peasant protagonists, so that the story can be told without apparent authorial intrusion.

That narrative discipline is not always attained in the stories with European themes to which Finlayson turned, in *Sweet Beulah Land* and subsequently; in these stories, the social thesis sometimes obstructs the imaginative realisation of life. Finlayson's intention is too didactic: characters become flat victims or oppressors, without the ambiguity of his Maori protagonists. If this is often so of the European short stories, however, Finlayson's novels largely avoid the tendency to polemic. Beneath the comic and anecdotal surface of *Tidal Creek*, the poetic ideal is made flesh in the peasant figure of Uncle Ted. There is considerable power, too, in Finlayson's treatment of the passionate puritan Hartman, in *The Schooner Came to Atia*, although the energy of this novel is partly dissipated by Finlayson's introduction of an anti-colonialist theme. Similar personal and social crises are better integrated in "Jim and Miri," the most successful of the three novellas published as *Other Lovers*.

Overall, Finlayson's work represents a problem in New Zealand fiction at large: it stems from a recognition of reality so alarming that its expression is often polemical rather than suggestive of its themes. But where Finlayson's sympathy provides a conduit for his imagination to work, as in the Maori stories, his moral awareness is held in check and his art becomes a subtle recreation of life. It is to these stories, republished in *Brown Man's Burden and Later Stories*, that the reader will return.

John Muirhead

FIRBANK, (Arthur Annesley) Ronald. English. Born in London, 17 January 1886. Educated at Mortimer Vicarage School; Eton College; Uppingham School, 1900–01; Howley Grange, Sainte-Tulle, France, 1901–02; St. Symphorien, Indre et Loire, France, 1903–04; Trinity Hall, Cambridge, 1906–09. Briefly served in the British Army, 1917. Lived in Oxford, 1914–19; thereafter lived and travelled on the Continent, in Italy, France, North Africa, and the West Indies. *Died 21 May 1926.*

PUBLICATIONS

Collections

Works. 8 vols., 1929–30.
The Complete Firbank. 1961.

Fiction

Odette d'Antrevernes, and A Study in Temperament.   1905; *Odette* revised as *Odette: A*
   Fairy Tale for Weary People, 1916.
Vainglory.   1915; revised edition, 1925.
Inclinations.   1916.
Caprice.   1917.
Valmouth: A Romantic Novel.   1919.
Santal.   1921.
The Flower Beneath the Foot, Being a Record of the Early Life of St. Laura de Nazianzi
   and the Times in Which She Lived.   1923.
Prancing Nigger.   1924; as *Sorrow in Sunlight,* 1924.
Concerning the Eccentricities of Cardinal Pirelli.   1926.
The Artificial Princess.   1934.
The New Rythum [sic] *and Other Pieces.*   1962.
Far Away.   1966.
La Princesse aux Soleils, and Harmonie (bilingual edition, translated by Edgell
   Rickword).   1973.

Play

The Princess Zoubaroff.   1920.

Verse

The Wind and the Roses.   1965.

Bibliography: *A Bibliography of Firbank* by Miriam J. Benkovitz, 1963.

Reading List: *Firbank* by Jocelyn Brooke, 1951; *Firbank: A Biography* by Miriam J.
Benkovitz, 1967; *Firbank* by James D. Merritt, 1969; *Prancing Novelist* by Brigid Brophy,
1972; *Firbank: Memoirs and Critiques* edited by Mervyn Horder, 1977.

*   *   *

   In his lifetime Ronald Firbank arranged for publication of nine pieces of juvenilia, one
play, and eight novels. Since his death, the incomplete "New York novel" on which he was at
work, *The Artificial Princess* (started many years earlier), and several juvenile works
including "Lady Appledore's Mésalliance" have appeared. Firbank's reputation as a writer of
fiction must rest on the eight novels and especially on the last three. He succeeded most
completely in those in presenting his delight in the beauty of the world and his amusement
and occasional regret at the disorder produced by human self-absorption and delusion.
   Firbank's early work was uncertain. The perspective of his fiction was first apparent in a
fragment called "Lila," written in 1896 when he was ten years old. But except for his self-
conscious concern with language, he gave no promise of his novels in his first publications,
"La Princesse aux Soleils Romance Parlée" and "Harmonie," which appeared in *Les Essais
Revue Mensuelle* in late 1904 and early 1905. Both are merely set pieces, as is *A Study in
Temperament,* also in 1905. *A Study* tells of an attempted seduction to which the lady
involved gives less importance than to the colour of her hair. Lacking the capacity for
emotion, she lives isolated in some private identity, as do all the characters. They fail to

communicate with each other despite their wit, and they exist in moral disorder.

Here were the subject and the direction characteristic of Firbank's novels. But he preferred the tale with which *A Study* was published, the saccharine and derivative *Odette d'Antrevernes*. (Partly because his mother admired *Odette*, he produced a similar piece, *Santal*, as late as 1921, a story of the orphan boy Cherif and his search for Allah.) But throughout his experimental years, Firbank turned more and more to the subject and method which inform his mature work. This fact is evident in still unpublished sketches such as "When Widows Love" or "A Tragedy in Green" as well as the two publications of his Cambridge days, "The Wavering Disciple" and "A Study in Opal" and the posthumously published "Lady Appledore's Mésalliance." Then at the end of 1912, Firbank forced himself to commence his first full-length work, *Vainglory*, a novel carefully constructed from his own earlier pieces − "Lady Appledore's Mésalliance," "The Wavering Disciple," "A Study in Opal," and others − in a series of scenes set side by side so as to emphasize and evaluate each other.

Inclinations, a novel which progresses wholly by dialogue, *Caprice*, perhaps Firbank's most conventional novel, and *Valmouth* each marked an advance in subject matter and technique, so that by 1919 Firbank had a pattern for his fiction. He had learned to manipulate dialogue. He had developed a special type of heroine, what Nancy Cunard called a "sweet-sad or yearning" character such as Mrs. Shamefoot in *Vainglory*. He had settled on two modes of comment on his pervasive theme of order and disorder, the civil-savage and Christianity and its earthly manifestation, especially in the Church. He presented these, as Harold Nicolson said, by means of a "system of correlated planes."

Firbank refined these methods in *The Flower Beneath the Foot*, *Prancing Nigger*, and *Concerning the Eccentricities of Cardinal Pirelli*. Although in *The Flower* Firbank evaluates the Church with thematic and technical mastery and in *Prancing Nigger* he develops the civil-savage theme brilliantly, *Cardinal Pirelli* is the height of his achievement. *Cardinal Pirelli* has no story and it has only two pieces of action. It opens at the baptismal font of a cathedral in Seville as Pirelli administers the sacrament of baptism to a young dog. It ends when the naked Cardinal, on the eve of his departure for Rome and the Pope's discipline as a consequence of the baptism, falls dead chasing the boy Chicklet around the great empty Cathedral of Clemenza, the "Cage of God." Since these two actions are not elements of plot, of cause and effect, Firbank could keep time sequence to a minimum and organize spatially in a series of scenes reinforced by fragmented dialogue so that everything seems to sound at the same time. The scenes of *Cardinal Pirelli* create a pattern of reflexive meaning, fixing attention on no one group but on their total relationships and, by association, on the age-old values which they travesty. The cathedral sacristy, a place of business with an eye to profit and "quite the liveliest spot in the city" after the "tobacco-factory and the railway-station," provides an appropriate background for Pirelli. His character is equivocal. He acknowledges that moderation is a virtue, but it contradicts the beauty and temptation of the world, especially in the hot glory of summer. Repeatedly his thoughts stray from his hunger for God to his hunger for the world and often he can not distinguish between them. Even as he stands ready to rouse the sleeping Chicklet and set in motion the mad chase in the cathedral. Pirelli prays that he not be led into temptation.

The wild pursuit of the child mingles contrary desires, the concrete and the ideal, both of which Firbank found in "fairy childhood." But Chicklet's innocence is sadly imperfect, and his flight from the Cardinal is more tantalising than sincere. The boy hesitates once in his wild scamper to ask Pirelli what rewards he is prepared to offer. As for the Cardinal, his chasing the boy is contradictory on all sides; it is the final impotence of morality. For all his prayers, Pirelli can not turn from temptation; and his desire to capture and possess the doubtful purity of the boy has violation as its aim. The chase ends at dawn, when Cardinal Pirelli, his heart "in painful riot," falls dead before a painting of "the splendour of Christ's martyrdom." Having shed his crimson mantle, Pirelli lies "nude and elementary," dispossessed of everything except his mitre. Expressively, the chase ends when his flight from maturity, a transgression against order, brings Pirelli to his death. Then, freed from the world's systems of which the Church is one, he lies exposed, helpless, a man with God's hand – the mitre – on his brow.

Cardinal Pirelli is Firbank at his best. He has commented with the more profound of his two modes, Christianity and its earthly practice. His characters' speeches, whether monologue or dialogue, are subordinated to the demands of his fiction. The Cardinal, a "yearning" male, is both complex and consistent; and Firbank's "correlated planes" are brilliant and beautiful.

—Miriam J. Benkovitz

FISHER, Vardis (Alvero). American.f2Born in Annis, Idaho, 31 March 1895. Educated at Rigby High School, Idaho, graduated 1915; University of Utah, Salt Lake City, B.A. 1920; University of Chicago, A.M. 1922, Ph.D. (magna cum laude) 1925. Served in the United States Army Artillery Corps, 1918. Married 1) Leona McMurtrey in 1917 (died, 1924), two sons; 2) Margaret Trusler in 1928 (divorced, 1939), one son; 3) Opal Laurel Holmes in 1940. Assistant Professor of English at the University of Utah, 1925–28, and New York University, 1928–31; full-time writer from 1931; taught at Montana State University, Bozeman, Summer 1932, 1933; Director, Idaho Writers' Project and Historical Records Project of the Works Progress Administration, 1935–39; Syndicated Columnist ("Vardis Fisher Says") in Idaho newspapers, 1941–68. *Died 9 July 1968.*

PUBLICATIONS

Fiction

Toilers of the Hills. 1928.
Dark Bridwell. 1931.
In Tragic Life. 1932; as *I See No Sin,* 1934; as *The Wild Ones,* 1958.
Passions Spin the Plot. 1934.
We Are Betrayed. 1935.
No Villain Need Be. 1936.
April: A Fable of Love. 1937.
Odyssey of a Hero. 1937.
Forgive Us Our Virtues: A Comedy of Evasions. 1938.
Children of God. 1939.
City of Illusion. 1941.
The Mothers. 1943.
Darkness and the Deep. 1943.
The Golden Rooms. 1944.
Intimations of Eve. 1946.
Adam and the Serpent. 1947.
The Divine Passion. 1948.
The Valley of Vision. 1951.
The Island of the Innocent. 1952.
Jesus Came Again: A Parable. 1956.

A Goat for Azazel. 1956.
Pemmican: A Novel of the Hudson's Bay Company. 1956.
Peace Like a River. 1957.
My Holy Satan: A Novel of Christian Twilight. 1958.
Tale of Valor: A Novel of the Lewis and Clark Expedition. 1958.
Love and Death: The Complete Stories. 1959.
Orphans in Gethsemane. 1960.
Mountain Man. 1965.

Verse

Sonnets to an Imaginary Madonna. 1927.

Other

The Neurotic Nightingale. 1935.
The Caxton Printers in Idaho: A Short History. 1944.
God or Caesar? The Writing of Fiction for Beginners. 1953.
Suicide or Murder? The Strange Death of Governor Meriwether Lewis. 1962.
Thomas Wolfe as I Knew Him and Other Essays. 1963.
Gold Rushes and Mining Camps of the Early American West, with Opal Laurel Holmes. 1968.

Editor, *Idaho: A Guide in Word and Picture.* 1937.
Editor, *The Idaho Encyclopedia.* 1938.
Editor, *Idaho Lore.* 1939.

Bibliography: "Fisher: A Bibliography" by George Kellogg, in *Western American Literature,* Spring 1970.

Reading List: "Fisher Issue" of *American Book Collector,* September 1963; *Fisher* by Joseph M. Flora, 1965; *Fisher: The Frontier and Regional Works* by Wayne Chatterton, 1972; "The Primitive World of Fisher: The Idaho Novels" by John R. Milton, in *Midwest Quarterly,* Summer 1976.

*   *   *

Vardis Fisher is usually placed with the naturalists in American literature and among the strident voices of protest in the 1930's. While his greatest fame came in the depression years – climaxed with the Harper Prize in 1939 for *Children of God* – he was a prolific writer whose work spanned four decades. He wore no labels easily and relished defying definition. Not interested in literary trends, he stuck doggedly to the goals he set himself. He survived numerous battles with publishers and lived to see a modest but genuine revival of interest in his work.

Fisher's youth in an isolated area along the Snake River in Idaho was lonely and terrifying. Alfred Kazin called him America's last authentic novelist of the frontier. More importantly, Fisher was the first to write significant novels of the Rocky Mountain West. His passionate, sometimes violent and ambiguous, response to his mountain country produced his best work. His first published novel, *Toilers of the Hills,* gave a poignant rendering of pioneer efforts to farm the difficult Antelope Hills bordering the South Fork of the Snake. The sense of place and people was even stronger in his second novel, *Dark Bridwell* – his most satisfying work of fiction. Fisher seemed on the way to founding a Western counterpart to Faulkner's Yoknapatawpha County, for he was also writing short stories and poems about the people of the Antelope Hills. Vridar Hunter, the protagonist of *In Tragic Life*, had already appeared as a minor character in *Dark Bridwell*; and Dock Hunter, the farmer of *Toilers*, is Vridar's uncle.

But Vridar was not simply a character who had played a part in the earlier novel. As his name indicates, he was also an autobiographical figure. *In Tragic Life* renders Fisher's first eighteen, largely agonized, years forcefully. The book became the first volume of an autobiographical tetralogy – and as the other volumes appeared Antelope became less significant. It became clear that Fisher was intent on exploring his own agonies more than a region. His first wife had committed suicide while he was a graduate student, and there were major psychological problems he had to work out. The confessional aspect of his work is large. Vridar made an unusual hero, for Fisher was often castigating him. Hence, the tetralogy becomes increasingly intellectual and loaded with indictments of a world Vridar never made – the final volume being decidedly a novel of ideas.

Not overly concerned with critical objections to his tetralogy, Fisher felt that his autobiographical searches had not led him to understand Vridar as he would have liked. Even as he finished the tetralogy, Fisher made plans for his *Testament of Man* novels – a series to be based on extended research into man's evolutionary development, particularly his ideas about divinity. Beginning with *Darkness and the Deep*, when man is little more than an ape and possessed only the simplest speech, Fisher traces man's "progress" until he eventually retells Vridar's story as the final volume in the series of twelve. The most successful books are the first two and the final one. The later volumes become increasingly discursive and the presentation of research as experience less successfully integrated.

Still, Fisher has an important place among the American writers of historical novels. The impetus behind his famous *Children of God* was a search into his most immediate religious heritage – Mormonism. He focuses directly on the lives of Joseph Smith and Brigham Young for the major part of his long novel. His intention was to be as accurate as possible. The success of *Children of God* led Fisher to pursue other aspects of the Western American past, with the goal of accurate rendering a prime consideration. He also wrote non-fictional works about the West as well as about writing.

Fisher's final novel, *Mountain Man*, is vastly different from his other historical novels of the West. Although based on an actual mountain man, "Liver-eating" Johnson, the novel is markedly different from Fisher's more factual novels like *Children of God* or *The Mothers*. It is patterned on music and highlights the romantic spirit more carefully hidden in his other work.

—Joseph M. Flora

FITZGERALD, F(rancis) Scott (Key). American. Born in St. Paul, Minnesota, 24 September 1896. Educated at the St. Paul Academy, 1908–11; Newman School, Hackensack, New Jersey, 1911–13; Princeton University, New Jersey, 1913–17. Served in the United States Army, 1917–19: 2nd Lieutenant. Married Zelda Sayre in 1920; one daughter. Advertising Copywriter for Barron Collier Agency, New York, 1919–20; full-time writer from 1920; lived in Europe, 1924–26, 1929–31; screenwriter for Metro-Goldwyn-Mayer, 1937–38. *Died 21 December 1940.*

Publications

Collections

The Bodley Head Fitzgerald, edited by Malcolm Cowley and J. B. Priestley.   6 vols.,
   1958–63.
The Fitzgerald Reader, edited by Arthur Mizener.   1963.
Letters, edited by Andrew Turnbull.   1963; excerpts, as Letters to His Daughter, 1965.

Fiction

This Side of Paradise.   1920.
Flappers and Philosophers (stories).   1920.
The Beautiful and Damned.   1922.
Tales of the Jazz Age.   1922.
John Jackson's Arcady, edited by Lilian Holmes Stack.   1924.
The Great Gatsby.   1925; A Facsimile of the Manuscript edited by Matthew J. Bruccoli,
   1973; Apparatus edited by Matthew J. Bruccoli, 1974.
All the Sad Young Men (stories).   1926.
Tender Is the Night: A Romance.   1934; revised edition, 1951.
Taps at Reveille (stories).   1935.
The Last Tycoon: An Unfinished Novel, Together with The Great Gatsby and Selected
   Writings.   1941.
The Mystery of the Raymond Mortgage (story).   1960.
The Pat Hobby Stories.   1962.
The Apprentice Fiction of Fitzgerald, edited by John Kuehl.   1965.
Dearly Beloved.   1969.
Bits of Paradise: 21 Uncollected Stories, with Zelda Fitzgerald, edited by Matthew J.
   Bruccoli and Scottie Fitzgerald Smith.   1973.
The Basil and Josephine Stories, edited by Jackson R. Bryer and John Kuehl.   1973.

Plays

Fie! Fie! Fi-Fi! (plot and lyrics only), book by Walker M. Ellis, music by D. D. Griffin,
   A. L. Booth, and P. B. Dickey (produced 1914).   1914.
The Evil Eye (lyrics only), book by Edmund Wilson, music by P. B. Dickey and F.
   Warburton Guilbert (produced 1915).   1915.
Safety First (lyrics only), book by J.F. Bohmfalk and J. Biggs, Jr., music by P. B. Dickey,
   F. Warburton Guilbert, and E. Harris (produced 1916).   1916.
The Vegetable; or, From President to Postman (produced 1923).   1923.
Screenplay for Three Comrades, edited by Matthew J. Bruccoli.   1978.

Screenplays: A Yank at Oxford, with others, 1938; Three Comrades, with Edward E.
Paramore, 1938.

Radio Play: Let's Go Out and Play, 1935.

Other

The Crack-Up, with Other Uncollected Pieces, Note-Books, and Unpublished Letters,
   edited by Edmund Wilson.   1945.

Afternoon of an Author: A Selection of Uncollected Stories and Essays, edited by Arthur
    Mizener.   1957.
Thoughtbook, edited by John Kuehl.   1965.
Fitzgerald in His Own Time: A Miscellany, edited by Matthew J. Bruccoli and Jackson R.
    Bryer.   1971.
Dear Scott/Dear Max: The Fitzgerald-Perkins Correspondence, edited by John Kuehl
    and Jackson R. Bryer.   1971.
*As Ever, Scott Fitz–: Letters Between Fitzgerald and His Literary Agent Howard Ober
    1919–1940*, edited by Matthew J. Bruccoli.   1972.
Ledger.   1972.
The Cruise of the Rolling Junk (travel).   1976.
The Notebooks, edited by Matthew J. Bruccoli.   1978.

Bibliography: *Fitzgerald: A Descriptive Bibliography* by Matthew J. Bruccoli, 1972.

Reading List: *The Far Side of Paradise* (biography), by Arthur Mizener, 1951, revised
edition, 1965; *The Fictional Technique of Fitzgerald* by James E. Miller, 1957, revised
edition, as *Fitzgerald: His Art and His Technique*, 1964; *Beloved Infidel*, 1958, and *The Real
Fitzgerald: Thirty-Five Years Later*, 1976, both by Sheila Graham; *Fitzgerald*, by Kenneth
Eble, 1963; *Fitzgerald: A Collection of Critical Essays* edited by Arthur Mizener, 1963;
Fitzgerald and His Contemporaries by William F. Goldhurst, 1963; *Fitzgerald: A Critical
Portrait* by Henry Dan Piper, 1965; *Fitzgerald and the Craft of Fiction* by Richard D. Lehan,
1966; *Fitzgerald: The Last Laocoön* by Robert Sklar, 1967; *Fitzgerald: An Introduction and
Interpretation* by Milton Hindus, 1968; *Fitzgerald* by Andrew Turnbull, 1975.

*   *   *

Like so many modern American writers, F. Scott Fitzgerald created a public image of
himself as a representative figure of his times, which may have been a part of the promotional
campaign to sell his fiction. It worked for a while, with such success that any effort to evoke
the Jazz Age or the Roaring Twenties is inevitably accompanied by a reference to or a
photograph of Fitzgerald. But the public memory is fickle, and after he and Zelda had left the
big stage and the gossip columnists no longer had their reckless antics to report, people forgot
that he was once considered a writer of great promise and talent, and few realised that he had
produced a body of work that bids well to bring him status as a writer for all times.
    When Fitzgerald appeared on the literary scene in 1920 with *This Side of Paradise*, a semi-
autobiographical guide to life at Princeton and the story of a sensitive young man who is
trying to find his place in society, the critics were taken with its sophisticated style, its use of
the social milieu, its honest treatment of emotional experience, and its somewhat bold
portrayal of the younger generation. His readers, then, looked for even better writing in the
following five years, but few would agree that he fulfilled his promise. Neither of the two
collections of intriguing, skillful, but often uneven short stories, *Flappers and Philosophers*
and *Tales of the Jazz Age*, nor the weak play *The Vegetable* seemed to satisfy their
expectations. His second novel, *The Beautiful and Damned*, was looked to more eagerly and
was more widely reviewed than any other work by the author. The hero, Fitzgerald said in a
letter to his publisher, was intended as "one of those many with the tastes and weaknesses of
an artist but with no actual creative inspiration," and the novel related how he and his
beautiful young wife were "wrecked on the shoals of dissipation." The use of
autobiographical details again occasioned some speculation and caused the book to sell well,
but many critics found it an unsuccessful effort at a somber tragedy of a typical American
sensibility and thought that it lacked organization or focus. Some recent critics, however,
have felt it to be a better novel than contemporary readers realized.
    Whatever faults one may find in Fitzgerald's early work, with the publication of *The Great*

Gatsby he fulfilled his highest promise and gave to American literature one of its masterworks. On the surface, of course, *The Great Gatsby* is much a part of its age as a brilliant dramatization of the social and economic corruptions of the jazz age, marked by Prohibition, gangsterism, blasé flappers, and uprootedness. American morality was marked by questionable business ethics, commercial criteria for success, and ultraconservatism in social and political thinking. Historians like Charles Beard were insisting that materialistic and economic factors rather than idealistic motives had determined the course of American history. Through character and theme, Fitzgerald dealt in one way or another with all of these historic factors with such a sensitivity that one can even intuit in the text slight prophetic reverberations of the stock market crash of 1929 and the Great Depression in the offing.

Beyond these surface concerns, the novel deals symbolically with the failure of the American dream of success, which in Fitzgerald's time was still best-known through the Horatio Alger novels. Like Benjamin Franklin before him, Horatio Alger expounded, by way of his dime novels, the possibility of rising from rags to riches through industry, ambition, self-reliance, honesty, and temperance. In this myth, and the frontier tradition of self-reliance, lies the genesis of what impels Gatsby. Behind his simple and touching study and work schedule in the copy of *Hopalong Cassidy* cherished by his father lies the childhood dreams of a Franklin or a Thomas Edison, the lectures on self-improvement of a Russell Conwell or a Dale Carnegie, the lessons on bodily development of a Charles Atlas, and the tradition that every American boy could make a million dollars or become President. But what an ironic reversal! By imitating the great American moralists, Gatsby rises to be a rich and powerful criminal.

A second significant thematic concern of the novel relates to its symbolic use of the Mid-West as a contrast with the East. In his nostalgic reverie on the Mid-West near the end of the novel, Nick Carraway concludes, "I see now that this has been a story of the West, after all — Tom and Gatsby, Daisy, Jordan, and I, were all Westerners, and perhaps we possessed some deficiency in common which made us subtly unadaptable to Eastern life." This last line is ironic, because Nick left his Minnesota home originally because it "seemed like the ragged edge of the universe," but by the end of the novel it is the place to which he returns to regain a sense of balance and moral equilibrium. Fitzgerald is playing with the traditional American dichotomy between the East as a model of European sophistication and corruption and the West as a repository of the fundamental decencies and virtues derived from contact with the American soil, the new Garden of Eden.

A figure who lurks in the background of the novel is Dan Cody, whose name suggests the mythic traditions surrounding Daniel Boone and Buffalo Bill Cody. Cody had helped settle the nation and made a fortune besides, and therefore he represents the energies that sparked the Western frontier movement. But as Frederick Jackson Turner had reminded everyone in 1893, the frontier had been closed and no longer carried the significance it once had as the source of sudden wealth and the place of refuge for those seeking a second chance. By the time Gatsby met him, Dan Cody had degenerated into a senile old man subject to the advances of opportunists and gold-diggers. Gatsby takes him as his ideal, nevertheless, and, like the romantic that he is, he refuses to let historic circumstance stand in his way. Rather than wrest his fortune from the raw earth, he pioneers eastward and conquers the urban wilderness through adapting its devious means to the romantic end of recapturing the past. But history cannot be repeated, and the historic promise that Gatsby learned from Cody was, Nick notes, "already behind him, somewhere back in that vast obscurity beyond the city, where the dark fields of the republic rolled on under the night."

Jay Gatsby, then, is the ultimate American arch-romantic. Because he lacked the wealth and timing, he missed the girl on whom he had focused what Nick calls his "heightened sensitivity to the promises of life." After obtaining the wealth through corrupt means, he returns five years later to fulfill his "incorruptible dream" by attempting to repeat the one golden moment of his life when he possessed that "elusive rhythm," that "fragment of lost words" which we all seek to recall in this mundane existence from a former life, time or world. Not since Don Quixote's pursuit of Dulcinea has literature seen such a noble, heartbreaking, and impossible quest.

Adopting a modified first-person narrative form from Conrad, Fitzgerald unfolds Gatsby's tragedy for us through the eyes of the narrator, Nick Carraway. What we learn through Nick is that pure will power divorced from rationality and decency leads to destruction, and that a merely selfish dream or notion is insufficient to justify the enormous amount of energy and life expended by Gatsby. It is a lesson that this nation would not learn for almost another fifty years, and a suggestion that Fitzgerald's prophetic vision saw farther into the future than the Depression years. When Gatsby is viewed against the moral decadence and cowardly conduct of the Buchanans – "You're worth the whole damn bunch put together," Nick tells him – his unassailable romanticism makes him appear heroic. As an individual, then, who dreams higher than he can achieve, whose reach exceeds his grasp, Gatsby is at the heart of the tragic condition and thus shares certain characteristics with Oedipus, Hamlet, and other tragic heroes of Western literature. Unlike Arthur Miller's modern tragic figure, Willy Loman, Gatsby doesn't evoke mere pity and disgust at the end, as he faithfully waits for a phone call that will never come.

Aside from its concern with social and moral questions of continuing consequence, *The Great Gatsby* is one of the most carefully constructed and precisely written novels in American literature. The subtle complexity of the language; the calculated use of colors, references, and connotations; the striking configurations of verbal patterns and repetitions – all lead the reader to read and reread sentences time and time again to catch the multi-level nuances of meaning. The style is poetic and repays the application of the techniques of studied explication.

Because of the disarray of his personal life, his dwindling financial resources, and his increasing self-doubts as a writer, Fitzgerald was unable to bring his artistry to such a perfect pitch again. His numerous short stories written primarily for pay (some of which were collected in *All the Sad Young Men* and *Taps at Reveille* and his indifferent work for Hollywood only occasionally encouraged his best talents. His next novel, *Tender Is the Night*, which came nine years after *Gatsby*, used European locales and his experiences with his wife's mental illness, another foray into autobiographical materials. What some critics felt was an unresolved problem in structure and a failure to provide clear character motivation caused many to overlook its impressive sweep of characters and its admirable effort to deal with significant psychological and social themes. After his death, the fragments of a novel, *The Last Tycoon*, were found, many pages of which suggest that Fitzgerald was regaining control of his creative skills at the last. Despite his lapses and occasional self-indulgence, the high quality of his best work, and most certainly the striking achievement in *The Great Gatsby*, has brought his achievement the success which eluded his grasp during his own lifetime.

—M. Thomas Inge

FLEMING, Ian (Lancaster). English. Born in London, 28 May 1908. Educated at Eton College and the Royal Military Academy, Sandhurst; studied languages at the University of Munich and the University of Geneva. Served in the Royal Naval Volunteer Reserve, as personal assistant to the Director of Naval Intelligence, 1939–45; Lieutenant. Married Anne Geraldine Charteris in 1952; one son. Moscow Correspondent for Reuters Ltd., London, 1929–33; associated with Cull and Company, merchant bankers, London, 1933–35; stockbroker with Rowe and Pitman, London, 1935–39; Moscow Correspondent for *The*

Times, London, 1939; Foreign Manager, Kemsley, later Thomson, Newspapers, 1945–49; Publisher, *The Book Collector*, London, 1949 until his death. Awarded Order of Dannebrog, 1945. *Died 12 August 1964.*

PUBLICATIONS

Fiction

> *Casino Royale.* 1953; as *You Asked for It*, 1955.
> *Live and Let Die.* 1954.
> *Moonraker.* 1955; as *Too Hot to Handle*, 1957.
> *Diamonds Are Forever.* 1956.
> *The Diamond Smugglers.* 1957.
> *From Russia, With Love.* 1957.
> *Doctor No.* 1958.
> *Goldfinger.* 1959.
> *For Your Eyes Only: Five Secret Exploits of James Bond.* 1960.
> *Thunderball.* 1961.
> *The Spy Who Loved Me.* 1962.
> *On Her Majesty's Secret Service.* 1963.
> *You Only Live Twice.* 1964.
> *Chitty-Chitty-Bang-Bang* (juvenile). 1964.
> *The Man with the Golden Gun.* 1965.
> *Octopussy, and The Living Daylights.* 1966.

Other

> *Thrilling Cities.* 1963.
> *Ian Fleming Introduces Jamaica*, edited by Morris Cargill. 1966.

Bibliography: *Fleming: A Catalogue of a Collection: Preliminary to a Bibliography* by Iain Campbell, 1978.

Reading List: *The James Bond Dossier* by Kingsley Amis, 1965; *The Life of Fleming* by John Pearson, 1966; *Fleming: The Man with the Golden Pen* by Richard Gant, 1966.

*   *   *

After a varied career in journalism, the City, newspaper management, and as Personal Assistant to the Director of Naval Intelligence during the Second World War, Ian Fleming scored an immediate success as the author of a series of spy thrillers which sold over forty million copies in his lifetime. Several of his tales were turned into equally successful films, while the central character he created, James Bond, Secret Agent 007, became so valuable a commercial property that other authors were commissioned to exploit him in further adventures after Fleming's untimely death.

The earlier James Bond novels were among the fore-runners of a renewed taste for spy stories in the 1950's and 1960's. They are built around swiftly moving plots, crammed with action but straightforward in plan: though Fleming was fully aware of the activities of the wartime XX Committee in turning enemy agents, and is said to have modelled James Bond on the double agent Dusko Popov, he did not go in for the convoluted deceptions that later practitioners of the spy story have sometimes imposed on their readers as well as on their fictional characters. Instead, he preferred to increase the level of excitement of his thrillers by involving his hero in macabre dangers, violent combat, and encounters with alluring and sexually uninhibited young women.

There is undoubtedly a strong strain of brutality in the fantasy world which Fleming created. Bond is portrayed as a ruthless professional who is wholly dedicated to the Service which employs him as a double-O agent, i.e., one licensed to kill in the performance of his duties. The character-drawing is simple, and content to be superficial, with heroes and villains clearly distinguished, the latter usually physically repulsive as well as ideologically menacing and morally unacceptable.

Other ingredients in the Bond novels should be noted as setting patterns for Fleming's imitators, sometimes to the point of unintended parody, sometimes as elegantly deliberate "send-ups" of an increasingly fashionable genre of popular fiction. Fleming indulged his hero in the satisfaction of expensive tastes, particularly in such matters as food and drink, motor-cars, and personal belongings: precisely proportioned dry Martinis, eggs Benedict, Corniche convertibles, and Girard-Perregaux wrist-watches give an extra romantic gloss to the surface of his stories. They also dwell expertly on details of fire-arms and ammunition; and if some of the more ingenious equipment and devices employed in the novels struck sober-minded readers at the time as barely credible, they have subsequently proved, in the light of recent revelations of the workings of the CIA, to be less fantastic than the realities of certain actual or projected Intelligence operations.

The excellence of Fleming's achievement in an admittedly minor branch of literature may be measured thus: the forgetful reader who picks up one of the James Bond novels again after ten or twenty years will find it as fresh and engaging as ever.

—Stewart F. Sanderson

FORD, Ford Madox. English. Born Ford Madox Hueffer in Merton, Surrey, 17 December 1873; grandson of the artist Ford Madox Brown; changed name to Ford, 1923. Educated privately, in Folkestone, Kent, and at University College School, London. Served in France as an officer in the Welch Regiment in World War I. Married Elsie Martindale in 1894 (separated, 1909); two daughters. Writer from 1892; settled in Kent, 1894; collaborated with Joseph Conrad, 1900–03; returned to London, 1907: Founding Editor, *The English Review*, London, 1908–10; moved to Paris after World War I: Founding Editor, *Transatlantic Review*, Paris, 1924; in later years lived in the South of France and in New York City. *Died 26 June 1939.*

PUBLICATIONS

Collections

The Bodley Head Ford. 5 vols., 1962–71.
Letters, edited by Richard M. Ludwig. 1965.

Fiction

> *The Shifting of the Fire.* 1892.
> *The Queen Who Flew: A Fairy Tale.* 1894.
> *The Inheritors: An Extravagant Story,* with Joseph Conrad. 1901.
> *Romance,* with Joseph Conrad. 1903.
> *The Benefactor: A Tale of a Small Circle.* 1905.
> *The Fifth Queen: The Fifth Queen and How She Came to Court, Privy Seal: His Last Venture,* and *The Fifth Queen Crowned: A Romance.* 3 vols., 1906–08.
> *An English Girl: A Romance.* 1907.
> *Mr. Apollo: A Just Possible Story.* 1908.
> *The "Half Moon": A Romance of the Old World and the New.* 1909.
> *A Call: The Tale of Two Passions.* 1910.
> *The Portrait.* 1910.
> *The Simple Life Limited.* 1911.
> *Ladies Whose Bright Eyes: A Romance.* 1911; revised edition, 1935.
> *The Panel: A Sheer Comedy.* 1912; revised edition, as *Ring for Nancy,* 1913.
> *The New Humpty-Dumpty.* 1912.
> *Mr. Fleight.* 1913.
> *The Young Lovell: A Romance.* 1913.
> *Zeppelin Nights: A London Entertainment,* with Violet Hunt. 1915.
> *The Good Soldier: A Tale of Passion.* 1915.
> *The Marsden Case: A Romance.* 1923.
> *The Tietjens Tetralogy: Some Do Not, No More Parades, A Man Could Stand Up, Last Post.* 4 vols., 1924–28; as *Parade's End,* 1950.
> *The Nature of a Crime,* with Joseph Conrad. 1924.
> *A Little Less Than Gods: A Romance.* 1928.
> *When the Wicked Man.* 1931.
> *The Rash Act.* 1933.
> *Henry for Hugh.* 1934.
> *Vive le Roy.* 1936.

Play

> *The Fifth Queen Crowned,* with F. N. Connell, from the novel by Ford (produced 1909).

Verse

> *The Questions at the Well, with Sundry Other Verses for Notes of Music.* 1893.
> *Poems for Pictures and for Notes of Music.* 1900.
> *The Face of the Night: A Second Series of Poems for Pictures.* 1904.
> *From Inland and Other Poems.* 1907.
> *Songs from London.* 1910.
> *High Germany: Eleven Sets of Verse.* 1911.
> *Collected Poems.* 1913.
> *Antwerp.* 1914.
> *On Heaven, and Poems Written on Active Service.* 1918.
> *A House.* 1921.
> *New Poems.* 1927.
> *Collected Poems.* 1936.
> *Buckshee.* 1966.

Other

The Brown Owl: A Fairy Story (juvenile).   1892.
The Feather (juvenile).   1892.
Ford Madox Brown: A Record of His Life and Work.   1896.
The Cinque Ports: A Historical and Descriptive Record.   1900.
Rossetti: A Critical Essay on His Art.   1902.
The Soul of London: A Survey of a Modern City.   1905.
The Heart of the Country: A Survey of a Modern Land.   1906.
Christina's Fairy Book (juvenile).   1906.
England and the English: An Interpretation.   1907.
The Pre-Raphaelite Brotherhood: A Critical Monograph.   1907.
Ancient Lights and Certain New Reflections.   1911; as *Memories and Impressions: A
    Study in Atmospheres,* 1911.
The Critical Attitude.   1911.
This Monstrous Regiment of Women.   1913.
The Desirable Alien: At Home in Germany, with Violet Hunt.   1913.
Henry James: A Critical Study.   1913.
When Blood Is Their Argument: An Analysis of Prussian Culture.   1915.
Between St. Dennis and St. George: A Sketch of Three Civilizations.   1915.
Thus to Revisit: Some Reminiscences.   1921.
Mister Bosphorus and the Muses; or, A Short History of Poetry in Britain.   1923.
Women and Men.   1923.
Joseph Conrad: A Personal Remembrance.   1924.
A Mirror to France.   1926.
New York Is Not America.   1927.
New York Essays.   1927.
No Enemy: A Tale of Reconstruction.   1929.
The English Novel from the Earliest Days to the Death of Conrad.   1930.
Return of Yesterday (Reminiscences 1894–1914).   1931.
It Was the Nightingale (autobiography).   1933.
Provence, from Minstrels to the Machine.   1935.
Great Trade Route.   1937.
Portraits from Life: Memories and Criticisms.   1937; as *Mightier Than the Sword,* 1938.
The March of Literature from Confucius to Modern Times.   1938.
Critical Writings, edited by Frank MacShane.   1964.
Your Mirror to My Times (reminiscences), edited by Michael Killigrew.   1970.

Translator, *The Trail of the Barbarians,* by Pierre Loti.   1917.
Translator, *Perversity,* by Francis Carco.   1928.

Bibliography: *Ford: A Bibliography of Works and Criticism* by D. D. Harvey, 1962; "Ford"
by P. Armato, in *English Literature in Transition 10,* 1967.

Reading List: *Ford: A Study of His Novels* by Richard A. Cassell, 1961; *Ford's Novels* by
John A. Meixner, 1962; *The Life and Works of Ford* by Frank MacShane, 1965; *The Limited
Hero in the Novels of Ford* by N. Leer, 1967; *Ford* by C. G. Hoffman, 1967; *The Saddest
Story* (biography) by Arthur Mizener, 1971; *Ford: The Critical Heritage* edited by Frank
MacShane, 1972; *Ford: Modern Judgements* edited by Richard A. Cassell, 1972; *Ford* by
Sondra J. Stang, 1977.

*   *   *

Ford Madox Ford was born into an artistic and literary circle – his uncle by marriage was William Rossetti, brother of Dante Gabriel and Christina; he was a part of English literary life from the beginning. He published his first book, *The Brown Owl*, at the age of eighteen. It was a fairy story, illustrated by his grandfather. His first volumes of poetry and fiction attracted little notice, but in 1898 he accepted Conrad's invitation to collaborate with him on two novels, *The Inheritors* and *Romance*. This experience deepened his understanding of literary technique. At the same time, Ford continued his own work, writing books on the countryside where he was farming, on urban life in London, as well as a trilogy of historical novels called *The Fifth Queen*, about Katherine Howard, wife of Henry VIII.

He returned to London in 1907, and a year later founded *The English Review*, a remarkable monthly magazine in which he published the work of James, Wells, Hudson, Bennett, Hardy, Galsworthy, Yeats, and Belloc. He was the first to publish Ezra Pound, D. H. Lawrence, Wyndham Lewis and Norman Douglas. During this period, Ford also developed as a poet and exercised a profound influence on Pound and others of a group that came to be known as the Imagists. These successes were interrupted by his separation from his wife and a romance with Violet Hunt. The resulting scandal came on top of his loss of *The English Review* which was bought from under him after one year. Ford suffered an emotional crisis, but he was able to surmount his difficulties and even wrote his most successful single novel, *The Good Soldier*, during this period of stress.

Ford's admiration of the great French novelists, Stendhal, Flaubert and Maupassant, whom he looked upon as his antecedents, made him a champion of literary impressionism, a method of writing that attempts to render experience through surface observations without obtrusive comments by the author. *The Good Soldier* is narrated by one of the characters and is a study of sexual pressures on four characters from an upper-middle class background whose codes of behavior inhibit them from dealing successfully with these pressures. Gentility and propriety cannot cover up the insanity and cruelty that lie beneath the surface.

During World War I, Ford wrote several books of propaganda for the allied cause and, although he was over-age, he also served in France as an officer in the Welch Regiment. Afterwards, he moved to Paris where he befriended James Joyce, Gertrude Stein, Ernest Hemingway and numerous other expatriate writers, including his old companion Ezra Pound. Here Ford established another magazine, *Transatlantic Review*, which published these and other writers, mainly of the avant-garde. By now, Ford was living with Stella Bowen, an Australian painter. During this period he continued writing literary reminiscences as well as fiction and poetry. His most important work consisted of four novels, *Some Do Not*, *No More Parades*, *A Man Could Stand Up* and *Last Post*. This tetralogy, which later came to be known as *Parade's End*, centers on the life of Christopher Tietjens, a Yorkshire squire who gradually shed his accepted gentlemanly notions in the course of a psychological war waged against him by his estranged wife, Sylvia. This personal struggle takes place against the collapse of a society that had been corrupted by the commercial values and careerism that also led to four years of bloodshed in the trenches. A panoramic work covering many levels of society, *Parade's End* shows that it is necessary to abandon social forms and privilege to preserve the old values that gave England its character. Tietjens retreats with a new wife to a small farm in the country where he survives on what he can grow, much as a peasant does. Generally acknowledged to be the best portrayal of the effect of the World War on Great Britain, the Tietjens tetralogy is at once a psychological and sociological work. The books do not follow chronology but are narrated in Ford's impressionistic manner so as to hold the reader's attention to immediate experience.

Despite his enormous literary output, Ford never achieved financial security. Many of his books failed to cover their advances and he was forced to move from one publisher to another. During the last decade of his life he spent most of his time on a small farm near Toulon in the south of France and in New York where he was a figure of some standing, along with such contemporaries as Theodore Dreiser and Sherwood Anderson. Always interested in the younger generation, Ford befriended many American writers, mostly southerners, including Allen Tate, Caroline Gordon, Katherine Anne Porter, Edward

Dahlberg, William Carlos Williams, Jean Stafford, and Robert Lowell. Although he continued with fiction, he also wrote books that deal impressionistically with the southern regions of France and the United States. *Provence* and *Great Trade Route* celebrate the unpretentious life of self-sufficient small-hold farmers and criticise mass production and big business. Ford also wrote memorably about other writers, continued his memoirs and completed a series of literary portraits of such friends as James, Conrad, Crane, Hudson, and Lawrence. His last book, *The March of Literature*, was a monumental and loving survey of great writers from ancient China and Greece to modern times. It is an idiosyncratic book testifying to his taste and humanity. Ford always believed in clarity and simplicity; he favored realists above romantics and sided with conscious literary artists against inspired amateurs. His nature was Mediterranean rather than Nordic, and he was always generous and sympathetic to the young.

—Frank MacShane

FORESTER, C(ecil) S(cott).   English.   Born in Cairo, Egypt, 27 August 1899; grew up in the London suburbs. Educated at Alleyne's School, London, and Dulwich College, London, 1910–17; studied medicine at Guy's Hospital, London, but left without qualifying. Married 1) Kathleen Belcher in 1926 (divorced, 1944), two sons; 2) Dorothy Ellen Foster in 1947. Writer from 1917; screenwriter, in Hollywood, 1932; War Correspondent for *The Times*, London, in Spain, 1936–37, and subsequently in Czechoslovakia during the Nazi occupation; in later life lived in Berkeley, California. Recipient: Black Memorial Prize, 1940. *Died 2 April 1966.*

PUBLICATIONS

Fiction

> *Napoleon and His Court.* 1924.
> *The Paid Piper.* 1924.
> *A Pawn among Kings.* 1924.
> *Josephine, Napoleon's Empress.* 1925.
> *Payment Deferred.* 1926.
> *Love Lies Dreaming.* 1927.
> *Victor Emmanuel II and the Union of Italy.* 1927.
> *The Wonderful Week.* 1927; as *One Wonderful Week*,1927.
> *Louis XIV, King of France and Navarre.* 1928.
> *The Shadow of the Hawk.* 1928; as *The Daughter of the Hawk,* 1928.
> *Brown on Resolution.* 1929; as *Single-Handed,* 1929.
> *Nelson.* 1929; as *Lord Nelson,* 1929.
> *Plain Murder.* 1930.
> *Two-and-Twenty.* 1931.
> *Death to the French.* 1932.
> *The Gun.* 1933; as *Rifleman Dodd,* 1933.
> *The Peacemaker.* 1934.
> *The African Queen.* 1935.

The General. 1936.
The Happy Return. 1937; as *Beat to Quarters,* 1937.
Flying Colours. 1938.
A Ship of the Line. 1938.
The Captain from Connecticut. 1941.
Poo-Poo and the Dragons (juvenile). 1942.
The Ship. 1943.
The Commodore. 1945; as *Commodore Hornblower,* 1945.
Lord Hornblower. 1946.
The Sky and the Forest. 1948.
Mr. Midshipman Hornblower. 1950.
Randall and the River of Time. 1950.
Lieutenant Hornblower. 1952.
The Barbary Pirates (juvenile). 1953.
Hornblower and the Atropos. 1953.
The Nightmare. 1954.
The Good Shepherd. 1955.
Hornblower in the West Indies. 1958; as *Admiral Hornblower in the West Indies,* 1958.
Hunting the Bismarck. 1959; as *The Last Nine Days of the Bismarck,* 1959.
Hornblower and the Hotspur. 1962.
The Hornblower Companion. 1964.
Hornblower and the Crisis: An Unfinished Novel. 1967.
The Man in the Yellow Raft (stories). 1969.

Plays

U 97. 1931.
Nurse Cavell, with C. E. B. Roberts (produced 1934). 1933.

Screenplays: *Forever and a Day,* with others, 1944; *Captain Horatio Hornblower,* with others, 1951.

Other

The Voyage of the Annie Marble. 1929.
The Annie Marble in Germany. 1930.
Marionettes at Home. 1936.
The Earthly Paradise. 1940; as *To the Indies,* 1940.
The Age of Fighting Sail: The Story of the Naval War of 1812. 1956.
Long Before Forty (autobiography). 1967.

Editor, *The Adventures of John Wetherell.* 1953.

Reading List: *The Life and Times of Horatio Hornblower* by Cyril N. Parkinson, 1971.

*   *   *

In 1932, C. S. Forester began writing scripts for the Hollywood screen, a transition in media which has proven disastrous for many a successful novelist. For Forester, however, the result was happy, for perhaps no single factor better explains his great achievement as a novelist of adventure and the sea than his successful work as a screenwriter. In an autobiographical article included in *The Hornblower Companion*, Forester states that his words record a "series of visualizations." The scene is perceived as a stage drama with Forester as an omniscient ghost moving among the players. Once created, the author reviews the product "like a Hollywood director in his chair in a projector room." The footage is then put aside, and the process is repeated with the next scene. The result is a story which is at once episodic and very easy to visualize.

Like the exacting director of a historical spectacular, Forester demands absolutely accurate detail. An avid reader of history and nautical works, he acquired vast technical knowledge on all aspects of life at sea and naval military science. His achievement, however, is in his ability to integrate accurate technical information with the narrative. We learn about ships, but we are not really aware of being taught about ships. Rather the effect is that of a well-directed cinematic episode: the detail is precise, but what strikes the viewer is a unified image with all components in proper subordination. Indeed, Forester presents the necessary naval data much less obtrusively than Melville imparts the facts about whaling.

But for Forester the novel is only what it seems to be; sea captains are sea captains and whales are whales. Characters have virtues, strengths, and faults enough to make them seem as real as the realistic scenes of history and adventure in which they move, but we are never led to suspect that the novel is in fact a metaphor for a different level of philosophy and profound cosmic truth. Instead, Forester vividly shows us other people and other times; he lets us share adventure, and – a greater virtue for a writer than profundity – he never bores us.

—William J. Heim

FORSTER, E(dward) M(organ). English. Born in London, 1 January 1879. Educated at Tonbridge School, and at King's College, Cambridge, B.A. 1901, M.A. 1910. Lived in Greece and Italy, 1901–07; helped found, and contributed to, the *Independent Review*, London, 1903; lectured at the Working Men's College, London, 1907; visited India, 1912; Red Cross Volunteer Worker in Egypt, 1914–18; Literary Editor, *The Daily Herald*, London, 1920–21; Private Secretary to the Maharajah of Dewas, India, 1922; Fellow of King's College, Cambridge, and Clark Lecturer, Trinity College, Cambridge, 1927; Honorary Fellow of King's College, 1946, until his death. Vice-President, London Library; Member, General Advisory Council, BBC; President, Cambridge Humanists. Recipient: Black Memorial Prize, 1925; Prix Femina Vie Heureuse, 1925; Royal Society of Literature Benson Medal, 1937, and Companion of Literature, 1961. LL.D.: University of Aberdeen, 1931; Litt.D.: University of Liverpool, 1947; Hamilton College, Clinton, New York, 1949; Cambridge University, 1950; University of Nottingham, 1951; University of Manchester, 1954; Leyden University, Holland, 1954; University of Leicester, 1958. Honorary Member, American Academy of Arts and Letters, and Bavarian Academy of Fine Arts. Companion of Honour, 1953; Order of Merit, 1968. *Died 7 June 1970.*

PUBLICATIONS

Collections

(Works) (Abinger Edition), edited by Oliver Stallybrass. 1972–

Fiction

> *Where Angels Fear to Tread.* 1905.
> *The Longest Journey.* 1907.
> *A Room with a View.* 1908.
> *Howards End.* 1910; *Manuscripts* edited by Oliver Stallybrass, 1973.
> *The Celestial Omnibus and Other Stories.* 1911.
> *The Story of the Siren.* 1920.
> *A Passage to India.* 1924.
> *The Eternal Moment and Other Stories.* 1928.
> *The Collected Tales.* 1947; as *The Collected Short Stories,* 1948.
> *Maurice.* 1971.
> *The Life to Come and Other Stories.* 1972.

Plays

> *Pageant of Abinger,* music by Ralph Vaughan Williams (produced 1934). 1934.
> *England's Pleasant Land: A Pageant Play* (produced 1938). 1940.
> *Billy Budd,* with Eric Crozier, music by Benjamin Britten, from the story by Herman
>   Melville (produced 1952). 1951; revised version (produced 1964), 1961.

Screenplay: *A Diary for Timothy* (documentary), 1945.

Other

> *Egypt.* 1920.
> *Alexandria: A History and a Guide.* 1922; revised edition, 1938.
> *Pharos and Pharillon.* 1923.
> *Anonymity: An Enquiry.* 1925.
> *Aspects of the Novel.* 1927.
> *A Letter to Madan Blanchard.* 1931.
> *Sinclair Lewis Interprets America.* 1932.
> *Goldsworthy Lowes Dickinson* (biography). 1934.
> *Abinger Harvest.* 1936.
> *What I Believe.* 1939.
> *Nordic Twilight.* 1940.
> *The New Disorder.* 1949.
> *The Hill of Devi, Being Letters from Dewas State Senior.* 1953.
> *Two Cheers for Democracy.* 1951.
> *Desmond MacCarthy.* 1952.
> *I Assert That There Is an Alternative to Humanism.* 1955.
> *Battersea Rise.* 1955.
> *Marianne Thornton 1797–1887: A Domestic Biography.* 1956.
> *Albergo Empedocle and Other Writings,* edited by George H. Thomson. 1971.
> *A View Without a Room.* 1973.
> *Aspects of the Novel and Related Writings,* edited by Oliver Stallybrass. 1974.
> *Letters to Donald Windham.* 1976.
> *Commonplace Book.* 1978.

Bibliography: *A Bibliography of Forster* by B. J. Kirkpatrick, 1965; *Forster: An Annotated Bibliography of Writing about Him* edited by Frederick P. W. McDowell, 1977.

Reading List: *Forster* by Lionel Trilling, 1944; *The Novels of Forster* by James McConkey, 1957; *The Art of Forster* by H. J. Oliver, 1960; *The Achievement of Forster* by J. B. Beer, 1962; *Forster: The Perils of Humanism* by Frederick Crews, 1962; *Art and Order: A Study of Forster* by Alan Wilde, 1964; *Forster: A Collection of Critical Essays* edited by Malcolm Bradbury, 1966; *The Cave and the Mountain: A Study of Forster* by Wilfred Stone, 1966; *Forster: The Critical Heritage* edited by P. Gardner, 1973; *Forster: The Personal Voice* by John Colmer, 1975; *Forster: A Life* by P. N. Furbank, 2 vols., 1977–78.

*   *   *

In all his writings E. M. Forster championed freedom, tolerance, and individualism. From the start he discovered a wholly personal voice to express his view of life. Never attached to any literary school or movement – not even to the Bloomsbury group, of which he was only a peripheral member – he achieved a symbolic importance for generations of readers and writers as the voice of their unofficial selves, the self that refuses to be regimented or made to conform to social conventions. His writings celebrate the importance of beauty, personal relations, and the quest for harmony. They also expose the characteristic weaknesses of the English middle classes: their neglect of the imagination and their distrust of emotion. Although opposed to novels with a message, Forster offers the ideal of "only connect" as a solution to the "undeveloped heart" of the average Englishman, the way of culture as a counterpoise to a life of "telegrams and anger" without, and "panic and emptiness" within. Through an original blend of moral realism and poetic insight, he creates a vision of possible but elusive harmony.

Travel made Forster a writer. Italy, which he visited with his mother after leaving Cambridge in 1901, provided the inspiration for several short stories, travel sketches, and two novels. The short stories celebrate the spirit of place and the eternal moment. The two novels, *Where Angels Fear to Tread* and *A Room with a View*, contrast the instinctive life of Italy with the stifling conventions of English suburban life. Already in his early fiction can be seen what were to become his master themes: personal relations, money, salvation through love, imagination, and the wisdom of the body. The Italian novels have a Mozartian exuberance, a youthful zest in creation. Taking Jane Austen as his model and adding a malicious dash of Samuel Butler, he expands the form to accommodate the unconscious and the infinite. Beneath the shrewdly observed details of character and incident runs a mysterious subterranean life, felt especially in the two heroines, Lucy and Caroline, but also in the ambiguous relations of Philip and Gino. The Forster papers in King's College Library reveal that Forster was displacing his homosexual preoccupations through the conventions of English domestic comedy, but not without some distortion and strain.

Three novels, *The Longest Journey* (Forster's favourite), *Howards End*, and the posthumously published homosexual novel *Maurice*, are all concerned with the theme of continuity and the future of England. The first, a story of the artist as a young man that predates Joyce's classic, is partly autobiographical. Although flawed by occasional sentimentality and melodrama, it presents a radiant ideal of comradeship, especially in the Cambridge chapters. The weak idealistic hero, Rickie Elliot, is destroyed through compromise and deceit, but dies saving his step-brother's life. The novel ends with the young English pagan Stephen and his child as the true inheritors of England. In *Howards End* the polarities are no longer Life and Art, as they are in the first three novels, but Business and Culture, Doing and Being. The "Condition of England" and its future becomes a major theme, and, by the use of an elaborate pattern of imagery (later called "Rhythm" in *Aspects of the Novel*), Forster gives a resonance and expansion of meaning that most Edwardian social novels lack. The epigraph of the novel, "only connect," embraces both personal relations and the class structure. The inheritance of a house, a symbolic marriage, and an improbable union are the means used to suggest a new psychic and social harmony. The house, Howards End, which is based on Forster's early home Rooksnest, comes to represent an idealised England, so that the question who will inherit Howards End takes on a wider significance.

Ultimately, though, the renewal of harmony between the two estranged Schlegel sisters is far more convincing than the promise of social unity conveyed by the contrived details of plot and imagery. Brilliantly successful as the portrayal of the women in this novel is, Forster soon tried to escape from "the swish of the skirts" in an unfinished social novel, *Arctic Summer*, which contrasted two types of men, the heroic and the intellectual, and in *Maurice*, conceived through an incident at Edward Carpenter's house in 1913, which explored the themes of homosexual love and the future of England as a classless society through the love of the stockbroker Maurice Hall and the gamekeeper Alec Scudder.

For the making of his masterpiece, *A Passage to India*, Forster had intimate knowledge of the tensions between the rulers and the ruled and between Muslims and Hindus as the result of his two widely separated visits to India, the first in 1912–13 and the second in 1921. Moreover, his Red Cross service in Alexandria from 1915 to 1918 expanded the range of his personal relations and knowledge of eastern thought. Later, as Private Secretary to the Maharajah of Dewas, he witnessed Hindu ceremonies, lived close to deeply religious men, and felt the terror and beauty of the Indian landscape. *A Passage to India*, Forster repeatedly insisted, "is not really about politics," but aspires to be "poetic and philosophic." Essentially, it explores the difficulties men face in trying to understand each other and the universe. The disastrous visit to the Marabar Caves not only precipitates the series of misunderstandings between the Indian doctor Aziz and the English educator Fielding, but also, through Mrs. Moore's terrible nihilistic vision, suggests that there may be only an echoing void at the heart of the universe. The three-part symphonic structure of the novel, Mosque, Caves, Temple, the dominant pattern of promise and withdrawal, seen both in the false dawns of the landscape and the elusive appeals of friendship, the recurrent imagery of caves and overarching sky, all serve to hold in tension the major polarities of man's existence. *A Passage to India* represents a great expansion in Forster's art and vision. By setting the quest for truth in an alien environment where the cherished ideals of Western humanism were challenged, he freed himself from the limited insular values of Cambridge and Bloomsbury.

After *A Passage to India* Forster wrote no further novels. The reason for his silence was not simply that he felt out of touch with the world that came into existence after the First World War, but that he wanted to write about homosexual relations and this the external and internal censor would not allow. Instead of novels, he wrote occasional short stories (posthumously published as *The Life to Come and Other Stories*), numerous essays, reviews, and two biographies: of his Cambridge friend, G. L. Dickinson, and of his great-aunt, Marianne Thornton, who left the £8,000 that made his career as a writer possible and whose influence, he confessed, "in a most tangible sense" followed him "beyond the grave." He perhaps overpaid the debt in his portraits of the elderly sybils Mrs. Wilcox and Mrs. Moore, who live on in other characters' lives after their deaths.

With the rise of Hitler and the outbreak of war, Forster achieved new success as a popular broadcaster when he distilled the essence of his liberal humanism in memorable fashion on home and overseas services. Some of his radio talks and lectures appear in *Two Cheers for Democracy*, but many have still to be published in book form. Our picture of Forster the man and Forster the artist is rapidly changing as scholars draw on new material in the Forster Archive at Cambridge and as the various volumes of the splendid new Abinger Edition appear. His dilemma as a homosexual writer is now clearer, his conscious artistry more apparent, the facts of his sheltered, female-dominated world fuller. But there is some danger that his fame may be undermined by irrelevant biographical detail. The discovery that Forster did not know the facts of human copulation until he was over thirty can hardly detract from the astonishing maturity of his early fiction, though it does certainly cast an ironic light on his ardent celebration of the wisdom of the body. And nothing can detract from his achievement in writing two of the greatest twentieth-century novels in *Howards End* and *A Passage to India*. Although not an experimental writer like Joyce or Virginia Woolf, it seems certain that he will survive with D. H. Lawrence, as one of the two most original novelists of the first half of this century.

—John Colmer

FOSTER, Hannah (Webster). American. Born in Boston in 1759. Nothing is known about her early life and education. Married the Reverend John Foster in 1785; two daughters. Writer from c. 1780; lived in her husband's parish of Brighton, Massachusetts, until his death, then settled with her daughters in Montreal. *Died 17 April 1840.*

PUBLICATIONS

Fiction

The Coquette; or, The History of Eliza Wharton. 1797.
The Boarding School; or, Lessons of a Preceptress to Her Pupils. 1798.

Bibliography: in *Bibliography of American Literature* by Jacob Blanck, 1959.

*   *   *

Two of the earliest essays into American fiction were designed to "expose the dangerous consequences of seduction." William Hill Brown's *The Power of Sympathy* and Hannah Foster's *The Coquette* are cut from the same Richardsonian pattern. Of the two the more convincing and more durable is the Foster book. Better constructed and more single-minded in its purpose, it can still appeal to readers today.

Moreover, *The Coquette* is based on fact and thus achieves a kind of realism that was more becoming to American rather than English taste. Eliza Wharton, the heroine, was in reality Elizabeth Whitman and her lover was Pierpont Edwards, both of good Massachusetts families. The newspaper accounts tell of her elopement with him and of her death in the Bell Tavern in Danvers, Massachusetts. A secret marriage is hinted at, but that part of the story remains a mystery. These events took place ten years before the appearance of the novel; but even more compelling is the fact that Hannah Foster's husband was the cousin of the wife of Deacon John Whitman of Stow, himself a cousin of Elizabeth Whitman's father. It seems probable that Hannah Foster, through these family connections was in possession of the facts.

The Coquette is an imitation of Richardson's *Clarissa Harlowe*, but it is one of the most successful in a long series of seduction novels written in that period. The characters of Major Peter Sanford, the seducer, and Eliza Wharton are convincing and straightforward. The other characters are skillfully used to build the plot and comment on the unfortunate lovers, so that the reader's attention never moves away from the unfolding tragedy. The motivation is real and the moments of tortured self-revelation raise the novel above the sensationalism and sentimentality of many novels of this genre. Moreover, Foster does not fall into the obvious excesses of the epistolary form; she does not tax the credulity of the reader, nor does she intrude with tedious editorializing.

—Dominic J. Bisignano

FRAME, Janet (Paterson). New Zealander. Born in Dunedin, 28 August 1924. Educated at Oamaru North School; Waitaki Girls' High School; Otago University Teachers Training College, Dunedin. Recipient: Church Memorial Award, 1951, 1954; New Zealand Literary Fund Award, 1960; New Zealand Scholarship in Letters, 1964; Robert Burns Fellowship, Otago University, 1965. Lives in Dunedin.

PUBLICATIONS

Fiction

> The Lagoon: Stories.   1951; revised edition, as The Lagoon and Other Stories, 1961.
> Owls Do Cry.   1957.
> Faces in the Water.   1961.
> The Edge of the Alphabet.   1962.
> The Reservoir: Stories and Sketches.   1963.
> Snowman, Snowman: Fables and Fantasies.   1963.
> Scented Gardens for the Blind.   1963.
> The Adaptable Man.   1965.
> The Reservoir and Other Stories.   1966.
> A State of Siege.   1966.
> The Rainbirds.   1968; as Yellow Flowers in the Antipodean Room, 1969.
> Intensive Care.   1970.
> Daughter Buffalo.   1972.

Verse

> The Pocket Mirror.   1967.

Other

> Mona Minim and the Smell of the Sun (juvenile).   1969.

Reading List: An Inward Sun: The Novels of Frame, 1971, and Frame, 1977, both by J. A. Downie; "Preludes and Parables" by H. Winston Rhodes, in Landfall 102, 1973.

                              *   *   *

Janet Frame's best-liked novel, certainly in her own country, is her first, Owls Do Cry, a strongly autobiographical account of childhood in a small, rural New Zealand town. But before writing this she dealt with similar experiences in her first collection of short stories, The Lagoon, which presents several recollections of an idyllic childhood threatened, like her own, by bereavement and pain. Two of her sisters were drowned in separate accidents during her own girlhood; these tragedies are given to the Withers family of Owls Do Cry, becoming conflated in the burning of the oldest child, Francie, a tragedy which comes to symbolize the extinction of innocence and imagination by adult society. A parallel tragedy, linked to this by images, occurs later when Daphne, the second Withers child, is given a leucotomy after being forced into a mental hospital when her only "illness" is possession of a vividly lyrical imagination.

Some of the unresolved themes of this novel are treated in her next two, Faces in the Water and The Edge of the Alphabet, which complete a trilogy devoted to the Withers family. In Faces in the Water, Daphne, concealed behind the name of Istina Mavet, is a young woman who has entered a mental hospital after long periods of confusion and unhappiness. The novel is a descent into hell, and carries Istina from a ward of near-normal patients through others to a ward full of wild, deranged figures. Her recovery and eventual discharge have echoes of Orpheus's quest for Eurydice. These echoes occur again in The Edge of the Alphabet, the story of the journey to England made by Toby, the doltish son of the Withers family, who is seeking both his ancestry and the chance to write a novel. His failure to do either is balanced by the success of his friend, Zoe Bryce, in creating a small sculpture, a forest made of silver paper, that symbolizes the imaginative world both characters have found so difficult to capture in words.

The fugitive nature of written words becomes the dominant subject of Janet Frame's next two novels, *Scented Gardens for the Blind* and *The Adaptable Man*. H. Winston Rhodes has pointed to the parabolic relationship of all her stories of this period, collected in *The Reservoir* and *Snowman, Snowman*, to her other fiction; he refers particularly to the metaphor of blindness in her stories and its importance in the fourth novel, which deals with humans' refusal to see the harsh light of reality, and their preference for the scented gardens of civilization. The novel's three narrators are revealed finally to have been one, an ancient mute in a mental hospital; the incoherent grunts with which she ends the work suggest some return to a primitive communion and lead to the linguistic concerns of *The Adaptable Man*, a novel concerned again with a quest for a new language that will heal humans instead of dividing them. The only one of her novels to be set entirely in England, this work shows great control, confidence, and maturity, and may well come to be regarded as her finest and most significant work. Its theme of adaptability has evolutionary and linguistic implications alike, and the historical perspective of the novel gives her writing new dignity and compassion. In addition, it continues her concern with the form and techniques of writing, issues which she dextrously makes the subject of the novel.

A State of Siege and *The Rainbirds* have the simple directness of the parabolic form they use; the first concerns a spinster schoolteacher who retires to a cottage on an island in the north of New Zealand to learn to paint authentically but finds herself besieged by her imagination and memory instead, and is destroyed; the second is about an undistinguished immigrant from England who is knocked over by a car in a New Zealand town, deemed dead but comes to life again in hospital, and finds that his family and friends shun him as if he were diseased, that his job has been taken by someone else, and finally that actual death will be his only reward.

Intensive Care and *Daughter Buffalo* are products of periods spent at writers' colonies in the U.S.A. during the protests against the Vietnam War. *Intensive Care* is a substantial work, partly retrospective and partly visionary, which examines New Zealand's obsession with war and the kind of society this obsession produces; its final section is a nightmare vision of New Zealand as Vietnam, swarming with American soldiers who are to execute all local inhabitants whose imagination and intellect make them unusual and hence suspect. *Daughter Buffalo* is a slighter work, set almost entirely in New York, and is a kind of dialogue between Edelman, an American-Jewish doctor who specializes in studying death, and Turnlung, an elderly New Zealand writer whose interests are much the same. The earlier ruse of revealing a novel to have been written by a single figure occurs here, but by the time this is shown the book has comprehensively surveyed modern man's obsession with death, not simply in the U.S.A. but in New Zealand as well, and, by implication, throughout the world.

It is this wide range of significance that most distinguishes Janet Frame's best writing, which develops from personal concerns to a general compassion for human suffering and the kind of ignorance that prevents people from developing into whole human beings. It is distinguished, too, by her advocacy of a language charged with imagination and insight as an anodyne for these problems. Her occasional tendencies toward obsessiveness and obscurity are far outweighed by these distinctive qualities.

—Patrick Evans

FRANK, Waldo (David).   American.   Born in Long Branch, New Jersey, 25 August 1889. Educated at De Witt Clinton High School, New York, 1902–06; Les Chamettes Pensionnat, Lausanne, Switzerland, 1906–07; Yale University, New Haven, Connecticut, B.A. and M.A. 1911. Married 1) Margaret Naumberg in 1916 (divorced, 1926), one son; 2) Alma Magoon in 1927 (divorced, 1943), two daughters; 3) Jean Klempner in 1943, two sons. Theatre Critic, *Courier-Journal*, New Haven, 1910–11; Reporter, *New York Evening Post*, 1911–12, and *New York Times*, 1912; lived abroad, 1913–14; Founding Editor, *Seven Arts*, New York, 1916; conscientious objector during World War I; member of staff of the *Ellsworth County Leader*, Kansas, 1919; Contributing Editor, *New Republic*, New York, 1925–40, and *New Masses*, New York, 1926; Lecturer, New School for Social Research, New York, 1927; Honorary Professor, Central University of Ecuador, 1949. Chairman, Independent Miners' Relief Committee, 1932; First Chairman, League of American Writers, 1935. Litt.D.: Universidad Nacional de San Marcos, Lima, Peru, 1929. Member, National Institute of Arts and Letters, 1952. *Died 9 January 1967.*

PUBLICATIONS

Fiction

    The Unwelcome Man.   1917.
    The Dark Mother.   1920.
    Rahab.   1922.
    City Block.   1922.
    Holiday.   1923.
    Chalk Face.   1924.
    The Death and Birth of David Markand.   1934.
    The Bridegroom Cometh.   1938.
    Summer Never Ends.   1941.
    Island in the Atlantic.   1946.
    Invaders.   1948.
    Not Heaven.   1953.

Play

    New Year's Eve.   1929.

Other

    The Art of the Vieux Colombier: A Contribution of France to the Contemporary Stage.   1918.
    Our America.   1919; as *The New America*, 1922.
    Salvos: An Informal Book about Books and Plays.   1924.
    Time Exposure, By Search-Light.   1926.
    Virgin Spain: Scenes from the Spiritual Drama of a Great People.   1926; revised edition, 1942.
    Five Arts, with others.   1929.
    The Re-Discovery of America: An Introduction to a Philosophy of American Life.   1929.
    America Hispana: A Portrait and a Prospect.   1931.
    Dawn in Russia: The Record of a Journey.   1932.

In the American Jungle 1925–1936. 1937.
Chart for Rough Water: Our Role in a New World. 1940.
South American Journey. 1943.
The Jew in Our Day. 1944.
Birth of a World: Bolívar in Terms of His Peoples. 1951.
Bridgehead: The Drama of Israel. 1957.
The Rediscovery of Man: A Memoir and a Methodology of Modern Life. 1958.
Cuba, Prophetic Island. 1961.

Editor, *Tales from the Argentine,* translated by Anita Brenner. 1930.
Editor, *The Collected Poems of Hart Crane.* 1933; revised edition, as *The Complete Poems,* 1958.
Editor, with others, *America and Alfred Stieglitz: A Collective Portrait.* 1934.

Translator, *Lucienne,* by Jules Romains. 1925.

Reading List: *The Novels of Frank* by William R. Bittner, 1958; *The Shared Vision of Frank and Hart Crane* by Robert L. Perry, 1966; *Frank* by Paul J. Carter, 1967.

*   *   *

Although Waldo Frank produced a large and varied body of work in prose – history, fiction, essays – he considered himself a poet. In his memoirs, he refers to himself as a poet, describes his novels as lyrical, and says that *Virgin Spain* represents a subjective, lyrical expression of the author. The memoirs provide a useful introduction to the man and to the genesis and the attitudes informing some of his important books.

Surprisingly, his important books are history, not fiction or essays. Frank's essays were written for periodicals, and consist principally of commentary on literature, the theatre, the current American scene, and the position of the Jew in the modern world. Occasionally they are listed as criticism, but Frank lacked the tools of criticism. He also lacked wit and humor, as is painfully evident in a collection of brief "Profiles," first published in *The New Yorker.* Like his history and fiction, his essays offer a poet's vision and use of language. In the best, in the introduction to Hart Crane's poems, for example, this vision enlarges the reader's understanding. It tends to vitiate much of his other writing, especially his fiction.

At the heart of Frank's work is his vision of a social and personal Whole – variously termed Cosmos or Being or The Great Tradition – achieved in western Europe in the middle ages by the church, through the teaching of Jesus. In succeeding ages, according to Frank, this very teaching – that the Kingdom of God is within man – gave rise to an ego which, particularly in America, replaced the Ptolemaic universe with a secular, mechanistic multiverse. The chaos of the multiverse is but a stage, however, in man's history, which must culminate in the Whole once more, the knowledge that God, the universal, is within man, whose life therefore has purpose and direction.

The timeless, spaceless nature of this vision of the Whole precludes the development of character and situation in Frank's fiction, as he himself asserts. Consequently, his short stories are made up essentially of moments of epiphany, and his novels contain inert ideological and symbolic material. Like a poet, he attempts to re-create language, using nouns as verbs and adjectives as nouns. These usages and his poetic descriptions unhappily abound to the point of embarrassment in his writing.

On account of his vision, his histories of North and South America, Russia, and Spain must be accepted on his terms, as works of art. His considerable research gives substance to some that otherwise would amount to little more than poetic travel books. As history, *Birth of a World* is his best, undoubtedly in part because it was commissioned by the Venezuelan

Government and because Bolívar, not Frank, is at the center of the narrative. Most important for the reader's comprehension and intelligent assessment of Frank's work is *The Rediscovery of America*. For it presents his vision, interpreting religion and history from a poet's perspectives, with a poet's insights.

—Robert F. Richards

FREDERIC, Harold. American. Born in Utica, New York, 19 August 1856. Educated at the Advanced School, Utica, graduated 1871. Married Grace Williams in 1877, one daughter and three sons; also had two daughters and one son by Kate Lyon. Worked in Boston, 1873–74; Proofreader, *Utica Morning Herald*, 1875; Reporter, 1875–80, and Editor, 1880–81, *Utica Observer*; Editor, *Evening Journal*, Albany, New York, 1882–84; settled in London, 1884: London Correspondent of the *New York Times*, 1884 until his death. *Died 19 October 1898.*

PUBLICATIONS

Collections

Stories of York State, edited by Thomas F. O'Donnell. 1966.

Fiction

Seth's Brother's Wife: A Study of Life in the Greater New York. 1887.
The Lawton Girl. 1890
In the Valley. 1890.
The Return of the O'Mahony. 1892.
The Copperhead. 1893.
The Copperhead and Other Stories of the North During the American War. 1894.
Marsena and Other Stories of the Wartime. 1894.
The Damnation of Theron Ware. 1896; as *Illumination*, 1896; edited by Everett Carter, 1960.
Mrs. Albert Grundy: Observations in Philistia. 1896.
March Hares. 1896.
In the Sixties (stories). 1897.
Gloria Mundi. 1898; abridged version, as *Pomps and Vanities*, 1913.
The Deserter and Other Stories: A Book of Two Wars. 1898.
The Market-Place. 1899.

Other

The Young Emperor William II of Germany: A Study in Character Development on a Throne. 1891.
The New Exodus: A Study of Israel in Russia. 1892.

Bibliography: *A Bibliography of Writings by and about Frederic* by Thomas F. O'Donnell, Stanton Garner, and Robert H. Woodward, 1975.

Reading List: *Frederic* by Thomas F. O'Donnell and Hoyt C. Franchere, 1961; *The Novels of Frederic* by Austin E. Briggs, 1969; *Frederic* by Stanton Garner, 1969.

*   *   *

Two distinct strains, realistic and romantic, intermix in Harold Frederic's fiction. He regarded Erckmann-Chatrian and Hawthorne as the principal influences on his own work. His reading of popular romance, together with qualities inherent in his temperament and the pattern of his career, manifests itself in certain romantic effects. He lapses into melodrama and sentimentality and recurrently draws central figures who are young, hopeful, naive, and embarked on fairy-tale adventures of personal fulfilment. Frederic's romanticism matures in the brief course of his writing career, however, from an initial school-boy emulation of Erckmann-Chatrian in the earliest stories towards a Hawthorne-like probing of the ambiguities manifest in human character, and of the inner and outer pressures that determine behavior. Frederic's reputation and his distinctive character as a writer depend primarily on his talents as a realist who exploited materials pertaining to the Mohawk Valley region of New York. In the autobiographical derivation of his fiction, in his faithful representation of everyday language, behavior, and scene, and in his dramatic method (i.e., his letting the tale tell itself rather than interpreting it for the reader) Frederic has been compared to William Dean Howells, whom he greatly admired. His essentially comic vision also associates him with Howells and with an underlying American optimism ultimately deriving from Emerson.

Frederic's first novel, *Seth's Brother's Wife*, his masterwork *The Damnation of Theron Ware*, and his best stories are all realistic. They draw upon his childhood experiences in a working-class, Methodist home during the Civil War era and upon his subsequent observations as a photographer's apprentice and a journalist in upstate New York. Seth is a young journalist variously involved with his job, politics, and his brother's wife, his story enacted against the dreary background of a poor upstate farming district. Theron Ware is a small-town Methodist minister whose intellectual, aesthetic, and sexual initiations under the influence of town sophisticates paradoxically result in both *éclaircissement* and moral degeneration. Here as elsewhere Frederic's overt treatment of sexuality and his preoccupation with the type of the modern woman are manifest. The Civil War stories are highly original, dealing with ambivalent attitudes toward the war and with its effects upon civilians at home rather than celebrating military heroics. Written in 1891–92, these have been collected in a modern edition as *Harold Frederic's Stories of York State*. *The Lawton Girl*, a moderately successful sequel to *Seth*, and *In the Valley*, a historical romance of the Revolutionary War, are also set in the Mohawk Valley.

Frederic was a highly successful foreign correspondent, and this activity represented a second career in part motivated by financial objectives. All his fiction except the early stories was written in England, and he initially attempted to assimilate European materials in *The Return of the O'Mahony*. This far-fetched, comical, trivial romance is Frederic's deepest plunge into Irish folk materials, although folklore, legend, and genealogy interested him throughout his career, and his interest in the New York Irish predated his journalistic immersion in Irish politics. *March Hares*, set in London, is believed to be a fictional celebration of Frederic's liaison with Kate Lyon. Its deft, urbane, and comic tone, characteristic of Frederic's mature voice, is reminiscent of that of his bachelor narrator in *Mrs. Albert Grundy*, a series of fictionalized satirical sketches orginally published in the *National Observer* as "Observations in Philistia."

In his last two novels, *Gloria Mundi* and *The Market-Place*, Frederic makes his most serious attempts to discover European materials of sufficient richness to replace the New York regionalist material that he had substantially worked through. Of these *Gloria Mundi*, a

Cinderella tale of a young man's coming into a dukedom and an inheritance, is the less successful. Frederic was ill-advised to attempt the depiction of a social milieu inaccessible to him, and the novel lacks the authenticity that characterizes his scene-painting of rural New York. In *The Market-Place*, however, a romance of commercial enterprise dealing with life in the City and with the interaction of political and philanthropic motives, Frederic opens up a vein of material that he might easily have exploited thereafter. Taken together, the central figures of *Theron Ware*, *Gloria Mundi*, and *The Market-Place* manifest a deepening psychological insight and an ever-increasing subtlety and ambiguity in rendering the relationships between character and environment. The peculiar strength of *Theron Ware*, which is generally regarded as a minor classic, may in fact derive from its bringing together the New York regionalist material at which Frederic was a sure hand, with his increasingly subtle probing into the forces that shape and thwart human development.

Frederic's novels reveal curious intermixtures of disparate treatment, material, and attitudes within individual works. Some of the inconsistencies might result from lack of revision, but a sort of intellectual omnivorousness characterizes Frederic. Nonetheless, the diversity of his talents, attitudes, and experiments is in itself remarkable. His novels characteristically reveal multiple perspectives, a tendency to view experience from more than one point of view. The problem of distinguishing between mere inconsistencies and calculated ironies is a crux in assessing individual works fairly and in forming a conclusive judgment of his achievement as a novelist.

—Jean Frantz Blackall

FREEMAN, Mary E(leanor) Wilkins. American. Born in Randolph, Massachusetts, 31 October 1852; brought up in Randolph, then in Brattleboro, Vermont; returned to Randolph, 1883. Educated at Brattleboro High School, graduated 1870; Mount Holyoke Female Seminary, South Hadley, Massachusetts, 1870–71; Glenwood Seminary, West Brattleboro, 1871. Married Dr. Charles M. Freeman in 1902 (separated, 1922; died, 1923). Settled in Metuchen, New Jersey, 1902, and remained there for the rest of her life. Recipient: Howells Medal, 1925. Member, National Institue of Arts and Letters, 1926. *Died 13 March 1930.*

PUBLICATIONS

Fiction

    A Humble Romance and Other Stories. 1887; as *A Far-Away Melody and Other Stories*, 1890.
    A New England Nun and Other Stories. 1891.
    Jane Field. 1892.
    Pembroke. 1894; edited by P. D. Westbrook, 1971.
    Madelon. 1896.
    Jerome, A Poor Man. 1897.
    Silence and Other Stories. 1898.
    The People of Our Neighbourhood. 1898; as *Some of Our Neighbours*, 1898.
    The Jamesons. 1899.

In Colonial Times. 1899.
The Heart's Highway: A Romance of Virginia in the Seventeenth Century. 1900.
The Love of Parson Lord and Other Stories. 1900.
Understudies (stories). 1901.
The Portion of Labor. 1901.
Six Trees (stories). 1903.
The Wind in the Rose-Bush and Other Stories of the Supernatural. 1903.
The Givers (stories). 1904.
The Debtor. 1905.
"Doc" Gordon. 1906.
By the Light of the Soul. 1907.
The Fair Lavinia and Others. 1907.
The Shoulders of Atlas. 1908.
The Winning Lady and Others. 1909.
The Butterfly House. 1912.
The Yates Pride. 1912.
The Copy-Cat and Other Stories. 1914.
An Alabaster Box, with Florence Morse Kingsley. 1917.
Edgewater People (stories). 1918.
The Best Stories, edited by Henry Wysham Lanier. 1927.

Play

Giles Corey, Yeoman. 1893.

Other

Goody Two-Shoes and Other Famous Nursery Tales, with Clara Doty Bates. 1883.
Decorative Plaques (juvenile verse), designs by George F. Barnes. 1883.
The Cow with Golden Horns and Other Stories (juvenile). 1884(?).
The Adventures of Ann: Stories of Colonial Times (juvenile). 1886.
The Pot of Gold and Other Stories (juvenile). 1892.
Young Lucretia and Other Stories (juvenile). 1892.
Comfort Pease and Her Gold Ring (juvenile). 1895.
Once upon a Time and Other Child-Verses. 1897.
The Green Door (juvenile). 1910.

Bibliography: in *Bibliography of American Literature* by Jacob Blanck, 1959.

Reading List: *Freeman* by Edward Foster, 1956; *Freeman* by P. D. Westbrook, 1967.

*   *   *

Mary E. Wilkins Freeman, who wrote almost exclusively about rural and village life in New England, ranks among the foremost American local colorists or regionalists. Brought up in a family of modest means and station in the small towns of Randolph, Massachusetts, and Brattleboro, Vermont, she drew the material for her fiction from her own experience; and when she started, in her early twenties, to write stories with New England settings she was hailed as an expert in the dialect, customs, and character traits of the people of her region. Thus she won a place among the early realists in American literature, receiving laudatory comments from William Dean Howells, a leader in the realist movement.

Freeman's keenest personal interest and her greatest strength were in the psychological analysis of characters representative of the final phase of Puritanism. In her day the old religion and culture lingered in the back-country, but in an advanced state of decay. This was a period in the rural areas that one literary historian felicitously described as "the terminal moraine of New England Puritanism." Among the people the old Puritan strengths had degenerated into eccentricity, neurosis, and worse; and these warpings of personality are portrayed unforgettably in Freeman's works. Especially fascinating to her was the transformation of the Puritan will — once considered to be under God's direction — into pathological compulsions and obsessions: a man who will not enter his church but sits on its porch for ten years during Sabbath services because of a minor doctrinal difference with the minister ("A Conflict Ended"); a village seamstress who faints from hunger rather than receive payment for two patchwork quilts because she keeps misplacing one rag and forces herself to redo her work twice ("An Honest Soul"); a woman who waits fifteen years for her lover to return from Australia, finds on his return that he is in love with another girl, and lives out the rest of her life in self-imposed solitude ("A New England Nun"); a young farmer who breaks his engagement with his fiancée because of an insignificant political disagreement with her father and postpones reconciliation for ten years (Pembroke).

Freeman's best writing is in the form of short fiction, which from the beginning of her career found ready acceptance in periodicals like Harper's New Monthly. The best known among the many volumes of her tales were the first two to be published — A Humble Romance and Other Stories and A New England Nun and Other Stories. Freeman also wrote a number of novels, the most notable of which are Jane Field and Pembroke, both dealing with New England village life. The latter is a powerful novel, which received the highest praise from Arthur Machen and Conan Doyle. In all her writing Freeman's style is simple and direct, though at times she proves herself adept at using symbols (the chained dog and caged canary in "A New England Nun"). At present, because of her sympathetic and realistic fictional treatment of women, she has aroused considerable interest among feminist critics in America.

—P. D. Westbrook

FULLER, Henry Blake.   American.   Born in Chicago, Illinois, 9 January 1857. Educated at South Division High School, Chicago, 1872, 1875–76, and Allison Classical Academy, Oconomowoc, Wisconsin, 1873–74. Worked at Ovington's Crockery, Chicago, 1876, and the Home National Bank, Chicago, 1877–78; toured Europe and on his return to Chicago became a full-time writer; contributed to the Chicago Tribune, 1884, and to the book review section of the Chicago Evening Post, 1901–02; editorial writer for the Chicago Record-Herald, 1911–13. Member, Advisory Committee, Poetry, Chicago, 1912–29. Died 28 July 1929.

PUBLICATIONS

Fiction

The Chevalier of Pensieri-Vani (stories).   1890; revised edition, 1892.
The Chatelaine of La Trinité.   1892.
The Cliff-Dwellers.   1893.

With the Procession. 1895.
From the Other Side: Stories of Transatlantic Travel. 1898.
The New Flag: Satires. 1899.
The Last Refuge: A Sicilian Romance. 1900.
Under the Skylights (stories). 1901.
Waldo Trench and Others: Stories of Americans in Italy. 1908.
Lines Long and Short: Biographical Sketches in Various Rhythms (stories). 1917.
On the Stairs. 1918.
Bertram Cope's Year. 1919.
Gardens of This World. 1929.
Not on the Screen. 1930.

Plays

O, That Way Madness Lies: A Play for Marionettes, in *Chapbook 4,* December 1895.
The Puppet-Booth: Twelve Plays. 1896.
The Coffee-House, and *The Fan,* from plays by Goldoni. 2 vols., 1925–26.
The Red Carpet, in *Fuller: A Critical Biography* by Constance Griffin. 1939.

Other

Editor, *The So-Called Human Race,* by Bert Leston Taylor. 1922.

Bibliography: *Fuller and Hamlin Garland: A Reference Guide* by Charles L. P. Silet, 1977.

Reading List: *Fuller: A Critical Biography* by Constance Griffin, 1939; *Fuller* by John Pilkington, 1970; *Fuller of Chicago: The Ordeal of a Genteel Realist in Ungenteel America* by Bernard R. Bowron, Jr., 1974.

                              *   *   *

An American writer whose work suggests Henry James or William Dean Howells, but without the former's strength and without the latter's variety, Henry Blake Fuller strikes his admirers as subtle and his detractors as dull. In his best novels the style is elegant and spare, distinguished by a dry wit; in verse and drama, and in his last two novels, however, the performance is uncertain and even embarrassing. An "unconquerable reticence," in Harriet Monroe's phrase, and the "deliberate flatness" which Edmund Wilson observed do not encourage many readers to pursue this decorous writer. Three novels and several stories, however, do not deserve their present neglect.

Fuller's fictions pass in Italy or in Chicago. In the first group, somewhat vulgar Americans encounter sophisticated Europeans in a series of books beginning with *The Chevalier of Pensieri-Vani.* An elderly American woman, for example, longs to escape her crass new country for the older, presumably better one; an Italian nobleman is persuaded to alter his family's villa to suit the whims of tasteless Americans; on a train, an American encounters a travelling theatrical troupe and mistakes it for royalty. These ironic miniatures are finely honed and atmospheric, but they are less persuasive than the best of the Chicago novels.

With the Procession traces a middle-class family's pathetic attempts to social climb. An older generation has made the modest family fortune which a younger one wastes. The son is a posturing dilettante, the daughter a fatuous spinster, each aspiring to join Chicago's social "procession." *On the Stairs* follows the equally mediocre lives of two boys, the rise of one and the fall of the other, through two generations that blur the social distinctions which separated them in youth and separate them through economic ones.

Fuller's preoccupation with failures – despite his wry humor – may account, in part, for the indifference with which his best novel was greeted. *Bertram Cope's Year* attempts to overcome Fuller's "unconquerable reticence" in dealing with homosexuals, but in a manner sufficiently elliptical to obscure its intentions. Cope, an androgynous young man of surpassing good looks, attracts everyone despite his seeming diffidence and lack of marked intellect, but the attraction is only superficial. Cope is the *beau ideal* with little to offer, and his catastrophic effect on a variety of people is emotional rather than physical, spun in Fuller's most indirect manner. Critics seem to have misunderstood the novel, and Fuller's friends were embarrassed by it. A decade later he wrote two other novels, but at the time of the failure of *Bertram Cope's Year* he said, "No further novels likely: too much effort and too little return – often none." It deserves attention.

—Bruce Kellner

FURPHY, Joseph. Pseudonym: Tom Collins.   Australian.   Born at Yering Station, near Yarra Glen, Victoria, 26 September 1843. Educated at home, and at schools in Kangaroo Ground and Kyneton. Married Leonie Germain in 1867; two sons and one daughter. Farmer, later teamster in northern Victoria; bullock-driver in Riverina for about seven years; worked in his brother's foundry at Shepparton, 1884–1904; contributor to the *Bulletin* from 1889; lived in Fremantle, Western Australia, 1905 until his death. *Died 13 September 1912.*

PUBLICATIONS

Fiction

　　Such Is Life, Being Certain Extracts from the Diary of Tom Collins.   1903; abridged and
　　　　edited by Vance Palmer, 1937.
　　Rigby's Romance.   1921; complete version, 1946.
　　The Buln-Buln and the Brolga.   1948.

Verse

　　Poems, edited by Kate Baker.   1916.

Bibliography: *Furphy: An Annotated Bibliography* by Walter W. Stone, 1955.

Reading List: *Furphy: The Legend of the Man and His Book* by Miles Franklin, 1944: *Furphy* by John Barnes, 1963.

*   *   *

No Australian novelist of the nineteenth century is held in higher esteem today than Joseph Furphy, who wrote under the pseudonym of Tom Collins. Yet his *Such Is Life*, not published until 1903, had only a small devoted following until towards the end of World War II when, with increasing frequency, his name became linked to Henry Lawson's as one of the founders of a native literary tradition.

Apart from some poems and stories, Furphy's writing was contained in the original manuscript of *Such Is Life* which he sent to A. G. Stephens of the *Bulletin* in 1897. This manuscript, which drew on his experiences as a bullock driver in the Riverina and his voluminous reading, became through excisions and revisions *Such Is Life*, *Rigby's Romance* (serialized in 1905, but first complete book publication in 1946) and *The Buln-Buln and the Brolga*.

Such Is Life was taken to be mainly a work of reminiscence for the first forty years after publication, until the critical climate for its recognition as a novel with a fictional view of life developed. Furphy's love of literature, and especially his affection for Fielding and Sterne, inspired him to narrative playfulness and stylistic parody. In the post war period, these characteristics answered to critical interests in self-conscious fictionalizing, experiments with points of view, and form as a means of perception. The novel's strengths are sufficiently diverse for it to answer to future critical demands. It is an encyclopaedic study of provincial life as a microcosm focusing universal issues, as well as a comic demonstration of the vanity of philosophic speculation on such issues. Furphy's literary erudition, at times pedantic, combines with a forceful vernacular realism to make the work unique – and irreducible to critical formulae.

Furphy held nationalistic and social attitudes similar to those of his contemporary Henry Lawson, and described his original manuscript as having "temper, democratic; bias, offensively Australian." Like Lawson, he was concerned to discover a form that would express the reality he had observed, and to reject the romantic conventions that he felt falsified life. *Such Is Life* purports to be a recollection of the comic picaro Tom Collins as he randomly turns up entries in his diary for 1883: it seems a realistically unstructured collection of sketches, remembered conversations (in various dialects), tales, and incessant philosophical reflections from Collins – some in interior monologue, some in direct address to the reader. Collins seizes every opportunity to ridicule "romance" and the conventions he associates with popular fiction, especially melodramatic plot. Henry Kingsley's *Geoffry Hamlyn*, the classic "colonial romance," is his favourite target. Art, though, has its revenge, because a maze of relationships and intricate coincidences lie beneath the apparently random surface, undetected or unacknowledged by Collins.

The Buln-Buln and the Brolga and *Rigby's Romance* were both expanded from discarded chapters of *Such Is Life*. The first highlights Furphy's parody of prevailing literary clichés, and provides a very good introduction to his work. Its antagonists, Fred Falkland-Pritchard and Barefoot Bob, compete to tell the tallest tale. As their names suggest, they draw on different traditions – that of the literary romance and that of the oral yarn. As narrator, Tom Collins provides a background of humorous realism through his recollection of childhood in a country town. As with some of Lawson's work, there are correspondences with what Mark Twain and other western humorists had been doing in America. *Rigby's Romance* emphasizes Furphy's interest in social theory. Structurally it consists of exemplary tales told during a protracted discussion of socialism around a camp-fire. Once it is appreciated that the American Rigby will evade his chance of romance through theorizing to Collins and others, the book can be appreciated for its polysyllabic humour and its sly engagement with the ideals of Christian Socialism.

—Brian Kiernan

GADDIS, William. American. Born in New York City in 1922. Educated at Harvard University, Cambridge, Massachusetts. Recipient: National Institute of Arts and Letters grant, 1963; National Endowment for the Arts grant, 1966, 1974; National Book Award, 1976.

PUBLICATIONS

Fiction

The Recognitions. 1955.
JR. 1975.

* * *

William Gaddis's *The Recognitions* and *JR* are both huge works, and the reputation they have earned for Gaddis testifies to the intrinsic interest of these difficult novels. The reputation also testifies to a widespread impatience with old fashions of narrative and a thirst for other ways of presenting experience. Among these "other ways" – ways that can also be observed in John Barth, Thomas Pynchon, Richard Brautigan, and others – are the modes of transmuting reality, perhaps of getting at its essence by stringent rearrangement, which the reader meets in *The Recognitions* and *JR*.

JR is, as a story, an account of the fraudulent manipulation of stocks by a sixth-grader in a Long Island school for delinquents. The boy (JR) uses adults as agents and exploits for his own benefit the fatuities and self-deceptions of the great American world of trade and "development." An amusing anecdote. But Gaddis opens it out to deal with all that takes place in the universe that is composed of stock flotation, management of industry, manipulation of bequests, and even in the arts, which are not independent of the commercial textures that surround them. In these tossing seas, the little craft of the boy JR often vanishes from view to reappear a hundred pages later.

All this is presented in a way that leaves a realistic copying of the world to one side. Interminable conversations, by telephone or face-to-face, blend with other conversations, and one learns by osmosis rather than by explicit statement which characters are speaking on a certain page. Moreover, many characters are endowed with knowledge they would not have in "real life"; obscure Christian heresies or reference to Eliot's *Waste Land* occasionally sum up what a fumbling speaker is trying to say. To some readers, the result of all this is just confusion; others will find *JR* an often comic and revealing view of a world in which conventional pieties, familial and sexual, conform to the laws of trade. From this point of view, the novel is a confident innovation that refines a reader's awareness and encourages his detachment from what the bulk of mankind regard as important.

The earlier novel, *The Recognitions*, also views a great variety of persons and settings, but under the sign of religion rather than money. Persons try to see the sum of human meaning expressed by the various religions of the world and express some of these meanings in works of art and, even, in personal involvements. If Gaddis himself has an attitude toward the motley adventures and aspirations he reports, it is perhaps indicated by several references to Frazer's *Golden Bough*, where the effort of a scholar's mind to free itself from delusion is displayed. But such a firm center to *The Recognitions* becomes dim as endless inconsequence and violence mingle, undoing the "noble" hope of this character or that one. Scenes of great comic power alternate with interminable discussion.

In both the novels there is an odor of spoilt culture. Money, religion, and even sex are played off against each other and become the subjects of contemptuous regard. The two novels are an ambitious report on the dubious achievements of the human imagination. To none of these achievements does Gaddis commit himself, either by the design of his fiction or by sympathy with what he relates.

—Harold H. Watts

GALE, Zona. American. Born in Portage, Wisconsin, 26 August 1874. Educated in Portage public schools, and at the University of Wisconsin, Madison, 1891–95, B.L. 1895, M.L. 1899. Married William L. Breese in 1928; one adopted daughter. Reporter for the Milwaukee *Evening Wisconsin*, 1895–96, the *Milwaukee Journal*, 1896–1901, and the New York *Evening World*, 1901–03; returned to Portage, 1904; thereafter a full-time writer. Member, Wisconsin Library Commission, 1920–32; Member of the Board of Regents, 1923–29, and of the Board of Visitors, 1936–38, University of Wisconsin; Delegate from Wisconsin, International Congress of Women, Chicago, 1933. Recipient: Butterick Prize, 1911; Pulitzer Prize, for drama, 1921. D.Litt.: Ripon College, Wisconsin, 1922; University of Wisconsin, 1929; Rollins College, Winter Park, Florida, 1930. Honorary Member, Phi Beta Kappa, Western Reserve University, Cleveland, 1925. *Died 27 December 1938.*

PUBLICATIONS

Fiction

> *Romance Island.* 1906.
> *The Loves of Pelleas and Etarre* (stories). 1907.
> *Friendship Village* (stories). 1908.
> *Friendship Village Love Stories.* 1909.
> *Mothers to Men.* 1911.
> *Christmas: A Story.* 1912.
> *Neighborhood Stories.* 1914.
> *Heart's Kindred.* 1915.
> *A Daughter of the Morning.* 1917.
> *Birth.* 1918.
> *Peace in Friendship Village* (stories). 1919.
> *Miss Lulu Bett.* 1920; edited by Lella B. Kelsey, 1928.
> *Faint Perfume.* 1923.
> *Preface to a Life.* 1926.
> *Yellow Gentians and Blue* (stories). 1927.
> *Borgia.* 1929.
> *Bridal Pond* (stories). 1930.
> *Papa La Fleur.* 1933.
> *Old-Fashioned Tales.* 1933.
> *Light Woman.* 1937.
> *Magna.* 1939.

Plays

>   *The Neighbours* (produced 1912).   1926.
>   *Miss Lulu Bett*, from her own novel (produced 1920).   1921.
>   *Uncle Jimmy*.   1922.
>   *Mister Pitt* (produced 1925).   1925.
>   *Evening Clothes*.   1932.
>   *Faint Perfume*, from her own novel.   1934.
>   *The Clouds*.   1936.

Verse

>   *The Secret Way*.   1921.

Other

>   *Civic Improvement in Little Towns*.   1913.
>   *When I Was a Little Girl*.   1913.
>   *What Women Won in Wisconsin*.   1922.
>   *Portage, Wisconsin, and Other Essays*.   1928.
>   *Frank Miller of Mission Inn*.   1938.

Bibliography: "Gale" by Harold P. Simonson, in *American Literary Realism 3*, 1968.

Reading List: *Still Small Voice: The Biography of Gale* by August Derleth, 1940; *Gale* by Harold P. Simonson, 1962.

*   *   *

"There is no contemporary author," wrote Joseph Wood Krutch in 1929, "whose evolution is more interesting than that of Zona Gale." Although she lived most of her life in the village of her birth — Portage, Wisconsin — and wrote largely in the village vein that attracted the talents of so many other writers of her generation, she was nevertheless a child of her age who responded to the astonishing variety of its pressures.

After four years in New York, during which she wrote *Romance Island* and *The Loves of Pelleas and Etarre*, two books of saccharine sentimentality, Gale returned to Portage to write a series of novels and tales, including *Friendship Village*, *Friendship Village Love Stories*, *Neighborhood Stories*, and *Peace in Friendship Village*. Unlike the meanness of Lewis's Gopher Prairie, the grotesquery of Anderson's Winesburg, or the enervation of Garland's Middle Border, Gale's Friendship Village, though not so sentimentally drawn as her earlier Romance Island, was an idyllic and hospitable town dedicated to children, family, and community.

However, her pastoral rendering of Friendship Village obscured her growing concerns with the issues and movements of her day — pacifism, women's rights, prohibition, civil liberties, progressivism, and others — even as it did her labors in their behalf: writing pamphlets and delivering speeches, campaigning for the progressive La Follettes of her native Wisconsin, joining the ill-fated protest against the execution of Sacco and Vanzetti. In truth, Gale's increasingly realistic image of the world found its way even into the Friendship Village tales, which by the decade's end had begun to compromise the idyll with an occasional suggestion of reform. More important, her growing politicization was signaled in three novels of social relevance, all written during the Friendship Village period: *Heart's*

Kindred, a pacifist piece; *A Daughter of the Morning*, a portrait of the working woman's plight; and what is perhaps her best work, *Birth*. In the last of these three, readers found a vision of small-town Americana whose acerbity approaches that of the better-known realist writers of her time. Indeed, *Birth*, along with *Miss Lulu Bett*, an equally acerbic novel of village life for which, after dramatization, Gale was awarded the Pulitzer Prize, nearly established their author as an authentic if minor realist writer.

Zona Gale soon moved on, however. Prompted on a personal level by the death of her doting mother and more generally by the rise of a variety of New Thought movements in which she took interest, Gale moved from realism to spiritualism and the occult, a vantage point from which she wrote a number of short stories and also *Preface to a Life*, a novel whose major character, though living on some higher astral plane, is understood by his fellow villagers to be insane.

Her talent having been a modest one, Zona Gale has fallen into the obscurity which most critics agree she deserves. Still, she was in tune with many of the social currents of her day. And had her powers of imagination been greater, had her artistic control been stronger, her contribution to American letters might well have been of a higher rank.

—Bruce A. Lohof

GALSWORTHY, John.   English.   Born in Combe, Surrey, 14 August 1867. Educated at the Sangeen School, Bournemouth, 1876; Harrow School, 1881–86; New College, Oxford, 1886–89; entered Lincoln's Inn, London, 1889: called to the Bar, 1890. Married Ada Cooper in 1905. Travelled in the United States, Canada, Australia, New Zealand, and the South Seas, then briefly practised law until 1895; thereafter a full-time writer. President, P.E.N. Club, 1921. Recipient: Nobel Prize for Literature, 1932. D.Litt.: Oxford University, 1931. Honorary Fellow, New College, Oxford. Honorary Member, American Academy of Arts and Sciences, 1931. Order of Merit, 1929. *Died 31 January 1933.*

PUBLICATIONS

Collections

The Galsworthy Reader, edited by Anthony West.   1967.

Fiction

From the Four Winds (stories).   1897.
Jocelyn.   1898.
Villa Rubein.   1900; revised edition, 1909.
A Man of Devon.   1901; revised edition, with *Villa Rubein*, 1909.
The Island Pharisees.   1904; revised edition, 1908.
The Man of Property.   1906; *In Chancery*, 1920; *Awakening*, 1920; *To Let*, 1921; complete version as *The Forsyte Saga*, 1922.
The Country House.   1907.

Fraternity. 1909.
The Patrician. 1911.
The Dark Flower. 1913.
The Freelands. 1915.
Beyond. 1917.
Five Tales. 1918; as *The First and the Last,* and *The Stoic,* 2 vols., 1920; as *The Apple Tree and Other Tales,* 1965.
The Burning Spear, Being the Adventures of Mr. John Lavender in Time of War. 1919.
Saint's Progress. 1919.
Tatterdemalion (stories). 1920.
Captures (stories). 1923.
The White Monkey. 1924; *The Silver Spoon,* 1926; *Swan Song,* 1928; complete version as *A Modern Comedy,* 1929.
Caravan: The Assembled Tales. 1925.
Two Forsyte Interludes. 1927.
On Forsyte 'change. 1930.
Soames and Flag. 1930.
Maid in Waiting. 1931; *Flowering Wilderness,* 1932; *Over the River,* 1933 (as *One More River,* 1933); complete version as *End of the Chapter,* 1934.
Corduroys. 1937.
The Rocks. 1937.
'Nyasha. 1939.

Plays

The Silver Box (produced 1906). 1909; edited by John Hampden, 1964.
Joy: A Play on the Letter I (produced 1907). 1909.
Strife (produced 1909). 1909.
Justice (produced 1910). 1910; edited by John Hampden, 1964.
The Little Dream: An Allegory (produced 1911). 1911; revised edition, 1912.
The Pigeon: A Fantasy (produced 1912). 1912.
The Eldest Son: A Domestic Drama (produced 1912). 1912.
The Fugitive (produced 1913). 1913.
The Mob (produced 1914). 1914.
The Little Man (produced 1915). In *Six Short Plays,* 1921.
A Bit o' Love (produced 1915). 1915.
The Foundations: An Extravagant Play (produced 1917). 1920.
The Skin Game (produced 1920). 1920.
The Defeat (produced 1920) In *Six Short Plays,* 1921.
A Family Man (produced 1921). 1922.
The First and the Last (produced 1921). In *Six Short Plays,* 1921.
Six Short Plays (includes *The First and the Last, The Little Man, Hallmarked, Defeat, The Sun, Punch and Go*). 1921.
The Sun (produced 1922). In *Six Short Plays,* 1921.
Punch and Go (produced 1924). In *Six Short Plays,* 1921.
Loyalties (produced 1922). 1922.
Windows: A Comedy for Idealists and Others (produced 1922). 1922.
The Forest, from his own story "A Stoic" (produced 1924). 1924.
Old English (produced 1924). 1924.
The Show (produced 1925). 1925.
Escape: An Episodic Play (produced 1926). 1926; edited by John Hampden, 1964.
Plays. 1928.
Exiled: An Evolutionary Comedy (produced 1929). 1929.

The Roof (produced 1929). 1929.
Carmen, with Ada Galsworthy, from the opera by Henri Meilhac and Ludovic Halevy,
music by Bizet. 1932.
The Winter Garden: Four Dramatic Pieces (includes *Escape – Episode VII, The Golden
Eggs, Similes, The Winter Garden*). 1935.

Verse

Moods, Songs, and Doggerels. 1912.
Five Poems. 1919.
Verses New and Old. 1926.
Collected Poems, edited by Ada Galsworthy. 1934.

Other

A Commentary. 1908.
A Justification of the Censorship of Plays. 1909.
A Motley. 1910.
The Inn of Tranquillity: Studies and Essays. 1912.
The Little Man and Other Satires. 1915; as *Abracadabra and Other Satires*, 1924.
A Sheaf. 1916.
The Land: A Plea. 1917.
Addresses in America. 1919.
Another Sheaf. 1919.
Memorable Days. 1924.
Castles in Spain and Other Screeds. 1927.
Works. 26 vols., 1927–34.
Two Essays on Conrad. 1930.
Author and Critic. 1935.
Glimpses and Reflections. 1937.
Forsytes, Pendyces, and Others, edited by Ada Galsworthy. 1935.
Autobiographical Letters: A Correspondence with Frank Harris. 1933.
Letters 1900–1932, edited by Edward Garnett. 1934.
My Galsworthy Story (letters), by Margaret Morris. 1967.

Editor, with Ada Galsworthy, *Ex Libris John Galsworthy.* 1933.

Bibliography: *A Bibliography of the Works of Galsworthy* by H. V. Marrot, 1928; *Galsworthy:
His First Editions* by G. H. Fabes, 1932; "Galsworthy: An Annotated Bibliography of
Writings about Him" by H. E. Gerber, with continuation by E. E. Stevens, in *English
Literature in Transition 1* and 7, 1958, 1967; *Galsworthy the Dramatist: A Bibliography of
Criticism* by E. H. Mikhail, 1971.

Reading List: *The Life and Letters of Galsworthy* by H. V. Marrot, 1935; *Galsworthy* by
Ralph H. Mottram, 1953; *The Man of Principle: A View of Galsworthy* by Dudley Barker,
1963; *Galsworthy* by David Holloway, 1968; *Galsworthy: A Biography* by Catherine Dupré,
1976.

*   *   *

John Galsworthy's reputation, like that of many writers, fell steeply in the twenty years after his death, partly for the purely snobbish reason that he was not born working-class. Today it has greatly recovered, and he is recognized as standing no less high than such of his near-contemporaries as Wells, Ford, and Bennett, and in the theatrical field not so far below the mighty Shaw. Galsworthy's recovery of reputation is in part due to the immensely successful television dramatization of *The Forsyte Saga* which went – and is probably still going – round the world. In addition, there has recently been a more sober reassessment of writers of Galsworthy's heyday. The former glib dismissals of him as genteel, a moralising humanitarian, a man too aware of the "claims of niceness" will not do for those who have been reawakened to *The Forsyte Saga*, or who have seen some of the splendid revivals of his plays.

The Forsyte Saga itself and its pendants (two trilogies and additional single works), gradually written and assembled over more than twenty years, is far from consistent in tone and style. Its early volumes picture a largely departed way of life – of the upper business and professional classes in late Victorian and early Edwardian times – and its later books are a unique evocation of the lives of those same classes in the 1920's. But today's fashionable interest in Victoriana, and nostalgia generally – including perhaps a bit of envy among middle-class readers for the picture of a spacious and expansive world – are not enough to explain the interest in Galsworthy's novels. The books are full of interesting characters in a changing and developing time, resulting in an almost documentary view of the period. There are strong dramatic situations, with a rich series of plots. And though Galsworthy is short on humour, he is strong on irony. Even outside the strongly focused story of *The Forsyte Saga* itself (*The Man of Property*, *In Chancery*, *Awakening*, and *To Let*), the story of the family and its acquaintances and relations continue in later volumes which are far from negligible as fiction.

His plays have made an even greater come-back in the 1960's and 1970's, largely based on successes on the stage. Young critics acclaim his dramatic talent, his rich and subtle realism and, as Gareth Lloyd Evans in *The Language of Modern Drama* says, "a quality of associativeness in the language." Evans notes that he is a great master of the pause in dialogue, in creating *tableaux vivants*, and in stage directions which are both evocative and of great practical help to the actor.

Often his plays take a theme of the day, almost from a newspaper account, and present it as a problem, but with a wide imaginative and intellectual breadth. The treatment sometimes attains something approaching poetry, and one may detect the cadences of Synge. In this, in fact, he has been compared to Pinter. Galsworthy himself points out in an essay in the collection *Candelabra* (in *Works*, 1932) that though he sets problems in many of his best plays – *Strife*, *Justice*, *The Silver Box*, and *The Skin Game* – he does not try to solve them or to effect direct reform; he seeks only "to present truth and, gripping with it his readers or his audience, to produce in them a sort of mental and moral fermenting, whereby vision may be enlarged, imagination livened, and understanding promoted." Like Shaw, Galsworthy shows society to itself. "He was perhaps," writes Gareth Lloyd Evans, "the last prose dramatist of undoubted importance who realized that prose itself need not be the servant alone of the world of public man but can minister to matters more deeply interfused and less palpable."

—Kenneth Young

GALT, John. Scottish. Born in Irvine, Ayrshire, 2 May 1779. Educated at Irvine Grammar School; schools in Greenock; Lincoln's Inn, London, 1809–12. Married Elizabeth Tilloch in 1813; three sons. Clerk, Greenock Customs House, 1796, and for James Miller and Company, Greenock, 1796–1804; engaged in business ventures in London, 1805–08; travelled with Byron from Gibraltar to Malta, 1809; agent for a merchant in Gibraltar,

1812–13; Editor, *Political Review*, London, 1812, and *New British Theatre* monthly, London, 1814–15; Secretary, Royal Caledonian Society, 1815; regular contributor to the *Monthly Magazine*, 1817–23, and to *Blackwoods's Magazine* from 1819; lobbyist for the Edinburgh and Glasgow Union Canal Company, 1819–20, and later for other clients; Secretary, 1823–26, and Superintendent, resident in Canada, 1826–29, to the Canada Company, formed for the purchase of crown land; founded the town of Guelph, Ontario; imprisoned for debt after his return to England, 1829; Editor, *The Courier* newspaper, London, 1830; contributor to *Fraser's Magazine* from 1830; lived in Greenock, 1834 until his death. *Died 11 April 1839.*

PUBLICATIONS

Collections

> *Works*, edited by D. S. Meldrum and William Roughead.   10 vols., 1936.
> *Poems: A Selection*, edited by G. H. Needler.   1954.
> *Collected Poems*, edited by Hamilton Baird Timothy.   1969.

Fiction

> *The Majolo: A Tale.*   1816.
> *The Earthquake: A Tale.*   1820.
> *Glenfell; or, Macdonalds and Campbells.*   1820.
> *Annals of the Parish; or, The Chronicle of Dalmailing During the Ministry of the Reverend Micah Balwhidder.*   1821; edited by James Kinsley, 1967.
> *The Ayrshire Legatees; or, The Pringle Family.*   1821.
> *Sir Andrew Wylie of That Ilk.*   1822.
> *The Provost.*   1822; edited by Ian A. Gordon, 1973.
> *The Steam-Boat.*   1822.
> *The Entail; or, The Lairds of Grippy*, edited by David M. Moir.   1822; edited by Ian A. Gordon, 1970.
> *The Gathering of the West; or, We've Come to See the King*, with *The Ayrshire Legatee.*   1823; edited by Bradford A. Booth, 1939.
> *Ringan Gilhaize; or, The Covenanters.*   1823; edited by George Douglas, 1899.
> *The Spaewife: A Tale of the Scottish Chronicles.*   1823.
> *Rothelan: A Romance of the English Histories* (stories).   1824.
> *The Omen.*   1826.
> *The Last of the Lairds; or, The Life and Opinions of Malachi Mailings, Esq., of Auldbiggins*, completed by David M. Moir.   1826.
> *Lawrie Todd; or, The Settlers in the Woods.*   1830; revised edition, 1849.
> *Southennan.*   1830.
> *Bogle Corbet; or, The Emigrants.*   1831.
> *The Member.*   1832; edited by Ian A. Gordon, 1976.
> *The Radical.*   1832.
> *Stanley Buxton; or, The Schoolfellows.*   1832.
> *Eben Erskine; or, The Traveller.*   1833.
> *The Stolen Child: A Tale of the Town.*   1833.
> *The Ouranoulogos; or, The Celestial Volume.*   1833.
> *Stories of the Study.*   1833.
> *The Howdie and Other Tales*, edited by William Roughead.   1923.
> *A Rich Man and Other Stories*, edited by William Roughead.   1925.

Plays

> The Tragedies of Maddelen, Agamemnon, Lady Macbeth, Antonia, and
> Clytemnestra. 1812.
> The Apostate; Hector; Love, Honour, and Interest; The Masquerade; The Mermaid;
> Orpheus; The Prophetess; The Watchhouse; The Witness, in The New British
> Theatre. 1814–15.
> The Appeal (produced 1818). 1818.

Verse

> The Battle of Largs: A Gothic Poem, with Several Miscellaneous Pieces. 1804.
> The Crusade. 1816.
> Poems. 1833.
> Efforts by an Invalid. 1835.
> A Contribution to the Greenock Calamity Fund. 1835.
> The Demon of Destiny and Other Poems. 1839.

Other

> Cursory Reflections on Political and Commercial Topics. 1812.
> Voyages and Travels in the Years 1809, 1810, and 1811. 1812.
> The Life and Administration of Cardinal Wolsey. 1812.
> Letters from the Levant. 1813.
> The Life and Studies of Benjamin West. 2 vols., 1816–20; as The Progress of Genius,
> 1832; edited by Nathalia Wright, 1960.
> The Wandering Jew; or, The Travels and Observations of Hareach the Prolonged
> (juvenile). 1820.
> All the Voyages round the World. 1820.
> A Tour of Europe and Asia. 2 vols., 1820.
> George the Third, His Court and Family. 2 vols., 1820.
> Pictures Historical and Biographical, Drawn from English, Scottish, and Irish History
> (juvenile). 2 vols., 1821.
> The National Reader and Spelling Book. 2 vols., 1821.
> A New General School Atlas. 1822.
> The English Mother's First Catechism for Her Children. 1822.
> Modern Geography and History. 1823.
> The Bachelor's Wife: A Selection of Curious and Interesting Extracts (essays). 1824.
> The Life of Lord Byron. 1830.
> The Lives of the Players. 2 vols., 1831.
> The Canadas as They at Present Commend Themselves to the Enterprise of Emigrants,
> Colonists, and Capitalists, edited by Andrew Picken. 1832.
> The Autobiography. 2 vols., 1833.
> The Literary Life and Miscellanies. 3 vols., 1834.

> Editor, The Original and Rejected Theatre, and The New British Theatre. 4 vols.,
> 1814–15.
> Editor, Diary Illustrative of the Times of George the Fourth, vols. 3–4, by Lady Charlotte
> Bury. 1838.
> Editor, Records of Real Life in the Palace and Cottage, by Harriet Pigott. 1839.

Reading List: *Galt* by Jennie W. Aberdein, 1936; *Galt and 18th Century Scottish Philosophy,* 1954, and *Galt's Scottish Stories,* 1959, both by Erik Frykman; *Susan Ferrier and Galt* by William M. Parker, 1965; *Galt: The Life of a Writer* by Ian A. Gordon, 1972.

*   *   *

John Galt was the author of well over forty volumes, ranging from novels and biography to travel, art criticism, drama, and verse. The reader has to discriminate between those (written under financial pressure) of slight literary interest and a central group of novels of distinctive quality. Recent evaluative criticism and publication for the first time of accurate texts have led to a revival of interest in Galt and a consequent revaluation of his work as a novelist.

Galt's major contribution to the novel was his sensitive and yet ironic portrayal of the rural Scotland of the late eighteenth century, a period when an agricultural society was giving way to the new industrial growth. Galt welcomed the advantages of industrial development, while at the same time regretting the passing of the old order and the decline of the rural sense of community. He had an acute ear for Scottish dialect speech and a sharp eye for eccentricities of character. The result in his best novels is an ironic blend of realistic comedy and a romantic nostalgia for a disappearing rural society. *Annals of the Parish* records fifty years of change, narrated by the shrewd parish minister Micah Balwhidder; *The Entail* is a three-generation study of obsession, the avaricious Claud and his wife Leddy Grippy (an indefatigable and loquacious survivor) both memorable portraits; in *The Last of the Lairds* the elderly Malachi Mailings wages a comic rearguard action against the new age of improvements.

The three other novels in Galt's Scottish group are variations on his main theme. In *The Ayrshire Legatees* and *The Steam-Boat* Galt transports his rural characters to metropolitan London, for the sake of comic contrast. *The Provost* (highly praised by Coleridge and regarded by Galt as his best work) is an acute study of the machiavellian politics of power, set in a small Scottish town. The theme was later expanded by Galt for a wider stage in *The Member*, the first political novel in English and a devastating study of the unreformed House of Commons. On its republication in 1976, a contemporary critic found it "comes close to the sublime on many pages." Two other Galt novels are worth noting: *Ringan Gilhaize*, a powerful historical novel written as a rebuttal of Scott's *Old Mortality*, and *Bogle Corbet*, republished in Canada in 1977 as illustrating "the first and still typical Canadian anti-hero."

Galt's characterisation and his handling of pithy Scots dialect has always ensured him a place as a comic writer. The recent revival of interest in Galt's work, following the republication of novels long out of print, has led to a concentration on the more serious sociological implications of his fiction. Galt's forte is the short "autobiographical" novel in which the central character, self-deceived, reveals himself. Though the comedy of *Annals of the Parish* continues to appeal, *The Provost* is the best example of Galt's ironic technique and skill as a novelist.

—Ian A. Gordon

GARDNER, Erle Stanley. Pseudonyms: A. A. Fair, Carleton Kendrake, and Charles J. Kenny. American. Born in Malden, Massachusetts, 17 July 1889; as a child lived with his family in mining camps in California, Oregon, and the Klondike. Educated at Palo Alto High School, California; studied law in the offices of various California lawyers; admitted to the California bar, 1911. Married 1) Natalie Talbert in 1912 (died, 1968), one daughter; 2) Agnes

Jean Bethell in 1968. Lawyer in Oxnard, California, 1911–16, and in Ventura, California, 1916–33; also, President, Consolidated Sales Company, San Francisco, 1918–21; began to write in 1921; visited China, 1931; full-time writer from 1933. Served as President of the Ventura County Bar Association; Co-Founder, "Court of Last Resort," *Argosy* magazine. Recipient: Mystery Writers of America Grand Master Award, 1961. Honorary alumnus: Kansas City University, 1955; D.L.: McGeorge College of Law, Sacramento, California, 1956. *Died 11 March 1970.*

PUBLICATIONS

Fiction

> *The Case of the Velvet Claws.* 1933.
> *The Case of the Sulky Girl.* 1933.
> *The Case of the Curious Bride.* 1934.
> *The Case of the Howling Dog.* 1934.
> *The Case of the Lucky Legs.* 1934.
> *The Case of the Counterfeit Eye.* 1935.
> *The Case of the Caretaker's Cat.* 1935.
> *The Clue of the Forgotten Murder.* 1935.
> *This Is Murder.* 1935.
> *The Case of the Sleepwalker's Niece.* 1936.
> *The Case of the Stuttering Bishop.* 1937.
> *The Case of the Dangerous Dowager.* 1937.
> *The Case of the Lame Canary.* 1937.
> *The D.A. Calls It Murder.* 1937.
> *Murder up My Sleeve.* 1937.
> *The Case of the Shoplifter's Shoe.* 1938.
> *The Case of the Substitute Face.* 1938.
> *The D.A. Holds a Candle.* 1938.
> *The Case of the Perjured Parrot.* 1939.
> *The Case of the Rolling Bones.* 1939.
> *The D.A. Draws a Circle.* 1939.
> *The Bigger They Come.* 1939; as *Lam to the Slaughter,* 1939.
> *The Case of the Baited Hook.* 1940.
> *Gold Comes in Bricks.* 1940.
> *Turn on the Heat.* 1940.
> *The Case of the Silent Partner.* 1940.
> *The D.A. Goes to Trial.* 1940.
> *The Case of the Haunted Husband.* 1941.
> *The Case of the Turning Tide.* 1941.
> *The Case of the Empty Tin.* 1941.
> *Double or Quits.* 1941.
> *Spill the Jackpot!* 1941.
> *Bats Fly at Dusk.* 1942.
> *Owls Don't Blink.* 1942.
> *The Case of the Careless Kitten.* 1942.
> *The Case of the Drowning Duck.* 1942.
> *The D.A. Cooks a Goose.* 1942.
> *The Case of the Buried Clock.* 1943.
> *The Case of the Drowsy Mosquito.* 1943.

The Case of the Smoking Chimney. 1943.
Cats Prowl at Night. 1943.
Give 'em the Ax. 1944; as *An Axe to Grind.* 1951.
The D.A. Calls a Turn. 1944.
The Case of the Crooked Candle. 1944.
The Case of the Black-Eyed Blonde. 1944.
The Case of the Half-Wakened Wife. 1945.
The Case of the Golddigger's Purse. 1945.
The Case of the Borrowed Brunette. 1946.
The Case of the Backward Mule. 1946.
The D.A. Breaks the Seal. 1946.
Crows Don't Count. 1946.
Fools Die on Friday. 1947.
The Case of the Fan-Dancer's Horse. 1947.
The Case of the Lazy Lover. 1947.
Two Clues: The Clue of the Runaway Blonde, The Clue of the Hungry Horse. 1947.
The D.A. Takes a Chance. 1948.
The Case of the Vagabond Virgin. 1948.
The Case of the Lonely Heiress. 1948.
The Case of the Dubious Bridegroom. 1949.
The D.A. Breaks an Egg. 1949.
Bedrooms Have Windows. 1949.
The Case of the Cautious Coquette. 1949.
The Case of the Musical Cow. 1950.
The Case of the Negligent Nymph. 1950.
The Case of the One-Eyed Witness. 1951.
The Case of the Angry Mourner. 1951.
The Case of the Fiery Fingers. 1951.
The Case of the Moth-Eaten Mink. 1952.
The Case of the Grinning Gorilla. 1952.
Top of the Heap. 1952.
Some Women Won't Wait. 1953.
The Case of the Green-Eyed Sister. 1953.
The Case of the Hesitant Hostess. 1953.
The Case of the Runaway Corpse. 1954.
The Case of the Fugitive Nurse. 1954.
The Case of the Restless Redhead. 1954.
The Case of the Glamorous Ghost. 1955.
The Case of the Sun Bather's Diary. 1955.
The Case of the Nervous Accomplice. 1955.
The Case of the Terrified Typist. 1956.
The Case of the Gilded Lily. 1956.
The Case of the Demure Defendant. 1956.
Beware the Curves. 1956.
Some Slips Don't Show. 1957.
You Can Die Laughing. 1957.
The Case of the Daring Decoy. 1957.
The Case of the Lucky Loser. 1957.
The Case of the Screaming Woman. 1957.
The Case of the Long-Legged Models. 1958.
The Case of the Foot-Loose Doll. 1958.
The Case of the Calendar Girl. 1958.
The Count of Nine. 1958.
Pass the Gravy. 1959.

The Case of the Waylaid Wolf. 1960.
The Case of the Singing Skirt. 1959.
The Case of the Mythical Monkeys. 1959.
The Case of the Deadly Toy. 1959.
The Case of the Shapely Shadow. 1960.
The Case of the Duplicate Daughter. 1960.
Kept Women Can't Quit. 1960.
Bachelors Get Lonely. 1961.
Shills Can't Cash Chips. 1961; as *Stop at the Red Light,* 1962.
The Case of the Bigamous Spouse. 1961.
The Case of the Spurious Spinster. 1961.
The Case of the Reluctant Model. 1961.
The Case of the Blonde Bonanza. 1962.
The Case of the Ice-Cold Hands. 1962.
Try Anything Once. 1962.
Fish or Cut Bait. 1963.
The Case of the Amorous Aunt. 1963.
The Case of the Mischievous Doll. 1963.
The Case of the Stepdaughter's Secret. 1963.
The Case of the Phantom Fortune. 1964.
Up for Grabs. 1964.
The Case of the Horrified Heirs. 1964.
The Case of the Daring Divorcee. 1964.
The Case of the Crimson Kiss (stories). 1964; augmented edition, 1971.
The Case of the Beautiful Beggar. 1965.
Cut Thin to Win. 1965.
The Case of the Troubled Trustee. 1965.
Widows Wear Weeds. 1966.
The Case of the Worried Waitress. 1966.
The Case of the Queenly Contestant. 1967.
Traps Need New Bait. 1967.
The Case of the Careless Cupid. 1968.
The Case of the Murderer's Bride and Other Stories, edited by Ellery Queen. 1969.
The Case of the Fabulous Fake. 1969.
All Grass Isn't Green. 1970.
The Case of the Crying Swallow (stories). 1971.
The Case of the Fenced-In Woman. 1972.
The Case of the Irate Witness (stories). 1972.
The Case of the Postponed Murder. 1973.

Other

The Land of Shorter Shadows. 1948.
The Court of Last Resort. 1952.
Neighborhood Frontiers. 1954.
Hunting the Desert Whale. 1960.
Hovering over Baja. 1961.
The Hidden Heart of Baja. 1962.
The Desert Is Yours. 1963.
The World of Water. 1965.
Hunting Lost Mines by Helicopter. 1965.
Off the Beaten Track in Baja. 1967.
Gypsy Days on the Delta. 1967.

Mexico's Magic Square. 1968.
Host with the Big Hat (on Mexico). 1969.
Drifting Down the Delta. 1969.
Cops on Campus and Crime in the Street. 1970.

Bibliography: *Gardner: A Checklist* by E. H. Mundell, 1968.

Reading List: *The Case of Gardner* by Alva Johnston, 1947; *Gardner: The Case of the Real Perry Mason* (includes bibliography) by Dorothy B. Hughes, 1978.

*   *   *

Erle Stanley Gardner spent much of his childhood traveling with his mining-engineer father through the remote regions of California, Oregon, and the Klondike. In his teens he not only boxed for money but promoted a number of unlicensed matches. Soon after entering college he was, by his own account, expelled for slugging a professor. But in the practice of law he found the form of combat he seemed born to master. He was admitted to the California bar in 1911 and opened an office in Oxnard, where he represented the Chinese community and gained a reputation for flamboyant trial tactics. In one case, for instance, he had dozens of Chinese merchants exchange identities so that he could discredit a policeman's identification of a client. In the early 1920's he began to write western and mystery stories for magazines, and eventually he was turning out and selling the equivalent of a short novel every three nights while still lawyering during the business day. With the sale of his first novel in 1933 he gave up the practice of law and devoted himself to full-time writing, or more precisely to dictating. Thanks to the popularity of his series characters — lawyer-detective Perry Mason, his loyal secretary Della Street, his private detective Paul Drake, and the foxy trio of Sergeant Holcomb, Lieutenant Tragg and District Attorney Hamilton Burger — Gardner became one of the wealthiest mystery writers of all time.

The 82 Mason adventures from *The Case of the Velvet Claws* (1933) to the posthumously published *The Case of the Postponed Murder* (1973) contain few of the literary graces. Characterization and description are perfunctory and often reduced to a few lines that are repeated in similar situations book after book. Indeed virtually every word not within quotation marks could be deleted and little would be lost. For what vivifies these novels is the sheer readability, the breakneck pacing, the involuted plots, the fireworks displays of courtroom tactics (many based on gimmicks Gardner used in his own law practice), and the dialogue, where each line is a jab in a complex form of oral combat.

The first nine Masons are steeped in the hardboiled tradition of *Black Mask* magazine, their taut understated realism leavened with raw wit, sentimentality, and a positive zest for the dog-eat-dog milieu of the free enterprise system during its worst depression. The Mason of these novels is a tiger in the social-Darwinian jungle, totally self-reliant, asking no favors, despising the weaklings who want society to care for them, willing to take any risk for a client no matter how unfairly the client plays the game with him. Asked what he does for a living, he replies: "I fight!" or "I am a paid gladiator." He will bribe policemen for information, loosen a hostile witness' tongue by pretending to frame him for a murder, twist the evidence to get a guilty client acquitted and manipulate estate funds to prevent a guilty non-client from obtaining money for his defense. Besides *Velvet Claws*, perhaps the best early Mason novels are *The Case of the Howling Dog* and *The Case of the Curious Bride* (both 1934).

From the late 1930's to the late 1950's the main influence on Gardner was not *Black Mask* but the *Saturday Evening Post*, which serialized most of the Mason novels before book publication. In these novels the tough-guy notes are muted, "love interest" plays a stronger role, and Mason is less willing to play fast and loose with the law. Still the oral combat remains breathlessly exciting, the pace never slackens and the plots are as labyrinthine as before, most of them centering on various sharp-witted and greedy people battling over control of capital. Mason, of course, is Gardner's alter ego throughout the series, but in several novels of the second period another author-surrogate arrives on the scene in the person of a philosophical old desert rat or prospector who delights in living alone in the wilderness, discrediting by his example the greed of the urban wealth – and power-hunters. Among the best cases of this period are *Lazy Lover*; *Hesitant Hostess*, which deals with Mason's breaking down a single prosecution witness; and *Lucky Loser* and *Foot-Loose Doll* with their spectacularly complex plots.

Gardner worked without credit as script supervisor for the long-running *Perry Mason* television series (1957–66), starring Raymond Burr, and within a few years television's restrictive influence had infiltrated the new Mason novels. The lawyer evolved into a ponderous bureaucrat mindful of the law's nicetices, just as Burr played him, and the plots became chaotic and the courtroom sequences mediocre, as happened all too often in the TV scripts. But by the mid-1960's the libertarian decisions of the Supreme Court under Chief Justice Earl Warren had already undermined a basic premise of the Mason novels, namely that defendants menaced by the sneaky tactics of police and prosecutors needed a pyrotechnician like Mason in their corner. Once the Court ruled that such tactics required reversal of convictions gained thereby, Mason had lost his *raison d'être*.

Several other detective series sprang from Gardner's dictating machine during his peak years. The 29 novels he wrote under the by-line of A.A. Fair about diminutive private eye Donald Lam and his huge irascible partner Bertha Cool are often preferred over the Masons because of their fusion of corkscrew plots with fresh writing, characterizations, and humor. The high spots of the series are *The Bigger They Come* and *Beware the Curves*. And in his nine books about small-town district attorney Doug Selby Gardner reversed the polarities of the Mason series, making the prosecutor his hero and the defense lawyer the oft-confounded trickster. But most of Gardner's reputation stems from Perry Mason, and his best novels in both this and his other series offer abundant evidence of his natural storytelling talent, which is likely to retain its appeal as long as people read at all.

—Francis M. Nevins, Jr.

GARLAND, (Hannibal) Hamlin. American. Born near West Salem, Wisconsin, 16 September 1860; as a boy worked with his father on a farm in Iowa. Educated at the Cedar Valley Seminary, Osage, Iowa, graduated 1881. Married Zuline Taft in 1899; two daughters. Homesteader in the Dakotas, 1883–84; Teacher, Boston School of Oratory, 1884–91; full-time writer from 1891; lived in Chicago, 1893–1916, and in New York City from 1916. Founder/President, Cliff Dwellers, Chicago, 1907. Recipient: Pulitzer Prize, for biography, 1922; Roosevelt Memorial Association Gold Medal for Literature, 1931. Honorary degrees: University of Wisconsin, Madison, 1926; Northwestern University, Evanston, Illinois, 1933. Member, 1918, and Director, 1920, American Academy of Arts and Letters. *Died 4 March 1940.*

PUBLICATIONS

Fiction

Main-Travelled Roads: Six Mississippi Valley Stories. 1891; revised edition, 1907; edited by Thomas A. Bledsoe, 1954.

A Member of the Third House. 1892.
Jason Edwards: An Average Man. 1892.
A Little Norsk; or, Ol' Pap's Flaxen. 1892.
A Spoil of Office. 1892.
Prairie Folks (stories). 1892; revised edition, 1899.
Rose of Dutcher's Coolly. 1895; revised edition, 1899; edited by Donald Pizer, 1969.
Wayside Courtships (stories). 1897.
The Spirit of Sweetwater. 1898; revised edition, as *Witch's Gold,* 1906.
The Eagle's Heart. 1900.
Her Mountain Lover. 1901.
The Captain of the Gray-Horse Troop. 1902.
Hesper. 1903.
The Light of the Star. 1904.
The Tyranny of the Dark. 1905.
Money Magic. 1907; as *Mart Haney's Mate,* 1922.
The Moccasin Ranch. 1909.
Cavanagh, Forest Ranger. 1910.
Other Main-Travelled Roads (includes *Prairie Folks* and *Wayside Courtships*). 1910.
Victor Ollnee's Discipline. 1911.
The Forester's Daughter. 1914.
They of the High Trails (stories). 1916.

Play

Under the Wheel. 1890.

Verse

Prairie Songs. 1893.
Iowa, O Iowa! 1935.

Other

Crumbling Idols: Twelve Essays on Art. 1894; edited by Jane Johnson, 1960.
Ulysses S. Grant: His Life and Character. 1898.
The Trail of the Goldseekers: A Record of Travel in Prose and Verse. 1899.
Boy Life on the Prairie. 1899; revised edition, 1908.
The Long Trail (juvenile). 1907.
The Shadow World. 1908.
A Son of the Middle Border. 1917; edited by Henry M. Christman, 1962.
A Daughter of the Middle Border. 1921.
The Book of the American Indian. 1923.
Trail-Makers of the Middle Border. 1926.
The Westward March of American Settlement. 1927.
Back-Trailers from the Middle Border. 1928.
Roadside Meetings. 1930.
Companions on the Trail: A Literary Chronicle. 1931.
My Friendly Contemporaries: A Literary Log. 1932.
Afternoon Neighbors: Further Excerpts from a Literary Log. 1934.
Joys of the Trail. 1935.
Forty Years of Psychic Research: A Plain Narrative of Fact. 1936.

The Mystery of the Buried Crosses: A Narrative of Psychic Exploration. 1939. *Diaries*, edited by Donald Pizer. 1968.

Bibliography: *Henry Blake Fuller and Garland: A Reference Guide* by Charles L. P. Silet, 1977.

Reading List: *Garland: A Biography* by Jean Holloway, 1960; *Garland's Early Work and Career* by Donald Pizer, 1960; *Garland: L'Homme et l'Oeuvre* by Robert Mane, 1968.

*   *   *

Hamlin Garland played an important role in the development of realism in America, but the work of enduring significance that he bequeathed to the last half of the 20th century is modest. One volume of stories, one novel, and his autobiography are all that a contemporary reader need bother about. Garland is one of the most uneven of American writers, for the gulf is wide between the stories in *Main-Travelled Roads* and the popular fiction he later turned out for the *Saturday Evening Post*. His fall from realism into sentimental romance is simply embarrassing.

After Garland left the Midwest and went to Boston to become a writer, he was encouraged by Joseph Kirkland, a realist writer, to make use of his farm background. No authentic farmer yet had appeared in American literature, and the subject was virgin. This advice came in 1887 as Garland was returning from a visit to see his mother, who had had a stroke, and he was burning with indignation over the privations and injustices of farm life. In addition, the 1880's were a period of farm depression, for too much new land had been opened up too fast and the invention of farm machinery had over-stimulated production. Out of this context came the six stories that made up the original edition of *Main-Travelled Roads*. They are "A Branch Road," "Up the Coulé," "Among the Corn Rows," "The Return of a Private," "Under the Lion's Paw," and "Mrs. Ripley's Trip." Some take place in Wisconsin where Garland was born, some in Iowa where the Garlands homesteaded after the Civil War, and one makes use of the Dakotas where Garland homesteaded himself before leaving for Boston to become a writer. The general theme is the hard lot of the farmer, and especially the farm wife, but the stories are not all somber. "Mrs. Ripley's Trip" is bucolic comedy, and "Among the Corn Rows" ends with an elopement and high hopes. All of the stories, however, are filled with closely observed detail that make them good examples of literary realism. There are some naturalistic elements in the victimization of the characters by forces beyond their control, but Garland is not really a naturalist. It is above all the intensity of his feeling that carries these stories.

That Garland's compulsion to write these stories lay mostly in his anger of the moment and not in deeply held convictions is shown by subsequent developments. After he settled his mother in Wisconsin and began to prosper, he lost his zeal for social criticism. He was not dishonest, but he saw the world in terms of himself and later lapsed into a terrible respectability. He continued to write stories, however, and the six stories in *Main-Travelled Roads* eventually grew to twelve, but the later tales are inferior and lapse into sentimentality. He also produced another volume of somber tales, *Prairie Folks*, before his indignation abated, and he wrote four novels worth mentioning. The first, *A Little Norsk*, has something of the hard Dakota farm life in it, but it is marred by sentimentality. His best novel, and one that still can be recommended, is *Rose of Dutcher's Coolly*, the story of a farm girl who goes to the state university and then to Chicago to pursue a career. The detail is good, especially the childhood and adolescence of Rose on the farm, and it deals with feminist problems of the 1890's. *Jason Edwards* is single-tax propaganda written after Garland had met Henry George and become a supporter of the single-tax panacea for economic ills. *A Spoil of Office* is a populist novel attacking political corruption and reminding modern readers who stumble on

449

it that 1892 was the year that James Weaver led the United States' most successful third party movement.

Garland made a literary comeback in 1917 when he wrote his autobiography, *A Son of the Middle Border*. This is a first-rate work that ranks with the best that Garland accomplished in the 1890's. He followed this with three other volumes of family history: *A Daughter of the Middle Border*, *Trail-Makers of the Middle Border* (this one fictionalized), and *Back-Trailers from the Middle Border*, but these are less interesting than the first. Because Garland lived a long time and made a point of meeting writers and public figures, students of literary history will find considerable interest in his literary reminiscences: *Roadside Meetings*, *Companions on the Trail*, *My Friendly Contemporaries*, and *Afternoon Neighbors*. Also noteworthy is Garland's one venture into literary criticism, *Crumbling Idols*, in which he makes a strong defense of realism.

—James Woodress

GARNETT, David. English. Born in Brighton, Sussex, 9 March 1892; son of the writer Edward Garnett and the translator Constance Garnett. Educated at University College School, London, 1906–08; studied botany at the Royal College of Science, now Imperial College of Science and Technology, London, 1910–15, A.R.C.S. 1913, D.I.C. 1915. Conscientious objector during World War I: involved with the Friends' War Victims Relief Expedition; served as a Flight Lieutenant in the Royal Air Force Volunteer Reserve, 1939–40; Planning Officer and Historian, Political Warfare Executive, 1941–46. Married 1) Ray Marshall in 1921 (died, 1940); 2) Angelica Bell in 1942; six children. Partner, with Francis Birrell, in Birrell and Garnett, booksellers, London, 1920–24; Partner, with Birrell and Francis Meynell, Nonesuch Press, London, 1923–35; Literary Editor, *New Statesman and Nation*, London, 1932–34; Director, Rupert Hart-Davis Ltd., publishers, London, 1946–52. Recipient: Hawthornden Prize, 1923; Black Memorial Prize, 1923. Fellow, Imperial College, 1956. Companion of Literature, Royal Society of Literature, 1977. C.B.E. (Commander, Order of the British Empire), 1952. Lives in Montcuq, France.

PUBLICATIONS

Fiction

Dope Darling. 1919.
Lady into Fox. 1922.
A Man in the Zoo. 1924.
The Sailor's Return. 1925.
Go She Must! 1927.
The Old Dovecote and Other Stories. 1928.
No Love. 1929.
The Grasshoppers Come. 1931.
A Terrible Day (story). 1932.
Pocahontas; or, The Nonparell of Virginia. 1933.
Beany-Eye. 1935.

Aspects of Love. 1955.
A Shot in the Dark. 1958.
A Net for Venus. 1959.
Two by Two: A Story of Survival. 1963.
Ulterior Motives. 1966.
An Old Master and Other Stories. 1967.
A Clean Slate. 1971.
The Sons of the Falcon. 1972.
Purl and Plain and Other Stories. 1973.
Plough over the Bones. 1973.
The Master Cat: The True and Unexpurgated Story of Puss in Boots. 1974.
Up She Rises. 1977.

Other

A Rabbit in the Air: Notes from a Diary Kept While Learning to Handle an Aeroplane. 1932.
War in the Air, September 1939–May 1941. 1941.
The Golden Echo (autobiography): *The Golden Echo.* 1953; *Flowers of the Forest,* 1955; *The Familiar Faces,* 1962.
The White/Garnett Letters, with T. H. White, edited by Garnett. 1968.
First "Hippy" Revolution. 1970.

Editor, with others, *The Week-End Book.* 1924.
Editor, *The Letters of T. E. Lawrence.* 1938; as *The Selected Letters of T. E. Lawrence,* 1952.
Editor, *Fourteen Stories,* by Henry James. 1946.
Editor, *The Novels of Thomas Love Peacock.* 1948.
Editor, *The Essential T. E. Lawrence.* 1951.
Editor, *Carrington: Letters and Extracts from Her Diaries.* 1970.

Translator, *The Kitchen Garden and Its Management,* by Professor Gressent. 1919.
Translator, *A Voyage to the Island of the Articoles,* by André Maurois. 1929.
Translator, *338171 (Lawrence of Arabia),* by Victoria Ocampo. 1963.

*   *   *

In *Lady into Fox* the heroine becomes a vixen. In *A Man in the Zoo* the hero is exhibited as an example of *homo sapiens.* David Garnett, however, denies that he writes fantasy; he prefers the description "poetic realist." Certainly in the works which followed he has tended to describe the fantastic element of ordinary experience. Where the first two novels were fables, conjectural allegories (*Lady into Fox* he describes as the *reductio ad absurdum* of the problem of fidelity in love), the later work appears dispassionately to outline a world in which fact is stranger than fiction.

The fiction lies more in the romantic imagination, the fears, prejudices, and submerged animal nature, of his characters. In *The Sailor's Return* the negro wife is ironically depicted as a calm and civilized force attacked by the ignorance and barbarism of English villagers. In *Go She Must!* Ann Dunnock's escape from provincial life to bohemian Paris brings sensual fulfilment which in turn demands sorrow for Richard, the friend who had facilitated the move. Every gain represents another's loss; the human animal's territory is constantly threatened and he defends it with refined and devious savagery. Ann's father, after a life of repression and frustration as the village vicar, goes mad and, removing the windows, converts the vicarage into an open aviary. The primal need to live in closer harmony with nature (with truth), it is suggested, cannot be denied. Ann feels "no shame or anger, ... no irritation against the outside world but only pity." As a rationalist, an atheist and an admitted "libertine," Garnett saw the 1920's as an age of hope, although his novels usually record the interference of the old prejudices with that hope. He believed that "an age of reason and of love was succeeding one of madness, of suspicion and of hate."

It is this guarded optimism, expressing a positive delight in physical sensation, that colours his more important work. A friend of Lawrence, he shared the desire to celebrate the animal nature of man. But he is less willing to lambast those characters trapped by social hypocrisy. "I realised," he says in *The Golden Echo*, "I was a savage and an embarrassment to my friends." *No Love* is his *bildungsroman* about two boyhood friends, Benedict and Simon, the first educated by atheistical liberal parents, the second by strict conservative principles. On Tinder Island, their home, they begin equal and free yet ultimately the insensitivity and philistinism of Simon's father's world claims him. "What's wrong with Simon" is that "there's No Love. No Love in his heart. He has never learned what it is from other people." Garnett considers this "one of the best of my books ... there hangs about the whole story the indefinable melancholy and hopelessness of life." His "optimism," then, is relative. He looks forward to a world where eternal compromise and heartbreak will be accepted as the natural order. It is the optimism of one who loves truth above all things and finds solace in its acceptance. Resignation and despair he sees as the result of frustrated romanticism.

The moral structure of the earlier work relies, then, on a temperate rejection of the old world of clergymen, admirals, and provincial dignitaries and an assertion of the noble savagery of man. The romantic aeroplane expedition in *The Grasshoppers Come* results in the death of the lovers and the pilot's gruelling and strangely beautiful fight for survival. In *Beany-Eye* Joe Starling's insanity is largely the result of collective ignorance and persecution. He is "like a mortally wounded gorilla encompassed by pigmy enemies." Throughout, the straightforward, honest savage in all men is worried and tortured, his survival dependent upon "liberal" agencies.

Garnett's rebellion, however, is not angry; it is against his "birthright as a rebel and a puritan." He distrusts fanaticism and revolution; his affinities lie with the liberalism of Bloomsbury, and, like Waugh, he dislikes the Age of the Common Man. After a long gap, he began writing novels again in the 1950's. But these, while evoking the same melancholy acceptance of the relativity of human experience, express more the urbanity of a man of the world than the primitive force of his early work. Controlling and distorting passion now appears only as the charming naivety of *un souvenir léger*. Always a conscious artist, he maintains structural unity but has lost that disappointment at man's outraged innocence which before sharpened his irony.

—Martin Stannard

GASKELL, Elizabeth (Cleghorn, née Stevenson). English. Born in Chelsea, London, 29 September 1810; brought up in Knutsford, Cheshire, by her aunt. Educated at Miss Byerley's school in Stratford upon Avon, 1824–27. Married the Unitarian minister William Gaskell in 1832; one son and four daughters. Lived in Manchester from 1832; contributed to Dickens's *Household Words*, 1850–58; met and became a friend of Charlotte Brontë, 1850: visited her at Haworth, 1853; organized sewing-rooms during the cotton famine of 1862–63; contributed to the *Cornhill Magazine*, 1860–65. *Died 12 November 1865.*

PUBLICATIONS

Collections

Novels and Tales, edited by C. K. Shorter. 11 vols., 1906–19.
Letters, edited by J. A. V. Chapple and Arthur Pollard. 1966.
Tales of Mystery and Horror, edited by Michael Ashley. 1978.

Fiction

Mary Barton: A Tale of Manchester Life. 1848; edited by Stephen Gill, 1970.
The Moorland Cottage. 1850.
Ruth. 1853.
Cranford. 1853; edited by Peter Keating, with Cousin Phillis, 1976.
Lizzie Leigh and Other Tales. 1855.
North and South. 1855; edited by Angus Easson, 1973.
Round the Sofa. 1859; as My Lady Ludlow and Other Tales, 1861.
Right at Last and Other Tales. 1860.
Lois the Witch and Other Tales. 1861.
A Dark Night's Work. 1863.
Sylvia's Lovers. 1863; edited by Arthur Pollard, 1964.
Cousin Phillis. 1864; edited by Peter Keating, with Cranford, 1976.
Cousin Phillis and Other Tales. 1865.
The Grey Woman and Other Tales. 1865.
Wives and Daughters. 1866; edited by F. Glover Smith, 1969.

Other

The Life of Charlotte Brontë. 2 vols., 1857; revised edition, 1857; edited by Alan
    Shelston, 1975.
My Diary: The Early Years of My Daughter Marianne. 1923.

Editor, Mabel Vaughan, by Maria S. Cummins. 1857.

Bibliography: by Clark S. Northrup in Gaskell by Gerald DeWitt Sanders, 1929; Gaskell: An
Annotated Bibliography 1929–1975 by Jeffrey Welch, 1977.

Reading List: Gaskell: Her Life and Work by Annette B. Hopkins, 1952; Gaskell, Novelist
and Biographer by Arthur Pollard, 1965; Gaskell: The Basis for Reassessment by Edgar
Wright, 1965; Gaskell, The Artist in Conflict by Margaret L. Ganz, 1969; Gaskell's
Observation and Invention by John G. Sharps, 1970; Gaskell by John McVeagh, 1970;
Gaskell and the English Provincial Novel by Wendy A. Craik, 1974; Gaskell: The Novel of
Social Crisis by Coral Lansburg, 1975; Gaskell: A Biography by Winifred Gérin, 1976.

*   *   *

The two best known works of Elizabeth Gaskell are not novels in the strictest sense of the
term. Cranford is really a collection of short stories linked together by their common location
in Cranford, modelled on the Cheshire town of Knutsford. Mrs. Gaskell wrote several other

short stories, many of which, like "The Old Nurse's Story" and "Lois the Witch," have a powerful impact, but *Cranford* is marred by sentimentality, and owes much of its appeal to the consolation it offers to the elderly that their old age will be a happy one. Mrs. Gaskell's *Life of Charlotte Brontë*, in contrast, is a sad story, in which, though Mrs. Gaskell did her best to write the truth, she sometimes, as in suppressing Charlotte's love affair with Monsieur Heger, sacrificed truth in an effort to preserve Charlotte's reputation; at other times the novelist in her overcame the biographer. *Cranford* and *The Life of Charlotte Brontë* have had an important if adverse effect on Mrs. Gaskell's standing as a novelist. As a result of *Cranford* we tend to think of her as a pleasant lightweight writer of escapist fiction with little of value to offer in commenting on real life, while her biographical work has meant that we tend to look on her novels as records of social history, ignoring her artistic achievement. These slighting and contradictory verdicts can be shown to be false by an examination of her five major novels.

Mary Barton was published in the year of Revolutions, 1848, and reflects contemporary preoccupation with the threatened Chartist rebellion. Mary Barton is the daughter of a poor but respectable worker, John Barton, who is gradually driven to despair and murder by the refusal of the authorities to do anything to alleviate the condition of the workers. His victim is Harry Carson, who has tried to seduce Mary, and for a time Mary's other lover, Jem Wilson, is suspected of the murder; but Mary's aunt Esther, a prostitute, supplies evidence which points to the real murderer's guilt, and a deathbed confession by John Barton enables Jem and Mary to start a new life in Canada. Mary Barton's independence is the most notable feature of a somewhat unreal heroine; her levelheadedness in saving one lover from taking the blame for a crime her father has committed is commendable but improbable. John Barton is the real hero of the novel, and his decline is treated with compassion but without sentimentality, just as the nostalgic yearnings of the Manchester workers for the countryside before the Industrial Revolution can provide no solution to the problems of the future. Like many of Mrs. Gaskell's novels, *Mary Barton* asks many questions, but provides no easy answers.

Mrs. Gaskell's handling of prostitution in *Mary Barton* met with little adverse comment, but *Ruth* was attacked because it appeared to be sympathetic to a fallen woman. Ruth's fall from grace is delicately handled, and she appears to modern readers as almost entirely innocent, whereas her seducer Mr. Bellingham seems cruel and callow. Ruth, abandoned pregnant by Bellingham, is rescued by a dissenting clergyman and his sister. Mr. and Miss Benson pass her off as a young widow, and as such she meets with the approval of Benson's richest parishioner, Mr. Bradshaw, but her real identity is discovered when Bellingham reappears as a parliamentary candidate. Mr. Bradshaw is furious at Ruth and the Bensons, but they meet his onslaught calmly, and Ruth becomes a nurse, eventually dying through her courage in nursing Bellingham. This conclusion may seem a little contrived, just as the division between the virtuous unworldly Benson and Ruth herself, and the selfish Bellingham and self-righteous Bradshaw, is a little too clear-cut. Mrs. Gaskell is more successful with minor characters like the Benson's servant Sally, Bradshaw's daughter Jemima, and his partner Farquhar, who is initially in love with Ruth but eventually marries Jemima.

There is less black and white in Mrs. Gaskell's next novel, *North and South*, originally written as a serial for *Household Words*. Mrs. Gaskell did not get on well with Dickens, the editor of *Household Words*, but the novel does not show many traces of their differences. Margaret Hale is forced to leave Helstone, a Southern village, for the smoky metropolis of Milton, modelled on Manchester, because her father has religious doubts. These doubts are never explored, and Mr. Hale's vacillating behaviour is never overtly criticised, whereas the stubbornness of Margaret and her lover John Thornton, the rich Milton manufacturer, is more than once attacked. Eventually Margaret learns to abandon some of her Southern snobbery, and Thornton becomes a little more conciliatory to his workers, although the note of compromise on which the novel ends is not a very hopeful one. There is a melodramatic subplot involving Margaret's brother Frederick, who is accused of murder. *North and South* veers rather uneasily between the sexual struggle involving Margaret and Thornton and the social struggle involving Thornton and his workers, but in many ways this is Mrs. Gaskell's richest novel.

In *Sylvia's Lovers* Mrs. Gaskell crossed the Pennines to set her novel in Monkshaven, based on the Yorkshire port of Whitby. She also went back in time to the era of the Napoleonic wars when press-gangs seized the crews of the Yorkshire whalers to serve in the Navy. Charlie Kinraid, a dashing young sailor, is seized by the press-gang, though Philip Hepburn, Sylvia Robson's other lover, who has witnessed the incident, does not deny the general report that Charlie has been drowned. When Sylvia's father Daniel is executed for an attack on the press-gang, Sylvia reluctantly marries Philip. But she has not forgotten Charlie, and once the facts are known she turns against Philip. After melodramatically saving Charlie's life at the siege of Acre, Philip returns home unrecognized, eventually dying of poverty and gaining Sylvia's forgiveness. Between writing *North and South* and *Sylvia's Lovers* Mrs. Gaskell had been concerned with Charlotte Brontë's biography, and it is possible that it was the influence of the Brontës which led her to this attempt to give her novels the powerful romantic aura of *Wuthering Heights* and *Jane Eyre*. Charlie Kinraid is a pale imitation of Heathcliff, Sylvia's dilemma is never explored as fully as that of Jane Eyre, the melodramatic coincidences and reappearances are less convincing than parallel incidents in the Brontë novels – and yet in the dark, brooding, obsessive Hepburn, conventionally kind and, apart from his single lie about Kinraid's disappearance, scrupulously well-behaved, Mrs. Gaskell created a major character, the equal of any other in nineteenth-century fiction.

In *Wives and Daughters*, unfinished at the time of Mrs. Gaskell's death, there appears to be a retreat from high romance and social history to the homely world of Cranford, but, though set vaguely in the past, *Wives and Daughters* has a message for the confused squirearchy, who refused to read the signs of the times, and for their wives and daughters, who still lived in an unreal world where their empty beauty could win them instant admiration. The hero, Roger Hamley, a scientific explorer, and the heroine, Molly Gibson, shrewd, strong and sensitive, are admirable characters, admirably presented.

Mrs. Gaskell is hard to place. While obviously not in the first division of novelists she is equally obviously no minor figure. Her novels cover a more varied range than those of Thackeray, are better plotted than those of Dickens, and are more realistic than those of the Brontës; and yet, perhaps because she is trying to do too many things at once, she does not match any of these great names in spite of her considerable achievement.

—T. J. Winnifrith

GERHARDIE, William (Alexander). English. Born in St. Petersburg, now Leningrad, Russia, 21 November 1895, of British parents. Educated at the St. Annen Schule, and Reformierte Schule, St. Petersburg, 1900–13; Kensington College, London, 1913–16; Worcester College, Oxford, 1920–23, M.A. (honours), B.Litt. Served in the British Army in the Royal Scots Greys in World War I: Assistant Military Attaché at the British Embassy, Petrograd, 1917–18, and served in the British military missions to Siberia, 1918–20; demobilised with rank of Captain; O.B.E. (Officer, Order of the British Empire), 1920; served in the Officers' Emergency Reserve, 1940. Editor, "English by Radio," BBC, London, 1942–45. Recipient: Phoenix Award, 1965; Arts Council Bursary, 1966. *Died 15 July 1977.*

PUBLICATIONS

Fiction

Futility: A Novel on Russian Themes. 1922.
The Polyglots. 1925.
A Bad End (stories). 1926.
The Vanity-Bag (stories). 1927.
Pretty Creatures (stories). 1927.
Jazz and Jasper: The Story of Adams and Eva. 1928; as *Eva's Apples: A Story of Jazz and Jasper,* 1928; revised edition, as *My Sinful Earth,* 1947; as *Doom,* 1971.
Pending Heaven. 1930.
The Memoirs of Satan, with Brian Lunn. 1932.
Resurrection. 1934.
The Casanova Fable: A Satirical Revaluation, with Hugh Kingsmill. 1934.
Of Mortal Love. 1936.
My Wife's the Least of It. 1938.

Plays

Perfectly Scandalous; or, "The Immorality Lady" (produced 1968). 1927; as *Donna Quixote; or, Perfectly Scandalous,* 1929.
I Was a King in Babylon (produced 1948).
Rasputin: The Ironical Tragedy (produced 1960).

Other

Anton Chekhov: A Critical Study. 1923.
Memoirs of a Polyglot (autobiography). 1931.
Meet Yourself As You Really Are: About Three Million Detailed Character Studies Through Self-Analysis, with Prince Leopold of Loewenstein. 1936; as *Analyze Yourself: How to See Yourself as You Really Are,* adapted by Victor Rosen, 1955; revised edition, as *Meet Yourself As You Really Are,* 1972.
The Romanovs: Evocation of the Past as a Mirror for the Present. 1939.
My Literary Credo: An Introduction to the First Collected Uniform Revised Edition of the Works of William Gerhardie. 1947.

Reading List: *Scholars of the Heart* by S. Gorley Putt, 1962; *Tradition and Dream* by Walter Allen, 1964; "Gerhardie Lives" by James Parkhill-Rathbone, in *Twentieth Century,* 1969.

*   *   *

The titles of three of William Gerhardie's books – *Futility, Pretty Creatures,* and *Pending Heaven* – perhaps best illustrate his major themes. With a detached, amused curiosity he describes the antics of his characters, each vainly struggling to fulfil a dream, each doomed to failure. His criticisms are less bitter than Waugh's, his attitude to absurdity less frivolous than Michael Arlen's. Gerhardie is arguably the last "undiscovered" major author of the 1920's and 1930's.

The earliest influence was Russian literature – Turgenev, Dostoevsky, Tolstoy, and, in particular, Chekhov. *Futility* and *The Polyglots* echo Chekhovian themes throughout, describing Russian society as pervaded by the myths of persistently deferred expectation. In *Futility*, plans are eagerly laid – for Andrei Andreich and Nina's wedding, for the restoration of Nikolai Vasilievich's fortunes through his mines – but nothing ever comes of them and the resultant compromise tortures the protagonists. Micawberish optimism is seen almost as a form of masochism. The author is infuriated by this willed denial of pragmatism and yet in love with his characters' naïvety, their fantasy and melodrama. At this stage, while wary of enthusiasm, he is nevertheless infatuated by it.

The critical success of *Futility* and *The Polyglots* drew him into the political and literary establishment where he met Bennett, Shaw, Wells, and Beaverbrook. Their influence tempered his romantic enthusiasm. "Long before I knew I was to be a writer," he says in *Memoirs of a Polyglot*, "I felt instinctively that what we human beings yearn for are the general things, and the particular things come to you *by the way*, when you are not looking." He learnt from Tolstoy that a literary artist cannot invent the psychology of his characters; he was indifferent to "political," didactic literature and resented interference in others' business, yet not until his last novel, *My Wife's the Least of It*, did he succeed in re-creating the "life" of his early work. The intervening books are Shavian linguistic and philosophic games, *Jazz and Jasper* clearly marking the transition. It is half "a novel on Russian themes," half a Wellsian utopian extravaganza (although it was Lawrence who sketched the means for employing the extraordinary climax). We are distanced from the characters, as in *Pending Heaven*, by their constant intellectual assessment of their situation and by deliberately facetious linguistic devices "The original sin was when man wrapped himself up in the visible world. The ultimate sin was when he shed it." *Pending Heaven* describes both sins in Max Fisher's desperate search for the right woman. He collects a harem (stealing two lovers from his best friend), each member of which is largely indifferent to him; he tries the Lawrencian "blood contact" of living in the desert. When eventually he does find someone who suits him physically and financially he asks her, out of kindness to the others and moral cowardice, to join the household. She objects and marries his best friend. It is partly a serious psychological investigation, partly a joke at the expense of Lawrence and Hugh Kingsmill (the model for Max).

The "heaven" each individual awaits in Gerhardie's work is confused with the "visible universe" and sought for with the shoddiest self-deception. Ultimately it is seen as "an empty restaurant where you arrive having lost your appetite." The impossibility of completion, in Lawrencian terms, is at once man's torture and delight; his hopeless struggle towards this goal is both heroic and egotistical. Gerhardie, like Chekhov and Beckett, charts the complexities of an eternal source of anxiety, waiting in false hope, which is epitomised by romantic love and the confusion of sexual and spiritual longing. From this he distils a sad humour: "My wife's the least of it, ... the least I have to complain of in life," says Mr. Baldridge in the last novel – his wife is insane.

—Martin Stannard

GIBBON, Edward. English. Born in Putney, London, 27 April 1737. Educated at a day school in Putney; Dr. Wooddeson's school in Kingston-on-Thames, Surrey, 1746; Westminster School, London, 1749–50; Magdalen College, Oxford (gentleman commoner), 1752–53; with Reverend M. Pavillard in Lausanne, 1753–58. Served in the Hampshire Militia, 1759–70: Major and Colonel Commandant. Toured Italy, 1764–65; settled in London, 1772, and began to write his history; joined Dr. Johnson's Literary Club, 1774; became Professor of Ancient History at the Royal Academy, 1774; Member of Parliament for Liskeard, 1774–80, and for Lymington, 1781–83: Commissioner of Trade and Plantations, 1779–82; lived in Lausanne, 1783–93, then returned to London. *Died 16 January 1794.*

PUBLICATIONS

Collections

Letters, edited by J. E. Norton.   3 vols., 1956.

Prose

Essai sur l'Etude de la Littérature.   1761; translated, as *An Essay on the Study of Literature,* 1764; revised edition, in *Miscellaneous Works,* 1837.
Mémoires Littéraires de la Grand Bretagne pour l'An 1767, with Jacques Georges Deyverdun.   1768.
Critical Observations on the Sixth Book of the Aeneid.   1770.
The History of the Decline and Fall of the Roman Empire.   6 vols., 1761–88; edited by J. B. Bury, 7 vols., 1926–29.
A Vindication of Some Passages in the Decline and Fall of the Roman Empire.   1779; revised edition, 1779.
Miscellaneous Works.   2 vols., 1796; revised edition, 1814, 1837.
Memoirs.   2 vols., 1827; edited by Georges A. Bonnard, 1966.
Journal to January 28th 1763, My Journal 1, 2, and 3, and Ephemerides.   1929.
Le Journal à Lausanne 17 Août 1763 19 Avril 1764, edited by Georges A. Bonnard.   1945.
Miscellanea Gibboniana, edited by G. R. de Beer, Georges A. Bonnard, and L. Junod.   1952.
Gibbon's Journey from Geneva to Rome: His Journal from 20 April to 2 October 1764, edited by Georges A. Bonnard.   1961.
Autobiography, edited by M. M. Reese.   1970.
The English Essays, edited by Patricia Craddock.   1972.

Bibliography: *A Bibliography of the Works of Gibbon* by Jane E. Norton, 1940; *Gibbon: A Handlist of Critical Notices and Studies* by F. Cordasco, 1950.

Reading List: *Gibbon* by Michael Joyce, 1953; *Gibbon* by C. V. Wedgwood, 1955; *The Literary Art of Gibbon* by H. L. Bond, 1960; *Gibbon the Historian* by Joseph W. Swain, 1966; *Gibbon and His World* by G. R. de Beer, 1968; *Narrative Form in History and Fiction* by Leo Braudy, 1970.

*   *   *

   The last great English tragedy, according to E. M. W. Tillyard, was Edward Gibbon's *Decline and Fall.* It is a tragedy without a hero, though there are several candidates, and without even a villain. But it portrays the destruction of something great and beautiful, doomed more by its own fatal flaws than by the efforts of its enemies. And it is embellished by three qualities of great literature: brilliantly clear and exciting narrative, ironic wit, and majestically beautiful prose.
   To sustain the intensity of a tragic drama for six volumes would of course be impossible for writer or reader. Instead, Gibbon divided the story into a number of discrete episodes, each with its own tragic action, its temporary relief, its finally inadequate heroes. After a three-chapter prologue describing the Roman Empire in the age of the Antonines, "the period in the history of the world in which the condition of the human race was most happy," the first three volumes are devoted to the successive stages of decline before the capture of Italy by the

barbarians that marks the end of the Roman Empire in the West. The three volumes end with an epilogue, the "General Observations on the Fall of the Roman Empire in the West." The theme here discovered and pronounced is certainly worthy of tragedy: "the decline of Rome was the natural and inevitable effect of immoderate greatness."

The last three volumes, the account of the Eastern Empire, have a similar structure. Introductory chapters describe transient hopes and achievements, a Gothic king in Italy "who might have deserved a statue among the best and bravest of the ancient Romans," and the achievements of Justinian, Emperor of the East for nearly forty years, and his great general Belisarius. A final chapter again completes the frame, this time with a chronicle of the fortunes and decay of the city of Rome itself, a vast metonymy for Roman civilization. Although this latter half of the *Decline and Fall* suffered most from Gibbon's ignorance and biasses and has therefore been most fully superseded for historians by subsequent histories, its presentation of the theme that the rise of new cultural syntheses is experienced as the loss and destruction of the old is timeless. "I have described the triumphs of barbarism and religion," says Gibbon in the final chapter. In the glaring irony of the coupled causes, it is sometimes overlooked that he confesses to having described triumphs.

Though the *Decline and Fall* far outshines his other work, Gibbon is not a one-book author. Of the two other English works he published in his lifetime, the *Vindication* is a masterpiece of polemic. More important, however, is Gibbon's posthumous masterpiece, his history of himself. This work, which André Maurois called one of the few "perfect examples" of autobiography, gives the reader the literary pleasures of relating character and fate to experience, of the wit and elegance of Gibbon's prose, together with the interest of honest historical testimony. It is unmatched as an account of the growth of a great scholar's mind. Thus the *Memoirs*, like the *Decline and Fall*, is not merely a contribution to our knowledge of the past, but permanently valuable literature.

—Patricia Craddock

GIBBON, Lewis Grassic. Pseudonym for James Leslie Mitchell. Scottish. Born near Auchterless, Aberdeenshire, 13 February 1901; grew up in Arbuthnott, Kincardineshire. Educated at the Arbuthnott school and Mackie Academy, Stonehaven. Married R. Middleton in 1925; one son and one daughter. Journalist on local newspapers, 1917–18; Clerk in the Army, 1918–22, and Air Force, 1923–29; also an explorer and archaeologist from 1922; lived in Welwyn Garden City, 1930 until his death. *Died 21 February 1935.*

PUBLICATIONS

Fiction

Stained Radiance: A Fictionist's Prelude. 1930.
The Thirteenth Disciple, Being Portrait and Saga of Malcolm Maudslay in His Adventure Through the Dark Corridor. 1931.
The Calends of Cairo. 1931.
Three Go Back. 1932.
The Lost Trumpet. 1932.

459

A Scots Quair: Sunset Song, Cloud Howe, Grey Granite. 3 vols., 1932–34; *Sunset Song* edited by J. T. Low, 1971.
Persian Dawns, Egyptian Nights: Two Story-Cycles. 1933.
Image and Superscription. 1933.
Spartacus. 1933.
Gay Hunter. 1934.
A Scots Hairst: Essays and Short Stories, edited by I. S. Munro. 1967.

Other

Hanno; or, The Future of Exploration. 1928.
Niger: The Life of Mungo Park. 1934.
The Conquest of the Maya. 1934.
Scottish Scene; or, The Intelligent Man's Guide to Albyn, with Hugh MacDiarmid. 1934.
Nine Against the Unknown: A Record of Geographical Exploration, with J. L. Mitchell. 1934.

Reading List: *Leslie Mitchell: Lewis Grassic Gibbon* by I. S. Munro, 1966; *Beyond the Sunset: A Study of Gibbon* by Douglas F. Young, 1973.

* * *

There are three works by Lewis Grassic Gibbon in print at the present time, and for once critical opinion would tend to endorse the commercial instincts of publishers. In spite of the biographies, archaeological studies, essays, short stories, and novels published in an almost frantically busy brief career, Gibbon's claim to be regarded as an interesting and important figure rests almost entirely upon the Scottish novels and short stories set in his native place, the Mearns of Kincardineshire. These are Scottish not only in their setting and themes, but in the innovatory use of a Scottish prose based on speech rhythms which has proved unique. Of the other fiction some, such as *The Thirteenth Disciple*, is autobiographical, but he also used his fiction as propaganda for the Diffusionist views which are a constant theme in all his work from *The Conquest of the Maya* and the archaeological essays to *Three Go Back*, *The Lost Trumpet*, and *Image and Superscription*.

Gibbon's greatest achievement is undoubtedly the trilogy, *A Scots Quair*. The story is set entirely in the Mearns during the period from 1911 to the 1930's and follows the fortunes of Chris Guthrie, daughter of a peasant farmer, from girlhood to middle-age, through three marriages and against three different settings, from farm to small town to city. Of the three volumes, the first, *Sunset Song*, is the most successful, perhaps because it is rooted in the land itself, which in turn binds together the personal, social, and mythic dimensions of the novel. The land of the Mearns is a dour, red clay; the living wrested from it is hard-won. For all its moods of lyric sweetness, it is the land's harshness that has conditioned the men who work the small farms. It has coarsened them, made them bitter and mean-spirited. Calvinism is a natural religion to John Guthrie, her father. Repelled by what her father has become, the young Chris sees her escape in education. But the harshness and cruelty that characterise the struggle to survive on the farms, and the viciousness and scandal-mongering that mark the life of the community are countered by the kindness and generosity of characters like Long Rob of the Mill and Chae Strachan, and by the hard beauty of the land itself. Writing in his essay on "The Land" he said of the northern harvest that it is "harder and slower ... and lovelier in its austerity." Chris is torn between an "English Chris" who hates this life, and a "Scottish Chris" who loves it. In the end it is the land that wins, but the book is elegiac; the way of life she chooses is dying, the war brings it to an end. It is in that sense that the novel is a sunset song.

Throughout the trilogy, Gibbon employs two interesting technical devices. The first is highly original: the use of a second-person narrator. It can be the voice of the community, expressing communal hopes, fears, and delights, or, used satirically, can give the measure of its depravity as it criticises, judges, and gossips. At other times it carries Chris's inner life, but viewed with the objectivity that moving out of the first person allows. It is in this ability to combine both inner intimacy and common gossip, to convey both first person and third, that Gibbon secured a vehicle admirably suited to the exploration of his themes. The second device is flashback, in itself no innovation and tending, for me, to become increasingly artificial as the trilogy proceeds, but performing a crucial thematic function. The chapters in *Sunset Song* are a series of recollections which take place on successive visits to Blawearie loch with its ancient stone circle. The stones provide a perspective which takes us out of the day-to-day linear time of the novel, and is distinct even from the rhythmical time pattern of the farming year which provides the chapter headings. They represent a universal or geological time which establishes a mythic dimension to Chris's character, and presides over her personal and social identities. The sense of time involved here is related very clearly to the archaeological and diffusionist interests apparent in all his work, but the historical sense is also to be linked to his communism, as it is in the trilogy through Ewan Tavendale, Chris's son, for communism takes account of that sense of time in which nothing endures but the endurance of the peasant himself.

The second volume, *Cloud Howe*, finds Chris married to Robert Colquhoun, minister of Segget. The novel is concerned with the dreams and ideas – the clouds – that men pursue through the world. Robert is a Christian Socialist who seeks change through socialism. His hopes are crushed in the failure of the General Strike of 1926, and the symbolic still-birth of Chris's child. The thematic exploration of endurance and change is taken further in the relationship of Robert and Chris. She, like the land, represents a more enduring order of time than Robert, who follows the ever-changing clouds. He is therefore the more vulnerable, and when he cracks he flees to a meek mystical Christianity.

The son of her first marriage, Ewan Tavendale, becomes the real hero of *Grey Granite*, the final novel. He is the one character whom Chris recognises as perhaps older than herself; if she is the land, he is the grey granite beneath. This is linked with his problematical coldness as a character and with the historicist aspect of the communist creed to which he moves as the novel proceeds. The action now takes place in the city in the bleak atmosphere of the strikes, hunger marches, and unemployment that mark the Depression. The conception of this final novel is perhaps the most ambitious, and if it is not entirely satisfactory it remains a work of considerable interest and importance.

—Brian W. M. Scobie

GISSING, George (Robert). English. Born in Wakefield, Yorkshire, 22 November 1857. Educated at private day schools in Wakefield; Lindow Grove, a Quaker boarding school in Alderley Edge, Cheshire; Owens College, Manchester, 1872 (Ward's English Poem Prize). Married 1) Helen Harrison in 1879 (died, 1888); 2) Edith Underwood in 1891, one son; 3) Gabrielle Fleury in 1899. Clerk in Liverpool, then travelled to America, worked as a tutor and gas fitter in Boston, and travelled as far west as Chicago; failed to find work as a journalist in America, and returned to England in 1877; began writing in 1878; tutor to the sons of Frederic Harrison, 1882, then obtained other pupils and began contributing to the *Pall Mall Gazette* and other periodicals; full-time writer from 1890; lived in the South of France, 1901 until his death. *Died 28 December 1903.*

PUBLICATIONS

Collections

Stories and Sketches, edited by A. C. Gissing. 1938.

Fiction

Workers in the Dawn. 1880; edited by Robert Shafer, 1935.
The Unclassed. 1884; revised edition, 1895.
Isabel Clarendon. 1886.
Demos. 1886.
Thyrza. 1887.
A Life's Morning. 1888.
The Nether World. 1889.
The Emancipated. 1890.
New Grub Street. 1891; edited by Irving Howe, 1962.
Denzil Quarrier. 1892.
Born in Exile. 1892.
The Odd Women. 1893.
In the Year of Jubilee. 1894.
Eve's Ransom. 1895.
The Paying Guest. 1895.
Sleeping Fires. 1895.
The Whirlpool. 1897.
Human Odds and Ends: Stories and Sketches. 1898.
The Town Traveller. 1898.
The Crown of Life. 1899.
Our Friend the Charlatan. 1901.
The Private Papers of Henry Ryecroft. 1903.
Veranilda. 1904.
Will Warburton. 1905.
The House of Cobwebs and Other Stories. 1906.
An Heiress on Condition (story). 1923.
Sins of the Fathers and Other Tales, edited by Vincent Starrett. 1924.
A Victim of Circumstance and Other Stories. 1927.
A Yorkshire Lass (story). 1928.
My First Rehearsal, and My Clerical Rival, edited by Pierre Coustillas. 1970.

Verse

Hope in Vain. 1930.

Other

Charles Dickens: A Critical Study. 1898.
By the Ionian Sea: Notes of a Ramble in Southern Italy. 1901.
Letters to Edward Clodd. 1914; edited by Pierre Coustillas, 1973.
Letters to an Editor, edited by C. K. Shorter. 1915.
Critical Studies of the Works of Dickens, edited by T. Scott. 1924.

The Immortal Dickens. 1925.

Letters to Members of His Family, edited by Algernon and Ellen Gissing. 1927.

Letters to Eduard Bertz 1887–1903, edited by A. C. Young. 1961.

Gissing and H. G. Wells: Their Friendship and Correspondence, edited by R. A. Gettmann. 1961.

Commonplace Book, edited by Jacob Korg. 1962.

Letters to Gabrielle Fleury, edited by Pierre Coustillas. 1965.

Notes on Social Democracy. 1968.

Essays and Fiction, edited by Pierre Coustillas. 1970.

London and the Life of Literature in Late Victorian England: Diary 1887–1902, edited by Pierre Coustillas. 1977.

Editor, *Forster's Life of Dickens*, abridged and revised. 1903.

Bibliography: *Gissing: An Annotated Bibliography of Writings about Him* by Joseph Wolff, 1974; *Gissing: A Bibliography* by Michael Collie, 1975.

Reading List: *Gissing: Grave Comedian* by Mabel C. Donnelly, 1954; *Gissing* by A. C. Ward, 1959; *Gissing: A Critical Biography* by Jacob Korg, 1963; *Gissing: A Study in Literary Leanings* by O. H. Davis, 1966; *Gissing: The Critical Heritage* edited by Pierre Coustillas and Colin Partridge, 1972; *Gissing* (biography) by Gillian Tindall, 1973, as *The Born Exile*, 1974; *Gissing in Context* by Adrian Poole, 1975; *Gissing: A Biography*, 1977, and *The Alien Art: A Critical Study of Gissing's Novels*, 1978, both by Michael Collie.

*　　*　　*

There are two different ways of reading George Gissing, and, though the same reader may possibly adopt both, they are so incompatible that he will do so only by means of a deliberate choice to alter from one to the other. He can be read as a sociological novelist, a painstaking latter-day imitator of Dickens (whose work he adored) without the genius or the humour of Dickens, but like him in his vivid sense of the London scene and his subtle portrayal of class differences. Or he can be read as a tortured romantic who poured out in scorn and bitterness his disillusionment with life, his dissatisfaction with his own lot, and his contempt for all those millions, especially the poor and uneducated, who did not value art and literature above crude satisfactions.

His career was that of the talented and studious meritocrat, spoiled and thwarted in part by class inferiority and lack of opportunity, but much more by his own intemperance and unwisdom. He made two disastrous marriages; he always had a grudge. Beginning as an idealistic socialist (a side of him that produced the very early *Workers in the Dawn*) he soon reverted to extreme distrust and contempt for the class just below that in which he was born — his father was a bookish pharmaceutical chemist. He writes always as if men like himself, struggling to rise by intellect and literature, were being dragged down by a gross, ignorant, and heartless populace into an intolerable nether pit of squalor and mediocrity. Perhaps he maintained this all the more passionately because he knew in his heart that it was not so. He got a good education, won scholarships, and recklessly wasted opportunities for advancement.

One has only to think of Samuel Johnson, so similar to him in circumstances of birth and early education, so utterly unlike him in generous feeling for the poor, unfortunate, and ignorant to discount a good deal of Gissing's spleen. Yet his unfairness and one-sidedness were by no means an unmixed loss to him as a writer. Snobbery, admiration for the rich and well-born, anxiety about money, fear of the gutter are very powerful emotions; and in Gissing they found their poet. He carried them to a point of intensity where they seem to be purified of a good part of their pettiness; in the presentation of these feelings he has few equals. And so, though he is never a brilliant and often not even a lively writer, he contributes something irreplaceable to the canon of English literature.

Like most self-absorbed and socially inept young writers, he vastly overrated the effect he would have on the public. Already in the early 1880's he was a disappointed man. In *The Unclassed* he attempted, with partial success, to present an unvarnished account of the social and moral consequences of prostitution, implying a criticism of the sentimental treatment of the subject by the novelists of the generation before. With *Demos*, a bitter warning against trusting or trying to improve the poor, he attained his first modest success, and with the proceeds fulfilled the great ambition of his life in travelling to Italy and Greece. (It was very characteristic of him to describe his first sight of Vesuvius as the greatest moment of his life.) A later journey, made in the company of H. G. Wells, resulted in his nearest approach to a happy book, *By the Ionian Sea*.

The books which form the core of his achievement were written in quick succession between 1889 and 1893. *The Nether World* is a powerful and painful study of life among the London poor, more notable for indignation than for pity. In *New Grub Street*, though his personal feelings of envy and chagrin are not hidden, he achieved perhaps his most truthful and original sociological study. The title recalls the phrase commonly used for the literary world in the time of Alexander Pope, and both the similarities to this and the differences from it are presented in masterly style. One notices, when Gissing is writing in this vein, that it is the whole scene, not individual characters or incidents, that remains memorable. The author appears rather to be recording than creating. *The Odd Women* is an original study of the life of single women cut off from family ties and trying to make their way in what is still mainly a man's world.

We need not be surprised that he lost inspiration after this. He had always lacked high creative talent, and a certain weariness and repetitiveness creep into the later writing. Bad health also took its toll. But the rather slight *Private Papers of Henry Ryecroft* attained a surprising readership and remains one of his two or three best-known books. It is free from the tormented longings of so many earlier books, and presents in simple and sober style the easy, quiet, bookish life of a man with a small private income. It was a life Gissing never attained; but he may well have been wrong in his conviction that, if he had, he would have been a better writer. The anguish of his disappointment is the very stuff of his literary achievement.

—A. O. J. Cockshut

GLASGOW, Ellen (Anderson Gholson). American. Born in Richmond, Virginia, 22 April 1874, and lived there for all of her life. Educated at home, and in private schools in Richmond; began to lose her hearing at age 16, and eventually went deaf. Writer from 1896. President, Richmond Society for the Prevention of Cruelty to Animals. Recipient: Howells Medal, 1941; Pulitzer Prize, 1942. D.Litt.: University of North Carolina, Chapel Hill, 1930; D.L.: University of Richmond, 1938; Duke University, Durham, North Carolina, 1938; College of William and Mary, Williamsburg, Virginia, 1939. Member, American Academy of Arts and Letters, 1938. *Died 21 November 1945.*

PUBLICATIONS

Collections

> *Letters,* edited by Blair Rouse.   1958.
> *Collected Stories,* edited by Richard K. Meeker.   1963.

Fiction

> *The Descendent.*   1897.
> *Phases of an Inferior Planet.*   1898.
> *The Voice of the People.*   1900; edited by William L. Godshalk, 1972.
> *The Battle-Ground.*   1902.
> *The Deliverance.*   1904.
> *The Wheel of Life.*   1906.
> *The Ancient Law.*   1908.
> *The Romance of a Plain Man.*   1909.
> *The Miller of Old Church.*   1911.
> *Virginia.*   1913.
> *Life and Gabriella.*   1916.
> *The Builders.*   1919.
> *One Man in His Time.*   1922.
> *The Shadowy Third and Other Stories.*   1923; as *Dare's Gift and Other Stories,* 1924.
> *Barren Ground.*   1925.
> *The Romantic Comedians.*   1926.
> *They Stooped to Folly: A Comedy of Morals.*   1929.
> *The Sheltered Life.*   1932.
> *Vein of Iron.*   1935.
> *In This Our Life.*   1941.
> *Beyond Defeat: An Epilogue to an Era,* edited by Luther Y. Gore.   1966.

Verse

> *The Freeman and Other Poems.*   1902.

Other

> *Works.*   8 vols., 1929–33; revised edition, 12 vols., 1938.
> *A Certain Measure: An Interpretation of Prose Fiction.*   1943.
> *The Woman Within* (autobiography).   1954.

Bibliography: *Glasgow: A Bibliography* by William L. Kelley, edited by Oliver L. Steele, 1964.

Reading List: *Glasgow and the Ironic Art of Fiction* by Frederick P. W. McDowell, 1960; *Glasgow* by Blair Rouse, 1962; *Glasgow* by Louis Auchincloss, 1964; *Glasgow's American Dream* by Joan Foster Santas, 1966; *Three Modes of Modern Southern Fiction: Glasgow, Faulkner, and Wolfe* by C. Hugh Holman, 1966; *Without Shelter: The Early Career of*

Glasgow by J. R. Raper, 1971; *Glasgow's Development as a Novelist* by Marion K. Richards, 1971; *Glasgow and the Woman Within* by E. S. Godbold, 1972.

* * *

Ellen Glasgow was the first clear voice in the movement that became known as the American Southern Renascence. She was the first writer to apply the principles of critical realism and a detached and ironic point of view to the people, the region, and the problems of the American South. Beginning with her first novel, *The Descendent*, in 1897, and ending with *Beyond Defeat*, posthumously published in 1966, she produced twenty novels in which with varying degrees of success she brought to Virginia and the South what she felt it most needed, "blood and irony." In addition to these novels, she published a volume of critical introductions to a collected edition of her novels, *A Certain Measure*; a volume of undistinguished verse, *The Freeman and Other Poems*; and a collection of mediocre short stories, *The Shadowy Third*.

Her first two novels, both laid in New York, point to her later work only in attempting a clear-eyed realism and in having southern characters. But beginning in 1900, with *The Voice of the People*, and continuing through *The Battle-Ground*, *The Deliverance*, *The Romance of a Plain Man*, *The Miller of Old Church*, *Virginia*, and *Life and Gabriella*, Ellen Glasgow constructed a fictional social history of the Commonwealth of Virginia from the Civil War to the First World War, placing a particular emphasis upon the transition from a ruling aristocracy to the rise of the middle class to political and economic power. In this series of novels, she traced the petrifaction of the aristocratic ideals of pre-war Virginia and recorded through the lives of fictional characters the major social revolution which the rise of the middle class produced. These novels are historical only in the sense that all historical novels deal with issues of manners, politics, and economic forces in an earlier age, for they do not deal with historical personages or actual events. She treated social history with detachment, irony, and a self-consciously witty style. In 1925 she published *Barren Ground*, a novel of a lower-middle-class country woman, Dorinda Oakley, in her struggle with self, circumstance, and the soil. In this novel Ellen Glasgow reached the highest expression of her historical view, although there are no historical events as such in the novel. *Barren Ground* is a grim story, reminiscent of the works of Thomas Hardy, whom she greatly admired. It recounts, she declared, events that could happen "wherever the spirit of fortitude has triumphed over the sense of futility." She also said that it demonstrated that "one may learn to live, one may even learn to live gallantly without delight." Though she was acquainted with modern scientific, social, and anthropological views of man and society, her fundamental view of life remained shaped, as this statement suggests, by a firm but non-theological Calvinistic determinism.

Barren Ground not only summed up the first period in her active career, a period which had seen, in addition to the works named, the publication of four minor novels and her short stories and poetry; it also launched the most productive and artistically successful period in her career. In 1926 she published *The Romantic Comedians*, an almost perfectly constructed novel of manners, laid in Queenborough, her name for her native city of Richmond. The novel, centered in the marriage of an old man to a young girl, is a witty and amusing attack upon the social customs of the surviving Virginia aristocracy. She followed *The Romantic Comedians* with *They Stooped to Folly*, another comedy of manners laid in Queenborough, which plays amusing variations on the idea of the ruined woman through three generations of a Virginia family. *The Sheltered Life*, a tragi-comedy which concludes the Queenborough trilogy, ranks with *Barren Ground* as one of her two best works. *The Sheltered Life* is particularly noteworthy for its treatment of time and memory. "The Deep Past," a section of the novel consisting of the recollections of a very old man, is her finest single piece of work. Two other novels published during her life-time portray the growing darkness of her view of life. *Vein of Iron* is a grim picture of life in the Virginia mountains, a story which she called "a drama of mortal conflict with fate." *In This Our Life*, a Pulitzer Prize winner, is a despairing view of modern life in Queenborough, a book which, she said, shows "that character is an end in itself." *Beyond Defeat*, written as a sequel to it, strongly supports this view.

Ellen Glasgow was a committed realist with a tragic view of human potentialities. Her world view was strongly shaped by a sense of imperfection and failure in all human efforts. Supremely the novelist and fictional historian of her native Virginia, she maintained toward the places in which she lived and the people whom she loved an ironic detachment largely the result of her witty and polished and consciously fashioned style. A half-dozen of her novels, including *Virginia*, *Barren Ground*, the Queenborough trilogy, and *Vein of Iron* are works of considerable distinction. In her own time, she enjoyed both popular and critical respect. Since her death she has received little attention, but she deserves to be better known and more widely read.

—C. Hugh Holman

GODWIN, William. English. Born in Wisbech, Cambridgeshire, 3 March 1756; moved with his family to Debenham, Suffolk, 1758, and Guestwick, Norfolk, 1760. Educated at a dame school in Guestwick; Robert Akers's school at Hindolveston, 1764–67; Rev. Samuel Newton's school in Norwich, 1767–71; usher in Akers's school, 1771–72; Hoxton Academy, London, 1773–78. Married 1) the writer Mary Wollstonecraft in 1797 (died, 1797), one daughter, Mary, who married Shelley; 2) Mary Jane Clairmont in 1801, one son; three adopted children. Calvinist minister at Ware, Hertfordshire, 1778–79, and Stowmarket, Suffolk, 1780–82; began to write in 1782; on trial as minister at Beaconsfield, 1783, then gave up the ministry for a career as a writer; settled in London: contributed to the *English Review* and the *New Annual Register*, and occasionally took on pupils; became known, after 1793, as a spokesman for English radicalism; bookseller and publisher, with his wife, 1805 until they went bankrupt, 1822; full-time writer, 1824–33; Yeoman Usher of the Exchequer, 1833–36. *Died 7 April 1836.*

PUBLICATIONS

Collections

An Enquiry Concerning Political Justice (and other writings), edited by K. Codell Carter. 1971.

Fiction

Italian Letters; or, The History of the Count de St. Julian. 1783; edited by Burton R. Pollin, 1965.
Imogen: A Pastoral Romance. 1784.
Things As They Are; or, The Adventures of Caleb Williams. 1794, revised edition, 1796, 1797, 1816, 1831; edited by David McCracken, 1970.
St. Leon: A Tale of the Sixteenth Century. 1799.
Fleetwood; or, The New Man of Feeling. 1805; revised edition, 1832.

Mandeville: A Tale of the Seventeenth Century in England. 1817.
Cloudesley. 1830.
Deloraine. 1833.

Plays

Antonio (produced 1800). 1800.
Faulkener (produced 1807). 1807.

Other

A Defence of the Rockingham Party, in Their Late Coalition with Lord North. 1783.
An Account of the Seminary That Will Be Opened at Epsom. 1783.
The History of the Life of William Pitt. 1784.
The Herald of Literature. 1784.
Sketches of History in Six Sermons. 1784.
Instructions to a Statesman, Humbly Inscribed to the Earl Temple. 1784.
An Enquiry Concerning the Principles of Political Justice and Its Influence on General Virtue and Happiness. 2 vols., 1793; edited by F. E. L. Priestley, 1946.
Considerations on Grenville's and Pitt's Bills Concerning Treasonable and Seditious Practices. 1795.
The Enquirer: Reflections on Education, Manners, and Literature. 1797.
Memoirs of the Author of A Vindication of the Rights of Woman. 1798; edited by J. M. Murray, 1928.
Thoughts Occasioned by Dr. Parr's Spital Sermon. 1801.
Life of Geoffrey Chaucer, Including Memoirs of John of Gaunt. 2 vols., 1803.
Fables Ancient and Modern Adapted for the Use of Children. 1805.
The Looking Glass: A True History of the Early Years of an Artist. 1805.
The Pantheon; or, Ancient History of the Gods of Greece and Rome (juvenile). 1806.
The History of England (juvenile). 1806.
The Life of Lady Jane Grey and Guildford Dudley Her Husband. 1806.
Essay on Sepulchres. 1809.
History of Rome (juvenile). 1809.
Dramas for Children, Imitated from the French of L. F. Jauffret. 1809.
The Lives of Edward and John Philips, Nephews and Pupils of Milton. 1815.
Letters of Verax (on Napoleon). 1815.
Letter of Advice to a Young American. 1818.
Of Population: An Answer to Mr. Malthus's Essay. 1820.
History of the Commonwealth of England from Its Commencement to the Restoration of Charles the Second. 4 vols., 1824–28.
History of Greece (juvenile). 1828.
Thoughts on Man, His Nature, Productions, and Discoveries. 1831.
Lives of the Necromancers. 1834.
The Moral Effects of Aristocracy, with *The Spirit of Monarchy,* by William Hazlitt. 1835(?).
Essays Never Before Published, edited by C. K. Paul. 1873.
Godwin and Mary: Letters of Godwin and Mary Wollstonecraft, edited by Ralph M. Wardle. 1966.
Uncollected Writings 1785 1822, edited by Jack Marken and Burton R. Pollin. 1968.

Bibliography: *Godwin: A Synoptic Bibliography* by Burton R. Pollin, 1967.

Reading List: *Godwin: His Friends and Contemporaries* (life and letters) by C. Kegan Paul, 1876; *Godwin: A Biographical Study* by George Woodcock, 1946; *Godwin: A Study in Liberalism* by D. Fleisher, 1951; *Godwin and the Age of Transition* by A. E. Rodway, 1952; *Godwin and His World* by R. G. Grylls, 1953; *Education and Enlightenment in the Works of Godwin* by Burton R. Pollin, 1962; *Godwin's Novels: Theme and Craft* by G. McCelvey, 1964; *Godwin* by E. E. and E. G. Smith, 1966; *The Philosophical Anarchism of Godwin* by John R. Clark, 1977.

*   *   *

William Godwin's novels exhibit a peculiar combination of rootedness in historical circumstance with universalizing, even "mythic" form. His earliest fictions, *Imogen* and *Italian Letters*, show at once his idealizing tendency, his perception of history as a form of romance, and his restless interest in the problem of how to give moral ideas fictional form. These very different experiments in resolving that problem were then forgotten as Godwin attempted to make his fame, and transform the world, through moral philosophy and "philosophical history," and when he returned to fiction he had just become the leading intellectual influence on "English Jacobinism" with his *Enquiry Concerning Political Justice* (1793). Here he had found exactly the style and form of discourse of express his mind, as he reflected on the political history of mankind, and strove to put the events of the early 1790's into a universal historical perspective, and so take the heat out of political controversy and social conflict.

But he clearly wanted a more popular, more moving form of writing to express the same historical vision, the same hopes and fears for the future, and almost immediately after finishing his treatise he began *Things As They Are*, better known by its original subtitle, *The Adventures of Caleb Williams*. Godwin turned to fiction rather than history because it was a more popular form, more universal, and, as he expressed it in an unpublished essay three years later, more open to the expression of the meaning of history because it was free from merely historical facts. And so in *Caleb Williams* Godwin uses names from the history of revolutions, and from the struggle of reason against feudal and chivalric custom. At the same time, he creates a form which embodies the materialist and necessitarian philosophy of *Political Justice*. He uses first person narrative for immediacy and retrospective inset narrative to show how circumstances have created character. He gives over much of the novel to the description of psychological states, thus combining the necessitarian "science of mind" with the psychological realism of Richardson, or his friend Elizabeth Inchbald (*A Simple Story*). Godwin also borrowed from the picaresque novel and criminal biographies, giving their form a greater coherence and intensity by turning it into "adventures of flight and pursuit," and dwelling on imprisonment as a universal metaphor for the relationship between the individual and social institutions. Finally, he enriched the symbolic structure of his narrative by using the language of religion (he was after all a lapsed Calvinist) to describe the crises of his hero's social rebellion, and his remorse. The achievement of *Caleb Williams*, then, is to unify several levels of meaning in a vision of the continuing struggle of truth against tyranny. He could do this because, as he wrote the novel in 1793–4, he, like many others, was straining reason, knowledge, and imagination to prophesy the outcome of the age of Revolution.

By the time he wrote his next novel many of his worst fears had been realized. *St. Leon* is coloured by elegiac sentiment, the sense that the heroic age was past; in its choice of Reformation Europe as a setting, its use of historical characters from the French religious wars, and its insistence on the isolation of those whose knowledge gives them power to help mankind, the novel is a comment on events of the recent past. At the same time Godwin's historical conception was even grander here than in *Caleb Williams*, revealing his recent interest in and attempt to write heroic drama. Perhaps most significant, Godwin also used the novel to acknowledge his own and his fellow Jacobins' errors in ignoring the "domestic affections" and cultivation of individual sensibility. However, the novel is a failure because Godwin's execution, his style, fell far short of his design. It was only in his next novel, *Fleetwood*, that Godwin regained the power of his abstract and often heavy prose style, and only in *Fleetwood* did he successfully combine the themes, ideas, and attitudes of Wordsworthian Romanticism (received via Coleridge) with his own reconstructed philosophy of necessity. The price he paid, however, was a lessening of the intensity and a partial abandonment of the unity of plot and design which had been the strengths of *Caleb Williams*.

After *Fleetwood* Godwin turned to still other ways of spreading his ideas, writing and publishing children's books, history, biography, and essays such as the interesting *Essay on Sepulchres* and *Thoughts on Man*. These works all carry the same ideas into diverse literary modes, but he was most successful in the relaxed form of the long essay. His last three novels do not make any great advance on what he had already achieved in that form. *Mandeville* was largely a response to the fiction of Scott. After another long interval Godwin returned to fiction which resembles that of his momentary follower Bulwer Lytton. *Cloudesley* and *Deloraine* combine elements from *Fleetwood*, his heroic dramas, and his earliest novels. The truth is, Godwin had made his most substantial contribution to the development of the English novel in *Caleb Williams*, and, significantly, it was this novel which Godwin continued to revise for successive editions, the last of which was published as a contemporary of his very last novels. *Caleb Williams*, created in the midst of a universal historical crisis, synthesized the achievements of the English fiction of the past, and anticipated the achievements of the future.

—Gary Kelly

GOLD, Michael. American. Born Irving Granich in New York City, 12 April 1894; changed his name when he began writing. Educated in local schools until age 13. Married. Worked as a night porter, clerk, and driver for an express company, 1907–11; carpenter's helper, section gang laborer, shipping clerk, and factory hand, 1911–15; settled in Boston, 1915, and lived there for several years; returned to New York, and worked as a copy reader for the New York *Call*; joined the Communist Party after the Russian Revolution, and was thereafter associated with various radical publications: Assistant Editor, *Masses*; Founder and Editor, *Liberator*, 1920–22; Founder, with Hugo Gellert, *New Masses*, 1926, and Editor until 1948; also contributed to the *Daily Worker*; in later years, Contributing Editor, *Masses and Mainstream*. Died 14 May 1967.

PUBLICATIONS

Collections

A Literary Anthology, edited by Michael Folsom. 1972.

Fiction

The Damned Agitator and Other Stories. 1926.
Jews Without Money. 1930.

Plays

Hoboken Blues (produced 1928).
Fiesta (produced 1929).
Money. 1930.
Battle Hymn, with Michael Blankfort (produced 1936).   1936.

Other

Life of John Brown.   1924.
120 Million.   1929.
Charlie Chaplin's Parade (juvenile).   1930.
Change the World!   1937.
The Hollow Men.   1941.

Editor, with others, Proletarian Literature in the United States: An Anthology.   1935.

*   *   *

Michael Gold's passion for the flowering of a truly proletarian culture was the direct outcome of the life he had known in the ghetto. "When I hope it is the tenement hoping ...," he reminisced in his celebrated essay, "Towards Proletarian Art," "I am all that the tenement group poured into me during those early years of my spiritual travail." His semi-autobiographical novel, Jews Without Money, which vividly and poignantly evoked the squalid and suffocating reality of his boyhood world, with its stench and filth, hoodlums and prostitutes, bugs, sweatshops, and swarming immigrants, was in itself intended as a model of the kind of art he was keen to see in vogue in the United States. A proletarian movement in art could take root, he felt, only if there was a spontaneous resurgence of creativity among workers at all levels – when "in every American factory there is a dramatic group ... when mechanics paint in their leisure, and farmers write sonnets." It was, therefore, necessary that preference in art be given to the sufferings of the hungry and persecuted masses over the "precious silly little agonies" of bourgeois writers. Workers, he maintained, must employ "swift action, clear form, the direct line, cinema in words" to create an art imbued with social purpose and bristling with the complex nuances of their lives. The New Masses, which he helped to start in 1926 with the express aim of publishing and popularising the contributions of working men and women, did succeed, to a limited extent, in providing a forum of artistic expression to obscure worker-poets such as H. H. Lewis and Martin Russak, but the experiment could not be sustained and continued for long. His plays, Hoboken Blues, describing with intimate nearness the Harlem poor in the jazz-age, and Fiesta, dealing with the life of the peons and patricians of Mexico countryside, though not successful commercially, at least attested to his earnestness in providing a scathing critique of a literary culture desperately struggling to arrive at a meaningful comprehension of its aims and values.

Gold, never a stickler for stylistic perfection, staked his trust in the absolute sovereignty of the "message" of art, and, in spite of his well-known fondness for Shakespeare and Schiller, often insisted that the artists of the working-class had nothing to learn from the great literature of the bourgeois past. If in his poetry he resorted to the direct statement – with a view to dramatising the predicament of "Vanzetti in the Death House" or celebrating the raw pleasures of ordinary life in "Bucket of Blood" – he generally inclined, Whitmanlike, toward lyricism and prophetic bursts of eloquence in his prose to invoke the grandeur of the Marxist apocalypse awaiting the decay of the old economic order: "For out of our death shall arise glories, and out of the final corruption of this old civilization we have loved shall spring the new race – the supermen." His political sympathies notwithstanding, he could display real glimmerings of objectivity and candour in his literary criticism. His admiration for Upton Sinclair, for instance, was always tempered by his awareness that Sinclair's vision was limited by a fuzzy and unrealistic idealising of the working class and an inbred puritanism that grudged "the poor little jug of wine and hopeful song of the worker." Likewise, his criticism of Hemingway's "colourful if sterile world ... completely divorced from the experience of the great majority of mankind" never overlooked the great American writer's stylistic and narrative accomplishments.

Though faded in appearance, Gold's writings today serve as a powerful reminder of the often forgotten truth that artistic possibilities can be discovered even in the most neglected sections of society and that it is mostly the writers "corrupted by all the money floating everywhere" that find it "unfashionable to believe in human progress ... to work for a better world."

—Chirantan Kulshrestha

GOLDING, William (Gerald). English. Born in St. Columb Minor, Cornwall, 19 September 1911. Educated at Marlborough Grammar School; Brasenose College, Oxford, B.A. 1935. Served in the Royal Navy, 1940–45. Married Ann Brookfield in 1939; two children. Writer, actor, and producer in small theatre companies, 1934–40, 1945–54; Schoolmaster, Bishop Wordsworth's School, Salisbury, Wiltshire, 1939–40, 1945–61; Visiting Professor, Hollins College, Virginia, 1961–62. M.A.: Oxford University, 1961; Honorary Fellow, Brasenose College, 1966; D.Litt.: University of Sussex, Brighton, 1970. Fellow of the Royal Society of Literature, 1955. C.B.E. (Commander, Order of the British Empire), 1966. Lives in Bowerchalke, Wiltshire.

PUBLICATIONS

Fiction

> *Lord of the Flies.* 1954.
> *The Inheritors.* 1955.
> *Pincher Martin.* 1956; as *The Two Deaths of Christopher Martin,* 1957.
> *Free Fall.* 1960.
> *The Spire.* 1964.
> *The Pyramid.* 1967.
> *The Scorpion God* (stories). 1971.

Plays

> *The Brass Butterfly* (produced 1958). 1958.

> Radio Plays: *Miss Pulkinhorn,* 1960; *Break My Heart,* 1962.

Verse

> *Poems.* 1934.

Other

The Hot Gates and Other Occasional Pieces. 1965.

Reading List: *The Art of Golding* by Bernard S. Oldsey and Stanley Weintraub, 1965; *Golding* by Bernard F. Dick, 1967; *The Novels of Golding* by Howard S. Babb, 1970; *Golding: A Critical Study* by Mark Kinkead-Weekes and Ian Gregor, 1970; *Golding: The Dark Fields of Discovery* by Virginia Tiger, 1974; *Golding* by Stephen Medcalf, 1975.

*   *   *

In an essay entitled "Crosses," William Golding revealed that one of the afflictions he has had to bear in life has been "the inability to write poetry." Instead, he has produced six novels and three stories (one of which, "Envoy Extraordinary," he later re-worked as a play, *The Brass Butterfly*). Though at first sight rather various, all of these fictions conform to a type. They are works deliberately designed "to inculcate a moral lesson," and the teaching methods that they use are those of parable: characters of a schematic kind are so displayed as to spell out a clear theme; symbol periodically underlines a meaning which the patterning of incident has been set up to demonstrate.

Basically, what these fictions have to say is that "man produces evil as a bee produces honey." They are books about "the terrible disease of being human"; their unaltering aim is to make man face "the sad fact of his own cruelty and lust." What they all proclaim is the fixed conviction that "Man is a fallen being. He is gripped by original sin. His nature is sinful and his state perilous."

As Golding has recognised, this is an announcement that lacks novelty. But, he contends, "what is trite is true, and a truism can become more than a truism when it is a belief passionately held." His writing could be seen as an attempt to justify this claim – with varying results. There are times when what he calls his "savage grasp on life" appears to be no more than a rather heavy-handed clutching at standard religious props; but there are others where it has taken imaginative hold, and then, under its pressure, his material is moulded into memorably fierce contours.

In subject-matter, Golding's fiction is ambitious and diverse. Chronologically, the range is wide, taking in Neanderthal victims of *homo sapiens* at one extreme, and human victims of nuclear war at the other. Intermediate stopping-points include a Pharaoh's court, imperial Rome, a medieval cathedral community, and a small town in the 1920's. A devotee of archaeology, Golding reconstructs these little worlds with vivid precision. Strewn with sharp-edged detail, the physical settings of his novels always have a satisfying actuality. And much effort obviously goes into establishing the social structure of a period, setting up the different totems and taboos whose shadows are then shown to fall across the characters.

But these are not documentary books. Alongside the archaeologist in Golding – and more dominant – is a moralist: the allegorist soon makes didactic use of what the anthropologist provides. In *Lord of the Flies*, for instance, the activities of schoolboys on a desert island are not merely recorded. They are made to trace harsh diagrams of human history, chart social evolution as a grisly collapse from fruit-eating commune to totalitarian butchery. Jetsam from a nuclear war, the children re-enact the process that has brought them to this state: restored to an Eden, they convert it to an abattoir. And no devil pushes them towards this fall. Evil – though hysterically externalised as "The Beast" – turns out to have a human face. As the novel finishes, a boy brought to awareness weeps "for the end of innocence, the darkness of man's heart."

Merging fast-paced narrative into a streamlined, semi-allegoric structure that moves with increasing impetus through scenes of savagery to a terminating pessimism about man, *Lord of the Flies* much resembles *The Inheritors*, another myth-like story that can be glossed in both political and religious terms. These two novels, Golding's most successful, deal with humanity and evil in a generalised, panoramic way. In each, human corruption shows itself most fearsomely through mob-atrocity. The subsequent books focus more on individuals and private relationships, particularly ones of a sexually exploitative kind. This presents Golding with material of greater emotional and psychological complexity, which he does not seem equipped to handle well. Moral intricacies are soon ironed out under the dead-weight of a continually imposed didacticism. Character flattens into stereotype and is left uninterestingly rigid.

Often so acute when scrutinising physical phenomena, Golding's eye does not penetrate particularly far when observing human personality. Able to convey sensory experience with a raw immediacy, he shows himself much feebler at portraying thought, speech, or emotional response. And so his last four novels and his stories offer an unusual collage of blur and precision, cliché and originality. In *Pincher Martin* – Golding's first attempt at studying an individual – what is strong and what is weak weirdly polarise. The phantasmagoria sections of this novel – where the efforts of dead Martin's ego to remain intact are presented as a struggle for survival on a rock in the Atlantic – carry intense physical conviction as exposure and attrition scour at their victim; but the "real-life" sections of the book are populated with pasteboard; the flash-backs to Martin's past relationships merely light up a lifeless series of crudely posed moral tableaux.

A weakness at characterisation – something he skilfully by-passed in *Lord of the Flies* and *The Inheritors* by concentrating on protagonists who were not mature human beings – is one of Golding's most disabling defects. Repetition is another. Character-types recur throughout his fiction, as do bits of plot-mechanism and the same technical devices – *Lord of the Flies*, *The Inheritors*, *Pincher Martin*, *The Spire*, and "Clonk Clonk" all attempt to gain swift shock from a dramatic shift of viewpoint at their end.

Most limiting to Golding's achievement, though, is the predictability of moral observation, the thematic monotony of his fiction. There is a virtuoso variety about the material from which he shapes his fables; but the lessons drawn from it – that man is fallen, savage, and selfish, a creature who perverts the power of love – are rather repetitive and conventional.

—Peter Kemp

GOLDSMITH, Oliver. Irish.   Born in Pallas, near Ballymahon, Longford, 10 November 1728. Educated at the village school in Lissoy, West Meath, 1734–37; Elphin School, 1738; a school in Athlone, 1739–41, and in Edgeworthstown, Longford, 1741–44; Trinity College, Dublin (sizar; Smyth exhibitioner, 1747), 1745–49 B.A. 1749; studied medicine at the University of Edinburgh, 1752–53; travelled on the Continent, in Switzerland, Italy, and France, 1753–56, and may have obtained a medical degree. Settled in London, 1756; tried unsuccessfully to support himself as a physician in Southwark; worked as an usher in Dr. Milner's classical academy in Peckham, 1756, and as a writer for Ralph Griffiths, proprietor of the *Monthly Review*, 1757–58; Editor, *The Bee*, 1759; contributed to the *British Magazine*, 1760; Editor, *The Lady's Magazine*, 1761; also worked for the publisher Edward Newbery; worked as a proof-reader and preface writer, contributed to the *Public Ledger*, 1760, and prepared a *Compendium of Biography*, 7 volumes, 1762; after 1763 earned increasingly substantial sums from his own writing; one of the founder members of Dr. Johnson's Literary Club, 1764. *Died 4 April 1774.*

PUBLICATIONS

Collections

Collected Letters, edited by Katharine C. Balderston. 1928.
Collected Works, edited by Arthur Friedman. 5 vols., 1966.
Poems and Plays, edited by Tom Davis. 1975.

Fiction

The Vicar of Wakefield. 1766; edited by Arthur Friedman, 1974.

Plays

The Good Natured Man (produced 1768). 1768.
The Grumbler, from a translation by Charles Sedley of a work by Brueys (produced
    1773). Edited by Alice I. P. Wood, 1931.
She Stoops to Conquer; or, The Mistakes of a Night (produced 1773). 1773; edited by
    Arthur Friedman, 1968.
Threnodia Augustalis, Sacred to the Memory of the Princess Dowager of Wales, music by
    Mattia Vento (produced 1772). 1772.
The Captivity (oratorio), in Miscellaneous Works. 1820.

Verse

The Traveller; or, A Prospect of Society. 1764.
Poems for Young Ladies in Three Parts, Devotional, Moral, and Entertaining. 1767.
The Deserted Village. 1770.
Retaliation. 1774.
The Haunch of Venison: A Poetical Epistle to Lord Clare. 1776.

Other

An Enquiry into the Present State of Polite Learning in Europe. 1759.
The Bee. 1759.
The Mystery Revealed. 1762.
The Citizen of the World; or, Letters from a Chinese Philosopher Residing in London to
    His Friends in the East. 2 vols., 1762.
The Life of Richard Nash of Bath. 1762.
An History of England in a Series of Letters from a Nobleman to His Son. 2 vols., 1764.
An History of the Martyrs and Primitive Fathers of the Church. 1764.
Essays. 1765; revised edition, 1766.
The Present State of the British Empire in Europe, America, Africa, and Asia. 1768.
The Roman History, from the Foundation of the City of Rome to the Destruction of the
    Western Empire. 2 vols., 1769; abridged edition, 1772.
The Life of Thomas Parnell. 1770.
The Life of Henry St. John, Lord Viscount Bolingbroke. 1770.
The History of England, from the Earliest Times to the Death of George II. 4 vols.,
    1771; abridged edition, 1774.

The Grecian History, from the Earliest State to the Death of Alexander the Great. 2 vols., 1774.
An History of the Earth and Animated Nature. 8 vols., 1774.
A Survey of Experimental Philosophy, Considered in Its Present State of Improvement. 2 vols., 1776.

Editor, *The Beauties of English Poesy.* 2 vols., 1767.

Translator, *The Memoirs of a Protestant,* by J. Marteilhe. 2 vols., 1758; edited by A. Dobson, 1895.
Translator, *Plutarch's Lives.* 4 vols., 1762.
Translator, *A Concise History of Philosophy and Philosophers,* by M. Formey. 1766.
Translator, *The Comic Romance of Scarron.* 2 vols., 1775.

Bibliography: *Goldsmith Bibliographically and Biographically Considered* by Temple Scott, 1928.

Reading List: *Goldsmith* by Ralph Wardle, 1957; *Goldsmith* by Clara M. Kirk, 1967; *Goldsmith: A Georgian Study* by Ricardo Quintana, 1967; *Life of Goldsmith* by Henry A. Dobson, 1972; *Goldsmith* by A. Lytton Sells, 1974; *Goldsmith: The Critical Heritage,* edited by George S. Rousseau, 1974; *The Notable Man: The Life and Times of Goldsmith* by John Ginger, 1977.

*   *   *

Oliver Goldsmith's reputation is made up of paradox. His blundering, improvident nature nevertheless won him the loyalty and friendship of figures like Dr. Johnson, Sir Joshua Reynolds, and Edmund Burke. While in society he was a buffoon, his writing testifies to personal charm and an ironic awareness of his own and others' absurdity. Critical opinion of his work similarly varies from acceptance of Goldsmith as the sensitive apologist for past values to appraisal of him as an accomplished social and literary satirist. Indeed, his work can operate on both levels, a fact perhaps recognised by the young Jane Austen in her *Juvenilia* when she took Goldsmith's abridgements of history for young persons as a model for her own exercise in irony.

Drifting into authorship after a mis-spent youth (as Macaulay notes in his disapproving *Life*), Goldsmith turned to hack writing, contributing articles to the *Monthly* and *Critical Reviews* from 1757. His more ambitious *Inquiry into the Present State of Polite Learning* of 1759 won him the reputation of a man of learning and elegant expression. In this last essay he reveals his fundamental dislike of the contemporary cult of sensibility which was to generate not only his own "laughing" form of comedy in the drama but also *The Vicar of Wakefield.* Meeting Smollett, then editor of the *British Magazine,* Goldsmith was encouraged to expand his contributions to literary journalism. He produced the weekly periodical *The Bee*; many papers collected and published in 1765 and 1766 as *Essays*; and, most important, the "Chinese Letters" of 1760–61 collected as *The Citizen of the World.*

The "citizen" is, of course, an Oriental traveller, observing the fashions and foibles of the *bon ton* in London with wide-eyed innocence that carries within it implicit comment and criticism not unmixed with humour. The device was borrowed from the French, notably Montesquieu's *Lettres Persanes* (1721). In each essay the absurdities of behaviour are marked, the whole inter-woven by continuing narratives around the Man in Black, Beau Tibbs, the story of Hingo and Zelis, for instance. In many ways the ironies, improbabilities, and apparent innocence of the Chinese letters prefigure the extended prose romance of *The Vicar of Wakefield.*

This could be seen as Goldsmith's answer to Sterne's *Tristram Shandy* (1759). He had attacked Sterne's sentimental fiction as "obscene and pert" in *The Citizen*; in many ways *The Vicar* parodies Sterne's novel but with such a light hand that it has been taken on face value for many generations as the tale indeed of a family "generous, credulous, simple, and inoffensive." However, Goldsmith early establishes for the observant the manifest danger of complacency in such apparent virtues. His Yorkshire parson displays the moral duplicity of a feeling heart, for Goldsmith's approach to life and art is the opposite of Sterne's relativism and dilettante values.

Goldsmith's moral seriousness (while softened by genial good humour) dominates that other work now considered "classic," *The Deserted Village*. His earlier sortie in the genre of topographical/philosophical verse, *The Traveller*, did much to establish his reputation. It is an accomplished use of convention, where the poet climbs an eminence only to have his mind expanded into contemplation of universal questions. In *The Deserted Village*, however, the poet comes to terms with a particular social problem in a particular landscape as opposed to former abstract musings above imaginary solitudes. "Sweet Auburn" can be identified closely with the village of Nuneham Courtenay, where the local land-owner had recently moved the whole community out in order to extend and improve his landscape park. The fact becomes a catalyst for Goldsmith in a consideration of where aesthetic values and irresponsible wealth lead: a symbol taken from life and not from poetic convention.

Goldsmith's rhymed couplets have grace and ease, particularly when his verse is unlaboured, as in the prologues and epilogues to his own and others' plays. The charm and humour of these can be observed in his later poem *Retaliation*, which has a pointed raciness born out of the settling of personal scores. Always the butt of jokes in the group known as The Club, here he gets his own back with a series of comic epitaphs for the other members. Notable is that for Garrick – "On the stage he was natural, simple, affecting; Twas only that when he was off he was acting" – but he labels himself the "gooseberry fool."

As a dramatist, Goldsmith exploited both verbal dexterity and the comedy of situation, looking back to Shakespeare in the rejection of the so-called genteel comedy of Hugh Kelly or Richard Cumberland. Affected and strained in tone and action, the drama of sentiment offered to Goldsmith nothing of the "nature and humour" that he saw as the first principle of theatre. However he might despise the sentimental school, he cannot avoid using some of its conventions, the good-natured hero, of course, and the device of paired lovers, but the way these are treated is particular to himself. Together with Sheridan, Goldsmith exploits the theatrical unreality of comedy, using the stage as a separate world of experience with its own laws and therefore demanding the suspension of disbelief in order that farcical unreality might unmask farcical reality. His character Honeydew in *The Good Natured Man* has something in common with Charles Surface in *School for Scandal*, but the tone of Goldsmith's comedy is less brittle than that of Sheridan's. This mellow tone, a fundamental wholesomeness, is magnificently encapsulated in *She Stoops to Conquer*.

Goldsmith's first play met with a poor response, as being too "low" in its matter (especially the bailiffs scene), and, though *She Stoops to Conquer* was open to similar criticism, its riotous humour overcame prejudice. In short, it was good theatre and this is testified by its continuing popularity in production. Characters like Tony Lumpkin, Mrs. Hardcastle, and the old Squire have become literary personalities, while the pivot of the plot, Marlow's loss of diffidence in apparently more relaxed circumstances, holds true to human nature. The character of Kate is a liberated heroine in the Shakespearean style, contrasted as in the older comedy with a foil. One is able to relate Goldsmith's "laughing" comedy to that of Shakespeare in many ways, for the Lord of Misrule dominates both.

The range of Goldsmith's work is touched by this same humour and sensitivity, the good heart that is so easily squandered as he himself acknowledged in *The Good Natured Man*, but is just as easily extended with purpose to the reader. As Walter Scott observed, no man contrived "so well to reconcile us to human nature."

—B. C. Oliver-Morden

GOODMAN, Paul. American. Born in New York City, 9 September 1911. Educated at the City College of New York, B.A. 1931; University of Chicago, Ph.D. 1940 (received, 1954). Married twice; two daughters and one son. Reader for Metro-Goldwyn-Mayer, 1931; Instructor, University of Chicago, 1939–40; Teacher of Latin, physics, history, and mathematics, Manumit School of Progressive Education, Pawling, New York, 1942; also taught at New York University, 1948, Black Mountain College, North Carolina, 1950, and Sarah Lawrence College, Bronxville, New York, 1961; Knapp Professor, University of Wisconsin, Madison, 1964; taught at the Experimental College of San Francisco State College, 1966, and at the University of Hawaii, Honolulu, 1969, 1971. Editor, *Complex* magazine, New York; Film Editor, *Partisan Review*, New Brunswick, New Jersey; Television Critic, *New Republic*, Washington, D.C.; Editor, *Liberation* magazine, New York, 1962–70. Recipient: American Council of Learned Societies Fellowship, 1940; National Institute of Arts and Letters grant, 1953. Fellow, New York Institute for Gestalt Therapy, 1953, and Institute of Policy Studies, Washington, D.C., 1965. *Died 3 August 1972.*

PUBLICATIONS

Collections

> *Collected Poems*, edited by Taylor Stoehr.   1973.
> *Collected Stories and Sketches.*   vol. 1 (of 4), 1978.

Fiction

> *The Grand Piano; or, The Almanac of Alienation.*   1942.
> *The Facts of Life* (stories).   1945.
> *The State of Nature.*   1946.
> *The Break-Up of Our Camp and Other Stories.*   1949.
> *The Dead of Spring.*   1950.
> *Parents' Day.*   1951.
> *The Empire City.*   1959.
> *Our Visit to Niagara* (stories).   1960.
> *Making Do.*   1963.
> *Adam and His Works: Collected Stories.*   1968.
> *Don Juan; or, The Continuum of the Libido.*   1977.

Plays

> *The Tower of Babel,* in *New Directions in Poetry and Prose.*   1940.
> *2 Noh Plays* (produced 1950).   In *Stop-Light,* 1941.
> *Stop-Light* (5 Noh plays: *Dusk: A Noh Play, The Birthday, The Three Disciples, The Cyclist, The Stop Light*).   1941.
> *The Witch of En-Dor,* in *New Directions 1944.*   1944.
> *Theory of Tragedy,* in *Quarterly Review of Literature 5.*   1950.
> *Faustina* (produced 1952).   In *Three Plays,* 1965.
> *Abraham* (cycle of Abraham plays: produced 1953).   *Abraham and Isaac* in *Cambridge Review,* November 1955.
> *The Young Disciple* (produced 1955).   In *Three Plays,* 1965.
> *Little Hero* (produced 1957).   In *Tragedy and Comedy: 4 Cubist Plays,* 1970.

The Cave at Machpelah (produced 1959).   In *Commentary*, June 1958.
Three Plays. 1965.
Jonah (produced 1966).   In *Three Plays*, 1965.
Tragedy and Comedy: 4 Cubist Plays (includes *Structure of Tragedy, After Aeschylus;
    Structure of Tragedy, After Sophocles; Structure of Pathos, After Euripides; Little
    Hero, After Molière*).   1970.

Verse

Ten Lyric Poems. 1934.
12 Ethical Sonnets. 1935.
15 Poems with Time Expressions.   1936.
Homecoming and Departure. 1937.
Childish Jokes: Crying Backstage.   1938.
A Warning at My Leisure. 1939.
Pieces of Three, with Meyer Liben and Edouard Roditi.   1942.
Five Young American Poets, with others.   1945.
The Copernican Revolution. 1946.
Day and Other Poems.   1954.
Red Jacket. 1956.
Berg Goodman Mezey. 1957.
The Well of Bethlehem. 1959.
The Lordly Hudson (Collected Poems).   1963.
Hawkweed. 1967.
North Percy. 1968.
Homespun of Oatmeal Gray.   1970.
Two Sentences. 1970.

Other

Art and Social Nature (essays).   1946.
Kafka's Prayer. 1947.
Communitas: Means of Livelihood and Ways of Life, with Percival Goodman.   1947;
    revised edition, 1960.
Gestalt Therapy: Excitement and Growth in the Human Personality, with Frederick Perls
    and Ralph Hefferline. 1951.
The Structure of Literature. 1954.
*Censorship and Pornography on the Stage, and Are Writers Shirking Their Political
    Duty?* 1959.
Growing Up Absurd: Problems of Youth in the Organized Society.   1960.
The Community of Scholars. 1962.
Utopian Essays and Practical Proposals. 1962.
Drawing the Line. 1962.
The Society I Live in Is Mine. 1963.
Compulsory Mis-Education. 1964; revised edition, 1971.
People or Personnel: Decentralizing and the Mixed System.   1965.
Mass Education in Science. 1966.
Five Years: Thoughts During a Useless Time.   1966.
Like a Conquered Province: The Moral Ambiguity of America.   1967.
The Open Look. 1969.
New Reformation: Notes of a Neolithic Conservative.   1970.
Speaking and Language: Defence of Poetry.   1971.

Little Prayers and Finite Experience. 1972.
Drawing the Line: Political Essays, edited by Taylor Stoehr. 1977.
Nature Heals: Psychological Essays, edited by Taylor Stoehr. 1977.
Creator Spirit, Come: Literary Essays, edited by Taylor Stoehr. 1977.

Editor, *Seeds of Liberation.* 1965.

*   *   *

Towards the end of his life Paul Goodman became a cult figure among young, disaffected Americans. His writings were in favour of sexual liberation (he was avowedly bi-sexual) and freedom from planners' control, and they passionately protested against American involvement in Vietnam – these were all causes that could be and were embraced by a large number of students and their sympathisers. Goodman became suddenly famous, his books went into paperback, he led marches, received many offers to speak on and off campus; and in a sense he wore himself out trying to make the armies of the night into an efficient fighting force against corporation America.

Cult figures rise and fall. But Goodman is a far more substantial figure than his momentary status might make him appear. I would guess that comparatively few of those who began buying his books in the 1960's managed to work their way through them. And this is not because the books are poor, or badly written, but because Goodman is a tough-minded thinker, a man of real intellectual distinction, who refuses to be caught out in simplistic postures, and who never pandered to popular demands that he should become a generation's guru. In short, Goodman is in no way to be blamed for the odd, upward turn of his reputation during those last hopeful, bewildering, and finally sad years of his life. (The sadness was caused by a series of heart attacks and more grievously by the death of his beloved son, Matty, about which he writes in a series of moving poems in his volume of poetry *Homespun of Oatmeal Gray.*)

Perhaps the single work that did most to endear him to the young was *Growing Up Absurd,* which he subtitled "Problems of youth in the organised society." Yet this is not a glib tract for the times: on the contrary, it clearly grew out of Goodman's lifelong dedication to his own particular brand of intellectual anarchism, his deeply-held and passionately-argued for belief that the life of the individual was being more and more threatened by the state. Goodman is really a descendant of John Stuart Mill and Walt Whitman: he longs to invite his soul to loaf, but he fears that the time for loafing may well be past. The themes of *Growing Up Absurd* are also presented in fictional form in many of his stories, in *The Empire City,* and, particularly, in *Making Do.*

Behind *Growing Up Absurd* is a quite magnificent study of the American city as it is and as it might be, *Communitas,* written with his brother Percival. Wonderfully well-written, rigorous in method, in argument, and in detailed application, *Communitas* seems to me a deeply sane and wise book. And the same may be said for most of the essays in *Utopian Essays and Practical Proposals.* Goodman is indeed an extraordinarily good essayist, better, I would say, than Orwell; he is also a minor poet of some distinction (his posthumous *Little Prayers and Finite Experience* is an interesting experiment in intercutting small lyrical prayers-in-verse with longer prose meditations); and also, though not so successfully, a writer of fiction. Reviewing *Growing Up Absurd,* Webster Schott pointed out that Goodman is "a rational Utopian who has most of the analytical apparatus and theoretical formulations of modern sociology, psychology, historiography and aesthetics at his finger tips."

This almost terrifying breadth and depth – along with his warm and loving heart – help give Goodman his distinction.

—John Lucas

GORDIMER, Nadine. South African. Born in Springs, Transvaal, 20 November 1923. Educated at the Convent School, and the University of the Witwatersrand, Johannesburg. Married 1) G. Gavron in 1949; 2) Reinhold Cassirer in 1954; one son and one daughter. Visiting Lecturer, Institute of Contemporary Arts, Washington, D.C., 1961, Harvard University, Cambridge, Massachusetts, 1969, Princeton University, New Jersey, 1969, Northwestern University, Evanston, Illinois, 1969, and the University of Michigan, Ann Arbor, 1970; Adjunct Professor of Writing, Columbia University, New York, 1971. Recipient: Smith Literary Award, 1961; Thomas Pringle Award, 1969; Black Memorial Prize, 1972; Booker Prize, 1974; Grand Aigle d'Or Prize, France, 1975; CNA Literary Award, 1975. Lives in Johannesburg.

PUBLICATIONS

Fiction

Face to Face: Short Stories. 1949.
The Soft Voice of the Serpent and Other Stories. 1952.
The Lying Days. 1953.
Six Feet of the Country (stories). 1956.
A World of Strangers. 1958.
Friday's Footprint and Other Stories. 1960.
Occasion for Loving. 1963.
Not for Publication and Other Stories. 1965.
The Late Bourgeois World. 1966.
A Guest of Honour. 1970.
Livingstone's Companions: Stories. 1971.
The Conservationist. 1974.
Selected Stories. 1975.
Some Monday for Sure (stories). 1976.

Other

On the Mines, with David Goldblatt. 1973.
The Black Interpreters (literary criticism). 1973.

Editor, with Lionel Abrahams, *South African Writing Today.* 1967.

Bibliography: *Gordimer, Novelist and Short Story Writer: A Bibliography of Her Works* by Racilia Jilian Nell, 1964.

Reading List: *Gordimer* by Robert F. Haugh, 1974; *Gordimer* by Michael Wade, 1978.

*   *   *

Nadine Gordimer is one of the foremost fiction-writers in South Africa. Her short stories and novels capture the stresses and ironies of life in that authoritarian, segregated society. Although her fiction deals mainly with the lives of English-speaking whites, she is one of the few South African writers who creates equally convincing sketches of black Africans, Asians, and Afrikaners.

Her writing is closely involved with politics yet seldom explicitly political. Not only is she a hauntingly accurate recorder of the sclerotic effects of white domination, but also the pre-eminent portraitist of white, English-speaking middle-class life. Gordimer both knows that society intimately and remains detached from it in her writing. This element of detachment has resulted in her being unjustly considered cold by some critics. But the accuracy and detail of her observations are moulded by a profoundly sympathetic intelligence. Gordimer seldom recreates for their own sake the quirks of comfortable, provincial, white, South African society. In her novels and short stories the relentless accuracy of detail is almost invariably tied to an emotional reaction: a sense of loss, of impotence, and – rarely – of vitality or courage.

It is because Gordimer deals so closely with individuals in observed situations that politics form a menacing background to almost all her writing. As she remarked in an interview with Alan Ross in the *London Magazine* (May 1965): "whites among themselves are shaped by their peculiar position, just as black people are by theirs. I write about their private selves; often, even in the most private situations, they are what they are because their lives are regulated and their mores formed by the political situation."

The emphases in the private lives of Nadine Gordimer's fictional characters change with the age. One can trace the deterioration in the South African political situation throughout her writing career of more than thirty years. The short stories in particular illustrate the growing powerlessness of the "decent," "liberal" white minority.

In the early volumes, many tales reveal the grotesque inequalities inherent in white supremacy. Both blacks and whites are portrayed as helpless victims of a brutally stratified society: "civilised" whites are capable of little more than token sympathy for their black servants; the private tragedies of blacks rarely perturb more than the surface of a bland, decorous white world. In *Not for Publication* and *Livingstone's Companions* the atmosphere has changed. There are still marvellously evocative accounts of the slightly bewildered social antics of an increasingly outdated, isolated white culture. But the growth of the police state in the later stories brings with it a relentless ossifying of liberal responses, a steady cheapening of defiant gestures, and an inexorable dwindling of determined political opposition from black and white. The short stories are not uniformly bleak, however. Nadine Gordimer frequently builds a personal tale around a fleeting but sharply focused moment of revelation or insight. These concise evocations of the vital, the ephemeral, or the corrosive element in various relationships give a range to her writing far beyond that of the social themes for which she is best known.

Her novels follow the same pattern of development as her short stories. *The Lying Days* describes the struggle of the heroine to break free, first from the taboos of the mining community in which she grows up, and second from the facile group of intellectual whites with whom she later mixes in Johannesburg. She encounters racial violence and a feeling of impotence after the Afrikaner Nationalist victory of 1948, but decides not to run away from her disillusion and guilt.

This beautifully observed *bildungsroman* is Nadine Gordimer's most optimistic book. Disillusion itself and the increasingly fragmented nature of life in a segregated society are the pressing themes of her later novels. In *A World of Strangers* a visiting Englishman tries unsuccessfully to move both in affluent white Johannesburg and in the fast, illicit world of the black townships. Real contact between the two is, however, impossible. *Occasion for Loving* records the corrosive effects of a love affair between a black man and a white woman in a society which brands such a relationship illegal.

The next novel is even darker. *The Late Bourgeois World* is a steely examination of the entombed white English-speaking world in post-Sharpeville South Africa. Through its protagonist, a young divorced woman, the novel records the futile sabotage attempts of her leftist ex-husband and her own terror in the face of an appeal for help from a member of the black underground. Her bland, white society provides a fog-like emotional foreground through which the fear and impotence of her position loom sharp and menacing.

There is a turning away from this dead end in *A Guest of Honour*. Set in an unidentified

African country, the novel examines the problems of newly won independence. The central character is a sympathetic Englishman working as a special consultant. His life is complicated by an unexpected passion for a young white woman, which is described with poignant vitality. His frustrations in the new state are paralleled by growing strife, and he is killed in an arbitrary act of violence.

South Africa is again the setting of *The Conservationist*. Mehring, the successful white industrialist through whose consciousness most of the book unfolds, is perplexed by the unsatisfying nature of his possessions. In particular, his weekend farm is obtruded upon by memories (of his callow, liberal son and his smug ex-lover) and by itinerant blacks. In this world of chimera and unfulfilment only the land remains tangible and stable. Yet it too eludes Mehring. A black corpse buried on his farm has a more legitimate claim to be part of it than any guilt-laden lien Mehring can command. The aridity of *The Conservationist* suggests a new kind of dead end. But its haunting evocation of atrophy is only a further step in the author's remarkable chronicling of decay in her society.

—Rowland Smith

GORDON, Caroline. American. Born in Trenton, Kentucky, 6 October 1895. Educated at Bethany College, West Virginia, A.B. 1916. Married the poet Allen Tate in 1924 (divorced, 1954); one daughter. Reporter, *Chattanooga News*, Tennessee, 1920–24; Lecturer in English, University of North Carolina Woman's College, Greensboro, 1938–39; Lecturer in Creative Writing, School of General Studies, Columbia University, New York, from 1946; Visiting Professor of English, University of Washington, Seattle, 1953; Writer-in-Residence, University of Kansas, Lawrence, 1956, and University of California at Davis, 1962–63. Recipient: Guggenheim Fellowship, 1932; O. Henry Award, 1934; National Institute of Arts and Letters grant, 1950; National Endowment for the Arts grant, 1966, D.Litt.: Bethany College, 1946; St. Mary's College, Notre Dame, Indiana, 1964. Lives in Princeton, New Jersey.

PUBLICATIONS

Fiction

Penhally. 1931.
Aleck Maury, Sportsman. 1934; as *The Pastimes of Aleck Maury: The Life of a True Sportsman,* 1935.
None Shall Look Back. 1937.
The Garden of Adonis. 1937.
Green Centuries. 1941.
The Women on the Porch. 1944.
The Forest of the South (stories). 1945.
The Strange Children. 1951.
The Malefactors. 1956.
Old Red and Other Stories. 1963.
The Glory of Hera. 1972.

Other

How to Read a Novel.   1957.
A Good Soldier: A Key to the Novels of Ford Madox Ford.   1963.

Editor, with Allen Tate, *The House of Fiction: An Anthology of the Short Story.*   1950;
revised edition, 1960.

Bibliography: *Flannery O'Connor and Gordon: A Reference Guide* by Robert E. Golden and
Mary C. Sullivan, 1977.

Reading List: *Gordon* by Frederick P. W. McDowell, 1966; *Gordon* by W. J. Stuckey, 1972.

*   *   *

Caroline Gordon is rightly grouped with writers of the so-called Southern Literary
Renaissance, but is sometimes inappropriately called a regionalist. Most of her novels and
short stories are set in her native Kentucky and in other nearby regions of the South, but her
fiction strives toward the kind of universality achieved by the writers she most admires:
Flaubert, Henry James, and James Joyce. She is an artist of the "dramatic" school, that is, she
attempts to efface herself as author and allow her fiction to speak for itself. In addition to her
nine novels and two short story collections, *Forest of the South* and *Old Red and Other
Stories*, Caroline Gordon has written a critical book, *How to Read a Novel*, in which she sets
down the theoretical basis for her own fiction. With Allen Tate she is also editor of *The House
of Fiction*, a widely used anthology of the short story with critical commentary on the craft
and teaching of the short story form.

Gordon is a novelist, however, not a critic. Her life-long theme has been the quest for
heroic paradigms, a search that has lead her back to pioneer Kentucky (*Green Centuries*), to
the pre-Civil War South (*Penhally*), to the War itself (*None Shall Look Back*) and, in modern
times, to a Southern plantation in the 1930's (*Garden of Adonis*) ruined by drouth and the
depression. Gordon's heros are men or women who, on principle or out of commitment to a
cause, stand up for what they believe to be right. This quest, as her fictions moved toward the
20th century, necessarily involved her with the widespread modern preference for the anti-
hero and its attendant cultural implications, particularly with the view that meaningful action
is impossible to an intellectually aware individual. In *The Women on the Porch*, set in New
York and Kentucky, she takes as her hero a deracinated intellectual-poet and "saves" him
from emotional detachment through a final reconciliation with his estranged wife, a
resolution that points toward the next stage in Gordon's development. In *Strange Children*,
narrated by a young girl, the hero – also an intellectual – comes to the realization that what is
missing from his life is religious faith. *The Malefactors* carries this resolution a step farther:
the hero, Thomas Claiborne, cures his emotional paralysis by entering the Catholic Church.
In *The Glory of Hera*, Miss Gordon returns once more to the past, finding her hero and her
heroic paradigm in Hercules of Greek myth; she sets forth his story with all the sharpness of
detail and dramatic enactment that characterized her earlier work.

The fiction of Caroline Gordon has much in common with the major fiction of the modern
period, particularly with Hemingway's tightly controlled, dramatic, impersonal symbolic
novels and stories, and it reflects the same attachment to the natural world and traditional
values to be found in southern writers generally and Faulkner in particular. The chief
difference, perhaps, between the work of Caroline Gordon and that of her contemporaries is
in her lack of moral ambiguity. Her fiction is less a discovery of acceptable shades of meaning
than a bodying forth in enigmatic form of timeless moral truths.

—W. J. Stuckey

GORE, Catherine (Grace Frances, née Moody). English. Born in East Retford, Nottinghamshire, in 1799. Educated privately. Married Captain Charles Gore in 1823; ten children. Composer from 1827; settled in France, 1832, later returned to England. *Died 29 January 1861.*

PUBLICATIONS

Fiction

Theresa Marchmont; or, The Maid of Honour. 1824.
Richelieu; or, The Broken Heart. 1826.
The Lettre de Cachet; The Reign of Terror. 1827.
Hungarian Tales. 1829.
Romances of Real Life. 1829.
Women as They Are; or, The Manners of the Day. 1830.
Pin-Money. 1831.
The Tuileries. 1831; as *The Soldier of Lyons,* 1841.
Mothers and Daughters. 1831.
The Opera. 1832.
The Fair of Mayfair. 1832; as *The Miseries of Marriage,* 1834.
The Sketch Book of Fashion. 1833.
Polish Tales. 1833.
The Hamiltons; or, The New Era. 1834.
The Diary of a Désennuyée. 1836.
Mrs. Armytage; or, Female Domination. 1836.
Memoirs of a Peeress; or, The Days of Fox. 1837; revised edition, 1859.
Stokeshill Place; or, The Man of Business. 1837.
The Heir of Selwood; or, Three Epochs of a Life. 1838.
Mary Raymond and Other Tales. 1838.
The Woman of the World. 1838.
The Cabinet Minister. 1839.
The Courtier of the Days of Charles II, with Other Tales. 1839.
The Dowager; or, The New School for Scandal. 1840.
Preferment; or, My Uncle the Earl. 1840.
The Abbey and Other Tales. 1840.
Greville; or, A Season in Paris. 1841.
Cecil; or, The Adventures of a Coxcomb. 1841.
Cecil a Peer. 1841; as *Ormington,* 1842.
The Man of Fortune and Other Tales. 1842.
The Ambassador's Wife. 1842.
The Money-Lender. 1843; as *Abednego,* 1854.
Modern Chivalry; or, A New Orlando Furioso, edited by William Harrison
    Ainsworth. 1843.
The Banker's Wife; or, Court and City. 1843.
Agathonia. 1844.
The Birthright and Other Tales. 1844.
The Popular Member; The Wheel of Fortune. 1844.
Self. 1845.
The Story of a Royal Favourite. 1845.
The Snow Storm. 1845.
Peers and Parvenus. 1846.

New Year's Day. 1846.
Men of Capital. 1846.
The Débutante; or, The London Season. 1846.
Castles in the Air. 1847.
Temptation and Atonement and Other Tales. 1847.
The Inundation; or, Pardon and Peace. 1847.
The Diamond and the Pearl. 1848.
The Dean's Daughter; or, The Days We Live In. 1853.
The Lost Son. 1854.
Transmutation; or, The Lord and the Lout. 1854.
Progress and Prejudice. 1854.
Mammon; or, The Hardships of an Heiress. 1855.
A Life's Lessons. 1856.
The Two Aristocracies. 1857.
Heckington. 1858.

Plays

The School for Coquettes (produced 1831).
Lords and Commons (produced 1831).
The Queen's Champion, from a play by Scribe (produced 1834).   1886.
Modern Honour; or, The Sharpers of High Life (produced 1834).
The King's Seal, with James Kenney (produced 1835).   1835.
The Maid of Croissey; or, Theresa's Vow (produced 1835).   N.d.
King O'Neil; or, The Irish Brigade (produced 1835).   N.d.
King John of Austria, from a play by Casimir Delavigne (produced 1836).
A Tale of a Tub (produced 1837).
A Good Night's Rest; or, Two in the Morning (produced 1839).   1883(?).
Dacre of the South; or, The Olden Time.   1840.
Quid pro Quo; or, The Day of Dupes (produced 1844).   1844.

Verse

The Two Broken Hearts.   1823.
The Bond: A Dramatic Poem.   1824.

Other

The Historical Traveller, Comprising Narratives Connected with European History.   2
    vols., 1831.
The Rose Fancier's Manual.   1838.
Paris in 1841.   1842.
Sketches of English Character.   2 vols., 1846.
Adventures in Borneo.   1849.

Editor, *Picciola; or, Captivity Captive,* by X. B. Saintine.   1837.
Editor, *The Lover and the Husband,* by Charles de Bernard.   3 vols., 1841.
Editor, *Modern French Life.*   3 vols., 1842.
Editor, *Fascination and Other Tales.*   3 vols., 1842.
Editor, *The Queen of Denmark,* by T. C. Heiberg.   3 vols., 1846.

Bibliography: in *XIX Century Fiction* by Michael Sadleir, 2 vols., 1951.

Reading List: *The Silver-Fork School: Novels of Fashion Preceding Vanity Fair* by Matthew Whiting Rosa, 1936; *A Victorian Album* by Lucy Poate Stebbins, 1946.

*   *   *

"Silver-fork" novels, popular between 1825 and 1850, are exclusively devoted to detailed and realistic representations of fashionable life. Catherine Gore compensated for her late start in the genre in 1830 by her prolific output. In 1841 she published her masterpiece *Cecil* anonymously because her novel *Greville* appeared the same week and because her name was already staled by custom. The undisputed mistress of the fashionable novel, Mrs. Gore outdid her contemporaries in relentlessly poking fun at the world she depicted so accurately. Although conscious of the dubious literary merit of her "rubbish" – her "sickly progeniture" of lightweight fiction – Mrs. Gore sought to be an historian of the ephemera and caprices, the proprieties and vices of upper-crust society. Her basic theme is simply that of man's adjustment to his environment; behind her artistic detachment from her worldlings is a considerable and sympathetic understanding of human nature. Mrs. Gore excels in portraying the uppermost middle classes, whose unique traits are modified by their peculiar social position. She sagaciously exposes the life beneath the façade while tracing political, social, and domestic relations firmly and subtly. The masculine viewpoint and fearless energy of her novels distinguish her from Jane Austen, to whom she felt intellectually akin. Mrs. Gore's preface to *Pin-Money* expresses her "attempt to transfer the familiar narrative of Miss Austen to a higher sphere of society," and she is similar to her predecessor in her subjects, and her irony in describing many of her memorable characters. But Jane Austen's delicate clarity is very different from Mrs. Gore's elaborate verbosity.

The inexhaustibility of Mrs. Gore's imagination qualifies her literary reputation. Her satire and epigrammatic wit, however swift and subtle, are incessant, and her prose is a motley of foreign tags, quotations, allusions, pompous vocabulary, and circumlocution. The combination initially dazzles but eventually hypnotizes. Mrs. Gore's genius can easily be underestimated because of the abundance – and redundance – of her works themselves. She successfully created popular songs, etchings, comedies, dramas, melodramas, farces, poems, travel books, garden manuals, historical tales, and several novels extending beyond the confines of fashionable life. Her best books include *Mothers and Daughters*, *The Hamiltons*, *Mrs. Armytage*, *Cecil* and its sequel *Cecil a Peer*, and *The Banker's Wife*.

Mrs. Gore made the most of a genre whose formulaic situations and superficial characters precluded profound depth or universal appeal. She is superb at the comedy of artificial life; her style at its best is quick, elastic, and buoyant; her novels sometimes exhibit true pathos. She was famous both as a witty conversationalist and as a truthful and commonsensical writer. Bulwer claimed that her satire made Thackeray's look like caricature, while Thackeray reacted by parodying her work in his "Novels by Eminent Hands." Mrs. Gore's importance remains historical rather than literary – when her own audience tired of silver-fork novels, the critics predicted that future generations would re-discover her subject matter and restore her prestige.

—Janice M. Cauwels

GRAHAM, R(obert) B(ontine) Cunninghame. Scottish. Born in London, 24 May 1852; son of the laird of Ardoch, Dumbartonshire; succeeded to the family estates, 1883. Educated at Harrow School and at a private school in Brussels. Married the poet Gabriela Balmondière in 1879 (died, 1900). Travelled extensively in South and Central America, and in Spain, from

1869; Liberal Member of Parliament for North-West Lanarkshire, 1886–92, but became a socialist and follower of William Morris; Co-Founder, with Keir Hardie, and first President, Scottish Labour Party, 1888; contested the Camlachie division of Glasgow, 1892, and Western Stirling and Clackmannan, 1918; Founder Member, and first President, Scottish National Party, 1928. Justice of the Peace and Deputy Lieutenant for Dunbartonshire; Justice of the Peace for Perth and Stirling. *Died 20 March 1936.*

PUBLICATIONS

Collections

    The Essential Graham, edited by Paul Bloomfield.   1952.

Fiction and Sketches

    Father Archangel of Scotland and Other Essays, with Gabriela Graham.   1896.
    The Ipané.   1899.
    Thirteen Stories.   1900.
    Success.   1902.
    Progress and Other Sketches.   1905.
    His People.   1906.
    Faith.   1909.
    Hope.   1910.
    Charity.   1912.
    A Hatchment.   1913.
    El Rio de la Plata (stories in Spanish).   1914.
    Scottish Stories.   1914.
    Brought Forward.   1916.
    The Dream of the Magi.   1923.
    Redeemed and Other Sketches.   1927.
    Thirty Tales and Sketches, edited by Edward Garnett.   1929.
    Writ in Sand.   1932.
    Mirages.   1936.
    Rodeo: A Collection of Tales and Sketches, edited by A. F. Tschiffely.   1936.
    The South American Sketches, edited by John Walker.   1978.

Other

    Notes on the District of Menteith for Tourists and Others.   1895.
    Aurora la Cujiñi: A Realistic Sketch in Seville.   1898.
    Mogreb-El-Acksa: A Journey in Morocco.   1898.
    A Vanished Arcadia, Being Some Account of the Jesuits in Paraguay 1607 to 1767.   1901.
    Hernando de Soto.   1903.
    Bernal Diaz del Castillo.   1915.
    A Brazilian Mystic, Being the Life and Miracles of Antonio Conselheiro.   1920.
    Cartagena and the Banks of the Sinú.   1920.
    The Conquest of New Granada, Being the Life of Gonzalo Jimenez de Quesada.   1922.

The Conquest of the River Plate. 1924.
Inveni Portam: Joseph Conrad. 1924.
Doughty Deeds: An Account of the Life of Robert Graham of Gartmore, Poet and Politician 1735–97. 1925.
Pedro de Valdivia, Conqueror of Chile. 1926.
José Antonio Páez. 1929.
Bibi. 1929.
The Horses of the Conquest. 1930; edited by R. M. Denhardt, 1949.
Portrait of a Dictator: Francisco Solano Lopez (Paraguay 1865–70). 1933.
With the North West Wind. 1937.
Three Fugitive Pieces, edited by H. F. West. 1960.

Translator, *Mapirunga*, by Gustavo Barroso. 1924.

Bibliography: *A Bibliography of the First Editions of Graham* by Leslie Chaundy, 1924; *The Herbert Faulkner West Collection of Graham*, 1938.

Reading List: *Don Roberto* by H. F. West, 1936; *Don Roberto, Being an Account of the Life and Works of Graham* by A. F. Tschiffely, 1937, as *Tornado Cavalier*, 1955; *Graham: A Centenary Study* by Hugh MacDiarmid, 1952; *Prince-Errant and Evocator of Horizons: A Reading of Graham* by R. E. Haymaker, 1967.

*   *   *

Literature was for "Don Roberto" – his nickname in South America – as for his ancestor, Robert Graham of Gartmore, author of "If doughty deeds my lady please," but one department of living. Nevertheless, R. B. Cunninghame Graham made himself a minor master in the craft of the travel book and the art of the short story.

His travel books, notably *Mogreb-el-Acksa* about Morocco, and *El Rio de la Plata*, breathe the enthusiasm and sharp insights of a man of action who happened also to have a vigorous and clear prose style. His short stories, often with settings in the distant lands he travelled, are to be found in the collections *Faith, Hope, Charity, Success,* and *Scottish Stories*. His particular skill as a story-teller is to involve the reader through a compelling and sometimes exotic opening, and then to lay a hand on his arm and keep him listening. He is not a subtle writer, but a man of wide experience in the ways of the world who knows what to interpret and how to interpret it. The much-anthologised "Beattock for Moffat" admirably sets out the case of the dying man who has spent all his life abroad, yet wants to end his days in his native land, a common nineteenth-century phenomenon.

Cunninghame Graham's main influence on Scotland was not a literary one. Co-founder with Keir Hardie of the Scottish Labour Party, Cunninghame Graham was also a founder member and, in 1928, first President of the Scottish National Party. He is thus commonly thought of as one of the "founding fathers" behind the twentieth-century Scottish Renaissance Movement.

—Maurice Lindsay

GRAHAME, Kenneth. Scottish. Born in Edinburgh, 8 March 1859. Educated at St. Edward's School, Oxford, 1868–75. Married Elspeth Thomson in 1899; one son. Worked for Grahame, Currie, and Spens, parliamentary agents, London, 1875–79; Gentleman-Clerk, 1879–98, and Secretary, 1898–1908, Bank of England, London. Secretary of the New Shakespere Society, London, 1877–91. *Died 6 July 1932.*

PUBLICATIONS

Fiction

The Golden Age. 1895.
Dream Days. 1898; revised edition, 1899.
The Headswoman (stories). 1898.
The Wind in the Willows. 1908.
First Whisper of "The Wind in the Willows," edited by Elspeth Grahame. 1944.

Other

Pagan Papers. 1893.
The Grahame Day Book, edited by Margery Coleman. 1937.

Editor, *Lullaby-Land: Songs of Childhood,* by Eugene Field. 1897.
Editor, *The Cambridge Book of Poetry for Children.* 2 vols., 1916.

Reading List: *Grahame: Life, Letters, and Unpublished Work* by P. R. Chalmers, 1933; *Grahame: A Study of His Life, Work, and Times* by Peter Green, 1959 (includes bibliography); *Grahame* by Eleanor Graham, 1963.

*   *   *

Although he wrote only four books, a short story, and enough uncollected essays to fill one more volume, Kenneth Grahame can be claimed as a major author in two branches of literature. He is now best known for *The Wind in the Willows,* one of the greatest children's books in our language, but without it he would still hold a high place for his essays and stories *about* children collected in two volumes, *The Golden Age* and *Dream Days.*

These two volumes grew out of his first book, *Pagan Papers,* a collection of essays written in a literary style brought into fashion by such writers as Walter Pater and Robert Louis Stevenson, too exotic and precious for many readers today. This early volume (suitably adorned with an Aubrey Beardsley frontispiece) concluded with six sketches subtitled "The Golden Age," which were reprinted with twelve others as a separate book under that title. It was followed by *Dream Days,* containing eight longer stories.

These two collections brought about a revolution in children's literature by dealing with the contemporary child in every-day surroundings. They tell of a family of children (based on his own childhood) whose parents are dead and who are being brought up by maiden aunts – the "Olympians" – with whom they consider themselves permanently at war. The children live their own life of mingled reality and make-believe, pitying the Olympians and scoring off them whenever possible; the children accept their commands when they must, but consider them arbitrary and incomprehensible whims of an alien order of beings.

Grahame's ornate style is here perfectly suited to his subject and makes each sketch or episode into a literary jewel for the fastidious adult – "Well nigh too praiseworthy for praise," was Swinburne's famous description. Those readers to whom this ornate style appeals find the sketches a never-ending delight, and read them again and again.

Their effect on children's literature was to present childhood as a state in itself, and children as a distinct race of beings in their own right rather than as miniature adults to be guided up the steep path to Olympus: they opened the way for such writers as E. Nesbit, Arthur Ransome, and numerous lesser practitioners. But it must be stressed that these two books which hold so much of the precious essence of childhood are not books for children. It is not merely the style which puts off the child reader, but in some subtle way the deeper content which seems a kind of violation of the precious secrets of childhood, a trespassing of adult, Olympian feet into a land that they have no right to enter.

Writing *for* children, and using stories told to his own small son, Grahame conquered this other kingdom with *The Wind in the Willows* – a book loved by both adults and children, a fantasy set in a natural fairyland of the inner life of the river-side: "with his ear to the reed-stems he caught, at intervals, something of what the wind was whispering, so constantly among them." The "intervals" of prose-poetry may appeal mainly to the adult reader, but the riverside adventures of Toad and Mole and Rat and Badger (which A. A. Milne made into a play *Toad of Toad Hall*) appeal to the younger reader as well as the adult.

—Roger Lancelyn Green

GRAVES, Richard. English. Born in Mickleton, Gloucestershire, 4 May 1715. Educated privately, and at Roysse's Grammar School, Abingdon, Oxfordshire, 1728–32; Pembroke College, Oxford, 1732–36; All Souls College, Oxford, 1736–40, M.A. in divinity 1740; also studied medicine in London, 1736. Married Lucy Bartholomew c. 1744 (died, 1777); four sons and one daughter. Fellow of All Souls, 1736–44; chaplain to the William Fitzherbert family, at Tissington, near Ashbourne, Derbyshire, 1741–44; Curate, possibly at Aldworth, near Reading, 1744, and at Whitchurch, Oxfordshire, 1749; Rector of Claverton, near Bath, 1749 until his death; also ran a school at Claverton from the 1760's, and held the living of Croscombe, 1802–04. *Died 23 November 1804.*

PUBLICATIONS

Fiction

The Spiritual Quixote; or, The Summer's Ramble of Mr. Geoffry Wildgoose: A Comic Romance. 1773; edited by Clarence Tracy, 1967.
Columella; or, The Distressed Anchoret: A Colloquial Tale. 1779.
Eugenius; or, Anecdotes of the Golden Vale: An Embellished Narrative of Real Facts. 1785.
Plexippus; or, The Aspiring Plebeian. 1790.

Play

The Coalition; or, The Opera Rehearsed (produced 1793?). 1794.

Verse

The Love of Order: A Poetical Essay. 1773.
The Progress of Gallantry: A Poetical Essay. 1774.
Euphrosyne; or, Amusements on the Road of Life. 2 vols., 1776–80.
Lucubrations, Consisting of Essays, Reveries in Prose and Verse. 1786.
The Rout; or, A Sketch of Modern Life, from an Academic in the Metropolis to His Friend in the Country. 1789.
The Farmer's Son: A Moral Tale. 1795.

Other

A Letter from a Father to His Son at the University. 1787.
Recollections of Some Particulars in the Life of the Late William Shenstone. 1788.
The Reveries of Solitude, Consisting of Essays in Prose, A New Translation of the Muscipula, and Original Pieces in Verse. 1793.
Sermons. 1799.
Senilities; or, Solitary Amusements in Prose and Verse. 1801.
The Invalid, with the Obvious Means of Enjoying Health and a Long Life. 1804.
The Triflers; Consisting of Trifling Essays, Trifling Anecdotes, and a Few Poetical Trifles. 1805.

Editor, *The Festoon: A Collection of Epigrams, Ancient and Modern, with an Essay on That Species of Composition.* 1765; revised edition, 1767.

Translator, *Galateo; or, A Treatise on Politeness and Delicacy of Manners,* by Giovanni della Casa. 1774.
Translator, *The Sorrows of Werter,* by Goethe. 1779.
Translator, *The Heir Apparent; or, The Life of Commodus,* by Herodian. 1789.
Translator, *The Meditations of the Emperor Marcus Aurelius.* 1792.
Translator, *Hiero on the Condition of Royalty: A Conversation,* by Xenophon. 1793.

Reading List: *The Literary Career of Graves* by Charles Jarvis Hill, 1935 (includes bibliography).

*   *   *

Though Richard Graves habitually dismissed his writings as "trifling," all the best of them have an intellectual core. *Columella,* for example, illustrates the evils that may befall a man who steps out of the role in life proper to one of his class by withdrawing into himself. The plot of *Plexippus* was meant to show that a man of "genius, learning, or industry" is better entitled to respect than one who has only an hereditary title to boast of. *Eugenius* explores the "paradox" that modern manners are better than those of earlier times. *The Spiritual Quixote,* the first and best of the novels, is a satire on Methodism. Geoffry Wildgoose, its hero, goes out quixotically on the road to preach Whitefield's theology: faith rather than good works, the new birth, and the total depravity of the natural man. Wesley is also satirized for laying claim to apostolical grace, but, as his theological position was closer than Whitefield's to Graves's own, he is treated less severely. Wildgoose has many adventures of the *Joseph Andrews* type, and in the end is reconciled to the church of his ancestors by the experience of falling in love. Nature comes into conflict with grace, at least with grace as defined by the more austere of the Methodist preachers, and is triumphant.

Graves found it hard to develop a coherent plot in any of his novels. That of *Plexippus,* for example, is spoiled when the "man of genius" who is its hero turns out to have also been well born, and that of the *Spiritual Quixote* is weakened by many digressions and by Wildgoose's being diverted from his pious aims rather than disillusioned with them. Graves's love of a good story, which he tells well, combined with a heavy reliance on his own experience, makes his novels look like episodic memoirs. The best parts of the *Spiritual Quixote*, for example, are Mr. Rivers's interpolated story, in which the author tells the only slightly edited version of his own courtship and marriage, and the scenes in Bath and the Peak country, which are drawn from the life. Moreover, it has often been suggested that the character of Geoffry Wildgoose is modelled on that of the author's brother, Charles Caspar, who for a time was an itinerant Methodist preacher, and that several of the other characters are also based on Graves's friends and associates, just as Columella, in the novel of that name, is William Shenstone. Though many of those identifications are plausible, their implications must not be pressed too far: Columella, Wildgoose, and the others are not pictures of Graves's friends and relations, but characters created for his own fictional purposes. It is as wrong to underrate his imaginative powers as to overrate them.

Graves has a gift for striking words and clever turns of phrase, and apt allusions and quotations pour out in his books and letters. He is often too wordy; most of his works would have benefitted from cutting. Often he seems most successful in miniature forms like the epigram: *The Festoon*, which he edited, contains a number of his own epigrams as well as a collection of epigrams by others, and had a wide circulation. In his novels, the wit and the shrewd comments attract one now rather than the larger elements of design. An amusing talker, he gives the best of his works the liveliness and charm that mark the man himself.

—Clarence Tracy

GRAVES, Robert (Ranke). English. Born in London, 24 July 1895. Educated at Charterhouse School, Surrey; St. John's College, Oxford, B.Litt. 1926. Served in France with the Royal Welch Fusiliers in World War 1; was refused admittance into the armed forces in World War II. Married 1) Nancy Nicholson, one son and two daughters; 2) Beryl Pritchard, three sons and one daughter. Professor of English, Egyptian University, Cairo, 1926. Settled in Deya, Majorca; with the poet Laura Riding established the Seizen Press and *Epilogue* magazine. Left Majorca during the Spanish Civil War; settled in Glampton-Brixton, Devon during World War II; returned to Majorca after the war. Clark Lecturer, Trinity College, Cambridge, 1954; Professor of Poetry, Oxford University, 1961–66; Arthur Dehon Little Memorial Lecturer, Massachusetts Institute of Technology, Cambridge, 1963. Recipient: Bronze Medal for Poetry, Olympic Games, Paris, 1924; Hawthornden Prize, 1935; Black Memorial Prize, 1935; Femina Vie Heureuse-Stock Prize, 1939; Russell Loines Award, 1958; National Poetry Society of America Gold Medal, 1960; Foyle Poetry Prize, 1960; Arts Council Poetry Award, 1962; Italia Prize, for radio play, 1965; Queen's Gold Medal for Poetry, 1968; Gold Medal for Poetry, Cultural Olympics, Mexico City, 1968. M.A.: Oxford University, 1961. Honorary Fellow, St. John's College, Oxford, 1971. Honorary Member, American Academy of Arts and Sciences, 1970. Lives in Majorca.

PUBLICATIONS

Fiction

The Shout. 1929.
No Decency Left, with Laura Riding. 1932.

The Real David Copperfield. 1933; as *David Copperfield by Charles Dickens, Condensed by Robert Graves,* edited by Merrill P. Paine. 1934.

I, Claudius: From the Autobiography of Tiberius Claudius, Emperor of the Romans, Born B.C. 10, Murdered and Deified A.D. 54. 1934.

Claudius the God and His Wife Messalina: The Troublesome Reign of Tiberius Claudius Caesar, Emperor of the Romans (Born B.C. 10, Died A.D. 54), As Described by Himself; Also His Murder at the Hands of the Notorious Agrippina (Mother of the Emperor Nero) and His Subsequent Deification, As Described by Others. 1934.

"Antigua, Penny, Puce." 1936; as *The Antigua Stamp.* 1937.

Count Belisarius. 1938.

Sergeant Lamb of the Ninth. 1940; as *Sergeant Lamb's America,* 1940.

Proceed, Sergeant Lamb. 1941.

The Story of Marie Powell: Wife to Mr. Milton. 1943; as *Wife to Mr. Milton: The Story of Marie Powell,* 1944.

The Golden Fleece. 1944; as *Hercules, My Shipmate,* 1945.

King Jesus. 1946.

Watch the North Wind Rise. 1949; as *Seven Days in New Crete,* 1949.

The Islands of Unwisdom. 1949; as *The Isles of Unwisdom,* 1950.

Homer's Daughter. 1955.

¡Catacrok! Mostly Stories, Mostly Funny. 1956.

Collected Short Stories. 1964.

Plays

John Kemp's Wager: A Ballad Opera. 1925.

Much Ado about Nothing, from the play by Shakespeare, textual revisions by Graves (produced 1965).

Radio Play: *The Anger of Achilles,* 1964.

Verse

Over the Brazier. 1916.

Goliath and David. 1916.

Fairies and Fusiliers. 1917.

Treasure Box. 1919.

Country Sentiment. 1920.

The Pier-Glass. 1921.

Whipperginny. 1923.

The Feather Bed. 1923.

Mock Beggar Hall. 1924.

Welchman's Hose. 1925.

(Poems). 1925.

The Marmosite's Miscellany. 1925.

Poems (1914–1926). 1927.

Poems (1914–1927). 1927.

Poems 1929. 1929.

Ten Poems More. 1930.

Poems 1926–1930. 1931.

To Whom Else? 1931.

Poems 1930–1933. 1933.

Collected Poems. 1938.

No More Ghosts: Selected Poems.   1940.
Work in Hand, with Alan Hodge and Norman Cameron.   1942.
(Poems).   1943.
Poems 1938–1945.   1946.
Collected Poems (1914–1947).   1948.
Poems and Satires 1951.   1951.
Poems 1953.   1953.
Collected Poems 1955.   1955.
Poems Selected by Himself.   1957; revised edition, 1961, 1966.
The Poems.   1958.
Collected Poems 1959.   1959.
More Poems 1961.   1961.
Collected Poems.   1961.
New Poems 1962.   1962.
The More Deserving Cases: Eighteen Old Poems for Reconsideration.   1962.
Man Does, Woman Is 1964.   1964.
Love Respelt.   1965.
Collected Poems 1965.   1965.
Seventeen Poems Missing from "Love Respelt."   1966.
Colophon to "Love Respelt."   1967.
(Poems), with D. H. Lawrence, edited by Leonard Clark.   1967.
Poems 1965–1968.   1968.
Poems about Love.   1969.
Love Respelt Again.   1969.
Beyond Giving: Poems.   1969.
Poems 1968–1970.   1970.
The Green-Sailed Vessel.   1971.
Poems 1970–1972.   1972.
Deyá.   1973.
Timeless Meeting: Poems.   1973.
At the Gate   1974.
Collected Poems 1975.   1975.
New Collected Poems.   1977.

Other

On English Poetry, Being an Irregular Approach to the Psychology of This Art, from Evidence Mainly Subjective.   1922.
The Meaning of Dreams.   1924.
Poetic Unreason and Other Studies.   1925.
My Head! My Head! Being the History of Elisha and the Shumanite Woman; With the History of Moses as Elisha Related It, and Her Questions to Him.   1925.
Contemporary Techniques of Poetry: A Political Analogy.   1925.
Another Future of Poetry.   1926.
Impenetrability; or, The Proper Habit of English.   1927.
The English Ballad: A Short Critical Survey.   1927.
Lars Porsena; or, The Future of Swearing and Improper Language.   1927; revised edition, as *The Future of Swearing and Improper Language,* 1936.
A Survey of Modernist Poetry, with Laura Riding.   1927.
Lawrence and the Arabs.   1927; as *Lawrence and the Arabian Adventure,* 1928.
A Pamphlet Against Anthologies, with Laura Riding.   1928; as *Against Anthologies,* 1928.
Mrs. Fisher; or, The Future of Humour.   1928.

Goodbye to All That: An Autobiography.   1929; revised edition, 1957, 1960.

But It Still Goes On: An Accumulation.   1930.

Epilogue: A Critical Summary, vols. 1, 2, and 3, with Laura Riding and others.   1935–37.

T. E. Lawrence to His Biographer Robert Graves.   1938.

The Long Week-end: A Social History of Great Britain 1918–1939, with Alan Hodge.   1940.

The Reader over Your Shoulder: A Handbook for Writers of English Prose, with Alan Hodge.   1943.

The White Goddess: A Historical Grammar of Poetic Myth.   1948; revised edition, 1958.

The Common Asphodel: Collected Essays on Poetry 1922–1949.   1949.

Occupation: Writer.   1950.

The Nazarene Gospel Restored, with Joshua Podro.   1953.

The Crowning Privilege: The Clark Lectures 1954–1955; Also Various Essays on Poetry and Sixteen New Poems.   1955; as *The Crowning Privilege: Collected Essays on Poetry,* 1956.

Adam's Rib and Other Anomalous Elements in the Hebrew Creation Myth: A New View.   1955.

The Greek Myths.   2 vols., 1955.

Jesus in Rome: A Historical Conjecture, with Joshua Podro.   1957.

They Hanged My Saintly Billy.   1957; as *They Hanged My Saintly Billy: The Life and Death of Dr. William Palmer,* 1957.

Steps: Stories, Talks, Essays, Poems, Studies in History.   1958.

Five Pens in Hand.   1958.

Food for Centaurs: Stories, Talks, Critical Studies, Poems.   1960.

The Penny Fiddle: Poems for Children.   1960.

Greek Gods and Heroes.   1960; as *Myths of Ancient Greece,* 1961.

Selected Poetry and Prose, edited by James Reeves.   1961.

The Siege and Fall of Troy (juvenile).   1962.

The Big Green Book.   1962.

Oxford Addresses on Poetry.   1962.

The Hebrew Myths: The Book of Genesis, with Raphael Patai.   1964.

Ann at Highwood Hall: Poems for Children.   1964.

Majorca Observed.   1965.

Mammon and the Black Goddess.   1965.

Two Wise Children (juvenile).   1966.

Poetic Craft and Principle: Lectures and Talks.   1967.

Spiritual Quixote.   1967.

The Poor Boy Who Followed His Star (juvenile).   1968.

The Crane Bag and Other Disputed Subjects.   1969.

On Poetry: Collected Talks and Essays.   1969.

Poems: Abridged for Dolls and Princes (juvenile).   1971.

Difficult Questions, Easy Answers.   1972.

Editor, with Alan Porter and Richard Hughes, *Oxford Poetry, 1921.*   1921.

Editor, *John Skelton (Laureate), 1460(?)–1529.*   1927.

Editor, *The Less Familiar Nursery Rhymes.*   1927.

Editor, *Old Soldiers Never Die,* by Frank Richards.   1933.

Editor, *Old Soldier Sahib,* by Frank Richards.   1936.

Editor, *The Comedies of Terence,* translated by Echard.   1962.

Translator, with Laura Riding, *Almost Forgotten Germany,* by George Schwarz.   1936.

Translator, *The Transformations of Lucius, Otherwise Known as The Golden Ass,* by Apuleius.   1950.

Translator, *The Cross and the Sword,* by Manuel de Jesus Galvan. 1954.
Translator, *The Infant with the Globe,* by Pedro Antonio de Alarcon. 1955.
Translator, *Winter in Majorca,* by George Sand. 1956.
Translator, *Pharsalia: Dramatic Episodes of the Civil Wars,* by Lucan. 1956.
Translator, *The Twelve Caesars,* by Suetonius. 1957.
Translator, *The Anger of Achilles: Homer's Iliad.* 1959.
Translator, with Omar Ali-Shah, *Rubaiyyat of Omar Khayaam.* 1967.
Translator, *The Song of Songs.* 1973.

Bibliography: *A Bibliography of the Works of Graves* by Fred H. Higginson, 1966.

Reading List: *Graves* by Martin Seymour-Smith, 1956, revised edition, 1965, 1970; *Graves* by J. M. Cohen, 1960; *Swifter than Reason: The Poetry and Criticism of Graves* by Douglas Day, 1963; *Graves* by George Stade, 1967; *Barbarous Knowledge: Myth in the Poetry of Yeats, Graves, and Muir* by Daniel Hoffman, 1967; *The Poetry of Graves* by Michael Kirkham, 1969; *The Third Book of Criticism* by Randall Jarrell, 1969.

*   *   *

Robert Graves's prolific writings in prose and verse express his own conflicting characteristics. He is at once a Romantic primitive and a classicist; a seeker of ecstasy and of formal perfection. Committed to the life of feeling and the rule of intuition, he is a compulsive systematizer and puzzle-solver. Indeed, Graves is a confirming example of what T. S. Eliot diagnosed as the characteristic modern condition: dissociation of sensibility from thought. Graves's entire career expresses his inspired, inventive, and ingenious efforts to express either side of this essential self; in his best work, both are intertwined.

Graves's childhood and adolescence were typical of his class and time. Son of A. P. Graves, a facile verse-writer and translator from the Irish who was inspector of schools in Dublin, Robert had a proper Edwardian childhood and was schooled at Charterhouse. At the outbreak of the first World War he volunteered and was comissioned in the Royal Welch Fusiliers. His choice of regiment reflects his desire to find his own Celtic roots elsewhere than in the Ireland preempted by his father's literary activity. The immediate result of service was his exposure to the horror of trench warfare, severe wounds, being reported dead, return to duty, subsequent hospitalization in England where he was treated for shell-shock by Dr. W. H. R. Rivers, whose patients included Siegfried Sassoon and Wilfred Owen and whose psychiatric theories influenced Graves's aesthetic in the 1920's. The war experience and its aftermath are memorably stated in his autobiography, *Goodbye to All That,* his aesthetic in *Poetic Unreason.*

By 1916 Graves had published his first book of poems, *Over the Brazier,* rather vapid stuff compared to what he would write within a decade. As a war poet Graves did not deal, as did Owen, Sassoon, and Isaac Rosenberg, with reality; his desperately self-protective imagination held fast to nursery and nature images, the pieties of Georgianism. Not until the war was over could Graves grapple with its nightmarish revelation of the madness of reality, as he does in such poems as "In Procession," "Warning to Children," "Alice," "The Cool Web," "In Broken Images," and many others. These are among the most powerful reflections of the disintegration of certainty, the blasting apart of pre-war norms, the guilt of survivors, the desperation of man deprived of the traditional and institutional props of his culture.

With tenacity Graves refused, however, to surrender certain of those institutions and traditions. As a poet he resisted the modernist break-up of meter, form, and linguistic decorum. In its conventional craft his work is thus nearer to that of Hardy and Yeats than to Eliot or Pound. In theme, however, he has not essayed the range of any of these. Besides his poems of psychomachia mentioned above, his principal theme has been the recording of romantic love. In this his work shows affinities to Donne and the Cavalier poets, but Graves's view of love is unique. From the beginning he viewed love as a transcendent ecstasy immutably linked with doom, as in "Love Without Hope" (1925):

> Love without hope, as when the young bird-catcher
> Swept off his tall hat to the Squire's own daughter,
> So let the imprisoned larks escape and fly
> Singing about her head, as she rode by.

This quatrain encapsulates the convictions Graves would raise into myth in *The White Goddess*, that stupendous "Historic grammar of poetic myth" which explicates what in his poem "To Juan at the Winter Solstice" he called the "one story and one story only / That will prove worth your telling." The Squire's daughter will become a queen, a goddess, while remaining the mortal woman whom the poet is fated to love; the young bird-catcher is of course the poet whose singing larks were imprisoned in his head (under his tall hat) until he gave them freedom to declare his hopeless adoration. The beloved is in fact the poet's Muse who appears to him as Mother, Lover, and Layer-out, a tripartite pattern of significance Graves traces to the once-universal matriarchal religious states that preceded the patriarchy, repressive of the life of feeling, which the Judeo-Christian tradition has foisted upon the world.

Accept this historiography (with its roots in Celtic and Classical paganism) or not; what is incontestable is that Graves has written a body of love poetry without rival in our time for its intensity, elegance, and occasional lubricity.

As novelist and essayist Graves demonstrates the erudition and intellectual ingenuity that characterize *The White Goddess*. Many of his fictions offer "answers" to conundrums historians not gifted with a poet's intuition have been unable to solve, just as Graves's discursive books often "restore" defective literary or sacred texts (e.g., the ballads, the Bible). His most admired novels, *I, Claudius* and *Claudius the God*, provide the hitherto secret memoirs of Claudius himself and give an even more intimate view than did Suetonius of the depravities of Rome's first family between the reigns of Caesar Augustus and Claudius himself. The latter, shy, stammering, introspective, and wise, has a poet's understanding of the social and personal catastrophes enacted around him. To the alert reader Graves is writing about the decline and fall of the British as well as the Roman empire, as he does overtly in *The Long Week-end*. Other novels present historical cruces from similarly unexpected points of view. *Wife to Mr. Milton* exonerates its heroine against the received calumnies of a poet Graves dislikes intensely. *Sergeant Lamb's America* treats the American Revolution as seen by a predecessor in Graves's own regiment.

Graves's measure for other poets, as for himself, is their participation in "The poetic trance derive[d] from ecstatic worship of the age-old matriarchal Greek Muse, who ruled Sky, Earth, Underworld in triad." In his Oxford lectures, *Mammon and the Black Goddess*, Graves discovers a further stage in his anatomy of love, the stations of the poet's progress. "The Black Goddess ... promises a new pacific bond between men and women, corresponding to a final reality of love, in which the patriarchal marriage bond will fade away.... Faithful as Vesta, gay and adventurous as the White Goddess, she will lead man back to that sure instinct of love which he long ago forfeited by intellectual pride." Robert Graves has continued to pour forth poems on his "one story only" past his eightieth year.

—Daniel Hoffman

GREEN, Henry. Pseudonym for Henry Vincent Yorke. English. Born near Tewkesbury, Gloucestershire, in 1905. Educated at Eton College; Oxford University. Served in the Fire Service, London, 1939–43. Married the Hon. Mary Adelaide Biddulph in 1929; one son. Writer from 1926; Managing Director, H. Pontifex and Company, Birmingham, after the war. *Died 13 December 1973.*

PUBLICATIONS

Fiction

> *Blindness.* 1926.
> *Living.* 1929.
> *Party Going.* 1939.
> *Caught.* 1943.
> *Loving.* 1945.
> *Back.* 1946.
> *Concluding.* 1948.
> *Nothing.* 1950.
> *Doting.* 1952.

Other

> *Pack My Bag: A Self-Portrait.* 1940.

Reading List: *The Novels of Green* by Edward Stokes, 1959; *Green: Nine Novels and an Unpacked Bag* by John Russell, 1960; *A Reading of Green* by A. K. Weatherhead, 1961; *Green* by Robert S. Ryf, 1967; *Toward "Loving": The Poetics of the Novel and the Practice of Green* by Bruce Bassoff, 1975.

*   *   *

While Henry Green's novels reveal stylistic characteristics and habits of composition which make them unmistakably the work of the same man, they all (with the partial exception of *Nothing* and *Doting*) deal with widely different aspects of human experience. Partly, no doubt, as a result of his having spent some time on the shop floor of the family business of which he was later to become head, he was equally at home with people of many different kinds: aristocrats, professionals, the *nouveaux riches*, servants, factory workers. Coupled with the breadth of his sympathies is a many-sided technical virtuosity which is not ostentatiously displayed, but is partially concealed beneath essentially realist surfaces. Preferring not to reveal himself directly in his books, Green expresses his materials by unemphatic uses of recurrent motif and imagery, by startling juxtapositions and symmetries, and by a careful orchestration of third-person narrative voices.

Green's first novel, *Blindness*, begun when he was a schoolboy, was continued during the two years which he spent at Oxford and was published when he was 21. For the work of so young a writer, it is a *tour de force* of the creative imagination. Green's choice of a theme without direct autobiographical implication (adjustment to accidental blindness at an early age) is in keeping with the detachment which is characteristic of all of his work. Despite his own later judgement, several times reiterated ("*Blindness* is no good"), the novel contains some remarkably penetrating passages. *Living*, which followed three years later, is more decidedly successful. Its depiction of life in a Birmingham foundry is impressive both for Green's structural control and for his mature insights into bosses and workers alike. Late in the composition of *Living*, Green decided to make a minor stylistic experiment by omitting most of the definite and indefinite articles. The effect, unexpectedly successful, is to create a general impression of dialect and of closeness to life.

Living is a rich, dense book, full of imagery, of people, of action. *Party Going*, published ten years later, is, by comparison, sparser, harder, more schematic. Although the upper and lower classes are still set off against each other, Green devotes most of his attention to a group of wealthy young people who had hoped to get to France to enjoy themselves but are temporarily confined to a railway station by fog. While they are waiting, they play a series of elaborate social games which Green analyses with a mixture of malice and sympathy. Despite the nature of the subject matter, the novel is far more than a social comedy. The empty personal lives of the main characters are set in a powerfully symbolic context in which Green makes especially interesting use of sharply defined physical objects: a dead pigeon wrapped in brown paper, gulls flying under a bridge, streamers of fog inside the station building, steam rising from whisky thrown on to a fire. The whole is tantalisingly suggestive and serves as a forerunner of the work of Alain Robbe-Grillet and other *nouveaux romanciers*, some of whom have looked upon Green as an important precursor.

In the three novels which he wrote during World War II, *Caught, Loving*, and *Back*, Green further consolidated the technical assurance of *Party Going*. *Caught*, his most powerful expression of human anguish, is a remarkably taut account of conflicting needs among those who served in the fire service during the war. The structure makes use of complex time schemes which lend the book a highly modern, even cubist tone.

Loving is the most highly coloured, and in some respects the most human and tender of Green's books. Beginning and ending as a fairy tale ("Once upon a day ... lived happily ever after"), it deals with life in remote and neutral Ireland during the war. A group of expatriate Britishers, including both masters and servants, lives in an isolated country castle. Along with much that is superficially idyllic – the brilliant peacocks which strut on the green lawns – there is a great deal that is petty, distressing, and even violent. Green's evocation of life below stairs is extraordinarily acute – perceptive without being aggressive, compassionate without being sentimental.

A concern with the contrast between subjective and objective perceptions of reality, begun in *Caught*, is fully developed in *Back*, a sensitive account of the return from the war of a physically and mentally shattered soldier, Charley Summers. Rose, the woman whom Charley had loved, is dead. As Charley's disturbed mind cannot accept the reality of the situation, he begins, with varying degrees of personal conviction, to transfer her identity to another girl. Green makes much use of the conflict of illusion and reality, developing it mainly through intensive use of a single dominant symbol, the rose.

Concluding, written in response to the growing importance of state control after the war, is concerned with personal relations rather than with political creeds. It is the most thoroughly symbolic of Green's novels, using flowers, animals, birds, the dance, and social rituals to suggest unspecified anxieties and tensions. As in Green's earlier books, many significant problems of human existence are treated sympathetically but entirely without programmatic or didactic intent.

In contrast to his lack of political or social dogmatism, Green held very strong views about the craft of writing. Towards the end of his active career he became increasingly convinced that the most effective way in which a novelist could create the illusion of life was by allowing the reader to hear the characters speak, without authorial intervention. The novelist, he believed, "has no business with the story he is writing" (BBC talk, published in *The Listener*, 9 November 1950); he should not undertake the impossible task of explaining what the characters are thinking: "do we know, in life, what other people are really like? I very much doubt it. We certainly do not know what other people are thinking and feeling. How then can the novelist be so sure?" Green's last two novels, *Nothing* and *Doting*, are accordingly dominated by dialogue of a remarkably realistic but also highly organised character. The significance of the dialogue is largely determined by its arrangement into patterns of a schematic, almost geometric kind, in which actors exchange roles, scenes echo and repeat each other, and suggestive leitmotifs recur. In writing these "abstract novels," as he himself called them, Green brought his crisp, detached, economical art to some kind of technical culmination. After them he wrote nothing more, and although they do not represent his finest work, they are among the most interesting experiments in British prose.

—Clive Hart

GREENE, Graham. English. Born in Berkhamsted, Hertfordshire, 2 October 1904. Educated at Berkhamsted School; Balliol College, Oxford. Served in the Foreign Office, London, 1941–44. Married Vivien Dayrell-Browning in 1927; one son and one daughter. Staff Member, *The Times*, London, 1926–30; Film Critic, 1937–40, and Literary Editor, 1940–41, *Spectator*, London; Director, Eyre and Spottiswoode, publishers, London, 1944–48, and The Bodley Head, publishers, London, 1958–68. Recipient: Hawthornden Prize, 1941; Black Memorial Prize, 1949; Shakespeare Prize, Hamburg, 1968; Thomas More Medal, 1973; Mystery Writers of America Grand Master Award, 1975. Litt.D.: Cambridge University, 1962; D.Litt.: University of Edinburgh, 1967. Honorary Fellow, Balliol College, 1963. Chevalier of the Legion of Honour, 1969. Companion of Honour, 1966.

PUBLICATIONS

Fiction

The Man Within. 1929.
The Name of Action. 1930.
Rumour at Nightfall. 1931.
Stamboul Train: An Entertainment. 1932; as *Orient Express*, 1933.
It's a Battlefield. 1934.
England Made Me. 1935; as *The Shipwrecked*, 1953.
The Basement Room and Other Stories. 1935.
The Bear Fell Free (story). 1935.
A Gun for Sale: An Entertainment. 1936; as *This Gun for Hire*, 1936.
Brighton Rock. 1938.
The Confidential Agent. 1939.
Twenty-four Stories, with James Laver and Sylvia Townsend Warner. 1939.
The Power and the Glory. 1940; as *The Labyrinthine Ways*, 1940; as *The Power and the Glory*, edited by R. W. B. Lewis, 1970.
The Ministry of Fear: An Entertainment. 1943.
Nineteen Stories. 1947; augmented edition, as *Twenty-one Stories*, 1954.
The Heart of the Matter. 1948.
The Third Man: An Entertainment. 1950.
The Third Man, and The Fallen Idol. 1950.

The End of the Affair. 1951.
Loser Takes All: An Entertainment. 1955.
The Quiet American. 1955.
Our Man in Havana: An Entertainment. 1958.
A Visit to Morin (story). 1959.
A Burnt-Out Case. 1961.
A Sense of Reality (stories). 1963.
The Comedians. 1966.
May We Borrow Your Husband? and Other Comedies of the Sexual Life. 1967.
Travels with My Aunt. 1969.
The Collected Stories. 1972.
The Honorary Consul. 1973.
The Human Factor. 1978.

Plays

The Living Room (produced 1953). 1953.
The Potting Shed (produced 1957). 1957.
The Complaisant Lover (produced 1959). 1959.
Carving a Statue (produced 1964). 1964.
The Third Man: A Film, with Carol Reed. 1968.
Alas, Poor Maling, from his own story (broadcast 1975). In *Shades of Greene,* 1975.
The Return of A. J. Raffles: An Edwardian Comedy Based Somewhat Loosely on E. W. Hornung's Characters in "The Amateur Cracksman" (produced 1975). 1975.

Screenplays: *The First and the Last* (*21 Days*), 1937; *The New Britain,* 1940; *Brighton Rock* (*Young Scarface*), with Terence Rattigan, 1947; *The Fallen Idol,* with Lesley Storm and William Templeton, 1948; *The Third Man,* with Carol Reed, 1950; *The Stranger's Hand,* with Guy Elmes and Giorgio Bassani, 1954; *Loser Takes All,* 1956; *Saint Joan,* 1957; *Our Man in Havana,* 1960; *The Comedians,* 1967.

Radio Play: *Alas, Poor Maling,* from his own story, 1975.

Verse

Babbling April. 1925.

Other

Journey Without Maps: A Travel Book. 1936.
The Lawless Roads: A Mexican Journey. 1939; as *Another Mexico,* 1939.
British Dramatists. 1942.
The Little Train (juvenile). 1946.
Why Do I Write? An Exchange of Views Between Elizabeth Bowen, Greene and V. S. Pritchett. 1948.
After Two Years. 1949.
The Little Fire Engine (juvenile). 1950; as *The Little Red Fire Engine,* 1952.
The Lost Childhood and Other Essays. 1951.
The Little Horse Bus (juvenile). 1952.
The Little Steam Roller: A Story of Mystery and Detection (juvenile). 1953.
Essais Catholiques, translated by Marcelle Sibon. 1953.

In Search of a Character: Two African Journals.   1961.
The Revenge: An Autobiographical Fragment.   1963.
Victorian Detective Fiction: A Catalogue of the Collection Made by Dorothy Glover and
     Greene, Introduced by John Carter.   1966.
Collected Essays.   1969.
A Sort of Life (autobiography).   1971.
The Pleasure-Dome: The Collected Film Criticism of Greene, 1935–1940, edited by John
     Russell Taylor.   1972; as Greene on Film, 1972.
The Portable Greene, edited by Philip Stratford.   1973.
Lord Rochester's Monkey, Being the Life of John Wilmot, Second Earl of
     Rochester.   1974.

Editor, The Old School: Essays by Divers Hands.   1934.
Editor, The Best of Saki.   1950.
Editor, with Hugh Greene, The Spy's Bedside Book: An Anthology.   1957.
Editor, The Bodley Head Ford Madox Ford.   4 vols., 1962–63.
Editor, An Impossible Woman: The Memories of Dottoressa Moor of Capri.   1975.

Bibliography: Greene: A Checklist of Criticism by J. D. Vann, 1970.

Reading List: Greene by Francis Wyndham, 1955, revised edition, 1958; Greene by J. A.
Atkins, 1957, revised edition, 1966; Greene: The Major Novels by Lynette Kohn, 1961;
Greene by David Pryce-Jones, 1963; Greene: Some Critical Considerations edited by R. O.
Evans, 1963 (includes bibliography by N. Brennan); Greene by David Lodge, 1966; Greene:
The Aesthetics of Exploration by Gwenn R. Boardman, 1971; Greene the Entertainer by Peter
Wolfe, 1972; Greene: A Collection of Critical Essays edited by Samuel Hynes, 1973.

                               *   *   *

Graham Greene is an inveterate visitor and revisitor. Travel, the dominant fact of his life, is
also the central theme and metaphor of his work: places visited, people met, and ideas
pursued are certain to reappear in his later writings. In 1938, for example, Greene toured
Mexico, and in 1939 published a reflective travel book based on his experiences. The Power
and the Glory, the fictional transformation of his encounter with Mexico, appeared in 1940.
Similarly, his journeys to Africa have yielded two travel books, Journey Without Maps and In
Search of a Character, and two novels, The Heart of the Matter and A Burnt-Out Case. Travel
in Greene, however, is internal as well as external, temporal as well as spatial. In Journey
Without Maps, he compares his own expedition to Liberia with the psychoanalyst's attempts
to penetrate the darkness of the human heart: "The method of psychoanalysis is to bring the
patient back to the idea he is repressing: a long journey backwards without maps … until one
has to face the general idea, the pain or the memory.…" This provides the rationale for
Greene's own explorations. The voyager travels to another land; the man searches uncharted
territories within his own psyche; and the artist analyses the springs and processes of his own
creativity. Life and art are mutually catalytic, and Greene notes their interaction in Journey
Without Maps as he recalls one particular Liberian native: "He was called Wordsworth.…
Already he was intent on joining that odd assortment of 'characters' … damned by their
unselfconsciousness to be material for the novelist.…" More than thirty years later, this
comment is dramatised in Travels with My Aunt, where the central character has a negro
lover named Wordsworth. Even Greene's conversion to Catholicism is part of this process of
revisitation, another backward journey to find a new way forward: "I had got somewhere by
way of memories I hadn't known I possessed. I had taken up the thread of life from very far
back, from as far back as innocence." The general corollary of this is a deterministic view of
the human condition: "No one," writes Greene, "— the theologians and psychologists agree —

is responsible for his own character: he can make only small modifications for good or ill." It is precisely the nature and extent of those "small modifications" that constitute the essence of Greene's work.

In his autobiography, *A Sort of Life*, Greene offers "an epigraph for all the novels I have written" in a quotation from Browning's "Bishop Blougram's Apology":

> Our interest's on the dangerous edge of things.
> The honest thief, the tender murderer ...
> We watch while these in equilibrium keep
> The giddy line midway.

These lines are particularly relevant to the earliest phase of Greene's career, from his first novel, *The Man Within*, to *Brighton Rock*. During this decade, Greene produced, among other writings, five "novels" and two "entertainments" (a self-imposed and shifting classification finally dissolved in the 1960's). These share a cast of characters whose internal chaos is produced and mirrored by their environments: smugglers, strikers, political assassins – cousins of the morally ambiguous beings in the Browning quotation. Andrews, the "honest" smuggler of *The Man Within*, betrays his best friend; and Raven, the murderer in *A Gun for Sale*, emerges as both pitiless and pitiable. In all these early stories, Greene's rhetoric manouevres the reader into a questioning of conventional notions of good and evil, and into a sympathetic understanding of the failure and the criminal.

The second period of Greene's career is marked by the introduction of a more explicitly religious dimension into the world created in the novels of the 1930's. Greene had become a Roman Catholic in 1926, but not until *Brighton Rock*, *The Power and the Glory*, and *The Heart of the Matter* does he begin to explore the dilemmas of Catholic characters. He has repeatedly denied that he is a "catholic novelist," and the importance of religion in these novels is that it gives the characters a deeper, more tragic awareness of the human condition. In 1938, Greene had criticised the lack of such a dimension in Somerset Maugham's characters: "Rob human beings of their heavenly and their infernal importance, and you rob your characters of their individuality." The individuality of Greene's Catholic characters lies in their divided natures: they are torn between their religious belief, whether residual or active, and the human demands of existence. Pinkie, the teenage gangster of *Brighton Rock*, has a spiritual sense of "good" and "evil" which seems to transcend the secular values of "right" and "wrong." The Whiskey Priest in *The Power and the Glory*, though he has betrayed his priestly office, appears to be redeemed by his pity for human suffering. Scobie, the hero of *The Heart of the Matter*, is similarly split between divine decree and human compassion. All three die, but whether they are saved or damned is left open because, as the priest puts it in *Brighton Rock*, we cannot comprehend "the appalling strangeness of the mercy of God."

The End of the Affair marks the transition to Greene's later work. In that novel, the divided character of the 1940's is finally split, and the book consists of two accounts of an apparent miracle, one by a believer and one by a non-believer. Bendrix, the unsympathetic novelist-narrator, is the precursor of the anti-heroes of the later Greene. During this third phase of his career, there are changes of direction, or at least of emphasis. Greene's fictive universe becomes comic rather than tragic. He had foreshadowed such a shift as early as 1936 when he wrote that "truth is seldom tragic, for human beings are not made in that grand way.... Truth is nearly always grotesque." Greene's own comedies lean towards the grotesque: indeed, one might apply to them a word which increasingly figures in his writing – "absurd," which he seems to use in the modernist sense of "meaningless." The move from tragedy to comedy is paralleled by a concentration on secular themes (in this phase, only the stage-plays *The Living Room* and *The Potting Shed* are explicitly concerned with the religious experience). In the "catholic" novels, the central conflict is between human and divine wills, and tragedy emerges from their irreconcilability. Pinkie, the Whiskey Priest, and Scobie ultimately define themselves in relation to God: their true identities are achieved beyond this world. The later novels adopt different criteria for the definition of identity. Greene the psychologist supersedes Greene the theologian, and the quest for identity-with-God becomes a quest for secular identity. This explains the intensification of Greene's use of the picaresque-*bildungsroman* form, and his increased interest in first-person narration.

Secular identity proves no easier to achieve than spiritual. The central figures in the later fiction – Fowler in *The Quiet American*, Brown in *The Comedians*, Plarr in *The Honorary Consul* – are rootless, faithless men existing in the familiar strife-torn environments – Vietnam, a leper-colony, Duvalier's corrupt Haiti. These characters are committed to no social or religious faith, and are also unable to give themselves fully in any human relationship. They are hollow men, unable to find, or even to seek, something with which to fill the void left by the disappearance of God. Brown, in *The Comedians*, thinking about his dead father, sums this up:

> ... my real father? Presumably he was dead, but I wasn't sure.... But I felt no genuine curiosity about him; nor had I any wish to seek him out or to find his tombstone, which was possibly, but not certainly, marked with the name of Brown. Yet my lack of curiosity was a hollow where a hollow should not have been. I had not plugged the hollow with a substitute.... No priest had come to represent a father to me, and no region of the earth had taken the place of home. I was a citizen of Monaco, that was all.

Brown's identity problem is placed squarely on his detachment. But he, and the heroes of the later fiction generally, undergoes a process by which they are shaken into curiosity, and sometimes commitment – often through confrontation with a character who epitomises all that is good and bad in such commitment: Alden Pyle in *The Quiet American*, Messrs. Smith and Jones in *The Comedians*, Aunt Augusta in *Travels with My Aunt*.

"The symmetry of his thought lends the whole body of his work the importance of a system," wrote Greene of one of his acknowledged masters, Henry James. The statement is just as applicable to his own work, for it too has a uniformity of vision. The consistency of Greene's fictive world is partly rooted in the recurrence of certain themes, symbols, and settings. Seediness and failure, loyalty and betrayal, the lingering influence of childhood: these are some of the elements which render Greene's writings so instantly recognizable that W. H. Auden could confidently coin the term "grahamgreeneish." Yet within this framework Greene's work has changed and developed, not least because he is such a highly self-conscious scrutineer of his own "obsessions."

—J. C. Hilson

GREENE, Robert. English. Born in Norwich, Norfolk, baptized 11 July 1558. Educated at St. John's College, Cambridge, 1575–78, B.A. 1578; Clare Hall, Cambridge, M.A. 1583; incorporated at Oxford, 1588. Married in 1585, but later deserted his wife; one illegitimate son. Travelled in Italy and Spain, 1579–80; writer from 1580; settled in London, 1586, and quickly became known as a pamphleteer and romancer; associated with the University Wits; known for his profligate life. *Died 2 or 3 September 1592.*

Collections

Life and Complete Works in Prose and Verse, edited by A. B. Grosart.   15 vols.,
   1881–86.
Plays and Poems, edited by J. C. Collins.   2 vols., 1905.
Complete Plays, edited by T. H. Dickinson.   1909.

Fiction

Mamillia: A Mirror or Looking Glass for the Ladies of England.   1583; augmented
   edition, 1583(?).
Arbasto: The Anatomy of Fortune.   1584.
Gwydonius: The Card of Fancy.   1584; edited by George Saintsbury, in *Shorter Novels
   1,* 1929.
Morando the Tritameron of Love.   1584; augmented edition, 1587.
The Mirror of Modesty.   1584.
Planetomachia.   1585.
Euphues His Censure to Philautus.   1587.
Penelope's Web.   1587.
Pandosto: The Triumph of Time.   1588; as *Dorastus and Fawnia,* 1636; edited by
   James Winny, in *The Descent of Euphues,* 1957.
Perimedes the Blacksmith.   1588.
Ciceronis Amor: Tullie's Love.   1589; edited by Charles Howard Larson, 1974.
The Spanish Masquerado.   1589.
Menaphon: Camilla's Alarum to Slumbering Euphues.   1589; as *Greene's Arcadia,*
   1610; edited by G. B. Harrison, with *A Margarite of America* by Thomas Lodge,
   1927.
Greene's Never Too Late.   1590.
Greene's Mourning Garment.   1590.
Greene's Farewell to Folly.   1591.
The Black Book's Messenger: The Life and Death of Ned Browne.   1592; edited by A.
   V. Judges, in *The Elizabethan Underworld,* 1930.
Philomela: The Lady Fitzwater's Nightingale.   1592.
Greene's Groatsworth of Wit, Bought with a Million of Repentance.   1592; edited by A.
   C. Ward, 1927.
*Greene's Orpharion, Wherein Is Discovered a Musical Concord of Pleasant
   Histories.*   1599 (first extant edition).
Alcida: Greene's Metamorphosis.   1617 (first extant edition).

Plays

Alphonsus, King of Aragon (produced 1587?).   1599; edited by W. W. Greg, 1926.
Friar Bacon and Friar Bungay (produced 1589?).   1594; edited by J. A. Lavin, 1969.
A Looking Glass for London and England, with Thomas Lodge (produced
   1590?).   1594; edited by T. Hayashi, 1970.
Orlando Furioso, One of the Twelve Peers of France (produced 1591?).   1594; edited by
   W. W. Greg, in *Two Elizabethan Stage Abridgements,* 1923.
The Scottish History of James the Fourth (produced 1591?).   1598; edited by Norman
   Sanders, 1970.

A Knack to Know a Knave (produced 1592).   1594.
George à Greene, The Pinner of Wakefield (produced before 1593).   1599; edited by E. A. Horsman, 1956.

Verse

A Maiden's Dream: Upon the Death of Sir Christopher Hatton.   1591.

Other

A Notable Discovery of Cozenage.   1591; *The Second Part of Cony-Catching,* 1591; *Third and Last Part,* 1592; edited by A. V. Judges, in *The Elizabethan Underworld,* 1930.
A Disputation Between a He Cony-Catcher and a She Cony-Catcher.   1592; as *Thieves Falling Out, True Men Come by Their Goods,* 1615; edited by A. V. Judges, in *The Elizabethan Underworld,* 1930.
A Quip for an Upstart Courtier.   1592.
The Repentance of Robert Greene, Master of Arts.   1592; edited by G. B. Harrison, with *Greene's Groatsworth of Wit,* 1923.

Translator, *An Oration at the Burial of Gregory the 13th,* from the French.   1585.
Translator, *The Royal Exchange,* by Orazio Rinaldi.   1590.

Bibliography: *Greene Criticism: A Comprehensive Bibliography* by T. Hayashi, 1971; *Greene* by A. F. Allison, 1975.

Reading List: *Greene* by J. C. Jordan, 1915; *The Professional Writer in Elizabethan England* by E. H. Miller, 1959; *L'Opera Narrativa di Greene* by F. Ferrara, 1960; *The Aphorisms of Orazio Rinaldi, Greene, and Lucas Gracian Dantisco* by C. Speroni, 1968.

*   *   *

Robert Greene, in the few years between his graduation with an M.A. from Cambridge in 1583 and his early death in 1592, was a restless and indefatigable free-lance writer with a massive output. He turned his hand to several currently popular genres in succession. Beginning with prose romances (of which he wrote some dozen), he was then briefly involved in the Marprelate controversy, an angry exchange of theological pamphlets written for popular appeal deliberately in colloquial style. This led him to experiment with a series of prose pamphlets on "conny catching," for which he drew on his considerable knowledge of the seamy (and criminal) side of London life. These pamphlets, ostensibly designed to expose the "cosenages and villainies" of the Elizabethan underworld, met with great popular success as lively pieces of crime fiction.

Greene was associated with Lodge, Nashe, and other of the "university wits" and was inescapably drawn into working for the theatre. The full extent of his involvement (considering the collaborative writing common at the time) is not exactly determinable, but he is the certain author of five plays, four of them comedies produced by Queen Elizabeth's Men between 1589 and 1591.

Greene began by writing for a leisured and cultured audience – his romance, *Menaphon,* is, typically, dedicated to a noble lady and its preface is addressed "To the Gentlemen Readers." For these he wrote his prose romances (the best-known are *Menaphon* and *Pandosto,* the source of Shakespeare's *The Winter's Tale*), Arcadian love-tales marked by lively plotting, pastoral settings, interspersed lyrics, and a highly mannered prose style. His involvement with public controversy led to a great change in his attitude to writing. The later conny-catching and other pamphlets exploit the resources of a colloquial prose based on the speech of ordinary Londoners. With his friend Nashe, Greene expanded "downwards" the whole range of vocabulary and prose structures that could be admitted into literary English, and so paved the way for Defoe and the establishment of the English novel.

His skill in plotting, acquired in his prose fiction, is evident in all his work for the theatre. His best-known comedy, *Friar Bacon and Friar Bungay*, owes something to the magic scenes in Marlowe's *Faustus*, but Greene shows an independent mastery of the resources of the Elizabethan stage (the inset "glass perspective" scene, where he presents simultaneously scenes in two different places, both actions integrated into the forward movement of the plot). His portraits, in prose and drama, of lively and independent-minded young women (Margaret in *Friar Bacon*, Fawnia in *Pandosto*) foreshadow, and perhaps helped towards creating, the Rosalinds and Beatrices of Shakespeare; in one of his early works he announced himself as a "Homer of women."

Like many Elizabethan writers of any genre, in an age when poetry and music went hand-in-hand, he had an instinctive facility for lyric poetry. Twenty of his lyrics (from his plays and his prose romances) are included in the *Oxford Book of Sixteenth Century Verse*.

—Ian A. Gordon

GREY, Zane. American. Born Pearl Zane Gray in Zanesville, Ohio, 31 January 1872. Educated at Moore High School, Zanesville; University of Pennsylvania, Philadelphia, D.D.S. 1896. Married Lena Elise Roth in 1905; two sons and one daughter. Practised dentistry in New York City, 1896–1904; thereafter a full-time writer; traveled in the West, 1907–18; settled in California, 1918. *Died 23 October 1939.*

PUBLICATIONS

Fiction

Betty Zane. 1903.
The Spirit of the Border. 1906.
The Last of the Plainsmen. 1908.
The Last Trail. 1909.
The Short Stop. 1909.
The Heritage of the Desert. 1910.
The Young Forester. 1910.
The Young Pitcher. 1911.
The Young Lion Hunter. 1911.
Riders of the Purple Sage. 1912.
Ken Ward in the Jungle. 1912.
Desert Gold. 1913.
The Light of Western Stars. 1914.
The Lone Star Ranger. 1915.

The Rainbow Trail. 1915.
The Border Legion. 1916.
Wildfire. 1917.
The U.P. Trail. 1918.
The Desert of Wheat. 1919.
The Man of the Forest. 1920.
The Red-Headed Outfield and Other Stories. 1920.
The Mysterious Rider. 1921.
To the Last Man. 1922.
The Day of the Beast. 1922.
Wanderer of the Wasteland. 1923.
Tappan's Burro and Other Stories. 1923.
The Call of the Canyon. 1924.
Roping Lions in the Grand Canyon. 1924.
The Thundering Herd. 1925.
The Deer Stalker. 1925.
The Vanishing American. 1925.
Under the Tonto Rim. 1926.
Forlorn River. 1927.
Nevada. 1928.
Wild Horse Mesa. 1928.
Don: The Story of a Dog. 1928.
Rogue River Feud. 1929.
Fighting Caravans. 1929.
The Wolf Tracker. 1930.
The Shepherd of Guadaloupe. 1930.
Sunset Pass. 1931.
Arizona Ames. 1932.
Robber's Roost. 1932.
The Drift Fence. 1933.
The Hash Knife Outfit. 1933.
The Code of the West. 1934.
Thunder Mountain. 1935.
The Trail Driver. 1936.
The Lost Wagon Train. 1936.
King of the Royal Mounted [and the Northern Treasure, in the Far North, Gets His Man, Policing the Far North, and the Great Jewel Mystery, and the Ghost Guns of Roaring River]. 7 vols., 1936–46.
West of the Pecos. 1937.
Tex Thorne Comes Out of the West. 1937.
Majesty's Rancho. 1938.
Raiders of the Spanish Peaks. 1938.
Western Union. 1939.
Knights of the Range. 1939.
30,000 on the Hoof. 1940.
Twin Sombreros. 1941.
Stairs of Sand. 1943.
The Wilderness Trek. 1944.
Shadow of the Trail. 1946.
Valley of Wild Horses. 1947.
The Maverick Queen. 1950.
The Dude Ranger. 1951.
Captives of the Desert. 1952.
Wyoming. 1953.

Lost Pueblo. 1954.
Black Mesa. 1955.
Stranger from the Tonto. 1956.
The Fugitive Trail. 1957.
The Arizona Clan. 1958.
Horse Heaven Hill. 1959.
The Ranger and Other Stories. 1960.
Blue Feather and Other Stories. 1961.
Boulder Dam. 1963.
Zane Grey, Outdoorsman: Best Hunting and Fishing Stories, edited by George
     Reiger. 1972.

Other

Last of the Great Scouts (Buffalo Bill), with Helen Cody Wetmore. 1918.
*Tales of Fishes [Lonely Trails, Southern Rivers, Fishing Virgin Seas, the Angler's
     Eldorado, Swordfish and Tuna, Fresh Water Fishing, Tahitian Waters].* 8 vols.,
     1919–31.
Book of Camps and Trails. 1931.
An American Angler in Australia. 1937.
Adventures in Fishing, edited by Ed Zern. 1952.

Reading List: *Grey* by Carlton Jackson, 1973; *Grey* by Ann Ronald, 1975.

*   *   *

Zane Grey's literary career typifies the American Horatio Alger success story, and Grey helped to perpetuate the Horatio Alger myth, using striking settings in the American West. Grey struggled for several years in New York City and near Lackawaxen, Pennsylvania, writing essays on fishing and a trilogy based on the Zane family history in the settlement of the Ohio Valley. But Grey received little encouragement, save from his wife, and gathered rejection slips until he found his subject in the American West as a result of a visit to Arizona at the request of C. J. "Buffalo" Jones, a business entrepreneur.

Grey's own taste in literature was for the romantic, and he realized that the West was still close enough to frontier conditions for him to use it as a splendid testing ground of a man's worth. Owen Wister had discovered the cowboy as romantic hero with *The Virginian* (1902), and Grey was quick to capitalize on Wister's discovery. He paid his debt to Wister by using the subtitle of Wister's famous novel as the title for his first book about the West, *The Last of the Plainsmen.*

That book was largely a narrative of travel and was followed by his first proper novel of the West, *The Heritage of the Desert.* The success in sales was moderate, but in the story of the rise to manhood of an Eastern misfit, John Hare, Grey had found those elements of adventure, suspense, and history that were to make him the most popular writer of his time. *Riders of the Purple Sage,* his next Western, was to insure that Grey's struggles to establish himself as a writer were at an end. From then on he easily outdistanced other American writers in sales and popular, although not critical, appreciation.

Grey was bothered by the reaction of critics to his work. There is, however, much of the formula in Grey. He is often melodramatic and sentimental, and his style is stilted or awkward. But his fiction has emphasized the importance of the West to the American psyche, and embodied values in American life that those given critical acclaim frequently scoffed at or ignored. Grey was concerned about changing mores in American society. His *The Call of the Canyon,* for example, is contemporary in its concern for the plight of the returned soldier and in its objection to the "new woman." Grey's views, obviously, reflected a large segment of popular opinion in the 1920's, when he was frequently at or near the top of the best-seller lists.

While Grey also wrote many books for boys and books about the outdoors, he will continue to be known for his Western fiction. His energies were so great that new Grey titles were published for years after his death. His work is perennially popular.

—Joseph M. Flora

———————————

GRIFFIN, Gerald. Irish. Born in Limerick, 12 December 1803. Educated at local schools in Limerick. Lived with his brother in Adare, where he began writing, 1820–23; settled in London, to pursue a literary career, 1823; contributed to the *Literary Gazette* and other periodicals; tried, unsuccessfully, to achieve success as a dramatist; conceived of, and presented, an opera in recitative, and in English, at the English Opera-House, London, 1826; returned to Ireland, 1827; briefly studied law at the University of London, then returned to full-time writing; again returned to Ireland, 1838, and subsequently became a member of the Roman Catholic Society of Christian Brothers. *Died 12 June 1840.*

PUBLICATIONS

Collections

Poetical Works (includes the play *Gisippus*). 1926.

Fiction

Holland-Tide; or, Munster Popular Tales. 1827.
Tales of the Munster Festivals. 1827.
The Collegians; or, The Colleen Bawn: A Tale of Garryowen. 1829; edited by Padraic Colum, 1918.
The Rivals; Tracy's Ambition. 1830; edited by John Cronin, 1978.
The Christian Physiologist: Tales Illustrative of the Five Senses. 1830; as *The Offering of Friendship,* 1854.
The Invasion. 1832.
Tales of My Neighbourhood. 1835.
The Duke of Monmouth. 1836.
Talis Qualis; or, Tales of the Jury Room. 1842.
The Beautiful Queen of Leix; or, The Self-Consumed. 1853.
The Day of Trial. 1853.
The Voluptuary Cured. 1853.
The Young Milesian and the Selfish Crotarie. 1853.
The Kelp-Gatherer. 1854.
A Story of Psyche. 1854.
Card-Drawing, The Half Sir, and Suil Dhuv the Coiner. 1857.

Plays

The Noyades (produced 1826).
Gisippus; or, The Forgotten Friend (produced 1842).   1842.

Verse

Poetical Works.   1851.

Reading List: *The Life of Griffin* by D. Griffin, 1843; *Griffin, Poet, Novelist, Christian Brother* by W. S. Gill, 1940; *Two Studies in Integrity: Griffin and the Reverend Francis Mahoney* by Ethel Mannin, 1954; *The Irish Novelists 1800–1850* by Thomas Flanagan, 1959; *Griffin: A Critical Biography* by John Cronin, 1978.

*   *   *

Poet, dramatist, and novelist, Gerald Griffin was among the most talented of early nineteenth-century Irish writers, though in his lifetime one of the least successful of that unhappy tribe. A number of poems and unpublished plays have their date of composition in his adolescence, among them *Gisippus*, later produced by Macready. Griffin's main literary training, however, took place in the demanding world of London hack journalism, in the company of, among other expatriates, John Banim. Although most of his best work was done after he quit that world, its tempo, palette, and sense of proportion remains substantially indebted to the models encountered during those years of apprenticeship, a period not generally noted for the quality of its fiction.

Today, Griffin's reputation rests almost solely on one novel, and that largely because it was the basis of Boucicault's well-known melodrama, *The Colleen Bawn*. He deserves better. The novel in question, *The Collegians*, is the most successful contemporary attempt to depict the moral range of Irish Catholic society. The story moves comparatively easily from drawing-room to cabin; the peasant characters are well differentiated, and the middle-classes seem somewhat less stilted than usual; a strictly contemporary note is dispensed with, so that psychological issues supersede historical ones, uncharacteristically for the Irish novel of the day. Moreover, in the character of Hardress Cregan, the hapless and gifted protagonist, Griffin has created one of the most complete embodiments of the cultural tensions obtaining in the Ireland of the author's own time, and from which he was far from immune. The style of *The Collegians* is needlessly uneven, and some of the episodes are preposterously melodramatic or intolerably sentimental. But its interest overrides its faults.

Griffin's other fiction is on the whole less impressive, being more flaccid in its scene-painting, less compressed in its use of documentary material, and not as well provided with a striking range of characters. Those with explicit historical themes are undoubtedly the weakest. Of the remainder, *Tracy's Ambition* is arguably the most noteworthy. Griffin also has his place in the development of the Irish short story as the intimate though somewhat formless *Tales of the Munster Festivals* shows. In general, while not in any real sense an unsung genius, Griffin has more to offer, particularly in the context of the development of Irish fiction in the nineteenth century, than has been usually recognised.

—George O'Brien

GROSSMAN, Edith (Howitt, née) Searle. New Zealander. Born in Beechworth, Victoria, Australia, in 1863. Educated at Invercargill Grammar School; Christchurch Girls' High School; Canterbury College (junior university scholar), 1881–85, B.A. 1884, M.A. (honours) 1885. Married Joseph Penfound Grossman. Teacher at Wellington Girls' College; writer from 1890. Founding Member, Canterbury Women's Institute. *Died 28 February 1931.*

PUBLICATIONS

Fiction

In Revolt. 1892.
A Knight of the Holy Ghost. 1907.
Hermione. 1908.
The Heart of the Bush. 1910.

Other

In Memoriam Helen Macmillan Brown. 1903.
Life of Helen Macmillan Brown. 1905.

Reading List: "Informing the Void: Initial Cultural Displacement in New Zealand Writing" by Peter Alcock, in *Journal of Commonwealth Literature 6,* 1971.

                                    x   *   x

Of Edith Searle Grossman's four novels only the last need detain us. As one of the early woman graduates of the University of New Zealand she was naturally involved in the vigorous feminism of the nineties (New Zealand women gained the vote in 1893) as well as the contemporary and allied temperance movement (it was said there were then two causes of death in the colony, drink and drowning – while drunk). It is only in *The Heart of the Bush* that her writing transcends the narrow crusading dogmatism and often crude (though contemporarily relevant) exaggeration of her earlier fiction.

This book has three parts: "Between two hemispheres," "The hidden vale," "The book of Dennis and Adelaide." The first gave its title to the original chapter six of E. II. McCormick's *Letters and Art in New Zealand* (1940), which suggests its value as model treatment of our crisis of "Home" (England) or "home" (New Zealand?!). In this part the heroine, Adelaide Borlase, returned from ten years' European education, must choose between Dennis MacDiarmid, the hired man with whom she had plighted childish troth, and the "faultlessly got up Englishman" Horace Brandon: "somehow, re-entering the scenes of her childhood gave her the sensation of being the same child again, or rather of being two distinct persons who did not agree with each other." MacDiarmid spells out sound colonial sense: "Little girl ..., what have they done to you over there in England?" Adelaide soon comes right – "Dennis, Dennis, I never will be Horace Brandon's wife" – but not without some convincing explanation and inoffensive moralising: the magnificent trees in the bush (sub-tropical vegetation) "mocked old architecture with their own richer loveliness and life," and "you cannot see nearly so far in England," she said, "You are always looking through a kind of film. And there are no heights there and no depths."

"The hidden vale" presents their "bush" honeymoon in strange, presumably Freudian,

513

incidents that climax in a chaste but plainly eucharistic meal ("some hard bread and some of Emmeline's home-made wine") well above the vegetation line when Adelaide is rescued from a glacial crevasse. The highly sentimental part 3 reveals the brisk colonial practicality of Dennis, a virtue in part 1, as a threat to their marriage when he neglects Adelaide for local affairs in the form of a developing dairy factory and frozen meat works. This time it is Dennis who sees the error of his ways and settles for idyllic domesticity. E. H. McCormick points out this is precisely the opposite of the national decision.

Over-written at times, naïve in characterisation, *The Heart of the Bush* is still honest, economic, and concentrates in 300 pages a lively, intelligent, convincing dramatisation of some central problems of this young country then – and now.

—Peter Alcock

GROSSMITH, George. English. Born in London, 9 December 1847. Educated at the North London Collegiate School. Married Rosa Noyce in 1873 (died, 1905); two sons and two daughters. Reporter at Bow Street Police Court for *The Times*, London, 1866; made debut as an actor and singer, 1870; leading singer in the Gilbert and Sullivan Operas, at the Savoy Theatre, London, 1877–89; toured, with his own show, *Humorous and Musical Recitals*, in Britain, Ireland, Canada, and the United States, 1889–1906; retired from the stage, 1908. Composer: wrote more than 600 songs and sketches. *Died 1 March 1912.*

PUBLICATIONS

Fiction

    The Diary of a Nobody, with Weedon Grossmith.   1892.

Plays

    No Thoroughfare (produced 1869).
    "Two" Much Alike, with A. R. Rogers (produced 1870).
    Cups and Saucers, music by Grossmith (produced 1878).
    Mr. Guffin's Elopement, with Arthur Law (produced 1882).
    The Real Case of Hide and Seekyl (produced 1888).

Other

    A Society Clown: Reminiscences.   1888.
    Piano and I: Further Remembrances.   1910.
    G.G. (miscellany).   1933.

*   *   *

Many people have approached the Victorian novel through George and Weedon Grossmith's *The Diary of a Nobody*, and from this deceptively simple account of the aspirations, anxieties, pleasures, and humiliations of a London clerk of the 1880's have had their first taste of the class structure and tabus of Victorian society. Mr. Pooter and his neat little wife Carrie live in modest, contented comfort in Brickfield Terrace, Holloway, in a nice six-roomed residence with little back garden and a maid servant in the basement. The Grossmiths record the Pooters' menage, their circle of irritating, sometimes embarrassing friends, their pastimes, their taste in clothes and in furniture with affectionate humour that never lapses into mockery. We watch Mr. Pooter put up the plaster of Paris stags' heads which are to give tone to the hall and are never tempted to sneer. It is a way of life that we sense was vanishing even then, to be overtaken soon by the more raffish late Victorian style represented by young Lupin Pooter and his flashy, moneyed acquaintances, but there is no sentimentality in the Grossmiths' account of it.

A child can appreciate the humour; an adult sees the poignancy: the hat that blows away as Mr. Pooter is about to address himself to a superior lady, the cabman who insults him, the young men who mock his clothes, the theatre party where the guests he so wants to impress finish by paying for the hosts – all mortifications that he survives, after the first chagrin, with undeflatable optimism. Continual re-reading can only make one marvel at the economy with which the Grossmiths convey the complexity of the Victorian class system, where everybody was in the comfortable position of being able to look down on somebody else and few (certainly none at the Pooter level) were without a higher class to which to pay tremulous deference. Their gift for characterisation was considerable; *The Diary of a Nobody* contains a gallery of portraits, some of which like the silent Mr. Padge and his "That's right" have passed into the national mythology. No doubt many of them were used by George Grossmith in his stage character sketches before they were written down for *Punch*. Few ephemeral writings of this sort have been so successfully welded together into permanent literary form. (Weedon Grossmith, who collaborated with his brother in the text, provided the illustrations.)

—Gillian Avery

GROVE, Frederick Philip. Canadian. Born Felix Paul Berthold Friedrich Greve, in Radomno, Prussia-Poland, 14 February 1879; naturalized citizen, 1921. Educated at St. Pauli school, Hamburg, 1886–95; Gymnasium des Johanneums, Hamburg, 1895–98; University of Bonn, 1898–1900; Maximiliens University, Munich, 1901–02; University of Manitoba, Winnipeg, B.A. 1921. Married Catherine Wiens in 1914; one daughter, one son. Writer and translator in Germany, 1902–09; imprisoned for fraud, 1903–04; emigrated to Canada c. 1909; settled in Manitoba: taught in Haskett, 1913, Winkler, 1913–15, Virdin, 1915–16, Gladstone, 1916–17; Ferguson, 1918, Eden, 1919–22, and Rapid City, 1922–24; Editor, Graphic Press, Ottawa, 1929–31, and Associate Editor, *Canadian Nation*, 1929; manager of a farm in Simcoe, Ontario, 1931–38, and lived on the farm after his retirement. Recipient: Lorne Pierce Gold Medal, 1934; Canadian Writers' Federation Pension, 1944; Governor-General's Award, for non-fiction, 1947. D.Litt.: University of Manitoba, 1945. Fellow, Royal Society of Canada, 1941. *Died 19 August 1948.*

PUBLICATIONS

Collections

    Letters, edited by Desmond Pacey. 1975.

Fiction

    Fanny Essler (in German). 1905.
    Maurermeister Ihles Haus. 1906; translated as *The Master Mason's House,* 1976.
    Settlers of the Marsh. 1925.
    A Search for America. 1927.
    Our Daily Bread. 1928.
    The Yoke of Life. 1930.
    Fruits of the Earth. 1933.
    Two Generations: A Story of Present-Day Ontario. 1939.
    The Master of the Mill. 1944.
    Consider Her Ways. 1947.
    Tales from the Margin: The Selected Short Stories, edited by Desmond Pacey. 1971.

Verse

    Wanderungen. 1902.
    Helena und Damon (verse drama). 1902.

Other

    Oscar Wilde (in German). 1903.
    Randarabesken zu Oscar Wilde. 1903.
    Over Prairie Trails. 1922.
    The Turn of the Year. 1923.
    It Needs to Be Said.... 1929.
    In Search of Myself. 1946.

Translator of works by Balzac, Robert and Elizabeth Barrett Browning, Cervantes, Ernest Dowson, Dumas, Flaubert, Gide, Le Sage, Meredith, Henri Murger, Pater, Wells, and Wilde into German, 1903–9.

Reading List: *Grove,* 1969, and *FPG: The European Years,* 1973 (includes bibliography), both by Douglas O. Spettigue; *Grove* by Ronald Sutherland, 1969; *Grove* by Desmond Pacey, 1970; *Grove* by Margaret R. Stobie, 1973.

*   *   *

    The Canadian Frederick Philip Grove is now known to have begun his career as the minor German author Felix Paul Greve. Brilliant literary detective work by Douglas Spettigue has established that Greve published at least two novels, a volume of poetry and a verse-drama, two critical works on Oscar Wilde, and numerous translations from English and French. Most of this work in German has passed into obscurity or anonymity, although

Maurermeister Ihles Haus has been published in English as *The Master Mason's House*. A slightly belated example of European naturalism, the novel foreshadows some of Grove's Canadian fiction in its concern for close description and the conflict between sexes and generations.

The years between 1909, when Grove left Europe in mysterious circumstances and his appearance as a teacher on the Canadian prairies in 1912, are a blank. Events recorded in his autobiography and biographical fiction are entirely untrustworthy before 1912, and frequently after, except as they bear on his novels or as data for psychoanalytic criticism. Of his first two Canadian works, each a series of essays responding to Canadian seasons, *Over Prairie Trails* has been recognised as a significant statement on the implications of man's direct confrontation with the harsh environment of Manitoba in winter. Twenty-five of the 68 short stories he also began writing in the 1920's were collected posthumously as *Tales from the Margin*; as with his novels – his uncollected poetry in English shares only the theme – their strength lies in his description of "the generally tragic reaction of the human soul to the fundamental conditions of man's life on earth." This phrase from *It Needs to Be Said*, essays on literature and nationality, is characteristic of Grove's fiction, particularly the four prairie chronicles which are the source of his contemporary reputation.

That Grove's tragic heroes were usually men and most often pioneers reflects his preoccupation with the eventual futility of human will opposed to a fate dictated by circumstances. Both *Settlers of the Marsh* and *The Yoke of Life* see young men struggling with fate in the form of sexual desire, innocence, and their swampy marginal farmland. The two older men of *Fruits of the Earth* and *Our Daily Bread* are both agrarian patriarchs, tragic in their isolation from their families, their economic success ironic because both are left only with their autocratic wills to sustain them. And each feels betrayed because his wife appears to encourage his children to challenge him by abandoning the farm, a pattern echoed in the slighter *Two Generations*, set in Ontario.

The Master of the Mill carries the idea of will to an extreme through industrial capitalism; a family dynasty and a whole town are enslaved by the mechanical evolution of a flour mill, despite one son's attempt to use it to create a miniature welfare state. *Consider Her Ways*, a science fantasy, postulates the evolution of a species of ants whose intellect is higher than that of man; humans have devolved by choosing the evolutionary path of materialistic "slave-makers." Despite Grove's glacial style, both works are increasingly associated with the beginnings of modernism in Canadian fiction.

—Bruce Nesbitt

GUNN, Neil M(iller). Scottish. Born in Dunbeath, Caithness, 8 November 1891. Educated at the Highland School, and privately. Married Jessie Dallas Frew in 1921. Civil Servant until 1937, latterly as an officer of Customs and Excise; thereafter a full-time writer. Recipient: Black Memorial Prize, 1938. LL.D.: University of Edinburgh. *Died 15 January 1973.*

PUBLICATIONS

Fiction

The Grey Coast. 1926.
Hidden Doors (stories). 1929.

Morning Tide. 1931.
The Lost Glen. 1932.
Sun Circle. 1933.
Butcher's Broom. 1934; as *Highland Night,* 1935.
Highland River. 1937.
Wild Geese Overhead. 1939.
Second Sight. 1940.
The Silver Darlings. 1941.
Young Art and Old Hector. 1942.
The Serpent. 1943; as *Man Goes Alone,* 1944.
The Green Isle of the Great Deep. 1944.
The Key of the Chest. 1945.
The Drinking Well. 1946.
The Shadow. 1948.
The Silver Bough. 1948.
The Lost Chart. 1949.
The White Hour and Other Stories. 1950.
The Well at the World's End. 1951.
Blood Hunt. 1952.
The Other Landscape. 1954.

Plays

Back Home. 1932.
The Ancient Fire (produced in the 1930's).
Choosing a Play: A Comedy of Community Drama. 1938.
Old Music. 1939.
Net Results. 1939.

Other

Whisky and Scotland: A Practical and Spiritual Survey. 1935.
Off in a Boat (travel). 1938.
Storm and Precipice and Other Pieces. 1942.
Highland Pack (travel). 1949.
The Atom of Delight (autobiography). 1956.

Bibliography: in *The Bibliotheck 3,* 1961.

Reading List: *Essays on Gunn* edited by David Morrison, 1971; *Gunn: The Man and the Writer* edited by Alexander Scott and Douglas Gifford, 1973.

*   *   *

Until the publication of Neil M. Gunn's first novel, *The Grey Coast,* in 1926, no Scottish novelist had written fiction about the Highlands from the inside. That novel, like *The Lost Glen,* would have been remembered with interest if Gunn had not done greater things. But with *Morning Tide,* which in date of composition lies between these two, Gunn showed himself concerned with the slow economic disintegration of the old Highland way of life, though ostensibly the book is about the growing up of Hugh, a boy bred for the sea. When Hugh's brother, Alan, sets sail for Australia, leaving behind him the regrets and the implications of social defeat that emigration implies: "a great slackness came upon the people. They stood in groups, moved listlessly, drifted away, talking all the time in easy tones. 'Oh, they'll get on all right, the same lads!' They smiled. 'Trust them for that!' But their smiles were weary, as though there was in them a final element of defeat."

Mythology, the "swallow of life" in the hand of the young, "the human mother carrying on her ancient solitary business with the earth," and the persistent influence of the old archetypal world with the fire as its centre – these occupy Gunn not only in *Butcher's Broom* but throughout much of his work.

The finest of Gunn's early novels, if not the best of them all, is *The Silver Darlings*, a magnificent tribute to the indomitable spirit of the Gael, yet at the same time an adventure story with the terrible pace and authority of authenticity. Its theme is the social situation resulting from the sweeping of the people from strath to coast during the Clearances, and the resultant development of the fishing industry, particularly on the Moray Coast.

The middle period Gunn novels leave behind them even the trappings of history and explore entirely the landscape of the mind. Sometimes, as in *The Green Isle of the Great Deep*, the symbolism is carried to such a length that it becomes incredible. With *The Drinking Well*, Gunn's basic inability to deal with the modern urban situation once again results in an ultimate lack of credibility.

In his later novels, like *The Shadow* and *The Key of the Chest*, Gunn is no longer concerned with "the swallow of life" in the hand of an adolescent, but with the gun in the hand of an adult: with the problem of violence and its implications on individuals and society. Yet his slow-moving image-carrying prose style, so effective in his half-dozen earlier masterpieces, seems unsuited to the fast pace endemic to this particular contemporary preoccupation.

After British acclaim and a spell of curious (and, to the author, embarrassing) popularity in Nazi Germany, Gunn's reputation slumped, both in Scotland and elsewhere. In recent years, however, an awakened Scottish national consciousness and the availability of paper-back editions of his finest novels have led to a welcome reappraisal of Gunn's powerful and individual qualities.

—Maurice Lindsay

HAGGARD, Sir H(enry) Rider. English. Born in Bradenham, Norfolk, 22 June 1856. Educated at Ipswich Grammar School, Suffolk; Lincoln's Inn, London, 1880–84: called to the Bar, 1884. Married Mariana Margitson in 1880; three daughters. Lived in South Africa, as Secretary to Sir Henry Bulwer, Governor of Natal, 1875–77, member of the staff of Sir Theophilus Shepstone, Special Commissioner in the Transvaal, 1877, and Master of the High Court of the Transvaal, 1877–79; returned to England, 1879; managed his wife's estate in Norfolk from 1880; travelled throughout England investigating condition of agriculture and the rural population, 1901–02; British Government Special Commissioner to report on Salvation Army settlements in the United States, 1905; Chairman, Reclamation and Unemployed Labour Committee, Royal Commission on Coast Erosion and Afforestation, 1906–11; travelled around the world as a Member of the Dominions Royal Commission, 1912–17. Chairman of the Committee, Society of Authors, 1896–98; Vice-President, Royal Colonial Institute, 1917. Knighted, 1912; K.B.E. (Knight Commander, Order of the British Empire), 1919. *Died 14 May 1925.*

PUBLICATIONS

Fiction

> *Dawn.* 1884.
> *The Witch's Head.* 1885.
> *King Solomon's Mines.* 1885.
> *She.* 1887.
> *Allan Quatermain.* 1887.
> *A Tale of Three Lions.* 1887.
> *Mr. Meeson's Will.* 1888.
> *Maiwa's Revenge; or, The War of the Little Hand.* 1888.
> *My Fellow Laborer and the Wreck of the Copeland.* 1888.
> *Colonel Quaritch, V.C.* 1888.
> *Cleopatra.* 1889.
> *Allan's Wife and Other Tales.* 1889.
> *Beatrice.* 1890.
> *The World's Desire.* with Andrew Lang. 1890.
> *Eric Brighteyes.* 1891.
> *Nada the Lily.* 1892.
> *Montezuma's Daughter.* 1893.
> *The People of the Mist.* 1894.
> *Joan Haste.* 1895.
> *Heart of the World.* 1895.
> *The Wizard.* 1896.
> *Dr. Therne.* 1898.
> *Swallow.* 1899.
> *Black and White Heart, and Other Stories.* 1900.
> *Lysbeth.* 1901.
> *Pearl Maiden.* 1903.
> *Stella Fregelius.* 1904.
> *The Brethren.* 1904.
> *Ayesha: The Return of She.* 1905.
> *The Way of the Spirit.* 1906.
> *Benita.* 1906.
> *Fair Margaret.* 1907.

The Ghost Kings.   1908.
The Yellow God.   1908.
The Lady of Blossholme.   1909.
Morning Star.   1910.
Queen Sheba's Ring.   1910.
The Mahatma and the Hare.   1911.
Red Eve.   1911.
Marie.   1912.
Child of Storm.   1913.
The Wanderer's Necklace.   1914.
The Holy Flower.   1915; as Allan and the Holy Flower, 1915.
The Ivory Child.   1916.
Elissa; or, The Doom of Zimbabwe.   1917.
Finished.   1917.
Love Eternal.   1918.
Moon of Israel.   1918.
When the World Shook.   1919.
The Ancient Allan.   1920.
Smith and the Pharaohs and Other Tales.   1920.
She and Allan.   1921.
The Virgin of the Sun.   1922.
Wisdom's Daughter.   1923.
Heu-Heu; or, The Monster.   1924.
Queen of the Dawn.   1925.
Treasure of the Lake.   1926.
Allan and the Ice Gods.   1927.
Mary of Marion Isle.   1929.
Belshazzar.   1930.

Other

Cetywayo and His White Neighbours; or, Remarks on Recent Events in Zululand, Natal,
     and the Transvaal.   1882; revised edition, 1888.
Church and State.   1895.
The Spring of the Lion.   1899.
A Farmer's Year.   1899.
The Last Boer War.   1899.
A Winter Pilgrimage.   1901.
Rural England.   2 vols., 1902.
A Gardener's Year.   1905.
Report on the Salvation Army Colonies.   1905; revised edition, as The Poor and the
     Land, 1905.
Regeneration: An Account of the Social Work of the Salvation Army.   1910.
Rural Denmark and Its Lessons.   1911.
A Call to Arms.   1914.
The After-War Settlement and the Employment of Ex-Service Men.   1916.
The Days of My Life: An Autobiography, edited by C. J. Longman.   2 vols., 1926.

Bibliography: A Bibliography of the Writings of Haggard by J. E. Scott, 1947.

Reading List: Haggard: His Life and Work by Morton N. Cohen, 1960, revised edition, 1968,
and Kipling to Haggard: The Record of a Friendship edited by Cohen, 1965; Haggard: A
Voice from the Infinite by Peter Berresford Ellis, 1978.

*   *   *

The book that made H. Rider Haggard's reputation, *King Solomon's Mines*, was modelled on Stevenson's *Treasure Island*, but it substituted Africa, then still the "Dark Continent," for the Spanish main. Two years later, Haggard followed this initial success with a more unusual tale, *She*, which took African adventure beyond external reality into a land of hidden civilization where the supernatural held sway. Tribal Africa and mysterious culture soon became a Haggard speciality, and for over forty years, he spun one adventure tale after another, enthralling a vast English reading public hungry for armchair escape from a humdrum European existence. Haggard never styled himself a literary man or even a novelist, and in fact characterized himself aptly as a storyteller. He never aspired to the refinements and subtleties that might have taken his works into an artistic realm; he would not interrupt a flashy succession of incidents to delineate or develop character; nor did he take the pains to shape the spontaneous rush of words. Still, his virile imagination and his uncanny knack for telling a story with its own inner force have won him deep respect, and his brand of adventure, the first to exploit Africa in fiction, still claims a large audience.

—Morton N. Cohen

HALIBURTON, Thomas Chandler. Canadian. Born in Windsor, Nova Scotia, 17 December 1796. Educated at the King's College School, Windsor, Ontario, and King's College, Windsor, B.A. 1815; studied law: admitted to the Nova Scotia bar, 1820. Married 1) Louisa Neville in 1816 (died, 1840), eleven children; 2) Sarah Harriet Williams in 1856. Practised law in Annapolis Royal, Nova Scotia, from 1820; Member for Annapolis Royal, Nova Scotia House of Assembly, 1826–29; Chief Justice of the Inferior Court of Common Pleas, Nova Scotia, 1829–41; Justice of the Nova Scotia Supreme Court, 1841–56; retired to England, 1856, to Isleworth, Middlesex, 1859; Member of Parliament (U.K.) for Launceton, 1859–65. Chairman, Canadian Land and Emigration Company. Member of the Board, British North American Association of London. D.C.L.: Oxford University, 1858. *Died 27 August 1865.*

PUBLICATIONS

Collections

Sam Slick in Pictures: The Best of the Humour of Haliburton, edited by Lorne Pierce. 1956.

Fiction

The Clockmaker; or, The Sayings and Doings of Samuel Slick of Slickville. 3 vols., 1836–40.
The Letter-Bag of the Great Western; or, Life in a Steamer. 1840.
The Attaché; or, Sam Slick in England. 1843.
The Old Judge; or, Life in a Colony. 1849.
Yankee Yarns and Yankee Letters. 1852.

Sam Slick's Wise Saws and Modern Instances; or, What He Said, Did, or Invented.   2
   vols., 1853; as Sam Slick in Search of a Wife, 1855.
Nature and Human Nature.   1855.
The Season Ticket.   1860.
The Courtship and Adventures of Jonathan Hombred; or, The Scrapes and Escapes of a
   Live Yankee.   1860.

Other

A General Description of Nova Scotia.   1823.
An Historical and Statistical Account of Nova Scotia.   2 vols., 1829.
The Bubbles of Canada.   1839.
A Reply to the Report of the Earl of Durham.   1839.
The English in America.   2 vols., 1851; as Rule and Misrule of the English in America.
   1851.
An Address on the Present Condition, Resources, and Prospects of British North
   America.   1857.

Editor, Traits of American Humor by Native Americans.   3 vols., 1852.
Editor, The Americans at Home; or, Byeways, Backwoods, and Prairies.   3 vols., 1854.

Reading List: Haliburton by V. L. Chittick, 1924 (includes bibliography); Language and
Vocabulary of Sam Slick by Elna Bengtsson, 1956; Canadian History and Haliburton by Stan
Bodvar Liljegren, 1969.

*   *   *

Thomas Chandler Haliburton, the staunch Canadian Tory and author of numerous
nineteenth-century political satires, continues to be read today because of his central
character, Sam Slick. In seven volumes of sketches, Haliburton grants the Connecticut
Yankee Slick a varied career first as a pedlar in Nova Scotia, then as an American diplomat in
England, and finally as a United States Fisheries Commissioner. But Slick is most successful
as a literary character in Haliburton's early works. Most notably, in The Clockmaker, First
Series, Slick effectively voices Haliburton's own criticism of Nova Scotians and of democratic
tendencies in colonial government. Slick notes that though provincials or Bluenoses possess
vast natural resources, their lives consist of "only one-third work and two-thirds 'blowing
time.' " He tells his travelling companion the Squire that "a false pride ... is the ruin of this
country. I hope I may be skinned if it ain't." And he mocks the typical Nova Scotian who in
chasing his wayward horse "runs fourteen miles to ride two because he is in a tarnation
hurry." Furthermore, Slick all but labels the politicians in Halifax as con men. They are, he
says, as full of smiles, compliments, and promises as "a dog is full of fleas," and he adds that
the Bluenoses who can be fooled by this "deserve to be duped." Through Slick, Haliburton
thus shows the Nova Scotians to be victims of their own laziness, false pride, and inefficiency,
and he suggests, as he does more forcefully in later volumes, that full-fledged democracy for
Nova Scotia is undesirable.
    Yet Slick is not merely a spokesman for Haliburton. His Yankee trickery and excessive
pride come in for their own share of ridicule. When Slick, using "soft sawder and human
natur'," sells a clock worth $6.50 for $40 and a horse worth £10 for £50, the reader's
reaction to him is surely ambivalent. And the reader also shares the Squire's observation that
"With all his shrewdness to discover, and his humor to ridicule the foibles of others, Mr.
Slick was blind to the many defects of his own character, and ... exhibited in all he said and
all he did the most overweening conceit himself."

Sam Slick is then clearly of interest to the modern reader as a somewhat complex comic character. He is, however, also interesting for the place he occupies in the history of American humor. Indeed, Slick is, as V. L. Chittick observes in his critical biography of Haliburton, a direct descendent of two very different figures in American humorous writing – Jack Downing and Davy Crockett. Haliburton's use of a Yankee to advise the Nova Scotians and his choice of comic techniques were derived from the Jack Downing stories of Seba Smith. And Haliburton combines these "down-East" traits with the traditions of old Southwestern humor, for Slick's extravagant language and his clock peddling were suggested by the Davy Crockett yarns. Slick is as truly a "ring-tail roarer" as he is a Connecticut Yankee. In fact, this very conbination helped make him a folk hero who, as both Chittick and Richard Chase have commented, influenced Herman Melville's *Moby-Dick*.

Haliburton's distinctive, though largely outdated and reactionary, satiric position and his use of both Downing and Crockett make Sam Slick a rather intriguing creation. Nineteenth-century readers were so interested in this character that the volumes about him went through more than one hundred editions. And modern students of American humor continue to read Thomas Chandler Haliburton's sketches about Sam Slick, for Slick is a character who can command both personal and historical interest.

—Suzanne Marrs

HAMMETT, (Samuel) Dashiell. American. Born in St. Mary's County, Maryland, 27 May 1894. Educated at the Baltimore Polytechnic Institute to age 13. Served as a sergeant with the Motor Ambulance Corps of the Unites States Army in World War I, 1918–19, and with the United States Army Signal Corps in World War II, 1942–45. Married Josephine Annas Dolan in 1920 (divorced, 1937); two daughters. Worked as a clerk, stevedore, advertising manager, and as a private detective for the Pinkerton Agency, 1908–22; full-time writer from 1922; Instructor, Jefferson School of Social Science, New York, 1946–47. President, Civil Rights Congress of New York, 1946–47; Member, Advisory Board, *Soviet Russia Today*; President, League of American Writers. *Died 10 January 1961.*

PUBLICATIONS

Collections

The Big Knockover: Selected Stories and Short Novels, edited by Lillian Hellman. 1966; as *The Hammett Story Omnibus*, 1966.

Fiction

$106,000 Blood Money. 1927; as *Blood Money*, 1943.
The Dain Curse. 1929.
Red Harvest. 1929.
The Maltese Falcon. 1930.
The Glass Key. 1931.

Secret Agent X-9 (comic strip), illustrated by Alex Raymond.   1934.
The Thin Man.   1934.
The Adventures of Sam Spade and Other Stories.   1944.
The Continental Op.   1945.
The Return of the Continental Op.   1945.
A Man Called Spade and Other Stories.   1945(?).
Hammett Homicides, edited by Ellery Queen.   1946
Dead Yellow Women, edited by Ellery Queen.   1947.
Nightmare Town, edited by Ellery Queen.   1948.
The Creeping Siamese, edited by Ellery Queen.   1950.
Woman in the Dark: More Adventures of the Continental Op, edited by Ellery Queen.   1951.
A Man Called Thin, and Other Stories, edited by Ellery Queen.   1962.

Plays

Watch on the Rhine (screenplay), with Lillian Hellman, in *Best Film Plays of 1943–44*, edited by John Gassner and Dudley Nichols.   1945.

Screenplays: *After the Thin Man*, with Frances Goodrich and Albert Hackett, 1937; *Another Thin Man*, with Frances Goodrich and Albert Hackett, 1939; *Watch on the Rhine*, with Lillian Hellman, 1943.

Other

Editor, *Creeps by Night: Chills and Thrills.*   1931.
Editor, *Modern Tales of Horror.*   1932.
Editor, *The Red Brain and Other Thrillers.*   1961; as *Breakdown and Other Thrillers*, 1968.

Bibliography: *A List of the Original Appearances of Hammett's Magazine Work* by E. H. Mundell, 1968.

Reading List: "The Black Mask School" by Philip Durham and "The Poetics of the Private-Eye: The Novels of Hammett" by Robert I. Edenbaum, both in *Tough Guy Writers of the Thirties* edited by David Madden, 1968; *Hammett: A Casebook* edited by William F. Nolan, 1969; *Unfinished Woman*, 1969, *Pentimento*, 1974, and *Scoundrel Time*, 1976, all by Lillian Hellman; Introduction by Steven Marcus to *The Continental Op*, 1974.

*   *   *

In the same year (1923) that he began publishing his stories of the Continental Op in *Black Mask*, the monthly pulp magazine founded by H. L. Mencken and George Jean Nathan, Dashiell Hammett contributed to their more sophisticated *Smart Set* a collection of terse observations about his career as a Pinkerton agent under a title echoing the writings of his former employer: "From the Memoirs of a Private Detective." In form these "memoirs" play against familiar conventions of detective literature. A wry remark such as "I know a forger who left his wife because she had learned to smoke cigarettes while he was serving a term in prison" diminishes the categorical morality of crime literature, and other comments on the inadequacy of fingerprints as clues or the number of unsolved cases in a detective's files disparage all accounts of infallible detective procedures. Since the stories of the Continental

Op, Ned Beaumont, Sam Spade, and Nick Charles similarly transgress familiar conventions, it is not hard to see why readers, like Raymond Chandler in his famous essay "The Simple Art of Murder," consider Hammett to have added realism to a form grown effete by its emphasis on the myths of ratiocinative detection.

Hammett is notable for the versimilitude in his use of criminal argot and the description of underworld life, but that cannot be confused with imitation of *the real world*. And his use of American vernacular speech in the first person narrations of the Continental Op or Nick Charles and the density of action and dialogue in the futile quest for the Maltese falcon or the political crimes of *The Glass Key* should be seen as the requirement of the contract between author and reader of fiction that there be a specific world within the fiction. The extraordinarily complicated, and unlikely, plotting even in the novelettes about the Op, are as incongruent with the reader's known world as the private detectives are unlike their real-life counterparts who occupy themselves with tawdry divorce cases or employee theft.

What, then, is Hammett's achievement, if it is not in mimetic narrative? The answer seems to be that he supplants the mystery puzzle and idealized heroes of earlier detective fiction with themes that codify a modern sense of urban disorder. He achieves this, first of all, by creation of a milieu of pervasive corruption. In his novels – all but *The Thin Man* originally serialized in *Black Mask* – and short stories the socially reputable are as criminal as the gangsters with whom they often collaborate. The action of plot necessarily follows. Everyone becomes involved in crime, while the force of violence is the common expression of will for those who recognize no law but their own domination, and for the detective because his reason is insufficient alone. When the systems of our social and political myths cannot account for the feel of confusion and menace in urban life, the caricature of a naturalistic world in Hammett's fiction becomes a plausible image.

Similarly, Hammett's stylized representation of hard-boiled detectives offers an appropriate common-sense theme of behavior. Sam Spade repressing sentiment, Ned Beaumont acting on motives that are unclear even to himself, the Continental Op just doing his job, and Nick Charles affecting sophistication are all masked figures. Behind the tough and cool face they maintain before their world, as though there were no such thing as subjective psychology, we sense a vulnerability that becomes justification for wariness and a disposition to violence. We are intrigued by the thought that Hammett's detectives are what Huck Finn would have become when he found the Territory where he hoped to escape civilization dotted with cities, and in adulthood converted his sense of complicity in events beyond his control into a principle of behavior.

—John M. Reilly

HANLEY, James. Irish. Born in Dublin in 1901; brother of the writer Gerald Hanley. Served in the Canadian Navy during World War I. Married Dorothy Enid Heathcot; one son. Worked as a merchant seaman and journalist.

PUBLICATIONS

Fiction

The German Prisoner (story). N.d.
A Passion Before Death (story). 1930.
Drift. 1930.

Boy. 1931.
The Last Voyage (story). 1931.
Men in Darkness: Five Stories. 1931.
Stoker Haslett (story). 1932.
Aria and Finale (stories). 1932.
Ebb and Flood. 1932.
Captain Bottell. 1933.
Resurrexit Dominus. 1934.
Quartermaster Clausen (stories). 1934.
At Bay (story). 1935.
The Furys: *The Furys,* 1935; *The Secret Journey,* 1936; *Our Time Is Gone,* 1940;
    Winter Song, 1950; *An End and a Beginning,* 1958.
Stoker Bush. 1935.
Half an Eye: Sea Stories. 1937.
People Are Curious (stories). 1938.
Hollow Sea. 1938.
The Ocean. 1941.
No Directions. 1943.
Sailor's Song. 1943.
At Bay and Other Stories. 1944.
Crilley and Other Stories. 1945.
What Farrar Saw. 1946.
Selected Stories. 1947.
Emily. 1948.
A Walk in the Wilderness (stories). 1950.
The House in the Valley. 1951.
The Closed Harbour. 1952.
Collected Stories. 1953.
Don Quixote Drowned (stories). 1953.
The Welsh Sonata: Variations on a Theme. 1954.
Levine. 1956.
Say Nothing. 1962.
Another World. 1972.
Darkness (story). 1973.
A Woman in the Sky. 1973.
A Dream Journey. 1976.
A Kingdom. 1978.

Plays

Say Nothing (broadcast 1961; produced 1962).   In *Plays of the Year 27,* 1963.
The Inner Journey (produced 1967).   1965.
Forever and Ever (produced 1966).
Plays One (includes *The Inner Journey* and *A Stone Flower).*   1968.
It Wasn't Me (produced 1968).
Leave Us Alone (produced 1972).

Radio Plays: *S.S. Elizabethan,* 1941; *Freedom's Ferry* series, 1941; *Open Boat* series,
1941; *Return to Danger,* 1942; *A Winter Journey,* 1958; *I Talk to Myself,* 1958; *A Letter
in the Desert,* 1958; *Gobbet,* 1959; *The Queen of Ireland,* 1960; *Miss Williams,* 1960;
Say Nothing, 1961; *A Pillar of Fire,* 1962; *A Walk in the World,* 1962; *A Dream,* 1963;
The Silence, 1968; *Sailor's Song,* 1970; *One Way Only,* 1970; *A Terrible Day,* 1973; *A
Dream Journey,* 1974.

Television Plays: *The Inner World of Miss Vaughan,* 1964; *Another Port, Another Town,* 1964; *Mr. Ponge,* 1965; *Day Out for Lucy,* 1965; *A Walk in the Sea,* 1966; *That Woman,* 1967; *Nothing Will Be the Same Again,* 1968.

Other

Broken Water: An Autobiographical Excursion. 1937.
Grey Children: A Study in Humbug and Misery. 1937.
Between the Tides. 1939; as *Towards the Horizons,* 1949(?).
John Cowper Powys: A Man in the Corner. 1969.
The Face of Winter (sketch). 1969.
Herman Melville: A Man in the Customs House. 1971.

Reading List: *The Novels of Hanley* by Edward Stokes, 1964.

*   *   *

James Hanley is one of the most prolific of contemporary novelists. But, though praised by leading writers and critics (including W. H. Auden, E. M. Forster, Herbert Read and C. P. Snow) as "one of the most important of living writers," Hanley has been little read, and has received little critical notice.

Hanley's work is undeniably uneven, and the nature of his subject-matter (usually the world of the urban and sea-going proletariat) has probably had little popular appeal. But the main reason for the neglect of his work may be the mistaken assumption that he is a realist, in a period when realism has been generally considered an inferior fictional mode. "Realist," however, is a no more adequate label for Hanley than for Faulkner, whom he resembles in his selective and prevailingly sombre but compassionate vision of human life; in his power to create larger-than-life characters which achieve an almost mythic stature; and in his surrealistic experiments with language, especially in some of the shorter novels, like *Sailor's Song, No Directions* and *The Welsh Sonata.* Even in the longer novels like *The Furys* and *Hollow Sea,* with their masses of realistic detail, Hanley's primary interest is always in what goes on in the minds of his characters, in their private dreams, fantasies, obsessions and nightmare dreads.

Of the three earliest novels the second, *Boy,* is the most important. An angry and appalling study of outraged, humiliated and victimized adolescence, it is also Hanley's first novel of the sea.

Dennis Fury, a main character in the Fury saga has also been a seaman for most of his life. But it is his wife, Fanny, who is the most memorable figure in this gargantuan cycle. She is both prosaic and legendary, at once a middle-aged, dowdy, toil-worn, intensely respectable and bigoted housewife, and a creature as vital, passionate and a-moral as a heroine of Celtic myth. Despite faults of diffuseness and melodrama, the first four novels, held together by the dominating central figure of Mrs. Fury, have an impressive sweeping movement, through growing conflict within the family to the climax in the murder of a lustful money-lender, by the son, Peter, a failed priest, then through the fragmentation of the family to the slow knitting together of the surviving parents and their achievement of some degree of tranquillity. The final volume, centred on Peter Fury, released after fifteen years in prison, is one of Hanley's most successful technical experiments in the fusing of past and present; it really belongs with other studies of loneliness, unfulfillment and inability to communicate written in the fifties.

The three novels about sailors, ships and the sea in time of war represent one of the peaks of Hanley's creative achievement. Though published within five years (1938–43) they are very different in scale, subject and treatment. The formidably long *Hollow Sea,* concerned with the 1914–18 war, depends far more heavily on Hanley's memories of his own experiences than does *The Ocean*, concerned with the 1939–45 war. *Sailor's Song*, by a remarkable feat, brings into the compass of a short novel the two wars at sea, and the quarter-century between. The first two are, in the main, straightforwardly realistic, but *Sailor's Song* is one of Hanley's most experimental novels, in language and technique.

Hanley's only novel of the war on land, *No Directions*, has similarity to *The Ocean* and in quality ranks with it. The setting is a single Chelsea house, divided into five flats; the time-scheme is restricted to a single evening during the blitz. But it is more like *Sailor's Song* in its fusion of realism and fantasy; it is a haunting fantasia rather than a story. The reality that Hanley sought to present was itself a nightmare, and his mingling of wild poetry and bleak naturalism conveys the terror, the macabre confusion, and the horrifying grandeur of the blitz with superb effectiveness.

Of Hanley's post-war novels two are particularly impressive – *The Closed Harbour* and *Levine*. They are very different in tone and atmosphere (the sticky heat of Marseilles is as important in *The Closed Harbour* as the wintry bleakness of northern England in *Levine*) but they are alike in that their chief characters are war-scarred ex-sailors who are obsessed by the desire to get back to sea. Both the French merchant captain, Eugene Marius, and the Polish ordinary seaman, Felix Levine, are sole survivors of ships sunk during the war, and both are distrusted outcasts – Marius because he is suspected of the murder of his nephew, Levine because he has no provable past or identity. The end for Marius is insanity, for Levine the murder of the English woman who marries him, and stifles him by the devouring possessiveness of her devotion. These two novels embody, in a pure form, Hanley's vision of human beings as solitary, unable to communicate with one another, the victims of obsessions and compulsive drives. Tragic vision, masterful technical control and the sheer distinction of the writing combine to make these two of the finest English works of the fifties.

James Hanley developed strikingly during his career as a novelist, though his Hardyesque vision – bleak but never misanthropic – remained essentially the same. The melodramatic violence of his earlier work was eliminated without any loss of real power; its clumsiness, crudity, and turgidity give way to a style spare, strong, disciplined but flexible, evocative and individual. Despite the neglect of his work, few of his British contemporaries have equalled his achievement.

— Edward Stokes

HARDY, Thomas. English. Born in Upper Bockhampton, Dorset, 2 June 1840. Educated in local schools, 1848–54, and privately, 1854–56; articled to the ecclesiastical architect, John Hicks, in Dorchester, 1856–61; studied in evening classes at King's College, London, 1861–67. Married 1) Emma Lavinia Gifford in 1874 (died, 1912); 2) Florence Emily Dugdale in 1914. Settled in London, 1861, to practice architecture, and worked as Assistant to Sir Arthur Blomfield, 1862–67; gave up architecture to become full-time writer from c. 1873; lived in Max Gate, Dorchester, after 1883. Justice of the Peace for Dorset; Member of the Council of Justice to Animals. Recipient: Royal Institute of British Architects medal, for essay, 1863; Architecture Association prize, for design, 1863; Royal Society of Literature Gold Medal, 1912. LL.D.: University of Aberdeen; University of St. Andrews; University of Bristol; Litt.D.: Cambridge University; D.Litt.: Oxford University. Honorary Fellow: Magdalene College, Cambridge; Queen's College, Oxford. Honorary Fellow of the Royal Institute of British Architects, 1920. Order of Merit, 1910. *Died 11 January 1928.*

Collections

New Wessex Edition of the Works. 1974– .
Complete Poems, edited by James Gibson. 1976; revised *Variorum Edition*, 1978.
The Portable Hardy, edited by Julian Moynahan. 1977.
Collected Letters, edited by Richard Little Purdy and Michael Millgate. vol. 1 (of 7), 1978.

Fiction

Desperate Remedies. 1871; revised edition, 1896, 1912.
Under the Greenwood Tree: A Rural Painting of the Dutch School. 1872; revised edition, 1896, 1912; edited by Anna Winchcombe, 1975.
A Pair of Blue Eyes. 1873; revised edition, 1895, 1912, 1920.
Ear from the Madding Crowd. 1874; revised edition, 1875, 1902; edited by James Gibson, 1975.
The Hand of Ethelberta: A Comedy in Chapters. 1876; revised edition, 1895, 1912.
The Return of the Native. 1878; revised edition, 1895, 1912; edited by Colin Temblett-Wood, 1975.
Fellow Townsmen. 1880.
The Trumpet-Major: A Tale. 1880; revised edition, 1895; edited by Ray Evans, 1975.
A Laodicean; or, The Castle of the De Stancys. 1881; revised edition, 1881, 1896, 1912.
Two on a Tower. 1882; revised edition, 1883, 1883, 1895, 1912.
The Romantic Adventures of a Milkmaid. 1883; revised edition, 1913.
The Mayor of Casterbridge: The Life and Death of a Man of Character. 1886; revised edition, 1895, 1912; edited by F. B. Pinion, 1975; edited by James K. Robinson, 1977.
The Woodlanders. 1887; revised edition, 1895, 1912; edited by F. B. Pinion, 1975.
Wessex Tales, Strange, Lively and Commonplace. 1888; revised edition, 1896, 1912.
Tess of the d'Urbervilles: A Pure Woman Faithfully Presented. 1891; revised edition, 1892, 1895, 1912; edited by Scott Elledge, 1965, revised 1977.
A Group of Noble Dames. 1891; revised edition, 1896.
Life's Little Ironies: A Set of Tales. 1894; revised edition, 1896, 1912.
Wessex Novels. 16 vols, 1895–96.
Jude the Obscure. 1896; revised edition, 1912; edited by Norman Page, 1978.
The Well-Beloved: A Sketch of Temperament. 1897; revised edition, 1912.
A Changed Man, The Waiting Supper, and Other Tales. 1913.
An Indiscretion in the Life of an Heiress. 1934; edited by Carl J. Weber, 1935.
Our Exploits at West Poley, edited by R. L. Purdy. 1952.

Plays

Far from the Madding Crowd, with J. Comyns Carr, from the novel by Hardy (produced 1882).
The Three Wayfarers, from his own story "The Three Strangers" (produced 1893). 1893; revised edition, 1935.
Tess of the d'Urbervilles, from his own novel (produced 1897; revised version, produced 1924). In *Tess in the Theatre*, edited by Marguerite Roberts, 1950.
The Dynasts: A Drama of the Napoleonic Wars. 3 vols., 1903–08; vol. 1 revised, 1904.

The Play of Saint George.   1921.
The Famous Tragedy of the Queen of Cornwall (produced 1923).   1923; revised edition,
    1924.

Verse

Wessex Poems and Other Verses.   1898.
Poems of the Past and the Present.   1902; revised edition, 1902.
Time's Laughingstocks and Other Verses.   1909.
Satires of Circumstance: Lyrics and Reveries, with Miscellaneous Pieces.   1914.
Selected Poems.   1916; revised edition, as Chosen Poems, 1929.
Moments of Vision and Miscellaneous Poems.   1917.
Collected Poems.   1919.
Late Lyrics and Earlier, with Many Other Verses.   1922.
Human Shows, Far Phantasies, Songs, and Trifles.   1925.
Winter Words in Various Moods and Metres.   1928.

Other

The Dorset Farm Labourer, Past and Present.   1884.
Works (Wessex Edition).   24 vols., 1912–31.
Works (Mellstock Edition).   37 vols., 1919–20.
Life and Art: Essays, Notes, and Letters, edited by Ernest Brennecke, Jr.   1925.
The Early Life of Hardy 1840–91, by Florence Hardy.   1928; The Later Years of
    Hardy, 1892–1928, 1930 (dictated to his wife Florence).
Letters of Hardy, edited by Carl J. Weber.   1954.
Notebooks and Some Letters from Julia Augusta Martin, edited by Evelyn
    Hardy.   1955.
"Dearest Emmie": Letters to His First Wife, edited by Carl J. Weber.   1963.
The Architectural Notebook, edited by C. J. P. Beatty.   1966.
Personal Writings: Prefaces, Literary Opinions, Reminiscences, edited by Harold
    Orel.   1966.
One Rare Fair Woman (letters to Florence Henniker), edited by Evelyn Hardy and F. B.
    Pinion.   1972.
The Personal Notebooks, edited by Richard H. Taylor.   1978.

Editor, Select Poems of William Barnes.   1908.

Bibliography: Hardy: A Bibliographical Study by R. L. Purdy, 1954, revised edition, 1968;
Hardy: An Annotated Bibliography of Writings about Him edited by Helmut E. Gerber and
W. Eugene Davis, 1973.

Reading List: Hardy of Wessex by Carl J. Weber, 1940, revised edition, 1965; Hardy the
Novelist by David Cecil, 1943; Hardy: The Novels and Stories by Albert Guerard, 1949,
revised edition, 1964; The Pattern of Hardy's Poetry by Samuel Hynes, 1961; Hardy: A
Collection of Critical Essays edited by Albert Guerard, 1963; Hardy by Irving Howe, 1967; A
Hardy Companion, 1968, revised edition, 1976, and Hardy: Art and Thought, 1977, both by
F. B. Pinion; Hardy: His Career as a Novelist by Michael Millgate, 1971; Hardy and British
Poetry by Donald Davie, 1972; Hardy and History by R. J. White, 1974; Young Hardy, 1975,
and The Older Hardy, 1978, both by Robert Gittings; An Essay on Hardy by John Bayley,
1978.

*   *   *

In his early twenties Thomas Hardy aspired to be a country curate and poet, like William Barnes. Yet, after a period of intense reading in London, he rejected belief in Providence for scientific philosophy, based largely on the writings of J. S. Mill, Darwin's *The Origin of Species*, and readings in geology and astronomy. Like Mill, Hardy was impressed with Auguste Comte's emphasis on the need for altruism and a programme of reform based on education and science. Hardy never forfeited his belief in the Christian ethic; he was convinced that there was little hope for humanity without enlightened co-operation and charity. His preface to *The Woodlanders* suggests that his conscious aim in his last major novels was to further amelioration through enlisting the sympathetic awareness of his readers. Humanitarianism combines with his scientific outlook in imaginatively visualized presentations to maintain his appeal today.

Hardy's basic ideas did not change greatly and, as his London poems of 1865–67 show, they were formed early. Events are the result primarily of circumstance or chance, which is all that is immediately apparent in an evolving network of cause-effect relationships extending through space and time. In *The Woodlanders* the "web" which is for ever weaving shows, for example, a link between the death of Mrs. Charmond and the American Civil War. Chance includes heredity and character; only when reason prevails is man free to influence the course of events. Such philosophical ideas are inherent, and sometimes explicit, in Hardy's first published novel, *Desperate Remedies*. His previous novel, *The Poor Man and the Lady* (which survives only in scenes adapted to other novels and in "An Indiscretion in the Life of an Heiress"), had been loosely constructed, and too satirical, of London society and contemporary Christianity in particular, to gain acceptance.

In *Desperate Remedies* Hardy merged, for the sake of publication, a tragic situation with a thriller story and a complicated plot (in the manner of Wilkie Collins). Until the sensational dénouement takes over, the writing in enriched with poetical quotations and effects, Shelley's wintry image of adversity determining crisis settings, as in later Hardy novels. A reviewer's commendation of his rustic scenes led to *Under the Greenwood Tree*, which Hardy wrote rapidly, with notable economy, in a happy mood kindled by love of Emma Gifford, a church organist whose blue dress and vanity are the subject of light satire in a novel remarkable for its rustic humour. Though the story of *A Pair of Blue Eyes* was planned before Hardy's first Cornish visit, and its characters are almost wholly fictional, this tragic romance is based on Cornish memories. Often poetic in conception, it suffered from the pressures of serial demands. The heroine's crisis anticipates *Tess*. Writing anonymously for *The Cornhill Magazine*, Hardy was more ambitious in *Far from the Madding Crowd*, showing marked development in Wessex humour and the dramatization of passion. A suggestion that this pastoral work was written by George Eliot made Hardy put aside the story which became *The Woodlanders* for *The Hand of Ethelberta*, a comedy directed by Darwinian ideas and social satire. After a respite, during which he read a great deal, Hardy began *The Return of the Native*, but difficulties with magazine editors made him rewrite much in the first two books. Partly inspired by Arnold, more by Pater's essay on Winckelmann, his theme is hedonism (with a Greek slant) versus altruistic idealism. Life as something to be endured (and avoided by the hedonist) is represented by Egdon Heath. The insignificance of the individual in time (with reference to Egdon) is stressed in a number of scenes, the most important being Darwinian and closely associated with Mrs. Yeobright's death.

Hardy's next novels suggest that he was still searching for the direction his genius should take. After *The Trumpet-Major*, a story dependent for relief on traditional comic types and situations, against a background of threatened Napoleonic invasion, he experimented with a second novel of ideas in *A Laodicean*. Handicapped by prolonged illness, he failed to give artistic cohesion to the theme of Arnold's "imaginative reason," in resolving the conflict between modern technology and a *prédilection d'artiste* for the romantic splendours of the past. Mephistophelian villainy contributes to the counterplot, and continues on a minor scale in *Two on a Tower*, where the story, set against the immensities of stellar space, reveals Hardy's maturing emphasis on altruism. In *The Mayor of Casterbridge* he solved the problem of catering for weekly serialization without detriment to tragic grandeur, his standards being set by the great masterpieces of the past, from classical times onwards. Some of the most moving scenes are in prose of Biblical simplicity or in the vernacular of the unlettered poor. After Henchard's death, Whittle emerges more noble of heart than the shrewd Farfrae or the philosophical Elizabeth-Jane. Hardy had found where his deepest sympathies lay.

Thenceforward his tragedy is centred in the deprivation or ill-chance of the underprivileged: Marty South and Tess, Giles Winterborne and Jude. The tragedy of *The Woodlanders* hinges on false social values which induce Grace Melbury to marry a philanderer whose hypocrisy is veiled in Shelleyan idealism. Tess, as a victim of chance and the embodiment of Christian charity (which suffereth long), is a pure (but not perfect) woman. "Once victim, always victim" echoes Richardson's *Clarissa*, the most important creative influence on *Tess. Jude*, the most ambitious and complex of Hardy's tragedies, was not finished to his satisfaction. The Christminster-Crucifixion parallel seems forced at the critical juncture, and hereditary traits of Jude and Sue, with reference to marriage, are too exceptional and peripheral to create convincing tragedy, though the novel contains the most moving dramatic scenes Hardy ever wrote, possibly with his own domestic situation in mind.

He had reason at this time to realize more than ever his readiness to fall imaginatively in love with beautiful women, and he had made it the subject of his satirical fantasy *The Well-Beloved*. One result of this tendency is that his heroines are generally more attractive than his men, Henchard excepted.

Hardy's most characteristic natural settings are psychological rather than scenic, expressing the feelings or situations of his principal characters. His visualizing techniques serve to make his critical scenes more impressive and memorable.

Such was Hardy's sense of the relativity of things that he rarely lost his sense of humour, as may be seen in "A Few Crusted Characters," written as a relief from *Tess*. Among his short stories, there are several, ranging from anecdote to novelette, from humour to satire and tragedy, which rank high in Hardy's fiction.

Violent criticism of *Jude* made Hardy relinquish prose fiction, and return to poetry, sooner than he intended. He had time to prepare for *The Dynasts*, a work he had contemplated in various forms for many years. In this epic drama of the Napoleonic wars, with nations swayed by forces beyond the control of reason, Hardy regards the conflict philosophically through the Spirit of the Years, and tragically through the Spirit of the Pities. It is a work of immense scholarship and artistic proportion, containing some of Hardy's finest prose pictures and some moving lyrics. Its main weaknesses are in the verse, however, as well as in the visual and over-mechanical presentation of the Will.

Much of Hardy's early poetry (before and after his novel writing period) suggests that he did not write it with ease. Rigorously rejecting poetical lushness, he achieved an independence of style reflecting his own observation, thought, vision, and feeling. Integrity shines through his verse even when it is oddly laboured. Impressed by the best of Wordsworth and Browning, he disciplined himself to write lyrical poetry as little removed as possible from the idiom of spoken English; and it is this quality, combined with his personal appeal, which explains the hold he has on modern readers. Most of his poems (and most of his greatest) were composed after he had reached the age of seventy. The autobiographical element is considerable.

Fortified by Arnold's declaration that "what distinguishes the greatest poets is their powerful and profound application of ideas to life," Hardy used verse to promulgate beliefs which he hoped would help to prepare a way for the Positivist religion of humanity. He remained an "evolutionary meliorist" until, in his last years, the prospect of another European war made him place the blame for the Unfulfilled Intention in human affairs, not on an abstract Immanent Will, but on the folly of mankind.

His personal poetry has deeper resonances, as may be found particularly in "Poems of 1912–13," written after the death of his first wife. Hardy wrote many narrative poems in dramatic or ballad form. Unusual events and ironies of chance attracted him as much as in his prose; but more important is the poetry which he found in everyday life. "There is enough poetry in what is left, after all the false romance has been extracted, to make a sweet pattern," he affirmed. Many of his poems were composed with song-music in mind, and in stanzas demanding high manipulative skill. So imaginatively sensitive is Hardy to experience that even readers familiar with his poetry continually find something new to admire in movement, expression, or image. His finer poems are surprisingly varied and numerous; in them and elsewhere he modulates language with exquisite art to convey a living voice. The rare distinction of being both a major poet and a major novelist belongs to Thomas Hardy.

—F. B. Pinion

HARRIS, George Washington. American. Born in Allegheny City, Pennsylvania, 20 March 1814; grew up in Knoxville, Tennessee. Educated in local schools; apprenticed to a metalworker, Knoxville, 1826–33. Married 1) Mary Emeline Nance in 1835 (died, 1867), six children; 2) Jane E. Pride in 1869. Captain of the *Knoxville*, a Tennessee River boat, 1833–38; wrote for the Knoxville *Argus* in the late 1830's; farmer in Tucaleeche Cove, Tennessee, 1839–43; contributor to the *Spirit of the Times*, New York, 1843; opened a metalworking shop in Knoxville, 1843; Superintendent, Holston Glass Works, 1849; Captain of the steamboat *Alida*, Tennessee River, 1854; coppermine surveyor in Ducktown, Tennessee, 1854; Alderman, Fourth Ward of Knoxville, 1856; Postmaster of Knoxville, 1857; wrote for the *Union and American*, Nashville, Tennessee, 1858–61; moved to Nashville, 1859 until it was occupied by Union troops, 1862, and lived in various parts of the South during the Civil War, 1862–65; worked for the Wills Valley Railroad, 1866–69; contributed to the *Daily American*, Chattanooga, Tennessee, 1867–68. Delegate, Southern Commercial Convention, Savannah, Georgia, 1856; Member, Democratic State Central Committee, Tennessee, 1859. *Died 11 December 1869.*

PUBLICATIONS

Collections

   Sut Lovingood's Yarns, and High Times and Hard Times, edited by M. Thomas Inge. 2 vols., 1966–67.

Prose

   Sut Lovingood: Yarns Spun by a "Nat'ral Born Durn'd Fool: Warped and Wove for Public Wear." 1867.
   Interesting Biographical Sketch. 1867.
   Sut Lovingood: Travels with Old Abe Lincoln. 1937.

Bibliography: in *Bibliography of American Literature* by Jacob Blanck, 1959.

Reading List: *Harris* by Milton Rickels, 1966.

*   *   *

   George Washington Harris was neither a writer by trade nor a Southerner by birth. Yet he contributed to American literature one of its most distinctively Southern comic figures in Sut

Lovingood and brought the American literary vernacular to its highest level of achievement before Mark Twain.

Harris had been brought as a child to Knoxville, Tennessee, by his half-brother from the place of his birth in Allegheny City, Pennsylvania, and he adapted to the attitudes and mores of the ante-bellum South with spirited enthusiasm. With little education in the formal sense, he had a wide cross-section of occupations, including metal working, captaining a steamboat, farming, running a glass works and a sawmill, surveying, running for political office, serving as a postmaster, and working for the railroad. Such diverse experience gave Harris a large reservoir of material from which to draw in his writing.

Writing was a leisure time activity for Harris, who began as an author of political sketches for local newspapers and sporting epistles for the New York *Spirit of the Times*. He quickly developed a facility for local color and dialect and a skill for bringing backwoods scenes and events to life on the printed page. When he contributed the first Sut Lovingood sketch to the *Spirit* (4 November 1854), he outdistanced all the other humorists of the Old Southwest by allowing one central character to tell his own stories in his own vernacular and by granting him (without authorial comment) a lease on life according to the integrity and consistency of that character's independence in thought and action. Mark Twain would learn this lesson well from Harris, whose one collection of stories, *Sut Lovingood: Yarns*, he reviewed, and put it to effective use in *Adventures of Huckleberry Finn*.

While authors and critics such as William Dean Howells and Edmund Wilson have found Sut Lovingood repugnant, others such as Mark Twain, William Faulkner, and F. O. Matthiessen have paid tribute to Harris's genius. What makes Sut distinctive is the combination in his character of such human failings as bigotry, vulgarity, cowardice, brutality, and offensive behavior, along with a steadfast opposition to hypocrisy, dishonesty, and all limitations set on personal and social freedom. Many readers find it difficult to like Sut, but few find it possible to resist the appeal he has, especially those who enjoy seeing hypocritic sins revealed and those who take advantage of innocence appropriately and brutally punished. Sut is a minister of justice in coarse Southern homespun whose wildly funny pranks and incorrigible attitudes make him one of the most intriguing characters in American literary history.

—M. Thomas Inge

HARRIS, Joel Chandler. American. Born near Eatonton, Georgia, 9 December 1848. Educated at local schools. Married Esther LaRose in 1873; three daughters and two sons. Printer's devil and typesetter for *The Countryman* weekly, published at the Turnwold Plantation, 1862–66; member of staff of the *Telegraph*, Macon, Georgia, 1866, the *Crescent Monthly*, New Orleans, 1866–67, the *Monroe Advertiser*, Forsyth, Georgia, 1867–70, the *Morning News*, Savannah, Georgia, 1870–76, and the *Atlanta Constitution*, 1876–1900; Founder, with his son Julian, *Uncle Remus's Magazine* later *Uncle Remus – The Home Magazine*, 1907–08. Member, American Academy of Arts and Letters, 1905. *Died 2 July 1908.*

PUBLICATIONS

Collections

The Complete Tales of Uncle Remus, edited by Richard Chase. 1955.

Fiction

Uncle Remus: His Songs and His Sayings: The Folklore of the Old Plantation. 1880; as *Uncle Remus and His Legends of the Old Plantation,* 1881; as *Uncle Remus; or, Mr. Fox, Mr. Rabbit, and Mr. Terrapin,* 1881; revised edition, 1895.
Nights with Uncle Remus: Myths and Legends of the Old Plantation. 1883.
Mingo and Other Sketches in Black and White. 1884.
Free Joe and Other Georgian Sketches. 1887.
Daddy Jack the Runaway and Short Stories Told after Dark. 1889.
Balaam and His Master and Other Sketches and Stories. 1891.
A Plantation Printer: The Adventures of a Georgia Boy During the War. 1892; as *On the Plantation,* 1892.
Uncle Remus and His Friends: Old Plantation Stories, Songs, and Ballads, with Sketches of Negro Character. 1892.
Little Mr. Thimblefinger and His Queer Country: What the Children Saw and Heard There. 1894.
Mr. Rabbit at Home. 1895.
The Story of Aaron (So Named), The Son of Ben Ali, Told by His Friends and Acquaintances. 1896.
Sister Jane, Her Friends and Acquaintances. 1896.
Stories of Georgia. 1896; revised edition, 1896.
Aaron in the Wildwoods. 1897.
Tales of the Home Folks in Peace and War. 1898.
Plantation Pageants. 1899.
The Chronicles of Aunt Minervy Ann. 1899.
On the Wings of Occasions. 1900.
Gabriel Tolliver: A Story of Reconstruction. 1902.
The Making of a Statesman and Other Stories. 1902.
Wally Wanderoon and His Story-Telling Machine. 1903.
A Little Union Scout: A Tale of Tennessee During the Civil War. 1904.
Told by Uncle Remus: New Stories of the Old Plantation. 1905.
Uncle Remus and Brer Rabbit. 1907.
The Bishop and the Boogerman. 1909.
The Shadow Between His Shoulder-Blades. 1909.
Uncle Remus and the Little Boy. 1910.
Uncle Remus Returns. 1918.
The Witch Wolf: An Uncle Remus Story. 1921.
Qua: A Romance of the Revolution, edited by Thomas H. English. 1946.

Verse

The Tar-Baby and Other Rhymes of Uncle Remus. 1904.

Other

Editor and Essayist: Miscellaneous Literary, Political, and Social Writings, edited by Julia C. Harris. 1931.

Editor, *Life of Henry W. Grady, Including His Writings and Speeches: A Memorial Volume.* 1890.
Editor, *The Book of Fun and Frolic.* 1901; as *Merrymaker,* 1902.
Editor, *World's Wit and Humor.* 1904.

Translator, *Evening Tales*, by Frederic Ortoli.   1893.

Bibliography: in *Bibliography of American Literature* by Jacob Blanck, 1959.

Reading List: *The Life and Letters of Harris* by Julia C. Harris, 1918; *Harris, Folklorist* by Stella Brewer Brookes, 1950; *Harris: A Biography* by Paul M. Cousins, 1968.

*   *   *

Joel Chandler Harris's reputation as a writer of the Uncle Remus stories for children is somewhat misplaced. His first book, though deliberately illustrated and published as a volume in the publisher's "humorous" catalogue, was introduced by Harris as having a "perfectly serious" intention. He wanted to preserve the legends in their "original simplicity, and to wed them permanently to the quaint dialect ... through the medium of which they have become a part of the domestic history of every Southern family." He had heard them originally on the Turnwold Plantation from characters similar to Uncle Remus himself, and he was careful to present the dialect accurately. Indeed, the original publication of the tales in the Atlanta *Constitution* (and reprinted in northern newspapers) had aroused anthropological interest even before they were published in book form. Harris's introduction also emphasizes the universality of the tales, and the African origin of the adventures of the rabbit, terrapin, fox, tortoise, bear, deer used by Uncle Remus. In a later volume, Harris introduced another Negro character, African Jack, who sometimes tells the same stories as Uncle Remus has told, but in different versions and in a different (Gullah) dialect.

What is often remembered by later readers of the tales is the picture, perhaps overly sweetened by various illustrators of the stories, of the white-haired 80-year-old ex-slave, Uncle Remus, and the little 7-year-old white boy (never named) to whom he tells his stories. Perhaps Uncle Remus is patching his coat, or blowing the ashes off a yam roasted in some hot coals to share with the boy, as he introduces his story. The stories are often used to point up a moral lesson for the boy (he shouldn't be stingy, or disturb others' property), but the tales themselves are always amusing, and often ____, and even the moral lessons are sometimes tart. Harris, in short, is not merely a transcriber of folk-lore, but an artist. Mark Twain, in fact, realized the tales' oral potentialities, and successfully used them in his own readings; he even suggested a joint reading-tour with Harris.

But Harris wrote other things besides the Uncle Remus stories. Though his literary views demanded that proper "American" writing should deal with common people, preferably in a rural setting, he created a wide range of white and black characters, from the mountains and the lowlands. And the story "Free Joe and the Rest of the World" shows something of the harshness of slavery. Free Joe is a free Negro in a small community of slaves and masters, simple and friendless, a misfit, in fact. His wife is a slave, and, once her owner realizes that Joe has been visiting her, she is sold to a distant master. Joe is described as "the embodiment of that vague and mysterious danger that seemed to be forever lurking on the outskirts of slavery, ... a danger always threatening, and yet never assuming shape; intangible, and yet real; impossible, and yet not improbable," suggesting something of the unspoken fears of the southern slave-owner society. Harris also championed a spirit of reconciliation of North and South after the Civil war, suggested in his fiction by the fact that he more than once used the motif of a southern girl marrying a northern man who had fought against the South. These writings, along with the Uncle Remus tales, show Harris as perhaps the first writer to present a comprehensive view of the southern Negro "befo' the war, endurin' the war, en atterwards."

—George Walsh

HARRIS, (Theodore) Wilson. Guyanese. Born in New Amsterdam, British Guiana, now Guyana, 24 March 1921. Educated at Queen's College, Georgetown, 1934–39; started land surveying, under government auspices, 1939–42; subsequently licensed to practise. Married 1) Cecily Carew in 1945; 2) Margaret Burns Whitaker in 1959. Government Surveyor, 1942–54, and Senior Surveyor, 1955–58, Government of British Guiana; settled in London, 1959; Visiting Lecturer, State University of New York at Buffalo, 1970; Writer-in-Residence, University of the West Indies, and Scarborough College, University of Toronto, 1970; Commonwealth Fellow in Caribbean Literature, University of Leeds, 1971; Visiting Professor, University of Texas, Austin, 1972, and University of Aarhus, 1973; Henfield Writing Fellow, University of East Anglia, Norwich, 1974. Delegate to the National Identity Conference, Brisbane, 1968, and to the Unesco Symposium on Caribbean Literature, Cuba, 1968. Recipient: Arts Council grant, 1968, 1970; Guggenheim Fellowship, 1973.

PUBLICATIONS

Fiction

> *The Guiana Quartet: Palace of the Peacock*, 1960; *The Far Journey of Oudin*, 1961; *The Whole Armour*, 1962; *The Secret Ladder*, 1964.
> *Heartland*. 1964.
> *The Eye of the Scarecrow*. 1965.
> *The Waiting Room*. 1967.
> *Tumatumari*. 1968.
> *The Sleepers of Roraima* (stories). 1970.
> *Ascent to Omai*. 1970.
> *The Age of the Rainmakers* (stories). 1971.
> *Black Marsden*. 1972.
> *Companions of the Day and Night*. 1975.
> *Genesis of the Clowns*. 1975.
> *Da Silva Da Silva's Cultivated Wilderness, and Genesis of the Clowns*. 1977.
> *The Tree of the Sun*. 1978.

Verse

> *Fetish*. 1951.
> *Eternity to Season*. 1954.

Other

> *Tradition and the West Indian Novel*. 1965.
> *Tradition, The Writer and Society: Critical Essays*. 1967.

Reading List: *Harris and the Caribbaean Novel* by Michael Gilkes, 1975; *Enigma of Values* edited by Kirsten Holst Petersen and Anna Rutherford, 1975; *The Naked Design* by Hena Maes-Jelinek, 1976.

*   *   *

Though written some ten to twelve years before his first novel was published, Wilson Harris's poetry is shaped by the vision that was to inspire the form and content of his now considerable fictional "work in progress." This vision has its source in the contrasts, the perpetual motions, and the grandiose nature of his native Guyana which, for him, is informed by the two dimensions of eternity and season and by a spirit born of a history of repetitive conquest. *Eternity to Season* brings together two widely remote civilizations, the Mediterranean presented in "Troy" and the Amerindian evoked in "Behring Straits." Their meeting is indirectly recorded in a third poem called "Amazon," which brings to light the creative potentiality of a people so far divided into oppressor and oppressed, the nameless folk that figures so prominently in much of Harris's fiction. The characters in this modern epic – ordinary Guyanese labourers – are called after Greek mythological heroes, faced with the same fundamental issues as their namesakes and moved by similar aspirations. But the interplay of extremes in nature (which can either merely reflect, or else inspire a deeper vision of, man's own states), the weaving and unravelling of its seasonal manifestations, are incentives to a freedom of spirit and a reconciliation of the heterogeneous elements within themselves and their society that should help them grow out of the fixed postures imposed by history. Thus, using universal myths, Harris adapts them to the West Indian experience (as he was later to elicit new meaning from Amerindian myths in *The Sleepers of Roraima* and *The Age of the Rainmakers*) and shows man's power to change his destiny. Through his poetic sequence a Guyanese consciousness becomes attuned to its own environment (see "Recreation of the Senses") and recognizes in it the native complex of phenomena that must feed the sensibility and the imagination of individual and community. Both strongly philosophical (concerned with concepts of space and time/timelessness) and highly sensuous, this poetry is built on paradoxes; it juxtaposes contradictory images and epithets which create a configuration of material and immaterial perspectives and convey the constant interaction between outer and inner reality. Declaring the imperfection of both heaven and earth, if offers an essentially dynamic and open-ended view of existence seen as a process of reunion and separation, of alternating rebirth and death, with which man must learn to move.

This essential fluidity and its meaning are more clearly realized in Harris's fiction, for they manifest themselves through more individualized and concrete setting and characters. The first cycle of his novels, *The Guiana Quartet* and *Heartland*, offers a composite picture of the country's landscapes and its multi-racial communities. They recreate the major feats and trials of the Guyanese experience in both past and present (conquest, slavery, exploitation, violence, the suppression of racial groups). But as much as historical facts and their consequences, Harris brings to light the basic impulses and motives that generated them and the more insidious and deceptive forms of their contemporary effects. Although Harris's novels differ widely from one another in both form and content, there is a sense in which *Palace of the Peacock*, as "novel of expedition" relating a journey into both outer and inner psychological heartland, prefigures them all. It describes the dislocation of personality, the disintegration of conscious or unconscious attitudes of conquest, that his main characters experience as they progress towards the state of void and namelessness suffered by the victims of history or of individual possessiveness.

This necessary shattering of rigid ways of being leads to partial and unfinished reconstructions in the protagonist's consciousness, unfinished because the dynamic duality achieved between dissolution and recreation is, according to Harris, in the very nature of life. The predicament of Caribbean peoples (or of any individual in a given community), their eclipse and possibility of rebirth through the breakdown of totalitarian assumptions, has inspired Harris's philosophy of existence as illustrated in his fiction. It is also the source of his conception of characters, the structure of his novels and their narrative texture, and his dualistic use of imagery. Harris equates dominant forms in art with static and dominant social structures, and he tries to break out of them. The result is, in his second cycle of novels (from *The Eye of the Scarecrow* to *Ascent to Omai*), a surface fragmentation matched with an underlying sense of unity conveyed through a language that aims at reproducing the interrelatedness of all life, human and natural. In these novels Harris's double preoccupation with the creation of a genuine community and an "art of community" is more evident than ever. The protagonist's consciousness (which is also an artist's) contains the world it explores and envisages a reconciliation of its opposites through a regenerating (and regenerated) imagination and through what is presented in a more recent novel as a "Copernican revolution of sentiment."

This has led to new developments in a third cycle of novels initiated with *Black Marsden*. Here the horizons of the individual consciousness are further widened to contain mankind's "global theatre" within which an attempt is made to bridge the gap between contrasting civilizations and to throw light (as in *Companions of the Day and Night*) on the mutation by which eclipsed peoples are beginning to emerge from their buried condition. This mutation is brought to light by the capacity of individual characters to transform ("revise") given images or "paintings" of the past and harmonize them into a vision of heterogeneous wholeness (as opposed to one-sided totality). In Harris's latest novels this wholeness is perceived through a mosaic of characters and motifs who represent and bring together the two faces of tradition, one assertive and oppressive, the other hardly perceptible and usually ignored because it has grown out of the sufferings of the nameless and the oppressed.

—Hena Maes-Jelinek

HARTE, (Francis) Bret.   American.   Born in Albany, New York, 25 August 1836; lived with his family in various cities in the northeast, then settled in New York City, 1845. Educated in local shcools to age 13. Married Anna Griswold in 1862. Worked in New York in a lawyer's office, then in a merchant's counting room; moved to California, 1854, and taught school, worked as a clerk for an apothecary, and as an expressman in various California towns; writer for the *Northern Californian*, Arcata, 1857–60; settled in San Francisco: typesetter for the *Golden Era*, 1860; clerk in the Surveyor-General's Office, 1861–63; Secretary of the United States branch mint, 1863–69; contributor and, occasionally, Acting Editor, *Californian*, 1864–66; first Editor, *Overland Monthly*, 1868–70; full-time writer from 1870; lived in New York, 1871–78; tried unsuccessfully to establish *Capitol* magazine, 1877; United States Commercial Agent in Krefeld, Germany, 1878–80, and Consul in Glasgow, 1880–85; lived in London, 1885 until his death. *Died 5 May 1902.*

PUBLICATIONS

Collections

> *Works.*   25 vols., 1914.
> *Letters*, edited by Geoffrey Bret Harte.   1926.
> *Representative Selections*, edited by Joseph B. Harrison.   1941.
> *The Best Short Stories*, edited by Robert N. Linscott.   1967.

Fiction

> *Condensed Novels and Other Papers.*   1867; revised edition, 1871.
> *The Lost Galleon and Other Tales.*   1867.
> *The Luck of Roaring Camp and Other Sketches.*   1870; revised edition, 1871.

Stories of the Sierras and Other Sketches. 1872.
The Little Drummer; or, The Christmas Gift That Came to Rupert: A Story for Children. 1872.
Mrs. Skaggs's Husbands and Other Sketches. 1873.
An Episode of Fiddletown and Other Sketches. 1873.
Idyls of the Foothills. 1874.
Tales of the Argonauts and Other Sketches. 1875.
Wan Lee, The Pagan and Other Sketches. 1876.
Gabriel Conroy. 1876.
Thankful Blossom: A Romance of the Jerseys 1779. 1877.
Thankful Blossom and Other Tales. 1877.
My Friend, The Tramp (stories). 1877
The Story of a Mine. 1877.
The Man on the Beach (stories). 1878.
Jinny (stories). 1878.
Drift from Two Shores. 1878; as The Hoodlum Bard and Other Stories, 1878.
An Heiress of Red Dog and Other Sketches. 1879.
The Twins of Table Mountain (stories). 1879.
Jeff Briggs's Love Story and Other Sketches. 1880.
Flip and Other Stories. 1882.
In the Carquinez Woods. 1883.
California Stories. 1884.
On the Frontier (stories). 1884.
By Shore and Sedge. 1885.
Maruja. 1885.
Snow-Bound at Eagle's. 1886.
The Queen of the Pirate Isle. 1886.
A Millionaire of Rough-and-Ready, and Devil's Ford. 1887.
The Crusade of the Excelsior. 1887.
A Phyllis of the Sierras, and A Drift from Redwood Camp. 1888.
The Argonauts of North Liberty. 1888.
Cressy. 1889.
Captain Jim's Friend, and The Argonauts of North Liberty. 1889.
The Heritage of Dedlow Marsh and Other Tales. 1889.
A Waif of the Plains. 1890.
A Ward of the Golden Gate. 1890.
A Sappho of Green Springs and Other Tales. 1891.
A First Family of Tasajara. 1891.
Colonel Starbottle's Client and Some Other People. 1892.
Susy: A Story of the Plains. 1893.
Sally Dows, Etc. (stories). 1893.
A Protegee of Jack Hamlin's and Other Stories. 1894.
The Bell-Ringer of Angel's and Other Stories. 1894.
Clarence. 1895.
In a Hollow of the Hills. 1895.
Barker's Luck and Other Stories. 1896.
Three Partners; or, The Big Strike on Heavy Tree Hill. 1897.
The Ancestors of Peter Atherly and Other Tales. 1897.
Tales of Trail and Town. 1898.
Stories in Light and Shadow. 1898.
Mr. Jack Hamlin's Meditation and Other Stories. 1899.
From Sand Hill to Pine. 1900.
Under the Redwoods. 1901.
Openings in the Old Trail. 1902; as On the Old Trail, 1902.

Condensed Novels: Second Series: New Burlesques.   1902.
Trent's Trust and Other Stories.   1903.

Plays

Two Men of Sandy Bar, from his own story "Mr. Thompson's Prodigal."   1876.
Ah Sin, with Mark Twain (produced 1877).   Edited by Frederick Anderson, 1961.
Sue, with T. Edgar Pemberton, from the story "The Judgment of Bolinas Plain" by
    Harte (produced 1896).   1902; as Held Up (produced 1903).

Verse

The Heathen Chinee.   1870.
Poems.   1871.
That Heathen Chinee and Other Poems, Mostly Humorous.   1871.
East and West Poems.   1871.
Poetical Works.   1872; revised edition, 1896, 1902.
Echoes of the Foot-Hills.   1874.
Some Later Verses.   1898.
Unpublished Limericks and Cartoons.   1933.

Other

Complete Works.   1872.
Prose and Poetry.   2 vols., 1872.
Lectures, edited by Charles Meeker Kozlay.   1909.
Stories and Poems and Other Uncollected Writings, edited by Charles Meeker
    Kozlay.   1914.
Sketches of the Sixties by Harte and Mark Twain from "The Californian" 1864–67,
    edited by Charles Meeker Kozlay.   1926; revised edition, 1927.
San Francisco in 1866, Being Letters to the Springfield Republican, edited by George R.
    Stewart and Edwin S. Fussell.   1951.

Editor, Outcroppings, Being Selections of California Verse.   1866.
Editor, Poems, by Charles Warren Stoddard.   1867.

Bibliography: in Bibliography of American Literature by Jacob Blanck, 1959.

Reading List: Harte, Argonaut and Exile by George R. Stewart, 1931; Mark Twain and Harte
by Margaret Duckett, 1964; Harte: A Biography by Richard O'Connor, 1966; Harte by
Patrick David Morrow, 1972.

*   *   *

Because of the nature of his fiction and the timing of his publication of "The Luck of
Roaring Camp" (1868), Bret Harte is often remembered as the earliest of American local
colorists. Insofar as his craftsmanship is concerned, however, Harte may be considered the
logical extension of earlier Southern humorists like Augustus Baldwin Longstreet, William
Tappan Thompson, Johnson Jones Hooper, and Joseph Glover Baldwin, all of whom were
realists writing with broad humor of the more primitive moments of Southern frontier life.

Critics have consistently pointed out the influence of Dickens on Harte's work. Joseph B. Harrison in his introduction to *Bret Harte: Representative Selections*, has pinpointed several Dickens influences, e.g., the mixture of humor and sentiment, the exploitation of unique characters in unique situations and environment, the simplification of character to the point of caricature, extravagant dialect and names (Hash, Starbottle, Rats), the love of stupid but good people, opposition to the hypocritical, and satire on injustice.

Harte's literary career lends itself to easy if not simplistic geographic division, i.e., stories composed while the author was in residence in California, in New York, and in Europe. Scholars point out somewhat consistently the gradual deterioration of the artist as he moved further and further from California. In any event, the scholarly consensus is that Harte's literary reputation rests largely on his work completed before the end of 1871 when he returned to the East to write for magazines. Work completed after 1878, when Harte sailed to Europe to be a consul in Prussia, is generally considered hack work and is all but ignored today.

The use of contrast is perhaps the most genuine hallmark of Harte's fiction. Arthur Hobson Quinn, for example, has noted Harte's use of "moral contrast," and John Erskine in *Leading American Novelists* has attributed Harte's successful humor to Harte's perception of contrast in American life itself. "The Outcasts of Poker Flat," which vies with "The Luck of Roaring Camp" for the honor of Harte's best work, centers on use of contrasts: four degenerates are juxtaposed with two innocents, a harlot starves herself to death in order to save a virgin, the gambler Oakhurst gives up his chance for safety to the Innocent and then commits suicide. Erskine notes that Harte perceives the good qualities in the life of the lowly as in "Tennessee's Partner" and that his use of parody in *Condensed Novels*, which satirizes popular sentimental and idealistic novels, is comparable to that of Swinburne.

Local color stories, because of their nature, depend to a large extent upon their fidelity to detail. Harte's stories like "The Outcasts of Poker Flat" or "Miggles," are, therefore, frequently praised for their meaningful use of detail. Some of the best short stories Harte ever wrote were written for *The Overland*: "The Outcasts of Poker Flat," " Miggles," "Tennessee's Partner," "The Idyl of Red Gulch," and "Brown of Calaveras." Scholars generally agree that Harte never again equalled their freshness, spontaneity, compression, and unity.

"Tennessee's Partner" is the third most frequently anthologized Harte story. Here, Harte makes chance, fate, and accident the normal, the customary. The sentimentality in the story satisfied the taste of the reading audience of the late nineteenth century.

Of the more than two hundred poems in the standard edition of Harte, more than one half are narrative, one third humorous or satirical, and one third entirely or partially dialect. Although the great strength of Harte's poetry is his brevity, he fails, on the other hand, to unite brevity and symbolism and emotional implication, a unity necessary to successful poetry. Harte's best poetry is always his satirical and humorous verse. Harte's best two poems and his most frequently reprinted ones are "Plain Language from Truthful James" and "The Society upon the Stanislaus." As a novelist, Harte has generally been judged superficial, for his characters, like many of Dickens' poorer characters, are wooden and puppet-like. The characters, for example, in *Gabriel Conroy*, *A Waif of the Plains*, and *In the Carquinez Woods* have neither ideas nor passions to be sustained or complicated.

Bret Harte's real achievement, then, is to be found in his local color stories written, for the most part, before 1871, stories which bear his hallmark of brevity, dramatic action reporting, the new morality of the far West, humor, contrast, and uncluttered style. G. K. Chesterton (quoted by Erskine) has observed that Harte's fiction serves, realistically, to remind us that "while it is very rare indeed in the world to find a thoroughly good man, it is rarer still, rare to the point of monstrosity, to find a man who does not either desire to be one or imagine that he is one already."

—George C. Longest

HARTLEY, L(eslie) P(oles).   English.   Born in Whittlesey, Cambridgeshire, 30 December 1895. Educated at Harrow School; Balliol College, Oxford, B.A. 1922. Served in World War I, 1916–18. Fiction Reviewer for *Spectator, Week-end Review, Weekly Sketch, Time and Tide, The Observer*, and *Sunday Times*, all in London, 1923–72. Clark Lecturer, Trinity College, Cambridge, 1964. Recipient: Black Memorial Prize, 1948; Heinemann Award, 1954. Companion of Literature, Royal Society of Literature, 1972. C.B.E. (Commander, Order of the British Empire), 1956. *Died 13 December 1972.*

PUBLICATIONS

Collections

The Complete Short Stories.   1973.

Fiction

Night Fears and Other Stories.   1924.
Simonetta Perkins.   1925.
The Killing Bottle (stories).   1932.
The Shrimp and the Anemone.   1944 (as *The West Window*, 1945); *The Sixth Heaven*, 1946; *Eustace and Hilda*, 1947; complete version, as *Eustace and Hilda*, 1958.
The Travelling Grave and Other Stories.   1948.
The Boat.   1949.
My Fellow Devils.   1951.
The Go-Between.   1953.
The White Wand and Other Stories.   1954.
A Perfect Woman.   1955.
The Hireling.   1957.
Facial Justice.   1960.
Two for the River and Other Stories.   1961.
The Brickfield.   1964.
The Betrayal.   1966.
The Collected Short Stories.   1968.
Poor Clare.   1968.
The Love-Adept: A Variation on a Theme.   1969.
My Sister's Keeper.   1970.
Mrs. Carteret Receives and Other Stories.   1971.
The Harness Room.   1971.
The Collections.   1972.
The Will and the Way.   1973.

Other

The Novelist's Responsiblity: Lectures and Essays.   1967.

Reading List: *Hartley* by Paul Bloomfield, 1962, revised edition, 1970; *Hartley* by Peter Bien, 1963; *Wild Thyme, Winter Lightning* by Anne Mulkeen, 1974.

*   *   *

The novels of L. P. Hartley compose a various and complex body of work about which, however, certain generalizations can be made. The most inclusive observation is one that puts Hartley in opposition to some writers of a later generation than his. Underlying Hartley's almost tireless variety is a conviction that the fiction he creates is an ingenious yet faithful reflection of a real world that both Hartley and his readers experience; it is the function and indeed the duty of the novelist to recreate that reality. Hartley's novels are submitted to readers both to illuminate the reality in question and to win from each reader an assent to what the novels report.

Such a faith in what fiction can offer is now less common than Hartley himself, for example, assumes. At any rate, fiction that discards assiduous appeals to the real world, parodies that world, or holds it at an ironic distance is alien to Hartley's work. By his own estimate, Hartley works in the tradition established by Henry James in which a novelist traces the delicate complexities of human relationships – relationships that exist both within a novel and inside the human society to which the novel is offered. For Hartley, at least, a novel is not just a surface report of a world that is present and dependable; a work of fiction is an ingenious and deft investigation of the aspects of that world which escape the blunt intelligence of a novelist like Arnold Bennett.

All this can be seen in Hartley's longest work, the trilogy *Eustace and Hilda*. The long tale of the relation between a middle-class English boy and his older sister begins with a tireless inspection of the early years of the brother and sister, with accounts of their amusements, their limited social contacts in an English coastal town, and the unspoken contest for supremacy between the two children. This section of the novel is entitled *The Shrimp and the Anemone*; the title refers to an incident in which, to Eustace's horror, one seaside creature, the anemone, devours another, the shrimp. It is fair to say that the devoured creature stands for the boy and the voracious one for the older sister. Indeed, Hartley uses the metaphor on the last page of his trilogy where, in a vision, Eustace senses that the anemone closes around his finger. " 'I shall wake up now,' thought Eustace, who had wakened from many dreads." Hartley adds: "But the cold crept onwards and he did not wake."

But before this sinister moment is reached, Hartley provides a selective chronicle of Eustace's progress from childhood to adult life. Eustace is sent through the British version of upward mobility: there are contacts with the upper class; Eustace goes to Oxford and wins admiration for his literary abilities: he travels to Venice and spends a summer with the privileged. But in the months before his death, he returns to his old home and tries to deliver his sister Hilda from the paralysis for which he is responsible (he has, not intentionally, sacrificed her in his quest for self-knowledge and maturity). Hilda – one might say – forces her brother to deliver her, at the cost of his own life.

The pattern of psychological interest which spreads itself out in *Eustace and Hilda* comes into sharper focus in Hartley's later work. There, as in the trilogy, the techniques of presenting the real – that is, the psychologically real – world vary. Hartley uses dream, events, and dialogues that stand for the imaginative life of a character, and prolonged meditations of Hartley's own upon the choices a character has made. All these devices alternate with each other and also with sharp re-creations of the external world, physical and social, through which a character is moving. Thus in *The Go-Between*, a young boy spends a summer in a household socially superior to his own and becomes a messenger who advances the liaison between a charming girl and a local farmer; the liaison ends in tragedy, and part of the tragedy is the boy's withdrawal from his own future. Like Hartley's Eustace, the boy also encounters an anemone. The fate of the boy is compelling because both his inner world and the setting which surrounds it are regarded by Hartley as having an existence somehow actual.

So also in *The Hireling*, to take one more example. *The Hireling* is, like *The Go-Between*, a brilliant and economical sketch of the collision of states of mind; a hired driver and a neurotic noble lady give comfort to each other. Hartley's account charts the ebb and flow of the strange relationship. The two persons are comprehended not because Hartley imports some rigorous system of explanation, Freudian, Jungian, or other. Hartley's analysis, delicate and sympathetic as it is, is closer to the aperçus of La Rochefoucauld and *cartes de tendresse* than it is to the dogmatisms of modern formal explanations of human behavior.

To one side of the main body of Hartley's work is *Facial Justice*. This novel is Hartley's *Brave New World*. The well-worn machinery of novels of the future is, however, put to work by Hartley to illustrate theses of his own, spoken and unspoken. The reshaping of faces into conventional prettiness, the intolerable supervision of individual lives, and the sterility of an imposed taste are negative demonstrations of what the rest of the novels suggest. To be human is, for Hartley, to be open to the perceptions of error and success in the relations between persons and classes. And *The Go-Between* and *The Hireling* are examples of the work of a moralist who is unwilling to preach but who is tireless as he practices his arts of demonstration.

—Harold H. Watts

HAWKES, John (Clendennin Burne, Jr.).   American.   Born in Stamford, Connecticut, 17 August 1925. Educated at Trinity School, 1940–41; Pawling High School, 1941–43; Harvard University, Cambridge, Massachusetts, 1943–49, A.B. 1949. Served as an ambulance driver with the American Field Service in Italy and Germany, 1944–45. Married Sophie Goode Tazewell in 1947; three sons and one daughter. Assistant to the Production Manager, Harvard University Press, 1949–55; Visiting Lecturer, 1955–56, and Instructor in English, 1956–58, Harvard University. Assistant Professor, 1958–62, Associate Professor, 1962–67, Professor of English, 1967–73, and since 1973 University Professor, Brown University, Providence, Rhode Island. Special Guest, Aspen Institute for Humanistic Studies, Colorado, 1962; member of the staff of the Utah Writers Conference, summer 1962, and Bread Loaf Writers Conference, Vermont, summer 1963; Visiting Professor of Creative Writing, Stanford University, California, 1966–67; Visiting Distinguished Professor of Creative Writing, City College of the City University of New York, 1971–72. Member, Panel on Educational Innovation, Washington, D.C., 1966–67. Recipient: National Institute of Arts and Letters grant, 1962; Guggenheim Fellowship, 1962; Ford Fellowship, for drama, 1964; Rockefeller Fellowship, 1968; Prix du Meilleur Livre Etranger, 1973. Lives in Providence, Rhode Island.

PUBLICATIONS

Fiction

The Cannibal. 1949.
The Beetle Leg. 1951.
The Goose on the Grave, and The Owl: Two Short Novels. 1954.
The Lime Twig. 1961.
Second Skin. 1964.
Lunar Landscapes: Stories and Short Novels 1949–1963. 1969.
The Blood Oranges. 1971.
Death, Sleep, and the Traveler. 1974.
Travesty. 1976.

Plays

The Wax Museum (produced 1966).   In The Innocent Party, 1966.
The Questions (produced 1966).   In The Innocent Party, 1966.
The Innocent Party: Four Short Plays.   1966.
The Undertaker (produced 1967).   In The Innocent Party, 1966.
The Innocent Party (produced 1968).   In The Innocent Party, 1966.

Other

Editor, with others, The Personal Voice: A Contemporary Prose Reader.   1964.
Editor, with others, The American Literary Anthology 1: The 1st Annual Collection of the
    Best from the Literary Magazines.   1968.

Bibliography: Three Comtemporary Novelists: An Annotated Bibliography by Robert M.
Scotto, 1977; Hawkes: An Annotated Bibliography by Carol A. Hryciw, 1977.

Reading List: The Fabulators by Robert Scholes, 1967; City of Words by Tony Tanner, 1971;
Comic Terror: The Novels of Hawkes by Donald J. Greiner, 1973; Hawkes and the Craft of
Conflict by John Kuehl, 1975.

                                *   *   *

American letters has not, on the whole, been particularly receptive to the cultivation of
truly esoteric talents, probably because some appeal to a general audience is almost morally as
well as commercially compulsory in American culture. John Hawkes, however, comes close
to being a writer whose intransigent dedication to a special conception of art provides the
exception to this rule. But if he has colonized for himself a separate place in contemporary
fiction, he has done so not through the promulgation of an exotic or cultist philosophy, nor
through the projection of a public personality that cuts against the grain of conventional
mores, but pre-eminently as a prose stylist. In his first full-length novel, The Cannibal, he
staked out the literary area which he would make uniquely his own: the creation of an
uncompromising verbal artifice that aims at rendering sensuously and in the modern idiom
the melodramatic atmosphere of traditional Gothic materials in a manner designed to
implicate the reader in ambivalent sado-masochistic responses. That is, Hawkes has
deliberately conceived of his fiction as a premeditated assault against a victimized reader. The
establishment of a powerful tension between the outrageously unacceptable behavior of the
plot and characters and the equally undeniable visceral reactions of the individual reader
results in that impasse of aesthetic distortion that is usually assumed to be within the
provenance of "the grotesque." And in Hawkes's work the largest part of the burden in
achieving this goal is entrusted to his style – a lean, elusive, visual-kinetic succession of
images that alternately beguiles, frustrates, and shocks the reader's expectations.
    Set in a fantastic post-World War II Occupied Germany, The Cannibal ignores
conventional time-sequences, character development, and cause-effect probabilities to
describe the triumphant uprising of the defeated nation in the persons of a crippled handful of
mutated life-forms tortuously emerging from the debris of their own corruption. Belying its
own stoic bitterness, the novel moves casually back and forth through time, dispassionately
issuing a series of vividly etched vignettes of murder, betrayal, cannibalism, and destructive
perversions of love. And although the work occasionally suggests the experimentalism of
Dada and Surrealism, its rigorous stylistic attachment to the matter-of-fact conventions of
realism forces it on the reader with the imperative of a personal nightmare.
    After The Cannibal, Hawkes experimented with a bleak parody of the Western (The Beetle

Leg) and a grim excursion in archaism (*The Goose on the Grave*) before producing the masterful *The Lime Twig*. Partly indebted to *Brighton Rock* and the post-war British movies, and partly a sardonic parody of the detective novel, *The Lime Twig* depicts brilliantly the ironic confluence of banal bourgeois fantasies (Hencher, Margaret and Michael Banks) and a ruthless underworld gang that brings those fantasies to terrible realization as it endeavors to make a fortune on a horse-race. Hawkes's uncanny evocation of the seedy atmosphere of the British demi-monde and his persuasive characterization of the twisted loneliness of Hencher and the semi-voluntary brutalization of the Bankses give this novel a quality of sadistic and yet poetic grotesquerie remarkable in its integrity to its own cruel aesthetic purposes.

With *Second Skin* Hawkes inaugurates a new direction in narrative focus, restricting himself to the consciousness of the first-person point of view (the Skipper's), throwing some doubt on the reliability of that point of view, and adding an element of playfulness to the chronicle of the horrible events (rape, sodomy, suicide) that mark the Skipper's journey toward ambiguous self-understanding. And in the trilogy of novels that has followed (*Blood Oranges, Death, Sleep, and the Traveler*, and *Travesty*), this use of an increasingly unreliable narrator and a playfulness that sometimes borders on the frivolous have become even more marked. But if the last three or four novels show a falling-off from the concentrated purity of Hawkes's earlier excursions in seductive horror, his prose style has remained as sensuous, supple, and shocking as it was in the beginning. He remains well outside the mainstream of contemporary fiction, but he has settled a small but solid island of stylistic rigor which stands as a kind of navigational guide for his contemporaries and those who are voyaging after him.

—Earl Rovit

HAWTHORNE, Nathaniel. American. Born Nathaniel Hathorne in Salem, Massachusetts, 4 July 1804. Educated at Samuel Archer's School, Salem, 1819; Bowdoin College, Brunswick, Maine, 1821–25. Married Sophia Peabody in 1842; two daughters and one son. Lived with his mother in Salem, writing and contributing to periodicals, 1825–36; Editor, *American Magazine of Useful and Entertaining Knowledge*, Boston, 1836; weigher and gager in the Boston Customs House, 1839–41; invested in the Brook Farm Commune, West Roxbury, Massachusetts, and lived there, 1841–42; moved to Concord, Massachusetts, 1842–45; Surveyor, Salem Customs House, 1845–49; lived in Lenox, Massachusetts, 1850–51, West Newton, Massachusetts, 1851, and settled again in Concord, 1852; United States Consul in Liverpool, 1853–57; lived in Italy, 1858–59, and London, 1859–60, then returned to Concord. *Died 17 May 1864.*

PUBLICATIONS

Collections

Complete Writings. 22 vols., 1900.
Representative Selections, edited by Austin Warren. 1934
Complete Novels and Selected Tales, edited by Norman Holmes Pearson. 1937.
Works, edited by William Charvat and others. 1963 –
Poems, edited by Richard E. Peck. 1967.

Fiction

Fanshawe: A Tale.   1828; with *The Blithedale Romance*, in *Works*, 1965.

Twice-Told Tales.   1837; revised edition, 1842; in *Works*, 1974.

The Celestial Rail-Road.   1843.

Mosses from an Old Manse.   1843; in *Works*, 1974.

The Scarlet Letter: A Romance.   1850; edited by Sculley Bradley and others, 1962, revised edition, 1978.

The House of the Seven Gables: A Romance.   1851; edited by Seymour L. Gross, 1967.

The Snow-Image and Other Twice-Told Tales.   1851; in *Works*, 1974.

The Blithedale Romance.   1852; edited by Seymour L. Gross and Rosalie Murphy, 1977.

Transformation; or, The Romance of Monte Beni.   1860; as *The Marble Faun*, 1860; edited by Richard H. Rupp, 1971.

Pansie: A Fragment.   1864.

Septimus: A Romance, edited by Una Hawthorne and Robert Browning.   1872; as *Septimus Felton; or, The Elixir of Life*, 1872.

The Dolliver Romance and Other Pieces, edited by Sophia Hawthorne.   1876.

Fanshawe and Other Pieces.   1876.

Dr. Grimshaw's Secret: A Romance, edited by Julian Hawthorne.   1883; edited by Edward H. Davidson, 1954.

The Ghost of Dr. Harris.   1900.

Other

Grandfather's Chair: A History for Youth.   1841; *Famous Old People, Being the Second Epoch of Grandfather's Chair*, 1841; *Liberty Tree, with the Last Words of Grandfather's Chair*, 1841, revised edition, 1842.

Biographical Stories for Children.   1842.

True Stories from History and Biography.   1851.

A Wonder-Book for Girls and Boys.   1851; with *Tanglewood Tales*, in *Works*, 1972.

Life of Franklin Pierce.   1852.

Tanglewood Tales for Girls and Boys, Being a Second Wonder-Book.   1853; with *A Wonder-Book*, in *Works*, 1972.

Our Old Home: A Series of English Sketches.   1863; in *Works*, 1970.

Passages from the American Note-Books, edited by Sophia Hawthorne.   2 vols., 1868.

Passages from the English Note-Books, edited by Sophia Hawthorne.   2 vols., 1870.

Passages from the French and Italian Note-Books, edited by Una Hawthorne.   2 vols., 1871.

Twenty Days with Julian and Little Bunny: A Dairy.   1904.

Love Letters.   2 vols., 1907.

Letters to William D. Ticknor.   2 vols., 1910.

The Heart of Hawthorne's Journal, edited by Newton Arvin.   1929.

The American Notebooks, edited by Randall Stewart.   1932; in *Works*, 1972.

The English Notebook, edited by Randall Stewart.   1941.

Hawthorne as Editor: Selections from His Writings in the American Magazine of Useful and Entertaining Knowledge, edited by Arlin Turner.   1941.

Editor, with Elizabeth Hawthorne, *Peter Parley's Universal History.*   2 vols., 1837; as *Peter Parley's Common School History*, 1838.

Editor, *Journal of an African Cruiser*, by Horatio Bridge.   1845.

Editor, *The Yarn of a Yankee Privateer*, by Benjamin Frederick Browne(?).   1926.

Bibliography: *Hawthorne: A Descriptive Bibliography* by C. E. Frazer Clark, Jr., 1977.

Reading List: *Hawthorne* by Henry James, 1879; *Hawthorne: A Biography* by Randall Stewart, 1948; *Hawthorne's Fiction: The Light and the Dark* by Richard H. Fogle, 1952, revised edition, 1964; *Hawthorne: A Critical Study* by Hyatt A. Waggoner, 1955; *Hawthorne's Tragic Vision* by Roy R. Male, 1957; *Hawthorne, Man and Writer* by Edward Wagenknecht, 1961; *Hawthorne: An Introduction and an Interpretation* by Arlin Turner, 1961; *The Sins of the Fathers: Hawthorne's Psychological Themes* by Frederick Crews, 1966; *Hawthorne, Transcendental Symbolist* by Marjorie Elder, 1969; *The Recognition of Hawthorne: Selected Criticism since 1828* edited by B. Bernard Cohen, 1969; *The Shape of Hawthorne's Career* by Nina Baym, 1976; *Hawthorne: The Poetics of Enchantment* by Edgar A. Dryden, 1977; *Rediscovering Hawthorne* by Kenneth Dauber, 1977.

*   *   *

Nathaniel Hawthorne's fiction is unique in two important respects. He was the first major novelist in English to combine high moral seriousness with transcendent dedication to art. He was also the first major novelist in English to insist upon the basic unreality of his works. An imaginative genius gifted with considerable linguistic skill, he opened a path in literature that few have followed with comparable success. Like all great writers he was original in that fundamental sense in which the work resists duplication because it remains identified with the creative individuality of the author. George Eliot followed Hawthorne in the attempt to wed morality to art, but she attempted the fusion within a framework of realistic verisimilitude. Most writers since Hawthorne who have worked outside of the framework of realism have been less concerned than he with the moral seriousness of their works.

Isolation stands at the heart of his development as an artist. For twelve years after his graduation from Bowdoin College he lived in his mother's house in Salem, publishing *Fanshawe* at his own expense and numerous tales and sketches in magazines and gift annuals at rates so low that the income from the twenty-seven tales he published in the *Token* amounted to less than $350. Since all of this early material was published either anonymously or under pseudonyms, he achieved no reputation and acquired no literary friends. In terms of financial success, indeed, it probably would not have mattered much if he had acquired friends and a reputation early. Like other American writers of his time he suffered even during the years of his greatest popularity from the lack of an international copyright law; he could neither compete at home with cheap editions of famous English authors nor reap much income from his sales in England. Although *The Scarlet Letter* made him a name, it earned him a pitifully small income (probably not more than $1,500 from the American sales during his lifetime). Under the circumstances, it is not surprising that he developed a literary aesthetic in which mass appeal had no place. He wrote to please himself and also that occasional isolated reader who would share with him his aesthetic and moral sensibilities.

He early formed the habit of working from the inside outward. Unlike his friend Melville he possessed no well of exotic experience to draw his subject matter from. His material came from his thoughts, his reading, his brooding upon New England and its history. Coming to believe that all truth that matters is inner ("the truth," as he expressed it, "of the human heart"), he considered externalities to be inherently deceptive. Consequently he considered verisimilitude, in the sense of faithfulness to the world of actuality, to be a highly questionable merit in fiction. Much more important to him was the construction of a fictive world that remained faithful to the artist's inmost vision. Hence his insistence that his works were to be judged as romances rather than novels. Hence, too, the considerable drive toward symbol and allegory.

He is a romantic writer, but not because his material is distant in time and place. Among his longer fictions, *The House of the Seven Gables*, *The Blithedale Romance*, and *The Marble Faun* are contemporary with his own time. *The Scarlet Letter* and many of the Tales are set in that Puritan New England that he knew so intimately. He is romantic in the more important sense of considering verifiable fact to be a less important commodity in the world than the unverifiable discoveries of imagination and intuition. He is also romantic in the particularly American sense of possessing a visionary idea of a society in which perfect freedom, equality, and justice might one day prevail, though no such society has yet appeared on earth. It is against such a vision that *The Scarlet Letter* especially must be read; it is the vision that places Hawthorne, for all his idiosyncrasy, in the direct line of American novelists from Cooper through Melville, Twain, and James.

His most frequent themes revolve around the sanctity of the individual, the necessity for warm human relationships, the nature of sin, a distrust of science and the intellect, and a belief in the fundamental ambiguity of earthly phenonema. All are closely related in his work, with an exploration of the nature of sin the tie that binds the others together. Thus the characters of Rappaccini ("Rappaccini's Daughter"), Ethan Brand ("Ethan Brand"), and Roger Chillingworth (*The Scarlet Letter*) mix their sin from the same ingredients: all are coldly intellectual, scientifically detached individuals who possess no effectively warm human relationships, are willing and even eager to intrude upon the privacy of others, and are convinced of the possibility of ultimate triumph over the mysteries of the phenomenal world. The sin of adultery that Hester Prynne of *The Scarlet Letter* has committed is much less sweeping than this. The result of a natural need for human warmth, it is clothed in ambiguity. There are sins and sins. In a more perfect society Hester's act would be no sin. If there exists, however, the unpardonable sin that Ethan Brand seeks it is very close to that attributed to Roger Chillingworth by Arthur Dimmesdale in *The Scarlet Letter*: "He has violated, in cold blood, the sanctity of a human heart."

The terrific "power of blackness" that Melville saw in Hawthorne begins in the isolation of the artist and ends in the ambiguity of his work. As artist he must break through the isolation or remain self-incased and unread. His artistry drives him inward, away from the human contact that is necessary for survival both as a writer and as a man. In his works he must remain true to his deepest vision, including for Hawthorne an abiding sense of the world's unshakeable ambiguities, but he must also make this vision accessible to others. In "The Minister's Black Veil" and "Young Goodman Brown" the touchstones of isolation and ambiguity are given splendid emphasis, but they remain important to the effect of large numbers of other works as well, from deceptively simple sketches such as "Wakefield" or "The Ambitious Guest" through the relative lightness of *The House of the Seven Gables* to the dark complexities of *The Marble Faun*.

In the end, the peculiar conditions of his creative life served him well. Steeped in the New England that he depicted so effectively in the majority of his works, he created masterly short fiction because the form came naturally to him. He probed beneath the surfaces of his subjects because he saw so little in the outward appearances that was of lasting interest. Without the financial support of the British three-decker tradition, he wrote much shorter novels than Dickens or Eliot, but his works gain in impact through compression. Few novelists in English have accomplished so much in so few words as is accomplished in *The Scarlet Letter*. Few have displayed better than Hawthorne does in his best works the power of romance, or, by inference, the limitations of superficial realism. Seldom have the modes of symbol and allegory been so effectively rendered in prose.

—George Perkins

HAYWOOD, Eliza (née Fowler). English. Born in London, probably in 1693. Married Valentine Haywood in 1711 (who deserted her, 1721); two children. Writer from childhood; praised by Steele as "Sappho," 1709; actress, in Dublin, then in London, from 1715; successful as a novelist from 1724; ridiculed by Pope in the *Dunciad*, 1728; Editor, *The Female Spectator*, London, 1744–46, and *The Parrot*, London, 1746. *Died 25 February 1756.*

PUBLICATIONS

Fiction

Love in Excess; or, The Fatal Enquiry. 3 vols., 1719–20.
The British Recluse; or, The Secret History of Cleomira, Supposed Dead. 1722.
Idalia; or, The Unfortunate Mistress. 1723.
The Injured Husband; or, The Mistaken Resentment. 1723.
The Fatal Secret; or, Constancy in Distress. 1724.
Lasselia; or, The Self-Abandoned. 1724.
The Masqueraders; or, Fatal Curiosity. 1724.
The Rash Resolve; or, The Untimely Discovery. 1724.
A Spy upon the Conjuror. 1724.
The Arragonian Queen. 1724.
The Surprise; or, Constancy Rewarded. 1724.
Bath Intrigues, in Four Letters to a Friend in London. 1725.
The Unequal Conflict; or, Nature Triumphant. 1725.
Fantomina; or, Love in a Maze. 1725.
Memoirs of a Certain Island Adjacent to the Kingdom of Utopia. 1725.
The Dumb Projector. 1725.
Dalinda; or, The Double Marriage. 1725.
Fatal Fondness; or, Love Its Own Opposer. 1725.
Memoirs of the Baron de Brosse. 1725.
The City Jilt; or, The Alderman Turned Beau. 1726.
The Mercenary Lover; or, The Unfortunate Heiresses. 1726.
The Distressed Orphan; or, Love in a Madhouse. 1726(?).
The Double Marriage; or, The Fatal Release. 1726.
Cleomelia; or, The Generous Mistress. 1727.
The Fruitless Enquiry. 1727.
Letters from the Palace of Fame. 1727.
The Life of Madam De Villesache. 1727.
Love in Its Variety (stories). 1727.
The Perplexed Duchess; or, Treachery Rewarded, Being Some Memoirs of the Court of Malfy. 1727.
Philidore and Placentia; or, L'Amour Trop Delicat. 1727; edited by W. M. McBurney, in *Four Before Richardson*, 1963.
The Secret History of the Present Intrigues of the Court of Carimania. 1727.
Persecuted Virtue; or, The Cruel Lover. 1728.
The Agreeable Caledonian; or Memoirs of Signiora di Morella, A Roman Lady. 2 vols., 1728–29; as *Clementina; or, The History of an Italian Lady*, 1768.
The Disguised Prince; or, The Beautiful Parisian. 1728.
Irish Artifice; or, The History of Clarina. 1728.
The Fair Hebrew. 1729.
Love-Letters on All Occasions Lately Passed Between Persons of Distinction (stories). 1730.

Adventures of Eovaai, Princess of Ijaveo.   1736; as *The Unfortunate Princess*, 1741.
The Fortunate Foundlings, Being the Genuine History of Colonel M——rs and His Sister Madame Du P——y.   1744.
Epistles for the Ladies.   2 vols., 1749–50.
Life's Progress Through the Passions; or, The Adventures of Natura.   1748.
The History of Miss Betsy Thoughtless.   1751.
The History of Jemmy and Jenny Jessamy.   1753.
The Invisible Spy.   1755.
The Wife.   1756.
The Husband, in Answer to the Wife.   1756.

Plays

The Fair Captive, from a work by a Captain Hurst (produced 1721).   1721.
A Wife to Be Let (produced 1723).   1724.
Frederick, Duke of Brunswick-Lunenburgh (produced 1729).   1729.
The Opera of Operas; or, Tom Thumb the Great, with William Hatchett, music by Thomas Arne, from the play by Fielding (produced 1733).   1733.

Verse

Poems on Several Occasions.   1724.

Other

The Tea Table (magazine).   1724.
Works.   4 vols., 1724.
Secret Histories, Novels, and Poems.   6 vols., 1725–27.
Reflections on the Various Effects of Love.   1726.
A Present for a Servant Maid.   1743.
The Female Spectator (magazine).   4 vols., 1747; selections edited by J. B. Priestley, 1929.

Translator, *Mary Stuart, Queen of Scots.*   1725.
Translator, *La Belle Assemblée; or, The Adventures of Six Days,* by Madeleine Gomez.   1725.
Translator, *The Lady's Philosopher's Stone,* by Louis Adrien Duperron de Castera.   1725.
Translator, *L'Entretien des Beaux Esprits, Being a Sequel to La Belle Assemblée,* by Madeleine Gomez.   1734.
Translator, *The Virtuous Villagers,* by de Mouhy.   1742.
Translator, *The Busy Body: A Successful Spy.*   1742.
Translator, *Letters from a Lady of Quality to a Chevalier,* by Edme Boursault.   N.d.

Reading List: *The Life and Romance of Haywood* by George Frisbie Whicher, 1915 (includes bibliography).

*   *   *

As the successor to Aphra Behn and Mrs. Manley, Eliza Haywood was probably the most well-known and certainly the most prolific female writer of the 1720's. She began her career in 1719–20 with a novel, *Love in Excess; or, The Fatal Enquiry*, and during the decade which followed she published some forty original works, translated a number of French novellas, and wrote three plays. She seems to have turned to writing after leaving her husband, and she became a sophisticated professional writer who turned out book after book according to a clearly visible and highly successsful popular format. Her work in that busy decade took two separate if closely related forms: the secret history and the novel. Her *Memoirs of a Certain Island Adjacent to the Kingdom of Utopia* was a fairly successful imitation of Mrs. Manley's popular and notorious *New Atlantis* (1709). Both these books were collections of highly embellished gossip, scandal, and libel about prominent people of the day. Haywood's book combines sexual sensationalism with a vigorus satirical rhetoric in which Cupid denounces the perversion of his worship by avarice, adultery, and the exploitation and betrayal of women by a corrupt male-dominated society. The so-called "South-Sea Bubble" financial disaster of 1722 is the basis of Haywood's denunciations of the rich and the powerful, but the main appeal of the book was clearly the near-pornographic intensity and lurid melodrama of its recurring sexual scenes. Haywood's secret histories contain, in fact, nothing more than localized and abridged versions of the story she told over and over again in her novels, some of which were given the label of secret history as well. From *Love in Excess* through such works as *Idalia, Lasselia, The Fatal Secret*, and *Philidore and Placentia* Haywood repeated with unfailing energy and only slight variations an apparently popular formula story which featured genteel and euphemistic but effectively pornographic descriptions of female passion and male lust.

Typically, a young girl is pursued by a treacherous suitor in a complicated social or moral situation which often features incest as well as adultery. Seduction or outright rape is a standard incident, and terrible consequences invariably follow, even violent death and sometimes grim revenge on the seducer. At the center of all this operatic melodrama is the "power of love," an irresistible but destructive urge whose thrilling and forbidden intensities Haywood's novels were designed to evoke in their readers. A scene such as this one from *Love in Excess* is entirely representative of Haywood's style and method. The heroine, Melliora, is asleep: her "Gown and the rest of her Garments were white, all ungirt, and loosely flowing, discover'd a Thousand Beauties, which modish Formalities conceal." Melliora dreams of the handsome D'Elmont, and he enters to steal a chaste good-night kiss; but the scene quickly turns into a typical Haywoodian erotic moment, complicated by moral melodrama:

> ... he tore open his Waistcoat, and joyn'd his panting Breast to hers, with such a Tumultuous Eagerness! Seiz'd her with such a Rapidity of Transported hope Crown'd Passion, as immediately wak'd her from an imaginary Felicity, to the Approaches of a Solid One. Where have I been? (said she, just opening her Eyes) where am I? – (And then coming more perfectly to her self) Heaven! What's this? – I am D'Elmont (Cry'd the O'erjoy'd Count) the happy D'Elmont! Melliora's, the Charming Melliora's D'Elmont! O, all ye Saints, (Resum'd the surpriz'd Trembling fair) ye Ministring Angels! Whose Business 'tis to guard the Innocent! Protect and Shield my Virtue! ... Come, come no more Reluctance (Continu'd he, gathering Kisses from her soft Snowy Breast at every Word) Damp not the fires thou hast rais'd with seeming Coiness! I know thou art mine! All mine! And thus I – Yet think (said she Interrupting him, and Strugling in his Arms) think what 'tis that you wou'd do, nor for a Moments Joy, hazard your Peace for Ever. By Heaven, cry'd he: I will this Night be Master of my Wishes, no Matter what to Morrow may bring forth.

Haywood became famous for writing what the 18th century called "warm" scenes like this one, and a prefatory poem in her 1732 collected *Secret Histories, Novels and Poems* begins its praise of her thus: "Persuasion waits on all your bright Designs,/And where you point the

Varying Soul Inclines:/See! Love and Friendship, the fair Theme inspires,/We glow with Zeal, we melt in soft Desires!" Not so soft, we might be tempted to add, for there is nothing very mysterious about the commercial success of Haywood's works. Her stories were English versions of the amatory novellas popular on the continent in the latter half of the 17th century, and they provided her apparently large and eager audience with a satisfying fantasy world filled with lust and pathos and with an exotic aristocratic elegance and corruption. Her stories are as rich with popular fantasies about the upper classes as they are thick with soft eroticism. They also very clearly expressed a sort of instinctive feminism, and in a strange and untypical novel called *The British Recluse* two ruined ladies articulate a coherent and eloquent response to male exploitation and go off to live together in virtuous seclusion in the country.

Haywood's novels of the 1720's are important (if virtually unreadable), for they are a symptom (and perhaps even a cause) of the increasing popularity of fiction in England during that period. The tradition of popular narrative she helped form is a key part of the literary context in which Richardson and Fielding and the other major novelists of the century were to operate in the 1740's. Mrs. Haywood herself outlived her fame and published little in the 1730's and '40's.

But she was shrewdly professional to the end and responded to the fashion created by Richardson's novels by writing two "domestic" novels, *The History of Miss Betsy Thoughtless* and *The History of Jemmy and Jenny Jessamy*, which remained popular until the end of the century.

—John Richetti

HAZLITT, William. English. Born in Maidstone, Kent, 10 April 1778; lived with his family in the United States, 1783–87, and in Wem, Shropshire, from 1787. Educated privately at home; studied for the Unitarian ministry at Hackney Theological College, London, 1793–94, then returned to his father's house at Wem, and continued his studies, mainly in philosophy, on his own; met Coleridge, 1798, subsequently visited him at Stowey, and, with Coleridge, visited Wordsworth at Lynton; gave up theological studies; studied painting with his brother and in Paris, 1802–03; gave up art in 1805. Married 1) Sarah Stoddart in 1808 (separated, 1819; divorced, 1822), one son; 2) Mrs. Bridgewater in 1824 (separated, 1825). Writer from 1792; divided his time between Wem and London, 1805–08; through Coleridge and Wordsworth, met Lamb and Godwin; supported Godwin in the controversy with Malthus, 1807; settled in Winterslow, near Salisbury, 1808; returned to London, 1812; lectured on philosophy at the Russell Institution; Parliamentary Reporter, 1812–13, and Dramatic Critic, 1814, for the *Morning Chronicle*; contributed to the *Edinburgh Review*, 1814 until his death; also wrote for the *Champion, The Times*, Leigh Hunt's *Examiner, London Magazine, Liberal*, and the *New Monthly*; lectured at the Surrey Institution, 1818–20; toured France and Italy, 1824–25. *Died 18 September 1830.*

PUBLICATIONS

Collections

    Complete Works, edited by P. P. Howe.   21 vols., 1930–34.
    Selected Writings, edited by Ronald Blythe.   1970.

Prose

An Essay on the Principles of Human Action, Being an Argument in Favour of the Natural Disinterestedness of the Human Mind.   1805.
Free Thoughts on Public Affairs; or, Advice to a Patriot.   1806.
A Reply to the Essay on Population by Malthus, in a Series of Letters.   1807.
A New and Improved Grammar of the English Tongue for the Use of Schools.   1810.
Memoirs of the Late Thomas Holcroft, completed by Hazlitt.   3 vols., 1816; edited by Elbridge Colby, as *The Life of Holcroft,* 2 vols., 1925.
The Round Table: A Collection of Essays on Literature, Men, and Manners, with Leigh Hunt.   2 vols., 1817.
Characters of Shakespeare's Plays.   1817; edited by C. Morgan, in *Liber Amoris and Dramatic Criticisms,* 1948.
A View of the English Stage; or, A Series of Dramatic Criticisms.   1818.
Lectures on the English Poets.   1818.
A Letter to William Gifford.   1819.
Lectures on the English Comic Writers.   1819; edited by A. Johnson,   1965.
Political Essays.   1819.
Lectures, Chiefly on the Dramatic Literature of the Age of Elizabeth.   1820.
Table-Talk; or, Original Essays.   2 vols., 1821–22.
Liber Amoris; or, The New Pygmalion.   1823; edited by C. Morgan, 1948.
Characteristics, in the Manner of Rochefoucault's Maxims.   1823.
Sketches of the Principal Picture Galleries in England with a Criticism on Marriage A-la-mode.   1824.
The Spirit of the Age; or, Contemporary Portraits.   1825; edited by E. D. Mackerness, 1969.
The Plain Speaker: Opinions on Books, Men, and Things.   2 vols., 1826.
Notes of a Journey Through France and Italy.   1826.
The Life of Napoleon Buonaparte.   4 vols., 1828–30.
Conversations of James Northcote, R.A.   1830; edited by Frank Swinnerton, 1949.
Literary Remains.   2 vols., 1836.
Sketches and Essays, Now First Collected by His Son.   1839; as *Men and Manners,* 1852.
Criticisms on Art and Sketches of the Picture Galleries of England, edited by William Hazlitt, Jr.   2 vols., 1843–44; as *Essays on the Fine Arts,* 1873.
Winterslow: Essays and Characters Written There, edited by William Hazlitt, Jr.   1850.
A Reply to Z, edited by Charles Whibley.   1923.
New Writings, edited by P. P. Howe.   2 vols., 1925–27.
Hazlitt in the Workshop: The Manuscript of "The Fight," edited by Stewart C. Wilcox.   1943.

Editor, *An Abridgement of the Light of Nature Pursued,* by Abraham Tucker.   1807.
Editor, *The Eloquence of the British Senate.*   2 vols., 1807.
Editor, *Select British Poets.*   1824.

Bibliography: *Bibliography of Hazlitt* by Geoffrey Keynes, 1931.

Reading List: *Hazlitt* by J. B. Priestley, 1960; *Hazlitt* by Herschel Baker, 1962; *Hazlitt and the Creative Imagination* by W. P. Albrecht, 1965; *Hazlitt and the Spirit of the Age* by Roy Park, 1971; *Hazlitt* by Ralph M. Wardle, 1971; *Hazlitt, Critic of Power* by John Kinnaird, 1978.

*   *   *

William Hazlitt was an essayist pure and simple. He never published poems or fiction or drama, and his only excursion into the so-called creative arts was an abortive attempt as a young man to become a painter, which left him with a deep understanding of a craft he found he could not practice and thus made him one of the best early art critics in England and a true precursor of Ruskin. Yet, though he mainly restricted himself to criticism and reminiscence, with an occasional foray into political radicalism (to which he remained faithful when many of his friends, like Wordsworth and Coleridge, were alarmed by events in France into turning to the Right), Hazlitt raised the personal essay to the level of an art, and it is difficult to think of anyone except his friend and contemporary Charles Lamb who has excelled him in this genre.

Hazlitt was condemned by his poverty to be a perpetual journalist. He found the time to write few long, sustained books, and those which he did complete, like his amateurish *Essay on the Principles of Human Action*, his ponderous *Life of Napoleon* and the Rousseauish confessions of *Liber Amoris*, the tale of his unhappy love affair with Sarah Walker, are all relative failures. It was the lengthy essay — often a long review article — of the type which literary magazines of the time favoured, that showed Hazlitt at his best. There he could develop his flashes of insight without becoming involved in scholarly elaborations that would have revealed the lack of education and broad reading of which his enemies — with some justice — often accused him. Certainly he made up for these deficiencies by a strong intuitive understanding of both painters and writers. He stressed the importance of the emotion aroused by an open-hearted response to a work of literature or art, and declared that his critic's role was "to feel what is good and give reasons for the faith that is in me." He tended to ignore what other critics might have said, and made a virtue out of this by claiming that he was trying to show an original response to original work — to "that which was never imagined or expressed before."

Hazlitt's best books are all collections of essays and lectures, often with a unity of approach that links them, and within the limitations of such a form he acted not merely as a pioneer critic but also as a pioneer literary historian, reaching back into almost the whole past and present of English literature. Much of his best writing is about men he knew and their work. In essays like "My First Acquaintance with Poets" and "The Conversation of Poets" he not only portrays his own development as a young writer fascinated with the personality of Coleridge, but he also gives insights into the personalities of the Lake poets that go beyond the biographical into an understanding of the sources of their poetry.

At the same time, in volumes like *Characters of Shakespeare's Plays*, *Lectures on the English Poets*, *Lectures on the English Comic Writers*, and *Lectures on the Dramatic Literature of the Age of Elizabeth*, Hazlitt contributed greatly to the nineteenth-century rehabilitation of English writers of the sixteenth, seventeenth and early eighteenth centuries. He wrote very well on men he understood empathically, such as Milton, Fielding and Cervantes (whom Hazlitt cavalierly included among the English comic writers), and the Restoration comedians of manners like Wycherley and Congreve, but where his sympathies did not reach he was inclined to be silent, and perhaps his greatest omission as a critic-historian of English writing up to his time lay in his neglect of the Metaphysical poets.

Yet, for all his perceptiveness in understanding writers of the past, Hazlitt was undoubtedly at his best in writing of the world he knew from direct experience. *The Spirit of the Age*, with its sharp critical portraits of his contemporaries, despite occasional flashes of prejudice, is one of the best books to give the flavour of the English literary world at the end of the Napoleonic Wars, making verdicts on men and their works which posterity has on the whole sustained, and *The Plain Speaker*, ranging somewhat more widely, is equally fresh in its approach.

"Well, I've had a happy life," are Hazlitt's recorded last words. To those who knew the difficulties and disappointments he had endured, it seemed an astonishing statement. Yet an indefatigable zest for life was part of Hazlitt's nature, emerging in some of his best essays, like the splendid piece "On Going a Journey" (which begins characteristically: "One of the pleasantest things in the world is going a journey; but I like to go by myself"), the robust accounts of popular pleasures in "The Fight" and "The Indian Jugglers," and the two essays that balance each other, "On the Feeling of Immortality in Youth" and "On the Fear of Death," which concludes that "The most rational cure after all for the inordinate fear of death is to set a just value on life." The value Hazlitt set on life is shown in his love of English words and the rhythms of speech, in his love of the common life of Englishmen, and in his power to enter the mind of a creator, whether writer or artist, whether Wordsworth or Poussin.

In the way meant by Wilde, Hazlitt was pre-eminently the critic as artist; he never merely dissected or described, but in the best sense recreated what he discussed.

—George Woodcock

HEARN, (Patricio) Lafcadio (Carlos Tessima).   Japanese.   Born on the island of Santa Maura, Greece, 27 June 1850; raised in Dublin; emigrated to Japan, 1890; naturalized, 1895. Educated at St. Cuthbert's College, Ushaw, County Durham, England, 1863–66; Petits Precepteurs, Yvetot, near Rouen, France, 1867. Married 1) a mulatto c. 1875; 2) Setsu Koizumi in 1891; three sons and one daughter. Settled in the United States, 1869, and worked at various menial jobs in Cincinnati, Ohio; became a proofreader for Robert Clarke Company, then a member of staff of *Trade List* weekly, and a reporter for the *Cincinnati Enquirer*, 1873–75; lost this job because of the miscegenation laws; member of staff of the *Cincinnati Commercial*, 1875–78; Assistant Editor, *New Orleans Item*, 1878–81; member of staff of the *New Orleans Times-Democrat*, 1881–87; lived in Martinique and wrote for *Harper's*, 1887–89, then went to Japan: teacher in the Ordinary Middle School, Matsue, 1890–91, and the Government College, Kumamoto, 1891–94; worked for *Kobe Chronicle*, 1894–95; Professor of English Literature, Imperial University, Tokyo, 1896–1903; English Teacher, Waseda University, 1904. *Died 26 September 1904.*

PUBLICATIONS

Collections

Writings.   16 vols., 1922.
Selected Writings, edited by Henry Goodman.   1949.

Fiction

Chita: A Memory of Last Island.   1889.
Youma: The Story of a West-Indian Slave.   1890.
Barbarous Barbers and Other Stories, edited by Ichiro Nishizaki.   1939.

Other

Stray Leaves from Strange Literature.   1884.
Some Chinese Ghosts.   1887.
Two Years in the French West Indies.   1890.

Glimpses of Unfamiliar Japan.   2 vols., 1894.
Out of the East: Reveries and Studies in New Japan.   1895.
Kokoro: Hints and Echoes of Japanese Inner Life.   1896.
Gleanings in Buddha-Fields: Studies of Hand and Soul in the Far East.   1897.
Exotics and Retrospectives.   1898.
In Ghostly Japan.   1899.
Shadowings.   1900.
A Japanese Miscellany.   1901.
Kotto, Being Japanese Curios, with Sundry Cobwebs.   1902.
Kwaidan: Stories and Studies of Strange Things.   1904.
Japan: An Attempt at Interpretation.   1904.
The Romance of the Milky Way and Other Studies and Stories.   1905.
Letters from the Raven, Being the Correspondence of Hearn with Henry Watkin, edited by Milton Bronner.   1907.
The Japanese Letters, edited by Elizabeth Bisland.   1910.
Leaves from the Diary of an Impressionist: Early Writings, edited by Ferris Greenslet.   1911.
Editorials from the Kobe Chronicle, edited by Merle Johnson.   1913; edited by Makoto Sangu, 1960.
Fantastics and Other Fancies, edited by Charles Woodward Hutson.   1914.
Karma, edited by Albert Mordell.   1918.
Essays in European and Oriental Literature, edited by Albert Mordell.   1923.
Creole Sketches, edited by Charles Woodward Hutson.   1924.
An American Miscellany: Articles and Stories Now First Collected, edited by Albert Mordell.   2 vols., 1924.
Occidental Gleanings: Sketches and Essays Now First Collected, edited by Albert Mordell.   2 vols., 1925.
Some New Letters and Writings, edited by Sanki Ichikawa.   1925.
Editorials, edited by Charles Woodward Hutson.   1926.
Facts and Fancies, edited by R. Tanabé.   1929.
Essays on American Literature, edited by Sanki Ichikawa.   1929.
Gibbeted: Execution of a Youthful Murderer, edited by P. D. Perkins.   1933.
Spirit Photography, edited by P. D. Perkins.   1933.
Letters to a Pagan, edited by R. B. Powers.   1933.
Letters from Shimane and Kyushu.   1935.
American Articles, edited by Ichiro Nishizaki.   4 vols., 1939.
Buying Christmas Toys and Other Essays, edited by Ichiro Nishizaki.   1939.
Literary Essays, edited by Ichiro Nishizaki.   1939.
The New Radiance and Other Scientific Sketches, edited by Ichiro Nishizaki.   1939.
Oriental Articles, edited by Ichiro Nishizaki.   1939.
An Orange Christmas.   1941.
Children of the Levee, edited by O. W. Frost.   1957.
Japan's Religions: Shinto and Buddhism, edited by Kazumitsu Kato.   1966.

Editor, *La Cuisine Creole: A Collection of Recipes.*   1885.

Translator, *One of Cleopatra's Nights,* by Gautier.   1882.
Translator, *Gombo Zhèbes: Little Dictionary of Creole Proverbs.*   1885.
Translator, *The Crime of Sylvestre Bonnard,* by Anatole France.   1890.
Translator, *Japanese Fairy Tale* series.   5 vols., 1898–1922.
Translator, *The Temptation of St. Anthony,* by Flaubert.   1910.
Translator, *Japanese Lyrics.*   1915.
Translator, *Saint Anthony and Other Stories,* by de Maupassant, edited by Albert Mordell.   1924.

Translator, *The Adventures of Walter Schnaffs and Other Stories*, by de Maupassant, edited by Albert Mordell. 1931.
Translator, *Stories*, by Pierre Loti, edited by Albert Mordell.   1933.
Translator, *Stories*, by Zola, edited by Albert Mordell.   1935.
Translator, *Sketches and Tales from the French*, edited by Albert Mordell.   1935.

Lecture notes of Hearn's Japanese students published: *Interpretations of Literature*, 2 vols., 1915, *Appreciations of Poetry*, 1916, *Life and Literature*, 1917, and *Pre-Raphaelite and Other Poets*, 1922, all edited by John Erskine; *A History of English Literature*, 2 vols., 1927, supplement, 1927, revised edition, 1941, *Complete Lectures on Art, Literature, and Philosophy*, 1932, *On Poetry*, 1934, and *On Poets*, 1934, all edited by R. Tanabé; *Lectures on Shakespeare*, edited by Sanki Ichikawa, 1928; *Lectures on Prosody*, 1929; *Victorian Philosophy*, 1930; *Lectures on Tennyson*, edited by Shigetsugu Kishi, 1941.

Bibliography: *Hearn: A Bibliography of His Writings* by F. R. and Ione Perkins, 1934; in *Bibliography of American Literature* by Jacob Blanck, 1963.

Reading List; *Life and Letters* by Elizabeth Bisland, 2 vols., 1906; *Hearn* by Marcel Robert, 2 vols., 1950–51; *Young Hearn* by O. W. Frost, 1958; *Hearn* by Elizabeth Stevenson, 1961; *An Ape of Gods: The Art and Thought of Hearn* by Beongcheon Yu, 1964; *Discoveries: Essays on Hearn* by Albert Mordell, 1964; *Hearn* by Arthur E. Kunst, 1969.

*   *   *

Parental desertion and a rootless, restless childhood left Lafcadio Hearn with a heart "like a bird fluttering impatiently for the migrating season," spurning the "egotistical individualism," "constitutional morality," and scientific positivism of an Anglo-Saxon world from which he "considered [him]self ostracized, tabooed, outlawed." Initially he sought in creole New Orleans ("the paradise of the South") and the tropical Caribbean that "sensuous life …, the life desire" which would favour "the development of a morbid nervous sensibility to material impressions, … absolute loss of thinking, … numbing and clouding of memory." But it was the less languid, more ascetic culture of the Orient which finally offered him the refuge of "feelings, so strangely far away from all the nineteenth century part of me, that the faint blind stirrings of them make one afraid – deliciously afraid."

At his best, Hearn evokes both in form and content an ethos "as gentle as the light of dreams," "the all-temperate world," "soft serenity" and "passionless tenderness" and "the vague but immeasurable emotion of Shinto" of his adoptive homeland. "Depth does not exist in the Japanese soulstream," he observed, and the evocative, picturesque surfaces of his essays seem to gain from his own ocular deficiency: "a landscape necessarily suggests less to the keen-sighted man than to the myope. The keener the view the less depth in the impression produced." His *penchant*, derived from a journalistic training, was for the quick sketch and fleeting *aperçu*; *Two Years in the French West Indies* he described as "simple note-making," "impressions of the moment," a method disclosed by the very titles of his later work: *Glimpses of Unfamiliar Japan*, *Gleanings in Buddha Fields*, *Stray Leaves from Strange Literature*, the latter being "reconstructions of what impressed me as most fantastically beautiful in the most exotic literature." *Some Chinese Ghosts*, *Shadowings*, *In Ghostly Japan* likewise retell a society through its most impalpable manifestations. Herbert Spencer's evolutionary vitalism taught him "a new reverence for all kinds of faith" which Hearn transferred to the cult of ancestor-worship. Seeking to reconcile his western sense of fragmentary but unique identity with oriental quietism and self-abnegation, he came to believe that "We are, each and all, infinite compounds of anterior lives" (*Gleanings*), and that "the thoughts and acts of each being, projected beyond the individual existence, shape other lives unborn" (*Out of the East*). He saw the past as subliminal echoes investing the present, and in the Japanese Festival of the Dead found a ceremonious symbolism of the human condition: "Are we not ourselves as lanterns launched upon a deeper and a dimmer sea, and ever separating further and further one from another as we drift to the inevitable dissolution?" (*In Ghostly Japan*).

Hearn's style, like that he admired in Poe and Gautier, is an "engraved gem-work of words," rich with "voluptuous delicacy" – exquisite, precious, given to elaborate catalogues of isolated details and a self-conscious, sesquipedalian cadence which can overwhelm the sense ("mesmeric lentor," "the stridulous telegraphy of crickets," "a limpid magnificence of light indescribable"). In his sympathy for the intangible and evanescent he can also rise to poignancy and at times a sharp, racy vigour.

—Stan Smith

HELLER, Joseph. American. Born in Brooklyn, New York, 1 May 1923. Educated at New York University, B.A. 1948; Columbia University, New York, M.A. 1949; Oxford University (Fulbright Scholar), 1949–50. Served in the United States Army Air Force in World War II: Lieutenant. Married Shirley Held in 1945; one son and one daughter. Instructor in English, Pennsylvania State University, University Park, 1950–52; Advertising Writer, *Time* magazine, New York, 1952–56, and *Look* magazine, New York, 1956–58; Promotion Manager, *McCall's* magazine, New York, 1958–61; full-time writer from 1961. Recipient: National Institute of Arts and Letters grant, 1963. Member, National Institute of Arts and Letters, 1977.

PUBLICATIONS

Fiction

    Catch-22. 1961.
    Something Happened. 1974.

Plays

    We Bombed in New Haven (produced 1967). 1968.
    Catch-22, from his own novel. 1971.
    Clevinger's Trial, adaptation of chapter 8 of his novel *Catch-22* (produced 1974). 1973.

    Screenplays: *Sex and the Single Girl,* with David R. Schwartz, 1964; *Casino Royale* (uncredited), with others, 1967; *Dirty Dingus Magee,* with others, 1970.

Bibliography: *Three Contemporary Novelists: An Annotated Bibliography* by Robert M. Scotto, 1977.

Reading List: "Heller's *Catch-22*" by Burr Dodd, in *Approaches to the Novel* edited by John Colmer, 1967; "The Sanity of *Catch-22*" by Robert Protherough, in *The Human World,* May

1971; *Critical Essays on Catch-22* edited by James Nagel, 1974; *"Something Happened:* A New Direction" by George J. Searles, in *Critique 18,* 1977.

*   *   *

Joseph Heller's fame rests firmly on a single novel, *Catch-22.* His play, *We Bombed in New Haven,* which dramatizes similar material, is a failure, while his second novel, *Something Happened,* with its unattractive hero and deliberately pedestrian style, lacks the originality and linguistic vitality of its predecessor.

Catch-22 is not, as has often been supposed, just another anti-war novel in the Remarque, Frederick Manning, Norman Mailer tradition. Its theme is altogether more comprehensive. Heller invents a series of lunatic incidents to show that the comic formula "Catch-22" applies not only to the insanity of war but to love, business, and even religion. Thus early in the novel the hero, Yossarian, a flyer in World War Two, discovers that in war a man cannot plead madness to escape from further missions because, as Doc Daneeka says, "anyone who wants to get out of combat missions isn't really crazy." Later he finds that the same catch prevents him from marrying the girl he loves. "You won't marry me because I'm crazy, and you say I'm crazy because I want to marry you? Is that right?" The same circular formula extends beyond love and war to big business and even religion. Through the unscrupulous Milo Minderbinder, it touches the roots of capitalist enterprise, revealing that behind the compulsive acquisitiveness of capitalism lies a completely amoral destructive force, blind in its operation and totally unconcerned with human consequences. At the highest level the formula "Catch-22" seems to apply to God's laws as well as to man's; or, rather, men project their own irrationality on God. Heller's comprehensive indictment of society achieves its amazing breadth through his suggestion that a single unifying mental structure underlies the human predicament. We are caught. Although we may enjoy an illusion of freedom, as soon as we reach out to grasp it we become more firmly enslaved.

In order to enforce this dilemma Heller carefully manipulates patterns of logic and language to lay bare two opposite structures of behaviour and belief. On the one hand there is the system of irrational conformity represented by the generals. On the other hand there is the system of rational revolt typified by the rebels Yossarian and Orr. Each group regards the other an insane and often a single word may express the contrasting mental structures. An equally ingenious manipulation of time schemes serves to create a sense of an absurd universe and to embody comprehensive criticism of society. Yossarian's visits to hospital establish some framework of clock-time, but the main narrative sequence is not chronological but psychological. All events are described as if they were equally present in the hero's mind. The fact that it is impossible to reconcile the time schemes that apply to Yossarian's and Minderbinder's experiences and the fact that their paths cross at significant moments reinforce the contrast between Yossarian's unsuccessful rebellion against authority and Minderbinder's unprincipled triumph. When the narrative comes spiralling round to the last account of Snowden's death alongside Yossarian, Minderbinder's message in place of the stolen morphine tablets, "What is good for M & M Enterprises is good for the country" (a parody of an American President's phrase about General Motors), brings home the inhuman consequences of blind, selfish commercialism. This harrowing memory provides the ultimate justification for Yossarian's decision to desert to neutral Sweden.

Catch-22 is a bawdy, gimmicky novel that owes much of its popular success to its attacks on authority, its deliberate shock tactics, its inspired moments of farce, its gallery of comic characters, and its fashionable invitation to opt out of the system. Yet it stands up to rigorous analysis surprisingly well. Indeed it only yields up its full meaning when the intricacies of the time schemes and the inversions of language and logic have been fully grasped. It offers a model proof that the secret of truth-telling lies in form-making just as *Something Happened* proves that the choice of a dull hero and a dull style may produce a dull book

—John Colmer

HEMINGWAY, Ernest.   American.   Born in Oak Park, Illinois, 21 July 1899. Educated at Oak Park High School, graduated 1917. Served as a Red Cross Ambulance driver in Italy, 1918; also served on the western front with the Italian Arditi: wounded in action: Medaglia d'Argento al Valore Militare; Croce di Guerra; involved in anti-submarine patrol duty off the coast of Cuba, 1942–44. Married 1) Hadley Richardson in 1921 (divorced, 1927), one son: 2) Pauline Pfeiffer in 1927 (divorced, 1940), two sons; 3) the writer Martha Gellhorn in 1940 (divorced, 1946); 4) Mary Welsh in 1946. Reporter, *Kansas City Star*, 1917; Reporter, then Foreign Correspondent, Toronto *Star* and *Star Weekly*, 1920–24; covered the Greco-Turkish War, 1922; settled in Paris, 1921, and became associated with the expatriate community, including Gertrude Stein and Ezra Pound; Correspondent in Paris for the Hearst newspapers, 1924–27; full-time writer from 1927; settled in Key West, Florida, 1928, later moved to Cuba, then to Idaho; War Correspondent for the North American Newspaper Alliance, in Spain, 1937–38; War Correspondent for *Collier's* in Europe, 1944–45. Recipient: Pulitzer Prize, 1953; Nobel Prize for Literature, 1954; American Academy of Arts and Letters Award of Merit, 1954. *Died* (by suicide) *2 July 1961.*

PUBLICATIONS

Collections

A Hemingway Selection, edited by Denniś Pepper.   1972.

Fiction

Three Stories and Ten Poems.   1923.
In Our Time: Stories.   1924; revised edition, 1925.
The Torrents of Spring: A Romantic Novel in Honor of the Passing of a Great Race.   1926.
The Sun Also Rises.   1926; as *Fiesta,* 1927.
Men Without Women (stories).   1927.
A Farewell to Arms.   1929.
God Rest You Merry Gentlemen (stories).   1933.
Winner Take Nothing (stories).   1933.
To Have and Have Not.   1937.
The Fifth Column and the First Forty-Nine Stories (includes play).   1938.
For Whom the Bell Tolls.   1940.
The Portable Hemingway, edited by Malcolm Cowley.   1944.
The Essential Hemingway.   1947.
Across the River and into the Trees.   1950.
The Old Man and the Sea.   1952.
Hemingway in Michigan (stories), edited by Constance Cappel Montgomery.   1966.
The Fifth Column and Four Stories of the Spanish Civil War.   1969.
Islands in the Stream.   1970.
The Nick Adams Stories, edited by Philip Young.   1972.
A Divine Gesture: A Fable.   1974.

Plays

Today Is Friday.   1926.

The Spanish Earth (screenplay).   1938.
The Fifth Column (produced 1940).   In *The Fifth Column ...*, 1938.

Screenplay: *The Spanish Earth* (documentary).   1937.

Verse

Collected Poems.   1960.

Other

Death in the Afternoon.   1932.
Green Hills of Africa.   1935.
The Hemingway Reader, edited by Charles Poore.   1953.
The Wild Years (newspaper articles), edited by Gene Z. Hanrahan.   1962.
A Moveable Feast (autobiography).   1964.
By-Line: Selected Articles and Dispatches of Four Decades, edited by William
    White.   1967.
Cub Reporter: "Kansas City Star" Stories, edited by Matthew J. Bruccoli.   1970.

Editor, *Men at War: The Best War Stories of All Time.*   1942.

Bibliography: *Hemingway: A Comprehensive Bibliography* by Audre Hanneman, 1967, and
supplement, 1975; *Hemingway: A Reference Guide* by Linda Wagner, 1977.

Reading List: *Hemingway: The Writer as Artist* by Carlos Baker, 1952, revised edition, 1972;
Hemingway by Philip Young, 1952, revised edition, as *Hemingway: A Reconsideration,* 1966;
Hemingway and His Critics: An International Anthology edited by Carlos Baker, 1961;
Hemingway: A Collection of Critical Essays edited by Robert P. Weeks, 1962; *Hemingway* by
Earl Rovit, 1963; *Hemingway: An Introduction and Interpretation* by Sheridan Baker, 1967;
Hemingway and the Pursuit of Heroism by Leo Gurko, 1968; *Hemingway: The Inward
Terrain* by Richard B. Hovey, 1968; *Hemingway's Heroes* by Delbert E. Wylder, 1969;
Hemingway and His World by Anthony Burgess, 1978.

*   *   *

When Ernest Hemingway was awarded the Nobel Prize for Literature the Swedish
Academy commented on the central themes of his work. Courage and compassion in a world
of violence and death were seen as the distinguishing marks of "one of the great writers of
our time ... who, honestly and undauntedly, reproduces the genuine features of the hard
countenance of the age." These comments sum up perceptively the characteristic
preoccupations of Hemingway's fiction and of the heroic code of behaviour which it
explores. But they do less than justice to another aspect of his writing. Hemingway was also a
deliberate and careful artist, for whom every book was, in his own words, "a new
beginning" in which the writer "should always try for something that has never been done."
    Hemingway started his working life as a newspaper reporter, an excellent training in
writing graphic declaratory prose. Covering crime stories was one introduction to a violent
world, service with a Red Cross ambulance unit in Italy another. Severely wounded just
before his nineteenth birthday, he received further emotional wounds when rejected by an
American nurse with whom he fell in love. These experiences epitomise themes he was to

explore in his short stories and novels, in prose which he deliberately stripped bare of adjectival colouring and rhetorical flourishes.

His first books, *Three Stories and Ten Poems* and *In Our Time*, were slim volumes which attracted coterie attention. The second of them consisted of twelve stark vignettes – scenes of war, bull-fighting, murder – which in a later edition were interleaved between lengthier short stories in which the Hemingway hero, and the heroic code of grace under pressure, first appear. Seven of the stories are episodes in the experience of a young man whose sensitivity has been violated in various ways, physically, emotionally, and spiritually. One day, he knows, his traumata will be healed; but this will take time, courage, and an effort of will. In the meantime he holds on stoically.

The Torrents of Spring, an uncharacteristic burlesque, is unimportant except as an indication of Hemingway's considerable skill as a comic satirist: it foreshadows the very funny ironical humour in, for instance, passages of *Death in the Afternoon* and *A Moveable Feast. In Our Time*, however, is the matrix from which the rest of his fiction is cast, both the later volumes of short stories and the succession of brilliantly finished, though occasionally flawed, novels.

The Sun Also Rises established Hemingway beyond question as a significant new novelist. Narrated in the first person, it deals with the predicament of the hero, emasculated by an unlucky war wound, in his frustrated love for an Englishwoman whom time and misfortune have driven into alcoholism, nymphomania, and self-destructive irresponsibility. Charting the mores of Paris cafe society playboys and would-be artists, Hemingway for some readers obscured the moral seriousness of his novel through the brilliance of his writing, especially in the scenes at the fiesta in Pamplona. But the message is there. The hero has learnt to accept his plight with honesty and courage; and even the heroine, though morally ruined, is honest with herself and in her own fashion also honourable. The hero's own moral strength allows him to treat her with compassion.

In his next novel Hemingway settled for third person narration. A romantic tragedy of love and war, *A Farewell to Arms* shows considerable technical development. Formally constructed in five acts, it is closely knit by complex sub-structures beneath the surface of the story. Symbols of weather and topography unobstrusively counterpoint the action, while contrasts of profane and sacred love are made both overtly and covertly in the evolving relationship between the hero and the novel's innocent tragic heroine. In this novel, too, Hemingway tried to communicate directly his own experience of being wounded by trench-mortar fire, in a cardinal passage which supports his occasionally expressed view that writing is a kind of self-therapy.

Hemingway's views on fiction, which incidentally show how closely he had studied the English, French, and Russian novelists, are for the most part woven into his classic study of bull-fighting, *Death in the Afternoon*. In brief, his aim was to write simply and directly about directly received experience. The more precisely a writer can express the essential impact of experience, the more precisely he will impress that experience on his readers. His task is to set down "the sequence of motion and fact which made the emotion," which "with luck and if you stated it purely enough" should remain valid always. By concentrating on describing his characters in action a writer should be able to communicate unwritten emotional reverberations, whereas to write as an omniscient commentator is to spoil his fiction by adding what is structurally unnecessary and undesirable. In a famous comparison, Hemingway likens the artist's work to the tip of an iceberg, whose dignity of movement is due to only one-eighth of it being above water. It is an austere approach to the writer's craft, but one whose discipline gives Hemingway's work unmistakable authority and strength.

While many writers in the early 1930's were as much concerned with political as with literary preoccupations, Hemingway fed his experience and his literary production by big-game hunting, fishing, and shooting. This is the period of some of his best short stories, including "The Snows of Kilimanjaro," technically superb in its accumulated moves from reality to illusory vision. His novel *To Have and Have Not* is less satisfying. An attempt to portray characters under economic stress in the depression, it was cobbled together from two earlier short stories and was written hastily between visits to Spain during the Civil War. This also is the period of *The Fifth Column*, an undistinguished venture into the theatre.

The Spanish Civil War, however, provided Hemingway with the theme of another outstanding novel, *For Whom the Bell Tolls*, in which again he extended his techniques. The story is built around twin themes, the dynamiting of a bridge by a guerilla group and the love affair of an American partisan and a girl in the group. The action is restricted to some seventy hours, the location to a single valley, the personae to a handful; but by dipping into the stream of the hero's thoughts about his former life and by having various characters recount their memories, Hemingway works beyond these confines to create an ample but tightly organised novel of epic dimensions. There is an optimistic shift, too, in the heroic code, in that the Hero is now in command of himself and meets death alone but fearless. Contemporary judgments of this novel were often politically coloured, ranging from allegations that Hemingway had "largely sloughed off his Stalinism" to accusations of Fascist sympathies: today these reflect clearly Hemingway's sypathetic treatment of the complexity of political and human predicaments. Of the novel's literary quality there has never been any doubt.

His next two novels, *Across the River and into the Trees* and *The Old Man and the Sea*, take the heroic code further. The latter's message that a man can be destroyed but not defeated carries a suggestion of Christian salvation. Though *Across the River and into the Trees* contains some of Hemingway's intensest writing (e.g., the description of the duck-shoot with which the novel opens), it is flawed by occasional obtrusions of the author's own personality and by his as yet incomplete mastery of new modes of symbolism operating at multiple levels. These are under perfect control in *The Old Man and the Sea*, a work of flawless craftsmanship that can be read literally, or as an allegory of human life, or of the Crucifixion, or of the artist's struggle to dominate his material.

The posthumous publication of the long, uneven *Islands in the Stream*, unrevised by his skilled hand, neither adds to nor detracts from the reputation of a dedicated and sensitive artist, one of the greatest and most influential prose writers of the twentieth century.

—Stewart F. Sanderson

HENRY, O. Pseudonym for William Sydney, or Sidney, Porter. American. Born in Greensboro, North Carolina, 11 September 1862. Educated in a private school in Greensboro to age 15; apprentice pharmacist in Greensboro, 1877–81: licensed by the North Carolina Pharmaceutical Association, 1881. Married 1) Athol Estes in 1887 (died, 1897), one son and one daughter; 2) Sara Lindsay Coleman in 1907. Moved to Texas, 1882, and worked on a ranch in LaSalle County, 1882–84; bookkeeper in Austin, 1884–86; contributed to the *Detroit Free Press*, 1887; Draftsman, Texas Land Office, Austin, 1887–91; Teller, First National Bank, Austin, 1891–94; Founder/Editor, *The Iconoclast*, later the *Rolling Stone* magazine, Houston, 1894–95; Columnist ("Tales of the Town," later "Some Postscripts"), *Houston Post*, 1895–96; accused of embezzling funds from his previous employers, First National Bank, Austin, 1896; fled to Honduras; returned to Austin because of wife's illness, 1897; jailed for embezzling in the Federal Penitentiary, Columbus, Ohio, 1898–1901; while in prison began publishing stories as O. Henry; moved to New York, 1902; thereafter a full-time writer; regular contributor to the New York *Sunday World*, 1903–05. O. Henry Memorial Award established by the Society of Arts and Sciences, 1918. *Died 5 June 1910.*

PUBLICATIONS

Collections

> *The Complete Works.* 1937.
> *Stories*, edited by Harry Hansen. 1965.

Fiction (stories)

> *Cabbages and Kings.* 1904.
> *The Four Million.* 1906.
> *The Trimmed Lamp.* 1907.
> *Heart of the West.* 1907.
> *The Voice of the City.* 1908.
> *The Gentle Grafter.* 1908.
> *Roads of Destiny.* 1909.
> *Options.* 1909.
> *Strictly Business: More Stories of the Four Million.* 1910.
> *Whirligigs.* 1910.
> *Let Me Feel Your Pulse.* 1910.
> *Sixes and Sevens.* 1911.
> *Rolling Stones.* 1912.
> *Waifs and Strays.* 1917.

Other

> *Letters to Lithopolos from O. Henry to Mabel Wagnalls.* 1922.
> *Postscripts* (from *Houston Post*), edited by Florence Stratton. 1923.
> *O. Henry Encore: Stories and Illustrations* (from *Houston Post*), edited by Mary Sunlock Harrell. 1939.

Bibliography: *A Bibliography of O. Henry* by Paul S. Clarkson, 1938.

Reading List: *Henry Biography* by C. Alphonso Smith, 1916; *The Caliph of Bagdad* by Robert H. Davis and Arthur B. Maurice, 1931; *Henry: The Man and His Work*, 1949, and *Henry, American Regionalist*, 1969, both by Eugene Hudson Long; *The Heart of Henry* by Dale Kramer, 1954; *Alias O. Henry: A Biography* by Gerald Langford, 1957; *Henry from Polecat Creek* by Ethel Stephen Arnett, 1962; *Henry* by Eugene Current-Garcia, 1965; *Henry: The Legendary Life* by Richard O'Connor, 1970.

*   *   *

William Sydney Porter's first story to appear in a national magazine was published in September 1898 while he was in prison, and it was in prison that he began writing in earnest. Following his release, Porter moved to New York where he wrote prodigiously; during 1904 and 1905 he is said to have produced a story a week for the New York *World*. Fame and notoriety, which he shunned, came to him quickly, as did money, which he spent lavishly and usually unwisely. *Cabbages and Kings*, his first collection of stories, established him as an author to be taken seriously. By 1908, with the publication of *The Voice of the City*, he was hailed as having "breathed new life into the short story; the stigma of the genre is wearing off, and for its rehabilitation ... [Porter] is responsible"; and in 1914, in a symposium conducted by the New York *Times*, "A Municipal Report" was voted "the greatest American short story ever written."

By 1920, ten years after his death, five million volumes of Porter's stories had been sold, but the current of critical opinion had turned against them and their author: not uncharacteristic is H. L. Mencken's pronouncement that "in the whole canon of O. Henry's work you will not find a single recognizable human character." A just estimate of Porter's fiction lies somewhere between such extremes. O. Henry brought verve, excitement, and humor to the genre. Enormously interested in people, he is capable of swift and compassionate insights into the average person, and his sympathy for the under-dog, the little man or woman dwarfed in the maze of comtemporary life, to a degree accounted for his enormous popularity. He was a good reporter with a keen eye for the significant detail, and he had a feeling for setting unmatched by most of his contemporaries. His brisk openings and the engrossing narrative pace of even his least successful stories are perhaps the major reasons for his instant appeal. Perhaps most important of all, he influenced an entire generation of writers and helped provide an enthusiastic audience for their work.

Porter's faults are as conspicuous as his assets – contrivance, sentimentality, repetition, and melodrama; his trick endings, particularly, seemed patently dated in the context of the new realism of the Twenties. He wrote rapidly – "once I begin a yarn I must finish it without stopping or it kinda goes dead on me" – and revised seldom. Haunted by memories of the past, increasingly engulfed in alcohol, Porter had no illusions about his literary shortcomings. "I'm a failure," he wrote to a friend. "My stories? No, they don't satisfy me. It depresses me to have people point me out as 'a celebrated author.' It seems such a big label for such picayune goods."

Porter's work, as one of his contemporaries commented, never did justice to his talents. Perhaps the soundest estimate of his contribution has been made by one of the most important English fiction writers of the twentieth century, H. E. Bates. However one belittles O. Henry, Bates comments in *The Modern Short Story*, "he still emerges, by his huge achievement and the immense popularity of his particular method, as an astonishingly persistent influence on the short story of almost every decade since his day."

—William Peden

HENTY, G(eorge) A(lfred). English. Born in Trumpington, Cambridge, 8 December 1832. Educated at Westminster School, London, 1847–52; Caius College, Cambridge, 1852. Served in the Hospital Commisariat and the Purveyor's Department during the Crimean War: helped organize Italian hospitals, 1859; served in Belfast and Portsmouth: Turkish Order of the Medjidie. Married 1) Elizabeth Finucane in 1858, two sons and two daughters; 2) Bessie Keylock. Crimean War Correspondent, *Morning Advertiser*, London; Special Correspondent, in Europe, Africa, Asia, and North America, *The Standard*, London, 1865–76; Editor, *Union Jack* magazine, London, 1880–83, and *Beeton's Boy's Own Magazine*, London, 1888–90, and later annuals, 1890–93. *Died 16 November 1902.*

PUBLICATIONS

Fiction

A Search for a Secret. 1867.

All But Lost. 1869.

Out on the Pampas; or, The Young Settlers. 1871.

. *The Young Franc-Tireurs and Their Adventures in the Franco-Prussian War.* 1872.

' *The Young Buglers: A Tale of the Peninsular War.* 1879.

Seaside Maidens. 1880.

In Times of Peril: A Tale of India. 1881.

The Cornet of Horse: A Tale of Marlborough's Wars. 1881.

Winning His Spurs: A Tale of the Crusades. 1882; as *The Boy Knight,* 1883; as *Fighting the Saracens,* 1892.

Facing Death; or, The Hero of the Vaughan Pit: A Tale of the Coal Mines. 1882.

Under Drake's Flag: A Tale of the Spanish Main. 1882.

With Clive in India; or, The Beginnings of an Empire. 1883.

By Sheer Pluck: A Tale of the Ashanti Wars. 1883.

Jack Archer: A Tale of the Crimea. 1883; as *The Fall of Sebastopol,* 1892.

Friends, Though Divided: A Tale of the Civil War. 1883.

True to the Old Flag: A Tale of the American War of Independence. 1884.

In Freedom's Cause: A Story of Wallace and Bruce. 1884.

St. George for England: A Tale of Cressy and Poitiers. 1884.

The Lion of the North: A Tale of the Times of Gustavus Adolphus and the Wars of Religion. 1885.

The Young Colonists. 1885.

The Dragon and the Raven; or, The Days of King Alfred. 1885.

For Name and Fame; or, Through the Afghan Passes. 1885.

Through the Fray: A Tale of the Luddite Riots. 1885.

Yarns on the Beach: A Bundle of Tales. 1885.

With Wolfe in Canada; or, The Winning of a Continent. 1886.

The Bravest of the Brave; or, With Peterborough in Spain. 1886.

A Final Reckoning: A Tale of Bush Life in Australia. 1886.

The Young Carthaginian; or, A Struggle for Empire. 1886.

Bonnie Prince Charlie: A Tale of Fontenoy and Culloden. 1887.

For the Temple: A Tale of the Fall of Jerusalem. 1887.

In the Reign of Terror: The Adventures of a Westminster Lad. 1887.

Sturdy and Strong; or, How George Andrews Made His Way. 1887.

The Cat of Bubastes: A Tale of Ancient Egypt. 1888.

The Lion of St. Mark: A Tale of Venice. 1888.

Captain Bayley's Heir: A Tale of the Gold Fields of California. 1888.

Orange and Green: A Tale of the Boyne and Limerick. 1888.

Gabriel Allen, M.P. 1888.

The Curse of Carne's Hold: A Tale of Adventure. 1889.

One of the 28th: A Tale of Waterloo. 1889.

By Pike and Dyke: A Tale of the Rise of the Dutch Republic. 1889.

Camps and Quarters, with Archibald Forbes and Charles Williams. 1889.

Tales of Daring and Dangers. 1889.

The Plague Ship. 1889.

With Lee in Virginia: A Story of the American Civil War. 1889.

A Hidden Foe. 1890.

By Right of Conquest; or, With Cortez in Mexico. 1890.

By England's Aid; or, The Freeing of the Netherlands (1585–1604). 1890.

A Chapter of Adventures; or, Through the Bombardment of Alexandria. 1890; as *The Young Midshipman: A Story of the Bombardment of Alexandria,* 1902.

Maori and Settler: A Story of the New Zealand Wars. 1890.

Redskin and Cowboy: A Tale of the Western Plains. 1891.

The Dash for Khartoum: A Tale of the Nile Expedition. 1891.

Held Fast for England: A Tale of the Siege of Gibraltar (1779–1883). 1891.

In Greek Waters: A Story of the Grecian War of Independence (1821–1827). 1892.
Beric the Briton: A Story of the Roman Invasion. 1892.
Condemned as a Nihilist: A Story of Escape from Siberia. 1892.
The Ranche in the Valley. 1892.
A Jacobite Exile: Being the Adventures of a Young Englishman in the Service of Charles XII of Sweden. 1893.
Tales from the Works of Henty. 1893; as *Tales from Henty,* 1925.
St. Bartholomew's Eve: A Tale of the Huguenot Wars. 1893.
Through the Sikh War: A Tale of the Conquest of the Punjaub. 1893.
Rujub, The Juggler. 1893; as *In the Days of the Mutiny: A Military Novel,* 1893.
Dorothy's Double. 1894.
In the Heart of the Rockies: A Story of Adventure in Colorado. 1894.
When London Burned: A Story of Restoration Times and the Great Fire. 1894.
Wulf the Saxon: A Story of the Norman Conquest. 1894.
The Tiger of Mysore: A Story of the War with Tippoo Saib. 1895.
A Woman of the Commune: A Tale of the Two Sieges of Paris. 1895; as *Cuthbert Hartington: A Tale of the Siege of Paris,* 1899; as *A Girl of the Commune,* n.d.; as *Two Sieges of Paris; or, A Girl of the Commune,* n.d.
A Knight of the White Cross: A Tale of the Siege of Rhodes. 1895.
Through Russian Snows: A Story of Napoleon's Retreat from Moscow. 1895.
On the Irrawaddy: A Story of the First Burmese War. 1896.
At Agincourt: A Tale of the White Hoods of Paris. 1896
Bears and Decoits and Other Stories. 1896.
With Cochrane the Dauntless: A Tale of the Exploits of Lord Cochrane in South American Waters. 1896.
In Battle and Breeze: Sea Stories, with George Manville Fenn and W. Clark Russell. 1896.
With Moore at Corunna: A Tale of the South African War. 1897.
A March on London, Being the Story of Wat Tyler's Insurrection. 1897.
With Frederick the Great: A Story of the Seven Years' War. 1897.
Among Malay Pirates. 1897; as *Among the Malays,* 1900(?).
The Queen's Cup. 1897.
Colonel Thorndyke's Secret. 1898; as *The Brahmin's Treasure,* 1899.
At Aboukir and Acre: A Story of Napoleon's Invasion of Egypt. 1898.
Both Sides the Border: A Tale of Hotspur and Glendower. 1898.
Under Wellington's Command: A Tale of the Peninsular War. 1898.
The Golden Cañon. 1899.
No Surrender! A Tale of the Rising in La Vendée. 1899.
On the Spanish Main. 1899.
Won by the Sword: A Tale of the Thirty Years' War. 1899.
The Lost Heir. 1899.
In the Irish Brigade: A Tale of War in Flanders and Spain. 1900.
In the Hands of the Cave-Dwellers. 1900.
With Buller in Natal; or, A Born Leader. 1900.
Out with Garibaldi: A Story of the Liberation of Italy. 1900.
A Roving Commission; or, Through the Black Insurrection of Hayti. 1900.
The Sole Survivors. 1901.
With Roberts to Pretoria: A Tale of the South African War. 1901.
At the Point of the Bayonet: A Tale of the Mahratta War. 1901.
John Hawke's Fortune: A Story of Monmouth's Rebellion. 1901.
To Herat and Cabul: A Story of the First Afghan War. 1901.
With Kitchener in the Soudan: A Story of Atbara and Omdurman. 1902.
With the British Legion: A Story of the Carlist Wars. 1902.
The Treasure of the Incas: A Tale of Adventure in Peru. 1902.

With the Allies to Pekin: A Tale of the Relief of the Legations. 1903.
Through Three Compaigns: A Story of Chitral, Tirah, and Ashantee. 1903.
By Conduct and Courage: A Story of Nelson's Days, edited by C. G. Henty. 1904.
Gallant Deeds. 1905.
In the Hands of the Malays and Other Stories. 1905.
Redskins and Colonists; or, A Boy's Adventures in the Early Days of Virginia; Burton and Son; The Ranche in the Valley; Sole Survivors. 1905.
A Soldier's Daughter and Other Stories. 1906.

Other

The March to Magdala. 1868.
The March to Coomassie. 1874.
Those Other Animals. 1891.
The Sovereign Reader: Scenes from the Life and Reign of Queen Victoria. 1887; revised edition, as *Queen Victoria: Scenes from Her Life and Reign,* 1901.

Editor, *Our Sailors,* by William H. G. Kingston, continued by Henty. 1882.
Editor, *Our Soldiers,* by William H. G. Kingston, continued by Henty. 1886.
Editor, *Yule Logs.* 1898.
Editor, *Yule-Tide Yarns.* 1899.
Editor, *Famous Travels.* 1902.

Bibliography: *Bibliography of Henty and Hentyana* by R. S. Kennedy and B. J. Farmer, 1956; *Henty: A Bibliography* by Robert L. Dartt, 1971.

Reading List: *Henty: The Story of an Active Life* by G. Manville Fenn, 1907.

*   *   *

At the head of innumerable copies of Blackie & Sons list of books for the young stands a quotation from the *Athenaeum*: "English boys owe a debt of gratitude to Mr. Henty." It could almost claim that the very idea of "English boys," as a special breed, was his creation; how far the youths who were moulded to embody the idea should have been grateful has been a matter of some debate. Inescapably, Henty's books have been seen as an influence, the epitome of the values of British Imperialism, and powerful weapons in the transmission of its ideology. Prolific himself, Henty also had many imitators who repeated his message and his narrative patterns, with obvious historical and geographical didactic intent, and scarcely less obvious presentation of heroic character models.

Henty's work, however, was not original or even unusual in its deliberate transmission of certain cultural values; since the beginning, the overwhelming majority of writers and purchasers of children's books have had didactic intentions. Henty's adventure stories are the descendants of evangelical tracts, with a shift of emphasis from the virtues of submission, piety, and holy dying to independence, pluck, and courage, reflecting a shift in social values. Henty's artistic contribution was his invention of a formulaic narrative pattern into which old stories and subjects were absorbed and redirected. He took a young, middle-class hero (presented as typical rather than exceptional amongst Englishmen, so that the reader could readily identify with him and his successes) and placed him in exciting situations where he could exhibit his sterling qualities and have them substantially rewarded. The situations adaptable for this purpose included the exotic outposts of Empire, where the heroes of Ballantyne and Mayne Reid had fought, explored, and hunted; the sea settings long used by Marryat and W. H. G. Kingston; and even the city streets of the old industrious apprentice tale, transmuted by the influence of Samuel Smiles. All were grist to Henty's mill, and when he had exhausted these, and the military settings suggested by his personal experience as a war correspondent, he turned to history, and made the historical adventure story particularly his own. Of course he sought only local colour in the carefully correct historical incidents he used: he had neither Scott's perception of the significance of historical difference, nor Kipling's near-mystical vision of its oneness with the present. Similarly his stories of the Empire are devoid of Kipling's Indian atmosphere, and his sea stories are jolly rather than ecstatic like, say, John Masefield's. But intensities were no part of his purpose. In his better books, those with enough motor power to burn up their factual fuel and keep the adventure moving fast, he performs well the task he set himself of providing the young Englishman with an image of himself which would help him to become a self-respecting adult in the role society gave him. The passing of that society has left his books, so closely bound up with it, without a purpose, and inevitably unread.

—J. S. Bratton

HERBERT, (Alfred Francis) Xavier. Australian. Born in Port Hedland, Western Australia, 15 May 1901; moved with his family to Geraldton. Educated in local schools; Christian Brothers College, Fremantle; Technical College, Perth; University of Melbourne, diploma in pharmacy. Served in the Australian Imperial Forces in the Pacific, 1942–44. Began career as a pharmacist; also worked as a deep-sea diver, sailor, miner, and stock rider; free-lance writer from 1925; Superintendent of Aborigines, Darwin, 1935–36. Recipient: Australian Literary Society's Gold Medal, 1939; Miles Franklin Award, 1976. Lives in Redlynch, Queensland.

PUBLICATIONS

Fiction

  Capricornia. 1937.
  Seven Emus. 1959.
  Soldiers' Women. 1961.
  Larger Than Life: Twenty Short Stories. 1963.
  Poor Fellow My Country. 1975.

Other

  Disturbing Element (autobiography). 1963.

Reading List: Introduction by L. T. Hergenham to *Capricornia*, 1972; *Herbert* by Harry P. Heseltine, 1973; "*Poor Fellow My Country:* Herbert's Masterpiece?" by Laurie Clancy, in *Southerly*, 1977.

*   *   *

What is principally striking about Xavier Herbert's writing is its energy, often rough but compellingly forceful. The reverse of the medal is an unfortunate tendency to garrulousness (a quantitative, not a qualitative fault), leading to charges of overwriting, first in *Capricornia*, increasingly with *Soldiers' Women*, and finally and most notably – because it is the most sensitive of his books – with *Poor Fellow My Country*. The first and the last are works of major importance. (*Soldiers' Women* is perhaps not major, though it is a record of Australian war-time experience under various social pressures, and does not lack vigour, which is inseparable from Herbert's explosive indignation, on any subject; but its bulk is without the drive which animates the other two.)

Capricornia and *Poor Fellow* are vehicles of a passionate nationalism thwarted by bungling, the point of view being very much Herbert's own, yet unquestionably sincere and unfadingly vehement. There are affinities with the Jindyworobak school of writers in the 1930's, now due for revision and reassessment. Herbert's attachment is to the Australian *land* (a quasi-mystical concept) and, as its animating principle, to the Aborigines seen as a displaced and degraded race. *Capricornia*, with its focus on the Top End, dwells, with political implications, on the ruthless dispossession of the tribes, the relentless devastation of the country for profit and the waste it entails, white and often absentee capitalist exploitation, corruption through miscegenation (epitomized in the story of No-name/Nawnim/Norman Shillingsworth), and the wooden-headed industrialization process exhibited in the building of the railway which goes south but ends nowhere. Herbert's handling of character is often masterly in a satirical manner (there is tremendous comic gusto in the burial service near the beginning of *Capricornia*); the model is obviously Dickens, but the eighteenth-century picaresque is discernible through it too. The impact of *Capricornia* was tremendous in the thirties and remained controversial; after it appeared Herbert was said to be *persona non grata* in certain Top End circles. Nevertheless his heart and interest remained grounded in the north, and the same subject matter provided the motivation for the more seriously and elaborately conceived *Poor Fellow My Country*. This work is also concerned with national issues, the land, the Aborigines (whom he had in the meantime studied much more closely), and the black/white problem, here given a more complex dimension. *Poor Fellow My Country* is Herbert's *apologia*. It is an unwieldy book, of an exuberance hard to do justice to; but certainly it stands out as one of the most remarkable achievements by any Australian writer, whether for its weight or its sometimes superb imaginative insights. Its narrative interest is secondary to its intense, passionate purposiveness: in the end it is a huge, gross poem rather than a story. Its compassion is enormous. So also is its truculence – but that is the man, the style, and inescapable.

Seven Emus is a slight but attractive story not without affinities with Arthur Upfield; it has a texture of odd aboriginal mysteries. *Disturbing Element* is frank, entertaining autobiography, and perhaps the bow is not too coarsely overdrawn. The short stories are lively and readable, with an economy the longer works do not aim at.

—Brian Elliott

HERGESHEIMER, Joseph. American. Born in Philadelphia, Pennsylvania, 15 February 1880. Educated at a Quaker school in Germantown, Philadelphia; studied painting at the Pennsylvania Academy of Fine Arts, Philadelphia. Married Dorothy Hemphill in 1907. Settled in Virginia, and began to write, 1900; subsequently moved to West Chester, Pennsylvania, and later to Stone Harbor, New Jersey. *Died 25 April 1954.*

<small>Publications</small>

Fiction

> *The Lay Anthony.*   1914.
> *Mountain Blood.*   1915.
> *The Three Black Pennys.*   1917.
> *Gold and Iron.*   1918.
> *The Happy End* (stories).   1919.
> *Linda Condon.*   1919.
> *Java Head.*   1919.
> *Cytherea.*   1922.
> *The Bright Shawl.*   1922.
> *Balisand.*   1924.
> *Tol'able David* (stories).   1923.
> *Merry Dale.*   1924.
> *Tampico.*   1926.
> *Quiet Cities* (stories).   1928.
> *Triall by Armes* (stories).   1929.
> *The Party Dress.*   1930.
> *The Limestone Tree.*   1931.
> *Love in the United States, and The Big Shot.*   1932.
> *Tropical Winter* (stories).   1933.
> *The Foolscap Rose.*   1934.

Play

> Screenplay: *Flower of Night*, with Willis Goldbeck, 1925.

Other

> *Hugh Walpole: An Appreciation.*   1919.
> *San Cristóbal de la Habana.*   1920.
> *The Presbyterian Child* (autobiography).   1923.
> *From an Old House* (autobiography).   1925.
> *Swords and Roses.*   1929.
> *Sheridan: A Military Narrative.*   1931.
> *Berlin.*   1932.

Bibliography: "Hergesheimer: A Selected Bibliography 1913–45" by James J. Napier, in *Bulletin of Bibliography 24*, 1963–64.

Reading List: *Hergesheimer: The Man and His Books* by Llewellyn Jones, 1920; *Hergesheimer* by James Branch Cabell, 1921; *The Fiction of Hergesheimer* by Ronald E. Martin, 1965; *Ingenue among the Lions: Letters of Emily Clark to Hergesheimer*, 1965.

*   *   *

James Branch Cabell called Joseph Hergesheimer "the most insistently superficial of writers" and meant it as a compliment; half a century later the remark speaks unintentionally for his detractors. Writing from "aspiration hopelessly in advance of accomplishment," as Hergesheimer described his endeavors, he was reputed one of America's foremost novelists; today he is almost forgotten, and many readers would think deservedly so. After several quasi-historical novels, Hergesheimer turned to his immediate milieu – the American 1920's – and made the subject glossily his own. Later, his attempts at *belles lettres* – travel books and descriptions of old houses in fancy prose – blurred into his fiction, and flesh and blood disappeared into the architecture.

Of his early books, *Java Head* is an excellent adventure story of clipper ships and miscegenation in eighteenth-century Salem, with a Manchu princess as catalyst. *The Three Black Pennys* is an underrated novel about a Pennsylvania coal mining family, tracing an emotional decline from the eldest, sober and hard-working, to the youngest, a dilettante; finely written, even moving, it is undeserving of its present neglect.

The later novels "flash and glitter like so many fricaseed rainbows," according to George Jean Nathan. *Linda Condon* and *Cytherea* trace the hedonism of the twenties – prohibition, permanent waves, "extraordinary qualities of superlative jewels and superfine textures" – with ironic detachment. In *The Party Dress*, however, written at the end of the decade, Hergesheimer detailed the mystique of golf – not only the shots in a game but the look of the greens and the quality of the clubs – in deadly earnest, and he lavished as much attention on his characters' houses, clothing, table manners, including the silver and crystal, as he did on their love affairs. Later historical novels, *Balisand* and *The Limestone Tree*, for example, had not even the glamour of the twenties to enliven them.

Alfred Kazin spotted the quintessential Hergesheimer passage in *Cytherea*: " 'I want to be outraged!' Her low ringing cry seemed suppressed, deadened as though the damasked and florid gilt and rosewood, now inexpressibly shocked, had combined to muffle the expression, the agony, of her body." Kazin called Hergesheimer's passion "vulgar"; Wilson Follett called it an "aristocratic distinction" although "a distinctly un-American trait."

Readers in an audio-visual age may grow impatient with Hergesheimer's tales of beautiful women and wise men stifled by sybaritic description; but many of the novels accurately reflect their own time, however meretricious that time was. Hergesheimer still has much to say, by the fact of his reputation during the twenties, to a later period preoccupied with pop culture.

—Bruce Kellner

HERRICK, Robert. American. Born in Cambridge, Massachusetts, 26 April 1868. Educated at Cambridge High School, 1881–85; Harvard University, Cambridge, Massachusetts, 1885–90 (Editor, Harvard *Advocate* and *Monthly*). Married Harriet Emery in 1894 (divorced, 1916); two children. Instructor in Rhetoric, Massachusetts Institute of Technology, Cambridge, 1890–93; joined faculty of the University of Chicago, 1893; Professor of English, 1905–23; Teacher, Rollins College, Winter Park, Florida, 1931; Secretary to the Governor of the Virgin Islands, 1935–38. *Died 23 December 1938.*

PUBLICATIONS

Fiction

Literary Love-Letters and Other Stories.   1897.
The Man Who Wins.   1897.

The Gospel of Freedom. 1898.
Love's Dilemmas (stories). 1898.
The Web of Life. 1900.
The Real World. 1901; as *Jock o' Dreams,* 1908.
Their Child (stories). 1903.
The Common Lot. 1904.
The Memoirs of an American Citizen. 1905; edited by Daniel Aaron, 1963.
The Master of the Inn (stories). 1908.
Together. 1908.
A Life for a Life. 1910.
The Healer. 1911.
His Great Adventure. 1913.
One Woman's Life. 1913.
Clark's Field. 1914.
The Conscript Mother (stories). 1916.
Homely Lilla. 1923.
Waste. 1924.
Wanderings (stories). 1925.
Chimes. 1926.
The End of Desire. 1932.
Sometime. 1933.

Other

Composition and Rhetoric for Schools, with Lindsay Todd Damon. 1899; revised
    edition, 1911.
Teaching English, with May Estelle Cook and Lindsay Todd Damon. 1899.
The World Decision. 1916.
Little Black Dog. 1931.

Reading List: *Herrick: The Development of a Novelist* by Blake Nevius, 1962; *Herrick* by
Louis J. Budd, 1971.

*   *   *

In his first novelette, *The Man Who Wins,* Robert Herrick dealt with the question which
was to be central to his entire work: what is success? A dedicated medical researcher is
diverted into a lucrative practice, but late in life he sees his mistake and encourages young
men not to seek material gain. Similarly, in *The Web of Life* a doctor samples and rejects the
luxurious life of a society physician and refuses to marry the daughter of a capitalist until she
renounces her wealth. *The Master of the Inn* presents a doctor who heals with simple
methods in a rural hospital although he commands a knowledge of modern medicine. *The
Healer* deals with a Canadian doctor who is traduced by his wife into leaving his spiritually
rewarding life in the wild for a financially rewarding practice in Chicago. Disgusted by the
avarice of city doctors, the doctor recommends that the professions all become "great
monastic orders," and returns to his home.
    Other novels contrast the proper use of technical knowledge to help mankind with the use
of knowledge for selfish gain. An architect in *The Common Lot* exploits his profession until
his shady practices cause several people to be killed in a fire. Business executives climb to the
top in their fields before realizing the hollowness of their triumphs in *The Real World, A Life
for a Life,* and *Waste.* All the executives atone by working for small, struggling businesses
and crusading against trusts. Only the central character of *Memoirs of an American Citizen,* a

meat-packer named Van Harrington who claws his way to a fortune and a seat in the Senate, seems to have few regrets. Herrick was more proud of this characterization than any other, and it is doubtless his best. Herrick enlivened these novels with interesting details from the worlds of business and the professions, freighting them with symbolic weight which skillfully clarified the conflict between the central figures. However, it is not always clear why small businesses in the West are more moral and rewarding than large ones in the East.

In all these novels, Herrick buttressed the main plot with a sub-plot contrasting the sordid family relationships of the rich with the more loving and simple ones of the lower classes. In *Together, One Woman's Life, Homely Lilla*, and *The End of Desire*, he placed his main emphasis on the problem of women's rights, sexual liberation, and modern marriage. Advanced for his day in these matters, Herrick recommended that women share men's work and that men relieve women from the drudgery of housework and child-rearing. As with business, Herrick finds greed the enemy of good marriages.

Clark's Field shows why private property should not be allowed to restrict urban growth, while *Chimes* deals with academic life. Herrick's views on many subjects are summarized in his Utopian novel of the future, *Sometime*.

Even if his novels are occasionally resolved by flimsy devices such as earthquakes or fires, Herrick deserves serious attention for his incisive criticism of his culture and his accurate picture of it.

—William Higgins

HEYWARD, DuBose. American. Born in Charleston, South Carolina, 31 August 1885. Educated in local schools until age 14. Married the playwright Dorothy Hartzell Kuhns in 1923; one daughter. Worked from 1899 in a hardware store, as a clerk with a Charleston steamboat line, and as a checker in a cotton shed; later formed an insurance business with a friend; Founder, with Hervey Allen, The Poetry Society of South Carolina, 1920, and subsequently lectured and read his works for the Society throughout the South; gave up the insurance business to become a full-time writer, 1924. Recipient: Pulitzer Prize, for drama, 1927. Litt.D.: University of North Carolina, Chapel Hill, 1928; College of Charleston, 1929. Honorary Member, Phi Beta Kappa; Member, National Institue of Arts and Letters. Lived in Charleston all his life. *Died 16 June 1940.*

PUBLICATIONS

Fiction

Porgy. 1925.
Angel. 1926.
The Half Pint Flask (story). 1929.
Mamba's Daughters. 1929.
Peter Ashley. 1932.
Lost Morning. 1936.
Star Spangled Virgin. 1939.

Plays

Porgy, with Dorothy Heyward, from the novel by DuBose Heyward (produced
   1927).   1928.
Brass Ankle (produced 1931).   1931.
Porgy and Bess, with Ira Gershwin, music by George Gershwin (produced
   1935).   1935.
Mamba's Daughters, with Dorothy Heyward, from the novel by DuBose Heyward
   (produced 1939).   1939.

Verse

Carolina Chansons: Legends of the Low Country, with Hervey Allen.   1922.
Skylines and Horizons.   1924.
Jasbo Brown and Selected Poems.   1931.

Other

Fort Sumter, with Herbert Ravenal Sass.   1938.
The Country Bunny and the Little Gold Shoes (juvenile).   1939.

Editor, with others, Year Book of the Poetry Society of South Carolina, 1921–24.   4
   vols., 1921–24.

Reading List: Heyward, The Man Who Wrote Porgy by Frank Durham, 1965.

*   *   *

    Novelist, storywriter, playwright, and poet, DuBose Heyward was a sensitive romantic
artist whose earnest but realistic humanitarianism, sympathetic understanding of the Negro,
and lyrical evocations of the landscape, folklore, and legends of his region made him a forerunner of the Southern literary movement which the Poetry Society of South Carolina, under
his leadership, helped to initiate among writers' groups and little magazines in the 1920's. His
poetry, dealing mainly with the grim battle for survival on the mountains, nostalgic
descriptions of low country life, and the mystery and vitality of the Negro personality,
brought him early recognition and served as a crucible for experimenting with the settings,
themes, incidents, and tones he was to exploit later in his fiction and drama. It is not hard to
see how crucially his novel Angel and short-story "Brute" – to think of two instances –
depend on poems such as "A Mountain Woman" and "A Yoke of Steers" for their vivid
scenic particulars, characterization, and treatment of the innate strength and resilience of the
human spirit engaged in a fierce and near-impossible struggle with a hostile environment.
    Porgy, Heyward's most popular and accomplished novel, makes full use of his poetic and
narrative gifts. Heyward subtly intertwines the developing stages of his narrative with the
cycle of seasons to provide symbolic elevation to his story of a beggar-murderer whose futile
search for stability and peace eventually leads to the recognition that the inexorable pressure
of a contrary, even malevolent, fate can be withstood, if not substantially minimised, by an
attitude of acceptance. In Mamba's Daughters, a more ambitious though less competently
executed novel, a variant of the same theme is employed in recounting the trials of three
generations of a Negro family in their upward climb toward social security and prosperity.
    But, to Heyward, the Negro was more than a symbol of resistance against overwhelming
odds: he was, in most events, conceived as an emissary from an enchanting world of exotic

customs and beliefs, possessing an inimitable primitive aura and energy that are vulnerable to the forces of modernization. This view of the Negro is given eloquent expression in "The Half-Pint Flask," a haunting story about the erosion of rational and scientific attitudes in the face of time-honoured superstitions. Approaching the same issue in an altered context in *Star Spangled Virgin*, Heyward makes use of entertaining but biting satire to expose the inadequacy of all reformist measures that ignore the intractable rhythms and perceptions of Negro life. Such views are also symptomatic of his whole-hearted agreement with a primary assumption of Southern writing that art belongs more to the realm of the heart than of the head.

An uneven writer whose later performance, despite occasional enthusiastic responses, never really measured up to the expectations aroused by his early promise, Heyward wrote at his best when he employed dramatic contrivances such as violence and natural calamities to lend pace to the narrative. His treatment of ideas in art generally tended to be feeble and often regressed to the level of dull pontification. *Porgy* is the single work for which he is likely to be remembered, for it has become, in Frank Durham's words, "a part of native folklore, its characters and their romantic story having gradually so embedded themselves into the group consciousness that the name of their creator is almost forgotten. Not many authors have gained such enduring, if increasingly anonymous, immortality."

—Chirantan Kulshrestha

HOBBES, Thomas. English. Born in Westport, Wiltshire, 5 April 1588. Educated at a church school in Westport from age 4; Robert Latimer's school, 1599–1603; Magdalen Hall, Oxford, 1603–08, B.A. 1608. Had one illegitimate daughter. Tutor and Travelling Secretary to William Cavendish, later 2nd Earl of Devonshire, 1608–28; travelled with Sir Gervase Clinton's son, 1629–31; Tutor and Travelling Companion to William Cavendish, 3rd Earl of Devonshire, 1631–40; lived in Paris, 1640–51: tutored Charles II in mathematics, 1646–48; received a pension from the Earl of Devonshire, 1651; returned to England, 1652, and settled in London; granted a pension from the king, 1660. *Died 4 December 1679.*

PUBLICATIONS

Collections

English and Latin Works, edited by William Molesworth. 16 vols., 1839–45.
Selections, edited by J. E. Woodbridge. 1930.

Prose

A Brief of the Art of Rhetoric (on Aristotle). 1635(?).
Elementorum Philosophiae:
  1. *De Corpore.* 1655; edited by C. von Brockdorff, 1934; translated as *Philosophical Rudiments Concerning Government and Society*, 1651.
  2. *De Homine.* 1658.

3. *De Cive.* 1642; edited by Sterling P. Lamprecht, 1949.

Human Nature; or, The Fundamental Elements of Policy. 1650.

De Corpore Politico; or, The Elements of Law, Moral and Politic. 1650; edited by Ferdinand Tönnies, 1889.

Epistolica Dissertatio de Principiis Justis et Decori. 1651.

Leviathan; or, The Matter, Form, and Power of a Commonwealth. 1651; edited by C. B. MacPherson, 1968.

Of Liberty and Necessity. 1654; edited by C. von Brockdorff, 1938.

The Questions Concerning Liberty, Necessity, and Chance. 1656.

Aretelogia; or, Marks of the Absurd Geometry of John Wallis. 1657.

Examinatio et Emendatio Mathematicae Hodiernae Qualis Explicatur in Libris Johannis Wallisii. 1660.

Dialogus Physicus: Sive de Nature Aeris. 1661.

Problemata Physica. 1662.

Mr. Hobbes Considered in His Loyalty, Religion, Reputation, and Manners. 1662.

De Principiis et Ratiocinatione Geometrarum. 1666.

Quadratura Circuli. 1669.

Rosetum Geometricum cum Censura Brevi Doctrinae Wallisianae de Motu. 1671.

Three Papers Presented to the Royal Society Against Dr. Wallis. 1671.

Lux Mathematica Excussa Collisionibus Johannis Wallisii et Thomae Hobbesii. 1672.

Principia et Problemata Aliquot Geometrica. 1674.

A Letter about Liberty and Necessity. 1676.

Decameron Physiologicum; or, Ten Dialogues of Natural Philosophy. 1678.

Behemoth; or, An Epitome of the Civil Wars of England. 1679; edited by Ferdinand Tönnies, 1889.

An Historical Narration Concerning Heresy and the Punishment Thereof. 1680.

A Dialogue Between a Philosopher and a Student of the Common Laws of England. 1681; edited by Joseph Cropsey, 1971.

Historia Ecclesiastica Carmine Elegiaco Concinnata. 1688.

Verse

De Mirabilibus Pecci Carmen (in Latin). 1666(?).

Other

Translator, *Eight Books of the Peloponnesian War*, by Thucydides. 1629; edited by Richard Schlatter, 1975.

Translator, *The Iliads and Odyssey of Homer.* 1673.

Bibliography: *Hobbes: A Bibliography* by Hugh Macdonald and M. Hargeaves, 1952.

Reading List: *Sir William Davenant's "Gondibert," Its Preface, and Hobbes's Answer: A Study in English Neo-Classicism* by Cornell March Dowlin, 1934; *The Hunting of Leviathan* by Samuel I. Mintz, 1962; *The Divine Politics of Hobbes: An Interpretation of Leviathan* by F. C. Hood, 1964; *The Anatomy of Leviathan* by F. S. McNeilly, 1968; *The Logic of Leviathan* by D. P. Gautheir, 1969; *Hobbes and the Epic Tradition of Political Theory* by Sheldon S. Wolin, 1970; *Hobbes in His Time* edited by Ralph Ross, Herbert W. Schneider, and Theodore Waldman, 1975; *The Golden Lands of Hobbes* by Miriam M. Reik, 1977.

*   *   *

"Mr. Hobbes is and will in future ages be accounted the best writer at this day in the world." If James Harrington's contemporary assessment of the merits of Hobbes's prose style appears a little fulsome, it is as well to remember that it was not untypical. Harrington disliked the political philosophy propounded by Hobbes, but he recognised the lucidity and forcefulness of the language in which his "noxious and combustible" doctrines were made public. Perhaps Hobbes is known today first and foremost for his pessimistic view of human nature – an opinion which profoundly influenced several generations of English writers – the consequence of which was the belief that, without strong government, "the life of man" would degenerate to a state in which it was "solitary, poore, nasty, brutish, and short." But, in addition to his philosophy, his psychology, and his mathematics, he was a literary critic of some weight, and a translator of not merely Thucydides, but of Homer's epics, the *Iliad* and the *Odyssey*. His literary significance was such that Sir William Davenant worked on Hobbes's aesthetic theories in the heroic poem *Gondibert*. Not only did Hobbes scrutinise Davenant's composition daily, as it was being written, but the publication of the first two books of *Gondibert* were accompanied, in 1650, by a preface by the poet addressed to Hobbes, and by an answer from the pen of Hobbes himself. Together, these critical essays formulated "a manifesto from the classical school" of some critical importance (Edmund Gosse, *From Shakespeare to Pope*, 1885). In his tersely argued essay, Hobbes asserted that it was the role of the poet, "by imitating humane life in delightful and measur'd lines, to avert men from vice and incline them to vertuous and honorable actions," and he put forward the critical axioms on which the "New Aesthetics" should be based.

But Hobbes's criticism and translations should be put into perspective alongside his thought. Pierre Bayle, in his *Dictionary*, referred to Hobbes as "one of the greatest minds of the seventeenth century," while Hobbes himself claimed that his translation of the *Odyssey* was published merely to "take off my Adversaries from shewing their folly upon my more serious Writings, and set them upon my Verses to shew their wisdom." It is these "more serious Writings," and *Leviathan* in particular, that still interest us today. His philosophy was consistent, but the definitive version was given in 1651 in *Leviathan*. When Hobbes was writing, England had been plunged into the turmoil of civil war, and he was in exile in France. The firmness of the bonds which held society together within its hierarchical framework was being tested to the utmost. Anarchy threatened, and, once law and order was submerged, property would be unprotected. Basing his system on a shrewd list of psychological truisms, Hobbes postulated the consequences of anarchy in a vision of total and incessant war of every man against every man. He sought to analyse society and social behaviour in scientific terms, to demonstrate what would happen should society fall apart, or cease to function properly.

At the root of all of Hobbes's theories is the truism that man is a rational egoist. From this starting-point, he works on three quasiaxiomatic observations: that men perpetually seek power; that, to all intents and purposes, men are equal "in the faculties of body, and mind"; and that there is a scarcity of resources. From these propositions, he deduces his system. Without the restraints imposed upon society by a sovereign power which maintains law and order, a state of war would exist, because "Competition of Riches, Honour, Command, or other power, enclineth to Contention, Enmity, and War." But because man is a *rational* egoist, he can see that it is in his interests to escape from the prevalent conditions of a "state of nature." Reason "suggesteth convenient Articles of Peace" – the so-called laws of nature. By surrendering to a sovereign, along with all other men, his natural right to do anything that is in any way conducive to self-preservation, man can get round this impasse. The social contract – "the mutuall transferring of Right" – is the crux of Hobbes's system. Once the sovereign has been set up, he has the power and authority to ensure that no-one breaks the contract, punishing transgressors impartially. In Hobbes's view this was, in effect, the situation in England in 1651. He was a royalist, but the sovereign did not necessarily have to be a king, simply an absolute power able to maintain law and order. The sovereign was the Leviathan, or artificial man, "a common Power to keep them all in awe," without which society would quickly decline into a state of nature.

It was Hobbes's horrific view of human nature, rather than his totalitarianism, which troubled his contemporaries. As proof of his psychological analysis, he asked men to observe the lack of real altruism in society. He denied that man was a social or sociable animal, and in so doing he had contrived to render God irrelevant to his system. In 1676 one clergyman suggested that his doctrines had been "the debauching of this generation." Although, as Quentin Skinner points out (in *The Historical Journal*, September 1966), Hobbes's opinions were not unique, he was the figure at which all darts were levelled. We can sense a reaction to Hobbes in the literature of the Augustan age, in the thought of Shaftesbury, and in the cult of sentimentality, which was not only anti-Puritan and anti-Stoic, but implicitly anti-Hobbesian (see R. S. Crane in *Journal of English Literary History*, December 1934). It is possible that in *Gulliver's Travels* the Yahoos are the epitome of the popular view of Hobbesian man, while in *Tom Jones* Blifil is a perfect specimen of the rational egoist, in contrast to the good-nature, benevolence, and altruism of Tom himself. It is a measure of the influence of Hobbes's opinions on human nature that they are reflected and refuted in many works of the Augustan imagination, and that they were recognisable as Hobbesian without explicit statement.

—J. A. Downie

HOGG, James. Scottish. Born in Ettrick, Selkirkshire, baptized 9 December 1770. Attended the local school for one year; apprentice shepherd from the age of 6; largely self-educated. Married Margaret Phillips in 1820. Shepherd at Willanslee, 1787–90, and at Yarrow, 1790–1800; poet and songwriter from 1796; managed his parents' farm at Ettrick, 1800–03; met Sir Walter Scott, who encouraged his writing and subsequently arranged for publication of his verse, 1802; shepherd at Mitchelstacks, Nithsdale, 1803–07; farmer in Dumfriesshire, 1808; went bankrupt and returned to Ettrick; settled in Edinburgh, 1810, and thereafter devoted himself to writing; Editor, *The Spy*, Edinburgh, 1810–11; inherited a farm, Altrive Lake in Yarrow, from a patron, 1816, and lived there for the rest of his life; contributor to *Blackwood's Magazine*, Edinburgh. *Died 21 November 1835.*

PUBLICATIONS

Collections

Tales and Sketches.   6 vols., 1837.
Poetical Works.   5 vols., 1838–40.
Works, Letters, and Manuscripts, edited by R. B. Adam.   1930.
Selected Poems, edited by Douglas S. Mack.   1970.

Fiction

The Hunting of Badlewe: A Dramatic Tale.   1814.
The Long Pack: A Northumbrian Tale.   1817.
The Brownie of Bodsbeck and Other Tales.   1818; *The Brownie of Bodsbeck* edited by
     Douglas S. Mack, 1976.
Winter Evening Tales.   1820.
The Three Perils of Man; or, War, Women, and Witchcraft: A Border Romance.   1822;

as *The Siege of Roxburgh*, in *Tales and Sketches*, 1837; edited by Douglas Gifford, 1972.
The Three Perils of Woman; or, Love, Leasing, and Jealousy: A Series of Domestic Scottish Tales. 1823.
The Private Memoirs and Confessions of a Justified Sinner. 1824; as *The Suicide's Grave*, 1828; as *Confessions of a Fanatic*, in *Tales and Sketches*, 1837; edited by John Carey, 1969.
Altrive Tales Collected among the Peasantry of Scotland and from Foreign Adventurers. 1832.
Tales of the Wars of Montrose. 1835; edited by J. E. H. Thomson, 1909.
Kilmeny. 1905.

Plays

Dramatic Tales. 2 vols., 1817.
The Royal Jubilee: A Scottish Mask. 1822.

Verse

Scottish Pastorals, Poems, Songs. 1801.
The Mountain Bard, Consisting of Ballads and Songs Founded on Facts and Legendary Tales. 1807; revised edition, 1821.
The Forest Minstrel: A Selection of Songs, with others. 1810.
The Queen's Wake: A Legendary Poem. 1813.
A Selection of German Hebrew Melodies. 1815(?).
The Pilgrims of the Sun. 1815.
The Ettrick Garland, Being Two Excellent New Songs, with Scott. 1815.
Mador of the Moor. 1816.
A Border Garland. 1819(?).
Poetical Works. 4 vols., 1822.
Queen Hynde. 1825.
The Shepherd's Calendar. 2 vols., 1829.
Songs by the Ettrick Shepherd. 1831.
A Queer Book. 1832.

Other

The Shepherd's Guide, Being a Practical Treatise on the Diseases of Sheep. 1807.
Critical Remarks on the Psalms of David, with W. Tennant. 1830.
A Series of Lay Sermons on Good Principles and Good Breeding. 1834.
The Domestic Manners and Private Life of Sir Walter Scott. 1834; as *Familiar Anecdotes of Scott*, 1834.
A Tour in the Highlands in 1803: A Series of Letters to Scott. 1888.
Memoirs of the Author's Life, and Familiar Anecdotes of Scott, edited by Douglas S. Mack. 1972.

Editor, *The Poetic Mirror; or, The Living Bards of Britain.* 1816; edited by T. E. Welby, 1929.
Editor, *The Jacobite Relics of Scotland.* 2 vols., 1819–21.
Editor, *Select and Rare Scottish Melodies.* 1829.
Editor, *Songs Now First Collected.* · 1831.

Editor, with William Motherwell, *The Works of Robert Burns.*   5 vols., 1834–36.

Bibliography: "Hogg" by F. E. Pierce, in *Yale University Library Gazette 5,* 1931.

Reading List: *The Ettrick Shepherd: A Biography* by H. T. Stephenson, 1922; *The Ettrick Shepherd* by E. C. Batho, 1927; *Life and Letters of Hogg,* vol. 1, by A. L. Strout, 1946; *Hogg: A Critical Study* by L. Simpson, 1962; *Hogg* by Douglas Gifford, 1976.

*   *   *

James Hogg's masterpiece is *The Private Memoirs and Confessions of a Justified Sinner,* a novel set in Scotland at the beginning of the eighteenth century. Like Scott's *Old Mortality,* Hogg's novel deals with the political and religious conflicts between Whig and Tory, Covenanter and Royalist. The *Justified Sinner* begins with a description of the marriage of the Tory Laird of Dalcastle, George Colwan, and a fanatically religious woman of extreme Whig views. The marriage is a disastrous failure, and the couple soon agree to live apart, in different parts of the Laird's house. Two sons are born to Lady Dalcastle. The first is named George and is brought up by his father, but the Laird refuses to recognise the second boy as his own, and this child is brought up by his mother and the Rev. Robert Wringhim, a clergyman who shares her extreme religious views. Indeed, Lady Dalcastle's second son is eventually named Robert Wringhim after the man who, it is strongly implied, is his real father. The brothers Robert and George, by now young men, meet for the first time in Edinburgh during a session of the Scottish Parliament. This meeting provokes a public quarrel which sparks off a more general conflict between the Whig and Tory factions, and in due course Robert murders his brother outside a brothel. The first section of the novel, which is narrated by an "Editor" of Tory sympathies, ends when Robert contrives to make his escape from justice, after his guilt as a murderer has been established.

The second section of the novel consists of Robert Wringhim's own Private Memoirs and Confessions, in which Robert describes how he came to believe himself to be one of the elect, a "justified person" unalterably chosen by God for salvation, and incapable of falling from his justified state through any sinful act. Robert is then befriended by a mysterious stranger, Gil-Martin, who is recognised by the reader as the Devil in disguise. At Gil-Martin's instigation, Robert sets out to purify the world by murdering the enemies of true religion. His first victim is Mr. Blanchard, a worthy minister who opposes Robert's extreme theological views. Robert then murders his brother George, and he later seals his damnation by committing suicide.

The *Justified Sinner* is a complex and powerful novel, and the portrait of Robert Wringhim is remarkable for its psychological insight. Hogg's other works do not reach the same heights, although *The Brownie of Bodsbeck* and *The Three Perils of Man* are rich and vigorous (although loosely constructed) novels which are based largely on traditional folk material. Hogg also used folk material in his short stories, of which "The Brownie of the Black Haggs" is a particularly fine example.

As a poet, Hogg's best work was influenced by the eighteenth-century Scottish vernacular tradition of Ramsay, Fergusson, and Burns, as well as by the traditional ballads of his native Ettrick. Hogg made a distinguished contribution to the Scottish song tradition, and he also produced "The Witch of Fife," a magnificent comic poem based, like Burns's "Tam o' Shanter," on the distinctive feeling of the old Scottish peasantry for the supernatural. Hogg's outstanding achievement in verse, however, is probably "Kilmeny," a religious poem based on traditional folk tales of abduction to fairyland. Both "Kilmeny" and "The Witch of Fife" were included in *The Queen's Wake,* a long poem in which Hogg tells of a contest among the poets held to celebrate the return of Mary Queen of Scots from France.

—Douglas S. Mack

HOLCROFT, Thomas. English. Born in London, 10 December 1745. Self-educated. Married four times, lastly to Louisa Mercier; one son and two daughters. Worked as a stableboy in Newmarket, Suffolk, 1757–60, and in his father's cobbler's stall, London, 1761–64; taught school in Liverpool, 1764; resumed his trade of shoemaker, London, 1764–69, and contributed to the *Whitehall Evening Post*; tutor in the family of Granville Sharp, 1769; prompter at a Dublin theatre, 1770–71; strolling player in the provinces in England, 1771–78; returned to London, 1778, and thereafter a prolific writer: contributed to the *Westminster Magazine, Wit's Magazine, Town and Country*, and early numbers of the *English Review*; actor and playwright at Drury Lane Theatre, 1778–84; Correspondent in Paris for the *Morning Herald*, 1783; joined the Society for Constitutional Information, 1792: indicted for treason, imprisoned, then discharged, 1794; moved to Hamburg, 1799, and tried, unsuccessfully, to establish the *European Repository*; lived in Paris, 1801–03, then returned to London: set up a printing business with his brother-in-law, 1803, which subsequently failed. *Died 23 March 1809.*

PUBLICATIONS

Fiction

Alwyn; or, The Gentleman Comedian, with William Nicholson. 1780.
The Family Picture; or, Domestic Dialogues on Amiable Subjects. 1783.
An Amorous Tale of the Chaste Loves of Peter the Long and His Most Honoured Friend Dame Blanche Bazu. 1786.
Anna St. Ives. 1792; edited by Peter Faulkner, 1970.
The Adventures of Hugh Trevor. 1794; edited by Seamus Deane, 1973.
Memoirs of Bryan Perdue. 1805.

Plays

The Crisis; or, Love and Fear (produced 1778).
Duplicity (produced 1781). 1781; as *The Masked Friend* (produced 1796).
The Noble Peasant, music by William Shield (produced 1784). 1784.
The Follies of a Day; or, The Marriage of Figaro, from a play by Beaumarchais (produced 1784). 1785; revised version, 1881; revised version, from the opera by da Ponte, music by Mozart (produced 1819), 1819.
The Choleric Fathers, music by William Shield (produced 1785). 1785.
Sacred Dramas Written in French by la Comtesse de Genlis. 1785.
Seduction (produced 1787). 1787.
The School for Arrogance, from a play by Destouches (produced 1791). 1791.
The Road to Ruin (produced 1792). 1792; edited by Ruth I. Aldrich, 1968.
Love's Frailties (produced 1794). 1794.
Heigh-Ho! for a Husband. 1794.
The Rival Queens; or, Drury Lane and Covent Garden (produced 1794).
The Deserted Daughter, from a work by Diderot (produced 1795). 1795.
The Man of Ten Thousand (produced 1796). 1796.
The Force of Ridicule (produced 1796).
Knave or Not?, from plays by Goldoni (produced 1798). 1798.
He's Much to Blame (produced 1798). 1798.
The Inquisitor (produced 1798). 1798.
The Old Clothesman, music by Thomas Attwood (produced 1799). Songs published 1799(?).

Deaf and Dumb; or, The Orphan Protected, from a play by de Bouilly (produced 1801). 1801.
The Escapes; or, The Water-Carrier, music by Thomas Attwood, songs by T. J. Dibdin, from an opera by J. N. Nouilly, music by Cherubini (produced 1801).
A Tale of Mystery, from a play by Pixérécourt (produced 1802). 1802.
Hear Both Sides (produced 1803). 1803.
The Lady of the Rock (produced 1805). 1805.
The Vindictive Man (produced 1806). 1806.

Verse

Elegies. 1777.
Human Happiness; or, The Sceptic. 1783.
Tales in Verse, Critical, Satirical, Humorous. 1806.

Other

A Plain and Succinct Narrative of the Late [Gordon] Riots. 1780; edited by Garland Garvey Smith, 1944.
The Trial of the Hon. George Gordon. 1781.
Memoirs of Baron de Tott, Containing the State of the Turkish Empire and the Crimea. 2 vols., 1785.
The Secret History of the Court of Berlin. 2 vols., 1789.
A Narrative of Facts Relating to a Prosecution for High Treason. 2 vols., 1795.
A Letter to William Windham on the Intemperance and Danger of His Public Conduct. 1795.
Travels from Hamburg Through Westphalia, Holland, and the Netherlands. 2 vols., 1804.
Memoirs, completed by William Hazlitt. 3 vols., 1816; edited by Elbridge Colby, as *The Life of Holcroft*, 2 vols., 1925.

Editor, *Letter on Egypt*, by Mr. Savary. 2 vols., 1786.
Editor, and Translator, *Posthumous Works of Frederick, King of Prussia.* 13 vols., 1789.
Editor, *The Theatrical Recorder.* 2 vols., 1805–06.

Translator, *Philosophical Essays with Observations on the Laws and Customs of Several Eastern Nations*, by Foucher d'Osbornville. 1784.
Translator, *Tales of the Castle*, by la Comtesse de Genlis. 5 vols., 1785.
Translator, *Caroline of Lichtfield*, by Baroness de Montolieu. 2 vols., 1786.
Translator, *Historical and Critical Memoirs of the Life and Writings of Voltaire*, by Chaudon. 1786.
Translator, *The Present State of the Empire of Morocco*, by Chenier. 2 vols., 1788.
Translator, *The Life of Baron Frederick Trenck.* 3 vols., 1788.
Translator, *Essays on Physiognomy*, by J. C. Lavater. 3 vols., 1789.
Translator, *Travels Through Germany, Switzerland, and Italy*, by Frederick Leopold, Count Stolberg. 2 vols., 1796–97.
Translator, *Herman and Dorothea*, by Goethe. 1801.

Bibliography: *A Bibliography of Holcroft* by Elbridge Colby, 1922.

Reading List: *Holcroft and the Revolutionary Novel* by Rodney M. Baine, 1965; *The English Jacobin Novel* by Gary Kelly, 1976.

*   *   *

Thomas Holcroft was a self-taught man of letters, and one of the leading radical writers of the period of the French Revolution. His early writing was mostly for the theatre, and both *The School for Arrogance* and *The Road to Ruin* were successful in combining sentimental melodrama with the new philosophy. But with changing theatrical taste, Holcroft's plays passed into an oblivion from which they are yet to be restored. He chose to use the novel form for the fuller exposition of his political outlook, an outlook clearly influenced by his friendship with William Godwin, the most famous radical intellectual of the day, and his acquaintance with other radicals like Tom Paine and Mary Wollstonecraft.

Holcroft's two major novels are *Anna St. Ives* and *The Adventures of Hugh Trevor. Anna St. Ives* may be regarded as the equivalent in fiction of Godwin's *Political Justice*. It expresses its criticism of society through the contrasting contenders for the hand of the heroine, Anna: the rationalist Frank Henley, the virtuous son of the steward of Anna's father, and the aristocratic rake Coke Clifton. Clifton is a character in the line of Richardson's Lovelace in *Clarissa*, confident, witty, and unprincipled. He is allowed to express himself with a theatrical exuberance which gives the novel some vitality: "Should I be obliged to come like Jove to Semele, in flames, and should we both be reduced to ashes in the conflict, I will enjoy her!" However, the novel has a clear doctrinaire intention, which results in the defeat of Clifton and the marriage of Frank and Anna. The extravagance of Holcroft's idealism comes out in the final conversion of Clifton himself to the high-minded radicalism of his two unfailing friends.

Hugh Trevor is less diagrammatic in its rendering of life, but no less didactic in intention. The story of Trevor's life is basically picaresque, with a variety of adventures and events, but the moral of his experiences is clear: society is corrupt, and reason must guide the individual if he is to avoid its coercions. But there is also some psychological development, which would seem to have an autobiographical origin, in Trevor's gradual development of control over his original impulsiveness. When this is allied with a vigorous satirical attack on various aspects of society, including the Church, the law and reactionary politicians, the overall effect is a novel of considerable interest. Together with *Anna*, it justifies Holcroft's claim to be considered as a significant participant in an important tradition of rationalist social idealism.

—Peter Faulkner

HOLMES, Oliver Wendell. American. Born in Cambridge, Massachusetts, 29 August 1809. Educated at Phillips Academy, Andover, Massachusetts; studied law at Harvard University, Cambridge, Massachusetts, graduated 1829; studied medicine for two years in Europe, then at Harvard Medical School, M.D. 1836. Married Amelia Lee Jackson in 1840; three children. Practised medicine in Boston; Professor of Anatomy and Physiology, Dartmouth College, Hanover, New Hampshire, 1838–40; discovered that Puerperal Fever was contagious, 1843; Professor of Anatomy, Harvard Medical School, 1847–82. Honorary degrees: Oxford, Cambridge, and Edinburgh universities, 1886. *Died 7 October 1894.*

Collections

Complete Poetical Works, edited by Horace E. Scudder. 1895.
Representative Selections, edited by S. I. Hayakawa and Howard Mumford
  Jones. 1939.

Fiction

Elsie Venner: A Romance of Destiny. 1861.
The Guardian Angel. 1867.
A Mortal Antipathy: First Opening of the New Portfolio. 1885.

Verse

The Harbinger: A May-Gift. 1833.
Poems. 1836; revised edition, 1846, 1848, 1849.
Urania: A Rhymed Lesson. 1846.
Astraea: The Balance of Illusions. 1850.
Poetical Works. 1852.
Songs and Poems of the Class of 1829, second edition. 1859; revised edition, 1868.
Songs in Many Keys. 1861.
Poems. 1862.
Humorous Poems. 1865.
Songs of Many Seasons 1862–1874. 1874.
Poetical Works. 1877.
The Iron Gate and Other Poems. 1880.
Poetical Works. 2 vols., 1881.
Illustrated Poems. 1885.
Before the Curfew and Other Poems, Chiefly Occasional. 1888.
At Dartmouth: The Phi Beta Kappa Poem 1839. 1940.

Other

Boylston Prize Dissertations for 1836 and 1837. 1838.
Homoeopathy and Its Kindred Delusions (lectures). 1842.
The Autocrat of the Breakfast-Table. 1858.
The Professor at the Breakfast-Table, with the Story of Iris. 1860.
*Currents and Counter-Currents in Medical Science, with Other Addresses and
  Essays.* 1861.
Soundings from the Atlantic. 1863.
*The Poet at the Breakfast-Table: His Talks with His Fellow-Boarders and the
  Reader.* 1872.
John Lothrop Motley: A Memoir. 1878.
The School-Boy. 1879.
Poems and Prose Passages, edited by Josephine E. Hodgdon. 1881.
Medical Essays 1842–1882. 1883.
Pages from an Old Volume of Life: A Collection of Essays 1857–1881. 1883.
Ralph Waldo Emerson. 1884.

Our Hundred Days in Europe. 1887.
Over the Teacups. 1890.
Writings. 14 vols., 1891–92.
A Dissertation on Acute Pericarditis. 1937.
The Autocrat's Miscellanies (miscellany), edited by Albert Mordell. 1959.

Editor, with Jacob Bigelow, *Principles of the Theory and Practice of Medicine*, by Marshall Hall. 1839.
Editor, with Donald G. Mitchell, *The Atlantic Almanac 1868.* 1867.

Bibliography: *Bibliography of Holmes* by Thomas Franklin Currier and Eleanor M. Tilton, 1953; in *Bibliography of American Literature* by Jacob Blanck, 1963.

Reading List: *Life and Letters of Holmes* by John T. Morse, Jr., 2 vols., 1896; *Holmes of the Breakfast-Table* by Mark A. De Wolfe Howe, 1936; *Amiable Autocrat: A Biography of Holmes* by Eleanor M. Tilton, 1947; *Holmes* by Miriam R. Small, 1963.

*   *   *

The great popular reputation of Oliver Wendell Holmes in the nineteenth century receded with the eclipse of New England pre-eminence. Except for the rural Whittier, Holmes was the most provincial of the New England writers, and unlike the others he did not espouse causes. The Boston of his occasional verse and genial essays was not (according to the editors of *Representative Selections*) "the rebellious Boston, out of which came the antislavery societies, transcendentalism, and the feminist movement." In the opening chapter of his first novel (*Elsie Venner*) Holmes describes and provides a lasting label for cultured, mercantile Bostonians with Bulfinch houses, Beacon Street addresses, and ancestral portraits. He became the spokesman for this "Brahmin Caste of New England" when his *Autocrat of the Breakfast-Table* began to appear in the *Atlantic Monthly* in 1857. Although his public had read his occasional poems ever since he was a Harvard undergraduate, his new image as "the Autocrat" established Holmes's reputation as a major American writer.

There had been little time for writing prose between 1830 and 1857, for Holmes had become an M.D. and held professorships of anatomy at Dartmouth and Harvard. But Holmes was a brilliant and incessant talker, and when he hit upon the scheme of jotting down his own talk, he had the matter for his essay series. Literary historians agree that his personality imposed itself upon and gave unity to his writing – poetry, essays, and fiction alike. There is a consistent mental set in his writing also: he was a clear-headed rationalist who disliked even the "bullying" of science and abhorred the dogmatism of theology. His attacks on Calvinism were his closest approximation to taking up a cause, but it seems strange now that Boston thought of him as an American Voltaire. However, Holmes liked to point out the parallels between his own life and Dr. Johnson's. Johnson was born in 1709, Holmes in 1809; both were urban beings, and Holmes's devotion to Boston matched Johnson's love of London. Both were great talkers and were devoted to common sense; and, though his wit has not survived as well as Johnson's, one, at least, of Holmes's remarks is remembered: "Boston State-House is the hub of the solar system. You couldn't pry that out of a Boston man if you had the tire of all creation straightened out for a crowbar."

The *Atlantic Monthly* version of *The Autocrat of the Breakfast Table* begins, "I was just going to say, when I was interrupted." After the twelve *Atlantic* installments had become a book in 1858, the author explains that the interruption had lasted a quarter of a century, since two articles entitled "The Autocrat of the Breakfast Table" had appeared in the *New England Magazine* in 1831 and 1832. He had matured and gained confidence in the twenty-five-year interval; along with his medical practice and professorships, he had published important medical essays – and a volume of poems. His Harvard lectures were as celebrated for their

589

wit as for their learning, and from 1841 to 1857 he was a sought-after lyceum lecturer on literary as well as medical subjects. But Dr. Holmes was becoming even better known in Boston and Cambridge as a genial humorist and master of conversation.

His fellow-Brahmin, James Russell Lowell, accepted the editorship of the *Atlantic Monthly* on the condition that Holmes become a regular contributor. Holmes had suggested the name for the new magazine; and there were Holmes's poems, essays, and reviews or installments of novels in the magazine every year until 1893. The *Atlantic* published sixty-five Holmes poems, each of his three novels, three series of *Autocrat* sequels – *The Professor at the Breakfast-Table*, *The Poet at the Breakfast-Table*, and *Over the Teacups* – and *Our Hundred Days in Europe*.

It is difficult to evaluate Holmes's writing on medical subjects, or determine how his role as a doctor and professor of anatomy related to his literary career. Scientific medicine was just beginning a phenomenal advance in Holmes's day, but it is generally agreed that his own chief claim to medical distinction was his excellence as a teacher. Most interest in recent years has focused on his three "medicated novels" (Holmes accepted the term of a "dear old lady" who refused to read them): *Elsie Venner*, *The Guardian Angel*, and *A Moral Antipathy*. None of them contributed much to the development of the novel, though they fit into a kind of American novel vacuum – Hawthorne and Melville coming before, Howells and James after. *Elsie Venner* still gets respectful attention, but the plot of *A Moral Antipathy* has been judged "so absurd that it hardly bears repetition." Psychologists and psychiatrists have found validity and importance in the neuroses pictured in these novels, some of them profoundly shocking to Holmes's readers a hundred years ago.

To the twentieth century, Oliver Wendell Holmes was a writer of verse, not poetry – which even his contemporaries might have conceded. Significantly, both "The Deacon's Masterpiece" (or "One Hoss Shay" – sometimes interpreted as an allegory of New England Calvinism) and "The Chambered Nautilus," his acknowledged masterpiece, were both "recited" by the Autocrat of the Breakfast Table.

To the generations growing up in the first half of the twentieth century, the name Oliver Wendell Holmes meant the distinguished jurist whom F. D. Roosevelt had hailed in 1933 as "the greatest living American." This son and namesake, the only member of his family to outlive Dr. Holmes, had his father's clear-headed rationalistic turn of mind – but none of his other traits. Nearly a half century after the son's death, the elder Holmes is again emerging as a distinct figure: the conservative but clear-sighted, talkative Brahmin, who liked mill-owners better than abolitionists and transcendentalists, and who lived long enough to write graceful poetic tributes to nearly all of the nineteenth-century New England worthies.

—Clarence A. Glasrud

HOOK, Theodore (Edward).   English.   Born in London, 22 September 1788; son of the composer James Hook. Educated at private schools, and at Harrow School for one year; later attended Oxford University for two terms. Achieved fame as a boy as a writer, generally with his father, of numerous successful comic operas, 1805–11; a member of the Prince of Wales' circle; Accountant-General and Treasurer of Mauritius, 1813–17: discharged on a charge of embezzling; returned to London; attempted, unsuccessfully, to establish a magazine, *The Arcadian*, 1818–19; Editor, *John Bull*, from 1820; imprisoned for debt, London, and property confiscated, on the Mauritius charge, 1823–25; Editor, *New Monthly Magazine*, 1836–41. *Died 24 August 1841.*

PUBLICATIONS

Collections

Choice Humorous Works. 1873.

Fiction

The Man of Sorrow. 1808; as *Ned Musgrave; or, The Most Unfortunate Man in the World*, 1842.
Sayings and Doings: A Series of Sketches from Life. 9 vols., 1824–28.
Maxwell. 1830.
Gervase Skinner; or, The Sin of Economy. 1830.
Love and Pride. 1833; as *The Widow and the Marquess*, 1842.
The Parson's Daughter. 1833; revised edition, 1835.
Gilbert Gurney. 1836.
Jack Brag. 1837.
Gurney Married: A Sequel to Gilbert Gurney. 1838.
Precepts and Practice. 1840.
Births, Deaths, and Marriages. 1839; as *All in the Wrong*, 1842.
Fathers and Sons. 1842.
Peregrine Bunce; or, Settled at Last. 1842.

Plays

The Soldier's Return; or, What Can Beauty Do?, music by James Hook (produced 1805). 1805.
The Invisible Girl, music by James Hook, from a French play (produced 1806). 1806.
Catch Him Who Can!, music by James Hook (produced 1806). 1806.
Tekeli; or, The Siege of Montgatz, music by James Hook, from a play by Pixérécourt (produced 1806). 1806.
The Fortress, music by James Hook, from a play by Pixérécourt (produced 1807). 1807.
Music-Mad, music by James Hook (produced 1807). 1808.
The Siege of St. Quentin; or, Spanish Heroism, music by James Hook (produced 1808).
Killing No Murder, music by James Hook (produced 1809). 1809; revised version, as *A Day at the Inn* (produced 1823), with *The Gentleman in Black* by Mark Lemon, 1886.
Safe and Sound, music by James Hook (produced 1809). 1809.
Ass-ass-ination (produced 1810).
The Will or the Widow; or, Puns in Plenty (produced 1810).
Darkness Visible (produced 1811). 1811.
The Trial by Jury (produced 1811). 1811.
Exchange No Robbery; or, The Diamond Ring (produced 1820). 1820.
Over the Water (produced 1820).
A Joke's a Joke; or, Too Much for Friendship (produced 1830).

Other

Facts Illustrative of the Treatment of Napoleon Buonaparte in Saint Helena. 1819.
Tentamen; or, An Essay Towards the History of Whittington. 1820.

The Life of General Sir David Baird.   2 vols., 1832.
The Ramsbottom Letters.   1872; revised edition, 1874.

Editor, *Reminiscences of Michael Kelly the Singer.*   2 vols., 1826.
Editor, *Pascal Bruno*, by Dumas.   1837.
Editor, *Cousin Geoffrey, The Old Bachelor*, by H. M. G. Smythies.   3 vols., 1840.
Editor, *The French Stage and the French People*, by J. A. Benard.   1841.
Editor, *Peter Priggins*, by J. T. J. Hewlett.   3 vols., 1841.
Editor, *The Parish Clerk*, by J. T. J. Hewlett.   3 vols., 1841.

Bibliography: in *XIX Century Fiction: A Bibliographical Record* by Michael Sadleir, 2 vols., 1951.

Reading List: *Life and Remains of Hook* by R. H. D. Barham, 2 vols., 1849, revised edition, 1853, 1877; *Hook and His Novels* by M. F. Brightfield, 1928.

*   *   *

Theodore Hook is ranked as a forerunner of Charles Dickens. Like Dickens, whose vast audience he helped to cultivate, he never seems to have rested, forever compelled to supply copy, eager to observe and to inform. But with him the journalist proved stronger than the narrator, though he could spell out the human predicament and had a sure grasp of the narrative potential of a situation. In his numerous novels and novellas he never genuinely probes a relationship or fully explores a personality. Doubtless there is some curiosity and concern on his part, but very little compassion, or even engagement, goes into his lively and smooth-running accounts.

Hook makes little effort to develop a plausible action. His plots are contrived and abound in coincidence, whose spuriousness he may even ironically concede. When he resorts to the pattern of the didactic tale much is made of the avowed authenticity of the events described, while the inherent logic of the parable remains largely unheeded. His novels proper must have required more application, yet here we are again struck by a facility of composition which never integrates or even shapes the material employed.

Hook lacked creative genius, but excelled in observation. There are qualities of vividness and fluency about his sketches that will still hold us. Sometimes the documentation seems too detailed, but then his readers were avid for information of any kind, and the wide range of his descriptions makes for diversity. His realism, conversely, never amounts to a detached representation of men and manners. There is an abundance of oddities and cranks among his manifold characters, who owe more to Hook's acumen than to the literary models of his great predecessors. No incongruity would escape him, and he was too much a satirist to forego a sarcastic censure when the occasion arose. Nevertheless, his social criticism remains strangely abortive throughout. In an age striving for reforms Hook closed his eyes to any change that might disturb the social set-up. His heroes usually claim aristocratic descent or adhere to an upper-middle-class background. Anyone below that station can fulfil a minor role only, unless he offers material for caricature, and the most scathing comment is indeed reserved for the social climber.

This is not to say that his work is entirely subordinated to a purpose. There is considerable variety in his scenes and the ever present criticism is often blended with humour or even elevated to pathos. But satire and caricature remain the most striking elements of Theodore Hook's narrative style and may be assumed to have influenced the Victorian novel of manners. Indirectly, such an influence may even extend to a much later period.

—Herbert Foltinek

HOOPER, Johnson Jones. American. Born in Wilmington, North Carolina, 9 June 1815. Educated in local schools. Married a Miss Brantley. Worked on newspapers in Charleston, 1830–35; travelled and lived in the Gulf States of America, 1835–40, read law under his brother in Lafayette, Alabama, 1840–45; writer from 1845; edited the *Dadeville Banner*, and the Wetumpka *Whig*, and helped to edit the Montgomery *Journal*, all Alabama, 1846, then returned to Lafayette; Solicitor, 9th Alabama Judicial Circuit, 1849–53; Editor, *The Mail*, Montgomery, 1853–61; Secretary, Provisional Congress of the Southern States, 1861–62. Died 7 June 1862.

PUBLICATIONS

Fiction and Sketches

Some Adventures of Captain Simon Suggs, Late of the Tallapoosa Volunteers, Together with Taking the Census and Other Alabama Sketches. 1845; augmented edition, 1848.
A Ride with Old Kit Kuncher and Other Sketches and Scenes of Alabama. 1849.
The Widow Rugby's Husband, A Night at the Ugly Man's, and Other Tales of Alabama. 1851.
Dog and Gun: A Few Loose Chapters on Shooting. 1856.

Reading List: *The Southern Poor-White from Lubberland to Tobacco Road* by Shields McIlwaine, 1939; *Alias Simon Suggs: The Life and Times of Hooper* by W. Stanley Hoole, 1952; *Hooper: A Critical Study* by Howard Winston Smith, 1963; Introduction by Manly Wade Wellman to *Adventures of Captain Simon Suggs*, 1969.

*   *   *

The achievement of Johnson Jones Hooper is rooted in his contributions to nineteenth-century Southwest humor, a broadly realistic, often satiric, sometimes cold-blooded, oral-vernacular taletelling revealing a near absence of civilized standards of conduct. Some establishment critics of the early twentieth century tended virtually to dismiss Hooper's art as "discomfiture" – an "ancient, primitive, anti-social kind of merry-making" (*Library of Southern Literature*). Despite such narrow judgment, Hooper's work was well received in its own day, appearing in such popular American humor anthologies as *The Big Bear of Arkansas* and *Polly Peablossom's Wedding and Other Tales*. Moreover, within an eighteen-year period twenty-one editions of Hooper's books appeared, eleven editions of his masterpiece, *Some Adventures of Captain Simon Suggs*, appearing between 1845 and 1856.

In form, the work has long been viewed as campaign biography, and hence tied to the political machinations of frontier folk. The work, however, can be taken as a burlesque of campaign biography, with specific events based on Andrew Jackson's military career.

Suggs himself is perhaps the "bad boy" of American literature, a man proficient in the art of drinking, joking, and staying just a step ahead of his creditors. Hooper's biographer, W. Stanley Hoole, cites Bird Young of Tallapoosa County as the historical model for Suggs. As fictional creation, Suggs, however, is the epitome of the poor-white. Shields McIlwaine notes that the adventurer has a "long nose hung above a mouth stained by the filthy weed ...," his family living in "woolhat poverty." As a cultural-sociological phenomenon, Suggs originates perhaps in the Lubberland of William Byrd.

More than any other character from frontier humor, however, Suggs is indebted to the European tradition of the picaresque. As Howard Winston Smith has noted in his helpful critical study, both Suggs and Don Quixote undergo imitation promotions (Suggs to captaincy and Quixote to knighthood), and both works are episodic in nature. The general picaresque trait of the "picaro and the priest," moreover, originating in *Lazarillo de Tormes*, accounts in large part for Hooper's greatest moment in his most frequently anthologized chapter, "The Captain Attends a Camp Meeting." That particular chapter ultimately became the source for chapter twenty of *Huckleberry Finn*. Hooper ties together the many episodes by having each end in the triumph of frontier rascality over both innocence and sophistication.

None of Hooper's later writings has been judged equal to his first book. Both *The Widow Rugby's Husband, A Night at the Ugly Man's, and Other Tales of Alabama* and *Dog and Gun* attest to the author's love of the life he knew, but neither work reveals the real Hooper that Thackeray judged the "most promising writer of his day."

—George C. Longest

HOPE, Anthony. Pseudonym for Sir Anthony Hope Hawkins. English. Born in London, 9 February 1863. Educated at St. John's Foundation School, London and, subsequently, Leatherhead, Surrey; Balliol College, Oxford, 1881–85 (graduated with honours); called to the Bar, Middle Temple, London, 1887. Served the government in the Editorial and Public Branch Department, 1914–18. Married Elizabeth Somerville Sheldon in 1903; two sons and one daughter. Practised law in London, 1887–94; thereafter a full-time writer. Member of the Committee for twelve years, Chairman for four years, and a founder of the pension scheme, the Authors' Society, London. Knighted, 1918. *Died 8 July 1933.*

PUBLICATIONS

Fiction

A Man of Mark. 1890.
Father Stafford. 1891.
Mr. Witt's Widow. 1892.
A Change of Air. 1893.
Half a Hero. 1893.
Sport Royal and Other Stories. 1893.
The Dolly Dialogues. 1894.
The God in the Car. 1894.
The Indiscretion of the Duchess. 1894.
The Prisoner of Zenda. 1894.
The Chronicles of Count Antonio. 1895.
Comedies of Courtship. 1896.
The Heart of Princess Osra and Other Stories. 1896.
Phroso. 1897.
Rupert of Hentzau. 1898.
Simon Dale. 1898.
The King's Mirror. 1899.
Quisante. 1900.

Tristam of Blent. 1901.
The Intrusions of Peggy. 1902.
Double Harness. 1904.
A Servant of the Public. 1905.
Sophy of Kravonia. 1906.
Tales of Two People. 1907.
The Great Miss Driver. 1908.
Second String. 1910.
Mrs. Maxon Protests. 1911.
A Young Man's Year. 1915.
Captain Dieppe. 1918.
Beaumaroy Home from the Wars. 1919.
Lucinda. 1920.
Little Tiger. 1925.

Plays

The Price of Empire (produced 1896).
The Adventure of Lady Ursula (produced 1898). 1898.
When a Man's in Love, with Edward Rose (produced 1898).
Rupert of Hentzau, from his own novel (produced 1899).
English Nell, with Edward Rose, from the novel *Simon Dale* by Hope (produced 1900).
Pilkerton's Peerage (produced 1902). 1918.
Captain Dieppe, with Harrison Rhodes (produced 1904).
Helena's Path, with Cosmo Gordon-Lennox (produced 1910).
Love's Song (produced 1916).
The Philosopher in the Apple Orchard: A Pastoral. 1936.

Other

The New (German) Testament: Some Texts and a Commentary. 1914.
Militarism, German and British. 1915.
Why Italy Is with the Allies. 1917.
Selected Works. 10 vols., 1925.
Memories and Notes. 1927.

Reading List: *Hope and His Books* by Charles E. Mallett, 1935; "The Prisoner of the Prisoner of Zenda: Hope and the Novel of Society" by S. G. Putt, in *Essays in Criticism 6*, 1956.

*   *   *

The name of Anthony Hope creeps into histories of late Victorian literature almost by virtue of a single book, *The Prisoner of Zenda*, one of the most popular novels of the period, and indeed of all time. Yet Hope was a prolific writer, author of thirty-two works of fiction, a dozen or so plays, some political pamphlets written during World War I when he was employed by the Ministry of Information, and an autobiography. Trained as a barrister, Hope first took to writing in his spare time, achieving a modest success with a series of whimsical sketches contributed to the *Westminster Gazette*, later gathered together and published under the title *The Dolly Dialogues*. However, after the public's enthusiastic reception of *The Prisoner of Zenda* in 1894 he became a professional writer, endeavoring to repeat the success of this novel with a sequel entitled *Rupert of Hentzau*. He also wrote several other historical romances and some novels set in his own day, none of which deserves more than passing attention.

In a sense it is unfortunate that Hope turned professional, for in his evident determination to make a decent living by his pen, much of the spark went out of his writing. True, the arch humor of *The Dolly Dialogues* may strike modern readers as exceedingly tiresome and the social adventures he describes appallingly trivial, yet in this book his prose skips along at an easy pace, and at his best Hope can match the accomplished Ada Leverson, who covers the same social territory and writes in a similar vein.

Sprightliness and good humor are also apparent in *The Prisoner of Zenda*, an improbable tale concerning Rudolf Rassendyll, an English gentleman of Ruritania, who impersonates the king at his coronation, thereby thwarting a plot to remove him from the throne. Later, he falls in love with the King's betrothed; this is described in *Rupert of Hentzau*, and there we follow the lovers' fortunes until Rassendyll finally gives up both his life and the Princess Flavia for their love and her honor. Although the reader is swept along by the swashbuckling incidents of the fast-moving plot, sharing vicariously the romantic adventures of the hero, the ironic tone of the first book prevents him from identifying too closely with the characters, thus enabling him to experience the thrills aroused by the hero's adventures and laugh at them at the same time. In *Rupert of Hentzau*, however, Hope seems to take his improbable tale more seriously. The villains become more theatrically villainous, and the misfortunes of the lovers are described with an almost misanthropic intensity. While occasional flashes of mild cynicism add life to the story, it rarely captures the high spirits of its better known forbear.

Hope belongs to that age of story-tellers described by Roger Lancelyn Green in his book *Tellers of Tales* (1965), which includes Robert Louis Stevenson and Rider Haggard, Conan Doyle and A. E. W. Mason, and, while it may be argued that his total achievement falls short of that of his more illustrious tale-telling contemporaries, his name will no doubt endure, at least as long as "Ruritania" remains a word in the English language.

—John M. Munro

HOWE, E(dgar) W(atson). American. Born in Treaty, Indiana, 3 May 1853. Educated in local schools; apprenticed, as a printer, to his father, 1865–68. Married Clara L. Frank in 1875 (divorced, 1901); two sons and one daughter. Worked as a printer in Indiana, Missouri, Iowa, Nebraska, and Utah, 1868–72; Publisher, *Globe*, Golden, Colorado, 1872; Founder, with his brother James, and Editor, *Daily Globe*, Atchison, Kansas, 1877–1911; Editor and Publisher of *E. W. Howe's Monthly*, Atchison, 1911–33. Litt.D.: Rollins College, Winter Park, Florida, 1926; Washburn College, Topeka, Kansas, 1927. *Died 3 October 1937.*

PUBLICATIONS

Fiction

The Story of a Country Town. 1883; edited by Brom Weber, 1964.
The Mystery of The Locks. 1885.
A Moonlight Boy. 1886.

A Man Story. 1889.
An Ante-Mortem Statement. 1891.
The Confessions of John Whitlock, Late Preacher of the Gospel. 1891.
Dying Like a Gentleman and Other Stories. 1926.
The Covered Wagon and the West (stories). 1928.
Her Fifth Marriage and Other Stories. 1928.
When a Woman Enjoys Herself and Other Tales of a Small Town. 1928.

Other

Mark Antony De Wolfe Howe 1808–1895: A Brief Record of a Long Life. 1897.
Daily Notes on a Trip Around the World. 2 vols., 1907.
A Trip to the West Indies. 1910.
Country Town Sayings: A Collection of Paragraphs from the Atchison Globe. 1911.
Travel Letters from New Zealand, Australia, and Africa. 1913.
Success Easier Than Failure. 1917.
The Blessing of Business. 1918.
Ventures in Common Sense, edited by H. L. Mencken. 1919.
The Anthology of Another Town. 1920.
Adventures in Common Sense. 1922.
Notes for My Biographer: Terse Paragraphs on Life and Letters. 1926.
Preaching from the Audience: Candid Comments on Life. 1926.
Sinner Sermons: A Selection of the Best Paragraphs of Howe. 1926.
Plain People (autobiography). 1929.
The Indignation of Howe. 1933.

Reading List: *Howe, Country Town Philosopher* by Calder M. Rickett, 1968; *Howe* by S. J. Sackett, 1972.

*   *   *

"I come of a long line of plain people," E. W. Howe writes at the beginning of his autobiography *Plain People,* but as a famous editor in the days of personal journalism and as a minor novelist of the late 19th century, Howe achieved a measure of distinction in his own day and a small niche in the history of American life and culture. He is the author of one novel that continues to be reprinted and read, and his autobiography, long out of print, deserves to be better known. Howe is an authentic bit of Americana woven into the fabric of national experience – a figure to be compared in this respect with Benjamin Franklin, Horatio Alger, H. L. Mencken, and Will Rogers.

After establishing himself as a newspaper editor, Howe turned toward literature. For months in the early 1880's he worked over the manuscript of *The Story of a Country Town* at the kitchen table after finishing a long day in the newspaper office. When commercial publishers turned down his book, he published it himself. The novel was an immediate success and encouraged him to write several more, all of which were failures and never have been reprinted. Eventually he resigned himself to filling his newspaper columns with aphoristic paragraphs that attracted national attention. He published additional books during the rest of his life, but they are mostly forgotten travel letters, tracts on business, and collections of his newspaper and magazine paragraphs. One other, however, is worth reading: *The Anthology of Another Town,* a prose version of and answer to Edgar Lee Masters's *Spoon River Anthology.*

The Story of a Country Town draws on the life of Howe's father and his own experience growing up in northwest Missouri where the novel takes place. It's basically a melodramatic tragedy of a backwoods Othello who becomes insanely jealous when he discovers that his wife once was in love with another man. As a work of art, it is full of crudities, but the story is told with such a passionate intensity by Howe's persona, young Ned Westlake, who observes the action, that readers are swept along by it.

Both Howells and Twain, who received copies from the author, wrote flattering letters about the novel. Howells thought it a "very remarkable piece of realism" and praised the fidelity of the country town setting, although he objected to the sentimentality of the tragic romance. The novel generally has been classed with early examples of realism, but it is only partly realistic, and Howe's later novels demonstrated that he was really a sentimental romancer at heart. *The Story of a Country Town* can be seen, with its bitter memories of the narrator's youth, as a forerunner of the revolt-from-the-village literature of Sinclair Lewis, Sherwood Anderson, and Masters, but Howe during his later years filled his newspaper columns with the most blatant Chamber-of-Commerce puffery and really believed that all virtue resided in the small town and rural life.

—James Woodress

HOWELLS, William Dean.   American.   Born in Martin's Ferry, Ohio, 1 March 1837. Largely self-educated. Married Elinor Mead in 1862 (died, 1910); one son and two daughters. Compositor, 1851–58, Reporter, 1858–60, and News Editor, 1860–61, *Ohio State Journal*, Columbus; also correspondent, in Columbus, for the Cincinnati *Gazette*, 1857; contributor to his father's newspaper, *The Sentinel*, Jefferson, Ohio, from 1852, and wrote for various national magazines from 1860; United States Consul in Venice, 1861–65; Assistant Editor, 1866–71, and Editor-in-Chief, 1871–81, *Atlantic Monthly*, Boston; Professor of Modern Languages, Harvard University, Cambridge, Massachusetts, 1869–71; wrote the "Editor's Study" column for *Harper's* magazine, 1886–92; Co-Editor, *Cosmopolitan* magazine, 1892. Recipient: American Academy of Arts and Letters Gold Medal, 1915. M.A.: Harvard University, Cambridge, Massachusetts, 1867; Litt.D.: Yale University, New Haven, Connecticut, 1901; Oxford University, 1904; Columbia University, New York, 1905; L.H.D.: Princeton University, New Jersey, 1912. President, American Academy of Arts and Letters, 1908–20. *Died 11 May 1920.*

PUBLICATIONS

Collections

 Representative Selections, edited by Clara Marburg Kirk and Rudolf Kirk.   1950.
 Selected Writings, edited by Henry Steele Commager.   1950.
 Complete Plays, edited by Walter J. Meserve.   1960.
 Selected Edition, edited by Ronald Gottesman.   1968—

Fiction

 Their Wedding Journey.   1872; edited by John K. Reeves, in *Selected Edition*, 1968.
 A Chance Acquaintance.   1873; edited by Ronald Gottesman, David J. Nordloh, and

Jonathan Thomas, in *Selected Edition*, 1971.

A Foregone Conclusion. 1874.

The Lady of the Aroostook. 1879.

The Undiscovered Country. 1880.

A Fearful Responsibility and Other Stories. 1881.

Doctor Breen's Practice. 1881.

A Modern Instance. 1882; edited by David J. Nordloh and David Kleinman, in *Selected Edition*, 1978.

A Woman's Reason. 1883.

The Rise of Silas Lapham. 1885; edited by Walter J. Meserve and David J. Nordloh, in *Selected Edition*, 1971.

Indian Summer. 1886; edited by Scott Bennett and David J. Nordloh, in *Selected Edition*, 1971.

The Minister's Charge; or, The Apprenticeship of Lemuel Barker. 1886; edited by David J. Nordloh and David Kleinman, in *Selected Edition*, 1968.

April Hopes. 1888.

Annie Kilburn. 1888.

A Hazard of New Fortunes. 1889; edited by David J. Nordloh, in *Selected Edition*, 1976.

The Shadow of a Dream. 1890; with *An Imperative Duty*, edited by Martha Banta, Ronald Gottesman, and David J. Nordloh, in *Selected Edition*, 1970.

An Imperative Duty. 1891; with *The Shadow of a Dream*, edited by Martha Banta, Ronald Gottesman, and David J. Nordloh, in *Selected Edition*, 1970.

Mercy. 1892; as *The Quality of Mercy*, 1892.

The World of Chance. 1893.

The Coast of Bohemia. 1893.

A Traveler from Altruria. 1894; complete edition, edited by Clara Marburg Kirk and Rudolf Kirk, as *Letters of an Altrurian Traveller (1893–1894)*, 1961; with *Between the Dark and the Daylight*, in *Selected Edition*, 1968.

The Day of Their Wedding. 1896.

A Parting and a Meeting. 1896; with *The Day of Their Wedding*, as *Idyls in Drab*, 1896.

The Landlord at Lion's Head. 1897.

An Open-Eyed Conspiracy: An Idyl of Saratoga. 1897.

The Story of a Play. 1898.

Ragged Lady. 1899.

Their Silver Wedding Journey. 1899.

A Pair of Patient Lovers (stories). 1901.

The Kentons. 1902; in *Selected Edition*, 1971.

The Flight of Pony Baker: A Boy's Town Story. 1902.

Questionable Shapes. 1903.

Letters Home. 1903.

The Son of Royal Langbrith. 1904; edited by David Burrows, Ronald Gottesman, and David J. Nordloh, in *Selected Edition*, 1969.

Miss Bellard's Inspiration. 1905.

Through the Eye of a Needle. 1907.

Between the Dark and the Daylight: Romances. 1907; with *A Traveler from Altruria*, in *Selected Edition*, 1968.

Fennel and Rue. 1908.

New Leaf Mills: A Chronicle. 1913.

The Daughter of the Storage and Other Things in Prose and Verse. 1916.

The Leatherwood God. 1916; in *Selected Edition*, 1976.

The Vacation of the Kelwyns: An Idyl of the Middle Eighteen-Seventies. 1920.

Mrs. Farrell. 1921.

Plays

Samson, from the play by Ippolito d'Este (produced 1874).   1889.
The Parlor Car.   1876.
Out of the Question.   1877.
A Counterfeit Presentment.   1877.
Yorick's Love (produced 1878).   In Complete Plays, 1960.
The Sleeping-Car (produced 1887).   1883.
The Register.   1884.
The Elevator (produced 1885).   1885.
The Garroters (produced 1886).   1886.
A Foregone Conclusion, with William Poel, from the novel by Howells (produced 1886).   In Complete Plays, 1960.
Colonel Sellers as a Scientist, with Mark Twain, from the novel The Gilded Age by Twain and Charles Dudley Warner (produced 1887).   In Complete Plays, 1960.
A Sea Change; or, Love's Stowaway: A Lyricated Farce, music by George Henschel.   1887.
The Mouse Trap (produced 1887–88?).   In The Mouse Trap and Other Farces, 1889.
The Mouse Trap and Other Farces (includes A Likely Story, Five O'Clock Tea, The Garroters).   1889.
The Sleeping-Car and Other Farces.   1889.
The Albany Depot.   1892.
A Letter of Introduction.   1892.
The Unexpected Guests.   1893.
Evening Dress (produced 1894).   1893.
Bride Roses (produced 1894).   1900.
A Previous Engagement.   1897.
Room Forty-Five.   1900.
The Smoking Car.   1900.
An Indian Giver.   1900.
Minor Dramas (includes A Masterpiece of Diplomacy and Her Opinion of His Story).   2 vols., 1907.
The Mother and the Father.   1909.
Parting Friends.   1911.

Verse

Poems of Two Friends, with John J. Piatt.   1860.
No Love Lost: A Romance of Travel.   1869.
Poems.   1873.
Stops of Various Quills.   1895.

Other

Lives and Speeches of Abraham Lincoln and Hannibal Hamlin.   1860.
Venetian Life.   1866; revised edition, 1872, 1907.
Italian Journeys.   1867; revised edition, 1872, 1901.
Suburban Sketches.   1871; revised edition, 1872; as A Day's Pleasure and Other Sketches, 1876.
Sketch of the Life and Character of Rutherford B. Hayes.   1876.

A Little Girl among the Old Masters. 1884.

Three Villages. 1884.

Tuscan Cities. 1886.

Modern Italian Poets: Essays and Versions. 1887.

A Boy's Town (juvenile). 1890.

Criticism and Fiction. 1891.

A Little Swiss Sojourn. 1892.

Christmas Every Day and Other Stories Told for Children. 1892.

My Year in a Log Cabin. 1893.

My Literary Passions. 1895.

Impressions and Experiences. 1896.

Stories of Ohio. 1897.

Doorstep Acquaintance and Other Sketches. 1900.

Literary Friends and Acquaintance: A Personal Retrospect of American Authorship. 1900; edited by David F. Hiatt and Edwin H. Cady, in *Selected Edition,* 1968.

Heroines of Fiction. 2 vols., 1901.

Literature and Life: Studies. 1902.

London Films. 1905.

Certain Delightful English Towns. 1906.

Roman Holidays and Others. 1908.

Seven English Cities. 1909.

My Mark Twain: Reminiscences and Criticisms. 1910; edited by Marilyn Austin Baldwin, 1967.

Imaginary Interviews. 1910.

Familiar Spanish Travels. 1913.

The Seen and Unseen at Stratford-on-Avon: A Fantasy. 1914.

Years of My Youth (autobiography). 1916; in *Selected Edition,* 1975.

Life in Letters, edited by Mildred Howells. 2 vols., 1928.

Prefaces to Contemporaries (1882–1920), edited by George Arms, William M. Gibson, and Frederick C. Marston, Jr., 1957.

Criticism and Fiction and Other Essays, edited by Clara Marburg Kirk and Rudolf Kirk. 1959.

The Mark Twain–Howells Letters 1872–1910, edited by Henry Nash Smith and William M. Gibson. 2 vols., 1960.

Discovery of a Genius: Howells and Henry James, edited by Albert Mordell. 1961.

Howells as Critic, edited by Edwin H. Cady. 1973.

Editor, *Three Years in Chili,* by Mrs. C. B. Merwin. 1861; as *Chili Through American Spectacles,* n.d.

Editor, *Choice Autobiographies.* 8 vols., 1877–78.

Editor, with Thomas Sergeant Perry, *Library of Universal Adventure by Sea and Land.* 1888.

Editor, *Mark Twain's Library of Humor.* 1888.

Editor, *The Poems of George Pellew.* 1892.

Editor, *Recollections of Life in Ohio from 1813 to 1840,* by William Cooper Howells. 1895.

Editor, with Russell Sturgis, *Florence in Art and Literature.* 1901.

Editor, with Henry Mills Alden, *Southern Lights and Shadows* (stories). 1907.

Editor, *The Great Modern American Short Stories: An Anthology.* 1920.

Editor, *Don Quixote by Cervantes,* translated by Charles Jarvis. 1923.

Translator, *Venice, Her Art Treasures and Historical Associations: A Guide,* by Adalbert Müller. 1864.

Bibliography: *A Bibliography of Howells* by William M. Gibson and George Arms, 1948; in *Bibliography of American Literature* by Jacob Blanck, 1963.

Reading List: *The Road to Realism*, 1956, and *The Realist at War*, 1958, both by Edwin H. Cady; *Howells: His Life and World* by Van Wyck Brooks, 1959; *Howells: A Century of Criticism* edited by Kenneth E. Eble, 1962; *Howells and the Art of His Times* by Clara Marburg Kirk, 1965; *The Immense Complex Drama: The World and Art of the Howells Novel*, by George C. Carrington, Jr., 1966; *The Literary Realism of Howells* by William McMurray, 1967; *Howells* by William M. Gibson, 1967; *The Achievement of Howells* by Kermit Vanderbilt, 1968; *Howells: The Friendly Eye* by Edward Wagenknecht, 1969; *Howells: An American Life* by Kenneth S. Lynn, 1971; *The Realism of Howells* by George N. Bennett, 1973.

*   *   *

William Dean Howells's literary career was remarkable not only for its length and variousness but for its continuous and conscientious productivity. For more than fifty years, extending from the nineteenth well into the twentieth century, Howells appeared in print as a journalist, a poet, a sensitively observant but unsentimental traveler, a novelist, a playwright, a critic and a polemicist in the cause of realism (these last two functions merging in *Criticism and Fiction*), a publicist and explicator of foreign writers for an ill-informed American public, and the educator of that same public to the greatness of its own writers like James and Twain.

The experience behind this writing was also rich and varied, directly furnishing much of the material for the immense productivity. Moreover, it was an experience that had its public occasions, most notably Howells's outspoken opposition to the treatment of the Chicago anarchists in the Haymarket affair. Beneath the surface of a life that moved from midwestern printshops and newspapers through the consulship at Venice and the editorship of the *Atlantic* to the new center of literary activity in New York, and brought varied relationships with the literary giants of New England and deep literary and personal friendships with the new giants of American literature, James and Twain, there was profound personal experience: the challenge of Darwinian science to religious faith, and an increasing awareness of cultural dislocations, political corruptions, and economic inequities. Thus, Howells's writing became a permanently valuable record of a broad spectrum of the American literary, social, economic, religious, and moral experience. Even more importantly, in an impressive number of his fictions Howells achieved the transmutation of actual and vicarious experience into realistic art, met his own criterion of "dispersing the conventional acceptations by which men live on easy terms with themselves" without falling into the error of claiming thereby to have solved "the riddle of the painful earth."

Howells's relatively late decision to become a novelist kept him close to his own experience and to the unsophisticated literary devices in the early novels. The tentatively novelistic *Their Wedding Journey* stated his intention to deal with "poor Real life," but the pronouncement stemmed more from his distrust of his ability to manage a sustained narrative and his desire to employ the methods of the travel book than from a theory of realism. *A Chance Acquaintance* also employed the narrative structure of the journey, but it also developed a situation in which the moral spontaneity of an unsophisticated American girl (a portrait highly praised by James) served to reveal the stultifying snobbishness of a proper Bostonian, and, to the dissatisfaction of many, chose the "realistic" mode of an "unhappy" ending in which the girl rejected the ungentlemanly gentleman. Throughout this apprenticeship period, Howells continued to exploit the kind of confrontation labelled by Edwin H. Cady the "conventional-unconventional formula." He also put to use his own experience in summer boarding houses in *Mrs. Farrell* (serialized as *Private Theatricals*) and in pre-Jamesian versions of the international novel in *A Foregone Conclusion* and *The Lady of the Aroostook*. The former is often cited as a benchmark in the terrain of Howells's early novels because of its skillful dramatic development (a lesson learned from Turgenev) of a "tragic" involvement of an Italian priest and another of Howells's radically innocent American girls.

Beginning in 1880 with *The Undiscovered Country*, Howells's fiction began to take account of issues not easily confined within the limits of the novel of manners (the terminology most frequently applied to the pre- and post-"economic" fiction). That novel has begun to receive deserved attention as an original transformation of Hawthornian themes into a probing study of the problem of religious faith and as Howells's first major attempt to achieve a reconciliation of the American present with its past through a pastoral vision. It was followed by *A Modern Instance*, in any accounting, including Howells's own, one of his most penetrating studies of American life. In spite of general contemporary misunderstanding, it was a contemporary reviewer who noted that the novel was not an anti-divorce tract but "a demonstration of a state of society of which divorce was the index." As the novel expands from a brilliant study of the disintegration of a marriage through a failure of moral discipline, that state of society is depicted as one marked by the decay of vital religious faith, of family solidarity as the nexus of social stability, of the social ethic which is being displaced by purely commercial principles. *The Rise of Silas Lapham* also involves a questioning of American commercial society as Lapham's moral rise is achieved by the sacrifice of the materialistic success for which he very nearly sold his soul. It was so far, moreover, from being a mere comedy of manners – as many readers have termed it because of Lapham's attempts to gain entrance into Boston society and because of the apparent submergence of the moral issue to the romantic sub-plot (the relationship of the plots is a point of extensive critical debate) – that Howells suffered some kind of psychic breakdown in being confronted with the issues it raised: the degree and nature of his commitment to a democracy which included the Irish and Jews; his own relationship with proper Bostonians and New England literati, most of whom had little appreciation for the realistic art to which he had committed himself. The increasing doubts about the America about which he had once been thoroughly optimistic but which he came to feel, as he told James, was "coming out all wrong in the end" made him ripe for the reading of Tolstoy (begun in 1885) and for the expression of a newly open radicalism in the novels of the 1890's which Everett Carter has distinguished as works of "critical realism."

The most important of these was *A Hazard of New Fortunes*. It was preceded by *Annie Kilburn*, a demonstration of the Tolstoyan lesson of the necessity for "*justice* not *alms*" as the corrective for the economic and social ills of the polity. It was followed by *The Quality of Mercy*, an accusation of a system of which embezzlers were merely symptomatic, and *The World of Chance*, an examination of the malfunctioning or absence of causality in not only the business world but in all human involvements. Howells then abandoned the realistic novel as the vehicle of his socialistic ideas and turned to an openly dialectical form in two Altrurian (Utopian) romances.

The recovery of a "usable" Howells after a period in which he was the largely unread touchstone of timid gentility and Victorian morality for writers and critics like Sinclair Lewis and H. L. Mencken was directly due to the rediscovery of these two Utopias, with their socio-economic criticisms of American life. Critical debate continues today concerning their artistic quality and their significance to the totality of Howells's career: they have often been seen, even in approaches modified from the doctrinaire criticism of the 1930's, as marking the limit of Howells's artistic growth, and as evidencing a "tragic vision" absent from his other work (and shaped not only by Tolstoy but a number of profound personal experiences, including the hazard of his career in defense of the Haymarket anarchists and the protracted illness and agonizing death of his daughter). Consequently, his career has been seen as a growth through the comedy of manners to social realism to a unique critical realism and then a falling away. That falling away has been variously explained as simply an exhaustion of the creative impulse; as a failure of nerve in questioning the values and value of American society; as a recognition of his inability to provide solutions to the problems he examined; as a deliberate return to the intellectually and financially safe fiction of his earlier career. The complications of Howells's reputation can be seen in the various interpretations of *A Hazard of New*

Fortunes, a key novel. It has been seen variously as a comedy of manners, a symbolic myth of Christian atonement, a realistic tragedy, a treatise on aesthetics, and a combined "psychological" and "economic" novel.

After 1893, Howells still had twenty-seven years of productive life during which he published a dozen or so novels. Of these, almost half – *The Landlord at Lion's Head, The Kentons, The Son of Royal Langbrith, The Leatherwood God*, and the posthumous *The Vacation of the Kelwyns* – have, from various critical perspectives, been judged worthy to be included in the permanent Howells canon. If that canon is initiated by *A Modern Instance* – indeed, a case may be made for the earlier *A Foregone Conclusion* or *The Undiscovered Country* – the continuous excellence of Howells's realistic fiction throughout his career assures him an important place in the history of the development of American fiction. And, if there is added to that assessment his also continuous and influential role in his associations with the *Atlantic, Harper's*, and other journals, his importance as a *force* in American literature is difficult to overstate.

—George N. Bennett

HUDSON, W(illiam) H(enry).   British.   Born in Quilmes, near Buenos Aires, Argentina, 4 August 1841, of American parents; emigrated to England, 1869; naturalized, 1900. Served in the Argentinian Army, 1866. Married Emily Wingrave in 1877 (died, 1921). Naturalist: collected birds for the Smithsonian Institution and the London Zoological Society, 1866–69; settled in London, 1869, where he and his wife kept a series of unsuccessful boarding houses in Bayswater; began writing in 1880; lived in Westbourne Park, London, 1886–1921. Granted Civil List pension, 1901. Bird sanctuary erected in his memory, Hyde Park, London, 1925. *Died 18 August 1922.*

PUBLICATIONS

Collections

> *Works.*   7 vols., 1951–54.
> *Birds and Green Places: A Selection*, edited by P. E. Brown and P. H. T. Hartley.   1964.

Fiction

> *The Purple Land That England Lost: Travels and Adventures in the Banda Oriental, South America.*   1885.
> *A Crystal Age.*   1887.
> *Fan: The Story of a Young Girl's Life.*   1892.
> *El Ombú.*   1902; as *South American Sketches*, 1909; as *Tales of the Pampas*, 1916.
> *Green Mansions: A Romance of the Tropical Forest.*   1904.
> *A Little Boy Lost.*   1905.
> *Dead Man's Plack, and An Old Thorn.*   1920.

Other

Argentine Ornithology, with P. L. Sclater.   2 vols., 1888–89; shortened version, as Birds
of La Plata, 2 vols., 1920.
The Naturalist in La Plata.   1892.
Birds in a Village.   1893.
Idle Days in Patagonia.   1893.
British Birds, with Frank E. Beddard.   1895.
Birds in London.   1898.
Nature in Downland.   1900.
Birds and Man.   1901.
Hampshire Days.   1903.
The Land's End: A Naturalist's Impressions in West Cornwall.   1908.
Afoot in England.   1909.
A Shepherd's Life: Impressions of the South Wiltshire Downs.   1910.
Adventures among Birds.   1913.
Far Away and Long Ago: A History of My Early Life.   1918; revised edition, 1931.
Birds in Town and Village.   1919.
The Book of a Naturalist.   1919.
A Traveller in Little Things.   1921.
A Hind in Richmond Park, edited by Morley Roberts.   1922.
Collected Works.   24 vols., 1922–23.
Rare, Vanishing, and Lost British Birds, edited by Linda Gardiner.   1923.
153 Letters, edited by Edward Garnett.   1923; as Letters to Garnett, 1925.
Men, Books, and Birds, edited by Morley Roberts.   1925.
Letters to R. B. Cunninghame Graham, edited by Richard Curle.   1941.
Letters on the Ornithology of Buenos Ayres, edited by David R. Bewar.   1951.
Diary Concerning His Voyage from Buenos Aires to Southampton 1874, edited by Jorge
Cesares.   1958.

Bibliography: Hudson: A Bibliography by John R. Payne, 1976.

Reading List: Hudson by Robert Hamilton, 1946; Hudson's Reading by H. F. West, 1947;
From Pampas to Hedgerows and Downs: A Study of Hudson by R. E. Haymaker, 1954;
Hudson by Ruth Tomalin, 1954; Hudson by John T. Frederick, 1972.

*   *   *

W. H. Hudson was a prolific writer; his collected works ran to twenty-four volumes, and
did not include all his writings. But in spite of this large production Hudson's books fall into
no more than two main thematic categories, those in which he recalls the pampas of the
Argentine where he lived as a child and a young man, and those in which he records the rural
life of England seen through the eyes of a peripatetic field naturalist. There is an underlying
link between the two groups; in his wanderings through the less spoilt areas of the English
countryside Hudson – who detested urban civilisation – was seeking to recover the simplicity
and the pristine quality of life on the pampas.

Yet the writings relating to South America remain the most interesting of Hudson's works,
perhaps because they were written out of vivid memories that haunted the years of poverty
and solitude after Hudson came to England in 1874. They include an autobiographical
volume about childhood in Argentina (Far Away and Long Ago) and also Hudson's works of
fiction, The Purple Land, Green Mansions, and El Ombú.

Hudson did not think of himself as primarily a novelist; his chosen role was that of
naturalist, and he was a pioneer in agitating for the protection of species of wild birds which

he saw vanishing from the English countryside. But his few works of fiction have an artless power that comes from their being written in the kind of clear strong prose so many of the nineteenth-century naturalists used in the accounts of their travels.

The Purple Land is a narrative of revolution in Uruguay, and one has only to compare it with Conrad's *Nostromo*, which deals with a similar situation, to realize that Hudson was a simple tale-teller rather than a true novelist. The narrative is direct but without subtlety, and the book holds one's interest to the end mainly for its recreation of remembered scenes in vividly descriptive passages. There is the same kind of authenticity about the sketches of gaucho life collected in *El Ombú*; they are too simple to be classed as short stories, and yet they give the kind of vivid sense a good travel book might project of the cruelty and deprivation – and also the enviable freedom – of the gaucho life. Hudson's most ambitious and most imaginative work of fiction is *Green Mansions*, a romance about the jungles of Venezuela, to which Hudson had never been; in the character of the bird-girl Rima, a fairy-tale figure, it clearly projects Hudson's sense of the need to achieve some kind of harmony between man and the natural world. It is through its evocation of the feel and texture of the natural world that *Green Mansions* still appeals; Hudson did not have the inventive power to make its central fantasy convincing or to validate its pantheism.

—George Woodcock

HUGHES, Richard (Arthur Warren). English. Born in Weybridge, Surrey, 19 April 1900. Educated at Charterhouse School, Surrey; Oriel College, Oxford, B.A. 1922. Served in the British Army, 1918; in the Admiralty, London, 1940–45; O.B.E. (Officer, Order of the British Empire), 1946. Married Frances C. R. Bazley in 1932; five children. Co-Founder and Director, Portmadoc Players, Wales, 1922–25; Vice-Chairman, Welsh National Theatre, 1924–36; Petty Constable of Langharne, 1936; Filmwriter, Ealing Studios, London, 1945–55. Recipient: Femina Vie Heureuse Prize, 1929; Arts Council award, 1961; Welsh Arts Council award, 1973. D.Litt.: University of Wales, Cardiff, 1956. Fellow, Royal Society of Literature, 1962. Honorary Member, American Academy of Arts and Letters, 1963; gave Blashfield Foundation Address, 1969. *Died 28 April 1976.*

PUBLICATIONS

Fiction

A Moment of Time (stories).   1926.
A High Wind in Jamaica.   1929; as *The Innocent Voyage,* 1929.
Burial, and The Dark Child (verse and story).   1930.
In Hazard: A Sea Story.   1938.
The Human Predicament: The Fox in the Attic.   1961; *The Wooden Shepherdess,* 1973.

Plays

The Sisters' Tragedy (produced 1922).   1922.
The Man Born to Be Hanged (produced 1923).   In *The Sisters' Tragedy and Other Plays,* 1924.

A Comedy of Good and Evil (produced 1924; as *Minnie and Mr. Williams*, produced 1948). In *The Sisters' Tragedy and Other Plays*, 1924.
Danger (broadcast 1924). In *The Sisters' Tragedy and Other Plays*, 1924.
The Sisters' Tragedy and Three Other Plays. 1924; as *A Rabbit and a Leg: Collected Plays*, 1924; as *Plays*, 1966.

Screenplays: *A Run for Your Money*, with others, 1949; *The Divided Heart*, with Jack Whittingham, 1954.

Radio Play: *Danger*, 1924.

Verse

Lines Written upon First Observing an Elephant Devoured by a Roc. 1922.
Gipsy-Night and Other Poems. 1922.
Ecstatic Ode on Vision. 1923.
Meditative Ode on Vision. 1923.
Confessio Juvenis: Collected Poems. 1926.

Other

Hughes: An Omnibus. 1931.
The Spider's Palace and Other Stories (juvenile). 1931.
Don't Blame Me! and Other Stories (juvenile). 1940.
The Administration of War Production, with J. D. Scott. 1955.
Gertrude's Child (juvenile). 1966.
The Wonder-Dog: Collected Stories for Children. 1977.

Editor, with Robert Graves and Alan Porter, *Oxford Poetry 1921*. 1921.
Editor, *Poems*, by John Skelton. 1924.

Reading List: *Hughes* by Peter Thomas, 1973.

*   *   *

The first and most obvious feature of Richard Hughes's career as a novelist is the extreme paucity of his output. In more than fifty years as a professional writer he published only two novels and the magnificent torso of a third. The second feature is equally obvious. From novel to novel he was completely unpredictable, in a way that astonished. That he seemingly wrote so little is in part explained by the way he wrote. He was a perfectionist who sought perfection by constant rewriting, and as he rewrote, time and time again, so he reduced and eliminated. While writing his unfinished novel, *The Human Predicament*, of which two sections, *The Fox in the Attic* and *The Wooden Shepherdess*, were published, he would say that in order to finish it he would need to live to be 120.

The originality and brilliance of his first novel, *A High Wind in Jamaica*, were immediately recognised, and within a matter of years by general consent it was accorded classic status as a novel of childhood. Hughes shows his children as it were in experimental conditions. Emily Bas-Thornton and her brothers and sisters are kidnapped by pirates while sailing from Jamaica to England in the 1860's. The pirates are rendered no more conventionally than the children; they seem curiously reluctant pirates, the last pygmy remnants of a giant race, as much at the mercy of the children as the children are at theirs. But it is the presentation of the children that astonishes. Children, Hughes implies, are mad, and grown-ups have no more chance of "intellectual sympathy" with them than they have with animals. And this is brought out time and again in the kinship between children and animals, in the scene, for instance, in which Emily goes to sleep one night with a baby alligator for company. "Alligators," Hughes tells us, "are utterly untamable." The irony of the novel reaches its climax in the trial of the pirates at the Old Bailey. After almost fifty years, *A High Wind in Jamaica* remains curiously disconcerting. Reading it, one feels in the presence of fantasy; but it is not fantasy; children and pirates alike are too real and convincing for that. And the terror and violence are real too. There is a strange hallucinated quality, a quality of what has been called domesticated bizarreness.

Hughes's second novel, *In Hazard*, appeared after an interval of nine years and again its mastery was immediately recognised. Since it is a story of a battle with a hurricane it had to stand up to comparison with Conrad's *Typhoon*, which it does entirely successfully. Throughout the novel there is a Defoe-like quality which provides the book with its special ambience. As with Conrad, Hughes's real theme is not the storm as such but the human response to it. The novel is in essence a celebration of virtue in the old Roman, not the Victorian, sense, the conscious acceptance and practice of duty in terms of work. "Changing a jib in a stiff breeze is a microcosm, as it were, of saving a ship in a storm."

The novel enters another, quite unexpected dimension when Ao Ling, a young Chinese member of the crew is arrested and put in irons, for a mutiny of the Chinese crew is feared. He is arrested for the wrong reasons but he is indeed a Communist agitator wanted by the Hong Kong police. Hughes's sympathy for him is such that we are forced to realise that Ao Ling may well represent another variant of virtue.

The Human Predicament has to be considered as a fragment. Inspirations for the work came to Hughes when he was working in the Admiralty in London during the war; it was borne in on him that the war, its origins and consequences, was the only theme worth a novelist's attention. So, in Hughes's own words, it was to be "a historical novel of my own times." *The Fox in the Attic* begins in 1923 with a superbly written episode in the life of Augustine Penry-Herbert, a young Welsh squire just out of Oxford, haunted by the war he has so narrowly missed. Bewildered, innocent, uncomprehending, full of the vague liberal notions of the early 1920's he sets out to discover at first hand the "New Germany" of the Weimar Republic, and stays in the Bavarian castle of a remote cousin, some of whose occupants are caught up in the incipient Nazi movement. Absurdly, Augustine falls in love with his cousin Mitzi, who, almost blind, destined to be a nun, is almost unaware of him. Her life as a nun is touched upon in *The Wooden Shepherdess*, and it seems clear that the religious and spiritual life was to be no less the province of *The Human Predicament* than the secular and political.

What we have of the novel, however, is dominated by the historic figures and events that stalk through its midst, Hitler himself and Ludendorff mounting their seemingly farcical *putsch* in Munich, Hitler skulking half-crazed afterwards in the Hanfdtaengls' country cottage. It was Hughes's triumph as a historical novelist that the figures from history and the fictitious characters are equally convincing and in no sense in competition with one another, just as the renderings of life in rural Wales, England, New England and Germany ring with equal truth.

During the 1920's Hughes had some reputation as a poet; his collected poems, *Confessio Juvenis*, poems reminiscent of the early work of Robert Graves, with whom he was associated at Oxford, appeared in 1926. As a young man he was also prominent in the Welsh dramatic revival and his play, *A Comedy of Good and Evil*, set in rural Wales, was produced both in London and New York. His short play, *Danger*, was the first play specifically written for sound broadcasting to be produced by the BBC.

—Walter Allen

HUGHES, Thomas. English. Born in Uffington, Berkshire, 20 October 1822. Educated at Rugby School, 1834–42; Oriel College, Oxford, 1842–45 (played cricket for Oxford, 1842), B.A. 1845; entered Lincoln's Inn, London, 1845, migrated to the Inner Temple, and called to the Bar, 1848. Married Frances Ford in 1848; three sons and three daughters. Practised law in London from 1848: Queen's Counsel, 1869; associated with F. D. Maurice and the Christian Socialists who subsequently helped to create the co-operative movement: contributed to the *Christian Socialist* and *Tracts on Christian Socialism* and acted as Editor of the *Journal of Association*; Chairman of the first Co-operative Congress, 1869; helped to pass the Industrial and Provident Societies Act, 1893; involved in the founding of the Working Men's College, Great Ormond Street, London, 1854, and served as its Principal, 1872–83; Liberal Member of Parliament for Lambeth, 1865–68, and Frome, 1868–74; Founder Member of the Church Reform Union, 1870; established model community in Tennessee which proved unsuccessful, 1879; County Court Judge in Chester, 1882 until his death. *Died 22 March 1896.*

Publications

Fiction

Tom Brown's School Days, by an Old Boy. 1857; edited by Charles Swain Thomas, 1920.
The Scouring of the White Horse; or, The Long Vacation Ramble of a London Clerk. 1859.
Tom Brown at Oxford. 1861.

Other

History of the Working Tailors' Association. 1850.
Account of the Lock-Out of Engineers 1851–52. 1860.
Tracts for Priests and People. 1861.
The Cause of Freedom: Which Is Its Champion in America, The North or the South? 1863.
A Layman's Faith. 1868.
Alfred the Great. 3 vols., 1869.
Memoirs of a Brother. 1873.
The Old Church: What Shall We Do with It? 1878.
The Manliness of Christ. 1879.
True Manliness (selections), edited by E. E. Brown. 1880.
Rugby, Tennessee, Being Some Account of the Settlement Founded on the Cumberland Plateau by the Board of Aid to Land Ownership. 1881.
Memoir of Daniel Macmillan. 1882.
Life and Times of Peter Cooper. 1886.
James Fraser, Second Bishop of Manchester: A Memoir 1818–85. 1887.
David Livingstone. 1889.
Vacation Rambles. 1895.
Early Memories of Childhood. 1899.

Editor, *The Biglow Papers,* by James Russell Lowell. 1859.
Editor, *The Trades' Unions of England,* by Louis Philip d'Orleans. 1869.
Editor, *The Friendship of Books,* by F. D. Maurice. 1874.

609

Editor, with E. V. Neale, *A Manual for Co-Operators*.   1881.
Editor, *G.T.T.: Gone to Texas: Letters from Our Boys*.   1884.

Bibliography: *Charles Kingsley and Hughes: First Editions in the Library at Dormy House* by M. L. Parrish and B. K. Mann, 1936.

Reading List: *Hughes and His American Rugby* by M. B. Harmer, 1928; *Hughes: The Life of the Author of Tom Brown's School Days* by E. C. Mack and W. H. G. Armytage, 1953.

*   *   *

As a novelist Thomas Hughes is remembered for a single book. *Tom Brown's School Days* is an admirable work, written with fire and enthusiasm, presenting the reaction of an ordinary boy imbued with "animal life in its fullest measure, good nature and honest impulses, hatred of injustice and meanness, and thoughtlessness in its fullest measure," to the regime of Thomas Arnold, headmaster and reformer of Rugby, whose principles and ideals he barely understands, though he reverences him to the point of worship. From *Tom Brown* all later schoolboy literature sprang, though through the decades the Arnold ideal of Christian manliness became more and more distorted until it denoted just pluck and team-spirit – the aspects of schoolboy life that Dr. Arnold found so particularly distasteful and dangerous.

Tom Brown at Oxford never achieved such popularity. The *Saturday Review* called it a failure which gets "more dull, purposeless and depressing as it proceeds." We can read it now as a minor piece of social history, showing us university life in the 1840's, where the gentlemen commoners in their silk gowns and velvet caps dine aloof at High Table, where unpopular tutors are screwed into their rooms, and boisterous undergraduates play quoits with the college silver. It was the background presence of Dr. Arnold that had been the *raison d'être* of the *School Days*. There is no such figure to provide a solution to the problems that Tom Brown meets at Oxford. He finds it unsatisfying, a place where young men are tossed and left unsupervised and unoccupied to sow their wild oats, where the tradition of learning has largely departed leaving a vacuum for ordinary people such as himself who are not natural scholars, who feel distaste for the raffish dissipation of the idle rich, and who are not attracted to the High Church movement. Sport and mild Christian Socialism help to pass the time, but for Tom, as for the reader, the university year plods along wearily. Town and gown riots, fishing trips, boat races, and the lack-lustre romantic episodes are no substitute for the evocation of boyhood in the *School Days*; the warm friendships, the passionate hatreds, the hero-worship, and the Oxford personalities are pale shadows beside Harry East, Flashman, young Arthur.

The Scouring of the White Horse is even less successful – a sentimental lauding of the glories of the English countryside, where the manly, bluff, kindly squires work and play side by side with their loyal and devoted cottagers. Much of this is, in fact, an expansion of the earlier chapters of the *School Days*, which the far more powerful Rugby scenes tempt us to overlook.

—Gillian Avery

HUNEKER, James (Gibbons). American. Born in Philadelphia, Pennsylvania, 31 January 1860. Educated at Roth's Military Academy, Philadelphia, subsequently studied law; studied piano in Paris with Georges Mathias, and in New York City with Rafael Joseffy.

Teacher of piano at the National Conservatory, New York, 1886–98; Art Critic for the New York *Sun*, 1900–12; Music Critic for the New York *Times*, 1912–19, and the *Sun*, 1919–21. *Died 9 February 1921.*

PUBLICATIONS

Collections

> *Letters* and *Intimate Letters*, edited by Josephine Huneker. 2 vols., 1922–24.
> *Essays*, edited by H. L. Mencken. 1929.

Fiction

> *Melomaniacs* (stories). 1902.
> *Visionaries* (stories). 1905.
> *Painted Veils.* 1921.

Other

> *Mezzotints in Modern Music.* 1899.
> *Chopin: The Man and His Music.* 1900.
> *Overtones: A Book of Temperaments.* 1904.
> *Iconoclasts: A Book of Dramatists.* 1905.
> *Egoists: A Book of Supermen.* 1909.
> *Promenades of an Impressionist.* 1910.
> *Franz Liszt.* 1911.
> *The Pathos of Distance: A Book of a Thousand and One Moments.* 1913.
> *Old Fogy: His Musical Opinions and Grotesques.* 1913.
> *New Cosmopolis: A Book of Images.* 1915.
> *Ivory, Apes, and Peacocks.* 1915.
> *Unicorns.* 1917.
> *The Philharmonic Society of New York and Its Seventy-Fifth Anniversary: A Retrospect.* 1917(?).
> *The Steinway Collection of Paintings by American Artists.* 1919.
> *Bedouins; Mary Garden* (essays and stories). 1920.
> *Steeplejack* (autobiography). 2 vols., 1920.
> *Variations.* 1921.

> Music editions: *Forty Piano Compositions* by Chopin, 1902; *Forty Songs* by Brahms, 1903; *The Greater Chopin*, 1908; *Forty Songs* by Strauss, 1910; *Forty Songs* by Tchaikovsky, 1912; *Romantic Preludes and Studies for Piano*, 1919.

Bibliography: in *Bibliography of American Literature* by Jacob Blanck, 1963.

Reading List: *Huneker* by Benjamin DeCasseres, 1925; *Huneker, Critic of the Seven Arts* by Arnold T. Schwab, 1963.

*   *   *

James Huneker is probably America's most versatile critic. Beginning in the late 1880's as a music critic, he acquired an international reputation in the next fifteen years, especially for his writings on Chopin, Liszt, and Richard Strauss. The musical associations of Baudelaire, Gautier, Huysmans, George Moore, and others led him to their non-musical books and thus into literary criticism, of which his best book was *Egoists*. His deep interest in the new psychology quickly attuned him to the work of Ibsen, Strindberg, Shaw, Maeterlinck, Hauptmann, and Sudermann, and his *Iconoclasts* was the most brilliant study of these playwrights to appear in America.

Best known for popularizing contemporary or near-contemporary Continental writers, Huneker also singled out the best American novelists of his day – James, Howells, Wharton, Norris, Dreiser – and called attention to Whitman, Poe, Dickinson, and Robinson at a time when these poets were either vilified or ignored by many other critics. But his talent in detecting the most enduring of early twentieth-century American artists was most notably reflected, perhaps, in his praise of painters such as Bellows, Davies, Henri, Luks, Marin, Maurer, Prendergast, Shinn, and Sloan.

As a critic, Huneker was probably most comfortable, technically, in music (he had studied and taught piano) and least secure, despite his perspicacity, in art. Fond of anecdotes, puns, and parodies, he produced essays admired for their wit, humor, urbanity, and range. His tendency to dart from topic to topic, idea to idea, name to name, paying little attention to connecting links and logical development, sometimes made him seem superficial or irritating to those who valued clear, sustained reasoning above the picturesque phrase and the evocative association. But the staccato manner and the incessant allusions sprang from a mind richly loaded with gleanings from life and literature and quick with intuitive perception and sympathy. Not hesitating to pass judgment, in an undogmatic way, on artists of his own day, he was usually right: few of his swans turned out to be geese.

In his short stories – collected in *Melomaniacs, Visionaries,* and *Bedouins* – and in his one novel, *Painted Veils,* Huneker displayed the wide reading, powerful curiosity about the artist as a human being, the fascination with sexual or sensory abnormality, and the colorful, epigrammatic style reflected in his criticism. If the stories smack a bit too much of the grotesqueries of Hoffman and Poe, they achieve some originality in Huneker's attempt to penetrate and portray the emotional life of the musician. In coming to grips with sexual themes, he was clearly ahead of his time in his fiction as well as his criticism. His plots reveal his flair for the humorously bizarre, and touches of comic description accompany his lively imagination. If his skill in execution – especially in characterization and dialogue – had matched his inventive facility, Huneker might have become the outstanding writer of fiction he always wanted to be.

—Arnold T. Schwab

HUNT, (James Henry) Leigh.   English.   Born in Southgate, Middlesex, 19 October 1784. Educated at Christ's Hospital, London. Married Marianne Kent; seven children. Journalist for all of his life: contributor to the *Traveller,* before 1805; Editor, *The News,* 1805–07; contributor to the *Statesman,* 1806, and the *Times,* 1807; Editor, *The Examiner: A Sunday Paper,* 1808–21, and contributor until 1825; Editor, *The Reflector,* 1810–11; imprisoned for libelling the Prince Regent, 1813–15; Editor, *The Indicator,* 1819–21, and *The Literary Pocket-Book; or, Companion for the Lover of Nature and Art,* 1819–23; joined Shelley in Italy to establish *The Liberal: Verse and Prose from the South,* 1822; after Shelley's death lived with Byron at Pisa; returned to London, 1825; contributor to the *New Monthly Magazine,*

1825–26, and occasionally until 1850; Editor, *The Companion*, 1828; contributor to *Atlas*, 1828–30; Editor, *The Chat of the Week*, 1830, and *The Tatler: A Daily Journal of Literature and the Stage*, 1830–32; contributor to *True Sun* and *Weekly True Sun*, 1833–34; Editor, *Leigh Hunt's London Journal*, 1834–35, *The Monthly Repository*, 1837–38, and *Leigh Hunt's Journal*, 1850–51; Contributor to *Spectator*, 1858–59, and to the *Morning Chronicle* throughout his career. Granted Civil List pension, 1847. *Died 28 August 1859.*

PUBLICATIONS

Collections

Poetical Works, edited by H. S. Milford.   1923.

Fiction

Sir Ralph Esher; or, Adventures of a Gentleman of the Court of Charles II.   1832.
Tales, edited by William Knight.   1891.

Play

A Legend of Florence (produced 1840).   1840.

Verse

Juvenilia.   1801.
The Feast of the Poets and Other Pieces.   1814; revised edition, 1815.
The Descent of Liberty: A Mask.   1815.
The Story of Rimini.   1816.
Foliage; or, Poems Original and Translated.   1818.
Hero and Leander, and Bacchus and Ariadne.   1819.
Poetical Works.   3 vols., 1819; revised edition, 1832, 1844.
Amyntas: A Tale of the Woods, from the Italian of Tasso.   1820.
Ultra-Crepidarius · A Satire on William Gifford.   1823.
Bacchus in Tuscany: A Dithyrambic Poem, from the Italian of Redi.   1825.
Captain Sword and Captain Pen.   1835.
The Palfrey: A Love-Story of Old Times.   1842.
Stories in Verse Now First Collected.   1855.
Ballads of Robin Hood, edited by L. A. Brewer.   1922.

Other

Critical Essays on the Performers of the London Theatres.   1807.
An Attempt to Show the Folly and Danger of Methodism.   1809.
The Prince of Wales v. The Examiner: A Full Report of the Trial of John and Leigh Hunt.   1812.
The Reflector (periodical, 1810–11).   2 vols., 1812.
Musical Copyright: Whitaker Versus Hume.   1816.

The Round Table: A Collection of Essays on Literature, Men, and Manners, with William Hazlitt.   2 vols., 1817.
The Months, Descriptive of the Successive Beauties of the Year.   1821; edited by R. H. Bath, 1929.
The Indicator.   1822.
Lord Byron and Some of His Contemporaries.   1828; revised edition, 1828.
Christianism; or, Belief and Unbelief Reconciled, edited by John Forster.   1832; revised edition, as *The Religion of the Heart*, 1853.
The Indicator and The Companion: A Miscellany for the Fields and Fireside.   2 vols., 1834.
Hunt's London Journal 1834–35.   2 vols., 1834–35.
The Seer; or, Commonplaces Refreshed.   2 vols., 1840–41.
Imagination and Fancy, with an Essay in Answer to the Question What Is Poetry?   1844; edited by Edmund Gosse, 1907.
Stories from the Italian Poets.   2 vols., 1846.
Men, Women, and Books.   2 vols., 1847.
A Jar of Honey from Mount Hybla.   1848.
The Town: Its Memorable Characters and Events.   2 vols., 1848.
Autobiography.   3 vols., 1850; revised edition, 1860; edited by J. E. Morpurgo, 1949; *The Earliest Sketches* edited by Stephen F. Fogle, 1959.
Table Talk.   1851.
The Old Court Suburb; or, Memorials of Kensington.   2 vols., 1855; revised edition, 1855.
A Saunter Through the West End.   1861.
Correspondence, edited by Thornton Hunt.   2 vols., 1862.
A Tale for a Chimney Corner and Other Essays, edited by E. Ollier.   1869.
A Day by the Fire and Other Papers Hitherto Uncollected, edited by J. E. Babson.   1870.
The Wishing-Cap Papers, Now First Collected, edited by J. E. Babson.   1873.
Essays and Poems, edited by R. B. Johnson.   2 vols., 1891.
Dramatic Essays, edited by William Archer and R. W. Lowe.   1894.
The Love of Books, edited by L. A. and E. T. Brewer.   1923.
Marginalia, edited by L. A. Brewer.   1926.
Prefaces, Mainly to His Periodicals, edited by R. B. Johnson.   1927.
My Hunt Library: The Holograph Letters, edited by L. A. Brewer.   1938.
The Dissidence of Dissent (Monthly Repository 1837–38), edited by F. E. Mineka.   1944.
Dramatic Criticism, Literary Criticism, and *Political and Occasional Essays*, edited by L. H. and C. W. Houtchens.   3 vols., 1949–62.
Musical Evenings; or, Selections, Vocal and Instrumental, edited by David R. Cheney.   1964.
Hunt on Eight Sonnets of Dante, edited by D. Rhodes.   1965.

Editor, *Classic Tales, Serious and Lively, with Critical Essays.*   5 vols., 1806–07.
Editor, *The Masque of Anarchy*, by Shelley.   1832.
Editor, *The Dramatic Works of Sheridan.*   1840.
Editor, *The Dramatic Works of Wycherley, Congreve, Vanbrugh, and Farquhar.*   1840.
Editor, with R. H. Horne, *The Poems of Chaucer Modernized.*   1841.
Editor, *One Hundred Romances of Real Life.*   1843.
Editor, *The Foster Brothers: A Tale of the Wars of Chiozza*, by Thornton Hunt.   3 vols., 1845.
Editor, *Wit and Humour, Selected from the English Poets.*   1846.
Editor, with J. B. Syme, *Readings for Railways.*   2 vols., 1849–53.
Editor, *A Book for a Corner.*   1849.
Editor, *Beaumont and Fletcher* (selections).   1855.
Editor, with S. Adams Lee, *The Book of the Sonnet.*   2 vols., 1867.

Reading List: *Hunt and His Circle* by Edmund Blunden, 1930; *Hunt* by Louis Landré, 1936 (includes bibliography); *Byron, Shelley, Hunt, and The Examiner* by W. H. Marshall, 1960.

*   *   *

It is impossible to ignore Leigh Hunt, yet it is uncommonly difficult to "place" his contribution to Literature. He was a splendidly competent editor whose journals failed to realise their potential. He was an essayist overshadowed by Lamb, a critic overshadowed by Hazlitt and a poet overshadowed by Shelley, Byron, Keats, Wordsworth, and Tennyson among others. As a reformer he had the moral courage to accept imprisonment for his views and to remain true to his beliefs. His only reward for this was a Civil List pension when the party of "Reform" became the government.

Dickens pilloried him as Skimpole in *Bleak House*, drawing him as "a sentimentalist, brilliant, vivacious and engaging, but thoroughly selfish and unprincipled." Byron thought him boring and prosaic, yet Shelley considered him "gentle, honourable, innocent and brave" and Carlyle made no bones about referring to him as "a Man of Genius." The Victorians over-praised his verse; today it appears the work of a competent man-of-letters. There is no doubting the generosity of his critical judgement even though the sceptic might claim that he picked winners by backing every horse in the race. It was his lack of judgement in supporting his claims which was damaging, the indiscriminate nature of his enthusiasm.

Nevertheless he has left at least one book of considerable interest. Carlyle rated *The Autobiography of Leigh Hunt* as "by far the best book of the autobiographic kind ... in the English language," and it is likely to remain his most lasting achievement. It is a surprisingly cool look at literature, politics, and society by a man who knew most of the literary figures of the first half of the nineteenth century. It is written with charm and perception and it is, as J. E. Morpurgo has rightly said, "a magnificently arranged selection of journalistic writing."

He has been called a hack. If his response to the need to provide for himself and his family lays him open to this charge, he was surely the most splendid hack in literary journalism.

—John Stuart Williams

HURSTON, Zora Neale. American. Born in Eatonville, Florida, 7 January 1903. Educated at a primary school in Eatonville; Morgan Academy of Morgan College, Baltimore, graduated 1921; Howard University, Washington, D.C., 1924–26; Barnard College, New York, 1926–28, B.A. 1928. Researcher in American folklore (Rosenwald Foundation grant), 1928–32; writer from 1932; researcher in Haiti and the British West Indies (Guggenheim Fellowship), 1936–38; subsequently Professor of Drama, North Carolina College for Negroes. Recipient: Anisfield Wolf Award, 1943; Howard University Alumni Award, 1943. Litt.D.: Morgan State College, Baltimore, 1939. *Died 28 January 1960.*

PUBLICATIONS

Fiction

Jonah's Gourd Vine. 1934.
Their Eyes Were Watching God. 1937.
Moses, Man of the Mountain. 1939.
Seraph on the Suwanee. 1948.

Play

> *The First One*, in *Ebony and Topaz: A Collectanea*, edited by Charles S. Johnson. 1927.

Other

> *Mules and Men.* 1935.
> *Tell My Horse.* 1938; as *Voodoo Gods: An Inquiry into Native Myths and Magic in Jamaica and Haiti.* 1939.
> *Dust Tracks on a Road: An Autobiography.* 1942.

> Editor, *Caribbean Melodies.* 1947.

Reading List: *In A Minor Chord* (on Hurston, Cullen and Toomer) by Darwin T. Turner, 1971; *Hurston: A Literary Biography* by Robert E. Hemenway, 1977.

*   *   *

The leading fact about Zora Neale Hurston is her identification with black folklore. She spent her childhood in the black town of Eatonville, Florida. As a student in anthropology, she recorded the oral literature of the black South and Caribbean, and her best writing employs the intangible artifacts of traditional culture. Yet the preoccupation with folk life had ambivalence. As Robert E. Hemenway has shown, she experienced conflict between her role as a scientific observer of culture and the need to express her feelings as an intuitive participant. She never denied the value of science, but eventually art alone claimed her talents.

Art, however, had its own ambivalence. For, while the substance of Hurston's work derived from spontaneous folk life, she was, of course, a deliberate literary writer. *Mules and Men* represents an early effort to resolve the consequent aesthetic problem. In it Hurston adapts folklore to the requirements of written literature by creating a persona and framing folktales in the context of a return home. This structure provides readers with a sense of entry into the community. One feels a privileged listener, but it must be remembered that one actually hears Hurston's selectively condensed version of the tales. Several years later, in *Moses, Man of the Mountain*, Hurston's confidence in her ability to reshape folk matter permitted her to assume the role openly. Taking as her premise the traditional parallel between the children of Israel and enslaved Africans she synthesizes legends and images to establish Moses as a humanized Afro-American.

Still more literary ways of using folk life appear in *Jonah's Gourd Vine* and *Their Eyes Were Watching God*. The first book presents as its central figure a preacher endowed with magnificent command of poetic language who thereby typifies the creativity of folk culture. At the same time he is morally flawed by a sexual drive that continually brings him low. Possibly through this flaw Hurston meant to create a tragic figure, but there can be no doubt that with the preacher's wife she touched the theme of her most distinguished book. *Their Eyes Were Watching God*, a novel about Janie Crawford's disappointing marriages and exhilirating love affair with the ebullient Tea Cake fully merges author and folk subject. The theme of a woman struggling to realize herself was inevitable for a female artist as independent as Hurston. That Janie becomes free within the culture of the black South, however, represents both a social and an aesthetic resolution. The social resolution appears as preference for black cultural values despite shortcomings, the aesthetic resolution as the assimilation of folk to the consciousness of a modern artist.

—John M. Reilly

HUXLEY, Aldous (Leonard).   English.   Born in Godalming, Surrey, 26 July 1894; son of the scientist T. H. Huxley; brother of the scientist and writer Julien Huxley. Educated at Hillside School, Godalming, 1903–08; Eton College, 1908–13; Balliol College, Oxford, 1913–15, B.A. (honours) in English 1915. Married 1) Maria Nys in 1919 (died, 1955); 2) Laura Archera in 1956; one son. Worked in the War Office, 1917; taught at Eton College, 1918; member of the editorial staff of the *Athenaeum*, London, 1919–20; Drama Critic, *Westminster Gazette*, 1920–21; full-time writer from 1921; travelled and lived in France, Italy, and the United States, 1923–37; settled in California, 1937, and worked as a free-lance screenwriter. Recipient: American Academy of Arts and Letters Award, 1959. Companion of Literature, Royal Society of Literature, 1962. *Died 22 November 1963.*

PUBLICATIONS

Collections

The World of Huxley: An Omnibus of His Fiction and Non-Fiction over Three Decades, edited by Charles J. Rolo.   1947.
Letters, edited by Grover Smith.   1969.
Collected Poetry, edited by Donald Watt.   1971.

Fiction

Limbo (stories).   1920.
Crome Yellow.   1921.
Mortal Coils (stories).   1922.
Antic Hay.   1923.
Little Mexican and Other Stories.   1924; as *Young Archimedes,* 1924.
Those Barren Leaves.   1925.
Two or Three Graces and Other Stories.   1926.
Point Counter Point.   1928.
Brief Candles: Stories.   1930.
Brave New World.   1932.
Eyeless in Gaza.   1936.
After Many a Summer.   1939; as *After Many a Summer Dies the Swan,* 1939.
Twice Seven: Fourteen Selected Stories.   1944.
Time Must Have a Stop.   1944.
Ape and Essence.   1948.
The Genius and the Goddess.   1955.
Collected Short Stories.   1957.
Island.   1962.
The Crows of Pearblossom (juvenile).   1967.

Plays

The Discovery, from the play by Frances Sheridan (produced 1924).   1924.
The World of Light (produced 1931).   1931.
The Giocanda Smile, from his own story (produced 1948).   1948; as *Mortal Coils,* 1948.

Screenplays: *Pride and Prejudice,* with Jane Murfin, 1940; *Jane Eyre,* with John Houseman and Robert Stevenson, 1944; *A Woman's Vengeance,* 1947.

Verse

The Burning Wheel. 1916.
Jonah. 1917.
The Defeat of Youth and Other Poems. 1918.
Leda. 1920.
Selected Poems. 1925.
Arabia Infelix and Other Poems. 1929.
The Cicadas and Other Poems. 1931.
Verses and a Comedy. 1946.

Other

On the Margin: Notes and Essays. 1923.
Along the Road: Notes and Essays of a Tourist. 1925.
Essays New and Old. 1926.
Jesting Pilate: The Diary of a Journey. 1926.
Proper Studies. 1927.
Do What You Will: Essays. 1929.
Holy Face and Other Essays. 1929.
Vulgarity in Literature: Digressions from a Theme. 1930.
Music at Night and Other Essays. 1931.
Rotunda (selection). 1932.
Retrospect (selection). 1933.
Beyond the Mexique Bay. 1934.
The Olive Tree and Other Essays. 1936.
What Are You Going to Do about It? The Case for Reconstructive Peace. 1936.
Stories, Essays, and Poems. 1937.
*Ends and Means: An Enquiry into the Nature of Ideals and into the Methods Employed for
    Their Realization.* 1937.
The Most Agreeable Vice. 1938.
Words and Their Meanings. 1940.
Gray Eminence: A Study in Religion and Politics. 1941.
The Art of Seeing. 1942.
The Perennial Philosophy. 1945.
Science, Liberty, and Peace. 1946.
Food and People, with John Russell. 1949.
Prisons, with the Carceri Etchings by Piranesi. 1949.
Themes and Variations. 1950.
The Devils of Loudun. 1952.
Joyce the Artificer: Two Studies of Joyce's Methods, with Stuart Gilbert. 1952.
A Day in Windsor, with J. A. Kings. 1953.
The Doors of Perception. 1954.
Adonis and the Alphabet, and Other Essays. 1956; as *Tomorrow and Tomorrow and
    Tomorrow and Other Essays,* 1956.
Heaven and Hell. 1956.
Brave New World Revisited. 1958.
Collected Essays. 1959.
On Art and Artists, edited by Morris Philipson. 1960.

Selected Essays, edited by Harold Raymond.   1961.
Literature and Science.   1963.
The Politics of Ecology: The Question of Survival.   1963.
Moksha: Writings on Psychedelics and the Visionary Experience (1953–1963), edited by Michael Horowitz and Cynthia Palmer.   1976.
The Human Situation: Lectures at Santa Barbara 1959, edited by Piero Ferrucci.   1977.

Editor, with W. R. Childe and T. W. Earp, *Oxford Poetry 1916.*   1916.
Editor, *Texts and Pretexts: An Anthology with Commentaries.*   1932.
Editor, *The Letters of D. H. Lawrence.*   1932.
Editor, *An Encyclopedia of Pacifism.*   1937.

Translator, *A Virgin Heart*, by Rémy de Gourmont.   1921.
Translator, *L'Apres-Midi d'un Faune*, by Mallarmé.   1956.

Bibliography: *Huxley: A Bibliography 1916–59* by Claire J. Eschelbach and Joyce Lee Shober, 1961; supplement by Thomas D. Clarson and Carolyn S. Andrews, in *Extrapolation 6*, 1964.

Reading List: *Huxley: A Literary Study* by J. A. Atkins, 1956, revised edition, 1967; *Huxley: A Study of the Major Novels* by Peter Bowering, 1968; *Huxley: Satire and Structure* by Jerome Meckier, 1969; *Huxley* by Harold H. Watts, 1969; *Dawn and the Darkest Hour: A Study of Huxley* by George Woodcock, 1972; *Huxley* (biography) by Sybille Bedford, 2 vols., 1973–74; *Huxley: A Collection of Critical Essays* edited by Robert E. Kuehn, 1974; *Huxley: The Critical Heritage* edited by Donald Watt, 1975; *The Timeless Moment: A Personal View of Huxley* by Laura Huxley, 1975.

*   *   *

One of the most unexpected turns of literary fortune during the present century has been the sharp decline in the repute of Aldous Huxley, who in the 1920's and even the 1930's appeared to be one of the most important modern writers. The process cannot be blamed on posterity; it began during Huxley's lifetime. Nor was it entirely due to the diminution in quality of his final novels and novellas, like *Island* or *The Genius and the Goddess*, or to the fact that in his later years he turned towards mysticism, experimentation with drugs, and environmentalism, for these are the very interests that have burgeoned in recent years among the young. Rather it was due to a lapse of interest in the kind of novels on which he made his name and which he wrote during his most productive period, the elaborate novels of manners which carried the ironic viewpoint and the conversational brilliance of Thomas Love Peacock's heritage into the modern age. It was not that Huxley's novels fell into total neglect, for they are still reprinted; but their standing in comparison with – say – those of Huxley's friend and contemporary D. H. Lawrence has fallen so notably that Huxley appears as a minor novelist of limited scope rather than the major novelist which, on the strength of books like *Eyeless in Gaza* and *Point Counter Point*, many of his contemporaries imagined him to be.

Huxley's earliest novels, *Crome Yellow, Antic Hay*, and *Those Barren Leaves*, are populated with writers, artists, intellectuals, and the inhabitants of the wealthy and degenerate quasi-bohemia that patronized artists in the 1920's and provided a background of large houses in the country and in Italy, of clubs and cafes, of fashionably artistic events. It is a milieu to which the sharp, cynical pattern of conversation devised by Peacock can be admirably adapted, and Huxley does it with great verve and gaiety, adding interest by introducing – under the thinnest disguises – well-known people of the real artistic world

(Bertrand Russell, Lawrence, Lady Ottoline Morrell) and not neglecting at appropriate times to remind us of the skull beneath the laughing face, for evil is as much talked about as good, and the gayer a character appears the more tragic his true predicament is likely to be. These early novels are brilliantly written and acerbically intelligent without being profound, and the glittering surface tends to disguise the fact that the characters are less substantial than the ideas they express. Even when they are shown from the inside, the ironic view is at work, and we tend to laugh at or to pity them rather than to feel with them.

As Huxley moves into deeper philosophic speculation, and hence into a graver kind of fiction, more direct in its moral criticism, more searching in its enquiries into human destiny, the deficiencies in Huxley's creative power become evident. He cannot invent a structure that will carry great moral themes; he does not have the kind of generative empathy that creates the characters to live through great moral battles; and so even the most ambitious of his books, *Point Counter Point* and *Eyeless in Gaza*, though they impressively unmask the social pretences of Huxley's world, appear as noble failures in comparison with the novels of, say, Dostoevsky, whom Huxley at this period sought to emulate. Indeed, insofar as these novels were tendentious, they seemed to be self-defeating, since they tended to project a Yeatsian situation where "The best lack all conviction, while the worst/Are full of passionate intensity."

The novels that followed *Eyeless in Gaza*, like *After Many a Summer* and *Time Must Have a Stop*, show a progressive decline, since they lose the verbal brilliance of the earlier works, and are inhabited by puppets who merely expound varying aspects of Huxley's philosophic and moral speculations. The only novel that Huxley published after the 1920's which still retains a considerable appeal is *Brave New World*, a brilliant utopia-in-reverse where the somewhat synthetic quality of the characters seems appropriate to the fantasy vision of the future that is Huxley's warning to modern man.

—George Woodcock

HYDE, Robin. Pseudonym for Iris Guiver Wilkinson. New Zealander. Born in Cape Town, South Africa, 19 January 1906; emigrated to New Zealand, with her family, as an infant. Educated at Berhampore School, Wellington; Wellington Girls' College; Victoria College, Wellington. Had two children. Staff Member, *Dominion*, Wellington, 1923–26; thereafter worked as a free-lance writer and journalist; Editor, *New Zealand Observer*, 1931–33; lived in China, 1938; settled in England, 1938. *Died* (by suicide) *23 August 1939*.

PUBLICATIONS

Fiction

Passport to Hell: The Story of James Douglas Stark. 1936.
Check to Your King: The Life History of Charles, Baron de Thierry. 1936.
Wednesday's Children. 1937.
Nor the Years Condemn. 1938.
The Godwits Fly. 1938.

Verse

The Desolate Star and Other Poems. 1929.
The Conquerors and Other Poems. 1935.

Persephone in Winter. 1937.
Houses by the Sea and the Later Poems. 1952.

Other

Journalese (reminiscences). 1934.
Dragon Rampant: Reminiscences of the Sino-Japanese War. 1939.

Reading List: *Hyde* by Gloria Rawlinson, 1978.

*   *   *

Robin Hyde was one of the first to explore the New Zealand experience as a poet, novelist and journalist. The mid-1930's marked a transition from the colonial outlook to a growing sense of national identity, and Robin Hyde's place in this context is as vital as it was individualistic. Her prose style, evolved from a diversity of talents and attitudes, is notable for its idiosyncratic blend of poetic imagery, humour, compassionate insight, and journalistic sense of pace. Her present reputation rests largely on two books, *Check to Your King* and *The Godwits Fly*, and a number of anthologised poems.

Check to Your King remains a unique contribution to antipodean history as the first, and to date only, full-length biography of that quixotic character, Charles, Baron de Thierry. De Thierry came to New Zealand in 1837 to claim the 40,000 acre property he had purchased in 1822 through an obliging missionary. Here he intended to found a Utopia for English settlers and Maori people alike, with himself as Sovereign Chief. The collapse of his dreams is told with Robin Hyde's own mixture of humour and sympathy in a narrative that weaves 20th-century hindsight into the 19th-century background. *The Godwits Fly* was acknowledged by Robin Hyde as autobiographical. Eliza Hannay is the central character in this poetic but often acidulous story of suburban life in New Zealand. Eliza's childhood, schooldays, love affairs, and traumatic experience as a single girl escaping to Australia for the birth of a still-born child, are all vividly related. But for most readers Eliza's story is somewhat up-staged by the brilliant portraits of the Hannay parents, the socialistic father and ultra-conservative mother, within whose domestic arena are fought out the social and political arguments that continue to plague our troubled century.

Robin Hyde's other books bear witness to her versatile outlook. *Passport to Hell* recounts the early life of John Douglas Stark, a teenage Bomber in World War I. The often brutal frankness of this book still shocks even post-World War II critics. *Wednesday's Children*, by contrast, mingles shrewd humour and tenderness in its fantasy story of a lonely spinster's dreamed-up children. Robin Hyde's last book, *Dragon Rampant*, relates her travels and experiences in China during the 1938 phase of the Sino-Japanese War, including a horrific account of her life in, and escape from, the Japanese-occupied city of Hsuchowfu.

Robin Hyde's poetry had its own distinctive voice, despite the early influences of Shelley, Yeats, and the Georgian poets. She was hostile to the intellectualism of the 1930's, but even so extended her language and imagery to meet the challenge of modernism, and her own increasing consciousness of the "New Zealand experience." The result was such notable poems as "Thirsty Land," "Journey from New Zealand," and the evocative sequence "Houses by the Sea." Her travels in China also inspired some memorable poems, including a poignant essay on inter-cultural relationships, "What Is It Makes the Stranger?," which has been described by Allen Curnow (in his Introduction to *The Penquin Book of New Zealand Verse*) as "that best of poems by a New Zealander on a pilgrimage of self-discovery."

—Gloria Rawlinson

INCHBALD, Elizabeth (née Simpson). English. Born in Stanningfield, near Bury St. Edmunds, Suffolk, 15 October 1753. Married the actor and painter Joseph Inchbald in 1772 (died, 1779). Settled in London, 1772; debut as an actress, playing opposite her husband, Bristol, 1772; subsequently appeared in various Scottish towns, 1772–76, various English towns, 1776–78, and under Tate Wilkinson in Yorkshire, 1778–80; appeared on the London stage, 1780 until her retirement, 1789. *Died 1 August 1821.*

PUBLICATIONS

Fiction

> *A Simple Story.* 1791; edited by J. M. S. Tompkins, 1967.
> *Nature and Art.* 1796; edited by W. B. Scott, 1886.

Plays

> *A Mogul Tale; or, The Descent of the Balloon* (produced 1784). 1788.
> *I'll Tell You What* (produced 1785). 1786.
> *Appearance Is Against Them* (produced 1785). 1785.
> *The Widow's Vow,* from a play by Patrat (produced 1786). 1786.
> *Such Things Are* (produced 1787). 1788.
> *The Midnight Hour; or, War of Wits,* from a play by Dumaniant (produced 1787). 1787.
> *All on a Summer's Day* (produced 1787).
> *Animal Magnetism* (produced 1788). 1788(?).
> *The Child of Nature,* from a play by Mme. de Genlis (produced 1788). 1788.
> *The Married Man,* from a play by Philippe Néricault-Destouches (produced 1789). 1789.
> *The Hue and Cry,* from a play by Dumaniant (produced 1791).
> *Next Door Neighbours,* from plays by L. S. Mercier and Philippe Néricault-Destouches (produced 1791). 1791.
> *Young Men and Old Women,* from a play by Gresset (produced 1792).
> *Every One Has His Fault* (produced 1793). 1792; edited by Allardyce Nicoll in *Lesser English Comedies of the Eighteenth Century,* 1931.
> *The Wedding Day* (produced 1794). 1794.
> *Wives as They Were and Maids as They Are* (produced 1797). 1797.
> *Lovers' Vows,* from a play by Kotzebue (produced 1798). 1798.
> *The Wise Men of the East,* from a play by Kotzebue (produced 1799). 1799.
> *To Marry, or Not to Marry* (produced 1805). 1805.
> *The Massacre* and *A Case of Conscience,* in *Memoirs of Mrs. Inchbald* by James Boaden. 2 vols., 1833.

Other

> Editor, *The British Theatre; or, A Collection of Plays with Biographical and Critical Remarks.* 25 vols., 1808.
> Editor, *A Collection of Farces and Other Afterpieces.* 7 vols., 1809.
> Editor, *The Modern Theatre.* 10 vols., 1809.

Bibliography: "An Inchbald Bibliography" by George L. Joughlin, in *Studies in English*, 1934.

Reading List: *Memoirs of Mrs. Inchbald* by James Boaden, 2 vols., 1833; *Inchbald and Her Circle* by Samuel R. Littlewood, 1921; *Inchbald, Novelist* by William MacKee, 1935; *Inchbald et la Comédie "Sentimentale" Anglaise au XVIII Siècle* by Françoise Moreux, 1971.

*   *   *

"Now Mrs. Inchbald was all heart," said James Boaden, her biographer, and the statement is as true of her writings as of her life. It is not the whole truth, of course; Boaden's memoir bears ample evidence of her independent spirit, her chasteness of mind and morals, her political liberalism, her candour, and her ardent and life-long pursuit of intellectual self-improvement. These too went to shape her plays and novels. Her plays reveal a fairly constant moral interest, combined with concern for domestic virtues set against the temptations of fashionable society, and working on the conventions of sentimental comedy and the social, scientific, religious, political, and literary topics of the day. She kept well abreast of changing theatrical tastes in the last two decades of the century, but constantly strove to give her slender subjects, complicated plots, and conventional characters some serious moral content. So, as the writer of an epilogue to one of her adaptations from French put it, her version had "the merit/Of giving Gallic Froth – true BRITISH SPIRIT." Her dramas, even those taken from French or German originals (such as Kotzebue's *Lovers' Vows*), were made her own not so much by their themes or techniques as by her thorough subordination of her borrowed materials to her personal version of the moral and aesthetic values of the time. As J. Taylor put it in his prologue to her last play, *To Marry or Not to Marry*, "In all, her anxious hope was still to find,/Some useful moral for the feeling mind."

Her novels were her real achievement, however, and to them she devoted the painstaking care of the conscious artist. These fictions carry many of the same themes and techniques as her plays, and her skill at stagecraft is everywhere apparent in dialogue and the management of scenes, but what she adds in her novels to the technical proficiency of the experienced playwright is an acutely observed sentimental realism. For in both her novels, but especially in the first, *A Simple Story*, can be felt the pressure of autobiography, of the many hours the young woman, wife, and widow had devoted not just to study, but to reflection, and to the practice of that candour which was self-knowledge. From her knowledge of herself, combined with her varied social experience, and informed by her reading in moral writers of all kinds, came that authenticity of psychological observation which made her novels so admired by the likes of William Godwin and Maria Edgeworth. For her, as for so many of the women writers of her day, moral education, the chastening of sensibility by experience, reflection, reason, and reading, was the basic form to be sought in life. In her first novel this form is given all the symmetry, deployed through parallels and contrasts in plot, character, and incident, that could be expected from a kind, even a fictitious kind, of moral discourse. In her second novel, moral education is made more of a public issue, diffused into a satire on the institutions of society, but still shaped by the kind of antithesis represented by the novel's title, *Nature and Art*. Autobiography and moral and social issues are not separate in her novels, then, but fused successfully in fictional form. It was this achievement that won her novels admiration in her own day, and makes them still worth reading now.

—Gary Kelly

INGRAHAM, Joseph Holt. American. Born in Portland, Maine, 25 January 1809. Possibly educated at Bowdoin College, Brunswick, Maine. Married Mary Brooks in 1849; three daughters and one son, the writer Prentiss Ingraham. Teacher at Jefferson College, Washington, Mississippi; writer of romances from 1835; established a girls school at

Nashville, Tennessee, 1849; began theological studies: ordained deacon, 1851, and priest, 1852, in the Protestant Episcopal Church, and thereafter wrote only books with religious themes; missionary in Aberdeen, Mississippi, 1852–54; Rector, St. John's Church, Mobile, Alabama, 1855–58, and Christ Church, Holly Springs, Mississippi, 1859 until his death. *Died 18 December 1860.*

PUBLICATIONS

Fiction

Lafitte, The Pirate of the Gulf. 1836; as *The Pirate,* 1839.
Burton; or, The Sieges. 1838; as *Quebec and New York; or, The Three Beauties,* 1839.
Captain Kyd; or, The Wizard of the Sea. 1839; as *Kyd the Buccaneer,* 1839.
The American Lounger; or, Tales, Sketches, and Legends Gathered in Sundry Journeyings. 1839.
The Quadroone; or, St. Michael's Day. 1840.
The Dancing Feather; or, The Amateur Freebooters: A Romance of New York. 1842; as *The Pirate Schooner,* 1877.
Edward Austin; or, The Hunting Flask: A Tale of the Forest and Town. 1842.
The Gipsy of the Highlands; or, The Jew and the Heir. 1843.
Jemmy Daily; or, The Little News Vender. 1843.
Morris Graeme; or, The Cruise of the Sea-Slipper: A Sequel to The Dancing Feather. 1843.
Fanny H——; or, The Hunchback and the Roué. 1843.
Mark Manly; or, The Skipper's Lad: A Tale of Boston in the Olden Times. 1843.
Frank Rivers; or, The Dangers of the Town. 1843.
The Young Genius; or, Trials and Triumphs. 1843.
Howard; or, The Mysterious Disappearance: A Romance of the Tripolitanian War. 1843.
Black Ralph; or, The Helmsman of Hurlgate. 1844.
Theodore; or, The Child of the Sea, Being a Sequel to Lafitte. 1844.
Rodolphe in Boston! 1844.
Billy Woodhull; or, The Pretty Haymaker. 1844.
The Corsair of Casco Bay; or, The Pilot's Daughter. 1844.
Ellen Hart; or, The Forger's Daughter. 1844.
The Miseries of New York; or, The Burglar and Counsellor. 1844.
Steel Belt; or, The Three Masted Goleta: A Tale of Boston Bay. 1844.
Arnold; or, The British Spy! (includes *The Bold Insurgent*). 1844; as *The Treason of Arnold,* 1847.
The Midshipman; or, The Corvette and Brigantine. 1844.
La Bonita Cigarera; or, The Beautiful Cigar Vendor: A Tale of New York. 1844.
The Spanish Galleon; or, The Pirate of the Mediterranean: A Romance of the Corsair Kidd. 1844.
Estelle; or, The Conspirator of the Isle: A Tale of the West Indian Seas. 1844.
The Silver Bottle; or, The Adventures of Little Marlboro in Search of His Father. 1844.
Herman de Ruyter; or, The Mystery Unveiled: A Sequel to The Beautiful Cigar Vendor. 1844.
The Diary of a Hackney Coachman. 1844.
Santa Claus; or, The Merry King of Christmas. 1844.
Caroline Archer; or, The Milliner's Apprentice. 1844.
Eleanor Sherwood, The Beautiful Temptress! 1844.

The Clipper-Yacht; or, Moloch the Money-Lender: A Tale of London and the Thames. 1845.

Marie; or, The Fugitive: A Romance of Mount Benedict. 1845.

Freemantle; or, The Privateersman! A Nautical Romance of the Last War. 1845.

Scarlet Feather; or, The Young Chief of the Abenaquies: A Romance of the Wilderness of Maine. 1845.

Forrestal; or, The Light of the Reef. 1845.

Rafael. 1845.

The Knights of Seven Lands. 1845; as *The Seven Knights,* 1845.

Montezuma, The Serf; or, The Revolt of the Mexitili: A Tale of the Last Days of the Aztec Dynasty. 1845.

Will Terril; or, The Adventures of a Young Gentleman Born in a Cellar. 1845.

Norman; or, The Privateersman's Bride: A Sequel to Freemantle. 1845.

Neal Nelson; or, The Siege of Boston: A Tale of the Revolution. 1845; as *Sons of Liberty,* 1887.

A Romance of the Sunny South; or, Feathers from a Traveller's Wing. 1845.

Paul Deverell; or, Two Judgments for One Crime: A Tale of the Present Day. 1845.

Paul Perril, The Merchant's Son; or, The Adventures of a New-England Boy Launched upon Life. 2 vols., 1845–46(?).

The Adventures of Will Wizard! Corporal of the Saccarapa Volunteers. 1845.

Alice May, and Bruising Bill (stories). 1845.

Bertrand; or, The Story of Marie de Heywode, Being a Sequel to Marie. 1845.

Charles Blackford; or, The Adventures of a Student in Search of a Profession. 1845.

The Cruiser of the Mist. 1845.

Fleming Field; or, The Young Artisan: A Tale of the Days of the Stamp Act. 1845.

Grace Weldon; or, Frederica the Bonnet-Girl: A Tale of Boston and Its Bay. 1845.

Harry Harefoot; or, The Three Temptations: A Story of City Scenes. 1845.

Henry Howard; or, Two Noes Make One Yes (includes *Trout-Fishing*). 1845.

Mary Wilbur; or, The Deacon and the Widow's Daughter. 1845.

The Mast-Ship; or, The Bombardment of Falmouth. 1845.

The Wing of the Wind. 1845.

Arthur Denwood; or, The Maiden of the Inn: A Tale of the War of 1812. 1846.

The Lady of the Gulf. 1846; as *Josephene,* 1853(?).

Leisler; or, The Rebel and the King's Man: A Tale of the Rebellion of 1689. 1846.

Ramero; or, The Prince and the Prisoner! 1846.

Bonfield; or, The Outlaw of the Bermudas. 1846.

The Silver Ship of Mexico. 1846.

Berkeley; or, The Lost and Redeemed. 1846.

Mate Burke; or, The Foundlings of the Sea. 1846.

The Mysterious State-Room: A Tale of the Mississippi. 1846.

The Odd Fellow; or, The Secret Association, and Foraging Peter (stories). 1846.

Pierce Fenning; or, The Lugger's Chase. 1846; as *The Rebel Coaster,* 1867.

The Ringdove; or, The Privateer and the Cutter. 1846(?); as *A Yankee Blue-Jacket,* 1888.

The Slave King; or, The Triumph of Liberty. 1846.

The Spectre Steamer and Other Tales. 1846.

The Young Artist, and The Bold Insurgent (stories). 1846.

The Surf Skiff; or, The Heroines of the Kennebec (includes *Captain Velasco*). 1847.

The Truce; or, On and Off Soundings: A Tale of the Coast of Maine. 1847.

Blanche Talbot; or, The Maiden's Hand: A Romance of the War of 1812 (includes *Henry Temple*). 1847.

The Brigantine; or, Guitierro and the Castilian: A Tale Both of Boston and Cuba (includes *The Old Bean*). 1847.

Edward Manning; or, The Bride and the Maiden. 1847.

Beatrice, The Goldsmith's Daughter: A Story of the Reign of the Last Charles.   1847.
Ringold Griffitt; or, The Raftsman of the Susquehannah: A Tale of Pennsylvania.   1847.
The Free-Trader; or, The Cruiser of Narragansett Bay.   1847.
The Texan Ranger; or, The Maid of Matamoras (includes *Alice Brandon*).   1847.
Wildash; or, The Cruiser of the Capes.   1847.
Jennette Alison; or, The Young Strawberry Girl.   1848.
Nobody's Son; or, The Life and Adventures of Percival Mayberry.   1851.
The Arrow of Gold; or, The Shell Gatherer.   1854(?).
The Prince of the House of David; or, Three Years in the Holy City.   1855.
Rivingstone; or, The Young Ranger Hussar: A Romance of the Revolution.   1855.
The Pillar of Fire; or, Israel in Bondage.   1859.
The Throne of David: From the Consecration of the Shepherd of Bethlehem to the Rebellion of Prince Absalom.   1860.
The Sunny South; or, The Southerner at Home.   1860; as *Not "A Fool's Errand,"* 1880; as *Kate's Experiences,* 1880.
Mortimer; or, The Bankrupt's Heiress.   1865.
Wildbird; or, The Three Chances.   1869.
The Avenging Brother; or, The Two Maidens.   1869.
The Pirate Chief; or, The Cutter of the Ocean.   N.d.

Other

The South-West.   1835.
Pamphlets for the People, in Illustration of the Claims of the Church and Methodism.   1854.

Bibliography: in *Bibliography of American Literature* by Jacob Blanck, 1963.

Reading List: *Ingraham* by Robert W. Weatherby II, 1978.

*   *   *

Joseph Holt Ingraham was one of the first Americans to try to make a living by writing fiction, and his career provides a paradigm of the forms to which early would-be professionals turned in their efforts to meet the destructive competition from imported works in the days before international copyright.

After achieving success with his non-fiction account of his travels in Louisiana and Mississippi (*The South-West*), he turned to the then favorite two-volume historical novel after the manner of Scott and Cooper. His first, *Lafitte, The Pirate of the Gulf*, a conventional romance about a patriotic Louisiana pirate who turns out to have been highborn, was his most successful and remained in print well into the twentieth century. *Burton* (which is about the Canadian campaign of Aaron Burr during the American Revolution) and *Captain Kyd* (another fantasy about a famous pirate) were less successful; despite the appeal of the subjects, the stories were too preposterous and chaotically constructed even for readers accustomed to Gothic fiction. A fourth double-decker, *The Quadroone*, another tale of baby-switching during the Spanish occupation of New Orleans in the eighteenth century, was coldly received; and a projected fifth, *The Dancing Feather*, an unlikely tale of contemporary piracy in New York harbor, had to be ended abruptly after the tenth chapter of a planned fifty and published as a cheap paperback.

During the next five years, Ingraham led in productivity a pack of hungry writers churning out the hundred-page pamphlets that new high-speed printing presses made it possible to sell for a quarter. Ingraham wrote at least sixty; most were stories of pirates and other nautical adventurers, though some were early tales of the shady side of big city life. Typical and most interesting are *The Beautiful Cigar Vendor* and its sequel *Herman de Ruyter*, in which Ingraham provides his own solution to the mystery of the disappearance of Mary Cecilia Rogers, a New York girl who inspired also Poe's "The Mystery of Marie Roget."

When Ingraham entered the work of the Protestant Episcopal church in 1847, what the *Knickerbocker* magazine called his "cheap and nasty," "immoral" stories ceased to flow from his pen, although in 1851 he produced a final short work, *Nobody's Son*, protesting the mistreatment of orphans in the manner of Dickens' popular fictions.

Ingraham's greatest success and major contribution to literature came late in his life, however, when, as he was engaged in the ministry, he began to write a life of Christ in the form of a series of letters from an impressionable young Egyptian girl visiting the Holy Lands in Christ's time. These developed into *The Prince of the House of David*, the first religious best-seller, and the prototype of a vein that has flourished through the works of Lew Wallace, Lloyd Douglas, and others to the present day. Further attempts, however, to tell the story of Moses (*The Pillar of Fire*) and the founding of the Hebrew kingdom (*The Throne of David*) were less successful because the novels became too long-winded and clumsily constructed. He failed to find a publisher for a projected fourth novel, *St. Paul, The Roman Citizen*, before his sudden and still mysterious death.

—Warren French

IRVING, Washington. American. Born in New York City, 3 April 1783. Educated in local schools; studied law in the offices of Henry Masterton, 1799, of Brockholst Livingstone, 1801, and of Josiah Ogden Hoffman, 1802; admitted to the New York Bar, 1806, but never practised. Served as a Staff Colonel in the United States Army during the war of 1812. Travelled in Europe, 1804–06; became partner, with his brothers, in family hardware business, New York and Liverpool, 1810: representative of the business in England, 1815 until the firm collapsed, 1818; thereafter a full-time writer: lived in Dresden, 1822–23, London, 1824, Paris, 1825, and Madrid, as member of the United States Legation, 1826–29; Secretary, United States Legation in London, 1829–32; returned to New York, then toured the southern and western United States, 1832; lived at the manor house "Sunnyside," Tarrytown-on-Hudson, New York, 1836–42; United States Ambassador to Spain, 1842–45, then returned to Tarrytown. Recipient: Royal Society of Literature medal, 1830. D.C.L.: Oxford University, 1831. *Died 28 November 1859.*

PUBLICATIONS

Collections

    Works (Author's Revised Edition).　21 vols., 1860–61.
    Representative Selections, edited by Henry A. Pochmann.　1934.
    Complete Works, edited by Henry A. Pochmann.　1969–.
    Complete Tales, edited by Charles Neider.　1975.

Fiction and Sketches

Salmagundi; or, The Whim-Whams and Opinions of Launcelot Langstaff, Esq., and Others, with James Kirke Paulding and William Irving.   2 vols., 1807–08.
The Sketch Book of Geoffrey Crayon, Gent.   7 vols., 1819–20; revised edition, 2 vols., 1820.
Bracebridge Hall; or, The Humourists: A Medley.   1822; edited by J. D. Colclough, 1898.
Letters of Jonathan Oldstyle, Gent.   1824; edited by Stanley T. Williams, 1941.
Tales of a Traveller.   1824.
The Alhambra: A Series of Tales and Sketches of the Moors and Spaniards.   1832.
Essays and Sketches.   1837.
Chronicles of Wolfert's Roost and Other Papers.   1855.

Plays

Charles the Second; or, The Merry Monarch, with John Howard Payne, from a play by A. V. P. Duval (produced 1824).   1824.
Richelieu: A Domestic Comedy, with John Howard Payne, from a play by A. V. P. Duval (produced 1826; as *The French Libertine*, produced 1826).   1826.
Abu Hassan.   1924.
The Wild Huntsman, from a play by Friedrich Kind.   1924.
An Unwritten Play of Lord Byron.   1925.

Verse

The Poems, edited by William R. Langfeld.   1931.

Other

A History of New York from the Beginning of the World to the End of the Dutch Dynasty.   2 vols., 1809; revised edition, 1812, 1848; edited by Edwin T. Bowden, 1964.
A History of the Life and Voyages of Christopher Columbus.   4 vols., 1828; edited by Winifred Hulbert, as *The Voyages of Columbus*, 1931.
A Chronicle of the Conquest of Granada.   2 vols., 1829.
Voyages and Discoveries of the Companions of Columbus.   1831.
Miscellanies (A Tour on the Prairies, Abbotsford and Newstead Abbey, Legends of the Conquest of Spain).   3 vols., 1835; *A Tour of the Prairies* edited by John Francis McDermott, 1956.
Astoria; or, Anecdotes of an Enterprise Beyond the Rocky Mountains.   2 vols., 1836; edited by Edgeley W. Todd, 1964.
Adventures of Captain Bonneville; or, Scenes Beyond the Rocky Mountains of the Far West, based on journals of B. L. E. Bonneville.   1837; as *The Rocky Mountains*, 1837; edited by Edgeley W. Todd, 1961.
The Life of Oliver Goldsmith, with Selections from His Writings.   2 vols., 1840; edited by G. S. Blakely, 1916.
Biography and Poetical Remains of the Late Margaret Miller Davidson.   1841.
A Book of the Hudson.   1849.
Mahomet and His Successors, in *Works.*   2 vols., 1850; in *Works*, 1970.

Life of George Washington. 5 vols., 1855–59; abridged and edited by Charles Neider, 1976.

Spanish Papers and Other Miscellanies, edited by Pierre M. Irving. 2 vols., 1866.

Letters to Mrs. William Renwick and to Her Son James Renwick. 1915.

Letters to Henry Brevoort, edited by George S. Hellman. 2 vols., 1915.

Journals (Hitherto Unpublished), edited by William P. Trent and George S. Hellman. 3 vols., 1920.

Notes and Journals of Travel in Europe 1804–1805. 3 vols., 1921.

Diary: Spain 1828–1829, edited by Clara Louisa Penney. 1926.

Notes While Preparing Sketch Book 1817, edited by Stanley T. Williams. 1927.

Tour in Scotland 1817, and Other Manuscript Notes, edited by Stanley T. Williams. 1927.

Letters from Sunnyside and Spain, edited by Stanley T. Williams. 1928.

Journal (1823–1824), edited by Stanley T. Williams. 1931.

Irving and the Storrows: Letters from England and the Continent 1821–1828, edited by Stanley T. Williams. 1933.

Journal 1803, edited by Stanley T. Williams. 1934.

Journal 1828, and Miscellaneous Notes on Moorish Legend and History, edited by Stanley T. Williams. 1937.

The Western Journals, edited by John Francis McDermott. 1944.

Contributions to the Corrector, edited by Martin Roth. 1968.

Irving and the House of Murray (letters), edited by Ben Harris McClary. 1969.

Editor, *The Miscellaneous Works of Goldsmith.* 4 vols., 1825.

Editor, *Poems,* by William Cullen Bryant. 1832.

Editor, *Harvey's Scenes of the Primitive Forest of America.* 1841.

Translator, with Peter Irving and Georges Caines, *A Voyage to the Eastern Part of Terra Firma; or, The Spanish Main,* by F. Depons. 3 vols., 1806.

Bibliography: *A Bibliography of the Writings of Irving* by Stanley T. Williams and Mary Allen Edge, 1936; in *Bibliography of American Literature* by Jacob Blanck, 1963.

Reading List: *Life and Letters of Irving* by Pierre M. Irving, 4 vols., 1862–64 *The Life of Irving* by Stanley T. Williams, 2 vols., 1935; *The World of Irving* by Van Wyck Brooks, 1944; *Irving and Germany* by Walter A. Reichart, 1957; *Irving: Moderation Displayed* by Edward Wagenknecht, 1962; *Irving* by Lewis Leary, 1963; *Irving: An American Study* by William L. Hedges, 1965; *Irving Reconsidered: A Symposium* edited by Ralph Aderman, 1969; *Irving: A Tribute,* 1972, and *A Century of Commentary on the Works of Irving,* 1976, both edited by Andrew B. Myers.

*   *   *

Born in 1783, the year in which the American Revolution ended, Washington Irving, son of a prosperous New York hardware merchant, became the first author of the new country to be acclaimed in England. Although he never wrote a novel – indeed, his chief achievement resides in perhaps a dozen sketches and short stories – he must be acknowledged as the first man of letters in the United States. He lived until 1859, much admired by Poe and Hawthorne, whose grapplings with the darker side of human nature were as foreign to his own sanguine temperament as were their respective interests in ideas and in the extended development of plot and character. Yet Irving had managed to win not only their admiration but also that of Scott, Coleridge, and Byron. By the time he published *The Sketch Book of*

Geoffrey Crayon, Gent. in 1819–20, his best work had been done. In the succeeding forty years he, like his contemporary William Cullen Bryant, became enshrined as a living figurehead of literary culture in America, though the conditions of American life rapidly outstripped his preparation or inclination to treat them in his writing.

In the event, however, Irving did bring to his vocation a belletristic sensibility, and a style that combined grace and poise with an inimitable pictorial quality. This style seems a fusion of Augustan balance with the sentiments of early Romanticism; it is among the first purely literary artifacts in the culture of the new republic. Irving's stylistic influence is visible in Hawthorne, in the tales of Bret Harte set in Spanish California, and even in Henry James (e.g., the description of Gardencourt in *The Portrait of a Lady*). But a decade before achieving the grace and strength of this style in *The Sketch Book*, Irving had scored a literary triumph of a different stripe with *A History of New York* (as the pseudonymous Diedrich Knickerbocker). This burlesque, Hudibrastic in its energy, is a satiric debunking of the Colonial history of Dutch New York, published in 1809, its author's and its country's twenty-sixth year. Although Irving was not to be so boldly satirical again, this youthful extravagance exhibits also another aspect of his sensibility which stayed with him to the end: his fascination with the past.

Never one to stay tied to the family hardware business, he served in the War of 1812 as a staff colonel, and in 1815 returned to Europe (he had taken a grand tour in 1804) – little knowing that he would not see New York again for seventeen years. Arriving in England, he sought out Scott, who had admired his *History*. Irving quickly became Scott's disciple, and, as is seen in *The Sketch Book*, he turned, in his most memorable stories, to the local settings and legends of the same Dutch ancestors whose political figures he had, as Diedrich Knickerbocker, lampooned a decade earlier. But Irving, although he anticipates by half a century the local color movement in fiction, was not merely a local colorist. He used the color of his native locale, the Hudson Valley, to impart the tinge of native realism to fables he deftly appropriated from European literature. "Rip Van Winkle," the tale which would bring Irving world-wide fame, is in part a nearly literal rendering from Otmar's *Volkssagen*. "The Legend of Sleepy Hollow," Irving's other masterpiece, is similarly based on Bürger's *Der Wilde Jäger* and one of the Rübezahl tales. Yet Irving did more than give these Germanic folk motifs a local habitation and a name. He infused them with subliminal universal significance, and at the same time, by an authorial alchemy no doubt unconscious on his part, expressed in them the very spirit of his nation and of his time.

In "Rip Van Winkle" the localization of the ancient German tale is perfect. Rip, a shrew-bedevilled husband, is a stock comic figure seeking regressive freedom in his bottle and in the wilderness of the mountaintop. There, encountering the ghosts of Hendrik Hudson's crew, he drinks their magical draught – and awakens as an old man, his fowling gun rusted beside him. In the meantime, however, life had gone on in the village below: that life included the American Revolution. So Rip's return from the blessed otherworld of the irretrievable past is to a new, busy, bustling nation he cannot understand, or enter. Irving's pervasive theme of nostalgia for the unrecoverable past is here at once mythologized and made unforgettable.

In "The Legend of Sleepy Hollow" Irving again appropriates a comic stereotype, for his Ichabod Crane, the Yankee schoolmaster, is akin to satirical versions of the Puritan character – calculating, narrow-gauged, lacking in spontaneity – found in the popular culture of the time. With intuitive prescience Irving puts Ichabod in opposition to Brom Bones, a brawny, forthright Dutchman whose character resembles that of such frontier folk heroes yet to come as Mike Fink or Davy Crockett. Thus at the beginning of American literature Irving anticipates the regional conflict between East and West, between the Puritan, urban, prudential character and the freedom of the natural man. He further imbeds this story in the expressive energies of popular culture by making the plot hinge on a tall tale that is also the frontiersman's hoax. Ichabod, known to be superstitious, is run out of town by the headless horseman. Brom Bones, in the saddle with the pumpkinhead in his lap, stays in Kinderhook to marry the girl. Thus Irving bestows his favor on an American of the coming century. In his own life, however, Irving was not as lucky as Brom Bones. His fiancée, Matilda Hoffman, daughter of a judge, died, and it may be that this early loss colored Irving's Romantic nostalgia.

Elsewhere in *The Sketch Book* Irving wrote at lower levels of intensity, exploring the folk customs of English Christmas, describing "A Country Church," "A Sunday in London," and the like. These at best are gentle impressionistic evocations of nostalgic moods. In *Bracebridge Hall* and *Tales of a Traveller* he reiterated similar subjects; *Chronicles of Wolfert's Roost* draws on Irving's travels in Germany and Spain, but the best tales are "Kidd the Pirate" and "The Devil and Tom Walker," the one an American legend, the other a native adaptation of the Faustian theme. Little in these books has lived, though in their time they doubtless enriched American literature with an antiquarian's love of the vanished or vanishing folkways of Europe.

Irving spent the winter of 1825 in Dresden, the next three years in Madrid, and then served from 1829 until his return in 1832 as Secretary of the American legation in London. His Spanish sojourn led to his writing the tales in *The Alhambra* and to his lengthy biographies of Mahomet and Columbus. These, as Stanley Williams has observed, are really romances rather than factual accounts of their subjects. After returning to the States, Irving, aware of the public's desire for fictional treatments of the West, took a tour of the wilds and provided them with *A Tour of the Prairies*, *Astoria* (an account of John Jacob Astor's success in the fur trade) and *Adventures of Captain Bonneville*. Thus the famous writer tried to obviate suspicion of his long exile, but these writings bring to the West only the pictorialist's eye trained in London and Madrid. Irving could not romanticize such subjects.

It was characteristic of this genial author's temperament that he chose as his primary vehicle the sketch during the decades when the short story was supplanting it in popularity. In fact his own tales served as models for Poe, Hawthorne, and other authors whose fictions hurried the genre of the sketch into oblivion. If Irving's works of lasting value are but few and those few brief, his career is nonetheless significant; not only did he write some incomparable tales, and prove that authorship was a possible profession in a new country, but at the very moment when American literary consciousness was first developing he enriched his nation's culture with his cosmopolitan reflection of the themes and modes of British and continental Romanticism.

—Daniel Hoffman

ISHERWOOD, Christopher (William Bradshaw). American. Born in High Lane, Cheshire, England, 26 August 1904; emigrated to the United States, 1939; naturalized, 1946. Educated at Repton School, 1919–22; Corpus Christi College, Cambridge, 1924–25; King's College, London, as a medical student, 1928–29. Private Tutor, and Secretary to André Mangeot and his Music Society String Quartet, London, 1926–27; writer from 1928; taught English in Berlin, 1930–33; travelled in Europe, 1933–37, and in China, with W. H. Auden, 1938; reviewer, *The Listener*, London, 1935–37; screenwriter, in Hollywood, for Metro-Goldwyn-Mayer, Warner Brothers, and 20th Century Fox, from 1939; worked with the American Friends Service Committee, Haverford, Pennsylvania, 1941–42; Resident Student, Vedanta Society of Southern California: Editor, with Swami Prabhavananda, *Vedanta and the West*, Hollywood, 1943–44; Guest Professor of Modern English Literature, Los Angeles State College, and the University of California at Santa Barbara, 1959–62; Regents Professor, University of California at Los Angeles, 1965–66, and University of California at Riverside, 1966–67. Recipient: Brandeis University Creative Arts Award, 1975. Member, National Institute of Arts and Letters, 1949. Lives in Santa Monica, California.

PUBLICATIONS

Fiction

All the Conspirators. 1928.
The Memorial: Portrait of a Family. 1932.
Mr. Norris Changes Trains. 1935 (as *The Last of Mr. Norris*, 1935); *Sally Bowles*,
   1937; *Goodbye to Berlin*, 1939; complete version, as *The Berlin Stories*, 1946.
Prater Violet. 1945.
The World in the Evening. 1954.
Down There on a Visit. 1962.
A Single Man. 1964.
A Meeting by the River. 1967.

Plays

The Dog Beneath the Skin; or, Where is Francis?, with W. H. Auden (produced 1936;
   revised version, produced 1937). 1935.
The Ascent of F6, with W. H. Auden (produced 1937). 1936; revised version, 1937.
On the Frontier, with W. H. Auden (produced 1938). 1938.
The Adventures of the Black Girl in Her Search for God, from the novel by G. B. Shaw
   (produced 1969).
A Meeting by the River, with Don Bachardy, from the novel by Isherwood (produced
   1972).
Frankenstein: The True Story (screenplay), with Don Bachardy, based on the novel by
   Mary Shelley. 1973.

Screenplays: *Little Friend*, with Margaret Kennedy, 1934; *Rage in Heaven*, with Robert
Thoeren, 1941; *Forever and a Day*, with others, 1944; *Adventure in Baltimore*, with
Lionel Houser and Lesser Samuels, 1949; *The Great Sinner*, with Ladislas Fodor and
Rene Fulop-Miller, 1949; *Diane*, 1955; *The Loved One*, with Terry Southern, 1965; *The
Sailor from Gibraltar*, with Don Magner and Tony Richardson, 1967; *Frankenstein:
The True Story*, with Don Bachardy, 1972.

Other

Lions and Shadows: An Education in the Twenties. 1938.
Journey to a War, with W. H. Auden (on China). 1939.
The Condor and the Cows: A South American Travel Diary. 1950.
An Approach to Vedanta. 1963.
Ramakrishna and His Disciples. 1965.
Exhumations: Stories, Articles, Verse. 1966.
Essentials of Vedanta. 1969.
Kathleen and Frank (autobiographical). 1971.
Christopher and His Kind (autobiography). 1976.

Editor, *Vedanta for the Western World.* 1945.
Editor, *Vedanta for Modern Man.* 1951.
Editor, *Great English Short Stories.* 1957.

Translator, *Intimate Journals*, by Charles Baudelaire. 1930.

Translator (verse only), *Penny for the Poor,* by Bertolt Brecht. 1937; as *Threepenny Novel,* 1956.

Translator, with Swami Prabhavananda, *Bhagavad-Gita: The Song of God.* 1944.

Translator, with Swami Prabhavananda, *Crest-Jewel of Discrimination,* by Shankara. N.d.

Translator, with Swami Prabhavananda, *How to Know God: The Yoga Aphorisms of Patanjali.* 1953.

Bibliography: *Isherwood: A Bibliography, 1923–1967* by Selmer Westby and Clayton M. Brown, 1968.

Reading List: *Isherwood* by Carolyn G. Heilbrun, 1970; *Isherwood* by Alan Wilde, 1971; *Isherwood* by Francis King, 1976; *Isherwood: A Biography* by Jonathan Fryer, 1977; *Isherwood: Myth and Anti-Myth* by Paul Piazza, 1978.

*   *   *

Cyril Connolly considered Christopher Isherwood's first novel, *All the Conspirators,* to be "the key to Isherwood and the 'twenties. It is as mature, as readable, as concentrated as anything he has written since." Certainly, many of the themes which were to pre-occupy him during his "European" period (the 1930's) are reflected here – oppression by the older generation, the moral aftermath of the Great War, the striving towards a more relevant literary aesthetic. But his own 1957 Foreword is ruthlessly accurate in analysing its faults – "the author's chauvinism," his deliberate stylistic imitation of Joyce, Woolf, Forster, and Mansfield. There is a wilful obscurity which is clearly another, and largely irrelevant, part of his challenge to the self-satisfaction of the Establishment and the world of Georgian *littérateurs.* Ultimately it represents a condemnation of weakness, an attempt to exorcise that insecurity described in *Lions and Shadows* as "a feeling of shame that we hadn't been old enough to take part in the European War," the failure to have exercised one's potential "heroism" in the "test." In keeping with Ford Madox Ford, Waugh, and Forster, conventional heroism is invalidated and replaced by a personal struggle against social pressure. In 1928 Isherwood saw this in sinister terms. The concept of a deliberate conspiracy against youth and truth by the "poshocracy" led him initially into fantasy. At Cambridge with Edward Upward (the Chalmers of *Lions and Shadows*), he constructed an imaginative underworld, Mortmere, which allowed escape through malicious humour, rejecting outright all "movements," romanticism and even the Labour Government. It was the need to combine this phantasmagoric vision with a positive left-wing approach that eventually produced the more mature Berlin stories. *All the Conspirators* and his second novel, *The Memorial,* never escape the egotism of their author ruthlessly striving for "objectivity."

In *Down There on a Visit* Mr. Lancaster suggests that the hero write "a series of stories which do not describe an emotion but create it." This aesthetic advance is successfully achieved in *Mr. Norris Changes Trains* and *Goodbye to Berlin.* The latter is a collection of separate pieces with a basic cast of characters – "A Berlin Diary (Autumn 1930)," "On Ruegen Island (Summer 1931)," "The Nowaks," "The Landauers," "A Berlin Diary (Winter 1932–3)," and the short novel *Sally Bowles.* The first piece sets the new tone: "I am a camera with its shutter open, quite passive, recording, not thinking...." The whole celebrates the life-force of conventionally immoral or unimportant characters – Mr. Norris is a spy and a flagellant, Sally Bowles an indifferent cabaret singer of easy virtue, Frl. Schroeder a gossip and a snob, Otto Nowak a homosexual. In the lurid perversity and crushing penury of Berlin during the death throes of the Weimar Republic Isherwood discovered a menagerie which satisfied both his sense of fantasy and his moral indignation at the poshocracy. The conspiracy is now between himself and these extraordinary figures against despair, philistinism, and brutality (epitomised at this stage by Nazism), and he became what he has remained ever since, the "writer of autobiographical novels" described in *Kathleen and Frank*.

Goodbye to Berlin is, however, prefaced by the statement that " 'Christopher Isherwood' is a convenient ventriloquist's dummy, nothing more." All his major work has been written in the first person, and, while not "purely autobiographical," the novels which follow in the "American" period – *Prater Violet, The World in the Evening, Down There on a Visit, A Single Man*, and *A Meeting by the River* – are undeniably explorations of personal motivation. His own development is a limitless source of fictional material – as the malcontent in the illusory world of cinema people, as the child of Bloomsbury, and as the perpetual outsider, the homosexual, intellectual-aesthete pre-occupied with the injustices of a heterosexual society and the eradication of his own ego. The imprisonment of youth and "life" by the conspirators of the establishment is replaced as a theme by the imprisonment of the self by the ego. "*Down There*," he states, "refers to that nether world within the individual which is the place of loneliness, alienation and hatred. This novel ... describes four characters shut up in private hells of their own making, self-dedicated to the lifelong struggle with The Others." *A Meeting by the River* maintains the scrupulous objectivity of the Berlin stories with its letter and diary format, eschewing authorial description, but it is a distinctly "moral" tale openly advocating Isherwood's pre-occupation with the mystical Hindu philosophy of Vedanta.

The later work generally suffers from a plethora of vacuous philosophical discussion attempting to rationalise his earlier "dread of the Future" and even stronger "dread of the Past with its prestige, its traditions," its "implied challenge and reproach." It advocates the here and now, sensuous fulfilment, spontaneity and personal commitment, but lacks the objectivity and compelling vivacity of the Berlin stories. Friedrich Bergmann in *Prater Violet* is the last of these garish and lovable figures; on a larger canvas, attempting to trace the complex psychological permutations of personal relations, Isherwood is less successful. His homosexuality bothered him first with guilt and then with justification. In writing of Elizabeth Rydal and Stephen Monk's marriage in *The World in the Evening* he is sentimental and ill at ease; it was not until *A Meeting by the River* that he could create a wholly unpleasant homosexual in the selfish and irresponsible Patrick. And even here we sense it to be a forced gesture towards denying the authorial ego.

In *Prater Violet* we see Isherwood at his finest:

> A traveller, a wanderer. I was aware of Bergmann, my fellow-traveller, pacing beside me, a separate secret consciousness, locked away within itself, distant as Betelgeuse, yet for a short while sharing my wanderings. ...
> There is one question which we seldom ask each other directly: it is too brutal. And yet it is the only question worth asking our fellow-travellers – What makes you go on living? Why don't you kill yourself? Why is all this bearable? What makes you bear it?

These questions are answered by ironical implication in this novel and the Berlin stories. It is the shared sacrifice, the love of life, the company of fellow-travellers as well as the mundanity of doing "whatever was next on the list." The pain and delight behind the façade, the terse humour, the jewelled fantasy punctuating *la vie quotidienne*, described but never explained by his "camera," result in allusive and powerful sketches, economical yet redolent with suggestion.

—Martin Stannard

JACKSON, Helen (Maria) Hunt (née Fiske). American. Born in Amherst, Massachusetts, 15 October 1830. Educated at Ipswich Female Seminary, Massachusetts, and at Abbott Brothers School, New York City. Married 1) Edward Bissell Hunt in 1852 (died, 1863), two sons; 2) William Sharpless Jackson in 1875. Neighbor and schoolmate of Emily Dickinson, who remained her life-long friend; after her first marriage, travelled throughout the United States with her husband, an officer in the Army Corps of Engineers; after his death, settled in Newport, Rhode Island, 1866, and thereafter became a full-time writer; travelled in Europe, 1868–70; moved to Colorado Springs, 1875; became interested in Indian affairs: appointed United States Special Commissioner to investigate conditions of the Mission Indians of California, 1882–83. *Died 12 August 1885.*

PUBLICATIONS

Fiction

Saxe Holm's Stories. 2 vols., 1874–78.
The Story of Boon. 1874.
Mercy Philbrick's Choice. 1876.
Hetty's Strange History. 1877.
Nelly's Silver Mine: A Story of Colorado Life. 1878.
The Hunter Cats of Connorloa. 1884.
Ramona. 1884.
Zeph: A Posthumous Story. 1885.
Pansy Billings and Popsy: Two Stories of Girl Life. 1898.

Verse

Verses. 1870; revised edition, 1871, 1874.
Easter Bells. 1884.
Pansies and Orchids, edited by Susie B. Skelding. 1884.
Sonnets and Lyrics. 1886.

Other

Bits of Travel. 1872.
Bits of Talk about Home Matters. 1873.
Bits of Talk, in Verse and Prose, for Young Folks. 1876.
Bits of Travel at Home. 1878.
A Century of Dishonor: A Sketch of the United States Government's Dealings with Some of the Indian Tribes. 1881; edited by Andrew F. Rolle, 1965.
Mammy Tittleback and Family: A True Story of Seventeen Cats. 1881.
The Training of Children. 1882.
Report on the Condition and Needs of the Mission Indians of California, with Abbot Kinney. 1883; *Father Junipero and His Work* edited by Richard B. Yale, 1966.
Glimpses of Three Coasts. 1886.
Between Whiles. 1887.

Editor, *Letters from a Cat,* by Deborah Fiske. 1879.

Translator, *Bathmendi,* by J. P. C. de Florian. 1867.

Bibliography: in *Bibliography of American Literature* by Jacob Blanck, 1963.

Reading List: *Jackson* by Ruth Odell, 1939; by Allan Nevins, in *American Scholar*, 1941; *Jackson* by Evelyn I. Banning, 1973.

*   *   *

When Helen Hunt Jackson died in 1885 Emily Dickinson promised her immortality: "Helen of Troy will die, but Helen of Colorado, never." At the time of her death her reputation was at its height as the result of two works, *A Century of Dishonor* and *Ramona*, both produced partly in consequence of Mrs. Jackson's move to Colorado and the West after her second marriage in 1875. Thomas Wentworth Higginson compared her to George Eliot; another critic thought her verse in some respects superior to that of Elizabeth Barrett Browning. *A Century of Dishonor* went out of print in 1885 and remained so until 1965 but *Ramona* went through over three hundred printings in the intervening years and was transferred to both stage and screen.

Paradoxically these two works alone do not give much understanding of either the writer's background or of her cultural and literary drives. In essence she was a New Englander whose closest friends and influences included not only Emily Dickinson and Higginson but Nathaniel Hawthorne, Horace Greeley, and the sculptors Horace Greenough and William Wetmore Story. Much of her verse and prose was filled by preoccupations with sin and morality, with the evil in man and the need for moral struggle. Allan Nevins had argued in *American Scholar* (1941) that *A Century of Dishonor* is too sentimental, and he is correct in that its purpose was polemical rather than literary or historical. But there is far less sentimentality in the main body of her work. Though her descriptions are often close to cosy, her sympathies are defined by a rationalism and an individualism that make her characters in the end fully responsible for their own fates, and she does not bring excess emotion to the telling of their destinies. Her characters survive and struggle on after what in other novelists of the day would have been the final and crippling climax, as can be seen in both *Hetty's Strange History* and *Mercy Philbrick's Choice*.

Such a modern sounding quality is linked to what some of her contemporary critics felt needed apology: a devaluing of narrative in some of her work. At times the results are anti-climactic, for it is difficult to sustain the dramatic tension once the central focus of the plot has been passed. The difference in the characters' lives before and after this point is described is often too extremely presented, but the great advantage is escape from dénouement. It is possible that the emphasis on the continuity of life was one aspect of an outlook that was partly formed by a vigorous and intelligent sense of humour, though this quality is to be found more in her ephemeral writings like *Bits of Travel at Home* than in the more formal works.

Modern readers would be attracted not only by her sympathy for the Native American but also by her strong feminism. Her heroines are the prime movers of her plots; the men revolve about them. Her women tend to be socially committed, fulfilling themselves through the exercise of their talents in the world, and, if introspective, only in a way that strengthens them when in contact with others. The women she describes would not have been at home among the New England mill-workers; their freedom of action depended on their freedom from poverty. Her lack of interest in this connection prevented her being swamped by naturalism and has deprived her of readers in a century that demands it.

In life Helen Hunt Jackson was vivacious, articulate, intelligent, and active. Her work deserves respect as that of a modern woman in the thirty years after the Civil War.

—R. A. Burchell

JACKSON, Shirley. American. Born in San Francisco, California, 14 December 1919. Educated at Syracuse University, New York, B.A. 1940. Married the writer Stanley Edgar Hyman in 1940; two daughters and two sons. Recipient: Edgar Allan Poe Award, 1961. *Died 8 August 1965.*

PUBLICATIONS

Collections

 The Magic of Jackson, edited by Stanley Edgar Hyman. 1966.

Fiction

 The Road Through the Wall. 1948; as *The Other Side of the Street,* 1956.
 The Lottery; or, The Adventures of James Harris (stories). 1949.
 Hangsaman. 1951.
 The Bird's Nest. 1954; as *Lizzie,* 1957.
 The Sundial. 1958.
 The Haunting of Hill House. 1959.
 We Have Always Lived in the Castle. 1962.

Plays

 The Lottery, from her own story, in *Best Television Plays 1950–51,* edited by William I.
  Kauffman. 1952.
 The Bad Children: A Play in One Act for Bad Children. 1959.

Other

 Life among the Savages. 1953.
 The Witchcraft of Salem Village (juvenile). 1956.
 Raising Demons. 1957.
 Special Delivery: A Useful Book for Brand-New Mothers. 1960; as *And Baby Makes Three,* 1960.
 9 Magic Wishes (juvenile). 1963.
 Famous Sally (juvenile). 1966.
 Come Along with Me: Part of a Novel, Sixteen Stories, and Three Lectures, edited by
  Stanley Edgar Hyman. 1968.

Reading List: *Jackson* by Lenemaja Friedman, 1975.

* * *

 Throughout her work Shirley Jackson focuses on incongruities in an everyday setting, whether for comic or sinister effect. This is as true of her "disrespectful memoir" of her children, *Life among the Savages,* and its equally hilarious sequel, *Raising Demons,* as of the dark psychological explorations of her novels and short stories. In her later fiction she wrote about extraordinary characters and situations, but these were always located in an everyday setting, whose juxtaposition provided her staple ingredient of incongruity.

Much of Jackson's work is concerned with an attempt to gain, or regain, an identity. *The Bird's Nest* concerns a mentally disturbed girl who has four different voices and identities. It is triumphantly structured, but, like the earlier *Hangsaman*, the positive note on which it ends fails to remove our doubts about the future of its main character. In *The Sundial* Jackson focuses on an eccentric group of characters in the Halloran family house, where, directed by a dead relative, they await the end of the world in the belief that they alone will be saved. Allegorical relationships emerge between the characters, and the narrative, characteristically both comic and macabre, develops baroque motifs of sundial and maze.

Like *The Sundial* and her famous spine-chiller *The Haunting of Hill House* (with its "clashing disharmonies"), *We Have Always Lived in the Castle* centres on a house. Even more than in *The Sundial* the reader is induced to identify with its inhabitants – eccentric or criminal though they may be – against "them" in the world outside. Eighteen-year-old "Merricat" describes her life with her sister Constance after the latter's acquittal from a charge of poisoning the rest of the family – a charge of which the local people believe her to be guilty. The destructive invasion of the world outside parallels the set-piece of the peaceable invasion of the locals invited to the final barbeque in *The Sundial*. The portrayal of the sisters' loving relationship, albeit in macabre circumstances, makes *We Have Always Lived in the Castle* the most remarkable of Jackson's books.

A few of Jackson's short stories delight in the incongruous for its own sake; however, most of her stories, including the title story of *The Lottery* (which caused a sensation on its publication in the *New Yorker* in 1948), are informed by a genuine sense of evil. The stories generally centre on an isolated female, often the inadequate victim of a daemon lover (such as James Harris in *The Lottery*). These characters are lost in the concrete jungle of the Kafkaesque city or are on long-distance journeys "to the end of the night." This theme is habitually announced by laughter, lines from songs and poems, or nursery rhymes, transmuted to sinister leitmotivs.

To portray the fragmented personality Jackson resorted to a kind of zany verbal logic and semantic irony. Yet though there are passages in her work reminiscent of Borges, she kept any experimental tendency in her writing subordinated to the demands of story-telling, her prime consideration as the lectures in *Come Along with Me* make clear.

—Val Warner

JACOBS, W(illiam) W(ymark). English. Born in Wapping, London, 8 September 1863. Educated privately. Married Agnes Eleanor Williams in 1900; two sons and two daughters. Worked in the Savings Bank Department of the Civil Service, London, 1883–99; thereafter a full-time writer. *Died 1 September 1943.*

PUBLICATIONS

Collections

Selected Short Stories, edited by Hugh Greene.   1975.

Fiction

> *Many Cargoes* (stories). 1896.
> *The Skipper's Wooing, and The Brown Man's Servant.* 1897.
> *Sea Urchins* (stories). 1898; as *More Cargoes*, 1898.
> *A Master of Craft.* 1900.
> *Light Freights* (stories). 1901.
> *At Sunwich Port.* 1902.
> *The Lady of the Barge and Other Stories.* 1902.
> *Odd Craft* (stories). 1903.
> *Dialstone Lane.* 1904.
> *Captains All* (stories). 1905.
> *Short Cruises* (stories). 1907.
> *Salthaven* 1908.
> *Sailors' Knots* (stories). 1909.
> *Ship's Company* (stories). 1911.
> *Night Watches* (stories). 1914.
> *The Castaways.* 1916.
> *Deep Waters* (stories). 1919.
> *Fifteen Stories.* 1926.
> *Sea Whisper* (stories). 1926.
> *Snug Harbour: Collected Stories.* 1931.
> *The Night-Watchman and Other Longshoremen.* 1932.
> *Cruises and Cargoes* (omnibus). 1934.

Plays

> *The Grey Parrot*, with Charles Rock (produced 1899). 1908.
> *Beauty and the Barge*, with L. N. Parker, from the story by Jacobs (produced 1904). 1910.
> *The Temptation of Samuel Burge*, with Frederick Fenn (produced 1905).
> *The Boatswain's Mate*, with Herbert C. Sargent (produced 1907). 1907; revised version, music by Ethel Smyth (produced 1916).
> *The Changeling*, with Herbert C. Sargent, from the story by Jacobs (produced 1908). 1908.
> *The Ghost of Jerry Bundler*, with Charles Rock. 1908.
> *Admiral Peters*, with Horace Mills (produced 1908). 1909.
> *A Love Passage*, with P. E. Hubbard (produced 1913). 1913.
> *In the Library*, with Herbert C. Sargent, from the story by Jacobs (produced 1913). 1913.
> *Keeping Up Appearances* (produced 1915). 1919.
> *The Castaway*, with Herbert C. Sargent, from the story by Jacobs. 1924.
> *Establishing Relations.* 1925.
> *The Warming Pan.* 1929.
> *A Distant Relative.* 1930.
> *Master Mariners.* 1930.
> *Matrimonial Openings.* 1931.
> *Dixon's Return.* 1932.
> *Double Dealing.* 1935.

Bibliography: "Epitome of a Bibliography of Jacobs" by E. A. Osborne, in *American Book Collector*, 1934.

Reading List: *Books in General* by V. S. Pritchett, 1953.

*   *   *

W. W. Jacobs began his literary career while employed in the Post Office Savings Bank, but his father was a wharf manager at Wapping, and he set most of his comic short stories among London's wharves and dockland, in harbour towns, or on board tugs and steamers plying the Thames Estuary. His first successes were won in magazines before he published his earliest collection in volume form, and he eventually produced almost twenty books, including a number of light novels. He also adapted several of his tales as efficient one-act plays, mostly in collaboration, *The Boatswain's Mate* providing the libretto for an opera by Ethel Smyth. Many of Jacobs's stories were devised while on walking tours with his illustrator Will Owen, whose bluff, easily recognized drawings contributed to the writer's popularity.

Jacobs's principal figures are generally male – longshoremen, sailors, nightwatchmen (one is often employed as narrator), and others having to do with the sea and shipping, although their domestic tribulations feature nearly as frequently as their professional occupations, and a conflict between the demands of ship and shore is often a point of departure. Stereotypes such as sharp-tongued wives, flirtatious widows, crooked landlords, downtrodden clerks, saucy errand-boys, pert daughters of retired skippers, and dashing junior partners frequently occupy the supporting roles; conjugal and monetary hazards are a perennial concern, while the perils of courtship are also amply demonstrated. A small but important group of stories centres around a public-house in Claybury, a feud-ridden country village where the plausible rogue Bob Pretty usually outwits his opponents in the local raffle or church flower-show. An even smaller place is reserved for some excellent ghost-stories and tales of horror, including the justly celebrated "Monkey's Paw," surely one of the most masterly stories of the macabre ever produced.

Jacobs's plots are anecdotal, generally involving intrigues and deceit and often concluding with an unexpected twist which catches characters and readers unaware. His narrative method is commendably brisk and straightforward, with a minimum of scene-setting, and, although his humour partly relies on Dickensian circumlocution, there is a welcome economy about his style. His lively dialogue is similarly pithy, insult veiled or overt constituting its principal keynote since his characters rarely enjoy a harmonious relationship for long. One may admit that Jacobs's is not an extensive range and that structural and thematic monotony can set in after a time, yet one cannot deny the attraction of his unexacting but inventive anecdotes, his unmalicious humour, his unwearied devotion to coaxing variations from a basic set of ingredients. Jacobs is not a major comic artist, but for those prepared to scale down their demands, he can prove a very satisfying one.

—William M. Tydeman

JAMES, Henry. English. Born in New York City, 15 April 1843; brother of the philosopher William James; emigrated to England; naturalized, 1915. Educated at the Richard Pulling Jenks School, New York; travelled, with his family, in Europe from an early age: studied with tutors in Geneva, London, Paris, and Boulogne, 1855–58, Geneva, 1859, and Bonn, 1860; lived with his family in Newport, Rhode Island, 1860–62; attended Harvard Law School, Cambridge, Massachusetts, 1862–65. Settled with his family in Cambridge,

1866, and wrote for the *Nation* and *Atlantic Monthly*, 1866–69; toured Europe, 1869; returned to Cambridge, 1870–72; wrote art criticism for the *Atlantic Monthly*, 1871–72; lived in Europe, 1872–74, Cambridge, 1875, and Paris, 1875–76: writer for the *New York Tribune*, Paris, 1875–76; settled in London, 1876, and lived in England for the rest of his life; settled in Rye, Sussex, 1896; travelled throughout the United States, 1904–05. L.H.D.: Harvard University, 1911; Oxford University, 1912. Order of Merit, 1916. *Died 28 February 1916.*

PUBLICATIONS

Collections

Novels and Stories, edited by Percy Lubbock.   35 vols., 1921–24.
Complete Plays, edited by Leon Edel.   1949.
Complete Tales, edited by Leon Edel.   12 vols., 1962–65.
Representative Selections, revised edition, edited by Lyon N. Richardson.   1966.
Letters, edited by Leon Edel.   1974–

Fiction

A Passionate Pilgrim and Other Tales.   1875.
Roderick Hudson.   1875; edited by Leon Edel, 1960.
The American.   1877; edited by James W. Tuttleton, 1978.
Watch and Ward.   1878; edited by Leon Edel, 1960.
The Europeans: A Sketch.   1878; edited by Leon Edel, with *Washington Square*, 1967.
Daisy Miller: A Study.   1879.
An International Episode.   1879.
The Madonna of the Future and Other Tales.   1879.
Confidence.   1880; edited by Herbert Ruhm, 1962.
A Bundle of Letters.   1880.
The Diary of a Man of Fifty, and A Bundle of Letters.   1880.
Washington Square.   1881; edited by Gerald Willen, 1970.
The Portrait of a Lady.   1881; edited by Robert D. Bamberg, 1975.
The Siege of London, The Pension Beaurepas, and The Point of View.   1883; revised edition, 1884.
Novels and Tales.   14 vols., 1883.
Tales of Three Cities.   1884.
The Author of Beltraffio, Pandora, Georgina's Reasons, The Path of Duty, Four Meetings.   1885.
Stories Revived.   1885.
The Bostonians.   1886; edited by Leon Edel, 1967.
The Princess Casamassima.   1886.
The Reverberator.   1888.
The Aspern Papers, Louisa Pallant, The Modern Warning.   1888.
A London Life, The Patagonia, The Liar, Mrs. Temperly.   1889.
The Tragic Muse.   1890.
The Lesson of the Master, The Marriages, The Pupil, Brooksmith, The Solution, Sir Edmund Orme.   1892.
The Real Thing and Other Tales.   1893.
The Private Life, The Wheel of Time, Lord Beaupre, The Visits, Collaboration, Owen Wingrave.   1893.

Terminations, The Death of the Lion, The Coxon Fund, The Middle Years, The Altar of the Dead. 1895.

Embarrassments, The Figure in the Carpet, Glasses, The Next Time, The Way It Came. 1896.

The Other House. 1896.

The Spoils of Poynton. 1897; edited by Leon Edel, 1967.

What Maisie Knew. 1897; edited by Douglas Jefferson, 1966.

In the Cage. 1898; edited by Morton Dauwen Zabel, 1958.

The Two Magics, The Turn of the Screw, Covering End. 1898; *The Turn of the Screw* edited by Robert Kimbrough, 1966.

The Awkward Age. 1899; edited by Leon Edel, 1967.

The Soft Side (stories). 1900.

The Sacred Fount. 1901; edited by Leon Edel, 1953.

The Wings of the Dove. 1902; edited by J. Donald Crowley and Richard A. Hocks, 1978.

The Better Sort (stories). 1903.

The Ambassadors. 1903; edited by S. P. Rosenbaum, 1966.

The Golden Bowl. 1904.

Novels and Tales (New York Edition), revised by James. 24 vols., 1907–09.

Julia Bride. 1909.

The Finer Grain. 1910.

The Outcry. 1911.

The Ivory Tower, edited by Percy Lubbock. 1917.

The Sense of the Past, edited by Percy Lubbock. 1917.

Gabrielle de Bergerac, edited by Albert Mordell. 1918.

Travelling Companions (stories). 1919.

A Landscape Painter (stories). 1919.

Master Eustace (stories). 1920.

Eight Uncollected Tales, edited by Edna Kenton. 1950.

Plays

Daisy Miller, from his own story. 1883.

The American, from his own novel (produced 1891). 1891.

Guy Domville (produced 1895). 1894.

Theatricals (includes *Tenants, Disengaged*) (produced 1909). 1894.

Theatricals: Second Series (includes *The Album, The Reprobate*) (produced 1919). 1894.

The High Bid (produced 1908). In *Complete Plays,* 1949.

The Saloon (produced 1911). In *Complete Plays,* 1949.

The Outcry (produced 1917). In *Complete Plays,* 1949.

Other

Transatlantic Sketches. 1875; revised edition, as *Foreign Parts,* 1883.

French Poets and Novelists. 1878; revised edition, 1883; edited by Leon Edel, 1964.

Hawthorne. 1879; edited by William M. Sale, Jr., 1956.

Portraits of Places. 1883.

Notes on a Collection of Drawings by George du Maurier. 1884.

A Little Tour in France. 1884.

The Art of Fiction, with Walter Besant. 1885; edited by Leon Edel, in *The House of Fiction,* 1956.

Partial Portraits. 1888.

Picture and Text. 1893.

Essays in London and Elsewhere. 1893.

William Wetmore Story and His Friends. 2 vols., 1903.

The Question of Our Speech, The Lesson of Balzac: Two Lectures. 1905.

English Hours. 1905; edited by Alma Louise Lowe, 1960.

The American Scene. 1907; edited by Leon Edel, 1968.

Views and Reviews. 1908.

Italian Hours. 1909.

The Henry James Year Book, edited by Evelyn Garnaut Smalley. 1911.

A Small Boy and Others (autobiography). 1913.

Notes of a Son and Brother (autobiography). 1914.

Notes on Novelists and Some Other Notes. 1914.

Letters to an Editor. 1916.

Within the Rim and Other Essays 1914–1915. 1919.

The Middle Years (autobiography), edited by Percy Lubbock. 1917.

Letters, edited by Percy Lubbock. 2 vols., 1920.

Notes and Reviews. 1921.

A Most Unholy Trade, Being Letters on the Drama. 1923.

Three Letters to Joseph Conrad, edited by Gerard Jean-Aubry. 1926.

Letters to Walter Berry. 1928.

Letters to A. C. Benson and Auguste Monod, edited by E. F. Benson. 1930.

Theatre and Friendship: Some James Letters, edited by Elizabeth Robins. 1932.

The Art of the Novel: Critical Prefaces, edited by R. P. Blackmur. 1934.

Notebooks, edited by F. O. Matthiessen and Kenneth B. Murdock. 1947.

The Art of Fiction and Other Essays, edited by Morris Roberts. 1948.

James and Robert Louis Stevenson: A Record of Friendship and Criticism, edited by Janet Adam Smith. 1948.

The Scenic Art: Notes on Acting and the Drama 1872–1901, edited by Allan Wade. 1948.

Daumier, Caricaturist. 1954.

Selected Letters, edited by Leon Edel, 1955.

The American Essays, edited by Leon Edel. 1956.

The Future of the Novel: Essays on the Art of the Novel, edited by Leon Edel. 1956; as *The House of Fiction,* 1957.

The Painter's Eye: Notes and Essays on the Pictorial Arts, edited by John L. Sweeney. 1956.

Parisian Sketches: Letters to the New York Tribune 1875–1876, edited by Leon Edel and Ilse Dusoir Lind. 1957.

Literary Reviews and Essays on American, English, and French Literature, edited by Albert Mordell. 1957.

James and H. G. Wells: A Record of Their Friendship, Their Debate on the Art of Fiction, and Their Quarrel, edited by Leon Edel and Gordon N. Ray. 1958.

French Writers and American Women: Essays, edited by Peter Buitenhuis. 1960.

James and John Hay: The Record of a Friendship, edited by George Monteiro. 1965.

Switzerland in the Life and Work of James: The Clare Benedict Collection of Letters from James, edited by Jörg Hasler. 1966.

Translator, *Port Tarascon,* by Alphonse Daudet. 1891.

Bibliography: *A Bibliography of James* by Leon Edel and D. H. Laurence, 1957; revised edition, 1961; in *Bibliography of American Literature* by Jacob Blanck, 1968.

Reading List: *James: The Major Phase* by F. O. Matthiessen, 1944; *James* (biography) by Leon Edel, 5 vols., 1953–72, revised edition, 2 vols., 1978; *The American James* by Quentin Anderson, 1957; *The Comic Sense of James* by Richard Poirier, 1960; *The Novels of James* by Oscar Cargill, 1961; *The Ordeal of Consciousness in James* by Dorothea Crook, 1962; *The Expanse of Vision: Essays on the Craft of James* by Lawrence B. Holland, 1964; *The Imagination of Loving: James's Legacy to the Novel* by Naomi Lebowitz, 1965; *James: A Reader's Guide* by S. Gorley Putt, 1966; *James: The Critical Heritage* edited by Roger Gard, 1968; *James* by Tony Tanner, 1968; *The Negative Imagination: Form and Perspective in the Novels of James* by Sallie Sears, 1969; *Reading James* by Louis Auchincloss, 1975; *Language and Knowledge in the Late Novels of James* by Ruth Bernard Yeazell, 1976.

*   *   *

Few who accord the novels and short stories of Henry James the attention they deserve come away from the experience unmoved by the subject matter and unenlightened by the artistry, yet it is probably true that James would be little read today if it were not for the continuing enthusiasm of individuals who discover him first as a reading assignment in a college or university course. More than almost any other great novelist, James is a writer whose best works require a sympathetic power of attention that the casual reader is not disposed to give. For most people James is an acquired taste. Unless they approach him in the right spirit they never acquire the taste at all. Yet he is certainly one of the great writers in English, one of those artists of another era who nevertheless seems most perennially modern.

His dedication to literature for fifty years from the Civil War until his death in 1916 produced a body of work of monumental scope. He never married, never carried on anything resembling a conventional courtship. His friendships were virtually all rooted in shared literary or artistic enthusiasms. He travelled – often, it seems, merely to reinvigorate himself for a new assault upon his artistic problems. With less talent and similar dedication he might have produced novels and tales that consisted mainly of the same stories retold, the same techniques exploited again and again in order to recapture prior successes. Something of this tendency resides in his work, as it does in the work of all masters, but there is also an extraordinary continual development that reaches its peak in three late masterpieces: *The Wings of the Dove*, *The Ambassadors*, and *The Golden Bowl*. The late work of some poets can best be read largely in the light of the education gained by studying their earlier efforts: James is one of a relatively few novelists whose work cries out to be approached in a similar manner.

"It's a complex fate being an American," James once wrote, "and one of the responsibilities it entails is fighting against a superstitious valuation of Europe." Herein is expressed the essence of the "international theme" that runs through much of his work. In a time when more than a few novelists were making capital out of the social complications that arise when individuals from one side of the Atlantic confront the natives of the other side upon their home ground, James made this subject peculiarly his own by returning to it in work after work. So doing, he lifted it outside the confines of drawing room comedy and placed it squarely at the crossroads of the two great traditions of the nineteenth-century novel in English. Among the best of James's international novels and tales are *The American*, *The Europeans*, *Daisy Miller*, *The Portrait of a Lady*, *The Wings of the Dove*, *The Ambassadors*, and *The Golden Bowl*. In these works the central concerns of previous novelists in English come together in a confrontation almost mythic in its implications. Simply expressed, the central concern of English novelists from Austen through Scott, Dickens, and Eliot was the accommodation of individual aspirations within the sheltering embrace of the social framework; both their social view and their art were shaped by a realistic vision of compromise. Just as simply expressed, the central concern of American novelists from Cooper through Hawthorne, Melville, and Twain, was with those individual aspirations that are incapable of accommodation within any social framework except the as-yet-unrealized American dream of perfect freedom, equality, and justice; their social view and their art were shaped by a vision that looked toward a world considerably more ideal than the world they lived in. James brought these visions together in an amalgamation inherently tragic. His best works express in metaphor how much the condition of modern man hangs continually in the balance between the European dream of social accommodation and the American dream of perfect freedom.

Closely related to the international theme is James's continual emphasis upon partial perspectives. Human knowledge, he insists, and consequently human action, is sharply limited by inescapable conditions of time and place. From Christopher Newman to Lambert Strether his Americans achieve their destiny because the perspectives forced upon them by birth and education allow them no choices except the ones they inevitably make. From Madame de Cintré to Madame de Vionnet his Europeans are similarly limited. This at least is the theory: the novel is realistic, as James most often intended it should be, when the fates of the characters follow inevitably from the conditions that surround them; it is romantic, as James sometimes allowed, when the fates evolve from conditions imposed by the author that are quite distinct from the facts of observable reality. The realistic effect that he intended for most of his novels derives from the success with which he developed techniques for objectifying the partial perspectives from which humans direct their lives.

An important part of his work is also the theme of awareness that comes too late. His people are concerned above all with the question of how to live, but most of them have not any clear idea of how to begin. Sometimes they are wealthy, like Christopher Newman in *The American*, Milly Theale in *The Wings of the Dove*, and Maggie Verver in *The Golden Bowl*. Sometimes they become wealthy, like Isabel Archer in *The Portrait of a Lady*. Sometimes they live in expectation of wealth, like Kate Croy in *The Wings of the Dove*. In most instances they have at least, like Lambert Strether in *The Ambassadors*, enough to enable them to live comfortably, though it is often true of the less attractive figures that they suppose themselves in need of more than they possess. In any event they are mostly free of the more mundane cares of life and have nearly total leisure in which to pursue happiness through courtship, marriage, liaisons, social activity, travel, the search for culture: whatever, in short, seems most attractive to them. To live most fully, James makes clear in a number of places, is to be most fully aware of one's possibilities so that one may make the best of them. Since, however, the most interesting possibilities come from human relationships which are inherently a tissue of subtle complexities, to be most fully aware is to possess a depth of sympathetic insight that comes to few people until it is too late to take advantage of it. Total freedom for James's characters involves the freedom to make social commitments different from those that all too often they make, wrongly, in bondage to some mistaken understanding, or do not make at all because, sadly, they fail to perceive the opportunity that lies before them.

A great critic, James is also a great technical experimenter. The best of his criticism is preserved in individual essays such as "The Art of Fiction" and in his *Notebooks* and the prefaces that he wrote for the New York edition of his works. All are read most profitably in conjunction with the example of his fiction. His technical experiments are most readily approached through those many fictions in which he enforces the theme of partial perspectives by contriving severely limited perspectives from which to narrate. Some of the easier works in which this theme and this method are important are the early *Daisy Miller* and the late "The Beast in the Jungle." Because Daisy is never seen except from the partial view that Winterbourne enjoys, the reader remains in danger of sharing Winterbourne's misunderstanding of her character. Because May Bartram, in "The Beast in the Jungle," is never seen except in a view accessible to Marcher, the same potential problem exists. Fundamentally simple in these works, both theme and technique become more complex in "The Aspern Papers," *The Turn of the Screw*, and *The Sacred Fount*. In all three the careful reader is aware that there may be some aspect of the truth that remains dark to the central character. In "The Aspern Papers" most readers believe they can see beyond the limited vision of the narrator; in *The Turn of the Screw* there are good reasons to suppose both that the ghosts do and do not exist; in *The Sacred Fount* the puzzle that begins the novel becomes not less but more of a puzzle as it ends. In *The Portrait of a Lady, The Wings of the Dove, The Ambassadors*, and *The Golden Bowl* the theme of partial perspectives (which involves often the theme of too late awareness) merges with the international theme to provide the substance of James's most lasting achievement.

Many of James's fictions conclude upon a sense of loss. In his deepest vision human life is fundamentally tragic because of the eternal tension between the individual's sense of his vast human opportunities and his frequently inadequate awareness of his personal limitations. Like Isabel Archer or Lambert Strether, twentieth-century readers, too, are possessed by dreams of boundless freedom. Like both, they make in the end the choices that they *can* make – which are often not at all the choices that they would make if they lived in a world in which a just and equal perfect freedom came less insistently into conflict with the requirements of social accommodation.

—George Perkins

JAMES, M(ontague) R(hodes). English. Born in Goodnestone, Kent, 1 August 1862. Educated at Eton College (King's Scholar), 1876–82 (Editor, *Eton College Chronicle*, 1881–82; Wilder Divinity Prize, and Newcastle Scholarship, 1882); King's College, Cambridge (Eton Scholar; Carus Divinity Prize, 1882; Bell Scholarship, 1883; Craven Scholarship, and Septuagint Prize, 1884), 1882–85, first class degrees in classical tripos, 1884–85. At Cambridge University: Assistant to the Director of the Fitzwilliam Museum, 1886–87; Fellow of King's College, from 1887; Lecturer in Divinity, 1888; Dean of King's College, 1889–1900; Director of the Fitzwilliam Museum, 1893–1908; tutor at King's College, 1900–02; Sandars Reader in Bibliography, 1903, 1923; Provost of King's College, 1905–18; Vice-Chancellor of the University, 1913–15; Provost of Eton College, 1918–36; Donnellan Lecturer, Trinity College, Dublin, 1927; Schweich Lecturer, British Academy, London, 1927; David Murray Lecturer, University of Glasgow, 1931. President, Buckinghamshire Archaeological Society; Trustee, British Museum; member of the royal commissions on Public Records, on the Universities of Oxford and Cambridge, and on Historical Monuments. Recipient: Bibliographical Society gold medal, 1929. D.Litt.: Trinity College, Dublin; LL.D.: University of St. Andrews; D.C.L.: Oxford University. Commander of the Order of Leopold, Belgium. Fellow of the British Academy, 1903; Honorary Member of the Royal Irish Academy. Order of Merit, 1930. *Died 12 June 1936.*

PUBLICATIONS

Collections

Ghost Stories, edited by Nigel Kneale.   1973.

Fiction

Ghost-Stories of an Antiquary.   1904.
More Ghost Stories of an Antiquary.   1911.
A Thin Ghost and Others.   1919.

The Five Jars. 1922.
A Warning to the Curious and Other Ghost-Stories. 1925.
Wailing Well. 1928.
Collected Ghost Stories. 1931.

Play

The Founder's Pageant and Play of St. Nicholas, with A. B. Ramsay. 1919.

Other

The Sculptures in the Lady Chapel at Ely. 1895.
Guide to the Windows of King's College Chapel, Cambridge. 1899.
Description of an Illuminated Manuscript of the 13th Century. 1904.
Notes on the Glass in Ashridge Chapel. 1906.
The Sculptured Bosses in the Roof of the Bauchun Chapel, Norwich Cathedral. 1908;
    Cloisters, 1911.
*Old Testament Legends, Being Stories Out of Some of the Less-Known Apocryphal
    Books.* 1913.
The Wanderings and Homes of Manuscripts. 1919.
Eton College Chapel: The Wall Paintings. 1923.
Bibliotheca Pepysiana, part 3. 1923.
Eton and King's: Recollections, Mostly Trivial 1875–1925. 1926.
Suffolk and Norfolk: A Perambulation of the Two Counties. 1930.
The Apocalypse in Art. 1931.
St. George's Chapel, Windsor: The Woodwork of the Choir. 1933.
Letters to a Friend, edited by Gwendolen McBryde. 1956.

Editor, with J. W. Clark, *The Will of King Henry VI.* 1896.
Editor, with A. Jessopp, *Life and Miracles of St. William of Norwich*, by Thomas of
    Monmouth. 1896.
Editor, *The Ancient Libraries of Canterbury and Dover.* 1903.
Editor, *The Second Epistle General of Peter, and The General Epistle of Jude.* 1912.
Editor, *The Chaundler Manuscripts.* 1916.
Editor, *Madam Crowl's Ghost and Other Tales of Mystery*, by Sheridan Le Fanu. 1923.
Editor, *Latin Infancy Gospels: A New Text.* 1927.
Editor, *The Bestiary.* 1928.
Editor, with A. B. Ramsay, *Letters of H. E. Luxmoore.* 1929.
Editor, *The Dublin Apocalypse.* 1932.
Editor, *The New Testament.* 4 vols., 1934–35.

Translator, with H. E. Ryle, *Psalms of the Pharisees.* 1891.
Translator, *The Biblical Antiquities of Philo.* 1917.
Translator, *Henry the Sixth*, by Joannes Blacman. 1919.
Translator, *The Lost Apocrypha of the Old Testament.* 1920.
Translator, *De Nugis Curialium*, by Walter Map. 1923.
Translator, *The Apocryphal New Testament.* 1924.
Translator, with others, *Excluded Books of the New Testament.* 1927.
Translator, *Forty Stories*, by Hans Christian Andersen. 1930; augmented edition, as
    Forty-Two Stories, 1953.

Descriptive Catalogues of manuscripts in Eton College, Fitzwilliam Museum, the collection of H. V. Thompson, Rylands Library, University College, Aberdeen, and Oxford and Cambridge universities, 35 vols., 1895–1932.

Bibliography: "James: An Annotated Bibliography of Writings about Him" by J. R. Cox, in *English Literature in Transition 12*, 1969.

Reading List: *A Memoir of James* by S. G. Lubbock, 1939 (includes bibliography by A. F. Scholfield).

*   *   *

M. R. James was supreme in at least three specialised fields – as a scholar of apocryphal Biblical literature and of medieval illuminated manuscripts, and as a writer of ghost stories. The first two no doubt contributed to the last, as did a mastery of folklore and of medieval archaeology, and a life spent in Gothic surroundings as Provost of Eton and of King's College, Cambridge.

His first volume was called *Ghost Stories of an Antiquary*, and many of the plots arise from just the kind of situation when an antiquary might suddenly ask himself, "Is this curiosity about the past decent or even well-advised? Where am I trespassing?" Moreover, the density of reference – true or fictional – derived from antiquarian knowledge and upholding the stories contributes immensely to their power of convincing: nothing could be further from the ambiguities of Henry James, except in respect of knowing precisely how much to show, how much to leave at that corner of the eye which provokes nervous terror. Again, he fulfills his claim to make his ghosts act consistently with the ghosts of folklore. Part of this consistency is a kind of double motivation: most of his beings have a clear function, many indeed have been set as guardians or sent as avengers, yet themselves seem lost, driven, or searching with malignity indeed but with no other motive corresponding to human motives. The fear – and it is always fear, for James knows of no beneficent ghost – is heightened by a certain confidence, solidity, and even benevolence about the donnish and squirearchic society set in a pastoral landscape, the environment in which the cracks develop that reveal the supernatural, and about the clarity of prose style and the humorous observation with which James renders this environment.

It is relevant that he was a brilliant mimic, that the stories were mostly composed for friends as Christmas entertainment, and particularly that he was a calmly believing Christian. His belief in wandering spirits and revenants went no further, he said, than a willingness to consider evidence; but he talked of dead friends, where his serious beliefs were involved, as of fellow guests waiting to welcome him into unfamiliar surroundings. Fundamentally, his stories convey a sense of the totally other set in the totally familiar, and leave one therefore with a sense, in their own small sphere, or something aesthetically and spiritually absolute.

—Stephen Medcalf

JEFFERIES, Richard. English. Born at Coate Farm, near Swindon, Wiltshire, 6 November 1848. Educated at schools in Sydenham, Kent, and Swindon, to age 15. Married in 1874. Travelled in France, 1865, attempted unsuccessfully to travel to America, then returned to Swindon; wrote for the *North Wilts Herald*, 1866–70: became its regular reporter and local correspondent for a Gloucestershire paper; travelled in Belgium, 1870; returned to England and worked as a free-lance writer; settled in London, 1876, and wrote for the *Pall Mall Gazette;* in later life settled in Sussex. *Died 14 August 1887.*

PUBLICATIONS

Collections

> *Works*, edited by C. Henry Warren.   6 vols., 1948–49.
> *The Essential Jefferies*, edited by M. Elwin.   1948.

Fiction

> *The Scarlet Shawl*.   1874.
> *Restless Human Hearts*.   1875.
> *World's End*.   1877.
> *Wood Magic: A Fable*.   1880.
> *Greene-Ferne Farm*.   1880.
> *Bevis: The Story of a Boy*.   1882.
> *The Dewy Morn*.   1884.
> *After London; or, Wild England*.   1885.
> *Amaryllis at the Fair*.   1887.
> *The Early Fiction*, edited by G. Toplis.   1896.
> *T.T.T.*   1896.

Other

> *Reporting, Editing, and Authorship*.   1873.
> *Jack Brass, Emperor of England*.   1873.
> *A Memoir of the Goddards of North Wilts*.   1873.
> *Suez-cide! or, How Miss Britannia Bought a Dirty Puddle and Lost Her Sugarplums*.   1876.
> *The Gamekeeper at Home: Sketches of Natural History and Rural Life*.   1878.
> *Wild Life in a Southern County*.   1879.
> *The Amateur Poacher*.   1879.
> *Hodge and His Masters*.   2 vols., 1880; edited by Henry Williamson, 1937.
> *Round about a Great Estate*.   1880.
> *Nature near London*.   1883.
> *The Story of My Heart: My Autobiography*.   1883; edited by Samuel J. Looker, 1947.
> *The Life of the Fields*.   1884.
> *Red Deer*.   1884.
> *The Open Air*.   1885.
> *Field and Hedgegrow, Being the Last Essays*, edited by J. Jefferies.   1889.
> *The Toilers of the Field*.   1892.
> *Jefferies' Land: A History of Swindon and Its Environs*, edited by G. Toplis.   1896.
> *Nature and Eternity and Other Uncollected Papers*.   1907.
> *The Nature Diaries and Notebooks*, edited by Samuel J. Looker.   1941.
> *Beauty Is Immortal, Felise of "The Dewy Morn," with Some Hitherto Uncollected Essays and Manuscripts*, edited by Samuel J. Looker.   1948.
> *The Old House at Coate, and Hitherto Unpublished Essays*, edited by Samuel J. Looker.   1948.

Reading List: *Jefferies: His Life and Work* by Edward Thomas, 1909; *Jefferies: A Tribute* edited by Samuel J. Looker, 1946; *Jefferies, Man of the Fields: A Biography and Letters* by

Samuel J. Looker and Crichton Porteous, 1965; *Jefferies: A Critical Study* by W. J. Keith, 1966.

*   *   *

Richard Jefferies's earliest society novels are ill-conceived, whereas *Greene-Ferne Farm* and *The Dewy Morn* have been appreciated for their natural freshness. His last novel, *Amaryllis at the Fair*, is clearly the strongest, drawing on his family background and developed with naturalistic techniques "absolutely true to nature and fact." Characters come alive when Jefferies probes the rooted tensions within the family. Outstanding sketches appear of Farmer Iden's nervous wife, his ninety-year-old father, and Iden himself (a genius bent on failure) in his rituals of potato planting, dining, and napping after dinner, when he pretends to sleep while mice climb his knee for crumbs. As story, however, the novel is continually fragmented by digressions. Toward the close the plot breaks loose and then breaks off, and we sense the underlying frustrations of the dying author.

Jefferies's excellence is to be found in his essays on nature and rural life, most of these following one of three prevalent tendencies. Some of the earliest, such as appeared in *The Amateur Poacher*, are personal essays, enabling the reader to live over boyhood experiences with the author. Very similar are numerous familiar essays, descriptive encounters with people and landscapes, birds, animals, wild flowers, and golden wheat under a burning sun. Finally, social essays range from the early conservative letters to the *Times* on the Wiltshire labourer to the more radical views of "Rural Dynamite" or "One of the New Voters." Rural characters include farmers and gamekeepers, gipsies and poachers, and always the figures of Hodge and his field-faring women, on whose backs the burden of agricultural life rested. Jefferies the journalist strove for facts, and, as facts accumulated, his voice rose, "pleading for more humane treatment of the poor." With his sympathies grew his commitment to naturalism, culminating in "A True Tale of the Wiltshire Labourer." Yet he will best be remembered for familiar essays with their many descriptions of rural life executed in a transparent style.

The Story of My Heart is a unique contribution of the nature essayist. Plotless, lacking autobiographical facts, it searches out the spirit of life and conceives a realm of idea beyond the circle of the known. Many contributing thoughts are hardly original. Like Carlyle, Jefferies finds miracle in natural phenomena, casts off time and takes "now" for eternity, and focuses upon what Carlyle had considered the essential "Me." Like Mill or Hardy, he sees nature as ultra-human, lacking mind. Like Pater, he condemns asceticism and aims to enjoy all that is possible in life. What is original is perhaps Jefferies's uniting of nature and spirit, flesh and "soul life," not as philosophy but personal experience. The pantheist discovers that the mystery lies not in nature but in himself, and his spirit is darkened by the insights and aches of modernism. Still Jefferies looks beyond his problem: "full well aware that all has failed, ... there lives on in me an unquenchable belief, thought burning like the sun, that there is yet something to be found."

—William J. Hyde

JEROME, Jerome K(lapka).   English.   Born in Walsall, Staffordshire, 2 May 1858; grew up in London. Educated at Marylebone Grammar School, London. Served as an ambulance driver on the Western front during World War I. Married Georgina Henrietta Stanley in 1888; one daughter. Left school at 14 and worked, successively, as a railway clerk, schoolmaster, actor, and journalist; writer from 1885; Co-Founder and Editor, with Robert Barr and George Brown Burgin, *The Idler* magazine, London, 1892–97; Founding Editor, *To-Day* weekly newspaper, London, 1893–97. *Died 14 June 1927.*

Fiction

Three Men in a Boat (To Say Nothing of the Dog). 1889.
Told after Supper. 1891.
John Ingerfield and Other Stories. 1894.
Sketches in Lavender, Blue, and Green. 1897.
Three Men on the Bummel. 1900.
The Observations of Henry. 1901.
Paul Kelver. 1902.
American Wives and Others. 1904.
Tommy and Co. 1904.
The Passing of the Third Floor Back and Other Stories. 1907.
The Angel and the Author and Others. 1908.
Malvina of Brittany. 1916.
Anthony John: A Biography. 1923.

Plays

Barbara (produced 1886). 1886.
Sunset (produced 1888). 1888.
Fennel, from a play by François Coppée (produced 1888). 1888.
Woodbarrow Farm (produced 1888). 1921.
Pity Is Akin to Love (produced 1888).
New Lamps for Old (produced 1890).
Ruth, with A. Addison Bright (produced 1890).
What Women Will Do (produced 1890).
Birth and Breeding (produced 1890). 1895.
The Prude's Progress, with Eden Phillpotts (produced 1895). 1895.
The Rise of Dick Halward (produced 1895).
Biarritz, with Adrian Ross, music by F. O. Carr (produced 1896).
The MacHaggis, with Eden Phillpotts (produced 1897).
Miss Hobbs (produced 1899). 1902.
Tommy (produced 1906).
The Passing of the Third Floor Back, from his own story (produced 1908). 1910.
Fanny and the Servant Problem (produced 1908). 1909.
The Master of Mrs. Chilvers (produced 1911). 1911.
Esther Castways (produced 1913).
Robina in Search of a Husband (produced 1913). 1914.
The Great Gamble (produced 1914).
The Three Patriots (produced 1915).
The Celebrity (as *Cook,* produced 1917; as *The Celebrity,* produced 1928). 1926.
The Soul of Nicholas Snyders (produced 1927). 1927.

Other

The Idle Thoughts of an Idle Fellow: A Book for an Idle Holiday. 1886.
On Stage and Off: The Brief Career of a Would-Be Actor. 1888.
Stage-Land: Curious Habits and Customs of Its Inhabitants. 1889.
Diary of a Pilgrimage, and Six Essays. 1891.

Novel Notes. 1893.
The Second Thoughts of an Idle Fellow. 1898.
Tea-Table Talk. 1903.
Idle Ideas in 1905. 1905.
They and I. 1909.
All Roads Lead to Calvary. 1919.
A Miscellany of Sense and Nonsense. 1923.
My Life and Times. 1926.

Reading List: *Jerome: His Life and Works* by A. Moss, 1929; *Jerome* by W. Gutkess, 1930.

*   *   *

Jerome K. Jerome always believed that a literary gentleman whom he met in an East London park as a boy, and who refused to give his name, was Charles Dickens. He told the gentleman that what he liked in the novels of Dickens was the humour, and that his favourite character was Mr. Pickwick; and the gentleman said, "Oh, damn Mr. Pickwick.... I like him well enough – or used to. I'm a bit tired of him, that's all."

There would have been justice in this: for Jerome later accepted reluctantly that his own fame was based on his humour, and indeed on a book which is one of the worthiest successors of *The Pickwick Papers* – *Three Men in a Boat (To Say Nothing of the Dog).* Its sequels – *Three Men on the Bummel* and *Diary of a Pilgrimage* – and his humorous journalistic essays *The Idle Thoughts of an Idle Fellow* remain enjoyable. His play *The Passing of the Third Floor Back* (about the redemption of the shabby and dubious inhabitants of a London lodging house by a man who offers them a sense of their better selves, and whom audiences think of as Christ, though Jerome preferred a vaguer identification), though sentimental, is still heard of. And *Paul Kelver*, his *David Copperfield*, an autobiographical picaresque novel set in East End, lodging house, and Bohemian London, is excellent reading, and most unjustly neglected.

But *Three Men in a Boat* is unique. Partly, as Jerome himself says, this is because of its "hopeless and incurable veracity." In fact, much of it is a record of holidays taken by Jerome with Carl Hentschel (Harris) and George Wingrave, though Montmorency the dog is imaginary; and few people can have gone on a boating, or indeed walking or camping, holiday, without something reminding them of the book. But the process whereby particular facts become universal and delightful truth is no less strange here than in any other literature. The style is important: Jerome has Chaucer's china-blue eye, a gift for portraying the principal narrator – himself – as both devastatingly naive and annihilatingly observant. The sentiment which surprises one in odd detachable passages, though rather feeble, seems to express some quite deep level of the book: perhaps the concluding reflection of Paul Kelver that "this fortress of laughter that a few of you have been set aside to guard" may, trivial as it seems, be the key to the battle against suffering. Moreover, the most obvious difference of *Three Men in a Boat* from Jerome's other anecdotal comedies is that the river journey does duty in it for a plot. Perhaps as Arthur Machen observed of *The Pickwick Papers* that its magic comes from its sharing the essential ecstasy, the withdrawal from life, of the *Odyssey* or the myth of Dionysus, so even in the less daemonic *Three Men in a Boat* the symbolic quality of the river journey may echo. Certainly no book conveys better the bursting happiness of a summer holiday: and isn't that ecstasy?

—Stephen Medcalf

JEWETT, Sarah Orne. American. Born in South Berwick, Maine, 3 September 1849, and lived there for all of her life. Educated at Miss Rayne's School, 1855, and the Berwick Academy, 1861–65; graduated 1865. Full-time writer from 1865; contributed to the *Atlantic Monthly* from 1869; through association with the editor, William Dean Howells, came to know the Boston literary circle of Lowell and Whittier; later travelled abroad and met Tennyson, Christina Rossetti, and Henry James. Litt.D.: Bowdoin College, Brunswick, Maine, 1901. *Died 24 June 1909.*

PUBLICATIONS

Collections

    Stories and Tales. 7 vols., 1910.
    Letters, edited by Richard Cary. 1956; revised edition, 1967.
    The Country of the Pointed Firs and Other Stories, edited by Mary Ellen Chase. 1968.

Fiction

    Deephaven. 1877; edited by Richard Cary, with other stories, 1966.
    Old Friends and New (stories). 1879.
    Country By-Ways. 1881.
    The Mate of the Daylight and Friends Ashore (stories). 1883.
    A Country Doctor. 1884.
    A Marsh Island. 1885.
    A White Heron and Other Stories. 1886.
    The King of Folly Island and Other People. 1888.
    Strangers and Wayfarers. 1890.
    Tales of New England. 1890.
    A Native of Winby and Other Tales. 1893.
    The Life of Nancy (stories). 1895.
    The Country of the Pointed Firs. 1896.
    The Queen's Twin and Other Stories. 1899.
    The Tory Lover. 1901.
    An Empty Purse: A Christmas Story. 1905.
    Uncollected Short Stories, edited by Richard Cary. 1971.

Verse

    Verses, edited by M. A. DeWolfe Howe. 1916.

Other

    Play Days: A Book of Stories for Children. 1878.
    The Story of the Normans (juvenile). 1887.
    Betty Leicester: A Story for Girls. 1890.
    Betty Leicester's English Xmas (juvenile). 1894; as *Betty Leicester's Christmas,* 1899.
    Letters, edited by Annie Fields. 1911.
    Letters Now in Colby College Library, edited by Carl J. Weber. 1947.

Editor, *Stories and Poems for Children,* by Celia Thaxter.   1895.
Editor, *The Poems of Celia Thaxter.*   1896.
Editor, *Letters of Sarah Wyman Whitman.*   1907.

Bibliography: *A Bibliography of the Published Writings of Jewett* by Clara Carter Weber and Carl J. Weber, 1949; in *Bibliography of American Literature* by Jacob Blanck, 1969.

Reading List: *Jewett* by F. O. Matthiessen, 1929; *Jewett* by John Eldridge Frost, 1960; *Jewett* by Richard Cary, 1962; *Jewett* by Margaret Farrand Thorp, 1966.

*   *   *

The American novelist Willa Cather ranked Sarah Orne Jewett's *The Country of the Pointed Firs* with Nathaniel Hawthorne's *The Scarlet Letter* and Mark Twain's *Huckleberry Finn* as one of the three American prose literary works most likely to endure. The estimate is probably overenthusiastic; yet *The Country of the Pointed Firs,* a loosely constructed episodic novel laid on the Maine Coast in America, is at least a minor classic and will continue to be read for many years to come. Jewett was an eminently successful literary regionalist – a depicter of setting and character in the area where she had been born and brought up in a patrician family whose sympathies had been Tory during the Revolutionary War. Yet her somewhat aristocratic viewpoint – she was inordinately proud of her Anglo-Norman ancestry – in no way affected her understanding and admiration of the fishing and farming people about whom she wrote in her best work.

Her first book, *Deephaven,* fashioned from sketches that had previously appeared in the *Atlantic Monthly,* deals with life among all classes in a typical Maine seaport, with emphasis upon social and economic decay as commerce and shipping became more and more concentrated in the larger ports like Boston and New York. Jewett's tone in this volume, as in much of her writing, is one of nostalgia for a time when her region had figured vitally in the maritime life of the nation and had nurtured a population of hardy seafarers who sailed their vessels to all the great ports of the world. These days, regrettably, were past, but Jewett still found much to praise among the Maine folk of her time. *The Country of the Pointed Firs* is her major tribute to these quiet, resourceful, hard-working people, the significance of whose lives, now that the adventurous sea-faring days were gone, Jewett found to be in the success with which they had adjusted to a harsh environment. The women especially (and most of Jewett's strong characters are women) had learned to live in harmony with their native region – a rocky, island-studded coast with steep pastures and forested mountains rising close back from the water. The most notable of these women, the widow Elmira Todd, subsisted as an herbalist, thus personifying the Maine folks' ability to draw life-giving strength from a seemingly sterile land.

Jewett, in her Preface to *Deephaven,* stated that she considered one of her functions as a regional writer was to make the rest of the nation acquainted with the lives and characteristics of a little-known segment of the population. But more important, taking her cue from a statement by George Sand regarding the French peasantry, Jewett believed that the scrutiny to which she, as a writer, subjected her Maine neighbors would reveal a human worth and gentle heroism rarely found elsewhere. Jewett, indeed, saw a physical resemblance between the Maine Coast and the coast and isles of Greece, and she saw classical qualities in her Maine characters. Thus Mrs. Todd, standing on an Atlantic headland and mourning her husband drowned in shipwreck, reminds Jewett of Antigone "alone on the Theban plain." Elsewhere Mrs. Todd as an herbalist reminds Jewett of the enchantress Medea. Such allusions, inserted in passing, underline Jewett's point in this and other books: that the simplest persons can attain a dignity, even a tragic grandeur, essentially the same as that found in the literary records of the classic ages. She did not always find these qualities only among maritime people. The persons in her fiction include up-country farmers, elderly ladies in elm-shaded inland towns, and Irish maid-servants, and almost invariably she presents them as possessing, and exhibiting, a potential for the full range of human experience from tragedy to ecstasy.

Jewett's prose is notable for its purity and variety. Her descriptions of land and sea are lyrically evocative. Her narrative style is direct and flowing. In her dialogue she succeeds better than any other New England writer in reproducing the accents and, especially, the rhythms of the speech of her region. Unlike many local-colorists, she does not strive for phonetic renderings of dialect – efforts that usually result in grotesque and nearly unintelligible manglings of spelling. Jewett emphasizes regional diction, idiom, and cadence with only minor alterations of spelling. The result is not only readable but authentic.

Jewett in her lifetime was an admired and popular writer, publishing a sizable number of novels and collections of tales and sketches. Among the novels *A Country Doctor*, which draws from her experiences in accompanying her physician father on his rounds, deserves mention, as does *A Marsh Island*, an idyllic celebration of life on a coastal farm. Among her volumes of short fiction and sketches three of the richest are *Country By-Ways*, *A White Heron and Other Stories* (the title piece being her most famous story), and *The King of Folly Island and Other People*, containing the superb story "Miss Tempy's Watchers."

Though born and brought up in a small Maine town and always fiercely loyal to the place of her birth, Jewett was very much in touch with, and an influence in, the literary life of her times. A close friend of Mrs. James Fields, wife of the prominent Boston publisher, she was active in Boston literary circles and met many of the nation's and world's great writers as they visited the publisher's home. Eventually she became recognized as the author who carried local color, or regionalism, to the highest artistic level it has attained in America. Her writing has served as a model for other American authors, not all of them local-colorists, especially women of her and later generations. For example, Willa Cather, following Jewett's example and personal advice, redirected her early efforts from rather mediocre fiction in the manner of Henry James to the writing of highly successful competent novels based on life in the midwestern farmlands where she had been brought up. Jewett always held that an author's chief source of material should be his or her own locale and personal experience. To this conviction she remained faithful throughout her writing career.

—P. D. Westbrook

JHABVALA, Ruth Prawer.   British.   Born in Cologne, Germany, of Polish parents, 7 May 1927; emigrated to England, as a refugee, 1939; naturalized, 1948. Educated at Hendon County School, London; Queen Mary College, University of London, 1945–51, M.A. in English literature 1951. Married the architect C. S. H. Jhabvala in 1951; three daughters. Lived in India, 1951–77. Recipient: Booker Prize, 1975; Guggenheim grant, 1976.

P<small>UBLICATIONS</small>

Fiction

> *To Whom She Will.*   1955; as *Amrita*, 1956.
> *The Nature of Passion.*   1956.
> *Esmond in India.*   1957.
> *The Householder.*   1960.

Get Ready for Battle.   1962.
Like Birds, Like Fishes and Other Stories.   1963.
A Backward Place.   1965.
A Stronger Climate: 9 Stories.   1968.
An Experience of India (stories).   1971.
A New Dominion.   1973.
Heat and Dust.   1975.
How I Became a Holy Mother and Other Stories.   1976.

Plays

Shakespeare Wallah: A Film, with James Ivory, with *Savages,* by Ivory.   1973.
Autobiography of a Princess, Also Being the Adventures of an American Film Director in the Land of the Maharajas, with James Ivory and John Swope.   1975.

Screenplays: *The Householder,* 1963; *Shakespeare Wallah,* with James Ivory, 1965; *The Guru,* 1968; *Bombay Talkie,* 1970; *Roseland,* 1978; *Hullabaloo over Georgie and Bonnie's Pictures,* 1978.

Television Play: *The Place of Peace,* 1975.

Reading List: *The Fiction of Jhabvala* by Haydu M. Williams, 1973.

*   *   *

Ruth Prawer Jhabvala was born of Polish parents in Germany in 1927. She moved to England in 1939 and when she was twenty-four she married an Indian architect and went to live in India. All her work up to date, both her novels and short stories, has been concerned with her experience of India. At first Ruth Jhabvala was mesmerised by India; she endeavoured to steep herself completely in Indian life, and her first novels are peopled completely by Indians. This euphoria she said lasted for a decade; then the poverty, hunger, and appalling conditions of which she had at first been oblivious suddenly became visible. This led her to write *Get Ready for Battle,* her one novel that deals with India's social problems.

Ruth Jhabvala is a natural satirist with a sharp eye for hypocrisy and inconsistency. With a delicate irony that reminds one, on occasions, of Jane Austen, she exposes the foibles, weaknesses, and prejudices of her English characters while at the same time acknowledging the problems of those who come to India. Her criticism hardens when she turns to the westernized Indians. "Fashionable chatterers," is how she describes them, "hybrids, neither Western nor Indian, whose days are numbered." She is even more scathing about the latest group of travellers to India, those who belong to the westernized hippy movement. "They're the new sahibs," she says. "They detest India, they speak in the rudest way about the dirt and people cheating them, they're all day hanging outside American Express where their money comes from, then they exchange it on the black market, buy drugs, sell them and move around in filthy, torn clothes, which is a mockery of poverty in India. They're like parasites. Indians detest them and rightly so."

Since 1961 Ruth Jhabvala has collaborated with the film director James Ivory. She has scripted five films for him, including *Shakespeare Wallah* and *Autobiography of a Princess.* There is a close relationship between the latter and *Heat and Dust,* the novel that won Ruth Jhabvala the Booker prize in 1975. In the film and the novel she has turned back to the Raj. In both she has interwoven past and present, counterpointed in such a way as to pick up the slightest nuance and so achieve the maximum effect. Both are minor masterpieces conjuring up a whole world of allusion and illusion.

One has felt in Ruth Jhabvala's writing a continuing and ever-growing sense of alienation and an increasing urgency to leave India. She has now done so. This does not mean she has discarded or rejected her Indian experience. As a critic of her work, Yasmine Gooneratne, has pointed out (in *Kunapipi*, 1978), "She is not the first, nor will she be the last, writer for whom India has provided inspiration, experience, and a starting point; for perhaps her 'Indian' novel will, in the final count, represent merely a milestone along her path to the greatness for which she has the potential."

—Anna Rutherford

JOHNSON, Pamela Hansford. English. Born in London, 29 May 1912. Educated at Clapham County Secondary School, London. Married 1) Gordon Neil Stewart in 1936, one son and one daughter; 2) C. P. Snow, *q.v.*, in 1950, one son. Writer and critic since 1935; Fellow, Center for Advanced Studies, Wesleyan University, Middletown, Connecticut, and Honorary Fellow, Timothy Dwight College, Yale University, New Haven, Connecticut, 1961. Litt.D.: Temple University, Philadelphia, 1963; York University, Toronto, 1967; Widener College, Chester, Pennsylvania, 1970. Fellow, Royal Society of Literature, 1951. C.B.E. (Commander, Order of the British Empire), 1975. Lives in London.

PUBLICATIONS

Fiction

This Bed Thy Centre. 1935.
Blessed above Woman. 1936.
Here Today. 1937.
World's End. 1937.
The Monument. 1938.
Girdle of Venus. 1939.
Too Dear for My Possessing. 1940.
Tidy Death, with Neil Stewart. 1940.
The Family Pattern. 1942.
Winter Quarters. 1943.
Murder's A Swine, with Neil Stewart. 1943; as *The Grinning Pig*, 1943.
The Trojan Brothers. 1944.
An Avenue of Stone. 1947.
A Summer to Decide. 1948.
The Philistines. 1949.
Catherine Carter. 1952.
An Impossible Marriage. 1954.
The Last Resort. 1956; as *The Sea and the Wedding*, 1957.
The Humbler Creation. 1959.
The Unspeakable Skipton. 1959.

657

An Error of Judgement. 1962.
Night and Silence, Who Is Here? An American Comedy. 1963.
Cork Street, Next to the Hatter's: A Novel in Bad Taste. 1965.
The Survival of the Fittest. 1968.
The Honours Board. 1970.
The Holiday Friend. 1972.
The Good Listener. 1975.

Plays

Corinth House (produced 1948). 1954.
The Supper Dance, with C. P. Snow. 1951.
Family Party, with C. P. Snow. 1951.
Spare the Rod, with C. P. Snow. 1951.
To Murder Mrs. Mortimer, with C. P. Snow. 1951.
The Pigeon with the Silver Foot, with C. P. Snow. 1951.
Her Best Foot Forward, with C. P. Snow. 1951.
Six Proust Reconstructions (broadcast 1948–56). 1958; as *Proust Recaptured: Six Radio Sketches, Based on the Author's Characters,* 1958.
The Rehearsal, with Kitty Black, from a play by Jean Anouilh (produced 1961). 1961.
The Public Prosecutor, with C. P. Snow, from a play by Georgi Dzhagarov, translated by Marguerite Alexieva (produced 1967). 1969.

Radio Plays: *Six Proust Reconstructions: The Duchess at Sunset,* 1948, *Swann in Love,* 1952, *Madame de Charlus,* 1954, *Albertine Regained,* 1954, *Saint-Loup,* 1955, and *A Window at Montjaurain,* 1956.

Verse

Symphony for Full Orchestra. 1934.

Other

Thomas Wolfe: A Critical Study. 1947; as *Hungry Gulliver: An English Critical Appraisal of Thomas Wolfe,* 1948.
Ivy Compton-Burnett. 1951.
On Iniquity: Some Personal Reflections Arising Out of the Moors Murder Trial. 1967.
Important to Me: Personalia. 1974.

Editor, with C. P. Snow, *Winter's Tales 7.* 1961; as *Stories from Modern Russia,* 1962.

Reading List: *Johnson* by Isabel Quigly, 1968.

*   *   *

As deeply, in her individual way, as Graham Greene or William Golding, Pamela Hansford Johnson is concerned with the nature of good and evil, the complexity of moral problems and choices. She presents without simplification or censure such thought-provoking dilemmas as that of her consultant-physician in *An Error of Judgement.* Shocked to discover within himself a sadistic fascination with pain, he abandons his practice: only to be forced into a still more drastic course of action, when his self-tormenting conscience is confronted with a total lack of it in the brutal young delinquent he has befriended. Responsibility, in its various guises, is the central theme of many of Pamela Hansford Johnson's novels. In *The Last Resort* she investigates the obligations of filial duty to possessively devouring parents. Conflicts of loyalty, between love and ambition and between religious vocation and personal fulfilment respectively, are explored in *Catherine Carter* and *The Humbler Creation*.

Yet even the most serious of her novels abounds in incisive humorous observation. The richness of her comic gift is most fully exemplified in *The Unspeakable Skipton*, based on the career of Baron Corvo. The adventures and absurdities of this disreputable expatriate, preying outrageously on an unappreciative society in the name of art, are depicted with devastating wit. Rather less successful, but still delectably funny, are the related novels about the pretentious poetess Dorothy Merlin and her circle in *Night and Silence, Who is Here?*, set on a New Hampshire campus, and *Cork Street, Next to the Hatter's*, a satire on literary London.

Pamela Hansford Johnson's varied backgrounds show an unerring sense of atmosphere and eye for detail. Her beloved Bruges is precisely and poetically evoked in both *The Unspeakable Skipton* and *Too Dear for My Possessing*, while a later novel, *The Holiday Friend*, also returns to Belgium. Avowing herself "unregenerately urban, obstinately a Londoner," she portrays the streets of the city with vigorous realism in her first novel, *This Bed Thy Centre*, in the drab, unfashionable parish of her vicar in *The Humbler Creation*, and in *The Survival of the Fittest*. This vividly documented picture of London between the 1930's and early 1960's illustrates a sense of period as accurate and authentic as that of place. So also do the meticulously observed Victorian theatrical background of *Catherine Carter*, and the changing socio-political scene through the progress of the experience related in *Too Dear for My Possessing*, *An Avenue of Stone*, and *A Summer to Decide*.

The narrator of that trilogy is a man; and it is noteworthy how many other novels – among them *The Unspeakable Skipton*, *The Survival of the Fittest*, and *The Good Listener* – have male central characters. Pamela Hansford Johnson has a talent, comparatively rare among women novelists, for subtle and convincing depiction of the viewpoints, thought-processes, and emotional responses of the opposite sex. Indeed her whole breadth of subject and treatment is peculiarly masculine in its detachment, expressing a shrewd yet compassionate acceptance of many aspects of human frailty.

—Margaret Willy

JOHNSON, Samuel. English. Born in Lichfield, Staffordshire, 18 September 1709. Educated at Lichfield Grammar School, and at the Stourbridge School, to age 16; Pembroke College, Oxford, 1728–29, left without taking a degree. Married Elizabeth Porter in 1735 (died, 1752). Usher in a grammar school in Market Bosworth, Leicestershire; worked for the publisher of the *Birmingham Journal*, 1732; took pupils at Edial, Staffordshire, among them David Garrick, 1736–37; travelled with Garrick to London, and settled there, 1737; supported himself by writing for Cave's *Gentleman's Magazine*, 1734–44, for which he wrote reports on debates in Parliament, 1740–44; catalogued the library of the second Earl of Oxford, 1742; worked on his *Dictionary*, 1747–55; formed the Ivy Lane Club, 1749; Author/Editor, *The Rambler*, 1750–52; contributed to *The Adventurer*, 1753–54; arrested for debt, but released on a loan from Samuel Richardson, 1756; contributed to the *Literary Magazine*, 1756–58; wrote "The Idler" for the *Universal Chronicle*, 1758–60; moved to Inner Temple Lane, now Johnson's Buildings, 1759; pensioned by the crown, 1762; founded

The Literary Club, 1764; wrote pamphlets against Wilkes, 1770, a defense of government policy in the Falkland Islands, 1771, and in America, 1775; toured Scotland with James Boswell, subsequently his biographer, 1773; travelled to Wales, 1774, and Paris, 1775; formed the Essex Head Club, 1783. M.A.: Oxford University, 1775; LL.D.: Trinity College, Dublin, 1765; Oxford University, 1775. *Died 13 December 1784.*

PUBLICATIONS

Collections

Works. 16 vols., 1903.
Letters, edited by R. W. Chapman. 3 vols., 1952.
Works, edited by A. T. Hazen and others. 1958–
Complete English Poems, edited by J. D. Fleeman. 1971.
Selected Poetry and Prose, edited by Frank Brady and William K. Wimsatt. 1977.

Fiction

The Prince of Abyssinia: A Tale. 1759; revised edition, 1759; as *The History of Rasselas, Prince of Abyssinia: An Asian Tale,* 1768; edited by Geoffrey Tillotson and Brian Jenkins, 1971.

Play

Irene (produced 1749). 1749; as *Mahomet and Irene* (produced 1749).

Verse

London: A Poem in Imitation of the Third Satire of Juvenal. 1738.
The Vanity of Human Wishes: The Tenth Satire of Juvenal Imitated. 1749.

Other

A Complete Vindication of the Licensers of the Stage. 1739.
The Life of Admiral Blake. 1740.
An Account of the Life of Mr. Richard Savage, Son of the Earl Rivers. 1744; edited by Clarence Tracy, 1971.
An Account of the Life of John Philip Barretier. 1744.
Miscellaneous Observations on the Tragedy of Macbeth. 1745.
The Plan of a Dictionary of the English Language, Addressed to the Earl of Chesterfield. 1747.
The Rambler. 8 vols., 1750–52; edited by A. B. Strauss and Walter Jackson Bate, in *Works,* 1969.
The Adventurer, with others. 2 vols., 1753–54; in *Works,* 1963.
A Dictionary of the English Language. 2 vols., 1755; revised edition, 1773.
The Idler. 2 vols., 1761; edited by Walter Jackson Bate and J. M. Bullitt, in *Works,* 1963.

Preface to His Edition of Shakespeare's Plays. 1765.

The False Alarm. 1770.

Thoughts on the Late Transactions Respecting Falkland's Islands. 1771.

The Patriot, Addressed to the Electors of Great Britain. 1774.

Taxation No Tyranny: An Answer to the Resolutions and Address of the American Congress. 1775.

A Journey to the Western Islands of Scotland. 1775; edited by D. L. Murray, 1931.

Prefaces, Biographical and Critical, to the Works of the English Poets. 10 vols., 1779–81; as *The Lives of the English Poets*, 1781; revised edition, 1783; edited by G. B. Hill, 3 vols., 1905; selection edited by J. P. Hardy, 1972.

Prayers and Meditations, edited by George Strahan. 1785; revised edition, 1785, 1796; edited by D. and M. Hyde, in *Works*, 1958.

Debates in Parliament, edited by George Chalmers. 2 vols., 1787.

Letters to and from Johnson, by Hester Lynch Piozzo. 2 vols., 1788.

The Celebrated Letter to the Earl of Chesterfield, edited by James Boswell. 1790.

An Account of the Life of Johnson to His Eleventh Year, Written by Himself, edited by Richard Wright. 1805.

A Diary of a Journey into North Wales in the Year 1774, edited by R. Duppa. 1816; in *Works*, 1958.

Johnson: His Life in Letters, edited by David Littlejohn. 1965.

Literary Criticism, edited by R. D. Stock. 1974.

Editor, *The Plays of Shakespeare.* 8 vols., 1765

Editor, *The Works of Richard Savage, with an Account of the Author.* 1775.

Translator, *A Voyage to Abyssinia*, by Father Jerome Lobo. 1735.

Translator, *A Commentary on Pope's Principles of Morality; or, An Essay on Man*, by Crousaz. 1739.

Bibliography: *A Bibliography of Johnson* by W. P. Courtney and D. N. Smith, 1915; *Johnsonian Studies 1887–1950: A Survey and Bibliography* by James L. Clifford, 1951, supplement by M. Wahba, in *Johnsonian Studies 1950–60*, 1962.

Reading List: *Life of Johnson* by James Boswell, 1791, edited by R. W. Chapman, 1953; *Passionate Intelligence: Imagination and Reason in the Work of Johnson* by Arieh Sachs, 1967; *Johnson as Critic*, 1973, and *Johnson* (biography), 1974, both by John Wain; *The Ascent of Parnassus* by Arthur Bryant, 1975; *Johnson and Poetic Style* by William Edinger, 1977; *The Stylistic Life of Johnson* by William Vesterman, 1977; *Johnson* by Walter Jackson Bate, 1978.

*   *   *

Johnson was regarded in his own time as the dominant figure of the English literary world; his achievement covers an extraordinary range: he was scholar and critic, moralist and essayist, poet and prose stylist, all in the first degree of merit.

With his verse-tragedy *Irene* in his pocket, and David Garrick as travelling companion, Johnson came from Lichfield to London in 1737. *Irene* was not published and produced until 1749, and was no great success, but Johnson's heroic couplet satire *London*, based on Juvenal's third satire, appeared in 1738, on the same day as Pope's *Epilogue to the Satires*. *London* criticises the values of the city in general, and of Whig London in particular; here Johnson wears Pope's mantle of the conservative (and Tory) satirist. Johnson's first London years were spent partly in the company of such Grub Street inhabitants as Richard Savage;

the *Account of the Life of Richard Savage* is a product of this friendship, and is an important early essay by Johnson in the art of biography.

Johnson turned again to verse satire in *The Vanity of Human Wishes*, based on Juvenal's tenth satire. This poem, Johnson's greatest, states a favourite theme: the inevitable unhappiness of human existence whatever choice in life is made. In turn Johnson considers mankind's yearnings for the various gifts of power, learning, military fame, long life, beauty, even virtue, and gives a melancholy account, with individual examples, of the misfortunes attendant upon each. This is not, however, mere pessimism. Johnson's Christian modification of Juvenal's stoic "mens sana in corpore sano" finds in religious faith a hard-fought-for consolation: "Still raise for good the supplicating voice,/But leave to heav'n the measure and the choice."

The theme of *Rasselas*, a moral tale set in Abyssinia and Egypt which has some similarities with Voltaire's *Candide*, is again the choice of life. Johnson's princely young hero escapes, with his sister and the poet Imlac, from the secluded innocence of the Happy Valley, and makes trial of various schemes of life. One after another the delusions and inconveniences of the pastoral life and the hermit's life, the life of the stoic and the life "according to nature," the family life and the scholar's life, are exposed. Life is found to be "every where a state in which much is to be endured, and little to be enjoyed"; the moral enforced is that no choice can be happy, but a choice must be made. Johnson may perhaps be seen returning to this theme with greater hope in his moving brief elegy "On the Death of Dr. Robert Levet" (1783), whose central message is that man finds fulfilment in the steady daily application of his particular talent: "The modest wants of ev'ry day/The toil of ev'ry day supplied."

It was with the 208 issues of *The Rambler* (1750–52), periodical essays on the pattern established earlier in the century by *The Spectator* and *The Tatler*, though more serious in tone and content, that Johnson became a major literary figure in contemporary estimation. In *The Rambler*, explicitly, it was Johnson's intention "to inculcate wisdom or piety," to teach both a reasonable and a religious attitude to life, dealing with topics as fundamental to human experience as youth and old age, marriage and death, grief and sorrow. In a small number of the *Rambler* essays Johnson is a literary critic, considering notably the topics of the novel (issue 4), biography (60), prejudice and the rules in criticism (93, 156, 158), and tragedy and comedy (125). Johnson's essays in *The Adventurer* and *The Idler* are in a rather lighter vein.

In the periodical essays and *Rasselas* may already be found the characteristic Johnsonian prose style, legislative and authoritative, often imitated, though far more flexible and exact than facile imitation would suggest. Careful judgements of life are crystallised in a precisely chosen diction, and ideas are given their relations by the balanced rhythms of clause echoing clause within the sentence. To this Johnson's weighty and pointed heroic couplets in *The Vanity of Human Wishes* and *London* are a poetic equivalent.

The reputation begun by *The Rambler* was established, in a different field, by the *Dictionary*, a triumph of individual scholarship and labour. Johnson as a lexicographer is distinguished by his accurate definitions of the meanings of words, and by his use of the historical principle. Words are illustrated by passages chosen not only for their semantic aptness, but also for their literary and moral qualities. The choice of passages reveals the enormous range of Johnson's reading, and, strikingly, his admiration for and knowledge of Elizabethan literature. The *Dictionary* is more descriptive than prescriptive; though he acknowledged that "there is in constancy and stability a general and lasting advantage," Johnson was too realistic to believe (with Swift, for example), that it is possible to fix and enforce linguistic usage.

Johnson's next major project was his edition of Shakespeare, remarkable for a commentary which shows Johnson's response to have been not only informed but also sometimes intensely personal, and for the theoretically and historically important preface. In the preface Johnson judges Shakespeare in a partly conservative light, approving of his "just representations of general nature" (a neo-classical position Johnson had already enunciated in the tenth chapter of *Rasselas*), and disapproving of his failure to provide a consistent and complete moral vision. Johnson shows a robust open-mindedness in defending Shakespeare against accusations that he mixes dramatic kinds and fails to observe the unities. Shakespeare's plays "are not in the rigorous and critical sense either tragedies or comedies" because they depict the mingled conditions of real life. The unities of time and place need not be observed because "the spectators are always in their senses and know ... that the stage is only a stage, and that the players are only players." Johnson rejects arbitrary prescription, steadily insisting that the primary aim of literature is a moral one, to be secured through delighting the reader: "there is always an appeal open from criticism to nature. The end of writing is to instruct; the end of poetry is to instruct by pleasing."

Johnson's literary output decreased in the late 1760's and 1770's. This is the period of gladiatorial conversation and literary dictatorship portrayed by James Boswell, whom Johnson had met in 1763. Johnson's main arena was the Club, founded at Joshua Reynolds's suggestion in 1764 and including, at its inception or in later years, many of the most eminent literary men of the time, among them Goldsmith and Garrick, Boswell and Burke, Edward Gibbon and Adam Smith.

To these years belong Johnson's most significant political writings, eloquent expressions of a personally consistent and conscientious conservatism. In *The False Alarm* Johnson defends Parliament's refusal to seat the radical John Wilkes. In *Taxation No Tyranny* he asserts the right of the British government to impose taxes upon the American colonists.

The *Journey to the Western Islands of Scotland* is a record of the tour, dangerous and adventurous for so old a man, that Johnson undertook with Boswell in 1773. If Johnson's account lacks the anecdotal vividness of Boswell's, there is here nonetheless the accustomed Johnsonian nobility of general moral reflection, in a social and physical landscape new to his experience.

Perhaps Johnson's greatest literary achievement came towards the end of his life, when he was commissioned by a group of London booksellers to provide a set of introductory essays for a collection of the works of the English poets. Each of the *Lives* consists of a detailed biography and brief character sketch, and a critical account of the poet. These critical passages are the fruition of a lifetime's reading and hard thought, providing a judicial assessment of the English poetic tradition against the twin standards of delight and truth to nature. Not surprisingly, Johnson's "great tradition" (though he has a wide range of interest and liking) is the line of satirical and ethical heroic couplet verse originating with Denham and Waller and perfected by Dryden and Pope, clear in expression and moral in intent. His aversion is poetry, whether by John Donne or Thomas Gray, which in his opinion fails to promote truth or express its meanings perspicuously. Though Johnson admired Milton's verse, and especially *Paradise Lost*, even so great a poem as *Lycidas* is attacked for what Johnson considered its harsh and unpleasing diction and metre, and its submergence of true feeling in an artificial pastoral allegory. Though the modern critical consensus does not accept all of Johnson's valuations, his criticism has the crucial virtues of exact and generally sympathetic understanding of what he reads, and the constant application of a systematic literary judgement. Johnson may seem to us sometimes too unwilling to compromise with historical relativism, or apparently insensitive to such of our favourite literary values as irony, ambiguity, imagination, and metaphor; yet his criticism is the work of a great and superbly stocked mind, always identifying the major questions, and the modern who takes issue with him needs to be armed with reasons.

—Marcus Walsh

JONES, James. American. Born in Robinson, Illinois, 6 November 1921. Educated at the University of Hawaii, Honolulu, 1942; New York University, 1945. Served in the United States Army, 1939–44: Bronze Star; Purple Heart. Married Gloria Mosolino in 1957; one son and one daughter. Recipient: National Book Award, 1952. *Died 9 May 1977.*

PUBLICATIONS

Fiction

From Here to Eternity. 1951.
Some Came Running. 1957
The Pistol. 1959.
The Thin Red Line. 1962.
Go to the Widow-Maker. 1967.
The Ice-Cream Headache and Other Stories. 1968.
The Merry Month of May. 1971.
A Touch of Danger. 1973.
Whistle: A Work-in-Progress. 1974; complete version, 1978.

Other

Viet Journal. 1974.
WWII: A Chronicle of Soldiering, with Art Weithas. 1975.

Bibliography: *Jones: A Checklist* by John R. Hopkins, 1974.

*   *   *

Generally regarded as the most successful "war-novelist" to emerge from World War II, James Jones, at his best, writes the way a good combat infantryman serves out a campaign. His prose is direct, muscular, prepared to take advantage of tactical opportunities, efficient, cynical without being pessimistic, and cannily aware of the ambiguous areas where fear mingles with bravery, and self-interest and self-sacrifice shade together. One of the few modern writers to depict the character of man-as-warrior sympathetically and without romantic illusions, Jones will probably be remembered for *From Here to Eternity, The Thin Red Line,* and his acute nonfictional study, *WWII: A Chronicle of Soldiering.*

In *From Here to Eternity,* Jones found a story perfectly adequate to his thematic interests: the heroic struggle of the warrior-individual trying to maintain his sense of self against the pressures of the very system that provides him with his cherished identity. Prewitt, the doomed protagonist, becomes an indelible figure in the gallery of American fictional soldiers that runs from Crane's Henry Fleming through Hemingway's Frederic Henry to Joseph Heller's Yossarian. Unlike the others, however, Prewitt is a soldier by choice and devotion; he is neither a rebel against, nor a victim of, the institution in which he finds his fullest realization. Jones's non-military fiction – including *Some Came Running, Go to the Widow-Maker,* and *The Merry Month of May* – tends to lack the controlled narrative focus of his war novels; characteristically, the prose is much looser, the action moves toward the melodramatic and sensational, and the novels suffer from a combination of verbosity and sentimentality.

—Earl Rovit

JOYCE, James (Augustine Aloysius).   Irish.   Born in Dublin, 2 February 1882. Educated at Clongowes Wood College, Dublin, 1888–91; Belvedere College, Dublin, 1893–98; University College, Dublin, 1898–1902, B.A. in modern languages 1902; studied medicine in Paris, 1903. Lived with Nora Barnacle from 1904; they married, 1931; one son and one daughter. Taught briefly in Dublin, 1903, then left Ireland for the Continent; taught English in Trieste, 1905–15, Zurich, 1915–18, and again in Trieste, 1918–20; full-time writer from 1920; lived in Paris, 1920–39, and Zurich, 1939–41; suffered from failing eyesight: nearly blind in later life. *Died 13 January 1941.*

PUBLICATIONS

Collections

>   *The Portable Joyce,* edited by Harry Levin.   1947; revised edition, 1966; as *The Essential Joyce,* 1948.
>   *Letters,* edited by Stuart Gilbert and Richard Ellmann.   3 vols., 1957–66; *Selected Letters,* edited by Ellmann, 1975.

Fiction

>   *Dubliners* (stories).   1914; edited by Robert Scholes and W. Litz, 1969.
>   *A Portrait of the Artist as a Young Man.*   1916; edited by C. G. Anderson, 1968.
>   *Ulysses.*   1922; edited by Richard Ellmann, 1969; facsimile of the manuscript, 3 vols., 1975.
>   *Anna Livia Plurabelle; Tales Told of Shem and Shaun; Haveth Childers Everywhere; Two Tales of Shem and Shaun; The Mime of Mick, Nick, and the Maggies* (fragments from *Work in Progress*).   5 vols., 1928–34.
>   *Finnegans Wake.*   1939; revised edition, 1950, 1964.
>   *Stephen Hero* (first draft of *A Portrait of the Artist*), edited by Theodore Spencer.   1944; edited by John J. Slocum and Herbert Cahoon, 1955, 1963.
>   *Anna Livia Plurabelle: The Making of a Chapter,* edited by Fred H. Higginson.   1960.
>   *Scribbledehobble: The Ur-Workbook for Finnegans Wake,* edited by Thomas E. Connolly.   1961.
>   *A First-Draft Version of Finnegans Wake,* edited by David Hayman.   1963.
>   *The Cat and the Devil* (juvenile), edited by Richard Ellmann.   1964.

Play

>   *Exiles* (produced in German 1919; in English 1925).   1918.

Verse

>   *Chamber Music.*   1907; edited by William York Tindall, 1954.
>   *Pomes Penyeach.*   1927.
>   *Collected Poems.*   1936.

Other

James Clarence Mangan. 1930.
The Early Joyce: The Book Reviews 1902–03, edited by Stanislaus Joyce and Ellsworth
    Mason. 1955.
Critical Writings, edited by Ellsworth Mason and Richard Ellmann. 1959.
Giacomo Joyce, edited by Richard Ellmann. 1968.

Bibliography: *A Bibliography of Joyce* by John J. Slocum and Herbert Cahoon, 1953; *A Bibliography of Joyce Studies* by Richard H. Deming, 1964, revised edition, 1978.

Reading List: *Joyce's Ulysses* by Stuart Gilbert, 1930, revised edition, 1952; *Joyce: A Critical Introduction* by Harry Levin, 1941, revised edition, 1960; *A Reader's Guide to Joyce*, 1959, and *A Reader's Guide to Finnegans Wake*, 1969, both by William York Tindall; *Joyce* (biography), 1959, and *The Consciousness of Joyce*, 1977, both by Richard Ellmann; *The Art of Joyce: Method and Design in Ulysses and Finnegans Wake* by W. Litz, 1961; *The Classical Temper: A Study of Joyce's Ulysses* by S. L. Goldberg, 1961; *Surface and Symbol: The Consistency of Joyce's Ulysses*, 1962, and *Joyce: Common Sense and Beyond*, 1966, both by Robert Martin Adams; *Structure and Motif in Finnegans Wake*, 1962, and *A Concordance to Finnegans Wake*, 1963, both by Clive Hart; *The Conscience of Joyce* by Brendan O Hehir, 1967; *Joyce: The Critical Heritage 1902–41* edited by Robert H. Deming, 2 vols., 1970.

*   *   *

Although James Joyce left Dublin very early in his career to establish himself on the Continent, where the radical literary experimentalists of the 1920's and 1930's were later to look upon him as a leader, he never lost his respect for the ordering principles and sense of cultural continuity which he had learned from his traditional Irish Jesuit education. Not only are all of his works, even *Finnegans Wake*, closely controlled and rationally planned, but all of them have firm roots in the literature of the past: *Dubliners* is influenced by French short stories, *A Portrait of the Artist* is written in the tradition of the *Bildungsroman*, *Exiles* could not have existed without the example of Ibsen, *Ulysses* is a transformation into modern terms of the *Odyssey*, *Finnegans Wake* makes explicit use of many sources from earlier dream-literature. Joyce was a great innovator, but part of his greatness lies in his capacity to rejuvenate and develop familiar forms.

Although in his earliest years Joyce tried his hand at all the major literary *genres*, his first fully formed works were short lyric poems. A loosely organised sequence of thirty-six make up his first published volume (*Chamber Music*), and while in later years he devoted himself almost entirely to prose, he continued to write occasional lyrics, some of which were collected as *Pomes Penyeach*. Most of the poems are brief, simple, direct, and unambiguous. Although one or two have a pleasing rhythmic quality coupled with an unusually delicate balance of imagery, they are comparatively unimportant by-products of a talent which needed a different vehicle of expression.

Indirection, ambiguity, intricate structural patterning, and far-reaching stylistic experimentation characterise Joyce's mature prose. If the stories in *Dubliners*, his first prose volume, show little of the linguistic complexity which became so evident a feature of *Ulysses* and *Finnegans Wake*, their deceptive simplicity conceals a subtle precision in the use of diction which grows fully apparent only after much re-reading. While the stories are essentially independent of one another, they are given structural unity by their arrangement into grouped sequences in which the characteristics of Joyce's fellow citizens are scrutinised from four main points of view: childhood, adolescence, maturity, and public life. The last of the stories, "The Dead," the longest and finest of the set, explores the accumulation of psychological pressures which lead to the recognition by Gabriel Conroy, a cultivated

Dubliner, that he is not altogether so central to his wife's emotional experience as he had hitherto imagined. A similar growth of self-awareness, with the consequent need for adjustment, marks the climactic moments of *Exiles* and *Ulysses*, and to some degree also of *Finnegans Wake*.

Exiles, Joyce's only published play, has never been popular with theatre-goers or readers. Until long after his death it was commonly dismissed as a stiff and essentially undramatic work, unattractive in theme, unconvincing in characterisation, and difficult to stage effectively. *Exiles* nevertheless explores in penetrating and original ways some of the problems of personal relationships which were to remain central to Joyce's later work: sexual fidelity, personal betrayal, physical and spiritual freedom. Successful performances in the 1960's and 1970's, including a notable production directed by Harold Pinter, have begun to show that, despite some awkward dialogue and a structural debt to Ibsen, *Exiles* marks a significant stage in Joyce's development of his themes.

While he was writing his early poems and the first stories of *Dubliners*, Joyce experimented with autobiography. A long draft, part of which was posthumously published as *Stephen Hero*, was discarded as too crude, too direct, too full of circumstantial detail. In its place Joyce wrote *A Portrait of the Artist as a Young Man*, which, although based on the events of his life between infancy and his departure for Paris at the age of twenty, is autobiographical in only a qualified sense. Stephen Dedalus, the central figure, is a highly fictionalised version of the author, more intense and less human than Joyce himself, and serving many other ends than that of realistic self-portraiture. Stephen is an embodiment of the artistic temperament in general, seen as a special kind of individual singled out from the rest of the world by an innate and almost sacred mission. Not only is Stephen associated with the creative power of his mythical forebear Daedalus, the "great artificer," but he is led by his artistic vocation to think of himself as "a priest of the eternal imagination, transmuting the daily bread of experience into the radiant body of everliving life." Joyce's attitude to this grandiose and solemn formulation is ambiguous: depicting Stephen with a mixture of irony and sympathy, he suggests the special importance of the artist in the modern world while refraining from making a full commitment to his hero. *A Portrait of the Artist* explores the development of Stephen's artistic awareness through a sequence of five main phases during which he confronts paternal authority, subjugation by the flesh, the dominance of the Church, the attraction of an immature lyricism, and finally discovers the liberation of a true artistic vocation born from a marriage of aesthetic judgment and logical order. Each of the five chapters has a clearly symmetrical shape, with a crucial central scene, and each explores possibilities of language in keeping with the development of Stephen's consciousness.

Ulysses, the long and complex novel on which for many readers Joyce's reputation largely depends, had surprisingly modest beginnings. Joyce first conceived of it as another short story in the *Dubliners* mode, and the earliest passages that he drafted were imagined as material for a continuation of *A Portrait of the Artist*. While these origins remain apparent both in the limited scope of the physical events, all of which occur on 16 June 1904 ("the dailiest day possible," as Arnold Bennett put it), and in the reappearance of Stephen Dedalus as a secondary character, *Ulysses* expanded during the seven years of its composition to become a massive scrutiny both of the most fundamental of human concerns and of the linguistic means whereby those concerns may be analysed and presented. Among the most attractive of the book's virtues is the vitality of its "felt life": Joyce creates a remarkably realistic image of the city of Dublin and of its inhabitants. Throughout his life, but especially in mid-career, factual accuracy mattered greatly to Joyce. *Ulysses* depicts a solid three-dimensional world directly derived from the realist fiction of the nineteenth century. It also, however, reflects a world in which language provides boundless possibilities for the perception of truth. The comparatively simple events of its eighteen chapters are presented through styles and techniques of increasing complexity, leading to a multiplicity of vision which looks forward to the new French novels of the 1950's and 1960's.

Although the realism of *Ulysses* remains one of the constituent elements of *Finnegans Wake*, relativism of language and of perception wholly dominates the later book. The clarity of waking thought which helps the reader to find his bearings in *Ulysses* gives way to the fluidity of the dream as images mutate, coalesce, are replaced by their contraries. The themes of the earlier books are still evident: a Dublin pub-keeper and his family are troubled by aggressions, rivalries, and guilts which they attempt to resolve by playing out in the imagination a series of archetypal scenes. As in a dream, the characters continually reappear in different guises, only to be continually confronted with the same irreducible problems. The language is exuberant, full of distortions and compressions which echo and express the fluid content.

Both *Ulysses* and *Finnegans Wake* require the reader to work hard for complete understanding. *Finnegans Wake* is by far the more difficult of the two, making demands which many have been unwilling to try to meet. The difficulties of both books are not merely linguistic, but result in large measure from Joyce's inclusion of many allusions: local Irish events, comparatively esoteric book-learning, and matters arising from personal rivalries and jealousies. While one's understanding of *Ulysses* is undoubtedly enriched by elucidation of such materials, which do not in any case dominate the content, it is not clear that patient elucidation of private and local allusions is the most fruitful approach to *Finnegans Wake*. Consciously allowing some references to remain blurred contributes to one's sense of the book's dream-like quality and is in keeping with the extraordinary music of Joyce's prose.

—Clive Hart

KAVAN, Anna. English. Born in Cannes, France, in 1904; brought up in California. Educated privately and in Church of England schools. Married 1) Donald Ferguson (divorced); 2) Stuart Edmonds. Lived in the United States, Burma, Europe, Australia, and New Zealand; settled in London. *Died 5 December 1968.*

PUBLICATIONS

Fiction

A Charmed Circle. 1929.
The Dark Sisters. 1930.
Let Me Alone. 1930.
A Stranger Still. 1935.
Goose Cross. 1936.
Rich Get Rich. 1937.
Asylum Piece and Other Stories. 1940.
Change the Name. 1941.
I Am Lazarus: Short Stories. 1941.
The House of Sleep. 1947; as Sleep Has His House, 1948.
A Scarcity of Love. 1956.
Eagles' Nest. 1957.
A Bright Green Field and Other Stories. 1958.
Who Are You? 1963.
Ice. 1967.
Julia and the Bazooka (stories), edited by Rhys Davies. 1970.
My Soul in China (stories), edited by Rhys Davies. 1975.

Other

The Horse's Tale, with K. T. Bluth. 1949.

*   *   *

Anna Kavan was a writer of distinction. According to Rhys Davies, who edited and wrote the introduction to the posthumous volume of her stories collected under the title *Julia and the Bazooka*, she was a heroin addict for the last thirty years of her life and a syringe lay in her hand when her body was found. On reflection, he is probably right to begin his account of Anna Kavan's art with some such straightforward acknowledgement of her drug dependence.

I do not know if the use of heroin could be made to account for the febrile and highly coloured brilliance of some of her texts – it seems on the whole more likely that she was a woman of clairvoyant imaginative power who used drugs to cope with the comparative drabness of world *outside* her writing. What certainly emerges from the stories in *Julia and the Bazooka* is the boredom and the cold, the inner emptiness and death-wishing deadness of the hardened addict. "Hardened" indeed is in this context merely a descriptive word.

At her best, Anna Kavan was as vulnerable and sensitive as any of the writers of the "great subjective-feminine tradition" to which Lawrence Durrell has claimed she belonged. The title story of *Julia and the Bazooka* – a summing-up of her life, the "bazooka" being her pet name for the syringe – tells how far she felt she had fallen from that tradition, into dullness, monotony, death. "There is no more Julia anywhere. Where she was there is only nothing."

Some of the stories fail to rise above the level of an organised hysteria. Others – e.g., "Fog," "The Mercedes," and "Experimental" – are urgent and moving without quite satisfying, as stories, the tensions they postulate. Some half dozen things here, however, are as fine as the best sketches in *Asylum Piece*, the first book she wrote as Anna Kavan, and should not be missed by anyone who cares for contemporary writing. Chief among these I would place "A Visit," a near-perfect piece of work with a quality of *rightness* to its illogic that can only be termed poetic.

Anna Kavan's novel *A Scarcity of Love* has been described by Rhys Davies as "a kind of prelude" to these stories in which the central metaphor is the author's own drug addiction. It is indeed possible to feel in the presence of the same metaphor here, as the female protagonist gropes towards an experience of evil that is never quite defined, but it seems to me that an abbreviated acquaintance with the world is in this case padded out to give it a substance not naturally its own. Anna Kavan was best when she faced her delicate and dangerous material most directly. There are moments in *A Scarcity of Love* where her conscious mind seems extinguished by what it is trying to say, but these occur mostly in the early chapters, which owe a debt to Kafka, and the book becomes garrulous and deliberate before it is half over.

Two other novels and an autobiographical text deserve attention. *Who Are You?* is a puzzling, disturbing, beautifully written minor piece. Set down in a tropical hell, three characters – an intelligent young girl, her husband, and a stranger nicknamed "Suede Boots" – live twice through the same situations. The girl suffers; the husband torments her, rapes her, and plays tennis using a rat instead of a ball; the stranger sympathises with the girl and encourages her to escape. The girl's hesitations are punctuated by the endless enquiring cry of a bird in the tamerind trees behind the house: *Who-are-you? Who-are-you? Who-are-you?* Put thus, it may sound pretentious. I can only suggest that to write about this finely economical book in any terms other than its own is cruelly to distort the excellence of the original text. Anna Kavan takes nothing for granted in it, and her determination to show the horror of the emptiness beneath the skull beneath the skin is truly dismaying.

The novel *Ice*, in its paperback reissue, bears an interesting introduction by Brian Aldiss, in which he relates this novel to the speculative world of science fiction and adjudges it Anna Kavan's finest achievement on the grounds that its cleverly extended metaphor of a world being enclosed and eroded by ice makes the perfect objective correlative for its author's addiction to heroin. *Ice* is indeed a strange and strong book, but its groping towards a never-quite-defined experience of evil remains groping.

Sleep Has His House was neglected when it was first published. It is a testament of remarkable if feverish beauty, recounting the experiences of an unhappy childhood in a heightened prose that tugs those experiences free of their gloom. A transfer is pressed on memory, and Anna Kavan's pleasure in words and images transforms the given scenes until they resemble the slighter moments in Rimbaud's *Les Illuminations*.

In summary, one may say that Anna Kavan, underestimated in her lifetime, is now gradually being recognised as a lyricist and a fantasist of importance. If, as we now know, her fantasies had their root in drug addiction, then all the more reason to see her as part of that Romantic sub-school which includes major writers such as Coleridge and De Quincey as well as minor ones such as Francis Thompson, writers whose apprehension of reality finds an emblem and an idiom in drugs.

—Robert Nye

KENEALLY, Thomas (Michael).   Australian.   Born in Sydney, New South Wales, 7 October 1935. Educated at St. Patrick's College, Strathfield, New South Wales; studied for the priesthood and studied law. Served in the Australian Citizens Military Forces. Married Judith Martin in 1965; two daughters. High school teacher in Sydney, 1960–64; Lecturer in Drama, University of New England, Armidale, New South Wales, 1968–70. Recipient: Commonwealth Literary Fund Fellowship, 1966, 1968, 1972; Miles Franklin Award, 1967, 1968; Captain Cook Bi-Centenary Prize, 1970. Fellow, Royal Society of Literature, 1973.

PUBLICATIONS

Fiction

> *The Place at Whitton.*   1964.
> *The Fear.*   1965.
> *Bring Larks and Heroes.*   1967.
> *Three Cheers for the Paraclete.*   1968.
> *The Survivor.*   1969.
> *A Dutiful Daughter.*   1971.
> *The Chant of Jimmie Blacksmith.*   1972.
> *Blood Red, Sister Rose.*   1974.
> *Gossip from the Forest.*   1975.
> *Moses the Lawgiver.*   1975.
> *Season in Purgatory.*   1976.
> *Victim of the Aurora.*   1977.
> *Passenger.*   1979.

Plays

> *Halloran's Little Boat* (produced 1966).
> *Childermass* (produced 1968).
> *An Awful Rose* (produced 1972).

> Television Play: *Essington*, 1974.

Other

> *Ned Kelly and the City of Bees* (juvenile).   1978.

*   *   *

Thomas Keneally, most prolific among contemporary Australian novelists, was first concerned with situations related more or less closely to his own experience – *The Place at Whitton*, a horror-story set in a Catholic seminary, *The Fear*, recalling a wartime childhood, and *Three Cheers for the Paraclete*, a tale of a liberal Catholic priest's conflicts with his superiors.

His third novel, *Bring Larks and Heroes*, made his name. It is set in early Australian convict society, exploring what Keneally has called "the working or absence of conscience" among characters in an intolerable but also inescapable situation. In the same passage he speaks of being "obsessed with the notion of Australia as a country alien to the people who live in it," and something of this informs *The Chant of Jimmie Blacksmith*, the story of a half-aborigine who sought a place in white society, was rebuffed, went berserk, and was pursued to his death by outraged white Australians.

Vitality and vivacity characterise Keneally, the man and the author. He always has a story to tell and is keen to find new ways of telling it, whether in grotesque allegory as in *A Dutiful Daughter*, quasi-historical narrative in *Blood Red, Sister Rose*, the account of Joan of Arc, who fascinates him, or the staccato passages of *Gossip from the Forest* about the Armistice of 1918. Recent novels are *Season in Purgatory*, the story of an English doctor with Yugoslav partisans, and *Victim of the Aurora*, in which Keneally returns to Antarctic exploration, a theme which he had already used in *The Survivor*. *Victim of the Aurora* betrays that tendency to the sensational which characterised some of his earlier work.

He has also written plays. *An Awful Rose* is about a psychological disorientated religious, and *Halloran's Little Boat* derives from *Bring Larks and Heroes*.

—Arthur Pollard

KENNEDY, John Pendleton. American. Born in Baltimore, Maryland, 25 October 1795. Educated at the Sinclair Academy, Baltimore, and Baltimore College, graduated 1812; studied law: admitted to the Maryland bar, 1816. Served in the United States Army during the War of 1812. Married 1) Mary Tennant in 1824 (died, 1825); 2) Elizabeth Gray in 1829. Practised law in Baltimore from 1816; Member, Maryland House of Delegates, 1820–23; inherited large income from an uncle c. 1830 and increasingly gave up the law for literature and politics; Member from Maryland, United States House of Representatives, 1838, 1840–44: Chairman of the Congressional Committee on Commerce; Member of the Maryland House of Delegates, and Speaker of the House, 1846–48; Secretary of the Navy, under President Fillmore, 1852–53: organized Commodore Perry's expedition to Japan, 1852. Provost, University of Maryland; President, Board of Trustees, Peabody Institute, Baltimore. *Died 18 August 1870.*

PUBLICATIONS

Collections

   Collected Works. 10 vols., 1871–72.

Fiction

   Swallow Barn; or, A Sojourn in the Old Dominion. 1832; edited by Ernest E. Leisy, 1937.
   Horse Shoe Robinson: A Tale of the Tory Ascendency. 1835; edited by Ernest E. Leisy, 1937.
   Rob of the Bowl: A Legend of St. Inigoe's. 1838; edited by William S. Osborne, 1965.
   Quodlibet, Containing Some Annals Thereof. 1840.

Other

The Red Book, with Peter Hoffman Cruse.   2 vols., 1820–21.
Defense of the Whigs.   1843.
Memoirs of the Life of William Wirt, Attorney General of the United States.   1849.
The Border States.   1860.
Mr. Ambrose's Letters on the Rebellion.   1865.

Editor, with Alexander Bliss, *Autograph Leaves of Our Country's Authors.*   1864.

Bibliography: in *Bibliography of American Literature* by Jacob Blanck, 1969.

Reading List: *The Life of Kennedy* by Henry T. Tuckerman, in *Collected Works,* 1871; *Kennedy, Gentleman from Baltimore* by Charles H. Bohner, 1961; *Kennedy* by Joseph V. Ridgely, 1966.

*   *   *

Only two of John Pendleton Kennedy's four works of fiction can really be called novels. Much like Washington Irving's *Bracebridge Hall,* which it both resembles and satirizes, *Swallow Barn* is hardly more than a series of sketches loosely held together by common characters and a pair of shadowy plot lines, and *Quodlibet* is a satire on Jacksonian politics and policies of the 1830's projected through a history of the imaginary borough of Quodlibet. *Horse Shoe Robinson* and *Rob of the Bowl* are thus his only true novels. Both are historical romances of the kind made popular by Scott and Cooper.

Swallow Barn is in many ways his most attractive book. Hardly the realistic work it has sometimes been called, it makes good-natured fun of a group of Virginia planters in the early nineteenth century, burlesques their chivalric ideals and pretensions, yet also treats with respect many of the gentlemanly values they attempt to preserve. *Quodlibet,* by contrast, attacks the leveling democrats through one of their number. Solomon Secondthoughts recounts the history of Quodlibet in such a way as to damn the very policies and practices he thinks he is upholding. The work is thus a clever, if dated, piece of satire.

Horse Shoe Robinson and *Rob of the Bowl,* on the other hand, develop their themes through the use of history. Kennedy sought to maintain historical accuracy in both, but like other historical romances, the books are concerned not so much with demonstrable fact as with the meaning to be found in the events of the past. Thus, *Horse Shoe Robinson* portrays the American Revolution as a desperate struggle by young patrician leaders and their yeoman supporters to establish a free society, and *Rob of the Bowl* depicts the successful defense of seventeenth-century Maryland against both Puritan rebels and lawless buccaneers as the maintenance of established order against the threat of disruption.

Kennedy's four books would thus seem to work at cross purposes: *Horse Shoe Robinson* affirming the need for progressive social change, and *Rob of the Bowl* upholding the value of social stability; *Swallow Barn* satirizing Virginia aristocrats, and *Quodlibet* attacking leveling democrats. Yet the books are not so diverse in meaning as they may seem. The issues they present are those that troubled thinking Americans during the 1830's, and Kennedy seems to suggest that some kind of balance among the conflicting ideas should be maintained: though American society must progress, it should not change so radically as to destroy the important personal and social values that had come to it from the past. Taken together, then, his four works of fiction indicate the skill with which Kennedy, who did not think of himself as a professional man of letters, was able to develop a complex social theme.

—Donald A. Ringe

KEROUAC, Jack. American. Born Jean Louis Lebris de Kerouac in Lowell, Massachusetts, 12 March 1922. Educated at Horace Mann School, New York; Columbia University, New York, 1940–41, 1942. Served in the United States Merchant Marine, and Navy, during World War II. Married in 1944 (annulled), and 1950 (divorced); married Stella Sampas in 1966; one daughter. Sports Reporter for the Lowell *Sun*, 1942; became a writer after the war, supporting himself by various odd jobs; worked as brakeman with the Southern Pacific Railroad, San Francisco, 1952–53; travelled throughout the United States and Mexico, 1953–56; fire lookout for the United States Agricultural Service in Washington state, 1956; full-time writer from 1957. *Died 21 October 1969.*

PUBLICATIONS

Fiction

> *The Town and the City.* 1950.
> *On the Road.* 1957; edited by Scott Donaldson, 1978.
> *The Subterraneans.* 1958.
> *The Dharma Bums.* 1958.
> *Doctor Sax: Faust Part Three.* 1959.
> *Maggie Cassidy.* 1960.
> *Excerpts from "Visions of Cody."* 1959; complete version, 1972.
> *Tristessa.* 1960.
> *Book of Dreams.* 1960.
> *Big Sur.* 1962.
> *Visions of Gerard.* 1963.
> *Desolation Angels.* 1965.
> *Satori in Paris.* 1966.
> *Vanity of Duluoz: An Adventurous Education 1935–46.* 1968.
> *Pic.* 1971.
> *Two Early Stories.* 1973.

Play

> *Pull My Daisy* (screenplay). 1961.

> Screenplay: *Pull My Daisy,* 1959.

Verse

> *Mexico City Blues.* 1959.
> *Hymn – God Pray for Me.* 1959.
> *Rimbaud.* 1960.
> *The Scripture of the Golden Eternity.* 1960; revised edition, 1970.
> *Poem.* 1962.
> *A Pun for Al Gelpi.* 1966.
> *Hugo Weber.* 1967.
> *Scattered Poems.* 1971.
> *Trip, Trap: Haiku along the Road from San Francisco to New York, 1959,* with Albert
>   Saijo and Lew Welch. 1973.
> *Heaven and Other Poems,* edited by Donald Allen. 1977.

Other

Lonesome Traveler, drawings by Larry Rivers.   1960.

Bibliography: *A Bibliography of Works by Kerouac* by Ann Charters, 1967; revised edition, 1975.

Reading List: *No Pie in the Sky: The Hobo as American Culture Hero in the Works of Jack London, John Dos Passos, and Kerouac* by Frederick Feied, 1964; *Kerouac: A Biography*, by Ann Charters, 1973; *Jack's Book: An Oral Biography* by Barry Gifford and Lawrence Lee, 1978.

*   *   *

Along with Gary Snyder, Allen Ginsberg, William Burroughs, Neal Cassady, and their compatriots, Jack Kerouac was an unlikely cultural hero. Each, in his own very different way, was a thread in the vast social ethnic called the United States. Kerouac was rooted more than most in a traditional American *mythos*. Raised in a working-class Catholic family in Lowell, Massachusetts, given to normal boyhood fantasies of early greatness as a football star (he very nearly recognized them in his brief stay at Columbia University), he later became the leading prose writer of the Beat Movement. His group and its substantial youthful following sparked a cultural renaissance in mid-century United States – in literature, music, painting, and the larger realms of society and politics – that will not soon be forgotten.

Kerouac's favourite early nickname was "memory babe," suggestive of his own prodigious memory and the accompanying later desire to preserve, in a weakly fictionalized pickle, the experiences of childhood and youth in Lowell, his days on the road in the heart of America, and particularly his friends and exploits along the way. From his first and most conventional work, *The Town and the City*, he sought to preserve in their essences: himself (as Peter Martin, Sal Paradise, and Jack Duluoz), Snyder (as Japhy Ryder), Ginsberg (as Carlo Marx and Irwin Garden), Burroughs (as Old Bull Lee and Bull Hubbard), and Neal Cassady (as Dean Moriarity and Cody Pomeray). He had hoped, in later life, to collect his works – uniformly bound as multi-volumes of a single gigantic work, with real names and places restored.

Kerouac, the man and the writer, represented a revitalization of the romantic spirit in America. He idealized a return to a more essential and authentic life and intense existence in the present, be it in the streets of his fictional Lowell (*The Town and the City, Doctor Sax*), along the streams and firetrails of his fictional Oregon (*The Dharma Bums*), in the *barrios* of his fictional California and Mexico (*On the Road, Big Sur, Mexico City Blues*), or in subterranean clubs of New York, Denver, San Francisco, and points along the way. His biographers, particularly Ann Charters and Charles Marcus, document his own fierce and often troubled individualism, recurrent optimism, and reverence for sentient life, and the tragedy of his later years – virtually alone in Florida and finally Lowell.

Jack Kerouac's work depicted both the ideals of the "hot" beats – those like Neal Cassady who burned their lives as filaments in a quest for "IT!," "kicks," pure ecstatic existence in what Norman Mailer calls "the enormous present" – and the "cool" beats – Gary Snyder and kindred spirits who sought a return to essence in the more Eastern detached, ascetic realms of Zen and allied philosophies. A keynote of his fiction and poetry is the notion that the act of creating literature is in itself a performance, an authentic act testifying to intensely-felt experience. (We should recall the great popularity of poetry as a *declaimed* form, a *song* as well as a text, often combined with jazz, during the Beat years.) Thus Kerouac's work rarely responds well to the techniques of close textual reading. He claimed to have written *On the Road* "at white heat" in several weeks on an unbroken roll of teletype paper; his later work is rarely revised, very loose in form, episodic and lyrical at best, improvised like the jazz the Beats so admired, given to humor and nostalgia and the crests and valleys of romantic fiction.

Like many of his fellow Beats (a predominantly masculine group), Kerouac was widely lauded and damned – in his own day and in the present. Like Burroughs and Cassady and Ginsberg, Kerouac lived his life as a kind of work of art, an action painting, a jazz riff. Their experiments in sexuality, with drugs, with the many and often frightening potentialities of psychic and social order and disorder, their bold and often naïve desires to re-awaken dormant chords in American life and writing – these have rarely been met with balanced opinions. And Kerouac, as the central figure of the most well-defined literary movement in twentieth-century America, like most truly revolutionary figures, found no final peace in his life and will not soon rest easily in mass thought or literary history.

—Jack Hicks

KINGSLEY, Charles. English.   Born in Holne, Devonshire, 12 June 1819; brother of Henry Kingsley, *q.v.* Educated in preparatory school in Clifton, Bristol, 1831–33; Helston Grammar School, Cornwall, 1833–35; King's College School, London, 1835–38; Magdalene College, Cambridge, 1838–42, B.A. (honours) in classics 1842, M.A. 1860. Married Fanny Grenfell in 1844; two daughters and two sons. Took holy orders: Curate, 1842–44, and Rector, 1844 until his death, Eversley, Hampshire; Lecturer at Queen's College, London, 1848; Regius Professor of Modern History, Cambridge University, 1860–69; History Tutor to the Prince of Wales, 1861; toured the West Indies, 1869–70; Canon of Chester Cathedral, 1869–73; made a lecture tour of the United States, 1873–74; Canon of Westminster Abbey, London, and Chaplain to the Queen, 1873–75. *Died 23 January 1875.*

PUBLICATIONS

Collections

Works.   28 vols., 1880–85.

Fiction

Alton Locke, Tailor and Poet: An Autobiography.   1850.
Yeast: A Problem.   1851.
Hypatia; or, New Foes with an Old Face.   1853.
Westward Ho! or, The Voyages and Adventures of Sir Amyas Leigh.   1855; edited by
    M. W. and G. Thomas, 1957.
Two Years Ago.   1857.
The Water-Babies: A Fairy Tale for a Land-Baby.   1863; edited by Robert Harding,
    with *The Heroes,*1947.
Hereward the Wake, "Last of the English."   1866; edited by Herbert Van Thal, 1967.
The Tutor's Story, completed by Mary St. Leger Harrison.   1916.

Play

The Saint's Tragedy.   1848.

Verse

Andromeda and Other Poems.   1858.
Poems: Collected Edition.   1872; revised edition, 1878, 1880, 1884.

Other

Twenty-Five Village Sermons.   1849; revised edition, as Town and Country Sermons, 1861.
Cheap Clothes and Nasty.   1850.
Phaethon; or, Loose Thoughts for Loose Thinkers.   1852.
Sermons on National Subjects.   2 vols., 1852–54; revised edition, as The King of the Earth and Other Sermons, 1872.
Alexandria and Her Schools.   1854.
Who Causes Pestilence?   1854.
Glaucus; or, The Wonders of the Shore.   1855; revised edition, 1856, 1858.
Sermons for the Times.   1855.
Sermons for Sailors.   1855; as Sea Sermons, 1885.
The Heroes; or, Greek Fairy Tales for My Children, illustrated by the author.   1855; edited by M. W. and G. Thomas, 1961.
Miscellanies.   2 vols., 1859.
The Good News of God: Sermons.   1859.
The Gospel of the Pentateuch: A Set of Parish Sermons.   1863.
Hints to Stammerers, by a Minute Philosopher.   1864.
The Roman and the Teuton (lectures).   1864.
Mr. Kingsley and Dr. Newman: A Correspondence on the Question Whether Dr. Newman Teaches That Truth Is No Virtue.   1864.
David: Four Sermons.   1865; revised edition, 1874.
Three Lectures.   1867.
The Water of Life and Other Sermons.   1867.
Discipline and Other Sermons.   1868.
The Hermits.   3 vols., 1868.
Madam How and Lady Why; or, First Lessons in Earth-Lore for Children.   1870.
At Last: A Christmas in the West Indies.   2 vols., 1871.
Town Geology.   1872.
Plays and Puritans, and Other Historical Essays.   1873.
Prose Idylls New and Old.   1873.
Westminster Sermons.   1874.
Health and Education.   1874.
Lectures Delivered in America in 1874.   1875.
Letters to Young Men on Betting and Gambling.   1877.
True Words for Brave Men.   1878.
All Saints' Day and Other Sermons, edited by W. Harrison.   1878.
From Death to Life: Fragments of Teaching to a Village Congregation with Letters on the Life after Death, edited by Frances E. Kingsley.   1887.
Words of Advice to Schoolboys, edited by E. F. Johns.   1912.
American Notes: Letters from a Lecture Tour in 1874, edited by R. B. Martin.   1958.

Editor, *South by West; or, Winter in the Rocky Mountains and Spring in Mexico.* 1874.

Bibliography: *Kingsley and Thomas Hughes: First Editions in the Library at Dormy House* by M. L. Parrish and B. K. Mann, 1936.

Reading List: *Kingsley: His Letters and Memories of His Life* by Frances E. Kingsley, 2 vols., 1877; *Kingsley* by Margaret Farrand Thorp, 1937; *Kingsley and His Ideas* by Guy Kendall, 1947; *Canon Kingsley* by Una Pope-Hennessy, 1948; *Apologia pro Kingsley* by P. J. Fitzpatrick, 1969; *The Beast and the Monk: A Life of Kingsley* by Susan Chitty, 1974; *Kingsley; The Lion of Eversley* by Brenda Colloms, 1975.

*   *   *

Gerard Manley Hopkins once wittily remarked that whenever he thought of Charles Kingsley – and we may be sure it would not be too often – he imagined a man leaping up from the table, with his mouth full of bread and cheese, spluttering that he wasn't going to have any more of this damned nonsense. Probably at the forefront of Hopkins's mind was Kingsley's rash attack on Newman for going over from Anglicanism to Rome (the attack brought in reply one of the great apologies of all time, *Apologia Pro Sua Vita*), but there is a sense in which Kingsley is *always* rash.

Kingsley deserves some credit for being the founder, in the 1840's, with his subtler friend, the Rev. F. D. Maurice, of "muscular Christianity," which also became known as Christian Socialism. Both men were alarmed by the drift away from the Anglican church among working-class men; and the 1851 Religious Census confirmed just how few working-class people went to church. Kingsley rightly held the church itself to blame for this state of affairs. He saw that industrialisation had created enormous problems for its victims – as working-class people were thought of – and that the church had dismally failed to address itself to any of the problems. Kingsley had a genuine compassion for the working-classes, and he wanted fuller and happier lives to be open to them – "a life of bathhouses and cricket" as contemporaries perhaps unkindly referred to it.

A stream of novels and essays came from Kingsley's fatally fluent pen, nearly all of them concerned with the effort to reconcile class to class, to explain people to each other, to preach the brotherhood of man. *The Water-Babies* is a children's story with an adult meaning: Tom is to be understood as a social outcast, a version of Oliver Twist or the chimney sweep of Blake's great poem in *Songs of Innocence*, and Kingsley wanted his audience to be shocked into pity and compassion over his fate. The same is true of *Alton Locke*, perhaps his best and certainly his most often discussed novel. It is told by the eponymous hero, a chartist tailor, and, as I have pointed out in my essay in *Tradition and Tolerance in Nineteenth Century Fiction*, Kingsley goes out of his way to insist on Alton's being a blood brother of the middle-class audience which might be expected to read the novel. As a result, of course, he ends up by denying any conditioning factors in Alton's life that could explain his character or actions. Alton is simply an "Englishman."

Kingsley's naive form of patriotism comes out in his historical writings, which nowadays have an embarrassingly jingoistic air to them. No wonder that serious historians were appalled when he was appointed to the chair of history at Cambridge. Even Kingsley seems to have had some doubts about the wisdom of his appointment, and he was not a man given to self-doubt. Had he been, he would undoubtedly have written better books. As it is, we may be grateful to him for so vigorously drawing attention to problems and complexities which finer minds than his found difficult to understand or resolve.

—John Lucas

KINGSLEY, Henry. English. Born in Barnack, Northamptonshire, 2 January 1830; brother of Charles Kingsley, *q.v.* Educated at King's College School, London, 1844–50; Worcester College, Oxford, 1850–53. Married his cousin Sarah Kingsley in 1864. Left university, with other students, to work in the Australian goldmines: worked in Australia, possibly as a drover on a sheep and cattle station in Victoria, as a mounted policeman in Sydney, and as a miner at the Caledonian Goldfields, near Melbourne, 1853–57, then returned to England; settled in Wargrave, near Henley-on-Thames, 1864; Editor, *Edinburgh Daily Review*, 1869–71; settled in London; full-time novelist from 1871. *Died 24 May 1876.*

PUBLICATIONS

Collections

    Novels, edited by C. K. Shorter. 8 vols., 1894–95.

Fiction

    The Recollections of Geoffry Hamlyn. 1859.
    Ravenshoe. 1862.
    Austin Elliot. 1863.
    The Hillyars and the Burtons. 1865.
    Leighton Court. 1866.
    Silcote of Silcotes. 1867.
    Mademoiselle Mathilde. 1868.
    Stretton. 1869.
    Old Margaret. 1871.
    Hetty and Other Stories. 1871.
    The Harveys. 1872.
    Hornby Mills and Other Stories. 1872.
    Oakshott Castle. 1873.
    Reginald Hetherege. 1874.
    Number Seventeen. 1875.
    The Grange Garden. 1876.
    The Mystery of the Island. 1877.

Other

    Tales of Old Travel Re-Narrated. 1869.
    The Lost Child (juvenile). 1871.
    The Boy in Grey and Other Stories and Sketches (juvenile). 1871.
    Valentin: A French Boy's Story of Sedan (juvenile). 1872; revised edition, 1874.
    Fireside Studies. 1876.

    Editor, *Robinson Crusoe,* by Defoe. 1868.

Reading List: *Kingsley: Towards a Vindication* by S. M. Ellis, 1931 (includes bibliography); *Some Novels of Kingsley* by Leonie Kramer, 1954; *Kingsley and Colonial Fiction* by John Barnes, 1971; *The Neglected Brother: A Study of Kingsley* by William H. Scheverle, 1971.

                *   *   *

Although he has always been overshadowed by his elder brother, Charles, Henry Kingsley has had a special significance for Australian readers because of his first novel, *Geoffry Hamlyn*. This romance of Australian pioneering was for generations of Australians "the best Australian novel that has been, and probably will be written," as the novelist, Marcus Clarke, wrote. However, to the "offensively Australian" novelist, Joseph Furphy, at the turn of the century, it seemed "an exceedingly trashy and misleading novel," and he dismissed Kingsley's heroes as "slender-witted, virgin-souled, overgrown schoolboys." The very force of Furphy's attack was indicative of the novel's continuing appeal, which lies essentially in its idealised and heroic version of pioneering life. Kingsley transplanted in Australia his ideal of English country life, a group of landed families maintaining the traditional standards of the "big house," and with considerable skill incorporated in his narrative the more picturesque and dramatic elements of Australian station life: a bushfire, a kangaroo hunt, cattle branding, a child lost in the bush, and encounters with aborigines and bushrangers.

Kingsley had gone to the colonies during the gold rushes, and had known only hardship and disappointment during his stay of over four years. In the novel, published on his return to England, he wrote of the years before the gold discoveries in the character of an elderly and successful colonist, looking back in a spirit of affectionate reminiscence on the experiences he shared with his friends. The first volume of *Geoffry Hamlyn* (it was the usual three-volume length) is set in England, and reads like stock romance, written under the strong influence of Walter Scott. It is only when Kingsley moves his characters to Australia at the beginning of the second volume that it becomes more than that. In general, novels about life in the colonies in the mid-nineteenth century tended to be fact — more or less accurate — dressed up as fiction. Of those writing about Australia, Kingsley best realised the possibilities of the subject for romantic fiction.

None of Kingsley's later novels was as good as *Geoffry Hamlyn*, and as a writer he declined rather than matured. In his second novel, *Ravenshoe*, he turned from the land of "sunshine and adventure" to write of what he called, at the end of *Geoffry Hamlyn*, "that charming English country life, the like of which, I take it, no other country can show." This novel has been the most highly praised of all his work, but it is more notable for what it promises than for what it achieves in its handling of the theme of loss of identity which is worked out in a series of complicated family relationships. In *The Hillyars and the Burtons*, which contains a finely evocative account of Chelsea where Kingsley spent his childhood, he again traced the fortunes of a group of colonists, and here he gets closer to the realities of colonial life of his time than he does in *Geoffry Hamlyn*.

Kingsley was not a strong or original writer; increasingly, his fiction was lacking in formal integrity and derivative in its notions of character and motive. Yet, however defective his later work, he never wholly lost his power to create an exciting episode and to evoke the beauty of the landscapes in England and Australia which he had viewed with the eyes of an amateur painter and naturalist. He lacked the intellectual depth and moral stamina of his famous brother, but he had a genuine, if minor, talent for romance. And because of the accident of history he has had an influence on the development of writing in Australia, where he is still read and studied widely.

—John Barnes

KIPLING, (Joseph) Rudyard.   English.   Born in Bombay, India, 30 December 1865, of English parents. Educated at the United Services College, Westward Ho!, Devon, 1878–82. Married Caroline Starr Balestier in 1892; three children. Assistant Editor, *Civil and Military Gazette*, Lahore, 1882–87; Editor and Contributor, "Week's News," *Pioneer*, Allahabad, 1887–89; returned to England, and settled in London: full-time writer from 1889; lived in

Brattleboro, Vermont, 1892–96, then returned to England; settled in Burwash, Sussex, 1902. Rector, University of St. Andrews, 1922–25. Recipient: Nobel Prize for Literature, 1907; Royal Society of Literature Gold Medal, 1926. LL.D.: McGill University, Montreal, 1899; D.Litt.: University of Durham, 1907; Oxford University, 1907; Cambridge University, 1908; University of Edinburgh, 1920; the Sorbonne, Paris, 1921; University of Strasbourg, 1921; D.Phil.: University of Athens, 1924. Honorary Fellow, Magdalene College, Cambridge, 1932. Associate Member, Académie des Sciences Morales et Politiques, 1933. Refused the Poet Laureateship, 1895, and the Order of Merit. *Died 18 January 1936.*

PUBLICATIONS

Collections

> *Complete Works* (Sussex Edition).   35 vols., 1937–39; as *Collected Works* (Burwash Edition), 28 vols., 1941.
> *Verse: Definitive Edition.*   1940.
> *The Best Short Stories,* edited by Randall Jarrell.   1961; as *In the Vernacular: The English in India* and *The English in England,* 2 vols., 1963.
> *Stories and Poems,* edited by Roger Lancelyn Green.   1970.
> *Short Stories,* edited by Andrew Rutherford.   1971.
> *Selected Verse,* edited by James Cochrane.   1977.

Fiction

> *Plain Tales from the Hills.*   1888.
> *Soldiers Three: A Collection of Stories.*   1888.
> *The Stories of the Gadsbys: A Tale Without a Plot.*   1888.
> *In Black and White.*   1888.
> *Under the Deodars.*   1888; revised edition, 1890.
> *The Phantom 'Rickshaw and Other Tales.*   1888; revised edition, 1890.
> *Wee Willie Winkie and Other Child Stories.*   1888; revised edition, 1890.
> *The Light That Failed.*   1890.
> *The Courting of Dinah Shadd and Other Stories.*   1890.
> *Mine Own People.*   1891.
> *The Naulahka: A Story of West and East,* with Wolcott Balestier.   1892.
> *Many Inventions.*   1893.
> *Soldier Tales.*   1896; as *Soldier Stories,* 1896.
> *The Day's Work.*   1898.
> *The Kipling Reader.*   1900; as *Selected Stories,* 1925.
> *Traffics and Discoveries.*   1904.
> *Actions and Reactions.*   1909.
> *Abaft the Funnel.*   1909.
> *A Diversity of Creatures.*   1917.
> *Selected Stories,* edited by William Lyon Phelps.   1921.
> *Debits and Credits.*   1926.
> *Selected Stories.*   1929.
> *Thy Servant a Dog, Told by Boots.*   1930; revised edition, as *Thy Servant a Dog and Other Dog Stories,* 1938.
> *Humorous Tales.*   1931.
> *Animal Stories.*   1932.
> *Limits and Renewals.*   1932.

All the Mowgli Stories.   1933.
Collected Dog Stories.   1934.

Play

The Harbour Watch (produced 1913; revised version, as *Gow's Watch*, produced 1924).

Verse

Schoolboy Lyrics.   1881.
Echoes, with Alice Kipling.   1884.
Departmental Ditties and Other Verses.   1886.
Departmental Ditties, Barrack-Room Ballads, and Other Verse.   1890.
Barrack-Room Ballads and Other Verses.   1892.
Ballads and Barrack-Room Ballads.   1893.
The Seven Seas.   1896.
Recessional.   1897.
An Almanac of Twelve Sports.   1898.
Poems, edited by Wallace Rice.   1899.
Recessional and Other Poems.   1899.
The Absent-Minded Beggar.   1899.
With Number Three, Surgical and Medical, and New Poems.   1900.
Occasional Poems.   1900.
The Five Nations.   1903.
The Muse among the Motors.   1904.
Collected Verse.   1907.
A History of England (verse only), with C. R. L. Fletcher.   1911; revised edition, 1930.
Songs from Books.   1912.
Twenty Poems.   1918.
The Years Between.   1919.
Verse: Inclusive Edition, 1885–1918.   3 vols., 1919; revised edition, 1921, 1927, 1933.
A Kipling Anthology: Verse.   1922.
A Choice of Songs.   1925.
Sea and Sussex.   1926.
Songs of the Sea.   1927.
Poems 1886–1929.   3 vols., 1929.
Selected Poems.   1931.
East of Suez, Being a Selection of Eastern Verses.   1931.
The Complete Barrack-Room Ballads, edited by C. E. Carrington.   1973.

Other

Quartette, with others.   1885.
The City of Dreadful Night and Other Sketches.   1890.
The City of Dreadful Night and Other Places.   1891.
The Smith Administration.   1891.
Letters of Marque.   1891.
American Notes, with *The Bottle Imp*, by Robert Louis Stevenson.   1891.
The Jungle Book (juvenile).   1894; *The Second Jungle Book*, 1895.
*Out of India: Things I Saw, and Failed to See, in Certain Days and Nights at Jeypore and
    Elsewhere.*   1895.

The Kipling Birthday Book, edited by Joseph Finn. 1896.
"Captain Courageous": A Story of the Grand Banks (juvenile). 1897; edited by J. de L. Ferguson, 1959.
A Fleet in Being: Notes on Two Trips with the Channel Squadron. 1898.
Stalky & Co. (juvenile). 1899; revised edition, as *The Complete Stalky & Co.*, 1929; edited by Steven Marcus, 1962.
From Sea to Sea: Letters of Travel. 1899; as *From Sea to Sea and Other Sketches*, 1900.
Works (Swastika Edition). 15 vols., 1899.
Kim (juvenile). 1901.
Just So Stories for Little Children. 1902.
Puck of Pook's Hill (juvenile). 1906.
Letters to the Family (Notes on a Recent Trip to Canada). 1908.
Kipling Stories and Poems Every Child Should Know, edited by Mary E. Burt and W. T. Chapin. 1909.
Rewards and Fairies (juvenile). 1910.
The Kipling Reader. 1912.
The New Army in Training. 1915.
France at War. 1915.
The Fringes of the Fleet. 1915.
Tales of "The Trade." 1916.
Sea Warfare. 1916.
The War in the Mountains. 1917.
The Eyes of Asia. 1918.
The Graves of the Fallen. 1919.
Letters of Travel (1892–1913). 1920.
A Kipling Anthology: Prose. 1922.
Land and Sea Tales for Scouts and Guides. 1923.
The Irish Guards in the Great War. 2 vols., 1923.
Works (Mandalay Edition). 26 vols., 1925–26.
A Book of Words: Selections from Speeches and Addresses Delivered Between 1906 and 1927. 1928.
The One Volume Kipling. 1928.
Souvenirs of France. 1933.
Ham and the Porcupine (juvenile). 1935.
A Kipling Pageant. 1935.
Something of Myself for My Friends Known and Unknown. 1937.
Letters from Japan, edited by Donald Richie and Yoshimori Harashima. 1962.
Kipling to Rider Haggard: The Record of a Friendship, edited by Morton Cohen. 1965.

Bibliography: *Kipling: A Bibliographical Catalogue* by J. McG. Stewart, edited by A. W. Keats, 1959; "Kipling: An Annotated Bibliography of Writings about Him" by H. E. Gerber and E. Lauterbach, in *English Fiction in Transition 3*, 1960, and *8*, 1965.

Reading List: *Kipling: His Life and Work* by C. E. Carrington, 1955; *A Reader's Guide to Kipling's Work* by Roger Lancelyn Green, 1961, and *Kipling: The Critical Heritage* edited by Green, 1971; *Kipling's Mind and Art* edited by Andrew Rutherford, 1964; *Kipling and the Critics* edited by E. L. Gilbert, 1965; *Kipling* by J. I. M. Stewart, 1966; *Kipling: Realist and Fabulist* by Bonamy Dobrée, 1967; *Kipling and His World* by Kingsley Amis, 1975; *Kipling: The Glass, The Shadow, and the Fire* by Philip Mason, 1975; *The Strange Ride of Kipling: His Life and Works* by Angus Wilson, 1977.

*   *   *

T. S. Eliot called Rudyard Kipling "the most inscrutable of authors ... a writer impossible to belittle." On the face of it, it was an extraordinary judgement to pass on an author who was the idol of the plain, philistine, notably non-literary public, suggesting that he was as difficult, almost as hermetic to popular understanding as Eliot himself might be construed to be, and that if it was impossible to belittle him it had not been for want of many people trying. As the celebrant of British imperialism and "the white man's burden," which was one of his own phrases, in his lifetime Kipling was anathema to all good liberals both with a large and a small initial letter, and even today, forty years after his death, fairness to him is not easy.

Part of the difficulty in making a judgement lies in the complexity of his character, part in the disconcerting range of his subject-matter. It is impossible to read *Plain Tales from the Hills* without being forced partially to agree with the nineteenth-century critic who accused him of honouring "everywhere the brute and the bully." At the same time it is impossible not to be struck with the warmth of his sympathy both for children and for those men and women, white and brown alike, caught up in interracial sexual relations, as in "Without Benefit of Clergy." He appears, indeed, in these stories as, to borrow Bagehot's phrase for Dickens, the "special correspondent for posterity" reporting the day-to-day life of the British Raj in the last decades of Victoria's reign. That he was an unillusioned observer of the nature of imperialism emerges clearly in what is probably the finest of his Indian stories, "The Man Born to Be King," in which two down-at-heel adventurers seize a country to the north of Afghanistan and only fail to establish a dynasty there because of the character-defects of one of them. It is an ironically grim fable on the nature of empire-building.

Though in his lifetime Kipling was seen as above all a writer about India, in fact he spent less than ten years of his adult life in the country, and it seems clear that his imagination widened and deepened after leaving it. His range is extraordinary, so much so that it is impossible to pick out any one story as typical of Kipling; instead, there are peaks of excellence, each *sui generis*, and in a narrow space all one can do is give instances. There is "Mrs. Bathurst," a study in sexual magic, and, in its subtlety and indirection and mastery of the rendering of character through dialogue, possibly the most remarkable story in the language. It compels realisation that Kipling was not only a modern but at times even a modernist writer.

There are the great mythopoeic stories of Sussex life, in particular "Friendly Brook," a story very pagan in tone about what in effect is a local deity of the kind we find in Latin poetry, and "The Wish-House," a beautiful story of self-sacrifice in which something like an instance of ancient folk-lore is astonishingly invented. There are stories based in scientific invention, such as "The Eye of Allah," in which the microscope is invented – and smashed to bits – in a medieval monastery, and "Wireless," in which an early experiment in transmission by radio is magically tied up with the presence of an apothecary's assistant, whose mind in a trance is invaded by the spirit of John Keats. There are stories of morbid psychology like the chilling and in my view often misunderstood "Mary Postgate." There is the haunting story of phantom children, "They," which so influenced Eliot in the writing of "Burnt Norton."

That he was the greatest of English short-story writers can scarcely be doubted. He was never a successful novelist, though *Kim* is a case on its own, a wonderfully sympathetic evocation of Indian native life. He was, obviously, one of the great children's writers, and it was precisely in such works as *The Jungle Book*, *Puck of Pook's Hill* and *Stalky & Co.* that he most unambiguously dramatised his moral values, what he called the Law, which "lesser breeds" were without. Above all, perhaps, with his younger contemporaries Joyce and Lawrence, with whom one feels he would have had little sympathy, he was one of the undisputed masters of specifically modern English prose.

A definitive critical estimate of Kipling as a poet is still awaited. He stood apart from the general poetic theories and practice current in his lifetime and forged his own characteristic expression in poems like "Danny Deever" and "Mandalay" out of the music hall ballad, which he brought into literature. His most famous poem, "Recessional," is obviously one of the great hymns. He was in a very real sense that rarest of beings, a genuine popular poet, and whatever his final place in our poetry may prove to be, one thing is certain. More lines and phrases from his verse have passed into the common mind and speech than those of any other English poet of the century.

—Walter Allen

KIRKLAND, Joseph. American. Born in Geneva, New York, 7 January 1830; grew up in Michigan and Illinois. Received little formal education; studied law, 1873–80; admitted to the Illinois bar, 1880. Served in the American Civil War, in the Illinois 12th Regiment, 1861, as Aide-de-Camp, Adjutant-General's Department, Washington, D.C., 1861, and on the staff of Generals Fitz-John Porter and McClellan, 1862–63: Major. Married Theodosia Burr Wilkinson in 1863; four children. Sailor on a packet ship, 1847; Clerk and Reader, *Putnam's Monthly*, 1852; Auditor, Illinois Central Railroad, Chicago, 1856–58; Supervisor, Carbon Coal Company, Tilton, Illinois, 1858; established coal mining business, in Tilton, 1863, and a retail coal business, in Chicago, 1868; bankrupt, 1877; worked for the United States Revenue Service, 1875–80; practised law, in partnership with Mark Bangs, Chicago, 1880–90; Special Correspondent and Literary Editor, *Chicago Tribune*, 1889 until his death. Member, Committee on the World Exposition in Chicago, 1893. *Died 29 April 1894.*

PUBLICATIONS

Fiction

Zury, The Meanest Man in Spring County: A Novel of Western Life. 1887.
The McVeys (An Episode). 1888.
The Captain of Company K. 1891.

Play

Sidonie, The Married Flirt, with James B. Runnion, from a novel by Daudet (produced 1877).

Other

The Story of Chicago, completed by Caroline Kirkland. 2 vols., 1892–94.
The Chicago Massacre of 1812. 1893.

Editor, *Lily Pearl and the Mistress of Rosedale,* by Ida Glenwood. 1892.
Editor, with John Moses, *The History of Chicago.* 2 vols., 1895.

Bibliography: in *Bibliography of American Literature* by Jacob Blanck, 1969.

Reading List: *Kirkland* by Clyde E. Henson, 1962.

*   *   *

Joseph Kirkland's claim to fame rests entirely on one book, *Zury*, and a superficial reading of it is likely to be misleading. Literary historians have been too quick to classify Kirkland with other "agrarian realists" and "protest novelists." It is true that *Zury* contains many details conveying the narrowness, brutality, and deprivation of midwestern farm life in the middle of the nineteenth century. Zury (the name is short for Usury) has a beloved sister who dies as a result of the primitive conditions on the farm, and the family has no coins with which to weight her eyelids. Since she dies in mid-winter, the family has no choice but to let the body freeze and wait for the spring thaw to bury her.

The novel also forcefully describes the cruelty and niggardliness Zury must possess to accumulate his modest fortune. Having been made selfish by his environment, he seeks to avoid his responsibility for making pregnant the young and innocent school teacher from the East, Anne Sparrow. He arranges to marry her to a local idler, John McVey.

However, to emphasize these details is to neglect the end of *Zury* and the entirety of the sequel, *The McVeys*. The second volume followed soon after the first, and in it Zury sees his error and takes an interest in his and Anne's twin children (McVey has conveniently died). Although she at first rejects him, Zury and Anne eventually marry and symbolically combine the vitality and toughness of Zury's West with the culture and refinement of Anne's East, and the last scene of *The McVeys* finds them cozy and happy in a prosperous farmhouse. One might suggest that Kirkland was ultimately more "realistic" than some of his more bitter contemporaries, and certainly more entertaining.

After writing *The Captain of Company K*, an episodic but vivid story of the Civil War, Kirkland showed little interest in artistic creation, and devoted himself to editorial and historical work.

—William Higgins

KOESTLER, Arthur. English. Born in Budapest, Hungary, 5 September 1905; became a British subject after World War II. Educated at the University of Vienna, 1922–26. Married 1) Dorothy Asher in 1935 (divorced, 1950); 2) Mamaine Paget in 1950 (divorced 1953); 3) Cynthia Jefferies in 1965; one daughter. Foreign Correspondent for the Ullstein chain, Berlin, in the Middle East, 1927–29, and in Paris, 1929–30; Foreign Editor, *B.Z. am Mittag*, and Science Editor, *Vossische Zeitung*, Berlin, 1930–32; member of the Graf Zeppelin polar expedition, 1931; travelled in Russia, 1932–33; member of the Communist Party, 1932–38; free-lance writer, in Paris, London, and Zurich, 1933–36; War Correspondent for the *News Chronicle*, London, in Spain, 1936–37; imprisoned by the Nationalists, then exchanged through intervention of the British government; imprisoned in France, 1939–40, then joined the French Foreign Legion, 1940–41, escaped to Britain, and served in the British Pioneer Corps, 1941–42; after discharge, worked for the Ministry of Information, London, and as a night ambulance driver; Special Correspondent, in Palestine, for *The Times*, London, 1945, and for the *Manchester Guardian* and *New York Herald Tribune*, 1948; Visiting Chubb Fellow, Yale University, New Haven, Connecticut, 1950; Fellow, Center for Advanced Study in the Behavioral Sciences, Stanford University, California, 1964–65. Recipient: Sonning Prize, University of Copenhagen, 1968. LL.D.: Queen's University, Kingston, Ontario. Fellow, 1957, and Companion of Literature, 1974, Royal Society of Literature. C.B.E. (Commander, Order of the British Empire), 1972. Lives in London.

PUBLICATIONS

Novels

The Gladiators, translated by Edith Simon.   1939.
Darkness at Noon, translated by Daphne Hardy.   1940.
Arrival and Departure.   1943.
Thieves in the Night: Chronicle of an Experiment.   1946.
The Age of Longing.   1951.
The Call-Girls: A Tragi-Comedy with Prologue and Epilogue.   1972.

Plays

Twilight Bar: An Escapade in Four Acts (produced 1946).   1945.

Screenplay: *Lift Your Head, Comrade* (documentary), 1944.

Other

Von Weissen Nächten und Roten Tagen.   1933.
Encyclopédie de la Vie Sexuelle, with Dr. Levy-Lenz and A. Willy.   1934; as *Encyclopedia of Sexual Knowledge*, edited by Norman Haire, 1934.
Menschenopfer Unerhört.   1937; English version, in *Spanish Testament*, 1937.
Spanish Testament (autobiography).   1937; excerpt, as *Dialogue with Death*, 1942; revised edition, 1954.
Scum of the Earth (autobiography).   1941.
The Yogi and the Commissar and Other Essays.   1945.
Sexual Anomalies and Perversions: A Summary of the Works of Magnus Hirschfeld.   1946; revised edition, edited by Norman Haire, 1952.
L'Encyclopédie de la Famille, with Manes Sperber.   N.d.
Insight and Outlook: An Inquiry into the Common Foundations of Science, Art, and Social Ethics.   1949.
Promise and Fulfillment: Palestine 1917–1949.   1949.
Arrow in the Blue (autobiography).   1952.
The Invisible Writing (autobiography).   1954.
The Trail of the Dinosaur and Other Essays.   1955.
Reflections on Hanging.   1956.
The Sleepwalkers: A History of Man's Changing Vision of the Universe.   1959; section published as *The Watershed: A Biography of Johannes Kepler*, 1960.
The Lotus and the Robot.   1960.
Hanged by the Neck: An Exposure of Capital Punishment in England, with C. H. Rolph.   1961.
The Act of Creation.   1964.
The Ghost in the Machine.   1967.
Drinkers of Infinity: Essays 1955–1967.   1968.
The Case of the Midwife Toad.   1971.
The Roots of Coincidence.   1972.
The Challenge of Chance: Experiments and Speculations.   1973; as *The Challenge of Chance: A Mass Experiment in Telepathy and Its Unexpected Outcome*, 1975.
The Heel of Achilles: Essays 1968–1973.   1974.
The Thirteenth Tribe: The Khazar Empire and Its Heritage.   1976.
Janus: A Summing Up.   1978.

Editor, *Suicide of a Nation? An Enquiry into the State of Britain Today.* 1963.
Editor, with J. R. Smythies, *Beyond Reductionism: New Perspectives in the Life Sciences: The Alpbach Symposium.* 1969.

Reading List: *Koestler* by J. Nedava, 1948; *Koestler* by John Atkins, 1956; *Koestler: Das Literarische Werk* by Peter Alfred Huber, 1962; *Chronicles of Conscience: A Study of Orwell and Koestler* by Jenni Calder, 1968; *Koestler* by Wolfe Mays, 1973; *Koestler: A Collection of Critical Essays* edited by Murray A. Sperber, 1977.

*   *   *

Arthur Koestler is a writer whose work in fiction, in polemic essays, and in books that rather exhaustively investigate the implications of scientific theory embodies a concern for man's present condition and his immediate future. In this variety, Koestler is not unlike the somewhat older writer Aldous Huxley, who did not hesitate to express his concerns for man in a variety of forms, often with brilliance and always with pertinacity. In Koestler's work the central note is that of horror for the events that have already occurred in this century and a desperate hope that further horror may be averted and that man may truly become the thinking animal that he sometimes gives promise of being. What matters for Koestler is less the particular artistic form that he takes up than the use he may make of it as he continues pursuing his central preoccupation.

Koestler first won international attention with his novel *Darkness at Noon.* This novel, which tells of the imprisonment and interrogation and, finally, the liquidation of an "old Bolshevik" named Rubashov — a figure perhaps modelled on Trotsky — offered readers an effective synthesis of two elements: one man's betrayal by a dream he had held, and an analysis of the ambiguities of Marxian hope as it moves from prospect to realization. The novel is full of compelling analyses of the hardening of hope into party dogma and authoritarianism. These analyses have been repeated elsewhere by Koestler — for example, in his contribution to a collection of essays entitled *The God That Failed.* But in *Darkness at Noon,* at least, there is no great disharmony between what is dramatically represented and what is argued. This harmony diminishes in later novels like *Arrival and Departure* and *The Age of Longing,* where the characters and the dramatic action are chiefly means of representing the various winds of doctrine that Koestler puts before us for judgement.

After *The Age of Longing* Koestler abandoned for many years the creation of fiction. A much later novel, *The Call Girls,* is close to the polemic and expository work which engaged the writer's attention after *The Age of Longing.* In this novel members of a learned seminar convened to avert world disaster — an event that Koestler brings on the scene in *The Age of Longing* — meet and offer an incoherent collection of solutions that will avert a holocaust. Attempts are made to relate the solutions to the characters of the persons who offer them, but it is plain that the conflict of human character has a minor interest for Koestler. The "solutions" are, in fact, possibilities that Koestler has followed ever since the time, during the 1930's when he was a science editor for a German paper, and was horrified by the rise of the Nazis to power. At this time he became a member of the Communist party — a relationship that he terminated before he wrote *Darkness at Noon* which is, in fact a record of disgust for the authoritarianism of the Left.

Pursuit of solutions has led Koestler in many directions. But they are all only slightly tangential to the main path he has followed. Koestler has written books of social and political analysis. In *The Yogi and the Commissar* he pits the wisdom of the guru against that of the Marxian theorist. In *The Lotus and the Robot* he makes a careful assessment of the "wisdom" of the East and finds it closes off options that are still open in the distressed West. In a series of other books, Koestler measures the resources that lie in the various scientific explorations that have taken place in the culture to which he — and most of his readers — belong. In *The Act of*

Creation, for example, Koestler makes a study of scientific and artistic creation, drawing on whatever help psychology and neuro-physiology can offer. In *The Ghost in the Machine* he tries to underline the importance of the human mind (the "ghost") for which some of the sciences of man — behaviorism, laboratory psychology — have little patience because the "mind" notably resists quantification and controls that are overt and rigorous. Koestler urges us, in relation to the mind and the uses we can make of it, to move "beyond reductionism."

This summary of Koestler's concerns has omitted specific mention of many of his books: e.g., his autobiography which begins with the volume *Arrow in the Blue*, his careful estimate of extra-sensory perception and related matters in *The Roots of Coincidence*, and other works. But these books are also part of the difficult balancing act by which Koestler tries to find a basis for continued human resistance to horror and collapse. The human effort takes place on grounds that lie between extremes. One extreme sees man as a material composite that is readily manipulable (by other men, of course). The alternate view suggests that man is the one creature that can lose himself in mystical "occanic experience" (a term that Koestler has taken from Freud). The human mind (and the being it enlives) is a whole in relation to that which it rises from (material substance, evolutionary history, personal psychoses); and it is — or can be — a part of that which it moves toward but is not likely to reach: a better form of humanity where emotion and reason have an interplay that at present escapes us.

—Harold H. Watts

KOSINSKI, Jerzy (Nikodem). American. Born in Lodz, Poland, 14 June 1933; emigrated to the United States, 1957; naturalized, 1965. Educated at the University of Lodz, 1950–55, M.A. in history 1953, M.A. in political science 1955; Columbia University, New York, 1958–64; New School for Social Research, New York, 1962–65. Married Mary Hayward Weir in 1962 (died, 1968). Aspirant (Associate Professor), Polish Academy of Sciences, Warsaw, 1955–57; Fellow, Center for Advanced Studies, Wesleyan University, Middletown, Connecticut, 1968–69; Senior Fellow, Council for the Humanities, and Visiting Lecturer in English Prose, Princetown University, New Jersey, 1969–70; Professor of English Prose and Criticism, School of Drama, and Resident Fellow, Davenport College, Yale University, New Haven, Connecticut, 1970–72. President, American P.E.N. Club, 1973. Member of the Executive Board, National Writers Club; Director, International League for the Rights of Man. Recipient: Polish Academy of Sciences grant, 1955; Ford Fellowship, 1958; Prix du Meilleur Livre Etranger, France, 1966; Guggenheim Fellowship, 1967; National Book Award, 1969; American Academy of Arts and Letters grant, 1970; John Golden Fellowship in Playwriting, 1970. Lives in New York City.

PUBLICATIONS

Fiction

    The Painted Bird. 1965; revised edition, 1970.
    Steps. 1968.
    Being There. 1971.
    The Devil Tree. 1973.
    Cockpit. 1975.
    Blind Date. 1977.

Other

The Future Is Ours, Comrade. 1960.
No Third Path. 1962.
Notes of the Author on "The Painted Bird" 1965. 1965.
The Art of the Self: Essays à propos "Steps." 1968.
The Time of Life: The Time of Art (essays; in Dutch). 1970.

*   *   *

In Jerzy Kosinski's first novel, *The Painted Bird*, there is an incident that sums up not only the thrust of the novel in which it appears; the incident points to the core of the great variety of experiences that appear in Kosinski's later novels. A peasant catches a raven, paints it with brilliant colors, and releases it to return to its fellows. But the other birds will not accept it and tear it to pieces. This image is a metaphor which expresses the experience of the narrator in the novel, a child of dark aspect ("gypsy" or "Jewish" by turns) who wanders through Poland, deprived of his parents and depending on the ungentle mercies of the peasants he encounters; the peasants, blond and stupid, regard the child as full of evil magic. And the "painted" child learns to survive by duplicity; he endures a solitude that he has not chosen; the only morality he knows is that of survival.

It is a morality which, with appropriate alterations, the central figures of the other novels sense; just so do they define and experience their existences. Such a morality is tested — admired from several angles — in *Steps*, a collection of narrative fragments and mostly unlocalized amorous dialogues. Much of this material is linked with the education and migration to a foreign country of a young man who is, like the child in *The Painted Bird*, on the run, exploited and exploiting wherever he goes. To him every new acquaintance is both an affront and an opportunity.

For a change of pace, the hero of *Being There* is no person displaced by war; rather, he is an orphan without identity, unable to read, skillful only as a gardener. But when he leaves the Eden where he has learned his only skills, his oddity and peculiar vulnerability arouse wonder and respect, rather than antipathy as in *The Painted Bird*. His trivial remarks about gardening are taken as profound and enigmatic insights by those he encounters; business men, TV reporters, and others surround him with an aura of ultimate authority. In *The Devil Tree*, a young man named Jonathan James Whalen wanders through another landscape of solitude, this one created by his great inherited wealth. There is practically nothing that he cannot purchase and manipulate, and the absolute control he can exercise separates him from other persons as fully as does, for example, the "gypsy" aspect of the child in *The Painted Bird*. Whatever can be purchased can also be thrown away; this is the core of Whalen's experience.

The wanderings presented in *Cockpit* are those of a secret agent named Tarden. Born in a Communist country, he soon learns what *his* precious endowment is: intelligence and guile that surpass the intelligence and guile of all other persons. Every person he meets is a predestined victim whom Tarden can mislead and abuse, all with the intent of showing that Tarden is one "painted bird" whom his hostile peers cannot destroy.

Each of Kosinski's novels is a demonstration of one variety of solipsism. Community of any kind is a figment that misleads inferior imaginations. Each of Kosinski's novels dissolves such illusions. Innocence, wealth, and guile are alternate strategies, but they have a common goal. All confirm that each human being is alone, and those who have a degree of wisdom recognize their solitude and enforce it.

—Harold H. Watts

LA FARGE, Oliver (Hazard Perry). American. Born in New York City, 19 December 1901. Educated at the Groton School, Connecticut, graduated 1920; Harvard University, Cambridge, Massachusetts (Editor, *Harvard Lampoon*; President, *Advocate*; Class Poet), 1920–24, graduated 1924, then did graduate work in anthropology (Hemenway Fellow), M.A. 1929. Served in the United States Army, 1942–46: Lieutenant-Colonel; Legion of Merit, 1946. Married 1) Wanden E. Mathews in 1929 (divorced), one son and one daughter; 2) Consuelo Otille C. de Baca in 1939, one son. Anthropologist: involved in expeditions for the Peabody Museum, Harvard, in Arizona, 1921, 1922, 1924; Assistant in Ethnology, Department of Middle American Research, Tulane University, New Orleans, 1925–26; involved in research expeditions to Mexico and Guatemala, 1926–28; Research Associate in Ethnology, Columbia University, New York, 1931; Director of the Columbia University expedition to Guatemala, 1932; thereafter a full-time writer and historian. President, Association on American Indian Affairs, 1932–41, 1948. Recipient: Pulitzer Prize, 1930; O. Henry Prize, 1931; Guggenheim Fellowship, 1941. A.M.: Brown University, Providence, Rhode Island, 1932. Fellow, American Association for the Advancement of Science, 1938, American Anthropological Association, 1947, and American Academy of Arts and Sciences, 1953. Member, National Institute of Arts and Letters, 1957. *Died 2 August 1963.*

PUBLICATIONS

Fiction

Laughing Boy. 1929.
Sparks Fly Upward. 1931.
Long Pennant. 1933.
All the Young Men (stories). 1935.
The Enemy Gods. 1937.
The Copper Pot. 1942.
A Pause in the Desert (stories). 1957.
The Door in the Wall (stories). 1965.

Other

Tribes and Temples: A Record of the Expedition to Middle America Conducted in 1925, with Frans Blom. 2 vols., 1926–27.
The Year Bearer's People, with Douglas Byers. 1931.
As Long as the Grass Shall Grow. 1940.
War below Zero: The Battle for Greenland, with B. Balchen and C. Ford. 1944.
Raw Material (autobiography). 1945.
Santa Eulalia: The Religion of the Cuchumatán Indian Town. 1947.
The Eagle in the Egg. 1949.
Cochise of Arizona: The Pipe of Peace Is Broken (juvenile). 1953.
Mother Ditch. 1954.
A Pictorial History of the American Indian. 1956.
Behind the Mountains. 1956.
Santa Fe: The Autobiography of a Southwestern Town, with Arthur N. Morgan. 1959.
American Indian. 1960.
The Man with the Calabash Pipe (essays), edited by Winfield Townley Scott. 1966.

Editor, with Jay Bryan Nash, *The New Day for the Indians.* 1938.
Editor, *The Changing Indian.* 1940.

Translator, *A Man's Place,* by Ramón Sender.   1940.

*   *   *

Of the more than twenty books by Oliver La Farge, nearly half are scientific or historical, and a third are fiction. Yet he is generally known as the author of but one book, his first novel, *Laughing Boy.*

It is not surprising that his histories are virtually unknown. Of those concerning Indians, his most important is *A Pictorial History of the American Indian,* which offers a wealth of material about the various tribes to a public aware of the minority question. Other histories, however – about World War II, the city of Santa Fe, the events of La Farge's own life – are too specialized to be of general interest.

For a similar reason, his scientific work is all but unknown. Not only has the subsequent accumulation of knowledge dwarfed his contributions to ethnology, but as he notes in his personal history, *Raw Material,* the details that absorb the scientist are unlikely to interest more than a handful of fellow scientists. The accounts of expeditions to Central America in which he took part – *Tribes and Temples, The Year Bearer's People, Santa Eulalia* – are highly readable, but too narrowly concerned with the Indian to interest the public for which they were intended.

On the other hand, his second novel, *Sparks Fly Upward,* using the same Indian material, was a best seller. This and *The Enemy Gods,* dealing with the Navajos in the Southwest, reveal the plight of the Indian caught between two cultures. The theme is also explored in a collection of short stories, *All the Young Men.*

With his fifth novel, *The Copper Pot,* La Farge attempted to avoid being typecast as a writer about Indians. This story of an artist in New Orleans is more an affectionate memoir, however, than a novel. Two short story collections, *A Pause in the Desert* and *The Door in the Wall,* use other than Indian material, as does *The Long Pennant,* a novel about the aftermath of piracy by a New England vessel.

Yet it is La Farge's knowledgeable use of Indian material that distinguishes his fiction. A symbiotic relationship exists between the scientific and the creative in his work, the former providing it with substance and originality. Although a first-rate story teller, he exhibits no particularly original turn of mind. He breaks no new ground in his use of language or fictional techniques. As he makes plain in his newspaper columns, collected in *The Man with the Calabash Pipe,* he wished to preserve traditional values, in language and elsewhere – an attitude reflected in his lifelong involvement with the Indian.

This attitude and his unique material are most happily met in his two finest novels, *Laughing Boy* and *The Enemy Gods.* The latter is considered superior, presenting more information and dealing with weightier problems. Yet it is unremittingly melancholy and gray compared with *Laughing Boy,* whose young lovers in an Indian Eden are likely to continue to make it the book by which Oliver La Farge will be known.

—Robert F. Richards

LAMB, Charles.   English.   Born in the Inner Temple, London, 10 February 1775. Educated at Christ's Hospital, London, 1782–89. Worked in the office of the merchant Joseph Paice, 1790, and in the Examiner's Office of South Sea House, 1791–92; worked in the Accountant's Office of the East India Company, 1792 until he retired, with a pension, 1825; writer from 1795; a friend of Wordsworth, Coleridge, and Hazlitt; guardian of his sister Mary, who was periodically insane, from 1796; contributed to *London Magazine,* 1820–25. *Died 27 December 1834.*

PUBLICATIONS

Collections

Works, edited by T. Hutchinson.   2 vols., 1908.
The Letters of Lamb, to Which Are Added Those of His Sister Mary Lamb, edited by E.
   V. Lucas.   3 vols., 1935.
The Portable Lamb, edited by John Mason Brown.   1964.
A Lamb Selection: Letters and Essays, edited by F. B. Pinion.   1965.
Letters of Charles and Mary Anne Lamb, edited by Edwin W. Marrs, Jr.   1975–

Fiction

A Tale of Rosamund Gray and Old Blind Margaret.   1798.

Plays

John Woodvil: A Tragedy.   1802.
Mr. H—; or, Beware a Bad Name (produced 1806).   1813.
The Wife's Trial; or, The Intruding Widow, in *Blackwood's Magazine,* December 1828.
The Pawn-Broker's Daughter, in *Blackwood's Magazine,* January 1830.

Verse

Blank Verse, with Charles Lloyd.   1798.
Poetry for Children, Entirely Original, with Mary Lamb.   2 vols., 1809; edited by A. W.
   Tuer, 2 vols., 1892.
Prince Dorus; or, Flattery Put Out of Countenance: A Poetical Version of an Ancient Tale
   (juvenile).   1811; edited by J. P. Broscoe, 1896.
Beauty and the Beast; or, A Rough Outside with a Gentle Heart: A Poetical Version of an
   Ancient Tale (juvenile).   1811.
Album Verses.   1830.
Satan in Search of His Wife.   1831.

Other

Original Letters of Sir John Falstaff and His Friends, with J. White.   1796; edited by
   Israel Gollancz, 1907 (possibly not by Lamb).
The King and Queen of Hearts (juvenile).   1805; edited by E. V. Lucas, 1902.
Tales from Shakespeare Designed for the Use of Young Persons, with Mary Lamb.   2
   vols., 1807; edited by J. C. Trewin, 1964.
The Adventures of Ulysses (juvenile).   1808; edited by Ernest A. Gardner, 1921.
Mrs. Leicester's School; or, The History of Several Young Ladies Related by Themselves
   (juvenile), with Mary Lamb.   1809.
Works.   2 vols., 1818.
Elia: Essays Which Have Appeared under That Signature in the London
   Magazine.   1823; *Second Series,* 1828; both series, 2 vols., 1835; edited by W.
   Macdonald, 2 vols., 1929.
The Last Essays of Elia.   1833.

Recollections of Christ's Hospital. 1835.
Eliana, Being Hitherto Uncollected Writings, edited by J. E. Babson. 1864.
Mary and Charles Lamb: Poems, Letters, and Remains, edited by W. C. Hazlitt. 1874.
Lamb on Shakespeare, edited by Joan Coldwell. 1978.

Editor, *Sentimental Tablets of the Good Pamphile,* by J. C. Gorjy, translated by P. S. Dupuy. 1795.
Editor, *Specimens of English Dramatic Poets Who Lived about the Time of Shakespeare.* 1808; edited by Israel Gollancz, 1893.

Bibliography: *Bibliography of the Writings of Charles and Mary Lamb* by J. C. Thomson, 1908.

Reading List: *The Lambs: A Study of Pre-Victorian England* by K. Anthony, 1945; *Lamb* by Edmund Blunden, 1954; *The Life of Lamb* by R. Fukuhara, 1963; *A Study of Lamb's Essays of Elia* by T. Fukuda, 1964; *Lamb and the Theatre* by Wayne McKenna, 1978.

*　　　*　　　*

Charles Lamb's life has become universal property both from his autobiographical genius (often mischievously perverted) and from the circle of literary greatness that looked to him as to its focus. "His genius is talent," wrote Coleridge, "and his talent is genius, and his heart is as whole and one as his head." Both the admiration and the affection were echoed by Wordsworth, Hazlitt, Hunt, Hood, and De Quincey.

Loved by his friends and reverenced by his admirers as *sui generis,* nevertheless, Lamb displayed, qualities that appeal to the English zeal for convention. He was essentially middle-class, born away from the handicap of poverty and never achieving the shame of riches. In practical terms he was as unadventurous as he was daring in imagination. He worked for thirty years as a clerk in the East India House. He lived all his life in London or its suburbs, venturing only once to the Continent, and he went to the country only when he could not avoid the invitations of friends, confessing himself to be "not romance-bit about *Nature.*"

Conservative in his love of familiar things, friends, books, and places, he was nevertheless ardent to reform wrongs done or intended, and his early lampoons, written mostly for Leigh Hunt's *Examiner,* were as vitriolic as anything produced in an age of sharp political satire.

Lamb made his literary debut as a poet, contributing four sonnets to Coleridge's *Poems on Various Subjects* (1796), and in 1798 Lamb with Charles Lloyd published *Blank Verse,* a collection which included his most memorable poem, "The Old Familiar Faces." Also in 1798 he tried his hand at a novel, *Rosamund Gray,* an effort that is best forgotten even by his most fervent admirers. His attempts to make his mark as a dramatist are scarcely more admirable. *John Woodvil* is a dubious imitation of Jacobean tragedy and *Mr. H—* was hissed off the stage, "the author hissing as loud as any."

The *Tales from Shakespeare* has retained a certain world-wide popularity from 1807 to the present day but (perhaps fortunately for his reputation) most of the book is by Charles's sister Mary; his part in it was contributed rather from a sense of duty – of support for a tragic woman who had brought tragedy into his life but whom he loved dearly – than from any literary enthusiasm.

He was still at hack work, editing a volume of selections from Elizabethan and Jacobean dramatists when at last he found the subject-matter which allowed him the scope of his originality. The critical essays which he added to his selection (and a subsequent series written for Hunt's *Reflector*) reinstated the English in their own domain, resurrected for them the beauties of the English Renaissance, "saving and salving Webster, Jonson, Marlowe, Middleton – even Shakespeare himself" after two centuries of neglect or ill-usage by iconoclasts. Lamb's friends Coleridge and Hazlitt were shrewder and perhaps finer critics, but Lamb was more truly a man of the theatre.

By 1818 he had made his reputation, but not his fortune. His reputation was enhanced but his fortune not at all when in that year his scattered contributions in verse and prose were gathered together under the portentous title of *The Works of Charles Lamb*. There followed an invitation to contribute occasional essays to the *London Magazine* and (though he said later that he wished to be remembered "as the first to draw the public attention to the old English dramatists") it was these "Elia" essays (collected as *Essays* and *The Last Essays of Elia*) which made his fame with his contemporaries and have held it against all changes in taste, settling him amongst the incomparable few of English literature.

Humour was his consolation for sorrow but, as with all great men, his apprehension of humanistic pathos and even tragedy were never quite submerged by his sense of comedy. Before he became Elia, he had masked himself with a number of pseudonyms, he had written of Charles Lamb as if he were a chance acquaintance, and he even borrowed the person though not the personality of Coleridge, but at last in the cheerful pen-life of Elia he escaped the burdensome sadness of life as Lamb. There is no writer like Elia. His English "stammers like his speech" but the consequence is beauty. He chases an insignificant idea and makes it significant; he "makes of an interloping inspiration a literary occasion." He relishes archaisms, scholarly asides, private jokes, but he is never precious.

And if Elia is not enough, there are still Lamb's letters to buy for him a palace high on the slopes of the English Parnassus.

—J. E. Morpurgo

LAMMING, George (Eric). Barbadian. Born in Barbados in 1927. Taught school in Trinidad and Venezuela; host of a book review programme for the West Indian Service of the BBC, London, 1951; member of the faculty of the University of the West Indies, Kingston, Jamaica, 1968. Recipient: Guggenheim Fellowship, 1954; Maugham Award, 1957. Lives in London.

PUBLICATIONS

Fiction

In the Castle of My Skin. 1953.
The Emigrants. 1954.
Of Age and Innocence. 1958.
Season of Adventure. 1960.
Water with Berries. 1971.
Natives of My Person. 1972.

Other

The Pleasures of Exile. 1960.

Editor, *Cannon Shot and Glass Beads.* 1974.

* * *

George Lamming's main subject is the development of West Indian society. He seeks to give an imaginative insight into the growth of West Indian sensibility and through that to offer an interpretation of West Indian history. The history of the West Indies consists of a series of journeys, explored by Lamming both as metaphors and as historical facts.

In the Castle of My Skin is a recreation of the world that came into being as a result of the first journey. It recreates the childhood hopes and dreams of a poor West Indian boy with great tenderness, and at the same time it traces the gradual destruction of a village community and the emergence of a new black middle class. *The Emigrants* looks at the meaning of the journey to England which was undertaken by thousands of West Indians during the 1950's. The book explores the clash between the idea of England and the reality as it was experienced by the emigrants. *Of Age and Innocence* is concerned with the voyage back to the West Indies and the journey into independence. It is very concretely a political novel. Lamming says himself that it is "a study in the last stages of colonialism." *Season of Adventure* takes the form of an interior journey, a quest for identity sparked off by the ceremony of souls which is witnessed by the main character. The book is a search for what is to be the cultural base of a true West Indian identity. *Natives of My Person* ends the cycle with the beginning. Set in the sixteenth century, it tells the story of the original journey which was responsible for the society and aspirations of *In the Castle of My Skin*.

In his books Lamming grapples with vital issues, and he has made a major contribution to the understanding of the West Indian psyche. The novels are written with great care and attention to minute details; in this way action, symbol, and metaphor are carefully worked into a coherent pattern. There is, however, a tendency for this carefulness to be overdone which accounts for the occasional heavy and overwritten passages.

—Kirsten Holst Petersen

LANDOR, Walter Savage. English. Born in Warwick, 30 January 1775. Educated at Rugby School, and privately; Trinity College, Oxford, 1793–94 (rusticated). Led a private regiment against Napoleon in Spain, 1808. Married Julia Thuillier in 1811 (separated, 1835). Writer from 1793; lived in South Wales on an income from his father from 1795, then inherited considerable wealth on his father's death, 1805; purchased Llanthony Abbey, 1809; lived in France, 1814, and in Italy, 1815–35, in Florence, 1821–35; returned to England, and lived in Bath, 1835–58; involved in an action for libel, 1858, and resided in Italy again until his death. *Died 17 September 1864.*

PUBLICATIONS

Collections

Letters, edited by Stephen Wheeler. 1899.
The Complete Works, edited by T. Earle Welby and Stephen Wheeler. 16 vols., 1927–36.
Poems (selection), edited by Geoffrey Grigson. 1964.
A Biographical Anthology, edited by Herbert Van Thal. 1973.

Prose

To the Burgesses of Warwick. 1797; edited by R. H. Super, 1949.

Three Letters Written in Spain to D. Francisco Riguelme. 1809.

Commentary on Memoirs of Mr. Fox. 1812; edited by Stephen Wheeler, as *Charles James Fox: A Commentary on His Life and Character,* 1907.

Letters Addressed to Lord Liverpool and the Parliament on the Preliminaries of Peace. 1814.

Letter from Mr. Landor to Mr. Jervis. 1814.

Imaginary Conversations of Literary Men and Statesmen. 5 vols., 1824–29; edited by R. H. Boothroyd, 1936.

Citation and Examination of William Shakespeare Before the Worshipful Sir Thomas Lucy Knight Touching Deer Stealing, to Which Is Added a Conference of Master Edmund Spenser, a Gentleman of Note, with the Earl of Essex Touching the State of Ireland. 1834.

Pericles and Aspasia. 2 vols., 1836; edited by G. Ravenscroft Dennis, 1903.

The Letters of a Conservative, in Which Are Shown the Only Means of Saving What Is Left of the English Church. 1836.

The Pentameron and Pentalogia. 1837.

To Robert Browning. 1845.

The Works. 2 vols., 1846.

Imaginary Conversation of King Carlo-Alberto and the Duchess Belgioioso on the Affairs and Prospects of Italy. 1848.

Popery, British and Foreign. 1851.

On Kossuth's Voyage to America. 1851.

Tyrannicide, Published for the Benefit of the Hungarians in America. 1851.

Imaginary Conversations of Greeks and Romans. 1853.

The Last Fruit Off an Old Tree. 1853.

Letters of an American Mainly on Russia and Revolution. 1854.

Antony and Octavius: Scenes for the Study. 1856.

Letter to Emerson. 1856.

Selections from the Writings (prose), edited by G. S. Hilliard. 1856.

Collection of Autograph Letters and Historical Documents: The Blessington Papers, edited by A. Morrison. 1895.

Letters and Other Unpublished Writings, edited by Stephen Wheeler. 1897.

An Address to the Fellows of Trinity College Oxford on the Alarm of Invasion. 1917.

Landor: Last Days, Letters, and Conversations, edited by H. C. Minchin. 1934.

Plays

Count Julian. 1812.

Andrea of Hungary and Giovanni of Naples. 1839.

Fra Rupert. 1840.

The Siege of Ancona, in *Works.* 1846.

Verse

Poems. 1795.

Moral Epistle Respectfully Dedicated to Earl Stanhope. 1795.

Gebir: A Poem in Seven Books. 1798; translated by Landor, as *Gebirus Poema,* 1803; edited by Arthur Symons, with *The Hellenics,* 1907.

Poems from the Arabic and Persian. 1800.

Poetry.   1800; augmented edition, 1802.
Iambi Incerto Auctore.   1802(?).
Simonidea.   1806.
Ode ad Gustavum Regem: Ode ad Gustavum Exulem.   1810.
Idyllia Nove Quinque Heroum atque Heroidum.   1815.
Sponsalia Polyxenae.   1819.
Idyllia Heroica Decem Librum Phaleuciorum Unum.   1820.
Gebir, Count Julian, and Other Poems.   1831.
Terry Hogan: An Eclogue.   1836.
A Satire on Satirists and Admonition to Detractors.   1836.
Poemata et Inscriptiones.   1847.
The Hellenics Enlarged and Completed.   1847; revised edition, 1859; edited by Arthur
   Symons, with *Gebir*, 1907.
The Italics.   1848.
Savagius Landor Lamartino.   1848.
Epistola ad Pium IX Pontificem.   1849.
Ad Cossuthum et Bemum.   1849.
Dry Sticks, Fagoted by Landor.   1858.
Savonarola e il Priore di San Marco.   1860.
Heroic Idyls with Additional Poems.   1863.
A Modern Greek Idyl.   1917.
To Elizabeth Barrett Browning and Other Verses.   1917.

Bibliography: *The Publication of Landor's Works* by R. H. Super, 1954.

Reading List: *Landor* by M. Elwin, 1941, revised edition, as *Landor: A Replevin*, 1958; *Landor: A Biography* by R. H. Super, 1954; *Landor* by G. R. Hamilton, 1960; *L'Oeuvre de Landor* by P. Vitoux, 1964; *Landor* by E. Dilworth, 1971.

*   *   *

According to Ezra Pound in *How to Read*, "the decline of England began on the day when Landor packed his trunks and departed to Tuscany." And Yeats concluded his fine poem "To a Young Beauty" with the proud claim:

> There is not a fool can call me friend,
> And I may dine at journey's end
> With Landor and with Donne.

Yet Landor remains little read. We may indeed feel that what both Pound and Yeats were primarily responding to was a certain patrician high-handedness in Landor's character which found its neatest expression in his "Dying Speech of an Old Philosopher":

> I strove with none, for none was worth my strife:
>   Nature I loved, and next to Nature, Art:
> I warmed both hands before the fire of life;
>   It sinks; and I am ready to depart.

This has an admirable crispness and clarity, the qualities which Landor found most congenial in the Classics that he knew so well. But it may be doubted whether it shows much depth of self-knowledge in one whose whole life was spent in striving with others usually for very good reasons. After all, Landor was rusticated from Oxford for shooting his fowling-piece at the windows of an "obnoxious Tory" who was making too much noise, and served as the original of Dickens's Boythorn in *Bleak House* who sets his estate about with notices warning "That any person or persons audaciously presuming to trespass on this property will be punished with the utmost severity of private chastisement, and prosecuted with the utmost rigour of the law."

Nevertheless, as if in proof of Yeats's belief that a writer expresses a view of life antithetical to his public behaviour, Landor sought a style in prose and verse which would embody the classical ideas of lucidity and balance. Outside the epigrams – including the well-known tribute to his loved Rose Aylmer – Landor succeeded best in prose. The early blank-verse narrative poem *Gebir* lacks the force of either narrative or characterisation to sustain it, and the same is true of his plays, which lack dramatic power and can hardly be envisaged on the stage.

It was in the *Imaginary Conversations* that Landor, perhaps encouraged by his friend Southey who was then beginning his Colloquies, found his appropriate form. In these he could bring together related or contrasting historical characters and use the juxtaposition to bring out what seems to him significant ideas about life and conduct. At first sight, the *Conversations* might seem to parallel the dramatic monologues of his later friend Browning, but in fact their aims were different. Whereas Browning was interested above all in the varieties of human character, Landor's interest lay in the presentation of ideas and attitudes. Yet there is enough variety in Landor's knowledge of history and his breadth of interests to sustain these literary dialogues, some of which have been effectively broadcast. At his best, as in "Elizabeth and Cecil," "Southey and Porson," "Washington and Franklin," "Epictetus and Seneca," and the longer *Pericles and Aspasia*, Landor shows great skill in giving expression to what is basically his own philosophy, a high-toned classical republicanism, sweetened by a sense of beauty and transience.

A neglected aspect of Landor is his excellence as a letter writer. Should the reader begin to lose interest on the formality of the *Conversations*, he will find in the letters more of the ebullient character who appealed to many close friends throughout a long life. The published *Letter to Emerson* was an expression of Landor's pleasure and interest in Emerson's recent *English Traits*. Characteristically Landor was both polite and firm in his response, going through the references to his own conversation and explaining their implications. He also clarified his own political attitude: "I was always Conservative; but I would eradicate any species of evil, political, moral or religious, as soon as it springs up, with no reference to the blockheads who cry out, '*What would you substitute in its place?*' When I pluck up a dock or a thistle, do I ask any such question?"

It is in his less formal letters that Landor's unique combination of scholarship, irascibility, and humanity finds its fullest expression.

—Peter Faulkner

LARDNER, Ring(old Wilmer). American. Born in Niles, Michigan, 6 March 1885. Educated at Niles High School, graduated 1901; Armour Institute of Technology, now Illinois Institute of Technology, Chicago, 1901–02. Married Ellis Abbott in 1911; four sons. Worked as a freight clerk and bookkeeper in Niles, 1902–05; Reporter, *South Bend Times*, Indiana, 1905–07; Sportswriter for *Inter Ocean*, Chicago, 1907, *Chicago Examiner*, 1908, and the *Chicago Tribune*, 1909–10; Editor, *Sporting News*, St. Louis, 1910–11; Sportswriter, *Boston American*, 1911, *Chicago American*, 1911–12, and *Chicago Examiner*, 1912–13; Columnist ("In the Wake of the News"), *Chicago Tribune*, 1913–19; moved to Long Island, New York, 1919; thereafter a writer for the Bell Syndicate; later wrote radio reviews for *The New Yorker*. Died 25 September 1933.

PUBLICATIONS

Collections

> *The Lardner Reader*, edited by Maxwell Geismar. 1963.

Fiction

> *You Know Me Al: A Busher's Letters.* 1916.
> *Gullible's Travels* (stories). 1917.
> *Own Your Own Home.* 1919.
> *The Real Dope.* 1919.
> *The Big Town.* 1921.
> *How to Write Short Stories (with Samples).* 1924.
> *The Love Nest and Other Stories.* 1926.
> *Round Up: The Stories.* 1929; as *Collected Short Stories*, 1941.
> *First and Last.* 1934.
> *Some Champions: Sketches and Fiction*, edited by Matthew J. Bruccoli and Richard
>   Layman. 1976.

Plays

> *Zanzibar*, music and lyrics by Harry Schmidt (produced 1903). 1903.
> *Elmer the Great* (produced 1928).
> *June Moon*, with George S. Kaufman (produced 1929). 1930.

> Screenplay: *The New Klondike*, with Tom Geraghty, 1926.

Verse

> *Bib Ballads.* 1915.

Other

> *My Four Weeks in France.* 1918.
> *Treat 'Em Rough: Letters from Jack the Kaiser Killer.* 1918.
> *Regular Fellows I Have Met.* 1919.
> *The Young Immigrunts.* 1920.
> *Symptoms of Being 35.* 1921.
> *Say It with Oil: A Few Remarks about Wives*, with *Say It with Bricks: A Few Remarks
>   about Husbands*, by Nina Wilcox Putnam. 1923.
> *What of It?* 1925.
> *The Story of a Wonder Man.* 1927.
> *Lose with a Smile.* 1933.
> *Ring Around Max: The Correspondence of Lardner and Max Perkins*, edited by Clifford
>   M. Caruthers. 1973.

> Editor, with Edward G. Heeman, *March 6th, 1914: The Home Coming of Charles A.
>   Comisky, John J. McGraw, James J. Callahan.* 1914.

Bibliography: *Lardner: A Descriptive Bibliography* by Matthew J. Bruccoli and Richard Layman, 1977.

Reading List: *Lardner* by Donald Elder, 1956; *Lardner* by Walton R. Patrick, 1963; *Lardner* by Otto A. Friedrich, 1965; *Ring: A Biography of Lardner* by Jonathan Yardley, 1977.

*   *   *

Ring Lardner wrote in the tradition of a long line of American popular journalists and humourists who exploited slang and the illiteracies of vernacular speech for comic ends. In doing so, he transmuted what was initially a stock comic device into something much more, an instrument of satire. At the same time, he was, however unwittingly, one of those writers, of whom Mark Twain is the great exemplar, whose sensitivity to the value of the spoken word helped to liberate American prose from the artificial diction that marked so much nineteenth-century writing.

Beginning as a sports writer on an Indiana paper, in 1913 he took over the "In the Wake of the News" column in the *Chicago Tribune*. The Jack Keefe letters were meanwhile appearing in magazines, purporting to be written by an oafish, semi-literate baseball player who through his own words all-unconsciously exposes himself in all his obnoxiousness. Published as an epistolary novel, *You Know Me Al*, they brought him the attention of a wider public, and *How to Write Short Stories*, the title of which has been seen as typical of his inability to believe that he was a serious writer, brought critical acclaim. Edmund Wilson, for example, commenting on the discrepancy between the matter of the book and the jokey way in which it was presented, wrote, "what one finds in *How to Write Short Stories* is a series of studies of American types almost equal in importance to those of Sherwood Anderson and Sinclair Lewis."

Among the stories appearing in the volume were "Some Like Them Cold," an exchange of letters wonderfully funny in their dead-pan way between an aspiring popular song-writer on the make in New York City and a girl he has met by chance in the LaSalle Street railway station in Chicago, and "The Golden Honeymoon," in which an elderly middle-class American, from Trenton, New Jersey, father-in-law of "John H. Kramer, the real estate man," recounts the holiday he and his wife spent in Florida to celebrate their golden wedding.

These stories illustrate two things. The first is that Lardner, as Wilson pointed out in his *Dial* review, had "an unexcelled, a perhaps unrivalled, mastery" of the American language, that he knew equally well the language of the popular-song writer and the "whole vocabulary of adolescent clichés of the middle-aged man from New Jersey," and that he understood the difference between the spoken language of these types and the language they used for writing. The other thing is that, as all his critics have pointed out, Lardner's is nothing if not a reductive art. His characters expose themselves unerringly in their speech and letters in all the grossness of their complacency and self-regard. No element of affection or compassion is allowed to creep into their delineation. It measures the difference between Lardner's art and Sinclair Lewis's on the one hand and Sherwood Anderson's on the other.

In other words, Lardner was essentially a satirist, and increasingly since his death he has been seen as one of the major American satirists. In this respect he has, perhaps, been over-rated. In his 1924 review Edmund Wilson, who had put Lardner forward as in some sense a latter-day Mark Twain, asked: "Will Ring Lardner then, go on to his *Huckleberry Finn* or has he already told all he knows?" The appearance of *The Love Nest and Other Stories* two years later, though it contained the merciless "Haircut," showed in effect that he had already told us all he knew. Admirable as his satire is, it seems time once again to emphasise the part he played in the liberation of American prose by bringing back into it the rhythms of native speech.

—Walter Allen

LAURENCE, (Jean) Margaret. Canadian. Born in Neepawa, Manitoba, 18 July 1926. Educated at the University of Manitoba, Winnipeg, B.A. 1947. Married John F. Laurence in 1947 (divorced, 1969); one son and one daughter. Lived in Somali and Ghana, 1950–57, and in England; Writer-in-Residence, University of Toronto, 1969–70. Recipient: Beta Sigma Phi award, 1960; President's Medal, University of Western Ontario, 1961, 1962, 1964; Governor-General's Award, 1967, 1975; Canada Council Senior Fellowship, 1967, 1971; Molson Prize, 1974, 1975. Lives in Penn, Buckinghamshire.

PUBLICATIONS

Fiction

> *This Side Jordan.* 1960.
> *The Tomorrow-Tamer: Stories.* 1963.
> *The Stone Angel.* 1964.
> *A Jest of God.* 1966; as *Rachel, Rachel*, n.d.
> *The Fire-Dwellers.* 1969.
> *A Bird in the House* (stories). 1970.
> *The Diviners.* 1974.
> *Heart of a Stranger* (stories). 1977.

Other

> *The Prophet's Camel Bell* (travel). 1963; as *New Wind in a Dry Land*, 1964.
> *Long Drums and Cannons: Nigerian Dramatists and Novelists, 1952–66.* 1968.
> *Jason's Quest* (juvenile). 1970.

> Editor, *A Tree for Poverty.* 1954.

Reading List: *Laurence* by Clara Thomas, 1969 (includes bibliography).

*   *   *

Although nearly half of Margaret Laurence's work has been prompted by her seven years in Africa, her major accomplishment in fiction is an inter-related cycle of short stories and four novels centred in Manawaka, Manitoba, a fictional small town on the Canadian prairies.

Her African experience in Somaliland (Somalia) and the Gold Coast (Ghana) eventually resulted in a volume of translations, a travel memoir, a novel, a collection of short stories, and a series of critical essays. Laurence's book for children, *Jason's Quest*, is a moral fable set in London. *Heart of a Stranger* brings together 19 sketches written between 1964 and 1975 as "travels and entertainments ... a record of the long journey back home."

   A Tree for Poverty, translations of Somali oral poetry and prose published by the government of the Protectorate, includes examples of formal poetic *gabei*, oral folk-tales, and love-poems, *belwo*. *The Prophet's Camel Bell*, a conventional travel narrative, reflects her recurrent urge to view "the whole of life through different eyes." Laurence's attempts to break out of her preconceptions as an anglophone Canadian in Africa, together with her anti-imperialist sentiments, were strengthened during her five years in Ghana. Her first novel, *This Side Jordan*, dramatises the complexities of the strained racial truce existing in the Gold Coast immediately before independence. The mixed success of her seeing with "different eyes" and experimenting with different voices is also suggested in *The Tomorrow-Tamer*, stories first published between 1956 and 1963. The figure of exile is dominant, whether expatriate or Ghanaian; political statement – particularly deft in the allegory of "Godman's Master" – emerges through both oral tale and tightly constructed Western narrative. The title of Laurence's only book of literary criticism, essays on Nigerian dramatists and novelists writing from 1952 to 1966, is taken from a poem by the late Christopher Okigbo: "long drums and cannons:/the spirit in the ascent." Written before the Biafran War, the longer essays on Soyinka, Clark, Achebe, Tutuola, and Ekwensi (six other authors are considered briefly) explore the ambiguities of language, religion and culture inherent in that difficult "ascent."

   Laurence's Canadian fiction may not originally have been conceived as an organic cycle, but the five works taken together comprise an unusually coherent examination of five generations of women. The stories collected as *A Bird in the House* are told by Vanessa MacLeod, a girl growing through the ten terrifying years from childhood to adolescence. Laurence has called the book "fictionalized autobiography"; it is a sensitive tracing of one woman's view of the social history of western Canada during the depression and the Second World War. The small town of Manawaka, with its claustrophobic social structure, immigrant mix, and comfortably visible signs of ancestry, becomes a place which must be escaped in *A Jest of God*. In her late thirties and unmarried, Rachel Cameron is haunted by her mother and religion and sexual frustration. (A film version, *Rachel, Rachel*, inexplicably transposed the location of the novel to the New England area of the United States, thus missing the peculiarly Canadian inhibitions of the 1960's which were vividly evoked by the text.) Rachel's older sister, Stacey MacAindra, is a 39-year-old housewife in Vancouver, smothered by her four children and husband in *The Fire-Dwellers*. Her bitter and humorous memories, fantasies, conversation, and inner thoughts end only in acceptance of her entrapment, despite the ostensible freedom offered by an affair and her life away from Manawaka.

   The Diviners, Laurence's most ambitious novel, is recounted by a 47-year-old novelist, Morag Gunn. Her illegitimate teen-age daughter, Pique, was deliberately conceived with a Métis father (mixed French-Canadian and native Indian), and represents the most important of Morag's three quests: for her immediate past, through her own adoptive parents in Manawaka; for her ancestral past, by living in England and taking a Scots lover; and for herself, through her fiction and Pique. The daughter unknowingly brings these three together by melding a series of symbols begun early in Laurence's career. *The Stone Angel*, chronologically her second novel and perhaps her finest, completes the cycle. Hagar Shipley's dying memories are compressed into two or three weeks, when she is 90. Indomitable, sensual, and crusty, she escapes incarceration in an old age home by running away from her elderly children; she finally accepts that her pride has been destructive, and her raging against death comes to be an affirmation of love, both past and present.

—Bruce Nesbitt

LAVIN, Mary. Irish. Born in East Walpole, Massachusetts, 11 June 1912; moved with her family to Ireland as a child. Educated at East Walpole schools; Loreto Convent, Dublin; National University of Ireland, Dublin, M.A. (honours) 1938. Married 1) William Walsh in 1942 (died, 1954), one son and two daughters; 2) Michael MacDonald Scott in 1969. Writer from 1938. President, Irish P.E.N., 1964–65. Recipient: Black Memorial Prize, 1944; Guggenheim Fellowship, 1959, 1961, 1962; Katherine Mansfield Prize, 1962; Ella Lynam Cabot Fellowship, 1971; Eire Society Gold Medal, U.S.A., 1974; Gregory Medal, 1974. D.Litt.: National University of Ireland, 1968. Member, Irish Academy of Letters: President, 1971–73. Lives in Bective, County Meath.

PUBLICATIONS

Fiction

> *Tales from Bective Bridge.* 1942.
> *The Long Ago and Other Stories.* 1944.
> *The House in Clewe Street.* 1945.
> *The Becker Wives and Other Stories.* 1946; as *At Sallygap and Other Stories,* 1947.
> *Mary O'Grady.* 1950.
> *A Single Lady and Other Stories.* 1951.
> *The Patriot Son and Other Stories.* 1956.
> *Selected Stories.* 1959.
> *The Great Wave and Other Stories.* 1961.
> *The Stories.* 2 vols., 1964–74.
> *In the Middle of the Fields and Other Stories.* 1967.
> *Happiness and Other Stories.* 1969.
> *Collected Stories.* 1971.
> *A Memory and Other Stories.* 1972.
> *The Shrine and Other Stories.* 1977.

Other

> *A Likely Story* (juvenile). 1957.
> *The Second Best Children in the World* (juvenile). 1972.

Bibliography: "Lavin: A Checklist" by Paul A. Doyle, in *Papers of the Bibliographical Society of America 63,* 1969.

Reading List: "A Skeleton Key to the Stories of Lavin" by Augustine Martin, in *Studies 52,* Winter 1963; *Lavin* by Zack R. Bowen, 1975.

*   *   *

Mary Lavin is unique in Irish literature for her devotion to the short story. Apart from two novels, of which she now speaks dismissively, and some early, uncollected verse, her artistic life has been entirely given over to short fiction, in the art of which Liam O'Flaherty alone, among Irish writers, is her superior. Yet she remains one of the least-known modern Irish writers, due partly perhaps to her lack of public involvement in contemporary cultural politics.

The world of her stories is largely private, and at times remote. Countryside or small towns provide the typical settings. Some of her work reveals an anti-metropolitan slant. Intimate relationships, usually marital or familial, are almost invariably the basis of her stories, though much of her strongest work deals with the severing of intimate ties seen from the standpoint of the female character involved. Particularly impressive among such stories are those dealing with bereavement and widowhood. On the whole, her female characters outnumber the male, and are more strikingly drawn, more firmly installed in the frequently asocial domain of their own sensibilities. However, her work is certainly not above social concerns, and, while her predominant interest is the moral range of provincial life, many of her stories, as well as the better of her two novels, *The House in Clewe Street*, are sharply critical of *petit-bourgeois* society.

Recurring exploration of this fictional terrain has occasioned charges of narrowness. But what her work may lack in breadth it makes up for in depth. Notable among her artistic effects are a tendency to dwell upon ostensibly trivial or irrelevant gestures, words, or objects which become the fulcrum of the story; a sense of the irregular movement of time, which makes her stories develop in an uneven, almost wayward but very lifelike manner; and an emphasis on change as a fact of life, the true force of which is revealed in her characters' typically partial and uneasy accommodation of it. These features combine to make Mary Lavin's work at its best unself-conscious, free of determinism, and fully sensitive to the glad quirks, the sad contingencies, and the idiosyncratic uncanniness of existence (a sense of the uncanny being perhaps an inheritance from her early mentor, Lord Dunsany). She is a supple and resourceful stylist. Her *oeuvre*, however, is decidedly uneven, and has numerous lapses into whimsy, arch humour, and impatience, together with occasional manipulation of character. However, readers of such stories as "The Long Ago," "The Becker Wives," "The Nun's Mother," and "Happiness," for example, must agree that Mary Lavin has most impressively and rewardingly carried out her intention of "looking closer than normal into the human heart."

—George O'Brien

LAWRENCE, D(avid) H(erbert). English. Born in Eastwood, Nottinghamshire, 11 September 1885. Educated at Nottingham High School, 1898–1901; University College, Nottingham, now University of Nottingham, 1906–08: teacher's certificate, 1908. Eloped with Frieda Weekley in 1912, married in 1914. Worked for a firm of surgical appliance makers, Nottingham, 1901; teacher in Eastwood and Ilkeston, Nottinghamshire, 1902–06; teacher at the Davidson Road School, Croydon, Surrey, 1908–12; full-time writer from 1912; lived in Germany, 1912–14; in England, 1914–19; Editor, with Katherine Mansfield and John Middleton Murry, *The Signature* magazine, 1915; prosecuted for obscenity (*The Rainbow*), 1915; left England, 1919, and travelled in Australia, Mexico, Sicily, and Sardinia; lived in the southwestern United States, Mexico, and Italy. Also a painter: one-man show, London, 1929 (closed by the police). Recipient: Black Memorial Prize, 1921. *Died 2 March 1930.*

Collections

Collected Letters, edited by Harry T. Moore.   2 vols., 1962.
Complete Poems, edited by Vivian de Sola Pinto and F. Warren Roberts.   2 vols., 1964.
Complete Plays.   1965.
A Selection, edited by R. H. Poole and P. J. Shepherd.   1970.

Fiction

The White Peacock.   1911; edited by Harry T. Moore, 1966.
The Trespasser.   1912.
Sons and Lovers.   1913; edited by Julian Moynahan, 1968; *A Facsimile of a Manuscript*, edited by Mark Schorer, 1978.
The Prussian Officer and Other Stories.   1914.
The Rainbow.   1915.
Women in Love.   1920.
The Lost Girl.   1920.
Aaron's Rod.   1922.
England My England and Other Stories.   1922.
The Ladybird, The Fox, The Captain's Doll.   1923; as *The Captain's Doll: Three Novelettes*, 1923.
Kangaroo.   1923.
The Boy in the Bush, with M. L. Skinner.   1924.
St. Mawr, Together with The Princess.   1925.
The Plumed Serpent (Quetzalcoatl).   1926.
Sun (story).   1926; unexpurgated edition, 1928.
Glad Ghosts (story).   1926.
Rawdon's Roof (story).   1928.
The Woman Who Rode Away and Other Stories.   1928.
Lady Chatterley's Lover.   1928; *The First Lady Chatterley* (first version), 1944; *La Tre Lady Chatterley* (three versions), in Italian, 1954; *John Thomas and Lady Jane* (second version), 1972.
The Escaped Cock.   1929; as *The Man Who Died*, 1931.
The Virgin and the Gipsy.   1930.
Love among the Haystacks and Other Pieces.   1930.
The Lovely Lady (stories).   1933.
A Modern Lover (stories).   1934.
A Prelude (story).   1949.
The Princess and Other Stories, and *The Mortal Coil and Other Stories*, edited by Keith Sagar.   2 vols., 1971.

Plays

The Widowing of Mrs. Holroyd (produced 1920).   1914.
Touch and Go.   1920.
David (produced 1927).   1926.
A Collier's Friday Night (produced 1965).   1934.
The Daughter-in-Law (produced 1967).   In *Complete Plays*, 1965.
The Fight for Barbara (produced 1967).   In *Complete Plays*, 1965.
The Married Man, and *The Merry-Go-Round*, in *Complete Plays*.   1965.

Verse

Love Poems and Others. 1913.
Amores. 1916.
Look! We Have Come Through! 1917.
New Poems. 1918.
Bay. 1919.
Tortoises. 1921.
Birds, Beasts, and Flowers. 1923.
Collected Poems. 2 vols., 1928.
Pansies. 1929.
Nettles. 1930.
Last Poems, edited by Richard Aldington and Giuseppe Orioli. 1932.
Fire and Other Poems. 1940.

Other

Twilight in Italy. 1916.
Movements in European History. 1921; revised edition, 1926.
Psychoanalysis and the Unconscious. 1921.
Sea and Sardinia. 1921.
Fantasia of the Unconscious. 1922.
Studies in Classic American Literature. 1923; edited by Armin Arnold, as *The Symbolic Meaning: The Uncollected Versions,* 1962.
Reflections on the Death of a Porcupine and Other Essays. 1925.
Mornings in Mexico. 1927.
The Paintings of Lawrence. 1929.
My Skirmish with Jolly Roger (introduction to *Lady Chatterley's Lover*). 1929; as *A propos of Lady Chatterley's Lover,* 1930.
Pornography and Obscenity. 1929.
Assorted Articles. 1930.
Apocalypse. 1931.
Letters, edited by Aldous Huxley. 1932.
Etruscan Places. 1932.
We Need One Another. 1933.
Phoenix: The Posthumous Papers, edited by Edward D. McDonald. 1936.
The Paintings, edited by Mervyn Levy. 1964.
Phoenix II: Uncollected, Unpublished, and Other Prose Works, edited by F. Warren Roberts and Harry T. Moore. 1968.
Lawrence in Love: Letters to Louie Burrows, edited by James T. Boulton. 1968.
Centaur Letters, edited by Edward D. McDonald. 1970.
Letters to Martin Secker, 1911–30, edited by Martin Secker. 1970.
The Quest for Ranamin: Letters to S. S. Koteliansky, 1914–30, edited by G. J. Zytaruk. 1970.
Letters to Thomas and Adele Seltzer: Letters to His American Publishers, edited by Gerald M. Lacy. 1976.

Translator, with S. S. Koteliansky, *All Things Are Possible*, by Leo Shestov. 1920.
Translator, *Mastro-Don Gesualdo*, by Giovanni Verga. 1923.
Translator, *Little Novels of Sicily*, by Giovanni Verga. 1925.
Translator, *Cavalleria Rusticana and Other Stories*, by Giovanni Verga. 1928.
Translator, *The Story of Doctor Manente*, by A. F. Grazzini. 1929.
Translator, with S. S. Koteliansky, *The Grand Inquisitor*, by Dostoevsky. 1930.

Bibliography: *A Bibliography of Lawrence* by F. Warren Roberts, 1963.

Reading List: *The Intelligent Heart*, 1954, revised edition, as *The Priest of Love*, 1974, and *The Life and Works of Lawrence*, revised edition, 1964, both by Harry T. Moore; *Lawrence, Novelist* by F. R. Leavis, 1955; *The Love Ethic of Lawrence* by Mark Spilka, 1955, and *Lawrence: A Collection of Critical Essays* edited by Spilka, 1963; *The Dark Sun: A Study of Lawrence* by Graham Hough, 1956; *Lawrence: A Composite Biography* edited by Edward Nehls, 3 vols., 1957–59; *The Deed of Life: The Novels and Tales of Lawrence* by Julian Moynahan, 1963; *Lawrence* by R. P. Draper, 1964, and *Lawrence: The Critical Heritage* edited by Draper, 1970; *Double Measure: A Study of the Novels and Stories of Lawrence* by George H. Ford, 1965; *The Art of Lawrence* by Keith Sagar, 1966; *Acts of Attention: The Poems of Lawrence* by Sandra M. Gilbert, 1972; *Lawrence* by Frank Kermode, 1973.

*   *   *

D. H. Lawrence's background, which was an important influence on his work, is best described in his own essay "Nottingham and the Mining Countryside." Life in late nineteenth-century Eastwood, he says, "was a curious cross between industrialism and the old agricultural England of Shakespeare and Milton and Fielding and George Eliot." His father, a semi-literate miner who spoke the Nottinghamshire and Derbyshire dialect, was essentially working-class in habits and outlook, but his mother, who had been a schoolteacher, spoke "King's English" and prided herself on her superiority to the world into which she had married. Their son owed much to both. It was his mother who encouraged him to develop his intelligence and took pride in his educational achievements, but it was from his father's sensuousness and the "intimate community" of the miners that he derived his later belief in the overriding importance of non-intellectual contact between men and women and of intuitive awareness rather than scientific knowledge.

Lawrence's first important novel, *Sons and Lovers*, is a study of working-class life seen from within. In it he draws extensively on his own background and personal experiences. Mr. and Mrs. Morel are fictional portraits of his mother and father, and their son Paul has much in common with Lawrence himself. Similarly, his youthful sweetheart, Jessie Chambers, is reflected in the character of Miriam Leivers, and the farm where she lives is based on the Haggs', near Eastwood, which helped to give Lawrence his deep understanding of, and passion for, English country life. The theme of the novel is mother-love as a dominating and destructive force. Lawrence himself comments that Mrs. Morel's sons, William and Paul, are "urged into life by their reciprocal love of their mother.... But when they come to manhood, they can't love, because their mother is the strongest power in their lives, and holds them" (letter of 14 November 1912). But the mother is also a vital, energetic force in Paul's life. Although her opposition to Miriam as a sweetheart for her son is in part the result of jealousy (they compete for the same intellectual interest), it is also based on a shrewd recognition that Miriam's soulful possessiveness is inimical to her son's fulfilment.

The sensuousness which Paul Morel inherits from his father finds expression in his purely physical relationship with Clara. In this part of the novel, as in certain passages of natural description which have a powerful, but indefinable, symbolic quality, Lawrence anticipates the exploration of unconscious influences on human relationships which becomes the primary theme of his two greatest novels, *The Rainbow* and *Women in Love*. Here Lawrence makes important innovations in characterization. The emphasis on analysis of motives and moral choice typical of nineteenth-century realism gives way to a sense that a subterranean life force takes over and directs the main characters at critical moments in their relations with each other. As Lawrence puts it, "You mustn't look in my novel [*The Rainbow*] for the old stable *ego* – of the character ... don't look for the development of the novel to follow the lines of certain characters: the characters fall into the form of some other rhythmic form, as when one draws a fiddle bow across a fine tray delicately sanded, the sand takes lines unknown" (letter of 5 June 1914).

In *The Rainbow* three generations of the Brangwen family struggle successively to find a balanced relationship in which their strong, instinctive sense of oneness with the natural world is harmonised with the conscious intelligence and mechanical sophistication which are increasingly the marks of modern industrialised society. A tentative resolution is achieved in the first generation when Tom and Lydia meet, like a rainbow, "to the span of the heavens" with their child Anna "free to play in the space beneath, between"; but in the succeeding generations the struggle is both intensified and less satisfactory in outcome, culminating in the complete collapse of the relationship between Ursula and Skrebensky in the third generation.

The method Lawrence employs in *The Rainbow* is highly original, and yet the result is not an obviously "experimental" novel such as Joyce's *Ulysses* or Virginia Woolf's *The Waves*. It is still, like *Sons and Lovers*, in many respects a vivid record of life in the English midlands of the late nineteenth and early twentieth century, and it has many scenes of compelling emotional realism; but it transcends these to become a symbolist exploration of human relations seen in the context of the natural rhythm of life itself, and expressed in a language which has strong biblical overtones. The result is a work which is often repetitive, sometimes obscure, and occasionally pretentious, but always bristling with a compelling immediacy of experience which demands an intensely personal response from the reader.

Women in Love (originally conceived as an integral part of *The Rainbow*) continues the experiences of Ursula into a new relationship with Rupert Birkin, which is presented as the creative counterpoint to the destructive relationship between her sister, Gudrun, and Birkin's friend, Gerald Crich. Marriage and personal fulfilment through the sexual relationship remains the theme of this novel, but a further dimension is added to it by Birkin's role as prophet of a new conception of "polarity" between man and woman, which involves both mutual commitment and a balanced independence. Birkin also believes in the need for a relationship of "blood brotherhood" between man and man to complement the marital relationship between man and woman. Altogether *Women in Love* is the most ambitious of Lawrence's novels. Criticism of social and economic conditions, a major preoccupation with Lawrence during and after the war years, mounts here to a sweeping denunciation of the devitalised materialism of contemporary England, and is skilfully interlocked with symbolic scenes which, like those of *Sons and Lovers* and *The Rainbow*, remain mysteriously evocative while being more purposefully organised in accordance with an almost epic, or mythic, design. Some of the faults of *The Rainbow* remain, and Lawrence's didacticism is at times excessive (though this is qualified by the self-criticism which is incorporated into the character of Birkin), but despite these flaws *Women in Love* is Lawrence's masterpiece and one of the undoubted classics of modern literature.

The novels which follow *Women in Love* are disappointingly inferior. The best of these is *Lady Chatterley's Lover* which has a tautness of structure and clarity of theme lacking in *Aaron's Rod* and *Kangaroo*, while its return to the treatment of the sexual relationship in warm, personal terms is a welcome contrast to the doctrinaire abstractions and the pseudo-religious revivalism of *The Plumed Serpent*. But even *Lady Chatterley* has an unsatisfactorily simplified schematic quality compared with *Sons and Lovers*, *The Rainbow*, and *Women in Love*.

There is, however, no reason to suspect a flagging of creative effort if one takes into account the tales, poems, travel books, and critical essays, and the marvellous spontaneity of the stream of letters, written without any thought of publication, which continued to flow from Lawrence's pen in the years after 1916. His special flair for the short story genre is apparent in his earliest work, in tales of the Nottingham environment such as "Odour of Chrysanthemums" and "Daughters of the Vicar," which show remarkable skill in combining atmosphere, psychological truth, and moral discrimination in terms of what makes for and against living fulfilment. These qualities are continued in the "long short stories" of his middle period, but joined with a more highly developed capacity for conveying levels of meaning which are subversive of conventionally accepted standards. In "The Ladybird" this is suggested through the dark, hypnotic influence of Count Psanek on Lady Daphne, a forerunner of the relationship between Mellors and Connie in *Lady Chatterley*, though the story is marred by the self-consciously "poetic" prose in which it is written. (A more successful attempt at the same theme is made in *The Virgin and the Gipsy*.) The colloquial freedom and syntactic naturalness of "The Fox" and "The Captain's Doll" are more characteristic of Lawrence's short story style, though in themselves they have quite separate and distinct virtues. "The Fox" is a powerful fusion of realism and symbolism, while "The Captain's Doll" is a triumph of tone and humour, looking forward to the more specifically satirical short stories such as "Things" and "The Man Who Loved Islands."

The best of Lawrence's prose work in his last years is to be found in *The Man Who Died* (first printed as *The Escaped Cock*), a re-interpretation of Christianity through the story of Jesus risen in the flesh to a new appreciation of the sensuous world and physical love. Like the travel book *Etruscan Places*, it is essentially a visionary work, offering a criticism of the modern world, but indirectly through an imaginative re-creation of a way of life enhanced by the vitality and sense of wonder which have all but disappeared from the present. In this respect it is akin to the poetry of Lawrence's *Last Poems*, which meditate on death, but in so doing heighten his keen sense of the lambent, instantaneous quality of life.

The rare achievement of Lawrence's poetry has still not been given the recognition which it deserves. When writing in traditional forms, i.e., mostly in his early verse, he often seems ill-at-ease, struggling to say something for which his medium is unsuited, but in the more fluent mode of free verse, which he used with an instinctive sense of rhythm and appropriate line length that exerted its own flexible control, he found the perfect means for communicating "direct utterance from the instant whole man" (Preface to the American edition of *New Poems*). The themes are often those of the novels and stories, but the implicit disclaimer of finality enables him to give those themes a freshness and tentativeness of expression which is a welcome relief from the assertiveness of the prose. "End of Another Home Holiday," for example, achieves a delicacy of poise between disapproval of, and sympathy for, maternal love which is perhaps finer than that of *Sons and Lovers*; and the poems of *Birds, Beasts, and Flowers*, especially "Snake" and the first part of "Fish," communicate (better than, for example, the short novel *St. Mawr* does) that sense of the inviolable otherness of the living, non-human world which acts by its very presence as a criticism of man's abuse of his own instinctual being.

His early dialect verse, like the best of his plays (*The Widowing of Mrs. Holroyd* and especially *The Daughter-in-Law*), faithfully reflects the mocking, un-stuffy, working-class voice of his Nottinghamshire background; and it is this tone of voice which gives the verse of *Pansies* and *Nettles* (labelled "satirical doggerel" by W. H. Auden) its mocking, deflationary humour. Here Lawrence, the prophet, brings himself down to earth and saves himself from his own messianic over-assertiveness. As he puts it in the poem "St. Matthew":

> So I will be lifted up, Saviour,
> But put me down again in time Master,
> Before my heart stops beating, and I become what I am not.

—R. P. Draper

LAWSON, Henry (Hertzberg).   Australian.   Born in Grenfell, New South Wales, 17 June 1867. Educated at the Eurunderee Public School, 1876; became deaf at age 9. Married Bertha Bredt in 1896 (separated, 1902), one son and one daughter. Held various jobs from age 13 — builder, apprentice to a railway contractor, house painter, and clerk; contributed to his mother's magazines, *Republican* and *Dawn*, Sydney, in the 1880's, and to the *Bulletin*,

Sydney, in the 1890's; worked for the labour paper *Brisbane Boomerang* in 1892; laborer in Bourke, 1892–93; telegraph lineman in New Zealand, 1893–94; gold prospector in Western Australia, 1896; teacher, Mangamauna Maori School, 1897–99; returned to Sydney, 1900; lived in London, 1900–03, then settled in Sydney. *Died 2 September 1922.*

PUBLICATIONS

Collections

> *Prose Works.* 2 vols., 1935.
> *Stories,* edited by Cecil Mann. 3 vols., 1964.
> *Collected Verse,* edited by Colin Roderick. 3 vols., 1967–69.
> *Letters, 1890–1922,* edited by Colin Roderick. 1970.
> *Short Stories and Sketches, 1888–1922,* edited by Colin Roderick. 1972.
> *Autobiographical and Other Writings, 1887–1922,* edited by Colin Roderick. 1972.
> *The Portable Lawson,* edited by Brian Kiernan. 1976.

Fiction

> *Short Stories in Prose and Verse.* 1894.
> *While the Billy Boils* (stories). 1896.
> *On the Track, and Over the Sliprails* (stories). 1900.
> *The Country I Come From* (stories). 1901.
> *Joe Wilson and His Mates* (stories). 1901.
> *Children of the Bush* (stories and poems). 1902; as *Send Round the Hat* and *The Romance of the Swag,* 2 vols., 1907.
> *The Rising of the Court and Other Sketches in Prose and Verse.* 1910.
> *Mateship: A Discursive Yarn.* 1911.
> *The Strangers' Friend.* 1911.
> *Triangles of Life and Other Stories.* 1913.

Verse

> *In the Days When the World Was Wide and Other Verses.* 1896.
> *Verses, Popular and Humorous.* 1900.
> *When I Was King and Other Verses.* 1905.
> *The Elder Son.* 1905.
> *The Skyline Riders and Other Verses.* 1910.
> *A Coronation Ode and Retrospect.* 1911.
> *For Australia and Other Poems.* 1913.
> *My Army, O, My Army! and Other Songs.* 1915; as *Songs of the Dardanelles and Other Verses,* 1916.
> *Selected Poems.* 1918.
> *The Auld Shop and the New.* 1923.
> *Joseph's Dream.* 1923.
> *Winnowed Verse.* 1924.
> *Popular Verses.* 1924.
> *Humorous Verses.* 1924.
> *Poetical Works.* 3 vols., 1925.
> *The Men Who Made Australia.* 1950.

Other

A Selection from the Prose Works, edited by George Mackaness.   1928.

Bibliography: *An Annotated Bibliography of Lawson* by George Mackaness, 1951.

Reading List: *Lawson* by Stephen Murray-Smith, 1962; *Lawson: The Grey Dreamer* by Denton Prout, 1963; *Lawson* by Colin Roderick, 1966, and *Lawson: Criticism 1894–1971* edited by Roderick, 1972; *Lawson among Maoris* by Bill Pearson, 1968; *The Receding Wave: Lawson's Prose* by Brian E. Matthews, 1972.

*   *   *

In his verses, sketches, stories, and journalistic pieces, Henry Lawson wrote from his experiences as a worker in both country and city. He was seen as the most representative of Australian writers by his own and later generations: the founder of a native, vernacular literary tradition, and the imaginative historian of the decades between the gold rushes and Federation, the period of transition between a rural and an urban-industrial Australia.

Although he first gained recognition for his ballads, which remain popular, his high critical reputation today rests on the best of his stories. From his early writing, it is apparent that Lawson had two models for fiction. One was the conventional magazine story with a heavily contrived situation and resounding ending – whether melodramatic or humorous. The other was the journalistic sketch, ostensibly not fictional at all. An early example is the genre piece "A Day on a Selection," published in the *Bulletin*, a weekly to which readers contributed paragraph-length sketches and anecdotes typical of Australian life.

Lawson continued to write conventionally plotted stories. Such humorous examples as "The Loaded Dog" and "The Iron Bark Chip" are still entertaining. His artistic development, however, can be seen in terms of his extending, without contrivance, the realistic sketch towards fuller, more rounded stories. His most frequently anthologized story, "The Drover's Wife," is an early example: it is a sketch of a typical bushwoman's experiences shaped around an anecdote.

In 1892, assisted by the *Bulletin*, Lawson visited the real "bush" for the first time. Appalled by the reality that conflicted with its conventional depiction, he determined, like his contemporary Joseph Furphy, to reject "literary" falsification. "The Union Buries Its Dead," a developed sketch of an up-country funeral, explicitly rejects "literary" sentimentality. Still a strikingly modern story, it is an imaginatively realistic appraisal of men on the margin of human existence. Lawson employs an involved narrator speaking colloquially, so avoiding the sense of a patronizing presentation of "low" characters, and the conventional representation of "low" speech found in earlier stories. From this time on, apart from humorous stories, he was to prefer such narration, and to move the sketch towards fuller dramatic and thematic complexity.

The typical Lawson story, which blends reportage with an unobtrusive imaginative structuring, is about adversity in the bush or the city, the consolation of mateship, and the temptation to escape into drink or nostalgia. Two good examples are "Going Blind" and "Telling Mrs. Baker": these illustrate his concern with the need for sympathy in a harsh world, and, particularly, the ambiguous role of the imagination. The imagination can sustain but it can also delude – an underlying personal preoccupation throughout Lawson's work.

The height of his achievement is the sequence of four "Joe Wilson" stories. (Lawson frequently wrote clusters of stories with common characters or themes, but complained that editors disregarded his intentions.) First published in England while he was there in 1901, the sequence brings together all his major themes and presents them with dramatic amplitude. Through Joe Wilson's narration, Lawson resolves his own romantic and realistic tendencies in a recognition of the transient nature of happiness in an adverse world. The sequence contains the greatest single example of his fiction, "Water Them Geraniums." Nothing else in Australian writing, of whatever length, sees further into the disappointments of life yet manages also to find its redeeming significance.

—Brian Kiernan

LEACOCK, Stephen (Butler). Canadian. Born in Swanmoor, Isle of Wight, Hampshire, England, 30 December 1869; emigrated to Canada with his family, 1876. Educated at Upper Canada College, Toronto, until 1887; University of Toronto, 1887–91, B.A. 1891; University of Chicago, 1899–1903, Ph.D. in political economy 1903. Married Beatrix Hamilton in 1900 (died, 1925), one son. Taught at Uxbridge High School, 1889, Upper Canada College, 1891–99, and the University of Chicago, 1899–1903; Lecturer in Political Science, 1903–06, Associate Professor of Political Science and History, 1906–08, William Dow Professor of Political Economy, and Head of the Department of Political Science and Economics, 1908–36, and Professor Emeritus, 1936–44, McGill University, Montreal. Toured the Empire as a Rhodes Trust Lecturer, 1907–08. Recipient: Lorne Pierce Medal, 1937. Litt.D: Brown University, Providence, Rhode Island, 1917; D.Litt.: University of Toronto, 1919; D.H.L.: Dartmouth College, Hanover, New Hampshire, 1920. Fellow, Royal Society of Canada, 1910. *Died 28 March 1944.*

PUBLICATIONS

Collections

The Best of Leacock, edited by J. B. Priestley. 1957; as *The Bodley Head Leacock,* 1957.

Fiction and Sketches

Literary Lapses: A Book of Sketches. 1910.
Nonsense Novels. 1911.
Sunshine Sketches of a Little Town. 1912.
Behind the Beyond, and Other Contributions to Human Knowledge. 1913.
Arcadian Adventures with the Idle Rich. 1914.
The Methods of Mr. Sellyer: A Book Store Study. 1914.
Moonbeams from the Larger Lunacy. 1915.
Further Foolishness: Sketches and Satires on the Follies of the Day. 1916.
Frenzied Fiction. 1918.
The Hohenzollerns in America, with the Bolsheviks in Berlin and Other Impossibilities. 1918.
Winsome Winnie and Other New Nonsense Novels. 1920.

Over the Footlights. 1923.
College Days. 1923.
The Garden of Folly. 1924.
Winnowed Wisdom. 1926.
Short Circuits. 1928.
The Iron Man and the Tin Woman, with Other Such Futurities. 1929.
Laugh with Leacock: An Anthology. 1930.
The Leacock Book, edited by Ben Travers. 1930.
Wet Wit and Dry Humour. 1931.
Afternoons in Utopia. 1932.
The Dry Pickwick and Other Incongruities. 1932.
The Perfect Salesman, edited by E. V. Knox. 1934.
Funny Pieces. 1936.
Here Are My Lectures and Stories. 1937.
Model Memoirs and Other Sketches from Simple to Serious. 1938.
Too Much College; or, Education Eating Up Life. 1939.
Laugh Parade. 1940.
My Remarkable Uncle and Other Sketches. 1942.
Happy Stories, Just to Laugh At. 1943.
Last Leaves. 1945.

Play

Q, with Basil Macdonald Hastings (produced 1915). 1915.

Verse

Marionettes' Calendar 1916. 1915.
*Hellements of Hickonomics in Hiccoughs of Verse Done in Our Social Planning
Mill.* 1936.

Other

Elements of Political Science. 1906; revised edition, 1921.
Baldwin, LaFontaine, Hincks: Responsible Government. 1907; revised edition, as
Mackenzie, Baldwin, LaFontaine, Hincks, 1926.
Adventures of the Far North. 1914.
The Dawn of Canadian History. 1914.
The Mariner of St. Malo: A Chronicle of the Voyages of Jacques Cartier. 1914.
Essays and Literary Studies. 1916.
The Unsolved Riddle of Social Justice. 1920.
My Discovery of England. 1922.
Economic Prosperity in the British Empire. 1930.
Mark Twain. 1932.
Back to Prosperity: The Great Opportunity of the Empire Conference. 1932.
Charles Dickens: His Life and Work. 1933.
Lincoln Frees the Slaves. 1934.
Humor, Its Theory and Technique. 1935.
Humor and Humanity. 1937.
My Discovery of the West: A Discussion of East and West in Canada. 1937.
All Right, Mr. Roosevelt. 1939.

Our British Empire: Its Structure, Its History, Its Strength. 1940.
Canada: The Foundations of Its Future. 1941.
Montreal, Seaport and City. 1942.
How to Write. 1943.
My Old College, 1843–1943. 1943.
Canada and the Sea. 1944.
While There Is Time: The Case Against Social Catastrophe. 1945.
The Boy I Left Behind Me (autobiography). 1946.

Editor, *Lahontan's Voyages.* 1932.
Editor, *The Greatest Pages of Dickens.* 1934.
Editor, *The Greatest Pages of American Humor.* 1936.

Bibliography: *Leacock: A Check-List and Index of His Writings* by Gerhard R. Lomer, 1954.

Reading List: *Leacock, Humorist and Humanist* by Ralph L. Curry, 1959; *Leacock: A Biography* by David M. Legate, 1970.

*   *   *

The first sketch in Stephen Leacock's first humorous work, *Literary Lapses*, describes the narrator's panic-stricken attempt to open a bank account, and money and the antics of those who possess it are the most prominent *leitmotifs* in his subsequent writing. He made his first career as a lecturer in economics, and his second as a quick-witted observer of the quirks and blemishes of the life-style of the brave new world of transatlantic consumerism. When he says, blandly, in *The Garden of Folly*, "Business having become the most important thing in life, it is quite clear that it is destined to swallow up the feeble things that we used to call literature and art," he is recording an uneasy possibility.

Those who admire Leacock have stressed the satirical edge in his writing; others have insisted that he let himself be blunted by success. Certainly his portrait-caricatures of the rogues of big-city as of small-town business are affectionate and even admiring. Perhaps that means that his strength is in irony rather than satire. That could certainly be argued of the best pieces in *Sunshine Sketches of a Little Town*, *Arcadian Adventures with the Idle Rich*, and *The Garden of Folly*. The first of these is set in Mariposa, a "typical" Canadian small-town, the second among the inhabitants of Plutoria Avenue in a "typical" North American city. The stories in each are elaborate anecdotes, spun out by Leacock's ingenuity. He is a raconteur, not, as some have believed, a novelist *manqué*. He is also a parodist, a punster, a compiler of comic lists, and frequently the inventor of spurious documents. *The Garden of Folly* is an example of Leacock's non-fictional style, that of the moral (or mock-moral) essayist. *Nonsense Novels*, *Frenzied Fiction*, and *Winsome Winnie* contain some of his happiest frolics. The ideal reader of Leacock is one who is willing to be silly and ready to indulge an urge to chuckle like the would-be compositors of his first two books, who, he says, found it impossible to print them because they kept falling back "suffocated with laughter and gasping for air."

—Peter Thomson

LEE, John (Alexander). New Zealander. Born in Dunedin, 31 October 1891. Educated in local schools. Served as a sergeant in the New Zealand Expeditionary Forces in World War I, 1915–18: lost an arm in combat; Distinguished Conduct Medal. Married Marie E. Guy in 1919; three children. Farm and factory worker until 1909; joined the New Zealand Public Works Department, 1910; Labour Member of Parliament for Auckland East, 1922–28, and for Grey Lynn, 1931–43: Under-Secretary to the Minister of Finance, 1936–39; Controller of the State Housing Department, 1939–40; expelled from the Labour Party, 1940; Director, Printing Service Ltd., and Democratic Property Ltd., Auckland, 1940–46; Managing Director, Vital Books Ltd., Auckland, from 1950. President, Auckland Rugby League, 1935–40; Member of the Council, New Zealand Booksellers Association, 1959–61; Honorary President, New Zealand Branch, P.E.N., 1969. LL.D.: University of Otago, Dunedin, 1965. Lives in Auckland.

PUBLICATIONS

Fiction

    Children of the Poor. 1934.
    The Hunted. 1936.
    Civilian into Soldier. 1937.
    The Yanks Are Coming. 1943.
    Shining with the Shiner (stories). 1944.
    Shiner Slattery. 1964.

Other

    Four Years of Failure: A History of the Smash-and-Grab Government. 1935.
    Labour and Prosperity. 1935.
    Labour Has a Plan. 1935.
    Returned Soldiers – Vote Labour. 1935.
    Banking and the New Zealand Labour Government. 1937.
    Money Power for the People. 1937.
    Socialism in New Zealand. 1938.
    A Letter Which Every New Zealander Should Read. 1939.
    Debt-Hold, Leasehold, Bankhold, or Prosperityhold. 1940.
    The Democratic Labour Party in Business and the Home. 1940.
    Expelled from the Labour Party for Telling the Truth. 1940.
    Hitler. 1940.
    I Fight for New Zealand. 1940.
    Mussolini, Apostle of Violence. 1940.
    This Debt Slavery (speeches). 1940.
    Manufacture or Perish. 1941.
    Simple on a Soap-Box (autobiography). 1964.
    Rhetoric at the Red Dawn. 1965.
    The Lee Way of Speech Training. 1965; as *The Lee Way to Public Speaking,* 1965.
    Delinquent Days (autobiography). 1967.
    Political Notebooks. 1973.

*   *   *

John Lee wrote both fact and fiction, and it is not easy to draw a sharp line between the two. The reason for this is that all his fictional works have a strong autobiographical element.

He first rose to fame as a writer in 1934 when *Children of the Poor* was published. The narrator-protagonist is the child Albany Porcello, who grows up in the slums of Dunedin in the 1890's. It is a story of a stunted childhood, and of the unremitting poverty which eventually leads to Albany's being made a ward of the state. The book was published anonymously, and created a scandal when it was revealed that it was written by Lee, who was by then a Labour member of parliament. The conservative New Zealand public found it offensive that one of their leading figures and representatives should admit to a delinquent past, a prostitute sister, a drunken grandmother, and a childhood of squalor and poverty. For John Lee made it clear that it was his own past he was revealing through the story of Albany Porcello. No doubt it was the conditions of the 1930's that reminded Lee of his own deprived childhood and led him to write his first novel. He followed it with a sequel, *The Hunted*, which continued the story of Albany and followed his career through reform school, his escape and final recapture. In 1967 Lee published his autobiography, *Delinquent Days*. If one compares the dedication to this work with that of *Children of the Poor* the very close link between fact and fiction is made obvious:

> "To daughters of the poor. To errant brats and guttersnipes. To eaters of left-overs, the wearers of cast-offs. To slaves of the wash-tub and scrub-brush, whose children, nevertheless, go to hell. To teachers who adopt, through compulsion or desire, the method of the barrack square. To juvenile culprits fleeing from the inescapable hand of the law, sometimes called justice ... THIS STORY OF THE GUTTER." (*Children of the Poor*)

> "To Welfare and Probation Officers, Magistrates and Judges, Jailors and Police, Enlightened or Obscurantist Ministers of Justice and Attorney Generals ... is dedicated this book of one who somehow survived." (*Delinquent Days*)

Lee wrote other works — including a series of very successful sketches, *Shining with the Shiner* and *Shiner Slattery*, which tell of his days when he roamed the New Zealand countryside carrying his swag — but his chief importance lies in his two socially committed novels, *Children of the Poor* and *The Hunted*. In these two works he drew a distinction, not between the good and the bad, but between the "haves" and the "have-nots," and showed that social injustice and poverty could exist as easily in the New World as in the Old.

—Anna Rutherford

LE FANU, (Joseph) Sheridan. Irish. Born in Dublin, 28 August 1814. Educated privately, and at Trinity College, Dublin, 1833–37; called to the Irish Bar, 1839, but never practised. Married Susan Bennett in 1843 (died, 1858). Member of the staff of the *Dublin University Magazine* from 1837; Editor and Proprietor, 1861–69; purchased the Dublin newspaper *The Warder*, 1839, and subsequently took over the *Evening Packet* and later the *Dublin Evening Mail*. Active in radical conservative politics, 1838–48. Went into semi-retirement on wife's death. *Died 7 February 1873.*

PUBLICATIONS

Collections

> The Poems, edited by A. P. Groves. 1896.
> Madam Crowl's Ghost and Other Tales of Mystery, edited by M. R. James. 1923.
> Ghost Stories and Mysteries, edited by E. F. Bleiler. 1975.

Fiction

> The Cock and Anchor, Being a Chronicle of Old Dublin City. 1845; edited by B. S. Le Fanu, 1895.
> The Fortunes of Colonel Torlogh O'Brien. 1847.
> Ghost Stories and Tales of Mystery. 1851.
> The House by the Church-Yard. 1863.
> Wylder's Hand. 1864.
> Uncle Silas: A Tale of Bartram-Haugh. 1864.
> Guy Deverell. 1865.
> All in the Dark. 1866.
> The Tenants of Malory. 1867.
> A Lost Name. 1868.
> Haunted Lives. 1868.
> The Wyvern Mystery. 1869.
> Checkmate. 1871.
> The Rose and the Key. 1871.
> Chronicles of Golden Friars (stories). 1871.
> In a Glass Darkly (stories). 1872.
> Willing to Die. 1873.
> The Purcell Papers (stories). 1880.

Reading List: Wilkie Collins, Le Fanu, and Others by Stewart M. Ellis, 1931 (includes bibliography); Le Fanu by Nelson Browne, 1951; "Le Fanu's Richard Marston (1848): The History of an Anglo-Irish Text" by W. J. McCormack, in 1848: The Sociology of Literature edited by Francis Barker and others, 1978.

*   *   *

Sheridan Le Fanu is best understood as Maria Edgeworth's successor as a novelist of the Irish gentry. Like her, he is preoccupied with the past; but whereas she attempts imaginatively to reconstitute the past, Le Fanu sees it as an inexorable pressure on the present. Given his recurring and anxious concern with religious speculation, we may say that he substitutes the patterns of original sin for the dynamics of history.

This anxiety is given a Gothic expression in the stories of 1838–40, later collected as The Purcell Papers. With the short-lived political optimism of the early 1840's, Le Fanu wrote two historical novels, The Cock and Anchor and Torlogh O'Brien, in which a diminished interest in the supernatural is paralleled by a more flexible approach to Irish history and the possibility of social change. The events of 1848, however, combined with a deteriorating domestic life – the two are mordantly reflected in "Richard Marston" – destroyed Le Fanu's new found (and perhaps fragile) confidence. It was only fifteen years later that he resumed an active career as a novelist.

A ten-year frenzy of activity began with The House by the Church-Yard, which retains an

Irish historical setting. From *Wylder's Hand* and *Uncle Silas* onwards he was obliged for commercial reasons to use a contemporary English setting. In *Uncle Silas*, this imposition is transformed into a further dimension of exile and dislocation, but the remaining novels — loosely identifiable with the "sensational" school of Wilkie Collins and Charles Reade — are of negligible interest. Among the later fiction the tales in *Chronicles of Golden Friars* and *In a Glass Darkly* are Le Fanu's most controlled and impressive work.

The principal difference between the full-length novels and these tales lies in the explicit operation of supernatural agencies in the short fiction. The novels recurringly present a hero whose fate is conditioned by a past offence against society or family; the tales translate this plot into the terms of a sensational theology. The overriding pattern, however, is one of implosion, of diffused self-destruction. *Uncle Silas* describes Hell and the condition of the damned as "depraved gregariousness, and isolation too"; the words also aptly describe the diminished status of the Irish ascendancy in the Victorian period, as reflected in Le Fanu's life and work.

—W. J. McCormack

LEHMANN, Rosamond (Nina). English. Born in Bourne End, Buckinghamshire, in 1901; sister of the writer John Lehmann and the actress Beatrix Lehmann. Educated at Girton College, Cambridge (scholar). Married 1) Leslie Runciman; 2) the Honorable Wogen Philipps, later Lord Milford, in 1928 (divorced); one son. Past President, English Centre, P.E.N., and International Vice-President, International P.E.N.; Member of the Council, Society of Authors, London. Commandeur dans l'Ordre des Arts et Lettres, 1968. Lives in London.

PUBLICATIONS

Fiction

Dusty Answer. 1927.
A Note in Music. 1930.
Invitation to the Waltz. 1932.
The Weather in the Streets. 1936.
The Ballad and the Source. 1944.
The Gipsy's Baby and Other Stories. 1946.
The Echoing Grove. 1953.
The Sea-Grape Tree. 1976.

Play

No More Music (produced 1938). 1939.

Other

A Letter to a Sister. 1931.
A Man Seen Afar, with W. Tudor Pole. 1965.

The Swan in the Evening: Fragments of an Inner Life. 1967.
Letters from Our Daughters, with Cynthia Hill Sandys. 1972.

Editor, with others, *Orion: A Miscellany 1–3.* 3 vols., 1945–46.

Translator, *Geneviève,* by Jacques Lemarchand. 1947.
Translator, *Children of the Game,* by Jean Cocteau. 1955; as *The Holy Terrors,* 1957.

Bibliography: "Lehmann: A Bibliography" by M. T. Gustafson, in *Twentieth Century Literature 4,* 1959.

Reading List: *Lehmann* by D. E. Lestourgeion, 1965; *Subjective Vision and Human Relationships in the Novels of Lehmann* by Wiktoria Dorosz, 1975.

*   *   *

Rosamond Lehmann's subjects are infidelity and its ramifications, glamour, infatuation, and the kind of emotional distress that results from moral and aesthetic scruples. Each of the early novels has as its point of contrast a dazzling, scintillating family that epitomises style and personal advantage for the heroine. Judith, in *Dusty Answer,* idolises the next-door children but ends by establishing her own integrity and power: "she ... had broken in among them and taken them one by one for herself. She had been stronger than their combined force, after all." But it has been a process of disillusion with a climax of humiliation when Judith's devotion is flung back in her dumbfounded face. Like any breathless, impressionable girl she has allowed herself to be taken in, reading more into a simple sexual act than her seducer intends. "I thought that was what you wanted: what you were asking for," self-contained Roddy states with tactless bewilderment.

Another moment of total insensitivity, painful for the reader, occurs in *The Weather in the Streets*: Olivia and Rollo are staying illicitly in a country hotel when Rollo spots an acquaintance accompanied by a person whom he describes without thinking as "a very hot bit." "I couldn't bear Rollo saying that," Olivia muses. But the heroine of this novel and the earlier *Invitation to the Waltz* is ultimately a more complex, more coherent character than Judith, and the author has achieved a kind of dramatic concentration by focusing only on the major relationship.

The two novels, *Invitation to the Waltz* and its sequel, complement each other perfectly, though the second is by far the more ambitious, scrutinising with passionate sympathy and dispassionate thoroughness and realism the whole course of an adulterous liaison. Rollo Spencer is the son of an upper-class family whose gaiety, kindness, and social assurance have made them irresistible to intelligent but vulnerable Olivia. Rollo's sister Marigold corresponds to Mariella in *Dusty Answer* and Clare in *A Note in Music* – the society butterfly whose function is to enthrall and amuse. Many of Rosamond Lehmann's characters are the stereotypes of light fiction, standard romantic figures into which she infuses a quality of liveliness or vitality that makes them, for the moment of their appearance, acceptable. A gentle narrative mockery intervenes between the reader and the excesses of sentimentality or affectation.

The novels are intensely subjective, rarely concerning themselves with issues unrelated to the central theme. The shifts of consciousness, ellipses, transcription of thoughts, impressions, fragments of memory, and moments of prognosis are all technical devices used principally to convey the protagonist's state of mind. Symbolism is kept to a minimum, though one characteristic motif is the dead child which can be said to represent fatal inadequacies in a relationship or a failure of growth at some fundamental level. Thus, Rollo's beautiful but ailing wife embarks on a pregnancy while Olivia goes through with an abortion. Dinah, in *The Echoing Grove,* gives birth to a stillborn baby like the earlier heroine of *A Note in Music.*

And in "The Gipsy's Baby" (the title story in a short story collection) a sense of secretiveness and malignancy is disseminated by the supposed discovery of a gruesome little object in a clump of brambles.

The literary virtues of economy and wit are largely absent from the novels of Rosamond Lehmann; instead there is a peculiar sensitivity to nuances of emotional feeling which is expressed analytically as the writing progresses. The central characters all possess a delicate independence of spirit which makes them especially attractive to a present-day reader.

—Patricia Craig

LENNOX, Charlotte (née Ramsay). English. Born in New York, possibly in Albany, c. 1729–30. Went to England, 1743, and remained there for the rest of her life. Married Alexander Lennox in 1747 (died c. 1797), one son and one daughter. Appeared on the stage, 1749–50; thereafter supported herself by writing and translating; befriended by Samuel Johnson and Richardson; Editor, *Lady's Museum*, London, 1760–61. Granted Royal Literary Fund pension, 1792. *Died 4 January 1804.*

PUBLICATIONS

Fiction

 The Life of Harriot Stuart. 1750.
 The Female Quixote; or, The Adventures of Arabella. 1752; edited by Margaret Dalziel, 1970.
 Henrietta. 1758.
 Sophia. 1762.
 The History of the Marquis of Lussan and Isabella. 1764.
 Euphemia. 1790.

Plays

 Philander: A Dramatic Pastoral. 1757.
 Oedipus, Electra, and *Philoctetes,* in *The Greek Theatre.* 3 vols., 1759.
 The Sister, from her own novel *Henrietta* (produced 1769). 1769.
 Old City Manners, from *Eastward Ho* by Jonson, Chapman, and Marston (produced 1775). 1775.

Verse

 Poems on Several Occasions. 1747.

Other

Shakespeare Illustrated; or, The Novels and Histories, on Which the Plays Are Founded, Collected and Translated. 3 vols., 1753–54.
The Lady's Museum, 1760–61 (periodical). 2 vols., 1760–61 (some material not by Lennox).

Translator, The Memoirs of the Countess of Bercy. 1756.
Translator, The Memoirs of M. de Bethune, Duke of Sully. 1756.
Translator, Memoirs for the History of Madame de Maintenon, by L. Angliviel de la Beaumelle. 1757.
Translator, Meditations and Penitential Prayers, by the Duchess de la Vallière. 1774.

Reading List: Lennox: An Eighteenth-Century Lady of Letters by Miriam R. Small, 1935; The First American Novelist? by G. H. Maynadier, 1940; The Mystery of Lennox, First Novelist of Colonial America by Philippe Séjourné, 1967.

*   *   *

Charlotte Lennox's reputation is based on a single novel, The Female Quixote, and, although she wrote other work of some merit, her strength as an author is closely related to her insight into the mind of her Quixotic Arabella, living in a private world constructed out of the French heroic romances written in the previous century, where pure and constant passion inspires deeds of prodigious valour. Her first novel, Harriot Stuart, also has a romantic heroine, familiar with the attentions of admirers whose ardour was incompatible with the prosaic decencies of common life, but the element of self-delusion is less prominent. Almost anything might happen in the wilds of New York province, where Charlotte Lennox spent her childhood, and where the most attractive part of the novel is set. In The Female Quixote the heroine's illusions are elaborately conjured up, and artfully juxtaposed with the world of rural England and the manners of polite society. For much of the time (and here one detects the influence of her friend Samuel Johnson) the novel might be taken as a long case-history from the files of a psychiatrist. But although Arabella's preconceptions lead her continually astray, they also sustain a character that is in many ways admirable. She is benevolent, generous, and – romance apart – sufficiently intelligent. She is contrasted favourably with the petty-minded and ungenerous Miss Glanville, whose sanity could never be in doubt. The novel is evidence of a contemporary fascination with "enthusiasm" and the pleasures of imagination.

A later work, Henrietta, reduces the devotee of romance to a mere object of satire. Miss Woodby's passion for "violent friendships" anticipates the pretensions of Isabella Thorpe in Jane Austen's Northanger Abbey. The heroine herself is a sensible young woman whose perceptions are sharpened by her inferior and dependent station in life. Sophia provides another variation on the author's favourite theme, with a heroine whose unwearied application to reading produces only good sense and virtue.

Charlotte Lennox also wrote a few pieces for the stage. The Sister, based on part of Henrietta, includes a fine elderly female Quixote (Lady Autumn), but it is otherwise undistinguished.

—Geoffrey Carnall

LESSING, Doris (May). British. Born in Kermanshah, Persia, now Iran, 22 October 1919; moved with her family to a farm in Rhodesia, 1925. Educated at the Girls High School, Salisbury. Married 1) Frank Charles Wisdom in 1939 (divorced, 1943), one son and one daughter; 2) Gottfried Lessing in 1945 (divorced, 1949). Settled in London in 1949; thereafter a full-time writer. Recipient: Maugham Award, 1954. Associate Member, American Academy of Arts and Letters, 1974; Honorary Fellow, Modern Language Association, 1974.

PUBLICATIONS

Fiction

The Grass Is Singing. 1950.
This Was the Old Chief's Country: Stories. 1951.
Children of Violence: Martha Quest. 1952; *A Proper Marriage,* 1954; *A Ripple from the Storm,* 1958; *Landlocked,* 1965; *The Four-Gated City,* 1969.
Five: Short Novels. 1953.
Retreat to Innocence. 1956.
No Witchcraft for Sale: Stories and Short Novels. 1956.
The Habit of Loving (stories). 1957.
The Golden Notebook. 1962.
A Man and Two Women: Stories. 1963.
African Stories. 1964.
Winter in July (stories). 1966.
The Black Madonna (stories). 1966.
Nine African Stories. 1968.
Briefing for a Descent into Hell. 1971.
The Story of a Non-Marrying Man and Other Stories. 1972.
The Temptation of Jack Orkney and Other Stories. 1972.
The Summer Before the Dark. 1973.
Collected African Stories: This Was the Old Chief's Country and *The Sun Between Their Feet.* 2 vols., 1973.
The Memoirs of a Survivor. 1974.
Collected Stories: To Room Nineteen and *The Temptation of Jack Orkney.* 2 vols., 1978.
Stories. 1978.

Plays

Before the Deluge (produced 1953).
Mr. Dolinger (produced 1958).
Each His Own Wilderness (produced 1958). In *New English Dramatists,* 1959.
The Truth about Billy Newton (produced 1960).
Play with a Tiger (produced 1962). 1962.
The Storm, from a play by Alexander Ostrowsky (produced 1966).
The Singing Door, in *Second Playbill 2,* edited by Alan Durband. 1973.

Television Plays: *The Grass Is Singing,* 1962; *Please Do Not Disturb,* 1966; *Care and Protection,* 1966; *Between Men,* 1967.

Verse

Fourteen Poems. 1959.

Other

Going Home. 1957.
In Pursuit of the English: A Documentary. 1960.
Particularly Cats. 1967.
A Small Personal Voice: Essays, Reviews, Interviews, edited by Paul Schlueter. 1974.

Bibliography: *Lessing: A Bibliography* by Catharina Ipp, 1967; *Lessing: A Checklist of Primary and Secondary Sources* by Selma R. Burkom and Margaret Williams, 1973.

Reading List: *Lessing* by Dorothy Brewster, 1965; *Lessing,* 1973, and *Lessing's Africa,* 1978, both by Michael Thorpe; *The Novels of Lessing* by Paul Schlueter, 1973; *Lessing: Critical Studies* edited by Annis Pratt and L. S. Dembo, 1974.

*   *   *

In an interview in 1962 Doris Lessing declared, "I feel the best thing that ever happened to me was that I was brought up out of England. I took for granted kinds of experience that would be impossible to a middle-class girl here." It was her African experience that provided the material for her first novel, *The Grass Is Singing.* Owing to her isolation in the African bush, the illness of her farmer-husband, and her own overwork in nursing him, Mary Turner, a white woman, loses her authority over her black houseboy, Moses. A personal, sexual relationship is established between them. When, however, Mary reneges on this and tries to send Moses away, he murders her. In this situation Doris Lessing concentrates a theme which recurs in much of her later work. The connection between Mary and Moses breaks the great taboo of the colour bar between the black and white races, with disastrous results, and yet in a way that both emphasises the decadence and sterility of the life in which Mary is trapped, and hints that her only hope of renewal is through the forbidden bond which is being created with Moses.

This possibility of life breaking into an alien and sterile form is echoed in the way human beings are seen in relation to the natural forces of the African bush, to which Doris Lessing is deeply responsive. It is symbolised in the ridgepole which holds up the roof of the Quests' house in *Martha Quest*: "It had lain for weeks in a bath of strong chemicals to protect it from ants and insects; but now it was riddled with tiny holes, and if one put one's ear to it there could be heard a myriad tiny jaws at work, and from the holes slid a perpetual trickle of faint white dust." The image is one of decay, but also of busy, and weirdly beautiful, life, which the white man's chemical tries, but fails, to exclude. More positively, in the short story, "A Mild Attack of Locusts" (from *The Habit of Loving*), the heroine, who had felt herself an alien in the bush, and loathed above all the threat of a plague of locusts, nevertheless manages to endure one; she sees the locusts in the morning light clinging to the vegetation so that "it looked as if every tree, every bush, all the earth, were lit with pale flames." In the capacity to connect with the bush lies the hope of fulfilment; isolation from it spells sterility.

A parallel recurrent theme in Doris Lessing's work is that of connection with, or severance from, society. It is the theme of *Children of Violence*, "a study," in Doris Lessing's own description of it, "of the individual conscience in its relations with the collective." This is a five-part *bildungsroman* showing the development of a young rebellious Rhodesian girl, Martha Quest, reacting against her white, colonial, middle-class background in both its social and political aspects. Her first, "proper" marriage to Douglas Knowell comes to grief because of Martha's refusal to conform to her husband's establishment ideas; her second, to Anton Hesse, leader of a small communist cell in Zambesia, shows the equal futility of her political allegiances. There is friendship within the group, but no real contact with the black Africans. In *Landlocked* a more passionate love-affair with the communist Thomas Stern is counterpointed with the emergence of a new, younger group – idealistic left-wingers who seem set to repeat Martha's own errors of illusion and hope. Finally, in *The Four-Gated City* Martha has left Zambesia for London. The political activities of the isolated "group" are superseded by the English and European events of the 1950's and 1960's (defections from the Communist Party after Hungary, the anti-nuclear warfare campaigns of the C.N.D., etc.) and a life of feminist freedom which continues, however, to be frustrating and discordant. This book brings Martha's story up to the date of writing (1969), then shoots beyond it into an imagined future of nuclear holocaust, social collapse, and the tentative emergence of a race of tender, rather than muscle-bound, supermen. This gives *Children of Violence* an optimistic ending rather like that of D. H. Lawrence's *The Rainbow*.

Although *The Four-Gated City* is part of this *bildungsroman* sequence it also marks a significant new development in Doris Lessing's use of fiction. A new theme, that of madness (heralded in *The Golden Notebook*, which appeared between *A Ripple from the Storm* and *Landlocked*), breaks the surface. The flat, prosaic realism of the preceding volumes gives way to more hectic evocation of the disorientated world of schizophrenia, presented, however, as being in some way more valuable than the "sane" impressions of normality. Martha and her neurotic friend Lynda begin to use the fantasies of madness as "maps or signposts for a country which lay just beyond or alongside, or within the landscape they could see and touch." *Memoirs of a Survivor* is a later variation on this same theme, the collapse of a high-technology civilisation running parallel with the delusions of a "survivor" that another world exists in Alice-in-Wonderland form through the opaque wall of her living-room.

The influence of R. D. Laing is apparent here, but so, it should be added, is the influence of the romantic movement, not least of William Blake. In challenging standard assumptions about mental illness, Lessing is re-affirming the romantic belief in the paradoxical illumination which may come from the shadow side of consciousness, and using it as a means of reinforcing her radical attacks on the received values of modern western society. Her seeming break with her own past as a writer is thus, in fact, an assertion of continuity. What had seemed defeated and blocked by disillusionment is renewed in the more startling form of subversive creative fantasy. This is especially evident in *Briefing for a Descent into Hell*. The debt to Romanticism can be seen in the neo-Wordsworthian situation of the hero, Charles Watkins, Professor of Classics, who suffers from a breakdown which gives him both "intimations of immortality" and a horrifying vision of twentieth-century man's pollution of his environment and his own self-destruction. On the realistic level these are delusive fantasies from which he must finally be rescued and restored to normality; but, as in James's *The Turn of the Screw*, the ambiguous narrative of *Briefing* enables Watkins to be interpreted either as a potential liberator who is being stunned into conformity by society's conditioning apparatus, or as a sick escapist who is being brought back to reality and responsibility. Unlike James, however, Lessing preserves a far less inscrutable detachment. Her radicalism allows only the liberating hypothesis to seem the valid one.

The latter part of *The Four-Gated City*, and the whole of *Briefing* and *Memoirs of a Survivor* represent the new direction in which Doris Lessing's work is now moving, but *The Golden Notebook* remains her most successful and most technically sophisticated achievement so far. It stands at the junction of the two main paths that her fiction has taken, the realistically reportorial and the visionary fantastic. The central figure, Anna, a novelist suffering from a writer's block, compartmentalizes her life into four notebooks dealing with areas of experience which readers of Lessing's other stories and novels will recognize as highly characteristic of the author: African memories, communist political activities, intimate personal experiences (recorded in diary form), and the novel that Anna is attempting to write within the novel which is *The Golden Notebook*.

The dominant theme, if one theme can be separated out from the complicated interweavings of this book, is the theme of the free woman – the struggle of woman to live in a new style of independence from, and equality with, man, and yet her experience of being constantly undermined by the psychological and social conditioning, and possibly inherent needs, which constitute her femininity. As with *Children of Violence*, the movement of this novel is towards disintegrative collapse, though at the level of the individual personal life rather than the life of one entire society. This is counterbalanced, however, by an optimism which is embodied in the possibility of a fifth, "golden" notebook containing and combining the separated experiences of her four other notebooks. The strength of this novel is in its honesty, immediacy, and vibrant contemporaneity – the strength of *Children of Violence*, in short, but intensified and concentrated in a more effectively located theme and situation – combined with a complexity of organisation (owing much to the experimentalism of early "modernists" such as Gide, Joyce, and Virginia Woolf) which formally matches the psychological incoherence to which the pursuit of its feminist theme leads.

It remains for future readers to decide whether form and subject have, in fact, been perfectly married in this novel, but there is little doubt that this is the most ambitious attempt Doris Lessing has yet made to give the full range of her experience unified expression; and if she seems in her latest work to be more concerned with extending the range of that experience, the time will no doubt come when she will again feel the need to re-integrate the old with the new, and so attempt a second *Golden Notebook*.

—R. P. Draper

LEVER, Charles (James). Irish. Born in Dublin, 31 August 1806. Educated at Trinity College, Dublin, 1823–28; studied medicine in Göttingen; awarded M.B. by Trinity College, 1831. Married Catherine Baker in 1833 (died, 1870); one daughter. Served as a surgeon on an emigrant ship to Canada, 1828, then practised medicine in various Irish towns; physician for the Board of Health in County Clare; dispensary doctor at Port Stewart; practised in Brussels, 1839–42; Editor, *Dublin University Magazine*, 1842–45; lived in Italy from 1845; Vice-Consul at Spezia, 1858–67, and Consul at Trieste, 1867–72. *Died 1 June 1872.*

PUBLICATIONS

Collections

Works. 34 vols., 1876–78.
Novels, edited by Julia Kate Neville. 37 vols., 1897–99.

Fiction

The Confessions of Harry Lorrequer. 1839; edited by L. S. Benjamin, 1907.
Charles O'Malley, The Irish Dragoon. 1841.
Our Mess (Jack Hinton and *Tom Burke of "Ours").* 3 vols., 1843–44.
Arthur O'Leary: His Wanderings and Ponderings in Many Lands. 1844; as *Adventures of Arthur O'Leary*, 1856.

St. Patrick's Eve. 1845.
Nuts and Nutcrackers. 1845.
Tales of the Trains. 1845.
The O'Donoghue. 1845.
The Knight of Gwynne. 1847.
The Martins of Cro' Martin. 1847.
Diary and Notes of Horace Templeton, Late Secretary of Legation at —. 1848.
Confessions of Con Cregan, The Irish Gil Blas. 1849.
Roland Cashel. 1850.
The Daltons; or, Three Roads in Life. 2 vols., 1850–52.
Maurice Tierney. 1852.
The Dodd Family Abroad. 2 vols., 1852–54.
Sir Jasper Carew: His Life and Experiences. 1855.
The Fortunes of Glencore. 1857.
Davenport Dunn; or, The Man of the Day. 1859.
One of Them. 1861.
A Day's Ride. 1863.
Barrington. 1863.
Luttrell of Arran. 1863.
Cornelius O'Dowd upon Men, Women, and Other Things in General. 3 vols., 1864–65.
A Rent in the Cloud. 1865.
Tony Butler. 1865.
Sir Brook Fossbrooke. 1866.
The Bramleighs of Bishop's Folly. 1868.
Paul Gosslett's Confessions in Law and the Civil Service. 1868.
The Boy of Norcott's. 1869.
Lord Kilgobbin. 1872.
The Military Novels. 9 vols., n.d.
Gerald Fitzgerald the Chevalier. 1899.

Reading List: Lever: His Life in His Letters by Edmund Downey, 2 vols., 1906; "Lever" by Roger McHugh, in Studies 27, 1938; Dr. Quicksilver: The Life of Lever by Lionel Stevenson, 1939.

*   *   *

Charles Lever wrote some thirty novels in the thirty-five years between 1837 and 1872. His early novels, Harry Lorrequer, Charles O'Malley, and Jack Hinton, were light-hearted, full of incident, sometimes farcical, always ebullient; they have been attacked by Irish literary critics – and politicians – for their stage-Irish characters, their presentation of the lighter side of garrison life in Ireland. When Lever left Ireland in 1845 the attacks largely ceased. He then began to write novels with more historical than military interest, he explored the social and political milieu of Europe, and he deepened his understanding of life and capacity for comment on it. He also developed his style and novelistic techniques in the middle 1840's and 1850's. Thus Roland Cashel and Sir Jasper Carew take a broad view of Irish problems, while The Knight of Gwynne, which owed something to Lever's friendship with Maria Edgeworth, examines the extravagant recklessness which sapped the foundations of the Anglo-Irish. His characters are now more realistic, more balanced.

Shaw's preface to Major Barbara acknowledges his debt to Lever's poignant sense of the tragi-comedy of Ireland – most developed in his middle period – his ironic, impartial view of the conflict between life and romantic imagination. But Yeats, Lady Gregory, and more recent commentators seem only to have noticed (and disliked) the stage-Irish element in his work. Had they read Barrington, Sir Brook Fossbrooke, and Lord Kilgobbin, which give a full and tragic view of Ireland in the latter part of the nineteenth century? These novels are influenced in their scope by Scott and Balzac, and convey a sense that the ascendancy's power had long vanished, a fierce indignation about the faults of British administration, and a melancholic foreboding of great catastrophe to come.

—A. Norman Jeffares

LEVERSON, Ada (née Beddington). English. Born in London in 1865. Educated privately. Married Ernest Leverson in 1884; one son and one daughter. Writer from 1885; a friend of George Moore, Oscar Wilde (who nicknamed her "The Sphinx"), Max Beerbohm, and the Sitwells; contributed sketches and parodies to *The Yellow Book* and *Punch* in the 1890's; Woman's Columnist, as "Elaine," in the Sunday newspaper *The Referee*; wrote for *The Criterion*, 1926; lived abroad, mainly in Italy, in later years. *Died in 1936.*

PUBLICATIONS

Fiction

   The Twelfth Hour. 1907.
   Love's Shadow. 1908.
   The Limit. 1911.
   Tenterhooks. 1912.
   Bird of Paradise. 1914.
   Love at Second Sight. 1916.
   The Little Ottleys (Love's Shadow, Tenterhooks, Love at Second Sight). 1962.

Reading List: Introduction by Colin MacInnes to *The Little Ottleys*, 1962; *The Sphinx and Her Circle: A Biographical Sketch of Leverson* by Violet Wyndham, 1963.

                              *   *   *

Ada Leverson's six novels can be divided into two halves: those which are about the Ottleys, and those which are not. *The Twelfth Hour, The Limit*, and *Bird of Paradise* are in the latter category, and have many features in common. Each is concerned with a marriage which has reached the point of being under threat. In each there is a marital relationship which is as intense for those concerned as are the pre-marital relationships of the conventional love story. In each, the woman is beautiful and much courted by society, particularly male society, while herself being deeply in love with her husband: "Had her many friends and acquaintances been told that the chief wish of the pretty Mrs. Kellynch was the more complete and absolute conquest of her own husband ... they would have been surprised, incredulous, perhaps even a little shocked." Much of the life of the novels is the attempt of the wife to be recognised by a distracted, often absent, husband. In *The Twelfth Hour* the husband is absorbed in racing and antique-collecting, and tends to take his wife Felicity for granted. By the end of the novel he has been wooed into some admissions of love.

In *Bird of Paradise* Bertha is wooed by a would-be lover at the same time that she woos her own husband. Her realisation that her husband is, finally, jealous comes as a joyful recognition, and the marriage is saved from disruption. The interest in these two novels is in the tension between the flow of marital love from the woman to the man, and the extra-marital and social pressures: will her husband realise she loves him in time to save her from the outside world? *The Limit* is a more conventional story of marital jealousy, with the husband wooing the wife back into the safety of marriage.

Leverson's strength as a novelist is best seen in *Love's Shadow*, *Tenterhooks*, and *Love at Second Sight*. *Love's Shadow* looks as if it began as a pre-marital love story, something unusual for Leverson. As the novel proceeds more and more space is given to Edith and Bruce Ottley, and the young lovers recede into a sub-plot. By the end of the novel, Leverson has realised Edith's and Bruce's possibilities, and the next two novels focus on them. Edith is an intelligent sensible woman, who matures throughout the trilogy. Bruce is vain, boastful, casually amorous, hypochondriac and selfish. Together they are very funny indeed. In *Tenterhooks*, Edith meets her ideal man, good-looking, intelligent, sensitive, patriotic, and by the end of *Love at Second Sight* her absurd marriage is ended when Bruce runs off with a farcical figure called Madame Frabelle.

All Leverson's best writing is dialogue, in which she is heavily influenced, though not drowned, by Oscar Wilde. Some whole chapters are done in this mode, with brilliant characterisations, though she never completed a stage play. Had she lived in the mid-twentieth century, television would have been her medium – and her scripts for situation comedy would have been sophisticated, intelligent, and compulsively viewable.

—Gabriel Bergonzi

LEWIS, C(live) S(taples).   English.   Born in Belfast, Northern Ireland, 29 November 1898. Educated at Wynyard School, Hertfordshire, 1908–10; Campbell College, Northern Ireland, 1910; Cherbourg School, Malvern, 1911–13; privately, 1914–17; University College, Oxford (scholar), 1917, 1919–23 (Chancellor's English Essay Prize, 1921), B.A. (honours) 1922. Served in the Somerset Light Infantry, 1917–19: First Lieutenant. Married Joy Davidman Gresham in 1956 (died, 1960). Philosophy Tutor, 1924, and Lecturer in English, 1924, University College, Oxford; Fellow and Tutor in English, Magdalen College, Oxford, 1924–54; Professor of Medieval and Renaissance English, Cambridge University, 1954–63. Riddell Lecturer, University of Durham, 1943; Clark Lecturer, Cambridge University, 1944. Recipient: Gollancz Prize for Literature, 1937; Library Association Carnegie Medal, 1957. D.D.: University of St. Andrews, Scotland, 1946; Docteur-ès-Lettres, Laval University, Quebec, 1952; D.Litt.: University of Manchester, 1959; Hon. Dr.: University of Dijon, 1962; University of Lyons, 1963. Honorary Fellow, Magdalen College, Oxford, 1955; University College, Oxford, 1958; Magdalene College, Cambridge, 1963. Fellow of the Royal Society of Literature, 1948; Fellow of the British Academy, 1955. *Died 22 November 1963.*

PUBLICATIONS

Collections

Letters, edited by W. H. Lewis.   1966.
A Mind Awake: An Anthology of Lewis, edited by Clyde S. Kilby.   1968.

Fiction

Out of the Silent Planet. 1938.
Perelandra. 1943; as *Voyage to Venus,* 1953.
That Hideous Strength: A Modern Fairy-Tale for Grown-Ups. 1945.
Till We Have Faces: A Myth Retold. 1956.
The Dark Tower and Other Stories, edited by Walter Hooper. 1977.

Verse

Spirits in Bondage: A Cycle of Lyrics. 1919.
Dymer. 1926.
Poems, edited by Walter Hooper. 1964.
Narrative Poems, edited by Walter Hooper. 1969.

Other

The Pilgrim's Regress: An Allegorical Apology for Christianity, Reason and Romanticism. 1933; revised edition, 1943.
The Allegory of Love: A Study in Medieval Tradition. 1936.
Rehabilitations and Other Essays. 1939.
The Personal Heresy: A Controversy, with E. M. W. Tillyard. 1939.
The Problem of Pain. 1940.
The Weight of Glory. 1942.
The Screwtape Letters. 1942; revised edition, 1961.
A Preface to Paradise Lost. 1942.
Broadcast Talks: Right and Wrong: A Clue to the Meaning of the Universe, and What Christians Believe. 1942; as *The Case for Christianity,* 1943.
Christian Behaviour: A Further Series of Broadcast Talks. 1943.
The Abolition of Man: or, Reflections on Education with Special Reference to the Teaching of English in the Upper Forms of Schools. 1943.
Beyond Personality: The Christian Idea of God. 1944.
The Great Divorce: A Dream. 1945.
Miracles: A Preliminary Study. 1947.
Vivisection. 1947(?).
Transposition and Other Addresses. 1949; as *The Weight of Glory and Other Addresses,* 1949.
The Lion, The Witch, and the Wardrobe (juvenile). 1950.
Prince Caspian: The Return to Narnia (juvenile). 1951.
The Voyage of the "Dawn Treader" (juvenile). 1952.
Mere Christianity. 1952.
The Silver Chair (juvenile). 1953.
English Literature in the Sixteenth Century, Excluding Drama. 1954.
The Horse and His Boy (juvenile). 1954.
The Magician's Nephew (juvenile). 1955.
Surprised by Joy: The Shape of My Early Life. 1955.
The Last Battle (juvenile). 1956.
Reflections on the Pslams. 1958.
Shall We Lose God in Outer Space? 1959.
The Four Loves. 1960.
The World's Last Night and Other Essays. 1960.
Studies in Words. 1960; revised edition, 1967.
An Experiment in Criticism. 1961.

A Grief Observed (autobiography).   1961.
They Asked for a Paper: Papers and Addresses.   1962.
Beyond the Bright Blue (letters).   1963.
Letters to Malcolm, Chiefly on Prayer.   1964.
The Discarded Image: An Introduction to Medieval and Renaissance Literature.   1964.
Screwtape Proposes a Toast and Other Pieces.   1965.
Of Other Worlds: Essays and Stories, edited by Walter Hooper.   1966.
Studies in Medieval and Renaissance Literature, edited by Walter Hooper.   1966.
Spenser's Images of Life, edited by Alastair Fowler.   1967.
Christian Reflections, edited by Walter Hooper.   1967.
Letters to an American Lady, edited by Clyde S. Kilby.   1967.
Mark vs. Tristram: Correspondence Between C. S. Lewis and Owen Barfield, edited by
    Walter Hooper.   1967.
Selected Literary Essays, edited by Walter Hooper.   1969.
God in the Dock: Essays on Theology and Ethics, edited by Walter Hooper.   1970; as
    Undeceptions: Essays on Theology and Ethics, 1971.
The Humanitarian Theory of Punishment.   1972.
The Joyful Christian: 128 Readings, edited by William Griffin.   1977.

Editor, *George MacDonald: An Anthology.*   1946.
Editor, *Arthurian Torso, Containing the Posthumous Fragment of "The Figure of
    Arthur,"* by Charles Williams.   1948.

Bibliography: *Lewis An Annotated Checklist of Writings about Him and His Works* by Joe R.
Christopher and Joan K. Ostlin, 1974.

Reading List: *Lewis: Apostle to the Sceptics* by Chad Walsh, 1949; *The Christian World of
Lewis* edited by Clyde S. Kilby, 1964; *Light on Lewis* edited by Jocelyn Gibb, 1965 (includes
bibliography by Walter Hooper); *Lewis: A Biography* by Roger Lancelyn Green and Walter
Hooper, 1974; *The Secret Country of Lewis* by Anne Arnott, 1974; *Bright Shadow of Reality:
Lewis and the Feeling Intellect* by Corbin S. Carnall, 1974; *The Longing for Form: Essays on
the Fiction of Lewis* edited by Peter J. Shakel, 1977.

*   *   *

It will remain hard during this century to do justice to C. S. Lewis for three reasons: 1) his
Irish polemicism, 2) his insisting on tradition in the sense of what has been done, which
placed him in the head-on conflict with the age, superbly expressed in his lecture "De
Descriptione Temporum," 3) his deliberate scorn for what has been the wellspring of modern
literature, the exploring of the foundations and boundaries of consciousness.

In his professional field, literary history, these qualities make for brilliantly provocative
writing, and *The Allegory of Love, A Preface to Paradise Lost, English Literature in the
Sixteenth Century, The Discarded Image,* and *Spenser's Images of Life* – a wide variety of
books but all celebrating the joyfully hierarchic, symbolic, and ritual world which he thought
we have lost – will be read as long as anyone reads literary history. But to put such a question
as "After all, is not *The Screwtape Letters,* both in the design – letters of temptation from a
senior to a junior devil – and in the execution, as good as *A Tale of a Tub*?" leaves one uneasy
and irresolute about answering either way. They quite probably are equally good, and it
might be fair to describe Lewis as a modern Swift – only a little too much at ease in Zion. The
best of his science-fiction, *Perelandra,* and his retelling of the myth of Cupid and Psyche, *Till
We Have Faces,* may probably meet the proof of time as well as *Gulliver's Travels.*

But it is significant that each of these was accompanied by a work which promises equally
well but remained a fragment – the alternative world of "The Dark Tower" and the retelling

of Helen of Troy's life called "After Ten Years." Lewis had an active and probably disturbed unconscious mind which brought forth both remarkable dreams and pictures round which he wrote his fiction, but it seems to have been kept firmly under control by his brilliant conscious carapace. The two fragments both concern a duality of beloveds, a false Helen and a true, and were probably in danger of going askew – either by letting free something too definitely erotic, or by unbalancing Lewis's central concern – the coincidence of myth, truth, and fact which was at the heart of his acceptance of Christianity and the incarnation. A certain subduing of fact to idea is observable in his too-smoothly written exploratory theology in *The Problem of Pain* and *Miracles*, and even in the vivid autobiography, *Surprised by Joy*, in which he recounts how he was led to awareness of God by meditation on romantic longing. (The expository *Mere Christianity* and the overt fable of *The Screwtape Letters* and *The Great Divorce* escape this criticism.) His science-fiction, much of his literary history (especially where allegory is the subject), and his admirable Narnia series (for children) all follow this urge to present a universe at once factual and symbolic. But the most satisfactory reconciliation of these two sides of truth comes in the books written after he had met Joy Gresham (later his wife), which include, as well as *Till We Have Faces*, his record of his grief at her death, *A Grief Observed*. Not only in this classic and shattering book, but also in his academically revolutionary *An Experiment in Criticism* (which anticipates later, French-influenced attempts to turn critical attention from the book to the act of reading), he allows full rein to the skill at introspection which previously he had on principle kept curbed. This new impulse is embodied not only in the story but in the title of *Till We Have Faces*. It is a pity that his earlier reputation – not wholly correct, though sedulously cultivated by himself, his enemies, and some of his friends – as a straightforward reactionary, has hindered these remarkable books from achieving their proper fame.

—Stephen Medcalf

LEWIS, Matthew Gregory ("Monk" Lewis). English. Born in London, 9 July 1775. Educated at Dr. Fountaine's School, London; Westminster School, London; Christ Church, Oxford. Writer from 1791; visited Weimar, and met Goethe, 1792–93; Attaché to the British Embassy in The Hague, 1794–95; famous as a writer from the age of 20; Member of Parliament for Hindon, Wiltshire, 1796–1802; inherited his father's properties, 1812; visited his estates in Jamaica, to arrange for the welfare of his slaves, 1815–16; visited Byron and Shelley in Geneva, 1816; toured Italy, 1817. *Died 14 May 1818.*

PUBLICATIONS

Collections

   Tales in Verse of Terror and Wonder, edited by L. E. Smith.   1925.

Fiction

   The Monk: A Romance.   1796; expurgated edition, as *Ambrosio; or, The Monk*, 1798;
      edited by Howard Anderson, 1973.
   Romantic Tales.   1808.

Plays

Village Virtue: A Dramatic Satire. 1796.
The Minister, from a play by Schiller. 1797; revised version, as *The Harper's Daughter; or, Love and Ambition* (produced 1803), 1813.
The Castle Spectre, music by Michael Kelly (produced 1797). 1798.
Rolla; or, The Peruvian Hero, from a play by Kotzebue. 1799.
The Twins; or, Is It He or His Brother? (produced 1799). Edited by Karl S. Guthke, in *Huntington Library Quarterly 25*, 1962.
The East Indian, from a play by Kotzebue (produced 1799). 1800; as *Rivers; or, The East Indian*, 1800; as *Rich and Poor* (produced 1812), n.d.
Adelmorn the Outlaw, music by Michael Kelly (produced 1801). 1801.
Alfonso, King of Castile (produced 1802). 1801.
The Captive (produced 1803). In *Life and Correspondence* by Margaret Baron-Wilson, 2 vols., 1839.
Rugantino: The Bravo of Venice, from a play by Pixérécourt. 1805.
Adelgitha; or, The Fruits of a Single Error, music by Michael Kelly (produced 1807). 1806.
The Wood Demon; or, The Clock Has Struck, music by Michael Kelly (produced 1807); revised version, as *One O'Clock! or, The Knight and the Wood Demon*, music by Michael Kelly and M. P. King (produced 1811).
Venoni; or, The Novice of St. Mark's, music by Michael Kelly, from a play by Bouhet (produced 1808). 1809.
Raymond and Agnes (produced 1809). N.d.
Temper; or, The Domestic Tyrant (produced 1809).
Timour the Tartar (produced 1811). 1811.
The Enchanted Fire of the Invisible Island; or, The Golden Gallery (produced 1824).

Verse

Tales of Terror, with others. 1799.
The Love of Gain: A Poem Imitated from Juvenal. 1799.
Tales of Wonder, written and collected by Lewis and others. 2 vols., 1801.
Monody on the Death of Sir John Moore. 1809.
Poems. 1812.
The Isle of Devils: A Historical Tale Founded on an Anecdote in the Annals of Portugal. 1827.
Crazy Jane 1830(?).

Other

Journal of a West India Proprietor Kept During a Residence in the Island of Jamaica. 1834; as *Journal of a Residence among the Negroes in the West Indies*, 1845; edited by M. Wilson, 1929.

Translator, *The Bravo of Venice: A Romance*, by J. H. D. Zschokke. 1805; abridged edition, as *Rugantino: The Bravo of Venice*, 1805.
Translator, *Feudal Tyrants; or, The Counts of Carlsheim and Sargans: A Romance, Taken from the German.* 4 vols., 1806.
Translator, *The Four Facardins*, by Count Anthony Hamilton, in *Fairy Tales and Romances.* 1849.

733

Bibliography: in *Gothic Bibliography* by Montague Summers, 1941.

Reading List: *Life and Correspondence* by Margaret Baron-Wilson, 2 vols., 1839; Introduction by John Berryman to *The Monk*, 1952; *A Life of Lewis* by Louis F. Peck, 1961.

*   *   *

The Monk, written by a nineteen-year-old diplomat as a stay against boredom, established the fame and notoriety of Matthew Gregory Lewis, a humane, generous, rather boring little man who could scarcely be more different from his creation, with its horrific reveling in lust, incest, rape, murder, and the supernatural. In spite of the defects of a sometimes wooden style, only loosely connected episodes, and lack of depth in character, *The Monk* is a prime specimen of the Gothic horror novel, with genuine energy and lasting power. Set during the time of the Inquisition in Spain and Germany, the novel explores the mysterious evils that lie beneath the surface of normal reality. Ambrosio, the eloquent, pious monk at the peak of his career, has within him elements of vanity, hypocrisy, and lust which explode beyond control as he becomes entangled in a web of complicated events: the illicit love of Raymond and Agnes, the heartless, criminal power of a prioress, and the devoted, ultimately diabolical, passion of Matilda, who has entered Ambrosio's service disguised as a page. Lewis's narration of the progress of Ambrosio's destruction, as his lust leads him to atrocious crimes, minutely described, assumes a vigor which impels the reader into the realm of shocking chaos and nightmarish evil.

No other of Lewis's works approached the success of *The Monk*, but Lewis's literary accomplishments do not end with that novel. Some of his dramas were popular for a time, but none has been revived; his favorite forms were tragedy and what he called "Grand Romantic Melo-Drama." The most successful, *The Castle Spectre*, is typically Gothic, with an ancient castle, underground passages, a gloomy dungeon, a bloody ghost, and elaborate light and sound effects for maximum shock and melodrama. His poems have considerable merit, displaying great variety in subject and technique, often with striking rhythmic power. Sir Walter Scott said of Lewis, "He had the finest ear for the rhythm of verse I ever heard — finer even than Byron's." He was also an accomplished translator and adaptor of French and German, and orally translated Goethe's *Faust* while visiting Byron in Italy. The posthumous *Journal of a West India Proprietor*, a record of Lewis's visits to Jamaica to oversee property inherited from his father, shows Lewis as a sensible, humane observer of human life. Totally unlike his Gothic productions, it is — according to Coleridge, who found *The Monk* too "minutely libidinous" and blasphemous — "by far his best work."

—David McCracken

LEWIS, (Harry) Sinclair. American. Born in Sauk Center, Minnesota, 7 February 1885. Educated at Sauk Center High School; Oberlin Academy, Ohio, 1902–03; Yale University, New Haven, Connecticut (Editor, *Yale Literary Magazine*), 1903–06, 1907–08, A.B. 1908. Married 1) Grace Livingston Hegger in 1914 (divorced, 1925), one son; 2) the columnist Dorothy Thompson in 1928 (divorced, 1942), one son. Worked as a janitor in Upton Sinclair's socialist community at Helicon Hall, Englewood, New Jersey, 1906–07; Assistant Editor, *Transatlantic Tales*, New York, 1907; successively, reporter on a newspaper in Waterloo, Iowa, promoter for a charity organization in New York, secretary to Alice MacGowan and Grace MacGowan Cook in Carmel, California, writer for the Associated

Press and the *Bulletin* in San Francisco, Assistant Editor of the *Volta Review* in Washington, D.C., and, in New York, manuscript reader for the publishers Frederick A. Stokes, Assistant Editor of *Adventure*, Editor for the Publishers' Newspaper Syndicate, and Editor for the George H. Doran Company, 1908–16; full-time writer from 1916; reported the Viennese Revolution for the New York *Evening Post* and Philadelphia *Ledger*, 1918. Recipient: Pulitzer Prize, 1926 (refused); Nobel Prize for Literature, 1930. Litt.D.: Yale University, 1936. Member, American Academy of Arts and Letters, 1938. Lived in Vermont and, in later years, in Europe. *Died 10 January 1951.*

PUBLICATIONS

Collections

    The Man from Main Street: Selected Essays and Other Writings 1904–1950, edited by Harry E. Maule and Melville H. Cane. 1953.

Fiction

    Hike and the Aeroplane (juvenile). 1912.
    Our Mr. Wrenn. 1914.
    The Trail of the Hawk. 1915.
    The Job. 1917.
    The Innocents. 1917.
    Free Air. 1919.
    Main Street. 1920.
    Babbitt. 1922.
    Arrowsmith. 1925; as *Martin Arrowsmith,* 1925; edited by Barbara G. Spayd, 1933.
    Mantrap. 1926.
    Elmer Gantry. 1927.
    The Man Who Knew Coolidge. 1928.
    Dodsworth. 1929.
    Ann Vickers. 1933.
    Work of Art. 1934.
    Selected Short Stories. 1935.
    It Can't Happen Here. 1935.
    The Prodigal Parents. 1938.
    Bethel Merriday. 1940.
    Gideon Planish. 1943.
    Cass Timberlane. 1945.
    Kingsblood Royal. 1947.
    The God-Seeker. 1949.
    World So Wide. 1951.

Plays

    Hobohemia (produced 1919).
    Jayhawker, with Lloyd Lewis (produced 1934). 1935.
    It Can't Happen Here, from his own novel (produced 1936). 1938.
    Storm in the West (screenplay), with Dore Schary. 1963.

Other

John Dos Passos' "Manhattan Transfer." 1926.
Cheap and Contented Labor: The Picture of a Southern Mill Town in 1929. 1929.
From Main Street to Stockholm: Letters of Lewis 1919–1930, edited by Harrison Smith.
   1952.

Bibliography: *A Lewis Checklist* by James Lundquist, 1970.

Reading List: *Lewis: An American Life,* 1961 (includes bibliography), and *Lewis,* 1963, both
by Mark Schorer; *Lewis* by Sheldon Norman Grebstein, 1962; *Dorothy and Red* by Vincent
Sheean, 1963; *The Art of Lewis* by D. J. Dooley, 1967; *The Quixotic Vision of Lewis* by
Martin Light, 1974.

*   *   *

   Sinclair Lewis, the first American Nobel Laureate in Literature, was recognized with
justice by the Nobel Prize committee for the accuracy and the detail with which he portrayed
American life. He applied the concepts of critical realism as they had been developed in the
nineteenth century to the subject of the American midwest, and, using a gift for satiric
caricature and a remarkable skill at mimicry, created a vivid picture of middle-class America
and its values, ideals, and assumptions in the early twentieth century. He portrayed with
devastating satiric power and sardonic force the lack of beauty, dignity, and value in
America's materialistic culture. Lewis, although he was hailed in his own day as the
spokesman of a new literary movement, was actually a culmination of the movement of
critical realism which had begun in the decades immediately after the Civil War. He came as
the summarizing expression of moods and methods typical of the midwestern "revolt from
the village" that had produced such writers as Hamlin Garland, E. W. Howe, and Edgar Lee
Masters. Like many other midwest writers, Lewis moved from the West to the East – in his
case from Minnesota to Connecticut and New York – and then used the land of his childhood
as his chief subject and often his principal target.
   Between 1914 and 1920 he published five novels, the best being *The Job* and *Free Air,* and
a number of short stories in popular periodicals. Critical hindsight now shows us that these
early works, although clearly in the tradition of the popular fiction of their time, also
adumbrated in theme, treatment, and character the major work which was to come. In 1920
he published *Main Street,* a corruscating picture of the dullness, drabness, conformity, and
materialism of a small, midwestern town. With it his career was brilliantly launched to the
acclaim of the nation and the world. He followed it with *Babbitt,* a portrayal of a petit-
bourgeois businessman in a middle-sized midwestern city, a weak man who vainly attempts
to break out of the pattern of conformity which shapes his days and to understand himself
and achieve his own freedom. This plot pattern was to be recurrent in most of Lewis's work.
Babbitt, perhaps his most satisfactory single work, was the first of a long series of novels each
of which examined a specific business or profession. After publishing it, he started collecting
material for a novel on the labor movement, but that book was never written. *Arrowsmith,*
written with the aid of the biologist Paul DeKruif, and in its own time regarded by many as
his finest single piece of work, studied the profession of medicine and contrasted it with the
idealized view of scientific research. Lewis pointed his satiric guns at the Protestant ministry
in *Elmer Gantry,* a howling comedy of extravagant and slashing satire; and he
sympathetically portrayed the American businessman abroad and satirized the cultural
pretensions of his wife in *Dodsworth.* This novel begins Lewis's significant shift from the
harsh treatment of his middle-class American subjects to a steadily growing sympathy for
them.
   In 1930, he received the Nobel Prize for literature and in his acceptance speech attacked

Howells, whose critical movement he was himself the product of, and praised a group of young writers, such as Thomas Wolfe and Ernest Hemingway, who were soon to be important in advancing novelistic innovations that quickly dated his own work. In the 1920's Lewis had defined America, or at least important aspects of it, for itself and had produced vital, lively, original, and important satiric portraits of America's middle-class failings. The Nobel Prize came as the crowning accolade on one of the major accomplishments in the social novel which any American has ever achieved. But it came when that accomplishment was virtually complete. For following 1930, Lewis's career seems almost to be a search for subject matter.

In *Ann Vickers*, a book much influenced by his admiration for and exasperation with his second wife, the famous journalist Dorothy Thompson, Lewis examined the career woman, but with clearly mixed feelings. He examined the hotel industry in *Work of Art*, the first of his "major" works which was, as Mark Schorer declared, "completely without distinction." *It Can't Happen Here* re-established an important position for him with the American public. This study of the potentiality for American fascism seemed to be a political warning that spoke directly and responsibly to major issues in American life. Today, however, it seems thin and surprisingly conservative. That Lewis was indeed becoming increasingly conservative despite his attacks upon fascism was evident in *Prodigal Parents*, a book about radical and irresponsible children, in which he draws what is almost a comic strip view of communism. Its protagonist, Fred Cornplow, whom Lewis admires, is essentially the same middle-class businessman he had earlier satirized as Babbitt and the denizens of *Main Street*. *Bethel Merriday* is the story of the education of a young actress in summer stock and touring companies. It is embarrassingly sentimental. *Gideon Planish* is an attack on organized philanthrophy. More like *Elmer Gantry* than any book Lewis had written since 1927, it is angry and intemperate, an example of slashing satire and violent comedy; yet it is so overdrawn that it seems almost a parody of Lewis's earlier work. *Cass Timberlane* is an account of American marriage. *Kingsblood Royal* takes up the issue of race in a mechanical and unconvincing parable. *The God-Seeker* is a historical novel laid in Minnesota in the days of its early settlement. Although it can be considered the first novel in an unfinished panel of labor books, it is too much like costume romance to be taken seriously. In *World So Wide*, published posthumously in 1951, the year of his death, Lewis returns to the theme of the American in Europe in a book which is virtually a rewriting of *Dodsworth*, though now the satiric edge is gone, and the European culture that he once supported has become the target of his attack. The characters in this last sad work seemed, as Malcolm Cowley said, "survivors from a vanished world."

Sinclair Lewis's work falls easily into three periods – the early apprenticeship work, followed by the great accomplishment of the 1920's in which in five novels he gives a vigorous and emphatic picture of his world, followed by a long, sad, groping toward suitable subjects. Few American writers have had a greater impact on their world than Lewis during his ten great years, 1920–29. As Mark Schorer said, "He gave us a vigorous, perhaps unique thrust into the imagination of ourselves." But after this great success he was increasingly removed from the materials which were his primary subject matter, and he wrote out of memory rather than direct experience, so that his later novels were increasingly the memorials to a world and an age that was past. He was a very good social novelist but not a truly great writer. Nevertheless, it was appropriate that the first American Nobel Laureate in Literature should have been a man intimately committed to using literature to portray his fellow countrymen and to instruct them through satiric portraiture.

—C. Hugh Holman

LEWIS, (Percy) Wyndham. English. Born in a yacht in the Bay of Fundy, off Nova Scotia, 18 November 1882. Educated at Rugby School, 1897–98; Slade School of Art, London, 1898–1901. Served with the Royal Artillery, 1916; War Artist, 1917–19. Married Gladys Anne Hoskyns in 1929. Travelled on the Continent, 1902–08, then settled in London; artist: Co-Founder, Camden Town Group, 1911; Member, Roger Fry's Omega Workshops, 1913; a Founder, Vorticist Group, 1913, and Founder, with Ezra Pound, and Editor, *Blast*, 1914–15; Founder, Group X, 1920; travelled with T. S. Eliot in France, 1921; Editor, *The Tyro* review, 1921–22, and *The Enemy*, 1927–29; lived in Canada, 1940–45; Lecturer, Assumption College, Windsor, Ontario, 1943–45; returned to London; Art Critic for *The Listener*, 1946–50. Works included in the Tate Gallery, and Victoria and Albert Museum, London; Museum of Modern Art, New York; Toronto Art Museum; Detroit Art Museum; etc. Lit.D.: University of Leeds, 1952. Granted Civil List pension, 1952. *Died 7 March 1957.*

PUBLICATIONS

Collections

> *Letters*, edited by W. K. Rose. 1963.
> *A Soldier of Humor and Selected Writings*, edited by Raymond Rosenthal. 1966.
> *Lewis: An Anthology of His Prose*, edited by E.W. F. Tomlin. 1969.
> *Collected Poems and Plays*, edited by Alan Munton. 1978.

Fiction

> *Tarr.* 1918; revised edition, 1928.
> *The Wild Body, A Soldier of Humor, and Other Stories.* 1927.
> *The Human Age: The Childermass.* 1928 (revised edition, 1956); *Monstre Gai, Malign Fiesta*, 1955.
> *The Apes of God.* 1930.
> *Snooty Baronet.* 1932.
> *The Revenge for Love.* 1937.
> *The Vulgar Streak.* 1941.
> *Rotting Hill* (stories). 1951.
> *Self Condemned.* 1954.
> *The Red Priest.* 1956.
> *The Roaring Queen*, edited by Walter Allen. 1973.
> *Mrs. Dukes' Million*, edited by Frank Davey. 1977.

Plays

> *The Ideal Giant*, in *The Ideal Giant, The Code of a Herdsman, Cantelman's Springmate.* 1917.
> *Enemy of the Stars.* 1932.

> Radio Plays: *Monstre Gai* and *Malign Fiesta*, with D. G. Bridson, from the novels by Lewis, 1955.

Verse

Engine-Fight Talk [One-Way Song].   1933.

Other

The Ideal Giant, The Code of a Herdsman, Cantelman's Springmate.   1917.
Harold Gilman: An Appreciation, with Louis F. Fergusson.   1919.
The Caliph's Design: Architects! Where Is Your Vortex?   1919.
Fifteen Drawings.   1920.
The Art of Being Ruled.   1926.
The Lion and the Fox: The Role of Hero in the Plays of Shakespeare.   1927.
Time and Western Man.   1927.
Paleface: The Philosophy of the "Melting Pot."   1929.
Satire and Fiction, with *The History of a Rejected Review,* by Roy Campbell.   1930.
Hitler.   1931.
The Diabolical Principle, and The Dithyrambic Spectator.   1931.
Thirty Personalities and a Self-Portrait (drawings).   1932.
Doom of Youth.   1932.
Filibusters in Barbary: Record of a Visit to the Sous.   1932.
The Old Gang and the New Gang.   1933.
Men Without Art.   1934.
Left Wings over Europe; or, How to Make a War about Nothing.   1936.
Count Your Dead: They Are Alive! or, A New War in the Making.   1937.
Blasting and Bombardiering (autobiography).   1937; revised edition, 1967.
The Mysterious Mr. Bull.   1938.
The Jews: Are They Human?   1939.
The Hitler Cult, and How It Will End.   1939.
Lewis the Artist: From "Blast" to Burlington House.   1939.
America, I Presume.   1940.
Anglosaxony: A League That Works.   1941.
America and Cosmic Man.   1948.
Rude Assignment: A Narrative of My Career Up-to-Date.   1949.
The Writer and the Absolute.   1952.
The Demon of Progress in the Arts.   1954.
Enemy Salvoes: Selected Literary Criticism, edited by C. J. Fox.   1975.

Editor, *Blast: Review of the Great English Vortex.*   2 vols., 1914–15.
Editor, *The Tyro: A Review of the Arts of Painting, Sculpture, and Design.*   2 vols., 1921–22.
Editor, *The Enemy: A Review of Art and Literature.*   3 vols., 1927–29.

Bibliography: *Lewis: A Descriptive Bibliography* by Omar S. Pound and Philip Grover, 1978.

Reading List: *The Art of Lewis* by C. Handley-Reed, 1951; *A Master of Our Time: A Study of Lewis* by Geoffrey Grigson, 1951; *Lewis* by Hugh Kenner, 1953; *Lewis* by E. W. F. Tomlin, 1955; *Lewis: A Portrait of the Artist as the Enemy* by G. Wagner, 1957 (includes bibliography); *Lewis* by W. H. Pritchard, 1968; *Lewis: Fictions and Satires* by Robert T. Chapman, 1973; *Lewis the Novelist* by Timothy Materer, 1975.

*   *   *

Novelist, poet, playwright, philosopher, art critic, autobiographer, editor, pamphleteer, social observer, and commentator on public affairs, Wyndham Lewis was one of the most versatile writers of his time. In addition, he was a painter of major importance. He was early associated with Pound, Eliot, and Joyce as one of the pioneers of the modern movement in letters; and, although he never enjoyed a success comparable to that achieved by Eliot or Joyce, and was spared the notoriety of Pound, his posthumous reputation grew rapidly until his place as an author of the first importance was firmly established.

Except in his short stories and in parts of the novels, Lewis is not an easy writer; but he devised a style of unmistakable originality, and his best work is characterized by a primal energy and an intellectual penetration which led Eliot to describe it as combining "the thought of the modern and the energy of the cave man."

Early in his career, Lewis, who was receptive to the ideas of several cultures, formulated his own "metaphysic." This ran counter to the prevailing notions of the intelligentsia, which were essentially pragmatic and above all relativistic or, as Lewis would say, "time-conscious." In his *Time and Western Man*, the most original and certainly the most influential of his books, Lewis asserts the primacy of the intellect and the objectivity of values — in short, the classical ideal. As he had said earlier, in *The Art of Being Ruled*: "Life itself is not important. Our values make it so; but they are, mostly, the important ones, non-human values, although the intenser they are the more they imply a supreme vital connotation. To attach, as the humanitarian does, a mystical value to life *itself*, for its own sake, is as much a treachery to spiritual truth as it is a gesture to 'humanity.' " Here may be detected the influence of T. E. Hulme, whose *Speculations*, posthumously published in 1924, initiated a reaction against all forms of romanticism. Lewis's earlier championship of Vorticism (a term originated by Pound) had reflected his attempts to apply such principles in the sphere of art. The flamboyant magazine *Blast* was intended to identify and disinfect, in a comminatory manner, what Lewis considered to be the debilitating influences in British society. Thus: "BLAST HUMOUR: QUACK ENGLISH drug for stupidity and sleepiness.... BLAST SPORT: HUMOUR'S first cousin and accomplice.... BLAST DIABOLICS: rapture and roses of the erotic bookshelves, culminating in PURGATORY OF PUTNEY." These denunciations, distributed over the page with typographical eccentricity, were paralleled by a series of "blessings," and there were a few cases of a movement or a personality appearing under both heads.

A certain veneration for authority, first apparent in *The Caliph's Design*, became more explicit in *The Art of Being Ruled*, his major politico-sociological treatise. This attitude, together with some denunciations of the Left in *Left Wings over Europe*, not to mention the slighter *Hitler*, led to his being classed as a crypto-fascist; but a study of Lewis's writings as a whole, including the important *The Hitler Cult, and How It Will End*, reveals him as at heart an enemy of totalitarianism. Moreover, he was a humane and gentle personality; and it is known that he much resented the attempts of pre-war political right-wingers to secure his support for their various movements. Perhaps the best statement of his mature position is in *Rude Assignment* (1949): "At a time when everyone was for a fanatical *étatisme*, I was not. It seemed to me to promise no good to anybody — to kick out kings and queens and put masters in their place with a hundred times their power."

To approach Lewis's prose work for the first time is to be confronted with a bewildering variety from which to choose. The uninitiated might well begin with the collection of short stories, *The Wild Body*, which has worn extremely well and in which his particular brand of tough, satirical humour first showed itself, together with his view of laughter as something "primitive, hard, and unchangeable." This might be followed by the later collection, *Rotting Hill*, which evokes almost uncannily the mood of post-war London. The first novel, *Tarr*, was considered a landmark in fiction on account of its radical departure from the conventional wish-fulfilling love-cum-adventure story; but its knotty, elliptical style and surgically unsentimental treatment of character may be less digestible than *The Revenge for Love*, a chilling story of politics in England and Spain before the Spanish Civil War. *The Apes of God*, a gigantic satire on Bloomsbury, though containing passages of great brilliance, numbs finally by an excess of impersonal mockery; it was aptly described as a "massacre of the insignificants." Despite a slow start, *Self Condemned* is perhaps the most powerful of the novels, because Lewis here laid bare his private anguish during a self-imposed wartime exile. A parallel but distinct series of imaginative works begins with the play *Enemy of the Stars*, written in 1914 but published in 1932, and continues with *The Childermass* (1928), completed with *Monstre Gai* and *Malign Fiesta* (1955) under the general title of *The Human Age*. These works possess an incandescent, hallucinatory quality which calls to mind Blake's Prophetic Books, even though the prose is in the tradition of Swift, and the dream sometimes turns to nightmare. The two later volumes were described as being the best novel to come out of the Cold War. Much of the remainder of Lewis's work is polemical.

—E. W. F. Tomlin

LINDSAY, Jack. Australian. Born in Melbourne, Victoria, 20 October 1900; son of the writer and artist Norman Lindsay. Educated at Brisbane Grammar School; University of Queensland, Brisbane, 1918–21, B.A. (honours) in classics 1921. Served in the British Army, 1941–45, in the Royal Corps of Signals, 1941–43, and as a scriptwriter in the War Office, 1943–45. Married Meta Waterdrinker in 1956; one son and one daughter. Editor, with Kenneth Slessor and F. Johnson, *Vision*, Sydney, 1923–24; settled in England, 1926; Proprietor and Director, Fanfrolico Press, London, 1927–30; Editor, with P. R. Stephensen, *London Aphrodite*, 1928–29; Editor, *Poetry and the People*, London, 1938–39; Editor, *Anvil*, London, 1947; Editor, with John Davenport and Randall Swingler, *Arena*, London, 1949–51. Recipient: Australian Literature Society Couch Gold Medal, 1960; Order of Merit, U.S.S.R., 1968. D.Litt.; University of Queensland. Fellow of the Royal Society of Literature, 1945, and of the Ancient Monuments Society, 1961. Lives in Castle Hedingham, Essex.

PUBLICATIONS

Fiction

Cressida's First Lover: A Tale of Ancient Greece. 1932.
Rome for Sale. 1934.
Caesar Is Dead. 1934.
Last Days with Cleopatra. 1935.
Despoiling Venus. 1935.
Storm at Sea. 1935.
The Wanderings of Wenamen: 1115–1114 B.C. 1936.
Come Home at Last and Other Stories. 1936.
Shadow and Flame. 1936.
Adam of a New World. 1936.
Sue Verney. 1937.
End of Cornwall. 1937.
1649: A Novel of a Year. 1938.
Brief Light: A Novel of Catullus. 1939.
Lost Birthright. 1939.

Guiliano the Magnificent, adapted from a work by D. Johnson.   1940.
Light in Italy.   1941.
Hannibal Takes a Hand.   1941.
The Stormy Violence.   1941.
We Shall Return: A Novel of Dunkirk and the French Campaign.   1942.
Beyond Terror: A Novel of the Battle of Crete.   1943.
The Barriers Are Down: A Tale of the Collapse of a Civilisation.   1945.
Hullo Stranger.   1945.
Time to Live.   1946.
The Subtle Knot.   1947.
Men of Forty-Eight.   1948.
Fires in Smithfield.   1950.
The Passionate Pastoral.   1951.
Betrayed Spring: A Novel of the British Way.   1953.
Rising Tide.   1953.
The Moment of Choice.   1955.
A Local Habitation: A Novel of the British Way.   1957.
The Great Oak: A Story of 1549.   1957.
The Revolt of the Sons.   1960.
All on the Never-Never: A Novel of the British Way of Life.   1961.
The Way the Ball Bounces.   1962.
Masks and Faces.   1963.
Choice of Times.   1964.
Thunder Underground: A Story of Nero's Rome.   1965.
Death of a Spartan King and Two Other Stories of the Ancient World.   1974.

Plays

Marino Faliero: A Verse-Play.   1927.
Helen Comes of Age: Three Original Plays in Verse.   1927.
Hereward: A Verse Drama.   1930.
The Whole Armour of God (produced 1944).
Robin of England (produced 1945).
The Face of Coal, with B. Coombes (produced 1946).
Iphigeneia in Aulis, from a play by Euripides (produced 1967).
Hecuba, from a play by Euripides (produced 1967).
Electra, from a play by Euripides (produced 1967).
Orestes, from a play by Euripides (produced 1967).
Nathan the Wise, from a play by Lessing (produced 1967).

Verse

Fauns and Ladies.   1923.
The Passionate Neatherd.   1930.
Into Action: The Battle of Dieppe: A Poem.   1942.
Second Front: Poems.   1944.
Clue of Darkness.   1949.
Peace Is Our Answer.   1950.
Three Letters to Nikolai Tikhonov.   1951.
Three Elegies.   1957.

Other

William Blake: Creative Will and the Poetic Image. 1927; revised edition, 1929.
Dionysos: or, Nietzsche contra Nietzsche: An Essay in Lyrical Philosophy. 1928.
The Romans. 1935.
Runaway (juvenile). 1935.
Rebels of the Goldfields (juvenile). 1936.
Marc Antony: His World and His Contemporaries. 1936.
John Bunyan: Maker of Myths. 1937.
The Anatomy of Spirit: An Enquiry into the Origins of Religious Emotions. 1937.
To Arms! A Story of Ancient Gaul (juvenile). 1938.
England, My England. 1939.
A Short History of Culture. 1939; revised edition, 1962.
The Dons Sight Devon: A Story of the Defeat of the Invincible Armada (juvenile). 1942.
Perspective for Poetry. 1944.
British Achievement in Art and Music. 1945.
Mulk Raj Anand: A Critical Essay. 1948.
Song of a Falling World: Culture During the Break-up of the Roman Empire (A.D. 350–600). 1948.
Marxism and Contemporary Science; or, The Fulness of Life. 1949.
A World Ahead: Journal of a Soviet Journey. 1950.
Charles Dickens: A Biographical and Critical Study. 1950.
Byzantium into Europe: The Story of Byzantium as the First Europe (362–1204 A.D.) and Its Further Contribution till 1453 A.D. 1952.
Rumanian Summer, with M. Cornforth. 1953.
The Lotus and the Elephant. 1954.
Civil War in England: The Cromwellian Revolution. 1954.
George Meredith: His Life and Work. 1956.
The Romans Were Here: The Roman Period in Britain and Its Place in Our History. 1956.
After the Thirties: The Novel in Britain and Its Future. 1956.
Life Rarely Tells: An Autobiographical Account Ending in the Year 1921 and Situated Mostly in Brisbane, Queensland. 1958.
Arthur and His Times: Britain in the Dark Ages. 1958.
The Discovery of Britain: A Guide to Archaeology. 1958.
1764: The Hurly-Burly of Daily Life Exemplified in One Year of the 18th Century. 1959.
The Writing on the Wall: An Account of Pompeii in Its Last Days. 1960.
The Roaring Twenties: Literary Life in Sydney, New South Wales, in the Years 1921–26. 1960.
Death of the Hero: French Painting from David to Delacroix. 1960.
William Morris: Writer. 1961.
Our Celtic Heritage. 1962.
Fanfrolico and After (autobiography). 1962.
Daily Life in Roman Egypt. 1963.
Nine Days' Hero: Wat Tyler. 1964.
The Clashing Rocks: A Study of Early Greek Religion and Culture, and the Origins of Drama. 1965.
Leisure and Pleasure in Roman Egypt. 1965.
Our Anglo-Saxon Heritage. 1965.
J. M. W. Turner: His Life and Work: A Critical Biography. 1966.
Our Roman Heritage. 1967.
Meetings with Poets: Memories of Dylan Thomas, Edith Sitwell, Louis Aragon, Paul Eluard, Tristan Tzara. 1968.

Men and Gods on the Roman Nile. 1968.
The Ancient World: Manners and Morals. 1968.
Cézanne: His Life and Art. 1969.
The Origins of Alchemy in Graeco-Roman Egypt. 1970.
Cleopatra. 1971.
The Origins of Astrology. 1971.
Gustave Courbet: His Life and Work. 1973.
Helen of Troy: Woman and Goddess. 1974.
Blastpower and Ballistics: Concepts of Force and Energy in the Ancient World. 1974.
The Normans and Their World. 1974.
William Morris: His Life and Work. 1975.
The Troubadours and Their World of the Twelfth and Thirteenth Centuries. 1976.
Hogarth: His Art and World. 1977.
Decay and Renewal: Critical Essays on Twentieth Century Writing. 1977.
William Blake. 1978.
The Monster City: Defoe's London 1688–1730. 1978.

Editor, with Kenneth Slessor, *Poetry in Australia.* 1923.
Editor, with P. Warlock, *Loving Mad Tom: Bedlamite Verses of the XVI and XVII Centuries.* 1927.
Editor, *Metamorphosis of Aiax,* by John Harington. 1928.
Editor, *Parlement of Pratlers.* 1928.
Editor, *Delighted Earth,* by Robert Herrick. 1928.
Editor, *Inspiration.* 1928.
Editor, *Letters of Philip Stanhope, Second Earl of Chesterfield.* 1930.
Editor, with Edgell Rickword, *A Handbook of Freedom: A Record of English Democracy Through Twelve Centuries.* 1939.
Editor, with others, *New Lyrical Ballads.* 1945.
Editor, *Anvil: Life and the Arts: A Miscellany.* 1947.
Editor, *New Development Series.* 1947–48.
Editor, *Herrick: A Selection.* 1948.
Editor, *William Morris: A Selection.* 1948.
Editor, with Randall Swingler, *Key Poets.* 1950.
Editor, *Barefoot,* by Z. Stancu. 1950.
Editor, *Paintings and Drawings of Leslie Hurry.* 1952.
Editor, *The Sunset Ship: Poems of J. M. W. Turner.* 1966.
Editor, *The Autobiography of Joseph Priestley.* 1970.
Editor, *Clara's Lovers; or, A Novel on Blue Paper,* by William Morris. 1974.

Translator, *Lysistrata,* by Aristophanes. 1925.
Translator, *Satyricon and Poems,* by Petronius. 1927, revised edition, 1960.
Translator, *Homage to Sappho.* 1928.
Translator, *Complete Poems of Theocritus.* 1929.
Translator, *Hymns to Aphrodite,* by Homer. 1929.
Translator, *Women in Parliament,* by Aristophanes. 1929.
Translator, *The Mimiambs of Herondas.* 1929.
Translator, *The Complete Poetry of Gaius Catullus.* 1930.
Translator, *Sulpicia's Garland: Roman Poems.* 1930.
Translator, *Patchwork Quilt: Poems by Ausonius.* 1930.
Translator, *The Golden Ass,* by Apuleius. 1931; revised edition, 1960.
Translator, *I Am a Roman.* 1934.
Translator, *Medieval Latin Poets.* 1934.
Translator, *Daphnis and Chloe,* by Longus. 1948.
Translator, with S. Jolly, *Song of Peace,* by V. Nezval. 1951.

Translator, *Poems of Adam Mickiewicz.* 1957.
Translator, *Russian Poetry, 1917–1955.* 1957.
Translator, *Asklepiades in Love.* 1960.
Translator, *Modern Russian Poetry.* 1960.
Translator, *Cause, Principle, and Unity: 5 Dialogues,* by Giordano Bruno. 1962.
Translator, *Ribaldry of Ancient Greece.* 1965.
Translator, *Ribaldry of Ancient Rome.* 1965.
Translator, *The Elegy of Haido,* by Teferos Anthias. 1966.
Translator, *The Age of Akhenaten,* by Eleonore Bille-de-Mot. 1967.
Translator, *Greece, I Keep My Vigil for You,* by Teferos Anthias. 1968.

Reading List: *Mountain in the Sunlight* by Alick West, 1958.

*　　　*　　　*

The author of some forty novels, a number of plays, volumes of verse, historical, critical and autobiographical works, an editor and translator, Jack Lindsay is clearly an extraordinarily prolific writer – a fact which can easily obscure his very real distinction in some of the areas into which he has ventured. His co-editorship of *Vision* in Sydney in the early 1920's, for example, is still felt to have introduced a significant period in Australian culture, while his study of Dickens written in 1950 is highly regarded. But of all his work it is probably the novel to which he has made his most significant contribution.

Since 1936 when, to use his own words in *Fanfrolico and After,* he "reached bedrock," Lindsay has maintained a consistent Marxist viewpoint – and it is this viewpoint which if nothing else has guaranteed his novels a minor but certainly not negligible place in modern British literature. Feeling that "the historical novel is a form that has a limitless future as a fighting weapon and as a cultural instrument" (*New Masses,* January 1937), Lindsay first attempted to formulate his Marxist convictions in fiction mainly set in the past: particularly in his trilogy in English novels – *1649* (dealing with the Digger and Leveller movements), *Lost Birthright* (the Wilkesite agitations), and *Men of Forty-Eight* (written in 1939, the Chartist and revolutionary uprisings in Europe). Basically these works set out, with most success in the first volume, to vivify the historical traditions behind English Socialism and attempted to demonstrate that it stood, in Lindsay's words, for the "true completion of the national destiny."

Although the war years saw the virtual disintegration of the left-wing writing movement of the 1930's, Lindsay himself carried on: delving into contemporary affairs in *We Shall Return* and *Beyond Terror,* novels in which the epithets formerly reserved for the evil capitalists or Franco's soldiers have been transferred rather crudely to the German troops. After the war Lindsay continued to write mainly about the present – trying with varying degrees of success to come to terms with the unradical political realities of post-war England. In the series of novels known collectively as "the British Way," and beginning with *Betrayed Spring* in 1953, it seemed at first as if his solution was simply to resort to more and more obvious authorial manipulation and heavy-handed didacticism. Fortunately, however, from *Revolt of the Sons,* this process was reversed, as Lindsay began to show an increasing tendency to ignore party solutions, to fail indeed to give anything but the most elementary political consciousness to his characters, so that in his latest (and what appears to be his last) contemporary novel, *Choice of Times,* his hero, Colin, ends on a note of desperation: "Everything must be different, I can't live this way any longer. But how can I change it, how?" To his credit as an artist, Lindsay doesn't give him any explicit answer.

—David J. Smith

LINKLATER, Eric (Robert Russell). Scottish. Born in Dounby, Orkney, 8 March 1899. Educated at Aberdeen Grammar School; studied medicine, then English at the University of Aberdeen, M.A. 1925. Served as a private in the Black Watch, 1917–19; Major in the Royal Engineers, commanding the Royal Engineers Orkney Fortress, 1939–41; Member of Staff, Directorate of Public Relations, War Office, 1941–45; temporary Lieutenant-Colonel in Korea, 1951; Territorial Decoration. Married Marjorie MacIntyre in 1933; two sons and two daughters. Assistant Editor, *The Times of India*, Bombay, 1925–27; Assistant to the Professor of English Literature, University of Aberdeen, 1927–28; Commonwealth Fellow, Cornell University, Ithaca, New York, and the University of California, Berkeley, 1928–30; full-time writer from 1930. Rector of the University of Aberdeen, 1945–48; Deputy Lieutenant of Ross and Cromarty, Scotland, 1968–73. Recipient: Carnegie Medal, 1945. LL.D.: University of Aberdeen, 1946. Fellow of the Royal Society of Edinburgh, 1971. C.B.E. (Commander, Order of the British Empire), 1954. *Died 7 November 1974.*

PUBLICATIONS

Fiction

White-Maa's Saga. 1929.
Poet's Pub. 1929.
Juan in America. 1931.
The Men of Ness: The Saga of Thorlief Coalbiter's Sons. 1932.
The Crusader's Key (stories). 1933.
Magnus Merriman. 1934.
The Revolution (stories). 1934.
God Likes Them Plain: Short Stories. 1935.
Ripeness Is All. 1935.
Juan in China. 1937.
The Sailor's Holiday. 1937.
The Impregnable Women. 1938.
Judas. 1939.
Private Angelo. 1946.
Sealskin Trousers and Other Stories. 1947.
A Spell for Old Bones. 1949.
Mr. Byculla. 1950.
Laxdale Hall. 1951.
The House of Gair. 1953.
The Faithful Ally. 1954; as *The Sultan and the Lady,* 1955.
The Dark of Summer. 1956.
A Sociable Plover and Other Stories and Conceits. 1957.
Position at Noon. 1958; as *My Father and I,* 1959.
The Merry Muse. 1959.
Roll of Honour. 1961.
Husband of Delilah. 1962.
A Man over Forty. 1963.
A Terrible Freedom. 1966.
The Stories. 1968.

Plays

The Devil's in the News (produced in 1930's). 1934.
Crisis in Heaven (produced 1944). 1944.

To Meet the MacGregors (produced 1946?).   In *Two Comedies*, 1950.
Love in Albania (produced 1948).   1950.
Two Comedies.   1950.
The Mortimer Touch (as *The Atom Doctor*, produced 1950; as *The Mortimer Touch*, produced 1952).   1952.
Breakspear in Gascony.   1958.

Screenplay: *The Man Between*, with Harry Kurnitz, 1953.

Verse

A Dragon Laughed and Other Poems.   1930.

Other

Ben Jonson and King James: Biography and Portrait.   1931.
Mary, Queen of Scots.   1933.
Robert the Bruce.   1934.
The Lion and the Unicorn; or, What England Has Meant to Scotland.   1935.
The Cornerstones: A Conversation in Elysium.   1941.
The Defence of Calais.   1941.
The Man on My Back (autobiography).   1941.
The Northern Garrisons: The Defence of Iceland and the Faroe, Orkney and Shetland Islands.   1941.
The Raft, and Socrates Asks Why: Two Conversations.   1942.
The Highland Division.   1942.
The Great Ship, and Rabelais Replies: Two Conversations.   1944.
The Wind on the Moon (juvenile).   1944.
The Art of Adventure (essays).   1947.
The Pirates in the Deep Green Sea (juvenile).   1949.
The Campaign in Italy.   1951.
Our Men in Korea.   1952.
A Year of Space: A Chapter in Autobiography.   1953.
The Ultimate Viking (essays).   1955.
Karina with Love (juvenile).   1958.
Edinburgh.   1960.
Sweden, photographs by Karl Werner Gullers.   1964.
Orkney and Shetland: An Historical, Geographical, Social and Scenic Survey.   1965.
The Prince in the Heather.   1965.
The Conquest of England.   1966.
The Survival of Scotland: A Review of Scottish History from Roman Times to the Present Day.   1968.
Scotland.   1968.
The Secret Larder.   1969.
The Royal House of Scotland.   1970.
Fanfare for a Tin Hat (autobiography).   1970.
The Music of the North.   1970.
A Corpse on Clapham Common: A Tale of Sixty Years Ago.   1971.
Voyage of the "Challenger."   1972.
The Black Watch, with Andro Linklater.   1976.

Editor, *The Thistle and the Pen: An Anthology of Modern Scottish Writers*.   1950.
Editor, *John Moore's England: A Selection from His Writings*.   1970.

*   *   *

A professional writer in the fullest sense of the term, Eric Linklater turned his hand successfully to fiction, history, essays, drama, children's books, and autobiography, delighting a wide range of readers with his elegant prose and robust intelligence.

As a historian he was particularly concerned with Scotland, with the Viking world of his Orkney forebears, and with the British Army. He wrote of soldiering with a historian's grasp of strategy and an infantry officer's eye for tactics; of soldiers he wrote with the compassion of one who had roistered as a Private in the Black Watch and known chill fear in his bowels as a sniper in No-man's-land. If two paradoxical extremes seem to co-exist here, the same is true of his attitude to Scottish history. A patriotic (even sometimes romantically patriotic) Orkneyman and Scot, he nevertheless maintained that Scotland's history before 1707 was but an epic tale and that Scotland's greatest glory, her intellectual flowering in the 18th and 19th centuries, was nurtured in large measure by the stability the Union brought about. Such extremes are also reflected in his work as a novelist, for he explored a variety of themes and experimented at different times with a variety of narrative techniques.

His early comic success in *Poet's Pub* was followed by *Juan in America* and *Juan in China*, which recount the adventures in love and war of an English descendant of Byron's Don Juan. Full of exuberant invention, these picaresque novels are as good as anything in their kind. But he also wrote at this time *The Men of Ness*, cast in the spare stylistic mould of Norse saga, and a stark contrast to his other prose of that period (he himself wrote in *The Man on My Back* that he earlier "drank deeply of the Elizabethan writers, and the fumes of their prodigious eloquence hung in my brain for years"). Later he was also to experiment, not too successfully, with alternating structures of prose and verse in the sombre pages of *Roll of Honour*.

In *Magnus Merriman* Linklater turned to the Scottish scene, to satirise the ongoings at a by-election and take ranging shots at Edinburgh and London society in the 1930's. Other books set in Scotland include *The Merry Muse*, an uproarious novel about the discovery of bawdy poems written by Robert Burns; *The Dark of Summer*, a strange tale of espionage and politics in the northern isles; and the Highland comedy *Laxdale Hall*.

Behind the apparent diversity of his later novels, both comic and more serious, lie two unifying themes. The first is the problem of freedom and independence in a world dominated by bureaucratic institutions; the second is the nature of personal heredity. The hero of *Private Angelo* is in conflict with organised society in the shape of military discipline. He deserts from the Italian army, escapes from the German, and is abducted from the British, ending up as a free man in his own *paese* – but free only within the rule of his forceful young wife. The neatly contrived *Position at Noon* presents an emotionally and financially bankrupt figure who blames his predicament on his booby of a father, and then traces the predicaments of successive generations backwards to the energetic ruffian who founded the family. The firm historical sense, the irony and wit, are held in perfect balance; and the blend of fact and fantasy in the chapter in which Wordsworth and Coleridge figure is one of the most hilarious inventions in English fiction.

Eric Linklater exhibited in marked degree "the Caledonian anti-syzygy," the yoking together of conflicting qualities; a precise and literal vision, and a strain of wild fantasy; an unlikely conjunction of sober-siddedness and a quick sense of the ludicrous. All this was controlled by intellect, discipline, and careful craftsmanship; and his work is in consequence always both entertaining and thought-provoking.

—Stewart F. Sanderson

LOCKE, David Ross. See **NASBY, Petroleum V.**

LOCKRIDGE, Ross. American. Born in Bloomington, Indiana, 25 April 1914. Educated at Indiana University, Bloomington, B.A. in English 1935; did post-graduate work at Harvard University, Cambridge, Massachusetts, 1940–41. Married Vernice Baker in 1937; four children. Instructor in English at Indiana University, 1936–40, and at Simmons College, Boston, 1941–47. *Died* (by suicide) *6 March 1948.*

PUBLICATIONS

Fiction

   Raintree County. 1948.

Reading List: *Ross and Tom: Two American Tragedies* by John Leggett, 1974.

*   *   *

   Ross Lockridge's one published work, the sprawling thousand-page novel *Raintree County*, was a huge popular and critical success in 1948. Praised as "a novel of rare stature," the first American epic since *Moby-Dick*, then increasingly disparaged as "an amalgam of undigested Wolfe, murky Faulkner, and watery Whitman," it is now rarely read or mentioned. Periodically literary historians try to restore it to prominence, even eminence, but with lean results, perhaps because the novel's sunny optimism, frontier humor, and abiding faith in the American dream are not congenial to contemporary readers. On all its many layers, *Raintree County* is an exuberant Fourth of July festival of Americana.
   On the Fourth of July, 1892, in the small town of Waycross, Indiana, the townspeople join together for a holiday of celebration, oratory, reminiscence, as observed by John Wickliff Shawnessy, a 53-year-old schoolteacher reunited with his boyhood friends – a sleek senator, an ailing railroad tycoon, a wry journalist. Flash-backs re-create their common past, which eventuates in montage: structurally, events in John's life contrast with national events (his wedding is counterpointed with John Brown's execution, the birth of his son with the firing on Fort Sumter), and stylistically each event is viewed in the contrasting styles of fictitious newspaper accounts, old diaries and letters, blustering gossips and salty frontiersmen. The montages build into a panoramic view of American history and a critique of the 19th-century corrosion of the Declaration of Independence. The omniscient, disillusioned, but still hopeful narrator implies that the second American Revolution was the Civil War, epic atonement for slavery, and that the third was the Rail Strike of 1877, epic industrialism and enslavement of the poor. The urbane, witty journalist (a fine comic character) is the hero's Darwinian alter ego, cosmopolitan theoretician of the American experiences that Hoosier Johnny must undergo and struggle to understand – such as soldiering against the South, watching the first trains arrive in the Mid-West. The hero himself, a Jeffersonian idealist, is also America's

fledgling poet, the modern Johnny Appleseed restoring the national earth with his words, his ideals, and his faith. Ringed with comic Bunyanesque characters and somber Lincolnesque tragedies, Johnny is in many ways the uncorruptible soul of epic America, and his life documents the century's "contest for my soul." On multiple levels of historical and literary allusion, each level complete with its contrapuntal movements of personal and national life, Lockridge weaves a kaleidoscopic epic, striving to be myth, that owes obvious debts to Joyce, Melville, Whitman. Lockridge's America is "mancreated," "greatchested," "buntinghung." Though the symbolism is sometimes muddled, and the sentiment sometimes saccharine, Lockridge's gigantesque conception and his technical virtuosity were perhaps unparalleled in America until Pynchon's *Gravity's Rainbow*. There is ample reason to consider *Raintree County* an important novel for its era and a substantial achievement.

—Jan Hokenson

LODGE, Thomas. English. Born in West Ham, London, c. 1558. Educated at the Merchant Taylors' School, London, 1571–73; Trinity College, Oxford, matriculated 1573, B.A. 1577, M.A. 1581; entered Lincoln's Inn, London, 1578; later studied medicine at Avignon: M.D. 1600; awarded M.D. at Oxford, 1602; admitted to the College of Physicians, London, 1610. Married 1) Joan Lodge in 1583, one daughter; 2) Mrs. Jane Aldred. Settled in London, 1578; gave up study of law for a literary career, c. 1580; a friend of Robert Greene, and probably of Rich, Daniel, Drayton, and Lyly; served with Captain Clarke on an expedition to the Terceras and Canary Islands, 1588, and with Thomas Cavendish on an expedition to Brazil and the Straits of Magellan, 1591–93; returned to London, and resumed literary career, 1593–96; converted to Roman catholicism; abandoned literature, and practised medicine, in London, from 1600. *Died in September 1625.*

PUBLICATIONS

Collections

Complete Works, edited by Edmund Gosse.   4 vols., 1883.

Fiction

An Alarum Against Usurers, The Delectable History of Forbonius and Prisceria, The Lamentable Complaint of Truth over England.   1584.
Rosalynde: Euphues' Golden Legacy.   1590; as *Euphues' Golden Legacy,* 1612; edited by Geoffrey Bullough, in *Narrative and Dramatic Sources of Shakespeare 2,* 1958.
The Famous, True, and Historical Life of Robert Second Duke of Normandy.   1591.
Euphues' Shadow, The Battle of the Senses, The Deaf Man's Dialogue.   1592.
The Life and Death of William Long Beard, with Many Other Histories.   1593.
A Margarite of America.   1596; edited by G. B. Harrison, 1927.

Plays

> The Wounds of Civil War, Lively Set Forth in the True Tragedies of Marius and Sylla (produced 1588?). 1594; edited by Joseph W. Houppert, 1969.
> A Looking Glass for London and England, with Robert Greene (produced 1590?). 1594; edited by T. Hayashi, 1970.

Verse

> Scilla's Metamorphosis, Interlaced with the Unfortunate Love of Glaucus, with Sundry Other Poems and Sonnets. 1589; as A Most Pleasant History of Glaucus and Scilla, 1610; edited by N. Alexander, 1967.
> Phillis: Honoured with Pastoral Sonnets, Elegies, and Amorous Delights; The Tragical Complaint of Elstred. 1593; edited by M. F. Crow, 1896.
> A Fig for Momus, Containing Satires, Eclogues, and Epistles. 1595.

Other

> A Defence of Poetry, Music, and Stage Plays. 1579(?).
> Catharos: Diogenes in His Singularity. 1591.
> The Devil Conjured. 1596.
> Wit's Misery and the World's Madness. 1596.
> Prosopopoeia: Containing the Tears of the Mother of God. 1596.
> The Poor Man's Talent, in Complete Works. 1883.

> Translator, The Flowers of Lodowicke of Granado, by Michael ab Isselt. 1601.
> Translator, The Famous Works of Josephus. 1602.
> Translator, A Treatise of the Plague, by F. Valleriole. 1603.
> Translator, The Works of Seneca. 1614; selections edited by W. Clode, 1888, and by W. H. D. Rouse, 1899.
> Translator, A Learned Summary upon the Famous Poem of William of Saluste, Lord of Bartas, Translated Out of French. 1621.

Bibliography: Lodge: A Concise Bibliography by S. A. Tannenbaum, 1940; Lodge 1939–65 by R. C. Johnson, 1968.

Reading List: Lodge by Edward A. Tenney, 1935; Lodge, Gentleman by Pat M. Ryan, 1958; Lodge by W. D. Rae, 1967.

*   *   *

Thomas Lodge's main claim to literary recognition lies in his pastoral romance, Rosalynde: Euphues Golden Legacie. For all the title's apparent indebtedness to Lyly, the work derives less from Euphues itself than from classical sources common to both Lyly and Lodge. Two fables intertwine in Rosalynde. Dominant much of the time is the narrative concerning the fates of two girls, Rosalynde and Alinda, who escape into the Forest of Arden to avoid the wrath of King Torismond, Alinda's father and Rosalynde's uncle. In the Forest they encounter Rosader, one of the three sons of Sir John of Bordeaux. Rosalynde is secretly in love with Rosader, and he with her; but because Rosalynde is disguised as a page, calling herself Ganymede, she is naturally unrecognized by her lover. The second narrative concerns Sir John's sons and the ways in which they succeed or fail in living up to their dead father's precepts. With the meeting of Rosalynde and Rosader, the two narratives combine. The lovers compete in impromptu versifying, after Rosalynde has challenged Rosader to demonstrate, in "some amorous eclogue," the depth of his love for the mistress he cannot see in her.

Rosalynde is, of course, the source for Shakespeare's *As You Like It*, but it is important to acknowledge the work for its own merits. Lodge's medium, a highly polished prose interspersed with gentle songs, is appropriate for the stories he has to tell and for his neat, if conventional, antithesis of court and country. His pastoral idyll knows few hardships, as the philosophical Corydon tells Alinda: "Envy stirs not us, we covet not to climb, our desires mount not above our degrees, nor our thoughts above our fortunes. Care cannot harbour in our cottages, nor do homely couches know broken slumbers: as we exceed not in diet, so we have enough to satisfy: and, mistress, I have so much Latin, *Satis est quod sufficit*." As well as the thought, the style of this passage speaks proudly of its origins; in the sentence "Care cannot harbour in our cottages, nor do homely couches know broken slumbers," Lodge achieves with the uninflected language a chiastic symmetry that Ovid would have approved.

Lodge treats the lovers' verses with a delicate seriousness. The situation, with Alinda playing on her pipe while Rosalynde and Rosader vie with each other in lyrics, is, in the extreme, artificial. Yet Lodge's tact in avoiding excess, either in the verse or in the prose, is such that the comedy is gentle, but never ludicrous; disbelief is always willingly suspended.

> Love in my bosom like a bee
> Doth suck his sweet:
> Now with his wings he plays with me,
> Now with his feet.
> Within mine eyes he makes his nest,
> His bed amidst my tender breast;
> My kisses are his daily feast,
> And yet he robs me of my rest.
> Ah, wanton, will ye?

Lyrics such as this deserve a place in the Elizabethan anthology. Lighter in touch than some of Wyatt's, they have also a whimsical humour which his poems often lack.

In *A Looking Glass for London*, which he wrote with Robert Greene, Lodge takes a stern look at the sorry state of the nation. A conqueror who rivals Tamburlaine ("*Rasni* is God on earth and none but he") indulges his lust for women; his extravagant wife scents herself with all the perfumes of Arabia; a usurer deprives a poor man of his cow and then bribes the judge to pervert the course of justice; the blacksmith's servant beats his master — all are comically exaggerated characters, and all, of course, are properly punished. Jonah's Nineveh is the meeting-place for these incongruous characters, and there is always at hand the doom-laden prophet Oseas, who can extend the moral to sixteenth-century London:

> If such escapes ô London raigne in thee:
> Repent, for why each sin shall punisht bee.
> Repent, amend, repent, the houre is nie,
> Defer not time, who knowes when he shall die?

Lodge also attempted writings in other popular Renaissance genres, and although there is nothing especially striking about, for instance, his satires in *A Fig for Momus* there is, equally, nothing to be ashamed of. He is always careful and competent, applying the best of his skill to the matter in hand, whether as a pastoral sonneteer in *Phillis*, or as a medical practitioner in a pamphlet giving advice to the poor and sick on the management of the plague. Like other writers of his time, he held literature in the highest esteem; in his *Reply* to Stephen Gosson's attack on the stage, he wrote: "Poetes were the first raysors of cities, prescribers of good lawes, mayntayners of religion, disturbors of the wicked, advancers of the wel disposed, inventors of laws, and lastly the very fot-paths to knowledge, and understanding."

—Roma Gill

LONDON, Jack (John Griffith London). American. Born in San Francisco, California, 12 January 1876. Educated at a grammar school in Oakland, California; Oakland High School, 1895–96; University of California, Berkeley, 1896–97. Married 1) Bessie Maddern in 1900 (separated, 1903; divorced, 1905), two daughters; 2) Charmian Kittredge in 1905. Worked in a cannery in Oakland, 1890; sailor on the *Sophie Sutherland*, sailing to Japan and Siberia, 1893; returned to Oakland, wrote for the local paper, and held various odd jobs, 1893–94; tramped the United States and Canada, 1894–96: arrested for vagrancy in Niagara Falls, New York; joined the gold rush to the Klondike, 1897–98, then returned to Oakland and became a full-time writer; visited London, 1902; War Correspondent in the Russo-Japanese War for the *San Francisco Examiner*, 1904; settled on a ranch in Sonoma County, California, 1906, and lived there for the rest of his life; attempted to sail round the world on a 45-foot yacht, 1907–09; War Correspondent in Mexico, 1914. *Died 22 November 1916.*

PUBLICATIONS

Collections

> *Short Stories*, edited by Maxwell Geismar. 1960.
> *(Works)*, edited by I. O. Evans. 18 vols., 1962–68.
> *The Bodley Head London*, edited by Arthur Calder-Marshall. 4 vols., 1963–66.

Fiction

> *The Son of the Wolf: Tales of the Far North.* 1900; as *An Odyssey of the North*, 1915.
> *The God of His Fathers and Other Stories.* 1901; as *The God of His Fathers: Tales of the Klondike*, 1902.
> *Children of the Frost* (stories). 1902.
> *The Cruise of the Dazzler.* 1902.
> *A Daughter of the Snows.* 1902.
> *The Kempton-Wace Letters*, with Anna Strumsky. 1903.
> *The Call of the Wild.* 1903.
> *The Sea-Wolf.* 1904.
> *The Faith of Men and Other Stories.* 1904.
> *Tales of the Fish Patrol.* 1905.
> *The Game.* 1905.
> *White Fang.* 1906.

Moon-Face and Other Stories.   1906.
Love of Life and Other Stories.   1907.
Before Adam.   1907.
The Road (stories).   1907.
The Iron Heel.   1908.
Martin Eden.   1909.
Burning Daylight.   1910.
Lost Face (stories).   1910.
When God Laughs and Other Stories.   1911.
South Sea Tales.   1911.
Adventure.   1911.
The Strength of the Strong (story).   1911.
The House of Pride and Other Tales of Hawaii.   1912.
A Son of the Sun (stories).   1912; as *The Adventures of Captain Grief,* 1954.
Smoke Bellew (stories).   1912; as *Smoke and Shorty,* 1920.
The Night-Born, and Also The Madness of John Horned, When the World Was Young,
    The Benefit of the Doubt, Winged Blackmail, Bunches of Knuckles, War, Under the
    Deck Awnings, To Kill a Man, The Mexican.   1913.
The Abysmal Brute.   1913.
John Barleycorn.   1913; as *John Barleycorn; or, Alcoholic Memoirs,* 1914.
The Valley of the Moon.   1913.
The Mutiny of the Elsinore.   1914.
The Strength of the Strong (collection).   1914.
The Scarlet Plague.   1915.
The Jacket (The Star Rover).   1915.
The Little Lady of the Big House.   1916.
The Turtles of Tasman (stories).   1916.
The Human Drift.   1917.
Jerry of the Islands.   1917.
Michael, Brother of Jerry.   1917.
Hearts of Three.   1918.
The Red One (stories).   1918.
On the Makaloa Mat.   1919; as *Island Tales,* 1920.
Dutch Courage and Other Stories.   1922.
The Assassination Bureau Ltd., completed by Robert L. Fish.   1963.
Stories of Hawaii, edited by A. Grove Day.   1965.

Plays

Scorn of Woman.   1906.
Theft.   1910.
The Acorn-Planters: A California Forest Play.   1916.
Daughters of the Rich, edited by James E. Sisson.   1971.

Other

The People of the Abyss.   1903.
War of the Classes.   1905.
London: A Sketch of His Life and Work.   1905.
Revolution.   1909.
Revolution and Other Essays.   1910.
The Cruise of the Snark.   1911.

754

London by Himself. 1913.
Letters from Jack London, Containing an Unpublished Correspondence Between London and Sinclair Lewis, edited by King Hendricks and Irving Shepard. 1965.

Bibliography: *London: A Bibliography* by Hensley C. Woodbridge, John London, and George H. Tweney, 1966, supplement by Woodbridge, 1973; in *Bibliography of American Literature* by Jacob Blanck, 1969.

Reading List: *Sailor on Horseback: The Biography of London* by Irving Stone, 1938; *London: A Biography* by Richard O'Connor, 1964; *London, American Rebel* by Philip S. Foner, 1964; *London* by Earle Labor, 1974; *London: The Man, The Writer, The Rebel* by Robert Barltrop, 1977; *Jack: A Biography* by Andrew Sinclair, 1977.

* * *

Jack London was a talented writer so caught up in certain myths that they were part of what destroyed him. The illegitimate son of an impoverished spiritualist, Flora Wellman, he early learned self-reliance. Although he attended high school and, briefly, college, he was largely self-educated. London's university was the world he experienced and subsequently wrote about: San Francisco Bay, first as an oyster pirate and then as a member of the State Fish Patrol; the Pacific, the Orient, and the Bering Sea as an able seaman on a schooner hunting seals; the nation, across which he tramped as a vagabond; Alaska, where he prospected for gold; and California, where eventually he was a wealthy landowner burdened by the problems of maintaining a large ranch. London saw himself as an exemplar of the rags-to-riches story, an Anglo-Saxon superman who succeeded because of his superior intelligence and physical prowess, who took pride in his individualism, yet sympathized with the masses and believed that some form of socialism was the cure for the inequities of capitalist society.

To assert that his deprived childhood and his personal adventures were central to his development is not to deny that he was profoundly influenced by what he read as a young man. Early in his adolescence he delved into the seminal thinkers of the nineteenth century; his biographer Andrew Sinclair writes that during a winter in the Alaskan Klondike London absorbed "the books that became the bedrock of his thought and writing, underlying even the socialism which was his faith." Among London's readings that winter were the works of Darwin, Thomas Huxley, Spencer, and Kipling. "Charles Darwin and Herbert Spencer, messiahs of the new creed, became his intellectual mentors, along with Frederich Nietzsche and Karl Marx," Charles Child Walcutt wrote in a pamphlet about London, declaring that the author's struggles came to seem to himself "an epitome of the Darwinian Struggle for Existence, his success an example of the Spencerian Survival of the Fittest." Natural laws governed everything, London decided, so his problem became to reconcile the unimportance of the individual in a Darwinian universe and the Marxist certainty of social revolution with his equal certainty that he had the force and intelligence to rise above his fellow men.

His writing constantly reflects these contradictory beliefs, sometimes emphasizing one, sometimes another. In a succession of essays, short stories, novels, plays, travel books, and autobiographical tracts — during his forty years of life he wrote more than fifty books, too many for them all to be good — he portrayed the immutable laws of nature and man's need for community, while at the same time creating heroic figures who dominated both people and environment. As London's success grew, he heeded his socialist beliefs less, ultimately in his fiction painting what he liked to think were self-portraits of supermen defying the forces of nature and the demands of capitalism or of the masses. At his best London was able to hold these contradictions in balance; and technically his work, as H. L. Mencken wrote in *Prejudices: First Series,* contained "all the elements of sound fiction: clear thinking, a sense of character, the dramatic instinct, and, above all, the adept putting together of words —

words charming and slyly significant, words arranged, in the French phrase, for the respiration and the ear." But finally his techniques could not sustain work that had lost its thematic equilibrium. He was an individualist, not a socialist. His lip service to socialism, wrote Walcutt, was "a protest against his early poverty"; London, he added, never dwelled on what might be the benefits of socialism.

London's heroes and heroines are individualists who survive the challenges of nature and society if they are strong enough, or are defeated if they are not – or, one might add, if London was pained by his socialist conscience. Thus in what is perhaps his best and best known story, *The Call of the Wild*, the powerful dog Buck, snatched from an easy life and submitted to brutal treatment and a harsh environment in the Klondike, survives because he is the superior individual. Buck, returned to the world of his ancestors, eventually runs with a pack of wolves, but he is at their head, where his intelligence and strength have put him. Wolf Larsen, the superman figure of *The Sea-Wolf*, both attracts and repels the beautiful, fragile poetess Maud Brewster and the effete Humphrey Van Weyden, whom Larsen rescues aboard his ship, the *Ghost*. Antagonized by Larsen, the two escape to an island, only to have him reappear aboard the wrecked *Ghost*. The arrogant individualist Larsen eventually dies, but it is his strength and skill that are admirable; the other two survive because they become strong like Wolf, yet lack his utter egotism. London would later assert that his point had been that a Wolf Larsen could not survive in modern society; but clearly he empathized with the arch-individualist, and Van Weyden's victory comes only after he has assimilated Larsen's qualities.

Another of London's heroes, Martin Eden, would die because of his individualism, but his death by suicide seems gratuitous, not, as London claimed, the result of Eden's believing in nothing and not accepting the socialism the author professed to favor. London could not portray a socialist state even before he abandoned socialism, which he did in his fiction when – as in the novels *Burning Daylight*, *The Valley of the Moon*, and *The Little Lady of the Big House* – he blatantly espoused Aryan supermen and escape from the urban masses. His socialist novel *The Iron Heel* takes the form of a text discovered long after socialism has triumphed. What the novel describes, however, is not a socialist utopia, but the violent rise of a repressive totalitarian state opposed by small cadres of insurgents led by a blond superman, Ernest Everhard. By 1914, when London reported for *Collier's* magazine on the revolution in Mexico, he "no longer spoke as the compassionate revolutionary," notes Andrew Sinclair, "but as the racist and jingoist supporter of the American oil interests – a man of property, a man used to servants, who was echoing the views of other men used to property and servants."

London died in 1916, by then severely ill and depressed by the recognition that he could not live out the myths he portrayed in his fiction. Still, he had not failed; his best work is vivid and dramatic; and his hyperbole, if annoying, nevertheless tells the reader much about United States culture.

—Townsend Ludington

LONGSTREET, Augustus Baldwin. American. Born in Augusta, Georgia, 22 September 1790. Educated at the Waddell Academy, Willington, South Carolina, 1808–11; Yale University, New Haven, Connecticut, 1811–13, graduated 1813; Litchfield, Connecticut Law School, 1813–14; admitted to the Georgia bar, 1815. Married Frances Eliza Parke in 1816. Practised law in Greensboro, Georgia, from 1816; Member, Georgia Legislature, 1821; Circuit Judge, Superior Court of Georgia, 1822–25; settled in Augusta, 1827;

contributed to the *Southern Recorder*, Milledgeville, Georgia, and various other newspapers, 1827–30; Founding Editor, *The Sentinel*, Augusta, 1834–36; ordained Methodist minister, 1838; President, Emory College, Oxford, Georgia, 1839–48, Centenary College, Jackson, Louisiana, 1849, University of Mississippi, 1849–56, and the University of South Carolina, Columbia, 1857–65; settled in Mississippi, 1865. *Died 9 July 1870.*

PUBLICATIONS

Fiction and Sketches

Georgia Scenes, Characters, and Incidents, etc. 1835.
Master William Mitten; or, A Youth of Brilliant Talents Who Was Ruined by Bad Luck. 1864.
Stories with a Moral, Humorous and Descriptive of Southern Life a Century Ago, edited by Fitz. R. Longstreet. 1912.

Other

A Voice from the South. 1847.

Bibliography: in *Bibliography of American Literature* by Jacob Blanck, 1973.

Reading List: *Judge Longstreet: A Life Sketch* by O. P. Fitzgerald, 1891 (includes letters and unpublished material); *Longstreet: A Study of the Development of Culture in the South* by John Donald Wade, 1924, edited by M. Thomas Inge, 1969.

*   *   *

Augustus Baldwin Longstreet's reputation rests primarily on *Georgia Scenes*, a collection of sketches and tales about life in Middle Georgia in the early nineteenth century. *Georgia Scenes* contrasted with the plantation literary tradition which focused on wealthy slaveholding landowners. As a circuit-court judge, Longstreet visited many rural communities and collected humorous stories and anecdotes of rough but colorful country people. Their simple amusements such as barn dances, horse-swapping, and shooting matches are affectionately recorded, along with a slightly more brutal side of life (gander-pulling, fights, and political disputes). Overt cruelty and violence are generally overlooked. For example, in "The Fight" the maiming of the combatants is treated in an almost slapstick vein. In his close attention to physical details and settings and in his attempts to write colloquial dialogue, Longstreet anticipated the local color writers of the post-civil war period. His best works, such as "Turn-Out," in which unruly country boys playfully "force" their schoolmaster to give them a day's vacation, are based on folk traditions and rituals and possess an archetypal power. Poe praised Longstreet because he was anxious to see American writers use native materials in their stories.

Longstreet was forty before he turned his hand to fiction. First his legal career, then his work as newspaper owner and editor, and later his ministry in the Methodist Church took precedence over authorship. He sometimes feared his comic sketches were undignified; in fact, everything he wrote expressed firm religious beliefs and conservative political views. In *Georgia Scenes* his narrator, Hall, describes rural escapades, while the character Baldwin ridicules the affectations of newly rich townspeople. Both are aloof and frequently disapproving, like the author. Blacks, although they seldom appear in the stories, are treated comically or with contempt. Later essays, such as those collected in *A Voice from the South*, were devoted to defending slavery.

In his own day Longstreet was best known as the president of four different Southern universities. Some of his experiences with students are included in his only novel, *William Mitten*. As a record of the times this neglected work is as informative as *Georgia Scenes*; and the author's characterizations of William and William's mother and uncle reveal a surer sense of satire and of the dynamics of family life than one finds in the earlier work. His essays on religious and political subjects and the posthumously collected tales in *Stories with a Moral* are elegantly phrased but discursive and tedious. He eventually considered himself more of a moral guide or social historian than a story-teller. Although some critics consider Longstreet a frontier humorist, he is primarily a Southern writer, highly didactic, constructing a value system unique to his region.

—Kimball King

LOVECRAFT, H(oward) P(hillips).   American.   Born in Providence, Rhode Island, 20 August 1890, and lived there for the rest of his life. Educated in local schools. Married the writer Sonia Greene in 1924 (divorced, 1929). Writer from 1908, supporting himself by ghost writing and working as a revisionist; regular contributor to *Weird Tales* from 1923. *Died 15 March 1937.*

PUBLICATIONS

Collections

> *Collected Poems.*   1963.
> *Selected Letters 1911–1931*, edited by August Derleth and Donald Wandrei.   3 vols., 1965–71.

Fiction

> *The Shadow over Innsmouth.*   1936.
> *The Outsider and Others*, edited by August Derleth and Donald Wandrei.   1939.
> *The Survivor and Others*, with August Derleth.   1957.
> *Dreams and Fancies.*   1962.
> *Dagon and Other Macabre Tales.*   1965.
> *The Dark Brotherhood.*   1966.

Other

> *Beyond the Wall of Sleep* (miscellany), edited by August Derleth and Donald Wandrei.   1943.

Marginalia, edited by August Derleth and Donald Wandrei. 1944.
Something about Cats and Other Pieces, edited by August Derleth. 1949.
The Shuttered Room and Other Pieces, with others, edited by August Derleth. 1959.

Bibliography: *The New Lovecraft Bibliography* by Jack Chalker, 1962, revised edition, as *Mirage on Lovecraft,* 1965.

Reading List: *H. P. L.: A Memoir,* 1945, and *Some Notes on Lovecraft,* 1959, both by August Derleth; "Lovecraft Issue" of *Fresco,* Spring 1958; *Lovecraft: A Biography* by L. Sprague de Camp, 1975; *The Lovecraft Companion* by Philip A. Shreffler, 1977.

*   *   *

    H. P. Lovecraft's reputation depends not so much on any particular one of the sixty-odd fantastic stories that he published, mostly in the pulp magazine *Weird Tales,* but rather on the way in which most of these stories contribute to what has become known since the author's death as the "Cthulhu Mythos." Although the stories are not consistent with each other and although Lovecraft never codified his cosmology (he was a visionary, not a blueprint-maker), the basic construct of the Mythos is that, in the days before mankind, this planet was inhabited by a group of fish-like beings called the "Old Ones," who worshipped Cthulhu, represented in "The Call of Cthulhu" as a gigantic, gelatinous form. Apparently because their culture decayed, the "Old Ones" were driven from the earth by man; but they were not destroyed. Led by the apparently immortal Yog-Sothoth, they retreated to the remote, dark planet Yogguth, where they still conspire to regain control of the earth. Sometimes, as in "The Whisperer in Darkness," they contemplate an attack on a decadent mankind; but more often, as in Lovecraft's longest work, "The Case of Charles Dexter Ward," they seek, through unspeakable rites of black magic, to mate with human beings through the connivance of dissolute human collaborators.
    The generally suppressed knowledge of the Cthulhuites has been hinted at only in the forbidden *Necronomicon* of the mad Arab Abdul Alhazred, one Latin copy of which is preserved at Miskatonic University in Arkham, a mouldering New England seaport that is the setting of many of Lovecraft's tales. When the plots of the "Old Ones" are foiled, the earthly invaders or fishy-looking halfbreeds dissolve leaving behind only a pool of noxious-smelling, jelly-like material. Those who are willfully or inadvertently involved in the conspiracies – like those in "The Dunwich Horror" and "The Color Out of Space" – usually face madness and inevitable destruction. The Mythos, despite vagueness and inconsistencies, is a remarkable fictional manifestation of the mentality that has produced many conspiratorial theories about local and extra-terrestrial threats to human societies. At first Lovecraft had difficulty finding readers, but he found his advocate to the world in 1926 when he attracted the attention of August Derleth. Derleth expanded and regularized the mythos, kept it in print, and even invited others to contribute to it; and Lovecraft attracted a small but fanatical band of cultists in the United States and abroad, especially in France.
    Ordinary critical standards are irrelevant to such an enterprise. Lovecraft's fables were often awkwardly plotted and obscurely worded, but so are many "scriptures." Critics complained that he did not write novels, but, like Poe, his visions were best suited to shorter forms. Although many find his fantasies preposterous, he did create one of the most remarkable imaginative constructs of the twentieth century – an original myth that arises from a child's enormous fascination with sex and his repressive fear of it. Lovecraft's uniqueness lies in his ability to preserve – if perhaps only through dreams – and to articulate in adulthood the fantasies that provide a child's internal defense against inscrutable threats.

—Warren French

LOVER, Samuel. Irish. Born in Dublin, 24 February 1797. Educated privately. Married 1) Miss Berrel in 1827 (died, 1847); 2) Miss Wandby in 1852. Worked in his father's stock brokerage, Dublin, but left to become a painter: miniaturist, marine painter, and illustrator, in Dublin, 1818–33: elected to the Royal Hibernian Academy, 1828, and became its Secretary, 1830; exhibited at the Academy, 1832, and at the Royal Academy, London, 1833; also a song writer, librettist, and singer, from 1818; a Founder, 1833, and contributor to the *Dublin University Magazine*; settled in London, 1835: worked as a painter, and contributed to various periodicals; one of the founders of *Bentley's Miscellany*; gave up painting because of failing eyesight, 1844; devised a one-man show of his own works, "Irish Evenings," and presented it in London, 1844–46, and in America, 1846–48; returned to London, and devised a second one-man show, "Paddy's Portfolio," 1848, then resumed his earlier occupation of opera librettist; devoted himself mainly to song writing, 1852–64; retired to Dublin. *Died 6 July 1868.*

PUBLICATIONS

Collections

    Poetical Works. 1880.
    Collected Writings, edited by J. J. Roche. 10 vols., 1901–13.
    Works, edited by J. J. Roche. 6 vols., 1902.

Fiction

    Legends and Stories of Ireland. 2 vols., 1831–34; edited by D. J. O'Donoghue, 1899.
    Rory O'More: A National Romance. 1837; revised edition, 1839; edited by D. J. O'Donoghue, 1898.
    Handy Andy. 1842; edited by E. Rhys, 1907; abridgement edited by Sean O'Faolain, 1945.
    Treasure Trove. 1844; as *He Would Be a Gentleman; or, Treasure Trove,* 1877; edited by D. J. O'Donoghue, 1899.
    Tom Crosbie and His Friends. 1878.
    Further Stories of Ireland, edited by D. J. O'Donoghue. 1899.

Plays

    Grana Uile; or, The Island Queen, music by William Penson (produced 1832).
    The Beau Isle (produced 1835).
    The Olympic Pic-Nic (produced 1835).
    Rory O'More, from his own novel (produced 1837). N.d.
    The White Horse of the Peppers (produced 1838). 1838.
    The Hall Porter (produced 1839). 1839.
    The Happy Man (produced 1839). 1858(?).
    Snap Apple Night; or, A Kick-Up in Kerry (produced 1839).
    The Greek Boy (produced 1840). 1884.
    Il Paddy Whack in Italia (produced 1841). N.d.
    The Sentinel of the Alma (produced 1854).
    Barney the Baron; or, The Haunted Chamber (produced 1857). With *The Happy Man,* 1883.

MacCarthy More; or Possession Nine Points of the Law (produced 1861).   N.d.
Barney the Baron; The Happy Man.   1883.

Verse

Songs and Ballads.   1839.
The Low Back Car.   1855.
Metrical Tales and Other Poems.   1860.
Original Songs for the Rifle Volunteers, with C. Mackay and T. Miller.   1861.

Other

The Parson's Horn-Book.   2 vols., 1831.

Editor, Popular Tales and Legends of the Irish Peasantry.   1834.
Editor, The Lyrics of Ireland.   1858; as Poems of Ireland, 1884.
Editor, Rival Rhymes in Honour of Burns.   1859.

Reading List: The Life of Lover: Artistic, Literary, and Musical by W. B. Bernard, 2 vols.,
1874; Lover by Andrew J. Symington, 1880.

*   *   *

It was Samuel Lover's misfortune that the publication of his best known novel, Handy
Andy, coincided with the emergence of an articulate cultural nationalism in the Young
Ireland movement. The novel was a harmless, and indeed remains a humorous, exercise in
stage-Irish comedy, but the new self-conscious dignity of Irish public opinion rejected
Lover's work as a travesty. Despite this hostile reception in his homeland, he is probably
remembered principally for Handy Andy. An earlier novel, Rory O'More, deserves more
attention; by taking the name of a leading aristocratic insurgent of the 1641 rebellion, and
giving it to a humble character in a novel centred on the 1798 rebellion, Lover was
attempting to make a general statement about Irish history and the manner in which fiction
treats it. The conceit, however, was rather better managed than the execution of the novel as
a whole.

If present-day interest in Lover is expressed principally by critics concerned with the
development of the novel in nineteenth-century Ireland, in his time he had a reputation in
Great Britain and America as an entertainer who produced drama, ballad poetry, and song
with equal facility. Together with his collection of folksong and his paintings, his work is a
large if ill-organised monument to Victorian industry and prolixity. The central problem,
affecting the fiction with special gravity, was Lover's uncertain notion of what Irish culture
was and how it might be presented to the world. Too often he concentrated on the question of
presentation, and accepted hand-me-down notions of national character and humour.

—W. J. McCormack

LOWRY, (Clarence) Malcolm (Boden). English. Born in Liscard, Cheshire, 28 July 1909. Educated at the Braeside School, Cheshire; Caldicote School, Hitchin, Hertfordshire, 1915–23; Leys School, Cambridge, 1927; Weber's School of Modern German, Bonn, 1928; St. Catharine's College, Cambridge, 1929–32, B.A. in English 1932. Married 1) Jan Gabrial in 1934 (divorced, 1940); 2) Margerie Bonner in 1940. Lived in Mexico, 1937–39, Canada, 1940–54, and Sussex, England, 1954–57. Recipient: Governor-General's Award, Canada, 1962. *Died 27 June 1957.*

PUBLICATIONS

Collections

Selected Poems, edited by Earle Birney and Margerie Lowry. 1962.
Selected Letters, edited by Harvey Breit and Margerie Lowry. 1965.

Fiction

Ultramarine. 1933; revised edition, 1962.
Under the Volcano. 1947.
Hear Us, O Lord, from Heaven Thy Dwelling Place (stories). 1961.
Lunar Caustic, edited by Earle Birney and Margerie Lowry. 1968.
Dark as the Grave Wherein My Friend Is Laid, edited by Douglas Day and Margerie Lowry. 1968.
October Ferry to Gabriola, edited by Margerie Lowry. 1970.
China, and Kristbjorg's Story in the Black Hills. 1974.

Play

Notes on a Screenplay for F. Scott Fitzgerald's Tender Is the Night, with Margerie Lowry. 1967.

Verse

Psalms and Songs, edited by Margerie Lowry. 1975.

Bibliography: by Earle Birney, in *Canadian Literature 8,* Spring 1961.

Reading List: *Lowry* by Daniel B. Dodson, 1970; *Lowry: The Man and His Work* edited by George Woodcock, 1971; *Lowry* by W. H. New, 1972; *Lowry: A Biography* by Douglas Day, 1973; *Lowry: His Art and Early Life* by Muriel Bradbrook, 1974; *The Art of Lowry* edited by Anne Smith, 1978.

*   *   *

Many novelists – Balzac, Zola and Proust among them – have thought of their novels as being parts of some larger life work that would provide an imaginative portrait of their age but would also make some major social or philosophic or psychological statement about the condition of man. Malcolm Lowry, whose reading was vast and whose philosophical wanderings were adventurous and wide, was such an author, but, unlike the other writers I have mentioned, he completed little of the great structure he had foreseen when he conceived the fictional cycle "The Voyage That Never Ends." In fact, during his lifetime Lowry published only two books, *Ultramarine* and, fourteen years later, *Under the Volcano*, the novel on which his reputation now rests. He also published a few stories and poems in periodicals. One novel that appears to have been virtually complete – *In Ballast to the White Sea* – was destroyed when his cabin on Burrard Inlet in British Columbia was burnt down. But the greater part of Lowry's work remained unfinished and unpublished at the time of his death in 1957.

The reasons why Lowry never completed a book after he finished *Under the Volcano* in 1945 are obviously complex, and his alcoholism was probably less a cause than a concurrent symptom of the monumental unsureness that prevented him from being satisfied with almost everything he wrote in his later years. Yet was it unsureness? Could it not have been also a sense that life was continually revising itself? Interpreted in either way, Lowry's failure to complete the ambitious works with which his later years were consumed suggests that he had come to a point when the barriers between art and life were so shredded that they hardly existed.

Certainly this view is borne out by a study of Lowry's books, both those he passed for publication and those which after his death were revised by others and published in his name. *Ultramarine*, written in his very early twenties, is patently autobiographical, based on the voyage which Lowry himself undertook as cabin boy in 1928 on a freighter bound for the China Seas. Only in *Under the Volcano* and in a few of the short stories – notably "The Forest Path to the Spring" – does one have a sense of emerging from the self that was Malcolm Lowry. *Under the Volcano* has often been treated – justly I think – as Lowry's only successful novel. In this story of the almost self-induced murder of Geoffrey Firmin, an alcoholic British consul, the human drama is integrated in a closely knit formal and metaphorical structure, largely cabbalistic in its origins, and the sinister aspects of Mexican life combine with the splendour of the country's topography to symbolize the metaphysical overtones. The strong autobiographical element – for the Consul's disintegrating marriage and his alcoholic adventures in a small Mexican town can easily be correlated to Lowry's own experiences – is exemplarily subsumed in the fictional.

In other words, one can believe in the Consul and his world in the sense of crediting them with an autonomous existence, which is more than one can say for the two novels published after Lowry's death, *Dark as the Grave Wherein My Friend Is Laid* and *October Ferry to Gabriola*. Both of these novels were put together by Lowry's widow Margerie, in one case with the co-operation of Douglas Day, out of a chaos of varying drafts, so that in neither case is one sure that the published version really represents Lowry's final wishes. What is quite clear is that both novels, for all their passages of splendid writing, are amazingly unresolved when one considers how long Lowry was working on them. Wilderness, the leading character of *Dark as the Grave*, and Ethan Llewelyn in *October Ferry*, are all too palpably varying personae who have never completely detached themselves from their creator, and the adventures they undergo, on a trip to Mexico and a trip to Vancouver Island respectively, are elaborations of narratives already contained in Lowry's notebooks, and never sufficiently detached for us to be confident about describing them as fiction. Curiously enough, the very journey symbolism, the escape that in each case does not succeed, is indicative of Lowry's desire to escape from himself, and his difficulty in doing so. It is perhaps significant that the one piece among the works published after his death which stands complete as a work of fictional art is "The Forest Path to the Spring," an extraordinarily evocative novella whose territory never goes beyond the woods and the sea around the little shack in Canada which he loved so deeply. For once, Lowry was not trying frantically – and, because of his eagerness, failing – to escape from himself. More than anything else he wrote in his later years, this brief work is the true *Paradiso* that balances the *Inferno* of *Under the Volcano*.

—George Woodcock

LYLY, John. English. Born in the Weald of Kent c. 1553. Educated at King's School, Canterbury, Kent; Magdalen College, Oxford, B.A. 1573, M.A. 1575; also studied at Cambridge University, M.A. 1579. Married Beatrice Browne in 1583; two sons and one daughter. In the service of Lord Delawarr, 1575–80, and the Earl of Oxford, from 1580; leased Blackfriars Theatre, London, 1584, but subsequently gaoled for debt in the same year; wrote for the children's acting companies of the Chapel Royal and St. Paul's, London, until 1591; Member of Parliament for Hindon, Aylesbury, and Appleby, 1589–1601. *Died* (buried) *30 November 1606.*

PUBLICATIONS

Collections

> *Dramatic Works,* edited by F. W. Fairholt.   2 vols., 1858–92.
> *Complete Works,* edited by R. W. Bond.   1902.

Fiction

> *Euphues: The Anatomy of Wit.*   1578; augmented edition, 1579; edited by J. Winny, 1957; *Euphues and His England,* 1580; *Euphues* (both parts), 1617; edited by M. W. Croll and H. Clemons, 1916.

Plays

> *Alexander, Campaspe, and Diogenes* (produced 1584).   1584; as *Campaspe,* 1584; edited by W. W. Greg, 1933.
> *Sappho and Phao* (produced 1584).   1584.
> *Galathea* (produced 1584–88?).   1592; edited by A. B. Lancashire, with *Midas,* 1969.
> *Mother Bombie* (produced 1587–90?).   1594; edited by A. Harriette Andreadis, 1975.
> *Endymion, The Man in the Moon* (produced 1588).   1591; edited by W. H. Neilson, 1911.
> *Love's Metamorphosis* (produced 1589–90?).   1601.
> *Midas* (produced 1590?).   1592; edited by A. B. Lancashire, with *Galathea,* 1969.
> *The Woman in the Moon* (produced 1590–95?).   1597.

Other

> *Pap with a Hatchet, Alias a Fig for My Godson; or, Crack Me This Nut; or, A Country Cuff, That Is, A Sound Box of the Ear, for the Idiot Martin.*   1589.

Bibliography: *Lyly: A Concise Bibliography* by S. A. Tannenbaum, 1940; *Lyly 1935–65* by R. C. Johnson, 1968.

Reading List: *Lyly and the Italian Renaissance* by V. M. Jeffery, 1928; *Lyly: The Humanist and Courtier,* 1962, and *Lyly and Peele,* 1968, both by George K. Hunter; *The Court Comedies of Lyly; A Study in Allegorical Dramaturgy* by Peter Saccio, 1969.

*   *   *

John Lyly graduated as Master of Arts from Oxford, where he had enjoyed the patronage of Lord Burleigh, Queen Elizabeth's Lord High Treasurer. He gained a position as secretary to the Earl of Oxford, Burleigh's son-in-law and a supporter of a company of boy actors. Lyly's humanistic education, and his entry as a young man to court circles, determined both his audience and his entire literary output. He first appeared in print with a pastoral prose romance *Euphues: The Anatomy of Wit* and followed it up with an even more successful sequel *Euphues and his England*, both parts continuing during his lifetime to be regularly reprinted.

He was appointed vice-master of Paul's Boys (the cathedral choristers who also acted as boy actors) and later to a position in the Revels Office, which was responsible for mounting the Queen's entertainments. He was (with Nashe) drawn in for a time on the side of the bishops in the theological Marprelate controversy to which he contributed one pamphlet *Pappe with an Hatchet* in colloquial prose. But unlike Nashe, who found in the pamphlet a new and effective prose style, Lyly preferred the prose style of which he was a master and the audience with which he was familiar. His later work, all theatrical, was written to be acted (and sung) by Paul's Boys for performance before Elizabeth and her court.

Euphues, a love-romance, was directed particularly towards an audience of leisured ladies. "*Euphues* had rather lie shut in a lady's casket than open in a scholar's study," claims its preface. Lyly drew on the stylistic devices of medieval and renaissance rhetoric to produce a skilled, highly mannered, prose (which has always since Lyly's time been termed Euphuism, the sentence quoted above being a relatively simple example). Euphuism was characterised by (a) a balance of similar parts of speech in successive clauses, the matching words generally reinforced by alliteration or by "like endings," (b) equal-length phrases or clauses used in a parallel series, (c) the repetition of words derived from the same stem, (d) the use of antithesis, and (e) frequent far-fetched similes many of them drawn from the natural world and derived from Pliny's *Natural History*. The style was much admired and was fashionable for a few years. It was brilliantly parodied by Shakespeare in a speech by Falstaff, and echoes of it can be found in mannered prose as late as that of Dr. Johnson.

When Lyly came to write for the theatre, he generally used some variation of his Euphuistic prose style, though he could vary it with a more colloquial (but never vulgar) idiom if the situation demanded. Apart from *Campaspe* (derived from Classical history) and *Mother Bombie* (a Terence-type comedy on an English folk-theme), his plays are fantasies based on themes and characters from Classical mythology. The format encouraged lavish spectacle, allegorical references to current affairs in court (in *Endymion*, Cynthia and Endymion could be readily interpreted as Elizabeth and Leicester), aristocratic comedy to evoke what the preface to *Sapho and Phao* called "soft smiling, not loud laughing"; and it could very easily (as in the close of *Endymion*) be diverted to open praise of the monarch who was present at the performance. All was presented with a high degree of wit and dazzling verbal displays.

With a cast of boy actors and choristers, and an audience who demanded glitter, Lyly made no attempt to present real human feelings. His comedy was pantomimic and non-realistic, and (given the terms in which it was written) extremely effective. He made full use of the resources at his disposal. *Endymion*, for instance, contains several lyrics for his choristers, a dumb-show representing a dream, a dance of fairies for his troop of boy actors, and indications in the stage directions for spectacular costumes, changing scenic effects, and a final transformation in full view ("Bagoa recovers human shape").

The drama of the Elizabethan and Jacobean period ranges over a spectrum. At one end is the "drumming decasyllabon" of Marlowe's *Doctor Faustus* and *Tamburlaine* and the poetry and human insights of Shakespeare. Lyly's plays are at the other end of the spectrum. They are scripts for a kind of extended *commedia dell' arte*, and their real affinities are with the later Court Masque of Inigo Jones and Ben Jonson.

—Ian A. Gordon

LYTLE, Andrew (Nelson). American. Born in Murfreesboro, Tennessee, 26 December 1902. Educated at Sewanee Military Academy, Tennessee; Exeter College, Oxford, 1920; Vanderbilt University, Nashville, B.A. 1925; Yale University School of Drama, New Haven, Connecticut, 1927–29. Married Edna Langdon Barker in 1938 (died, 1963); three daughters. Writer from 1930; Professor of History, Southwestern College, Memphis, Tennessee, 1936; Professor of History, University of the South, Sewanee, Tennessee, and Managing Editor of the *Sewanee Review*, 1942–43; Lecturer, 1946–48, and Acting Head, 1947–48, University of Iowa School of Writing, Iowa City; Lecturer in Creative Writing, University of Florida, Gainesville, 1948–61; Lecturer in English, 1961–67, and Professor of English, 1968–73, University of the South, Sewanee, and Editor of the *Sewanee Review*, 1961–73. Recipient: Guggenheim Fellowship, 1940, 1941, 1960; National Endowment for the Arts grant, 1966. Litt.D.: Kenyon College, Gambier, Ohio, 1965; University of Florida, 1970; University of the South, 1973. Lives in Monteagle, Tennessee.

PUBLICATIONS

Fiction

The Long Night. 1936.
At the Moon's Inn. 1941.
A Name for Evil. 1947.
The Velvet Horn. 1957.
A Novel, A Novella and Four Stories. 1958.

Other

Bedford Forrest and His Critter Company (biography). 1931; revised edition, 1960.
The Hero with the Private Parts: Essays (literary criticism). 1966.
A Wake for the Living: A Family Chronicle. 1975.

Editor, *Craft and Vision: The Best Fiction from "The Sewanee Review."* 1971.

Reading List: "Lytle Issue" of *Mississippi Quarterly*, Fall 1970; *The Form Discovered: Essays on the Achievement of Lytle* edited by M. E. Bradford, 1973.

*   *   *

Andrew Lytle's family on both sides was prominent in Middle Tennessee, and in fact Murfreesboro, the town where he was born, was founded on land given by his ancestor. His family chronicle, *A Wake for the Living*, traces the course of their history for almost two centuries. Lytle's movement into the writing of fiction was gradual. His undergraduate years at Vanderbilt University coincided with the heyday of the Fugitive group, and the friendships he formed with these poets led him into his own literary career. His main interest during the 1920's, however, was theater; he studied playwriting at the Yale School of Drama, and in New York he had a brief career as an actor.

Even before he left New York he had begun the research on his first book, *Bedford Forrest and His Critter Company*. He thus followed his friends Allen Tate and Robert Penn Warren, whose first prose works were likewise Civil War biographies. In 1930 these men and nine of their friends, led by their former teacher John Crowe Ransom, published *I'll Take My Stand*.

This famous symposium inaugurated the Agrarian movement, to which Lytle was passionately committed. He was indeed about the only Agrarian who actually practiced farming during the 1930's, and for a few years he attempted to combine this with the literary profession. His great interest in the history of his region led to his first novel, *The Long Night*, a tragedy of revenge set against the background of the Civil War.

Although Lytle is usually identified with Tennessee, where three of his four novels are set, he is keenly aware of the larger clash of cultures. *At the Moon's Inn* brings the Spanish explorer De Soto to his fate in North America as he attempts to overcome the vast wilderness through an act of will. The short novel "Alchemy" likewise has Pizarro confronting the Inca world of Peru. In the foreword to *A Novel, A Novella, and Four Stories* Lytle comments that "The westward movement of Europeans, beginning with Columbus, not only shattered the narrow physical boundaries of Christendom but, like all extension, weakened it by reducing a union composite of spiritual and temporal parts to the predominance of material ends." This statement might serve as the theme that links all of Lytle's books. His third novel, *A Name for Evil*, is about a modern Southerner who brings ruin upon himself and his family in an abortive effort to restore the past; the fictional convention here is the ghost story. *The Velvet Horn*, which is set in the Cumberland Mountains soon after the Civil War, involves a boy's initiation into manhood and an extraordinary tangle of family relationships. It is the richest of Lytle's books and one of the masterpieces of Southern fiction.

—Ashley Brown

LYTTON OF KNEBWORTH, Baron. See **BULWER-LYTTON, Edward.**

MACAULAY, Dame (Emilie) Rose. English. Born in Rugby, Warwickshire, 1 August 1881; lived with her family in Varazze, Italy, 1887–94. Educated at Oxford High School for Girls, 1894–99; Somerville College, Oxford, 1900–03. Full-time writer from 1903; lived in Cambridgeshire, 1903–16, Beaconsfield, 1916–25, and in London from 1925; worked in a hospital, as a land girl, in the War Office, and in the Ministry of Information, during World War I; publisher's reader for Constable, London, 1919; Special Reporter for the *Daily Chronicle*, in Geneva, 1925; Columnist ("Marginal Comments"), *Spectator*, London, 1935–36. Recipient: Femina-Vie Heureuse Prize, 1922; Black Memorial Prize, 1957. D.Litt.: Cambridge University, 1951. D.B.E. (Dame Commander, Order of the British Empire), 1958. *Died 30 October 1958.*

PUBLICATIONS

Fiction

> *Abbots Verney.* 1906.
> *The Furnace.* 1907.
> *The Secret River.* 1909.
> *The Valley Captives.* 1911.
> *Views and Vagabonds.* 1912.
> *The Lee Shore.* 1912.
> *The Making of a Bigot.* 1914.
> *Non-Combatants and Others.* 1916.
> *What Not: A Prophetic Comedy.* 1918.
> *Potterism: A Tragi-Farcical Tract.* 1920.
> *Dangerous Ages.* 1921.
> *Mystery at Geneva.* 1922.
> *Told by an Idiot.* 1923.
> *Orphan Island.* 1924.
> *Crewe Train.* 1926.
> *Keeping Up Appearances.* 1928; as *Daphne and Daisy,* 1928.
> *Staying with Relations.* 1930.
> *They Were Defeated.* 1932; as *The Shadow Flies,* 1932.
> *Going Abroad.* 1934.
> *I Would Be Private.* 1937.
> *And No Man's Wit.* 1940.
> *The World My Wilderness.* 1950.
> *The Towers of Trebizond.* 1956.

Verse

> *The Two Blind Countries.* 1914.
> *Three Days.* 1919.

Other

> *A Casual Commentary* (articles). 1925.
> *Catchwords and Claptrap.* 1926.
> *Some Religious Elements in English Literature.* 1931.

Milton. 1934; revised edition, 1957.
Personal Pleasures. 1935.
An Open Letter to a Non-Pacificist. 1937.
The Writings of E. M. Forster. 1938.
Life among the English. 1942.
They Went to Portugal. 1946.
Fabled Shore: From the Pyrenees to Portugal. 1949.
Pleasure of Ruins. 1953; edited by Constance Babington Smith, 1977.
Letters to a Friend, 1950–52, and *Last Letters to a Friend, 1952–58,* edited by Constance Babington Smith. 2 vols., 1961–62.
Letters to a Sister, edited by Constance Babington Smith. 1964.

Editor, *The Minor Pleasures of Life.* 1934.
Editor, with Daniel George, *All in a Maze: A Collection of Prose and Verse.* 1938.

Reading List: *Macaulay* by Alice R. Bensen, 1969; *Macaulay* (biography) by Constance Babington Smith, 1972.

                              *   *   *

Rose Macaulay was verging on forty when she published *Potterism,* the first of her books to achieve wide popularity. The novel displayed the gift for story-telling and for satire aiming at surface follies rather than the deep structure of society which marked most of her work. In fact, with her passion for travel and conversation, she found herself essentially happy in the society she knew. She had an occasional gift for pure fantastic satire, best shown, perhaps, in *Orphan Island,* a story about a shipload of orphans wrecked with their spinster governess on a South Sea island, and breeding a race of descendants clinging to the strictest Victorian shibboleths. Her most moving novel is probably *They Were Defeated,* a sad love story, and a lament for the defeat of the Cavaliers in the Civil War. Her best novel is probably *The Towers of Trebizond,* published two years before her death, brilliantly conversational in tone, but also reflecting a private grief, a love affair with a married man whose death in an accident had led her back to the practice of a strict High Anglicanism. Some letters to her spiritual guide were published after her death. Never dull and always honest, she deserves to be more widely read than she now is.

                                                                    —G. S. Fraser

MACAULAY, Thomas Babington; 1st Baron Macaulay. English. Born in Rothley Temple, Leicestershire, 25 October 1800. Educated at a private school in Little Shelford, Cambridgeshire, 1812–14; Aspenden Hall, Hertfordshire, 1814–18; Trinity College, Cambridge (Chancellor's Medal for English verse, 1819, 1821), 1818–22, B.A. 1822; called to the Bar, 1826. Fellow of Trinity College, 1824–31; contributor to the *Edinburgh Review,* 1825–45; practised as a barrister on the Northern Circuit; Commissioner of bankruptcy, 1828–30; elected Whig Member of Parliament for Calne, 1830; Commissioner of the Board of Control, 1832–34; Legal Adviser to the Supreme Council of India, 1834–38; Member of Parliament for Edinburgh, 1839–47, 1852–56; Secretary of War, 1839–41; Paymaster-General, 1846–47. Lord Rector of the University of Glasgow, 1849. Created Baron Macaulay of Rothley, 1857. *Died 28 December 1859.*

PUBLICATIONS

Collections

Works.   12 vols., 1898.
Works, edited by Thomas F. Henderson.   9 vols., 1905–07.
Prose and Poetry, edited by G. M. Young.   1967.
Selected Writings, edited by John Clive and Thomas Pinney.   1972.
Letters, edited by Thomas Pinney.   4 vols. (of 8), 1975–77.

Verse

Pompeii.   1819.
Evening.   1821.
Lays of Ancient Rome.   1842; edited by G. M. Trevelyan, 1928.
Hymn, edited by L. Horton-Smith.   1902.

Other

Critical and Miscellaneous Essays.   3 vols., 1840–41.
Critical and Historical Essays Contributed to the Edinburgh Review.   3 vols., 1843; edited by Hugh Trevor-Roper, 1965.
Scenes and Characters from the Writings.   1846.
The History of England from the Accession of James II.   5 vols., 1849–61 (vol. 5 edited by Lady Trevelyan); edited by T. F. Henderson, 5 vols., 1931.
Speeches, Parliamentary and Miscellaneous.   2 vols., 1853.
Speeches.   1854; edited by G. M. Young, 1935.
The Indian Civil Service, with others.   1855.
Selections from Essays and Speeches.   2 vols., 1856.
Biographical and Historical Sketches.   1857.
Were Human Sacrifices in Use among the Romans? A Correspondence Between Macaulay, Sir Robert Peel, and Lord Mahon.   1860; as *Some Inquiries Concerning Human Sacrifice among the Romans,* edited by T. Thayer, 1878.
Correspondence Between the Bishop of Exeter and Macaulay on Certain Statements Respecting the Church of England.   1860.
The Indian Election Minutes, edited by H. Woodrow.   1862.
Marginal Notes, edited by G. O. Trevelyan.   1907.
Essay and Speech on Jewish Disabilities, edited by I. Abrahams and S. Levy.   1910.
What Did Macaulay Say about America?, edited by H. M. Lydenberg.   1925.
Legislative Minutes, edited by C. D. Dharker.   1946.
Napoleon and the Restoration of the Bourbons, edited by Joseph Hamburger.   1978.

Editor, *A Penal Code Prepared by the Indian Law Commissioners.*   1837.

Reading List: *The Life and Letters* by G. O. Trevelyan, 2 vols., 1876, revised edition, 1877, edited by G. M. Trevelyan, 2 vols., 1932; *Macaulay,* 1932 (includes bibliography), and *Macaulay,* 1978, both by Arthur Bryant; *Macaulay* by G. R. Potter, 1959; "Macaulay Issue" of *Review of English Studies,* 1960; *The Boundaries of Fiction: Carlyle, Macaulay, Newman* by George L. Levine, 1968; *Macaulay: The Shaping of an Historian* by John Clive, 1973; *Macaulay* by Jane Millgate, 1973.

*   *   *

Thomas Babington Macaulay was essayist, poet, and historian, a best-seller in each mode. His greatest, perhaps most lasting work is his so-called *History of England* which to all intents and purposes began with the Revolution of 1688 and tailed away into the reign of Queen Anne which he did not complete. What remains is inevitably not the balanced conception he had in mind, and a number of discoveries since his time must radically change some of his attitudes to personages (such as Judge Jefferies, William Penn, and King William himself who is a hero to Macaulay) and events, yet a properly annotated edition of his work is still perhaps the best introduction to this period of English history. The reasons for this are the sheer luminous brilliance of his writing, the scope of his historical outlook, and his imaginative powers. Some of the best pieces are the scenes during the trial of Richard Baxter (Macaulay was himself a barrister for a time in the Northern circuit). As Bagehot put it, "He throws over matters which are in their nature dry and dull – transactions, budgets, bills – the charm of fancy which a poetical mind employs to enhance and set forth the charm of which is beautiful." His reading and research were of an almost fabulous thoroughness: if, for example, his history required him to describe a still extant town he would visit it, measure it, look at its relics, make a note of such things as the time it took to get from one point to another so as to be more exact in his description of, say, military movements.

Macaulay made his literary name early in his career by his contribution of essays, often in the form of extended reviews, to the monthlies then in vogue, in particular the *Edinburgh Review*. These essays were not the short sheets favoured by Addison, Steele, or Dr. Johnson; his contributions sometimes tended to be the length of a short book. The *Edinburgh Review*, though not rigidly political, had a Whig tendency and Macaulay became a Whig M.P. The best known of his critical essays is that on Milton, quite brilliant in expression though he later thought it rather too shrill and showy. Each reader will find his own favourite: from every essay they read they will learn something. He is particularly vivacious and thought-provoking on the playwrights of the Restoration (in the early 19th century far from being a subject of polite discussion) or the long study of Francis Bacon, and he makes splendid fun of Robert Southey. His great gift of judgment is perhaps best seen in his work on Byron or Warren Hastings.

Best known of all Macaulay's works are some of his *Lays of Ancient Rome*, which he printed to great acclaim in 1842. They were a result of his wide and deep classical reading combined with his passion for English ballads, which in his early days were still being composed, re-written, and printed for sale at every street corner, certainly in London:

> Then out spake brave Horatius
> The Captain of the Gate:
> "To every man upon this earth
> Death cometh soon or late.
> And how can man die better
> Than facing fearful odds,
> For the ashes of his father
> And the temples of his Gods."

He left also the brief, echoing "Epitaph on a Jacobite" who for his "true King" threw away "lands, honours, wealth, sway" –

> And one dear hope, that was more prized than they.
> For him I languished in a foreign clime,
> Grey-haired with sorrow in my manhood's prime;
> Heard on Lavernia Scargill's whispering trees,
> And pined by Arno for my lovelier Tees....

Here Macaulay's historical imagination touches the keys of pathos and lost endeavour which adorn some pages of his *History* and move us there as here.

—Kenneth Young

MacDONALD, George. Scottish. Born near Huntly, Aberdeenshire, 10 December 1824. Educated at King's College, University of Aberdeen, 1840–45, M.A. 1845; Congregationalist Theological College, Highbury, London, 1848–50. Married Louisa Powell in 1850 (died, 1902); eleven children. Private tutor in London, 1845–48; Minister, Trinity Congregational Church, Arundel, Sussex, 1850–53; lecturer and preacher in Manchester, 1855–56, Hastings, Sussex, 1857–59, and London, from 1859; Editor, with Norman MacLeod, *Good Words for the Young* magazine, 1870–72; lectured in England and America, 1872; lived in Bordighera, Italy in later life. LL.D.: University of Aberdeen, 1868. Granted Civil List pension, 1877. *Died 18 September 1905.*

PUBLICATIONS

Collections

> *MacDonald: An Anthology*, edited by C. S. Lewis. 1946.
> *The Light Princess and Other Tales of Fantasy*, edited by Roger Lancelyn Green. 1961.
> *The Gifts of the Child Christ: Fairy Tales and Stories for the Childlike*, edited by Glenn Edward Sadler. 2 vols., 1973.

Fiction

> *Phantastes: A Faerie Romance for Men and Women.* 1858.
> *David Elginbrod.* 1863.
> *Adela Cathcart.* 1864.
> *The Portent: A Story of the Inner Vision of the Highlanders, Commonly Called the Second Sight.* 1864.
> *Alec Forbes of Howglen.* 1865.
> *Annals of a Quiet Neighbourhood.* 1867.
> *Dealings with the Fairies.* 1867.
> *Guild Court.* 1867.
> *Robert Falconer.* 1868.
> *The Seaboard Parish.* 1868.
> *At the Back of the North Wind.* 1870.
> *Ranald Bannerman's Boyhood.* 1871.
> *The Princess and the Goblin.* 1871.
> *The Vicar's Daughter: An Autobiographical Story.* 1871.
> *Wilfrid Cumbermede.* 1872.
> *Gutta-Percha Willie, The Working Genius.* 1873.
> *The Wise Woman: A Parable.* 1875; as *A Double Story*, 1876; as *The Lost Princess*, 1895; edited by Elizabeth Yates, 1965.
> *Malcolm.* 1875.
> *St. George and St. Michael.* 1876.
> *Thomas Wingfield, Curate.* 1876.
> *The Marquis of Lossie.* 1877.
> *Sir Gibbie.* 1879; edited by Elizabeth Yates, 1965.
> *Paul Faber, Surgeon.* 1879.
> *Mary Marston.* 1881.
> *Warlock o' Glen Warlock.* 1881; as *Castle Warlock: A Homely Romance*, 1882.
> *Weighed and Wanting.* 1882.
> *The Princess and the Curdie.* 1882.

The Gifts of the Child Christ and Other Tales. 1882; as *Stephen Archer and Other Tales,* 1883.
Donal Grant. 1883.
What's Mine's Mine. 1886.
Home Again. 1887.
The Elect Lady. 1888.
A Rough Shaking. 1890.
There and Back. 1891.
The Flight of the Shadow. 1891.
Heather and Snow. 1893.
The Light Princess and Other Fairy Tales. 1893.
Lilith: A Romance. 1895.
Salted with Fire. 1897.
Far above Rubies (stories). 1899.
The Fairy Tales, edited by Greville MacDonald. 5 vols., 1904.

Verse

Within and Without: A Dramatic Poem. 1855.
Poems. 1857.
A Hidden Life and Other Poems. 1864.
The Disciple and Other Poems. 1867.
Dramatic and Miscellaneous Poems. 2 vols., 1876.
A Book of Strife, in the Form of the Diary of an Old Soul. 1880.
A Threefold Cord: Poems by Three Friends, with John Hill MacDonald and Greville Matheson, edited by George MacDonald. 1883.
The Poetical Works. 2 vols., 1893.
Rampolli: Growths from a Long-Planted Root, Being Translations Chiefly from the German, Along with a "Year's Diary of an Old Soul." 1897.

Other

Unspoken Sermons. 3 vols., 1867–89.
The Miracles of Our Lord. 1870.
Works of Fancy and Imagination. 10 vols., 1871.
England's Antiphon. 1874.
Orts. 1882; as *The Imagination and Other Essays,* 1883; revised edition, as *A Dish of Orts,* 1893.
The Tragedie of Hamlet, Prince of Denmark: A Study of the Text of the Folio of 1623. 1885.
The Hope of the Gospel (sermons). 1892.
The Hope of the Universe. 1896.

Editor, *A Cabinet of Gems, Cut and Polished by Sir Philip Sidney, Now for the More Radiance Presented Without Their Setting.* 1892.

Translator, *Twelve of the Spiritual Songs of Novalis.* 1851.
Translator, *Exotics: A Translation of the Spiritual Songs of Novalis, The Hymn Book of Luther, and Other Poems from the German and Italian.* 1876.

Bibliography: *A Centennial Bibliography of MacDonald* by John Malcolm Bullock, 1925.

Reading List: *MacDonald and His Wife* by Greville MacDonald, 1924; *The Visionary Novels of MacDonald* by A. Freemantle, 1954; *The Golden Key: A Study of the Fiction of MacDonald* by R. L. Wolfe, 1961.

*   *   *

George MacDonald wrote fairy tales and fantasies for adults and children. Modern writers like C. S. Lewis and J. R. R. Tolkien have asserted his importance in inspiring their own fantasy worlds. He in turn drew upon the visionary writing of Crashaw, Novalis, and Fouqué, and fairy-tale and legend. He sought to establish allegorical or parabolic ways of writing through which he could give the strength of traditional image and symbolism to his own moral vision, and impress its beauty on readers. Such a method is, even for as delicate an imagination as MacDonald's, fraught with problems: the simple moral lessons of the fairy-tale may be conveyed successfully even by the self-conscious imitator of the form, as MacDonald does most elegantly in the Princess stories and the tales of *Dealings with the Fairies*; but the other-worlds he constructs out of strings of parables and verses in *Phantastes* and *Lilith* can be confusing and inconsistent on a symbolic level, and indeed the symbolic power of the writing becomes dissociated from the philosophy it is intended to express.

The centre of this philosophy was MacDonald's belief in the importance of the child and a childlike approach to life and death, to human relationships, and to God. His vision of the child was as holy idiot, humankind in a natural loving relationship with all creation and its Creator. To express this idea, parable forms and fairy-tales, relegated by the wordly-wise to the entertainment of children, were an obvious choice. He also, however, embodied his message in the child hero of more conventional stories. *At the Back of the North Wind* includes both homely detail of Diamond's family life and his spiritual adventures with the North Wind; as in *Lilith*, the door between the two is in fact the door between this unsatisfactory life and the real life beyond death, and Diamond's trips with North Wind culminate in his permanent translation to the land at her back. This is MacDonald's personal version of the common tract story in which the poor child is released after much instructive suffering into a better world; his imaginative realisation of death as a cold, awesome, but loving preceptress lifts the commonplace to a different plane, but its origin is clear. The writer's own faith was founded upon a Scottish Calvinist upbringing, and other novels such as *Sir Gibbie* and *David Elginbrod* concentrate on the rich texture of Scottish life, with its simple piety, as the cradle of his holy innocents. In *Sir Gibbie*, as in *A Rough Shaking*, the rather fay saintliness of the central character is made interesting for the reader by its ability to preserve him unharmed through perilous adventures. Similarly, we are held by conventional novelists' tools of description and characterisation in MacDonald's autobiographically based novels like *Ranald Bannerman's Boyhood* and *Robert Falconer*. It is in the fantasies, however, that the modern reader finds the child-worship of this peculiarly Victorian imagination expresses itself with lasting effectiveness.

—J. S. Bratton

MACHEN, Arthur (Llewellyn Jones). Welsh. Born in Caerleon-on-Usk, 3 March 1863. Educated at Hereford Cathedral School, 1874–80. Married twice; one son and one daughter. Writer from 1880; clerk for a publisher in London, 1883; actor with the Benson Shakespearian Repertory Company from 1902: toured with the company for several years; regular contributor to the *Evening News*, London, from 1912. Granted Civil List pension, 1933. *Died 15 December 1947.*

Collections

> *Tales of Horror and the Supernatural,* edited by Philip Van Doren Stern.   1948.
> *The Strange World of Machen.*   1960.

Fiction

> *A Chapter from a Book Called the Ingenious Gentleman Don Quijote de la Mancha Not till Now Printed.*   1887.
> *The Chronicle of Clemendy; or, The History of the IX Joyous Journeys* (stories).   1888.
> *Thesaurus Incantatus: The Enchanted Treasure; or, The Spagyric Quest of Beroaldus Cosmopolita.*   1888.
> *The Great God Pan, and The Inmost Light.*   1894.
> *The Three Impostors; or, The Transmutations* (stories).   1895.
> *The House of the Hidden Light.*   1904.
> *The House of Souls* (stories).   1906.
> *The Hill of Dreams.*   1907.
> *Parsifal: The Story of the Holy Graal.*   1913.
> *The Angel of Mons: The Bowmen and Other Legends of the War.*   1915; revised edition, 1915.
> *The Great Return.*   1915.
> *The Terror: A Fantasy.*   1917; revised edition, 1927.
> *The Secret Glory.*   1922.
> *The Shining Pyramid* (stories and essays).   1923; revised edition, 1925.
> *The Glorious Mystery* (stories and essays), edited by Vincent Starrett.   1924.
> *Ornaments in Jade* (stories).   1924.
> *The Green Round.*   1933.
> *The Cosy Room and Other Stories.*   1936.
> *The Children of the Pool and Other Stories.*   1936.

Verse

> *Eleusinia.*   1881.
> *An Excellent Ballad of the Armed Man.*   1963.

Other

> *The Anatomy of Tobacco; or, Smoking Methodised, Divided, and Considered after a New Fashion.*   1884.
> *Hieroglyphics.*   1902; revised edition, 1912.
> *Dr. Stiggins: His Views and Principles.*   1906.
> *War and the Christian Faith.*   1918.
> *Far Off Things* (autobiography).   1922.
> *Things Near and Far* (autobiography).   1923.
> *The Collector's Craft.*   1923.
> *Strange Roads.*   1923.
> *Works.*   9 vols., 1923.
> *The Grande Trouvaille: A Legend of Pentonville.*   1923.

775

Dog and Duck (essays).   1924.
The London Adventure; or, The Art of Wandering (autobiography).   1924.
Precious Balms.   1924.
The Canning Wonder.   1925.
Dreads and Drolls (essays).   1926.
Notes and Queries.   1926.
A Souvenir of Cadby Hall.   1927.
Parish of Amersham.   1930.
Tom o' Bedlam and His Song.   1930.
A Few Letters.   1932.
The Glitter of the Brook (essays).   1932.
Autobiography (includes *Far Off Things* and *Things Far and Near*).   1951.
Brindles and Spurs (essays).   1951.
A Note on Poetry.   1959.
From the London Evening News (essays).   1959.

Editor, *A Handy Dickens: Selections.*   1941.

Translator, *The Heptameron of Marguerite Queen of Navarre.*   1886.
Translator, *Fantastic Tales*, by François Béroalde de Verville.   1890.
Translator, *The Memoirs of Casanova.*   12 vols., 1894.
Translator, *Casanova's Escape from the Leads, Being His Own Account.*   1925.

Bibliography: *Machen: A Bibliography* by H. Danielson, 1923; *A Bibliography of Machen* by Wesley D. Sweetser, 1965.

Reading List: *Machen: Novelist of Ecstasy and Sin* by Vincent Starrett, 1918; *A Machen Miscellany* edited by William F. Gekle, 1957; *Machen: Essays by Various Hands* edited by Brocard Sewell, 1960; *Machen: A Short Account of His Life and Works* by S. A. Reynolds and W. E. Charlton, 1963; *Machen* by Wesley D. Sweetser, 1964; *Machen* by David P. M. Michael, 1971.

*   *   *

Arthur Machen achieved little acclaim until the 1920's, although he composed some of his major works in the 1890's. He disclaimed, however, being a part of the aesthetic-decadent movement and declared himself primarily influenced by his Welsh birthplace, Caerleon-on-Usk. In the autobiographical *Far Off Things*, he attributes his impulse to write to the fact that when his eyes "first opened in earliest childhood they had before them the vision of an enchanted land." His works, therefore, are pervasively romantic, often infused with mysticism and symbolism and frequently couched in terms of the weird and occult. Even his satire – of big business, industrialization, science, naturalistic determinism, democracy, Puritanism, Protestantism, atheism, and Communism – denounces attitudes and beliefs destructive and antithetical to the romantic spirit. His view of nature was essentially sacramental, and his purpose was to suggest the eternal realities behind the veil of sensible appearances or, like the alchemist, to transmute everyday reality into a world of magic and wonder, to convey the naked transcendental forces behind human existence.

A masterful stylist and voluminous writer, Machen covers a wide spectrum of genres – translations, notably the classic rendition of Casanova's *Memoirs*; medieval tales; an anatomy; tales of terror and the supernatural; impressionistic criticism in *Hieroglyphics*; sagacious and tolerant personal essays, like *Dog and Duck*, seemingly ingenuous, though artful; satire; experimental novels; mystical prose poems, like "The Rose Garden"; and autobiography. His major fictional works present a study of good and evil in progression from pure diabolism to the attainment of sanctity and the occurrence of miracles.

Not quite a novel, *The Hill of Dreams* imperfectly fuses elements of satire, mysticism, and symbolism. Lacking realistic conversation and "round" characters, the work is significant, however, as an experimental forerunner of the stream-of-consciousness school. In the judgment of Madeleine L. Cazamian, it is "without doubt the most decadent book in all of English literature" (*L' Anti-Intellectualisme et L' Esthétisme: 1880–1900*, my translation). Upon his tales of terror and the supernatural, which he, ironically, considered potboilers and which constitute a major portion of his total canon, his fame and influence are largely based. Among those frequently anthologized are *The Great God Pan*, a study of diabolism utilizing Roman symbols; "The Novel of the Black Seal," on the same theme of omnipresent evil, using symbols from Celtic folklore; "The Novel of the White Powder," on perichoresis and instantaneous evolutionary reversion, effected by chemical means; "The White People," on the fine line between sorcery and sanctity, between Black and White Magic; and "The Bowmen," a tale of miraculous intervention. A longer work, *The Terror*, is a transcendental murder mystery of greater amplitude than du Maurier's "The Birds."

Because of his peculiar knowledge of demonology, witchcraft, folklore, and occultism and his unique talent for suggesting the indescribable through the creation of atmosphere, Machen has never been surpassed in the small area of psychological and transcendental supernatural. He is the spokesman without peer for sorcery and sanctity existing behind the veil of the ineffable mystery; and his mastery has been acknowledged by H. P. Lovecraft, Ray Bradbury, and Henry Miller. Machen is the kind of author who is perpetually being rediscovered and, in a limited but continuing way, he has survived.

—Wesley D. Sweetser

MacINNES, Colin. English. Born in London in 1914; son of the singer James MacInnes and the writer Angela Thirkell. Educated in Australia. Served as a sergeant in the Intelligence Corps in World War II. *Died 22 April 1976.*

PUBLICATIONS

Fiction

To the Victors the Spoils. 1950.
June in Her Spring. 1952.
City of Spades. 1957.
Absolute Beginners. 1959.
Mr. Love and Justice. 1960.
All Day Saturday. 1966.
Westward to Laughter. 1969.
Three Years to Play. 1970.
Out of the Garden. 1974.
A Chair to the Spirit. 1978.

Other

England, Half English (essays).   1961.
London: City of Any Dream.   1962.
Australia and New Zealand, with the editors of *Life.*   1964.
Sweet Saturday Night.   1967.
Loving Them Both: A Study of Bisexuality and Bisexuals.   1974.
"No Novel Reader" (on Rudyard Kipling).   1975.
Out of the Way: Later Essays.   1978.

*   *   *

Colin MacInnes's novels appeared in three batches: two at the start of the fifties, five years' silence followed by the three London novels, six years without any published fiction and then five more. The first, *To the Victors the Spoils,* is an autobiographical account of army experiences in Holland and Germany in the closing stages of the war. *June in Her Spring* looks back earlier, to Australia, where he spent his childhood, and is a sheep-station romance of young love frustrated, with a sub-plot of a psychopathic delinquent.

These works are no preparation for the great achievement which followed, the London books. In them MacInnes reports on much-discussed facets of contemporary London life: race relations, youth, and the police. His fascination with understanding his times is shown in the essays collected in *England, Half English,* where his topics include pop music, drinking clubs, and teenage fashions.

In the first, *City of Spades* narration is alternately by an ebullient young Nigerian, Johnny Fortune, who has come to London in search of fortune and adventure, and a well-meaning, naive Colonial Welfare Officer, who follows Johnny as he goes to dubious pubs and clubs, and mixes with hemp-smokers and peddlers, gamblers and ponces. After two experiences with the law, Johnny decides to return to Africa. MacInnes appears to prefer the cheerful, amoral, living-in-the-present of his characters to dull, sedate English behaviour. And though he has no illusions about fighting, drinking and drug addiction, he recommends tolerance.

"Absolute beginners" are teenagers, and MacInnes assumes they are a strange new world, since for the first time they have the money to create their own culture. The story is told in the first person by a boy of eighteen, who describes such different scenes as a smart Chelsea party, a TV studio, a Soho drinking club and a look at the country on a trip up river from Windsor to Marlow. He loves jazz, and we read of a club and a big concert. The date is the late Summer of 1958 and the last episode, detached from the rest, is the race riot of Notting Hill. Because the youth is an individual (he makes big money taking pornographic pictures), he is not wholly convincing as a typical figure, with articulate opinions on everything from politics to television. MacInnes is always there, aware and tender, alive and compassionate.

Mr. Love and Justice tells the stories of Frankie Love, the ex-seaman who picks up a Stepney tart and becomes a ponce, and Ted Justice, the plainclothes policeman. Their paths intersect, their roles become blurred and the men are friends in hospital at the end. Literary artistry is more marked than in previous works, with the deliberate pairing, and the names prompting us to ask whether this is a fable showing Love may be the more just and Justice the more loving.

Some critics place the novels as no more than painless sociology, with information of a particular date (*Absolute Beginners* especially is dated). The books, however, remain full of energy, of character and of language. MacInnes says "I chose a language for 'coloured people,' or for teenagers, that was almost entirely an invented one; though true, so far as I could make it, to the minds and spirits of the characters I was describing." So the language is English Runyon, and one notes, variously, Cockney, Yiddish, Salinger, underworld terms, and jazz and beatnik idiom. No other writer (critics have invoked Mayhew, Defoe, Hogarth, and Genet to try to convey the flavour) has achieved MacInnes's kind of exuberant, sometimes titillating, fictionalized fact.

All Day Saturday, the sixth novel, returns to pre-war Australian sheep-farming country, but with a maturer view than shown in *June in Her Spring*. The next two books are a surprise, looking much further back, feats of storytelling which reconstruct the mid-eighteenth century and Elizabethan London. *Westward to Laughter* is a yarn about a Highland youth who goes to sea, travels to the West Indian island of St. Laughter, is unjustly convicted, becomes a slave and runs away, joins a pirate ship and is finally hanged. *Three Years to Play* (which is the working life of a boy actor), the longest of his novels, presents yet another boy in search of fortune in London. He is involved in underworld gangs, acts out a real-life inspiration for *As You Like It* in Epping Forest, and meets Shakespeare and hears of other writers. *Out of the Garden* concerns Rattler, an ex-army officer, taking over a big Victorian "ruin" to convert as an amusement park. This plan proves to be a cover for selling arms to Northern Irish Protestants, to lead to an army dictatorship in Britain (presciently, MacInnes's book was published several months *before* this possibility began to be seriously discussed). More important, MacInnes returned to the 1970's to comment on Britain, on youth, money, sex, class, stylizing the idioms and catch-phrases of the time.

—Malcolm Page

MACKENZIE, Sir (Edward Montague) Compton. English. Born in West Hartlepool, County Durham, 17 January 1883; brother of the actress Fay Compton. Educated at St. Paul's School, London; Magdalen College, Oxford (Editor, *Oxford Point of View*; Business Manager, Oxford Dramatic Society), B.A. (honours) in modern history 1904. Second Lieutenant, 1st Volunteer Battalion, Hertfordshire Regiment, 1900–02; Lieutenant, 1915, and Captain, 1916, in the Royal Marines: served in the Dardanelles Expedition, 1915; Military Control Officer, Athens, 1916; Director, Aegean Intelligence Service, 1917; O.B.E. (Officer, Order of the British Empire), 1919; Chevalier, Legion of Honour; Captain in the Home Guard, 1940–44. Married 1) Faith Stone in 1905 (died, 1960); 2) Christina MacSween in 1962 (died, 1963); 3) Lilian MacSween in 1965. Founder, 1923, and Editor, 1923–61, *The Gramophone*, London; Literary Critic, *Daily Mail*, London, 1931–35. Rector, University of Glasgow, 1931–34; President, Siamese Cat Club, 1928–72, Dickens Fellowship, 1939–46, Wexford Festival, 1951–72, and The Croquet Association, 1954–66; President, 1961–64, and Patron, 1964–72, The Poetry Society, London; Governor-General, Royal Stuart Society, 1961–72; President, Guild of Independent Publishers, 1969. LL.D.: University of Glasgow, 1932; St. Francis Xavier University, Antigonish, Nova Scotia, 1961. Knight Commander, Royal Order of the Phoenix, Greece, 1966. Fellow, 1945, and Companion of Literature, 1968, Royal Society of Literature; Honorary Royal Scottish Academician. Knighted in 1952. *Died 30 November 1972.*

PUBLICATIONS

Fiction

The Passionate Elopement. 1911.
Carnival. 1912.
Sinister Street. 2 vols., 1913–14; as *Youth's Encounter* and *Sinister Street*, 1913–14.

Guy and Pauline.   1915; as *Plashers Mead*, 1915.
The Early Life and Adventures of Sylvia Scarlett.   1918.
Sylvia and Michael: The Later Adventures of Sylvia Scarlett.   1919.
Poor Relations.   1919.
The Vanity Girl.   1920.
Rich Relatives.   1921.
The Altar Steps.   1922.
The Parson's Progress.   1923.
The Seven Ages of Woman.   1923.
The Old Men of the Sea: A Romance of Adventure in the South Pacific.   1924; revised
    edition, as *Paradise for Sale*, 1963.
The Heavenly Ladder.   1924.
Coral: A Sequel to "Carnival."   1925.
Fairy Gold.   1926.
Rogues and Vagabonds.   1927.
Vestal Fire.   1927.
Extremes Meet.   1928.
Extraordinary Women: Theme and Variations.   1928.
The Three Couriers.   1929.
April Fools: A Farce of Manners.   1930.
Buttercups and Daisies.   1931; as *For Sale*, 1931.
Our Street.   1931.
Water on the Brain.   1933.
The Darkening Green.   1934.
Figure of Eight.   1936.
The Four Winds of Love: The East Wind of Love.   1937 (as *The East Wind*, 1937); *The
    South Wind of Love*, 1937; *The West Wind of Love*, 1940; *West to North*, 1940; *The
    North Wind of Love*, 2 vols., 1944–45 (as *The North Wind of Love* and *Again to the
    North*, 1945–46).
The Red Tapeworm.   1941.
The Monarch of the Glen.   1941.
Keep the Home Guard Turning.   1943.
Whisky Galore.   1947; as *Tight Little Island*, 1950.
Hunting the Fairies.   1949.
The Rival Monster.   1952.
Ben Nevis Goes East.   1954.
Thin Ice.   1956.
Rockets Galore.   1957.
The Lunatic Republic.   1959.
Mezzotint.   1961.
The Stolen Soprano.   1965.
Paper Lives.   1966.

Plays

The Gentleman in Gray (produced 1907).
Carnival, from his own novel (produced 1912; as *Columbine*, produced 1920).
The Lost Cause: A Jacobite Play (broadcast, 1931).   1933.

Screenplay: *Whisky Galore* (*Tight Little Island*), with Angus Macphail, 1949.

Radio Play: *The Lost Cause*, 1931.

Verse

    Poems. 1907.

Other

    Kensington Rhymes (juvenile). 1912.
    Gramophone Nights, with Archibald Marshall. 1923.
    Santa Claus in Summer (juvenile). 1924.
    Mabel in Queer Street (juvenile). 1927.
    The Unpleasant Visitors, with *Posset's Toby Jub* by Mabel Marlowe (juvenile). 1928.
    The Adventures of Two Chairs (juvenile). 1929.
    Gallipoli Memories 1929.
    The Enchanted Blanket (juvenile). 1930.
    Told: Children's Tales and Verses. 1930.
    First Athenian Memories. 1931.
    The Conceited Doll (juvenile). 1931.
    The Fairy in the Window-Box (juvenile). 1932.
    Prince Charlie: De Jure Charles III, King of Scotland, England, France and Ireland. 1932.
    Unconsidered Trifles. 1932.
    Greek Memories. 1932.
    Reaped and Bound: Collected Essays. 1933.
    Literature in My Time. 1933.
    The Dining-Room Battle (juvenile). 1933.
    Prince Charlie and His Ladies. 1934.
    Marathon and Salamis. 1934.
    The Enchanted Island (juvenile). 1934.
    Catholicism and Scotland. 1936.
    The Book of Barra, with J. L. Campbell. 1936.
    The Naughtymobile (juvenile). 1936.
    Pericles. 1937.
    The Stairs That Kept On Going Down (juvenile). 1937.
    The Windsor Tapestry, Being a Study of the Life, Heritage and Abdication of H.R.H. the Duke of Windsor, K.G. 1938.
    A Musical Chair. 1939.
    Aegean Memories. 1940.
    Cavalry, with Faith Compton Mackenzie. 1942.
    Wind of Freedom: The History of the Invasion of Greece by the Axis Powers, 1940–1941. 1943.
    Mr. Roosevelt. 1943.
    Brockhouse. 1944.
    Dr. Beneš. 1946.
    The Vital Flame. 1947.
    All over the Place: Fifty Thousand Miles by Sea, Road and Rail. 1948.
    Eastern Epic I: An Account of the Part Played by the Indian Army in the Second World War. 1951.
    The Mackenzie Birthday Book. 1951.
    I Took a Journey: A Tour of the National Trust Properties. 1951.
    The House of Coalport, 1750–1950. 1951.
    The Queen's House: A History of Buckingham Palace. 1953.
    The Savoy of London. 1953.
    Echoes. 1954.

Realms of Silver: One Hundred Years of Banking in the East.   1954.
My Record of Music.   1955.
Sublime Tobacco.   1957.
Cats' Company.   1960.
Greece in My Life.   1960.
Catmint.   1961.
On Moral Courage.   1962; as *Certain Aspects of Moral Courage,* 1962.
Look at Cats.   1963.
My Life and Times: Octave One: 1883–1891, 1963; *Octave Two: 1891–1900,* 1963;
    Octave Three: 1900–1907, 1964; *Octave Four: 1907–1914,* 1965; *Octave Five:
    1915–1923,* 1966; *Octave Six: 1923–1930,* 1967; *Octave Seven: 1930–1938,* 1968;
    Octave Eight: 1939–1946, 1969; *Octave Nine: 1946–1953,* 1970; *Octave Ten:
    1953–1963,* 1971.
Little Cat Lost (juvenile).   1965.
The Strongest Man on Earth: Based on the BBC Television Jackanory Programme
    (juvenile).   1968.
Robert Louis Stevenson.   1968.
The Secret Island (juvenile).   1969.
Butterfly Hill (juvenile).   1970.
Achilles (juvenile).   1972.
Theseus (juvenile).   1972.
Jason (juvenile).   1972.
Perseus (juvenile).   1972.
Golden Tales of Greece (juvenile).   1974.

Reading List: *Mackenzie: An Appraisal of His Literary Work* by Leo Robertson, 1954;
Mackenzie by Kenneth Young, 1968; *Mackenzie* by David T. Dooley, 1974.

*   *   *

Born into a family noted in the annals of the British and American stage, Compton Mackenzie had a keen eye for details of appearance and character, a well-tuned ear for niceties of speech, and a considerable skill in constructing a plot and managing a scene. He also believed that the chief business of the artist is to engage the attention and sympathy of his audience. Professionally committed to a career as a writer, and endowed with abundant vitality, he tackled many kinds of literature including journalism, exercised his voice and his pen in private causes and public controversies, and in the course of a long life published over a hundred books.

His prodigious memory served him well in his autobiographical works, such as the volumes recounting his activities as a British Intelligence Officer in the Aegean and the ten *Octaves*, which teem with the acquaintance, incidents, and observations of an astonishingly varied life's experience. His memory was an asset in his fiction also, linked as it was with a power of imagination which allowed him to enter fully into the minds and emotions of a wide variety of people. Herein lies the secret of his successful children's books like *Santa Claus in Summer*: not only adults, but also the very young, respond to the gift that Henry James perceived in Mackenzie, "the ability to receive the direct impact of life so that you can return it directly to your readers."

His protean output of novels falls mainly into a number of groups – the romantic novels from *Carnival* to the *Sylvia Scarlett* sequence, the comic novels, and the under-rated masterpiece *The Four Winds of Love*. *Carnival*, the story of a young Cockney dancer's life, *Coral*, and *Figure of Eight*, explore the passing world of the London variety theatre. The first of these met with immediate success, but Mackenzie's fame was finally established by *Sinister Street*, a vivid tale of a young man's growth from infancy through schooldays and Oxford to his adventures in the London underworld. A classic delineation of a section of English society at that period, it has never been out of print. This was followed by *Guy and Pauline*, an idyll of romantic love fore-doomed, while in *Poor Relations* and *Rich Relatives* Mackenzie branched out in a new direction with the first of his purely comic novels. *Water on the Brain* and *The Red Tapeworm*, satirical and farcical, led to what the author called his "Highland romps," of which the best-known, *Whisky Galore*, and its hilarious film version, won him a new and appreciative generation of readers. His earlier trilogy of novels on the Anglo-Catholic movement, *The Altar Steps*, *The Parson's Progress*, and *The Heavenly Ladder*, is little noticed today, but *Thin Ice*, a firmly delicate study of the public and private disaster of a homosexual, has recently been reprinted after twenty years.

The reception of *The Four Winds of Love* by both the public and the critics was without doubt adversely affected by the circumstances of its publication. Issued in six volumes between 1937 and 1945, it is a sweeping panorama of the intellectual, artistic, and political life of the first half of the twentieth century in Europe and the United States, seen through the eyes of the central character as he grows from childhood to maturity in the changing world. A massive novel with a multiplicity of scenes and a large cast of characters, written at the height of the author's powers, *The Four Winds* seems assured, with *Sinister Street*, of a permanent place in the history of the English novel.

—Stewart F. Sanderson

MACKENZIE, Henry. Scottish. Born in Edinburgh, 26 August 1745. Educated at Edinburgh High School, and the University of Edinburgh. Married Penuel Grant in 1776; eleven children. Articled to a solicitor, George Inglis, in Redhall, to learn the exchequer business; went to London to learn English exchequer practice in 1765, then returned to Edinburgh · became a partner of Inglis, whom he later succeeded as attorney for the crown in Scotland; wrote, unsuccessfully, for the Edinburgh and London stage, 1773–89; Editor, *The Mirror*, Edinburgh, 1779–80, and *The Lounger*, Edinburgh, 1785–87; wrote extensively on contemporary politics, supporting the "constitutional cause"; Comptroller of Taxes for Scotland, 1804 until his death. One of the first members of the Royal Society of Edinburgh; Member of the Highland Society of Scotland: chairman of its committee to enquire into the authenticity of the Ossian poems. *Died 14 January 1831*.

PUBLICATIONS

Fiction

The Man of Feeling. 1771; edited by Brian Vickers, 1967.
The Man of the World. 1773.
Julia de Roubigné. 1777.

Plays

The Prince of Tunis (produced 1773). 1773.
The Shipwreck; or, Fatal Curiosity, from the play *Fatal Curiosity* by Lillo (produced 1784). 1784.

The Force of Fashion (produced 1789).
Virginia; or, The Roman Father.   1820(?).

Verse

The Pursuits of Happiness.   1771.

Other

Letters of Brutus to Certain Celebrated Political Characters.   1791.
Works.   3 vols., 1807.
Miscellaneous Works.   3 vols., 1819.
Account of the Life and Writings of John Home.   1822.
Anecdotes and Egotisms, edited by Harold W. Thompson.   1927.
Letters to Elizabeth Rose of Kilravock, on Literature, Events, and People, 1768–1815,
   edited by Horst W. Drescher.   1967.

Editor, *The Life of Thomas Paine,* by Francis Oldys.   1793.

Reading List: *A Scottish Man of Feeling* by Harold W. Thompson, 1931; *Mackenzie* by
Gerard A. Barker, 1975.

                                *   *   *

        Although Henry Mackenzie's influence spread in various directions, he is remembered
today as a minor novelist who profited from a major trend. The novel that made and
preserves his fame is *The Man of Feeling,* an episodic story in the same sentimental vein as
Goldsmith's *The Vicar of Wakefield* (1766) and Sterne's *Sentimental Journey* (1768). *The Man
of Feeling,* the story of the mortally sensitive Harley, who, after a series of encounters in
London with ruined maidens, pathetic Bedlamites, an old soldier, and a grieving family,
returns to his country home and swoons to death because his favorite, Miss Walton, requites
his love, was immensely popular. This brief synopsis sounds reductive and pejorative, and by
today's standards and tastes *The Man of Feeling* is indeed melodramatic and incredible. But
perhaps because of the popularity of such writers as Sterne and Goldsmith, perhaps because
of the growing cult of the individual, or because of Pelagian-latitudinarian trends in
eighteenth-century Christianity, or because of some combination of these, it made
Mackenzie, for two or three decades, a popular and influential man of letters.
        Mackenzie wrote two other novels, *The Man of the World* and *Julia de Roubigné.* Neither
received the acclaim of *The Man of Feeling,* although *Julia de Roubigné* drew some applause.
The generic influence of Samuel Richardson is apparent in both – in *The Man of the World*
Mackenzie attempts to create in Sindall a counterpart to Harley in *The Man of Feeling,* a
genteel villain like Lovelace in *Clarissa. Julia de Roubigné* has a more credible plot than *The
Man of the World* and is in the epistolary style, a structural strategy resulting in a sense of
psychological immediacy, as in Richardson at his best.
        Although he lived until 1831, Mackenzie's "creative" writing career had effectively ended
by around 1800. Declining health and increased involvement in his career as a lawyer were
probably the reasons. His *Letters of Brutus* were topical and soon forgotten. He remained
widely respected, however, particularly in the polite literary circles of Edinburgh, as a critic
of perceptive taste. He was influential in furthering the reputations of Burns and Scott at

crucial points early in their careers, and his "Account of the German Theatre" (1790) helped augment the growing popularity in Great Britain of German authors, Schiller in particular. His critical biography of the playwright John Home (1822) is sympathetic and intelligent. Mackenzie was very much a man of his times and was sensitive and thoughtful in literary matters. His canon includes poetry of the ballad-revival sort as well as dramatic tragedy and comedy. But he remained unassuming, modest, and, after some early success, not highly ambitious.

—Paul D. McGlynn

MacLENNAN, (John) Hugh. Canadian. Born in Glace Bay, Nova Scotia, 20 March 1907. Educated at Halifax Academy; Dalhousie University, Halifax, B.A. 1928; Oriel College, Oxford (Rhodes Scholar), B.A., M.A. 1932; Princeton University, New Jersey, Ph.D. 1935. Married 1) Dorothy Duncan in 1936 (died, 1957); 2) Frances Walker in 1959. Classics Master, Lower Canada College, Montreal, 1935–45; full-time writer, 1945–51; Associate Professor, 1951–67, and since 1967 Professor of English, McGill University, Montreal. Recipient: Guggenheim Fellowship, 1943; Governor-General's Award, 1946, 1949, 1960, for nonfiction, 1950, 1955; Lorne Pierce Gold Medal, 1952; Molson Prize, 1966. D.Litt.: University of Western Ontario, London, 1953; University of Manitoba, Winnipeg, 1955; Waterloo Lutheran University, Ontario, 1961; Carleton University, Ottawa, 1967; LL.D.: Dalhousie University, 1956; University of Saskatchewan, Saskatoon, 1959; McMaster University, Hamilton, Ontario, 1965; University of Toronto, 1966; Laurentian University, Sudbury, Ontario, 1966; University of Sherbrooke, Quebec, 1967; University of British Columbia, Vancouver, 1968; St. Mary's University, Halifax, 1968; Mount Alison University, Sackville, New Brunswick, 1969; D.C.L.: Bishop's University, Lennoxville, Quebec, 1965. Fellow, Royal Society of Canada, 1953, and the Royal Society of Literature, England, 1959. C.C. (Companion, Order of Canada), 1967. Lives in Montreal.

PUBLICATIONS

Fiction

Barometer Rising. 1941.
Two Solitudes. 1945.
The Precipice. 1948.
Each Man's Son. 1951.
The Watch That Ends the Night. 1959.
Return of the Sphinx. 1967.

Other

Oxyrhynchus: An Economic and Social Study. 1935.
Cross Country. 1948.
Thirty and Three (essays). 1954.

Scotchman's Return and Other Essays.   1960; as *Scotsman's Return and Other Essays,*
   1960.
Seven Rivers of Canada.   1961; as *The Rivers of Canada,* 1961.
The Colour of Canada.   1967.

Editor, *McGill: The Story of a University.*   1960.

Reading List: *MacLennan* by George Woodcock, 1969; *MacLennan* by Peter Buitenhuis,
1969; *MacLennan* by Alec Lucas, 1970; *The Novels of MacLennan* by Robert H. Cockburn,
1970.

                                    *   *   *

   Canadian writers in the English language suffer disadvantages that are unknown to men of
letters of other countries. The long and rich history of British literature is part of their heritage
but they cannot write as Englishmen lest they become foreigners in their own country. They
are North Americans, and the economic, cultural and political influence of the United States
is to them immediate and powerful, but as Canadians they cannot themselves participate in
the exercise of that influence. They belong to a nation of two languages but to one which, for
all that the politicians have decreed, is still far from being bilingual and so they are cut off
from the support of their fellow-Canadians who write in French and from a substantial
minority of readers in a country which even in its entirety is not plush with enthusiasm for its
artists. Faced with all these handicaps and inevitably attracted to one or the other of the two
powerful magnets of English-language publishing, London and New York, many Canadian
writers have turned their backs on Canadianism while others have been obsessed by it and
have become little more than brash heralds of Canadian chauvinism. Among Canadian
novelists only Hugh MacLennan has been consistent in his ability to create an essentially
Canadian mythology without abdicating the novelist's responsibility to be at once
idiosyncratic and universally comprehensible.
   It is one of the persistent paradoxes of Canadian literature that so many of its leading
exponents are typically Canadian, in that it is a notable trait among Canada's intelligentsia
that they have in their heredity and upbringing so many strains that are extra-Canadian.
MacLennan, for example, is a fourth generation Nova Scotian, but his father still spoke
Gaelic, and the fatalism, the religious fervour, and the mythology of the Highland Scots are as
real in the novels of Hugh MacLennan – above all in *Each Man's Son* and *Return of the
Sphinx* – as they are in the novels of Scotland-based Scotsmen such as Neil Gunn and Eric
Linklater. But if, as has been said, "several of his novels ... can be regarded as transatlantic
epilogues to the history of Scottish literature, and the records of a pastoral people battered and
bewildered by urban society," nevertheless the most obvious influences on his literary
personality are not Scottish, and certainly not Nova Scotian, but Oxford and Princeton, the
two great centres of elegant intellectualism in which he was educated.
   A dedicated classical scholar, MacLennan has never lacked the courage to attempt in his
novels the grandeur of Greek tragedy. The sense of guilt that prevades *The Precipice* is
explicitly derived from Canadian Puritanism. *Two Solitudes* is the most complete
representation in fictional form of the division between English and French Canada, the
schism which, above all others, makes the concept of Canadianism an illusion. *Each Man's
Son* mourns the fate of MacLennan's own race, the Highland Scots thrust out of Scotland by
poverty and in Nova Scotia damned to abandon their rural tradition and to live by coal-
mining. All these are Canadian themes, but they are also parables of man's estate, and in all
his work MacLennan holds to his ambition to fuse realism and symbolism.
   MacLennan said of his early novels, "I was writing out of a country at that time unknown
even to itself," and that consequently he was forced to explore and to explain in detail many
aspects of the Canadian character. In the same passage he claims that by the time he came to

write his later novels exegesis of this kind was no longer necessary. Yet if there is a blemish in MacLennan's craftsmanship, it springs from his skill as an essayist, and if that blemish exists it is most apparent in the novels written in the 1950's and 1960's, above all in *The Watch That Ends the Night*, in which the narrative is frequently broken by didactic interpolations. And perversely MacLennan's first novel *Barometer Rising* is almost entirely free from expository asides.

Already when he wrote *Barometer Rising* MacLennan was a superior craftsman, capable of handling plot, characterisation, and setting, and already he was concerned to find the parable behind the chronicle. But he would never again find historical events so pliable to his purpose as those which he chronicles in *Barometer Rising*, the Great War and the explosion that wrecked Halifax in 1917. Perhaps no Canadian ever will − for the symbolism of the Halifax disaster is both dramatic and inevitable, and it was the Great War, more even than Confederation, which aroused Canadians to aspirations of nationhood.

—J. E. Morpurgo

MACLEOD, Fiona.   See SHARP, William.

MAILER, Norman.   American.   Born in Long Branch, New Jersey, 31 January 1923. Educated at Harvard University, Cambridge, Massachusetts, S.B. in aeronautical engineering 1943; did postgraduate work at the Sorbonne, Paris, 1944. Served in the United States Army Infantry, 1944–46. Married 1) Beatrice Silverman in 1944 (divorced, 1951), one daughter; 2) Adele Morales in 1954 (divorced, 1962), two daughters; 3) Lady Jeanne Campbell in 1962 (divorced, 1963), one daughter; 4) Beverly Bentley in 1963 (divorced, 1971), two sons; 5) Carol Stevens in 1971, one daughter. Co-Editor, *Dissent*, New York, 1953–63; Co-Founding Editor, *Village Voice*, New York, 1954; Columnist, *Esquire* magazine, New York, 1962–63; Independent Candidate for Mayor of New York City, 1968; film director. Recipient: National Institute of Arts and Letters grant, 1960; Pulitzer Prize, for non-fiction, 1969; National Book Award, for non-fiction, 1969; Edward MacDowell Medal, 1973; National Art Club's Gold Medal for Literature, 1976. Member, National Institute of Arts and Letters. Lives in Brooklyn, New York.

PUBLICATIONS

Fiction

   The Naked and the Dead.   1948.
   Barbary Shore.   1951.
   The Deer Park.   1955.

Advertisements for Myself (includes essays and verse).   1959.
An American Dream.   1965.
The Short Fiction.   1967.
Why Are We in Vietnam?   1967.
A Transit to Narcissus, edited by Howard Fertig.   1978.

Plays

The Deer Park (produced 1967).   1967.
Maidstone: A Mystery (screenplay).   1971.

Screenplays: *Wild 90,* 1967; *Beyond the Law,* 1967; *Maidstone,* 1968.

Verse

Deaths for the Ladies and Other Disasters.   1962.

Other

The White Negro.   1959.
The Presidential Papers.   1963.
Cannibals and Christians.   1966.
The Bullfight.   1967.
The Armies of the Night: History as a Novel, The Novel as History.   1968.
Miami and the Siege of Chicago: An Informal History of the Republican and Democratic Conventions of 1968.   1969.
The Idol and the Octopus: Political Writings on the Kennedy and Johnson Administrations.   1968.
Of a Fire on the Moon.   1970.
The Prisoner of Sex.   1971.
The Long Patrol: 25 Years of Writing from the Works of Mailer, edited by Robert Lucid.   1971.
Existential Errands.   1972.
St. George and the Godfather.   1972.
Marilyn.   1973.
The Faith of Graffiti, with Mervyn Kurlansky and Jon Naar.   1974; as *Watching My Name Go By,* 1975.
The Fight.   1975.
Some Honorable Men: Political Conventions 1960–1972.   1976.
Genius and Lust: A Journey Through the Major Writings of Henry Miller, with Henry Miller.   1976.

Bibliography: *Mailer: A Comprehensive Bibliography* by Laura Adams, 1974.

Reading List: *Mailer* by Richard J. Foster, 1968; *The Structured Vision of Mailer* by Barry H. Leeds, 1969; *Mailer: The Man and His Work* edited by Robert Lucid, 1970; *Mailer* by Richard Poirier, 1972; *Mailer: A Critical Study* by Jean Radford, 1974; *Down Mailer's Way* by Robert Solotaroff, 1974; *Existential Battles: The Growth of Mailer* by Laura Adams, 1975; *Mailer* by Philip Bufithis, 1978.

*   *   *

Even in the ferment of the American literary scene since 1950 few novelists have provoked – from deans of criticism as from common readers – the ferment of praise and attack that greets every new work by Norman Mailer. A definitive assesment of Mailer cannot yet be written, both because each work must be considered part of the whole, the *oeuvre* that Mailer is still extending and defining in his own terms, and because many people (not excluding Mailer), consider his present writings preparation for, indeed perhaps part of, the greatest American novel of his generation. His objective has not changed since 1959, when he wrote that he "will settle for nothing less than making a revolution in the consciousness of our time." The young James Joyce couched such hyperbole in the third person, but Mailer is obstreperously the artist as "I." It is typical of Mailer's caustic, profoundly ironic aggrandizement of himself as artist, America's seer and clown, to have added, "I could be wrong, and if I am, then I'm the fool who will pay the bill" (*Advertisements for Myself*). Even Mailer's fiercest detractors agree that he has by now more than met his own challenge, and the question is whether he has yet to write, or has already written, his great work.

Provisionally Mailer's canon can be described in four stages: an apprenticeship from 1948–58 including his first three novels; a difficult transition from 1959–64 in public self-criticism; the mastery of prose fiction culminating in the works of 1965–67; and the period since 1968 which, to appropriate his subtitle to *Armies of the Night*, consists in his explorations of "History as a Novel, the Novel as History."

The Naked and the Dead is the work of a young social realist indebted to Dos Passos: on a Pacific island in World War II an American platoon (an ethnic composite) is sent on a hopeless mission by a disdainful general for personal reasons of vindictiveness, and under the immediate command of a brutal illiterate sergeant, proletarian homologue of the fascistic general; deftly Mailer evokes the past lives and the present ordeals of the platoon, the intense, but purposeless valor of little men enmeshed in tycoons' wars. Thereafter Mailer turned away from naturalist techniques and from focus on character to develop the allegorical tendencies that underlay his first study of Americans at war. Just as the island was a metaphor for America, so in *Barbary Shore* a madcap urban boardinghouse is context for the allegorical collisions of national political and social forces; artistically unsuccessful, because the tight political framework is overwhelmed by unaccountable fears and inconsistencies in the characters, *Barbary Shore* remains the experimental keystone of all Mailer's later use of metaphorical structures. In *The Deer Park* he drew back into more traditional modes, for the realistic account of a young writer's apprenticeship in a film colony among embattled Hollywood idealists and nihilists, victims and agents of both America's cinema-induced fantasies and the McCarthy Committee; confused in crucial ways, *The Deer Park* initiates Mailer's supple use of clashing rhetorical styles and introduces Marion Faye, a theologian of evil who prefigures major issues in the later fiction. The *warfare*, the political then increasingly moral and aesthetic combat between opposing aspects of American culture (nature and technology, creativity and waste, Christian humanism and capitalist lust), shapes the form and tone of all three novels, their dualistic structures and their still discordant mix of stridency and sentiment. The three novels concern extinction of spirit and creative energy by the capitalist system, as its antagonists confront their own terrors, at the limits of sanity, in opposing it. Chronologically Mailer structures his novels less and less on the dualities inherent in the American political system and more on those in the self as participant in the system.

Advertisements for Myself burst the constraints that had kept Mailer's work so anxious, both daring and tentative, through most of the 1950's. The volume is a collection of all his work to date (in entirety or excerpt) and, through meticulous prefaces, his assessment of himself as creator of it. He publicly adopts the first person as the "voice" of his work (most later third-person work will feature his character "Mailer," a novelist), he works out his aesthetic as America's artist, he fixes his political position as (vestigial Marxist) Existentialist "moral anarchism," he announces his program for himself, and – as in all subsequent works – he attempts to divine the future from the present state of culture, literature, and himself. *Advertisements* is the fulcrum, the self-scrutiny enabling Mailer to move away from mentors

(Hemingway, the naturalists, Malraux) to fiction uniquely his own. Three short pieces inform that transition. "The Man Who Studied Yoga" gently mocks Sam Slovoda, defeated writer and middle-class conformist, and marks a terminus, Mailer's last calm moment before his fiery (some say foul-mouthed barroom brawling) rebellion against such passive death. "The White Negro" posits creative self-assertion, announcing "Mailer" the Hipster of literature: Hip (modulated in the 1960's to Protest and in the 1970's to Aquarius) fascinates him as active, anarchic opposition to the WASP fascism that threatens to appropriate human freedom and even dignity; Hip entails obscenity, which Mailer values as active assault on hypocrisy and thus as the linguistic essence of street-based democracy, and *machismo*, Mailer's prized – and much maligned – assertion of the masculine. His story "The Time of Her Time" is both a mock-epic battle of the sexes and a serious refusal to deny instinct as the price of civilization, even if that means virtually raping a Freudian co-ed. The Advertisements led Mailer to excesses (many since modified), but the important base is "Mailer" the novelist addressing the dichotomies in the culture and in himself, the artist as antagonist of his own cultural and literary past and as its interpreter, hero of the creative effort – denied by the forces of corporate power – to interpret, indeed to shape history.

An American Dream and *Why Are We in Vietnam?* are masterful dramatizations of his cultural and artistic argument, in consummate styles. In the first novel middle-aged Rojack, radical intellectual married to a tycoon's daughter, murders her and then, for 32 hours, tries to locate in himself as in the world the "fine divide" between madness and sanity. He tries to poise himself between the daily world of newspaper lies, CIA, police, and the nightmare world of psychotic imaginings, death, hallucination (thus *in* the schizophrenia that is the heart of the American dream, as in the rapidly shifting, telescoped languages of these milieux), only to find that they are contemporaneous and coextensive, that there is no safe parapet overlooking the incoherence, neither in the city nor in himself. In the second novel D.J., 18-year-old son of a Dallas millionaire, recounts (as if in the electronically broadcast chatter of a Texas disc jockey) going bear hunting with his Pa in Alaska and welcoming that greatest of American puberty rites with a slavering satisfaction. Vietnam is mentioned only in the last sentence, in searing fillip to this horrific allegory of the greater atrocity that is the character of the nation. The novel is a comic masterwork forcing the reader to poise on Mailer's fine edge between laughter and dread, where the ghastly implications of the title corrode the Huckleberry Finn humor. The hyped style is in the end a devaluation of language (always an ironic operation in Mailer), the media blasting the human mind. In the two novels, in complex metaphors and a rhetorical virtuosity as rich as Faulkner's, Mailer dismantles the American self-image, dramatizing the dualisms that entrap his villainous hero and his heroic villain.

All Mailer's fiction played character against context, dialectically observing character as both creator-of and created-by the event in which he is participant. Moving in the late 1960's from fiction to real people and events, Mailer developed that technique into a methodology for exploring the "fine divide" between history and the novel. Bringing to journalism both the techniques of fiction-writing and the subjective moral seriousness of the novelist, Mailer now writes about extraordinary spectacles in American public life. He does so as "Mailer," "the Historian" or "the Novelist," interchangeably, both participant and observer, citizen and artist. One such report won rebel Mailer respectability, the Pulitzer Prize for "Non-Fiction," but the aesthetic status of his "Reports" is still far from decided; certain readers (such as John Hollowell in *Fact & Fiction*) hail Mailer as progenitor of the new "non-fiction novel," and others term Mailer's late work a renegade form of autobiography. With great deftness of historical and literary allusion, "the Reporter" describes his thoughts and feelings in the midst of political or other public extravaganzas, which he sees as epic battles of forces in the American psyche, manifesting to public view elements of the national character which otherwise remain concealed. *The Armies of the Night* (perhaps the best among these works) chronicles the anti-war march on the Pentagon; "Superman Comes to the Supermarket," "In the Red Light," *Miami and the Siege of Chicago*, *St. George and the Godfather* describe the political conventions of 1960–72; *Of a Fire on the Moon* details the moonshot and queries the possibility of personal heroism in a technocracy; *The Fight* and *The Faith of Graffiti* concern two famous prize fighters and a host of famous ghetto street artists, personal combat and personal name as public spectacle. Richard Poirier in *Norman Mailer* (the finest critical study to date) explains the significance of "Mailer": "We are invited to see him in these books within intricately related fields of force, and then to watch him act simultaneously as participant, witness, and writer, who evokes in the clashes of his style a 'war' among the various elements that constitute the life of the country and of the self." In cunning interplay between history and memoir, "Mailer" the novelist blunders through events, dissecting their significance and pondering the ambivalences in his own response as participant-observer, until "Mailer" effectively constitutes the narrative field as the archetypally American duality of dream and dread, angel and swine.

There are now signs that Mailer has exhausted his reporter's mode. Distaste and new experimentation began before *St. George and the Godfather*, a disaffected testament whose patent dualisms bored even Mailer. There is no doubt that to "Mailer," quintessential American sensibility, Watergate was a horror; in the 1976 preface to *Some Honorable Men* he chides, too severely, his old belief in history as the product of forces visible to the skilled observer ("So we are obliged to recognize that much of what we looked on as history is, in fact, not much related to the facts"), and therefore redoubles his insistence that the world of fiction be brought to bear on the facts of journalism. His recent work focuses on the multiple selves warring within the public individual, notably Marilyn Monroe and Henry Miller, embodiments of the worlds of sex and aestheticism that continue to absorb him. One sign of his turning away from public spectacle was the shift of voice in *Graffiti* to "Aesthetic Investigator"; the text is a brief, deeply disturbed investigation of correlatives between street kids' graffiti and the modern artist's disappearance from the work of art (Rauschenberg erasing De Kooning and selling the signed erasure) as a last defiance against the corporate take-over of art. The aesthetics of defiance are also a subject of *Marilyn* concerning cinema and of *Genius and Lust* concerning autobiographical fiction.

Now under contract to complete a major novel "large in scope" by 1981, Mailer is writing his first fictional work in many years. In the 1976 preface to the political writings he notes, "How much America becomes the character, no, the protagonist of that novel no genius is large enough to write," adding, not so typically, "Shakespeare would grow modest before America." The new novel may not prove to be the masterwork expected, nor so immodest as once predicted, but it is certain to be praised and attacked on grounds of greatness.

—Jan Hokenson

MAIS, Roger. Jamaican. Born in 1905. Educated at Calabar High School. Worked as civil servant and journalist; also a photographer and painter. Associated with the political activist Norman W. Manley in the 1930's and 1940's: imprisoned for anti-colonial essay for six months in 1944; lived abroad, 1951–54. *Died in 1955.*

PUBLICATIONS

Fiction

And Most of All Man (stories and verse).   1939.
Face and Other Stories.   1942.

The Hills Were Joyful Together.   1953.
Brother Man.   1954.
Black Lightning.   1955.

Play

Atalanta in Calydon, from the play by Swinburne (produced 1950).

Reading List: Introduction by Norman Manley to *Three Novels,* 1966; *Mais* by Jean D'Costa, 1979.

*   *   *

Some understanding of Roger Mais's generation is helpful in the reading of his fiction. He belonged to that group of middle-class intellectuals and political activists who assumed the leadership of mass labour and nationalist movements throughout much of the West Indies during the 1930's and 1940's. This is the group that dominated the slow movement towards nationhood in Jamaica, Trinidad, Barbados, and Guyana, among others. It is therefore no coincidence that Jamaica's late Prime Minister, Norman Manley, wrote the introduction to Mais's *Three Novels* (a reprint of his three major works) for both Manley the political leader and Mais the writer belonged to what Manley describes as "the National Movement." By a similar token it is to be expected that Mais's fiction is marked by a socio-political commitment (to the poor, to the working classes, and to national identity) which he shares with political counterparts like Manley. And this commitment is best exemplified by the three novels on which much of his reputation rests, *The Hills Were Joyful Together, Brother Man,* and *Black Lightning.*

The Hills Were Joyful Together is a novel about victimization, and the victims are the slum dwellers of Jamaica's capital, Kingston. The slum "yard" is a cage, confining its members to a closed cycle of poverty which breeds crime and which in turn removes the slum dweller even further from socio-economic opportunities. And it is also a cage of indiscriminate brutality, the kind that arises from perpetual poverty and involves even the gentle hero, Surjue. In his case poverty leads to a bungled burglary attempt, and to prison where he is shot to death in an attempted escape. Moreover the circumstances of Surjue's imprisonment and death emphasize that the slum yard is not an isolated phenomenon but a symbol of a pervasive social malaise that corrupts all social institutions, including a rather brutish judicial system.

Despite the emphasis on institutional failures in a work like *The Hills* Mais's fiction is not merely one-dimensional social protest. The work also suggests that the human tragedy is compounded by an inscrutable universal fate, but that in the final analysis the individual's salvation, from hostile environment and fate alike, lies in his or her own hands. Thus although he is a failure in one sense, Surjue nevertheless emerges with heroic dimensions because he embodies a certain integrity and nobility which are heightened rather than diminished by his conflict with a brutal world. Similarly, notwithstanding the *public* downfall of the folk preacher, Bra Man, in *Brother Man,* he and his woman Minette enjoy a triumph of sorts, a triumph which flows from their individual strength and from the integrity of their relationship. The practical attempts at brotherhood fail, but Bra Man's dreams of brotherhood are validated by the moral strength of Bra Man the dreamer. And, conversely, Bra Man's *individual* integrity is confirmed by his capacity to seek brotherhood on behalf of his fellow creatures. Finally, this insistence on that inner strength and on those private resources which are necessary for survival in a hostile world is most explicit in the most introspective of the novels, *Black Lightning.* In this work the setting shifts from urban

Kingston to rural Jamaica which becomes the background for an intense analysis of private relationships between a selected number of characters. In effect Mais's fiction is simultaneously an act of socio-political commitment and an exploration of that inner life which is essential to the individual who attempts to deal with the world outside.

—Lloyd W. Brown

MALAMUD, Bernard. American. Born in Brooklyn, New York, 26 April 1914. Educated at Erasmus Hall, New York; City College of New York, 1932–36, B.A. 1936; Columbia University, New York, 1937–38, M.A. 1942. Married Ann de Chiara in 1945; one son and one daughter. Teacher, New York high schools, evenings 1940–49; Instructor to Associate Professor of English, Oregon State University, Corvallis, 1949–61. Since 1961, Member of the Division of Language and Literature, Bennington College, Vermont. Visiting Lecturer, Harvard University, Cambridge, Massachusetts, 1966–68. Recipient: Rosenthal Award, 1958; Daroff Memorial Award, 1958; Ford Fellowship, 1959, 1960; National Book Award, 1959, 1967; Pulitzer Prize, 1967; O. Henry Award, 1969, 1973. Member, National Institute of Arts and Letters, 1964; American Academy of Arts and Sciences, 1967.

PUBLICATIONS

Fiction

    The Natural. 1952.
    The Assistant. 1957.
    The Magic Barrel (stories). 1958.
    A New Life. 1961.
    Idiots First (stories). 1963.
    The Fixer. 1966.
    Pictures of Fidelman: An Exhibition. 1969.
    The Tenants. 1971.
    Rembrandt's Hat (stories). 1973.

Other

    A Malamud Reader, edited by Philip Rahv. 1967.

Bibliography: *Malamud: An Annotated Checklist* by R. N. Kosofsky, 1969.

Reading List: *Malamud* by Sidney Richman, 1966; *Malamud: A Collection of Critical Essays* edited by Joyce and Leslie Field, 1974; *Art and Idea in the Novels of Malamud* by Robert Ducharme, 1974; *Malamud and the Trial by Love* by Sandy Cohen, 1974.

*   *   *

Bernard Malamud, one of the most popular contemporary writers of Jewish-American fiction, contributes significantly to the growth in ethnic consciousness in American letters. He raises serious questions about the American dream and the American tradition. The luckless and bungling heroes who populate his fiction are twentieth-century replies to the supernatural powers of Natty Bumpo, the heroic stature of Captain Ahab, and the moral development of Isabel Archer.

Malamud's short stories and novels derive from two essential aspects of his past: his Jewish upbringing and his secular education. The Jewish past provides Malamud with much surface detail (setting, dialect) and with the ironic tone and biting humor of much of his fiction. Also Malamud is a careful student of the Western Christian literary tradition which often provides him with symbol sets and literary parallels. It even colors his theme of redemption through suffering to the extent that his characters appear more as Christian martyrs than as Yiddish-speaking immigrants.

His first novel, *The Natural*, is his most ingenious adaptation of Christian legend. A story of the baseball hero, Roy Hobbs, it is a conflation of the American myth of the sports hero, specifically the baseball hero, and the medieval legends of the Fisher King and the Grail. A natural athlete, Roy is plagued by false goddesses and unworthy goals. In the end, when promised the opportunity to redeem the dry land, the unsuccessful team, Roy fails morally. He helps fix the game.

The Assistant, also a novel of striving after new gods, is one of Malamud's most oppressive: it is, however, not a story of hopelessness. Frank Alpine, a Gentile who participates in the robbery of Morris Bober's grocery and rapes Helen Bober, learns to repent for his earlier self. An admirer of St. Francis, Frank is redeemed through his suffering – he becomes a Jew like his former employer Morris Bober. One of the most effective aspects of this novel is the vividly evoked setting. The Bobers are living a life of poverty and desperation. Into this darkened vision beam the lights of Frank's love for Helen and his gradual salvation through the laws of self-sacrifice.

A New Life, a barely disguised *roman à clef* of Malamud's years at Oregon State University, chronicles the growth of Sam Levin from loser to father. He arrives at a first teaching position; he is approaching thirty, anxious to please, yet filled with aspirations. Only after he gets to Cascadia College does he discover that the school is not a liberal arts school but a technical institute. This is only the first of a series of disappointments and reversals in his original plan. In his first year, he has an affair with the wife of the chairman of the English department and is forced to leave Cascadia and the profession of teaching. He takes with him a pregnant woman whom he no longer loves, her two adopted children, and a mature vision of the responsibility of the individual.

In *The Fixer*, Malamud turns from the American landscape to the Russian countryside. The plot of the novel is based on the Mendel Belis case of the early twentieth century. But the character Yakov Bok is a production of the imagination of Malamud. A simple, irreligious Jew, Yakov attempts to escape the *shtetl*, Jewishness, and an unfaithful wife by slipping out of the Pale of Settlement. He is discovered living in a Christian area and accused to the ritual murder of a Gentile boy. The development of his Jewish and humanitarian consciousness is a direct result of his torture in the Russian prison. His victory over disease, death, and insanity is more than a physical one and more than an individual one.

In *Pictures of Fidelman*, a picaresque novel, Arthur Fidelman travels to Italy, first to study art, then to paint, finally simply to become human. Three of the episodes collected in this novel had been previously published as short stories. By collecting them into a single volume and adding new episodes, Malamud rounds out the bungling and lost character that is Fidelman. In this foreign setting, an American innocent, like many American innocents before him, learns what Europe has to offer. But, more than that, he learns what his own inadequacies are.

The Tenants, an experimental novel, suggests some of the complexities of the relationship between blacks and Jews in mid-twentieth-century America. Malamud's ambivalence about this relationship is apparent in the three suggested endings to the novel. Added to the problems of black-white interaction are the deprived atmosphere of the setting (an abandoned tenement house) and the jealousy of competitors (both main characters are novelists). As the conflict intensifies between Harry Lesser and Willie Spearmint, Malamud develops social, sexual, political, and even aesthetic implications of their argument. In the end, they represent also the struggle between the formalist writer and the Marxist writer.

The tales in Malamud's collections run the gamut from sheer fantasy to painful realism. These short stories are most often peopled by the Jews of Malamud's experience – immigrants and second generation Americans. Even in the most fantastic of the tales, the quality of the Yiddish past filters through the fiction, either in the turn of a phrase or in the detail of a setting or biographical background or in a thematic concern with the holiness of intellectuality.

In the best examples of his short fiction the main characters share more with the Yiddish past than do the main characters of his novels. Whether that hero be an unfeeling *yeshive* student ("Magic Barrel"), a father protecting an idiot son ("Idiots First"), a modern-day Job confronted by a black Jewish angel ("Angel Levine"), a talking bird ("The Jewbird"), a guilty son duped by a fake miracle rabbi ("The Silver Crown"), a frightened American in Russia accosted by a censored writer ("Man in the Drawer"), or a talking horse ("The Talking Horse"), each of these individuals is clearly indebted to the Jewish past in the Diaspora. Each is specifically indebted to the feelings of ambivalent chosenness that is the position of the Jew in Europe since the first century.

—Barbara Gitenstein

MALLOCK, William Hurrell. English. Born in Cheriton Bishop, Devon, 7 February 1849. Educated privately under Reverend Philpot at Littlehampton; Balliol College, Oxford (Newdigate Prize, 1871), 1869–74, degrees 1871, 1874. Novelist and political and philosophical polemicist from 1875; lectured in the United States, 1907. *Died 2 April 1923.*

PUBLICATIONS

Fiction

> *The New Republic; or, Culture, Faith, and Philosophy in an English Country House.* 1877; edited by John Lucas, 1975.
> *The New Paul and Virginia; or, Positivism on an Island.* 1878.
> *A Romance of the Nineteenth Century.* 1881.
> *The Old Order Changes.* 1886.
> *A Human Document.* 1892.
> *The Heart of Life.* 1895.
> *The Individualist.* 1899.
> *The Veil of the Temple; or, From Night to Twilight.* 1904.
> *An Immortal Soul.* 1908.

Verse

> *Poems.* 1867.
> *The Parting of the Ways: A Poetic Epistle.* 1867.

The Isthmus of Suez. 1871.
Poems. 1880.
Verses. 1893.
Lucretius on Life and Death. 1900.

Other

Every Man His Own Poet; or, The Inspired Singer's Recipe Book. 1872.
Is Life Worth Living? (essays). 1879.
Social Equality: A Short Study in a Missing Science. 1882.
Atheism and the Value of Life: Five Studies in Contemporary Literature. 1884.
Property and Progress; or, A Brief Enquiry into Contemporary Social Agitation in England. 1884.
In an Enchanted Island; or, A Winter Retreat in Cyprus. 1889.
The Landlords and the National Income: A Chart Showing the Proportion Borne by the Rental of the Landlords to the Gross Income of the People. 1884.
Labour and the Popular Welfare. 1893.
Studies of Contemporary Superstition. 1895.
Classes and Masses; or, Wealth, Wages, and Welfare in the United Kingdom: A Handbook of Social Facts for Political Thinkers and Speakers. 1896.
Aristocracy and Evolution. 1898.
Doctrine and Doctrinal Disruption, Being an Examination of the Intellectual Position of the Church of England. 1900.
Religion as a Credible Doctrine. 1902.
The Fiscal Dispute Made Easy. 1903.
The Reconstruction of Belief. 1905.
A Critical Examination of Socialism. 1907.
The Nation as a Business Firm: An Attempt to Cut a Path Through the Jungle. 1910.
Social Reform as Related to Realities and Delusions: An Examination of the Increase and Distribution of Wealth from 1801 to 1910. 1914.
The Limits of Pure Democracy. 1819; abridgement, as *Democracy,* 1924.
Capital, War, and Wages: Three Questions in Outline. 1918.
Memoirs of Life and Literature. 1920.

Editor, *Lucretius* (selections). 1878.
Editor, *Letters, Remains, and Memoirs of E. A. Seymour, 12th Duke of Somerset.* 1893.

Reading List: *The Novels of Mallock* by Amy B. Adams, 1934; "The Novels of Mallock" by Charles C. Nickerson, in *English Literature in Transition 6,* 1963 (includes bibliography); *Literature and Politics in the Nineteenth Century* by John Lucas, 1971.

*   *   *

William Hurrell Mallock became an overnight sensation with his first published work, *The New Republic.* He continued to find readers and stir controversy throughout the closing years of the nineteenth century, but died virtually forgotten in 1923. Byron asserted that he was born for opposition, and the same may be said of Mallock. Fortunately for Byron, he died before old age could make some of his attitudes irrelevant. Unfortunately for Mallock, he did not. As a result, he often gives the impression in his later years of tilting at windmills or, worse, of fighting a purely phantom enemy.

Mallock was by nature, one might say, a conservative in politics, in literature, and in religious matters. Although he never became a Catholic, he revered the Roman church; he loathed the Broad Church movement, and had a lasting contempt for its leaders, especially for Jowett, Master of Mallock's college, Balliol, even when those leaders were dead or superseded. He had an equally strong detestation for Liberals in politics, and he thought that all socialists were either madmen or frauds. In literary matters he admired the Roman poets and satirists, had little good to say of nineteenth-century writers, and thought Swinburne should have been horsewhipped for his *Songs Before Sunrise*. In short, Mallock appears as everyone's favourite caricature of the crusty, out-of-touch blimp, growling his way through a life of almost comic irrelevance.

Yet Mallock at his best is a formidable satirist, an important spokesman for Conservatism, and an elegant essayist, whose *In an Enchanted Island* must be one of the best travel books ever written. In a long life, he published volumes of poetry, novels, political treatises, works of religious polemic, social critiques, collections of literary criticism: in fact, there was scarcely anything that he did not touch on at some time or another. At the end of his life he published *Memoirs of Life and Literature*, a typically contentious, witty volume, full of valuable anecdotes.

His masterpiece is undoubtedly *The New Republic*. It is a *roman à clef* in which Mallock brilliantly holds up for inspection and, usually, ridicule, the ideas and beliefs of famous contemporaries. Among them are Jowett, Matthew Arnold, Walter Pater, Thomas Huxley and William Tyndall. (For a full list of the characters, and a key to their originals, the reader should consult my edition of the work, 1975.) Only one man is allowed to escape censure. John Ruskin appears lightly disguised as Mr. Herbert, breathing woe and damnation to his assembled audience. Ruskin was delighted by the portrait and told a friend that Mallock understood him better than any man living. Mallock himself came to have doubts about Ruskin, mostly because of Ruskin's interest in working-class politics (he took particular exception to *Unto This Last* and *Fors Clavigera*), and in his later works tended to play the role of Mr. Herbert himself. That is to say that, whether writing novel, polemic, or straightforward propaganda, he appears as the prophet of doom, telling his audience how unhappy they are because God is being killed off, how unfortunate because society is being levelled down to a common greyness, how lacking in cultural resource because the great writers of the past are increasingly neglected. It was a role he clearly enjoyed.

Mallock is often outrageous, frequently silly, and sometimes shrill and spiteful. But he is always readable, and at his best he is a weighty adversary.

—John Lucas

MALORY, Sir Thomas.   Identification of the author is not certain: English; lived in the 15th century; from the late 19th century claimed by some scholars to be Sir Thomas Malory of Newbold Revell – a claim now disputed.

PUBLICATIONS

Prose

    Le Morte Darthur Reduced into English.   1485; edited by Eugène Vinaver, 3 vols., 1947; revised edition, 1967.

Reading List: *Malory* by M. C. Bradbrook, 1958; *Essays on Malory* edited by J. A. W. Bennett, 1963; *Malory's Originality* by R. M. Lumiansky, 1964; *The Book of Kyng Arthur: The Unity of Malory's Morte Darthur* by C. Moorman, 1965; *Romance and Chronicle: A Study of Malory's Prose Style* by P. J. C. Field, 1971; *Malory: Style and Vision in Le Morte Darthur* by Mark Lambert, 1975; *Malory's Morte Darthur* by Larry D. Benson, 1976.

* * *

Sir Thomas Malory's *Le Morte Darthur* is the basic source of our view of Lancelot, Arthur, and Gawain, of the Grail legend and of the Round Table. Although he did not invent most of his material, Malory abridged the monstrous bulk of the sources, simplified the narrative structure, modernized the tone and themes, and devised a coherent framework for these important tales. Camelot would not be one of the principal mythical settings of Western culture if Malory had not rescued the tales from extinction by organizing them in a vernacular prose version which focuses strongly on humanistic values, is couched in a graceful style, and is accessible to a large body of readers. The earlier romances glorified the epic virtues of *comitatus* and battlefield prowess as well as the medieval ideal of renunciation of worldly values. By focusing on individuals and their inner conflicts and placing high values on secular honor and political order, Malory modernized the basic themes. Particularly through his restructuring of the tales around the character of Lancelot, the best of worldly men, Malory transformed the tales for a modern reader. Malory's identity remains uncertain, but whoever he was, he did his work well.

William Caxton edited and printed the book he chose to call *Le Morte Darthur* because he thought of it as an exemplar: "that noble men may see and lerne the noble actes of chyvalrye, the jentyl and vertuous dedes that somme knyghtes used in tho dayes, by whyche they came to honour, and how they that were vycious were punysshed and ofte put to shame and rebuke." The work was known only in Caxton's version until W. F. Oakeshott discovered a fifteenth-century manuscript version in the Fellows' Library of Winchester College in 1934. Eugène Vinaver then edited the standard version, using the Caxton and Winchester texts.

The court of King Arthur is a central myth of human idealism, and it has occupied that place in Western thought for 500 years. Spenser, Tennyson, the Pre-Raphaelite painters, Sidney Lanier, John Steinbeck and others have drawn from the Malory canon, but none has rivalled the contribution he made. Because he combined material from French and Middle English romances, some scholars have dismissed him as a mere compiler, but a careful study of his work shows that in his abridging and organizing of the tales, Malory improved them and wove them into a pattern with rich symbolic threads. C. S. Lewis likened the result to a medieval cathedral. "Though every part of it was made by a man, the whole has rather grown than been made. Such things have a kind of existence that is almost midway between the works of art and those of nature."

One of the major techniques Malory used to gain coherence is the elimination of many minor characters and the reassignment of key adventures to knights he wished to emphasize. Thus some encounters undertaken by Gawain, Cador, and others in the sources are attributed in Malory to Lancelot. The mythic tale of the exiled nobleman who finds his heritage and proves his lineage, which is associated with Parzival among others in continental tales, is used to flesh out the story of Gareth, who is only an alliterative name in the sources.

Malory's small cast is headed by Merlin, the figures of the Tristram cycle, the families of King Lot and King Pellinore, the characters associated with the Grail, and Arthur, Guenevere, and Lancelot. He achieves a coordinating effect by using characters and incidents from one set of adventures to foreshadow or symbolize events and themes in another. He capitalizes on the similarities of incident between the Tristram story and the central love triangle to ennoble the character of Arthur; the feuding between the families of Lot and Pellinore demonstrates a major weakness of the knightly bond which will be dissolved by the last campaign; the ethos of the Grail quest stands in stark contrast to the accepted behavior of merely adventurous questers.

Lancelot is the fulcrum on which Malory's work turns. His pre-eminence among knights is predicted before the founding of the Round Table, and he is the last of the major figures left alive. His trials and internal struggles are at the centre of many of the individual episodes and are the key to the major conflicts of the work. Sir Ector's lament over his body is an elegy for an entire era. Gawain's character suffers most from the advancement of Lancelot. In early stories Gawain was a noble knight and, as Arthur's nephew, foremost in the fellowship; in Malory's version Gawain is noted for violence and vengeance. He is noble only in his deathbed reconciliation with Lancelot.

Even Lancelot's failings are related to triumph. His illegitimate son, Galahad, is the finest of other-worldly knights and achieves completely the Grail quest Lancelot achieves partially. Though Lancelot slips back into the love affair with Guenevere after the Grail quest, he alone is able to heal Sir Urry, who can be healed only by the best knight in the world.

In the French account of the Grail quest, Lancelot is a symbol of sin. The hermits he meets deliver long and cruel lectures on his weakness and guilt. Malory omits the most condemnatory passages and focuses on instability as Lancelot's fatal weakness. His Lancelot has a limited vision of the Grail and develops spiritual awareness as he realizes the limitations of the earthly code of which he is the outstanding proponent. His failure to hold to that higher vision is a tragedy, but Lancelot remains a hero.

This careful development of Lancelot as a sympathetic and admirable character is related to the overall humanistic theme. In contrast to the renunciation-of-the-world theme of the French source, Malory emphasizes his view of chivalry as the closest man can come to a perfect society. Since he worked during the turbulent years of the War of the Roses, finishing in 1469–70, the reader can appreciate his enthusiasm for stability and idealism. His ideals are put forth in the oath sworn yearly by Arthur's knights:

> never to do outerage nothir morthir, and allwayes to fle treson, and to gyff mercy unto hym that askith mercy, uppon payne of forfiture [of their] worship and lordship of kynge Arthure for evirmore; and allwayes to do ladyes, damesels, and jantilwomen and wydowes [socour:] strengthe hem in hir rightes, and never to enforce them, uppon payne of dethe. Also that no man take no batayles in a wrongefull quarell for no love ne for no worldis goodis.

Malory saw the crumbling of that world not as a punishment of sin but as a tragedy brought on by instability, a flaw he found in his main character, Lancelot, and in the Englishmen of his own tempestuous time.

—Barbara M. Perkins

MANDER, Jane.   New Zealander.   Born in 1877. *Died in 1949.*

PUBLICATIONS

Fiction

The Story of a New Zealand River.   1920.
The Passionate Puritan.   1921.
The Strange Attraction.   1922.

Allen Adair.   1925; edited by Dorothea Turner, 1971.
The Besieging City.   1926.
Pins and Pinnacles.   1928.

Reading List: *Mander,* 1972, and *"The Story of a New Zealand River:* Perceptions and Prophecies in an Unfixed Society," in *Critical Essays on the New Zealand Novel* edited by Cherry Hankin, 1976, both by Dorothea Turner.

*   *   *

The slender output and belated recognition of Jane Mander have until recently disguised her importance as a seminal figure in New Zealand literature. As her novels were largely ignored on first publication, so did her artistic purposes change, with the result that three of her six novels are of slight critical significance. *The Strange Attraction* now reads like a strident attempt at sensationalism, while in *The Besieging City* and *Pins and Pinnacles* she used New York and London locations in an apparent attempt to extend her readership.

It is on the other three novels with a New Zealand location that Jane Mander's literary stature must rest. *The Story of a New Zealand River* has some of the obvious technical clumsiness of a first novel, in particular a very awkward handling of narrative perspective; yet it remains the definitive fictional study of the puritanism which until recently has dominated New Zealand society, and its naturalistic emphasis on environmental conditioning anticipates the brilliant documentary sections of the undeservedly neglected *The Passionate Puritan.* Mander's fourth novel is, however, her masterpiece. *Allen Adair* deals, like its predecessors, with emergent society in the northern areas of New Zealand, but the texture of human relationships is much more subtle. Here, the former themes of puritanism, self-induced isolation, and frigid marriage are again prominent, but there is also an undercurrent of latent homosexuality between the best-conceived male characters in Jane Mander's essentially feminist fictional world.

It is not surprising that restricted library access and related social attitudes left Jane Mander at her death virtually unknown in her own country, but recent responses indicate that her place is beside Katherine Mansfield and Frank Sargeson as pioneers in the fictional dissection of New Zealand colonial culture.

—Howard McNaughton

MANLEY, Delariviere; also known as Mary Manley.   English.   Born in the Channel Islands, probably in Jersey, 7 April 1663. Married her cousin John Manley c. 1688 (already married; subsequently deserted her; died, 1714). Lived with the Duchess of Cleveland, then travelled in England, 1694–96; writer from 1695; involved in an attempt to defraud the estate of a man named Pheasant, 1705; wrote romances from 1705; arrested for libel (*New Atalantis*), 1709, released 1710; contributed to *The Examiner* from 1711. *Died 11 July 1724.*

PUBLICATIONS

Collections

Novels (The Secret History of Queen Zarah and the Zarazians, The New Atalantis, Memoirs of Europe, The Adventures of Rivella), edited by Patricia Köster.   2 vols., 1971.

Fiction

Letters, to Which Is Added a Letter from a Supposed Nun in Portugal. 1696; as *A Stage-Coach Journey to Exeter*, 1725.
The Secret History of Queen Zarah and the Zarazians. 1705.
The Lady's Packet of Letters, Taken from Her by a French Privateer in Her Passage to Holland. 1707.
Secret Memoirs and Manners of Several Persons of Quality of Both Sexes from the New Atalantis, an Island in the Mediterranean. 1709.
Memoirs of Europe, Towards the Close of the Eighth Century. 1710.
Court Intrigues. 1711.
The Adventures of Rivella; or, The History of the Author of the Atalantis. 1714.
The Power of Love, in *Seven Novels.* 1720.

Plays

The Lost Lover; or, The Jealous (produced 1696). 1696.
The Royal Mischief (produced 1696). 1696.
Almyna; or, The Arabian Vow (produced 1706). 1707.
Lucius, The First Christian King of Britain (produced 1717). 1717.

Other

A True Narrative of the Examination of the Marquis de Guiscard. 1711.
A True Relation of the Intended Riot on Queen Elizabeth's Birthday. 1711.
A Modest Inquiry. 1714.

Reading List: *Five Queer Women* by Walter and Clare Jerrold, 1929; *Popular Fiction Before Richardson* by John Richetti, 1969.

*   *   *

Delariviere Manley achieved fame and notoriety in 1709 with the publication of *Secret Memoirs and Manners of several Persons of Quality of Both Sexes from the New Atalantis*, a collection of scandalous narratives about prominent Whig nobles and politicians. The enormous success of this book is easy to understand; the scandals it provided were mostly sexual, and Manley had a talent for the vivid rendition of what the 18th century called "warm" scenes. Like many sensational and erotic narratives of the age, *The New Atalantis* has an elaborate moral facade and claims to be an outraged satiric attack on the corruption of the times. Manley begins Part II by calling her book a satire "on different Subjects, Tales, Stories, and Characters of Invention, after the Manner of Lucian, who copy'd from Varro." The best parts of the book are precisely the satiric ones, those recurring and energetic denunciations of the age which add up to a lively and often grotesque panorama of intrigue, lust, betrayal, and even crime. Manley's stories were based on some facts, and the book was designed as Tory political propaganda to undermine public confidence in the Whig ministry, which fell from power in 1710. But *The New Atalantis* was reprinted several times until 1736, long after its political scandals had faded, suggesting that Manley's real achievement was the effective imagining of a mythical world of corruption and immorality in which readers found satisfactions that were neither satiric nor political.

In a way, Manley's abilities as a writer of narrative lagged behind her intelligence as a satirist and political writer. She wrote an interesting preface to her 1705 scandal novel about the Duchess of Marlborough, *The History of Queen Zarah*, in which she speaks with sense and clarity of the need for the probable and the natural in those "little histories" such as her book which she claims are now replacing the once popular French romances. And yet the characters in *Queen Zarah* are monsters of vice, the language they speak rhetorically swollen, and the scenes and actions depicted are wildly exaggerated. In *The Adventures of Rivella*, a thinly fictionalized version of her own curiously melodramatic private life (seduced into a bigamous marriage by her cousin and then deserted), Manley manages a restrained and even touching account of female suffering. But her other books are of little intrinsic literary value; they are vigorous and often lively but clumsy and generally incoherent narratives. Though she apparently aspired to narrative virtues such as consistency of character and probability of situation which the masters of the English novel were shortly to achieve, Manley could only describe a world of blasted female innocence and brutal male lust. But she managed to present such moral and sexual melodrama very effectively, and her works give us access to an imaginary world which had a powerful hold on a large audience for a good part of the 18th century.

—John Richetti

MANNING, Olivia. English. Born in Portsmouth, Hampshire. Educated in private schools. Married Reginald Donald Smith in 1939. Press Officer, United States Embassy, Cairo, 1942; Press Assistant, Public Information Office, Jerusalem, 1943–44, and British Council, Jerusalem, 1944–45; novel reviewer for *Spectator*, London, 1949–50, and *The Sunday Times*, London, 1965–66. Recipient: Tom-Gallon Trust Award, 1949. C.B.E. (Commander, Order of the British Empire), 1976. Lives in London.

Publications

Fiction

The Wind Changes. 1937.
Growing Up: A Collection of Short Stories. 1948.
Artist among the Missing. 1949.
School for Love. 1951.
A Different Face. 1953.
The Doves of Venus. 1955.
My Husband Cartwright (stories). 1956.
The Balkan Trilogy: *The Great Fortune.* 1960; *The Spoilt City,* 1962; *Friends and Heroes,* 1965.
A Romantic Hero and Other Stories. 1967.
The Play Room. 1969; as *The Camperlea Girls,* 1969.
The Rain Forest. 1974.
The Danger Tree. 1977.
The Battle Lost and Won. 1978.

Plays

Screenplay: *The Play Room*, 1970.

Radio Plays: *The Little Ottleys*, from novels by Ada Leverson, 1964; *The Card*, from the novel by Arnold Bennett, 1964; *Futility*, 1973, and *The Polyglots*, 1977, from novels by William Gerhardie.

Other

The Remarkable Expedition: The Story of Stanley's Rescue of Emin Pasha from Equatorial Africa. 1947; as *The Reluctant Rescue*, 1947.
The Dreaming Shore (travel). 1950.
Extraordinary Cats. 1967.

Reading List: *Continuance and Change: The Contemporary British Novel Sequence* by Robert K. Morris, 1972.

* * *

Like Somerset Maugham, Olivia Manning admits her debt as a novelist to life as she knows it. "I write out of experience," she says, "I have no fantasy." Living much abroad has enriched her fictional resources with a variety of foreign backgrounds. The story of *Artist among the Missing* is set in the Middle East, and *School for Love* is about war-time Jerusalem seen through the eyes of an adolescent English boy. In her most important work, the "Balkan Trilogy," the events of *The Great Fortune* and *The Spoilt City* take place in Romania between the beginning of the last war and the German occupation of the country; the final volume, *Friends and Heroes*, moves to Athens, and ends, after the fall of Crete, with escape to Alexandria. Miss Manning's recent novel, *The Danger Tree*, continues the adventures of these characters in war-time Egypt. In an intervening book, *The Rain Forest*, she depicts sinister forces at work on a fictional island in the Indian Ocean.

A notable aspect of Olivia Manning's art is the intricate interplay she achieves between her backgrounds and the conflicts of personal relationship among the characters who inhabit them. Thus, in *The Rain Forest*, the seething political intrigue and unrest of the island, and the charged, sultry presence of the primeval forest itself, intensify the emotional tensions between the married couple who remain obstinately separate in their individualities, yet need each other with the wry, accepting love of long mutual knowledge, compromise, and lack of illusion. This interaction of public with private, each strengthening the credibility and conviction of the other, is most triumphantly realized in the "Balkan Trilogy," the culmination of Olivia Manning's formidable gifts and one of the major contributions to post-war English fiction.

Hitherto the writer's clarity and precision of style and cool, ironic detachment had sometimes tended to resemble hardness; but here it deepens, without losing any of its biting edge, into a greater warmth of human sympathy. The story unfolds through the sharp yet compassionate consciousness of Harriet Pringle: newly married, a stranger in Bucharest, and painfully attempting to understand the complexities not only of an alien political situation and people, but of her own ambivalent attitude towards her husband, who works for a British cultural organization in the city. The authenticity of atmosphere and detail in this authoritative picture of a nation's slow corruption and disintegration into foredoomed collapse is at once meticulous and comprehensive. So too is the subtle observation of character, from the contrarieties of the admirable yet maddening Guy to the comic absurdities of the aristocratic emigré Yakimov – a portrait of a charming, amoral rogue who makes a worthy companion for Pamela Hansford Johnson's Daniel Skipton. The breadth and command of her historical range, her vividly visual sense of place, and her psychological perspicacity, place Olivia Manning among the most skilful fictional chroniclers of our troubled time.

—Margaret Willy

MANSFIELD, Katherine. Pseudonym for Kathleen Mansfield Beauchamp. New Zealander. Born in Wellington, 14 October 1888. Educated at a school in Karori; Girls' High School, Wellington, 1898–99; Miss Swainson's School, Wellington, 1900–03; Queen's College, London, 1903–06; Royal Academy of Music, Wellington, 1906–08. Married George Bowden in 1909 (separated, 1909; divorced, 1918); lived with John Middleton Murry from 1912; married him, 1918. Settled in London, 1908; contributed to *The New Age*, 1910–11; contributed to Murry's *Rhythm*, and its successor, *The Blue Review*, and later became his partner, 1911–13; reviewer for the *Westminster Gazette*, 1911–15; Founder, with Murry and D. H. Lawrence, *Signature* magazine, 1916; tubercular: lived for part of each year in the South of France, then Switzerland, from 1916; contributed to the *Athenaeum*, edited by Murry, 1919–20. Recipient: Femina-Vie Heureuse Prize, 1921. *Died 9 January 1923.*

PUBLICATIONS

Collections

Letters, edited by J. Middleton Murry.   2 vols., 1928.
Collected Stories.   1945.
Selected Stories, edited by Dan Davin.   1953.
Letters and Journals: A Selection, edited by C. K. Stead.   1977.

Fiction

In a German Pension (stories).   1911.
Je Ne Parle Pas Français.   1918.
Bliss and Other Stories.   1920.
The Garden Party and Other Stories.   1922.
The Dove's Nest and Other Stories.   1923.
Something Childish and Other Stories.   1924; as *The Little Girl and Other Stories*, 1924.
The Aloe.   1930.
The Mystery of Maata: A Novel, edited by Patrick A. Lawlor.   1946.
Undiscovered Country: The New Zealand Stories, edited by Ian A. Gordon.   1974.

Verse

Poems.   1923.

Other

Journal, edited by J. Middleton Murry. 1927; revised edition, 1934.
Novels and Novelists (reviews), edited by J. Middleton Murry. 1930.
Scrapbook, edited by J. Middleton Murry. 1939.
Letters to John Middleton Murry, 1913–1922, edited by Murry. 1951.
Passionate Pilgrimage: A Love Affair in Letters: Mansfield's Letters to John Middleton
    Murry from the South of France 1915–1920, edited by Helen McNeish. 1976.
The Urewera Notebook, edited by Ian A. Gordon. 1978.

Translator, with S. S. Koteliansky, Reminiscences of Leonid Andreyev, by
    Gorky. 1928.

Bibliography: The Critical Bibliography of Mansfield by Ruth C. Mantz, 1931; Mansfieldiana:
A Brief Mansfield Bibliography by G. N. Morris, 1948; Mansfield: Publications in Australia
1907–1909 by Jean E. Stone, 1977.

Reading List: The Loneliness of Mansfield by Patrick A. Lawlor, 1950; Mansfield: A Critical
Study by Sylvia Berkman, 1951; Mansfield: A Biography by Antony Alpers, 1953; Mansfield
by Ian A. Gordon, 1954; Mansfield by Saralyn R. Daly, 1965; Mansfield: An Appraisal by
Nariman Hormasji, 1967; The Edwardianism of Mansfield by Frederick J. Foot, 1969; The
Fiction of Mansfield by Marvin Magalaner, 1971; Mansfield: A Biography by Jeffrey Meyers,
1978.

*   *   *

Katherine Mansfield was the daughter of Harold Beauchamp, a New Zealand merchant
and banker. She was educated in various schools in Wellington, and in Queen's College,
London, where she had already begun to write. Back in Wellington at the age of 18, she
persuaded her family to allow her return to London, and she settled there before she was 20.
It took her two years to find an outlet for her short stories. Early in 1910 she was accepted by
The New Age, for which she produced a series of tartly satirical stories with settings that were
familiar from her experiences in England, Belgium, and Bavaria. The Bavarian stories,
unsympathetic portrayals of German provincial life, were collected in a volume In a German
Pension, which was well reviewed.
    Katherine Mansfield was by now dissatisfied with the narrow range of story which The
New Age expected of her (the editor rejected her more romantic writing). A chance meeting
with John Middleton Murry, then editing the periodical Rhythm, led to an invitation to
contribute something different. With the help of one of her old New Zealand diaries, she
wrote her first recognisably New Zealand story "The Woman at the Store," and during 1912
and 1913 she provided Rhythm and its successor, The Blue Review, with a group of stories
based on memories of her native country and of her family. She became Murry's lover (they
were later married) and his partner. Stories of this period, like "An Indiscreet Journey" and
"The Little Governess," show advances both in technique and in sympathy, very different
from the brittle satire of her New Age contributions.
    Early in 1915, her brother arrived from New Zealand on his way to the British army. He
was killed in a training accident towards the end of the year and the shock of his death sent
Katherine Mansfield into a self-imposed exile in the south of France, where she began writing
"recollections of my own country." The first version of this new story was called The Aloe. It
was later revised and entitled "Prelude," first published in 1918 by Virginia and Leonard
Woolf at their Hogarth Press. "The Prelude method" – a plotless series of episodes that (in her
own words) "just unfolds and opens" – was something quite new in the English short story;
and when "Prelude" first appeared in book form in Bliss and Other Stories in 1920, Katherine

Mansfield was recognised as one of the significant writers in the literary scene of the time. Virginia Woolf, as her recently published letters indicate, was unable to repress feelings of jealousy at this rival talent.

Periodicals were now more hospitable. She returned to *The New Age*, and other journals took her work. Murry's accession in 1919 to the editorship of *The Athenaeum* provided her with the readiest outlet in periodical form for her later work. But by now she had turned ill and had to spend every winter, separated from Murry, in the south of France. Her last year, 1922, was spent in Switzerland, in a vain search for health.

The stories written after the appearance of *Bliss* appeared in the volume that consolidated her reputation, *The Garden Party and Other Stories*. It contained most of her best New Zealand stories ("At the Bay," "The Garden Party," "The Voyage," "The Stranger") but her new stories written with English or continental backgrounds (notably "The Daughters of the Late Colonel" and "Miss Brill") are written with equal sensitivity. After her death, in early 1923, Murry published two more volumes, collected from the periodicals and from her manuscripts.

Technically, Katherine Mansfield made the kind of advance in short-story writing that her contemporaries James Joyce and Virginia Woolf were making in the novel. She was a pioneer in the interior monologue and in the presentation of shifting viewpoints. Most of her best short stories are, without being mere photographic replicas, shaped-up recollections of her family and her New Zealand childhood. Her studies of children (seen through their own eyes and not those of adults) have few equals. Her stories are written in a carefully evolved prose that owes something to the techniques of poetic language: and her best stories measure up to the close analysis that is usually reserved for lyric poetry. Her range of material is not great – children on their own, children reacting to adults, the lonely and isolated woman in a hostile world, these are her main preoccupations. But, granted the narrowness of her range, she is penetrating and superbly effective. Her work has continued to attract.

After her death, Murry collected some of her manuscripts and portions of her notebooks, and published them as the *Journal of Katherine Mansfield*. The quality of the writing ensured it a great success and it became one of the important "confessional" writings of the period. Recent research on her manuscripts has demonstrated that his selection of material was very partial and pietistic. The saintly wraith that emerges from the *Journal* is largely the creation of selective editing. The real Katherine Mansfield was made of much tougher material, a hard-working professional at her trade, and the *Journal* should be regarded with caution by readers seeking biographical enlightenment.

—Ian A. Gordon

MARQUAND, John P(hillips). American. Born in Wilmington, Delaware, 10 November 1893. Educated at Newburyport High School, Massachusetts; Harvard University, Cambridge, Massachusetts, 1912–15, A.B. 1915. Served with the Massachusetts National Guard in the Mexican Border Service, 1916; student, Camp Plattsburg, 1917; commissioned 1st Lieutenant in the Field Artillery, and served with the 4th Brigade of the American Expeditionary Forces in France, 1917–18; Special Consultant to the Secretary of War, Washington, D.C., 1944–45; War Correspondent for the United States Navy, 1945. Married 1) Christina Davenport Sedgwick in 1922 (divorced, 1935), one son and one daughter; 2) Adelaide Hooker in 1937 (divorced, 1958), two sons and one daughter. Assistant Magazine Editor, *Boston Transcript*, 1915–17; with the Sunday Magazine Department, *New York Tribune*, 1919–20; advertising copywriter for the J. Walter Thompson Company, New

York, 1920–21; full-time writer from 1921. Member, Board of Overseers, Harvard University; Member, Editorial Board, Book-of-the-Month Club, New York. Litt.D.: University of Maine, Orono, 1941; University of Rochester, New York, 1944: Yale University, New Haven, Connecticut, 1950; D.H.L.: Bates College, Lewiston, Maine, 1954. Member, National Institute of Arts and Letters. *Died 16 July 1960.*

PUBLICATIONS

Fiction

The Unspeakable Gentleman. 1922.
Four of a Kind (stories). 1923.
The Black Cargo. 1925.
Do Tell Me, Doctor Johnson. 1928.
Warning Hill. 1930.
Haven's End (stories). 1933.
Ming Yellow. 1935.
No Hero. 1935.
Thank You, Mr. Moto. 1936.
The Late George Apley: A Novel in the Form of a Memoir. 1937.
Think Fast, Mr. Moto. 1937.
Mr. Moto Is So Sorry. 1938.
Wickford Point. 1939.
Mr. Moto Takes a Hand. 1940.
Don't Ask Questions. 1941.
H.M. Pulham, Esquire. 1941.
Last Laugh, Mr. Moto. 1942.
So Little Time. 1943.
Repent in Haste. 1945.
B.F.'s Daughter. 1946; as *Polly Fulton*, 1947.
Point of No Return. 1949.
It's Loaded, Mr. Bauer. 1949.
Melville Goodwin, USA. 1951.
Sincerely, Willis Wayde. 1955.
North of Grand Central (omnibus). 1956.
Mr. Moto's Three Aces (omnibus). 1956.
Stopover: Tokyo. 1957.
Life at Happy Knoll (stories). 1957.
Women and Thomas Harrow. 1958.

Play

The Late George Apley, with George S. Kaufman, from the novel by Marquand (produced 1944). 1946.

Other

Prince and Boatswain: Sea Tales from the Recollections of Rear-Admiral Charles Clark, with James Morris Morgan. 1915.

Lord Timothy Dexter of Newburyport, Mass. 1925.
Federalist Newburyport; or, Can Historical Fiction Remove a Fly from Amber? 1952.
Thirty Years (miscellany). 1954.
Timothy Dexter Revisited. 1960.

Reading List: *Marquand* by John J. Gross, 1963; *Marquand* by C. Hugh Holman, 1965; *The Late J. P. Marquand* by Stephen Birmingham, 1972.

*   *   *

John P. Marquand was a popular professional writer who whetted the skills of realistic and gently satiric writing to a very fine edge in several popular novels and scores of short stories in the mass circulation magazines before, in 1937, he set out to employ these skills with affectionate irony and gentle satire to the society of affluent upper-middle-class America in its seats of influence and power. For the twenty years that followed he was not only a practiced portrayer of American life but also one of the most popular novelists that America has produced.

The Late George Apley, which in 1937 broke the pattern of Marquand's popular fiction, is a parody of "collected letters with commentary" of distinguished people. It is a satiric picture of a very proper Bostonian and the ways in which the constraints of his society kept him in line and made him a good but stuffy and frustrated man. It received the Pulitzer Prize and launched Marquand's career as an important American social novelist. It was the first of three novels in which Marquand explored in contrasting panels aspects of the life of Boston. *Wickford Point* is the story of a decaying family loosely bound to the Transcendentalists, a comic picture of the diminishment of greatness and the sadness of the Indian summer of the spirit, and *H. M. Pulham, Esquire* is a self-portrait by a contemporary Bostonian, a post-World War I businessman, and the account of his ineffectual revolt against his class and its customs. These three novels form a triptych of New England life and utilize a variety of satiric skills, largely resulting from ironic points of view and the extensive use of the device of narrative flashback.

Like Sinclair Lewis, whom he greatly admired, Marquand moved on, after his complex portrait of Boston, to other cities and other professions in his growing list of studies of American life. *So Little Time* explores the vulgarly opulent world of West Coast movie-makers. It is laid during World War II, and suggests the inexorable passage of time. His other wartime novel, *B.F.'s Daughter*, deals with big business and the Washington bureaucracy, and is only a limited success. (A short novel *Repent in Haste* also deals with the war, but it is very slight.) *Point of No Return* is, after *The Late George Apley*, Marquand's best novel. It is the story of a banker who explores his New England small-town roots in an effort to find bases for a decision he must make, only to discover that all the decisions had already been made without his being aware of it, and that he has passed "the point of no return," a conclusion that most Marquand protagonists reach after painfully reviewing their lives. In addition to many amusing social caricatures, the book contains a serious examination of the sociology of New England towns, and to some degree of New York City. It and the Boston trilogy are Marquand's works which seem most likely to survive.

Melville Goodwin, USA is a portrayal of a General seen through the admiring eyes of a popular journalist. The journalist is a devastating portrait of the shallowness of the view of man held by the popular media, but, at the time the book was published, few critics recognised that it was an ironic novel that cut both ways, and they made the mistake of assuming that Marquand approved of the military officer and his decisions. It represents, after *The Late George Apley*, Marquand's most complex use of narrative point of view for satire, and indicates that his use of technical devices and his skill as a satiric novelist continued to grow through much of his long career. *Sincerely, Willis Wayde* is that Marquand novel most obviously like the Sinclair Lewis of the 1920's. It is a devastating portrait of a big business promoter, a man utterly without character. In 1958 Marquand published what he declared in advance would be his last novel, *Women and Thomas Harrow*, the story of a very successful playwright and his three marriages. This novel is a kind of self-consciously ironic *Tempest* to John P. Marquand's career.

Marquand is particularly notable for the double vision through which he could be in his world and still see it and himself from the vantage point of a detached on-looker. The result was that his portraits of American citizens, their frustrations, the extent to which their lives had already been determined by a structure of social decisions made by others without their awareness, and the sort of quiet desperation in which they lived out their days was particularly powerful. The reader who sees himself in some of his more absurd actions and postures in Marquand's novels has the feeling that he is also seeing Marquand as well. Like Sinclair Lewis he is the chronicler of men who make ineffectual revolts, of men who lack the stature of character and mind to be in any significant sense heroes; thus his ultimate view is comic. He examined the social conditions of American lives with irony and grace, and his "badgered American male" captures in his recurrent problems and poses not only how we behave, but also how hollow our lives often are at the core. He speaks both to our social-historical sense and to an unslaked spiritual thirst which our aridity creates. He never was capable of poetic soaring, but to his own age, at least, he spoke with ease and skill, with irony and wit, but, above all, with the authority of unsentimental knowledge.

—C. Hugh Holman

MARQUIS, Don(ald Robert Perry).   American.   Born in Walnut, Illinois, 29 July 1878. Educated at Walnut High School until age 15; worked at various jobs, then studied at the Corcoran Art School, Washington, D.C., 1899–1900. Married 1) Reina Melcher in 1909 (died, 1923), one son and one daughter; 2) the actress Marjorie Vonnegut in 1926. Worked as a clerk in the United States Customs Bureau, Washington, D.C., and as a reporter for the *Washington Times*, 1900–02; moved to Atlanta, Georgia: Associate Editor, *Atlanta News*, 1902–04; Editorial Writer, *Atlanta Journal*, 1904–07; Assistant Editor, to Joel Chandler Harris, on *Uncle Remus's Magazine*, Atlanta, 1907–09; moved to New York City, 1909; worked as a reporter on the New York *American* and the *Brooklyn Daily Eagle*, 1909–12; member of the editorial staff, 1912, and Columnist ("The Sun Dial"), 1912–20, New York *Evening Sun*; Columnist ("The Lantern"), *New York Tribune*, 1920–22; full-time writer from 1922. Recipient: Mark Twain Medal. Member, National Institute of Arts and Letters, 1923. *Died 29 December 1937.*

PUBLICATIONS

Collections

   The Best of Marquis, edited by Christopher Morley.   1939.

Fiction

   Danny's Own Story.   1912.
   The Cruise of the Jasper B.   1916.
   Carter and Other People (stories).   1921.

Pandora Lifts the Lid, with Christopher Morley. 1924.
When the Turtles Sing and Other Unusual Tales. 1928.
A Variety of People (stories). 1929.
Off the Arm. 1930.
Chapters for the Orthodox (stories). 1934.
Sun Dial Time (stories). 1936.
Sons of the Puritans. 1939.

Plays

The Old Soak (produced 1922). 1924.
The Dark Hours: Five Scenes from a History (produced 1932). 1924.
Words and Thoughts. 1924.
Out of the Sea (produced 1927). 1927.
Master of the Revels. 1934.

Verse

Dreams and Dust. 1915.
Noah an' Jonah an' Cap'n John Smith. 1921.
Poems and Portraits. 1922.
*Sonnets to a Red-Haired Lady (from a Gentleman with a Blue Beard) and Famous Love
    Affairs*. 1922.
The Awakening and Other Poems. 1924.
Archy and Mehitabel. 1927.
Love Sonnets of a Cave Man and Other Verses. 1928.
An Ode to Hollywood. 1929.
Archys Life of Mehitabel. 1933.
Archy Does His Part. 1935.

Other

Hermione and Her Little Group of Serious Thinkers. 1916.
Prefaces. 1919.
The Old Soak, and Hail and Farewell. 1921.
The Revolt of the Oyster. 1922.
Mr. Hawley Breaks into Song. 1923.
*The Old Soak's History of the World with Occasional Glances at Baycliff, L.I., and Paris,
    France*. 1924.
The Almost Perfect State (essays). 1927.
Her Foot Is on the Brass Rail. 1935.

Reading List: *O Rare Don Marquis: A Biography* by Edward Anthony, 1962.

*   *   *

Don Marquis is remembered as a humorist, but he wrote both humorous and serious
plays, poetry, and fiction. His last novel, *Sons of the Puritans*, is serious. Although unfinished,
this autobiographical narrative about a boy who grows to manhood in a small midwestern
town presents greater depth of feeling and complexity of character and situation than

Marquis's earlier, lighter novels. Like most of his work, it is well written and interesting. Like his other serious short work, however, it possibly suffers from Marquis's constant depression over having to do hack work to survive.

His serious poetry in particular sounds like the well written, graceful verse of other poets on the same well-worn themes. Yet his first collection of serious poems, *Dreams and Dust*, served a purpose; for the effect of much of his later comic verse – *Love Sonnets of a Cave Man*, for example – depends upon his sure knowledge of such themes in just such terms. Even his parodies of free verse, over the name of "Archy the Cockroach," occasionally contain poems that are comic largely on account of their sprightly elegant meter and rhyme.

Marquis is remembered chiefly for his creation of Archy, whose ideas and adventures first filled his newspaper columns and then were collected in books. Other columns, collected in *The Almost Perfect State*, deal lightly, humorously, sometimes seriously, with Marquis's notions concerning that State. Still other columns resulted in books about "The Old Soak," who became the central character in Marquis's only successful play.

The Old Soak, Archy the Cockroach, and Mehitabel the Cat reveal Marquis's comic capabilities at their best. As Archy, Marquis views life from the underside, that is, the side from which it appears ridiculous and therefore not to be taken seriously. So the incongruities, discrepancies, paradoxes, involved in this view – whether of man's morality and politics, Mehitabel's social and artistic pretensions, or any other matter – strike the reader as comic. Further, Archy's literary efforts make him ridiculous in turn, both because he is a cockroach and because he has the quite human soul of a free verse poet. For his broken typographic lines, without punctuation or capital letters, could not have been written by a cockroach and should not have been written by a poet. The comic effect is increased by the mockery of free verse and its maker.

Similarly, the Old Soak can not be taken seriously. His views of history, the Good Book, and prohibition, together with his misspellings and malapropisms, expose his ignorance and turn him into a figure of fun. For good reason, the play about him succeeded, banal as it is, whereas Marquis's more serious plays – mainly derived from legend and history – failed. Marquis's strength lies not in development of character, but in "characters," not in suspenseful action, but in absurd situations. These express his real gift, rare and rewarding in literature, the truly comic angle of vision.

—Robert F. Richards

MARRYAT, Frederick. English. Born in Westminster, London, 10 July 1792. Educated privately. Married Catherine Shairp in 1819; four sons and seven daughters, including the novelist Florence Marryat. Joined the Royal Navy, 1806; sailed as a midshipman on the *Impérieuse*, under Lord Cochrane, 1806–09, in the flagship *Centaur*, in the Mediterranean, 1810, and on the *Aeolus* and *Spartan* in the West Indies and off the coast of North America, 1811–12; sailed to the West Indies on the *Espiègle*, 1813; Lieutenant of the *Newcastle*, off the coast of North America, 1814 until invalided home, 1815; appointed Commander, 1815; commanded othe sloop *Beaver* cruising off St. Helena to guard against the escape of Napoleon, 1820–22; involved in suppression of Channel smuggling, on the *Rosario*, 1822; sailed in the *Larne* to the East Indies, 1823, and served in the Burmese war: Senior Naval Officer at Rangoon, 1824; commanded expedition up the Bassein River, 1825; appointed Captain of the *Tees*, 1825, and returned in her to England, 1826: C.B. (Companion, Order of the Bath), for services in Burma, 1826; commanded the *Adriadne* in the Atlantic service, 1828 until he retired to devote himself to writing, 1830; Editor, *Metropolitan Magazine*, London, 1832–35; lived in Brussels, 1836, Canada and the United States, 1837–39, and London, 1839–43; settled on a farm, Langham Manor, in Norfolk, 1843. Recipient: Royal

Humane Society gold medal, 1818. Fellow of the Royal Society, 1819; Member, Legion of Honour, 1833. *Died 9 August 1848.*

PUBLICATIONS

Collections

> *Novels,* edited by R. Brimley Johnson.   24 vols., 1896–98; revised edition, 26 vols., 1929–30.

Fiction

> *The Naval Officer; or, Scenes and Adventures in the Life of Frank Mildmay.*   1829.
> *The King's Own.*   1830.
> *Newton Forster; or, The Merchant Service.*   1832.
> *Peter Simple.*   3 vols., 1833–34.
> *Jacob Faithful.*   1834.
> *The Pacha of Many Tales.*   1835.
> *Japhet in Search of a Father.*   4 vols., 1835–36.
> *The Diary of a Blasé.*   1836; as *Diary on the Continent,* in *Olla Podrida,* 1840.
> *The Pirate, and The Three Cutters.*   1836; as *Stories of the Sea,* 1836.
> *Mr. Midshipman Easy.*   1836.
> *Snarleyyow; or, The Dog Fiend.*   1837; as *The Dog Fiend,* 1847.
> *The Phantom Ship.*   1839; edited by M. W. Disher, 1948.
> *Olla Podrida* (stories).   1840.
> *Poor Jack.*   1840.
> *Masterman Ready; or, The Wreck of the Pacific, Written for Young People.*   3 vols., 1841–42.
> *Joseph Rushbrook; or, The Poacher.*   1841; as *The Poacher,* 1846.
> *Percival Keene.*   1842.
> *The Settlers in Canada, Written for Young People.*   1844; edited by O. Warner, 1956.
> *The Mission; or, Scenes in Africa.*   1845.
> *The Privateer's-Man One Hundred Years Ago.*   1846.
> *The Children of the New Forest.*   1847.
> *The Little Savage,* completed by Frank S. Marryat.   2 vols., 1848–49.

Other

> *A Code of Signals for the Use of Vessels Employed in the Merchant Services.*   1817; revised edition, 1837, 1841.
> *A Suggestion for the Abolition of the Present System of Impressment in the Naval Service.*   1822.
> *The Floral Telegraph: A New Mode of Communication by Floral Signals.*   1836 (possibly not by Marryat).
> *The Diary in America, with Remarks on Its Institutions.*   6 vols., 1839; edited by Sydney Jackman, 1963.
> *Narrative of the Travels and Adventures of Monsieur Violet in California, Sonora, and Western Texas.*   1853; as *Travels and Romantic Adventures of Monsieur Violet among the Snake Indians,* 1843.
> *Valerie: An Autobiography* (not completed by Marryat).   2 vols., 1849.

Reading List: *Life and Letters of Marryat* by F. Church, 1872; *Marryat and the Old Navy* by Christopher Lloyd, 1939; *Marryat: A Rediscovery* by O. Warner, 1953; *Marryat: L'Homme et l'Oeuvre* by Maurice P. Gautier, 1973.

*   *   *

Though he is remembered as a children's author, Frederick Marryat began his fiction-writing as a novelist, and before that spent over twenty years at sea. His earliest books, in fact, are pamphlets on naval subjects. The material for his fiction was a career in the exotic world of Nelson's navy, the source of the potent English myth of Jack Tar: his writing owed little, therefore, to the latest literary fashions. One may perhaps compare him to Scott, who also felt himself to be an amateur, and was similarly reduced to writing desperately for money to maintain that position in his latter days. Neither author can be read with pleasure unless one accepts the convention of expansive, slow-moving story-telling. Scott's novels develop more profoundly within this plan, but Marryat was not without insights into contemporary concerns. Like Scott, he found history imaginatively exciting, and recreated it vividly; and he showed the Romantic sense of the importance of childhood and education, inflected towards a concern for moral training rather than in the Wordsworthian mystical direction, but still imaginatively handled. In, for example, *The Little Savage* the Rousseau-inspired motif of the child growing up cut off from civilisation is treated with considerable psychological grasp.

It was his concern for the accuracy of information conveyed to the young which led Marryat to writing for children: he was disgusted at the fantastic seamanship of *The Swiss Family Robinson*, and set out to improve upon it in *Masterman Ready*. Victorian boys were very lucky in this, for it opened to them the whole range of his sea stories, and his writing for children is itself free from the condescension and over-simplification of many boys' books. The novels are racy and vigorous, full of facts; the children's writing has a layer of simple piety, but also the charm of real information and practical instructions. In this he shows a grasp of the primitive bases of narrative satisfaction: his books all deal with situations in which he can make absorbing use of practical detail. The model may well be Defoe. He uses the desert-island story, where civilisation is rebuilt from nothing, in *Masterman Ready* and *The Little Savage*; he uses, in *The Settlers in Canada* and *The Children of the New Forest*, the similar outline of a civilised family improvising in a wild and dangerous setting; and in *Poor Jack* he takes the alternative design of a deprived individual living like a savage in the jungle of the city, as in Defoe's *Colonel Jack*. And always, like Defoe, Marryat tells us the details of how they did it, how it worked, and what it cost. In this kind of book looseness of design is not important: Carlyle's criticism of Marryat's writing as concerned with trivia is less true to our experience than Dr. Johnson's remark that no one ever put down *Robinson Crusoe* without wishing it was longer. Marryat's writing may be uneven, ill-planned, rambling – but it is also absorbing and delightful.

—J. S. Bratton

MARSH, Dame (Edith) Ngaio. New Zealander. Born in Christchurch, 23 April 1899. Educated at St. Margaret's College, Christchurch, 1910–14; Canterbury University College School of Art, Christchurch, 1915–20. Actress, 1920–23; theatrical producer, 1923–27; interior designer, London, 1928–32; thereafter a full-time writer; served in a Red Cross Unit in World War II; theatrical producer for O'Connor Theatre Management, New Zealand,

1944–52, and Canterbury University; Honorary Lecturer in Drama, Canterbury University, 1948. Recipient: Mystery Writers of America Grand Master Award, 1978. D.Litt.: University of Canterbury, 1963. O.B.E. (Officer, Order of the British Empire), 1948; D.B.E. (Dame Commander, Order of the British Empire), 1966. Fellow, Royal Society of Arts. Lives in Christchurch.

PUBLICATIONS

Fiction

A Man Lay Dead. 1934.
Enter a Murderer. 1935.
Death in Ecstasy. 1936.
The Nursing Home Mystery, with Henry Jellett. 1936.
Vintage Murder. 1937.
Artists in Crime. 1938.
Death in a White Tie. 1938.
Overture to Death. 1939.
Death at the Bar. 1940.
Death of a Peer. 1940; as Surfeit of Lampreys, 1941.
Death and the Dancing Footman. 1941.
Colour Scheme. 1943.
Died in the Wool. 1945.
The Final Curtain. 1947.
Swing Brother Swing. 1949; as A Wreath for Rivera, 1949.
Opening Night. 1951; as Night at the Vulcan, 1951.
Spinsters in Jeopardy. 1953.
Scales of Justice. 1955.
Death of a Fool. 1956; as Off with His Head, 1957.
Singing in the Shrouds. 1958.
False Scent. 1959.
Hand in Glove. 1962.
Dead Water. 1963.
Killer Dolphin. 1966; as Death at the Dolphin, 1967.
Clutch of Constables. 1968.
When in Rome. 1970.
Tied Up in Tinsel. 1972.
Black As He's Painted. 1974.
Last Ditch. 1977.
Grave Mistake. 1978.

Plays

Surfeit of Lampreys, with Owen B. Howell, from the novel by Marsh (produced 1950).
False Scent, from her own novel (produced 1961).
The Christmas Tree (juvenile). 1962.
A Unicorn for Christmas, music by David Farquhar (produced 1965).
Murder Sails at Midnight (produced 1972).

Television Play: Evil Liver, 1975.

Other

New Zealand, with R. M. Burdon.   1942.
A Play Toward: A Note on Play Production.   1946.
Perspectives: The New Zealander and the Visual Arts.   1960.
Play Production.   1960.
New Zealand.   1964.
Black Beech and Honeydew (autobiography).   1965.

*   *   *

Ngaio Marsh's *Black Beech and Honeydew* is principally about her life as a director-producer in the theatre and includes only passing references to her work as a mystery novelist. One such reference is a modest defence for the work she appears to consider only a means of livelihood rather than a vocation: "Intellectual New Zealand friends tactfully avoid all mention of my published work.... So it was astonishing, that time in England, to find myself broadcasting and being televised and interviewed and it was pleasant to find detective fiction being discussed as a tolerable form of reading by people whose opinion one valued. I suppose the one thing that can always be said in favour of the genre is that inside the convention the author may write with as good a style as he or she can command." Dame Ngaio's command of the genre has enabled her to create a body of work that is in quality, quantity, and popular appeal second only to the achievement of Agatha Christie. She resembles Christie also in the variety and richness of her backgrounds and in the good-humoured tone maintained throughout the novels.

Dame Ngaio has explained in a 1977 edition of *The Writer* that one rainy afternoon in 1933, having read a book by Christie or Sayers, she thought it would be "highly original" to write a mystery novel using the popular parlor game called "Murder" as a plot device. Thus *A Man Lay Dead* is a significant first novel in that it establishes those characteristics that have come to be Marsh's hall-marks: the attitude that fictional murder is primarily a game whose first obligation is to amuse, the interest in the habitations of the gently eccentric British middle and upper classes as locales, and the presentation of her perdurable detective, Roderick Alleyn.

Alleyn, who appears to be a more substantial, less quixotic version of Sayers's Lord Peter Wimsey, dominates virtually all of Dame Ngaio's mystery novels. He is occasionally joined by Nigel Bathgate and Inspector Fox, who play his Watsons. While he shows a remarkable inability to age, he nevertheless manifests a broadening of interests and represents (according to Earl F. Bargainnier in *Armchair Detective*, 1978) the combination of the aristocratic gentleman-detective of the 1930's and the hard-nosed cop of the later police procedurals.

Dame Ngaio has written some travel books about New Zealand and has used her native country as a background for a few of her thrillers, but most often she sets her novels in the British Isles and uses the theatre or a theatrical situation for backgrounds, such as *Opening Night (Night at the Vulcan)* and *Overture to Death.* Her experience in the theatre is also reflected in her sharp ear for dialogue and dialect.

—Nancy C. Joyner

MARTINEAU, Harriet. English.   Born in Norwich, Norfolk, 12 June 1802; sister of the theologian James Martineau. Educated at home, and at the Reverend Perry's school, in Norwich, to age 15, then continued classical studies on her own. Became partially deaf while still in her teens, and suffered from poor health for all of her life; writer from 1821; went through long illness and was left destitute, 1829; lived in London, 1832–39; became successful writer; visited America, 1834–36; invalid at Tynemouth, 1839–44; settled at

Clappersgate, Westmorland, 1845; became a friend of Wordsworth's; visited Egypt and Palestine, 1846–47; regular contributor to the *Daily News*, London, 1852–66; also contributed to the *Edinburgh Review* from 1859. Refused government pension, 1841, 1873. *Died 27 June 1876.*

PUBLICATIONS

Fiction

> *Five Years of Youth; or, Sense and Sentiment.* 1831.
> *Illustrations of Political Economy* (stories). 9 vols., 1832–34.
> *Poor Laws and Paupers Illustrated.* 4 vols., 1833–34.
> *Illustrations of Taxation.* 1834.
> *Deerbrook.* 1839.
> *The Hour and the Man.* 1841.
> *The Playfellow, Containing The Settlers at Home, Feats on the Fiord, The Peasant and the Prince, The Crofton Boys.* 4 vols., 1841.
> *The Rioters.* N.d.
> *Dawn Island.* 1845.
> *Forest and Game-Law Tales.* 3 vols., 1845–46.
> *The Billow and the Rock.* 1846.
> *Merdhen, The Manor and the Eyrie, and Old Landmarks and Old Laws.* 1852.
> *The Hampdens: A Historiette.* 1880.

Other

> *Devotional Exercises for the Use of Young Persons.* 1823; revised edition, as *Devotional Exercises, To Which Is Added A Guide to the Study of the Scriptures,* 1832.
> *Addresses with Prayers and Original Hymns for the Use of Families.* 1826.
> *Essential Faith of the Universal Church Deduced from Sacred Records.* 1831.
> *The Faith as Unfolded by Many Prophets: An Essay Addressed to the Disciples of Mohammed.* 1832.
> *Providence as Manifested Through Israel.* 1832.
> *Miscellanies.* 2 vols., 1836.
> *Society in America.* 3 vols., 1837; edited by Seymour Martin Lipset, 1968.
> *A Retrospect of Western Travel.* 3 vols., 1838.
> *How to Observe: Morals and Manners.* 1838.
> *Guides to Service.* 1839(?).
> *The Martyr Age of the United States of America.* 1840.
> *Life in the Sick-Room; or, Essays by an Invalid.* 1844.
> *Letters on Mesmerism.* 1845.
> *Eastern Life, Past and Present.* 3 vols., 1848.
> *Household Education.* 1849.
> *History of England During the Thirty Years' Peace 1816–46.* 2 vols., 1849–50; revised edition, 1855.
> *Two Letters on Cow-Keeping.* 1850(?).
> *Letters on the Laws of Man's Nature and Development,* with H. G. Atkinson. 1851.
> *Introduction to the History of the Peace from 1800 to 1815.* 1851.
> *Half a Century of the British Empire: A History of the Kingdom and the People from 1800 to 1850,* part 1. 1851.

Letters from Ireland. 1853.

Complete Guide to the Lakes. 1854.

Guide to Windermere, with Tours of Neighbouring Lakes and Other Interesting Places. 1854.

The Factory Controversy: A Warning Against Meddling Legislation. 1855.

A History of the American Compromises. 1856.

Corporate Traditions and National Rights: Local Dues on Shipping. 1857.

Guide to Keswick and Its Environs. 1857.

Suggestions Towards the Future Government of India. 1858.

Endowed Schools of Ireland. 1859.

England and Her Soldiers. 1859.

Survey of the Lake District. 1860.

Health, Husbandry, and Handicraft. 1861.

Biographical Sketches. 1869; revised edition, 1876.

Autobiography. 3 vols., 1877.

Editor, *Traditions of Palestine.* 1830.

Translator, *The Positive Philosophy of Auguste Comte.* 2 vols., 1853.

Bibliography: "Martineau: A Bibliography of the Separately Printed Books" by J. B. Rivlin, in *Bulletin of the New York Public Library,* 1946–47.

Reading List: *Martineau: An Example of Victorian Conflict* by Narola E. Rivenburg, 1932; *Martineau* by John C. Nevill, 1943; *The Life and Work of Martineau* by Vera Wheatley, 1957; *Martineau: A Radical Victorian* by Robert K. Webb, 1960; *Martineau* by Florence F. Miller, 1972.

*   *   *

A writer of eclectic works and of unflagging enthusiasms, Harriet Martineau was a novelist, political economist, journalist, travel writer, essayist, historian, translator, editor, and autobiographer. Her prodigious writing sometimes resulted in works of uneven quality but she never limited her pursuits, which ranged from children's books like *The Playfellow* to studies on the future government of India and the soldiers of England. Throughout her long, illness-plagued life – she was born without a sense of smell, gradually lost her hearing and was an invalid for five years until cured by mesmerism – Harriet Martineau was a teacher. Two curious but fascinating books describe her illness and miraculous recovery: *Life in the Sickroom* and *Letters on Mesmerism.* Literature for Harriet Martineau was a didactic vehicle to explain to readers the complex workings of society or the individual. She wrote books on American society, English morals, and Middle East religions. No subject was too arcane, no topic too abstruse for her popularizing.

The greatest success of Harriet Martineau was *Illustrations of Political Economy,* one of her earliest books. It was a series of stories that exemplified various economic principles. Summaries of the doctrinal points appear at the end of each fictional adventure. Demands for a free money market, for example, is the subject of "Berkely the Banker" while the argument for free trade is the theme of "The Loom and the Lugger." *Elements of Political Economy* by James Mill was the major source for Martineau's economic concepts. *Illustrations of Political Economy* was immensely popular, went through numerous printings and established Martineau as a prominent literary figure in London. She continued to be successful with short fictional tracts for social and political issues such as *Poor Laws and Paupers Illustrated* and *Forest and Game-Law Tales.* Her most sustained, mature attempt at novel writing was

Deerbrook, a didactic novel of English provincial life that shares certain general similarities with the work of Jane Austen and George Eliot.

Harriet Martineau was brought up a devout Unitarian but became a Free Thinker with an enthusiasm for science. In 1853 she translated Comte's influential work on Positivist philosophy. Her greatest subject, however, was herself, and her most significant work is her candid *Autobiography* begun in 1855 at the beginning of what she thought to be a fatal illness. The work did not appear until 1877, following her death. This lively, critical book, replete with comments on the major intellectual figures of the age and the difficulties of maintaining a literary career, is one of the most important autobiographies by a woman in the nineteenth century. With her energy, optimism, and passions, Harriet Martineau remains a vibrant although at times eccentric embodiment of the woman as Victorian man-of-letters.

—I. B. Nadel

MASON, A(lfred) E(dward) W(oodley).   English.   Born in Camberwell, London, 7 May 1865. Educated at Dulwich College, London, 1878–84; Trinity College, Oxford (exhibitioner in classics, 1887), 1884–87, degrees in classics 1886, 1888. Served with the Royal Marine Light Infantry in World War I, and was involved in secret service missions in Spain, Morocco, and Mexico: Major. Actor, in provincial touring companies, 1888–94; writer from 1895; Liberal Member of Parliament for Coventry, 1906–10. Honorary Fellow of Trinity College, 1943. *Died 22 November 1948.*

PUBLICATIONS

Fiction

A Romance of Wastdale.   1895.
The Courtship of Morrice Buckler: A Romance.   1896.
Lawrence Clavering.   1897.
The Philanderers.   1897.
Miranda of the Balcony.   1899.
Parson Kelly, with Andrew Lang.   1899.
The Watchers.   1899.
Clementina.   1901.
Ensign Knightley and Other Stories.   1901.
The Four Feathers.   1902.
The Truants.   1904.
The Broken Road.   1907.
Running Water.   1907.
At the Villa Rose.   1910.
The Clock.   1910.
Making Good.   1910.
The Turnstile.   1912.
The Witness for the Defence.   1913.
The Affair at the Semiramis Hotel.   1917.

The Four Corners of the World (stories).   1917.
The Episode of the Thermometer.   1918.
The Summons.   1920.
The Winding Stair.   1923.
The House of the Arrow.   1924.
No Other Tiger.   1927.
The Prisoner in the Opal.   1928.
The Dean's Elbow.   1930.
The Three Gentlemen.   1932.
The Sapphire.   1933.
Dilemmas (stories).   1934.
They Wouldn't Be Chessmen.   1935.
Fire over England.   1936.
The Drum.   1937.
Königsmark.   1938.
The Secret Fear.   1940.
Muck and Amber.   1942.
The House in Lordship Lane.   1946.

Plays

Blanche de Malètroit, from the story by R. L. Stevenson (produced 1894).   1894.
The Courtship of Morrice Buckler, with Isabel Bateman, from the novel by Mason (produced 1897).
Marjory Strode (produced 1908).
Col. Smith (produced 1909).
The Witness for the Defence (produced 1911).   1913.
Open Windows (produced 1913).
Green Stockings.   1914.
At the Villa Rose, from his own novel (produced 1920).   1928.
Running Water (produced 1922).
The House of the Arrow, from his own novel (produced 1928).
No Other Tiger, from his own novel (produced 1928).
A Present from Margate, with Ian Hay (produced 1933).   1934.

Other

The Royal Exchange.   1920.
Sir George Alexander and the St. James's Theatre.   1935.
The Life of Francis Drake.   1941.

Reading List: *Mason: The Adventures of a Story Teller* by Roger Lancelyn Green, 1952 (includes bibliography).

*   *   *

To think of A. E. W. Mason is to think of the swift, breathless, joyous rush of the adventures which he described so well – backed by the authenticity of his own adventurous life. After five years as an actor he turned to literature, achieving sudden fame with his second book, the swashbuckling *Courtship of Morrice Buckler,* followed by several others of the kind, and contemporary "adventure novels," the best known being *Miranda of the*

Balcony. A more subtle Jacobite romance, *Parson Kelly*, which he wrote with Andrew Lang, and its companion, *Clementina*, ended Mason's first period of historical romances.

By now he was able to go adventuring himself, notably into the Sudan not long after the Battle of Omdurman, which gave him the setting for his best-known book, *The Four Feathers*. This is an adventure story which is also a psychological study – notably of the hero, Harry Feversham, who, believing himself to be a coward, resigns his commission in the Army when his regiment is ordered on active service, and discovers while regaining his honour and his fiancée that he is braver than most when the actual moment of action comes. It contains also a character, John Durrance, who nearly usurps the role of hero as his powers of observation grow after he has become blind and he develops unexpected powers of detection.

This idea of detection by noticing reactions of all sorts in the people observed or suspected led Mason to the creation of his French detective, Inspector Hanaud, who made his first appearance in *At the Villa Rose* and reached his greatest powers in *The House of the Arrow* and *The Prisoner in the Opal*. These show the development of the detective story into the detective novel – the detailed presentation and study in depth of the characters, criminal and otherwise, concerned in the ingenious and exciting mystery to be solved.

Mason's other interests and experiences supplied the vivid setting for other novels and romances, most of them of a high level. His prowess as a mountaineer – sixteen hours on the Brenva Ridge of Mont Blanc – resulted in *Running Water*; his skill as a yachtsman, his early explorations in Morocco, his five years as Liberal M.P. for Coventry, his experiences in M.I.5 in the First World War – each inspired one or more books.

Towards the end of his life he turned back to historical fiction. His fine romance of the Spanish Armada, *Fire over England*, was made into one of the most popular films of its day. But his historical novel *Musk and Amber*, concerning the fortunes of an English nobleman who becomes one of the great *castrati* singers in an eighteenth-century setting in England and Venice, and achieves his vengeance on the man who sold him to this fate to cheat him of his inheritance, touches his highest peak. He will surely be remembered for this, for *The Four Feathers*, and for the best of the Inspector Hanaud stories.

—Roger Lancelyn Green

MATURIN, Charles Robert. Irish. Born in Dublin in 1782. Educated at Trinity College, Dublin, B.A. 1800. Married Henrietta Kingsbury in 1802; two sons. Took holy orders; served as Curate of Loughrea, and afterwards of St. Peter's, Dublin; also maintained a school in addition to his curacy, 1807–13; writer from 1806. *Died 30 October 1824.*

Publications

Fiction

Fatal Revenge; or, The Family of Montorio.   1807.
The Wild Irish Boy.   1808.
The Milesian Chief: A Romance.   1812.
Women; or, Pour et Contre.   1818.

Melmoth the Wanderer: A Tale.   1820; edited by Alethea Hayter, 1977,
The Albigenses · A Romance.   1824.
Leixlip Castle.   1825.

Plays

Bertram; or, The Castle of St. Aldobrand (produced 1816).   1816.
Manuel (produced 1817).   1817.
Fredolfo (produced 1819).   1819.
Osmyn the Renegade; or, The Siege of Salerno (produced 1830).

Verse

Lines on the Battle of Waterloo: A Prize Poem.   1816.

Other

Sermons.   1819.
Five Sermons on the Errors of the Roman Catholic Church.   1824.
The Correspondence of Scott and Maturin, edited by F. E. Ratchford and W. H.
    McCarthy.   1937.

Reading List: Maturin by Dale Kramer, 1973; Maturin: L'Homme et l'Oeuvre by Claude
Fierobe, 2 vols., 1974.

*   *   *

Charles Robert Maturin's Melmoth the Wanderer has every right to be considered the finest
Gothic novel in English. Earlier, Maturin had been known as a novelist – Walter Scott
praised Fatal Revenge in the Quarterly Review in May 1810 – and as a playwright – Edmund
Kean made a success in Bertram at Drury Lane – but his literary fortunes had then declined.
His two later plays, Manuel and Fredolfo, failed, and Coleridge published a scathing criticism
of Bertram in Biographia Literaria in 1817. But Melmoth was to fascinate Baudelaire, who
referred to "la grande création satanique du révérend Maturin" and proposed to translate it
into French; and as late as 1965 André Breton the Surrealist wrote an introduction for a new
translation into French.
    The success of Melmoth lies in its emotional intensity. The structure is far from tight, but
offers a good opportunity for Maturin's best effects. The hero sells his soul to the devil in
return for longer life, and the events of the novel concern his attempts to find and persuade
others in moments of intense suffering and despair to change places with him. The resulting
stories vary in time from the seventeenth century onwards and in place from the West Coast
of Ireland to a romantic island in the Indian Ocean. But the reader's persistent awareness of
Melmoth's plight gives unity and also a sense of the inevitable.
    Earlier Gothic novels like The Castle of Otranto or The Mysteries of Udolpho often give an
impression of fantasy, of the author's playing a literary game. But Melmoth is a much more
disturbing work in which sadism and violence are conveyed in such a way that they cannot
be ignored. The description of the death of the parricide monk, torn to pieces by the mob in
view of hidden, frightened Monçada, is particularly horrifying, and its power is no doubt
related to the fact that it was based partly on Maturin's memories of street violence in Dublin.
He had no need to invent aspects of human wickedness; he knew them from observation and

experience. The scene ends: "The officer who headed the troop dashed his horse's hoofs into a bloody formless mass, and demanded, 'Where was the victim?' He was answered, 'Beneath your horse's feet'; and they departed."

It is arguable that the Gothic novel is a limited form because of its concentration on the darker aspects of experience and its tendency to melodrama. In *Melmoth the Wanderer* Maturin was able to take the form to its limits because of the intensity of his feelings and the intermittent poetic power of his prose.

—Peter Faulkner

MAUGHAM, W(illiam) Somerset.   English.   Born in Paris, 25 January 1874, of English parents. Educated at King's School, Canterbury, Kent, 1887–91; University of Heidelberg, 1891–92; studied medicine at St. Thomas's Hospital, London, 1892–97; interned in Lambeth, London; qualified as a surgeon, L.R.C.P., M.R.C.S., 1897, but never practised. Served with the Red Cross Ambulance Unit, later with the British Intelligence Corps, in World War I. Married Syrie Barnardo Wellcome in 1915 (divorced, 1927), one daughter. Writer from 1896; lived abroad, mainly in Paris, 1897–1907; travelled widely during the 1920's, in the South Seas, Malaya, and China; lived at Cap Ferrat in the south of France from 1928; lived in the United States during World War II; instituted annual prize for promising young British writer, 1947. D.Litt.: Oxford University; University of Toulouse. Fellow, and Companion of Literature, 1961, Royal Society of Literature. Commander, Legion of Honour; Honorary Senator, University of Heidelberg; Honorary Fellow, Library of Congress, Washington, D.C.; Honorary Member, American Academy of Arts and Letters. Companion of Honour, 1954. *Died 16 December 1965.*

PUBLICATIONS

Fiction

> *Liza of Lambeth.*   1897; revised edition, 1904.
> *The Making of a Saint.*   1898.
> *Orientations* (stories).   1899.
> *The Hero.*   1901.
> *Mrs. Craddock.*   1902.
> *The Merry-Go-Round.*   1904.
> *The Bishop's Apron: A Study in the Origins of a Great Family.*   1906.
> *The Explorer.*   1907.
> *The Magician.*   1908.
> *Of Human Bondage.*   1915.
> *The Moon and Sixpence.*   1919.
> *The Trembling of the Leaf: Little Stories of the South Sea Islands.*   1921; as *Sadie Thompson and Other Stories,* 1928; as *Rain and Other Stories,* 1933.
> *The Painted Veil.*   1925.
> *The Casuarina Tree: Six Stories.*   1926; as *The Letter: Stories of Crime,* 1930.
> *Ashenden; or, The British Agent.*   1928.

Cakes and Ale; or, The Skeleton in the Cupboard. 1930.
Six Stories Written in the First Person Singular. 1931.
The Book-Bag. 1932.
The Narrow Corner. 1932.
Ah King: Six Stories. 1933.
The Judgement Seat (story). 1934.
East and West: The Collected Short Stories. 1934; as *Altogether,* 1934.
Cosmopolitans (stories). 1936.
Favorite Short Stories. 1937.
Theatre. 1937.
The Round Dozen (stories). 1939.
Christmas Holiday. 1939.
The Mixture as Before: Short Stories. 1940 as *Great Stories of Love and Intrigue,* 1947.
Up at the Villa. 1941.
The Hour Before the Dawn. 1942.
The Unconquered (story). 1944.
The Razor's Edge. 1944.
Then and Now. 1946.
Creatures of Circumstance: Short Stories. 1947.
Catalina: A Romance. 1948.
East of Suez: Great Stories of the Tropics. 1948.
Here and There (stories). 1948.
Complete Short Stories. 3 vols., 1951.
The World Over: Stories of Manifold Places and People. 1952.
Selected Novels. 3 vols., 1953.
Best Short Stories, edited by John Beecroft. 1957.
A Maugham Twelve: Stories, edited by Angus Wilson. 1960.
Malaysian Stories, edited by Anthony Burgess. 1969.
Seventeen Lost Stories, edited by Craig V. Showalter. 1969.

Plays

Marriages Are Made in Heaven (as *Schiffbrüchig,* produced 1902). Published in
     Venture, 1903.
A Man of Honour (produced 1903). 1903.
Mademoiselle Zampa (produced 1904).
Lady Frederick (produced 1907). 1911.
Jack Straw (produced 1908). 1911.
Mrs. Dot (produced 1908). 1912.
The Explorer: A Melodrama (produced 1908). 1912.
Penelope (produced 1909). 1912.
The Noble Spaniard, from a work by Ernest Grenet-Dancourt (produced 1909). 1953.
Smith (produced 1909). 1913.
The Tenth Man (produced 1910). 1913.
Landed Gentry (as *Grace,* produced 1910). 1913.
Loaves and Fishes (produced 1911). 1924.
A Trip to Brighton, from a play by Abel Tarride (produced 1911).
The Perfect Gentleman, from a play by Molière (produced 1913). Published in *Theatre
     Arts,* November 1955.
The Land of Promise (produced 1913). 1913.
The Unattainable (as *Caroline,* produced 1916). 1923.
Our Betters (produced 1917). 1923.
Love in a Cottage (produced 1918).

Caesar's Wife (produced 1919). 1922.
Home and Beauty (produced 1919; as *Too Many Husbands*, produced 1919). 1923.
The Unknown (produced 1920). 1920.
The Circle (produced 1921). 1921.
East of Suez (produced 1922). 1922.
The Camel's Back (produced 1923).
The Constant Wife (produced 1926). 1927.
The Letter, from his own story (produced 1927). 1927.
The Sacred Flame (produced 1928). 1928.
The Bread-Winner (produced 1930). 1930.
Dramatic Works. 6 vols., 1931–34; as *Collected Plays*, 3 vols., 1952.
For Services Rendered (produced 1932). 1932.
The Mask and the Face: A Satire, from a play by Luigi Chiarelli (produced 1933).
Sheppey (produced 1933). 1933.
Trio: Stories and Screen Adaptations, with R. C. Sherriff and Noel Langley. 1950.

Screen plays: *The Ordeal*, with Beulah Marie Dix, 1922; *The Verger*, in *Trio*, 1950.

Other

The Land of the Blessed Virgin: Sketches and Impressions of Andalusia. 1905.
On a Chinese Screen. 1922.
The Gentleman in the Parlour: A Record of a Journey from Rangoon to Haiphong. 1930.
Non-Dramatic Works. 28 vols., 1934–69.
Don Fernando; or, Variations on Some Spanish Themes. 1935.
My South Sea Island. 1936.
The Summing Up. 1938.
Books and You. 1940.
France at War. 1940.
Strictly Personal. 1941.
The Somerset Maugham Sampler, edited by Jerome Weidman. 1943; as *The Somerset Maugham Pocket Book*, 1944.
Great Novelists and Their Novels: Essays on the Ten Greatest Novels of the World and the Men and Women Who Wrote Them. 1948; revised edition, as *Ten Novels and Their Authors*, 1954; as *The Art of Fiction*, 1955.
A Writer's Notebook. 1949.
The Maugham Reader, edited by Glenway Wescott. 1950.
The Vagrant Mood: Six Essays. 1952.
Mr. Maugham Himself, edited by John Beecroft. 1954.
The Partial View (includes *The Summing Up* and *A Writer's Notebook*). 1954.
The Travel Books. 1955.
Points of View. 1958.
Purely for Pleasure. 1962.
Selected Prefaces and Introductions. 1963.
Essays on Literature. 1967.

Editor, with Laurence Housman, *Venture: An Annual of Art and Literature.* 2 vols., 1903–05.
Editor, *The Truth at Last*, by Charles Hawtrey. 1924.
Editor, *The Travellers' Library.* 1933; as *Fifty Modern English Writers*, 1933.
Editor, *Tellers of Tales: 100 Short Stories.* 1939; as *The Greatest Stories of All Time*, 1943.

Editor, *A Choice of Kipling's Prose.* 1952: as *Maugham's Choice of Kipling's Best: Sixteen Stories*, 1953.

Bibliography: *A Bibliography of the Works of Maugham* by Raymond Toole Stott, 1956; revised edition, 1973.

Reading List: *The Maugham Enigma*, 1954, and *The World of Maugham*, 1959, both edited by K. W. Jonas; *Maugham* by J. Brophy, revised edition, 1958; *Maugham: A Candid Portrait* by K. G. Pfeiffer, 1959; *Maugham: A Guide* by Laurence Brander, 1963; *The Two Worlds of Maugham* by W. Menard, 1965; *Maugham* by M. K. Naik, 1966; *The Dramatic Comedy of Maugham* by R. E. Barnes, 1968; *Maugham: A Biographical and Critical Study* by R. A. Cordell, revised edition, 1969; *Maugham and the Quest for Freedom* by Robert L. Calder, 1972; *The Pattern of Maugham: A Critical Portrait*, 1974, and *Maugham*, 1977, both by Anthony Curtis; *Maugham and His World* by Frederic Raphael, 1976.

*   *   *

"Every writer who has any sense," said W. Somerset Maugham in a press interview, "writes about the circumstances in which he himself has lived. What else can he write about with authority?" That statement is well illustrated by the closeness with which a long and varied life is reflected in Maugham's equally versatile achievement as short-story writer, novelist, dramatist, critic, essayist, and autobiographer. Upbringing in Paris and an early familiarity with the work of the French naturalists profoundly influenced his style and method, giving him a classical sense of form, lucidity, and Gallic detachment of attitude to human frailty and the ironies of existence. Later experiences as a medical student in London provided material for a realistic portrayal of slum life in his first novel, *Liza of Lambeth*, and, as a British intelligence agent during the First World War, for the Ashenden stories. Above all Maugham's extensive foreign travels, in search of new backgrounds and ways of life, proved inexhaustibly fruitful. He paints exotic Eastern scenes with economy and exactitude; and observes a wealth of bizarre incident and human idiosyncrasy – on liners, in clubs, in the bungalows of the white man in the tropics, where passions are stripped of the masks of conformity and convention demanded by more civilized communities – with amused tolerance and an unerring eye for the significant detail. Unlike his contemporaries Bennett, Galsworthy, and Wells, Maugham was not interested in fiction as the vehicle of social criticism. Savouring instead the singularity, paradox, and sheer unexpectedness of individual lives, he proclaimed his subject, in his short stories, novels, and plays alike, "the personal drama of human relationships."

Maugham's career as a dramatist spanned three decades, beginning with *A Man of Honour* in 1903 and ending in 1933 with *Sheppey*. His comedies of manners in the tradition of Oscar Wilde were less immediately successful than his fiction. Within a year of the production of *Lady Frederick* in 1907, however, he was rivalling the popularity of Shaw with four plays running in London. Such caustic, wittily satirical portrayals of elegant society as *Home and Beauty*, *The Circle*, *Our Betters*, and *The Bread-Winner*, with their dexterous craftsmanship and sparkling epigrammatic dialogue, continued to enjoy a steady stage success.

Maugham's achievement as a novelist is distinctly uneven. The authenticity of deep feeling in perhaps his most popular work, the long autobiographical *Of Human Bondage*, is vitiated by prolixity and that sentimentality which in many of his short stories masquerades as cynicism. In *The Razor's Edge*, written when he was over seventy, and *Catalina*, he is perceptibly out of his native element in ambitious explorations of uncharacteristic themes. The moral confusions and simplifications, lapses in taste, and overall implausibility in these novels show Maugham less at ease as an anatomist of spiritual struggles and values than in his accustomed role of shrewd and worldly observer of his fellow men. Essentially a master of shorter forms of fiction, he makes far greater impact in *The Moon and Sixpence*, based on the career of Gauguin, and *Cakes and Ale*, his own favourite. This astringent picture of London literary life introduces thinly disguised, maliciously acute portraits of two eminent contemporaries; and the engaging personality of Rosie, the maternal, warm-hearted barmaid, is in a clear line of descent from an earlier Maugham heroine, Liza. In its narrative expertise, perception, and credibility of characterization, *Cakes and Ale* is indisputably Maugham's most completely realized novel.

But it is in the short-story form that his individual gifts are most satisfyingly exemplified. Temperamentally and technically out of tune with Chekhov and his methods, Maugham from the first made Maupassant his model. His avowed aim was the "compact, dramatic story," tightly knit, sharply characterized, ending "with a full-stop rather than a straggle of dots," which could hold the attention of listeners over a dinner-table or in a ship's smoking room. To this end he developed with consummate skill the device of the narrator: his own urbane, ubiquitous presence, as ringside spectator rather than active participant, lending his tales the heightened verisimilitude of the conversational eye-witness account. Maugham's factual first-person narratives not only invest with veracity what might otherwise seem incredible (as he cunningly allows at the opening of "The Kite"); the deliberate tone of dry understatement intensifies by contrast the violent, often tragic events related by this suave, unobtrusive commentator. Sometimes, indeed, his "shock" climax seems calculated enough to be over-simplified and superficial. Compared with the psychological penetration and compassion in a story like Maupassant's "Boule de Suif," Maugham's situations and characterization lack subtlety and depth. His ironical revelations can be more effective in such lighter vein as the delectable disclosure of "The Colonel's Lady."

One of Maugham's favourite and most typical themes, in his sardonic clinical diagnoses of human folly in "Before the Party," "The Door of Opportunity," "The Lion's Skin," and many other stories, is the disillusioning disparity between the outward appearances of a relationship and its underlying reality. Not only amorous frailty is relentlessly exposed, but also the humbug of moral conventions and literary pretentiousness. Yet Maugham never explicitly moralizes. He presents life, as he sees it, dispassionately: almost – for his very lack of comment can carry its own acid implication. His cool, fastidious detachment is that of the outsider remote from the complexities and disasters of ordinary living. Disarmingly aware of his own limitations, both personal and literary, he acknowledges in his autobiographies his lack of that emotional warmth and sympathetic involvement which would, as he says, have given his work "intimacy, the broad human touch."

Maugham saw himself primarily as an entertainer; and he was indeed a supremely successful one, with his work broadcast, televised, filmed, and translated into many languages. In the light of his serious lifelong dedication to the writer's craft, he felt he had been consistently undervalued by the "intellectual" critics. Certainly his reputation has always stood higher abroad than in England; but an appreciative world-wide readership has made him possibly the most popular storyteller who has ever lived.

—Margaret Willy

McCARTHY, Mary (Therese). American. Born in Seattle, Washington, 21 June 1912. Educated at Forest Ridge Convent, Seattle; Annie Wright Seminary, Tacoma, Washington; Vassar College, Poughkeepsie, New York, A.B. 1933 (Phi Beta Kappa). Married 1) Harold Johnsrud in 1933; 2) Edmund Wilson, *q.v.*, in 1938, one son; 3) Bowden Broadwater in 1946; 4) James Raymond West in 1961. Editor, Covici Friede, publishers, New York, 1936–38; Editor, 1937–38, and Drama Critic, 1937–62, *Partisan Review*, New Brunswick,

New Jersey; Instructor, Bard College, Annandale-on-Hudson, New York, 1945–46, and Sarah Lawrence College, Bronxville, New York, 1948. Recipient: Guggenheim Fellowship, 1949, 1959; National Institute of Arts and Letters grant, 1957. D.Litt.: Syracuse University, New York, 1973; University of Hull, Yorkshire, 1974. Lives in Paris.

PUBLICATIONS

Fiction

> *The Company She Keeps.* 1942.
> *The Oasis.* 1949; as *A Source of Embarrassment,* 1950.
> *Cast a Cold Eye* (stories). 1950.
> *The Groves of Academe.* 1952.
> *A Charmed Life.* 1955.
> *The Group.* 1963.
> *Birds of America.* 1971.

Other

> *Sights and Spectacles, 1937–56.* 1956; as *Sights and Spectacles: Theatre Chronicles, 1937–58,* 1959; augmented edition, as *McCarthy's Theatre Chronicles, 1937–62,* 1963.
> *Venice Observed: Comments on Venetian Civilization.* 1956.
> *Memories of a Catholic Girlhood.* 1957.
> *The Stones of Florence.* 1959.
> *On the Contrary* (essays). 1961.
> *Vietnam.* 1967.
> *Hanoi.* 1968.
> *The Writing on the Wall* (essays). 1970.
> *Medina.* 1972.
> *The Mask of State: Watergate Portraits.* 1974.
> *The Seventeenth Degree.* 1974.

> Translator, *The Iliad; or, The Poem of Force,* by Simone Weil. 1948.
> Translator, *On the Iliad,* by Rachel Bespaloff. 1948.

Bibliography: *McCarthy: A Bibliography* by Sherli Goldman, 1968.

Reading List: *McCarthy* by Barbara McKenzie, 1966; *The Company She Kept* by Doris Grumbach, 1967; *McCarthy* by Irvin Stock, 1968.

*   *   *

Mary McCarthy belongs to that set of modern American authors who appear at first to be circumscribed by the time in which they write. Her first novel, *The Company She Keeps*, is the most charming and vigorous of her novels in spite of being almost too conscious of the political and social milieu of Greenwich Village. *The Company She Keeps* is light reading, but, in terms of plot, a daring experiment. It contains six chapters, each differing from the other in time and place, with one personality to hold the stories together. The strength of the personality, of the viewing eye, and the consistency of outlook which that eye provides, form the only cohesion to the "novel." It has about it the feel of the early experiments with surrealist fiction and at the same time the freshness and youthful vitality one sees in the early stories of Fitzgerald. McCarthy has captured, through details, the spirit of her generation just as surely. In the historical-social context, one learns more from writers like McCarthy and Fitzgerald than one can from our more literary authors. *The Company She Keeps* also offers a fascinating glimpse of McCarthy's powers as a journalist. Her critical essays are collected in *On the Contrary* and *The Writing on the Wall*. Her *Theatre Chronicles*, also begun early, offer the same strong command and vigor along with a truly original understanding and analysis of the theatre. Her essay on *Macbeth* in *The Writing on the Wall* is a perfect example of the way McCarthy's critical eye catches out similarities and modern relevancy that are startling and revealing to the reader. Her essays show what kind of professor she must have been: funny, inventive, clever, determined to catch at the sparkling threads of every idea. With *The Groves of Academe*, she created a small scandal with a biting portrait of a college President struggling with the politics of his English Department. *The Groves of Academe* and her fourth novel, *A Charmed Life*, are probably meant to be allegories — the former of Senator McCarthy's communist hunts, and the latter of a moral and philosophical sort where generalizations are drawn out of a small community that are meant to apply to all of us. *A Charmed Life* is a magnificent book — unlimited by time or distracting political concepts, it concerns what happens to people who retire from the world, to devote themselves to something, in this case Art. It is a gentle but shocking reminder to modern man that he cannot hide from the world out of sensibility or devotion to an unworldly goal; life remains dangerous. The characters in this novel come to life more thoroughly than the eight heroines of *The Group*, her most famous novel. *The Group* was a great success when it appeared: its vision of life affected an entire generation. Her own autobiography, *Memories of a Catholic Girlhood*, is a beautiful, classic, searching piece of writing. Along with *A Charmed Life*, *Memories* is the best showcase for her prose.

Mary McCarthy has always walked a very delicate line between her knowledge that the modern novel is plotless and between her love for the world and its myriad details. *The Company She Keeps* is a very carefully plotted novel, but it does not follow a time-line; *The Groves of Academe* has a traditional novelistic conception but, lacking the freewheeling movement of *Company*, is less successful; *A Charmed Life* is positioned insecurely but brilliantly on the line between the Dickensian novel of action and detail and the plotless modern impressionistic novel: it is a written play where the dramatic conflict is between clashing ideas and philosophies; *The Group* returns to a novel form that is more disjointed but richer of plot. Her last novel, *Birds of America*, is an interesting idea that somehow has not taken form, but it is sweet, funny, and very clever.

—Brady Nordland

McCULLERS, (Lula) Carson (née Smith). American. Born in Columbus, Georgia, 19 February 1917. Educated at Columbia University, New York; New York University, 1935–36. Married Reeves McCullers in 1937 (divorced, 1940); remarried Reeves McCullers in 1945 (died, 1953). Recipient: Guggenheim Fellowship, 1943; National Institute of Arts and Letters grant, 1943; New York Drama Critics Circle Award, 1950; Donaldson Award, for drama, 1950. Member, National Institute of Arts and Letters. *Died 29 September 1967.*

Publications

Fiction

The Heart Is a Lonely Hunter. 1940.
Reflections in a Golden Eye. 1941.
The Member of the Wedding. 1946.
The Ballad of the Sad Cafe: The Novels and Stories. 1951.
Seven (stories). 1954.
Clock Without Hands. 1961.

Plays

The Twisted Trinity, music by David Diamond. 1946.
The Member of the Wedding, from her own novel (produced 1950). 1957.
The Square Root of Wonderful (produced 1957). 1958.

Other

Sweet as a Pickle and Clean as a Pig (juvenile). 1964.
The Mortgaged Heart (uncollected writings), edited by Margarita G. Smith. 1971.

Bibliography: *Katherine Anne Porter and McCullers: A Reference Guide* by Robert F. Kiernan, 1976.

Reading List: *The Ballad of McCullers* by Oliver Evans, 1966, as *McCullers: Her Life and Work,* 1968; *McCullers* by Lawrence S. Graver, 1969; *The Lonely Hunter: A Biography of McCullers* by Virginia Spencer Carr, 1975; *McCullers* by Richard M. Cook, 1975.

*   *   *

Carson McCullers, though a person whom nearly all her friends found charming, was through much of her life an invalid, suffering from melancholia and loneliness. In spite of a remarkably full production for a comparatively short life, she only occasionally gathered energy to write with the perfection of style and structure she demanded of herself the narratives – in their essence long *nouvelles* rather than short novels – on which (though the dramatisation of her story *The Member of the Wedding* was very successful) her reputation rests. Her early novel *Reflections in a Golden Eye*, which made her famous, is set in an army post in peacetime, whose dullness and ordinariness she emphasises. But nothing is really dull and ordinary in McCullers's works, and there is mounting horror from the moment when the bewildered heroine's frustrated and slightly mad husband puts a tiny live kitten into a freezing post box till the moment when the heroine (who has had a love affair with a common soldier for whom her husband has a sadistic hatred) is seen sick in hospital having, in desperation, sheared off her nipples. The heroine, like many of McCullers's heroines, is simple, generous, and childlike, and it is a mark of McCullers's fine talent and charity that she does not force us to condemn anyone, even the husband. The horror of life is something coolly and charitably accepted by her, like its frustration, even like its innocence and fulfilment. She is a most moving and disturbing writer precisely because it seems not her purpose to move or disturb, or to make the reader share pain as he often does, but to present events and characters with coolness and precision.

The tone is in fact often near that of comedy (McCullers is always an amusing writer), even when the material verges on the tragic. *The Ballad of the Sad Cafe* has a grotesquerie, for instance, that makes one both cry and laugh. In a dull little southern town, a gruff young woman, grotesquely tall, with a kind heart which she conceals even from herself, runs a little cafe which gradually becomes a refuge for all the eccentric, lonely, and absurd characters in the town, and thus unconsciously has its own distinction. The awkward, clumsy heroine takes them all in, and is generous about credit, for they are not so very different – are mostly less odd, in fact – than herself. Unfortunately, she is susceptible to love, and falls in love with a malicious dwarf. He is ready enough to exploit her generosity, but hates everybody, and comes to hate the heroine with special intensity when he realises that she loves him. If anybody could at all attract him it would be a man with the normal height, the athletic bearing, the easy self-confidence, which he himself as a little monster so singularly lacks. And such men, of course, will treat him with contempt. There is almost a philosophy in this short novel, the philosophy that some people at least are drawn to love those who cannot love them, and that unwanted love can arouse not pity but resentment and malice.

The Member of the Wedding is a gentler book, about a girl in adolescence excited by a wedding in her family and vaguely ambitious to become "a member of the wedding," an organic part of it, in a way that is not physically or psychologically possible. Fortunately, in this story the heroine's troubles are responded to with love and understanding. But the novel makes us realise that both the attractiveness and the misfortunes of McCullers's heroines spring from an essential innocence in their nature.

Her later writing tended more towards comedy and revealed even more vividly her detailed, half-mocking, half-loving, knowledge of the *mores* of the American south. She was not a great writer, but a very good and original one, with the classic virtues. To turn to her from the wordy rhetorical improvisations of a major figure, William Faulkner, is to become refreshingly aware that McCullers's grace and economy are a model of how prose ought to be written. It is like turning from Dostoevsky to Turgenev.

—G. S. Fraser

MELVILLE, Herman. American. Born in New York City, 1 August 1819. Educated at the Albany Academy to age 13. Married Elizabeth Shaw in 1847; two sons and two daughters. Worked from age 15 as a clerk, farmhand, and schoolteacher; went to sea as a cabin boy on the *Highlander*, bound for Liverpool, 1839–40; served on the whaler *Acushnet*, 1841 until he jumped ship in the Marquesas, 1842; left the island on the Sydney schooner *Lucy Ann*, and jumped ship in Tahiti, 1842; sailed to Honolulu, and worked as a clerk and bookkeeper, 1843; shipped back to Boston on the frigate *United States*, 1843–44; devoted himself to writing from 1844; lived in New York, 1847–50, and Pittsfield, Massachusetts, 1850–63; travelled in the Near East and Europe, 1856–57; lectured in the United States, 1857–60; returned to New York, and served as District Inspector of Customs, 1866–85. *Died 28 September 1891.*

PUBLICATIONS

Collections

Works. 16 vols., 1922–24.
Representative Selections, edited by Willard Thorp. 1938.

Collected Poems, edited by Howard P. Vincent. 1947.
The Portable Melville, edited by Jay Leyda. 1952.
Letters, edited by Merrill R. Davis and William H. Gilman. 1960.
Selected Poems, edited by Hennig Cohen. 1964.
Great Short Works, edited by Warner Berthoff. 1966.
Writings, edited by Harrison Hayford, Hershel Parker, and G. Thomas Tanselle. 1968–

Fiction

Narrative of Four Months' Residence among the Natives of a Valley in the Marquesas Islands; or, A Peep at Polynesian Life. 1846; as *Typee*, 1846; revised edition, 1846; in *Writings*, 1968; edited by George Woodcock, 1972.
Omoo: A Narrative of Adventures in the South Seas. 1847; in *Writings*, 1968.
Mardi, and a Voyage Thither. 1849; in *Writings*, 1970.
Redburn, His First Voyage. 1849; in *Writngs*, 1969.
White Jacket; or, The World in a Man-of-War. 1850; edited by Hennig Cohen, 1967; in *Writings*, 1970.
The Whale. 1851; as *Moby-Dick; or, The Whale*, 1851; edited by Harrison Hayford and Hershel Parker, 1967.
Pierre; or, The Ambiguities. 1852; edited by H. A. Murray, 1957.
Israel Potter, His First Fifty Years of Exile. 1855; as *The Refuge*, 1865.
The Piazza Tales. 1856; edited by Egbert S. Oliver, 1948.
The Confidence-Man, His Masquerade. 1857; edited by Hershel Parker, 1971.
The Apple-Tree Table and Other Sketches. 1922.
Billy Budd and Other Prose Pieces, edited by Raymond M. Weaver, in *Works*. 1924; *Billy Budd* edited by Harrison Hayford and Merton M. Sealts, Jr., 1962.

Verse

Battle-Pieces and Aspects of War. 1866; edited by Hennig Cohen, 1963.
Clarel: A Poem, and Pilgrimage in the Holy Land. 1876; edited by Walter E. Bezanson, 1960.
John Marr and Other Sailors, with Some Sea-Pieces. 1888.
Timoleon. 1891.

Other

Journal up the Straits October 11, 1856–May 5, 1857, edited by Raymond M. Weaver. 1935; edited by Howard C. Horsford, as *Journal of a Visit to Europe and the Levant*, 1955.
Journal of a Visit to London and the Continent 1848–1850, edited by Eleanor Melville Metcalf. 1948.

Bibliography: *The Merrill Checklist of Melville* by Howard P. Vincent, 1969; in *Bibliography of American Literature* by Jacob Blanck, 1973.

Reading List: *Melville: The Tragedy of Mind* by William E. Sedgwick, 1944; *Melville* by Richard Chase, 1949; *Melville* by Newton Arvin, 1950; *The Melville Log: A Documentary Life of the Melvilles* by Jay Leyda, 2 vols., 1951, revised edition, 1969; *Melville* by Leon

Howard, 1951; *Melville's Quarrel with God* by Lawrance Thompson, 1952; *The Fine-Hammered Steel of Melville* by Milton R. Stern, 1957; *The Example of Melville* by Warner Berthoff, 1962; *Melville: The Ironic Diagram* by John D. Seelye, 1970; *An Artist in the Rigging: The Early Work of Melville*, 1972, and *Melville's Short Fiction*, 1977, both by William Dillingham; *Melville: The Critical Heritage* edited by Watson G. Branch, 1974; *Melville* (biography) by Edwin Haviland Miller, 1975.

*   *   *

What characterizes Herman Melville's novels from *Typee* through *Moby-Dick* is the sense of an immanent personality, the author through his narrator, examining himself, his experiences, and the world about him. This personality seeks categorical answers and finds none, and, when his quest fails, seeks ways to survive in an inscrutable universe. In these novels, the theme of the autobiographical quest is signalled by the presence of a first person narrator and by the easy identification of setting and events with the facts of Melville's life as a sailor. If the writings after *Moby-Dick* seem less autobiographical, it is because Melville places more distance between himself and his stories. Their subjects are more obviously interior, spiritual voyages to less romantic places, and an omniscient author, skeptical though compassionate, has displaced the roving, questing youth who spins high-spirited tales of his travels.

Soon after he returned from his voyage to the Pacific, Melville began to write. His first books, *Typee* and *Omoo*, are sailor's yarns based on his adventures in the Marquesas Islands and Tahiti after he jumped ship to sojourn with cannibals, to comb the beaches, and, when his Polynesian paradise began to pall, to go back to the sea. Hindsight reveals hints of themes which were to preoccupy him later, such as man's capacity for evil, appearance and reality, or the dubious blessings of both civilization and its opposite, primitivism; for it was typical of Melville to present another side of the question as a way of stating the complexity and uncertainty of things. They also show a capacity for quiet comedy, delight in word play, and penchant for social criticism. But in the main these books are light-hearted, colorful adventure, mildly fictionalized. Actually, *Typee* follows the facts closely, exploiting the potentiality for suspense in the uncertainty of the Typee's eating habits, the temptations of the narrator's situation as their petted prisoner, and the accumulating pressure to escape from being culturally if not physically consumed by them. An Australian whaler in need of hands rescues him, and he sails off toward the horizon. At this point the sequel, *Omoo* (the name means "wanderer"), begins. The captain proves incompetent and the mate a drunkard, so the sailors refuse duty. They are confined to a casually kept jail in Tahiti from which the young narrator wanders to a nearby island. After more wanderings of a picaresque sort, he goes back to sea.

Such open-endedness suggests uncertainty, or at least open-mindedness, and it encourages sequels. By this time Melville had been taken up by Evert and George Duyckinck, influential New York editors. He began to imbibe their ideas on literary nationalism and liberal politics and to borrow from their extensive collection of Renaissance books, reading Rabelais, Montaigne, Burton, Browne, and the British dramatists. This was heady stuff, and along with the chagrin he felt because publishers and critics questioned the authenticity of his realistic narratives, it caused him to try another tack. His third narrative, *Mardi*, begins realistically. On board a whaler in the South Seas two sailors contemplate desertion. However, theirs soon becomes "a chartless voyage" among allegorical islands of a mythical archipelago. The sailor-narrator rescues a symbolically provocative white captive, loves her, loses her, and pursues her beyond the ends of the earth. He is as relentless as Ahab in quest of the white whale and as self-destructive, but the search is put aside from time to time for intervals of philosophizing, rhapsodizing, and satirizing on topics of contemporary political, theological, artistic and scientific interest. *Mardi* is a thing of patches, some of which presage the bravura passages of *Moby-Dick* and *The Confidence-Man*. Melville's family and friends advised that he forego his mental travelling, and to the accompaniment of grumbling about financial necessities, he restrained himself in *Redburn* and *White Jacket*.

Redburn recalls Melville's first voyage, a summer's service on a trader carrying cotton to Liverpool. *White Jacket* reflects his experiences as an ordinary seaman on a "homeward bound" American frigate. They contributed to his bank account and reputation. In *Redburn* the titular narrator is a callow lad who grows up, discarding his social pretension, encountering misery and evil about which he can do little, yet learning to stand on his own. *White Jacket* is likewise an initiation story but more. Its titular character is named for a non-regulation pea jacket he is issued, which distinguishes him in a way that he first finds flattering yet proves so disadvantageous that the plot concerns his efforts to rid himself of it. His ship is treated as a microcosm of his nation, a professedly democratic state but one sustained by an authoritarian hierarchy which abuses "the people," as the ratings are called, and which is corrupt or inept. Despite this irony, *White Jacket*, with its emphasis on the brotherhood of the common seaman and the prospect that "Our Lord Admiral" above will right earthly wrongs, is Melville's most optimistic book.

Apparently *Moby-Dick* was conceived in the pattern of its predecessors – a sailor recalling, in a realistic and casual way, his experiences aboard a whaler on a Pacific cruise. But it grew from narrative to novel, encompassing drama and epic and a number of lesser genres (e.g., sermon, natural history, tall tale, technical manual); expanding its tonal range to include low comedy, high wit, and lofty tragedy; and posing questions both metaphysical and pragmatic. If the theme of this leviathanic book must be simplistically stated, one could say that it is a quest for a way to live with dignity in a world in which the only certainty is uncertainty. Superficially, it is the melodramatic tale of the search for an albino whale by a mad sea captain whom it had maimed, but the book is so rich that it encourages many interpretations. Indeed this seems the intention of the author, supporting its essential nature as an epistemological quest.

Pierre is a departure from Melville's six sea narratives. It opposes an Edenic countryside and a postlapsarian city, settings in which Pierre, an idealistic young patrician, attempts to attack the evil he discovers, the sin of his father, with the weapons of Christian rectitude. In a memorable analogy, Melville suggests that clocks on earth are only relatively accurate because they must be made applicable to earthly contours. Absolutely perfect time obtains in heaven alone. Pierre's attempt to apply celestial time to earth is disastrously out of joint. Badly received, *Pierre* compels, in the words of its subtitle, for "the ambiguities" laid bare through its psychological and ethical probing.

Melville now turned magazinist. *Israel Potter*, the fictionalized biography of a soldier during the Revolutionary War and later adrift in London, explores the endurance of the common man. *Piazza Tales* is distinguished for "Bartleby," an account of the response of a worldly lawyer whose copyist gently declines to exist; "Benito Cereno," the gothic adventure of a goodnatured American sea captain who encounters a ship deviously controlled by its cargo of slaves; and "The Encantadas," sketches of the Galapagos Islands, a volcanic waste in the thrall of an evil spell. The last prose fiction Melville published, *The Confidence-Man*, is a darkly comic work of such originality of concept, technique, and verbal dexterity that it seems a prototype of the modern American novel. The setting is a Mississippi River steamboat on April Fool's Day. The action is a series of confidence men (though perhaps only one, variously guised) in ritualistic confrontation with their marks who are vulnerable because of their faith, hope, and charity. The book satirizes American types and deflates American beliefs through the device of the confidence man who preaches trust apparently for some selfish reason. But one is never sure. This, Melville's most ingenious book, was a failure. Thereafter he never attempted to write for a popular audience.

Always self-taught, Melville studied poetry. Near the end of the Civil War he undertook a verse sequence, *Battle-Pieces*, which sought to comprehend this national tragedy. It begins with "The Portent," on the hanging of the abolitionist firebrand John Brown, and ends with elegies to the dead of both sides. Walt Whitman's "Drum-Taps" is the only comparable body of verse. A decade later he published *Clarel*, an ambitious narrative poem about a party of "pilgrims" of diverse background and persuasion who tour the Holy Land. The framework permits discussions of science, religion, and the future of the New World. While on the whole they do not lift the spirits and the tetrameter couplets grow wearisome, the poem has a stony integrity and curious, digressive cantos on such subjects as Piranesi's prison etchings and the Hindu god Rama. His shorter verses, issued privately, draw from his early life as a sailor, his travels in Europe and the Levant, and his literary explorations. They are uneven, but the most flawed are not without interest for their tensions, juxtapositions, and sense of tragedy, for what they attempt rather than what they achieve.

Melville's last work is a short novel, *Billy Budd*. A handsome sailor on a warship strikes down a petty officer. There are mitigating circumstances, but he is hanged so that the discipline of the crew might be secured. The tale is sensitive to every complexity and delicately controlled, but as always with Melville its emphasis is on questions rather than answers.

—Hennig Cohen

MENCKEN, H(enry) L(ouis). American. Born in Baltimore, Maryland, 12 September 1880, and lived there for the rest of his life. Educated at Knapp's Institute, Baltimore, and the Baltimore Polytechnic Institute. Married Sara Powell Haardt in 1930 (died, 1935). Reporter, *Baltimore Morning Herald*, 1899–1903; City Editor, 1903–05, and Chief Editor, 1905–06, *Baltimore Evening Herald*; member of the editorial staff of the *Baltimore Sun* and *Evening Sun*, 1906–41; Columnist ("The Free Lance"), 1910–16; War Correspondent in Germany, 1916–18; Literary Critic, 1908–23, and Editor, with George Jean Nathan, 1914–23, *Smart Set*, New York; Literary Adviser to Alfred A. Knopf, publishers, New York, from 1917; Contributing Editor, *The Nation*, New York, 1931–32; Co-Founder, with Nathan, 1923, and Editor, 1924–33, *American Mercury*, New York. Recipient: American Academy of Arts and Letters Gold Medal, 1950. *Died 29 January 1956.*

PUBLICATIONS

Collections

    Letters, edited by Guy J. Forgue. 1961.
    The American Scene: A Reader, edited by Huntington Cairns. 1965.

Fiction

    Christmas Story. 1946.

Plays

    The Artist (produced 1927). 1912.
    Heliogabalus: A Buffoonery, with George Jean Nathan. 1920.

Verse

Ventures into Verse. 1903.

Other

George Bernard Shaw: His Plays. 1905.
The Philosophy of Friedrich Nietzsche. 1908.
What You Ought to Know about Your Baby, with Leonard Keene Hirshberg. 1910.
Men Versus the Man: A Conversation Between Robert Rives La Monte, Socialist, and Mencken, Individualist. 1910.
Europe after 8:15, with George Jean Nathan and Willard Huntington Wright (travel). 1914.
A Little Book in C Major. 1916.
A Book of Burlesques. 1916.
A Book of Prefaces. 1917.
Pistols for Two, with George Jean Nathan. 1917.
Damn! A Book of Calumny. 1918.
In Defense of Women. 1918; revised edition, 1922.
The American Language. 1919; revised edition, 1921, 1923, 1936; supplement, 1945, 1948.
Prejudices, First Series. 1919; *Second Series,* 1920; *Third Series,* 1922; *Fourth Series,* 1924; *Fifth Series,* 1926; *Sixth Series,* 1927; *Selected Prejudices,* 1927; edited by James T. Farrell, as *Prejudices: A Selection,* 1958.
The American Credo, with George Jean Nathan. 1920.
Notes on Democracy. 1926.
Treatise on the Gods. 1930; revised edition, 1946.
Making a President: A Footnote to the Saga of Democracy. 1932.
Treatise on Right and Wrong. 1934.
Happy Days 1880–1892 (autobiography). 1940.
Newspaper Days 1899–1906 (autobiography). 1941.
A New Dictionary of Quotations on Historical Principles. 1942.
Heathen Days 1890–1936 (autobiography). 1943.
A Mencken Chrestomathy. 1949.
The Vintage Mencken, edited by Alistair Cooke. 1955.
Minority Report: Mencken's Notebooks. 1956.
A Carnival of Buncombe (essays), edited by Malcolm Moos. 1956; as *On Politics,* 1960.
The Bathtub Hoax and Other Blasts and Bravos from the Chicago Tribune, edited by Robert McHugh. 1958.
Mencken on Music: A Selection of His Writings on Music, Together with an Account of Mencken's Musical Life and a History of the Saturday Night Club, edited by Louis Cheslock. 1961.
Smart Set Criticism, edited by William H. Nolte. 1968.
New Letters, edited by Carl Bode. 1976.

Editor, *A Doll's House, Little Eyolf,* by Ibsen. 2 vols., 1909.
Editor, *The Gist of Nietzsche.* 1910.
Editor, *The Free Lance Books.* 5 vols., 1919–21.
Editor, *Americana.* 1925.
Editor, *Essays,* by James Gibbons Huneker. 1929.
Editor, *The American Democrat,* by James Fenimore Cooper. 1931.
Editor, *Southern Album,* by Sara Haardt. 1936.
Editor, *The Sunpapers of Baltimore.* 1937.

Translator, *The Antichrist,* by Nietzsche.   1920.

Bibliography: *Mencken: The Bibliography* by Betty Adler, 1961.

Reading List: *Mencken: A Portrait from Memory* by Charles Angoff, 1956; *Mencken: Literary Critic* by William H. Nolte, 1966; *Mencken* by Philip Wagner, 1966; *The Constant Circle: Mencken and His Friends* by Sara Mayfield, 1968; *Mencken* by Carl Bode, 1969; *Serpent in Eden: Mencken and the South* by Fred C. Hobson, Jr., 1974; *Mencken: A Study of His Thought* by Charles A. Fecher, 1978; *Mencken: Critic of American Life* by George H. Douglas, 1978.

*   *   *

H. L. Mencken's reputation was etched by the acidic wit that characterized his commentary on the American culture of his day. Trained as a newspaperman, Mencken reached the height of his powers in the 1920's when, as an associate of the *Sun* papers in Baltimore and an editor first of *The Smart Set* and then of *The American Mercury,* he became one the nation's most influential critics.

A prodigious writer, he published some twenty-five books – not to mention literally thousands of articles, essays, stories, editorials, book reviews – during the course of his career, beginning curiously with the now-forgotten *Ventures into Verse* in 1903 and moving in 1905 and 1908 respectively to the more representative *George Bernard Shaw: His Plays* and *The Philosophy of Friedrich Nietzsche.* Throughout, however, his style and his messages were those found in *Prejudices,* his most representative work, a six-volume collection of opinion published between 1919 and 1927. The messages were intensely iconoclastic: American culture had become stultified by its rigid adherence to a peculiarly "Puritan" form of Christian morality, and the quality of American politics – and, indeed, of American life – was being compromised by a foolish but persistent belief in egalitarianism. These messages and their many corollaries he published again and again, employing a style which became his particular signature, a style whose ingredients were the acerbic allusion, the caustic joke, the unusual word, the irreverent comparison. However, a story like "The Girl from Red Lion, P.A." is essentially a good-natured look at an ignorant country girl, with more than a hint of compassion.

With the advent of the 1930's depression, the popularity of Mencken's social commentary waned. In 1919, however, he had published *The American Language,* a book which he revised and supplemented at various times until 1948. In *The American Language* Mencken sought, as he said in his sub-title, to inquire "into the development of English in the United States." The volume was quickly accepted by linguists, and continues today as a standard reference work in the field. Indeed, it may well account for Mencken's fame long after his other work has become dated and been forgotten.

—Bruce A. Lohof

MEREDITH, George.   English.   Born in Portsmouth, Hampshire, 12 February 1828. Educated at Paul's Church School, Southsea, Hampshire; Moravian School, Neuwied sur Rhine, Germany, 1843–44; articled to a solicitor in London, 1845. Married 1) Mary Ellen Nicholls, daughter of the novelist Thomas Love Peacock, in 1849 (died, 1861), one son; 2) Marie Vulliamy in 1864 (died, 1885), one son and one daughter. Abandoned the law for journalism; settled in London, then in Surrey; writer from 1848; with others, edited *The*

Monthly Observer, London, 1848–49; contributed to *Chambers Journal*, London, 1849, and to *Fraser's Magazine*, London, 1851–52; leader writer for the *Ipswich Journal* from 1860; literary adviser to Chapman and Hall, publishers, London, 1862–94; Special Foreign Correspondent for the London *Morning Post* during the Austro-Italian War, 1866; Editor, 1867–68, and Contributor, 1867–1909, *Fortnightly Review*, London; lectured on comedy at the London Institution, 1877. Recipient: Royal Society of Literature gold medal, 1905. President, Society of Authors, 1892; Vice-President, London Library, 1902. Order of Merit, 1905. *Died 18 May 1909.*

PUBLICATIONS

Collections

> *Works.* 27 vols., 1909–11.
> *Letters*, edited by C. L. Cline. 3 vols., 1968.
> *Poems*, edited by Phyllis B. Bartlett. 2 vols., 1977.

Fiction

> *The Shaving of Shagpat: An Arabian Entertainment.* 1855; edited by F. M. Meynell, 1955.
> *Farina: A Legend of Cologne.* 1857.
> *The Ordeal of Richard Feverel: A History of Father and Son.* 1859; revised edition, 1878; edited by Norman Kelvin, 1961.
> *Evan Harrington; or, He Would Be a Gentleman.* 1861; edited by G. F. Reynolds, 1922.
> *Emilia in England.* 1864; as *Sandra Belloni*, 1886.
> *Rhoda Fleming.* 1865.
> *Vittoria.* 1867.
> *The Adventures of Harry Richmond.* 1871.
> *Beauchamp's Career.* 1875; edited by G. M. Young, 1950.
> *The House on the Beach.* 1877.
> *The Egoist: A Comedy in Narrative.* 1879; edited by Robert M. Adams, 1977.
> *The Tragic Comedians.* 1880; revised edition, edited by C. K. Shorter, 1891.
> *Diana of the Crossways.* 1885.
> *The Case of General Ople and Lady Camper.* 1890.
> *The Tale of Chloe.* 1890.
> *One of Our Conquerors.* 1891.
> *Lord Ormont and His Aminta.* 1894.
> *The Tale of Chloe and Other Stories.* 1894.
> *The Amazing Marriage.* 1895.
> *(Novels).* 39 vols., 1896–1912 (includes miscellaneous prose and bibliography).
> *Short Stories.* 1898.
> *Celt and Saxon.* 1910.

Play

> *The Sentimentalists* (produced 1910).

Verse

Poems. 1851.
Modern Love, and Poems of the English Roadside, with Poems and Ballads. 1862;
  revised edition, 1892.
Poems and Lyrics of the Joy of Earth. 1883.
Ballads and Poems of Tragic Life. 1887.
A Reading of Earth. 1888.
Jump-to-Glory Jane: A Poem. 1889.
*Poems: The Empty Purse, with Odes to the Comic Spirit, to Youth in Memory, and
  Verses.* 1892.
Selected Poems. 1897.
Odes in Contribution to the Song of French History. 1898.
A Reading of Life. 1901.
Last Poems. 1909.
Poems Written in Early Youth, Poems from Modern Love, and Scattered Poems. 1909.

Other

Works. 34 vols., 1896.
An Essay on Comedy and the Uses of the Comic Spirit. 1897; edited by Lane Cooper,
  1956.
Up to the Midnight: A Series of Dialogues Contributed to the Graphic. 1913.
The Contributions to the Monthly Observer, edited by H. Buxton Forman. 1928.

Bibliography: *A Bibliography of the Writings in Prose and Verse by Meredith,* 1922, and
Meredithiana, 1924, both by H. Buxton Forman; supplement by H. Lewis Sawin, in *Bulletin
of Bibliography,* 1955.

Reading List: *Meredith: Les Cinquante Premières Années* by René Galland, 1923; *The Ordeal
of Meredith* by Lionel Stevenson, 1954; *Meredith: His Life and Work* by Jack Lindsay, 1956;
A Troubled Eden: Nature and Society in the Works of Meredith by Norman Kelvin, 1961;
Meredith and English Comedy by V. S. Pritchett, 1970; *Meredith: The Critical Heritage* edited
by Ioan Williams, 1971; *Meredith Now* edited by Ian Fletcher, 1971; *The Readable People of
Meredith* by Judith Wilt, 1975; *Meredith: His Life and Lost Love* by David Williams, 1977.

*   *   *

In the year before his death, George Meredith, in an interview with Constantin Photiadès,
remarked, "my name is celebrated, but no one reads my books." Never greatly popular in his
own day, Meredith's work was nonetheless singular.

His first notable achievement was *The Ordeal of Richard Feverel.* Sir Austen Feverel,
bruised by his wife's infidelity and desertion, applies the Great Shaddock Dogma, a woman-
hating doctrine, to the scientific education of his son, Richard. Designed to bring him through
the puppy-love stage, the Blossoming Season, and the Magnetic Age free from the
temptations of Eve, or "the Apple Disease," it has disastrous consequences. Richard marries
Lucy Desborough without permission, leaves her temporarily to gain his father's
approbation, engages meanwhile in rescuing fallen women – and falls himself. A tragic
dénouement points up the insufferability of imposing a rigid code or of systematizing human
beings. Yet, at the end, incorrigible Sir Austen is plotting a program for his grandson. *The
Ordeal* is stylistically unique, an amalgam of high and low comedy, of romance, and of tragi-
comedy. In addition to the interesting narrative structure, the epigrammatic and aphoristic

wit, and the comic dialogue, there are numerous memorable characters, fewer autobiographical and more purely literary creations than in his later works. The unbalanced ones are Sir Austen's parasites – Adrian Harley, a seedy intellectual; the purely physical Algernon; and Uncle Hippias, a hypochondriacal dipsomaniac. Those who read earth right are Mrs. Berry, Lucy's counsellor ("Kissing don't last. Cookery do"); the independent, determined, and intuitive Lucy; and Austin Wentworth, Richard's spiritual guide. Finally, the cryptic and fluid symbolism of the "ordeal" broadening as the novel progresses, lends the masterful touch.

In the comic romance *Evan Harrington*, Meredith adopted a form – the *Bildungsroman* – and a subject – the illusions of class distinction – which he followed to an extent in *Emilia in England*, *The Adventures of Harry Richmond*, and *Beauchamp's Career*. Ashamed of his birth and aspiring to social status, Evan, brought ultimately to realize the distinction between a true gentleman and a sham, is able to acknowledge his lowly origins as son of a tailor. Meredith, drawing many of the characters from his family and acquaintances, suggests not merely class snobbery, but the broader scope of Carlyle's *Sartor Resartus*, as he had done in the earlier allegorical work *The Shaving of Shagpat*.

Modern Love (1862), a sequence of near-sonnets, is a psychological analysis of incompatibility in marriage. The wife has taken a lover; the husband, whose ego is battered, takes a mistress in retaliation. The study centers on the anguish and hypocrisy of physical closeness without mental communion:

> Like sculptured effigies they might be seen
> Upon their marriage-tomb, the sword between;
> Each wishing for the sword that severs all.

Love, "the crowning sun," had initially brought a oneness to intelligence and instinct; but they looked backward instead of forward and love became physical: "We are betrayed by what is false within." They at last hold "honest speech," but the wife, unable to act rationally, commits suicide to free her husband for the other woman. The omniscient narrator summarizes with a probable cause of the personal tragedy:

> Then each applied to each the fatal knife,
> Deep questioning, which probes to endless dole.
> Ah, what a dusty answer gets the soul
> When hot for certainties in this our life!

Modern Love is Meredith's most perceptive psychological study, written in his most penetrating language.

Emilia in England still displays some freshness, but the thematic thrust against sentimentalism and social climbing is a common one, and, increasingly thereafter, Meredith's work is, with a few exceptions, tired writing. *Vittoria*, the sequel to *Emilia*, deals with the Italian struggle for independence, and places the central character, now an opera diva, at the mercy of revolutionary events. *Harry Richmond* casts some oblique cross-cultural light on England through Harry's love for a German princess, Ottilia. *Beauchamp's Career* is a philosophic-political novel, with Carlyle's *Heroes and Hero Worship* in mind. Young Nevil enters politics as a Liberal, paralleling Meredith's own sympathies. This work, like many others, is flawed by a contemptuous, suspense-destroying, retrogressive narrative technique.

An Essay on Comedy gives Meredith's conception of comedy as a corrective device for pointing out right action based on reason rather than on sentimentality. Unlike satire or ridicule, it is detached and Olympian, so that it calls forth no resentment, only "volleys of silvery laughter."

The Egoist is a sustained high comedy of manners, with a style as fitted to the vain and shallow egoist, Sir Willoughby Patterne, as his trousers: "*You see he has a leg.*" While seeking a worthy match, he exercises *le driot de seigneur* by trifling with Laetitia Dale. Clara

Middleton, his bride elect, gradually detects his artificial sentiment, and breaks off with him. To save face, he proposes to Laetitia, who, with delightful irony, forces him to accept her on her own terms as a disillusioned critic of his faults. There is no narrative-impeding straining for the witty phrase and comic situation of his lesser works in this novel, usually considered his masterpiece.

"The Woods of Westermain," a poem of 1883, comes closest to consolidating Meredith's optimistic evolutionary theory emerging from his total canon. "Blood and brain and spirit, three .../ Join for true felicity." Instincts, intellect, and spirit are interdependent and derive nourishment and grow like the roots, limbs, and leaves on a tree. Any failure to read earth right results in imbalance of character, the anti-social disease of egoism. Such a theory perhaps explains the limitations of Meredith's work: the stereotyping of characters in terms of defects and the restriction to personal limitations within the social veneer. As an explanation of evil, it lacks cosmic import and complexity.

Nevertheless, as an unconventional, anti-Victorian experimentalist, as a humanistic free thinker, as a liberal reformer who championed equality for women, democratic political institutions, and freedom for oppressed nations – despite the fact that many of his other causes are now outdated – Meredith left to the reader of today three works of great distinction – *The Ordeal of Richard Feverel, Modern Love,* and *The Egoist.*

—Wesley D. Sweetser

MILLER, Henry (Valentine). American. Born in Yorkville, New York City, 26 December 1891. Attended the City College of New York, 1909. Married 1) Beatrice Sylvas Wickens in 1917 (divorced, 1924); 2) June Edith Smith in 1924 (divorced, 1934); 3) Martha Lepska in 1944 (divorced, 1952); 4) Eve McClure in 1953 (divorced); 5) Hoki Tokuda in 1967; one son and two daughters. Has held many jobs: with the Atlas Portland Cement Company, New York, 1909; Reporter, Washington, D.C., 1917; with the Bureau of Economic Research, New York, 1919; Employment Manager, Western Union Telegraph Company, 1920–24; lived in Europe, 1930–39: Proofreader, *Chicago Tribune* Paris edition, 1932; teacher at the Lycée Carnot, Dijon, 1932; Psychoanalyst, 1936; Editor, with Lawrence Durrell and Alfred Perlès, *The Booster,* later *Delta,* Paris, 1937–38; Continental Editor, *Volontes,* Paris, 1938–39; European Editor, *Phoenix,* Woodstock, New York, 1938–39; returned to the United States in 1940; settled in California, 1942. Also an artist: has exhibited water colors in New York, 1927, London, 1944, and Los Angeles, 1966. Recipient: Formentor Prize Committee Citation, 1961. Member, National Institute of Arts and Letters, 1957.

PUBLICATIONS

Fiction

Tropic of Cancer. 1934.
Black Spring. 1936.
Tropic of Capricorn. 1939.
The Rosy Crucifixion: Sexus. 1949; *Plexus,* 1953; *Nexus,* 1960.
Quiet Days in Clichy. 1956.

Plays

> Scenario: A Film with Sound.   1937.
> Just Wild about Harry: A Melo-Melo in 7 Scenes (produced 1963).   1963.

Other

> What Are You Going to Do About Alf?   1935.
> Aller Retour New York.   1935.
> Money and How It Gets That Way.   1938.
> Max and the White Phagocytes.   1938.
> The Cosmological Eye.   1939.
> Hamlet, with Michael Fraenkel.   2 vols., 1939–41.
> The World of Sex.   1940; revised edition, 1957.
> Wisdom of the Heart.   1941.
> The Colossus of Maroussi; or, The Spirit of Greece.   1941.
> The Angel Is My Watermark.   1944.
> Sunday after the War.   1944.
> The Plight of the Creative Artist in the United States of America.   1944.
> Semblance of a Devoted Past.   1944; unexpurgated edition, with To Paint Is to Love Again, 1968.
> Echolalia: Reproductions of Water Colors by Miller.   1945.
> Why Abstract?, with Hilaire Hiler and William Saroyan.   1945.
> Miller Miscellanea.   1945.
> The Air-Conditioned Nightmare.   1945; vol. 2, Remember to Remember, 1947.
> Obscenity and the Law of Reflection.   1945.
> Maurizius Forever.   1946; abridged edition, as Reflections on the Maurizius Case, 1974.
> Patchen: Man of Anger and Light, with A Letter to God by Kenneth Patchen.   1947.
> Of, By and About Miller: A Collection of Pieces by Miller, Herbert Read, and Others.   1947.
> Portrait of General Grant.   1947.
> Varda: The Master Builder.   1947.
> The Smile at the Foot of the Ladder.   1948.
> The Waters Reglitterized (includes reproductions of pictures by Miller).   1950.
> The Books in My Life.   1952.
> Nights of Love and Laughter.   1955.
> A Devil in Paradise: The Story of Conrad Mourand, Born Paris, 7 or 7:15pm, January 17, 1887, Died Paris, 10:30pm, August 31, 1954.   1956.
> Argument about Astrology.   1956.
> The Time of the Assassins: A Study of Rimbaud.   1956.
> Big Sur and the Oranges of Hieronymus Bosch.   1957.
> The Red Notebook.   1959.
> Art and Outrage: A Correspondence about Miller Between Alfred Perlès and Lawrence Durrell, with an Intermission by Miller.   1959.
> A Miller Reader, edited by Lawrence Durrell.   1959; as The Best of Miller, 1960.
> The Intimate Miller.   1959.
> To Paint Is To Love Again (includes reproductions of pictures by Miller).   1960.
> Stand Still like the Hummingbird.   1962.
> Watercolors, Drawings and His Essay "The Angel Is My Watermark."   1962.
> Lawrence Durrell and Miller: A Private Correspondence, edited by George Wickes.   1963.
> Books Tangent to Circle: Reviews.   1963.

Greece. 1964.
Miller on Writing. 1964.
Letters to Anaïs Nin. 1965.
Selected Prose. 2 vols., 1965.
Order and Chaos chez Hans Reichel. 1966.
Writer and Critic: A Correspondence, with W. A. Gordon. 1968.
Collector's Quest: Correspondence, 1947–1965, with J. R. Child. 1968.
Insomnia; or, The Devil at Large. 1970.
My Life and Times, edited by Bradley Smith. 1971.
Journey to an Antique Land. 1972.
Reflections on the Death of Mishima. 1972.
On Turning Eighty. 1972.
Miller in Conversation with Georges Belmont. 1972.
The Immortal Bard (on John Cowper Powys). 1973.
First Impressions of Greece. 1973.
This Is Henry – Henry Miller from Brooklyn, by Robert Snyder. 1974.
Letters of Miller and Wallace Fowlie 1943–1972. 1975.
The Nightmare Notebook. 1975.
Genius and Lust: A Journey Through the Major Writings of Miller, with Norman
    Mailer. 1976.
Four Visions of America, with others. 1977.
Miller's Book of Friends (memoirs). 1976; vol. 2, *My Bike and Other Friends,* 1978.
*Miller: Years of Trial and Triumph 1962–1964: The Correspondence of Miller and Elmer
    Gertz,* edited by Gertz and Felice Flanery Lewis. 1978.

Bibliography: *Miller: A Chronology and Bibliography* by Bern Porter, 1945; *Bibliography of
Miller* edited by Thomas H. Moore, 1961; *A Bibliography of Miller, 1945–1961* by Maxine
Renken, 1962.

Reading List: *Miller* by Kingsley Widmer, 1963; *Miller* by Frédéric Temple, 1965; *The Mind
and Art of Miller* by W. A. Gordon, 1967; *The Literature of Silence: Miller and Beckett* by
Ihab Hassan, 1968; *Miller: Three Decades of Criticism* edited by Edward B. Mitchell,
1971.

*   *   *

   Henry Miller's name became known to a wider public than that of a fashionable, rather
trendy literary *élite* largely as an unexpected result of the Allied Forces in Paris after 1944.
The soldiers and the civilians who accompanied them discovered his books – *Tropic of
Cancer, Black Spring, Tropic of Capricorn* – most of which had been refused publication in
the Anglo-Saxon countries because of their blatantly sexual matter. But they were available in
Paris published by Girodias's Obelisk Press, and were eagerly seized on by Americans and
Britons, many of whom succeeded in smuggling their finds into their home countries. Later
on, many of these books were published in England and America.
   Too often they were large, inchoate, rambling works with an autobiographical thread.
They passed rapidly, like a rushing, uncontrolled stream, from the rhapsodic to the sordid to
the pornographic. Miller's freedom of language and subject had a deep influence on the
thousands of writers who benefitted from the literary emancipation from censorship. Miller
himself may have been influenced by much of the *erotica* of the ages. But he was influenced
also by such American writers as Whitman and Robinson Jeffers, by the back-to-nature
animists such as Thoreau and D. H. Lawrence (about whom he wrote an unpublished study),
and by all the European writers who in one way or another contributed to such movements
as Dadaism and Surrealism. He praises such not always well-known writers as Céline,

Cingria, Blaise Cendrars, Milosz, Knut Hamsun, and Rimbaud, whose *Season in Hell* he translated. He has a sort of American-Irish dislike of Britons, except for Durrell and John Cowper Powys (whose novels he claims to understand, but whose real virtue was that he had written *In Defence of Sensuality*, and sensuality was a habit to which Miller always gave a high priority).

Miller as a writer is for freedom in every possible sense, an indecent Shelley, a Tom Paine with the lid off. He expresses, too, a semi-mystical belief that everything links with everything else and that the Creator will arrange that "If there is a genuine need it will be met." Miller, indeed, has himself had amazing luck in becoming a highly saleable writer. He always suffered from logorrhea – and, when he realized that he could earn real money by writing, from appalling over-production. He can be funny in a boisterous sort of way; he is a *farceur*; he can even convince one from time to time that he is genuinely perceptive, though the conviction seldom lasts long. He had a gift for assimilating trendy names and attitudes; Zen, Hokusai, the Essenes, Restif de la Bretonne, astrology, the occult, Milarepa the Tibetan monk. But paradoxically he can still react salutarily against the fashionable, against the claims, for example, of American medicine and the endless, self-defeating "don'ts" of urban Western societies – don't over-eat, don't walk if you can run, don't listen to the radio or watch television, don't get vaccinated or inoculated, don't get frightened if you are over or under weight. And, he concludes: "The great hoax which we are perpetuating every day of our lives is that we are making life easier, more comfortable, more enjoyable, more profitable. We are doing just the contrary. We are making life stale, flat and unprofitable every day in every way...." His attitude is far from new. It is certainly as old as the time of the Romantic poets. Nor does it advance our perceptions to keep on saying these things. Miller is not a great writer, and he can *en masse* be a great bore.

His best literary work, written with skill and *brio*, is *The Colossus of Maroussi*, for it carries to us the whole flavour of Athens in the months immediately preceding the Second World War, and the sense of the Greek-ness of Greeks. In general his early works are much the best for he was then really trying. *The Tropic of Cancer* is a gay, racy account of his life as a poor, often hungry, always lustful, writer in the Paris suburbs, just as *Sexus* (part of *The Rosy Crucifixion* trilogy) does give a picture of the lower middle class, working class, and prostitutes' life in New York in the years before the first World War. There are some rather fine passages in these books – "Easter came in like a frozen hare – but it was fairly warm in bed." Nor can one deny that he achieves at least novelty in his descriptions, sometimes quite comic, of sexual organs and of varieties of the sexual act. But the characters in his long autobiographical reminiscences are seldom visualised, except occasionally as extreme oddities when we see them like comic caricatures. There is little consideration of motives and less of psychology. The men and women move and act but we know only that it is because of the prime, crude instincts – sexual and the desire for food of which Miller makes a great deal.

Miller has been a copious letter writer all his life and an entertaining one. The correspondence between him and Durrell makes excellent reading, and there are vast stores of Miller letters in the archives of the University of California at Los Angeles.

—Kenneth Young

MILNE, A(lan) A(lexander). English. Born in London, 18 January 1882. Educated at Westminster School, London (Queen's Scholar), 1893–1900; Trinity College, Cambridge (Editor, *Granta*, 1902), 1900–03, B.A. in mathematics 1903. Served in the Royal Warwickshire Regiment, 1914–18. Married Dorothy de Sélincourt in 1913; one son. Free-lance journalist in London, 1903–06; Assistant Editor, *Punch*, London, 1906–14; full-time writer from 1918. *Died 31 January 1956.*

PUBLICATIONS

Fiction

Once on a Time. 1917.
Mr. Pim. 1921; as *Mr. Pim Passes By*, 1929.
The Red House Mystery. 1922.
A Gallery of Children. 1925.
Winnie-the-Pooh. 1926.
The House at Pooh Corner. 1928.
The Secret and Other Stories. 1929.
Two People. 1931.
Four Days' Wonder. 1933.
One Year's Time. 1942.
Chloe Marr. 1946.
Birthday Party and Other Stories. 1948.
A Table near the Band and Other Stories. 1950.
Prince Rabbit, and The Princess Who Could Not Laugh. 1966.

Plays

Wurzel-Flummery (produced 1917). 1921; revised version, in *First Plays*, 1919.
Make-Believe, music by George Dorlay, lyrics by C. E. Burton (produced 1918). In *Second Plays*, 1921.
Belinda: An April Folly (produced 1918). In *First Plays*, 1919.
The Boy Comes Home (produced 1918). In *First Plays*, 1919.
First Plays. 1919.
The Red Feathers (produced 1920). In *First Plays*, 1919.
The Lucky One (produced 1922). In *First Plays*, 1919.
The Camberley Triangle (produced 1919). In *Second Plays*, 1921.
Mr. Pim Passes By (produced 1919). In *Second Plays*, 1921.
The Romantic Age (produced 1920). In *Second Plays*, 1921.
The Stepmother (produced 1920). In *Second Plays*, 1921.
Second Plays. 1921.
The Great Broxopp: Four Chapters in Her Life (produced 1921). In *Three Plays*, 1922.
The Truth about Blayds (produced 1921). In *Three Plays*, 1922.
The Dover Road (produced 1921). In *Three Plays*, 1922.
Three Plays. 1922.
Berlud, Unlimited (produced 1922).
Success (produced 1923; as *Give Me Yesterday*, produced 1931). 1923.
The Artist: A Duologue. 1923.
The Man in the Bowler Hat: A Terribly Exciting Affair (produced 1924). 1923.
To Have the Honour (produced 1924; as *To Meet the Prince*, produced 1929). 1925.
Ariadne; or, Business First (produced 1924). 1925.
Portrait of a Gentleman in Slippers: A Fairy Tale (produced 1926). 1926.

The Princess and the Woodcutter, in Eight Modern Plays for Juniors, edited by John
  Hampden. 1927.
Miss Marlow at Play (produced 1927). 1936.
The Ivory Door: A Legend (produced 1927). 1928.
Let's All Talk about Gerald (produced 1928).
Gentleman Unknown (produced 1928).
The Fourth Wall: A Detective Story (produced 1928; as The Perfect Alibi, produced
  1928). 1929.
Toad of Toad Hall, music by H. Fraser-Simson, from the story The Wind in the Willows
  by Kenneth Grahame (produced 1929). 1929.
Michael and Mary (produced 1929). 1930.
They Don't Mean Any Harm (produced 1932).
Other People's Lives (produced 1933). 1935.
Miss Elizabeth Bennet, from the novel Pride and Prejudice by Jane Austen (produced
  1938). 1936.
Sarah Simple (produced 1937). 1939.
The Ugly Duckling. 1941.
Before the Flood. 1951.

Screenplays: The Bump, 1920; Five Pounds Reward, 1920; Twice Two, 1920; Birds of
Prey (The Perfect Alibi), with Basil Dean, 1930.

Verse

When We Were Very Young. 1924.
For the Luncheon Interval: Cricket and Other Verses. 1925.
Now We Are Six. 1927.
Behind the Lines. 1940.
Sneezles and Other Selections. 1947.
The Norman Church. 1948.

Other

Lovers in London. 1905.
The Day's Play (Punch sketches). 1910.
The Holiday Round (Punch sketches). 1912.
Once a Week (Punch sketches). 1914.
Happy Days (Punch sketches). 1915.
Not That It Matters. 1919.
If I May. 1920.
The Sunny Side. 1921.
(Selected Works). 7 vols., 1926.
The Ascent of Man. 1928.
By Way of Introduction. 1929.
Those Were the Days (omnibus). 1929.
When I Was Very Young (autobiography). 1930.
A. A. Milne (selections). 1933.
Peace with Honour: An Enquiry into the War Convention. 1934; revised edition, 1935.
It's Too Late Now: The Autobiography of a Writer. 1939; as Autobiography, 1939.
War with Honour. 1940.
War Aims Unlimited. 1941.
Going Abroad? 1947.

Books for Children: A Reader's Guide.   1948.
Year In, Year Out.   1952.
On Lewis Carroll.   1964.

Reading List: *Milne* by Thomas Burnett Swann, 1971; *The Enchanted Places* by Christopher Milne, 1974.

*   *   *

During his lifetime, A. A. Milne was famous for his plays and four children's books. He also published novels, short stories, poetry, and essays. Today, however, the general public knows only the children's books: *Winnie-the-Pooh*, the engaging story of a teddy bear and his friends, continued in a sequel, *The House at Pooh Corner*; and two volumes of light-hearted verse, *When We Were Very Young* and *Now We Are Six*.

His first collection of children's stories and his last, published posthumously, are deservedly unknown. The prince and princess of the latter are altogether more interesting in his fairy tale for grown-ups, *Once on a Time*, and in his plays, *The Ugly Duckling* and *The Ivory Door*. The fairy tale, now termed a "juvenile," still has readers; but the plays, like Milne's other plays, no longer have an audience – except *Toad of Toad Hall*, his delightful adaptation of *The Wind in the Willows*, which continues to entertain children.

Curiously, the qualities which distinguish Milne's successful children's books are among those that date and at times diminish his adult work. His technically excellent verse dances with rhythms and rhymes that undercut his serious adult poetry – of war and Nazism, for example, in *Behind the Lines*. Milne is, moreover, essentially a humorist, achieving his effects by exaggeration, gentle irony, understatement. His view is humane. As he writes in an introduction to his play *Michael and Mary*, he believes in cheerfulness and decency. These qualities enliven the everyday and freshen the banal. They have made small classics of his children's books and his fairy tale plays and fiction. They cannot, however, preserve even his best adult play, *Mr. Pim Passes By*, or his best novel, *Mr. Pim*, adapted from the play.

The reason for this is suggested in his autobiography, in which he observes that a man's life determines the kind of writer he is. Milne's pleasant, uneventful life is reflected in nearly all his writing. From the first trivial essays collected in *Those Were the Days* to the final good-humored, gracious collection, *Year In, Year Out*, conflict is hardly to be found in his work.

Except for well-bred exchanges of differing opinions, it is virtually nonexistent in his drama and fiction, including his pleasantly civilized mystery novel, *The Red House Mystery*. His best adult play, like many of his thirty-odd plays, is predictably a drawing room comedy, not so foolish as *Sarah Simple* and more amusing than the believable, but disappointing, *The Truth about Blayds*. *Mr. Pim Passes By* no longer has an audience, not only because Milne's borrowed situation – repeated in several of his failures – is old-fashioned; or because his characters are stock Milne characters, although more complex, with wider implications. Good plays have survived trite plots and stock characters; but Milne's audience no longer exists. It has been replaced by one that craves violent conflict, sitcoms, black comedy, and is not amused by the qualities that enchant the unchanging readers of his children's books.

—Robert F. Richards

MITCHELL, Donald Grant. Pseudonym: Ik Marvel. American. Born in Norwich, Connecticut, 12 April 1822. Educated at John Hall's School, Ellington, Connecticut,

1830–37; Yale University, New Haven, Connecticut (Editor, *Yale Literary Magazine*), 1837–41, graduated 1841. Married Mary Frances Pringle in 1853. Settled on the family farm in New London County, Connecticut, 1841, and devoted himself to farming and writing; clerk to the United States Consul in Liverpool, 1844–45; toured Europe, 1845–46; wrote for the *Morning Courier and New York Enquirer*, also studied law in the offices of John Osborne Sargent, New York, 1846–50; Editor, *Lorgnette*, New York, 1850; full-time writer from 1850; served as United States Consul in Venice, 1853–54; lived in Paris, 1855; returned to the United States, and settled on a farm, later called Edgewood, near New Haven, Connecticut. Recipient: New York Agricultural Society silver medal, 1843; New England Association of Park Superintendents silver cup, 1904. *Died 15 December 1908.*

PUBLICATIONS

Fiction

The Lorgnette; or, Studies of the Town by an Opera Lover. 1850; as *The Opera Goer,* 1852.
Reveries of a Bachelor; or, A Book of the Heart. 1850.
Dream Life: A Fable of the Seasons. 1851.
Fudge Doings, Being Tony Fudge's Record of the Same. 1855.
Seven Stories, with Basement and Attic. 1864.
Dr. Johns, Being a Narrative of Certain Events in the Life of an Orthodox Minister of Connecticut. 1866.

Other

Fresh Gleanings; or, A New Sheaf from the Old Fields of Continental Europe. 2 vols., 1847.
The Battle Summer, Being Transcripts from Personal Observation in Paris 1848. 1849.
My Farm of Edgewood: A Country Book. 1863.
Wet Days at Edgewood, with Old Farmers, Old Gardeners, and Old Pastorals. 1865.
Rural Studies, with Hints for Country Places. 1867; as *Out-of-Town Places,* 1884.
Pictures of Edgewood, photographs by Rockwood. 1868.
About Old Story-Tellers, of How and When They Lived, and What Stories They Told. 1878.
A Report to the Commissioners on Lay-Out of East Rock Park. 1882.
Bound Together: A Sheaf of Papers. 1884.
English Lands, Letters, and Kings. 4 vols., 1889–97.
American Lands and Letters. 2 vols., 1897–99.
Looking Back at Boyhood. 1906.
Works. 15 vols., 1907.
Louis Mitchell: A Sketch, edited by Waldo H. Dunn. 1947.

Editor, with Oliver Wendell Holmes, *The Atlantic Almanac 1868.* 1867.
Editor, *The Atlantic Almanac 1869.* 1868.
Editor, with Alfred Mitchell, *The Woodbridge Record, Being an Account of the Descendants of the Rev. John Woodbridge.* 1883.
Editor, *Daniel Tyler: A Memorial Volume.* 1883.

Bibliography: in *Bibliography of American Literature* by Jacob Blanck, 1973.

Reading List: *The Life of Mitchell* by Waldo H. Dunn, 1922.

*   *   *

There was perhaps no writer in nineteenth-century America who could more appropriately be labelled "genteel" than Donald Grant Mitchell. There was also perhaps no writer who more fully expressed the ambitions and mores of middle-class Americans. Like his contemporaries Richard Watson Gilder, Thomas Bailey Aldrich, and Richard Henry Stoddard, Mitchell addressed a middle-class audience that in both public and private life gave priority to "respectability," and nowhere was respectability more firmly entrenched than in the home. In a series of "country books" that included *My Farm of Edgewood*, *Wet Days at Edgewood*, and *Rural Studies*, Mitchell detailed an ideal respectable domestic life based on his own life at Edgewood, his home in rural Connecticut. The "country books" are long out of print, but for half a century they were highly regarded. At the time of Mitchell's death in 1908, surely few of his readers could have guessed that within a generation both Edgewood and its genial master would be forgotten.

Mitchell established his reputation in 1849 with the publication of *Reveries of a Bachelor* — a book utterly without original ideas but with a wealth of sentimental observations that gave it especial appeal for young women. Mitchell never disappointed his original audience; in book after book, they (and their husbands) found abundant sentiment and gentle advice. The formula extended even to his literary criticism, collected in, among other volumes, *American Lands and Letters*. Strictly speaking, it was not literary criticism but literary appreciation that he wrote.

Mitchell's genial, invariably pleasing writings deserve greater attention than they usually receive. As literature, they are of minor interest, yet as expositions of the aspirations and values of the genteel American they are invaluable. If a reader wishes to discover the ideal perimeters of life in middle-class America a century ago, Mitchell's books can show him.

—Edward Halsey Foster

MITCHELL, James Leslie.   See **GIBBON, Lewis Grassic**.

MITCHELL, Margaret (Munnerlyn).   American.   Born in Atlanta, Georgia, in 1900, and lived there for the rest of her life. Educated at the Washington Seminary, Atlanta, 1914–18; Smith College, Northampton, Massachusetts, 1918–19. Married John R. Marsh in 1925. Feature Writer and Reporter, *Atlanta Journal*, 1922–26. Recipient: Pulitzer Prize, 1937; Bohnenberger Memorial Award, 1938; New York Southern Society Gold Medal, 1938. M.A.: Smith College, 1939. *Died 16 August 1949.*

PUBLICATIONS

Fiction

Gone with the Wind. 1936.

Other

"Gone with the Wind" Letters 1936–1949, edited by Richard Harwell. 1976.

*   *   *

Margaret Mitchell wrote only one novel, *Gone with the Wind,* but it proved to be the most popular novel of her generation. At the time of her death in 1949, 3,800,000 copies were in print, and it continues to attract a large number of readers. *Gone with the Wind* was also made into a motion picture that at the time broke all attendance records and has since been revived more than once.

The continuing popularity of *Gone with the Wind* is not hard to account for. The tempestuous love affair of Scarlet O'Hara and Rhett Butler is in the great popular tradition. The Civil War background, the pathos of the South's defeat, the poverty and suffering (with its clear parallels to the 1930's depression) and eventual economic triumph of Scarlet, so cheering to readers with little to feel cheerful about, and then the "realistic" ending with its bitter-sweet parting of Rhett and Scarlet, contained more excitement than a dozen lesser novels. When one adds to the plethora of homely details about Southern life, the humor, the dozens of colorful minor characters all presented in competent if somewhat florid prose, one understands how even a writer as discriminating as F. Scott Fitzgerald would be impressed with what Margaret Mitchell had been able to pull off.

Literary critics also found things to admire in *Gone with the Wind*; some even felt it deserved the Pulitzer prize it won in 1937 by nosing out George Santayana's *The Last Puritan.* In *Cavalcade of the American Novel,* Edward Wagenknecht praised it for undercutting the "futilitarianism" and "deflation of values" that had been so smart in the 1920's. One can see how a political message could be extracted from Scarlet O'Hara's willingness to do anything (exploit convict labor, seduce her sister's fiancé) to get the money to save the family plantation. Even more significant, however, is the contrast afforded between Margaret Mitchell's vision of Southern history and William Faulkner's, particularly Mitchell's pragmatism and Faulkner's traditionalism. If one considers Faulkner's Flem Snopes one side of the moral coin, on the other side of which is Scarlet O'Hara, Margaret Mitchell's pragmatic history takes on an even deeper significance.

—W. J. Stuckey

MITCHELL, S(ilas) Weir. American. Born in Philadelphia, Pennsylvania, 15 February 1829; son of the physician John Kearsley Mitchell. Educated at the University Grammar School, Philadelphia; University of Pennsylvania, Philadelphia, 1844–48, left because of illness without taking a degree, subsequently awarded a B.A. as of Class of 1848, 1906; Jefferson Medical College, Philadelphia, M.D. 1850; studied medicine in Europe, 1850–51.

Served as a Surgeon with the Union Army during the Civil War. Married 1) Mary Middleton Elwyn in 1858 (died, 1862), two sons, including the dramatist Langdon Mitchell; 2) Mary Cadwalader in 1875. Practised medicine in Philadelphia, initially as an assistant to his father, from 1851; member of staff of the Philadelphia Orthopaedic Hospital and Infirmary for Nervous Diseases for forty years, and Professor at the Philadelphia Polyclinic and College for Graduates in Medicine; also a researcher: published extensively on pharmacological, physiological, and toxicological subjects, and, most notably, on his research into nervous diseases: pioneered the application of psychology to medicine; renowned for developing the theory of the "rest cure" as treatment for various mental diseases; devoted himself increasingly to writing during the last decades of his life. Trustee, University of Pennsylvania, from 1875; Trustee, Carnegie Institution, Washington, D.C.; first President, Franklin Inn (writer's club of Philadelphia), 1902–14. M.D.: University of Bologna, 1888; LL.D.: Harvard University, Cambridge, Massachusetts, 1886; University of Edinburgh, 1895; Princeton University, New Jersey, 1896; University of Toronto, 1906; Jefferson Medical College, 1910. Fellow, American Academy of Arts and Sciences. *Died 4 January 1914.*

PUBLICATIONS

Fiction

The Children's Hour (juvenile), with Elizabeth Stevenson. 1864.
The Wonderful Stories of Fuz-Buz and Mother Grabem the Spider (juvenile). 1867.
Hephzibah Guinness, Thee and You, and A Draft on the Banks of Spain. 1880.
In War Time. 1885.
Roland Blake. 1886.
Prince Little Boy and Other Tales Out of Fairy-Land. 1888.
Far in the Forest. 1889.
Characteristics. 1892.
Mr. Kris Kringle: A Christmas Tale. 1893.
When All the Woods Are Green. 1894.
Philip Vernon: A Tale in Prose and Verse. 1895.
A Madeira Party. 1895.
Hugh Wynne, Free Quaker. 1897.
The Adventures of François, Foundling, Thief, Juggler, and Fencing-Master During the French Revolution. 1898.
The Autobiography of a Quack, and The Case of George Dedlow. 1900.
Dr. North and His Friends. 1900.
Circumstance. 1901.
The Autobiography of a Quack and Other Stories. 1901.
A Comedy of Conscience. 1903.
Little Stories. 1903.
New Samaria, and The Summer of St. Martin. 1904.
The Youth of Washington, Told in the Form of an Autobiography. 1904.
Constance Trescot. 1905.
A Diplomatic Adventure. 1906.
A Venture in 1777 (juvenile). 1908.
The Red City: A Novel of the Second Administration of President Washington. 1908.
The Guillotine Club and Other Stories. 1910.
John Sherwood's Ironmaster. 1911.
Westways: A Village Chronicle. 1913.

Play

Francis Drake: A Tragedy of the Sea. 1893.

Verse

The Hill of Stones and Other Poems. 1883.
A Masque and Other Poems. 1888.
The Cup of Youth and Other Poems. 1889.
A Psalm of Deaths and Other Poems. 1891.
The Mother. 1891.
The Mother and Other Poems. 1893.
Collected Poems. 1896.
Ode on a Lycian Tomb. 1899.
The Wager and Other Poems. 1900.
Selections from the Poems. 1901.
Pearl, Rendered into Modern English Verse. 1906.
The Comfort of the Hills. 1909.
The Comfort of the Hills and Other Poems. 1910.
Complete Poems. 1914.

Other

Researches upon the Venom of the Rattlesnake. 1861.
Gunshot Wounds and Other Injuries of Nerves, with George R. Morehouse and William
    W. Keen. 1864.
Wear and Tear; or, Hints for the Overworked. 1871.
Injuries of Nerves and Their Consequences. 1872.
Fat and Blood, and How to Make Them. 1877; revised edition, 1878, 1884.
Lectures on Diseases of the Nervous System, Especially in Women. 1881; revised
    edition, 1885.
Researches upon the Venom of Poisonous Serpents, with Edward T. Reichert. 1886.
Doctor and Patient. 1888.
Two Lectures on the Conduct of the Medical Life. 1893.
The Composition of Expired Air and Its Effects upon Animal Life, with J. S. Billings and
    D. H. Bergey. 1895.
Clinical Lessons on Nervous Diseases. 1897.
*A Brief History of Two Families: The Mitchells of Ayrshire and the Symons of
    Cornwall.* 1912.
Some Recently Discovered Letters of William Harvey, with Other Miscellanea. 1912.
Works. 13 vols., 1913.

Editor, *Five Essays,* by John Kearsley Mitchell. 1859.

Bibliography: in *Bibliography of American Literature* by Jacob Blanck, 1973.

Reading List: *Mitchell: His Life and Letters* by Anna Robeson Burr, 1929; *Mitchell: Novelist and Physician* by Ernest Earnest, 1950; *Mitchell as a Psychiatric Novelist* by David M. Rein, 1952; *Mitchell, M.D. — Neurologist: A Medical Biography* by Richard D. Walker, 1970.

*   *   *

S. Weir Mitchell enjoyed during his lifetime almost as wide an acclaim for his work as a physician as for his writing. The hand that produced hundreds of scientific medical treatises was no less prolific in this *other* imaginative area, as Mitchell viewed it, and he voluminously turned out novels, short fiction, and poetry. "He's a world-doctor for sure," but "I can't say that he's a world-author," said Walt Whitman. Contemporary praise that ranked one Mitchell novel with *The Scarlet Letter*, two others as superior to *Henry Esmond* and *A Tale of Two Cities*, and one of his poems as finer than "Lycidas" was sincere but excessive.

Preceding and then accompanying his novel writing, Mitchell's short fiction is noteworthy mainly for its foreshadowing and typifying. The tales of fantasy, a few O. Henryish pieces, and several Poe-esque stories of supernatural mystery are more distinctive, but traditional trappings prevail in others. Probably most memorable is "The Case of George Dedlow," the autobiography of a quadruple amputee whose legs return during a climactic seance.

Mitchell's primary success as a storyteller came from his "summer-born books," the thirteen novels which were largely vacation products of his last thirty years. More accurately labeled romances, these works reveal a pioneer physician but a literary conservative during the rise of American Realism. Mitchell made three distinct contributions to American fiction, each with important realistic implications but none with significant realistic achievement. Characterization grounded in the psychological knowledge of his clinical experience was first in time and remains first in import. His coup here, the obsessed, neurotic woman with a marked capacity for evil, is best seen in *Roland Blake*, *Circumstance*, and *Constance Trescot*. Mitchell chose his names carefully: Octopia Darnell is octopus-like in her demanding hold upon the Wynnes, Lucretia Hunter is an unscrupulous seeker of lucre, and Constance Trescot is relentless in driving her husband's killer to suicide. Mitchell rightly thought *Constance Trescot* the best of his novels. A second contribution was the creation of a convincing atmosphere of a definite past. His long works of historical fiction – *Hugh Wynne, Free Quaker*, a best-seller about the American Revolution; *The Adventures of François*, set during the French Revolution; and *The Red City*, a novel of Philadelphia in Washington's second administration – manifest the extensive research and historical immersion with which Mitchell prepared himself for their writing. His third contribution, like his first, is more suggestive than fully realized. *Characteristics* and its sequel, *Dr. North and His Friends*, have been called "conversation novels" and lauded for their experimental originality. Plainly autobiographical, they continue the tradition of Oliver Wendell Holmes's autocratic *Breakfast-Table* series but look toward the more sophisticated use of conversation and complex interpersonal relationships in more serious fiction.

Mitchell was always serious about his poetry, but the judgment he hoped it would be given by time has not been forthcoming. His own nomination for immortality was the "Ode on a Lycian Tomb," inspired by the *Les Pleureuses* monument and his deep grief for the death of a daughter.

—Bert Hitchcock

MITFORD, Nancy. English. Born in London, 28 November 1904; daughter of the 2nd Lord Redesdale; sister of the writer Jessica Mitford. Educated privately. Married the Honourable Peter Rodd in 1933 (divorced, 1958; died, 1968). Managed a London bookshop during World War II; lived in France, latterly in Versailles, 1945 until her death. Chevalier, Legion of Honour, 1972. C.B.E. (Commander, Order of the British Empire), 1972. *Died 30 June 1973.*

Publications

Fiction

>*Highland Fling.* 1931.
>*Christmas Pudding.* 1932.
>*Wigs on the Green.* 1935.
>*Pigeon Pie: A Wartime Receipt.* 1940.
>*The Pursuit of Love.* 1945.
>*Love in a Cold Climate.* 1949.
>*The Blessing.* 1951.
>*Don't Tell Alfred.* 1960.

Play

>*The Little Hut,* from a play by André Roussin (produced 1950). 1951.

Other

>*Madame de Pompadour.* 1954; revised edition, 1968.
>*Voltaire in Love.* 1957.
>*The Water Beetle* (essays). 1962.
>*The Sun King: Louis XIV at Versailles.* 1966.
>*Frederick the Great.* 1970.

>Editor, *The Ladies of Alderley: Being the Letters Between Maria Josepha, Lady Stanley of Alderley, and Her Daughter-in-Law Henrietta Maria Stanley, During the Years 1841–1850.* 1938.
>Editor, *Noblesse Oblige: An Enquiry into the Identifiable Characteristics of the English Aristocracy.* 1956.

>Translator, *The Princess of Clèves,* by Mme. de Lafayette. 1950.

Reading List: *Mitford: A Memoir* by Harold Acton, 1975.

*   *   *

It is nearly impossible to discuss Nancy Mitford's creative output without mentioning her extraordinary family. She was the eldest of seven children (six girls and a boy), and raised without formal education by parents considered to be extremely eccentric. That the children themselves grew to independence rapidly is beyond question. One, Jessica, became a communist; her public, private, and artistic life has been a protest against her aristocratic and privileged upbringing. Two of the sisters became fascists, one marrying the head of the British Union of Fascists, and infamously noted as having kept company with Hitler. Another sister married royalty.

Nancy Mitford, in her novel *The Pursuit of Love,* gives us an almost voyeuristic look into the peculiarities of her family. In it, she sees herself as relatively removed from the family furor, exempt from its excesses. It is with such characteristic aristocratic reserve that she handles the subjects of her most widely read novels and biographies. The subjects of her biographies are in themselves revealing of the author's classical bearing. In *Voltaire in Love, Frederick the Great,* and *Madame de Pompadour,* Mitford's comfort with and respect for form, tradition, and finery lead to detailed descriptions of houses and grounds, paintings, jewel and snuff boxes. Though she is not afraid of exposing human frailty, she does so with the grace and reluctance of a priest indulging secrets of the confessional.

Mitford is much more at home in those novels which resemble the old comedies of manners. There, as in her biographies, characters are revealed as types, and, though they do not emerge in any psychological depth, they come to life like the caricatures in a Dickens novel. The names of her characters often reveal their most predominant personality trait. Mr. Mockbar, for example, in *Don't Tell Alfred*, is a newspaper columnist, and, as his name suggests, he is usually mean and always wrongheaded. Many of the characters appear and reappear sometimes only to serve author's wit and penchant for anecdote, though most of them are true to some part of contemporary life.

Mitford's driving point in the novels is to mock pretensions and pretentious people, though she does this with a light-handedness that has given her a reputation for cleverness rather than serious criticism. Her satires are not weighted on the side of intellectual insight, but tend to be facile and rather lacking in astringency. *Don't Tell Alfred* begins with a satire of the Foreign Office in England which has recalled a remarkable career diplomat from his post in France, replacing him with a pastoral theologist unsure of his mission. But the author cannot be cruel for too long, and soon she is looking for the saving element in her characters again, the side that exhibits the grace and gentility so often lacking in modern man.

Mitford has an ear for anecdote that is rare, and it is only the well-groomed restraint of the books that saves them from being gossipy bores and preserves their effectiveness as tender satires. Mitford has a worthy eye for the particularities of character, place, and situation, and it is this strength that has made her novels, biographies, essays, and travel articles so amusing and so popular.

—Lawrence R. Broer

MITTELHOLZER, Edgar (Austin). Guyanan. Born in New Amsterdam, British Guiana, now Guyana, 16 December 1909. Educated at Berbice High School, New Amsterdam. Served in the Trinidad Navy during World War II. Married 1) Roma Halfhide in 1942 (divorced, 1958), two sons and two daughters; 2) Jacqueline Pointer in 1960, one son. Worked as a customs official, meteorological observer, and journalist, until 1941; settled in London after World War II; member of the Books Department, British Council, London, 1948–52; full-time writer from 1952. Recipient: Guggenheim Fellowship, 1952. *Died 6 May 1965.*

PUBLICATIONS

Fiction

> *Corentyne Thunder.* 1941.
> *A Morning at the Office.* 1950; as *A Morning in Trinidad,* 1950.
> *Shadows Move among Them.* 1951.
> *The Children of Kaywana.* 1952; as *Kaywana Heritage,* 1976.
> *The Weather at Middenshot.* 1952.

The Life and Death of Sylvia. 1953; as *Sylvia,* 1963.
The Harrowing of Hubertus. 1954; as *Hubertus,* 1955; as *Kaywana Stock,* 1968.
My Bones and My Flute: A Ghost Story in the Old-Fashioned Manner. 1955.
Of Trees and the Sea. 1956.
A Tale of Three Places. 1957.
Kaywana Blood. 1958; as *The Old Blood,* 1958.
The Weather Family. 1958.
The Mad MacMullochs. 1959.
A Tinkling in the Twilight. 1959.
Latticed Echoes: A Novel in the Leitmotiv Manner. 1960.
Eltonsbrody. 1960.
Thunder Returning: A Novel in the Leitmotiv Manner. 1961.
The Piling of Clouds. 1961.
The Wounded and the Worried. 1962.
Uncle Paul. 1963.
The Jilkington Drama. 1965.
The Aloneness of Mrs. Chatham. 1965.

Other

Creole Chips. 1937.
The Adding Machine: A Fable for Capitalists and Commercialists. 1954.
With a Carib Eye. 1958.
A Swarthy Boy (autobiography). 1963.

Reading List: *Mittelholzer: The Man and His Work* by A. J. Seymour, 1968.

*   *   *

After World War II when the British Empire began to break up, there was great critical interest in English-language fiction from the Commonwealth countries as a result of what can now be seen as the naive hope that a worldwide English-speaking union might be preserved not through politics, but literature. A particular beneficiary of this short-lived movement was Edgar Mittelholzer, a native of British Guiana, who failed to follow up an exciting start.

His first professional novel, *A Morning at the Office,* was kindly received both in Great Britain and the United States, although reviewers felt that this plotless account of the tensions in a business office where colored clerks outnumber the whites (a kind of microcosm of the dissolving empire) was too thin and unresolved.

Mittelholzer scored an enormous hit, however, with his next novel, *Shadows Move among Them,* a stylish, cryptically ironic tale about a neurotic young man's attempts to gain control of his feelings while visiting a British minister's wise and witty family amidst the ruins of the old Dutch culture in the Guyana jungle. Anthony West compared the work to Norman Douglas's *South Wind* as one which "under cover of light entertainment ... discusses serious ideas sensibly and rationally." The visitor is led, almost unwillingly, out of his manias, West maintained, by the eccentric British family because they were able to deal with the jungle "as something that is there, not as a malicious departure from an ideal setting" (*New Yorker,* 6 October 1951). Other enthusiastic reviewers agreed that this unique fable might provide a model for facing the problems of new cultures evolving from the ruins of old in a world obsessed with guilt and existential despair. Two years after its publication, the novel provided the basis for Moss Hart's popular play, *The Climate of Eden.*

Mittelholzer never returned, however, to the sophisticated vein of this most successful work. His next novel, *The Children of Kaywana*, initiated a long, plodding trilogy that recounts the history of Guyana from its Dutch settlement in the seventeenth century down to 1960 through the lurid and violent doings of the van Groenwegel family. Readers were shocked by its sadism and sensuality, but received more sympathetically its more restrained companion pieces, *The Harrowing of Hubertus* and *Kaywana Blood*, as effective portrayals of three-dimensional characters against the extraordinary background of a jungle society. Reviewers became uneasy, however, as the author neared the present and became involved with "obeah," a local form of voodoo, for the impact of the work dwindled. It remains more important as the picture of an otherwise unchronicled past than for its artistic significance.

Between the first and second volumes of this trilogy, Mittelholzer published two other novels that can now be seen as ominous foreshadowings of those to follow. In the second, *The Life and Death of Sylvia*, he tried again to deal with modern Guyana; but despite the authenticity of the exotic setting, the mixed-blood heroine proved vapid because the author seemed unable to penetrate a woman's mind. He seemed to be running out of materials from his native land. Casting about for a fresh scene to exploit, he had already produced, in *The Weather in Middenshot*, a confused horror story about rural England; but this and others of the same kind to follow proved unsuccessful, although these obscure late novels surely indicate the truth of his report just before his grotesque death (apparently self-inflicted) that his principal interests were oriental occultism and psychical research. His talent was not for constructing histories, but for evoking atmosphere. He won readers as long as he had a tangible new world to offer them; but when his attention shifted from the physical to the metaphysical, the results were disastrous.

—Warren French

MOORE, Brian. Canadian. Born in Belfast, Northern Ireland, 25 August 1921; emigrated to Canada in 1948; moved to the United States in 1959. Educated at St. Malachy's College, Belfast. Served with the British Ministry of War Transport, in North Africa, Italy, and France, 1943–45. Married 1) Jacqueline Scully in 1951; 2) Jean Denney in 1966; one child. Served with the United Nations Relief and Rehabilitation Administration (UNRRA) Mission to Poland, 1946–47; Reporter, *Montreal Gazette*, 1948–52; full-time writer since 1952. Recipient: Authors Club of Great Britain Award, 1956; Beta Sigma Phi Award, 1956; Guggenheim Fellowship, 1959; Governor-General's Award, 1961; National Institute of Arts and Letters grant, 1961; Canada Council Fellowship, 1962; Smith Literary Award, 1973; Black Memorial Award, 1976. Lives in California.

PUBLICATIONS

Fiction

Judith Hearne. 1955; as *The Lonely Passion of Judith Hearne*, 1956.
The Feast of Lupercal. 1957; as *A Moment of Love*, 1965.
The Luck of Ginger Coffey. 1960.
An Answer from Limbo. 1962.
The Emperor of Ice-Cream. 1965.

I Am Mary Dunne.   1968.
Fergus.   1970.
Catholics.   1972.
The Great Victorian Collection.   1975.
The Doctor's Wife.   1976.

Plays

Screenplays: *The Luck of Ginger Coffey,* 1964; *Torn Curtain,* 1966; *The Slave,* 1967; *Catholics,* 1973.

Other

Canada, with the editors of *Life.*   1963.
The Revolution Script.   1971.

Reading List: *Moore* by Hallvard Dahlie, 1969 (includes bibliography); *Odysseus Ever Returning* by George Woodcock, 1970.

*   *   *

Brian Moore's fiction falls into three groups: the Belfast novels (*Judith Hearne, The Feast of Lupercal,* and *The Emperor of Ice-Cream*); the early North American novels (*The Luck of Ginger Coffey, An Answer from Limbo,* and *I Am Mary Dunne*); and the more recent metaphysical novels (*Fergus, Catholics,* and *The Great Victorian Collection*) written since his move to California some years ago. *The Doctor's Wife* (1976) comes under none of these headings, and must be considered separately since, although touching on areas Moore has already explored in his earlier work, it seems to mark a new departure.

The Belfast novels revolve around crises in the lives of an alcoholic spinster, a bachelor schoolmaster, and an adolescent boy in revolt against his family. The society Moore depicts – the Belfast of the 1940's – is a bleak and terrible place for the outsider or the transgressor; for the lonely, despairing Judith Hearne, or the incautious Diarmid Devine, who pursues a scandalous if pathetic affair with a Protestant girl, although he is himself a Catholic. But in *The Emperor of Ice-Cream,* which belongs to this early period although written years later, Moore strikes a more optimistic note with his account of a few formative months in the life of a Catholic boy who takes a job as an air-raid warden, thus outraging his old-fashioned, nationalist parents. The job, however, provides him with much picaresque experience of the adult world, and the opportunity to stand on his own feet.

The protagonists of the Belfast novels know, all too well, who they are. Their relation to the closed society around them is fixed, almost immutable. But in the early North American novels the characters begin to drift away from fixed identity, all but losing themselves in the existential flux of modern life. Ginger Coffey, an Irish immigrant in Montreal, finds his mental categories dissolving as he struggles to land a decent job commensurate with what he assumes to be his social status. In *An Answer from Limbo* an Irish writer living in New York sacrifices his mother for the sake of his work; cuts himself off, as it were, from his own past in order to create himself anew. And in *I Am Mary Dunne* a young woman in the midst of pre-menstrual tension literally forgets her own name and later comes close to suicide.

A vein of metaphysical speculation, released in Moore by the American experience, is evident in *Fergus, Catholics,* and *The Great Victorian Collection,* in each of which the nature of reality is called into question, and the nature and significance of art or artifice held up for

857

inspection. "The final belief," said Wallace Stevens, evidently one of Moore's favourite poets, "is to believe in a fiction, which you know to be a fiction, there being nothing else"; and this is the theme of the metaphysical novels, where creative activity is itself brought into the centre of the action, literally or symbolically. But in his most recent novel, *The Doctor's Wife*, Moore put aside these considerations in order to revisit earlier scenes. The book is a sort of Irish *Madame Bovary*. The heroine, on holiday in France, breaks with her husband, a Belfast surgeon, and has an ill-fated affair with an American student some years her junior. She is the antithesis of Judith Hearne, with everything that Judith Hearne desired, and she throws it all away, finishing up penniless and alone, but with her integrity undiminished, in a London bedsitter. And if the simple narrative line and the absence of metaphysics seem to represent a regression, we must conclude that Moore is making his world mosaically, not linearly – perhaps a richer and more various way of proceeding.

—Derek Mahon

MOORE, George (Augustus).   Irish.   Born at Moore Hall, Ballyglass, County Mayo, 24 February 1852; son of the landowner and politician G. H. Moore; moved with his family to London, 1869. Educated at Oscott College, Birmingham, 1861–69, then studied with an army tutor in London; studied painting at the Académie Julian, Paris, 1873–74. Lived in Paris, 1873–74, 1875–79; returned to London, 1880, and gave up painting for literature; wrote for the *Spectator* and the *Examiner*; art critic for the *Speaker*, 1891–95; settled in Ireland, and lived at Moore Hall and in Dublin, 1899–1911; High Sheriff of Mayo, 1905; returned to London, 1911. *Died 21 January 1933.*

PUBLICATIONS

Collections

> *Works* (Carra Edition).   21 vols., 1922–24.
> *Works* (Uniform Edition).   20 vols., 1924–33.
> *Works* (Ebury Edition).   20 vols., 1937.

Fiction

> *A Modern Lover.*   1883; revised edition, 1885; as *Lewis Seymour and Some Women,* 1917.
> *A Mummer's Wife.*   1884; revised edition, 1886, 1917; as *An Actor's Wife,* 1889.
> *A Drama in Muslin: A Realistic Novel.*   1886; revised edition, as *Muslin,* 1915.
> *A Mere Accident.*   1887.
> *Spring Days: A Realistic Novel – A Prelude to Don Juan.*   1888; revised edition, 1912; as *Shifting Love,* 1891.
> *Mike Fletcher.*   1889.
> *Vain Fortune.*   1891; revised edition, 1892, 1895.
> *Esther Waters.*   1894; revised edition, 1899, 1920.

Celibates (stories).   1895.
Evelyn Innes.   1898; revised edition, 1898, 1901, 1908.
Sister Theresa.   1901; revised edition, 1909.
The Untilled Field (stories).   1903; revised edition, 1903, 1914, 1926, 1931.
The Lake.   1905; revised edition, 1906, 1921.
Memoirs of My Dead Life.   1906; revised edition, 1921.
The Brook Kerith: A Syrian Story.   1916; revised edition, 1927.
Héloise and Abélard.   1921; *Fragments,* 1921.
In Single Strictness (stories).   1922; revised edition, 1923; as *Celibate Lives,* 1927.
Peronnik the Fool (story).   1926; revised edition, 1928.
Ulick and Soracha.   1926.
A Flood (story).   1930.
Aphrodite in Aulis.   1930; revised edition, 1931.

Plays

Martin Luther, with Bernard Lopez.   1879.
The Fashionable Beauty, with J. M. Glover (produced 1885).
The Honeymoon in Eclipse (produced 1888).
Thérèse Raquin, from a play by A. Texeira de Mattos from the novel by Zola (produced
    1891).
The Strike at Arlingford (produced 1893).   1893.
Journeys End in Lovers Meeting, with John Oliver Hobbes (produced 1894).
The Bending of the Bough (produced 1900).   1900.
Diarmuid and Grania, with W. B. Yeats (produced 1901).   1951; edited by Anthony
    Farrow, 1974.
Esther Waters, from his own novel (produced 1911).   1913.
The Apostle.   1911; revised version, as *The Passing of the Essenes* (produced 1930),
    1930.
Elizabeth Cooper (produced 1913).   1913; revised version, as *The Coming of Gabrielle*
    (produced 1923), 1920.
The Making of an Immortal (produced 1928).   1927.

Verse

Flowers of Passion.   1877.
Pagan Poems.   1881.

Other

Literature at Nurse; or, Circulating Morals.   1885.
Parnell and His Island.   1887.
Confessions of a Young Man.   1888; revised edition, 1889, 1904, 1917, 1926.
Impressions and Opinions.   1891; revised edition, 1913.
Modern Painting.   1893; revised edition, 1896.
The Royal Academy.   1895.
Memoirs of My Dead Life.   1906; revised edition, 1921.
Reminiscences of the Impressionist Painters.   1906.
Hail and Farewell: A Trilogy (Ave, Salve, Vale) (autobiography).   3 vols., 1911–14.
    revised edition, 1925.

A Story-Teller's Holiday.   1918; revised edition, 2 vols., 1928.
Avowals (autobiography).   1919.
Moore Versus Harris (correspondence with Frank Harris).   1921.
Conversations in Ebury Street (autobiography).   1924; revised edition, 1930.
Letters to Edouard Dujardin 1866–1922 (in French), translated by John
   Eglinton.   1929.
The Talking Pine.   1931.
A Communication to My Friends.   1933.
Letters (to John Eglinton).   1942.
Letters to Lady Cunard 1895–1933, edited by Rupert Hart-Davis.   1957.
Moore in Transition: Letters to T. Fisher Unwin and Lena Milman 1894–1910.   1968.

Editor, *Pure Poetry: An Anthology.*   1924.

Translator, *The Pastoral Loves of Daphnis and Chloe,* by Longus.   1924.

Bibliography: *A Bibliography of Moore* by Edwin Gilcher, 1970.

Reading List: *The Life of Moore* by Joseph M. Hone, 1936 (includes bibliography); *Moore: A Reconsideration* by Malcolm J. Brown, 1955; *GM: Memories of Moore* by Nancy Cunard, 1956; *Moore* by A. Norman Jeffares, 1965; *Moore: L'Homme et l'Oeuvre* by J. C. Noel, 1966; *Moore: The Artist's Vision, The Storyteller's Art* by Janet Dunleavy, 1973.

                              *   *   *

   George Moore's kaleidoscopic literary enthusiasms, his quirky use of self-parody, and his seemingly compulsive redrafting of a protean "canon" make him something of an anomaly to literary historians, both as an author and a personality. The eldest son of a wealthy Irish landowner and M.P., he grew up an awkward, ill-educated boy, the despair of his parents and, sometimes, himself. Upon coming of age, he inherited the family estate and immediately asserted independence by leaving for Paris to study art; there he lived seven years, picking up a haphazard, bohemian education in the studios and cafes of Montmartre. He spent most of the next twenty years in England, largely in London, where he established a mercurial reputation as an obstreperously avant-garde novelist and art critic. Then in 1900 he moved to Dublin to contribute his knowledge of literature and the theater to the Irish cultural renaissance. Eventually estranged from the Irish literary establishment, he returned after ten years to London to settle into an active old age, turning out controversial reminiscences and historical novels narrated in a gradually developed, distinctive prose style, the "melodic line" of his last years.
   Though Moore resists facile assessment, his work is historically important – particularly his novels, short stories, and criticism/memoirs – because it mirrors significant aesthetic and technical changes in English prose fiction over a nearly fifty-year span. Both in subject and in structure his fiction champions three major late nineteenth-century art movements – Aestheticism, Naturalism, and Impressionism – and reflects his involvement in a wide spectrum of social and aesthetic "causes" – feminism and the Irish problem (*A Drama in Muslin*), the attack on the values of the middle-class English "villa" (*Spring Days*), the introduction of Ibsenesque drama in England (*Vain Fortune*), the turn-of-the-century enthusiasm for Wagnerian opera (*Evelyn Innes*), the stimulation of an endemic Irish literature (*The Untilled Field*), the pursuit of a stream-of-consciousness narrative style (*The Lake*), to name but the most obvious. Among his five books of memoirs his first, *Confessions of a Young Man*, is a revealing period piece of literary and aesthetic criticism, in its original

version. Of the others, the three volumes of *Hail and Farewell* maintain interest because of their puckish blend of Irish literary gossip, lampoons, and sometimes shrewd, sometimes irascible literary criticism (those volumes stirred up wide contemporary reaction and turned most of Moore's Irish friends into acquaintances). Unfortunately, Moore blurred the topical significance of all of his works by rewriting nearly every one (often several times) in his later method and from a later perspective, and his selecting from among them three quite different collected editions.

His fiction can be divided roughly into three chronological periods: the first, an experimental blend of French and English realism and Aestheticism, ends with his best-known novel, *Esther Waters*, 1894; the second, an attempt at an amorphous psychological "intentionalism," fades into the third, that of his "melodic line," sometime after his epistolary novel, *The Lake*, 1905, and before his biblical-historical novel, *The Brook Kerith*, 1916. Within these three periods fall Moore's fifteen proto-novels and five collections of short stories. Several transcend a purely historical interest to emerge important for their own sake.

One is his second novel, *A Mummer's Wife*, the first openly avowed English attempt at doctrinaire French naturalism. It was a *succès de scandale*, and its rejection by the circulating libraries allowed Moore to attack publicly the artistic assumptions behind their monopoly. The novel itself contains two powerful character studies in the actor Dick Lennox and his dipsomaniac wife, Kate, and is narrated with uncommon structural unity. Indeed, what is remarkable about the original version is how well Moore combines a Zolaesque attention to structure and detail with a Balzacian depth of authorial comment. His next novel, *A Drama in Muslin*, also has a life of its own. In it Moore reveals the tawdry values of the Irish gentry through the lives of five girls on display in the Irish marriage mart as set against the background of their strife-torn country in the early 1880's. Arnold Bennett, for example, commended it (in *Fame and Fiction*) "as a brilliant instance of the modern tendency to bring history, sociology and morals within the dominion of the novelist's art." But by far the best and most popular of Moore's novels is *Esther Waters*. It is the story of an English servant girl who, sustained by a simple religious faith, rears her illegitimate son to manhood against heavy odds. Moore tells her story with quiet realism and tight structural unity, with each detail, each character contributing to the overall thematic pattern of Esther's muted victory over circumstances. That pattern proved a landmark in the development of thematic form in the English realistic novel.

Another literary landmark was his collection of short stories about the Irish, *The Untilled Field*. Influenced somewhat by Turgenev, he explored in most of those stories a theme of human loneliness amid the spiritual and cultural wasteland of contemporary Ireland. That theme and its inherent tone of melancholy profoundly affected the modern Irish short story. A melancholy tone is also integral to his final prose style, a languid, continuously flowing narrative line that blends dialogue with interior monologue with authorial commentary, *The Brook Kerith* being the best-known example. In that novel, through Joseph of Arimathea Moore traces the life of Jesus after he is presumably nursed back to health after being crucified; the story culminates in Jesus's ironically accidental encounter with the Christian fanatic Paul. It was, of course, another *succès de scandale*, but it also contains several powerful character studies set against a thoughtfully evoked historical background, a narrative synthesis that succeeds, for the most part, because of Moore's unique late style, his final landmark achievement.

—Jay Jernigan

861

MOORE, John. Scottish. Born in Stirling, baptized 7 December 1729; moved with his mother to Glasgow, 1737. Educated at Glasgow Grammar School; studied medicine at the University of Glasgow, and was simultaneously apprenticed to the surgeon John Gordon; qualified, 1747; studied in Paris, 1749–51; awarded M.D., University of Glasgow, 1770. Married Miss Simson in 1757; one daughter and five sons. Surgeon's mate in the Duke of Argyll's Regiment, serving at hospitals in Maestricht, 1747; Assistant to the Surgeon of the Coldstream Guards, at Flushing and Breda, 1748–49; Surgeon to the British Ambassador in Paris, 1749–51; practised in Glasgow with his former teacher John Gordon, 1751–53, then on his own, 1753–72; travelled with the Duke of Hamilton on the Continent, 1772–78; practised in London from 1778. *Died 21 January 1802.*

PUBLICATIONS

Collections

Works, with *Memoirs* by Robert Anderson. 7 vols., 1820.

Fiction

Zeluco: Various Views of Human Nature. 1789.
Edward: Various Views of Human Nature. 1796.
Mordaunt, Being Sketches of Life, Character, and Manners in Various Countries, Including the Memoirs of a French Lady of Quality. 1800; edited by W. L. Renwick, 1965.

Other

A View of Society and Manners in France, Switzerland, and Germany. 2 vols., 1779.
A View of Society and Manners in Italy. 2 vols., 1781.
Medical Sketches. 1786.
A Journal During a Residence in France. 2 vols., 1793–94.
A View of the Causes and Progress of the French Revolution. 2 vols., 1795.
Memoirs (of Smollett), and *A View of the Commencement and Progress of Romance,* in *Works of Smollett.* 1797.

Reading List: *The Popular Novel in England 1770–1800* by J. M. S. Tompkins, 1932.

*   *   *

John Moore, described by Smollett's Jery Melford in *Humphry Clinker* as "an eminent surgeon ... a merry facetious companion, sensible and shrewd, with a considerable fund of humour," carried the Augustan literary tradition through to the end of the eighteenth century. His first publications, *A View of Society and Manners in France, Switzerland, and Germany* and *A View of Society and Manners in Italy* were the fruits of his thoughtful observations while travelling as physician to the Duke of Hamilton on a conventional Grand Tour. He then went on to write three novels, which combine the same kind of observant manner with their fictional elements.

Zeluco was the most exotic of these novels, and the only one to be reprinted in the nineteenth century. The account of Southern Italy is probably its main interest for the modern reader, but it was the villain Zeluco whose melodramatic panache and bad end appealed to popular taste. In *Edward* Moore wrote about English society, with a plot suggested by Marivaux's *La Vie de Marianne*, which perhaps accounts for the novel's lack of cohesion, but in *Mordaunt* he achieved a balanced expression of his interests.

Mordaunt is subtitled *Sketches of Life, Character, and Manners in Various Countries, Including the Memoirs of a French Lady of Quality*. In the first volume, Mordaunt is held up in Switzerland by a sprained ankle, and so has leisure for a correspondence which ranges interestingly over such topics as German military discipline, the leaders of the French Revolution, the sensationalism of German plays and ballads, and the sobriety of the Spanish court. On his recovery he rescues a French lady in Paris and takes her to London, and the Marquise's story constitutes Moore's Whig critique of the Revolution, with the destruction of the Gironde seen as the abandonment of constructive idealism. The final volume tells of Mordaunt's gradually overcoming his hostility to marriage with the aid of the virtuous and lovely Horatia Clifford and – more incisively – the entrapping of the arrogant aristocrat Deanport by a designing young woman from York, despite his ambitious mother the Countess. Moore shows a wit worthy of Fielding in a scene in which Lady Deanport's declamation about charity is interrupted by a beggar, who is dismissed as an "idle, intruding vagabond" before the panegyric on benevolence can be concluded.

Good humour and good sense are the qualities of Moore's novels, especially *Mordaunt*, which kept alive a certain masculine flavour in an era when the novel form was largely the preserve of women, who sometimes brought to it a sentimentality to which Moore is, at his best, a bracing antidote.

—Peter Faulkner

MORE, Hannah. English. Born in Stapleton, Gloucestershire, near Bristol, 2 February 1745. Educated at her eldest sister's boarding school in Bristol; subsequently lived with her four sisters in a house in Bristol, and taught at the school. Visited London, 1774, and became acquainted with Garrick and his wife, Burke, Reynolds, and Dr. Johnson; enjoyed success as a playwright; lived with Garrick's wife after his death in 1779, and from that time came increasingly to devote herself to reform and religious issues; moved to Cowslip Green, near Bristol, 1787; became acquainted with John Newton and Wilberforce, 1787; set up Sunday schools in Cheddar, 1789; after 1792 issued a series of "cheap repository tracts," which led to the formation of the Religious Tract Society, 1799; continued writing religious/moral treatises until 1819. *Died 7 September 1833.*

PUBLICATIONS

Fiction

> *Village Politics.* 1792.
> *Cheap Repository Tracts* (49 titles). 1795–97; revised version, as *Stories for the Middle Ranks of Society, and Tales for the Common People*, 1818.
> *Coelebs in Search of a Wife.* 1808.

Plays

A Search after Happiness: A Pastoral Drama.   1766(?); revised edition, 1796.
The Inflexible Captive (produced 1774).   1774.
Percy (produced 1777).   1778.
The Fatal Falsehood (produced 1779).   1779.
Sacred Dramas, Chiefly Intended for Young Persons, and Sensibility: A Poem (includes *Moses in the Bulrushes, Belshazzar, David and Goliath, Daniel*).   1782.

Verse

Sir Eldred of the Bower and The Bleeding Rock: Two Legendary Tales.   1776.
Ode to Dragon, Mr. Garrick's House-Dog at Hampton.   1777.
Florio: A Tale for Fine Gentlemen and Fine Ladies, and The Bas Bleu; or, Conversation.   1786.
Slavery.   1788.
Bishop Bonner's Ghost.   1789.
Poems.   1816.
The Twelfth of August; or, The Feast of Freedom.   1819; as *The Feast of Freedom; or, The Abolition of Domestic Slavery in Ceylon*, 1827.
Bible Rhymes on the Names of All the Books of the Old and New Testaments.   1821; revised edition, 1822.

Other

Essays on Various Subjects, Principally Designed for Young Ladies.   1777.
Thoughts on the Importance of the Manners of the Great to General Society.   1788.
An Estimate of the Religion of the Fashionable World.   1791.
Remarks on the Speech of M. Dumont on the Subjects of Religion and Education.   1793.
Questions and Answers for the Mendip and Sunday Schools.   1795.
Strictures on the Modern System of Female Education.   2 vols., 1799.
Works.   8 vols., 1801; revised edition, 19 vols., 1818–19; 11 vols., 1830.
Hints Towards Forming the Character of a Young Princess.   2 vols., 1805.
Practical Piety.   2 vols., 1811.
Christian Morals.   2 vols., 1813.
An Essay on the Character and Practical Writings of St. Paul.   2 vols., 1815.
Moral Sketches of Prevailing Opinions and Manners.   1819.
Letters to Zachary Macaulay, edited by A. Roberts.   1860.
Letters, edited by R. B. Johnson.   1925.

Editor, *The Spirit of Prayer.*   1825.

Reading List: *Memoirs of the Life and Correspondence of Mrs. More* by W. Roberts, 4 vols., 1834; *More*, by Charlotte Yonge, 1888; *More* by Annette B. Meakin, 1911; *More's Interest in Education and Government* by L. W. Courtney, 1929; *More's Cheap Repository Tracts in America* by Harry B. Weiss, 1946; *More and Her Circle* by Mary A. Hopkins, 1947; *More* by Mary Gwladys Jones, 1952; *Fiction for the Working Man* by Louis James, 1963.

*   *   *

Hannah More was the main literary exponent of the Evangelical movement within the Church of England in the later eighteenth and early nineteenth centuries, the ally of Wilberforce in his campaign for the moral improvement of the country. Her literary career began, however, in the freer atmosphere of the 1770's in London, where she associated with the Blue-Stockings, Mrs. Montagu's literary ladies, and with such celebrities as Burke, Reynolds, Walpole, Dr. Johnson, and Garrick. Garrick's friendship encouraged her to write *Percy*, which was successfully performed by him in 1777, but after his death she became increasingly involved in philanthropical and religious activity, and she refrained from even attending the revival of her play in 1787.

In her mood of increasing seriousness she became friendly with the Evangelical Bishop Porteus, and with the young Wilberforce himself, publishing in 1788 a criticism of the manners of the upper classes and a poem attacking the Slave Trade – a mainstay of the economy of Bristol, near which town she lived. On a visit to Cheddar with Wilberforce, she was so distressed by the lack of religious provision for the poor that she devoted her considerable energies to establishing a Sunday School, and became very involved in this attempt to provide religious education of a kind suited to the lower orders. For her political position was thoroughly conservative, and she responded to the French Revolution with horror. In 1792 she published *Village Politics*, an attack on the new radical ideas. She continued with an immensely successful series of *Cheap Repository Tracts* inculcating her political philosophy. The tracts were widely distributed, and their success helped to lead to the formation of the Religious Tract Society in 1799, part of the strenuous attempt by the religious and political establishment to contain the rising tide of social criticism and discontent.

Hannah More is more interesting as a representative figure in a significant social movement than exciting as a writer, but the *Tracts* are clear, and based on observation as well as ideology: they would not have been so widely known unless their unsophisticated readers had found something in them to hold their interest. Her *Strictures on the Modern System of Female Education* criticises both the narrowness of the prevailing system and the feminism of Mary Wollstonecraft, whose *Vindication of the Rights of Women* had appeared in 1792. Her most substantial fictional work, *Coelebs in Search of a Wife*, attacks the looseness of Regency morals and suggests the Evangelical ideal. Her attitudes thus form a significant part of the background to such a novel as Jane Austen's *Mansfield Park*, but the deliberately didactic Hannah More lacked the irony with which Jane Austen tempered her moral idealism.

—Peter Faulkner

MORGAN, Charles (Langbridge). English. Born in Kent, 22 January 1894; son of the civil engineer Sir Charles Morgan. Entered the Royal Navy as a cadet, 1907: educated at naval colleges in Osborne and Dartmouth; served in the Atlantic and in China, 1911–13, then resigned, 1913; rejoined, 1914, and interned in Holland after the retreat from Antwerp, 1914–18; studied at Brasenose College, Oxford (President, Oxford University Dramatic Society), 1918–21. Married the writer Hilda Vaughan in 1923; one son and one daughter. Assistant Drama Critic, 1921–26, and Principal Drama Critic, 1926–39, *The Times*, London; also contributed a weekly article on the London theatre to the *New York Times*; served at the Admiralty, with intervals in France and the United States, 1939–44; Ker Lecturer, University of Glasgow, 1945; Zaharoff Lecturer, Oxford University, 1948. President, English Association, 1953–54; International President, P.E.N., 1954–56. M.A.: Oxford University; LL.D.: University of St. Andrews. Officer, Legion of Honour; Member of the French Academy. Fellow, Royal Society of Literature. *Died 6 February 1958.*

<small>PUBLICATIONS</small>

Fiction

The Gunroom. 1919.
My Name Is Legion. 1925.
Portrait in a Mirror. 1929; as *First Love,* 1929.
The Fountain. 1932.
Sparkenbroke. 1936.
The Voyage. 1940.
The Empty Room. 1941.
The Judge's Story. 1947.
The River Line. 1949.
A Breeze of Morning. 1951.
Challenge to Venus. 1957.

Plays

The Flashing Stream (produced 1938). 1938.
The River Line, from his own novel (produced 1952). 1952.
The Burning Glass (produced 1954). 1953.

Verse

Ode to France. 1942.

Other

Epitaph on George Moore. 1935.
The House of Macmillan (1843–1943). 1943.
Reflections in a Mirror (essays). 2 vols., 1944–46.
Liberties of the Mind (essays). 1951.
The Writer and His World: Lectures and Essays. 1960.
Selected Letters, edited by E. Lewis. 1967.

Reading List: *Morgan* by A. Gérard, 1943; *A la Rencontre de Morgan* by M. Vincent, 1947; *The Novels and Plays of Morgan* by H. C. Duffin, 1959; *Notice sur la Vie et les Travaux de Morgan* by S. Madariaga, 1960; *Morgan* by V. de Pange, 1961 (includes bibliography).

*   *   *

The decline in Charles Morgan's reputation in the course of half a century provides a striking example of the vicissitudes of literary fashion. At the height of his celebrity during the 1930's and early 1940's, the distinction and permanence of his work was seldom in doubt, and he was hailed as one of the foremost living masters of English prose. After the success of *Portrait in a Mirror,* each new book was almost unanimously acclaimed by reviewers of standing in the leading journals, and three different novels were awarded the most coveted literary prizes of the time. Yet today Morgan is little read by an older generation, scarcely known to a younger, and discounted by the serious critics. Even in France, where his reputation always stood highest, it now seems in decline.

Such extreme reaction can be as untrustworthy as immoderate adulation. The over-literary pretentiousness of much of Morgan's writing, especially in its philosophical flights, is self-evident; as are the stilted, often solemnly inflated dialogue of his plays and Byronic theatricality of certain characters – in, for instance, the attitudes struck by the aristocratic Sparkenbroke in one of his most highly praised and popular novels. Nevertheless Morgan was a dedicated writer intent on the exploration of serious themes; a craftsman with a conscious care for style, which at its best, when not betrayed into preciosity, continues to give memorable expression to central truths.

His war-time and immediately post-war essays collected in the two volumes of *Reflections in a Mirror* survey different aspects of living in a troubled and restless time of transition, and are unified by a search for permanent values amid its insecurities and confusions. This acute, pervasive awareness of the corrupting pressures of contemporary society upon the individual is at the root of Morgan's most constant preoccupation in novels like *The Fountain*, *Sparkenbroke*, *The Empty Room*, and *The Voyage*, and in his three plays, most notably *The Flashing Stream*. He owed the background of *The Fountain* to his experiences during the First World War as an internee in Holland; and this book is his fullest and probably most successful investigation of the quest for what he calls "that contemplative stillness [which] is but the name for a state of invulnerability ... even amid the activity of the world." His central characters pursue their ideal of "singleness ... of mind," as Morgan also calls this spiritual freedom from the claims and conflicts of everyday life, with the zeal and discipline of mystics. Their struggles with the varied distractions from its achievement form the absorbing theme of work whose integrity of purpose, however frequently flawed its expression, cannot fairly be disputed.

—Margaret Willy

MORGAN, Lady (Sydney Morgan, née Owenson). Irish. Born in Dublin in 1783; daughter of the actor Robert Owenson. Educated in various schools in or near Dublin. Married Sir Thomas Charles Morgan in 1812 (died, 1843). Supported her family by working as a governess in the family of Featherstone, at Bracklin Castle, Westmeath, 1798–1800; may also have appeared on the stage; writer from 1801; later became a member of the household of the Marquis of Abercorn until her marriage; settled in Dublin, 1814; travelled in England, France, and Italy, 1818–20, France, 1829, and Belgium, 1835; granted a pension from Lord Melbourne, 1837; wrote for the *Athenaeum*, London, 1837–38; settled in London, 1839, and thereafter ceased to write. *Died 14 April 1859.*

PUBLICATIONS

Fiction

    St. Clair; or, The Heiress of Desmond.   1803; revised edition, 1812.
    The Novice of St. Dominick.   1805.
    The Wild Irish Girl: A National Tale.   1806.

Patriotic Sketches of Ireland, Written in Connaught.   1807.
Woman; or, Ida of Athens.   1809.
The Missionary: An Indian Tale.   1811; revised edition, as *Luxima, The Prophetess: A
   Tale of India,* 1859.
O'Donnel: A National Tale.   1814; revised edition, 1835.
Florence Macarthy: An Irish Tale.   1818.
The O'Briens and the O'Flahertys: A National Tale.   1827; edited by R. Shelton
   Mackenzie, 1856.
Dramatic Scenes from Real Life.   1833.
The Princess: or, The Beguine.   1835.

Verse

Poems.   1801.
Twelve Original Hibernian Melodies.   1805.
The Lay of an Irish Harp; or, Metrical Fragments.   1807.
The Mohawks: A Satirical Poem, with Sir Charles Morgan.   1822.

Other

A Few Reflections (on Irish theatre).   1804.
France.   2 vols., 1817; revised edition, 1818.
Italy.   2 vols., 1821; revised edition, 3 vols., 1821.
Letters to the Reviewers of Italy.   1821.
The Life and Times of Salvator Rosa.   2 vols., 1824.
Absenteeism.   1825.
The Book of the Boudoir (autobiographical sketches).   2 vols., 1829.
France in 1829–30.   2 vols., 1830.
Woman and Her Master.   2 vols., 1840.
The Book Without a Name, with Sir Charles Morgan.   2 vols., 1841.
Letter to Cardinal Wiseman.   1851.
Passages from My Autobiography.   1859.
An Odd Volume, Extracted from an Autobiography.   1859.
Memoirs: Autobiography, Diaries, and Correspondence, edited by W. Hepworth
   Dixon.   2 vols., 1862.

Reading List: *The Friends, Foes, and Adventures of Lady Morgan* by William John
Fitzpatrick, 1859; *The Wild Irish Girl: The Life of Lady Morgan* by Lionel Stevenson, 1936.

*   *   *

   The daughter of a well-known Irish actor, Robert Owenson, renowned in his day for
playing the lovable stage-Irishman, Lady Morgan added to his bequest of sentimentality a
histrionic flair of her own to become one of the literary curiosities of the age. Her first and
greatest success, *The Wild Irish Girl,* encouraged her to don the cloak and take up the harp of
her heroine, Glorvina, by which name she was known to habitués of Regency salons, whom
she entertained with sad songs of Erin (anticipating, incidentally, the success of Thomas
Moore some years later). She became an apologist for Irish nationalism, based on the
distinctiveness of native Irish culture, thereby giving picturesque stimulus to a train of
thought which has adherents yet. She developed Jacobin leanings. She became the object of
scurrilous attacks by John Wilson Croker (himself Irish) of the *Quarterly Review,* and of

extravagant patronage. Perhaps most importantly of all, in her own view, she became notorious.

Of her many literary productions, the most important are her Irish novels, and, for good or ill, except for Macpherson's *Ossian* they must be held most responsible for introducing Ireland to Romanticism. These novels, of which the most impressive feature is their passages of natural description, are set in a land which time has half-forgotten, peopled by remote, hill-dwelling clans led by men of fierce honour. Their themes are expressive of Ireland in the aftermath of the Act of Union – dispossession, defensiveness, social impotence. These afflictions are not presented as being important for themselves but as being the basis for a series of impossible escapes and resolutions. The novels portray deliverance from Irish reality, and as such are interesting early examples of Irish nationalist mythology. Their style is suitably rhetorical and rhapsodic. The most interesting – because of its uncharacteristic treatment of near-contemporary issues – is *The O'Briens and the O'Flahertys*.

Despite the widespread success of these and many of her other productions (notably *France*), Lady Morgan's career seems as much part of the history of taste as it is of literary history. Her contribution to Irish literature, though not without interest, is essentially spurious. The self-mythologising of her later works, her theatricality and sense of publicity, the novelty of her propaganda, even her quite original sensitivity to the moods of the literary marketplace, all seem to diminish her status as a writer, while at the same time emphasising her unique and phenomenal career.

—George O'Brien

MORLEY, Christopher (Darlington). American. Born in Haverford, Pennsylvania, 5 May 1890. Educated at Haverford College, 1906–10; New College, Oxford (Rhodes Scholar), 1910–13. Married Helen Booth Fairchild in 1914; one son and three daughters. Member of the staff of Doubleday, Page and Company, publishers, New York, 1913–17, *Ladies Home Journal*, New York, 1917–18, *Evening Public Ledger*, Philadelphia, 1918–20, and the *New York Evening Post*, 1920–24; a Founder, 1920, and Columnist ("The Bowling Green"), 1924–39, *The Saturday Review of Literature*, New York. D.Litt.: Haverford College, 1933. Member, National Institute of Arts and Letters. *Died 28 March 1957.*

PUBLICATIONS

Collections

Bright Cages (verse), edited by John Bracker. 1965.

Fiction

Parnassus on Wheels. 1917.
In the Sweet Dry and Dry, with Bert Haley. 1919.
The Haunted Bookshop. 1919.
Kathleen. 1920.

Tales from a Rolltop Desk. 1921.
Where the Blue Begins. 1922.
Pandora Lifts the Lid, with Don Marquis. 1924.
Thunder on the Left. 1925.
Pleased to Meet You. 1927.
The Arrow. 1927.
Rudolph and Amina; or, The Black Crook. 1930.
Human Being. 1932.
Swiss Family Manhattan. 1932.
The Trojan Horse. 1937.
Kitty Foyle. 1939.
Thorofare. 1942.
The Man Who Made Friends with Himself. 1949.

Plays

Thursday Evening (produced 1921). 1922.
Rehearsal. 1922.
One Act Plays (includes *Thursday Evening, Rehearsal, Bedroom Suite, On the Shelf, Walt, East of Eden*). 1924.
Where the Blue Begins, with E. S. Colling. 1925.
Good Theatre. 1926.
Really, My Dear.... 1928.
In Modern Dress. 1929.
The Blue and the Gray; or, War Is Hell, from the play *Allatoona* by Judson Kilpatrick and J. Owen Moore. 1930.
The Rag-Picker of Paris; or, The Modest Modiste, from the play by Edward Stirling. 1937.
Soft Shoulders (produced 1940).

Verse

The Eighth Sin. 1912.
Songs for a Little House. 1917.
The Rocking Horse. 1919.
Hide and Seek. 1920.
Chimneysmoke. 1921.
Translations from the Chinese. 1922.
Parson's Pleasure. 1923.
Toulemonde. 1928.
Poems. 1929.
Mandarin in Manhattan: Further Translations from the Chinese. 1933.
The Apologia of the Ampersand. 1936.
Footnotes for a Centennial. 1936.
The Middle Kingdom: Poems 1929–1944. 1944.
The Old Mandarin: More Translations from the Chinese. 1947.
Spirit Levels and Other Poems. 1946.
Poetry Package, with William Rose Benét. 1949.
The Ballad of New York, New York, and Other Poems, 1930–1950. 1950.
A Pride of Sonnets. 1951.
Gentlemen's Relish. 1955.

Other

Shandygaff. 1918.
Mince Pie: Adventures on the Sunny Side of Grub Street. 1919.
Travels in Philadelphia. 1920.
Pipefuls (essays). 1920.
Plum Pudding. 1921.
An Apology for Boccaccio. 1923.
Conrad and the Reporters. 1923.
Inward Ho! 1923.
The Powder of Sympathy. 1923.
Outward Bound. 1924.
Religio Journalistici. 1924.
Hostages to Fortune (miscellany). 1925.
Forty-four Essays. 1925; as *Safety Pins and Other Essays,* 1925.
Paumanok. 1926.
The Romany Stain. 1926.
I Know a Secret (juvenile). 1927.
The Case of Bouck White. 1927.
(Works). 12 vols., 1927.
The Tree That Didn't Get Trimmed. 1927.
Essays. 1928.
A Letter to Leonora. 1928.
Off the Deep End. 1928.
A Ride in the Cab of the Twentieth Century Limited. 1928.
The House of Dooner, with T. A. Daly. 1928.
The Worst Christmas Story. 1928.
Seacoast of Bohemia. 1929.
The Goldfish under the Ice (juvenile). 1930.
Apologia pro Sua Preoccupatione. 1930.
Born in a Beer Garden; or, She Troupes to Conquer: Sundry Ejaculations, with Ogden
    Nash and Cleon Throckmorton. 1930.
On the Nose. 1930.
Blythe Mountain, Vermont. 1931.
When We Speak of a Tenth –. 1931.
John Mistletoe (reminiscences). 1931.
Notes on Bermuda. 1931.
Ex Libris Carissimis (lectures). 1932.
Fifth Avenue Bus (miscellany). 1933.
Shakespeare and Hawaii (lectures). 1933.
Internal Revenue (essays). 1933.
"Effendi," Frank Nelson Doubleday, 1862–1934. 1934.
Hasta la Vista; or, A Postcard from Peru. 1935.
Old Loopy: A Love Letter for Chicago. 1935.
Rare Books: An Essay. 1935.
Streamlines (essays). 1936.
Morley's Briefcase. 1936.
Morley's Magnum. 1938.
History of an Autumn. 1938.
No Crabb, No Christmas. 1938.
Letters of Askance. 1939.
Another Letter to Lord Chesterfield. 1945.
The Ironing Board (essays). 1949.
Barometers and Bookshops. 1952.

Editor, *Record of the Class of 1910 of Haverford College.* 1910.
Editor, *American Rhodes Scholars, Oxford 1910–1913.* 1913.
Editor, *The Booksellers' Blue Book.* 2 vols., 1914.
Editor, *Making Books and Magazines.* 1916.
Editor, *Modern Essays.* 2 vols., 1921–24.
Editor, *The Bowling Green: An Anthology of Verse.* 1924.
Editor, *A Book of Days.* 1930.
Editor, *Ex Libris.* 1936.
Editor, with Louella D. Everett, *Bartlett's Familiar Quotations,* 11th edition. 1937;
   12th edition, 1948.
Editor, *Walt Whitman in Camden: A Selection of Prose from Specimen Days.* 1938.
Editor, *The Best of Don Marquis.* 1939.
Editor, *Leaves of Grass,* by Walt Whitman. 1940.
Editor, *Sherlock Holmes and Dr. Watson: A Textbook of Friendship.* 1944.

Translator, *Two Fables,* by Alfred de Musset and Wilhelm Hauff. 1925.
Translator, *Max and Moritz,* by Wilhelm Busch. 1932.

Reading List: *Morley* by Mark I Wallach, 1976; *Three Hours for Lunch: The Life and Times of Morley* by Helen McK. Oakley, 1976.

*   *   *

Christopher Morley was a distinguished and popular novelist, essayist, and poet, whose intense literary passions and promotions, such as his sponsorship of the writings of Joseph Conrad and his organization (with his brothers) of the Baker Street Irregulars, combine with his writings to make him one of the few genuine American "men of letters."

Morley's earliest novels, *Parnassus on Wheels* and *The Haunted Bookshop,* are brief, simple stories of booksellers in World War I America, yet they set the tone for the more sophisticated works to follow, many of which also revolve around characters involved in the literary world. *Where the Blue Begins,* an allegory about the human quest for meaning in life, is written as a dog story and enjoyed considerable success in a children's edition, but is actually a profoundly and successfully serious book. *Thunder on the Left,* which followed, is a thoughtful and controversial fantasy about the problems of children trying to come to terms with adulthood.

Kitty Foyle, Morley's best-selling novel, is an ambitious interior monologue told by a working-class girl from Philadelphia. Kitty is an atypical Morley protagonist, neither intellectual nor literary, yet *Kitty Foyle* represents Morley at the peak of his style. Derived from Morley's experiences with the "new generation" of New York career girls in the 1920's and 1930's, Kitty nonetheless displays a striking degree of individuality. Although *Kitty Foyle* largely abandons Morley's usual "mission" of bringing literature to the common man, it paradoxically comes closest of all of Morley's works to being great literature itself.

Morley's last novel, *The Man Who Made Friends with Himself,* embodies much of what is weakest and strongest in Morley's novels: it is intensely personal, extravagantly allusive, and rich with quotation. Somewhat autobiographical, it is a complex and demanding book to read, but worth the effort for lovers of English style.

While Morley is best remembered as a novelist, his frequent and polished essays in *The Saturday Review,* which he helped found in 1920, were perhaps as important in establishing his distinctive reputation among his contemporaries as a "man of letters." Collected into published volumes, such as *Streamlines* and *The Ironing Board,* many of these discuss people, places, and events with literary ties. While most are meant to be informative, Morley's essays always undertake the additional task of entertaining the reader, and are among his most enjoyable works.

Much of Morley's poetry reflects his predominant concern with literature. His earliest poems, however, following his marriage in 1914, are both domestic in subject and sentimental in tone, a blend Morley (with the concurrence of his critics) coined "dishpantheism." Perhaps his most important poetry is an original genre he called "Translations from the Chinese," which Morley first conceived as a burlesque of free verse, but later developed into a shrewd, ironic vehicle for social commentary. These "Translations" are among the most readable works of a writer who, while not of the first rank, was one of his era's most versatile and interesting literary figures.

—Mark I. Wallach

MORRIS, Wright (Marion). American. Born in Central City, Nebraska, 6 January 1910. Educated at Lakeview High School, Chicago; Crane College, Chicago; Pomona College, Claremont, California, 1930–33. Married 1) Mary Ellen Finfrock in 1934 (divorced, 1961); 2) Josephine Kantor in 1961. Has lectured at Haverford College, Pennsylvania, Sarah Lawrence College, Bronxville, New York, and Swarthmore College, Pennsylvania; Professor of English, California State University, San Francisco, 1962–75. Also a photographer. Recipient: Guggenheim Fellowship, 1942, 1946, 1954; National Book Award, 1957; National Institute of Arts and Letters grant, 1960; Rockefeller grant, 1967. Honorary degrees: Westminster College, Fulton, Missouri, 1968; University of Nebraska, Lincoln, 1968; Pomona College, Claremont, California, 1973. Member, National Institute of Arts and Letters, 1970. Lives in Mill Valley, California.

PUBLICATIONS

Fiction

My Uncle Dudley. 1942.
The Man Who Was There. 1945.
The World in the Attic. 1949.
Man and Boy. 1951.
The Works of Love. 1952.
The Deep Sleep. 1953.
The Huge Season. 1954.
The Field of Vision. 1956.
Love among the Cannibals. 1957.
Ceremony in Lone Tree. 1960.
What a Way to Go. 1962.
Cause for Wonder. 1963.
One Day. 1965.
In Orbit. 1967.
Green Grass, Blue Sky, White House (stories). 1970.
Fire Sermon. 1971.
War Games. 1972.
Here Is Einbaum (stories). 1973.
A Life. 1973.

Real Losses, Imaginary Gains. 1976.
The Fork River Space Project. 1977.

Other

The Inhabitants (photo-text). 1946.
The Home Place (photo-text). 1948.
The Territory Ahead (essays). 1958.
A Bill of Rites, A Bill of Wrongs, A Bill of Goods (essays). 1967.
God's Country and My People (photo-text). 1968.
Morris: A Reader. 1970.
Love Affair: A Venetian Journal (photo-text). 1972.
About Fiction: Reverent Reflections on the Nature of Fiction with Irreverent Observations on Writers, Readers, and Other Abuses. 1975.
Structures and Artifacts: Photographs 1933–1954. 1976.
Conversations with Morris: Critical Views and Responses, edited by Robert E. Knoll. 1977.

Editor, *The Mississippi River Reader.* 1962.

Reading List: *Morris* by David Madden, 1964; *Morris* by Leon Howard, 1968; *The Novels of Morris: A Critical Interpretation* by G.B. Crump, 1978.

*   *   *

Wright Morris, who has been called "the most major minor novelist in America," has had greater success with the critics than with the novel-reading public. He is also an important photographer: his four "photo-text" books are interspersed among the many novels he has published since 1942. In addition, Morris's critical essays on the art of fiction, and its relation to life and the modern reader, are unusually candid and stimulating. In all of his fiction the characters are vivid Americans, their talk salty and often funny; but these people also struggle with the issues and problems that beset the modern world. Morris recognizes his estrangement from other novelists and novel readers, and the reasons for it: "In my use of language there is an element that the narrative novelist has no interest in, might even find obstructive. He would say, 'One of the things that is wrong with this novel is that it holds the reader up. He has to read too carefully.' I would agree."

The Nebraska plains of Morris's first nine years haunt his imagination, and his first five books (novels and photo-texts) all take him "home" again. Then in his novels of the early 1950's, Morris portrays people cut off from the past (and often from love): they are monsters (like Mrs. Ormsby of *Man and Boy*), or suicidal (like Will Brady of *The Works of Love*). In *The Deep Sleep* the Porter house in suburban Philadelphia becomes a symbol of America, and the events in the novel become American experience in miniature. In the three "major" Morris novels that followed – *The Huge Season, The Field of Vision,* and *Ceremony in Lone Tree* – past and present are transformed through heroism, love, and the creative imagination.

In most of his fiction Morris contrasts old and young, and the revolution of the 1960's gave him exciting new matter. New frontiers of sex are explored in *Love among the Cannibals* and *What a Way to Go*: in both erotic love is overtly important. Although the action is focused upon the animal pound in a small California town in *One Day*, the day is November 22, 1963: Morris suggests, as he also does elsewhere, that nature might well abandon human civilization and make a new start with an animal (like the chipmunk in *The Huge Season*). In typical Morris fashion, too, the intellectual pessimism is leavened by his fascination with life, revealed most clearly through the hundreds of grotesque but vital characters that crowd his novels. *In Orbit* reveals age looking at youth: age sees the horrible but hopeful, living new day, envies and even admires. The prototypical motorcycle hoodlum rapes and pillages, albeit in a sometimes burlesque way; the victims, who are "upright citizens" of a small town, are unable – apparently unwilling – to identify the culprit. Then a tornado sweeps through the village, and the townspeople have no more hope of stopping the marauding youth than of halting the devastating wind storm. Both seem awful natural forces.

In *Fire Sermon* Morris returns to the picaresque auto trip of his first novel, *My Uncle Dudley*; the journey is still from California to the midwest, but the time has moved forward from the 1920's to the 1960's. Using a familiar Morris pair-up, *Fire Sermon* takes an old man and a boy back to Nebraska, plus two hitch-hikers picked up on the way. This young hippie couple, totally free, inspire admiration in both the man and the boy; though it means the end of his day for the old man, he accepts the inevitable, natural succession of youth. *A Life* completes the story of the old man, who now seeks and achieves death at the hands of an Indian and thus fulfills a ritual requirement of nature.

Characters recur in Morris novels, sometimes (but not always) retaining the same names. Thus, Tom Scanlon first appears in *The World in the Attic*, is one of the central figures in *The Field of Vision*, and survives as the remaining inhabitant of Lone Tree, Nebraska, in *Ceremony in Lone Tree*. Taken together, Morris's works are intent on seeking out a usable past and its impact on the present, asserting the continuity of the American character, and positing the creative and vital forces in nature.

—Clarence A. Glasrud

MORRISON, Arthur. English. Born in Kent, 1 November 1863. Educated in Kent schools. Married Elizabeth Adelaide Thatcher in 1892; one son. Journalist in London from the early 1880's; member of the staff of the *National Observer* during Henley's editorship; full-time writer from 1894; collector of Chinese and Japanese paintings which were acquired by the British Museum in 1913; Chief Inspector of the Special Constabulary of Epping Forest, Essex, during World War I. Fellow, and Member of the Council, of the Royal Society of Literature. *Died 4 December 1945.*

PUBLICATIONS

Fiction

> *The Shadows Around Us: Authentic Tales of the Supernatural.* 1891.
> *Martin Hewitt, Investigator* (stories). 1894.
> *Tales of Mean Streets.* 1894.
> *Chronicles of Martin Hewitt.* 1895.
> *Zig-Zags at the Zoo.* 1895.
> *A Child of the Jago.* 1896; edited by P. J. Keating, 1969.
> *Adventures of Martin Hewitt: Third Series.* 1896.
> *The Dorrington Deed-Box* (stories). 1897.
> *To London Town.* 1899.
> *Cunning Murrell.* 1900.
> *The Hole in the Wall.* 1902.

The Red Triangle, Being Some Further Chronicles of Martin Hewitt. 1903.
The Green Eye of Goona: Stories of a Case of Tokay. 1904; as *The Green Diamond,* 1904.
Divers Vanities (stories). 1905.
Green Ginger (stories). 1909.
(Stories). 1929.
Fiddle O'Dreams (stories). 1933.

Plays

That Brute Simmons, with Herbert C. Sargent, from the story by Morrison (produced 1904). 1904.
The Dumb-Cake, with Richard Pryce, from a story by Morrison (produced 1907). 1907.
A Stroke of Business, with Horace Newte (produced 1907).

Other

The Painters of Japan. 2 vols., 1911.

Reading List: "A Study of Morrison" by J. Bell, in *Essays and Studies 5,* 1952; *Four Realist Novelists* by Vincent Brome, 1965.

*   *   *

Arthur Morrison was perhaps the best of that group of writers – others were Israel Zangwill, Barry Pain, W. Pett Ridge, and Edwin Pugh – who in the last decade of the nineteenth century examined lower middle- and working-class London life more or less realistically in fiction. His reputation rests securely on *Tales of Mean Streets,* a collection of short stories, and on his novels *A Child of the Jago* and *The Hole in the Wall,* though he wrote several detective stories. The world he deals with is the East End, Stepney and Bethnal Green specifically. It has largely gone now, destroyed by the town-planners at the turn of the century and by Hitler's bombers forty years later, but it survives in a sentence in which Morrison describes the mean streets of his *Tales:* "And the effect is that of *stables.*"
   The stories are notably sardonic and contemptuous of their subject, very *fin-de-siècle.* Morrison's East End is anything but sentimentalised; we are never allowed to forget that the police patrol it in threes; the author's aim is to expose conditions. In *A Child of the Jago* he tells the story of a young thief in Bethnal Green. The picture it gives of street wars is unique and terrifying. As art, however, it is inferior to *The Hole in the Wall,* in which the story is shown mainly through the eyes of a child. Stephen Kemp goes to live with his grand-father, who keeps a pub at Wapping, and gradually discovers that the old man, whom he adores, is in fact a receiver of stolen goods. The old man comes by a wallet containing £800 which has been stolen from a murdered shipowner, and the plot turns on the attempts of various criminal characters to get the money back. The execution of the plot is as grim and relentless as anything in Zola, and gains greatly in effectiveness in being recorded through a child's eye. Morrison was a collector of Japanese prints – his collection is now in the British Museum – and it has been suggested that the clarity and restraint that mark the novel were derived from their study.
   One thing must be borne in mind, particularly since Zola has been referred to. Morrison was a realist, but very much an English realist; the characters in his fiction are like nothing in Naturalism. And just as the dockland of *The Hole in the Wall,* the river and the fogs, remind

us of the setting of *Our Mutual Friend*, so the characters, Captain Kemp, Mr. Cripps, Mrs. Grimes and the rest, seem either Dickens characters by nature or characters conceived by a novelist so deeply steeped in the Dickens tradition that automatically he turns his creations into Dickens figures. They look like them and speak like them, and though this does not undercut Morrison's genuinely realistic quality, it does remind us, as Wells and Bennett do a decade later, that realism in English fiction has native English as well as French roots.

—Walter Allen

MOTLEY, Willard (Francis). American. Born in Chicago, Illinois, 14 July 1912. Educated at elementary and high schools in Chicago. Married; two sons. Worked as a transient laborer, waiter, cook, ranch hand, etc., throughout the United States during the 1930's: served jail sentence for vagrancy, Cheyenne, Wyoming; writer from 1939; worked as a photographer, an interviewer for the Chicago Housing Authority, and as a writer for the Office of Civilian Defense, in Chicago, in the 1940's; moved to Mexico, 1951. *Died 5 March 1965.*

PUBLICATIONS

Fiction

Knock on Any Door. 1947.
We Fished All Night. 1951.
Let No Man Write My Epitaph. 1958.
Let Noon Be Fair. 1966.

Reading List: "Motley and the Sociological Novel" by Alfred Weissgärber, in *Studi Americani 7,* 1961.

*   *   *

A middle-class Black writer, Willard Motley refused to confine his work to racial subjects, deliberately moving into the Chicago slums in order to live in an amalgam of the backgrounds, religions, and races that later appear in his books. Sometimes called superior to Drieser's novels or Terkel's non-fiction studies, his novels are naturalist panoramas of slum conditions. He orchestrates a dozen lives together in the same appalling career from idealistic youth to death in defeat as "cop-killer," "junkie," "whore," society's labels for its weakest victims, Motley's protagonists. There are many echoes of Zola in Motley's Chicago, the devouring Beast. Few American social realists have written with Motley's angry brilliance on ghetto immigrants, drug addiction, jack-rolling, racketeering. In his finest novel, *We Fished All Night*, Motley widens his focus on social and economic conditions in the slum – the cycle of poverty and oppression that slowly transforms his gentle adolescent heroes into "punks" – to include corporate and political structures, indeed the gangsterism at the root of World War II which leaves the slum depopulated, its few "heroes" mutilated or insane. Motley's youths

(Italian, Polish, Mexican, Black) are driven from home by brutality and squalor onto the streets for companionship and understanding; if they stay on the streets (in "the leer of the neon night") they end as hunted criminals; and if they try to move on, they claw their way among bribe-taking police and vote-buying politicians, ending just as hunted by their political enemies and just as criminal.

Every reader notes the flaws in Motley's work, the simplistic thesis of determinant slum environment, and the flaccidity of the last two novels where the artistic rigor relaxes and the vibrant anger often dissolves into bathos. But no reader denies Motley's astonishing ability to depict the pained squalor of life in the tenement, the poolroom, the bookie joint, the bar, the death-row cell, the addict's gibbered revery. Traditional in form, using flashback and narrated monologue within a tight chronological frame, the novels inter-relate through recurring characters, including successive generations, underscoring the sameness, the suffocating immutability of their world.

—Jan Hokenson

MULGAN, John (Alan Edward). New Zealander. Born in Christchurch, 31 December 1911; son of the writer Alan Mulgan. Educated at Maungawhan School, 1917–25; Wellington College, 1925–27; Auckland Grammar School, 1927–30; Auckland University College, 1930–32, B.A. 1932; Oxford University, 1933–35. Served in the British Army in the Middle East and Greece, 1939–45: Lieutenant-Colonel. Married Gabrielle Wanklyn in 1937; one son. Regular contributor to the *Auckland Star*, 1934–37; worked for the Clarendon Press, Oxford, 1935–39. *Died* (by suicide) *25 April 1945.*

PUBLICATIONS

Fiction

Man Alone. 1939.

Other

The Emigrants: Early Travellers to the Antipodes, with Hector Bolitho. 1939.
An Introduction to English Literature, with Dan Davin. 1947.
Report on Experience (autobiography), edited by Jack Bennett. 1947.

Editor, *Poems of Freedom.* 1938.
Editor, *A Concise Oxford Dictionary of English Literature.* 1939.

Reading List: *Mulgan*, 1968, and *Mulgan* (booklet), 1978, both by Paul Day.

*   *   *

A month before his suicide in 1945, John Mulgan described the manuscript of *Report on Experience* as "only the draft and outline of a book I'd like to write." It was nevertheless published two years later, and, although the intended revision and expansion would undoubtedly have made it more substantial, the book reveals a good deal about the author of *Man Alone* and has the direct, transparent style of that remarkable novel. Its mode is autobiographical, but its subject matter goes beyond personal concerns. Social patterns in New Zealand and England between the wars are seen with a shrewd eye and limned with a steady hand, and the rest of the book contains Mulgan's reflections on army life, on the nature of modern warfare, on ideologies and ideals, on the *virtus* ethic, and on wartime Greece. There is a tendency to generalize without supporting evidence or precise definition, and it is in this respect that his report is most obviously incomplete. But it belongs authentically to its period and to the cultural attitudes which shaped Mulgan's imagination.

It is significant that, although the thirties were dominated by widespread economic stress and political struggle, Mulgan's survey of New Zealand life during those years invokes no concepts of class or system. "Doctrinaire allegiances he distrusted absolutely," one of his friends said of him; and the criteria of Mulgan's commentary in *Report on Experience* imply a mellow humanism based on simple communal values. Of the Depression's impact he has this kind of thing to say: "Certain changes came over New Zealand at this time.... It was noticeable that men stopped speaking openly to one another, and the majority favoured a doctrine that every man's duty was to look after himself. This, of course, was the fine old flavour of the pioneers and of rugged, economic liberalism, but I think, from what I have read, that the pioneers turned out to help their neighbours in distress and survived because they lived as a community, and not as men alone."

Accordingly the primary emphasis in *Man Alone* is on the inadequacies of most relationships between people, and between individuals and the land itself, in a country pervaded by mean-spirited materialism. Paul Day has remarked in an essay on *Man Alone* that it shows how, in New Zealand, economic exigencies "provide a grimly constricting rule over human destinies," yet they do so in Mulgan's view not because of political injustices so much as because people force themselves into a narrow, solitary, joyless existence through their own "lust to possess." It is a moral critique rather than a specifically political one that Mulgan offers. This needs emphasizing because the novel's central concerns were sometimes misread when it first appeared. Johnson, the protagonist, is a casual drifter, sceptical of all theories and commitments, and indeed most of the characters are to some degree solitaries. That fact is not changed when, in the brief second part of the novel, Johnson goes off to fight in the Spanish War. A contemporary reviewer misrepresented this ending when he said of Johnson: "It is a mature and conscious socialist who volunteers for the Brigade in Spain," and added that Mulgan's purpose was to reveal "the deepening capitalist crisis." On the contrary, the author continues to underline in this post-script section (written only at the publisher's request to bring the book up to "minimum novel length") Johnson's non-committal view of politics. He goes to Spain merely for the sake of company and excitement.

The original title of the novel was "Talking of War"; but that refers primarily not to any class struggle, nor to international conflict, but to the hostility generated between men and the land by acquisitive individualism.

—Ian Reid

MULOCK, Dinah Maria; also known as Mrs. Craik.   English.   Born in Stoke-on-Trent, Staffordshire, 20 April 1826. Educated privately and in local schools. Married the publisher

George Lillie Craik in 1865. Settled in London, 1846; thereafter a full-time writer; lived in Bromley, Kent, from 1865. *Died 12 October 1887.*

PUBLICATIONS

Fiction

The Ogilvies. 1849.
Cola Monti; or, The Story of a Genius. 1849.
Olive. 1850.
The Head of the Family. 1852.
Bread upon the Waters: A Governess's Life. 1852.
Avillion and Other Tales. 1853.
A Hero: Philip's Book. 1853.
Agatha's Husband. 1853.
The Little Lychetts. 1855.
John Halifax, Gentleman. 1856.
Nothing New: Tales. 1857.
A Life for a Life. 1859.
Romantic Tales. 1859.
Domestic Stories. 1860.
Studies from Life. 1860.
Mistress and Maid. 1862.
Christian's Mistake. 1865.
A Noble Life. 1866.
How to Win Love; or, Rhoda's Lesson: A Story for the Young. 1866(?).
Two Marriages. 1867.
The Woman's Kingdom. 1869.
A Brave Lady. 1870.
The Unkind Word and Other Stories. 1870.
Twenty Years Ago, from the Journal of a Girl in Her Teens. 1871.
Hannah. 1872.
Is It True? Tales Curious and Wonderful. 1872.
My Mother and I. 1874.
Will Denbigh, Nobleman. 1877.
The Laurel Bush. 1877.
Young Mrs. Jardine. 1879.
His Little Mother and Other Tales. 1881.
Miss Tommy. 1884.
Work for the Idle Hands. 1886.
King Arthur: Not a Love Story. 1886.
An Unknown Country. 1887.

Verse

Poems. 1859.
Thirty Years: Poems New and Old. 1881; as *Poems,* 1888.

Other

Alice Learmont: A Fairy Tale (juvenile). 1852; revised edition, 1884.
A Woman's Thoughts about Women. 1858.
Our Year: A Child's Book. 1860.
The Fairy Book: The Best Popular Fairy Stories Selected and Rendered Anew. 1863.
A New Year's Gift to Sick Children. 1865.
Fair France: Impressions of a Traveller. 1871.
Little Sunshine's Holiday (juvenile). 1871.
The Adventures of a Brownie as Told to My Child. 1872.
The Little Lame Prince (juvenile). 1875.
Sermons Out of Church. 1875.
Children's Poetry. 1881.
Plain Speaking. 1882.
An Unsentimental Journey Through Cornwall. 1884.
About Money and Other Things. 1886.
Fifty Golden Years: Incidents in the Queen's Reign. 1887.
Concerning Men and Other Papers. 1888.

Editor, *A Legacy, Being the Life and Remains of John Martin.* 2 vols., 1878.

Translator, *M. de Barante,* by F. P. G. Guizot. 1867.
Translator, *A French Country Family,* by H. de Witt. 1867.
Translator, *A Parisian Family,* by H. de Witt. 1871.
Translator, *An Only Sister,* by H. de Witt. 1873.

Reading List: "The Author of *John Halifax, Gentleman*" by A. L. Reade, in *Notes and Queries* 9, 1951.

*   *   *

"*John Halifax* may fairly be taken as 'standing' for Mrs. Craik," in the opinion of Richard Brimley Johnson (*The Women Novelists,* 1918). More modern readers would be unlikely to demur. "The Authoress of John Halifax, Gentleman," as Dinah Maria Mulock (Mrs. Craik) appeared on countless subsequent title pages, produced more than fifty volumes during her career – novels, stories for young people, poems, short stories, and miscellaneous articles and sketches. Yet her reputation, such as it is, rests on an idealistic, sentimental tale of a tanner's apprentice of obscure birth who rises by his own efforts to become a "gentleman" and in so doing proves that the essence of gentility is not social but moral. Johnson quite rightly sees *John Halifax, Gentleman* in Mrs. Craik's happiest vein of stories for young persons, rather than as a conventional novel. In the course of his steady rise, the hero quells a bread riot, foils a rigged election in a rotten borough, and successfully introduces a steam engine into his mills with the support of his workmen, thus fixing the novel in the pre-Reform Bill era. Copious references to contemporary events and personalities, including the Napoleonic Wars, the abolition of slavery, the death of Perceval, the Luddite riots, and the appearance in the novel itself of Lady Hamilton, Dr. Jenner, Mrs. Siddons, and Charles Kemble, further establish the book's period flavour.

Mrs. Craik's penchant for deliberately placing her novels is reflected also in *A Life for a Life,* which more than one of her contemporaries regarded as equal if not superior to *John Halifax.* This is the story of an army surgeon in the immediate post-Crimean period who sells his commission and becomes immersed in prison reform. Unfortunately any interest which might have been generated by the unusual epistolary style of the novel, involving both a masculine and a feminine narrator, is more than mitigated by the plot, a typical mixture of thwarted love and a dark past involving a murder. Other novels like *Agatha's Husband* and *The Head of the Family*, more domestic in setting, are equally marred by this all too familiar formula of frustrated or undeclared love, false marriages, and even escape from shipwreck.

Mrs. Craik published two volumes of poetry during her life, of which the two best known poems are "Philip My King" and "Douglas, Douglas, Tender and True," both of which were occasionally anthologized. Of her miscellaneous work the most notable is *A Woman's Thoughts about Women*, not a radical statement of women's rights but a practical assessment of the status quo, advocating more activity and purpose for women, but in their accepted spheres of teaching, writing, painting, and public entertainment.

—Joanne Shattock

MUNRO, Hector Hugh. See **SAKI.**

MURDOCH, (Jean) Iris. English. Born in Dublin, Ireland, 15 July 1919. Educated at the Froebel Educational Institute, London; Badminton School, Bristol; Somerville College, Oxford, 1938–42, B.A. (honours) 1942; Newnham College, Cambridge (Sarah Smithson Student in philosophy), 1947–48. Married the writer John Bayley in 1956. Assistant Principal in the Treasury, London, 1942–44; Administrative Officer with the United Nations Relief and Rehabilitation Administration (UNRRA) in London, Belgium, and Austria, 1944–46; Fellow, St. Anne's College, Oxford, and University Lecturer in Philosophy, Oxford University, 1948–63: Honorary Fellow of St. Anne's College since 1963; Lecturer, Royal College of Art, London, 1963–67. Recipient: Black Memorial Award, 1974; Whitbread Literary Award, 1974. Member, Irish Academy, 1970. Honorary Member, American Academy of Arts and Letters, 1975. Lives in Steeple Aston, Oxfordshire.

PUBLICATIONS

Fiction

Under the Net. 1954.
The Flight from the Enchanter. 1956.
The Sandcastle. 1957.
The Bell. 1958.
A Severed Head. 1961.
An Unofficial Rose. 1962.
The Unicorn. 1963.
The Italian Girl. 1964.
The Red and the Green. 1965.

    The Time of the Angels.   1966.
    The Nice and the Good.   1968.
    Bruno's Dream.   1969.
    A Fairly Honourable Defeat.   1970.
    An Accidental Man.   1971.
    The Black Prince.   1973.
    The Sacred and Profane Love Machine.   1974.
    A Word Child.   1975.
    Henry and Cato.   1976.
    The Sea, The Sea.   1978.

Plays

    A Severed Head, with J. B. Priestley, from the novel by Murdoch (produced 1963). 1964.
    The Italian Girl, with James Saunders, from the novel by Murdoch (produced 1967). 1969.
    The Servants and the Snow (produced 1970). In *The Three Arrows, and The Servants and the Snow,* 1973.
    The Three Arrows (produced 1972). In *The Three Arrows, and The Servants and the Snow,* 1973.
    The Three Arrows, and The Servants and the Snow: Two Plays. 1973.

Other

    Sartre: Romantic Rationalist. 1953.
    The Sovereignty of Good (essays). 1970.
    The Fire and the Sun: Why Plato Banished the Artists. 1977.

Bibliography: *Murdoch and Muriel Spark: A Bibliography* by Thomas T. Tominaga and Wilma Schneidermeyer, 1976.

Reading List: *Degrees of Freedom: The Novels of Murdoch* by A. S. Byatt, 1965; *The Disciplined Heart: Murdoch and Her Novels* by Peter Wolfe, 1966; *Murdoch* by Rubin Rabinovitz, 1968; *Murdoch* by Frank Baldanza, 1974.

*   *   *

    Iris Murdoch's first published work was not in fact a novel, but a philosophical and critical treatise, *Sartre: Romantic Rationalist,* published in 1953. In spite of the prolific series of novels that followed this work, a total of nineteen to date, Murdoch has retained her position as a professional philosopher with a number of philosophical essays to her credit. She has also collaborated with J. B. Priestley and James Saunders in adapting two of her novels for the stage, and has written two other plays. The basic aims of Murdoch's fiction are established in her early work on Sartre. In her acceptance of Sartre the philosopher and Sartre the novelist as one, Murdoch reveals her own interest in using the novel as a way of developing philosophical ideas. She criticizes Sartre, however, for wanting art to analyze, to set the world in order, and to reduce it to the intelligible; her own view, as expressed in her essay "Against Dryness" (1961), is that "what we require is a renewed sense of the difficulty and complexity of moral life and the opacity of persons."
    When Murdoch's first novel, *Under the Net,* was published in 1954, it was immediately

acclaimed for its wit, humour, and intelligence. Emerging at the time when the neo-naturalistic novels of the "Angry Young Men" were attracting critical attention, *Under the Net* opened up an astonishingly varied world which hovers just on the brink of fantasy. Technically, it owes much to contemporary film techniques, and it provides a curious mixture of detailed comedy, acute human observation, and unashamedly open philosophical theorising. This literary cocktail may sound alarming, but its final effect is exhilarating, and much less awkward than the heavy-handed symbolism of her later novels.

Murdoch's next four novels vary greatly in style, but closer study reveals that the novelist is exploring different ways of approaching her over-riding pre-occupations: freedom, responsibility, and the meaning of love, often fused together in the apparently contradictory concept of responsibility as an essential part of liberty. *The Flight from the Enchanter* develops an elaborate and fantastic plot which verges on the supernatural. The theme of the novel is power, and its central figure is an "enchanter," Mischa Fox, who attempts to control the lives of all the other characters in various ways. This "enchanter" figure is to become a leitmotif in all her novels, and is central to the schematization that affects her later works. *The Sandcastle* appears to be almost drab by comparison in its presentation of a tired, middle-aged school-master who falls in love with a young painter; although tempted to leave his wife and family, he abandons the world of ostensible freedom for the Murdochian variety of freedom linked to responsibility and a more complete understanding of other people. The symbolic background to the novel is undeveloped, although present; instead the emphasis is on the development of character in the realistic mode.

Much more successful in every way, and still probably the most artistically coherent of all Murdoch's novels, is *The Bell*. In this work her ideas are explored on the realistic and the symbolic level, with the central image of the convent bell embodying the theme of love and the struggle to achieve it, in both human and religious terms. The symbolic background is used to enhance our understanding of the characters, and although it is clear that each character is contributing to the author's overall consideration of the theme, they exist in their own right and never become overtly subjugated to the needs of the plot.

A Severed Head reverts to an even narrower world than that of *The Flight from the Enchanter*, and it opens up a series of entertaining, but regrettably shallow novels. Murdoch's considerable talent has been badly squandered in the creation of type characters and predictable, though immensely stylish, plots, nearly all centred in the same self-indulgent, cultivated world of London and the Home Counties. Only her two Irish novels, *The Unicorn* and *The Red and the Green*, provide her characters with a concrete setting away from this milieu, and, although *The Red and the Green* raises some interesting moral problems regarding the young Anglo-Irish soldier whose loyalties are divided during the Easter Rising of 1916, there is a fundamental shallowness about the relationships and a lethargic quality in the prose that minimizes her achievement. *The Unicorn*, on the other hand, is so over-burdened with melodramatic events and with artificial and self-conscious dialogue that the religious symbolism is rendered meaningless. Murdoch's attempt to combine what she once described in an essay as "a small compact crystalline self-contained myth about the human condition" with the plurality of characters she so admires in the great novels of the nineteenth century does not succeed in *The Unicorn*; her achievement was very much greater in *The Bell*.

The Unicorn ends in a flurry of violent deaths and natural disasters, and events of this sort have become a familiar feature of the later novels. Floods (*Bruno's Dream*), fire (*The Italian Girl*), fatal car accidents (*An Accidental Man* and *A Word Child*), murder (*The Black Prince* and *The Sacred and Profane Love Machine*), drownings (*A Fairly Honourable Defeat*), international terrorism (*The Sacred and Profane Love Machine*) and suicides in generous quantities are offered as proof of Murdoch's view that life is full of the arbitrary, the unexpected, and the violent. These events are invariably promulgated to purge or sweep away a typical network of characters who are grouped around a charismatic "enchanter" figure. The heavy weight of the author's "thumb in the scale," as Lawrence describes it, makes the reader increasingly dissatisfied with violent death being used as a deus ex machina to provide an easy solution to the human problems delineated earlier in the novels. A paradox has developed regarding a writer whose theories so convincingly stress the individuality of the characters in a novel, yet whose tightly-wound plots relentlessly impose a pattern on the characters she herself creates. As a pattern-maker Murdoch is enormously skilful, but too often the novel turns into an empty shell that lacks substance.

This disappointing trend may at last be coming to an end. Two of the recent novels, *The Black Prince* and *A Word Child*, suggest that, for all the overt formalism and the sense that an elaborate intellectual game is being played out, Murdoch has not lost her ability to illuminate the motives that lie beneath the surface of human behaviour. *A Word Child* brings out again the tragedy that results when a genuine cry for love is ignored. When Walter Allen suggested in 1964 that "more than any other novelist of her generation, she seems to have it in her to become a great novelist," he was thinking particularly of *The Bell*, and Murdoch may yet fulfil the potential that her early novels suggested.

—Margaret B. Lewis

MURFREE, Mary Noailles. Pseudonym: Charles Egbert Craddock. American. Born at Grantlands, the family estate near Murfreesboro, Tennessee, 24 January 1850; became lame as a child; moved with her family to Nashville, Tennessee, 1856. Educated at a school in Nashville and, after the Civil War, at boarding school in Philadelphia. Writer from 1874. *Died 31 July 1922.*

PUBLICATIONS

Fiction

In the Tennessee Mountains (stories). 1884.
Where the Battle Was Fought. 1884.
Down the Ravine. 1885.
The Prophet of the Great Smoky Mountains. 1885.
In the Clouds. 1886.
The Story of Keedon Bluffs. 1887.
The Despot of Broomsedge Cove. 1889.
In the "Stranger People's" Country. 1891.
His Vanished Star. 1894.
The Phantoms of the Foot-Bridge and Other Stories. 1895.
The Mystery of Witch-Face Mountain and Other Stories. 1895.
The Young Mountaineers: Short Stories. 1897.
The Juggler. 1897.
The Story of Old Fort Loudon. 1899.
The Bushwhackers and Other Stories. 1899.
The Champion. 1902.
A Spectre of Power. 1903.
The Frontiersmen (stories). 1904.
The Storm Centre. 1905.

The Amulet. 1906.
The Windfall. 1907.
The Fair Mississippian. 1908.
The Raid of the Guerilla and Other Stories. 1912.
The Ordeal: A Mountain Romance of Tennessee. 1912.
The Story of Duciehurst: A Tale of the Mississippi. 1914.

Bibliography: in *Bibliography of American Literature* by Jacob Blanck, 1973; "Murfree: An Annotated Bibliography" by Reese M. Carleton, in *American Literary Realism 1870–1910*, Autumn 1974.

Reading List: *Charles Egbert Craddock (Mary Noailles Murfree)* by Edd Winfield Parks, 1941; *Murfree* by Richard Cary, 1967.

*   *   *

Mary Noailles Murfree gained a deserved reputation in her day as an accurate and graphic local colorist. Her short stories and novels set in the mountains of Tennessee are distinguished for their accurate transcription of dialect and their vivid depictions of scenery. "I love to be particular," she frequently quoted, and in her attention to the detail of mountain background and speech she was indeed "particular."

The eight stories of *In the Tennessee Mountains*, published under the pseudonym of Charles Egbert Craddock, won immediate popularity and came to be regarded as significant contributions to the short story genre. In the books that followed, notably *Where the Battle Was Fought*, *The Prophet of the Great Smoky Mountains*, and *In the "Stranger People's" Country*, the meticulous portrayal of landscape and local color continued to be her forte.

Murfree's characterizations were sometimes stylized, and her lengthy descriptions occasionally impeded the flow of the narrative, especially in her novels. Her themes were in general restricted to a handful of set situations involving the legal tussles of mountainfolk and townspeople, the impact of the sophisticated stranger upon the mountain girl and her jealous lover, the complications that follow in the wake of the superstitious religious fanatic. None the less, many of her characters achieved a high degree of verisimilitude: her beauties and crones, her fugitives from justice, her blacksmiths and preachers. In narrating their frustrated lives against the picturesque setting of the Tennessee Mountains, Murfree captured the public imagination and gained for herself a niche in regional literature.

Her style matched her vigorous themes. It was straightforward, forceful, and robust. Thus the revelation that Charles Egbert Craddock was the pseudonym of a woman astounded not merely her readers but her editor, Thomas Bailey Aldrich of *The Atlantic Monthly*.

Although Murfree experimented with other literary genres, including the historical novel and the romance, she is remembered primarily for her local color stories of the Tennessee Mountains. Her work has been compared, in respect to its general portrayal of scenery and people, with that of other regional writers such as Bret Harte, George Washington Cable, and Sarah Orne Jewett.

—Madeleine B. Stern

MYERS, L(eopold) H(amilton).   English.   Born in Cambridge, 6 September 1881; son of the writer Frederick W. H. Myers. Educated at Eton College, 1894–99; in Germany, 1899–1900; Trinity College, Cambridge, 1900–01, left without taking a degree. Married Elsie Palmer in 1908; two daughters. Writer from 1908; settled in London; worked as a temporary clerk in the Foreign Office, London, during World War I; visited Ceylon, 1925; in later years lived in Buckinghamshire. Recipient: Black Memorial Prize, 1936; Femina-Vie Heureuse Prize, 1936. *Died* (by suicide) *8 April 1944.*

PUBLICATIONS

Fiction

The Orissers.   1922.
The Clio.   1925.
The Near and the Far.   1929; revised edition, in *The Root and the Flower*, 1935.
Prince Jali.   1931; revised edition, in *The Root and the Flower*, 1935.
The Root and the Flower.   1935.
Strange Glory.   1936.
The Pool of Vishnu (conclusion of *The Root and the Flower*).   1940.

Verse

Arvat: A Dramatic Poem.   1908.

Other

Editor, *Human Personality,* by F. W. H. Myers.   1907.

Reading List: *Myers: A Critical Study* by G. H. Bantock, 1956; *The Novels of Myers* by Irène Simon, 1956.

*   *   *

L. H. Myers was the son of a Cambridge don who founded in 1882 the Society for Psychical Research. His comparative affluence gave him a security which probably accounts for the superb poise of his best work. Myers, like Forster and Virginia Woolf, deals with aspects of society and human values; he is also concerned with truth and meaning. He owes a good deal to his study of contemporary Cambridge writers on ethics. Myers enters into his characters; rarified and fastidious though many of them are, he lives with and in them. He believes in the value of personality and the possibility of a spiritual revolution which will alter the shape of natural things.

The Orissers, has a sensational plot, but it is fundamentally a study of opposed groups and an analysis of psychological types, a contrast between the idealistic and the coarse. Myers's next novel, *The Clio*, deals with similar themes very differently. He isolates his world on a steam-yacht, "probably the most expensive ... in the world." *The Clio* is a light and would-be elegant study of a society party that voyages up the Amazon and finds a revolution; the death of Sir James Annesley is a masterpiece of intimate, sympathetic analysis. The short novel *Strange Glory* is a beautifully constructed book not unrelated to a mystical experience which he had in America when a young man. In *Strange Glory* Myers uses the forests and swamps of Louisiana as he uses the Amazon jungles (in *The Clio*) and the India of Akbar (in *The Near and the Far*) to create an environment outside the normal experiences and pre-conceptions of the reader.

The first of the Indian novels, *The Near and the Far* (the title later given to the whole work) was followed by *Prince Jali* and *The Pool of Vishnu*. Few novelists have made their intentions clearer than Myers in his preface to *The Near and the Far*, where he states that he is not writing historical fiction. The Indian novels are a journey to the meeting of the near and the far, to the place where *There* becomes *Here*. The style of Myers is workmanlike and well-adapted to the needs of his great sequence. At its best it has superb precision and weight and an incantatory quality.

In his later years Myers became an adherent to Communism. He was intellectually convinced, but he had no personal knowledge of the proletariat or the class-struggle. In the end the dichotomy became too great. His attempt to reconcile his moral vision with his new political views, his disappointment with his own class, and his breaking away from old friendships were too much for his already failing health. "Why should human beings continue to live?" he asked, and in 1944 he committed suicide. Myers is more than a humanist; he is a philosophical thinker who sees man in the universe. To his searching after truth he brought not only a fine moral sensibility, but also a strong religious (though not sectarian) faith and a deep spiritual conviction.

—Ronald Bottrall

NABOKOV, Vladimir.   Pseudonym: V. Sirin (for Russian works).   American.   Born in St. Petersburg, now Leningrad, Russia, 23 April 1899; left Russia in 1919, and lived in Berlin, 1922–37, and France, 1937–40; settled in the United States, 1940; naturalized, 1945. Educated at the Prince Tenishev School, St. Petersburg, 1910–17; Trinity College, Cambridge, B.A. 1922. Married Véra Slonim in 1925; one son. Instructor in Russian Literature and Creative Writing, Stanford University, California, Summer 1941; Lecturer in Russian, Wellesley College, Massachusetts, 1941–48; Research Fellow, Museum of Comparative Zoology, Harvard University, Cambridge, Massachusetts, 1942–48; Professor of Russian Literature, Cornell University, Ithaca, New York, 1948–59; Visiting Lecturer, Harvard University, Spring 1955. Lived in later life in Switzerland. Recipient: Guggenheim Fellowship, 1943, 1953; National Institute of Arts and Letters grant, 1951; Brandeis University Creative Arts Award, 1963; American Academy of Arts and Letters Award of Merit Medal, 1969; National Medal for Literature, 1973. *Died 2 July 1977.*

PUBLICATIONS

Fiction

Mashen'ka.   1926; translated by the author and Michael Glenny as *Mary*, 1970.
Korol', Dama, Valet.   1928; translated by the author and Dmitri Nabakov as *King, Queen, Knave*, 1968.
Zashchita Luzhina (The Luzhin Defense).   1930; translated by the author and Michael Scammell as *The Defense,* 1964.
Vozrashchenie Chorba (The Return of Chorb)(story).   1930.
Podvig' (The Exploit).   1932; translated by the author and Dmitri Nabokov as *Glory*, 1971.
Kamera Obskura.   1933; translated by W. Roy as *Camera Obscura,* 1937; revised and translated by the author as *Laughter in the Dark*, 1938.
Otchayanie.   1936; translated by the author as *Despair,* 1937; revised edition, 1966.
Soglyadatay (The Spy).   1938; translated by the author and Dmitri Nabokov as *The Eye,* 1965.
Priglashenie na Kazn'.   1938; translated by the author and Dmitri Nabokov as *Invitation to a Beheading,* 1959.
The Real Life of Sebastian Knight.   1941.
Bend Sinister.   1947.
Nine Stories.   1947.
Dar.   1952; translated by the author and Michael Scammell as *The Gift,* 1963.
Lolita.   1955; translated by the author into Russian, 1967.
Vesna v Fial'te i Drugie Rasskazi (Spring in Fialta and Other Stories).   1956.
Pnin.   1957.
Nabokov's Dozen: A Collection of 13 Stories.   1958.
Pale Fire.   1962.
Nabokov's Quartet (stories).   1966.
Ada; or Ardor: A Family Chronicle.   1969.
Transparent Things.   1973.
A Russian Beauty and Other Stories, translated by Dmitri Nabokov.   1973.
Look at the Harlequins!   1974.
Tyrants Destroyed and Other Stories, translated by the author and Dmitri Nabokov.   1975.
Details of a Sunset and Other Stories.   1976.

Plays

Smertj (Death), *Deduschka* (Grandfather), *Poljus* (The Pole), *Tragediya gospodina Morna*
   (The Tragedy of Mr. Morn), and *Chelovek iz SSSR* (The Man from the USSR), in *Rul,*
   1923–27.
Izobretenie Val'sa (produced 1968).   In *Russkiya Zapiski,* 1938; translated as *The
   Waltz Invention* (produced 1968), 1966.
Sobytie (The Event) (produced 1938).   In *Russkiya Zapiski,* 1938.
Lolita: A Screenplay.   1974.

Screenplay: *Lolita,*   1962.

Verse

(Poems).   1916.
(Two Paths).   1918.
Gorniy Put' (The Empyrean Path).   1923.
Grozd' (The Cluster).   1923.
Stikhotvoreniya, 1920–1951 (Poems).   1952.
Poems.   1959.
Poems and Problems.   1971.

Other

Nikolai Gogol.   1944.
Conclusive Evidence: A Memoir.   1951; as *Speak, Memory: A Memoir,* 1952; revised
   edition, as *Speak, Memory: An Autobiography Revisited,* 1966.
Nabokov's Congeries: An Anthology.   1968.
Strong Opinions (essays).   1973.

Editor and Translator, *Eugene Onegin,* by Aleksandr Pushkin.   4 vols., 1964; revised
   edition, 4 vols., 1976.

Translator, *Nikolka Persik* (Colas Breugnon), by Romain Rolland.   1922.
Translator, *Anya v Strane Chudes* (Alice in Wonderland), by Lewis Carroll.   1923.
Translator, *Three Russian Poets: Verse Translations from Pushkin, Lermontov and
   Tyutchev.*   1945; as *Poems by Pushkin, Lermontov and Tyutchev,* 1948.
Translator, with Dmitri Nabokov, *A Hero of Our Times,* by Mikhail Lermontov.   1958.
Translator, *The Song of Igor's Campaign: An Epic of the Twelfth Century.*   1960.

Bibliography: *Nabokov: Bibliographie des Gesantwerks* by Dieter E. Zimmer, 1963, revised
edition, 1964; *Nabokov: A Bibliography* by Andrew Field, 1974.

Reading List: *Escape into Aesthetics: The Art of Nabokov* by Page Stegner, 1966; *Nabokov:
His Life in Art,* 1967, and *Nabokov: A Biography,* 1975, both by Andrew Field; *Nabokov: The
Man and His Work* edited by L. S. Dembo, 1967; *Nabokov* by Julian Moynahan, 1971;
Nabokov's Deceptive World by W. Woodlin Rowe, 1971; *Nabokov* by Donald E. Morton,
1974; *Nabokov's Dark Cinema* by Alfred Appel, Jr., 1974; *Reading Nabokov* by Douglas
Fowler, 1974; *Nabokov* by L. L. Lee, 1976; *The Real Life of Nabokov* by Alex de Jonge, 1976.

*   *   *

The most fruitful way to approach the extensive and varied Nabokov canon (verse, plays, short stories, autobiography, translations, critical articles, and works on chess and lepidoptery) is undoubtedly through the novels, particularly the earlier Russian ones which are frequently overlooked but which contain the fundamental themes and devices of the later works. For what is striking about Nabokov's art is the consistency with which it develops, structurally and thematically, from the initial exploration of nostalgia and émigré life of Berlin in *Mary* to the celebration of language and artifice and the treatment of time in *Ada*.

Nabokov's second novel, *King, Queen, Knave*, is the first to juxtapose crime and art for parodic purposes and leaves its hero, Franz, a myopic character (literally and figuratively), stranded outside the bliss of his criminal fictions. *The Eye*, a novella whose émigré narrator is beset with split perceptions of his self, is, according to Nabokov, the first work where he develops that "involute abode" of his later fiction. Of the other novels of this Berlin/Paris period, *Despair* is the most important, since Herman Karlovich is a recognizable (though very different) predecessor to *Lolita*'s Humbert Humbert. Herman is a wily, self-conscious villain who devises a complex crime involving the murder of his double, who, however, does not resemble Herman at all. Herman's "perfect crime," and his journal which records that crime, are flawed by the same misconception; he fails to realize that contingent reality cannot be manipulated and that "the invention of art contains far more truth than life's reality."

The Gift is important for its exploration of biography as a fictional form, an exploration which is also prominent in his first English novel, *The Real Life of Sebastian Knight*. V., the narrator, attempts to write the biography of his brother, Sebastian Knight, but is foiled at every turn since Knight's life moves with that same obliqueness as the chess piece after which he is named. Ultimately, however, V.'s narrative approximates Sebastian's life by virtue of the dynamic character of the unfulfilled quest which utilizes parody as "a kind of springboard for leaping into the highest region of serious emotion."

Pnin is a warmly witty but sad portrait of Professor Timofey Pnin, an aging Russian exile attempting to master American language and culture at a New England university; the professorial politicking finally defeats him. Besides its preoccupation with cultural exile, the novel shows a self-consciousness of language, though never to the extent that we find in Nabokov's best-known novel, *Lolita*. In fact, given that Humbert Humbert, the narrator and hero, writes about his nympholeptic escapades with the twelve-year old Lolita in prison where he has "only words to play with," language frames the entire novel and is the vehicle through which Humbert and Lolita are finally relegated to the "bliss of fiction." Humbert's sexual desire becomes a metaphor for the artistic desire to create, though not until Humbert learns the hard lesson that it is desire and not possession which is the transcendent reality. So when Humbert possesses Lolita in part I of the novel (the crime), he is forced to protect her jealously in a motel trek across America in part II (the getaway). He has violated the "intangible island of entranced time" which is established early in the novel with his childhood love, Annabel Lee. It is Annabel Lee in her "kingdom by the sea" who establishes the initial rift between desire and possession. Ultimately, Lolita is abducted from Humbert by Quilty, Humbert's double, and the final chase scene culminates in Quilty's murder, a comic, grotesque exorcism that allows Humbert some measure of grace in the "bliss of fiction."

Pale Fire is the most experimental and enigmatic of Nabokov's novels, since its structure entails a 999-line poem by John Shade and a foreword, commentary with footnotes, and index by Charles Kinbote, the poet's homosexual neighbour who is really an exile from the distant northern land of Zembla (Russia). Beyond the obvious parody of pedantic scholarship, the novel explores the interdependencies of multi-layered worlds, each reflecting and refracting the other: Shade tells his story in verse; Kinbote uses Shade's poem to reveal his Zemblan past; Gradus, a secret agent intent on killing Kinbote, murders Shade by mistake; and of course, stalking through the work there is Nabokov, the arch-inventor of them all. Because the narrative of each layer is invented and sustained by the other, the final effect is a spiral of artifice.

Ada, Nabokov's most ambitious fiction (although its status among critics remains uncertain), fuses the novelist's earlier themes and techniques with greater scope and linguistic dexterity. The opening three chapters present a baroque invocation, a fanfare of language for the core of the novel which chronicles the incestuous love affair of the precocious hero, Van Veen, and his sister, Ada. Van's obsession with the past and the novel's eroticism culminate in part IV in a long lecture on time and space. Here the past becomes an inseparable link to the present, making a "glittering 'now' that is the only reality of Time's texture." Erotic desire, the art of inventing, and the butterfly's life cycle are metaphors for the constant metamorphosis of the present, while the future is relegated to an unknowable realm of space. The narrative moves across an imaginary geography of overlapping Russian, European, and American landscapes, with an equally overlaid texture of language. All the familiar Nabokovian motifs and devices are heaped against the aristocratic setting of the "ardors and arbors of Ardis Hall": butterflies and botany, dreams and doubles, puns, word games, nostalgia, false leads, and eroticism. It is undoubtedly Nabokov's most festive celebration of language, artifice, and, what should not be overlooked, love.

Transparent Things is a novella bordering on the metaphysical as it deals with the transparency of objects in the present, and finally of life itself, as death, abetted by chance, brings Hugh Person to a characteristic Nabokovian ending. *Look at the Harlequins!* is a first-person memoir of a writer whose life and works have disguised parallels with Nabokov's own. It is a fiction created out of fiction, a deepening of the labyrinth of inventing. And while these two works never surpass *Ada*, they do illustrate what has been evident in Nabokov from the start, namely, that fiction becomes the only sustained reality beyond contingent existence – even, no doubt, the sustenance of self.

—Brent MacLaine

NAIPAUL, V(idiadhar) S(urajprasad). Trinidadian. Born in Trinidad, 17 August 1932. Educated at Queen's Royal College, Port of Spain, Trinidad, 1943–48; University College, Oxford, 1950–54, B.A. (honours) in English 1953. Married Patricia Ann Hale in 1955. Settled in England, 1950; Editor, "Caribbean Voices," BBC, London, 1954–56; Fiction Reviewer, *New Statesman*, London, 1957–61; travelled in the West Indies and South America, 1961, India, 1962–63, Africa, 1966, and the United States and Canada, 1969. Recipient: Rhys Memorial Prize, 1958; Maugham Award, 1961; Phoenix Trust Award, 1962; Hawthornden Prize, 1964; Smith Literary Award, 1968; Arts Council grant, 1969; Booker Prize, 1971.

PUBLICATIONS

Fiction

The Mystic Masseur. 1957.
The Suffrage of Elvira. 1958.
Miguel Street. 1959.
A House for Mr. Biswas. 1961.
Mr. Stone and the Knights Companion. 1963.
The Mimic Men. 1967.
A Flag on the Island (stories). 1967.
In a Free State. 1971.
Guerrillas. 1975.

Other

The Middle Passage: Impressions of Five Societies – British, French and Dutch – in the
West Indies and South America.   1962.
An Area of Darkness: An Experience of India.   1964.
The Loss of El Dorado: A History.   1969.
The Overcrowded Barracoon and Other Articles.   1972.
India: A Wounded Civilization.   1977.

Reading List: *The West Indian Novel* by Kenneth Ramchand, 1970; *Naipaul: An Introduction to His Work* by Paul Theroux, 1972; *Naipaul* by Donald Hamner, 1973, and *Naipaul* edited by Hamner, 1978; *Naipaul: A Critical Introduction* by Landeg White, 1975; *Paradoxes of Order: Some Perspectives on the Fiction of Naipaul* by Robert K. Morris, 1975.

*   *   *

V. S. Naipaul's readers, both private and official, have not been unappreciative, and his publisher has honoured him with a collected edition, a prize usually awarded to the illustrious dead. So much esteem might well have sunk, or at least spoiled, a lesser talent. It has had no such effect on Naipaul, who is undoubtedly a writer of the utmost devotion, as well as a man of rare personal integrity.

It is the life of Trinidad, its workers, peasants, crooks, shopkeepers, local politicians, pundits, which is the body of Naipaul's early novels, *The Mystic Masseur*, *The Suffrage of Elvira*, and *Miguel Street*, treated with gaiety, malice, the clearest insight, and with an unfailingly lucid and elegant line. It is the world described discursively, and sometimes bitterly, in *The Middle Passage*, a place where neither civilization nor revolution had been created, only plantations and prosperity, neglect and decline. There are two contrasts in this early work: one between the huddled disorder of the place, and the unqualified sharpness and clarity of the writer's definition. The barely controlled chaos, both of place and sensibility, is outlined with a controlled and absolute clarity. It is as though the defining form is not just an instrument of the writer's perception, but a protest of the wholeness of his self against the neurotic muddle of the surroundings. The other contrast is between the flatness and dreariness of village and town, graceless, mean, wretchedly thin, like the village of Fuente Grove, and the brilliance and liveliness of the people, a folk with a genius for vivacity, expressed in an idiom of dancing vitality and wit. The intimate, energetic, sometimes brutal, speech of the people, contrasts with the silken run of the author's own voice, which has a near-Latin order and assurance, and which speaks out of a more inclusive intelligence and for a scheme of values in which judgment is an essential part of registration, and a detached and cultivated irony a key element in the sensibility.

Indian stability, West Indian mobility: not an inaccurate description of the feel of this work.

Naipaul's prose style lacks any awkwardness or arbitrary flush; it is wholly free of the gratuitous and the gesturing. Indeed, it may well seem mild and unemphatic. But it is also lithe, sharp, and definitive. Its grace is no block to a questing analytic capacity. It corresponds in its quiet firmness to some central assurance in the author, and it is this medium which makes it possible for him to fit together a variety of idioms and conversational habits. It corresponds, too, to an unbending honesty, the moral equivalent of clarity of perception; this is a power which enables Naipaul to see his characters in all their contradictory complexity and depth. He is a master of tone, with a capacity to differentiate one from another, and to assemble a variety of tones in consort.

Naipaul's comedy is not one of situation or plot; nor are the characters cartoons or puppets; and if it is satirical that is only so because of the author's sense of the ridiculous and his eye for dishonesty. It has been called malicious but it is hard to see why, since the attitude is neither contemputous nor patronising, and the author can hardly be condemned for not having as his purpose the wrapping up of reality in cosy illusion. It is a comedy essentially of the individual person in his damaged society, the actual person and the observed setting. But even the gayest, the most deliriously comic persons are frayed with anxieties and hunted by sickness and death.

Naipaul's masterpiece, *A House for Mr. Biswas*, was published early in his career. It is a novel in the grand manner, deliberate, large in scope, constructing a world with authoritative ease, with a central figure, a biographical line, a multitude of grasped minor characters, people seen from within so that they possess an intrinsic, spontaneous vitality, and from without, so that they are located in time and place and in a context of value and feeling. The distaste for certain aspects of humanity, faint in his earlier work, harsher in the discursive books and in his latest novels, is taken up here into a much more inclusive sensibility which is concerned with an essential humanity and which blends unsentimental accuracy in notation with a braced pity and tensed, athletic tolerance. It is a novel which has, too, a more profound value, a deep poetic truth. This is realised in the creative, encompassing metaphor which initiates and sustains the novel. At the root of the metaphor is the idea of slavery. Naipaul had mentioned in an earlier book, *The Middle Passage*, the difficulty of finding in Trinidad physical evidence of slavery. But that palpable absence of external institution does not mean that slavery had not inflicted an incurable wound on the national consciousness. The members of the community in *A House for Mr. Biswas*, even those like the Indians who were exempt from formal, historical slavery, carry about with them in their attitude and posture, in their management of life and feeling, the indelible mark of the slave, who is supremely the unnecessary man. All are impelled by the urgency to demonstrate, to themselves even more than to others, their human necessity. In the earlier novels they did this by bruising themselves absurdly and ineffectively against an indifferent universe. Mr. Biswas constructs the proof of his necessity in both a comic and a most moving way. Saturated as he is with the ethos of the given place, maltreated in peculiar deficiencies and cruelties, he is none the less realised with such complete conviction, so living a reality, that he becomes a model of man, just as the history and situation which formed him are seen to be a metaphor of the process which constitutes any man.

The society (with the history implicit in it) which would produce the wiry, flinching figure of Mr. Biswas (and having done so coldly demonstrate his superfluousness) is evoked with humour for its absurdity, sadness for its cruelty, and precision in everything. This capacity for definition which is also embodiment, for solid and refined denotation, lies at the heart of Naipaul's expressive power. His mind and his language work, not by any poetic murmuration or suggestiveness, but by pointing, by specifying, delimiting, detailing. To arrive at the utmost clarity is Naipaul's artistic purpose; to mark off the detail in its uniqueness, whether it be object or feeling or event, is his method. The details so defined are assembled with such unobtrusive tact, with such a fine sense of what is sufficient, that without display or excess or strain they make a composition lit by a level and equal light, as convincing and as self-endorsing as a natural substance.

The one limitation on the generality, the fullness of grasp, of Naipaul's strong, original work, is something I can only call an over-developed, on occasion even an overwrought, sense of human offensiveness. It corresponds to that flinching distaste for the human skin in *The Mimic Men*. The note is insistent and sometimes shrill. It suggests in the author some radical horror of human flesh. The bias against the ordinary grossness of human beings which is clearly part of Naipaul's sensibility becomes here a rejection of the flesh itself.

If this is weakness, as I think it is, it is also evidence of another, more positive quality of Naipaul's writing. That is his scrupulous honesty in reporting both the facts of the case and his reaction to them. He never fudges a state of affairs or fakes his feelings. He has an eye without prejudice as well as an eye unclouded by fear that he might be prejudiced, a timidity common enough among a number of English writers.

—William Walsh

NARAYAN, R(asipuram) K(rishnaswami). Indian. Born in Madras, 10 October 1906. Educated at Maharaja's College, Mysore, graduated 1930. Full-time writer. Recipient: National Prize of the Indian Literary Academy, 1958; Padma Bhushan, India, 1964; National Association of Independent Schools Award, U.S.A., 1965; English-Speaking Union of the United States award, 1975. Litt.D.: University of Leeds, Yorkshire, 1967. Lives in Mysore, India.

PUBLICATIONS

Fiction

Swami and Friends: A Novel of Malgudi. 1935.
The Bachelor of Arts. 1937.
The Dark Room. 1938.
Cyclone and Other Stories. N.d.
Malgudi Days (stories). 1943.
The English Teacher. 1945; as Grateful to Life and Death, 1953.
An Astrologer's Day and Other Stories. 1947.
Mr. Sampath. 1949; as The Printer of Malgudi, 1955.
Dodu and Other Stories. 1950(?).
The Financial Expert. 1952.
Waiting for the Mahatma. 1955.
Lawley Road (stories). 1956.
The Guide. 1958.
The Man-Eater of Malgudi. 1961.
Gods, Demons, and Others (stories). 1964.
The Vendor of Sweets. 1967; as The Sweet Vendor, 1967.
A Horse and Two Goats (stories). 1970.
The Painter of Signs. 1976.

Other

Mysore. 1944.
My Dateless Diary (travel in America). 1960.
The Ramayana: A Shortened Modern Prose Version of the Indian Epic. 1972.
Reluctant Guru (essays). 1974.
My Days: A Memoir. 1974.
The Mahabharata: A Shortened Modern Prose Version of the Indian Epic. 1978.

Reading List: Narayan: A Critical Study of His Works by Haris Raizada, 1969; The Novels of Narayan by Lakshmi Holmstrom, 1973; Narayan by P. S. Sundaram, 1973.

*   *   *

The most immediately striking aspects of the eleven novels of R. K. Narayan are their spatial identity, for all take part in the imagined town of Malgudi, and their temporal continuity, for they take us from the days of the Raj, when the first of them — Swami and Friends — was written, down to the independent India whose struggles for self- realization form the background to later books, down through four decades to The Painter of Signs.

As Narayan constructs it in the mind's eye from novel to novel, Malgudi is a medium-sized south Indian provincial town, reminiscent of both Mysore and Bangalore, which changes as time goes on; it has an imaginary river where boys can play, saints can bathe ritually, and wives try to drown themselves; behind it lie the equally imaginary Mempi Hills, where townsmen of Malgudi can become anchorites and others, like Vasu in *The Man-Eater of Malgudi*, can work out their rage by hunting.

Yet history has made Malgudi not merely Indian. One of Narayan's main themes is in fact the strange consequences of the continuing influence of a departed alien culture – the British – which offers perhaps the only means by which even an intensely conservative society like that of south India, proud of its traditions, can play a viable role in the modern world. Narayan himself, writing an English more eloquent than that of many English writers, is of course an example of this phenomenon, and it tends to dominate his early novels.

These early novels are all set within the educational system of the Raj, and are Narayan's most autobiographical works: *Swami and Friends* draws heavily on his experience as a mission school boy, *The Bachelor of Arts* on his years as a college student, and *The English Teacher* on his unsuccessful pedagogic career.

Swaminithan and his fellows in *Swami and Friends* are unwitting examples of the contradictions which even in the 1930's Narayan saw entering into the culturally divided lives of modern Indians. They attend a mission school which prepared them for the College in Malgudi where English is the only language of instruction. In this situation they become dedicated to the English game of cricket, and their special form of the quest that dominates all Narayan novels is a comic one, the creation on the waste lots of Malgudi of an M.C.C. which they hope may rival its English namesake.

The alternative to submersion in western models is of course withdrawal into one or other of the interlocking traditional worlds of the village and the life of the wandering holy man, who usually finds his warmest welcome among illiterate peasants. In Narayan's novels such withdrawal often provides a way to self-discovery if not self-transformation.

After winning his degree, Chandran, in *The Bachelor of Arts*, wanders for eight months as a *sanyasin* – a holy beggar – because conflicting horoscopes have prevented him from marrying the girl he fell in love with when he saw her on the riverbank. But he goes through the motions of the holy life without being holy, and his moment of revelation comes when – at a time of drought and starvation – he realizes the fraud he had been foisting on himself as well as on the villagers who have fed him out of their iron rations. He returns to the normal world, becomes a successful small businessman and marries a girl whose stars in their motions dance well with his.

Savitri, the misused wife of *The Dark Room*, runs away from home when her husband carries on a public affair with a young widow, his colleague at the Egladia Insurance Company. She tries to drown herself, but is rescued by a thief and taken to his village, where she becomes servant in the temple until she finds the love of her children calling her back and the middle-class, half-Indian-half-Western world reclaims her.

Raju, in *The Guide*, does not return. Guide to the cave temples of the Malgudi Hills, he becomes involved with a former temple dancer, is led to crime and imprisonment, and then retreats to an old riverside temple. The villages take him for a saint, and he becomes trapped in the role, so that he undertakes a quixotic fast to end a drought and dies when the rains come. Only Jagan, in *The Sweet Vendor*, old, tired of profitable trading, disillusioned and – as he believes – defiled by the behaviour of a westernized son, seems likely to find in his withdrawal the wise detachment he seeks.

On a different, political level, the search for fulfilment outside ordinary currents of middle-class Indian life is portrayed in *Waiting for the Mahatma*. Sriram, rich and immature, falls in love with Bharati, one of the young women devotees who follow the Mahatma on his wanderings, and, when Bharati goes to prison on Gandhi's command, he falls in with a violent revolutionary who leads him into acts of sabotage. Sriram himself is imprisoned, and released in time to join Bharati and witness Gandhi's assassination in 1948.

Gandhi and his death represent an incursion from the outside world that destroys the magic autonomy of Malgudi and makes *Waiting for the Mahatma* at once one of the most interesting and least satisfying of Narayan's novels, largely because of the difference in grain between Gandhi and the people of Malgudi. For if there is one characteristic Narayan's characters share, it is mediocrity. Malgudi is a city of the petty and the unfulfilled and, like Chekhov, Narayan has produced from their very inadequacies, from their weaknesses and shallow pretensions, a combination of sadness and comedy that is irresistibly appealing. And even when the people of Malgudi seek to break out of the circle of their mediocrity, they fail because their ambitions overleap their capacities. The eponymous hero of *Mr. Sampath* sets out to establish in Malgudi a film studio that will rival those of Bombay and Calcutta, but the great epic of Hindu mythology that is to be his first production is ruined by a series of farcical disasters arising out of the jealousies, passions, and sheer inadequacies of Sampath and his associates.

But the ancient Indian myths which Narayan began to read with attention in his middle years are not merely plots for films; his novels recreate them in real life. Weak and inexperienced characters fall under the influence of malign men who are little more than nature forces personified. Such is the evil Dr. Pal in *The Financial Expert*, who sets the money-lender Margyya on his course of prosperity by giving him the copyright on an erotic book, who later corrupts Margyya's son Balu, and who finally encompasses the "financial expert's" ruin by starting the rumours that destroy him. And such too is Vasu the hunter who disrupts the life of the modest little printer Nataraj in *The Man-Eater of Malgudi* and threatens the little town's prosperity by seeking to kill the temple elephant for its ivory. In the end Vasu kills himself with the superhuman power he has not the wisdom to control, and the elephant marches on unharmed while Malgudi settles down again into the peace of mediocrity, a middle-class town in which, creating an ambiance for the sad eccentric characters and their quasi-mythical adventures, the colours and smells of India are so powerfully evoked that anyone who knows India south of Bombay has only to pick up a Narayan novel and read a dozen pages for the whole setting to re-form in his mind's nostril and the chatter of Indian voices to echo again in his ear. In Malgudi's microcosmic Indianness lives the secret of its appeal to readers in so many countries.

—George Woodcock

NASBY, Petroleum V(esuvius). Pseudonym for David Ross Locke. American. Born in Vestal, near Binghamton, New York, 20 September 1833. Educated in local schools to age 10; apprentice printer at the *Democrat*, Cortland, New York, 1843–50. Married Martha H. Bodine; three sons. Itinerant printer in various American cities, 1850–52; Founding Editor, with James G. Robinson, *Plymouth Advertiser*, Ohio, 1852–56; subsequently worked for various Ohio newpapers; Editor, *Jeffersonian*, Findlay, Ohio, 1861–65 (wrote first Nasby letter for the paper, 1861); Editor and Proprietor of the *Toledo Blade*, 1865 until his death (wrote Nasby letters for the paper until 1887); Managing Editor, *Evening Mail*, New York, 1871; served as Alderman from the third ward, Toledo. *Died 15 February 1888.*

PUBLICATIONS

Collections

Let's Laugh (selections), edited by Lloyd E. Smith. 1924.

Fiction and Sketches

> *The Nasby Papers: Letters and Papers Containing Views on the Topics of the Day.* 1864.
> *Nasby: Divers Views, Opinions and Prophecies of Yoors Trooly.* 1866.
> *Swinging round the Circle; or, Andy's Trip to the West, Together with a Life of Its Hero.* 1866.
> *Swingin round the Cirkle.* 1867.
> *Ekkoes from Kentucky.* 1867.
> *The Impendin Crisis uv the Dimocracy.* 1868.
> *The Struggles (Social, Financial and Political) of Petroleum V. Nasby.* 1873; as *The Moral History of America's Life Struggle,* 1874; abridged edition, edited by Joseph Jones, 1963.
> *Eastern Fruit on Western Dishes: The Morals of Abou Ben Adhem.* 1875.
> *Inflation at the Cross Roads.* 1875; as *Nasby on Inflation,* 1876.
> *The President's Policy.* 1877.
> *A Paper City* (novel). 1878.
> *The Democratic John Bunyan, Being Eleven Dreams.* 1880.
> *The Diary of an Office Seeker.* 1881.
> *Nasby in Exile; or, Six Months of Travel in England, Ireland, Scotland, France, Germany, Switzerland, and Belgium.* 1882.
> *Beer and the Body.* 1884.
> *Prohibition.* 1886.
> *The Demagogue: A Political Novel.* 1891.
> *The Nasby Letters.* 1893.

Plays

> *Inflation,* with Charles Gayler (produced 1876).
> *Widow Bedott* (produced 1879).

Verse

> *Hannah Jane.* 1881.

Other

> *Civil War Letters,* edited by Harvey S. Ford. 1962.

Reading List: *Nasby* by James C. Austin, 1965; *The Man Who Made Nasby, David Ross Locke* by John M. Harrison, 1969.

*   *   *

Petroleum V. Nasby was the creation of David Ross Locke, one of America's greatest newspaper men. Beginning as a printer at the age of twelve and progressing successfully as writer, editor, and publisher of several New York and Ohio newspapers, he took over the Toledo, Ohio, *Blade* in 1865, and made it one of the most widely read papers in the midwest. He had very little schooling, but he developed a rough but powerful editorial style that contributed to the course of American history. He supported the Republican Party from its beginnings. His opposition to the Confederacy during the Civil War encouraged the Union cause and President Lincoln personally. His insistence on the rights of Negroes helped lead public opinion toward the Emancipation Proclamation and the Thirteenth, Fourteenth, and Fifteenth Amendments to the Constitution. His attacks on political corruption promoted Civil Service reform and the exposure of political fraud in the Gilded Age. He aided the causes of prohibition and women's rights which led long after his death to the Eighteenth and Nineteenth Amendments.

But his greatest and most lasting fame came from the Nasby letters – a series of newspaper columns written from 1862 until Locke's death in 1888. Petroleum Vesuvius Nasby, the fictitious writer of the letters, stood for everything that Locke was against. Nasby was an illiterate, drunken, bigoted, racist Democrat. The Nasby letters are considered part of the American tradition of crackerbox humor – journalistic humor expressed in a lowbrow, rustic dialect and with a common-sense philosophy. But they are not humorous in a strict sense of the term; they are bitterly satirical, violently partisan, grossly concrete pictures of the American political scene. With the exception of Benjamin Franklin, Locke was probably America's greatest political satirist.

The best-known Nasby letters were collected in various books beginning in 1864. The best of these is *Divers Views*, which exposed blatantly the pro-Southern views of the Ohio Copperhead, Nasby, during the Civil War. But each collection included parts of the earlier material, and *The Nasby Letters* is the most complete, comprising a panorama of Republican thought and action during the most critical quarter-century of United States history.

The Nasby letters were but a part of Locke's literary activities. He was one of the most popular lecturers in America in an age when public lecturing was as important as television is today. His three famous lectures, delivered throughout the country under the pseudonym of Nasby, were small masterpieces on the issues of civil rights for Negroes, women's rights, and political corruption. He was the author of two excellent political novels, *A Paper City* and *The Demagogue*; two plays, *Inflation* and *Widow Bedott*, the latter being performed continually into the twentieth century; a very popular, very sentimental poem, *Hannah Jane*; a number of quite creditable hymns; and an untold number of articles, editorials, stories, novels, verses, and essays in newspapers, magazines, and pamphlets.

Locke did not pretend to be a literary artist. He wrote for his times, and he believed that politics was the most important concern of a democracy. He was a significant editor and publisher. And his Nasby letters and his lectures deserve continued attention.

—James C. Austin

NASHE, Thomas. English. Born in Lowestoft, Suffolk, baptized November 1567. Educated at St. John's College, Cambridge (sizar), 1582–88, B.A. 1586. Travelled on the continent, then settled in London, 1588; thereafter a full-time writer; a friend of Greene, Lodge, Daniel, and Marlowe; pamphleteer, engaged in running battle with the Harveys in the 1590's, a controversy suppressed by the Archbishop of Canterbury, 1599; imprisoned for drawing attention to abuses in the theatre (*The Isle of Dogs*), 1597. *Died in 1601.*

PUBLICATIONS

Collections

> *Works,* edited by R. B. McKerrow. 5 vols., 1904–10; revised edition, edited by F. P. Wilson, 5 vols., 1958.
> *Selected Writings,* edited by Stanley Wells. 1964.
> *The Unfortunate Traveller and Other Works,* edited by J. B. Steane. 1972.

Fiction

> The Unfortunate Traveller; or, The Life of Jack Wilton. 1594; augmented edition, 1594; edited by John Berryman, 1960.

Play

> Summer's Last Will and Testament (produced 1592). 1600.

Verse

> The Choice of Valentines, edited by J. S. Farmer. 1899.

Other

> The Anatomy of Absurdity. 1589.
> An Almond for a Parrot. 1590.
> Pierce Penniless His Supplication to the Devil. 1592; edited by G. R. Hibbard, 1951.
> Strange News of the Intercepting Certain Letters. 1592; as The Apology of Pierce Penniless, 1593.
> Christ's Tears over Jerusalem. 1593; revised edition, 1594.
> The Terrors of the Night; or, A Discourse of Apparitions. 1594.
> Have with You to Saffron Walden; or, Gabriel Harvey's Hunt Is Up. 1596.
> Lenten Stuff, with The Praise of the Red Herring. 1599.

> Editor, Astrophel and Stella, by Sir Philip Sidney. 1591.

Bibliography: Nashe: A Concise Bibliography by S. A. Tannenbaum, 1941; Nashe 1941–65 by R. C. Johnson, 1968.

Reading List: Two Elizabethan Writers: Nashe and Deloney by Robert G. Howarth, 1956; Nashe: A Critical Introduction by G. R. Hibbard, 1962.

*   *   *

Thomas Nashe, a young Juvenal or an English Aretine according to his contemporaries, seemed something of a literary sport in his own age and has continued to seem so to literary historians. His writings touch on a wide variety of genres – literary criticism, social satire, mock encomia, and short fiction – they represent, in fact, a mixed bag of goods. Furthermore, many pieces seem to have no definite subject matter, depending on the slightest of scaffolding to support adumbrations on a diversity of topics. Yet within this generic and topical variety the recurrence of certain themes may be said to provide a kind of focus.

The first is the high esteem for poetry. Like other Elizabethans, Nashe uses the term broadly to include writing that is fictive in nature and allied to learning since the true poet is a true scholar. Related themes are the niggardliness of patrons (and here Nashe speaks directly out of his own experience as a university graduate earning a scant living by his pen) and the upstart Puritans who have brought both poetry and learning into disrepute.

In his first published work (1589) – a brash critical essay introducing Robert Greene's Menaphon – he promises to persecute those idiots and their heirs who have made art bankrupt and sent poetry begging, a promise he in part fulfills in his Anatomy of Absurdity. In adopting the term "anatomy," Nashe makes clear that he has taken on the role of a surgeon who is to dissect the diseases of art – broadly interpreted. These include a diatribe against women, a hit and miss attack on Puritans and writers of various sorts, and a defense of poetry and learning. This jumble of topics is set forth in the euphuistic style, but he soon developed his own distinctive manner.

When he arrived in London in the fall of 1588, the Puritan pamphleteer known as "Martin Marprelate" had just initiated the first of his lively assaults on the Anglican establishment. His technique was to charge his irreverent attacks with all the force and pungency of racy colloquial speech, a technique so successful that the ecclesiastical authorities enlisted professional writers to answer in kind. Although the extent of Nashe's contribution is uncertain, what he learned from this flurry of verbal combat reinforced his own predilection for a seemingly spontaneous, unstudied style. As early as the Preface to *Menaphon* he declared his preference for the man who could achieve the "extemporal vein" in *any* mode to the deliberate rhetorician, and in his most popular work, *Pierce Penniless His Supplication to the Devil*, he boasts, in Latin, that he writes whatever comes into his mouth "as fast as his hand can trot."

Pierce, that is, Purse, Penniless becomes Nashe's long-lived persona. Since the motive for writing is his poverty, stemming from the illiberality of patrons, he addresses his supplication to the devil. This is a recital of the seven deadly sins of London society as they are personified in current social types, a scheme which allows him to satirize foibles and follies by means of sharp caricature and to illustrate them with humorous tales.

Nashe's one extant dramatic text is an occasional piece entitled *Summer's Last Will and Testament* which was privately performed in 1592 during an outbreak of the plague. It is quite simply a pageant of seasonal change where, before yielding up his throne to Autumn, the dying Summer calls on various officers – Ver, Harvest, etc. – to give an account of their stewardship. These seasonal personifications are also representative of social types in a blending of the natural and the human. Appropriately garbed, they sing and dance; yet there is an elegiac undercurrent in the ominous references to death and the plague. *Summer's Last Will* includes Nashe's most poignant lyric as well as jocular songs, but its style is modulated by the deflating, if not abusive, prose comments of – thanks to his name – the ghostly Presenter, Will Summers, Henry VIII's jester.

In 1597 Nashe's share in the scandalous *Isle of Dogs*, a play no longer extant, forced him to skip out of London and take refuge at Yarmouth. As a token of gratitude to the citizens, he wrote *Lenten Stuff*. Taking his cue from scholars of all ages who turned molehills into mountains, Nashe follows up a chronicle history of the city with a mock encomium of the red herring, including an account of its origins by way of a burlesque treatment of Marlowe's *Hero and Leander*. This notably anticipates 17th-century handling of the once popular epyllion.

Nashe also showed his literary gratitude to the Carey family by dedicating his mocking discourse on apparitions, *The Terrors of the Night*, to Sir George's daughter and his fantastical prose treatise, *Christ's Tears over Jerusalem*, to his wife. For the latter piece, though "an infant in the mysteries of divinity," he composes a "collachrymate" oration in which Christ projects the fall of Jerusalem for the sins of the Jews. This is a highly effective, if disconcerting flourish of rhetoric. In its wealth of tropes and figures, its playing on single words in different contexts, its use of classical quotations and instances (Christ cites Herodotus and specifies the height of Mt. Tabor), it suggests spiritual parody. In its stress on the lachrymal, it looks forward to the "tear poetry" of the 17th Century. To this oration Nashe adds a ghastly recital of the desolation of the city through sword, famine, and pestilence. Like a "soul surgeon" he then runs through the sins of the populace.

In *The Unfortunate Traveller*, he essays "a clean different vein." A piece of short fiction, it is a variety show in terms of kind: partly jest book, chronicle history, and travelogue. Its roguish hero, Jack Wilton, a dapper page, attends Henry VIII's wars in France, returns to England as a fop, goes off to Northern Europe where he witnesses the slaughter (in 1534) of the Anabaptists, meets up with his late master the poet Surrey and continues to travel with him, finally reaching Italy, the acme of all European tours. With such a geographical and historical spread, Nashe has ample opportunity to ridicule many intellectual and social pretensions, but most of all he achieves "variety of mirth" by parodying literary styles and genres.

The sensational elements of chronicle history are mocked by the comic treatment of the horrors of war and the sweating sickness. The inanities of Petrarchan love are mocked in the extravagant language of Surrey, who woos a Venetian magnifico's wife as a surrogate for his Geraldine though it is Jack, relying on "simplicity and plainness," who catches the bird and gets her with child. The extremes of symbolic trappings and *imprese* are mocked by the flamboyant tournament in Florence where, on behalf of his beloved, Surrey challenges all comers – Christians, Turks, Jews, or Saracens. When Jack and his courtesan reach Rome, the literary parody becomes more skilful and complex. The travel account – "the shop dust of the sights" he sees – includes a baroque description of the artificial luxuriance of a merchant's summerhouse in a parody of "golden age" literature; the "complaint" of the matron raped on her dead husband's body parodies that form's rhetorical excesses, while the account of Cutwolfe's grisly pleasure in vengeance ("The farther we wade in revenge, the nearer we come to the throne of the Almighty") parodies popular tragedy though its moral value is mockingly acknowledged in that the execution of the revenger persuades Jack to marry his courtesan and flee the Sodom of Italy. Throughout the bewildering multiplicity of action and event, the one constant is the author's concern with manipulating language: rhetorical technique exists for its own sake quite devoid of value judgements. Stressing extravagant manner rather than serious matter in a variety of popular and mixed forms, Nashe illustrates the dilution of humanist theory in the 1590's and forecasts a new emphasis.

—Elizabeth Story Donno

NEAL, John.   American.   Born in Falmouth, now Portland, Maine, 25 August 1793. Educated for a brief period in local schools. Married Eleanor Hall in 1828; five children. Clerk in a succession of shops in Portland, then worked as an itinerant teacher of penmanship and drawing in various towns along the Kennebec River; settled in Baltimore: kept a dry goods store, with John Pierpont, 1814 until the business failed, 1816; studied law, while writing for a living (briefly edited the *Baltimore Telegraph*; contributed to *Portico*; assisted Paul Allen in compiling *A History of the American Revolution*; published novels), 1816–23; lived in England, contributing to the most prominent English periodicals, particularly *Blackwood's Magazine*, 1823–27; returned to America, 1827, settled in Portland, and practised law there; edited the *Yankee*, Portland, 1828–29; later briefly edited the *New England Galaxy*, Boston, and a Portland newspaper; Editor, *Brother Jonathan*, New York, 1843; active contributor to the *North American Review*, *Harper's*, and the *Atlantic Monthly*, from 1850. M.A.: Bowdoin College, Brunswick, Maine, 1836. *Died 20 June 1876.*

PUBLICATIONS

Collections

> *Observations on American Art: Selections from the Writings*, edited by Harold Edward
>   Dickson.   1943.

Fiction

> *Keep Cool: A Novel, Written in Hot Weather.* 1817.
> *Logan: A Family History.* 1822.
> *Errata; or, The Works of Will Adams.* 1823.
> *Randolph.* 1823.
> *Seventy-Six.* 1823.
> *Brother Jonathan; or The New Englanders.* 1825.
> *Rachel Dyer: A North American Story.* 1828.
> *Authorship: A Tale.* 1830.
> *The Down-Easters.* 1833.
> *True Womanhood: A Tale.* 1859.
> *The White-Faced Pacer; or, Before and After the Battle.* 1863.
> *The Moose-Hunter, or, Life in the Maine Woods.* 1864.
> *Little Mocassin; or, Along the Madawaska: A Story of Life and Love in the Lumber Region.* 1866.

Play

> *Otho.* 1819.

Verse

> *The Battle of Niagara.* 1818; revised edition, 1819.

Other

> *One Word More: Intended for the Reasoning and Thoughtful among Unbelievers.* 1854.
> *Account of the Great Conflagration in Portland.* 1866.
> *Wandering Recollections of a Somewhat Busy Life: An Autobiography.* 1869.
> *Great Mysteries and Little Plagues.* 1870.
> *Portland Illustrated.* 1874.
> *American Writers,* edited by Fred Lewis Pattee. 1937.
> *Critical Essays and Stories,* edited by Hans-Joachim Lang, in *Jahrbuch für Amerikastudien,* 1962.

Bibliography: in *Bibliography of American Literature* by Jacob Blanck, 1973.

Reading List: *A Down-East Yankee from the District of Maine* by Windsor Pratt Daggett, 1920; *That Wild Fellow Neal and the American Literary Revolution* by Benjamin Lease, 1972.

*   *   *

Strongly influenced by American nationalism following the War of 1812, John Neal developed a theory of literature that, put into practice in a series of unusual novels, has helped to win him a minor place in American literary history. Concerned that American writers like Charles Brockden Brown, Washington Irving, and James Fenimore Cooper were not sufficiently "American" in their writing, Neal sought to create an original body of fiction that would imitate no foreign models, that would accurately depict American persons and places, and that would faithfully reproduce the American language. He constructed his works, moreover, on a psychological theory that placed great stress on the "heart" and the "blood," as opposed to the mind, a theory that led him to write rather formless fictions that frequently lapse into incoherence.

He turned to the American past for some of his novels – Indian conflicts in *Logan*, the American Revolution in *Seventy-Six* and *Brother Jonathan*, and the Salem witch trials in *Rachel Dyer* – and he drew American characters and reproduced American speech with considerable skill. At his best, Neal achieved a degree of realism uncommon in his time and occasionally reached a depth of psychological penetration suggestive of Poe. At his worst, however, he strained too much for effect, descended to Byronic posturing, indulged in both Gothic and sentimental absurdities, and fell into melodrama. All of Neal's books suffer to some degree from his excesses, and from his unwillingness – or inability – to give form to his novels. Only *Rachel Dyer*, perhaps his best book, exhibits a sustained authorial control, but even it has a long and digressive passage in one of the courtroom scenes.

Neal's one significant contribution to American fiction is his style. Derived from the cadences of American speech, it ranges from local dialect through the more general vernacular to the Biblical or prophetic. At its best, it gives a sense of immediacy to his work, whether the story is told, like *Seventy-Six*, by a common man who uses his natural language, or, like *Rachel Dyer*, by a narrative voice appropriately attuned to the seriousness of the action and theme. Neal was especially skillful in moving his story forward through the speech of his characters, and in some of his works, the reader will find page after page containing little more than conversation. In both style and technique of narration, therefore, John Neal stands near the head of the vernacular tradition in American literature and dimly foreshadows the language of Mark Twain.

—Donald A. Ringe

NEWBY, P(ercy) H(oward). English. Born in Crowborough, Sussex, 25 June 1918. Educated at Hanley Castle Grammar School, Worcester; St. Paul's College, Cheltenham, 1936–38. Served in the Royal Army Medical Corps, in France and Egypt, 1939–42. Married Joan Thompson in 1945; two daughters. Lecturer in English Language and Literature, Fouad I University, Cairo, 1942–46; free-lance writer and journalist, 1946–49; joined the BBC, London, 1949: Producer, Talks Department, 1949–58; Controller of the Third Programme, subsequently Radio 3, 1958–71; Director of Programmes, Radio, 1971–75; and Managing Director of Radio from 1975. Recipient: Atlantic Award, 1946; Maugham Award, 1948; Smith-Mundt Fellowship, 1952; Booker Prize, 1969. C.B.E. (Commander, Order of the British Empire), 1972. Lives in Chalfont St. Giles, Buckinghamshire.

PUBLICATIONS

Fiction

A Journey to the Interior. 1945.
Agents and Witnesses. 1947.
Mariner Dances. 1948.
The Snow Pasture. 1949.

The Young May Moon. 1950.
A Season in England. 1951.
A Step to Silence. 1952.
The Retreat. 1953.
A Picnic at Sakkara. 1955.
Revolution and Roses. 1957.
Ten Miles from Anywhere and Other Stories. 1958.
A Guest and His Going. 1959.
The Barbary Light. 1962.
One of the Founders. 1965.
Something to Answer For. 1968.
A Lot to Ask. 1973.
Kith. 1977.

Play

Radio Play: *The Reunion*, 1970.

Other

The Spirit of Jem (juvenile). 1947.
The Loot Runners (juvenile). 1949.
Maria Edgeworth. 1950.
The Novel 1945–1950. 1951.

Editor, *Tales from the Arabian Nights.* 1967.

Reading List: *The Fiction of Newby* by F. X. Mathews, 1964; *Newby* by G. S. Fraser, 1974.

*   *   *

P. H. Newby is a writer whose work is chiefly farcical. Farce is the result of a representation of life which offers a succession of external events that do not have any strict linkage with each other. Farcical also, in a more subtle way, is a depiction of an interior human climate in which the "weather" of one period in a human life is discontinuous with that of an earlier or later time.

Newby is a distinguished master of both sorts of farce — the farce of discontinuous event and the farce of inconsecutive psychological states. The farce of discontinuous events, often as wildly funny as the door-slams of a French farce, is met in Newby's novels which put conventional Western people in contact with mildly exotic Middle Eastern persons and events. *Revolution and Roses*, *The Picnic at Sakkara*, and *Agents and Witnesses* are knock-about accounts of the collision of incompatible cultures and of the inability of anyone to make sense of the disastrous confrontations that occur in Athens, Alexandria, or elsewhere. Most of the characters, both Western and Middle Eastern, are descendants of Aziz and Mrs. Moore in Forster's *A Passage to India*, but they have lost the moral concern that led Forster's characters into their attempts to weigh what had happened to them. In Newby's outright farcical novels, there is no such weighing. In compensation, there is the author's own tireless and delicate notation.

Such notation continues in the novels that have an English setting: *The Snow Pasture, A Step to Silence, The Retreat*, and others. These novels, on a first reading, lack the direct appeal to mirth that exists in the novels of Middle Eastern encounter. But it can be seen that in this group of novels farce – existence viewed as inconsecutive and inconclusive – has simply moved inward and now manifests itself in the states of being Newby meets in the characters he has created. Husbands and wives and others simply pass through several mental and psychological "sets" that are no more coherent with each other than are the clashing cultures in the novels previously noted.

Such novels as *Something to Answer For* and *A Lot to Ask* combine all the modes of farce in which Newby excels. In these novels the farce of cultural contrast alternates with the more intimate grotesqueness of a person's uncertainty about what last year's identity was and what next year's may well be. Only infrequently, as in *A Season in England*, does Newby present an account of the meshing of two or three personalities that is deep and transforming for all concerned. Most of Newby's work ignores such a possibility and indeed suggests that a world free of external and internal farce is hardly worth considering.

—Harold H. Watts

NEWMAN, John Henry; Cardinal Newman. English. Born in London, 21 February 1801. Educated at Trinity College, Oxford, 1817–22. Fellow, Oriel College, Oxford, 1822; ordained in the Anglican Church, 1824: Curate, St. Clement's, Oxford, 1824–26; Tutor, Oriel College, 1826; Vicar, St. Mary's, Oxford, 1828–43; a leading figure of the Oxford Movement in the 1830's, contributed to *Tracts for the Times*, 1833–41; Editor, with John Keble, A Library of the Fathers of the Holy Catholic Church, 1838–85; converted to Roman Catholicism, 1845, ordained a priest, 1847; established the Oratory of St. Philip Neri in Birmingham, 1848; Rector, Catholic University of Ireland, 1851–58; Editor, *Rambler*, 1859; created Cardinal, 1879. *Died 11 August 1890.*

PUBLICATIONS

Collections

> *Works.* 41 vols., 1908–18.
> *Prose and Poetry*, edited by Geoffrey Tillotson. 1957.
> *Letters*, edited by C. S. Dessain and others. 11 vols., 1961–77.
> *Diaries*, edited by I. T. Ker and Thomas Gornall. 1978–

Fiction

> *Loss and Gain.* 1848.
> *Callista: A Sketch of the Third Century.* 1856.

Verse

> *St. Bartholomew's Eve: A Tale of the Sixteenth Century*, with J. W. Bowden. 1821.
> *Memorials of the Past.* 1832.

Lyra Apostolica, with others.   1836.
Verses on Religious Subjects.   1853.
The Dream of Gerontius.   1866; edited by M. Sargent, 1937.
Verses on Various Occasions.   1868.
Echoes from the Oratory: Selections.   1884.

Other

The Life of Apollonius Tyanaeus, with a Comparison Between the Miracles of Scriptures and Those Elsewhere Related.   1825.
Suggestions to Certain Resident Clergymen of the University in Behalf of the Church Missionary Society.   1830.
The Arians of the Fourth Century: Their Doctrine, Temper, and Conduct.   1833; edited by G. H. Forbes, 1854; revised edition, 1871, 1876.
Parochial Sermons.   6 vols., 1834–42; edited by W. J. Copeland, 6 vols., 1868; vol. 2 edited by Vernon Stanley, as *Sermons for the Festivals,* 1904.
The Restoration of Suffragan Bishops Recommended.   1835.
Elucidations of Dr. Hampden's Theological Statements.   1836.
Lectures on the Prophetical Office of the Church.   1837.
Lectures on Justification.   1838.
The Church of the Fathers.   1839.
The Tamworth Reading Room: Letters on an Address by Sir Robert Peel.   1841.
Sermons, Bearing on Subjects of the Day.   1843; edited by W. J. Copeland, 1869.
Sermons, Chiefly on the Theory of Religious Belief.   1843; as *Fifteen Sermons,* 1872.
Plain Sermons by Contributors to Tracts for the Times, vol. 5.   1843; edited by W. J. Copeland, 2 vols., 1868.
An Essay on the Development of Christian Doctrine.   1845; edited by G. Wiegel, 1960.
Discourses Addressed to Mixed Congregations.   1849.
Lectures on Certain Difficulties Felt by Anglicans in Submitting to the Catholic Church.   1850; revised edition, 1857.
Lectures on the Present Position of Catholics in England.   1851; edited by J. J. Daly, 1942.
Discourses on the Scope and Nature of University Education.   1852; revised edition, 1859.
Lectures on the History of the Turks in Its Relation to Christianity.   1854.
The Office and Work of Universities.   1856; edited by G. Sampson, as *University Sketches,* 1902; edited by Michael Tierney, 1964.
Sermons Preached on Various Occasions.   1857.
Lectures and Essays on University Subjects.   1859.
Mr. Kingsley and Mr. Newman: A Correspondence on the Question Whether Dr. Newman Teaches That Truth Is No Virtue?   1864.
Apologia pro Vita Sua, Being a Reply to a Pamphlet Entitled What, Then, Does Dr. Newman Mean?   1864; as *History of My Religious Opinions,* 1865; edited by Martin J. Svaglic, 1967.
An Essay in Aid of a Grammar of Assent.   1870; edited by D. Gilson, 1955.
Miscellanies from the Oxford Sermons and Other Writings.   1870.
Two Essays on Scripture Miracles and on Ecclesiastical.   1870.
Essays Critical and Historical.   2 vols., 1872.
Historical Sketches.   3 vols., 1872–73.
Discussions and Arguments on Various Subjects.   1872.
The Idea of a University Defined and Illustrated (includes *Discourses on the Scope and Nature of University Education* and *Lectures and Essays on University subjects*).   1873; edited by I. T. Ker, 1976.

Six Selections. 1874.
Tracts Theological and Ecclesiastical. 1874.
Characteristics from the Writings, edited by W. S. Lilly. 1875; as *A Newman Anthology,* 1949.
The Via Media of the Anglican Church, Illustrated in Lectures, Letters, and Tracts Written Between 1830 and 1841. 2 vols., 1877.
Sayings. 1890.
Stray Essays and Controversial Points. 1890.
Meditations and Devotions, edited by W. P. Neville. 1893.
My Campaign in Ireland, edited by W. P. Neville. 1896.
Sermon Notes 1849–1878, edited by the Fathers of the Birmingham Oratory. 1913.
Letters and Poems from Malta 1832–1833, edited by Joseph Galea. 1945.
Essays and Sketches, edited by C. F. Harrold. 1948.
Sermons and Discourses, edited by C. F. Harrold. 2 vols., 1949.
Autobiographical Writings, edited by Henry Tristram. 1956.
Faith and Prejudice and Other Unpublished Sermons, edited by C. S. Dessain. 1956.
Catholic Sermons. 1957.
On Consulting the Faithful on Matters of Doctrine, edited by John Coulson. 1961.
A Newman Companion to the Gospels: Sermons, edited by Armel J. Coupet. 1966.
Newman the Oratorian: Unpublished Oratory Papers, edited by Placid Murray. 1969.
The Philosophical Notebook, edited by Edward Sillem. 2 vols., 1969–70.
The Theological Papers on Faith and Certainty, edited by J. Derek Holmes. 1976.

Editor and Contributor, *Tracts for the Times.* 6 vols., 1833–41.
Editor, *The Cistercian Saints of England, Volume 1* and *2* (part of *Lives of the English Saints*). 1844–45.
Editor, with John Keble, *Remains of Rev. R. H. Froude.* 4 vols., 1838–39.
Editor, *Thoughts on the Work of the Six Days of Creation,* by J. W. Bowden. 1845.
Editor and Translator, *Phormio, Pincerna,* and *Andria,* by Terence. 3 vols., 1864–70.
Editor and Translator, *Auluaria,* by Plautus. 1866.
Editor, *Notes on a Visit to the Russian Church in the Years 1840, 1841,* by William Palmer. 1882.

Translator, *The Devotions of Bishop Andrewes,* part 1. 1842.
Translator, *The Ecclesiastical History of M. Abbé Fleury.* 1842.

Bibliography: by A. Läpple, in *Newman Studien 1* edited by H. Fries and W. Becker, 1948.

Reading List: *The Life of Newman* by Wilfrid Ward, 1912; *Newman* by C. F. Harrold, 1945; *The Imperial Intellect: A Study of Newman's Educational Ideal* by A. D. Culler, 1955; *Newman* (biography) by Meriol Trevor, 2 vols., 1962; *Newman* by C. S. Dessain, 1966 (includes bibliography); *The Boundaries of Fiction: Carlyle, Macaulay, Newman* by George L. Levine, 1968; *Hebrew and Hellene in Victorian England: Newman, Arnold, and Pater* by David J. DeLaura, 1969; *Newman and the Common Tradition* by John Coulson, 1970; *Newman: The Consolation of Mind* by T. Vargish, 1970; *The Principle of Reserve in the Writings of Newman* by Robin C. Selby, 1975.

*   *   *

As one of the seminal thinkers of the nineteenth century, John Henry Newman has had a profoundly formative influence on modern theology and he is now regarded as one of the greatest Catholic theologians. But Newman is also one of the major Victorian prose writers, whose work can be studied alongside that of Carlyle, Ruskin, and Arnold, although he surpasses them in the sheer variety of his subject matter. The works, in more than forty volumes, include sermons, theology, philosophy, history, novels, essays, and verse. Nearly all his writings were "occasional," not least his two literary masterpieces, his *Apologia pro Vita Sua* and *The Idea of a University*. The one notable exception is *An Essay in Aid of a Grammar of Assent*, his principal achievement in the philosophy of religion, whose psychological penetration invites comparison with the introspective analysis of the best Victorian novels. His vast correspondence, still in the process of being published, will when complete comprise more than thirty volumes.

It is not easy to classify Newman as a writer, but arguably he is the most brilliant controversialist in English literature. His tracts and lectures during the Oxford Movement, in which he eloquently maintained the primitive Catholic character of the Church of England against both Rome and Reformation, culminated finally in *An Essay on the Development of Christian Doctrine*, the most famous theological work in the English language, which refuted his previous position by invoking the contemporary idea of evolution to justify the legitimacy of the Roman claims.

All Newman's power and subtlety as a controversialist were now turned to the defence of his new church, in the context of a culture and society traditionally hostile to Catholicism. A fresh exuberance of satire characterizes the two sets of lectures *Difficulties Felt by Anglicans* and *The Present Position of Catholics*. The controversy with Charles Kingsley in 1864 produced his classic autobiography, the *Apologia*, in which he attempted to vindicate his conversion by recounting the development of his religious views. The self-portrait is remarkable for its detachment and austere reserve, from which it derives paradoxically so much of its personal and persuasive appeal. The last chapter, "Position of My Mind since 1845," which is one of the finest pieces of sustained rhetoric in English, reflects Newman's growing disenchantment with the policies and practices of the contemporary Catholic Church.

Increasingly as a Catholic, Newman found himself fighting on two fronts, on the one hand for a dogmatic Christianity, on the other for an honest and open Church. The effect can be felt not only in the deepening and maturing of his theology but also in the development of an even more subtly modulated and nuanced rhetoric which achieves its finest expression in *The Idea of a University* where Newman depicts the ideal reconciliation of culture and religion.

Newman's earliest published poems were included in the Tractarian collection *Lyra Apostolica*, the best known of which is "Lead, Kindly Light" (1833). His single long poem *The Dream of Gerontius* has been made famous by Elgar's music. His two religious novels, *Loss and Gain* and *Callista*, are successful examples of the genre.

—I. T. Ker

NIN, Anaïs. American. Born in Paris in February 1903; emigrated to the United States in 1914; later naturalized. Educated in elementary school in New York; thereafter self-taught. Married Hugh Guiler (also called Ian Hugo) in 1920. Worked as a fashion and artist's model, 1918–20; studied psychoanalysis, then practised under Otto Rank in Europe, and briefly in New York; lived in Paris, 1930–40; writer from 1932; established Siana Editions, Paris, 1935; returned to New York, 1940. Member of the Advisory Board, Feminist Book Club, Los Angeles. Recipient: Prix Sévigne, 1971. Member, National Institute of Arts and Letters. *Died 14 January 1977.*

PUBLICATIONS

Fiction

> *House of Incest.* 1936.
> *Winter of Artifice.* 1939.
> *Under a Glass Bell.* 1944; as *Under a Glass Bell and Other Stories,* 1947.
> *This Hunger.* 1945.
> *Ladders to Fire.* 1946.
> *Children of the Albatross.* 1947.
> *Four Chambered Heart.* 1950.
> *A Spy in the House of Love.* 1954.
> *Solar Barque.* 1958.
> *Cities of the Interior.* 1959.
> *Seduction of the Minotaur.* 1961.
> *Collages.* 1964.
> *Cities of the Interior* (collection). 1974.
> *Waste of Timelessness and Other Early Stories.* 1977.
> *Delta of Venus: Erotica.* 1977.

Other

> *D. H. Lawrence: An Unprofessional Study.* 1932.
> *Realism and Reality.* 1946.
> *On Writing.* 1947.
> *The Diary,* edited by Gunther Stuhlmann. 6 vols., 1966–76; as *The Journals,* 6 vols., 1966–77.
> *The Novel of the Future.* 1968.
> *Unpublished Selections from the Diary.* 1968.
> *Nuances.* 1970.
> *An Interview with Nin,* by Duane Schneider. 1970.
> *The Nin Reader.* 1973.
> *A Photographic Supplement to the Diary.* 1975.
> *A Woman Speaks: The Lectures, Seminars, and Interviews of Nin,* edited by Evelyn Hinz. 1975.
> *In Favor of the Sensitive Man and Other Essays.* 1976.
> *Aphrodisiac,* with John Boyce. 1978.
> *Linotte: The Early Diary 1914–1920,* translated by Jean Sherman. 1978.

Bibliography: *Nin: A Bibliography* by Benjamin Franklin, 1973.

Reading List: *Nin* by Oliver Evans, 1968; *The Mirror and the Garden: Realism and Reality in the Writings of Nin* by Evelyn Hinz, 1973; *A Casebook on Nin* edited by Robert Zaller, 1974; *Collage of Dreams: The Writings of Nin* by Sharon Spencer, 1977.

*   *   *

Anaïs Nin's fiction may best be described as symphonic tone poems in prose, with their programmatic intermingling of similar themes and characters from one novel to another. Her characters are dancers, actresses, artists, musicians, and writers, all impelled by inner visions, illusions, or frustrations, who play their solo parts contrapuntally and always return as in the rondo form to the central female protagonist, with whom they all interact. Also characteristic of tone poems, Nin's style is psychologically discursive and impressionistic, with dreams and interior monologues substituting for the realism, dialogue, and clearly delineated plots of more traditional narratives. And her language is rhythmic, rich in sensuous imagery, and symbolic.

Nin's interests and opinions weave in and out of her novels like leitmotifs as contrapuntally as her characters do. Haunting all her fiction are evocations of music – jazz, opera, symphony – which Nin views as the inevitable preserver of memory and thus a barrier to all efforts to escape the past. Her faith in psychoanalysis as a tool for plumbing that past for constructive creative resources pervades all the novels, as does her belief in the permanency of art in contrast to the ephemerality of politics. Her fiction is totally apolitical; it focuses instead on the intricacies of intense physical and emotional relationships. Through these relationships, Nin also manifests her strong conviction in the fundamentally different sensibilities of men and women. Her men are usually unable to accept emotional responsibilities, are frustrated by their inability to act, and are drawn to the vision and sensitivity of nurturing women. Her women are seductive, submissive, and vulnerable because of their need for men; at the same time, they struggle to overcome this dependency on authority figures and to develop into independent human beings. Nin's depiction of women's search for a synthesis of these contrary facets of their personality along with her explicit rendering of female responses to sexual and emotional encounters – traditionally described from the male perspective – have made her novels attractive to a wide audience.

While her fiction need not be read in any particular order, there is a gradual evolution of control over the structure and language of her novels during the thirty years of their composition. Her craft developed from the earliest, *House of Incest*, a random collection of poetic impressions, to later ones like *Collages* which are more complex in characterization and more ambitious in structure, artistically shaped cycles of portraits radiating from a central figure. If Nin's fiction is read chronologically and concurrently with her diaries of the same period, the essential function of the latter to her fictional mode becomes strikingly evident. It was from her experiences and the portraits delineated in her diaries that Nin drew the material for all her novels, sometimes rewritten, often lifted intact into them. And the characteristics of her diaries parallel those in her fiction: musically counterpointed themes and characters; mystical, sensual, and poetic prose; and an enduring faith in the artistic life, psychoanalysis, and the differing sensibilities of the male and the female.

—Estelle C. Jelinek

NORRIS, (Benjamin) Frank(lin).   American.   Born in Chicago, Illinois, 5 March 1870; moved with his family to San Francisco, 1884. Educated at a school in Belmont, California, 1885–87; studied art at the Atelier Julien, Paris, 1887–89; studied English literature at the University of California, Berkeley, 1890–94, and writing at Harvard University, Cambridge, Massachusetts, 1894–95. Married Jeanette Black in 1900; one daughter. War Correspondent for the *San Francisco Chronicle* in South Africa during the Uitlander insurrection, 1895–96; member of the editorial staff of the *Wave*, San Francisco, 1896–97; War Correspondent, in Cuba, for *McClure's Magazine*, New York, 1898; Reader for Doubleday, publishers, New York, 1899–1902; settled on a ranch near Gilroy, California, 1902. *Died 25 October 1902*

PUBLICATIONS

Collections

(Complete Works). 10 vols., 1928.
The Letters, edited by Franklin Walker.   1956.

Fiction

Moran of the Lady Letty: A Story of Adventure off the California Coast. 1898; as
    Shanghaied, 1899.
McTeague: A Story of San Francisco.   1899; edited by Donald Pizer, 1977.
Blix.   1899.
A Man's Woman.   1900.
The Epic of Wheat: The Octopus: A Story of California.   1901; edited by Kenneth S.
    Lynn, 1958; *The Pit: A Story of Chicago,* 1903.
A Deal in Wheat and Other Stories of the New and Old West.   1903.
The Joyous Miracle.   1906.
The Third Circle.   1909.
Vandover and the Brute, edited by Charles G. Norris.   1914.

Verse

Yvernelle: A Legend of Feudal France.   1891.

Other

The Responsibilities of the Novelist and Other Literary Essays.   1903.
*The Surrender of Santiago: An Account of the Historic Surrender of Santiago to General
    Shafter, July 17, 1898.*   1917.
Two Poems and "Kim" Reviewed.   1930.
*Norris of "The Wave": Stories and Sketches from the San Francisco Weekly, 1893 to
    1897,* edited by Oscar Lewis.   1931.
The Literary Criticism, edited by Donald Pizer.   1964.
*A Novelist in the Making: A Collection of Student Themes and the Novels Blix and
    Vandover and the Brute,* edited by James D. Hart.   1971.

Bibliography: *Norris: A Bibliography* by Kenneth A. Lohf and Eugene P. Sheehy, 1959; *The
Merrill Checklist of Norris* by John S. Hill, 1970; in *Bibliography of American Literature* by
Jacob Blanck, 1973.

Reading List: *Norris: A Study* by Ernest Marchand, 1942; *Norris* by Warren French, 1962;
The Novels of Norris by Donald Pizer, 1966; *Norris: Instinct and Art* by William D.
Dillingham, 1969.

*   *   *

Although Frank Norris never wrote a work that could be considered a masterpiece, he
occupies an important place in American literary history. He is an early practitioner of

naturalism, along with his contemporaries Crane and Dreiser; he is an example of the French influence on American letters; and he is a noteworthy creator of the fictional landscape of California. Norris was a very uneven writer and capable of writing both popular magazine romance as well as serious fiction in the realistic/naturalistic tradition. Only two or three of his novels have demonstrated survival power.

As a young man Norris studied art in Paris, but there is no evidence that he read the French realists/naturalists at that time. He then was interested in romance, and his first work was a narrative poem, *Yvernelle: A Legend of Feudal France*, published while he was a student at the University of California. In 1894, when he entered Harvard as a special student of writing under Lewis Gates, he discovered Balzac, Flaubert, and especially Zola. He worked on his first novel *McTeague* during that year but didn't finish it until later after returning to California.

McTeague is a remarkable first novel, the most important piece of naturalism produced in America up to that time. It shows a strong Zola influence but is thoroughly naturalized in the United States. It is the story of a San Francisco dentist who is victimized by his inability to cope with marriage and complex social relationships. McTeague is a man of great strength but under the influence of alcohol loses his self-control. He is too stupid to cope with his wife, who becomes a miser, and a former friend, who causes him to lose his dental practice. The San Francisco locale is well done, and the disintegration of McTeague under the impact of forces he cannot control makes this a powerful naturalistic novel. The ending, unfortunately, is melodramatic and the symbolism far too obvious.

The Octopus, however, is a more mature work and is generally regarded as Norris's best achievement. It was the first of a projected trilogy to be called *The Epic of Wheat*. *The Octopus* deals with the growing of the wheat and is laid in the San Joaquin Valley of California. The ranching scenes, especially the planting of the wheat, are rendered with a good eye for the local color. Although there are many characters and several sub-plots, the story basically concerns the struggle between the ranchers and the railroad (the octopus) over shipping rates and land prices. It is an unequal battle because the railroad holds all the trump cards, and in the climactic episode of the novel the ranchers are defeated in an armed confrontation with the railroad deputies. There are a good many romantic elements in the novel and it ends on a note of cosmic optimism, but the work falls mainly in the category of naturalism. After the railroad has won the struggle, the President of the company argues that the railroad is a "force born out of certain conditions." No man can stop or control it any more than anyone can stop the wheat from growing.

The second novel in the trilogy was *The Pit*, completed before Norris's fatal appendectomy and published posthumously. It depicts the trading of the wheat on the Chicago grain exchange, and, while it is inferior to *The Octopus*, it tells an absorbing story of the protagonist's unsuccessful efforts to corner the wheat market. The third volume in the trilogy, which was to be called *The Wolf* and was to deal with the distribution of the wheat in a famine-stricken Europe, was never written.

Another of Norris's novels that also deserves attention is *Vandover and the Brute*, a work that he wrote before *McTeague* but never could get published. It was issued with some cuts, and perhaps some additions by his brother Charles, in 1914. The novel, a powerful study of disintegrating character, was too advanced for Doubleday, McClure and Co. in 1899. Vandover is weak-willed, indolent, badly brought up, and after his father dies, leaving him a handsome legacy, he squanders his money, is victimized by a friend, and ends in abject degradation.

Norris is perhaps the most notable disciple of Zola in American literature. He praised Zola passionately and often reread his favorite novels, *L'Assommoir, La Terre, Germinal, La Bête Humaine*. He researched his novels as Zola did, studying a manual of dentistry before writing *McTeague*, visiting a wheat farm while planning *The Octopus*. So pervasive was the influence that he joked about it in the inscription he wrote in the flyleaf of his wife's copy of *The Octopus*: "To my boss, Jeanette Norris, most respectfully ... Mr. Norris (The Boy Zola)."

Although he was influenced by Zola, Norris never got over the original impulse towards romance. His critical views as outlined in *The Responsibilities of the Novelist* favor the spontaneous, improvising story-teller. He cites Dumas as an excellent example. He also believed that all good novels must have some significant pivotal event – such as the battle between the ranchers and the railroad deputies in *The Octopus*. It is no wonder that Norris is not a thorough-going naturalist. In addition, Norris never took himself very seriously. He wrote too fast and between *McTeague* and *The Octopus* there is much trash. He was torn between the Kipling-Richard Harding Davis tradition and Zola.

—James Woodress

O'BRIEN, (Michael) Fitz-James. Irish. Born in Ireland, probably in County Limerick, in 1828; emigrated to the United States, 1852. Served in the American Civil War in the 7th New York Regiment, 1861–62: Aide-de-Camp to General Lander; commissioned Lieutenant, 1862; died of wounds. Left Ireland for London, 1849: Editor of *The Parlour Magazine*, 1851; settled in New York, 1852: Staff Member, *New York Daily Times*, 1852–53; regular contributor to *Harper's Monthly*, 1853–62, and Assistant Editor and Columnist ("Man about Town"), *Harper's Weekly*, 1857; Drama Critic, *New York Saturday Press*, 1858–59; press agent for actress Matilda Heron, 1859; Columnist ("Here and There"), *Vanity Fair*, 1860. *Died 6 April 1862.*

PUBLICATIONS

Collections

    The Poems and Stories, edited by William Winter. 1881.
    The Golden Ingot, The Diamond Lens, A Terrible Night, What Was It? 1921.
    The Fantastic Tales, edited by Michael Hayes. 1977.

Plays

    My Christmas Dinner (produced 1852).
    A Gentleman from Ireland (produced 1854).
    The Sisters, from a French play (produced 1854).
    Duke Humphrey's Dinner (produced 1856).
    The Tycoon; or, Young America in Japan, with Charles G. Rosenberg (produced 1860).

Verse

    Sir Brasil's Falcon. 1853.

Bibliography: in *Bibliography of American Literature* by Jacob Blanck, 1973.

Reading List: *O'Brien: A Literary Bohemian of the Eighteen-Fifties* by Francis Wolle, 1944 (includes bibliography).

*   *   *

After education in Ireland, and a short stint in London on the literary fringes, Fitz-James O'Brien emigrated to the United States and soon became a prominent member of New York's literary Bohemia that frequented Pfaff's, the old Hone House, and Windust's. O'Brien contributed lavishly to a number of American periodicals over the next six years among them the *American Whig Review, Putnam's Magazine, Harper's Weekly* and *Monthly, Vanity Fair, The Atlantic Monthly*, the *New York Times*. O'Brien was also the author of several plays, one, *A Gentleman from Ireland*, being presented successfully as late as 1895. His most imaginative story, "The Diamond Lens," appeared in 1858, winning him some fame, but at that point O'Brien's career as dandy author and bohemian faltered. He had acted as literary agent to M. L. Bateman, a theatrical director, and became involved with Matilda Heron, who appears to have had some responsibility for the collapse of O'Brien's fortunes. His splendid clothes, extensive library, elegant furnishings, soon disappeared; even his attractive personal appearance suffered a change for the worse with a broken nose from a professional pugilist. But he retained all his ebullience, and his end was brilliant. When the Civil War broke out, he joined the 7th Regiment of the National Guard of New York and won special mention for gallantry at the Battle of Bloomery Gap. A few days later he was wounded in the shoulder, indifferently nursed, and died of tetanus in 1862.

The general judgment on O'Brien is that he is more significant as personality than as author. Certainly, he wrote with unfortunate facility, and his verse is jaunty and negligible. Several of his stories, however, suggest a minor Poe with a dash of Hoffman. O'Brien had an undisciplined but powerful Gothic imagination that ranged over such topics as abnormal psychology, mesmerism, magic, alchemy, revenants, along with sharp flashes of prophetic imagination. "The Diamond Lens," a study of a mad microscopist, "The Wondersmith," with its aggressive manikin robots, and the ectoplasmic visitor of "What Was It?" retain some power to "electrify" the reader.

—Ian Fletcher

O'BRIEN, Flann. Pseudonym for Brian O'Nolan (Brian O'Nualláin). Irish. Born in Strabane, County Tyrone, Northern Ireland, 5 October 1911. Educated at Synge Street School; Blackrock College, Dublin; University College, Dublin (Editor, *Blather* magazine), B.A. 1932, M.A. 1935; travelling scholarship to Germany, 1933–34. Married Evelyn MacDonnell in 1948. Civil Servant, Dublin, 1935–53; Columnist, as Myles na gCopaleen ("Cruiskeen Lawn"), *Irish Times*, Dublin, 1940–66. *Died 1 April 1966.*

PUBLICATIONS

Collections

An O'Brien Reader, edited by Stephen Jones.   1978.

Fiction

At Swim-Two-Birds.   1939.
An Béal Bocht: nó, An Milléanach.   1941; translated by Patrick C. Power as *The Poor Mouth: A Bad Story about the Hard Life,* 1973.
The Hard Life: An Exegesis of Squalor.   1961.
The Dalkey Archive.   1964.
The Third Policeman.   1967.
Stories and Plays.   1973.
The Various Lives of Keats and Chapman, and The Brother, edited by Benedict Kiely.   1976.

Plays

Thirst (sketch; produced 1942).   In *Stories and Plays,* 1973.

The Insect Play, from a play by Karel Capek (produced 1943).
Faustus Kelly (produced 1943). 1943.
Máiréad Gillan (in Irish), from a play by Brinsley MacNamara. 1943.

Other

Cruiskeen Lawn. 1943.
The Best of Myles: A Selection from Cruiskeen Lawn, edited by Kevin O'Nolan. 1968.
Further Cuttings from Cruiskeen Lawn, edited by Kevin O'Nolan. 1977.
The Hair of the Dogma (from Cruiskeen Lawn). 1977.
The Other Myles, edited and translated by Patrick C. Power. 1978.

Reading List: *Myles: Portraits of Brian O'Nolan* edited by Timothy O'Keefe, 1973; *O'Brien: A Critical Introduction* by Anne Clissmann, 1975.

*   *   *

Flann O'Brien is usually mentioned with James Joyce and Samuel Beckett as one of twentieth-century fiction's great Irish innovators. To a certain extent this reputation is justified, but it is exclusively based on his first two novels, *At Swim-Two-Birds* and *The Third Policeman* (published posthumously). Daring as these two novels are in form and theme, and legitimate as it is to regard them as important exemplars of contemporary fictional categories such as "anti-realism" and "the literature of exhaustion," they comprise only one aspect of a career, the complexity of which is best appreciated when viewed as a whole in an Irish context. It is misleading to regard Flann O'Brien as essentially a modernist, and he differs from Joyce and Beckett in two significant, and possibly related, respects. He chose not to leave Ireland, though largely at odds with the life he found there and almost obsessively satirical in his view of it. Secondly, it is at least arguable that his career deteriorated rather than developed. Unlike his expatriate *confrères*, he chose not to pursue the artistic course suggested by the early novels, in comparison to which his post-war fiction, *The Hard Life* and *The Dalkey Archive*, are quiescent in tone, conventional in structure, and conservative in outlook.

Flann O'Brien's literary career is exclusively that of a novelist. Brian O'Nolan's other literary work – plays, translations, and above all his celebrated *Irish Times* column, "Cruiskeen Lawn" (translation, "full little jug") – was written under the pseudonym Myles na gCopaleen (a name borrowed from a character in Gerald Griffin's *The Collegians*, meaning "Myles of the ponies"). The production of this column filled a twenty-year interruption in the novelist's career, and, due to the non-appearance of *The Third Policeman* in correct chronological sequence, O'Brien's contemporary reputation was launched by the notoriety of *At Swim-Two-Birds* and *An Béal Bocht* (*The Poor Mouth*). Both these novels are devastating satires on, among other things, the nation's Gaelic cultural inheritance and the ways in which it was being handled both at an official and a popular level. Ignorance on the one hand and sentimentality and ineptitude on the other were conspiring to downgrade the status of "the plain people of Ireland." The attack is sharpest in the more concentrated *Poor Mouth*, but its orientation is wider in the earlier novel, and includes many other popular literary forms, Westerns and courtroom dramas in particular, as well as folk-tales and the ancient art of storytelling itself. A sense of misgiving about the supposed relationship between form and uniformity is the basis of many interesting formal experiments presented as a series of brilliant pastiches, a flair for which is to the fore in all his work. In the context, this goes a long way towards making the novel the "self-evident sham" and "work of reference" its author claims contemporary novels should be.

The link between these novels and their successors consists of their enacting the same teasing doubts about the value of the imagination. The most unnerving, complex, and successful of them − O'Brien's best novel − is *The Third Policeman*. Set in the hereafter it contemplates in a serenely lucid style a condition in which consciousness is of no avail. This central theme is embodied in de Selby, O'Brien's great comic creation, a crazed savant whose theories illustrate the epistemological pitfalls of imaginative excess. With its aura of lucidity, its deeply subversive empty centre, its representation of fear, this novel makes O'Brien close kin to Kafka and Sterne. In view of this it must be regretted that the postwar novels both suggest that doubts about the value of the imagination have become hardened beliefs. The stronger of the two, and the author's own favourite, *The Dalkey Archive*, reintroduces de Selby as an evil genius and presents a renunciation by Joyce of all his works except *Dubliners* (the work most frequently echoed in O'Brien's prose). It is a strong attack on imaginative over-reaching.

Far from being a deviation from his main concerns, "Cruiskeen Lawn" may be thought of as the optimum expression of them. The unevenness and formal indifference of newspaper work suited his increasingly querulous state of mind. It offered the author an outlet for verbal pranks, scalding satire, mordant cultural commentary, and, cumulatively, provides a vivid record of Dublin and environs in one of its more provincial periods, as well as a great deal of enjoyment. Its fragmentary, haphazard, and essentially non-imaginative character is typical of an author whose remarks on Joyce may well be applied to himself: "Humour, the handmaid of sorrow and fear creeps out endlessly in all [his] works.... With laughs he palliates the sense of doom that is the heritage of the Irish Catholic."

—George O'Brien

O'CONNOR, (Mary) Flannery. American. Born in Savannah, Georgia, 25 March 1925. Educated at the Women's College of Georgia, now Georgia College at Milledgeville, A.B. 1945; University of Iowa, Iowa City, M.F.A. 1947. Recipient: National Institute of Arts and Letters grant, 1957; O. Henry Award, 1957, 1963, 1965; Ford Foundation grant, 1959; Henry H. Bellaman Foundation award, 1964; National Catholic Book Award, 1966; National Book Award, 1972. D.Litt.: St. Mary's College, Kentucky, 1962; Smith College, Northampton, Massachusetts, 1963. *Died 3 August 1964.*

PUBLICATIONS

Collections

The Complete Stories. 1971.
The Habit of Being: Letters, edited by Sally Fitzgerald. 1978

Fiction

Wise Blood. 1952.
A Good Man Is Hard to Find and Other Stories. 1955; as *The Artificial Nigger and Other Tales,* 1957.

918

The Violent Bear It Away.   1960.
Everything That Rises Must Converge.   1965.

Other

Mystery and Manners: Occasional Prose, edited by Sally and Robert Fitzgerald.   1969.

Editor, *Death of a Child.*   1961.

Bibliography: *O'Connor and Caroline Gordon: A Reference Guide* by Robert E. Golden and Mary C. Sullivan, 1977.

Reading List: *O'Connor* by Stanley Edgar Hyman, 1966; *The Added Dimension: The Art and Mind of O'Connor* edited by Melvin J. Friedman and Lewis A. Lawson, 1966 (includes bibliography by Lawson); *The True Country: Themes in the Fiction of O'Connor* by Carter W. Martin, 1969; *The World of O'Connor* by Josephine Hendin, 1970; *Invisible Parade: The Fiction of O'Connor* by Miles Orvell, 1972; *O'Connor* by Preston M. Browning, Jr., 1974; *O'Connor* by Dorothy Tuck McFarland, 1976; *The Pruning Word: The Parables of O'Connor* by John R. May, 1976.

*   *   *

Flannery O'Connor belongs to a small group of twentieth-century writers whose work is profoundly religious, not through direct statement or preachment but because its informing theme and structure are theological. Flannery O'Connor was raised as a Roman Catholic in the Protestant southern United States, and she found in the "Christ-haunted" fundamentalist religious beliefs of that region much that awoke responsive chords in her, despite her basic theological differences with the Protestant faith. She brought to the portrayal of the people of her region a clear, hard, witty style, an unblinking eye, and a sense of both the divine and the ridiculous; and she used her violent portrayals of grotesque people to express a deep and unsentimental religious faith. Fairly early in her career, she developed lupus, an incurable disease that progressed inexorably to its conclusion in her death at the age of 39. Much of her work was produced after this disease had initially struck, and a great deal of her best fiction is concerned with death, and often with death as a release or means of salvation. Although this is a limited theme, and the range of her work often seems distressingly narrow, Flannery O'Connor worked within the limits of her art with great commitment, artistic integrity, high technical skill, and frequent success.

She is primarily a writer of short stories. The collection *A Good Man Is Hard to Find* and the posthumous *Everything That Rises Must Converge* contained nineteen examples of her best work in this form. *The Complete Stories* added twelve more. Her first novel, *Wise Blood,* is a weaving together of material originally written in short story form. Her only other novel was *The Violent Bear It Away.* (She was working on a third novel at the time of her death but apparently without the expectation of ever completing it.) Despite excellent elements in both her novels, O'Connor will survive as a master of the short story form. Her stories were based on what she called "anagogical vision ... the kind of vision that is able to see different levels of reality in one image or one situation." It is this anagogical element which has led to very extensive examination of levels of meaning in her stories by many critics.

Wise Blood is the story of the preacher Hazel Motes, called, he believed, to preach "the Church without Christ," a man who is driven by acts of violent grace finally to accept the Jesus whom he had denied, to blind himself, and to die, and in his death to achieve a kind of salvation. *The Violent Bear It Away* is the record of the efforts of a boy, Francis Marion Tarwater, to escape the prophetic calling bequeathed for him by his dead great-uncle. A much more tightly organized work than *Wise Blood, The Violent Bear It Away* is really the harrowing chronicle of the struggle of cosmic forces, represented by the religious great-uncle and a very modern uncle, for the soul of Francis Tarwater. The great-uncle ultimately triumphs.

O'Connor's short stories deal with simple Georgia people, hungry with a passionate desire for a spiritual dimension which the nature of their lives and their beliefs deny them. The usual pattern in these stories is that of a desperate search through extreme, violent, and grotesque actions that usually culminate in the entry of divine grace through some instrumentality that bestows salvation in the moment of death. The frantic and misdirected struggles of these human beings result in a violent but comic representation that seems in many ways to reflect the long tradition of American southwestern humor, with its extreme portrayals of grotesque people in violent and unusual situations. Her work is most like that of Erskine Caldwell in terms of the grotesqueness of her characters, the extravagance of her actions, the sharp and vigorous starkness of her prose, and her kind of pervasive comic sense. However, where Caldwell presents his characters as people distorted as a result of economic deprivation, Flannery O'Connor's world is the world of people rendered grotesque by their inability to satisfy their spiritual hungers. All of her characters can be explained in one sense in St. Augustine's phrase, "Our souls are restless till they find rest in Thee." Among her short stories of particular distinction are "A Good Man Is Hard to Find," "Good Country People," "The Artificial Nigger," "The Lame Shall Enter First," "Revelation," "Greenleaf," and the short novel "The Displaced Person."

In her short life Flannery O'Connor accomplished much in her intense art. Narrow though her range and subjects are, they are pursued with great distinction and great force. Ultimately she will remain a minor figure in American letters, but a minor figure of enormous challenge, subtlety, and accomplishment.

—C. Hugh Holman

O'CONNOR, Frank. Pseudonym for Michael Francis O'Donovan. Irish. Born in Cork in 1903. Educated at the Christian Brothers College, Cork. Fought in the Irish Civil War; worked for the Ministry of Information in London during World War II. Married 1) Evelyn Bowen in 1939, two sons and one daughter; 2) Harriet Randolph Rich in 1953, one daughter. Librarian in Cork until 1928, then in Dublin, writer from 1930; Director of the Abbey Theatre, London; lived in the United States during the 1950's. Litt.D.: University of Dublin, 1962. *Died 10 March 1966.*

PUBLICATIONS

Collections

Day Dreams and Other Stories, and The Holy Door and Other Stories, edited by Harriet Sheehy. 2 vols., 1973.

Fiction

Guests of the Nation (stories).   1931.
The Saint and Mary Kate.   1932.

Bones of Contention and Other Stories.   1936.
Dutch Interior.   1940.
Three Tales.   1941.
Crab Apple Jelly: Stories and Tales.   1944.
Selected Stories.   1946.
The Common Chord: Stories and Tales.   1947.
Traveller's Samples: Stories and Tales.   1951.
The Stories.   1952.
More Stories.   1954.
Stories.   1956.
Domestic Relations: Short Stories.   1957.
My Oedipus Complex and Other Stories.   1963.
Collection Two and *Three* (stories).   2 vols., 1964–69.
A Set of Variations (stories).   1969.

Plays

The Invincibles, with Hugh Hunt (produced 1938).
Moses' Rock, with Hugh Hunt (produced 1938).
In the Train, with Hugh Hunt (produced 1954).   In *The Genius of the Irish Theatre,*
    edited by S. Barnet and others, 1960.
The Statue's Daughter (produced 1971).   In *Journal of Irish Literature 4,* January 1975.

Verse

Three Old Brothers and Other Poems.   1936.

Other

The Big Fellow: A Life of Michael Collins.   1937; as *Death in Dublin: Michael Collins
    and the Irish Revolution,* 1937; revised edition, 1965.
A Picture Book (on Ireland).   1943.
Towards an Appreciation of Literature.   1945.
The Art of the Theatre.   1947.
Irish Miles.   1947.
The Road to Stratford.   1948; revised edition, as *Shakespeare's Progress,* 1960.
Leinster, Munster and Connaught   1950.
The Mirror in the Roadway: A Study of the Modern Novel.   1956.
An Only Child (autobiography).   1961.
The Lonely Voice: A Study of the Short Story.   1963.
The Backward Look: A Survey of Irish Literature.   1967.
My Father's Son (autobiography).   1968.

Editor, *Modern Irish Short Stories.*   1957.
Editor, *A Book of Ireland.*   1959.
Editor and Translator, *Kings, Lords, and Commons: An Anthology from the Irish.*   1959.
Editor and Translator, with David Greene, *A Golden Treasury of Irish Poetry A.D. 600 to
    1200.*   1967.
Translator, *The Wild Bird's Nest.*   1932.
Translator, *Lords and Commons.*   1938.
Translator, *The Fountain of Magic.*   1939.

Translator, *A Lament for Art O'Leary*, by Eileen O'Connell. 1940.
Translator, *The Midnight Court: A Rhythmical Bacchanalia*, by Bryan Merriman. 1945.
Translator, *The Little Monasteries: Poems*. 1963.

Reading List: *Michael/Frank: Studies on O'Connor* edited by Maurice Sheehy, 1969 (includes bibliography); *O'Connor: An Introduction* by Maurice Wohlgelernter, 1977.

*   *   *

Although he was productive in many literary fields – translator, critic, novelist – Frank O'Connor's most notable achievement is in the short story. To him is largely due credit for putting the modern Irish short story on the international literary map. The recurrent themes of his short fiction are loneliness, the problematic quest for personal independence, and the difficulties of coping with inherited responsibilities. His characters are drawn largely from the somewhat dormant world of middle- and lower-middle-class Irish provincial life of the post-Independence period. They are, typically, caught in a network of circumstances created by the dominant presence of structures and institutions not entirely of their own making. The most prominent of these are marriage, family life, and the Church. It is comparatively rare for an O'Connor character to have full control over his life, and less common for such control to be used fruitfully.

O'Connor used these themes to serve various ends. They are a means of reflecting upon the new Ireland ("Fish for Friday"), to the creation of which O'Connor contributed (though haphazardly, as his volumes of autobiography insist) as a member of the Republican forces. In this light, thoughts on the pitfalls of idealism are also much in evidence ("Anchors," "A Story by Maupassant"), which gives the stories their celebrated Chekhovian colouring. Another feature is the revelation of the man behind the social role. O'Connor's later stories tend to dwell on the lives of priests and doctors, and the vulnerabilities of these professions. Perhaps O'Connor's best-known stories, however, are his studies of children ("My Oedipus Complex," "Babes in the Wood"), some of which are semi-autobiographical. These children are allowed successfully to negotiate social norms in a much more idiosyncratic and refreshingly animated manner than are the author's adults, though like them they are ultimately, and essentially, powerless.

As might be expected from a writer who more than once declared himself to be a nineteenth-century realist, O'Connor's stories are not notable for their technical innovations. His belief that a story should have the sound of a man speaking, however, is an interesting solution to problems of authorial presence, and lends to the stories – particularly those about children – an engaging tone, confirming a basically sympathetic attitude to his characters (or, to enlarge on his debt to Chekhov, perhaps one should say a critically sympathetic attitude). O'Connor's style in fiction is, like his material, prosaic, despite its attractive tone, and represses with surprising consistency the lyric and intuitive side of his talent present elsewhere in his output.

Next in order of significant achievement are his verse translations from the Irish. Here he touched very little that he did not adorn. These poems – and most of his translations are poems in their own right – have a winning deftness of form and economy of style. Of neither of his two novels can this be said, and of all his works these are probably least read. His criticism, while wide-ranging, is only very occasionally penetrating and is marred by hasty judgements and a thin central argument, showing the strengths and weaknesses of an almost wholly self-educated mind.

The extent of Frank O'Connor's enduring contribution to modern Irish literature must remain a matter of conjecture, despite his wide popularity. His translations will last, and the stories, at the very least, reveal a bemused and perhaps somewhat bitter mind coping with the vicissitudes of Irish life in a critical transitional period.

—George O'Brien

O'FAOLÁIN, Seán. Irish. Born in Cork, 22 February 1900. Educated at University College, Cork, M.A. 1925; Harvard University, Cambridge, Massachusetts (Commonwealth Fellow, 1926–28; John Harvard Fellow, 1928–29), 1926–29, M.A. 1929. Served in the Irish Republican Army. Married Eileen Gould in 1928; two children, including the writer Julia O'Faolain. Lecturer in English, Boston College, 1929, and St. Mary's College, Strawberry Hill, Twickenham, Middlesex, 1929–33; full-time writer from 1933; formerly Editor of *The Bell*, Dublin. Director, Arts Council of Ireland, 1957–59. Lives in County Dublin.

PUBLICATIONS

Fiction

Midsummer Night Madness and Other Stories.   1932.
A Nest of Simple Folk.   1933.
There's a Birdie in the Cage (story).   1935.
Bird Alone.   1936.
A Born Genius (story).   1936.
A Purse of Coppers: Short Stories.   1937.
Come Back to Erin.   1940.
Teresa and Other Stories.   1947; as *The Man Who Invented Sin and Other Stories*, 1948.
The Finest Stories.   1957; as *The Stories*, 1958.
I Remember! I Remember! (stories).   1961.
The Heat of the Sun: Stories and Tales.   1966.
The Talking Trees (stories).   1970.
Foreign Affairs and Other Stories.   1976.
Selected Stories.   1978.

Plays

She Had to Do Something (produced 1937).   1938.
The Train to Banbury (broadcast 1947).   In *Imaginary Conversations*, edited by Rayner Heppenstall, 1948.

Radio Play: *The Train to Banbury*, 1947.

Other

The Life Story of Eamon de Valera.   1933.
Constance Markievicz; or, The Average Revolutionary: A Biography.   1934.
King of the Beggars: A Life of Daniel O'Connell.   1938.
De Valera.   1939.
An Irish Journey.   1940.
The Great O'Neill: A Biography of Hugh O'Neill, Earl of Tyrone, 1550–1616.   1942.
The Story of Ireland.   1943.
The Irish: A Character Study.   1947; revised edition, 1970.
The Short Story.   1948.
A Summer in Italy.   1949.
Newman's Way: The Odyssey of John Henry Newman.   1952.

923

South to Sicily. 1953; as *Autumn in Italy.* 1953.
The Vanishing Hero: Studies in Novelists of the Twenties. 1956.
Vive Moi! (autobiography). 1964.

Editor, *Lyrics and Satires from Tom Moore.* 1929.
Editor, *Autobiography,* by Theobald Wolfe Tone. 1937.
Editor, *The Silver Branch: A Collection of the Best Old Irish Lyrics.* 1938.
Editor, *The Adventures of Handy Andy,* by Samuel Lover. 1945.
Editor, *Short Stories: A Study in Pleasure.* 1961.

Reading List: *O'Faoláin: A Critical Introduction* by Maurice Harmon, 1966; *O'Faoláin* by Paul A. Doyle, 1968; *The Short Stories of O'Faoláin: A Study in Descriptive Techniques* by Joseph Storey Rippier, 1976.

*   *   *

Seán O'Faoláin is the doyen of modern Irish letters. His journalism, criticism, and fiction have, over the past fifty years, argued for liberal, secular, pluralistic values to obtain in the state that he, as a member of the republican forces, had helped bring into being. More than any of his contemporaries, he has consistently argued for the distinctive importance of literature to society (particularly to one as philistine and defensive as the emerging Irish Free State), as well as for the necessarily radical role writers must adopt to keep their culture alive. Broadly speaking, O'Faoláin has conducted this argument in two ways: mainly by precept up to the late 1940's, and thereafter mainly by example.

Artistically speaking, O'Faoláin's reputation rests on his achievements in the short story. His novels, however, deserve attention (especially *Bird Alone*) if only for their articulation of the cultural impasse which nationalist rhetoric and a repressive Church had created. All three novels depict a protagonist who, try as he might, finds nothing to identify with but this impasse. The artistic result is a curious sense of incompleteness deriving, paradoxically, from the evident finality of the protagonist's condition. Some of the early stories – those collected in *A Purse of Coppers*, for example – are similarly limited. Taken as a whole, however, O'Faoláin's stories show his evolution as a writer, a sense of evolution itself noticeable in his increasing flexibility and mellowness of tone, a much more deft use of irony, and a growing interest in middle-class characters and international (usually Italian) settings. This development is paralleled in the different ways O'Faoláin handles his main theme, which in a general way might be said to be that individuality must be viewed as a challenge. In the early stories, the individual was used as an exemplification of his society's teething troubles. With frequently heavy-handed irony, individuality was presented as a liability. Later collections – those following *Teresa* – demand that the individual add the quirky impress of his own nature to whatever he encounters, implicitly asserting that he is free to do so: individuality is now a *sine qua non.*

O'Faoláin's biographies, which must be ranked next to his stories in terms of artistic achievement, are also concerned with individuality, and it is tempting to view them as intellectual quarries from which the material for the related, more delicately wrought perceptions of the stories were won. The biographies are of subjects whose careers crystallise a decisive turning point in the history of their times. In his ability to meet the historical and political demands of the day by his intellectual and emotional energy, the individual becomes a hero – an ideal exemplar – of his own culture. In contrast to the limpid style usually found in the fiction, these·studies are impressionistic and urgent in style and tone. The most impressive of them is *The Great O'Neill.*

More obviously than that of any of his contemporaries, Seán O'Faoláin is assured of a significant place in the history of modern Irish literature. His fiction is often marred by a sense of being animated by strictly intellectual concerns, and by a too obvious awareness of his characters' vulnerability. The "blend of reason and sensibility" which he has said his work aims for is, generally speaking, an aspiration rather than an attainment. However, given the range and quality of his contribution – including, as well as works of enduring literary value, his editorship of *The Bell*, travel books, and an autobiography – future generations may well gratefully conclude that his combative career is his greatest achievement.

—George O'Brien

O'FLAHERTY, Liam. Irish.   Born in the Aran Islands, County Galway, 28 August 1896. Educated at Rockwell College, Cashel, 1908–12; Blackrock College, 1912–13; University College, Dublin, 1913–14. Organized a Republican corps in 1913, and fought for the Republicans in the Irish Civil War; served with the British Army during World War I; invalided out of service, 1918. Travelled around the world, working as a deckhand, porter, filing clerk, and farm labourer, in Asia, South America, the United States and Canada, 1918–21; returned to Ireland, and settled in Dublin; full-time writer from 1922. Recipient: Black Memorial Prize, 1926.

PUBLICATIONS

Fiction

Thy Neighbour's Wife.   1923.
Spring Sowing (stories).   1924.
The Black Soul.   1924.
The Informer.   1925.
Mr. Gilhooley.   1926.
The Tent and Other Stories.   1926.
The Fairy-Goose and Two Other Stories.   1927.
Red Barbara and Other Stories.   1928.
The Assassin.   1928.
The House of Gold.   1929.
Return of the Brute.   1929.
The Mountain Tavern and Other Stories.   1929.
The Ecstasy of Angus (story).   1931.
The Puritan.   1931.
Skerrett.   1932.
The Wild Swan and Other Stories.   1932.
The Martyr.   1933.
Hollywood Cemetery.   1935.
Famine.   1937.
The Short Stories.   1937.
Land.   1946.
Two Lovely Beasts and Other Stories.   1948.
Insurrection.   1950.
Dúil (Desire) (story).   1953.

The Stories. 1956.
Selected Stories, edited by D. A. Garrity. 1958.
The Wounded Cormorant and Other Stories (selected stories). 1973.
The Pedlar's Revenge and Other Stories, edited by A. A. Kelly. 1976.
The Wilderness. 1978.

Plays

Darkness. 1926.

Screenplays: *The Devil's Playground*, with others, 1937; *Last Desire*, 1939.

Other

The Life of Tim Healy. 1927.
A Tourist's Guide to Ireland. 1929.
Two Years. 1930.
Joseph Conrad: An Appreciation. 1930.
I Went to Russia. 1931.
A Cure for Unemployment. 1931.
Shame the Devil (autobiography). 1934.

Bibliography: *O'Flaherty: An Annotated Bibliography* by Paul A. Doyle, 1972.

Reading List: *The Literary Vision of O'Flaherty* by John Zneimer, 1971; *O'Flaherty* by Paul A. Doyle, 1971; *The Novels of O'Flaherty: A Study in Romantic Realism* by Patrick F. Sheeran, 1974; *O'Flaherty, The Storyteller* by A. A. Kelly, 1977.

*   *   *

Chronologically speaking, Liam O'Flaherty is a member of the generation of Irish writers which emerged after the establishment of the Irish Free State in 1921. Yet, while his output is at least as significant as that of such notable contemporaries as Seán O'Faoláin and Frank O'Connor, it bears little thematic, stylistic, or formal relation to theirs. O'Flaherty is antagonistic to cultural determinism. His style is predominantly energetic. And he is virtually the sole Irish writer of his day to persist in using the novel as a quasi-philosophical vehicle.

O'Flaherty's novels are primarily concerned with matters of the mind, chiefly spiritual. This concern is characteristically presented as being problematic. The typical O'Flaherty protagonist – of, for example, *Mr. Gilhooley* and *Skerrett* – is tormented by impulses of transcendence, which he interprets as the only dependable means of realising his own nature. Because the idea of self-realisation is conceived of problematically, it receives its fictional enactment in terms of challenge. The vitality of O'Flaherty's novels derives from his characters' willingness to rise to this challenge, to identify with it, and to live out its demands, regardless of the usually enormous psychic cost. The vividness of this struggle is reinforced by an extremely strong narrative sense and tempestuous verbal flair. These two features not infrequently contrive an air of melodrama and bathos, from which none of O'Flaherty's novels is entirely free. Gripping as the spiritual struggle is, there is a sense of obsession attached to it, and its exemplars are generally maladjusted or otherwise flawed. The confrontation they enact invariably precipitates their ruin, which diminishes the novels' intellectual coherence, leaving the reader impressed by the rhetoric of struggle but confused as to its actual value.

926

By eschewing thought and dispensing with self-absorbed protagonists, O'Flaherty's short fiction dwells on the most telling artistic feature of the novels, their immediacy of impact and sense of presence. It is generally agreed that O'Flaherty is the greatest Irish short-story writer. His unique innovation was to conceive of stories (or, bearing their superbly visual effects in mind, to draw sketches) largely devoid of human beings — cameos of fish, birds, and other undomesticated creatures: "The Rockfish," "The Wild Swan." But even stories such as "Two Lovely Beasts" and "Red Barbara" which have thematic echoes of the novels tend to portray their characters as natural phenomena, largely immune from the trials of consciousness. As in the novels, the quality of O'Flaherty's stories is very erratic. At their best, however, they achieve a rapturous attentiveness more artistically complete than anything in the longer works.

Of O'Flaherty's other writings the most important are the volumes of autobiography — *Two Years, I Went to Russia* and *Shame the Devil* — depicting the subjectivity of his formative artistic years, and his attempts to offset it by questing for archetypal experiences. As well as acknowledging Dostoevsky's influence, these books, perhaps more subtly than the novels, show its extent.

O'Flaherty's existential and primitivist concerns, and the expressionistic vigour of his prose, ensure him of a small place in the history of Modernism. His contribution to Irish literature is more difficult to assess. At the very least however, his *oeuvre* represents a range of preoccupations new to Irish fiction, and, crude though his mode of investigating them may often appear, his work can be regarded as a stimulating and still largely undeveloped prototype.

—George O'Brien

O'HARA, John (Henry). American. Born in Pottsville, Pennsylvania, 31 January 1905. Educated at Fordham Preparatory School; Keystone State Normal School; Niagara Preparatory School, Niagara Falls, New York, 1923–24. Married 1) Helen Petit in 1931 (divorced, 1933); 2) Belle Mulford Wylie in 1937 (died, 1954), one daughter; 3) Katherine Barnes Bryan in 1955. Reporter for the *Pottsville Journal*, 1924–26 and for the *Tamaqua Courier*, Pennsylvania, 1927; Reporter for the *New York Herald-Tribune*, and for *Time* magazine, New York, 1928; rewrite man for the *New York Daily Mirror*, radio columnist (as Franey Delaney) for the *New York Morning Telegraph*, and Managing Editor of the *Bulletin Index* magazine, Pittsburgh, 1928–33; full-time writer from 1933; film writer, for Paramount and other studios, from 1934; Columnist ("Entertainment Week"), *Newsweek*, New York, 1940–42; Pacific War Correspondent for *Liberty* magazine, New York, 1944; Columnist ("Sweet and Sour"), *Trenton Sunday Times-Adviser*, New Jersey, 1953–54; lived in Princeton, New Jersey, from 1954; Columnist ("Appointment with O'Hara"), *Collier's*, New York, 1954–56, ("My Turn"), *Newsday*, Long Island, New York, 1964–65, and ("The Whistle Stop"), *Holiday*, New York, 1966–67. Recipient: New York Drama Critics Circle Award, 1952; Donaldson Award, 1952; National Book Award, 1956; American Academy of Arts and Letters Award of Merit Medal, 1964. Member, National Institute of Arts and Letters, 1957. *Died 11 April 1970.*

Collections

Selected Letters, edited by Matthew J. Bruccoli.   1978.

Fiction

Appointment in Samarra.   1934.
BUtterfield 8.   1935.
The Doctor's Son and Other Stories.   1935.
Hope of Heaven.   1938.
Files on Parade (stories).   1939.
Pal Joey (stories).   1940.
Pipe Night (stories).   1945.
Here's O'Hara (omnibus).   1946.
Hellbox (stories).   1947.
All the Girls He Wanted (stories).   1949.
A Rage to Live.   1949.
The Farmers Hotel.   1951.
Ten North Frederick.   1955.
A Family Party.   1956.
The Great Short Stories of O'Hara.   1956.
Selected Short Stories.   1956.
From the Terrace.   1958.
Ourselves to Know.   1960.
Sermons and Soda Water (includes *The Girl on the Baggage Truck, Imagine Kissing
    Pete, We're Friends Again*).   3 vols., 1960.
Assembly (stories).   1961.
The Cape Cod Lighter (stories).   1962.
The Big Laugh.   1962.
Elizabeth Appleton.   1963.
49 Stories.   1963.
The Hat on the Bed (stories).   1963.
The Horse Knows the Way (stories).   1964.
The Lockwood Concern.   1965.
Waiting for Winter (stories).   1966.
The Instrument.   1967.
And Other Stories.   1968.
Lovey Childs: A Philadelphian's Story.   1969.
The O'Hara Generation (stories).   1969.
The Ewings.   1972.
The Time Element and Other Stories, and *Good Samaritan and Other Stories*, edited by
    Albert Erskine.   2 vols., 1972–74.
The Second Ewings.   1977.

Plays

Pal Joey, music by Richard Rodgers, lyrics by Lorenz Hart, from the stories by O'Hara
    (produced 1940).   1952.
Five Plays (includes *The Farmers Hotel, The Searching Sun, The Champagne Pool,
    Veronique, The Way It Was*).   1961.

Screenplays: *I Was an Adventuress*, with Karl Tunberg and Don Ettlinger, 1940; *He Married His Wife*, with others, 1940; *Moontide*, 1942; *On Our Merry Way* (episode), 1948; *The Best Things in Life Are Free*, with William Bowers and Phoebe Ephron, 1956.

Other

Sweet and Sour (essays). 1954.
My Turn (newspaper columns). 1966.
A Cub Tells His Story. 1974.
An Artist Is His Own Fault: O'Hara On Writers and Writings, edited by Matthew J. Bruccoli. 1977.

Bibliography: *O'Hara: A Checklist*, 1972, and *O'Hara: A Descriptive Bibliography*, 1978, both by Matthew J. Bruccoli.

Reading List: *The Fiction of O'Hara* by Russell E. Carson, 1961; *O'Hara* by Sheldon Norman Grebstein, 1966; *O'Hara* by Charles C. Walcutt, 1969; *O'Hara* (biography) by Finis Farr, 1973; *The O'Hara Concern: A Biography* by Matthew J. Bruccoli, 1975.

*   *   *

John O'Hara's 374 short stories and 18 novels record the changing habits and values of the United States from World War I to the Viet Nam conflict. O'Hara began writing as a reporter, editor, press agent and script writer; he worked first in his native Eastern Pennsylvania coal region (Pottsville – his fictional Gibbsville), and later in New York and Hollywood. His short stories began appearing in the *New Yorker* in 1928, and his first novel, *Appointment in Samarra*, identified him as a first-rate writer. His short stories range from short monologues, reminiscent of Ring Lardner (whose influence he acknowledged), to hundred-page novellas that may be his finest work: O'Hara has been called America's best short-story writer. Through his involvement with the New York theatrical world – plus an acknowledged mastery of dialogue – he tried to write for the stage. Even though his *Pal Joey* became a hit Rodgers and Hart musical, O'Hara's *Five Plays* are a testament to his lack of success as a playwright.

As O'Hara's fame grew, it was often asserted that his first novel, *Appointment in Samarra*, was also his best. The fast pace and shifting point of view held the reader until the suicide of Julian English at the end, which is still being debated: did Gibbsville drive him to it (just after the Great Crash in 1929), or did the compulsion come from within him? Nearly all of O'Hara's stories hold the reader's interest in the same way: how will the characters develop and what will happen to them? O'Hara said he was picturing, as honestly as he could, how twentieth-century Americans were driven by money, sex, and a struggle for status – often to their own destruction. In 1935 O'Hara published *BUtterfield 8*, his only *roman à clef*. The heroine, Gloria Wandrous, is much like the Jazz Age celebrity Starr Faithfull, whose body was washed up on a Long Island beach in 1931. The novel was a popular success and extended O'Hara's fictional domain from Pennsylvania to New York City. *Hope of Heaven* pushed his range much farther, to Hollywood. But there is a link between all three of the first novels: the protagonist-narrator (and Hollywood scriptwriter) of *Hope of Heaven* is Jimmy Malloy, a former Gibbsville reporter who has covered the Gloria Wandrous murder/suicide/accident.

More than a hundred short stories and sketches were published in *The Doctor's Son and Other Stories*, *Files on Parade*, and *Pipe Night*. These tightly written stories present character and situation satirically, but O'Hara is not callous about the loneliness, misery, and degradation he reveals – on Broadway or in Gibbsville. The best-known of these stories are the heavily ironic monologues (in the form of letters) of Joey Evans, a night club master of ceremonies. *Pal Joey*, a collection of fourteen stories, became a Rodgers and Hart musical. Joey is a heel, an anti-hero, and the sexual innuendo was shocking in 1940; but *Pal Joey* also had a strong plot line and has been called the first realistic American musical.

A Rage to Live is the first of O'Hara's long and elaborately documented novels. The time period is 1900 to 1920 and the locale Fort Penn (Harrisburg, Pennsylvania), but the serious social history was obscured for many readers by his heroine's lack of sexual control. In *Ten North Frederick* O'Hara moved the setting back to Gibbsville, where Joe Chapin earns great wealth and prestige with the help of his family name, a Yale law degree, and considerable intelligence. But Chapin aspires to be President of the United States: he attempts to buy the lieutenant governorship, is duped by an Irish politician, and drinks himself to death in "the quiet, gentlemanly, gradual way in which he had lived his life," in Sheldon Norman Grebstein's words. *From the Terrace* is an even larger and more ambitious work: O'Hara tells the story of Alfred Eaton, a small-town Pennsylvania boy who goes to New York and Washington, becomes a great financier and government official, and finally discovers that his life is empty and meaningless. O'Hara regarded it as his masterpiece.

O'Hara wrote prodigiously in the last 15 years of his life. *Ourselves to Know*, a big novel set in Eastern Pennsylvania, uses a circular technique and shifting perspective in trying to understand and explain Robert Millhouser, who killed his wife and was acquitted in a murder trial. In the Foreword to *Sermons and Soda Water*, three novellas all filtered through the consciousness of Jimmy Malloy, O'Hara explains why he used this unpopular and unprofitable form instead of expanding each of the stories into a 350-page novel:

> I want to get it all down on paper while I can. I am now fifty-five years old and I have lived with as well as in the Twentieth Century from its earliest days. The United States in this Century is what I know, and it is my business to write about it to the best of my ability, with the sometimes special knowledge I have. The Twenties, the Thirties, and the Forties are already history, but I cannot be content to leave their story in the hands of the historians and the editors of picture books. I want to record the way people talked and thought and felt, and to do it with complete honesty and variety.

The Big Laugh is O'Hara's second Hollywood novel: his monologues of classic Hollywood types are bawdy, funny, and authentic. *Elizabeth Appleton* is an academic novel, focused on a weekend when the dean's wife sees her husband passed over for the presidency of a small Pennsylvania college. *The Lockwood Concern*, O'Hara's last major novel, is "a condensed big book" (400 pages): four generations of the family have lived in a small town near Gibbsville since 1840, but third-generation George Lockwood compulsively destroys the dynasty by driving his only son to a criminal career in California. Critics charged that O'Hara's protagonists often destroy themselves and their social fabric without explicable motivation.

There were three more novels to come. *The Instrument* explores the parasitism of playwright Yank Lucas: he deserts the star actress on opening night, writes a new play on their relationship, and she commits suicide. *Lovey Childs: A Philadelphian's Story* deals with a Main Line heiress and her playboy husband (Sky Childs), who became Twenties celebrities; after divorce she achieves a stable marriage with her proper Philadelphia cousin. This is O'Hara's weakest novel, but it aroused speculation about his interest in lesbianism. At his death in 1970 O'Hara had completed *The Ewings* and was at work on a sequel; better than the two previous novels, it is the story of a young Cleveland lawyer and his wife in the booming economy of World War I. Six short story collections appeared in the 1960's, and two more after O'Hara's death.

Before World War II an "official" review of O'Hara had been established. John Peale Bishop (1937) found him skillful but cynical, a post-Jazz Age follower of Hemingway and Fitzgerald. Edmund Wilson (1940) recognized that O'Hara was a social commentator and that his writing was "of an entirely different kind from Hemingway's." O'Hara resembles Fitzgerald more than any writer, and their friendship – O'Hara proof-read Fitzgerald's *Tender Is the Night* – was renewed during Fitzgerald's last bitter days in Hollywood. O'Hara was a staunch Fitzgerald champion when that was not a popular cause, and wrote the introduction to the *Viking Portable Fitzgerald* (1945). When the big O'Hara novels became best sellers in the 1950's and 1960's, critics objected to the "mere accuracy" of his dialogue and detail, to the "surface reality" of his American scenes, and to the social climbing and sexual conduct of his characters. But, even when they found him "a hack writer," critics continued to review his books, and John Steinbeck called O'Hara the most underrated writer in America. His work lives, no matter how unfashionably. Though some critics object that his characters are not worth writing about, O'Hara's readers do not agree; and they admire the clarity of his style even though the critics would like more complexity and ambiguity. The academic world objects to O'Hara's view of life and literature, but if future generations seek an American Balzac to lay bare life in the United States from 1900 to 1970, they will find John O'Hara the most complete, the most accurate, and the most readable chronicler.

—Clarence A. Glasrud

OLIPHANT, Margaret (Oliphant, née Wilson). Scottish. Born in Wallyford, Midlothian, 4 April 1828. Married Francis Wilson Oliphant in 1852; two sons. Full-time writer from 1849; regular contributor to *Blackwood's Magazine*, Edinburgh, 1852 until her death. *Died 25 June 1897.*

PUBLICATIONS

Fiction

Passages in the Life of Mrs. Margaret Maitland.   1849.
Caleb Field: A Tale of the Puritans.   1851.
Merkland; or, Self-Sacrifice.   1851.
Memoirs and Resolutions of Adam Graeme of Mossgray.   1852.
Katie Stewart.   1853.
Harry Muir: A Story of Scottish Life.   1853.
The Quiet Heart.   1854.
Magdalen Hepburn.   1854.
Lilliesleaf.   1855.
Zaidee.   1856.
The Athelings; or, The Three Gifts.   1857.
The Days of My Life.   1857.
Sundays.   1858.
The Laird of Norlaw.   1858.
Orphans.   1858.
Agnes Hopetoun's Schools and Holidays.   1859.
Lucy Crofton.   1860.
The House on the Moor.   1861.

The Last of the Mortimers. 1862.
Chronicles of Carlingford: The Rector and the Doctor's Family, Salem Chapel, The Perpetual Curate, Miss Marjoribanks, Phoebe, Junior. 14 vols., 1863–76.
Heart and Cross. 1863.
Agnes. 1865.
A Son of the Soil. 1865.
Madonna Mary. 1866.
The Brownlows. 1868.
The Minister's Wife. 1869.
John: A Love Story. 1870.
The Three Brothers. 1870.
Squire Arden. 1871.
At His Gates. 1872.
Ombra. 1872.
May. 1873.
Innocent. 1873.
A Rose in June. 1874.
For Love and Life. 1874.
The Story of Valentine and His Brother. 1875.
Whiteladies. 1875.
The Curate in Charge. 1876.
Carità. 1877.
Mrs. Arthur. 1877.
Young Musgrave. 1877.
The Primrose Path: A Chapter in the Annals of the Kingdom of Fife. 1878.
The Fugitives. 1879.
Within the Precincts. 1879.
The Two Mrs. Scudamores (stories). 1879.
The Greatest Heiress in England. 1879.
A Beleaguered City, with *The Awakening,* by Katharine S. Macquoid. 1879.
He That Will Not When He May. 1880.
Harry Joscelyn. 1881.
In Trust: The Story of a Lady and Her Lover. 1881.
A Little Pilgrim. 1882.
Hester. 1883.
It Was a Lover and His Lass. 1883.
The Ladies Lindores. 1883.
Sir Tom. 1883.
The Wizard's Son. 1883.
Two Stories of the Seen and the Unseen (*Old Lady Mary, The Open Door*). 1885.
Madam. 1885.
Oliver's Bride. 1885.
The Prodigals and Their Inheritance. 1885.
A Country Gentleman and His Family. 1886.
Effie Ogilvie: The Story of a Young Life. 1886.
A House Divided Against Itself. 1886.
A Poor Gentleman. 1886.
The Son of His Father. 1886.
The Land of Darkness, along with Some Further Chapters in the Experience of the Little Pilgrims. 1888.
Joyce. 1888.
The Second Son, with Thomas Bailey Aldrich. 1888.
Cousin Mary. 1888.
Neighbours on the Green: A Collection of Stories. 1889.

Lady Car. 1889.
Kirsteen: The Story of a Scotch Family Seventy Years Ago. 1890.
The Duke's Daughter, and The Fugitives. 1890.
Sons and Daughters. 1890.
The Mystery of Mrs. Blencarrow. 1890.
Janet. 1891.
The Railway Man and His Children. 1891.
The Heir Presumptive and the Heir Apparent. 1891.
Diana Trelawney. 1892; as *Diana,* 1892.
The Cuckoo in the Nest. 1892.
The Marriage of Elinor. 1892.
Lady William. 1893.
The Sorceress. 1893.
A House in Bloomsbury. 1894.
Who Was Lost and Is Found. 1894.
Sir Robert's Fortune. 1894.
Two Strangers. 1894.
Old Mrs. Tredgold. 1895.
The Two Marys (stories). 1896.
The Unjust Steward; or, The Minister's Debt. 1896.
The Lady's Walk (stories). 1897.
The Ways of Life: Two Stories. 1897.
A Widow's Tale and Other Stories. 1898.
That Little Cutty and Two Other Stories. 1898.

Other

The Life of Edward Irving, Minister of the National Scotch Church, London. 2 vols., 1862.
Francis of Assisi. 1868.
Historical Sketches of the Reign of George Second. 2 vols., 1869.
Memoir of Count de Montalembert: A Chapter of Recent French History. 1872.
The Makers of Florence: Dante, Giotto, Savonarola, and Their City. 1876.
Dress. 1876.
Dante. 1877.
Molière, with F. Tarver. 1879.
The Queen. 1880.
Cervantes. 1880.
The Literary History of England in the End of the Eighteenth and the Beginning of the Nineteenth Century. 3 vols., 1882.
Sheridan. 1883.
The Makers of Venice: Doges, Conquerors, Painters, and Men of Letters. 1887.
A Memoir of the Life of John Tulloch. 1888.
Royal Edinburgh: Her Saints, Kings, Prophets, and Poets. 1890.
Jerusalem, The Holy City: Its History and Hope. 1891; reprinted in part as *The House of David,* 1891.
Memoir of the Life of Laurence Oliphant and Alice Oliphant, His Wife. 1891.
The Victorian Age of English Literature, with F. R. Oliphant. 2 vols., 1892.
Thomas Chalmers, Preacher, Philosopher, and Statesman. 1893.
Historical Sketches of the Reign of Queen Anne. 1894; as *Historical Characters,* 1894.
A Child's History of Scotland. 1895; as *A History of Scotland for the Young,* 1895.
The Makers of Modern Rome. 1895.
Jeanne d'Arc: Her Life and Death. 1896.

Annals of a Publishing House: William Blackwood and His Sons, Their Magazine and Friends. 2 vols., 1897.
The Autobiography and Letters, edited by Mrs. Harry Coghill. 1899; revised edition, 1899.
Queen Victoria: A Personal Sketch. 1901.

Editor, *Memoirs of the Life of Anna Jameson,* by Geraldine Macpherson. 1878.

Reading List: "A Valiant Woman" by Katherine Moore, in *Blackwood's Magazine,* 1958; "Oliphant" by M. Lockhead, in *Quarterly Review,* 1961; *Everywhere Spoken Against* by Valentine Cunningham, 1975.

*   *   *

Margaret Oliphant was a minor writer in the best sense of that term. Her work at its finest displayed talent of a high order in a narrow range. What was not on a minor scale was her output – a prodigious number of novels, short stories, reviews, literary history, and biography – a monument to a full-time career as a woman of letters. The *Autobiography and Letters* is an attractive and moving document of such a literary life, of a talent forced into regular production in order to support a family virtually until her death.

Her contributions to *Blackwood's* over forty-six years represent the bulk of this effort. At its best her literary criticism is anything but hack work, perceptive assessments of a working novelist on her contemporaries. Several of her biographical sketches, on Edward Irving, and on John Tulloch, emerged as full scale biographies. Her literary histories, particularly *The Victorian Age of English Literature,* written with F. R. Oliphant, contains a wealth of detail and judgment which only a gargantuan amount of reading could have produced. But the best of her non-fiction, and probably the best known, is *Annals of a Publishing House: William Blackwood and His Sons, Their Magazine and Friends,* still the standard work on the publishing house and its famous magazine, and one of the most thorough studies of nineteenth-century publishing and periodical production.

But Mrs. Oliphant's reputation rests mainly and justifiably on her novels, ranging from early stories of Scottish life, *Passages in the Life of Mrs. Margaret Maitland* and *Katie Stewart,* to the blatant pot-boilers of the last years. Two notable strands emerge, the Scottish novels and the Chronicles of Carlingford. Of the later Scottish stories probably the best is *Kirsteen,* the story of a girl, driven from her highland home by a puritanical father, who establishes herself with full independence as a milliner in London – a heroine who exemplified Mrs. Oliphant's belief in the resourcefulness and independence of her sex.

But her place in literary history would have been secure had she written nothing but the Chronicles of Carlingford, stories of English provincial life set in a mythical town where everything is dominated by church and chapel. The novels were written hurriedly and sometimes during periods of acute personal stress. Yet despite these pressures the threads of the plots and the major characters for the entire series were established in the first two stories, "The Rector" and "The Doctor," published in three volumes as *The Rector and the Doctor's Family.* Mrs. Oliphant's fame as the chronicler of evangelical life rests on the disproportionate reputation of *Salem Chapel,* the second but by no means the best of the novels, which presents a series of affectionate portraits of a group of bacon and cheese merchants, poulterers, greengrocers, and dairymen, the pillars of the institution of the title. Their tea meetings, evening lectures, and congregational machinations over an erring pastor form the basis of the novel (unfortunately seriously marred by a "sensational" subplot), one of the few occasions in fiction where this stratum of society is so fully described. Mrs. Oliphant later confessed that much of her material was drawn from her observations of chapel life in Liverpool where she lived during the early years of her marriage. But she is equally acute on other spheres of clerical life – on the anxieties of an Oxford don unable to cope with the demands of parish life, on the agonies of the family of a High Churchman determined to abandon the Church of England for Rome, and on the trials of an impecunious clergyman, again of High Church persuasion, who is denied the family living in the gift of his evangelical aunts. *Miss Marjoribanks* and *Phoebe, Junior* concentrate on the laity of Carlingford – Miss Marjoribanks, the strong-willed, independent daughter of the town's doctor, and the much later life of the grandaughter of the butterman of Salem Chapel, raised in the highest echelons of metropolitan nonconformity in a style quite undreamed of by her grandparents.

Parallels with Trollope are almost irresistible, and in the case of one plot and title, quite apparent. So great was the fame of the Chronicles that George Eliot was forced to state publically that she was not the author. But despite obvious comparisons with more illustrious contemporaries Mrs. Oliphant's work retains a flavour, wit, and poise very much its own.

—Joanne Shattock

O'NOLAN, Brian. See O'BRIEN, Flann.

OPIE, Amelia (née Alderson).   English.   Born in Norwich, Norfolk, 12 November 1769. Married the painter John Opie in 1798. Writer from childhood, and novelist from 1800; a friend of Sydney Smith, Sheridan, and Madame de Stael; became a Quaker in 1825, and thereafter wrote only moral tracts and articles. *Died 2 December 1853.*

PUBLICATIONS

Fiction

Dangers of Coquetry.   1790.
The Father and Daughter: A Tale, with An Epistle from the Maid of Corinth and Other Poetical Pieces.   1801.
Adeline Mowbray; or, The Mother and Daughter.   1804.
Simple Tales.   1806.
Temper; or, Domestic Scenes.   1812.
Tales of Real Life.   1813.
Valentine's Eve.   1816.
New Tales.   1818.
Tales of the Heart.   1820.
Madeline.   1822.
Illustrations of Lying, in All Its Branches.   1825.
Tales of the Pemberton Family, for the Use of Children.   1825.
Miscellaneous Tales.   12 vols., 1845–47.

Verse

Twelve Hindoo Airs, music by E. S. Biggs.   1800(?); *Second Set,* 1800(?).
Poems.   1802.
Elegy to the Memory of the Late Duke of Bedford.   1802.
The Warrior's Return and Other Poems.   1808.
Lays for the Dead.   1834.

Other

Detraction Displayed.   1828; as *A Cure for Scandal,* 1839.
Works.   2 vols., 1835.
Works.   3 vols., 1841.
Memorials of the Life of Opie, from Her Letters, Diaries and Other Manuscripts, edited by
    Cecilia Lucy Brightwell.   1854.

Editor, *Lectures on Painting,* by John Opie.   1809.

Reading List: *Amelia Opie, Worldling and Friend* by M. E. Macgregor, 1933 (includes
bibliography); *Amelia: The Tale of a Plain Friend* by J. Menzies-Wilson and H. Lloyd, 1937.

*   *   *

Amelia Opie deliberately wrote "tales" and not novels. She had no interest in "strong
character, comic situation, bustle, and variety of incident" (preface to *The Father and
Daughter*). Like many women novelists of the eighteenth century she was only interested in
situations of intense emotion, and, in spite of the fact that her many volumes of tales present a
fair range of character, incident, dialogue, and narrative mode, there is one basic situation
which recurs again and again. A heroine of sensibility leaves or is banished from home, due
to her own moral inadequacies or those of home itself (a severe or profligate parent); the
result of her departure is a series of scenes of remorse, as the plot moves crookedly, usually
with the help of breathtaking coincidences, through these passages of penitence to a grand
reconciliation; and the heroine finally arrives "home" sadder and wiser, though home often
proves to be but death's door.

The tales (and many of the poems) deal in separations, then – daughter from father (*The
Father and Daughter*), daughter from mother (*Adeline Mowbray*), wife from husband
(*Valentine's Eve*) – and in secret sorrows, suspicions, and unfavourable appearances ("The
Black Velvet Pelisse" in *Simple Tales*), often arranged around the question of the chasteness
of the heroine, and always tied up with her good or bad moral judgment. The theme arose
from Mrs. Opie's own relationship with her mother, and is portrayed with directness,
poignancy, and intensity in her early poem "In Memory of My Mother" (1791), a kind of
miniature of the structure of feeling found in most of her tales. But she did not, in her life or
her fiction, give way to morbid sensibility, and what is interesting is what she did, as a writer,
with this biographical *donnée.* She had a sense of humour, an active and observant mind, and
a fascination for anecdotes, and much of her own experience of the social and historical
world of Norwich and London during several decades of political and intellectual crisis finds
its way into her fiction. Her tales refer to a wide range of the issues, ideas, and events of the
day, from Sensibility to East Anglian windstorms, from war and economic distress to the
latest cut of a coat, and they show the influence of her father, of William Godwin, the
Dissenting culture to which she belonged, and the events of the French Revolution, viewed
typologically. All this is transposed into her writing, and all too thoroughly rendered in the
language and conventions of both the literature of Sensibility and the popular but "serious"

fiction of the day. Like her celebrated singing voice, Mrs. Opie's fictional voice is limited in range, and unable to extend itself over any span of effort, but it is clear, simple, personal, and in its own time was considered quite moving.

—Gary Kelly

ORRERY, Earl of. See **BOYLE, Roger.**

ORWELL, George. Pseudonym for Eric Arthur Blair. English. Born in Motihari, Bengal, India, 25 June 1903, of English parents. Educated at Eton College (King's Scholar), 1917–21. Served with the Republicans in the Spanish Civil War, 1936: wounded in action. Married 1) Eileen O'Shaughnessy in 1936 (died, 1945); 2) Sonia Mary Brownell in 1949; one adopted son. Served in the Indian Imperial Police, in Burma, 1922–27; returned to Europe, and lived in poverty in Paris, then in London, working as a dishwasher, tutor, bookshop assistant, etc., 1928–34; full-time writer from 1935; settled in Hertfordshire, 1935, and ran a general store until 1936; Correspondent for the BBC and *The Observer*, London, during World War II. *Died 21 January 1950.*

PUBLICATIONS

Collections

> *The Orwell Reader,* edited by Richard H. Rovere.   1956.
> *Selected Writings,* edited by George Bott.   1958.
> *Collected Essays, Journalism and Letters,* edited by Sonia Orwell and Ian Angus.   4 vols., 1968.

Fiction

> *Burmese Days.*   1934.
> *A Clergyman's Daughter.*   1935.
> *Keep the Aspidistra Flying.*   1936.
> *Coming Up for Air.*   1939.
> *Animal Farm: A Fairy Story.*   1945.
> *Nineteen Eighty-Four.*   1949; edited by Irving Howe, 1963.

Other

> *Down and Out in Paris and London.*   1933.

The Road to Wigan Pier. 1937.
Homage to Catalonia. 1938.
Inside the Whale and Other Essays. 1940.
The Lion and the Unicorn: Socialism and the English Genius. 1941.
Critical Essays. 1946; as *Dickens, Dali, and Others: Studies in Popular Culture,* 1946.
James Burnham and the Managerial Revolution. 1946.
The English People. 1947.
Shooting an Elephant and Other Essays. 1950.
Such, Such Were the Joys. 1953; as *England, Your England and Other Essays,* 1953.

Editor, *Talking to India: A Selection of English Language Broadcasts to India.* 1943.
Editor, with Reginald Reynolds, *British Pamphleteers 1: From the Sixteenth Century to the French Revolution.* 1948.

Bibliography: "Orwell: A Selected Bibliography" by Z. G. Zeke and W. White, in *Bulletin of Bibliography,* 1961–62, supplements, 1963, 1965.

Reading List: *Orwell* by Tom Hopkinson, 1953, revised edition, 1962; *Orwell: A Literary Study* by John A. Atkins, 1954, revised edition, 1971; *A Study of Orwell, The Man and His Works* by Christopher Hollis, 1956; *The Crystal Spirit: A Study of Orwell* by George Woodcock, 1966; *The Making of Orwell: An Essay in Literary History* by Keith Aldritt, 1969; *Orwell's Fiction* by Robert A. Lee, 1969; *The World of Orwell* by Miriam Gross, 1971; *Orwell* by Raymond Williams, 1971; *The Unknown Orwell,* 1972, and *Orwell: The Transformation,* 1978 (2 vol. biography), by Peter Stansky and William Abrahams; *A Reader's Guide to Orwell,* 1975, and *Orwell: The Critical Heritage,* 1975, both edited by Jeffrey Myers.

*   *   *

George Orwell never legally changed his name. He was born Eric Blair, and so he remained to his family and his bank manager until his death, yet the assumption of a pseudonym for his first book did represent an important personal evolution: nothing less than the acquisition of a second, observing persona. It is significant that, in the world in which he lived creatively, Eric Blair vanished and his writer-friends never thought of him except as that recreated being, George Orwell.

This act of self-distancing was one manifestation of the obsession with objectivity which Orwell cultivated throughout his career, and which gave him – in his time – an almost unparalleled ability to project his own experiences outside himself and describe them with the vivid eye of an observer. One has only to consider his great works of reportage, like *Down and Out in Paris and London, Homage to Catalonia,* and those magnificent Burmese fragments "Shooting an Elephant" and "A Hanging," to see this process at work – the author engaging the reader as another spectator in a scene where all the action is vividly seen from the outside yet with the feelings of the participant clearly delineated and analyzed; the spectator, by this manifest candour, is drawn to identify himself with man who is talking to him.

The clear delineation and analysis are also aspects of the kind of self-distancing which Orwell sought to achieve. He sought, in fact, to achieve a way of writing – a "prose like a window pane" – in which the mannerisms of the writer would not in any way come between the reader and the reported events. Paradoxically, of course, in trying to eliminate any self-conscious style, Orwell became one of the great English stylists of his time.

Orwell was probably, at his best, an essayist, and there is a letter to Julian Symons in which he declares, "I am not a real novelist anyway...." This is true to the extent that all Orwell's novels are really written to present points of view rather than to follow one of the classic aims of fiction, which is to examine the complexities of human characters and relationships. The two main interests in all of Orwell's six works of fiction, from *Burmese Days* down to

Nineteen Eighty-Four are, first, to present in fairly overt terms a criticism of the human condition as it is – and, by implication, a picture of the human condition as it might be, and, second, to celebrate the splendour of the earth's surface. This delight is not absent even from *Nineteen Eighty-Four*, where Orwell expressed it with a passion and clarity equal to that of the great nineteenth-century travelling naturalists whom he so much admired.

Orwell believed that no writer could fail to be to some degree politically motivated, and his own convictions, from the anti-imperialism of *Burmese Days* to the anti-totalitarianism of *Animal Farm* and *Nineteen Eighty-Four*, become elements in his novels. They never distort them to the extent of transforming them into tracts, but they do tend to affect the characterisation, rather more than the action, of these books. Orwell finds himself with certain ideas to express, with certain areas of experience which he can – as he believes – best deal with in fiction, and he tends to create a character who will carry these ideas or experiences as both his mouthpiece and, in terms of action, his alter ego.

Flory, the melancholic timber merchant who is the leading character in *Burmese Days*, not only projects Orwell's antagonism to imperialism; but also lives through Orwell's own fascination with the Burmese and his failure to stand out firmly against the injustices he saw around him while he was still a police officer. Dorothy in *A Clergyman's Daughter* is a vehicle to work out Orwell's loss of religious faith, but also lives through experiences as a hop picker and a tramp which Orwell was not able to use in non-fictional works. Comstock in *Keep the Aspidistra Flying* and Bowling in *Coming Up for Air* speak with Orwell's voice when they attack the power of money and the destructiveness of capitalist society, and when they are not being vehement about such matters they seem rather ineffectual as human beings. It is significant that the most successful of Orwell's works of fiction was the fable *Animal Farm*, in which he did not feel the need to present well-rounded characters or to become concerned with personal human predicaments, which a kind of natural *pudeur* always prevented him from exploring or projecting with any intensity. The very simplicity of *Animal Farm* is its great virtue. It is a perfect essayist's novel.

—George Woodcock

OUIDA. Pseudonym for Marie Louise de la Ramée.   English.   Born in Bury St. Edmunds, Suffolk, 1 January 1839. Educated privately. Lived in London, 1857–71; writer from c. 1860; contributed to *Bentley's Miscellany, Fortnightly Review, Nineteenth Century, North American Review*, etc.; lived in or near Florence, 1871–93, and in or near Lucca, Italy, 1894 until her death. Granted Civil List pension. *Died 25 January 1908.*

PUBLICATIONS

Fiction

Held in Bondage.   1863.
Strathmore.   1865.
Chandos.   1866.
Under Two Flags.   1867.
Cecil Castlemaine's Gage and Other Novelettes.   1867.

Idalia.   1867.
Tricotrin.   1869.
Puck.   1870.
Folle-Farine.   1871.
Pascarel.   1873.
Two Little Wooden Shoes.   1874.
Signa.   1875.
In a Winter City.   1876.
Ariadne: The Story of a Dream.   1877.
Friendship.   1878.
Moths.   1880.
Pipistrello and Other Stories.   1880.
A Village Commune.   1881.
In Maremma.   1882.
Frescoes: Dramatic Sketches.   1883.
Wanda.   1883.
Princess Napraxine.   1884.
A Rainy June.   1885.
Othmar.   1885.
Don Gesualdo.   1886.
A House Party.   1887.
Guilderoy.   1889.
Ruffino (stories).   1890.
Syrlin.   1890.
Santa Barbara (stories).   1891.
The Tower of Taddeo.   1892.
Two Offenders (stories).   1894.
The Silver Christ, and A Lemon Tree.   1894.
Toxin.   1895.
Le Selve and Other Tales.   1896.
An Altruist.   1897.
The Massarenes.   1897.
La Strega and Other Stories.   1899.
The Waters of Edera.   1900.
Street Dust and Other Stories.   1901.
Helianthus (unfinished).   1908.

Other

A Dog of Flanders and Other Stories (juvenile).   1872.
Bimbi: Stories for Children.   1882.
The New Priesthood: A Protest Against Vivisection.   1893.
Views and Opinions.   1895.
Dogs.   1897.
Critical Studies.   1900.

Reading List: *Ouida: A Study in Ostentation* by Yvonne ffrench, 1938; *Ouida: The Passionate Victorian* by Eileen Bigland, 1950; *The Fine and the Wicked: The Life and Times of Ouida* by Monica Stirling, 1957.

*   *   *

Ouida has suffered a cruel, ironical fate. Her novels, stories, and essays have been largely forgotten while her life has become a legend. The mere mention of the name of Ouida evokes a dismissive smile or sneer; very few people have read her novels, and she is associated with highly fanciful and idealised descriptions of guardsmen. Yet Ruskin praised her, and Max Beerbohm was one of her most enthusiastic and serious admirers.

Her novels are infused with a European spirit; they are far removed from the insular and at times provincial novels of many of her English predecessors and contemporaries. If, after reading Charlotte Brontë, say, or Mrs. Gaskell, you plunge into a novel of Ouida, you seem to breathe the air of a wider, more civilised, more amusing world. The conversation sparkles, and you are treated to a cascade of wit. Nor did Ouida herself greatly revere the established English novelists of her time. She said Besant's stories contained too much Dickens and water, and felt Dickens's influence was generally too strong on later writers.

Under Two Flags is the finest of her novels about the Brigade of Guards and the life of its officers; it was also her greatest popular success. She carefully and deliberately built up an idealised picture of the Guards officer's life complete with an impecunious hero, a forged promissory note, and an illegitimate girl named Cigarette, a mascot of the Foreign Legion. *Moths*, too, has an international setting, and is brilliantly witty. In *Princess Napraxine*, *Othmar*, and *Frescoes*, we are reminded of the novels of Ronald Firbank. In *Princess Napraxine* — the title could well have been chosen by Firbank himself — we find the same world of fantasy, the strange juxtaposition of words as in a mosaic, the capacity to transport the reader into the world of the unconscious; indeed, she anticipated Firbank in many ways, and these are perhaps the novels which are most readable today.

Altogether different are her novels of Italian peasant life. She undoubtedly had an insight into the character of the Italian peasant, and in *A Village Commune, Ariadne, In Maremma*, and *Don Gesualdo* she describes peasant life in ways that foreshadow the realistic works of Verga and D'Annunzio. In *A Village Commune* she sets out to champion the cause of a small village against the over-powering Italian bureaucracy; the novel aroused great controversy, and many Italians took strong exception to it.

In many ways Ouida was ahead of her time. Her essays are trenchant and to the point. Her opposition to the spread of industrialism, to conscription, militarism, and colonialism, are in some ways prophetic. At the same time she had a genuine love of Italy and the Italian countryside, and her descriptions of landscape are unrivalled.

—Ian Greenlees

PAGE, Thomas Nelson. American. Born in Oakland Plantation, Hanover County, Virginia, 23 April 1853. Educated in local schools, and at Washington College, later Washington and Lee University, Lexington, Virginia, 1869–72; read law with his father, 1872–73; studied law at the University of Virginia, Charlottesville, 1873–74, LL.B. 1874. Married 1) Annie Seddon Bruce in 1886 (died, 1888); 2) Florence Lathrop Field in 1893 (died, 1921). Practiced law in Richmond, Virginia, 1875–93; writer, 1884–1910; settled in Washington, D.C., 1893; United States Ambassador to Italy, 1913–19. Litt.D.: Washington and Lee University, 1887; Yale University, New Haven, Connecticut, 1901; Harvard University, Cambridge, Massachusetts, 1913; LL.D.: Tulane University, New Orleans, 1899; College of William and Mary, Williamsburg, Virginia, 1906; Washington and Lee University, 1907. Member, American Academy of Arts and Letters. *Died 1 November 1922.*

PUBLICATIONS

Fiction

In Ole Virginia; or, Marse Chan and Other Stories.   1887.
Two Little Confederates.   1888.
On Newfound River.   1891.
Among the Camps; or, Young People's Stories of the War.   1891.
Elsket and Other Stories.   1891.
The Burial of the Guns.   1894.
Pastime Stories.   1894.
Unc' Edinburg: A Plantation Echo.   1895.
The Old Gentleman of the Black Stock.   1897.
Two Prisoners.   1898.
Red Rock: A Chronicle of Reconstruction.   1898.
Santa Claus's Partner.   1899.
Gordon Keith.   1903.
Bred in the Bone (stories).   1904.
Under the Crust (stories).   1907.
Tommy Trot's Visit to Santa Claus.   1908.
John Marvel, Assistant.   1909.
The Land of the Spirit (stories).   1913.
The Stranger's Pew (story).   1914.
The Red Riders.   1924.

Verse

Befo' de War: Echoes in Negro Dialect, with A. C. Gordon.   1888.
The Coast of Bohemia.   1906.

Other

The Old South: Essays Social and Political.   1892.
Social Life in Old Virginia Before the War.   1897.
The Negro: The Southerner's Problem.   1904.
The Novels, Stories, Sketches, and Poems.   18 vols., 1906–18.
Robert E. Lee: The Southerner.   1908; as *General Lee,* 1909.

The Old Dominion: Her Making and Her Manners.   1908.
Mount Vernon and Its Preservation.   1910.
Robert E. Lee: Man and Soldier.   1911.
Italy and the World War.   1920.
Dante and His Influence.   1922.
Washington and Its Romance.   1923.

Editor, *The Old Virginia Gentleman and Other Sketches,* by George W. Bagby.   1910.

Bibliography: by Theodore L. Gross, in *American Literary Realism 1,* 1967.

Reading List: *Page: A Memoir of a Virginia Gentleman* by Roswell Page, 1923; *Page* by Theodore L. Gross, 1967.

*   *   *

Thomas Nelson Page owed his popularity to the local color movement, the interest of Northern readers in the defeated South following the Civil War, and the growth of the family magazine. Although there were writers in the deep South and the mountain areas, the dominant literary image of the region was provided by accounts of life in the tidewater. Page and other writers in the plantation literary tradition increased the Southerner's pride in his past and dramatized his sense of victimization and self-sacrifice. Page's essays and dialect stories, published first in such magazines as *Scribner's* and *Century,* eulogized a civilization in which landlords abided by an almost medieval sense of *gentilesse,* women were exalted, and all the chivalric virtues prevailed. Sir Walter Scott's romances and stories by the Virginia writers George Bagby and Armistead Gordon had influenced Page's style and themes. His protagonists were typically those who had survived the war and were faced with the task of adjusting to a new and alien culture. He attempted to evoke a world that lived only in memory, and nostalgia was, therefore, the dominant mood of his most successful work.

The favorable reception in both North and South of "Marse Chan," "Meh Lady," and the other stories of *In Ole Virginia* convinced Page that authorship would prove a surer path to fame than the legal profession. Consequently, after his first wife died and he married a wealthy widow, Page devoted himself to full-time writing. He wrote several novels in which he experimented with urban settings and satirical dialogue. Even in these works, however, Page described the impact of Southern values on the rest of the nation. Each of the major novels written in his middle years (*Red Rock, Gordon Keith,* and *John Marvel, Assistant*) concerns Southern "missionaries," Virginia gentlemen who preach their Southern ideals and convert Yankees in the process. Part of their doctrine was a distrust of industrialization, a belief that aristocratic paternalism could still combat the grosser aspects of democracy, and a wistful agrarianism. It was the first decade of the new century that brought Page to the peak of his literary fame. After 1910 he all but retired from writing and devoted his time to political affairs in Washington, D.C.; he was a personal friend of Theodore Roosevelt, and eventually became ambassador to Italy.

Few writers after Page described Southern institutions so uncritically. Of the later writers Margaret Mitchell came closer than most to sharing the elegant Virginian's views, while Glasgow, Cabell, Faulkner, and their contemporaries perceived the ironies and injustices of the system Page had defended. At his best Page epitomized the plantation literary tradition, and the strengths and weaknesses of his prose provide an excellent illustration of a once popular literary genre.

—Kimball King

PALMER, (Edward) Vance. Australian. Born in Bundaberg, Queensland, 28 August 1885. Educated at Ipswich Boys' Grammar School, Queensland, 1899–1901. Served in the Australian Imperial Forces in World War I. Married Janet Higgins in 1914. Journalist in Brisbane, 1901–05; free-lance writer in London, 1905–08; worked as a tutor, bookkeeper, and bush worker, in Australia, 1909; returned to London, 1910, and wrote for *New Age*, *Guardian Fortnightly*, and *British Review*; lived in Melbourne, 1915–25; associated with *Fellowship* literary magazine from 1917; Founder, with Louis Esson, Pioneer Players, in the 1920's; settled temporarily in Caloundra, Queensland, 1925, but returned to Melbourne. Chairman of the Advisory Board, Commonwealth Literary Fund, 1947–53. Recipient: Australian Literature Society Medal, 1930. *Died 15 July 1959.*

PUBLICATIONS

Fiction

> *The World of Men* (stories). 1915.
> *The Shantykeeper's Daughter.* 1920.
> *The Boss of Killara.* 1922.
> *The Enchanted Island.* 1923.
> *The Outpost.* 1924; revised edition, as *Hurricane*, 1935.
> *Cronulla: A Story of Station Life.* 1924.
> *The Man Hamilton.* 1928.
> *Men Are Human.* 1930.
> *The Passage.* 1930.
> *Separate Lives* (stories). 1931.
> *Daybreak.* 1932.
> *The Swayne Family.* 1934.
> *Sea and Spinifex* (stories). 1934.
> *Legend for Sanderson.* 1937.
> *Cyclone.* 1947.
> *Golconda.* 1948.
> *Let the Birds Fly* (stories). 1955.
> *Seedtime.* 1957.
> *The Rainbow Bird and Other Stories*, edited by A. Edwards. 1957.
> *The Big Fellow.* 1959.

Plays

> *The Prisoner* (produced 1919). In *The Black Horse and Other Plays*, 1924.
> *A Happy Family* (produced 1921).
> *Telling Mrs. Baker*, from the story by Henry Lawson (produced 1922). In *The Black Horse and Other Plays*, 1924.
> *The Black Horse* (produced 1923). In *The Black Horse and Other Plays*, 1924.
> *Travellers* (produced 1923). In *The Black Horse and Other Plays*, 1924.
> *The Black Horse and Other Plays.* 1924.
> *Ancestors*, in *Best Australian One-Act Plays.* 1937.
> *Hail Tomorrow.* 1947.

Verse

> *The Forerunners.* 1915.
> *The Camp.* 1920.

Other

National Portraits. 1940; revised edition, 1954.
A. G. Stephens: His Life and Work. 1941.
Frank Wilmot (Furnley Maurice). 1942.
Louis Esson and the Australian Theatre. 1948.
The Legend of the Nineties. 1954.
Intimate Portraits and Other Pieces: Essays and Articles, edited by H. P.
   Heseltine. 1969.

Editor, Such Is Life, by Joseph Furphy. 1937.
Editor, Coast to Coast: Australian Stories 1944. 1945.
Editor, Old Australian Bush Ballads, music by Margaret Sutherland. 1951.

Reading List: in Meanjin 18, 1959; Palmer by H. P. Heseltine, 1970; Palmer, 1971, and Vance and Nettie Palmer, 1975, both by Vivian Smith; Dream and Disillusion by David Walker, 1976.

*   *   *

"There'll be little care for beauty in the world they build tomorrow,/But these are my people, and I'm with them to the end." These lines from an early poem of Vance Palmer's express the conscious commitment that governed the whole of his work as a writer. But though Palmer saw himself as contributing to the creation of a national culture by portraying what he regarded as "an Australia of the spirit," his writing was not distinctively Australian in its style or idiom. Unlike the nationalist writers of an earlier generation whom he so admired – Lawson and Furphy – he had limited command of the vernacular, and his identification with ordinary Australians was more a matter of intellectual choice than instinctive feeling. In the history of Australian writing, Palmer occupies a special place, because of his dedication to the cause of a national literature. As a man of letters, he saw himself as having a role to play in the shaping of national values.

Palmer's creative output included poems, plays, novels, short stories, essays, and broadcast talks. His poems and plays are minor work, though the plays have a continuing interest because of Palmer's association with the Pioneer Players group, which attempted to create a national theatre on the model of the Abbey Theatre in Dublin. His novels and short stories represent him at his strongest. Beginning with conventional station romances, he matured steadily, and with The Passage he established himself as a significant Australian novelist. This novel, centering on the figure of the fisherman Lew Callaway, exemplifies Palmer's concern with the inward life of ordinary people. "My task is to set down Australian rhythms," he once said, and this simple yet challenging ambition underlies all his fiction.

With the exception of The Big Fellow, none of Palmer's novels is wholly satisfying. They are well-made; they focus on interesting themes; they examine the texture of human experience with intelligence and delicacy; but, with all their craftsmanship, they do not get enough of the very feel of life. The Big Fellow, however, is a moving novel, in which Palmer expressed more fully than elsewhere his personal vision of things. It is the third volume of a trilogy, begun with Golconda and continued with Seedtime, dealing with the public themes that preoccupied him throughout his life – his conviction that the essential values of Australian society had been defined in the 1890's and his profound belief in the responsibility of the individual to the community. But what gives The Big Fellow its distinctive strength is its quiet revelation of the inner life of the central character, a politician facing a crisis in which all the values of his life are questioned. Through the character of Macy Donovan, Palmer presents more fully than anywhere else his personal vision of life's meanings.

The subtle understanding which Palmer shows in his portrayal of Donovan's sense of inescapable loneliness is more often to be found in his short stories, especially in Let the Birds

Fly. It was in the restricted scope of the short story that Palmer could best express his own sensitive, romantic yearning for beauty and his wry awareness of the inevitable defeats the romantic must face. His stories of childhood – notably "The Rainbow Bird," "The Foal," "Josie," and "Mathieson's Wife" – are especially attractive in their restrained and sympathetic evocation of immature states of feeling.

Alongside the best of Palmer's creative writing must be set the best of his non-fiction prose. He contributed to many journals on a variety of topics and was a very successful radio book-reviewer. The magazine article, the radio talk, and the public lecture were forms he handled with ease. He had a remarkable ability to present ideas in an easily understood form without distorting or over-simplifying them, and the best of his journalism, along with his book of literary history, *The Legend of the Nineties*, will continue to be read with pleasure by all conditions of men.

—John Barnes

PALTOCK, Robert. English. Born in Westminster, London, in 1697. Studied law. Married Anna Skinner (died, 1767); two sons and two daughters. Attorney: lived in Clement's Inn, London, for several years; moved to Lambeth, London, c. 1759; writer from 1750. *Died 20 March 1767.*

PUBLICATIONS

Fiction

The Life and Adventures of Peter Wilkins, A Cornish Man, Relating Particularly to His Shipwreck near the South Pole. 1750; edited by Christopher Bentley, 1973.

Reading List: *The Imaginary Voyage in Prose Fiction* by Philip Babcock Gove, 1941 (includes bibliography); *Voyages to the Moon* by Marjorie Hope Nicholson, 1948.

*   *   *

The only work for which Robert Paltock is remembered is *The Life and Adventures of Peter Wilkins*, a novel which appeared in 1750. Until 1835 his identity lurked behind the initials R. P., and even these bafflingly appeared as R. S. on the original title page. Ascription to Paltock of one and sometimes two or three other works is extremely dubious. It is therefore a measure of the attractions of *Peter Wilkins* that it emerged brightly from these authorial obscurities and has captivated occasional readers for two centuries.

The story purports to have been dictated to the author by the eponymous narrator, and it has at first something of the raconteur's mere chronological onwardness that we find in Defoe. A series of episodic adventures establishes, as in *Robinson Crusoe*, a register of realism and a sturdy reliability of witness which will render more persuasive the fantasies of a never-never land that are to follow. Cast away in Antarctic latitudes Wilkins is sportively visited by flocks of Flying Indians, and one of them, an enchanting maiden named Youwarkee, unnoticed by her soaring friends, falls from the blue into his enraptured arms. The means of flight have been acquired biologically: a cloak-like integument, called a "graundee," sheathing the body, may be sprung open into a sort of kite. (The aerodynamic details were soberly demonstrated in the first edition by engravings, reproduced in the 1973 edition.)

Alone in their earthly paradise Peter and Youwarkee live out a long idyll of chastest courtship and then of godly domestic bliss among their many children. Paltock's little Eden charmingly dismisses Marvell's sentiment that "Two paradises 'twere in one/To live in paradise alone."

There follows now a major development of the novel when Wilkins and his family, who have at length been visited by several of Youwarkee's people, fly away to her homeland. (Peter is borne aloft in a chair, complete with safety-belt, by eight Indians.) If the earlier part is a connubial *Robinson Crusoe*, this latter part is a bland *Gulliver's Travels*; and the domestic Eden may be ironically related to the political Utopia. In the stone-age culture of the Indians, Peter's technological knowledge gives him enormous power and prestige which he exerts in every sphere of life (most dramatically in warfare), convinced that the Christian basis of his enlightenment gives his interventions a missionary justification.

In its own day *Peter Wilkins* was sufficiently acceptable, in the prolific genre of the Voyage Imaginaire or Robinsonade, to be immediately reprinted and soon translated into French and German. Then it was hailed during the Romantic era as a work of striking imaginative power by such men as Coleridge, Scott, Shelley, Lamb, and Leigh Hunt. Latterly it has acquired new interest as a document indicative of European imperial assumptions that were already beginning to impose "progressive" regimes by the destruction of alternative cultures all over the world.

—R. A. Copland

PARKER, Dorothy (née Rothschild). American. Born in West End, New Jersey, 22 August 1893. Educated at Miss Dana's School, Morristown, New Jersey, and Blessed Sacrament Convent, New York City. Married 1) Edwin Pond Parker II in 1917 (divorced, 1928); 2) the film actor Alan Campbell in 1933 (divorced, 1947; remarried, 1950; died, 1963). Member of the editorial staff of *Vogue*, New York, 1916–17; member of the editorial staff and Drama Critic, *Vanity Fair*, New York, 1917–20; Book Reviewer ("Constant Reader" column), *The New Yorker*, 1925–27; free-lance writer from 1927; book reviewer for *Esquire*, New York, 1957–62. Founder, with Robert Benchley and Robert E. Sherwood, Algonquin Hotel Round Table, New York, in the 1930's. Recipient: O. Henry Award, 1929; Marjorie Waite Peabody Award, 1958. *Died 7 June 1967.*

PUBLICATIONS

Fiction

    Laments for the Living. 1930.
    After Such Pleasures. 1933.
    Here Lies: The Collected Stories. 1939.
    Collected Stories. 1942.

Plays

Close Harmony; or, The Lady Next Door, with Elmer Rice (produced 1924).   1929.
Round the Town (lyrics only; revue) (produced 1924).
Sketches, in *Shoot the Works* (revue) (produced 1931).
The Coast of Illyria, with Ross Evans (produced 1949).
The Ladies of the Corridor, with Arnaud d'Usseau (produced 1953).   1954.
Candide (lyrics only, with others), book by Lillian Hellman, music by Leonard
   Bernstein, from the story by Voltaire (produced 1956).   1957.

Screenplays: *Business Is Business*, with George S. Kaufman, 1925; *The Moon's Our
Home*, with others, 1936; *Lady Be Careful*, with others, 1936; *Three Married Men*, with
Alan Campbell and Owen Davis, Sr., 1936; *Suzy*, with others, 1936; *A Star Is Born*,
with others, 1937; *Sweethearts*, with Alan Campbell, 1938; *Trade Winds*, with others,
1938; *The Little Foxes*, with others, 1941; *Weekend for Three*, with Alan Campbell and
Budd Schulberg, 1941; *Saboteur*, with Peter Viertel and Joan Harrison, 1942; *Smash
Up – The Story of a Woman*, with others, 1947; *The Fan*, with Walter Reisch and Ross
Evans, 1949.

Verse

Enough Rope.   1926.
Sunset Gun.   1928.
Death and Taxes.   1931.
Collected Poetry.   1931.
Collected Poems: Not So Deep as a Well.   1936.

Other

High Society, with George S. Chappell and Frank Crowninshield.   1920.
Men I'm Not Married To, with *Women I'm Not Married To*, by Franklin P.
   Adams.   1922.
The Portable Dorothy Parker.   1944.
The Best of Dorothy Parker.   1952.

Editor, *The Portable F. Scott Fitzgerald*.   1945.
Editor, with Frederick B. Shroyer, *Short Story: A Thematic Anthology*.   1965.

Reading List: in *An Unfinished Woman: A Memoir* by Lillian Hellman, 1969; *You Might as
Well Live* (biography) by John Keats, 1970.

*   *   *

Dorothy Parker's writings were aptly characterized by Alexander Woollcott as "a potent
distillation of nectar and wormwood, of ambrosia and deadly nightshade." This assessment
covers her perennially popular volumes of short stories, *Laments for the Living* and *After
Such Pleasures*. It also encompasses her three best-selling volumes of wry, bittersweet verse
(not serious "poetry," she claimed), *Enough Rope*, *Sunset Gun*, and *Death and Taxes* – mostly
love lamentations. It could also apply to her crisp, tart book reviews for the *New Yorker*; she
dismissed Milne's *House at Pooh Corner* with "Tonstant Weader fwowed up."
   Her book reviews for *Esquire* (1957–62) are skimpier and less successful. Her major play,

The Ladies of the Corridor (with Arnaud d'Usseau), a slice-of-life portrayal of aging, pathetic women who have lost their central purpose for living (through departures of husbands, lovers, children) is better as dialogue than as drama.

Many of Parker's well-crafted short stories focus on upper class Manhattan women of the 1920's and 1930's. The economic comfort of these women, whether young, middle-aged, or old, is counteracted by their superficial, pointless lives, barren of goals, meaningful activities, and inner resources. Although they are often physically attractive and elegantly dressed ornaments at the parties they live for, without such external social props they collapse.

Other people in Parker's stories do the *real* work; the men earn the money, the maids rear the children. So these women are bored, neurotic, unhappy, pampered parasites. Their fate is the fate of those who live through others, excessive emotional dependency: "Please, God, let him telephone me now." This cripples their potentiality for gaiety and charm and transforms them into shrill, malicious shrews who drink too much, talk too much, think too shallowly, and do too little. These characters are their own most pathetic victims; they seldom deceive others as they delude themselves.

Dorothy Parker excels in economically incisive descriptions of personalities, settings, costumes: a honeymooning bride "looked as new as a peeled egg." Her dramatic monologues are devastating, ironic characterizations. Thus the hypocritical "Lady with a Lamp" offers cold comfort to her alleged friend, jilted and unhappily recuperating from a clandestine abortion: "I worry so about you, living in a little furnished apartment, with nothing that belongs to you, no roots, no nothing." Parker's dialogues capture the cadences of real speech and the subtle nuances of personality and values: "Good night, useless," says the spoiled mother to her firstborn infant.

The essence of such social satire is the author's implicit desire for reform of these empty lives into significant existences. Her best story, "Big Blonde," which won the O. Henry Prize in 1929, epitomizes Parker's mixture of love and anger, coalesced into an enduring work of art. Indeed, many of Dorothy Parker's stories are memorable cameos, etched in acid and polished to gemlike lustre.

—Lynn Z. Bloom

PATER, Walter (Horatio). English. Born in Shadwell, London, 4 August 1839. Educated at Enfield Grammer School; King's School, Canterbury, Kent; Queen's College, Oxford, 1858–62, graduated (honours) in classics 1862. Tutor in Oxford, 1862–64; Fellow, Brasenose College, Oxford, from 1864 (tutored until 1883); writer from 1866; lived in Rome, 1882, 1883; lived part of each year in London, 1885–93. D.Litt.: University of Glasgow, 1894. *Died 30 July 1894.*

PUBLICATIONS

Collections

Works. 10 vols., 1910.
Selected Works, edited by Richard Aldington. 1948.
Letters, edited by Lawrence Evans. 1970.

Fiction

Marius the Epicurean: His Sensations and Ideas.   1885; revised edition, 1892; edited
   by J. Sagmaster, 1935.
Gaston de Latour: An Unfinished Romance, edited by Charles L. Shadwell.   1896.

Verse

The Chant of the Celestial Sailors.   1928.

Other

Studies in the History of the Renaissance.   1873; revised edition, as *The Renaissance,*
   1877; edited by Kenneth Clark, 1961.
Imaginary Portraits.   1887; edited by E. J. Brzenk, 1962.
Appreciations, with an Essay on Style.   1889; revised edition, 1890.
Plato and Platonism: A Series of Lectures.   1893.
An Imaginary Portrait.   1894.
Greek Studies: A Series of Essays, edited by Charles L. Shadwell.   1895.
Miscellaneous Studies: A Series of Essays, edited by Charles L. Shadwell.   1895.
Essays from The Guardian.   1896.
Uncollected Essays.   1903.
Sketches and Reviews.   1919.

Bibliography: *A Bibliography of the Writings of Pater* by Samuel Wright, 1975.

Reading List: *Pater* by A. C. Benson, 1906; *The Writings of Pater: A Reflection of British
Philosophical Opinion from 1860 to 1890* by Helen Hawthorne Young, 1933; *Pater* by Ian
Fletcher, 1959; *Pater: L'Homme et l'Oeuvre* by Germain d'Hangest, 2 vols., 1961; "Pattern
in Pater's Fiction" by R. T. Lenaghan, in *Studies in Philology 58*, 1961; *The Literary
Character of Pater* by Gordon McKenzie, 1967; *Pater's Portraits: Mythic Pattern in the
Fiction of Pater,* 1967, and *Pater,* 1977, both by Gerald Monsman; *The Case of Pater* by
Michael Levey, 1978.

*   *   *

Walter Pater's early aestheticism was distorted or trivialized by his disciples and it was
barely recognised that his thought developed over the years. For Oscar Wilde, the
Renaissance of 1873 was a golden book: but it was not Pater's final truth. His later attitudes
nonetheless are implicit from the beginning, and his work whether in art or literary criticism,
fiction, or philosophical discourse, possesses an opaque but still perceptible coherence. An
early paper, read in 1864 to the Old Mortality Society at Oxford, "Diaphaniété," announces
the theme of transforming finite self, fragmented according to the witness of the
contemporary sciences of observation, into the self in history. Pater's work was to be the
record of an autobiographical search to locate the true self in past culture, through memory,
and to project it into the future so that the lower forms of the self could be transcended, so
that it could identify itself, as a recent critic puts it, "with the external world as no longer
foreign but as its own possession." The aim of life, then, is not an inert sensuousness, but the
pursuit of an ideal in which the material and the spiritual are fused, most memorably
conveyed in the famous metaphor of the "hard gem-like flame" of the "Conclusion" to the
Renaissance. Another metaphor Pater frequently employs in his earlier work is that of
weaving disparate threads, "forces" in the terms of physics, both "inward" and "outward,"

into a harmonious, but still dynamic condition. The new aesthetic hero of Pater's early essays, who can be compared with other nineteenth-century heroic types (Carlyle's tyrant or Nietzsche's superman), was to achieve the "perfection of the moral life through the idealization of sensuous beauty" or, as he himself puts it, "a sort or moral beauty ... in the forms and colours of things." Essentially the type was to be a transcendence of earlier types of human excellence – saint, artist, and philosopher – whose perfection necessarily could arrive at intensity only through sacrifice of human possibility. The aesthetic hero is lighted up by some spiritual ray within, infinitely striving after a moral ideal by which "the veil of an outer life not simply expressive of the inward becomes thinner and thinner." He is, in other words, a harbinger of renaissance; "a majority of such would be the regeneration of the world." But the reward of culture comes through peace, not rebellion.

As a consequence of discovering in Winckelmann, the eighteenth-century Hellenist, a model of the aesthetic hero, Pater was later led to see art rather than metaphysics as the principle mode through which diaphanousness and renewal became possible. Renaissance (rebirth) is first studied in the phase of culture which bears that title, though for Pater that period is a fiction: renaissance is possible at many times and in many cultures, and the historical spirit is sensed by Pater (in the terminology of Matthew Arnold) as a perpetual struggle of Hellenistic and Hebraic, and a cyclical movement which locates the first manifestation of the Renaissance in mediaeval France and its consummation in the France of the early Pléiade. Yet the phase of culture represented by the *Renaissance* was concluded by the earlier seventeenth century, and it is Winckelmann who transmits by his personality the possibility of a new culture to Goethe. For Pater, then, the personalities behind the art works he discusses in the *Renaissance* are "fragmented selves" held together merely by his own luminous memories of aesthetic experience. The "Conclusion" is dangerously near to solipsism. Though Pater never disowned it, his later work constitutes a wider sweep into the past, a more elaborate escape from the "flux" through memory and autobiography – as in the first of his "imaginary portraits," "The Child in the House" – and outward to biography and history.

In the new phase of culture, the new Renaissance, the religious sense will also be involved, and this is recorded in *Marius the Epicurean*, a species of "spiritual autobiography" (an elaborated "imaginary portrait"), a form Pater seems to have derived from Rossetti's *Hand and Soul. Marius* is the memorial not of actions but of significant perceptions, and its subject is "inner vision"; the second-century setting is clearly analogous with the later nineteenth century, where a new "rebirth" of culture is becoming possible. But Marius must realize that rebirth in sensuous terms. The literary experiences described – the composition of the *Pervigilium Veneris*, Apuleius's fable of Cupid and Psyche, Fronto, Lucian, and an epistle of the early Church – compose precisely that "weaving" together in Marius's experience which enables him to become the veritable "Diaphane," until the Divine Idea is found incarnated within history in finite and sensuous form. As Leonardo da Vinci discovers the force that obsessed his dreams in the Lady Lise in Giaconda's house, so Marius sees in the face of Cecilia "the beautiful vision of antiquity." The image of Mona Lisa experienced linguistically by Pater reaffirms Pater's fellowship with Leonardo and Leonardo's with the historical process. So Cecilia objectifies in person Marius's (and Pater's) links with the early church and makes possible for Pater the embodiment of a new "religious phase" for the late nineteenth century.

Pater's other "imaginary portraits" constitute further approaches to "Renaissance," but mainly in aborted form. They range from the "Hippolytus Veiled" of antiquity to "Emerald Uthwart" set in earlier nineteenth-century England. This has strong autobiographical overtones. Pater had intended two further extended portraits which were to treat of sixteenth- and late eighteenth-century England, but only the first, *Gaston de Latour*, was begun.

One of the difficulties experienced in reading and evaluating Pater lies in the nature of his prose. The "weaving" process is faithfully reflected in the anxious parentheses and liturgical rhythms. That he could write in a different though equally mannered way, *Plato and Platonism*, with its colloquialisms and informalities, testifies.

951

Pater's importance for twentieth-century art and literature has only recently been recognised. Such notions as the "epiphany" (Joyce) and "significant form" (Clive Bell), such themes as the solitariness of modern man, the importance of the moment as it lives in the memory (Proust), the revelation of personality in terms of mythical archetypes – all these may be found in his work, while there are many buried echoes of Pater's insights and actual phraseology in the work of the very critics who most vehemently deny his stature.

—Ian Fletcher

PATON, Alan (Stewart).   South African.   Born in Pietermaritzburg, Natal, 11 January 1903. Educated at Maritzburg College, University of Natal, B.Sc. 1923, B.Ed. 1966. Married 1) Doris Francis in 1928 (died, 1967), two sons; 2) Anne Hopkins in 1969. Schoolteacher in Natal, in a native school and at Pietermaritzburg College, 1925–35; Principal, Diepkloof Reformatory, Johannesburg, 1935–48; full-time writer since 1948. Honorary Commissioner, Toc H Southern Africa, Botha's Hill, Natal, 1949–58; President of the Convocation, University of Natal, 1951–55, 1957–59; Founder and President, Liberal Party of South Africa, 1958–68; Chubb Fellow, Yale University, New Haven, Connecticut, 1973. Since 1969, Honorary President, South African National Union of Students. Recipient: Anisfield-Wolf Award, 1948; Newspaper Guild of New York Award, 1949; Freedom House Award, 1960; Free Academy of Arts Medal, Hamburg, 1960; National Conference of Christians and Jews Brotherhood Award, 1962; International League for Human Rights prize, 1977. L.H.D.: Yale University, 1954; D.Litt.: Kenyon College, Gambier, Ohio, 1962; University of Natal, 1968; Harvard University, Cambridge, Massachusetts, 1971; Trent University, Peterborough, Ontario, 1971; Rhodes University, Grahamstown, South Africa, 1972; Willamette University, Salem, Oregon, 1974; D.D.: University of Edinburgh, 1971. Fellow, Royal Society of Literature, 1961; Honorary Member, Free Academy of Arts, Hamburg, 1961. Lives in Hillcrest, Natal.

PUBLICATIONS

Fiction

Meditation for a Young Boy Confirmed (story).   1944.
Cry, The Beloved Country.   1948.
Too Late the Phalarope.   1953.
Debbie Go Home: Stories.   1961; as *Tales from a Troubled Land,* 1965.

Play

Sponono, with Krishna Shah, from a story by Paton (produced 1964).   1965.

Other

South Africa Today.   1951.
The Land and the People of South Africa.   1955; as *South Africa and Her People,* 1955; revised edition, 1965, 1971.

South Africa in Transition.   1956.

Hope for South Africa.   1958.

Hofmeyr.   1964; abridged, as *South African Tragedy: The Life and Times of Jan Hofmeyr,* 1965.

The Long View.   1968.

Instrument of Thy Peace: The Prayer of St. Francis.   1968.

Kontakion for You Departed.   1969; as *For You Departed,* 1969.

Case History of a Pinky.   1972.

Apartheid and the Archbishop: The Life and Times of Geoffrey Clayton, Archbishop of Cape Town.   1973.

Knocking at the Door: Shorter Writings, edited by Colin Gardner.   1975.

Reading List: *Paton* by Edward Callan, 1968.

*   *   *

Alan Paton is a liberal white South African. He was national president of the Liberal Party in South Africa until its disbandment in 1968. The unenviable position not only colours his writing, it also provides the subject matter: apartheid and its moral, psychological, and economic consequences. In what is probably the most famous novel to come out of South Africa, *Cry, The Beloved Country,* Paton explores this theme from two points of view. The old, simple, and humble black priest Steven Kumalo goes to Johannesburg in search of his son who has become a juvenile delinquent. His descent into the underworld of Johannesburg is registered through his horrified and honest eyes in a biblical language of great simplicity and beauty. When he finds his son it is too late; the boy is on trial for the murder of a white man. The bitter irony of the situation becomes clear when it is revealed that the murdered man was a "good" white man who worked hard to change the apartheid system. The next part of the book is devoted to the father of the murdered man Jarvis, Sr., who tries to comprehend his son's ideas as he reads through his papers. In the final section Kumalo and Jarvis reach an understanding, and through this Paton advocates a solution to the South African situation based on a combination of black humility and honesty and white American-inspired democratic liberalism.

Paton's position as principal of a reformatory for delinquent African boys has given him an insight into the criminal world of Johannesburg which he uses in *Cry, The Beloved Country.* In his collection of short stories *Debbie Go Home,* he explores this world and its inhabitants in a realistic fashion which does not leave room for the humility of Steven Kumalo.

Paton is, however, at his very best when he explores the Calvinist Boer mind as he does in *Too Late the Phalarope,* an excellent but much ignored book. It tells the story of the policeman Pieter van Vlaanderen, a pillar of the Boer community, and his silent agonizing fight against his desire to sleep with the black girl Stephanie. He finally loses the battle, is inevitably discovered and destroyed. The reasons for his desires and actions are explained very convincingly as the short comings of Calvinist morality – lack of love, fear of sexuality, and perverse colour prejudice. The book deserves all the attention which has been showered upon the more popular *Cry, The Beloved Country.*

—Kirsten Holst Petersen

PAULDING, James Kirke. American. Born in Great Nine Partners, now Putnam County, New York, 22 August 1778; grew up in Tarrytown, New York. Educated for a brief period in a local school. Married Gertrude Kemble in 1818 (died, 1841); several children. Settled in New York City c. 1796, worked in a public office, and continued his studies on his own; writer from c. 1805; wrote for the *Analectic Magazine*, 1812; Secretary of the Board of Navy Commissioners, Washington, D.C., 1815–23; Naval Agent in New York City, 1823–38; Secretary of the Navy, in the administration of Martin Van Buren, 1838–41; returned to a country estate near Hyde Park, New York, 1846. *Died 6 April 1860.*

PUBLICATIONS

Collections

    Collected Works, edited by William I. Paulding. 4 vols., 1867–68.
    The Letters, edited by Ralph M. Aderman. 1962.

Fiction

    Salmagundi; or, The Whim-Whams and Opinions of Launcelot Langstaff, Esq., and Others, with Washington and William Irving. 2 vols., 1807–08: *Second Series* (by Paulding only), 2 vols., 1819–20.
    The Diverting History of John Bull and Brother Jonathan. 1812.
    Koningsmarke: The Long Finne: A Story of the New World. 1823.
    John Bull in America; or, The New Munchausen. 1825.
    The Merry Tales of the Three Wise Men of Gotham. 1826.
    Tales of the Good Woman. 1829.
    Chronicles of the City of Gotham from the Papers of a Retired Common Councilman. 1830.
    The Dutchman's Fireside: A Tale. 1831.
    Westward Ho! 1832; as *The Banks of the Ohio*, 1833.
    The Book of Saint Nicholas. 1836.
    A Gift from Fairy-Land. 1838; as *A Christmas Gift from Fairy Land*, 1838.
    The Old Continental; or, The Price of Liberty. 1846.
    The Puritan and His Daughter. 1849.
    A Book of Vagaries (selections), edited by William I. Paulding. 1868.

Plays

    The Lion of the West, revised by John Augustus Stone and William Bayle Bernard (produced 1831; as *The Kentuckian; or, A Trip to New York*, produced 1833). Edited by James N. Tidwell, 1954.
    The Bucktails; or, Americans in England. 1847.
    American Comedies (includes *The Bucktails; The Noble Exile; Madmen All, or, The Cure of Love; Antipathies, or, The Enthusiasts by Ear*). 1847.

Verse

    The Lay of the Scottish Fiddle: A Tale of Havre de Grace, Supposed to Be Written by Walter Scott, Esq. 1813.
    The Backwoodsman. 1818.

Other

> *Naval Biography.* 1815.
> *The United States and England.* 1815.
> *Letters from the South.* 1817.
> *A Sketch of Old New England.* 1822.
> *The New Mirror for Travellers, and a Guide to the Springs.* 1828.
> *Works.* 7 vols., 1834–37.
> *A Life of Washington.* 2 vols., 1835.
> *Slavery in the United States.* 1836.

Bibliography: "A Bibliography of the Separate Publications of Paulding" by Oscar Wegelin, in *Papers of the Bibliographical Society of America 12*, 1918.

Reading List: *The Literary Life of Paulding* by William I. Paulding, 1867; *Paulding: Versatile American* by Amos L. Herold, 1926 (includes bibliography).

*   *   *

Through the 1830's, James Kirke Paulding's popularity with American readers rivalled that of his somewhat younger contemporaries Irving and Cooper. His name was also well known not only in Britain, but on the continent, where two of his novels – *The Dutchman's Fireside* and *Westward Ho!* – appeared in numerous translations. Although his audience dwindled sharply after 1845, he is still remembered as perhaps the most versatile, if not the most graceful, American author of the generation that matured between the two wars with England. During his long career Paulding won fame as a poet, novelist, essayist, biographer, playwright, and critic. He also wrote scores of short stories and sketches for both American and British periodicals. Most of his writing was done while he followed another career as public servant that culminated with his appointment in 1838 as Secretary of the Navy by President Martin Van Buren, a long-time friend whose ancestral roots were, like Paulding's, in the Dutch-American Hudson River valley.

Paulding was always more concerned with ideas than with art. Unlike his friend Irving (to whom he was related by marriage and with whom he collaborated on *Salmagundi*) he never made peace with either England or the romantic movement, which he scorned as a British conspiracy designed to sap the fiber of sturdy new-world republicanism. In a series of satires, commencing with *The Diverting History of John Bull and Brother Jonathan* and concluding with *John Bull in America*, he vigorously defended his young country against printed attacks by British travelers and reviewers. During the same period he wrote *The Lay of the Scottish Fiddle*, a book-length parody of *The Lay of the Last Minstrel*, burlesquing not only Scott's verse but his copious notes, and *The Backwoodsman*, another lengthy, often clumsy poem in heroic couplets designed, according to Paulding, to inform young American writers of the "rich poetic resources" available to them on their native ground. His call for American literary independence continued in his best-remembered essay, "National Literature," which appeared in *Salmagundi, Second Series*.

Prompted by the success of Cooper's *The Spy* and *The Pioneers*, Paulding turned to the novel in 1823, with *Koningsmarke*. Here he continued his satirical attack on Scott and what he considered to be the excesses of romanticism. In this first novel, Paulding hoped to demonstrate that Fielding, rather than Scott, was the proper model for American novelists. When *Koningsmarke* was misread and praised for the wrong reasons, Paulding abandoned satire and modified his attitude toward romanticism. *The Dutchman's Fireside*, set in the 1750's and in an area (upstate New York) that Cooper had already celebrated, was widely praised – not only by Cooper himself but by British readers, including an anonymous critic for *The Westminster Review* who praised Paulding for being "neither too elaborate like

Irving, nor too diffuse like Cooper." Paulding's third novel, *Westward Ho!*, captured the sense of adventure that urged many of his contemporaries to move from a settled east to an unsettled and still dangerous west. A fourth novel, *The Old Continental*, is based on the Benedict Arnold episode of the American Revolution. This and *The Puritan and His Daughter* were poorly planned and awkwardly written; they deserve the neglect they received even in Paulding's time.

Although Paulding had great ambitions as a playwright, he wrote only two plays of note, both comedies that dramatized social tensions between the England and America of his time. The second of them, *The Lion of the West*, won him a national prize, and was successfully produced in America and in London. It is most memorable for the character of Nimrod Wildfire, who closely resembles the American frontier hero, Davy Crockett.

Paulding's greatest success as a biographer came with his *Life of Washington*, a work that appeared in numerous editions until it was superseded by Washington Irving's.

—Thomas F. O'Donnell

PEACOCK, Thomas Love. English. Born in Weymouth, Dorset, 18 October 1785; moved with his mother to Chertsey, Surrey, 1788. Educated at Mr. Wicks' school in Englefield Green, Surrey. Married Jane Gryffydh in 1820 (died, 1852); four children. Settled in London, 1802, continued his studies on his own, and worked for merchants to support himself while writing; Secretary to Sir Home Riggs Popham, at Flushing, 1808–09; lived in North Wales, 1810–11; met Shelley, 1812, accompanied him on a visit to Edinburgh, 1813, and settled near him at Great Marlow, 1816; received a pension from Shelley; subsequently acted as the executor of Shelley's estate; joined the East India Company, London, 1819: Chief Examiner, 1836 until he retired, 1856; contributed to *Fraser's Magazine* until 1860. Lived in Halliford, near Shepperton, Middlesex. *Died 23 January 1866.*

PUBLICATIONS

Collections

>   *Works*, edited by H. F. B. Brett-Smith and C. E. Jones.   10 vols., 1924–34.
>   *The Novels*, edited by David Garnett.   1948.
>   *A Selection*, edited by H. L. B. Moody.   1966.

Novels

>   *Headlong Hall*.   1816; revised edition, 1816, 1823, 1837.
>   *Melincourt*.   1817.
>   *Nightmare Abbey*.   1818; revised edition, 1837; edited by Raymond Wright, with
>   *Crotchet Castle*, 1969.
>   *Maid Marian*.   1822; revised edition, 1837.
>   *The Misfortunes of Elphin*.   1829.
>   *Crotchet Castle*.   1831; edited by Raymond Wright, with *Nightmare Abbey*, 1969.
>   *Gryll Grange*.   1861.

Plays

> Plays (includes *The Dilettanti, The Three Doctors, The Circle of Leda*), edited by A. B.
> Young. 1910.

Verse

> *The Monks of St. Marks.* 1804.
> *Palmyra and Other Poems.* 1806.
> *The Genius of the Thames: A Lyrical Poem in Two Parts.* 1810.
> *The Genius of the Thames, Palmyra, and Other Poems.* 1812.
> *The Philosophy of Melancholy · A Poem in Four Parts, with a Mythological One.* 1812.
> *Sir Hornbook; or, Childe Launcelot's Expedition: A Grammatico-Allegorical Ballad.* 1813.
> *Sir Proteus: A Satirical Ballad.* 1814.
> *The Round Table; or, King Arthur's Feast.* 1817.
> *Rhododaphne; or, The Thessalian Spell.* 1818.
> *The Stable Boy.* 1820.
> *Paper Money Lyrics and Other Poems.* 1837.
> *Songs from the Novels.* 1902.
> *A Bill for the Better Promotion of Oppression on the Sabbath Day.* 1926.

Other

> *The Four Ages of Poetry.* 1863; edited by J. E. Jordan, 1965.
> *A Whitebait Dinner at Lovegrove's at Blackwall* (Greek and Latin text by Peacock,
>   English version by John Cam Hobhouse). 1851.
> *Calidore and Miscellanea,* edited by Richard Garnett. 1891.
> *Memoirs of Shelley, with Shelley's Letters to Peacock,* edited by H. F. B. Brett-
>   Smith. 1909; edited by Humbert Wolfe, in *The Life of Shelley* by Peacock, Hogg,
>   and Trelawny, 1933.
> *Letters to Edward Hookham and Shelley, with Fragments of Unpublished Manuscripts,*
>   edited by Richard Garnett. 1910.
> *Memoirs of Shelley and Other Essays and Reviews,* edited by Howard Mills. 1970.

> Translator, *Gl'Ingannati, The Deceived: A Comedy Performed at Siena in 1531, and
>   Aelia Laelia Crispis.* 1862; edited by H. H. Furness, in *New Variorum Edition of
>   Shakespeare,* vol. 13, 1901.

Reading List: *The Critical Reputation of Peacock* by Bill Read, 1959 (includes bibliography);
Peacock by J. I. M. Stewart, 1963; *Peacock* by Lionel Madden, 1967; *Peacock: His Circle and
His Age* by Howard Mills, 1968; *His Fine Wit: A Study of Peacock* by Carl Dawson, 1970;
Peacock (biography) by Felix Felton, 1973.

*   *   *

Thomas Love Peacock is one of the small number of writers who have created a totally
personal and idiosyncratic type of fiction. Whatever he may have owed to Aristophanes, or
Rabelais, or Voltaire, or Robert Bage, Peacock wrote novels unique in their blend of comedy
and the play of ideas. *Headlong Hall* and *Melincourt* established this pattern, with their
caricature characters like Squire Headlong, Mr. Milestone, Sir Oran Haut-Ton (the nearly-

human parliamentary candidate) and Sir Telegraph Paxarett, who indulge in much conversation in which each is able to reveal his particular preoccupation (though Sir Oran maintains an impressive silence). The clash of ideas is usually so extreme that a kind of intellectual farce ensues. In *Nightmare Abbey*, *Crotchet Castle* and *Gryll Grange* Peacock exploited his form to the best effect, while *Maid Marian* and *The Misfortunes of Elphin* are more historical and more romantic.

Nightmare Abbey centres on a rendering of Peacock's friend Shelley in the character of Scythrop Glowry, a young man unable to make up his mind between the charms of two young ladies; but the interest is in the interplay of ideas between a number of entertaining characters, including Mr. Flosky, the transcendental philosopher (a caricature of Coleridge), and Mr. Cypress, the melancholy poet (based on Byron). Through the amusing dialogue Peacock suggests the latent absurdity of the romantic commitment to extremes. His own attitude may be inferred as based on the supremacy of common sense.

In fact some critics have felt that Peacock's scepticism about ideals amounts to a species of clever Philistinism, with no positive creative elements. But the evidence of the novels, and especially *Crotchet Castle*, is that the humour aroused by the extravagances of the contrasting characters constitutes a value of its own, from which the ideals of toleration and humanity emerge unscathed. Peacock's intelligent awareness of his own time is shown in *Crotchet Castle* by his choice of characters, who are well suited to satisfy their host's curiosity over current issues; Mr. Crotchet explains why he has invited his guests: "The sentimental against the rational, the intuitive against the inductive, the ornamental against the useful, the intense against the tranquil, the romantic against the classical; these are great and interesting controversies, which I should like, before I die, to see satisfactorily settled." The reader must not share Mr. Crotchet's eagerness for certainties if he is to enjoy the novel, but he will find in the Scots economist Mr. MacQuedy, the Utopian Mr. Toogood, the operatic Mr. Trillo, and the Gothic enthusiast Mr. Chainmail amusing exemplifications of contemporary interests. Peacock deals neatly with the problem of ending his novels by including an element of romance – in this case between Captain Fitzchrome and Lady Clarinda – which can find its consummation in music (Peacock is adept at providing suitable songs) and in marriage.

The most vivid presence in *Crotchet Castle*, though, is undoubtedly the genial *bon viveur* Dr. Folliott, whose robust common sense and addiction to the Classics offer a sane contrast to the evanescent enthusiasms of the other guests. He is a similar type of character to the Reverend Doctor Opimian in *Gryll Grange*, written some thirty years later but in precisely the same style as the earlier novels. Here Peacock is still astute and lively in his dismissal of the system-mongers, who were building the commercial world which the Victorians have bequeathed to later generations. Peacock's criticisms here have something of the mellowness of old age, and there is an attractive Elysian quality about the setting in the unenclosed New Forest. By this time Meredith had married Peacock's daughter, and Meredith was to give a sardonic picture of the old man as Dr. Middleton, the father of the heroine of *The Egoist*, ready to sacrifice his daughter for another glass of the exquisite Patterne port. The central characters of Peacock's creation, however, strike us as achieving a sound balance between humanity and hedonism, and so contribute to that sense of good order which gives strength to the comic structures of his novels.

The comedy of ideas has no better English practitioner, and although it may be a limited form, it is one which combines civilisation and entertainment in equal measure. Peacock thus fully deserves the tribute of F. R. Leavis's footnote in *The Great Tradition* where he is praised for having created books "that have permanent life as light reading – indefinitely re-readable – for minds with mature interests."

—Peter Faulkner

PEAKE, Mervyn (Laurence).   English.   Born in Kuling, China, 9 July 1911. Educated at Tientsin Grammar School; Eltham College, Kent, 1923–29; Croydon College of Art, Surrey, 1929; Royal Academy schools, London, 1929–33. Served in the British Army, 1941–43; military artist for the Ministry of Information, 1943–45. Married Maeve Gilmore in 1937; two sons and one daughter. Taught at Westminster School of Art, London, 1936–41, and Central School of Art, London, 1949–60. Book and magazine illustrator: one-man shows – Calman Gallery, London, 1943; Peter Jones Gallery, London, 1944; toured Europe as staff artist of *The Leader*, 1945. Hospitalized for encephalitis, 1964–68. Recipient: Royal Literary Fund bursary, 1948; Heinemann Award, 1951. Fellow, Royal Society of Literature. *Died 18 November 1968.*

PUBLICATIONS

Collections

Selected Poems.   1972.
Writings and Drawings, edited by Maeve Gilmore and Shelagh Johnson.   1975.

Fiction

The Gormenghast Trilogy: Titus Groan, 1946; *Gormenghast*, 1950; *Titus Alone*, 1959.
Mr. Pye.   1953.

Plays

The Connoisseurs (produced 1952).
The Wit to Woo (produced 1957).

Radio Plays and Talks: *The Artist's World*, 1947; *Book Illustrations*, 1947; *Alice and Tenniel and Me*, 1954; *Titus Groan*, from his own novel, 1956; *The Voice of One*, 1956; *For Mr. Pye – An Island*, from his own novel, 1957.

Verse

Shapes and Sounds.   1941.
Rhymes Without Reason.   1944.
The Glassblowers.   1950.
The Rhyme of the Flying Bomb.   1962.
Poems and Drawings.   1965.
A Reverie of Bone and Other Poems.   1967.
A Book of Nonsense.   1972.
Twelve Poems, 1939–1960.   1975.

Other

Captain Slaughterboard Drops Anchor (juvenile).   1939; revised edition, 1945, 1967.
The Craft of the Lead Pencil.   1946.

Letters from a Lost Uncle (juvenile).   1948.
Drawings.   1950.
Figures of Speech (drawings).   1954.
The Drawings, text by Hilary Spurling.   1974.
Peake's Progress, edited by Maeve Gilmore.   1978.

Reading List: *A World Away: A Memoir of Peake* by Maeve Gilmore, 1970; *Peake: A Biographical and Critical Examination* by John Batchelor, 1974; *Peake* (biography) by John Watney, 1976.

*   *   *

Mervyn Peake's is a visual imagination: the strength of his literary accomplishment lies in its realization of atmosphere by an obsessive attention to detail, while as a book-illustrator he ranks with Tenniel in illustrating *Alice,* and captures the literary grotesquerie of Dickens and the brothers Grimm as well. The essence of his artistic style is a fanciful interweaving of form where art and nature are distorted into a bizarre congruity.

His verse belongs generically to the nonsense school of Lewis Carroll and Edward Lear, the masters of the logical absurd. Equally, his work belongs to the traditions of painter-poets, for in any piece the written word is closely allied to the visual image. The *Letters from a Lost Uncle,* for example, bring the notion of an "illuminated manuscript" into contemporary focus, with a playful embellishment of ill-typed script by sketches and doodles, obeying an inconsequential humour. Indeed Peake's originality lies in the way that he combines the grinning gargoyles of whimsy with an artistic and moral coherence that gives an architectonic structure to his Gothic vision. This is magnificently achieved in the Gormenghast trilogy.

True to the traditions of Gothic romance (a tradition that begins with Walpole's *The Castle of Otranto* and takes in Radcliffe's *The Mysteries of Udolpho* to reach the nineteenth-century formula of crumbling ruins, bats, owls, and subterranean passages), *Titus Groan* and its sequels are concerned with power structures, with individuals threatened by or rebelling against absolute, rigorous authority (in this case, the ritual of inherited custom). The Gothic edifice externalizes the inner psyche. Gormenghast itself is the labyrinthine matrix of childhood fears, adolescent uncertainties, adult obsession, and social taboo. Peake's hero rejects these on acquiring the "stronghold" of self-determination at the close of the last book, and there the Bildungsroman is complete. By comparison, the other rebel of the series, Steerpike, aspiring from the lower kitchens to the topmost pinnacle of Gormenghast by working to the system and exploiting its weaknesses, fulfils a typical novelistic paradigm and takes on the mantle of Barquentine to become lord of ritual, the canker at the centre of the decaying and disintegrating Gormenghast. Apparent ironies or absurdities of name and accident are justified within the complete structure of Peake's cosmos, where nothing is lost to the sublime magnitude, sprawling in its putrefaction like the rhetorical desciptions that amplify it.

The epic weight of the trilogy overshadows Peake's other work, and earned him a cult following in the late 1960's, possibly in recognition of the way that he can rationalize the fantastic, the grotesque, and the violent in a congruent insanity of vision. As a war-artist, Peake entered Belsen to observe corruption there that exceeded the wildest flights of Gothic fancy. Even Peake's lighter fiction carries the mark of the author's view of humankind as tragic. The hero of *Mr. Pye* fails ridiculously to achieve humanity; he cannot resolve the paradoxes of morality and can live only as angel or devil. For Peake the tragedy of existence is relieved by the comic disproportion that exists between human beings and their belief: a grotesqueness encapsulated by the grinning gargoyles on a Gothic ruin.

—B. C. Oliver-Morden

PERCY, Walker.   American.   Born in Birmingham, Alabama, 28 May 1916. Educated at the University of North Carolina, Chapel Hill, B.A. 1937; Columbia University, New York, M.D. 1941; intern at Bellevue Hospital, New York, 1942. Married Mary Bernice Townsend in 1946; two daughters. Contracted tuberculosis, gave up medicine, and became a full-time writer, 1943. Recipient: National Book Award, 1962; National Institute of Arts and Letters grant, 1967. Fellow, American Academy of Arts and Sciences; Member, National Institute of Arts and Letters. Lives in Covington, Louisiana.

PUBLICATIONS

Fiction

The Moviegoer.   1961.
The Last Gentleman.   1966.
Love in the Ruins: The Adventures of a Bad Catholic at a Time Near the End of the World.   1971.
Lancelot.   1977.

Other

The Message in the Bottle: How Queer Man Is, How Queer Language Is, and What One Has to Do with the Other.   1975.

Reading List: *City of Words* by Tony Tanner, 1971.

*   *   *

Walker Percy belongs to the movement in modern Southern writing that derives from T. S. Eliot and includes, among others, Allen Tate, Caroline Gordon, Robert Penn Warren, and William Faulkner. Percy is a traditionalist in reaction against what is perceived as the decay of moral standards, the loss of a sense of community and of shared values. His ideas are given rather full intellectual scope in his work of non-fiction, *The Message in the Bottle*. In his novels the issue is focused on sexuality, and the problem, as expressed in his fiction, is how to square sexual desire with traditional ideas of love and responsibility, complicated by the modern confusion of love and sex. What used to be regarded as sin and perversion is now acceptable to, even sanctioned by, church and state. The traditional concept of love is too idealistic to provide Percy's protagonists with a satisfactory pattern of behavior. Inevitably his novels involve the setting up of the problem and the working out of a solution, the protagonist wrestling with his moral confusion, then, finally, creating for himself a synthesis in which love and lust – giving and taking – are appropriately balanced.

His first novel, *The Moviegoer*, concludes with the protagonist, a lusty bachelor, failing in his latest sexual escapade and marrying a young woman of his own class, partly out of affection, but also because they share a sense of experienced responsibility. In *The Last Gentleman*, the hero, who suffers emotional detachment (which Percy sees as the chief modern malady) cures himself through his personal devotion to a dying youth and in turn helps cure a confused young woman and her cynical older brother. *Love in the Ruins*, set in the future "at a time near the end of the world," deals with the collapse of modern technology and concludes with the responsible marriage of the protagonist who tries to save his doomed world but, failing that, gives himself over to whiskey and lust for three beautiful women. At the novel's close he marries the most responsible and moral of the three and begins to live a simple, natural, and properly lustful life in the shadow of the remnants of the old Catholic Church. In *Lancelot* the pessimism is deeper, the solution more tenuous. The hero, at first tolerant of his wife's sexual infidelity, finally kills her and her lover, is confined to a mental institution, is "cured" and then released into the world. For a time, he takes on the responsibility of a young woman raped and maimed by a gang of thugs, but is rebuffed by the young woman in language suggestive to radical feminist ideology. Percy's latest protagonist then stands alone against a world shown to be corrupt beyond redemption. Even the Church, it seems, has fallen into the modern abyss confusion. A slight ray of final hope is that the young woman may eventually join him in his exile.

Percy's rendering of characters and scenes is striking, vivid, and bitingly satirical. He is a moral and, ultimately, a religious writer, but a perceptive novelist of manners as well. His sensitive and poetic style elevates material that less subtly treated might appear contrived and moralistic.

—W. J. Stuckey

PERELMAN, S(idney) J(oseph).   American.   Born in Brooklyn, New York, 1 February 1904. Educated at Brown University, Providence, Rhode Island, 1921–25, B.A. 1925. Married Laura West in 1929 (died, 1970); one son and one daughter. Writer and artist for *Judge* magazine, 1925–29, and for *College Humor* magazine, 1929–30; full-time writer from 1930; contributor to *The New Yorker* from 1931; lived in London, 1970–72. Recipient: New York Film Critics Award, 1936; Academy Award, 1956. Member, National Institute of Arts and Letters. Lives in New York City.

PUBLICATIONS

Prose

>Dawn Ginsbergh's Revenge.   1929.
>Parlor, Bedlam and Bath, with Q. J. Reynolds.   1930.
>Strictly from Hunger.   1937.
>Look Who's Talking.   1940.
>The Dream Department.   1943.
>Crazy Like a Fox.   1944.
>Keep It Crisp.   1946.
>Acres and Pains.   1947.
>The Best of Perelman.   1947.
>Westward Ha! or, Around the World in Eighty Clichés.   1947.
>Listen to the Mocking Bird.   1949.
>The Swiss Family Perelman.   1950.
>The Ill-Tempered Clavicord.   1952.
>Perelman's Home Companion: A Collector's Item (the Collector Being S. J. Perelman) of
>   36 Otherwise Unavailable Pieces by Himself.   1955.
>The Road to Miltown; or, Under the Spreading Atrophy.   1957; as Bite on the Bullet; or,
>   Under the Spreading Atrophy, 1957.

The Most of Perelman.   1958.
The Rising Gorge.   1961.
Chicken Inspector No. 23.   1966.
Baby, It's Cold Inside.   1970.
Monkey Business.   1973.
Vinegar Puss.   1975.
Eastward Ha!   1977.
The Most of Perelman (omnibus).   1978.

Plays

Sketches in *The Third Little Show* (produced 1931).
Sketches, with Robert MacGunigle, in *Walk a Little Faster* (produced 1932).
All Good Americans, with Laura Perelman (produced 1933).
Sketches in *Two Weeks with Pay* (produced 1940).
The Night Before Christmas, with Laura Perelman (produced 1941).   1942.
One Touch of Venus, with Ogden Nash, music by Kurt Weill, based on *The Tinted Venus* by F. Anstey (produced 1943).   1944.
Sweet Bye and Bye, with Al Hirschfield, music by Vernon Duke, lyrics by Ogden Nash (produced 1946).
The Beauty Part, with Ogden Nash (produced 1961).   1963.

Screenplays: *Horse Feathers,* with others, 1932; *The Miracle Man,* with others, 1932; *Florida Special,* with others, 1936; *Boy Trouble,* with others, 1939; *Ambush,* with Laura Perelman and Robert Ray, 1939; *The Golden Fleecing,* with others, 1940; *Around the World in Eighty Days,* with James Poe and John Farrow, 1956.

*   *   *

As a screenwriter, a playwright, and, primarily, an essayist, S. J. Perelman has spent nearly fifty years perfecting a unique and surrealistic sytle of humor marked by an uncontrollable imagination and an enormous, arcane vocabulary. Perhaps best described as a mixture of Groucho Marx (with whom he worked) and James Joyce (whom he called "the comic writer of the century"), Perelman is a roman candle of language, firing off metaphors where the untrained eye might see only an unloaded verb: "Carstairs exchanged a quizzical glance with his manservant, fitted it into an ivory holder, and lit it abstractedly." At the extreme, Perelman's sentences leap from pillar to post with a sheerly linguistic logic, sneering at cliché: "On her dainty egg-shaped head was massed a crop of auburn curls; the cucumbers she had grown there the previous summer were forgotten in the pulsing rhythm of the moment." Perelman's distinguishing characteristic is his total imaginative control of the work, and consequently neither his film scripts nor his stage plays have the comic intensity of the meticulously crafted essays.

Perelman's distaste for the mediocrity of the everyday world has manifested itself in a complete disdain for broad political and social satire. A large number of his essays take aim at popular movies, magazines, and novels, at newspapers, at advertising – soft prose and soft thinking of all stripes. Increasingly, however, he has turned inward, spinning off exotic tales from the merest personal anecdotes. Perelman is pleased to call himself a *feuilletoniste,* a writer of lapidary prose, and a crank who only writes when sufficiently enraged. He once summed up his interest in humor with these words (*New York Times Magazine,* 26 January 1969): "For me, its chief merit is the use of the unexpected, the glancing allusion, the deflation of pomposity, and the constant repetition of one's helplessness in a majority of situations."

—Walter Bode

PHILLIPS, David Graham. American. Born in Madison, Indiana, 31 October 1867. Educated in local schools; Asbury University, later DePauw University, Greencastle, Indiana, 1883–85; College of New Jersey, later Princeton University, 1885–87, A.B. 1887. Reporter for the *Cincinnati Star Times*, 1888, and the *Cincinnati Commercial Gazette*, 1889–90; settled in New York City: member of the editorial staff of the *Sun*, 1890–93; London Correspondent, 1893, General Reporter, 1893–95, Feature Writer, 1895–97, and Member of the Editorial Department, 1897–1902, *New York World*; full-time writer from 1902; active contributor to various national magazines, especially the *Saturday Evening Post*, Philadelphia, and *Cosmopolitan*, New York. *Died* (murdered) *24 January 1911.*

PUBLICATIONS

Fiction

> *The Great God Success.* 1901.
> *Her Serene Highness.* 1902.
> *A Woman Ventures.* 1902.
> *Golden Fleece: The American Adventures of a Fortune-Hunting Earl.* 1903.
> *The Master-Rogue: The Confessions of a Croesus.* 1903.
> *The Cost.* 1904.
> *The Social Secretary.* 1905.
> *The Deluge.* 1905.
> *The Mother-Light.* 1905.
> *The Plum Tree.* 1905.
> *The Fortune Hunter.* 1906.
> *Light-Fingered Gentry.* 1907.
> *The Second Generation.* 1907.
> *Old Wives for New.* 1908.
> *The Fashionable Adventures of Joshua Craig.* 1909.
> *The Hungry Heart.* 1909.
> *White Magic.* 1910.
> *The Husband's Story.* 1911.
> *The Conflict.* 1911.
> *The Grain of Dust.* 1911.
> *George Helm.* 1912.
> *The Price She Paid.* 1912.
> *Degarmo's Wife and Other Stories.* 1913.
> *Susan Lenox: Her Fall and Rise.* 1917.

Play

> *The Worth of a Woman* (produced 1908). 1908.

Other

> *The Reign of Gilt.* 1905.
> *The Treason of the Senate* (essays). 1953.

* * *

David Graham Phillips's first novel, *The Great God Success*, concerns a newspaperman who gains fortune and power by championing the cause of the people against "the interests," but who sells out when he begins to identify with the rich. In *The Deluge, Light-Fingered Gentry, The Master-Rogue*, and *The Grain of Dust* Phillips also dealt with the corrupting influence of capitalism on essentially good men.

While in college, Phillips roomed with Albert Beveridge, who was later to serve as Senator from Indiana. They remained good friends for the rest of their lives, and Phillips used Beveridge as a model for his paragon of political virtues, Hampden Scarborough. In *The Cost*, Scarborough's career is contrasted with his rival in love, an evil industrialist named Dumont. Scarborough's legislation ultimately triumphs over the capitalist's trusts. In *The Plum Tree*, Scarborough becomes a foil to a dishonest political power-broker. In these, as in his other political novels, *The Fashionable Adventures of Joshua Craig* and *George Helm*, Phillips recommends a vague populism and a return to honesty as the answer to the enormous social and economic problems facing America. His interest seems to be in exposing corruption, not in solving problems.

In his two "economic" novels, Phillips was somewhat bolder. Victor Dorn, the hero of *The Conflict*, is a revolutionary who contends that Marx will dominate the next two thousand years as Christ has dominated the last two thousand. In *The Second Generation*, Phillips seems to recommend the abolition of inherited property because of the harm done to both society and property-owners themselves.

Yet Phillips's greatest achievement was in his novels dealing with women's place in modern society. In *A Woman Ventures, Old Wives for New, The Price She Paid*, and in his only play, *The Worth of a Woman*, he ridiculed the stereotypical weak, soft home-bodies and extolled the virtues of women who competed on equal terms with men. In *The Hungry Heart* he defended the rights of neglected women to seek sexual satisfaction outside the bonds of matrimony. Phillips's most impressive novel, *Susan Lenox: Her Fall and Rise*, published posthumously, chronicles the life of a girl who is condemned by social forces beyond her control to a life of vice and crime. Nothing in Dreiser or Sinclair can match the brutality of Phillips's pictures of slum life and the horrors of white slavery. Through all her degradation, Susan maintains her essential dignity. When she overcomes her poverty, she still rejects all offers of respectability and marriage.

When Roosevelt applied the term "Muckraker" to a certain kind of investigative reporting, he was specifically referring to Phillips and his *Treason of the Senate*, and it is for his reporting, not his literary work, that history will remember him. Yet his novels provide a valuable insight into the hopeful, optimistic America of his era.

—William Higgins

PLOMER, William (Charles Franklyn). South African. Born in Pietersburg, Transvaal, 10 December 1903. Educated at Spondon House School; Beechmont, Sevenoaks, Kent; Rugby School; St. John's College, Johannesburg. Served in the Navy Intelligence Division, 1940–45. Farmed in South Africa; taught in Japan in the 1920's; Editor, with Roy Campbell, *Voorslag*, 1928; Fiction Reviewer, *Spectator*, London, 1933–38; succeeded Edward Garnett as Literary Adviser to Jonathan Cape, publishers, London, 1937. President, Poetry Society, London, 1968–71; President, Kilvert Society, Hereford, 1968–73. Recipient: Queen's Gold Medal for Poetry, 1963; Whitbread Award, 1973. D.Litt.: University of Durham, 1958. Fellow, Royal Society of Literature, 1951. C.B.E. (Commander, Order of the British Empire), 1968. *Died 21 September 1973.*

PUBLICATIONS

Collections

> *Electric Delights* (selections), edited by Rupert Hart-Davis.   1978.

Fiction

> *Turbott Wolfe.*   1926.
> *I Speak for Africa* (stories).   1927.
> *Paper Houses* (stories).   1929.
> *Sado.*   1931; as *They Never Came Back*, 1932.
> *The Case Is Altered.*   1932.
> *The Child of Queen Victoria and Other Stories.*   1933.
> *The Invaders.*   1934.
> *Curious Relations* (stories), with Anthony Butts.   1945.
> *Four Countries* (stories).   1949.
> *Museum Pieces.*   1952.

Plays

> *Gloriana*, music by Benjamin Britten (produced 1953).   1953.
> *Curlew River: A Parable*, music by Benjamin Britten, from a play by Juro Motomasa
>   (produced 1964).   1964.
> *The Burning Fiery Furnace*, music by Benjamin Britten (produced 1966).   1966.
> *The Prodigal Son*, music by Benjamin Britten (produced 1968).   1968.

Verse

> *Notes for Poems.*   1927.
> *The Family Tree.*   1929.
> *The Fivefold Screen.*   1932.
> *Visiting the Caves.*   1936.
> *Selected Poems.*   1940.
> *The Dorking Thigh and Other Satires.*   1945.
> *A Shot in the Park.*   1955; as *Borderline Ballads*, 1955.
> *Collected Poems.*   1960; revised edition, 1973.
> *A Choice of Ballads.*   1960.
> *Taste and Remember.*   1966.
> *Celebrations.*   1972.

Other

> *Cecil Rhodes.*   1933.
> *Ali the Lion: Ali of Tebeleni, Pasha of Jannina, 1741–1822.*   1936; as *The Diamond of
>   Jannina: Ali Pasha 1741–1822*, 1970.
> *Double Lives: An Autobiography.*   1943.
> *At Home: Memoirs.*   1958.
> *Conversation with My Younger Self.*   1963.
> *The Butterfly Ball and the Grasshopper Feast* (juvenile).   1973.

The Autobiography (revised versions of *Double Lives* and *At Home*).   1975.

Editor, *Japanese Lady in Europe*, by Haruko Ichikawa.   1937.
Editor, *Kilvert's Diary 1870–1879*.   3 vols., 1938–40; abridged edition, 1944; revised edition, 3 vols., 1960.
Editor, *Selected Poems of Herman Melville*.   1943.
Editor, with Anthony Thwaite and Hilary Corke, *New Poems 1961: A P.E.N. Anthology*.   1961.
Editor, *A Message in Code: The Diary of Richard Rumbold, 1932–1960*.   1964.
Editor, *Burn These Letters: Alice Lemon to Winifred Nicol, 1959–62*.   1973.

Translator, with Jack Cope, *Selected Poems of Ingrid Jonker*.   1968.

Reading List: *Plomer* by John R. Doyle, 1969.

*   *   *

William Plomer was a poet, novelist, and short story writer. He also wrote biographies, *Cecil Rhodes* and *Ali Pasha*, four libretti for works by Benjamin Britten, and was the discoverer and editor of *Kilvert's Diary 1870–1879*. J. R. Ackerley, one of his closest friends, sometimes addressed him in letters as "S.W.," and when I asked Plomer if I was correct in guessing that this stood for "Sweet William," he replied, "Yes, but it seems immodest to admit it." When he turned to writing about his own life, modesty inhibited his two attempts: *Double Lives* and *At Home* add up to little more than a series of nicely told anecdotes about his family and literary friends. There is not a word about the homosexual undertones present in his work. Candour, he believed, could be both tiresome and uncivilized because it could make an author unduly self-centred.

Plomer was born of English immigrant parents in the Transvaal, and his school years were divided between being educated in England and holidays in South Africa. When he was 16 he helped his father run a Zulu trading station. His first novel, *Turbott Wolfe*, which he began in his late teens, is an angry young man's book that refuses to take apartheid for granted. Today it is regarded by liberal South Africans as a pioneer work – though banned in their country.

His next novel, *Sado*, contrasts Japanese and European attitudes to life, and forsees the dangers inherent in Japanese militarist nationalism. Plomer had gone to Japan in 1926, taught at various colleges, but declined the chair of English literature at Tokyo University. His remaining three novels are set in England. A real life murder in Bayswater is the subject of *The Case Is Altered*, and the effects of unemployment on those who flocked to London during the depression in the 1930's is the theme of *The Invaders*. *Museum Pieces*, which opens after the Second World War, is concerned with a group of propertied upper-middle-class characters whose insistence on living in an Edwardian past turns them into "museum pieces." These three novels have not the same force as Plomer's earlier ones: they are too urbane, too detached. Five volumes of short stories – many of them traveller's tales in effect – make up the rest of his fiction.

Plomer was an excellent, though often underrated, minor poet of his day. Many of his ballads, despite their outward wit, probe at our uneasy civilization and deal with its exploitation of sex, racism, and class. One about D'Arcy Honeybunn, "the playboy of the demi-world," contains a line that already has a place in several books of quotations – "A rose-red cissy half as old as time." "Death of a Hedge-Sparrow" is a fine example of Plomer as a nature poet. But he is at his most powerful when he describes the ironies of life in South Africa, noting how iced drinks are served to immigrant settlers by "white gloves [that] disguise black hands." "The Taste of the Fruit" is a bitter, eloquent elegy about the deaths of the Afrikaans poet Ingrid Jonker and the writer Nathaniel Nakasa. In a poem called "Another Old Man," in Plomer's last book of verse, *Celebrations*, the poet provides his own epitaph.

These are its concluding lines:

> HE WAS JOKY BY NATURE
> SAD, SCEPTICAL, PROUD.
> WHAT HE WOULD NEVER FOLLOW,
> OR LEAD, WAS A CROWD.

—Neville Braybrooke

POE, Edgar Allan. American. Born in Boston, Massachusetts, 19 January 1809; orphaned, and given a home by John Allan, 1812. Educated at the Dubourg sisters' boarding school, Chelsea, London, 1816–17; Manor House School, Stoke Newington, London, 1817–20; Joseph H. Clarke's School, Richmond, 1820–23; William Burke's School, Richmond, 1823–25; University of Virginia, Charlottesville, 1826; United States Military Academy, West Point, New York, 1830–31. Served in the United States Army, 1827–29: Sergeant-Major. Married his 13-year-old cousin Virginia Clemm in 1836 (died, 1847). Journalist and editor: Assistant Editor, 1835, and Editor, 1836–37, *Southern Literary Messenger*, Richmond; Assistant Editor, *Gentleman's Magazine*, Philadelphia, 1839–40; Editor, *Graham's Lady's and Gentleman's Magazine*, Philadelphia, 1841–42; Sub-Editor, *New York Evening Mirror*, 1844; Co-Editor, *Broadway Journal*, 1845–46, New York. Lecturer after 1844. *Died 7 October 1849.*

PUBLICATIONS

Collections

> *Complete Works*, edited by James A. Harrison. 17 vols., 1902.
> *The Letters*, edited by John Ward Ostrom. 1948; revised edition, 2 vols., 1966.
> *Poems*, edited by Floyd Stovall. 1965.
> *Collected Works*, edited by Thomas O. Mabbott. 1969–

Fiction

> *The Narrative of Arthur Gordon Pym of Nantucket.* 1838.
> *Tales of the Grotesque and Arabesque.* 1840.
> *The Murders in the Rue Morgue, and The Man That Was Used Up.* 1843.
> *Tales.* 1845.
> *The Literati.* 1850.

Play

> *Politian: An Unfinished Tragedy*, edited by Thomas O. Mabbott. 1923.

Verse

> *Tamerlane and Other Poems.* 1827.
> *Al Aaraaf, Tamerlane, and Minor Poems.* 1829.
> *Poems.* 1831.
> *The Raven and Other Poems.* 1845.

Other

> *The Conchologist's First Book* (revised by Poe). 1839.
> *Eureka: A Prose Poem.* 1848; edited by Richard P. Benton, 1973.
> *Literary Criticism,* edited by Robert L. Hough. 1965.

Bibliography: *Bibliography of the Writings of Poe* by John W. Robertson, 1934; *A Bibliography of First Printings of the Writings of Poe* by C. F. Heartman and J. R. Canny, 1941; *Poe: A Bibliography of Criticism 1827–1967* by J. Lesley Dameron and Irby B. Cauthen, Jr., 1974.

Reading List: *Poe: A Critical Biography* by Arthur H. Quinn, 1941; *Poe: A Critical Study* by Edward H. Davidson, 1957; *The French Face of Poe* by Patrick F. Quinn, 1957; *Poe the Poet: Essays New and Old on the Man and His Work* by Floyd Stovall, 1959; *Poe* by Vincent Buranelli, 1961; *Poe* by Geoffrey Rans, 1965; *The Recognition of Poe: Selected Criticism since 1829* edited by Eric W. Carlson, 1966; *Poe: A Collection of Critical Essays* edited by Robert Regan, 1967; *Poe, Journalist and Critic* by Robert D. Jacobs, 1969; *Poe Poe Poe Poe Poe Poe Poe* by Daniel Hoffman, 1972; *Poe's Fiction: Romantic Irony in the Gothic Tales* by G. R. Thompson, 1973; *Poe* by David Sinclair, 1977; *The Tell-Tale Heart: The Life and Works of Poe* by Julian Symons, 1978.

*   *   *

Although Edgar Allan Poe wrote that for him "poetry has been not a purpose but a passion," he wrote only some fifty poems (excluding his album verses, jingles, and acrostics). Obliged to work at drudging journalism, he never realized his dream of founding a literary magazine of his own. While grinding out scores of reviews of some of the most forgettable books of the nineteenth century he wrote the tales, poems, and essays on which his posthumous renown is based. Aiming his work "not above the popular, nor below the critical, taste," he made use, as a professional magazinist must, of the fictional conventions of his day, turning to his own obsessive needs the Gothic horror story ("Ligeia," "The Fall of the House of Usher," "Berenice") and the tale of exploration ("A Descent into the Maelstrom," *Narrative of A. Gordon Pym*). In "The Gold Bug," "The Murders in the Rue Morgue," and "The Purloined Letter" he virtually invented the modern detective story, and he set the mold upon science fiction with "Mesmeric Revelations," "The Facts in the Case of Monsieur Valdemar," and "The Balloon Hoax." He also wrote dozens of satirical sketches. His critical writings were the most systematic and intelligent produced in America until his time.

Despite the paucity of his productions as a poet, he proved a major influence upon Baudelaire, who translated several of his tales and wrote that if Poe had not existed, he would have had to invent him. Through Baudelaire, Poe's critical theories influenced the entire French Symbolist movement. Although Poe believed, with Tennyson, that imprecision of meaning was necessary for the creation of beauty, he also believed that the poet is a deliberate maker who devises all of his effects to contribute to the single aim of his poem. "The Philosophy of Composition," an essay purporting to demonstrate how Poe wrote "The

Raven," presents the creative process as an interlocked series of conscious choices. Although this would seem the opposite of the Romantic view of the poet as inspired seer, Poe's systematic process is in fact determined by Romantic necessity and is derived from Coleridge's aesthetic. That necessity is the excitation of the soul through the contemplation of the most melancholy of subjects – the death of a beautiful woman. The complex interaction in this theory between obsessive emotional need and what Poe in his detective stories called "ratiocination" is characteristic of all of his best work.

It seems ironic and cruel that a writer whose tales of guilt and terror won him the admiration of Dostoevsky had to live a hand-to-mouth existence and, after his death, was defamed by a hostile editor and reviled by readers who took as autobiographical the characters in his tales who were opium fiends and necrophiliacs. Allen Tate (in his essay "The Angelic Imagination") identifies what it is in Poe's work that really set on edge Victorian sensibility: the lack of any God save impersonal force, a fictive world without Christian morality. Far more evocatively than in the naturalistic novels of fifty years later, Poe imagined the nightmare of a universe without the consolations of faith.

This visionary author's life was unmitigatedly wretched. His parents were itinerant actors; the alcoholic father deserted, leaving Elizabeth Arnold Poe with three infant children. A brother and sister of Edgar's were adopted by connections in Baltimore but she kept young Eddie by her as she acted the heroine in plays no more melodramatic than his life would be. Stricken by tuberculosis, she died a lingering death in Richmond, Virginia, attended by kindly local matrons, when Edgar was only three. The boy was taken into the home of John Allan, a prosperous tobacco factor who brought Edgar to England when his business took him there and sent the boy to the school so vividly remembered in "William Wilson." Allan sent Poe to the new University of Virginia where, on a niggardly allowance among the scions of wealthy families, he ran up gambling debts and was expelled. Mrs. Allan, like Poe's natural mother, died of tuberculosis, and Poe, who had no inclination for the tobacco business, quarreled with his "Pa" (he had discovered Allan's infidelities while his wife was still alive). Allan withheld love from Edgar, never adopted him, and so Poe was cast adrift penniless to make his way as an author. Not even a hitch in the army or a later enlistment in the military academy at West Point mollified Allan. Poe, deciding to leave West Point, could not persuade "Pa" to intercede for his release and had to feign illness until he was expelled. By this time he had published two volumes of poems. One is dedicated to the Corps of Cadets.

Poe's career henceforth was as assistant or principal editor on several magazines in Richmond, Philadelphia, and New York. While so engaged, he wrote nearly 90 tales and sketches, countless critical columns and reviews, two novellas, and an astrophysical treatise on the nature of the universe, entitled *Eureka*, which he described as a poem.

Poe married his first cousin Virginia Clemm when she was thirteen and lived with her and her mother (his aunt) until Virginia too, died of tuberculosis at twenty-three. Thereafter Poe conducted frenzied courtships of several poetesses; at this time he well may have been mad with grief. He died in delirium, under unexplained circumstances, on a trip to Baltimore. Poe's biographers agree that he idealized women, and that sexual desire seems not to have had an overt part in any of his relationships.

Poe classified his own fiction into the categories of "Tales of the Grotesque and Arabesque." Borrowing these terms from Scott, Poe meant by them to describe satirical, bizarre, jocose writings on the one hand, and on the other the fictional equivalents of poems. These were his prose efforts to excite his readers' souls by the contemplation of beauty and terror. His review of Hawthorne outlines his theory of fiction. The tale, like the poem, must be all of a piece, each detail contributing to the desired unity of effect; symbolism (Poe in the nomenclature of the day calls it allegory) must be present as a "profound undercurrent" in the tale. His fiction will work by indirection.

In Poe's work there is a mysterious interpenetrability of the soul's excitation with subterranean dread. A *frisson* of horror runs through his most impassioned tales. The clue to Poe's contradictions may be in his sketch "The Imp of the Perverse," for the fiction frequently dramatizes its theme of man's irresistible urge toward self-destruction (a man is driven to commit a terrible crime, then to reveal his guilt). This connects also with the theme of double identity ("William Wilson," "The Cask of Amontillado") and Poe's strain of hoaxing, not entirely confined to his jocular productions. Poe delighted in tricking his readers. He would make them believe that his mesmerizer had really hypnotized a dying man so that the soul lingered and answered questions for months after the death of the body; or that his balloonists had actually crossed the Atlantic in three days, arriving in South Carolina. So too with fantastic descents into the maelstrom and journeys to the end of the earth and back. "The Philosophy of Composition" is in one respect such a hoax. Like his detective genius Monsieur Dupin, Poe demonstrates his intuitive intellectual superiority.

Although only in *Pym* did he write a successful fiction of more than thirty pages, Poe's significance is multifold. He is a systematic critic and theorist predictive of the Symbolist movement. His best poems and fictions embody his aesthetic intention that every part of the literary artifact must contribute to the unifying effect of the whole. His mastery of popular genres made him the unwitting godfather of much popular literature in the present century, as well as a major influence on films. His poetic theory passed from the Symbolists back into American poetry through T. S. Eliot and its influence continues in Allen Tate and Richard Wilbur, among others. His fiction is widely translated and widely read. Poe's work indeed has reached both the popular and the critical taste.

—Daniel Hoffman

PORTER, Hal. Australian. Born in Albert Park, Melbourne, Victoria, 16 February 1911. Educated at Kensington State School, 1917; Bairnsdale State School, Victoria, 1918–21; Bairnsdale High School, 1922–26. Married Olivia Parnham in 1939 (divorced, 1943). Cadet Reporter, *Bairnsdale Advertiser*, 1927; Schoolmaster, Victorian Education Department, 1927–37, 1940; Queen's College, Adelaide, 1941–42; Prince Alfred College, Kent Town, South Australia, 1943–46; Hutchins School, Hobart, Tasmania, 1946–47; Knox Grammar School, Sydney, 1947; Ballarat College, Victoria, 1948–49; Nijimura School, Kure, Japan (Australian Army Education), 1949–50; Director, National Theatre, Hobart, 1951–53; Chief Librarian of Bairnsdale and Shepparton, Victoria, 1953–61; full-time writer from 1961. Australian Writers Representative, Edinburgh Festival, 1962; Lecturer for the Australian Department of External Affairs, in Japan, 1967. Recipient: Sydney Sesquicentenary Prize, 1938; Commonwealth Literary Fund Fellowship, 1956, 1960, 1964, 1968, and Subsidy, 1957, 1962, 1967; Sydney Journalists' Club Prize, 1959, for drama, 1961; *Encyclopaedia Britannica* Award, 1967; Captain Cook Bi-Centenary Prize, 1970. Lives in Garvoc, Victoria.

PUBLICATIONS

Fiction

Short Stories. 1942.
A Handful of Pennies. 1958.
The Tilted Cross. 1961.
A Bachelor's Children. 1962.

The Cats of Venice (stories).   1965.
Mr. Butterfry and Other Tales of New Japan.   1970.
Selected Stories, edited by Leonie Kramer.   1971.
The Right Thing.   1971.
Fredo Fuss Love Life (stories).   1974.

Plays

The Tower (produced 1964).   1963.
The Professor (as *Toda-San,* produced 1965; as *The Professor,* produced 1965).   1966.
Eden House (produced 1969; as *Home on a Pig's Back,* produced 1972).   1969.
Parker (produced 1972).

Verse

The Hexagon.   1956.
Elijah's Ravens.   1968.
In an Australian Country Graveyard and Other Poems.   1973.

Other

The Watcher on the Cast-Iron Balcony (autobiography).   1963.
Australian Stars of Stage and Screen.   1965.
The Paper Chase (autobiography).   1966.
The Actors: An Image of the New Japan.   1968.
Criss-Cross (autobiography).   1973.
The Extra (autobiography).   1976.

Editor, *Australian Poetry 1957.*   1957.
Editor, *Coast to Coast 1961–1962.*   1963.
Editor, *It Could Be You.*   1972.

Bibliography: *A Bibliography of Porter* by Janette Finch, 1966.

Reading List: *Porter* by Mary Lord, 1974.

*   *   *

Hal Porter is not only one of Australia's finest short-story writers but he has also written one of the very best of all Australian autobiographies. The title of the first volume of this work is *The Watcher on the Cast-Iron Balcony*; the watcher is Porter, and it is in this role that we find him in both his autobiography and his fiction. The role itself creates a duality between Hal Porter the writer and Hal Porter the man. As the watcher, the artist, he is alone, isolated, detached, endeavouring always to be objective, to sift the real from the non-real. "This watching, this down-gazing, this faraway staring, is an exercise in solitude and non-involvement." But the community is there "to rob him of aloneness and content." For Porter is not only a spectator, he is also a participant; his fiction as well as his autobiography is written out of his own personal experience. He comments on his method of writing (in *Southerly,* 1969):

pure fiction, and flights of fancy are utterly beyond me. As a result another preoccupation is necessary. This is with the mechanics of transmuting actual personal experience, or the witnessed experiences of others, into what reads (I pray!) like true to life fiction.... Many characters, settings, and situations, already tied up in a "plot," are filched, holus-bolus, with the insolence of a shop-lifter, straight out of "life."

Of course, as an artist he will shape his material; he may be, as he writes in *The Paper Chase*, a "restless picker-up" but he is also a "ruthless pruner," and it is in the pruning that his imagination is at work — in the artist's sensitivity to the essentials, and in the ability to arrange "the million bits of the answer into One Answer." The One Answer is what Porter is seeking; the question he asks is: what is real? Rarely do his characters know the truth; many of them live, and some of them even die, with their illusions.

In the second volume of his autobiography, *The Paper Chase*, Porter tells of his methods when he is looking back on past experience. "As always, when writing of a past self, I try to put down what is felt 'then' even if 'now' has changed the feeling." "Francis Silver," one of the best known of Porter's stories, is an excellent example of Porter at work. The narration passes through several Hal Porters, the naïve boy, the romantic adolescent, the idealistic youth, the bitter and cynical young adult and the writer aware of "one disconcerting, even disenchanting thing: what one oneself remembers is not what others remember." The concern of the story is with the question of true identity; it deals with a moment of initiation when a youthful illusion is shattered by a harsh reality. Such moments occur quite frequently in Porter's work, and the often savage and grotesque nature of the reversal suggests the bitterness of one who feels that perhaps life is a fraud.

Any reader must be immediately aware that Porter has an eye that is gluttonous for details. He has said in the article already mentioned:

> In more intense forms of writing — the short story, for instance — effects must be made quickly, and often on many planes in immediately sequent sentences. Even if one splurge or over-express, one dares not falter on minutiae: dress, vehicles, customs, moral quirks, peculiar snobberies, atmospheric tone, and — above all — conversation.... To write down what is literally heard, to tape-record as it were in writing is to miss the point: the eye does not hear. The reader has to be tricked with a selection of words which "look" like what is supposed to be "heard." Acquiring the necessary illusionist's skill, ... has been another of my preoccupations.

Through his assembling of all the details Porter not only recaptures another age but also the people who lived in it. In *The Paper Chase* he said, "The quality of one's connection with people through their relation with things, tunes, scents, sounds, and so on is a subject of great allure, its existence a great blessing." This is the special significance of things for Porter; they are "evidences of humanity ... threads resistant to time and space." As such they are man's protection against mutability, against the destructive element in time, which so often creates an illusion out of what was once a reality. The details, the picture, the song, remain to defy time.

In "Francis Silver" the destruction of the lock of hair signifies the destruction of yet another illusion for the young man. The stench reminds us of the ugliness, perhaps the evil of reality; the agony is that of a youth stripped of one more romantic ideal. He goes out cynically to perform his first adult chore, which ironically enough is to perpetuate an illusion. Only the watcher will remain aware of the reality.

—Anna Rutherford

PORTER, Katherine Anne. American. Born in Indian Creek, Texas, 15 May 1890. Educated in Louisiana and Texas: at home, aged 3 to 8; in private school, 8 to 12; in an Ursuline Convent, 12 to 16. Married 1) Eugene Dove Pressly in 1933 (divorced, 1938); 2) Albert Russel Erskine, Jr., in 1938 (divorced, 1942). Reporter and Arts Critic, *Rocky Mountain News*, Denver, 1919; lived in Mexico and Europe between the wars; taught at Olivet College, Michigan, 1940; Lecturer in Writing, Stanford University, California, 1948–49; Guest Lecturer in Literature, University of Chicago, Spring 1951; Visiting Lecturer in Contemporary Poetry, University of Michigan, Ann Arbor, 1953–54; Fulbright Lecturer, University of Liège, Belgium, 1954–55; Writer-in-Residence, University of Virginia, Charlottesville, Autumn 1958; Glasgow Professor, Washington and Lee University, Lexington, Virginia, Spring 1959; Lecturer in American Literature for the United States Department of State, in Mexico, 1960, 1964; Ewing Lecturer, University of California at Los Angeles, 1960; Regents' Lecturer, University of California at Riverside, 1961. Library of Congress Fellow in Regional American Literature, 1944; United States Delegate, International Festival of the Arts, Paris, 1952; Member, Commission on Presidential Scholars, 1964; consultant in Poetry, Library of Congress, 1965–70. Recipient: Guggenheim Fellowship, 1931, 1938; New York University Libraries Gold Medal, 1940; Ford Foundation grant, 1959, 1960; O. Henry Award, 1962; Emerson-Thoreau Bronze Medal, 1962; Pulitzer Prize, 1966; National Book Award, 1966; National Institute of Arts and Letters Gold Medal, 1967; Mystery Writers of America Edgar Allan Poe Award, 1972. D.Litt.: University of North Carolina Woman's College, Greensboro, 1949; Smith College, Northampton, Massachusetts, 1958; Maryville College, St. Louis, 1968; D.H.L.: University of Michigan, Ann Arbor, 1954; University of Maryland, College Park, 1966; Maryland Institute, 1974; D.F.A.: La Salle College, Philadelphia, 1962. Vice-President, National Institute of Arts and Letters, 1950–52; Member, American Academy of Arts and Letters, 1967. Lives in College Park, Maryland.

PUBLICATIONS

Fiction

Flowering Judas. 1930; augmented edition, as *Flowering Judas and Other Stories,* 1935.
Hacienda: A Story of Mexico. 1934.
Noon Wine (story). 1937.
Pale Horse, Pale Rider: Three Short Novels. 1939.
The Leaning Tower and Other Stories. 1944.
Selected Short Stories. 1945.
The Old Order: Stories of the South. 1955.
A Christmas Story. 1958.
Ship of Fools. 1962.
The Collected Stories. 1964; augmented edition, 1967.

Other

My Chinese Marriage. 1921.
Outline of Mexican Popular Arts and Crafts. 1922.
What Price Marriage. 1927.
The Days Before: Collected Essays and Occasional Writings. 1952; augmented edition, as *The Collected Essays and Occasional Writings,* 1970.

A Defense of Circe. 1955.
The Never-Ending Wrong (on the Sacco-Vanzetti case). 1977.

Translator, *French Song Book.* 1933.
Translator, *The Itching Parrot,* by Fernandez de Lizárdi. 1942.

Bibliography: *A Bibliography of the Works of Porter* by Louise Waldrip and Shirley Ann Bauer, 1969: *Porter and Carson McCullers: A Reference Guide* by Robert F. Kiernan, 1976.

Reading List: *The Fiction and Criticism of Porter* by Harry John Mooney, Jr., 1957, revised edition, 1962; *Porter* by Ray B. West, Jr., 1963; *Porter and the Art of Rejection* by William L. Nance, 1964; *Porter* by George Hendrick, 1965; *Porter: The Regional Sources* by Winifred S. Emmons, 1967; *Porter: A Critical Symposium* edited by Lodwick Hartley and George Core, 1969; *Porter's Fiction* by M. M. Liberman, 1973.

*　　*　　*

Katherine Anne Porter was probably the finest writer of short stories and novellas of her time in the United States. Her last work of fiction, *Ship of Fools*, suggests either that the novel as such was not her form or that the hatred and contempt aroused in her by German behaviour under the Nazis had robbed her both of her usual skill and of her usual sense that life, in all its sadness and frustrations, is incurably poetic. Her collection of essays, *The Days Before*, however, is fascinating both in the excellence of its criticism and in the light it throws on her own work: "I am passionately involved with those individuals who populate all these enormous migrations, calamities, who fight wars and furnish life for the future." We see such an individual in Porter's own stories (in *The Leaning Tower*, for instance) as a quiet, imaginative, sad girl of old Southern family, aware of the past because of her grandmother and her old negro servant, aware of the grotesque because of a visit to a circus whose clowns frighten her, and aware of death and horror because of a brother who kills a pregnant rabbit and shows her the baby rabbits, who will now never be born in its womb. We see Miranda (in *Pale Horse, Pale Rider*,) as a young girl who has married to flee from her family and yet in some ways emotionally dried up. Other stories, like *Noon Wine*, evoke a sense of fatality, violence springing from heat and bewilderment.

Porter's great gift as a storyteller is to take material, particularly a wistfulness for the past, a sense of the strangeness, loneliness, cruelty, and treachery of life, the decay of love, or the failure to be able to love, and to avoid the twin temptations of treating this material with either sentimentality or a cheap cynicism. She evokes gravely and gracefully both the potential beauty and the bewildering lurking betrayal of life. Born in Texas in 1890, but maturing as a writer in the 1930's, she combined in an unusual way a solid sense of the past and the atmosphere of place with a fine sense of that ambivalence or complexity of attitude that we have in mind when we talk of "modernity" in fiction. Her proper readers will have the sense of reading in two ages at once, and of being presented with two possible standards of judgment, one the firm, exact, and unargued standard of the Old South, the other the modern standard which, more frighteningly, hands over the task of judgment to the reader.

—G. S. Fraser

PORTER, William Sydney. See **HENRY, O.**

POWELL, Anthony (Dymoke). English. Born in London, 21 December 1905. Educated at Eton College; Balliol College, Oxford, M.A. Served in the Welch Regiment, 1939–41, and in the Army Intelligence Corps, 1941–45: Major; Order of the White Lion, Czechoslovakia; Order of Leopold II, Belgium; Oaken Crown and Croix de Guerre, Luxembourg. Married the writer Lady Violet Pakenham in 1934; two sons. Worked for Duckworth, publishers, London, 1926–35; scriptwriter for Warner Brothers of Great Britain, 1936; full-time writer from 1936; Literary Editor, *Punch*, London, 1953–58; reviewer for the *Daily Telegraph*, *Times Literary Supplement*, and other London papers. Trustee, National Portrait Gallery, London, since 1962. Recipient: Black Memorial Prize, 1958; Smith Literary Prize, 1974. D.Litt.: University of Sussex, Brighton, 1971. Honorary Fellow, Balliol College, 1974. C.B.E. (Commander, Order of the British Empire), 1956. Lives near Frome, Somerset.

PUBLICATIONS

Fiction

Afternoon Men. 1931.
Venusberg. 1932.
From a View to a Death. 1933; as *Mr. Zouch: Superman: From a View of a Death*, 1934.
Agents and Patients. 1936.
What's Become of Waring. 1939.
A Dance to the Music of Time:
  A Question of Upbringing. 1951.
  A Buyer's Market. 1952.
  The Acceptance World. 1955.
  At Lady Molly's 1957.
  Casanova's Chinese Restaurant. 1960.
  The Kindly Ones. 1962.
  The Valley of Bones. 1964.
  The Soldier's Art. 1966.
  The Military Philosophers. 1968.
  Books Do Furnish a Room. 1971.
  Temporary Kings. 1973.
  Hearing Secret Harmonies. 1975.

Plays

The Garden God and The Rest I'll Whistle: The Text of Two Plays. 1971.

Verse

Caledonia: A Fragment. 1934.

Other

John Aubrey and His Friends. 1948; revised edition, 1963.
To Keep the Ball Rolling (autobiography): *Infants of the Spring*, 1976; *Messengers of Day*, 1978.

Editor, *Barnard Letters 1778–1884.* 1928.
Editor, *Novels of High Society from the Victorian Age.* 1947.
Editor, *Brief Lives and Other Selected Writings of John Aubrey.* 1949.

Reading List: *Powell* by Bernard Bergonzi, 1962; *The Novels of Powell* by Robert K. Morris, 1968; *Powell: A Quintet, Sextet and War* by John Russell, 1970; *Powell* by Neil F. Brennan, 1974; *The Novels of Powell* by James Tucker, 1976; *Invitation to the Dance: A Guide to Powell's A Dance to the Music of Time* by Hilary Spurling, 1977.

*   *   *

Anthony Powell's claim to be considered as a major novelist rests chiefly on his twelve-volume sequence *A Dance to the Music of Time*. He had, however, published five wholly re-readable novels in the 1930's while working first as a publisher and later as a writer of film scripts. While it is true that military service substantially interrupted his career as a novelist – after the war he at first got himself back into literary training as an editor and biographer, writing among other things a scholarly and entertaining book on John Aubrey and the literary, antiquarian, and philosophical scene of the seventeenth century – it is at least arguable that the fallow years contributed to a richer and riper eventual harvest.

His earlier novels, wittily contrived and always urbane in tone, take for their subject matter those social echelons observed and depicted contemporaneously by Aldous Huxley and Evelyn Waugh. *Afternoon Men* explores the communal distractions and private gambits, both social and sexual, of upper middle-class London society, if not wholly in decline and fall at any rate starting to break up. The fabric is beginning to look threadbare, the social garment both shabby and seedy. *Venusberg* carries the exploration further, both in terms of its thematic focus on Europe after the Bolshevik revolution and of its technically tighter organisation as a novel. In *From a View to a Death* Powell turned to English rural society, as yet rather less shaken by change; and, in the country-house setting and the theme of the artist who is determined to marry well, we find a presage of themes in the major work to come. *Agents and Patients* is a light-hearted comedy about the education of a rich but inexperienced young man by two less rich and inexperienced film producers on the make; and *What's Become of Waring* is a teasing story about an author who, for what turn out to be very good reasons, conceals his own life behind a screen of mystery.

While it is possible to find in these earlier novels sign-posts pointing towards *A Dance to the Music of Time*, it would be wrong to make too much of such discoveries, which are the result of critical hindsight. The fingerposts probably indicate parallel directions rather than point specifically to the final destinations.

When one considers *A Dance to the Music of Time* as a whole, one is conscious that Anthony Powell presents his readers with a brooding meditation on time and life and their evolving patterns, whose faintly melancholic mood is relieved by acceptance of the ultimate logic, though sequentially fragmented unpredictability, of human affairs. The major theme which emerges from this meditation is the contrast between sensitive imagination and bludgeoning force. Men of imagination survive creatively as members of the human family; men of power destroy and are finally destroyed along with their own transient creations. Yet if these somewhat cool, though less than chill, reflections are mirrored in the depths of the work as a whole, the surface texture of the novels, volume by volume and page by page, could hardly be in greater contrast. The wit, elegance, and irony, both amused and amusing, which were displayed in Powell's earlier novels are constantly deployed throughout each component part of the sequence; and it is this surface contrapuntalism which invests the work with the secret harmonies whose resolution finally is reached in the last volume, as its title metaphorically hints.

Large metaphorical reference is in fact one of the major devices Powell uses to underpin the structure of *A Dance to the Music of Time*. The cast of brilliantly presented major and minor characters – the decent, tolerant narrator Nick Jenkins (the man of imagination), the awful Widmerpool (a splendidly realised comic horror of the archetypal man of power), and all the lively company of thrusting, shrinking, scheming, muddled, pathetic, and ripely cheerful eccentric members of this middle and upper class comedy – is bound together in the metaphor derived from the Poussin painting at the beginning of the novel. Life is a dance in which individuals move now in recognisable evolutions, now in "seemingly meaningless gyrations, while partners disappear only to reappear again, once more giving pattern to the spectacle," as Powell with extraordinary skill handles a multitude of strands of characters, places, and events in order to weave his grand design. A very English novel, perhaps it could have been written only by an Englishman ironically distanced from his subject by being, as in Powell's case, Anglo-Welsh.

—Stewart F. Sanderson

POWERS, J(ames) F(arl). American. Born in Jacksonville, Illinois, 8 July 1917. Educated at Quincy College Academy, Illinois; Northwestern University, Chicago campus, 1938–40. Married the writer Betty Wahl in 1946; three daughters and two sons. Worked in Chicago, 1935–41; Editor, Illinois Historical Records Survey, 1938; worked as a hospital orderly during World War II; writer from 1943; taught at St. John's University, Collegeville, Minnesota, 1947; Marquette University, Milwaukee, Wisconsin, 1949–51; University of Michigan, Ann Arbor, 1956–57; Writer-in-Residence, Smith College, Northampton, Massachusetts, 1965–66. Recipient: National Institute of Arts and Letters grant, 1948; Guggenheim Fellowship, 1948; Rockefeller Fellowship, 1954, 1957, 1967; National Book Award, 1963. Member, National Institute of Arts and Letters.

PUBLICATIONS

Fiction

Prince of Darkness and Other Stories.   1947.
The Presence of Grace (stories).   1956.
Morte D'Urban.   1962.
Look How the Fish Live.   1975.

Reading List: *Powers* by John V. Hagopian, 1968.

*   *   *

J. F. Powers was frustrated trying to find work in Chicago during the depression years 1935–41. In the early years of World War II he met many social rebels in Chicago – workers, Blacks, and European exiles – and became a pacifist: he was appalled equally by the destructive war and patriotic propaganda. Early in 1943 he was the only lay person to attend a priests' retreat at St. John's Abbey in Collegeville, Minnesota. Following a period of reading and introspection Powers wrote "Lions, Harts, Leaping Does," in which Father Didymus attains true holiness as he dies, holding to his faith along with a strong sense of unworthiness. Three Powers sketches appeared in *The Catholic Worker* in 1943: "the upholstery of Christianity has held up better than the idea and practice.... Anyone who is not a saint is spiritually undersized – the world is full of spiritual midgets."

In *Prince of Darkness and Other Stories*, the best pieces have priest protagonists: the title story, "The Forks," "The Valiant Woman," and "Lions, Harts, Leaping Does." Among the eleven stories are three bitter tales about the plight of Chicago Blacks; "Jamesie," a story of adolescence that is probably autobiographical; and "Renner," a story of anti-Semitism. The critical reception of Powers's stories – especially among his fellow writers – was impressive. *The Presence of Grace* has nine stories, all but two of them about priests. The prevailing mood is mellow in these stories, and some reviewers found his clerical scenes deplorably picturesque instead of astringent.

Except for the story of Father Didymus, Powers used both humor and irony to expose priestly venality in his earlier stories: they reveal the dark side of "the endless struggle between religious idealism and selfish, worldly interests." Wit and subtle irony are still at work on priestly foibles in the nine stories of *The Presence of Grace*, but the absurdities seem less vicious and more forgivable. "Zeal" is a fair example: obtuse and bungling Father Early provokes his sophisticated bishop into a redeeming examination of his own soul.

Powers has published only one novel, *Morte D'Urban*, which grew out of a short story he had begun 15 years earlier. In "The Devil Was the Joker," the Order of St. Clement is a central concern; and some minor figures in the novel – Father Udovic, Monsignor Renton, and their Bishop – are the chief characters in "Dawn." For his novel Powers sets up two Minnesota dioceses, Great Plains and Ostergothenburg. Powers's own words best describe his intention: "The story is about Father Urban being sent to this foundation of the Order (Clementines) in Minnesota. He had been a big-time speaker, a poor man's Fulton Sheen. He was suddenly sent up here to this white elephant ... as one of the boys.... That's my story ... how he tried to put the place on its feet.... I thought it would be a nice little nut-brown novel, all kinds of irony." Though the critics reviewed *Morte D'Urban* favorably, most of them missed some levels of irony and even misinterpreted the point. Perhaps because parts of the novel had appeared in journals and Powers had an impressive reputation as a writer of short stories, many reviewers found *Morte D'Urban* episodic and lacking in unity as novel. Powers's ironic unifying devices were possibly too subtle.

Look How the Fish Live is uneven: half of the stories are clearly below Powers's usual high quality. Several of these inferior pieces, including the title story and "Tinkers," are new in subject matter and technique; but they fall far short of five stories in this collection that match Powers's best. These are stories of young, emancipated curates devoted to their creature comforts and with callow notions of how the Church should modernize; middle-aged priestly operators who specialize in efficiency, PR, and good housekeeping; elderly priests and dying bishops who clearly belong to another era but survive preposterously and precariously in an alien world. Through the agency of such Roman Catholic clerics, Powers views the modern world humorously and seriously at the same time – but always ironically.

Powers has always been a painstaking writer, and critics often praised his "structural finesse and verbal sensitivity," his "remarkable ear for the dialects and idioms of midwestern speech," and "the perfect fluency, realism, and economy" of his dialogue. The brilliant satire and subtle humor of *Morte D'Urban* have been recognized – though not widely enough; and Powers's use of the Arthurian matter has been variously interpreted and assessed. But one aspect of this and other Powers fiction has not been properly appreciated, perhaps because his Roman Catholic matter is probed so deeply and detailed so accurately. He uses the dilemma of Roman Catholicism in the middle years of the twentieth century to dramatize the impact of rampant materialism on a society trying to save – or find – its soul and sanity.

—Clarence A. Glasrud

POWYS, John Cowper. British. Born in Shirley, Derbyshire, 8 October 1872; brother of T. F. Powys, *q.v.*, and the writer Llewelyn Powys. Educated at the Sherborne School; Corpus Christi College, Cambridge. Married Margaret Alice Lyon in 1896 (died, 1947); one son. Writer from 1896; lectured on English literature in the United States, 1904–34: spent winters in America, returning to England each summer, 1910–28; lived permanently in New York and California, 1928–34; returned to England, 1934, and subsequently settled in North Wales. D.Litt.: University of Wales, 1962. *Died 17 June 1963.*

PUBLICATIONS

Fiction

Wood and Stone: A Romance. 1915.
Rodmoor: A Romance. 1916.
Ducdame. 1925.
Wolf Solent. 1929.
The Owl, The Duck, and – Miss Rowe! Miss Rowe! (story). 1930.
A Glastonbury Romance. 1932.
Weymouth Sands. 1934; as *Jobber Skald,* 1934.
Maiden Castle. 1936.
Morwyn; or, The Vengeance of God. 1937.
Owen Glendower: An Historical Novel. 1940.
Porius: A Romance of the Dark Ages. 1951.
The Inmates. 1952.
Atlantis. 1954.
The Brazen Head. 1956.
Up and Out (stories). 1957.
Homer and the Aether. 1959.
All or Nothing. 1960.

Play

The Idiot, with Reginald Pole, from the novel by Dostoevsky (produced 1922).

Verse

Odes and Other Poems. 1896.
Poems. 1899.
Wolf's Bane: Rhymes. 1916.
Mandragora. 1917.
Samphire. 1922.
Lucifer. 1956.
A Selection, edited by Kenneth Hopkins. 1964.

Other

The War and Culture: A Reply to Professor Münsterberg. 1914; as *The Menace of German Culture,* 1915.

Visions and Revisions: A Book of Literary Devotions. 1915.
Confessions of Two Brothers, with Llewelyn Powys. 1916.
One Hundred Best Books. 1916.
Suspended Judgments: Essays on Books and Sensations. 1916.
The Complex Vision. 1920.
The Art of Happiness. 1923.
Psychoanalysis and Morality. 1923.
The Religion of a Sceptic. 1925.
The Secret of Self Development. 1926.
The Art of Forgetting the Unpleasant. 1928.
The Meaning of Culture. 1929; revised edition, 1939.
Debate! Is Modern Marriage a Failure?, with Bertrand Russell. 1930.
In Defence of Sensuality. 1930.
Dorothy M. Richardson. 1931.
A Philosophy of Solitude. 1933.
Autobiography. 1934.
The Art of Happiness (not the same as the 1923 book). 1935.
The Enjoyment of Literature. 1938; revised edition, as *The Pleasures of Literature,* 1938.
Mortal Strife. 1942.
The Art of Growing Old. 1944.
Pair Dadeni; or, The Cauldron of Rebirth. 1946.
Dostoievsky. 1947.
Obstinate Cymric: Essays 1935–1947. 1947.
Rabelais. 1948.
In Spite Of: A Philosophy for Everyman. 1953.
Letters to Louis Wilkinson 1935–1956. 1958.
Letters to Glyn Hughes, edited by Bernard Jones. 1971.
Letters to Nicholas Ross, edited by Arthur Uphill. 1971.
Letters 1937–1954, edited by Iorweth C. Peate. 1974.
Letters to His Brother Llewelyn 1902–1925, edited by Malcolm Elwin. 1975.

Bibliography: *Powys: A Record of Achievement* by Derek Langridge, 1966.

Reading List: *Welsh Ambassadors: Powys Lives and Letters* by Louis Marlow, 1936, revised edition, 1971; *The Powys Brothers* by R. C. Churchill, 1962; *The Saturnian Quest: A Chart of the Prose Works of Powys* by G. Wilson Knight, 1964; *Powys: Old Earth-Man* by H. P. Collins, 1966; *The Powys Brothers: A Biographical Appreciation* by Kenneth Hopkins, 1967; *Powys, Novelist* by Glen Cavaliero, 1973; *The Demon Within: A Study of Powys's Novels* by John A. Brebner, 1973; *Powys* by Jeremy Hooker, 1973.

*   *   *

John Cowper Powys's writings have not been accorded the general recognition which their unusual range and power deserve. His achievement as a novelist substantially depends on *Wolf Solent* and *A Glastonbury Romance*, which together with *Weymouth Sands* and *Maiden Castle* depict west country scenes familiar to him from youth. The central theme of self-fulfilment links these novels with the fiction of Hardy and D. H. Lawrence. Powys knew Hardy personally, and his experience of America compares interestingly with Lawrence's. His perspective on English society is that of an exile who returns home but seems ill at ease. He shows exceptional insight into the eccentric in human behaviour, and suggests a point of view from which the strangeness of all terrestrial life can be perceived.

Powys's literary development is self-consistent. His taste in poetry is old-fashioned, and his verses are weakly conventional. The earlier novels, *Wood and Stone*, *Rodmoor*, and *Ducdame*, embody his elementalism in a more challenging form, and evolve the typical Powys hero: a harassed pedestrian figure with a stick, whose pleasures are mainly contemplative. Powys is concerned with the life of the imagination, and tries to demonstrate how wider forms of cultural awareness, including myth, can modify, perhaps transform, a commonplace or degrading routine of existence.

Essential to an understanding of Powys, and extraordinarily impressive in its own right, is his *Autobiography*. In it he outlines his imaginative strategy in a prose remarkable for its wide intellectual resources and ironic reservations. He does not disdain to speak of the particular, the personal, and even the unwholesome, his favourite philosopher being William James. Powys's writings on philosophy and culture range from the barren formality of *The Complex Vision* to the therapeutic cheerfulness of books like *The Art of Growing Old*. He is at his best when he argues for a highly eclectic and pragmatic view of culture, as in *The Meaning of Culture* and *A Philosophy of Solitude*, and when he illustrates it in the essays of *The Pleasures of Literature* and his book on Rabelais.

A deep commitment to Wales appears in *Owen Glendower* and *Porius*. Both exhibit Powys's love of an inordinately long story for its own sake, but the former is nearer to conventional historical romance than the latter. *Porius*, conceived as a challenge to various orthodox categories of thought, is a kind of Powysian reverie. The fictional environment it creates is concrete and particular, and yet deliberately remote and fantastic: a story about the Dark Ages based on the landscape the author could see from his doorstep. Digression is the main principle of narrative development, and this affords ample space for his passionate animism and his conception of a pluralistic universe.

The later years bring further fantasy and improvisation. Such works as *Atlantis*, *The Brazen Head*, and *All or Nothing* are whimsical elaborations on themes from classical and medieval legend and nursery tales. The complex voice of the *Autobiography* may be heard again in *Letters to Louis Wilkinson 1935–1956*.

—Peter Easingwood

POWYS, T(heodore) F(rancis).   British.   Born in Shirley, Derbyshire, 20 December 1875; brother of J. C. Powys, *q.v.*, and the writer Llewelyn Powys. Educated at private schools, and at Dorchester Grammar School. Married Violet Rosalie Bodds in 1905; two sons and one adopted daughter. Lived in Dorset for most of his life; writer from 1908. *Died 27 November 1953.*

PUBLICATIONS

Fiction

>*The Left Leg* (stories).   1923.
>*Black Bryony.*   1923.
>*Mark Only.*   1924.
>*Mr. Tasker's Gods.*   1925.
>*Mockery Gap.*   1925.

A Stubborn Tree (story).   1926.
Innocent Birds.   1926.
Feed My Swine (story).   1926.
A Strong Girl, and The Bride: Two Stories.   1926.
What Lack I Yet? (story).   1927.
Mr. Weston's Good Wine.   1927.
The Rival Pastors (story).   1927.
The House with the Echo: Twenty-Six Stories.   1928.
The Dewpond (story).   1928.
Fables.   1929; as *No Painted Plumage,* 1934.
Christ in the Cupboard (story).   1930.
The Key of the Field (story).   1930.
Kindness in a Corner.   1930.
The White Paternoster and Other Stories.   1930.
Uriah on the Hill (story).   1930.
Uncle Dottery: A Christmas Story.   1930.
The Only Penitent.   1931.
When Thou Wast Naked.   1931.
Unclay.   1931.
The Tithe Barn, and The Dove and the Eagle (stories).   1932.
The Two Thieves: In Good Earth, God, The Two Thieves.   1932.
Captain Patch: Twenty-One Stories.   1935.
Make Thyself Many (story).   1935.
Goat Green; or, The Better Gift (story).   1937.
Bottle's Path and Other Stories.   1946.
God's Eyes A-Twinkle (stories).   1947.
Rosie Plum and Other Stories, edited by Francis Powys.   1966.
Come and Dine, and Tadnol (stories), edited by Peter Riley.   1967.

Other

An Interpretation of Genesis.   1907.
The Soliloquy of a Hermit.   1916; as *Soliloquies of a Hermit,*   1918.

Bibliography: *A Bibliography of Powys* by Peter Riley, 1967.

Reading List: *The Novels and Stories of Powys* by W. Hunter, 1930; *Welsh Ambassadors: Powys Lives and Letters* by Louis Marlow, 1936, revised edition, 1971; *Powys* by H. Coombes, 1960; *The Powys Brothers* by R. C. Churchill, 1962; *Theodore: Essays on Powys* edited by Brocard Sewell, 1964; *The Powys Brothers: A Biographical Appreciation* by Kenneth Hopkins, 1967; *Powys* by R. C. Churchill, 1970.

*   *   *

T. F. Powys was one of a talented family of writers – his brothers included John Cowper and Llewelyn – who though of Welsh origin were brought up in Somerset and Dorset where their father was a Church of England minister. His books, once the delight of the literary connoisseur, have been out of fashion for some years though it is not quite clear why. His novels and short stories are simple, almost fabular in style, reflecting the richness of soil and character in that small coastal area between Wareham and Weymouth where he lived most of his mature life.

Yet he is not a realistic writer: whether peasants, farmers, or clergymen, his characters are.

983

as a critic of the time wrote, sometimes like gargoyles and sometimes like sculptured saints. The typical story often begins quite ordinarily as though it was about commonplace people in a commonplace rural situation, and then something odd emerges with a sense of overweening evil and horror or of simple goodness where it is least expected. In much of his narrative he imitates the oddities of Dorset country pronunciation: "old" is "wold," "that" is "thik," but there is nothing that will confuse any English reader; Powys does not write in the difficult Dorset dialect as did the poet William Barnes.

Much of Powys's writing has the effect of poetry; there is a half-hidden allegory through which the reader may glimpse beneath the simple situation some of life's profundities. His pages have, too, a curious way of recreating without obvious effort the very smell of a Dorset village in the 1920's.

The novel *Mr. Tasker's Gods* has a gruesome theme and an instinctive sense of character, though *Mr. Weston's Good Wine* has more artistry about it and has long been his most popular work. He is at his best in short stories which often have an uncanny power and collected titles which could only be his – *Christ in the Cupboard, Uncle Dottery, God's Eyes A-Twinkle.*

—Kenneth Young

PRICHARD, Katharine Susannah. Australian. Born in Levuka, Fiji, 4 December 1883; emigrated with her family to Australia, 1886. Educated at home, and at South Melbourne College. Married Hugo Throssell in 1919 (died, 1933); one son. Worked as a governess in South Gippsland, and as a teacher at Christ Church Grammar School, Melbourne; journalist for the Melbourne *Herald* and *New Idea*, Sydney; free-lance journalist in London and Europe, 1908; Editor, Melbourne *Herald*'s "Women's Work" column 1908–12; returned to London, and worked as a free-lance journalist, 1912–16: Correspondent in France, 1916; full-time writer from 1916; settled in Greenmount, Western Australia; member of the Australian Communist Party from 1920. *Died 20 October 1969.*

PUBLICATIONS

Fiction

    The Pioneers. 1915; revised edition, 1963.
    Windlestraws. 1916.
    The Black Opal. 1921.
    Working Bullocks. 1926.
    The Wild Oats of Han (juvenile). 1928; revised edition, 1968.
    Coonardoo, The Well in the Shadow. 1929.
    Haxby's Circus, The Lightest, Brightest Little Show on Earth. 1930; as *Fay's Circus,* 1931.
    Kiss on the Lips and Other Stories. 1932.
    Intimate Strangers. 1937.
    Moon of Desire. 1941.
    Potch and Colour (stories). 1944.

The Roaring Nineties: A Story of the Goldfields of Western Australia. 1946.
Golden Miles. 1948.
Winged Seeds. 1950.
N'Goola and Other Stories. 1959.
Subtle Flame. 1967.
Moggie and Her Circus Pony (juvenile). 1967.
Happiness: Selected Short Stories. 1967.

Plays

The Burglar (produced 1910).
The Pioneers (produced 1923). In *Best Australian One-Act Plays*, 1937.
Brumby Innes (produced 1972). 1927.

Verse

Clovelly Verses. 1913.
Earth Lover. 1930.
The Earth Lover and Other Verses. 1932.

Other

The New Order. 1921.
Marx: The Man and His Work. 1922.
The Materialist Conception. 1922.
The Real Russia. 1935.
Why I Am a Communist. 1950(?).
Child of the Hurricane: An Autobiography. 1963.
On Strenuous Wings: A Half-Century of Selected Writings, edited by Joan
    Williams. 1965.

Editor, with others, *Australian New Writing 1–3.* 3 vols., 1943–45.

Reading List: "Prichard Issue" of *Overland 12,* 1959; *Prichard* by H. Drake-Brockman,
1967.

*   *   *

In 1915 Katharine Susannah Prichard's first novel, *The Pioneers*, won the Hodder and
Stoughton prize in the Australian section of their prize for Dominion novels. She had done
what she had set out to do, namely, "proved ability to 'succeed' abroad." Having done so she
returned to Australia: "I wanted to live and write in Australia about the country and its
people." While in England she had been shocked by the appalling slum conditions. The
Russian revolution and the doctrines of Marx and Engels were to give direction to her
indignation, and when the Australian Communist Party was formed in 1920 she joined it. So,
added to her aim of "knowing the Australian people and interpreting them to themselves"
was the additional one of propagating the socialist doctrine both in her life and in her work.
As Jack Lindsay wrote, "[Her work] is a creative development of the Marxist concepts of
what humanises and what alienates, born out of an artist's deep sympathy for, and
understanding of, her fellow men."

She had inherited the democratic, humanist tradition of the 1890's. However, while she shared with the nationalist, realist writers of that period a firm belief in mateship, in the virtues of the working people, the ordinary Australians, she did not share Lawson's picture of "a grey and distressing country. I wanted," she said, "to bring a realisation of the beauty and vigour of our life to Australian literature." What impresses one is her evocative portrayal of the land in which her characters live and which she so obviously loved. Her settings were wide, varying from the opal fields in *The Black Opal*, the timber country in *Working Bullocks*, the small town circuit in *Haxby's Circus*, the outback station in *Coonardoo*, the gold fields in her trilogy *The Roaring Nineties*, *Golden Miles*, and *Winged Seeds*. But no matter how varied the setting the same theme emerged. Always her concern was for the little man in his struggle against exploitive capitalism: her aim was to show how under that system man became alienated not only from his fellow men but also from himself and nature. It is not surprising that Prichard should turn her attention to the most exploited group in Australia, the aborigines. *Coonardoo*, which was to have a powerful effect on the white conscience, is not simply the tragedy of a single person but of a whole people, a tragedy for which the white population was directly responsible.

It has been argued by some that her political commitment has been detrimental to her artistic achievement. In reply to such critics one could quote Lunuchansky: "Of what do you accuse me? Of the fact that the great flames of my fervour to transform the world are burning in my art too?" What inspires one in Prichard's works is the vitalism that informs them. There is in her writing an affirmation of a life force that will continue to struggle in spite of the most appalling conditions and against what seem to be insurmountable odds. As Sam told Han in the first work Katharine Susannah Prichard wrote (*The Wild Oats of Han*), "You've just got to shake your fist at Life and say: 'You can't break me. You can't!' "

While her reputation rests essentially on her novels and short stories, mention should also be made of the seventeen plays she wrote, three of which have been produced. One of them, *Brumby Innes* (1927), won the Triad competition and then waited forty-five years for production. When it was eventually produced in 1972 it was greeted with acclaim by the critics, one of whom wrote, "Anyone thinking of putting indigenous ingredients together and writing The Great Australian Play can screw the cap back on his pen and take himself off quietly to the pub. It has been belatedly discovered that Katharine Susannah Prichard wrote it in 1927." There is no doubt at all that she is assured of a permanent place in Australian literature.

—Anna Rutherford

* * *

PRIESTLEY, J(ohn) B(oynton). English. Born in Bradford, Yorkshire, 13 September 1894. Educated in Bradford schools, and at Trinity Hall, Cambridge, M.A. Served with the Duke of Wellington's and the Devon Regiments, 1914–19. Married 1) Patricia Tempest (died, 1925), two daughters; 2) Mary Wyndham Lewis (divorced, 1952), two daughters and one son; 3) the writer Jacquetta Hawkes in 1953. Writer from 1925; Director of the Mask Theatre, London, 1938–39; radio lecturer on the BBC programme "Postscripts" during World War II; regular contributor to the *New Statesman*, London. President, P.E.N., London, 1936–37; United Kingdom Delegate, and Chairman, UNESCO International

Theatre Conference, Paris, 1947, and Prague, 1948; Chairman, British Theatre Conference, 1948; President, International Theatre Institute, 1949; Member, National Theatre Board, London, 1966–67. Recipient: Black Memorial Prize, 1930; Ellen Terry Award, 1948. LL.D.: University of St. Andrews; D.Litt.: University of Birmingham; University of Bradford. Honorary Freeman of the City of Bradford, 1973. Order of Merit, 1977. Lives in Alveston, Warwickshire.

PUBLICATIONS

Fiction

Adam in Moonlight. 1927.
Benighted. 1927; as *The Old Dark House,* 1928.
Farthing Hall, with Hugh Walpole. 1929.
The Good Companions. 1929.
The Town Major of Miraucourt (story). 1930.
Angel Pavement. 1930.
Faraway. 1932.
Albert Goes Through (story). 1933.
I'll Tell You Everything: A Frolic, with Gerald Bullett. 1933.
Wonder Hero. 1933.
They Walk in the City: The Lovers in the Stone Forest. 1936.
The Doomsday Men: An Adventure. 1938.
Let the People Sing. 1939.
Black-Out in Gretley: A Story of – and for – Wartime. 1942.
Daylight on Saturday: A Novel about an Aircraft Factory. 1943.
Three Men in New Suits. 1945.
Bright Day. 1946.
Jenny Villiers: A Story of the Theatre. 1947.
Going Up: Stories and Sketches. 1950.
Festival at Farbridge. 1951; as *Festival,* 1951.
The Other Place and Other Stories of the Same Sort. 1953.
The Magicians. 1954.
Low Notes on a High Level: A Frolic. 1954.
Saturn over the Water: An Account of His Adventures in London, South America and Australia by Tim Bedford, Painter; Edited, with Some Preliminary and Concluding Remarks, By Henry Sulgrave and Here Presented to the Reading Public. 1961.
The Thirty-First of June: A Tale of True Love, Enterprise and Progress in the Arthurian and ad-Atomic Ages. 1961.
The Shapes of Sleep: A Topical Tale. 1962.
Sir Michael and Sir George: A Tale of COMSA and DISCUS and the New Elizabethans. 1964; as *Sir Michael and Sir George: A Comedy of the New Elizabethans,* 1965(?).
Lost Empires, Being Richard Herncastle's Account of His Life on the Variety Stage from November 1913 to August 1914, Together with a Prologue and Epilogue. 1965.
Salt Is Leaving. 1966.
It's an Old Country. 1967.
The Image Men: Out of Town, and London End. 2 vols., 1968; as *The Image Men,* 1969.
The Carfitt Crisis and Two Other Stories. 1975.
Found, Lost, Found; or, The English Way of Life. 1976.

Plays

The Good Companions, with Edward Knoblock, from the novel by Priestley (produced 1931).   1935.
Dangerous Corner (produced 1932).   1932.
The Roundabout (produced 1932).   1933.
Laburnum Grove: An Immoral Comedy (produced 1933).   1934.
Eden End (produced 1934).   1934.
Cornelius: A Business Affair in Three Transactions (produced 1935).   1935.
Duet in Floodlight (produced 1935).   1935.
Bees on the Boat Deck: A Farcical Tragedy (produced 1936).   1936.
Spring Tide, with George Billam (produced 1936).   1936.
The Bad Samaritan (produced 1937).
Time and the Conways (produced 1937).   1937.
I Have Been Here Before (produced 1937).   1937.
I'm a Stranger Here (produced 1937).
People at Sea (produced 1937).   1937.
Mystery at Greenfingers: A Comedy of Detection (produced 1938).   1937.
When We Are Married: A Yorkshire Farcical Comedy (produced 1938).   1938.
Music at Night (produced 1938).   In *Three Plays,* 1943.
Johnson over Jordan (produced 1939).   Published as *Johnson over Jordan: The Play, And All about It (An Essay),* 1939.
The Long Mirror (produced 1940).   In *Three Plays,* 1943.
Good Night Children: A Comedy of Broadcasting (produced 1942).   In *Three Comedies,* 1945.
Desert Highway (produced 1943).   1944.
They Came to a City (produced 1943).   In *Three Plays,* 1943.
Three Plays.   1943.
How Are They at Home? A Topical Comedy (produced 1944).   In *Three Comedies,* 1945.
The Golden Fleece (as *The Bull Market,* produced 1944).   In *Three Comedies,* 1945.
Three Comedies.   1945.
An Inspector Calls (produced 1945).   1945.
Jenny Villiers (produced 1946).
The Rose and Crown (televised 1946).   1947.
Ever since Paradise: An Entertainment, Chiefly Referring to Love and Marriage (produced 1946).   1949.
The Linden Tree (produced 1947).   1948.
The Plays of J. B. Priestley.   3 vols., 1948–50; vol. 1 as *Seven Plays,* 1950.
Home Is Tomorrow (produced 1948).   1949.
The High Toby: A Play for the Toy Theatre (produced 1954).   1948.
Summer Day's Dream (produced 1949).   In *Plays III,* 1950.
The Olympians, music by Arthur Bliss (produced 1949).   1949.
Bright Shadow: A Play of Detection (produced 1950).   1950.
Treasure on Pelican (as *Treasure on Pelican Island,* televised 1951; as *Treasure on Pelican,* produced 1952).   1953.
Dragon's Mouth: A Dramatic Quartet, with Jacquetta Hawkes (produced 1952).   1952.
Private Rooms: A One-Act Comedy in the Viennese Style.   1953.
Mother's Day.   1953.
Try It Again (produced 1965).   1953.
A Glass of Bitter.   1954.
The White Countess, with Jacquetta Hawkes (produced 1954).   1956.
The Scandalous Affair of Mr. Kettle and Mrs. Moon (produced 1955).   1956.
These Our Actors (produced 1956).

Take the Fool Away (produced 1956).
The Glass Cage (produced 1957).   1958.
The Thirty-First of June (produced 1957).
The Pavilion of Masks (produced 1963).   1958.
A Severed Head, with Iris Murdoch, from the novel by Murdoch (produced 1963).   1964.

Screenplays: *Sing As We Go*, with Gordon Wellesley, 1934; *We Live in Two Worlds*, 1937; *Jamaica Inn*, with Sidney Gilliat and Joan Harrison, 1939; *Britain at Bay*, 1940; *Our Russian Allies*, 1941; *The Foreman Went to France (Somewhere in France)*, with others, 1942; *Last Holiday*, 1950.

Radio Plays: *The Return of Jess Oakroyd*, 1941; *The Golden Entry*, 1955; *End Game at the Dolphin*, 1956; *An Arabian Night in Park Lane*, 1965.

Television Plays: *The Rose and Crown*, 1946; *Treasure on Pelican Island*, 1951; *The Stone Face*, 1957; *The Rack*, 1958; *Doomsday for Dyson*, 1958; *The Fortrose Incident*, 1959; *Level Seven*, 1966; *The Lost Peace* series, 1966; *Anyone for Tennis*, 1968; *Linda at Pulteneys*, 1969.

Verse

The Chapman of Rhymes (juvenilia).   1918.

Other

Brief Diversions, Being Tales, Travesties and Epigrams.   1922.
Papers from Lilliput.   1922.
I for One.   1923.
Figures in Modern Literature.   1924.
Fools and Philosophers: A Gallery of Comic Figures from English Literature.   1925; as *The English Comic Characters*, 1925.
George Meredith.   1926.
Talking: An Essay.   1926.
(Essays).   1926.
Open House: A Book of Essays.   1927.
Thomas Love Peacock.   1927.
The English Novel.   1927; revised edition, 1935.
Too Many People and Other Reflections.   1928.
Apes and Angels: A Book of Essays.   1928.
The Balconinny and Other Essays.   1929; as *The Balconinny*, 1930.
English Humour.   1929.
Self-Selected Essays.   1932.
Four-in-Hand (miscellany).   1934.
English Journey, Being a Rambling But Truthful Account of What One Man Saw and Heard and Felt and Thought During a Journey Through England During the Autumn of the Year 1933.   1934.
Midnight on the Desert: A Chapter of Autobiography.   1937; as *Midnight on the Desert, Being an Excursion into Autobiography During a Winter in America, 1935–36.*   1937.
Rain upon Godshill: A Further Chapter of Autobiography.   1939.
Britain Speaks (radio talks).   1940.

Postscripts (radio talks).   1940.
Out of the People.   1941.
Britain at War.   1942.
British Women Go to War.   1943.
Here Are Your Answers.   1944.
Letter to a Returning Serviceman.   1945.
The Secret Dream: An Essay on Britain, America and Russia.   1946.
Russian Journey.   1946.
Theatre Outlook.   1947.
Delight.   1949.
A Priestley Companion: A Selection from the Writings.   1951.
Journey down a Rainbow, with Jacquetta Hawkes (travel).   1955.
All about Ourselves and Other Essays, edited by Eric Gillett.   1956.
Thoughts in the Wilderness (essays).   1957.
Topside; or, The Future of England: A Dialogue.   1958.
The Story of Theatre (juvenile).   1959; as *The Wonderful World of the Theatre,* 1959;
    revised edition, 1969.
Literature and Western Man.   1960.
William Hazlitt.   1960.
Charles Dickens: A Pictorial Biography.   1961; as *Dickens and His World,* 1969.
Margin Released: A Writer's Reminiscences and Reflections.   1962.
Man and Time.   1964.
The Moments and Other Pieces.   1966.
The World of Priestley, edited by D. G. MacRae.   1967.
All England Listened: Priestley's Wartime Broadcasts.   1968.
Essays of Five Decades, edited by Susan Cooper.   1968.
*Trumpets over the Sea, Being a Rambling and Egotistical Account of the London
    Symphony Orchestra's Engagement at Daytona Beach, Florida, in July–August
    1967.*   1968.
The Prince of Pleasure and His Regency, 1811–1820.   1969.
The Edwardians.   1970.
Snoggle (juvenile).   1971.
Victoria's Heyday.   1972.
*Over the Long High Wall: Some Reflections and Speculations on Life, Death and
    Time.*   1972.
The English.   1973.
Outcries and Asides.   1974.
A Visit to New Zealand.   1974.
*Particular Pleasures, Being a Personal Record of Some Varied Arts and Many Different
    Artists.*   1975.
The Happy Dream (biography).   1976.
English Humour.   1976.
Instead of the Trees (autobiography).   1977.

Editor, *Essayists Past and Present: A Selection of English Essays.*   1925.
Editor, *Tom Moore's Diary: A Selection.*   1925.
Editor, *The Book of Bodley Head Verse.*   1926.
Editor, *The Female Spectator: Selections from Mrs. Eliza Haywood's Periodical,
    1744–1746.*   1929.
Editor, *Our Nation's Heritage.*   1939.
Editor, *Scenes of London Life, From Sketches by Boz by Charles Dickens.*   1947.
Editor, *The Best of Leacock.*   1957; as *The Bodley Head Leacock,* 1957.
Editor, with O. B. Davis, *Four English Novels.*   1960.
Editor, with O. B. Davis, *Four English Biographies.*   1961.

Editor, *Adventures in English Literature.* 1963.
Editor, *An Everyman Anthology.* 1966.

Reading List: *Priestley* by Ivor Brown, 1957, revised edition, 1964; *Priestley: An Informal Study of His Work* by David Hughes, 1958; *Mensch und Gesellschaft bei Priestley* by L. Löb, 1962 (includes bibliography); *Priestley the Dramatist* by G. L. Evans, 1964; *Priestley: Portrait of an Author* by Susan Cooper, 1970; *Priestley* by John Braine, 1978.

*   *   *

J. B. Priestley, born as long ago as 1894, is not only jack of most literary trades but master of quite a few: novels, plays, essays both historical and literary. He fully deserved his Order of Merit in 1977. During the second world war he became a skilled broadcaster with a large following.

After the first world war he was a widely appreciated essayist and reviewer. More recently he completed a remarkably readable autobiography. He was a superb journalist as he showed in the now classic *English Journey.* But it is probably as a novelist, translated into almost every known language and in the best-seller class, that he is best known. *The Good Companions,* a picaresque novel without a real picaro (rogue), describes on a broad Victorian-style canvas the adventures of a travelling concert party and those who attach themselves to it. It has a not-quite-happy ending. No less successful a year later was *Angel Pavement,* which had no happy ending at all and concerned the disasters brought upon a group of lower middle-class clerical workers in a City of London veneer firm by a predatory "sharp Alec" from the Baltic. There are a dozen or more pieces of fiction he wrote in the ensuing years, notably the superb, gently satirical study of the new universities and the advertising business in *The Image Men,* and *Bright Day,* which some regard as his best post-war novel. It harks back, as so often in his work, to the experiences of a family and others the narrator has known before the overwhelming and shattering experience of the first World War (in which Priestley fought) and which changed so many lives in many countries. Almost all his novels continue to be readable and are often stimulating, for example, *Let the People Sing, Daylight on Saturday,* and *Festival at Farbridge.* He discovered a fluent and often witty narrative style. He was obscure neither in subject matter nor character portrayal; yet he did not lack psychological penetration.

It is, however, for certain of his plays that he would claim real originality. Some, excellent though they are – and continually performed all over the world – are conventional in format – *Eden End* or *Laburnum Grove* or the moving *The Linden Tree.* But he carried out such stage experiments as *Ever since Paradise,* a comedy about love and marriage where each set of three couples are both actors and soliloquising commentators. The most powerful of the experimental plays is *Johnson over Jordan,* a sort of dramatic obituary of a recently deceased business man which has moments of great insight and moving intensity. It is full of Johnson's hopes and fears and, now, vain regrets. It is difficult, indeed, to stage, but as moving as any mid-20th-century drama.

Priestley's plays and other works were often centred on the theories popularized by J. W. M. Dunne, Carl Jung, and others about the nature of time, on which Priestley wrote with intelligence and imagination. Priestley has also always been sensitive to the, as he would regard it, untoward interference of politics in men's lives. He is not a party man, though until later years he would have regarded himself as anti-Conservative. Since 1950 or so, his essays became more and more polemical and opposed to authoritarian Socialism. He may be summed up as a centre radical if that is not a contradiction in terms. Radical, however, he certainly is in the sense that he believes changes may quickly be made to improve matters rather than having to wait for the slow processes of evolution. He has invented words which have become part and parcel of the common talk of his time; one such word was "admass" which conveyed the idea of the mindless majorities of "civilised" mankind helplessly persuaded by subtle advertising schemes to buy more and more goods they did not require.

By some of his contemporaries he was reputed to be of a contumacious nature. Certainly he was not one to be over-ruled or to allow his views to go unheard – and he had views and preferences on pictures (he himself painted) and on music as well as, of course, on the arts he himself practised. But despite his bluntness of speech he was not – as he himself repeatedly declared – quarrelsome. Most who knew him enjoyed his company; and to his millions of devoted followers he was a source of delight on the page and stage, a superb entertainer full of talent and here and there something of genius.

—Kenneth Young

PRITCHETT, Sir V(ictor) S(awdon). English. Born in Ipswich, Suffolk, 16 December 1900. Educated at Alleyn's School, Dulwich, London. Married Dorothy Rudge Roberts in 1936; one son and one daughter. Worked in the leather trade in London, 1916–20, and in the shellac, glue, and photographic trade in Paris, 1920–32; Correspondent in Ireland and Spain for the *Christian Science Monitor*, Boston, 1923–26; Critic from 1926, Permanent Critic from 1937, and Director from 1946, *New Statesman*, London; Christian Gauss Lecturer, Princeton University, New Jersey, 1953; Beckman Professor, University of California, Berkeley, 1962; Writer-in-Residence, Smith College, Northampton, Massachusetts, 1966, 1970–72; Visiting Professor, Brandeis University, Waltham, Massachusetts, 1968; Clark Lecturer, Cambridge University, 1969. President, P.E.N. Club, English Centre, 1970, and President of International P.E.N., 1974. Recipient: Heinemann Award, for non-fiction, 1969; P.E.N. Award for non-fiction, 1974. D.Lit.: University of Leeds, 1972. Fellow, Royal Society of Literature, 1969. Honorary Member, American Academy of Arts and Letters, 1971. C.B.E. (Commander, Order of the British Empire), 1969. Knighted, 1975. Lives in London.

PUBLICATIONS

Fiction

    Clare Drummer. 1929.
    The Spanish Virgin and Other Stories. 1930.
    Shirley Sanz. 1932; as *Elopement into Exile,* 1932.
    Nothing Like Leather. 1935.
    Dead Man Leading. 1937.
    You Make Your Own Life (stories). 1938.
    It May Never Happen and Other Stories. 1945.
    Mr. Beluncle. 1951.
    Collected Stories. 1956.
    The Sailor, The Sense of Humor, and Other Stories. 1956.
    When My Girl Comes Home (stories). 1961.
    The Key to My Heart (stories). 1963.
    The Saint and Other Stories. 1966.
    Blind Love and Other Stories. 1969.
    The Camberwell Beauty and Other Stories. 1974.
    Selected Stories. 1978.

Plays

>The Gambler (broadcast, 1947). In *Imaginary Conversations,* edited by Rayner Heppenstall, 1948.

>Screenplay: *Essential Jobs* (documentary), 1942.

>Radio Play: *The Gambler,* 1947.

Other

>*Marching Spain* (travel). 1928.
>*In My Good Books.* 1942.
>*The Living Novel.* 1946; revised edition, as *The Living Novel and Later Appreciations,* 1964.
>*Why Do I Write? An Exchange of Views Between Elizabeth Bowen, Graham Greene, and Pritchett.* 1948.
>*Books in General.* 1953.
>*The Spanish Temper* (travel). 1954.
>*London Perceived.* 1962.
>*Foreign Faces.* 1964; as *The Offensive Traveller,* 1964.
>*New York Proclaimed.* 1965.
>*The Working Novelist.* 1965.
>*Dublin: A Portrait.* 1967.
>*A Cab at the Door: Childhood and Youth, 1900–1920.* 1968.
>*George Meredith and English Comedy.* 1970.
>*Midnight Oil* (autobiography). 1971.
>*Balzac: A Biography.* 1973.
>*The Gentle Barbarian: The Life and Work of Turgenev.* 1977.
>*Great American Families,* with others. 1977.

>Editor, *This England.* 1938.
>Editor, *Novels and Stories,* by Robert Louis Stevenson. 1945.
>Editor, *Turnstile One: A Literary Miscellany from the New Statesman.* 1948.

*   *   *

There are few more distinguished men of letters alive today than V. S. Pritchett. Indeed, he may be said to be one of the last of his kind. And this is not only because of the variety of his output – travel literature, essays, criticism, short stories, novels, autobiography – but because nowadays very few writers can make a living by journalism of a serious kind, as he has done, and still find time to write on a more substantial scale.

Had Pritchett been born fifty years later he would, no doubt, have become a Professor of English at some university or other, and he would have been very good at it. For he is a first-rate critic. His *The Living Novel* has rightly become a standard book, and his study of Balzac will no doubt follow suit. Moreover, his regular book reviews in the *New Statesman* undoubtedly drew many readers to that journal, and must rank as among the best work that ever appeared in its pages. Pritchett wrote as a practitioner of fiction, but never as a blinkered or jaundiced one; and for this we must be grateful.

What of his fiction, by which, I would guess, Pritchett sets most store? Of the novels, *Dead Man Leading* seems to me the best, yet I confess that, although I find this story of exploration in South America to be elegantly written and carefully structured, it seems curiously lifeless: as though someone had constructed a perfect model of a human body, but could find no way

993

to make it breathe or move. The short stories are, however, more impressive, at their best. But Pritchett has been a prolific writer in this particular genre, having published many volumes plus a *Collected Stories*, and not all of the stories come up to the standard he achieves in, for example, "Blind Love" and "A Debt of Honour." At his best, Pritchett is a wryly comic observer of ordinary people caught in circumstances which they have to struggle to control, and which sometimes come to control them. He avoids the obviously bizarre, the eccentric, the outrageous: all his finest effects come from quiet, shrewd observation and understatement. In this, he reminds me very strongly of the late William Sansom, and of such American writers as John Cheever and John Updike. (It is no coincidence, I think, that all these writers found favour with *The New Yorker*.)

Pritchett has also published two remarkable volumes of autobiography, *A Cab at the Door* and *Midnight Oil*. The secret hero of the first of these is undoubtedly Pritchett's father, the kind of man who seems to have stepped straight out of a novel by H. G. Wells: constantly in financial difficulties, shifting from job to job, town to town, in order to escape furious creditors (hence the book's title), always on the look-out for a new dream to nourish, impossible and yet endlessly forgivable. Writing of his discovery of the world of books, when he was still a small child, Pritchett remarks that there was a small case of books at home, "usually kept in the backroom which was called my father's study. Why he had to have a study we could not see. There was an armchair, a gate-legged table, a small rug, piles of business magazines usually left in their wrappers; the floor boards were still bare as indeed were our stairs; Father had temporarily suppressed his weakness for buying on credit." The elegant, mercilessly keen-eyed, but savingly comic tone of that typifies Pritchett's style at its finest.

—John Lucas

PURDY, James (Otis). American. Born near Fremont, Ohio, 14th July 1923. Educated at the University of Chicago, 1941, 1946; University of Puebla, Mexico. Worked as an interpreter in Latin America, France, and Spain; taught at Lawrence College, Appleton, Wisconsin, 1949–53; full-time writer from 1953; Visiting Professor, University of Tulsa, Oklahoma, 1977. Recipient: National Institute of Arts and Letters grant, 1958; Guggenheim Fellowship, 1958, 1962; Ford Fellowship, for drama, 1961. Lives in Brooklyn, New York.

PUBLICATIONS

Fiction

Don't Call Me by My Right Name and Other Stories. 1956.
63: Dream Palace (stories). 1956; as *63: Dream Stories,* 1957.
Color of Darkness: Eleven Stories and a Novella. 1957.
Malcolm. 1959.
The Nephew. 1960.
Children Is All (stories and plays). 1961.
Cabot Wright Begins. 1964.
Eustace Chisholm and the Works. 1967.
An Oyster Is a Wealthy Beast (story and poems). 1967.
Mr. Evening: A Story and Nine Poems. 1968.
On the Rebound: A Story and Nine Poems. 1970.
Sleepers in Moon-Crowned Valleys: Jeremy's Version, 1970; *The House of the Solitary Maggot,* 1974.

I Am Elijah Thrush.   1972.
In a Shallow Grave.   1976.
A Day after the Fair (stories and play).   1977.
Narrow Rooms.   1978.

Plays

Mr. Cough Syrup and the Phantom Sex, in *December 8,* 1960.
Cracks (produced 1963).
Children Is All (produced 1965).   In *Children Is All,* 1961.
Wedding Finger, in *New Directions 28,* 1974.

Verse

The Running Sun.   1971.
Sunshine Is an Only Child.   1973.

Bibliography: "Purdy" by George E. Bush, in *Bulletin of Bibliography,* March 1971.

Reading List: *Purdy* by Henry Chupack, 1975; *Purdy* by Stephen D. Adams, 1976.

*   *   *

"We're all alike, inside, and we're all connected."

"You can't run away from yourself. You can run to the ends of the earth, but you'll be waiting for yourself there."

James Purdy is a much neglected writer who stands firm against the literary establishment which, as he has said, rejects his unconventional and often scalding portrayals of American society: "From the beginning my work has been greeted with a persistent and even passionate hostility." "The theme of American commercial culture," he adds, is "that man can be adjusted ... that to be 'in' is to exist. My work is the furthest from this definition of reality." Despite the difficulties in gaining publication ("Had it not been for Dame Edith Sitwell, who prevailed upon a British publisher," states Purdy, "I would never have been published in America and never heard of"), when *Color of Darkness* and, later, *Malcolm* appeared, Purdy was recognized as a writer of extraordinary imagination, a fantasist who, while concerned with matters common to the beats and the dramatists of the absurd – the isolation of youth from peers, parents, and society – brought to his form a unique style. Purdy combined surrealism with a meticulously rhetoric-free prose. He mixed realism, fairy tale, and allegory, and created an entirely new form; he transcribed and often poeticized native American speech within brutal satiric forms; he illustrated the exquisite varieties of suffering that society imposes upon the innocent, the nonconformist. In *63: Dream Palace, Color of Darkness, The Nephew,* and, perhaps his best-known work, *Malcolm,* he portrayed the inevitable and lethal possessiveness within both heterosexual and homosexual love; the need and yet fear of human companionship; man's failure in his struggle toward identity. Malcolm, typical of Purdy's orphaned heroes and prototype of all Purdy's men-children longing to belong and embrace an identity, becomes instead an appendage, an object – to be used, manipulated, brutalized, and ultimately discarded by the so-called caring people of his world. In *Children Is All, Cabot Wright Begins,* and *Eustace Chisholm and the Works,* Purdy remains for his readers frightening – indeed deeply troubling – as he treats in detail taboo subjects like homosexuality, abortion, rape, and incest, within ingenious frames. *Cabot Wright Begins*, which portrays an American automaton who can assert a human identity only through acts of rape, is one of America's most savage and grotesque comedies. Purdy's tone remains defiant. As one of his earliest critics, Warren French, later wrote of *Eustace Chisholm*, in *A Season of Promise*: "I was scarcely prepared for the violently compressed power, the exhausting vehemence, the almost superhuman exorcism of the wanton evil that destroys many innocents that sets Purdy's new effort far apart from the whining and cocktail chatter that often passes for serious fiction."

Jeremy's Version and *The House of the Solitary Maggot*, the first two parts of Purdy's trilogy, *Sleepers in Moon-Crowned Valleys*, combine Purdy's gift for realism with the erotic phantasmagorias of his more elliptical works. Again, scathing humor and caustic wit indict a society and its efforts to neuterize the human spirit. Purdy abandons the symbolic concretizations of the erotic, in order to draw more palpably flesh-and-blood characters, people with whom one identifies more immediately. Somewhat like Faulkner in *The Sound and the Fury*, Purdy here creates in a post-bellum family a parable of fallen America. He portrays in incredible and vivid detail a family whose growth and decline is underscored by excruciating pride and pain, where parents and children (in all combinations) visit upon one another an occasional kindness, but more often a persistent cruelty. Purdy's subject again is, on the one hand, man's struggle for love – specifically in the context of birthright and family – and on the other, the inevitable selfishness, violence, and destruction that are played out in parent (especially the mother) and child in payment for the bonds of incest.

In a Shallow Grave, about a war veteran whose incredibly disfigured body is both the grave from which he must daily survive and the world in which he must submit himself, was described by *The New York Times* reviewer as "a modern Book of Revelation," a gripping, imaginative, "powerful" novel "with prophecies, vision and demonic landscapes."

What has been called Purdy's unremitting bitterness and grotesqueness of vision is ultimately transcended by an exquisite poetic prose, and by the author's deep feeling for mankind. Purdy's style, based upon, as he has said, "the rhythms and accents of American speech," has about it, as the review just cited noted, "briers in his voice, as if he meant to tear at his readers with a kind of harsh music ... [a] deliberate scratching of the reader's ear" enabling the author "to mix evil and naiveté without spilling over into melodrama and tedious morality plays." Remarkable, in addition, is Purdy's richly textured, compressed, seemingly simple and direct prose which weaves together level upon level of symbol – often from nature (especially birds, flowers, animals, and light and dark), as well as from classical and biblical sources.

Finally, one is left with the author's profound compassion towards people. One may often feel anger, horror, and even repulsion towards Purdy's sadistic, licentious, and greedy people, but at the same time, one is haunted and overwhelmed by their loneliness and innocence. Purdy touches his readers on the deepest level, as he portrays, in every thing he writes, man's courage, dignity, and ultimate victory in the act of mere survival.

—Lois Gordon

PYNCHON, Thomas. American. Born in Glen Cove, New York, 8 May 1937. Educated at Cornell University, Ithaca, New York, 1954–58, B.A. 1958. Served in the United States Navy. Worked as an editorial writer for the Boeing Aircraft Corporation, Seattle, Washington; now a full-time writer. Recipient: Faulkner Award, 1964; Rosenthal Memorial Award, 1967; National Book Award, 1974; Howells Medal (refused), 1975.

PUBLICATIONS

Fiction

V. 1963.
The Crying of Lot 49. 1966.
Gravity's Rainbow. 1973.
Mortality and Mercy in Vienna (story). 1976.

Bibliography: *Three Contemporary Novelists: An Annotated Bibliography* by Robert M. Scotto, 1977.

Reading List: *Mindful Pleasures: Essays on Pynchon* edited by George Levine and David Leverenz, 1976; *The Grim Phoenix: Reconstructing Pynchon* by William M. Plater, 1978.

*   *   *

Thomas Pynchon's novels *V.*, *The Crying of Lot 49*, and *Gravity's Rainbow* have in common qualities that attract some readers and repel others. Both companies of readers are, however, likely to agree on what it is that they respond to in the work of Pynchon. It is an unremitting brilliance of invention, accompanied by a wide range of knowledge. The knowledge embraces the major course of European history over the past century, and it often deviates into nooks and crannies of the entire course of Western experience. In this respect, Pynchon has a novelist's plenty that makes him the peer of John Barth, William Gaddis, and others of his time. The consequence is that one has the sense of reading not only a novel but of progressing through pages from the *Britannica*, torn out at random.

The phrase "at random" is not entirely just. The assorted slices of erudition – scientific as well as cultural – are linked with Pynchon's often mad narrative sequences in ways that lead a reader to think, at a certain turn of a Pynchon novel, that he has come to the beating heart of the narrative. For throughout the tales are scattered clues that seem to lead from the witch's house of a particular novel – a place of confinement à la Hansel and Gretel – back to comprehension and mastery. But the clues to meaning – to the intent and often the animus of the novels – are scattered so generously that each reader is likely to follow a solitary path from the witch's hut (the novel as experienced) to some safe edge of a forest (the act of personal judgment).

Yet certain judgments are not wholly solitary. Each novel has a strand of interest that threads through scenes of great comic and satiric effect. There is, in *V.*, a decades-long pursuit of a mysterious being; one can hardly call this being a woman since her eyes are glass, her dentures precious metal, and her feet detachable. And there is, in *The Crying of Lot 49*, the effort of Mrs. Oedipa Maas to discover whether an ancient European secret society for distributing mail is still alive and functioning in today's California. In *Gravity's Rainbow* events in England and Germany during the closing years of World War II are concerned with English efforts to frustrate buzz bombs and other missiles and with German efforts to launch those missiles. (A young American named Slothrop has a sexual activity that seems linked with the arrival of the bombs. But this is only a small part of a variegated story.)

Such strands are obviously purloined from popular and facile tales of intrigue. In Pynchon's novels the strands become enmeshed in displays of language brilliance and events both grotesque and, if one has missed a clue or so, gratuitous. The clues – if that is what certain passages come to – sometimes do point to the identity of V., or the workings of the society that competes with the public mail systems of the world in *The Crying of Lot 49*, or that crisis of world order in *Gravity's Rainbow*. At other times, the clues are – or seem to be – self-subsistent rather than centers about which one can gather the motley contents of a novel.

997

V., for example, ranges from the 1910's to about 1956. European-based characters are touched by V. and "her" progress from being a human person to an assemblage of inanimate elements wondrously animated. In contrast, the American characters are known only in an immediate present; this is "The Crew," a collection of people united by their drinking and whoring and also by an uneasy but quite intermittent questioning of all they do. What is the relation between these two strands? Is the V. experience an account of the decadence that reached its terminus in Pynchon's boozy crew of young "Nueva Yorkers"? Similarly, is the Trystero group that Oedipa Maas pursues, come weal come woe, one that allures the heroine because it speaks, unclearly, of firm purpose asserting itself in a world where there is none? And is the action of the German rocket chief in *Gravity's Rainbow* – the launching of the body of his young lover inside one of the last rockets – a scream of despair for civilization or just one more comic incident among many such?

Pynchon, satiric and ironic at most times, moralistic in rare but intense passages, creates textures of narrative that distort – but do not much misrepresent – the society they mirror. Back and forth over this texture Pynchon's mind darts. It sometimes expresses an intellect that is disembodied and uninvolved. At other times, there is acknowledgement of a link between the novelist and what he sets down. But such a link is no sooner noted than it is severed.

—Harold H. Watts

QUEEN, Ellery. Pseudonym for the cousins Frederic Dannay and Manfred B. Lee; also used the pseudonym Barnaby Ross. Americans. **DANNAY, Frederic**: born in Brooklyn, New York, 20 October 1905. Educated at Boys' High School, Brooklyn. Married 1) Mary Beck in 1926 (died), two sons; 2) Hilda Wisenthal in 1947 (died, 1972), one son; 3) Rose Koppel in 1976. Writer and art director for a New York advertising agency prior to 1931; full-time writer, with Manfred B. Lee, 1931–71, and on his own from 1971. Visiting Professor, University of Texas, Austin, 1958–59. Lives in Larchmont, New York. **LEE, Manfred B.**: born in Brooklyn, New York, 11 January 1905. Educated at New York University. Married Catherine Brinker in 1942; four daughters and four sons. Publicity writer in New York for film companies prior to 1931; full-time writer, with Frederic Dannay, 1931 until his death. Justice of the Peace, Roxbury, Connecticut, 1957–58. *Died 3 April 1971.* Dannay and Lee edited *Mystery League* magazine, 1933–34, and *Ellery Queen's Mystery Magazine*, from 1941; they wrote the "Adventures of Ellery Queen" radio series, 1939–48; they were co-founders and co-presidents of Mystery Writers of America, and received Mystery Writers of America awards in 1945, 1947, 1949, Special Book Award, 1951, and Grand Master Award, 1961.

PUBLICATIONS

Fiction

The Roman Hat Mystery. 1929.
The French Powder Mystery. 1930.
The Dutch Shoe Mystery. 1931.
The Egyptian Cross Mystery. 1932.
The Greek Coffin Mystery. 1932.
The Tragedy of X: A Drury Lane Mystery. 1932.
The Tragedy of Y: A Drury Lane Mystery. 1932.
The Tragedy of Z: A Drury Lane Mystery. 1933.
Drury Lane's Last Case: The Tragedy of 1599. 1933.
The Siamese Twin Mystery. 1933.
The American Gun Mystery: Death at the Rodeo. 1933.
The Chinese Orange Mystery. 1934.
The Adventures of Ellery Queen (stories). 1934.
The Spanish Cape Mystery. 1935.
Halfway House. 1936.
The Door Between. 1937.
The Four of Hearts. 1938.
The Devil to Pay. 1938.
The Dragon's Teeth. 1939; as *The Virgin Heiresses*, 1954.
The New Adventures of Ellery Queen (stories). 1940.
Calamity Town. 1942.
There Was an Old Woman. 1943; as *The Quick and the Dead*, 1956.
The Case Book of Ellery Queen. 1945.
The Murderer Is a Fox. 1945.
Ten Days' Wonder. 1948.
Cat of Many Tails. 1949.
Double Double: A New Novel of Wrightsville. 1950; as *The Case of the Seven Murderers*, 1958.
The Origin of Evil. 1951.
Calendar of Crime (stories). 1952.

The King Is Dead. 1952.
The Scarlet Letters. 1953.
The Golden Summer (by Dannay). 1953.
The Glass Village. 1954.
Q.B.I.: Queen's Bureau of Investigation. 1955.
Inspector Queen's Own Case: November Song. 1956.
The Finishing Stroke. 1958.
The Player on the Other Side. 1963.
And on the Eighth Day. 1964.
The Fourth Side of the Triangle. 1965.
Queens Full (stories). 1965.
A Study in Terror. 1966; as *Sherlock Holmes Versus Jack the Ripper,* 1967.
Face to Face. 1967.
The House of Brass. 1968.
Cop Out. 1969.
The Last Woman in His Life. 1970.
A Fine and Private Place. 1971.

Play

Screenplay (by Lee): *Closed Gates,* with Frances Guihan, 1927.

Other

The Detective Short Story: A Bibliography. 1942; revised edition, 1969.
Queen's Quorum: A History of the Detective-Crime Short Story as Revealed by the 100 Most Important Books Published in the Field since 1845. 1951; revised edition, 1969.
In the Queens' Parlor and Other Leaves from the Editors' Notebook. 1957.

Editor, *Challenge to the Reader: An Anthology.* 1938.
Editor, *101 Years' Entertainment: The Great Detective Stories 1841–1941.* 1941.
Editor, *Sporting Blood: The Great Sports Detective Stories.* 1942; as *Sporting Detective Stories,* 1946.
Editor, *The Female of the Species: The Great Women Detectives and Criminals.* 1943; as *Ladies in Crime,* 1947.
Editor, *The Misadventures of Sherlock Holmes.* 1944.
Editor, *Best Stories from Ellery Queen's Mystery Magazine.* 1944.
Editor, *Rogues' Gallery: The Great Criminals of Modern Fiction.* 1945.
Editor, *To the Queen's Taste.* 1946.
Editor, *The Queen's Awards,* later *Mystery Annuals* and *Anthologies* (from *Ellery Queen's Mystery Magazine*). 29 vols., 1946–75.
Editor, *Murder by Experts.* 1947.
Editor, *20th Century Detective Stories.* 1948.
Editor, *The Literature of Crime: Stories by World-Famous Authors.* 1950.
Editor, *International Case Book.* 1964.
Editor, *The Woman in the Case.* 1966; as *Deadlier Than the Male,* 1967.
Editor, *Poetic Justice: 23 Stories of Crime, Mystery, and Detection by World-Famous Poets.* 1967.
Editor, *Minimysteries: 70 Short-Short Stories of Crime, Mystery, and Detection.* 1969.
Editor, *Japanese Golden Dozen: The Detective Story World in Japan.* 1978.

Also compiled volumes of stories by Dashiell Hammett and others, and other anthologies.

Reading List: *Royal Bloodline: Ellery Queen* by Francis M. Nevins, Jr., 1974 (includes bibliography).

*   *   *

Ellery Queen is both the pseudonym and the detective creation of two Brooklyn-born first cousins, Frederic Dannay and Manfred B. Lee. At the time they created Ellery Queen, Dannay was a copywriter and art director for a Manhattan advertising agency and Lee a publicity writer for the New York office of a film studio. The announcement of a $7500 prize contest for a detective novel catalyzed the cousins into literary action in 1928, and Ellery's first adventure was published the following year. Dannay's experience in advertising may have inspired the innovation of using the same name for the cousins' deductive protagonist and for their own joint byline – a device that, along with the excellence of the books themselves, turned Ellery Queen into a household name and his creators into wealthy men.

In the late 1920's the dominant figure in American detective fiction was S. S. Van Dine (Willard Huntington Wright), an erudite art critic whose novels about the impossibly intellectual aesthete-sleuth Philo Vance were consistent best-sellers. The early Ellery Queen novels, with their patterned titles and their scholarly dilettante detective forever dropping classical quotations, were heavily influenced by Van Dine, though superior in plotting, characterization, and style. Ellery is a professional mystery writer and amateur sleuth who assists his father, Inspector Richard Queen, whenever a murder puzzle becomes too complex for ordinary police methods. His first-period cases, from *The Roman Hat Mystery* (1929) through *The Spanish Cape Mystery* (1935), are richly plotted specimens of the Golden Age deductive puzzle at its zenith, full of bizarre circumstances, conflicting testimony, enigmatic clues, alternative solutions, fireworks displays of virtuoso reasoning, and a constant crackle of intellectual excitement. All the facts are presented, trickily but fairly, and the reader is formally challenged to solve the puzzle ahead of Ellery. Most of Queen's distinctive story motifs – the negative clue, the dying message, the murderer as Iagoesque manipulator, the patterned series of clues deliberately left at scenes of crimes, the false answer followed by the true and devastating solution – originated in these early novels. Perhaps the best works of the first period are *The Greek Coffin Mystery* and *The Egyptian Cross Mystery*, which both appeared in 1932, the same year in which, under the second pseudonym of Barnaby Ross, Dannay and Lee published the first and best two novels in the tetralogy dealing with actor-detective Drury Lane: *The Tragedy of X* and *The Tragedy of Y*.

By 1936 the Van Dine touches had left Queen's work and been replaced by the influence of the slick-paper magazines and the movies, to both of which the cousins had begun to sell. In second-period Queen the patterned titles vanish and Ellery gradually becomes less priggish and more human. In several stories of the period he is seen working as a Hollywood screenwriter, reflecting the cousins' brief stints at Columbia, Paramount, and MGM. Most of Queen's work in the late 1930's is thinly plotted, overburdened with "love interest," and too obviously written with film sales in mind, but the best book of the period, *The Four of Hearts*, is an excellent detective story as well as a many-faceted evocation of Hollywood in its peak years.

At the start of the new decade most of the cousins' energies went into writing a script a week for the long-running *Adventures of Ellery Queen* radio series (1939–48) and accumulating a vast library of detective short stories. Out of this collection came Queen's *101 Years' Entertainment*, the foremost anthology of the genre, and *Ellery Queen's Mystery Magazine*, which throughout its life from 1941 till today has been edited solely by Dannay. In 1942 the cousins returned to fiction with the superbly written and characterized *Calamity Town*, a semi-naturalistic detective novel in which Ellery solves a murder in the "typical small town" of Wrightsville, U.S.A. Their third and richest period as mystery writers lasted sixteen years and embraced twelve novels, two short story collections and Dannay's autobiographical novel *The Golden Summer* (1953), published as by Daniel Nathan. In third-period Queen the complex deductive puzzle is fused with in-depth character studies, magnificently detailed evocations of place and mood, occasional ventures into a topsy-turvy Alice in Wonderland otherworld reflecting Dannay's interest in Lewis Carroll, and explorations into historical, psychiatric, and religious dimensions. The best novels of this period are *Calamity Town* itself; *Ten Days' Wonder*, with its phantasmagoria of biblical symbolism; *Cat of Many Tails*, with its unforgettable images of New York City menaced by a heat wave, a mad strangler of what seem to be randomly chosen victims, and the threat of World War III; and *The Origin of Evil*, in which Darwinian motifs underlie the clues and deductions. Finally, in *The Finishing Stroke*, the cousins nostalgically recreated Ellery's young manhood in 1929, just after the publication of "his" first detective novel, *The Roman Hat Mystery*.

"In my end is my beginning," says Eliot; and the cousins apparently meant to retire as active writers after *The Finishing Stroke*. Five years later, however, they launched a fourth and final group of Ellery Queen novels, from *The Player on the Other Side* (1963), the best book of the period, to *A Fine and Private Place* (1971), published almost simultaneously with Manfred Lee's death of a heart attack. The novels and short stories of period four retreat from all semblance of naturalistic plausibility and rely on what Dannay has called "fun and games" – heavily stylized plots and characterizations and the repetition of dozens of motifs from the earlier periods.

No new novels have appeared since Lee's death and none is likely in the future, although Dannay remains active and perceptive as ever in his capacity as editor of the *Mystery Magazine*. But the reputation of Ellery Queen, author and detective, has long been assured. Of all America's mystery writers Queen is the supreme practitioner of that noble but now dying genre, the classic formal detective story.

—Francis M. Nevins, Jr.

QUILLER-COUCH, Sir Arthur (Thomas). Pseudonym: "Q." English. Born in Bodmin, Cornwall, 21 November 1863. Educated at Newton Abbot, Devon; Clifton College, Bristol; Trinity College, Oxford, 1882–86, honours degrees in classics, 1884, 1886. Married Louisa Amelia Hicks in 1889; one son and one daughter. Lecturer in Classics at Trinity College, 1886–87, then settled in London; worked as a free-lance journalist and for the publishing firm of Cassell: Assistant Editor of Cassell's Liberal weekly *The Speaker*, 1890–92, and contributor until 1899; settled in Fowey, Cornwall, 1892, and continued to work as a free-lance journalist until 1912; Fellow of Jesus College, Cambridge, and King Edward VII Professor of English, Cambridge University, 1912–44: with H. M. Chadwick and Dr. Hugh Fraser Stewart, established an independent honours school of English literature at Cambridge, 1917; Editor, King's Treasuries of Literature series, Dent, publishers, London, from 1920. Mayor of Fowey, 1937–38; also Justice of the Peace and County Alderman, Cornwall. Litt.D.: University of Bristol, 1912; LL.D.: University of Aberdeen, 1927; University of Edinburgh, 1930. Honorary Fellow, Trinity College, Oxford, 1926. Fellow, and Member of the Academic Committee, Royal Society of Literature. Knighted, 1910. *Died 12 May 1944.*

PUBLICATIONS

Fiction

Dead Man's Rock.   1887.
The Astonishing History of Troy Town.   1888; as *Troy Town*, 1928.

The Splendid Spur.   1889.
Noughts and Crosses: Stories, Studies, and Sketches.   1891.
The Blue Pavilions.   1891.
I Saw Three Ships and Other Winter's Tales.   1892.
The Delectable Duchy: Stories, Studies, and Sketches.   1893.
Fairy Tales, Far and Near.   1895.
Wandering Heath: Stories, Studies, and Sketches.   1895.
Ia: A Love Story.   1895.
St. Ives, Being the Adventures of a French Prisoner in England, with Robert Louis
    Stevenson (completed by Quiller-Couch).   1897.
The Ship of Stars.   1899.
Old Fires and Profitable Ghosts (stories).   1900.
The Laird's Luck and Other Fireside Tales.   1901.
The Westcotes.   1902.
The White Wolf and Other Fireside Tales.   1902.
The Adventures of Harry Revel.   1903.
Two Sides of the Face: Midwinter Tales.   1903.
The Collaborators; or, The Comedy That Wrote Itself.   1903.
Hetty Wesley.   1903.
Fort Amity.   1904.
Shakespeare's Christmas and Other Stories.   1904.
Shining Ferry.   1905.
Sir John Constantine.   1906.
The Mayor of Troy.   1906.
Poison Island.   1906.
Major Vigoureux.   1907.
Merry-Garden and Other Stories.   1907.
True Tilda.   1909.
Corporal Sam and Other Stories.   1910.
Lady Good for Nothing: A Man's Portrait of a Woman.   1910.
Brother Copas.   1911.
The Sleeping Beauty and Other Tales from the Old French.   1911.
Hocken and Hunken: A Tale of Troy.   1912.
My Best Book (stories).   1912.
In Powder and Crinoline: Old Fairy Tales Retold.   1913; as *The Twelve Dancing
    Princesses and Other Fairy Tales,* 1923.
News from the Duchy (stories).   1913.
Nicky-Nan, Reservist.   1915.
Mortallone and Aunt Trinidad: Tales of the Spanish Main.   1917.
Foe-Farrell · A Romance.   1918.
Selected Stories.   1921.
Tales and Romances.   30 vols., 1928.
Q's Mystery Stories.   1937.
Shorter Stories.   1946.
Castle Dor, completed by Daphne du Maurier.   1962.

Verse

Athens.   1881.
Green Bays: Verses and Parodies.   1893; revised edition, 1930.
Poems and Ballads.   1896.
The Vigil of Venus and Other Poems.   1912.
Poems.   1929.

Other

The Warwickshire Avon, illustrated by Alfred Parsons.   1891.
Adventures in Criticism.   1896.
Historical Tales from Shakespeare.   1899.
From a Cornish Window.   1906.
The Roll Call of Honour.   1912.
Poetry.   1914.
On the Art of Writing (lectures).   1916.
Memoir of Arthur John Butler.   1917.
Notes on Shakespeare's Workmanship.   1917; as Shakespeare's Workmanship, 1918.
Studies in Literature.   3 vols., 1918–29.
On the Art of Reading (lectures).   1920.
Charles Dickens and Other Victorians.   1925.
The Age of Chaucer.   1926.
A Lecture on Lectures.   1927.
A Further Approach to Shakespeare.   1934.
The Poet as Citizen and Other Papers.   1934.
The Jubilee of County Councils 1899–1939.   1939.
Cambridge Lectures.   1943.
Memories and Opinions: An Unfinished Autobiography, edited by S. C. Roberts.   1944.
Q Anthology, edited by Frederick Brittain.   1948.

Editor, The Golden Pomp: A Procession of English Lyrics from Surrey To Shirley.   1895.
Editor, The Story of the Sea.   2 vols., 1895–96.
Editor, English Sonnets.   1897; revised edition, 1935.
Editor, A Fowey Garland.   1899.
Editor, The Oxford Book of English Verse 1250–1900.   1900; revised edition, 1939.
Editor, The World of Adventure: A Collection of Stirring Scenes (The Black, Blue,
    Brown, Green, Grey, and Red Adventure Book).   6 vols., 1904–05.
Editor, The Pilgrim's Way: A Little Scrip of Good Counsel for Travellers.   1906.
Editor, Select English Classics.   32 vols., 1908–12.
Editor, The Oxford Book of Ballads.   1910.
Editor, The Oxford Book of Victorian Verse.   1912.
Editor, with J. Dover Wilson, Plays, by Shakespeare (Comedies in New Cambridge
    Edition).   14 vols., 1921–31.
Editor, A Bible Anthology.   1922.
Editor, The Oxford Book of English Prose.   1925.
Editor, with A. Nairne and T. R. Glover, The Cambridge Shorter Bible.   1928.
Editor, Felicities of Thomas Traherne.   1934.

Translator, with Paul M. Francke, A Blot of Ink, by René Bazin.   1892.

Reading List: The Q Tradition by Basil Willey, 1946; Quiller-Couch: A Biographical Study of Q by Frederick Brittain, 1947 (includes bibliography).

*   *   *

My first introduction to Arthur Quiller-Couch ("Q") was encountering in 1945 his books On the Art of Writing and On the Art of Reading, and wondering why the lectures I was hearing at McGill were not as sensible and stimulating as those of an earlier generation at Cambridge. Q's classical quotations and erudite allusions may have sounded a bit more pompous in the 1940's than they did when first delivered, but there were a genuine enthusiasm and a desire to offer truly practical advice. Others also stressed "plain words" in writing, and were perhaps better critics of literature, but few had Q's light touch with verse parody that contrived to be both imitation and devastating criticism. Perhaps his greatest contribution to scholarship was to bring to general and critical attention the poets he featured in his thoughtful anthologies (including *The Oxford Book of English Verse*). Though not exceptionally innovative, they were sound and widely used, and it is through them, and not his strictly critical works, that he made his useful contribution to the modern view of poetry.

Entertaining poet and influential critic that he was, it was in his own fiction that he did his best work. There is a wild Cornish romanticism in *Dead Man's Rock* and *The Astonishing History of Troy Town*, while *The Splendid Spur* and *The Ship of Stars* rival Neil Munro in catching the manner of Robert Louis Stevenson, and are, I think, better than Munro's *John Splendid* (1898). In fact, Q was chosen to finish *St. Ives*, the novel left incomplete at the death of Stevenson, and he did an admirable job in proving himself a master spinner of yarns. (His own unfinished novel, *Castle Dor*, was completed by another Cornish writer, Daphne du Maurier.)

It is as a writer of romantic fiction, and not as a critic, anthologist, journalist, professor, or local politician, that he has a small but secure place in history.

—Leonard R. N. Ashley

RADCLIFFE, Ann (née Ward). English. Born in London, 9 July 1764. Educated privately. Married William Radcliffe, subsequently editor of the *English Chronicle*, in 1787. Writer, 1789–1797; thereafter lived in retirement. *Died 7 February 1823.*

PUBLICATIONS

Collections

> *Poetical Works.* 2 vols., 1834.
> *Novels.* 1877.

Fiction

> *The Castles of Athlin and Dunbayne: A Highland Story.* 1789.
> *A Sicilian Romance.* 1790.
> *The Romance of the Forest, Interspersed with Some Pieces of Poetry.* 1791.
> *The Mysteries of Udolpho: A Romance, Interspersed with Some Pieces of Poetry.* 1794; edited by Bonamy Dobrée, 1966.
> *The Italian; or, The Confessional of the Black Penitents: A Romance.* 1797; edited by Frederick Garber, 1968.
> *Gaston de Blondeville; or, The Court of Henry III Keeping Festival in Ardenne; St. Alban's Abbey: A Metrical Tale; with Some Metrical Pieces.* 1826.

Verse

> *Poems.* 1815.

Other

> *A Journey Made in the Summer of 1794 Through Holland and the Western Frontier of Germany.* 1795.

Bibliography: in *Gothic Bibliography* by Montague Summers, 1941.

Reading List: *Radcliffe* by Aline Grant, 1952; *Sublimity in the Novels of Radcliffe: A Study of the Influence of Burke's Enquiry* by M. Ware, 1963.

*   *   *

Ann Radcliffe's novels are concerned with terror and reason, in their late eighteenth-century significations. She is uninterested in complex characterizations, rational plot, natural dialogue, or social themes. Instead, she tries to throw her idealized heroines into the greatest perplexity and fear as often and for as many reasons as possible, before she finally elucidates all obscurities, dispels all fears, and explains all mysteries. Thus she uses geographical and historical distance to achieve exotic effects, and her settings exploit most of the types of the sublime and picturesque set out in the standard treatises on those subjects. Her stories concern concealed or afflicted relationships between idealized heroes and heroines and virtuous but ineffectual parents or guardians on one hand, and vicious and tyrannical persecutors on the other. Her plots are unprogressive, rely heavily on various devices of retardation, function on the principle of linked complications, and are terminated by a *deus ex machina* or a grand coincidence. Her characters, with the exception of Schedoni in *The Italian*, are abstract and uninteresting; she cares little for individual psychology, only for opportunities to describe inner conflicts, or various ways of overthrowing reason by means of sublimity and terror. The only other modes of sensibility that interest her are the moral and aesthetic tastes of her heroes and heroines, seen in her descriptions of their responses to music, ruins, or picturesque nature. Dialogue too is abstract and artificial, and, where it is impassioned, relies heavily on the rhetorical clichés of heroic drama.

And so the novels are static in form. There is no development of character or theme, no argument embodied in a concatenation of character and circumstance, only a repetition in diverse forms of mystery, obscurity, terror, and perplexity, until finally what is feared – rape, murder, or some forced action such as marriage or transfer of property – is evaded. The double movement in the novels is from mystery and confinement to knowledge and freedom, as temperance, fortitude, chastity, and family loyalty triumph over passion, egotism, pride, and licentiousness. But the victory of reason and self-control over mystery and excess is guaranteed right from the beginning by the narrative voice. Even-tempered, lucid, and balanced, it rarely breaks down into expressiveness, and, through apparent mysteries, confusions, and terrors, works out the same values, and the same view of man and society, which are presented in the contemporaneous novel of manners and social life.

The tension between terror and reason, then, is the dominant characteristic of Mrs. Radcliffe's fiction. It was the source of her enormous popularity and she continued to develop the skill and complexity of her treatment of it from *The Castles of Athlin and Dunbayne* to *The Mysteries of Udolpho*. *The Italian* was probably meant as a criticism of the mass of inferior imitators of her own achievement, and therefore probably an afterthought, while *Gaston de Blondeville* and the verse romance *St. Alban's Abbey* were unsuccessful attempts to develop fictional modes different from that she had perfected, and exhausted, with *Udolpho* and *The Italian*.

—Gary Kelly

RAO, Raja. Indian. Born in Hassan, Mysore, 21 November 1909. Educated at Nizam College, Hyderabad, University of Madras, B.A. in English 1929; University of Montpellier, France, 1929–30; the Sorbonne, Paris, 1930–33. Married 1) Camille Mouly in 1931; 2) Katherine Jones in 1965; one son. Has spent half of his life in France; now lives half the year in India and half in Europe and the United States. Since 1965, Professor of Philosophy, teaching one semester a year, University of Texas, Austin. Recipient: Academy of Indian Literature Prize, 1964; Padma Bhushan, Government of India, 1969.

PUBLICATIONS

Fiction

Kanthapura. 1938.
The Cow of the Barricades and Other Stories. 1947.
The Serpent and the Rope. 1960.
The Cat and Shakespeare: A Tale of India. 1965.

Comrade Kirillov.   1976.
The Policeman and the Rose.   1977.

Other

Whither India, with Iqbal Singh.   1948.

Editor, with Iqbal Singh, *Changing India.*   1939.

Reading List: *Rao* by M. K. Naik, 1972; *Rao: A Critical Study of His Work* by C. D. Narasimhaiah, 1973.

*   *   *

As the author of only half a dozen published works, one of which is a collection of short-stories and two of which are of novella length, Raja Rao runs the risk of not having written enough to be regarded as a major Indian novelist. Yet the publication of his first novel, *Kanthapura,* established him as an important writer, while *The Serpent and the Rope,* on which he had been working for many years, has increasingly become the focal point of critical work on Indian fiction in English.

Rao has written short stories from his teens onwards. Some of them (including a few in French) are obscurely hidden away in esoteric magazines, but the best of his early work appeared in *The Cow of the Barricades and Other Stories.* Stories like "Javni," set in Rao's home city of Mysore, or "Akkayya" (the name means "elder sister") show his early preoccupation both with social conditions in India and with the values to be accorded womanhood. A third concern of Rao's later and maturer work, the encounter of Indian and European cultural history, is indicated by the story "Nimka."

Kanthapura is set in a village of that name in the valleys of Himavathi, some distance from Mysore in South India. In the Foreword to the novel Rao says, "The telling has not been easy. One has to convey in a language that is not one's own the spirit that is one's own." The novel deals with the impact of Gandhian principles upon a traditional community. Rao brings the village to life with remarkable feeling, though at times the English he uses seems to strain against the problems of unsophisticated people which he is trying to render. The result may seem a little cloudy or sometimes self-consciously poetic.

C. D. Narasimhaiah, an eminent Indian critic, writes at the start of his book on Rao, "That Raja Rao is India's most significant novelist writing in the English language today is now indisputable." The claim is based on the centrality in Indian fiction of *The Serpent and the Rope.* This novel is written on a more ambitious scale than any other English-language work from India. Drawing on traditional legends from *The Ramayana* and attempting at moments a linguistic synthesis of English meaning and Sanskrit rhythms, the novel explores the relationship of India and Europe through the marriage of its protagonists Rama and Madeleine. The novelist shows a deep awareness of the spiritual and historic links between European and Asian culture, between Catholicism, Hinduism, and Buddhism, between the heresies of east and west. Though the novel is primarily philosophical it does not read like an abstract treatise. Most criticism centres on whether Rao has created proper characters, or merely ideological symbols, on whether or not his interpretation of the Feminine Principle is sentimental, and on the degree to which a deliberately open-ended novel (for Rama does not fulfil his quest) can be considered an achieved work of art.

The Serpent and the Rope has been followed by two short novels, *The Cat and Shakespeare* and *Comrade Kirillov,* in which Rao writes philosophical explorations of the Indian-ness of India.

—Alastair Niven

RAWLINGS, Marjorie Kinnan. American. Born in Washington, D.C., 8 August 1896. Educated at Western High School, Washington, D.C.; University of Wisconsin, Madison, B.A. 1918 (Phi Beta Kappa). Married 1) Charles Rawlings in 1919 (divorced, 1933); 2) Norton Sanford Baskin in 1941. Editor, YWCA National Board, New York, 1918–19; Assistant Service Editor, *Home Sector* magazine, 1919; staff member, *Louisville Courier Journal*, Kentucky, and *Rochester Journal*, New York, 1920–28; syndicated verse writer ("Songs of a Housewife"), United Features, 1926–28; lived in Florida from 1928; thereafter a full-time writer. Recipient: O. Henry Award, 1933; Pulitzer Prize, 1939. LL.D.: Rollins College, Winter Park, Florida, 1939; L.H.D.: University of Florida, Gainesville, 1941. Member, National Institute of Arts and Letters, 1939. *Died 14 December 1953.*

PUBLICATIONS

Collections

The Rawlings Reader, edited by Julia Scribner Bigham. 1956.

Fiction

South Moon Under. 1933.
Golden Apples. 1935.
The Yearling. 1938.
When the Whippoorwill – (stories). 1940.
Jacob's Ladder. 1950.
The Sojourner. 1953.

Other

Cross Creek. 1942.
Cross Creek Cookery. 1942; as *The Rawlings Cookbook,* 1960.
The Secret River (juvenile). 1955.

Reading List: *Frontier Eden: The Literary Career of Rawlings* by Gordon F. Bigelow, 1972; *Rawlings* by Samuel I. Bellman, 1974.

* * *

Marjorie Kinnan Rawlings is a regional writer. Her work is inhabited by the simple people and natural settings of the Florida backwoods which she adopted as her home. Often paramount in her novels is the struggle against the vicissitudes of an uncertain existence by the poor white – the Florida cracker – commonly epitomized in an archetypal young protagonist with frontier virtues. These patterns are evident in her first four novels and in much of her short fiction.

South Moon Under depicts the difficulties of a hunter scratching out a living as a moonshiner in the Florida scrub country. The novel combines vividly descriptive scenes of rural existence with strong characterizations and an eventful plot. *Golden Apples* recounts the efforts of an orphaned and impoverished brother and sister to survive in late 19th-century northern Florida. They "squat" on the estate of an exiled and embittered young Englishman whom they patiently regenerate. The resourceful protagonist is a more convincing figure than the vaguely sketched Englishman in this flawed but dramatically forceful novel. In the novella *Jacob's Ladder* a rootless and destitute young cracker couple encounter adversities in luckless attempts to wrest a living from a bounteous but treacherous environment. The pair's deep mutual reliance and indomitable spirit are a poignant and emotionally powerful testament.

The author's internationally acclaimed novel *The Yearling* represents her finest achievement. The hero is 12-year-old Jody Baxter who lives with his parents in the Florida hammock country of the 1870's. As his family undergoes severe economic setbacks, Jody tames a fawn which becomes his forest-roaming companion. When, however, his pet cannot be restrained from eating the precious crops, it must be killed. The anguished boy feels betrayed by his father and severs their close relationship. Eventually they are reconciled. Tragedy has made a man of him. Throughout the story weave such themes as man's need to belong to the land which, in turn, belongs to those who lovingly cultivate it, and the inevitability of unfair and unexpected betrayal by man and nature. Rawlings's compellingly truthful portrait of a boy and his tender relationships is universally appealing. Her striking description of nature's elemental forces and the simple but significant events in the lives of people close to the land enrich an absorbingly ingenuous story. This distinguished novel stands as a classic of both adult and children's literature.

When the Whippoorwill –, a collection of the author's major short fiction, is highlighted by three richly amusing cracker comedies often told in the vernacular ("Benny and the Bird Dogs," "Cocks Must Crow," and "Varmints"), and also contains a serious portrayal of a wife exploited by a shiftless backwoods bootlegger ("Gal Young 'Un") as well as the novella "Jacob's Ladder." While the remaining stories are undistinguished, the overall collection displays the hand of an able story-teller. *The Sojourner*, an ambitious but imperfect novel, is a wooden family-chronicle centering on a Job-like farmer toiling on a New York state farm owned by an unloving mother reserving her affection for his wandering elder brother. Missed are the Florida locales of her earlier fiction, also detailed with verve and warmth in the autobiographical *Cross Creek*.

Marjorie Kinnan Rawlings is a pastoral writer of percipience and power whose blaze on the tree of American regional literature has been cut deep enough to last.

—Christian H. Moe

READE, Charles. English. Born in Ipsden, Oxfordshire, 8 June 1814. Educated privately by a clergyman at Rose Hill, near Iffley, 1822–27, and at the private school of Rev. Hearn at Staines, Middlesex, 1827–29; Magdalen College, Oxford, 1831–35, B.A. 1835, M.A. 1838, D.C.L. 1847; entered Lincoln's Inn, London, 1836; Vinerian Fellow, 1842; called to the Bar, 1843. Fellow of Magdalen College, Oxford, 1835 until his death, and held the posts of Bursar, 1844 (re-elected, 1849), Dean of Arts, 1845, and Vice-President, 1851; writer from 1850; thereafter gradually withdrew from university life and lived mainly in London. *Died 11 April 1884.*

PUBLICATIONS

Collections

(Works). 17 vols., 1895.

Fiction

Peg Woffington. 1852; edited by Emma Gollancz, 1901.
Christie Johnstone. 1853.
Clouds and Sunshine; Art: A Dramatic Tale. 1855.
It Is Never Too Late to Mend. 1856.
The Course of True Love Never Did Run Smooth (stories). 1857.
Propria Quae Maribus: A Jeu d'Esprit, and The Box Tunnel: A Fact. 1857.
White Lies. 1857; as *Double Marriage; or, White Lies,* 1868.
Cream (stories). 1858.
A Good Fight and Other Tales. 1859; *A Good Fight* edited by Andrew Lang, 1910.
Love Me Little, Love Me Long. 1859.
The Cloister and the Hearth. 1861.
Hard Cash. 1863.
Griffith Gaunt; or, Jealousy. 1866.
Foul Play, with Dion Boucicault. 1868.
Put Yourself in His Place. 1870.
A Terrible Temptation. 1871.
The Wandering Heir. 1872.
A Simpleton. 1873.
The Jilt. 1877.
A Woman-Hater. 1877.
Golden Crowns: Sunday Stories. 1877.
Singleheart and Doubleface. 1882.
Good Stories of Man and Other Animals. 1884.
The Jilt and Other Stories. 1884.
A Perilous Secret. 1884.

Plays

The Ladies' Battle; or, Un Duel en Amour, from a play by Scribe (produced 1851). 1851.
Peregrine Pickle, from the novel by Smollett (produced 1854). 1851.
Angelo, from the play by Victor Hugo (produced 1851). 1851.
Rachel the Reaper, from a work by George Sand (as *A Village Tale,* produced 1852; revised version, as *Rachel the Reaper,* produced 1872). 1871.
The Lost Husband, from a play by A. A. Bourgeois and A. M. B. Gaudichot Masson (produced 1852). 1852.
Masks and Faces; or, Before and Behind the Curtain, with Tom Taylor (produced 1852). 1854; edited by George Rowell, in *Nineteenth-Century Plays,* 1953.
Gold! (produced 1853). 1853.
The Courier of Lyons; or, The Attack upon the Mail, from a work by Moreau, Siraudin, and Delacour (produced 1854). 1854; as *The Lyons Mail* (produced 1877), 1895.
The King's Rival, with Tom Taylor (produced 1854). 1854.
Honour Before Titles; or, Nobs and Snobs (produced 1854).
Two Loves and a Life (produced 1854). 1854.
Nance Oldfield, from a play by Fournier (as *Art,* produced 1855; revised version, as *An Actress by Daylight,* produced 1871; as *Nance Oldfield,* produced 1883). 1883.
Poverty and Pride, from a play by Edward Brisebarre and Eugene Nus. 1856.
The First Printer, with Tom Taylor (produced 1856).
The Hypochondriac, from a play by Molière (produced 1858; as *The Robust Invalid,* produced 1870). 1857.
Le Faubourg Saint-Germain. 1859.

It's Never Too Late to Mend, from his own novel (produced 1864).   1865; edited by
   Léone Rives, 1940.
The Prurient Prude.   1866.
Dora, from a poem by Tennyson (produced 1867).   1867.
The Double Marriage, from a play by August Maquet (produced 1867).   1867; revised
   version (produced 1868).
Foul Play, with Dion Boucicault, from their own novel (produced 1868; revised version,
   produced 1868).   1871; revised by Reade, 1883; revised version, as *Our Seamen*
   (produced 1874); as *The Scuttled Ship* (produced 1877).
The Well-Born Workman; or, A Man of the Day, from his novel *Put Yourself in His Place*
   (as *Put Yourself in His Place*, produced 1870; as *Free Labour*, produced
   1870).   1878.
Kate Peyton; or, Jealousy, from his novel *Griffith Gaunt* (produced 1867; as *Kate
   Peyton's Lovers*, produced 1873).   1872.
Shilly Shally, from the novel *Ralph the Heir* by Anthony Trollope (produced 1872).
The Wandering Heir, from his own novel (produced 1873).
Joan, from the novel *That Lass o' Lowries* by Frances Hodgson Burnett (produced
   1878).
The Countess and the Dancer, from a play by Sardou (as *Jealousy*, produced 1878;
   revised version, as *The Countess and the Dancer*, produced 1886).   1883.
Drink, from a play by Zola, Busnach, and Gastineau (produced 1879).
Love and Money, with Henry Pettitt (produced 1882).   1883.
Single Heart and Double Face (produced 1882); as *Double Faces* (produced 1883).

Other

It Is Never Too Late to Mend: Proofs of Its Prison Revelations.   1859.
Monopoly Versus Property.   1860.
The Eighth Commandment.   1860.
To the Editor of the Daily Globe, Toronto: A Reply to Criticism.   1871.
The Legal Vocabulary.   1872.
Cremona Violins.   1873.
*A Hero and a Martyr: A True and Accurate Account of the Heroic Feats and Sad
   Calamity of James Lambert.*   1874.
Trade Malice: A Personal Narrative, and The Wandering Heir.   1875.
The Coming Man (letters).   1878.
Dora; or, The History of a Play.   1878.
Readiana: Comments on Current Events.   1882.
Bible Characters.   1888.

Bibliography: *Collins and Reade* by M. L. Parrish, 1940; *Collins and Reade: A Bibliography
of Critical Notices and Studies* by Francesco Cordasco and Kenneth Scott, 1949.

Reading List: *Dickens, Reade, and Collins: Sensation Novelists* by W. C. Phillips, 1919;
Reade: A Biography by Malcolm Elwin, 1931; *The Making of The Cloister and the Hearth* by
Albert Morton Turner, 1938; *Reade: Sa Vie, Ses Romans* by Léone Rives, 1940 (includes
bibliography); *Reade: A Study in Victorian Authorship* by Wayne Burns, 1961; *Reade* by
Elton E. Smith, 1977.

*   *   *

   William Dean Howells placed his finger on the pulse of Charles Reade's claim to greatness
and his singular weakness: "he might have been the master of a great school of English

realism; but ... he remained content to use the materials of realism and produce the effect of romanticism" (*My Literary Passions*, 1895). Nothing could be clearer than his excessive devotion to realism. His playscripts bristled with suggestions for stage business (*Gold*), descriptions of ingenious and realistic settings (*Dora*), and the most explicit stage directions (*The Scuttled Ship*). He thanked the London *Times* for news items that provided the plots for four of his most popular novels: *It Is Never Too Late to Mend*, *Hard Cash*, *Put Yourself in His Place*, and *A Terrible Temptation*. In his study he never got beyond arm's reach of his compendious notebooks, his index files, and the five-foot-tall notecards that leaned against his walls like screens. He frequently contended that true fiction should be as "solid" with fact as non-fiction.

But Reade's absorbed interest in facts was always hostage to essentially old-fashioned, sentimental ideals. Plays and novels both follow the same pattern: evil appears to triumph and good to fail, but do not fear — at the eleventh hour the kaleidoscope will be shaken by a Celestial Hand, and all the pieces will fall into rightful place and correct relationship.

Ironically, it was his taste for melodrama that makes his plays unplayed in an age dominated by that most melodramatic of media — television. In the novel it separated him from his greater contemporaries, Thackeray, Eliot, and Dickens, and linked him with the lesser purveyors of the "sensation novel," Collins, Bulwer-Lytton, and Braddon. Indeed so little did he differentiate between stage and novel that six of his plays were rewritten as novels (*Rachel the Reaper*, *Masks and Faces*, *Gold*, *Foul Play*, *Jealousy*, *Singleheart and Doubleface*), and in his prose fiction the acid test of a passage was to consider how it would play on the stage.

His best and most enduring novel, *The Cloister and the Hearth*, exactly exemplifies the tension between realism and romanticism. The Erasmus *Compendium* of 1524 provided the historical facts; seventy-nine medieval studies filled in the realistic background. The Erasmus autobiographical fragment was full of stirring event and Reade was the great master of eventful narrative. The plot was one long picaresque journey, and Reade liked to send his heroes far from home. The catastrophe was borne by a fraudulent letter, and Reade's novels are full of false letters bearing evil news. The hero of the *Compendium* and *The Cloister and the Hearth* is a semi-historical figure; but is he not equally as much another of that long line of Reade's "Resourceful Heroes"? And the heroine, frank, honest, faithful, is as Victorian as fifteenth-century Dutch. The author who loved fact found the perfect fact, and Reade's masterpiece resulted.

—Elton E. Smith

REEVE, Clara. English. Born in Ipswich, Suffolk, 23 January 1729. Educated at home. Settled with her family in Colchester, Essex, 1755; thereafter a full-time writer. *Died 3 December 1807.*

PUBLICATIONS

Fiction

> *The Champion of Virtue: A Gothic Story.* 1777; as *The Old English Baron*, 1778; edited by James Trainer, 1967.
> *The Two Mentors: A Modern Story.* 1783.
> *The Exiles; or, Memoirs of the Count de Cronstadt.* 1788.

The School for Widows. 1791.
Memoirs of Sir Roger de Clarendon, A Natural Son of Edward the Black Prince. 1793.
Destination; or, Memoirs of a Private Family. 1799.

Verse

Original Poems on Several Occasions. 1769.

Other

The Progress of Romance Through Times, Countries, and Manners. 2 vols., 1785.
Plans for Education, with Remarks on the Systems of Other Writers. 1792.

Translator, *The Phoenix,* by John Barclay. 1772.

*   *   *

The name of Clara Reeve is today associated almost exclusively with two works, one of them a gothic adventure story, the other a literary-historical review presented in dialogue form. The gothic story published under Reeve's name in 1778 as *The Old English Baron* had a year previously appeared anonymously as *The Champion of Virtue,* purporting to be an edition of an ancient manuscript. This device points back to the example of Horace Walpole in the preface to *The Castle of Otranto,* and although the pretence is no longer sustained in the second edition of Clara's novel, the preface openly confesses that "this story is the literary offspring of the Castle of Otranto, written upon the same plan, with a design to unite the most attractive and interesting circumstances of the ancient Romance and modern Novel." What is new is her stated intention to lessen the violent impact of Walpole's supernatural machinery which, she believed, dissolved the book's enchantment. Her pursuit of moderation embraced not only the presentation of the supernatural, but also the emotions and temperaments of the principal characters, whose function is most succinctly outlined in the exhortation that "this awful spectacle be a lesson to all present, that though wickedness may triumph for a season, a day of retribution will come!"

It is in her second major work, *The Progress of Romance,* that she discusses the process of development from romance to novel and presents in the form of a historical review "through times, countries and manners" a clear indication of her own ideals. The criteria include the portrayal of everyday events in familiar language, naturalness of manner, probability, simplicity, and moral improvement. Any analysis of her novels would show her concern with the promotion of social and domestic virtues, as in her second novel, *The Two Mentors,* where innate goodness triumphs over the worst that misguided education and evil advisers can do, up to her final work, *Destination; or, Memoirs of a Private Family,* with its high moral and didactic tone, again in a specifically educational context. As a convinced believer in the power of the written word to influence the mind, particularly of the young and immature, for good or evil, Reeve wrote in the circumspect and demure style to be expected of the modest gentlewoman that she was. (J. K. Reeves cites the use of the phrase "antiquated virgin" as evidence that Reeve was not the authoress at least of part of the novel *Fatherless Fanny* which was attributed to her, since he believed her incapable of coining such a phrase.) The absence of passion, the holding-back of the imagination, the fear of excess which characterise her work leave the reader with a feeling of a benevolent writer almost afraid of herself and of the possibility of giving offence or of weakening the moral fibre of society. Sir Walter Scott's verdict on her, with all that it does not say, still seems very appropriate: "The various novels of Clara Reeve are all marked by excellent good sense, pure morality, and a competent command of those qualities which constitute a good romance."

—James Trainer

REID, Vic(tor Stafford). Jamaican. Born in Jamaica, 1 May 1913. Educated in Jamaica. Married; four children. Reporter, editor, and foreign correspondent for various newspapers; worked in advertising; currently, managing director and chairman of a printing and publishing company in Kingston, Jamaica; has travelled extensively in the Americas, Africa, Europe, and the Middle East. Recipient: Guggenheim Fellowship, 1959; Canada Council Fellowship; Mexican Writers Fellowship. Lives in Kingston, Jamaica.

PUBLICATIONS

Fiction

New Day. 1949.
The Leopard. 1958.
Mount Ephraim. 1972.
The Sun and Juan de Bolas. 1974.

Other

Sixty-Five (juvenile). 1960.
The Young Warriors (juvenile). 1967.
Buildings in Jamaica. 1970.

*   *   *

Vic Reid's novel *New Day* is a landmark in Caribbean literature. As Gerald Moore remarked in *The Chosen Tongue*, "discovery in the cultural sense comes with a realization that one is neither a rootless being devoid of identity, nor a lost son of Africa or Asia, but a man made by this island now." For the people of Jamaica this discovery was made when Vic Reid's novel *New Day* was published in 1949.

The novel spans a period of eighty years, from the time of the Morant Bay Rebellion in 1865 when the constitution was abolished till 1944 when constitution rule was once more returned to the people, and there was a promise at least of a "new day." The narrator is the eighty-seven-year-old Johnny Campbell. On the eve of independence he looks back to the past, and it is through his reminiscences that we trace the history of Jamaica and its people. Through Johnny Campbell, Reid has given us an artist's interpretation of eighty years of Jamaican history and of the people and forces that have shaped this history.

The final section of the novel has come in for some criticism. Sylvia Wynter (in *Savacou 5*, 1971) writes:

> Garth is made to bear the weight of an expectation that can never be realized. Whilst the first part of the book parallels and patterns the structure of its society, and reflects its failure to satisfy human needs, the third part fails by ignoring the fact that a change in the superstructure of the plantation, a new Constitution, even Independence, were changes which left the basic system untouched; and which only prolonged the inevitable and inbuilt confrontation.

Reid ignores this situation. Unlike George Beckford in *Persistent Poverty* or George Lamming in his novel *Natives of My Person*, he fails to point out that what in fact has happened in Caribbean society is that the old masters and colonizers have been replaced by new ones. But as Mervyn Morris said, "That there was more to see ... does not invalidate the book."

The whole work is in dialect. By making the language of the people an acceptable literary medium, Reid paved the way for other writers such as Samuel Selvon.

Mention should also be made of Reid's novel *The Leopard*. The setting this time is Kenya; the book was written to counterbalance the flood of anti-Kikuyu literature that followed the Mau-Mau uprising. The narrator is Nebu, the African; the conflict between him and Gibson, the white settler, the leopard, the destroyer of harmony in the natural world, is symbolic of the black-white conflict in Africa. Interest centres eventually on Toto, the half-caste child of Nebu and Mrs. Gibson, who is alienated from both his European and Kikuyu ancestry. It is Toto's alienation that in Kenneth Ramchand's opinion makes "*The Leopard* in its finest aspect a parable on the relationship between alienated West Indian and embarrassing African ancestry" (*The West Indian Novel and Its Background*, 1970).

While *The Leopard* has been acclaimed by a number of critics it is almost certain that Vic Reid's reputation will rest on his novel *New Day*.

—Anna Rutherford

RENAULT, Mary. Pseudonym for Mary Challans. English. Born in London, 4 September 1905. Educated at Clifton High School, Bristol; St. Hugh's College, Oxford, M.A.; Radcliffe Infirmary, Oxford, S.R.N. 1936. Writer from 1939; worked as a nurse during World War II; emigrated to South Africa, 1948. National President, P.E.N. Club of South Africa, 1961. Recipient: National Association of Independent Schools Award, U.S.A., 1963; Silver Pen Award, 1971. Fellow, Royal Society of Literature, 1959. Lives in Cape Town.

PUBLICATIONS

Fiction

Purposes of Love.   1939; as *Promise of Love*, 1940.
Kind Are His Answers.   1940.
The Friendly Young Ladies.   1944; as *Middle Mist*, 1945.
Return to Night.   1947.
North Face.   1948.
The Charioteer.   1953.
The Last of the Wine.   1956.
The King Must Die.   1958.
The Bull from the Sea.   1962.
The Mask of Apollo.   1966.
Fire from Heaven.   1970.
The Persian Boy.   1972.
The Praise Singer.   1978.

Other

The Lion in the Gateway: Heroic Battles of the Greeks and Persians at Marathon, Salamis, and Thermopylae (juvenile).   1964.
The Nature of Alexander.   1975.

Reading List: *Renault* by Peter Wolfe, 1969; *The Hellenism of Renault* by Bernard F. Dick, 1972.

※   *   *

Mary Renault is famous for her novels with a Greek setting, beginning with *The Last of the Wine*, although she had previously written six books with a contemporary setting. All of the early novels have a slightly sentimental air except *The Charioteer*, a tough and poignant account of homosexual love in the Second World War. Homosexuality is a theme to which she reverts in the Greek novels, but her handling of it in a contemporary setting at a time when the subject was hardly discussed is both delicate and courageous. Of the Greek novels those dealing with Classical Greece, *The Last of the Wine* and *The Mask of Apollo*, are the least successful. Though Renault follows her classical sources faithfully she somehow fails to capture the atmosphere of Greece at its greatest. She is more successful in *The King Must Die* and *The Bull from the Sea*, perhaps because there are no literary sources to follow from the Minoan period and she has more scope to use her imagination. *Fire from Heaven* and *The Persian Boy* takes us to the world of Alexander the Great, where no Greek historical source can penetrate the romance and mystery surrounding Alexander's character; here Renault makes a brave attempt. It would seem that a historical novel is more successful as a novel when the history is more difficult.

—T. J. Winnifrith

RHYS, Jean (née Williams).   English.   Born in Dominica, West Indies, 24 August 1894; emigrated to England, 1910. Educated at The Convent, Rouseau, Dominica, and at the Royal Academy of Dramatic Art, London. Married three times; lastly to Max Hamer in 1947. Writer from 1919; lived in Paris between the wars, then returned to England; now lives in Devon. Recipient: Arts Council Bursary, 1967; Smith Literary Award, 1967; Heinemann Award, 1967. Fellow, Royal Society of Literature, 1966. C.B.E. (Commander, Order of the British Empire), 1978.

PUBLICATIONS

Fiction

The Left Bank and Other Stories.   1927.
Postures.   1928; as *Quartet*, 1929.
After Leaving Mr. Mackenzie.   1931.
Voyage in the Dark.   1934.
Good Morning, Midnight.   1939.
Wide Sargasso Sea.   1966.
Tigers Are Better-Looking, with a Selection from The Left Bank (stories).   1968.
Sleep It Off Lady (stories).   1976.

Reading List: "The Wide Sargasso Sea: A West Indian Reflection" by John Hearne, in *Cornhill,* Summer 1974; *Rhys* by Louis James, 1979.

*   *   *

Jean Rhys (a name adopted at the instigation of Ford Madox Ford) was born, and brought up until the age of sixteen, on the West Indian island of Dominica. Her father was a Welsh doctor called Williams, while her mother was a white creole, that is, of a family settled for several generations in the island. Dominica was British, and English was the language of her home and education, yet the popular language, and one she used with servants, was the French dialect of the island. Later, in Europe, she was to live and write about Paris quite as much as about London. The friction of the two languages is felt throughout her work.

At the age of sixteen she was sent to boarding school in England, hated it, and transferred to the Royal Academy of Dramatic Art, but her training there was stopped by her father's death after only a term, and it was only many years later, and then briefly, that she revisited Dominica. *Voyage in the Dark,* though not her first published book, is based on the first notebooks which she kept, she herself suggests, with a therapeutic or compensatory purpose: "I didn't want to write. I wanted to be happy. But you don't have much choice" (*Planet 33*). Anna Morgan, the heroine, is clearly very close to Jean Rhys's early experience. She has a West Indian background, becomes a chorus girl, is befriended, seduced, and abandoned by a middle-aged admirer, and floats off into a nightmare world of lonely hotels and rented rooms. Economically exploited, sexually exploited, yet with an element of self-destructiveness and inner violence, Anna is the prototype of the Jean Rhys heroine-victim who is nowhere more thoroughly and frighteningly portrayed than in the last of the pre-war novels, *Good Morning, Midnight.*

But one should not be misled by the autobiographical material and the helplessless of the heroines. Jean Rhys is not helpless, because she exerts a complete and precise control through her style. Short sentences, simple clauses pared of adjectives, remind one of Hemingway, while laconic understatement and a feeling for the absurd keep sentiment and self-pity at bay – but not all emotion. Indeed, one of the most remarkable things in her work is her ability, while identifying with the victim, to cross the barriers briefly and make us feel pity for the victimisers, armoured by power and property and at the same time emotionally stunted by them.

Since their re-issue in the 1960's her books have received some attention from women's movements, and rightly so, for Jean Rhys not only chronicles the exploitation of women, but seems conscious of them *as a group* in society, of their economic position and of the roles imposed on them by a male society. We see the problems of identity that arise when a woman tries to assert herself as a person against the mask of clothes, make-up, and the face put on to meet society. There are also several moving occasions when, breaking through all this, one woman shows real solidarity with another and succours her.

Yet Jean Rhys is not a reformist, though glad of reforms. She finds too much of what she calls "Fabianism" in an author such as Margaret Drabble, and thinks that some of her own earlier work may have erred in this direction. Her own position is much more akin to Conrad's (whose work she knew well through Ford): she finds the world tragic, though sometimes absurdly so, but this can be no exoneration of those who inflict suffering.

In each of Jean Rhys's novels up to 1939 there had been some reference to the West Indies, however passing – the story of a mulatto woman in London related by a minor character, or a French West Indian song, "Maladie d'Amour," played on a gramophone – and this seemed adequately explained as the bringing of a certain amount of Caribbean background into novels whose main themes were European and urban. Her next novel, *Wide Sargasso Sea,* did not appear until 1966. It not only has a West Indian setting, but makes the exploration of the heroine-victim inseparable from that setting, and leads one to a new estimate of the earlier works. The impulse to write the book arose from a reading of *Jane Eyre,* a phenomenon paralleled by the Nigerian Achebe's writing of *Things Fall Apart* as a kind of answer to Joyce

Cary's *Mister Johnson*. It is an impulse to tell the story from the other side. *Wide Sargasso Sea* is told largely from the point of view of the young Creole heiress who eventually becomes the mad first Mrs. Rochester of *Jane Eyre*. We see her impoverished childhood in the post-emancipation West Indies, the double rejection by negro and rich white society; then her inheritance, her marriage to Rochester, and the increasing sense of bewilderment, distress, and unreality which leads to the fire at Thornfield Hall. A close reading of the texts suggests that *Jane Eyre* was more than the occasion for *Wide Sargasso Sea*, which, while it is an alternative account, also echoes the Victorian novel in several details.

Wide Sargasso Sea is one of the major works of West Indian literature. Though some West Indian critics dismiss it as irrelevant to the islands' present concerns, others, such as John Hearne, have recognized in it a deep exploration of the psychological dimension of race and violence and slavery which have been so much a part of Caribbean experience. While Jean Rhys is still, in this book, master of the lucid and epigrammatic phrase, she now allows herself a richer and more adjectival prose, a more romantic treatment of experience, one might say. *Wide Sargasso Sea* yields to none of her other books in its depiction of pain, but there is a much stronger surge of trancendent, even triumphant feeling. The heroine dies in flames, but we remember the tree in the West Indies which bears flowers of flame: "If you are buried under the flamboyant tree ... your soul is lifted up when it flowers." And Grace Poole who looks after her at Thornfield says: "I'll say one thing, she hasn't lost her spirit."

Looking back at the other books, we understand that the West Indies are after all deeply present in the imagery and symbolic scenes. Domesticated English nature is judged by the intenser colours of the West Indies, as are the underdeveloped hearts of the European bourgeoisie by the islands' more intense and violent passions. A flame-tulip, a red hat or dress, recall, consciously or unconsciously, the bright flowers and sunsets of the islands, and often appear at moments when the heroines need something to hold on to. The Jean Rhys heroine can be destroyed but not broken. She can even say: "When we live, let us live; when we give, let us give."

—Ned Thomas

RICH, Barnaby.   English.   Born in Essex in 1542. Married in 1586. Soldier for all of his life: enlisted in the Army as a boy, c. 1555; served in Queen Mary's war with France, 1557–58, in the Le Havre siege, 1562, in Ireland, 1570–72, in The Netherlands, 1576, and in Ireland again, 1577–92: rose to the rank of Captain; impoverished during the 1590's; trained soldiers in London, 1600–06; helped put down the Essex rebellion, 1601; returned to Ireland c. 1608; granted pension by King James, 1616. *Died 10 November 1617.*

PUBLICATIONS

Fiction

> *A Right Excellent and Pleasant Dialogue Between Mercury and an English Soldier*.   1574.
> *Rich His Farewell to Military Profession*.   1581; revised edition, 1594, 1606; *Apolonius and Silla* edited by Morton Luce, 1907.
> *The Strange and Wonderful Adventures of Don Simonides*.   1581; second part, 1584.
> *The Adventures of Brusanus, Prince of Hungaria*.   1592.

Other

Alarm to England, Foreshowing What Perils Are Procured Where the People Live Without Regard of Martial Law. 1578.

The True Report of a Late Practice Enterprised by a Papist with a Young Maiden in Wales. 1582.

A Pathway to Military Practice. 1587.

Greene's News Both from Heaven and Hell. 1593; edited by R. B. McKerrow, 1922.

A Soldier's Wish to Britain's Welfare. 1604; as *The Fruits of Long Experience,* 1604.

Faults, Faults, and Nothing Else But Faults. 1606; *Room for a Gentleman; or, The Second Part of Faults, Collected for the True Meridian of Dublin,* 1609.

A Short Survey of Ireland Truly Discovering Who Hath Armed the Hearts of the People with Disobedience. 1609.

A New Description of Ireland, Wherein Is Described the Disposition of the Irish Whereunto They Are Inclined. 1610; as *A New Irish Prognostication,* 1624.

A True and Kind Excuse Written in Defence of That Book Entitled A New Description of Ireland. 1612.

A Catholic Conference Between Sir Tady MacMareall a Popish Priest and Patrick Plaine a Student. 1612.

The Excellency of Good Women. 1613.

Opinion Deified, Discovering the Engines, Traps, and Trains That Are Set to Catch Opinion. 1613.

The Honesty of This Age. 1614; edited by P. Cunningham, 1844.

My Lady's Looking Glass, Wherein May Be Discerned a Wise Man from a Fool, a Good Woman from a Bad. 1616.

The Irish Hubbub; or, The English Hue and Cry. 1617; revised edition, 1617.

Translator, *The Famous History of Herodotus.* 1584.

Reading List: *Rich: A Short Biography* by Thomas M. Cranfill and D. H. Bruce, 1953.

*   *   *

Barnaby Rich was a soldier, a government agent, a privateer (briefly), and an author with a passionate social conscience. His first two books sprang from his experience as a soldier, his wide reading, and the strongly anti-Catholic feeling which was to colour much of his writing; essentially they are arguments for national readiness for war with Spain. (He later wrote three more military tracts, one of them, *A Pathway to Military Practice,* containing invaluable descriptions of the different duties of army officers of the period.) Bored in dull Ireland, he turned to story-telling and wrote his most popular work, *Farewell to Military Profession;* three more romances followed, the tediously euphuistic *Don Simonides,* well-accepted enough to permit a second volume, and *Brusanus,* which in part allegorizes with dark humour the author's failure to gain court patronage. The *Farewell,* which had four editions during Rich's lifetime, contains eight tales which draw upon the Italians Cinthio and Strapola and the English writer/translators Golding, Painter, and Pettie. At least nine plays of the period have been shown to be indebted to the *Farewell,* most importantly Shakespeare's *Twelfth Night.* The stories differ in character, but all have realistic detail, a robust joviality, and dialogue which is usually free from the heavily ornamented style of many of Rich's contemporaries. His lightness and humour are at their best in the tales of "Two Brethren" and "Phylotus and Emelia."

Disappointment, poverty, and frustration after 1592 probably led to the aggressively bitter tone of much of his other work. *Faults, Faults* was modishly anti-feminist, *Opinion Deified* and the ironically named *Honesty of This Age* more general in their attack. To those books critical of the government and way of life of the Irish published in his lifetime can be added the confidential reports on the country which he sent to Cecil, Sir Julius Caesar, and King James. Although known best for his fiction, Rich is a valuable source of information and ideas concerning Ireland, military practice, and the society of his day. His vigorous style and lively wit ensure his place in the forefront of the minor Elizabethan prose writers.

—Alan Brissenden

RICHARDSON, Dorothy (Miller). English. Born in Abingdon, Berkshire, 17 May 1873. Educated in local day schools. Married the artist Alan Odle. Worked as a teacher and as a clerk; writer from 1913; settled in Cornwall. *Died 17 June 1957.*

PUBLICATIONS

Fiction

> *Pointed Roofs.* 1915; *Backwater,* 1916; *Honeycomb,* 1917; *The Tunnel,* 1919; *Interim,* 1919; *Deadlock,* 1921; *Revolving Lights,* 1923; *The Trap,* 1925; *Oberland,* 1927; *Dawn's Left Hand,* 1931; *Clear Horizon,* 1935; complete version, as *Pilgrimage* (includes *Dimple Hill*), 4 vols., 1938; augmented edition, including *March Moonlight,* 1967.

Other

> *The Quakers Past and Present.* 1914.
> *Gleanings from the Works of George Fox.* 1914.
> *Jane Austen and the Inseparables.* 1930.

> Translator, *Some Popular Foodstuffs Exposed,* by Paul Carton. 1913.
> Translator, *Man's Best Food: An Enquiry into the Case for a Non-Flesh Diet,* by Gustav Krüger. 1914.
> Translator, *The Du Barry,* by Karl von Schumacher. 1932.
> Translator, *Mammon,* by Robert Neumann. 1933.
> Translator, *Jews in Germany,* by Josef Kastein. 1934.
> Translator, *André Gide: His Life and His Work,* by Léon Pierre-Quint. 1934.
> Translator, *Silent Hours,* by R. de Traz. 1934.

Bibliography: by G. Glikin, in *English Literature in Transition,* 1965.

Reading List: *Richardson* by John Cowper Powys, 1931; *Richardson* by Caesar R. Blake, 1960; *Richardson: An Adventure in Self-Discovery* by Horace Gregory, 1967; *Richardson* by John Rosenberg, 1973; *Richardson* by Thomas F. Staley, 1976; *Richardson: A Biography* by Gloria G. Fromm, 1977.

*   *   *

Born in 1873, Dorothy M. Richardson was the oldest by almost ten years of those novelists, the others being Joyce, Lawrence, and Virginia Woolf, who in the first three decades of the century, working quite independently and with different ends in mind, reshaped the English novel. Her first novel, *Pointed Roofs*, appeared in 1915, her twelfth, *Dimple Hill*, in 1938. Together, with a kind of coda called *March Moonlight* not published until 1967, they compose what is in effect one novel called *Pilgrimage*, a *roman fleuve* in the truest sense of the word.

In *March Moonlight* Dorothy Richardson calls "current existence, the ultimate astonisher," and current existence, the current existence of her heroine Miriam Henderson, is the one theme of her sequence of novels. In a famous essay, "The Modern Novel," Virginia Woolf dreamed of a novel totally released from convention, in which there would be "no plot, no comedy, no tragedy, no love interest or catastrophe in the accepted sense, and perhaps not a single button sewn on as the Bond Street tailors would have it." *Pilgrimage* is that novel precisely. The day-to-day existence of Miriam is everything, and it was with reference to the manner of its rendering that the phrase "stream of consciousness" was first used in literary criticism, by the novelist May Sinclair, reviewing one of the volumes of the novel in 1918 and finding the key to Dorothy Richardson's method in a passage in William James's *Principles of Psychology*, published in 1890: "Consciousness does not appear to itself chopped up in bits.... It is nothing jointed; it flows.... Let us call it the stream of thought, of consciousness, or of subjective life."

Pilgrimage is a remarkable achievement. Its weakness lies in the fact that the method is everything. The first volumes, recording Miriam's life as a governess in a school in Germany, still excite, for the novelty of her experience and the flux of a very intelligent girl's responses to the world outside her are enchantingly caught. But when Miriam returns to England and the light of common day falls on the scene, boredom increasingly sets in, and there remains only the interest provided by a documentary account of the advanced political and artistic life in London in the first decade of the century and by glimpses of famous figures of the time, such as H. G. Wells, the Hypo Wilson of the novel.

And there is something else the consequences of which, given the technique, the modern reader with the best will in the world cannot escape. Just as William James's was a pre-Freudian psychology so is Miriam's psychology. Whole areas of a woman's experience are ignored, and the evasion is the more emphasised, it seems, because of the stream-of-consciousness technique. With the publication of *Ulysses*, it was inescapable that *Pilgrimage* should look old-fashioned, and it was inevitable that as an influence on later fiction Dorothy Richardson should be displaced by James Joyce.

—Walter Allen

RICHARDSON, Henry Handel. Pseudonym for Ethel Florence Lindesay Richardson Robertson. Australian. Born in Melbourne, Victoria, 3 January 1870. Educated at the Presbyterian Ladies' College, Melbourne; studied music at the Leipzig Conservatorium, 1887–90. Married John G. Robertson in 1895 (died, 1933). Lived in Strasbourg, 1895–1903, in London, 1903, and in Sussex from 1933; writer from 1908. Recipient: Australian Literature Society Gold Medal, 1929. *Died 20 March 1946.*

PUBLICATIONS

Fiction

> *Maurice Guest.* 1908.
> *The Getting of Wisdom.* 1910.
> *Australia Felix.* 1917; *The Way Home,* 1925; *Ultima Thule,* 1929; complete version,
>   as *The Fortunes of Richard Mahony,* 1930.
> *The End of a Childhood and Other Stories.* 1934.
> *The Young Cosima.* 1939.

Other

> *Two Studies.* 1931.
> *Myself When Young.* 1948.
> *Letters to Nettie Palmer,* edited by Karl-Johan Rossing. 1953.

> Translator, *Siren Voices,* by J. P. Jacobsen. 1896.
> Translator, *The Fisher Lass,* by B. Bjørnson. 1896.

Bibliography: "Richardson: An Annotated Bibliography of Writings about Her" by Verna D. Wittock, in *English Literature in Transition 6,* 1964.

Reading List: *Richardson: A Study* by Nettie Palmer, 1950; *Richardson and Some of Her Sources,* 1954, *A Companion to Australia Felix,* 1962, and *Richardson,* 1966, all by Leonie Kramer; *Richardson* by Vincent Buckley, 1961; *Ulysses Bound: Richardson and Her Fiction* by Dorothy Green, 1973 (includes bibliography).

*   *   *

Henry Handel Richardson's novels and short stories are at once intensely personal and part of a powerful literary tradition. As an expatriate in late 19th-century Germany, she found herself for the first time psychologically and intellectually at home in a milieu in which the polarities of existence, permanence and change, and the attempt to reconcile or transcend them were the dominant concerns of thinkers and artists. Her heroes (and heroines) are always "in flight"; even an old woman on her death-bed in the story "Mary Christina" wants to get up and go away, "far away." Richardson's true place, therefore, is within the German Romantic tradition that took its rise in Goethe, and no estimate of her achievement can afford to ignore the influence on her work of her husband, John George Robertson, for whom Goethe was the supreme artist. Robertson, one of the most distinguished German and Scandinavian scholars of his day, was for thirty years Professor of Germanic and Scandinavian Languages at London University, inaugurating the first systematic study of these subjects in Britain. It is not surprising that these are the influences felt most in Richardson's work, not those of the Russians or the French as is sometimes claimed.

Richardson's early childhood was tragic and her girlhood unhappy; her novels are the result of bringing to bear on these painful memories her later experience as a music-student in Leipzig and what she absorbed at the side of her husband. It was Robertson who first documented, as a philologist, the transition from the concept of art as mimesis to the assertion of the primacy of the imagination in artistic creation. Traces of Robertson's account of the relationship between truth and fiction and of the function of the imagination can be clearly discerned in Richardson's work, from *Maurice Guest* and *The Getting of Wisdom* to the late short stories. These new ideas shed light on her past and on her country's past, and enabled her to make symbolic use of both. Australia, and especially the Australia of the gold-rush period, was the perfect image of flux and instability, while the search for gold was itself an ancient symbol of the longing for wholeness, for permanence, which her divided nature craved. *The Fortunes of Richard Mahony* is only marginally a realistic period novel about an emigrant doctor; it is much more a novel about a state of mind and a metaphysic; its deceptively commonplace domestic mould, the skilled psychological presentation of the conflict of wills and purposes between husband and wife, have blinded many critics to its complexity.

Richardson had been writing for thirty years before the publication of the final volume of the trilogy, *Ultima Thule*, brought her sudden fame. The two previous volumes, *Australia Felix* and *The Way Home*, about Mahony's early struggles, his rise to unexpected riches, and his sudden loss of fortune, appeared too far apart in time to make the impact they deserved, and it is true their significance is not wholly clear without the third volume, which is much more self-contained.

Selected details from her father's life provided the scaffolding for the novel, but the temperament with which she endowed Mahony is much more her own than her father's. The fusing of fact and fiction results in a work of art which is a great parable of the deepest longings of the human spirit, embodied in Mahony and his wife Mary, by means of a narrative method which can be justly called dialectic. Richardson is a master of telling and climactic scenes, and the one in which Mahony finally goes out of his mind, as he burns his deeds, his scrip, his insurance policies – everything to do with money – is one of the most memorable images of the contradictions of rising capitalism in modern literature. At the same time, the relentless unfolding of the novel, its sombre tones, place it, if not on the same level, at least in the same category, as Sophoclean tragedy. The great Oedipean theme is inescapable Destiny; that of *Richard Mahony* is the limitless unpredictability of the genotype, the stubborn core of irrationality at the heart of things that all flesh must accept.

The same theme sounds in the first novel, *Maurice Guest*, though it is not yet a major one. Richardson was more concerned, when she began to write, about her two painful and impossible love-experiences, and the book is an exploration of the nature of love. On a surface level, it draws on her life as a music-student, and on her considerable professional competence as pianist and composer, for its realistic and figurative content. The book was as innovative as *Richard Mahony* was to be, though Richardson has never been given due credit for originality. *Maurice Guest* is one of the earliest full-length portraits of the "outsider" figure in English, and the first to treat homosexuality openly, though the term is not used; the first to treat Freudian ideas critically, the first to present Nietzschean ideas ironically – so subtly indeed that she was accused later of being a Nietzschean. The novel anatomizes a number of human relationships that normally come under the heading "love" and exposes them for what they are: different forms of narcissism. Real love, in which the one seeks the happiness of the other, is defined by its absence, though Richardson has something positive to say on behalf of the obsessive personality in her summing-up. The heroine of the book is modelled externally on Eleonora Duse, and her violinist lover, Schilsky, is an ironic portrait of the young Richard Strauss; the central character, Maurice, and the heroine are a composite, psychologically, of Richardson herself, but so detached and objective is her style that there is no way of knowing this without biographical assistance. The novel was deeply influenced by Jacobsen's *Niels Lyhne*, and, more superficially, by D'Annunzio's *Il Fuoco*, but, when all debts are acknowledged, *Maurice Guest* is unmistakably Richardson's own creation, felt upon her pulses. The book was one of the best pillaged works of its day, admired and imitated by fellow-novelists, and then ignored, its pioneering of the "outsider" theme unrecognised. *The Getting of Wisdom*, written concurrently with *Maurice Guest*, but published two years later, handles the same theme more lightly in the setting of a Melbourne girls' school. Its relationship with *Richard Mahony* is direct: the wisdom Laura learns so painfully is that which Mahony attempts to convey to his wife in *The Way Home*: "*Panta rei* is the eternal truth; *semper idem* the lie we long to see confirmed."

The short stories, *The End of a Childhood*, are conceived with great insight and beautifully shaped. With one or two exceptions, they arc sombre in tone, especially when dealing with sexual deviance or themes of alienation. The best of them is perhaps "Mary Christina," an early story originally entitled "Death." It is a powerful evocation of the physical sensations of dying and the nearest Richardson came to nihilism. (Her usual attitude to the "great mystery" she shared with Spiritualists like Sir Oliver Lodge; she was a member of the Society for Psychical Research for many years, but her temper was sceptical rather than dogmatic.)

Her prose is remarkable for its rhythms and its elegiac tone rather than for its diction and she is not to be judged according to the canons of lyric poetry but by the strengths proper to a novelist: characterisation and organisation. Through all the changes of literary fashion since the 1920's, Richardson has remained the most permanently satisfying of Australian novelists.

—Dorothy Green

RICHARDSON, Samuel. English. Born in Derbyshire in 1689. Little is known about his education: may have attended Christ's Hospital or Merchant Taylors' School. Married 1) Martha Wilde (died, 1731), five sons and one daughter; 2) Elizabeth Leake, one son and five daughters. Apprenticed to the stationer John Wilde, in London, 1706; thereafter worked for several years as a compositor and corrector in a London printing office; proprietor of his own printing firm in Fleet Street, afterwards in Salisbury Court, 1719 until the end of his life; became printer of the *Journals* of the House of Commons (26 volumes), of the *Daily Journal*, 1736–37, and the *Daily Gazetteer*, 1738; Master of the Stationers' Company, 1754; built new printing offices in Salisbury Court, 1755; bought half the patent of "law printer to his majesty," 1760. *Died 4 July 1761.*

PUBLICATIONS

Collections

The Novels. 18 vols., 1929–31.

Fiction

Pamela; or, Virtue Rewarded. 1740; second part, 1741; edited by M. Kinkead-Weekes, 1962.
Clarissa; or, The History of a Young Lady. 7 vols., 1747–48; augmented edition, 1749; edited by John Butt, 1962.
The History of Sir Charles Grandison. 7 vols., 1753–54; edited by Jocelyn Harris, 1972.

Other

The Apprentice's Vade Mecum. 1733; edited by Alan D. McKillop, 1975.
A Seasonable Examination of the Pleas and Pretensions of the Proprietors of, and Subscribers to, Play-Houses, Erected in Defiance of the Royal Licence. 1735.

Aesop's Fables. 1739.

Letters Written to and for Particular Friends, Directing the Requisite Style and Forms to Be Observed in Writing Familiar Letters. 1741; edited by B. W. Downs, as *Familiar Letters on Important Occasions,* 1928.

The Correspondence of Richardson, edited by Anna Laetitia Barbauld. 6 vols., 1806.

Selected Letters, edited by John Carroll. 1964.

The Richardson–Stinstra Correspondence, and Stinstra's Prefaces to Clarissa, edited by William C. Slattery. 1969.

Editor, with others, *The Negotiations of Sir Thomas Roe, in His Embassy to the Ottoman Porte.* 1740.

Editor, *A Tour Through the Whole Island of Great Britain,* by Daniel Defoe. 4 vols., 1742.

Bibliography: *Richardson: A Bibliographical Record of His Literary Career with Historical Notes* by W. M. Sale, 1936; *Richardson: A List of Critical Studies 1896–1946* by Francesco Cordasco, 1948.

Reading List: *Richardson, Printer and Novelist,* 1936, and *Early Masters of English Fiction,* 1956, both by Alan D. McKillop; *Richardson* by R. Brissenden, 1958; *Richardson* by A. Kearney, 1968; *Richardson: A Biography* by T. C. Duncan Eaves and Ben D. Kimpel, 1971; *Richardson and the Eighteenth-Century Puritan Character* by Cynthia Griffin Wolff, 1972; *Richardson: Dramatic Novelist* by M. Kinkead-Weekes, 1973; *A Natural Passion: A Study of the Novels by Richardson* by Margaret A. Doody, 1974.

*   *   *

Samuel Richardson is generally regarded as one of the founders of the English novel, and *Pamela* is one of the first authentically novelistic narratives in English. The reasons for this primacy are partly technical, as Richardson developed a method for rendering the psychological reality of his central character which has no equal in previous fiction. *Pamela* is an epistolary novel, a collection of letters which Richardson claims to be editing written to her parents by a young servant girl. Using letters to tell a story was not in itself a new strategy in 1740, but Richardson's originality lies in the detailed intensity with which Pamela's letters dramatize her situation and personality. Those letters are a young girl's record of a sexual ordeal, as she tells her parents the long story of her master's attempts first to seduce and then to rape her. The trials of persecuted female virtue were a popular theme in the early 18th century, the subject of numerous plays and novels which provided for their audience a mixture of moral pathos and erotic sensation. Like those works, *Pamela* presents isolated and improbably pure female innocence versus powerful and ruthless male lust. Richardson, however, transcends those sexual stereotypes by the simple but inspired device whereby Pamela tells her own story as it happens and in that process of immediate transcription reveals a personality which is far more complex than those of the paragons of popular literature. Indeed, some readers (including some of Richardson's 18th-century critics) have accused Pamela of hypocrisy and selfish calculation, of faking her innocence and holding out for marriage. Such criticism confirms Richardson's achievement, for Pamela is a complex and potentially contradictory character, self-consciously pure and innocent and at the same time strong and self-possessed, terrified of sex and yet clearly attracted to her master, humble and submissive to her social superiors and yet morally proud and socially ambitious. Those contradictions and the interesting personality they define are what Richardson managed brilliantly to convey in *Pamela,* although he might not have recognized this description of his book.

In all his novels, Richardson's intentions were strongly didactic and religious. *Pamela* grew out of a project undertaken at the request of several booksellers to compile a collection of model letters which uneducated persons could use on specific occasions. One of those imagined occasions required a letter written by her parents to a young female servant whose master had tried to seduce her. Richardson's imagination was fired by that hint, and he wrote *Pamela* in several months of intense activity. That intensity is apparent in the novel, and the remarkable complexity of its main character seems to be the result of Richardson's strong identification with her. Pamela describes events, situations, and emotions in careful detail as they happen to her; her letters sometimes turn into a spontaneous journal and she writes "instantaneous description," as Richardson later described his technique for making his characters come alive. Readers experience the world from Pamela's excited participation in it, and the effect is of immediacy and suspenseful, dramatic urgency. Richardson renders Pamela as a terrified teen-ager, menaced by her master's sexual violence, bewildered by her own ambivalence, and cut off from any effective legal redress against her persecutors. But Richardson also presents her as a moral heroine, trusting in God and praying for the spiritual strength to resist her own inclinations and to reform her master. Pamela triumphs in the end, as her Mr. B. becomes an adoring spouse and to the disgust of many modern readers "virtue" is rewarded, as the book's subtitle promises. The last pages of *Pamela* are thick with didacticism and moral sentiments, but Richardson is a pioneer of the realistic novel precisely because he shows us how religious belief and moral will interact with psychological and social factors which threaten to overwhelm them.

Pamela was a great success, so much so that several spurious continuations were published, and Richardson felt compelled to write his own sequel in which the now-married Pamela deals with her husband's infatuation with another woman. This second part of *Pamela* is virtually unreadable but marks in some ways an important step in Richardson's development as a self-consciously skillful novelist. The crude moral melodrama of the original story gives way to more complicated questions of manners, and this volume has a more varied cast of correspondents, each of whom writes letters according to character. This increased complexity of social situation and variety of character looks forward to Richardson's second and greatest work, *Clarissa; or, The History of a Young Lady*.

Clarissa is an immense work, the longest novel in the language, and yet its plot is simple enough in outline. Clarissa Harlowe is the beautiful and saintly daughter of an enormously wealthy but untitled family who press her to marry a man she despises, Roger Solmes. His rival is a young aristocratic rake, Robert Lovelace, who has entered the family circle as the suitor of Clarissa's sister, Arabella. Attracted by Clarissa's beauty and intrigued by her virtue, Lovelace declines to pursue his suit for Arabella and is challenged to a duel on this account by the brother in the family, James. After wounding James, Lovelace begins to court Clarissa, to the consternation and implacable opposition of the family. Lovelace corresponds secretly with Clarissa and tricks her into running away with him. Most of this occurs at the very beginning of the novel, and most of the letters revolve around Lovelace's attempts to seduce Clarissa. Eventually, he drugs and rapes her in the brothel where she is his prisoner; but Clarissa escapes soon after and dies with slow dignity in the course of several hundred pages, resisting Lovelace's offers of marriage and surrounded by tearful and worshipping admirers who marvel at her serene goodness. The book ends with Lovelace's death in a duel with her cousin, Colonel Morden.

As in *Pamela*, this melodramatic story is told in letters which describe events that have just happened, and again Richardson's special achievement is a dramatization of complicated personal and social relationships that leaves simple melodrama far behind. In place of the single viewpoint of *Pamela*'s letters, *Clarissa* is told by various characters, each of whom has a distinctive style as a writer and a special perspective on the action. The hundreds of letters which make up the novel are a constantly varied and shifting set of voices, and the scenes the letters describe are sharply observed and run from a witty comedy of manners to pathos and tragedy of the highest kind. Richardson's immersion in each of his large cast of characters is masterful, and in the case of Clarissa and Lovelace leads to a richness and complexity without parallel in previous fiction.

Clarissa is as good as she is beautiful, and yet her resistance to her family's demands and to Lovelace's seductions is carried out with a diplomatic skill and persuasive power that justify in one sense their claims that she is self-willed and bent upon her own pleasure. Indeed, for modern readers perhaps the book's most compelling feature is the buried sexuality implicit in Clarissa's strong aversion to Solmes and her cautious attraction to Lovelace. To read her letters is to experience a profoundly troubled personality struggling to resolve a tangle of conflicting emotions and allegiances. Lovelace possesses an equally complex personality, overtly self-obsessed and flamboyant in asserting its needs for sex and power. Richardson's art lets us see that Lovelace plays his role of aristocratic libertine insecurely and self-consciously. He is attracted and enraged by Clarissa's virtuous resistance and driven to revealing extremes of love and hatred. In fact, the greatness of *Clarissa* can be measured by its powerfully exact revelation of the divided personalities of its two main characters. The protracted struggle between them is a contest not simply of wills but an extravaganza of competing literary styles and modes of self-understanding and presentation. Richardson's revolutionary perfection of the epistolary novel enabled him to depict a world where the subjective forces of individual will and consciousness can be observed trying to shape and even to master objective social and historical forces which resist such manipulation.

Richardson thought of the dying Clarissa as a Christian martyr and a tragic heroine destroyed by an irreligious and materialistic culture. Her slow and intensely rendered death is genuinely moving even for modern readers; it is also a novelistically appropriate action, since it is her way as a character in a novel of re-asserting control over the world and justifying herself. *Clarissa* remains a novel of tragic status because it successfully dramatizes psychological and social conflicts that we now can understand were not resolvable. To some extent, the conflict between Clarissa and Lovelace is between complex individuals whose complexity is the result of their status as representatives of different social classes at a moment of historical transition. For Richardson and the 18th-century middle-classes who were his readers, Lovelace is a projection of an outlawed egoism and sexuality which they located in a dangerous opposing way of life; he represents energies they believed in suppressing. Clarissa is a character who heroically suppresses those same energies and rejects any personal or social ambitions, but she is also an embodiment of a purified and spiritualized middle-class individualism which is in its own way imperious and ambitious. In her heroic resistance and death, she aspires to remake the world in her own image.

In spite of Clarissa's heroism, many readers found themselves drawn to the irrepressible Lovelace, and in subsequent editions of the book Richardson tried to make him less attractive, partly by revisions and partly by footnotes instructing the reader not to be fooled by Lovelace's charms. Richardson's last novel, *Sir Charles Grandison* was his attempt to produce a virtuous hero as a contrast to Lovelace. Although it has found very few modern readers, *Grandison* was a successful and influential work until the middle of the 19th century. It features an even wider variety of scenes and characters than *Clarissa*, as Sir Charles spends a good deal of his time in Italy courting the beautiful Clementina della Porretta. There is melodrama here as well in the tortured refusal of that pious lady to marry the Protestant Sir Charles because of his religion and in the hero's rescue of his wife-to-be, Harriet Byron, from an abduction carried out by a villainous rake, Sir Hargrave Pollexfen. But the main charm of the book for its 18th-century audience was its reconciliation of upper-class gentility and a perfect moral delicacy. The psychological intensity and tragic social conflicts of *Clarissa* give way to the unfailing goodness of Sir Charles, to a neat and satisfying dramatization of moral sentiments, and to a mild comedy of manners which were to set the tone for the English novel for the next fifty years.

—John Richetti

RICHLER, Mordecai. Canadian. Born in Montreal, Quebec, 27 January 1931. Educated at the Montreal Hebrew Academy; Baron Byng High School, Montreal; Sir George Williams University, Montreal, 1948–50. Married Florence Wood in 1959; three sons and two daughters. Lived in Europe, 1959–72; Writer-in-Residence, Sir George Williams University, 1968–69; Visiting Professor, Carleton University, Ottawa, 1972–74. Member for Canada, Editorial Board, Book-of-the-Month Club, since 1976. Recipient: President's Medal, University of Western Ontario, for non-fiction, 1959; Canada Council Junior Arts Fellowship, 1959, 1960, and Senior Arts Fellowship, 1966; Guggenheim Fellowship, 1961; Governor-General's Award, 1969, 1971; Writers Guild of America award, 1974; British Film Festival Golden Bear, 1974; Canadian Library Association English Medal Award, for children's book, 1976. Lives in Montreal.

PUBLICATIONS

Fiction

> *The Acrobats.* 1954; as *Wicked We Love*, n.d.
> *Son of a Smaller Hero.* 1955.
> *A Choice of Enemies.* 1957.
> *The Apprenticeship of Duddy Kravitz.* 1959.
> *The Incomparable Atuk.* 1963; as *Stick Your Neck Out*, 1963.
> *Cocksure.* 1968.
> *The Street: Stories.* 1969.
> *St. Urbain's Horseman.* 1971.
> *Notes on an Endangered Species and Others* (stories). 1974.

Plays

> Screenplays: *Dearth of a Salesman*, 1957; *No Love for Johnnie*, with Nicholas Phipps, 1961; *Tiara Tahiti*, with Geoffrey Cotterell and Ivan Foxwell, 1962; *The Wild and the Willing (Young and Willing)*, with Nicholas Phipps, 1962; *Life at the Top*, 1965; *The Apprenticeship of Duddy Kravitz*, 1974; *Fun with Dick and Jane*, with David Giler and Jerry Belson, 1977.

> Radio Play: *It's Harder to Be Anybody*, 1961.

> Television Plays: *Trouble with Benny*, 1959; *The Apprenticeship of Duddy Kravitz*, from his own novel, 1961; *The Fall of Mendel Crick*, from a story by Isaac Babel, 1963.

Other

> *Hunting Tigers under Glass: Essays and Reports.* 1969.
> *Shovelling Trouble.* 1972.
> *Jacob Two-Two Meets the Hooded Fang* (juvenile). 1975.
> *Creativity and the University*, with André Fortier and Rollo May. 1975.
> *Images of Spain.* 1977.

> Editor, *Canadian Writing Today.* 1970.

Reading List: *Richler* by George Woodcock, 1970; *Richler* edited by G. David Sheps, 1970; *Richler* by Robert Fulford, 1971.

*   *   *

Mordecai Richler, the Canadian novelist and essayist, was born in Montreal of a Jewish family which originated in Russia and Poland. Of his novels, *The Apprenticeship of Duddy Kravitz* and *St. Urbain's Horseman* are not only the most ambitious in scale but the ones that have earned most critical praise. Many of his novels have enjoyed remarkable sales, especially the temptingly titled *Cocksure*, a bawdy and satirical fantasy about modish London. His collection of essays, *Hunting Tigers under Glass*, includes witty but perceptive pieces on Expo 67 and Norman Mailer, as well as the sharply ironic "Jews in Sport."

Jewishness is the subject and Jewish is the tone of all Richler's work. Though he knows the slicker business world of Jewish enterprise, mocking it with brio in several of his books, he writes more feelingly of the Jewish minority in French-speaking Montreal. Duddy Kravitz, who has also become the subject of a successful Canadian film based on Richler's novel, has been described as "a two-timing, trouble-making, self-pitying, anti-goy young Jew from a Montreal back-street." Richler portrays him with an almost total lack of sentimentality. Similar lives are presented in *St. Urbain's Horseman* and in a collection of short stories entitled *The Street*. In *St. Urbain's Horseman* Richler links Canadian experience with the Nazi treatment of the Jews, providing his novel with a deeper compassion than has been obvious in earlier work.

Richler's combination of abrasive humour and racy style can lead him into cynicism, even meretriciousness. *Cocksure*, like *The Incomparable Atuk* whose central character is an Eskimo poet taken up by a public relations officer, makes splendid fun of media techniques and of trendy attitudes. Both novels, however, partly fall victim to the superficiality they seek to satirise.

Richler enjoys great popular success but is regarded with some suspicion by critics for his apparent lack of seriousness. In his best work, however, he writes with such shrewd observation of minority groups that he is likely to be assured a lasting place among the leaders of Canadian fiction. He has also worked on several film scripts, including John Braine's *Life at the Top*, as a result of which the film world plays an important part in many of his writings. He lived mainly in Europe from 1959 to 1972, which may account for a sense of rootlessness running through some of his work.

—Alastair Niven

RICHTER, Conrad (Michael).   American.   Born in Pine Grove, Pennsylvania, 13 October 1890. Educated at the Susquehanna Academy and High School, Pennsylvania, graduated 1906. Married Harvena Achenbach in 1915; one daughter. Worked as a teamster, farm laborer, bank clerk, and journalist, in Pennsylvania, 1906–08; Editor, *Weekly Courier*, Patton, Pennsylvania, 1909–10; Reporter for the *Leader*, Johnstown, Pennsylvania, and the *Pittsburgh Dispatch*, 1910–11; private secretary in Cleveland, 1911–13; free-lance writer, in Pennsylvania, from 1914; settled in New Mexico, 1928. Recipient: New York University Society of Libraries gold medal, 1942; Pulitzer Prize, 1951; National Institute of Arts and Letters grant, 1959; National Book Award, 1960. Litt.D.: Susquehanna University, Selinsgrove, Pennsylvania, 1944; University of New Mexico, Albuquerque, 1958; Lafayette College, Easton, Pennsylvania, 1966; LL.D.: Temple University, Philadelphia, 1966; L.H.D.: Lebanon Valley College, Annville, Pennsylvania, 1966. Member, National Institute of Arts and Letters. *Died 30 October 1968.*

PUBLICATIONS

Fiction

Brothers of No Kin and Other Stories.   1924.
Early Americana (stories).   1936
The Sea of Grass.   1937.
The Trees.   1940; *The Fields,* 1946; *The Town,* 1950; complete version, as *The Awakening Land,* 1966.
Tacey Cromwell.   1942.
The Free Man.   1943.
Smoke over the Prairies and Other Stories.   1947.
Always Young and Fair.   1947.
The Light in the Forest.   1953.
The Lady.   1957.
Dona Ellen.   1959.
The Waters of Kronos.   1960.
A Simple Honorable Man.   1962.
The Grandfathers.   1964.
A Country of Strangers.   1966.
The Wanderer.   1966.
Over the Blue Mountain (juvenile).   1967.
The Aristocrat.   1968.
The Rawhide Knot and Other Short Stories.   1978.

Other

Human Vibration: The Mechanics of Life and Mind.   1925.
Principles in Bio-Physics.   1927.
The Mountain on the Desert: A Philosophical Journey.   1955.
Individualists under the Shade Trees in a Vanishing America.   1964.

Reading List: *Richter* by Edwin W. Gaston, 1965; *Richter* by Robert J. Barnes, 1968; *Richter's Ohio Trilogy: Its Ideas, Themes, and Relationship to Literary Tradition* by Clifford D. Edwards, 1970.

*   *   *

Conrad Richter is the latest and one of the best novelists of the American frontier, in the tradition of James Fenimore Cooper and Willa Cather. To this tradition he brings a deeper perspective and a more self-conscious artistry, as suggested by his choice of titles: his first novel was *The Sea of Grass*, and his second volume of short stories, *Early Americana*. But his best fiction, by far, is the trilogy *The Trees*, *The Fields*, and *The Town*. These three novels narrate the growth of an American family from its early struggle with the wilderness and the Indians, through its settlement and clearing of the fields, to the beginnings of an industrial America in the new town.

Perhaps the best and certainly the most original of these novels is *The Trees*, which follows the migration of Sayward Luckett and her family through the forests of Western Pennsylvania to the Ohio frontier. But more powerful than any human protagonist is the brooding presence of the primeval trees, which shadow the lives of all those beneath, until "the woodsies" adopt their dark and often savage ways in order to survive. In this world tragedy is inevitable: Sayward's mother dies of fever, her huntsman father deserts (or disappears), and she is left to bring up her younger siblings. There is no room in this world for romance, and the novel ends with Sayward's strange marriage to a drunken young lawyer, a fugitive from his New England past. The later two novels of the trilogy continue the story of the new family into the modern world.

After this Ohio trilogy Richter's most interesting novels are two which use autobiographical material to describe the conflict between a preacher father and his son. *The Waters of Kronos* tells of an early pioneer town which has been condemned to make way for a new reservoir, whose waters – like the waters of time – will drown the memory of its pioneer past. Underlying this is the ancient myth of Kronos, the titan father conquered by the son. A second novel, *A Simple Honorable Man*, describes the infinite complexity of the conflicts which create the "simple" character of the titular hero.

Richter's best early novel, *The Sea of Grass*, tells of the pioneer Southwest, as do many of his short stories. *The Light in the Forest* narrates the tragic conflict of a white boy, kidnapped and brought up by Indians, who tries to return to his own people. This same conflict informs *A Country of Strangers*, whose heroine had also been raised by Indians. Three novels, *Tacey Cromwell*, *Always Young and Fair*, and *The Lady*, describe heroines of different types who cope in different ways with the male-dominated society of the frontier. Finally, several volumes of non-fiction develop the philosophy which gives form to all Richter's creative writing. The best of these is *The Mountain on the Desert*.

—Frederic I. Carpenter

RINEHART, Mary Roberts. American. Born in Pittsburgh, Pennsylvania, in 1876. Educated in elementary and high schools in Pittsburgh, and at Pittsburgh Training School for nurses, graduated 1896. Married Dr. Stanley Marshall Rinehart in 1896 (died, 1932); three sons. Full-time writer from 1903; lived in Pittsburgh until 1920, in Washington, D.C., 1920–32, and in New York City from 1932. Litt.D.: George Washington University, Washington, D.C., 1923. *Died 22 September 1958.*

PUBLICATIONS

Fiction

    The Circular Staircase. 1908.
    The Man in Lower Ten. 1909.
    When a Man Marries. 1909.
    The Window at the White Cat. 1910.
    The Amazing Adventure of Letitia Carberry. 1911.
    Where There's a Will. 1912.
    The Case of Jennie Brice. 1913.
    The After House. 1914.
    The Street of Seven Stars. 1914.
    K. 1915.

Tish. 1916.
Bab, A Sub-Deb. 1917.
Long Live the King! 1917.
The Altar of Freedom. 1917.
The Amazing Interlude. 1918.
Twenty-Three and a Half Hours' Leave. 1918.
Love Stories. 1919.
Dangerous Days. 1919.
A Poor Wise Man. 1920.
The Truce of God. 1920.
Affinities and Other Stories. 1920.
Isn't That Just Like a Man! 1920.
More Tish. 1921.
Sight Unseen, and The Confession. 1921.
The Breaking Point. 1922.
The Out Trail. 1923.
Temperamental People (stories). 1924.
The Red Lamp. 1925.
Tish Plays the Game. 1926.
Nomad's Land (stories). 1926.
The Bat. 1926.
Lost Ecstasy. 1927.
Two Flights Up. 1928.
This Strange Adventure. 1929.
The Romantics (stories). 1929.
The Door. 1930.
Miss Pinkerton. 1932; as *The Double Alibi,* 1932.
The Album. 1933.
Mr. Cohen Takes a Walk. 1934.
The State Versus Elinor Norton. 1934.
The Doctor. 1936.
Married People (stories). 1937.
Tish Marches On. 1937.
The Wall. 1938.
The Great Mistake. 1940.
Familiar Faces: Stories of People You Know. 1941.
Haunted Lady. 1942.
Alibi for Israel and Other Stories. 1944.
The Yellow Room. 1945.
A Light in the Window. 1948.
Episode of the Wandering Knife: Three Mystery Tales. 1950.
The Swimming Pool. 1952.
The Frightened Wife and Other Murder Stories. 1953.

Plays

Double Life (produced 1906).
Seven Days, with Avery Hopwood (produced 1909). 1931.
Cheer Up (produced 1912).
The Bat, with Avery Hopwood, from novel *The Circular Staircase* by Rinehart (produced 1920). 1932.

Screenplay: *Aflame in the Sky,* with Ewart Anderson, 1927.

Other

Kings, Queens, and Pawns: An American Woman at the Front. 1915.
Through Glacier Park: Seeing America First, with Howard Eaton. 1916.
Tenting Tonight: A Chronicle of Sport and Adventure in Glacier Park and the Cascade Mountains. 1918.
My Story (autobiography). 1931; revised edition, 1948.
Writing Is Work. 1939.

*   *   *

Mary Roberts Rinehart, a successful writer of thrillers and of comic novels about the travels and adventures of a spinster, "Tish," modelled on herself and her friends, may be considered one of the founder figures of the American novel of mystery and suspense. From her first successful novel, *The Circular Staircase,* to a late work like *The Album,* she used the same pattern. The setting is usually in a more-or-less enclosed house, often a lodging house or block of houses deliberately shut off from the outer world. The heroine is usually either an inexperienced but bright young woman or a shrewd but eccentric spinster. By overhearing odd conversations or mysterious footsteps the heroine slowly tracks down a murderer, whose identity comes as a shock to her. But then a real detective, a minor character (he may have been posing as one of the lodgers), rescues her in time. Miss Rinehart's novels are still popular, especially in America, and their period and oddly wholesome flavour (one never really believes that the heroine will suffer the fate looming over her) make them agreeable reading. They were jocularly christened novels of the "Had I but known ..." school (they were always told in the first person), and Mignon C. Eberhart was her most distinguished successor.

—G. S. Fraser

ROBERTS, Elizabeth Madox. American. Born in Perryville, Kentucky, 30 October 1881; lived part of her childhood in Colorado. Educated at Covington Institute, Springfield, Kentucky; Covington High School, Kentucky, 1886–1900; University of Chicago (Fiske Prize, 1921), 1917–21, Ph.B. in English 1921 (Phi Beta Kappa). Private tutor and teacher in various public schools, 1900–10; writer from 1920. Recipient: O. Henry Prize, 1930. Member, National Institute of Arts and Letters, 1940. *Died 13 March 1941.*

PUBLICATIONS

Fiction

The Time of Man. 1926.
My Heart and My Flesh. 1927.
Jingling in the Wind. 1928.
The Great Meadow. 1930.
A Buried Treasure. 1931.

The Haunted Mirror: Stories. 1932.
He Sent Forth a Raven. 1935.
Black Is My Truelove's Hair. 1938.
Not by Strange Gods: Stories. 1941.

Verse

In the Great Steep's Garden. 1915.
Under the Tree (juvenile). 1922; revised edition, 1930.
Song in the Meadow. 1940.

Reading List: *Roberts: An Appraisal* by J. Donald Adams, 1938; *Roberts, American Novelist* by Harry Modean Campbell and Ruel E. Foster, 1956; *Herald to Chaos: The Novels of Roberts* by Earl Rovit, 1960; *Roberts* by Frederick P. W. McDowell, 1963 (includes bibliography).

                            *   *   *

The philosophic idealism of Bishop Berkeley, the realistic conventions of regional fiction, and a poetic talent for rendering sensuous impressions are the unlikely ingredients that conjoin in the making of Elizabeth Madox Roberts's novels. Her characteristic way of harmonizing these disparate materials is through the focus of an introspective female who serves as narrator-protagonist − a controlling consciousness that shapes the contours of her own growing personality and those of the outside world, interactively and simultaneously. Two of Roberts's novels, *The Time of Man* and *The Great Meadow*, attained considerable success when they were originally published. The first chronicles the sensibility of a Kentucky girl, Ellen Chesser, whose experience as a migrant farm-wife is measured by the eternal cycles of poverty, labor, and the universal portions of grief, pain, joy, and love. Deliberately conceived on the model of the *Odyssey*, *The Time of Man* aims at a kind of epic quality in its unsentimental depiction of the struggle between creative life-instincts and the implacable limitations of the human condition. *The Great Meadow* reworks this theme, but its heroine, Diony, is a more sophisticated consciousness; she is aware of herself and her role, and the journey-motif is not the twenty-year wanderings of an impoverished farm family, but the great Western trek from Virginia to the founding of Kentucky in the late 18th century. Both novels allowed Roberts to develop and display her strengths as a novelist: a supple, lyrical prose style, admirably suited to the particular feminine sensibility that she espoused; a sense of rhythmical narrative structure that moves in slow, undramatic accretions of episodic action; and an unforced, natural symbolism infusing the texture of events.

Although these two novels are regarded as Roberts's major achievements, *My Heart and My Flesh* and *He Sent Forth a Raven* are scarcely less accomplished. The first was meant to be an antithetical sequel to *The Time of Man*, the protagonist, in this case, being stripped of all buffers against adversity only to assert an indomitable will to live. The second is Roberts's most ambitious effort; *He Sent Forth a Raven* invokes the allegorical grandeur of the Biblical story of Noah and *Moby-Dick*, and, although the novel is not entirely able to control its materials, it is rich in meaning and strangely powerful. She also wrote three other novels, two collections of short stories, and three volumes of poetry. Her poems − fresh, vivid, and marked by their capacity to record a direct sensuous immediacy − are frequently anthologized in collections of verse for children.

                                                                                    —Earl Rovit

ROBERTS, Kenneth (Lewis). American. Born in Kennebunk, Maine, 8 December 1885. Educated in local schools and at Cornell University, Ithaca, New York (Editor, *Cornell Widow*), 1904–08, A.B. 1908. Served in the United States Army, in the Intelligence Section of the Siberian Expeditionary Force, 1918–19: Captain. Married Anna Seiberling Mosser in 1911. Reporter and Columnist, *Boston Globe*, 1909–17, and also member of the editorial staff of *Life* Magazine, New York, 1915–18; Correspondent, in Washington, D.C., and Europe, for the *Saturday Evening Post*, Philadelphia, 1919–28; thereafter a full-time writer; lived in Italy, 1928–37, then settled in Kennebunkport, Maine. Recipient: special Pulitzer Prize, 1957. Litt.D.: Dartmouth College, Hanover, New Hampshire, 1934; Colby College, Waterville, Maine, 1935; Bowdoin College, Brunswick, Maine, 1937; Middlebury College, Vermont, 1938; Northwestern University, Evanston, Illinois, 1945. Member, National Institute of Arts and Letters. *Died 21 July 1957.*

PUBLICATIONS

Fiction

Arundel. 1930.
The Lively Lady. 1931.
Rabble in Arms. 1933.
Captain Caution: A Chronicle of Arundel. 1934.
Northwest Passage. 1937.
Oliver Wiswell. 1940.
Lydia Bailey. 1947.
Boon Island. 1956.

Plays

Panatella, with Romeyn Berry, music by T. J. Lindorff and others (produced 1907). 1907.
The Brotherhood of Man, with Robert Garland. 1934.

Other

Europe's Morning After. 1921.
Sun Hunting: Adventures and Observations among the Native and Migratory Tribes of Florida. 1922.
Why Europe Leaves Home. 1922.
The Collector's Whatnot, with Booth Tarkington and Hugh Kahler. 1923.
Black Magic. 1924.
Concentrated New England: A Sketch of Calvin Coolidge. 1924.
Florida Loafing. 1925.
Florida. 1926.
Antiquamania. 1928.
For Authors Only and Other Gloomy Essays. 1935.
It Must Be Your Tonsils. 1936.
Trending into Maine. 1938.
The Kenneth Roberts Reader. 1945.
I Wanted to Write. 1949.

Don't Say That about Maine! 1951.
Henry Gross and His Dowsing Rod. 1951.
The Seventh Sense. 1953.
Cowpens: The Great Morale-Builder. 1957; as *The Battle of Cowpens,* 1958.
Water Unlimited. 1957.

Editor, *March to Quebec: Journals of the Members of Arnold's Expedition.* 1938.

*   *   *

Kenneth Roberts's reputation rests on his historical novels dealing with American history from the time of the French and Indian War to the War of 1812. These are long, character-and-action packed novels that succeed admirably in bringing history to life. Because Roberts brought to the writing of fiction two decades of newspaper and magazine journalism and a passion for accurate detail, his novels are noteworthy for their historical accuracy. His interest in historical fiction began with a curiosity about his own Maine ancestors who had been involved in the American Revolution.

Roberts went about his novels as though he were writing history. He borrowed trunk-loads of books from the Library of Congress and historical societies and ransacked the shelves of antiquarian book dealers. When he could not find what he wanted in printed sources, he went to the archives. In researching *Northwest Passage,* for example, he found in the British Public Record Office a large collection of previously unused letters, petitions, and reports written by Major Robert Rogers himself, who was to be the protagonist of the novel. When he was writing *Lively Lady* at his winter home off the coast of Tuscany he spent hours with Bowditch's *Navigator* and binoculars watching sailing ships in the harbor in order to master the details of sailing a brig.

Without the help of Booth Tarkington, his summer neighbor in Kennebunkport, Maine, however, Roberts might not have become a novelist. In 1928 Tarkington persuaded him to drop his journalism and begin his first novel. For the next 15 years Tarkington talked over plans, encouraged him and then, when the novels were in rough draft, acted as advisor and editor. Night after night Roberts read aloud from manuscripts and gratefully accepted suggestions for deletions and revisions. Roberts's diary shows that in one three-month period in 1936 he spent 58 nights reading the first 51 chapters of *Northwest Passage.*

Arundel is the story of Benedict Arnold's disastrous expedition against Quebec in 1775, narrated by a Richard Nason from Arundel, Maine. Nason's son is the protagonist of Roberts's next novel, *Lively Lady,* which deals with the operations of a privateer in the war of 1812. *Rabble in Arms* is also about men from Arundel who fight with Arnold, the hero of the novel, and ends with the Battle of Saratoga. *Captain Caution* is another sea story laid at the time of the War of 1812. *Northwest Passage* is Roberts's most memorable work and depicts the fascinating career of Major Rogers, Indian fighter during the French and Indian War, who dreamed of finding the Northwest Passage to the Pacific, was governor of Michilimackinac and later court-martialed. *Oliver Wiswell* is a novel of particular interest because it tells the story of the American Revolution from the viewpoint of a loyalist.

—James Woodress

ROLFE, Frederick (William).   Pseudonym: Baron Corvo.   English.   Born in London, 22 July 1860. Educated at North London Collegiate School to age 14; student and lay teacher at St. Mary's College, Oscott, Warwickshire, 1887–88; studied for the priesthood at Scots College, Rome, 1889–90. Apprentice teacher and schoolmaster at Stationers' Company

School, 1878–79, King Edward VI Grammar School, Saffron Walden, Essex, 1880–81, Winchester Modern School, Hampshire, 1881–82, Bartholomew's Grammar School, Newbury, Berkshire, 1882, Balsham Manor, Cambridge, 1883–84, and Grantham Grammar School, Lincolnshire, 1884–86, then a private tutor; Editor, *The Holywell Record*, Wales, 1897–98; lived in London, 1889–1907, and Venice, 1908 until his death. Recipient: Royal Literary Fund grant, 1902. *Died 25 October 1913.*

PUBLICATIONS

Collections

    Collected Poems, edited by Cecil Woolf. 1974.

Fiction

    Stories Toto Told Me. 1898.
    In His Own Image. 1901.
    Hadrian the Seventh. 1904.
    Don Tarquinio: A Kataleptic Phantasmatic Romance. 1905.
    The Weird of the Wanderer, Being the Papyrus Records of Some Incidents in One of the Previous Lives of Mr. Nicholas Crabbe, with C. H. C. Pirie-Gordon. 1912.
    The Desire and Pursuit of the Whole: A Romance of Modern Venice. 1934.
    Hubert's Arthur, Being Certain Curious Documents Found among the Literary Remains of Mr. N.C., with C. H. C. Pirie-Gordon. 1935.
    Three Tales of Venice. 1950.
    Amico di Sandro: A Fragment of a Novel. 1951.
    The Cardinal Prefect of Propaganda and Other Stories. 1957.
    Nicholas Crabbe; or, The One and the Many, edited by Cecil Woolf. 1958.
    Don Renato: An Ideal Content, edited by Cecil Woolf. 1963.

Verse

    Tarcissus: The Boy Martyr of Rome in the Diocletian Persecution. 1880.

Other

    Chronicles of the House of Borgia. 1901; as *A History of the Borgias*, 1931.
    Letters to Grant Richards. 1952.
    Letters to C. H. C. Pirie-Gordon, edited by Cecil Woolf. 1959.
    Letters to Leonard Moore, edited by Cecil Woolf and Bertram W. Korn. 1960.
    Letters to R. M. Dawkins, edited by Cecil Woolf. 1962.
    Without Prejudice: One Hundred Letters to John Lane, edited by Cecil Woolf. 1963.
    Letters to James Walsh, edited by Donald Weeks. 1972.
    The Venice Letters, edited by Cecil Woolf. 1974.
    The Armed Hands and Other Stories and Pieces, edited by Cecil Woolf. 1974.
    The Reverse Side of the Coin: Some Further Correspondence Between Rolfe and Grant Richards. 1974.
    Aberdeen Interval: Some Letters from Rolfe to Wilfrid Meynell. 1975.

Different Aspects: Rolfe and the Foreign Office. 1976.
Letters to Harry Bainbridge, edited by Miriam J. Benkovitz. 1977.

Translator, *The Rubáiyát of 'Umar Khaiyam* (from the French version of J. B. Nicolas). 1903.

Bibliography: *A Bibliography of Frederick Rolfe, Baron Corvo* by Cecil Woolf, 1957; revised edition, 1969, 1972.

Reading List: *The Quest for Corvo* by A. J. A. Symons, 1934; *Corvo 1860–1960: A Collection of Essays by Various Hands* edited by Cecil Woolf and Brocard Sewell, 1961, as *New Quests for Corvo,* 1965; *Corvo* by Donald Weeks, 1971; *Frederick Rolfe, Baron Corvo: A Biography* by Miriam J. Benkovitz, 1976.

*   *   *

Frederick Rolfe, self-styled Baron Corvo, was gifted and versatile. He began his literary career by writing verses such as "Seeking and Finding," a schoolboy's prize poem of 1877, or *Tarcissus: The Boy Martyr,* his first separate publication which appeared in 1880. He translated or helped translate poetry from Greek and French as in *The Songs of Meleager* and *The Rubáiyát of 'Umar Khaiyam* from the French of J. B. Nicolas. Rolfe wrote book reviews and other essays, often polemic. His letters demonstrate both his capacity for great good humour and his mastery of invective. He acted as ghost writer at least once. He wrote one gorgeous and elaborate history, *Chronicles of the House of Borgia.* But as a literary man, Rolfe excelled as a writer of fiction in the form of short stories and novels.

Rolfe's finest short fiction appeared first in *The Yellow Book* and subsequently as *Stories Toto Told Me* and its sequel, *In His Own Image.* These are stories of the saints as told to Rolfe by Toto, an Italian peasant boy whose person is as beautiful as his simple faith. The sustained range of these tales and their serene charm are products of an imaginative, skilled craftsman.

The full-length novel *Hadrian the Seventh* is Rolfe's best known work, partly owing to Peter Luke's dramatization. In *Hadrian,* Rolfe imagined himself not only a Catholic priest, his dearest wish, but also Pope. He depicted himself as a wise and humane prelate victimized by numerous associates. *Hadrian* is obviously autobiographical as is all Rolfe's fiction. Rolfe continued the account of himself in *Nicholas Crabbe* and *The Desire and Pursuit of the Whole,* a story of homosexual love. Less patently autobiographical are *Don Tarquinio* and *Hubert's Arthur,* the latter started in collaboration with Harry Pirie-Gordon but re-written on the canals of Venice. Even in *Stories Toto Told Me* and in other short pieces written at about the same time as well as in those composed in Venice toward the end of his life, Rolfe is his own hero enacting aspects of the Corvine character or his version of it. In turn, he was Hadrian, Nicholas Crabbe, Hubert, Dom Gheraldo in *Don Renato: An Ideal Content.*

Don Renato carries to an extreme Rolfe's passion for inventing his own vocabulary from Greek or Latin bases, but his persistence in coining or adapting words is apparent in much of his work. He gloried, too, in obscure learning exhibited most freely in *Don Renato* and *The Weird of the Wanderer,* of which Rolfe granted that Pirie-Gordon wrote a tenth. Often side by side with the learning and the contorted vocabulary is current slang. Rolfe constructed his sentences as A. J. A. Symons pointed out, so that he "set his adverbs as far before both parts of the verb" as he could. Thus, Rolfe marked whatever he wrote with Rolfean or Corvine individuality. He was capable of real artistry in construction, subject matter, and pitch. His sentences and his paragraphs are less idiosyncratic than skillful in their balance and variety. He was capable, in accordance with the demands of his fiction, of ferocity and power, of arrogance, disdain, humour, tenderness, and gentle simplicity; but he was never a bore.

—Miriam J. Benkovitz

RØLVAAG, O(le) E(dvart).   American.   Born on Donna Island, Helgeland, Norway, 22 April 1876; emigrated to the United States, 1896; naturalized, 1908. Educated in Donna schools to age 14; Augustana College, Canton, South Dakota, 1899-1901; St. Olaf College, Northfield, Minnesota, 1901–05, B.A. 1905, M.A. 1910; University of Oslo, 1905–06. Married Jennie Marie Berdahl in 1908; three sons and one daughter. Worked on his uncle's farm in South Dakota, 1896–99; Professor of Norwegian Language and Literature, 1906–31, and Head of the Norwegian Department, 1916–31, St. Olaf College; writer from 1912. Secretary, Norwegian-American Historical Association, 1925–31. Honorary degree: University of Wisconsin, Madison, 1929. Knight of the Order of St. Olaf, Norway, 1926. *Died 5 November 1931.*

PUBLICATIONS

Fiction

Amerika-breve (Letters from America).   1912; translated by Ella Tweet and Solveig Zempel, as *The Third Life of Per Smevik,* 1971.
Paa Glemte Veie (On Forgotten Paths).   1914.
To Tullinger: Et Billede fra Idag (Two Fools: A Picture of Our Time).   1920; revised edition, translated by Sivert Erdahl and Rølvaag, as *Pure Gold,* 1930.
Laengselens Baat.   1921; translated by Nora O. Solum, as *The Boat of Longing,* 1933.
I de Dage: Fortaelling om Norske Nykommere i Amerika (In Those Days: A Story of Norwegian Pioneering in America).   1924; *Ricket Grundlaegges* (The Founding of the Kingdom), 1925; both books translated by Lincoln Colcord and Rølvaag, as *Giants in the Earth,* 1927.
Peder Seier.   1928; translated by Rølvaag and Nora O. Solum, as *Peder Victorious,* 1929.
Den Signede Dag (The Blessed Day).   1931; translated by Trygve M. Ager, as *Their Fathers' God,* 1931.

Other

Ordforklaring til Nordahl Rolfsens Laesebok for Folkeskolen, II.   1909.
Haandbok i Norsk Retskrivning og uttale til Skolebruk og Selvstudium, with P. J. Eikeland.   1916.
Norsk Laesebok, with P. J. Eikeland.   3 vols., 1919–25.
Omkring Faedrearven (essays).   1922.

Editor, *Deklamationsboken.*   1918.

Reading List: *Rølvaag: A Biography* by Theodore Jorgenson and Nora O. Solum, 1939; *Rølvaag: His Life and Art* by Paul Reigstad, 1972.

*   *   *

O. E. Rølvaag's great achievement is *Giants in the Earth,* first published in Norway in 1924 and 1925, then translated into English by Rølvaag and Lincoln Colcord in 1927. The result is remarkable: to a bi-lingual reader the characters seem to be thinking and speaking in Norwegian patterns and cadence, even though the words are English and few Norwegian expressions are left untranslated. By common agreement, *Giants in the Earth* is America's best immigrant story, its great pioneering novel, and a towering documentary of the Middle West.

The events Rølvaag describes in *Giants in the Earth* occurred twenty-five years before he arrived in America. But the setting is the South Dakota he came to in 1896 at the age of twenty, the characters his own kind of Norwegian immigrants, and the events a composite of many accounts he had heard from Dakota pioneers. Writing the book in the 1920's, Rølvaag relied especially on the memory of his father-in-law, Andrew Berdahl. Although the prairie he describes is a formidable adversary for his pioneers, Rølvaag's characters are even more remarkable, especially the hard-driving, inventive, and irrepressible Per Hansa: he is the very type of the ideal American pioneer, yet also very Norwegian. But critics usually have even higher praise for Per's wife, Berit, who is neurotic, backward-looking, and fanatically religious. Rølvaag's pioneer has a dual struggle: against the unbroken prairie and a wife who thinks she has sinned unforgivably in disobeying her parents, in mating with Per Hansa, and in leaving Norway.

Per Hansa's story is heroic and tragic, rare qualities in twentieth century fiction. Berit lives on through the two sequels Rølvaag wrote – *Peder Victorious* and *Their Fathers' God* – and achieves a greatness of her own. The struggle to retain her Norwegian heritage in the new American settlements was a cause Rølvaag supported whole-heartedly. But the essential themes of the two later novels – assimilation and cultural clashes – lack the power and drama of the pioneering struggle. Of more interest is *Pure Gold*, a reworking of Rølvaag's 1920 novel *To Tullinger* (Two Fools): it is the stark tale of a pioneering couple who become monsters of greed. Rølvaag's own favorite was *Laengselens Baat*, which appeared in English translation as *The Boat of Longing* after his death. The strong note of pathos (perhaps pessimism) in this novel has two sources: Nils, a sensitive, artistic, young immigrant, encounters a materialistic America; and his Norwegian parents wait in vain for letters from their son.

Even though the greatness of *Giants in the Earth* was recognised at once, scholars and critics have been uneasy about assigning Ole Rølvaag a place in American literature: he wrote in Norwegian, not English. His psychological realism might owe something to Sherwood Anderson, but a greater influence stemmed from Knut Hamsun and Arne Garborg. As his correspondence reveals, Rølvaag wrote as fluently in English as in Norwegian. Working with translators in turning his novels into English, he weighed and considered each word and phrase. But Rølvaag taught Norwegian language and literature during most of his life in America. Despite Conrad's achievement in the English novel, Rølvaag thought that giving up his native language would require "a remaking of soul." Such a "spiritual readjustment" he would not undertake.

—Clarence A. Glasrud

ROSS, Martin. Pseudonym for Violet Florence Martin. Irish. Born at Ross House, County Galway, 11 June 1862; settled with her family in Dublin, 1872. Educated at home, and at Alexandra College, Dublin. Writer from 1886; lived with her cousin and collaborator, Edith Somerville, *q.v.*, in Drishane, County Cork, 1886 until her death; with Edith Somerville, travelled extensively on the Continent and lived at various times in Paris; in failing health from 1898. Vice-President, Munster Women's Franchise League. *Died 21 December 1915.*

See the entry for Edith Somerville.

ROSS, Sinclair. Canadian. Born in Shellbrook, Saskatchewan, 22 January 1908. Served in the Canadian Army, 1942–45. Worked for the Royal Bank of Canada for 43 years: in Winnipeg, 1931–42, and in Montreal, 1946–68; now retired. Lives in Malaga, Spain.

PUBLICATIONS

Fiction

As for Me and My House. 1941.
The Well. 1958.
The Lamp at Noon and Other Stories. 1968.
Whir of Gold. 1970.
Sawbones Memorial. 1974.

Reading List: "Ross's Ambivalent World" by W. H. New, in *Canadian Literature*, Spring 1969; "No Other Way: Ross's Stories and Novels" by Sandra Djwa, in *Canadian Literature*, Winter 1971.

                        *   *   *

Sinclair Ross has written chiefly about the harshness of life on the Canadian prairie. His early stories and first novel, *As for Me and My House*, set against the drought and depression of the 1930's are established classics of Canadian literature. Ross describes the wind, the dust storms, and the fierce extremes of climate with powerful accuracy, but what is remarkable is the way he uses the details of setting as symbolic counters for human emotions. For example, the drought and vast distances between prairie farms reflect the spiritual dryness and the loneliness felt by the characters. Ross describes the efforts of the farmers and the people of the small prairie towns to wrest a living from their bleak environment, and in his style there is a taut, spare quality which is the perfect measure of man's struggle to endure. Ross's stories focus on three main figures: the farmer, physically strong but inarticulate, who pits himself against the adversities of the land; the young wife and mother who longs for a closer relationship with her husband and dreams of their moving away from the lonely farm; and the child who escapes into an imaginative world of his own making suggested by a fragment of music or by the spirit and freedom of a horse.

"The Lamp at Noon," "Cornet at Night," and "One's a Heifer" are fine stories, yet Ross's masterpiece is the novel *As for Me and My House*, which documents the repressed lives of a preacher and his wife in a small town during the depression. The story is told in diary form by the wife, Mrs. Bentley, who craves for intimacy with her silent, aloof husband, and who plots their escape from the town. Her husband, however, effects his own escape by closing himself in his study where he tries to paint. The form of the novel is striking, for the repressed, claustrophobic existence of the characters is perfectly rendered by the secretive and repetitious entries Mrs. Bentley makes in her daybook. The artist's struggle to find himself gives the novel a universal theme, but the artist's story is told unconventionally by means of the wife's observations rather than through the artist's consciousness. What is more impressive, however, is the author's creation of his female narrator; seldom has a male writer portrayed a woman so credibly or sympathetically.

Ross's output has been small. *The Well* and *Whir of Gold*, conventionally plotted narratives, have added little to his reputation, but in writing *Sawbones Memorial*, the story of a small town doctor, Ross found another fictional structure which vividly renders the life of the prairies. There is no narration in *Sawbones Memorial*, only the drama-like presentation of conversations and memories on the night of the doctor's retirement party, but this unique form serves once again to chronicle man's struggle to survive in a harsh land and his instinct to dream of a better life.

—David Stouck

ROTH, Henry. American. Born in Tysmenica, Austria-Hungary, 8 February 1906. Educated at the City College of New York, B.S. 1928. Married Muriel Parker in 1939; two sons. Worked for the Works Progress Administration (WPA), 1939; teacher at Roosevelt High School, New York, 1939–41; precision metal grinder in New York, Providence, Rhode Island, and Boston, 1941–46; teacher in Montville, Maine, 1947–48; attendant at the Maine State Hospital, 1949–53; waterfowl farmer, 1953–62; private tutor, 1956–65. Recipient: National Institute of Arts and Letters grant, 1965; City College of New York's Townsend Harris Medal, 1965; D. H. Lawrence Fellowship, University of New Mexico, 1968. Lives in Albuquerque, New Mexico.

P∪BLICATIONS

Fiction

Call It Sleep. 1934.

Reading List: *Roth* by Bonnie Lyons, 1975.

* * *

The author of a single novel of intense power, Henry Roth has a minor but vital position in twentieth-century American writing. *Call It Sleep*, published in 1934 but neglected until reprinted in 1960, concentrates immigrant life, childhood experience, and Freudian theory in a striking, stream-of-consciousness narrative. Although Henry Roth has never published another novel – some short stories have appeared in periodicals – *Call It Sleep* remains an important work for its blending of Jewish myth, psychological symbol, and urban reality. A writer of the depression and part of a group to emerge in the 1930's in New York and Chicago (Michael Gold, Daniel Fuchs, Meyer Levin), Henry Roth nonetheless remains unique in his creation of a young hero caught between the foulness of life and the purity of dreams.

Call It Sleep appeared in the same year as the first American edition of *Ulysses*, and Roth, who was influenced by Joyce, employed the techniques of interior monologue, free association, and stylistic experimentation. Developing the myths of redemption and rebirth, Roth enlarged his novel from an autobiographical account of Jewish immigrants in Brooklyn and the Lower East Side to a dramatic exploration of childhood, family conflict, and Oedipal aggression. Four symbols dominate the novel: a cellar connoting dark, sexual fears, a picture with overtones of illicit sex, a piece of coal that is the key to flaming redemption and a trolley rail that is the means to a blinding, almost mystical power.

Language in the novel becomes a fascinating interweaving of English narrative, Yiddish speech, and idioms of the street. Emulating the tale of Isaiah and the burning coal of redemption, the young hero, David Schearl, in the climactic scene of the book virtually kills himself by forcing a milk ladle into the third rail of a trolley track. This act is the symbolic culmination of the hero's desperate effort to redeem himself and his world. His act of purification achieves his need for transcending the sordidness of everyday life — the family quarrels, beatings by his father, poverty of his neighborhood, mistreatment of his mother — that has plagued him.

Call It Sleep, for all its accuracy in portraying immigrant life and economic injustice, cannot be labeled a proletarian or radical novel. It is, rather, a work of vivid, imaginative power that surpasses the stereotypes of such fiction. But why has Henry Roth written no other major work? He explains this failure as not having to mature: "In *Call It Sleep* I stuck with the child, so I didn't have to mature.... I think I just failed at maturity, at adulthood." Shunning the life of a writer, Henry Roth has been a laborer, teacher, psychiatric attendant, and waterfowl farmer. But his distaste for literary life and small output does not detract from the value of his novel, which remains one of the most affecting works of American prose fiction.

—I. B. Nadel

ROTH, Philip (Milton). American. Born in Newark, New Jersey, 19 March 1933. Educated at Newark College, Rutgers University, 1950–51; Bucknell University, Lewisburg, Pennsylvania, 1951–54, A.B. 1954; University of Chicago, 1954–55, M.A. 1955. Served in the United States Army, 1955–56. Married Margaret Martinson in 1958 (died, 1968). Instructor in English, University of Chicago, 1956–58; full-time writer from 1958; Visiting Writer, University of Iowa, Iowa City, 1960–62; Writer-in-Residence, Princeton University, New Jersey, 1962–64; Visiting Writer, State University of New York at Stony Brook, 1966, 1967, and the University of Pennsylvania, Philadelphia, 1967, 1968, 1970, 1971. Member of the Corporation of Yaddo, Saratoga Springs, New York. Recipient: Guggenheim Fellowship, 1959; National Book Award, 1960; Daroff Award, 1960; National Institute of Arts and Letters grant, 1960; O. Henry Award, 1960; Ford Foundation grant, for drama, 1965; Rockefeller Fellowship, 1966. Member, National Institute of Arts and Letters, 1970.

PUBLICATIONS

Fiction

Goodbye, Columbus, and Five Short Stories.   1959.
Letting Go.   1962.
When She Was Good.   1967.
Portnoy's Complaint.   1969.
Our Gang (Starring Tricky and His Friends).   1971.
The Breast.   1972.

The Great American Novel.   1973.
My Life As a Man.   1974.
The Professor of Desire.   1977.

Plays

Heard Melodies Are Sweet, in *Esquire,* August 1958.
The President Addresses the Nation (sketch; produced 1973).

Other

Reading Myself and Others.   1975.

Bibliography: *Roth: A Bibliography* by Bernard F. Rodgers, Jr., 1974.

Reading List: *Bernard Malamud and Roth: A Critical Essay* by Glenn Meeter, 1968; "The Journey of Roth" by Theodore Solotaroff, in *The Red Hot Vacuum,* 1970.

*   *   *

"Sheer Playfulness and Deadly Seriousness are my closest friends," Philip Roth has remarked in interview; "I am also on friendly terms with Deadly Playfulness, Serious Playfulness, Serious Seriousness, and Sheer Sheerness. From the last, however, I get nothing; he just wrings my heart and leaves me speechless." Roth's early work explored with a tense and exasperated earnestness "the whole range of human connections ... between clannish solidarity ... and exclusion or rejection," the struggle of what he has called "the determined self" (in a double sense) against its contingent identity and environment. *When She Was Good* surprised his critics by delineating the self-deception and hypocrisy of small-town Gentile America with the same acid sharpness he brought to the anxieties, pieties, and suppressed hysteria of middle-class and metropolitan Jewry in *Goodbye, Columbus* and *Letting Go.* Roth's characters are usually painfully alert to the insistent and insidious dialogue of conscience with the unconscious: beneath the innocent and upright text of conversation and event lurks a subtext of amoral impulsions, disclosed through Freudian slips and misprisions, by displacement, gesture, and "unintended" innuendo. With *Portnoy's Complaint* the libido came into its own, redefining the ironic, self-conscious wit which enlivened the earlier works as the evasive strategy of "people [who] wear the old unconscious on their *sleeves.*" Portnoy complains that he is "the son in the Jewish joke – *only it ain't no joke!*", and the book mischievously ends with a "punch line" ("So. Now vee may perhaps to begin. Yes?") which brackets the whole confessional text as a pre-analysis warm-up on Dr. Spielvogel's couch. (This same psychoanalyst returns in *My Life as a Man* as representative of a grey, reassuring normalcy which frames the novelist-hero's outrageously self-dramatizing "life.")
Portnoy's compulsive onanism, fêted with Rabelaisian panache, provides a constant analogy for the art of fiction itself (a "complaint" is both physical disorder and literary device). Story-telling is also an autotelic act, a self-sufficient and finally inconsequential spilling of the beans; and the theme is extended in *The Breast,* where Kepesh wakes to find himself translated into the literary tradition he has been teaching, metamorphosed into a huge, almost self-enclosed mammary gland – "Beyond sublimation. I made the word flesh. I have outKafkaed Kafka." *The Great American Novel* (its very title self-reflexive) is a tissue of parody and pastiche which suggests that baseball is not only *a* theme but *the* supreme fiction of American culture (as Roth remarked in an essay, "the literature of my boyhood"). *My Life as a Man* has as its main text the "True Story" of the novelist Peter Tarnopol, preceded by

two "Useful Fictions" which are his short-story variations on the crisis of marital breakdown and blocked creativity which dominates his in-any-case fictitious "Life." Roth plays further games with the reader, alluding to previous writings of Tarnopol's that inevitably and teasingly recall his own earlier work. But if here narcissism in "life" (i.e., "content") becomes reflected in the auto-referentiality of the "text" (i.e., "form"), the sheer exuberance of Roth's invention makes it clear that he is not fixated in the dead-end "Sheer Sheerness" of his fictive analogue. If Tarnopol is only tangentially affected by the great historic events of his era, Roth has written of them at length in *Our Gang* (settling accounts in advance with the Nixon mafia) and in the essays collected as *Reading Myself and Others*. For Roth the introversions of contemporary fiction reflect a wider, social dilemma: "Defying a multitude of bizarre projections, or submitting to them," he has said, "would seem to me at the heart of everyday living in America." Adapting Philip Rahv's division of American writers into "redskins" and "palefaces" – the one rumbustious and anarchic, the other stiff and priggish – he has proposed his own third category, a subversive synthesis of the two, the "redface." Roth's is the poetry of embarrassment and exposure; by making *unease* both theme and narrative technique, he has fused play and seriousness into a style inimitably his own, which is not easily rendered "speechless."

—Stan Smith

ROWSON, Susanna (née Haswell). English. Born in Portsmouth, Hampshire, in 1762; grew up in Massachusetts where her father, a naval officer, was stationed; returned with her family to England, 1778. Educated privately. Married William Rowson in 1786. Full-time writer, 1786 until her husband went bankrupt, 1792; appeared with him on the stage, in Edinburgh, 1792–93, and with the Philadelphia Company, for which she also wrote, in Philadelphia, Baltimore, and Annapolis, Maryland, 1793–96; wrote and acted for the Federal Street Theatre Company, Boston, 1796–97; Founder and teacher at a young ladies' academy in Boston, 1797–1822; Editor, *Boston Weekly Magazine*, 1802–05. President, Boston Fatherless and Widows Association. *Died 2 March 1824.*

PUBLICATIONS

Fiction

    Victoria. 1786.
    The Inquisitor; or, Invisible Rambler. 1788.
    The Test of Honour. 1789.
    Charlotte: A Tale of Truth. 1791; as *Charlotte Temple*, 1794; edited by Clara M. and Rudolf Kirk, 1964; edited by William S. Kable, in *Three Early American Novels*, 1970.
    Mentoria; or, The Young Lady's Friend. 1791.
    Rebecca; or, The Fille de Chambre. 1792; as *The Fille de Chambre*, 1793.
    Trials of the Human Heart. 1795.
    Reuben and Rachel; or, Tales of Old Times. 1798.
    Sarah; or, The Exemplary Wife. 1813.

Charlotte's Daughter; or, The Three Orphans. 1828; as *Lucy Temple: One of the Three Orphans,* 1842 (?).
Love and Romance: Charlotte and Lucy Temple. 1854.

Plays

Slaves in Algiers; or, A Struggle for Freedom, music by Alexander Reinagle. 1794.
The Female Patriot; or, Nature's Rights, from the play *The Bondman* by Philip Massinger (produced 1795).
The Volunteers: A Musical Entertainment, music by Alexander Reinagle (produced 1795). 1795.
Americans in England; or, Lessons for Daughters (produced 1797). 1796; as *The Columbian Daughters; or, Americans in England* (produced 1800).
The American Tar (produced 1796).
Hearts of Oak, from the work by John Till Allingham (produced 1810–11?).

Verse

Poems on Various Subjects. 1788.
A Trip to Parnassus; or, The Judgment of Apollo on Dramatic Authors and Performers. 1788.
The Standard of Liberty: A Poetical Address. 1795.
Miscellaneous Poems. 1804.

Other

An Abridgement of Universal Geography, Together with Sketches of History. 1805.
A Spelling Dictionary. 1807.
A Present for Young Ladies (miscellany). 1811.
Youth's First Step in Geography. 1818.
Biblical Dialogues Between a Father and His Family. 1822.
Exercises in History, Chronology, and Biography, in Question and Answer. 1822.

Bibliography: "Rowson, The Author of *Charlotte Temple*: A Bibliographical Study" by R. W. G. Vail, in *Proceedings of the American Antiquarian Society 42,* April–October 1932.

Reading List: *Rowson, America's First Best-Selling Novelist* by Ellen B. Brandt, 1975; *In Defense of Women: Rowson* by Dorothy Weil, 1976.

*   *   *

Because of the popularity, variety, and number of Susanna Rowson's books, she may properly be considered the foremost woman of letters of her generation in the United States. The phenomenal success on both sides of the Atlantic of her novel *Charlotte Temple* has tended to obscure her other considerable accomplishments, but she also wrote other novels and a large number of plays, poetry, textbooks, and miscellanies which defy classification. Her literary career is even more remarkable in light of her prominence in her other occupations, those of actress and educator. She has the distinction of being not only one of America's first professional women but also one of the first advocates of women's rights in the United States.

Charlotte: A Tale of Truth has gone through over 200 editions since it was first published in 1791 and was, according to R. W. G. Vail, "the most popular of all early American novels." While detractors have dismissed it as being sentimental and formulaic, supporters have accounted for its popularity by insisting on its forthright realism within the sentimental convention. Rowson herself claimed that the story of seduction and betrayal is an actual one, and in the early 1800's the gravestone of the purported model, Charlotte Stanley, was changed to "Charlotte Temple." It still may be seen in Trinity Churchyard in New York City. No other novel by Rowson can approach the popularity of this best seller, but others were highly regarded, notably *The Fille de Chambre* and *Reuben and Rachel*.

One of her few extant plays, *Slaves in Algiers* is the first successfully produced play by a woman in America. A musical comedy, written in collaboration with Alexander Reinagle, it is of topical interest in that it was a protest against the capture of American ships off the Barbary coast from 1785 to 1794. The play is notable for its fervent nationalism and the insistence upon the equality of women in the new nation. Although it was well-received by play-goers, William Cobbett roundly attacked it for its feminist sentiments.

Rowson's poems and songs were not critically well-received, and today they seem florid and derivative. Nevertheless many of them were immensely popular, especially "America, Commerce, and Freedom." Her textbooks and miscellanies are of only historical interest today. In spite of her significant contributions to American letters, little critical attention has been paid her until quite recently, but two new studies of her career suggest that her work is worthy of serious consideration.

—Nancy C. Joyner

RUDD, Steele. Pseudonym for Arthur Hoey Davis. Australian. Born in Drayton, Queensland, 14 November 1868. Educated in the Emu Creek State School. Married twice; three sons and one daughter from the first marriage. Worked on sheep and cattle stations in Queensland, 1880–86; settled in Brisbane, 1886, and entered the Queensland Civil Service: Junior Clerk in the office of the Curator of Intestate Estates, 1886–88; Clerk in the Sheriff's Office, 1889–1902, and Under-Sheriff, 1902–03; full-time writer from 1903; columnist for newspapers in Brisbane, and for the Sydney *Bulletin*; Founding Editor, *Steele Rudd's Magazine*, Brisbane and Sydney, 1904–08, 1923–30. *Died 11 October 1935.*

PUBLICATIONS

Fiction

On Our Selection! 1899.
Our New Selection. 1903.
Sandy's Selection. 1904.
Back at Our Selection. 1906.
The Poor Parson. 1907.
In Australia. 1908.
Dad in Politics and Other Stories. 1908; as *For Life and Other Stories,* 1908.
Stocking Our Selection. 1909.

Duncan McClure. 1909.
From Selection to City. 1909.
On an Australian Farm. 1910.
The Dashwoods. 1911.
The Book of Dan. 1911.
The Old Homestead. 1917.
Memoirs of Corporal Keeley. 1918.
Grandpa's Selection. 1919.
We Kaytons. 1921; as *Kayton's Selection,* 1926.
On Emu Creek. 1923.
Me an' th' Son. 1924.
The Rudd Family. 1926.
The Miserable Clerk. 1926.
The Romance of Runnibede. 1927 (?).
Green Grey Homestead. 1934.

*   *   *

Arthur Hoey Davis's singular achievement was his creation, as "Steele Rudd," of an enduring Australian mythology. It epitomizes the struggle of the common man-on-the-land to accept and adapt to the basic rural environment; the "selector" (unlike the earlier and wealthier "squatter") was the nearest equivalent to a European peasant settler, dogged, independent, and hard-working, and he was endowed with a similar tenacity and energy. In modern times the character of Dad Rudd, with the rest of the Rudd family – Dan, Dave, Kate, Mabel, Joe, a colonially extensive tribe – is perhaps not so convincingly representative of the Australian farmer, who with time has become relatively more prosperous and relatively more conservative. But Davis's vision was of the selector's world in its primary phase, and the picture had great vigour. His characters were from the first grotesques; the humour was a horse-laugh. All this became easy to caricature, a fact which accounts for the (artistic) corruption which in its later days descended on the legend when it became the material for comic strip presentation in newspapers; but this was something outside Davis's invention, imposed by popular success itself. In order to preserve proportion a discriminating reader will always go to Davis's early books; those first stories have a colonial freshness that is as true as the characters are good. And it is a tribute to their integrity that, even in the corruption of the Rudds in later days, only the literary proprieties suffered – nothing could destroy their essential innocence or the warmth of their humanity. When Davis took his rural characters to town and Dad entered politics they still kept their rural identity and colour. Their truth, not their subtlety, preserves them; they are comic ghosts and phantoms and as such do not sustain for long – but phantoms also have great perdurability, and these will always remain ready to imaginative recall as long as Australians are disposed to turn back romantically to those phases of early history which represent their struggle to possess their own landscape, those bad old days of frustration and despair which, in their innermost hearts, they really treasure as the golden age of their national pride. To this mythological phenomenon, even now in these very different times, "Steele Rudd" still holds one of the essential keys.

—Brian Elliott

RUNYON, (Alfred) Damon. American. Born in Manhattan, Kansas, 4 October 1880; grew up in Pueblo, Colorado. Educated in Pueblo public schools. Served in the United States Army during the Spanish-American War, 1898–1900. Married 1) Ellen Egan in 1911 (died), one son and one daughter; 2) Patrice del Grande in 1932 (divorced, 1946). Reporter for, successively, the Pueblo *Chieftain*, Colorado Springs *Gazette*, Denver *News*, Denver *Post*, and San Francisco *Post*, 1900–10; Sportswriter for the New York *American*, 1911–18, and Correspondent for Hearst newspapers in Mexico, 1912, and in Europe during World War 1, 1917–18; columnist and feature writer for King Features/International News Service, from 1918; producer at RKO and 20th Century Fox, Hollywood, 1942–43; in later years lived in Florida. Recipient: National Headliners Club of New York Feature Writing Prize, 1939. Died of Cancer: Damon Runyon Memorial Fund for Cancer Research established shortly after his death. *Died 10 December 1946.*

PUBLICATIONS

Collections

    A Treasury of Runyon, edited by Clark Kinnaird. 1958.

Fiction (stories)

    Guys and Dolls. 1931.
    Blue Plate Special. 1934.
    Money From Home. 1935.
    More Than Somewhat. 1937.
    Furthermore. 1938.
    The Best of Damon Runyon, edited by E. C. Bentley. 1938.
    Take It Easy. 1938.
    My Old Man. 1939.
    My Wife Ethel. 1940.
    Damon Runyon Favorites. 1942.
    Runyon à la Carte. 1944.
    In Our Town. 1946.
    Short Takes. 1946.
    Trials and Other Tribulations. 1948.
    Runyon First and Last. 1949; as *All This and That,* 1950.
    The Turps. 1951.

Play

    A Slight Case of Murder, with Howard Lindsay (produced 1935). 1940.

Verse

    The Tents of Trouble. 1911.
    Rhymes of the Firing Line. 1912.
    Poems for Men. 1947.

Other

Captain Eddie Rickenbacker, with Walter Kiernan. 1942.

                            *   *   *

Damon Runyon belongs to that long line of American journalists who make copy out of the comic potentiality of life around them. Much of that comedy derives from the rich variety of speech patterns among the various immigrant communities spread across the U.S.: German, Dutch, Polish, Irish; and, in Runyon's case, the Jewish-Italian speech of the Bronx and related areas of New York. For what gives Runyon his special distinction is that he wrote about life in the big city, whereas previous journalist/fiction-writers in his mould had largely confined themselves to small-town midwestern communities.

Runyon's world is that of the seedy mafiosa, barflies, compulsive gamblers, womanisers, men who sport names such as "Society Max," "Harry the Horse," "Rusty Charlie," "Feet Samuels," "Dancing Dan." All the stories about these characters are written in the continuous present tense, as though Runyon himself is one of the barflies, spinning a yarn into his neighbour's ear, making a chuckly anecdote out of his friends' misfortunes and misadventures. For example: "This Heine Schmitz is a very influential citizen of Harlem, where he has large interests in beer, and it is by no means violating any confidence to tell you that Heine Schmitz will just as soon blow your brains out as look at you. In fact, I hear sooner."

Once he had discovered this raffishly, down-at-heels, yet defiantly stylish world (or sub-world), and had discovered a style of narrating its doings, there was really no reason why Runyon shouldn't go on and on recounting anecdotes about it (much as Wodehouse, having invented Wooster and Jeeves, could set them in motion time after time). Runyon was, in fact, a prolific author. Quite apart from volumes of light verse, there were numerous collections of his short stories and a play. The verse and play need not detain us. They are lightweight, the verse reminiscent of poets like James Whitcomb Riley and Eugene Field, in that they tell folksy tales of lovable low-life characters, although in Runyon's case the characters were often of the city rather than of the country.

Of the volumes of short stories, perhaps the pick are *More Than Somewhat, Take It Easy, Furthermore*, and *My Old Man*. The best of the stories are hilariously funny, and Runyon manages effortlessly to capture a style of speech which, in its aping of "polite" or "standard" American English, tells one only too graphically of the difficulties immigrant communities had in learning a new tongue, while desperately – or naturally – keeping to modes of expression that belonged to their mother-tongue. Who can forget Nathan Detroit's anxious questioning of ever-loving Adelaide: "Would you say that some doll might fall for some guy which you would not think she would do so?" Or Joe the Joker's remark that "Only last night, Frankie Ferocious sends for Ropes and tells him he will appreciate it as a special favour if Ropes will bring me to him in a sack"?

One could, of course, object that the real world of the Mafia is so cynically immoral that laughter about it is indefensible. Perhaps. But against that it has to be said that Runyon's world is no more real than the world of the Woosters, or of Blandings. In its own way, however, it is just as funny.

                                                              —John Lucas

RUSKIN, John. English. Born in London, 8 February 1819. Educated at the Reverend Dale's School, Peckham, London, 1834–35; Christ Church, Oxford (Newdigate Prize for poetry, 1839), 1836–42, B.A. 1842, M.A. 1843. Married Euphemia Chalmers Gray in 1848 (divorced, 1854; she subsequently married Millais). Writer on art, and subsequently on economics and social structure, from 1842; visited the Continent, especially Italy, on numerous occasions throughout his life; championed the Pre-Raphaelite Brotherhood from 1851; lectured throughout England, 1855–70; sorted and catalogued the Turner bequest to the National Gallery, 1857; Rede Lecturer, Cambridge, 1867; first Slade Professor of Fine Art, Oxford University, 1869–79, 1883–84; suffered from recurrent mental breakdowns from 1870; lived at Brantwood, on Coniston Lake, from 1871; founded the Company of St. George, to carry out his economic doctrines, 1871, and wrote the company's journal *Fors Clavigera*, 1871–84; founded an art school in Oxford, a school in Camberwell, London, and Whitelands College, Chelsea, London. D.C.L.: Oxford University, 1893. Honorary Student, Christ Church, Oxford, 1858; Honorary Fellow, Corpus Christi College, Oxford, 1871; Honorary Member, Royal Society of Painters in Water-Colours, 1873; Fellow, Royal Geological Society, Royal Zoological Society, and Royal Institute of British Architects. *Died 20 January 1900.*

PUBLICATIONS

Collections

> *Works,* edited by E. T. Cook and A. D. O. Wedderburn.   39 vols., 1903–12.
> *Ruskin Today* (selections), edited by Kenneth Clark.   1967.

Prose

> *Modern Painters: Their Superiority in the Art of Landscape Painting to All the Ancient Masters.*   5 vols., 1843–60.
> *The Seven Lamps of Architecture.*   1849.
> *The Stones of Venice.*   3 vols., 1851–53.
> *Notes on the Construction of Sheepfolds.*   1851.
> *Pre-Raphaelitism.*   1851; edited by Laurence Binyon, 1907.
> *The King of the Golden River; or, The Black Brothers: A Legend of Styrica* (juvenile).   1851; edited by M. L. Becker, 1946.
> *Giotto and His Works in Padua.*   3 vols., 1853–60.
> *Lectures on Architecture and Painting.*   1854.
> *The Harbours of England.*   1856.
> *The Elements of Drawing in Three Letters to Beginners.*   1857.
> *The Political Economy of Art.*   1857.
> *The Two Paths, Being Lectures on Art and Its Application to Decoration and Manufacture.*   1859.
> *The Elements of Perspective Arranged for the Use of Schools.*   1859.
> *Unto This Last: Four Essays on the First Principles of Political Economy.*   1862; edited by J. D. C. Monfries and G. E. Hollingsworth, 1931.
> *Sesame and Lilies: Two Lectures.*   1865.
> *An Inquiry into Some of the Conditions at Present Affecting the Study of Architecture in Our Schools.*   1865.
> *The Ethics of the Dust: Ten Lectures to Little Housewives on the Elements of Crystallisation.*   1866; edited by R. O. Morris, 1914.

The Crown of Wild Olive: Three Lectures on Work, Traffic, and War. 1866; edited by W. F. Melton, with *The Queen of the Air*, 1919.

Time and Tide by Weare and Tyne: Twenty-Five Letters to a Working Man of Sunderland on the Laws of Work. 1867; edited by P. Kaufman, 1928.

The Queen of the Air, Being a Study of the Greek Myths of Cloud and Storm. 1869; edited by W. F. Melton, with *The Crown of Wild Olive*, 1919.

Lectures on Art. 1870; revised edition, 1887.

Fors Clavigera: Letters to the Workmen and Labourers of Great Britain. 8 vols., 1871–84.

The Relation Between Michael Angelo and Tintoret. 1872.

The Sepulchral Monuments of Italy. 1872.

Proserpina: Studies of Wayside Flowers. 10 vols., 1875–86.

Deucalion: Collected Studies of the Lapse of Waves and Life of Stones. 9 vols., 1875–83.

Mornings in Florence, Being Simple Studies of Christian Art for English Travellers. 6 vols., 1876–77.

Guide to the Principal Pictures in the Academy of Fine Arts in Venice, Arranged for English Travellers. 2 vols., 1877; revised edition, 1891.

St. Mark's Rest: The History of Venice, Written for the Help of the Few Travellers Who Still Care for Her Monuments. 6 vols., 1877–84.

Notes on Drawings by Turner. 1878; revised edition, 1878.

Notes on Drawings by Ruskin. 1879.

The Laws of Fiesole: A Familiar Treatise on the Elementary Principles and Practice of Drawing and Painting. 1879.

Elements of English Prosody for Use in St. George's Schools. 1880.

Arrows of the Chace, Being a Collection of Scattered Letters Published Chiefly in the Daily Newspapers 1840–1880, edited by A. D. O. Wedderburn. 2 vols., 1880.

Our Fathers Have Told Us: Sketches of the History of Christendom for Boys and Girls. 5 vols., 1880–83.

The Art of England: Lectures. 1884.

The Pleasures of England: Lectures. 1884.

On the Old Road: A Collection of Miscellaneous Essays 1834–85, edited by A. D. O. Wedderburn. 2 vols., 1885; revised edition, 3 vols., 1899.

Praeterita: Outlines of Scenes and Thoughts Perhaps Worthy of Memory in My Past Life. 3 vols., 1886–89.

Dilecta: Correspondence, Diary Notes, and Extracts from Books, Illustrating Praeterita. 3 vols., 1886–1900.

Hortus Inclusus: Messages from the Wood to the Garden, edited by A. Fleming. 1887.

Ruskiniana (letters and lectures), edited by A. D. O. Wedderburn. 2 vols., 1890–92.

Letters upon Subjects of General Interest, edited by T. J. Wise. 1892.

Letters to William Ward, edited by T. J. Wise. 2 vols., 1892.

Stray Letters to a London Bibliophile, edited by T. J. Wise. 1892.

Three Letters and an Essay, edited by H. P. Dale. 1893.

Verona and Other Lectures, edited by W. H. Collingwood. 1894.

Letters on Art and Literature, edited by T. J. Wise. 1894.

Letters to Ernest Chesneau, edited by T. J. Wise. 1894.

Letters to a College Friend. 1894.

Letters to Rev. F. J. Faunthorpe, edited by T. J. Wise. 1894.

Ruskin on Music, edited by A. M. Wakefield. 1894.

Ruskin on Education, edited by W. Jolly. 1894.

Studies in Both Arts, Being Ten Subjects Drawn and Described by Ruskin, edited by W. G. Collingwood. 1895.

Letters to Rev. A. F. Malleson, edited by T. J. Wise. 1896.

Letters to F. J. Furnivall, edited by T. J. Wise. 1897.

Letters to MG and HG. 1903.
Letters to C. E. Norton, edited by Norton. 2 vols., 1903.
Comments on the Divina Commedia, edited by G. P. Huntington. 1903.
The Cestus of Aglaia. 1905.
The Solitary Warrior: New Letters, edited by John Howard Whitehouse. 1929.
Letters to Francesca, and Memoirs of the Alexanders, edited by L. G. Swett. 1931.
Letters to Bernard Quaritch 1867–88, edited by C. Q. Wrentmore. 1938.
Friends of a Lifetime: Letters to F.C.C., edited by V. Meynell. 1940.
The Gulf of Years: Letters to Kathleen Olander, edited by R. Unwin. 1953.
Letters from Venice 1851–52, edited by J. L. Bradley. 1955.
The Diaries, edited by Joan Evans and John Howard Whitehouse. 3 vols., 1956–59.
The Winnington Letters: Correspondence with Margaret Alexis Bell and the Children at Winnington Hall, edited by Van Akin Burd. 1969.
The Brantwood Diary, edited by Helen Gill Viljoen. 1971.
Ruskin in Italy: Letters to His Parents, edited by Harold L. Shapiro. 1972.
Sublime and Beautiful: Letters to Louisa, Marchioness of Waterford, Anna Blunden, and Ellen Heaton, edited by Virginia Surtees. 1972.

Verse

Salsette and Elephanta. 1839.
Poems. 1850.
Poems, edited by W. G. Collingwood. 2 vols., 1891.
Poems. 1906.
A Walk in Chamouni and Other Poems, edited by R. Tutin. 1908.

Other

Collected Works. 15 vols., 1861–63.
Collected Works. 11 vols., 1871–80.
Selected Works. 8 vols., 1885.
Collected Works (Brantwood Edition). 22 vols., 1891–92.
Selections, edited by W. G. Collingwood. 2 vols., 1893.

Editor, *The Story of Ida: Epitaph on an Etrurian Tomb,* by Francesca Alexander. 1883.
Editor, *Dame Wiggings of Lee and Her Seven Wonderful Cats.* 1885.

Bibliography: in *Works,* 1912; *Ruskin: A Bibliography 1900–74* by Kirk H. Beetz, 1976.

Reading List: *Ruskin: Renascence,* 1946, and *Ruskin, Prophet of the Good Life,* 1948, both edited by John Howard Whitehouse, and *Vindication of Ruskin,* 1950, by Whitehouse; *Ruskin, The Great Victorian* by D. Leon, 1949; *Ruskin: The Portrait of a Prophet* by Peter Quennell, 1949; *Ruskin* by Joan Evans, 1954; *The Darkening Glass: A Portrait of Ruskin's Genius* by J. D. Rosenberg, 1961; *Ruskin* by Quentin Bell, 1963, revised edition, 1977; *The Failing Distance: The Autobiographical Impulse in Ruskin* by Jay Fellows, 1975; *Ruskin and Venice* by Robert Hewison, 1978.

*   *   *

   John Ruskin is one of the great theorists and prose writers of the 19th century. His theories of beauty, form, and the ideal as he applied them to art and to life are essential to the modern concept of art as a primary expression of society. His revelation of abstract values in architecture, painting, and sculpture have led to our present terms "functionalism" and "organic form."

The first volume of his work *Modern Painters*, published when he was 24, is a romantic evocation of the grandeur of nature in the tradition of Wordsworth, as well as a detailed study of the paintings of J. M. W. Turner whom Ruskin defended from the prevalent schools of art. Ruskin's criteria of judgment combined with his precocious and persuasive literary style made him an instant success. He was greatly admired throughout his lifetime, though some of his later works were controversial.

The succeeding four volumes of *Modern Painters*, which he worked on over a period of eighteen years, continue intermittently his diverse themes of nature, beauty, and great art and their relations to moral values. Ruskin was a visionary: from the Alps to the cathedrals of Normandy he found examples of truth, fidelity to nature, and morality. He appreciated the handiwork of God as much as the gothic window traceries at Rouen; he analyzed both in detail, producing eloquent descriptions and evocations and, more importantly as he developed, moral lessons and meanings alike in the Alps as the Cathedral.

He made minute and encyclopedic studies of an area or an artist which prepared him to make grand generalizations when he wrote. He prepared drawings of many of the settings of Turner's own work so he was able to say with exactitude what changes Turner had made in the actual landscape. For *The Stones of Venice*, he studied every building and ornament in five square miles, making careful tracings or renderings of many, and so thoroughly acquainted himself with Venetian history that the history and the art it produced are woven together meaningfully in the text: he leads the reader to perceive that the two are inseparable in fact. In the society that created the Gothic architecture of Venice, the Catholic Middle Ages, Ruskin had found his dream society where the moral natures of society and its artists could be complementary, where men's souls could prosper.

His vision had shifted from "the art object to its creator," his biographer J. D. Rosenberg wrote, and from the creator to the society that formed him. Because "all great art is the work of the whole living creature, body and soul, and chiefly soul," Ruskin believed countries should cherish the human lives and energies which are their souls. His vision of morality involved the whole man, the whole production and tradition of a society. The art of living became his subject. In contrast to his early works that relate him to the romantic, aesthetic movements of the Victorian period, his later writings connect him to the magnificent Victorian tradition of social criticism and to men like Carlyle, Dickens, and William Morris. His first effort to raise the social conscience was *Unto This Last*, a book considered so radical that Ruskin was denounced as a subversive. He wrote inspired social criticism that vividly and persuasively communicated his outrage. His writings were influential in founding the British Labour Party, and most of his suggestions have been adopted since his death in 1900, among them free state education, social security funds, rent control, and the common market.

He remained essentially a poet and a dreamer: a popularizer, not an activist, who preferred to treat the whole man and the soul. He had preached for Turner, for the high seriousness of art, then preached for social reform; finally he turned his pen to reform the inner man. He commenced a series of lectures throughout England, ending with the Slade Professorship at Oxford, published later under the titles *Sesame and Lilies* and *The Crown of Wild Olive*; and he wrote a series of letters, *Time and Tide*, and *Munera Pulveris* (published in *Collected Works*, 1871) all in the attempt to awaken deadened moral sensations in mankind. He did not abandon his social conscience; he incorporated it into the entirety of his thought.

His mind collapsing under personal anguish and the frustration of his efforts to revolutionize England, Ruskin turned to more autobiographical writing. With his little masterpieces, "The Mystery of Life and Its Arts" and "Art and Morals," he found a medium for self-expression that loosed his mature powers – the personal essay. He wrote his new essays on a bewildering number of subjects – from art to ornithology. At this point his mind had split into opposing channels of hope and despair. While he wrote the gloomy, enraged *Fors Clavigera*, he also began his autobiography, *Praeterita*, which freed his mind from the misery of the present by recreating the harmonious and beautiful past. His final works, *Praeterita* and "The Bible of Amiens" (which influenced Proust profoundly), are masterpieces of style and individuality revealed. The greatness of *Praeterita*, apart from the personality it uncovers, is the uncanny and effortless eloquence that captures so movingly the child's mind: Ruskin observes himself as well as he had done works of art.

His isolated, puritanical childhood, described in his autobiography, had trained his mind to close observation and heightened visual pleasure; at the same time his mother's Scotch Protestantism gave him a sense of high moral purpose and seriousness. He would not tolerate the "Grand Style" of painters like Reynolds, or the blind, greedy capitalism of *The Wealth of Nations*, and he could not bear pretension in others or himself. His powerful words communicated his strange inner dreams of good and evil, his belief in nature as a vital, unstructured power, and his dreams for society. He devoted his life to persuading the eye and educating the public first in art and then in duty. He was a passionate revolutionary and a brilliant critic and artist apart from his crusades. His literary criticism, collected as *Fiction, Fair and Foul*, in *Works*, demonstrates the rare perception and insight he brought to everything. Although he has been criticized for obsessive, formless ranting, his mastery of English prose with the flexibility, richness and lyricism of his style and his highly personal point of view give his voluminous, digressive writings an organic unity.

—Brady Nordland

RUTHERFORD, Mark. Pseudonym for William Hale White. English. Born in Bedford, 22 December 1831. Educated at Bedford Modern School; studied for the ministry at the Countess of Huntingdon's College, Cheshunt, and at New College, St. John's Wood, London (expelled); in later years preached in Unitarian chapels. Married 1) Harriet Arthur in 1856 (died, 1891), five sons and one daughter; 2) Dorothy Vernon in 1911. Entered the Civil Service as a Clerk in the Office of the Registrar-General, Somerset House, London, 1854; transferred to the Admiralty, 1858; Assistant Director of Contracts, 1879 until he retired, 1891; briefly served as Registrar of Births, Marriages, and Deaths for the Borough of Marylebone; London Correspondent for *The Scotsman*. Died 14 March 1913.

PUBLICATIONS

Fiction

The Autobiography of Mark Rutherford, Dissenting Minister.   1881.
Mark Rutherford's Deliverance, Being the Second Part of His Autobiography.   1885; revised edition, 1888.
The Revolution in Tanner's Lane.   1887.
Miriam's Schooling and Other Papers.   1890.
Catharine Furze.   1893.
Clara Hopgood.   1896.

Other

An Argument for an Extension of the Franchise.   1866.
A Dream of Two Dimensions.   1884.

The Inner Life of the House of Commons.   2 vols., 1897.
*A Description of the Wordsworth and Coleridge Manuscripts in the Possession of Mr. T.
   North Longman.*   1897.
An Examination of the Charge of Apostasy Against Wordsworth.   1898.
Pages from a Journal, with Other Papers.   1900; *More Pages, with Other Papers,* 1910;
   Last Pages, edited by Dorothy V. White, 1915.
John Bunyan.   1904.
The Early Life of Mark Rutherford (William Hale White) (autobiography).   1913.
Letters to Three Friends, edited by Dorothy V. White.   1924.

Editor, *Selections from Dr. Johnson's Rambler.*   1907.
Editor, *The Life of John Sterling,* by Thomas Carlyle.   1907.

Translator, *Ethic,* by Spinoza.   1893.
Translator, *Tractatus de Intellectus Emendatione,* by Spinoza.   1895.

Bibliography: *Rutherford: A Bibliography of First Editions* by S. Nowell-Smith, 1930.

Reading List: *Religion and Art of White* by W. H. Stone, 1954; *Rutherford: A Biography of
White* by C. M. MacLean, 1955; *White (Rutherford)* by I. Stock, 1956; "The Novels of
Rutherford" by P. Thomson, in *Essays in Criticism 14,* 1964; *The Literature of Change:
Studies in the Nineteenth-Century Provincial Novel* (on Rutherford, Gaskell, and Hardy) by
John Lucas, 1978.

                              *   *   *

   Mark Rutherford (the pseudonym of William Hale White) was the author of six novels and
some notes and journals. His work provides a fine example of the puritan temper that is
widespread in English thought and character. Growing up in Victorian Bedfordshire, deeply
rooted in the traditions of radical dissent, he freely acknowledged his spiritual kinship with
John Bunyan. At the same time no contemporary dissenting creed could satisfy him, and he
was expelled from his theological college for doubting the literal truth of the Bible. He is
therefore a puritan outside the chapel walls and, with Bunyan, one of the rare examples of the
Puritan as novelist. If nothing else, his writing serves to remind us that a puritan need not be
a bore or a philistine.
   His novels are close to his own experience and distinguished by a profound moral
earnestness. Best known are his first two books, *The Autobiography of Mark Rutherford* and
its sequel *Mark Rutherford's Deliverance.* Of the remaining novels, *The Revolution in
Tanner's Lane* is the most wide-ranging and powerful, but each of the others, *Miriam's
Schooling, Catharine Furze, Clara Hopgood,* has something to recommend it. The Mark
Rutherford of *The Autobiography* and *Deliverance* grows up in a narrow provincial Victorian
world. He becomes a dissenting minister but is appalled at the narrow illiberal life of the
chapel community and turns away from it in search of a more genuine salvation. He is
profoundly influenced by Wordsworth and he finally finds peace in a kind of stoic, humanist
deism. Although the writer's interest is mainly in inner experience he has a shrewd eye for
the details of outward life also. He sharply observed and accurately recalled the social scene,
and he gives us vivid and authentic glimpses of the life of non-comformist communities in
provincial towns. The puritan honesty and integrity of his mind give a fine clarity and purity
to his prose. He has qualities of directness and simplicity that are rare in the Victorian period.
Although he admired Carlyle, his own writing belongs rather to the tradition of Bunyan,
Defoe, and Cobbett.

                                                                          —Alan Warner

SAKI. Pseudonym for Hector Hugh Munro. Scottish. Born in Akyab, Burma, 18 December 1870, of an English Army family; raised in Pilton, Devon. Educated at a private school in Exmouth, Devon, 1882–85; Bedford Grammar School, 1885–87. Served as a private, then corporal, in the 22nd Royal Fusiliers in World War I, 1914–16; died in action in France, 1916. Served in the military police in Burma, 1893–95, then returned to Devon; settled in London, 1900; thereafter a full-time writer; wrote political satires for the *Westminster Gazette*; Correspondent for the *Morning Post* in the Balkans, 1902, Warsaw and St. Petersburg, 1904–06, and Paris, 1906–08; wrote political and other sketches for various newspapers from 1908; parliamentary commentary writer for *Outlook*, 1914. *Died 13 November 1916.*

PUBLICATIONS

Collections

> *Works.* 8 vols., 1926–27.
> *Short Stories.* 1930.
> *The Novels and Plays.* 1933.
> *The Bodley Head Saki*, edited by J. W. Lambert. 1963.

Fiction and Sketches

> *Reginald* (stories). 1904.
> *Reginald in Russia and Other Sketches.* 1910.
> *The Chronicles of Clovis* (stories). 1911.
> *The Unbearable Bassington.* 1912.
> *When William Came: A Story of London under the Hohenzollerns.* 1913.
> *Beasts and Super-Beasts* (stories). 1914.
> *The Toys of Peace and Other Papers.* 1919.
> *The Square Egg and Other Sketches, with Three Plays.* 1924.

Plays

> *The East Wing*, in *Lucas' Annual*, 1914.
> *The Watched Pot*, with Cyril Maude (produced 1924). In *The Square Egg*, 1924.
> *The Death Trap*, and *Karl-Ludwig's Window*, in *The Square Egg.* 1924.
> *The Miracle-Merchant*, in *One-Act Plays for Stage and Study 8*, edited by Alice
>   Gerstenberg. 1934.

Other

> *The Rise of the Russian Empire.* 1900.
> *The Westminster Alice.* 1902.

Reading List: *The Satire of Saki* by G. J. Spears, 1963; "The Performing Lynx" by V. S. Pritchett, in *The Working Novelist*, 1965; *Munro (Saki)* by Charles H. Gillen, 1969.

*   *   *

Saki has no formula. His wit and imagination are fertile in many spheres – in creating amusing names (never too extravagant to be incredible), in turning a cliché or an idiom inside out, in deflating almost any sort of pretention or pomposity, even disillusion, in unexpected descriptions of nature. Yet there does seem to be a recurrent theme or subject for much of his fiction, both stories and novels – the incongruous, the pagan, the outsider.

Usually social incongruity is seen in the context of middle and upper class or intellectual life in London (or the country houses that serve it). Frivolity, the rivalries of hostesses, the petty gossip or secrets of the social butterflies (epitomized by Clovis Sangrail) are at the bottom of some of the cleverest stories. Tobermory, a cat who has been taught to speak, almost spoils a house-party by revealing all the secrets it has overheard in out-of-the-way places, until it is killed by "the big Tom from the Rectory." A pair of childhood sweethearts (in the playlet "The Baker's Dozen") meet aboard ship after many years and find themselves free to marry, only to have the union threatened by the fact that they have 13 children between them (the possibility of disowning one because of its depravity is disallowed: "You can't expect a boy to be vicious until he's been to a good school"). Lucas Croyden, a man about town, has it pointed out to him by his friends "that it was a doubtful kindness to initiate a boy from behind a drapery counter into the blessedness of the higher catering," only to have the boy taken up by Lucas's aunt ("Adrian"). The editor of the *Cathedral Monthly* is discovered to write music-hall songs ("The Secret Sin of Septimus Brope").

There is a touch of the bizarre in several stories. A man has himself tattooed by a brilliant Italian master of the craft with The Fall of Icarus (he had expected a battle scene, but was satisfied nonetheless), and is then prevented from leaving the country because of a law which forbids the export of Italian works of art ("The Background"). A painter makes a hit with *Ox in a Morning-Room, Late Autumn* and *Barbary Apes Wrecking a Boudoir* ("The Stalled Ox"). Other stories are even more bizarre. In "Sredni Bashtar," a young boy manages to have his hated guardian, Mrs. De Ropp, killed by his large polecat-ferret. The title character of "Gabriel-Ernest" is actually a werewolf, and Pan (with "golden and equivocal" laughter) lives in the woods near Yessney, and causes the death of Mortimer Seltoun's pugnacious wife ("The Music on the Hill").

Yet many of the characters Saki writes about are politicians, and this hints at an underlying seriousness. The fact that Saki was a parliamentary commentator gives point to remarks like "The public missed in him that touch of blatancy which it looks for in its rising public men" or "Behind his careful political flippancy and cynicism one might also detect a certain careless sincerity, which would probably in the long run save him from moderate success, and turn him into one of the brilliant failures of the day." And when Arlington Stringham makes a joke in the House of Commons, his wife immediately suspects him of seeing another woman; a later remark by Stringham ("the people of Crete unfortunately make more history than they can consume locally") puts paid to the marriage.

Saki's novels, *When William Came* and *The Unbearable Bassington*, are both in fact serious works. Each of them inspects the sort of incongruity the stories deal with, but from a different angle. *When William Came* (published in 1913) assumes a quick defeat of England by Germany in the coming war, and centers on Murray Yeovil, absent from England during the war, and not prepared to accept defeat and occupation with the same pragmatism his wife shows. Cicely, in fact, is a social hostess, eager to keep her salon in London at all costs; Murray retreats to the country, though not without compromise. *The Unbearable Bassington* centers on Comus Bassington and his mother, Francesca. Though Comus is rather like the frivolous Clovis Sangrail, his pagan name and description ("His large green-grey eyes seemed for ever asparkle with goblin mischief and the joy of revelry, and the curved lips might have been those of some wickedly-laughing faun; one almost expected to see embryo horns fretting the smoothness of his sleek dark hair") put him into a different category. Almost as if deliberately to spite his mother (a carefully observed character), he refuses to make his way in the compromising world of London society; he loves the sparkling world of London, but he courts the failure which sends him to one of the colonies, and his death. A hint of the strong love between himself and his mother gives psychological truth to the picture, even though

Francesca is controlled – on the surface, at least – by her social position and possessions. The ironical conclusion to the novel is that her treasured painting is revealed to be a copy at the same time that she learns of Comus's death; but her grief is for Comus, despite the "mockery of consolation" she receives from her brother.

Saki can be compared to Wilde, to Firbank, to Noël Coward, even to Orwell (because of the Burma connection); V. S. Pritchett calls *The Unbearable Bassington* a footnote to James's *The Spoils of Poynton*. But Saki is unmistakably himself: a witty and, despite his cruelty, a moving writer.

—George Walsh

SALINGER, J(erome) D(avid). American. Born in New York City, 1 January 1919. Educated in New York City public schools; at Valley Forge Military Academy, Pennsylvania; New York University; Columbia University, New York. Served as a Staff Sergeant in the 4th Infantry Division of the United States Army, 1942–46. Married Claire Douglas in 1953 (divorced, 1967); one son and one daughter. Writer from 1940; contributed to *The New Yorker*, 1948–59. Lives in New Hampshire.

PUBLICATIONS

Fiction

The Catcher in the Rye. 1951.
Nine Stories. 1953; as *For Esmé – With Love and Squalor, and Other Stories.* 1953.
Franny and Zooey (stories). 1961.
Raise High the Roof Beam, Carpenters, and Seymour: An Introduction. 1963.

Reading List: *The Fiction of Salinger* by Frederick L. Gwynn and Joseph L. Blotner, 1960; *Salinger and the Critics* edited by William F. Belcher and James W. Lee, 1962; *Salinger* by Warren French, 1963; *Studies in Salinger* edited by Marvin Laser and Norman Fruman, 1963; *Salinger: A Critical and Personal Portrait* by Henry A. Grunwald, 1964; *Salinger* by James E. Miller, 1965.

*   *   *

Of his writings, J. D. Salinger has so far wished to preserve only a novel and thirteen short stories, all published between 1948 and 1959, mostly in *The New Yorker*. Despite this limited body of work, Salinger was, at least between 1951 and 1963, the most popular American fiction writer among serious young persons and many alienated adults because of the way in which he served as a spokesman for the feelings of his generation. Thus his work is of unique interest as evidence of the sensibility of those times.

Salinger had taken a short-story writing course under Whit Burnett, the influential editor of *Story*, which gave many important American fiction writers their start. Salinger's first published work, "The Young Folks," appeared there in 1940. Like much of his later work, this slight piece contrasted the behavior of, on one hand, shy, sensitive and, on the other, tough, flippant, unfeeling young upper-middle-class urbanites. During the 1940's, Salinger published (in *Story* and most of the popular slick magazines like *Collier's*) another nineteen stories that he has not allowed to be collected. Some of these, like "This Sandwich Has No Mayonnaise," are of interest for introducing a character named Holden Caulfield, who resembles the later protagonist of *The Catcher in the Rye*, but who dies during World War II. Most are very short, heavily ironic tales about troubled young people defeated by what Holden Caulfield would call "the phony world." The only one of great interest in the light of Salinger's later achievement is the longest, "The Inverted Forest," a cryptic tale about an artist's relationship to society. The lines quoted from the poetry of the central figure, Raymond Ford — "Not wasteland, but a great inverted forest/with all the foliage underground" — suggest that all beauties are internal, so that the artist is exempt from external responsibilities.

The question of the sensitive individual's responsibility to the world remains the focal question in all of Salinger's better known fiction. *The Catcher in the Rye* is the comically grotesque account of Holden Caulfield's two-and-a-half-day odyssey through the waste land of New York City at Christmas time after he decides to quit his fashionable prep school. Holden dreams of escaping the city and going out west where he could build "a little cabin somewhere ... and live there for the rest of my life ... near the woods, but not right in them" (a description that foreshadows almost exactly the New England retreat where Salinger himself has lived for the past twenty years). In the speech that gives the novel its title, he tells his little sister Phoebe that the one thing he would like to do is stand guard over "all these little kids playing some game in this big field of rye and all" and "catch everybody if they start to go over the cliff." But Holden learns, when he sees obscenities scratched on the walls of Phoebe's elementary school, that "You can't ever find a place that's nice and peaceful, because there isn't any." And watching Phoebe ride the Central Park carousel, he realizes, "The thing with kids is, if they want to grab for the gold ring, you have to let them do it, and not say anything." Wiser but sadder, he decides that he must return home rather than take the responsibility for leading Phoebe astray.

Although Salinger is most often identified as the author of this novel, Holden Caulfield, who finally compromises with his social responsibilities, is not the typical hero in Salinger's work. The stories that the author has chosen to preserve begin and end with accounts of the suicide of Seymour Glass, oldest son and spiritual guide to his six siblings of a New York Irish-Jewish theatrical family. In "A Perfect Day for Bananafish," the first of *Nine Stories*, we learn only the circumstances of Seymour's suicide in a Miami Beach hotel. In "Seymour: An Introduction," his brother and interpreter Buddy offers at last the explanation for the event: "The true artist-seer ... is mainly dazzled to death by his own scruples, the blinding shapes and colors of his own sacred human conscience."

The eleven stories published between these two carry us from the account of the suicide to the illumination of its significance, and reflect along the way Salinger's increasing absorption in oriental philosophies, especially Zen Buddhism. Four of *Nine Stories* — "Uncle Wiggily in Connecticut," "The Laughing Man," "Just Before the War with the Eskimos," and "Pretty Mouth and Green My Eyes" — offer, like *The Catcher in the Rye*, depressing pictures of people trapped in the "phony" world, but dreaming of a "nice" world. In four of the later stories, however, Salinger suggests that the grim situation might be ameliorated — "Down at the Dinghy" portrays Seymour's sister's reconciliation of her small son to a threatening world; "For Esmé — With Love and Squalor" is a triumphant epithalamion for a young girl who has done meaningful good in a warring world; "DeDaumier-Smith's Blue Period" is an amazingly successful description of a mystical experience that leads a young man to forsake aggressive ambitions; and the famous concluding story, "Teddy," presents a boy who has truly absorbed the Buddhist concept of the illusoriness of material life and is prepared to move serenely beyond it.

In the longer "Glass Saga" stories, Salinger focuses on Seymour's siblings and presents, in "Franny," the story of the youngest child's breakdown when confronted with the "ego" of the squalid world of college and theater. In "Zooey," her brother literally talks her out of her breakdown by assuming the voice of the departed Seymour, and counselling, "An artist's only concern is to shoot for some kind of perfection, and *on his own terms*, not anyone else's." "Raise High the Roof Beam, Carpenters" prefaces "Seymour: An Introduction" with Buddy's fond recollection of Seymour's violent responses to beauty and his supreme affront to the rituals of his urban caste when he persuades his intended to run off with him on their wedding day instead of submitting to a fancy ceremony.

Since these stories were collected in 1963, Salinger has published only "Hapworth 16, 1924," a labored account of seven-year-old Seymour's prodigious sexual and intellectual proclivities as revealed by a letter home from summer camp. In the one interview he has granted in recent years – to protest an unauthorized edition of his uncollected stories – Salinger protested that he is still writing constantly, but he denounced publication as "a terrible invasion" of his privacy.

—Warren French

SALTUS, Edgar (Evertson). American. Born in New York City, 8 October 1855. Educated at St. Paul's School, Concord, New Hampshire; studied briefly at Yale University, New Haven, Connecticut, the Sorbonne, Paris, University of Heidelberg, and University of Munich, 1872–76; Columbia University Law School, New York, 1876–80, LL.B. 1880, but never practiced law. Married 1) Helen Sturgis Read in 1883 (divorced, 1891); 2) Elsie Welsh Smith in 1895 (separated, 1901; died, 1911), one daughter; 3) Marie Giles in 1911. Settled in New York; writer from 1884; worked as an editor and compiler for P. F. Collier and Son, publishers, in the late 1890's. *Died 31 July 1921.*

PUBLICATIONS

Fiction

    Mr. Incoul's Misadventure. 1887.
    The Truth about Tristrem Varick. 1888.
    Eden. 1888.
    A Transaction in Hearts. 1889.
    A Transient Guest and Other Episodes. 1889.
    The Pace That Kills. 1889.
    Mary Magdalen. 1891.
    Imperial Purple. 1892.
    The Facts in the Curious Case of H. Hyrtl, Esq. 1892.
    Madame Sapphira: A Fifth Avenue Story. 1893.
    Enthralled: A Story of International Life. 1894.
    When Dreams Come True: A Story of Emotional Life. 1894.
    Purple and Fine Women. 1903.
    The Perfume of Eros: A Fifth Avenue Incident. 1905.
    Vanity Square: A Story of Fifth Avenue Life. 1906.
    Daughters of the Rich. 1909.

The Monster. 1912.
The Paliser Case. 1919.
The Ghost Girl, edited by Marie Saltus. 1922.

Verse

Poppies and Mandragora, edited by Marie Saltus. 1926.

Other

Balzac. 1884.
The Philosophy of Disenchantment. 1885.
The Anatomy of Negation. 1886.
Love and Lore. 1890.
The Pomps of Satan (essays). 1904.
Historia Amoris, A History of Love. 1906.
The Lords of the Ghostland: A History of the Ideal. 1907.
Oscar Wilde: An Idler's Impression. 1917.
The Gardens of Aphrodite. 1920.
The Imperial Orgy: An Account of the Tsars from the First to the Last. 1920.
Parnassians Personally Encountered, edited by Marie Saltus. 1923.
The Uplands of Dream (essays and poems), edited by Charles Honce. 1925.
Victor Hugo, and Golgotha: Two Essays, edited by Marie Saltus. 1925.

Editor, The Lovers of the World. 3 vols., n.d.

Translator, After-Dinner Stories from Balzac. 1886.
Translator, Tales Before Supper from Gautier and Merimée. 1887.

Reading List: Saltus, The Man by Marie Saltus, 1925; Saltus by Claire Sprague, 1968.

*   *   *

In 1884 Edgar Saltus began his literary career with Balzac, an introductory study which witnesses to his predominantly European culture. This was followed by his elegant popularisations of German contemporary pessimists, Schopenhauer and Hartmann, in The Philosophy of Disenchantment and The Anatomy of Negation. His first novel, Mr. Incoul's Misadventure, inaugurates the first, most successful phase of his fiction.

In 1891 Saltus published Mary Magdalen, reportedly originating in conversations with Oscar Wilde, the first of his impressionist quasi-histories. Imperial Purple, high-coloured portraits of the Roman emperors from Caesar to Heliogabalus, was deservedly popular, but the attempted emulation in Imperial Orgy, which presented the Russian Czars from Ivan the Terrible to Nicholas "the last," is considerably less achieved.

Mr. Incoul's Misadventure, in fact, is typical of Saltus's novels, with its pessimism, self-conscious style, occasional authentic glimpses of upper class life, melodramatic themes, and loose plotting: a millionaire coldly and ingeniously revenges himself on his wife and the man who loves her. The Truth about Tristram Varick, is more lucid in structure, with a "point of view" presented by the hero, though the incidents are hardly less melodramatic. Eden is less successful, but introduces us to what was to become Saltus's standard types of women: blonde Eve and darkly passionate, "fatal" Lilith. A Transaction in Hearts has an interesting "new" woman and a powerful story line. The Pace That Kills has a suicidal villain-hero who is a less attractive version of Incoul, while *Enthralled* is an extravaganza owing something to Hugo and Wilde's *The Picture of Dorian Gray*. In *When Dreams Come True*, a *bildungsroman* of sorts, Saltus breaks through his own sterotypes – the "fatal woman" emerges as a witty and balanced wife – and produces his best novel. The relationship with his first wife, from whom he was divorced in 1891, underlies his virulent novel *Madame Sapphira*.

The later novels are less satisfying. *The Perfume of Eros*, the best of them, memorably portrays a slum child for whom the wages of sin are success; a charming flapper is killed off when her moral situation threatens to become too complex. *Vanity Square* promises that critique of a cultured and bored society Saltus was well endowed to write, but, though embodying entertaining discussion of ideas, disentegrates into fable. In *Daughters of the Rich* Saltus moves from New York to Southern California, but it is inhabited by the familiar Saltus types and situations: "new" women, murder, and misunderstandings in love. Incest, duels, two unconsummated marriages, theosophy, and mildly Wildean wit hardly redeem *The Monster*. *The Paliser Case* is a faded version of *The Perfume of Eros*, and *The Ghost Girl* a mediocre Gothic novel.

Saltus's sometimes amusing short stories were written largely for popular consumption and are more melodramatic in plot and exotic in setting than the novels. The poetry was collected in *Poppies and Mandragora*; chiselled in a Parnassian manner, it faintly recalls Hérédia. The brief essay *The Gardens of Aphrodite*, which discusses the god of love as Eros-Don Juan, is interesting in itself and for the light it casts on Saltus's fiction. *Lords of the Ghostland* examines the major religions of the world, introducing theosophy for the first time. *Oscar Wilde: An Idler's Impression* agreeably records a friendship, mainly through reported conversations. French literature is the subject of *Parnassians Personally Encountered* and *Victor Hugo and Golgotha*; Saltus also translated Balzac, Merimée, and Gautier.

Saltus's importance is largely that of populariser of European *fin de siècle* modes and topics in the United States. He produced no masterpiece, but his pessimism, determinism, use of fable, allegory, and paradox suggest a poor man's Oscar Wilde, a Wilde without the drama, but a dweller in a high, slightly flashy Bohemia.

—Ian Fletcher

SANSOM, William. English. Born in London, 18 January 1912. Educated at Uppingham School and in Europe. Served in the London Fire Service in World War II. Married Ruth Grundy in 1954; one son and one stepson. Worked in a bank and an advertising agency, and as a scriptwriter; full-time writer from 1944. Recipient: Society of Authors Scholarship, 1946, and Bursary, 1947. Fellow, Royal Society of Literature, 1951. *Died 20 April 1976.*

PUBLICATIONS

Fiction

Fireman Flower and Other Stories.   1944.
Three (stories).   1946.
South: Aspects and Images from Corsica, Italy and Southern France (stories).   1948.

The Equilibriad (story). 1948.
The Body. 1949.
Something Terrible, Something Lovely (stories). 1948.
The Passionate North: Short Stories. 1950.
The Face of Innocence. 1951.
A Touch of the Sun (stories). 1952.
A Bed of Roses. 1954.
Lord Love Us (stories). 1954.
A Contest of Ladies (stories). 1956.
The Loving Eye. 1956.
Among the Dahlias and Other Stories. 1957.
The Cautious Heart. 1958.
Selected Short Stories. 1960.
The Last Hours of Sandra Lee. 1961; as *The Wild Affair,* 1964.
The Stories. 1963.
Goodbye. 1966.
The Ulcerated Milkman (stories). 1966.
The Vertical Ladder and Other Stories. 1969.
Hans Feet in Love. 1971.
The Marmelade Bird (stories). 1973.
A Young Wife's Tale. 1974.

Other

Jim Braidy: The Story of Britain's Firemen, with James Gordon and Stephen Spender. 1943.
Westminster in War. 1947.
Pleasures Strange and Simple (essays). 1953.
It Was Really Charlie's Castle (juvenile). 1953.
The Light That Went Out (juvenile). 1953.
The Icicle and the Sun. 1958.
The Bay of Naples. 1960.
Blue Skies, Brown Studies. 1961.
Away to It All. 1964.
Grand Tour Today. 1968.
Christmas. 1968; as *A Book of Christmas,* 1968.
The Birth of a Story. 1972.
Proust and His World. 1973.
Skimpy (juvenile). 1974.
Grandville. 1975.

Editor, *Choice: Some New Stories and Prose.* 1946.
Editor, *The Tell-Tale Heart and Other Stories,* by Edgar Allan Poe. 1948.

Translator, *Chendru: The Boy and the Tiger,* by Astrid Bergman. 1960.

Reading List: *Sansom: A Critical Assessment* by Paulette Michel-Michot, 1971.

* * *

William Sansom himself was more interested in his short fiction than in his novels, and it is upon them that his fame rests most securely. His work in both the short and the longer forms is spectacular in its variety of subject matter, method, and mood; it ranges from tales of fantasy, terror, and the macabre to expanded anecdotes and reminiscences, and conventional realism. But perhaps his outstanding hallmark is his marvelous creation of mood, atmosphere, and a sense of place, whether he is writing about the nightmarish experiences of a husband and wife on holiday in the Western Highlands ("A Waning Mood"); two murderous barbers – hoodlums on the side, one of whom is "known to do things to night watchmen, unnecessarily, that do not bear repeating" – confronting each other with drawn razors in a Soho barbershop ("Impatience"); an ageing matinee idol playing host to a bizarre group of international beauties when the familiar and the customary momentarily become permeated with the terror of the "hour of sundowners ... when the human beast, old moon-monkey, awakes to the idea of night. Hour of day's death, and dark beginning, uneasy hour of change" ("A Contest of Ladies"); or the memorable novella about Count Ludwig de Boda, man of universal detachment, alone and lost on a snowy road in the Austrian Alps, a road as "uneventful and empty" as his own life has become ("Episode at Gastein").

In a frequently-quoted comment, Sansom has stated that "a writer of my sort lives in a state of continual wonder at life. Even if the subject or episode is sordid, or plain humdrum, that amazement is still there. It is the sense of this which I want to convey to others." And convey it he does, with dazzling skill and a narrative excitement rare among his contemporaries. Facile story teller, weaver of magic webs, and trenchant social commentator, Sansom at his best is a writer to be cherished, "a link in an unfinished chain of long-term literary history," as one British reviewer commented years ago; a "caretaker to keep the lost domain of Arnheim green, and prevent the crack in the House of Usher from closing."

—William Peden

SANTAYANA, George. Spanish. Born in Madrid, 16 December 1863; emigrated with his family to the United States, 1872, but retained Spanish nationality. Educated at the Brimmer School, Boston; Boston Latin School; Harvard University, Cambridge, Massachusetts, 1882–86, B.A. 1886; studied in Berlin, 1886–88, and at King's College, Cambridge, 1896–97. Taught philosophy at Harvard University, 1889–1912: Professor of Philosophy, 1907–12; writer from 1894; Hyde Lecturer, the Sorbonne, Paris, 1905–06; lived in Europe from 1912, in England, 1914–18, and in Rome from 1920; Spencer Lecturer, Oxford University, 1923; lived in the Convent of Santa Stefano Rotondo, Rome, from 1939. Recipient: Royal Society of Literature Benson Medal, 1928; Columbia University Butler Gold Medal, 1945. *Died 26 September 1952.*

PUBLICATIONS

Collections

The Letters, edited by Daniel Cory.   1955.
Complete Poems, edited by William G. Holzberger.   1978.

Fiction

The Last Puritan: A Memoir in the Form of a Novel.   1935.

Plays

> *Lucifer: A Theological Tragedy.*   1899; revised edition, 1924.
> *The Marriage of Venus,* and *Philosophers at Court,* in *The Poet's Testament.*   1953.

Verse

> *Sonnets and Other Verses.*   1894.
> *A Hermit of Carmel and Other Poems.*   1891.
> *Poems.*   1922.
> *The Poet's Testament: Poems and Plays.*   1953.

Other

> *Lotze's System of Philosophy.*   1889; edited by Paul Grimley Kuntz, 1971.
> *Platonism in the Italian Poets.*   1896.
> *The Sense of Beauty, Being the Outlines of Aesthetic Theory.*   1896.
> *Interpretations of Poetry and Religion.*   1900.
> *The Life of Reason; or, The Phases of Human Progress.*   5 vols., 1905–06; revised
>   edition, with Daniel Cory, 1954.
> *Three Philosophical Poets: Lucretius, Dante, and Goethe.*   1910.
> *Winds of Doctrine: Studies in Continental Opinion.*   1913.
> *Egotism in German Philosophy.*   1916; as *The German Mind,* 1968.
> *Character and Opinion in the United States.*   1920.
> *Little Essays,* edited by Logan Pearsall Smith.   1920.
> *Soliloquies in England and Later Soliloquies.*   1922.
> *Scepticism and Animal Faith.*   1923.
> *Dialogues in Limbo.*   1925; revised edition, 1948.
> *Platonism and the Spiritual Life.*   1927.
> *The Realm of Essence.*   1927; *The Realm of Matter,* 1930; *The Realm of Truth,* 1937;
>   *The Realm of Spirit,* 1940; complete version, as *The Realms of Being,* 4 vols., 1942.
> *The Genteel Tradition at Bay.*   1931.
> *Five Essays.*   1933; as *Some Turns of Thought in Modern Philosophy,* 1933.
> *Obiter Scripter: Lectures, Essays, Reviews,* edited by Justus Buchler and Benjamin
>   Schwartz.   1936.
> *The Works.*   14 vols., 1936–37.
> *The Philosophy of Santayana,* edited by Irwin Edman.   1936.
> *The Background of My Life.*   1944; *The Middle Span,* 1945; *My Host the World,* 1953;
>   complete version, as *Persons and Places,* 1963.
> *The Idea of Christ in the Gospels; or, God in Man.*   1946.
> *Atoms of Thought: An Anthology of Thoughts,* edited by Ira D. Cardiff.   1950; as *The*
>   *Wisdom of Santayana,* 1964.
> *Dominations and Powers: Reflections on Liberty, Society, and Government.*   1951.
> *Essays in Literary Criticism,* edited by Irving Singer.   1956.
> *The Idler and His Works, and Other Essays,* edited by Daniel Cory.   1957.
> *Vagabond Scholar* (letters and dialogues with Bruno Lind).   1962.
> *Animal Faith and Spiritual Faith* (essays), edited by John Lachs.   1967.
> *The Genteel Tradition: Nine Essays,* edited by Douglas L. Wilson.   1967.
> *Santayana's America: Essays on Literature and Culture,* edited by James
>   Ballowe.   1967.
> *Santayana on America,* edited by Richard Carlton Lyon.   1968.
> *Selected Critical Writings,* edited by Norman Henfrey.   2 vols., 1968.

The Birth of Reason and Other Essays, edited by Daniel Cory. 1968.
Physical Order and Moral Liberty: Previously Unpublished Essays, edited by John and
  Shirley Lachs. 1969.

Translator, with others, *The Writings of Alfred de Musset*, revised edition, vol. 2. 1907.

Reading List: *The Philosophy of Santayana* by Paul S. Schilpp, 1940 (includes bibliography by
Shonig Terzian); *Santayana and the Sense of Beauty* by Richard Butler, 1956; *Santayana's
Aesthetics: A Critical Introduction* by Irving Singer, 1957; *Santayana: The Laters Years* by
Daniel Cory, 1963; *Santayana, Art, and Aesthetics* by Jerome Ashmore, 1966; *Santayana* by
Willard E. Arnett, 1968.

*   *   *

Born in Spain of a Roman Catholic family, George Santayana was a philosopher, an atheist
and a materialist, but retained a deep affection for the Roman Catholic Church, and died in
his old age, as an invalid, cared for by nuns in a Convent hospital in Rome. His working life
was spent as Harvard where his colleague, the optimistic pragmatist William James, disliked
Santayana intensely and felt that his dry, cynical sadness was corrupting. Few philosophers
of his time, if any (the possible rivals are F. H. Bradley and Henri Bergson) have written with
more charm and elegance. The defect of such a style in a philosopher, however, is that it lulls
the reader who should be alert for logical flaws; as a result, it would be hard to summarise
Santayana's thought. He might be described, perhaps, as a Platonising materialist; only
matter was eternal, man was mortal, but man could abstract from matter intellectual essences
which (except that they were final products, not sources of being) resembled Plato's world of
forms and ideas. Santayana is perhaps at his best as a thinker when he steps away from
abstract thinking and applies his mind to literature, as in *Three Philosophical Poets*, or to a
place that appealed to him, as in *Soliloquies in England*. In his novel, *The Last Puritan*, based
on his knowledge of young Americans through his teaching at Harvard, he tries to do justice
to the best sides of that American tradition which, with his innately hierarchical and
conservative attitude, he on the whole rejected.

—G. S. Fraser

SARGESON, Frank. New Zealander. Born in Hamilton, 23 March 1903. Educated at
Hamilton High School; University of New Zealand; admitted as a Solicitor of the Supreme
Court of New Zealand, 1926. Estates Clerk, New Zealand Public Trust, Wellington,
1928–29; has also worked as a journalist. Recipient: Centennial Literary Competition prize,
1940; New Zealand Government literary pension, 1947–68; Hubert Church Prize, 1952,
1968; Katherine Mansfield Award, 1965. D.H.L.: University of Auckland, 1974. Lives in
Auckland.

PUBLICATIONS

Fiction

Conversation with My Uncle and Other Sketches. 1936.
A Man and His Wife (stories). 1940.

When the Wind Blows. 1945.
That Summer and Other Stories. 1946.
I Saw in My Dream. 1949.
I for One.... 1954.
Collected Stories 1935–1963, edited by Bill Pearson. 1964; revised edition, as *The Stories 1935–1973*, 1973.
Memoirs of a Peon. 1965.
The Hangover. 1967.
Joy of the Worm. 1969.
Man of England Now (includes *Game of Hide and Seek* and *I for One ...*). 1972.
Sunset Village. 1976.

Plays

A Time for Sowing (produced 1961). In *Wrestling with the Angel,* 1964.
The Cradle and the Egg (produced 1962). In *Wrestling with the Angel,* 1964.
Wrestling with the Angel: Two Plays. 1964.

Other

Once Is Enough: A Memoir. 1972.
More Than Enough. 1975.
Never Enough! (memoirs). 1977.

Editor, *Speaking for Ourselves: A Collection of New Zealand Stories.* 1945.

Bibliography: in *The Stories,* 1973.

Reading List: *The Puritan and the Wolf: A Symposium of Critical Essays on the Work of Sargeson* edited by Helen Shaw, 1955; *Sargeson* by H. Winston Rhodes, 1969; *Sargeson in His Time* by Dennis McEldowney, 1977.

*   *   *

Thirty years ago Frank Sargeson already occupied a pre-eminent position among New Zealand prose-writers on the strength of the unspectacular but carefully crafted short stories which he had been producing since the mid-1930's. Yet this body of work, though respected and influential, was very small, and he added only two book-length publications in the period up to 1964. As Sargeson had reached his sixties, it would have been pardonable then to suppose that his career was virtually over. But the publication of his *Collected Stories* in 1964 not only confirmed the excellence and exemplary quality of his achievement in the short-story form; it also initiated a remarkable late flowering: four novels, a brace of plays, two volumes of autobiography, novellas, and various contributions to periodicals. While extending his achievement, however, these writings of recent years have in general confirmed its nature and direction. Sargeson's chief virtues derive from a preoccupation with the distinctive contours of New Zealand speech, with language not as a mere tool for the writer but as his material, a medium which carries the imprint of a particular place and time.

Reading through his *Collected Stories*, arranged in chronological sequence, one notices an increasing sophistication of technique; yet throughout the steady development – from the direct and even moralistic sketches of early years, through the subtler artistry of stories like "A Man and His Wife," to the more inventive disposition of materials in stories of the 1950's and 1960's — certain essential elements stay constant. Most obviously, these are all very brief tales; they have a confined span of action; they deal with small groups of characters; they are almost always narrated from within the consciousness of one of these characters; and they keep strictly to an idiom appropriate to that consciousness, an idiom which is therefore often flat and muted. In short, the formal aspects of his stories are characterized by stringent limitation. Take for example "I've Lost My Pal" (*Conversation with My Uncle*). It contains only three characters, one of them the narrator, who simply relates how his friend came to be murdered by a fellow-worker. What gives it potency is the fact that we observe through eyes that do not see the whole truth. The very inadequacy of the narrator's concluding comments forces us to sift everything that has been said and make our own independent judgement about the attitudes of George the murderer, Tom the victim, and the narrator himself. This kind of experiment in attenuation is repeated in story after story, most impressively in the novella *That Summer*, in which a soft-hearted and almost simple-minded rolling stone called Bill recounts some of his experiences during a few weeks of the depression. He feels deeply, but cannot get beyond a formulaic slang in expressing his feelings. As he moves in random fashion from place to place we meet his few casual acquaintances; but although the setting is urban no sense of social relationships emerges, and although his dealings with other people are full of nuance he is not conscious of it. Sargeson's achievement in *That Summer* is to have utilized these self-imposed limitations in such a way that they give moving emphasis to the central thematic issues.

For his first novel, *I Saw in My Dream*, Sargeson abandoned the first-person narrative stance, but the point of view is still strictly limited. We remain within the narrow orbit of the central character's circumstances, and whatever occurs is refracted through his consciousness. The structure is essentially linear, having length without substantial breadth, and once again there is no attempt to depict directly an extensive social milieu. Society takes the shape of claustrophobic, puritanical family pressures.

Even more confined is the scale of *I for One ...*, a novella in diary form in which a very sheltered spinster reflects on her experiences over a brief period. The technique of narration is a little less reductive than in the earlier stories, since Katherine is sufficiently self-aware and articulate to be able to record happenings and feelings with some precision. But the action is as tightly circumscribed as ever; the little that does actually take place does so offstage.

Sargeson's most impressive single work is *Memoirs of a Peon*. Instead of the flat, laconic language of the short stories, he now couches his first-person narration in an elaborate style of comic circumlocution and bookish artifice. The wordy protagonist is Michael Newhouse, a latter-day suburban Casanova, and much of the story consists of his mock-heroic accounts of his amorous exploits and embarrassments. In an odd way, the verbosity becomes as limiting as the deadpan plainness had formerly been: since Newhouse processes his personal history periphrastically, there is a tendency for moral distinctions to be blurred while minutiae get focal attention.

In *The Hangover*, as in so much of his work, Sargeson directs his unblinking but not uncompassionate gaze towards an adolescent who is struggling to reconcile the disturbing facts of his widening world with the severe assumptions derived from a narrowly religious upbringing. Alan, with his hungover puritanism, is cast in the same mould as the central figures of "A Good Boy" (*Conversation with My Uncle*) and of *I Saw in My Dream*. Indeed, the anatomy of puritanism is Sargeson's obsessive subject. In *The Hangover* this familiarity of material is modified with some formal novelty: the narrative perspective shifts from time to time so that we are freed for a while from Alan's onion-peel mind to follow the thoughts or doings of some other person. Nevertheless, secondary characters are not numerous and are so treated that we regard them as subordinate parts of a simple design, economically drawn, whose main component is the frustrated Alan.

Joy of the Worm is an exercise in garrulity, and doesn't quite succeed. Material that might have made a fine sketch has been inflated to furnish 150 pages without acquiring real amplitude in the process. Sargeson has attempted something difficult: to sustain our interest in two bores, the Reverend James Bohun and his son Jeremy. Bohun senior is a bookworm whose chief joy is savouring Gibbon and Hooker – and reproducing their cadences in flatulent discourse of his own. (The "worm" of the title also signifies sexuality – both Bohuns are supposed to be splendidly potent – and mortality.) Bohun junior is a nonentity. There is something inert about this narrative; the inner action is as uneventful as the external. The relationship between father and son and the marital relationships of each are examined at some length, but nothing much is elicited. In an interview, Sargeson said he intended the book to be "a celebration of the Bohun vitality," but this quality fails to come through dramatically enough to be convincing. The novel is by no means merely tedious; Sargeson's mimic gift is amusingly displayed in the numerous letters, from various hands, which carry much of the story, and the reader who knows his Virgil and Catullus will relish some incidental allusions. But such things only thicken the texture without giving it a full-bodied flavour.

There is no room here for discussion of Sargeson's two plays, published together as *Wrestling with the Angel*, or of his three-part memoir. A fine capstone to his oeuvre appeared in 1976: *Sunset Village* is set in a cluster of pensioner flats which are suddenly exposed to public scrutiny when it seems that one of the inmates has been murdered. The old Sargesonian motif of sexual concealment reappears, and the satirical irony that pervades so much of his later work is again incisively present. In all, *Sunset Village* provides a pleasant blend of the formal economy which governed Sargeson's earliest writings and the mellow comedy which released such an unexpectedly prolific flow of new fiction in his autumnal years.

—Ian Reid

SAROYAN, William. American. Born in Fresno, California, 31 August 1908. Educated in Fresno public schools. Served in the United States Army, 1942–45. Married Carol Marcus in 1943 (divorced, 1949; remarried, 1951; divorced, 1952); one daughter and one son, the poet Aram Saroyan. Past occupations include grocery clerk, vineyard worker, post office employee; Clerk, Telegraph Operator, then Office Manager of the Postal Telegraph Company, San Francisco, 1926–28; Co-Founder, Conference Press, Los Angeles, 1936; Founder and Director, Saroyan Theatre, New York, 1942; Writer-in-Residence, Purdue University, Lafayette, Indiana, 1961. Recipient: New York Drama Critics Circle Award, 1940; Pulitzer Prize, 1940 (refused). Member, National Institute of Arts and Letters. Lives in Fresno, California.

PUBLICATIONS

Fiction

The Daring Young Man on the Flying Trapeze and Other Stories. 1934.
Inhale and Exhale (stories). 1936.
Three Times Three (stories). 1936.
Little Children (stories). 1937.
A Gay and Melancholy Flux: Short Stories. 1937.
Love, Here Is My Hat (stories). 1938.

A Native American (stories).   1938.
The Trouble with Tigers (stories).   1938.
Peace, It's Wonderful (stories).   1939.
3 Fragments and a Story.   1939.
My Name Is Aram (stories).   1940.
Saroyan's Fables.   1941.
The Insurance Salesman and Other Stories.   1941.
48 Saroyan Stories.   1942.
31 Selected Stories.   1943.
Some Day I'll Be a Millionaire: 34 More Great Stories.   1943.
The Human Comedy.   1943.
Dear Baby (stories).   1944.
The Adventures of Wesley Jackson.   1946.
The Saroyan Special: Selected Short Stories.   1948.
The Fiscal Hoboes (stories).   1949.
*The Twin Adventures: The Adventures of Saroyan: A Diary; The Adventures of Wesley
    Jackson: A Novel.*   1950.
The Assyrian and Other Stories.   1950.
Rock Wagram.   1951.
Tracy's Tiger.   1951.
The Laughing Matter.   1953; as *The Secret Story*, 1954.
The Whole Voyald and Other Stories.   1956.
Mama, I Love You.   1956.
Papa, You're Crazy.   1957.
Love (stories).   1959.
Boys and Girls Together.   1963.
One Day in the Afternoon of the World.   1964.
After Thirty Years: The Daring Young Man on the Flying Trapeze (includes
    essays).   1964.
Best Stories of Saroyan.   1964.
My Kind of Crazy Wonderful People: 17 Stories and a Play.   1966.

Plays

The Man with the Heart in the Highlands, in *Contemporary One-Act Plays*, edited by
    William Kozlenko.   1938; revised version, as *My Heart's in the Highlands* (produced
    1939), 1939.
The Time of Your Life (produced 1939).   1939.
The Hungerers (produced 1945).   1939.
A Special Announcement (broadcast 1940).   1940.
Love's Old Sweet Song (produced 1940).   In *Three Plays*, 1940.
*Three Plays: My Heart's in the Highlands, The Time of Your Life, Love's Old Sweet
    Song.*   1940.
Subway Circus.   1940.
Something about a Soldier (produced 1940).
Hero of the World (produced 1940).
The Great American Goof (ballet scenario; produced 1940).   In *Razzle Dazzle*, 1942.
Radio Play (broadcast 1940).   In *Razzle Dazzle*, 1942.
The Ping Pong Game (produced 1945).   1940.
Sweeney in the Trees (produced 1940).   In *Three Plays*, 1941.
The Beautiful People (produced 1941).   In *Three Plays*, 1941.
*Three Plays: The Beautiful People, Sweeney in the Trees, Across the Board on Tomorrow
    Morning.*   1941.

Across the Board on Tomorrow Morning (produced 1941). In *Three Plays*. 1941.

The People with Light Coming Out of Them (broadcast 1941). In *The Free Company Presents*, 1941.

There's Something I Got To Tell You (broadcast 1941). In *Razzle Dazzle*, 1942.

Hello, Out There (produced 1941). In *Razzle Dazzle*, 1942.

Jim Dandy (produced 1941). 1941; as *Jim Dandy: Fat Man in a Famine*, 1947.

Talking to You (produced 1942). In *Razzle Dazzle*, 1942.

Razzle Dazzle; or, The Human Opera, Ballet, and Circus; or, There's Something I Got to Tell You: Being Many Kinds of Short Plays As Well As the Story of the Writing of Them (includes *Hello, Out There, Coming Through the Rye, Talking to You, The Great American Goof, The Poetic Situation in America, Opera, Opera, Bad Men in the West, The Agony of Little Nations, A Special Announcement, Radio Play, The People with Light Coming Out of Them, There's Something I Got to Tell You, The Hungerers, Elmer and Lily, Subway Circus, The Ping Pong Players*). 1942.

Opera, Opera (produced 1955). In *Razzle Dazzle*, 1942.

Get Away Old Man (produced 1943). 1944.

Sam Ego's House (produced 1947–48?). In *Don't Go Away Mad and Two Other Plays*, 1949.

Don't Go Away Mad (produced 1949). In *Don't Go Away Mad and Two Other Plays*. 1949.

Don't Go Away Mad and Two Other Plays: Sam Ego's House; A Decent Birth, A Happy Funeral. 1949.

The Son (produced 1950).

The Slaughter of the Innocents (produced 1957). 1952.

The Oyster and the Pearl: A Play for Television (televised 1953). In *Perspectives USA*, Summer 1953.

Once Around the Block (produced 1956). 1959.

The Cave Dwellers (produced 1957). 1958.

Ever Been in Love with a Midget (produced 1957).

Cat, Mouse, Man, Woman; and The Accident, in *Contact 1*, 1958.

Settled Out of Court, with Henry Cecil, from the novel by Henry Cecil (produced 1960). 1962.

The Dogs; or, The Paris Comedy (as *Lily Dafon*, produced 1960). In *The Dogs; or, The Paris Comedy and Two Other Plays*, 1969.

Sam, The Highest Jumper of Them All; or, The London Comedy (produced 1960). 1961.

High Time along the Wabash (produced 1961).

Ah Man, music by Peter Fricker (produced 1962).

Four Plays: The Playwright and the Public, The Handshakers, The Doctor and the Patient, This I Believe, in *Atlantic*, April 1963.

Dentist and Patient, and Husband and Wife, in *The Best Short Plays 1968*, edited by Stanley Richards. 1968.

The Dogs; or, The Paris Comedy and Two Other Plays: Chris Sick; or, Happy New Year Anyway, Making Money, and Nineteen Other Very Short Plays. 1969.

The New Play, in *The Best Short Plays 1970*, edited by Stanley Richards. 1970.

Armenians (produced 1974).

The Rebirth Celebration of the Human Race at Artie Zabala's Off-Broadway Theatre (produced 1975).

Screenplay: *The Good Job*, 1942.

Radio Plays: *Radio Play*, 1940; *A Special Announcement*, 1940; *There's Something I Got to Tell You*, 1941; *The People with Light Coming Out of Them*, 1941.

Television Plays: *The Oyster and the Pearl*, 1953; *Ah Sweet Mystery of Mrs. Murphy*, 1959; *The Unstoppable Gray Fox*, 1962.

Ballet Scenario: *The Great American Goof*, 1940.

Other

The Time of Your Life (miscellany). 1939.
Harlem as Seen by Hirschfeld. 1941.
Hilltop Russians in San Francisco. 1941.
Why Abstract?, with Henry Miller and Hilaire Hiler. 1945.
The Bicycle Rider in Beverly Hills (autobiography). 1952.
Saroyan Reader. 1958.
Here Comes, There Goes, You Know Who (autobiography). 1961.
A Note on Hilaire Hiler. 1962.
Me (juvenile). 1963.
Not Dying (autobiography). 1963.
Short Drive, Sweet Chariot (autobiography). 1966.
Look at Us: Let's See: Here We Are: Look Hard: Speak Soft: I See, You See, We all See;
 Stop, Look, Listen; Beholder's Eye; Don't Look Now But Isn't That You? (us?
 U.S.?). 1967.
Horsey Gorsey and the Frog (juvenile). 1968.
I Used to Believe I Had Forever; Now I'm Not So Sure. 1968.
Letters from 74 rue Taitbout; or, Don't Go But if You Must Say Hello to
 Everybody. 1969; as *Don't Go But If You Must Say Hello to Everybody*, 1970.
Days of Life and Death and Escape to the Moon. 1970.
Places Where I've Done Time. 1972.
The Tooth and My Father (juvenile). 1974.
Famous Faces and Other Friends: A Personal Memoir. 1976.
Morris Hirshfield. 1976.
Sons Come and Go, Mothers Hang In Forever (memoirs). 1976.
Chance Meetings. 1978.

Editor, *Hairenik 1934–1939: An Anthology of Short Stories and Poems.* 1939.

Bibliography: *A Bibliography of Saroyan 1934–1963* by David Kherdian, 1965.

Reading List: *Saroyan* by Howard R. Floan, 1966.

*   *   *

Hailed by some as the greatest writer to come out of San Francisco since Frank Norris, William Saroyan is one of the striking paradoxes in 20th-century literary writing in America. If he has been dismissed for being non-literary, a critic of the eminence of Edmund Wilson has lauded him for his uncanny gift for creating atmosphere in his books: "Saroyan takes you to the bar, and he creates for you there a world which is the way the world would be if it conformed to the feeling instilled by drinks. In a word, he achieves the feat of making and keeping us boozy without the use of alcohol and purely by the action of art."

Saroyan never went beyond high school and thus exemplifies the successful homespun writer. *The Daring Young Man on the Flying Trapeze and Other Stories* was his first collection of short fiction, and many still consider it to be among his finest writing. A breathtakingly prolific writer (he produced about five hundred stories between 1934 and 1940), Saroyan is a short story writer, playwright, and novelist, but his claim to greatness rests essentially on plays like *My Heart's in the Highlands* and *The Time of Your Life* and on his short stories. He has been criticized for his pervasive sentimentality, but his retort to the charge is that it is a very sentimental thing to be a human being. And to the charge that his style is careless and sloppy, he responded: "I do not know a great deal about what the words come to, but the presence says, Now don't get funny; just sit down and say something: it'll be all right. Say it wrong; It'll be all right anyway. Half the time I *do* say it wrong, but somehow or other, just as the presence says, it's right anyway. I am always pleased about this."

One of his best stories, "A Daring Young Man on the Flying Trapeze," is an interior monologue revealing the recollections of a poor writer who lives in the troubled present while achieving distance from it by reaching back into the past centuries. Unperturbed on the conscious level by his problems, occasionally the young writer is embittered by such experiences as the need to sell his books to buy food. Finally, on returning to his room in the afternoon from his wanderings he dies a sudden and painless death. Saroyan's identification with his young protagonist is evident, despite the author's disclaimers. The story is suffused with pathos, though there is clearly an attempt to hold the sentimentality in check. The story would also appear to be a plea for sympathy and support for deprived writers. Among his plays, *The Time of Your Life* is the one that probably most fully reflects Saroyan the artist. It received both the Drama Critics Circle Award and the Pulitzer Prize, but Saroyan refused the latter as an expression of his contempt for commercial patronage of art. Despite its melodramatic plot the play, as Howard R. Floan admirably sums up, is "about a state of mind, illusive but real, whose readily recognizable components are, first, an awareness of America's youth – its undisciplined swaggering, unregulated early life – and, secondly, a pervasive sense of America in crisis: an America of big business, of labor strife, of depersonalized government, and, above all, of imminent war."

At seventy, Saroyan's interest in the comedy-tragedy of life remains undiminished: "Living is the only thing. It is an awful pain most of the time, but this compels comedy and dignity." What makes Saroyan stand out in American literary writing is his optimism about life despite the evidence to the contrary in the world around, especially as perceived by most American writers; and his buoyancy seems to work with his considerable reading public. But the major appeal of his writing comes from his characters, who are common people like gas station attendants, and from his heavily romantic emphasis on the individuality of man. With charming candour Saroyan not too long ago declared that his main purpose was to earn as much money as possible – a confession that has been used by adverse criticism to exaggerate the casualness of his writing and to withhold due recognition from him.

—J. N. Sharma

SAVERY, Henry. Australian. Born in Butcombe, Somerset, England, 4 August 1791; transported to Australia, 1825. Married Eliza Elliott in 1815 (separated, 1829); one son. Apprentice in Bristol; thereafter worked as a sugar refiner and newspaper editor; convicted of forgery, 1825: death sentence changed to transport to Hobart Town: worked as a clerk in the Colonial Secretary's and Colonial Treasurer's offices, 1825–27; worked for the Superintendent of Van Diemen's Land Establishment, 1827–29; imprisoned for debt, 1829–30; given ticket of leave, 1832; farmer, 1832–38; granted conditional pardon, 1838; convicted of forgery, 1840, and imprisoned in Port Arthur. *Died 6 February 1842.*

PUBLICATIONS

Fiction

The Hermit in Van Diemen's Land. 1829.
Quintus Servinton: A Tale Founded upon Incidents of Real Occurrence. 3 vols.,
   1830–31; edited by Cecil H. Hadgraft, 1962.

*   *   *

Henry Savery was a well-educated, rich Bristol merchant who, because of financial difficulties, committed forgery and was subsequently condemned to death. The day before he was to be executed the sentence was commuted to deportation for life to Australia. Seventeen years later he died in the notorious convict prison in Port Arthur. Doubt surrounds the manner of his death, namely whether he cut his throat or whether he suffered a stroke. What is certain is that he died in the most miserable of circumstances. His claim to fame lies in his authorship of the first Australian novel, *Quintus Servinton.*

Prior to writing the novel Savery had written another book, *The Hermit of Van Diemen's Land.* This consisted of a series of sketches written while serving a prison sentence and published separately at first in the *Colonial Times* under the pseudonym of Simon Stokeley. The pseudonym was necessary, as convicts were forbidden to write for the press and were punished with transportation to the dreaded Macquarie Harbour if they did so. It was modelled on a contemporary English work, *The Hermit in London.* The series were in letter form and bore some resemblance to Goldsmith's Chinese Letters (published in volume form as *The Citizen of the World*). There are also some undertones of *The Spectator.* The book is particularly interesting for the light it throws on the social life of Hobart under Governor Arthur's rule. The "hermit," under the guise of an Englishman visiting Tasmania, satirizes Hobart society and its leading citizens. The satire was a little too close to the bone, for it involved the publisher in a libel suit and cost him £80.

Two years later *Quintus Servinton* was published. The novel is obviously autobiographical. Picaresque in structure, it follows the events of Savery's own life. Up until his crime and deportation it is realistic, but when the facts become unpalatable Savery romanticizes, and the novel displays some of the worst excesses of the early 19th-century English novel of this kind. Fiction was much kinder than fate to Savery. Having done penance for his sins, Quintus is permitted to return to England where he lives happily ever after. "The stains that had marked him were removed by the discipline he had been made to endure." The moral preached is the typical Victorian moral, "crime does not pay," and the novel follows the pattern of several other books dealing with the convict theme. Sin is synonymous with crime; Australia is the purgatory where expiation must take place before one can return to "that other Paradise."

Its literary merit, though slight, lies in the power to tell a story. It is, however, an important social document because of the picture it gives of convict life and society in the early days of Australia's history.

—Anna Rutherford

SAYERS, Dorothy L(eigh). English. Born in Oxford, 13 July 1893. Educated at the Godolphin School, Salisbury, Wiltshire, 1909–11; Somerville College, Oxford (Gilchrist Scholar), 1912–15, B.A. (honours) in French 1915, M.A. 1920. Married Oswald Arthur Fleming in 1926 (died, 1950). Taught modern languages at Hull High School for Girls,

Yorkshire, 1915–17; Reader for Blackwell, publishers, Oxford, 1917–18; assistant at the Les Roches School, France, 1919–20; copywriter for Benson's advertising agency, London, 1921–31; full-time writer and broadcaster from 1931; Editor, with Muriel St. Clare Byrne, Bridgeheads series, Methuen, London, 1941–46. Vicar's Warden, St. Thomas's, Regent Street, London, 1952–54, and St. Paul's, Covent Garden, London, from 1954. President, Modern Language Association, 1939–45, and the Detection Club, 1949–57. *Died 17 December 1957.*

PUBLICATIONS

Collections

A Matter of Eternity: Selections, edited by Rosamond Kent Sprague.   1973.

Fiction

Whose Body?   1923.
Clouds of Witness.   1926.
Unnatural Death.   1927; as *The Dawson Pedigree,* 1928.
The Unpleasantness at the Bellona Club.   1928.
Lord Peter Views the Body.   1928.
The Documents in the Case, with Robert Eustace.   1930.
Strong Poison.   1930.
Five Red Herrings.   1931; as *Suspicious Characters,* 1931.
The Floating Admiral, with others.   1931.
Have His Carcase.   1932.
Hangman's Holiday.   1933.
Murder Must Advertise.   1933.
The Nine Tailors.   1934.
Gaudy Night.   1935.
Papers Relating to the Family of Wimsey.   1935.
Busman's Holiday.   1937.
Double Death, with others.   1939.
In the Teeth of the Evidence and Other Stories.   1939.
The Days of Christ's Coming (for children).   1960.

Plays

Busman's Holiday, with Muriel St. Clare Byrne (produced 1936).   In *Famous Plays of 1937,* 1937.
The Zeal of Thy House (produced 1937).   1937.
He That Should Come: A Nativity Play (broadcast 1938).   1939.
The Devil to Pay, Being the Famous Play of John Faustus (produced 1939).   1939.
Love All (produced 1940).
The Man Born to Be King: A Play-Cycle on the Life of Our Lord and Saviour Jesus Christ (broadcast 1941–42).   1943.
The Just Vengeance (produced 1946).   1946.
Where Do We Go from Here? (broadcast 1948).   1948.
The Emperor Constantine: A Chronicle (produced 1951).   1951.

Radio Plays: *Behind the Screen* (serial), with others, 1930; *The Scoop* (serial), with others, 1931; *He That Should Come*, 1938; *The Man Born to Be King*, 1941–42; *Where Do We Go from Here?*, 1948.

Verse

Op. 1.   1916.
Catholic Tales and Christian Songs.   1918.

Other

The Greatest Drama Ever Staged (on Easter).   1938.
Strong Meat.   1939.
Begin Here: A War-Time Essay.   1940.
The Mind of the Maker.   1941.
The Mysterious English.   1941.
Even the Parrot: Exemplary Conversations for Enlightened Children.   1944.
Unpopular Opinions: Twenty-One Essays.   1946.
Creed or Chaos? and Other Essays in Popular Theology.   1947.
The Story of Adam and Christ, illustrated by Fritz Wegner.   1953.
Introductory Essays on Dante.   1954.
The Story of Noah's Ark, illustrated by Fritz Wegner.   1956.
Further Papers on Dante.   1957.
The Poetry of Search and the Poetry of Statement, and Other Posthumous Essays on Literature, Religion, and Language.   1963.
The Wimsey Family (correspondence with C. W. Scott-Giles).   1977.
Wilkie Collins: A Critical and Biographical Study, edited by E. R. Gregory.   1977.

Editor, with T. W. Earp and E. F. A. Geach, *Oxford Poetry 1918.*   1918.
Editor, *Great Stories of Detection, Mystery, and Horror.*   3 vols., 1928–34; as *The Omnibus of Crime*, 1929; *Second* and *Third Omnibus*, 1932–35.
Editor, *Tales of Detection.*   1936.

Translator, *Tristan of Brittany*, by Thomas the Troubadour.   1929.
Translator, *Hell, Purgatory, and Paradise* (the last volume with Barbara Reynolds), by Dante.   3 vols., 1949–62.
Translator, *The Song of Roland.*   1957.

Bibliography: *An Annotated Guide to the Works of Sayers* by Robert R. Harmon and Margaret A. Burger, 1977.

Reading List: *The Emperor's Clothes* by Kathleen Nott, 1954; *Religion in Modern English Drama* by Gerald Weales, 1961; "Sayers, Lord Peter, and God" by Carolyn Heilbrun, in *American Scholar*, 1968; *Such a Strange Lady: An Introduction to Sayers* by Janet Hitchman, 1975.

*   *   *

Though Dorothy L. Sayers abandoned the detective novel in 1937 to concentrate exclusively on what she regarded as more important writing, she seems destined to be more widely remembered as the creator of Lord Peter Wimsey than for her plays, essays, or translations. Surprisingly, however, no agreement exists about which of the novels are the best. *The Documents in the Case*, a non-Wimsey novel written in collaboration with the pseudonymous Robert Eustace, *Murder Must Advertise*, and *The Nine Tailors* have been widely praised, as has *Gaudy Night*, which has received credit more for its theme, characterization, and novel-of-manners qualities than for its mystery plot. Her shorter detective fiction is considered inferior to her novels.

As a dramatist, Sayers constructed plays to serve as vehicles for Christianity. Best regarded is *The Man Born to Be King*, a twelve-play cycle on the life of Jesus. The most significant of Sayers's other plays is *The Zeal of Thy House*, which uses the rebuilding of the Choir of Canterbury Cathedral as the springboard for a discussion of the worth and meaning of work, a frequent theme in her non-fiction.

Sayers's medieval studies are intended for the general reader rather than for the specialist. While all reveal her sensitive grasp of the period, they have been criticized for seeming to link appreciation for medieval literature to acceptance of medieval Christianity. Her translations of *The Song of Roland* and *The Divine Comedy* were well-received upon publication and continue to enjoy considerable popularity; the latter has been characterized as idiosyncratic for the emphasis it places on Dante's humor as an important factor in the development of the work.

Sayers's other works are today read largely by those already committed to her conservative ideas on such topics as language, education, and religion. The sole exception is her introduction to *Great Stories of Detection, Mystery, and Horror* (published in the United States as the first *Omnibus of Crime*), in its day the best analysis of detective fiction and still one of the starting points for any serious study of the genre. Other works deserve greater attention. In *The Mind of the Maker* Sayers presents a unique analysis of the activity of the creative writer in terms of the Christian Trinity: the Idea which holds a work together; the Energy which brings a work into existence; and the Creative Power which communicates the Energy to the writer and to other readers and produces an effect in them. Finally, the combination of erudition and wit in such *jeux d'esprit* as "Dr. Watson's Christian Name" and "The Dates in 'The Red-headed League' " furnish illuminating glimpses of a too often neglected facet of Sayers's art and personality.

—William D. Reynolds

SCHREINER, Olive (Emilie Albertina).   South African.   Born in Wittebergen mission station, Cape of Good Hope, 24 March 1855. Largely self-educated. Married Samuel Cronwright in 1894; one daughter. Governess to the Orpen family children, in South Africa, 1874–81; lived in England, 1881–89; writer from 1882; lived in South Africa, 1890–1913; returned to England, 1913. *Died 10 December 1920.*

PUBLICATIONS

Collections

The Letters, edited by S. C. Cronwright-Schreiner.   1924.
A Selection, edited by Uys Krige.   1968.

Fiction

>*The Story of an African Farm.* 1883.
>*Dreams.* 1891.
>*Dream Life and Real Life.* 1893.
>*Trooper Peter Halket of Mashonaland.* 1897.
>*Stories, Dreams, and Allegories,* edited by S. C. Cronwright-Schreiner. 1923.
>*From Man to Man; or, Perhaps Only –.* 1926.
>*Undine.* 1928.

Other

>*The Political Situation in Cape Colony,* with S. C. Cronwright-Schreiner. 1896.
>*The English-South African's View of the Situation: Words in Season.* 1899.
>*Closer Union: A Letter on the South African Union and the Principles of Government.* 1909.
>*Woman and Labour.* 1911.
>*Thoughts on South Africa.* 1923.

Reading List: *The Life of Schreiner* by S. C. Cronwright-Schreiner, 1924; *Schreiner: A Study in Latent Meanings* by Marion V. Friedmann, 1954; *Schreiner* by Michael Harmel, 1955; *Schreiner, Her Friends and Times* by Daisy Adler, 1955; *Schreiner: Portrait of a South African Woman* by Johannes Meintjes, 1965; *Until the Heart Changes: A Garland for Schreiner* by Zelda Friedlander, 1967; *Schreiner: A Short Guide to Her Writings* by Ridley Beeton, 1974.

*   *   *

Olive Schreiner had her first novel, *The Story of an African Farm*, published when she was in her twenties. For the remaining years of her life, apart from occasional journalism and a few allegories, she produced one short propagandist novel about the Boer War, *Trooper Peter Halket of Mashonaland*, and a major non-fictional study, *Woman and Labour*. After her death her husband published a fairly disastrous forerunner to *The Story of an African Farm*, *Undine*, which she had written in early youth, and *From Man to Man* on which she had been working at the time of her death. All these works, apart from *The Story of an African Farm*, are almost entirely unread today, and even her most famous novel which won her instant celebrity is now neglected. Olive Schreiner's South African background has perhaps not helped her reputation. Pro-Boer in the Boer War and a pacifist in the World War she hardly curried favour with the English-speaking world, while her sympathy for all sections of the African population has not endeared her to the ruling party in South Africa. It would, however, be hard to deny her skill in evoking the harsh beauty of her native land. Her attacks on orthodox religion won her fame in 1883, but when *From Man to Man* was published they already seemed out of date. The loose allegorical structure of her novels full of long sermons in favour of feminism or against religious orthodoxy makes them difficult reading, and as novels they cannot be ranked very highly in spite of moments of inspired lyricism. As a feminist, however, Olive Schreiner deserves more recognition than she has been given: the predicament of Undine, of Lyndall in *The Story of an African Farm*, and of Rebekah in *From Man to Man*, all prevented from fulfilling their aspirations, is fairly and poignantly presented, and Olive Schreiner's shriller successors could learn much from her.

—T. J. Winnifrith

SCOTT, Sir Walter. Scottish. Born in Edinburgh, 15 August 1771; spent his childhood in the Border country. Educated at Edinburgh High School, and the University of Edinburgh; studied law as a clerk in his father's law office; admitted to the Faculty of Advocates, 1792. Married Charlotte Charpentier in 1797 (died, 1826); four children. Writer from 1796; Sheriff-Depute of Selkirkshire, 1799–1832; Clerk of the Court of Session, 1806–30; joined his brother and James Ballantyne as a partner in a printing company, Edinburgh, 1804, which went bankrupt in 1826, involving him in the discharge of its debts for the rest of his life; founded the *Quarterly Review*, 1809; built and lived at Abbotsford from 1812. Created a baronet, 1820. *Died 21 September 1832.*

PUBLICATIONS

Collections

> *Poetical Works,* edited by J. G. Lockhart. 12 vols., 1833–34; edited by J. Logie
> Robertson, 1904.
> *Miscellaneous Prose Works,* edited by J. G. Lockhart. 28 vols., 1834–36; 2 additional
> vols., 1871.
> *The Letters,* edited by Herbert Grierson. 12 vols., 1932–37.
> *Short Stories.* 1934.
> *Selected Poems,* edited by Thomas Crawford. 1972.

Fiction

> *Waverley; or, 'Tis Sixty Years Since.* 1814.
> *Guy Mannering; or, The Astrologer.* 1815.
> *The Antiquary.* 1816.
> *The Black Dwarf, Old Mortality.* 1817; *Old Mortality* edited by Angus Calder, 1975.
> *Rob Roy.* 1817.
> *The Heart of Mid-Lothian.* 1818.
> *The Bride of Lammermoor; A Legend of Montrose.* 1819.
> *Ivanhoe: A Romance.* 1819.
> *The Monastery.* 1820.
> *The Abbot; or, The Heir of Avenel.* 1820.
> *Kenilworth: A Romance.* 1821; edited by David Daiches, 1966.
> *The Pirate.* 1821.
> *The Fortunes of Nigel.* 1822.
> *Peveril of the Peak.* 1823.
> *Quentin Durward.* 1823; edited by M. W. and G. Thomas, 1966.
> *St. Ronan's Well.* 1823.
> *Redgauntlet: A Tale of the Eighteenth Century.* 1824.
> *Tales of the Crusaders (The Betrothed, The Talisman).* 1825.
> *Woodstock; or, The Cavalier.* 1826.
> *Chronicles of the Canongate: First Series: The Highland Widow, The Two Drovers, The
> Surgeon's Daughter.* 1827; *Second Series: The Fair Maid of Perth,* 1828.
> *My Aunt Margaret's Mirror, The Tapestried Chamber, Death of the Laird's Jock, A
> Scene at Abbotsford.* 1829.
> *Anne of Geierstein; or, The Maiden of the Mist.* 1829.
> *Waverley Novels* (Scott's final revision). 48 vols., 1829–33.
> *Count Robert of Paris, Castle Dangerous.* 1832.

Plays

Goetz of Berlichingen, with The Iron Hand, by Goethe.   1799.
Guy Mannering; or, The Gipsy's Prophecy, with Daniel Terry, music by Henry Bishop
    and others, from the novel by Scott (produced 1816).   1816.
Halidon Hill: A Dramatic Sketch from Scottish History.   1822.
MacDuff's Cross, in *A Collection of Poems*, edited by Joanna Baillie.   1823.
The House of Aspen (produced 1829).   In *Poetical Works*, 1830.
Auchindrane; or, The Ayrshire Tragedy (produced 1830).   In *The Doom of Devorgoil;
    Auchindrane*, 1830.
*The Doom of Devorgoil: A Melo-Drama; Auchindrane; or, The Ayrshire
    Tragedy*.   1830.

Verse

*The Chase, and William and Helen: Two Ballads from the German of Gottfried Augustus
    Bürger*.   1796.
The Eve of Saint John: A Border Ballad.   1800.
The Lay of the Last Minstrel.   1805.
Ballads and Lyrical Pieces.   1806.
Marmion: A Tale of Flodden Field.   1808.
The Lady of the Lake.   1810.
The Vision of Don Roderick.   1811.
Rokeby.   1813.
The Bridal of Triermain; or, The Vale of St. John, in Three Cantos.   1813.
The Lord of the Isles.   1815.
The Field of Waterloo.   1815.
The Ettrick Garland, Being Two Excellent New Songs, with James Hogg.   1815.
Harold the Dauntless.   1817.
New Love-Poems, edited by Davidson Cook.   1932.

Other

Paul's Letters to His Kinsfolk.   1816.
The Visionary.   1819.
Provincial Antiquities of Scotland.   2 vols., 1826.
*The Life of Napoleon Buonaparte: Emperor of the French, with a Preliminary View of the
    French Revolution*.   9 vols., 1827.
Tales of a Grandfather, Being Stories Taken from Scottish History.   9 vols., 1827–29.
Miscellaneous Prose Works.   6 vols., 1827.
Religious Discourses by a Layman.   1828.
The History of Scotland.   2 vols., 1829–30.
Letters on Demonology and Witchcraft.   1830.
Tales of a Grandfather, Being Stories Taken from the History of France.   3 vols., 1830.
Letters Addressed to Rev. R. Polwhele, D. Gilbert, F. Douce.   1832.
Letters Between James Ellis and Scott.   1850.
Journal 1825–32, edited by D. Douglas.   2 vols., 1890; edited by W. E. K. Anderson,
    1972.
Familiar Letters, edited by D. Douglas.   2 vols., 1894.
*The Letters of Scott and Charles Kirkpatrick Sharpe to Robert Chambers,
    1821–45*.   1903.
The Private Letter-Books, edited by W. Partington.   1930.

Sir Walter's Postbag: More Stories and Sidelights from the Collection in the Brotherton Library, edited by W. Partington. 1932.

Some Unpublished Letters from the Collection in the Brotherton Library, edited by J. A. Symington. 1932.

The Correspondence of Scott and Charles Robert Maturin, edited by F. E. Ratchford and W. H. McCarthy. 1937.

Private Letters of the Seventeenth Century, edited by D. Grant. 1948.

Editor, *An Apology for Tales of Terror*. 1799.

Editor, *Minstrelsy of the Scottish Border*. 2 vols., 1802; edited by Alfred Noyes, 1908.

Editor, *Sir Tristrem: A Metrical Romance*, by Thomas of Ercildoune. 1804.

Editor, *Original Memoirs Written During the Great Civil War*, by Sir H. Slingsby and Captain Hodgson. 1804.

Editor, *The Works of John Dryden*. 18 vols., 1808 (*Life of Dryden* published separately, 1808, edited by Bernard Kreissman, 1963).

Editor, *Memoirs of Captain George Carleton*. 1808.

Editor, *Queenhoo-Hall: A Romance, and Ancient Times: A Drama*, by Joseph Strutt. 4 vols., 1808.

Editor, *Memoirs of Robert Cary, Earl of Monmouth, and Fragmenta Regalia*, by Sir Robert Naunton. 1808.

Editor, *A Collection of Scarce and Valuable Tracts*. 13 vols., 1809–15.

Editor, *English Minstrelsy, Being a Collection of Fugitive Poetry*. 2 vols., 1810.

Editor, *The Poetical Works of Anna Seward*. 3 vols., 1810.

Editor, *Memoirs of Count Grammont*, by Anthony Hamilton. 2 vols., 1811.

Editor, *The Castle of Otranto*, by Horace Walpole. 1811.

Editor, *Secret History of the Court of King James the First*. 2 vols., 1811.

Editor, *The Works of Jonathan Swift*. 19 vols., 1814 (*Memoirs of Swift* published separately, 1826).

Editor, *The Letting of Humours Blood in the Head Vaine*, by S. Rowlands. 1814.

Editor, *Memorie of the Somervilles*. 2 vols., 1815.

Editor, *Trivial Poems and Triolets*, by Patrick Carey. 1820.

Editor, *Memorials of the Haliburtons*. 1820.

Editor, *Northern Memoirs Writ in the Year 1658*, by Richard Franck. 1821.

Editor, *Ballantyne's Novelist's Library*. 10 vols., 1821–24 (*Lives of the Novelists* published separately, 2 vols., 1825).

Editor, *Chronological Notes of Scottish Affairs from the Diary of Lord Fountainhall*. 1822.

Editor, *Military Memoirs of the Great Civil War*, by John Gwynne. 1822.

Editor, *Lays of the Lindsays*. 1824.

Editor, *Auld Robin Gray: A Ballad*, by Lady Anne Barnard. 1825.

Editor, with D. Laing, *The Bannatyne Miscellany*. 1827.

Editor, *Memoirs of the Marchioness de la Rochejaquelein*. 1827.

Editor, *Proceedings in the Court-Martial Held upon John, Master of Sinclair, 1708*. 1829.

Editor, *Memorials of George Bannatyne, 1545–1608*. 1829.

Editor, *Trial of Duncan Terig and Alexander Bane Macdonald, 1754*. 1831.

Editor, *Memoirs of the Insurrection*in Scotland in 1715*, by John, Master of Sinclair. 1858.

Bibliography: *Bibliography of the Waverley Novels* by G. Worthington, 1930; "A Bibliography of the Poetical Works of Scott 1796–1832" by W. Ruff, in *Transactions of the Edinburgh Bibliographical Society I*, 1938; *A Bibliography of Scott: A Classified and Annotated List of Books and Articles Relating to His Life and Works 1797–1940* by J. C. Corson, 1943.

Reading List: *Scott as a Critic of Literature* by M. Ball, 1907; *Scott: A New Life* by Herbert Grierson, 1938; *Scott* by Una Pope-Hennessy, 1948; *Scott: His Life and Personality* by H. Pearson, 1954; *Scott* by Ian Jack, 1958; *The Heyday of Scott* by Donald Davie, 1961; *Witchcraft and Demonology in Scott's Fiction* by C. O. Parsons, 1964; *Scott* by T. Crawford, 1965; *Scott's Novels* by F. R. Hart, 1966; *Scott: The Great Unknown* by Edgar Johnson, 2 vols., 1970; *The Wizard of the North: The Life of Scott* by Carola Oman, 1973; *"The Siege of Malta" Rediscovered* by Donald E. Sultana, 1977.

*   *   *

Walter Scott was born in Edinburgh in 1771. His father, who is affectionately satirized as Saunders Fairford, the "good old-fashioned man of method" in *Redgauntlet*, was a respected solicitor. His mother, the daughter of a well-known medical professor at the University, had brains and character, and it is tempting to believe that from her Scott inherited the ability which put him for a time at the very top of the tree. He had his education at the High School of Edinburgh and at Edinburgh University. Of formative importance, however, were the months he spent at his paternal grandfather's Border farm as a small boy recuperating from the illness (probably poliomyelitis) which left him permanently lame. The tales he heard there of old, unhappy, far-off things, and the skirmishes in which his own ancestors had fought, lit in him the love of the Scottish past which was the enduring passion of his life.

As Sheriff of Selkirkshire and a Clerk of the Court of Session, Scott was obliged to divide his time between Edinburgh and his Sherifdom; and it was near Selkirk that he built Abbotsford, the "Conundrum Castle" of a house which he embellished with all manner of historical trophies and curiosities. His two official salaries combined to give him a modest competence. They were not, however, enough to let him live in the style of the wealthier Edinburgh lawyers, the *noblesse de la robe* so important to Scottish society, nor of the landowners of the Border country round Abbotsford. That, literature alone could provide.

The literary task to which he devoted his youth was the collection of the Border ballads. His taste had run that way since early youth; he loved the country through whose remoter parts he rode in the quest for those who could recite or sing to him the old songs he wanted; he had a fantastically retentive memory and above all the endearing faculty of talking easily to people of all kinds. *The Minstrelsy of the Scottish Border*, inspired by the example of Percy's *Reliques*, is not, by modern standards, scholarly. There are valuable discursive notes, but modern imitations are accorded a place alongside genuine ballads, and Scott was not interested in variant readings, nor above improving or adding a verse or two. Nonetheless *The Minstrelsy* confirmed Scott's bent towards the historic past, and it established his reputation as a rising man.

One poem, originally intended for the *Minstrelsy*, grew under Scott's hand into his first major independent work. *The Lay of the Last Minstrel* is a narrative poem of magic and border chivalry which, although imperfect in construction and seldom rising to real poetry, exactly struck the growing taste for the mediaeval and the supernatural. The poem's successors *Marmion* and *The Lady of the Lake* were also instantly successful; *Rokeby*, *The Lord of the Isles*, and *Harold the Dauntless* were less so.

Although the range of Scott's poetry is narrow, it has considerable merits. It is muscular, manly verse; its galloping rhythms suit his subjects, and it passes the first test of narrative verse that it should tell the story well. The narrative poetry reaches its heights in moments of action:

> The stubborn spearmen still made good,
> Their Dark, impenetrable wood,
> Each stepping where his comrade stood,
> The instant that he fell

or in the elegiac sadness:

> Of the stern strife, and carnage drear,
> Of Flodden's fatal field,
> Where shiver'd was fair Scotland's spear,
> And broken was her shield.

Scott's best-known poems, however, are the songs interspersed with the narrative in both poems and novels. Thousands who have never read Scott are familiar with Schubert's settings of "Ave Maria" and the other lyrics from *The Lady of the Lake*.

In July 1814 a three-volume novel entitled *Waverley* was published anonymously in Edinburgh. Within five weeks it had sold out, and by the following January it was into its fifth edition. If Scott's real motive had been to protect his reputation as a poet should the novel fail, he had no need to keep up the mystery; but speculation about the unknown author amused him, and he did not acknowledge his authorship of the Waverley novels, which were published at the rate of two a year, until twelve years later.

Scott's reputation has suffered from judgements based on the mass of his work rather than the best of it. At his best – in *The Antiquary, Rob Roy, Old Mortality, The Heart of Mid-Lothian, The Bride of Lammermoor*, and *Redgauntlet* (some would add *Waverley, Guy Mannering* and *The Fair Maid of Perth*) – he was writing of a country whose history and people he knew intimately. *Redgauntlet* begins in the Edinburgh of his youth; the trial of Effie Deans is set in a court-room he knew well; Scott's grandmother remembered being carried as a child to a covenanters' field-preaching, and Scott himself had talked with a man who had been "out" with the Jacobites in 1715 and 1745. The Scottish novels are Scott's real achievement. They inspired writers as diverse as Hugo, George Eliot, Tolstoy, and James Fenimore Cooper. In a sense, they created Scotland as it is known today. They introduced to the world a new form of fiction, the historical novel.

The great historical characters – James VI, Cromwell, Mary and Elizabeth, Prince Charlie, Rob Roy – are seldom central to the novels in which they appear, for Scott's technique is to follow the fortunes of an ordinary man caught up in great events, but they are striking portraits of breathing, fallible human beings. "Sir Walter not only invented the historical novel," says Trevelyan, "but he enlarged the scope and revolutionized the study of history itself." After reading the Waverley novels men could no longer content themselves with broad generalizations about the past; Scott had taught them that it was peopled by real men and women.

As a creator of character his range is enormous. He is the first novelist in English to bring the lower orders of society to life on the page, not as figures of fun but as part of humanity. Fairservice, Ochiltree, Mucklebackit, Balderstone and Davie Deans – as well as Bailie Jarvie the merchant, lawyers like Pleydell and Fairfold, and small lairds like Dumbiedykes – are both of their age and for all time.

Scott's marvellous command of the Scottish dialect, his eye for the telling detail, and the humorous yet affectionate way in which he allows his characters to reveal themselves in speech, led his contemporaries to compare him with Shakespeare. "Not fit to tie his brogues," was Scott's characteristic disclaimer. In one respect, however, he is Shakespeare's superior. His common people – his servants and gardeners and beggars – are better. To Shakespeare they are seen *de haut en bas*. There is no similar condescension in Scott.

The subtleties of Jane Austen, whom he greatly admired, were not within Scott's range. As he said in his *Journal*, his was "the Big Bow-wow strain" of writing, and he prided himself on his "hurried frankness of composition." As a story-teller, he is at his best over the shorter distance of "Wandering Willie's Tale" in *Redgauntlet* or of great scenes like the trials of McIvor and Cuddie Headrigg, the appeal of Jeanie Deans to Queen Caroline, or the fight in the Clachan of Aberfoyle.

Again and again he returns to the conflict between old ways and new. By temperament and by upbringing Scott was both a romantic and a realist. In the novels he thrills to the

Jacobite past; but he settles ultimately for the age of reason, for Hume and Adam Smith rather than Rob Roy and Charles Edward Stuart. The tension of opposites characteristic of eighteenth-century Scotland remains his theme in the novels set further back in time or further off in place: Cavaliers and Roundheads in *Woodstock*, Saxons and Normans in *Ivanhoe*, Royalists and Covenanters in *Old Mortality*. The truth, for Scott, habitually lies somewhere between the extremes. He is one of the sanest of great writers.

"The greatest figure he ever drew is in the *Journal*," wrote John Buchan, "and it is the man Walter Scott." In 1825, when Scott began to keep a journal, his reputation was at its height. A few months later the slump of 1826 ruined his printer and publisher and, in those days before limited liablity, Scott himself. Legally he could have declared himself bankrupt, but he would not. "My own right hand shall do it," he said, and he set himself to work, mornings and evenings, week days and Sundays, term time and holidays, to pay off the joint debt of £126,000. Thanks mainly to the collected editions of his work to which he contributed notes, the debt was finally paid off, but Scott himself, hastened to an early grave by worry and overwork, did not live to see it. Carlyle's famous sentence was fully earned: "No sounder piece of British manhood was put together in that eighteenth century of Time."

—W. E. K. Anderson

SEDGWICK, Catharine Maria. American. Born in Stockbridge, Massachusetts, 28 December 1789. Educated at the district school, and at boarding schools in Boston and Albany, New York; also received private instruction in several languages. Lived in Albany and New York City, 1807–13; returned to Stockbridge, 1813; later lived in Lenox, Massachusetts, and New York; writer from 1822; travelled in Europe, 1839–40, and in the American Midwest, 1854. Active in the work of the Unitarian Church, and the Women's Prison Association of New York. *Died 31 July 1867.*

PUBLICATIONS

Fiction

> *A New-England Tale; or, Sketches of New England Character and Manners.* 1822; revised edition, as *A New England Tale, and Miscellanies,* 1852.
> *Redwood.* 1824.
> *The Travellers.* 1825.
> *Hope Leslie; or, Early Times in the Massachusetts.* 1827.
> *Clarence; or, A Tale of Our Own Times.* 1830.
> *The Linwoods; or, "Sixty Years Since" in America.* 1835.
> *Home.* 1835.
> *Tales and Sketches.* 2 vols., 1835–44.
> *Live and Let Live; or, Domestic Service Illustrated.* 1837.
> *Wilton Harvey.* .1845.
> *The Boy of Mount Rhigi* (juvenile). 1848.
> *Married or Single?* 1857.
> *The Poor Rich Man and the Rich Poor Man.* 1864.

Other

Means and Ends; or, Self-Training.   1839.
Letters from Abroad to Kindred at Home.   1841.
Morals of Manners; or, Hints for Our Young People.   1846.
Facts and Manners for School-Day Reading.   1848.
The Works.   3 vols., 1849.
Memoir of Joseph Curtis, A Model Man.   1858.

Reading List: Life and Letters edited by Mary E. Dewey, 1871.

*   *   *

The novels of Catharine Maria Sedgwick, the best of which include Redwood and Hope Leslie, are distinguished by close attention to realistic detail, especially regional customs and manners. They utilize American scenery, manners, customs, and materials, and are usually centered on moral circumstances of especially American interest. Redwood, for example, contrasts a Northern and a Southern family. Hope Leslie is set in Puritan New England, and aspects of New England history, scenery, and manners are finely detailed. In The Linwoods, the tensions that resulted in the American Revolution are dramatized in the conflicts between a family of colonists and a family of royalists. Clarence demonstrates the value of a natural aristocracy, an aristocracy of talent and virtue such as projected by Thomas Jefferson, over an aristocracy based solely on birth and wealth. A New-England Tale, the first of Sedgwick's novels, is partially a religious tract attacking the remnants of Calvinism in New England, and Married or Single? is one of the earliest feminist American pleas for socially equitable treatment of women.

Sedgwick's moral preoccupations are largely tied to social and political concerns of her day, and while these moral concerns are in many instances now of little interest (as well as obscure to readers without training in American social and political history), her novels have continuing literary value among the earliest and the best examples of regionalism in American writing. Sedgwick had an acute ear for American dialect and a fine sense of regional customs and manners. As a literary stylist, she was not especially remarkable, although superior to most of her contemporary American writers, but she was capable of detailing with precision regional characteristics, landscapes, and dialect. Furthermore, alone among her contemporary American novelists, she was capable of creating credible women in fiction. While it was common for American novelists to portray women as ideally (if improbably) passive and unambitious, Sedgwick portrayed heroines who were morally superior; all of her novels center on women whose superior moral judgment places them far above others – particularly men.

—Edward Halsey Foster

SELVON, Samuel (Dickson).   Trinidadian.   Born in Trinidad, 20 May 1923. Educated at Naparima College, Trinidad, 1935–39. Served as a wireless operator with the Trinidad Royal Naval Volunteer Reserve, 1940–45. Married 1) Draupadi Persaud in 1947, one son; 2) Althea Nesta Daroux in 1963, two sons and one daughter. Journalist, Trinidad Guardian, 1946–50; civil servant, in the High Commission, London, 1950–53; full-time writer from 1954. Recipient: Guggenheim Fellowship, 1954, 1968; Society of Authors Travelling Scholarship, 1958; Trinidad Government Scholarship, 1962; Arts Council of Great Britain grant, 1967, 1968; Humming Bird Medal, Trinidad, 1969. Lives in London.

Publications

Fiction

> *A Brighter Sun.* 1952.
> *An Island Is a World.* 1955.
> *The Lonely Londoners.* 1956.
> *Turn Again, Tiger.* 1958.
> *Ways of Sunlight* (stories). 1958.
> *I Hear Thunder.* 1963.
> *The Housing Lark.* 1965.
> *The Plains of Caroni.* 1969.
> *Those Who Eat the Cascadura.* 1972.
> *Moses Ascending.* 1975.

Plays

> Radio Plays: *Lost Property,* 1965; *A House for Teona,* 1965; *A Highway in the Sun,* 1967; *Rain Stop Play,* 1967; *You Right in the Smoke,* 1968; *Worse Than Their Bite,* 1968; *Bringing in the Sheaves,* 1969; *Perchance to Dream,* 1969; *Eldorado West One,* 1969; *Home Sweet India,* 1970; *Mary Shut Your Gate,* 1971; *The Magic Stick,* from work by I. Khan, 1971; *Voyage to Trinidad,* 1971; *Those Who Eat the Crocodile,* 1971; *Water for Veronica,* 1972; *Cry Baby Brackley,* 1972; *Harvest in Wilderness,* 1972; *Zeppi's Machine,* 1977.

Reading List: *The West Indian Novel* by Kenneth Ramchand, 1970.

*   *   *

In the 1950's there was a major exodus of writers from the Caribbean to London. These included V. S. Naipaul, Wilson Harris, George Lamming, Edgar Mittelholzer, Andrew Salkey, and Samuel Selvon. They left the Caribbean, like thousands of other West Indians, with the hope of a bright new future in the mother country. On arrival their hopes were soon dashed. Instead of a welcome they were met with open hostility, rejection, exploitation, and racial prejudice. Several of the above mentioned writers have written about the lives of these unwanted immigrants in England but none as successfully as Samuel Selvon. In books like *The Lonely Londoners, Ways of Sunlight,* and *The Housing Lark,* he describes in tragi-comic fashion the ordinary everyday lives of the simple West Indian immigrants in London and the loneliness that lies behind their lives. "It have people living in London," remarks one of Selvon's characters, "who don't know what happening in the room next to them, far more the street, or how other people living. London is a place like that" (*The Lonely Londoners*).

While Selvon is probably best known for his stories set amongst the West Indian community in London it could be argued that his finest work is his first novel, *A Brighter Sun.* The novel is set in Trinidad and describes the attempt of a young East Indian peasant, Tiger, to establish an identity. But the novel is not only a description of Tiger's growing awareness of self; it is also an attempt on Selvon's part to show the various ethnic groups in the Caribbean struggling to establish a single Caribbean identity. For, unlike V. S. Naipaul,

Selvon believes this to be a possibility if all the races co-operate. This single identity is symbolized by Tiger's house which the various races help him to build.

A Brighter Sun has another claim to fame, and that is because of Selvon's use of dialect. "It is in this novel," remarked the West Indian critic, Kenneth Ramchand, "that dialect first becomes the language of consciousness in West Indian fiction." Selvon was not only the first to use and explore dialect successfully in this way; he still remains without equal in this field.

—Anna Rutherford

SHADBOLT, Maurice (Francis Richard). New Zealander. Born in Auckland, 4 June 1932. Educated at Te Kuiti High School; Avondale College; University of Auckland. Married twice; three sons and one daughter. Journalist for various New Zealand publications, 1952–54; documentary scriptwriter and director for the New Zealand National Film Unit, 1954–57; full-time writer from 1957; lived in London and Spain, 1957–60, then returned to New Zealand. Recipient: Hubert Church Memorial Award, 1959; New Zealand State Literary Fellowship, 1960, 1970; Katherine Mansfield Award, 1963, 1967; Robert Burns Fellowship, Otago University, 1963; National Association of Independent Schools Award, U.S.A., 1966; Freda Buckland Award, 1969; Pacific Area Travel Association Award, for non-fiction, 1971; James Wattie Award, 1973. Lives in Auckland.

PUBLICATIONS

Fiction

The New Zealanders: A Sequence of Stories. 1959.
Summer Fires and Winter Country (stories). 1963.
Among the Cinders. 1965.
The Presence of Music: 3 Novellas. 1967.
This Summer's Dolphin. 1969.
An Ear of the Dragon. 1971.
Strangers and Journeys. 1972.
A Touch of Clay. 1974.
Danger Zone. 1976.

Other

New Zealand: Gift of the Sea, with Brian Blake. 1963.
The Shell Guide to New Zealand. 1968.
Isles of the South Pacific, with Olaf Ruhen. 1968.

Reading List: Shadbolt by Conrad Bollinger, 1975; "Ambition and Accomplishment in Shadbolt's Strangers and Journeys" by Lawrence Jones, in Critical Essays on the New Zealand Novel edited by Cherry Hankin, 1976.

*   *   *

Maurice Shadbolt has said of his work that "as a man of my time and place ... I have simply tried to make sense of it." Certainly his fiction, taken collectively, does attempt to make sense of contemporary New Zealand, forming a picture with three dimensions – social, historical, and personal.

Read as social documents, Shadbolt's works show the major currents of the time and place. The change from a rural to an urban society, with the resultant growth of urban and suburban discontents, is evident, especially in the stories of *Summer Fires and Winter Country*. The decline of political activism in the 1950's, discouraged both by the rigidities of the Cold War and the complacency engendered by the Welfare State, is seen in the stories of *The New Zealanders* and in the middle sections of *Strangers and Journeys*, while the last sections of that book and the more recent novels show the rebirth of political activism in the 1960's and 1970's in relation to Vietnam, ecological issues (*A Touch of Clay*), and French nuclear testing (*Danger Zone*). Another recurring theme, prominent in *The Presence of Music* and *Strangers and Journeys*, has been the place of the artist in helping to mould the national sensibility of a society that is still "shapeless, half-formed, indistinct."

Shadbolt's picture of the "bruised Eden" of contemporary New Zealand is given depth by the historical dimension, for, with his own family roots reaching back to the early European settlement, he sees the present as the result of past attempts to impose European dreams on Pacific islands. These dreams, the pioneer dream of a pastoral paradise and the political dream of the just city, are touched upon in *Among the Cinders* and *A Touch of Clay*, but they are developed most fully in *Strangers and Journeys*, where the failure of the dreams of the fathers is visited upon the sons.

Social and historical concerns, however, have merely formed a background to Shadbolt's primary theme of personal relationships – sexual, familial, and between male friends. In a society lacking the direction of a religious faith or a political ideology, and deprived of the challenge of the physical struggle for survival, personal relationships become the only source of meaning and the real "danger zone" in which one is tested. Repeatedly Shadbolt shows the weight that personal relations must carry, how fragile they are, how difficult it is to maintain relationships that are honest, mutual, responsible, non-exploiting.

Shadbolt's portrait of New Zealand is presented artfully, especially in the handling of multiple plots and time-levels and of recurring images and motifs. However, facility can pass into slickness, especially in the mannered style and in the tendency to melodramatic plotting and stereotyped characters. Only in such stories as "The Strangers," "The Room," and "Figures of Light" and in the first section of *Strangers and Journeys* is Shadbolt entirely successful, but all the books have impressive sequences and all contribute to his account of his time and place.

—Lawrence Jones

SHARP, William. Pseudonym: Fiona Macleod. Scottish. Born in Paisley, Renfrewshire, 12 September 1855. Educated at Blair Lodge School, Paisley, to 1868; Glasgow Academy, 1868–71; University of Glasgow, 1871–74. Married his cousin Elizabeth Amelia Sharp in 1884. Clerk in a law office in Glasgow, 1874–76; travelled to Australia, 1876–78; Clerk in the City of Melbourne Bank, London, 1878–81; thereafter supported himself by writing; visited Italy, and studied art, 1883–84; appointed Art Critic of the *Glasgow Herald*, 1884; Editor, *Canterbury Poets* series, 1884–90, and *Biographies of Great Writers* series, 1887–90; visited the United States and Canada, 1889; lived in Rome, 1890–91; again visited America, 1891–92; settled at Phenice Croft, Sussex, 1892; Editor, *The Pagan Review* (one number), 1892; wrote mystical prose and verse as Fiona Macleod from 1893. *Died 14 December 1905.*

Collections

Writings, edited by Elizabeth Amelia Sharp.   7 vols., 1909–10.

Fiction

The Sport of Chance.   1888.
Children of Tomorrow: A Romance.   1889.
A Fellowe and His Wife, with B. W. Howard.   1892.
Pharais: A Romance of the Isles.   1894.
The Mountain Lovers.   1895.
The Sin-Eater and Other Tales.   1895.
The Washer of the Ford and Other Legendary Moralities.   1896.
Green Fire: A Romance.   1896.
Madge o' the Pool, The Gypsy Christ, and Other Tales.   1896.
Wives in Exile.   1896.
The Laughter of Peterkin: A Retelling of Old Tales of the Celtic Wonderland.   1897.
The Shorter Stories.   1897.
Silence Farm.   1899.

Plays

The House of Usna (produced 1900).   1903.
The Immortal Hour (produced 1914).   1907.

Verse

The Human Inheritance, The New Hope, Motherhood.   1882.
Earth's Voices, Transcripts from Nature, Sospitra, and Other Poems.   1884.
Romantic Ballads and Poems of Phantasy.   1888.
Sospiri di Roma.   1891.
From the Hills of Dream: Mountain Songs and Island Runes.   1896; revised edition, as
    Threnodies and Songs, and Later Poems, 1907.
Songs and Poems, Old and New.   1909.

Other

D. G. Rossetti: A Record and a Study.   1882.
Life of Shelley.   1887.
Life of Heinrich Heine.   1888.
Life of Robert Browning.   1890.
The Life and Letters of Joseph Severn.   1892.
The Pagan Review (periodical), edited by W. H. Brooks.   1892.
Fair Women in Painting and Poetry.   1894.
Vistas.   1894.
Ecce Puella and Other Prose Imaginings.   1896.
The Dominion of Dreams.   1899.

The Divine Adventure, Iona, By Sundown Shores: Studies in Spiritual History.   1900.
Progress of Art in the Century.   1902.
The Winged Destiny: Studies in the Spiritual History of the Gael.   1904.
Literary Geography.   1904.
Where the Forest Murmurs: Nature Essays.   1906.
Poems and Dramas.   1910.

Editor, *The Songs, Poems, and Sonnets of Shakespeare.*   1885.
Editor, *Great English Painters,* by Allan Cunningham.   1886.
Editor, *Sonnets of This Century.*   1886.
Editor, *Song-Tide,* by P. B. Marston.   1888.
Editor, *American Sonnets.*   1889.
Editor, *Essays on Men and Women,* by Sainte-Beuve.   1890.
Editor, *Great Odes, English and American.*   1890.

Reading List: *William Sharp (Fiona Macleod): A Memoir Compiled by His Wife* by Elizabeth Amelia Sharp, 1912 (includes bibliography).

*   *   *

When William Sharp moved to London in 1878 from his family home in Glasgow, he was intent upon becoming a poet. He soon came under the influence of Dante Gabriel Rossetti and his circle, and that influence is apparent in his first volume of poems, *The Human Inheritance.* For the rest of the decade, he persisted with poetry, but earned his living as a critic, editor, and biographer. Other volumes of verse appeared during the 1880's but only in the phantasy poems of *Romantic Ballads and Poems of Phantasy* are there signs of the economy of language and the distinctive voice that characterized the poems he wrote in the late 1890's and published as Fiona Macleod.

During three months in Italy, he wrote a group of poems unlike any he had done, *Sospiri di Roma.* These poems are musical, sensuous, and filled with colorful, vivid imagery. They also portray with regret the ravages time has inflicted upon ancient Roman civilization, and inflicts always upon youthful love and passion. With echoes of Swinburne, these poems foreshadow a dominant motif of English poetry during the decade that was beginning.

The creative period which produced the works of Fiona Macleod began in 1894 with *Pharais: A Romance of the Isles,* which Sharp issued under that pseudonym. His original intent was to impart authenticity to the Celtic romance, and increase its chances for a favorable critical reception. The pseudonym had the effect of stimulating Sharp's imagination and releasing his deeper feelings. Although he continued until his death in 1905 to publish criticism and fictional works as William Sharp, he wrote most movingly and effectively as Fiona Macleod.

Pharais was followed by two other romances, *The Mountain Lovers* and *Green Fire,* but even as Fiona Macleod Sharp had trouble sustaining the reader's interest, or his own, through long narratives. They tend to break into vignettes. The best Fiona Macleod prose is in the short tales he collected in *The Sin-Eater* and *The Washer of the Ford.* Retellings of stories heard among the natives in the West of Scotland, these stories project the bleakness as well as the superstitions and the sense of mystery that characterized the lives of the people in the West. Celtic myths and legends inform the daily lives of the people in the tales. If Sharp frequently confused or misused the details of those legends, so, we may presume, did his informants. Many of these stories are compelling and moving even when their style becomes excessively florid.

The Fiona Macleod prose turned gradually to the essay form. With *The Divine Adventure, The Winged Destiny,* and *Where the Forest Murmurs,* the phantom author became a Celtic seer. These works are not without interest, but their philosophic content is thin and dated, and they lack the crisp reality and emotional power of the better tales.

Sharp's best work appeared in the poems in the successive editions of Fiona Macleod's *From the Hills of Dream*. The poems in this volume vary in quality; a few are very good. Just as Sharp's imagination had been quickened in Italy by the broken remains of Roman life and culture, so it was moved by the Celtic past of the western shores and islands of Scotland and the failures of love and loss of life he encountered there. In the poems of Fiona Macleod, Sharp turned from the strong musical cadences and brilliant imagery of *Sospiri di Roma* to the quieter, subtler music of the early Yeats. That more restrained voice produced greater control; and it more nearly suited the lamenting voices he heard and the dreary lives he observed in the West of Scotland. The best Fiona Macleod poems are marked by economy and precision of diction and a fine-tuned sense of the irony inherent in the loss of hope and the failure of dreams.

—William F. Halloran

SHAW, Henry Wheeler. Pseudonym: Josh Billings. American. Born in Lanesboro, Massachusetts, 21 April 1818. Educated at the Lenox Preparatory School, Massachusetts; Hamilton College, Clinton, New York, 1833–34. Married Zilpha Bradford in 1845. Worked at odd jobs in the Midwest, 1835–45, and in the East, 1845–54; settled in Poughkeepsie, New York, 1854; auctioneer and realtor in Poughkeepsie, 1854–66; Alderman, 1858; writer from 1859; contributed to the *Poughkeepsie Daily Press* from 1860; lecturer from 1863; contributed to the *New York Weekly*, 1867–85, and *Century Magazine*, 1884–85. *Died 14 October 1885.*

PUBLICATIONS

Collections

Complete Works. 1888.
Uncle Sam's Uncle Josh, edited by Donald Day. 1953.

Prose

Josh Billings, Hiz Sayings. 1865.
Josh Billings on Ice, and Other Things. 1868.
Josh Billings' Farmers' Allminax for the Year 1870. 1870 (and later volumes to 1879); 1870–79 sequence published in 1 vol., 1902.
Everybody's Friend; or, Josh Billings's Encyclopedia and Proverbial Philosophy of Wit and Humor. 1874.
Josh Billings, His Works Complete. 1876.
Josh Billings' Trump Kards: Blue Grass Philosophy. 1877.
Complete Comical Writings. 1877.
Old Probability: Perhaps Rain – Perhaps Not. 1879.

Josh Billings' Cook Book and Piktorial Proverbs.   1880.
Josh Billings Struggling with Things.   1881.
Josh Billings' Spice Box.   1881.

Reading List: *Shaw (Billings)* by David B. Kesterson, 1973.

*   *   *

Farmer, boatman, explorer, real-estate salesman, auctioneer, Henry Wheeler Shaw turned to writing in his middle age and leapt into national prominence in America with an "Essa on the Muel bi Josh Billings" ("The Muel is haf hoss and haf Jackass, and then kums to a full stop, natur diskovering her mistake"). He took a pen name but avoided the topical subjects of his contemporaries. Unfortunately for the modern reader, he did adopt the comic device of atrocious spelling, then considered in America to be a sure-fire laugh-getter. As with the Irish dialect of Finley Peter Dunne's "Mr. Dooley," however, it is often worth the extra effort in reading, for Josh Billings's cracker-barrel philosophy and "trump-kard" aphorisms are frequently hilarious. It's worth the trouble to meet characters such as Mehitable Saffron, "the virgin-hero ov wimmins' rights ... she spoke without notes, at arms' length."

Max Eastman declared that Josh Billings was "the father of imagism" and found nothing in New England poetry before Billings's time "quite comparable to his statement that goats 'know the way up a rock as natural as woodbine,' which is Homeric." Certainly Billings is a primitive La Bruyère, a rustic La Rochefoucauld, and an aphorist with a moralistic rather than a cynical streak. "Most people repent ov their sins bi thanking God they aint so wicked as their nabers." He stressed that "yu hav tew be wise before yu kan be witty" and there is plenty of wisdom in such comments as "There may cum a time when the Lion and the Lamb will lie down together – i shall be as glad to see it as enny body – but i am still betting on the Lion."

—Leonard R. N. Ashley

SHELLEY, Mary (Wollstonecraft).   English.   Born in Somers Town, London, 30 August 1797; daughter of the writers William Godwin, *q.v.*, and Mary Wollstonecraft Godwin. Married the poet Percy Bysshe Shelley in 1816 (died, 1822); two sons and one daughter. Lived in Dundee, 1812, 1813–14, then returned to London; eloped to the Continent with Shelley, 1814; writer from 1816; after Shelley's death lived at Genoa with the Leigh Hunts, 1822–23, then returned to England; supported herself by writing fiction and contributing to periodical. Travelled in Germany, 1840–41, and Italy, 1842– 43. *Died 1 February 1851.*

PUBLICATIONS

Collections

Letters, edited by Frederick L. Jones.   2 vols., 1944.
Collected Tales and Stories, edited by Charles E. Robinson.   1976.

Fiction

Frankenstein; or, The Modern Prometheus.   1818; revised edition, 1831; edited by M.
  K. Joseph, 1969; 1818 edition edited by James Rieger, 1974.
Valperga; or, The Life and Adventures of Castruccio, Prince of Lucca.   1823.
The Last Man.   1826; edited by Hugh J. Luke, 1965.
The Fortunes of Perkin Warbeck: A Romance.   1830; revised edition, 1830.
Lodore.   1835.
Falkner.   1837.
Mathilda, edited by Elizabeth Nitchie.   1959.

Plays

Proserpine and Midas: Mythological Dramas, edited by A. Koszul.   1922.

Verse

The Choice: A Poem on Shelley's Death, edited by H. Buxton Forman.   1876.

Other

*History of a Six Weeks' Tour Through a Part of France, Switzerland, Germany, and
  Holland*, with Percy Bysshe Shelley.   1817; abridgement edited by C. I. Elton, 1894.
Rambles in Germany and Italy in 1840, 1842, and 1843.   2 vols., 1844.
*Shelley and Mary: A Collection of Letters and Documents of a Biographical
  Character.*   3 vols., 1882.
Letters, Mostly Unpublished, edited by Henry H. Harper.   1918.
Journal, edited by Frederick L. Jones.   1947.
My Best Mary: The Selected Letters, edited by Muriel Spark and Derek Stanford.   1953.

Editor, *Posthumous Poems*, by Percy Bysshe Shelley.   1824.
Editor, *The Poetical Works of Percy Bysshe Shelley.*   4 vols., 1839.
Editor, *Essays, Letters from Abroad, Translations, and Fragments*, by Percy Bysshe
  Shelley.   2 vols., 1840.

Reading List: *Child of Light: A Reassessment of Shelley* by Muriel Spark, 1951; *Shelley,
Author of Frankenstein* by Elizabeth Nitchie, 1953; *Shelley* by E. Bigland, 1959; *Shelley dans
Son Oeuvre* by Jean de Palaccio, 1969; *Shelley's Frankenstein: Tracing the Myth* by
Christopher Small, 1973; *Shelley's Mary: A Life of Mary Godwin Shelley* by Margaret
Leighton, 1973.

*   *   *

In a busy life as professional author, Mary Shelley wrote seven novels and some two dozen
short stories, as well as travel-books, biographies, and reviews. Of all this, *The Last Man*, at
least, deserves to survive for its sombre apocalyptic vision; yet Mary Shelley is remembered
for one book only, *Frankenstein*, which she wrote at the age of nineteen. Its special quality
owes much to the stimulating influence of Byron and Shelley on a lively young mind, though
it is a book that neither of them could have written. Even its technical faults create

complexity, and its unresolved ideas turn what might have been a moralistic Gothic tale into a work of mythology.

The novel, as its subtitle indicates, is a reworking of the Prometheus-creator theme in a modern setting, using sensational reports of galvanism to supply fire from heaven. It thus becomes a parable of the Creator's responsibility for mankind, and more specifically of the scientist's power to restructure nature. Neither Frankenstein nor the Monster that he brings to life is inherently evil: Frankenstein is a noble character, surrounded and inspired by examples of benevolence, and the Monster is initially a noble savage who responds to the benign influence of nature. Yet Frankenstein, having created the Monster, cannot fulfil his obligations to his creature, who tells him, "I was benevolent and good; misery made me a fiend. Make me happy, and I shall again be virtuous."

The title-page quotation is the anguished question of Milton's Adam to his God: "Did I request thee, Maker, from my clay/To mould Me man?" Initially it is the Monster who asks this, and even forgives Frankenstein for his desertion, asking only to be given an Eve of his own kind and allowed to withdraw to the wilderness. Only when Frankenstein reneges on this does the Monster become, not Adam, but a fallen Satan who destroys everyone connected with his maker. But the Monster, as "demon," is also an anti-self, like Blake's Spectre, and this is expressed in the dream-like chase with which the story concludes. Frankenstein too has eaten the apple of knowledge and been expelled from Paradise; he in turn can confront his Maker with the same tragic question.

The ideas which Mary Shelley absorbed from her friends reflected their interest in the new scientific speculations on the nature and origin of life which were just beginning to take shape. In the next century and a half these were to transform our understanding of the world and our capacity to act upon it. By a rare feat of imaginative insight, she was able to suggest the two main consequences of this, an obscure or absent God and an ambivalent technology. Her handling of them has entered popular consciousness through continual reworking, imitation, and parody. If these have overlaid and sometimes debased the original, this is the price one pays for creating a myth.

—M. K. Joseph

SHORTHOUSE, Joseph Henry. English. Born in Birmingham, 9 September 1834. Educated at Grove House, Tottenham, London. Married Sarah Scott in 1857. Worked in his father's chemical business in Birmingham all his life; writer from 1880. *Died 4 March 1903.*

PUBLICATIONS

Fiction

John Inglesant: A Romance. 1880.
The Little Schoolmaster Mark: A Spiritual Romance. 2 vols., 1883–84.
Sir Percival: A Story of the Past and the Present. 1886.
A Teacher of the Violin and Other Tales. 1888.
The Countess Eve. 1888.
Blanche, Lady Falaise. 1891.

Other

On the Platonism of Wordsworth. 1882.

Reading List: *The Life and Letters of Shorthouse,* edited by Sarah Shorthouse, 2 vols., 1905; *The Historical, Philosophical, and Religious Aspects of John Inglesant* by M. Polak, 1934; *"John Inglesant* and Its Author" by M. Bishop, in *Essays by Divers Hands,* 1958.

*   *   *

In the eyes of more than one of his contemporaries Joseph Henry Shorthouse was unquestionably *homo unius libri* (P. E. More, *Shelburne Essays III,* 1905). More recent admirers have tended to agree. *John Inglesant,* the work of a reclusive Birmingham vitriol manufacturer, caught the public imagination in much the same way that Mrs. Humphry Ward's *Robert Elsmere* was to do a few years later. Having worked on the book for more than ten years, Shorthouse had a hundred copies privately printed and circulated in 1880. He would have let the matter rest, professing himself content that one hundred educated persons had read his work, had not Mrs. Ward seen the novel and drawn it to the attention of Alexander Macmillan, who published it commercially in 1881. Although it never achieved the enormous popular success of Mrs. Ward's novel, *John Inglesant* was seized upon by literary and intellectual circles, and Shorthouse appropriately lionized. Lord Acton declared he had read "nothing more thoughtful and suggestive since *Middlemarch*" (*Letters to Mary Gladstone,* 1904), and as the ultimate seal of approval Gladstone was photographed with a volume of the novel on his knee.

Nineteenth-century readers saw in this seventeenth-century spiritual odyssey an analogue of their own dilemma in the wake of the Oxford Movement. John Inglesant, the hero, is brought up a member of the English church in a family with strong Catholic sympathies. Because of this background he is trained by a Jesuit to act as a mediator between the English and Roman churches. In a series of adventures, many of them undertaken in support of Charles I, he becomes friendly with the followers of Nicholas Ferrar at Little Gidding, and later spends much of his time in Italy where he becomes a disciple of the quietist Molinos. Eventually he returns to England and the English church.

Nearly half the novel takes place in Italy, a detailed and evocative setting which was commented on by contemporary readers, particularly as Shorthouse was known never to have left England during his lifetime. The entire work, both the English and Italian sections, is saturated with seventeenth-century sources, the product, it was acknowledged, of years of reading. Rumblings about the book's accuracy, by Acton and others, continued until 1925, when W. K. Fleming, in an article in the *Quarterly Review,* showed that not only was Shorthouse immersed in seventeenth-century sources, the novel was an extraordinary collage of them. Fleming uncovered almost verbatim borrowings from Anthony à Wood, Aubrey's *Lives,* Burton's *Anatomy of Melancholy,* and Evelyn's *Diary.* The last in particular was relied on extensively for the Italian scenes. In the course of Inglesant's colloquy with the philosopher Hobbes, eleven lines of the *Leviathan* appeared directly. Much of the section showing the influence of Henry More the Platonist was taken blatantly from Ward's *Life of More.*

But such a "discovery" was anything but the unveiling of a gigantic literary hoax. Irrespective of Shorthouse's dubious methods the novel remains fascinating for its plot and historical colouring. Graham Hough (*New Statesman,* 3 August 1946) quite rightly places it in the picaresque tradition, a deliberate journey of the hero through the major political and intellectual circles of his time with corresponding adventures in each. Hough is perhaps too cynical in arguing that the novel has no conclusion, that Inglesant is always convinced by the last person with whom he speaks, and that he ends up in the Church of England because the novel happens to stop when he returns to England. Readers from Acton onwards, however, have commented on Inglesant's thinness as a character. We never quite come to grips with the peculiar personality which lends itself to be trained as a go-between of the two major churches without, it would appear, wholeheartedly committing himself to either. Certainly his abrupt return to England when Molinos is disgraced does not carry with it the comfort of firm conviction. Nevertheless the work remains one of the most interesting of the religious novels of the Victorian period as well as a unique "literary curiosity."

Shorthouse failed to sustain the literary momentum generated by John Inglesant. His later works, of which *The Little Schoolmaster Mark* and *Sir Percival* are the best known, are pallid fables of almost childlike simplicity. In all his work, but particularly in the later novels, it is possible to trace the faint influence of Hawthorne, his favourite author from the days of his youth.

—Joanne Shattock

* * *

SIDNEY, Sir Philip. English. Born in Penshurst, Kent, 30 November 1554. Educated at Shrewsbury School, Shropshire, 1564–68; Christ Church, Oxford (left without a degree). Married Frances Walsingham in 1583. Travelled in France, Germany, and Italy, as Gentleman of the Bedchamber to Charles IV, 1572–75; Member of Elizabeth's court: Ambassador to Emperor Rudolf and then to the Prince of Orange, 1577; in disfavor with the Queen, retired to his sister's estate at Wilton, 1580; Member of Parliament, 1581; knighted, 1582; Governor of Flushing, 1585; accompanied Leicester to the Netherlands to fight against Spain, and died in battle there. *Died 17 October 1586.*

PUBLICATIONS

Collections

> *Complete Works*, edited by Albert Feuillerat.   4 vols., 1912–26.
> *Poems*, edited by William A. Ringler, Jr.   1962.
> *Selected Poetry and Prose*, edited by David Kalstone.   1970.

Fiction

> *The Countess of Pembroke's Arcadia.*   1590; revised edition, including material from earlier version, 1593; edited by Albert Feuillerat, in *Complete Works*, 1922; earlier version, edited by Albert Feuillerat, in *Complete Works*, 1926; as *The Old Arcadia*, edited by J. Robertson, 1973; 1590 edition edited by Maurice Evans, 1977.

Verse

> *Astrophel* [i.e., *Astrophil*] *and Stella* (includes sonnets by other writers), edited by Thomas Nashe.   1591; revised edition, in *Arcadia*, 1598; edited by M. Putzel, 1967.
> *The Psalms of David*, with the Countess of Pembroke, edited by S. W. Singer.   1823; edited by J. C. A. Rathmell, 1963.

Other

The Defense of Poesy. 1595; as *An Apology for Poetry,* 1595; edited by Jan van Dorsten, 1966.

The Countess of Pembroke's Arcadia (miscellany; includes *Certain Sonnets, Defense of Poesy, Astrophel and Stella, The Lady of May*). 1598; augmented edition, including *A Dialogue Between Two Shepherds,* 1613.

Miscellaneous Prose, edited by Katherine Duncan-Jones and Jan van Dorsten. 1973.

Bibliography: *Sidney: A Concise Bibliography* by S. A. Tannenbaum, 1941, supplement by G. R. Guffey, 1967; *Sidney: An Annotated Bibliography of Modern Criticism, 1941–1970* by Mary A. Washington, 1972.

Reading List: *Sidney and the English Renaissance* by J. Buxton, 1954; *Sidney* by Kenneth Muir, 1960; *Symmetry and Sense: The Poetry of Sidney* by R. L. Montgomery, Jr., 1961; *Sidney's Poetry: Contexts and Interpretations* by David Kalstone, 1965; *The Epic Voice: Arcadia* by R. Delasanta, 1967; *Heroic Love: Studies in Sidney and Spenser* by Mark Rose, 1968; *Sidney* by Robert Kimbrough, 1970; *Young Sidney 1572–1577* by James M. Osborn, 1972; *The Poetry of Sidney: An Interpretation in the Context of His Life and Times* by John G. Nichols, 1974; *Sidney: A Study of His Life and Work* by A. C. Hamilton, 1977; *Sidney: The Maker's Mind* by Dorothy Connell, 1978.

*   *   *

The keynote of Sir Philip Sidney's work is self-conscious artistry in the service of psychological exploration. In his *Defense of Poesy,* he defined poetry as an art of imitation, as did theorists before him; but he insisted that the object of imitation exists not in nature but in the poet's mind, so that poetry becomes the giving form or image to ideas. Thus the poet becomes a maker of fictions, and fiction becomes the exercise of hypothesis, whereby the poet, "freely ranging within the zodiac of his own wit," explores "the divine consideration of what may be, or should be." The end of knowledge for Sidney is the repair of the Fall by implanting self-knowledge and action; and poetry does that better than philosophy or history, not only because it presents precepts of virtue in apprehensible images, but also because, by so doing, it causes delight which moves men to "take that goodness in hand which, without delight, they would flee as from a stranger." By casting his treatise into the form of a delightful classical oration – with its changes of tone from the relaxed humor of the opening to the passionate exhortation of the ending – Sidney made the defending of poetry itself an imaginary action, whereby his persuasion to love poetry became analogous to poetry's persuasion to embrace virtue.

Sidney's great prose romance, *Arcadia,* exists in two different forms. The *Old Arcadia* (ca. 1579–80) is a straight-forward narrative in five "books" or "acts" following the five-act structure of Terentian comedy; the books are separated by four verse interludes or entertainments by the Arcadian shepherds, each with its special theme which both ties together the various actions preceding it in the narrative and contrasts the main action tonally. The romance belongs to the pastoral tradition, with its concerns over humility, figured as man's harmony with nature, and pride, as man's attempt to rise above nature. It centers around questions of human control over events, and these dilate into parallel actions of love, in the private, and order, in the political, realms, book-by-book. Sidney's sophisticated narrative persona views these actions with objectivity and, frequently, with wry comedy.

The comic tone disappears in the incomplete *New Arcadia,* an extensive revision of the first two and one-half books (ca. 1583–4) which elaborated characterization, ideas, style, and especially plot. Sidney added thirteen new episodes that showed events in the main plot from a variety of angles and created thematic density whereby the three books of the revised romance became small disquisitions on love, reason against passion, and the nature of marriage. By focusing on a clearly articulated ideational structure thus, Sidney forged the pastoral romance into an ethical and psychological tool, according to the aims of poetry set out in the *Defense*. The verse interludes of both *Arcadias* are marked by interesting experiments with classical meters and Romance forms. Some of them – the sapphic "If mine eyes can speak," the great double sestina "Ye goatherd gods" – are really accomplished poems.

In *Astrophil and Stella* Sidney made his most telling experiments. He made the sonnet psychologically dramatic by emphasizing conflict in the form, specifically by polarizing octave and sestet to dramatize the clash of different states of mind. In sonnet 15 the octave parodies bookish modes of composition, while the sestet reverently presents the natural emergence of poetry from love. The stylistic clash in this and other sonnets suggests the replacement of a less by a more valid perception of a situation, usually an external viewpoint by an internal one. In sonnet 31, the contrast between the sentimental octave and the satiric sestet frames a dramatic action whereby the sentimental lover gradually reaches contact with the whole moral man. The histrionics of the Sidneyan sonnet come out strikingly in sonnets like 47, which reads like a soliloquy in a play, the internal argument of Astrophil suddenly crumbling with the appearance of Stella, and 74, wherein, after Astrophil's presentation of himself as bumbling poet, he suddenly emerges as the sophisticated lover-poet who teases the simple reader.

In the 108 sonnets and 11 songs of *Astrophil and Stella* we observe an anatomy of the mind of the lover in its infinite variety. When read consecutively, the collection outlines a psychological action, in a series of lyric moments, describing the influence of love on the relation between the self and reality. The first 22 sonnets lay out themes of love and poetry in a dispersed manner; with the twenty-third sonnet, interrelations become firmer by contiguous themes and rhyme links, and the action settles into the rejection of external reality for the sake of love. Sonnets 31 to 40 explore the precise nature of this love, its difficulty in the face of a real-life husband for Stella and the desire to retreat from it in sleep and dream. With Sonnet 41, we move from the "prospective musings" internal to Astrophil outward to his experience of the reality of life in love; sonnets are now directly addressed to Stella and describe experiences with her. From Sonnet 52 through the first Song (the songs presenting public events in the love experience), sensuality enters the sequence, and for a while external action determines the progress of the affair, first in a series of linked sonnets on hope (66–67), joy (68–70), and desire (71–72), then by a stolen kiss described in the Second Song and celebrated in the ensuing sonnets (79–82). This external action is shown directly in the Fourth through Ninth Songs describing a meeting, Astrophil's open declaration, and Stella's firm rejection of him. The sequence then returns to internal experience in a group of sonnets on absence (87–92) wherein Astrophil turns inward and Stella becomes abstract to him; the final movement shows Astrophil alone, bound up in his mind once more; night characterizes his state, as do images of the self as prison.

Sidney's works offer various hypotheses about love's influence on the mind. In both prose and verse he experimented with form as a means of conveying psychological insight. Whereas in the two *Arcadias* he infused fiction with poetic and dramatic devices, in *Astrophil and Stella* he welded lyrics together into a psychological fiction. The effects of such bold experimentation were quick to be grasped by Sidney's contemporaries, especially after the publication of his works in the early 1590's, and they can be seen especially in the fiction of Greene and Lodge, and in the poetry of Spenser, Greville, Campion, Daniel, Drayton, and Jonson.

—Walter R. Davis

SILLITOE, Alan. English. Born in Nottingham, 4 March 1928. Educated in local schools to age 14. Served as a radio operator in the Royal Air Force, 1946–49. Married the poet Ruth Fainlight in 1959; two children. Worked at various odd jobs in Nottingham, 1942–46; writer from 1948; travelled and lived in France, Italy, and Spain, 1952–58; Literary Adviser to W. H. Allen and Company, publishers, London, from 1970. Recipient: Authors Club prize, 1958; Hawthornden Prize, 1960. Lives in Wittersham, Kent.

PUBLICATIONS

Fiction

Saturday Night and Sunday Morning. 1958.
The Loneliness of the Long Distance Runner (stories). 1959.
The General. 1960.
Key to the Door. 1961.
The Ragman's Daughter (stories). 1963.
The Death of William Posters. 1965.
A Tree on Fire. 1967.
Guzman Go Home (stories). 1968.
A Start in Life. 1970.
Travels in Nihilon. 1971.
Raw Material. 1972.
Men, Women, and Children (stories). 1973.
The Flame of Life. 1974.
Down to the Bone (stories). 1976.
The Widower's Son. 1976.

Plays

The Ragman's Daughter (produced 1966).
All Citizens Are Soldiers, with Ruth Fainlight, from a play by Lope de Vega (produced 1967). 1969.
The Slot Machine (as *This Foreign Field,* produced 1970). In *Three Plays,* 1978.
Pit Strike (televised 1977). In *Three Plays,* 1978.
The Interview (produced 1978). In *Three Plays,* 1978.
Three Plays (includes *The Slot Machine, The Interview, Pit Strike).* 1978.

Screenplays: *Saturday Night and Sunday Morning,* 1960; *The Loneliness of the Long Distance Runner,* 1961; *The Ragman's Daughter,* 1974.

Television Play: *Pit Strike,* 1977.

Verse

Without Beer or Bread. 1957.
The Rats and Other Poems. 1960.
A Falling Out of Love and Other Poems. 1964.
Shaman and Other Poems. 1968.
Love in the Environs of Voronezh and Other Poems. 1968.

Poems, with Ted Hughes and Ruth Fainlight.   1971.
Barbarians and Other Poems.   1974.
Storm: New Poems.   1974.

Other

The Road to Volgograd (travel).   1964.
The City Adventures of Marmalade Jim (juvenile).   1967.
Mountains and Caverns: Selected Essays.   1975.
Big John and the Stars (juvenile).   1977.
The Incredible Fencing Fleas (juvenile).   1978.

Reading List: *Sillitoe* edited by Michael Marland, 1970; *Sillitoe* by Allen Richard Penner, 1972; "The Existential Dilemmas of Sillitoe's Working-Class Heroes" by A. R. Nordella, in *Studies in the Novel*, 1973; "Sillitoe's Political Novels" by M. Wielding, in *Cunning Exiles: Studies of Modern Prose Writers* edited by D. Anderson, 1975.

*   *   *

Anarchy, socialism, and sex are allied and recurrent themes in much of Alan Sillitoe's work. His Nottingham working-class home becomes the setting for rebellious characters who find the tentacles of government reaching even their intensely private, family-orientated lives through such things as form-filling, vote-catching, pay-as-you-earn taxation, or National Service, but who try to resist it with all the force of their traditionally bloody-minded individualism. Their archetypes are Arthur Seaton, the "young anarchic roughneck" of *Saturday Night and Sunday Morning*; Michael Cullen, the bastard-hero of the working-class picaresque novel *A Start in Life*; and Smith, the long-distance runner who prefers deliberately to lose society's race to security, recognition, and respectability.

The more orderly ideal of socialism is at least the apparent theme of such novels as *Travels in Nihilon* and *The Flame of Life*. The first is a satire, on the lines of such inverted Utopias as *Gulliver's Travels*, Book IV, and Samuel Butler's *Erewhon*, directed at the irrationality and irresponsible violence inherent in the capitalist, free-enterprise system of Nihilon. By the end of the novel, however, the Rational forces which have succeeded in "liberating" Nihilon from the tyranny of unreason are already succumbing to the anarchy which they have supposedly overthrown. Similarly, *The Flame of Life*, which concerns another form of experimental Utopia – an English kibbutz combining the ideal of the extended family with planning for a socialist revolution – ends in disintegration. Neither is cynical (indeed, Sillitoe writes with almost naive enthusiasm), but each seems to find the ideal of order incompatible with the need of chaos.

The myth of working-class potency is likewise a recurrent theme, but ambiguously exploited. Sillitoe's heroes seek to banish their frustrations in an orgy of sexual satisfaction which resolves neither their own nor their partners' problems. Sex becomes yet another form of anarchy, though with an undertow dragging the men against their will towards an order and responsibility which they resist like a threat of castration, and laying the women under the spell of a sensuality which in the end only exacerbates their demand for peace and security.

Order and anarchy represent a paradox which, according to Sillitoe himself, was present in his own childhood background. His relations on his mother's side, the Burtons, were "the simple men" in him, and the Sillitoes "the complex men." And the characters in his fiction are often simple men caught in the complicated cog-wheels of society against which their only defence is a loosely strung tirade of protest. At the same time he is fascinated by the structures of discipline, often crude and brutal, with which society tries to subdue and contain this chaos which is "the source of life and richness." Thus, in *The General* and *The Widower's Son* he focuses on the military life as it centres on men who, after submitting to all the externals of discipline, achieve impressive efficiency and success, and yet remain powerful misfits whose success is essentially self-defeating.

This paradox remains largely unresolved in Sillitoe's work. Such resolution as there is consists in the turbulent release of his demotic prose. Though he speaks (in *Raw Material*) with contempt of "the talkers" for whom there is "only one truth" and for whom "manic continual speech prevents self-knowledge and the threat of facing the wasteland," through the creation of manic first-person monologues he often makes comic exaggeration, prejudice, expletives, and sheer rage serve the needs of frustrated anarchy. The result is a primitive, but sometimes very effective, brand of catharsis.

—R. P. Draper

SIMMS, William Gilmore.   American.   Born in Charleston, South Carolina, 17 April 1806. Educated in public and private schools in Charleston; apprenticed to a druggist, then studied law; admitted to the South Carolina bar, 1827. Married 1) Anna Malcolm Giles in 1826 (died, 1832); 2) Chevillette Roach in 1836 (died, 1863); at least 15 children. Practiced law in Charleston from 1827, but subsequently gave up law for literature; Editor, *Charleston City Gazette*, 1830–32; visited the North and formed friendship with William Cullen Bryant; settled in New Haven, 1833; returned to Charleston, 1835; divided his time between his wife's family home, Woodlands Plantation, Barnwell County, and Charleston, from 1836; Editor, *Southern Quarterly Review*, 1849–54; advocate of slavery: lectured in New York, 1856; after the Civil War wrote serials for magazines in New York and Philadelphia. *Died 11 June 1870.*

PUBLICATIONS

Collections

> *The Letters,* edited by Mary C. Simms Oliphant, Alfred Taylor Odell, and T. C. Duncan Eaves.   5 vols., 1952–56; supplement, 1977.
> *Writings,* edited by John C. Guilds.   1969–

Fiction

> *The Book of My Lady: A Melange* (stories).   1833.
> *Martin Faber: The Story of a Criminal.*   1833; in *Writings 5,* 1974.
> *Guy Rivers: A Tale of Georgia.*   1834.
> *The Yemassee: A Romance of Carolina.*   1835; edited by C. Hugh Holman, 1961.
> *The Partisan: A Tale of the Revolution.*   1835.

Mellichampe: A Legend of the Santee.   1836.
Richard Hurdis; or, The Avenger of Blood.   1838.
Pelayo: A Story of the Goth.   1838.
Carl Werner: An Imaginative Story, with Other Tales.   1838; in *Writings 5*, 1974.
The Damsel of Darien.   1839.
Border Beagles: A Tale of Mississippi.   1840.
The Kinsmen; or, The Black Riders of Congaree.   1841; as *The Scout*, 1854.
Confession; or, The Blind Heart: A Domestic Story.   1841.
Beauchampe; or, The Kentucky Tragedy.   1842; portion revised, as *Charlemont; or, The Pride of the Village*, 1856.
Castle Dismal; or, The Bachelor's Christmas: A Dramatic Legend.   1844.
The Prima Donna: A Passage from City Life.   1844; in *Writings 5*, 1974.
Helen Halsey; or, The Swamp State of Conelachita: A Tale of the Borders.   1845; as *The Island Bride*, 1869.
Count Julian; or, The Last Days of the Goth.   1845.
The Wigwam and the Cabin (stories).   2 vols., 1845–46; as *Life in America*, 1848.
The Lily and the Totem; or, The Huguenots in Florida.   1850.
Flirtation at the Moultrie House.   1850; in *Writings 5*, 1974.
Katharine Walton; or, The Rebel of Dorchester.   1851.
The Golden Christmas: A Chronicle of St. John's, Berkeley.   1852.
The Sword and the Distaff; or, "Fair, Fat, and Forty." 1852; revised edition, as *Woodcraft; or, Hawks about the Dovecote*, 1854.
As Good as a Comedy; or, The Tennesseean's Story.   1852; in *Writings 3*, 1972.
Marie De Berniere (stories).   1853; as *The Maroon: A Legend of the Caribbees, and Other Stories*, 1855.
Vasconselos: A Romance of the New World.   1853.
Southward Ho! A Spell of Sunshine.   1854.
The Forayers; or, The Raid of the Dog-Days.   1855.
Eutaw.   1856.
The Cassique of Kiawah.   1859.
Cavalier of Old South Carolina: Simms's Captain Porgy, edited by Hugh W. Hetherington, 1966.
Voltmeier; or, The Mountain Men, edited by James B. Meriwether, in *Writings 1*.   1969.
Joscelyn: A Tale of the Revolution, edited by Keen Butterworth, in *Writings 16*.   1975.

Verse

Monody on the Death of General Charles Cotesworth Pinckney.   1825.
Lyrical and Other Poems.   1827.
Early Lays.   1827.
The Vision of Cortes, Cain, and Other Poems.   1829.
The Tri-Color; or, The Three Days of Blood in Paris.   1830.
Atalantis: A Story of the Sea.   1832.
Southern Passages and Pictures.   1839.
Donna Florida.   1843.
Grouped Thoughts and Scattered Fancies.   1845.
Areytos; or, Songs of the South.   1846.
Lays of the Palmetto.   1848.
Charleston and Her Satirists: A Scribblement.   1848.
The Cassique of Accabee, A Tale of Ashley River, with Other Pieces.   1849.
Sabbath Lyrics; or, Songs from Scripture.   1849.
The City of the Silent.   1850.
Norman Maurice; or, The Man of the People.   1851.

Michael Bonham; or, The Fall of Bexar.   1852.
Poems · Descriptive, Dramatic, Legendary, and Contemplative.   1853.

Other

The Remains of Maynard Davis Richardson.   1833.
Slavery in America.   1838.
The History of South Carolina.   1840.
The Geography of South Carolina.   1843.
The Life of Francis Marion.   1844.
Views and Reviews in American Literature, History, and Fiction.   1845; edited by C. Hugh Holman, 1962.
The Life of Captain John Smith.   1846.
The Life of the Chevalier Bayard.   1847.
The Life of Nathanael Greene.   1849.
Father Abbott; or, The Home Tourist.   1849.
South Carolina in the Revolutionary War.   1853.
Egeria; or, Voices of Thought and Counsel for the Woods and Wayside.   1853.
Works.   20 vols., 1853–66.
Sack and Destruction of the City of Columbia, S.C.   1865; edited by A. S. Salley, 1937.

Editor, *The Charleston Book: A Miscellany in Prose and Verse.*   1845.
Editor, *War Poetry of the South.*   1867.

Bibliography: *A Bibliography of the Separate Writings of Simms* by Oscar Wegelin, 1941.

Reading List: *Simms* by William P. Trent, 1892; *Simms as Literary Critic* by Edd Winfield Parks, 1961; *Simms* by Joseph V. Ridgely, 1962.

*   *   *

The most versatile and representative Southern writer of the 19th century and one of the more talented American writers of the period, William Gilmore Simms tried his hand at many literary forms and tasks. He published at least four biographies, the best of which, *The Life of Francis Marion,* is a consideration of sources and materials also used in several of his long fictions on the Revolution. He also wrote books on the geography and history of South Carolina.

Simms was early and late a journalist. He edited both newspapers and magazines and eventually possessed considerable influence, especially in the South, as editor and contributor of essays and criticism to such journals as the *Southern Literary Gazette, Southern Literary Messenger, Southern Literary Journal, Southern Quarterly Review*, and *Russell's Magazine.* He also contributed to many of the most consequential Northern magazines, including the *Knickerbocker, Democratic Review, Graham's, Harper's New Monthly,* and *Lippincott's.* Some of his best periodical criticism is collected in *Views and Reviews,* but, as Edd W. Parks has noted in *William Gilmore Simms as Literary Critic* (1961), there is also important criticism in prefaces and advertisements to novels and in letters. In the Advertisement to *The Yemassee* in 1835, for example, Simms elaborated on a distinction between the romance and the novel that allowed the writer of the former considerable latitude in the treatment of the possible and the probable; in long critical essays he discoursed learnedly on Cooper's writings in 1842 (and gave his chief American rival every bit of his due), and in 1845 he dealt effectively with "Americanism in Literature"; and in letters in 1842 and thereafter he discussed perceptively the place of realism in fiction and fairly characterized Poe as magazinist, story writer, and poet. Simms's letters have recently assumed their rightful place in any study of his canon as a result of their publication in five volumes (1952–1956), with a sixth supplementary volume.

Simms also wrote a number of plays, including two in blank verse (*Norman Maurice* and *Michael Bonham*), and his view of his own merit as a poet is indicated in a remark in a letter of 24 November 1853 that his "poetical work exhibits the highest phase of the Imaginative faculty which this Country has yet exhibited, and the most philosophical in connection with it." Few, including his friends Paul Hamilton Hayne and Henry Timrod, agreed with him then or subsequently.

Over the years, however, most critics have agreed that Simms's chief contribution was to the novel. This is still largely the case when one considers the size and scope of his accomplishment in the seven books of the Revolutionary Romances (1835–1856) or observes carefully the achievement in such individual works as *The Yemassee, Border Beagles, Katharine Walton, Woodcraft,* or *The Cassique of Kiawah.* But Simms was a significant writer of short fiction, and John C. Guilds maintains in his introduction to *Stories and Tales* (Volume 5 of the Centennial Edition of the Writings) that the "short story or tale" is Simms's "best genre," and the contents of this edition plus the better-known tales of the two volumes of *The Wigwam and the Cabin* clearly show that Simms did indeed make a consequential and varied contribution to short fiction.

Simms's versatility and prolificness, to say nothing of the adverse reaction of Northern readers to his political views during the Civil War and its aftermath, assuredly contributed to the decline in his literary reputation, which reached its nadir with World War II. With, however, studies of C. Hugh Holman in the late 1940's and thereafter, the edition of letters in the 1950's (including especially the critical evaluation of Simms's best work by Donald Davidson), the appraisal of Simms as man of letters by Jay B. Hubbell in *The South in American Literature* in 1954, and the beginning of the publication of the Centennial Edition, Simms's work has received and is continuing to receive the attention it has long merited.

—Rayburn S. Moore

SINCLAIR, May (Mary Amelia St. Clair Sinclair). English. Born in Rock Ferry, Cheshire, 24 August 1863. Educated at Cheltenham Ladies' College, 1881–82. Writer from 1895; lived in Sidmouth and London; served with the Belgian Red Cross Ambulance Corps during World War I; worked with the Hoover Relief Commission; settled in Bierton, near Aylesbury, Buckinghamshire, 1936; twice visited America. Fellow, Royal Society of Literature, 1916. *Died 14 November 1946.*

PUBLICATIONS

Fiction

Audrey Craven. 1897.
Mr. and Mrs. Nevill Tyson. 1898; as *The Tysons,* 1907.
Two Sides of a Question (stories). 1901.
The Divine Fire. 1904.
The Helpmate. 1907.

The Judgment of Eve. 1907.
Kitty Tailleur. 1908; as *The Immortal Moment,* 1908.
The Creators: A Comedy. 1910.
The Flaw in the Crystal. 1912.
The Combined Maze. 1913.
The Judgment of Eve and Other Stories. 1914; as *The Return of the Prodigal,* 1914.
The Three Sisters. 1914.
Tasker Jevons: The Real Story. 1916; as *The Belfry,* 1916.
The Tree of Heaven. 1917.
Mary Olivier: A Life. 1919.
The Romantic. 1920.
Mr. Waddington of Wyck. 1921.
Life and Death of Harriett Frean. 1922.
Anne Severn and the Fieldings. 1922.
Uncanny Stories. 1923.
Arnold Waterlow: A Life. 1924.
A Cure of Souls. 1924.
The Rector of Wyck. 1925.
Far End. 1926.
The Allinghams. 1927.
History of Anthony Waring. 1927.
Fame (story). 1929.
Tales Told by Simpson. 1930.
The Intercessor and Other Stories. 1931.

Verse

Nakiketos and Other Poems. 1886.
Essays in Verse. 1891.
The Dark Night (novel in verse). 1924.

Other

Feminism. 1912.
The Three Brontës. 1912.
A Journal of Impressions in Belgium. 1915.
A Defence of Idealism: Some Questions and Conclusions. 1917.
The New Idealism. 1922.

Translator, *Outlines of Church History,* by Rudolf Sohm. 1895.
Translator, *England's Danger,* by T. von Sosnosky. 1901.

Bibliography: "On the Sinclair Collection" by Theophilus E. M. Boll, in *University of Pennsylvania Library Chronicle,* 1961.

Reading List: *Sinclair, Novelist: A Biographical and Critical Introduction* by Theophilus E. M. Boll, 1973.

*   *   *

In 1904 Owen Seaman chided English critics for failing to recognize the magnificence of

May Sinclair's *The Divine Fire*. This critical neglect is still evident at the present day. She frightened many reviewers with her learning, her revelations about women, her knowledge of men, and her realism in regarding sex as so — or even too — often a decisive fact of life.

Her main work is her novels. Her first published novel, *Audrey Craven*, is a comedy observing the moves a woman makes unconsciously to shed the discomfort she feels over being an empty self, and to acquire a content her social sense would be proud of. *The Divine Fire*, her springboard to celebrity, anticipated Jung's concept of individuation. It brings together a Cockney poet, whose genius is encumbered by vulgar traits, and a socially polished and intellectually brilliant woman who resists her unconscious love for him while stimulating him to his finest work as an artist. *The Creators* is about a group of novelists and poets, single and married. The plot concerns the effects of unconsciously acted-upon suggestions, and the different influences of sex upon the creative genius. *The Combined Maze* is spun from the same theme: the sexual effect upon a youth of his lavishing his sympathetic love exclusively upon his mother.

Mary Olivier: A Life, May Sinclair's favorite and her psychological autobiography, centers on an intelligent self, the only girl in a family, as she passes from her first awareness of her mother's breast on through all the external and internal forces strengthening or limiting that self. She becomes a successful poet, a matured self, reconciled to the loss of her lover and experiencing beauty, reality, the full awareness of self, and the all-embracing, all-infusing presence of God. The defensive phase of the theme is spoken by Mary when she discovers what the sin against the Holy Ghost means: "Not adoring the self in people. Hating it. Trying to crush it." *Life and Death of Harriett Frean* is the obverse of *Mary Olivier*. With a lean style, but orchestrating a variety of moods, it tells the absurd tragedy of a daughter who allows her self to be thwarted in every veleity and finally obliterated into the shadow of her sweetly possessive mother. *A Cure of Souls* is a suave comedy whose central figure is a clergyman who, in guarding his refined self from every care for others, inflicts cruelty upon those who mistake his clerical collar as a symbol of trust.

Her novels show an intense interest in psychology, especially in the mystery of the will and the self, both conscious and unconscious (with dreams often used to throw light on what the intellect can't clearly see). But her novels are varied in mood and subject matter. Her ear for dramatically intent dialogue and eye for shaping each set scene suggest that she studied Pinero. By experimenting with her style, stripping accessories to make do with the simplest dress of words — dropping, for example, relative pronouns and conjunctions — she produced a lean, incisive prose.

—Theophilus E. M. Boll

SINCLAIR, Upton. American. Born in Baltimore, Maryland, 20 September 1878; moved with his family to New York City, 1888. Educated at the City College of New York, 1893–97, A.B. 1897; Columbia University, New York, 1897–1901. Married 1) Meta H. Fuller in 1900 (divorced, 1911); 2) Mary Craig Kimbrough in 1913 (died, 1961); 3) Mary Elizabeth Willis in 1961 (died, 1967). Writer from 1893, novelist from 1900; founded socialist community, Helicon Home Colony, Englewood, New Jersey, 1906–07; Socialist candidate for Congress, from New Jersey, 1906; settled in Pasadena, California, 1915; Socialist candidate for Congress, 1920, and for the United States Senate, 1922, from California, and for Governor of California, 1926, 1930; moved to Buckeye, Arizona, 1953. Recipient: Pulitzer Prize, 1943; American Newspaper Guild Award, 1962. *Died 25 November 1968.*

PUBLICATIONS

Fiction

Springtime and Harvest: A Romance. 1901; as *King Midas,* 1901.
The Journal of Arthur Stirling. 1903.
Prince Hagen. 1903.
Manassas: A Novel of the War. 1904; as *Theirs Be the Guilt,* 1959.
The Jungle. 1906.
A Captain of Industry. 1906.
The Metropolis. 1908.
The Moneychangers. 1908.
Samuel the Seeker. 1910.
Love's Pilgrimage. 1911.
Sylvia. 1913.
Damaged Goods. 1913.
Sylvia's Marriage. 1914.
King Coal. 1917.
Jimmie Higgins. 1918.
The Spy. 1919; as *100%: The Story of a Patriot,* 1920; excerpt, as *Peter Gudge
    Becomes a Secret Agent,* 1930.
They Call Me Carpenter. 1922.
Oil! 1927.
Boston. 1928; abridgement as *August 22nd,* 1965.
Mountain City. 1929.
Roman Holiday. 1931.
The Wet Parade. 1931.
Co-op: A Novel of Living Together. 1936.
*The Gnomobile: A Gnice Gnew Gnarrative with Gnonsense but Gnothing
    Gnaughty.* 1936.
Little Steel. 1938.
Marie Antoinette. 1939; as *Marie and Her Lover,* 1948.
World's End. 1940.
Between Two Worlds. 1941.
Dragon's Teeth. 1942.
Wide Is the Gate. 1943.
Presidential Agent. 1944.
Dragon Harvest. 1945.
A World to Win. 1946.
Presidential Mission. 1947.
One Clear Call. 1948.
O Shepherd, Speak! 1949.
Another Pamela; or, Virtue Still Rewarded. 1950.
The Return of Lanny Budd. 1953.
What Didymus Did. 1954; as *It Happened to Didymus,* 1958.
The Cup of Fury. 1956.
Affectionately Eve. 1961.
The Coal War: A Sequel to King Coal. 1977.

Plays

Prince Hagen, from his own novel (produced 1909). 1909.

Plays of Protest (includes *Prince Hagen, The Naturewoman, The Machine, The Second-Story Man*). 1912.
Hell: A Verse Drama and Photo-Play. 1923.
The Pot Boiler. 1924.
Singing Jailbirds (produced 1930). 1924.
Bill Porter. 1925.
Wally for Queen! The Private Life of Royalty. 1936.
A Giant's Strength (produced 1948). 1948.

Verse

Songs of Our Nation. 1941.

Other

The Toy and the Man. 1904.
Our Bourgeois Literature. 1905.
Colony Customs. 1906.
The Helicon Home Colony. 1906.
A Home Colony: A Prospectus. 1906.
What Life Means to Me. 1906.
The Industrial Republic. 1907.
The Overman. 1907.
Good Health and How We Won It. 1909; as *The Art of Health,* 1909; as *Strength and Health,* 1910.
War: A Manifesto Against It. 1909.
Four Letters about "Love's Pilgrimage." 1911.
The Fasting Cure. 1911.
The Sinclair-Astor Letters: Famous Correspondence Between Socialist and Millionaire. 1914.
The Social Problem as Seen from the Viewpoint of Trade Unionism, Capital, and Socialism, with others. 1914.
Sinclair: Biographical and Critical Opinions. 1917.
The Profits of Religion. 1918.
Russia: A Challenge. 1919.
The High Cost of Living (address), with *This Misery of Boots,* by H. G. Wells. 1919.
The Brass Check. 1919; section entitled *The Associated Press and Labor,* 1920.
Press-titution. 1920.
The Crimes of the "Times": A Test of Newspaper Decency. 1921.
The Book of Life: Mind and Body. 1921; revised edition, 4 vols., 1950; *Love and Society,* 1922; revised edition, 4 vols., n.d.
The McNeal-Sinclair Debate on Socialism. 1921.
The Goose-Step: A Study of American Education. 1922; revised edition, n.d.
Biographical Letter and Critical Opinions. 1922.
The Millennium: A Comedy of the Year 2000. 1924.
The Goslings. 1924; excerpt, as *The Schools of Los Angeles,* 1924.
Mammonart. 1925.
Letters to Judd. 1926; revised edition, as *This World of 1949 and What to Do about It,* 1949.
The Spokesman's Secretary. 1926.
Money Writes! 1927.
The Pulitzer Prize and "Special Pleading." 1929.

Mental Radio.   1930; revised edition, 1962.
Socialism and Culture.   1931.
Sinclair on "Comrade" Kautsky.   1931.
American Outpost.   1932; as *Candid Reminiscences: My First Thirty Years,* 1932.
I, Governor of California, and How I Ended Poverty.   1933.
Sinclair Presents William Fox.   1933.
The Way Out – What Lies Ahead for America?   1933; as *The Way Out: A Solution to
   Our Present Economic and Social Ills,* 1933; revised edition, as *Limbo on the Loose: A
   Midsummer Night's Dream,* 1948.
EPIC Plan for California.   1934.
EPIC Answers: How to End Poverty in California.   1934.
Immediate EPIC.   1934.
The Lie Factory Starts.   1934.
An Upton Sinclair Anthology, edited by I. O. Evans.   1934; revised edition, 1947.
Sinclair's Last Will and Testament.   1934.
We, People of America, and How We Ended Poverty: A True Story of the Future.   1934.
Depression Island.   1935.
I, Candidate for Governor, and How I Got Licked.   1935; as *How I Got Licked and Why,*
   1935.
What God Means to Me: An Attempt at a Working Religion.   1936.
The Flivver King.   1937.
No Pasoran! (They Shall Not Pass).   1937.
Our Lady.   1938.
Terror in Russia? Two Views, with Eugene Lyons.   1938.
Sinclair on the Soviet Union.   1938.
Expect No Peace!   1939.
Telling the World.   1939.
What Can Be Done about America's Economic Troubles?   1939.
Your Million Dollars.   1939; as *Letters to a Millionaire,* 1939.
*Is the American Form of Capitalism Essential to the American Form of
   Democracy?*   1940.
Peace or War in America.   1940.
Index to the Lanny Budd Story, with others.   1943.
To Solve the German Problem – A Free State?   1943.
The Enemy Had It Too.   1950.
A Personal Jesus: Portrait and Interpretation.   1952; as *Secret Life of Jesus,* 1962.
Radio Liberation Speech to the Peoples of the Soviet Union.   1955.
My Lifetime in Letters.   1960.
The Autobiography of Sinclair.   1962.

Editor, *The Cry for Justice* (anthology).   1915.

Bibliography: *Sinclair: An Annotated Checklist* by Ronald Gottesman, 1973.

Reading List: *This Is Sinclair* by James Lambert Harte, 1938; *The Literary Manuscripts of
Sinclair* by Ronald Gottesman and Charles L. P. Silet, 1972; *Sinclair* by Jon A. Yoder, 1975;
Sinclair: American Rebel by Leon Harris, 1975.

*   *   *

   No American author has produced more writing, had a greater influence on society, and
received less serious critical attention than Upton Sinclair. The depository of Sinclair
manuscripts, books, and letters at The Lilly Library, Indiana University, weighs more than

eight tons. More than 250,000 letters are included in the collection, letters to Shaw, Gandhi, Trotsky, Roosevelt, Kennedy, and countless letters to readers and critics concerning his own work and that of others. The material is available for work that might lead to a reassessment of Sinclair just as the discovery of the Malahide papers caused a radical change in critical opinion concerning James Boswell.

Upton Sinclair wrote on more subjects than we can catalogue; he was interested in extrasensory perception, religion, economics, alcoholism, and much more. He wrote ninety books and many pamphlets, and without his work the social world in which we live would probably lack many of the benefits we take for granted. But of those books, only one, *The Jungle*, has survived as an American classic, and critics are divided as to whether it is a classic of imaginative literature or a classic work of propaganda. Even the once popular Lanny Budd series (eleven novels, 1940–53), one of which, *Dragon's Teeth*, won the Pulitzer Prize, is all but forgotten. The key critical issue apparent in the rather limited Sinclair scholarship is whether Upton Sinclair is a genuine novelist or a very skilled and effective propagandist for social and Socialist reform. Most critics think the latter.

Van Wyck Brooks, in *The Confident Years*, acknowledged *The Jungle* as an outstanding example of muckraking literature; however, muckraking literature operates only on a level of social effect and falls short of the serious novel. *The Jungle* tells of the Lithuanian emigrant family of Jurgis Rudkus. Seeking the realization of the American Dream, the family settles in the Chicago of the early twentieth century. Jurgis goes to work in the stockyards (which provides Sinclair the opportunity to describe the filthy practices of the meat-packing industry) and the family moves into a ramshackle house, deceptively painted by the agent to appear new. There follows a series of tragedies and horrors as members of the family are killed or debased by a social system that cares nothing for the helpless people it exploits. Jurgis's futile attempts to strike back are rewarded with prison sentences. Finally, he learns of the Socialist movement. He finds a job in a hotel managed by a Socialist, and recaptures a sense of hope.

Despite certain well-constructed scenes of genuinely human life, such as the Lithuanian wedding of Jurgis and Ona, it is evident to most readers that Jurgis's family exists primarily as an index to gauge the failures of the social system that destroys them. They are acted upon; they do not act. Indeed, all we learn about human nature from *The Jungle*'s characters is that human nature can be perverted and debased by society. On the other hand, we learn a very great deal about the society. Readers in 1906 learned more than they imagined, and the conditions in the meat-packing industry, so well described by Sinclair, attracted the attention of reformers and presidents. The world of *The Jungle* is a naturalistic world, a world in which only the economically fit survive. Here, human lives are manipulated by an indifferent, if not hostile, scheme of things. But Sinclair's message is that the scheme can change. We have created or at least permitted the existence of the thing that oppresses us, and if enough are made aware of the full horror of that thing, the few who control and profit from it will have to surrender.

In *Upton Sinclair: American Rebel*, Leon Harris observes that successful propaganda must disappear. It seeks to make its ideas commonplace; it causes us to accept its message as the product of our own clear perception of the way things are. Then the actual organ of the propaganda fades in the glow of our self-satisfaction. Most of Sinclair's literature was, and was intended to be, just this kind of successful propaganda. The alteration in our lives and thinking has been tremendous, and we cannot imagine that it could ever be other than that society should care about the people who comprise it. Only on a very rare occasion does a piece of propaganda strike us with such impact that the work itself becomes part of the history that we study and remember, for it is dangerous to forget history. The result, as in the case of *The Jungle*, is a puzzle for critics who know that propaganda should fade away and novels should concern themselves with character development. Paradoxically, then, Upton Sinclair at his best fails in both genres and creates a work that the literate world insists is a classic.

—William J. Heim

SINGER, Isaac Bashevis. American. Born in Radzymin, Poland, 14 July 1904; emigrated to the United States in 1935, naturalized, 1943. Educated at the Tachkemoni Rabbinical Seminary, Warsaw, 1920–22. Married Alma Haimann in 1940; one son. Proofreader and translator for *Literarishe Bleter*, Warsaw, 1923–33; journalist for the *Jewish Daily Forward*, New York, from 1935. Recipient: Louis Lamed Prize, 1950, 1956: National Institute of Arts and Letters grant, 1959; Daroff Memorial Award, 1963; two National Endowment for the Arts grants, 1966; Brandeis University Creative Arts Award, 1969; National Book Award, for children's literature, 1970, and for fiction, 1974; Nobel Prize for Literature, 1978. D.H.L.: Hebrew Union College, Los Angeles, 1963; D.Lit.: Colgate University, Hamilton, New York, 1972; Litt.D.: Bard College, Annandale-on-Hudson, New York, 1974. Member, National Institute of Arts and Letters, 1965; American Academy of Arts and Sciences, 1969; Jewish Academy of Arts and Sciences; Polish Institute of Arts and Sciences. Lives in New York City.

PUBLICATIONS

Fiction

The Family Moskat, translated by A. H. Gross. 1950.
Satan in Goray, translated by Jacob Sloan. 1955.
Gimpel the Fool and Other Stories, translated by Saul Bellow and others. 1957.
The Magician of Lublin, translated by Elaine Gottlieb and Joseph Singer. 1960.
The Spinoza of Market Street and Other Stories, translated by Elaine Gottlieb and others. 1961.
The Slave, translated by the author and Cecil Hemley. 1962.
Short Friday and Other Stories, translated by Ruth Whitman and others. 1964.
Selected Short Stories. 1966.
The Manor, translated by Elaine Gottlieb and Joseph Singer. 1967.
The Séance and Other Stories, translated by Ruth Whitman and others. 1968.
The Estate, translated by Elaine Gottlieb, Joseph Singer, and Elizabeth Shub. 1970.
A Friend of Kafka and Other Stories. 1970.
Enemies: A Love Story, translated by Alizah Shevrin and Elizabeth Shub. 1972.
A Crown of Feathers and Other Stories. 1973.
Passions and Other Stories. 1975.
Shosha. 1978.

Plays

The Mirror (produced 1973).
Schlemiel the First (produced 1974).
Yentl, The Yeshiva Boy, with Leah Napolin, from a story by Singer (produced 1974).

Other

In My Father's Court (autobiography), translated by Channah Kleinerman-Goldstein and others. 1966.
Zlateh the Goat and Other Stories (juvenile), translated by the author and Elizabeth Shub. 1966.
Mazel and Schlimazel; or, The Milk of a Lioness (juvenile), translated by the author and Elizabeth Shub. 1967.

The Fearsome Inn (juvenile), translated by the author and Elizabeth Shub.   1967.
When Schlemiel Went to Warsaw and Other Stories (juvenile), translated by the author
    and Elizabeth Shub.   1968.
A Day of Pleasure: Stories of a Boy Growing Up in Warsaw (juvenile), translated by the
    author and Elizabeth Shub.   1969.
Elijah the Slave (juvenile), translated by the author and Elizabeth Shub.   1970.
Joseph and Koza; or, The Sacrifice to the Vistula (juvenile), translated by the author and
    Elizabeth Shub.   1970.
Alone in the Wild Forest (juvenile), translated by the author and Elizabeth Shub.   1971.
The Topsy-Turvy Emperor of China (juvenile), translated by the author and Elizabeth
    Shub.   1971.
The Wicked City (juvenile), translated by the author and Elizabeth Shub.   1972.
The Fools of Chelm and Their History (juvenile), translated by the author and Elizabeth
    Shub.   1973.
The Hasidin: Paintings, Drawings and Etchings, with Ira Moskowitz.   1973.
Why Noah Chose the Dove (juvenile), translated by Elizabeth Shub.   1974.
A Tale of Three Wishes (juvenile).   1976.
A Little Boy in Search of God: Mysticism in a Personal Light, with Ira
    Moskowitz.   1976.
Naftali the Storyteller and His Horse, Sus, and Other Stories (juvenile).   1976.
A Young Man in Search of Love, translated by Joseph Singer.   1978.

Editor, with Elaine Gottlieb, *Prism 2*.   1965.

Translator, *Pan*, by Knut Hamsun.   1928.
Translator, *All Quiet on the Western Front*, by Erich Maria Remarque.   1930.
Translator, *The Magic Mountain*, by Thomas Mann.   4 vols., 1930.
Translator, *The Road Back*, by Erich Maria Remarque.   1930.
Translator, *From Moscow to Jerusalem*, by Leon S. Glaser.   1938.

Bibliography: in *Bulletin of Bibliography*, January–March 1969.

Reading List: *Singer and the Eternal Past* by Irving Buchen, 1968; *The Achievement of Singer*
edited by Marcia Allentuck, 1969; *Critical Views of Singer* edited by Irving Malin, 1969;
Singer by Ben Siegel, 1969; *Singer* by Irving Malin, 1972.

*   *   *

   Isaac Bashevis Singer is an example of a strange phenomenon of American Jewish
literature – a Yiddish writer who in his later years gained international fame through the
English translation of his novels and short stories. The Yiddish audience for which Singer
wrote was never a very large one; he did not willingly ascribe to either the nostalgic
yearnings of one school of Yiddishists, or the socialistic diatribes of the other school of
Yiddishists.
   The divorce from the latter school was especially difficult for the young Singer, for it
implied a separation from his older brother, Israel Joshua, also an accomplished writer. This
older brother was the first to open the door to secular education and to the questions which
inevitably awakened Isaac to the narrowness of his father's world of Hasidism and the
inadequacy of his mother's more rational, but nevertheless medieval, normative Judaism.
Unlike his brother Israel Joshua, Isaac Bashevis was unwilling to discard his past altogether;
he was unwilling to choose between mysticism and rationality, between past and present, or
even between gothicism and realism. Singer's art is a marriage of these diverse elements in

his past; they are what afford his fiction such charm on the one hand and such sophistication on the other.

In his early years, Singer wrote solely for the Yiddish press, under several pseudonyms — for example, Varshavsky and Segal. Even his name Bashevis is a pseudonym in honor of his mother, Bathsheba. These early pieces included feuilletons, autobiographical sketches, short fiction, and novels. Some of these have been translated into English, but many remain unknown to the non-Yiddish reading public. By 1950, Singer had begun the process which was to give him such fame in the next twenty years; he began to publish in English translation as well as in the original Yiddish.

The first major venture in this double publication was his epic novel *The Family Moskat*, appearing simultaneously in English and Yiddish. The significant differences between the Yiddish original and the English translation reveal the problematic nature of Singer's existence as an English writer. In the English version, the main characters are left to their doom in Warsaw on the eve of the Nazi takeover. In the Yiddish version, a youthful remnant escapes to Israel. The symbolic significance of their escape and tenuous existence is not lost on the Yiddish writer Singer, nor the Yiddish reader.

As defined by Irving Malin, Singer's novels can be divided into two groups, open and closed. *The Family Moskat* is probably the best example of his open novels. It is an historical family chronicle; the scope of the tale is large and has significant sociological implication; the style is primarily realistic. For Singer, these chronicles are most often set in a time during which the confined *shtetl* life of the East European Jew is being questioned. Other novels in this manner include *The Manor* and *The Estate*.

Of the second (closed) type of Singer novel, *Satan in Goray* is probably the clearest example. It is short, condensed in time; there is an aura of mystery and irrationality; the style, the characters, the setting are all symbolic. Set in the distressing era of the anti-Semitic pogromist Chmielnicki and the false messiah Shabbatai Zevi, this novel relates the disintegration of personality and community that resulted from these horrors of the Jewish past. Other closed novels include *The Magician of Lublin* and *The Slave*. (*Enemies: A Love Story* does not fit well into either slot, but it is more closed than open.)

Singer's symbolism, which owes much to the structure and style of *kaballah*, is evident in many of his short stories as well as the closed novels. In the best of the stories, the author suggests the complex dichotomies, the multiple levels of human existence, and the ambivalent nature of life itself by the use of name symbolism, the supernatural, and multiple narrators. Before the reader can with assurance interpret a story, he must note who tells that story. The reader of "The Destruction of Kreshev" does a disservice to Singer's art if he overlooks the fact that the narrator is Satan, surely an untrustworthy narrator. If he reads the superstitious tale "Zeitl and Rickel," he must note that an uneducated old woman is speaking. The happenings of these tales are filtered through a perspective that colors subject, tone, and conclusion. Even in the masterpiece "Gimpel the Fool," we must recognize that Gimpel himself tells the tale; his naivety and good nature determine the conclusion.

Another important narrator type in Singer's fiction is the semi-autobiographical narrator. In the more belletristic of the tales, he uses this portrait of himself as a mirror reflecting another's story. In "A Friend of Kafka," Jacques Kohn tells the history of his peculiar life. But we do not hear the tale directly; rather we hear it from a man bearing many similarities to the young Isaac Singer. He knew Jacques; Jacques told him a story, and he tells us.

The more simply autobiographical pieces are collected in two books (*In My Father's Court*, *A Day of Pleasures*). These sketches give a clear impression of the life of the young Singer, of his awakening experiences in life, love, and education, and his movement away from his father's narrow past. However, it is the more recent *A Little Boy in Search of God* that most tellingly reveals the intellectual ferment that troubled the young Singer and led him to the development of his twentieth-century mysticism.

Singer is modern in his vision of humanity: his treatment of sexuality and insanity alienated him from many of his Yiddish readers while enhancing his stature in the modern American mind. This rift has caused many of the English critics to overemphasize the modernity of the writer. In so doing, they have overlooked the medieval method of symbolism which adds much of the depth and beauty to Singer's work. Such confusion is only a natural consequence of his position as a Jewish-American writer, a man born in Poland but writing in New York, a man writing in Yiddish but being read in English, and a man looking toward the past to tell of the future.

—Barbara Gitenstein

SINGH, Khushwant. Indian. Born in Hadali, India, now Pakistan, 2 February 1915. Educated at the Modern School, Delhi; St. Stephen's College, Delhi; Government College, Lahore, B.A. 1934; King's College, London, LL.B. 1938; called to the Bar, Inner Temple, London, 1938. Married Kaval Malik in 1939; two children. Practising lawyer, High Court, Lahore, 1939–47; Press Attaché, Indian Foreign Service, in London and Ottawa, 1947–51; member of the staff of the Department of Mass Communications, UNESCO, Paris, 1954–56; Editor, *Yejna*, an Indian government publication, New Delhi, 1956–58; Visiting Lecturer, Oxford University, 1964, University of Rochester, New York, 1965, Princetown University, New Jersey, 1967, University of Hawaii, Honolulu, 1967, and Swarthmore College, Pennsylvania, 1969; Editor of *The Illustrated Weekly of India*, Bombay, from 1969. Head of the Indian Delegation, Writers Conference, Manila, 1965. Recipient: Padma Bhushan, Government of India, 1974. Lives in Bombay.

PUBLICATIONS

Fiction

The Mark of Vishnu and Other Stories. 1950.
Train to Pakistan. 1955; as *Mano Majra*, 1956.
I Shall Not Hear the Nightingale. 1959.
The Voice of God and Other Stories. N.d.
A Bride for the Sahib and Other Stories. N.d.
Black Jasmine. 1971.

Other

The Sikhs. 1952.
Jupji: The Sikh Morning Prayer. 1959.
The Sikhs Today: Their Religion, History, Culture Customs, and Way of Life. 1959; revised edition, 1964.
Fall of the Kingdom of the Punjab. 1962.
A History of the Sikhs, 1469–1964. 2 vols., 1963–66.
Ranjit Singh: Maharajah of the Punjab, 1780–1839. 1963.
Shri Ram: A Biography, with Arun Joshi. 1963.
Ghadar, 1919: India's First Armed Revolution, with Satindra Singh. 1966.
Homage to Guru Gobind Singh, with Suneet Veer Singh. 1966.

Hymns of Nanak the Guru. 1969.
Singh's India (essays), edited by Rahul Singh. N.d.

Editor, *A Note on G. V. Desani's "All about H. Hatterr" and "Hali,"* with Peter Russell. 1952.
Editor, with Jays Thadani, *Land of the Five Rivers: Stories of the Punjab.* 1965.
Editor, *Sunset of the Sikh Empire,* by Sita Ram Kohli. 1967.
Editor, *I Believe.* 1971.
Editor, *Love and Friendship.* 1974.
Editor, *Sacred Writings of the Sikhs.* N.d.

Translator, with M. A. Husain, *Umrao Jan Ada: Courtesan of Lucknow,* by Mohammed Ruswa. 1961.
Translator, *The Skeleton,* by Amrita Pritam. 1964.
Translator, *I Take This Woman,* by Rajinder Singh Bedi. N.d.

Reading List: *Singh* by V. A. Shahane, 1972.

*   *   *

Although he is a prolific and distinguished Sikh historian and editor, Khushwant Singh's reputation as a fiction writer rests solely upon *Mano Majra* (also published in the United States under the title *Train to Pakistan*), a harrowing tale of events along the borders of the newly divided nations of India and Pakistan in the summer of 1947.

The atrocities that accompanied the division of these nations had an enormously depressing effect on a world that had just fought a long, bitter war to defeat practitioners of genocide. The somewhat artificial division of the subcontinent (the boundaries remain in dispute) had been strictly along religious lines: Pakistan was to be a nation of Moslems; India, of Hindus, Sikhs, and what Singh calls "pseudo Christians." There were, however, colonies of non-coreligionists left within each nation. Rather than settle down to peaceful coexistence or permit a passive exchange of populations, partisans on both sides set out on a violent campaign of annihilating the communities that were trapped on their ancestral lands beyond friendly borders.

Mano Majra is laid against a background of this ruthless and senseless mass destruction. This powerful novel derives its title from a squalid border town, where a rail line crosses from India into Pakistan. At first this mixed community of Sikhs and Moslems is undisturbed by the violence that is breaking out elsewhere on the frontier, but inevitably it, too, is caught up in the mass hysteria as ominous "ghost trains" of slain Sikhs begin to arrive in town from across the border. Agitation for reprisals follows when the Moslems of the town are at last rounded up and fanatics urge the Sikhs of the community to kill their former neighbors as the train carrying them to Pakistan passes through town.

Singh's story contrasts the ineffectualness of the educated and ruling classes with the power of the violent and irrational peasants. Singh's terse fable suggests a profound disillusionment with the power of law, reason, and intellect in the face of elemental human passions. The philosophy that sparked his tale seems to be expressed through the thoughts of Iqbal, the young radical, as he realizes his helplessness and drifts off into a drugged sleep the night of the climatic incident of the train's passing: "If you look at things as they are ... there does not seem to be a code either of man or of God on which one can pattern one's conduct. ... In such circumstances what can you do but cultivate an utter indifference to all values? Nothing matters."

The same disillusioned tone characterizes Singh's second novel, *I Shall Not Hear the Nightingale,* but the rather wooden tale is almost overwhelmed by heavy-handed ironies. The action occurs about five years before that of the earlier novel, at a time when the British are expressing a willingness to get out of India once the Axis nations have been defeated in World War II. The novel takes a much dimmer view of the human capacity for compassion and self-sacrifice than *Mano Majra* (at one point Sher Singh reflects that "for him loyalties were not as important as the ability to get away with the impression of having them").

His ironic stories resemble Angus Wilson's and express a similar disillusionment about man's rationality. Singh is a brilliant, sardonic observer of a world undergoing convulsive changes; and his novels provide a unique insight into one of the major political catastrophes of this century. His difficulties in fusing his editorial comments with the action in his stories, however, cause his novels to remain principally dramatized essays.

—Warren French

SMITH, Charlotte (née Turner). English. Born in London, 4 May 1749. Educated in local schools to age 12. Married Benjamin Smith in 1765 (separated, 1787); twelve children. Imprisoned with her husband for debt, 1783–84; settled in Normandy, 1784; full-time writer from 1787. *Died 28 October 1806.*

PUBLICATIONS

Fiction

> *Emmeline, The Orphan of the Castle.* 1788; edited by Anne Henry Ehrenpreis, 1971.
> *Ethelinde; or, The Recluse of the Lake.* 1789.
> *Celestina.* 1791.
> *Desmond.* 1792.
> *The Old Manor House.* 1793; edited by Anne Henry Ehrenpreis, 1969.
> *The Wanderings of Warwick.* 1794.
> *The Banished Man.* 1794.
> *Montalbert.* 1795.
> *Marchmont.* 1796.
> *The Young Philosopher.* 1798.
> *Letters of a Solitary Wanderer* (stories). 5 vols., 1800–02.

Play

> *What Is She?* (produced 1799). 1799.

Verse

> *Elegiac Sonnets and Other Sonnets.* 1784; augmented edition, 1786; 2 vols., 1789–97.
> *The Emigrants.* 1793.
> *Beachy Head, with Other Poems.* 1807.

Other

Rural Walks, in Dialogues for Young Persons.   2 vols., 1795.
Rambles Further: A Continuation of Rural Walks.   2 vols., 1796.
A Narrative of the Loss near Weymouth.   1796.
Minor Morals, Interspersed with Original Stories (juvenile).   2 vols., 1798.
Conversations Introducing Poetry, for the Use of Children.   2 vols., 1804.
History of England, in a Series of Letters to a Young Lady, vols. 1 and 2.   1806.
The Natural History of Birds (juvenile).   2 vols., 1807.

Translator, *Manon Lescaut,* by Prévost.   2 vols., 1786.
Translator, *The Romance of Real Life,* by Gayot de Pitaval.   1787.

Reading List: *The Popular Novel in England* by J. M. S. Tompkins, 1932, revised edition, 1969; *Smith, Poet and Novelist* by Florence M. A. Hilbish, 1941.

*   *   *

It was as a poet that Charlotte Smith wished to be remembered; she undertook novel-writing only because it was more profitable. She attained considerable proficiency in her sonnets, and, although purists objected to their non-Petrarchan form, they were admired by William Lisle Bowles, Wordsworth, and Coleridge. The best of them can still be read with pleasure. Her poems are suffused with a pensive melancholy that sometimes verges on the morbid, but her observation of nature is precisely and sensitively rendered. Generally the scene – a ruined castle, a barren island, a riverside meadow – suggests her present misery as contrasted with her former happiness.

If the *Elegiac Sonnets* contain her best poetic output, *The Emigrants* – a portrait of victims of the French Revolution – illustrates Mrs. Smith's liberal sympathies. Both here and in *Beachy Head* she paints the seaside background in Sussex with careful attention to detail.

As a novelist Mrs. Smith defies classification as "Gothic" – though she flirted with Radcliffean effects – or "Revolutionary" – though she sympathized with the radical views of William Godwin and his circle. She was obsessed, as they were, with the poor, the oppressed, and the ill-educated; and her novels – sometimes explicitly, more often implicitly through characterization – embody these concerns. Her first novel, *Emmeline,* a sentimental tale of thwarted love that was derived from Fanny Burney's *Cecilia,* was followed by two others in the same mode. But with *Desmond* (1792) she broke away to produce a work of avowed propaganda. In it she argued that conditions in revolutionary France were preferable to those under the old regime, and she used her title character as an instrument to chastise the abuses of English government. Two years later, in *The Banished Man,* Mrs. Smith expressed very different views when the bloodiness of revolutionary events had tempered her liberalism. And in her third didactic novel inspired by the Revolution, *The Young Philosopher,* she sought an intellectual justification, through her Rousseauesque hero, for the turmoil in France.

Her best novel, *The Old Manor House,* is marked by vigorous characterization and a plot that depends less on coincidence and artifice than on actions which derive directly from character. Walter Scott thought Mrs. Rayland – a capricious, domineering old snob – "without a rival." Mrs. Smith's descriptions of English landscape, in this novel and others, are unusual for their understated realism. Even more admirable is her moral realism: like her hero Fielding, she was intolerant of cant and pretension. Despite her tendency to heavy-handed satire, she possessed an underlying tolerance that commands our admiration.

—Anne Henry Ehrenpreis

SMITH, Seba. Pseudonym: Major Jack Downing. American. Born in Buckfield, Maine, 14 September 1792; moved with his family to Bridgton, Maine, 1799. Educated at a school in Bridgton; Bowdoin College, Brunswick, Maine, 1815–18, B.A. (honors) 1818. Married Elizabeth Oakes Prince (the writer Elizabeth Oakes Smith) in 1823; five children. Taught school in Portland, Maine, 1818–19; travelled in the South, and in Europe, 1819–20; Assistant Editor, *Eastern Argus*, Portland, 1820–26; Founding Editor, *Portland Courier*, 1829–34 (wrote Downing letters for the paper from 1830); wrote for various periodicals from 1834; moved to New York, 1842; Editor, *Rover*, 1843–45, and Emerson's *United States Magazine*, 1854–59; founded the *Great Republic* magazine, 1859; retired to Patchogue, Long Island, 1860. *Died 29 July 1868.*

PUBLICATIONS

Fiction

The Life and Writings of Major Jack Downing of Downingville. 1833.
Letters Written During the President's Tour "Down East." 1833.
The Select Letters of Major Jack Downing. 1834.
John Smith's Letters, with "Picters" to Match. 1839.
May-Day in New York; or, House-Hunting and Moving. 1845.
Dew-Drops of the Nineteenth Century. 1846.
'Way Down East; or, Portraitures of Yankee Life. 1854.
My Thirty Years Out of the Senate. 1859.
Speech of John Smith, Not Given. 1864.

Verse

Powhalan: A Metrical Romance. 1841.

Other

New Elements of Geometry. 1850.

Reading List: *Smith* by Milton and Patricia Rickels, 1977.

*   *   *

Jack Downing, the creation of Seba Smith, is the prototype of the Yankee critic and humourist, a racy character set against the rustic and picturesque New England background, yet clever enough to serve as confidant of an American President. This pattern of humour paved the way for such homey critics and philosophers as Sam Slick, Hosea Biglow, and Will Rogers.

Smith launched his Jack Downing in the *Portland Courier*, his own newspaper, the first daily to be issued in Maine, in 1830. Jack takes on the guise of a Yankee adventurer who left his native village of Downingville to trade in Portland. From bartering and bargaining, Jack turned to politics and wrote humorous accounts of his career and partners to the family back home. The Downing letters enjoyed a wide circulation in New England, which encouraged Smith to widen his horizons, so he sent Jack to Washington where he becomes counselor to the President. What poured from his pen was a scathing but humorous satire of Jacksonian Democracy. Singled out for criticism was the horde of job seekers that descended on Washington as well as the folly and disaster of land speculation and the national bank. One of the prime targets for his sarcastic venom was the Mexican War. Jack bitingly remarks to General Pierce: "Uncle Joshua always says, in nine cases out of ten, it costs more to rob an orchard than it would be to buy the apples."

His last series of Downing letters appeared under the title *My Thirty Years Out of the Senate*, a parody of Thomas Hart Benton's *Thirty Years View*. He also wrote a collection of tales on Yankee customs, *'Way Down East*.

—Dominic J. Bisignano

SMOLLETT, Tobias (George). Scottish. Born in Dalquhurn, Dunbartonshire, baptized 19 March 1721. Educated at Dumbarton Grammar School; studied medicine at the University of Glasgow, and apprenticed to William Stirling and John Gordon, Glasgow surgeons, 1736–39; awarded M.D. by Marischal College, Aberdeen, 1750. Married Anne Lascelles, probably in 1747; one daughter. Settled in London, 1739; sailed as a surgeon on the *Cumberland* in Ogle's West Indian Squadron, 1741–43; set up as a surgeon in Downing Street, London, 1744; writer from 1747; moved to Bath, 1751; returned to London, 1753; Founding Editor, *The Critical Review*, 1756–63; imprisoned for libel, 1759; Editor, *The British Magazine*, 1760–62, and *The Briton*, 1762–63; lived in Nice, 1763–65, and in Italy, 1769–71. *Died 17 September 1771.*

PUBLICATIONS

Collections

Works, edited by W. E. Henley and Thomas Seccombe. 12 vols., 1899–1901.
Novels. 11 vols., 1925–26.
Selected Writings, edited by Arthur Calder-Marshall. 1950.
Letters, edited by Lewis M. Knapp. 1970.

Fiction

The Adventures of Roderick Random. 1748.
The Adventures of Peregrine Pickle, in Which Are Included Memoirs of a Lady of Quality. 1751; revised edition, 1758; edited by James L. Clifford, 1964.
The Adventures of Ferdinand, Count Fathom. 1753; edited by Damian Grant, 1971.
The Life and Adventures of Sir Launcelot Greaves. 1762; edited by David L. Evans, 1973.
The History and Adventures of an Atom. 1769.
The Expedition of Humphry Clinker. 1771; edited by André Parreaux, 1968.

Plays

>   *The Regicide; or, James the First of Scotland.* 1749.
>   *The Reprisal; or, The Tars of Old England* (produced 1757). 1757.

Verse

>   *Advice: A Satire.* 1746.
>   *Reproof: A Satire.* 1747.
>   *Ode to Independence.* 1773.

Other

>   *An Essay on the External Use of Water.* 1752; edited by Claude E. Jones, in *Bulletin of the Institute of the History of Medicine,* 1935.
>   *A Complete History of England, Deduced from the Descent of Julius Caesar to the Treaty of Aix la Chapelle 1748.* 4 vols., 1757–58; *Continuation of the Complete History of England,* 4 vols., 1760–61.
>   *Travels Through France and Italy, Containing Observations on Character, Customs, Religion, Government, Police, Commerce, Arts, and Antiquities, with a Particular Description of the Town, Territory, and Climate of Nice.* 2 vols., 1766; edited by Thomas Seccombe, 1907.

>   Editor, *A Treatise on the Theory and Practice of Midwifery,* by W. Smellie. 1751.
>   Editor, *A Collection of Cases and Observations in Midwifery,* by W. Smellie. 1754.
>   Editor, *Travels Through Different Cities of Germany, Italy, Greece, and Several Parts of Asia,* by Alex Drummond. 1754.
>   Editor, *A Compendium of Authentic and Entertaining Voyages, Digested in a Chronological Series.* 7 vols., 1756.
>   Editor and Translator, with Thomas Francklin, *The Works of Voltaire.* 38 vols., 1761–74; *Candide and Other Tales,* edited by James Thornton, 1937.
>   Editor, *The Present State of All Nations, Containing a Geographical, Natural, Commercial, and Political History of All the Countries in the Known World.* 8 vols., 1768–69.

>   Translator, *The Adventures of Gil Blas of Santillane,* by Le Sage. 4 vols., 1748.
>   Translator, *Select Essays on Commerce, Agriculture, Mines, Fisheries, and Other Useful Subjects.* 1754.
>   Translator, *The History and Adventures of the Renowned Don Quixote,* by Cervantes. 2 vols., 1755.
>   Translator, *The Adventures of Telemachus, The Son of Ulysses,* by Fénelon. 2 vols., 1776.
>   Translator, *Select Essays, Containing the Manner of Raising and Dressing Flax and Hemp, Collected from the Dictionary of Arts and Sciences.* 1777.

Bibliography: *Smollett Criticism, 1925–45,* and *1770–1924* by F. Cordasco, 2 vols., 1947–48.

Reading List: *The Later Career of Smollett* by Louis L. Martz, 1942; *Smollett, Traveller-Novelist* by George M. Kahrl, 1945; *Smollett's Reputation as a Novelist* by F. W. Boege, 1947 (includes bibliography); *Smollett: Doctor of Men and Manners* by Lewis M. Knapp, 1949; *Smollett* by Laurence Brander, 1951; *Radical Doctor Smollett* by Donald J. Bruce, 1964; *The*

Tradition of Smollett by Robert Giddings, 1967; *Smollett* by R. D. Spector, 1969; *The Novels of Smollett* by Paul-Gabriel Boucé, translated 1976.

*   *   *

Labels like "novelist" and "novel" are at best problematic, and at worst dangerous, when applied to the writers and fictions of the eighteenth century. Not only did these words have different meanings than they do today, but none of the great quintumvirate – Defoe, Richardson, Fielding, Sterne, and Smollett – would have conceived of himself as "a novelist"; the literary output of all five covers most of the major literary kinds. The youngest of them, Tobias Smollett, comes closest to being a "professional" writer of fiction, though even his *œuvre* is staggeringly broad: he was dramatist, poet, journalist, historian, travel-writer, and translator as well as "novelist." What distinguishes him from the others is that he seems to have been working towards a concept of the novel as an autonomous literary kind. In his Dedication to *Ferdinand Count Fathom*, he presents the following definition:

> A novel is a large, diffused picture, comprehending the characters of life, disposed in different groups, and exhibited in various attitudes, for the purposes of an uniform plan, and general occurrence, to which every individual figure is subservient. But this plan cannot be executed with propriety, probability, or success, without a principal personage to attract the attention, unite the incidents, unwind the clue of the labyrinth, and at last close the scene, by virtue of his own importance.

This provides an important frame for the consideration of Smollett's own work. However faulty the execution, he was clearly engaged in the development of a theory of the novel and in its application.

Four of Smollett's novels have the word "adventures" in their titles, and that fact serves to identify the mode in which he characteristically worked. Samuel Johnson's *Dictionary* defines "adventure" as "an enterprise in which something must be left to hazard"; and Smollett's fictive world is ruled and misruled by hazard and fortune. His heroes attempt in different ways, and with varying degrees of success, to order their risky, deceptive, and sometimes hostile environments. The literary co-ordinates of this anarchic world are Cervantes's *Don Quixote* and LeSage's *Gil Blas*, both of which Smollett translated. From them he derives his journey-structures, his satiric vision of society, and his fascination with the psychology of quixotism, the solipsistic delusions which he sees as controlling all human minds.

In the Preface to *The Adventures of Roderick Random*, Smollett specifically cites *Don Quixote* and *Gil Blas* as his models for his own first attempt at combining romance and satire into fiction. His overall purpose in the first-person narrative of Roderick's escapades is, he writes, to show "modest merit struggling with every difficulty to which a friendless orphan is exposed, from his own want of experience as well as from the selfishness, envy, malice and base indifference of mankind." Most readers probably find the self-centred, revengeful, angry young man at the centre of this story less sympathetic than Smollett seems to have hoped. Roderick is a young Scotsman who (like Smollett) takes the high road to London only to find fame and fortune harder to come by than he expected. After a series of urban misadventures, he is press-ganged aboard a man of war, where the chicanery, corruption, and violence are only a more intense version of life on shore. Smollett eventually extricates his hero from a world which threatens to swamp him by the romance-device of the reappearing father, whom Roderick happens upon in Paraguay. Restored to his identity and estate, he can now marry his flawless romance-heroine, Narcissa.

In *The Adventures of Peregrine Pickle*, Smollett takes a figure not unlike Roderick and subjects him to the scrutiny of a third-person narrator. Like Fielding in *Tom Jones* (to which *Peregrine Pickle* bears some affinity – indeed, Smollett intemperately accused Fielding of purloining his ideas), Smollett in *Peregrine Pickle* attempts a substantial definition of the nature of true heroism. But Tom Jones is a good man who appears to be a rogue; Peregrine *is* a rogue and a trickster, albeit with a good heart and conscience buried under a penchant for elaborate and often nasty practical jokes. These two sides of his nature co-exist rather uneasily, and Smollett as narrator fails to exert the unifying, controlling influence of Fielding's narrative voice. Peregrine's career is plotted as a moral education, a struggle between reason and passion in which the former gradually emerges victor, though not always convincingly. As in *Roderick Random*, much of the book's frenetic energy is generated by its gallery of minor characters, particularly such naval grotesques as Commodore Trunnion and Tom Pipes.

The next two novels, *The Adventures of Ferdinand, Count Fathom* and *The Adventures of Sir Launcelot Greaves*, are experiments with different kinds of heroes. Ferdinand is an unalloyed villain, born to a camp-following whore in the midst of a war, and committed in later life to a Hobbesian vision of the human condition as a state of warfare. Like Peregrine Pickle he thrives on cheating and gulling those around him; but his unmitigated viciousness draws no sympathy from the reader. Fathom is born evil, not corrupted by society, and he cannot therefore be reformed by education. Smollett can save him only by an implausible and sentimental conversion following the exposure of his villainy at the end of the novel. By contrast, Sir Launcelot Greaves is a good and sane man in a world of badmen and madmen. A *rational* quixote, he roams the roads of mid-eighteenth-century England and affords Smollett a lively satiric vehicle for renewing his perennially scathing attacks on such contemporary institutions as the law, the prison system, and the literary establishment.

Smollett's last book, *The Expedition of Humphry Clinker*, differs from its predecessors in form, tone, and purpose right from its title-page. It is an *expedition*, not a series of adventures. The distinction is clear from Johnson's definition of "expedition": "a march or voyage with martial intentions." Matthew Bramble's journey is a consciously undertaken campaign for better health, and, while he is not exempt from hazard and accident, his route is clearly plotted from his Gloucestershire estate to Bath, London, Scotland, and back. From the first, too, the primary impulse of *Humphry Clinker* is comic rather than satiric. Its hero is the most fully developed example of the "benevolent misanthrope" type who had appeared in some of the earlier novels. Outwardly a sour critic of men, manners, and institutions, Matt Bramble is in reality good-hearted, compassionate, and magnanimous. Bramble's nostalgia for the lost world of his youth affords Smollett a sounding-board for his critique of modern life, but the attitude of mind the book recommends is a mellower and more tolerant one. This is underlined by Smollett's choice of the letter-method of narration: five of Bramble's party, of both sexes and different social standing, send accounts of persons, places, and events to friends. Each correspondent is limited by his or her own experience and point of view, and only the reader has the evidence to piece together a complete version of the expedition free from "the falsifying medium of prejudice and passion." The fusion of the Fieldingesque journey-structure with Richardson's epistolary technique points to another of Smollett's purposes in *Humphry Clinker*. The novel is an affectionate critical pastiche of the themes and conventions of eighteenth-century fiction (including those of Smollett's own earlier novels). *Humphry Clinker* self-consciously employs an eponymous hero whose role is secondary (compare *Joseph Andrews*), a romance-plot turning on revelations of true identity, and a multiple-marriage ending. The last of these encapsulates Smollett's shrewdest critical point. The last word on the four marriages which end the novel is given to the marvellously malapropistic Welsh maidservant, Win Jenkins, who, as so often, reaches truth *via* an orthographic vagary. When the marriage-knots are all tied, intending to write "our society is to separate," she produces "our satiety is to suppurate." There could be no more devastating comment on the happy-ever-after myth which ended so many eighteenth-century novels with marriage. It is a pity that Smollett did not live to attempt a post-marital study like Fielding's *Amelia*.

—J. C. Hilson

SNOW, C(harles) P(ercy); Baron Snow of Leicester. English. Born in Leicester, 15 October 1905. Educated at Alderman Newton's School, Leicester; University College, Leicester, now the University of Leicester, B.Sc. 1927, M.Sc. 1928; Christ's College, Cambridge, Ph.D. 1930. Married Pamela Hansford Johnson, *q.v.*, in 1950; one son. Fellow, 1930–50, and Tutor, 1935–45, Christ's College; Editor of *Discovery*, Cambridge, 1938–40; Technical Director, Ministry of Labour, London, 1940–44; C.B.E. (Commander, Order of the British Empire), 1943; Civil Service Commissioner, 1945–60; Director, English Electric Company, London, 1947–64; Parliamentary Secretary, Ministry of Technology, 1964–66. Rede Lecturer, Cambridge University, 1959; Godkin Lecturer, Harvard University, Cambridge, Massachusetts, 1960; Regents Professor, University of California, Berkeley, 1960. President, Library Association, 1961; Director, Educational Film Centre, London, 1961–64; Rector, University of St. Andrews, Scotland, 1961–64. Fellow, Yale University, New Haven, Connecticut; Extraordinary Fellow, Churchill College, Cambridge; Honorary Fellow, Christ's College, Cambridge. Recipient: Black Memorial Prize, 1955. LL.D.: University of Leicester, 1959; University of Liverpool, 1960; University of St. Andrews, 1962; Brooklyn Polytechnic Institute New York, 1962; University of Bridgeport, Connecticut, 1966; University of York, 1967; D.Litt.: Dartmouth College, Hanover, New Hampshire, 1960; Bard College, Annandale-on-Hudson, New York, 1962; Temple University, Philadelphia, 1963; Syracuse University, New York, 1963; University of Pittsburgh, 1964; D.H.L.: Kenyon College, Gambier, Ohio, 1961; Washington University, St. Louis, 1963; University of Michigan, Ann Arbor, 1963; D.Phil.Sc.: Rostov State University, East Germany, 1963; D.Sc.: Pennsylvania Military College, Chester, 1966. Fellow of the Royal Society of Literature, 1951. Honorary Member, American Academy of Arts and Letters. Knighted, 1957; created Baron Snow of Leicester, 1964. Lives in London.

PUBLICATIONS

Fiction

> *Death under Sail.* 1932; revised edition, 1959.
> *New Lives for Old.* 1933.
> *The Search.* 1934.
> *Strangers and Brothers:*
>> *Strangers and Brothers.* 1940; as *George Passant*, 1973.
>> *The Light and the Dark.* 1947.
>> *Time of Hope.* 1949.
>> *The Masters.* 1951.
>> *The New Men.* 1954.
>> *Homecomings.* 1956; as *Homecoming*, 1956.
>> *The Conscience of the Rich.* 1958.
>> *The Affair.* 1960.
>> *Corridors of Power.* 1964.
>> *The Sleep of Reason.* 1968.
>> *Last Things.* 1970.
> *The Malcontents.* 1972.
> *In Their Wisdom.* 1974.

Plays

> *The View over the Park* (produced 1950).

The Supper Dance, with Pamela Hansford Johnson.   1951.
Family Party, with Pamela Hansford Johnson.   1951.
Spare the Rod, with Pamela Hansford Johnson.   1951.
To Murder Mrs. Mortimer, with Pamela Hansford Johnson.   1951.
The Pigeon with the Silver Foot, with Pamela Hansford Johnson.   1951.
Her Best Foot Forward, with Pamela Hansford Johnson.   1951.
The Public Prosecutor, with Pamela Hansford Johnson, from a play by Georgi
  Dzhagarov, translated by Marguerite Alexieva (produced 1967).   1969.

Other

Richard Aldington: An Appreciation.   1938.
Writers and Readers of the Soviet Union.   1943.
The Two Cultures and the Scientific Revolution.   1959; revised edition, as *Two Cultures
  and a Second Look*, 1964.
Science and Government.   1961.
A Postscript to Science and Government.   1962.
Snow: A Spectrum: Science, Criticism, Fiction, edited by Stanley Weintraub.   1963.
Variety of Men.   1967.
The State of Siege.   1969.
Public Affairs.   1971.
Trollope: His Life and Art.   1975.
The Realists (essays).   1978.

Editor, with Pamela Hansford Johnson, *Winter's Tales 7.*   1961; as *Stories from
  Modern Russia*, 1962.

Reading List: *Snow* by William Cooper, 1959; *The World of Snow* by Robert Greacen, 1962
(includes bibliography by Bernard Stone); *Snow: The Politics of Conscience* by Frederick Karl,
1963; *Snow* by Jerome Thale, 1964; *Snow* by Robert Gorham Davis, 1965; *The Two Culture
Theory in Snow's Novels* by Nora C. Graves, 1971; *The Novels of Snow: A Critical
Introduction* by Suguna Ramanathan, 1978.

*   *   *

C. P. Snow, the author of *Strangers and Brothers*, a unique eleven-volume novel sequence,
as well as of many influential and provocative essays, began his career as a talented scientist;
later he interrupted his literary efforts to serve in the British government.
  Snow's non-fiction has created a significant amount of controversy. His best-known essay
is *The Two Cultures and the Scientific Revolution*, a brilliant analysis of the lack of
communication between the scientific and the literary-intellectual "cultures" in modern
society. In it, Snow calls for educational reform to permit the bridging of the "two cultures."
Another important essay, *Science and Government*, caused an uproar in Britain with its
graphic analysis of how large-scale strategic bombing was carried out in World War II,
despite the skepticism of most of the scientific community.
  Most of Snow's early fiction is interesting only for its demonstration of the various paths
his writing might have taken, including a detective story, *Death under Sail*, and an
anonymous science fiction novel, *New Lives for Old*. *The Search*, however, is a highly
regarded study of scientists at work that presages Snow's later fascination with "man in
committee"; it also confronts the issue of scientific fraud, which also reappears in later Snow
novels.
  The *Strangers and Brothers* sequence, planned and begun in the mid-1930's, and not

completed until 1970, is a series of interdependent novels, almost all of which, however, are capable of standing on their own. Each is narrated in the first person by Lewis Eliot, who is sometimes the major character and at other times merely an observer. Recurring themes of the sequence include the uses and abuses of power; the strength of human appetites and emotions, as opposed to the tenuous hold of reason; and the operation of men in committee settings, bureaucracies, and other organized environments. Many of these themes are first introduced through Eliot's insights into others and are later recapitulated in his own life. These are discussed in Snow's particularly lucid, uncomplicated style, avoiding densely symbolic prose.

Strangers and Brothers, the first novel published in the sequence (later retitled *George Passant*, after its main character), is set in Eliot's youth. It is distinguished primarily by the brilliant portrait of Passant, a gifted but irrational utopian, who is constantly frustrated by his attempts to take on established society, as well as by his powerful sensual appetites. *The Conscience of the Rich* offers another excellent character portrait, this time of Leonard March, a proud, dominating, aristocratic Jewish patriarch, whose possessive love (a recurring sub-theme of the sequence) for his son, Charles, drives Charles to hurt his father by "punishing" himself. *Time of Hope*, the first novel concerned directly with the experience of Lewis Eliot, takes him from his childhood to age 28, when he is a young lawyer married to his first wife, Sheila Knight. Sheila is one of Snow's most sharply drawn characters: a frustrated, neurotic woman, egocentric yet honest, she unintentionally exercises a magnetic attraction over Eliot which holds him despite damage to himself and to his career. The story of their marriage is excruciating – and quite masterfully portrayed. *The Light and the Dark* is largely the story of Roy Calvert, Snow's only attempt at a "tragic hero." Melancholy and brilliant, Calvert resembles Sheila in some respects, but never becomes as powerful or as convincing a character.

The Masters is probably Snow's finest novel. It is the study of a power struggle set in the unlikely arena of an unidentified Cambridge college, where a new Master (or head) is to be elected. Not only is *The Masters* full of the fascinating character portraits for which Snow is justly renowned; its scenes of college faculty committees in action constitute an intriguing paradigm of political life.

The New Men is another novel about a group – in this case a team of British scientists working to develop an atomic bomb. Lewis Eliot's younger brother, Martin, becomes a major character, setting the stage for another rebellion against possessive love: that of Lewis for his brother. *Homecomings* returns the focus to Lewis himself, depicting the end of his first marriage, when Sheila commits suicide, and the beginnings of his second. *The Affair* returns to a Cambridge setting, bringing back many of the characters introduced in *The Masters*. This time, the process of group decision-making is explored in the context of an alleged scientific fraud, raising important issues about the nature of justice.

Corridors of Power, set in Parliament, is a more traditionally political novel; it reflects Snow's own exposure to the world of high-level politics. An interesting study of "back room" bargaining and of the use of power, it is surprisingly low-keyed and slow-paced. *The Sleep of Reason*, based on the celebrated Moors Murders Trial, is a complex, sophisticated novel about the passions which hide behind the veneer of civilization. It also explores, with penetrating insight, the tensions between the generations, including those caused by possessive love. *Last Things* is just what its title implies, a final trot across the stage for many of the surviving characters from the preceding volumes.

One of the most fascinating aspects of the *Strangers and Brothers* sequence is the changing role of the narrator, Lewis Eliot. Not merely Snow's alter ego, Eliot is a developing personality whose observations become more mature and subtle. The interplay between Eliot's role as a character and his shifting perspective as narrator constitutes much of the uniqueness of Snow's accomplishment.

Since reaching the end of *Strangers and Brothers*, Snow has published two more novels. *The Malcontents* is his "1960's" work, focusing on "youth culture" and political turmoil, while pursuing the more usual Snow theme of the uses and abuses of power. *In Their*

Wisdom is a more interesting work, revolving around a legal battle over a disputed will, but confronting many hard questions of ageing – including illness, death, and inheritance. Like many of the volumes of *Strangers and Brothers*, it is thoughtful, entertaining, and finely crafted.

—Mark I. Wallach

SOMERVILLE, Edith (Anna Oenone). Irish. Born in Corfu, 2 May 1858; grew up at the family home at Drishane, County Cork, Ireland. Educated at home, and at Alexandra College, Dublin; studied painting at the Westminster School of Art, London, in Dusseldorf, and at the studios of Colarossi and Delecluse in Paris. Began career as an illustrator, and continued to illustrate her own books and to exhibit after becoming a writer (one-man shows of paintings in Dublin and London, and in New York City, 1929); organist at the parish church of Castlehaven, Drishane, 1875 until her death; lived with her cousin and collaborator, Martin Ross, *q.v.*, in Drishane, 1886 until Ross's death in 1915; with Ross, travelled extensively on the Continent and lived at various times in Paris; after Ross's death continued to write (as Somerville and Ross) on her own. Master of the West Carbery Foxhounds, 1903–19. Recipient: Irish Academy of Letters Gregory Medal, 1941. Litt.D.: Trinity College, Dublin, 1932. Founding Member, Irish Academy of Letters, 1933. *Died 8 October 1949.*

PUBLICATIONS (with Martin Ross)

Fiction

> *An Irish Cousin.* 1889; revised edition, 1903.
> *Naboth's Vineyard.* 1891.
> *The Real Charlotte.* 1894.
> *The Silver Fox.* 1898; revised edition, 1902.
> *Some Experiences of an Irish R.M.* (stories). 1899.
> *A Patrick's Day Hunt* (by Ross). 1902.
> *All on the Irish Shore: Irish Sketches.* 1903.
> *Further Experiences of an Irish R.M.* (stories). 1908.
> *Dan Russel the Fox: An Episode in the Life of Miss Rowan.* 1911.
> *The Story of the Discontented Little Elephant* (juvenile; by Somerville). 1912.
> *In Mr. Knox's Country* (stories). 1915.
> *Mount Music.* 1919.
> *An Enthusiast.* 1921.
> *The Big House of Inver.* 1925.
> *French Leave.* 1928.
> *Little Red Riding Hood in Kerry.* 1934.
> *The Sweet Cry of Hounds* (stories). 1936.
> *Sarah's Youth.* 1938.

Verse

Slipper's ABC of Foxhunting (by Somerville). 1903.

Other

Through Connemara in a Governess Cart. 1892.
In the Vine Country. 1893.
Beggars on Horseback: A Riding Tour of North Wales. 1895.
Some Irish Yesterdays. 1906.
Irish Memories. 1917.
Stray-Aways (essays). 1920.
Wheel-Tracks. 1923.
The States Through Irish Eyes (by Somerville). 1930.
An Incorruptible Irishman, Being an Account of Chief Justice Charles Kendal Bushe and of His Wife, Nancy Crampton, and Their Times, 1767–1843. 1932.
The Smile and the Tear (essays). 1933.
Records of the Somerville Family from 1174 to 1940 (by Somerville and Boyle Townshend Somerville). 1940.
Notions in Garrison (essays). 1941.
Happy Days! Essays of Sorts. 1946.

Editor (Somerville only), *The Mark Twain Birthday Book.* 1885.
Editor (Somerville only), *Notes of the Horn: Hunting Verse, Old and New.* 1934.

Bibliography: *A Bibliography of the First Editions of the Works of Somerville and Ross* by Elizabeth Hudson, 1942.

Reading List: *Somerville: A Biography* by G. Cummins, 1952; *Somerville and Ross: A Biography* by M. Collis, 1968; *Somerville and Ross: A Symposium,* 1969; *The Irish Cousins: The Books and Background of Somerville and Ross* by Violet Powell, 1970; *Somerville and Ross* by John Cronin, 1972.

*   *   *

Edith Somerville and Martin Ross were cousins, and they shared a common background in the "Big House" of the Anglo-Irish ascendancy. Their autobiographical memoirs, *Irish Memories,* give a fascinating picture of this background. When Martin died in 1915 Edith continued to publish her books under their joint names. Altogether they wrote some sixteen works of fiction and several travel books, but their reputation depends upon one or two novels and their humorous short stories.

The Real Charlotte presents, with astringent humour and ironic detachment, the Anglo-Irish world of Lismoyle, a small town in the south-west of Ireland at the end of the last century. At a time when Douglas Hyde was founding the Gaelic League and Yeats was rediscovering the world of Celtic legend and trying to foster an Irish national literature, Somerville and Ross described the Irish social scene as they viewed it from the windows of the "Big House." Their picture is not a flattering one, from the lunatic Sir Benjamin Dysart of Bruff House to the ailing and impoverished Julia Duffy of Gurthnamuckla. The authors have a skilful and witty command of language. At times their dry irony is reminiscent of Jane Austen; at other times there is a sharp astringency that catches the reader by surprise. On a gentle summer evening a carrion crow in a thorn-bush is "looking about him if haply he could see a wandering kid whose eyes would serve him for his supper." The Charlotte of the book's title, a plain, squat, middle-aged woman, is decidedly an anti-heroine, and her story disgusted many Victorian readers.

The Big House of Inver is another novel of considerable power, but the most popular and widely read of all their books was *Some Experiences of an Irish R.M.*, followed by *Further Experiences of an Irish R.M.*. With a few exceptions the stories are light-heartedly entertaining. The Irish Resident Magistrate of the title is Major Yeates, an ex-Indian Army man of Irish extraction, who is appointed to a post in a remote district of south-west Ireland. His misadventures, which frequently lead him into undignified and amusing positions, provide the staple material of the stories. Taken as a whole they reveal vividly the Anglo-Irish world of hunting, shooting, boating, point-to-point races, and occasional private balls. A range of amusing and eccentric characters are presented. Frank O'Connor said (in *Leinster, Munster, and Connaught*, 1950) that "with Joyce's *Dubliners* 'the R.M.' is the most closely observed of all Irish storybooks, but whereas Joyce observes with cruel detachment, the authors of 'the Irish R.M.' observe with love and glee."

—Alan Warner

SPARK, Muriel (Sarah).   Scottish.   Born in Edinburgh.   Educated at James Gillespie's School for Girls, Edinburgh. Married S. O. Spark in 1937 (divorced); one son. Worked in the Political Intelligence Department of the Foreign Office during World War II; General Secretary of the Poetry Society, and Editor of the *Poetry Review*, London, 1947–49; thereafter a full-time writer. Recipient: Prix Italia, for radio plays, 1962; Black Memorial Prize, 1966. LL.D.: University of Strathclyde, Glasgow, 1971. Fellow of the Royal Society of Literature, 1963. O.B.E. (Officer, Order of the British Empire), 1967. Lives in Rome.

PUBLICATIONS

Fiction

>*The Comforters.*   1957.
>*The Go-Away Bird and Other Stories.*   1958.
>*Robinson.*   1958.
>*Memento Mori.*   1959.
>*The Ballad of Peckham Rye.*   1960.
>*Voices at Play* (stories and radio plays).   1961.
>*The Bachelors.*   1960.
>*The Prime of Miss Jean Brodie.*   1961.
>*The Girls of Slender Means.*   1963.
>*The Mandelbaum Gate.*   1965.
>*Collected Stories 1.*   1967.
>*The Public Image.*   1968.
>*The Driver's Seat.*   1970.
>*Not to Disturb.*   1971.
>*The Hothouse by the East River.*   1972.
>*The Abbess of Crewe: A Modern Morality Tale.*   1974.
>*The Takeover.*   1976.

Plays

Voices at Play (stories and the radio plays *The Party Through the Wall, The Interview, The Dry River Bed, Danger Zone).* 1961.
Doctors of Philosophy (produced 1962).   1963.

Radio Plays: *The Party Through the Wall,* 1957; *The Interview,* 1958; *The Dry River Bed,* 1959; *The Ballad of Peckham Rye,* 1960; *Danger Zone,* 1961.

Verse

The Fanfarlo and Other Verse.   1952.
Collected Poems 1.   1967.

Other

Child of Light: A Reassessment of Mary Shelley.   1951.
Emily Brontë: Her Life and Work, with Derek Stanford.   1953.
John Masefield.   1953.
The Very Fine Clock (juvenile).   1958.

Editor, with Derek Stanford, *Tribute to Wordsworth.*   1950.
Editor, *A Selection of Poems,* by Emily Brontë.   1952.
Editor, with Derek Stanford, *My Best Mary: The Letters of Mary Shelley.*   1953.
Editor, *The Brontë Letters.*   1954.
Editor, with Derek Stanford, *Letters of John Henry Newman.*   1957.

Bibliography: *Iris Murdoch and Spark: A Bibliography* by Thomas T. Tominaga and Wilma Schneidermeyer, 1976.

Reading List: *Spark: A Biographical and Critical Study* by Derek Stanford, 1963; *Spark* by Karl Malkoff, 1968; *Spark* by Patricia Stubbs, 1973; *Spark* by Peter Kemp, 1974.

*   *   *

Economy has always fascinated Muriel Spark. What attracted her to writing novels in the first place was that the activity enabled her to do two things at once – "express the comic side of my mind and at the same time work out some serious theme." She achieves this by handling her material both as a satirist and an allegorist: the small worlds on which her novels concentrate are subjected to ironic scrutiny and, simultaneously, transformed into striking images, "glimpses that seem like a microcosm of reality."

The satiric element is perhaps most obvious. "Ridicule," Mrs. Spark has said, "is the only honourable weapon we have left." In her novels, it can glitter, wielded with a cutting elegance. Her strategy is to dissect rather closed societies, a wide variety of which are laid out in her fiction. Sometimes, their members are linked by a shared quality – old age, bachelorhood; sometimes, they are geographically restricted – girls and teachers in an Edinburgh school, the staff of a chateau outside Geneva; sometimes, they are both – divided characters in the divided Jerusalem of 1961. Always, though, they are subjected to sardonic probing. Captured with deft mimicry, their words and gestures are picked up and pointed out as symptomatic of corruption or of weakness. Small-scale mental and moral debilities are everywhere exposed, along with more malign disorders. Lies and treachery tend to have an epidemic hold on the worlds portrayed; jealousy festers; there are ugly knots of inflamed resentment; blackmail poisons numerous relationships; and, occasionally, homicidal violence bursts. All this is recorded in astringent prose, healthily full of wit and unexpected aptnesses. The precision and the balance of the writing, its intelligence, inventiveness, and vigour, act as damning counter-point. Tacitly, these qualities deride the squalors and inanities chronicled with such exhilarating accuracy. The satire is aided, too, by other kinds of juxtaposition. The inescapable realities of time, age, death − frequently referred to − throw into sharp relief the futility of much of the characters' behaviour, illuminate the transience of those rewards they are pursuing with deluded ingenuity. A Catholic writer, Mrs. Spark has said that her religion helps her satire in that it affords "a norm ... something to measure from." It also provides a useful eschatological backcloth, in front of which her characters − "the solemn crowds with their aimless purposes, their eternal life not far away" − can be put into a chastening perspective.

Catholicism influences this fiction in another way as well. It is a potent factor governing Mrs. Spark's allegorical procedures. It was only after her conversion to Catholicism that she started to write novels: largely, it seems, because she now "began to see life as a whole rather than as a series of disconnected happenings." The connection between this belief and her fiction is not hard to perceive. The doctrine she has accepted regards life as full of meaning, hallmarked by design and purpose. In her novels, she attempts to bring this out: she elaborately structures her material − organises her plot, choreographs her characters' actions, arranges salient aspects of the setting − so as to endow the sector of society that she is studying with an allegorical significance. In this way, the dictatorial behaviour of an Edinburgh schoolmistress is turned into an emblem of Fascism; a girls' hostel becomes a symbol of human effort to live communally and decently without selfish competition; a scandal in the Roman film world amidst a media circus of duplicitous publicity is worked into a garish image of man's efforts to deceive and self-deceive.

A book produced by one of the many writers in Mrs. Spark's fiction is entitled *The Transfiguration of the Commonplace*. And this is what she herself is much concerned to do: to transfigure the commonplace − the ordinary world she has submitted to sharp-eyed satiric survey − into something meaningfully patterned, purged of the redundant. To this end, relevance increasingly controls her work. In early books, such as *The Comforters* or *Memento Mori*, she draws an excluding line round characters who have something in common, a quality that can be isolated for examination. Then the physical settings of the novels start to take on an added significance: the London background is of considerable importance in *The Bachelors* and *The Ballad of Peckham Rye*, as is Edinburgh in *The Prime of Miss Jean Brodie* and Jerusalem in *The Mandelbaum Gate*. A further move towards tight coherence is to make the books' settings in time carefully appropriate: the 1930's witnessing the rise of European dictators, are crucial to the history of Miss Brodie; the story of *The Girls of Slender Means* is very aptly placed between V.E. and V.J. days. Later fiction shows another element being worked into the general accord: narrative modes are given a parodic suitability. *The Driver's Seat*, for instance, travesties the boy-meets-girl romance and the murder hunt; *Not to Disturb* satirically jumbles bits of Gothic novel with the conventions of Jacobean tragedy; *The Hothouse by the East River* is a ghost story strategically turned inside out.

Muriel Spark's recent novels have shown signs of structural wavering and some coarsening of satiric presentation. In the main, though, her achievement has been extremely impressive. Her fiction has brought attractively together formal elegance and lively comic documentary. It has managed to be both compact and various, consistent and developing. While always aiming to increase these books' economy of structure, Mrs. Spark has kept them generously stocked with a rich diversity of character and incident. In her novels, graceful form and vivid content very pleasurably coalesce.

—Peter Kemp

STAFFORD, Jean. American. Born in Covina, California, 1 July 1915. Educated at the University of Colorado, Boulder, B.A. 1936, M.A. 1936; University of Heidelberg, 1936–37. Married 1) the poet Robert Lowell in 1940 (divorced, 1948); 2) Oliver Jensen in 1950 (divorced, 1953); 3) the writer A. J. Liebling in 1959 (died, 1963). Instructor, Stephens College, Columbia, Missouri, 1937–38; Secretary, *Southern Review*, Baton Rouge, Louisiana, 1940–41; Lecturer, Queens College, Flushing, New York, Spring 1945; Fellow, Center for Advanced Studies, Wesleyan University, Middletown, Connecticut, 1964–65; Adjunct Professor, Columbia University, New York, 1967–69. Recipient: National Institute of Arts and Letters grant, 1945; Guggenheim Fellowship, 1945, 1948; National Press Club Award, 1948; O. Henry Award, 1955; Ingram-Merrill grant, 1969; Chapelbrook grant, 1969; Pulitzer Prize, 1970. Member, National Institute of Arts and Letters, 1970.

PUBLICATIONS

Fiction

>   *Boston Adventure.* 1944.
>   *The Mountain Lion.* 1947.
>   *The Catherine Wheel.* 1952.
>   *Children Are Bored on Sunday* (stories). 1953.
>   *Bad Characters* (stories). 1964.
>   *Collected Stories.* 1969.

Other

>   *Elephi: The Cat with the High I.Q.* (juvenile). 1962.
>   *The Lion and the Carpenter and Other Tales from the Arabian Nights Retold* (juvenile). 1962.
>   *A Mother in History.* 1966.

*   *   *

The art of Jean Stafford is the art of the miniaturist – the quickly realized short story, told with economy and control, is her ideal form. Many of her stories were published in *The New Yorker* and *The Saturday Evening Post*, and it is easy to detect the economy and tautness that come from the pressures of journalistic publication "Miss Bellamy was old and cold," begins "The Hope Chest" (*Collected Stories*), "and she lay quaking under an eiderdown which her mother had given her when she was a girl of seventeen." In a sense, the half-dozen pages which follow merely expand the implications of that sentence. Typically, the story is rooted in the old woman's memories of her childhood and years as a young woman: most of Jean Stafford's writing deals with loneliness perceived by the child who suffers it or by the adult who was once the child.

Her own artistic eye, in fact, is that of the child poised on the brink of adult experience and seeing largely the concrete details of surrounding life. Her most successful writing enlarges its range by suggesting wider experience through symbols such as the mountain lion of her second novel, which represents the untamed, authentic power of the natural world into which the two young children of the story are plunged. The horrific violence which concludes the novel comes not from the lion but from man; like many of the stories, the work simmers with a brooding though suppressed sense of the brutality of experience.

Jean Stafford's other novels, *Boston Adventure* and *The Catherine Wheel*, are possibly less successful because they lack such a convincing controlling symbol. As usual, they are concerned with young people, but the world these young grow into suggests imprisonment and failure rather than fulfilment and enrichment. But although these are not her best works, the standard of their prose remains as high as in any of her stories.

—Patrick Evans

STEAD, Christina (Ellen). Australian. Born in Rockdale, Sydney, New South Wales, 17 July 1902. Educated at Sydney University Teachers' College, graduated 1922. Married William James Blake in 1952 (died, 1968). Demonstrator, Sydney University Teachers' College, in Sydney schools, 1922–24; secretary in Sydney, 1925–28; moved to Europe, 1928, and worked as a clerk in offices in London, 1928–29, and in Paris, 1930–35; moved to the United States, 1935: Senior Writer, Metro-Goldwyn-Mayer, Hollywood, 1943; Instructor, New York University, 1943–44; returned to Australia. Since 1969, Fellow in Creative Arts, Australian National University, Canberra. Recipient: Arts Council of Great Britain grant, 1967; Patrick White Award, 1974. Lives in Hurstville, New South Wales.

PUBLICATIONS

Fiction

> *The Salzburg Tales.* 1934.
> *Seven Poor Men of Sydney.* 1934.
> *The Beauties and Furies.* 1936.
> *House of All Nations.* 1938.
> *The Man Who Loved Children.* 1940.
> *For Love Alone.* 1944.
> *Letty Fox: Her Luck.* 1946.
> *A Little Tea, A Little Chat.* 1948.
> *The People with the Dogs.* 1952.
> *Dark Places of the Heart.* 1966; as *Cotters' England,* 1967.
> *The Puzzleheaded Girl: 4 Novellas.* 1967.
> *The Little Hotel.* 1974.
> *Miss Herbert (The Suburban Wife).* 1976.

Other

> Editor, with William J. Blake, *Modern Women in Love.* 1945
> Editor, *Great Stories of the South Sea Islands.* 1956.

> Translator, *Colour of Asia,* by Fernand Gigon. 1955.
> Translator, *The Candid Killer,* by Jean Giltène. 1956.
> Translator, *In Balloon and Bathyscaphe,* by August Piccard. 1956.

Reading List: "Stead Issue" of *Southerly,* 1962; *Stead,* 1969, and *Stead,* 1969, both by R. G. Geering.

*   *   *

The author of the most powerful, brilliant and individual Australian novel during the last fifty years has been, like several of Australia's best novelists, an expatriate. Her *House of All Nations*, the most cosmopolitan of her books, has been generously acclaimed in America, but has attracted little serious criticism in her own country. Its complexity, its exuberant detail, its large cast of 159 characters, may have been too much for reviewers to handle, and its form (a series of 104 scenes) presents a kaleidoscopic surface bewildering to readers accustomed to the conventional linear development of a story. Equally baffling, perhaps, is the author's political and moral stance; the book is obviously the work of a radical with a knowledge of Marxism, but there is much in it which would not please the orthodox Marxist, however unflattering its picture of finance capitalism. One suspects that reviewers find Stead's X-ray eye unnerving.

Of all Australian novelists, Christina Stead is most unmistakably a novelist born. Others may surpass her in philosophic coherence or tighter organisation, but not in native genius which finds expression in prose of surpassing richness, ease, and variety, not in range and clarity of observation and in vivid, firm characterisation. With these gifts, which she exercises as easily as a virtuoso violinist playing cadenzas, are allied a penetrating intelligence, an intense curiosity with a sensual quality reminiscent of Tolstoy's, a vision entirely individual, rich with quirks and prejudices, and a compassionate tolerance that stops well short of facile indifference. She may observe rather than judge, but her mind is not an empty room for winds to blow through. There is a strong biological base to Christina Stead's approach to fiction, inherited from her naturalist father. It is discernible in all her books, but is openly present in *The Man Who Loved Children*, a novel based on Australian experience but set in America, in which she analyses dramatically the influences of heredity, association, environment, and circumstances, which combine to produce a genius. This book, and the earlier *The Salzburg Tales* and *Seven Poor Men of Sydney*, show that her interests, unlike those of her social realist contemporaries inside and outside Australia, were not in the common man but in the uncommon man. There is a strong ingredient of the fantastic, even of the grotesque or the supernatural, in her work, though she would probably argue, like Carlos Fuentes, that the "normal" is nowhere to be found. Be that as it may, it is impossible to agree with the American critic and poet Randall Jarrell that the Pollitt family in *The Man Who Loved Children* is in any sense typical or representative. If the "seven poor men" have any reality at all, they are certainly far from being ordinary, and the gallery of story-tellers who tell the tales in *The Salzburg Tales* are as rich and bizarre as the stories they tell.

Christina Stead is above all an observer of the human scene, whose eye is alive to every detail and nuance and who is a full, precise recorder of what she sees. The more unusual and intrinsically interesting the objects under her observation, the greater the heights to which she rises; she has no talent for glorifying domestic trivia. The magnificent *House of All Nations*, furthest removed from the terrain thought proper for female novelists, shows her genius uninhibited. The novel plunges us into the mythomaniac world of finance of the Banque Mercure and its fascinating director Jules Bertillon, charming, unmoral, imaginative, and a compelling talker, whose luck is fabulous and whose dominant instinct is play. Every facet of his world glitters on the pages: speculation, commercial deals, stock manipulations, tax frauds, gambling for control of others – in short a kind of financial totalitarianism analogous to the political totalitarianism spreading over Europe in the late 1930's. Yet all this is refracted through a transforming imagination which understands poetically the intoxication of financial power; the result is prose of a richness rare in modern times.

Most of her other books are in some way concerned with the fortunes of women, though it is a mistake to see her as a feminist: for her, love between men and women is the natural expression of the human libido. The point of view of Teresa in *For Love Alone* is still the basis of her philosophy of life: Teresa's search for the right to love and the right to personal freedom are aspects of the same quest. Love and life are indistinguishable and life without love is not life at all. But it should be noted that this quest is an affair of "exchange": the capacity to love does not imply a demand to be loved. Jonathan Crow's real sin in *For Love Alone* is not so much that he does not return Teresa's love, but that he is incapable of being touched by it, of accepting it; hence the identification of him with the diabolical, a state which is seen as pitiful, as much as malevolent. In *The Puzzleheaded Girl*, one of four novellas published under that title, Stead returned to the theme of incapacity for love, this time in a woman.

As a novelist, Christina Stead's truest begetter is perhaps Dickens. She has the same talent for creating freestanding characters who owe their reality to the element of caricature in their construction, and who, like Mr. Micawber, pass into the language and become independent of their origins. Sam Pollitt, "the man who loved children," is of this kind and so is his wife Henny. The novel in which they appear was probably the first to be designed as deliberately "ecological"; it is one of several examples of the innovatory qualities in Australian women novelists which have been given little recognition, either at home or abroad.

—Dorothy Green

STEELE, Sir Richard. Irish. Born in Dublin, baptized 12 March 1672. Educated at Charterhouse, London, where he met Joseph Addison, 1684–89; matriculated at Christ Church, Oxford, 1690; postmaster at Merton College, Oxford, 1691–94, but left without taking a degree. Enlisted as a cadet in the Duke of Ormonde's guards, 1694; Ensign in Lord Cutts's Regiment, 1695, and served as Cutts's confidential secretary, 1696–97; Captain, stationed at the Tower of London, by 1700; transferred as Captain to Lord Lucas's Regiment in 1702. Married 1) Margaret Ford Stretch in 1705 (died, 1706); 2) Mary Scurlock in 1707 (died, 1718), two sons and two daughters. Wrote extensively for the theatre, 1701–05; Gentleman-Writer to Prince George of Denmark, 1706–08; Gazetteer (i.e., Manager of the *Gazette*, the official government publication), 1707–10; Commissioner of Stamps, 1710–13; Editor, *The Tatler*, to which Addison was the major contributor, 1709–11; Editor, with Addison, *The Spectator*, 1711–12; Editor, *The Guardian*, 1713; elected Member of Parliament for Stockbridge, Hampshire, 1713, but expelled for anti-government views; Editor, *The Englishman*, 1713–14, *The Lover*, 1714, and *The Reader*, 1714; on accession of George I, 1714, appointed Justice of the Peace, Deputy Lieutenant for the County of Middlesex, Surveyor of the Royal Stables at Hampton Court, and Supervisor of the Drury Lane Theatre, London: granted life patent of Drury Lane, 1715; Member of Parliament for Boroughbridge, Yorkshire, 1715; Editor, *Town Talk*, 1715–16, *The Tea-Table*, and *Chit-Chat*, 1716; appointed Commissioner for Forfeited Estates in Scotland, 1716; quarrelled with Addison, 1719; Editor, *The Plebeian*, 1719, and *The Theatre*, 1720; Member of Parliament for Wendover, Buckinghamshire, 1722; retired to Wales, 1724. Knighted, 1715. *Died 1 September 1729.*

PUBLICATIONS

Collections

Correspondence, edited by R. Blanchard.   1941; revised edition, 1968.
Plays, edited by Shirley S. Kenny.   1971.

Essays and Prose Writings

The Christian Hero, An Argument Proving That No Principles But Those of Religion Are Sufficient to Make a Great Man. 1701; edited by R. Blanchard, 1932.

The Tatler, with Addison. 4 vols., 1710–11; edited by G. A. Aitken, 4 vols., 1898–99; selections edited by L. Gibbs, 1953.

The Spectator, with Addison. 8 vols., 1712–15; edited by D. F. Bond, 5 vols., 1965; selections edited by R. J. Allen, 1957.

An Englishman's Thanks to the Duke of Marlborough. 1712.

A Letter to Sir M. W[arton] Concerning Occasional Peers. 1713.

The Importance of Dunkirk. 1713.

The Guardian, with others. 2 vols., 1714; edited by Alexander Chalmers, 1802.

The Englishman (2 series, and an epistle). 3 vols., 1714–16; edited by R. Blanchard, 1955.

The Crisis, with Some Seasonable Remarks on the Danger of a Popish Successor. 1714.

The French Faith Represented in the Present State of Dunkirk. 1714.

A Letter Concerning the Bill for Preventing the Growth of Schism. 1714.

Mr. Steele's Apology for Himself and His Writings. 1714.

A Letter from the Earl of Mar to the King. 1715.

A Letter Concerning the Condemned Lords. 1716.

Account of Mr. Desagulier's New-Invented Chimneys. 1716.

An Account of the Fish Pool, with Joseph Gillmore. 1718.

The Joint and Humble Address to the Tories and Whigs Concerning the Intended Bill of Peerage. 1719.

A Letter to the Earl of O – d Concerning the Bill of Peerage. 1719.

The Plebeian. 1719; edited by R. Hurd, in Addison's *Works*, 1856.

The Spinster, in Defence of the Woollen Manufactures. 1719.

The Crisis of Property. 1720.

A Nation a Family; or, A Plan for the Improvement of the South-Sea Proposal. 1720.

The State of the Case Between the Lord Chamberlain and the Governor of the Royal Company of Comedians. 1720.

The Theatre. 1720; edited by John Loftis, 1962.

Tracts and Pamphlets, edited by R. Blanchard. 1944.

Steele's Periodical Journalism 1714–16: The Lover, The Reader, Town Talk, Chit-Chat, edited by R. Blanchard. 1959.

Plays

The Funeral; or, Grief a-la-Mode (produced 1701). 1702.

The Lying Lover; or, The Ladies' Friendship (produced 1703). 1704.

The Tender Husband; or, The Accomplished Fools (produced 1703). 1705.

The Conscious Lovers (produced 1722). 1723.

Verse

The Procession: A Poem on Her Majesty's Funeral. 1695.

Occasional Verse, edited by R. Blanchard. 1952.

Other

Editor, *The Ladies Library.* 3 vols., 1714.

Editor, *Poetical Miscellanies.* 1714.

Reading List: *Steele* by Willard Connely, 1934; *Steele at Drury Lane* by John Loftis, 1952; *Steele, Addison, and Their Periodical Essays* by Arthur R. Humphreys, 1959; *Steele: The Early Career*, 1964, and *The Later Career*, 1970, both by Calhoun Winton.

*   *   *

Though best remembered as a periodical essayist, Sir Richard Steele's literary career began in the theatre – if, that is, one forgets and forgives his moralizing tract *The Christian Hero*, an unsuccessful attempt at self-admonition. His plays were frank attempts to make piety more palatable, while avoiding the sexual excesses for which Collier had condemned the stage, and which increasingly middle-class audiences were also finding offensive.

The first, *The Funeral*, has several touches of originality, notably in its satire of the undertaking business, its sprightly yet sympathetic treatment of its female characters, and its liveliness of plotting. Indeed, two of the participants in Gildon's *A Comparison Between the Two Stages* allege that in this latter respect the play resembles a farce more than it does a comedy, and it may be regretted that Steele never successfully evaded formal considerations of this kind – though two fragments, *The School of Action* and *The Gentleman*, do begin to assert the kind of freedom from the rules that Gay and Fielding more happily achieved.

The Lying Lover was unalleviated by realism, displayed less comic spirit, and was, as Steele ruefully admitted, "damn'd for its piety." Loosely derived from Corneille's *Le Menteur*, it features a pathetic repentance scene, in which its hero, Young Bookwit, awakens in prison to find that he has killed a rival in a drunken duel. For this he is duly contrite in blank verse, to the extent of putting forgiveness before honour. There is some wit in the quixotic Bookwit's romancing in the earlier scenes, and his respectful welcome to Newgate by his fellow inmates hints at the inverted morality of *The Beggar's Opera*: yet, just a few scenes later, Steele perpetrates a double shift in the plot lacking any sense of its own fatal absurdity.

The Tender Husband, Steele's third play, also proved to be his last to reach the stage for nearly eighteen years. It has a female Quixote, or prototype Lydia Languish, as its heroine – and, indeed, the original of Tony Lumpkin in that heroine's cousin, Humphry Gubbin. Unfortunately, the sub-plot featuring the eponymous husband, who devises an unlikely test of his wife's faithfulness by disguising his own mistress as a suitor, disrupts the comic flow, and complicates the conclusion with a sentimental reconciliation.

In the following years, Steele was increasingly active as a Whig politician, his major literary achievement being, of course, the succession of periodicals he created, some written in collaboration with Joseph Addison. Of these, the best remembered are *The Spectator*, and *The Guardian*, with the irrelevantly titled *The Theatre* probably the most important of the later series. Whether or not Steele succeeded in his aim "to make the pulpit, the bar, and the stage all act in concert in the cause of piety, justice, and virtue" is arguable: but he certainly perfected a distinctive new form of clubable *belles lettres*, incidentally exploring techniques of characterization for his recurrent *personae* which were to be of significance to the early novelists, and publishing some first-rate dramatic criticism.

Although *The Conscious Lovers*, which did not reach the stage till 1722, was influential in the development of the *comédie larmoyante* in France, to the modern mind it merely demonstrates that, at its most sentimental, eighteenth-century comedy was no laughing matter. With the exception of its scenes below stairs – their purpose all too evidently to sugar a didactic pill – it is a distinctly unfunny play: yet, according to Steele, an audience's pleasure might be "too exquisite for laughter," and thus better expressed in the tears evoked by the inexpressibly virtuous behaviour of his hero, Young Bevil, and by the convenient reshufflings of the characters in the closing scene.

The mercantile morality of the play is at once over-explicit and interruptive, and its characters are neither in the humours nor the manners tradition, but mere ethical absolutes. No wonder that Fielding's Parson Adams considered it the first play fit for a Christian to read since the pagan tragedies – but then good Parson Adams lacked both irony and a sense of incongruity, as does *The Conscious Lovers*. Steele is better remembered by the feeling for both irony *and* incongruity in his earlier plays, and, of course, by his largeness of heart as a periodical essayist.

—Simon Trussler

STEELE, Wilbur Daniel. American. Born in Greensboro, North Carolina, 17 March 1886. Educated at kindergarten in Germany, 1889–92, and at schools in Colorado, 1892–1900; University of Denver Preparatory School, 1900–03; University of Denver, 1903–07, B.A. 1907; Boston Museum School of Fine Arts, 1907–08; Académie Julian, Paris, 1908. Married 1) Margaret Thurston in 1913 (died, 1931), two sons; 2) Norma Mitchell in 1932 (died, 1967). Free-lance writer; lived in Provincetown, Massachusetts, 1919–29; Co-Founder, Provincetown Players, 1915; lived in Chapel Hill, North Carolina, 1929–32, Hamburg, Connecticut, 1932–56, and Old Lyme, Connecticut, 1956–64; in rest home and hospital after 1964. D.Litt.: University of Denver, 1932. *Died 26 May 1970.*

PUBLICATIONS

Fiction

Storm. 1914.
Land's End and Other Stories. 1918.
The Shame Dance and Other Stories. 1923.
Isles of the Blest. 1924.
Taboo. 1925.
Urkey Island (stories). 1926.
The Man Who Saw Through Heaven and Other Stories. 1927.
Meat. 1928; as *The Third Generation,* 1929.
Tower of Sand and Other Stories. 1929.
Undertow. 1930.
Diamond Wedding. 1931.
Sound of Rowlocks. 1938.
That Girl from Memphis. 1945.
The Best Stories. 1945.
Full Cargo: More Stories. 1951.
Their Town. 1952.
The Way to the Gold. 1955.

Plays

Contemporaries (produced 1915).
Not Smart (produced 1916). In *The Terrible Woman ...* , 1925.
The Giants' Stair (produced 1924). 1924.

Ropes, in *The Terrible Woman* .... 1925.
The Terrible Woman and Other One Act Plays. 1925.
Post Road, with Norma Mitchell (produced 1934). 1935.
How Beautiful with Shoes, with Anthony Brown, from the story by Steele (produced 1935).
Luck, in *One Hundred Nonroyalty Plays*, edited by William Kozlenko. 1941.

Reading List: *Steele* by Martin Bucco, 1972.

*   *   *

Between the Great War and the Great Depression Wilbur Daniel Steele was America's recognized master of the popular short story. Many of his nearly two hundred published stories (an unschematized history of certain values prevailing in America at the time) transcend the formulas and clichés of mass fiction. Steele submitted to his day's conventions, but, like Poe, created a medley of dazzling variations. By wedding the "New Psychology" to his tight plots, melodramatic adventures, jagged coincidences, and surprise endings, he achieved a particular and celebrated perfection. But as magazines turned increasingly to social realism, sensational confession, and quicksilver style, demand for Steele's intricate stories declined.

Through exotic detail and vivid suggestion, *The Best Stories of Wilbur Daniel Steele* evokes the atmospheres of Cape Cod, the South, the Caribbean, North Africa, and the Middle East. With remarkable purity of concentration Steele exploits the temporality of literature, subordinates part to whole, and makes each yarn a *Gestalt*. "Romantic" themes like suspected innocence, revenge and retribution, power of love and friendship, premonition, and return from the "dead" intertwine with such "realistic" ideas as heredity versus environment, law and conscience, divided self, quest for identity, and awakening. Sophoclean symmetry heightens the commonplace, but sometimes Steele's heavy-handed "chance" destroys his grim illusions. Still, his sinewy twists and shock endings (less meretricious then O. Henry's) force us to *re-see* life's awesome ironies and literature's delightful ones.

"The Man Who Saw Through Heaven," one of his most effective stories, dramatizes the physical and spiritual evolution of mankind in a *tour de force* of condensation. The classic "How Beautiful with Shoes" (also a Broadway play) renders the emotional awakening of a cloddish Appalachian girl abducted by a runaway psychotic. "When Hell Froze" is a memorable period piece. For sheer ingenuity and suspense "Footfalls," a tale of paternal revenge, has few equals. "Conjuh," "Blue Murder," "Bubbles," "The Body of the Crime," "For They Know Not What They Do" – these stories and many others have received high praise.

Steele's Euclidian logic, detective imagination, and knotty style suited the shorter form far better than the novel. His longer fiction, labored and wooden, displays feeble narrative line, thematic fuzziness, clotted exegesis, and trite detail. Perhaps *Meat*, an early novel which boldly indicts the perpetuation of weakness, is his best.

Today Wilbur Daniel Steele's radiant prize stories crop up in anthologies, and historians of the American short story acknowledge his uniqueness, but he attracts little serious critical attention. An important transitional writer who bridges the Poe-O. Henry and the Anderson-Hemingway traditions, Wilbur Daniel Steele was a marvelous technician who occasionally compelled his stories to the level of high art.

—Martin Bucco

STEIN, Gertrude. American. Born in Allegheny, Pennsylvania, 3 Feburary 1874; as a child lived in Vienna, Paris, and Oakland, California. Educated at schools in Oakland and San Francisco; Radcliffe College, Cambridge, Massachusetts, 1893–97: studied philosophy under William James; studied medicine at Johns Hopkins Medical School, Baltimore, 1897–1901. Writer from 1902; lived in Paris from 1903, with her friend Alice B. Toklas from 1908; center of a circle of artists, including Picasso, Matisse, and Braque, and of writers, including Hemingway and Fitzgerald. *Died 27 July 1946.*

PUBLICATIONS

Collections

> *Writings and Lectures 1911–1945* (selection), edited by Patricia Meyerowitz. 1967; as *Look at Me Now and Here I Am,* 1971.
> *Selected Operas and Plays,* edited by John Malcolm Brinnin. 1970.

Fiction

> *Three Lives: Stories of the Good Anna, Melanctha, and the Gentle Lena.* 1909.
> *The Making of Americans, Being a History of a Family's Progress.* 1925.
> *A Book Concluding with As a Wife Has a Cow: A Love Story.* 1926.
> *Lucy Church Amiably.* 1931.
> *Ida: A Novel.* 1941.
> *Brewsie and Willie.* 1946.
> *Blood on the Dining Room Floor.* 1948.
> *Things as They Are: A Novel in Three Parts.* 1950.
> *Mrs. Reynolds, and Five Early Novelettes,* edited by Carl Van Vechten. 1952.
> *A Novel of Thank You,* edited by Carl Van Vechten. 1958.

Plays

> *Geography and Plays.* 1922.
> *A Village: Are You Ready Yet Not Yet.* 1928.
> *Operas and Plays.* 1932.
> *Four Saints in Three Acts,* music by Virgil Thomson (produced 1934). 1934.
> *A Wedding Bouquet: Ballet,* music by Lord Berners (produced 1936). 1936.
> *In Savoy; or, Yes Is for a Very Young Man* (produced 1946). 1946.
> *The Mother of Us All,* music by Virgil Thomson (produced 1947). 1947.
> *Last Operas and Plays,* edited by Carl Van Vechten. 1949.
> *In a Garden,* music by Meyer Kupferman (produced 1951). 1951.
> *Lucretia Borgia.* 1968.

Verse and Prose Poems

> *Tender Buttons: Objects, Food, Rooms.* 1914.
> *Have They Attacked Mary. He Giggled.* 1917.
> *Before the Flowers of Friendship Fade Friendship Faded.* 1931.
> *Two (Hitherto Unpublished) Poems.* 1948.

Stanzas in Meditation and Other Poems (1929–1933), edited by Carl Van Vechten. 1956.

Other

Portrait of Mabel Dodge. 1912.
Composition as Explanation. 1926.
Descriptions of Literature. 1926.
An Elucidation. 1927.
Useful Knowledge. 1928.
An Acquaintance with Description. 1929.
Dix Portraits. 1930.
How to Write. 1931.
The Autobiography of Alice B. Toklas. 1933.
Matisse, Picasso, and Gertrude Stein, with Two Shorter Stories. 1933.
Portraits and Prayers. 1934.
Chicago Inscriptions. 1934.
Lectures in America. 1935.
Narration: Four Lectures. 1935.
The Geographical History of America; or, The Relation of Human Nature to the Human Mind. 1936.
Everybody's Autobiography. 1937.
Picasso. 1938.
The World Is Round (juvenile). 1939.
Prothalamium. 1939.
Paris France. 1940.
What Are Masterpieces. 1940.
Wars I Have Seen. 1945.
The Stein First Reader, and Three Plays (juvenile). 1946.
Selected Writings, edited by Carl Van Vechten. 1946.
Four in America. 1947.
Kisses Can. 1947.
Literally True. 1947.
Two: Gertrude Stein and Her Brother and Other Early Portraits (1908–1912), edited by Carl Van Vechten. 1951.
Bee Time Vine and Other Pieces (1913–1927), edited by Carl Van Vechten. 1953.
As Fine as Melanctha (1914–1930), edited by Carl Van Vechten. 1954.
Painted Lace and Other Pieces (1914–1937), edited by Carl Van Vechten. 1955.
Absolutely Bob Brown; or, Bobbed Brown. 1955.
To Bobchen Haas. 1957.
Alphabets and Birthdays, edited by Carl Van Vechten. 1957.
On Our Way (letters). 1959.
Cultivated Motor Automatism, with Leon M. Solomons. 1969.
Fernhurst, Q.E.D., and Other Early Writings, edited by Leon Katz. 1972.
A Primer for the Gradual Understanding of Stein, edited by Robert Bartlett Haas. 1972.
Reflections on the Atomic Bomb (unpublished writings), edited by Robert Bartlett Haas. 1974.
Dear Sammy: Letters from Stein and Alice B. Toklas, edited by Samuel M. Steward. 1977.

Bibliography: *Stein: A Bibliography* by Robert Wilson, 1974.

Reading List: *Stein: Form and Intelligibility* by Rosalind S. Miller, 1949; *Stein: A Biography of Her Work* by Donald Sutherland, 1951; *The Flowers of Friendship* (letters to Stein) edited by Donald Gallup, 1953; *Stein: Her Life and Work* by Elizabeth Sprigge, 1957; *The Third Rose: Stein and Her World* by John Malcolm Brinnin, 1959; *Stein* by Frederick J. Hoffman, 1961; *What Is Remembered* by Alice B. Toklas, 1963; *The Development of Abstractionism in the Writings of Stein*, 1965, and *Stein*, 1976, both by Michael J. Hoffman; *Stein and the Literature of Modern Consciousness* by Norman Weinstein, 1970; *Stein in Pieces* by Richard Bridgman, 1970; *Charmed Circle* by James Mellow, 1974; *Exact Resemblance to Exact Resemblance: The Literary Portraiture of Stein* by Wendy Steiner, 1978.

*   *   *

If Paul Cézanne, of whom Gertrude Stein wrote a "portrait" in 1911, broke with traditional forms (such as perspective) and traditional modes (such as pictorial replication), he did so by accenting the verticals, horizontals, and diagonals that he saw in nature. He moved painting towards geometric forms, towards the abstract, and developed new spatial patterns in which, by showing an object simultaneously from several viewpoints, planes and surfaces interacted visually on the canvas. His paintings are not of nature, but provide a visualisation of the formal parts of what he saw. Cézanne said that he did not paint pictures; he painted *paint*. Gertrude Stein does the same thing with words.

Her work is largely a systematic investigation of the formal elements of language (syntax, parts of speech, grammar, etymology, punctuation) or of the formal elements of literature (narrative, poetry, dialogue, fiction, drama), in which we see the skeleton of the writing or of the form rather than the burden it carries. Apparent nonsense, her work has been the subject of much ridicule (yet it has influenced three generations of writers). "Nobody knows what I am trying to do but I do and I know when I succeed," she said, in *As Fine as Melanctha*. William Carlos Williams (*Selected Essays*) praised her for "cleansing" the language, for "tackling the fracture of stupidities bound in thoughtless phrases, in our calcified grammatical constructions, and in the subtle brainlessness of our ... rhythms which compel words to follow certain others without precision of thought." Her concern is for writing (or reading) as movement; for literature, seen as something other than a body of reference work; for writing (reading) envisioned as the first concern of the immediate and attentive moment.

It is convenient to divide Gertrude Stein's work into three more-or-less distinct groups. The first consists of such well-known and comparatively straightforward narratives as *The Autobiography of Alice B. Toklas*, *Wars I Have Seen*, and *Three Lives*, which includes the much-anthologized "Melanctha," in which we see (or, more accurately, hear) Melanctha simultaneously from several angles, as in a Cubist painting. Some of the dialogue between Melanctha and Jeff has an effect much like that of Marcel Duchamp's painting *Nude Descending a Staircase*. Richard Wright records reading the story to "a group of semi-literate Negro stockyard workers" who "slapped their thighs, howled, laughed, stomped, and interrupted me constantly to comment on the characters" (*PM*, 11 March 1945). It is the language of speech.

The second group contains Stein's critical and exegetical work, such as *Composition as Explanation*, *Narration*, *What Are Masterpieces*, and the celebrated *Lectures in America*, in which she discusses her own writing, and, offering general reflections on the forms, genres, modes, and periods of English literature, explains the principles on which much of her own work is based. The fruit of protracted meditation on language, her exegeses are at times difficult to follow; as Thornton Wilder observed, "Miss Stein pays her listeners the high compliment of dispensing for the most part with that apparatus of illustrative simile and anecdote that is so often employed to recommend ideas." And when, in *Lectures in America*, she says "more and more one does not use nouns," she is pointing to the very plasticity of language one finds in the third group of her work, the overtly experimental and difficult writing.

Work in this group, such as *Tender Buttons*, *Stanzas in Meditation*, *An Acquaintance with*

Description, or *How to Write*, may properly be thought of as "exemplary," since it demonstrates the principles enunciated in the exegetical work. While composing *How to Write* Stein called *Tender Buttons* "my first conscious struggle with the problem of correlating sight, sound and sense, and eliminating rhythm; – now I am trying grammar and eliminating sight and sound" (*Transition 14*, 1928), while in *Lectures in America* she said that in *Tender Buttons* "I struggled with the ridding of myself of nouns. I knew that nouns must go in poetry as they had gone in prose if anything that is everything was to go on meaning something." A noun is the name of a thing, and "if you feel what is inside that thing you do not call it by the name by which it is known"; instead, like Whitman, you "mean names without naming them." Breaking syntax, forcing words into multiple grammatical functions, in *Tender Buttons* or *Stanzas in Meditation* Stein seeks to write a poem which, taken as a whole, becomes itself a noun. For example, as Meredith Yearsley points out, under the title "A Box" the poem acts a box out linguistically by the quadruple repetition of a particular construction. The closedness of the box is caught by use of grammatical constructions which force the reader to rescan the sentence. Here, most clearly, Stein uses words the way Cézanne uses paint.

How to Write, originally entitled *Grammar, Paragraphs, Sentences, Vocabulary, Etcetera*, works similarly, through exploring the effect of semantic and syntactic anomalies in a prose which demands of the reader the expectation that words, the parts of speech, will hold their conventional position and function in the sentence. In a sentence like "It is very well a date which makes each separate in a leaf in a dismissal," the major source of difficulty is not in the lack of punctuation so much as in the ambiguous functions of words and phrases. In other sentences from "Arthur a Grammar" the reader need only supply punctuation to render the sentence wholly intelligible: "There is a difference between a grammar and a sentence this is grammar in a sentence I will agree to no map with which you may be dissatisfied and therefore beg you to point out what you regard as incorrect in the positions of the troops in my two sentences." In each case, the sentence acts out its meaning.

In such ways Stein's words remove themselves from the context in which they (may have) originated and acquire a new context in which they can assert their meaning by demonstrating it. The world of Gertrude Stein is one in which things are the cause rather than the content of language, and it is thus an interiorized world, where definitions are held in the process and in the moment of defining: Stein held that poetry is stasis, where the object, be it Melanctha or Roast Beef or Arthur a Grammar, fills all the available space, much as a Cubist object fills a crowded flat surface. The work is dense, and exuberant.

While the strength of Stein's personality might account for her influence on writers like Hemingway or Anderson, it does not account for her later influence, or for her friendship with painters like Picasso or Juan Gris. Later readers of her work, like Robert Duncan, George Bowering, or B. P. Nichol, find themselves, imitating her writing, turning to their own childhood. This is in part because Stein's language is devoid of allusion, seems to have no past, and things seem to speak directly, perceived in immediacy.

—Peter Quartermain

STEINBECK, John (Ernst). American. Born in Salinas, California, 27 February 1902. Educated at Salinas High School, graduated 1918; special student at Stanford University, California, 1919–25. Married 1) Carol Henning in 1930 (divorced, 1943); 2) Gwyn Conger in 1943 (divorced, 1949), two sons; 3) Elaine Scott in 1950. Worked at various jobs, including Reporter for the New York *American*, apprentice hod-carrier, apprentice painter, chemist, caretaker of an estate at Lake Tahoe, surveyor, and fruit picker, 1925–35; full-time writer from 1935; settled in Monterey, California, 1930, later moved to New York City; special writer for the United States Army Air Force during World War II; Correspondent in Europe for the New York *Herald Tribune*, 1943. Recipient: New York Drama Critics Circle Award, 1938; Pulitzer Prize, 1940; Nobel Prize for Literature, 1962. *Died 20 December 1968.*

PUBLICATIONS

Fiction

Cup of Gold: A Life of Henry Morgan, Buccaneer, with Occasional References to History. 1929.
The Pastures of Heaven. 1932.
To a God Unknown. 1933.
Tortilla Flat. 1935.
In Dubious Battle. 1936.
Of Mice and Men. 1937.
The Red Pony (stories). 1937.
The Long Valley (stories). 1938.
The Grapes of Wrath. 1938.
The Moon Is Down. 1942.
Cannery Row. 1945.
The Wayward Bus. 1947.
The Pearl. 1947.
Burning Bright. 1950.
East of Eden. 1952.
Sweet Thursday. 1954.
The Short Reign of Pippin IV: A Fabrication. 1957.
The Winter of Our Discontent. 1961.

Plays

Of Mice and Men (produced 1937). 1937.
The Forgotten Village (screenplay). 1941.
The Moon Is Down, from his own novel (produced 1942). 1943.
Burning Bright, from his own novel (produced 1950). 1951.
Viva Zapata! The Original Screenplay, edited by Robert E. Morsberger. 1974.

Screenplays: *The Forgotten Village,* 1941; *Lifeboat,* with Jo Swerling, 1944; *The Pearl,* with Emilio Fernandez and Jack Wagner, 1947; *The Red Pony,* 1949; *Viva Zapata!,* 1952.

Other

Their Blood Is Strong. 1938.
Sea of Cortez: A Leisurely Journal of Travel and Research, with Edward F. Ricketts. 1941.
Bombs Away: The Story of a Bomber Team. 1942.
The Portable Steinbeck, edited by Pascal Covici. 1943; revised edition, 1946, 1958; revised edition, edited by Pascal Covici, Jr., 1971.

Vanderbilt Clinic. 1947.
A Russian Journal, photographs by Robert Capa. 1948.
The Log from the Sea of Cortez. 1951.
Once There Was a War. 1958.
Travels with Charley in Search of America. 1962.
America and Americans. 1966.
The Journal of a Novel: The East of Eden Letters. 1969.
Steinbeck: A Life in Letters, edited by Elaine Steinbeck and Robert Wallsten. 1975.
The Acts of King Arthur and His Noble Knights, From the Winchester Manuscripts of Malory and Other Sources. 1977.

Bibliography: *A New Steinbeck Bibliography 1929–1971* by Tetsumaro Hayashi, 1973.

Reading List: *Steinbeck and His Critics* edited by E. W. Tedlock, Jr., and C. V. Wicker, 1957; *The Wide World of Steinbeck,* 1958, and *Steinbeck, Nature, and Myth,* 1978, both by Peter Lisca; *Steinbeck* by Warren French, 1961; *Steinbeck* by F. W. Watt, 1961; *Steinbeck* by Joseph Fontenrose, 1963; *Steinbeck and Edward F. Ricketts: The Shaping of a Novelist* by Richard Astro, 1973; *Steinbeck: The Errant Knight* by Nelson Valjean, 1975.

*   *   *

John Steinbeck often puzzled critics during his lifetime because early in his career his style and subject matter seemed to change with each new story, and after World War II there was a generally acknowledged but puzzling decline in his artistic prowess. Now, however, in a larger perspective we can see that underlying the apparent diversity of Steinbeck's work is a consistently developing vision of man's relation to his environment. This larger perspective is provided, in part, by the generally acknowledged end of the Age of Modernism, as described in Maurice Beebe's "What Modernism Was" (*Journal of Modern Literature,* July 1974). After offering a longer definition, Beebe approves Philip Stevick's observation that the modernist sensibility might almost be defined by "its irony, its implicit admiration for verbal precision and understatement." Marston LaFrance in *A Reading of Stephen Crane* (1971) traces this characteristic irony to Kierkegaard and describes its possessors as perceiving "a double realm of values where a different sort of mind would perceive only a single realm."

Steinbeck's varying works during the years of his greatest popularity and power in the 1930's were characterized by precisely this kind of irony. It is excellently illustrated by Sir Henry Morgan's speech at the end of Steinbeck's first novel, *Cup of Gold,* "Civilization will split up a character, and he who refuses to split goes under." Despite its importance in establishing Steinbeck's viewpoint, this apprentice work is strikingly different from his later books. A flamboyantly written historical costume drama about a Caribbean pirate who sacks the golden city of Panama to capture a legendary woman and then returns her to her husband for a ransom and sells out his piratical cohorts for high government position, *Cup of Gold* exudes the same disenchanted world-weariness as the abundant "Waste Land" literature of the 1920's.

A similar preoccupation with characters of mythical dimensions in a dying world colors one of Steinbeck's strangest novels, *To a God Unknown* (third published, it antedates the second). In this fantasy, Joseph Wayne – the leader among four brothers who allegorize lust, sanctimoniousness, animalism, and martyrdom – sacrifices himself to bring the needed rain to his parched valley. Here, as in the story-cycle called *The Pastures of Heaven,* Steinbeck discovers the beautiful, small valleys of his native California as the settings for his most powerful tales. But whereas *To a God Unknown* employs the same kind of baroque language and bizarre episodes as *Cup of Gold, The Pastures of Heaven* offers a lower-keyed, vernacular language and earthy tales of the defeat of good intentions in a Naturalistic manner that emphasizes the irony of man's sufferings in a paradisically beautiful setting.

Steinbeck continues to employ this Naturalistic viewpoint in his next works. *Tortilla Flat* seems at first glance much different from the others because of the archaic style arising from the effort to translate Malory's *Morte Darthur* into the language and actions of Mexican-American "paisanos" in Monterey, California; but beneath its surface of quaint humor, it, too, is an ironic fable of civilization "splitting up" a person: once the fabulous Danny abandons his "natural life" in the woods to become a property owner, he can never go back again and must die with a gesture of defiant despair. *In Dubious Battle*, which is often justifiably called the best American strike novel, deals realistically with tense labor problems among California apple growers and migrant pickers and ends as grimly as *Tortilla Flat*, with the disappearance of Doc Burton, the one man of objective good will in the story, and a murder that renders faceless a young labor organizer.

In *Of Mice and Men*, Steinbeck's first experiment in writing a play-novelette, Lennie, a tower of physical strength, must die because he has not the mentality to control his behavior and kills the soft things he loves to fondle. His death destroys also his protector George's dream of their some time finding security on a farm of their own. The stories collected in *The Long Valley* record similar helpless defeats – in the most familiar of them, "Chrysanthemums" and "Flight," we see first a love-starved woman exploited by a wily itinerant and then another young man whose mind is not strong enough to control his behavior driven to his death by shadowy pursuers. The collection concludes with one of Steinbeck's most popular and masterful works, *The Red Pony*. This four-story cycle depicts a sensitive boy's growing into maturity through his encounters on his father's ranch with the fallibility of man, the wearing out of man, the unreliability of nature, and the exhaustion of nature that leads to the extinguishing of man's dynamic urge for "Westering."

Steinbeck's next work after his success with *Of Mice and Men* was apparently planned as another ironic, defeatist tale entitled *L'Affaire Lettuceberg*, based on his observation of the outrageous plight of migrant workers who had fled the Midwestern Dust Bowl in hope of making a new start in California. During the writing, however, Steinbeck experienced a great change of heart, abandoned what he had written as "a smart-alec book," and, writing feverishly, recast his work as *The Grapes of Wrath*, his most popular and critically most highly acclaimed work.

The Grapes of Wrath alternates the story of the travails of the Joad family, share-croppers tractored out of Oklahoma who find only a hostile reception in the West, with inter-chapters that generalize this family history as a nation's tragedy. Through the inspiration of the martyred ex-preacher Jim Casy, the Joads at last learn the lesson of co-operation summed up by Ma's speech, "Use' ta be the fambly was fust. It ain't so now. It's anybody." Yet the novel is still modernist in sensibility, for the much discussed ending in which daughter Rosasharn offers breast milk intended for her own dead baby to a dying old man is ambiguous. The Joads have found temporary haven, but no security; the national tragedy can only be solved by the readers, not the writer. Steinbeck has, however, turned from characters who are helpless victims to those who learn to heighten their consciousnesses enough to transcend their afflictions.

After reshaping this key novel, Steinbeck would never revert completely to the ironical modernist point of view; but neither was he able consistently enough to contrive situations convincingly optimistic enough to provide an alternative. His two further play-novelettes, *The Moon Is Down* – written during World War II about the military occupation of a peaceful nation – and *Burning Bright* – a meditation on sterility that pleads that "the species must go staggering on" – suffered from "misplaced universalism." They were populated with two-dimensional allegorical figures from Medieval morality plays. Other works like the very popular *The Pearl*, *The Wayward Bus*, and the script for Elia Kazan's film *Viva Zapata!* – like the earlier short film *The Forgotten Village* – take Mexicans from underprivileged backgrounds and turn them into folk-Messiahs, "natural saints." (The driver of *The Wayward Bus* even has the initials J. C.) Kino's gesture in *The Pearl* of casting away the fabulous jewel that has brought only misery rather than promised fortune and the tribute at the end of Kazan's film to Zapata's indomitable spirit have heartened audiences, but they are theatricalized indications that Steinbeck, instead of looking ahead, seeks – as such later non-fiction works as *America and Americans* and the "Letters to Alicia" make clear – a return to simple, folk values of the past.

Only in *Cannery Row*, where Steinbeck again universalizes the comic story he tells through "inter-chapters," does he succeed in creating, through his portrait of Doc (based on his good friend Ed Ricketts), a remarkable figure who has both the selflessness and the sophistication to transcend the trials and temptations of the materialistic world through escape into "the cosmic Monterey" fragmentarily embodied in deathless art.

Steinbeck attempted to tell such a story of transcendence again in his most ambitious novel, *East of Eden*, by again alternating between two kinds of material, but this time they fail to fuse. The story of his own family returns to the lyrical Naturalism of his work of the 1930's, but the material is so heavily ironic that it fails to produce an affirmation; he seeks this through the labored fictional pursuit of the meaning of the Hebrew word "Timshel," which animates another allegorical fable – this one spiced up with much sensational material – about a modern Adam, his errant wife, and his twin sons who re-enact the Biblical account of man's first family.

His subsequent fiction was trivial. *Sweet Thursday* brought back Doc and other characters from *Cannery Row*, but reduced Doc to a confused sentimentalist ministered to principally by kindly whores. *The Short Reign of Pippin IV* was a very funny, timely attack on French politics and art during the years of Charles de Gaulle, but its sketchiness makes it dated. Finally in *The Winter of Our Discontent*, Steinbeck tried to make a fresh start by writing about a small Long Island town. The novel developed from a very funny short story, "How Mr. Hogan Robbed a Bank," but the humor disappeared in this account of Ethan Allen Hawley's struggles with his conscience about having been betrayed by others and betraying others. While the novel does not quite become simply another revelation of modernist alienation (Hawley makes the affirmative gesture of rejecting suicide in order to help his daughter live) he really makes for less selfish reasons the same kind of compromise that Henry Morgan makes in Steinbeck's first novel. Thus Steinbeck's fiction returns at last almost full circle to the point where it had begun after achieving but falling away from the triumphant visions of *The Grapes of Wrath* and *Cannery Row*.

—Warren French

STERNE, Laurence. English. Born in Clonmel, County Tipperary, Ireland, 24 November 1713, of an English Army family; as a child lived at various regimental posts in England and Ireland. Educated at a school in Halifax, Yorkshire, 1723–31; Jesus College, Cambridge, 1733–36 (sizar, 1733; scholar, 1734), matriculated 1735, B.A. 1737, M.A. 1740. Married Elizabeth Lumley in 1741 (separated, 1764), two daughters. Ordained Deacon, 1737: Curate of St. Ives, Huntingdonshire, 1737; Assistant Curate, Catton, Yorkshire, 1738; Ordained priest, 1738; Rector of Sutton-in-the-Forest, Yorkshire, 1738, and the adjoining parish Stillington from 1743 (retained both livings all his life; lived in Sutton until 1760); Prebendary of York Cathedral from 1741; writer from 1758; visited London, 1760: vilified by other writers for indecency (*Tristram Shandy*); received perpetual curacy of Coxwold, Yorkshire, and settled there, 1760; lived in France, 1762–64; travelled in France and Italy, 1765–66; met Mrs. Eliza Draper, 1767; lived in London, 1767. *Died 18 March 1768.*

Publications

Collections

> *Works,* edited by Wilbur L. Cross.   12 vols., 1904.
> *Works.*   7 vols., 1926–27.
> *Letters,* edited by Lewis P. Curtis.   1935.

Fiction

> *A Political Romance.*   1759; edited by Ian Jack, with *A Sentimental Journey* and *Journal to Eliza,* 1968.
> *The Life and Opinions of Tristram Shandy, Gentleman.*   9 vols., 1759–67; edited by James Aiken Work, 1940.
> *A Sentimental Journey Through France and Italy, by Mr. Yorick.*   1768; edited by Gardner D. Stout, Jr., 1967.

Other

> *The Sermons of Mr. Yorick.*   7 vols., 1760–69; selection edited by Marjorie David, 1973.
> *Letters to His Most Intimate Friends, with a Fragment in the Manner of Rabelais, to Which Are Prefixed Memoirs of His Life and Family Written by Himself.*   3 vols., 1775.

Bibliography: *Sterne in the Twentieth Century: An Essay and a Bibliography of Sternean Studies 1900–1965* by Lodwick Hartley, 1966, revised edition, 1968.

Reading List: *Life and Times of Sterne* by Wilbur L. Cross, 1909, revised edition, 1929; *The Politicks of Sterne* by Lewis P. Curtis, 1929; *Early Masters of English Fiction* by Alan D. McKillop, 1956; *Sterne: De l'Homme à l'Oeuvre* by Henri Fluchère, 1961, translated as *Sterne from Tristram to Yorick,* 1965; *Sterne* by W. S. Piper, 1965; *Sterne's Comedy of Moral Sentiment,* 1966, and *Sterne: The Early and Middle Years,* 1975, both by Arthur Cash, and *The Winged Skull* edited by Cash and J. M. Stedmond, 1971; *Sterne: A Collection of Critical Essays* edited by John Traugott, 1968; *Wild Excursions: The Life and Fiction of Sterne* by David Thompson, 1972; *Sterne: The Critical Heritage* edited by Alan B. Howes, 1974.

*   *   *

Tristram Shandy and *Sentimental Journey* brought Sterne immediate fame and notoriety and have continued to provoke controversy. He has been praised by some as the most innovative novelist of the eighteenth century, a humorist of genius, while damned by others as affected, shallow, and indecent. Nietzsche called Sterne "the freest writer of all times," and indeed both his novels play fast and loose with narrative conventions. The liberties of *Tristram Shandy* may strike readers as especially bewildering. What should we make of a book filled with Rabelaisian wit, in which digressions overwhelm plot, in which events and reflections seem governed by whim, in which chronology is so elastic that the novel ends several years before it begins, and in which the hero scarcely appears? First chapters normally serve to orient readers; the opening chapter of *Tristram Shandy,* with Mrs. Shandy's seemingly pointless question about winding the family clock, works to disorient us, to signal that we have entered a new world and must learn to find our way. As we read on we begin to see that the narrative is not, in fact, disjointed or random, that the story has its own principles of associative coherence.

Tristram Shandy ignores chronology because the treatment of time is psychological. Events unfold as they present themselves to Tristram's mind; the length of particular episodes depends on the number of memories, feelings, and ideas a given action or conversation evokes. The smallest incident may thus be whole chapters in the telling. The fluidity of Sterne's transitions from one subject to the next has encouraged comparisons of his method to stream-of-consciousness. Such comparisons are misleading, however, because everything presented in the novel assumes an audience. What we have in *Tristram Shandy*, and later in *Sentimental Journey*, is not interior monologue, not the flow of unspoken thoughts, but something closer to uninhibited conversation. Tristram addresses the reader as a new acquaintance who must be teased and cajoled into an understanding of how to read his book. A reader must learn, for example, that the digressions only appear to lead away from the story; usually they circle back to it in ingenious, instructive ways. As Tristram explains, "my work is digressive, and it is progressive too, – and at the same time." If Tristram interrupts Toby in mid-sentence for a thirty page excursion, that digression is by no means irrelevant. It tells us things about Toby which shed light on his singular character and which make us better able to appreciate what he has to say when Tristram finally returns to him.

Sterne's characters are no less striking than his devices of narrative. Walter, with his preposterous theories of names and noses, the gentle Toby with his passion for model fortifications, seem as single-minded as any humorous character of Jonsonian comedy. But as Sterne develops them they are neither so one-dimensional, nor so purely ridiculous. If Sterne delights in odd behavior, he wants also to know what lies behind it. He traces Toby's hobbyhorse to the days when, convalescing from a serious wound received at the siege of Namur, Toby tries to tell visitors precisely what has happened to him. First he buys a map of Namur, then he consults books on military science. One thing leads to another; before long he can think of nothing except battles. Character, Sterne suggests, is shaped by circumstances more than by choice. Men are at the mercy of events, and "the wisest men in all ages, not excepting *Solomon* himself," have had hobbyhorses. The hobbies of Walter and Toby may strike us as laughable, yet who can say that they are any more silly, or more avoidable, than those of the other characters, or any more silly than our own? In *Tristram Shandy* distinctions between the sensible and the ridiculous rapidly lose force.

Hobbyhorses do make communications between characters difficult. When every man perceives the world in an intensely personal way, how can talk fail to be at cross purposes? But Sterne steers clear of despairing reflections on human isolation. A spirit of genial tolerance informs his novel. At Shandy Hall the bonds of affection are strong enough to hold people together. Besides, breakdowns in communications are not always recognized: "He was a very great man! added my uncle *Toby*; (meaning *Stevinus*) – He was so, brother *Toby*, said my father, (meaning *Piereskius*)." The lives of Sterne's characters have little to do with their understanding of other people; they derive deepest satisfaction from their hobbyhorses. In this sense the world of *Tristram Shandy* borders on the solipsistic. Like Joyce or Virginia Woolf, Sterne stresses the primacy of subjective experience. It is not action that matters, it is the way actions are perceived. Toby may be only an invalid on half-pay, yet in imagination he is again a soldier fighting his country's battles. War games for him transcend play; they are a patriotic obligation.

We must remember that the full title of Sterne's novel is *The Life and Opinions of Tristram Shandy, Gentleman*. Tristram may scarcely appear as a character, but through his "opinions" he is everywhere; every scene is filtered through his consciousness. He says little about what has happened to him, a great deal about how he thinks and feels. We come, finally, to be on a more intimate footing with him than with many characters in fiction about whose activities we know far more. The sensibility revealed is a curious and often disconcerting amalgam of his father's licentious wit and out-of-the-way learning and his uncle's readiness to shed kindly tears. Tristram can solicit sympathy for a lovelorn maiden one moment and use her

for a laugh the next: "MARIA look'd wistfully for some time at me, and then at her goat —
and then at me — and then at her goat again, and so on alternately — Well, *Maria,* said I softly
— What resemblance do you find?" Should we take Maria seriously or as a joke? is Sterne, at
bottom, a sentimentalist or a jester? Nietzsche thought that at bottom he was *both,* and that
the most striking evidence of his freedom as a writer lay precisely in the lightening ease with
which he could move from pathos to mockery.

Though *Sentimental Journey* is a far less eccentric novel than *Tristram Shandy* it too
celebrates private sensibility and is complicated by still subtler ambiguities. Parson Yorick's
account of his travels through France transmutes small events — an encounter with a
mendicant friar, conversation with a grisette, dinner with a peasant family — into richly
imagined experiences. Yorick cares nothing for sights. He is a connoisseur of feeling. "Was I
in a desert," he declares, "I would find out wherewith in it to call forth my affections." No
reader would doubt him for a minute. What does raise doubt is the extent to which those
affections are sincere. As in *Tristram Shandy* it is hard to determine just where Sterne stands.
We can take a hint from Yorick's name and find evidence aplenty that he is a sentimental
fool, even an outright fraud. At the theatre in Paris he trembles with pity for a dwarf whose
view of the stage is blocked by an enormous German, but he lifts not a finger to help him.
While he does try to release the caged starling that has been taught to cry "I can't get out," he
abandons the attempt at the first difficulty, and later gives the bird away, cage and all.

Yet Sterne does not always undercut Yorick's feelings. There is nothing ludicrous, surely,
about his admiration for the peasants of the Bourbonnais. If Yorick is a fool he is a fool of
uncommon charm and insight. He knows, for instance, that his kindness to the *fille de
chambre* who visits him in his room is to some degree self-serving. But he defends himself
with a question which compels the reader to examine the purity of his own motives and to
consider whether motives *need* be pure: "If Nature has so wove her web of kindness, that
some threads of love and desire are entangled with the piece — must the whole web be rent in
drawing them out?" Sterne is ever an enemy to hasty judgment and facile moralizing. *A
Sentimental Journey* and *Tristram Shandy* invite us to look at the world anew, to find
complexity and strangeness in the familiar, and to recognize that what seems excessive or odd
may have closer ties to ordinary experience than we have thought.

—Michael DePorte

STEVENSON, Robert Louis (Robert Lewis Balfour Stevenson). Scottish. Born in
Edinburgh, 13 November 1850. Educated at the Edinburgh Academy; studied engineering at
the University of Edinburgh, 1866–71, then studied law in the office of Skene, Edwards, and
Gordon, Edinburgh: called to the Scottish Bar, 1875, but never practised. Married Fanny
Vandergrift Osbourne in 1880; two step-children, including the writer Lloyd Osbourne.
Travelled and lived on the Continent, chiefly in France, 1875–80; writer from 1876;
contributed to the *Cornhill Magazine,* 1876–82; travelled widely, partly in search for a cure
for tuberculosis, from 1880: lived in Davos, Switzerland, Hyères, France, Bournemouth,
England, and the South Seas; settled in Samoa, 1888. *Died 3 December 1894.*

PUBLICATIONS

Collections

> *The Letters of Stevenson to His Family and Friends*, edited by Sidney Colvin.   2 vols.,
>   1899; revised edition, 4 vols., 1911.
> *Works* (Vailima Edition), edited by Lloyd Osbourne and Fanny Stevenson.   26 vols.,
>   1922–23.
> *Selected Writings*, edited by Saxe Commins.   1947.
> *Collected Poems*, edited by Janet Adam Smith.   1950.
> *Essays*, edited by Malcolm Elwin.   1950.

Fiction

> *New Arabian Nights* (stories).   1882.
> *Treasure Island*.   1883.
> *More New Arabian Nights: The Dynamiter*, with Fanny Stevenson.   1885.
> *Prince Otto: A Romance*.   1885.
> *Strange Case of Dr. Jekyll and Mr. Hyde*.   1886.
> *Kidnapped, Being Memoirs of the Adventures of David Balfour in the Year 1751*.   1886.
> *The Merry Men and Other Tales and Fables*.   1887.
> *The Misadventures of John Nicholson: A Christmas Story*.   1887.
> *The Black Arrow: A Tale of the Two Roses*.   1888.
> *The Master of Ballantrae: A Winter's Tale*.   1889.
> *The Wrong Box*, with Lloyd Osbourne.   1889.
> *The Wrecker*, with Lloyd Osbourne.   1892.
> *Catriona: A Sequel to Kidnapped*.   1893; as *David Balfour*, 1893.
> *The Bottle Imp* (stories).   1893(?).
> *Island Nights' Entertainments* (stories).   1893.
> *The Ebb-Tide: A Trio and Quartette* (stories), with Lloyd Osbourne.   1894.
> *The Body-Snatcher* (stories).   1895.
> *The Amateur Emigrant from the Clyde to Sandy Hook* (stories).   1895.
> *The Strange Case of Dr. Jekyll and Mr. Hyde, with Other Fables*.   1896.
> *Fables*.   1896.
> *Weir of Hermiston*.   1896.
> *St. Ives, Being the Adventures of a French Prisoner in England*, completed by Arthur
>   Quiller-Couch.   1897.
> *The Waif Woman* (stories).   1916.
> *When the Devil Was Well* (stories).   1921.
> *The Suicide Club and Other Stories*, edited by J. Kenneth White.   1970.

Plays

> *Deacon Brodie; or, The Double Life: A Melodrama*, with W. E. Henley (produced
>   1882).   1880.
> *Admiral Guinea: A Melodrama*, with W. E. Henley (produced 1890).   1884.
> *Beau Austin*, with W. E. Henley (produced 1890).   1884.
> *Macaire: A Melodramatic Farce*, with W. E. Henley (produced 1900).   1885.
> *The Hanging Judge*, with Fanny Stevenson.   1887; edited by Edmund Gosse, 1914.
> *Monmouth*, edited by Charles Vale.   1928.

Verse

> *Penny Whistles* (juvenile). 1883.
> *A Child's Garden of Verses.* 1885.
> *Underwoods.* 1887.
> *Ticonderoga.* 1887.
> *Ballads.* 1890.
> *Songs of Travel and Other Verses.* 1895.
> *Poems Hitherto Unpublished,* edited by George S. Hellman. 2 vols., 1916; as *New Poems and Variant Readings,* 1918; additional volume, edited by Hellman and William P. Trent, 1921.

Other

> *The Pentland Rising: A Page of History, 1666.* 1866.
> *The Charity Bazaar: An Allegorical Dialogue.* 1871.
> *An Appeal to the Clergy.* 1875.
> *An Inland Voyage.* 1878.
> *Edinburgh: Picturesque Notes.* 1879.
> *Travels with a Donkey in the Cévennes.* 1879.
> *Virginibus Puerisque and Other Papers.* 1881.
> *Familiar Studies of Men and Books.* 1882.
> *The Silverado Squatters: Sketches from a Californian Mountain.* 1883.
> *Memoirs and Portraits.* 1887.
> *Thomas Stevenson, Civil Engineer.* 1887.
> *Memoir of Fleeming Jenkin.* 1887.
> *Father Damien: An Open Letter to the Reverend Dr. Hyde of Honolulu.* 1890.
> *The South Seas: A Record of Three Cruises.* 1890.
> *Across the Plains, with Other Memories and Essays,* edited by Sidney Colvin. 1892.
> *A Footnote to History: Eight Years of Trouble in Samoa.* 1892.
> *The Works* (Edinburgh Edition), edited by Sidney Colvin. 28 vols., 1894–98.
> *In the South Seas.* 1896.
> *A Mountain Town in France: A Fragment.* 1896.
> *The Morality of the Profession of Letters.* 1899.
> *Essays and Criticisms.* 1903.
> *Prayers Written at Vailima.* 1903.
> *Essays of Travel.* 1905.
> *Essays in the Art of Writing.* 1905.
> *Lay Morals and Other Papers.* 1911.
> *Records of a Family of Engineers.* 1912; unfinished chapters edited by J. Christian Bat, 1930.
> *Memoirs of Himself.* 1912.
> *Some Letters,* edited by Lloyd Osbourne. 1914.
> *On the Choice of a Profession.* 1916.
> *Diogenes in London.* 1920.
> *Hitherto Unpublished Prose Writings,* edited by Henry H. Harper. 1921.
> *Stevenson's Workshop, with Twenty-Nine MS. Facsimiles,* edited by William P. Trent. 1921.
> *Confessions of a Unionist: An Unpublished "Talk on Things Current," Written in the Year 1888,* edited by F. V. Livingston. 1921.
> *The Best Thing in Edinburgh,* edited by Katharine D. Osbourne. 1923.
> *The Castaways of Soledad,* edited by George S. Hellman. 1928.
> *Henry James and Stevenson: A Record of Friendship and Criticism,* edited by Janet Adam Smith. 1948.

Silverado Journal, edited by J. E. Jordan.   1954.
RLS: Stevenson's Letters to Charles Baxter, edited by De Lancey Ferguson and M. Waingrow.   1956.
From Scotland to Silverado, edited by J. D. Hart.   1966.
Travels in Hawaii, edited by A. Grove Day.   1973.
The Cévennes Journal: Notes on a Journey Through the French Highlands.   1978.

Bibliography: *The Stevenson Library of E. J. Beinecke* by G. L. McKay, 6 vols., 1951–64.

Reading List: *Stevenson,* 1947, and *Stevenson and His World,* 1973, both by David Daiches; *Voyage to Windward: The Life of Stevenson* by J. C. Furnas, 1951; *Portrait of a Rebel: The Life and Work of Stevenson* by Richard Aldington, 1957; *Stevenson and the Fiction of Adventure* by Robert Kiely, 1964; *Stevenson and the Romantic Tradition* by Edwin M. Eigner, 1966; *Stevenson* by James Pope-Hennessy, 1974; *Stevenson* by Paul M. Binding, 1974.

*   *   *

Robert Louis Stevenson was, in the best sense of that 19th century term, a man of letters. Unlike most of their kind, however, he achieved high distinction as a novelist, as an essayist, and as a poetic miniaturist.

His early novels are adventure stories, of which *Treasure Island* first won his fame. It is, by any standards, a masterly piece of story-telling, cleverly constructed, vividly drawn, and grasping the reader's attention from beginning to end. Taking an adult viewpoint, it has sometimes been criticised on the ground that the virtuous are saved almost by accident, by a boy who is hardly aware of what he is doing. It seems to me wrong to suggest that the story's resolution implies on this account some kind of Calvinistic ambiguity in Stevenson's make-up, though his understanding of the warp and woof of the temper of Calvinism was to be reflected in his last masterpiece.

The Black Arrow, though by no means "tushery" – the word Stevenson invented to define the false jargon usually to be found in historical novels set in mediaeval times – does not succeed in creating the sense of atmosphere which raises *Kidnapped* somewhat beyond the level of expert fabling for the young. The desire to provide adventure at boys' level was no doubt the prime intention in *Kidnapped,* the aftermath of Jacobitism and the affair of the Red Fox simply the historical springboard for the chase over Kinlochrannoch and the other strongly portrayed and fast-moving action scenes. But just as, in the six best Waverley novels, Scott dealt with the great moments of confrontation in Scottish history, in *Kidnapped* Stevenson shows himself capable of continuing Scott's tradition. What makes an historic novel worthwhile, as opposed to "tushery" or fancy-dress flummery, is its creation of credible tensions. The tension that holds *Kidnapped* together comes from an acute portrayal of constant clashes of conflicting loyalties, an age-old Scottish dilemma: that of the young Whig, David Balfour, for his romantic Jacobite friend, Alan Breck; that of the clansmen for Breck himself; that of Macpherson for his clan; and that of Breck for the King over the Water. Breck and Balfour are both moderately well drawn, and so is the Scrooge-like eccentric, miserly Uncle Ebenezer. The style throughout is mellifluous, Stevenson's instinctive ability to balance vocables within a period, and periods within a sentence, refined to suit the demands of fast action. The novel thus, to some extent, escapes the charge of being mannered – the style counting for more than the content – commonly applied to his earlier books, and to the sequel *Catriona,* which suffers not only from less vigorous action, but from its author's inability almost to the end of his life to create convincingly the character of a young woman.

Popular as these books are, especially with young people, Stevenson's reputation as a great writer rests not upon them. but on a handful of other works: *Dr. Jekyll and Mr. Hyde,* that macabre tale based on the double life of Edinburgh's notorious Deacon Brodie, and an excursion into the darker reaches of the Calvinist psyche; the fine Scots study in the exercise of the powers of darkness that is "Thrawn Janet" (in *The Merry Men*), a forerunner in miniature to Stevenson's masterful *Weir of Hermiston*; another story powerfully told, "The Beach of Falesá" from *Island Nights' Entertainment*; and his two late novels, *The Master of Ballantrae* and *Weir of Hermiston*.

Superficially, *The Master of Ballantrae* might appear to be yet another exercise in the swashbuckling vein of his earlier Scottish romances. Yet it is much more than that. For all its inequalities, and its thoroughly unsatisfactory ending – a fault to which the author admitted – it marks Stevenson's first success in the creating of character for its own sake, rather than the provision of characters who depend upon the action to give them their dimensions. The Durie brothers are interesting for what they are, rather than for what they do. Alison Graeme, later Mrs. Henry Durie, is in many ways Stevenson's first reasonably convincing woman. There is the cleverly handled device of triple narrative. The fact that all three narrators are in different ways biased provides a kind of verisimilitude with the confusion of daily life, which rarely allows three people who have witnessed even the same single incident to repeat it in terms that exactly correspond.

Good though the best things in *The Master of Ballantrae* are – not least being their evocation of Scottish scenery and weather – *Weir of Hermiston* is an enormous leap forward. Based on the life-story of the "hanging judge", Robert MacQueen, Lord Braxfield, the novel includes one of the great moments in Scottish fiction – Lord Weir's confrontation with his more sensitive but weaker son, Archie, after a courtroom scene. These two central characters apart, the complete success of the two Kirsties, aunt and niece, the free and frequent handling of Scots, and the telling economy of the writing combine to make the unfinished torso a masterpiece, the first depiction in fiction of the strength and the weakness of a clever man moulded by the hereditary effects of Scots Calvinism.

Much of Stevenson's prose output took the form of travel-books, like *Travels with a Donkey in the Cévennes* and *The Silverado Squatters*, or collections of essays, the most famous being *Virginibus Puerisque* and *Familiar Studies of Men and Books*. As a travel-writer, his eye was sharp, the setting down of his observations and reactions unfailingly elegant. His letter "to maidens and boys" derived its title from Horace, and comprises gracefully expressed common sense which might do much to ease the hurt of youth, were youth a condition capable of rational remedy.

Much of Stevenson's poetry shows a concern with style for its own sake, as in the well-known "Romance," where the prospect of a woman washing herself "white" in "dewfall at night" is prettily ridiculous. Yet the poem had become popular because of its graceful clarity. Escapism, usually kept in check in his fiction, is given freer rein in his verse. Perhaps for this reason his most delightful things are to be found in *A Child's Garden of Verses*, and in such expression of homeward longing as "In the Highlands" and "To S. R. Crockett."

Stevenson's poems in Scots helped to keep the language alive in the last quarter of the 19th century, and are certainly above the general ruck of rhyming vernacular sentimentality being produced at that time. The "Standard Habbie" stanza, however, seems to have affected him with a parochialism not usually manifested in his work.

Although his reputation has been somewhat down-valued during the past fifty years, he is still affectionately regarded in Scotland as belonging to the company of Burns and Scott, if perhaps not quite on the level of either of them.

—Maurice Lindsay

STOKER, Bram.   Irish.   Born Abraham Stoker in Dublin, 8 November 1847. Educated in a private school in Dublin; Trinity College, Dublin, 1866–70, B.A. 1870; entered Middle Temple, London: called to the Bar, 1890. Married Florence Anne Lemon Balcombe in 1878; one son. Civil Servant in Dublin, 1867–77; Drama Critic, *Dublin Mail*, 1871–78; Editor, The Halfpenny Press, Dublin, 1874; settled in London: Acting Manager for Henry Irving, 1878–1905, and Manager of Irving's Lyceum chain, 1878–1902; writer from 1880. President, Philosophical Society. *Died 20 April 1912.*

PUBLICATIONS

Collections

> *The Stoker Bedside Companion: Stories of Fantasy and Horror*, edited by Charles
>   Osborne.   1973.

Fiction

> *Under the Sunset* (juvenile).   1881.
> *The Snake's Pass.*   1890.
> *Crooken Sands.*   1894.
> *The Watter's Mou'.*   1894.
> *The Shoulder of Shasta.*   1895.
> *Dracula.*   1897.
> *Miss Betty.*   1898.
> *The Mystery of the Sea.*   1902.
> *The Jewel of Seven Stars.*   1903.
> *The Man.*   1905.
> *Lady Athlyne.*   1908.
> *Snowbound: The Record of a Theatrical Touring Party.*   1908.
> *The Lady of the Shroud.*   1909.
> *The Lair of the White Worm.*   1911.
> *Dracula's Guest and Other Weird Stories.*   1914.

Other

> *The Duties of Clerks of Petty Sessions in Ireland.*   1879.
> *Personal Reminiscences of Henry Irving.*   2 vols., 1906.
> *Famous Imposters.*   1910.

Reading List: *The Dracula Myth* by Gabriel Ronay, 1972; *The Annotated Dracula* by Leonard Wolf, 1975; *The Man Who Wrote Dracula: A Biography of Stoker* by Daniel Farson, 1975.

*   *   *

Cinema-goers are more familiar with Dracula's name than readers of literature with that of his creator, Bram Stoker. Apart from the much-filmed novel, Stoker's fiction is a noxious *pot-pourri* of plagiarism – "The Judge's House" and "Dracula's Guest" are borrowed from Le

Fanu – racism, and semi-conscious sexual titillation, the entire tincture being then suspended in sadistic violence and pseudo magic.

Yet even to its readers *Dracula* manages to stand above this dubious standard. Its principal theme, vampirism, had a longish history dating from the days of Byron and Polidori; its incidental concern with fetishism – the vampire can be repelled not only with the sign of the cross but with the physical application of the consecrated wafer to cracks in masonry – touches with its rough texture on the raw spot of Victorian religious unease. These purely external factors, however, do not wholly account for the novel's survival. In *Dracula* Stoker adapted the device more subtly employed by Wilkie Collins of attributing various strands of his narrative to various narrators; in Collins it contributes to a psychological mystery; in Stoker it heightens a fearful ignorance. The incorporation of telegrams, extracts from letters and diaries, even the use of broken English and transliterated short-hand, helps the author to disguise the appalling lack of coherent style which marks his other work. The result is an ever-shifting, discontinuous chronicle of fascination and pursuit, where sexual, religious, racial, and historical obsessions are intermittently indulged in and deplored.

The contrast between seemingly respectable London and the timeless horror of Transylvania is an integral part of Stoker's structure. Together with the virulent anti-Negro tirades of *The Lair of the White Worm*, this juxtaposition reminds us that the author was a contemporary of Conan Doyle and Rider Haggard, and wrote during the hey-day of British jingoism and colonial exploitation.

—W. J. McCormack

STOREY, David (Malcolm). English. Born in Wakefield, Yorkshire, 13 July 1933; brother of the novelist Anthony Storey. Educated at Queen Elizabeth Grammar School, Wakefield, 1943–51; Wakefield College of Art, 1951–53; Slade School on Fine Art, London, 1953–56, diploma in fine arts. Married Barbara Rudd Hamilton in 1956; two sons and two daughters. Played professionally for the Leeds Rugby League Club, 1952–56. Fellow, University College, London, 1974. Recipient: Rhys Memorial Award, 1961; Maugham Award, 1963; *Evening Standard* award, for drama, 1967, 1970; New York Drama Critics Circle Award, 1971, 1973, 1974; Faber Memorial Prize, 1973; Obie Award, 1974; Booker Prize, 1976. Lives in London.

PUBLICATIONS

Fiction

This Sporting Life. 1960.
Flight into Camden. 1961.
Radcliffe. 1963.
Pasmore. 1972.
A Temporary Life. 1973.
Saville. 1976.

Plays

> *The Restoration of Arnold Middleton* (produced 1966).   1975.
> *In Celebration* (produced 1969).   1969.
> *The Contractor* (produced 1969).   1970.
> *Home* (produced 1970).   1970.
> *The Changing Room* (produced 1971).   1972.
> *The Farm* (produced 1973).   1973.
> *Cromwell* (produced 1973).   1973.
> *Life Class* (produced 1974).   1975.
> *Mother's Day* (produced 1976).   1977.

Screenplays: *This Sporting Life*, 1963; *In Celebration*, 1974.

Television Play: *Grace*, from the story by James Joyce. 1974.

Other

> *Writers on Themselves*, with others.   1964.
> *Edward*, drawings by Donald Parker.   1973.

Reading List: *Revolutions in Modern English Drama* by K. J. Worth, 1972; *Playback* by Ronald Hayman, 1973; *Storey* by John Russell Taylor, 1974; *Playwrights' Theatre* by Terry Browne, 1975.

*   *   *

It is rare for a writer to claim attention equally as a dramatist and a novelist, but it is impossible to say that David Storey is a primarily one or the other. He had already published an accomplished novel of working-class experience, *This Sporting Life*, when a group of plays, all presented at the Royal Court Theatre and directed by Lindsay Anderson, established him as one of the two leading figures (Edward Bond, the other) in the "second wave" of contemporary British drama. More recently he has produced a series of further, prize-winning novels. There is considerable variation of tone across his work from the sombreness of *Radcliffe* or *Cromwell* to the sardonic persiflage of *Life Class* or *A Temporary Life*; but reticence and subjectivity complement each other in his writing in both genres.

His undeniable concern with social class has a moral and cultural rather than political focus. *In Celebration* most straightforwardly exposes the strains that social mobility has set up in a family of working-class origins. The influence of D. H. Lawrence shows clearly here, but Storey marks out his individual territory in the expression of bitter and painful feelings and extreme mental turmoil on the edge of breakdown. Though he can recreate social detail precisely, as in *This Sporting Life* and *Saville*, his avoidance of explicit general comment contributes to the impression that the major characters in his novels move somnambulistically through a pattern of events unconsciously chosen. They themselves are manifestations of tradition, or deep-rooted class experience – of manual labour, poverty, and deprivation (Mrs. Hammond, in *This Sporting Life*, an unappeasable figure of suffering and defeat, is an impressive early example). If they find themselves in comfortable middle-class circumstances, they compulsively reject and destroy the conformist role and drift into more fundamentally determined alignments and confrontations. In *Radcliffe*, the strength of the labouring class in seen with fascination from the point-of-view of the opposed and dependent high culture. The titles of the novels *Radcliffe* and *Saville* and of the play *Cromwell* denote the hold of tradition on individual life: *Saville* presents its main figure living out the experience of a family identified with a particular place in social history; *Radcliffe* is a Gothic novel in which an old house haunts and dominates the minds of a family; *Cromwell* stands for a complex of moral qualities and social ideals.

Though the plots of all Storey's novels and plays are quite distinct from each other, the reader is struck by the reworking of particular episodes (including a beating-up) again and again, in variant order and associated with different characters. The analogy that comes to mind is that of the painter (which Storey also is) who includes a number of motifs idiosyncratically in picture after picture. The play *Life Class* and the novel *A Temporary Life* draw specifically on his familiarity with art schools, and the latter is interestingly structured so that stages of the narrative are linked with current ideas (and practices) of the nature and status of visual art.

If Storey's interest in continuity is reminiscent of Raymond Williams's, his most distinguished plays suggest a structuralist model in the kind of integration they achieve. *The Contractor* and *The Changing Room* dispense with star parts and a conventional narrative plot in favour of theatrical teamwork to create a new version of the ancient notion of the theatre as microcosm. Stage business takes on the status of dramatic action and the dialogue is spare, laconic, half-articulate, close to being a neutral element from which no line can be abstracted and quoted to significant effect. It approximates to "writing degree zero" and serves a drama that has a more than usually tenuous existence as a literary work. In the theatre, the actors create the form of the play and, in *The Contractor*, it is their achievement that stands clear at the climax: the wedding marquee, an image of art and the play itself, not as an individual production, but emerging out of the communal work process. *The Changing Room* excludes the separate achievement, the sacred ritual of the Rugby League game, to trace the emergence − and later dissolution − of the team out of disparate individuals. *Home* moves closer to Absurdist drama (though Ewbank is no more the Contractor of the earlier play's title than Pozzo is Godot); but the idea of "home" from which the sense of alienation arises is here replaced by the reality which the characters (the actors in rehearsal and performance) make for themselves: the relationships they build, and communications they effect. The strict observance of the unities works both ways: preserving the effect of extreme naturalism and defining the plays as symbols. The richness of meaning arising from this inexplicit drama recalls Chekhov, as does the degree and quality of theatrical collaboration required.

—Margery Morgan

STOUT, Rex (Todhunter). American. Born in Noblesville, Indiana, 1 December 1886. Educated at Topeka High School, Kansas; University of Kansas, Lawrence. Served in the United States Navy, 1906–08. Married 1) Fay Kennedy in 1916 (divorced, 1933); 2) Pola Hoffman in 1933; two daughters. Worked as an office boy, store clerk, bookkeeper, sailor, and hotel manager, 1916–27; full-time writer from 1927; Founding Director, Vanguard Press, New York; Master of Ceremonies, "Speaking of Liberty," "Voice of Freedom," and "Our Secret Weapon" radio programs, 1941–43. Chairman of the Writers' War Board, 1941–46, and the World Government Writers Board, 1949–75; President, Friends of Democracy, 1941–51, Authors' Guild, 1943–45, and Society for the Prevention of World War III, 1943–46; President, 1951–55, 1962–69, and Vice-President, 1956–61, Authors League of America; Treasurer, Freedom House, 1957–75; President, Mystery Writers of America, 1958. Recipient: Mystery Writers of America Grand Master Award, 1959. *Died 27 October 1975.*

Fiction

How Like a God.   1929.
Seed on the Wind.   1930.
Golden Remedy.   1931.
Forest Fire.   1933.
Fer-de-Lance.   1934.
The President Vanishes.   1934.
The League of Frightened Men.   1935.
O Careless Love!   1935.
The Rubber Band.   1936; as To Kill Again, 1960.
The Red Box.   1937.
The Hand in the Glove.   1937; as Crime on Her Hands, 1939.
Too Many Cooks.   1938.
Mr. Cinderella.   1938.
Some Buried Caesar.   1939.
Mountain Cat.   1939; as The Mountain Cat Murders, 1964.
Red Threads.   1939.
Double for Death.   1939.
Over My Dead Body.   1940.
Bad for Business.   1940.
Where There's a Will.   1940.
The Broken Vase.   1941.
Alphabet Hicks.   1941; as Sounds of Murder, 1965.
Black Orchids (stories).   1942.
Booby Trap (stories).   1944.
Not Quite Dead Enough (stories).   1944.
The Silent Speaker.   1946.
Too Many Women.   1947.
And Be a Villain.   1948; as More Deaths Than One, 1949.
The Second Confession.   1949.
Trouble in Triplicate (stories).   1949.
Three Doors to Death (stories).   1950.
In the Best Families.   1950; as Even in the Best, 1951.
Murder by the Book.   1951.
Curtains for Three (stories).   1951.
Triple Jeopardy (stories).   1952.
Prisoner's Base.   1952; as Out Goes She, 1953.
The Golden Spiders.   1954.
Three Men Out (stories).   1954.
The Black Mountain.   1954.
Before Midnight.   1955.
Might as Well Be Dead.   1956.
Three Witnesses (stories).   1956.
Three for the Chair (stories).   1957.
If Death Ever Slept.   1957.
Champagne for One.   1958.
And Four to Go (stories).   1958.
Plot It Yourself.   1959.
Crime and Again.   1959.
Murder in Style.   1960.

Three at Wolfe's Door (stories).   1960.
Too Many Clients.   1960.
The Final Deduction.   1961.
Gambit.   1962.
Homicide Trinity (stories).   1962.
The Mother Hunt.   1963.
Trio for Blunt Instruments (stories).   1964.
A Right To Die.   1964.
The Doorbell Rang.   1965.
Death of a Doxy.   1966.
The Father Hunt.   1968.
Death of a Dude.   1969.
Please Pass the Guilt.   1973.
Three Trumps (stories).   1973.
Triple Zeck (stories).   1974.
A Family Affair.   1975.
Justice Ends at Home and Other Stories.   1977.

Other

The Nero Wolfe Cookbook, with others.   1973.

Editor, *The Illustrious Dunderheads* (on American isolationists).   1942.
Editor, with Louis Greenfield, *Rue Morgue 1.*   1946.
Editor, *Eat, Drink, and Be Buried.*   1956; revised edition, as *For Tomorrow We Die,*
1958.

Reading List: *Stout: A Biography* by John McAleer, 1977.

*   *   *

At the beginning of a career undertaken after he had earned enough money in business to permit full devotion to writing, Rex Stout published four critically acceptable but unpopular "straight" novels. Then, in the decade after he had committed himself to the detective genre with the publication of *Fer-de-Lance,* he developed a variety of sleuths: "Dol" Bonner and Sally Colt in *The Hand in the Glove,* Tecumseh Fox who appeared in three novels, Alphabet Hicks in one novel bearing his name, Delia Brand in *Mountain Cat,* and Inspector Cramer of *Red Threads.* Stout is known, however, almost entirely because he was the creator of Nero Wolfe.

Like Sherlock Holmes, Stout's evident model for a Great Detective, Nero Wolfe so dominates the tales in which he appears that enthusiasts refer to them as though they were authorless – they are simply Nero Wolfe stories; and, again like his model and a small handful of other fictional detectives such as Charlie Chan or Sam Spade, Nero Wolfe – the enormously fat, eccentric genius-recluse – has achieved independence of the tales themselves. He is an autonomous figure in the popular imagination, familiar even to those with the slightest literary knowledge of his exploits.

There can be no doubt it was Stout's intention to create a mythic detective. The constellation of traits attributed to Wolfe coupled with his mental infallibility are the formula of a character who dominates as well as presides, and the narrative voice of Archie Goodwin, though it is quite unlike Dr. Watson's, provides for the distancing that surrounds the solver of mysteries with his own aura of mystery. Moreover, Archie's speech develops the illusion of a case's history with the attendant suspense necessary to deflect our awareness that the only subject of the fiction is the detective.

It would be incorrect, however, to describe Stout only as an imitator of formulas pioneered by Arthur Conan Doyle, because he artfully manages the genre of detection fiction in his own way. It is just that his way involves simplication of the genre rather than the transgression of conventions we usually associate with innovation. A striking example of Stout's simplification is in the setting of the stories. Wolfe's household is central to every tale. He never goes abroad to the classic country house or to walk the city's mean streets; thus, in one stroke we get both ambience (W. 35th St. equals Baker St.) and intensification of the detective's prominence, since clients and aides with the guilty and innocent suspects must all subject themselves to the force of his orbit, their thoughts and acts entirely subordinate to Wolfe's interpretations.

Fundamentally, the plot of every tale of detection is epistemological. It progresses through scenes of a detective's methodical expansion of his knowledge of the reality of some mysterious events until it is concluded by a celebration of rationality in which all the secondary characters witness the detective's literal creation of truth through summary analysis of events and motives. In plot, too, Stout has simplified. With Wolfe working on cases in his own study – the consummate armchair detective – each scene prefigures the classical denouement, maintaining a dominance by Wolfe's mind over events that matches the supremacy of his personality.

The result of Stout's simplification of the detection story is to invest the saga of Nero Wolfe with an Augustan formality. The incidents of the stories and novels vary, but each repeats invariable movements extolling the nature of a Great Detective.

—John M. Reilly

STOW, (Julian) Randolph. Australian. Born in Geraldton, Western Australia, 28 November 1935. Educated at Guildford Grammar School, Western Australia; University of Western Australia, Nedlands, B.A. 1956. Formerly an anthropological assistant, working in Northwest Australia and Papua New Guinea; taught at the University of Adelaide, 1957; Lecturer in English Literature, University of Leeds, Yorkshire, 1962, and University of Western Australia, 1963–64; Lecturer in English and Commonwealth Literature, University of Leeds, 1968–69. Recipient: Australian Literary Society Gold Medal, 1957, 1958; Miles Franklin Award, 1958; Commonwealth Fund's Harkness Travelling Fellowship, 1964–66; Britannica Australia Award, 1966.

PUBLICATIONS

Fiction

A Haunted Land. 1956.
The Bystander. 1957.
To the Islands. 1958.
Tourmaline. 1963.
The Merry-Go-Round in the Sea. 1965.

Plays

> *Eight Songs for a Mad King,* music by Peter Maxwell Davies. 1969.
> *Miss Donnithorne's Maggot,* music by Peter Maxwell Davies. 1974.

Verse

> *Act One.* 1957.
> *Outrider: Poems 1956–1962.* 1962.
> *A Counterfeit Silence: Selected Poems.* 1969.

Other

> *Midnite: The Story of a Wild Colonial Boy* (juvenile). 1967.

> Editor, *Australian Poetry 1964.* 1964.

Bibliography: *Stow: A Bibliography* by P. A. O'Brien, 1968.

Reading List: "Outsider Looking Out" by W. H. New, in *Critique 9,* 1967; "Waste Places, Dry Souls" by Jennifer Wightman, in *Meanjin,* June 1969; *The Merry-Go-Round in the Sea* by Edriss Noall, 1971.

*   *   *

Randolph Stow's reputation as a novelist is based upon five novels which were published by the time he was thirty. These youthful works are rooted in his fascination with family, with the inescapable inheritance of the blood, and his intense feeling for the landscapes of childhood. "I say we have a bitter heritage, but that is not to run it down," says the narrator in *Tourmaline,* and that might serve as an epigraph for all of Stow's fiction. The theme of a "bitter heritage" is central to the first two novels, which are set in the West Australian countryside where Stow grew up. *A Haunted Land* is a vividly imagined but melodramatic story of the Maguire family last century. *The Bystander* concerns Maguire descendants, whose emotional lives are still clouded by the effects of the turbulent family past. This second novel, though it still has a Gothic flavour in places, is more firmly anchored in social observation and realistic psychology than the first, and indicates how rapidly Stow's talent developed.

With his third novel, *To the Islands,* Stow sought to extend his range and to escape the criticism of improbability that had been made of his first two attempts to write fiction. "This is not, by intention, a realistic novel" he announced in an Author's Note; and though the details are realistic, the action is boldly symbolic. The central figure is the aging missionary, Heriot, who leaves the Christian mission in north-western Australia, to which he has devoted his life, and wanders in search of the "islands of the dead" of aboriginal myth. His journey is a journey into the "strange country" of the self, but Stow does not succeed in giving his symbolism the dramatic substance and logic that Patrick White achieves in *Voss,* a novel with which it is inevitably compared.

In strikingly different ways the next two novels focus on the moral discoveries to be made in that "strange country" of a man's own being: their concern is with the meaning of selfhood. *Tourmaline* is Stow's most ambitious experiment in non-naturalistic fiction. Behind it lies his belief, expressed in an article in *Westerly,* 1961, that Australia is an "enormous symbol," and "because of its bareness, its absolute simplicity, a truer and broader symbol of the human environment than any European writer could create from the complex material of Europe." *Tourmaline*, a desolate country town to which the false hope of reviving life comes in the form of a supposed water diviner, is a kind of Australian waste land, which Stow pictures in images recalling some of Sidney Nolan's paintings. The novel is carefully composed in a mannered, almost ritualistic prose, aiming to direct the reader to the mythic dimensions of the setting and narrative.

More successful is *The Merry-Go-Round in the Sea*, Stow's most sustained piece of realism. With a strong autobiographical base, it is wonderfully evocative of the world as a child knows it. Stow traces the growth of Rob Coram from his earliest memories to adolescence with a warmth and sureness of insight. The boy is at the end made painfully aware that he must depend upon himself, when his loved older cousin, Rick Maplestead, decides to reject Australia and the family to which the boy feels himself proud to belong. With the recognition of his responsibility to himself the boy is ready for coming manhood: "The world and the clan and Australia had been a myth of his mind, and he had been, all the time, an individual." Whereas *Tourmaline* is a skeletal, allegorical work, shaped to express Stow's acceptance of the Taoist vision of existence, *Merry-Go-Round* has all the solidity of remembrance of things past, recreating places and atmospheres and personalities with a loving care for sensuous detail, while yet suggesting the symbolic values this experience holds. In this novel Stow seemed to have begun a new phase as a novelist, but so far no further novels have appeared.

Though he has – perhaps temporarily – ceased to write fiction, Stow has continued to write poetry. The themes of his poetry have been those of his fiction, the most striking correspondence being the series of variations on the themes of the Tao, which Stow entitled "The Testament of Tourmaline." Stow's poetry, always technically accomplished and free of modishness, has not received the recognition it deserves. It is a poetry of passionate utterance, controlled by a traditional sense of form and often distinguished by a memorable command of phrase and rhythm. Stow has written several fine sequences, such as "Stations" (a "suite for three voices and three generations") and "Thailand Railway"; and more recently *Eight Songs for a Mad King* (with music by Peter Maxwell Davies) and a libretto, *Miss Donnithorne's Maggot*. Stow is most often thought of as a poet of lyrical feeling, but he has a gift for parody and satire which finds expression in occasional poems and in his delightful children's story, *Midnite*. This tale of a bushranger with a gang of animals gives him opportunities to mock Australian literary preoccupations. The two sides of Stow can be seen by comparing a serious poem such as "The Singing Bones" with the hilarious treatment of the same theme in *Midnite*.

Now in his forties, Stow is a gifted writer whose achievements in fiction and poetry are already considerable. His recent interest in the relationship of poetry and music would seem to point to the possibility of a new development in his career.

—John Barnes

STOWE, Harriet (Elizabeth) Beecher. American. Born in Litchfield, Connecticut, 14 June 1811. Educated in the local dame school, and at Hartford, Connecticut Female Seminary, 1824. Married Reverend Calvin Ellis Stowe in 1836 (died. 1886); seven children. Moved with her family to Cincinnati, 1832; contributed sketches to the *Western Monthly Magazine* and *The Mayflower*; moved to Brunswick, Maine, 1850; became ardent abolitionist; full-time writer from 1850; famous and controversial as a writer from publication of *Uncle Tom's Cabin*, 1852; lived in Andover, Massachusetts, then Hartford,

Connecticut, and Mandarin, Florida, from 1852; visited England three times, and toured the Continent; a friend of Lady Byron, George Eliot, and Ruskin; contributed to the *Atlantic Monthly*, New York *Independent*, and the *Christian Union. Died 1 July 1896.*

PUBLICATIONS

Collections

> *The Writings.*   16 vols., 1896.
> *Collected Poems,* edited by John Michael Moran, Jr.   1967.

Fiction

> *Prize Tale: A New England Sketch.*   1834.
> *The Mayflower: or, Sketches of Scenes and Characters among the Descendants of the Pilgrims.*   1843; augmented edition, 1855.
> *Uncle Tom's Cabin; or, Life among the Lowly.*   1852; edited by Kenneth S. Lynn, 1962.
> *Uncle Sam's Emancipation* (stories).   1853.
> *Dred: A Tale of the Great Dismal Swamp.*   1856; as *Nina Gordon,* 1866.
> *The Minister's Wooing.*   1859.
> *Agnes of Sorrento.*   1862.
> *The Pearl of Orr's Island: A Story of the Coast of Maine.*   1862.
> *Daisy's First Winter and Other Stories.*   1867.
> *Oldtown Folks.*   1869; edited by Henry F. May, 1966.
> *My Wife and I; or, Harry Henderson's History.*   1871.
> *Pink and White Tyranny: A Society Novel.*   1871.
> *Sam Lawson's Oldtown Fireside Stories.*   1872.
> *We and Our Neighbors; or, The Records of an Unfashionable Street.*   1875.
> *Poganuc People: Their Loves and Lives.*   1878.

Play

> *The Christian Slave,* from her own novel *Uncle Tom's Cabin.*   1855.

Verse

> *Religious Poems.*   1867.

Other

> *An Elementary Geography.*   1835.
> *A Key to Uncle Tom's Cabin.*   1853.
> *Sunny Memories of Foreign Lands.*   2 vols., 1854.
> *The Two Altars; or, Two Pictures in One.*   1855.
> *Geography for My Children.*   1855.
> *Our Charley and What to Do with Him.*   1858.
> *A Reply in Behalf of the Women of America.*   1863.

The Ravages of a Carpet. 1865.
Stories about Our Dogs. 1865.
House and Home Papers. 1865.
Little Foxes. 1866.
Queer Little People. 1867.
The Chimney-Corner. 1868.
Men of Our Times. 1868.
The American Woman's Home. 1869.
Little Pussy Willow (juvenile). 1870.
Lady Byron Vindicated. 1870.
Woman in Sacred History. 1873; as *Bible Heroines,* 1878.
Palmetto-Leaves. 1873.
Betty's Bright Idea. 1876.
Footsteps of the Master. 1877.
A Dog's Mission. 1881.
Our Famous Women. 1884.

Bibliography: *Stowe: A Bibliography* by Margaret Holbrook Hildreth, 1976.

Reading List: *Life of Stowe from Her Letters and Journals* edited by Charles Edward Stowe, 1889; *Crusader in Crinoline: The Life of Stowe* by Forrest Wilson, 1941; *The Rungless Ladder: Stowe and New England Puritanism* by Charles H. Foster, 1954; *Stowe* by John R. Adams, 1963; *Stowe: The Known and the Unknown* by Edward Wagenknecht, 1965; *The Novels of Stowe* by Alice C. Crozier, 1969; *The Building of "Uncle Tom's Cabin"* by E. Bruce Kirkham, 1977.

*   *   *

Uncle Tom's Cabin, Harriet Beecher Stowe's masterpiece, has been said to have had a "social impact ... on the United States ... greater than that of any book before or since." There is no doubt that it was one of the few books which have changed the climate of public opinion and helped swing the political pendulum. While recent evaluations of the work tend to reveal in it not less but more literary craftsmanship, any critical analysis must consider this novel not so much as a literary production than as an instrument that led to action.

Mrs. Stowe grew up in "a kind of moral heaven, replete with moral oxygen – fully charged with intellectual electricity," and much of that "moral oxygen" and "intellectual electricity" was injected into *Uncle Tom's Cabin*. The guiding principles of self-abnegation, spiritual regeneration, and Christian purpose inculcated in her early training filtered into her writing. Coupled with her own high-minded interest in social reform, they were shaped into a powerful ethical weapon. The author had read of the atrocities of slavery, and, when the Fugitive Slave Law spurred her to action, she was finally metamorphosed into the instrument of the Lord who created an "epic of Negro bondage." This powerful narrative of damnation and salvation, with its bold message that slavery destroys both the master and the slave, electrified the nation. While *Uncle Tom's Cabin* is, on the one hand, a domestic novel, it is also a forceful, vital, original, and daring moral instrument.

Although its characters are sometimes symbols and some of its incidents are stylized, the figures of Simon Legree, Eliza, Mr. St. Clare, Little Eva, and Uncle Tom have joined a parade of unforgettable literary characters that have become part of the national consciousness. The author's reliance upon tact did not preclude her recourse to realism. Just how powerfully Mrs. Stowe's timely propaganda stirred the American conscience is revealed by its publishing history. Within a year of publication its sales topped 300,000, and before the Civil War the figure reached three million. It made its author famous overnight, inspired a spate of anti-*Uncle Tom* novels, and won the praise of such diverse critics as Henry Wadsworth

Longfellow and Henry James. According to one reviewer: "The mightiest princes of intellect, as well as those who have scarcely harbored a stray thought ... friends of slavery equally with the haters of that institution ... all ... bend with sweating eagerness over her magic pages." Emerson traced its power to the universality of its message when he commented: "We have seen an American woman write a novel of which a million copies were sold in all languages, and which had one merit, of speaking to the universal heart, and was read with equal interest to three audiences, namely, in the parlor, in the kitchen, and in the nursery of every house." *Uncle Tom's Cabin* still has the power of stirring conflicting emotions in its critics. James Baldwin's attribution of racial prejudice to the novel, for example, has met its effective rebutters. Although the novel is no longer widely read, it is unlikely that it will ever be forgotten.

Mrs. Stowe's earlier work consisted of sentimental and conventional sketches that reflected her belief in the sanctity of the home and woman's place in it. After the success of *Uncle Tom's Cabin* she replied to objectors with *A Key to Uncle Tom's Cabin* and returned to the theme of anti-slavery in *Dred*. Between 1862 and 1884, she produced at least a book a year; most of them consisted of essays on the home, domestic novels, stories of death and redemption, as well as a defense of Lady Byron.

She has recently, and surprisingly, been called "the only major feminine humorist nineteenth-century America produced," an attribution based less upon a sense of the jocular than upon an ear for idiom and an eye for actuality. The books that flowed from her tireless pen often reveal these qualities. They also reveal her dissection of the Calvinist ethic, and despite their sentimentality they provide considerable documentary insight into the moral climate of nineteenth-century New England.

The aptest description of Harriet Beecher Stowe was made by the biographer who dubbed her a "Crusader in Crinoline." For the most part, her crinolines have turned into period pieces, and her crusade has become historic. Yet she helped to document and advance that crusade, and in *Uncle Tom's Cabin* she created a book that shook the world.

—Madeleine B. Stern

STRIBLING, T(heodore) S(igismund). American. Born in Clifton, Tennessee, 4 March 1881. Educated at Clifton public schools; Normal College, Florence, Alabama, graduated 1903; studied law at the University of Alabama, LL.B. 1904. Married Louella Kloss in 1930. Practiced law in Florence, 1906; member of the staff of the *Taylor-Trotwood Magazine*, Nashville, Tennessee, 1906–07; thereafter a full-time writer; wrote moral stories for Sunday School magazines, the income from which allowed him to travel and live in South America and Europe; later lived in Clifton; Instructor in Creative Writing, Columbia University, New York, 1936, 1940. Recipient: Pulitzer Prize, 1933. LL.D.: Oglethorpe University, Atlanta, Georgia, 1936. *Died 10 July 1965.*

PUBLICATIONS

Fiction

The Cruise of the Dry Dock. 1917.
Birthright. 1922.
Fombombo. 1923.

Red Sand. 1924.
Teeftallow. 1926.
Bright Metal. 1928.
East Is East. 1928.
Clues of the Caribbees, Being Certain Criminal Investigations of Henry Poggioli, Ph.D. 1929.
Strange Moon. 1929.
Backwater. 1930.
The Forge. 1931.
The Store. 1932.
Unfinished Cathedral. 1934.
The Sound Wagon. 1935.
These Bars of Flesh. 1938.

Reading List: *Stribling* by Wilton Eckley, 1975.

* * *

T. S. Stribling, who began as a writer of moral adventure tales for Sunday School magazines and then moved on to the pulps and finally to serious fiction, is remembered chiefly for *The Store*, which won him the Pulitzer prize in 1933. It is the second volume of his trilogy (*The Forge* and *Unfinished Cathedral* are the other two) dealing with the fortunes of the Vaiden family, particularly with the rise of Miltaides Vaiden from poor man to rich landowner and cotton planter in the ante-bellum South. In this trilogy, as in his other serious novels (*Birthright, Teeftallow, Bright Metal, Sound Wagon, These Bars of Flesh*), Stribling is a social satirist and local colorist. His strong point is his gift of observation, of setting down in credible language the look and feel of a natural landscape and the poor whites and blacks who inhabit it. His weaknesses are his themes (which tend to be simplistic), his plots (melodramatic), and his style (often crudely pretentious). Like Sinclair Lewis, Stribling is a social critic and debunker, his locale the middle South (Tennessee, Alabama), and his chief concern prejudice against blacks and the general narrow-mindedness of ingrown Southern communities. In *Birthright*, he deals with a Harvard-educated black from Tennessee forced to live the stereotyped role of an uneducated black laborer. But he has also debunked the American scene of lawyers and businessmen (*Sound Wagon*) and the American education college (*These Bars of Flesh*). Much of his fiction is hackwork, quickly turned out melodrama with a slight satirical edge. *Fombombo, Red Sand,* and *Strange Moon* mix satire, South American politics, business, and romance. Stribling also wrote detective stories (*Clues of the Caribbees*).

Stribling is an "objective" observer who sees history as a mechanical process, individuals as pawns in the grip of economic and social forces. His fiction is interesting to the literary historian for the way he blends popular stereotypes with old-fashioned liberal political and social ideas, and for the contrast offered between his mechanistic histories of the South and William Faulkner's mythical histories, a contrast that helps make clear not only Stribling's appeal to liberal critics in the 1930's but also the reason Faulkner was disliked and undervalued.

—W. J. Stuckey

STRONG, L(eonard) A(lfred) G(eorge). Irish. Born in Plymouth, Devon, 8 March 1896. Educated at Brighton College, Sussex; Wadham College, Oxford (open classical scholar), 1915–16, 1919–20, B.A. 1920, M.A. Married Sylvia Brinton in 1926. Assistant Master, Summer Fields School, Oxford, 1920–30; full-time writer from 1930; series editor for the publishers Gollancz, Nelson, and Blackwell, in the 1930's; Visiting Tutor, Central School of Speech and Drama, London; Director, Methuen, publishers, London, 1938–58. Recipient: Black Memorial Prize, 1946. Member, Irish Academy of Letters; Fellow, Royal Society of Literature. *Died 17 August 1958.*

PUBLICATIONS

Fiction

Doyle's Rock and Other Stories. 1925.
The English Captain and Other Stories. 1929.
Dewer Rides. 1929.
The Jealous Ghost. 1930.
The Garden. 1931.
The Big Man (story). 1931.
Don Juan and the Wheelbarrow and Other Stories. 1932.
The Brothers. 1932.
Sea Wall. 1933.
Corporal Tune. 1934.
Tuesday Afternoon and Other Stories. 1935.
The Seven Arms. 1935.
The Last Enemy: A Study of Youth. 1936.
Two Stories. 1936.
The Swift Shadow. 1937; as *Laughter in the West,* 1937.
The Nice Cup o' Tea (stories). 1938.
The Open Sky. 1939.
Evening Piece (story). 1939.
Sun on the Water and Other Stories. 1940.
The Bay. 1941.
Slocombe Dies. 1942.
The Unpractised Heart. 1942.
All Fall Down. 1944.
The Director. 1944.
Othello's Occupation. 1945; as *Murder Plays an Ugly Scene,* 1945.
Travellers: Thirty-One Selected Short Stories. 1945.
The Doll (story). 1946.
Trevannion. 1948.
Which I Never: A Police Diversion. 1950.
Darling Tom and Other Stories. 1952.
The Hill of Howth. 1953.
Deliverance. 1955.
Light above the Lake. 1958.
Treason in the Egg: A Further Police Diversion. 1958.

Plays

The Absentee. 1939.

Trial and Error.   1939.
The Director, from his own novel (produced 1951).
Sea Winds with Norah Lloyd (produced 1954).
It's Not Very Nice.   1954.

Screenplay: *Mr. Perrin and Mr. Traill,* with T. J. Morrison, 1948.

Verse

Dallington Rhymes.   1919.
Twice Four.   1921.
Dublin Days.   1921.
Says the Muse to Me, Says She.   1922.
Eight Poems.   1923.
The Lowery Road.   1923.
Seven Verses: Christmas, 1924.   1924.
Seven Verses: Christmas, 1925.   1925.
Difficult Love.   1927.
At Glenan Cross: A Sequence.   1928.
Northern Light.   1930
Christmas 1930.   1930.
Selected Poems.   1931.
March Evening and Other Verses.   1932.
Amalia, Ye Aged Sow (juvenile).   1932.
Call to the Swan.   1936.
Low's Company: Fifty Portraits, with Helen Spalding.   1952.
The Body's Imperfection: The Collected Poems.   1957.

Other

Patricia Comes Home (juvenile).   1929.
The Old Argo (juvenile).   1931.
Common Sense about Poetry.   1931.
A Defence of Ignorance.   1932.
Life in English Literature: An Introduction for Beginners, with Monica Redlich.   3
    vols., 1932.
King Richard's Land: A Tale of the Peasants' Revolt (juvenile).   1933.
Fortnight South of Skye (juvenile).   1934.
The Westward Rock (juvenile).   1934.
Mr. Sheridan's Umbrella (juvenile).   1935.
*The Hansom Cab and the Pigeons, Being Random Reflections upon the Silver Jubilee of
    King George V.*   1935.
Common Sense about Drama.   1937.
The Minstrel Boy: A Portrait of Tom Moore.   1937.
Henry of Agincourt (juvenile).   1937.
The Man Who Asked Questions: The Story of Socrates (juvenile).   1937.
The Fifth of November (juvenile).   1937.
Odd Man In (juvenile).   1938.
Shake Hands and Come Out Fighting (on boxing).   1938.
They Went to the Island (juvenile).   1940.
Wrong Foot Foremost (juvenile).   1940.
House in Disorder (juvenile).   1941.

English for Pleasure (broadcasts for children). 1941.
John McCormack: The Story of a Singer. 1941.
John Millington Synge. 1941.
An Informal English Grammar. 1943.
Authorship. 1944.
Sink or Swim (juvenile). 1945.
A Tongue in Your Head. 1945.
Light Through the Cloud. 1946.
Maud Cherrill. 1949.
The Sacred River: An Approach to James Joyce. 1949.
John Masefield. 1952.
Personal Remarks (essays). 1953.
The Writer's Trade. 1953.
The Story of Sugar. 1954.
Dr. Quicksilver, 1660–1742: The Life and Times of Thomas Dover, M.D. 1955.
Flying Angel: The Story of the Missions to Seamen. 1956.
The Rolling Road: The Story of Travel on the Roads of Britain. 1956.
A Brewer's Progress, 1757–1957: A Survey of Charrington's Brewery. 1957.
Courtauld Tompson: A Memoir. 1958.
Instructions to Young Writers. 1958.
Green Memory (autobiography). 1961.

Editor, *Eighty Poems: An Anthology.* 1924; as *By Haunted Stream: An Anthology of Modern English Poets,* 1924.
Editor, *The Best Poems of 1923 to 1927.* 5 vols., 1924–28.
Editor, *The Furnival Book of Short Stories.* 1932.
Editor, *Beginnings* (anthology of autobiographical essays). 1935.
Editor, with C. Day Lewis, *A New Anthology of Modern Verse 1920–1940.* 1941.
Editor, *English Domestic Life During the Last 200 Years: An Anthology Selected from the Novelists.* 1942.
Editor, *Sixteen Portraits of People Whose Houses Have Been Preserved by the National Trust.* 1951.
Editor, *Fred Bason's Second Diary.* 1952.
Editor, *Lorna Doone,* by R. D. Blackmore. 1958.

*   *   *

L. A. G. Strong was a prolific writer whose versatility may have caused him to be somewhat underrated. Taken together, his short stories and early novels, and the poetry collected in *The Body's Imperfection* constitute a considerable achievement.

He was an assistant master at Summer Fields School, Oxford, until 1930, when the great success of his first novel *Dewer Rides* encouraged him to devote himself entirely to literary work. His childhood memories of Ireland and Devon – *Dewer Rides* was a story of Dartmoor – influenced his fiction, as did his instinct as a poet, and so did the spinal trouble which kept him from most sports and paradoxically induced an emphasis in his writing on physical strength and toughness.

Among the earlier novels which consolidated his reputation were *The Brothers,* a story of Highland fishermen; *Sea Wall,* chiefly set in Dublin; and *Corporal Tune.* The later novels included *The Director,* later adapted as a play for the Gate Theatre, Dublin. Strong's mastery of the short story can be sampled in such collections as *The English Captain* and *Travellers,* which was awarded the James Tait Black prize; he could turn expertly from comedy and sentiment to the macabre, the fearful, and the ironic.

By the skeptical, Strong came to be considered something of a literary chameleon, and indeed, being a hard worker, he was ready to take most of the opportunities that presented themselves. He wrote biographies, notably of Thomas Moore and John McCormack; he wrote books for children, school books, and one-act plays; he wrote a book on boxing, and even one on sugar. For a number of years he reviewed regularly in the *Spectator*; his literary criticism was shown at its best in his book on James Joyce, *The Sacred River*, and in his *Personal Remarks*, containing studies of Synge and Yeats.

Added to all this professional activity was a keen interest in singing and the theatre. Strong found time to teach drama and voice production and travelled widely as an adjudicator of amateur dramatics. He may have overestimated his strength, for he died suddenly after a minor operation at Guildford in 1958. The delightful autobiography of his early life, *Green Memory*, contains a characteristic photograph of "L.A.G.S.," with his quirky eyebrows and pleasant humorous features, a man widely loved for his modesty, kindliness, and constant willingness to help other writers and artists.

—Derek Hudson

STYRON, William. American. Born in Newport News, Virginia, 11 June 1925. Educated at Christchurch School, Virginia; Davidson College, North Carolina, 1942–43; Duke University, Durham, North Carolina, 1943–44, 1946–47, A.B. 1947. Served in the United States Marine Corps, 1944–45, 1951: 1st Lieutenant. Married Rose Burgunder in 1953; one son and three daughters. Associate Editor for McGraw Hill, publishers, New York, 1947; full-time writer from 1947; Advisory Editor, *Paris Review*, Paris and New York, since 1952; member of the Editorial Board of *The American Scholar*, Washington, D.C., since 1970. Fellow of Silliman College, Yale University, New Haven, Connecticut, since 1964. Recipient: American Academy of Arts and Letters Prix de Rome, 1952; Pulitzer Prize, 1968; Howells Medal, 1970. D.H.: Wilberforce University, Ohio, 1967: Litt.D.: Duke University, 1968; New School for Social Research, New York; Tufts University, Medford, Massachusetts. Member, National Institute of Arts and Letters, and American Academy of Arts and Sciences. Lives in Roxbury, Connecticut.

Publications

Fiction

Lie Down in Darkness. 1951.
The Long March. 1956.
Set This House on Fire. 1960.
The Confessions of Nat Turner. 1967.

Play

In the Clap Shack (produced 1972). 1973.

Other

Editor, *Best Short Stories from "The Paris Review."* 1959.

Reading List: *Styron* by Robert H. Fossum, 1968; *Styron* by Cooper R. Mackin, 1969; *Styron's "The Confessions of Nat Turner": A Critical Handbook* edited by Melvin J. Friedman and Irving Malin, 1970 (includes bibliography); *Styron* by Richard Pearce, 1971; *Styron* by Marc L. Ratner, 1972; *The Achievement of Styron* edited by Irving Malin and Robert K. Morris, 1974.

*   *   *

With the publication of *The Confessions of Nat Turner*, William Styron fulfilled — unwittingly and with great reluctance — early predictions that he would prove worthy of great national attention. The novel, based on the extracted confession of an insurrectionary leader of the Southampton, Virginia, slave revolt of 1803, was published in the midst of profound racial turmoil in the late 1960's of the United States. The considerable literary strengths of the book — Styron's talents as a story teller, stylist, dreamer of the interior psyche — were submerged under a torrent of larger sociological and cultural questions. Black and white historians, sociologists, psychologists debated a morass of questions, especially (1) the propriety of a Southern white liberal's depicting a black slave hero; (2) the psychic image of Nat Turner as a sexually tormented and driven figure; (3) the complex vision on black-white race relations offered in the novel. Black scholar John E. Clarke collected a major body of the criticism in *William Styron's "Nat Turner": Ten Black Writers Respond* (1968).

Styron's first novel, *Lie Down in Darkness*, was exceptionally well-reviewed (although the inescapable debts to Faulkner and Wolfe were acknowledged), and Maxwell Geismar led the way in hailing it as "maybe the best novel since World War II." As a writer of the American South, Styron owes a debt to a strong literary and cultural stream. Louis D. Rubin, Jr., sums it up: "It involved ... a reliance upon the resources of a sounding rhetoric rather than understatement, a dependence upon the old religious universals ('love and honor and pity and pride and sacrifice,' as Faulkner once termed them) rather than a suspicion of all such external moral formulations, and a profound belief in the reality of the past as importantly affecting present behavior — an 'historical sense,' as contrasted with the dismissal of history as irrelevant and meaningless."

Throughout Styron's three novels, and in his shorter works as well, there is a consistent and abiding interest in the press of human social, political, and allied institutions and mores on the individual consciousness, and in the human consequences thereof. Styron's work is heavily reliant on the figures of the mind — on dream and nightmare, on interior monologue and fantasy, on the densities of memory and reflection. The Loftis family of his first novel — Milton and Helen and especially their daughter Peyton — is a moving group portrait of a family dismembered by the bankruptcy and collapse of Old Southern ways of being. In Peyton Loftis's flight to the North and finally New York, we see particularly the psychic devastation resultant from the demands of a shadow world of "old religious universals," but one no longer able to offer the place and fixity and comfort that once justified it.

Styron's interest in the individual psyche's response to the demands of a culture are nowhere more apparent than in his portrait of Nat Turner. While his novel does offer a vivid and moving image of slave life, Styron's clear interest is in the psychology of this unlikely slave leader. Under Styron's pen — to the great anger of certain black hagiographers — Turner emerges as a religious visionary and repressed polymorph, yearning for sexual contact with his white masters and mistresses and loathing himself for doing so.

Styron's most consistent fictional interest has been in the individual psychic results of the emergence of the South into the modern world, but he has also manifested a second concern in his work: in the tensions between the private conscience and mature sensibility and the incessant demands of the modern military establishment, seen in its most extreme American form in the United States Marine Corps. An early novella, *The Long March*, demonstrates this interest, as do his most recently published excerpt from a novel-on-progress, "Marriott, The Marine" (part of a novel entitled *The Way of the Warrior*), and the play *In the Clap Shack*.

Styron works slowly and painfully, and no doubt the turmoil around *The Confessions of Nat Turner* interrupted and threatened his work. But, based on recent excerpts, particularly the strongly autobiographical "Marriott, The Marine," his most absorbing and least mannered work in a long time, I would judge that his best work – and it would be considerable to top *Lie Down in Darkness* – is yet to be written.

—Jack Hicks

SUCKOW, Ruth. American. Born in Hawarden, Iowa, 6 August 1892; grew up in various Iowa towns. Educated at Grinnell College, Iowa, 1910–13; Curry Dramatic School, Boston, 1914–15; University of Denver, 1915–18, B.A. 1917, M.A. 1918. Married the writer Ferner Nuhn in 1929. Writer from 1918; Editorial Assistant on *The Midland*, Iowa City, 1921–22; owner and manager of the Orchard Apiary, Earlsville, Iowa, in the 1920's; spent winters in New York City, 1924–34; lived in Cedar Falls, Iowa, 1934–52, and Claremont, California, from 1952. M.A.: Grinnell College, 1931. *Died 23 January 1960.*

PUBLICATIONS

Fiction

    Country People. 1924.
    The Odyssey of a Nice Girl. 1925.
    Iowa Interiors (stories). 1926; as *People and Houses*, 1927.
    The Bonney Family. 1928.
    Cora. 1929.
    The Kramer Girls. 1930.
    Children and Older People (stories). 1931.
    The Folks. 1934.
    Carry-Over. 1936.
    New Hope. 1942.
    Some Others and Myself: Seven Stories and a Memoir. 1952.
    The John Wood Case. 1959.

Reading List: *Suckow* by Leedice McAnnelly Kissane, 1969; *Suckow: A Critical Study of Her Fiction* by Margaret Stewart Omrcanin, 1972.

*   *   *

In the 1920's Ruth Suckow was considered a major talent, destined to write novels and short stories of distinction, possibly a great American writer. H. L. Mencken published her short fiction in his *Smart Set* and *American Mercury*, and praised her extravagantly. Suckow's stories seemed to fit somewhere between Willa Cather and Sinclair Lewis, but to many she was more honest and straightforward than either. Fifty years later Ruth Suckow is considered a minor figure: a good Iowa regionalist, an uncompromising, unsentimental realist who wrote about the ordinary, middle-class people of the American heartland at the beginning of the automotive age.

After the 1920's the literary standing of Cather and Lewis was eclipsed by Hemingway, Dos Passos, Steinbeck, Fitzgerald, and Faulkner. Literary fashion turned against Ruth Suckow, but more important factors were responsible for her decline in stature. Her quiet, uneventful accounts worked best in short stories, but novels were more profitable and more prestigious. Her most ambitious novel, *The Folks* (727 pages), was a Literary Guild selection in 1934. More than twenty years elapse in this account of an Iowa small-town banker and his wife, and the start in life of their four children. The action extends to New York and San Diego, but the point of view is always Iowa small-town. Departing from her earlier practice, in this novel Suckow interprets and comments on the actions and motivations of her characters. But though people, places, and events ring true, there is too little drama, conflict, or interest in the people to sustain the long story. Two later novels – *New Hope* and *The John Wood Case* – drew little critical attention.

The Folks reveals Ruth Suckow's shortcomings. The same weaknesses are found in her earlier novels: *Country People*, *The Odyssey of a Nice Girl*, *The Bonney Family*, *Cora*, and *The Kramer Girls*. The last two of this group reveal her new interest in feminism; the earlier novels reveal the texture of small-town life in Iowa seen through the eyes of a young girl.

The short stories of *Iowa Interiors* and *Children and Older People* are Suckow's best work. The stories in a third volume, *Some Others and Myself*, are admittedly inferior – more reflective and contemplative, less objective. As in her longer fiction, the point of view in these stories is restricted and revealing: as the daughter of a small-town clergyman, Suckow saw many lonely, elderly couples and frustrated spinsters. She describes the countless family gatherings and church affairs she had been a part of, not social, political, and economic machinations. There is no explicit sex, no violence, no drama or suspense.

In his *Midwestern Farm Novel* Roy Meyer finds Suckow unsatisfactory because she sees Iowa farms – their people and problems – from the point of view of a small-town preacher's daughter who occasionally came out to those farms. A fellow-Iowan, the socialist Josephine Herbst, objected to Suckow's blindness to social implications. A comparison with her slightly older contemporary, Sherwood Anderson, is revealing: like Suckow's, Anderson's short stories are far better than his novels, but the psychological insights in Anderson's stories contrast sharply with the flatness and simplicity of her honest realism.

—Clarence A. Glasrud

SURTEES, R(obert) S(mith). English. Born in Durham in 1803. Educated at Durham Grammar School until 1819; articled to a Durham solicitor, 1819, and subsequently qualified. Married Elizabeth Jane Fenwick in 1841; one son and two daughters. Settled in London, and bought a law partnership, then had difficulty in recovering the purchase money; took rooms in Lincoln's Inn, and began contributing to *Sporting Magazine* to support himself; also compiled a manual for horse buyers, 1830; Founder, with Rudolph Ackermann, 1831, and Editor, 1831–36, *New Sporting Magazine*; succeeded to his father's estate in Durham, 1838; became Justice of the Peace for Durham, Major of the Durham Militia, and High Sheriff of Durham, 1856. *Died 16 March 1864.*

Collections

> *Novels.* 10 vols., 1929–30.
> *Hunting Scenes,* edited by Lionel Gough. 1953.

Fiction

> *Jorrocks' Jaunts and Jollities; or, The Hunting, Racing, Driving, Sailing, Eating, Eccentric, and Extravagant Exploits of That Renowned Sporting Citizen, Mr. John Jorrocks.* 1838; revised edition, 1869.
> *Handley Cross; or, The Spa Hunt.* 1843.
> *Hillingdon Hall; or, The Cockney Squire.* 1845.
> *Hawbuck Grange; or, The Sporting Adventures of Thomas Scott, Esq.* 1847.
> *Mr. Sponge's Sporting Tour.* 1853.
> *"Ask Mamma"; or, The Richest Commoner in England.* 1858.
> *Plain or Ringlets.* 1860.
> *Mr. Romford's Hounds.* 1864.
> *Young Tom Hall,* edited by E. D. Cuming. 1926.

Other

> *The Horseman's Manual.* 1831.
> *The Analysis of the Hunting Field, Being a Series of Sketches of the Principal Characters That Compose One.* 1846.
> *Surtees by Himself and E. D. Cuming.* 1924.
> *Town and Country Papers,* edited by E. D. Cuming. 1929.

Reading List: *Surtees: A Critical Study* by Frederick Watson, 1933; *Surtees* (biography) by Leonard Cooper, 1952; *The England of Nimrod and Surtees* by Edward W. Bovill, 1959; *Surtees* by Horst W. Drescher, 1961; *A Jorrocks Handbook* by Robert L. W. Collison, 1964; *The Deathless Train: The Life and Work of Surtees* by David R. Johnston-Jones, 1974.

*   *   *

R. S. Surtees is *the* novelist of hunting, and is best remembered for his creation of Jorrocks, who may well have suggested the idea of Pickwick to Dickens. The contributions to *The New Sporting Magazine* (1831–34) which were collected as *Jorrocks' Jaunts and Jollities* are a series of picaresque adventures of the London grocer turned hunting-man. Fat, outspoken, self-confident and often comic, Jorrocks had in *Handley Cross*, Surtees's next novel, a foil in James Pigg, hard-riding and hard-drinking huntsman, but Pigg is more than this; he is also a "character" in his own right. *Handley Cross* creates a world of its own, a setting within a newly fashionable watering-place, possibly based on Leamington. In this novel also the characters display a greater fullness than in its predecessor. Surtees's third novel was *Hillingdon Hall*, which has didactic leanings; it has been called "a handbook to the farmer's progress."

Hawbuck Grange, like *Jorrocks*, also appeared as "Sporting Sketches" and is, if anything, even looser than *Jorrocks*. Its central character, Tom Scott, is much less rumbustious than

Jorrocks — a decent, honest hunting farmer; and a new element in Surtees is Scott's love-affair, but it does not come to anything.

The next novel, *Mr. Sponge's Sporting Tour*, is more powerful, with its main figure, "a good, pushing, free-and-easy sort of man, wishing to be a gentleman without knowing how," and a number of others — Benjamin Buckram, Jack Spraggon, Mr. Jogglebury Crowdey and Facey Romford — among Surtees's most memorable characters. It is here too that Lucy Glitters first appears, though her triumph will come later in *Mr. Romford's Hounds*. This, his last novel, is much better than its two predecessors, *Ask Mamma* and *Plain or Ringlets?* His one other novel, *Young Tom Hall*, was serialised in 1851–52, but not published complete until 1926.

Surtees's characters and dialogue are full-blooded; his plots are episodic, sometimes disjointed, but always vigorous; he is full of comedy and satire. His greatest quality is zest.

—Arthur Pollard

SWIFT, Jonathan. English. Born in Dublin, Ireland, 30 November 1667, of English parents. Educated at Kilkenny Grammar School, 1674–82; Trinity College, Dublin, 1682–88. Married Esther (Stella) Johnson in 1716 (died, 1728). Companion and Secretary to Sir William Temple at Moor Park, Farnham, Surrey, 1689–91, 1691–94, 1695–99; writer from 1695; ordained in the Anglican Church, in Dublin, 1695, and held first living at Kilroot, Northern Ireland, until 1698; Chaplain to the Earl of Berkeley, Lord Lieutenant of Ireland, 1700; vicar of Laracor; Prebend, St. Patrick's Cathedral, Dublin, 1701; editor of several volumes of Temple's works during the 1700's; aligned with the Tory ministry of Oxford and Bolingbroke, 1710; lived in London, wrote political pamphlets, and contributed to *The Examiner*, 1710–14; Dean of St. Patrick's Cathedral, Dublin, from 1713; a leader of the Irish resistance movement from 1724; visited London, 1726, 1727, but otherwise resided in Dublin until his death. D.D.: University of Dublin, 1701. *Died 19 October 1745*.

PUBLICATIONS

Collections

Poems, edited by Harold Williams. 3 vols., 1937.
Prose Works, edited by Herbert Davis. 14 vols., 1939–68.
Gulliver's Travels and Other Writings, edited by Louis A. Landa. 1960.
The Correspondence, edited by Harold Williams. 5 vols., 1963–65.
A Tale of a Tub and Other Satires, edited by Kathleen Williams. 1975.
Selected Poems, edited by C. H. Sisson. 1977.

Fiction

A Tale of a Tub, Written for the Universal Improvement of Mankind, to Which Is Added an Account of a Battle Between the Ancient and Modern Books in St. James's Library. 1704; revised edition, 1710; edited by G. C. Guthkelch and D. N. Smith, 1958.

Travels into Several Remote Nations of the World, by Captain Lemuel Gulliver. 1726;
    revised edition, 1735; edited by Angus Ross, 1972.

Verse

Baucis and Philemon, Imitated from Ovid. 1709.
Part of the Seventh Epistle of the First Book of Horace Imitated. 1713.
The First Ode of the Second Book of Horace Paraphrased. 1713.
The Bubble. 1721.
Cadenus and Vanessa. 1726.
Miscellanies in Prose and Verse, with others. 4 vols., 1727–32.
Horace, Book I, Ode XIV, Paraphrased. 1730.
The Lady's Dressing Room, to Which Is Added A Poem on Cutting Down the Old Thorn at
    Market Hill. 1732.
An Elegy on Dicky and Dolly. 1732.
The Life and Genuine Character of Doctor Swift, Written by Himself. 1733.
On Poetry: A Rhapsody. 1733.
An Epistle to a Lady. 1734.
A Beautiful Young Nymph Going to Bed, Written for the Honour of the Fair Sex. 1734.
An Imitation of the Sixth Satire of the Second Book of Horace, completed by
    Pope. 1738.
Verses on the Death of Dr. Swift. 1739.

Other

A Discourse of the Contests and Dissensions Between the Nobles and the Commons in
    Athens and Rome. 1701; edited by F. H. Ellis, 1967.
Predictions for the Year 1708. 1708.
A Project for the Advancement of Religion and the Reformation of Manners. 1709.
A New Journey to Paris. 1711.
The Conduct of the Allies. 1711.
Some Remarks on the Barrier Treaty. 1712.
A Proposal for Correcting, Improving, and Ascertaining the English Tongue. 1712.
Mr. Collin's Discourse of Free-Thinking. 1713.
The Public Spirit of the Whigs. 1714.
A Proposal for the Universal Use of Irish Manufacture. 1720.
Fraud Detected; or, The Hibernian Patriot, Containing All the Drapier's Letters to the
    People of Ireland. 1725; as *The Hibernian Patriot,* 1730.
A Short View of the Present State of Ireland. 1728.
A Modest Proposal for Preventing the Children of Poor People from Being Burthen to
    Their Parents or the Country. 1729.
An Examination of Certain Abuses, Corruptions, and Enormities in the City of
    Dublin. 1732.
The Works. 1735.
A Complete Collection of Genteel and Ingenious Conversation. 1738; edited by E.
    Partridge, 1963.
Some Free Thoughts upon the Present State of Affairs, Written in the Year 1714. 1741.
Three Sermons. 1744.
Directions to Servants. 1745.
The Last Will and Testament of Swift. 1746.
Brotherly Love: A Sermon. 1754.
The History of the Four Last Years of the Queen. 1758.

Editor, *Letters Written by Sir William Temple and Other Ministers of State.*   3 vols.,
1700–03.
Editor, *Miscellanea: The Third Part,* by William Temple.   1701.
Editor, *Memoirs: Part III,* by William Temple.   1709.

Bibliography: *A Bibliography of the Writings of Swift* by H. Teerink, 1937, revised edition,
edited by Arthur H. Scounten, 1963; *A Bibliography of Swift Studies 1945–1965* by J. J.
Stathis, 1967.

Reading List: *The Mind and Art of Swift* by Ricardo Quintana, 1936; *The Sin of Wit* by
Maurice Johnson, 1950; *Swift: The Man, His Works, and the Age* by Irvin Ehrenpreis, 2 vols.
(of 3), 1962–67; *Swift and the Satirist's Art* by E. W. Rosenheim, Jr., 1963; *Swift and the Age
of Compromise* by Kathleen Williams, 1968, and *Swift: The Critical Heritage* edited by
Williams, 1970; *Swift: A Critical Introduction* by Denis Donoghue, 1969; *Swift* edited by C.
J. Rawson, 1971, and *Gulliver and the Gentle Reader* by Rawson, 1973.

*   *   *

Jonathan Swift began as a poet, and wrote many poems throughout his life. His poetic
achievement has been overshadowed by his major prose satires, but deserves to be
recognised. After a brief early period of Cowleyan odes, Swift abandoned "serious" or
"lofty" styles (both terms are his own), and became one of the masters in a great English
tradition of "light" verse, informal but far from trivial, which includes the works of Skelton,
Samuel Butler, Prior, Byron, and Auden. Byron admired him especially, and said he "beats
us all hollow." Swift seldom wrote what he called "serious Couplets," avoiding a form which
his friend Pope was bringing to a high refinement of precision and masterfulness. He
preferred looser and more popular metres, and most often the loose octosyllabic couplet
chiefly associated with Butler's *Hudibras,* a poem Swift greatly admired. These looser forms
reflected the disorders of life, rather than seeming to subdue or iron out these disorders
within the reassuring contours of a style which overtly proclaimed the author's triumphant
and clarifying mastery. Even the few poems which, exceptionally, Swift wrote in the heroic
couplet, the "Description of the Morning" and the "Description of a City Shower," tend to
flatten that eloquently patterned metre into an idiom of bare realistic notation, registering the
chaotic and unstructured energies of common city scenes rather than any sense of the
satirist's control.

These two poems also parody some conventions of grand poetic description, and Swift's
impulse to undercut the loftier orderings of "serious" poets runs through virtually all his
work as a poet. The celebrated "excremental" poems ("The Lady's Dressing Room," "A
Beautiful Young Nymph Going to Bed," "Strephon and Chloe," "Cassinus and Peter") are
among other things parodies of the false idealisations of love-poetry. The famous plaintive cry
that "Celia, Celia, Celia shits," which occurs in two of the poems and has shocked healthy-
minded readers like D. H. Lawrence and Aldous Huxley, has this dimension of parody,
although more than mere parody is at work. The words are too playful to support any simple
view that Swift hated the human body or was a misogynist. Through his foolish Strephons,
Swift mocks those who cannot accept the physical facts and seek refuge in idealising
poeticisms. But he also tells us that the body is ugly and perishable, and that in matters of love
and of friendship the moral and intellectual virtues are a sounder guide. These themes also
run through many non-scatological poems which he wrote to women friends, notably the
moving and tender poems to Stella and the archly self-justifying "Cadenus and Vanessa."

The latter, a defence of his role in a one-sided love-affair, is one of several autobiographical
poems which Swift, at various periods, wrote as apologies for some aspect of his private or
public life. Of these, the most interesting are "The Author upon Himself" and *Verses on the
Death of Dr. Swift.* The latter is perhaps his best-known poem, a comprehensive and in many

places light-hearted and low-key defence of his literary and political career, rising towards the end to a pitch of self-praise which some readers have found distasteful. *An Epistle to a Lady* is a revealing poem about Swift's unwillingness to write in a "lofty Stile"; and *On Poetry: A Rapsody*, whose title implies a similar point, is in the main an angry and witty account of the world of bad poets and hireling politicians.

In the 1730's Swift also wrote a series of angry poems on Irish affairs, of which "The Legion Club" is the best known. These attacks on prominent public men in Ireland sometimes have the force of ritual curses, and are perhaps the only places where Swift attempts what is often (and almost always wrongly) attributed to him, a Juvenalian grandeur of denunciation.

Swift's earliest major work is the prose *Tale of a Tub* (published 1704, but began about 1696 and largely written by 1700), a brilliantly inventive and disturbing display of his satiric powers. It is the last and greatest English contribution to the long Renaissance debate on the relative merits of the Ancients and the Moderns. Through a deliberately diffuse and all-embracing parody, the *Tale* mimics the laxity, muddle, and arrogance of Modern thought, both in religion and in the various branches of literature and learning. This parody is sometimes very specific, as when Dryden's garrulous self-importance, or the mystical nonsense of some "*dark* Author" like Thomas Vaughan, is mocked. But it extends beyond specific examples to the whole contemporaneous republic of bad authors and to all deviant religions, which for Swift meant mainly the dissenting sects and Roman Catholicism. The cumulative force of its many-sided and probing irony reaches even further, however, transcending parody altogether and turning into a comprehensive anatomy of modern culture and indeed of human folly in general. Many readers, from Swift's time to our own, have felt that its effect was so destructive as to undermine even those things to which Swift claimed to be expressing loyalty, including the Church of England and indeed religion itself. Swift defended himself against such charges, but they stuck, and were to damage his career as a churchman. Whether or not Swift's defense is wholly accepted, the work shows Swift's deep and characteristic tendency to put his most powerful energies into the destructive or critical side of his vision, leaving the positive values to emerge by implication from the wreckage. The *Tale* was published with two accompanying pieces, *The Battle of the Books* and the *Discourse Concerning the Mechanical Operation of the Spirit*. The first extends the *Tale*'s satire on learning, the second on religious abuses.

In the years after 1704, Swift wrote a number of tracts on matters of religion and ecclesiastical politics. Of these, the "Argument Against Abolishing Christianity," has exceptional distinction as an ironic *tour de force*, subtle, inventive, slippery and playful, yet charged with an urgency of purpose and a sense of cherished values under threat.

During the period of Swift's early fame, 1710–14, Swift became a protégé of Harley and wrote many political tracts in support of his Tory ministry and of the controversial Peace of Utrecht. Harley put him in charge of the *Examiner*, for which he wrote some of his best brief polemical pieces, notably against the Duke of Marlborough, hero of the war against France. Of his other political writings in this period perhaps the most important is *The Conduct of the Allies*. Swift was one of the members of the Scriblerus club, a group of satirical wits associated with Harley (now Earl of Oxford), whose other regular members were Pope, Gay, Arbuthnot, and Thomas Parnell. The Club mostly met in 1714, and was effectively dispersed after Queen Anne's death in that year and the consequent collapse of the Tory administration. But the Club's activities not only resulted in the collectively composed *Memoirs of Martinus Scriblerus* (which Pope published much later, in 1741), but also influenced other writings by individual Scriblerians, including *Gulliver's Travels* (1726), and Pope's *Dunciad* (1728). In 1713, Swift became Dean of St. Patrick's Cathedral in Dublin, the highest preferment he could achieve in the Church. He regarded it as a blow to his hopes, and thought of his native Ireland as a place of exile.

After the Queen's death in 1714, he remained in Ireland for almost the whole of his life, and became actively involved in Irish political affairs. His Irish writings of the 1720's and (to a lesser degree) the 1730's earn him his honoured place as a defender of Ireland's rights. He was one of a series of great Anglo-Irishmen who fought to relieve Ireland's wrongs at the hands of the English oppressor: the list includes Charles Stewart Parnell and W. B. Yeats. The most important literary text among Swift's Irish writings is *A Modest Proposal*, an ironic pamphlet advocating the selling of Irish infants for food as a means of helping the economy. This *Proposal* is the climax of a whole series of tracts, which included *A Proposal for the Universal Use of Irish Manufacture*, the *Drapier's Letters*, and *A Short View of the State of Ireland*, in which the economic and political weaknesses of Ireland are bitterly exposed, and remedies suggested. The common view that these works are mainly or entirely anti-English is only partially true. It is becoming increasingly recognised that Swift was also concerned to expose the Irish for their failure to help themselves: their slavish temperament, economic fecklessness, commercial disreputability, the draining of the country's resources by absentee landlords. These criticisms underlie *A Modest Proposal*, which is more accurately read as a cry of exasperation against Irishmen of all classes and parties than as an attack on the English oppressor (although it is that too). Swift disliked the Irish while feeling called upon to defend their political rights. He thought of himself as English, accidentally "dropped" in Ireland by birth and kept there by an unhappy turn in his career. But he fought powerfully for Irish interests, achieved some practical successes (especially with the *Drapier's Letters*), and became and has remained a national hero.

Gulliver's Travels was published in 1726. It bears strong traces of Swift's involvement in Irish affairs. But its reach is, of course, much wider. Like *A Tale of a Tub*, it has a framework of parody (in this case mainly of travel-books), but its principal satiric concerns, unlike those of the *Tale*, are not in themselves enshrined in the parody. Neither work deals merely with bad books, and both are concerned with a fundamental exploration of the nature of man. But in the *Tale*, the follies of unregulated intellect and impulse are directly expressed in the kind of book and the features of style which Swift mimics, whereas in *Gulliver's Travels* the travel-book format is mainly a convenient framework for a consideration of human nature which is only marginally concerned with the character of travel-writers.

In the first two books, an allegory of human pride begins to establish itself. The tiny Lilliputians of Book I are a minuscule and self-important replica of the society of England; the giants of Book II demonstrate that in the eyes of larger creatures we ourselves seem as ludicrous as the Lilliputians seem to us. The two Books have a complementary relationship which is forceful and clear: a neat balancing of narrative structures which supports and illustrates the basic satiric irony, and is able to accommodate a wide range of detailed satiric observation about English and European mores and institutions.

This exceptionally tidy structural arrangement gives way in the rest of the work to something more complex and less predictable. Book III takes us to a miscellany of strange lands, all of them inhabited by humans of normal size, and between them illustrating particular social and political institutions (repressive government, insane and inhumane scientific research projects, wild follies of intellect). If the schematic relationship between Books I and II is not continued, much of Book III adds to or develops the exposure of particular human characteristics and institutions which had begun in the earlier books. But towards the end of Book III a new note is struck. Gulliver visits the land of the Struldbruggs, who have the gift of immortality but without perpetual youth. The horror which these hideous creatures arouse as they decay into increasing senility is no longer primarily concerned with moral culpability. It is a portrayal of certain grim features of the human situation which are independent of good and evil.

In Book IV the satire becomes absolute, transcending all mere particularities of vice and folly of the kind encountered so far. The savage Yahoos have most of the vices and follies satirised earlier, but they embody a sense of the radical ugliness of the human animal, in his moral and his physical nature, which amounts (or so it seems to many readers) to a more fundamental disenchantment. The Houyhnhnms, the horse-shaped rulers of the humanoid Yahoos, are by contrast absolutely reasonable and virtuous, as the Yahoos are absolutely irrational and vicious. Swift said that he wished to disprove the traditional definition of man as a "rational animal," and he did so partly by enshrining an ideal rationality in a beast commonly named in philosophical discourse as an example of the non-rational animal: the horse. Swift's analysis has usually been considered a bleak and disturbing one, although some recent critics have held that Swift really believed that man both was and ought to be a creature who came somewhere between Yahoo and Houyhnhnm, a liberal and humane though fallible creature of the sort exemplified by the good Portuguese captain, who appears briefly near the end. This latter view seems to me misguided.

—C. J. Rawson

TARKINGTON, (Newton) Booth. American. Born in Indianapolis, Indiana, 29 July 1869, and lived there for most of his life. Educated at Phillips Exeter Academy, New Hampshire; Purdue University, Lafayette, Indiana, 1888–89; Princeton University, 1889–93; did not graduate. Married 1) Laurel Louisa Fletcher in 1902 (divorced, 1911), one daughter; 2) Susannah Robinson in 1912. Writer from 1893; also an artist: illustrated *Character Sketches* by Riley and other works; member of the Indiana House of Representatives, 1902–03; in later life also lived in Kennebunkport, Maine. Recipient: Pulitzer Prize, 1919, 1922; National Institute of Arts and Letters Gold Medal, 1933; Boy Scouts of America Silver Buffalo, 1935; Roosevelt Distinguished Service Medal, 1942; Howells Medal, 1945. A.M.: Princeton University, 1899; Litt.D.: Princeton University, 1918; De Pauw University, Greencastle, Indiana, 1923; Columbia University, New York, 1924; L.H.D.: Purdue University, 1939. Member, American Academy of Arts and Letters. *Died 19 May 1946.*

PUBLICATIONS

Collections

The Gentleman from Indianapolis: A Treasury of Tarkington, edited by John Beecroft. 1957.

Fiction

The Gentleman from Indiana. 1899.
Monsieur Beaucaire. 1900.
The Two Vanrevels. 1902.
Cherry. 1903.
In the Arena: Stories of Political Life. 1905.
The Beautiful Lady. 1905.
The Conquest of Canaan. 1905.
His Own People. 1907.
The Guest of Quesnay. 1908.
Beasley's Christmas Party. 1909.
The Flirt. 1913.
Penrod. 1914; Penrod and Sam, 1916; Penrod Jashber, 1929; complete revised version, as Penrod: His Complete Story, 1931.
The Turmoil. 1915; The Magnificent Ambersons, 1918; The Midlander, 1923; complete version, as Growth, 1927.
Seventeen. 1916.
The Spring Concert (story). 1916.
Harlequin and Columbine and Other Stories. 1918.
Ramsey Milholland. 1919.
Alice Adams. 1921.
Gentle Julia. 1922.
The Fascinating Stranger and Other Stories. 1923.
Women. 1925.
Selections from Tarkington's Stories, edited by Lilian Holmes Strack. 1926.
The Plutocrat. 1927.
Claire Ambler. 1928.
Young Mrs. Greeley. 1929.

Mirthful Haven. 1930.
Mary's Neck. 1932.
Wanton Mally. 1932.
Presenting Lily Mars. 1933.
Little Orvie. 1934.
Mr. White, The Red Barn, Hell, and Bridewater. 1935.
The Lorenzo Bunch. 1936.
Rumbin Galleries. 1937.
The Heritage of Hatcher Ide. 1941.
The Fighting Littles. 1941.
Kate Fennigate. 1943.
Image of Josephine. 1945.
The Show Piece (unfinished). 1947.
Three Selected Short Novels (includes *Walterson, Uncertain Molly Collicut,* and *Rennie Peddigoe*). 1947.

Plays

The Guardian, with Harry Leon Wilson. 1907; as *The Man from Home* (produced 1908), 1908; revised version, 1934.
Cameo Kirby, with Harry Leon Wilson (produced 1908).
Foreign Exchange (produced 1909).
If I Had Money (produced 1909).
Springtime (produced 1909).
Your Humble Servant, with Harry Leon Wilson (produced 1909).
Beauty and the Jacobin: An Interlude of the French Revolution (produced 1912). 1912.
The Man on Horseback (produced 1912).
The Ohio Lady, with Julian Street. 1916; as *The Country Cousin* (produced 1921), 1921.
Mister Antonio (produced 1916). 1935.
The Gibson Upright, with Harry Leon Wilson (produced 1919). 1919.
Up from Nowhere, with Harry Leon Wilson (produced 1919).
Poldekin (produced 1920). In *McClure's,* March–July 1920.
Clarence (produced 1921). 1921.
The Intimate Strangers (produced 1921). 1921.
The Wren (produced 1922). 1922.
The Ghost Story (juvenile) (produced 1922). 1922.
Rose Briar (produced 1922).
The Trysting Place (produced 1923). 1923.
Magnolia (produced 1923).
Tweedles, with Harry Leon Wilson (produced 1924). 1924.
Bimbo, The Pirate (produced 1926). 1926.
The Travelers (produced 1927). 1927.
Station YYYY (produced 1927). 1927.
How's Your Health?, with Harry Leon Wilson (produced 1930). 1930.
Colonel Satan (produced 1932).
The Help Each Other Club (produced 1933). 1934.
Lady Hamilton and Her Nelson (produced 1945). 1945.

Screenplays: *Edgar and the Teacher's Pet,* 1920; *Edgar's Hamlet,* 1920; *Edgar's Little Saw,* 1920; *Edgar, The Explorer,* 1921; *Get Rich Quick Edgar,* 1921; *Pied Piper Malone,* with Tom Geraghty, 1924; *The Man Who Found Himself,* with Tom Geraghty, 1925.

Radio Plays: *Maud and Cousin Bill* series, 1932–33 (75 episodes).

Other

Works   21 vols., 1918–28.
The Works.   27 vols., 1922–32.
The Collector's Whatnot, with Hugh Kahler and Kenneth Roberts.   1923.
Looking Forward and Others (essays).   1926.
The World Does Move (reminiscences).   1928.
Some Old Portraits: A Book about Art and Human Beings.   1939.
Your Amiable Uncle: Letters to His Nephews.   1949.
*On Plays, Playwrights, and Playgoers: Selections from the Letters of Tarkington to George
    C. Tyler and John Peter Toolcy 1918–1925,* edited by Alan S. Downer.   1959.

Translator, *Samuel Brohl and Company,* by Victor Cherbuliez.   1902.

Bibliography: *A Bibliography of Tarkington* by Dorothy Ritter Russo and Thelma L. Sullivan,
1949, supplement in *Princeton University Library Chronicle 16,* 1955.

Reading List: *Tarkington: Gentleman from Indiana* by James Woodress, 1955; *Tarkington* by
Keith J. Fennimore, 1974.

*   *   *

Although Booth Tarkington was a very popular author during his lifetime, his reputation
has dimmed since his death, and today few of his works are read. Yet he was an excellent
fictional craftsman and a first-rate story teller, and his best novels are absorbing. Though
there are no sexual titillation and little tragedy in his books, he has a sense of humor and
observes and records the human comedy with a clear eye. His significance lies in his
depiction of urban, midwestern, middle-class America during the decades of intensely rapid
growth in the late 19th and early 20th centuries, and in his stories of children. He writes in
the tradition of commonplace realism as pioneered by Howells.

His trilogy published under the collective title *Growth* is important. These novels study the
social and economic life of a medium-sized midwestern city that may be identified as
Indianapolis. *The Turmoil,* which contains a very contemporary-sounding indictment of air
pollution and civic neglect in the pursuit of the dollar, is the story of an ascending family, the
first-generation makers of the new industrial wealth. *The Magnificent Ambersons,* winner of a
Pulitzer Prize, deals with an old family whose money was made in the Gilded Age. The
family is engulfed by the encroaching industrialism of the 20th Century, and the wealth is
dissipated by the second and third generations. *The Midlander,* which comes as close as
Tarkington ever came to tragedy, is the unhappy story of a promoter-developer of the urban
growth. Similar in subject and theme to the *Growth* trilogy is *Alice Adams,* perhaps
Tarkington's best novel. This story, which deserves to be better known, is a poignant comedy
of manners that details the unsuccessful efforts of a girl of modest circumstances to catch a
socially prominent husband. Character, plot, and the theme of social mobility all are skillfully
blended in this novel that won Tarkington a second Pulitzer Prize.

Tarkington's second major accomplishment lies in his boy stories, *Penrod, Penrod and
Sam,* and *Penrod Jashber.* These distinguished tales in the tradition of the realistic boy-story
begun by Mark Twain in *Tom Sawyer* appeal both to children and adults, are rich in
authentic detail and dialogue, and may turn out to be the author's most enduring work.
Tarkington also was adroit in depicting adolescents, but the vast change in teen-age mores

since *Seventeen* appeared in 1916 makes this once-popular novel a period piece rather than a story of perennial interest.

Tarkington was a playwright as well as a novelist, and any history of American drama must accord him a niche for some of his two dozen plays. *The Man from Home*, which he wrote with Harry Leon Wilson, enjoyed a long run on Broadway, and his play *Clarence*, which starred Alfred Lunt and Helen Hayes at the beginning of their careers, was a memorable success. Few American novelists have mastered the play form as well as Tarkington.

—James Woodress

TAYLOR, Elizabeth (née Coles). English. Born in Reading, Berkshire, 3 July 1912. Educated at the Abbey School, Reading. Married John William Kendall Taylor in 1936; one son and one daughter. Worked as a governess and librarian before her marriage; full-time writer from 1945. *Died 19 November 1975.*

PUBLICATIONS

Fiction

    At Mrs. Lippincote's. 1945.
    Palladian. 1946.
    A View of the Harbour. 1947.
    A Wreath of Roses. 1949.
    A Game of Hide-and-Seek. 1951.
    The Sleeping Beauty. 1953.
    Hester Lilly and Other Stories. 1954.
    Angel. 1957.
    The Blush and Other Stories. 1958.
    In a Summer Season. 1961.
    The Soul of Kindness. 1964.
    A Dedicated Man and Other Stories. 1965.
    The Wedding Group. 1968.
    Mrs. Palfrey at the Claremont. 1971.
    The Devastating Boys (stories). 1972.
    Blaming. 1976.

Other

    Mossy Trotter (juvenile). 1967.

Reading List: "The Novels of Taylor" by Robert Liddell, in *Review of English Literature*, April 1960; "Art in Miniature" by Paul Bailey, in *New Statesman*, 10 August 1973.

*   *   *

Critics have sometimes justly compared the shrewd, delicate ironies of Elizabeth Taylor with those of Jane Austen. Another attribute shared by these tolerantly amused, intensely feminine delineators of human foible was a distaste for sensational subject-matter and personal publicity alike. This perhaps in part accounts for the comparatively limited recognition, in favour of flashier fictional attractions, accorded to one of the most quietly distinguished talents of our time.

Like that of Jane Austen, Elizabeth Taylor's field of observation was chiefly confined to the social milieu she knew best – the educated, comfortably-off middle classes. But she has also a precise eye for the seedy and the shabby-genteel: the saloon-bar drinkers "in belted camel-hair coats, with trilby hats pulled forward over purple faces," or the house with "Fernlea" inscribed "in curly gilt letters on the fanlight" and standing "in a ferny, dusty garden, full of old iris-roots and broken terra-cotta path-edgings." That sharply selective perception of the significant detail of person and place is matched by an exact ear for the niceties of dialogue: the uncomfortably recognizable conversation of Amy's formidable grandchildren, for example, or the speech-habits of the delectable Ernie, her hypochondriacal housekeeper, in *Blaming*. Elizabeth Taylor's insights into human shortcomings, the unworthy motives which so often activate our behaviour, are disconcertingly acute. A favourite theme is the discrepancy between aspiration and mundane reality; and also the hypocrisies of self-deception so caustically pinpointed in the sententiously high-minded commune founded by Cressy's grandfather in *The Wedding Group*. This is a writer who thrives on incongruity, whether of situation – as in the unlikely marriage of *In a Summer Season* – or of character – Midge, the demonstratively unpossessive doting mother in *The Wedding Group*, or Flora in *The Soul of Kindness*, a menace to the happiness of her acquaintance through her ostensibly well-meaning interference in other people's lives.

Yet for all her wry sense of absurdity and gently relentless malice, Elizabeth Taylor is never unaware of the pathos and pain of existence so inextricably mixed with the humours of most lives. She brings a deep imaginative sympathy to the disappointments and insecurities of her three women, two young and one old, in the fine *A Wreath of Roses*. This extends throughout novels like *Mrs. Palfrey at the Claremont*, which so movingly depicts the predicament of unwanted old age courageously coping with indignity and loneliness, to her exploration of the problems of widowhood, the impact of bereavement upon a bored, self-absorbed woman, in her posthumous novel *Blaming*. Elizabeth Taylor's fastidious gift will continue to be missed by discriminating readers who value a civilized intelligence and refined sensibility, elegant economy of style, and a sophisticated ironical wit tempered always by compassion.

—Margaret Willy

TENNANT, Kylie. Australian. Born in Manly, New South Wales, 12 March 1912. Educated at Brighton College, Manly; University of Sydney, 1931. Married Lewis C. Rodd in 1932; two children. Full-time writer, 1935–59; worked as journalist, publisher's reader, literary adviser, and editor, 1959–69; resumed full-time writing career, 1969. Life Patron, Fellowship of Australian Writers; Member, Commonwealth Literary Fund Advisory Board, 1961–73. Recipient: S.H. Prior Memorial Prize, 1935, 1941; Australian Literary Society Gold Medal, 1941; Commonwealth Jubilee Stage Prize, 1951. Lives in Hunter's Hill, New South Wales.

Fiction

Tiburon. 1935.
Foveaux. 1939.
The Battlers. 1941.
Ride On Stranger. 1943.
Time Enough Later. 1943.
Lost Haven. 1945.
The Joyful Condemned. 1953; complete version, as *Tell Morning This,* 1967.
The Honey Flow. 1956.
Ma Jones and the Little White Cannibals (stories). 1967.

Plays

Tether a Dragon. 1952.
John o' the Forest and Other Plays (juvenile). 1952.
The Bells of the City and Other Plays (juvenile). 1955.
The Bushranger's Christmas Eve and Other Plays (juvenile). 1959.

Other

Australia: Her Story: Notes on a Nation. 1953; revised edition, 1964, 1971.
Long John Silver: The Story of the Film. 1953.
The Development of the Australian Novel. 1958.
All the Proud Tribesmen (juvenile). 1959.
Speak You So Gently (travel). 1959.
Trail Blazers of the Air. 1965.
The Australian Essay, with L. C. Rodd. 1968.
Evatt: Politics and Justice (biography). 1970.
The Man on the Headland (biography). 1971.

Editor, *Great Stories of Australia 1–7.* 7 vols., 1963–66.
Editor, *Summer's Tales 1* and *2.* 1964, 1965.

Reading List: *The Novels of Tennant* by Margaret Dick, 1966 (includes bibliography).

*   *   *

Kylie Tennant once remarked that the Australian novel "eats its peas with its knife," and her own fiction has been something of an embarrassment to those who want literature to be a well-mannered business. She shows on the one hand a capacity for inventive zest and intellectual alertness that few Australian novelists of her generation can match, yet on the other a disconcerting penchant for throwing aesthetic decorum to the winds. She would no doubt admit cheerfully that there are rough patches in her writing, that her techniques are often unsubtle, and that the usual structure of her narratives is casual to the point of untidiness.

Similarly she declines to be solemn about her convictions, or even to admit that she holds any creed. Told once that all serious writers should develop some philosophy, she quipped that it "sounded like growing a moustache to hide my weak mouth." A target for ridicule throughout her work is any pretentious or zealous brand of system-mongering; repeatedly the author mocks those intent on "gnawing and nagging and converting and proselytizing," as she puts it in *Ride On Stranger*, whose heroine Shannon is one of several Tennant characters engaged in steering an honest course between the Scylla of dogmatic idealism and the Charybdis of sterile cynicism. Like many Australian writers before her, she tends to extend her sympathy more readily to the underdog, the battler, than to the well-off and cultivated areas of society, and on that basis some critics have placed her within the so-called "democratic tradition" said to derive from Lawson, Furphy, and others. But as Xavier Pons demonstrates in an article on *The Battlers*, her best-known novel (*Australian Literary Studies*, October 1974), Tennant rejects the spirit of that tradition; it was essentially optimistic, anticipating a fine future for Australian society, whereas she implicitly suggests in her fiction that the facts of experience belie any meliorist faith. Like her character Shannon, Tennant apparently can "not believe that half a dozen changes in the social system would cleanse the sewers of human ignorance and stupidity." We are our own victims.

Compassionate humour is Tennant's response to this dismal spectacle. She admires resilience, unpretentious integrity, and vitality; but she can take a wry pleasure in depicting all sorts of vice and folly without becoming uncharitable towards her own creatures. Her novels swarm with a wide variety of people and activities, and, formally considered, they are more remarkable for profusion than for proportion. But they testify consistently, in the very inclusiveness of their structure, to the breadth of Kylie Tennant's concerns.

—Ian Reid

THACKERAY, William Makepeace.   English.   Born in Calcutta, India, 18 July 1811, of English parents; sent to England, 1817. Educated at schools in Hampshire, and Chiswick, London; Charterhouse, London, 1822–28; Trinity College, Cambridge, 1829–30, left without taking a degree; travelled abroad and visited Goethe at Weimar, 1830–31; entered Middle Temple, London, 1831, but soon abandoned legal studies. Married Isabella Shawe in 1836 (separated from her, when she went insane, 1842); three daughters. Purchased *The National Standard*, London, 1833, and became its editor until it failed, 1834; settled in Paris to study drawing, 1834–37: published satirical drawings, 1836; Paris Correspondent for *The Constitutional*, London, 1836–37; returned to England, 1837; thereafter a full-time writer; contributed to *The Times* and *Fraser's Magazine*; contributed articles and drawings to *Punch*, 1842–54; published an annual "Christmas Book," 1846–50; lectured on the "English Humourists," 1851, and lectured in America, 1852–53, 1855; stood for Parliament as Liberal candidate for Oxford, 1857; Editor, *Cornhill Magazine*, 1860–62. *Died 24 December 1863.*

PUBLICATIONS

Collections

Works, edited by George Saintsbury.   17 vols., 1908.
The Letters and Private Papers, edited by Gordon N. Ray.   4 vols., 1946.

Fiction

The Second Funeral of Napoleon, in Three Letters to Miss Smith of London, and The Chronicle of the Drum. 1841.

Jeames's Diary. 1846.

Mrs. Perkins's Ball. 1847.

Vanity Fair: A Novel Without a Hero. 1848; revised edition, 1853, 1863; edited by Geoffrey and Kathleen Tillotson, 1963.

The Great Hoggarty Diamond. 1848; as *The History of Samuel Titmarsh and the Great Hoggarty Diamond,* 1849.

Our Street. 1848.

The History of Pendennis: His Fortunes and Misfortunes, His Friends and His Greatest Enemy. 2 vols., 1849–50; revised edition, 1863; edited by Donald Hawes, 1972.

Doctor Birch and His Young Friends. 1849.

The Kickleburys on the Rhine. 1850.

Stubbs's Calendar; or, The Fatal Boots. 1850.

Rebecca and Rowena: A Romance upon Romance. 1850.

The History of Henry Esmond, Esq. 1852; revised edition, 1858; edited by Gordon N. Ray, 1950.

Men's Wives. 1852.

The Luck of Barry Lyndon: A Romance of the Last Century. 2 vols., 1852–53; revised edition, as *The Memoirs of Barry Lyndon, Esq.,* 1856; edited by Martin J. Anisman, 1970.

The Newcomes: Memoirs of a Most Respectable Family. 2 vols., 1854–55; revised edition, 1863.

The Rose and the Ring; or, The History of Prince Giglio and Prince Bulbo: A Fireside Pantomime for Great and Small Children. 1855; edited by Gordon N. Ray, 1947.

The Virginians: A Tale of the Last Century. 2 vols., 1858–59; revised edition, 1863; edited by George Saintsbury and J. L. Robinson, 1911.

Lovel the Widower. 1860; revised edition, 1861.

The Adventures of Philip on His Way Through the World. 1862.

Denis Duval. 1864.

Verse

The Loving Ballad of Lord Bateman. 1839.

Other

The Yellowplush Correspondence. 1838.

The Paris Sketch Book. 2 vols., 1840.

Comic Tales and Sketches. 2 vols., 1841.

The Irish Sketch Book. 2 vols., 1843.

Notes of a Journey from Cornhill to Grand Cairo, by Way of Lisbon, Athens, Constantinople, and Jerusalem, Performed in the Steamers of the Penninsular and Oriental Company. 1846.

The Book of Snobs. 1848; complete edition, 1852; edited by John Sutherland, 1978.

Miscellanies: Prose and Verse. 2 vols., 1849–51.

The Confessions of Fitz-Boodle, and Some Passages in the Life of Major Gahagan. 1852.

A Shabby Genteel Story and Other Tales. 1852.

Punch's Prize Novelists, The Fat Contributor, and Travels in London. 1853.

The English Humourists of the Eighteenth Century: A Series of Lectures.   1853; revised
   edition, 1853; edited by W. L. Phelps, 1900.
Miscellanies: Prose and Verse.   4 vols., 1855–57.
Christmas Books.   1857.
The Four Georges: Sketches of Manners, Morals, Court and Town Life.   1860.
Roundabout Papers.   1863; edited by J. E. Wells, 1925.
Early and Late Papers, edited by J. T. Fields.   1867.
Miscellanies, vol. 5.   1870.
The Students' Quarter; or, Paris Five and Thirty Years Since.   1874.
The Orphan of Pimlico and Other Sketches, Fragments, and Drawings.   1876.
Sultan Stork and Other Stories and Sketches (1829–1844), edited by R. H.
   Shepherd.   1887.
Reading a Poem.   1891.
Loose Sketches, An Eastern Adventure.   1894.
The Hitherto Unidentified Contributions to Punch, with a Complete Authoritative
   Bibliography from 1845 to 1848, edited by M. H. Spielmann.   1899.
Writings in the National Standard and the Constitutional, edited by W. T.
   Spencer.   1899.
Stray Papers, edited by Lewis Melville.   1901.
The New Sketch Book, Being Essays from the Foreign Quarterly Review, edited by R. S.
   Garnett.   1906.
Contributions to the Morning Chronicle, edited by Gordon N. Ray.   1955.

Bibliography: A Thackeray Library by Henry Sayre Van Duzer, 1919.

Reading List: Thackeray: A Biography by Lewis Melville, 2 vols., 1910; Thackeray: A
Critical Portrait by J. W. Dodds, 1941; Thackeray: A Reconsideration by J. Y. T. Grieg,
1950; Thackeray: The Sentimental Cynic by L. Ennis, 1950; Thackeray the Novelist by
Geoffrey Tillotson, 1954; Thackeray by Gordon N. Ray, 2 vols., 1955–58; Thackeray and
the Form of Fiction by J. Loofbourow, 1964; Thackeray: A Collection of Critical Essays
edited by Alexander Welsh, 1968; Thackeray: The Major Novels by Juliet MacMaster, 1971;
The Exposure of Luxury: Radical Themes in Thackeray by Barbara Hardy, 1972; Thackeray
at Work by John Sutherland, 1974; Thackeray: Prodigal Genius by John Carey, 1977; The
Language of Thackeray by K. C. Phillips, 1978.

*   *   *

   One of the main problems which faces the critic of Thackeray is to determine exactly
where the decline sets in, and how damaging that decline was. John Carey is most severe and
locates the critical point at 1848, consigning all the mature novels into an inferior place.
Carey relishes the savagely satirical early Thackeray of Barry Lyndon and The Book of Snobs.
The post-Vanity Fair fiction represents a "disastrous collapse ... into gentlemanliness and
cordiality." In Carey's diagnosis the calamities of Thackeray's youth were formative of his
genius; separation from his mother, exclusion from his class as a ruined young man, and a
tragic marriage may have been painful, but they were the making of a great writer. After
Vanity Fair "he was destroyed by success." Whether or not this is true, Thackeray was
certainly damaged severely in health after 1849 and not always capable of giving his best,
even if he had been so disposed. Nonetheless most commentators would see the first three
full-sized novels, Vanity Fair, Pendennis, and Esmond, as constituting a sustained major
achievement. Gordon Ray's authoritative opinion as the official biographer is that it was only
at this stage of his career that Thackeray developed a mature moral vision commensurate
with the panoramic range of his fiction and the energy of his satire. Esmond, coming at the
end of this brilliant five-year period, is also uniquely interesting in being the only major novel

which Thackeray wrote entire before publication, appearing as it did in the traditional three volumes rather than as a serial in the magazines or in monthly thirty-two page numbers. The "three-decker" *Esmond* is arguably more carefully executed than Thackeray's other month-to-month writing. The last novels have their supporters, too, and some recent scholars seem inclined to value the whole of Thackeray's output – even the previously maligned *The Virginians* and *Philip* where Thackeray's art is at its most relaxed and loose-knit.

It helps to section Thackeray's career into manageable units. The early phase (1837–47) is rich, heterogeneous, and composed of short pieces of writing for the journals and relatively slim books. (Much of this writing was published in book form only years later.) Since the convention of nineteenth-century magazine writing imposed anonymity on contributors, Thackeray turned a handicap into advantage by cultivating a virtuosity in comic pseudonyms. (His favourite persona was the amiable Michael Angelo Titmarsh; others include Ikey Solomons, Mr. Snob, Our Fat Contributor, Yellowplush, Jeames de la Pluche.) "Writing for his life" meant doing whatever work would pay, for whatever journal would hire him – whether the grand *Edinburgh Review* or Colburn's sublimely snobbish *New Monthly Magazine*. The range of Thackeray's writing at this stage of his life is bewildering. It includes historical and sociological essays, reviewing, reportage (the magnificent "Going to See a Man Hanged," *Fraser's Magazine*, August 1840, should be cited), travel books, literary polemics (especially against Bulwer-Lytton), burlesques (notably the famous 1847 *Punch* parodies, later collected as *Novels by Eminent Hands*), novellas, and illustration work (Thackeray was actually considered as a potential illustrator for *Pickwick Papers*; much of his early work is self-illustrated as are the major novels *Vanity Fair*, *Pendennis*, and *The Virginians*).

Thackeray's versatility at this stage of his writing life is extraordinary. Up to 1847 and the decisive triumph of *Vanity Fair*, it would have been difficult to foresee precisely what career this brilliant man would succeed in – if indeed his restless and often bitter temperament would allow him to succeed in anything. With hindsight, however, we can see two substantial blocks of work in this first decade's writing. First is the material Thackeray contributed to *Fraser's Magazine*, which comprises the bulk of the early fiction. Although Thackeray himself underrated or disavowed this work in later life it remains a major achievement in its own right. It is also clear that the tory-radical tone of *Fraser's* suited Thackeray the reviewer and essayist, and some of his best work of this kind was done in Fraser's columns. His involvement with *Fraser's* diminished in the early 1840's as his other great connection, with *Punch* (founded 1841), began. Thackeray was a staff writer for *Punch* for a number of years and the weekly journal furnished innumerable comic opportunities for his pen and pencil. In addition to myriad squibs (many of which are probably still unidentified) there are longer serial offerings, one of which, *The Snobs of England* (1846–47, later *The Book of Snobs*), stands out. The critique of "snobbery" (a term which Thackeray made current in its familiar sense) organises the often undisciplined hostilities of the younger Thackeray into a coherent analysis of English society. It leads naturally on to the novel whose opening numbers overlapped with *Snobs'* final chapters, *Vanity Fair*. Regrettably, however, *Snobs*, like all Thackeray's *Punch* work, is now more recondite than his *Fraser's* contributions by virtue of the topicality which weekly publication encouraged.

Vanity Fair deserves to be considered a transitional phase of Thackeray's career all by itself. It marks the turning point in his writing career, and possibly his personal life as well. *Vanity Fair* can be seen itself as a novel balanced between two views of life, embodied in the heroines – Becky all intelligence and no heart, Amelia all heart and no intelligence. Thackeray's supposed sympathies and antipathies for the personages in this novel have furnished rich critical debate. Nonetheless it is safe to say that with all its ambiguities this is his great achievement. In the omniscient manner that he was to make his own, Thackeray follows the fortunes of an intertwining group of characters over two decades, offering, in passing, a wonderfully solid panorama of early nineteenth-century England. (Like most mid-nineteenth-century novelists Thackeray preferred to antedate the action of his novels.) For the first time Thackeray indulges expansively in the famous "sermoning," stepping down, as he says, to speak with the reader confidentially. Yet the scenic and narrative responsibilities of the novelist are not evaded as, arguably, they are in some later novels.

After *Vanity Fair* Thackeray's novels conform to a characteristic pattern. All follow the career of a young man (more or less based on Thackeray himself) making his way through the world, gaining a wife and an education in life en route. Two settings predominate, early nineteenth century and eighteenth century. As an historical novelist Thackeray has affinities with Scott; his acquaintance with the eighteenth century was intimate and unforced. (At the time of his death his library was largely composed of volumes from the eighteenth century which he collected with a connoisseur's taste.) *Esmond*, *The Virginians*, *Denis Duval* and the two sets of lectures testify to his ambition, late in life, to write a history of Queen Anne's time. Unfortunately the only substantial realisation of this ambition was the house in Palace Green, Kensington, which was designed to his specification in the Queen Anne style, and to which he moved a year before his death.

It was denied to Thackeray to give up writing fiction; he needed the money too much. Bradbury and Evans paid him £60 a number for *Vanity Fair*, £100 a number for *Pendennis*, £200 a number for *The Newcomes*, and £250 for *The Virginians*. Even at these prices Thackeray was never really comfortably off, and he was facing something of a crisis in 1859, after Bradbury and Evans lost money on his American historical novel. At this stage the dynamic publisher George Smith (who had published *Esmond*, paying £1,200) re-entered Thackeray's professional life. He was made editor of the newly founded *Cornhill Magazine* at a princely salary, which made the last years of his life the most prosperous. Thackeray did not write top-rate fiction for Smith (though *Lovel the Widower* has recently found favour with the critics). On the other hand he did provide for the magazine the magnificent series of essays collected as *The Roundabout Papers*. These benign reflections on life are the best things of their kind Thackeray ever wrote.

—John Sutherland

THOREAU, Henry David. American. Born in Concord, Massachusetts, 12 July 1817. Educated at the Concord Academy, and at Harvard University, Cambridge, Massachusetts, 1833–37, graduated 1837. Writer from 1835; founded a school with his brother in Concord, 1838, also worked with his father in manufacturing lead pencils; began the walks and studies of nature that became the main occupation of his life, 1839; lived with Emerson, and helped him to edit *The Dial*, 1841–43; lived in a shanty in the woods by Walden Pond, 1845–47; again lived with Emerson, 1847; jailed for refusing to pay taxes, 1847; worked at various odd jobs, including gardening, fence building, and land surveying, also lectured and wrote for various periodicals; visited Canada, 1850, and the Maine woods, 1853, 1857; spent his last years in Concord. *Died 6 May 1862.*

PUBLICATIONS

Collections

Complete Works, edited by Harrison G. O. Blake.   5 vols., 1929.
Collected Poems, edited by Carl Bode.   1943; revised edition, 1964.
The Correspondence, edited by Walter Harding and Carl Bode.   1958.

Writings, edited by William L. Howarth.   1971–
Thoreau's Vision: The Major Essays, edited by Charles R. Anderson.   1973.
Selected Works, edited by Walter Harding.   1975.

Prose

A Week on the Concord and Merrimack Rivers.   1849; edited by Carl Hovde and
    others, in *Writings*, 1978.
Walden; or, Life in the Woods.   1854; edited by J. Lyndon Shanley, in *Writings*, 1971.
Excursions, edited by Ralph Waldo Emerson.   1863.
The Maine Woods.   1864; edited by Joseph J. Moldenhauer, in *Writings*, 1972.
Cape Cod.   1865.
Letters to Various Persons, edited by Ralph Waldo Emerson.   1865.
A Yankee in Canada, with Anti-Slavery and Reform Papers.   1865; *Reform Papers*
    edited by Wendell Clark, in *Writings*, 1973.
Early Spring in Massachusetts.   1881; *Summer*, 1884; *Autumn*, 1888; *Winter*, 1892.
Miscellanies.   1894.
The Service, edited by Frank B. Sanborn.   1902.
Sir Walter Raleigh, edited by Henry Aiken Metcalf.   1905.
The First and Last Journeys of Thoreau, edited by Frank B. Sanborn.   2 vols., 1905.
Journals, edited by Bradford Torrey.   14 vols., 1906; edited by Francis H. Allen, 1949;
    Selected Journals edited by Carl Bode, 1967, as *The Best of Thoreau's Journals*, 1971.
The Moon.   1927.
Consciousness at Concord: The Text of Thoreau's Hitherto Lost Journal (1840–1841),
    edited by Perry Miller.   1958.
Literary Notebook, edited by Kenneth Walter Cameron.   1964.
Over Thoreau's Desk: New Correspondence 1838–1861, edited by Kenneth Walter
    Cameron.   1965.
Fact Book, edited by Kenneth Walter Cameron.   2 vols., 1966.
Canadian Notebook, edited by Kenneth Walter Cameron.   1967.

Translator, *The Transmigration of the Seven Brahmans*, edited by Arthur E.
    Christy.   1932.
Translator, *Seven Against Thebes*, by Aeschylus, edited by Leo Max Kaiser.   1960.

Bibliography: *A Bibliography of Thoreau* by Francis H. Allen, 1908; *The Literary
Manuscripts of Thoreau* by William L. Howarth, 1974.

Reading List: *The Concord Saunterer* by Reginald Cook, 1940, revised edition, as *Passage to
Walden*, 1949; "From Emerson to Thoreau" by F. O. Matthiessen, in *American Renaissance:
Art and Expression in the Age of Emerson and Whitman*, 1941; *Thoreau: The Quest and the
Classics* by Ethel Seybold, 1951; *The Making of Walden* by J. Lyndon Shanley, 1957; *The
Shores of America: Thoreau's Inward Exploration* by Sherman Paul, 1958, and *Thoreau: A
Collection of Critical Essays* edited by Paul, 1962; *A Thoreau Handbook*, 1959, and *The Days
of Thoreau: A Biography*, 1965, both by Walter Harding; *The Recognition of Thoreau:
Selected Criticism since 1848* edited by Wendell Glick, 1969; *Thoreau* by Leon Edel, 1970;
Thoreau as Romantic Naturalist by James McIntosh, 1974.

*   *   *

Henry David Thoreau is still remembered in his native town of Concord in Massachusetts
as a quirky man, and indeed he was, but also as a bold economist. "Most men," he said, "lead

lives of quiet desperation," so intent on earning a living that they have no time to live. How much better, he thought, was one day of work and six days at more profitable occupation than six days of labor and one day of rest. Thoreau's work was for a brief period that of school teacher, for a longer time that of a helper in his father's pencil-making business, and latterly that of a surveyor. His occupation was that of an observer and recorder of nature, and of man's proper relation to the world in which he lived. Punning on the correct pronunciation of his name, he called himself a thorough man, and that he was, thoroughly attentive to his daily task of walking, observing, recording, and then painstakingly transcribing into his journals the profits that each day brought. These journals were his storehouse containing materials from which his writings were drawn, and remain a storehouse in which readers today discover quizzical nudgings toward truths.

For to Thoreau truths were not to be captured by declarative frontal attack. They must be warily approached, as any wild thing must be approached, circled cautiously, lest in fear they take flight, or, if sprung on too suddenly become caged in words which inevitably distort. "In wildness," Thoreau announced, "is the preservation of the world." But wildness did not mean wilderness. He was shocked to fear by wind-swept mountain tops, so like primordial chaos. Nature was better with man in it. Thoreau preferred the woodlands, swamplands, and waterways of a man-centered universe. He thought of himself as a "self-appointed inspector of snow-storms and rain-storms," a "surveyor, if not of highways, then of forest paths and across-lots routes," faithfully minding, he said, "my own business."

He had a large sense of drama. He dramatized himself, and he dramatized the world of nature. Though others have been imprisoned for cause of conscience, he is remembered as the one who spent a night in jail for refusal to pay taxes to support a tainted war, and who then wrote an essay in support of "Civil Disobedience" which still remains a handbook for young rebels. When he retired in 1845 to a cabin beside Walden Pond, he chose the 4th of July, the anniversary of America's Declaration of Independence, as the day to take residence there in token of his own independence. He was a supreme egotist, vauntingly unashamed of eccentricities of dress and deportment. His mission was, he said, to crow like Chanticleer, to wake his neighbors up.

He went to his cabin in the woods, not in surly withdrawal from a workaday world. Indeed, he often walked into town, if only to feast on his mother's delicious pies. While officially in residence beside Walden Pond, he took time off for an excursion to Mount Katahdin in Maine. But ordinarily he remained in residence, an eccentric man making daily eccentric pilgrimages around and beyond the still waters of the pond, his evenings spent in recording his daily adventures, culling from them and earlier recordings materials to be made into books or essays. For, like any sensible writer, he sought in his pond-side retreat the quiet and solitude necessary for writing.

While there, again dramatically for exactly two years, two months, and two days, he completed one book and the draft of another. The first was a reminiscent account of a two-week excursion which he and his brother, now deceased, had taken during the summer of 1839, travelling through waterways in a boat of their own construction to the White Mountains in New Hampshire. In composing *A Week on the Concord and Merrimack Rivers*, Thoreau telescoped those two weeks to one and limited himself almost entirely to river adventures. By many, the *Week* is considered Thoreau's most lively book, filled with youthful verve and sombre remembrances, and with observations on men and nature and books, and the livening power of each. "A basket," Thoreau later called it, "of delicate texture," the weaving so fine that, as basket, its strands fall apart to shower a reader with whimsical wisdom and insightful perceptions.

But *A Week* was not well-received when it appeared in 1849. Of an edition of a thousand copies more than seven hundred were returned to him by its publisher unsold. Meanwhile, Thoreau, in residence now in Concord, continued on small excursions, to Cape Cod, again to Maine, but mostly through the outskirts of his native town. He lectured occasionally, but not comfortably nor outstandingly well. He published accounts of his excursions and his essay on civil disobedience, first titled "Resistance to Civil Government." But, if not mostly, most importantly, he puttered over revisions of the second book which had occupied him during his residence beside Walden Pond.

When it appeared in 1854, *Walden; or, Life in the Woods* was better received than *A Week* had been, but the reception was not always enthusiastic, indeed was more than often mocking: who is this humbug, pretending to be a hermit, who has the insolence to tell us how we should live? But no book written in the nineteenth century, except perhaps Karl Marx's *Das Kapital*, has become more of a scripture, a guide, a handbook. Its long first chapter on "Economy" was often reprinted as a tract used by advocates of labor reform on both sides of the Atlantic. Other people built, and still build, secluded small hide-a-ways where work may be done, in art, literature, or contemplation. Many a busy, work-imprisoned person has lived vicariously in an imaginary pond-side retreat of his own. William Butler Yeats is said to have modeled his Innisfree on recollections of *Walden*. W. H. Hudson proclaimed Thoreau "without master or mate ... in the foremost ranks of the prophets."

He condenses his more than two-year residence beside Walden Pond into the four seasons of a single year, joyously through New England's brief summer for twelve chapters, then a single chapter on autumn and three more on winter, an exultant penultimate chapter on spring, moving toward a conclusion which gives final coherence to the cycle, which is not only seasonal but diurnal – day, evening, night, and morning – and which also suggests the ages of man through youth, manhood, old age, death, and finally, with spring and morning, resurrection. Though reprimanding people for work-filled sloth, *Walden* is also a compelling, ecstatic book, a manual of affirmation, confidently asserting in its final sentences, "There is more day to dawn. The Sun is but a morning star."

To most people Thoreau is *Walden*, and *Walden* Thoreau, or, if you wish, thorough. But there was more life to live and record, more excursions to make, more writing to be meticulously done. In his journals he made notes for a Book of the Seasons, which remains in embryo, never put together except by other people who have mined the journals for seasonal lore. When Thoreau died in his mid-fifties, he left sheaves of manuscript as his principal worldly legacy. Most of them have been variously edited by friends or admirers. *Excursions* in 1863 was made up of essays, many of them previously published. *The Maine Woods* in 1864 told of three excursions into the northern wilderness. *Cape Cod* in 1865 and *A Yankee in Canada* in 1866, though not without occasional delicately phrased insights, were, like most of *The Maine Woods*, narratives of travel rather than testaments to an ideal. Thoreau's journals have been published, though not in their entirety, and other people have culled books from them; his letters have been gathered, his poems and translations from the Greek, and his juvenile writings, often neither complete nor completely correct, until in 1971 the Princeton University Press inaugurated a new meticulous edition, now in progress, of his writings.

Thoreau represents many things to many people. To some he is the ultimate nonconformist who brings comfort to those who relish nonconformity in lifestyle or dress. To others, he is an escapist, unhindered by familial responsibilities. Still others suspect that his bachelorhood resulted from fear or distrust of women, or of himself. Naturalists have found him inexpert in identification of species. Ecologists claim him as a pioneer. Civil rebels, from Gandhi to Martin Luther King and beyond, have found him a spark igniting them to action. He was perhaps each of these, but was in total more than the sum of them all. He was a writer, a stylist quite equal to any who in his time or since has managed the flexible complexities of our language. The delicacy of the web that his words construct is too fine to provide the comfort of didacticism. His words fly free to allow each reader to pattern them to dimensions of his own. Everyone, it has been said, gets the Thoreau that he deserves.

—Lewis Leary

THORPE, Thomas Bangs. American. Born in Westfield, Massachusetts, 1 March 1815. Educated at Wesleyan University, Middletown, Connecticut, 1833–36. During the Civil War served as Staff Officer to General Butler, in the United States Volunteers, 1862: Colonel. Married. Painter: maintained a studio in Baton Rouge, Louisiana, 1835–53; writer from 1840; edited the Louisiana Whig newspapers, Concordia *Intelligencer*, 1843, New Orleans *Commercial Times*, 1845, New Orleans *Daily Tropic*, 1846, Baton Rouge *Conservator*, 1847, and New Orleans *National*, 1847; moved to New York City, 1853; contributed to numerous periodicals; Co-Proprietor and Co-Editor, *Spirit of the Times*, New York, 1859–60; Surveyor of the Port of New Orleans, 1862–63; City Surveyor of New York, 1865–69, and Chief of the Warehouse Department of the New York Customs House, 1869–78. *Died 20 September 1878.*

PUBLICATIONS

Fiction and Sketches

   The Mysteries of the Backwoods; or, Sketches of the Southwest. 1846.
   The Hive of the Bee-Hunter: A Repository of Sketches. 1854.
   The Master's House: A Tale of Southern Life. 1854.

Other

   Our Army on the Rio Grande. 1846.
   Our Army at Monterey. 1847.
   The Taylor Anecdote Book: Anecdotes and Letters of Zachary Taylor. 1848.
   Reminiscences of Charles L. Elliott, Artist. 1868.

Reading List: *Thorpe* by Milton Rickels, 1962.

*   *   *

   Thomas Bangs Thorpe, a Northerner who loved the South and lived in Louisiana for many years, is one of the finest writers in the group known as old Southwestern humorists. At his best Thorpe was able to relinquish a formal, educated, fashionable mode of writing for an informal, ungrammatical, humorous view of the old Southwest. Indeed, Thorpe's great talent was his ability to render frontier speech and humor vividly.
   In 1839, Thorpe, a portrait painter by trade, achieved national and international attention with his first essay about the frontier. "Tom Owen, The Bee-Hunter" described an eccentric whom Thorpe had met in the backwoods of Louisiana, a man whose primary interest in life was fearlessly pursuing bees and taking their honey. Unfortunately, in this essay Thorpe used a highly literary language, hardly the language of the frontier, and he thereby held himself and his readers at a considerable distance from his subject.
   This problem of authorial distance was completely solved, however, in Thorpe's masterpiece "The Big Bear of Arkansas," published in 1841. Although he began this tale with a predominantly formal description of the "heterogeneous" passengers on a Mississippi steamboat and ended it in an equally formal style, Thorpe permitted a rather uncouth passenger to tell a tall tale within this frame. Jim Doggett, an Arkansas frontiersman, speaks throughout most of "The Big Bear" and his language is far from literary. His pronunciation (as suggested by misspellings), the rhythms of his speech, his grammatical errors, the idioms

and metaphors he uses are all appropriate to the Western roarer, and form a purposeful, telling contrast to the relatively dull frame style. This contrast is intensified by the exaggerated nature of Jim's frontier humor: Jim reports that in Arkansas beets grow as large as cedar stumps and wild turkeys grow too fat to fly. But the primary exaggeration in this story is not particularly humorous. Doggett says that the big bear seems to raid his farm at will, to have almost supernatural powers, and to loom as large as a "black mist." None of these details sets one laughing. They do, however, suggest that this "creation bar," like Faulkner's bear, is a symbol of a once vast wilderness which itself is doomed. Indeed, Thorpe's bear seems to recognize his inevitable doom and to die, though at Jim's hands, only because "his time come." There is, nevertheless, a joke embedded within this rather melancholy strain. When the bear decides his time has come, he surprises Doggett at a most inopportune moment – the Arkansas hunter is literally caught with his "inexpressibles" down.

Thorpe never equalled this tale. His "second finest frontier story" (according to Milton Rickels), "Bob Herring, The Arkansas Bear Hunter," is certainly of interest. Though Bob Herring is not the ring-tail roarer that Jim Doggett is, he is a realistic frontiersman, and his language is both amusing and authentic. Yet the structure of this story lacks the technical brilliance of "The Big Bear." While "The Big Bear" encloses Jim's yarn within a frame, "Bob Herring" rather awkwardly juxtaposes two bear hunts told from different perspectives. Moreover, the latter story relies extensively upon an imaginative but gentlemanly narrator, and one longs to hear the voice of Bob Herring more pervasively.

Thorpe subsequently published two collections of stories and essays, edited a number of newspapers, wrote a history of the Mexican War, composed a mediocre reform novel, and contributed many articles to national periodicals. But his single most creative product came early in his career and was not to be matched by later works. "The Big Bear of Arkansas" was Thorpe's greatest achievement, one that abetted the rise of realism, dealt with the nature of the frontier, and guaranteed its author a place in American literary history.

—Suzanne Marrs

THURBER, James (Grover). American. Born in Columbus, Ohio, 8 December 1894. Educated at Ohio State University, Columbus. Married 1) Althea Adams in 1922 (divorced, 1935), one daughter; 2) Helen Wismer in 1935. Code Clerk, American Embassy, Paris, 1918–20; Reporter, *Columbus Dispatch,* 1920–24, Paris edition of the *Chicago Tribune,* 1924–26, and the *New York Evening Post,* 1926–27; Editor, then writer, 1927–38, then free-lance contributor, *The New Yorker* magazine; also an illustrator from 1929. Litt.D.: Kenyon College, Gambier, Ohio, 1950; Yale University, New Haven, Connecticut, 1953; L.H.D.: Williams College, Williamstown, Massachusetts, 1951. *Died 2 November 1961.*

PUBLICATIONS

Collections

Vintage Thurber: A Collection of the Best Writings and Drawings. 2 vols., 1963.

Short Stories and Sketches (illustrated by the author)

The Owl in the Attic and Other Perplexities. 1931.
The Seal in the Bedroom and Other Predicaments. 1932.
My Life and Hard Times. 1933.
The Middle-Aged Man on the Flying Trapeze: A Collection of Short Pieces. 1935.
Let Your Mind Alone! and Other More or Less Inspirational Pieces. 1937.
Cream of Thurber. 1939.
The Last Flower: A Parable in Pictures. 1939.
Fables for Our Time and Famous Poems Illustrated. 1940.
My World – and Welcome to It. 1942.
Men, Women, and Dogs: A Book of Drawings. 1943.
The Thurber Carnival. 1945.
The Beast in Me, and Other Animals: A New Collection of Pieces and Drawings about Human Beings and Less Alarming Creatures. 1948.
The Thurber Album: A New Collection of Pieces about People. 1952.
Thurber Country: A New Collection of Pieces about Males and Females, Mainly of Our Own Species. 1953.
Thurber's Dogs: A Collection of the Master's Dogs, Written and Drawn, Real and Imaginary, Living and Long Ago. 1955.
A Thurber Garland. 1955.
Further Fables for Our Time. 1956.
Alarms and Diversions. 1957.
Lanterns and Lances. 1961.
Credos and Curios. 1962.
Thurber and Company. 1966.

Plays

The Male Animal, with Elliott Nugent (produced 1940). 1940.
A Thurber Carnival, from his own stories (produced 1960). 1962.

Wrote the books for the following college musical comedies: *Oh My, Omar,* with Hayward M. Anderson, 1921; *Psychomania,* 1922; *Many Moons,* 1922; *A Twin Fix,* with Hayward M. Anderson, 1923; *The Cat and the Riddle,* 1924; *Nightingale,* 1924; *Tell Me Not,* 1924.

Other

Is Sex Necessary? or, Why You Feel the Way You Do, with E. B. White. 1929.
Many Moons (juvenile). 1943.
The Great Quillow (juvenile). 1944.
The White Deer (juvenile). 1945.
The 13 Clocks (juvenile). 1950.
Thurber on Humor. 1953(?).
The Wonderful O (juvenile). 1955.
The Years with Ross. 1959.

Bibliography: *Thurber: A Bibliography* by Edwin T. Bowden, 1968.

Reading List: *Thurber* by Robert E. Morsberger, 1964; *The Art of Thurber* by Richard C.

Tobias, 1969; *Thurber, His Masquerades: A Critical Study* by Stephen A. Black, 1970; *The Clocks of Columbus: The Literary Career of Thurber* by Charles S. Holmes, 1973, and *Thurber: A Collection of Essays* edited by Holmes, 1974; *Thurber: A Biography* by Burton Bernstein, 1975.

*   *   *

James Thurber, who was not destined to be one of America's celebrated poets, first turned up in the pages of *The New Yorker* on 26 February 1927 with two forgettable bits of verse. His third contribution (5 March 1927) was more indicative of what was to come. Called "An American Romance," it is the account of a "little man in an overcoat that fitted him badly," who stations himself in a revolving door, defying a number of authority figures, and stays there until he is rewarded with instant celebrity. An ur-Walter Mitty, then, caught in an American landscape which Thurber would eventually view more sardonically, almost a fable for our time.

Thurber had been a newspaperman on the Columbus *Dispatch* and the Paris edition of the Chicago *Tribune* and a free-lance contributor to a number of publications before he arrived at *The New Yorker*, but it was with that magazine that his reputation both as writer and cartoonist was made, a reputation that he sometimes saw as limiting to his artistic aspirations. He served on the staff until 1938 and remained a contributor until 1961; eventually he tried to define the quality of the place and his own ambiguous attachment to it in *The Years with Ross*, which E. B. White called "a sly exercise in denigration, beautifully concealed in words of sweetness and love."

Thurber's first book was a collaboration with White, the parody volume *Is Sex Necessary?* His second, *The Owl in the Attic*, initiated the practice of collecting his magazine pieces which he would follow for the rest of his writing life. Sometimes – *My Life and Hard Times*, *Let Your Mind Alone!*, *The Years with Ross* – the group of essays was obviously conceived as a book; in most cases, the mixture is fortuitous, although occasionally, as in *Thurber's Dogs*, held together by a common subject matter. Of his early books, *My Life and Hard Times*, a marvelously funny mock biography, is the most impressive, the more so when one considers that Thurber returned to the same Ohio home ground to do the completely different and equally successful *The Thurber Album*.

There are many Thurbers: the playwright (*The Male Animal*, *A Thurber Carnival*); the author of children's books, of which *The White Deer* and *The 13 Clocks* are the happiest inventions; the adult fabulist of *Fables for Our Time* and *Further Fables*; the canine celebrant (*Thurber's Dogs*); the social observer who could write so well about soap opera ("Soapland" in *The Beast in Me, and Other Animals*); the perceptive critic who could work through parody or direct comment and the concerned artist who defended humor from outside attack and inside timidity in the repressive atmosphere of the 1950's. Through all these, there is a persistent Thurber, the dark humorist who, one way or another, kept asking, as the moral of one of the *Further Fables* puts it, "Oh, why should the shattermyth have to be a crumplehope and a dampenglee?"

—Gerald Weales

TOLKIEN, J(ohn) R(onald) R(euel).   English.   Born in Bloemfontein, South Africa, 3 January 1892; emigrated to England in 1896. Educated at the King Edward VI School, Birmingham; Exeter College, Oxford, B.A. 1915, M.A. 1919. Served with the Lancashire

Fusiliers, 1915–18. Married Edith Mary Bratt in 1916; four children. Worked as an assistant on the Oxford English Dictionary, 1918–20; Reader in English, 1920–23, and Professor of English Language, 1924–25, University of Leeds; at Oxford University: Rawlinson and Bosworth Professor of Anglo-Saxon, 1925–45; Fellow, Pembroke College, 1926–45; Leverhulme Research Fellow, 1934–36; Merton Professor of English Language and Literature, 1945–59; thereafter Emeritus Fellow of Merton College, and Honorary Fellow of Exeter College. Andrew Lang Lecturer, St. Andrews University, 1939; W. P. Ker Lecturer, University of Glasgow, 1953. Also an artist: one-man show, Oxford, 1977. Recipient: *New York Herald Tribune* Children's Book Award, 1938; International Fantasy Award, 1957. D.Litt.: University College, Dublin, 1954; University of Nottingham, 1970; Dr. en Phil. et Lettres: University of Liège, 1954. Fellow, 1957, and Benson Medallist, 1966, Royal Society of Literature. C.B.E. (Commander, Order of the British Empire), 1972. *Died 2 September 1973.*

PUBLICATIONS

Fiction

The Hobbit; or, There and Back Again.   1937.
Farmer Giles of Ham.   1949.
The Lord of the Rings: The Fellowship of the Ring.   1954; *The Two Towers,* 1955; *The Return of the King,* 1956; revised edition, 1966.
Smith of Wootton Major.   1967.
The Father Christmas Letters (juvenile), edited by Baillie Tolkien.   1976.
The Silmarillion.   1977.

Verse

Songs for the Philologists, with others.   1936.
The Adventures of Tom Bombadil and Other Verses from the Red Book.   1962.
The Road Goes Ever On, music by Donald Swann.   1967.
Bilbo's Last Song.   1974.

Other

A Middle English Vocabulary.   1922.
Tree and Leaf (includes story and essay).   1964.
The Tolkien Reader.   1966.
Tree and Leaf, Smith of Wootton Major, The Homecoming of Beorhtnoth Beorhthelm's Son.   1975.

Editor, with E. V. Gordon, *Sir Gawain and the Green Knight.*   1925.
Editor, *Ancrene Wisse.*   1962.

Translator, *Sir Gawain and the Green Knight, Pearl, and Sir Orfeo,* edited by Christopher Tolkien.   1975.

Bibliography: *Tolkien Criticism: An Annotated Checklist* by Richard C. West, 1970; *Tolkien: A Bibliography* by Susan Barbara Melmed, 1972.

Reading List: *Tolkien and the Critics* edited by N. D. Isaacs and R. A. Zimbardo, 1968; *Master of Middle-Earth: The Fiction of Tolkien* by Paul Kocher, 1972; *Tolkien's World* by Randel Helms, 1974; *The Tolkien Companion* by J. E. A. Tyler, 1975; *Tolkien: A Biography* by Humphrey Carpenter, 1977 (includes bibliography).

*   *   *

What may be the central virtue of J. R. R. Tolkien's *The Lord of the Rings* had its origin in accident, but in an accident corresponding so closely to his life's direction as to seem inevitable. It is the sense of a world that, like reality, is dense, indefinitely various, and rooted in a history: a world that contains both an alien viewpoint which would annihilate it if it could comprehend it, and an inner world from which the total universe would be seen in its living and wonderful reality, if we could arrive there. The inner world is that of the elves: in their country, Lothlorien, Sam Gamgee says "I feel as if I were *inside* a song." We have fragments of their language, and the possibility of understanding it haunts the book. We also have fragments, finely conceived in their hideousness, of the speech of the opposed kingdom of Sauron, the language of the orcs. In contrast, the weakest point of the book, the unreliability of the narrative English – which varies from high fustian to banality, with a wide variety of better styles in between – has a Babel-like appropriateness. Roger Sale has suggested that this English is at its best when describing the variety of Tolkien's world, a variety revealed by light, and threatened with reduction to a monotonous, perpetually self-destroying darkness. In contrast, the chronicles of men's battles, where the powerful myth is less directly at work, are exercised on old legendary themes put in to fill out the frame, in which certain irritating mannerisms (e.g., inversion of word order) become conspicuous.

But there is another explanation for this unevenness. The depth and innerness of this world come from its being in origin a mere offshoot of another one. This other world is the actual history of the elves, and of the primitive men who were almost their peers. It was born of Tolkien's lifelong professional and personal absorption in language and myth as the ways in which man understands the actual world. That original history, conceived twenty years before *The Lord of the Rings*, but not published until twenty years after it, as *The Silmarillion*, lacks the continued innerness of its offshoot. What is impressive behind and within a story is not dealt with adequately when it is itself the story, when "the unimaginable hand and mind of Fëanor at their work, while both the White Tree and the Golden were in flower," which we long to perceive in *The Lord of the Rings*, are actually imagined. This is perhaps inevitable: as Tolkien's friend C. S. Lewis continually stressed, the power of romantic wonder is related to its expressing longing for the unimaginable. Tolkien maintained as part of the value of fairy story Chesterton's theory of its capacity to reawaken our sense of the wonder of the actual world (when Tolkien visited Venice, he wrote that it was *elvishly* lovely).

The Silmarillion could never have stood alone. But it is the innerness of *The Lord of the Rings*. The two books confer magnitude on each other; e.g., the discovery that Sauron's orcs were originally elves is a discovery of imagination in Coleridge's sense, of "the echo in the finite mind of the great I AM." Tolkien's own theory of imagination as "subcreation" closely follows Coleridge's. It is by Coleridgean standards that *The Lord of the Rings* should be judged.

Tolkien was persuaded to write it as a sequel to his smaller work, *The Hobbit*, which had been very little involved with his principal myths, just before the Second World War. The moral and emotional pressures of that war, cruelly renewing those of the first war in which his myths were first conceived, seem to have contributed to the imagination with which he transforms his old images in his new myth of the fatal ring of power. The total myth is dazzlingly reflected in microcosmic battles – the defeat of Shelob, for instance. Tom Bombadil arose in Tolkien's mind as the representative of the threatened Oxfordshire and Berkshire countryside: it is significant that at the end of the story it is said that Bombadil would probably take no interest in any of its adventures except in the visit to the Ents, which indeed is probably the most imaginative episode of the book. The Ents are a sort of tree, having the consciousness a tree would have if it waked up.

But the power of the book comes from its turning Tolkien's mythology inside out, so that we see not from the standpoint of the creator Iluvatar, nor of his angels the Valar, nor of elves, nor of men, but from that of something still further from the centre, and smaller, the hobbits. It is the freshness of the world, Ents, Bombadil, Shelob, elves, and all, breaking on their astonished eyes that is the book's freshness. And its morality is derived, as Donald Davie has pointed out, from a thorough-going refusal of the values of greatness and grandeur. In *The Silmarillion* even Beron, the figure who embodies the achievement of greatness from relative littleness, is a hero from the start and perpetually aided by elvish power. In *The Lord of the Rings* heroes, wizards, elves, and rulers cannot be trusted to carry the ring, which will corrupt them in proportion to their greatness. Their doings are relatively uninteresting, and for this reason sometimes uninterestingly told. The central story of the hobbits comes fully to life in the last stages of the carrying of the ring to its destruction by Frodo and Sam, of which the point is dogged determination described from step to step, and in which wonder is restricted to amazement at their success – what Tolkien called the "eucatastrophe" of fairy story and regarded as its religious message about the universe.

With all great romances (e.g., *Gawain and the Green Knight*), our wish-fulfilment fantasy of identification with the hero and entry into a world which finds glory in our common experience is paid for by imaginative hard work, and by the discovery of a fallibility which we are obliged to recognize as our own. I think we must concede the name of great romance to *The Lord of the Rings*.

—Stephen Medcalf

TOOMER, Jean (Nathan Eugene Toomer). American. Born in Washington, D.C., 26 December 1894. Educated at high schools in Brooklyn, New York, and Washington, D.C.; University of Wisconsin, Madison, 1914; American College of Physical Training, Chicago, 1916; New York University, summer 1917; City College of New York, 1917. Married 1) Margery Latimer in 1931 (died, 1932), one daughter; 2) Marjorie Content, 1934. Taught physical education in a school near Milwaukee, 1918; clerk in Acker, Merrall, and Conduit grocery company, New York, 1918; shipyard worker, New York; worked at Howard Theatre, Washington, D.C., 1920. Writer after 1922. Studied at Gurdjieff's Institute in Fontainebleau, France, 1924, 1926. *Died 30 March 1967.*

PUBLICATIONS

Fiction

Cane (includes verse). 1923.

Play

Balo, in *Plays of Negro Life,* edited by Alain Locke and Gregory Montgomery. 1927.

Other

Essentials (aphorisms).   1931.

Bibliography: "Toomer: An Annotated Checklist of Criticism" by John M. Reilly, in *Resources for American Literary Study*, Spring 1974.

Reading List: *In a Minor Chord* (on Toomer, Cullen, and Hurston) by Darwin T. Turner, 1971; *The Merrill Studies in Cane* edited by Frank Durham, 1971; *The Grotesque in American Negro Fiction: Toomer, Wright, and Ellison* by Fritz Gysin, 1975.

*   *   *

In a startling image of fulfillment Jean Toomer likened the descendants of slaves among whom he sought poetic motive to "purple ripened plums," the seed of one becoming "An everlasting song, a singing tree,/Caroling softly souls of slavery,/What they were, and what they are to me." The lyric containing this image, "Song of the Son," serves as one of the impressionistic epigraphs uniting *Cane* into a symbolic account of Toomer's effort to reconcile the technical sophistication of Harlem Renaissance art with folk life. His assertion that black rural life in Georgia provided him with the soil for a living literature ratified the cultural nationalism of the Renaissance, while the experimental form of this book demonstrated its kinship with literary modernism. For contemporaries, then, *Cane* promised a vitally new art.

Each of the stories, sketches, and poems making up *Cane* examines the possibility of intutive self-fulfillment. In the first part of the book, set in the South, a series of female characters achieve momentary redemption through expression of spontaneous feelings. The second part, set in Washington, D.C. variously represents characters whose feelings are blocked by social artifice. The whole concludes with a story-play in which the central figure, Kabnis, has internalized the violence and repression of caste relations so effectively that he is terrified of opening his senses at all. The complex intermingling of impressionism, expressionism, and generic forms in *Cane*, therefore, constitutes an argument for the spontaneity associated with "primitivism."

The tension between sophistication and spontaneity remained a dynamic source for Renaissance writers, but not for Toomer. Shortly after *Cane* was published he met Gurdjieff, had a mystical experience, and turned his life-long need for meaning toward a search for a transcendent principle of unity. One consequence was denial of the significance of racial identity. Another was production of writing increasingly distant from the sensual style of *Cane*. Toomer, once a harbinger of new art, became an enigmatic historical figure.

Only a small portion of his later writings was published. For critics the most notable piece has been "Blue Meridian," a long, visionary poem about a new American race, which at its best resonates with the inspiration of Whitman. One must conclude that in Toomer biographical experience overwhelmed creative imagination. A search for identity became so compelling that he could no longer gain the distance needed to convert the motive of his life into the substance of successful literature.

—John M. Reilly

TOURGÉE, Albion W(inegar). American. Born in Williamsfield, Ohio, 2 May 1838. Educated at Kingsville Academy, Ohio, 1854–59; University of Rochester, New York, 1859–61, B.A. 1862; studied law: admitted to the Ohio bar, 1864. Served in the 27th New York Volunteers, 1861: wounded at the first Battle of Bull Run, 1861; Lieutenant in the 105th Ohio Regiment, 1862–64: prisoner of war, 1863. Married Emma L. Kilbourne in 1863; one daughter. Assistant Principal of a school in Wilson, New York, 1861; taught and wrote for a newspaper in Erie, Pennsylvania, 1864–65; settled in Greensboro, North Carolina, 1865; practised law; entered politics for "carpet-bagger" interests, 1866; founded the *Union Register*, which failed, 1867; delegate to the "carpet-bag" conventions, 1868, 1875; Judge of the Superior Court of North Carolina, 1868–75; writer from 1874; Pension Agent at Raleigh, North Carolina, 1876–78; moved to New York, 1879, and settled in Mayville, 1881; Editor, *Our Continent*, Philadelphia, 1882–84; regular contributor to the *Daily Inter Ocean*, Chicago, 1885–98; founded *The Basis: A Journal of Citizenship*, Buffalo, New York, 1895–96; United States Consul-General at Bordeaux, 1897 until his death. Died 21 May 1905.

PUBLICATIONS

Fiction

> *Toinette.* 1874; as *A Royal Gentleman,* 1881.
> *Figs and Thistles: A Western Story.* 1879.
> *A Fool's Errand.* 1879; revised edition, incorporating *The Invisible Empire,* 1880; edited by John Hope Franklin, 1961.
> *Bricks Without Straw.* 1880; edited by Otto H. Olsen, 1969.
> *'Zouri's Christmas.* 1881.
> *John Eax and Marmelon; or, The South Without the Shadow.* 1882.
> *Hot Plowshares.* 1883.
> *Button's Inn.* 1887.
> *Black Ice.* 1888.
> *With Gauge and Swallow, Attorneys.* 1889.
> *Murvale Eastmas, Christian Socialist.* 1890.
> *Pactolus Prime.* 1890.
> *'89.* 1891.
> *A Son of Old Harry.* 1892.
> *Out of the Sunset Sea.* 1893.
> *An Outing with the Queen of Hearts.* 1894.
> *The Mortgage on the Hip-Roof House.* 1896.
> *The Man Who Outlived Himself* (stories). 1898.

Play

> *A Fool's Errand,* with Steele MacKaye, from the novel by Tourgée, edited by Dean H. Keller. 1969.

Other

> *The Code of Civil Procedure of North Carolina,* with Victor C. Barringer and Will B. Rodman. 1878.

An Appeal to Caesar. 1884.
The Veteran and His Pipe (essays). 1886.
Letters to a King. 1888.
The War of the Standards: Coin and Credit Versus Coin Without Credit. 1896.
The Story of a Thousand, Being a History of the 105th Volunteer Infantry, 1862 to 1865. 1896.
A Civil War Diary, edited by Dean H. Keller. 1965.

Bibliography: "A Checklist of the Writings of Tourgée" by Dean H. Keller, in *Studies in Bibliography 18,* 1965.

Reading List: *Tourgée* by Roy Floyd Dibble, 1921; *Tourgée* by Theodore L. Gross, 1963; *Carpetbagger's Crusade: The Life of Tourgée* by Otto H. Olsen, 1965.

*   *   *

Albion W. Tourgée's views on the art of the novel and his own practice as a novelist carry the unmistakable stamp of his active involvement as a journalist, polemicist, and judge in the political and public issues of the Reconstruction period in the United States. His unreserved preference for historical veracity, content, and social purpose (as implied in his criticism of James) always took precedence over the subtleties of technique and the nuances of character portrayal. Observing no separation between the role of the novelist and that of the historian, he conceived of the novel-form essentially as a frame for "a possible life ... in a true environment," insisting that the test of artistic success was inevitably the consistency with which such a life related to its milieu and to the dominant predispositions of the age. Interestingly enough, such a conviction did not bring him any closer to the writers of a realist and naturalist persuasion whose treatment of human depravity and poverty he found crude and repulsive. His admiration, sometimes carried to uncritical extremes, was for the realism of Cooper's descriptions, for there he found the ideals of love, truth, and purity that were worthy of emulation by the citizen of a New Republic. That he was the author of *The Code of Civil Procedure of North Carolina* and the editor of *The Union Register*, a newspaper firmly committed to radical reformist measures, also accounts for his fascination with such noble ideals.

Tourgée's best novels, *A Fool's Errand*, recounting a carpetbagger's grim struggle to work for the cause of equality and pacificism in the South, and *Bricks Without Straw*, concerned with an uneducated but enlightened black man's attempt to achieve selfhood, amplify and illustrate his prominent fictional themes and moral concerns – the possibility of social amelioration, the problem of vindicating one's cherished beliefs in a hostile society, the responses evoked by the tender and redemptive sentiment of love, sympathy for the Negroes, and the selflessness of the Republican set against the cupidity of the Southern white supremacist intent on denying political and civil rights to the Negro. To these are added a preacher's zeal and intensity, a penchant for melodrama, a forceful style and a penetrating if occasionally biased reading of the political climate in the South in the 1860's and 1870's. Tourgée's commitment to such themes and values places him securely, in Edmund Wilson's incontestable judgment, in the "second category of writers who aim primarily at social history. His narrative has spirit and movement; his insights are brilliantly revealing, and they are expressed with emotional conviction."

The inwardness of the imagination that Tourgée sought to exploit in his later fiction on his return to the North in 1879 produced poor and disappointing results. The absence of concrete historical, political, and social contexts often led him to write sentimental romantic tales abounding with improbable coincidences and permeated by an impractical ethical and religious humanitarianism. Thus, if in *Black Ice* a somnambulist, who has climbed to the top of a snowy mountain in search of her baby's grave, is heroically rescued, in *Button's Inn* the hero, an ex-murderer, is redeemed by conversion to Mormonism. The relative success of *'89*, in which Tourgée returned to his earlier themes in the original Southern setting, showed that he obviously was at ease in the comforts of a familiar environment and that he wrote most competently when called upon to provide a kind of fictional *apologia* of Radical Republicanism.

—Chirantan Kulshrestha

TRAVEN, B.   Pseudonym for a writer about whom very little is known. Most frequently identified with an American, Berwick Traven Torsvan: probably born in Chicago in 1890; lived in Germany during World War I; writer from 1926; lived in Mexico from the 1920's or 1930's until his death: Mexican citizen, 1951; married Rosa Elena Lujan in 1957. *Died 26 March 1969.*

Fiction

Das Totenschiff.   1926(?); as *The Death Ship,* 1934.
Der Wobbly.   1926; as *Die Baumwollpflücker,* 1929; as *The Cotton-Pickers,* 1956.
Der Schatz der Sierra Madre.   1927; as *The Treasure of the Sierra Madre,* 1934.
Der Busch (stories).   1928.
Die Brücke im Dschungel.   1929; as *The Bridge in the Jungle,* 1938.
Die Weisse Rose.   1929; as *The White Rose,* 1965.
Der Karren.   1930; as *The Carreta,* 1935.
Regierung.   1931; as *Government,* 1935.
Der Marsch ins Reich de Caoba: Ein Kriegsmarsch.   1933; as *March to Caobaland,* 1961; as *March to the Monteria,* 1963.
Die Rebellion der Gehenkten.   1936; as *The Rebellion of the Hanged,* 1952.
Die Troza.   1936.
Ein General Kommt aus dem Dschungel.   1940; as *The General from the Jungle,* 1954.
Macario (in German).   1950.
Aslan Norval (in German).   1960.
Stories by the Man Nobody Knows: Nine Tales.   1961.
The Night Visitor and Other Stories.   1966.
Maze of Love.   1967.
The Kidnapped Saint and Other Stories, edited by Rosa Elena Lujan and Mina C. and H. Arthur Klein.   1977.

Other

Land der Frühlings (on Mexico).   1928.
Sonnen-Schöpfung: Indianische Legende.   1936; as *The Creation of the Sun and the Moon,* 1968.

Bibliography: "A Checklist of the Work of Traven and the Critical Estimates and Biographical Essays on Him" by E. R. Hagemann, in *Papers of the Bibliographical Society of America 53,* 1959.

1207

Reading List: *Anonymity and Death: The Fiction of Traven* by Donald O. Chankin, 1975; *Traven: An Introduction* by Michael L. Baumann, 1976.

*   *   *

B. Traven kept his identity a closely guarded secret and never gave interviews to the press. He was probably born in Chicago of American Scandinavian parents; he had Marxist leanings, wrote usually in German, and died in Mexico City. His novel *The General from the Jungle* tells the story of a rebellion of Indians against a Mexican dictator. Among adventure writers he deserves a high place — on the same level as Jack London — while some of his themes bring to mind Conrad.

In all his fiction Traven is concerned with the problem of Mammon. "Gold is the devil," says one of the characters in *The Treasure of Sierra Madre* — a book on which John Huston based a successful film. Traven's most famous novel, and his finest, is *The Death Ship*. When it first came out in the mid-1930's in Germany, it sold over 200,000 copies before it was banned. Sub-titled "The Story of an American Sailor," it might be better described as the story of a hero without a name, for the author regards the sailor on a death ship as a gladiatorial hero whose Emperor is Mammon. Death ships are those which carry contraband, with ammunition and rifles hidden in crates labelled "Toys" or "Cocoa" or "Corned Beef." The crews are enlisted from men on the run — no names, no questions — or from seamen who have lost their papers and so have no status. This is what happens to Traven's hero, who is informed by the American consul in Paris: "I doubt your birth as long as you have no certificate of birth. The fact that you are sitting in front of me is no proof of your birth."

Later, Traven's hero, after a series of adventures with the Belgian and Dutch police and a short spell in a prison in Toulouse, finds himself aboard the *Yorikke*, a death ship that has put into Barcelona. Taken on as a fireman, he is made to work as a coal-shoveller. In a ship as old and patched up as the *Yorikke*, there is a constant danger that he may be burnt by the darts of scalding steam which continually escape from the pipes. He has to learn to slither from point to point like a snake. "Only the best snake dancers survived.... Others who had tried and failed were no longer alive." (In another novel, *March to Caobaland*, Traven writes: "Indian mahogany workers can be fed as royally as the stokers and oilers of a death ship where, as a rule, the food is of the lowest quality possible.")

The Nazis banned *The Death Ship* because they thought it Communist; some critics have made the same charge about Traven's other books. But this is to misinterpret them. Traven's fiction is as much an attack on bureaucrats, whatever their political creed, as it is a protest against the dictatorial power which money can invest in one man over another. Labour camps, no less than sweated labour, are both a part of the world of Mammon.

—Neville Braybrooke

TRESSELL, Robert. Pseudonym for Robert Noonan. Irish. Born in Dublin, probably in 1870. Educated in a grammar school in Dublin or, possibly, in London, until his mid-teens. Married in 1890 (separated, 1893); one daughter. Lived in Johannesburg, South Africa, 1897–99; in Hastings, Sussex, by 1902; employed as a painter and sign-writer in Hastings, 1902–10; writer from 1907. Member, Social Democratic Federation, 1906–07. Tubercular: *died 3 February 1911.*

Publications

Fiction

The Ragged Trousered Philanthropists, edited by Jessie Pope. 1914; edited by Frederick C. Ball, 1955.

Play

The Ragged Trousered Philanthropists, from his own novel (produced 1928). 1928.

Reading List: *Tressell of Mugsborough* by Frederick C. Ball, 1951, revised edition, as *One of the Damned: The Life and Times of Tressell*, 1973; *Tressell and the Ragged Trousered Philanthropists* by Jack Mitchell, 1969.

*   *   *

Robert Tressell's *The Ragged Trousered Philanthropists* is the first English novel in which working-class life is realistically depicted by a member of the working class, without condescension and without sentiment. The rather patronizing, moralistic attitude pervading such predecessors as Dickens's *Hard Times* and Gaskell's *Mary Barton* is abhorred in Tressell and overtly mocked. His depiction is at once more analytic and empathetic, and more detailed, verisimilar, and panoramic.

Dying of tuberculosis while working as a house painter, Tressell wrote the novel during the years 1907–10, partly in order to assure his daughter's financial security. She edited it for publication after his death, and excised a third of Tressell's manuscript, eliminated whole sections and characters, and transferred passages from one chapter to another, muting the workmen's profanity and the narrator's attacks on religion and capitalist morality. The original editor (and her successors) sought to bring the novel into line with the Naturalist literary fashions of the day, to the point where the abridged novel ends on the Socialist hero contemplating suicide. This novel was a best-seller in England in 1918, in 1925–27, and in the 1940's. The original work, restored and published in 1955, is steadily gaining acclaim as both "the classic working-class novel" and "the unique and memorable world" of a literary imagination that tends not toward Naturalism, but toward fable.

The title page reads "The Ragged Trousered Philanthropists, Being the story of twelve months in Hell, told by one of the damned, and written down by Robert Tressell." The inferno is the resort town of Mugsborough of 1903, its building industry and the destitution of the building-trades workers and their wives and children. The story is structured as a circle with a half dozen spokes, or sub-plots about individual families, converging upon a center, "the job," where the workmen gather daily to labor and, during breaks, exchange jokes and news. Action is minimal, consisting of the decline from a slight employment boom to a slump, punctuated with various illnesses, births, and deaths, a parliamentary election, and an occasional Church or Town Council meeting. Through extensive dialogue, the novel focuses upon the attitudes of the workers toward one another and their relations with their exploiters on all levels of British society.

Tressell derives much of his satirical strength from his framework of fable, recalling medieval moralities and Restoration comedies. Such leading citizens of Mugsborough as Mr. Sweater, Mr. Grinder, and Mr. Didlum grind and sweat the workers employed by such companies as Makehaste & Sloggitt and Snatchem & Graball. The sub-foreman Cross grovels to the foreman Hunter, whom the men mock as "Nimrod," and he in turn grovels to the owner Rushton. The capitalist caricatures interlock to constitute middle-class society, being not only employers but also store-owners, landlords, rate-setters, leaders of the Town Council and the Shining Light Chapel. The workmen enthusiastically elect Sweater to Parliament.

This satirical frame encloses the core of Tressell's novel, his detailed realistic depictions of the workmen's lives. The routine dread of unemployment, the debilitating squalor of poor housing, the fear of creditors, of illness, indeed of the precarious odds of survival, force the workmen to compete with one another as intensely as their employers compete for contracts. The ragged-trousered philanthropists are the typical workmen of the Edwardian era, who view such brutal conditions as natural, their lot in a well-ordered world, and consider fine meals and education "Not for the Likes of Us!," eagerly ratifying their oppression. Tressell's comic irony, of a subtlety rare in satirists, gives the novel its sinew and life. His motley team of house painters are engaged in decorating a home for someone else. Their lively discussions, during lunch breaks, dramatize both their clashing temperaments and their enduring vigor and humor as a class. No small part of the novel's popular appeal, even as abridged, has been Tressell's tragi-comic portrayal of working-class culture, its jokes and its politics. The Socialist protagonist Frank Owen makes little headway in lunch-time lectures on their condition, even as it worsens and as public events confirm his class thesis. He wins a few sympathizers, however, and the novel ends on their failing health and dogged hope.

Tressell is not a propagandist but a novelist using the resources of fable and satire to delineate a workingman's view of his colleagues and their condition. He constructs intricate sets of contrasts and parallels, as in the subtle analogies between the workmen Philpot and Slyme or the contrasts between Hunter-as-foreman on the job and Hunter-as-evangelist on a streetcorner. The return from a day's outing, in four carriages that soon are wildly racing one another, develops into a mock-epic stampede to the future with the capitalist carriage in the lead and the drinkers and the Christians and the Socialists all shrieking in pursuit. The symbolic overtones are incidental to the realism but pervasive, and the effect is a cumulative impression of a modern morality tale.

—Jan Hokenson

TRILLING, Lionel. American. Born in New York City, 4 July 1905. Educated at Columbia University, New York, B.A. 1925, M.A. 1926, Ph.D. 1938. Married the writer Diana Rubin in 1929; one child. Instructor in English, University of Wisconsin, Madison, 1926–27, and Hunter College, New York, 1927–32; Instructor, 1932–39, Assistant Professor, 1939–45, Associate Professor, 1945–48, Professor of English, 1948–70, Woodberry Professor of Literature and Criticism, 1965–70, University Professor, 1970–74, and University Professor Emeritus, 1974–75, Columbia University. George Eastman Visiting Professor, Oxford University, 1964–65; Norton Visiting Professor of Poetry, Harvard University, Cambridge, Massachusetts, 1969–70; Visiting Fellow, All Souls College, Oxford, 1972–73. Founder, with John Crowe Ransom and F. O. Matthiessen, and Senior Fellow, Kenyon School of Letters, Kenyon College, Gambier, Ohio, later the Indiana University School of Letters, Bloomington. Recipient: Brandeis University Creative Arts Award, 1968. D.Litt.: Trinity College, Hartford, Connecticut, 1955; Harvard University, 1962; Case-Western Reserve University, Cleveland, 1968; University of Durham, 1973; University of Leicester, 1973; L.H.D.: Northwestern University, Evanston, Illinois, 1963; Brandeis University, Waltham, Massachusetts, 1974; Yale University, New Haven, Connecticut, 1974. Member, National Institute of Arts and Letters, 1951; American Academy of Arts and Sciences, 1952. *Died 5 November 1975.*

PUBLICATIONS

Fiction

The Middle of the Journey.   1947.

Other

Matthew Arnold.   1939; revised edition, 1949.
E. M. Forster.   1943; revised edition, 1965.
The Liberal Imagination: Essays on Literature and Society.   1950.
The Opposing Self: Nine Essays in Criticism.   1955.
Freud and the Crisis of Our Culture.   1956.
A Gathering of Fugitives.   1956.
Beyond Culture: Essays on Literature and Learning.   1965.
Sincerity and Authenticity.   1972.
Mind in the Modern World.   1973.

Editor, *The Portable Matthew Arnold.*   1949; as *The Essential Matthew Arnold,* 1969.
Editor, *Selected Letters of John Keats.*   1951.
Editor, *Selected Short Stories of John O'Hara.*   1956.
Editor, with Steven Marcus, *The Life and Works of Sigmund Freud,* by Ernest
   Jones.   1961.
Editor, *The Experience of Literature: A Reader with Commentaries.*   1967.
Editor, *Literary Criticism: An Introductory Reader.*   1970.
Editor, with others, *The Oxford Anthology of English Literature.*   1972.

Reading List: *Three American Moralists: Mailer, Bellow, Trilling* by Nathan A. Scott, Jr.,
1973; *Trilling: Negative Capability and the Wisdom of Avoidance* by Robert Boyers, 1977.

*   *   *

Lionel Trilling was one of America's most distinguished literary critics. His first two books
were on Matthew Arnold and E. M. Forster, and these were followed by a number of essays
in which, like Arnold and Forster, he tried to show how liberal cultural values fostered by the
study of literature could help civilization. In some of his later works, especially perhaps in
Beyond Culture, this liberal stance, though aggressively stated, is maintained with a good deal
of pessimism.
   An equal pessimism is found in some of Trilling's short stories and his one novel, *The
Middle of the Journey.* The hero of this novel, John Laskell, recovering from a serious illness,
visits his friends the Crooms in a Connecticut village. He finds himself involved with a
woman in the village, Emily Caldwell, whose husband, Duck, works for the Crooms. A
fleeting affair with Emily has little chance of success as her daughter Susan dies, attacked by
the drunken Duck, though she has a weak heart and her death is accidental. The Crooms,
who are presented unsympathetically, maintain that it is society, not Duck, who is
responsible, whereas another friend of Laskell's, Gifford Maxim, a renegade communist who
has adopted a Christian stance and whose defection is bitterly resented by the Crooms, thinks
that Duck is guilty. Laskell takes up an indeterminate position, but does not feel that the
rejection of the dogmatism of his friends is particularly effective, any more than his gesture of
paying for Susan's funeral achieves anything. Written before the McCarthy witchhunts had
brought the issue of communism in America into the limelight, *The Middle of the Journey*

may seem a confusing novel at a time when McCarthy himself is virtually forgotten. But *The Middle of the Journey* is not just a novel about communism versus Christianity, as it might seem to be at first sight; it is, perhaps a little too obviously, a novel which strives to assert the liberal values of E. M. Forster and Matthew Arnold in an unsympathetic world, and as such, should take its place with Trilling's critical works.

—T. J. Winnifrith

TROLLOPE, Anthony. English. Born in London, 24 April 1815; son of the novelist Frances Trollope. Educated at Harrow School, 1822–25, 1831–33, and Winchester College, 1825–30. Married Rose Heseltine in 1844; two sons. Classical usher in a school in Brussels; joined the British Post Office, 1834: Surveyor's Clerk, later Deputy Surveyor, in Bangher, Clonmel, and Belfast, Northern Ireland, 1841–54; Chief Surveyor, Dublin, 1854–59; Chief Surveyor of the Eastern District, London, 1859–67: suggested the use of letter boxes; made official journeys to the West Indies, 1858, Egypt, 1858, and the United States, 1862; writer from 1843; one of the founders of the *Fortnightly Review*, 1865; Editor, *St. Paul's Magazine*, 1867–70; stood for Parliament as Liberal candidate for Beverley, 1868; travelled in Australia and New Zealand, 1871–72, and South Africa, 1878. *Died 6 December 1882.*

PUBLICATIONS

Collections

> *The Trollope Reader*, edited by Esther Cloudman Dunn and Marion E. Dodd. 1947.
> *Oxford Trollope*, edited by Michael Sadleir and Frederick Page. 15 vols., 1948–54.
> *Letters*, edited by Bradford A. Booth. 1951.

Fiction

> *The Macdermotts of Ballycloran.* 1847.
> *The Kellys and the O'Kellys; or, Landlords and Tenants: A Tale of Irish Life.* 1848.
> *La Vendée: A Historical Romance.* 1850.
> *The Warden.* 1855.
> *Barchester Towers.* 1857.
> *The Three Clerks.* 1858.
> *Doctor Thorne.* 1858.
> *The Bertrams.* 1859.
> *Castle Richmond.* 1860.
> *Framley Parsonage.* 1861.
> *Tales of All Countries.* 2 vols., 1861–63.
> *Orley Farm.* 2 vols., 1861–62.
> *The Struggles of Brown, Jones, and Robinson, by One of the Firm.* 1862.
> *Rachel Ray.* 1863.
> *The Small House at Allington.* 1864.

Can You Forgive Her? 1864.
Miss Mackenzie. 1865.
The Belton Estate. 1866.
The Claverings. 1867(?).
Nina Balatka. 1867.
The Last Chronicle of Barset. 1867; edited by Peter Fairclough, 1967.
Lotta Schmidt and Other Stories. 1867.
Linda Tressel. 1868.
Phineas Finn, The Irish Member. 1869.
He Knew He Was Right. 1869.
The Vicar of Bullhampton. 1870.
An Editor's Tales. 1870.
Sir Harry Hotspur of Humblethwaite. 1870.
Mary Gresley. 1871.
Ralph the Heir. 1871.
The Golden Lion of Granpère. 1872.
The Eustace Diamonds. 1872.
Lady Anna. 1873.
Phineas Redux. 1874.
Harry Heathcote of Gangoil: A Tale of Australian Bush Life. 1874.
The Way We Live Now. 1875.
The Prime Minister. 1876.
The American Senator. 1877.
Christmas at Thompson Hall. 1877; as *Thompson Hall*, 1885.
Is He Popenjoy? 1878.
How the Mastiffs Went to Iceland. 1878.
The Lady of Launay. 1878.
An Eye for an Eye. 1879.
John Caldigate. 1879.
Cousin Henry. 1879.
The Duke's Children. 1880.
Dr. Wortle's School. 1881.
Ayala's Angel. 1881.
Why Frau Frohmann Raised Her Prices and Other Stories. 1881.
The Fixed Period. 1882.
Marion Fay. 1882.
Kept in the Dark. 1882.
Not If I Know It. 1883.
The Two Heroines of Plumplington. 1882.
Mr. Scarborough's Family. 1883.
The Landleaguers. 1883.
An Old Man's Love. 1884.

Plays

Did He Steal It? 1869; edited by R. H. Taylor, 1952.
The Noble Jilt, edited by Michael Sadleir. 1923.

Other

The West Indies and the Spanish Main. 1859.
North America. 2 vols., 1862; edited by Robert Mason, 1968.

Hunting Sketches. 1865.
Travelling Sketches. 1866.
Clergymen of the Church of England. 1866.
The Commentaries of Caesar. 1870.
Australia and New Zealand.   2 vols., 1873; *Australia* edited by P. D. Edwards and R.
    B. Joyce, 1967.
Iceland. 1878.
South Africa.   2 vols., 1878; revised abridgement, 1879.
Thackeray. 1879.
The Life of Cicero.   2 vols., 1880.
Lord Palmerston. 1882.
An Autobiography, edited by H. M. Trollope.   2 vols., 1883; edited by Michael Sadleir,
    1947.
London Tradesmen, edited by Michael Sadleir.   1927.
Four Lectures, edited by Morris L. Parrish.   1938.
The Tireless Traveller: Twenty Letters to the Liverpool Mercury, 1875, edited by
    Bradford A. Booth.   1941.
The New Zealander, edited by N. John Hall.   1972.

Editor, *British Sports and Pastimes.*   1868.

Bibliography: *Trollope: A Bibliography* by Michael Sadleir, 1928, revised edition, 1934.

Reading List: *Trollope: A Commentary* by Michael Sadleir, 1927, revised edition, 1945;
Trollope by B. C. Brown, 1950; *Trollope: A Critical Study* by A. O. J. Cockshut, 1955;
Trollope: Aspects of His Life and Work by Bradford A. Booth, 1958; *The Changing World of
Trollope* by Robert M. Pohlemus, 1968; *Trollope's Political Novels,* 1968, and *Trollope,* 1978,
both by Arthur Pollard; *Trollope: The Critical Heritage* edited by Donald Smalley, 1969; *A
Guide to Trollope* by Winifred and James Gerould, 1975; *Trollope: His Life and Art* by C. P.
Snow, 1975; *The Novels of Trollope* by James R. Kincaid, 1977; *Trollope's Later Novels* by
Robert Tracy, 1978.

*   *   *

   Anthony Trollope was the most prolific of the great Victorian novelists. He produced 47
novels, more than any of his major contemporaries. The system behind Trollope's
unremitting industry was revealed in his *Autobiography,* where he attributed his success to
getting up early and writing by the clock; he aimed to do three hours work before breakfast,
composing 250 words every quarter an hour. The *Autobiography* also tots up Trollope's
literary earnings which then amounted to nearly £70,000; at his peak he could command
£3,000 for a three volume work. He describes this total as "comfortable, but not splendid."
The early hours were necessary because for the first 24 years of his writing life he was also an
official of the General Post Office in which he rose from scruffy beginnings to a high position.
His extensive journeys on business were turned to authorial advantage: he continued to write
on board ship and even in trains. Trollope's travel books, short stories, journalism, and other
non-fictional work filled out a life of intense activity. The solidity and wide range of
Trollope's fiction partly rests on the thorough knowledge of the world thus gained. Trollope
also had before him the example of his mother, who had made herself into a best-selling
author after the bankruptcy of his father; his brother T. A. Trollope also became a well-
known writer.
   Although reticent about such matters as his marriage and a near-fatal illness, the
Autobiography is generally notable for its candour, and Trollope would probably have felt it
dishonest to suppress any account of the methods by which his staggering output was kept

up. For those who take a romantic view of authorship, Trollope's insistence that writing novels is a trade like any other – shoe-making, for instance – will seem philistine. How can genuine art be combined with clock-watching? How can a writer who finishes one book only to start immediately on the next (as Trollope often did) be inspired or even serious? Trollope's industry might be excused on the grounds that he was simply writing for the market; he was certainly lucky in that a market for his kind of fiction was readily available. Even though three-volume novels were expensive, the circulating libraries spread the reputation and ensured the sales of authors who were prepared to work within mid-Victorian conventions and restraints, as Trollope largely was (although in one novel, *The Vicar of Bullhampton*, he did take a fallen woman as his subject). But the market was clearly not Trollope's only consideration; if it had been, he would not have glutted it so recklessly by over-production. In reality, his apparently effortless production was made possible by the incessant, even addictive activity of his imagination. Trollope was able to write so much so quickly because of the intense vitality of the people in his mind.

The origins of this fantasy-life lay in Trollope's unhappy youth. He had been miserable at both the schools he went to (Winchester and Harrow); his family hovered between gentility and destitution; he was separated for long periods from his mother and left with an increasingly unbalanced father. When he got a clerkship in the General Post Office he had to make his own way in London with little moral or economic support. For ten years he kept a journal (later destroyed) which taught him facility of expression, but more important for the future novelist was his habit of making up stories for himself. Although daydreams, these narratives were nevertheless bound by the laws of probability – "nothing impossible was ever introduced" – and were carried on for months and even years at a time. In this way Trollope learned "to dwell on a work created by my own imagination, and to live in a world altogether outside the world of my own material life."

When Trollope wrote about other novelists his main concern is the extent to which they knew their own personages; for him, fiction meant living with his characters "in the full reality of established intimacy." They should be with the author "as he lies down to sleep, and as he wakes from his dreams." At the same time, these imaginary creations must be exempted from the conditions of ordinary life: "on the last day of each month recorded, every person in his novel should be a month older than on the first."

With these criteria in mind, it is easy to see why Trollope's greatest achievements as a novelist depend on the completeness with which his characters are understood, an understanding which includes the ways in which their innate qualities are affected by the passage of time. A natural result of this was his unprecedented development of the novel series. His two sequences of inter-connected novels – the Barchester novels and the Palliser series – occupied him intermittently for twenty-four years of his writing life. *The Warden*, the first of the Barchester books, was actually the fourth Trollope wrote, following two Irish novels and a historical romance. It was topical, satirical, and some of the original reviewers thought it "clever." Its successor, *Barchester Towers*, develops Trollope's command of social comedy, while the next in the sequence, *Doctor Thorne*, finds Trollope grappling with a plot given him by his brother (elaborate plots were not favoured by Trollope since they brought excitement at the cost of truth to life). These novels have always been popular, but the later books in the series show an increasingly masterly command of character in action, which is not the less revealing for being precipitated by conventional dilemmas, mostly concerning love and marriage, but often involving the over-riding difficulty of how to make one's way in the world successfully but honestly. Throughout Trollope's work, characters show an almost obsessive concern with their own integrity, a concern equally apparent in their love-lives and in their professional struggles. It is in *Framley Parsonage*, *The Small House at Allington* and *The Last Chronicle of Barset*, too, that Trollope begins to reap the full advantage of his characters' reappearance. Mr. Crawley, who enters in the first of these, is developed in *The Last Chronicle* into a figure of near-tragic power. It is typical of the realism of Trollope's method that his superbly conveyed anguish is caused by something as trivial as a mislaid cheque for £20 which he is accused of stealing. Mr. Crawley does not go exactly mad, but neither is he always quite sane; he is the most striking of a number of characters in Trollope's work (Louis Trevelyan in *He Knew He Was Right* is another) whose instability is analysed with an unflustered empathy quite remarkable for its period.

The last two Barchester novels are also linked by the story of Lily Dale, jilted in the first of them, and unable even in the second to console herself with the faithful admiration of John Eames. It is a tribute to Trollope's ability to create people that seemed real that for the rest of his life he continued to get letters begging him to unite the couple at last – although, as Trollope himself pointed out, it is precisely because Lily can't get over her troubles that she is endearing. Eames's experiences as a civil servant have been said to reflect Trollope's own, but the character is not given privileged treatment or portrayed with particular intensity (as, say, the autobiographical characters of David Copperfield and Maggie Tulliver are by Dickens and George Eliot). Trollope's innate modesty did not allow him to think of himself as someone special.

This does not mean that he lacked self-assertion – he was noted in life for his bluster – or ambition. He nursed for a long time an "almost insane" desire to get into Parliament; at the age of 53 he unsuccessfully contested Beverley in Yorkshire as a Liberal. His longing to sit in the House of Commons was frustrated to good literary effect, since it resulted in the Palliser series. Trollope's interest, however, is much more in the behaviour of men in political life (and in the women who influence them) than in political ideas. There is virtually no propaganda in Trollope's as there is in Disraeli's fiction, which Trollope scorned. The two public careers that Trollope follows most closely are those of a young Irish member, Phineas Finn, whose means are slender and who depends on getting office, and Plantagenet Palliser, heir to the immense wealth of the Duke of Omnium whom he later succeeds. Plantagenet's acute sense of public responsibility leads him, in *The Prime Minister*, to head a coalition government – a task which calls for just that gift for personal relationships which, for all his genuine nobility, he lacks (and which his wife possesses so abundantly). The novel provides what is perhaps Trollope's most searching study of the interaction of private temperament and public pressure. Palliser was partly designed by Trollope as the type of the English gentleman but, though he is never less than that, his behaviour towards his wife and children, as presented in *Can You Forgive Her?* and *The Duke's Children*, is shown with a subtle understanding of the contradictions in his personality which far outruns any merely didactic intention. Palliser's rectitude and vulnerability are constantly exposed to the volatile and reckless spontaneities of his wife, Lady Glencora. They irritate each other because their personalities are so different, but they also need each other for the same reason. Their marriage, as chronicled through the whole sequence of novels, is deeply established in Trollope's imagination, so that he finds it easy, in many of its critical passages, simply to transcribe the characters' own words, rather than intervene and analyse as the theoretically all-seeing author. Trollope's personal intrusions in his own books are far from being a full guide to his characters' natures and how we should think about them; in his best work, it is the dialogue, the dramatisation, that reveals most fully the life that his books contain. Trollope rightly regarded the string of characters that run through the Palliser novels as the best work he ever did; certainly the Palliser marriage is studied with an intimacy of understanding and a lack of pretension that perhaps no other novelist of his period can match.

Part of its reality comes from the densely populated social world which Trollope accumulates round it. The great length of many of his novels allowed Trollope plenty of room in which to run several stories concurrently. The connections between these narratives are sometimes tenuous, and modern critical attempts to show that they all relate to some abstract theme or master-idea have often seemed implausible. What has attracted readers, both in his own time and subsequently, has rather been Trollope's inexhaustible interest in and capacity to register familiar fact and daily habit. Trollope knew that no-one is unimportant to himself; he treats his characters with the respect that is their due. As Henry James put it, in what is perhaps still the best essay yet written on Trollope (in *Partial Portraits*, 1888), "His great, his inestimable merit was his complete appreciation of the usual." What might be added to this generous tribute is the proviso that for Trollope "the usual" was an extraordinarily hospitable category. Trollope lived with his characters on their terms rather than on his, and as a result his fictional world has a far wider range of temperament and variety of personality than the conventional format of his novels might lead one to suppose.

—Stephen Wall

TUTUOLA, Amos. Nigerian. Born in Abeokuta, Western Nigeria, in June 1920. Educated at the Anglican Central School, Abeokuta. Served as a blacksmith in the Royal Air Force, in Lagos, 1943–46. Married Victoria Tutuola in 1947; four sons and four daughters. Since 1956, Stores Officer, Nigerian Broadcasting Corporation, Ibadan. Founder, Mbari Club of Nigerian Writers. Lives in Ibadan.

PUBLICATIONS

Fiction

The Palm-Wine Drinkard and His Dead Palm-Wine Tapster in the Dead's Town.   1952.
My Life in the Bush of Ghosts.   1954.
Simbi and the Satyr of the Dark Jungle.   1955.
The Brave African Huntress.   1958.
The Feather Woman of the Jungle.   1962.
Abaiyi and His Inherited Poverty.   1967.

Reading List: Tutuola by Harold R. Collins, 1969; Tutuola edited by Bernth Lindfors, 1978.

*   *   *

Amos Tutuola's writing is, in a sense, a historical accident. A Yoruba who was taught English for six years at primary school level in colonial Nigeria, he chose to write his stories in English and was published in England largely as a curiosity – not so much for his tales, which are wholly African, but for the entertainment value of his highly idiosyncratic English. Praised by Dylan Thomas for the originality of his language, he was nonetheless read in Europe chiefly as a primitive. He was praised for what was called his "mixture of sophistication, superstition and primitivism, and above all for the incantatory juggling with the English language" (Times Literary Supplement, 1962). Consequently he was at first condemned in Africa, on the grounds that he misrepresented his country and his culture. He is a historical accident because the combination of his peculiar talent and the patronising colonial attitude which found entertainment in his English and so brought him into print was a chance conjunction of unique circumstances.

At a distance from the tensions of colonial Nigeria and the early days of independence it is possible to locate qualities in Tutuola which derive less from his use of English than from his free-flowing way of telling a story. His English does have a refreshing vigour and originality, involving for instance an occasional redeployment of stock phrases with precision as well as force (Ajaiyi's inherited poverty is one example). Omolara Leslie (*Journal of Commonwealth Literature 9*, 1970) calls it speaking Yoruba in English words. It has a freedom and confidence, a flow, which further years of learning English in a pedagogic situation would certainly have impeded. The same unselfconsciousness gives the episodic stories and their background a powerful coherence. No less a voice than Chinua Achebe (*Morning Yet on Creation Day*, 1975) has warmly defended Tutuola's integrity as an African writing of his time and for his culture.

—Andrew Gurr

TWAIN, Mark. Pseudonym for Samuel Langhorne Clemens. American. Born in Florida, Missouri, 30 November 1835; grew up in Hannibal, Missouri. Married Olivia Langdon in 1870 (died, 1904); one son and three daughters. Printer's apprentice from age 12; helped brother with Hannibal newspapers, 1850–52; worked in St. Louis, New York, Philadelphia, Keokuk, Iowa, and Cincinnati, 1853–57; river pilot's apprentice, on the Mississippi, 1857: licensed as a pilot, 1859; went to Nevada as secretary to his brother, then in the service of the governor, and also worked as a goldminer, 1861; staff member, *Territorial Enterprise*, Virginia City, Nevada, 1862–64; moved to San Francisco, 1864; visited France, Italy, and Palestine, 1867; writer from 1867, lecturer from 1868; Editor, *Buffalo Express*, New York, 1868–71; moved to Hartford, Connecticut, and became associated with the Charles L. Webster Publishing Company, 1884: went bankrupt, 1894 (last debts paid, 1898). M.A.: Yale University, New Haven, Connecticut, 1888; Litt.D.: Yale University, 1901; Oxford University, 1907; LL.D.: University of Missouri, Columbia, 1902. *Died 21 April 1910.*

PUBLICATIONS

Collections

> *Letters*, edited by Albert B. Paine. 2 vols., 1917.
> *The Writings*, edited by Albert B. Paine. 37 vols., 1922–25.
> *The Portable Twain*, edited by Bernard De Voto. 1946.
> *The Complete Short Stories*, edited by Charles Neider. 1957.
> *Selected Shorter Writings*, edited by Walter Blair. 1962.
> *The Complete Novels*, edited by Charles Neider. 2 vols., 1964.
> *Works*, edited by John C. Gerber and others. 1972–

Fiction

> *The Celebrated Jumping Frog of Calaveras County and Other Sketches*, edited by John Paul. 1867.
> *The Innocents Abroad; or, The New Pilgrims' Progress.* 1869.
> *The Innocents at Home.* 1872.

The Gilded Age: A Tale of Today, with Charles Dudley Warner. 1873; *The Adventures of Colonel Sellers, Being Twain's Share of The Gilded Age*, edited by Charles Neider, 1965: complete text, edited by Bryant Morey French, 1972.
The Adventures of Tom Sawyer. 1876.
A True Story and the Recent Carnival of Crime. 1877.
Date 1601: Conversation as It Was by the Social Fireside in the Time of the Tudors. 1880; edited by Franklin J. Meine, 1939.
A Tramp Abroad. 1880.
The Prince and the Pauper. 1881.
The Stolen White Elephant etc. 1882.
The Adventures of Huckleberry Finn (Tom Sawyer's Companion). 1884; edited by Sculley Bradley and others, 1977.
A Connecticut Yankee in King Arthur's Court. 1889; edited by W. N. Otto, 1930.
The American Claimant. 1892.
Merry Tales. 1892.
The £1,000,000 Bank-Note and Other New Stories. 1893.
Pudd'nhead Wilson. 1894; as *The Tragedy of Pudd'nhead Wilson*, 1894; with *Those Extraordinary Twins*, edited by Malcolm Bradbury, 1969.
Tom Sawyer Abroad. 1894.
Tom Sawyer Abroad, Tom Sawyer, Detective, and Other Stories. 1896; as *Tom Sawyer, Detective, and Other Tales*, 1897.
Personal Recollections of Joan of Arc. 1896.
The Man That Corrupted Hadleyburg and Other Stories and Essays. 1900.
A Double Barrelled Detective Story. 1902.
Extracts from Adam's Diary. 1904.
A Dog's Tale. 1904.
The $30,000 Bequest and Other Stories. 1906.
Eve's Diary. 1906.
A Horse's Tale. 1907.
Extract from Captain Stormfield's Visit to Heaven. 1909; revised edition, as *Report from Paradise*, edited by Dixon Wecter, 1952.
The Mysterious Stranger: A Romance. 1916; *Mysterious Stranger Manuscripts* edited by William M. Gibson, 1969.
The Curious Republic of Gondour and Other Whimsical Sketches. 1919.
The Mysterious Stranger and Other Stories. 1922.
A Boy's Adventure. 1928.
The Adventures of Thomas Jefferson Snodgrass, edited by Charles Honce. 1928.
Jim Smiley and His Jumping Frog, edited by Albert B. Paine. 1940.
A Murder, A Mystery, and a Marriage. 1945.
The Complete Humorous Sketches and Tales, edited by Charles Neider. 1961.
Simon Wheeler, Detective, edited by Franklin R. Rogers. 1963.
Twain's Hannibal, Huck, and Tom, edited by Walter Blair. 1969.
Twain's Quarrel with Heaven: Captain Stormfield's Visit to Heaven and Other Sketches, edited by Roy B. Browne. 1970.

Plays

Colonel Sellers (produced 1874; as *The Gilded Age*, produced 1880).
Ah Sin, with Bret Harte (produced 1877). Edited by Frederick Anderson, 1961.
Colonel Sellers as a Scientist, with William Dean Howells (produced 1887). Edited by Walter J. Meserve, in *Complete Plays of Howells*, 1960.
The Quaker City Holy Land Excursion: An Unfinished Play. 1927.

Verse

> On the Poetry of Twain, with Selections from His Verse, edited by Arthur L. Scott. 1966.

Other

> Twain's (Burlesque) Autobiography and First Romance. 1871.
> Memoranda: From the Galaxy. 1871.
> Roughing It. 1872; edited by Franklin R. Rogers, in Works 2, 1972.
> A Curious Dream and Other Sketches. 1872.
> Screamers: A Gathering of Scraps of Humour, Delicious Bits, and Short Stories. 1872.
> Sketches. 1874.
> Sketches, New and Old. 1875.
> Old Times on the Mississippi. 1876.
> Punch, Brothers, Punch! and Other Sketches. 1878.
> An Idle Excursion. 1878.
> A Curious Experience. 1881.
> Life on the Mississippi. 1883.
> Facts for Twain's Memory Builder. 1891.
> How to Tell a Story and Other Essays. 1897; revised edition, 1900.
> Following the Equator: A Journey Around the World. 1897; as More Tramps Abroad, 1897.
> The Pains of Lowly Life. 1900.
> English as She Is Taught. 1900; revised edition, 1901.
> To the Person Sitting in Darkness. 1901.
> My Début as a Literary Person, with Other Essays and Stories. 1903.
> Twain on Vivisection. 1905(?).
> King Leopold's Soliloquy: A Defense of His Congo Rule. 1905: revised edition, 1906.
> Editorial Wild Oats. 1905.
> What Is Man? 1906.
> Christian Science, with Notes Containing Corrections to Date. 1907.
> Is Shakespeare Dead? From My Autobiography. 1909.
> Speeches, edited by F. A. Nast. 1910; revised edition, 1923.
> Queen Victoria's Jubilee. 1910.
> Letter to the California Pioneers. 1911.
> What Is Man? and Other Essays. 1917.
> Europe and Elsewhere. 1923.
> Autobiography, edited by Albert B. Paine. 2 vols., 1924.
> Sketches of the Sixties by Bret Harte and Mark Twain ... from "The Californian," 1864–67. 1926.
> The Suppressed Chapter of "Following the Equator." 1928.
> Twain the Letter Writer, edited by Cyril Clemens. 1932.
> Notebook, edited by Albert B. Paine. 1935.
> Letters from the Sandwich Islands, Written for the "Sacramento Union," edited by G. Ezra Dane. 1937.
> The Washoe Giant in San Francisco, Being Heretofore Uncollected Sketches, edited by Franklin Walker. 1938.
> Twain's Western Years, Together with Hitherto Unreprinted Clemens Western Items, by Ivan Benson. 1938.
> Letters from Honolulu Written for the "Sacramento Union," edited by Thomas Nickerson. 1939.

Twain in Eruption: Hitherto Unpublished Pages about Men and Events, edited by
Bernard De Voto. 1940.

*Travels with Mr. Brown, Being Heretofore Uncollected Sketches Written for the San
Francisco "Alta California" in 1866 and 1867*, edited by Franklin Walker and G. Ezra
Dane. 1940.

Republican Letters, edited by Cyril Clemens. 1941.

Letters to Will Brown, edited by Theodore Hornberger. 1941.

Letters in the "Muscatine Journal," edited by Edgar M. Branch. 1942.

Washington in 1868, edited by Cyril Clemens. 1943.

Twain, Business Man, edited by Samuel Charles Webster. 1946.

Letters of Quintus Curtius Snodgrass, edited by Ernest E. Leisy. 1946.

Twain in Three Moods: Three New Items of Twainiana, edited by Dixon Wecter. 1948.

The Love Letters, edited by Dixon Wecter. 1949.

Twain to Mrs. Fairbanks, edited by Dixon Wecter. 1949.

Twain to Uncle Remus, 1881–1885, edited by Thomas H. English. 1953.

Twins of Genius (letters to George Washington Cable), edited by Guy A.
Cardwell. 1953.

Mark Twain of the "Enterprise," edited by Henry Nash Smith and Frederick
Anderson. 1957.

*Traveling with Innocents Abroad: Twain's Original Reports from Europe and the Holy
Land*, edited by Daniel Morley McKeithan. 1958.

The Autobiography, edited by Charles Neider. 1959.

The Art, Humor, and Humanity of Twain, edited by Minnie M. Brashear and Robert M.
Rodney. 1959.

Twain and the Government, edited by Svend Petersen. 1960.

The Twain-Howells Letters 1872–1910, edited by Henry Nash Smith and William M.
Gibson. 2 vols., 1960.

Life as I Find It: Essays, Sketches, Tales, and Other Material, edited by Charles
Neider. 1961.

The Travels of Twain, edited by Charles Neider. 1961.

Contributions to "The Galaxy," 1868–1871, edited by Bruce R. McElderry. 1961.

Twain on the Art of Writing, edited by Martin B. Fried. 1961.

Letters to Mary, edited by Lewis Leary. 1961.

*The Pattern for Twain's "Roughing It": Letters from Nevada by Samuel and Orion
Clemens, 1861–1862*, edited by Franklin R. Rogers. 1961.

Letters from the Earth, edited by Bernard De Voto. 1962.

Twain on the Damned Human Race, edited by Janet Smith. 1962.

The Complete Essays, edited by Charles Neider. 1963.

Twain's San Francisco, edited by Bernard Taper. 1963.

The Forgotten Writings of Twain, edited by Henry Duskus. 1963.

Letters from Hawaii, edited by A. Grove Day. 1966.

Which Was the Dream? and Other Symbolic Writings of the Later Years, edited by John
S. Tuckey. 1967.

The Complete Travel Books, edited by Charles Neider. 1967.

Letters to His Publishers, 1867–1894, edited by Hamlin Hill. 1967.

Clemens of the "Call": Twain in California, edited by Edgar M. Branch. 1969.

Correspondence with Henry Huttleston Rogers, 1893–1909, edited by Lewis
Leary. 1969.

Fables of Man, edited by John S. Tuckey. 1973.

What Is Man? and Other Philosophical Writings, edited by Paul Baender, in
Works. 1973.

Journals and Notebooks, edited by Frederick Anderson and others. 1975–

Translator, *Slovenly Peter (Der Struwwelpeter)*. 1935.

Bibliography: *A Bibliography of the Works of Twain* by Merle Johnson, revised edition, 1935; in *Bibliography of American Literature* by Jacob Blanck, 1957.

Reading List: *Mark Twain: A Biography* by Albert B. Paine, 3 vols., 1912; *Twain: The Man and His Work* by Edward Wagenknecht, 1935, revised edition, 1961, 1967; *Twain: Man and Legend* by De Lancey Ferguson, 1943; *Mark Twain and Huck Finn* by Walter Blair, 1960; *A Casebook on Twain's Wound* edited by Lewis Leary, 1962; *Discussions of Twain* edited by Guy A. Cardwell, 1963; *Mr. Clemens and Mark Twain* by Justin Kaplan, 1966; *Twain: The Fate of Humor* by James M. Cox, 1966; *The Art of Twain* by William M. Gibson, 1976.

*   *   *

Samuel Langhorne Clemens, better known as Mark Twain, remains one of America's most widely read authors. To a great extent his popularity has rested upon his humor. It would be a mistake, however, to think of him simply as a humorist. To do so is to overlook the sharpness of his observation, the trenchancy of his social criticism, the depth of his concern for human suffering, and the clarity and extraordinary beauty of his style.

Story-telling came easily to Mark Twain because he grew up in the little town of Hannibal on the Mississippi river where the telling of "tall tales" was one of the chief pastimes. Even as a boy he developed a reputation for yarnspinning, a reputation he strengthened while a pilot on the Mississippi and a newspaperman in Nevada and California. Before he left California for the East in 1867 he had begun to deliver humorous lectures, a practice that he continued on and off until almost the end of his life. Oral story telling was immensely useful to him as a writer, for it taught him the value of such stylistic elements as point of view, proportion, timing, climax, concreteness, and dialogue that suggests real talk. He learned that the ear can catch much that the eye will miss; before finishing *Huckleberry Finn*, for example, he read it aloud over and over to make sure that it *sounded* right.

It should not be thought, however, that Mark Twain was an untutored genius who became a fine writer simply because he could tell a good tale. To be sure he had only a few years of formal schooling. But he worked in newspaper offices under some of the finest journalists of the time. More importantly he was a steady reader. A limited list of his reading would include American newspaper humor; popular fiction, as well as juvenile fiction; parodies and burlesques; travel books; the novels of such writers as Cervantes and Dickens (whom he admired) and Austen and Scott (whom he did not admire); history, biography, and autobiography; scientific works; and the writings of such persons as Hobbes, Bentham, Paine, Jefferson, Macaulay, Darwin, Carlyle, and especially W. E. H. Lecky. Most of Mark Twain's important works are a blend of his reading and his personal experience given form by his imagination.

Naturally enough he began his literary career by writing humorous sketches for midwestern and western newspapers. These apprentice pieces are derivative, satiric, and often gamy. About the only one that shows Twain's real promise as a literary figure is "The Celebrated Jumping Frog of Calaveras County." Significantly he wrote it for eastern instead of western publication. Van Wyck Brooks has argued that an eastern wife and eastern literary friends stunted Mark Twain's artistic growth, even emasculated it. But most critics agree with Bernard De Voto that Twain would probably have remained little more than a newspaper humorist without the influence of eastern readers and writers. One fact is certain: once Mark Twain began writing for an eastern audience he dropped the gaminess that had characterized his earlier work. Mrs. Clemens has been criticized for being too much of the moral censor, but the facts seem to indicate that Mark Twain censored himself far more than did his wife or any of his friends. Ribald in some of his speeches at men's banquets and in a few works meant only for men readers (e.g., *1601*) he rarely in his major works alludes even to romance between the sexes except in conventional Victorian ways.

Mark Twain continued to write short humorous sketches all through his life. His first longer works were travel books: *Innocents Abroad* and *Roughing It* – followed later by *A*

Tramp Abroad, *Life on the Mississippi*, and *Following the Equator*. Actually, the shift from short sketches to travel books was minimal since Twain's travel works were simply series of sketches, tales, and anecdotes strung together by loose chronological threads. Based largely on letters he wrote for the *Alta California*, *Innocents Abroad* relates episodes from a trip Mark Twain took to the Holy Land in 1867. It is not a tightly constructed book but a literary vaudeville show in which the reader's pleasure comes from the variety rather than the cohesion. As narrator, Twain shifts his role back and forth from a superior person (e.g., a gentleman or a teacher) to an inferior person (e.g., a simpleton or a sufferer) with unexpected and hilarious results. The appeal of *Innocents Abroad* lies mainly in its humor, but in its time it also satisfied a growing curiosity in America about foreign lands, and in treating European culture without the customary deference it gave Americans an opportunity to feel less inferior about their own culture. Sold from door to door by agents of the American Publishing Company, a subscription house that published Twain's early books, it was an extraordinary success even though the times were hard.

  Roughing It was even more successful and has continued to be one of Twain's best sellers. It is an account of his experiences in Nevada, California, and the Hawaiian Islands from 1861 through 1866. A somewhat more coherent account than *Innocents*, it is still primarily a series of sketches, actual and imagined, salted with old anecdotes and folklore. Although as narrator he again plays a variety of roles for comic effect, there is in *Roughing It* a basic consistency as he shows himself developing from a callow greenhorn to the experienced old-timer. *A Tramp Abroad* recounts a trip with Joseph Twichell, a Hartford minister, through parts of Germany, Switzerland, and Italy in 1878. It also contains such famous set-pieces as "Baker's Blue-Jay Yarn" and "The Awful German Language." *Life on the Mississippi* is the most disconnected of the travel books. The best portion, chapters IV–XVII, was published in seven installments in the *Atlantic Monthly* in 1875 under the title "Old Times on the Mississippi." These chapters offer comic glimpses of Twain's experience as an apprentice pilot. The remainder of the book, sprinkled with many irrelevancies, tells of a trip down and up the Mississippi from New Orleans to St. Paul taken in 1882. *Following the Equator* narrates the story of the around-the-world lecture tour Twain took in 1895–96 with Mrs. Clemens and his daughter Clara in an attempt to recoup some of the fortune he had just lost. Financially the trip was a success, but it was hard on his health and ended in misery when news came to them in England that their oldest daughter, Susy, was dying of meningitis. The book, Mark Twain said, was written to forget.

  Mark Twain collaborated with Charles Dudley Warner in writing his first novel, *The Gilded Age*. The work is poorly constructed and in places reads like the worst of sentimental novels, but it contains one of Twain's most memorable characters – Colonel Sellers, the incurable optimist – and some of his finest satire. His attacks on current get-rich-quick schemes and on political corruption were so trenchant that it is hardly an accident that the post Civil War period in America has been called "the gilded age."

  Next came the great books about boys. *The Adventures of Tom Sawyer* is his best constructed work since in it Twain manages to keep three narrative strands carefully interwoven: the family complication involving Tom and Aunt Polly; the love story between Tom and Becky; and the murder plot involving Tom, Huck, and Injun Joe. *Tom Sawyer* has been called "an idyll of boyhood," and as such it has never been surpassed. *The Prince and the Pauper*, the story of a mix-up in identity between Edward VI and the ragamuffin Tom Canty, was a happy addition to the children's literature of the time. *Adventures of Huckleberry Finn*, however, was an addition to the world's classics. This picaresque narrative is a modified frame story with Tom Sawyer being the focal center in the first three chapters and the last ten, and Huck and Jim being the center of interest in the middle twenty-nine chapters dealing with the journey down the river on a raft. Episodic in nature, the story nevertheless holds together because of the river, the constant presence of Huck as narrator, and perhaps especially because of Huck's growing awareness of Jim's humanity. The emotional climax of the book occurs where Huck resolves to save Jim from slavery even if he must go to hell for doing so. Many readers believe that the book goes downhill from that point to the end. Despite its humor and picturesque qualities the work is at bottom an unrelenting indictment of Mississippi river society in the 1840's – and of humanity in general at any time. But probably the most notable aspect of *Huckleberry Finn* is its style. Letting Huck tell the story forced Mark Twain to do what he did best: report concrete happenings in colloquial language. The result is what can properly be called folk poetry. It was this colloquial style that caused Ernest Hemingway to say that modern American literature began with *Huckleberry Finn*.

A Connecticut Yankee in King Arthur's Court begins as a spoof of Malory's *Morte Darthur* but quickly turns into an indictment of human tyranny: political, religious, and economic. As the sixth-century "boss," the nineteenth-century Yankee mechanic has one comic experience after another, but the work is essentially social satire, not so much of English history as contemporary industrialized society. The Yankee becomes less and less interesting as Twain uses him increasingly as a mouthpiece for his own views, especially the view that we are all the products of our training. The book is prophetic in its suggestion at the end that technology renders us insensitive to human suffering.

In the last twenty years of his life Twain's work fell off artistically though his political and social concerns continued to expand. In a work of potential greatness, *Pudd'nhead Wilson*, he confronted for the first time the more brutal aspects of slavery. His *Personal Recollections of Joan of Arc* is embarrassingly sentimental but more accurate in depicting the political forces at work than many other biographies of Joan. Shorter pieces attack such aspects of the time as American imperialism, Christian Science, the role of the Western powers in the Boxer Rebellion, King Leopold's treatment of the Congolese, and the lynching of blacks in the Southern states. *The Mysterious Stranger*, a work that Twain started at least three times and never finished, exhibits his philosophy of mechanical determinism and his growing belief that life is only a dream. *What Is Man?*, a dialogue in which an elderly cynic invariably bests a young idealist, argues that man is a machine and that choice is only an illusion. There is no doubt that the pessimism and bitterness, latent in Twain throughout most of his life, finally surfaced in these last twenty years. Financial difficulties and the deaths of his wife and two daughters seemed at times to be more than he could bear. Nevertheless his perceptions remained sharp and his writing controlled. Besides, he was sustained by honors from home and abroad such as no other American writer had ever enjoyed.

Much that Mark Twain wrote was topical and overwrought and is sliding into oblivion. But his best works remain unrivalled in their depiction of the comic and the pathetic in life – and of the inevitable relation between the two. William Dean Howells, Twain's best friend for forty years, composed a fitting epitaph when he wrote that Mark Twain was "sole, incomparable, the Lincoln of our literature."

—John C. Gerber

UPDIKE, John (Hoyer). American. Born in Shillington, Pennsylvania, 18 March 1932. Educated in Shillington public schools; Harvard University, Cambridge, Massachusetts, A.B. (summa cum laude) 1954; Ruskin School of Drawing and Fine Arts, Oxford, 1954–55. Married Mary Pennington in 1953; two sons and two daughters. Staff Reporter, *The New Yorker*, 1955–57; full-time writer from 1957. Recipient: Guggenheim Fellowship, 1959; Rosenthal Award, 1960; National Association of Independent Schools Award, 1963; National Book Award, 1964; O. Henry Award, 1966. Member, National Institute of Arts and Letters. Lives in Ipswich, Massachusetts.

PUBLICATIONS

Fiction

> *The Poorhouse Fair.* 1959.
> *The Same Door* (stories). 1959.
> *Rabbit, Run.* 1960.
> *Pigeon Feathers* (stories). 1962.
> *The Centaur.* 1963.
> *Of the Farm.* 1965.
> *The Music School* (stories). 1966.
> *Couples.* 1968.
> *Bech: A Book* (stories). 1970.
> *Rabbit Redux.* 1971.
> *Museums and Women and Other Stories.* 1972.
> *Warm Wine: An Idyll* (story). 1973.
> *A Month of Sundays.* 1975.
> *Picked-Up Pieces* (stories). 1975.
> *Marry Me: A Romance.* 1976.
> *The Coup.* 1978.

Plays

> *Three Texts from Early Ipswich: A Pageant.* 1968.
> *Buchanan Dying.* 1974.

Verse

> *The Carpentered Hen and Other Tame Creature.* 1958; as *Hoping for a Hoopoe*, 1959.
> *Telephone Poles and Other Poems.* 1963.
> *Bath after Sailing.* 1968.
> *Midpoint and Other Poems.* 1969.
> *Seventy Poems.* 1972.
> *Six Poems.* 1973.
> *Tossing and Turning.* 1977.

Other

> *The Magic Flute* (juvenile), with Warren Chappell. 1962.

The Ring (juvenile), with Warren Chappell.   1964.
Assorted Prose.   1965.
A Child's Calendar.   1966.
Bottom's Dream: Adapted from Shakespeare's "A Midsummer Night's Dream."   1969.
A Good Place.   1973.

Editor, Pens and Needles, by David Levine.   1970.

Bibliography: Updike: A Comprehensive Bibliography by B. A. Sokoloff and Mark E. Posner, 1973.

Reading List: Updike by Charles Thomas Samuels, 1969; The Elements of Updike by Alice and Kenneth Hamilton, 1970; Pastoral and Anti-Pastoral Elements in Updike's Fiction by Laura E. Taylor, 1971; Updike: Yea Sayings by Rachael C. Burchard, 1971; Updike by Robert Detweiler, 1972; Rainstorms and Fire: Ritual in the Novels of Updike by Edward P. Vargo, 1973; Fighters and Lovers: Theme in the Novels of Updike by Joyce B. Markle, 1974.

*   *   *

The successes of John Updike are linked with The New Yorker, a magazine for which he was once a staff member and for which he has remained a frequent contributor. But many of his novels go beyond the limits of interest that are frequently attributed to the journal: a well-bred scepticism as to what is possible for human sensibility in our time. It is true that Updike's novels and, even more, his short stories sometimes conform to these limits which see all human effort as subject to the ironies of cross-purpose. But Updike's sensibility, particularly as it unfolds in his longer works, is not that of a writer who has fully acquiesced in the general decay and uncertainty of an era. Rather Updike takes shape as a writer who keeps circling around the modern detritus with a sharp eye for some fragmented persistence of meaning and order. He is a moralist out of season. The season for confident reading of meaning may be completed, but the desire for such activity persists in much of Updike's work.

This may not be immediately apparent to some readers who can doubt that there is any link between a continuing moral curiosity and the many passages in the novels which give explicit accounts of sexual success and sexual impotence. Yet the sexual adventures of the minister in A Month of Sundays are no more exactly set down than are the "spiritual" aspirations that lead the minister to compose discourses that link the presence of sexuality with the advent of Grace. For Updike is not the kind of Stoic moralist familiar to us in the eighteenth century and elsewhere who seeks to detect and defend a purely humanistic code of excellence. The code of excellence that reveals itself intermittently in the Updike novels is one that has its roots in the O altitudos that had their traditional expression in the transports of mystics and in the teaching of the New Testament itself. The minister of A Month of Sundays thinks of Barth and Tillich when he is not fornicating and sometimes when he is. Updike provides some of his novels with epigraphs from the New Testament and Pascal. And, in the midst of a reported life which seems quite discontinuous with these august phrases, Updike provides flickers of light and inchoate illuminations that direct attention beyond traditional common sense and the current doubt that there is any sense whatever to the lives that a novelist may at present describe.

There is, in several of the novels, a central figure that sums up the moral situation in which modern persons live and make their Updike-sponsored effort to enjoy their lives and understand them. In The Centaur Updike speaks of a sequence – priest, teacher, and artist – that links the present to the past. The central figure in The Centaur is a frustrated teacher of science in a high school; his prototype is the ancient centaur, Chiron, who tried to reveal to his recalcitrant pupils the wisdom that had come to the early Greek oracles and the priests of holy places. The ancient centaur was mocked and wounded by his pupils; so also is the high school teacher by *his* students. But the modern centaur's son, Peter, responds to the harassed and comic nobility of his father. And when that son becomes an artist – when he has left his father behind him – the son wonders whether his service of esthetic excellence continues or cancels the pursuits of his father. (Earlier, the father had wondered about the relation of his teaching activity to his father's career as a clergyman.) Is the artist son the last link in a chain that extends backwards in time and moral-religious experience? Or is he a link that is independent of the earlier ones, a servant of a good that has no contact with the earlier excellences that his father and grandfather were devoted to?

This is a question that much of Updike's work raises but does not answer. The question is not asked monotonously. In his first novel, *The Poorhouse Fair*, Updike contrasts the humanitarian Connor, the director of the poor house, with a ninety-year-old man who maintains touch with older sources of moral illumination. In *Rabbit Run* and *Rabbit Redux* the centre of awareness is Harry Angstrom, an ill-educated and adulterous printer who would, it seems, be singularly cut off from "priest" and "teacher." Yet Rabbit Angstrom is subject to malaises that have only a feeble source in his parents and that rather rise from his changes of partners, his ill-fulfilled obligations to his son, and his contact with a rebellious black. In the midst of a life that is badly broken up, Angstrom demands not only sexual gratification but moral illumination from persons who are as confused as he is. The illumination is transient and is usually lost in a subsequent catastrophic event. But the event that is more than event – that is illumination – has occurred. This is all that Updike can report in his *Rabbit* narratives and elsewhere. In *Marry Me* Updike leads his chief character, who is about to dissolve a "good" marriage, to observe that we are in the midst of "the twilight of the old morality, and there's just enough to torment us, and not enough to hold us in."

Such are most of Updike's novels: clever narratives that move from narrative to meditation. At first encounter, Updike's work seems to be devoted to the reproduction of textures that are self-evident: textures of the inconsecutive, textures composed by the crass indifference of most men to each other. All this is done with brilliance and is "right." But through this neatly comprehended terrain move "priestly" and academic ghosts, the shades of Updike's "centaur" and the "centaur's" father.

—Harold H. Watts

UPWARD, Edward (Falaise). English. Born in Romford, Essex, 9 September 1903. Educated at the Repton School, 1917–21; Corpus Christi College, Cambridge (Chancellor's Medal for Verse), 1922–24, M.A. Married Hilda Maude Percival; two children. Schoolmaster, 1928–62; member of the editorial board of *The Ploughshare,* 1936–39.

PUBLICATIONS

Fiction

Journey to the Border. 1938.
In the Thirties. 1962; *The Rotten Elements,* 1969; complete version (including *No Home But the Struggle*), as *The Spiral Ascent,* 1977.
The Railway Accident and Other Stories. 1969.

Verse

Buddha.   1924.

Reading List: Introduction by W. H. Sellers to *The Railway Accident and Other Stories,* 1969; *The Auden Generation* by Samuel Hynes, 1976.

*   *   *

Edward Upward was a legendary figure among young writers associated with Auden in the 1930's. The fantastic picture of a diseased English culture in his early writing is mirrored in Auden's early poems, and was admired by Isherwood. At Cambridge, Upward and Isherwood invented a fantasy-village called Mortmere. They peopled it with bizarre characters and events in a series of anarchic tales in which conventional English values were playfully and threateningly inverted. The only surviving Mortmere story is Upward's "The Railway Accident," written in 1928. In it the narrator embarks upon a nightmare train journey ending in a disastrous accident from which he escapes to attend the Mortmere Rector's treasure hunt. The narrator himself is neurotic; the situations he observes are chaotic and menacing.

A neurotic and alienated protagonist is to be found in "The Colleagues" (1929) and "Sunday" (1931), as well as in Upward's most substantial pre-war work, *Journey to the Border.* These are not fantastic, Mortmere pieces. But in each the central character has fears about his inability to cope with the daily routines of his work. The narrators are on the verge of breakdown. All have hallucinatory glimpses of the "vile," "putrescent" nature of the society from which they are alienated. In his essay "Sketch for a Marxist Interpretation of Literature" (1937), Upward revealed a rigid political outlook. Fantasy was a retreat from the real world; only by recognising the inevitability of revolution could a modern book be true to life. This clash between his doctrinaire creed and his distinctive imaginative gifts dominates Upward's subsequent work.

Both the danger of fantasy and the decadence of society are central themes in *Journey to the Border.* The protagonist is the neurotic tutor to a wealthy family. Unable to bear his life as a subordinate member of the household, the tutor has a series of hallucinations during an outing to a country racecourse. Finally he realises that his retreat into fantasy is as deadly as the doomed world of his employer. He determines to take action in the real world and join the workers' movement.

Upward's next book appeared in 1962 after a prolonged silence. *In The Thirties* is the first volume of a trilogy entitled *The Spiral Ascent.* It describes the decision of a young middle-class schoolteacher to join the Communist Party in the 1930's and abandon his attempts at personal fulfilment as a poet. In the second volume, *The Rotten Elements,* the schoolteacher and his equally committed wife leave the Party in the 1940's because they feel it is no longer truly Marxist. In the final volume, *No Home But the Struggle,* the hero retires from schoolteaching to pursue the imaginative, poetic life. Through memory and flashback he relives his struggle to preserve emotional equilibrium in or out of the Party.

This partly autobiographical trilogy reworks the central conflict between private fulfilment and public action in Upward's more exciting (and more uneven) pre-war work. There, as Master of Mortmere, he can lay claim to being a seminal writer of the 1930's.

—Rowland Smith

van der POST, Laurens (Jan). South African. Born in Philippolis, 13 December 1906. Educated at Grey College, Bloemfontein. Served in the British Army, in the Western Desert and the Far East, in World War II; Prisoner of War, in Java, 1943–45; Military Attaché to the British Minister, Batavia, 1945–47: C.B.E. (Commander, Order of the British Empire), 1947. Married 1) Marjorie Wendt in 1929 (divorced, 1947), one son and one daughter; 2) the writer Ingaret Giffard in 1949. Farmer in the Orange Free State, South Africa, 1948–65. Explorer: has made several missions to Africa for the Colonial Development Corporation and the British Government, including a mission to Kalahari, 1952. Recipient: Anisfield-Wolf Award, 1951; National Association of Independent Schools Award, U.S.A., 1959; South African Central News Agency Prize, 1963, 1967. D.Litt.: University of Natal, Pietermaritzburg, 1965. Fellow, Royal Society of Literature, 1955. Lives in London and in Aldeburgh, Suffolk.

PUBLICATIONS

Fiction

In a Province. 1934.
The Face Beside the Fire. 1953.
Flamingo Feather. 1955.
A Bar of Shadow. 1956.
The Seed and the Sower (includes *A Bar of Shadow* and *The Sword and the Doll*). 1963.
The Hunter and the Whale: A Tale of Africa. 1967.
A Story like the Wind. 1972.
A Far-Off Place. 1974.
A Mantis Carol. 1975.

Plays

Screenplays: *The Lost World of the Kalahari,* 1956; *A Region of Shadow,* 1971; *The Story of Carl Gustav Jung,* 1971.

Other

Venture to the Interior. 1951.
The Dark Eye in Africa. 1955.
The Lost World of the Kalahari. 1958.
The Heart of the Hunter. 1961.
Journey into Russia. 1964; as *A View of All the Russias,* 1964.
A Portrait of All the Russias. 1967.
A Portrait of Japan. 1968.
The Night of the New Moon: August 6, 1945 ... Hiroshima. 1970.
African Cooking, with the editors of *Time-Life.* 1970.
Man and the Shadow. 1971.
Jung and the Story of Our Time: A Personal Experience. 1975.
First Catch Your Eland: A Taste of Africa. 1977.

Reading List: *van der Post* by Frederic I. Carpenter, 1969.

*   *   *

Laurens van der Post's fictional world is, like his real one, an intensely masculine world concerned with war, exploration, and adventure. It is for the most part set in his native South Africa and his main attraction as a writer lies in his capacity to recreate the South African landscape and fauna with a vividness and enthusiasm which are obviously born out of a great love for, and knowledge of, the country. However, van der Post also deals with social tensions. In *In a Province* a young white South African and his black friend who gets into trouble with the law become involved with communists and are finally killed. Though van der Post deplores racial discrimination, he has fought a life-long battle against what he sees as "communist subversion." This theme reappears in *Flamingo Feather* which, with its fast, exciting action and romantic/mystic tone, should appeal to the adventurer in each of us. *The Face Beside the Fire* is an altogether different novel, dealing with the problems of a South African writer in London and attempting an understanding of the psychological problems of alienation. *The Seed and the Sower* consists of three long short stories dealing with war and focussing on the life of a prisoner-of-war. They all draw their material from the author's experience as a prisoner-of-war in Japan during the Second World War. Van der Post's most widely read books, however, remain his accounts of expeditions into remote parts of Africa (*Venture to the Interior* and *The Lost World of the Kalahari*) in which he does not attempt any fictionalization of his material but describes his adventures as they happened.

—Kirsten Holst Petersen

VAN VECHTEN, Carl. American. Born in Cedar Rapids, Iowa, 17 June 1880. Educated at Cedar Rapids High School; University of Chicago, Ph.B. 1903. Married 1) Anna Elizabeth Snyder in 1907 (divorced, 1912); 2) the Russian actress Fania Marinoff in 1914. Composer and journalist: Reporter, *Chicago American*, 1903–05; Assistant Music Critic, 1906–07, Paris Correspondent, 1908–09, *New York Times*; author of the program notes for the Symphony Society of New York, 1910–11; Drama Critic, *New York Press*, 1913–14. Member of the Board of the Cosmopolitan Symphony Orchestra, and the W. C. Handy Foundation for the Blind; Founder, 1941, and Honorary Curator, 1946, James Weldon Johnson Memorial Collection of Negro Arts and Letters, Yale University Library, New Haven, Connecticut. D.Litt.: Fisk University, Nashville, Tennessee, 1955. Member, National Institute of Arts and Letters, 1961. *Died 21 December 1964.*

PUBLICATIONS

Fiction

Peter Whiffle, His Life and Works. 1922.
The Blind Bow-Boy. 1923.
The Tattooed Countess. 1924.
Firecrackers. 1925.
Nigger Heaven. 1926.
Spider Boy: A Scenario for a Moving Picture. 1928.
Parties: Scenes from Contemporary New York Life. 1930.

Other

Music after the Great War and Other Studies.   1915.
Music and Bad Manners.   1916.
Interpreters and Interpretations.   1917; revised edition, as Interpreters, 1920.
The Merry-Go-Round.   1918.
The Music of Spain.   1918.
In the Garret.   1920.
The Tiger in the House.   1920.
Red: Papers on Musical Subjects.   1925.
Excavations: A Book of Advocacies.   1926.
Feathers.   1930.
Sacred and Profane Memories (essays).   1932.
Ex Libris, in Dance Index (triple issue).   1942.
Fragments from an Unwritten Autobiography.   2 vols., 1955.
With Formality and Elegance (on photography).   1977.

Editor, Lords of the Housetops: Thirteen Cat Tales.   1921.
Editor, My Musical Life, by Nikolay Rimsky-Korsakoff, translated by Judah A. Joffe.
    1923; revised edition, 1942.
Editor, Gertrude Stein: Selected Writings.   1946.
Editor, Last Operas and Plays, by Gertrude Stein.   1949.
Editor, Unpublished Writings of Gertrude Stein.   8 vols., 1951–58.

Bibliography: Van Vechten: A Bibliography by Klaus W. Jonas, 1955.

Reading List: Van Vechten and the Twenties, 1955, and Van Vechten, 1965, both by Edward Leuders; Van Vechten and the Irreverent Decaaes by Bruce Kellner, 1968.

*   *   *

Carl Van Vechten's personal flamboyance in manner and dress, as well as his frequent enthusiasm for both the avant garde and the patently old-fashioned, labelled him a dilettante in his own time. The range and foresight in several distinct careers, however, mark him a unique and underestimated American writer.

A partial list of his discoveries is staggering. As a newspaper critic he endorsed the first performances in America of Isadora Duncan, Anna Pavlova, Mary Garden, Feodor Chaliapin, and Sergei Rachmaninoff, and he was the earliest American admirer of the music of Erik Satie, Richard Strauss, and Igor Stravinsky. In a series of volumes of musical and literary criticism – Interpreters and Excavations are particularly rewarding – his perceptions are startlingly fresh. He advocated musical scores for films by serious composers, the value of popular music and ragtime, ballet, Spanish music – all far in advance of other writers. He was one of the first to rediscover Herman Melville, and Ronald Firbank and Arthur Machen owe their American reputations to him. Van Vechten's tireless efforts on behalf of Gertrude Stein are well known; he was instrumental in placing the first books of Wallace Stevens and Langston Hughes; he fostered the careers of George Gershwin, Ethel Waters, Paul Robeson among musicians, and James Purdy among writers. His book about cats, The Tiger in the House, is seminal. He was largely responsible for the popular recognition of the Negro as a creative artist during the Harlem Renaissance.

Van Vechten is probably too analytical and discursive, too involved with amassing and cataloging outré material, to have written fiction of the first order, although all seven of his novels are variously engaging. Few books catch the charm of New York and Paris before the First World War so well as Peter Whiffle. None serves as such a good introduction to Harlem during the 1920's as *Nigger Heaven. The Tattooed Countess* criticizes small-town life at the turn of the century with a gently cheerful malice denied more resolute realists. Three novels document Van Vechten's "splendid drunken Twenties," as he called the period: *The Blind Bow-Boy*, *Firecrackers*, and *Parties* form a serious social trilogy in the disguise of buffoonery and farce, written with slinky elegance and wit.

Van Vechten gave up writing in favor of photography to document the century's celebrities for various collections he established: The James Weldon Johnson Memorial Collection of Negro Arts and Letters, at Yale, and The George Gershwin Memorial Collection of Music and Musical Literature, at Fisk, among others.

His work has dated very little; writing from the perspective of middle age, Van Vechten's evaluations of the 1920's are perhaps more solidly grounded than those of several more celebrated younger writers of the period.

—Bruce Kellner

VIDAL, Gore. American. Born in West Point, New York, 3 October 1925. Educated at Phillips Exeter Academy, New Hampshire, graduated 1943. Served in the United States Army, 1943–46. Full-time writer from 1944; Drama Critic, *Reporter* magazine, 1959; Democratic-Liberal Candidate for Congress, from New York, 1960. Member, Advisory Board, *Partisan Review*, New Brunswick, New Jersey, 1960–61; Member, President Kennedy's Advisory Committee on the Arts, 1961–63; Co-Chairman, The New Party, 1968–71. Lives in Rome.

PUBLICATIONS

Fiction

Williwaw. 1946.
In a Yellow Wood. 1947.
The City and the Pillar. 1948; revised edition, 1965.
The Season of Comfort. 1949.
A Search for the King: A Twelfth Century Legend. 1950.
Dark Green, Bright Red. 1950.
The Judgment of Paris. 1952.
Messiah. 1954; revised edition, 1965.
A Thirsty Evil: 7 Short Stories. 1956.
Julian. 1964.
Washington, D.C. 1967.
Myra Breckinridge. 1968.
Two Sisters: A Novel in the Form of a Memoir. 1970.
Burr. 1974.
Myron. 1975.
1876. 1976.
Kalki. 1978.

Fiction (as Edgar Box)

>Death in the Fifth Position. 1952.
>Death Before Bedtime. 1953.
>Death Likes It Hot. 1954.

Plays

>Visit to a Small Planet (televised, 1955). In Visit to a Small Planet and Other Television
>Plays, 1957; revised version (produced 1957), 1957.
>Honor (televised, 1956). In Television Plays for Writers: Eight Television Plays, edited
>by A. S. Burack, 1957; revised version as On the March to the Sea: A Southron
>Comedy (produced 1962), in Three Plays, 1962.
>Visit to a Small Planet and Other Television Plays (includes Barn Burning, Dark
>Possession, The Death of Billy the Kid, A Sense of Justice, Smoke, Summer Pavilion,
>The Turn of the Screw). 1957.
>The Best Man: A Play of Politics (produced 1960). 1960.
>Three Plays (Visit to a Small Planet, The Best Man, On the March to the Sea). 1962.
>Romulus: A New Comedy, from the play by Friedrich Dürrenmatt (produced
>1962). 1962.
>Weekend (produced 1968). 1968.
>An Evening with Richard Nixon and ... (produced 1972). 1972.

>Screenplays: The Catered Affair, 1956; I Accuse, 1958; The Scapegoat, with Robert
>Hamer, 1959; Suddenly Last Summer, with Tennessee Williams, 1960; The Best Man,
>1964; Is Paris Burning?, with Francis Ford Coppola, 1966; Last of the Mobile Hot-Shots,
>1970.

>Television Plays: Barn Burning, 1954; Dark Possession, 1954; Smoke, 1954; Visit to a
>Small Planet, 1955; The Death of Billy the Kid, 1955; A Sense of Justice, 1955; Summer
>Pavilion, 1955; The Turn of the Screw, 1955; Honor, 1956; The Indestructible Mr. Gore,
>1960.

Other

>Rocking the Boat (essays). 1962.
>Reflections upon a Sinking Ship (essays). 1969.
>Homage to Daniel Shays: Collected Essays 1952–1972. 1972; as Collected Essays
>1952–1972, 1974.
>Great American Families, with others. 1977.
>Matters of Fact and Fiction: Essays 1973–1976. 1977.

>Editor, Best Television Plays. 1956.

Reading List: Vidal by Ray Lewis White, 1968; The Apostate Angel: A Critical Study of Vidal
by Bernard F. Dick, 1974.

*   *   *

Of all the critical overviews of the wide-ranging work of the American writer Gore Vidal, his own appraisal may be as straightforward as one could hope for. In a foreword to a 1956 collection of his TV plays (*Visit to a Small Planet and Other Television Plays*), he says: "I am at heart a propagandist, a tremendous hater, a tiresome nag, complacently positive that there is no human problem which could not be solved if people would simply do as I advise." There is a determined strain of social criticism – always articulate, often vituperative, and sometimes just bitchy – at the center of most of his fiction, drama, and film scripts, especially in his most recent work. Consumed by American political history, Vidal has fashioned characters and situations that often serve as frontispieces for his heretical suspicions about the past and his unrelieved cynicism with regard to the future. Fortunately, there is almost always evidence of his considerable literary skill as well.

Since the publication of *Williwaw* in the author's twenty-first year, Vidal has prompted enthusiasm from critics lauding his early "promise." Whether that promise has been satisfied after thirty years of work in popular American literature is still the central question in most Gore Vidal reviews. But it is certain that the writer has managed to keep his name in contention the whole time. He has found popular and critical success in fiction – first with *Williwaw*, then with bestsellers like *The City and the Pillar, Julian, Washington, D.C., Myra Breckinridge, Burr,* and *1876*. He turned to television in its formative years, in the era of live tele-drama, and produced well-received plays for Omnibus, Studio One, and the Philco Television Playhouse (including the highly praised "Visit to a Small Planet"). His *The Best Man*, written for the Broadway stage in 1960, was a major success, encouraging an adaptation for film in 1964, followed by other film adaptations (including "Suddenly Last Summer," co-written with Tennessee Williams) and original screenplays.

But critics familiar with Gore Vidal's style and prolific outpourings seem to think that the writer's talent lies with the perfection of the essay. Indeed, the 1977 publication of a collection of his recent essays – *Matters of Fact and Fiction* – was greeted with all-around good notices, even if some reviewers had reservations. Vidal's skill with the essay form is hardly surprising in view of the usual criticisms of his other work as too polemical. It may well be, as Vidal himself has suggested informally, that at the heart of his dramatic and fictional efforts there is an essay, not only beating at the core of the work, but sometimes overwhelming the conventions of the form that seeks to contain it.

The elements of Vidal's creative polemic seem to be characterized by his gift for language, his "wit" (in the classical sense), and his strong reactionary instincts. This last tendency, Vidal's reactionary bent, seems puzzling at first, given his documented liberalism in social and political affairs (television networks have used him as a representative "liberal intellectual," and he actually ran for one of New York's Congressional seats on a suicidally liberal platform). But the contradiction might be a natural consequence of being Gore Vidal, grandson the T. P. Gore, respected Senator from Oklahoma, and son of a much admired college athlete who was an instructor at West Point when Vidal was born. The reactionary strain might be a case of his natural predispositions – based upon his aristocratic origins, his attraction to money and power and his unshakeable suspicions about the stupidity of the American public – overwhelming whatever ideological hopes he claims.

What emerges, in the words of P. N. Furbank (in a 1974 piece in *The Listener*), is "a sort of patriotic gloom." Rooted as he was in the school-book traditions of American history and its institutions, Vidal seems to have been particularly embittered by the unflattering lessons of his historical scholarship and his personal experience. He is stuck with the residue of his expectations about American innocence and morality, confounded by what he knows about political history. So to do justice to both the dream and the informed reality, he has developed an articulate, even lyrical, cynicism about the direction of modern letters and the final collision of the Republic with the world it has, in part, created.

—Lawrence R. Broer

VONNEGUT, Kurt, Jr. American. Born in Indianapolis, Indiana, 11 November 1922. Educated at Cornell University, Ithaca, New York, 1940–42; University of Chicago, 1945–47. Served in the United States Army Infantry, 1942–45: Purple Heart. Married Jane Marie Cox in 1945; two daughters and one son. Police Reporter, City News Bureau, Chicago, 1946; worked in public relations for the General Electric Company, Schenectady, New York, 1947–50; free-lance writer from 1950; teacher at the Hopefield School, Sandwich, Massachusetts, from 1965; Visiting Lecturer, Writers Workshop, University of Iowa, Iowa City, 1965–67, and Harvard University, Cambridge, Massachusetts, 1970–71. Recipient: Guggenheim Fellowship, 1967; National Institute of Arts and Letters grant, 1970. Litt.D.: Hobart and William Smith Colleges, Geneva, New York, 1974. Member, National Institute of Arts and Letters, 1973. Lives in West Barnstable, Massachusetts.

PUBLICATIONS

Fiction

Player Piano. 1952.
The Sirens of Titan. 1959.
Canary in a Cathouse (stories). 1961.
Mother Night. 1961.
Cat's Cradle. 1963.
God Bless You, Mrs. Rosewater; or, Pearls Before Swine. 1965.
Welcome to the Monkey House: A Collection of Short Works. 1968.
Slaughterhouse-Five; or, The Children's Crusade. 1969.
Breakfast of Champions; or, Goodbye, Blue Monday. 1973.
Slapstick; or, Lonesome No More. 1976.

Plays

The Very First Christmas Morning, in *Better Homes and Gardens,* December 1962.
Fortitude, in *Playboy,* September 1968.
Happy Birthday, Wanda June (produced 1970). 1971.
Between Time and Timbuktu; or, Prometheus-5: A Space Fantasy (televised, 1972; produced 1975). 1972.

Television Play: *Between Time and Timbuktu,* 1972.

Other

Wampeters, Foma, and Granfalloons: Opinions. 1974.

Bibliography: *Vonnegut: A Descriptive Bibliography and Annotated Secondary Checklist* by Asa B. Pieratt, Jr., and Jerome Klinkowitz, 1974.

Reading List: *Vonnegut: Fantasist of Fire and Ice* by David H. Goldsmith, 1972; *The Vonnegut Statement,* edited by Jerome Klinkowitz and John Somer, 1973; *Vonnegut in America: An Introduction to the Life and Work of Vonnegut* by Jerome Klinkowitz and

Donald L. Lawler, 1977; *Vonnegut* by James Lundquist, 1977; *Vonnegut* by Clark Mayo, 1977; *Vonnegut* by Richard Giannone, 1977.

*   *   *

In *Slaughterhouse-Five*, Vonnegut summarizes a science fiction novel by Kilgore Trout in which a time traveler goes back to the crucifixion and, with a stethoscope, listens to Christ's heart. The Savior, alas, is dead, stone dead. Trout is a character in several of Vonnegut's books, but his novel might well have been written by Vonnegut, for, like it, Vonnegut's novels portray a world in which there is no hope, no purpose, no salvation for the universe. Vonnegut is a moralist, but one who begins with the premise that morality, like civilization, merely expresses wishful thinking and chance. In this universe, divine intention is only imagined; it does not really exist.

Vonnegut's novels describe a deterministic, mechanistic world — a world of cause and effect with no overriding purpose or goal. The major novels and other works center on innocents like Billy Pilgrim (in *Slaughterhouse-Five*) and Dwayne Hoover (in *Breakfast of Champions*) who are victims both of other people and, more particularly, of an inability meaningfully to affect their own lives. For Vonnegut, civilization's problem is not that people don't, strictly speaking, take responsibility for their lives, but that they can't. *Breakfast of Champions* suggests that art offers at least temporary salvation, but it is more characteristic of Vonnegut's books to suggest that if there is any salvation for men, it lies in their innocence or their stupidity — and consequently their inability to understand how totally they are the product of circumstance, not free will.

Vonnegut's early reputation was largely among readers of science fiction. His books emphasize the obvious, if often overlooked, fact that the elaborate theoretical structures devised by modern technology and science have important moral implications. Since these structures tend to be entirely deterministic, they suggest that objective views of the universe have no room for chance or inspiration: everything has its immediate, ascertainable cause. True moral choice is, therefore, impossible.

In *Slapstick*, the most recent of his novels, Vonnegut argues that, at the least, "common decency" should characterize human relations. This conclusion may make his bleak moral view palatable to some readers, but it is also deeply sentimental. Vonnegut can appear sentimental even in his best work, but it may be this, together with his comic sense, that allows his work to escape the bitterness, if not the resignation, that his bleak view of experience would encourage.

—Edward Halsey Foster

WALLACE, (Richard Horatio) Edgar. English. Born in Greenwich, London, 1 April 1875. Educated at St. Peter's School, London; Board School, Camberwell, London, to age 12. Served in the Royal West Kent Regiment in England, 1893–96, and in the Medical Staff Corps in South Africa, 1896–99: bought his discharge, 1899; served in the Lincoln's Inn branch of the Special Constabulary, and as a special interrogator for the War Office, during World War I. Married 1) Ivy Caldecott in 1901 (divorced, 1919), two daughters and two sons; 2) Violet King in 1921, one daughter. Worked in a printing firm, shoe shop, rubber factory, and as a merchant seaman, plasterer, and milk delivery boy, in London, 1886–91; South African Correspondent for Reuter's, 1899–1902, and the London *Daily Mail,* 1900–02; Editor, *Rand Daily News,* Johannesburg, 1902–03; returned to London: Reporter, *Daily Mail,* 1903–07, and *Standard,* 1910; Racing Editor, and later Editor, *The Week-End,* later *The Week-End Racing Supplement,* 1910–12; Racing Editor and Special Writer, *Evening News,* 1910–12; founded *Bibury's Weekly* and *R. E. Walton's Weekly,* both racing papers; Editor, *Ideas* and *The Story Journal,* 1913; Writer, and later Editor, *Town Topics,* 1913–16; regular contributor to the *Birmingham Post,* and *Thomson's Weekly News,* Dundee; Racing Columnist, *The Star,* 1927–32, and *Daily Mail,* 1930–32; Drama Critic, *Morning Post,* 1928; Founder, *The Bucks Mail,* 1930; Editor, *Sunday News,* 1931. Chairman of the Board of Directors, and film writer/director, British Lion Film Corporation. President, Press Club, London, 1923–24. *Died 10 February 1932.*

PUBLICATIONS

Fiction

> *The Four Just Men.* 1905.
> *Smithy.* 1905.
> *Angel Esquire.* 1908.
> *The Council of Justice.* 1908.
> *Captain Tatham of Tatham Island.* 1909; revised edition, as *The Island of Galloping Gold,* 1916; as *Eve's Island,* 1926.
> *Smithy Abroad: Barrack Room Sketches.* 1909.
> *The Duke in the Suburbs.* 1909.
> *The Nine Bears.* 1910; as *The Other Man,* 1911; revised edition, as *The Secret House,* 1917; as *Silinski, Master Criminal,* 1930; as *The Cheaters,* 1964.
> *Sanders of the River* (stories). 1911.
> *The People of the River* (stories). 1912.
> *Private Selby.* 1912.
> *The Fourth Plague.* 1913.
> *Grey Timothy.* 1913; as *Pallard the Punter,* 1914.
> *The River of Stars.* 1913.
> *The Admirable Carfew* (stories). 1914.
> *Bosambo of the River* (stories). 1914.
> *Smithy's Friend Nobby.* 1914; as *Nobby,* 1916.
> *Bones, Being Further Adventures in Mr. Commissioner Sanders' Country* (stories). 1915.
> *The Man Who Bought London.* 1915.
> *The Melody of Death.* 1915.
> *1925: The Story of a Fatal Peace.* 1915.
> *Smithy and the Hun* (stories). 1915.
> *The Clue of the Twisted Candle.* 1916.
> *A Debt Discharged.* 1916.

The Tomb of Ts'in.   1916.
The Just Men of Cordova.   1917.
Kate Plus 10.   1917.
The Keepers of the King's Peace (stories).   1917.
Down under Donovan.   1918.
Lieutenant Bones (stories).   1918.
Tam o' the Scouts.   1918; as *Tam,* 1928.
Those Folk of Bulboro.   1918.
The Adventures of Heine (stories).   1919.
The Fighting Scouts.   1919.
The Green Rust.   1919.
The Man Who Knew.   1919.
The Daffodil Mystery.   1920; as *The Daffodil Murder,* 1921.
Jack o' Judgment.   1920.
Bones in London (stories).   1921.
The Book of All-Power.   1921.
The Law of the Four Just Men (stories).   1921.
The Angel of Terror.   1922; as *The Destroying Angel,* 1959.
Captains of Souls.   1922.
The Crimson Circle.   1922.
The Flying Fifty-Five.   1922.
Mr. Justice Maxell.   1922.
Sandi, The King-Maker.   1922.
The Valley of Ghosts.   1922.
Bones of the River (stories).   1923.
The Books of Bart.   1923.
Chick (stories).   1923.
The Clue of the New Pin.   1923.
The Green Archer.   1923.
The Missing Million.   1923.
The Dark Eyes of London.   1924.
Double Dan.   1924; as *Diana of Kara-Kara,* 1924.
Educated Evans (stories).   1924.
The Face in the Night.   1924.
Flat 2.   1924.
Room 13.   1924.
The Sinister Man.   1924.
The Three Oak Mystery.   1924.
The Black Avons.   1925.
Blue Hand.   1925.
The Daughters of the Night.   1925.
The Fellowship of the Frog.   1925.
The Gaunt Stranger.   1925; revised edition, as *The Ringer,* 1926.
The Hairy Arm.   1925; as *The Avenger,* 1926.
A King by Night.   1925.
The Mind of Mr. J. G. Reeder (stories).   1925; as *The Murder Book of J. G. Reeder,*
    1929.
The Strange Countess.   1925.
Barbara on Her Own.   1926.
The Black Abbot.   1926.
The Day of Uniting.   1926.
The Door with Seven Locks.   1926.
The Joker.   1926; as *The Colossus,* 1932.
The Man from Morocco.   1926; as *The Black,* 1930.

The Million-Dollar Story. 1926.
More Educated Evans (stories). 1926.
The Northing Tramp. 1926; as *The Tramp,* 1965.
Penelope of the Polyantha. 1926.
Sanders (stories). 1926; as *Mr. Commissioner Sanders,* 1930.
The Square Emerald. 1926; as *The Girl from Scotland Yard,* 1927.
The Terrible People. 1926.
The Three Just Men. 1926.
We Shall See! 1926; as *The Gaol-Breakers,* 1931.
The Yellow Snake. 1926.
Big Foot. 1927.
The Brigand (stories). 1927.
The Feathered Serpent. 1927.
The Forger. 1927; as *The Clever One,* 1928.
Good Evans! (stories). 1927; as *The Educated Man – Good Evans!,* 1929.
The Hand of Power. 1927.
The Man Who Was Nobody. 1927.
The Traitor's Gate. 1927.
The Mixer (stories). 1927.
Number Six. 1927.
The Squeaker. 1927; as *The Squealer,* 1928.
Terror Keep. 1927.
Again Sanders (stories). 1928.
Again the Three Just Men (stories). 1928; as *The Law of the Three Just Men,* 1931.
The Double. 1928.
Elegant Edward (stories). 1928.
The Flying Squad. 1928.
The Gunner. 1928; as *Gunman's Bluff,* 1929.
The Orator (stories). 1928.
The Thief in the Night (stories). 1928.
The Twister. 1928.
Again the Ringer (stories). 1929; as *The Ringer Returns,* 1931.
The Big Four (stories). 1929.
The Black (stories; not the same as the 1930 book). 1929.
For Information Received (stories). 1929.
Four Square Jane. 1929.
The Ghost of Down Hill, and The Queen of Sheba's Belt (stories). 1929.
The Golden Hades. 1929.
The Green Ribbon. 1929.
The India-Rubber Man. 1929.
The Lady of Little Hell (stories). 1929.
The Lone House Mystery (stories). 1929.
Planetoid 127, and The Sweizer Pump (stories). 1929.
Red Aces, Being Three Cases of Mr. Reeder (stories). 1929.
The Reporter (stories). 1929.
Forty-Eight Short Stories. 1929; selections published as *The Cat Burglar,* 1929, *Circumstantial Evidence,* 1929, *Fighting Snub Reilly,* 1929, *The Governor of Chi-Foo,* 1929, *The Little Green Man,* 1929, and *The Prison-Breakers,* 1929.
The Terror. 1929.
The Calendar. 1930.
The Clue of the Silver Key. 1930; as *The Silver Key,* 1930.
The Iron Grip (stories). 1930.
Killer Kay (stories). 1930.
The Lady Called Nita (stories). 1930.

The Lady of Ascot.   1930.
Mrs. William Jones and Bill (stories).   1930.
White Face.   1930.
On the Spot.   1931.
The Coat of Arms.   1931; as *The Arranways Mystery,* 1932.
The Devil Man.   1931.
The Man at the Carlton.   1931.
The Frightened Lady.   1932; as *The Mystery of the Frightened Lady,* 1933.
The Guv'nor and Other Stories.   1932; as *Mr. Reeder Returns,* 1932.
Sergeant Sir Peter (stories).   1932; as *Sergeant Dunn, CID,* 1962.
The Steward (stories).   1932.
When the Gangs Came to London.   1932.
The Stretelli Case and Other Mystery Stories.   1933.
The Last Adventure (stories).   1934.
The Woman from the East and Other Stories.   1934.
The Undisclosed Client (stories).   1963.

Plays

The African Millionaire (produced 1904).   1972.
Sketches, in *Hullo, Ragtime* (produced 1912).
Sketches, in *Hullo, Tango!* (produced 1913).
The Manager's Dream (sketch; produced 1913).
Hello, Exchange! (sketch; produced 1913).
Sketches, in *Business as Usual* (produced 1914).
The Forest of Happy Dreams (produced 1914).   In *One-Act Play Parade,* 1935.
The Whirligig (revue), with Wal Pink and Albert de Courville, music by Frederick
    Chappelle (produced 1919).
M'Lady (produced 1921).
The Ringer, from his novel *The Gaunt Stranger* (produced 1926).   1929.
The Mystery of Room 45 (produced 1926).
The Terror (produced 1927).   1929.
Double Dan, from his own novel (produced 1927).
A Perfect Gentleman (produced 1927).
The Yellow Mask, music by Vernon Duke (produced 1927).
The Lad (produced 1928).
The Flying Squad, from his own novel (produced 1928).   1929.
The Man Who Changed His Name (produced 1928).   1929.
The Squeaker, from his own novel (produced 1928).   1929.
Reasons Unknown (produced 1929).
The Calendar, from his own novel (produced 1929).   1932.
On the Spot (produced 1930).
The Mouthpiece (produced 1930).
Smoky Cell (produced 1930).
Charles III, from a play by Curt Götz (produced 1931).
The Old Man (produced 1931).
The Case of the Frightened Lady (produced 1931).   1932; as *Criminal at Large,* 1934.
The Green Pack (produced 1932).   1933.

Screenplays: *Edith Cavell,* 1917; *The Ringer,* 1928; *Valley of the Ghosts,* 1928; *The
Forger,* 1928; *Red Aces,* 1929; *The Squeaker,* 1930; *Should a Doctor Tell?,* 1930; *The
Hound of the Baskervilles,* with V. Gareth Gundrey, 1931; *The Old Man,* 1931.

Verse

> *The Mission That Failed! A Tale of the Raid and Other Poems.* 1898.
> *War! and Other Poems.* 1900.
> *Writ in Barracks.* 1900.

Other

> *Unofficial Despatches.* 1901.
> *The Council of Justice.* 1908.
> *Famous Scottish Regiments.* 1914.
> *Field Marshal Sir John French and His Campaigns.* 1914.
> *Heroes All: Gallant Deeds of the War.* 1914.
> *The Standard History of the War.* 4 vols., 1914–15.
> *Kitchener's Army and the Territorial Forces: The Full Story of a Great Achievement.* 6 vols., 1915.
> *War of the Nations,* vols. 2–11. 1915–19.
> *People: A Short Autobiography.* 1926.
> *This England.* 1927.
> *My Hollywood Diary.* 1932.

Bibliography: *The British Bibliography of Wallace* by W. O. G. Lofts and Derek Adley, 1969.

Reading List: *Wallace: Each Way* by Robert G. Curtis, 1932; *Wallace* by Ethel V. Wallace, 1932; *Wallace: The Biography of a Phenomenon* by Margaret Lane, 1938, revised edition, 1964.

*   *   *

The fact that Edgar Wallace was the most popular writer of his time should not necessarily be taken as evidence that he had no talent or merely varied one simple formula. He served in the ranks in the Boer War, and the experience gave him material for a volume of verses for which he was dubbed somewhat ambiguously "The Ranker Kipling." He wrote also some yarns of barrack-room life modelled on Kipling's *Soldiers Three.* Among his later fiction, *Sanders of the River, Bones of the River, Bosambo of the River,* stories of the struggles and stratagems of lonely British administrators on a river station in what might be Nigeria, attracted readers who disdained his thrillers. Some of these, however, like *The Mind of Mr J. G. Reeder,* showed ingenuity and a sense of character, and did not depend entirely on thrills. Once at least he cheated his readers, giving his hero the name Jasper, typical of villains of melodrama, and making his villain an attractive cleanlimbed Englishman. He had some real success on the stage with plays like *The Ringer.* But it must be admitted that most of his works, often written or dictated in a few days, were ephemeral, and that Margaret Lane's excellent biography of 1938 is likely to outlast Wallace's own works. For his time, he was a good time-killer, but his time is not ours.

—G. S. Fraser

WALLACE, Lew(is).   American.   Born in Brookville, Indiana, 10 April 1827; moved with his family to Indianapolis, 1837. Largely self-educated; studied law in his father's office in Indianapolis: admitted to the Indiana bar, 1849. Raised a company, and served as a 2nd Lieutenant in the United States Army Infantry, in the Mexican War, 1846–47; appointed Adjutant General of Indiana at the beginning of the Civil War: served as a Colonel in the 11th Indiana Volunteers; promoted to Brigadier General, 1861, and Major General, 1862; prepared the defense of Cincinnati, 1863; given command of the Middle Division and VIII Army Corps, with headquarters at Baltimore, 1863; fought battle of Monocracy, and saved Washington, D.C. from capture, 1864; member of the court that tried Lincoln's assassins, and President of the court that tried the commandant of the Andersonville prison; mustered out, 1865. Married Susan Arnold Elston in 1852. Edited a free soil paper in Indianapolis, 1848; practiced law in Indianapolis, 1849; moved to Covington, 1850: prosecuting attorney, 1850–53; moved to Crawfordsville, 1853; member of the Indiana State Senate, 1856; returned to Crawfordsville and his law practice after the Civil War; Republican candidate for Congress, for Indiana, 1870; writer from 1870, also an illustrator; Governor of the New Mexico Territory, 1878–81; served as United States Minister to Turkey, 1881–85, then returned to Crawfordsville. *Died 15 February 1905.*

PUBLICATIONS

Fiction

The Fair God; or, The Last of the 'Tzins: A Tale of the Conquest of Mexico.   1873.
Ben-Hur: A Tale of the Christ.   1880.
The Boyhood of Christ.   1888.
The Prince of India: or, Why Constantinople Fell.   1893.

Play

Commodus.   1876.

Verse

The Wooing of Malkatoon, Commodus.   1898.

Other

Life of General Ben Harrison.   1888.
An Autobiography.   2 vols., 1906.

Editor, *Famous Paintings of the World.*   1894.

Reading List: *"Ben-Hur" Wallace* by Irving McKee, 1947.

*   *   *

Though famous in his day as a soldier, governor, lawyer, and diplomat, Lew Wallace is mainly remembered as the author of *Ben-Hur*, one of the three best-selling American novels of the 19th century. Indeed, the novel is known by many who could not name the author. *Ben-Hur* occupies a unique place in American cultural history; subtitled "A Tale of the Christ," it was the first and in some cases the only novel to be read by many puritanical fundamentalists who considered other fiction to be a sinful and idle waste of time. Dramatized in 1899 by William Young, *Ben-Hur* was an immense success for 20 years as a stage spectacle complete with chariot race run on treadmills. The play further broke down puritan inhibitions by introducing many to the theatre, and a colossal 1925 film version accomplished the same thing for the movies. Wallace wrote two other successful historical novels, *The Fair God* and *The Prince of India*; a blank verse drama, *Commodus*; a long narrative poem, *The Wooing of Malkatoon*, about the founder of the Ottoman Empire; a campaign biography of Benjamin Harrison; an account of Fort Donelson for *Battles and Leaders of the Civil War*; and an autobiography completed by his wife after his death in 1905.

Though the reading public considered *Ben-Hur* a supplement to sacred scripture and went to the dramatizations as to a passion play, Wallace was not a churchgoer, and the novel is closer in spirit to Jacobean revenge tragedy than to the New Testament. Wallace claimed, however, that he wrote it in part to refute the agnosticism of Robert Ingersol, and that during its composition he became convinced of the divinity of Jesus. All his novels deal with the clash of religions and cultures: *The Fair God* with the conflict of Aztec and Catholic conquistadors; *The Prince of India* with Moslem and Christian during the fall of Constantinople; and *Ben-Hur* with Jewish, pagan Roman, and Christian. Wallace's heroes are an Aztec prince, a prince of Judea, and a Turkish Sultan – all unusual for a 19th-century Anglo-Saxon to champion. A thorough researcher and a careful stylist, Wallace blended exotic romanticism with realistic detail. Though his own life was as dramatic as any of his fiction, he felt himself in some ways a failure and wrote about the romantic past as an escape from the routine of the law, the army, and political and diplomatic posts.

—Robert E. and Katharine M. Morsberger

WALLANT, Edward Lewis. American. Born in New Haven, Connecticut, 19 October 1926. Educated at the Pratt Institute, New York, 1947–50; New School for Social Research, New York, 1954–55. Served as a gunner's mate in the United States Navy, 1944–46. Married Joyce Fromkin in 1948; two daughters and one son. Worked as a graphic designer for various advertising agencies, New York, 1950–62. Recipient: Bread Loaf Writers' Conference Fellowship, 1960; Daroff Memorial Award, 1961; Guggenheim Fellowship, 1962. *Died 5 December 1962.*

PUBLICATIONS

Fiction

The Human Season. 1960.
The Pawnbroker. 1961.

The Tenants of Moonbloom.   1963.
The Children at the Gate.   1964.

Reading List: *The Landscape of Nightmare: Studies in the Contemporary American Novel* by
Jonathan Baumbach, 1965.

*   *   *

Edward Lewis Wallant died at thirty-six, just as he was becoming known as a promising
novelist. The four novels of this brief career center around two dominant motifs: the quest
for family connections and the search for a viable religious-philosophical position. In *The
Tenants of Moonbloom*, a spokesman comments, "There is a Trinity of survival, and it
consists of Courage, Dream, and Love ... he who possesses all three, or two, or at least one of
these things wins whatever there is to win. ..." All four of Wallant's protagonists become
winners, in these terms, but first they must go through painful rebirths or births.

Joe Berman, a middle-aged plumber whose wife has just died in *The Human Season*,
Wallant's first novel, curses his Jewish God for a time but then loses his belief in an
anthropomorphic deity. In place of this, he comes to insist on the importance of the human
capacity for wonder and love and to accept his own failings in family relationships. Thus he
lays the ghosts of his god-like father, whom he loved too well, and his son, whom he feels he
did not love enough. *The Pawnbroker*, Wallant's second novel, presents Sol Nazerman,
whose wife and children died in a Nazi concentration camp, and where he was a subject of
experimental surgery. Nazerman affects total cynicism and a harshness comparable to that of
his Nazi tormentors, but his protective shell is broken by his young assistant in the
pawnshop, Jesus Ortiz, who, with three other black men, plans to rob Sol. During the
attempted robbery, Jesus, who has developed a confused filial love for Sol, takes the bullet
intended for the pawnbroker, and Sol is spiritually reborn. This is not, however, an easy or
sentimental resolution. Nazerman's rebirth is into "the crowding filth" of humanity, wherein
he feels "hopeless, wretched, strangely proud."

Though published last due to an arrangement Wallant made before he died, *The Children
at the Gate* was written third and is transitional. Here the protagonist, Angelo DeMarco, at
eighteen, has never been emotionally alive. The agent of his awakening is a Jewish hospital
orderly, a benevolent drug pusher and comic Christ figure whose symbol is the bedpan rather
than the cross. The characters in this novel tend to be overdrawn, and the humor is
sometimes forced, but the book provides a bridge to *The Tenants of Moonbloom*. Norman
Moonbloom is another character in the process of becoming. After a protracted, cocoon-like
education, his first job is as rental agent for his brother, owner of four tenement houses.
Norman begins to empathize with the miserable tenants, and, though knowing it will do no
real good, he sets out to repair everything in the tenements, as an act of personal affirmation.
Norman's labors are preparatory to birth, and, as is the case in the other novels, coming to
life includes recognition of death's inevitability, but for Norman this is not important.
Through ritual initiation he has become identified with humanity and has thus achieved a
kind of immortality.

In these novels, Wallant progressed from family concerns and questions of Jewish belief to
Moonbloom's identification with the human family and an affirmation of the worldly value
of the most inclusive religious ritual, the initiation rite. He progressed, also, from the rather
grim acceptance of the first novel through reluctant affirmation in the second and third to
joyful and comic belonging in the last, in which Moonbloom, at thirty-three, loses his
virginity and learns to laugh. Near that last novel's end, Norman Moonbloom, covered with
filth from a bathroom wall he is repairing, shouts, "I'M BORN!"

—James Angle

WALPOLE, Horace (or Horatio); 4th Earl of Orford. English. Born in London, 24 September 1717; son of the politician Sir Robert Walpole. Educated at Eton College, 1727–34; King's College, Cambridge, 1735–39, left without taking a degree. Travelled in France and Italy, with the poet Thomas Gray, 1739–41, then returned to England and settled in London; Member of Parliament for Callington, Cornwall, 1741–53, Castle Rising, Norfolk, 1754–57, and King's Lynn, Norfolk, 1757–67; purchased an estate at Twickenham, Middlesex, 1747, which he subsequently named Strawberry Hill and gradually gothicized, 1753–76; established a printing press at Strawberry Hill, on which he printed his own works and those of other authors, 1757–89; visited Paris, 1765, 1767, 1775; succeeded to the earldom of Orford, 1791. *Died 2 March 1797.*

PUBLICATIONS

Collections

    Works, edited by Mary Berry and others. 9 vols., 1798–1825.
    Letters, edited by Mrs. Paget Toynbee. 16 vols., 1903–05; supplement edited by Paget Toynbee, 3 vols., 1918–25.
    Fugitive Verses, edited by W. S. Lewis. 1931.
    Correspondence, edited by W. S. Lewis and others. 1937 –

Fiction

    The Castle of Otranto. 1765; edited by W. S. Lewis, 1964.
    Hieroglyphic Tales. 1785.

Plays

    The Mysterious Mother. 1768; edited by Montague Summers, with *The Castle of Otranto,* 1924.
    Nature Will Prevail (produced 1778). In *Works,* 1798.
    The Fashionable Friends (produced 1802). 1802.

Other

    The Lesson for the Day. 1742.
    The Beauties. 1746.
    Epilogue to Tamerlane. 1746.
    Aedes Walpolianae. 1747; revised edition, 1752.
    A Letter from Xo Ho. 1757.
    Fugitive Pieces in Verse and Prose. 1758; augmented edition, 1770.
    A Catalogue of the Royal and Noble Authors of England, Scotland, and Ireland. 2 vols., 1758; *Postscript,* 1786.
    A Dialogue Between Two Great Ladies. 1760.
    Catalogue of the Pictures and Drawings in the Holbein Chamber. 1760.
    Catalogue of the Pictures of the Duke of Devonshire. 1760.
    Anecdotes of Painting in England, and A Catalogue of Engravers (based on material collected by G. Vertue). 4 vols., 1762–63; additional vol. of *Anecdotes,* 1780;

additional vol. of *Anecdotes* edited by F. W. Hilles and P. B. Daghlian, 1937.
The Magpie and Her Brood. 1764.
An Account of the Giants Lately Discovered. 1766.
Historic Doubts on Richard III. 1768; edited by P. M. Kendall, 1965.
A Description of the Villa of Horace Walpole. 1774.
Essay on Modern Gardening. 1785; edited by W. S. Lewis, 1931.
Notes to the Portraits at Woburn Abbey. 1800.
Reminiscences Written for Mary and Agnes Berry. 1805; edited by Paget Toynbee, 1924.
Memoirs of the Last Ten Years of the Reign of George II, edited by Lord Holland. 2 vols., 1822.
Memoirs of George III, edited by Denis Le Marchant. 4 vols., 1845; edited by G. F. R. Barker, 1894.
Journal of George III, edited by J. Doran. 2 vols., 1859; as *Last Journals,* edited by A. Francis Steuart, 1910.
Manuscript Common-Place Book, edited by W. S. Lewis. 1927.
Memoirs and Portraits (selection), edited by Matthew Hodgart. 1963; revised edition, 1963.
Miscellany 1786–1795, edited by Lars E. Troide. 1978.

Editor, *The Life of Lord Herbert of Cherbury Written by Himself.* 1765.

Bibliography: *A Bibliography of Walpole* by Allen T. Hazen, 1948.

Reading List: *The Life of Walpole* by Stephen Gwynn, 1932; *Walpole and the English Novel* by K. K. Mehrota, 1934; *Walpole* by R. W. Ketton-Cremer, 1940; *Walpole's Memoirs* by Gerrit P. Judd, 1959; *Walpole* by W. S. Lewis, 1961; "Walpole" by Bonamy Dobrée, in *Restoration and Eighteenth Century Literature: Essays in Honor of A. D. McKillop* edited by Carroll Camden, 1963; *Walpole: Writer, Politician, and Connoisseur: Essays* edited by Warren H. Smith, 1968; *Walpole* by Martin Kallich, 1971.

*   *   *

Horace Walpole is significant for his contributions to history, literature, and art. His literary reputation rests principally on his letters (about 6000 in the correspondence, 4000 by Walpole himself) in which he vividly chronicles his times. On his continental tour he had initiated his friendship with Sir Horace Mann with whom, for example, he corresponded regularly for nearly fifty years. In a visit to Paris, 1765, he met Madame du Deffand whose friendship was confirmed in an extensive correspondence till her death in 1780. Other correspondents were William Mason, the poet and biographer of Gray; William Cole, the antiquary; and, among many others, George Montagu, his friend at Eton.

At Eton Walpole had made many lasting friends, among them the politician Henry Seymour Conway and the poet Thomas Gray. Gray accompanied Walpole on his tour, and his early poems were first published at Walpole's press at Strawberry Hill. At King's College, Cambridge, Walpole came under the influence of Conyers Middleton, whose deistic rationalism he adopted and maintained throughout his life. Walpole's "Verses in Memory of Henry VI, the Founder of King's College, Cambridge" praises the Gothic college chapel, providing evidence of a very early esthetic commitment to the Gothic architectural style. In his verse "Epistle to Ashton," Walpole emphasizes his distaste for religious bigotry and fanaticism.

In addition to his letters, Walpole also kept numerous journals in which he presented his well-informed views on the politics of the reigns of George II and George III for forty years, 1751–1791. With Burke and Conway, Walpole opposed the war against the American colonies; and, later, he believed Burke was right to oppose the egalitarian ideals of the French Revolution. In the realm of art, Walpole was a taste-maker with his innovative transformation of his country estate into the celebrated Gothic restoration at Strawberry Hill. His *Anecdotes of Painting* is a standard source of information about English art before 1750.

In his two most important literary works, the novel *The Castle of Otranto* and the tragedy *The Mysterious Mother*, Walpole exploited the possibility of violence and the supernatural in the medieval milieu, thereby setting the taste for the Gothic in narrative and drama. The chief feature of this romantic literature is terror, terror effected by the atmospheric gloom of a forbidding castle and all its appurtenances calculated to produce sensation, chilling and thrilling: skeletons and haunting ghosts in secret rooms, trap doors with creaking hinges, dark corridors, threats of violence, pursuit of a lovely damsel in distress by a satanic and lustful villain, and the like. In the novel the tyrannical villain is inexplicably motivated to sadistic cruelty, thereby creating the suspense that inevitably explodes in a catastrophic climax. In his play, Walpole evokes terror through an artful priest and horror by grounding the action upon incest, which turns out to be the mysterious sin haunting the gloomy castle.

Ironically, Walpole's esthetic medievalism resulted in the tarnishing of his reputation. For when Chatterton attempted in 1769 to make the author of *Otranto* and the builder of Strawberry Hill his patron, only to be rejected, Walpole was blamed for his untimely death as an apparent suicide. In view of what is known of Walpole's generous character, his reputation as a cold and heartless aristocrat is undeserved.

—Martin Kallich

WALPOLE, Sir Hugh (Seymour). English. Born in Auckland, New Zealand, 13 March 1884, of English parents. Educated at King's School, Canterbury, Kent, and Durham School; Emmanuel College, Cambridge, 1903–06, graduated (honours in historical tripos) 1906. Served with the Russian Red Cross in Galicia, 1914–16; Director of the Anglo-Russian Propaganda Bureau in Petrograd, 1916–17. Member of the staff of the Mersey Mission to Seamen, 1906; travelled in France and Germany, 1907; Assistant Master at Epsom College, Surrey, 1908; full-time writer, in London, from 1909; subsequently a friend of Henry James and Arnold Bennett; undertook first of a series of lecture tours in the United States, 1919; Rede Lecturer, Cambridge University, 1925. First Chairman of the Selection Committee of the Book Society, London, from 1929; first Chairman, Society of Bookmen, London, now the National Book League. Recipient: Black Memorial Prize, 1919, 1920. Fellow, Royal Society of Literature. C.B.E. (Commander, Order of the British Empire), 1918. Knighted, 1937. *Died 1 June 1941.*

PUBLICATIONS

Fiction

The Wooden Horse. 1909.
Maradick at Forty: A Transition. 1910.
Mr. Perrin and Mr. Traill: A Tragi-Comedy. 1911; as *The Gods and Mr. Perrin,* 1911.
The Prelude to Adventure. 1912.

Fortitude, Being a True and Faithful Account of the Education of an Explorer. 1913.
The Duchess of Wrexe, Her Decline and Death: A Romantic Commentary. 1914.
The Golden Scarecrow. 1915.
The Dark Forest. 1916.
The Green Mirror: A Quiet Story. 1917.
Jeremy. 1919.
The Secret City. 1919.
The Captives. 1920.
The Thirteen Travellers (stories). 1921.
The Young Enchanted: A Romantic Story. 1921.
The Cathedral. 1922.
Jeremy and Hamlet. 1923.
The Old Ladies. 1924.
Portrait of a Man with Red Hair: A Romantic Macabre. 1925.
Harmer John: An Unworldly Story. 1926.
Jeremy at Crale. 1927.
The Silver Thorn (stories). 1928.
Winterspoon: Passages in the Lives of Two Sisters, Janet and Rosalind Grandison. 1928.
Farthing Hall, with J. B. Priestley. 1929.
Hans Frost. 1929.
The Herries Chronicle: Rogue Herries, Judith Paris, The Fortress, Vanessa, The Bright Pavilions, Katherine Christian. 6 vols., 1930–43.
Above the Dark Circus: An Adventure. 1931; as *Above the Dark Tumult,* 1931.
All Souls' Night (stories). 1933.
Captain Nicholas: A Modern Comedy. 1934.
Cathedral Carol Service (story). 1934.
The Inquisitor. 1935.
A Prayer for My Son. 1936.
John Cornelius, His Life and Adventures. 1937.
Head in Green Bronze and Other Stories. 1938.
The Joyful Delaneys. 1938.
The Sea Tower: A Love Story. 1939.
The Blind Man's House: A Quiet Story. 1941.
The Killer and the Slain: A Strange Story. 1942.
Mr. Huffam and Other Stories. 1948.

Plays

Robin's Father, with Rudolf Besier (produced 1918).
The Cathedral, from his own novel (produced 1932). 1937.
The Haxtons. 1939.

Screenplays: *Vanessa: Her Love Story,* 1935; *David Copperfield,* with Howard Estabrook, 1935; *Little Lord Fauntleroy,* 1936.

Radio Play: *Behind the Screen* (serial), with others, 1930.

Other

Joseph Conrad. 1916; revised edition, 1924.
The Art of James Branch Cabell. 1920.

A Walpole Anthology. 1921.
The Crystal Box. 1924.
Reading: An Essay. 1926.
A Stranger (juvenile), with *Red Pepper,* by Thomas Quayle. 1926.
Anthony Trollope. 1928.
My Religious Experience. 1928.
The Apple Trees: Four Reminiscences. 1932.
A Letter to a Modern Novelist. 1932.
Extracts from a Diary. 1934.
Roman Fountain. 1940.
A Note on the Origins of the Herries Chronicle. 1940.
The Freedom of Books. 1940.
Open Letter of an Optimist. 1941.
Women Are Motherly. 1943

Editor, *The Waverley Pageant: The Best Passages from the Novels of Scott.* 1932.
Editor, *Essays and Studies,* vol. 18. 1933.
Editor, with Wilfred Partington, *Famous Stories of Five Centuries.* 1934.
Editor, with others, *The Nonesuch Dickens.* 23 vols., 1937–38.
Editor, *A Second Century of Creepy Stories.* 1937.

Reading List: *Walpole: A Study* by Marguerite Steen, 1933; *Walpole and His Writings* by A. Wall, 1947; *Walpole: A Biography* by Rupert Hart-Davis, 1952.

*   *   *

Hugh Walpole is a comparatively prolific author of fiction – mainly novels – who began writing before the First World War but whose reputation received a considerable boost from a long article by Henry James in the *Times Literary Supplement.* Although James's own novels sold only slowly, his reputation as literary judge and critic was very high. Hugh Walpole was a friend or acquaintance of most of the novelists of this period. To the popular and influential Arnold Bennett, Walpole was the "authentic" novelist. He went to the war front in Burma where he served in a variety of functions and continued to write, particularly *The Dark Forest,* which was well-received and regarded by Walpole himself as his best novel.

The taste for Walpole's once enormously popular work has largely vanished. This is a pity, since there is much good reading in him. It needs only a successful television serial to make his long series of books about his Lake District family, the Herries, as familiar as Galsworthy's Forsytes, though the two long sagas bear no resemblance. Besides this saga, there is his immortal school story, *Mr. Perrin and Mr. Traill:* there are also his sub-Trollope genre (e.g., *The Cathedral*) and his fantastic-thriller stories, which usually have a half-hidden psychiatric theme; among the best of these are *Portrait of a Man with Red Hair* and *Above the Dark Circus.* He wrote many short stories, particularly for children, and studies of authors, among them *Trollope.* Largely to bring financial help to the young J. B. Priestley, he collaborated with him in a novel called *Farthing Hall.*

Walpole, though one of his obituarists declared him lacking in talent, was an adept writer, but little of his work was fashionable or innovative. The young could find in him nothing to emulate. This was perhaps what made Maugham's picture of him as Alroy Kear in *Cakes and Ale* the more bitter. Walpole knew that he was no more than a journeyman of letters, however much money he made.

—Kenneth Young

WALTON, Izaak. English. Born in Stafford, 9 August 1593. Married 1) Rachel Floud in 1626 (died, 1640), seven children; 2) Anne Ken in 1647 (died, 1662), one daughter and two sons. Apprenticed to a London sempstress c. 1610; set up as a draper in Fleet Street, 1614; Freeman of the Ironmongers' Company, 1618; retired, 1644; lived with Bishop George Morley at Farnham, Surrey, 1662–78, and with his son-in-law at Winchester, 1678 until his death. *Died 15 December 1683.*

PUBLICATIONS

Collections

The Compleat Walton, edited by Geoffrey Keynes. 1929.

Prose

The Life of John Donne. 1658; revised edition, in *Lives,* 1670.
The Compleat Angler; or, The Contemplative Man's Recreation. 1653; revised edition, 1658, 1661; in *The Universal Angler,* 1676.
The Life of Mr. Rich. Hooker. 1665; revised edition, in *Lives,* 1670.
The Life of Dr. Sanderson, with tracts by Sanderson and a sermon by Hooker. 1678; edited by W. Jacobson, in *Works of Sanderson,* vol. 6, 1854.
The Lives of Dr. John Donne, Sir Henry Wotton, Mr. Richard Hooker, Mr. George Herbert. 1670; revised edition, 1675; edited by George Saintsbury, 1927.
Love and Truth. 1680.

Editor, *Reliquiae Wottonianae; or, A Collection of Lives, Letters, Poems,* by Sir Henry Wotton. 1651; revised edition, 1654, 1685.

Bibliography: in *The Compleat Walton,* 1929.

Reading List: *Walton* by Margaret Bottrall, 1955; *The Making of Walton's Lives* by D. Novarr, 1958; *Biography in the Hands of Walton, Johnson, and Boswell* by J. E. Butt, 1966; *The Art of the Compleat Angler* by J. R. Cooper, 1968.

*   *   *

Chance rather than design led Izaak Walton to a literary career. He was a London tradesman who had enjoyed no educational advantages. A man of great integrity, a traditionalist in religion and politics, he must have possessed a genius for friendship. It was through the encouragement of such high-ranking friends as Sir Henry Wotton, Bishop Morley, and Charles Cotton that he became a writer of real distinction.

Walton was a pioneer in biography, and his *Lives,* particularly those of Herbert and Donne, are small masterpieces; but by far his most famous book is *The Compleat Angler.* It was not, however, until its pastoral charm caught the fancy of Charles Lamb and other Romantic critics that it became something of a best-seller as well as a classic. His original readers certainly welcomed the book, and Walton revised it several times; but to them it was primarily a fishing manual, though diversified by many songs and poems, anecdotes and snatches of moralising. Only posterity could fully appreciate the idyllic quality of Walton's portrayal of innocent country pastimes and pleasures in an unspoilt English landscape, or relish the quaintness of his credulity in matters of natural history.

To the author, the book was a recreation, written during the Cromwellian interregnum to solace himself for the loss of happier bygone times. He had already published his lives of Donne and Wotton. Both men had been personally known to him. He had gone fishing with Wotton, and was familiar enough with the Dean of St Paul's to receive one of his emblematic seals and to be present at his death-bed. Izaak Walton devoted much patient labour to the compilation of these and three subsequent biographies (Hooker, Herbert, and Sanderson). They were published collectively in 1670, a proof that they were quickly recognised as possessing merits quite beyond those of the ordinary prefatory life or commemorative eulogy. Dr. Johnson, himself a master of the brief biography, regarded Walton's *Lives* as one of his favourite books.

Izaak Walton's standards of accuracy naturally differ greatly from those of modern academic researchers. He did, however, set down straightforwardly what he took to be facts, and he relied whenever possible on personal testimony, thus achieving an impression of intimacy that is particularly engaging. When occasion required it, he could be impressively eloquent, and he handled both narrative and digression with great skill. Walton has been criticised for treating his subjects with too much veneration, and for reducing them all to a sameness of gentle piety. The charge is not unfounded. He was himself a pious conformist, and a rather sententious moralist. His experience of public life was limited. But if the testimony of his extant portraits can be trusted, he was, as all his writings suggest, a strong, genial and intelligent man, who deserved the appellation of "honest Izaak." Few seventeenth-century writers of prose have left behind them a more attractive legacy.

—Margaret Bottrall

WARD, Artemus. Pseudonym for Charles Farrar Browne. American. Born in Waterford, Maine, 26 April 1834. Largely self-educated; learned printer's trade on the *Weekly Democrat*, Lancaster, New Hampshire, 1847–48. Worked as a compositor and reporter on various New England newspapers from 1848, and worked in the printing trade in Boston for three years; writer from 1852; Reporter, then Columnist (as Artemus Ward), *Cleveland Plain Dealer*, 1852–59; member of the staff of *Vanity Fair*, New York, 1859–62; lecturer (performances of selections from his own works) in Boston and New York, 1861, Washington, D.C., 1862, California and Nevada, 1863, New York and Canada, 1864, and London, 1866–67; contributed to *Punch*, London, 1866–67. *Died 6 March 1867.*

PUBLICATIONS

Collections

Selected Works, edited by Albert Jay Nock. 1924.

Prose

Artemus Ward, His Book. 1862.
Artemus Ward, His Travels. 1865.
Artemus Ward among the Fenians. 1866.

Artemus Ward in London and Other Papers. 1867.

Artemus Ward's Lecture, edited by T. W. Robertson and E. P. Hingston.   1869; as *Artemus Ward's Panorama*, 1869.

Letters of Artemus Ward to Charles E. Wilson, 1858–1861.   1900.

Bibliography: in *Bibliography of American Literature* by Jacob Blanck, 1955.

Reading List: *Ward: A Biography and Bibliography* by Don C. Seitz, 1919; *Ward* by James C. Austin, 1964.

*   *   *

Charles Farrar Browne, better known as Artemus Ward, was a Yankee humorist and a foremost representative of native American humor. During the decades of the 1850's and 1860's he was so phenomenally popular that he became the national jester of the Civil War period. He reached national prominence with his Artemus Ward pieces, which first appeared in his column in the Cleveland *Plain Dealer* in 1858. As editor of *Vanity Fair* (1861–62), he became the unofficial dean of American humor. Finally, he turned to lecturing and founded the comic lecture as an enduring American institution.

Browne's literary reputation rests largely on the humor he published in the *Plain Dealer* and *Vanity Fair*. Basic to his technique in the best of this humor is his use of Artemus Ward, an old side-showman and rascal, as his alter ego. Using the side-showman's point of view and colloquial language, Browne commented on a great variety of subjects. The literary forms which he employed most extensively were the anecdote and the mock letter to the editor. His favorite humorous device was misspelling, and he used it expertly.

The Artemus Ward pieces generally treat national figures, subjects, and issues; few significant aspects of mid-nineteenth-century culture escaped his scrutiny. Reformers and cultists caught his attention early, and he directed some of him most pungent satire at the fanatics among them. He satirized militant feminists, zealous temperance advocates, Mormons, Shakers, and proponents of free love; his biggest guns, however, he reserved for unceasing war on the Abolitionists. A strong northern Democrat, he commented extensively, too, on the subject of national politics; a strong supporter of the Union, he gave much attention to the Civil War. During the war he repeatedly attacked Congress, the inept leadership of the Union Army, draft-dodgers, profiteers, and pseudo-patriots.

Throughout his career Browne expressed freely his socio-economic views, generally those of the Democratic Party. He was constantly critical of questionable business practices, the mania for making money, speculation, and the excesses of capitalism in general. The false ideals of his age he attacked again and again. In a number of his burlesques of the popular romance, for example, he satirized not only the style of the genre itself, but also the sentimentality, the questionable values, and superficial moralism which pervaded popular culture.

Basically burlesques of the serious lyceum lecture, Browne's lectures were pure popular entertainment. By careful planning and cautious experimentation he succeeded in appealing to a large segment of the American people, and, at the end of his career, to British audiences as well. By making comic lecturing both respectable and profitable he paved the way for Mark Twain and the numerous other literary comedians who followed him. His best and most famous lecture was "Artemus Ward among the Mormons."

For almost two decades, Charles F. Browne held the attention, affection, and respect of countless Americans, including Abraham Lincoln. Browne not only entertained Americans, but, pleading for sanity, common sense, and moderation, he helped to shape public opinion during a most critical period in American life. Finally, his success abroad helped to bring about a reappraisal by Americans of their native humorists.

—John Q. Reed

WARD, Mrs. Humphry (née Mary Augusta Arnold). English. Born in Hobart, Tasmania, 11 June 1851, of English parents; grand-daughter of Dr. Arnold of Rugby, and niece of the poet Matthew Arnold; returned to England with her family, 1856. Educated in English boarding schools, 1858–67. Married Thomas Humphry Ward in 1872; one son and two daughters. Settled in Oxford with her family, 1867, and continued her studies on her own; contributed to the *Dictionary of Christian Biography,*1877; Secretary to Somerville College, Oxford, 1879; moved to London, 1881; contributed to *The Times, Pall Mall Gazette,* and *Macmillan's Magazine;* founded a social settlement at University Hall, Gordon Square, 1890, which developed into the Passmore Edwards Settlement, 1897; Founder, Women's National Anti-Suffrage League, 1908; appointed one of the first 7 women magistrates, 1920. LL.D.: University of Edinburgh. *Died 24 March 1920.*

PUBLICATIONS

Fiction

Milly and Olly; or, A Holiday among the Mountains (juvenile). 1881.
Miss Bretherton. 1884.
Robert Elsmere. 1883.
The History of David Grieve. 1892.
Marcella. 1894.
The Story of Bessie Costrell. 1895.
Sir George Tressady. 1896.
Helbeck of Bannisdale. 1898.
Eleanor. 1900.
Lady Rose's Daughter. 1903.
The Marriage of William Ashe. 1905.
Fenwick's Career. 1906.
Diana Mallory. 1908.
Daphne; or, Marriage à la Mode. 1909.
Canadian Born. 1910.
The Case of Richard Meynell. 1911.
The Mating of Lydia. 1913.
The Coryston Family. 1913.
Delia Blanchflower. 1915.
Eltham House. 1915.
A Great Success. 1916.
Lady Connie. 1916.
Missing. 1917.
Cousin Philip. 1919.
Harvest. 1920; as *Love's Harvest,* 1929.

Plays

Eleanor, from her own novel (produced 1902). 1903; (revised version produced 1905).
Agatha, with L. N. Parker, from the novel *Lady Rose's Daughter* by Mrs. Ward (produced 1905). 1904.
The Marriage of William Ashe, with Margaret Mayo, from the novel by Mrs. Ward (produced 1908).

Other

The Play-Time of the Poor. 1906.
William Thomas Arnold, Journalist and Historian, with C. E. Montague. 1907.
Letters to My Neighbours on the Present Election. 1910; revised edition, 1910.
Writings. 16 vols., 1911–12.
England's Effort: Six Letters to an American Friend. 1916.
Towards the Goal. 1917.
A Writer's Recollections. 1918.
The War and Elizabeth. 1918.
Fields of Victory. 1919.

Translator, *Amiel's Journal.* 2 vols., 1885.

Reading List: *The Life of Mrs. Ward* by Janet P. Trevelyan, 1923; "Mrs. Ward and the Victorian Ideal" by C. Lederer, in *Nineteenth-Century Fiction 6,* 1951; *Mrs. Ward* by Enid Huws Jones, 1973.

*   *   *

Mrs. Humphry Ward was the granddaughter of Thomas Arnold and the niece of Matthew Arnold, and she displays in her novels the moral earnestness of both her grandfather and her uncle. Her own father, Thomas Arnold, Jr., whose flirtation with Roman Catholicism was an embarrassment to his family, may have influenced her in portraying many of her heroes as men tormented by indecision and religious doubt. The most notable hero of this kind is Robert Elsmere. His struggle to resist the intellectual pressure to abandon orthodoxy in favour of humanitarian secular religion, very much on the same lines as that preached by Matthew Arnold, was recorded in *Robert Elsmere,* an instant best-seller. *Robert Elsmere* is less impressive as a novel than as a record of religious doubt, although the predicament of Robert Elsmere's wife, Catherine, who appears in a sequel, *The Case of Richard Meynell,* is outlined with great sensitivity. On the other hand a sub-plot involving a love affair between Catherine's sister Rose and a dreary Oxford don, Langham, is a distinctly lightweight affair. Sub-plots are also an irritation in *The History of David Grieve,* the record of a working man's struggle to rise in the world while abandoning the support of orthodox religion. *Helbeck of Bannisdale* is considered by many as Mrs. Ward's best novel, in that the love affair between the sceptical Laura Fountain and the devout Catholic, Alan Helbeck, is an integral part of the novel's religious investigation.

Mrs. Ward's later novels are more concerned with social than religious issues. *Marcella, Sir George Tressady,* and *Lady Rose's Daughter* were all concerned with the need to do something for the poor, a cause in which Mrs. Ward herself laboured strongly, although she resisted any radical solution, just as she was opposed to the Suffragette movement. The anti-suffragette novels, *Delia Blanchflower* and *Cousin Philip,* like the novels in favour of social reform, are marred by too much propaganda in favour of or against a cause, long since won and lost, but in spite of this propaganda element Mrs. Humphry Ward deserves more credit than she now receives.

—T. J. Winnifrith

WARNER, Charles Dudley. American. Born in Plainsfield, Massachusetts, 12 September 1829; moved with his family to Charlemont, Massachusetts, 1837, and Cazenovia, New York, 1841. Educated at the Oneida Conference Seminary, Cazenovia; Hamilton College, Clinton, New York, B.A. 1851; worked as a railway surveyor in Missouri, 1853–54; joined a friend in business in Philadelphia, 1855; studied law at the University of Pennsylvania, Philadelphia, 1856–58, LL.B. 1858. Married Susan Lee in 1856. Writer from 1851; practiced law in Chicago, 1858–60; moved to Hartford, Connecticut, 1860, and established life-long partnership with Joseph R. Hawley: Assistant Editor to Hawley, 1860, then Editor, 1861–67, of Hawley's *Evening Press*; Editor and Proprietor, with Hawley, of the *Courant* (which consolidated with the *Press*), 1867 until his death; also wrote "The Editor's Drawer," 1884–98, and "The Editor's Study," 1894–98, for *Harper's* magazine; with his brother, George Warner, edited the *Library of the World's Best Literature*, 1896–97. Member, Hartford Park Commission, and Connecticut State Commission on Sculpture; Vice-President, National Prison Association. President, American Social Science Association, and National Institute of Arts and Letters. *Died 20 October 1900.*

PUBLICATIONS

Collections

Complete Writings, edited by Thomas R. Lounsbury.   15 vols., 1904.

Fiction

The Gilded Age: A Tale of Today, with Mark Twain.   1873; edited by Bryant Morey French, 1972.
A Little Journey in the World.   1889.
The Golden House.   1895.
That Fortune.   1899.

Other

My Summer in a Garden.   1871.
Saunterings (travel).   1872.
Backlog Studies.   1873.
Baddeck and That Sort of Thing (travel).   1874.
My Winter on the Nile, Among the Mummies and Moslems.   1876.
In the Levant.   1877.
In the Wilderness.   1878.
Being a Boy.   1878.
Washington Irving (biography).   1881.
Captain John Smith (1579–1631), Sometime Governor of Virginia, and Admiral of New England.   1881.
A Roundabout Journey.   1883.
A Study of Prison Reform.   1886.
Their Pilgrimage.   1887.
On Horseback: A Tour of Virginia, North Carolina, and Tennessee.   1888.
A-Hunting of the Deer and Other Essays.   1888.
Studies in the South and West, with Comments on Canada.   1889.

Our Italy. 1891; as *The American Italy,* 1892.
As We Were Saying. 1891.
As We Go. 1893.
The Relation of Literature to Life. 1896.
The People for Whom Shakespeare Wrote. 1897.
Fashions in Literature and Other Literary and Social Essays and Addresses. 1902.
Charles Dickens: An Appreciation. 1913.

Editor, *The Book of Eloquence.* 1851.
Editor, *The Warner Classics.* 4 vols., 1897.
Editor, *Dictionary of Authors, Ancient and Modern,* and *Synopsis of Books, Ancient and Modern.* 2 vols., 1910.

Reading List: *Warner* by Annie Fields, 1904; *Nook Farm: Mark Twain's Hartford Circle* by Kenneth R. Andrews, 1950.

*   *   *

Charles Dudley Warner was a competent essayist and editor whose high reputation from 1870 to 1900 is matched by an equally undeserved neglect in the present century. About half of his books are pot-boilers, especially the ten travel books that dealt first with Europe and the Near East and later with America. For example, *Our Italy* was subsidized to encourage travel to California. Only through his collaboration with Mark Twain in *The Gilded Age* is Warner known to most readers today. But his 1904 biographer dismissed *The Gilded Age*: "With all its ingenuities and cleverness, the book can hardly be called a literary success." The three novels Warner published from 1889 to 1899 were also passed over without much attention.

But in recent years these novels have been reprinted for their commentary on American society. In the trilogy, a great fortune is built up and finally lost, an indictment of the new American plutocracy which accumulated wealth and sacrificed values. Warner knew the threat posed by the Robber Barons in the period called the "Gilded Age," but he had confidence in the eventual triumph of New England-based morality and middle-class idealism. These novels are the culmination of Warner's observations, and his most serious studies of American society. As fiction they are less notable: Warner was an essayist, not a novelist.

Warner's literary criticism reflects conservative American cultural attitudes at the end of the nineteenth century. His two biographies are workmanlike: *Washington Irving* was his own volume in the "American Men of Letters" series he edited in the 1880's; and *Captain John Smith* was written as a semi-humorous contribution to the abortive "Lives of American Worthies" planned by a rival publisher. With his brother, he edited *The Library of the World's Best Literature,* but they document the literary taste of another day.

Although Warner's literary output was varied, his point of view remained consistent throughout his career. Warner was genial, idealistic, and temperate, a conservative in morals, literary tastes, and business matters. He was a thoroughly professional journalist-literary man, at his natural best in the personal essay. When his modest newspaper pieces collected into *My Summer in a Garden* made a tremendous success, he published the more elaborate *Backlog Studies* and was called a fit successor to Charles Lamb and Washington Irving. *In the Wilderness* and *Their Pilgrimage* are travel books about the Adirondacks and fashionable resorts, but more notable for their essays on manners. *As We Were Saying* and *As We Go* are collections of Warner's *Harper's* essays: American individuality is threatened by materialism and refinement. *Being a Boy* is Warner's nostalgic memories of a farm in the Berkshires in the 1830's. This reminiscence and *My Summer in a Garden* ought to be reprinted: Warner's unpretentious style and mellow mood might charm readers today.

—Clarence A. Glasrud

WARNER, Rex (Ernest). English. Born in Birmingham, 9 March 1905. Educated at St. George's School, Harpenden, Hertfordshire; Wadham College, Oxford, B.A. (honours) in classics and English literature 1928. Served in the Home Guard, London, 1942–45. Married 1) Frances Chamier Grove in 1929, two sons and one daughter; 2) Barbara, Lady Rothschild, in 1949, one daughter; 3) remarried Frances Chamier Grove in 1966. Schoolmaster in Egypt and England, 1928–45; worked for the Allied Control Commission in Berlin, 1945; Director, British Institute, Athens, 1945–47; Tallman Professor of Classics, Bowdoin College, Brunswick, Maine, 1962–63; University Professor of English, University of Connecticut, Storrs, 1964–74. Recipient: Black Memorial Prize, 1961. D.Litt.: Rider College, Trenton, New Jersey, 1968. Honorary Fellow, Wadham College, 1973. Commander, Royal Order of the Phoenix, Greece, 1963. Honorary Member, New England Classical Association. Lives in Wallingford, Oxfordshire.

PUBLICATIONS

Fiction

The Wild Goose Chase. 1937.
The Professor. 1938.
The Aerodrome. 1941.
Why Was I Killed? A Dramatic Dialogue. 1943; as Return of the Traveller, 1944.
Men of Stones: A Melodrama. 1949.
Escapade: A Tale of Average. 1953.
The Young Caesar. 1958.
Imperial Caesar. 1960.
Pericles the Athenian. 1963.
The Converts. 1967.

Plays

Screenplays (documentaries): World Without End, 1953; The Immortal Land, 1958.

Verse

Poems. 1937; revised edition, as Poems and Contradictions, 1945.

Other

The Kite (juvenile). 1936; revised edition, 1963.
English Public Schools. 1945.
The Cult of Power: Essays. 1946.
John Milton. 1949.
Views of Attica and Its Surroundings. 1950.
E. M. Forster. 1950; revised edition, 1960.
Men and Gods. 1950.
Ashes to Ashes: A Post-Mortem on the 1950–51 Tests, with Lyle Blair. 1951.
Greeks and Trojans. 1951.
Eternal Greece, photographs by Martin Hurlimann. 1953.

The Vengeance of the Gods (juvenile).   1954.
Athens.   1956.
The Greek Philosophers.   1958.
Look at Birds (juvenile).   1962.
Athens at War: Retold from The History of the Peloponnesian War of Thucydides.   1970.
Men of Athens: The Story of Fifth-Century Athens.   1972.
The Stories of the Greeks.   1978.

Editor, with Laurie Lee and Christopher Hassall, *New Poems 1954.*   1954.
Editor, *Look Up at the Skies! Poems and Prose*, by Gerard Manley Hopkins.   1972.

Translator, *The Medea of Euripides.*   1944.
Translator, *Prometheus Bound*, by Aeschylus.   1947.
Translator, *The Persian Expedition*, by Xenophon.   1949.
Translator, *Hippolytus*, by Euripides.   1949.
Translator, *Helen*, by Euripides.   1951.
Translator, *The Peloponnesian War*, by Thucydides.   1954.
Translator, *Fall of the Roman Republic: Marius, Sulla, Crassus, Pompey, Caesar, Cicero: Six Lives*, by Plutarch.   1958; revised edition, 1972.
Translator, *Poems of George Seferis.*   1960.
Translator, *War Commentaries of Caesar.*   1960.
Translator, *Confessions of St. Augustine.*   1963.
Translator, with Th. D. Frangopoulos, *On the Greek Style: Selected Essays in Poetry and Hellenism*, by George Seferis.   1966.
Translator, *History of My Times*, by Xenophon.   1967.
Translator, *Moral Essays*, by Plutarch.   1971.

Reading List: *Warner, Writer* by A. L. McLeod, 1960, and *The Achievement of Warner* edited by McLeod, 1965 (includes bibliography).

*   *   *

Of all the writers who belonged to what has become known as "the Auden generation," Rex Warner is the one whose work most clearly shows the influence of classical studies. He has translated many classic Greek and Roman authors – Aeschylus, Euripides, Xenophon, Thucydides, and others – as well as the modern Greek writer George Seferis. Since World War II he has written historical novels set in the classic period, including two "autobiographies" of Julius Caesar, a "biography" of Pericles by a "contemporary," and "a novel of early Christianity" entitled *The Converts*. At the same time he is a careful observer of nature, as his many poems about birds indicate, and, in contemporary matters, he is fascinated by the problem of power; a collection of his essays is entitled *The Cult of Power*.

This theme of political power is central to the three novels for which Warner is best known, all written when the last war was imminent or had just begun: *The Wild Goose Chase*, *The Professor*, and *The Aerodrome*. The first is an allegory expressing the experiences of a young man crossing a "frontier" (a frequent symbol in the literature of the 1930's) and travelling in a grotesque and irrational world like "K." in Kafka's novel *The Castle*. Warner is frequently compared with Kafka, although his technique of grotesquerie is integrated with recognisable political and ethical concern. A Marxist orientation is evident in the ultimate victory of the peasants and "comrades" over the "King," who, like Sir Oswald Mosley of the British Union of Fascists, is a lover of fencing and organiser of a "New Party."

Warner integrates his allegorical fictional technique and "message" more successfully in *The Professor*. The hero, a professor of classics who believes in "abstract justice" and an honorable code of conduct, is so greatly respected that he is appointed head of a national government at a time when there is an "enemy on the frontier." However, his courageous honesty is no match for the unscrupulous intrigues of a party which is brutally Fascist in policy and method. Throughout the political melodrama, Warner is able to sustain our empathy with the professor, liberal and high-minded but increasingly powerless and tragic. *The Aerodrome* is perhaps Warner's most successful novel. The basic theme is simple – the superiority and eventual victory of human love, with all its vagaries and inefficiency, over a superbly organised but ruthless totalitarian state – but the story is told with such literary skill and understanding that it remains exciting and culturally relevant.

—Ernest Griffin

WARNER, Sylvia Townsend.   English.   Born in Harrow, Middlesex, 6 December 1893. Educated privately. Member of the Editorial Committee of *Tudor Church Music* (Oxford University Press), 1916–26; full-time writer from 1926; contributor to *The New Yorker* from 1935. Recipient: Prix Menton, 1968. Fellow, Royal Society of Literature, 1967; Honorary Member, American Academy of Arts and Letters, 1972. *Died 1 May 1978.*

PUBLICATIONS

Fiction

> *Lolly Willowes; or, The Loving Huntsman.*   1926.
> *Mr. Fortune's Maggot.*   1927.
> *The Maze: A Story to Be Read Aloud.*   1928.
> *The True Heart.*   1929.
> *Some World Far from Ours, and Stay, Corydon, Thou Swain* (stories).   1929.
> *Elinor Barley* (stories).   1930.
> *A Moral Ending and Other Stories.*   1931.
> *The Salutation* (stories).   1932.
> *More Joy in Heaven and Other Stories.*   1935.
> *Summer Will Show.*   1936.
> *After the Death of Don Juan.*   1938.
> *The Cat's Cradle Book* (stories).   1940.
> *A Garland of Straw and Other Stories.*   1943.
> *The Museum of Cheats: Stories.*   1947.
> *The Corner That Held Them.*   1948.
> *The Flint Anchor.*   1954.
> *Winter in the Air and Other Stories.*   1955.
> *A Spirit Rises: Short Stories.*   1962.
> *A Stranger with a Bag and Other Stories.*   1966; as *Swans on an Autumn River: Stories,* 1966.
> *The Innocent and the Guilty: Stories.*   1971.
> *Kingdom of Elfin* (stories).   1976.

Verse

The Espalier. 1925.
Time Importuned. 1928.
Opus 7: A Poem. 1931.
Rainbow. 1932.
Whether a Dove or Seagull: Poems, with Valentine Ackland. 1933.
Boxwood: Sixteen Engravings by Reynolds Stone Illustrated in Verse. 1960

Other

The Portrait of a Tortoise: Extracted from the Journals and Letters of Gilbert White. 1946.
Somerset. 1949.
Jane Austen. 1951; revised edition, 1957.
Sketches from Nature (reminiscences). 1963.
T. H. White: A Biography. 1967.

Editor, *The Week-end Dickens.* 1932.

Translator, *By Way of Sainte-Beuve,* by Proust. 1958; as *On Art and Literature 1896–1917,* 1964.
Translator, *A Place of Shipwreck,* by Jean René Huguenin. 1963.

*   *   *

All critics are unanimous in extolling Sylvia Townsend Warner's exquisite style, but not all critics agree that the content of her work justified this unique quality. In her first two novels, *Lolly Willowes* and *Mr. Fortune's Maggot,* she dealt with subjects that are now very contemporary. The heroine of the first novel is a very independent woman who willingly and even eagerly is transformed into a witch, ready to contend with the Devil. If the reader wants to see in it a blow for women's liberation, Warner supplies him with ample material. The charm of the book lies in its semi-serious blend of reality and fantasy. *Mr. Fortune's Maggot* is a delicate study in psycho-sexuality, exploring the relationship between a middle-aged clergyman and a young native boy.

Her next book, *The True Heart,* is another delightful blend of reality and fantasy. Sukey Bond, a young orphan girl, falls in love with a slightly retarded young man who is the son of her idol. The reader is prepared for a pastoral tragedy in the manner of Hardy, but fantasy wins out. In an audience with Queen Victoria, Sukey successfully pleads for the right to her lover.

In the volumes that follow, Warner delves into historical fiction with a background of France at the time of the revolution of 1848 in *Summer Will Show,* perhaps the least successful of the series in spite of the excellent portrayal of the heroine. The legend of Don Juan is the subject of *After the Death of Don Juan,* in which the characters of Mozart's opera confront each other in a desolate but charming Spanish town. The wily Don shows himself to be a reactionary, and some critics saw in this a parable of modern Spain on the eve of revolution. Of the four historical books, the most successful, and truly a minor masterpiece, is *The Corner That Held Them,* the story of Oby, a fourteenth-century nunnery in Catholic England. She blends the trials of Black Death and the Peasants' Revolt with the study of medieval literature and the Ars Nova with special mention of Guillaume de Machaut. As a reconstruction of medieval life, it invites comparisons with Zoe Oldenberg and Sigrid Unset. Her last novel, *The Flint Anchor,* was suggested by her own family background: "Round about 1800 my great-great-grandfather, John Warner, married a Miss Townsend. They had a son, and soon after his birth the young wife went back to her father's house. Nothing more is known of John Warner, because his memory was obliterated under the statement that he was a wicked young man who must never be spoken of. That is the germ of *The Flint Anchor*." Although it is a chronicle of family life in the first half of the nineteenth century, it is a novel of many moods and structurally perhaps the best.

—Dominic J. Bisignano

WARREN, Robert Penn. American. Born in Guthrie, Kentucky, 24 April 1905. Educated at Guthrie High School; Vanderbilt University, Nashville, Tennessee, B.A. (summa cum laude) 1925; University of California, Berkeley, M.A. 1927; Yale University, New Haven, Connecticut, 1927–28; Oxford University (Rhodes Scholar), B.Litt. 1930. Married 1) Emma Brescia in 1930 (divorced, 1950); 2) the writer Eleanor Clark in 1952, one son and one daughter. Member of the Fugitive Group of poets: Co-Founding Editor, *The Fugitive*, Nashville, 1922–25; Assistant Professor, Southwestern College, Memphis, Tennessee, 1930–31, and Vanderbilt University, 1931–34; Assistant and Associate Professor, Louisiana State University, Baton Rouge, 1934–42, and Founding Editor, *Southern Review*, Baton Rouge, 1935–42; Professor of English, University of Minnesota, Minneapolis, 1942–50; Professor of Playwriting, 1950–56, and Professor of English, 1962–73, Yale University; now Professor Emeritus. Consultant in Poetry, Library of Congress, Washington, D.C., 1944–45; Jefferson Lecturer, National Endowment for the Arts, 1974. Recipient: Caroline Sinkler Award, 1936, 1937, 1938; Guggenheim Fellowship, 1939, 1947; Shelley Memorial Award, 1943; Pulitzer Prize, for fiction, 1947, for poetry, 1958; Screenwriters Guild Robert Meltzer Award, 1949; Sidney Hillman Prize, 1957; Edna St. Vincent Millay Memorial Prize, 1958; National Book Award, for poetry, 1958; Bollingen Prize, for poetry, 1967; National Endowment for the Arts grant, 1968; Henry A. Bellaman Prize, 1970; Van Wyck Brooks Award, for poetry, 1970; National Medal for Literature, 1970; Emerson-Thoreau Medal, 1975. D.Litt.: University of Louisville, Kentucky, 1949; Kenyon College, Gambier, Ohio, 1952; University of Kentucky, Lexington, 1955; Colby College, Waterville, Maine, 1956; Swarthmore College, Pennsylvania, 1958; Yale University, 1959; Fairfield University, Connecticut, 1969; Wesleyan University, Middletown, Connecticut, 1970; Harvard University, Cambridge, Massachusetts, 1973; LL.D.: University of Bridgeport, Connecticut, 1965. Member, American Academy of Arts and Letters; Chancellor, Academy of American Poets, 1972. Lives in Fairfield, Connecticut.

PUBLICATIONS

Fiction

Night Rider. 1939.
At Heaven's Gate. 1943.
All the King's Men. 1946.
Blackberry Winter (stories). 1946.
The Circus in the Attic and Other Stories. 1947.
World Enough and Time: A Romantic Novel. 1950.

Band of Angels. 1955.
The Cave. 1959.
Wilderness: A Tale of the Civil War. 1961.
Flood: A Romance of Our Times. 1964.
Meet Me in the Green Glen. 1971.
A Place to Come To. 1977.

Plays

Proud Flesh (in verse, produced 1947; revised [prose] version, produced 1948).
All the King's Men (produced 1959). 1960.

Verse

Thirty-Six Poems. 1935.
Eleven Poems on the Same Theme. 1942.
Selected Poems 1923–1943. 1944.
Brother to Dragons: A Tale in Verse and Voices. 1953.
Promises: Poems 1954–1956. 1957.
You, Emperors and Others: Poems 1957–1960. 1960.
Selected Poems: New and Old 1923–1966. 1966.
Incarnations: Poems 1966–1968. 1968.
Audubon: A Vision. 1969.
Or Else: Poem/Poems 1968–1974. 1974.
Selected Poems 1923–1975. 1977.

Other

John Brown: The Making of a Martyr. 1929.
I'll Take My Stand: The South and the Agrarian Tradition, with others. 1930.
Understanding Poetry: An Anthology for College Students, with Cleanth Brooks. 1938;
    revised edition, 1950, 1960.
Understanding Fiction, with Cleanth Brooks. 1943; revised edition, 1959.
A Poem of Pure Imagination: An Experiment in Reading, in *The Rime of the Ancient
    Mariner,* by Samuel Taylor Coleridge. 1946.
Modern Rhetoric: With Readings, with Cleanth Brooks. 1949; revised edition, 1958.
Fundamentals of Good Writing: A Handbook of Modern Rhetoric, with Cleanth
    Brooks. 1950; revised edition, 1956.
Segregation: The Inner Conflict in the South. 1956.
Remember the Alamo! 1958.
Selected Essays. 1958.
The Gods of Mount Olympus. 1959.
The Legacy of the Civil War: Meditations on the Centennial. 1961.
Who Speaks for the Negro? 1965.
A Plea in Mitigation: Modern Poetry and the End of an Era. 1966.
Homage to Theodore Dreiser. 1971.
John Greenleaf Whittier's Poetry: An Appraisal and a Selection. 1971.
A Conversation with Warren, edited by Frank Gado. 1972.
Democracy and Poetry. 1975.

Editor, with Cleanth Brooks and J. T. Purser, *An Approach to Literature: A Collection of*

Prose and Verse with Analyses and Discussions.   1936; revised edition, 1939, 1952.
Editor, *A Southern Harvest: Short Stories by Southern Writers.*   1937.
Editor, with Cleanth Brooks, *An Anthology of Stories from the Southern Review.*   1953.
Editor, with Albert Erskine, *Short Story Masterpieces.*   1954.
Editor, with Albert Erskine, *Six Centuries of Great Poetry.*   1955.
Editor, with Albert Erskine, *A New Southern Harvest.*   1957.
Editor, with Allen Tate, *Selected Poems,* by Denis Devlin.   1963.
Editor, *Faulkner: A Collection of Critical Essays.*   1966.
Editor, with Robert Lowell and Peter Taylor, *Randall Jarrell 1914–1965.*   1967.
Editor, *Selected Poems of Herman Melville.*   1971.
Editor, with Cleanth Brooks and R. W. B. Lewis, *American Literature: The Makers and the Making.*   2 vols., 1974.

Bibliography: *Warren: A Bibliography* by Mary Nancy Huff, 1968.

Reading List: *Warren: The Dark and Bloody Ground* by Leonard Casper, 1960; *Warren* by Paul West, 1964; *Warren: A Collection of Critical Essays* edited by John Lewis Longley, Jr., 1965; *A Colder Fire: The Poetry of Warren,* 1965, and *The Poetic Vision of Warren,* 1977, both by Victor H. Strandberg; *Web of Being: The Novels of Warren* by Barnett Guttenberg, 1975.

*   *   *

Robert Penn Warren is a distinguished American writer in at least three genres: the novel, poetry, and the essay. Although he has lived outside the South since 1942, he has so consistently written novels, essays, and poetry on southern subjects, in southern settings, and about southern themes that he must be regarded still as a southern writer. Over much of his work there is a typically southern brooding sense of darkness, evil, and human failure, and he employs a Gothicism of form and an extravagance of language and technique of a sort often associated with writing in the southeastern United States. Warren is a profoundly philosophical writer in all aspects of his work. Writing of Joseph Conrad, he once said, "The philosophical novelist, or poet, is one for whom the documentation of the world is constantly striving to rise to the level of generalization about values ... for whom the urgency of experience ... is the urgency to know the meaning of experience." The description fits him well.

In Warren's principal work in the novel and poetry, there are a persistent obsession with time and with history, a sense of man's imperfection and failure, and an awareness that innocence is always lost in the acts of achieving maturity and growth. His characters are usually men who destroy themselves through seeking an absolute in a relative universe. From his first book, a biography of John Brown (1929), to Percy Munn, the protagonist of *Night Rider* (1939), to Willie Stark of *All the King's Men* (1946), to Jeremiah Beaumont of *World Enough and Time* (1950), to Lilburn Lewis in the poem-play *Brother to Dragons* (1953), to Jed Tewksbury in *A Place to Come To* (1977) – Warren's protagonists repeat this pattern of the obsessive and ultimately self-destructive search for the impossible ideal.

His work usually rests on actual events from history or at least on actual historical situations – *Night Rider* on the Kentucky tobacco wars, *At Heaven's Gate* on a Nashville political murder, *All the King's Men* on the career of Huey Long, *World Enough and Time* on an 1825 Kentucky murder, *Band of Angels* and *Wilderness* on the Civil War, *The Cave* on Floyd Collins's cave entombment, *Flood* on the inundating of towns by the Tennessee Valley Authority, *A Place to Come To* to at least some extent on his own experiences as a college teacher, although the story can hardly be considered autobiographical. The poem *Brother to Dragons* is based on an atrocious crime committed by Thomas Jefferson's nephews. This concern with history and the individual implications of social and political events is also present in his nonfiction, such as *Segregation: The Inner Conflict in the South*, *The Legacy of the Civil War*, and *Who Speaks for the Negro?* These works, too, deal with fundamental issues of southern history.

In order to present the philosophical meaning of his novels and poems, Warren uses highly individualized narrators, such as Jack Burden in *All the King's Men*; special techniques of narrative point of view, as in *World Enough and Time*; frequently a metaphysical style; the illumination of events through contrast with enclosed and frequently recollected narratives, as in *Night Rider* and *All the King's Men*; and highly melodramatic plots which become elaborate workings out of abstract statements, as in *Band of Angels*.

His poetry reiterates essentially the same view of man. He began as an undergraduate at Vanderbilt University writing poetry with the Fugitive poetry group – John Crowe Ransom, Allen Tate, and Donald Davidson – and he continued to write a relatively fixed form, tightly constructed, ironic lyric verse until about 1943. Between 1943 and 1953 he concentrated predominantly on the novel. With *Brother to Dragons* he returned to poetic expression, and since that time has written extensively in both poetic and novelistic forms. The verse forms that he has used since 1953 have been much looser, marked by broken rhythms, clusters of lines arranged in patterns dictated by emotion, and frequent alternations in the level of diction. Behind his poetry, as behind his fiction, there is usually an implied, if not explicit, narrative pattern. This narrative pattern is often historical, as in "The Ballad of Billy Potts," *Brother to Dragons*, or *Audubon*. In his recent verse, Warren contrasts man's weaknesses and imperfections with the enduring stars, with time, and with eternity.

As a critic and teacher, Warren has had a profound influence on the study and criticism of literature. His textbook *Understanding Poetry*, written with Cleanth Brooks, a presentation of poetry in New Critical terms emphasizing the poem as an independent work of art, went a long way toward creating a revolution in how literature was taught in American colleges. He has written many other textbooks and critical studies such as *Homage to Theodore Dreiser*, *John Greenleaf Whittier's Poetry*, and *Democracy and Poetry*.

Warren is still very active; during his 72nd year he published *Selected Poems 1923–1975* and a distinctive and distinguished novel *A Place to Come To*. Warren's work in all genres is marked by a high concern with language, a depth of philosophical statement, a firm and rigorous commitment to a moral-ethical view of man, and a willingness to experiment often beyond the limits of artistic safety with the forms in which he works. Warren is a peculiarly indigenous American writer of great intelligence and of significant accomplishment. He can, with justice, be called our most distinguished living man of letters.

—C. Hugh Holman

WARUNG, Price. Pseudonym for William Astley. Australian. Born in Liverpool, Lancashire, England, 13 August 1855; emigrated with his family to Australia in 1859, and settled in Richmond, Victoria. Educated at St. Stephen's School, Richmond, and at the Model School, Carlton, Victoria. Married Louisa Frances Cape in 1884. Founding Editor, *Richmond Guardian*, 1875; member of staff of the *Riverine Herald*, Echuca, 1876–77; suffered a nervous breakdown, 1878–80; correspondent in Casterton and Melbourne, 1881–82; Editor, *Australian Graphic*, Sydney, 1883; reporter for the Warnambool *Standard*, Sydney *Globe*, Bathurst *Times*, Tumut *Independent*, and the Bathurst *Free Press*, 1884–90; settled in Sydney, 1891; columnist for the Sydney *Bulletin*, 1890–93; Managing Editor, *Australian Workman*, 1893. Granted Commonwealth Literary Fund pension, 1908. *Died 5 October 1911.*

PUBLICATIONS

Fiction

Tales of the Convict System. 1892.
Tales of the Early Days. 1894.
Tales of the Old Regime, and The Bullet of the Fated Ten. 1897.
Tales of the Isle of Death (Norfolk Island). 1898.
Half-Crown Bob and Tales of the Riverine. 1898.

Other

Labor in Politics: A Criticism and Appeal. 1893.
The Federal Capital: An Argument for the Western Site. 1903.

*   *   *

Price Warung was the pseudonym used by William Astley whose main claim to fame lies in his tales of the Australian convict system. Astley wrote ninety-four stories of convict life which, with few exceptions, were published between the years 1890 and 1892 in *The Bulletin*, the journal which played a major role in the creation of an indigenous literature in Australia. *The Bulletin*'s motto was "Temper, democratic; bias, offensively Australian," and it was one that Astley could agree with wholeheartedly. Astley was a radical and a nationalist. He saw himself as a missionary who was going to help bring about a new Australia in which capitalism would be replaced by socialism and the wealth taken from the few and shared out among the many.

Not all of Astley's stories are set in a penal colony – they move from free settlements to places of secondary punishment – but they are all concerned in some way or other with convict life and present a similar thesis. Astley's aim was to show that the convicts were more sinned against than sinning, and that the real villains were the British capitalists and imperialists. In a period of increasing nationalistic fervour it is easy to see the reason for the popularity of his stories. His stories all reveal the horror of a cruel and corrupt system and on a larger scale the inhumanity of man to man. Such a theme easily lends itself to the macabre and the melodramatic, and, striving for powerful effects, Astley made full use of both, unfortunately too much so. He was so involved with his thesis, of bringing home the message, that he lacked the detachment so necessary for artistic achievement. The artist is swamped by the polemicist. His plots are contrived, his characters stereotyped. Even his stories which have not got a convict theme (for example, *Tales of the Riverine*) reveal the same flaws.

There has been a recent revival of interest in Astley's work, not because of its literary merit but because of the renewed interest by Australians in their past and of any interpretation of it that might reveal the truth behind the fiction.

—Anna Rutherford

WAUGH, Evelyn (Arthur St. John). English. Born in London, 28 October 1903; brother of the writer Alec Waugh. Educated at Lancing College, Sussex (edited the school paper); Hertford College, Oxford (senior history scholar); Hatherley's Art School, London, 1924. Served with the Royal Marines, then with the Commandos, 1939–42: Major; served with the Royal Horse Guards, 1942–45. Married 1) the Hon. Evelyn Gardner in 1928 (divorced, 1930; marriage annulled, 1936); 2) Laura Herbert in 1937, three daughters and three sons, including the writer Auberon Waugh. Settled in London, 1924; taught school, and worked on the *Daily Express*; full-time writer from 1928; convert to Roman Catholicism, 1930; settled in Combe Florey, near Taunton, Somerset. Recipient: Hawthornden Prize, 1936; Black Memorial Prize, 1953. Fellow, and Companion of Literature, 1963, Royal Society of Literature. *Died 10 April 1966.*

PUBLICATIONS

Fiction

Decline and Fall: An Illustrated Novelette.   1928.
Vile Bodies.   1930.
Black Mischief.   1932.
A Handful of Dust.   1934.
Mr. Loveday's Little Outing and Other Sad Stories.   1936.
Scoop: A Novel about Journalists.   1938.
Put Out More Flags.   1942.
Work Suspended: Two Chapters of an Unfinished Novel.   1942.
Brideshead Revisited: The Sacred and Profane Memories of Captain Charles Ryder.   1945.
Scott-King's Modern Europe.   1947.
The Loved One: An Anglo-American Tragedy.   1948.
Work Suspended and Other Stories Written Before the Second World War.   1949.
Helena.   1950.
Men at Arms.   1952; *Officers and Gentlemen*, 1955; *Unconditional Surrender* 1961 (as *The End of the Battle*, 1962); complete revised version, as *Sword of Honour*, 1965.
Love among the Ruins: A Romance of the Near Future.   1953.
Tactical Exercise.   1954.
The Ordeal of Gilbert Pinfold: A Conversation Piece.   1957.
Basil Seal Rides Again; or, The Rake's Regress.   1963.

Verse

The World to Come.   1916.

Other

PRB: An Essay on the Pre-Raphaelite Brotherhood 1847–52.   1926.
Rossetti: His Life and Works.   1928.
Labels: A Mediterranean Journal.   1930; as *A Bachelor Abroad*, 1930.
Remote People.   1931; as *They Were Still Dancing*, 1932.
Ninety-Two Days: The Account of a Tropical Journey Through British Guiana and Part of Brazil.   1934.
Edmund Campion.   1935; revised edition, 1946, 1961.
Waugh in Abyssinia.   1936.
Robbery under Law: The Mexican Object-Lesson.   1939; as *Mexico: An Object Lesson*, 1939.

When the Going Was Good. 1946.
Wine in Peace and War. 1947.
The Holy Places (essays). 1952.
The World of Waugh, edited by C. J. Rolo. 1958.
The Life of Ronald Knox. 1959.
A Tourist in Africa. 1960.
A Little Learning (autobiography). 1964.
Diaries, edited by Michael Davie. 1976.
A Little Order: A Selection from His Journalism, edited by Donat Gallagher. 1977.

Editor, *A Selection from the Occasional Sermons of Ronald Knox.* 1949.

Bibliography: *Waugh: A Checklist of Primary and Secondary Material* by R. M. Davis and others, 1972; supplement by Alain Blayac, in *Book Collector,* Spring 1976.

Reading List: *Waugh* by Christopher Hollis, 1954; *Waugh: Portrait of the Artist* by F. J. Stopp, 1958; *Waugh* by Malcolm Bradbury, 1964; *The Satiric Art of Waugh* by James F. Carens, 1966; *Waugh: A Critical Essay* by Paul A. Doyle, 1969; *Waugh* edited by R. M. Davis, 1969; *Masks, Modes, and Morals: The Art of Waugh* by William J. Cook, 1971; *Waugh and His World* by David Pryce-Jones, 1973; *Waugh: A Biography* by Christopher Sykes, 1975; *Waugh's Officers, Gentlemen, and Rogues: The Fact Behind the Fiction* by Gene D. Phillips, 1976.

*   *   *

As a young man Evelyn Waugh aspired to "the dedicated world of the handcraftsman" and he would have preferred to illustrate, to decorate, to carpenter, or to print had not penury driven him to literature. "Evelyn," his brother wrote, "is almost the only writer I know who does not like writing." The idea of this workmanlike professionalism disturbs our normal concept of "The Writer," whose fingers constantly itch for a pen. In the autobiographical *The Ordeal of Gilbert Pinfold* he stated that "He regarded his books as things quite external to himself to be used and judged by others. He thought them well-made, better than many reputed works of genius, but he was not vain of his accomplishment, still less of his reputation...." Deliberately oblique and obstructive in later life to protect his privacy, he nevertheless took writing (and art in general) very seriously. It was simply that his aesthetic emphasis on craftsmanship was, and still is, unfashionable. What is often ignored is that he was responsible for perfecting certain technical innovations in the English novel and that, at the beginning of his career, he was an ardent advocate of *avant-garde* methods.

At Oxford he met Harold Acton and through him became interested in T. S. Eliot and Firbank. From Eliot he borrowed the epic quality of mundanity; from Firbank a style of allusive, "structural" humour. In an important 1929 essay ("Ronald Firbank," *Life and Letters,* March 1929) he explains that "In quite diverse ways Mr. Osbert Sitwell, Mr. Carl Van Vechten, Mr. Harold Acton, Mr. William Gerhardi and Mr. Ernest Hemingway are developing the technical discoveries upon which Mr. Ronald Firbank so negligently stumbled." Waugh considered Firbank to be "the first quite modern writer to solve for himself, quite unobtrusively ... the aesthetic problem of representation in fiction; to achieve ... a new, balanced interrelation of subject and form. Nineteenth-century novelists achieved a balance only by complete submission to the idea of the succession of events in an arbitrarily limited period of time ... the novelist was fettered by cause and effect." Waugh's answer to this problem represents a general philosophical statement as well as an aesthetic experiment. With Acton he rejected outright the effusive romanticism of the Victorians, the effete *poseurs* of the 1890's (especially Wilde), and the pastoral follies and chauvinism of the Georgians. The art of their fathers and grandfathers they considered to be distorted by a world view based on the concepts of material and spiritual "Progress," cause and effect working to the ultimate good of mankind. But the world to Waugh was not a composite of discernible facts; it was a "bodiless harlequinade," a Websterian madhouse in which, before 1930, fantasy was the only relief. Consequently we find in his first novel, *Decline and Fall*, a comedy structured on the unreliable nature of fate in which innocence is ruthlessly carbonadoed by experience. His first wife deserted him when he was in the middle of writing *Vile Bodies*, and the frenetic force of the harlequinade turns to tragedy. The shock at this infidelity hastened his conversion to Catholicism and in September 1930 he was received into the Church.

Before this time Waugh was an atheist and an iconoclast. Catholicism allowed him a secure philosophical position from which he could continue to write acerbic comedies of manners without succumbing to despair. Life on earth was irrelevant and by definition obscure; there was no question before 1945 of writing propagandist "religious" novels. More important, perhaps, Catholicism allowed pattern and form to his aesthetic predilection for the warmth and ebullience of "Southern" art and his distaste for the "narrow, scrambling, specialised life of a northern megalopolitan culture." In a 1930 article he clearly states the reasons for his conversion. They are not connected with the aesthetic appeal of the ceremony but nevertheless are aesthetic in origin. "Civilisation – and by this I do not mean talking cinemas and tinned food, nor even surgery and hygienic houses, but the whole moral and artistic organisation of Europe – has not in itself the power of survival. It came into being through Christianity and without it has no power to command allegiance."

What Waugh learned, then, from Firbank, Eliot, and Hemingway was an allusive style, rich in colloquialisms, structured on "refrains" rather than authorial description, using dialogue heavily to convey a sense of vacuity and impermanence, but which was nevertheless so carefully structured that behind the farce and the hopelessness there lies the solidity of a permanent tragedy. In Waugh this tragedy rests largely on an analysis of human vanity seen through the distorting lens of a central *naif*. The parties in *Vile Bodies* and the arbitrary nature of Adam and Nina's proposed marriage, the "Progress Through Sterility" of Seth's absurd imitation of "civilisation" (*Black Mischief*), Brenda Last's fashionable affair and Tony's fatuous journey to Brazil (*A Handful of Dust*), the depraved sycophancy and competition of journalists scrambling to provide distorted "news" (*Scoop*) – in all this, man's dignity is ironically asserted by implication. Catholicism, the "whole moral and artistic organisation of Europe," is barely mentioned, but its morality underpins the cruel image of contemporary man in the pre-1939 novels.

Waugh saw the struggle as quite simply between "civilisation" and the "barbarians." With the increasing possibility of communist government in the late 1930's he moved more to the Right and openly supported Italian (but not German) Fascism. By now he was in step with other Catholic apologists – Chesterton, Belloc, and Knox – and he greeted the advent of World War II as an opportunity for action.

He was writing a novel in 1939 about a writer undergoing, as he was, a "climacteric." It is in a more conventional style, attempting for the first time to describe emotion, to experiment with controlled sentimentality. This became *Work Suspended* and is one of Waugh's finest (although ostensibly unfinished) pieces: "For the civilised man there are none of those swift transitions of joy and pain which possess the savage; words form slowly like pus about his hurts; there are no clean wounds for him.... Not until they have assumed the livery of defence can his emotions pass through the Lines.... Sabotage behind the Lines, a blind raised and lowered at a lighted window, a wire cut, a bolt loosened, a file disordered – that is how civilised man is undone." "Civilised man" is a strange, hybrid creature so conditioned as not to be able to attack his enemies. With the onset of the war, that shyness was now abandoned. The problem had been to pinpoint the aggressors. Now, as he expressed it (ironically) in *Men at Arms*, "splendidly, everything had become clear. The enemy was plain in view, huge and hateful, all disguise cast off. It was the Modern Age in arms. Whatever the outcome there was a place for him [Guy Crouchback] in that battle."

The new tone and literary style are at once more sympathetic and more aggressive. *Brideshead Revisited* was to be his "Magnum Opus," the first novel to which he had been wholly committed, yet it largely lost him his literary reputation. "Mr. Edmund Wilson," he wrote afterwards, "was outraged ... at feeling God introduced into my story. I believe that you can only leave God out by making your characters pure abstractions.... So in future in my books there will be two things to make them unpopular: a pre-occupation with style and an attempt to represent man more fully which, to me, means only one thing: man in relation to God."

From this point, then, Waugh openly attacks the "barbarians" – Hooper and Mottram in *Brideshead*, American culture in *The Loved One*, Apthorpe in *Men at Arms*, "Fido" Hound and Ludovic in *Officers and Gentlemen* and *Unconditional Surrender*. As the title of the final volume of the *Sword of Honour* trilogy implies, no victory in material terms is possible. Political and military solutions by the "enlightened" Allies are as subject to outrageously immoral compromise as the anarchic world of the 1920's and 1930's. The individual is still submerged in the mob and swept along by circumstance over which he has no control. The difference now is that the arbitrary nature of fate has been replaced by the operation of Divine Grace; God working in wondrous ways quietly provides a form of justice: Lord Marchmain's death-bed conversion, Helena's mission, and Guy's ultimate happiness. Gervase Crouchback states at one point: "The Mystical Body doesn't strike attitudes.... Quantitative judgments don't apply."

Rationalist critics were of course horrified at this development. But what they saw as a regression into religiosity Waugh considered the only reality, and in that sense we must allow him to describe it, as we must with Milton or Donne. His later novels should stand or fall on the quality of their characterisation which is, if anything, more powerful than in the early work.

Work Suspended, he considered, described a world which no longer existed. The war represented the long-awaited advent of a Dark Age; the refugees, numberless anonymous hordes without papers, tramp the world in his later work like John Plant and Guy Crouchback, homeless, not *sympatico* with their age. Traditional values – aesthetic and moral – are undermined, respectively, by abstraction and corruption. The "real" no longer exists in a world of substitutes and façades. It is a depressing vision enlivened only by cruel humour at the expense of the Common Man, the socialists, and modern aesthetics. In order to "pass through the Lines" his savage critique had to abandon those delightful abstractions, his earlier *naïfs*, and the aggressive assertion of "absolute" standards occasionally causes us to shudder at its simplistic generalisations and arrogance. Nevertheless, the artistic, if not the social, humility is always present. The trilogy, for all its bitterness, is perhaps the best novel to come out of the war and the earlier work ranks among the highest achievements of British fiction between 1928 and 1960.

—Martin Stannard

WELCH, (Maurice) Denton. English. Born in Shanghai, China, 29 March 1915. Educated at St. Michael's School, Uckfield, Sussex; Repton School, to age 17; Goldsmith School of Art, London, for four years. Artist: illustrated some of his books; injured in an accident, 1935; thereafter a partial invalid. *Died 30 December 1948.*

PUBLICATIONS

Collections

Welch: Extracts from His Published Works, edited by Jocelyn Brooke. 1963.

Fiction

Maiden Voyage. 1943.
In Youth Is Pleasure. 1944.
Brave and Cruel, and Other Stories. 1948.
A Voice Through a Cloud. 1950.

Verse

Dumb Instrument: Poems and Fragments, edited by Jean-Louis Chevalier. 1977.

Other

A Last Sheaf (miscellany), edited by Eric Oliver. 1951.
Journals, edited by Jocelyn Brooke. 1952.
I Left My Grandfather's House: An Account of His First Walking Tour. 1958.

Reading List: "A Few Novel Techniques of Welch" by Ruby Cohn, in *Perspective*, 1958; *Welch* by Robert S. Phillips, 1974.

*   *   *

The three novels and the stories by Denton Welch are almost purely autobiographical, so that the name of fiction seems inappropriate to them: there is almost no generic threshold between them and the *Journals*. Central to all the work is the sentience of the author-protagonist whose most natural mode of narration is in the first person, and whose own names (Denton and Maurice) are sometimes retained.

All Welch's work was written between his road accident at the age of twenty and his painful early death. Some of his books were decorated by his own paintings, end-papers, and chapter-headings whose rococo ingenuities complement the text. *Maiden Voyage* provides immediate access to the special obsessions of Welch's mind and senses, as well as to the social rejections he seemed compelled to make. The sixteen-year-old boy runs away from his public school and travels out to join his father and to meet the commercial and diplomatic community in pre-revolutionary China. The train of events, particularly the exotic richness of an eastern country, becomes symbolic of the author's flight from conventionality and his life-long ecstasy of the senses. *In Youth Is Pleasure* retreats a year or two to trace the younger boy's displacement in an English environment of hotels and smart people. *A Voice Through a Cloud* recounts the agony and the endurance of the man of twenty after his spine has been irreparably damaged. The power of the book lies in the preternatural susceptibility to pain and indignity of the victim. *Brave and Cruel* is a collection of stories placed at various points in the author's experience and almost all related in the first person. *A Last Sheaf* contains nearly all the stories, poems and pictures remaining unpublished at his death. The *Journals* were also edited and published posthumously.

The fascination of Welch's work, which is undeniably high, depends almost wholly upon the intricacy and vividness of the author's receptive and reflective sensibility. His senses are exposed, pleasantly or painfully, to the impact of colour, sound, smell, shape, and lustre. The phenomenal world takes on a psychedelic radiance. This acuity of the senses is associated with an engaging liberty of thought and action in the narrator, whose manner of reporting is, however, restrained and unaffected. He deliberately explores sensations, whipping himself, painting his body, eavesdropping, stealing, prying through windows, ransacking others' wardrobes and drawers, wearing women's clothing. He is a passionate social misfit, seeking random friendships but constantly repelled by those he meets. Adoration of his mother who has died, and dislike of his father who is wealthy and worldly, suggest a classical psychic disability. The abnormality is patent, but Welch's courage and independence, the clarity of his self-examination, his amused penetration of others' motives, and the educated refinement of his aesthetic responses proclaim in him a most lucid sanity.

—R. A. Copland

WELLS, H(erbert) G(eorge). English. Born in Bromley, Kent, 21 September 1866. Educated at Mr. Morley's Commercial Academy, Bromley, until age 13: certificate in book-keeping; apprentice draper in Windsor, 1880; student teacher at a school in Wookey, Somerset, 1880; apprentice chemist in Midhurst, Sussex, 1880–81; apprentice draper at Hyde's Emporium, Southsea, Hampshire, 1881–83; student/assistant at Midhurst Grammar School, 1883–84; studied at the Royal College of Science, London, 1884–87 (failed examinations); taught at Holt Academy, Wrexham, 1887–88, and at Henley House School, Kilburn, London, 1888–89; awarded B.Sc., University of London, 1890. Married 1) his cousin Isabel Mary Wells in 1891 (separated, 1893; divorced, 1895); 2) Amy Catherine Robbins in 1895 (died, 1927), two sons; had a son by Rebecca West, *q.v.*, the writer Anthony West. Tutor at the University Tutorial College, London, 1891–92; full-time writer from 1893; Labour candidate for Parliament, for the University of London, 1922, 1923. Member of the Fabian Society, 1903–08. D.Lit.: University of London, 1936; Honorary Fellow, Imperial College of Science and Technology, London. *Died 13 August 1946.*

PUBLICATIONS

Collections

Selected Short Stories. 1958.

Fiction

Select Conversations with an Uncle, Now Extinct, and Two Other Reminiscences. 1895.
The Time Machine: An Invention. 1895.
The Wonderful Visit. 1895.
The Stolen Bacillus and Other Incidents. 1895.
The Island of Dr. Moreau. 1896.
The Wheels of Chance: A Holiday Adventure. 1896.
The Plattner Story and Others. 1897.
The Invisible Man: A Grotesque Romance. 1897.
Thirty Strange Stories. 1897.
The War of the Worlds. 1898.
When the Sleeper Wakes: A Story of the Years to Come. 1899; revised edition, as *The Sleeper Awakes,* 1910.
Tales of Space and Time. 1899.

A Cure for Love (story).   1899.
The Vacant Country (story).   1899.
Love and Mr. Lewisham.   1900.
The First Men in the Moon.   1901.
The Sea Lady: A Tissue of Moonshine.   1902.
Twelve Stories and a Dream.   1903.
The Food of the Gods, and How It Came to Earth.   1904.
A Modern Utopia.   1905.
Kipps: The Story of a Simple Soul.   1905.
In the Days of the Comet.   1906.
The War in the Air, and Particularly How Mr. Bert Smallways Fared While It Lasted.   1908.
Tono-Bungay.   1908; edited by Bernard Bergonzi, 1966.
Ann Veronica: A Modern Love Story.   1909.
The New Machiavelli.   1910.
The History of Mr. Polly.   1910; edited by Gordon N. Ray, 1960.
The Country of the Blind and Other Stories.   1911; revised edition of *The Country of the Blind*, 1939.
The Door in the Wall and Other Stories.   1911.
Marriage.   1912.
The Passionate Friends.   1913.
The World Set Free: A Story of Mankind.   1914.
The Wife of Sir Isaac Harman.   1914.
Boon: The Mind of the Race, The Wild Asses of the Devil, and The Last Trump, Being a Selection from the Literary Remains of George Boon, Appropriate to the Times.   1915.
Bealby: A Holiday.   1915.
The Research Magnificent.   1915.
Mr. Britling Sees It Through.   1916.
The Soul of a Bishop: A Novel – with Just a Little Love in It – about Conscience and Religion and the Real Trouble of Life.   1917.
Joan and Peter: The Story of an Education.   1918.
The Undying Fire: A Contemporary Novel.   1919.
The Secret Places of the Heart.   1922.
Men Like Gods.   1923.
The Dream.   1924.
Christina Alberta's Father.   1925.
The World of William Clissold: A Novel at a New Angle.   1926.
Short Stories.   1927; as *Complete Short Stories*, 1966.
Meanwhile: The Picture of a Lady.   1927.
Mr. Blettsworthy on Rampole Island.   1928.
The King Who Was a King: The Book of a Film.   1929.
The Adventures of Tommy (juvenile).   1929.
The Autocracy of Mr. Parham: His Remarkable Adventure in This Changing World.   1930.
The Bulpington of Blup.   1932.
The Shape of Things to Come: The Ultimate Resolution.   1933; revised edition, as *Things to Come* (film story), 1935.
The Croquet Player.   1936.
The Man Who Could Work Miracles (film story).   1936.
Star Begotten: A Biological Fantasia.   1937.
Brynhild.   1937.
The Camford Visitation.   1937.
The Brothers.   1938.
Apropos of Dolores.   1938.

The Holy Terror. 1939.
Babes in the Darkling Wood. 1940.
All Aboard for Ararat. 1940.
You Can't Be Too Careful: A Sample of Life 1901–1951. 1941.
The Desert Daisy, edited by Gordon N. Ray. 1957.
The Wealth of Mr. Waddy, edited by Harris Wilson. 1969.

Plays

Kipps, with Rudolf Besier, from the novel by Wells (produced 1912).
The Wonderful Visit, with St. John Ervine, from the novel by Wells (produced 1921).
Hoopdriver's Holiday, from his novel *The Wheels of Chance,* edited by M. Timko, in
    English Literature in Transition, 1964.

Screenplays: *H. G. Wells Comedies (Bluebottles, The Tonic, Daydreams),* with Frank
Wells, 1928; *Things to Come,* 1936; *The Man Who Could Work Miracles,* 1936.

Other

Text-Book of Biology. 2 vols., 1893; vol. 1 revised, 1894.
Honours Physiography, with R. A. Gregory. 1893.
Certain Personal Matters: A Collection of Material, Mainly Autobiographical. 1897.
*Anticipations of the Reaction of Mechanical and Scientific Progress upon Human Life and
    Thought.* 1901.
Mankind in the Making. 1903.
The Future in America: A Search after Realities. 1906.
Faults of the Fabian. 1906.
Reconstruction of the Fabian Society. 1906.
Socialism and the Family. 1906.
This Misery of Boots. 1907.
Will Socialism Destroy the Home? 1907.
New Worlds for Old. 1908; revised edition, 1917.
First and Last Things: A Confession of Faith and Rule of Life. 1908; revised edition,
    1917, 1929.
Floor Games (juvenile). 1911.
Liberalism and Its Party: What Are We Liberals to Do? 1913.
Little Wars (children's games). 1913; revised edition, 1931.
*An Englishman Looks at the World, Being a Series of Unrestrained Remarks upon
    Contemporary Matters.* 1914; as *Social Forces in England and America,* 1914.
The War That Will End War. 1914.
The Peace of the World. 1915.
What Is Coming? A Forecast of Things after the War. 1916.
The Elements of Reconstruction. 1916.
War and The Future: Italy, France, and Britain at War. 1917.
God the Invisible King. 1917.
In the Fourth Year: Anticipations of a World Peace. 1918.
British Nationalism and the League of Nations. 1918.
Memorandum on Propaganda of Policy Against Germany. 1918.
History Is One. 1919.
The Outline of History, Being a Plain History of Life and Mankind. 1920.
Russia in the Shadows. 1920.
The Salvaging of Civilisation. 1921.

The New Teaching of History. 1921.
Washington and the Hope of Peace. 1922; as *Washington and the Riddle of Peace*, 1922.
Two Letters to Joseph Conrad. 1922.
What H. G. Wells Thinks about "The Mind in the Making" by James Harvey Robinson. 1922.
A Short History of the World. 1922.
The Story of a Great Schoolmaster, Being a Plain Account of the Life and Ideas of Sanderson of Oundle. 1924.
A Year of Prophesying. 1924.
Works. 26 vols., 1924–27.
Mr. Belloc Objects to "The Outline of History." 1926.
Wells' Social Anticipations, edited by H. W. Laidler. 1927.
The Way the World Is Going: Guesses and Forecasts of the Years Ahead. 1928.
The Open Conspiracy: Blue Prints for a World Revolution. 1928; revised edition, 1930; revised edition, as *What Are We to Do with Our Lives?*, 1931.
Imperialism and the Open Conspiracy. 1929.
The Science of Life: A Summary of Contemporary Knowledge about Life and Its Possibilities, with Julian Huxley and G. P. Wells. 3 vols., 1929–30; revised edition, as *Science of Life Series,* 9 vols., 1934–37; revised edition, 1938.
The Way to World Peace. 1930.
The Work, Wealth, and Happiness of Mankind. 2 vols., 1931; revised edition, 1934; as *The Outline of Man's Work and Wealth,* 1936.
After Democracy: Addresses and Papers on the Present World Situation. 1932.
Experiment in Autobiography: Discoveries and Conclusions of a Very Ordinary Brain since 1866. 2 vols., 1934.
The New America: The New World. 1935.
The Anatomy of Frustration: A Modern Synthesis. 1936.
World Brain. 1938.
Travels of a Republican Radical in Search of Hot Water. 1939.
The Fate of Homo Sapiens. 1939.
The New World Order. 1940.
The Rights of Man; or, What Are We Fighting For? 1940.
The Common Sense of War and Peace: World Revolution or War Unending. 1940.
Two Hemispheres or One World? 1940.
Guide to the New World: A Handbook of Constructive World Revolution. 1941.
The Outlook for Homo Sapiens. 1942.
Science and the World-Mind. 1942.
Phoenix: A Summary of the Inescapable Conditions of World Reorganization. 1942.
A Thesis on the Quality of Illusion in the Continuity of Individual Life of the Higher Metazoa, with Particular Reference to the Species Homo Sapiens. 1942; abridged version, as *The Illusion of Personality,* 1944.
The Conquest of Time. 1942.
The New Rights of Man. 1942.
Crux Ansata: An Indictment of the Roman Catholic Church. 1943.
The Mosley Outrage. 1943.
'42 to '44: A Contemporary Memoir upon Human Behaviour During the Crisis of the World Revolution. 1944.
The Happy Turning: A Dream of Life. 1945; edited by G. P. Wells, in *The Last Books,* 1968.
Mind at the End of Its Tether. 1945; edited by G. P. Wells, in *The Last Books,* 1968.
Journalism and Prophecy 1893–1946, edited by W. Warren Wagar. 1964.
Henry James and Wells: A Record of Their Friendship, Their Debate on the Art of Fiction, and Their Quarrel, edited by Leon Edel and Gordon N. Ray. 1958.

Arnold Bennett and Wells: A Record of Their Personal and Literary Friendship, edited by Harris Wilson. 1960.
George Gissing and Wells: Their Friendship and Correspondence, edited by R. A. Gettmann. 1961.

Bibliography: *Wells: A Comprehensive Bibliography*, 1966, revised edition, 1968.

Reading List: *Wells: A Biography* by Vincent Brome, 1951; *The Early Wells: A Study of the Scientific Romances* by Bernard Bergonzi, 1961, and *Wells: A Collection of Critical Essays* edited by Bergonzi, 1975; *Wells: An Outline* by F. K. Chaplin, 1961; *Wells and the World State* by W. Warren Wagar, 1961; *Wells: His Turbulent Life and Times* by Lovat Dickson, 1969; *Wells: The Critical Heritage* edited by Patrick Parrinder, 1972; *The Time Traveller: The Life of Wells* by Norman and Jeanne MacKenzie, 1973; *Wells and Rebecca West* by Gordon N. Ray, 1974; *Anatomies of Egotism: A Reading of the Last Novels of Wells* by Robert Bloom, 1977.

*   *   *

H. G. Wells wrote more than fifty novels and volumes of short stories and many non-fiction books besides, some of great distinction and influence: prodigality was part of his genius. The fiction falls broadly into three phases in roughly chronological sequence, the scientific romances, the comic novels, and the novels of ideas, and of course the three categories overlap, notably in *Tono-Bungay*. Of their kind the scientific romances are still unsurpassed, and the earliest, *The Time Machine*, one draft of which was written when he was still a student, remains the most remarkable and becomes the more so as the years pass. It shows, as one critic has written, "that evolution may produce degenerates, that the future may belong to giant crabs, and that, according to the second law of thermodynamics, sun and earth must die." Indeed, it seems now in some sense to be the one substitute we have for the great poem on evolution that the nineteenth-century poets failed to write. And it rebukes, as the scientific romances do generally, the view that Wells was a naive optimist with an unbounded belief in the beneficence of science. On the contrary, the scientific romances are minatory. At the same time, in the sheer creative high spirits they display, the delight in invention and the brilliance of imagination, works like *The Island of Dr. Moreau*, *The First Men in the Moon*, *The Invisible Man*, and *The War of the Worlds* are reminiscent of no other writer so strongly as the Swift who created Lilliput, Brobdingnag, and Laputa.

Wells's comic novels, *The Wheels of Chance*, *Kipps*, *The History of Mr. Polly*, are all rooted in his early background, which was suburban lower-middle-class, conservative, respectable, repressive. He escaped it, almost miraculously, by the hunger of his imagination and his zest for knowledge, and henceforth he was its sworn enemy. The hero is always a character very much like Wells himself, but a Wells who has not succeeded in getting away and who still half-heartedly subscribes to the tenets of that early background. Best of these novels is *The History of Mr. Polly*, which is delightful, comic, moving, and by implication Wells's most effective criticism of the society of his day: its theme is education or, rather, the inadequacies of popular education, summed up in the endearing figure of Mr. Polly, who, in his delight in language and in the exuberance of his imagination, might be an uneducated Wells. *Mr. Polly* is very much in the English tradition of fiction; behind it, we feel Dickens, whom Wells acknowledged as his master, and Fielding, for like *Joseph Andrews* it is a comic epic. When one thinks of the account of Polly's father's funeral, of Polly's wedding, of the wonderful character of Uncle Pentstemon, of Polly's linguistic flights, and of his Homeric fight with Uncle Jim at the Potwell Inn, one realises that though he may have been less than Dickens and Fielding he was of their kidney.

His quarrel with Henry James about the art of fiction is well-known and his reaction against James's attempts to convert him to the aesthetic view of the novel was petulant and indeed brutal. Years later, in his *Experiment in Autobiography*, he more or less disowned the title of novelist, saying, "I would rather be regarded as a journalist." Increasingly, he had come to see the novel as essentially a medium of ideas. The first overt example of this must be *Tono-Bungay*, which is an attempt, and an almost successful one, at a great novel on the grand scale.

It begins brilliantly, with the account of life in a great country house seen from the vantage-point of George Ponderevo, the housekeeper's son. An older England is evoked with astonishing sympathy; the great house, Bladesover, is almost as much a symbol of England as Forster's Howards End. George escapes, to become assistant in his Uncle Ponderevo's chemist's shop in a small country town and a science student in London, from which he is rescued by his uncle in order to help him exploit his patent medicine, Tono-Bungay. Uncle Ponderevo becomes a pinch-beck Napoleon of commerce and a millionaire and dies a bankrupt fugitive from justice. He is a Mr. Polly given a larger stage and allowed to translate his fantasies into action, and, like Polly, he steals our affections. George goes on to become a scientist and a pioneer in aviation. It is he who tries to save Ponderevo's fortunes by bringing back the Quap, radio-active earth, from a tropical island. It is George, too, commenting on the waste, irresponsibility, and inefficiency of capitalism, who is the conscience of the novel.

In *Tono-Bungay* ideas are made manifest in character, criticism of society embodied in action. After it, however, in the novel of ideas there is a progressive lack of interest in character and action. The roots of *The New Machiavelli* and *Ann Veronica* probably go down deeply enough into the life of their time to give them a permanent interest to students of social and political life in the first half of the twentieth century. In later novels, like *The World of William Clissold* and *Babes in the Darkling Wood*, interest in character has all but disappeared altogether. It should be said, however, that the passion the ideas arouse in Wells remains impressive; and that all the novels of Wells's last thirty years are not to be automatically discarded is shown by *The Bulpington of Blup*, written as late as 1932, a most exciting and entertaining satire on the consequences of following an exclusively aesthetic approach to oneself and the world.

—Walter Allen

WELTY, Eudora. American. Born in Jackson, Mississippi, 13 April 1909. Educated at Mississippi State College for Women, Columbus, 1926–27; University of Wisconsin, Madison, B.A. 1929; Columbia University School of Advertising, New York, 1930–31. Staff member, *The New York Times Book Review*, during World War II. Honorary Consultant in American Letters, Library of Congress, Washington, D.C., 1958. Recipient: O. Henry Award, 1942, 1943, 1968; Guggenheim Fellowship, 1942, 1948; National Institute of Arts and Letters grant, 1944, Howells Medal, 1955, and Gold Medal, 1972; Ford Fellowship, for drama; Brandeis University Creative Arts Award, 1965; Edward MacDowell Medal, 1970; Pulitzer Prize, 1973. D.Litt.: Denison University, Granville, Ohio, 1971; Smith College, Northampton, Massachusetts; University of Wisconsin, Madison; University of the South, Sewanee, Tennessee; Washington and Lee University, Lexington, Virginia. Member, American Academy of Arts and Letters, 1971. Lives in Jackson, Mississippi.

PUBLICATIONS

Fiction

A Curtain of Green and Other Stories. 1941.
The Robber Bridegroom. 1942.
The Wide Net and Other Stories. 1943.
Delta Wedding. 1946.
The Golden Apples (stories). 1949.
Selected Stories. 1954.
The Ponder Heart. 1954.
The Bride of Innisfallen and Other Stories. 1955.
Thirteen Stories, edited by Ruth M. Vande Kieft. 1965.
Losing Battles. 1970.
The Optimist's Daughter. 1972.

Other

Music from Spain. 1948.
Short Stories. 1949.
Place in Fiction. 1957.
Three Papers on Fiction. 1962.
The Shoe Bird (juvenile). 1964.
A Sweet Devouring (essay). 1969.
One Time, One Place: Mississippi in the Depression: A Snapshot Album. 1971.
A Pageant of Birds. 1974.
The Eye of the Story: Selected Essays and Reviews. 1978.

Bibliography: *Welty: A Reference Guide* by Victor H. Thompson, 1976.

Reading List: *Welty* by Ruth M. Vande Kieft, 1962; *A Season of Dreams: The Fiction of Welty* by Alfred Appel, Jr., 1965; *Welty* by J. A. Bryant, Jr., 1968.

*   *   *

Eudora Welty is a party to the great outpouring of fiction that is often referred to as the southern Renaissance, the discovery of solid traditions and uneasy tensions that color the work of William Faulkner, Katherine Anne Porter, Caroline Gordon, William Styron, and others. Welty's terrain overlaps that of Faulkner – the State of Mississippi. But it offers a contrasting appearance – indeed, a predominantly sunny one despite the shadows of ancient pain, present injustice, and future uncertainty that both Faulkner and Welty discover in their part of the South. But Welty's imaginative world maintains its special rules: rules of civility and of affection that protect the continuance of human meaning and human dignity. It is a continuance that may well be a "losing battle" (*Losing Battles* is the title of one of her novels), but it is never really a lost battle. The majority of the writer's characters reel under blows that chance, inheritance, and environment deal them, but they rise to hope and love another day. The compulsions they face and partly master are less awesome than those many a Faulkner person meets. True, there is guilt, but the guilt is personal rather than one which several generations have piled up. There are also authoritative patterns of life. But these patterns, in contrast to those of Faulkner, are familiar and easily identifiable rather than occult and mysterious. There is no "bear" or any other symbol of aboriginal compulsion moving back and forth in the delta and the hill country which Welty recollects and recreates in her short stories and her novels. The minds of her characters – rednecks, cotton aristocrats, and the "just folks" of small county seats – are indeed challenged by the events that overtake them. But the contests between minds and events issues in a draw, and sometimes better than a draw.

This can be seen in the many short stories, simple of surface but calculating in their approach to a revelatory conclusion. The story "Keela, The Outcast Indian Maiden" (in *A Curtain of Green*) seems, for most of its course, to be a study of the guilt a young man feels for his share in the exploitation of a little black man who has been kidnapped and exhibited as a freak in a sideshow. But by the end of the story the young man has made a sort of expiation of his share of guilt; this is a draw. But suddenly attention shifts to the little black man; *he* is only amused by the antics of his visitor and sits down to supper with his children; out of abasement the black man has won a minor victory.

The reverses and complexities that Welty meditates on are the stuff of her many stories. Such reverses and complexities also furnish out the longer works, with the possible exception of the early tale, *The Robber Bridegroom*, which is a pious salute to the violent times when Mississippi land was being invaded by white men, farmers, riverboat men, and robbers who attacked travellers on the Natchez Trace. This narrative has the willed simplicity of folk tale, as indeed do many of the short stories. But it is a simplicity that appears only intermittently in the longer novels, where the writer's imagination engages itself with a more or less contemporary milieu and the sensibilities educated there. *Delta Wedding* is a salute to the "cotton aristocrats" and their experience of power and complacency in the twenties of this century. Some characters in the novel enjoy their privileges, and others try to measure them and test them. The careless "lose" their battle; the thoughtful attain to an uneasy survival: a comprehension of their situation. It is a comprehension that, unfortunately, has to be recast from day to day.

This recasting is, in *Delta Wedding*, complex and difficult to express in a phrase. So it continues to be in shorter novels like *The Ponder Heart* and *The Optimist's Daughter*, two tales of matrimonial misadventures which are observed and studied by women – centers of awareness – who are sufficient vehicles for Welty's own discriminations. A more difficult book is *Losing Battles*. In this long account of a family reunion up in the Mississippi hills, the novelist for the most part dispenses with the fairly refined and privileged observers of her other novels. She also gives up the comic discriminations of *Delta Wedding* and *The Ponder Heart*. *Losing Battles* is, in sheer event, not far removed from the farce of Li'l Abner's Dogpatch; there are mad car accidents, watermelon fights, and gargantuan feastings. Nor does Miss Welty allow her own prose to reproduce the thoughts of her mostly back-country characters. The interminable conversations, fashioned from rural clichés, nevertheless become transparent envelopes through which appear the "contents" of each red-neck existence with a range of sensitivity almost as complex as that which is represented in *Delta Wedding*.

In short, Miss Welty has a wide range of strategies. But these all serve a concern that is strict, narrow, and unwavering: how persons respond to their opportunity to live, what comment they are able to make, the deep interest that lies in almost any such comment when it is carefully reproduced and charitably understood.

—Harold H. Watts

WESCOTT, Glenway. American. Born in Kewaskum, Wisconsin, 11 April 1901. Educated at the University of Chicago (President of the Poetry Society), 1917–19. Lived briefly in New Mexico, New York City and State, England, and Germany, 1919–25; lived in France and Germany, 1925–33; full-time writer from 1921. D.Litt.: Rutgers University, New Brunswick, New Jersey, 1963. President, National Institute of Arts and Letters, 1959–62; Member, American Academy of Arts and Letters. Lives in Rosemont, New Jersey.

PUBLICATIONS

Fiction

The Apple of the Eye. 1924.
... Like a Lover (stories). 1926.
The Grandmothers: A Family Portrait. 1927; as *A Family Portrait*, 1927.
Good-bye, Wisconsin (stories). 1928.
The Babe's Bed (story). 1930.
The Pilgrim Hawk: A Love Story. 1940.
Apartment in Athens. 1945; as *Household in Athens*, 1945.

Verse

The Bitterns: A Book of Twelve Poems. 1920.
Native of Rock: XX Poems, 1921–1922. 1925.

Other

Elizabeth Madox Roberts: A Personal Note. 1930.
Fear and Trembling (essays). 1932.
A Calendar of Saints for Unbelievers. 1932.
12 Fables of Aesop, Newly Narrated. 1954.
Images of Truth: Remembrances and Criticism. 1962.

Editor, *The Maugham Reader.* 1950.
Editor, *Short Novels of Colette.* 1951.

Bibliography: "Wescott: A Bibliography" by Sy Myron Kahn, in *Bulletin of Bibliography 22,* 1956.

Reading List: *Classics and Commercials* by Edmund Wilson, 1950; *Wescott* by William Rueckert, 1965; *Wescott: The Paradox of Voice* by Ira Johnson, 1971.

*   *   *

Glenway Wescott, a classmate of Yvor Winters and Vincent Sheean, was president of the Poetry Society at the University of Chicago. His Imagist lyrics appeared in *Poetry* and were later printed privately in two small volumes. He turned away from poetry after he came of age, and because of ill health left the university in 1919; for six restless years he lived briefly in New Mexico, the Berkshires, New York City, England, and Germany, usually with his lifelong friend Monroe Wheeler. Wescott's precocity, striking appearance (tall, blond), and cultivated British accent marked him during his expatriate years from 1925 to 1933, when he lived in Paris, at Villefrance-sur-Mer, and in Germany. In *The Autobiography of Alice B. Toklas*, Gertrude Stein records his first visit: "Glenway impressed us with his English accent. Hemingway explained. He said, when you matriculate at the University of Chicago, you write down just what accent you will have and they give it to you when you graduate." In the 1920's Wescott published impressive critical reviews (chiefly in *The Dial* and *The New Republic*), two novels, and a collection of short stories, though he has published very little in the succeeding 50 years.

Wescott was 23 when *The Apple of the Eye* was published. The story of Hannah Madoc, a Wisconsin farm woman, is told from various perspectives. It is a novel of initiation and of revolt against the hostile environment of farm and town – especially against repressive Puritanism. *The Grandmothers* was Wescott's greatest popular success. Alwyn Tower, reliving in France his Wisconsin childhood, is "a participating narrator, identical to the author's second (artistic) self" (Ira Johnson). His curiosity aroused by an old family album, the young man pieces together the story of his three grandmothers (one grandfather married twice). Cadenced prose and high sensitivity present the pioneer experience, always focused on Wescott's major themes of love and the self.

An introductory essay lent its title to *Good-bye Wisconsin*, a short story collection. The ten stories, and *The Babe's Bed*, a slightly longer short story published in a limited Paris edition, show Wisconsin as hostile to the realization of the self. Wescott published only five more short stories, from 1932 to 1942, none of them noteworthy. He is often classified as a midwestern realist and regionalist, and these stories obviously connect him with the "Revolt from the Village" writing of Edgar Lee Masters, Sherwood Anderson, and Sinclair Lewis. But Wescott's fiction also demonstrates his abandonment of realism, regionalism, and the provincial midwest for a European aesthetic existence and artistic ideal. Among his friends were Ford Madox Ford, Jean Cocteau, Elly Ney, and Rebecca West.

Wescott's current reputation as a stylist is based primarily on *The Pilgrim Hawk: A Love Story*, which first appeared in two issues of *Harper's Magazine* and has been reprinted and anthologized. Alwyn Tower, now in America, recounts a day's incident in France in 1940 which involves Irish and American expatriates and their servants. Tower's nostalgic reminiscence is heavily ironic, and the falcon is central to the love story Tower narrates. In addition to the two physical love triangles, a third appears to perceptive readers, a subtle examination of the conflict between appetite and control; as James Korges puts it (in *Contemporary Novelists*, 1976), "The reader is not told about the conflict of love and art; instead he receives it, as a powerful undercurrent in the story of an Irish couple and a hawk, which is also a story about love and art, freedom and captivity."

Wescott considered *Apartment in Athens* his contribution to the war effort. A German officer is billeted in the apartment of a Greek middle class intellectual. "The cramped physical and moral conditions, the readjustments in the relationships of the family, the whole distortion of the social organism by the unassimilable presence of the foreigner – all this is most successfully created" (Edmund Wilson). The novel, however, is marred by its ending, a long letter smuggled out of the prison cell of the condemned Greek father, and the anti-Nazi editorializing violates the fictional illusion.

Images of Truth collects the critical essays Wescott had published since 1939. His long essays on Katherine Anne Porter, Elizabeth Madox Roberts, Mann, Colette, Maugham, and Wilder are highly personal expressions of Wescott's own idiosyncratic views on life and literature. Wescott's Imagist poetry, which he abandoned early, has been long forgotten. His essentially lyric talent finds expression in his prose.

—Clarence A. Glasrud

WEST, Nathanael. Pseudonym for Nathan Wallenstein Weinstein. American. Born in New York City, 17 October 1906. Educated at Brown University, Providence, Rhode Island, Ph.B. 1924. Married Eileen McKenney in 1940. Writer from 1930; managed a residential club hotel in Sutton Place, New York, in the early 1930's; assistant to William Carlos Williams in editing *Contact*, 1932; writer, in Hollywood, for Columbia Pictures, 1933, 1938, Republic Pictures, 1936–38, RKO Pictures, 1938, 1939, and Universal Pictures, 1938. *Died* (in an auto accident) *22 December 1940.*

PUBLICATIONS

Collections

The Collected Works. 1957.

Fiction

The Dream Life of Balso Snell. 1931.
Miss Lonelyhearts. 1933.
A Cool Million: The Dismantling of Lemuel Pitkin. 1934.
The Day of the Locust. 1939.

Plays

Good Hunting: A Satire, with Joseph Shrank (produced 1938).

Screenplays: *The President's Mystery,* with Lester Cole, 1936; *Follow Your Heart,* with others, 1936; *Ticket to Paradise,* with others, 1936; *It Could Happen to You,* with Samuel Ornitz, 1937; *Rhythm in the Clouds,* with others, 1937; *Gangs of New York* (uncredited), 1938; *Orphans of the Street* (uncredited), 1938; *Born to Be Wild,* 1938; *Five Came Back,* with others, 1939; *I Stole a Million,* with Lester Cole, 1939; *The Spirit of Culver,* with others, 1939; *Men Against the Sky,* with John Twist, 1940; *Let's Make Music,* 1940.

Bibliography: *West: A Comprehensive Bibliography* by William White, 1975.

Reading List: *West: An Interpretive Study* by James F. Light, 1961; *West* by Stanley Edgar Hyman, 1962; *West: The Ironic Prophet* by Victor Comerchero, 1964; *The Fiction of West* by Randall Reid, 1967; *West: The Art of His Life* by Jay Martin, 1970, and *West: A Collection of Critical Essays* edited by Martin, 1971; *West: A Critical Essay* by Nathan A. Scott, 1971; *West's Novels* by Irving Malin, 1972.

*   *   *

While many of the writers of the 1930's found in the naturalistic tradition a form which would directly express their protest at what seemed to be the collapse or corruption of the American Dream, Nathanael West developed an oblique vision that may prove more lasting than the products of many of his contemporaries. A statement by his painter-protagonist, Tod Hackett (*The Day of the Locust*), provides a reasonable thematic definition of West's artistic intentions: "It is hard to laugh at the need for beauty and romance, no matter how tasteless, even horrible, the results of that are. But it is easy to sigh. Few things are sadder than the truly monstrous." Focusing relentlessly on the radical disparity between the romantic expectations pandered to by the mass-media and the actual limited portion which is the human lot, West's talent is to delineate "the truly monstrous" in a grotesque world that hovers ambiguously between the hilarious and the heartbreaking. Accepting more or less the same premises that underlie Eliot's *The Waste Land*, West's work is equally hallucinatory and probably more pessimistic, as well as more comic. It is partly indebted to the techniques of Surrealism that West absorbed in a brief post-college sojourn in Paris where he wrote his first novel (*The Dream Life of Balso Snell*), and its energy, I think, derives from a deep moral exasperation that could be a result of his youthful training in Judaism. Relatively overlooked when it was published, West's fiction brought the sub-genre of "Black Humor" into prominence after World War II when it served as a model of encouragement for such writers as Carson McCullers, James Purdy, Flannery O'Connor, and John Hawkes.

Although West wrote four novels in his abruptly ended career, he is remembered primarily for *Miss Lonelyhearts* and *The Day of the Locust*. In both novels West cultivates a stripped cinematic style, advancing his narrative in a spastic sequence of intense and fragmented scenes. As a Hollywood screenwriter for the last years of his life, West clearly found the discipline of the film compatible with his own penchant for constructing stories out of dominantly visual images, and *The Day of the Locust* is generally regarded as the premiere "Hollywood novel" in American fiction.

In *Miss Lonelyhearts*, the un-named protagonist is a bachelor newspaper columnist assigned to the job of giving advice to the lovelorn. Worn down by the barrage of unabated and insoluble misery that pours in on him and bedeviled by the savage nihilism of his city editor, Shrike, he finds himself unable even to imagine palliative possibilities for those who write to him. Further, his defensive cynicism and detachment erode as he begins to recognize his own condition in the broken human beings who are his suppliants. Killed finally in a ludicrous comedy of errors, he becomes a futile immolated Christ whose death is merely another addition to the crumpled heap of frustrated hopes that the novel assembles. West's dark mockery is pointed in all directions. The manipulators are as crippled and impotent as are the manipulated; nor does the novel permit any socio-political resolution of the problems it presents. Lacking a sane religious option for satisfying "the need for beauty and romance," the frenetic improvisations of the spiritually dispossessed can only be freakishly monstrous and sad.

The Day of the Locust displaces a greater imaginative volume, just as its setting − Hollywood at the time when it was dream-factory to the world − is a larger milieu than the newspaper office and bars of *Miss Lonelyhearts*. Here West places his artist-protagonist on the margins of the action and structures the novel on what might be termed the principle of "an image within an image." Tod Hackett is engaged in painting "The Burning of Los Angeles," a giant canvas that he intends to be prophetic in the Old Testament sense; and the novel as a whole duplicates on a greatly magnified screen his apocalyptic vision of a holocaust. Unlike the multitude of victims in *Miss Lonelyhearts*, the grotesques of *The Day of the Locust*, mindless as lemmings, purposeless as falling rain, seek vengeance for the rootlessness, disappointment, and excruciating boredom of their lives in random unprovoked destruction. If the keynote of *Miss Lonelyhearts* is a profound sadness wrested out of grotesque comedy, *The Day of the Locust* re-orchestrates that sadness with chords of terror. And the bitter humor of the earlier novel takes on accents of insane laughter in the later one.

—Earl Rovit

WEST, Dame Rebecca. Pseudonym for Cicily Fairfield Andrews. English. Born in County Kerry, Ireland, 25 December 1892. Educated at George Watson's Ladies College, Edinburgh. Had one son by H. G. Wells, *q.v.*, the writer Anthony West; married Henry Maxwell Andrews in 1930 (died, 1968). Writer from 1911; reviewer and political writer for *Freewoman*, London, 1911, and *Clarion*, London, 1912; Talks Supervisor, BBC, London, during World War II. Fellow of Saybrook College, Yale University, New Haven, Connecticut. D.Litt.: New York University. Member, Order of St. Sava, 1937; Chevalier, Legion of Honour, 1957. Fellow, 1947, Benson Medallist, 1967, and Companion of Literature, 1968, Royal Society of Literature. Member, American Academy of Arts and Letters. C.B.E. (Commander, Order of the British Empire), 1949; D.B.E. (Dame Commander, Order of the British Empire), 1959. Lives in Ibstone, Buckinghamshire.

PUBLICATIONS

Fiction

The Return of the Soldier. 1918.
The Judge. 1922.
Harriet Hume: A London Fantasy. 1929.
War Nurse: The True Story of a Woman Who Lived, Loved, and Suffered on the Western Front. 1930.
The Harsh Voice: Four Short Novels. 1935.
The Thinking Reed. 1936.
The Fountain Overflows. 1956.
The Birds Fall Down. 1966.

Other

Henry James. 1916.
The Strange Necessity: Essays and Reviews. 1928.
Lions and Lambs, with Low. 1928.
D. H. Lawrence. 1930; as *Elegy*, 1930.
Arnold Bennett Himself. 1931.
Ending in Earnest: A Literary Log. 1931.
St. Augustine. 1933.
A Letter to a Grandfather. 1933.
The Modern "Rake's Progress," with Low. 1934.
Black Lamb and Grey Falcon: A Journey Through Yugoslavia. 2 vols., 1941.
Rebecca's Cookbook. 1942.
The Meaning of Treason. 1947; revised edition, as *The New Meaning of Treason,* 1964.
A Train of Powder (essays). 1955.
The Court and the Castle: Some Treatments of a Recurrent Theme. 1957.
The Vassall Affair. 1963.
McLuhan and the Future of Literature. 1969.
West – A Celebration: A Selection of Her Writing. 1977.

Editor, *Carl Sandburg: Selected Poems.* 1926.

Reading List: *West: Artist and Thinker* by Peter Wolfe, 1971; *H. G. Wells and West* by Gordon N. Ray, 1974.

*   *   *

Rebecca West is a brilliant, opinionated woman who, besides being a novelist, writes with sure, deep conviction on many subjects. Her output during a busy career that started in 1911 includes political journalism, literary criticism, biography, history, travel writing, and fiction.

If this vast and varied output holds together, its unifying core must be the Augustinian doctrine of original sin. All of Rebecca West's books claim that there is more evil than good in the world and that the evil is more vivid. Her belief in man's depravity saturates her reading of Shakespeare in *The Court and the Castle*; the palace intrigues in the histories and tragedies show what happens when the will acts in a milieu where it counts as nothing.

History proves that people favor the unpleasant over the pleasant. Not only Augustine, but also Paul, Luther, and the Mithraic cultists promoted ugliness and cruelty. But renunciation merely aggravates loss; pain, while failing to purify sin, prolongs sin; sacrifice is a rite that drips with the blood of centuries. Rebecca West advises us to ignore this wreckage and to pursue pleasure instead. To follow her advice is harder than it appears. The pleasure seeker must be original, self-confident, and compassionate. It is much easier to court pain. Thus the pleasure principle builds moral fiber. To protect the sacredness of joy, we must repress the hatred and cruelty ingrained in us all and encourage others to do the same.

Only pleasure fosters the life-giving harmony between organisms and their environment that Rebecca West calls process. Process is her most encompassing doctrine. It may be defined as the sum of man's civilized energies, or, perhaps more accurately, as the application of civilized energies for civilizing purposes. Cumulative in character, it draws strength from two main sources: a close acquaintance with many related things over a long time and an openness to new experience. Her dislike of gambling, disorder, and violence makes slowness a virtue to her conservative skepticism: cream does not pour quickly.

Her crafting of her leading ideas has prompted some readers to rank her as the outstanding nonfiction writer in the language; Kenneth Tynan calls her "the best journalist alive, the only one who can record both the facts and their flavour without loss of grace or vigour." As has been said, her achievement as a documentary writer covers a wide range. Although no literary critic per se, she wrote the first systematic critical studies of Henry James and James Joyce, and, in *The Court and the Castle*, yoked Shakespeare to movements in European politics. Accordingly, *Black Lamb and Grey Falcon* stands as the masterpiece of travel literature of our century, and the magazine essays comprising *A Train of Powder* and *The New Meaning of Treason* bring to court reporting a heft and a command it never knew before.

Rebecca West's fiction lacks this uniformity of distinction. The four novels she published between 1918 and 1936 – *The Return of the Soldier*, *The Judge*, *Harriet Hume*, and *The Thinking Reed* – sag under the weight of their labored tonal effects. Their warm, golden curves fuse well with their moral seriousness, and their well-knit interior logic offers civilized, intellectual pleasure. But their violation of probablility and neglect of incident makes them literary exercises rather than novels. Though novelistically designed, they are only imitations of novels.

The two late works, *The Fountain Overflows* and *The Birds Fall Down*, surpass by far the four early ones. By waiting twenty years between her fourth and fifth novels, Rebecca West developed the artistry to do justice to the wealth of knowledge distinguishing her nonfiction. Both of the late novels center around a sensitive girl growing up in a deteriorating family. The malaise corroding the families is also undermining western culture at large. Both books pulsate with images of collapse, noncommunication, and incoherence; both, finally, turn on the irony of a female growing up in a crumbling, male-dominated world.

Though set in the early 1900's, these novels speak to our time. They impart a vision of life rather than a message. Solid, serious, and committed, they show, along with Rebecca West's best nonfiction, the interweaving of the moral, the political, and the religious. To neglect them is to miss the meanings behind much of our century's terror and beauty.

—Peter Wolfe

WHARTON, Edith (Newbold, née Jones). American. Born in New York City, 24 January 1862. Travelled in Italy, Spain, and France as a child; educated privately. Married Edward Wharton in 1885 (divorced, 1913). Lived in Newport, Rhode Island, after her marriage, and in Europe from 1907; a close frind of Henry James; helped organize the American Hostel for Refugees, and the Children of Flanders Rescue Committee, during World War I. Recipient: Pulitzer Prize, 1921; National Institute of Art and Letters Gold Medal, 1924. Litt.D.: Yale University, New Haven, Connecticut, 1923. Chevalier, Legion of Honour, 1916, and Order of Leopold, 1919. Member, American Academy of Arts and Letters, 1930. *Died 11 August 1937.*

PUBLICATIONS

Collections

> *A Wharton Reader,* edited by Louis Auchincloss. 1965.
> *The Collected Short Stories,* edited by R. W. B. Lewis. 1968.

Fiction

> *The Greater Inclination* (stories). 1899.
> *The Touchstone.* 1900; as *A Gift from the Grave,* 1900.
> *Crucial Instances* (stories). 1901.
> *The Valley of Decision.* 1902.
> *Sanctuary.* 1903.
> *The Descent of Man and Other Stories.* 1904.
> *The House of Mirth.* 1905; edited by R. W. B. Lewis, 1963.
> *Madame de Treymes.* 1907.
> *The Fruit of the Tree.* 1907.
> *The Hermit and the Wild Woman, and Other Stories.* 1908.
> *Tales of Men and Ghosts.* 1910.
> *Ethan Frome.* 1911; edited by Blake Nevius, 1968.
> *The Reef.* 1912.
> *The Custom of the Country.* 1913.
> *Xingu and Other Stories.* 1916.
> *Summer.* 1917.
> *The Marne.* 1918.
> *The Age of Innocence.* 1920.

The Glimpses of the Moon. 1922.
A Son at the Front. 1923.
Old New York: False Dawn (The 'forties), The Old Maid (The 'fifties), The Spark (The
   'sixties), New Year's Day (The 'seventies). 1924.
The Mother's Recompense. 1925.
Here and Beyond (stories). 1926.
Twilight Sleep. 1927.
The Children. 1928.
Hudson River Bracketed. 1929.
Certain People (stories). 1930.
The Gods Arrive. 1932.
Human Nature (stories). 1933.
The World Over (stories). 1936.
Ghosts (stories). 1937.
The Buccaneers. 1938.

Plays

The Joy of Living, from a play by Hermann Sudermann (produced 1902). 1902.
The House of Mirth, with Clyde Fitch, from the novel by Wharton (produced 1906).

Verse

Verses. 1878.
Artemis to Actaeon and Other Verse. 1909.
Twelve Poems. 1926.

Other

The Decoration of Houses, with Ogden Codman, Jr. 1897.
Italian Villas and Their Gardens. 1904.
Italian Backgrounds. 1905.
A Motor Flight Through France. 1908.
Fighting France: From Dunkerque to Belfort. 1915.
Wharton's War Charities in France. 1918.
L'Amérique en Guerre. 1918.
French Ways and Their Meaning. 1919.
In Morocco. 1920.
The Writing of Fiction. 1925.
A Backward Glance (autobiography). 1934.

Editor, The Book of the Homeless: Original Articles in Verse and Prose. 1916.
Editor, with Robert Norton, Eternal Passion in English Poetry. 1939.

Bibliography: Wharton: A Bibliography by Vito J. Brenni, 1966; Wharton and Kate Chopin:
A Reference Guide by Marlene Springer, 1976.

Reading List: Wharton: A Study of Her Fiction by Blake Nevius, 1953; Wharton: Convention
and Morality in the Work of a Novelist by Marilyn Jones Lyde, 1959; Wharton by Louis
Auchincloss, 1961; Wharton: A Collection of Critical Essays edited by Irving Howe, 1962;

Wharton and James: The Story of Their Friendship by Millicent Bell, 1965; *Wharton: A Biography* by R. W. B. Lewis, 1975; *Wharton* by Richard H. Lawson, 1977; *A Feast of Words: The Triumph of Wharton* by Cynthia Griffin Wolff, 1978.

*   *   *

Edith Wharton was a versatile as well as a prolific writer. During her lifetime, she published over forty books, including some twenty novels, ten collections of short stories, books of verse, a pioneer work in interior design (with Ogden Codman, Jr.) *The Decoration of Houses*, several books of travel, an autobiography, and books on Italian villas, France, and fictional theory. It is by her fiction, however, that her importance as a writer must be judged. Mrs. Wharton was an admirer and close friend of Henry James. Because of that friendship and because of certain parallels between their lives (both New Yorkers, both expatriates) and between their fictions (both with an interest in the manners of the rich, and in Americans living abroad), as well as aesthetic principles Mrs. Wharton appears to have got from "the master," she has been called a disciple of James, an allegation that has obscured significant differences between them. James was a metaphysical writer, Mrs. Wharton a novelist of manners. James's method was to remove his characters from the effects of social forces and to locate his story in the minds of his characters, Mrs. Wharton's was to deal with the impact of social and moral forces on the lives of her protagonists. Conflict in James is usually internal. In Mrs. Wharton, it is almost always external, involving a superior individual in a struggle with the representatives of a social world with which the individual is fundamentally at odds.

The grand exception is *The Reef*, Mrs. Wharton's most Jamesian novel. Here the action is confined almost exclusively to a chateau in France and the issue narrowed to a psychological struggle in the mind of the heroine, Anna Leath, who discovers that the man she has agreed to marry has had an affair with the young woman who is about to marry her step-son. Despite the economy, the tightness, the remoteness from the usual social forces that move through Mrs. Wharton's pages, the conflict is much like that to be found in other Wharton novels, except that here it is treated as a psychological problem rather than a social and moral struggle. Anna Leath, the protagonist, cannot accept her fiancé's promiscuity nor can she give him up; and so, at the end of the novel, she is reduced to a state of tormented indecision.

In the first of her major novels, *The House of Mirth*, Lily Bart, a young woman from an old New York family ruined by financial reverses and extravagance, is caught between her love of beauty and luxury and her moral fastidiousness. If she should marry the man she loves she would live in what to her would be physical squalor; if she marries a man she does not love in order to get the material things essential to her sense of well being, she would violate her deepest nature. She manages to salvage her moral integrity but slides into poverty and, then, death, and a pathetic moral triumph.

Ethan Frome, a short novel that differs in some ways (a New England setting, impoverished rural characters) from Mrs. Wharton's typical fiction, nonetheless deals with an issue similar to the one that confronts Lily Bart: the conflict between social and moral conventions and the deep desires of the individual. Ethan Frome, married to a homely neuresthenic woman several years older than himself, falls in love with his wife's pretty cousin. Although he contemplates eloping with the girl, Mattie Wills, social pressures win out. Ethan and Mattie's attempt to escape their fate through suicide ends with them maimed for life and left in the care of the grim woman they had tried to foil.

Both *Ethan Frome* and *Summer*, Mrs. Wharton's other short New England novel, give fuller rein to sexual passion than other Wharton novels. Ethan and Mattie have to pay for their passion in a cruelly ironic way; Charity Royal, protagonist of *Summer*, is allowed a kind of idyllic bliss in the arms of her lover before the score is reckoned and she is obliged to marry her elderly guardian, a good, solid man who will give her a respectable place in the town of North Dormer and a name for her unborn child, but a passionless marriage.

In *The Age of Innocence*, the last of Edith Wharton's important novels, the same issue is

1287

dealt with in a lightly ironic way. Newland Archer has two choices: he can marry the conventional young woman to whom he is engaged or he can break with her and live with Ellen Olenska, a Europeanized American shown to be emotionally and aesthetically more attractive to Archer. The choice is between what is socially acceptable to old New York society and what most engages Archer's deepest feelings. Again, convention triumphs. Archer marries May. Ellen returns to Europe. Years later, in a kind of wistful epilogue, Archer visits Europe and, with his wife dead, might re-establish his relationship with Ellen. Archer fails to visit Ellen, however, and takes comfort from the knowledge that his life with May has had its compensations. Thus, it seems, Mrs. Wharton has made a kind of peace with the vexing conflict between personal desire and social obligation.

Custom of the Country, which appeared in 1913, strikes a note that was to be echoed increasingly after 1920. It is Mrs. Wharton's major satire on American life and its lays out in a manner that anticipates the cruder satires of Sinclair Lewis the rise of vulgar Americans from the West. Undine Sprague is the feminine version, Elmer Moffat the male. With neither taste nor moral scruple, they assail the old monied New York aristocracy, conquer it, and move on to Europe and repeat their triumph. Undine marries and divorces Ralph Marvel of New York, marries and divorces a French aristocrat and, then, marries Elmer Moffat who is now a multi-millionaire settled in Europe and buying up rare antique art. In this novel Mrs. Wharton's usual theme – the impingement of social and economic forces on the lives of sensitive individuals – is relegated to a minor role. Ralph Marvel's suicide (precipitated by Undine's greed) is but one of the brutal blows inflicted by Undine during her upward scramble.

After 1920 the satirical note predominated in novels such as *Twilight Sleep*, *The Children*, *Hudson River Bracketed*, and *The Gods Arrive*. In all of these novels there was a decided falling off both of artistic integrity and of imaginative energy. The brilliant, lucid style of the early work was scarcely visible now, except in *The Mother's Recompense* and in the non-satirical parts of *The Children*. *Glimpses of the Moon* was not much above the level of soap opera, and *Twilight Sleep* was a broader and less convincing satire on current representatives of American women than *Custom of the Country*. *Hudson River Bracketed* and *The Gods Arrive* deal with the career of an American novelist, Vance Weston, tracing his rise from obscurity in Euphoria, Illinois, to international fame in London and Paris, but they fail to bring his story into significant focus. In *The Buccaneers* Mrs. Wharton returned once more to the scene of her earlier and best triumphs, old New York before the turn of the century, but the novel remained unfinished at her death.

Among the seventy or so published short stories at least a dozen appear to have enduring quality, including "The Other Two," "Xingu," "Kerfol," "The Bunner Sisters," "The Triumph of Night," "Bewitched," "A Bottle of Perrier," "After Holbein," "Mr. Jones," "Pomegranate Seed," "Roman Fever," and "Joy in the House," and "The Eyes."

In 1934 Mrs. Wharton published her autobiography, an engaging though carefully selective account of her life, which referred only briefly to her disastrous marriage and dealt humorously and ironically with her eminent friend Henry James. Even before her death in 1937 Edith Wharton's literary reputation had begun to decline. It is only recently that interest in her work has revived, partly as the result of the new feminine consciousness. Still, even now, her novels and stories are not so highly regarded as they once were nor as seriously treated by literary critics as they deserve to be. What were once regarded as her strengths – her firm grasp of the social realities of her time and place, and her ready accessibility – now appear to be her chief limitations. However, her two novels about New England life, *Ethan Frome* and *Summer*, along with *The House of Mirth*, *The Reef* and *The Age of Innocence* are among the best novels of their time and constitute an impressive body of work.

—W. J. Stuckey

WHITE, E(lwyn) B(rooks). American. Born in Mt. Vernon, New York, 11 July 1899. Educated at Mt. Vernon High School; Cornell University, Ithaca, New York, A.B. 1921. Served as a private in the United States Army, 1918. Married Katharine Sergeant Angell in 1929 (died, 1977); one son. Reporter, *Seattle Times*, 1922–23; advertising copywriter, 1924–25; Contributing Editor, *The New Yorker*, from 1927; Columnist ("One Man's Meat"), *Harper's*, New York, 1937–43. Recipient: National Association of Independent Schools Award, 1955; American Academy of Arts and Letters Gold Medal, 1960; Presidential Medal of Freedom, 1963; American Library Association Laura Ingalls Wilder Award, 1970; George G. Stone Center for Children's Books Award, 1970; National Medal for Literature, 1971. Litt.D.: Dartmouth College, Hanover, New Hampshire, 1948; University of Maine, Orono, 1948; Yale University, New Haven, Connecticut, 1948; Bowdoin College, Brunswick, Maine, 1950; Hamilton College, Clinton, New York 1952; Harvard University, Cambridge, Massachusetts, 1954; L.H.D.: Colby College, Waterville, Maine, 1954. Fellow, American Academy of Arts and Sciences; Member, American Academy of Arts and Letters, 1974. Lives in North Brooklin, Maine.

PUBLICATIONS

Sketches and Prose

Is Sex Necessary? or, Why You Feel the Way You Do, with James Thurber. 1929.
Ho Hum. 1931.
Another Ho Hum. 1932.
Alice Through the Cellophane. 1933.
Every Day Is Saturday. 1934.
Farewell to Model T. 1936.
Quo Vadimus? or, The Case for the Bicycle. 1939.
One Man's Meat. 1942; augmented edition, 1944.
The Wild Flag: Editorials from the New Yorker on Federal World Government and Other Matters. 1946.
Here Is New York. 1949.
The Second Tree from the Corner. 1954.
The Points of My Compass: Letters from the East, The West, The North, The South. 1962.
A White Reader, edited by William W. Watt and Robert W. Bradford. 1966.
Essays. 1977.

Verse

The Lady Is Cold. 1929.
The Fox of Peapack and Other Poems. 1938.

Other

Stuart Little (juvenile). 1945.
Charlotte's Web (juvenile). 1952.
The Trumpet of the Swan (juvenile). 1970.
Letters, edited by Dorothy Lobrano Guth. 1976.

Editor, with Katharine S. White, *A Subtreasury of American Humor.* 1941.

Reading List: *White* by Edward C. Sampson, 1974.

*   *   *

In an editorial headnote in *Letters*, E. B. White refers to the "squibs and poems" that he began submitting to *The New Yorker* shortly after it was founded in 1925. He joined the staff of the magazine two years later and retained a real, if sometimes tenuous, connection with it for the rest of his writing life. His poems are conventional light verse, rather weak examples of a genre that tends toward wry sentiment, easy irony, and even easier rhyme. His important literary work is the care and feeding of the "squib," its transformation from fragile sketch to full-bodied essay. One of the tools in effecting that change was the discipline involved in writing the unsigned editorials, the "Notes and Comments" that he once called "my weekly sermon," samples of which have been collected in *Every Day Is Saturday* and *The Wild Flag*. It was the signed pieces, the "casuals" to use the *New Yorker* term, for which White became best known. As with most of the *New Yorker* humorists, he worked in a variety of styles (including the parody volume *Is Sex Necessary?* that he wrote with James Thurber), but he is at his most characteristic sketching ordinary incidents with affection and mild surprise, colored occasionally by outright fantasy. Most of his early work never escaped the pages of the magazine for which it was written, but the best of these pieces can be found in *Quo Vadimus?*

As early as 1929, in a letter to his brother, he wrote, "I discovered a long time ago that writing of the small things of the day, the trivial matters of the heart, the inconsequential but near things of this living, was the only kind of creative work which I could accomplish with any sincerity or grace." Although he never ceased to be concerned with "the small occasions," as he once called them, he came to know that the trivial and the inconsequential are inextricably bound with the vital, to write about everyday life with the awareness that it involved everyday death. The deepening tone in White's work began with "One Man's Meat," the monthly essay he started contributing to *Harper's* in 1937; it can be heard in later volumes like *The Second Tree from the Corner* and *The Points of My Compass*. In *Essays*, a retrospective gathering of more than forty years, White can be found at his saddest, his richest, his finest.

There is another White, but the author of the books for children is simply a gentler variation on the man who wrote *Essays*, as can be seen in the death of Charlotte and the rebirth made explicit in the arrival of all those baby spiders. *Charlotte's Web* is the most complex of White's children's books, placing a fantasy rescue in a realistic setting, using artifice to celebrate natural processes. Both *Stuart Little* and *The Trumpet of the Swan* are quest stories, but the first of these is probably White's most enduring book for children, not simply for the charm of its hero, but because it has an ending that does not end, a close that leaves Stuart – like White, like any good writer – still in search of beauty.

—Gerald Weales

WHITE, Patrick (Victor Martindale). Australian. Born in London, England, 28 May 1912. Educated at schools in Australia, 1919–25; Cheltenham College, 1925–29; King's College, Cambridge, 1932–35, B.A. in modern languages 1935. Served in the Royal Air Force as an Intelligence Officer, in the Middle East, 1940–45. Travelled in Europe and the

United States, and lived in London, before World War II; writer from 1938; returned to Australia after the war. Recipient: Australian Literary Society Gold Medal, 1956; Miles Franklin Award, 1958, 1962; Smith Literary Award, 1959; National Conference of Christians and Jews' Brotherhood Award, 1962; Nobel Prize for Literature, 1973. A.C. (Companion, Order of Australia), 1975. Lives in Sydney.

PUBLICATIONS

Fiction

    Happy Valley. 1939.
    The Living and the Dead. 1941.
    The Aunt's Story. 1948.
    The Tree of Man. 1955.
    Voss. 1957.
    Riders in the Chariot. 1961.
    The Burnt Ones (stories). 1964.
    The Solid Mandala. 1966.
    The Vivisector. 1970.
    The Eye of the Storm. 1973.
    The Cockatoos: Shorter Novels and Stories. 1974.
    A Fringe of Leaves. 1976.

Plays

    Return to Abyssinia (produced 1947).
    The Ham Funeral (produced 1961). In *Four Plays,* 1965.
    The Season at Sarsaparilla (produced 1962). In *Four Plays,* 1965.
    A Cheery Soul (produced 1963). In *Four Plays,* 1965.
    Night on Bald Mountain (produced 1964). In *Four Plays,* 1965.
    Four Plays. 1965.
    Big Toys (produced 1977).

Verse

    The Ploughman and Other Poems. 1935.

Bibliography: *A Bibliography of White* by Janette Finch, 1966.

Reading List: *White* by Geoffrey Dutton, 1961; *White* by Robert F. Brissenden, 1966; *White* by Barry Argyle, 1967; *The Mystery of Unity: Theme and Technique in the Novels of White* by Patricia A. Morley, 1972; *The Eye in the Mandala: White, A Vision of Man and God* by Peter Beatson, 1976; *White's Fiction* by William Walsh, 1978.

*   *   *

    Patrick White comes from a pioneering Australian family, although he was born in London. He travelled widely in Europe and the U.S.A. before World War II, and also lived in

London where he was much involved with the theatre, a life-long passion. Part of the depth and intensity of his view of the world comes from his experience of its newer and older civilizations.

His first novel, *Happy Valley* (which he will not allow to be reprinted), was highly praised by some of the most eminent contemporary English critics and writers. It is an uneven but powerful work, set in the high, cold country of southern New South Wales, where he had worked as a jackeroo (an Australian term for a young man learning the skills of managing sheep or cattle). Its immaturity shows in the strong stylistic influence of Joyce, its maturity in its characteristic searching assessment of the causes of human failure.

The Living and the Dead is set in the England of the second and third decades of the twentieth century, and is a harsh judgement of a society more dead than living, softened by the refusal of some of the characters, especially female, to "behave in the convention of a clever age that encouraged corrosiveness, destruction." It is also the first of White's many onslaughts on "the disgusting, the nauseating aspect of the human ego." White's deepest and most consistent purpose in all his work is the offering of signposts on the road to humility. He is a profoundly religious writer, not bound to any creed.

White's original genius appears unmistakably in his next novel, *The Aunt's Story*. The aunt is a spinster, Theodora Goodman, who although lonely and "leathery" has an extraordinarily rich understanding of life and people. Her story moves from reality to illusion, in Australia, Europe and the U.S.A.; she is broken by her longing, but inability, to reconcile the two.

White's next novel, *The Tree of Man*, is the result of his decision to return to Australia after the war, where he settled on a farm near Castle Hill, on the edge of Sydney, with a Greek friend and partner, Manoly Lascaris. All his subsequent books are, in a sense, his attempts to populate what he once called "The Great Australian Emptiness." His love-hate relationship with his own country (for some years now he has lived in Sydney) has in recent years extended to an active involvement in public issues, especially over the constitutional crisis of 1975, surprising perhaps in someone who guards his privacy so fiercely.

The Tree of Man is White's tribute to the ability of ordinary men and women to survive against the elemental and inhuman forces of nature in Australia; ironically, the action takes place on the outskirts of Sydney, and not in the immensities of the outback. Into these surroundings White plunged his next hero. *Voss* is a novel about a German explorer in New South Wales, Queensland, and the Northern Territory, some of the inspiration for which came from White's reading of the journals of the explorers E. J. Eyre and Ludwig Leichhardt. With *The Tree of Man* and *Voss* White secured his international reputation. In *The Tree of Man* he attempted to explain the ordinary. In *Voss* he took an extraordinary hero into an extraordinary country, with the Aborigines leading Voss on to further mysteries of magic and death. But the explorer's real journey is in the purification of his soul through torments of both agony and joy, understood only by the partner of his spiritual life, Laura Trevelyan, who remains in Sydney.

However, no discussion of White's work should be involved exclusively with the spiritual. White is also a master of social comedy, with a classical eye and ear for pretension and vulgarity, and an equally classical, if perhaps surprising, love of knockabout farce and bawdry.

White's next novel, *Riders in the Chariot*, brings a European experience of war and racial persecution into the stifling bourgeois normality of White's mythical Sydney suburb, Sarsaparilla. But, as the title indicates, understanding is only achieved by those who see that life is "streaming with implications," those with the vision of the Chariot. The range of the book may be hinted at by the individuality of the "Riders": Himmelfarb, the Jewish migrant; Miss Hare, a slightly dotty old lady; Mrs. Godbold, a working-class woman (and one of White's great gallery of women without whom the world would collapse); and Alf Dubbo, an Aboriginal artist who is also familiar with booze and the brothel.

In the early 1960's White's energies shifted temporarily to the theatre and the short story. An early (1947) play, *The Ham Funeral*, was produced in Adelaide for the first time in 1961, followed in rapid succession by *The Season at Sarsaparilla*, *A Cheery Soul* (adapted from a short story), and *Night on Bald Mountain*. These plays came from a deep and long-felt passion for the theatre, but White, disillusioned with the intrigues of theatrical life, turned his back on the stage until 1976, when spurred on by contemporary Australian social and political corruption, he wrote *Big Toys*, which had a long run in various Australian capital cities in 1977.

The Solid Mandala, set in Sydney, is perhaps the most tightly knit, difficult, yet rewarding of White's novels. The twin brothers, Waldo and Arthur Brown, are in many ways the two halves of human nature, knowledge and intuition, fancy and imagination.

The Vivisector, a novel about an artist and the nature of art itself, is the most unsparing and uncompromising of White's works. As the title suggests, no compromise is possible for a true artist, doomed to loneliness, uncomforted by love or sex because both are in competition with art. It is a bleak philosophy, but, as so often with White, it must be emphasized that there is always comedy, from wit to bawdry, from irony to hilarity, which is present not for light relief but because White is always conscious of the human comedy beyond the individual tragedy.

White's recent novel *A Fringe of Leaves* is immediately accessible, with an unexpected tenderness considering the violence of the action: 19th-century shipwreck and murder, and the ordeal of a white woman, naked except for a fringe of leaves, among wild Aborigines, who may be "wild" but in fact have plenty to teach her.

White's genius shows no sign of slackening in its attack or invention. He has more novels on the way, and a film (based on a short story), *The Night the Prowler*, was made in 1977. His intense individuality comes in life from his depth and clarity of vision, and in literature from his unmistakable style, which is based on the widest expansion of metaphor; to adapt De Quincey's words, his style "cannot be regarded as a *dress* or alien covering, but it becomes the *incarnation* of his thoughts."

—Geoffrey Dutton

WHITE, T(erence) H(anbury).   English.   Born in Bombay, India, 29 May 1906. Educated at Cheltenham College, 1920–24; Queens' College, Cambridge (exhibitioner), 1925–27, 1928–29, B.A. 1929. Taught at a preparatory school, 1930–32, and Stowe School, Buckinghamshire, 1932–36; full-time writer from 1936; lived in Ireland, 1939–46, and in the Channel Islands, from 1946. *Died 17 January 1964.*

PUBLICATIONS

Fiction

   Dead Mr. Nixon, with R. McNair Scott.   1931.
   Darkness at Pemberley.   1932.
   They Winter Abroad.   1932.
   First Lesson.   1932.
   Farewell Victoria.   1933.
   Earth Stopped; or, Mr. Marx's Sporting Tour.   1934.
   Gone to Ground.   1935.

The Sword in the Stone.   1938; revised edition, in *The Once and Future King,* 1958.
The Witch in the Wood.   1939; revised edition, as *The Queen of Air and Darkness,* in
   The Once and Future King, 1958.
The Ill-Made Knight.   1940; revised edition, in *The Once and Future King,* 1958.
The Elephant and the Kangaroo.   1947.
The Master: An Adventure Story.   1957; edited by Vincent Whitcombe, 1967.
The Once and Future King.   1958.
The Book of Merlyn.   1977.

Verse

Loved Helen and Other Poems.   1929.
The Green Bay Tree; or, The Wicked Man Touches Wood.   1929.
Verses.   1962.

Other

England Have My Bones (essays).   1936.
*Burke's Steerage; or, The Amateur Gentleman's Introduction to Noble Sports and
   Pastimes.*   1938.
Mistress Masham's Repose (juvenile).   1946.
The Age of Scandal: An Excursion Through a Minor Period.   1950.
The Goshawk (on falconry).   1951.
The Scandalmonger (on English scandals).   1952.
The Godstone and the Blackymor (on Ireland).   1959.
America at Last: The American Journal of White.   1965.
The White/Garnett Letters, edited by David Garnett.   1968.

Editor and Translator, *The Book of Beasts, Being a Translation from a Latin Bestiary of
   the Twelfth Century.*   1954.

Reading List: *White: A Biography* by Sylvia Townsend Warner, 1967; *White* by John K.
Crane, 1974.

                                    *   *   *

   T. H. White was a passionately imaginative and humorous writer who was not good at
making things up. In his best work he transforms existing stories, historical material, or the
details of his life by his intense enthusiasm and love. Characteristically, he regarded *The Book
of Beasts* (clearly a transformation rather than a creation since it is translated from the Latin)
as his most serious work. He probably preferred it because, while he often wrote too easily,
translating was a difficult skill and, like a landed salmon or a trained hawk, gave him proof of
his own worth. The need for such achievements was at the root of his well-known assertion
that the best cure for unhappiness is to learn something.
   The many things that he learnt were the material of his writing and his life. He turned to
objects and animals rather than to people, and loved things. One of the best of his early
verses, in *Loved Helen,* is addressed to cows, "organic lumps," telling them, "You are
security." His poetry is intricately elaborate, an exercise in skill. Verses may be revealing,
however; the quasi-objective skill of the historian was one White pursued more
wholeheartedly, from the early success of *Farewell Victoria* to *The Age of Scandal,* written in
1950. The former is a sustained feat of the historical imagination, creating a Victorian mood

through the story of a life, more unified than most of his pre-war books. The *Age of Scandal* essays are often brilliantly funny, a display of quirky erudition appropriate to their subject. In *Mistress Masham's Repose* he goes further, working imaginatively on material drawn from the mythopoeic borderland between history and literature, using Swift's Lilliputians in a children's story by turns instructive, gruesome, and hilarious.

Bookish skills were balanced, White held, by manual ones; like Kipling, his need to grasp mysteries included those of trades and sports as well as of the past. In *The Goshawk* and *England Have My Bones* he writes about the things making up "the tangible side of country life." White's impulse to learn to plough, for contact with "the various world," appeals to the modern reader; but his minute accounts of fishing, hunting, shooting, and flying small aircraft have become remote. For all these skills, though, he found an ultimate use in the fabric of his major work.

The Once and Future King, like Mervyn Peake's fantasies, is in some sense a product of the Second World War. Under that pressure, White's transforming imagination became that of the mythmaker, working on our major myth, the Matter of Britain. Into these books he directed his feeling for the history, people, animals, and landscapes of England and Ireland, and his love for arcane skills from Latinity to falconry, creating an imaginary world of childlike, logical brilliance. Beneath this level, the archetypal story gave creative expression to White's tangled moral problems, so that the paradoxes of pain and guilt, and goodness, fun, and gaiety within his character are harnessed, making his an emotionally satisfying, as well as an enchanting and funny, version of the story of Arthur.

—J. S. Bratton

WHITE, William Hale.   See **RUTHERFORD, Mark.**

WILDER, Thornton (Niven).   American.   Born in Madison, Wisconsin, 17 April 1897. Educated at Oberlin College, Ohio, 1915–17; Yale University, New Haven, Connecticut, A.B. 1920; American Academy in Rome, 1920–21; Princeton University, New Jersey, A.M. 1926. Served in the United States Coast Artillery Corps, 1918–19; in the United States Army Air Intelligence, rising to the rank of Lieutenent-Colonel, 1942–45: honorary M.B.E. (Member, Order of the British Empire), 1945. Teacher, 1921–28, and House Master, 1927–28, Lawrenceville School, New Jersey. Full-time writer from 1928. Lecturer in Comparative Literature, University of Chicago, 1930–36; Visiting Professor, University of Hawaii, Honolulu, 1935; Charles Eliot Norton Professor of Poetry, Harvard University, Cambridge, Massachusetts, 1950–51. United States Delegate: Institut de Cooperation Intellectuelle, Paris, 1937; with John Dos Passos, International P.E.N. Club Congress, England, 1941; UNESCO Conference of the Arts, Venice, 1952. Recipient: Pulitzer Prize, for fiction, 1928, for drama, 1938, 1943; National Institute of Arts and Letters Gold Medal, 1952; Friedenpreis des Deutschen Buchhandels, 1957; Austrian Ehrenmedaille, 1959; Goethe-Plakette, 1959; Brandeis University Creative Arts Award, 1959: Edward MacDowell Medal, 1960; Presidential Medal of Freedom, 1963; National Book Committee's National

Medal for Literature, 1965; Century Association Art Medal; National Book Award, for fiction, 1968. D. Litt.: New York University, 1930; Yale University, 1947; Kenyon College, Gambier, Ohio, 1948; College of Wooster, Ohio, 1950; Northeastern University, Boston, 1951; Oberlin College, 1952; University of New Hampshire, Durham, 1953; Goethe University, Frankfurt, 1957; University of Zurich, 1961; LL.D.: Harvard University, 1951. Chevalier, Legion of Honor, 1951; Member, Order of Merit, Peru; Order of Merit, Bonn, 1957; Honorary Member, Bavarian Academy of Fine Arts; Mainz Academy of Science and Literature. Member, American Academy of Arts and Letters. *Died 7 December 1975.*

PUBLICATIONS

Fiction

The Cabala. 1926.
The Bridge of San Luis Rey. 1927.
The Woman of Andros. 1930.
Heaven's My Destination. 1934.
The Ides of March. 1948.
The Eighth Day. 1967.
Theophilus North. 1973.

Plays

The Trumpet Shall Sound (produced 1927).
The Angel That Troubled the Waters and Other Plays (includes *Nascuntur Poetae, Proserpina and the Devil, Fanny Otcott, Brother Fire, The Penny That Beauty Spent, The Angel on the Ship, The Message and Jehanne, Childe Roland to the Dark Tower Came, Centaurs, Leviathan, And the Sea Shall Give Up Its Dead, Now the Servant's Name Was Malchus, Mozart and the Gray Steward, Hast Thou Considered My Servant Job?, The Flight into Egypt*). 1928.
The Long Christmas Dinner (produced 1931). In *The Long Christmas Dinner and Other Plays,* 1931; libretto, music by Paul Hindemith (produced 1961), libretto published, 1961.
The Happy Journey to Trenton and Camden (produced 1931). In *The Long Christmas Dinner and Other Plays,* 1931; revised version, as *The Happy Journey,* 1934.
Such Things Only Happen in Books (produced 1931). In *The Long Christmas Dinner and Other Plays,* 1931.
Love and How to Cure It (produced 1931). In *The Long Christmas Dinner and Other Plays,* 1931.
The Long Christmas Dinner and Other Plays in One Act. 1931.
Queens of France (produced 1932). In *The Long Christmas Dinner and Other Plays,* 1931.
Pullman Car Hiawatha (produced 1962). In *The Long Christmas Dinner and Other Plays,* 1931.
Lucrece, from a play by André Obey (produced 1932). 1933.
A Doll's House, from a play by Ibsen (produced 1937).
Our Town (produced 1938). 1938.
The Merchant of Yonkers, from a play by Johann Nostroy, based on *A Well-Spent Day* by John Oxenford (produced 1938). 1939; revised version, as *The Matchmaker* (produced 1954), 1955.

The Skin of Our Teeth (produced 1942). 1942.
Our Century. 1947.
The Victors, from a play by Sartre (produced 1949).
A Life in the Sun (produced 1955); as *The Alcestiad*, music by L. Talma (produced
   1962). Published as *Die Alkestiade*, 1958; as *The Alcestaid; or, A Life in the Sun,
   and The Drunken Sisters: A Satyr Play*, 1977.
The Drunken Sisters. 1957.
Bernice (produced 1957).
The Wreck of the 5:25 (produced 1957).
Plays for Bleecker Street (includes *Infancy, Childhood,* and *Someone from Assisi*)
   (produced 1962). 3 vols., 1960–61.

Screenplays: *Our Town*, 1940; *Shadow of a Doubt*, 1943.

Other

The Intent of the Artist, with others. 1941.
Kultur in einer Demokratie. 1957.
Goethe und die Weltliteratur. 1958.

Bibliography: *A Bibliographical Checklist of the Writings of Wilder* by J. M Edelstein, 1959.

Reading List: *Wilder* by Rex Burbank, 1961; *Wilder* by Helmut Papajewski, 1961, translated
by John Conway, 1968; *Wilder* by Bernard Grebanier, 1964; *The Art of Wilder* by Malcolm
Goldstein, 1965; *The Plays of Wilder: A Critical Study* by Donald Haberman, 1967.

*   *   *

Many recent American writers have written both plays and fiction, but no other has
achieved such a distinguished reputation for both as Thornton Wilder. He is distinguished
also for the uniqueness of his works: each is a fresh formal experiment that contributes to his
persistent conception of the artist's re-inventing the world by revivifying our preceptions of
the universal elements of human experience.

Wilder's earliest published works in *The Angel That Troubled the Waters and Other Plays*
are short pieces presenting usually fantastic situations in an arch, cryptic style employed by
such favored writers of the 1920's as Elinor Wylie. A number of the plays deal with the
special burden that falls upon persons who discover that they possess artistic gifts, and most
of them demand staging too complex for actual performance.

Before he became a successful playwright, Wilder was a novelist. His first novel *The
Cabala*, displays much the same preciosity as the early plays. It describes through loosely
linked episodes the effort of an aspiring young American writer to be accepted by the Cabala,
"members of a circle so powerful and exclusive that ... Romans refer to them with bated
breath." These elegant figures turn out to be contemporary embodiments of the ancient
Roman gods, and the veiled point of the work is that the United States is to succeed a
decaying Rome as the next abiding place of these gods.

This fantasy did not attract many readers, but Wilder achieved an astonishing success with
his next short novel, *The Bridge of San Luis Rey*, which became a surprise best seller. This
episodic story about the perishability of material things and the endurance of love is
exquisitely structured. It tells the stories of the five persons who die in the collapse of a
famous Peruvian bridge with a framework provided by the narrative of a Brother Juniper,
who investigates the accident to learn whether "we live by accident and die by accident, or

live by plan and die by plan." For his efforts, both he and his book are publicly burned. The last sentence stresses that the only bridge that survives is love.

Wilder's third novel, *The Woman of Andros*, was attacked by socially-minded critics of the 1930's for evading present realities and retreating to the classical world; but this subtle fictionalization of Terence's *Andria* actually relates closely to Wilder's own seemingly dying world through its presentation of the death of the Greek world at the time of the coming of Christ because its commercial and artistic communities had become alienated. With his next novel, *Heaven's My Destination*, Wilder returned to contemporary America to create one of his most beguiling characters, George Brush, a high-school textbook salesman in the midwest, who fails comically and pathetically in his constant efforts to uplift other people and who recovers his faith only when he realizes that he must remain an isolated wanderer, happy only in the world that he makes for himself.

The world that we make for ourselves is the subject again of one of Wilder's most admired works and one of his major contributions to a myth of American community, the play *Our Town*. Wilder explained in *The Intent of the Artist* that he turned from the novel to the stage in the 1930's because "the theater carries the art of narration to a higher power than the novel or the epic poem." He was impatient, however, with the elaborate stage settings of the naturalistic theater, and he had already sought in short plays like *The Long Christmas Dinner* to tell a fundamental human story with only the simplest of props. His culminating experiment with this technique was *Our Town*, a chronicle of the value of "the smallest events in our daily life" in a traditional New England village.

Wilder next experimented with updating a nineteenth-century farce that had been popular in both English and German versions as *The Merchant of Yonkers*. Unsuccessful when first ponderously presented by Max Reinhardt, the play in a revised version entitled *The Matchmaker* was a popular success that subsequently provided the basis for the enormously popular musical comedy, *Hello, Dolly!* Wilder did enjoy enormous immediate success with his third major play, *The Skin of Our Teeth*, an expressionist fantasy about man's struggles for survival through the Ice Age, the Flood, and the Napoleonic Wars as symbolized by the travails of the Antrobus family. Again Wilder's timing was superb. A world reduced to doubt and despair by World War II responded enthusiastically to this affirmative vision of man's possible survival despite his destructive propensities.

Wilder served with American Intelligence units in Italy during World War II, and for his first post-war work returned to the novel and to a classical Roman setting for *The Ides of March*. This pseudo-history, which Malcolm Goldstein compares to "a set of bowls placed one within another," centers on the assassination of Julius Caesar, but traces through four overlapping sections an ever widening circle of events in order to present "the tragic difference between Caesar's idealistic visions and the sordid events for which they are finally responsible" – a subject fraught with implications for the mid-twentieth century.

After the comparatively cool reception of this work, Wilder published little for twenty years. Although his plays remained popular, he was generally too lightly regarded after World War II when existential *angst* dominated literary criticism. His writings were felt to be too affirmative and optimistic, and his long silence caused him to be regarded as an artist whose time had passed. Literary mandarins were startled, therefore, by the appearance in 1967 of his longest and most complex work, *The Eighth Day*. This novel jumps back and forth in time as it resurrects the events relating to a murder in a southern Illinois coal town early in the twentieth century, the false conviction of a man who escapes, and the eventual solution of the cunning crime. This mystery plot, however, provided only a backdrop for Wilder's observation that all history is one "enormous tapestry" and that "there are no Golden Ages and no Dark Ages. There is the oceanlike monotony of the generations of men under the alternations of fair and foul weather." At the center of the work stands the falsely accused John Ashley, who avoids succumbing to despair over this inescapable cycle by "inventing" afresh such fossilized institutions as marriage and fatherhood as he also invents small practical objects to make man's work easier. An old woman whom he meets sums up the sensibility that informs the novel, "The human race gets no better. Mankind is vicious, slothful, quarrelsome, and self-centered. . . .[But] you and I have a certain quality that is rare as teeth in a hen. We work. And we forget ourselves in our work."

The Eighth Day triumphantly capped Wilder's "re-invention" of mankind, but he had one final delight for readers. Perhaps to complement James Joyce's and others' portraits of the artist as a young man *by* a young man, Wilder presented in his last published work, *Theophilus North*, an episodic novel about the artist as a young man *by* an old man. The seemingly loosely connected tales are actually – as in his other works – parts of an intricate mosaic that discloses against a background of the "nine cities" of Newport, Rhode Island, the nine career possibilities that a young man explores before discovering that being a writer will encompass all of them.

—Warren French

WILLIAMS, Charles (Walter Stansby). English. Born in London, 20 September 1886. Educated at the St. Albans School, Hertfordshire; University College, University of London. Married Florence Conway in 1917; one son. Joined Oxford University Press as a Reader, 1908, and remained a member of staff until his death; writer from 1908. M.A.: Oxford University, 1943. *Died 15 May 1945.*

PUBLICATIONS

Collections

  Selected Writings, edited by Anne Ridler. 1961.
  Collected Plays. 1963.

Fiction

  War in Heaven. 1930.
  Many Dimensions. 1931.
  The Place of the Lion. 1931.
  The Greater Trumps. 1932.
  Shadows of Ecstasy. 1933.
  Descent into Hell. 1937.
  All Hallows' Eve. 1945.

Plays

  The Moon: A Cantata, music by William G. Whittaker. 1923.
  The Masque of the Manuscript, music by Hubert Foss. 1927.
  A Myth of Shakespeare. 1928.
  The Masque of Perusal, music by Hubert Foss. 1929.
  Three Plays (includes *The Witch, The Chaste Woman, The Rite of Passion*). 1931.

Thomas Cranmer of Canterbury (produced 1936). 1936.
Judgement at Chelmsford: A Pageant Play (produced 1939). 1939.
The House of the Octopus. 1945.
Seed of Adam and Other Plays (includes *The Death of Good Fortune, The House by the Stable, Grab and Grace*). 1948.

Verse

The Silver Stair. 1912.
Poems of Conformity. 1917.
Divorce. 1920.
Windows of Night. 1924.
An Urbanity. 1927 (?).
Heroes and Kings. 1930.
Taliessin Through Logres. 1938.
The Region of the Summer Stars. 1944.
Arthurian Torso, Containing the Posthumous Fragment of The Figure of Arthur, edited by C. S. Lewis. 1948.

Other

Poetry at Present. 1930.
The English Poetic Mind. 1932.
Bacon. 1933.
Reason and Beauty in the Poetic Mind. 1933.
James I. 1934.
The Ring and the Book, Retold, by Robert Browning. 1934.
Rochester. 1935.
Queen Elizabeth. 1936.
The Story of the Aeneid, Retold, by Virgil. 1936.
Stories of Great Names. 1937.
Henry VII. 1937.
He Came Down from Heaven. 1938.
The Descent of the Dove: A Short History of the Holy Spirit in the Church. 1939
The Way of Exchange. 1941.
Religion and Love in Dante: The Theology of Romantic Love. 1941.
Witchcraft. 1941.
The Forgiveness of Sins. 1942.
The Figure of Beatrice: A Study of Dante. 1943.
Flecker of Dean Close. 1946.
The Image of the City and Other Essays, edited by Anne Ridler. 1958.

Editor, with V. H. Collins, *Poems of Home and Overseas.* 1921.
Editor, *A Book of Victorian Narrative Verse.* 1927.
Editor, with H. S. Milford, *The Oxford Book of Regency Verse.* 1928.
Editor, *Poems of G. M. Hopkins*, revised edition. 1930.
Editor, *A Short Life of Shakespeare*, by Edmund Chambers. 1933.
Editor, *The New Book of English Verse.* 1935.
Editor, *The Passion of Christ.* 1939.
Editor, *The New Christian Year.* 1941.
Editor, *The Letters of Evelyn Underhill.* 1943.
Editor, *Solway Ford and Other Poems* by Wilfred Gibson. 1945.

Bibliography: *Williams: A Checklist* by Lois Glenn, 1975.

Reading List: *An Immortality for Its Own Sake: A Study of the Concept of Poetry in the Writings of Williams* by John P. Gigrich, 1954; *Williams* by John Heath-Stubbs, 1955; *An Introduction to Williams* by A. M. Hadfield, 1959; *The Theology of Romantic Love: A Study of the Writings of Williams*, 1962 (includes bibliography), and *Williams: A Critical Essay*, 1966, both by Mary M. Shideler; *Shadows of the Imagination: The Fantasies of C. S. Lewis, Tolkien, and Williams* edited by M. R. Hillegas, 1969; *Shadows of Heaven: Religion and Fantasy in the Writings of C. S. Lewis, Williams and Tolkien* by Gunnar Urang, 1971; *Romantic Religion: A Study of Barfield, Lewis, Williams, and Tolkien* by Robert J. Reilly, 1971.

*   *   *

Charles Williams has perhaps the best claim to be described as the Blake of the twentieth century. Their imaginations were similar, and both were men uneasy with the literary modes available to them; both were slighted by their eras. Quentin Bell's praise of Blake as "a Cockney who had seen God" applies to Williams. But unfortunately it is hard to point to anything in Williams's work having the perfection which has made it impossible to ignore Blake's lyrics. Perhaps the best candidate is the novel *Descent into Hell*, whose theme of the relation of a man and girl to their other selves (probably responsible for the doppelgänger scenes in T. S. Eliot's *Little Gidding* and *The Cocktail Party*) was close to the heart of Williams's thought. "Heart of his thought" is the just phrase, since Williams's work is characterised by a passionate realisation of metaphysical intuitions. "We must," he said, "examine the pattern of the glory." One feels persuaded during the reading of the passage in *Descent into Hell* in which the girl, Pauline, meets her double that one is hearing the word which Dostoevsky's Ivan Karamazov imagined, which will show (as Williams said shortly before his death) that "when we are dead we shall find that we enjoyed everything, even if we were murdered."

The best way, indeed, into Williams's work is to appreciate the union in him of two opposite convictions – the agonised apprehension of pain and evil expressed in such poems as "Domesticity" (in *Windows of Night*), in his essay "The Cross" (in *The Image of the City*), and in his history *Witchcraft* – and his conviction that the whole universe is to be known as good. These are fused together by two further polarised characteristics of his – scepticism and a sense of glory – and the quartet of qualities are perhaps best seen in four books which he grouped together, all published 1937–39 – *Descent into Hell*, the poems called *Taliessin Through Logres*, the idiosyncratic romantic theology of *He Came Down from Heaven*, and a history of the action of the Holy Ghost, *The Descent of the Dove*. The last is perhaps the only unscriptural book which can persuade its readers to feel that all history is the work of God.

To use expressions of uniqueness about Williams's communication of his vision is mere justice. "There are passages in his novels," says T. S. Eliot, "which describe, with extraordinary precision, the kind of unexplainable experience which many of us have had, once or twice in our lives, and been unable to put into words." Williams's own struggle with words was hard, varying from the use of quotations clumsily interposed as a kind of shorthand, and of words with an obscure weight of private meaning, to inspired language which (as Eliot again says) communicates "an extraordinary sense of glory." The variety of genre in the books already mentioned is characteristic. Perhaps no single kind of book could capture what he saw, and all genres tend to break in his hands. One can recommend not only *Descent into Hell* but all the novels, provided that the reader is willing to accept a subtle and profound rendering of the depths of such characters as are at the centre of the story, side by side with a stylised version of their manner of speech, and shorthand sketches of the minor characters. The same applies to his poetic dramas such as *Thomas Cranmer of Canterbury* and *The House of the Octopus*. His criticism – especially the chapter on Shakespeare in *The English Poetic Mind*, his preface to the World's Classics *Milton's Poetry*, and his book on

Dante, *The Figure of Beatrice* — is no different from other men's criticism in that he is superb on what he finds corresponds to his own inner life — crisis, inner subversion, a symbolic perception of the world — and its principal peculiarity, that he rarely criticises adversely, is no disadvantage. But the same characteristics can be limiting in his biographies, as of Rochester, Bacon, James I. He thought of himself as primarily a poet, and his poetry can be magnificent. But his writing, even in the noblest passages, displays an eccentric ear, partly conditioned by the interplay in him of a gorgeous imagination and abstract scepticism, and has a complexity of tone hard to catch. People who knew him personally have no difficulty in hearing him through his writings, and many writers — Eliot, Auden, John Wain, Anne Ridler, John Heath-Stubbs, and others — have testified to a uniqueness of personality — trembling with life— which gave a meaning to the word saint. C. S. Lewis observed that "When the idea of death and the idea of Williams met in my mind, it was the idea of death that was changed." The tone of this extraordinary vitality can be caught by later readers either from knowing a wide range of work, or from hitting soon on that particular book which speaks to their condition. For those who believe that they have caught the right tone, reading Williams has impact and power of transforming experience comparable to that of the greatest literature.

—Stephen Medcalf

WILLIAMSON, Henry.   English.   Born in Parkstone, Dorset, 1 December 1895; grew up in London. Educated at Colfe's Grammar School, Lewisham, London. Served as an infantryman and officer in the Bedfordshire Regiment of the British Army during World War I, 1914–19. Married Ida Letitia Hibbert in 1925 (divorced, 1947), four sons and one daughter; remarried in 1948, one son. Settled in London, 1919; worked briefly in the advertising department of *The Times*; thereafter a full-time writer; settled in Devon, 1921; broadcaster, for the Western Region of the BBC, Bristol, on farming and country life, during the 1930's; lived on a farm in Stiffkey, Norfolk, in the late 1930's and until 1945, then returned to Devon; briefly interned at the outbreak of World War II for Fascist sympathies. Recipient: Hawthornden Prize, 1928. *Died 13 August 1977.*

PUBLICATIONS

Fiction

> *The Flax of Dream.*   1936.
> > *The Beautiful Years.*   1921; revised edition, 1929.
> > *Dandelion Days.*   1922; revised edition, 1930.
> > *The Dream of Fair Women.*   1924; revised edition, 1931.
> > *The Pathway.*   1928.
> *The Peregrine's Saga and Other Stories of the Country Green.*   1923; as *Sun Brothers,*
> > 1925.
> *The Old Stag: Stories.*   1926.
> *Tarka the Otter, Being His Joyful Water-Life and Death in the Country of the Two*
> > *Rivers.*   1927.
> *The Linhay on the Downs* (stories).   1929.

The Ackymals (story).   1929.
The Village Book (stories).   1930.
The Patriot's Progress, Being the Vicissitudes of Pte. John Bullock.   1930.
The Star-Born.   1933; revised edition, 1948.
The Labouring Life (stories).   1932; as *As the Sun Shines*, 1933.
On Foot in Devon; or, Guidance and Gossip, Being a Monologue in Two Reels.   1933.
The Gold Falcon; or, The Haggard of Love.   1933; revised edition, 1947.
The Linhay on the Downs and Other Adventures in the Old and New World.   1934.
Salar the Salmon.   1935.
The Sun in the Sands.   1945.
Life in a Devon Village (based on material in *The Village Book* and *The Labouring Life*).   1945.
Tales of a Devon Village (based on material in *The Village Book* and *The Labouring Life*).   1945.
The Phasian Bird.   1948.
A Chronicle of Ancient Sunlight:
    The Dark Lantern.   1951.
    Donkey Boy.   1952.
    Young Phillip Maddison.   1953.
    How Dear Is Life.   1954.
    A Fox under My Cloak.   1955.
    The Golden Virgin.   1957.
    Love and the Loveless: A Soldier's Tale.   1958.
    A Test to Destruction.   1960.
    The Innocent Moon.   1961.
    It Was the Nightingale.   1962.
    The Power of the Dead.   1963.
    The Phoenix Generation.   1965.
    A Solitary War.   1966.
    Lucifer Before Sunrise.   1967.
    The Gale of the World.   1969.
Tales of Moorland and Estuary.   1953.
In the Woods (stories).   1960.
Collected Nature Stories.   1970.
The Scandaroon.   1972.
Animal Saga (stories).   1974.

Play

Television Documentary: *The Vanishing Hedgerow*, 1972.

Other

The Lone Swallows.   1922; revised edition, as *The Lone Swallows and Other Essays of Boyhood and Youth*, 1933.
The Wet Flanders Plain.   1929; revised edition, 1929.
The Wild Red Deer of Exmoor: A Digression of the Logic and Ethics and Economics of Stag-Hunting in England Today.   1931.
Devon Holiday.   1935.
Goodbye West Country.   1937.
The Children of Shallowford (autobiography).   1939; revised edition, 1959.
As the Sun Shines: Selections.   1941.

The Story of a Norfolk Farm (autobiography).   1941.
Genius of Friendship: "T. E. Lawrence."   1941.
Norfolk Life, with L. R. Haggard.   1943.
Scribbling Lark (juvenile).   1949.
A Clear Water Stream (autobiography).   1958.

Editor, *A Soldier's Diary of the Great War,* by Douglas Herbert Bell.   1929.
Editor, *An Anthology of Modern Nature Writing.*   1936.
Editor, *Richard Jefferies: Selections of His Work.*   1937.
Editor, *Hodge and His Masters,* by Richard Jefferies.   1937.
Editor, *My Favourite Country Stories.*   1946.
Editor, *Unreturning Spring, Being the Poems, Sketches, Stories, and Letters* of James
    Farrar.   1950.

Bibliography: *A Bibliography and a Critical Survey of the Works of Williamson* by I.
Waveney Girvan, 1931.

*   *   *

Henry Williamson was a gifted story teller, and a superb nature writer in the tradition of
Jefferies and Hudson. His early nature articles in the *Daily Express* were reprinted in *The
Lone Swallows*; his first novel, *The Beautiful Years,* the opening volume of the tetralogy *The
Flax of Dream,* appeared in the same year. Two more collections of nature stories, *The
Peregrine's Saga* and *The Old Stag,* led up to his two novel-length stories of animal life,
Tarka the Otter and *Salar the Salmon.* In presenting Williamson with the Hawthornden Prize
for *Tarka,* John Galsworthy gave high praise to this "work of imagination fortified by
endless patient observation." *Tarka* and *Salar* were acclaimed on publication as modern
classics, a verdict that time has confirmed.

During the whole of the 1914–18 war Williamson served as an officer in the British Army.
At Christmas 1914 he was present at the spontaneous truce when British and German troops
fraternized in No Man's Land. This incident changed Williamson's thinking, and it became
his chief aim as a writer to expose the inherited mental attitudes that are among the deepest
causes of war. Thus his *Flax of Dream* novels – *The Beautiful Years, Dandelion Days, The
Dream of Fair Women,* and *The Pathway* – trace the life story of a disorientated, idealistic ex-
officer of the 1914 war from his early childhood until his death by drowning after he has
completed a book that he hopes will change the world. *The Pathway* was published in 1928,
and was at once recognized as "almost" a great novel.

Williamson's later novel-series, in fifteen volumes, *A Chronicle of Ancient Sunlight,* sets
out to present more objectively and classically the themes dealt with subjectively and
romantically in *The Flax of Dream.* These novels follow the life of Willie Maddison's cousin
Phillip, another idealistic ex-soldier, who believes that he must take up Willie's unfulfilled
mission. The new series begins in late Victorian London (*The Dark Lantern*), and covers both
the Great War (*How Dear Is Life, A Fox under My Cloak, The Golden Virgin, A Test to
Destruction*) and the war years 1939–1945, when Phillip is farming in East Anglia. The final
volume, *The Gale of the World,* brings the story down to the 1950's. In an apocalyptic
dénouement Phillip finds the psychic and spiritual wholeness that his cousin Willie never
achieved, and the long saga ends on a note of joy. *A Chronicle of Ancient Sunlight* may be
seen as a vast work of autobiography transmuted by imagination.

Between the wars Williamson published several volumes of miscellaneous essays and
sketches of rural life. Some of the best of these were reprinted in *Life in a Devon Village* and
Tales of a Devon Village. His farming years are graphically recorded in *The Story of a Norfolk
Farm.*

—Brocard Sewell

WILLIS, Nathaniel Parker. American. Born in Portland, Maine, 20 January 1806. Educated at Boston Latin School; Phillips Academy, Andover, Massachusetts; Yale University, New Haven, Connecticut, graduated 1827. Married 1) Mary Stace in 1835 (died, 1845); 2) Cornelia Grinnell in 1846, three daughters and two sons. Became known as a writer while still an undergraduate; edited 2 issues of *The Legendary*, 1828, and an annual *The Token*, 1829; Founding Editor, *American Monthly Magazine*, Boston, 1829–31; settled in New York, 1831; lived in Europe, as Foreign Correspondent for the *New York Mirror*, edited by George Pope Morris, 1831–36; returned to New York, and continued to travel and write for the *Mirror*, 1836–39; with D. T. O. Porter, Founding Editor of the *Corsair*, New York, 1839; Proprietor and Editor, with Morris, of the weekly *New Mirror*, subsequently the daily *Evening Mirror*, 1840–45; visited Europe, 1845, then returned to New York and joined Morris as editor and proprietor of his *National Press*, which they renamed the *Home Journal*, 1846–64, as sole owner and editor, 1864–67; settled at Idlewild, a country seat on the Hudson, 1853. *Died 20 January 1867.*

PUBLICATIONS

Collections

    Prose Writings, edited by Henry A. Beers. 1885.
    Poetical Works. 1888.

Fiction

    Inklings of Adventure. 1836.
    Loiterings of Travel. 1840.
    Romance of Travel (stories). 1840.
    Dashes at Life with a Free Pencil. 1845.
    People I Have Met (stories). 1850.
    Life Here and There (stories). 1850.
    Fun-Jottings; or, Laughs I Have Taken a Pen To (stories). 1853.
    Paul Fane; or, Parts of a Life Else Untold. 1857.

Plays

    Bianca Visconti; or, The Heart Overtasked (produced 1837). 1839.
    Tortesa; or, The Usurer Matched (produced 1839). 1839.

Verse

    Sketches. 1827.
    Fugitive Poetry. 1829.
    Poem Delivered Before the Society of the United Brothers, with Other Poems. 1831.
    Melanie and Other Poems. 1835.
    The Sacred Poems. 1843.
    Poems of Passion. 1843.
    The Lady Jane and Other Poems. 1843.
    Poems Sacred, Passionate, and Humorous. 1845; revised edition, 1849.

Poems of Early and After Years.   1848.

Other

   Pencillings by the Way.   3 vols., 1835; revised edition, 1844; reprinted in part as
      Summer Cruise in the Mediterranean, 1853.
   A l'Abri; or, The Tent Pitched.   1839; revised edition, as *Letters from under a Bridge,*
      and Poems, 1840.
   American Scenery, drawings by W. H. Bartlett.   2 vols., 1840.
   Canadian Scenery Illustrated, drawings by W. H. Bartlett.   2 vols., 1842.
   The Scenery and Antiquities of Ireland, with J. Stirling Coyne, drawings by W. H.
      Bartlett.   2 vols., 1842.
   Lectures on Fashion.   1844.
   Rural Letters and Other Records of Thought at Leisure.   1849.
   Hurry-Graphs; or, Sketches of Scenery, Celebrities, and Society.   1851.
   Memoranda of the Life of Jenny Lind.   1853.
   Health Trip to the Tropics.   1853.
   Famous Persons and Famous Places.   1854.
   Out-Doors at Idlewild.   1855.
   The Rag-Bag: A Collection of Ephemera.   1855.
   The Convalescent.   1859.

   Editor, *The Legendary.*   1828.
   Editor, *Trenton Falls, Picturesque and Descriptive.*   1851.

Reading List: *Willis* by Henry A. Beers, 1885 (includes bibliography); *The World of Washington Irving* by Van Wyck Brooks, 1944; *Willis* by Cortland P. Auser, 1969.

                              *   *   *

   Nathaniel Parker Willis was in his day the most famous recorder of the details of social life and customs in America. In a sense, he was to his age what Tom Wolfe is to ours, but he was, in a way that Wolfe is not, sympathetic to most of the signs of status that he found around him – the resorts, homes, clothes, and so forth.
   Willis seldom dealt with old established families. He generally concerned himself with the newly rich in search of the means through which they could express their status. He provided them with newspaper and magazine columns describing exactly the things they wanted to know and collected his observations in a series of volumes that were quite popular at the time. His books about fashionable life can be divided into three categories: (1) books dealing with fashionable life abroad (a subject of endless fascination for newly rich Americans who, as a measure of their recently acquired status, adopted European standards, customs, and even diction – although few such people had crossed the Atlantic), (2) books concerning fashionable life in America, especially in New York and in such watering-places as Saratoga Springs, New York, and (3), most significantly, books detailing rural, middle-class life. *Pencillings by the Way* is an excellent account of his observations abroad, and *Hurry-Graphs* is typical of his volumes on life in America. His books on rural life include *A l'Abri, Out-Doors at Idlewild,* and *The Convalescent* and are of major importance to social as well as cultural historians as three of the earliest and most influential expressions of middle-class obsession with rural and suburban life. Willis, together with the essayist and landscape gardener Andrew Jackson Downing, was among the first to popularize this way of life in America. He also worked with the picturesque painter W. H. Bartlett.
   Willis was also a poet (albeit a minor one), a playwright, a novelist, and a short story

writer. His short stories, such as those collected in *Dashes at Life with a Free Pencil*, have from time to time attracted critical attention, and his novel *Paul Fane* has been considered a forerunner of Henry James's international novels, but it was as a journalist, critics generally agree, that he was most successful. In particular, it is his documents of fashionable life for which he should be remembered.

—Edward Halsey Foster

WILSON, Angus (Frank Johnstone). English. Born in Bexhill, Sussex, 11 August 1913. Educated at Westminster School, London, 1927–31; Merton College, Oxford, B.A. (honours) in medieval and modern history 1936. Served in the Foreign Office, 1942–46. Staff Member, British Museum, London, 1937–55: Deputy Superintendent of the Reading Room, 1949–55; Lecturer, 1963–66, and since 1966 Professor of English Literature, University of East Anglia, Norwich; Ewing Lecturer, University of California at Los Angeles, 1960; Bergen Lecturer, Yale University, New Haven, Connecticut, 1960; Moody Lecturer, University of Chicago, 1960; Northcliffe Lecturer, University College, London, 1961; Leslie Stephen Lecturer, Cambridge University, 1962–63; Beckman Professor, University of California, Berkeley, 1967; John Hinkley Visiting Professor, Johns Hopkins University, Baltimore, 1974. Member of the Committee, Royal Literary Fund, 1966; Member of the Arts Council of Great Britain, 1966–69; Chairman, National Book League, London, 1971–74; President, Dickens Fellowship, London, 1974–75. Recipient: Black Memorial Prize, 1959; Prix de Meilleur Roman Etranger, 1960. Honorary Fellow, Cowell College, University of California at Santa Cruz, 1968. Fellow, 1958, and Companion of Literature, 1972, Royal Society of Literature. C.B.E. (Commander, Order of the British Empire), 1968. Lives in Bradfield St. George, Suffolk.

PUBLICATIONS

Fiction

The Wrong Set and Other Stories. 1949.
Such Darling Dodos and Other Stories. 1950.
Hemlock and After. 1952.
Anglo-Saxon Attitudes. 1956.
A Bit off the Map and Other Stories. 1957.
The Middle Age of Mrs. Eliot. 1958.
The Old Men at the Zoo. 1961.
Late Call. 1964.
No Laughing Matter. 1967.
Death Dance: 25 Stories. 1969.
As If by Magic. 1973.

Play

    The Mulberry Bush (produced 1956). 1956.

Other

    Emile Zola: An Introductory Study of His Novels. 1952; revised edition, 1965.
    For Whom the Cloche Tolls: A Scrapbook of the Twenties, illustrated by Philippe
       Jullian. 1953.
    The Wild Garden; or, Speaking of Writing. 1963.
    Tempo: The Impact of Television on the Arts. 1964.
    The World of Charles Dickens. 1970.
    The Naughty Nineties. 1976.
    The Strange Ride of Rudyard Kipling: His Life and Works. 1977.

    Editor, *A Maugham Twelve,* by W. Somerset Maugham. 1966.
    Editor, *Cakes and Ale, and Twelve Short Stories,* by W. Somerset Maugham. 1967.
    Editor, *Writers of East Anglia.* 1977.

Reading List: *Wilson* by Jay Halio, 1964; *Wilson* by K. W. Gransden, 1969; *Harvest of a Quiet Eye: The Novel of Compassion* by James Gindin, 1971.

*   *   *

    Both his admirers and his detractors have always agreed that Angus Wilson is an uncomfortable writer. His intelligence, his sharp eye for social comedy and incongruity, his contempt for stupidity, his dislike of most of his own characters have been apparent ever since the appearance of his first impressively accomplished volume of stories, *The Wrong Set* in 1949. The reasons for his uncomfortableness are various and have become apparent gradually. First, perhaps, should be placed his deeply ambivalent attitude to the Victorian age and its great writers. Unlike many novelists of our century, who blithely assumed that they knew much more of life than the Victorians, Wilson understood from the first that the nineteenth century was the great unrepeatable classic age of the English novel. He saw, as others refused to do, that Jane Austen and Dickens were great classic monuments of art, compared with which later writers were either crude or puny or both. But on the other hand he was deeply distrustful of many of the beliefs and attitudes shared by nineteenth-century novelists and their readers. He disliked or ignored Christianity. He was suspicious of moral rhetoric, distrustful of patriotism. He was constantly aware of the problem of unconscious motives, took Freud very seriously, and was habitually self-analytical. To a man of this temperament, Jane Austen must have seemed incurious, and Dickens naive and complacent, in their attitudes to the self.
    Next should be placed his long and painful inner debate, reflected in many of his writings (especially the story "Such Darling Dodos," the play *The Mulberry Bush,* and the novel *The Middle Age of Mrs. Eliot*) about the liberal and progressive values which apparently satisfied so many educated people down to 1914. Born in 1913, and growing up in the rackety, uncertain inter-war years, he was both fascinated by the apparent stability and exasperated by the complacency and self-contradictions of the generation contemporary with his own parents. Much of his work might be described as a running debate with E. M. Forster, a man so like himself in being clever, sceptical, comfortably provided with unearned income, and homosexual; but so unlike him in his naive country primitivism, his bland unawareness that most people have to work for a living, and his complacent oblivion of depths and contradictions in the self. Wilson is never content with a comfortable opposition between the

nice and the nasty people in his books. Even the characters with whom he most closely identifies (like Bernard Sands in *Hemlock and After*) have terrifying flaws, which, often, the course of the story forces them to realize. The scene in which Bernard Sands, though himself homosexual, realizes that he has a sadistic impulse towards a fellow-homosexual, from which the police officer sent to arrest him is free, can stand as typical of many others. Wilson can be angry, one-sided, unfair. He is never complacent.

A third source of uneasiness lies in the changing standards of reticence and decency during Wilson's writing life. The change in what can acceptably be said in public between 1949 and 1977 is so great as to be paralleled only perhaps by the period 1820 to 1850. Wilson feels he ought to welcome the decline of reticence. Words like "puritan," "stuffy," "respectable" flow from his pen with an easy contempt which occasionally makes one wonder whether his undoubtedly powerful intelligence is not on this point a little in abeyance. But when one considers his art it is a different story. The difficulty of speaking openly about sexual inversion and perversion was a clear gain to his early work; his later work is marred by boring desire to leave nothing unsaid, and a desperate desire to shock an apparently almost unshockable audience.

This is one reason, perhaps, among others which cannot be fully known for the catastrophic decline in the quality of his work since about 1960, when he was still under fifty, and might have hoped to remain in his prime for many more years. He established himself as a notably sharp and pointed writer of short stories with *The Wrong Set* and *Such Darling Dodos*. *Hemlock and After* and *Anglo-Saxon Attitudes* had their faults but were notable for their variety, intelligent observation, and resourcefulness. *The Middle Age of Mrs. Eliot* seemed to herald the arrival of a major novelist. He achieved real empathy with a woman character (he is quite justified in claiming his own greater understanding of women as a notable point of superiority to Forster); the petulance and unfairness of much of his earlier work was muted, and the perennial homosexual dilemma was presented in a more intelligent and feeling way than before. One waited eagerly for his next book. When it came, *The Old Men at the Zoo* was disappointing in its unsupported fantasies, its refusal to be bound by the necessary formal principle of the realistic novel. But it was, nevertheless intelligent, inventive, and readable. *Late Call* was dull and tired, and *No Laughing Matter* and *As If by Magic* showed a failure of creative powers, which had perhaps at no time been quite equal to his general intellectual and critical powers. Nevertheless in his rather short creative period (about 1949–61) he made a contribution of lasting value to the English novel.

—A. O. J. Cockshut

WILSON, Edmund. American. Born in Red Bank, New Jersey, 8 May 1895. Educated at Hill School, Pottstown, Pennsylvania, 1909–12; Princeton University, New Jersey, 1912–16, A.B. 1916. Served in the United States Army, in the Intelligence Corps, 1917–19. Married 1) Mary Blair in 1923; 2) Margaret Candy in 1930; 3) Mary McCarthy, *q.v.*, in 1938; 4) Elena Thornton in 1946; three children. Reporter, *New York Evening Sun*, 1916–17; Managing Editor, *Vanity Fair*, New York, 1920–21; Associate Editor, *New Republic*, New York, 1926–31; Book Reviewer, *The New Yorker*, 1944–48, and occasionally thereafter. Recipient: Guggenheim Fellowship, 1935; National Institute of Arts and Letters Gold Medal, for non-fiction, 1955; Presidential Medal of Freedom, 1963; Edward MacDowell Medal, 1964; Emerson-Thoreau Medal, 1966; National Book Committee's National Medal for Literature, 1966; Aspen Award, 1968. *Died 12 June 1972.*

Collections

Letters on Literature and Politics 1912–1972, edited by Elena Wilson.   1977.
A Wilson Celebration, edited by John Wain.   1978.

Fiction

I Thought of Daisy.   1929; revised edition, with *Galahad,* 1957.
Memoirs of Hecate County (stories).   1946; revised edition, 1958.
Galahad, with I Thought of Daisy.   1957.

Plays

The Evil Eye: A Musical Comedy, lyrics by F. Scott Fitzgerald (produced 1915).
The Crime in the Whistler Room (produced 1924).   In *This Room and This Gin and These Sandwiches,* 1937.
Discordant Encounters: Plays and Dialogues.   1926.
This Room and This Gin and These Sandwiches: Three Plays (includes *The Crime in the Whistler Room, A Winter in Beech Street,* and *Beppo and Beth*).   1937.
The Little Blue Light (produced 1950).   1950.
Five Plays: Cyprian's Prayer, The Crime in the Whistler Room, This Room and This Gin and These Sandwiches, Beppo and Beth, The Little Blue Light.   1954.
The Duke of Palermo and Other Plays, with an Open Letter to Mike Nichols (includes *Dr. McGrath* and *Osbert's Career; or, The Poet's Progress*).   1969.

Verse

The Undertaker's Garland, with John Peale Bishop.   1922.
Poets, Farewell! (poems and essays).   1929.
Note-Books of Night (poems, essays and stories).   1942.
Three Reliques of Ancient Western Poetry Collected by Wilson from the Ruins.   1951.
Wilson's Christmas Stocking: Fun for Young and Old.   1953.
A Christmas Delerium.   1955.
Night Thoughts.   1961.
Holiday Greetings 1966.   1966.

Other

Axel's Castle: A Study in the Imaginative Literature of 1870–1930.   1931.
The American Jitters: A Year of the Slump (essays).   1932; as *Devil Take the Hindmost,* 1932.
Travels in Two Democracies (dialogues, essays, and story).   1936.
The Triple Thinkers: Ten Essays on Literature.   1938; augmented edition, as *The Triple Thinkers: Twelve Essays on Literary Subjects,* 1948.
To the Finland Station: A Study in the Writing and Acting of History.   1940.
The Boys in the Back Room: Notes on California Novelists.   1941.
The Wound and the Bow: Seven Studies in Literature.   1941.

Europe Without Baedeker: Sketches among the Ruins of Italy, Greece, and England. 1947; revised edition, 1966.

Classics and Commercials: A Literary Chronicle of the Forties. 1950.

The Shores of Light: A Literary Chronicle of the Twenties and Thirties. 1952.

The Scrolls from the Dead Sea. 1955; revised edition, as *The Dead Sea Scrolls 1947–1969,* 1969.

Red, Black, Blond, and Olive: Studies in Four Civilizations: Zuñi, Haiti, Soviet Russia, Israel. 1956.

A Piece of My Mind: Reflections at Sixty. 1956.

The American Earthquake: A Documentary of the Twenties and Thirties. 1958.

Apologies to the Iroquois. 1960.

Patriotic Gore: Studies in the Literature of the American Civil War. 1962.

The Cold War and the Income Tax: A Protest. 1963.

The Bit Between My Teeth: A Literary Chronicle of 1950–1965. 1965.

O Canada: An American's Notes on Canadian Culture. 1965.

A Prelude: Landscapes, Characters and Conversations from the Earlier Years of My Life. 1967.

The Fruits of the MLA. 1968.

Upstate: Records and Recollections of Northern New York. 1971.

A Window on Russia for the Use of Foreign Readers. 1972.

The Devils and Canon Barham: Ten Essays on Poets, Novelists, and Monsters. 1973.

The Twenties: From Notebooks and Diaries of the Period, edited by Leon Edel. 1975.

Israel, and The Dead Sea Scrolls. 1978.

Editor, *The Last Tycoon: An Unfinished Novel by F. Scott Fitzgerald, Together with The Great Gatsby and Selected Stories.* 1941.

Editor, *The Shock of Recognition: The Development of Literature in the United States Recorded by the Men Who Made It.* 1943; enlarged edition, 1955.

Editor, *The Crack-Up: With Other Uncollected Pieces, Note-Books and Unpublished Letters,* by F. Scott Fitzgerald. 1945.

Editor, *The Collected Essays of John Peale Bishop.* 1948.

Editor, *Peasants and Other Stories,* by Chekhov. 1956.

Bibliography: *Wilson: A Bibliography* by Richard David Ramsey, 1971.

Reading List: *Wilson: A Study of the Literary Vocation in Our Time* by Sherman Paul, 1965; *Wilson* by Warner Berthoff, 1968; *Wilson* by Charles P. Frank, 1970; *Wilson* by Leonard Kriegel, 1971.

*   *   *

Edmund Wilson is a kind of American equivalent to Cyril Connolly, a critic who is learned (Wilson was influenced at Princeton, by his French Professor, Christian Gauss) but prefers high journalism to academic teaching as his medium, and whose deliberately easy, witty, and colloquial style disguises his learning. He was the critic to whom writers of his time turned for both advice and friendship, and his correspondence shows both his frankness and his generosity with his advice and his time. Occasionally, perhaps, his friendship with other writers – as with Edna St. Vincent Millay, with whom in his youth he was in love – may have a little softened his critical judgment, but only very rarely. Of his many books of critical essays, *Axel's Castle* (the first clear introduction in the title essay to French Symbolism and its influence on great modern poets), *The Triple Thinkers,* and *The Wound and the Bow* are the deepest and most distinguished, but collections of his shorter pieces, largely written for *The New Yorker*, like *Classics and Commercials*, make perhaps even racier reading. His excellent book on the origins of the Russian Revolution, *To the Finland Station*, reflects an interest in Marxism that did not last.

He wrote minor but sometimes witty verses, and one of his two works of fiction, *I Thought of Daisy*, has a wit, a warmth, and an evocation both of the character of the heroine and of the older Bohemian world of New York that make it a novel one frequently re-reads. An anthology of responses to great American writers by their great contemporaries, *The Shock of Recognition*, is indispensable to any student of American literature. What one remembers most, however, of Wilson (whose interests stretched to the Dead Sea Scrolls, to read which he learned Hebrew in middle age, and the plight of the American Indian) is less any single book than a personality which combined a startling honesty, a rather frightening tartness, and a great generosity of spirit.

—G. S. Fraser

WILSON, Ethel.   English/Canadian.   Born in South Africa, 20 January 1888. Educated at Trinity Hall, Southport, Lancashire. Married Dr. Wallace Wilson (died). Taught in the public schools of Vancouver, British Columbia. Recipient: Canada Council Medal, 1962; Lorne Pierce Medal, 1964. D.Litt.: University of British Columbia, Vancouver, 1955. Medal of Service, Order of Canada, 1970. Lives in Vancouver.

PUBLICATIONS

Fiction

Hetty Dorval.   1947.
The Innocent Traveller.   1949.
The Equations of Love, with Tuesday and Wednesday, and Lilly's Story.   1952.
Swamp Angel.   1954.
Love and Salt Water.   1956.
Mrs. Golightly and Other Stories.   1961.

Reading List: *Wilson* by Desmond Pacey, 1967.

*   *   *

The Canadian writer Ethel Wilson sets her novels and stories largely in her home province of British Columbia. The ocean, the mountains, and the rain forests form a backdrop to her fiction and frequently carry symbolic associations in the development of a story. But while Mrs. Wilson is a realist, faithful to her region, her fiction is informed throughout by the universal problem of human relationships – their complexity, their difficulty. Mrs. Wilson's fictional world is peopled with eccentrics and lonely individuals who do not easily relate to others, but who experience nonetheless a profound need for some form of human community. The concern with communication is imbedded in Mrs. Wilson's style. She has said she likes best the formal and simple sentence, clear and unloaded; but while the simple style forms the matrix of her prose, her writing is nonetheless marked by stylistic quirks — curious repetitions, illogical statements, ellipses. The failure of men to communicate with each other is the thematic corollary to this style and the gaps in Mrs. Wilson's writing represent forms of arrest and discontinuity in the flow of human relationships.

The recurrent drama in Mrs. Wilson's fiction is the lonely quest of a young woman, orphaned and cut off from familiar surroundings, to discover her identity and to forge a link with the human community at large. The link is hard to establish, and Mrs. Wilson reveals the many ways by which human contacts are broken. In *Hetty Dorval* jealousy and guilt bring the girl narrator to a state of bitter isolation at the end of the novel, while in the story "Mrs. Golightly and the First Convention" shyness keeps the heroine from enjoying her holiday and the company of other women. In *Swamp Angel* the heroine's desire for mastery in every situation prevents her from forming lasting human ties until near the end of the novel when she begins to test an old woman's observation that we are all part of "the everlasting web" of creation. Mrs. Wilson is fascinated with lonely, anonymous individuals who retreat from human contacts and she gives us on a philosophical level a complementary vision of the universe as an ungoverned void subject to accident and chance. But at the same time she refers us frequently in her writing to Donne's admonition that "No man is an Island," and insists on the humanist's values of love, faith, and responsibility. Mrs. Wilson's fiction is of a consistently high level artistically and to single out her masterwork would be simply to indicate a personal preference.

—David Stouck

WISTER, Owen. American. Born in Germantown, Philadelphia, Pennsylvania, 14 July 1860. Educated at schools in Switzerland and England; Germantown Academy; St. Paul's School, Concord, New Hampshire, 1873–78; Harvard University, Cambridge, Massachusetts, 1878–82, B.A. (summa cum laude) in music 1882; studied music in Europe, 1882–84, then studied at the Harvard Law School, 1885–88, LL.B. 1888; admitted to the Pennsylvania bar, 1889. Married his second cousin Mary Channing Wister in 1898 (died, 1913); three sons and three daughters. Practised law in Philadelphia, 1889–91; thereafter a full-time writer; settled in Charleston, South Carolina, 1902. Overseer, Harvard University, 1912–18, 1919–25. Fellow, American Academy of Arts and Letters. Honorary Member, Société des Lettres, Paris; Honorary Fellow, Royal Society of Literature, London. *Died 21 July 1938.*

PUBLICATIONS

Fiction

The New Swiss Family Robinson. 1882.
The Dragon of Wantley. 1892.
Red Men and White (stories). 1895.
Lin McLean. 1897.

The Jimmyjohn Boss and Other Stories.   1900.
The Virginian: A Horseman of the Plains.   1902.
Philosophy 4: A Story of Harvard University.   1903.
Lady Baltimore.   1906.
How Doth the Simple Spelling Bee.   1907.
Mother.   1907.
Members of the Family.   1911.
When West Was West.   1928.

Verse

Done in the Open, illustrated by Frederic Remington.   1902.
Musk-Ox, Bison, Sheep, and Goat, with Caspar W. Whitney and George Bird
    Grinnell.   1904.
Indispensable Information for Infants.   1921.

Other

Ulysses S. Grant.   1900.
The Seven Ages of Washington: A Biography.   1907.
The Pentecost of Calamity (essay).   1918.
A Straight Deal; or, An Ancient Grudge (essay).   1920.
Neighbors Henceforth.   1922.
Watch Your Thirst: A Dry Opera in Three Acts.   1923.
Roosevelt: The Story of a Friendship, 1880–1919.   1930.
The Writings.   11 vols., 1928.
Wister Out West: His Journals and Letters, edited by Fanny Kemble Wister.   1958.

Reading List: *The Eastern Establishment and the Western Experience: The West of Frederic Remington, Theodore Roosevelt, and Wister* by G. Edward White, 1968; *Wister* by Richard W. Etulain, 1973.

                        *   *   *

Although he never gave himself fully to the American West, the West was the making of Owen Wister as a man and as a writer. Born into an aristocratic Philadelphia family, educated in eastern schools and abroad, Wister initially sought a career in music. His practical father encouraged a business career, then law. Uncertain of himself, Wister took the advice of his physician in 1885 and went to Wyoming for the summer. Then and in succeeding summers in the West, he found health, and a frontier and cowboy milieu that he knew was about to end and deserved to be put into fiction. Wister saw great romantic possibilities in the cowboy, known to fiction only in dime novels.

Wister had published a burlesque of *Swiss Family Robinson* the year he graduated from Harvard. Shortly thereafter he and a cousin wrote a novel, but he took the advice of William Dean Howells, who found the book too bold, and did not submit it for publication. Wister's instinct was for the actual and the concrete, and he might have been a better writer had he not acquiesced repeatedly to the genteel tradition. The habit of writing ingrained, he kept detailed journal entries on his Western summers – the factual basis for many of his stories. The journals, published twenty years after Wister's death, are well worth reading.

In 1891 Wister wrote "Hank's Woman," his first Western story. *Harper's* accepted it and encouraged Wister to write about the West. His stories were full of local color interest when the local color movement was still important in American literature. *Red Men and White*, his first short story collection, was published in 1896, followed by *Lin McLean*. The cowboy McLean gave some unity to the book, but it is hardly a novel. *The Virginian*, the novel that is Wister's most important achievement, was likewise based on earlier published stories. It, too, has problems of point of view. The Eastern tenderfoot who arrives in Wyoming and "grows up" there could not possibly know all the material he relates. The novel's structure is episodic. The contrast of East and West, however, gave embodiment to Wister's sense of the romantic possibility of the cowpuncher, possibilities that became legion in Western novels and movies. Wister's hero is a natural aristocrat who is capable of showing his inner fiber in a land with its own rules for law and order. Wister was not particularly interested in portraying the inside of ranch life; rather he wished to show his hero grow and adjust to the closing frontier, proving himself worthy of the aristocratic Molly Stark Wood of Vermont who has come to Wyoming to teach school.

However attractive the West might be for summer hunting and adventure, Wister became increasingly pulled to the East and to Europe, and to the South. He had moved to Charleston, South Carolina, in 1902, where the southern aristocratic codes were congenial to Wister's temperament. *Lady Baltimore* is Wister's Jamesian comedy of manners. The Jamesian narrator comes from the North to Kings Port (Charleston) to engage in genealogical research. The love story he narrates, and plays a part in, enables Wister to juxtapose culture against culture. The novel is pleasant reading, convincing in its portrayal of Southern attitudes of the time, and indicative of the reservations Wister had about the cruder West. Thereafter, Wister wrote other stories about the West, but he ceased to visit it, and by the time of World War I his main concern was his family, Europe, and politics.

—Joseph M. Flora

WODEHOUSE, Sir P(elham) G(renville). American. Born in Guildford, Surrey, England, 15 October 1881; emigrated to the United States in 1910; naturalized, 1955. Educated at Dulwich College, London, 1894–1900. Married Ethel Rowley Wayman in 1914. Bank Clerk, Hong Kong and Shanghai Bank, London, 1900–02; full-time writer from 1902; Columnist ("By the Way"), *The Globe*, London, 1903–09; Drama Critic, *Vanity Fair*, New York, 1915–19; worked as a scriptwriter in Hollywood; interned by the Germans during World War II; settled on Long Island, New York, after the war. D.L.: Oxford University, 1939. Knighted, 1975. *Died 14 February 1975.*

PUBLICATIONS

Collections

Vintage Wodehouse, edited by Richard Usborne.   1977.

Fiction

The Pothunters.   1902.
A Prefect's Uncle.   1903.
Tales of St. Austin's.   1903.

The Gold Bat. 1904.

The Head of Kay's. 1905.

Love among the Chickens. 1906; revised edition, 1921.

The White Feather. 1907.

The Swoop: How Clarence Saved England: A Tale of the Great Invasion. 1909.

Mike: A Public School Story. 1909; part 2 reprinted as *Enter Psmith*, 1935; revised edition, as *Mike at Wrykyn* and *Mike and Psmith*, 2 vols., 1953.

The Intrusion of Jimmy. 1910; as *A Gentleman of Leisure*, 1910.

Psmith in the City: A Sequel to Mike. 1910.

The Prince and Betty. 1912; revised edition, as *Psmith, Journalist*, 1915.

The Prince and Betty (different book from the previous title). 1912.

The Little Nugget. 1913.

The Man Upstairs and Other Stories. 1914.

Something New. 1915; as *Something Fresh*, 1915.

Uneasy Money. 1916.

Piccadilly Jim. 1917.

The Man with Two Left Feet and Other Stories. 1917.

Their Mutual Child. 1919; as *The Coming of Bill*, 1920.

A Damsel in Distress. 1919.

My Man Jeeves (stories). 1919.

The Little Warrior. 1920; as *Jill the Reckless*, 1921.

Indiscretions of Archie (stories). 1921.

The Clicking of Cuthbert (stories). 1922; as *Golf Without Tears*, 1924.

Three Men and a Maid. 1922; as *The Girl on the Boat*, 1922.

The Adventures of Sally. 1922; as *Mostly Sally*, 1923.

The Inimitable Jeeves (stories). 1923; as *Jeeves*, 1923.

Leave It to Psmith. 1923.

Bill the Conqueror: His Invasion of England in the Springtime. 1924.

Ukridge (stories). 1924; as *He Rather Enjoyed It*, 1926.

Carry On, Jeeves! (stories). 1925.

Sam the Sudden. 1925; as *Sam in the Suburbs*, 1925.

The Heart of a Goof. 1926; as *Divots*, 1927.

Meet Mr. Mulliner (stories). 1927.

The Small Bachelor. 1927.

Money for Nothing. 1928.

Fish Preferred. 1929; as *Summer Lightning*, 1929; as *Fish Deferred*, 1929.

Mr. Mulliner Speaking (stories). 1929.

Very Good, Jeeves! (stories). 1930.

Big Money. 1931.

If I Were You. 1931.

Doctor Sally. 1932.

Hot Water. 1932.

Mulliner Nights (stories). 1933.

Heavy Weather. 1933.

Thank You, Jeeves. 1934.

Right Ho, Jeeves. 1934; as *Brinkley Manor*, 1934.

Mulliner Omnibus (stories). 1935; revised edition, as *The World of Mr. Mulliner*, 1972.

Blandings Castle and Elsewhere (stories). 1935.

The Luck of the Bodkins. 1935.

Laughing Gas. 1936.

Young Men in Spats (stories). 1936.

Lord Emsworth and Others (stories). 1937; as *The Crime Wave at Blandings and Other Stories*, 1937.

Summer Moonshine. 1937.

The Code of the Woosters. 1938.
Uncle Fred in the Springtime. 1939.
Quick Service. 1940.
Eggs, Beans, and Crumpets (stories). 1940.
Dudley Is Back to Normal (stories). 1940.
Money in the Bank. 1942.
Joy in the Morning. 1946.
Full Moon. 1947.
Spring Fever. 1948.
Uncle Dynamite. 1948.
The Mating Season. 1949.
Nothing Serious (stories). 1950.
The Old Reliable. 1951.
Barmy in Wonderland. 1952; as *Angel Cake,* 1952.
Pigs Have Wings. 1952.
Ring for Jeeves. 1953; as *The Return of Jeeves,* 1954.
Jeeves and the Feudal Spirit. 1954; as *Bertie Wooster Sees It Through,* 1955.
French Leave. 1956.
Something Fishy. 1957; as *The Butler Did It,* 1957.
Cocktail Time. 1958.
Selected Stories, edited by John W. Aldridge. 1958.
A Few Quick Ones (stories). 1959.
How Right You Are, Jeeves. 1960; as *Jeeves in the Offing,* 1960.
The Ice in the Bedroom. 1961; as *Ice in the Bedroom,* 1961.
Service with a Smile. 1961.
Stiff Upper Lip, Jeeves. 1963.
Biffen's Millions. 1964; as *Frozen Assets,* 1964.
The Brinkmanship of Galahad Threepwood. 1965; as *Galahad at Blandings,* 1965.
Plum Pie (stories). 1966.
The World of Jeeves (stories). 1967.
The Purloined Paperweight. 1967; as *Company for Henry,* 1967.
Do Butlers Burgle Banks? 1968.
A Pelican at Blandings. 1969; as *No Nudes Is Good Nudes,* 1970.
The Girl in Blue. 1970.
Much Obliged, Jeeves. 1971; as *Jeeves and the Tie That Binds,* 1971.
Pearls, Girls, and Monty Bodkin. 1972; as *The Plot That Thickened,* 1973.
Bachelors Anonymous. 1973.
The Golf Omnibus: Thirty-One Selected Golfing Short Stories. 1973.
The World of Psmith (stories). 1974.
Aunts Aren't Gentlemen. 1974; as *The Cat-Nappers,* 1974.
The World of Ukridge (stories). 1975.
Sunset at Blandings. 1977.

Plays

The Bandit's Daughter (sketch), with Herbert Westbrook, music by Ella King-Hall (produced 1907).
A Gentleman of Leisure, with John Stapleton (produced 1911); as *A Thief for a Night* (produced 1913).
After the Show, with Herbert Westbrook (produced 1913).
Brother Alfred, with Herbert Westbrook (produced 1913).
Nuts and Wine, with C. H. Bovill, music by Frank Tours (produced 1914).
Pom Pom, with Anne Caldwell, music by Hugo Felix (produced 1916).

Miss Springtime (lyrics only, with Herbert Reynolds), book by Guy Bolton, music by Emmerich Kalman and Jerome Kern (produced 1916).

Have a Heart, with Guy Bolton, music by Jerome Kern (produced 1917). 1917.

Oh, Boy!, with Guy Bolton, music by Jerome Kern (produced 1917); as *Oh, Joy* (produced 1919).

Leave It to Jane, with Guy Bolton, music by Jerome Kern (produced 1917).

Kitty Darlin' (lyrics only), book by Guy Bolton, music by Rudolf Friml (produced 1917).

The Riviera Girl (lyrics only), book by Guy Bolton, music by Emmerich Kalman and Jerome Kern (produced 1917).

Miss 1917, with Guy Bolton, music by Jerome Kern and Victor Herbert (produced 1917).

Oh, Lady! Lady!, with Guy Bolton, music by Jerome Kern (produced 1918).

See You Later, with Guy Bolton, music by Jean Schwartz and Joseph Szulc (produced 1918).

The Girl Behind the Gun, with Guy Bolton, music by Ivan Caryll (produced 1918); as *Kissing Time* (produced 1919).

Oh, My Dear!, with Guy Bolton, music by Louis Hirsch (produced 1918).

The Rose of China (lyrics only), book by Guy Bolton, music by Armand Vecsey (produced 1919).

The Golden Moth, with Fred Thompson, music by Ivor Novello (produced 1921).

The Cabaret Girl, with George Grossmith, Jr., music by Jerome Kern (produced 1922).

The Beauty Prize, with George Grossmith, Jr., music by Jerome Kern (produced 1923).

Sitting Pretty, with Guy Bolton, music by Jerome Kern (produced 1924).

Hearts and Diamonds, with Laurie Wylie, music by Bruno Granichstaedten, lyrics by Graham John (produced 1926). 1926.

Oh, Kay!, with Guy Bolton, music by George Gershwin, lyrics by Ira Gershwin (produced 1926).

The Play's the Thing, from a play by Molnar (produced 1926). 1927.

Her Cardboard Lover, with Valerie Wyngate, from a play by Jacques Deval (produced 1927).

Good Morning, Bill, from a play by Ladislaus Fodor (produced 1927). 1928.

The Nightingale, with Guy Bolton, music by Armand Vecsey (produced 1927).

Rosalie (lyrics only, with Ira Gershwin), book by Guy Bolton and Bill McGuire, music by George Gershwin and Sigmund Romberg (produced 1928).

A Damsel in Distress, with Ian Hay (produced 1928). 1930.

The Three Musketeers (lyrics only, with Clifford Grey), book by Bill McGuire, music by Rudolf Friml (produced 1928). 1937.

Baa, Baa, Black Sheep, with Ian Hay (produced 1929). 1930.

Candle-Light, from a play by Siegfried Geyer (produced 1929). 1934.

Leave It to Psmith, with Ian Hay (produced 1930). 1932.

Who's Who, with Guy Bolton (produced 1934).

Anything Goes, with Guy Bolton, music by Cole Porter (produced 1934). 1936.

The Inside Stand (produced 1935).

Don't Listen Ladies, with Guy Bolton, from a play by Sacha Guitry (produced 1948).

Nothing Serious (produced 1950; also produced as *Springboard to Nowhere*, and *House on a Cliff*).

Come On, Jeeves, with Guy Bolton (produced 1956). 1956.

Screenplays: *Oh, Kay!*, with Carey Wilson and Elsie Janis, 1928; *Those Three French Girls*, with others, 1930; *The Man in Possession*, 1931; *Damsel in Distress*, with Ernest Pagano and S. K. Lauren, 1937; *Her Cardboard Lover*, with others, 1942.

Television Play: *Arthur*, from a play by Molnar.

Other

William Tell Told Again. 1904.
Not George Washington, with Herbert Westbrook. 1907.
The Globe "By the Way" Book: A Literary Quick-Lunch for People Who Have Only Got Five Minutes to Spare, with Herbert Westbrook. 1908.
Louder and Funnier (essays). 1932.
Nothing But Wodehouse, edited by Ogden Nash. 1932.
Wodehouse (selection). 1934.
Bring on the Girls: The Improbable Story of Our Life in Musical Comedy, with Pictures to Prove It, with Guy Bolton. 1953.
Performing Flea: A Self-Portrait in Letters, edited by W. Townend. 1953; revised edition, as *Author! Author!,* 1962.
America, I Like You. 1956; revised edition, as *Over Seventy: An Autobiography with Digressions,* 1957.
The Uncollected Wodehouse, edited by David A. Jasen. 1976.

Editor, *A Century of Humour.* 1934.
Editor, with Scott Meredith, *The Best of Modern Humor.* 1952.
Editor, with Scott Meredith, *The Week-End Book of Humor.* 1952.
Editor, with Scott Meredith, *A Carnival of Modern Humor.* 1967.

Bibliography: *A Bibliography and Reader's Guide to the First Editions of Wodehouse* by David A. Jasen, 1971.

Reading List: *Wodehouse at Work: A Study of the Books and Characters* by Richard Usborne 1961 (includes bibliography), revised edition, as *Wodehouse at Work to the End,* 1977; *Wodehouse* by Richard J. Voorhees, 1966; *Wodehouse* by R. B. D. French, 1966; *Homage to Wodehouse* edited by Thelma Cazalet-Keir, 1973; *Wodehouse: A Portrait of a Master* by David A. Jasen, 1973; *Comic Style of Wodehouse* by Robert A. Hall, Jr., 1974.

*   *   *

P. G. Wodehouse was born to write, and he wrote for eighty years. Fame, fortune, or old age made no difference. He wrote on for "the pleasure of turning out the stuff," and because nature told him to do so. Extremely conscientious, he took great pains, always polishing or rewriting. He insists that he has no message for humanity. It was not his business to "brood over the cosmos," but he has the good sense and observation of a comedian, and his kindly satire exposes the pretentious and the unreal. His achievement is unique in our time.

His school stories were his first success. In revolt against the mawkishness of books for boys in his time, he cheerfully mocks their weaknesses. He tells the truth about school life as he knows it, without sentimentality or avuncular advice on the problems of youth. In their naturalness, good sense, and humour, the school stories remain classics of their kind. In them he created Psmith, his first great comic character, with his elaborate stylized diction, his quick eye for the affected and ridiculous, and his social conscience. His deplorable Ukridge, created about the same time, has no conscience at all. Concerned only with himself and his lunatic plans to make a colossal fortune, he is a rogue, but then there is a kind of childlike innocence about him. Wodehouse loved him, and wrote stories about him for sixty years.

He became an established and popular author when he wrote his stories for the *Saturday Evening Post.* His public was a vast one, mostly made up by women and girls. He gave them love stories, but he did not give them sentimentality, melodrama, or burning passion. The falseness to life of romantic fiction is shown up. His young men and girls are of this world. They must learn that if they are to find happiness and fulfillment in life they must understand their world and understand themselves. Their guide is nature, and the dictates of nature must never be contravened.

Before he wrote these serials, Wodehouse had embarked on his long and highly successful career in the theatre. He enjoyed it enormously, except for two periods in Hollywood, where he complained of being given too much money for too little work. In his many short stories about Hollywood, his treatment of the tycoons of the studio is indulgent but not flattering. His theatrical experience affected his books. He now thought of every episode as a "scene" and the characters as actors. This was rather too marked at first, but his use of dramatic dialogue in later novels gives the effect of naturalness and intimacy.

In the novels and short stories that follow, Wodehouse reached his full maturity. He was now master of his craft as a story-teller, and master of the English language. The perfect turn of phrase is always there unless he wants the most ludicrous, as in the butterflies "loafing about" at Blandings. It is often said that Wodehouse remained all his life a belated Edwardian. He did not, though his affection for the period is obvious. These are stories of modern life, and reflect its changes in manners and outlook. There is a new sense of urgency about them. The plots become less simple, and so do the characters. The girls are less demure, the young men more demanding. There is now very little description, and the stories move more quickly. That the plots, situations, and characters become familiar is perfectly true, but that is rather a delight than a weakness to be deplored. When we are in Wodehouse territory we know its ways. We do not expect or wish for change or surprise. Our pleasure comes from the satisfying of expectation.

A critic once said of a book he was reviewing that it contained all the old Wodehouse characters under different names. Wodehouse struck back in the preface to his next book. "With my superior intelligence," he said, "I have outgeneralled the man by putting in all the old Wodehouse characters with the same names." For many readers, the peaks of his achievement are the series of novels and short stories about Bertie Wooster and his valet Jeeves, and those about Lord Emsworth and Blandings, in which we have the same characters and their associates for sixty years, never growing older though the world changes.

Bertie, if he is a nitwit, must be the most endearing nitwit in literature. Constantly plunged into situations of a kind calculated to make humanity shudder, he is the victim of his own chivalry and his loyalty to his friends. Jeeves, who gets him out of the situations, has more than ingenuity of invention in thinking out the elaborate designs by which this is brought about. He has a profound understanding of human nature and is widely read in philosophy and the arts. Constant references to English literature are a diverting feature of the series. The Blandings stories, which have their moments of seriousness and tenderness, are related chronicles of a great house. It is permissible to believe that the down-trodden Emsworth, always pestered by being drawn into confusing family affairs when he wants to be alone with his pig, the prize-winning Empress of Blandings, and always revealing a fuller richness of absurdity, was Wodehouse's most loved character, and Blandings his spiritual home.

—— R. B. D. French

WOLFE, Thomas (Clayton).   American.   Born in Asheville, North Carolina, 3 October 1900. Educated at the Orange Street grade school, Asheville, to age 11; North State Fitting School, Asheville, 1912–16; University of North Carolina, Chapel Hill (editor of the college magazine), 1916–20, B.A. 1920; Harvard University, Cambridge, Massachusetts, where he studied playwriting in George Pierce Baker's "47 Workshop", 1920–22, M.A. in English

1922. Instructor in English, Washington Square College, New York University, 1924–30; full-time writer from 1930; made several trips to Europe and lived briefly in London; travelled in the Pacific Northwest, 1938: contracted pneumonia. Recipient: Guggenheim Fellowship, 1930. Member, National Institute of Arts and Letters. *Died 15 September 1938.*

PUBLICATIONS

Collections

The Letters, edited by Elizabeth Nowell.   1956; selection, 1958.
The Wolfe Reader, edited by C. Hugh Holman.   1962.

Fiction

Look Homeward, Angel: A Story of the Buried Life.   1929.
Of Time and the River: A Legend of Man's Hunger in His Youth.   1935.
From Death to Morning (stories).   1935.
The Web and the Rock, edited by Edward C. Aswell.   1939.
You Can't Go Home Again, edited by Edward C. Aswell.   1940.
The Hills Beyond (stories), edited by Edward C. Aswell.   1941.
The Short Novels, edited by C. Hugh Holman.   1961.

Plays

The Return of Buck Gavin (produced 1919).   In Carolina Folk-Plays, second series, 1924.
The Third Night (produced 1919).   In The Carolina Play Book, September 1938.
Welcome to Our City (produced 1923).
Gentlemen of the Press (produced 1928).   1942.
Mannerhouse.   1948.

Verse

A Stone, A Leaf, A Door: Poems, edited by John S. Barnes.   1945.

Other

The Crisis in Industry.   1919.
The Story of a Novel.   1936.
A Note on Experts: Dexter Vespasian Joyner.   1939.
Letters to His Mother, Julia Elizabeth Wolfe, edited by John S. Terry.   1943.
The Years of Wandering in Many Lands and Cities.   1949.
A Western Journal: A Daily Log of the Great Parks Trip, June 20–July 2, 1938.   1951.
Wolfe's Purdue Speech, "Writing and Living," edited by William Braswell and Leslie A. Field.   1964.
The Letters to His Mother, Newly Edited from the Original Manuscripts, edited by C. Hugh Holman and Sue Fields Ross.   1968.

The Notebooks, edited by Richard S. Kennedy and Paschal Reeves.   2 vols., 1970.
The Mountains, edited by Pat M. Ryan.   1970.

Bibliography: *Of Time and Thomas Wolfe: A Bibliography with a Character Index*, 1959, and *Wolfe: A Checklist*, 1970, both by Elmer D. Johnson.

Reading List: *Wolfe: A Critical Study* by Pamela Hansford Johnson, 1947, as *Hungry Gulliver: An English Critical Appraisal of Wolfe*, 1948; *Wolfe: The Weather of His Youth* by Louis D. Rubin, Jr., 1955, and *Wolfe: A Collection of Critical Essays* edited by Rubin, 1973; *Wolfe* by Elizabeth Nowell, 1960; *Wolfe*, 1960, and *The Loneliness at the Core: Studies in Wolfe*, 1975, both by C. Hugh Holman, and *The World of Wolfe* edited by Holman, 1962; *The Window of Memory: The Literary Career of Wolfe* by Richard S. Kennedy, 1962; *Wolfe's Albatross: Race and Nationality in America* by Paschal Reeves, 1969.

*   *   *

With the publication in 1929 of *Look Homeward, Angel*, American fiction was invested with a fresh talent quite unlike that of any writer of the past. On its narrative level, it was a story of maturation, covering the first twenty years in the life of a youth in conflict with his family and his small North Carolina town, but it was no novel in the usual sense, but a loose chronicle held together with an assemblage of some of the most memorable characters in fiction. Noticeable throughout were vestiges of thwarted careers in playwriting and poetry which Wolfe would have preferred. Availing himself of the titanism then permitted in American fiction, and gifted with a Proustian power of nearly total recall of sights and sounds, Wolfe lacquered the narrative of *Look Homeward, Angel* with dithyrambic luxuriance and a sensuous Whitmanian prose, twisting easily from the rhetorical to the dramatic. At his command, too, was a bent for caricature, even burlesque, and satire. His comic exaggeration in depicting characters was never understood by those acquainted with the models on whom they were based. Symbols – the angel, the ghost, trains, mountains, and those images in the haunting refrain "a stone, a leaf, an unfound door" – underscored Wolfe's intent in characterization and meaning.

Its sequel, *Of Time and the River*, took Wolfe's autobiographical hero, Eugene Gant, to Harvard, New York, and Europe. For his thesis, Wolfe appropriated the Joycean wanderer's search for the father, and imposed an epic framework upon the narrative by intoning names from famous Greek legends. In such a novel as this, Wolfe became, according to one ecstatic comment, "our closest approach to Homer." Allied with the search for the father was an attempt to discover America's greatness through the intensity of one man's experience, and to reveal to Americans as totally as possible the loneliness and transiency of their lives. In order to accomplish this, the hero was provided with a Faustian hunger, an obsessive and unquenchable desire for achievement and knowledge. There must be, he proclaimed, "*never* an end to curiosity! ... I must think. I must mix it all with myself and with America." *The Story of a Novel*, Wolfe's confessional monograph of how *Of Time and the River* was written, tells of a "great black cloud" within him which poured forth "a torrential and ungovernable flood" about "night and darkness in America." The result was a novel of apparent formlessness, but it was an intentional formlessness, symbolically parallel to the formlessness of life itself and of his native land.

Though Wolfe's second book was a great success, so sensitive was he to charges of excessive emotional energy and lyricism that for his third, *The Web and the Rock*, he promised to write an "objective" account of his hero, now named George Webber. Webber was given a somewhat different background and young manhood, but in midstream Webber took on the familiar traits of Eugene Gant – that is to say, Thomas Wolfe himself. A love affair with a woman much older than Webber led directly into *You Can't Go Home Again*, by the end of which Wolfe's promise of objectivity was realized, his understanding of social problems effected, and his transformation completed: from romantic egocentricity to a clearer vision of the realities of life, from chaos to order, from uncertainty to assurance, from self, in short, to mankind. In the development of a social consciousness, Wolfe's hero was propelled into a rejection of a number of youthful ambitions. No longer sufficient were success and fame and romantic love; of ultimate primacy was one's belief "that America and the people in it are deathless, undiscovered, and immortal, and must live."

After the publication of his first novel, Wolfe had only nine years to finish his writing. Since he was resolved on a one-man vision of life, everything was part of the "single" book, including his early plays, two volumes of *Letters*, his *Notebooks*, two collections of short stories, the excerpts and essays, and *A Western Journal*. That he produced such an abundance in so short a time was due to a compulsion to write almost continuously. He rarely took vacations, was annoyed by intrusions, and was committed wholly to his "work," as he called it. It has been argued that Wolfe should be read in isolated segments, as tone poems perhaps, or as short novels where his control can easily be observed. His books, according to another view, were rather a "fictional thesaurus," composed of many diverse elements – theatrical dialogue, choral ode, essay, travelogue, biography, oratory, lyric poetry, dramatic episode. Though his four major books were no more autobiographical than many single works by Melville and Twain, Fitzgerald and Hemingway, his persistent chronological continuum affronted some readers and critics in a way the practices of other novelists had not.

As an American writer – and he may turn out to be the most American writer – Wolfe was in the tradition of Emerson, Thoreau, Melville, Twain, Dreiser, Sandburg, and Sherwood Anderson. He shared the idealism of Jefferson and Whitman, especially in their projection of the American Dream in which lay the hopes of young men and women everywhere to do the best that was within them to do. His pages were often a sheer symbolic poetry of time and the river, of the web and the rock. Yet his greatest attainment was a fiction of scenes and characters remarkably vital, bountiful, and rich.

—Richard Walser

WOOLF, (Adeline) Virginia.   English.   Born in London, 25 January 1882; daughter of the scholar and writer Leslie Stephen. Educated privately. Married the writer Leonard Woolf in 1912. Settled in Bloomsbury, 1904; associated with the biographer Lytton Strachey, the economist J. M. Keynes, the art critic Roger Fry, the novelist E. M. Forster, and others, later known as the Bloomsbury Group; reviewer for the *Times Literary Supplement*, London, and other periodicals; Founder, with Leonard Woolf, of the Hogarth Press, Richmond, Surrey, later London, 1917–41. *Died* (by suicide) *28 March 1941.*

PUBLICATIONS

Collections

   The Letters, edited by Nigel Nicolson and Joanne Trautman.   1975–

Fiction

   The Voyage Out.   1915.
   Two Stories, with Leonard Woolf.   1917.

Night and Day. 1919.
Kew Gardens (story). 1919.
Monday or Tuesday (stories). 1921.
Jacob's Room. 1922.
Mrs. Dalloway. 1925.
To the Lighthouse. 1927.
Orlando: A Biography. 1928.
The Waves. 1931; draft versions edited by J. W. Graham, 1976.
Flush: A Biography. 1933.
The Years. 1937.
Between the Acts. 1941.
A Haunted House and Other Short Stories. 1944.
Mrs. Dalloway's Party: A Short Story Sequence, edited by Stella McNichol. 1973.
The Pargiters: The Novel-Essay Portion of The Years, edited by Mitchell Leaska. 1978.

Play

Freshwater, edited by Lucio P. Ruotolo. 1976.

Other

Mr. Bennett and Mrs. Brown. 1924.
The Common Reader. 1925; second series, 1932.
A Room of One's Own. 1929.
Street Haunting. 1930.
On Being Ill. 1930.
Beau Brummell. 1930.
A Letter to a Young Poet. 1932.
Walter Sickert: A Conversation. 1934.
Three Guineas. 1938.
Reviewing. 1939.
Roger Fry: A Biography. 1940.
The Death of the Moth and Other Essays. 1942.
The Moment and Other Essays. 1942.
The Captain's Death Bed and Other Essays. 1950.
A Writer's Diary, Being Extracts from the Diary of Woolf, edited by Leonard
    Woolf. 1953.
Woolf and Lytton Strachey: Letters, edited by Leonard Woolf and James
    Strachey. 1956.
Hours in a Library. 1958.
Granite and Rainbow: Essays. 1958.
Contemporary Writers, edited by Jean Guiguet. 1965.
Nurse Lugton's Golden Thimble (juvenile). 1966.
Collected Essays, edited by Leonard Woolf. 4 vols., 1966–67.
Moments of Being: Unpublished Autobiographical Writings, edited by Jeanne
    Schulkind. 1976.
The Diary, edited by Anne Olivier Bell. 1977–
*Books and Portraits: Some Further Selections from the Literary and Biographical
    Writings,* edited by Mary Lyon. 1977.

Translator, with S. S. Koteliansky, *Stavrogin's Confession,* by Dostoevsky. 1922.
Translator, with S. S. Koteliansky, *Tolstoi's Love Letters.* 1923.

Translator, with S. S. Kotelianisky, *Talks with Tolstoy,* by A. D. Goldenveizer.   1923.

Bibliography: *A Bibliography of Woolf* by B. J. Kirkpartick, 1957, revised edition, 1967.

Reading List: *Woolf* by David Daiches, 1942, revised edition, 1963; *Woolf: Her Art as a Novelist* by Joan Bennett, 1945, revised edition, 1964; *Woolf: A Commentary* by Bernard Blackstone, 1949; *Woolf's London,* 1959, and *Woolf,* 1963, both by Dorothy Brewster; *Woolf et Son Oeuvre* by Jean Guiguet, 1962, translated by Jean Stewart as *Woolf and Her Works,* 1965; *Feminism and Art: A Study of Woolf* by Herbert Marder, 1968; *Woolf: A Biography* by Quentin Bell, 2 vols., 1972; *Woolf: A Critical Reading* by Avrom Fleishman, 1975; *Woolf: The Critical Heritage* edited by Robin Majumdar and Allen McLaurin, 1975; *The Novels of Woolf* by Hermione Lee, 1977; *Woolf: Sources of Madness and Art* by Jean O. Love, 1977; *A Marriage of True Minds: An Intimate Biography of Leonard and Virginia Woolf* by George Spater and Ian Parsons, 1977.

*   *   *

Virginia Woolf, with E. M. Forster, is one of the two novelists of the Bloomsbury Group, which also included Lytton Strachey, John Maynard Keynes, Roger Fry, and Clive Bell. The group took its name from the house in Bloomsbury to which Virginia moved when her sister Vanessa married Clive Bell. From her father, Sir Leslie Stephen (Mr. Ramsay in *To the Lighthouse*), Virginia had inherited a sharp critical sense, and from her mother, Julia Duckworth, who died when her daughters were young, a feeling for the opulence and richness of life (her mother is Mrs. Ramsay). With Leonard Woolf, whom she married, she was to found the Hogarth Press, which published her own books and much other important work. Her most distinguished books outside her fiction are probably her biography of her friend Roger Fry, the two volumes of *The Common Reader* (her quotations are often inaccurate, and books are used as a way of exploring personality with a novelist's penetration, but there is distinction throughout), and the short plea for women's independence, *A Room of One's Own* (a longer book on the same subject, *Three Guineas*, is distressingly bad). Virginia Woolf suffered all her life from recurrent nervous breakdowns and at the beginning of the war drowned herself. Some of her books are bad, like *Three Guineas*, trivial, like *Flush*, or successful in a self-indulgent way, like *Orlando*, but though there is an intense sensibility – a sensibility that might be called a mystical atheism or a transfiguration of death – especially notable in her most original work, *The Waves*, her written work is completely sane.

Her first novel, *The Voyage Out*, is quite traditional in structure, though the theme, a young girl's acceptance of death after her discovery of love, is one that looks forward to the mood of the later work. *Night and Day*, essentially a comedy about the difficulty in approach to each other of two lovers of different social classes – though the difference is not violent (intellectual upper-middle and intellectual lower-middle) – is perhaps an attempt at something in the manner of her friend Forster. It has passages that are very funny, especially those about the heroine's aunt eternally and untidily engaged on a biography of the family genius who is also the family scandal, yet it is a little stodgy. *Jacob's Room*, an attempt to construct a young man through his surroundings and the impressions he has left, though the hardest reading of all Woolf's novels is also her break-through to a new mode. This reaches complete success in *Mrs. Dalloway*, though not all readers have felt the frail charm of the heroine whose uncertain sense of self-identity consummates itself in her mystical feeling for evening parties. Septimus Smith, a shell-shock case who commits suicide, never meets Mrs. Dalloway but is in a sense the tragic alternative version of her.

Woolf's next novel, *To the Lighthouse*, a loving recreation of her mother and father and childhood, has remained her best-loved book. The middle chapter, with the brief sentence about Mrs. Ramsay's death and the evocation of the life of an empty and uninhabited house over many years, is one of the most original and haunting things in English fiction. Lily Briscoe finishing her painting as Virginia Woolf is finishing her novel (one thinks of the "It is finished" from the Cross) is a masterly picture of the passion of the artist. *The Waves*, consisting of monologues of a group of characters from childhood to old age and the contemplation of death, is the novel almost transfigured into poetry. It has been argued that the novel is merely, in all its characters, a stylised reverie by Woolf in various disguises, and Elizabeth Hardwick has complained that, after one has said it is very beautiful, there is little more to say. But it is here that Woolf has most purely distilled her vision. *Orlando* is light-hearted relief from this effort; here Woolf is frank about the dual attraction to her of both men and women (though in life she was flirtatious but sexually frigid). *The Years* is an attempt to achieve a more conventional success with a family chronicle, and has perhaps been a little underrated, as the posthumous *Between the Acts*, essentially about English history and centred on a village pageant, has been perhaps a little overrated.

After long neglect, Virginia Woolf is now enjoying a period of revival. Undergraduates both in Great Britain and the United States are showing for her the enthusiasm which ten years or so ago they might have shown for D. H. Lawrence. This is not merely because she is a precursor of women's liberation, but also because of her respect for sensibility, personal vision, and the inner life. There were perhaps greater novelists in her period, and certainly novelists with a wider social range and more experience of inner turmoil and violence. But there was no finer spirit. Quentin Bell's biography and recent collections of her letters make irresponsible gossip. But one's sense of the fine spirit remains.

—G. S. Fraser

WOOLSON, Constance Fenimore. American. Born in Claremont, New Hampshire, 5 March 1840; while still an infant moved with her family to Cleveland. Educated at Miss Hayden's School, Cleveland, and the Cleveland Seminary; Madame Chegary's School, New York City, graduated 1858. Returned to the family home in Cleveland, 1858; writer from 1862, full-time writer from 1869; lived in the Carolinas and Florida, 1873–79; wrote criticism for the *Atlantic Monthly*, Boston, 1877–79; lived in Europe after 1879, in England, 1883–86, Florence, 1887–89, Oxford, 1891–93, and Venice, 1893–94. *Died 24 January 1894.*

PUBLICATIONS

Collections

(Selection), edited by Claire Benedict.   1932.

Fiction

The Old Stone House (juvenile).   1872.
Castle Nowhere: Lake Country Sketches.   1875.
Rodman the Keeper: Southern Sketches.   1880.
For the Major.   1883.

Anne.   1883.
East Angels.   1886.
Jupiter Lights.   1889.
Horace Chase.   1894.
The Front Yard and Other Italian Stories.   1895.
Dorothy and Other Italian Stories.   1896.

Verse

Two Women: 1862.   1877.

Other

Mentone, Cairo, and Corfu.   1895.

Reading List: *Woolson: Literary Pioneer* by John D. Kern, 1934; *Woolson* by Rayburn S. Moore, 1963.

*   *   *

Although Constance Fenimore Woolson contributed verse to the magazines and published a long poem, wrote a children's story, and collected some of her travel sketches for a volume that appeared posthumously, she was best known in her own day as a writer of fiction, and to one Boston critic at least as the "novelist laureate" of America. Such a characterization is likely to strike present readers as a bit off the mark, but in the late nineteenth century her stories and novels struck many reviewers and critics, including Henry James, as an important contribution to literature.

Even present readers must concede that Woolson made a contribution to the short fiction of her period. Her best stories – "The Lady of Little Fishing," "Rodman the Keeper," "King David," "The Front Yard," and "A Transplanted Boy," among others – demonstrate her capacity to deal with scenes as varied as the Great Lakes country, the South, and Europe and with universally valid characters. She was not an innovator in technique, but her best tales suggest that she was mindful of the work of George Eliot, Turgenev, and Henry James.

As a novelist she was less successful. Though the scenes and characters are, as in the short stories, handled ably, the structure of her novels (except *Horace Chase*) seems episodic and infrequently functional. This weakness in structure is ironically pointed up by her success with *For the Major*, her only novella, a minor classic in many ways, and her most successful sustained piece of fiction. Still, each novel has its individual merits and *East Angels*, as James maintained in *Harper's Weekly* in 1887, "is a performance which does Miss Woolson the highest honour."

Her best work belongs to the development of realism in America, as regards both local color and the psychological analysis of character, and it offers, as I have noted in *Constance Fenimore Woolson*, "a sympathetic understanding and treatment of character in authentic surroundings by one whose vision was broad enough and whose insight was deep enough to include not only her own country but Europe as well."

—Rayburn S. Moore

WRIGHT, Richard (Nathaniel).   American.   Born near Natchez, Mississippi, 4 September 1908; brought up in an orphanage. Educated in local schools through junior high school. Married 1) Rose Dhima Meadman in 1938; 2) Ellen Poplar; two daughters. Worked in the post office in Memphis, Tennessee, at age 15; later moved to New York; worked for the Federal Writers Project, and the Federal Negro Theatre Project; member of the Communist Party, 1932–44; Harlem Editor, *Daily Worker*, New York; lived in Paris from 1947. Recipient: Guggenheim Fellowship, 1939; Spingarn Medal, 1941. *Died 28 November 1960.*

PUBLICATIONS

Collections

   The Wright Reader, edited by Ellen Wright and Michel Fabre.   1978.

Fiction

   Uncle Tom's Children: Four Novellas.   1938; augmented edition, 1940.
   Native Son.   1940.
   The Outsider.   1953.
   Savage Holiday.   1954.
   The Long Dream.   1958.
   Eight Men (stories).   1961.
   Lawd Today.   1963.
   The Man Who Lived Underground (story; bilingual edition), translated by Claude Edmonde Magny, edited by Michel Fabre.   1971.

Plays

   Native Son (The Biography of a Young American), with Paul Green, from the novel by Wright (produced 1941).   1941.
   Daddy Goodness, from a play by Louis Sapin (produced 1968).

   Screenplay: *Native Son,* 1951.

Other

   How Bigger Was Born: The Story of "Native Son."   1940.
   The Negro and Parkway Community House.   1941.
   Black Boy: A Record of Childhood and Youth.   1945.
   12 Million Black Voices: A Folk History of the Negro in the United States.   1941.
   Black Power: A Record of Reactions in a Land of Pathos.   1954.
   Bandoeng: 1.500.000.000 Hommes, translated by Helene Claireau.   1955; as *The Color Curtain: A Report on the Bandung Conference,* 1956.
   Pagan Spain.   1956.
   White Man, Listen!   1957.
   Letters to Joe C. Brown, edited by Thomas Knipp.   1968.
   American Hunger (autobiography).   1977.

Bibliography: "A Bibliography of Wright's Words" by Michel Fabre and Edward Margolies, in *New Letters 38*, Winter 1971; "Wright: An Essay in Bibliography" by John M. Reilly, in *Resources for American Literary Study*, Autumn 1971.

Reading List: *Wright* by Constance Webb, 1968; *The Art of Wright* by Edward Margolies, 1969; *The Most Native of Sons* (biography) by John A. Williams, 1970; *The Emergence of Wright: A Study of Literature and Society* by Keneth Kinnamon, 1972; *Wright* by David Bakish, 1973; *The Unfinished Quest of Wright* by Michel Fabre, translated by Isabel Barzun, 1973 (includes bibliography); *Wright: Impressions and Perspectives* edited by David Ray and R. M. Farnsworth, 1973.

*   *   *

Richard Wright's career can be described in terms of three reputations he has earned: the realist protesting racial oppression, the typifier of the experience of entry into modern history, and the author who makes his themes seem inevitable by the power of artistic craft. In the best recent criticism these three reputations coalesce, appearing as the figure of different levels of significance to be found in his writing; but while he was alive the fact of his race and his dissent from the culture of his native land, first as radical, then as expatriate, concentrated attention upon the thematic burden of his works.

Wright served a literary apprenticeship made harsh because of his poverty and the restrictions of Jim Crow but otherwise similar to other American authors'; yet he seemed to leap into literary prominence when his collection of stories, *Uncle Tom's Children*, won first prize in a contest sponsored by *Story* magazine for writers on the Federal Writers Project. The four novellas in that volume are arranged to depict the struggles of Southern black peasants in resistance to a caste system dependent upon lynch violence for its sanction and efficacy. For most reviewers the book was a shocking rendition of the facts of racial conflict in affecting narrative, its distinction not so much that the author was black, though reviews made as much of that as they did of the prize the book had won, but rather that *Uncle Tom's Children* told its stories from within the black experience. The book brought news that blacks could effectively articulate their victimization.

As though to match horror with horror, Wright's first published novel, *Native Son*, carried the story of racial conflict to the North where Bigger Thomas, Chicago-born and bred, acts out his role in the American racial drama by his murder of a white woman. At the risk of fulfilling racist expectations in his portrayal of Bigger, Wright completed his inversion of the stereotype of the black victim by showing violence as the necessary prelude to self-realization for his protagonist. Again Wright had written a book that brought news to its audience; *Native Son* was a cautionary tale for whites.

With the popular success of *Native Son* Wright became a public figure called upon to lecture and write as a spokesman for the American Negro. He was qualified for the role not only by literary success but also by a childhood in Mississippi and an adulthood in northern cities similar in pattern to the life of thousands of other black migrants, so it was appropriate that he organize that experience in literature: first with *12 Million Black Voices*, a documentary history of black peasants transplanted into urban life told in the poetic prose of a collective first person narration, and then with his own autobiography, *Black Boy*.

It is unusual for a person not yet forty to write an autobiography and to end the story even before he had established himself in adulthood, but Wright justifies his book by presenting it as at once his own and his people's story. For many other blacks this latter point was dubious. They charged that he had been extremely selective by omitting any positive portrayal of black cultural and family life. The point has merit, but *Black Boy* enhanced Wright's reputation as the realist who showed more profoundly than anyone before him the human waste that is the heritage of North American slavery.

There can be no doubt Wright felt personally threatened by racism in a way that literary success could not ameliorate. It was the motive for his move to Paris in 1947. Though objectively different, Wright's experience in the Communist Party (described in a portion of the original manuscript of *Black Boy*, cut from the book on advice of editors, published separately in 1944, and issued in the excised section of autobiography titled *American Hunger* in 1977) seems to have been psychologically as problematic as racism, so that when he exiled himself from America he was also without the political committment that had informed his work until 1944.

The first book he wrote in exile augmented Wright's second reputation. *The Outsider* portentously invites reading as philosophical fiction. Cross Damon seizes upon the accident of a false report of his death to embark upon a life free of contingency, where action is self-sanctioned and alienation grants perception of mankind in a world of dead myths. Cross, however, can neither escape anguish nor achieve disalienation in his version of freedom. In that respect his problem reflects the author's. Wright described himself in publicity for the novel as a man without ideological burdens for the first time in his life, but his own characteristic feeling of alienation produced an interesting novel undermined by its nihilism.

Wright needed new premises for his writing and found them in the Third World. The four non-fictional books he published from 1954 to 1957 derive from Wright's belief that his own experience was being repeated in the history of Africans and Asians moving from a pre-industrial, traditional society into a modern, mass world. On the assumption of this congruity he wrote the accounts of Ghana, the Bandung Conference, Spain – which represented the world not yet touched by modernism – and the lectures published as *White Man, Listen!* All blend reportage and subjective response to show Richard Wright looking at, feeling with the world in change, and defining himself again as typical, though this time on a world-wide stage.

Wright's exile has sometimes been described as though it were the fag end of his career. In fact, it was a creative period twice as long as he had in the United States. Besides his non-fictional reports, he published three novels and compiled a collection of short stories, issued posthumously. *Savage Holiday* extends Wright's interest in extreme narrative situations to the plight of a white man trapped by psychosis and an accidental death for which he feels responsible. *The Long Dream*, meant to open a trilogy tracing the movement of a young man from Mississippi into life in Europe, is a tightly written *bildungsroman* neatly synthesizing Wright's conception of the psychological trauma of social experience in the person of "Fish" Tucker.

None of Wright's exile writings, however, received the critical or popular acclaim of his first works. There may be a variety of explanations for this, besides the possibility of their lesser quality, but a leading reason for the slump in his popular reputation must be that he no longer wrote as the realistic bringer of news about America and that his performance in the role of typifier of modern life had less authority than the writing by acknowledged "experts." Nevertheless, the exile works alert us to the importance of Wright as an artist.

Examining *The Outsider* and *Savage Holiday*, for instance, we find that their structures are inversions and parodies of the thriller genre, that the expressionistic parable "The Man Who Lived Underground," as well as the stories in *Eight Men*, include experiments in narrative stripped down to bare dialogue. Intrigued by these findings, we return to the early writings and find that they, too, are constructed so that transgression of the conventions of genre constitute meaning, with imagery and controlled narrative voice accounting for the impact of such stories as *Native Son* which we read at first without awareness of literary craft, and that the mediations of ideology in *Uncle Tom's Children* and the portrait of the artist in *Black Boy* are masterfully subordinated in character and plot. In short, we complete the survey of Wright's career by recognizing that the themes which won him fame as a realist and attention as an intellectual are the products of art. So, now we are ready to study Richard Wright in earnest.

—John M. Reilly

YERBY, Frank (Garvin). American. Born in Augusta, Georgia, 5 September 1916. Educated at Paine College, Augusta, A.B. 1937; Fisk University, Nashville, Tennessee, M.A. 1938; University of Chicago, 1939. Married 1) Flora Helen Claire Williams in 1941 (divorced), two sons and two daughters; 2) Blanca Calle Perez in 1956. Instructor, Florida Agricultural and Mechanical College, Tallahassee, 1938–39, and Southern University and A. and M. College, Baton Rouge, Louisiana, 1939–41; Laboratory Technician, Ford Motor Company, Dearborn, Michigan, 1941–44; Magnaflux Inspector, Ranger (Fairchild) Aircraft, Jamaica, New York, 1944–45; full-time writer from 1945; settled in Madrid, 1954. Recipient: O. Henry Award, 1944.

PUBLICATIONS

Fiction

>   *The Foxes of Harrow.* 1946.
>   *The Vixens.* 1947.
>   *The Golden Hawk.* 1948.
>   *Pride's Castle.* 1949.
>   *Floodtide.* 1950.
>   *A Woman Called Fancy.* 1951.
>   *The Saracen Blade.* 1952.
>   *The Devil's Laughter.* 1953.
>   *Benton's Row.* 1954.
>   *Bride of Liberty.* 1954.
>   *The Treasure of Pleasant Valley.* 1955.
>   *Captain Rebel.* 1956.
>   *Fairoaks.* 1957.
>   *The Serpent and the Staff.* 1958.
>   *Jarrett's Jade.* 1959.
>   *Gillian.* 1960.
>   *The Garfield Honor.* 1961.
>   *Griffin's Way.* 1962.
>   *The Old Gods Laugh: A Modern Romance.* 1964.
>   *An Odor of Sanctity.* 1965.
>   *Goat Song: A Novel of Ancient Greece.* 1968.
>   *Judas, My Brother: The Story of the Thirteenth Disciple.* 1968.
>   *Speak Now.* 1969.
>   *The Dahomean.* 1971; as *The Man from Dahomey,* 1971.
>   *The Girl from Storyville: A Victorian Novel.* 1972.
>   *The Voyage Unplanned.* 1974.
>   *Tobias and the Angel.* 1975.
>   *A Rose for Ana María.* 1976.
>   *Hail the Conquering Hero.* 1977.

Reading List: *The Unembarrassed Muse* by Russel B. Nye, 1970.

*   *   *

Readers of his many best-selling romances are still amazed to discover that Frank Yerby began his career as a militant writer of black protest fiction. Perhaps a more surprising activity of his early years was his poetry writing. The careful and painstaking construction of sonnets does not seem a practice this supposedly inartistic teller of racy, swashbuckling tales would spend much time on. But Yerby is a writer and a person filled with curious complexities, and the more one studies his career the more one observes a fascinating and paradoxical phenomenon.

His first published short stories in the forties were outspoken and bitter works about the predicament of contemporary black Americans. "Homecoming" (*Common Ground*, 1946) ironically portrays the return to his home in the rural South of a young black veteran who has lost a leg defending democracy. His white neighbors view him as just another uppity nigger too big for his britches, and instead of receiving a hero's welcome he is almost lynched. "Health Card" (*Harper's*, May 1944), another early story, won an O. Henry Award. The work relates the humiliation a black soldier and his wife are forced to face in the South during World War II: it is assumed in the camp town where the protagonist is stationed that any black woman seen with a black man is probably a whore needing a "health card."

Around the time World War II ended, Yerby's life as a writer took a totally unpredictable turn. He had written an apparently realistic novel about black life but no publisher was interested in printing it. And so, according to a very cynical article he wrote for *Harper's* in 1959, he set out quite coolly and rationally to become a popular author. He studied those novels that had high sales over a period of years, and derived from them what almost amounts to a formula to ensure popularity. He would create escapist costume novels containing no dominating social problems. He would construct relatively tightly plotted stories about strong sexy men and vivacious sexy women.

Obviously, few writers who attempt to write racy adventurous novels become best sellers. But Yerby succeeded in an unprecedented fashion. Since his first published novel and first smash popular success, *The Foxes of Harrow*, Yerby has written hit after hit, many of which have been made into films. Around the mid-1950's his very high popularity began to decline, but it is still claimed that he has been on the best-seller lists more times since 1900 than any other American novelist, except for Mary Roberts Rinehart. This achievement seems even more remarkable when it is considered that since the 1960's his novels have rarely been reviewed in the major mass-circulation magazines. The audience he has built up apparently needs no stimulation beyond his books themselves.

The few critics who have taken his work seriously point out that he writes something closer to anti-romance than romance. Both his heroes and heroines are more apt to be cunning opportunists than virtuous aristocrats. The fantasy worlds his characters operate in — the Spanish Main, the Holy Land, the reconstruction South — are rather dirty and unglamorous places as he describes them. Moreover, the frequently restated charge that he has turned his back on his race (in *Anger and Beyond*, for example, Saunders Redding claimed that in ignoring his racial heritage Yerby was revealing "pathological overtones" in his fiction) is absolutely false. In many of his most popular novels, such as *Griffin's Way*, or *A Woman Called Fancy*, Yerby deals quite accurately with the treatment of blacks in the South. Yerby now distinguishes between his serious works (such as *Speak Now*) and his entertainments (practically any of his hits) and claims that in the future he is going to concentrate on the serious work. His distinction seems something of an apologetic defense, however, and perhaps an unnecessary one. For several decades he has been the most popular novelist in America addressing the racial theme.

—Jack B. Moore

YONGE, Charlotte (Mary).   English.   Born in Otterbourne, Hampshire, 13 August 1823, and lived there for the rest of her life. Writer from 1837; Editor, 1851–90, and Assistant Editor, 1891–95, *The Monthly Packet*; Editor, *The Monthly Paper of Sunday Teaching*, 1860–75, and *Mothers in Council*, 1890–1900. *Died 24 March 1901.*

PUBLICATIONS

Fiction

Le Château de Melville; ou, Récreations du Cabinet d'Etude.   1838.
Abbey Church; or, Self-Control and Self-Conceit.   1844.
Scenes and Characters; or, Eighteen Months at Beechcroft.   1847; as *Beechcroft*, 1871.
Henrietta's Wish; or, Domineering.   1850.
Kenneth; or, The Rear Guard of the Grand Army.   1850.
Langley School.   1850.
The Two Guardians; or, Home in This World.   1852.
The Heir of Redclyffe.   1853.
The Herb of the Field.   1853.
The Castle Builders; or, The Deferred Confirmation.   1854.
Heartsease; or, The Brother's Wife.   1854.
The Little Duke; or, Richard the Fearless.   1854; as *Richard the Fearless*, 1856.
The History of Sir Thomas Thumb.   1855.
The Lances of Lynwood.   1855.
The Railroad Children.   1855.
Ben Sylvester's Word.   1856.
The Daisy Chain; or, Aspirations: A Family Chronicle.   1856.
Harriet and Her Sister.   1856.
Leonard the Lion-Heart.   1856.
Dynevor Terrace; or, The Clue of Life.   1857.
The Christmas Mummers.   1858.
Friarswood Post Office.   1860.
Hopes and Fears; or, Scenes from the Life of a Spinster.   1860.
The Mice at Play.   1860.
The Strayed Falcon.   1860.
The Pigeon Pie.   1860.
The Stokesley Secret.   1861.
The Young Stepmother; or, A Chronicle of Mistakes.   1861.
Countess Kate.   1862.
Sea Spleenwort and Other Stories.   1862.
Last Heartsease Leaves.   1862 (?).
The Trial: More Links of the Daisy Chain.   1864.
The Wars of Wapsburgh.   1864.
The Clever Woman of the Family.   1865.
The Dove in the Eagle's Nest.   1866.
The Prince and the Page: A Story of the Last Crusade.   1866.
The Danvers Papers: An Invention.   1867.
The Six Cushions.   1867.
The Chaplet of Pearls; or, The White and Black Ribaumont.   1868.
Kaffir Land; or, New Ground.   1868.
The Caged Lion.   1870.
Little Lucy's Wonderful Globe.   1871.

P's and Q's; or, The Question of Putting Upon. 1872.
The Pillars of the House; or, Under Wode, Under Rode. 1873.
Lady Hester; or, Ursula's Narrative. 1874.
My Young Alcides: A Faded Photograph. 1875.
The Three Brides. 1876.
The Disturbing Element; or, Chronicles of the Blue-Bell Society. 1878.
Burnt Out: A Story for Mothers' Meetings. 1879.
Magnus Bonum; or, Mother Carey's Brood. 1879.
Bye-Words: A Collection of Tales New and Old. 1880.
Love and Life: An Old Story in Eighteenth-Century Costume. 1880.
Mary and Norah; or, Queen Katharine's School, with *Nelly and Margaret.* 1880(?).
Cheap Jack. 1881.
Frank's Debt. 1881.
Lads and Lasses of Langley. 1881.
Wolf. 1881.
Given to Hospitality. 1882.
Langley Little Ones: Six Stories. 1882.
Pickle and His Page Boy; or, Unlooked For. 1882.
Sowing and Sewing: A Sexagesima Story. 1882.
Unknown to History: A Story of the Captivity of Mary of Scotland. 1882.
Stray Pearls: Memoirs of Margaret de Ribaumont, Viscountess of Bellaise. 1883.
Langley Adventures. 1884.
The Armourer's 'Prentices. 1884.
Nuttie's Father. 1885.
The Two Sides of the Shield. 1885.
Astray: A Tale of a Country Town, with others. 1886.
Chantry House. 1886.
The Little Rick-Burners. 1886.
A Modern Telemachus. 1886.
Under the Storm; or, Steadfast's Charge. 1887.
Beechcroft at Rockstone. 1888.
Nurse's Memories. 1888.
Our New Mistress; or, Changes at Brookfield Earl. 1888.
The Cunning Woman's Grandson: A Tale of Cheddar a Hundred Years Ago. 1889.
A Reputed Changeling; or, Three Seventh Years Two Centuries Ago. 1889.
The Slaves of Sabinus: Jew and Gentile. 1890.
More Bywords (stories and poems). 1890.
The Constable's Tower; or, The Times of Magna Carta. 1891.
Two Penniless Princesses. 1891.
The Cross Roads; or, A Choice in Life. 1892.
That Stick. 1892.
Grisly Grisell; or, The Laidly Lady of Whitburn: A Tale of the Wars of the Roses. 1893.
Strolling Players: A Harmony of Contrasts, with Christabel Coleridge. 1893.
The Treasures in the Marshes. 1893.
The Cook and the Captive; or, Attalus the Hostage. 1894.
The Rubies of St. Lô. 1894.
The Carbonels. 1895.
The Long Vacation. 1895.
The Release; or, Caroline's French Kindred. 1896.
The Wardship of Steepcombe. 1896.
The Pilgrimage of the Ben Beriah. 1897.
Founded on Paper; or, Uphill and Downhill Between the Two Jubilees. 1897.
The Patriots of Palestine: A Story of the Maccabees. 1898.
Scenes from "Kenneth." 1899.

The Herd Boy and His Hermit. 1899.
The Making of a Missionary; or, Daydreams in Earnest. 1900.
Modern Broods; or, Developments Unlooked For. 1900.

Plays

The Apple of Discord. 1864.
Historical Dramas. 1864.

Verse

Verses on the Gospel for Sundays and Holidays. 1880.

Other

Kings of England: A History for Young Children. 1848.
Landmarks of History. 3 vols., 1852–57.
The Instructive Picture Book; or, Lessons from the Vegetable World. 1857.
The Chosen People: A Compendium of Sacred and Church History for School Children. 1861.
A History of Christian Names. 1863; revised edition, 1884.
A Book of Golden Deeds of All Times and All Lands. 1864.
Cameos from English History. 9 vols., 1868–99.
The Pupils of St. John the Divine. 1868.
A Book of Worthies, Gathered from the Old Histories and Now Written Out Anew. 1869.
Keynotes of the First Lessons for Every Day in the Year. 1869.
Musings over the "Christian Year" and "Lyra Innocentium." 1871.
A Parallel History of France and England. 1871.
Pioneers and Founders; or, Recent Works in the Mission Field. 1871.
Scripture Readings for Schools, with Comments. 5 vols., 1871–79.
Questions on the Prayer-Book [Collects, Epistles, Gospels, Psalms]. 5 vols., 1872–81.
In Memoriam Bishop Patteson. 1872.
Aunt Charlotte's Stories of English [French, Bible, Greek, German, Roman] History for the Little One. 6 vols., 1873–77; as *Young Folks' History*, 6 vols., 1878–80.
Life of John Coleridge Patteson, Missionary Bishop to the Melanesian Islands. 2 vols., 1874.
Hints on the Religious Education of Children of the Wealthier Classes. N.d.
Womankind. 1875.
Eighteen Centuries of Beginnings of Church History. 1876.
The Story of the Christians and the Moors in Spain. 1878.
Short English Grammar for Use in Schools. 1879.
Aunt Charlotte's Evenings at Home with the Poets. 1880.
How to Teach the New Testament. 1881.
Practical Work in Sunday Schools. 1881.
English History Reading Books. 6 vols., 1881–83; as *Westminster Historical Reading Books*, 6 vols., 1891–92.
Talks about the Laws We Live Under; or, At Langley Night-School. 1882.
A Pictorial History of the World's Great Nations. 1882.
Aunt Charlotte's Stories of American History, with J. H. Hastings Weld. 1883.
English Church History. 1883.
Landmarks of Recent History 1770–1883. 1883.

The Daisy Chain Birthday Book, edited by Eadgyth.   1884.
A Key to the Waverley Novels, vol. 1.   1885.
Teachings on the Catechism: For the Little Ones.   1886.
The Victorian Half-Century: A Jubilee Book.   1886.
What Books to Lend and What to Give.   1887.
Hannah More (biography).   1888.
Preparation of Prayer-Book Lessons.   1888.
Conversations on the Prayer Book.   1888.
Deacon's Book of Dates: A Manual of the World's Chief Historical Landmarks and an Outline of Universal History.   1888.
Life of H.R.H. the Prince Consort.   1890.
Seven Heroines of Christendom.   1891.
Simple Stories Relating to English History.   1891.
Twelve Stories from Early English History.   1891.
Twenty Stories and Biographies from 1066 to 1485.   1891.
Old Times at Otterbourne.   1891.
An Old Woman's Outlook in a Hampshire Village.   1892.
The Hanoverian [Tudor, Stuart] Period, with Biographies of Leading Persons.   3 vols., 1892.
Chimes for Mothers: A Reading for Each Week in the Year.   1893.
The Girl's Little Book.   1893.
The Story of Easter.   1894.
John Keble's Parishes: A History of Hursley and Otterbourne.   1898.
Reasons Why I Am a Catholic and Not a Roman Catholic.   1901.

Editor, *Biographies of Good Women.*   2 vols., 1862–65.
Editor, *Readings from Standard Authors.*   1864.
Editor, with E. Sewell, *Historical Selections: A Series of Readings in English and European History.*   2 vols., 1868–70; as *European History,* 2 vols., 1872–73.
Editor, *A Storehouse of Stories.*   2 vols., 1870–72.
Editor, *Beneath the Cross: Readings for Children in Our Lord's Seven Sayings.*   1881.
Editor, *Historical Ballads.*   3 vols., 1882–83.
Editor, *Shakespeare's Plays for Schools, Abridged and Annotated.*   1883.
Editor, *Higher Reading Book for Schools, Colleges and General Use.*   1885.
Editor, *Chips from the Royal Image Being Fragments of the "Eikon Basilike" of Charles I,* by A. E. M. Anderson Morshead.   1887.

Translator, *Marie Thérèse de Lamourous, Foundress of the House of La Miséricorde at Bordeaux,* by Abbé Pouget.   1858.
Translator, *Two Years of School Life,* by Elise de Pressensé.   1869.
Translator, *The Population of an Old Pear Tree; or, Stories of Insect Life,* by E. van Bruyssel.   1870.
Translator, *Life and Adventures of Count Beugnot, Minister of State under Napoleon I,* by Count H. d'Ideville.   1871.
Translator, *Dames of High Estate,* by H. de Witt.   1872.
Translator, *Recollections of a Page at the Court of Louis XVI,* by Felix Count de France d'Hézecques.   1873.
Translator, *Recollections of Colonel de Gonville.*   1875.
Translator, *A Man of Other Days: Recollections of the Marquis Henry Joseph Costa de Beauregard.*   1877.
Translator, *The Youth of Queen Elizabeth, 1533–58,* by L. Wiesener.   2 vols., 1879.
Translator, *Catherine of Aragon, and the Sources of the English Reformation,* by Albert du Boys.   1881.
Translator, *Behind the Hedges; or, The War in the Vendee,* by H. de Witt.   1882.

Translator, *Sparks of Light for Every Day,* by H. de Witt. 1882.

Reading List: *Yonge: Her Life and Letters* by Christabel Coleridge, 1903; *Yonge: The Story of an Uneventful Life* by Georgina Battiscombe, 1943; *Victorian Best-Seller* by Margaret Mare and Alicia C. Percival, 1947; *A Chaplet for Yonge* edited by Georgina Battiscombe and Marghanita Laski, 1965.

*   *   *

The world that Charlotte Yonge describes is one that was small and rarified even in her time; she shows us a Tory squirearchy served by a loyal, dutiful, and unambitious tenantry; an upper middle class of unimpeachable descent, high-principled, highly educated, and High Church. She herself never cared to stray beyond these confines. She once ventured in middle age as far as France, to stay with a family who were as nearly the equivalent of her own family as French Protestants could be. Otherwise her whole life was passed in the Hampshire village near Winchester where she had been born. Here she devoted herself to her parents and to the parish organizations to which her writing, voluminous though it was, came second in her mind.

She disliked any ideas that she suspected might disturb the equilibrium of the old order which she upheld so staunchly. She abhorred, for instance, extreme Protestantism, the Roman church, biblical criticism, women's rights, socialism; she disapproved of the novels of Dickens and George Eliot. Her literary career spanned some 50 years, but she did not develop with them. To the end she clung to outmoded early Victorian proprieties, and wrote from the viewpoint of the dutiful daughter, true to the rules of conduct that her mother and John Keble, who had prepared her for confirmation, had laid down for her.

Within these limitations she succeeded, nevertheless, in creating a wholly credible society. We can walk in the landscapes she describes, and listen to those eager young women and high-minded young men enthusiastically discussing medieval chivalry, the poems of Southey, Schiller, foreign missions, a new project for the parish school, and know that these indeed are the voices of such families as Bishop Moberly's and her own cousinhood. Her gift for characterisation makes the reader overlook the formlessness of the plot which usually – outside the historical fiction, intended for younger readers – takes the form of domestic chronicles, many of whose personalities reappear as minor characters in other sagas. She particularly favoured huge families where the mother is dead; one remembers, for instance, the Mays of *The Daisy Chain* and *The Trial*, and the Underwoods of *The Pillars of the House*. She excelled at presenting young women, though she was never able to follow them very successfully into courtship or marriage, and it was for young, unmarried women that her adult works were specifically written, urging them to dedicate themselves to the welfare of their families (the needs of their parents being paramount). But she has left some shrewdly observed male portraits. Most memorable is the testy, impetuous Dr. May, but there are many more, including a wide range of clerics, bluff country squires, even worthless scapegraces like Arthur Martindale in *Heartsease* (though betting and extravagance are the only vices she can impute to them).

None of her novels was received with greater enthusiasm than *The Heir of Redclyffe* in 1853, which was eagerly read by bishops, undergraduates, guards officers, and royalty. It fitted the early Victorian mood, making virtue, self-sacrifice, and piety seem infinitely romantic. She maintained this ardent spirit in her later works, but. though to the end she had a large and devoted readership, it was among an older generation who, like her, preferred to look back with nostalgia.

—Gillian Avery

ZANGWILL, Israel. English. Born in the East End of London, 21 January 1864. Educated at schools in Plymouth and Bristol; Jews' Free School, Spitalfields, London; University of London, B.A. (honours). Married the writer Edith Ayrton in 1903; two sons and one daughter. Taught at the Jews' Free School, then worked as a journalist; edited the humorous periodical *Ariel*; writer from 1881. President, Jewish Territorial Organisation for the Settlement of Jews Within the British Empire, Jewish Historical Society, and Jewish Drama League. *Died 1 August 1926.*

PUBLICATIONS

Fiction

The Premier and the Painter, with Louis Cowen. 1888.
The Bachelors' Club. 1891.
The Big Bow Mystery. 1892.
Children of the Ghetto. 1892; reprinted in part as *Grandchildren of the Ghetto,* 1914.
The Old Maid's Club. 1892.
Ghetto Tragedies. 1893.
The King of Schnorrers: Grotesques and Fantasies. 1894.
Joseph the Dreamer. 1895.
The Master. 1895.
The Celibates' Club. 1898.
Dreamers of the Ghetto. 1898.
They That Walk in Darkness: Ghetto Tragedies. 1899.
The Mantle of Elijah. 1900.
The Grey Wig: Stories and Novelettes. 1903.
Ghetto Comedies. 1907.
Jinny the Carrier. 1919.

Plays

The Great Demonstration, with Louis Cowen (produced 1892). 1892.
Aladdin at Sea (produced 1893).
The Lady Journalist (produced 1893).
Six Persons (produced 1893). 1899.
Threepenny Bits (produced 1895).
Children of the Ghetto, from his own novel (produced 1899).
The Revolted Daughter (produced 1901).
Merely Mary Ann, from his own novel (produced 1904). 1921.
The Melting Pot (produced 1912). 1909.
The War God (produced 1911). 1911.
The Next Religion. 1912.
Plaster Saints (produced 1914). 1914.
The Moment Before: A Psychical Melodrama (produced 1916).
Too Much Money (produced 1918). 1924.
The Cockpit. 1921.
The Forcing House; or, The Cockpit Continued (produced 1926). 1922.
We Moderns (produced 1922). 1926.
The King of Schnorrers, from his own novel (produced 1925).

Verse

Blind Children.   1903.

Other

Without Prejudice.   1896.
Italian Fantasies.   1910.
The War for the World.   1916.
The Voice of Jerusalem.   1920.
Works.   14 vols., 1925.
Speeches, Articles, and Letters, edited by Maurice Simon.   1937.

Translator, *Selected Religious Poems,* by ben Judah Aben Gabirol Solomon.   1924.

Bibliography: "Zangwill: A Selected Bibliography" by A. Peterson, in *Bulletin of Bibliography 23,* 1961.

Reading List: *Zangwill: A Biography* by Joseph Leftwich, 1957; *Zangwill: A Study* by Maurice Wohlgelernter, 1964; *Zangwill* by Elsie Bonita Adams, 1971.

*   *   *

Israel Zangwill was a Jew in England. As such, he attempted, in great measure successfully, to integrate in his life and works the best of both civilizations, projecting them later to his people and all mankind. This he accomplished because of his versatility, a great deal of industry, and a conceit strong enough to enable him to disregard superiors, equals, and critics, as well as the fancied demands of the public. A child of two worlds, he was able to extend universally the boundaries of both these ideas he loved passionately: the Jewish and the English.

Born to poor immigrants in London's East End, he made a brief attempt at teaching, and then collaborated with a friend in writing one of the shilling books popular at the time. Some short stories and a long essay, "English Judaism," brought him to the attention of the newly organized Jewish Publication Society of America which invited him to produce a "big" Jewish novel. Accepting, Zangwill wrote *Children of the Ghetto,* an instant success which "woke all England to applause; with a bound Zangwill was on the heights."

From those heights flowed a stream of books – all reflecting the polarity within his own mind between the two worlds through which he forever moved: the Jewish and the English. For his proved to be, indeed, the antipodal mind that reveals admiration for apparently contradictory ideas. On the one hand, he wrote works which extol the belief that the ghetto, in which as a writer he seemed most successful, was no dungeon to the Jew as had been pictured by his contemporaries. In fact, Zangwill's dreamers of the ghetto, the flower of the Jewish intelligence, were often able to exchange the narrow life of their ghetto for the unrestricted ways of the outside world. On the other hand, Zangwill published some significant works of literary criticism, non-ghetto fiction, and drama with the declared attempt "to build Jerusalem in England's 'green and pleasant land,' " and, also, the world. For central to Zangwill's aesthetic is the basic concept that it is the duty of the artist *not* to divorce art from life but, rather, in the great war for the world, to use it to benefit mankind. In these works, as well as in his many essays, speeches, and articles, he is anxious not only to preach social humanism but to act as the conscience of mankind. The importance of art, he believed, necessitates that the artist sacrifice himself, a sacrifice which will, however, grant him not only truth but love. These must, he argued, inevitably improve the condition of man and mankind.

If, as Ben Jonson said, "in short circles life may perfect be," Zangwill's circles, marked, paradoxically, by the imaginary inner walls of the ghetto and the unchained world beyond, carried a light that, if not bright, was always illuminating. That light was spread by a dreamer whose soul, because it constantly assumed a dualistic form, was that of a Jewish Englishman.

—Maurice Wohlgelernter

NOTES
ON
ADVISERS
AND
CONTRIBUTORS

ALCOCK, Peter. Senior Lecturer in English, Massey University, Palmerston North, New Zealand; Associate Editor of *World Literature Written in English* and bibliographer for *Journal of Commonwealth Literature.* Member of the Executive Committee, Association for Commonwealth Literature and Language, 1968–77. **Essay:** Edith Searle Grossman.

ALLEN, Walter. Novelist and Literary Critic. Author of six novels (the most recent being *All in a Lifetime,* 1959); several critical works, including *Arnold Bennett,* 1948; *Reading a Novel,* 1949 (revised, 1956); *Joyce Cary,* 1953 (revised, 1971); *The English Novel,* 1954; *Six Great Novelists,* 1955; *The Novel Today,* 1955 (revised, 1966); *George Eliot,* 1964; and *The Modern Novel in Britain and the United States,* 1964; and of travel books, social history, and books for children. Editor of *Writers on Writing,* 1948, and of *The Roaring Queen* by Wyndham Lewis, 1973. Has taught at several universities in Britain, the United States, and Canada, and been an editor of the *New Statesman.* **Essays:** George Eliot; Richard Hughes; Rudyard Kipling; Ring Lardner; Arthur Morrison; Dorothy Richardson; H. G. Wells.

ANDERSON, David D. Professor of American Thought and Language, Michigan State University, East Lansing; Editor of *University College Quarterly* and *Midamerica.* Author of *Louis Bromfield,* 1964; *Critical Studies in American Literature,* 1964; *Sherwood Anderson,* 1967; *Anderson's "Winesburg, Ohio,"* 1967; *Brand Whitlock,* 1968; *Abraham Lincoln,* 1970; *Robert Ingersoll,* 1972; *Woodrow Wilson,* 1975. Editor or Co-Editor of *The Black Experience,* 1969; *The Literary Works of Lincoln,* 1970; *The Dark and Tangled Path,* 1971; *Sunshine and Smoke,* 1971. **Essay:** Louis Bromfield.

ANDERSON, W. E. K. Headmaster, Shrewsbury School, Shropshire. Editor of *The Journal of Sir Walter Scott,* 1972. **Essay:** Sir Walter Scott.

ANGLE, James. Assistant Professor of English, Eastern Michigan University, Ypsilanti. Author of verse and fiction in periodicals, and of an article on Edward Lewis Wallant in *Kansas Quarterly,* Fall 1975. **Essay:** Edward Lewis Wallant.

ASHLEY, Leonard R. N. Professor of English, Brooklyn College, City University of New York. Author of *Colley Cibber,* 1965; *19th-Century British Drama,* 1967; *Authorship and Evidence: A Study of Attribution and the Renaissance Drama,* 1968; *History of the Short Story,* 1968; *George Peele: The Man and His Work,* 1970. Editor of the *Enriched Classics* series, several anthologies of fiction and drama, and a number of facsimile editions. **Essays:** Maurice Baring; Ludwig Bemelmans; G. K. Chesterton; Sir Arthur Quiller-Couch; Henry Wheeler Shaw.

AUSTIN, James C. Professor of English Language and Literature, Southern Illinois University, Edwardsville. Author of *Fields of the Atlantic Monthly,* 1953; *Artemus Ward,* 1964; *Petroleum V. Nasby,* 1965; *Bill Arp,* 1970; *Popular Literature in America,* 1972, and of many articles on American literature, humor, and dialect; also author of the words and lyrics for four musical shows. **Essay:** Petroleum V. Nasby.

AVERY, Gillian. Author of more than 15 books for children (the most recent being *Huck and Her Time Machine,* 1977, and *Mouldy's Orphan,* 1978), and of critical works for adults, including *Mrs. Ewing,* 1961, *Nineteenth-Century Children* (with Angela Bull), 1965, and *Childhood's Pattern,* 1975. Editor of several anthologies for children and of works by Mrs. Ewing, Andrew Lang, Charlotte Yonge, Frances Hodgson Burnett, Mrs. Molesworth, E. V. Lucas, and other writers. **Essays:** George Grossmith; Thomas Hughes; Charlotte Yonge.

BARNES, John. Chairman of the Department of English, La Trobe University, Bundoora, Australia. Author of articles on Peter Cowan, Hal Porter, and Patrick White. **Essays:** Henry Kingsley; Vance Palmer; Randolph Stow.

BATESON, F. W.   Emeritus Fellow and Tutor in English Literature, Corpus Christi College, Oxford. Formerly, Founding-Editor of *Essays in Criticism.* Author of many books, including *English Comic Drama 1700–1750,* 1929; *English Poetry and the English Language,* 1934 (revised, 1973); *English Poetry: A Critical Introduction,* 1950 (revised, 1966); *Wordsworth: A Re-interpretation,* 1954; *A Guide to English Literature,* 1965 (revised, 1976); *Essays in Critical Dissent,* 1972; *The Scholar Critic,* 1972. Editor of *Pope's Epistles to Several Persons,* 1951 (revised, 1961), and *Selected Poems of Blake,* 1957.

BATTESTIN, Martin C.   William R. Kenan, Jr., Professor of English, University of Virginia, Charlottesville. Author of *The Moral Basis of Fielding's Art,* 1959, *The Providence of Wit: Aspects of Form in Augustan Literature and the Arts,* 1974, and a forthcoming biography of Fielding. Editor of the Wesleyan Edition of Fielding's works, and of *Joseph Andrews, Tom Jones,* and *Amelia.* **Essay:** Henry Fielding.

BENKOVITZ, Miriam J.   Professor of English, Skidmore College, Saratoga Springs, New York. Author of *Ronald Firbank: A Bibliography,* 1963 (and supplement), and *Firbank: A Biography,* 1969. Editor of *Edwy and Elgiva,* by Fanny Burney, and *A Passionate Prodigality,* 1975. **Essays:** Ronald Firbank; Frederick Rolfe.

BENNETT, George N.   Professor of English, Vanderbilt University, Nashville, Tennessee. Author of *The Realism of William Dean Howells, 1889–1920,* 1973. **Essay:** William Dean Howells.

BERGONZI, Bernard.   Senior Lecturer in English, University of Warwick, Coventry. Author of *Descartes and the Animals,* 1954; *The Early H. G. Wells,* 1961; *Heroes' Twilight,* 1965; *The Situation of the Novel,* 1970; *T. S. Eliot,* 1971; *Gerard Manley Hopkins,* 1977; *Reading the Thirties,* 1978. Contributor to *The Observer, Times Literary Supplement,* and other periodicals.

BERGONZI, Gabriel.   Free-lance Writer and Lecturer. **Essay:** Ada Leverson.

BIRNEY, Earle.   Free-lance Writer and Lecturer. Formerly, Professor of English at the University of British Columbia, Vancouver. Author of many volumes of verse (*Collected Poems,* 2 vols., 1974), two novels, and a play. Editor of several anthologies of verse and of works by Malcolm Lowry.

BISIGNANO, Dominic J.   Associate Professor of English, Indiana University-Purdue University, Indianapolis. **Essays:** Stella Benson; Hannah Foster; Seba Smith; Sylvia Townsend Warner.

BLACKALL, Jean Frantz.   Professor of English, Cornell University, Ithaca, New York. Author of *Jamesian Ambiguity and The Sacred Fount,* 1966, and of articles on Harold Frederic and Charlotte Brontë in *PMLA, Markham Review, Notes and Queries, Journal of Narrative Technique,* and *Journal of English and Germanic Philology.* **Essay:** Harold Frederic.

BLOOM, Edward A.   Professor of English, Brown University, Providence, Rhode Island; Editor of *Novel: A Forum on Fiction.* Author of *Samuel Johnson in Grub Street,* 1957; *The Order of Poetry* (with C. H. Philbrick and E. M. Blistein), 1961; *Willa Cather's Gift of Sympathy* (with Lillian D. Bloom), 1962; *The Order of Fiction,* 1964; *Joseph Addison's Sociable Animal* (with Lillian D. Bloom), 1971. Editor of *The Letters and Journals of Frances Burney,* vol. 8 (with Lillian D. Bloom), 1978. **Essay:** Fanny Burney.

BLOOM, Lynn Z.   Associate Professor of English, University of New Mexico,

Albuquerque. Author of *Doctor Spock: Biography of a Conservative Radical*, 1972; *The New Assertive Woman* (with K. Coburn and J. Pearlman), 1975; *Strategies for Composition*, 1979; and of articles, reviews, and poetry in periodicals. Editor, with others, of *Bear, Man, and God: Approaches to Faulkner's The Bear*, 1964 (revised, 1971), and *Symposium*, 1969. **Essay:** Dorothy Parker.

BLOTNER, Joseph.   Professor of English, University of Michigan, Ann Arbor. Author of *The Political Novel*, 1955; *The Fiction of J. D. Salinger* (with F. L. Gwynn), 1959; *The Modern American Political Novel, 1900–1960*, 1966; *Faulkner: A Biography*, 2 vols., 1974. Editor of *Faulkner in the University* (with F. L. Gwynn), 1959, and *Faulkner's Library: A Catalogue*, 1964. **Essay:** William Faulkner.

BODE, Walter.   Editor in the Chemistry Department, University of California, Berkeley; Assistant Editor of *San Francisco Theatre Magazine*, and free-lance theatre and film critic. **Essays:** Roark Bradford; S. J. Perelman.

BOGDANOR, Vernon.   Fellow and Tutor in Politics, Brasenose College, Oxford; Review Editor, *Political Studies*. Author of *Devolution*, 1978, and of articles in *The Conservative Opportunity*, 1976, and *Parliamentary Affairs*, *Political Quarterly*, and other periodicals. Editor of *The Age of Affluence, 1951–1964*, 1970, and *Lothair*, by Disraeli, 1974. **Essay:** Benjamin Disraeli.

BOLL, Theophilus E. M.   Emeritus Professor of English, University of Pennsylvania, Philadelphia; Research Consultant, *English Literature in Transition*. Author of *The Works of Edwin Pugh: A Chapter in the Novel of Humble London Life*, 1934, *Miss May Sinclair, Novelist: A Biographical and Critical Introduction*, 1973, and an essay on Stephen Hudson in *Richard, Myrtle and I*, edited by Violet Schiff, 1962. **Essay:** May Sinclair.

BOTTRALL, Margaret.   Biographer and Critic. University Lecturer, Department of Education, and Senior Tutor, Hughes Hall, University of Cambridge, until 1972. Author of *George Herbert*, 1954, and *Every Man a Phoenix: Studies in Seventeenth-Century Autobiography*, 1958. Editor of *Personal Records*, 1961, and *Songs of Innocence and Experience* by Blake, 1970. **Essay:** Izaak Walton.

BOTTRALL, Ronald.   Poet and Travel Writer. Has been a teacher and a member of the British Council or U.N. staffs in Finland, Singapore, Italy, Sweden, Brazil, Greece, and Japan. Author of several books of verse, the most recent being *Poems 1955–1973*, 1974, and of *Rome*, 1968. Co-Editor of works by T. S. Eliot and of verse anthologies. **Essay:** L. H. Myers.

BRATTON, J. S.   Lecturer in English, Bedford College, University of London. Author of *The Victorian Popular Ballad*, 1975. **Essays:** Lewis Carroll; G. A. Henty; George MacDonald; Frederick Marryat; T. H. White.

BRAYBROOKE, Neville.   Writer and Editor; contributor to *The Times*, *T.L.S.*, *Guardian*, *Saturday Review*, and *Sunday Telegraph*. Editor of the quarterly *The Wind and the Rain*, 1941–51. Author of *This Is London*, 1953; *London Green*, 1959; *London*, 1961; the novel *The Idler*, 1961; the play *The Delicate Investigation*, 1969. Editor of *T. S. Eliot: A Symposium*, 1958; *A Partridge in a Pear Tree: A Celebration for Christmas*, 1960; *Pilgrim of the Future: A Teilhard de Chardin Symposium*, 1966; *The Letters of J. R. Ackerley*, 1975. **Essays:** Djuna Barnes; William Plomer; B. Traven.

BRISSENDEN, Alan.   Senior Lecturer in English, University of Adelaide, Australia; Joint General Editor, Tudor and Stuart Text series. Author of *Rolf Boldrewood*, 1972. Editor of *A*

Chaste Maid in Cheapside by Thomas Middleton, 1968, *Shakespeare and Some Others*, 1976, and *The Portable Boldrewood*, 1978. **Essays:** Rolf Boldrewood; Barnaby Rich.

BROER, Lawrence R.   Associate Professor of English, University of South Florida, Tampa. Author of *Hemingway's Spanish Tragedy*, 1973, and of many essays and reviews in journals. Editor of *Counter Currents*, 1973, and *The Great Escape of the '20's*, 1977, and Co-Editor of *The First Time: Initial Sexual Experience in Fiction*, 1974. **Essays:** Nancy Mitford; Gore Vidal.

BROWN, Ashley.   Professor of English, University of South Carolina, Columbia; contributor to *Sewanee Review, Shenandoah, Southern Review, Spectator*, and other periodicals. Editor of *The Achievement of Wallace Stevens* (with R. S. Haller), 1962, *Modes of Literature* (with John L. Kimmey), 1968, and *Satire: An Anthology* (with Kimmey), 1977. **Essay:** Andrew Lytle.

BROWN, Lloyd W.   Member of the Department of Comparative Literature, University of Southern California, Los Angeles. Editor of *The Black Writer in Africa and the Americas*, 1973. **Essay:** Roger Mais.

BROWN, Mary.   Lecturer in English Studies, New University of Ulster, Coleraine. **Essay:** Ivy Compton-Burnett.

BUCCO, Martin.   Professor of English, Colorado State University, Fort Collins. Former Assistant Editor, *Western American Literature*. Author of *The Voluntary Tongue* (verse), 1957, *Frank Waters*, 1969, *Wilbur Daniel Steele*, 1972, and of verse, fiction, and criticism in *Colorado State Review, Occident, Studies in the Novel*, and other periodicals. **Essay:** Wilbur Daniel Steele.

BURCHELL, R. A.   Lecturer in American History and Institutions, University of Manchester. Author of *Westward Expansion*, 1975, "American Immigration in the Nineteenth and Twentieth Centuries" in *History of the United States*, edited by W. P. Adams, 1977, and of articles in *Journal of American Studies, California Historical Quarterly*, and *Southern California Quarterly*. **Essay:** Helen Hunt Jackson.

CAMPBELL, Ian.   Lecturer in English Literature, University of Edinburgh. Author of *Thomas Carlyle*, 1974, and of articles on Scottish literature since 1750. Associate Editor of the Duke-Edinburgh edition of *Carlyle Letters*, and editor of Carlyle's *Reminiscences* and *Selected Essays*. **Essays:** John Buchan; Thomas Carlyle.

CARNALL, Geoffrey.   Reader in English Literature, University of Edinburgh. Author of *Robert Southey and His Age*, 1960, *Robert Southey*, 1964, and *The Mid-Eighteenth Century* (with John Butt), a volume in the Oxford History of English Literature, 1978. **Essay:** Charlotte Lennox.

CARPENTER, Frederic I.   Author of *Emerson and Asia*, 1930; *Emerson Handbook*, 1953; *American Literature and the Dream*, 1955; *Robinson Jeffers*, 1962; *Eugene O'Neill*, 1964; *Laurens van der Post*, 1969. Has taught at the University of Chicago, Harvard University, and the University of California, Berkeley. **Essay:** Conrad Richter.

CAUWELS, Janice M.   Visiting Assistant Professor of English, University of Minnesota, Minneapolis. Author of "Authorial 'Caprice' vs. Editorial 'Calculation': The Text of Elizabeth Inchbald's *Nature and Art*," in *Publication of the Bibliographical Society of America*. **Essay:** Catherine Gore.

CLARK, John R. Professor and Chairman, Department of English, University of South Florida, Tampa. Author of *Form and Frenzy in Swift's "Tale of a Tub,"* 1970, and of many essays, reviews, and translations in periodicals. Editor of *Satire — That Blasted Art* (anthology), 1971, and of the satire issue of *Seventeenth-Century News*, 1975. **Essay:** Tom Brown.

COCKSHUT, A. O. J. G. M. Young Lecturer in Nineteenth-Century Literature, Oxford University. Author of *Anthony Trollope: A Critical Study*, 1955; *Anglican Attitudes*, 1959; *The Imagination of Charles Dickens*, 1961; *The Unbelievers: English Agnostic Thought, 1840–90*, 1964; *The Achievement of Walter Scott*, 1969; *Truth to Life*, 1974. **Essays:** Jane Austen; Elizabeth Bowen; Charles Dickens; George Gissing; Angus Wilson.

COHEN, Hennig. John Welsh Centennial Professor of History and Literature, University of Pennsylvania, Philadelphia. Former Editor of *American Quarterly* and President of the Melville Society. Author of *The South Carolina Gazette*, 1953, and *The Parade of Heroes: Legendary Figures in American Lore* (with Tristram Potter Coffin), 1978. Editor or Co-Editor of *The Battle Pieces*, 1963, *Selected Poems*, 1964, and *White Jacket*, 1967, all by Melville; *Humor of the Old Southwest*, 1964; *Folklore in America*, 1966; *The American Culture*, 1968; *Landmarks in American Writing*, 1969; *Folklore from the Working Folk of America*, 1973; *The Indians and Their Captives*, 1977. **Essay:** Herman Melville.

COHEN, Morton N. Professor of English, City University of New York. Author of *Rider Haggard: His Life and Work*, 1960 (revised, 1968). Editor of *Kipling to Haggard: The Record of a Friendship*, 1965, and *The Letters of Lewis Carroll*, 2 vols., 1978. **Essay:** H. Rider Haggard.

COHN, Ruby. Professor of Comparative Drama, University of California, Davis; Editor of *Modern Drama*, and Associate Editor of *Educational Theatre Journal*. Author of *Samuel Beckett: The Comic Gamut*, 1962; *Currents in Contemporary Drama*, 1969; *Edward Albee*, 1970; *Dialogue in American Drama*, 1971; *Back to Beckett*, 1973; *Modern Shakespeare Offshoots*, 1976. **Essay:** Samuel Beckett.

COLMER, John. Professor of English, University of Adelaide, Australia; General Editor of *Studies in Australian Culture*. Author of *Coleridge: Critic of Society*, 1959; *Approaches to the Novel*, 1967; *E. M. Forster: "A Passage to India,"* 1967; *Forster: The Personal Voice*, 1975; *Patrick White: "Riders in the Chariot,"* 1977; *Coleridge to "Catch-22": Images of Society*, 1978. **Essays:** E. M. Forster; Joseph Heller.

COPLAND, R. A. Former Member of the Department of English, University of Canterbury, Christchurch, New Zealand. **Essays:** James Courage; Robert Paltock; Denton Welch.

CORCORAN, Neil. Member of the Department of English, University of Sheffield. **Essay:** Conrad Aiken.

COX, Martha Heasley. Professor of English and Director of the Steinbeck Research Center, San Jose State University, California. Author of *Maxwell Anderson Bibliography*, 1958; *A Reading Approach to College Writing*, 1959 (and later editions); *Writing: Form, Process, Purpose*, 1962; *Image and Value: An Invitation to Literature*, 1966; *Nelson Algren* (with Wayne Chatterton), 1975; and articles on Algren, Anderson, and John Steinbeck. Editor of *Classic American Short Stories*, 1969; Guest Editor of *Steinbeck Quarterly*, Summer 1971, and *San Jose Studies*, November 1975. **Essay:** Nelson Algren.

CRADDOCK, Patricia. Associate Professor of English, Boston University. Author of

"Gibbon: The Man in His Letters," in *The Familiar Letter in the Eighteenth Century*, edited by H. Anderson and others, 1966; "Gibbon's Revisions of *The Decline and Fall*," in *Studies in Bibliography 21*, 1968; "An Approach to the Distinction of Similar Styles: Two English Historians," in *Style 2*, Spring 1968. Editor of *The English Essays of Gibbon*, 1972, and editor and translator, with N. Murstein, of *Gibbon's Essai sur l'étude de la littérature* (forthcoming). **Essay:** Edward Gibbon.

CRAIG, Patricia. Free-lance writer. Author of *You're a Brick, Angela: A New Look at Girls' Fiction from 1839 to 1975*, 1976, and *Women and Children First: Aspects of War and Literature*, 1978 (both with Mary Cadogan). **Essay:** Rosamond Lehmann.

CURNOW, Allen. Associate Professor of English, University of Auckland, New Zealand. Author of many volumes of verse (*Collected Poems 1933–1973*, 1974), and six plays. Editor of two anthologies of New Zealand verse.

DAHL, Curtis. Samuel Valentine Cole Professor of English, Wheaton College, Norton, Massachusetts. Author of *Robert Montgomery Bird*, 1966, and of articles on William Cullen Bryant, Edward Bulwer-Lytton, and Benjamin Disraeli. **Essay:** Edward Bulwer-Lytton.

DAVIS, Walter, R. Professor of English, University of Notre Dame, Indiana. Author of *A Map of Arcadia*, 1965, and of articles on Surrey, Lodge, Spenser, Drayton, Bacon, and Browne. Editor of *The Works of Thomas Campion*, 1967; *Idea and Act in Elizabethan Fiction*, 1969; *Twentieth-Century Interpretations of "Much Ado about Nothing,"* 1969. **Essays:** Francis Bacon; Sir Philip Sidney.

DePORTE, Michael. Associate Professor of English, University of New Hampshire, Durham. Author of *Nightmares and Hobbyhorses: Swift, Sterne, and Augustan Ideas of Madness*, 1974, a chapter on William Davenant in *The Later Jacobean and Caroline Dramatists* edited by Terence P. Logan and Denzell S. Smith, 1978, and an article on Byron in *Modern Language Quarterly*, 1972. Editor of *Enthusiasmus Triumphatus* by Henry More, 1966, *Discourse on Madness* by Thomas Tryon, 1973, and *Lucida Intervalla* by James Carkesse (forthcoming). **Essay:** Laurence Sterne.

DONNO, Elizabeth Story. Professor of English, Columbia University, New York; Editor of *Renaissance Quarterly*. Editor of *Metamorphosis of Ajax* by Sir John Harington, 1962; *Elizabethan Minor Epics*, 1963; *The Complete Poetry of Andrew Marvell*, 1972; *An Elizabethan in 1582: The Diary of Richard Madox*, 1976; *Marvell: The Critical Heritage*, 1977. **Essay:** Thomas Nashe.

DONOVAN, Dennis G. Professor of English, University of North Carolina, Chapel Hill; Editor of *Renaissance Papers*. Editor of bibliographies of Sir Thomas Browne and Robert Burton, and of checklists on other seventeenth-century writers. **Essay:** Robert Burton.

DOWNIE, J. A. Lecturer in English Literature, University of Leeds. Author of *An Inward Sun: The Novels of Janet Frame*, 1971; *Janet Frame*, 1977; "Political Characterization in *Gulliver's Travels*," in *Yearbook of English Studies 7*, 1977; *Robert Harley and the Press: Propaganda and Public Opinion in the Age of Swift and Defoe* (forthcoming). **Essay:** Thomas Hobbes.

DOYLE, Charles. Professor of English, and Director of the Division of American and Commonwealth Literature, University of Victoria, British Columbia. Author (as Mike Doyle) of several books of poetry, the most recent being *Going On*, 1974, and of critical studies of New Zealand poetry, R. A. K. Mason, and James K. Baxter. Editor of *Recent Poetry in New Zealand*, 1965. **Essay:** Richard Aldington.

DRAPER, R. P. Professor of English, University of Aberdeen, Scotland. Author of two books on Lawrence, and editor of *Lawrence: The Critical Heritage*, 1970, and *Hardy: The Tragic Novels: A Casebook*, 1975. **Essays:** D. H. Lawrence; Doris Lessing; Alan Sillitoe.

DUTTON, Geoffrey. Author of more than 25 books, including verse (most recently *New Poems to 1972*, 1972), novels (most recently *Queen Emma of the South Seas*, 1977), travel books, biographies, art criticism, and critical works, including *Patrick White*, 1961, and *Walt Whitman*, 1961. Editor of anthologies of Australian writing and translator of works by Yevtushenko and Bella Akhmadulina. **Essay:** Patrick White.

DUUS, Louise. Lecturer in American Studies, Douglass College, Rutgers University, New Brunswick, New Jersey. **Essay:** Rebecca Harding Davis.

EASINGWOOD, Peter. Member of the Department of English, University of Dundee, Scotland. **Essay:** John Cowper Powys.

EHRENPREIS, Anne Henry. Private Scholar. Editor of *The Literary Ballad*, 1966; *The Old Manor House*, 1969, and *Emmeline*, 1971, both by Charlotte Smith; *Northanger Abbey* by Jane Austen, 1972. **Essay:** Charlotte Smith.

EICHELBERGER, Clayton L. Professor of American Literature, University of Texas, Arlington; Editor of *American Literary Realism*. Author of *A Guide to Critical Reviews of United States Fiction, 1870–1910*, 2 vols., 1971–73, *William Dean Howells: A Research Bibliography*, 1976, and *Harper's Lost Reviews: The Literary Notes by Laurence Hutton, John Kendrick Bangs, and Others*, 1976. **Essay:** Richard Harding Davis.

EISINGER, Chester E. Professor of English, Purdue University, Lafayette, Indiana. Author of *Fiction of the Forties*, 1963, and of articles in *Proletarian Writers of the Thirties*, 1968, and the *Saturday Review*. Editor of *The 1940's: Profile of a Nation in Crisis*, 1969. **Essay:** Louis Auchincloss.

ELLIOTT, Brian. Reader in Austrialian Literary Studies, University of Adelaide. Author of the novel *Leviathan's Inch*, 1946; *Singing to the Cattle and Other Australian Essays*, 1947; *Marcus Clarke*, 1958; *The Landscape of Australian Poetry*, 1967. Editor of *Coast to Coast: Australian Stories 1948*, 1949, and *Bards in the Wilderness: Australian Poetry to 1920* (with Adrian Mitchell), 1970. **Essays:** Martin Boyd; Xavier Herbert; Steele Rudd.

EVANS, Patrick. Lecturer in English and American Studies, University of Canterbury, Christchurch, New Zealand. **Essays:** Paul Bowles; Janet Frame; Jean Stafford.

FANNING, Charles. Assistant Professor of English, Bridgewater State College, Massachusetts. Author of *Finley Peter Dunne and Mr. Dooley: The Chicago Years*, 1978, and of articles on Dunne, the Chicago Irish, and Robert Lowell. Editor of *Mr. Dooley and the Chicago Irish: An Anthology*, 1976. **Essays:** George Ade; Finley Peter Dunne; James T. Farrell.

FARMER, Philip José. Free-lance writer. Author of more than 20 novels, the most recent being *The Dark Design*, 1977, and of *Tarzan Alive: A Definitive Biography of Lord Greystoke*, 1972. **Essays:** L. Frank Baum; Edgar Rice Burroughs.

FAULKNER, Peter. Member of the Department of English, University of Exeter, Devon. Author of *William Morris and W. B. Yeats*, 1962; *Yeats and the Irish Eighteenth Century*, 1965; *Humanism in the English Novel*, 1976; *Modernism*, 1977. Editor of *William Morris: The Critical Heritage*, 1973, and of works by Morris. **Essays:** R. D. Blackmore; Samuel

Butler; Thomas Holcroft; Walter Savage Landor; Charles Robert Maturin; John Moore; Hannah More; Thomas Love Peacock.

FLETCHER, Ian. Reader in English Literature, University of Reading, Berkshire. Author of plays and verse, and of *Walter Pater*, 1959 (revised, 1970); *A Catalogue of Imagist Poets*, 1966; *Beaumont and Fletcher*, 1967; *Meredith Now*, 1971; *Swinburne*, 1972. Editor of anthologies of verse and drama, and of works by Lionel Johnson, Victor Plarr, and John Gray. **Essays:** Sir Max Beerbohm; Fitz-James O'Brien; Walter Pater; Edgar Saltus.

FLORA, Joseph M. Professor of English, University of North Carolina, Chapel Hill. Author of *Vardis Fisher*, 1965, *William Ernest Henley*, 1974, and *Frederick Manfred*, 1974. Editor of *The Cream of the Jest* by James Branch Cabell, 1975, and *A Biographical Guide to Southern Literature* (with R. A. Bain and Louis D. Rubin, Jr.), 1978. **Essays:** James Branch Cabell; Vardis Fisher; Zane Grey; Owen Wister.

FOLTINEK, Herbert. Professor of English and American Literature, University of Vienna. Author of *Vorstufen zum Viktorianischen Realismus*, 1968, *Fieldings Tom Jones und das österreichische Drama*, 1976, and articles in periodicals. Editor of *Arthur Schnitzler: Grosse Szene*, 1959, and *Marriage* by Susan Ferrier, 1971. **Essays:** Susan Ferrier, Theodore Hook.

FOSTER, Edward Halsey. Associate Professor and Director of the American Studies Program, Stevens Institute of Technology, Hoboken, New Jersey. Author of *Catharine Maria Sedgwick*, 1974; *The Civilized Wilderness*, 1975; *Josiah Gregg and Lewis Hector Garrard*, 1977; *Susan and Anna Warner*, 1978; and of articles on American literature and American studies. Editor of *Hoboken: A Collection of Essays* (with Geoffrey W. Clark), 1976. **Essays:** Richard Henry Dana, Jr.; Donald Grant Mitchell; Catharine Maria Sedgwick; Kurt Vonnegut, Jr.; Nathaniel Parker Willis.

FRASER, G. S. Reader in Modern English Literature, University of Leicester. Author several books of verse, the most recent being *Conditions*, 1969; travel books; critical studies of Yeats, Dylan Thomas, Pound, Durrell, and Pope; and of *The Modern Writer and His World*, 1953, *Vision and Rhetoric*, 1959, and *Metre, Rhythm, and Free Verse*, 1970. Editor of works by Keith Douglas and Robert Burns, and of verse anthologies. **Essays:** E. F. Benson; George du Maurier; Lawrence Durrell; Rose Macaulay; Carson McCullers; Katherine Anne Porter; Mary Roberts Rinehart; George Santayana; Edgar Wallace; Edmund Wilson; Virginia Woolf.

FRENCH, R. B. D. Former Senior Lecturer in English Literature, Trinity College, Dublin; correspondent for *The Times*, and contributor to other newspapers and periodicals. Author of *P. G. Wodehouse*, 1967, and of screenplays and revues. **Essay:** P. G. Wodehouse.

FRENCH, Warren. Professor of English and Director of the Center for American Studies, Indiana University-Purdue University, Indianapolis; Member of the Editorial Board, *American Literature* and *Twentieth-Century Literature*; series editor for Twayne publishers. Author of *John Steinbeck*, 1961; *Frank Norris*, 1962; *J. D. Salinger*, 1963; *A Companion to "The Grapes of Wrath,"* 1963; *The Social Novel at the End of an Era*, 1966; and a series on American fiction, poetry, and drama, *The Thirties*, 1967, *The Forties*, 1968, *The Fifties*, 1971, and *The Twenties*, 1975. **Essays:** Timothy Shay Arthur; Joseph Holt Ingraham; H. P. Lovecraft; Edgar Mittelholzer; J. D. Salinger; Khushwant Singh; John Steinbeck; Thornton Wilder.

GERBER, John C. Chairman of the Department of English, State University of New York, Albany; Member of the Editorial Board, *Resources for American Literary Study*. Formerly

Chairman of the Department of English, University of Iowa. Author of *Factual Prose* (with Walter Blair), 1945, *Literature*, 1948, *Writers Resource Book*, 1953, and other works on writing and speaking. Editor of *Twentieth-Century Interpretations of "The Scarlet Letter,"* 1968, and *Studies in Huckleberry Finn*, 1971; General Editor of the Iowa-California edition of the works of Mark Twain. **Essays:** Ralph Waldo Emerson; Mark Twain.

GÉRIN, Winifred. Biographer and Critic. Author of *Anne Brontë*, 1959; *Branwell Brontë*, 1961; *Charlotte Brontë*, 1967; *Horatia Nelson*, 1970; *Emily Brontë*, 1971; *The Brontës*, 2 vols., 1973; *Elizabeth Gaskell: A Biography*, 1976. Editor of *Five Novelettes* by Charlotte Brontë, 1971. **Essays:** Anne Brontë; Charlotte Brontë; Emily Brontë.

GILL, Roma. Member of the Department of English, University of Sheffield, Yorkshire. Editor of *The Plays of Christopher Marlowe*, 1971, *William Empson: The Man and His Work*, 1974, and of works by Middleton and Tourneur. **Essay:** Thomas Lodge.

GITENSTEIN, Barbara. Assistant Professor of English, Central Missouri State University, Warrensburg. Author of articles on Nathaniel Hawthorne and Isaac Bashevis Singer in *The Comparatist* and *Yiddish*. **Essays:** Saul Bellow; Abraham Cahan; Bernard Malamud; Isaac Bashevis Singer.

GLASRUD, Clarence A. Professor of English Emeritus, Moorhead State University, Minnesota; Advisory Editor, *Studies in American Fiction*; Member of the Board of Publications, Norwegian-American Historical Association. Author of *Hjalmar Hjorth Boyesen: A Biographical and Critical Study*, 1963. Editor of *The Age of Anxiety*, 1960. **Essays:** H. H. Boyesen; F. Marion Crawford; Mazo de la Roche; Oliver Wendell Holmes; Wright Morris; John O'Hara; J. F. Powers; O. E. Rølvaag; Ruth Suckow; Charles Dudley Warner; Glenway Wescott.

GORDON, Ian A. Professor of English, University of Wellington, 1936–74. Has taught at the University of Leeds and the University of Edinburgh. Author of *John Skelton*, 1943; *The Teaching of English*, 1947; *Katherine Mansfield*, 1954; *The Movement of English Prose*, 1966, *John Galt*, 1972. Editor of *English Prose Technique*, 1948, and of works by William Shenstone, John Galt, and Katherine Mansfield. **Essays:** John Galt; Robert Greene; John Lyly; Katherine Mansfield.

GORDON, Lois. Professor of English and Comparative Literature, Fairleigh Dickinson University, Teaneck, New Jersey. Author of *Stratagems to Uncover Nakedness: The Dramas of Harold Pinter*, 1969, and of articles on Richard Eberhart, Randall Jarrell, Faulkner, T. S. Eliot, and Philip Roth. **Essay:** James Purdy.

GREEN, Dorothy. Member of the Faculty, Humanities Research Centre, Australian National University, Canberra. Author of books of verse, including *The Dolphin*, 1967, and of articles on Australian literature. **Essays:** Henry Handel Richardson; Christina Stead.

GREEN, Roger Lancelyn. Author of more than 50 books including fiction and verse for children and adults, retellings of folk and fairy tales, and critical studies of Andrew Lang, A. E. W. Mason, Lewis Carroll, J. M. Barrie, Mrs. Molesworth, C. S. Lewis, and Rudyard Kipling; also editor of works by these authors and others, and translator of plays by Sophocles. **Essays:** Arthur Conan Doyle; Kenneth Grahame; A. E. W. Mason.

GREENLESS, Ian. Director of the British Institute, Florence. Author of *Norman Douglas*, 1957. **Essays:** Norman Douglas; Ouida.

GRIFFIN, Ernest. Professor of English, York University, Downsview, Ontario; Co-Editor of *Modernist Studies*. Author of *Manual of English Prose Composition*, 1958; *The Dramatic Chorus in English Literary Theory and Practice*, 1959; *Bibliography of Literature and Religion*, 1967; *John Middleton Murry*, 1969. Editor of *Eugene O'Neill: A Collection of Criticism*, 1976. **Essay**: Rex Warner.

GURR, Andrew. Professor of English Language and Literature, University of Reading, Berkshire. Author of *The Shakespearean Stage*, 1970. Editor of several plays by Beaumont and Fletcher. **Essay**: Amos Tutuola.

HALLORAN, William F. Dean of the College of Letters and Science, University of Wisconsin, Milwaukee. **Essay**: William Sharp.

HART, Clive. Professor of Literature, University of Essex, Colchester; Editor of *A Wake Newslitter* since 1962. Author of *Structure and Motif in Finnegans Wake*, 1962, *Joyce's Ulysses*, 1968, and *A Topographical Guide to Joyce's Ulysses* (with Leo Knuth), 1975. Editor of *Joyce's Dubliners: Critical Essays*, 1969. **Essays**: Henry Green; James Joyce.

HATTON, Gwynneth. Teacher and free-lance editor. **Essay**: William De Morgan.

HEIM, William J. Associate Professor and Associate Chairperson of the Department of English, University of South Florida, Tampa; Assistant to the Editor, *Florida English Journal*. Author of "More Gold in Them Hills," in *Freshman English News*, Fall 1973, and "Letters from Young Dreiser," in *American Literary Realism*, 1975. **Essays**: C. S. Forester; Upton Sinclair.

HICKS, Jack. Assistant Professor of English, University of California, Davis. Fulbright-Hays Lecturer, University of Paris XII, 1977–78; past editor of *Carolina Quarterly* and *California Quarterly*. Author of *Cutting Edges: Young American Fiction for the 1970's*, 1973. **Essays**: Donald Barthelme; William S. Burroughs; Jack Kerouac; William Styron.

HIGGINS, William. Member of the Department of English, Western Carolina University, Cullowhee, North Carolina. **Essays**: Winston Churchill; Robert Herrick; Joseph Kirkland; David Graham Phillips.

HILSON, J. C. Lecturer in English, University of Leicester. Editor of *Augustan Worlds* (with M. M. B. Jones and J. R. Watson), 1978, and *An Essay on Historial Composition*, by James Moor, 1978. Author of articles on Hume, Richardson, Smollett, and Conrad. **Essays**: Roger Boyle, Earl of Orrery; John Cleland; Graham Greene, Tobias Smollett.

HITCHCOCK, Bert. Associate Professor and Head of the Department of English, Auburn University, Alabama; member of the bibliography committee, Society for the Study of Southern Literature. Author of "Whitman: The Pedagogue as Poet," in *Walt Whitman Review*, 1974. **Essay**: S. Weir Mitchell.

HOEFER, Jacqueline. Free-lance Writer. Author of essays on Beckett and other modern writers. **Essay**: Kay Boyle.

HOFFMAN, Daniel. Professor of English, University of Pennsylvania, Philadelphia. Author of several books of verse, the most recent being *Able Was I Ere I Saw Elba*, 1977, and of critical works including *The Poetry of Stephen Crane*, 1957, *Form and Fable in American Fiction*, 1961, *Poe Poe Poe Poe Poe Poe Poe*, 1972, and *Barbarous Knowledge: Myth in the Poetry of Yeats, Graves, and Muir*, 1973. Editor of anthologies and of works by Crane and Robert Frost. **Essays**: Stephen Crane; Robert Graves; Washington Irving; Edgar Allan Poe.

HOKENSON, Jan. Lecturer in Comparative Literature, University of California, Davis. Author of articles on Beckett, Céline, and Proust, in *James Joyce Quarterly, L'Esprit Créateur, Far-Western Forum,* and *Samuel Beckett: An Anthology of Criticism,* edited by Ruby Cohn, 1975. **Essays:** Ross Lockridge; Norman Mailer; Willard Motley; Robert Tressell.

HOLMAN, C. Hugh. Kenan Professor of English, Chairman of the Division of Humanities, and Special Assistant to the Chancellor, University of North Carolina, Chapel Hill; Editor of *Southern Literary Journal.* Author or co-author of several books, including five detective novels; *The Development of American Criticism,* 1955; *The Southerner as American,* 1960; *Thomas Wolfe,* 1960; *Seven Modern American Novelists,* 1964; *The American Novel Through Henry James: A Bibliography,* 1966; *Three Modes of Modern Southern Fiction,* 1966; *Roots of Southern Writing,* 1972; *The Loneliness at the Core,* 1975. Editor of works by Wolfe, William Gilmore Simms, and others. **Essays:** Ellen Glasgow; Sinclair Lewis; John P. Marquand; Flannery O'Connor; Robert Penn Warren.

HUDSON, Derek. Free-lance writer and editor. Author of books on Winthrop Mackworth Praed, Thomas Barnes, Norman O'Neill, Charles Keene, Martin Tupper, James Pryde, Lewis Carroll, Joshua Reynolds, Arthur Rackham, and others, and on journalism and topography. Editor of anthologies and of the diary of Henry Crabb Robinson. **Essay:** L. A. G. Strong.

HYDE, William J. Professor of English, University of Wisconsin, La Crosse. Author of articles on George Eliot, Hardy, Richard Jefferies, and Sabine Baring-Gould, in *PMLA, Victorian Studies, Victorian Newsletter,* and other periodicals. **Essays:** Sabine Baring-Gould; Richard Jefferies.

INGE, M. Thomas. Professor and Chairman of the Department of English, Virginia Commonwealth University, Richmond; Founding Editor of *Resources for American Literary Study* and *American Humor.* Author of *Donald Davidson: An Essay and a Bibliography,* 1965, and *Davidson,* 1971 (both with T. D. Young). Editor of works by George Washington Harris and William Faulkner, and of *Agrarianism in American Literature,* 1969; *The Black Experience,* 1969; *Studies in Light in August,* 1971; *Ellen Glasgow: Centennial Essays,* 1975. **Essays:** F. Scott Fitzgerald; George Washington Harris.

IVY, Randolph. Director of the Randolph Macon Woman's College Program at Reading, England. **Essays:** Mary Elizabeth Braddon; Wilkie Collins.

JAMES, Louis. Senior Lecturer in English and American Literature, University of Kent, Canterbury. Author of *The Islands in Between,* 1968, and *Fiction for the Working Class Man 1830–1850,* 1974.

JEFFARES, A. Norman. Professor of English Studies, University of Stirling, Scotland; Editor of *Ariel: A Review of International English Literature,* and General Editor of the Writers and Critics series and the New Oxford English series. Past Editor of *A Review of English Studies.* Author of *Yeats: Man and Poet,* 1949; *Seven Centuries of Poetry,* 1956; *A Commentary on the Collected Poems* (1958) and *Collected Plays* (1975) *of Yeats.* Editor of *Restoration Comedy,* 1974, and *Yeats: The Critical Heritage,* 1977. **Essays:** Joyce Cary; Charles Lever.

JELINEK, Estelle C. Instructor in English, San Francisco State University. Author of "Teaching Women's Autobiographies," in *College English,* September 1976, and "Anaïs Nin: A Critical Evaluation," in *Feminist Criticism: Essays on Theory, Poetry and Prose* edited by Karen Olson and Cheryl L. Brown, 1978. **Essay:** Anaïs Nin.

JERNIGAN, Jay. Professor of English, Eastern Michigan University, Ypsilanti; Associate Editor of *The Journal of Narrative Technique*. Author of *Henry Demarest Lloyd*, 1976, and of articles on George Moore and Yeats in *Michigan Academician*, *Bulletin of the New York Public Library*, and *Kansas Quarterly*. **Essay:** George Moore.

JONES, Lawrence. Associate Professor of English, University of Otago, Dunedin, New Zealand. Author of articles on Maurice Shadbolt and Thomas Hardy in *Landfall*, *Studies in the Novel*, *Journal of English Literary History*, and other periodicals, and of the introduction to *Roads from Home* by Dan Davin, 1976. **Essays:** Dan Davin; Maurice Duggan, Maurice Shadbolt.

JOSEPH, M. K. Professor of English, University of Auckland, New Zealand. Author of books of verse, most recently *Inscription on a Paper Dart*, 1974; novels, most recently *A Soldier's Tale*, 1976; and of *Byron the Poet*, 1964. Editor of *Frankenstein* by Mary Shelley, 1969. **Essay:** Mary Shelley.

JOYNER, Nancy C. Member of the Department of English, Western Carolina University, Cullowhee, North Carolina. **Essays:** Ngaio Marsh; Susanna Rowson.

KALLICH, Martin. Professor of English, Northern Illinois University, De Kalb. Author of *The Psychological Milieu of Lytton Strachey*, 1961; *The American Revolution Through British Eyes* (with others), 1962; *Heav'n's First Law: Rhetoric and Order in Pope's Essay on Man*, 1967; *Oedipus: Myth and Drama* (with others), 1968; *The Other End of the Egg: Religious Satire in Gulliver's Travels*, 1970; *The Association of Ideas and Critical Theory in 18th-Century England*, 1970; *Horace Walpole*, 1971; *The Book of the Sonnet* (with others), 1972. **Essays:** Edmund Burke; Horace Walpole.

KELLNER, Bruce. Associate Professor of English, Millersville State College, Pennsylvania. Author of *Carl Van Vechten and the Irreverent Decades*, 1968; *The Wormwood Poems of Thomas Kinsella*, 1972; *The Poet as Translator*, 1973; *Alfred Kazin's Exquisites: An Excavation*, 1975. Editor of *Selected Writings of Van Vechten about Negro Arts and Letters*, 1978. **Essays:** Hortense Calisher; Henry Blake Fuller; Joseph Hergesheimer; Carl Van Vechten.

KELLY, Gary. Member of the Department of English, University of Alberta, Edmonton. Author of *The English Jacobin Novel 1780–1805*, 1976. Editor of *Mary, and The Wrongs of Women* by Mary Wollstonecraft, 1976. **Essays:** Robert Bage; William Godwin; Elizabeth Inchbald; Amelia Opie; Ann Radcliffe.

KELSALL, Malcolm. Professor of English, University College, Cardiff; Advisory Editor of *Byron Journal*. Editor of *The Adventures of David Simple* by Sarah Fielding, 1969, *Venice Preserved* by Thomas Otway, 1969 and *Love for Love* by William Congreve, 1970. **Essays:** Joseph Addison; Sarah Fielding.

KEMP, Peter. Lecturer in English and American Literature, Middlesex Polytechnic, London. Author of *Muriel Spark*, 1974. **Essays:** William Golding; Muriel Spark.

KENDLE, Burton. Associate Professor of English, Roosevelt University, Chicago. Author of articles on D. H. Lawrence, John Cheever, and Chekhov. **Essay:** Thomas Deloney.

KER, I. T. Former Lecturer in English, York University. Editor of *The Idea of a University* by Newman, 1976, and of *Letters and Diaries of Newman*, 10 vols. (forthcoming). **Essay:** John Henry Newman.

KIERNAN, Brian. Senior Lecturer in English, University of Sydney. Author of *Images of Society and Nature* (on the Australian Novel), 1971; *Criticism*, 1974; "Patrick White," in *The Literature of Australia*, edited by Geoffrey Dutton, 1976; *Considerations: New Essays on Slessor, White, Stewart*, 1977. Editor of *The Portable Henry Lawson*, 1976, and *The Most Beautiful Lies* (anthology), 1978. **Essays:** Joseph Furphy; Henry Lawson.

KING, Kimball. Member of the Department of English, University of North Carolina, Chapel Hill. **Essays:** George Washington Cable; Augustus Baldwin Longstreet; Thomas Nelson Page.

KINNAMON, Keneth. Professor and Associate Head of the English Department, University of Illinois, Champaign-Urbana. Author of *The Emergence of Richard Wright*, 1972, and of articles on Wright. Editor of *Black Writers on America: A Comprehensive Anthology* (with Richard K. Barksdale), 1972, and of *James Baldwin: A Collection of Critical Essays*, 1974. **Essays:** James Baldwin; Ralph Ellison.

KULSHRESTHA, Chirantan. Reader in English, University of Hyderabad, India. Author of *The Saul Bellow Estate*, 1976; *Bellow: The Problem of Affirmation*, 1978; chapters in *Considerations*, edited by Meenakshi Mukherjee, 1977, and *Through the Eyes of the World: International Essays in American Literature*, edited by Bruce A. Lohof, 1978; and articles in *Chicago Review, American Review, Quest, Indian Literature*, and other periodicals. Editor of *Not by Politics Alone!* (with V. V. John), 1978. **Essays:** Michael Gold; DuBose Heyward; Albion W. Tourgée.

LEARY, Lewis. Kenan Professor Emeritus of English, University of North Carolina, Chapel Hill. Author of *Idiomatic Mistakes in English*, 1932; *That Rascal Freneau: A Study in Literary Failure*, 1941; *The Literary Career of Nathaniel Tucker*, 1951; *Mark Twain*, 1960; *Twain's Letters to Mary*, 1961; *John Greenleaf Whittier*, 1962; *Washington Irving*, 1963; *Norman Douglas*, 1967; *Southern Excursions*, 1971; *Faulkner of Yoknapatawpha County*, 1973; *Soundings: Some Early American Writers*, 1975; *American Literature: A Study and Research Guide*, 1976. Editor of works by Freneau and Twain, and several collections of essays. **Essay:** Henry David Thoreau.

LEWIS, Margaret B. Part-time teacher at the University of Durham and the Open University. **Essay:** Iris Murdoch.

LINDSAY, Maurice. Director of the Scottish Civic Trust, Glasgow, and Managing Editor of *The Scottish Review*. Author of several books of verse, the most recent being *Walking Without an Overcoat*, 1977; plays; travel and historical works; and critical studies including *Robert Burns: The Man, His Work, The Legend*, 1954 (revised, 1968), *The Burns Encyclopedia*, 1959 (revised, 1970), and *A History of Scottish Literature*, 1977. Editor of the Saltire Modern Poets series, several anthologies of Scottish writing, and works by Sir Alexander Gray, Sir David Lyndsay, Marion Angus, and John Davidson. **Essays:** Thomas De Quincey; R. B. Cunninghame Graham; Neil M. Gunn; Robert Louis Stevenson.

LODGE, David. Reader in English, University of Birmingham. Author of five novels (the most recent being *Changing Places*, 1975), *Language of Fiction*, 1966, *The Novelist at the Crossroads*, 1971, and studies of Graham Greene and Evelyn Waugh. Editor of novels by Jane Austen, George Eliot, Hardy, and *Twentieth Century Literary Criticism: A Reader*, 1972.

LOHOF, Bruce A. Associate Professor and Chairman of the Department of History, University of Miami; Joint Editor of the *Indian Journal of American Studies*, and member of the editorial board of *Journal of Popular Culture*. Former Senior Fulbright-Hays Scholar and

Director of the American Studies Research Centre, Hyderabad, India. Author of articles for *Social Studies Bulletin, Industrial Archeology, Centennial Review*, and other periodicals, and of papers for the American Studies Association and the Popular Culture Association. **Essays:** James Agee; Horatio Alger; Margaret Deland; Edward Eggleston; Zona Gale; H. L. Mencken.

LONGEST, George C. Associate Professor and Assistant to the Chairman of the Department of English, Virginia Commonwealth University, Richmond. Author of *Three Virginia Writers: Mary Johnston, Thomas Nelson Page, and Amélie Rives Troubetzkoy*, 1978, and of many articles and reviews **Essays:** James Lane Allen; Joseph G. Baldwin; Erskine Caldwell; Truman Capote; Bret Harte; Johnson Jones Hooper.

LUCAS, John. Professor of English and Drama, Loughborough University, Leicestershire; Advisory Editor of *Victorian Studies, Literature and History*, and *Journal of European Studies*. Author of *Tradition and Tolerance in 19th-Century Fiction*, 1966; *The Melancholy Man: A Study of Dickens*, 1970; *Arnold Bennett*, 1975; *Egilssaga: The Poems*, 1975; *The Literature of Change*, 1977; *The 1930's: Challenge to Orthodoxy*, 1978. Editor of *Literature and Politics in the 19th Century*, 1971, and of works by George Crabbe and Jane Austen. **Essays:** Arnold Bennett; Sir Walter Besant; Marie Corelli; Paul Goodman; Charles Kingsley; William Hurrell Mallock; V. S. Pritchett; Damon Runyon.

LUDINGTON, Townsend. Associate Professor of English, and Director of the Curriculum in Peace, War, and Defense, University of North Carolina, Chapel Hill. Editor of *The Fourteenth Chronicle: Letters and Diaries of John Dos Passos*, 1973. **Essays:** John Dos Passos; Jack London.

MACK, Douglas S. Assistant Librarian, University of Stirling Library, Scotland; Editor of *The Bibliotheck*. **Essay:** James Hogg.

MacLAINE, Brent. Graduate Student in the Department of English, University of British Columbia, Vancouver. **Essay:** Vladimir Nabokov.

MACLEOD, Norman. Lecturer in English, University of Edinburgh. Author of "This Familiar Repressive Series: Aspects of Style in the Novels of Kingsley Amis," 1971. **Essay:** Kingsley Amis.

MacSHANE, Frank. Professor and Chairman of the Writing Division, School of the Arts, Columbia University, New York; Co-Editor of *Translation*. Author of *Many Golden Ages*, 1963; *The Life and Work of Ford Madox Ford*, 1965; *The Life of Raymond Chandler*, 1976. Editor of works by Ford Madox Ford and translator of several books by Miguel Serrano and works by Jorge Luis Borges. **Essays:** Raymond Chandler; Edward Dahlberg; Ford Madox Ford.

MADDEN, David. Writer-in-Residence, Louisiana State University, Baton Rouge. Author of novels (the most recent being *Bijou*, 1974), short stories, plays, and critical works, including *Wright Morris*, 1964; *The Poetic Image in Six Genres*, 1969; *James M. Cain*, 1970; *Harlequin's Stick, Charlie's Cane*, 1975. Editor of works by Nathanael West and James Agee, and of several collections and anthologies. **Essay:** James M. Cain.

MAES-JELINEK, Hena. Chargé de Cours, University of Liège, Belgium. Author of *Criticism of Society in the English Novel Between the Wars*, 1970, *The Naked Design*, 1976, and articles on Peter Abrahams, V. S. Naipaul, Patrick White, and Wilson Harris. Editor of *Commonwealth Literature and the Modern World*, 1975. **Essay:** Wilson Harris.

MAHON, Derek. Writer-in-Residence, New University of Ulster, Coleraine. Author of seven books of verse, including *Night-Crossing*, 1968, *Lives*, 1972, and *The Snow Party*, 1975. Editor of *Modern Irish Poetry*, 1972. **Essay:** Brian Moore.

MARRS, Suzanne. Assistant Professor of English, State University of New York, Oswego. **Essays:** Thomas Chandler Haliburton; Thomas Bangs Thorpe.

McCORMACK, W. J. Member of the Faculty, School of English, University of Leeds. Editor of *A Festschrift for Francis Stuart on His Seventieth Birthday*, 1972. **Essays:** Maria Edgeworth; Sheridan Le Fanu; Samuel Lover; Bram Stoker.

McCRACKEN, David. Associate Professor of English, University of Washington, Seattle. Author of articles on Samuel Johnson, William Godwin, Edmund Burke, and others, in *Modern Philology*, *Philological Quarterly*, *Yearbook of English Studies*, *Western Speech Communications*, and other periodicals. Editor of *Caleb Williams* by William Godwin, 1970. **Essays:** William Beckford; Matthew Gregory Lewis.

McGLYNN, Paul D. Member of the Department of English, Eastern Michigan University, Ypsilanti. **Essay:** Henry Mackenzie.

McNAUGHTON, Howard. Senior Lecturer in English, University of Canterbury, Christchurch, New Zealand; Theatre Critic, *The Press* since 1968; Advisory Editor, *Act* since 1976. Author of *New Zealand Drama: A Bibliographical Guide*, 1974, and *Bruce Mason*, 1976. Editor of *Contemporary New Zealand Plays*, 1976. **Essay:** Jane Mander.

MEDCALF, Stephen. Member of the Faculty, School of European Studies, University of Sussex, Brighton. Author of articles on G. K. Chesterton, P. G. Wodehouse, William Golding, and other writers. Editor of *The Vanity of Dogmatizing: The Three Versions* by Joseph Glanvill, 1970. **Essays:** M. R. James; Jerome K. Jerome; C. S. Lewis; J. R. R. Tolkien; Charles Williams.

MOE, Christian H. Professor of Theatre, Southern Illinois University, Carbondale; Member of the Advisory Board, Institute of Outdoor Drama; Bibliographer, American Theatre Association. Author of *Creating Historical Drama* (with George McCalmon), 1965, an essay on D. H. Lawrence as playwright, and of several plays for children. **Essay:** Marjorie Kinnan Rawlings.

MOORE, Jack B. Professor of English, University of South Florida, Tampa. Author of *The Literature of Early America*, 1968; *The Literature of the American Renaissance*, 1969; *Guide to "Idylls of the King,"* 1969; *Maxwell Bodenheim*, 1970; *The Literature of the American Realistic Period*, 1971; *Guide to "Last of the Mohicans,"* 1971. **Essays:** Maxwell Bodenheim; Ignatius Donnelly; Frank Yerby.

MOORE, Rayburn S. Professor of English and Chairman, Division of Language and Literature, University of Georgia, Athens; Member of the Editorial Board, *Georgia Review*. Author of *Constance Fenimore Woolson*, 1963, *Paul Hamilton Hayne*, 1972, and many articles and reviews. Editor of *The Major and Selected Short Stories of Woolson*, 1967. **Essays:** John Esten Cooke; William Gilmore Simms; Constance Fenimore Woolson.

MORGAN, Margery. Reader in English, University of Lancaster. Author of *A Drama of Political Man: A Study in the Plays of Harley Granville-Barker*, 1961, and *The Shavian Playground: An Exploration of the Art of G. B. Shaw*, 1972. Editor of *You Never Can Tell* by Shaw, 1967, and *The Madras House* by Granville-Barker, 1977. **Essay:** David Storey.

MORPURGO, J. E.   Professor of American Literature, University of Leeds. Author and editor of many books, including the *Pelican History of the United States*, 1955 (third edition, 1970), and volumes on Cooper, Lamb, Trelawny, Barnes Wallis, and on Venice, Athens, and rugby football. **Essays:** Robertson Davies; Charles Lamb; Hugh MacLennan.

MORSBERGER, Katharine M.   Feature Writer, Pitzer College, Claremont, California. Author of articles on Nathaniel Hawthorne, Lew Wallace, and John Steinbeck. **Essay** (with Robert E. Morsberger): Lew Wallace.

MORSBERGER, Robert E.   Professor and Chairman of the Department of English, California State Polytechnic University, Pomona. Author of *James Thurber*, 1964; *Commonsense Grammar and Style*, 1965; *Swordplay and the Elizabethan and Jacobean Stage*, 1974; and of articles on Lew Wallace. Editor of *Viva Zapata!* by John Steinbeck, 1975. **Essay** (with Katharine M. Morsberger): Lew Wallace.

MUIRHEAD, John.   Lecturer in English, Massey University, Palmerston North, New Zealand. **Essay:** Roderick Finlayson.

MUNRO, John M.   Professor of English, American University of Beirut, Lebanon. Author of *English Poetry in Transition*, 1968; *Arthur Symons*, 1969; *Decadent Poetry in the 1890's*, 1970; *The Royal Aquarium: Failure of a Victorian Compromise*, 1971; *James Elroy Flecker*, 1976; *A Mutual Concern*, 1977; and other books. Editor of *Selected Poems of Theo. Marzials*, 1973. **Essay:** Anthony Hope.

NADEL, I. B.   Associate Professor of English, University of British Columbia, Vancouver. Author of articles on Victorian writing and Jewish fiction in *University of Toronto Quarterly*, *Criticism*, *Mosaic*, *Midstream*, *Event*, and other periodicals. **Essays:** Harriet Martineau; Henry Roth.

NESBITT, Bruce.   Member of the Department of English, Simon Fraser University, Burnaby, British Columbia. Author of *Earle Birney*, 1975. **Essays:** Frederick Philip Grove; Margaret Laurence.

NEVINS, Francis M., Jr.   Assistant Professor of Law, St. Louis University Law School, Missouri. Author of *The Mystery Writer's Art*, 1970, *Royal Bloodline: Ellery Queen, Author and Detective*, 1974, a novel *Publish or Perish*, 1975, and articles in *Detectionary*, *Journal of Popular Culture*, *Armchair Detective*, and other collections and periodicals. Editor of *Nightwebs: A Collection of Stories* by Cornell Woolrich, 1974. **Essays:** Erle Stanley Gardner; Ellery Queen.

NEW, W. H.   Associate Professor of English, University of British Columbia, Vancouver; Associate Editor of *Canadian Literature* and *World Literature Written in English*. Author of *Four Hemispheres*, 1971, and *Malcolm Lowry*, 1971.

NIVEN, Alastair.   Member of the Department of English Studies, University of Stirling, Scotland. Author of *D. H. Lawrence: The Novels*, 1978. **Essays:** Raja Rao; Mordecai Richler.

NORDLAND, Brady.   Free-lance Writer and Researcher. **Essays:** Mary McCarthy; John Ruskin.

NYE, Robert.   Free-lance Writer; Poetry Editor of *The Scotsman* and Poetry Critic for *The Times*, London. Author of several volumes of verse, a novel and short stories, plays, and books for children. Editor of selections of verse by Ralegh, William Barnes, and Swinburne, and translator of *Beowulf*. **Essay:** Anna Kavan.

O'BRIEN, George. Lecturer in English, University of Warwick. **Essays:** John Banim; Gerald Griffin; Mary Lavin; Sydney Owenson, Lady Morgan; Flann O'Brien; Frank O'Connor; Seán O'Faoláin; Liam O'Flaherty.

O'DONNELL, Thomas F. Professor of English, State University of New York, Brockport. Author of *Harold Frederic* (with Hoyt C. Franchere), 1961, and of articles on American writers, especially those of New York State, for *American Transcendental Quarterly* and other periodicals. Joint Editor of *A Bibliography of Harold Frederic*, 1975, and editor of works by Frederic, James Kirke Paulding, and Adriaen Van Der Donck. **Essay:** James Kirke Paulding.

OLIVER-MORDEN, B. C. Teacher at the Open University and the University of Keele. Editor of the 18th-Century section of *The Year's Work in English 1973.* **Essays:** Oliver Goldsmith; Mervyn Peake.

PAGE, Malcolm. Associate Professor of English, Simon Fraser University, Burnaby, British Columbia. Author of articles on John Arden, Arnold Wesker, English television drama and experimental drama, London's Unity Theatre, Canadian drama, and West Indian fiction, in *Modern Drama, Drama Survey, Theatre Quarterly, Novel, Twentieth-Century Literature,* and other periodicals. **Essay:** Colin MacInnes.

PATRIDES, C. A. Professor of English, University of Michigan, Ann Arbor. Formerly, Professor of English, University of York, England. Author of *Milton and the Christian Tradition,* 1966, and *The Grand Design of God: The Literary Form of the Christian View of History,* 1972. Editor of *Approaches to Paradise Lost,* 1968; *The Cambridge Platonists,* 1969; *History of the World* by Sir Walter Ralegh, 1971; *English Poems* by George Herbert, 1974; *Selected Prose* by Milton, 1974; *Major Works* by Sir Thomas Browne, 1977; *Approaches to Marvell,* 1978. **Essay:** Sir Thomas Browne.

PEARCE, Roy Harvey. Professor of English, University of California at San Diego. Author of *Colonial American Writing,* 1951, *The Savages of America,* 1953 (revised, 1965), and *The Continuity of American Poetry,* 1961. Co-Editor of the Centennial Edition of the Writings of Hawthorne, and of anthologies of essays on Hawthorne and Whitman.

PEDEN, William. Professor of English, University of Missouri, Columbia. Author of *Night in Funland and Other Stories,* 1968; *Twilight at Monticello* (novel), 1973; *The American Short Story: Continuity and Change 1940–1975,* 1975. **Essays:** O. Henry; William Sansom.

PERKINS, Barbara M. Director of Writing Improvement, Humanities Program, Eastern Michigan University, Ypsilanti. **Essays:** John William De Forest; Sir Thomas Malory.

PERKINS, George. Professor of English, Eastern Michigan University, Ypsilanti. Author or editor of *Writing Clear Prose,* 1964; *Varieties of Prose,* 1966; *The Theory of the American Novel,* 1970; *Realistic American Short Fiction,* 1972; *American Poetic Theory,* 1972; *The American Tradition in Literature* (with others), fourth edition, 1974. **Essays:** Nathaniel Hawthorne; Henry James.

PETERSEN, Kirsten Holst. Member of the Commonwealth Literature Division of the English Department, University of Aarhus, Denmark; reviewer for *Danida.* Editor of *Enigma of Values* (with Anna Rutherford), 1975. **Essays:** Cyprian Ekwensi; George Lamming; Alan Paton; Laurens van der Post.

PINION, F. B. Former Sub-Dean and Reader in English Studies, University of Sheffield, Yorkshire; Editor of the *Thomas Hardy Society Review.* Author of *A Hardy Companion,*

1968; *A Jane Austen Companion*, 1973; *A Brontë Companion*, 1975; *A Commentary on the Poems of Hardy*, 1976; *Hardy: Art and Thought*, 1977. Editor of *Two on a Tower* by Hardy, and of his complete short stories. **Essay:** Thomas Hardy.

POLLARD, Arthur. Professor of English, University of Hull, Yorkshire. Author of *Mrs. Gaskell, Novelist and Biographer*, 1965, and *Anthony Trollope*, 1978. Editor of *The Letters of Mrs. Gaskell* (with J. A. V. Chapple), 1966; *The Victorians* (Sphere History of Literature in English), 1970; *Crabbe: The Critical Heritage*, 1972; *Thackeray: Vanity Fair* (casebook), 1978. **Essays:** Thomas Keneally; R. S. Surtees.

POTOKER, Edward Martin. Professor of English, Baruch College, City University of New York. Author of *Ronald Firbank*, 1969, the article on German Literature since World War II in *Encyclopedia International*, and of essays on Nathanael West, Carl Van Vechten, John Braine, Colin Spencer, Judith Rossner, and other modern writers in *Saturday Review, The Nation, Ramparts, New York Times Book Review*, and other periodicals. **Essay:** John Braine.

QUARTERMAIN, Peter. Associate Professor of English, University of British Columbia, Vancouver. Author of "Louis Zukofsky: Re Location" in *Open Letter*, 1973, and "Romantic Offensive: *Tish*" in *Canadian Literature*, 1977. **Essay:** Gertrude Stein.

QUAYLE, Eric. Free-lance Writer. Author of *Ballantyne the Brave*, 1967, and a bibliography of Ballantyne; *The Ruin of Sir Walter Scott*, 1968; *The Collector's Book of Books, Children Books, Detective Fiction*, and *Boys' Stories*, 4 vols., 1971–73; *Old Cook Books: An Illustrated History*, 1978. **Essay:** R. M. Ballantyne.

RAWLINSON, Gloria. Free-lance Writer. Author of two books of verse, *The Island Where I Was Born*, 1955, and *Of Clouds and Pebbles*, 1963. Editor of *Houses by the Sea*, 1952, and *The Godwits Fly*, 1970, both by Robin Hyde. **Essay:** Robin Hyde.

RAWSON, C. J. Professor of English, University of Warwick, Coventry; Joint Editor of *Modern Language Review* and *Yearbook of English Studies*, and General Editor of the Unwin Critical Library. Author of *Henry Fielding*, 1968; *Fielding and the Augustan Ideal under Stress*, 1972; *Gulliver and the Gentle Reader*, 1973; *Focus: Swift*, 1978. Editor of *Fielding: A Critical Anthology*, 1973, and *Yeats and Anglo-Irish Literature: Critical Essays* by Peter Ure, 1973. **Essay:** Jonathan Swift.

REED, John Q. Chairman of the Department of English, Pittsburg State University, Kansas. Author of *Benjamin Penhallow Shillaber*, 1972, and of articles on Artemus Ward, Henry James, Faulkner, and Twain, in *American Literature, Midcontinent American Studies Journal, Encyclopaedia Britannica, Civil War History*, and *Midwest Quarterly*. **Essay:** Artemus Ward.

REID, Ian. Senior Lecturer in English, Adelaide University, Australia; Editorial Consultant, *Meanjin*. Author of *The Short Story*, 1977, and *Fiction and the Depression in Australia and New Zealand*, 1978. **Essays:** John Mulgan; Frank Sargeson; Kylie Tennant.

REILLY, John M. Associate Professor of English, State University of New York, Albany; Advisory Editor, *Obsidian: Black Literature in Review*, and *Melus*. Author of the bibliographical essay on Richard Wright in *Black American Writers* and of articles on Wright and other Afro-American writers, and on detective fiction, in *Colorado Quarterly, Phylon, CLA Journal, Journal of Black Studies, Armchair Detective, Journal of Popular Culture*, and other periodicals. Editor of *Twentieth-Century Interpretations of "Invisible Man,"* 1970, *Richard Wright: The Critical Reception*, 1978, and of the reference book *Detective and Crime*

Writers, 1980. **Essays:** William Wells Brown; W. F. B. Du Bois; Dashiell Hammett; Zora Neale Hurston; Rex Stout; Jean Toomer; Richard Wright.

RENDER, Sylvia Lyons. Specialist in Afro-American History and Culture, Manuscript Division, Library of Congress, Washington, D.C. Author of the introduction to Charles Waddell Chesnutt's *The Marrow of Tradition*, 1969, and of articles in *Encyclopaedia Britannica*, *CLA Journal*, *North Carolina Folklore*, and *Tennessee Folklore Society Bulletin*. Editor of *The Short Fiction of Chesnutt*, 1974. **Essay:** Charles Waddell Chesnutt.

REYNOLDS, William D. Associate Professor of English, Hope College, Holland, Michigan. Author of articles on Dorothy L. Sayers and J. R. R. Tolkien. **Essay:** Dorothy L. Sayers.

RHODES, H. Winston. Professor of English (retired), University of Canterbury, Christchurch. Past Editor of *New Zealand Monthly Review*. His books include *New Zealand Fiction since 1945*, 1968, *Frank Sargeson*, 1969, and six edited volumes of Rewi Alley's prose and verse.

RICHARDS, Robert F. Associate Professor of English, University of Denver, Colorado. Author of articles on Ralph Hodgson and Thomas Hornsby Ferril, and the introduction to *Words for Denver and Other Poems* by Ferril, 1966. Editor of *Concise Dictionary of American Literature*, 1969. **Essays:** Waldo Frank; Oliver La Farge; Don Marquis; A. A. Milne.

RICHETTI, John. Professor of English, Rutgers University, New Brunswick, New Jersey. Author of *Popular Fiction Before Richardson: Narrative Patterns 1700–1739*, 1969, and *Defoe's Narratives: Situations and Structures*, 1975. **Essays:** Eliza Haywood; Delariviere Manley; Samuel Richardson.

RINGE, Donald A. Professor of English, University of Kentucky, Lexington. Author of *James Fenimore Cooper*, 1962, *Charles Brockden Brown*, 1966, and *The Pictorial Mode: Space and Time in the Art of Bryant, Irving, and Cooper*, 1971. Member of the Editorial Board for *The Writings of James Fenimore Cooper*. **Essays:** Hugh Henry Brackenridge; Charles Brockden Brown; James Fenimore Cooper; John Pendleton Kennedy; John Neal.

ROGERS, Pat. Professor of English, University of Bristol. Author of *Grub Street: Studies in a Subculture*, 1972, and *The Augustan Vision*, 1974. Editor of *A Tour Through Great Britain* by Daniel Defoe, 1971, *Defoe: The Critical Heritage*, 1972, and *The Eighteenth Century*, 1978. **Essay:** Daniel Defoe.

ROVIT, Earl. Professor of English, City College of New York. Author of *Herald to Chaos: The Novels of Elizabeth Madox Roberts*, 1960; *Ernest Hemingway*, 1963; *The Player King*, 1965; *Saul Bellow*, 1967; *A Far Cry*, 1967; *Crossings*, 1973. **Essays:** Henry Adams; John Barth; Theodore Dreiser; John Hawkes; James Jones; Elizabeth Madox Roberts; Nathanael West.

RUOFF, James E. Associate Professor of English, City College of New York. Author of *Elizabethan Poetry and Prose*, 1972, *Crowell Handbook of Elizabethan and Stuart Literature*, 1973, and *Major Shakespearean Tragedies* (with Edward G. Quinn), 1973. **Essay:** John Bunyan.

RUTHERFORD, Anna. Head of the Commonwealth Literature Division, University of Aarhus, Denmark. Editor of *Kunapipi*, and Chairman of the European branch of the Commonwealth Literature and Language Association. Editor of *Commonwealth Short Stories* (with Donald Hannah), 1971, *Commonwealth* (essays), 1972, and *Enigma of Values* (with

Kirsten Holst Petersen), 1975. **Essays:** Peter Abrahams; Mulk Raj Anand; Ruth Prawer Jhabvala; John Lee; Hal Porter; Katharine Susannah Prichard; Vic Reid; Henry Savary; Samuel Selvon; Price Warung.

SALGÁDO, Gâmini. Professor of English, University of Exeter, Devon. Author of *Eyewitnesses of Shakespeare: Firsthand Accounts of Performances, 1590–1890,* 1975, and *The Elizabethan Underworld,* 1977. Editor of *Sons and Lovers: A Collection of Critical Essays,* 1969, *Cony Catchers and Bawdy Baskets,* 1973, works by D. H. Lawrence and Shakespeare, and collections of Jacobean and Restoration plays.

SAMBROOK, A. J. Senior Lecturer in English, University of Southampton, Hampshire. Author of *A Poet Hidden: The Life of Richard Watson Dixon,* 1962, and *William Cobbett: An Author Guide,* 1973. Editor of *The Scribleriad,* 1967, *The Seasons and The Castle of Indolence* by James Thomson, 1972 and *Pre-Raphaelitism: Patterns of Literary Criticism,* 1974. **Essay:** William Cobbett.

SANDERSON, Stewart F. Director of the Institute of Dialect and Folk Life Studies, University of Leeds. Author of *Hemingway,* 1961 (revised, 1970), and of many articles on British and comparative folklore and ethnology, and on modern literature. Editor of *The Secret Common-Wealth* by Robert Kirk, 1970, and *The Linguistic Atlas of England* (with others), 1978. **Essays:** George Borrow; Ian Fleming; Ernest Hemingway; Eric Linklater; Sir Compton Mackenzie; Anthony Powell.

SAUL, George Brandon. Professor Emeritus of English, University of Connecticut, Storrs; Contributing Editor, *Journal of Irish Literature.* Author of fiction (*The Wild Queen,* 1967), verse (*Hound and Unicorn,* 1969, and *Adam Unregenerate,* 1977), and of critical works, including *Prolegomena to the Study of Yeats's Poems* (1957) and *Plays* (1958), *Traditional Irish Literature and Its Backgrounds,* 1970, and *In Praise of the Half-Forgotten: Essays,* 1976. Also a composer. **Essay:** A. E. Coppard.

SCHWAB, Arnold T. Professor of English, California State University, Long Beach. Author of *James Gibbons Huneker: Critic of the Seven Arts,* 1963, *The Sound of Huneker* (forthcoming), and articles on Huneker, George Moore, and Joseph Conrad, in *American Literature, Nineteenth-Century Fiction,* and *Modern Philology.* **Essay:** James Huneker.

SCHWARZ, Daniel R. Associate Professor of English, Cornell University, Ithaca, New York. Author of articles on T. S. Eliot, Conrad, Hardy, and Dylan Thomas in *Studies in the Novel, Modern Fiction Studies, Twentieth-Century Literature,* and other periodicals. **Essay:** Joseph Conrad.

SCOBIE, Brian W. M. Member of the Faculty, School of English, University of Leeds. **Essay:** Lewis Grassic Gibbon.

SEWELL, Brocard. Lecturer in English, Mount Carmel College, Niagara Falls, Ontario; Priest of the Carmelite Order (English Province). Former Editor of *Aylesford Review.* Author of *Montague Summers: A Memoir,* 1966; *Footnote to the Nineties,* 1968; *The Vatican Oracle,* 1970; *Olive Custance,* 1975; *Cecil Chesterton,* 1975. **Essay:** Henry Williamson.

SEYERSTED, Per. Professor of American Literature and Director of the American Institute, University of Oslo; Chairman of the Nordic Association for American Studies. Author of *Gilgamesj,* 1967, and *Kate Chopin: A Critical Biography,* 1969. Editor of *The Complete Works of Kate Chopin,* 1969. **Essay:** Kate Chopin.

SHARMA, J. N. Academic Associate, American Studies Research Centre, Hyderabad. **Essays:** Ambrose Bierce; William Saroyan.

SHATTOCK, Joanne. Bibliographer, Victorian Studies Centre, University of Leicester. Author of articles on Victorian periodicals and reviewing, literary piracy, and the public readings of Dickens and Thackeray; contributor to *The Wellesley Index to Victorian Periodicals.* Currently editing *The Perpetual Curate* by Mrs. Oliphant, and a volume on Victorian periodicals. **Essays:** Dinah Maria Mulock; Margaret Oliphant; Joseph Henry Shorthouse.

SHUCARD, Alan R. Associate Professor of English, University of Wisconsin – Parkside, Kenosha. Author of two books of verse – *The Gorgon Bog,* 1970, and *The Louse on the Head of the Lord,* 1972. **Essay:** Walter Van Tilburg Clark.

SMITH, David J. Lecturer in English, University of Adelaide, Australia. Author of *Socialist Propaganda in the Twentieth-Century British Novel* (forthcoming). **Essay:** Jack Lindsay.

SMITH, Elton E. Professor of English and Bible, University of South Florida, Tampa. Author of *"The Two Voices": A Tennyson Study,* 1964; *William Godwin* (with Esther Marian Greenwell Smith), 1965; *Louis MacNeice,* 1970; *"The Angry Young Men" of the Thirties,* 1975; *Charles Reade,* 1977. **Essay:** Charles Reade.

SMITH, Esther Marian Greenwell. Professor of Language Arts, Polk Community College, Winter Haven, Florida. Author of *William Godwin* (with Elton E. Smith), 1965, articles on Melville and Hawthorne, and youth fiction for religious publishers. **Essay:** Pearl S. Buck.

SMITH, Rowland. Chairman of the Department of English, Dalhousie University, Halifax, Nova Scotia. Author of *Lyric and Polemic: The Literary Personality of Roy Campbell,* 1972. Editor of *Exile and Tradition: Studies in African and Caribbean Literature,* 1976. **Essays:** Nadine Gordimer; Edward Upward.

SMITH, Stan. Lecturer in English, University of Dundee, Scotland. Author of the forthcoming book *A Superfluous Man* (on Edward Thomas), and of articles on modern literature for *Critical Quarterly, Literature and History, Irish University Review, Scottish International Review,* and other periodicals. **Essays:** Lafcadio Hearn; Philip Roth.

STANNARD, Martin. Leverhulme Research Fellow in English Literature, University of Edinburgh. **Essays:** Michael Arlen; David Garnett; William Gerhardie; Christopher Isherwood; Evelyn Waugh.

STEAD, C. K. Professor of English, University of Auckland, New Zealand. Author of three volumes of verse – *Whether the Will Is Free,* 1964, *Crossing the Bar,* 1972, and *Quesada,* 1975 – a novel, *Smith's Dream,* 1971; and *The New Poetic: Yeats to Eliot,* 1964. Editor of *New Zealand Short Stories: Second Series,* 1966, a casebook on Shakespeare's *Measure for Measure,* 1971; and *The Letters and Journals of Katherine Mansfield: A Selection,* 1977.

STERN, Madeleine B. Free-lance Writer; Partner in Leona Rostenberg-Rare Books, New York. Author of *Louisa May Alcott,* 1950; *Imprints on History: Book Publishers and American Frontiers,* 1956; *We the Women: Career Firsts of 19th-Century America,* 1963; *Heads and Headlines: The Phrenological Fowlers,* 1971; *Old and Rare: Thirty Years in the Book Business* (with Leona Rostenberg), 1975, and of several biographies for adults and for children. Editor of *Women on the Move*, 1972; *The Victoria Woodhull Reader*, 1974; and *Louisa's Wonder Book*, 1975, *Behind a Mask*, 1975, and *Plots and Counterplots*, 1976, all by Louisa May Alcott. **Essays:** Louisa May Alcott; Mary Noailles Murfree; Harriet Beecher Stowe.

STOKES, Edward. Reader in English, University of Tasmania, Hobart; Co-Editor of *Australian Literary Studies*. Author of *The Novels of Henry Green*, 1959, and *The Novels of James Hanley*, 1964. **Essay:** James Hanley.

STOUCK, David. Associate Professor of English, Simon Fraser University, Burnaby, British Columbia. Author of *Willa Cather's Imagination*, 1975, and of articles in *American Literary Scholarship*. **Essays:** Sherwood Anderson; Sinclair Ross; Ethel Wilson.

STUCKEY, W. J. Associate Professor of English, Purdue University, Lafayette, Indiana; Founding Editor, *Minnesota Review*; Fiction Editor for *Quartet*, and Reader for *Modern Fiction Studies*. Author of *Pulitzer Prize Novels*, 1966, and *Caroline Gordon*, 1972. **Essays:** Edna Ferber; Caroline Gordon; Margaret Mitchell; Walker Percy; T. S. Stribling; Edith Wharton.

SUTHERLAND, James. Emeritus Professor of Modern English Literature, University College, London. Formerly, Editor of *Review of English Studies*. Author of many books, including *Leucocholy* (poems), 1926; *The Medium of Poetry*, 1934; *Defoe*, 1937; *A Preface to Eighteenth Century Poetry*, 1948; *The English Critic*, 1952; *On English Prose*, 1957; *English Satire*, 1958; *English Literature in the Late Seventeenth Century*, 1969; *Daniel Defoe: A Critical Study*, 1971. Editor of plays by Rowe, Dekker, Shakespeare, and Dryden, *The Dunciad* by Pope, 1943, and *The Oxford Book of Literary Anecdotes*, 1975.

SUTHERLAND, John. Member of the Department of English, University College, London. Author of *Thackeray at Work*, 1974. Editor, with Michael Greenfield of *Henry Esmond* by Thackeray, 1970. **Essay:** William Makepeace Thackeray.

SWEETSER, Wesley D. Professor of English, State University of New York, Oswego. Author of *Arthur Machen*, 1964, *A Bibliography of Machen* (with A. Goldstone), 1965, and *Ralph Hodgson: A Bibliography*, 1974. **Essays:** Marcus Clarke; Arthur Machen; George Meredith.

TANSELLE, G. T. Professor of English, University of Wisconsin, Madison; Bibliographical Editor of *The Writings of Herman Melville* since 1968 (6 vols. so far published). Author of *Royall Tyler*, 1967; *Guide to the Study of United States Imprints*, 2 vols., 1971; *The Editing of Historical Documents*, 1978; and two series of articles on descriptive bibliography and scholarly editing in *Studies in Bibliography*, *The Library*, *Papers of the Bibliographical Society of America*, and *Book Collector*. **Essay:** Floyd Dell.

THOMAS, Ned. Lecturer in English, University College of Wales, Aberystwyth; Founding Editor of *Planet* magazine. Author of *George Orwell*, 1965, and *The Welsh Extremist: Essays on Modern Welsh Literature and Society*, 1971. **Essay:** Jean Rhys.

THOMSON, Peter. Professor of Drama, University of Exeter, Devon. Author of *Ideas in Action*, 1977. Editor of *Julius Caesar* by Shakespeare, 1970; *Essays on Nineteenth-Century British Theatre* (with Kenneth Richards), 1971; *The Eighteenth-Century English Stage*, 1973; *Lord Byron's Family*, 1975. **Essays:** Pierce Egan; Stephen Leacock.

THWAITE, Ann. Free-lance Writer; Contributing Editor of *Cricket* magazine. Author of 15 books for children, the most recent being *Chatterbox*, 1978, and of *Waiting for the Party:*

The Life of Frances Hodgson Burnett, 1974; currently working on a book on Edmund Gosse. Editor of the *Allsorts* series for children and of *My Oxford*, 1977. **Essay:** Frances Hodgson Burnett.

TOMLIN, E. W. F. Free-lance Writer, Broadcaster, and Lecturer. Author of *The Approach to Metaphysics*, 1947; *The Western Philosophers*, 1950; *The Eastern Philosophers*, 1952; *Simone Weil*, 1954; *Living and Knowing*, 1955; *Wyndham Lewis*, 1955; *R. G. Collingwood*, 1956; *Tokyo Essays*, 1967; and books on Turkey and Japan. Editor of *Wyndham Lewis: An Anthology*, 1969, *Dickens: A Centenary Volume*, 1970, and *Arnold Toynbee: A Selection from His Works*, 1979. **Essay:** Wyndam Lewis.

TRACY, Clarence. Visiting Professor of English, University of Toronto. Author of *Artificial Bastard: The Life of Richard Savage*, 1953. Editor of *Poetical Works of Richard Savage*, 1962; *The Spiritual Quixote* by Richard Graves, 1968; *Browning's Mind and Art: Essays*, 1968; *Johnson's Life of Savage*, 1971; *The Rape Observed* by Alexander Pope, 1974. **Essay:** Richard Graves.

TRAINER, James. Professor of German, University of Stirling, Scotland. Editor of *The Old English Baron* by Clara Reeve, 1967. **Essay:** Clara Reeve.

TRAVERSI, Derek A. Professor of English, Swarthmore College, Pennsylvania. Author of *An Approach to Shakespeare*, 1938 (revised, 1968); *Shakespeare: The Last Phase*, 1954; *Shakespeare: From Richard II to Henry V*, 1957; *Shakespeare: The Roman Plays*, 1963; *T. S. Eliot: The Longer Poems*, 1976.

TRUSSLER, Simon. Editor of *Theatre Quarterly*. Theatre Critic, *Tribune*, 1969–76. Author of several books on theatre and drama, including studies of John Osborne, Arnold Wesker, John Whiting, Harold Pinter, and Edward Bond, and of articles on theatre bibliography and classification. Editor of two collections of eighteenth-century plays and of *The Oxford Companion to the Theatre*, 1969. **Essay:** Sir Richard Steele.

TYDEMAN, William M. Senior Lecturer in English, University College of North Wales, Bangor. Author of *The Theatre in the Middle Ages*, 1978, and of the chapter on the earlier 16th century in *Year's Work in English Studies*, 1971–74. Editor of *English Poetry 1400–1800*, 1970, and of casebooks on Wordsworth and Coleridge. **Essay:** W. W. Jacobs.

WALL, Stephen. Fellow of Keble College, Oxford; Co-Editor of *Essays in Criticism*. Editor of *Charles Dickens: A Critical Anthology*, 1970. **Essay:** Anthony Trollope.

WALLACH, Mark I. Associate Attorney, Baker, Hostetler and Patterson, Cleveland, Ohio. Author of *Christopher Morley*, 1976, and of articles on Morley in *Markham Review*, February 1972, and cable television in *Case Western Reserve Law Review*, Winter 1975. **Essays:** Christopher Morley; C. P. Snow.

WALSER, Richard. Professor Emeritus of English, North Carolina State University, Raleigh. Author of *North Carolina Drama*, 1956; *Thomas Wolfe: An Introduction and Interpretation*, 1961; *Literary North Carolina*, 1970; *Thomas Wolfe, Undergraduate*, 1977. **Essays:** James Boyd; Thomas Wolfe.

WALSH, George. Publisher and Free-lance Writer. **Essays:** Joel Chandler Harris; Saki.

WALSH, Marcus. Lecturer in English, University of Birmingham. Editor of *The Religious Poetry of Christopher Smart*, 1972. **Essays:** James Boswell; Samuel Johnson.

WALSH, William. Professor of Commonwealth Literature and Chairman of the School of English, University of Leeds. Author of *Use of Imagination*, 1958; *A Human Idiom*, 1964; *Coleridge*, 1967; *A Manifold Voice*, 1970; *R. K. Narayan*, 1972; *V. S. Naipaul*, 1973; *Patrick White's Fiction*, 1978. **Essay:** V. S. Naipaul.

WARNER, Alan. Professor of English, New University of Ulster, Coleraine. Author of *A Short Guide to English Style*, 1961, *Clay Is the Word* (on Patrick Kavanagh), 1961; *William Allingham*, 1975. **Essays:** William Carleton; Mark Rutherford; Edith Somerville and Martin Ross.

WARNER, Val. Free-lance Writer. Author of *Under the Penthouse* (verse), 1973. Editor of *Centenary Corbière*, 1974. **Essay:** Shirley Jackson.

WATTS, Harold H. Professor of English, Purdue University, Lafayette, Indiana. Author of *The Modern Reader's Guide to the Bible*, 1949; *Ezra Pound and the Cantos*, 1951; *Hound and Quary*, 1953; *The Modern Reader's Guide to Religions*, 1964; *Aldous Huxley*, 1969. **Essays:** John Cheever; James Gould Cozzens; William Gaddis; L. P. Hartley; Arthur Koestler; Jerzy Kosinksi; P. H. Newby; Thomas Pynchon; John Updike; Eudora Welty.

WEALES, Gerald. Professor of English, University of Pennsylvania, Philadelphia; Drama Critic for *The Reporter* and *Commonweal*. Author of *Religion in Modern English Drama*, 1961; *American Drama since World War II*, 1962; *A Play and Its Parts*, 1964; *The Jumping-Off Place: American Drama in the 1960's*, 1969; *Clifford Odets*, 1971. Editor of *The Complete Plays of William Wycherley*, 1966, and, with Robert J. Nelson, of the collections *Enclosure*, 1975, and *Revolution*, 1975. Recipient of the George Jean Nathan Award for Dramatic Criticism, 1965. **Essays:** Robert Benchley; James Thurber; E. B. White.

WEIR, Sybil B. Professor of English and American Studies, San Jose State University, California. Author of articles on Theodore Dreiser, Gertrude Atherton, Constance Fenimore Woolson, and Elizabeth Drew Stoddard. **Essay:** Gertrude Atherton.

WESTBROOK P. D. Professor of English, State University of New York, Albany. Author of *Acres of Flint: Writers of Rural New England*, 1951; *Biography of an Island*, 1958; *The Greatness of Man: An Essay on Dostoevsky and Whitman*, 1961; *Mary Ellen Chase*, 1966; *Mary Wilkins Freeman*, 1967. **Essays:** Edward Bellamy; Mary E. Wilkins Freeman; Sarah Orne Jewett.

WILLIAMS, John Stuart. Head of the Communications Department, South Glamorgan Institute of Higher Education, Cardiff. Author of four books of verse, the most recent being *Banna Strand*, 1975. Editor of three verse anthologies. **Essay:** Leigh Hunt.

WILLY, Margaret. Free-lance Writer and Lecturer. Author of two books of verse – *The Invisible Sun*, 1946, and *Every Star a Tongue*, 1951 – and of several critical works, including *Life Was Their Cry*, 1950; *Three Metaphysical Poets: Crashaw, Vaughan, Traherne*, 1961; *Three Women Diarists: Celia Fiennes, Dorothy Wordsworth, Katherine Mansfield*, 1964; *A Critical Commentary on "Wutherine Heights,"* 1966; and *A Critical Commentary on Browning's "Men and Women,"* 1968. Editor of two anthologies and of works by Goldsmith. **Essays:** H. E. Bates; Pamela Hansford Johnson; Olivia Manning; W. Somerset Maugham; Charles Morgan; Elizabeth Taylor.

WINNIFRITH, T. J. Member of the Department of English, University of Warwick, Coventry. Author of *The Brontës and Their Background: Romance and Reality*, 1973. **Essays:** Chinua Achebe; Agatha Christie; Daphne du Maurier; Elizabeth Gaskell; Mary Renault; Olive Schreiner; Lionel Trilling; Mrs. Humphry Ward.

WOHLGELERNTER, Maurice. Professor of English, Baruch College, City University of New York. Author of *Israel Zangwill: A Study*, 1964, and *Frank O'Connor: An Introduction*, 1977. Editor of *History, Philosophy, and Spiritual Democracy: Essays in Honor of Joseph L. Blau*, 1979. **Essay:** Israel Zangwill.

WOLFE, Peter. Professor of English, University of Missouri, St. Louis; Editor of *Virginia Woolf Quarterly*. Author of *The Disciplined Heart: Iris Murdoch and Her Novels*, 1966; *Mary Renault*, 1969; *Rebecca West: Artist and Thinker*, 1971; *Graham Greene: The Entertainer*, 1972; *John Fowles: Magus and Moralist*, 1976. **Essay:** Rebecca West.

WOODCOCK, George. Free-lance Writer, Lecturer, and Editor. Author of verse (*Selected Poems*, 1967), plays, travel books, biographies, and works on history and politics; critical works include *William Godwin*, 1946, *The Incomparable Aphra*, 1948, *The Paradox of Oscar Wilde*, 1949, *The Crystal Spirit* (on Orwell), 1966, *Hugh MacLennan*, 1969, *Odysseus Ever Returning: Canadian Writers and Writing*, 1970, *Mordecai Richler*, 1970, *Dawn and the Darkest Hour* (on Aldous Huxley), 1972, *Herbert Road*, 1972, and *Thomas Merton*, 1978. Editor of anthologies, and of works by Charles Lamb, Malcolm Lowry, Wyndham Lewis, and others. **Essays:** Morley Callaghan; William Hazlitt; W. H. Hudson; Aldous Huxley; Malcolm Lowry; R. K. Narayan; George Orwell.

WOODRESS, James. Professor of English, University of California, Davis; Editor of *American Literary Scholarship*. Author of *Howells and Italy*, 1952; *Booth Tarkington*, 1955; *A Yankee's Odyssey: The Life of Joel Barlow*, 1958; *Willa Cather: Her Life and Art*, 1970; *American Fiction 1900–1950*, 1974. Editor of *Voices from America's Past* (with Richard Morris), 1961, and *Eight American Authors*, 1971. **Essays:** Willa Cather; Hamlin Garland; E. W. Howe; Frank Norris; Kenneth Roberts; Booth Tarkington.

WORTH, George J. Professor and Chairman of the Department of English, University of Kansas, Lawrence. Author of *John Hannay: His Life and Works*, 1964. Editor of *Six Studies in Nineteenth-Century English Literature and Thought* (with Harold Orel), 1962. **Essay:** William Henry Ainsworth.

WRIGHT, Judith. Honours Tutor in English, University of Queensland, Brisbane. Author of a dozen books of verse – including *Collected Poems 1942–1970*, 1971, and *The Double Tree: Selected Poems*, 1978 – a novel, *The Nature of Love*, 1966; several juveniles; and books on Australian poetry, Shaw Neilson, Charles Harpur, and Henry Lawson. Editor of several anthologies of Australian verse and verse by Neilson.

YOUNG, Kenneth. Literary and Political Adviser, Beaverbrook Newspapers. Author of *John Dryden*, 1954; *A. J. Balfour*, 1963; *Churchill and Beaverbrook*, 1966; *The Greek Passion*, 1969; *Stanley Baldwin*, 1976; and other biographies and works on political and social history. Editor of the diaries of Sir R. Bruce Lochart. **Essays:** John Galsworthy; Thomas Babington Macaulay; Henry Miller; T. F. Powys; J. B. Priestley; Hugh Walpole.